The
Bedford
Introduction
to Drama

The Bedford Introduction to Drama

THIRD EDITION

Lee A. Jacobus
University of Connecticut

BEDFORD BOOKS ◆ BOSTON

For Bedford Books

President and Publisher: Charles H. Christensen
General Manager and Associate Publisher: Joan E. Feinberg
Managing Editor: Elizabeth M. Schaaf
Developmental Editor: Karen S. Henry
Editorial Assistants: Rebecca Jerman and Kate O'Sullivan
Production Editor: Bridget Leahy
Production Assistants: Stasia Zomkowski and Jocelyn Humelsine
Copyeditor: Mary Mitiguy
Text Design: Claire Seng-Niemoeller
Cover Design: Hannus Design Associates
Cover Photo (from left to right): From the *Oresteia* and *A Midsummer Night's Dream.* Photographs by Donald Cooper/Photostage. From *Angels in America.* Photograph by Joan Marcus.

Library of Congress Catalog Card Number: 96–84933

For information, write: Bedford Books, 75 Arlington Street, Boston, MA 02116 (617-426-7440)

ISBN: 0–312–13404–5

Acknowledgments

Greek Drama

Figure 1. Theater at Epidaurus from *The Theatre of Dionysus in Athens* by Arthur Wallace Pickard-Cambridge. Reprinted by permission of Oxford University Press.
Agamemnon, The Libation Bearers, The Eumenides from *The* Oresteia *by Aeschylus: A New Translation for the State,* by David Grene and Wendy Doniger O'Flaherty. Copyright © 1989 by The University of Chicago. Reprinted by permission of The University of Chicago Press. *Photos:* © Richard Feldman (pp. 73, 92).
"Orestes and the Gods" excerpt from *A History of Greek Literature,* translated by Clare Krojzl. Reprinted by permission of Routledge.
Excerpt from *The Art of Aeschylus* by Thomas Rosenmeyer. Copyright © 1982 The Regents of the University of California. Reprinted by permission of the University of California Press.
"*Oresteia:* Trilogy Preserved" from *Aeschylus* by Lois S. Spatz. Copyright © 1982 by G.K. Hall & Co. Reprinted by permission of Twayne Publishers, an imprint of Simon & Schuster Macmillan.
The Oedipus Rex from *Sophocles: The Oedipus Cycle, An English Version* by Dudley Fitts and Robert Fitzgerald. Copyright 1949 by Harcourt Brace & Company; renewed 1977 by Cornelia Fitts and Robert Fitzgerald. Reprinted by permission of the publisher. *Photos:* Henry S. Kranzler, all rights reserved (pp. 116–17); The Guthrie Theater (p. 130); © Dr. Jaromir Svoboda (p. 120); Museum fur Gestaltung Zurich (p. 117).
The Antigone from *Sophocles, The Oedipus Cycle, An English Version* by Dudley Fitts and Robert Fitzgerald. Copyright 1939 by Harcourt Brace & Company; renewed 1967 by Dudley Fitts and Robert Fitzgerald. Reprinted by permission of the publisher. CAUTION: All rights, including profes-

Acknowledgments and copyrights are continued at the back of the book on pages 1792–97, which constitute an extension of the copyright page.

Preface for Instructors

In its third edition, *The Bedford Introduction to Drama* remains first and foremost the most comprehensive anthology available: a collection of forty-eight important plays that have shaped dramatic literature from the time of the early Greek dramatists to the present. The book incorporates a number of features that distinguish it from other introductions to drama. Most notably, it presents five major playwrights in greater than usual depth, with three plays by Shakespeare and two each by Sophocles, Ibsen, Tennessee Williams, and August Wilson. Commentaries by playwrights, directors, actors, reviewers and critics, thorough biographical and critical introductions, brief production histories, and photographs of landmark productions accompany these and all the plays in the book and offer drama students a unique opportunity to study and write about major figures in the development of drama.

Seventeen plays are new to this edition; among them are Aeschylus's *Oresteia* (*Agamemnon*, *The Libation Bearers*, and *The Eumenides*), Marlowe's *Doctor Faustus*, Bernard Shaw's *Pygmalion*, Federico García Lorca's *The House of Bernarda Alba*, Bertolt Brecht's *Mother Courage*, Harold Pinter's *Betrayal*, David Mamet's *Oleanna*, and Tony Kushner's *Angels in America: Millennium Approaches*.

Also new to this edition is a large selection of classic and contemporary reviews of plays and a new section entitled How to Write a Drama Review, which analyzes professional reviews and offers suggestions for students writing reviews. These reviews complement the abundant collection of other kinds of commentary in the book—works by theater practitioners and literary and dramatic theorists. Thirty-one of the seventy-four commentaries are new to this edition.

The third edition continues the tradition of offering a strong representation of minority and women playwrights, including Aphra Behn's *The Rover*, Lady Gregory's *The Rising of the Moon*, Susan Glaspell's *Trifles*, Lorraine Hansberry's *A Raisin in the Sun*, Wole Soyinka's *The Strong Breed*, Caryl Churchill's *Top Girls*, David Henry Hwang's *The Dance and the Railroad*, Marsha Norman's *'night, Mother*, María Irene

Fornés's *The Conduct of Life,* August Wilson's *Fences* and *The Piano Lesson,* Suzan-Lori Parks's *The Death of the Last Black Man in the Whole Entire World,* and Anna Deavere Smith's *Twilight: Los Angeles, 1992.*

The Bedford Introduction to Drama offers a succinct but thorough history of Western drama. Even when it appears most timeless, all drama (like, of course, all literature) is a product of a language, an era, and a complex range of political, social, and ethnic influences. *The Bedford Introduction to Drama* highlights such influences. A general introduction gives an overview of the great ages of drama, the major genres and elements, and the cultural value of drama. Throughout the book, introductions to significant periods of drama, the playwrights, and the plays focus on the cultural contexts of the works and on their stage history.

Finally, *The Bedford Introduction to Drama* is a complete resource book for the beginning student of drama. In the general introduction, a discussion of the elements of drama defines the important terms and concepts and demonstrates these concepts in action, drawing its examples from Lady Gregory's one-act play *The Rising of the Moon.* The unusually large collection of theater photographs was increased by a third in this edition. Now nearly every play is accompanied by one or more striking photographs, and the plays by playwrights treated in depth are illustrated by photo essays often featuring more than one production to help students understand the plays as texts to be interpreted through performance.

Writing about Drama, the first appendix, shows students possible approaches to commenting on dramatic literature and points the way to developing ideas that can result in probing critical essays. From prewriting to outlining and drafting, the process of writing about drama is illustrated by reference to Lady Gregory's play, and a sample essay on the play provides one example of drama criticism. The new section, How to Write a Drama Review, will be especially useful for assignments involving attendance at theater productions.

The second appendix, Timelines for each period of drama, offers students a quick reference for noting the dates of important events in theater history, social and cultural history, and political history. This appendix, new to the third edition, can help students place events in theater history in a larger cultural context.

A third appendix, the Glossary of Dramatic Terms, defines concepts and terms clearly and concisely. When these terms are first introduced and defined in the text, they appear in small capital letters.

The Selected Bibliography, a fourth appendix, includes a list of reference works for the major periods of drama, the playwrights, and the plays by the five playwrights treated in depth. The cited general references, histories, biographies, critical studies, journal articles, reviews, and collections of plays are especially useful for research in drama.

While the book emphasizes the plays as texts to be read, a fifth appendix, the Selected List of Film, Video, and Audiocassette Resources, reinforces the element of performance. This list, accompanied by a list of distributors, can help instructors and students find an illuminating treatment of the plays in performance.

Acknowledgments

First, I would like to thank those who offered their advice on what to include in the first edition of this book: Jeff Glauner, Park College; Susan Smith, University of Pittsburgh; and Jordan Miller, University of Rhode Island. Second, I am grateful to those who read the introductions and commentaries in the first edition and who gave me the advantage of their knowledge and wisdom. G. Jennifer Wilson, University of California, Los Angeles; William Carroll, Boston University; Ronald Bryden, Graduate Centre for the Study of Drama, University of Toronto; Robert Dial, University of Akron; Jonnie Guerra, Mount Vernon College; and John Timpane, Lafayette College, were all unhesitating in offering suggestions and improvements.

For the second edition, experts in specific historical periods examined the introductions for accuracy and comprehensiveness. Each of the introductions was revised with their suggestions in mind. These reviewers were Michael Cadden, Princeton University; Mary Coogan, University of Colorado, Boulder; Anthony Graham-White, University of Illinois, Chicago; C. Fenno Hoffman; Robert D. Hume, Pennsylvania State University; Paul G. Reeve, University of Houston, University Park; Laurence Senelick, Tufts University; and Timothy Wiles, Indiana University, Bloomington.

I am also grateful to Keith Hull of the University of Wyoming for the warmth of his response to the book. Especially helpful in preparing the second edition were Elias Abdou, Community College of Allegheny, Pittsburgh; Robert E. Aldridge, Kirkwood Community College; Katya Amato, Portland State University; Keith Appler, University of Illinois, Urbana; Nora Bicki, University of Illinois, Champaign; Reverend Doctor Nadean Bishop, Eastern Michigan University; François Bonneville, State University of New York, Albany; Michael Boudreau, University of Illinois, Urbana; David Bratt, Winona State University; Marianne Cooley, University of Houston, University Park; Walter Creed, University of Hawaii, Manoa; Mary Beth Culp, Marymount College; Merilee Cunningham, University of Houston; Joan D'Antoni, University of Louisville; Wayne G. Deahl, Eastern Wyoming College; Charlotte Doctor, Los Angeles Pierce College; Janet Dow, Western Connecticut State University; Jerry D. Eisenhour, Eastern Illinois University; Fred M. Fetrow, United States Naval Academy; Jane E. Fisher, Canisius College; Charles Frey, University of Washington; Robert W. Funk, Eastern Illinois University; Stephen R. Grecco, Pennsylvania State University; L. W. Harrison, Santa Rosa Junior College; Dave Hartley, Central Florida

Community College; Andrew Jay Hoffman, Central Connecticut State University; Claudia L. Johnson, Marquette University; Ellen Redding Kaler, University of Kansas; Harvey Kassebaum, Cuyahoga Community College; Dorothy Louise, Franklin and Marshall College; Annette McGregor, Purdue University; Jack Mahoney, Vincennes University; James Marlow, Southeastern Massachusetts University; Christy Minadeo, Eastern Michigan University; Carol A. Moore, Louisiana State University; Roark Mulligan, University of Oregon; Eric Pederson, Butler County Community College; M. Bernice Pepke, Manatee Community College; Patrick Quade, Saint Olaf College; Carol Replogle, Loyola University, Chicago; William Reynolds, Hope College; Mark Rocha, California State University, Northridge; Matthew C. Roudane, Georgia State University; Dolores J. Sarafinski, Gannon University; Carol Scklenica, Marquette University; Rodney Simard, California State University, San Bernardino; James Stephens, Marquette University; Jeannie B. Thomas, University of Oregon; Gregory Ulmer, Kearney State College; Susan Vick, Worcester Polytechnic Institute; Linda Wells, Boston University; Keith Welsh, Webster University; Virginia West, Franklin and Marshall College; Paul Wood, Villanova University; and J. S. Wszalek, James Madison University.

For the third edition, Samuel Abel of Dartmouth College reviewed the historical material for accuracy and offered a number of very useful suggestions that I incorporated into the text. I am grateful for his help and for the response of those who offered suggestions and advice for improving the book, especially Cora Agatucci, Central Oregon Community College; Joan D'Antoni, University of Louisville; Harold J. Baxter, Trinity International University; Irene Blakely, Northland College; Cynthia Bowers, Loyola University, Chicago; Jody D. Brown, Ferrum College; Mark Browning, Johnson County Community College; William D. Buckley, Indiana University NW; William J. Campbell, SUNY College of Technology at Delhi; Heather S. Collins, Mott Community College; Ruth Contrell, New Mexico State University; Kenneth Cox, Oklahoma State University; Judith P. Cronk, Oklahoma State University; Marsha Cummins, Bronx Community College; James D. Cunningham, Florida Southern College; Tom DeSpain, Chemeketa Community College; Dexter Roger Dixon, University of Arkansas; Nancy Eddy, Indiana University—Purdue University at Indianapolis; Tom Empy, Casper College; Shawn Paul Evans, University of Tennessee at Chattanooga; Harry Feiner, Queens College; Monika Fischer, University of Oregon; James Fisher, Wabash College; Kay Forston, Phillips University; Wilma Hahn Hasse, Mitchell University; John E. Hallwas, Western Illinois University; David Henry, El Paso Community College; Kirsten F. Herdd, Eastern Michigan University; D. E. Jukes, Community College of Allegheny County; E. Kahn, Lehigh University; Jackson Kesler, Western Kentucky University; Lawrence Kinsman, New Hampshire College; Terry A. Klenk, Santa Fe Community College; Marcia K. Morrison, Genesee

Community College; Eva Patton, Fordham University; Richard Pettergill, University of Illinois at Chicago; David Pinner, Colgate University; Joseph Rice, University of Cincinnati; Deborah A. Ring, Case Western Reserve University; Hans H. Rudnick, Southern Illinois University; Samuel Schuman, University of North Carolina; William O. Scott, University of Kansas; Rita Smilkstein, North Seattle Community College; Gerald F. Snelson, Frostburg State University; N. J. Stanley, Agnes Scott College; Catherine Stevenson, University of Hartford; John S. Terhes, Chemeketa Community College; Charles Trainor, Siena College; Anita J. Turpin, Roanoke College; Joy Walsh, Butler County Community College; Gladdy White, Notre Dame College; Celeste Wiggins, Ursuline College; Salaam Yousif, California State University; and Ruth Zielke, Concordia College.

I owe a special debt of gratitude to the people at Bedford Books who worked behind the scenes to produce this book. Among the editorial assistants were Kate O'Sullivan, who helped prepare the manuscript, and Rebecca Jerman, who formatted the timelines, did editorial research, and moved the manuscript into production. The production editors, Bridget Leahy and Ann Sweeney, both moved mountains to keep this book on schedule. Stasia Zomkowski, production assistant, helped them make deadlines. The copyeditor, Mary Mitiguy, and proofreaders, Andrea Champlin, Sherri Dietrich, Anthony Perriello, and Ara Salibian, attended to the task of making sure the details were in order. The promotion people, Donna Dennison and Miranda Pinckert, worked on the cover to make the book beautiful, and Ellen Kuhl handled the brochure and direct mailing to help inform potential users of the book's existence. Laura Arcari began the revision process and helped launch the book. M. Beth Meszaros, a freelance research assistant, updated the bibliography and the audio-visual materials. She was assisted by two gifted librarians, Carol Poulliotte, Media Specialist at the Snell Library at Northeastern University, and Colleen Murphy, Media Specialist at Bentley College. Finally, I wish to thank Lyn Dohaney, who researched performance histories, found reviews, and drafted the timelines. She provided me with hundreds of pages of useful material, all of which helped make this book richer and better. I am deeply grateful for the combined efforts of this amazing crew, and for the expertise of Virginia Creeden, who cleared permissions. Special mention must go to Charles Christensen and Joan Feinberg, whose guiding hands have made this project smart, imaginative, and truly ambitious. Great publishers are rare in all times, and it is essential that their contributions to a project as immense as this be recognized. And finally I mention my alter ego and friend, Karen S. Henry, whose passion for theater matches my own and whose counsel and wisdom I rely on every step of the way. Karen has been the editor on this book since its inception. She has cared for it as one cares for something precious and personal and in this sense has matched me step for step. I am deeply in her debt.

Closer to home, I want to thank colleagues Regina Barreca, whose insights and careful critiques of drama are inspiring; Michael Meyer, with whom I have extensive discussions about drama; Brenda Murphy, whose expertise and good humor are virtually inexhaustible; and Jack Manning, whose wide-ranging knowledge of theater is a constant inspiration. Among those who helped prepare this and earlier editions, I wish to thank Kathleen Girard, Nevil Parker, Amy Page, and Jacqueline McCurry.

Contents

Appendices

The
Bedford
Introduction
to Drama

Introduction: Thinking About Drama

What Is Drama?

DRAMA is the art of representing for the pleasure of others events that happened or that we imagine happening. The primary ingredients of drama are characters, represented by players; action, described by gestures and movement; thought, implied by dialogue, words, and action; spectacle, represented by scenery, music, and costume; and, finally, audiences, who respond to this complex mixture.

When we are in the theater, we see the actors, hear the lines, are aware of the setting, and sense the theatrical community of which we are a part. Even when reading a play, we should imagine actors speaking lines and visualize a setting in which those lines are spoken. Drama is an experience in which we participate on many levels simultaneously. On one level, we may believe that what we see is really happening; on another level, we know it is only make-believe. On one level we may be amused, but on another level we realize that serious statements about our society are being made. Drama both entertains and instructs.

When Aristotle wrote about drama in the *Poetics*, a work providing one of the earliest and most influential theories of drama, he began by explaining it as the imitation of an action (MIMESIS). Those analyzing his work have interpreted this statement in several ways. One interpretation is that drama imitates life. On the surface, such an observation may seem simple, even obvious. But on reflection we begin to find complex significance in his comment. The drama of the Greeks, for example, with its intense mythic structure, its formidable speeches, and its profound actions, often seems larger than life or other than life. Yet we recognize characters saying words that we ourselves are capable of saying, doing things that we ourselves might do. The great Greek tragedies are certainly lifelike and certainly offer literary mirrors in which we can examine human nature. And the same is true of Greek comedies.

The relationship between drama and life has always been subtle and

1

complex. In some plays, such as Luigi Pirandello's *Six Characters in Search of an Author,* it is one of the central issues. We begin our reading or viewing of most plays knowing that the dramatic experience is not absolutely real in the sense that, for example, the actor playing Hamlet does not truly die or truly see a ghost or truly frighten his mother. The play imitates those imagined actions, but when done properly it is realistic enough to make us fear, if only for a moment, that they could be real.

We see significance in the actions Hamlet imitates; his actions help us live our own lives more deeply, more intensely, because they give us insight into the possibilities of life. We are all restricted to living this life as ourselves; drama is one art form that helps us realize the potential of life, for both the good and the bad. In an important sense, we can share the experience of a character such as Hamlet when he soliloquizes over the question of whether it is better to die than to live in a world filled with sin and crime.

Drama and Ritual

Such imaginative participation is only a part of what we derive from drama. In its origins, drama may have evolved from ancient Egyptian and Greek rituals, ceremonies that were performed the same way again and again and were thought to have a propitious effect on the relationship between the people and their gods.

In ancient Egypt some religious rituals evolved into repeated passion plays, such as those celebrating Isis and Osiris at the festivals of Heb-Seb in Abydos some three thousand years ago. Greek drama was first performed during yearly religious celebrations dedicated to the god Dionysus. The early Greek playwrights, such as Sophocles in *Oedipus Rex* and *Antigone,* emphasized the interaction between the will of the gods and the will of human beings, often pitting the truths of men and women against the truths of the gods.

The rebirth of drama in the Middle Ages — after the fall of Rome and the loss of classical artistic traditions — took place first in monasteries, then later in the cathedrals of Europe. It evolved from medieval religious ceremonies that helped the faithful understand more about their own moral predicament. *Everyman,* a late play in the medieval theater (it was written about 1500), concerns itself with the central issue of reward and punishment after this life because the soul is immortal.

Drama: The Illusion of Reality

From the beginning, drama has had the capacity to hold up an illusion of reality like the reflection in a mirror — we take the reality for granted while recognizing that it is nonetheless illusory. As we have seen, Aristotle described DRAMATIC ILLUSION as an imitation of an action. But unlike the reflection in a mirror, the action of most drama is not drawn from our actual experience of life, but from our potential or imagined experience. In the great Greek drama, the illusion includes the narratives of ancient myths that were thought to offer profound illumination. The interpretation of the myths by the Greek playwrights over a two-hundred-year period helped the Greek people participate in the myths, understand them, and apply their values to their daily lives.

Different ages have had different approaches to representing reality onstage. Greek actors spoke in verse and wore masks. The staging consisted of very little setting and no special costumes except for some comedies and satyr plays. Medieval drama was sometimes acted on pushwagons and carts, but the special machinery developed to suggest hellfire and the presence of devils was said to be so realistic as to be frightening. Elizabethan audiences were accustomed to actors who spoke directly to the crowds at their feet near the apron of the stage. All Elizabethan plays were done in essentially contemporary clothing, often with no more scenery than the suggestion of it in the spoken descriptions of the players. The actors recited their lines in verse, except when the author had a particular reason to use prose, for example to imply that the speaker was of low social station. Yet Elizabethans reported that their theater was much like life itself.

In Shakespeare's *A Midsummer Night's Dream,* fairies, enchantments, an ass's head on the shoulders of a man — all these are presented as illusions, and we accept them. They inform the audience — in Shakespeare's day and in modern times — not by showing us ourselves in a mirror but by demonstrating that even fantastic realities have significance for us.

Certainly *A Midsummer Night's Dream* gives us insight into the profound range of human emotions. We learn about the pains of rejection when we see Helena longing for Demetrius, who in turn longs for Hermia. We learn about jealousy and possessiveness when we see Oberon cast a spell on his wife, Titania, over a dispute concerning a changeling. And we learn, too, about the worldly ambitions of the "rude mechanicals" who themselves put on a play whose reality they fear might frighten their audience. They solve the problem by reminding their audience that it is only a play and that they need not fear that reality will spoil their pleasure.

In modern drama the dramatic illusion of reality includes not just the shape of an action, the events, and character but also the details of everyday life. In Bernard Shaw's *Major Barbara* we see Barbara in front of a Salvation Army band and we hear the music. When the action changes locale, the setting changes as well. Some contemporary playwrights make an effort to re-create a reality close to the one we live in. Some modern plays, like August Wilson's *Fences,* make a precise representation of reality a primary purpose, shaping the tone of the language to reflect the way modern people speak, re-creating contemporary reality in the setting, language, and other elements of the drama.

But describing a play as an illusion of reality in no way means that it represents the precise reality that we take for granted in our everyday experience. Rather, drama ranges widely and explores multiple realities, some of which may seem very close to our own and some of which may seem improbably removed from our everyday experience.

Seeing a Play Onstage

For an audience, drama is one of the most powerful artistic experiences. When we speak about participating in drama, we mean that as a member of the audience we become a part of the action that unfolds. This is a mysterious phenomenon.

When we see a play today, we are usually seated in a darkened theater looking at a lighted stage. In ages past, this contrast was not the norm. Greek plays took place outdoors during the morning and the afternoon; most Elizabethan plays were staged outdoors in the afternoon; in the Renaissance, some plays began to be staged indoors with ingenious systems of lighting that involved candles and reflectors. In the early nineteenth century most theaters used gaslight onstage; electricity took over in the later part of the century, and its use has grown increasingly complex: In most large theaters today computerized lighting boards have replaced Renaissance candles.

Sitting in the darkness has made our experience of seeing Greek and Elizabethan plays much different for us than it was for the original audiences. We do not worry about being seen by the "right people" or about studying the quality of the audience, as people did during the Restoration in the late seventeenth century. The darkness isolates us from all except those who sit adjacent to us. Yet we instantly respond when others in the audience laugh, when they gasp, when they shift restlessly. We recognize in those moments that we are part of a larger community drawn together by theater and that we are all involved in the dramatic experience.

Theaters and Their Effect

Different kinds of theaters make differing demands on actors and audiences. Despite its huge size, the open ARENA style theater of the early Greeks brought the audience into a special kind of intimacy with the actors. The players came very close to the first rows of seats, and the acoustics permitted even a whisper onstage to be audible in the far seats. The Greek theater also imparted a sense of formality to the occasion of drama. For one thing, its regularity and circularity was accompanied by a relatively rigid seating plan. The officials and nobility sat in special seats. Then each section of the theater was given over to specific families, with the edges of the seating area devoted to travelers and strangers to the town. One knew one's place in the Greek theater. Its regularity gave the community a sense of order.

Medieval theater also gave its audiences a sense of community, both when it used playing areas called mansions inside and outside the churches and when it used wagons wheeled about in processions in the streets or outside the city walls. That the medieval theater repeated the same cycles of plays again and again for about two hundred years, to the delight of many European communities, tells us something about the stability of those communities. Their drama was integrated with their religion, and both helped them express their sense of belonging to the church and the community.

In some medieval performances the actors came into the audience, breaking the sense of distance or the illusion of separation. It is difficult for us to know how much participation and involvement in the action the medieval audience felt. Modern audiences have responded very well to productions of medieval plays such as *The Second Shepherds' Play*, *Noah's Flood*, and *Everyman*, and we have every reason to think that medieval audiences enjoyed their dramas immensely. The guilds that performed them took pride in making their plays as exciting and involving as possible.

The Elizabethan playhouse was a wooden structure providing an enclosed space around a courtyard open to the sky. A covered stage thrust into the courtyard. As in the Greek theater, the audience was arranged somewhat by social station. Around the stage, which was about five feet off the ground, stood the groundlings, those who paid least for their entrance. Then in covered galleries in the building itself sat patrons who paid extra for a seat. The effect of the enclosed structure was of a small, contained world. Actors were in the habit of speaking directly to members of the audience, and the audience rarely kept a polite silence. It was a busy, humming theater that generated intimacy and involvement between actors and audience.

The proscenium stage of the nineteenth century — and our century as well — distances the audience from the play, providing a clear frame (the PROSCENIUM) behind which the performers act out their scenes. This detachment is especially effective for plays that demand a high degree of realism because the effect of the proscenium is to make the audience feel that it is witnessing the action as a silent observer, looking in as if through an imaginary fourth wall on a living room or other intimate space in which the action takes place. The proscenium arch gives the illusion that the actors are in a world of their own, unaware of the audience's presence.

In the twentieth century some of the virtues of the Greek arena theater, or THEATER IN THE ROUND, were rediscovered. In an effort to close the distance between audience and players, Antonin Artaud, the French actor and director, developed in the 1920s and 1930s a concept called the theater of cruelty. Using theater in the round, Artaud robbed the audience of the comfort of watching a distant stage and pressed his actors into the space of the viewers. His purpose was to force theatergoers to deal with the primary issues of the drama by stripping them of the security of darkness and anonymity. Theaters in Russia and Britain developed similar spaces in the 1930s and 1940s, and since the 1950s the

Arena Theater in Washington and the Circle in the Square in New York have continued the tradition.

Twentieth-century theater is eclectic. It uses thrust, arena, proscenium, and every other kind of stage already described. Some contemporary theater also converts nontheatrical space, such as warehouses or city streets, into space for performance.

Reading a Play

Reading a play is a different experience from seeing it enacted. For one thing, readers do not have the benefit of the interpretations made by a director, actors, and scene designers in presenting a performance. These interpretations are all critical judgments based on directors' ideas of how the play should be presented and on actors' insights into the meaning of the play.

A reading of a play produces an interpretation that remains in our heads and is not translated to the stage. The dramatic effect of the staging is lost to us unless we make a genuine effort to visualize it and to understand its contribution to the dramatic experience. For a fuller experience of the drama when reading plays, one should keep in mind the historical period and the conventions of staging that are appropriate to the period and that are specified by the playwright.

Some plays were prepared by their authors for reading as well as for staging, as evident in plays whose stage directions supply information that would be unavailable to an audience, such as the color of the characters' eyes, characters' secret motives, and other such details. Occasionally, stage directions, such as those of Bernard Shaw and Tennessee Williams, are written in a poetic prose that can be appreciated only by a reader.

It is not a certainty that seeing a play will produce an experience more "true" to the play's meaning than reading it. Every act of reading silently or speaking the lines aloud is an act of interpretation. No one can say which is the best interpretation. Each has its own merits, and the ideal is probably to read and see any play.

The Great Ages of Drama

Certain historical periods have produced great plays and great playwrights, although why some periods generate more dramatic activity than others is still a matter of conjecture for scholars examining the social, historical, and religious conditions of the times. Each of the great ages of drama has affected the way plays are written, acted, and staged in successive ages. In every age, drama borrows important elements from each earlier period.

Greek Drama

The Greeks of the fifth century B.C. are credited with the first masterful dramatic age, which lasted from the birth of Aeschylus (c. 525 B.C.) to the death of Aristophanes (c. 385 B.C.). Their theaters were supported by public funds, and the playwrights competed for prizes during the great festivals of Dionysus. Sometimes as many as ten to fifteen thousand people sat in the theaters and watched with a sense of delight and awe as the actors played out their tales.

Theater was extremely important to the Greeks as a way of interpreting their relationships with their gods and of reinforcing their sense of community. The fifth-century B.C. audience, mostly wealthy citizens, came early in the morning and spent the entire day in the theater. Drama for the Greeks was not mere escapism or entertainment, not a frill or a luxury. Connected as it was with religious festivals, it was a cultural necessity.

Sophocles' plays *Oedipus Rex* and *Antigone* are examples of the powerful tragedies that have transfixed audiences for centuries. Euripides, slightly younger than Sophocles, was also a prize-winning tragedian. His *Trojan Women, Alcestis, Medea, Bacchae,* and *Elektra [Electra]* are still performed and still exert an influence on today's drama. The same is true of Aeschylus, who was slightly older than both and whose *Agamemnon, The Libation Bearers, The Eumenides* (known collectively as the *Oresteia*), and *Prometheus Bound* have all been among the most lasting of plays.

In addition to such great tragedians, the Greeks also produced the important comedians Aristophanes and Menander (late fourth century B.C.), whose work has been plundered for plays as diverse as a Shakespeare comedy and a Broadway musical. Aristophanes' *Lysistrata,* in which the Athenian and Spartan women agree to withhold sex from their husbands until the men promise to stop making war, is a powerful social comedy. Menander produced a more subtle type of comedy that made the culture laugh at itself. Both styles of comedy are the staple of popular entertainment even today. Menander's social comedies were the basis of the comedy of manners, in which society's ways of behavior are criticized. The comedy of manners is exemplified in William Congreve's eighteenth-century *The Way of the World* and Molière's *The Misanthrope.*

Roman Drama

The Romans became aware of Greek drama in the third century B.C. and began to import Greek actors and playwrights. Because of many social and cultural differences between the societies, however, drama never took a central role in the life of the average Roman. Seneca, who is now viewed as Rome's most important tragedian, almost certainly wrote his plays to be read rather than to be seen onstage.

Roman comedy produced two great playwrights, Plautus and Terence, who helped develop the STOCK (or type) CHARACTER, such as the skinflint or the prude. Plautus was the great Roman comedian in the tradition of Menander's comedy of manners. Plautus's best-known plays are *The Braggart Warrior* and *The Twin Menaechmi;* and during the Renaissance, when all European schoolchildren read Latin, his works were favorites.

Terence's work was praised during the Middle Ages and the Renaissance as being smoother, more elegant, and more polished and refined than Plautus's. In his own age Terence was less admired by the general populace but more admired by connoisseurs of drama. His best-known plays — *The Woman of Andros, Phormio,* and *The Brothers* — are rarely performed today.

Drama took its place beside many other forms of entertainment in Roman culture — sports events, gladiator battles to the death, chariot races, the slaughter of wild beasts, and sacrifices of Christians and others to animals. The Roman public, when it did attend plays, enjoyed farces and relatively coarse humor. The audiences for Plautus and Terence, aristocratic in taste, may not have represented the cross-section of the community that was typical of Greek audiences.

Medieval Drama

After the fall of Rome and the spread of the Goths and Visigoths across southern Europe in the fifth century, Europe experienced a total breakdown of the strong central government Rome had provided. When Rome fell, Greek and Roman culture virtually disappeared. The great classical texts went largely unread until the end of the medieval period in the fourteenth and fifteenth centuries; however, expressions of culture, including art forms such as drama, did not entirely disappear. During the medieval period the church's power and influence grew extensively, and it tried to fill the gap left by the demise of the Roman Empire. The church became a focus of both religious and secular activity for people all over Europe.

After almost five centuries of relative inactivity, European drama was reborn in religious ceremonies in monasteries. It moved inside churches, then out of doors by the twelfth century, perhaps because its own demands outgrew its circumstances: Drama had become more than an adjunct of the religious ceremonies that had spawned it.

One reason that the medieval European communities regarded their drama so highly is that it expressed many of their concerns and values. The age was highly religious; in addition, the people who produced the plays were members of guilds whose personal pride was represented in their work. Their plays came to be called MYSTERY PLAYS because the trade that each guild represented was a special skill — a mystery to the average person. Of course, the pun on religious mystery was understood by most audiences.

Many of these plays told stories drawn from the Bible. The tales of Noah's Ark, Abraham and Isaac, and Samson and Delilah all had dramatic potential, and the mystery plays capitalized on that potential, as did plays on the life and crucifixion of Christ. Among mystery plays, *The Second Shepherds' Play* and *Abraham and Isaac* are still performed regularly.

Most mystery plays were gathered into groups of plays called CYCLES dramatizing incidents from the Bible, among other sources. They were usually performed outdoors, at times on movable wagons that doubled as stages. The audience either moved from wagon to wagon to see each play in a cycle, or the wagons moved among the audience.

By the fifteenth and sixteenth centuries, another form of play developed that was not associated with cycles or with the guilds. These were the MORALITY PLAYS, and their purpose was to touch on larger contemporary issues that had a moral overtone. *Everyman,* the best known of the morality plays, was performed in many nations in various languages.

Renaissance Drama

The revival of learning in the Renaissance, beginning in Italy in the fourteenth century, had considerable effect on drama because classical Greek and Roman plays were discovered and studied. In the academies in Italy, some experiments in re-creating Greek and Roman plays introduced music into drama. New theaters, such as Teatro Olympico in Vicenza (1579), were built to produce these plays; they allow us to see how the Renaissance reconceived the classical stage. Some of these experiments developed into modern opera. The late medieval traditions of the Italian theater's COMMEDIA DELL'ARTE, a stylized improvisational slapstick comedy performed by actors' guilds, began to move outside Italy into other European nations. The *commedia*'s stock characters, Harlequins and Pulcinellas, began to appear in many countries in Europe.

Elizabethan and Jacobean (named for King James I, who succeeded Elizabeth and reigned from 1603 to 1625) drama developed most fully during the fifty years from approximately 1590 to 1640. Audiences poured into the playhouses eager for plays about history and for the great tragedies of Christopher Marlowe, such as *Doctor Faustus,* and of Shakespeare, including *Macbeth, Hamlet, Othello, Julius Caesar,* and *King Lear.* But there were others as well: Middleton and Rowley's *The Changeling,* Cyril Tourneur's *Revenger's Tragedy,* and John Webster's *The White Devil* and his sensational *The Duchess of Malfi.*

The great comedies of the age came mostly from the pen of William Shakespeare: *A Midsummer Night's Dream, The Comedy of Errors, As You Like It, Much Ado About Nothing, The Taming of the Shrew,* and *Twelfth Night.* Many of these plays derived from Italian originals, usually novellas or popular poems and sometimes comedies. But Shakespeare, of course, elevated and vastly improved everything he borrowed.

Ben Jonson, a playwright who was significantly influenced by the classical writers, was also well represented on the Elizabethan stage, with *Volpone, The Alchemist, Everyman in His Humour, Bartholomew Fair,* and other durable comedies. Jonson is also important for his contributions to the MASQUE, an aristocratic entertainment that featured music, dance, and fantastic costuming.

The Elizabethan stage sometimes grew bloody, with playwrights and audiences showing a passion for tragedies that, like *Hamlet,* centered on revenge and often ended with most of the characters meeting a premature death. Elizabethan plays also show considerable variety, with many plays detailing the history of English kings and, therefore, the history of England. It was a theater of powerful effect, and contemporary diaries indicate that the audiences delighted in it. Theaters also flourished in

Spain in this period, producing Lope de Vega (1562–1635), who may have written as many as seventeen hundred plays.

Vega's immediate successor, Pedro Calderón de la Barca (1600–1681), is sometimes considered to be more polished in style, but also more stiffly aristocratic in appeal. He wrote fewer plays than Vega, but still produced an amazing body of work. He is said to have written at least one hundred eleven dramas and seventy or eighty *auto sacramentales,* the Spanish equivalent of religious morality plays designed for special religious ceremonies. Calderón is best known for *La vida es sueño, Life Is a Dream,* which is still performed today.

Theaters in Shakespeare's day were built outside city limits in seamy neighborhoods near brothels and bear-baiting pits, where chained bears were set upon by large dogs for the crowd's amusement. Happily, the theaters' business was good; the plays were constructed of remarkable language that seems to have fascinated all social classes, since all flocked to the theater by the thousands.

Late Seventeenth- and Eighteenth-Century Drama

After the Puritan reign in England from 1642 (when the theaters were closed) to 1660, during which dramatic productions were almost nonexistent, the theater was suddenly revived. In 1660 Prince Charles, sent to France by his father during the English Civil War, was invited back to be king, thus beginning what was known in England as the Restoration. It was a gay, exciting period in stark contrast to the gray Puritan era. During the period new indoor theaters modeled on those in France were built, and a new generation of actors and actresses (women took part in plays for the first time in England) came forth to participate in the dramatic revival.

Since the mid 1600s, French writers, interpreting Aristotle's description of Greek drama, had leaned toward development of a classical theater, which was supposed to observe the "unities" of time, place, and action: A play had one plot and one setting and covered the action of one day. In 1637 Pierre Corneille wrote *Le Cid,* using relatively modern Spanish history as his theme and following certain classical techniques. Jean-Baptiste Racine was Corneille's successor, and his plays became even more classical by centering on classical topics. His work includes *Andromache, Britannicus,* and, possibly his best play, *Phaedra.* Racine retired from the stage at the end of the century, but he left a powerful legacy of classicism that reached well into the eighteenth century.

Molière, an actor and producer, was the best comedian of seventeenth-century France. Among his plays, *The Misanthrope* and several others are still produced regularly in the West. Molière was classical in his way, borrowing ancient comedy's technique of using type, or stock, characters in his social satires.

Among the important playwrights of the new generation were Aphra Behn, the first professional English female writer, whose play *The Rover* was one of the most popular plays of the late seventeenth century, and

William Congreve, whose best-known play, *The Way of the World,* is often still produced. The latter is a lively comedy that aimed to chasten as well as entertain Congreve's audiences.

The eighteenth century saw the tradition of the comedy of manners continued in Richard Brinsley Sheridan's *School for Scandal* and Oliver Goldsmith's *She Stoops to Conquer.* The drama of this period focuses on social manners, and much of it is SATIRE, that is, drama that offers mild criticism of society and holds society up to comic ridicule. But underlying that ridicule is the relatively noble motive of reforming society. We can see some of that motive at work in the plays of Molière and Congreve.

During much of the eighteenth century, theater in France centered on the court and was controlled by a small coterie of snobbish people. The situation in England was not quite the same, although the audiences were snobbish and socially conscious. They went to the theater to be seen, and they often went in claques — groups of like-minded patrons who applauded or booed together to express their views. Theater was important, but attendance at it was like a material possession, something to be displayed for others to admire.

Nineteenth-Century Drama through the Turn of the Century

English playwrights alone produced more than thirty thousand plays during the nineteenth century. Most of the plays were sentimental, melodramatic, and dominated by a few very powerful actors, stars who often overwhelmed the works written for them. The audiences were quite different from those of the seventeenth and eighteenth centuries. The upwardly mobile urban middle classes and the moneyed factory and mill owners who had benefited economically from the industrial revolution demanded a drama that would entertain them.

The new audiences were not especially well educated, nor were they interested in plays that were intellectually demanding. Instead, they wanted escapist and sentimental entertainment that was easy to respond to and did not challenge their basic values. Revivals of old plays and adaptations of Shakespeare were also common in the age, with great stars like Edmund Kean, Sir Henry Irving, Edwin Forrest, Edwin Booth, and William Macready using the plays as platforms for overwhelming, and sometimes overbearing, performances. Thrillers were especially popular, as were historical plays and melodramatic plays featuring a helpless heroine.

As an antidote to such a diet, the new Realist movement in literature, marked by the achievements of French novelists Émile Zola and Gustave Flaubert, finally struck the stage in the 1870s and 1880s in plays by August Strindberg and Henrik Ibsen. Revolutionizing Western drama, these Scandinavians forced their audiences to pay attention to important issues and deeper psychological concerns than earlier audiences had done.

Strindberg's *Miss Julie,* a psychological study, challenged social complacency based on class and social differences. Ibsen's *A Doll House* was a blow struck for feminism, but it did not amuse all audiences. Some were horrified at the thought that Nora Helmer was to be taken as seriously as her husband. Such a view was heretical, but it was also thrilling for a newly awakened European conscience. Those intellectuals and writers who responded positively to Ibsen, including Bernard Shaw, acted as the new conscience and began a move that soon transformed drama. Feminism is also a theme, but perhaps less directly, of Ibsen's *Hedda Gabler,* the story of a woman whose frustration at being cast into an inferior role contributes toward a destructive — and ultimately self-destructive — impulse. Both plays are acted in a physical setting that seems to be as ordinary as a nineteenth-century sitting room, with characters as small — and yet as large — as the people who watched them.

The Russian Anton Chekhov's plays *Three Sisters, Uncle Vanya,* and *The Cherry Orchard,* written at the turn of the twentieth century, are realistic as well, but they are also patient examinations of character rather than primarily problem plays — like Ibsen's successful dramas *Ghosts* and *The Master Builder.* Chekhov is aware of social change in Russia, especially the changes that revealed a hitherto repressed class of peasants evolving into landowners and merchants. *The Cherry Orchard* is suffused with an overpowering sense of inevitability through which Chekhov depicts the conflict between the necessity for change and a nostalgia for the past.

These plays introduced a modern realism of a kind that was rare in earlier drama. Melodrama of the nineteenth century was especially satisfying to mass audiences because the good characters were very good, the bad characters were very bad, and justice was meted out at the end. But it is difficult in Chekhov to be sure who the heroes and villains are. Nothing is as clear-cut in these plays as it is in popular melodramas. Instead, Chekhov's plays are as complicated as life itself. Such difficulties of distinction have become the norm of the most important drama of the twentieth century.

Drama in the Early and Mid-Twentieth Century

The drama of the early twentieth century nurtured the seeds of nineteenth-century realism into bloom, but sometimes this drama experimented with audience expectations. John Millington Synge, for example, used the techniques of realism in *Riders to the Sea,* which might best be described as peasant tragedy. Synge contradicted the expectation of audiences that tragedy should focus on those who are elevated in social station. Maurya, the peasant mother who loses the last of her sons in the course of the play, is as tragic a figure as any in modern drama.

Eugene O'Neill's *Desire Under the Elms* is another tragedy that features the ordinary citizen rather than the noble. This play, while not a peasant tragedy, focuses on New England farmers as tragic characters. Arthur Miller's *Death of a Salesman* invokes a sense of dreadful inevitability within the world of the commercial salesman, the ordinary man. As in many other twentieth-century tragedies, the point is that the life of the ordinary man can be as tragic as Oedipus's life.

Luigi Pirandello experiments with reality in *Six Characters in Search of an Author,* a play that has a distinctly absurd quality, since it expects us to accept the notion that the characters on the stage are waiting for an author to put them into a play. Pirandello plays with our sense of illusion and of expectation and realism to such an extent that he forces us to reexamine our concepts of reality.

Bertolt Brecht's *Mother Courage,* an example of what the playwright called EPIC DRAMA, explores war from a complex series of viewpoints. On the one hand Courage is a powerful figure who has been seen as a model of endurance, but Brecht also wanted his audience to see that Courage brings on much of her own suffering by trying to profit from war. The sole act of self-sacrifice in the play comes at the end, when Kattrin beats her drum to warn villagers of the approach of a destroying army. Brecht produced the play early in World War II as a protest. Playwrights around the world responded to events such as World War I, the Communist revolution, and the Great Depression by writing plays that no longer permitted audiences to sit comfortably and securely in darkened theaters. Brecht and other playwrights instead came out to get their audiences, to make them feel and think, to make them realize their true condition.

Samuel Beckett's dramatic career began with *Waiting for Godot,* which audiences interpreted as an examination of humans' eternal vigilance for the revelation of God or of some transcendent meaning in their lives. In the play, Godot never comes, yet the characters do not give up hope. *Endgame*'s characters seem to be awaiting the end of the world: In the 1950s the shadow of nuclear extinction cast by the cold war dominated most people's imagination.

Tennessee Williams examines a physically and psychically frail young woman's withdrawal from life in *The Glass Menagerie.* The play derives from personal experience: Williams's sister was such a woman. Personal experience may also inform his *Cat on a Hot Tin Roof,* which portrays themes of homosexuality and marital sexual tension — themes that were not openly discussed in contemporary American theater except in veiled mythic terms, in the manner, for example, of O'Neill's *Desire Under the Elms.*

Nigerian playwright Wole Soyinka, who won the Nobel Prize for literature in 1986, portrays the complex intersection of a person's past and the present in his play *The Strong Breed,* set in an African village reminiscent of the Greek *polis.* Indeed, he has experimented with Greek tragic forms in *The Bacchae of Euripides,* which is also set in Africa. Soyinka's insights into the nature of culture and drama provide us with a new way of reflecting on drama's power in our lives.

Modern dramatists from the turn of the century to the Korean War explored in many different directions and developed new approaches to themes of dramatic illusion as well as to questions concerning the relationship of an audience to the stage and the players.

Contemporary Drama   As we approach the twenty-first century, the stage is vibrant. Although the commercial theaters in England and America are beset by high costs, they are producing remarkable plays. In Latin America, Germany, and France, the theater is active and exciting. Poland produced unusual experimental drama in the 1960s. The former Soviet Union, too, produced a number of plays that have been given a worldwide currency.

The hallmark of many of these plays has been experimentalism. Caryl Churchill's *Top Girls* includes a scene in which great women of the past hold a discussion as if there were no historical distinctions between them. Top Girls is an employment agency and a pun useful for a treatment of the feminist issues that concern Churchill in many of her plays.

Sam Shepard is well known as an actor in films, but he is also a contemporary playwright. His Pulitzer Prize–winning *Buried Child* appears serene and calm on the surface — especially at first — but Shepard is a master at probing beneath apparently ordinary surfaces and finding both surprises and shock in what people take for granted. The family is Shepard's true subject, and his portrait of the family, with its various psychic disfigurements, provides us with surprising insights into contemporary life.

In *'night, Mother*, Marsha Norman portrays two women whose lives are constricted, limited, and painful. Thelma, the mother, is desperately trying to keep Jessie, her daughter, from committing suicide. The structure of the play is traditional, but the material is highly controversial. The people in these modern plays have been given a bad deal and have given themselves a bad deal, and the drama compels us both to examine characters from whom we might otherwise turn away and to confront what those characters represent in our own lives.

Not all modern theater is experimental, however. August Wilson's *Fences* shows us the pain of life at the lower end of the economic ladder and in a form that is recognizably realistic and plausible. The play is set in the 1950s and focuses on Troy Maxon, a black man, and his relationship with his son and his wife. Tenement life is one subject of the play, but the most important subject is the courage it takes to keep going after tasting defeat. The entire drama develops within the bounds of conventional nineteenth-century realism.

Wilson's *The Piano Lesson* is somewhat less traditional and more experimental than his earlier work. The reference to the supernatural, and the strongly implied presence of a ghost connects the play with the tradition of "magical realism" in contemporary Latin American literature. Suzan-Lori Parks is a highly experimental playwright, generally forsaking the structure of the conventional realistic drama. Her *The Death of the Last Black Man in the Whole Entire World,* like its title, is blissfully excessive. She employs some of Brecht's techniques by structuring the play in "panels" — brief, intense scenes that connect imaginatively. Tony Kushner employs similar techniques in *Angels in America*. Its brilliantly staged scenes are filled with emotional intensity and the audience is carried on waves of imaginative speculation on America's history as well as on America's present. Anna Deavere Smith brings an interesting experimentation to a logical conclusion: She writes and performs her work, assuming the parts of multiple characters of every race and gender. Her *Twilight in Los Angeles: 1992*, an example of PERFORMANCE ART, is a form of drama becoming popular in many parts of the world. Laurie Anderson, Karen Finley, and Eric Bogosian are a few of the best-known performance artists. Experimentation is probably at the heart of the work of many playwrights, although it still does not please mainstream audiences on the scale of traditional drama.

Genres of Drama
Tragedy

Drama since the great age of the Greeks has taken several different forms. As we have seen, tragedies were one genre that pleased Greek audiences, and comedies pleased the Romans. In later ages, a blend of the comic and the tragic produced a hybrid genre: tragicomedy. In our time, unless a play is modeled on the Greek or Shakespearean tragedies, as is O'Neill's *Desire Under the Elms*, it is usually considered tragicomic rather than tragic. Our age still enjoys the kind of comedy that people laugh at, although most plays that are strictly comedy are frothy, temporarily entertaining, and not lasting.

TRAGEDY demands a specific worldview. Aristotle, in his *Poetics*, points out that the tragic hero or heroine should be noble of birth, perhaps a king like Oedipus or a princess like Antigone. This has often been interpreted to mean that the tragic hero or heroine should be more magnanimous, more daring, larger in spirit than the average person.

Modern tragedies have rediscovered tragic principles, and while Synge, O'Neill, and Miller rely on Aristotle's precepts, they have shown that in a modern society shorn of the distinctions between noble and peasant it is possible for audiences to see the greatness in all classes. This has given us a new way of orienting ourselves to the concept of fate; to HAMARTIA, the wrong act that leads people to a tragic end; and to the hero's or heroine's relationship to the social order.

Aristotle suggested that plot was the heart and soul of tragedy and that character came second. But most older tragedies take the name of the tragic hero or heroine as their title; this signifies the importance that dramatists invested in their tragic characters. Yet they also heeded Aristotle's stipulation that tragic action should have one plot rather than the double or triple plots that often characterize comedies. (Shakespeare was soundly criticized in the eighteenth century for breaking this rule in his tragedies.) And they paid attention to the concept of PERIPETEIA, which specifies that the progress of the tragic characters sometimes leads them to a reversal: They get what they want, but what they want turns out to be destructive. Aristotle especially valued a plot in which the reversal takes place simultaneously with the recognition of the truth, or the shift from ignorance to awareness, as it does in Sophocles' *Oedipus Rex*.

Playwrights in the seventeenth and eighteenth centuries in France were especially interested in following classical precepts. They were certain that Greek tragedy and Roman comedy were the epitome of excellence in drama. They interpreted Aristotle's discussion of dramatic integrity to be a set of rules governing dramatic form. These became known as the dramatic UNITIES specifying one plot, a single action that takes place in one day in a single setting. The neoclassical reinterpretation of the unities was probably much stricter than Aristotle intended.

Comedy

Two kinds of comedy developed among the ancient Greeks: OLD COMEDY, which resembles FARCE (light drama characterized by broad satirical comedy and an improbable plot) and often pokes fun at individuals with social and political power; and NEW COMEDY, which is a more refined commentary on the condition of society.

Old Comedy survives in the masterful works of Aristophanes, such as *Lysistrata,* while New Comedy hearkens back to the lost plays of Menander and resurfaces in plays such as Molière's *The Misanthrope*. Molière uses humor but mixes it with a serious level of social commentary. Modern COMEDY OF MANNERS studies and sometimes ridicules modern society as in Oscar Wilde's *The Importance of Being Earnest*.

Comedy is not always funny. Chekhov thought *The Cherry Orchard* was a comedy, while his producer, the great Konstantin Stanislavsky, who trained actors to interpret his lines and who acted in other Chekhov plays, thought it was a tragedy. The argument may have centered on the ultimate effect of the play on its audiences, but it may also have centered on the question of laughter. There are laughs in *The Cherry Orchard,* but they usually come at the expense of a character or a social group. This is true, as well, of Samuel Beckett's *Endgame*. We may laugh, but we also know that the play is at heart very serious.

Tragicomedy

Since the early seventeenth century, serious plays have been called TRAGICOMEDIES when they do not adhere strictly to the structure of tragedy, which emphasizes the nobility of the hero or heroine, fate, the wrong action of the hero or heroine, and a resolution that includes death, exile, or a similar end. Many serious plays have these qualities, but they also have some of the qualities of comedy: a commentary on society, raucous behavior that draws laughs, and a relatively happy ending. Yet their darkness is such that we can hardly feel comfortable regarding them as comedies.

Plays such as Sam Shepard's *Buried Child* and Lorraine Hansberry's *A Raisin in the Sun* can be considered tragicomedy. Indeed, the modern temperament has especially relied on the mixture of comic and tragic elements for its most serious plays. Eugene O'Neill, Tennessee Williams, Harold Pinter, Marsha Norman, and Caryl Churchill have all been masters of tragicomedy.

In contemporary drama tragicomedy takes several forms. One is the play whose seriousness is relieved by comic moments; another is a play whose comic structure absorbs a tragic moment and continues to express affirmation. Yet another is the dark comedy whose sardonic humor leaves us wondering how we can laugh at something that is ultimately frightening. This is the case with some absurdist comedies, which insist that there is no meaning in events other than the meaning we invent for ourselves. Pinter's *Betrayal* and Beckett's *Endgame* are such plays. They are funny yet sardonic, and when we laugh we do so uneasily.

Other genres of drama exist, although they are generally versions of tragedy, comedy, and tragicomedy. Improvisational theater, in which actors use no scripts and may switch roles at any moment, defies generic description. Musical comedies and operas are dramatic entertainments that have established their own genres related in some ways to the standard genres of drama.

Genre distinctions are useful primarily because they establish expectations in the minds of audiences with theatrical experience. Tragedies and comedies make different demands on an audience. According to Marsha Norman's explanation of the "rules" of drama: You have to know in a play just what is at stake. Understanding the principles that have developed over the centuries to create the genres of drama helps us know what is at stake.

Elements of Drama

All plays share some basic elements with which playwrights and producers work: plots, characters, settings, dialogue, movement, and themes. In addition, many modern plays pay close attention to lighting, costuming, and props. When we respond to a play, we observe the elements of drama in action together, and the total experience is rich, complex, and subtle. Occasionally, we respond primarily to an individual element — the theme or characterization, for instance — but that is rare. Our awareness of the elements of drama is most useful when we are thinking analytically about a play and the way it affects us.

For the sake of discussion, we will consider the way the basic elements of drama function in Lady Gregory's one-act play *The Rising of the Moon* (which follows this section). It has all the elements we expect from drama, and it is both a brief and a very successful play.

Plot

PLOT is a term for the action of a drama. Plot implies that the ACTION has a shape and form that will ultimately prove satisfying to the audience. Generally, a carefully plotted play begins with EXPOSITION, an explanation of what happened before the play began and of how the characters arrived at their present situation. The play then continues, using SUSPENSE to build tension in the audience and in the characters and to develop further the pattern of RISING ACTION. The audience wonders what is going to happen, sees the characters set in motion, and then watches as certain questions implied by the drama are answered one by one. The action achieves its greatest tension as it moves to a point of CLIMAX, when a revelation is experienced, usually by the chief characters. Once the climax has been reached, the plot continues, sometimes very briefly, in a pattern of FALLING ACTION as the drama reaches its conclusion and the characters understand their circumstances and themselves better than they did at the beginning of the play.

The function of plot is to give action a form that helps us understand elements of the drama in relation to one another. Plays can have several interrelated plots or only one. Lady Gregory's *The Rising of the Moon* has one very simple plot: A police sergeant is sent out with two policemen to make sure a political rebel does not escape from the area. The effect of the single plot is that the entire play focuses intensely on the interaction between the rebel, disguised as a ballad singer, and the sergeant. The sergeant meets the rebel, listens to him sing ballads, and then recognizes in him certain qualities they share. The audience wonders if a reward of one hundred pounds will encourage the sergeant to arrest the ballad singer or if, instead, the ballad singer's sense that his cause is just will convince the sergeant to let him go. The climax of the action occurs when the sergeant's two policemen return, as the ballad singer hides behind a barrel, and ask if the sergeant has seen any signs of the rebel. Not until that moment does the audience know for sure what the sergeant will do. When he gives his answer, the falling action begins.

Plots depend on CONFLICT between characters, and in *The Rising of the Moon* the conflict is very deep. It is built into the characters themselves, but it is also part of the institution of law that the sergeant serves and the ongoing struggle for justice that the ballad singer serves. This conflict, still evident today, was a very significant national issue in Ireland when the play was first produced in Dublin in 1907.

Lady Gregory works subtly with the conflict between the sergeant and the ballad singer, showing that although they are on completely opposite sides of the law — and of the important political issues — they are more alike than they are different. The ballad singer begins to sing the "Granuaile," a revolutionary song about England's unlawful dominance over Ireland through seven centuries; when he leaves out a line, the sergeant supplies it. In that action the sergeant reveals that, although he is paid by the English to keep law and order, his roots lie with the Irish people. By his knowledge of the revolutionary songs he reveals his sympathies.

Characterization

Lady Gregory has effectively joined CHARACTER and conflict in *The Rising of the Moon*: As the conflict is revealed, the characters of the sergeant and the ballad singer are also revealed. At first the sergeant seems eager to get the reward, and he acts bossy with Policeman X and Policeman B. And when he first meets the ballad singer he seems demanding and policemanlike. It is only when he begins to sense who the ballad singer really is that he changes and reveals a deep, sympathetic streak.

Lady Gregory, in a note to the play, said that in Ireland when the play was first produced, those who wanted Ireland to become part of England were incensed to see a policeman portrayed so as to show his sympathies with rebels. Those who wished Ireland to become a separate nation from England were equally shocked to see a policeman portrayed so sympathetically.

The sergeant and the ballad singer are both major characters in the play, but it is not clear that either is the villain or the hero. When the play begins, the sergeant seems to be the hero because he represents the law and the ballad singer appears to be the villain because he has escaped from prison. But as the action develops, those characterizations change. What replaces them is an awareness of the complications that underlie the relationship between the law and the lawbreaker in some circumstances. This is part of the point of Lady Gregory's play.

Lady Gregory has given a very detailed portrait of both main characters, although in a one-act play she does not have enough space to be absolutely thorough in developing them. Yet we get an understanding of the personal ambitions of each character, and we understand both their relationship to Ireland and their particular allegiances as individuals. They speak with each other in enough detail to show that they understand each other, and when the ballad singer hides behind the barrel at the approach of the other two policemen, he indicates that he trusts the sergeant not to reveal him.

Policeman X and Policeman B are only sketched in. Yet their presence is important. It is with them that the sergeant reveals his official personality, and it is their presence at the end that represents the most important threat to the security of the ballad singer. We know, though, little or nothing about them personally. They are characters who are functionaries, a little like Rosencrantz and Guildenstern in *Hamlet,* but without the differentiating characterizations that Shakespeare was able to give minor players in his full-length play.

The plays in this collection have some of the most remarkable characters ever created in literature. Tragedy usually demands complex characters, such as Oedipus, Antigone, Medea, Hamlet, and Willy

Loman. We come to know them through their own words, through their interaction with other characters, through their expression of feelings, through their decisions, and through their presence onstage depicted in movement and gesture.

Characters in tragicomedies are individualized and complexly portrayed, such as Madame Ranevskaya in *The Cherry Orchard*, Hedda Gabler, Miss Julie, and Nora Helmer in *A Doll House*. But just as effective in certain kinds of drama are characters drawn as types, such as Alceste, the misanthrope in Molière's play, and Everyman in medieval drama.

In many plays we see that the entire shape of the action derives from the characters, from their strengths and weaknesses. In such plays we do not feel that the action lies outside the characters and that they must live through an arbitrary sequence of events. Instead we feel that they create their own opportunities and problems.

Setting

The SETTING of a play includes many things. First, it refers to the time and place in which the action occurs. Second, it refers to the scenery, the physical elements that appear onstage to vivify the author's stage directions. In Lady Gregory's play, we have a dock with barrels to suggest the locale, and darkness to suggest night. These are important details that influence the emotional reaction of the audience.

Some plays make use of very elaborate settings, as does August Wilson's *Fences*, which is produced with a detailed tenement backyard onstage. Others make use of simple settings, such as the empty stage of Pirandello's *Six Characters in Search of an Author*.

Lady Gregory's setting derives from her inspiration for the play. She visited the quays — places where boats dock and leave with goods — as a young girl and imagined how someone might escape from the nearby prison and make his getaway "under a load of kelp" in one of the ships. The quay represents the meeting of the land and water, and it represents the getaway, the possibility of freedom. The barrel is a symbol of trade, and the sergeant and the ballad singer sit on its top and trade the words of a revolutionary song with each other.

The title of the play refers to another element of the setting: the moonlight. The night protects the ballad singer, and it permits the sergeant to bend his sworn principles a bit. The rising of the moon, as a rebel song suggests, signifies a change in society, the time when "the small shall rise up and the big shall fall down." Lady Gregory uses these elements in the play in a very effective way, interrelating them so that their significance becomes increasingly apparent as the play progresses.

Dialogue

Plays depend for their unfolding on dialogue. The DIALOGUE is the verbal exchanges between the characters. Since there is no description or commentary on the action, as there is in most novels, the dialogue must tell the whole story. Fine playwrights have developed ways of revealing character, advancing action, and introducing themes by a highly efficient use of dialogue.

Dialogue is spoken by one character to another, who then responds. But sometimes, as in Shakespeare's *Hamlet,* a character delivers a SOLIL-OQUY, in which he or she speaks onstage to him- or herself. Ordinarily, such speeches take on importance because they are thought to be especially true. Characters, when they speak to each other, may well wish to deceive, but generally when they speak to themselves, they have no reason to say anything but the truth.

In *The Rising of the Moon* Lady Gregory has written an unusual form of dialogue that reveals a regional way of speech. Lady Gregory was Anglo-Irish, but she lived in the west of Ireland and was familiar with the speech patterns that the characters in this play would have used. She has been recognized for her ability to re-create the speech of the rural Irish, and passages such as the following are meant to reveal the peculiarities of the rhythms and syntax of English as it was spoken in Ireland at the turn of the century:

SERGEANT: Is he as bad as that?
MAN: He is then.
SERGEANT: Do you tell me so?

Lady Gregory makes a considerable effort to create dialogue that is rich in local color as well as in spirit. John Millington Synge, another Irish playwright, whose dialogue in *Riders to the Sea* is also an effort to re-create the sounds and rhythms of rural Irish speech, once said: "In a good play every speech should be as fully flavored as a nut or apple, and such speeches cannot be written by anyone who works among people who have shut their lips on poetry." Lady Gregory, who produced the plays of Synge at the Abbey Theatre in Dublin, would certainly agree, as her dialogue in *The Rising of the Moon* amply shows.

Music

Lady Gregory introduces another dramatic element: music. In *The Rising of the Moon* the music is integral to the plot because it allows the ballad singer, by omitting a line of a rebel song, gradually to expose the sergeant's sympathies with the rebel cause. The sergeant is at first mindful of his duty and insists that the balladeer stop, but eventually he is captivated by the music. As the ballad singer continues, he sings a song containing the title of the play, and the audience or reader realizes that the title exposes the play's rebel sympathies.

Movement

We as readers or witnesses are energized by the movement of the characters in a play. As we read, stage directions inform us where the characters are, when they move, how they move, and perhaps even what the significance of their movement is. In modern plays the author may give many directions for the action; in earlier plays stage directions are few and often supplemented by those of a modern editor. In performance the movements that you see may well have been invented by the director, although the text of a play often requires certain actions, as in the ghost scene and final dueling scene in *Hamlet*. In some kinds of drama, such as musical comedy and Greek drama, part of the action may be danced.

Lady Gregory moves the ballad singer and the sergeant in telling ways. They move physically closer to one another as they become closer in their thinking. Their movement seems to pivot around the barrel, and in one of the most charming moments of the play, they meet each other's eyes when the ballad singer sits on the barrel and comments on the way the sergeant is pacing back and forth. They then both sit on the barrel, facing in opposite directions, and share a pipe between them, almost as a peace offering.

Theme

The theme of a play is its message, its central concerns — in short, what it is about. It is by no means a simple thing to decide what the theme of a play is, and many plays contain several rather than just a single theme. Often, the search for a theme tempts us to oversimplify and to reduce a complex play to a relatively simple catchphrase.

Sophocles' *Antigone* focuses on the conflict between human law and the law of the gods when following both sets of laws seems to be impossible. Antigone wishes to honor the gods by burying her brother, but the law of Kreon decrees that he shall have no burial, since her brother is technically a traitor to the state. Similar themes are present in other Greek plays. *Hamlet* has many themes. On a very elementary level, the main theme of *Hamlet* is revenge. This is played out in the obligation of a son to avenge the murder of a father, even when the murderer is a kinsman. Another theme centers on corruption in the state of Denmark.

Lady Gregory's play has revolution as one theme. The rising of the moon is a sign for "the rising" or revolution of the people against their English oppressors. The sergeant is an especially English emblem of oppression because the police were established by an Englishman, Robert Peele. At one point the balladeer suggests a song, "The Peeler and the Goat," but rejects it because in slang a peeler is a policeman.

Another important theme in *The Rising of the Moon* is that of unity among the Irish people. The sergeant seems to be at an opposite pole from the ballad singer when the play opens. He is posting signs announcing a reward that he could well use, since he is a family man. But as the play proceeds, the sergeant moves closer in thought to the Irish people, represented by the rebel, the ballad singer.

If concerned that readers and viewers will miss their thematic intentions, playwrights sometimes reveal these in one or two speeches. Usually, a careful reader or viewer has already divined the theme, and the speeches are intrusive. But Lady Gregory is able to introduce thematic material in certain moments of dialogue, as in this comment by the sergeant, revealing that the police are necessary to prevent a revolution:

SERGEANT: Well, we have to do our duty in the force. Haven't we the whole country depending on us to keep law and order? It's those that are down would be up and those that are up would be down, if it wasn't for us.

But the thematic material in *The Rising of the Moon* is spread evenly throughout, as is the case in most good plays.

In every play, the elements of drama will work differently, sometimes giving us the feeling that character is dominant over theme, or plot over character, or setting over both. Ordinarily, critics feel that character, plot, and theme are the most important elements of drama, while setting, dialogue, music, and movement come next. But in the best of dramas each has its importance and each balances the others. The plays in this collection strive for that harmony; most achieve it memorably.

Lady Gregory

Isabella Augusta Persse (1852–1932) was born in the west of Ireland. Her family was known as "ascendancy stock," that is, it was educated, wealthy, and Protestant living in a land that was largely uneducated, poverty-ridden, and Roman Catholic. A gulf existed between the rich ascendancy families, who lived in great houses with considerable style, partaking in lavish hunts and balls, and the impoverished Irish, who lived in one-room straw-roofed homes and worked the soil with primitive tools.

Lady Gregory took a strong interest in the Irish language, stimulated in part by a nurse who often spoke the language to her when she was a child. Her nurse was an important source of Irish folklore and a contact with the people who lived in the modest cottages around her family estate. It was extraordinary for any wealthy Protestant to pay attention to the language or the life of the poor laborers of the west of Ireland. Yet these are the very people who figure most importantly in the plays that Lady Gregory wrote in later life.

Isabella Persse met Sir William Gregory when she was on a family trip to Nice and Rome. They were actually neighbors in Ireland, but only slightly acquainted. He was also of Irish ascendancy stock and had been a governor of Ceylon. They were married the following year, when she was twenty-eight and he was sixty-three. Their marriage was apparently quite successful, and in 1881, their son, Robert Gregory, was born. They used the family home, Coole Park, as a retreat for short periods, but most of their time was spent traveling and living in London, where Sir William was a trustee of the National Gallery of Art. W. B. Yeats, Bernard Shaw, and numerous other important literary figures spent time in Coole Park and its beautiful great house in the early part of the twentieth century.

Lady Gregory led a relatively conventional life until Sir William Gregory died in 1892. According to the laws of that time, the estate passed to her son, so she anticipated a life of relatively modest circumstances. In the process of finishing Sir William's memoirs, she found herself to be a gifted writer. She used some of her spare time to learn Irish well enough to talk with the old cottagers in the hills, where she went to gather folklore and old songs. Although W. B. Yeats and others had collected volumes of Irish stories and poems, they did not know Irish well enough to authenticate what they heard. Lady Gregory published her Kiltartan tales (she had dubbed her neighborhood Kiltartan) as a way of preserving the rapidly disappearing myths and stories that were still told around the hearth as a matter of course in rural Ireland.

She was already an accomplished writer when she met W. B. Yeats in 1894. Their meeting was of immense importance for the history of drama, since they decided to forge their complementary talents and abilities to create an Irish theater. Their discussions included certain Irish neighbors, among them Edward Martyn, a Catholic whose early plays were very successful. They also talked with Dr. Douglas Hyde, a mythographer and linguist and the first president of modern Ireland. Another neighbor who took part, the flamboyant George Moore, was a well-established novelist and playwright.

The group's first plays — Yeats's *The Countess Cathleen* and Martyn's *The Heather Field* — were performed on May 8 and 9, 1899, under the auspices of the Irish Literary Theatre in Dublin at the Ancient Concert Rooms. Dedicated to producing plays by Irish playwrights on Irish themes, the Irish Literary Theatre became an immediate success. The greatest problem the founders faced was finding more plays. Lady Gregory tried her own hand and discovered herself, at age fifty, to be a playwright.

Her ear for people's speech was unusually good — good enough that she was able to give the great poet Yeats lessons in dialogue and to help him prepare his own plays for the stage. She collaborated with Yeats on *The Pot of Broth* in 1902, the year she wrote her first plays, *The Jackdaw* and *A Losing Game.* Her first produced play, *Twenty-Five,* was put on in 1903. By 1904 the group had rented the historic Abbey Theatre. Some of her plays were quite popular and were successful even in later revivals: *Spreading the News* (1904); *Kincora* and *The White Cockade* (1905); and *Hyacinth Halvey, The Doctor in Spite of Himself, The Gaol Gate,* and *The Canavans* (all 1906). In the next year, there were troubles at the Abbey over John Millington Synge's *Playboy of the Western World.* The middle-class audience resented the portrait of the Irish peasants as people who would celebrate a self-confessed father-killer, even though he had not actually done the "gallous deed." Lady Gregory faced down a rioting audience who were protesting what she felt was excellent drama.

In 1918 her son, a World War I pilot, was shot down over Italy. The years that followed were to some extent years of struggle. Lady Gregory managed the Abbey Theatre, directed its affairs, and developed new playwrights, among them Sean O'Casey. During the Irish Civil War (1920–1922), she was physically threatened, and eventually her family home, Roxborough, was burned. In 1926, after discovering that she had cancer, she made arrangements to sell Coole Park to the government with the agreement that she could remain there for life. She died in 1932, the writer of a large number of satisfying plays and the prime mover in developing one of the century's most important literary theaters.

THE RISING OF THE MOON

One of Lady Gregory's shortest but most popular plays, *The Rising of the Moon* is openly political in its themes. Lady Gregory had been writing plays only a short time, and she had been directing the Irish Literary Theatre when it became the Abbey Theatre Company and produced this play in 1907. Her interest in Irish politics developed, she said, when she was going through the papers of a distant relative of her husband. That man had been in the Castle, the offices of the English authorities given the task of ruling Ireland from Dublin. She said that the underhanded dealings revealed in those papers convinced her that Ireland should be a nation apart from England if justice were ever to be done.

In 1907 the question of union with England or separation and nationhood was on everyone's lips. Ireland was calm, and the people in Dublin were relatively prosperous and by no means readying for a fight or a revolution. Yet there had been a tradition of risings against the English dating back to the Elizabethan age and earlier. In 1907 the average Irish person believed that revolution was a thing of the past; actually, it was less than ten years in the future. Certain organizations had been developing, notably the widespread Gaelic League and the less-known Sinn Féin (We Ourselves), to promote Irish lore, language, and culture. English was the dominant language in Ireland, since it was the language of commerce, but it tended to obliterate the Irish culture. Lady Gregory's work with the Abbey Theatre, which was making one of the age's most important contributions to Irish culture, thus coincided with growing interest in the rest of Ireland in rediscovering its literary past.

The title *The Rising of the Moon* comes from a popular old rebel song that pointed to the rising of the moon as the signal for the rising of peoples against oppression. The main characters of the play represent the two opposing forces in Ireland: freedom and independence, personified by the ballad singer ("a Ragged Man"); and law and order, represented by the sergeant. The ballad singer is aligned with those who want to change the social structure of Ireland so that the people now on the bottom will be on top. The sergeant's job is to preserve the status quo and avoid such a turning of the tables.

In an important way, the sergeant and the ballad singer represent the two alternatives that face the modern Irish — now as in the past. One alternative is to accept the power of the English and be in their pay, like the sergeant; one would then be well fed and capable of supporting a family. The other alternative is to follow the revolutionary path of the ballad singer and risk prison, scorn, and impoverishment. The ballad singer is a ragged man because he has been totally reduced in circumstances by his political choices.

For Lady Gregory, this play was a serious political statement. She and W. B. Yeats — both aristocratic Protestant Irish — were sympathetic to the Irish revolutionary causes. They each wrote plays that struck a revolutionary note during this period. Neither truly expected a revolution; when the Easter Uprising of 1916 was put down with considerable loss of life and immense destruction of central Dublin, Yeats lamented that his plays may have sent some young men to their deaths.

It is possible that if either Yeats or Lady Gregory had thought there would be a revolution they would not have written such plays. They opposed violence, but it was clear to some that violence was the only means by which Ireland would be made into a separate nation.

The success of *The Rising of the Moon* lies in Lady Gregory's exceptional ear for dialogue. She captures the way people speak, and she also manages to draw the characters of the sergeant and ballad singer so as to gain our sympathies for both. In a remarkably economic fashion she dramatizes the problem of politics in Ireland, characterizing the two polarities and revealing some of the complexities that face anyone who tries to understand them.

Lady Gregory (1852–1932)
THE RISING OF THE MOON

1907

Persons

SERGEANT   POLICEMAN B
POLICEMAN X   A RAGGED MAN

Scene: *Side of a quay in a seaport town. Some posts and chains. A large barrel. Enter three policemen. Moonlight.*

(Sergeant, who is older than the others, crosses the stage to right and looks down steps. The others put down a pastepot and unroll a bundle of placards.)

POLICEMAN B: I think this would be a good place to put up a notice. (*He points to barrel.*)
POLICEMAN X: Better ask him. (*Calls to Sergeant.*) Will this be a good place for a placard?

(No answer.)

POLICEMAN B: Will we put up a notice here on the barrel?

(No answer.)

SERGEANT: There's a flight of steps here that leads to the water. This is a place that should be minded well. If he got down here, his friends might have a boat to meet him; they might send it in here from outside.
POLICEMAN B: Would the barrel be a good place to put a notice up?
SERGEANT: It might; you can put it there.

(They paste the notice up.)

SERGEANT (*reading it*): Dark hair — dark eyes, smooth face, height five feet five — there's not much to take hold of in that — It's a pity I had no chance of seeing him before he broke out of jail. They say he's a wonder, that it's he makes all the plans for the whole organization. There isn't another man in Ireland would have broken jail the way he did. He must have some friends among the jailers.

POLICEMAN B: A hundred pounds is little enough for the Government to offer for him. You may be sure any man in the force that takes him will get promotion.

SERGEANT: I'll mind this place myself. I wouldn't wonder at all if he came this way. He might come slipping along there (*points to side of quay*), and his friends might be waiting for him there (*points down steps*), and once he got away it's little chance we'd have of finding him; it's maybe under a load of kelp he'd be in a fishing boat, and not one to help a married man that wants it to the reward.

POLICEMAN X: And if we get him itself, nothing but abuse on our heads for it from the people, and maybe from our own relations.

SERGEANT: Well, we have to do our duty in the force. Haven't we the whole country depending on us to keep law and order? It's those that are down would be up and those that are up would be down, if it wasn't for us. Well, hurry on, you have plenty of other places to placard yet, and come back here then to me. You can take the lantern. Don't be too long now. It's very lonesome here with nothing but the moon.

POLICEMAN B: It's a pity we can't stop with you. The Government should have brought more police into the town, with *him* in jail, and at assize° time too. Well, good luck to your watch.

(*They go out.*)

SERGEANT (*walks up and down once or twice and looks at placard*): A hundred pounds and promotion sure. There must be a great deal of spending in a hundred pounds. It's a pity some honest man not to be better of that.

(*A Ragged Man appears at left and tries to slip past. Sergeant suddenly turns.*)

SERGEANT: Where are you going?

MAN: I'm a poor ballad-singer, your honor. I thought to sell some of these (*holds out bundle of ballads*) to the sailors.

(*He goes on.*)

SERGEANT: Stop! Didn't I tell you to stop? You can't go on there.

assize: Judicial inquest.

MAN: Oh, very well. It's a hard thing to be poor. All the world's against the poor!

SERGEANT: Who are you?

MAN: You'd be as wise as myself if I told you, but I don't mind. I'm one Jimmy Walsh, a ballad-singer.

SERGEANT: Jimmy Walsh? I don't know that name.

MAN: Ah, sure, they know it well enough in Ennis. Were you ever in Ennis, sergeant?

SERGEANT: What brought you here?

MAN: Sure, it's to the assizes I came, thinking I might make a few shillings here or there. It's in the one train with the judges I came.

SERGEANT: Well, if you came so far, you may as well go farther, for you'll walk out of this.

MAN: I will, I will; I'll just go on where I was going.

(*Goes toward steps.*)

SERGEANT: Come back from those steps; no one has leave to pass down them tonight.

MAN: I'll just sit on the top of the steps till I see will some sailor buy a ballad off me that would give me my supper. They do be late going back to the ship. It's often I saw them in Cork carried down the quay in a handcart.

SERGEANT: Move on, I tell you. I won't have anyone lingering about the quay tonight.

MAN: Well, I'll go. It's the poor have the hard life! Maybe yourself might like one, sergeant. Here's a good sheet now. (*Turns one over.*) "Content and a pipe" — that's not much. "The Peeler and the goat" — you wouldn't like that. "Johnny Hart" — that's a lovely song.

SERGEANT: Move on.

MAN: Ah, wait till you hear it. (*Sings.*)
There was a rich farmer's daughter lived near the town of Ross;
She courted a Highland soldier, his name was Johnny Hart;
Says the mother to her daughter, "I'll go distracted mad
If you marry that Highland soldier dressed up in Highland plaid."

SERGEANT: Stop that noise.

(*Man wraps up his ballads and shuffles toward the steps.*)

SERGEANT: Where are you going?

MAN: Sure you told me to be going, and I am going.

SERGEANT: Don't be a fool. I didn't tell you to go that way; I told you to go back to the town.

MAN: Back to the town, is it?

SERGEANT (*taking him by the shoulder and shoving him before him*): Here, I'll show you the way. Be off with you. What are you stopping for?

MAN (*who has been keeping his eye on the notice,*

points to it): I think I know what you're waiting for, sergeant.

SERGEANT: What's that to you?

MAN: And I know well the man you're waiting for — I know him well — I'll be going.

(*He shuffles on.*)

SERGEANT: You know him? Come back here. What sort is he?

MAN: Come back is it, sergeant? Do you want to have me killed?

SERGEANT: Why do you say that?

MAN: Never mind. I'm going. I wouldn't be in your shoes if the reward was ten times as much. (*Goes on off stage to left.*) Not if it was ten times as much.

SERGEANT (*rushing after him*): Come back here, come back. (*Drags him back.*) What sort is he? Where did you see him?

MAN: I saw him in my own place, in the County Clare. I tell you you wouldn't like to be looking at him. You'd be afraid to be in the one place with him. There isn't a weapon he doesn't know the use of, and as to strength, his muscles are as hard as that board (*slaps barrel*).

SERGEANT: Is he as bad as that?

MAN: He is then.

SERGEANT: Do you tell me so?

MAN: There was a poor man in our place, a sergeant from Ballyvaughan. — It was with a lump of stone he did it.

SERGEANT: I never heard of that.

MAN: And you wouldn't, sergeant. It's not everything that happens gets into the papers. And there was a policeman in plain clothes, too. . . . It is in Limerick he was. . . . It was after the time of the attack on the police barrack at Kilmallock. . . . Moonlight . . . just like this . . . waterside. . . . Nothing was known for certain.

SERGEANT: Do you say so? It's a terrible county to belong to.

MAN: That's so, indeed! You might be standing there, looking out that way, thinking you saw him coming up this side of the quay (*points*), and he might be coming up this other side (*points*), and he'd be on you before you knew where you were.

SERGEANT: It's a whole troop of police they ought to put here to stop a man like that.

MAN: But if you'd like me to stop with you, I could be looking down this side. I could be sitting up here on this barrel.

SERGEANT: And you know him well, too?

MAN: I'd know him a mile off, sergeant.

SERGEANT: But you wouldn't want to share the reward?

MAN: Is it a poor man like me, that has to be going the roads and singing in fairs, to have the name on him that he took a reward? But you don't want me. I'll be safer in the town.

SERGEANT: Well, you can stop.

MAN (*getting up on barrel*): All right, sergeant. I wonder, now, you're not tired out, sergeant, walking up and down the way you are.

SERGEANT: If I'm tired I'm used to it.

MAN: You might have hard work before you tonight yet. Take it easy while you can. There's plenty of room up here on the barrel, and you see farther when you're higher up.

SERGEANT: Maybe so. (*Gets up beside him on barrel, facing right. They sit back to back, looking different ways.*) You made me feel a bit queer with the way you talked.

MAN: Give me a match, sergeant (*he gives it and man lights pipe*); take a draw yourself? It'll quiet you. Wait now till I give you a light, but you needn't turn round. Don't take your eye off the quay for the life of you.

SERGEANT: Never fear, I won't. (*Lights pipe. They both smoke.*) Indeed it's a hard thing to be in the force, out at night and no thanks for it, for all the danger we're in. And it's little we get but abuse from the people, and no choice but to obey our orders, and never asked when a man is sent into danger, if you are a married man with a family.

MAN (*sings*): As through the hills I walked to view the hills and shamrock plain,
I stood awhile where nature smiles to view the rocks and streams,
On a matron fair I fixed my eyes beneath a fertile vale,
And she sang her song it was on the wrong of poor old Granuaile.

SERGEANT: Stop that; that's no song to be singing in these times.

MAN: Ah, sergeant, I was only singing to keep my heart up. It sinks when I think of him. To think of us two sitting here, and he creeping up the quay, maybe, to get to us.

SERGEANT: Are you keeping a good lookout?

MAN: I am; and for no reward too. Amn't I the foolish man? But when I saw a man in trouble, I never could help trying to get him out of it. What's that? Did something hit me?

(*Rubs his heart.*)

SERGEANT (*patting him on the shoulder*): You will get your reward in heaven.

MAN: I know that, I know that, sergeant, but life is precious.

SERGEANT: Well, you can sing if it gives you more courage.

MAN (*sings*): Her head was bare, her hands and feet with iron bands were bound,
Her pensive strain and plaintive wail mingles with the evening gale,
And the song she sang with mournful air, I am old Granuaile.
Her lips so sweet that monarchs kissed . . .

SERGEANT: That's not it. . . . "Her gown she wore was stained with gore." . . . That's it — you missed that.

MAN: You're right, sergeant, so it is; I missed it. (*Repeats line.*) But to think of a man like you knowing a song like that.

SERGEANT: There's many a thing a man might know and might not have any wish for.

MAN: Now, I daresay, sergeant, in your youth, you used to be sitting up on a wall, the way you are sitting up on this barrel now, and the other lads beside you, and you singing "Granuaile"? . . .

SERGEANT: I did then.

MAN: And the "Shan Van Vocht"? . . .

SERGEANT: I did then.

MAN: And the "Green on the Cape"?

SERGEANT: That was one of them.

MAN: And maybe the man you are watching for tonight used to be sitting on the wall, when he was young, and singing those same songs. . . . It's a queer world. . . .

SERGEANT: Whisht! . . . I think I see something coming. . . . It's only a dog.

MAN: And isn't it a queer world? . . . Maybe it's one of the boys you used to be singing with that time you will be arresting today or tomorrow, and sending into the dock. . . .

SERGEANT: That's true indeed.

MAN: And maybe one night, after you had been singing, if the other boys had told you some plan they had, some plan to free the country, you might have joined with them . . . and maybe it is you might be in trouble now.

SERGEANT: Well, who knows but I might? I had a great spirit in those days.

MAN: It's a queer world, sergeant, and it's little any mother knows when she sees her child creeping on the floor what might happen to it before it has gone through its life, or who will be who in the end.

SERGEANT: That's a queer thought now, and a true thought. Wait now till I think it out. . . . If it wasn't for the sense I have, and for my wife and family, and for me joining the force the time I did, it might be myself now would be after breaking jail and hiding in the dark, and it might be him that's hid-ing in the dark and that got out of jail would be sitting up here where I am on this barrel. . . . And it might be myself would be creeping up trying to make my escape from himself, and it might be himself would be keeping the law, and myself would be breaking it, and myself would be trying to put a bullet in his head, or to take up a lump of stone the way you said he did . . . no, that myself did. . . . Oh! (*Gasps. After a pause.*) What's that? (*Grasps man's arm.*)

MAN (*jumps off barrel and listens, looking out over water*): It's nothing, sergeant.

SERGEANT: I thought it might be a boat. I had a notion there might be friends of his coming about the quays with a boat.

MAN: Sergeant, I am thinking it was with the people you were, and not with the law you were, when you were a young man.

SERGEANT: Well, if I was foolish then, that time's gone.

MAN: Maybe, sergeant, it comes into your head sometimes, in spite of your belt and your tunic, that it might have been as well for you to have followed Granuaile.

SERGEANT: It's no business of yours what I think.

MAN: Maybe, sergeant, you'll be on the side of the country yet.

SERGEANT (*gets off barrel*): Don't talk to me like that. I have my duties and I know them. (*Looks round.*) That was a boat; I hear the oars.

(*Goes to the steps and looks down.*)

MAN (*sings*): O, then, tell me, Shawn O'Farrell,
Where the gathering is to be.
In the old spot by the river
Right well known to you and me!

SERGEANT: Stop that! Stop that, I tell you!

MAN (*sings louder*): One word more, for signal token,
Whistle up the marching tune,
With your pike upon your shoulder,
At the Rising of the Moon.

SERGEANT: If you don't stop that, I'll arrest you.

(*A whistle from below answers, repeating the air.*)

SERGEANT: That's a signal. (*Stands between him and steps.*) You must not pass this way. . . . Step farther back. . . . Who are you? You are no ballad-singer.

MAN: You needn't ask who I am; that placard will tell you. (*Points to placard.*)

SERGEANT: You are the man I am looking for.

MAN (*takes off hat and wig. Sergeant seizes them*): I am. There's a hundred pounds on my head. There is a friend of mine below in a boat. He knows a safe place to bring me to.

SERGEANT (*looking still at hat and wig*): It's a pity! It's a pity. You deceived me. You deceived me well.

MAN: I am a friend of Granuaile. There is a hundred pounds on my head.

SERGEANT: It's a pity, it's a pity!

MAN: Will you let me pass, or must I make you let me?

SERGEANT: I am in the force. I will not let you pass.

MAN: I thought to do it with my tongue. (*Puts hand in breast.*) What is that?

VOICE OF POLICEMAN X (*outside*): Here, this is where we left him.

SERGEANT: It's my comrades coming.

MAN: You won't betray me . . . the friend of Granuaile. (*Slips behind barrel.*)

VOICE OF POLICEMAN B: That was the last of the placards.

POLICEMAN X (*as they come in*): If he makes his escape it won't be unknown he'll make it.

(*Sergeant puts hat and wig behind his back.*)

POLICEMAN B: Did anyone come this way?

SERGEANT (*after a pause*): No one.

POLICEMAN B: No one at all?

SERGEANT: No one at all.

POLICEMAN B: We had no orders to go back to the station; we can stop along with you.

SERGEANT: I don't want you. There is nothing for you to do here.

POLICEMAN B: You bade us to come back here and keep watch with you.

SERGEANT: I'd sooner be alone. Would any man come this way and you making all that talk? It is better the place to be quiet.

POLICEMAN B: Well, we'll leave you the lantern anyhow.

(*Hands it to him.*)

SERGEANT: I don't want it. Bring it with you.

POLICEMAN B: You might want it. There are clouds coming up and you have the darkness of the night before you yet. I'll leave it over here on the barrel. (*Goes to barrel.*)

SERGEANT: Bring it with you, I tell you. No more talk.

POLICEMAN B: Well, I thought it might be a comfort to you. I often think when I have it in my hand and can be flashing it about into every dark corner (*doing so*) that it's the same as being beside the fire at home, and the bits of bogwood blazing up now and again.

(*Flashes it about, now on the barrel, now on Sergeant.*)

SERGEANT (*furious*): Be off the two of you, yourselves and your lantern!

(*They go out. Man comes from behind barrel. He and Sergeant stand looking at one another.*)

SERGEANT: What are you waiting for?

MAN: For my hat, of course, and my wig. You wouldn't wish me to get my death of cold?

(*Sergeant gives them.*)

MAN (*going toward steps*): Well, good night, comrade, and thank you. You did me a good turn tonight, and I'm obliged to you. Maybe I'll be able to do as much for you when the small rise up and the big fall down . . . when we all change places at the Rising (*waves his hand and disappears*) of the Moon.

SERGEANT (*turning his back to audience and reading placard*): A hundred pounds reward! A hundred pounds! (*Turns toward audience.*) I wonder, now, am I as great a fool as I think I am?

Greek Drama

Origins of Greek Drama

Because our historical knowledge of Greek drama is limited by the available contemporary commentaries and by partial archaeological remains — in the form of ruined theaters — we do not know when Greek theater began or what its original impulses were. Our best information points to 534 B.C. as the beginning of the formal competitions among playwrights for coveted prizes that continued to be awarded for several centuries. Thespis, credited as the first tragedy writer, seems to have changed the nature of the form by stepping out of the chorus and taking a solo part. But the origin of *tragedy*, which translates in Greek as "goat-song" or "song for the sacrificial goat," is obscure. One theory is that tragedy may have developed from the rites of rural cults that sacrificed a she-goat at some Dionysian festivals or from masked animal dances at certain cult celebrations.

One source that may well have influenced the Greeks was the Egyptian civilization of the first millennium B.C. Egyptian culture was fully formed, brilliant, and complex. And while Egyptologists do not credit it with having a formal theater, certain ceremonies, repeated annually at major festivals, seem to have counterparts in later Greek rituals and drama. The most important and most impressive Egyptian ritual, described by some scholars as a passion play, concerned the dramatic story of Isis and Osiris and the treachery of Osiris's brother Set.

The closest Greek counterpart to Osiris was DIONYSUS, who inspired orgiastic celebrations that found their way into early Greek drama. Dionysus was an agricultural deity, the Greek god of wine and the symbol of life-giving power. In several myths he, like Osiris, was ritually killed and dismembered and his parts scattered through the land. These myths paralleled the agricultural cycle of death and disintegration during the winter, followed by cultivation and rebirth in the spring, and reinforced the Greeks' understanding of the meaning of birth, life, and death.

Drama developed in ancient Greece in close connection with the Dionysia, religious celebrations dedicated to Dionysus. Four Dionysiac celebrations were held each winter in Athens beginning at the grape harvest and culminating during the first wine tastings: the Rural Dionysia in December, the Lenaia in January, the Anthesteria in February, and the City Dionysia in March. Except for the Anthesteria, the festivals featured drama contests among playwrights, and some of the works performed in those competitions have endured through the centuries. Theories that connect the origins of drama with religion hypothesize that one function of the religious festivals within which the drama competitions took place was the ritual attempt to guarantee fertility and the growth of the crops, upon which the society depended.

The CITY DIONYSIA, the most lavish of the festivals, lasted from five to seven days. It was open to non-Athenians and therefore offered Athenians the opportunity to show off their wealth, their glorious history, and their heroes, who were often honored in parades the day before the plays began. There is some question about what was presented on each day. Two days were probably taken up with dithyrambic contests among the ten tribes of Athens. Generally each tribe presented two choruses — one of men and one of boys — each singing a narrative lyric called a DITHYRAMB. A prize was awarded the best performers. Three days were devoted to contests among tragedians, most of whom worked for half the year on three tragedies and a SATYR PLAY, an erotic piece of comic relief that ended the day's performance. A tragedian's three plays sometimes shared related themes or myths, but often they did not. The tragedians wrote the plays, trained and rehearsed the actors, composed music, and created setting, dances, costumes, and masks. After 486 B.C. the first comedy competition was held, when five, then later three comedies were also presented during the festival. The performances were paid for by wealthy Athenians as part of their civic duty. The great Greek plays thus were not commercial enterprises, but an important part of civic and religious festivals.

Judges chosen by lottery awarded prizes, usually basing their decisions on the merits of the dramas. First prize went to the tragedian whose four plays were most powerful and most beautifully conceived.

The Greek Stage

At the center of the Greek theater was the ORCHESTRA, where the chorus sang and danced (*orches* is derived from the Greek for "dancing place"). The audience, sometimes numbering fifteen thousand, sat in rising rows on three sides of the orchestra. The steep sides of a hill formed a natural amphitheater for Greek audiences. Eventually, on the rim of the orchestra, an oblong building called the SKENE, or scene house, developed as a space for the actors and a background for the action. The term PROSKENION was sometimes used to refer to a raised stage added in later times in front of the *skene* where the actors performed. The theater at Epidaurus (Figure 1) was a model for the Greek theater plan.

Figure 1. Theater at Epidaurus

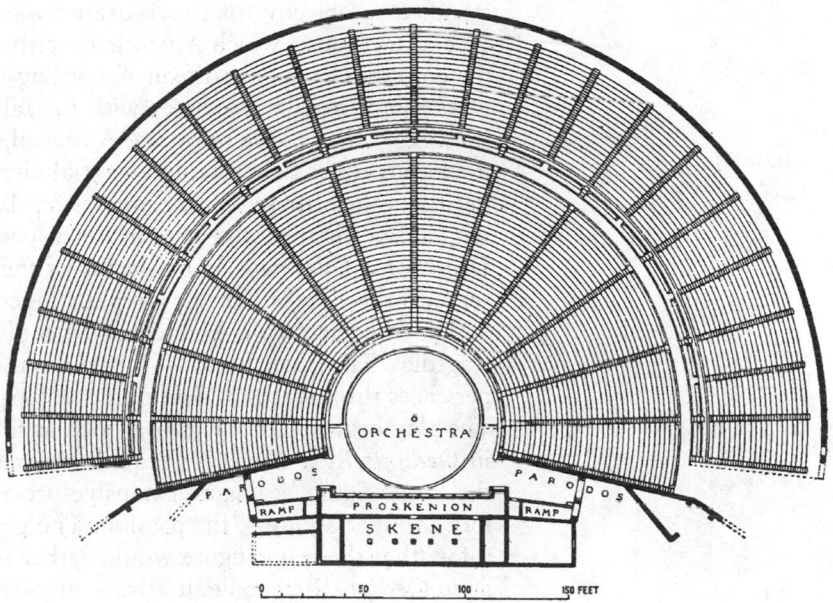

Greek theaters were widely dispersed from Greece to present-day Turkey, to Sicily, and even to southern France. Wherever the Greeks developed new colonies and city-states, they built theaters. In many of the surviving theaters the acoustics are so fine that a human voice onstage can be heard from any seat in the theater.

Perhaps the most spectacular theatrical device used by the Greek playwrights, the MEKANE ("machine"), was implemented onstage by means of elaborate booms or derricks. Actors were lowered onto the stage to enact the roles of Olympian gods intervening in the affairs of humans. Some commentators, such as Aristotle (384–322 B.C.), felt that the *mekane* should be used only if the intercession of deities was in keeping with the character of the play. The last of the great Greek tragedians, Euripides (c. 485–c. 406 B.C.), used the device in almost half of his tragedies. In *Medea* Euripides uses the *mekane* to lift Medea to the roof of the *skene* and into her dragon chariot as a means of resolving the play's conflict. At the end of the play Medea is beyond her persecutors' reach and is headed for safety in another country. Modern dramatists use a version of this, called *deus ex machina,* literally, "the god from the machine," when they rescue characters at the last moment by improbable accidents or strokes of luck. Usually, these are unsatisfying means of solving dramatic problems.

Genres of Greek Drama
Tragedy

Greek tragedy focused on a person of noble birth who in some cases had risen to a great height and then fell precipitately. Tragedies showed humans at the mercy of MOIRA, their fate, which they only partly understood. One objective of Greek drama was to have the audience experience a CATHARSIS, which Aristotle describes as a purging or purifying of the emotions of pity and fear. According to the Greeks, these are emotions that a person associates with the fall of someone in a high social station, such as a king or queen. A central character, or PROTAGONIST, of noble birth was therefore an essential element for the playwright striving to evoke catharsis in an audience. Twentieth-century experiments with tragic figures who are ordinary people, such as Arthur Miller's *Death of a Salesman,* as masterful as they are, would not have made sense to the Greeks. For the Greeks, tragedy could befall only the great.

The modern critic Kenneth Burke identified a pattern for Greek tragedies. The tragic figure — for whom the play is usually named — experiences three stages of development: purpose, passion, and perception. The play begins with a purpose, such as finding the source of the plague in *Oedipus Rex.* Then, as the path becomes tangled and events unfold, the tragic figure begins an extensive process of soul-searching and suffers an inner agony — the passion. The perception of the truth involves a fate that the tragic figure would rather not face. It might be death or, as in *Oedipus Rex,* exile. It always involves separation from the human community. For the Greeks, that was the greatest punishment.

According to Aristotle, the tragic hero's perception of the truth was the most intense moment in the drama. He called it ANAGNORISIS, or recognition. When it came at the same moment that the tragic figure's fortunes reversed — the PERIPETEIA — Aristotle felt that the tragedy was most fulfilling for the audience. This is the case in *Oedipus Rex.* Aristotle's comments in his *Poetics* on the structure and effect of *Oedipus Rex* remain the most significant critical observations made by a contemporary on Greek theater. (See the excerpt from the *Poetics* on page 160.)

The Structure of Greek Tragedies. The earliest tragedies seem to have developed from the emotional, intense dithyrambs sung by Athenian choruses. The CHORUS in most tragedies numbered twelve or fifteen men. They usually represented the citizenry in the drama. They dressed simply, and their song was sometimes sung in unison, sometimes delivered by the chorus leader. Originally, there were no actors separate from the chorus.

According to legend, Thespis (sixth century B.C.) was the first actor — the first to step from the chorus to act in dialogue with it — thus creating the AGON, or dramatic confrontation. He won the first prize for tragedy in 532 B.C. As the only actor, he took several parts, wearing MASKS to distinguish the different characters. One actor was the norm in tragedies until Aeschylus (525–456 B.C.), the first important Greek tragedian whose work survives, introduced a second actor, and then Sophocles (c. 496–c. 406 B.C.) added a third. (Only comedy used more: four actors.)

Like the actors, the members of the chorus wore masks. At first the masks were simple, but they became more ornate, often trimmed with hair and decorated with details that established the gender, age, or station of each character. The chorus and all the actors were male.

Eventually the structure of the plays became elaborated into a series of alternations between the characters' dialogue and the choral odes, with each speaking part developing the action or responding to it. Often crucial information furthering the action came from the mouth of a messenger, as in *Oedipus Rex*. The tragedies were structured in three parts: The PROLOGUE established the conflict; the episodes or agons developed the dramatic relationships between characters; and the EXODOS concluded the action. Between these sections the chorus performed different songs: PARODOS while moving onto the stage and STASIMA while standing still. In some plays the chorus sang choral ODES called the STROPHE as it moved from right to left. It sang the ANTISTROPHE while moving back to the right. The actors' episodes consisted of dialogue with each other and with the chorus. The scholar Bernhard Zimmerman has plotted the structure of *Oedipus Rex* in this fashion:

Prologue: Dialogue with Oedipus, the Priests, and Kreon establishing that the plague afflicting Thebes will cease when Laios's murderer is found.

Parodos: The opening hymn of the Chorus appealing to the gods.

First Episode: Oedipus seeks the murderer; Teiresias says it is Oedipus.

First Stasimon: The Chorus supports Oedipus, disbelieving Teiresias.

Second Episode: Oedipus accuses Kreon of being in league with Teiresias and the real murderer. Iokaste pleads for Kreon and tells the oracle of Oedipus's birth and of the death of Laios at the fork of a road. Oedipus sends for the eyewitness of the murder.

Second Stasimon: The Chorus, in a song, grows agitated for Oedipus.

Third Episode: The messenger from Oedipus's "hometown" tells him that his adoptive father has died and is not his real father. Iokaste guesses the truth and Oedipus becomes deeply worried.

Third Stasimon: The Chorus delivers a reassuring, hopeful song.

Fourth Episode: Oedipus, the Shepherd, and the Messenger confront the facts and Oedipus experiences the turning point of the play: He realizes he is the murderer he seeks.

Fourth Stasimon: The Chorus sings of the illusion of human happiness.

Exodos: Iokaste kills herself; Oedipus puts out his eyes; the Chorus and Kreon try to decide the best future action.

As this brief structural outline of *Oedipus Rex* demonstrates, the chorus assumed an important part in the tragedies. In Aeschylus's *Aga-*

memnon it represents the elders of the community. In Sophocles' *Oedipus Rex* it is a group of concerned citizens who give Oedipus advice and make demands on him. In *Antigone* the chorus consists of men loyal to the state. In Euripides' *Medea* the chorus is a group of the important women of Corinth.

Satyr Plays

The drama competitions held regularly from 534 B.C. consisted usually of the work of three playwrights who each produced three tragedies and one satyr play, a form of comic relief. In a satyr play, the chorus dressed as satyrs, comic half-beast, half-man figures who cavorted with a PHALLUS, a mock penis, and engaged in riotous, almost slapstick antics. The characters were not psychologically developed, as they were in tragedy; the situations were not socially instructive, as they were in comedy. Rough-hewn and lighthearted, the satyr plays may have been a necessary antidote to the intensity of the tragedies.

Only one satyr play survives, perhaps an indication that the form was not as highly valued as tragedy. In Euripides' *Cyclops,* based on Odysseus's confrontation with the one-eyed giant who dined on a number of his men, Odysseus outwits the giant with the aid of a well-filled wineskin. The powers of Bacchus (Dionysus) are often alluded to, and drunkenness is a prime ingredient. The play is witty, entertaining, and brief. It might well have been the perfect way to end an otherwise serious drama festival.

Comedy

No coherent Greek theories on comedy have come down to us. (Aristotle is said to have written a lost treatise on comedy.) In the *Poetics,* Aristotle points out that comedy shows people from a lower social order than the nobility, who are the main figures in tragedy.

The two greatest Greek comic writers were Aristophanes (c. 448–c. 385 B.C.), whose *Lysistrata* appears in this collection, and Menander (c. 342–c. 291 B.C.). The first was a master of OLD COMEDY (which lasted from c. 486 to c. 400 B.C.), in which individuals — sometimes well known to the audience — could be attacked personally. The nature of the humor was often ribald, coarse, and brassy, but, according to Aristotle, it was not vicious. Physical devices onstage, such as the erect phalluses beneath the men's garments in *Lysistrata,* accompanied ribald lines, and Athenian audiences were mightily entertained. Comedy appears to have provided release, but for entirely different emotions than those evoked by tragedy.

The Old Comedy of Aristophanes concentrated on buffoonery and farce. The NEW COMEDY of Menander and others whose work is now lost provided a less ribald humor that centered on the shortcomings of the middle classes. Although Menander enjoyed a great reputation in his own time and was highly regarded by Roman playwrights much later, very little of his work has survived. He is said to have written a few more than one hundred plays, but only one, *The Grouch,* survives intact. Twenty-three of his plays existed in a manuscript in Constantinople in the sixteenth century, but nothing of that volume seems to have survived. We know a number of titles, such as *The Lady from Andros, The Flatterer,* and *The Suspicious Man.* And we know that the Romans pilfered liberally from his plays. Beyond that we know little.

Menander's New Comedy concentrated on social manners. Instead of attacking individuals, as Aristophanes frequently did, Menander was more likely to attack a vice, such as vanity, or to portray the foibles of a social class. He aimed at his own middle class and established the pattern of parents or guardians struggling, usually over the issue of marriage, against the wishes of their children. The children ordinarily foil their parents' wishes, frequently with the help of an acerbic slave who provides the comedy with most of its humor. This pattern has proved so durable that it is used virtually every day in modern situation comedies on television.

Both Old and New Comedy have influenced theater from the time of the Greeks to the present. The nineteenth-century comedy of Oscar Wilde (in this collection) is an example of New Comedy, while the Marx Brothers' movies are examples of Old Comedy.

The Great Age of Greek Drama

The fifth century B.C. was not only the great creative age of Athenian theater but also the age of Athenian power in Greek politics. By the beginning of the century, Greece dominated trade in the Mediterranean and therefore in many of the major civilized urban centers of the world. The most important threat to Greek power came from the Persians, living to the east. After the Persians attacked in 490, Greek city-states such as Athens formed the Delian League to defend themselves, pouring their funds into the treasury at Delos. When the Persians threatened again in 483 B.C., Themistocles (525?–460? B.C.), Athenian soldier and statesman, realized he could not win a battle on land. By skillful political moves he managed to create a powerful navy. When the Persians attacked Athens in 480 B.C., Themistocles left a small rear guard to defend the Akropolis, the city's religious fortress. The Persians took the fortress, burned everything, and were lured by a clever ruse to Salamis, where they thought that a puny Athenian navy was making a getaway. Once the Persians set sail for Salamis, Themistocles turned on them and revealed a powerful fighting force that defeated the Persians once and for all.

In the years immediately following, Athens overstated its role in the Persian defeat and assumed an air of imperial importance. It appropriated the gold in the Delian League treasury, using it to rebuild the Akropolis beginning in 448 B.C. The great Greek general and leader Pericles (495?–429? B.C.) chose his friend Phidias to supervise the construction of the Parthenon and the other main buildings that are on the Akropolis even today. The threat of Athenian domination seems to have triggered the Peloponnesian Wars (432–406 B.C.), which pitted the Spartan alliance against the Athenian alliance. Athens eventually lost the war and its democratic government.

The events of these years, dominated by interminable wars, threats of a return to tyranny, and cultural instability, are coterminous with the great flourishing of Greek art, drama, and philosophy. The geniuses of Greek drama cluster in the period dating from the birth of Aeschylus (c. 525 B.C.) to the death of the philosopher Socrates (399 B.C.). Aeschylus wrote *The Persians* (472 B.C.); *Seven Against Thebes* (467 B.C.); and the *Oresteia* (458 B.C.), a trilogy centering on Orestes and consisting of *Agamemnon, The Libation Bearers,* and *The Eumenides. The Suppliants* and *Prometheus Bound* are of uncertain dates.

Aeschylus's introduction of a second actor made it possible to intensify the dramatic value of each *agon,* the confrontation between ANTAGONISTS. He is also notable for giving minor characters, such as the watchman who opens *Agamemnon,* both dimension and depth. Aeschylus's *Oresteia,* the only surviving trilogy, tells of the death of Agamemnon and the efforts of his son Orestes to avenge that death.

Sophocles (c. 496–c. 406 B.C.) and Euripides (c. 485–406 B.C.) learned from Aeschylus and from each other since they were all sometimes rivals. In addition to *Oedipus Rex* (c. 429 B.C.), Sophocles is known today for *Ajax* (c. 442 B.C.), *Philoctetes* (c. 409 B.C.), *Oedipus at Colonus* (406 B.C.), and *Electra* (date uncertain).

Euripides, the last of the great tragedians, may have written as many as ninety-two plays. Of the nineteen that survive, the best known are *Alcestis* (438 B.C.), *Medea* (431 B.C.), *Electra* (date uncertain), *The Trojan Women* (415 B.C.), and *The Bacchae* (produced in 405 B.C.). He is especially noteworthy for his portrayal of women and for his experimental approach to theater.

These three tragedians, along with Aristophanes, provide us with insight into the Greek dramatic imagination. They also reveal something of our common humanity, since their achievement — lost though it was for many centuries — shapes our current dramatic practice. The Greeks give us not only the beginnings of drama but the basis of drama. We build on it today whenever a play is written, whenever we witness a play.

Aeschylus

Very little is known for certain about the life of Aeschylus (c. 525–456 B.C.) despite a first attempt at a biographical sketch in 300 B.C. What is known is that he was born in Eleusis near Athens at a time that marked Athens's beginning as an important power in Greece and as the cradle of Western art and thought. When Aeschylus was born, Athens was under the control of tyrants, a control that ended in 510–508 B.C.; when he died, Athens was a democracy and one of the strongest states in the Greek confederation. The great threat to Athens's security came from the Persians, powerful Eastern warriors whose aim was the destruction of Greek economic power. Of the three great playwrights who lived in these times, Aeschylus is the only one who actually went to war against the Persians.

The records reveal that in 490 B.C. Aeschylus fought at the battle of Marathon, in which his brother was killed. The Persians were defeated at Marathon, and their king, Darius, died shortly thereafter. For ten years the Athenians enjoyed an uneasy peace, but in 480 B.C. the Persians returned under King Xerxes with a powerful fleet and army. Aeschylus fought at Salamis and probably also at a later victory in Plataea.

He seems to have been writing tragedies for fifteen years before his first victory in the drama competitions. He began competing in 499–496 B.C.; he won his first victory in 484 B.C. Aeschylus went on to win a total of thirteen competitions with thirteen tetralogies: groups of three tragedies and a satyr play. He may have written as many as ninety plays; the titles of eighty-three have come down to us, with seven plays and many fragments surviving. The *Oresteia* is the only surviving trilogy of Greek tragedies that we know were produced together. Sophocles' Oedipus plays were, by contrast, composed over a long period of time and never performed as a trilogy until recent times.

Many efforts have been made to connect Aeschylus's plays to his life and times, but on the whole such efforts have been unprofitable. Clearly, though, he wrote some plays that spoke to the times, such as *The Persians* (472 B.C.), undoubtedly inspired by Athenian success in the Persian wars. He also wrote plays associated with specific places, as in *The Women of Aetna,* produced in Sicily near Mount Aetna. *The Persians* won first prize and its expenses were paid for by Athens's ruler, Pericles, who, after the battle of Salamis, rebuilt the Acropolis with the Parthenon and the other important buildings, such as the Erectheum, that still stand there.

Aeschylus is sometimes credited with a rough and powerful style expressed in a language that sometimes forced him to make up new words. The power of his language is always remarked upon by those who know his Greek original, and his translators have often been poets in their own right. By contrast, the younger Sophocles uses a language that is smoother, more lyrical, and more graceful. Some critics have asserted that the younger playwrights profited from Aeschylus's development of tragic style.

Aeschylus died at age sixty-eight in Gela, Sicily, where he spent time at the request of a friendly tyrant, Hieron. The story surrounding Aeschylus's death has been told many times and is probably only legend. It was said that an eagle grasping a tortoise flew high into the air and accidentally dropped the tortoise on Aeschylus's head, killing him. His death came at the height of the development of Greek tragedy.

THE ORESTEIA

The *Oresteia*, the only extant trilogy of Greek tragedies, was performed in 458 B.C., winning first prize in the competition. As its name implies, it concerns the fate of Orestes, son of Agamemnon, even though Orestes is not present during the first of the three plays, *Agamemnon*. He does not enter until *The Libation Bearers* but becomes the center of the action in the third play, *The Eumenides*. As many commentators have observed, the three plays are in essence three acts of one larger play.

Lying behind the action of the three plays is a memory of the horror that has befallen the House of Atreus, the family to which Agamemnon and Aegisthus and Orestes belong. Centuries before Aeschylus, Homer had told part of the story, which was a myth of significant proportions by the time Aeschylus dramatized it. It is recounted by Aegisthus near the end of *Agamemnon* (lines 1731–1766), although he omits at least one important detail. Pelops, son of Tantalus, had two sons: Atreus and Thyestes. The legend has several forms, but in essence Atreus and Thyestes have a falling out over the throne of their father. In addition Atreus suspects that Thyestes has slept with his wife. With Atreus in control of the kingdom, Thyestes is invited to return for a reconciliation, but Atreus plans a fearful revenge. Pretending to prepare a feast of slaughtered animals, Atreus serves Thyestes his own two children chopped into a stew. Once he has eaten, Thyestes is shown the heads, hands, and feet of his children and vomits. He then flees into exile with his remaining infant son, Aegisthus.

Atreus's sons were Menelaus, who led the Greeks to Troy to regain his errant wife, Helen; and Agamemnon, who returned victorious from Troy. Agamemnon's children were Iphigenia, Electra, who figures in *The Libation Bearers;* and Orestes. The *Oresteia*, then, works out the curse on the house of Atreus.

The *Oresteia* in Performance

The first production of Aeschylus's trilogy in 458 B.C. won first prize in the drama competitions. Although tragedies were not usually revived, it seems that this trilogy was played again at Greek festivals some few years after Aeschylus's death in 456 B.C. Unfortunately, after the demise of the Greek festivals, Aeschylus was not performed again until the sixteenth century. Early in the twentieth century the *Oresteia* was produced in Greek in the United States to a limited but enthusiastic audience. Harvard University produced *Agamemnon* in 1906, using all male actors, who spoke the lines in Greek. Max Reinhardt produced the trilogy in Berlin in 1915, but problems with the size of the theater and the nature of the stage resulted in an unsuccessful production. In 1968 the Minnesota Theater Company adapted the trilogy as *The House of Atreus,* directed by Tyrone Guthrie, taking it to Broadway at the Billy Rose Theater. Beginning in 1977 in New York, Andrei Serban experimented with performing parts of the trilogy in a mixture of English and Greek because, as he said, "Greek sounds have the power to catch the real emotional experience of the text." Serban produced the plays at the Vivian Beaumont Theatre in Lincoln Center, New York. The high-tech staging, with exposed metal mesh floors and walls, created powerful effects. The Royal Shakespeare Company in 1980 put together an eleven-hour sequence of plays of Aeschylus, Euripides, and Sophocles on the fall of Troy, calling it *The Greeks;* it was successful both in England and abroad. The National Theatre in London produced the *Oresteia* in 1981 to considerable acclaim. Interestingly, the reviews of that production describe *Agamemnon* as having been eclipsed in dramatic importance by *The Libation Bearers,* which "becomes the great dramatic moment of the trilogy." Combining Euripides' *Iphigenia in Aulis* with the trilogy, the French Théâtre du Soleil performed *Les Atrides* in Paris, Montreal, and New York in 1992. Ariane Mnouchkine directed and conceived the production (in French with simultaneous translation), using only five actors. Paul Nadler compared *Les Atrides* with bullfights, which "deal with killers and victims acting out their fates upon fields of honor."

AGAMEMNON

The first play in the trilogy reveals several forceful characters. Clytemnestra, the wife of Agamemnon, presents herself as a faithful, long-suffering wife waiting patiently for her husband's return from war. However, the Chorus, composed of older men, knows that she has taken a lover, Aegisthus. Clytemnestra faces up to the rumors of her infidelity when Agamemnon returns, daring anyone to contradict her. Secretly, though, she plans (with the help of Aegisthus) to kill Agamemnon. Her discovery that her husband is returning with a female slave, the prophetess Cassandra, as his concubine gives her further motivation. When she confesses to the murder of Agamemnon and Cassandra, she tells the Chorus that she is exacting revenge against Agamemnon for sacrificing their daughter Iphigenia in order to get a favorable wind to sail to Troy. Later, Aegisthus justifies his role in the killing as revenge against the crimes of Agamemnon's father, Atreus.

To ensnare Agamemnon, Clytemnestra has woven an intricate web — the image of the spider is invoked in the play. She is warned of his return by the pillars of fire that are set from Troy to Greece as Agamemnon returns, so she is prepared. She produces a richly woven purple cloth — the equivalent of what we call a red carpet — on which she expects Agamemnon to walk into the palace. Knowing that to do so could offend the gods, he at first refuses. Ultimately he yields to her entreaties and enters the palace, leaving Cassandra outside to prophesy his death — and hers — to the unbelieving Chorus. Inside, Clytemnestra continues the pattern by winding a regal cloak about Agamemnon as he is in the bath, disabling him so that she is able to stab him mortally.

Throughout, the *Oresteia* emphasizes issues of gender. Often the Chorus comments on Clytemnestra's speaking with the authority of a man. The invocation of the god Apollo throughout the trilogy has been taken to imply an important cultural shift that Aeschylus recognizes. Is he referring to a distant past in which female deities were dominant but then were replaced by masculine deities? Such speculation is impossible to verify (see Lois Spatz's commentary on p. 103), but it is clear that the women in the *Oresteia* are powerful in their presence, demanding in their actions, and insistent in their demand for justice. *Agamemnon* ends with Clytemnestra facing down an angry and mistrustful Chorus and with Aegisthus claiming the throne and governing as a tyrant.

Aeschylus *(c. 525–456 B.C.)*

AGAMEMNON   458 B.C.

TRANSLATED BY DAVID GRENE AND WENDY DONIGER O'FLAHERTY

Dramatis Personae

SENTRY
CHORUS, *old men of Argos left behind after the Argives went to Troy*
CLYTEMNESTRA, *queen of Argos in the absence of King Agamemnon at Troy*
HERALD *from the Greek army*
KING AGAMEMNON
CASSANDRA, *princess of Troy, daughter of King Priam*
AEGISTHUS

SENTRY: You gods, release me.
    Crouched like a dog, I watch always, all year long,
    on the tower of the sons of Atreus.
    I have come to know the nightly gathering of the stars
    and those radiant dynasts of the firmament that
5   lead them.
    They bring winter and summer to men.
    Now I watch for a flaming light,
    the beacon fire, the tell-tale witness that Troy is captured.
    Such are my orders, orders from a hopeful queen
10   who thinks with the mind of a man.
    I have a bed here, soaked with dew, always shifting.
    But no dreams. Fear is my visitor, not sleep.
    I cannot close my eyes for fear.
    Sometimes I whistle or hum;
15   the tunes are my drug against my sleepiness.
    But then the sorrow comes.
    This house is in bitter trouble.
    Once it was well governed; not now.
    Still, may the fire of good news light the darkness
20   to be the lucky release from our troubles.

    The beacon! Day out of night!
    The dances everywhere in Argos!
    Thanks, good beacon!
    My lady, Agamemnon's wife, get out of bed!
25   Cry aloud a blessing on this beacon,
    since Troy is surely captured.
    I will myself begin the dance, for I'll score to myself, too,

the winning dice that the beacon threw for my master.
Oh, that I could touch with this hand of mine
the hand that I love, my lord's.   30
As for the rest, I haven't a word;
a great ox stands on my tongue.
If the house itself had a voice to speak,
it would tell the clearest story.
I choose to speak to those who understand;   35
for the others, I am all forgetfulness.
CHORUS: This is the tenth year
since they launched from this land
the Greek fleet of a thousand ships
to help right wrongs done.   40
They launched it, King Menelaus,
great plaintiff against Priam,
and Agamemnon his brother;
twin the yoke joining them in honor and throne,
twin their shared grace of God.   45

From their hearts the great war cry;
they screamed like eagles,
that wheel and wheel high above their eyries,
driven by the oarage of their wings,
in lonely agony for the loss of their nestlings,   50
and all the watchful care they had spent guarding them.

But One yet higher up, some Apollo or Pan or Zeus,°
hears the shrill-voiced sorrow of these settlers in his kingdom
and sends on the evildoers
the Fury that brings punishment, however late.   55
So a Lord greater than the kings, Zeus god of guest-friends,
sends the sons of Atreus on Alexander;°

---

52. Apollo or Pan or Zeus: Greek gods with the power to avenge crimes.   **57. Alexander:** Also known as Paris, Alexander was the son of King Priam and Queen Hecuba of Troy. He carried off Helen, the wife of Greek commander Menelaus (Agamemnon's brother), and this action caused the Trojan war.

in this quarrel over a woman of many men,
he would lay upon Greeks and Trojans alike
60   many wrestlings where the limbs grow heavy
and the knee is pressed into the dust
and the spear is shattered in the first rites of
    engagement.
Yet it is now as it is.
Fulfillment moves toward what is fated.
And not with burnt offerings nor with pouring
65   on of wine
nor sacrifice to the gods below
will you assuage that stubborn anger.

But we, dishonored for the ancientness of our
    flesh,
were left behind then when the army went;
we remain, propping on staffs a strength like a
70   child's.
For the child's marrow, too, leaps within his
    breast
but is only the match of an old man's;
the god of war is not there either.
And the overold, the leafage already withering,
walks his three-footed way,° no stronger than a
75   child;
wanders, a dream in the daylight.

You, daughter of Tyndareus, Queen
    Clytemnestra,
What's the matter? What's the news? What have
    you heard?
What message do you trust, that you order
    sacrifices
80   at all the altars?
Of all the gods that hold our city,
of those above and those beneath the earth,
of those at the doorpost and those at the
    marketplace,
the altars blaze with offerings.
85   Here one torch sends its flames to the sky,
and another raises its light,
charmed by the soft, guileless urgings of pure
    streams of oil
drawn from the depth of the royal store.
Tell us what you can and what may be said
90   about all these things.
Cure this care that now broods darkly on our
    minds.
But then hope, shining out of the sacrifice,
turns away the insatiable thoughts that might
    otherwise
eat out the heart in sorrow.

75. three-footed way: Walking with a cane or staff.

It is mine to declare the omens of victory   95
given to princely men on the journey.
For by God's grace, old age, which grows with
    life, my life,
still breathes on my lips persuasion,
the strength of song.
I tell how the princes of the Achaeans,   100
twin-throned, single-hearted
lords of the youth of Greece,
were sent against the land of Troy
with spear in hand to exact vengeance.
The furious omen-birds° sent them,   105
one black eagle, one white-tail,
the kings of birds to the kings of the ships.
Near the palace they came on the spear-striking
    side,
perched where all could see them
as they fed on the womb's gravid load of
    leverets,°   110
mother and all, pulled down in the hare's last
    course.
Cry sorrow, sorrow, but let the good prevail.

Yet the honest prophet of the army saw
the two sons of Atreus,
twin in military spirit,   115
and knew the princely leaders and hare-
    devourers —
knew that they were one and the same.
And so he declared in his prophecy,
"In time, this journey will capture Troy, Priam's°
    city;
and all the communal herds that graze before her
    towers   120
shall Fate give violently to plunder.
I only pray that no anger from the God will cast
    a cloud
upon this army forged from before to be
a great iron bit in the mouth of Troy.
For Queen Artemis° is full of pity out of
    jealousy   125
against those winged hounds of her father
who devour in sacrifice
the unhappy cowering mother with her brood
before they come to birth.

105. omen-birds: Eagles, thought to be messengers of the
gods.   110. leverets: Young hares.   119. Priam: King of
Troy at the time of the Trojan war.   125. Artemis: Greek
goddess, who was the daughter of Zeus and sister of Apollo.
Artemis was the protector of young animals. Angered at the
slaughter of the leverets, she caused contrary winds to prevent the Greeks from sailing for Troy. Agamemnon was
forced to sacrifice his daughter Iphigeneia to appease
Artemis and secure favorable winds.

130 She hates the eagles' feast.
     Cry sorrow, sorrow, but let the good prevail.

     Yes, she is kindly, that beautiful one,
     to cubs, scarcely crawling, of savage lions,
     and she finds her delight in all the breast-loving
         infants
135 of wild things of the field.
     Yet she grants fulfillment of what the omens
         imply:
     grant, Lady, favorable fulfillment, and void the
         other.
     I call on Apollo the Healer
     to keep her from setting against the Greeks
140 those contrary winds, winds that hold ships,
     staying winds, winds that stop sailing altogether.
     She might do this in eagerness for a different
         sacrifice,
     one that is lawless and horrible,
     a trueborn craftsman of quarrels,
145 that has no awe of a husband.
     For full of terrors it lurks,
     house keeping, crafty, long-memoried,
     an anger that punishes child-slaughter."

     Such were the prophecies of Calchas's° voice,
150 mingled with the good things,
     and all predicted for our royal house
     from omens on the way.
     In harmony with these,
     cry sorrow, sorrow, but let the good prevail.

155 Zeus, whoever he is,
     if it is dear to him to be so called,
     this is how I call him.
     I have thrown all into the scale,
     but cannot find his likeness —
160 there is only Zeus,
     if I must cast my burden of vain care from the
         heart
     in honest truth.

     Not he that once was great,
     swelling with daring, challenging all comers,
165 shall even be spoken of, for he is of the past.
     And he that came after him
     has had his three falls wrestling,
     and is gone.
     But whoever sings to Zeus
170 the victory song from a full heart,
     he shall win all that his heart desires.

     Zeus it is that has made man's road;
     he it is who has laid down the rule
     that understanding comes through suffering.
     Instead of sleep, there drips before the heart   175
     the recollected sorrow of past pain.
     It is against our wills that we become wise.
     Forced indeed upon us is the grace of our gods
     that sit on their solemn thrones.

     So on that day, the old leader of the Greek ships, 180
     faulting no prophet, caught his breath at his
         sudden calamity,
     when the Greek host was burdened
     with ships halted and empty holds,
     as they held the coast over against Chalcis,°
     at Aulis° where the tides roar to and fro.   185

     The hurricane that came from Strymon,°
     breeding deadly delays, starvation, lost
         anchorages,
     driving crews to aimless wanderings,
     sparing neither ships nor cables,
     wore down the flower of the Argives,   190
     doubling their time with enforced lingering.
     So when the prophet's voice rang out,
     proclaiming to the princes another cure for the
         bitter storm,
     a cure yet heavier to bear,
     he backed his prophecies with Artemis's name,   195
     and the twin sons of Atreus beat the ground with
         their staves
     and could not hold back their tears.
     Then the old king spoke and said,
     "Heavy indeed my fate if I disobey,
     but heavy, too, if I must butcher my child,   200
     the glory of my house, polluting a father's hands
     with streams of a virgin's blood beside the altar.
     Which of these two things is without evil?
     How shall I become a deserter of my fleet and
         fail my allies?
     There is sacred law on their side, that they
         passionately covet   205
     a virgin's blood as sacrifice to quell the winds.
     May it turn out well."

     When he put on the harness of Necessity,
     his spirit veered in a breath of change —
     to impiety, to unholiness, to desecration,   210
     and from it he drew audacity for his heart

---

184. **Chalcis:** City in Asia Minor across the straits from Aulis, where the Greeks were detained by contrary winds. 185. **Aulis:** City where the Greek fleet collected before sailing to Troy.   186. **Strymon:** River in Asia Minor across from Aulis.

149. **Calchas:** A prophet who accompanied the Greek army to Troy.

to stop at nothing.
For indeed there is a wretched distraction of the
    wits,
a primal source of ruin,
215   that puts recklessness in man's mind
and counsels ugliness.
So he dared to become his daughter's sacrificer
to aid the war waged for a woman —
first rites of deliverance for the ships.
Her prayers, and her cries of "Father," and her
220   maiden life
they set at nothing, those military umpires.
Her father ordered his servants to lift her
carefully over the altar
after the prayer, swooning, her clothes all round
    her,
225   like a young goat,
and with a gag on her beautiful lips
to restrain the cry that would curse his house.
Constrained to voicelessness by the violence of
    the bit,
she slipped to the ground her saffron robes,
and with darting, pitiful eyes struck each of her
230   sacrificers.
She stood out, like a figure in a picture,
    struggling to speak,
for often she had sung in her father's hospitable
    halls,
and with pure maiden voice lovingly honored
her beloved father's victory hymn,
235   with its triple libation to bring good luck.
What happened after that I neither saw nor tell.
But Calchas's divining art bore fruit;
the scales of justice have come down and brought,
with suffering, understanding.
240   You will learn the future when it happens.
Till then, let it be.
To do otherwise is to have sorrow before you
    need.
For it will come clear with the dawn's light.

(*Enter Clytemnestra.*)

But at the end of all this let there be good
    fortune.
Surely that is the wish of this (*turning to the*
245   *queen*)
our sole and closest bulwark against trouble in
    Argos.
I have come, Queen Clytemnestra, to pay you my
    respects;
for it is right, in the absence of the prince,
to honor the wife of the man whose throne is
    empty.
250   I would be glad to know

if you are sure of good tidings or not.
Is it in the hope of happy news
that you are ordering sacrifice?
But I won't resent it if you must be silent.
CLYTEMNESTRA: As the proverb goes,   255
    "May dawn be the dawn of good news
as she comes from her mother night" —
you shall learn of a joy greater than you hope.
For the Argives have captured Priam's city.
CHORUS: What? I cannot believe you; I cannot
    understand.   260
CLYTEMNESTRA: Troy is the Greeks' city now. Are
    my words clear?
CHORUS: Joy steals over me, and calls out tears, too.
CLYTEMNESTRA: Your eyes proclaim you a subject
    true and loyal.
CHORUS: What makes you trust the news? Have you
    proof of it?
CLYTEMNESTRA: I have, of course — unless the gods
    deceived me.   265
CHORUS: Dream visions? Do you believe in them?
CLYTEMNESTRA: No sleeping mind for me, no, nor
    its fancies.
CHORUS: Have flying rumors bloated you?
CLYTEMNESTRA: As if I were a child, you taunt me.
CHORUS: But when was it that the city was sacked?   270
CLYTEMNESTRA: In this last night that brought this
    dawn to birth.
CHORUS: What messenger can be as quick as that?
CLYTEMNESTRA: The god of fire, sending his brilliant
    glow from Mount Ida.°
Beacon sent beacon here with courier fires,
Ida to the crag of Hermes in Lemnos;°   275
then from that island a third flame sent on
was welcomed by the heights of Athos that
    belong to Zeus;
and high, spanning the sea's back,
the strength of the escorting flame went joyously
    onward.
The pine fire sent its golden blaze, almost a sun, 280
to the watchtowers of Macistus.
He didn't hesitate nor carelessly succumb to
    sleep,
but passed his share of the message,
and from afar, over the streams of Euripus,
he gave to the sentries of Messapion   285
the sign that the beacon's light had traveled to him.

273–275. **Mount Ida ... Lemnos:** Mountain in Asia Minor
southeast of Troy from which the gods could view the battles. The place names that follow trace the course of beacon
fires set to bring the news of the Greek victory from Troy to
Greece.

They in their turn lit up and sent the message
        farther,
firing a great heap of ancient gorse.
Still strong, the beacon's light never flagged,
but leapt over the plain of Asopus like a radiant
290   moon,
to Mount Cithaeron, and there awakened
another relay of traveling fire.
The guard station did not refuse the far-escorted
        flame;
it kindled more than was ordered, and launched
        its light
295   over the Gorgon lake; and coming to
the goat-haunted mountain,
urged the watchman not to scant the ordinance
        of fire.
They lit a huge beard of flame that burnt
        ungrudgingly,
and sent it over the Saronic gulf, now become its
        mirror,
beyond the headland, till it struck the heights of
300   Arachnus,
our neighboring sentry post here, and then again
struck right here on this roof of the sons of
        Atreus —
this fire that is the grandchild of that fire on
        Mount Ida.
Such were the courses of the torchbearers,
305   one from the other in relays,
and victor is he that ran first and last.
Such proof I have and such confirmation,
sent me out of Troy by my man.
CHORUS: My lady, to the gods once again
310   I shall give my prayer of thanks,
but I would like you to tell me all this again,
that I might hear the words and marvel at them
from beginning to end.
CLYTEMNESTRA: Troy is captured; this is the day; the
        Greeks hold it.
315   Within that city there rings out
a volume of cries that do not mingle.
This is how I see it.
Mix oil and vinegar in the same jar
and you could not call them friends;
320   they will not be at one.
So in Troy you might hear two sorts of crying:
the conquered and the conquerors.
The act is single, the meaning double.
Here are these:
325   throwing themselves on the dead bodies
of husbands and brothers,
children on the bodies of their fathers,
all sorrowing for the destiny of their dead,
they cry from throats no longer free.
330   Then there are the others:

roving all night after the fight
sets them down hungry to breakfast
on such foods as the city has;
they all share, no rank or place assigned,
but as each has got the luck of the draw.   335
They are already living in Troy's captured houses,
free of the frost beneath the sky, free of the
        dews.
They will sleep all night long without a guard,
like happy men.
If they revere the gods of that city in that
        captured land,   340
if they revere the gods' sacred places,
they who are conquerors will not be
        reconquered.
Only let no lust seize the army first,
let no greed conquer them,
to make them ravish what they should not.   345
They must still make the home voyage safely,
travel the other leg of the double track.
But even if the army came through offenseless
in the sight of the gods,
the wrong done to the dead may yet awaken,   350
seeking to contrive some sudden mischief.
This is what you hear from me, a woman.
But may the good prevail for all to see, past
        dispute.
Of the many good things I might have,
this is what I would choose.   355
CHORUS: My lady, you talk wisely, like a sensible
        man.
I have learned from you your convincing proofs,
and now again I prepare to greet the gods.
Surely we should thank them for what they have
        done for us.
O Zeus the king, and friendly night,   360
that has endowed us with great glory,
you that have cast upon the towers of Troy
a close-fitting mesh so that no one young or old
can overleap the great net of slavery,
the all-catching trap of ruin —   365
great Zeus of guest-friends I revere.
He has done all this. He has forever bent his
        bow
against Alexander, that no bolt should fail,
neither missing the mark nor scaling the stars.
They can say, "It is the stroke of Zeus";   370
the track of it is clear to see.
Zeus has acted as he has determined.
Someone has said,
"The gods do not deign to take heed of mortals
who trample underfoot the grace of holiness."   375
But he that said that had no piety in him.
The recklessness stands revealed
of those who breathe war beyond justice.

It is a recklessness that breeds consequences
380 when houses are overcrammed
beyond the measure of the best.
So I escape harm, let but a sufficiency be mine,
with abundance of good judgment.
For wealth gives no defense
385 for the man insolent with gorging,
who kicks the great altar of justice
to where none can see it.
Wretched persuasion,
intolerable child of forecounseling ruin,
390 drives him on violently.
And all cure is vain. It is not hidden, no —
the mischief shines, a lamp of evil light.
The black grain in Paris° shows through the test,
like base copper rubbed bare with use.
395 He has been like a child that chases a bird;
he has brought on this city an intolerable
        infection,
and no one of the gods will hear his prayer —
rather, pull down the unjust man
conversant with such things.
400 Such a one is Paris, who came
to the house of the sons of Atreus
and stained with shame the table of his host
by the theft of that host's wife.
She has left to her fellow citizens
the clanging of shields, the arming of sailors,
405 ambushes.
To Ilium she has brought ruin instead of dowry.
Her daring defying all limits,
she darted quickly through the gates.
And many a groan there was
410 among those that spoke for the palace:
"Ah me, ah me, for the house, the house and the
        princes.
Ah me for the bed and the tracks of the love of
        men on it."
There one can see the silence —
dishonored, unreviling, inexorable —
415 of him that sits apart.
Through yearning for the one gone over the sea,
a ghost will seem to rule the house.
The grace of beautiful statues is hateful to the
        man.
Their eyes are empty, and before them
420 all passionate love falls dead.
Fancies haunt him in dreams persuasively;
theirs is a grace without substance.
Unsubstantial it is, when one sees,
and dreaming reaches to the touch,

and the phantom is gone, quickly slipping
        through his hands,   425
as it follows the winged paths of sleep.
Such are the sorrows at home at the hearth;
but there are worse than these for all,
for those who joined the fleet and left the land of
        Greece.
In the house of every one of these   430
preeminent there is grief that reaches the heart.
They know whom they have sent forth, but
        instead of men
there come home urns and ashes to each house.
The war god is a money changer;
men's bodies are his money.   435
He holds the scales in the battle of the spear.
From Ilium he sends back to those who loved
        them
the scrapings of dust made heavy with their
        tears;
he loads the elegant urns with the dust that was
        once a man.
They mourn this man as they praise him —   440
how skilled he was in the fight — and another —
how gallantly he fell in his blood —
for another man's woman.
That is what they whisper and snarl;
and pain creeps about, full of ill will   445
toward the plaintiffs, the sons of Atreus.
But those others keep to their graves in all their
        beauty,
where they were, around the walls of Troy.
The enemy land that they have taken at last
has taken them, hidden them in itself.   450
The malicious speech of citizens is hard to bear;
it is the equal of a public curse.
And still I am troubled, lest I come to hear
something hidden in dark night.

For watchful are the gods' eyes   455
for those that kill by the thousands.
The black Furies reduce to dim nothingness
the man whose success has no justice in it,
wear him down, reversing his life's fortune.
And when he is among those we cannot see,   460
there is no help for him.
To be too well spoken of is heavy indeed.
For the thunderbolt is hurled from the eyes of
        Zeus.
May I not be a city-sacker, nor yet look upon my
        own life,
captured by others.   465
Swift is the rumor coursing through the city,
spurred by the fire of good tidings.
But whether it is true, who knows, or whether
somehow the gods deceive us.

---

393. Paris: A prince of Troy, Paris abducted Helen of Greece,
thus defying Zeus's law of hospitality.

470 Who is there so childish, so maimed of wit,
that the messages of fire should kindle his heart
only to sicken later when the news changes?
It is like the mettle of a woman's spirit
to praise the gracious gift before it is certainly
there.
475 The limits of a woman's belief can be
as easily and quickly crossed
as cattle graze across a boundary.
But quickly, too, dies the report
a woman utters.
Soon we shall know about the lights from the
480 beacons
and all the exchange of watch fires:
whether they are true or whether, like dreams,
a light of joy has stolen upon us and cheated our
minds.
Here I see the herald coming from the shore,
485 shaded with twigs of olive.
The thirsty dust, twin sister of mud across the
boundary,
is my witness; it witnesses to me that he has a
real voice,
and so his testimony is not one of the smoky fire
of some wood on the hillside.
490 He will rather speak out and tell us to be glad,
or — God forbid it is the contrary message.
There *have* been good things that have shown
through;
grant that this is their consummation.
Whoever prays anything else for this city,
I would he might reap the fruit of his mistaken
495 thoughts.

(*Enter a herald.*)

HERALD: O my fathers' earth, Argos, Argos,
ten long years and I have come to you;
so many shipwrecked hopes, and one a winner.
I never dreamed that I would have for my share
in death
500 a piece of dearest Argive land.
Now welcome earth, welcome the light of sun,
and Zeus supreme lord; and the Pythian King,°
no longer shooting his arrows against us;
you were harsh enough along Scamander's banks,
but now you are different, now you are savior
505 and healer,
King Apollo. My greetings to all the gods in
assembly.
My greeting to my patron god, Hermes, dear
herald,
whom all heralds worship.

502. **Pythian King:** The god Apollo.

My greetings to the heroes that sent us out
and kindly welcome back what's left of us after
the fight.   510
Hail, royal halls, roofs I have loved,
hail, holy seats and you divinities that face the
sunlight.
Receive now with faces bright in joy —
if ever you did in days gone by —
now receive the king in glory after so long.   515
He comes and brings light after night's darkness,
a light to you and to all these —
King Agamemnon.
Give him true welcome; truly it belongs to him,
the king who dug down Troy with the spade of
God's justice,   520
made plowland of Troy;
and the seed has perished from all their country.
Their altars and the shrines of their gods are
gone.
Such a yoking chain has he cast on Troy,
the king, Atreus's son, the old and happy man.   525
And now he comes here, most worthy of all
that now live and die.
Neither Paris nor the city that supports him
can boast that they have done more than they
have paid for.
He was condemned for rape and theft —   530
lost what he carried off.
He has reaped for harvest
the utter ruin of his father's house.
And doubly have the sons of Priam paid for their
offenses.
CHORUS: Herald of the Argive army, joy on your
homecoming!   535
HERALD: Joy, indeed. If the gods should end my life
now,
I'd not deny them.
CHORUS: Has the love of your lost homeland
tortured you so?
HERALD: Yes; the tears you see are tears of joy.
CHORUS: That disease had its pleasure for you, all
the same.   540
HERALD: What disease? What should I understand
by that?
CHORUS: Love's stroke. But you got love for the
love you gave.
HERALD: You mean this land has missed the army
as we missed you?
CHORUS: We were faint and weak and so have
groaned for you.
HERALD: Why so uneasy? What horror was in your
mind?   545
CHORUS: I say nothing and am safe — a long, long
silence.

HERALD: How could that be? Your king was away;
　　did you fear others?
CHORUS: As you said just now, I would have
　　welcomed death.
HERALD: It *has* been a success. Of course, in the
　　length of time,
　　one must say some things have gone well, some
550　　ill.
　　Who except the gods lives the whole span of his
　　　life
　　without trouble?
　　Yes, if I were to speak of the hard work
　　and the bad quarters,
555　the narrow gangways and the hard beds,
　　there's plenty to complain about.
　　Then there were the troubles on land,
　　disgusting things, too.
　　Our beds were under the enemy's walls.
　　Rain from the sky and dew from the grass
560　　soaked us
　　and kept rotting our clothing
　　and bred lice in our hair.
　　I could talk about the winter, which killed the
　　　birds;
　　Mount Ida and its snow made that intolerable.
565　And then there was the heat,
　　when the sea fell on its noontide bed and slept.
　　Not a breath of wind, not a stir on the waves —
　　Oh, why should I still feel pain for all this?
　　It's over, isn't it, all the trouble?
570　It's over indeed, for them, too, the dead;
　　they'll never have to trouble about getting up
　　　again.
　　Why should I reckon up the numbers of those
　　　who are gone?
　　Why should the living grieve because
　　fortune turned against us?
　　I'm ready to say a long goodbye to all that's
575　　happened.
　　For us that are left of the Greek army,
　　the gain certainly wins out,
　　and the bad side of things doesn't weigh it down.
　　So, those of us who have sped over land and sea
　　can stand facing the sunlight and make our
580　　boast:
　　"There was a day when the Argive army took
　　　Troy.
　　They have nailed the spoils of it
　　on the homes of the gods throughout Greece
　　to be a glory forever and ever."
585　When they hear this, men must praise
　　the city and its generals.
　　We shall also honor the grace of God
　　who brought it to pass.

　　That's my whole speech.
CHORUS: What you say wins me over; I admit it.　590
　　To be ready to learn is what makes a young man
　　out of an old one.
　　But it is this house and Clytemnestra
　　that the news most concerns,
　　though I, too, am the richer for it.　　　　595
CLYTEMNESTRA: I rejoiced long ago,
　　and raised the cry of joy over the news,
　　when first the fire came as my messenger in the
　　　night,
　　telling of Troy's capture and destruction.
　　That was when everyone found fault with me:　600
　　"Is it beacon fires that convince you
　　that Troy has now been sacked?
　　How like a woman's heart to be so lifted up."
　　In rumors such as these I appeared
　　to have gone astray in my wits.　　　　　605
　　But yet I made the sacrifices,
　　and following this "woman's fashion"
　　they all raised the chant, now here, now there,
　　throughout the city,
　　the songs of blessing at the gods' shrines,　610
　　and there they lulled to sleep
　　the sweet-smelling sacrificial fires.
　　Why *now* should I depend on you to tell me
　　　more?
　　I shall learn the whole story from my lord himself.
　　How shall I make best haste to receive him home,　615
　　my honored husband?
　　What sweeter day for a wife's eye to see
　　than when she opens the doors to her man
　　coming from the army,
　　when the gods have brought him safely back to
　　　her?　　　　　　　　　　　　　　620
　　Tell my husband this:
　　bid him come as quick as he can,
　　the city's darling.
　　And when he comes may he find his wife
　　true as he left her,　　　　　　　　　625
　　the watchdog of his house,
　　devoted to him, enemy to his enemies,
　　the same always and ever.
　　I never broke the seal
　　in all those years.　　　　　　　　　630
　　I know of no pleasure with another man
　　nor any talk or evil gossip against me,
　　anymore than I know how to dip this blade
　　to temper it.
　　Such is my boast, so full of truth　　　635
　　that even a well-bred wife
　　need not blush to utter it.

(*Exit Clytemnestra.*)

CHORUS: She has spoken very suitably
for those who understand her.
640 But tell me, Herald,
what of Menelaus?
Was he among the returning army?
Is he safe among you?
And will he come back home again, our dear
prince?
HERALD: I don't know how to put a fair face on
645 lies:
my friends would only have good of it
for a short time anyway.
CHORUS: Why can't you tell news that is both good
and true?
When you separate them, you can't get away
with it.
HERALD: Then — the man has vanished from the
650 Greek army,
he and his ship. *That* is not a lie.
CHORUS: Did you see him set forth from Ilium on
his own?
Or did some storm that struck you all together
snatch him away?
655 HERALD: You've hit it exactly;
in a few words you've covered a long, sad
story.
CHORUS: What do the rest of his shipmates think?
Do they say he's alive or dead?
HERALD: No one knows how to tell the news
clearly —
660 except the sun, there, that gives life to the world.
CHORUS: What do you mean? Was there a storm
that came upon the fleet by the gods' anger
and then ended?
HERALD: A day of good news — one should not
infect it
665 with the tongue of bad news.
The honor due to the two kinds of gods
is separate.
When a messenger with a gloomy face bears
cursed news
of an army's downfall,
670 there is one common injury which is public,
and then, besides, many a man is banned from
his home;
this is the double lash that the god of war
loves,
a two-speared ruin, a bloody pair.
When, I say, a messenger is loaded with such
calamities,
675 he must sing his news as his hymn to the Furies.
But when the saving messenger of good news
comes to a city that rejoices in well-being
— how should I mingle good with bad

in telling you of this storm
which surely did proceed from the gods' anger   680
against the Greeks?
For fire and sea, those two oldest and deepest of
enemies,
swore a conspiracy and pledged their common
allegiance
to destroy the wretched Greek army.
In the night, waves lashed by the storm   685
arose to plague us.
For the Thracian winds battered ship on ship.
Butting one another savagely
in the hurricane and sheets of hail,
they sank from sight, as our evil shepherd   690
drove us here and there.
When the clear light of the day came back,
we saw the sea blooming,
and its flowers were dead Greeks and wrecks.
For ourselves and our boat, we went unharmed;   695
some god stole us through it or begged us off;
he must have steered us himself,
for no man touched the steering oar.
Luck chose to become our savior, and sat on our
ship,
so that we missed the driving waves when we
were at anchor,   700
nor were driven aground on the rugged land.
Afterward, when we had escaped our watery
hell,
in the white light of day, we hardly dared to
trust our luck;
and in our own thoughts we were constantly
shepherds of some new calamity,   705
seeing how the fleet had been pounded and
ground to pieces.
Now, if any of them still breathes,
they speak of us as lost; of course they do.
We have much the same idea about them.
Let it turn out well. For Menelaus,   710
in all likelihood you may expect him back.
For if the beams of the sun discover him living
and seeing,
through the workings of God —
for surely God will not yet blot out
the whole family —   715
there is some hope that he'll come home again.
This is really the truth that you have heard.

(Exit herald.)

CHORUS: Who can have named her so,
with such truth, utterly?
Could it be someone we cannot see,   720
with foreknowledge of destiny,
that used his tongue in harmony with fortune?

She was called Helen,°
the bride won by the spear, sought in strife.
725 Helen means death, and death indeed she was,
death to ships and men and city
as she sailed out of the delicate fabrics of her
curtained room,
fanned by the breeze of giant Zephyr;°
and the man-swarm of shield-bearing hunters
730 came on the track of her,
the vanished track of the oar blades
which beached on the ever-green shores of
Simoeis
on the heels of their bloody quarrel.

To Ilium it drove her,
735 the wrath that brings fulfillment,
and again the word proved true, that equates
marriage and mourning,
for the wrath exacted vengeance at the last
for the guest-table dishonored at the hearth
shared by Zeus.
740 Wrath punished as victims those men,
the new marriage kinsmen,
who on that day must celebrate,
sing out of full throats
the hymn that honored the bride.
745 Perhaps that ancient city of Priam
has learned another tune now,
a tuneful dirge that calls him
Paris the dismally bedded;
the city has endured the ruin of its life,
750 the voice of countless lamentations,
through the wretched bloodletting of its citizens.
Once on a time there was a man
who raised a lion cub in his home.
It was a little thing, starved of milk,
755 still a suckling, still in the first rituals of its life,
gentle, a friend of children,
and a delight to the old.
Many a time it lay in their arms,
like a young baby;
760 its face was bright as it fawned on the hand
at the dictates of its belly's needs.
But time passed, and it showed
what disposition it had from its breeding;
it requited the grace of those that brought it up
765 by horrid slaughtering of their sheep,
an unbidden dinner guest.

723. **Helen:** Daughter of Zeus and Leda, a mortal woman, Helen was the wife of the Greek commander Menelaus before she was abducted by Paris and brought to Troy. 728. **Zephyr:** God of the west wind.

And the house was confused and befouled with
blood;
an evil it was that the servants couldn't fight,
a very murderous mischief.
God reared the lion in the house to become   770
an additional priest of ruin.
But on that first day — as I tell the story —
she came to the city of Ilium
a spirit of windless calm,
the delicate glory of wealth,   775
the soft arrow darting from her eyes,
the flower of love that bites the heart.
Then she changed direction, and brought
a bitter ending to the marriage,
hastening to the daughters of Priam   780
to sit with them and live with them
to their ruin.
Zeus, the god of guests, brought her there,
a Fury to make wives weep.
There is an old saying among men, first spoken
long ago,   785
that a man's great prosperity, when perfected,
gives birth and doesn't die childless,
but from that good fortune in true descent
there grows an ever-greedy misery.
In this, my mind is different from others'.   790
No, I say, it is the wicked deed
that breeds more wickedness, and like to its own
kind.
For the house that is straight-dealing and just
is fated always to have good children.
The ancient deed of sacrilege always breeds a
young one,   795
full of disaster for man, now or then,
when comes the dawn appointed for its birth.
A spirit but a clansman —
one cannot war against him nor fight him —
he is a thing unholy,   800
a daring, a black ruin to the halls,
and very like his parents.
For justice shines in houses grimed with smoke,
and she honors the good man.
And those gilded palaces where hands are dirty   805
she leaves, averting her eyes;
she goes to what is clean,
for she doesn't honor power
whose coinage is misstamped by the praise of the
rich.
And she guides everything to its due end.   810

(*Enter Agamemnon and Cassandra.*)

My lord, conqueror of Troy, descendant of
Atreus,
how shall I greet you, how do you reverence,

neither exceeding nor scanting due measure of
    praise?
Many men, indeed, who transgress justice,
honor appearance over reality.
Everyone is ready to cry over the unfortunate,
but the bite of that sorrow doesn't reach the
    heart.
So, too, there are those that seem to share joy,
yet the faces that they force have no laughter in
    them.
When one is a good judge of stock,
one doesn't miss the meaning of the man's eyes,
fawning in watery friendship
when they seem all loyalty.
In the days when you led the expedition from
    Greece,
for Helen's sake,
I saw you painted in ugly colors —
I will not hide that from you —
as one who had an unskillful hand
on the rudder of his wits
when you tried to win back through men's dying
a willing whore.
But now from the depth of my heart, in true
    friendship,
I say, May the work be kind to those who did it
    so well.
In time you shall know by enquiry
which of your citizens that stayed here at home
dealt justly, and which did wrong.

AGAMEMNON: First Argos and my country's gods,
I must address you; you and I are coauthors
of my home return and the justice
I exacted from Priam's city.
The causes were not spoken aloud,
but the gods heard them
and cast their votes with no opposing voices
into the bloody urn: for Ilium's destruction
and the deaths of men.
To the other urn nothing drew near
but the shadowy hope of a hand;
there was no filling that urn.
You can still see the smoke from the city's
    capture.
The hot blasts of ruin live there yet,
but there is ash, too, dying
as it sends into the air its breaths fattened on
    rich things.
For all of this we should pay our gods
much-remembering thanks.
We have taken vengeance for insolent robbery.
And for the sake of a woman a city has been
    leveled
by the biting beast of Argos, the colt,
the shield-bearing host,

that made its leap about the time of the setting
    Pleiades.
A ravening lion leaped over the wall
and licked its fill of royal blood.
So far my prelude stretches; that's for the gods.
What you've said of your feelings, I've heard and
    remember.
I say the same. You have me as your advocate.
In very few men is it native
to admire a successful friend without envying
    him.
For the poison of malice, settling on the heart,
doubles its weight in one who is stricken with
    envy.
He suffers under the load of his own troubles,
and groans to see the prosperity of the other
    man.
I know of what I speak; I very well understand
the glassy mirror of comradeship, that shadow of
    a shade,
which those prove to be who seemed my truest
    friends.
Only Odysseus,° who joined the fleet unwillingly,
once he was yoked was for me a ready trace
    horse.
Even as I speak of him, I do not know
if I speak of the dead or the living.
For other matters, we will set up public meetings
and take counsel in full assembly.
What is now well shall remain well; we shall see
    to it.
But where there is need for healing medicines,
we will try by surgery or cautery°
intelligently to avert the disease.
Now I will go in, into my halls, my hearth, my
    home,
and there I will first greet the gods
who sent me forth and brought me back again.
Victory has followed us;
let her be ours still, constantly!

(*Enter Clytemnestra.*)

CLYTEMNESTRA: You citizens, elders of Argos,
I will not be ashamed of speaking to you
of how I love my husband.
Modest inhibition is something
that dies away in human dealings.
I will tell of how wretched my life has been
while this man was in Troy —
at first hand I will tell it; it has been *my* life.

---

874. Odysseus: Throughout the *Iliad*, Homer's story of the
Trojan war, Odysseus is a brave soldier. He gives wise, even
wily advice to the Greeks.   **882. cautery:** The process of
burning with a hot iron in order to heal.

First, that a woman should sit in her house,
lonely without her male,
is something terrifying.
900 She hears so many hateful rumors;
here's one has come, and then another,
announcing a greater disaster still,
mouthing the ruin of the house.
If this man here had had as many wounds
905 as streams of rumor would have it,
he would have had more holes in him than a net.
If he had died, as his deaths multiplied in stories
   of him,
he must have had three bodies, like Geryon;
he would have boasted of taking a triple
910 shroud of earth to himself.
It was because of these hateful reports
that others, not I, have loosened many a cord
as it tightened round my neck.
And that is why your son
915 doesn't stand beside me as he should,
the proof of our trust, mine to you, yours to me,
our Orestes.
Do not wonder at this; a loyal ally keeps him
   safe,
Strophius the Phocian.°
920 He spoke to me of twin troubles:
your danger at Ilium, and then that here, too,
the anarchy of the people's voices
might overturn good counsel.
Indeed, it is inbred in men
925 to kick the man that's down.
That's the advice of Strophius, and there's no
   deceit in it.
For my own part, the gushing springs of my grief
have dried up;
there's not a drop left.
930 My eyes are in pain from late watching,
weeping for the beacons that should tell of you,
but never called for firing.
In my dreams, I have started up,
roused by the light strokes of the gnat's flight;
935 I have seen so much more happen to you
than could be contained within the time
with which I shared my sleep.
But now I have come through all this;
my heart is free of sorrow;
940 and so I can describe this man of mine —
a watchdog of the house,
the saving forestay of the ship,
the rooted pillar of the towering roof,
the single child of a father,

the land seen by sailors when they had given
   over hope,   945
the fairest day to see after the storm,
the springwater stream for the thirsty traveler.
It is sweet indeed to escape the harsh stroke of
   necessity.
Such terms of address would, I think, belong to
   him.
But let no one be jealous.   950
Many, indeed, were the evils we endured before.
Now, dear heart,
step from the carriage, but do not place on earth,
   my king,
this foot that trod Troy to destruction.
Servants, to whom I have commanded the task   955
of strewing his path to the house with
   tapestries —
let his way lie straight before him strewn with
   purple,
that justice may guide him to the home he never
   hoped for.
Everything else earned by fate
an unsleeping mind, with the help of the gods,   960
will arrange justly.
AGAMEMNON: Daughter of Leda,° guardian of my
   house,
your speech is a good fit for my absence:
both have stretched out long.
But to praise me in due fashion   965
is an honor that others should give.
Besides, do not make much of me in this
   woman's fashion,
nor grovel and gape flatteringly, like some
   foreigner,
nor strew my path with garments that would
   make it
an object of ill will;   970
it is the gods one should honor with such things.
For one who is mortal, for me certainly,
to walk on subtly woven beauties like these
cannot be without fear.
I tell you, honor me as man, not god.   975
Footmats and embroideries — they sound
   differently,
they are different.
Not to be presumptuous
is the greatest gift the gods can give you.
It's only when a life has ended, and ended well, 980
that one dare say, "Well done."
I would be cheerful if my life
were like this in everything.

---

919. **Strophius the Phocian:** A family friend with whom Orestes stayed at the time of Agamemnon's murder.

962. **Leda:** Mother of Clytemnestra by her husband, Tyndareus, and of Helen by Zeus, who approached Leda in the form of a swan.

CLYTEMNESTRA: Then tell me this, and let it be your own true judgment.

AGAMEMNON: Be sure, I will not falsify that judgment.

985

CLYTEMNESTRA: Was it through fear of the gods that you made this vow?

AGAMEMNON: I said, if any man ever did, what I knew would happen.

CLYTEMNESTRA: And what of Priam, if he had conquered as you have?

AGAMEMNON: He would certainly have trodden on the tapestry.

990

CLYTEMNESTRA: Don't be ashamed, then, of human reproach.

AGAMEMNON: Yes, but the ill repute of the people's voices
has a great power.

CLYTEMNESTRA: He that is not envied is also not admired.

AGAMEMNON: A woman should not long so for a fight.

995

CLYTEMNESTRA: In those that win, yielding is graceful.

AGAMEMNON: Do you set such store on victory in this dispute?

CLYTEMNESTRA: Let me have my way. You are the victor
if you yield readily.

AGAMEMNON: Well, if you will — here, someone undo my sandals,

1000

that are like slaves for the treading of my foot.
And as I walk upon these lovely cloths,
I pray against the envious eye of the gods
lest from afar it strike me.

1005

It's a great shame to spoil a house's wealth,
these weavings so dear in price, with the dirt of treading feet.
Enough of this.
Bring in this stranger here, and use her kindly.
The god looks from afar with approval

1010

on the merciful conqueror.
No one chooses to become a slave.
This woman is the very flower, picked out
from the spoils of war;
as a gift from the army to me, she followed me.

1015

Well, since I've been subdued to listen to you,
I will go into my house, treading on purple.

CLYTEMNESTRA: There is a sea — and who shall drain it dry? —
nourishing a spring, always new, an abundance of purple
to be bought with silver for the dyeing of garments.

1020

This house, my lord, has store enough of it,
thanks be to the gods.

This house does not know poverty.
I would have vowed the treading of many garments,
had I been so ordered by the shrines of the oracles,
to win the safe return of your life.   1025
When the root is there, the leaf comes to the house,
and stretches its shade against the dog star's heat.
And when you came to this house and hearth of yours,
it meant what heat means in the winter time.
And when Zeus makes wine from the bitter grape,   1030
it is still cool within the house,
when its perfected lord paces through the halls.
Zeus, Zeus, that brings all to perfection,
perfect my prayer.
Bring to perfection all you have to do.   1035

CHORUS: Why this fluttering, insistent terror
that keeps guard before my heart?
Is the song prophetic
that rises unhired and unbidden?
My grounded mind has no confidence to dismiss it   1040
like an obscure nightmare.
Time has grown old since the boats,
their hawsers all thrown out along the sands,
set out to Ilium.
With my eyes I am my own witness   1045
to their homecoming.
But nonetheless, my spirit within me
drones this tune of the Furies,
accompanied by no lyre,
a song taught by none but itself.   1050
It has none of the dear confidence of hope.
Not for nothing is the boding of my entrails,
the whirling of my heart, harmonized with
eddies of my mind that will surely bring fulfillment.
But I pray that what I expect may fall away,   1055
a lie, into unfulfillment.
There is no limit in health;
it is insatiable.
For disease is its next-door neighbor;
there is but a single wall between them.   1060
A man's destiny, facing straight ahead,
often crashes on the hidden reef.
Yet, if beforehand in prudent fear,
he casts overboard part of what he owns
with the derrick of good measure,   1065
his whole house does not sink utterly,
though overloaded to overflowing,
nor does the frame of the ship sink.
Many times the generous gifts of Zeus,

1070 and those of the furrows yearly tilled,
banish the disease of hunger.
But the black blood of a man,
when once it has fallen to the earth in his death,
who shall conjure it back again with any
      incantation?
1075 Did not Zeus, for the safety of the world,
stop the wizard who would raise the dead?
If there were no fates appointed by the gods
which checked other fates from having
      overmuch,
my heart would have outstripped my tongue
1080 and poured this out.
But now in the dark it mutters, in heart-anguish,
with never a hope of spinning out of my burning
      mind
what is right for this moment.
CLYTEMNESTRA: In with you too, now, Cassandra,
1085 since Zeus (you cannot be angry with Zeus)
has made you a sharer in the sacrifices in our
      house,
standing near the altar with many slaves that we
      own.
Get down from that carriage;
none of your high spirit of pride.
1090 They say that Heracles, Alcmene's son,°
was sold and forced to eat the bread of slavery.
If then the necessity of fate's scales
has forced this on you,
you should be very grateful for masters anciently
      rich.
Those who have reaped a harvest they never
1095   expected
are always excessive in harshness toward their
      slaves.
From us you will have all the usual treatment.
CHORUS: She has finished; it is to you she spoke,
and what she says is clear enough.
1100 You are taken, a quarry in fate's net;
obey her, then —
though I will understand if you don't.
CLYTEMNESTRA: If she has anything besides her
      swallow twitterings,
a barbaric speech that no one knows,
1105 I'll try to persuade her within her understanding.
CHORUS: Follow her. What she says is the best there
      is for you;
leave the carriage; obey her.
CLYTEMNESTRA: I have no time to waste here with
      her
outside the palace.

1090. **Heracles, Alcmene's son:** Heracles was a popular
Greek hero. According to legend, he was sold into slavery to
Omphale, Queen of Lydia.

The sheep stand ready for slaughter   1110
in front of the hearth at the center of the house.

(*To Cassandra.*)

You, if you're going to do anything that I tell
      you,
do it quickly.
But if you disobey because you don't take in my
      words —

(*To Chorus.*)

Here, you!   1115
Don't speak to her any more; use your hands;
that's all these foreigners understand.
CHORUS: I think the woman needs a good
      interpreter;
she looks like a wild thing newly caught.
CLYTEMNESTRA: She's crazy; she hears only her
      distraught mind.   1120
Of course she does, she that has left her newly
      captured city,
come here not yet knowing how to wear the
      curb bit,
till she's frothed out her spirit in blood.
I won't throw any more words at her to be
      belittled.

(*Exit Clytemnestra.*)

CHORUS: I pity her, and so I won't be angry.   1125
Come, you poor girl, desert your place in the
      carriage;
yield to what must be; wear your yoke for the
      first time.
CASSANDRA: Oh! Oh! Oh! Oh, the land!
Lord Apollo! Lord Apollo!
CHORUS: Why do you raise such dismal cries to
      Apollo?   1130
He is no god for the singer of dirges.
CASSANDRA: Oh! Oh! Oh! Oh, the land!
Lord Apollo! Lord Apollo!
CHORUS: Again she calls with her ill omens
upon the god who has no suitable place   1135
at scenes of mourning.
CASSANDRA: Lord Apollo! Lord Apollo! God of the
      streets,
god of destruction! Now again, god of my
      destruction,
and so easily.
CHORUS: She seems to me about to prophesy her
      own misfortunes.   1140
The gift of prophecy still sticks
even though the mind is now a slave's.
CASSANDRA: Lord Apollo! Lord Apollo!

God of my destruction! God of the streets!
1145 Through what streets have you led me now,
to what house?
CHORUS: To that of the sons of Atreus. If you don't
know that,
that I can tell you. And you won't say it's a lie.
CASSANDRA: Yes, to a house the gods hate;
1150 it has been witness of so many
murders of kin, butcheries,
bowl full of man's blood, ground soaked in shed
blood.
CHORUS: The stranger has a nose as keen as a hound;
she's on the trail of a murder and will find it.
1155 CASSANDRA: What convinces me are the witnesses —
the children, the babies screaming of their cut
throats,
of their flesh roasted and eaten by their father.
CHORUS: We have heard of your fame as a prophet;
but we need no foretellers here.
1160 CASSANDRA: Oh, what does she plan?
What is the great new grief?
It is a great evil against the house
that she is planning.
It is unbearable for its friends, uncurable.
1165 Defense stands aloof and keeps away.
CHORUS: These last foretellings are quite beyond my
understanding;
the others I know — indeed the whole city cries
them aloud.
CASSANDRA: Oh, you wretched woman,
is this what you bring to consummation?
1170 You have cleaned him in the bath
till his skin shined,
the husband to share your bed.
And how shall I tell the consummation?
It would be quick: the line of clutching hands,
1175 stretching out, one hooked to another.
CHORUS: I don't understand that yet;
you spoke riddles before,
but now what baffles me is the dimness
of what comes from the gods in words.
CASSANDRA: Oh! Oh! Oh! What is this that
1180 appears?
A net, a net of death. Can it be so?
But the meshes are the bedfellow, the accomplice
in murder.
Let the pack that ravens insatiate against the
family
bay for a sacrifice that merits death by stoning.
1185 CHORUS: What Fury is this you bid raise its cries
against the house?
I find no cleaning in your words.
To my heart rush back the blood drops of
yellowing stain,
as when the eyes grow dim at the setting of a
life's day,

a man falling by the point of a spear. 1190
And destruction comes quick.
CASSANDRA: Look at that! Look at that!
Keep away the bull from the cow!
She will take him in the folds of the robe
with the trick of the black horn. 1195
She strikes! He falls! He falls
in the water of the bath.
That is his end, I tell you,
a treacherous murder in a cauldron.
CHORUS: I will not boast of being a keen judge of
prophecy, 1200
but this certainly looks like something evil.
Anyway, what good word ever came to
mankind
from the prophets?
It is through evils that the wordy tricks of the
prophets
bring terrors for us to understand. 1205
CASSANDRA: Oh, the ill boding of my own sad fate!
For it is my own suffering, on top of his,
that my tongue spills out.

(*To the god.*)

Where is this you have brought me to in my
sorrow?
For nothing but to share his death; what else? 1210
CHORUS: You are someone god-possessed;
the god carries you along.
It is for yourself you cry out this tuneless tune.
Like the brown nightingale,° that can never have
enough of song, 1215
as she cries "Itys! Itys!" for her life rich in
sorrows,
and her mind loves pity for herself.
CASSANDRA: Oh! The life of the shrill-voiced
nightingale!
The gods covered *her* with a feathered body;
I tell you, they gave her a *sweet* life, 1220
and her cries are not cries of sorrow.
But what remains for me
is the splitting of the flesh with the two-edged
spear.
CHORUS: Where do they come from, these rushes
of useless agony carried by the god? 1225
You make music that is a mixture,

1214–21. Like the brown nightingale: The chorus alludes to
the story of Philomela, who was raped by her brother-in-law,
Tereus. Although her tongue was cut out to prevent her from
telling anyone of the crime, Philomela sent her sister a piece
of embroidery that revealed all. The sisters took their revenge upon Tereus by tricking him into eating his son, Itys.
According to some accounts, the gods turned Philomela into
a nightingale.

ugly cries of terror and high-pitched melodies.
Where did you get the milestones of evil words
that mark your prophetic journey?

1230 CASSANDRA: The marriage! The marriage of Paris,
deadly to those who loved him.
Scamander, river that my fathers drank of,
in that time I was raised on your shores;
but now around the banks of Cocytus and
Acheron,°

1235 the rivers of death, I am likely to prophesy,
and soon.

CHORUS: What is this word you have spoken all too
clearly?
A newborn child could understand.
The bite of murder has pierced me

1240 as you whimper at your painful fortune.
It is a heartbreak to hear you.

CASSANDRA: The agony, agony of the city utterly
ruined.
The sacrifices that my father made before the
walls,
the multiplied slaughter of cattle and woolly
sheep.

1245 None of it helped; it was no cure.
The city suffered as it was fated to suffer.
And I shall soon be thrown on the ground
in my own warm blood.

CHORUS: What you say now follows what you said
before.
Some malevolent god who falls on you with

1250 fearful weight
makes you a singer of these deadly mournful
things.
But as for the end — I am at a loss.

CASSANDRA: Now my prophecy shall no longer peer
from behind veils
like a newly married bride.

1255 No, it will rush on, a wind brightly blowing
into the sun's rising,
to send disaster surging like a wave to meet the
sunbeams,
a disaster yet greater than this.
I will not school you in riddles any longer.

1260 And do you be my witness that my nose is keen
and my tracking by shortcuts
on the path of crimes committed long ago.
Never do they leave the house,
that chorus that sings in ugly harmony.

1265 For their speech is of evil.
The revelers have drunk, to whet their courage
more,

man's blood, and so they abide in the house,
and none shall expel them: they are the Furies,
that attend on the murder of kin.

The song they sing as they beleaguer the house   1270
is the song of the primal destruction,
when the mind is blinded.
And each of the Furies has spat in disgust
on the brother's bed that hates its violator.
Hah! Am I an archer that missed,   1275
or have I hit the mark?
Or am I a false prophet
that raps on doors and babbles?
Be my witness, you, but first make your sworn
oath
that I know the story of the ancient sins   1280
of this house.

CHORUS: How would such an oath, even plighted in
all honesty,
serve as any kind of cure?
True, I do wonder at you,
that you, reared beyond the sea and speaking a
strange tongue   1285
should talk of these things as if you had been
there.

CASSANDRA: It was Apollo the prophet
that charged me with the office of prophecy.

CHORUS: He fell in love with you?
Is that possible for a god?   1290

CASSANDRA: Till now I was ashamed to speak of it.

CHORUS: As long as things go well, one has one's
delicacy.

CASSANDRA: He was a wrestler, that breathed his
grace into me.

CHORUS: Did you come to the breeding of children,
like other couples?   1295

CASSANDRA: I promised the god and cheated him.

CHORUS: Had you already got your gift of
prophecy?

CASSANDRA: Oh yes, I used to tell my countrymen
all that would happen.

CHORUS: How did you escape the god's anger?   1300

CASSANDRA: Since my offense against him,
no one believed a word of mine.

CHORUS: Ah, but to us right now, you seem to
prophesy truly.

CASSANDRA: Oh, oh, my agony! There it is again!
The fearful pain of true prophecy   1305
that twists me, that drives me wild;
and it is still only prelude.
Look! Look! You see them! The young ones,
sitting on the house like dream phantoms.
They are the likenesses of those children dead
and gone,   1310
killed by those they loved;
their hands are full of meat, their own flesh.
You can see it clearly; they carry the pitiful load

1234. Cocytus and Acheron: Rivers flowing together at the
entrance to the kingdom of death.

of their guts, and their father has tasted them.
1315 I tell you, there is punishment for this,
and someone is plotting it,
a lion, but a coward, that wallows, a
    housekeeper
in the bed of the returning lord—
O mine, *my* lord—for I must bear the yoke of
    slavery.
1320 The captain of the ships, the sacker of Ilium,
he knows not what tongue is licking him,
the tongue of the hateful bitch, her ears pricked,
like a secret blind vengeance,
that will work out his evil fate.
1325 So far her daring reaches:
the woman will murder the man.
She is—what shall I call her and be right?
this monstrous, biting creature.
A snake with poison at both ends;
1330 some Scylla° living in the rocks, death to sailors;
some murderous, raging mother of hell;
some truceless god of war;
a war she has declared upon her loved ones!
So let her cry her war cry,
1335 whose daring knows no limit,
as at the moment when the battle turns.
Yet she seems to rejoice that he has come safe
    home.
It is all one to me, if you do not believe any of
    this;
what difference?
1340 It is to be and will come.
Soon you will stand here and say of me, in pity,
she was too true a prophet.
CHORUS: The feast of Thyestes, and the flesh of the
    children,
I understand and shudder; fear is on me
1345 as I hear the truth, and no mere likenesses.
But for the rest I heard from you,
I have fallen off the course and run wide.
CASSANDRA: I tell you, you will live to see
Agamemnon's death.
CHORUS: Wretched girl, hold your tongue in piety.
CASSANDRA: No, no holy god of healing presides
1350 over this story.
CHORUS: True, if what you say is so; but God
forbid it should be.
CASSANDRA: You are all for God forbidding;
but their job is killing.
CHORUS: What man is he that furnishes this grief?
CASSANDRA: You have surely fallen astray of my
1355 prophecies.

1330. Scylla: A sea monster living in a cave opposite the
whirlpool, Charybdis. Ships could not escape the double
threat.

CHORUS: Yes, for I do not understand how the
    plotter
will make his plan work.
CASSANDRA: Yet I know Greek rather too well.
CHORUS: So does the Delphic oracle;° but it's hard
    to understand,
all the same.   1360
CASSANDRA: Oh! It attacks me like fire!
Oh! Oh! O god! O Lycian Apollo!
There she is, the lioness, two-footed bedfellow of
    the wolf,
in the absence of the true-bred lion.
She will kill me. Like one that brews a potion,   1365
She will put my reward, too, in the drink.
She cries her glee in triumph, as she whets the
    knife
for a man, to pay him in murder for bringing me
    here.

(She starts tearing off her robe and garlands.)

Why should I have these mockeries about me,
this staff, the prophet's garlands round my neck?   1370
Before I die myself, I shall at least destroy you.
Go; you shall be no more. Lie on the ground as
    you fall.
Thus I requite you.
Enrich some other girl with blinded madness,
some other girl than me.   1375
Look, Apollo himself undoes his prophetess
of her prophetic mantle; he has watched me
laughed to scorn even in this trumpery,
laughed at by friends turned foes,
with never a quiver in the scale—what
    hollowness!   1380
Ill-treated like a wandering beggar priest,
in misery half-starved to death, I still endured.
But now the prophet has unmade the prophet
and brought me here to meet my chance death.
No father's altar, but a chopping block, waits
    for me,   1385
to be warmed with my blood as I am butchered,
the preliminary victim. Yet, all the same, I shall
    not die
dishonored by the gods.
But another will come° to take vengeance for me;
he will kill the mother in whom he was seeded,   1390
and will avenge his father.
A wanderer outcast, grown alien to this land,

1359. Delphic oracle: The chief oracle of ancient Greece,
presided over by Apollo. The utterings of the oracle were
ambiguous and had to be interpreted.   1389. another will
come: Reference to Orestes, who avenges his father's murder
in the second part of the trilogy by Aeschylus.

who will return from exile
to put a coping stone of ruin for those he loved,
1395 for he has sworn a great oath by the gods
that his father's corpse shall bring him home
      again.
Why do I go on this way, crying, full of self-
      pity? —
now that I have seen Troy's ruin, as I saw it,
now as Troy's conquerors come off in the god's
      judgment,
1400 as I see them now.
I will go and face it; I will face my death.
These gates before me here, I call you now by
      name:
the gates of death.
But I pray that the stroke that reaches me
1405 may be a mortal stroke,
that without struggle, as the blood runs freely,
in easy death I may close these eyes of mine.
CHORUS: You are a woman that has suffered much,
and have understood much; and you have said
      much.
1410 But if you truly know your fate,
why do you walk up to the altar steadfastly,
like an ox?
CASSANDRA: There is no escape, my friends; the time
      is full.
CHORUS: Yet the latest moment has a special value.
CASSANDRA: This day has come; there is little I
1415 would gain by flight.
CHORUS: How courageous and steadfast!
CASSANDRA: No one who's happy hears these
      compliments.
CHORUS: But death, if fame comes with it,
comes still with grace to those that must die
      anyway.
CASSANDRA: I weep for you, father, and for your
1420 noble children.

(*She recoils.*)

CHORUS: What is it? What is the fear that turns you
      back?

(*Cassandra shudders.*)

CHORUS: What made you shudder?
Is it something in your mind that disgusts you?
CASSANDRA: The house! It reeks of murder, of
      dripping blood!
CHORUS: What? It's just the blood of sacrificed
1425 animals.
CASSANDRA: No, it is just like the smell of a grave.
CHORUS: It is no delicate Syrian incense in the house
      that you speak of.
CASSANDRA: Still — I will go into the house,

to mourn with cries my own and Agamemnon's
      deaths.   1430
I have enough of life.
My friends, I'm not scared
like a bird startled at a bush
in empty terror.
When I die, you will be my witness to this,   1435
when a woman dies to match my woman's death,
when a man falls to match that other man,
whose wife was his assassin.
This friendly office I lay on you, as I die now.
CHORUS: Poor girl, I pity you for your death,   1440
that the god predicted.
CASSANDRA: I have one more speech to make,
or shall I call it a dirge, just for myself.
As I face this last sunlight,
I call on those who shall be my avengers   1445
to make my enemies pay for *my* murder too,
only a dead slave, such an easy victory.
Men's fortunes, when they are good,
one might say of them, "They are like shadows
      only."
When they're bad, a wet sponge   1450
with one stroke wipes it all out.
The first truth has my pity, far more than the
      second.

(*Exit Cassandra.*)

CHORUS: To be successful is to be endlessly hungry
      for more;
all men are so.
There is no one who banishes good fortune from
      his house,   1455
so long as fingers point at it.
No man says, "Do not come here again, good
      fortune."
Here is this king, to whom the blessed gods
      granted
the sacking of Priam's city;
he came home with all the honors that the gods
      gave him.   1460
But now, if he shall pay for the blood of the past
and dying render the price of others' deaths,
who that hears this and must die himself
dare boast that a man may be born
to live a whole life unharmed?   1465
AGAMEMNON (*from within*): I've been hit! I am hurt
      to death.
CHORUS: Hush! Who is it that cries out, hurt to
      death?
AGAMEMNON: I'm hit again!
CHORUS: It is the king crying out; I think all is over.
But let us plan safety for ourselves — if we can. 1470
  1. My vote is to cry, Help! to the citizens

to come to the palace.
2. Yes, and at once, I think,
to catch them red-handed with dripping sword.
3. I think you're right; at least we should do
1475   something.
It certainly isn't the moment for hesitation.
4. But we can see. This is a kind of first act;
it looks like the beginning of a tyranny.
5. Yes, it does — because we're wasting time.
Their hands don't sleep, and they trample
1480   underfoot
the good reputation of delay.
6. I really do not know what would be best.
Those who do the deed of course find it easy to
plan.
7. Yes, I am with you. Anyhow,
one cannot by talking bring the dead to life
1485   again.
8. Are we then, in order to stretch our own lives,
to yield to a government that shames our royal
house?
9. No, that is awful. Death is better than that.
Death is better than subjection to a tyranny.
1490   10. Is the evidence of the cries good enough?
Are we right to predict that the man is dead?
11. Yes, one must know before one gets angry.
Knowing the truth is very far from guessing.
12. I have the support of many voices among
you:
that we should be told clearly how it is with
1495   Agamemnon.

(*Enter Clytemnestra.*)

CLYTEMNESTRA: Till now I have said much to meet
the occasion,
but now I will not be ashamed to say the
opposite.
How could one, rendering hate to those who
hated
but looked like loved ones,
hedge the trap about with sides too high to be
1500   leapt over?
This was my day of trial; I have thought of it
enough and long enough, a trial of an old
quarrel
years and years old.
Now I stand here where I have struck him.
1505   He is dead, and the sequence ended.
This is how I managed — I will not disavow it —
that he should not escape, nor defend himself
from death.
I threw about him an encompassing net,
as it might be for fish, all-entangling,
1510   an evil wealth of cloak.
I struck him twice. He gave two groans,

and his body went limp;
as he lay there, I gave him a third,
in honor of the Zeus that keeps the dead
securely in the underworld.   1515
This was my grace and prayer for him.
So, as he lay there, he gasped out his spirit,
choking, poured out a sharp stream of his blood
and struck me with the dark bloody shower.
I rejoiced as much as the new-sown earth   1520
rejoices in the glad rain of Zeus,
when the buds strike in earth's womb.
So it is, you old men of Argos here;
be glad, if you can. I triumph in it.
If it were right to pour libations   1525
on a dead man's body, I would have done so to
him,
and more than justly done so.
Here's a bowl of horrors, cursed horrors,
that he filled within our house,
and then he came and drank it off himself.   1530
CHORUS: I wonder at your tongue, how boldly it
wags,
that you should boast like this over a dead
husband.
CLYTEMNESTRA: You try me out as if I were
a woman that cannot think.
But my heart doesn't tremble,   1535
and I speak to you who know;
whether you wish to praise or blame me is all
one to me.
Here is Agamemnon, my husband, now a
corpse —
his death the work of this right hand of mine,
an efficient craftsman.   1540
That is how *that* is.
CHORUS: Woman, what evil thing have you eaten
that grows in the earth,
what draught have you tasted that comes from
the salt sea,
that you have taken upon you so horrible a
sacrifice   1545
and the curse of the people's voice?
You have cast away, you have torn apart,
and you shall be cast and torn away from the
city,
a monstrous object of hate to the citizens.
CLYTEMNESTRA: Now it's against me that you
proclaim banishment,   1550
that the hatred and curses of the citizens shall be
mine,
but in the old days you brought nothing against
that man,
who, with all the indifference of one whose
pastures are full
of teeming flocks, rich in wool,
had no care for the death of a lamb.   1555

He sacrificed his own daughter,
dearest pain of my womb,
to charm the contrariness of Thracian winds.
For this, should you not have banished him,
1560 payment for his polluting wickedness?
No, you are a careful hearer and harsh judge
only of *my* acts.
Threaten away! I tell you now, if once you
conquer me
in a fair fight, I'll be your subject;
1565 but if God gives another outcome,
you will get an education in discretion
and learn it thoroughly, though the knowledge
comes very late.
CHORUS: You think big thoughts, and you scream
proud defiance,
1570 as though the bloody smear of your success
had maddened your mind.
The smear of blood — I can see it in your eyes.
But still you must pay stroke for stroke,
with no friend to take your part.
CLYTEMNESTRA: You may now hear the solemn
1575 swearing of my oath:
By the justice due to my child, and now
perfected,
by the Spirit of Destruction and the Fury,
in whose honor I cut this man's throat,
my hope treads not within the hall of Fear
1580 so long as Aegisthus lights the hearth fire for me,
my loyal friend, as he has always been,
shield for my daring — no small one.
There lies Agamemnon, this girl's seducer —
he was the darling of all the women of Troy —
1585 and there she is, our prophet, prisoner of war,
that shared his bed, a faithful whore
that spoke her auguries for him, and knew as
well
the rubbing of the sailors' benches.
Both have suffered as they deserved.
He died as I said, and she has sung her swan
1590 song in death,
and lies with him, her lover.
But to me she has brought an additional side
dish
to *my* pleasure in bed.
CHORUS: What day of doom may I look for soon,
one with not too much pain, not too long
1595 bedridden,
that shall bring me the sleep that has no ending,
now that my kindest of guardians has been
overcome,
suffering so much at a woman's hands.
By a woman his life has perished.
Curse on you, crazy Helen, that were the single
1600 murderess
of all those lives, those many lives,

lost under Troy's walls;
now you have made the fulfillment,
the fine flowering, of whatever it was,
that quarrel within the house   1605
built to bring a man to misery.
You have perfected it,
through bloodshed that cannot be washed out.
CLYTEMNESTRA: Do not pray for your end in death
because of the burden of your grief in this,   1610
nor turn your anger against Helen,
as the man-killer who destroyed
those many lives of the Greeks,
and brought into being an incurable pain.
CHORUS: Spirit that attacks the house of the sons of
Atreus,   1615
you master me to the breaking of my heart;
your power is wielded by two women of like
soul.
And now you stand like an evil raven,
and croak over the dead a lawless hymn of
victory.
CLYTEMNESTRA: Now indeed you have made right   1620
the judgment of your mouth,
as you name the thrice-glutted spirit of this race.
It is through him that the love of blood-licking
is nourished in the belly,
and before the old wound has healed,   1625
new pus comes.
CHORUS: Yes, the one you name is indeed great,
the spirit whose anger lies heavy on this house.
And the tale you have to tell is evil;
it has an endless appetite for the events of blind
madness.   1630
But surely these are through Zeus,
who is cause of all, who brings all to pass.
For what is there that is fulfilled for man,
except through Zeus?
What is there of all this   1635
that is not of God's accomplishment?
O my king, my king,
how shall I sorrow for you?
What shall I say from a heart that loves you?
You lie there in that spider's web,   1640
gasping out your life in an unholy death.
Oh, oh! Conquered by deadly treachery,
to fall to such an ignoble bed
by a wife's hand and a double-edged blade.
CLYTEMNESTRA: You cry aloud on this as *my* work;   1645
but do not call me Agamemnon's wife.
No, it is the old, bitter, Evil Genius
of Atreus, giver of the cruel feast,
that has likened himself to the wife of this dead
man
and has paid him off, sacrificing a full-grown
victim   1650
in fulfillment for those young children.

CHORUS: But who will bear you witness
   that you are guiltless of the murder?
   How, how so? It is true, there may be,
1655   on his father's side, the Evil Genius to help you.
   And the black god of war presses on
   through tides of kindred blood
   to the place of his advance,
   where he pays just requital
1660   for the congealed fragments of the eaten children.
   O my king, my king,
   how shall I sorrow for you?
   What shall I say from a heart that loves you?
   You lie there in that spider's web,
1665   gasping out your life in an unholy death.
   Oh, oh! Conquered by deadly treachery,
   to fall to such an ignoble bed
   by a wife's hand and a double-edged blade.
CLYTEMNESTRA: Did *he* not also lay upon the house
1670   a treacherous destruction?
   The victim, my daughter, raised from his loins,
   Iphigeneia, whom I mourn for.
   What he did is what he suffered for.
   Let him not boast of anything in the house of
      death,
1675   for he paid for what he had done
   with death by the mischief of the sword.
CHORUS: I am all bewildered about what road to
      take
   as the house falls;
   my wits are deserted by their skillful carefulness.
1680   I fear the crash of the bloody torrent of rain
   that will shake the house to its foundation.
   Now it is a shower no longer.
   Fate is whetting its justice on other whetstones
   for another deed of injury.
1685   Earth, Earth, would you had received me
   before I lived to see him in his lowly couch
   in a silver-sided bath.
   Who shall bury him? Who shall keen him?
   Will you dare to do this, to make lament for him,
   you who killed him, your husband?
1690   Will you accomplish for his soul a grace no grace
   as thanks for his great deeds?
   Who shall stand at the grave and chant
   a praise of the hero
   with tears in the eye and truthful sorrow at
1695   heart?
CLYTEMNESTRA: The care of that concerns you not
      at all.
   It is by our hand that he fell, that he died,
   and we shall bury him
   with no cries of mourning from this house.
1700   But his daughter Iphigeneia, as is right,
   will welcome her father by the swift-flowing
      passage

over the River of Sorrows
   and throw her arms around him and kiss him.
CHORUS: This is but the exchange of insult for
      insult;
   it is hard to judge the issue of such a fight.   1705
   The pirate plunders the pirate,
   the killer pays for the killing.
   Still there remains, as long as Zeus remains on
      his throne,
   the rule that he who has acted shall suffer
      accordingly.
   That is the divine law.   1710
   Who shall expel from the house the brood of
      curses?
   The whole race is welded to destruction.
CLYTEMNESTRA: In what you say now, the prophecy
      has become truth.
   For my part, I am willing to make a sworn
      compact
   with the evil spirit of this house   1715
   to be satisfied with things as they are, however
      bad,
   on condition that he, in the days to come,
   may go from our house and wear out some other
      breed
   with murders of one another in the family.
   I will be utterly content with a small part of
      wealth,   1720
   if I can banish from these halls
   the madness of mutual bloodletting.

(*Enter Aegisthus.*)

AEGISTHUS: O happy light, day of justified revenge!
   Now I will say that the gods
   in watchfulness so high above the earth   1725
   still bear an eye on the sorrows of mortals to
      avenge them.
   Now I take pleasure to have seen this man
   lying here in the robes that were
   the nets of the Furies for him,
   paying for the plots his father's hand contrived.   1730
   For Atreus, ruler of this land, was this man's
      father,
   and his brother Thyestes was my father.
   Both were Pelops's sons; this is the plain story.
   The two of them were in dispute about the
      throne,
   and Atreus banished my father from city and
      home.   1735
   The unlucky Thyestes later returned,
   a suppliant at Atreus's hearth, and found safety
      there —
   I mean for his own part, for he did not die
   nor stained his fatherland with blood.
   But the vile Atreus, father of the dead man here,   1740

with show of eagerness rather than love,
gave my father a banquet of welcome.
He pretended to celebrate a day of feasting
on flesh slaughtered for meat,
1745 in all hospitality,
but the meat he gave my father was his own
    children's.
The feet and the ends of the fingers he put apart
    and hid,
as the guests sat man by man at separate tables.
So Thyestes in ignorance ate the other parts,
a meal that brought a curse, as you see, on all
1750   the race.
Later, when he discovered what awful act he had
    committed,
he moaned aloud, recoiled, and vomited up the
    bloody mess.
"A doom intolerable will overtake," he said,
"the house of Pelops."
1755 He kicked the dinner over to back the oath,
crying, "So perish every one of all your breed."
That is why you can see this man fallen dead
    here,
and I am justly the one who stitched together his
    murder.
I was the third son, and while I was still in
    swaddling clothes
1760 he drove me out along with my luckless father.
But when I grew to manhood, justice brought me
    back.
And so I laid my hand on him, though not face
    to face;
mine was the whole contriving of the evil plot.
So glorious the result,
1765 that now I would welcome death itself,
having seen him in the traps of justice.
CHORUS: Aegisthus, I do not respect insolence
at the moment of calamity.
Do you say that with aforethought you killed
    Agamemnon,
1770 that you alone planned this miserable murder?
In that case, I do not think your life will escape
the justice of the public curse, the stoning.
That's what I think.
AEGISTHUS: Do you talk back to me, you who sit at
    the lower oar,
1775 when we are in possession of the upper deck?
You will find out, despite your age,
how uncomfortable such learning is for an old
    man,
when discretion is the lesson set.
Chains in old age and hunger's pangs
are the very sharpest healing prophets of the
1780   mind.
Don't you see this when you see?

Kick not against the pricks, lest your own
    striking hurt you.
CHORUS: Woman, you who were his housekeeper
and at the same time sullied his bed,
did you plot his death when the victors were
    newly home   1785
and he had been their general?
AEGISTHUS: These words of yours are true
    progenitors of sorrows.
Yours is a tongue the opposite of Orpheus's:
he led all things his captive through the joy of
    his own voice,
but you with silly yappings arouse others to lead
    you captive.   1790
Once you are mastered, you'll be a tamer animal.
CHORUS: I suppose you'll be the sovereign of the
    Argives,
you, who when you plotted this man's murder
didn't dare to do the deed with your own hand.
AEGISTHUS: Well, no. The treachery was a woman's
    part,   1795
clearly so. I would be suspected as his old enemy.
But his wealth will give me a base to rule the
    citizens,
and the disobedient man I will yoke in heavy
    chains;
he will not be, I assure you, like a full-fed young
    trace horse.
No, unwelcome hunger and a dark cell   1800
will see him through into submission.
CHORUS: Why didn't you kill him yourself, with
    your cowardly soul?
No, your partner, the woman, did the killing,
to be the pollution of the land and of the gods of
    the land.
But I tell you, Orestes still sees the light of day, 1805
that he may come home, and with good luck on
    his side
be conquerer and the death of both of you.
AEGISTHUS: Since you're resolved to act and talk like
    this,
you'll soon know —
here, my bodyguards, this is your work, right
    here.   1810
CHORUS: Here, let each one of you be ready,
    hand on
sword hilt.
AEGISTHUS: I, too, hold the hilt of my sword.
I will face my death.
CHORUS: You talk of death; I welcome it. But I will
    try my chances.   1815
CLYTEMNESTRA: No, dearest, no. Let us do no
    further evils.
Those that there are, are many, a bloody harvest;
we have a good store of calamity.

No, no bloodletting.

1820 Good old men, off with you to your houses.
Yield to what must be, before you suffer.
What we did had to be done.
If this should be all of troubles, I would gladly
    welcome it,
though struck with misfortune
1825 by the heavy hoof of the evil spirit.
That is a woman's word, if anyone should
    think it
worth heeding.

AEGISTHUS: No, but to have them letting their
    tongues
blossom in insolence, to throw their empty
    threats about —
1830 "That they would try their chances" —
You lack all brains, so to abuse your master.

CHORUS: It does not fit an Argive to fawn on a
    villain.
AEGISTHUS: I will get even with you in the days to
    come.
CHORUS: Not if the Spirit brings Orestes home.
AEGISTHUS: I know the diet of exiles is rich in hope.   1835
CHORUS: Yes, do things, grow fat, pollute justice —
    while you can.
AEGISTHUS: You know you will pay me for your
    foolishness.
CHORUS: Boast, do; be bold — a cock beside your
    hen.
CLYTEMNESTRA: Do not pay heed to their vain
    yappings. I
and you together will make all things well,   1840
for we are masters of this house.

THE LIBATION BEARERS

The Greek title for this play is *Choephori,* which comes from the opening scene when Electra goes to the grave of her father with an offering for the dead (*choë*). The offering is a libation, a cupful of "rich wine" spilled on the grave in tribute. In tending her father's grave, Electra sees signs of her brother's presence, and she realizes that he has returned to take revenge on their father's killers. Revealing himself, Orestes plans then with Electra to kill Aegisthus and their mother, Clytemnestra. The Chorus, having suffered under Aegisthus's tyranny, applauds the plan.

Orestes has come back from exile having been dispossessed of all his rightful belongings. Moreover, the prophecy from Pythia, the guardian protecting the shrine of Apollo at Delphi, has declared that both Aegisthus and Clytemnestra must die for the killing of Agamemnon. Orestes and his friend Pylades pretend to be strangers come with news of Orestes' death and are admitted to the palace. Orestes kills Aegisthus but he hesitates before killing his mother.

Clytemnestra defends her actions and berates him; when Orestes hesitates, Pylades speaks his only three lines (941–43), reminding Orestes that if he does not kill his mother the prophecy of Pythia will be unfulfilled. Those words convince him, and despite his mother's threat to loose her hounds on him, he kills her. Taking her body and Aegisthus's body out to the Chorus, he claims to have enacted justice. He ultimately flees, hounded by the Furies, who torment him mercilessly. In its original production, the Furies wore terrifying masks specifically designed by Aeschylus to make the scene unusually frightening.

Aeschylus (c. 525–456 B.C.)

THE LIBATION BEARERS

(458 B.C.)

TRANSLATED BY DAVID GRENE AND WENDY DONIGER O'FLAHERTY

Dramatis Personae

ORESTES, *son of King Agamemnon*
PYLADES, *friend of Orestes*
ELECTRA, *daughter of King Agamemnon*
CHORUS, *captives of war in Argos, friends of Electra*
SERVANT *of the house*
NURSE *of Orestes*

CLYTEMNESTRA
AEGISTHUS

(*Enter Orestes and Pylades.*)

ORESTES: Hermes, god of the underworld,
Hermes, protector of my father's sovereign rights,
be now my savior, my ally, as I supplicate you.

For I come to this land a returned exile,
5   and here upon this mound, my father's grave,
I call on him to give ear to me and hear.
I dedicated a lock of my hair to Inachus for
      nurture,
and here is another, this time for mourning.
For, father, I wasn't there to raise my voice
10   in sorrow at your death.
I did not stretch out my hand
in the funeral greeting.

(*Enter Electra and Chorus.*)

What is this I see?
What is this band of women
15   all in black, marching by so conspicuously?
What can have happened? What does it look like?
What new disaster can have struck the house?
They seem to be bringing soothing libations for
      the dead;
that must be it.
20   For I see my sister Electra coming,
in deep mourning as she would be.
O Zeus, grant that I may avenge my father!
Be my ally, in all graciousness.
Pylades, let us stand aside here,
25   so we may find out truly what this is,
this procession of women.

(*They stand aside.*)

CHORUS: From the house I was sent to lead the
      procession
which brings the libations.
You can see our sharp fingernails are weary
30   from plowing new furrows on our cheeks
till they're torn and bloody.
Always the heart finds its meat in endless
      lamentation.
The robes at our breasts torn to linen shreds,
the sound of the tearing rags speaks our grief.
But we are stricken with sorrow for what
35   happens,
and our faces laugh no more.
Sharp and hair-raising the cry of a prophetic
      dream,
raising from sleep at dead of night, breathing
      anger,
it screams terror from the depths of the house;
40   it falls heavily on the women's quarters.
The dream-interpreters trusted to speak for the
      gods
scream, "The dead beneath the earth blame us;
they are angry against their killers."
O Mother Earth, here is a graceless grace to
      avert evil,
45   sought by this godless woman who has sent us.

I fear to utter this word.
For how can one expiate blood fallen on the
      earth?
O hearth in utter misery,
O house dug down in ruin,
sunless darkness that hates mankind   50
envelops the house in the deaths of its lords.
In the old days there was reverence,
something stronger than fighting, war, or
      conquest.
It penetrated the ears and minds of the people.
It is gone now. There is fear — yes.   55
There is success, and that among men
is a god, and more than a god.
But there is a balance-scale of justice that keeps
      watch,
quickly on some in the light of day,
and pain waits for others between light and
      darkness,   60
and still others are held by the night of
      unfulfillment.
For blood that the earth has drunk into itself,
a murder of requital has been fixed and will not
      dissolve.
It continues to haunt the guilty man with ruin,
in a disease always luxuriant.   65
For him also that pollutes the bed of bridal love,
there is no remedy;
all tracks lead to the one road,
and in vain would they cleanse
the hand that is infected.   70
On me the god has brought the constraint
of belonging to two cities — from my father's
      house
to this slavery; and in just things and unjust
I must submit to authority fiercely carried.
I will control the bitterness of my heart.   75
But beneath my cloak I weep
at the lechery of my masters,
and I am chilled with secret sorrow.
ELECTRA: Ladies in waiting that tend my house,
since you are here as part of the procession,   80
give me your counsel in this matter.
What am I to say as I pour the libation of
      mourning?
How can I speak with good will, how pray to
      my father?
Can I say, coming from *my* mother,
"A gift from a loving wife to loving husband"? 85
I haven't the audacity for that.
I cannot tell what I should say,
as I pour the oils on my father's grave.
Shall it be the usual prayer of mankind? —
"Grant to those that sent the garlands an
      antidote   90

to match the evils that occasioned the gifts."
Or shall I, in dishonoring silence
— as indeed my father died —
throw the liquid for earth to drink
95 and go away like someone throwing out dirt,
and with it hurl the vessel, with averted eyes?
My friends, be my partners in counsel.
For ours is a common grief for the house;
do not through fear of anyone
100 hide your thoughts in your heart.
For fate awaits alike the free
and the one who lives under a master's hand.
Speak, if you've anything better to say
than I have said.
105 CHORUS: I will speak then, since you bid me,
for this grave of your father I revere like an altar,
and my words will be what's in my mind.
ELECTRA: Speak, just as you revere my father's
grave.
CHORUS: Pour the holy oils, and say:
110 "To those that are his well-wishers —"
ELECTRA: Whom shall I address as that,
amongst his friends?
CHORUS: First yourself, and then whoever hates
Aegisthus.
ELECTRA: So my prayer will be for me and for you?
CHORUS: You know this yourself; speak it
115 immediately.
ELECTRA: Whom shall I add besides, to our faction?
CHORUS: Remember Orestes, even if he is not here.
ELECTRA: Good, good! How well you do instruct
me.
CHORUS: Then remember — "On those guilty of the
murder —"
120 ELECTRA: What shall I say? I don't know. Tell me.
CHORUS: Pray that on them there come a god or a
man —
ELECTRA: As judge or as avenger? Which shall I
say?
CHORUS: Say simply, "Who will kill to answer
killing?"
ELECTRA: Can I with piety ask the gods for that?
125 CHORUS: Yes, giving evil for evil to an enemy.
ELECTRA: Greatest herald of all above or below the
earth,
Hermes of the underworld,
summon the spirits under earth, who keep their
watch
over my father's house, to hear my prayer.
130 And Earth herself, that brings all things to birth,
and having raised them takes again from them
the fruit of their fertility —
here I, that pour to the dead this oil,
call to my father: Father, have pity on me.
135 Kindle dear Orestes to be a light to the house.

For as it is, both of us are exiles,
sold by our mother, who has traded us for her
man,
Aegisthus, her partner in our father's murder.
Myself, I might as well be a slave.
Orestes is banished from his property,   140
while they grow rich and insolent amidst our
troubles.
I pray you that Orestes may come here
with luck to back him.
O my father, hear me.
Grant that I may be more chaste than my
mother,   145
and have a hand more reverent than hers.
So far, my prayers for us; but upon our enemies
I pray, my father, that you come avenging
and bring a death with justice on the killers.
I set this prayer for evil, speaking against my
enemies,   150
in the midst of the prayer for good.
But Hermes be the bringer of good to us in the
upper world,
with the help of the gods and earth and
conquering justice.

(*She pours out the libations.*)

These are my prayers, and there the libation
poured.

(*Speaking to the Chorus.*)

It is the custom that you sing the hymn   155
to crown the mourning in honor of the dead.
CHORUS: Drop the streaming tear for a death,
for dead is our lord;
drop the tear that shall be a shield for us
to help the good avert the ill,   160
the curse of terror;
for now the offerings are poured.
Hear me, lord whom I revere,
hear me in the infirmity of my mind.
Let one come to redeem the house,   165
a man strong with the spear;
let him brandish in his hand a Scythian bow;
let him wield as well
the sword for fighting hand to hand.
ELECTRA: My father has the oils;   170
the earth has drunk them.

(*She sees the lock of Orestes' hair.*)

But here is new matter for a story;
share this, also with me.
CHORUS: Speak. My heart is dancing with fear.
ELECTRA: I see on the grave a lock of newly cut hair. 175
CHORUS: From what man's head, or what deep-
breasted girl's?

ELECTRA: That is a riddle anyone could guess.
CHORUS: Not I; tell me. I am old and you are
young.
ELECTRA: No one but myself could have cut off this
hair.
180 CHORUS: True, those who should mourn him so
are all his enemies.
ELECTRA: Yet certainly it looks very like —
CHORUS: Like whose hair? Tell me what you see in it.
ELECTRA: Certainly it much *resembles* mine.
CHORUS: Could it be a secret gift from him,
185   Orestes?
ELECTRA: It is very, very like his hair.
CHORUS: How could he have dared to come here?
ELECTRA: He *sent* it — this hair,
a mourning tribute to his father.
190 CHORUS: We have as much occasion to cry as ever,
if his foot shall never touch this land again.
ELECTRA: A wave of bitter gall has settled on my
heart;
it is as if a sword had pierced me through.
The thirsty drops fall from my eyes —
they cannot be held back, flood tide of winter
195   water —
as I look at this hair.
How can I believe that someone else among the
people here
owns hair like this? Surely, she that killed him
would hardly cut her hair to mourn him —
200   my mother, whose godless spirit disowns
the name of mother for her children.
But how can I say without a doubt
that this precious thing must belong to Orestes —
dearest to me in all the world?
205 Surely, hope begins to flatter me.
Oh, if only the hair could take a human voice
and play the messenger,
that I might not, as now, be in two minds and
waver;
then either it would bid me clearly
210   cast out this hair in loathing,
if it were truly a cutting from an enemy's head,
or, being kindred, it could mourn with me,
a decoration to this grave and honor to my
father.
We call on gods that know
215 in what storms, like sailors,
we are tossed and twisted. If we are to be saved,
a small seed may grow into a mighty trunk.
Look, look! Here is some more evidence —
footprints, and they are also like mine.
220 Here are two pairs of tracks
outlined — his, and some other traveler's with
him.
The imprint of the heels and the arches

measures exactly with mine
when I place my foot in the prints.
This is agony and craziness.   225

(*Orestes enters.*)

ORESTES: Pray for the rest, that it may turn out
well,
acknowledging the prayers that are fulfilled.
ELECTRA: As of now, what have I got with the help
of the gods?
ORESTES: You have come in sight of
what you long have prayed for.   230
ELECTRA: Do you know whom I have called upon?
ORESTES: I know that you dearly love Orestes.
ELECTRA: And how does that mean my prayers are
answered?
ORESTES: I am he. Do not look for any man
more loved than me.   235
ELECTRA: Is this some trick, sir, that you are playing
upon me?
ORESTES: If so, it is a trick upon myself.
ELECTRA: You want to make a mockery of my
sorrows.
ORESTES: If I mock your sorrows, I would mock my
own.
ELECTRA: Can I be talking to you, the real Orestes?   240
ORESTES: You see me in person, and don't know me.
But you saw the mourning lock of hair,
you trod in my footprints, tracking me out,
and then you were ecstatic, you were sure you
saw me.
Look here, put the lock of cut hair next to your
own;   245
and *this* (*indicating a lock of his hair*) is a match,
your brother's hair.
Look at this piece of woven cloth, your
handiwork,
your shuttle struck it on the loom;
the beasts are your embroidered pictures.   250
Control yourself. Do not let joy
quite overcome your wits.
For those who should be dearest
hate us both.
ELECTRA: O dearest darling of your father's house,   255
the tearful hope of the saving seed,
trust in your strength and you will still
win back that house.
O delightful face that has
all four shares of my love: 260
I must call you father, and to you belongs
the love due to a mother, too —
I hate her, quite justly —
and to you belongs, as well,
the love for my sister, ruthlessly sacrificed;   265

and you are my brother, trusted and honored
as no one else. May Victory, Justice,
and Zeus, making the third, greatest of all,
be your helpers; so I would have it.

270 ORESTES: Zeus, Zeus, look down and save us!
    Behold the brood who have lost their eagle
       father,
    killed in the folds and coils of the deadly viper.
    We are orphaned nestlings, and the hunger
       pinches;
    we are not yet fit to bring home what our fathers
       hunted.
275 So I and you, dear Electra, can be seen here —
    a family without a father —
    both sharers of the same exile at home.
    Yet, Zeus, my father was your worshiper,
    honored you greatly with his sacrifices,
280 and if you now destroy his children,
    where will you find a hand so generous to give
       feasts?
    If you blot out the eagle's breed, you will
       nevermore
    have signs to send to mortals such as will win
       belief.
    Nor will this trunk, this princely stock,
285 if wholly withered, serve your altars
    on days of sacrifice of cattle.
    Save us! You will lift this house to greatness
    that now is small, indeed would seem quite fallen.

CHORUS: Children, saviors of your father's hearth,
    silence, lest someone hear you, children,   290
    and through delight in talking bring the news
    to the masters of the house — Oh, to see *them*
    dead in a fiery ooze of pitch!
ORESTES: The strong oracle of Apollo will not let
    me down,
    that oracle that bade me run this risk.   295
    He spoke of many things in his warning voice,
    of chill destruction under the warm heart,
    if I should fail to pursue my father's murderers
    in their own fashion;
    "Kill them," he said, "to match their killings,   300
    you who are driven to madness
    by the loss of your inheritance."
    Otherwise, he said, with my own life
    I myself would pay, with a multitude of dreadful
       sufferings.
    Some of what he told me was of the anger of
       evil spirits   305
    from under the earth, malignant against mortals,
    diseases on us both, that would climb on our
       flesh
    with savage jaws, cankers that eat into our
       bodies' nature,
    and a white down on top of the sick parts.
    Of all assaults of the Furies° he spoke,   310
    that my father's blood would bring to bear
    upon me

A scene from the American Repertory
Theatre's 1994 production of the
Oresteia, directed by François Rochaix.

as I gaze clearly into the darkness, with eyebrows
   active.
For the arrow of those below, that flies in
   darkness,
winged by the prayers of the kindred of those
   dead,
315 and madness, and empty terrors waking at night,
drive with the bronze-plated scourge, haunt,
and chase from the city the tortured body.
Such people have no share nor partnership
in the libation bowl, nor the rich wine poured out.
The unseen anger of the father bars his son from
320   the altars;
none may welcome him nor lodge with him.
And at the last, unhonored and unloved,
in utter ruin, wasted to dryness, death.
Should I not believe the truth of oracles like
   these?
325 Even if I didn't believe, the deed must be done.
For there are many desires converging in one,
the gods' commands, my great grief for my
   father —
and I am pinched by loss of my property —
the thought that those most famous of mankind,
the citizens who devastated Troy in spirit of
330   glory,
shall become subjects of two women.
His (i.e., Aegisthus's) spirit is womanish. If it is
   not,
he will soon know what he is.
CHORUS: O great fates, bring all to fulfillment
through Zeus in the way that the path of
335   justice is.
Let enemy tongue pay for enemy tongue;
justice in exaction of a debt has a loud voice.
For bloody stroke, let a bloody stroke be paid.
"He who acts shall suffer" —
340 this is the voice of the story grown old in time.
ORESTES: Father, father most dread,
what shall I say or do
to bring you here from your far land
where the bed of the grave holds you,
345 where darkness is your share of the light,
where the eulogy of the mourners
is called joy and comfort
for the sons of Atreus, former princes of this
   house?
CHORUS: Child, the fierce, devouring jaw of fire
350 does not devour the spirit of the dead man;
no, he shows his anger later.

The dying man is mourned,
he that did the injury is discovered;
the due mourning of fathers and parents,
poured in abundance overflowing,   355
shall set the hunt on.
ELECTRA: Hear, O my father, in turn,
my grief and my tears.
Hear the twin dirge of your children by the
   graveside.
The grave has welcomed us,   360
as suppliant and exile, both alike.
What of this is well? What is without evil?
What is not our destruction,
our third fall in wrestling?
CHORUS: Yet still from all this, if the god so wills, 365
he may bring to pass more tuneful songs,
and instead of dirges at the grave
a hymn of welcome shall greet
the loving cup in the royal palace.
ORESTES: Would that under Troy's walls, father, 370
you had been cut down by the spear of some
   Lycian° soldier.
Then you would have left in your house
a fair fame, and established for your children
in their goings to and fro
a life for all to admire.   375
And you yourself would have had
a mounded grave in the land overseas
that your house could support with honor.
CHORUS: Then would you be loved of those whom
   you loved
who are in the house of death, who have died
   gloriously;   380
beneath the earth, you would be a prince of
   dreadful honor,
presiding among the greatest
of those kings of the underworld;
for you were a king in life,
even one of those whose hands were filled 385
with the giving of the doom of death
and the scepter that wins men's allegiance.
ELECTRA: Yes, father, would that beneath Troy's
   walls
you had died with the rest of the spear-
   slaughtered host,
and found your burial by the ford of
   Scamander.°   390
But I had rather those who killed you
should have died as you died,

---

310. **Furies:** Associated with the earth, the Furies or Erinyes
are spirits who punish murderers, especially if the victim is a
blood relative.

371. **Lycian:** The Lycians were allies of the Trojans.
390. **Scamander:** A river rising in Mount Ida and flowing into
the Hellespont, a strait dividing Europe from Asia (the modern strait of Dardanelles).

and some of us from afar off heard of it
as a tale of things that never touched us.

395 CHORUS: In that, my child, you speak of something
greater than gold, a great chance
and a greater bliss.
Certainly you can *speak* of it,
but there comes the sound of the stroke
400 of the double lash.
The champions of the one side are even now
under the earth,
and the hands of the masters of the house are
unholy —
those hateful creatures —
and grow more so against the children.

ORESTES: This has struck me to the heart like an
405 arrow.
Zeus, O Zeus, send up to us from the world
below
revenge, even though it be late in coming,
on the violent sacrilegious hand —
revenge to be perfected again for the parents.

CHORUS: May it be mine to sing a strong cry of
410 triumph
over a man stricken and a woman dying.
Why should I hide the hope which flutters in my
breast
despite me?
Sharp blows the rage before the portals of my
heart —
415 long-cherished hatred.

ELECTRA: When will the hand of Zeus strike with
power?
When will he split the head?
Let it come in such form as the land can believe.
After the days of injustice I demand justice.
Hear me, Earth, and you dignitaries of the
420 underworld.

CHORUS: It is the law that the drops of blood
fallen on the ground demand more blood.
The plague of the Furies calls aloud
on behalf of those already dead
425 for another destruction to crown the first.

ORESTES: Alas, Earth, sovereignties of the
underworld,
you all-mastering curses of the dead,
look upon us, look upon the remnants
of the stock of Atreus, so perplexed.
430 Look upon the dishonor of the house.
Whom shall one turn to, O Zeus?

CHORUS: My loving heart is shaken again
when I hear this pitiable cry;
my hope fails me; my heart grows blacker
435 as I listen. But when I see you
armed for action,
lightly my hope has torn away sorrow

as I greet the appearance of good fortune.

ELECTRA: What shall we say and win our prayer?
Shall it be all we have suffered from our mother? 440
We can flatter, but the others are not charmed.
I have a spirit like a ravening wolf's;
I got it from my savage-minded mother.

CHORUS: Like a woman of the East, and with
Oriental dirges,
I beat my breast, mourning.   445
The strokes of my hand come thick and fast;
one can see the traces of the gripping, tearing
nails,
up and down, up and down, and my wretched
head rings
in answering the sound of the blows.

ELECTRA: O mother, all-daring, you were his enemy, 450
and you dared to give him an enemy's funeral;
without citizens for the carrying forth of their
king,
without dirge you buried him, unmourned.

ORESTES: Indeed, utterly without honor is
the burying you tell of;   455
but she shall pay for the dishonoring of my
father,
by favor of the gods, by favor of these hands of
mine.
When I have cut my foes away from life,
may my death come upon me.

CHORUS: She cut off his hands to stuff in his
armpits,   460
let me tell you; she did that,
she who buried him as you say,
seeking to render his death something
unbearable to you, his children.
What I tell you is your father's dishonored
agony.   465

ELECTRA: You speak of my father's death; but I
stood apart,
dishonored, worthless. I was shut up
in a corner of the house, like a vicious dog.
I found a stream of tears readier than laughter;
I poured out my tears in flood in secret.   470
Hear me, this my father, and write it
in the tablets of your mind.

CHORUS: Drive the word through the ears
to the steadying pace of the mind.
These things are surely so;   475
but more one would wish to learn.
We must proceed with unbending spirit.

ORESTES: I bid you, father, come to us —
we love you.

ELECTRA: I have given you my tears;   480
I invite you.

CHORUS: And we chime in, a band of friends
that joins with them.

Hear us and come to the light,
485   come to us against your enemies.
ORESTES: War god will clash with war god,
Justice with Justice.
ELECTRA: O gods, grant just fulfillment!
CHORUS: I begin to tremble as I hear these prayers.
490   The fated moment has waited so long,
but it may come in answer to their prayers.
O evil, bred in the stock,
harsh bloody stroke of destruction,
mournful agony unbearable,
495   pain that cannot be put to rest!
The cure for these sorrows is in the house;
it must come from them, not from outside;
it must come from savage bloody strife itself.
This is the hymn of the Powers beneath the
earth.
500   Hear me, you Blessed Ones of the Underworld;
give helpful escort to these children's prayers
and lead them graciously to victory!
ORESTES: Father, killed in ways unroyal,
give me control of the house that was yours!
505   ELECTRA: I, too, Father, need this from you —
to destroy Aegisthus and to escape.
ORESTES: If this should be, then will your feasts
be kept among mankind in all due order.
But if it should not be so, then will you be
510   without honor among the well-feasted gods
on earth, without a share in the fat sacrifices.
ELECTRA: I, too, will bring you out of my dowry
libations from my father's house,
at my marriage.
515   This grave will have the primacy of honor.
ORESTES: O Earth, send up my father to oversee the
fight!
ELECTRA: Persephone, grant us a graceful victory!
ORESTES: Remember the bath in which you died, my
father.
ELECTRA: Remember the robes, put to new use as a
net.
520   ORESTES: Chains not of bronze held you, my father,
hunted to death.
ELECTRA: Caught you shamefully in treacherous
robes,
as in a trap.
ORESTES: Will these taunts rouse you from your
sleep, my father?
525   ELECTRA: Will you lift up your beloved head?
ORESTES: Send us Justice, as an ally to those who
love you!
Grant us a handhold to match *their* hands
if you, now conquered, want your
turn for victory!
530   ELECTRA: Hear this last cry of all, my father:
Look on the nestlings, here upon your grave.
Have pity on your brood, both male and female.

ORESTES: Do not blot out this seed of Pelops's
children.
For if they live you are not dead, in death.
Children are voices of salvation to a dead man;   535
they are like corks that keep the nets afloat,
saving the woven meshes from the depths.
ELECTRA: Hear — it is for you we raise our
sorrowful song.
You will save yourself if you listen to our
prayers.
CHORUS: Truly, this honor to the unsorrowed grave   540
has lasted long enough,
though none can fault you two for that.
But now, since you are rightly set on action,
you should try your fortune at once, and act.
ORESTES: We will, but it is not amiss to know   545
why she has sent the offerings, what story moved
her
to pay for an inexpiable crime
so many years after. Surely, a wretched favor
is this, sent to the insensitive dead man.
I cannot guess the meaning of these offerings,   550
but they are surely less than the offense.
If one were to spill everything in the world
to cure the bloodletting of one man,
the labor is lost, men say. But tell me what I ask,
if so be that you know it.   555
CHORUS: Yes, I know it,
my son, for I was there. That godless woman
was driven by dreams and by night-wandering
terrors
to send these offerings.
ORESTES: Did you find out about her dream,   560
to be able to tell it rightly?
CHORUS: She thought that she gave birth to a
snake —
that is how she told it.
ORESTES: How did her story end? How did it come
out?
CHORUS: She wrapped the snake in swaddling
clothes,   565
like a baby.
ORESTES: What food did it need, this newborn
monster?
CHORUS: She gave it the breast, in her dream.
ORESTES: How did the hateful thing not hurt the
nipple?
CHORUS: It did. It drew clots of blood with the milk.   570
ORESTES: This is not meaningless! It is a vision of a
man.
CHORUS: She started out of her sleep and cried in
terror,
and many a lamp that was blinded in darkness
blazed in the palace walls to pleasure its
mistress.
And after that, she sent these funeral offerings;   575

she hoped that they would cure all that was
   wrong.
ORESTES: This is *my* prayer, by this land,
   by my father's grave:
   may this dream find fulfillment for me!
580 I judge it will, too; all of it fits.
   For if the snake came from the same place *I* did,
   and wore my swaddling clothes, and sucked the
      breast
   that gave me sustenance, mixed the dear milk
   with clots of blood, and she was terrified
585 at what had happened — then, it must be so that,
   as she raised this fearful monster,
   she must die violently!
   For I that became that very snake will kill her,
   even as the dream has said.
590 CHORUS: I'll take your reading of these signs,
   and so may it turn out! For the rest,
   instruct us that are your friends —
   tell some what to do, and others what not to do.
   ORESTES: It is a simple story. My sister must go
      inside —
595 I tell her, hide this plan we have arranged —
   that those who killed with treachery a prince
   may themselves be caught with treachery and die
   in the same snare — as Loxias has prophesied,
   our Lord, Apollo, that from old times never lied.
600 I will disguise myself as a foreigner,
   with all the traveler's gear,
   and come with Pylades here to the courtyard
      gates.
   I will be a guest-friend and ally of the house.
   We will both speak with a Parnassian accent.
   Even if none of the sentries will be eager to
605   receive us,
   as the house is so bedeviled with trouble
   — yet we will stand and wait, until
   some passerby will guess at who we are
   and say, "Why does Aegisthus bar his door
610 against a suppliant — if he is really at home
   and knows of it?"
   And if once I cross the threshold
   of the courtyard gates, if once I find him
   upon my father's throne, or if he comes to speak
615 to me, face to face, or calls me to his presence,
   before he says, "Where is this foreigner from?"
   with my quick blade I will send him to his death.
   The Fury unstinted of murder will now drink
   a third draught of blood full strength, undiluted.
620 Do you, Electra, keep careful watch in the house,
   so that our plans will fit with one another.
   You, my friends, keep
   a very heedful hold upon your tongue.
   There is a season for silence and for necessary
      speech.
625 The rest Pylades here must oversee,

who has guided my sword to success in other
   contests.
      (*Exeunt Orestes, Pylades, Electra.*)
CHORUS: Many indeed are the terrors
   the earth breeds, causes for fear;
   and the bosom of the deep teems
   with monsters repulsive;   630
   overhead hang the lights
   that menace in midair;
   and all creatures, winged and earthbound,
   can tell of the wrath of the wind-driven
      hurricane.
   But who shall tell the tale   635
   of man's overbold spirit?
   And who can tell how far those passionate loves
   can dare, that live in the minds of perverse
      women,
   passions that keep company with man's crazed
      destruction?
   The love passion of the woman, winning victory, 640
   unloving, perverts the coupling companionship
   of beasts and men alike.
   Let him whose thoughts give him no wings
   still know, by learning, of dread Althaea's craft,
   the device of the burning torch: 645
   she kindled the red brand that was to live
   as long as her son, from the moment
   he came from his mother,
   crying, and made it measure with his life
   till it ended in the doom of death.   650
   There again, for your hate, is the story of Scylla,°
   a bloody murderess,
   who, on her foes' behalf, destroyed her own kin,
   persuaded by the Cretan necklace of wrought
      gold,
   the gift of Minos: plotting malice, she sheared 655
   the immortal hair from Nisus in his deep sleep —
   she was a bitch at heart.
   And so Hermes took possession of him.
   Since I have embarked on the tale
   of unsavory crimes — what of *this* vile marriage
      tie   660
   accursed by the house, what of the designs
   that the woman crafted against her soldier-
      husband?
   For my part, I honor the hearth unfired by
      passion,
   the spirit of a woman meek and kindly.
   But the worst thing told about in any story   665
   is the Lemnian deed; with groaning and the spit
      of contempt

---

651. Scylla: Daughter of Nisus, king of Megara. Nisus's life
and the safety of his kingdom depended on a lock of red hair
that grew on his head. Scylla cut off this lock of hair and betrayed the city to the king of Crete.

the public voice denounces it. Ever since then,
men speak of what is horrible as "like the
     Lemnian crime."
The breed of them is gone, dishonored of men,
670 because God hated them and cursed them,
and no one respects what is hated of God.
In this list of mine, what is wrongly included?
There is a sharp sword, and by the action of
     Justice,
herself trampled under foot unlawfully,
675 it strikes through and through, near the vitals,
those who violated the majesty of Zeus,
sinning against it all.
Deep-rooted is the trunk of Justice's tree,
and fate forges her sword on her behalf,
and to the house the glorious Fury, deeply
680   brooding,
brings a child at long last to exact
penalty for the pollution of old bloodshed in the
     past.

(*Enter Orestes and Pylades.*)

ORESTES: Hello, within there! Do you hear me
     knocking?
Who is there? Hello, again! Who is at home?
685 For the last time, come out, do!
if this house of Aegisthus has any hospitality.

(*Enter servant.*)

SERVANT: Very well; I hear you.
What is your country? Where do you come
     from?
ORESTES: Take a message to your masters,
690 to whom I come. I have news for them.
Hurry, for night's car hastens on to dark,
and it is time for travelers to cast anchor
at some house where strangers are welcomed.
Will someone in authority come out?
695 A lady? A man might be better;
there is a necessary modesty in talking with
     women
which blurs what one has to say. One can be
     franker
talking man to man; one can deliver clearly
a clearer message.
          (*Exit servant; enter Clytemnestra.*)
700 CLYTEMNESTRA: Sirs, say what you have to say.
You shall have all that fits this house to give —
warm baths, and comfortable beds after your
     labors,
and properly respectful faces to tend you.
If you must deal with matters of greater concern,
705 that *is* men's business, and I will tell them.
ORESTES: I am Daulieus, a stranger out of Phocis;
I was going to Argos, on my private business,

with my own equipment — I am here, as you see
     me now.
A man met me as I journeyed, a man unknown
     to me before,
as I to him — and asked me about the road   710
(his name was Strophius the Phocian,° so he told
     me):
"If, sir, you are going to Argos in any case,
would you remember, truly, to tell Orestes'
     parents
'Orestes is dead' — please
do not forget this message.   715
Whether his friends shall choose to bring him
     home
or to leave him here forever a foreigner —
a permanent resident — bring me back word
     again
what their decision is. For now the ribs
of the brazen urn hide the dust of this man much
     mourned."   720
I have told you what I heard.
But whether I speak to the masters and his
     kinfolk,
I do not know. His parents should be told.
CLYTEMNESTRA: Ah! Your story tells our utter ruin.
Curse of this house, how tough a wrestler   725
     you are against us!
How many things, even safely hidden away,
your watchfulness takes in,
your shafts launched from afar bring down.
You have stripped me of those I loved;   730
and now Orestes —
he had been wise, he had been taken away
and kept his foot out of destruction's mud.
He was one hope, a healer for the house's
     craziness,
and now you may cancel the entry in the ledger.   735
ORESTES: I would I could have
made the acquaintance of such noble hosts
through happy events, and so been entertained.
What is more agreeable than guest and host
in mutual entertainment!   740
But my mind scrupled at not completing this
     thing
for friends, once I had promised and pledged my
     word.
CLYTEMNESTRA: You will be treated with just as
     much dignity,
you will be just as good a friend to the house.

---

711. Strophius the Phocian: A family friend with whom
Orestes stayed at the time of Agamemnon's murder. See
Agamemnon 1. 922.

745 If you had not, another would have come and
given the news.
But now it's time that strangers who have
endured
the long day's travel should have suitable
welcome.

(*To a servant.*)

Here, bring this man to the men's guest
chambers;
bring in also his servants and fellow travelers.
And there let them be given the comforts of this
750 house.
I bid you do this as you shall answer it.
We ourselves will give your message to
the master of the house,
and with friends — which we have in plenty —
755 we will take counsel about this mischance.

(*Exeunt all but Chorus.*)

CHORUS: You dear girls, servants of this house,
when shall we show
the strength of our voices for Orestes?
O sacred land, o sacred eminence,
760 this tomb, where our king lies, that led the fleet,
now hear our words, now come to our help;
for now is the time for crafty Persuasion
to support our side, for Hermes of the
Underworld,
a nightly presence, to watch, to preside
765 over our deadly conflicts of the sword.
The stranger is like one that contrives mischief.

(*Enter nurse.*)

But here I see Orestes' nurse in tears.
Where are you going, Cilissa, out of doors?
The grief that goes with you is no hired mourning.
770 NURSE: The mistress bade me call Aegisthus speedily
to meet these strangers, that as man to man
he may come and understand this news of theirs.
To the servants she shows a solemn face of
sorrow,
but behind the eyes there is a lurking smile
775 in honor of events that have turned out well —
for her — but for the house a sheer disaster,
in the message that the strangers bring — so
clearly.
He surely too will hear and will rejoice
when he has grasped the story. Ah me! Ah me!
780 So much has happened in the past to the house
that was hard to bear — a mingled draught of
sorrow
that made my heart in my breast an agony.
But never did I endure the like of this;
all the rest of the cup I have drained with
patience,

but my Orestes, my life's work,   785
whom I took from his mother's hand and raised
him up!
My nights broken with his crying, all the many
tasks so uselessly performed — I bore them all;
for a baby is so helpless; you must tend him like
an animal,
the nurse's mind instead of his own; swaddled,   790
it does not say what ails it — hunger or thirst
or a wet diaper — the child's young belly
is autonomous! I was the prophet
of his needs, but often deceived, you may be
sure,
and so the laundress that made all white again;   795
a nurse is often nurse and cleaner both,
and *I* doubled in both trades, as I took Orestes
to raise as his father's heir. And now I hear
he is dead — O my God!
And I go to fetch this man, this very infection   800
of our house. He will be right glad to hear the
news.
CHORUS: You say she bade him come to her. But
how?
NURSE: What do you mean by "how"? I don't
understand.
CHORUS: Was he to come with his retinue or on his
own?
NURSE: She bade him bring his personal guards with
him.   805
CHORUS: Tell our cursed master nothing of the
sort;
tell him to come by himself, without a fear,
and listen; tell him to come quickly, gladly.
For a messenger may straighten out a crooked
signal.
NURSE: Are you a friend to this our present news?   810
CHORUS: Yes, but what if Zeus means to change
our present ill weather?
NURSE: How can that be? The house's hope,
Orestes, is gone.
CHORUS: Not yet. Only a bad prophet would read
it so.
NURSE: What! Do you have news different from
what is said?   815
CHORUS: Go, give your message; do what your
mistress told you.
NURSE: I will obey your words and go.
May all be for the best, as the gods will give it!

(*Exit nurse.*)

CHORUS: You, Zeus, father of the heavenly gods,
grant my prayer: that those who wish to see   820
propriety again in the lords of the house
win good success! All I have spoken is justly
spoken;
O Zeus, protect us.

825
Alas! Make our champion winner over his
   enemies
within the house. When you make him great,
you shall be repaid, two- and threefold,
for your graciousness.
Know that the son of your friend
is a colt yoked to the chariot of misfortune;

830
but you, if you impose a measured pace
on the running, you keep his rhythm on to
   safety;
you will see the reach of the striding
paces over the plain.
You temperate gods that haunt

835
the recesses of the house that delights in wealth,
   hear us;
with fresh judgment abolish
the blood of ancient deeds;
let no murder of long ago

840
breed another sequence in the house.
You that dwell in the great, fair-established
mouth of the cave,
grant the crowning of the house of the hero;
grant that he may see the radiant

845
light of freedom with welcoming eyes
as it comes out of the veil of dark mist.
May Hermes, the child of Maia,° as he justly
   should,
help him; may he give him a fair wind for what
   he does!
Many blind utterances he brings to light, if he
   will,

850
but when he utters obscure speech
he pulls the darkness of night over the eyes,
and by day it is not much clearer.
Then for the deliverance of the house's wealth
we shall raise the shout of female voices;

855
we shall strike up the magic cry, "She sails well!"
My profit shall increase in this,
and ruin no longer encompass my friends.
But do you, when the share of action comes,
bolder, in answer to her cry of "Child!"

860
cry, "Father!" and bring to pass
a destruction none can blame.
Keep within your breast
a heart like that of Perseus,
and with love to some beneath the earth
and to others above, hold the robe against the

865
   Gorgon.°

---

847. Maia: Daughter of Atlas and mother of Hermes (by
Zeus).   **863–65. Perseus . . . Gorgon:** Perseus is a mythological hero who, with the help of Athena, cut off the head of the
Gorgon Medusa, a monster whose eyes could turn human beings into stone.

Set bloody destruction within the house,
and with a glance blot out utterly the guilty.

(*Enter Aegisthus.*)

AEGISTHUS: I was summoned; my wife's message
   brought me here. I learn that there is news
   which some strangers have brought,   870
   very unpleasant news — the death of Orestes.
   It will be another bloody grief laid for the house
      to bear,
   a house already bitten by an old wound.
   How may I judge that this news is living and
      true?
   Or can it be the terrified tales of women   875
   which leap, winged, in the air, and then die vainly?
   What can you tell me of this that is clear to the
      mind?
CHORUS: Yes, we have heard. But go into the house,
   and make your own inquiry of the strangers.
   There is no strength in messengers   880
   like the personal inquiry of man to man on the
      spot.
AEGISTHUS: I am very anxious
   to see and test the messenger thoroughly —
   whether he was present, beside the man as he
      died,
   or only said what he knew from a dim rumor.   885
   I am wide awake; I will not be easily cheated.
                              (*Exit Aegisthus.*)
CHORUS: Zeus, Zeus, what shall I say, from where
      begin
   with prayers and invocations?
   How can I find words to express
   the loyalty I feel?   890
   For now the befouled points
   of knives that butcher men
   will either achieve the eternal ruin
   of Agamemnon's house,
   or there shall be one that kindles   895
   the fire and light in freedom's honor,
   and will rule throughout the city;
   he shall have the great wealth of his fathers.
   It shall be Orestes, the beloved of God,
   Orestes, that always as the third against the two   900
   shall lock in conflict. May it be for victory!
AEGISTHUS (*offstage*): Oh! Oh!
CHORUS: 1. O my God!
   2. What is it? How has it ended?
   3. Let us hold off, as the thing is being finished,   905
   that we may appear guiltless of the evil,
   for now the end of the battle is here.

(*Enter servant.*)

SERVANT: O sorrow, sorrow! Our master is killed.
   Sorrow again, the third cry of lament.

910 Aegisthus is no more. Open the doors, I say, and
hurry.
Pull the bolts back from the women's quarters.
It needs a strong young man to be able for that —
but hardly strong enough to help the dead.
That cannot be.
915 Oh! Oh!
It is the deaf I speak to; surely they sleep,
to whom I cry so unavailingly! Where is
Clytemnestra?
My cry has no effect.
What is she doing?
920 It seems that now *her* neck is on the block
to fall, as she has deserved it should.

(*Enter Clytemnestra.*)

CLYTEMNESTRA: What is this? What does your
shouting mean?
SERVANT: It is, I tell you, the dead killing the living.
CLYTEMNESTRA: I understand the truth of your
riddle.
925 We killed by cunning; now we die by cunning.
Here, someone, quick, bring me an ax.
Let us find out
if we will conquer or ourselves be conquered.
This is exactly the bad moment I have come to.

(*Enter Orestes and Pylades.*)

930 ORESTES: Yes, it is *you* I seek. *He* has had enough.
CLYTEMNESTRA: My God, he is dead — dearest,
strongest Aegisthus.
ORESTES: You love him, do you? In the same grave
you'll lie
along with him. You'll not prove false to him
even in death.
CLYTEMNESTRA: Stop, my child. Have some
935 reverence for this breast
which often, sleeping, you milked to your good,
squeezing it with your gums.
ORESTES: O Pylades, what shall I do?
I cannot kill my mother.
940 PYLADES: Where then will be Apollo's prophecies
spoken by the Pythia,° and the sworn compact?
Have everyone as enemy rather than the gods.
ORESTES: You win; in my judgment, your advice is
good.

(*To Clytemnestra.*)

Follow me, for I mean to kill you beside him.
945 You rated him in life above my father;

941. **Pythia:** Possessed by the god Apollo, the Pythia, like a
priestess, responded for Apollo when petitioners called upon
the god at the Delphic Oracle.

now in death sleep with him. Between the two
men,
you love and hate the wrong ones.
CLYTEMNESTRA: I raised you and would grow old
with you.
ORESTES: You killed my father. Would you live with
his son?
CLYTEMNESTRA: Fate, my child, was a partner in all
this.   950
ORESTES: And fate it is that brings this death on
you.
CLYTEMNESTRA: Do you not fear your mother's
curses, child?
ORESTES: You brought me to birth, and threw me
away to ruin.
CLYTEMNESTRA: No no! I "threw you away" to a
friend's house.
ORESTES: I was a free man's son; you sold me
shamelessly.   955
CLYTEMNESTRA: What was the price I got for you?
ORESTES: I am ashamed to insult you openly with
that.
CLYTEMNESTRA: Then you must speak equally of *his*
lechery.
ORESTES: Do not taunt the worker, when you sit
inside.
CLYTEMNESTRA: It is hard for a woman to live
without a man.   960
ORESTES: It is the man's work that supports
the woman in the house.
CLYTEMNESTRA: I see, my child, you mean to kill
your mother.
ORESTES: It is you who kill yourself, not I who kill
you.
CLYTEMNESTRA: Watch out; guard yourself against   965
your mother's furious hounds.
ORESTES: If I let you go, shall I not fear
my mother's furious hounds?
CLYTEMNESTRA: I think I am singing my dirge at the
grave's edge,
and that is vain.   970
ORESTES: It is my father's fate has brought your
death.
CLYTEMNESTRA: This is the snake I brought to birth
and suckled.
ORESTES: The fear in your dream was a true
prophet; yes.
You violated in killing; you are
violated in suffering.   975
(*Exeunt Orestes, Clytemnestra, Pylades.*)
CHORUS: I do bewail indeed the death of those two.
But since the brave Orestes has put the coping
stone
on many bloodlettings, I prefer this end to the
other,

that the eye of this house shall not be lost
    forever.
980 Justice has come at last
on the children of Priam of Troy.
Justice has come, and its heavy revenge
to Agamemnon's house also,
the double lion, the double war god.
985 That banished exile, by Apollo's word,
has obtained all his destined lot;
he yielded so prudently
to what the god told him to do.
Cry, cry hurrah!
990 for our ruling house, for escape from its woes,
for escape from its wastage of wealth
by two so foul, escape from its past
of ill luck.
There has come, too, the god whose concern
995 is crafty revenge and a secret fight;
and the trueborn daughter of Zeus
took Orestes' hand
and guided him; rightly we call her
Justice — apt is the name —
1000 and the anger she breathes against her enemies
is pure destruction.
Even as the Lord Apollo cried
from deep inside his shrine in Parnassus,°
so he struck the corruption, grown ingrained,
1005 and none can blame him there.
The might of the gods is always master
in action against the wicked.
Worthy it is to worship
the power that supports the heavens.
1010 There is the light for us to see;
there the great curb
is taken away from the house.
Arise, O house! For far too long a time
you have lain level with the earth.
1015 Soon time that brings all to accomplishment
shall cross the threshold of the palace,
when from the hearth she banishes
the ruin of infatuation; she has purification to
    expel it,
and all shall be there to be seen
1020 in smiling-faced fortune;
and we shall cry aloud,
"The strangers have fallen! They have vanished
from the palace they tenanted!"
There is light for us to see.

(*Enter Orestes and Pylades, with the bodies.*)

1025 ORESTES: See there, the two princes of this land.
They killed my father, plundered the house.

1003. **Parnassus:** A sacred mountain.

They were solemn as they sat on their thrones.
They are dear friends to one another still —

(*He points at the two bodies.*)

so at least you would think from how they are
    now.
Their plighted oath stands fast still, which they
    swore   1030
to work the murder of my wretched father
and die themselves, together.
Yes, they have kept their oaths well.
And look you, now, those that have heard
the sad story,   1035

(*He holds up an imaginary robe.*)

look at the traps for my poor father,
the tyings of his feet,
the fetters of his hands, the linkage of his legs.
Spread the garment out, and show it to all that
    stand
around here: this was the covering of the man.   1040
Let the father see it — not my father, of course,
but the father that looks down upon
all that is done here, the Sun-Father.
These are the deeds, the filthy deeds, of my
    mother;
let them be a testimony to Justice, one day,   1045
that this murder which I have done
was justly done: my mother's murder.
(I do not even speak about Aegisthus and his
    death;
he had what is legally come to him,
the justice due to an adulterer.)   1050
She it was who planned this hateful act upon
    him,
on him whose child she had carried heavy within
    her,
a child once loved but now, in the event,
a hating enemy.
How does she seem to you? Was she a viper,   1055
or a sea serpent, whose very touch brings
    corruption
though the hand was not bitten? Shall we so call
    her,
for her bold and vicious spirit?
What shall I say of the robe? What shall I call it
and make the name good? Was it a snare   1060
for a wild thing, or a covering for a corpse,
a bathrobe for him, trailing to his feet?
No, not a snare, but a net, you might say,
and a robe that fell to his feet.
Maybe the sort of thing a highwayman   1065
might use, to make a living, robbing travelers;
with such equipment he might gladden his heart,
as he plundered many.

May never a woman like her share house of
    mine!
1070   May the gods curse me rather to have no child!
CHORUS (*addressing the corpse of Clytemnestra*):
    Oh for the wretched act!
    You have ended in pitiful death.
    You waited and at the end
    retribution flowered.
1075   ORESTES: Did she do it, or didn't she?
    This robe is my witness
    that the sword of Aegisthus stained it.
    Time has deepened the stain of murdered blood
    that, joining in, has spoiled
1080   the many other dyes in the embroidery.
    I praise my father; now I am here to lament him.
    You I address, you woven cloth that murdered
    my father. Yes, I have pain
    for the deed, for the suffering, for our whole
    race.
1085   I have the pollution, the undesirable
    fruits of my victory.
CHORUS: No one of all mankind shall cross the end
    of his life and know no mischief, nor loss of
    honor.
    Ah me, for this present trouble — and now there
    is another.
1090   ORESTES: I want you to know —
    for how it will end I don't know —
    it is as if I were driving
    a team of horses clear out of the course.
    They are bolting with me, they have the better of
    me!
    It is my wits I mean; I cannot control them.
1095   There is fear
    in my heart that is ready to sing;
    I have a dance there under my anger.
    So while I am still in my senses I proclaim
    to you that are my friends — yes, I confess
1100   I killed my mother, and I did so justly.
    She was my father's murderer, a pollution
    she was, and one that the gods loathed.
    I cite as the chief cure for this awful thing I
    did —
    Apollo and his prophecies.
1105   He spoke to me and said: "If you do this,
    you shall be clear of evil blame; neglect it —"
    I will not say what punishment he promised;
    no one is archer enough to hit the target
    of that misery.
1110   And now behold me! Here, I am ready;
    with flocks of wool in the garland I will go
    to Loxias's shrine, his seat at the navel of the
    earth,

that which is called the immortal light of fire,
striving to escape the taint of kindred blood.
Apollo bade me seek no other hearth.   1115
In days to come I charge all Argives keep
within their memory how these evils happened,
and bear me testimony, when Menelaus comes.
I myself a wanderer, from this land outcast,
living and dead, leaving my repute to them . . .   1120
CHORUS: But what you did was right! Do not unite
your lips to evil utterance; do not blame yourself.
You gave its freedom to all the city of Argos;
you neatly cut off the heads of the two dragons.
ORESTES: Oh! Oh!   1125
Can these be women? Look! They are like
    Gorgons.
Their robes are dark, and they themselves a mass
of writhing snakes! I cannot stand and face them.
CHORUS: Your father's dearest son!
What are these visions that torment you?   1130
Stop. Do not fear.
You have won the victory.
ORESTES: These are not haunting *visions* of terror;
they are clearly what they are —
my mother's furious hounds.   1135
CHORUS: It is the fresh blood on your hand that
    does it.
It is from this your mind's distraction comes.
ORESTES: O Lord Apollo, how they are crowding in!
And from their eyes flow streams of loathsome
    blood!
CHORUS: One cleansing for you only —   1140
Apollo with a touch
shall make you free of these torments.
ORESTES: You don't see them, but *I* do.
I am driven. I cannot stay.

    (*Exit Orestes.*)

CHORUS: Good luck go with you! May the god look
    on you   1145
with kindly aspect, guarding you throughout
the perils of the happenings you must meet!
Here is the third storm
brought to fulfillment on the royal house,
savage in its blast.   1150
In the beginning was the child-eating
and the sufferings of Thyestes.
Then, second, came the murder of the king,
our general-in-chief, cut down in his bath.
And now the third — Is it a rescuer,   1155
or must I call him a destruction?
When will it find completion? When will it end?
When will the fierceness of our ruin
fall again to its sleep?

THE EUMENIDES

The last play in the trilogy resolves issues that are present in the opening scenes of *Agamemnon*. The Furies become the Chorus and are described as hideous and fearful, loathed by the gods. That the Furies represent the old gods is clear when they speak with Athena; they express their resentment at being thrust aside by the younger gods, of whom both Athena and Apollo are chief. After killing Clytemnestra, Orestes flees to the shrine of Apollo at Delphi and takes refuge on the omphalos, the great carved stone that was said to be the navel of the world. Because Orestes killed his mother, the Furies want his blood; but Athena holds them back with the promise of a trial on the hill of Ares, where the Amazons had once "pitched their tents." She refers to the Areopagus, a court of elders in Athens, recently reconstituted in Aeschylus's time to judge murder cases. Apollo represents the defense, and the Furies the prosecution. Before the judgment can be handed down, Athena explains that since she is born only from her father (she sprang fully grown and armed from Zeus's forehead), she must cast her vote on the side of the male if there is a tie vote. There is a tie, and she votes for Orestes' freedom.

The Furies in response threaten to poison the land, but Athena works out a compromise in presenting them with sacred land near the Erectheum on the Akropolis, where they will be revered by the citizens of Athens for all time. She gives them certain powers and mollifies them by changing them from hated deities to deities that the people will worship. The Furies accept the offer and ultimately sing the praises of Athens. Indeed, the play ends with the Furies praising Athens and promising to watch over the city. Ultimately, the *Oresteia* becomes an elaborate testament to the renewal of a great city — the Persians had burned everything to the ground in 480 B.C. — a city that had magnificently rebuilt itself. It is also a testament to a new order of deities led by the god of the muses, Apollo.

Aeschylus (c. 525–456 B.C.)

THE EUMENIDES   458 B.C.

TRANSLATED BY DAVID GRENE AND WENDY DONIGER O'FLAHERTY

Dramatis Personae

PRIESTESS OF APOLLO
ORESTES
APOLLO
GHOST OF CLYTEMNESTRA
CHORUS, THE FURIES
ATHENA

PRIESTESS: First, in my prayer, I give to Earth first
        place
    among the gods; first prophetess was she.
    Second, Eternal Law — second was she
    to sit on her mother's oracular seat, as the story
        goes.
5   In third allotment, one more Titan°
    daughter of Earth sat there,
    Phoebe° — a willing successor, not perforce.
    She gave the oracle to Phoebus,°
    a birthday gift — his name, too, echoed hers.
10 He left the lake and ridge of Delos°
    and beached his ship on the shores of Attica,
    and to this land he came, to his dwelling in
        Parnassus.
    He was attended and greatly glorified
    by the children of Hephaestus.° They were his
        road-makers;
    they made the wild land tame for him. The
15   people
    honored him mightily, as did Delphos also,
    their king and ruler. Zeus seized his mind,
    filled it with god, giving him the art to be
    the prophet, fourth upon this seat of prophecy,
20 Apollo, Zeus's spokesman and his son.
    These are the gods with whom my prayer begins.
    In my account the primacy is hers,

Athena of the Fore-Temple; then I reverence
the nymphs of the Corycian cavern,
hollow, bird-haunted, the resort of spirits;   25
Bromius° lives there — I do not forget him —
from there he led his Bacchanals,° as god,
contriving the death of Pentheus,° like snaring a
    hare.
I call as well upon the springs of Pleistus,
and the power of Poseidon,°   30
and highest and supreme perfecter, Zeus.
Now as prophet I assume my seat.
Grant that, of all my previous enterings here,
the gods make this the very best.
If there are any Greeks among you,   35
let them come forward after casting lots,
as is the custom, for I will conduct my
    prophecies
just as the god prescribes.

(She enters and then reemerges, on hands and knees.)

Horrors to tell! Horrors my eyes have seen!
They drove me from Apollo's house   40
back out again, so that I have no strength,
nor power to stand; look, I run on my hands,
no quickness in my feet — a terrified old woman
is nothing — indeed, the equal of a child.
I went to the inner shrine,   45
which was covered in garlands; there at the
    earth's navel
I saw a man, God's stain of guilt upon him,
sitting as suppliant on the very navel stone;
the blood was dripping
from his hands, and his sword was newly drawn;   50
he wore the olive twigs grown at the treetop,
chastely decked out with lavish flocks of wool,

---

5. **Titan:** One of the older gods who ruled before the Olympian gods defeated them.   7. **Phoebe:** Associated with the moon, this Titan was the mother of Leto, and thus grandmother of Apollo.   8. **Phoebus:** Another name for Apollo.   10. **Delos:** A small island, reputed to be the birthplace of Apollo and Artemis.   14. **Hephaestus:** Also known as Vulcan, Hephaestus was the god of fire, associated with the forge.

26. **Bromius:** Another name for Dionysus or Bacchus, a fertility god associated with orgiastic celebration and with wine.   27. **Bacchanals:** Orgiastic cult celebrations associated with Bacchus.   28. **Pentheus:** Pentheus denied the divinity of Bacchus and forbade the Thebans to worship him. When Pentheus went to spy on the Bacchic rites, Bacchus stirred the worshipers into a frenzy, and this band of women, including Pentheus's mother, tore Pentheus apart.   30. **Poseidon:** Greek god of water and the sea.

shining white fleece wool. So far I can speak
     clearly.
But in front of the man there slept, upon the
     benches,
55 a dreadful troop of women.
No, I won't say they were women, but Gorgons;
no, not that, either; their shapes did not seem
     to me
like Gorgons' shapes.
I saw a picture, once, of those, as they brought
60 the feast for Phineus,° but these I saw now
were wingless, black and utterly repulsive.
They snored, the smell of their breaths
was not to be borne,
and from their eyes there trickled a loathsome
     gum.
65 The gear upon them was not fit to wear
before God's images, nor within men's houses.
I never saw the tribe like to this company,
nor have I seen the land that could support them
without cause to regret the pain they cost her.
70 From here on it must be Loxias himself,
strong lord of this house,
that should take all this in charge.
He is a healing prophet, and can read portents,
and is, for all other things of this kind,
75 a force of purification.
               (*She leaves; enter Orestes and Apollo.*)
ORESTES: O King Apollo, you know not to be
     unjust;
since you know this, learn not to be neglectful.
Your strength is our best warranty for good-
     ness.
APOLLO: I will not desert you; to the end your
     guardian,
80 beside you and afar, I shall prove myself
not gentle to your enemies.
Now you see these crazed creatures,
sunk in sleep, its prisoners,
these filthy virgins, ancient, old children;
85 nor god nor man nor beast will touch them.
Their birth, too, was for evil, for evil darkness
is where they live, Tartarus° beneath the earth.
They are hated objects of men and the Olympian
     gods.
I will protect you; but you must flee from them.
90 Do not spare yourself. For they will hunt you

through all the length of the earth, as you stride
     onward,
over the ground worn by your feet,
over the seas, and then, over the island cities.
This task of yours will herd you on — do not
     weary
before it ends; go to the city of Pallas Athena;   95
there clasp your arms around the ancient image,
and sit. In that place we will find judges,
and speeches as our engine to enchant them;
so you shall be freed entirely from your troubles.
Yes, true, I *did* persuade you to kill your mother.   100
Remember that; do not let fear conquer your
     mind.
You, Hermes,° my blood-brother —
for your father is mine, too —
guard him and be to him, as your title is,
a very escort, a protection;   105
be his shepherd, for he is my suppliant.
Zeus honors the reverence due to outlaws,
with safe conduct to success, as it is astir
among mortal men.
     (*Exeunt Orestes and Apollo; enter Clytemnestra.*)
CLYTEMNESTRA'S GHOST: You sleep! Aha! What need
     have I of sleepers?   110
Because of you I am so dishonored among
the other dead; those dead that I have killed
never let up their insults against me.
I wander, shamed, among the perished people.
I tell you, I have the greatest blame among
     them,   115
I that have suffered such outrages from those
dearest to me,
and no god shows his anger on my behalf,
though I was slaughtered by hands that killed
     their mother.
Look here, look at that wound upon my heart.   120
For when the mind is asleep, its eyes are bright;
by day men have less vision of what is destined.
You have licked up many of my offerings,
wineless libations, sweet without wine.
To you I used to sacrifice by night   125
those feasts on the altar, shared with no other
     god.
Now I see all this trodden underfoot,
neglected. He has slipped away, like a fawn,
lightly — even from the closest drawn of nets.
He has escaped, heartily mocking us.   130
Hear how I plead for my very soul!
Take heed, you goddesses beneath the earth.
For it is I that call you, in a dream,

60. Phineus: King of Thrace who was plagued by Harpies, winged supernatural creatures, who stole or defiled his food. There are various versions of the crime for which Phineus was punished. Some accounts say he blinded his sons; others say that he allowed their stepmother to blind them.
87. Tartarus: Located below the kingdom of the dead ruled by Hades, Tartarus was where the Titans were imprisoned.

102. Hermes: Son of Zeus, Hermes is the younger brother of Apollo. He is a messenger of the more powerful gods, and a guide of souls.

Clytemnestra.
CHORUS (*they whimper like hounds, like dogs
      dreaming in sleep*)
135 CLYTEMNESTRA: You would whimper, would you? —
      but the man has escaped, gone far;
      his friends are not at all like mine!
CHORUS (*whimpers*)
CLYTEMNESTRA: You are too sleepy; you don't pity
      me!
      Orestes was his mother's murderer,
140 and he is fled and gone.
CHORUS (*now yelps, with meaningless sounds*)
CLYTEMNESTRA: Yelping, are you, but still sleepy?
      Get up and go!
      What is your destined work, but to bring ill to
      pass?
CHORUS (*sharp yelp*)
CLYTEMNESTRA: Sleep and work-weariness, sworn
      conspirators,
145 have drained the dreadful dragon of her vigor.
CHORUS (*the yelping growing more, and sharper*):
      Catch him, catch him, catch him! Mark him
      down!
CLYTEMNESTRA: You are hunting your quarry, but it
      is in a dream!
      There you give tongue, like a hound true to the
      scent.
      What are you *doing*? Up now, forget your
      weariness!
150 Do not grow soft in sleep, neglecting my wrongs.
      Let your heart respond to just reproach; to the
      dutiful,
      such reproaches serve as goads. Direct your
      bloody breath
      on the man that he
      may wither under its blast, under the belly's
      fire.
155 Follow him, follow him, hunt him again,
      and waste him.
                              (*Exit Clytemnestra.*)
CHORUS: Wake up; you wake her, as I wake you.
      What, are you sleepy? Up, kick off your sleep!
      Let us see if what begins now has any meaning.

(*The Chorus here may be variously divided; this is
only one guess how to do it.*)

160 1. Ah me, ah me! My friends, we have suffered!
      2. I indeed have suffered — and in vain!
      We have suffered a hurt most painful,
      and evil beyond enduring!
      He has slipped from the net; the quarry has
      gone.
165 3. Sleep overcame me; I lost my prey.
      4. O child of Zeus, what a thief you are.
      You are young and have ridden down

the ancient gods, through reverence for your
      suppliant,
a man godless, and bitter foe to his parents.
You are a god, but you stole away   170
a mother-murderer.
5. Who will say that any of this is just?
From my dream has come a reproach;
it struck me like the driver's whip,
when he grips it in the middle and urges his
      team;   175
it struck me below the heart and below the belly.
I can still feel the deadly chill,
of the savage public scourge.
6. This is what the new gods do,
who dominate all, overriding justice.   180
The seat dripping with blood,
hand and foot . . .
You can see earth's navel in blood,
taking on itself a massive curse.
The Prophet° has defiled his innermost shrine;   185
the pollution sits at the hearth;
he did it of his own will.
None but himself summoned him to act;
against the law of the gods he has honored the
      things
of mortal men, and destroyed   190
what was fated long ago.
Apollo shall have my bitterness,
and Orestes he shall not deliver;
though he flee underground he shall not be free;
defiled, he shall go where he will find   195
another avenger upon his head.

(*Enter Apollo.*)

APOLLO: Out with you! And be quick about it!
      Go, rid the prophetic sanctuary of your presence,
      lest the winged gleaming snake,
      sped by the golden bowstring, overtake you!   200
      Then in your agony you will vomit
      black foam from your lungs; you will spew out
      those lumps of congealed blood you have
      drawn in.
      It is not fit your feet should touch my house
      here.
      You belong where sentences of execution   205
      are carried out, the gouging of eyes,
      cutting of throats, castration of young boys,
      mutilation, stoning; where the whimperings
      of men impaled cry pity.
      Do you hear my description   210
      of your favorite festival? It fills you with delight
      but makes the gods loathe you!

185. Prophet: A reference to Apollo.

The whole aspect of your shape is a sure guide.
You are such things as ought to haunt the cave
215 of the blood-gulping lion; you should not rub
your infection off on a nearby oracle.
Be gone, unshepherded by any herdsman!
To such a flock as you, no god feels kindly.
CHORUS: My lord Apollo, hear me, in your turn;
220 you are no joint sharer in these acts;
you are the one main culprit —
you have done everything!
APOLLO: How so? Talk long enough to tell me that,
no more!
225 CHORUS: You gave an oracle that the stranger
should kill his mother.
APOLLO: I gave an oracle that he should
avenge his father. Certainly, I did.
CHORUS: And so you promised to accept new blood.
APOLLO: And I have bade him to approach this
230 house.
CHORUS: — insulting us, who dogged him here.
APOLLO: You are not fit to approach a shrine like
this.
CHORUS: But this is our appointed task.
APOLLO: What is this fine appointed task you
boast of?
235 CHORUS: We drive from their houses
those that kill their mothers.
APOLLO: What of the woman who has killed her
man?
CHORUS: She is no murderer of blood kin with the
murdered.
APOLLO: So, you would have made of no account,
dishonored,
those pledges of Zeus, and of Hera° the
240 Perfecter!
In your argument, Aphrodite° is discounted
utterly —
yet from her the very dearest things come to
human kind;
for man and woman, the bed,
when justly kept, their fated bed,
245 is greater than any oath that can be sworn.
If you give rein to men and women that kill each
other,
neither visiting them with wrath nor exacting
vengeance —
I declare you are unjust to harry Orestes.
For I know you take to heart what the one does,
250 but neglect the open doings of the other.
The goddess Athena shall oversee this trial.
CHORUS: As for this man, I will never let him alone.

240. **Hera:** Wife of Zeus, and a goddess of marriage.
241. **Aphrodite:** Greek goddess of love and fertility.

APOLLO: Pursue him, then; that's so much more
work for you!
CHORUS: Do not cut down my powers by your   255
words.
APOLLO: I would not choose to *have* your powers.
CHORUS: Yes, even without them you are counted
great,
by the throne of almighty Zeus.
But I am drawn by the blood,
the mother's blood, and I will seek due penalty.   260
I will hunt out this man.
APOLLO: But I will come to the rescue of my
suppliant;
I will protect him. Terrible is the anger
of a suppliant betrayed, if I should do so willingly,
either among men or gods.   265

(*The scene changes to Athens and Athena's temple;
enter Orestes.*)

ORESTES: Lady Athena, by the command of Apollo
I come; receive me kindly, though I am guilty;
still, my hand's undefiled and unpolluted;
the infection's dull, worn off in other houses
and wanderings among men.   270
I have crossed over dry land and over sea,
keeping Apollo's orders, from his oracle,
and so I approach your house and image,
goddess.
Here I watch and wait decision of my case.
CHORUS: Enough; here are the man's clear tracks.   275
Follow the pointings of the voiceless informer
against him,
for we trace him out, following blood fresh and
clotted,
as a hound does a fawn sorely wounded.
My chest gasps under the stress of many labors,
man-wearying. All earth's expanse   280
I have haunted. I have come, passing over the sea,
in wingless swoops as fast as any ship.
Now *he* is here, cowering some place or other;
the smell of human blood smiles to greet me.
Look, look, look again!   285
Let your eyes be everywhere,
that he may not give us the slip, and so
be a mother-murderer unpunished.
Here he is! He has twined his hands
round the image of the goddess immortal.   290
He is seeking protection; he wishes to be
subject to *trial* for what his hands did . . .
But that may *not* be! His mother's blood
has fallen to earth; it cannot be recalled.
It was shed and spread on the ground and is
gone.   295

(*To Orestes.*)

But blood to match that blood
you must give me to gulp from your living self,
rich blood-cake from your limbs.
From you I will gain in that horrid draught
300 fodder for my life.
Living as you are, I will waste you,
and haul you beneath the earth,
that you may pay for your mother's agony
with pains that shall match hers.
And under the earth you shall see those who
305   sinned,
that offended god or stranger
or loving parent — all such, each one
shall have what he justly suffers.
For Hades° is the great auditor —
310 under the earth — of mortal men;
he surveys all, written down in the tablets of his
     mind.
ORESTES: I have learned in the school of suffering
and come to know many purifications — when
     one must speak
and when be silent. In this matter now,
315 a wise master has instructed me to speak.
For the blood is falling asleep;
it is melting off my hand,
and the taint of mother-killing has washed away.
Yes, it *was* fresh once, and at the hearth
320 of Phoebus Apollo
it was expelled by pig sacrifices.
It would be much too long a story
to tell from the beginning with how many
I have shared company, and they never the
     worse.
325 Time, aging, pulls down everything alike.
So now with holy lips I call, in reverence,
Athena, queen of this land, to come and help me.
With never a spear stirred, she will win to her
     side
myself, my country, and my people of Argos,
330 loyal and dutiful, utterly her allies.
Now, whether Athena is in Libyan country,
or around the stream of Triton where she was
     born
and sets her foot, upright or draped,
a helper to those she loves; or whether in Phlegra
335 she looks on the plain like a stout captain of
     troops —
may she come to *me*
— she's a god and can hear from afar —
To deliver me from evil.
CHORUS: No, neither Apollo, nor Athena's strength
340 will rescue you, perishing, uncared for,

knowing in your heart no whereabouts of joy,
the blood sucked from you, fodder for ghosts,
a shade.
Answer me now! Do you despise my words?
You, raised to be mine, a victim sacred to me!   345
You shall be my feast while still the life is in you,
your throat not cut at the altar. You shall hear
the chant, the chant of the binding chains.
Come join the dance; let us join in it!
for we have made our decision   350
to reveal the song of hatred:
how we, the Furies' regiment,
administer men's fated lives.
We think we are straight in our dealings;
there is no one whose hands are clean,   355
ever visited by our anger.
Such a one lives his life out uninjured.
But against a sinner like this man,
who keeps secret his murderous hands,
we are upright witnesses for those dead,   360
exacters of blood in revenge against him —
to that man we appear, in the end.
Mother who bore me, O Mother Night,
how we punish those in the dark
and those who still see, oh hear!   365
For Leto's son° has dishonored me,
has stolen this cowering hare of mine,
this thing that is truly sacred to me,
because of his mother's blood.
Over the one to be sacrificed   370
here is our hymn, driving mind askew,
wrenching it from its course,
working its mischief:
This is the Furies' song,
chains on the mind, no sound of the lyre,   375
it wastes away mortal men.
This is the order for life of the world
that Fate, throughout, has spun
to abide forever:
that for mortal men whose lot was to do   380
the wanton murder of their own kin —
we shall attend these until
they enter the clay of earth;
and dead, too, such a one,
will not be free too much.   385
Over the one to be sacrificed
here is our hymn, driving mind askew,
wrenching it from its course,
working its mischief:
This is the Furies' song,   390
chains on the mind, no sound of the lyre,
it wastes away mortal men.

309. Hades: One of the sons of Cronos, Hades rules the
kingdom of the dead.

366. Leto's son: Reference to Apollo.

These were the tasks allotted
to us on the day we were born —
395   to keep our hands away from the deathless gods,
that none of *them* shall have feasts with us,
that we shall have neither scot nor lot
in the all-white robes.
For houses' overthrow is my choice,
400   where the *tame* war god kills his own;
hot in pursuit of that criminal,
however mighty he is, we will quench him
beneath the tide of new blood.
It is our aim to save other powers
405   from these concerns of ours,
and by our prayers to make sure
that none of the gods shall meddle with this,
nor come to dispute it with us.
But to Zeus we are a blood-dripping breed
410   against whom hatred is just;
he will have no discourse with us.
For houses' overthrow is my choice,
where the *tame* war god kills his own;
hot in pursuit of that criminal,
415   however mighty he is, we will quench him
beneath the tide of new blood.
Men's good reports are solemn indeed
when the reports live under the sky,
but they waste away, and their honor dies,
420   under the earth,
before the charge of our black robes,
and the dancing pounding of hating feet.
I leapt on high and came crashing down;
I brought all the weight of my foot to bear.
425   They ran their fastest, but I tripped up
their limbs in distracted ruin.
He falls and knows not his fall;
for the mischief has stolen his mind away,
so thick a mist of pollution
430   has spread all over him.
He is now a story men tell in sorrow
of a house beset by a thick dark fog.
I leapt on high and came crashing down;
I brought all the weight of my foot to bear.
435   They ran their fastest, but I tripped up
their limbs in distracted ruin.
It all abides; we are the contrivers,
the perfecters of evil, keen-memoried,
holy, inaccessible to mortal prayers.
440   We follow a task dishonored,
a function quite separate from the gods',
under a light that knows no sun;
the ways we follow are difficult roads,
alike for them that still have their eyes
445   and those who see only darkness.
Who, then, of mortal men,
does not reverence, has not feared,

when he hears of the ordinance sanctioned by
fate,
given me by gods in perfectness?
There still abides my ancient office;   450
I have known no demotion, although
it is under the earth where I hold my rank
and dwell in the darkness without sun.

(*Enter Athena.*)

ATHENA: I have heard a cry from afar,
from Scamander, where I took possession   455
of land which the leaders and chiefs of the
Achaeans
conceded to me, a great share of captured booty,
entirely for myself forever and ever,
a choice gift for the sons of Theseus.
From there I came driving my feet unwearied,   460
wingless, whirling my deep-bosomed aegis,
driving the car to which the eager colts are
yoked —
and here I see this company,
new to this land. I am not afraid, but wonder;
I look and wonder. Who can they be? I speak   465
to all of you — to you, and to the stranger
seated at my image. You there, who are
not like to anything begotten,
neither among goddesses whom the gods have
seen
nor similar to mortal shape — yet it is wrong   470
to speak ill to one that meets you without
offense;
that is not justice nor the sacred law.
CHORUS: Daughter of Zeus, you shall know all, and
quickly,
for we are Night's dark children; we are called
the Curses in our places under the earth.   475
ATHENA: I know your race and know your titles,
too.
CHORUS: Then, in a moment, you will know my
function.
ATHENA: I will, if what you have to say is clear.
CHORUS: We drive from their houses those that
murdered others.
ATHENA: What is the limit of this hunt for the
killer?   480
CHORUS: Where joy can never more be part of life.
ATHENA: Is this the hunt you set upon this man?
CHORUS: Yes; he confessed he was his mother's
killer.
ATHENA: Was he not subject to the force of
another's anger?
CHORUS: What is the force that drives to matricide?   485
ATHENA: This is one half of the case; there are two
sides.

CHORUS: He will not accept an oath, for he'll not
    give one.
ATHENA: You want to be *called* just
    rather than act justly.
CHORUS: How so? Instruct me. You are surely wise
490   enough.
ATHENA: Do not use the matter of the oaths, I tell
    you,
    to win unjustly.
CHORUS: Then, try the case, you; give a straight
    judgment.
ATHENA: Will the settlement of the case, then, rest
    with *me?*
495 CHORUS: Why not? We find you worthy,
    and those you spring from.
ATHENA: What have you to say, in turn, stranger, to
    this?
    Tell us your country and your family
    and your circumstances; and then fight the case
    against their slander of you — that is, if you sit
500   here
    confident in justice, beside my hearth, holding
    my image,
    a holy suppliant, as Ixion did.
    On all these matters give me a clear answer.
ORESTES: O Queen Athena:
505   first, from the last of what you said
    I will remove one great concern of yours.
    I am not in need of purification; it was not
    because
    I had pollution on my hand that I sat at your
    image.
    I will give you solid evidence of that.
510   The law is that the blood-guilty must be silent
    until, in the presence of a purifier,
    the slaughter of young victims stains him with
    blood.
    Long since, at other shrines, I have been so
    purified,
    both with victims and with water from running
    streams.
515   This care for me, then, you may leave aside.
    As for my race, here is what you should know:
    I am an Argive; and my father's name —
    I am glad you ask it — it is Agamemnon,
    the supreme marshal of our forces at sea.
520   With him you yourself rendered cityless that city
    of Ilium, Troy. But he, my father, died,
    shamefully, when he came to his own house. My
    mother,
    black-hearted mother, killed him, with cunning
    nets,
    hiding what proclaimed the murder in the bath.
525   I myself was in exile before this, but I returned
    and killed my mother — I will not deny it —

killing to quit the killing of my dear father.
Apollo bore his share of the guilt for all this
    with me,
for to spur me on, he threatened agonies
if I should not act against the guilty murderers.   530
Whether I did so justly or unjustly,
is now for you to judge.
However I fare, I am in your hands, content.
ATHENA: This is too great an issue
to pronounce judgment for men,   535
if any think *that* should be done,
nor is it in accordance with sacred law
that I should decide the issue of murder,
where anger is sharp — especially since you
(*she points at Orestes*)
have been in due submission to the law,   540
have approached my house, a suppliant purified
    and harmless.
So I would judge you blameless for the city.
But *these* have functions not lightly to be
    dismissed,
and if the judgment does not go their way,
afterward the poison that drips from their minds   545
will fall to the ground and be a pestilence
deadly and dark.
So the matter stands.
The outcome for both sides —
to let them stay or to send them away —   550
contains helpless disaster.
But since the case has fallen to me,
I will choose judges of murder
who have proper respect for an oath,
and so I will set up an ordinance forever.   555
So, now, you (*pointing to both Orestes and the
    Furies*)
summon witnesses and evidence
as aids to the sworn truth of the case.
I will come again, when I have chosen the best
from among my people to decide on what to do,
    truly,   560
without in their hearts infringing their sworn
    oaths
to the doing of injustice.
CHORUS: Here now is an outcome
of the new institutions,
if the plea and the crime   565
of the mother-killer shall prevail.
For, immediately, this act shall fit
all men for easiness of hand.
Besides, there await parents, in days to come,
many a wounding stroke dealt   570
by their truly begotten children.
For there will be no brooding wrath
of the Furies, that watch mankind,
to attend upon such deeds;

François Rochaix's production
of the *Oresteia* emphasized
multilevels of action. This scene
is from *The Eumenides* section
of the American Repertory
Theatre's production.

575   to all deadly things I will throw a loose rein.
As one tells another of a neighbor's suffering,
he may hear of ceasing or abatement
of such crimes — but it is all emptiness,
this advice. The cures do not avail.
580   Let no one struck by such calamity
call aloud, using the phrase,
"O Justice, O Throne of the Furies."
This is the kind of pitiful cry
that a father or mother, when the suffering is
    fresh,
585   will utter, when the house of Justice
comes crashing down.
There is a place where terror is good;

it should sit and watch over the mind.
Wisdom comes through
the cramping of limits.   590
Where there is a man who in light of day
fears nothing in his heart;
where there is a city of such men — which men,
    what city,
fears Justice as once they did?
Do not praise   595
the life anarchic
nor the life ruled by a master.
God has granted
the supremacy in everything
to the mean   600

between the two; though in his overseeing
he inclines now this way, now that.
The word I speak is a balanced word.
Arrogance is truly the child
605 of impiety, and from health of mind
comes that well-being which all men love
and all men pray for.
I say it all, when I say:
reverence the altar of Justice;
610 do not when you see gain,
kick that altar aside,
spurning it with your foot that knows not God.
For there shall be a penalty set on that —
the end remains fixed.
615 So let a man give heedful respect
to the reverence due to parents,
and to the honored comings and goings
of strangers within the house.
Let him be careful of them, too.
620 The man who is willingly just,
under no force of compulsion,
shall not fail of well-being;
no total destruction shall ever attend him.
But I say of the sinner who sets his boldness
625 in opposition, who carries a load
piled high in confusion,
won with injustice and violence,
to him the day will come
when he pulls down his sail, when the mast
    cracks
630 and his ship labors.
He cannot cope with the whirling eddies.
He calls on them that hear nothing.
The God has his laugh at that bold spirit,
when he sees him crippled in hopeless pain,
635 that he never thought would be his.
He cannot breast the waves.
At last he has foundered his early well-being
on the reef of Justice.
None are at hand to see him die
640 nor give him a tear of pity.
ATHENA: Make your announcement, herald,
and keep back the throng.
Let the clear Etruscan trumpet, filled with man's
    breath,
proclaim to the crowd its sharp-tongued message.
645 While the council chamber is filling, it helps
to have silence, to have the whole city
observe my laws, and for these two
to have their case well decided.
CHORUS: My Lord Apollo, rule in those matters
650 that belong to you;
tell me, what have you to do with this?
APOLLO: I have come
to give witness; this man in process of law

is my suppliant, and as such sits in my house,
and it is I have purified him of murder.   655
So I will be his advocate, for I too have the blame
for his mother's murder.

(*He speaks to Athena.*)

Introduce the case and judge it,
according to your knowledge.
ATHENA (*to the Furies*): It is for you to make your
    speech.   660
I declare the proceedings open.
The prosecutor should speak first; that way
he may properly inform us of the matter.
CHORUS: We are many, but we will speak in short
    compass.

(*To Orestes.*)

Answer us, in turn, after each question: 665
First, declare whether you *did* kill your mother.
ORESTES: Yes, I killed her. I do not deny that.
CHORUS: There is one of the three wrestling falls
    already.
ORESTES: I am not yet on the ground
for you to boast over me.   670
CHORUS: Very well; then tell us how you killed her.
ORESTES: I will; with sword in hand I cut her
    throat.
CHORUS: At whose incentive and by whose plans?
ORESTES: By Apollo's oracles; he is here, my witness.
CHORUS: The prophet instructed you to kill your
    mother?   675
ORESTES: Yes, and so far I do not fault what has
    happened.
CHORUS: You will, however, if the vote condemns
    you.
ORESTES: I have my trust; from the grave my father
will help me.
CHORUS: *You* trust the dead — when you have killed
    your mother!
ORESTES: Yes, for she was stained   680
with double blood-guiltiness.
CHORUS: How was that? Inform your judges here.
ORESTES: She killed, in the same man,
her husband and my father.
CHORUS: But you are alive — and she now quit of
    the murder!   685
ORESTES: Why did you not hunt *her* to banishment
when she was alive?
CHORUS: Because she was no blood kin to him she
    killed.
ORESTES: *I* am blood kin, then, to my mother?
CHORUS: How else did she raise you, murderer, in
    her womb?   690
Your dearest blood tie, to your mother, do you
    disown it?

ORESTES: Apollo, now bear witness, now expose
   how I have killed her justly. For the action,
   as action, I will not deny.
   Whether this bloodshed is in your eyes just or
695   unjust,
   do you now judge, that I may tell it to these
   (*pointing to the jury*).
APOLLO: I will speak to *you* (*he motions to the
   whole assembly*),
   this great court of Athens.
   I will speak justly, for I am a prophet and will
     not lie.
700 Upon my prophet's throne
   I never yet spoke of man or woman or city
   a word that was not bidden me by Zeus,
   father of the Olympians. Be advised
   how strong that justice is; I bid you follow his
     will.
705 There is no oath stronger than Zeus.
CHORUS: Zeus, you say, Zeus gave you this oracle
   to tell Orestes here that in avenging
   his father's murder he should forever dishonor
   his mother!
APOLLO: It is not the same for a nobleman to die —
   honored with the scepter, which the gods give
710   princes —
   as to die by a woman's hand, not with furious
     arrows
   launched by an Amazon, from afar, but, as you
     will hear —
   you, Pallas Athena, and you who have your seats
   to make your votes decide upon this matter.
715 He had come from war where he had fared
   for the most part well; he was received with
     loyalty;
   then as he went through his bath and she
     enfolded him,
   at the end, with a robe, and had him fettered
   in those embroidered folds, she struck him down.
720 This which I now have told you was the end
   of majesty and the great fleet's commander.
   Such was this woman; so I have described her,
   to move the people appointed to judge the case.
CHORUS: According to your story, Zeus gives
     precedence
725 to the fate of a father, but he himself
   fettered his father, ancient Cronos. How
   does your account, then, fail to be inconsistent?
   I call the judges to witness, to hear this.
APOLLO: You loathsome creatures, hated by the gods,
   one may break *fetters* — there are cures for
730   that —
   and expiation is often a potent engine.
   But when the dust has snatched to itself the
     blood

of a man once dead, there is no resurrection.
   My father has made no spells for *that;* all other
     things
   effortlessly he turns now this way and now that.   735
CHORUS: Look to how you defend acquittal of this
     man.
   He has shed on the ground his mother's blood —
   will he then live in his father's house in Argos?
   What public altars will he use? What lustration
   of brothers will receive him?   740
APOLLO: This I will tell you; mark how clear my
     words.
   She that is called the mother of the child
   is not its parent, but the nurse of the new seed;
   it is the stallion's thrust that is the parent;
   the woman saves the young living plant for a
     stranger,   745
   as she is a stranger to him, saves it among those
   couples whom the gods do not blight with
     stillbirth.
   I will give you proof of what I say; a father
   may generate without a mother; see —
   here is at hand my witness — the child of
     Olympian Zeus.   750
   She never lay in the womb's dark recesses;
   she is a living plant, such as no goddess could
     bear.
   Pallas, as I know all other things,
   I will make your city and your people great,
   and so I sent this man to sit in your house   755
   that there might be trust between you always,
   that you might have him as your ally, goddess,
   and those his children in the days to come;
   and so it be forever and forever
   a faithful covenant of both your peoples.   760
ATHENA: Am I now to bid the judges in all honesty
   give a true judgment? Has enough been said?
CHORUS: We have shot our bolt altogether. I remain
   to hear how the decision shall be made.
ATHENA (*speaking to the jury*):
   Now, how shall I act to be clear of blame from
     you?   765
APOLLO: You have heard what you have heard;
   in the truth of your hearts,
   sirs, give your votes —
   and respect the oaths you have sworn.
ATHENA: Here is my ruling now, you men of
     Athens: 770
   you who judge this first trial of bloodshed.
   This shall be for all time to come for the people
     of Aegeus
   the judges' council chamber.
   For this is Ares' hill, place of the Amazons;
   here their tents stood when they came here
     campaigning   775

in hatred against Theseus; here they built
tower against tower, a new city against the City.
They sacrificed to Ares, and the rock
and crag was hence called Areopagus.
Here is the city's Reverence, and her brother,
780   Fear,
shall check among the citizens injustice
night and day alike, providing that they
do not themselves make innovation
with influx of mischief on the laws. Pure
    water —
785   foul it with mud, you will never have it to drink.
My counsel to you citizens is this:
do not set amongst you for your honor
either anarchy or a master's rule.
Do not cast terror utterly
790   out of your city; for what man is just
that has no fear of anything?
If the citizens
fear what they honor, justly, they shall have
a saving fortress in their land and city
795   such as no other people of mankind
possess, neither among the Scythians
nor those in Pelops's country.
This shall be a council chamber untouched by
    gain,
revered, high-spirited, a true guard
800   over your land, watchful for those who sleep.
As such I shall create it.
At this length I advise my citizens
for days to come; for *now,* be upright,
bear your vote and decide the case
805   with reverence for your oath. My speech is done.

(*They cast their votes.*)

CHORUS: Yes, I shall give you counsel; do not
    dishonor
this company of ours; we can be dangerous.
APOLLO: And I bid you fear those oracles
that are both mine and Zeus's; let them not be
    fruitless.
CHORUS (*to Apollo*): Bloodshed is not your
810   function,
but you honor it.
Henceforth the oracles you give will be impure.
APOLLO: And so my father stumbled in his judgment
    when
Ixion, the first murderer, made his appeal?
CHORUS: You may have your say, but if I lose the
815   case,
I will be a danger to this land henceforth.
APOLLO: Neither among the gods that are new or old
do you find honor. I shall win over you.
CHORUS: Just such a thing you did in Pheres' house,
820   persuading the Fates to make a *man* immortal.

APOLLO: Is it not just to benefit a worshiper,
especially when he is in greatest need?
CHORUS: You destroyed all the old ways of the world
when you made drunk and cheated the old
    goddesses.
APOLLO: You will not win the settlement of this case,   825
and then will you vomit your poison,
but it will not hurt those you hate.
CHORUS: You have ridden me down, young god as I
    am old.
I wait to hear the settlement.
I have two minds still about my hate for the city.   830
ATHENA: It is my task to render final judgment:
this vote which I possess
I will give on Orestes' side.
For no mother had a part in *my* birth;
I am entirely for the male, with all my heart,   835
except in marriage; I am entirely my father's.
I will never give precedence in honor
to a woman who killed her man, the guardian of
    her house.
So if the votes are but equal, Orestes wins.
Let the judges now proceed   840
to cast out the votes from the urns that contain
    them.
ORESTES: O Phoebus Apollo, how will the
    decision go?
CHORUS: O Night, dark Mother, are you watching?
ORESTES: For me, it is death by hanging, or the light
    of life.
CHORUS: For us, destruction or continued honor.   845
APOLLO: Count out the thrown votes, sirs;
be careful not to wrong anyone in sorting them
    out.
One missed decision can mean a great mischief;
one vote cast often saves a house.

(*Silence.*)

ATHENA: The man has been acquitted in the murder
    suit,   850
for the number of the votes is equal.
ORESTES: Pallas, you have saved my house.
I that had lost a fatherland am restored to my
    house
by you. Truly, some Greek will say,
"There is an Argive who once again is home   855
in all his father owned, thanks to *them,*
Athena and Apollo and that Third,
the Savior who rules all."
He it was who out of regard for my father's death
saved me, when he saw these as my mother's
    advocates.   860
Now I shall go to my home again, but first
I shall pledge my oath to this land and to this
    people

for all the multiplying time to come,
that never shall a prince of Argos come
865 to raise an enemy's spear against your country.
On that day shall ourselves be in the grave
but against those who contravene this oath
we shall loose mischief that will cripple them,
make their wayfarings desperate and their
journeys
870 full of ill omen, that they shall repent
of what they strove to do.
But if they keep our covenant and honor
this city of Pallas, with their spears as allies,
we shall be all the kinder to them, ourselves.
Farewell then, goddess, and governors of this
875 city,
may all your struggles show no enemy escaping,
but safety to yourselves and victory always.

CHORUS: O you young gods, you have ridden down
the old ways; you have snatched them out of my
hands.
880 I have no more honor, but in my wretchedness
my anger will be heavy; on this land
I will relieve my heart's pain, drops on the earth,
poison, overbearing poison.
A blight will come of it — no leaves, no
children —
885 O Justice! The blight will attack the land
and cast upon it infections which kill its people.
Shall I weep? What shall I do?
I am mocked with laughter; among the citizens
I have intolerable sufferings.
890 O great unlucky daughters of Night,
dishonored in your sorrow.

ATHENA: Let my words prevail on you
not to take this so ill.
You have not been conquered — the suit has
truly ended
895 with equal votes; you have no dishonor in that.
But there was the clearest testimony from
Zeus —
he gave the oracles and was himself the
witness —
that Orestes should come to no harm from his act.
Will you then vomit your dark hate against
900 this land? Reflect; do not rage so, do not
bring infertility upon them, letting fall
the drops of divine hatred, keen cutting edges
that cruelly gnaw the seed away. For I
make an absolute promise to you, in all justice,
905 of a seat and a hiding place within this country
to be rightly yours, and you may sit at the hearth
on gleaming thrones, and be honored
by all the citizens.

CHORUS: O you young gods, you have ridden down
the old ways; you have snatched them out of my
910 hands.

I have no more honor, but in my wretchedness
my anger will be heavy; on this land
I will relieve my heart's pain, drops on the earth,
poison, overbearing poison.
A blight will come of it — no leaves, no
children — 915
O Justice! The blight will attack the land
and cast upon it infections which kill its people.
Shall I weep? What shall I do?
I am mocked with laughter; among the citizens
I have intolerable sufferings. 920
O great unlucky daughters of Night,
dishonored in your sorrow.

ATHENA: You are *not* dishonored; do not haughtily
ruin this land — you are gods and they are
mortal.
I myself trust in Zeus, and — why should I speak
of it? — 925
I am the only one among the gods
that knows the keys of the house wherein is
sealed
the lightning bolt — but there's no need of that.
Be persuaded by me; do not pour out
vain words against this country, words to bear, 930
as fruit, a general blight of all who bear fruit,
but lull to sleep the bitter strength of the dark
blood;
for you can share my majesty and peace;
you can have the firstfruits of this large land
as sacrifices for children and for marriage; 935
and when you have these forever, you will say
that I was right.

CHORUS: That I should suffer so!
I with my thoughts of ancient times,
that I should dwell beneath the earth, 940
an unhonored vile thing.
My breath is all anger and malignity.
Who assails my body? What pain is in my spirit?
Hear me, Mother Night.
For the ancient honors of the gods 945
have been snatched away and made nothing of
by cunning treachery.

ATHENA: I will bear with your moods for you are
older,
and though, for that, you are wiser than I,
Zeus has given me, too, a mind to perceive. 950
If you go to alien nations, I tell you,
you will find how much you loved this land,
for the on-flowing course of time shall see more
honors
for these my citizens. If you have your place
of honor beside the temple of Erechtheus, 955
you shall have from men and women worshiping
what you will never obtain from any others.
Only, I pray you, in this country of mine
do not cast sharp provocations to draw blood,

960 making mischief in the hearts of the young,
crazing the wits with never a drop of wine;
nor, as one takes the heart out of fighting cocks,
set among my citizens civil war, that turns their
courage
against one another. Let there be war indeed —
965 it will come easily enough — but war outside
in which they shall find their dangerous love of
glory.
I do not want my fighting cocks at home.
All this you can have, if you will, from me.
Be good to us, take good from us, take honor
970 and share with us this land much loved of God.
CHORUS: That I should suffer so!
I with my thoughts of ancient times,
that I should dwell beneath the earth,
an unhonored vile thing.
975 My breath is all anger and malignity.
Who assails my body? What pain is in my spirit?
Hear me, Mother Night.
For the ancient honors of the gods
have been snatched away and made nothing of
980 by cunning treachery.
ATHENA: I will not weary of telling you your
benefits,
that you may never say, being old,
and a goddess, you were dishonored and
destroyed
by me that am younger, and by men, my citizens,
985 driven abroad from this our land, an outcast.
If you find sacred the honor of Persuasion,
the sweetness of my tongue, its power to charm,
then remain here with us; if you will not,
you will be wrong to turn upon my land
990 your rage and malignity, or damage
my people; for you may certainly
be our land's lord, justly honored for ever.
CHORUS: Lady Athena, what is the home you
speak of?
ATHENA: One free of all unhappiness; only receive
the gift.
995 CHORUS: Suppose I do. What honor continues mine?
ATHENA: No household will thrive without you.
CHORUS: Will you indeed allow me so much power?
ATHENA: I shall prosper the enterprises of your
worshipers.
CHORUS: And you will guarantee this for all time?
1000 ATHENA: I do not promise what I will not perform.
CHORUS: There speaks your enchantment indeed!
I give over my anger.
ATHENA: If you stay here, you will find you gain
new friends.
CHORUS: What song would you have me chant over
this land?
ATHENA: A song of all that waits upon good
1005 victory.

From land and sea and sky may breezes and
sunshine
enfold our land. May the earth yield crops
and cattle their offspring in plenty for the
citizens,
all flourishing without stint, and all the safety
that goes with multitude of children. 1010
Prosper the enterprises of the pious. I
like a good gardener am happy when my plants,
the breed of just men here, know no sorrow.
So may your actions be. For my part,
in warlike contests I will not hold back 1015
until I have honor for this city for victories
throughout the world.
CHORUS: I shall accept joint tenancy with Pallas.
I shall not dishonor the city
which Zeus Almighty and the god of war 1020
hold as the guard station of the gods,
the glory of heavenly beings who are Greek.
For this city,
I give my prophecy with kind good will,
and I pray that the sun's bright radiance 1025
bring from the earth abundantly
all goods of life that depend on Fortune.
ATHENA: I have acted out of good will to my
citizens
in giving a home here to these divinities,
so great, so dangerous in their displeasure. 1030
These powers have for their allotted function
everything in human life.
He who has met them in ill humor
knows not whence the blows assail his life.
For the offences of the ancestors 1035
hale him before Them; his destruction is silent
but grinds him to dust, for all his loud talk,
under the Furies' hatred.
CHORUS: May no harmful winds blight your trees —
here is my litany of favor — 1040
may no blinding flame
working evil on the plants
cross the frontier of the seasons.
May no disease, destroying the fruitfulness
of the crops, steal darkly upon you. 1045
But let Pan
nourish your prosperous flocks
with twin lambs in due time.
May what the earth brings forth
in richest soil, as the gods' gift, 1050
give of its bounty.

(*Athena turns to the citizens.*)

ATHENA: Do you hear this,
you that are the city's guardians?
What consummation of good!
For great is the power of the dread Fury, 1055
amongst the immortals and also beneath the earth;

and amongst men, especially,
they bring to perfection for all to see
what they have provided:
1060   for some, occasions for song;
for others, a life rich in tears.
CHORUS: The chances that bring about men's deaths
before their time —
may nothing such be yours!
1065 You goddesses, the Fates,
my mother's sisters, grant —
yours is the power —
that young girls ripe for love
will find the men for their lives.
1070 You are the upright-dealing spirits
that have a part in every home,
that bear a weight in every time,
most honored among every one of the gods,
where the just dwell together.
1075 ATHENA: That you bring such good to fulfillment
for my country, out of your kindness,
I am heartily glad.
The face of Persuasion I revere
because she looked upon
1080 my tongue and mouth, as I spoke against
these, who were then angry and rejecting;
but Zeus of the Assembly was victorious,
and the victory we won was in the contest
for blessings for all time.
1085 CHORUS: This is my prayer:
that never in this city shall stir the noise
of faction, that is never sated with evils.
May the dust never drink the black blood
of fellow citizens, in their lust for revenge,
1090 hunting for murder to answer murder,
to the ruin of the city.
Rather let them give joy for joy
in harmony, a community united.
Let them hate, too, with one mind —
1095 for among mankind, this, too, cures much.
ATHENA: How minded are they to find the road
of a gracious tongue!
From these fearful countenances
I see great blessing come to my citizens;
1100 for if you kindly honor the Kindly Ones,
always and greatly honor them,
you shall live for all time
with land and city straight in its justice —
and all shall see it as such.
CHORUS: Farewell to you in the wealth that is your
1105   right!
Farewell, you people of this town,
that sit near Zeus, loved by
the Maiden Goddess who is loved.
You are wise
1110 in the course of time.

The Father reveres
those that shelter under her wings.
ATHENA: Farewell to you, too. I must go before you
to show you your palace, in the sacred light
of your escort of worshipers.   1115
Hasten to your place under the earth
attended by solemn sacrifices.
Keep away, restrain all destruction,
but send to our city all profit
for victory.   1120

(*Athena turns to the second chorus, a band of citizens
that lead the Furies to their new home.*)

  Guide them on their way,
you citizens, children of Cranaus;
guide these Powers that will settle among you.
And good among the citizens be the thought
that attends upon good received.   1125
CHORUS: Farewell, farewell again — I say it twice —
all you of this city,
Heavenly Ones and mortal men
that live in the city of Pallas.
While you show piety   1130
for my sharing in your lives
you shall find fault with nothing that befalls you.
ATHENA: I praise you for the meanings of your
  prayers
I shall send you on your way with light
of radiant torches to those places   1135
underneath, beneath our earth. Your escort
will be those who guard my image, a just escort.
For the eye of all this land of Theseus
must come forth, this glorious crowd
of children, wives, and the band of elder women.   1140
With clothes of scarlet dye honor them,
and let the light of fire set them on the road,
that this kindly company, favoring us, shall show
for time to come, gallantry in our sons.
THE ESCORT: Advance, in order, great and venerable,   1145
you virgin daughters of Night.
This is your loyal escort.
Hush, holy silence, all you who attend.
Beneath the ancient caverns of the earth,
be glorified, in honor, in sacrifice, and in Fortune.   1150
Hush, holy silence, all the people.
In graciousness and in just thought
for our land, come hither, Holy Ones,
rejoicing on your road with torches eaten by
  flame.
Now, now, sing in songs of praise.   1155
Peace be forever on the houses and citizens of
  Athens.
For Zeus who Sees All and the Fates
on these terms have come together.
Now, now, sing in songs of praise.

COMMENTARIES

Albrecht Dihle (b. 1923)

ORESTES AND THE GODS   *Tr. 1994*

TRANSLATED BY CLARE KROJZL

Dihle, in his A History of Greek Literature, *takes up the role of the old and the new gods in the* Oresteia. *In Dihle's view the question of interpretation of the will of the gods and of the law becomes central to the drama.*

The act of vengeance perpetrated by Orestes is by the express orders of the god Apollo, but the deed draws the attention of other deities responsible for the sanctity of the bond between mother and child. These, the Erinyes or Furies (goddesses of curses), hound the matricide mercilessly from one town to the next. He finds only fleeting refuge with Apollo in the temple at Delphi. The third play in the trilogy, *The Eumenides,* resolves this apparently hopeless conflict. A legal battle is fought out at the Areopagus, the time-honored murder court of the city of Athens, which convenes under the aegis of the goddess Athena. Apollo, representing the new order established by the Olympian gods, defends the deed of Orestes by pointing out the necessity of punishing the murder of a husband and king. The Erinyes, on the other hand, invoke the earlier order, calling for the expiation of matricide. The Areopagus dismisses the case against Orestes, at the same time mollifying the Erinyes by introducing their cult into Athens, where they are henceforth to dwell as *The Eumenides,* the gracious bestowers of blessings.

Aeschylus's theological interpretation of myth is based on a firm belief in the essential justice of the divine order of the universe. The idea of this justice making the gods into defenders of law and order among humankind had already been put forward by Hesiod, and later with a heightened sense of political responsibility by Solon. The notion that the actions of gods and heroes related in myth ought to correspond to the moral standards of his own day had moreover been the most important motif in the mythical interpretations of Pindar. What was new about Aeschylus's conception is that the law established by Zeus was more than a body of fixed rules whose observance was watched over by the gods with a system of reward and punishment. Instead, it was seen as a vital force constantly proving itself in ever new manifestations, and even able to resolve conflict which seemed hopeless from the human viewpoint. Apollo's claim is as valid as that of the Erinyes, so that Orestes, who must satisfy both, seems bound to be destroyed by this dilemma, as two divine powers conduct a mutual conflict with each other through his action and suffering, without releasing him from his moral responsibility. The trial instigated by Athena, the motherless daughter of Zeus, allows the dynamic nature of his law to manifest itself clearly, thereby resolving a unique, unforeseeable conflict through a decision that is specific to the situation, but also creates a new order, while at the same time reconciling two equally valid claims that had seemed to be hopelessly at odds. Nevertheless, it is in human action, carried out with a consciousness of responsibility, that this conflict between divine powers is acted out and resolved. Were it not for human beings, as is demonstrated using the metaphor of the court of Athenian citizens, the law of Zeus would have no scope in which to unfold. Human dignity consists in becoming the necessary partner of the gods, and in the right order of human society matching the divine order as closely as possible.

Thomas G. Rosenmeyer (b. 1920)
The Art of Aeschylus

1982

In examining the unity of the three plays of the Oresteia, *Rosenmeyer shows how they can be considered an interrelated trilogy. Looking at details in each play shows us that there is a subtle and crucial development of ideas from* Agamemnon *to* The Eumenides. *The proof that Aeschylus aimed at a coherent relationship among the three plays lies, as Rosenmeyer says in his first sentence, in the examination of "the dramatic trilogy."*

Aeschylean drama furnishes a particularly promising instrument of proof: the dramatic trilogy. Sophocles and Euripides, also, offered their plays in bundles of three. But it appears that the later playwrights normally regarded the bundling as a purely mechanical matter, without the least obligation to the author to make the individual plays hang together.[1] Aeschylus himself offered some "disconnected" trilogies, packages of plays put together only for the sake of institutional convenience. *Persians,* for example, was apparently flanked by two plays whose plots derive from legend, and though it could be argued that all three plays showed an unusual interest in monsters and monstrous behavior, it is quite out of the question that the spectators could have perceived them as constituting a larger whole. Aeschylus's most famous productions, on the other hand, were "connected" trilogies, aggregates of three (or, counting the satyr play, four) dramas linked in plot, cast of characters, and, it is assumed, artistic concept. Only one of them, the *Oresteia,* has survived. It will be useful to take a close look at it, to check out the assumption that in composing a connected trilogy Aeschylus meant to create a coherent structure.

The assumption is, indeed, a plausible one. For those who are interested in a measurable design, it will not be an accident that half way through the Great Exchange of *The Libation Bearers* — and that means roughly in the middle of the play and hence roughly in the center of the trilogy — the chorus chants the following (400–404):[2]

[1] But Euripides' trilogy of 415 B.C., consisting of *Alexandros, Palamedes,* and *Trojan Women,* seems to have been a connected one. The trilogy of 438 B.C., consisting of *Cretan Women, Alcmaeon in Psophis,* and *Telephus,* may have possessed certain thematic connections, but nothing definite is known.

[2] This translation is keyed to the line numbers in Greek. See lines 421–25 in *The Libation Bearers.* — ED.

It is the rule that drops of blood
Shed on the ground summon another
Death. Murder invokes the Fury; she
Brings from those who died before
Blight to pile on blight.

With some justice, it could be said that this is the central theme of the *Oresteia*. It is a drama, not of men acting, but of a whole world thrusting up representative shapes and voices to reveal its inner life through the interconnectedness of crime and outrage. We begin with a darkness that is illuminated by a war signal, and we end in a darkness, with the torches of peace heralding new possibilities of friction. All three plays open on a note of weariness, shaken off temporarily for illusory gains. The release prayed for by the watchman and promised to Orestes by Apollo (*Eum.* 100) appears to have been granted at the end of the last play. But given the central conviction voiced by the chorus, how much faith are we to put in that release?

Unity is, of course, not just a matter of parallels, but also the function of some kind of development. The expository style of the prologues helps us to trace the stages of one possible development, unless it turns out that the development is nothing more than subtle variations upon a common theme. The prologue of *Agamemnon* begins: "I ask the gods to ... for...." An avowal of worship addressed to the world at large, including the spectators, is followed by an explanatory phrase which starts the exposition, such as it is. In *The Libation Bearers,* the speaker turns directly to the god: "Hermes ... help me ... for...."; the ensuing exposition is now largely lost. In *The Eumenides,* the avowal is once again to the world at large: "I pay my respects to Gaia ...," but instead of a for clause, it is a relative clause, " ... Themis, who ...," that leads into the exposition — a historical survey which on the surface has rather little to do with the ostensible plot. ... Thus the beginning of *The Libation Bearers* is the most dramatic; the beginning of *The Eumenides* least so. The watchman of *Agamemnon* is only lightly involved, Orestes is deeply committed, while the priestess of the last play is little more than a mechanism to get the action moving. The dramatic weight of the trilogy rests within the middle piece. Framed as it is by two plays featuring unstable relations and large masses of people, *The Libation Bearers* settles down to converge upon individuals, on Orestes and his commitment. The trilogy as a whole gets its name from the character who dominates the central section (one may assume that it was Aeschylus himself who was responsible for the title attached to the trilogy).

Thematically, also, there are parallels and variations that appear to support the notion of a developing unity. The clot of blood that Clytemnestra offers along with her milk in the dream narrated by the chorus (*Lib.* 570) inevitably reminds us of the spray of blood in which Clytemnestra reveals herself toward the end of *Agamemnon*. The prayer of the Furies for the good health of the flocks (*Eum.* 1041–1053) and other similar blessings called down upon the commonwealth as a whole seem to be conceived as a reparation for the evil omens pervasive in *Agamemnon*: the healthy lambs make up for the blighted hare's offspring. Read in this fashion, the trilogy traces the difficulties attached to the tempering of a savage humanity that finally learns to live with itself. The meshing of sameness and evolution is maintained to the end when, after the pacification of the Furies, Athena, the seeming embodiment of temperance, can still break out in a flash of fury that recalls the old savagery. There is progress, but also a stubborn retention of the old.

Agamemnon and *The Libation Bearers* are full of pictures of children killed and eaten. With the nurse of *The Libation Bearers,* however, we find ourselves in the more homely atmosphere of an arrangement which allows the fondling and cherishing of children. In *The Eumenides,* children become an issue for a medical debate, and it may well be asked whether the pseudo-scientific objectivity with which Apollo and Athena conduct their argument is more humane than the waste of offspring heralded in the first two plays. The speech of the nurse is the realistic heart of the trilogy, and also its greatest unbending from the cruelties of the mythological vision. Beginning with the obsessive lyricism of *Agamemnon,* and ending with the evasive allegories of *The Eumenides,* we stop off briefly in the middle to watch, for one fleeting moment, domestic gentleness and warmth, embodied in a woman whose social status is further evidence of the marginality of that warmth. But it is real nonetheless, just as real as is the concentration in *The Libation Bearers* upon the moral fate of one man, a narrowing from the circling seasons, celestial processions and astral principalities advertised in the watchman's speech, and a brief respite before the scene broadens out again, but now into the world of politics, legal regulations, and institutional settlements.

It is understood that the conceptual development of the trilogy is toward a more and more civilized world. The catalogue of divine politics at the beginning of *The Eumenides* alerts us to the notion that we are leaving the larger cosmos, with its jealous personal divinities, behind us and are entering upon the canton diplomacy presided over by local gods. Apollo's advent is said (*Eum.* 15–17) to have been facilitated by the "sons of Hephaestus," shadowy culture heroes who built roads and cleared the country. The compacted synthesis of generations in the first play gives way before a willingness to accept the before and the after, the change from barbarism to culture. This at least is the mode in which *The Eumenides* presents itself, regardless of whether it means that the whole trilogy is a record of continuous progress and whether the playwright was concerned with the amelioration of man and his institutions. Again, the house, which looms so large in the first two plays and which functions as the principal locus of the clan solidarity whose injury cries out for blood, is dismissed quite unceremoniously in the last play, to be replaced by the nuclear family — the household consisting of father, mother, and children — and the city-state. Zeus and Apollo come to stand for city law, while Moira and the Furies represent clan practice: this neat distinction argued by the Marxist anthropologists, George Thomson among them, has much to be said in its favor, in spite of the purely speculative assertions about the tensions between a matrilineal and a patrilineal world which are usually associated with it.[3]

By the same token, comparing the choral lyrics of *The Eumenides* with those of the first two plays suggests a shift toward mimetic immediacy and personal relevance. The Furies have, after all, a role to play and a position to defend, which invests their singing with an authority that is lacking in *Agamemnon* and *The Libation Bearers,* even though the slave women of the latter, in the sequence of the Great Exchange, develop a surprising measure of authority. The movement towards immediacy and greater concreteness is most

---

[3] G. Thomson, *Aeschylus and Athens* (London, 1966), pp. 47 ff., 259 ff.

obviously experienced on the level of imagery. The lyric images of the two earlier plays are translated into tangibles and visible events. The trope of war as a lawsuit becomes the trial scene, that of hunting and the net issues in actual pursuit, the serpent of Clytemnestra's dream emerges in the ghostly costuming (to be imagined only?) of the Furies. Much of what was earlier expressed in the evocative multiplicity of the lyric is, in the last play, channeled into immediate visual impact. Similar progressions from lyric density to openness of action enliven the final portions of *Agamemnon* and *The Libation Bearers;* the poetic movement of the trilogy is mirrored in the movement of each of its parts. This dovetailing increases the effectiveness of the pattern. But it is only in the third play, as barbarism and clan-concrescence are abandoned, that the greater discursiveness of the presentation becomes an appropriate vehicle for the meaning. *The Eumenides* is, of course, a minor trilogy in its own right: the sequence of Delphi, trial, and conversion repeats, in a fashion, the larger sequence of prophetic lyricism, personal intrigue, and political resolution offered in the total structure. Yet we must remain careful not to interpret the sequence and the gradual loosening of the coil as if they signalled a historical evolution. The recalcitrance of the Furies and their ascendance in the ultimate compromise should be sufficient warning.

Lois Spatz *(b. 1940)*
ORESTEIA: TRILOGY PRESERVED   *1982*

In her examination of Aeschylus, Lois Spatz discusses how he conceived of the three plays of the Oresteia as a unified whole. She also provides some of the key background information that most of the original Greek audience would have known. Spatz connects the plays to events of the time in Athens, so we can better understand Aeschylus's innovations in treating the myths upon which he built his drama.

The *Oresteia* won first prize at the Great Dionysia of 458 B.C., just two years before Aeschylus's death. The three tragedies, *Agamemnon, The Libation Bearers (Choephoroi),* and *The Eumenides,* were presented in a sequence which concluded with a lost satyr play, *Proteus,* about the wanderings of Agamemnon's brother, Menelaus. Modern readers often study *Agamemnon* alone, although it is extremely difficult to follow and does not resolve the dramatic questions it raises, but the ancient spectators would have considered the drama as a first act in a larger whole. The trilogy is composed so that the *Agamemnon* and *The Libation Bearers* define a conflict which can only be resolved by a third and different action. *Agamemnon,* taken alone, seems an obscure play, for the extreme complexity of image, diction, and action is a dramatic device which conveys the moral, emotional, and political confusion of the initial situation. In the second play, where the next generation of characters better understand their positions and motivations, the action is clearer. In *The Eumenides,* Aeschylus illuminates the issues underlying the action and resolves them.

Because one must study the parts together to appreciate the whole, the trilogy will be treated as a single play. Although Aeschylus begins his drama *in medias res*, as Agamemnon is about to return from Troy, the audience was familiar with the stories concerning the crimes of Agamemnon's father, Atreus. Therefore, it would have suspected with increasing dread some relationship between the events of the present generation and the horrors of the past, which the poet does not mention directly until the last third of the play, when the curse on the House of Atreus becomes a central theme of the trilogy. Atreus was head of the house and ruler of Argos when Thyestes, his brother, raped his wife and attempted to steal his property and power. First Atreus exiled his brother, but judging that penalty inadequate, he invited him home and cooked and served Thyestes' children to him at a feast celebrating the reunion. When Thyestes discovered he had eaten his own sons, he cursed Atreus, promising revenge, and left Argos with his one remaining son, Aegisthus.

The curse arising from this horrible act brought misfortune to the next generation. Atreus's sons, Agamemnon and Menelaus, had married sisters, Clytemnestra and Helen, respectively. Helen, the most beautiful woman in Greece, was seduced and stolen away from the hearth of the House of Atreus by their guest, Paris (Alexander), son of King Priam of Troy. Paris's adultery was a violation of the sacred relationship between guest and host protected by Zeus Xenios ("Guest-Friend"). Therefore, the Argives considered it a serious crime demanding revenge, and launched the Trojan War, subject of the *Iliad* and epic cycle.

The Greek warriors who had sworn to support Menelaus met at Aulis under the leadership of Agamemnon, elder brother of the wronged husband and most powerful king in Greece. When rough seas prevented the fleet's passage to Troy, the priest Calchas informed Agamemnon that he must sacrifice his daughter, Iphigenia, to the goddess Artemis in order to calm the winds. Agamemnon, confident of the justice of the war and fearful of his restive troops, decided to slaughter Iphigenia so that the expedition could set sail.

Aeschylus begins his drama just as the Argives receive the news that Agamemnon has defeated Troy. The audience would know, however, from such sources as the *Odyssey*, the return stories of the cycle, and the *Oresteia* by the lyric poet Stesichorus, that, during these ten years of war, Clytemnestra had sent her son Orestes away and taken Aegisthus as a lover, and that the Greek soldiers in Troy had committed crimes which were punished on the return voyages. Aeschylus's gradual and sparing presentation of this background increases the mystery surrounding the events of the play itself.

Act I and Act II are both return and revenge stories. In *Agamemnon* several characters in sequence, the watchman, citizen/chorus, Queen Clytemnestra, and the herald, express hope and anxiety about the general's experiences in the Trojan War and his safe victorious return. Tension builds because the expectation of victory as the just punishment of Troy is constantly undercut by suggestions that the general and his men have themselves committed atrocities to insure victory. In fact, the Greek fleet has already been punished, destroyed by a god-sent storm at sea. At the mid-point in the drama, Agamemnon enters in triumph with his war prize, Cassandra, and is welcomed with Eastern pomp by his queen, Clytemnestra, who entices him to enter the palace on a luxurious tapestry. This greeting initiates the revenge story. After Agamemnon's entrance into the palace, Cassandra, the Trojan priestess of Apollo, predicts his murder and hers and relates it to the bloody history of the House of Atreus. Then Clytemnestra murders Agamemnon and his mistress and justifies her deed to the citizens as divine retribution for his sacrifice of their daughter, Iphigenia. Aegisthus, Clytemnestra's lover, later explains that history more precisely, justifying his part in Agamemnon's death as revenge for his uncle Atreus's slaughter of his brothers. Thus, the cycle of revenge as punishment which demands further revenge is clearly established by the end of the play. It is equally clear that Clytemnestra's act of revenge cannot break the cycle. She and her lover plan to replace Agamemnon as rulers of Argos, but they respond with threats of violence to the chorus's protests against their tyranny. *Agamemnon* ends with the chorus cowed for the moment, but predicting that Orestes, Agamemnon's son, sent away by Clytemnestra, will someday return to avenge the death of his father and assume his rightful place as head of the family and ruler of the state.

Act II, *The Libation Bearers,* also exhibits the return and revenge patterns, in dramatizing the murder of Agamemnon's murderers. First Orestes returns, fulfilling the hopes of his sister, Electra, and the chorus of household slaves, captives from Troy loyal to their conqueror, Agamemnon. Orestes later learns that his return has also fulfilled the nightmares of his mother, Clytemnestra. He enters, not as a conquering hero like his father, to be warmly welcomed and then duped, but as an exile in disguise, announcing his own death in order to deceive his mother and her lover. He has been spurred on by Apollo's demand that he avenge his father's death or suffer dire punishments, but he also acts from private motives as son, disinherited heir, and legitimate ruler of Argos. After praying with his sister and the chorus at the tomb of Agamemnon to invoke the aid of the gods and the powerful dead, he tricks Clytemnestra, kills Aegisthus, and then confronts his mother again. She tries to dissuade him, but he leads her into the house for the slaughter. When Orestes afterwards proclaims the justice of the matricide to the satisfied chorus, he does not gloat, as his mother before him did, for he recognizes that his deed was a crime as well as a necessity. He confesses that his pollution is a danger to himself and his community and prepares to leave Argos to be purified of blood guilt by Apollo. As he announces his plans, however, madness overtakes him; he seems to see the very Furies (Erinyes) from Hell descending on him to avenge his matricide. The chorus is puzzled that this act has not ended the chain of reciprocal revenge in the House of Atreus, but sends him forward to Apollo with prayers for success.

Act III, *The Eumenides,* introduces a new story pattern, "suppliant received"; a new setting, the shrines of the gods in Delphi and Athens; and new characters, the gods themselves — Apollo, the Furies, and Athena. The play begins at the shrine of Apollo in Delphi, where Orestes has arrived as a suppliant begging asylum from the Furies and release from blood guilt. Although Apollo has temporarily drugged the Furies into sleep, he cannot permanently protect Orestes from their vengeance. The god directs the matricide to the shrine of Athena in the Acropolis of Athens, where the goddess will release him from the curse. Once Orestes has fled, the ghost of Clytemnestra angrily arouses the sleeping Furies and sends them to track their prey. Orestes arrives in Athens and clings to the goddess's shrine, but the Furies enter soon after and threaten to destroy him. Athena returns just in time, and after questioning Orestes and the chorus of Furies, she decides the conflict is too important for her to resolve alone. Instead, she establishes a homicide court (modeled on the murder trials of the Court of the Areopagus) where citizen-judges (dicasts) will hear arguments for both sides and decide between them. The two present their cases, with Apollo supporting

Orestes' plea. When the jury's vote is equally split, Orestes is set free by Athena's order. Before he returns home, he thanks Apollo, Athena, and the court, promising eternal peace between Argos and Athens and wishing the city prosperity and victory forever. The Furies, incensed by the verdict, call down curses on Athens, but Athena persuades them to become honored participants in the new procedure, ever punishing injustice, but showering blessings on the good as well. When they accept her offer, they exchange their loathsome black garments for the red robes of metics (foreign residents in Athens), a visible sign of their transformation from Furies to Eumenides ("Kindly Ones"). The trilogy ends with a torchlight procession, similar to the Panathenaic Festival, in which the citizens escort the goddesses to their new home, a hallowed cave at the foot of the Acropolis.

It is a long way from the polluted House of Atreus in Argos, whose bloody Furies roost like metics on the roof (*L.B.*, 1023), to the clear bright light of Athens, with its court system, public festivals, rites of Apollo, and the patronage of Zeus's daughter, Athena. Aeschylus has chosen a primitive myth about a blood-vendetta which extends for generations and includes cannibalism and child sacrifice. But he has dramatized the saga in a way which makes it relevant to his fifth-century audience. In none of the earlier versions of the story (i.e., *Odyssey, Cypria, Nostoi,* Stesichorus's *Oresteia*) was Orestes freed by a verdict of the Court of the Areopagus in Athens. Aeschylus originated this resolution so that he could trace the development of human justice — from the blood-vendetta carried out by the family with the support of the Furies who automatically avenge kindred bloodshed, through the purification rituals performed at the shrines of Apollo, to its culmination in the state court system, established by Athena with Zeus's blessing.[1] In dramatizing the progress of justice from vendetta to trial, he is also tracing the evolution of social institutions, from family and clan united by kindred blood, through cult united by ritual and a common patron, up to its perfection in the democratic polls, exemplified by Athens, where the families were ruled by law, the gods supported the new institutions, and the citizens united into a harmonious and effective whole.[2] No Athenian could sit unmoved while Athena voted like a citizen according to the procedures established in mythic time, but still in effect in 458 B.C. Nor could he watch without pride the imitation of his great Panathenaic Festival and the respectful acceptance of the dread Furies as metics in his own state. Thus would the contemporary Athenian recognize the ideals and glory of his city in the resolution of the myth.

But if this resolution represents the culmination of human progress, at least two problems disturbed the polls in 458. The Court of the Areopagus (the aris-

[1] For a different opinion of Apollo's place, see Thomson, *Aeschylus,* pp. 259–61, and R. P. Winnington-Ingram, "The Role of Apollo in the *Oresteia*," *Classical Review* 47 (1933): 97–104. On the relation of purification to the laws on homicide, see D. M. MacDowell, *Athenian Homicide Law in the Age of the Orators* (Manchester: University of Manchester Press, 1963), pp. 4–5, 141–50.

[2] The family remained important, however, even in the legal prosecution for homicide, as MacDowell points out (*Athenian Homicide*, pp. 8–30). For a study of this evolution, see Richard Kuhns, *The House, the City, and the Judge: The Growth of Moral Awareness in the "Oresteia"* (Indianapolis: Bobbs-Merrill, 1962). George Thomson also traces the development from tribe to state and its influence on the form and ideas of drama, and on the *Oresteia* in particular (*Aeschylus,* pp. 229–78).

tocratic body of ex-archons which once functioned as supreme overseer of the laws of the land) had recently been a target of the democratic reform. In 462, Ephialtes and Pericles carried through the Assembly an act which removed the court's right to interfere with democratic legislation and reduced its jurisdiction to cases of premeditated murder. The aristocrats were incensed and Ephialtes himself was assassinated. Although Aeschylus's own position on this democratic reform cannot be determined with certainty, in *The Eumenides* the court's function as a tribunal for murder is given a divine validation. Ephialtes and Pericles had also favored challenging Spartan hegemony in Greece by allying with Argos, Sparta's main rival in the Peloponnese. In 461, the leader of the aristocrats, Cimon, was ostracized and the alliance with Argos approved. This change, which also produced fierce debate in the ensuing years, received attention from Aeschylus in the *Oresteia*. Orestes is clearly a political representative of Argos who allies himself with Athens, seemingly with Aeschylus's approval.[3]

It is not as important to label Aeschylus an aristocrat or radical as it is to recognize in the entire trilogy a paradigm for necessary compromise between disparate elements in the state.[4] If political vendettas are not controlled, there can be no civil order and consequently no peace and prosperity. Traditional groups like the Furies must be reconciled to the new system, treated with honor, and allowed to serve the state so that they can preserve for themselves and the community whichever of their principles remain valuable. Athena, establishing the Court of the Areopagus, defines its functions in words which echo the Furies' defense of their grim penalties:

> Here the reverence
> of citizens, their fear and kindred do-no-wrong
> shall hold by day and in the blessing of night alike
> all while the people do not muddy their own laws
> with foul infusions. But if bright water you stain
> with mud, you nevermore will find it fit to drink.
> No anarchy, no rule of a single master. Thus
> I advise my citizens to govern and to grace,
> and not to cast fear utterly from your city. What
> man who fears nothing at all is ever righteous? Such
> be your just terrors, and you may deserve and have
> salvation for your citadel, your land's defence
> such as is nowhere else found among men ...
> (*The Eumenides*, 11. 690–702)[5]

Her admonitions provide not only an eternal definition of good government, but also a timely warning to a population recently embroiled in civil strife.

[3] The debate about Aeschylus's position on the reforms is summarized by Podlecki, *Political Background*, pp. 81–92.

[4] Dodds, "Morals and Politics," is a forceful spokesman for this view.

[5] I have used the translation of Richmond Lattimore which appears in *The Complete Greek Tragedies: Aeschylus I* (New York, n.d.).

Sophocles

Sophocles (c. 496–c. 406 B.C.) won more prizes than any other tragedian in the Greek drama competitions, and he never came in lower than
second place. His first victory was against the grand old master Aeschylus in 468 B.C. Sophocles' last plays, which he wrote in his eighties, were
among his greatest. We have fragments of some ninety plays or poems
and seven complete tragedies, while records suggest that his output
numbered something over a hundred twenty plays.

Sophocles lived in interesting times. He would have recalled the first
defeat of the Persians in 490 B.C., when the news came by a messenger
who had run twenty-six miles from Marathon to Athens. In his adolescence, Athens achieved its astonishing and decisive victory over the
Persians at Salamis. His popularity as a tragedian and as a statesman coincided with the development of an imperial attitude in Athens. Athenian society honored the greatness of men like Aeschylus, Sophocles,
Euripides, the historian Herodotus, and all the politicians and artists
that Pericles drew to Athens for its rebuilding. It was a golden age shad-
owed by war.

Sophocles was both sociable and religious, serving as the priest of
several religious cults. He was also a man of action, popular enough to
be elected as one of Athens's twelve generals; he participated with Pericles in the Samian War (440–439 B.C.). His plays — especially *Antigone*
(441 B.C.), which preceded his election to generalship — often have deep
political concerns. One of his primary themes concerns the relation of
the individual to the *polis,* the state itself. Since the Greeks valued the
individual and at the same time regarded the *polis* as a sacred bulwark
against a return to barbarism, conflicts between the individual and the
polis were immensely painful.

When Sophocles began writing, he broke with an old tradition. From
the time of Thespis (mid-sixth century B.C.), each playwright acted in his
own plays. Aeschylus probably did so, but it is on record that Sophocles'
voice was not strong enough to permit him to take a part in his plays. He
played the lyre well enough to appear onstage, and he participated in a
game of ball in one of his plays, but he did not appear as an actor. He also
introduced innovations in the structure of his plays by changing the size
of the chorus to fifteen and by adding painted scenery, more props, and a
third actor to the two that Aeschylus and other tragedians had used.
Sophocles wrote some of his plays with specific actors in mind, much as
Shakespeare, Molière, and many other first-rank playwrights have done.

Sophocles was versed in the epics of Homer. Some of his plays derive from the *Iliad* or the *Odyssey*, although Sophocles always adapted the material of others to his own purposes. His nickname was the Attic Bee because he could investigate wonderful pieces of literature and always return with a useful idea. The approach he took to the structure of the play, measuring the effect of the rising action of complication and then ensuring that the moment of recognition occurred at the same time the falling action began, was recognized as a supremely elegant skill. Nowhere is this illustrated with more completeness than in *Oedipus Rex*.

The plays of Aeschylus, powerful though they are, do not have the same delicacy of construction as do Sophocles'. They are forceful but, in terms of structure, somewhat simpler. The structure of the plays of Euripides, Sophocles' successor, was never as fully worked out; and when Aristotle discussed the nature of tragedy in his *Poetics,* it was to Sophocles he turned for a model, not to the other two master playwrights of the genre.

Besides the Oedipus plays, Sophocles' other surviving plays are *Philoctetes, Ajax, Trachiniae,* and *Elektra*.

OEDIPUS REX

Oedipus Rex is one of three plays by Sophocles that treat the fate of Oedipus and his children. The plays were written over a period of thirty years: *Antigone* (first produced in 441 B.C.), *Oedipus Rex* (produced approximately fifteen years later, between 430 and 427 B.C.), and *Oedipus at Colonus* (produced in 401 B.C., after Sophocles' death). When these plays are produced together today, they are usually given in an order that follows the events of Oedipus's and Antigone's lives — *Oedipus Rex, Oedipus at Colonus,* and *Antigone* — almost like the trilogies that Athenian audiences often viewed in the early years of the drama competitions. In fact, they were never a unified trilogy, and one of Sophocles' distinctions is that he did not present as trilogies plays that were thematically related, as poets before him had done.

The original narratives of the Oedipus plays were known to Sophocles' audience — with the possible exception of the story of Antigone — and one of the special pleasures for the audience watching the action of *Oedipus Rex* was that they knew the outcome. They watched for the steps, the choices, that led Oedipus to his fate.

Oedipus Rex is the story of a noble man who seeks knowledge that in the end destroys him. His greatness is measured in part by the fact that the gods have prophesied his fate: The gods do not take interest in insignificant men. Before the action of the play begins, Oedipus has set out to discover whether he is truly the son of Polybos and Merope, the people who have reared him. He learns from the oracle of Apollo at Delphi, the most powerful interpreter of the voice and the will of the gods, that he will kill his father and marry his mother. His response is overwhelmingly human: He has seen his *moira,* his fate, and he cannot accept it. His reaction is to do everything he can, including leaving his homeland as quickly as possible, to avoid the possibility of killing Polybos and marrying Merope.

The Greek audience would have known that Oedipus was a descendant of Kadmos, founder of Thebes, who had sown the dragon teeth that produced the Spartoi (the sown men). Legend determined that the rulership of Thebes would be in dispute, with fraternal rivalry resembling that of the Spartoi, who fought and killed each other. This bloody legacy follows Oedipus, but it also reaches into all the plays of the trilogy. For example, in *Antigone* we learn that Antigone's brothers Polyneices and Eteocles killed each other in the shadow of the city walls. Thus, the fate Oedipus attempts to avoid actually dooms most of the characters in the three plays, including his true father, Laios, and his daughter Antigone.

Sophocles develops the drama in terms of IRONY — the disjunction between what seems to be true and what is true. Knowing the outcome of the action, the audience savors the ironic moments from the beginning of the play to the end. Oedipus flees his homeland to avoid fulfilling the prophecy, only to run headlong into the fate foretold by the oracle. He unwittingly returns to his original home, Thebes, and to his parents, murdering Laios, his true father, at a crossroads on the way and marrying Iokaste, his true mother, and becoming king of Thebes. The blind seer Teiresias warns Oedipus not to pursue the truth but, in human fashion, Oedipus refuses to heed Teiresias's warnings. When the complete truth becomes clear to Oedipus, he physically blinds himself in horror and expiation. Like the blind Teiresias, Oedipus must now look inward for the truth, without the distractions of surface experiences.

The belief that the moral health of the ruler directly affected the security of the *polis* was widespread in Athenian Greece. Indeed, the Athenians regarded their state as fragile — like a human being whose health, physical and moral, could change suddenly. Because the Greeks were concerned for the well-being of their state, the *polis* often figures in the tragedies. The Sophoclean Oedipus trilogy is usually called the Theban plays, a nomenclature that reminds us that the story of Oedipus can be read as the story of an individual or as the story of a state.

Oedipus Rex examines the tension between and interdependence of the individual and the state. The agricultural and ritual basis of the

Dionysian festivals — in which Greek drama developed — underscores the importance the Greeks attached to the individual's dependence on the state that feeds him and on the proper ways of doing things. This could be planting and harvesting or worshiping the gods or living as part of a political entity.

The underlying conflict in the play is political. The political relationship of human beings to the gods, the arbiters of their fate, is dramatized in Oedipus's relationship with the seer Teiresias. If he had his way, Oedipus might disregard Teiresias entirely. But Oedipus cannot command everything, even as ruler. His incomplete knowledge, despite his wisdom, is symptomatic of the limitations of every individual.

The contrast of Oedipus and Kreon, Iokaste's brother, is one of political style. Oedipus is a fully developed character who reveals himself as sympathetic but willful. He acts on his misunderstanding of the prophecy without reconsulting the oracle. He marries Iokaste and blinds himself without reconsulting the oracle. Kreon, who is much less complicated, never acts without consulting the oracle and thoughtfully reflecting on the oracle's message. Oedipus sometimes behaves tyrannically, and he appears eager for power. Kreon takes power only when forced to do so.

The depth of Sophocles' character development was unmatched, except by his contemporary Euripides, for almost two thousand years. Sophocles' drama is one of psychological development. His audiences saw Oedipus as a model for human greatness but also as a model for the human capacity to fall from a great height. The play is about the limits of human knowledge; it is also about the limits and frailty of human happiness.

Oedipus Rex in Performance

Oedipus Rex has enjoyed great popularity since its first performance. The Greeks, who originally restricted their plays to one performance, eventually began to revive plays of the masters. Oedipus was one of the most popular. In modern times, performance has been almost constant since the seventeenth century. Great dramatists have produced it in their own adaptations — Corneille (1659), John Dryden (1679), Voltaire (1718), William Butler Yeats (1923), and Jean Cocteau (1931) — proving the durability of the themes and the adaptability of the play. The early American performances (beginning in 1881) were in Greek but soon gave way to English. Modern versions have been both very traditional, such as those developed by the Royal Shakespeare Company in the 1970s, and experimental, such as that of Peter Brook (1968). Brook's production began with a huge golden cube reflecting brilliant light like the sun and ended with the ritual unveiling of a giant phallus. John Gielgud played Oedipus and Irene Worth, all in black, played Iokaste. Currently, Greek companies perform the play regularly in the theater of Dionysus in Athens as well as in Epidaurus and elsewhere.

Sophocles (c. 496–c. 406 B.C.)

OEDIPUS REX   *c. 430 B.C.*

TRANSLATED BY DUDLEY FITTS AND ROBERT FITZGERALD

Characters

OEDIPUS, *King of Thebes, supposed son of Polybos*
  and Merope, King and Queen of Corinth
IOKASTE, *wife of Oedipus and widow of the late King*
  Laios
KREON, *brother of Iokaste, a prince of Thebes*
TEIRESIAS, *a blind seer who serves Apollo*
PRIEST
MESSENGER, *from Corinth*
SHEPHERD, *former servant of Laios*
SECOND MESSENGER, *from the palace*
CHORUS OF THEBAN ELDERS
CHORAGOS, *leader of the Chorus*
ANTIGONE *and* ISMENE, *young daughters of Oedipus*
  and Iokaste. They appear in the Exodos but do not
  speak.
SUPPLIANTS, GUARDS, SERVANTS

The Scene: *Before the palace of Oedipus, King of*
Thebes. A central door and two lateral doors open
onto a platform which runs the length of the facade.
On the platform, right and left, are altars; and three
steps lead down into the orchestra, or chorus-ground.
At the beginning of the action these steps are crowded
by suppliants who have brought branches and chap-
lets of olive leaves and who sit in various attitudes of
despair. Oedipus enters.

PROLOGUE°

OEDIPUS: My children, generations of the living
  In the line of Kadmos,° nursed at his ancient
    hearth:
  Why have you strewn yourselves before these
    altars
  In supplication, with your boughs and garlands?
5 The breath of incense rises from the city

With a sound of prayer and lamentation.
                                        Children,
I would not have you speak through messengers,
And therefore I have come myself to hear you—
I, Oedipus, who bear the famous name.
(*To a Priest.*) You, there, since you are eldest in
    the company,   10
Speak for them all, tell me what preys upon you,
Whether you come in dread, or crave some
    blessing:
Tell me, and never doubt that I will help you
In every way I can; I should be heartless
Were I not moved to find you suppliant here.   15
PRIEST: Great Oedipus, O powerful king of Thebes!
You see how all the ages of our people
Cling to your altar steps: here are boys
Who can barely stand alone, and here are priests
By weight of age, as I am a priest of God,   20
And young men chosen from those yet
    unmarried;
As for the others, all that multitude,
They wait with olive chaplets in the squares,
At the two shrines of Pallas,° and where Apollo°
Speaks in the glowing embers.
                                Your own eyes   25
Must tell you: Thebes is tossed on a murdering
    sea
And can not lift her head from the death surge.
A rust consumes the buds and fruits of the earth;
The herds are sick; children die unborn,
And labor is vain. The god of plague and pyre   30
Raids like detestable lightning through the city,
And all the house of Kadmos is laid waste,
All emptied, and all darkened: Death alone
Battens upon the misery of Thebes.

You are not one of the immortal gods, we know;   35
Yet we have come to you to make our prayer
As to the man surest in mortal ways
And wisest in the ways of God. You saved us

Prologue: Portion of the play explaining the background and
current action.   **2. Kadmos:** Founder of Thebes.

24. Pallas: Pallas Athene, daughter of Zeus and goddess of
wisdom.   **Apollo:** Son of Zeus and god of the sun, of light
and truth.

From the Sphinx,° that flinty singer, and the
    tribute
40   We paid to her so long; yet you were never
    Better informed than we, nor could we teach
      you:
    A god's touch, it seems, enabled you to help us.

    Therefore, O mighty power, we turn to you:
    Find us our safety, find us a remedy,
45   Whether by counsel of the gods or of men.
    A king of wisdom tested in the past
    Can act in a time of troubles, and act well.
    Noblest of men, restore
    Life to your city! Think how all men call you
50   Liberator for your boldness long ago;
    Ah, when your years of kingship are
      remembered,
    Let them not say *We rose, but later fell* —
    Keep the State from going down in the storm!
    Once, years ago, with happy augury,
55   You brought us fortune; be the same again!
    No man questions your power to rule the land:
    But rule over men, not over a dead city!
    Ships are only hulls, high walls are nothing,
    When no life moves in the empty passageways.
60 OEDIPUS: Poor children! You may be sure I know
    All that you longed for in your coming here.
    I know that you are deathly sick; and yet,
    Sick as you are, not one is as sick as I.
    Each of you suffers in himself alone
65   His anguish, not another's; but my spirit
    Groans for the city, for myself, for you.

    I was not sleeping, you are not waking me.
    No, I have been in tears for a long while
    And in my restless thought walked many ways.
70   In all my search I found one remedy,
    And I have adopted it: I have sent Kreon,
    Son of Menoikeus, brother of the queen,
    To Delphi,° Apollo's place of revelation,
    To learn there, if he can,
75   What act or pledge of mine may save the city.
    I have counted the days, and now, this very day,
    I am troubled, for he has overstayed his time.
    What is he doing? He has been gone too long.
    Yet whenever he comes back, I should do ill
80   Not to take any action the god orders.
  PRIEST: It is a timely promise. At this instant

---

39. **Sphinx:** A winged monster with the body of a lion and the
face of a woman, the Sphinx had tormented Thebes with her
riddle, killing those who could not solve it. When Oedipus
solved the riddle, the Sphinx killed herself.   **73. Delphi:** Site
of the oracle, source of religious authority and prophecy, under the protection of Apollo.

They tell me Kreon is here.
OEDIPUS: O Lord Apollo!
    May his news be fair as his face is radiant!
PRIEST: Good news, I gather! he is crowned with
      bay,
    The chaplet is thick with berries.
OEDIPUS: We shall soon know; 85
    He is near enough to hear us now. (*Enter
    Kreon.*) O prince:
    Brother: son of Menoikeus:
    What answer do you bring us from the god?
KREON: A strong one. I can tell you, great afflictions
    Will turn out well, if they are taken well. 90
OEDIPUS: What was the oracle? These vague words
    Leave me still hanging between hope and fear.
KREON: Is it your pleasure to hear me with all
      these
    Gathered around us? I am prepared to speak,
    But should we not go in?
OEDIPUS: Speak to them all, 95
    It is for them I suffer, more than for myself.
KREON: Then I will tell you what I heard at Delphi.
    In plain words
    The god commands us to expel from the land of
      Thebes
    An old defilement we are sheltering. 100
    It is a deathly thing, beyond cure;
    We must not let it feed upon us longer.
OEDIPUS: What defilement? How shall we rid
    ourselves of it?
KREON: By exile or death, blood for blood. It was
    Murder that brought the plague-wind on the city. 105
OEDIPUS: Murder of whom? Surely the god has
    named him?
KREON: My Lord: Laios once ruled this land,
    Before you came to govern us.
OEDIPUS: I know;
    I learned of him from others; I never saw him.
KREON: He was murdered; and Apollo commands
    us now 110
    To take revenge upon whoever killed him.
OEDIPUS: Upon whom? Where are they? Where shall
    we find a clue
    To solve that crime, after so many years?
KREON: Here in this land, he said. Search reveals
    Things that escape an inattentive man. 115
OEDIPUS: Tell me: Was Laios murdered in his house,
    Or in the fields, or in some foreign country?
KREON: He said he planned to make a pilgrimage.
    He did not come home again.
OEDIPUS: And was there no one,
    No witness, no companion, to tell what
    happened? 120
KREON: They were all killed but one, and he got
    away

So frightened that he could remember one thing
    only.
OEDIPUS: What was that one thing? One may be the
    key
To everything, if we resolve to use it.
KREON: He said that a band of highwaymen
125   attacked them,
    Outnumbered them, and overwhelmed the king.
OEDIPUS: Strange, that a highwayman should be so
    daring—
    Unless some faction here bribed him to do it.
KREON: We thought of that. But after Laios' death
130   New troubles arose and we had no avenger.
OEDIPUS: What troubles could prevent your hunting
    down the killers?
KREON: The riddling Sphinx's song
    Made us deaf to all mysteries but her own.
OEDIPUS: Then once more I must bring what is dark
    to light.
135   It is most fitting that Apollo shows,
    As you do, this compunction for the dead.
    You shall see how I stand by you, as I should,
    Avenging this country and the god as well,
    And not as though it were for some distant friend,
140   But for my own sake, to be rid of evil.
    Whoever killed King Laios might — who
        knows? —
    Lay violent hands even on me — and soon.
    I act for the murdered king in my own interest.

    Come, then, my children: leave the altar steps,
    Lift up your olive boughs!
145   One of you go
    And summon the people of Kadmos to gather
        here.
    I will do all that I can; you may tell them that.
                                (Exit a Page.)
    So, with the help of God,
    We shall be saved — or else indeed we are lost.
150 PRIEST: Let us rise, children. It was for this we came,
    And now the king has promised it.
    Phoibos° has sent us an oracle; may he descend
    Himself to save us and drive out the plague.
*(Exeunt° Oedipus and Kreon into the palace by the
central door. The Priest and the Suppliants disperse
right and left. After a short pause the Chorus enters
the orchestra.)*

PARODOS° • Strophe° 1

CHORUS: What is God singing in his profound
    Delphi of gold and shadow?
    What oracle for Thebes, the Sunwhipped city?
    Fear unjoints me, the roots of my heart tremble.
    Now I remember, O Healer, your power, and
        wonder: 5
    Will you send doom like a sudden cloud, or
        weave it
    Like nightfall of the past?
    Speak to me, tell me, O
    Child of golden Hope, immortal Voice.

Antistrophe° 1

    Let me pray to Athene, the immortal daughter of
        Zeus,   10
    And to Artemis° her sister
    Who keeps her famous throne in the market ring,
    And to Apollo, archer from distant heaven —
    O gods, descend! Like three streams leap against
    The fires of our grief, the fires of darkness;   15
    Be swift to bring us rest!
    As in the old time from the brilliant house
    Of air you stepped to save us, come again!

Strophe 2

    Now our afflictions have no end,
    Now all our stricken host lies down   20
    And no man fights off death with his mind;
    The noble plowland bears no grain,
    And groaning mothers can not bear —
    See, how our lives like birds take wing,
    Like sparks that fly when a fire soars,   25
    To the shore of the god of evening.

Antistrophe 2

    The plague burns on, it is pitiless,
    Though pallid children laden with death
    Lie unwept in the stony ways,
    And old gray women by every path   30

Parodos: The song or ode chanted by the Chorus on their entry.   Strophe: Song sung by the Chorus as they danced from
stage right to stage left.   Antistrophe: Song sung by the
Chorus following the Strophe, as they danced back from stage
left to stage right.   11. Artemis: The huntress, daughter of
Zeus, twin sister of Apollo.

152. Phoibos: Apollo.   **154.** [S.D.] *Exeunt:* Latin for "they
go out."

Flock to the strand about the altars
There to strike their breasts and cry
Worship of Phoibos in wailing prayers:
Be kind, God's golden child!

Strophe 3

35   There are no swords in this attack by fire,
No shields, but we are ringed with cries.
Send the besieger plunging from our homes
Into the vast sea-room of the Atlantic
Or into the waves that foam eastward of
    Thrace —
40   For the day ravages what the night spares —
Destroy our enemy, lord of the thunder!
Let him be riven by lightning from heaven!

Antistrophe 3

Phoibos Apollo, stretch the sun's bowstring,
That golden cord, until it sing for us,
Flashing arrows in heaven!
                          Artemis, Huntress,
45   Race with flaring lights upon our mountains!
O scarlet god,° O golden-banded brow,
O Theban Bacchos in a storm of Maenads,°

(Enter Oedipus, center.)

Whirl upon Death, that all the Undying hate!
50   Come with blinding torches, come in joy!

SCENE 1

OEDIPUS: Is this your prayer? It may be answered.
    Come,
Listen to me, act as the crisis demands,
And you shall have relief from all these evils.

Until now I was a stranger to this tale,
5   As I had been a stranger to the crime.
Could I track down the murderer without a clue?
But now, friends,
As one who became a citizen after the murder,
I make this proclamation to all Thebans:
If any man knows by whose hand Laios, son of
10   Labdakos,

---

47. scarlet god: Bacchus, god of wine and revelry; also called
Dionysus.   **48. Maenads:** Female worshipers of Bacchus
(Dionysus).

Met his death, I direct that man to tell me
    everything,
No matter what he fears for having so long
    withheld it.
Let it stand as promised that no further trouble
Will come to him, but he may leave the land in
    safety.
Moreover: If anyone knows the murderer to be
    foreign,   15
Let him not keep silent: he shall have his reward
    from me.
However, if he does conceal it; if any man
Fearing for his friend or for himself disobeys this
    edict,
Hear what I propose to do:

I solemnly forbid the people of this country,   20
Where power and throne are mine, ever to
    receive that man
Or speak to him, no matter who he is, or let him
Join in sacrifice, lustration, or in prayer.
I decree that he be driven from every house,
Being, as he is, corruption itself to us: the
    Delphic   25
Voice of Apollo has pronounced this revelation.
Thus I associate myself with the oracle
And take the side of the murdered king.

As for the criminal, I pray to God —
Whether it be a lurking thief, or one of a
    number —   30
I pray that that man's life be consumed in evil
    and wretchedness.
And as for me, this curse applies no less
If it should turn out that the culprit is my guest
    here,
Sharing my hearth.
                      You have heard the penalty.
I lay it on you now to attend to this   35
For my sake, for Apollo's, for the sick
Sterile city that heaven has abandoned.
Suppose the oracle had given you no command:
Should this defilement go uncleansed for ever?
You should have found the murderer: your king,   40
A noble king, had been destroyed!
                              Now I,
Having the power that he held before me,
Having his bed, begetting children there
Upon his wife, as he would have, had he lived —
Their son would have been my children's brother,   45
If Laios had had luck in fatherhood!
(And now his bad fortune has struck him
    down) —
I say I take the son's part, just as though
I were his son, to press the fight for him

I did not do the murder, I can not name
The murderer. Phoibos ordained the search;
Why did he not say who the culprit was?
OEDIPUS: An honest question. But no man in the
world
   Can make the gods do more than the gods will.   65
CHORAGOS: There is an alternative, I think —
OEDIPUS: Tell me.
   Any or all, you must not fail to tell me.
CHORAGOS: A lord clairvoyant to the lord Apollo,
   As we all know, is the skilled Teiresias.
   One might learn much about this from him,
      Oedipus.   70
OEDIPUS: I am not wasting time:
   Kreon spoke of this, and I have sent for him —
   Twice, in fact; it is strange that he is not here.
CHORAGOS: The other matter — that old report —
   seems useless.
OEDIPUS: What was that? I am interested in all
   reports.   75
CHORAGOS: The king was said to have been killed
   by highwaymen.
OEDIPUS: I know. But we have no witnesses to that.
CHORAGOS: If the killer can feel a particle of dread,
   Your curse will bring him out of hiding!
OEDIPUS: No.
   The man who dared that act will fear no curse.   80

(*Enter the blind seer Teiresias, led by a Page.*)

CHORAGOS: But there is one man who may detect
   the criminal.
   This is Teiresias, this is the holy prophet
   In whom, alone of all men, truth was born.
OEDIPUS: Teiresias: seer: student of mysteries,
   Of all that's taught and all that no man tells,   85
   Secrets of Heaven and secrets of the earth:
   Blind though you are, you know the city lies
   Sick with plague; and from this plague, my lord,
   We find that you alone can guard or save us.

Possibly you did not hear the messengers?   90
Apollo, when we sent to him,
Sent us back word that this great pestilence
Would lift, but only if we established clearly
The identity of those who murdered Laios.
They must be killed or exiled.
                          Can you use   95
Birdflight° or any art of divination
To purify yourself, and Thebes, and me
From this contagion? We are in your hands.
There is no fairer duty
Than that of helping others in distress.   100

96. Birdflight: Prophets used the flight of birds to predict the future.

50   And see it won! I'll find the hand that brought
    Death to Labdakos' and Polydoros' child,
    Heir of Kadmos' and Agenor's line.°
    And as for those who fail me,
    May the gods deny them the fruit of the earth,
55   Fruit of the womb, and may they rot utterly!
    Let them be wretched as we are wretched, and
     worse!

    For you, for loyal Thebans, and for all
    Who find my actions right, I pray the favor
    Of justice, and of all the immortal gods.
60   CHORAGOS: Since I am under oath, my lord, I swear

51–52. Labdakos, Polydoros, Kadmos, and Agenor: Father, grandfather, great-grandfather, and great-great-grandfather of Laios.

FAR LEFT: Le Clanche Du Rand as Iokaste in Donald Sutherland and Robert Loper's production of *Oedipus Rex* at the 1975 Oregon Shakespeare Festival in Ashland. RIGHT: Philip L. Jones as the Shepherd. (Photos by Henry S. Kranzler.) BELOW: Franz Mertz's design for a 1952 production of *Oedipus Rex* directed by G. R. Sellner at Darmstadt, Landestheater.

TEIRESIAS: How dreadful knowledge of the truth can
    be
    When there's no help in truth! I knew this well,
    But did not act on it; else I should not have
    come.
OEDIPUS: What is troubling you? Why are your eyes
    so cold?
TEIRESIAS: Let me go home. Bear your own fate, and
105   I'll
    Bear mine. It is better so: trust what I say.
OEDIPUS: What you say is ungracious and unhelpful
    To your native country. Do not refuse to speak.
TEIRESIAS: When it comes to speech, your own is
    neither temperate
110   Nor opportune. I wish to be more prudent.
OEDIPUS: In God's name, we all beg you —
TEIRESIAS: You are all ignorant.
    No; I will never tell you what I know.
    Now it is my misery; then, it would be yours.
OEDIPUS: What! You do know something, and will
    not tell us?
115   You would betray us all and wreck the State?
TEIRESIAS: I do not intend to torture myself, or you.
    Why persist in asking? You will not persuade me.
OEDIPUS: What a wicked old man you are! You'd
    try a stone's
    Patience! Out with it! Have you no feeling at all?
TEIRESIAS: You call me unfeeling. If you could only
120   see
    The nature of your own feelings . . .
OEDIPUS: Why,
    Who would not feel as I do? Who could endure
    Your arrogance toward the city?
TEIRESIAS: What does it matter?
    Whether I speak or not, it is bound to come.
OEDIPUS: Then, if "it" is bound to come, you are
125   bound to tell me.
TEIRESIAS: No, I will not go on. Rage as you please.
OEDIPUS: Rage? Why not!
                    And I'll tell you what I think:
    You planned it, you had it done, you all but
    Killed him with your own hands: if you had eyes,
130   I'd say the crime was yours, and yours alone.
TEIRESIAS: So? I charge you, then,
    Abide by the proclamation you have made:
    From this day forth
    Never speak again to these men or to me;
135   You yourself are the pollution of this country.
OEDIPUS: You dare say that! Can you possibly think
    you have
    Some way of going free, after such insolence?
TEIRESIAS: I have gone free. It is the truth sustains
    me.
OEDIPUS: Who taught you shamelessness? It was not
    your craft.

TEIRESIAS: You did. You made me speak. I did not
    want to.   140
OEDIPUS: Speak what? Let me hear it again more
    clearly.
TEIRESIAS: Was it not clear before? Are you tempting
    me?
OEDIPUS: I did not understand it. Say it again.
TEIRESIAS: I say that you are the murderer whom
    you seek.
OEDIPUS: Now twice you have spat out infamy.
    You'll pay for it!   145
TEIRESIAS: Would you care for more? Do you wish
    to be really angry?
OEDIPUS: Say what you will. Whatever you say is
    worthless.
TEIRESIAS: I say you live in hideous shame with
    those
    Most dear to you. You can not see the evil.
OEDIPUS: Can you go on babbling like this for ever? 150
TEIRESIAS: I can, if there is power in truth.
OEDIPUS: There is:
    But not for you, not for you,
    You sightless, witless, senseless, mad old man!
TEIRESIAS: You are the madman. There is no one
    here
    Who will not curse you soon, as you curse me. 155
OEDIPUS: You child of total night! I would not
    touch you;
    Neither would any man who sees the sun.
TEIRESIAS: True: it is not from you my fate will
    come.
    That lies within Apollo's competence,
    As it is his concern.
OEDIPUS: Tell me, who made   160
    These fine discoveries? Kreon? or someone else?
TEIRESIAS: Kreon is no threat. You weave your own
    doom.
OEDIPUS: Wealth, power, craft of statemanship!
    Kingly position, everywhere admired!
    What savage envy is stored up against these, 165
    If Kreon, whom I trusted, Kreon my friend,
    For this great office which the city once
    Put in my hands unsought — if for this power
    Kreon desires in secret to destroy me!

    He has bought this decrepit fortune-teller, this 170
    Collector of dirty pennies, this prophet fraud —
    Why, he is no more clairvoyant than I am!
                            Tell us:
    Has your mystic mummery ever approached the
    truth?
    When that hellcat the Sphinx was performing here,
    What help were you to these people?   175
    Her magic was not for the first man who came
    along:

It demanded a real exorcist. Your birds —
What good were they? or the gods, for the
matter of that?
But I came by,
180 Oedipus, the simple man, who knows nothing —
I thought it out for myself, no birds helped me!
And this is the man you think you can destroy,
That you may be close to Kreon when he's king!
Well, you and your friend Kreon, it seems to me,
185 Will suffer most. If you were not an old man,
You would have paid already for your plot.

CHORAGOS: We can not see that his words or yours
Have been spoken except in anger, Oedipus,
And of anger we have no need. How to
accomplish
The god's will best: that is what most concerns
190 us.

TEIRESIAS: You are a king. But where argument's
concerned
I am your man, as much a king as you.
I am not your servant, but Apollo's.
I have no need of Kreon or Kreon's name.

195 Listen to me. You mock my blindness, do you?
But I say that you, with both your eyes, are
blind:
You can not see the wretchedness of your life,
Nor in whose house you live, no, nor with
whom.
Who are your father and mother? Can you tell
me?
200 You do not even know the blind wrongs
That you have done them, on earth and in the
world below.
But the double lash of your parents' curse will
whip you
Out of this land some day, with only night
Upon your precious eyes.
205 Your cries then — where will they not be heard?
What fastness of Kithairon° will not echo them?
And that bridal-descant of yours — you'll know
it then,
The song they sang when you came here to
Thebes
And found your misguided berthing.
All this, and more, that you can not guess at
210 now,
Will bring you to yourself among your children.

Be angry, then. Curse Kreon. Curse my words.
I tell you, no man that walks upon the earth

Shall be rooted out more horribly than you.   215
OEDIPUS: Am I to bear this from him? — Damnation
Take you! Out of this place! Out of my sight!
TEIRESIAS: I would not have come at all if you had
not asked me.
OEDIPUS: Could I have told that you'd talk
nonsense, that
You'd come here to make a fool of yourself, and
of me?
TEIRESIAS: A fool? Your parents thought me sane   220
enough.
OEDIPUS: My parents again! — Wait: who were my
parents?
TEIRESIAS: This day will give you a father, and break
your heart.
OEDIPUS: Your infantile riddles! Your damned
abracadabra!
TEIRESIAS: You were a great man once at solving
riddles.
OEDIPUS: Mock me with that if you like; you will   225
find it true.
TEIRESIAS: It was true enough. It brought about your
ruin.
OEDIPUS: But if it saved this town?
TEIRESIAS (to the Page):   Boy, give me your hand.
OEDIPUS: Yes, boy; lead him away.
                                    — While you are here
We can do nothing. Go; leave us in peace.
TEIRESIAS: I will go when I have said what I have to   230
say.
How can you hurt me? And I tell you again.
The man you have been looking for all this
time,
The damned man, the murderer of Laïos,
That man is in Thebes. To your mind he is
foreign-born,   235
But it will soon be shown that he is a Theban,
A revelation that will fail to please.
                                    A blind man,
Who has his eyes now; a penniless man, who is
rich now;
And he will go tapping the strange earth with his
staff.
To the children with whom he lives now he will
be   240
Brother and father — the very same; to her
Who bore him, son and husband — the very
same
Who came to his father's bed, wet with his
father's blood.
Enough. Go think that over.
If later you find error in what I have said,   245
You may say that I have no skill in prophecy.
(Exit Teiresias, led by his Page. Oedipus goes into the
palace.)

---

206. **Kithairon:** The mountain where Oedipus was abandoned
as an infant.

ODE° 1 • *Strophe 1*

CHORUS: The Delphic stone of prophecies
    Remembers ancient regicide
    And a still bloody hand.
    That killer's hour of flight has come.
5   He must be stronger than riderless
    Coursers of untiring wind,
    For the son of Zeus° armed with his father's
      thunder

Leaps in lightning after him;
And the Furies° hold his track, the sad Furies.

Antistrophe 1

Holy Parnassos'° peak of snow   10
Flashes and blinds that secret man,
That all shall hunt him down:
Though he may roam the forest shade
Like a bull gone wild from pasture

Ode: Song sung by the Chorus.   **7. son of Zeus:** Apollo.

9. Furies: Spirits called upon to avenge crimes, especially against kin.   **10. Parnassos:** Mountain sacred to Apollo.

Josef Svoboda's stage design
for M. Machacek's 1963
production of *Oedipus Rex*
in Prague.

15 To rage through glooms of stone.
    Doom comes down on him; flight will not avail
        him;
    For the world's heart calls him desolate,
    And the immortal voices follow, for ever follow.

Strophe 2

    But now a wilder thing is heard
    From the old man skilled at hearing Fate in the
20   wing-beat of a bird.
    Bewildered as a blown bird, my soul hovers and
        can not find
    Foothold in this debate, or any reason or rest of
        mind.
    But no man ever brought — none can bring
    Proof of strife between Thebes' royal house,
25 Labdakos' line, and the son of Polybos;°
    And never until now has any man brought word
    Of Laios' dark death staining Oedipus the King.

Antistrophe 2

    Divine Zeus and Apollo hold
    Perfect intelligence alone of all tales ever told;
    And well though this diviner works, he works in
30   his own night;
    No man can judge that rough unknown or trust
        in second sight,
    For wisdom changes hands among the wise.
    Shall I believe my great lord criminal
    At a raging word that a blind old man let fall?
    I saw him, when the carrion woman° faced him
35   of old,
    Prove his heroic mind. These evil words are lies.

SCENE 2

KREON: Men of Thebes:
    I am told that heavy accusations
    Have been brought against me by King Oedipus.

    I am not the kind of man to bear this tamely.

5   If in these present difficulties
    He holds me accountable for any harm to him
    Through anything I have said or done — why,
        then,

25. Polybos: King who adopted Oedipus.   **35. woman:** The
Sphinx.

I do not value life in this dishonor.
It is not as though this rumor touched upon
Some private indiscretion. The matter is grave.   10
The fact is that I am being called disloyal
To the State, to my fellow citizens, to my friends.
CHORAGOS: He may have spoken in anger, not from
        his mind.
KREON: But did you not hear him say I was the one
    Who seduced the old prophet into lying?   15
CHORAGOS: The thing was said; I do not know how
        seriously.
KREON: But you were watching him! Were his eyes
        steady?
    Did he look like a man in his right mind?
CHORAGOS: I do not know.
    I can not judge the behavior of great men.
    But here is the king himself.

(*Enter Oedipus.*)

OEDIPUS: So you dared come back.   20
    Why? How brazen of you to come to my house,
    You murderer!
                    Do you think I do not know
    That you plotted to kill me, plotted to steal my
        throne?
    Tell me, in God's name: am I coward, a fool,
    That you should dream you could accomplish
        this?   25
    A fool who could not see your slippery game?
    A coward, not to fight back when I saw it?
    You are the fool, Kreon, are you not? hoping
    Without support or friends to get a throne?
    Thrones may be won or bought: you could do
        neither.   30
KREON: Now listen to me. You have talked; let me
        talk, too.
    You can not judge unless you know the facts.
OEDIPUS: You speak well: there is one fact; but I
        find it hard
    To learn from the deadliest enemy I have.
KREON: That above all I must dispute with you.   35
OEDIPUS: That above all I will not hear you deny.
KREON: If you think there is anything good in being
        stubborn
    Against all reason, then I say you are wrong.
OEDIPUS: If you think a man can sin against his own
        kind
    And not be punished for it, I say you are mad.   40
KREON: I agree. But tell me: what have I done to
        you?
OEDIPUS: You advised me to send for that wizard,
        did you not?
KREON: I did. I should do it again.
OEDIPUS: Very well. Now tell me:
    How long has it been since Laios —

KREON: What of Laios?

OEDIPUS: Since he vanished in that onset by the
45   road?

KREON: It was long ago, a long time.

OEDIPUS: And this prophet,
   Was he practicing here then?

KREON: He was; and with honor, as now.

OEDIPUS: Did he speak of me at that time?

KREON: He never did,
   At least, not when I was present.

OEDIPUS: But . . . the enquiry?
   I suppose you held one?

50 KREON: We did, but we learned nothing.

OEDIPUS: Why did the prophet not speak against me
   then?

KREON: I do not know; and I am the kind of man
   Who holds his tongue when he has no facts to
   go on.

OEDIPUS: There's one fact that you know, and you
   could tell it.

KREON: What fact is that? If I know it, you shall
55   have it.

OEDIPUS: If he were not involved with you, he could
   not say
   That it was I who murdered Laios.

KREON: If he says that, you are the one that knows
   it! —
   But now it is my turn to question you.

60 OEDIPUS: Put your questions. I am no murderer.

KREON: First, then: You married my sister?

OEDIPUS: I married your sister.

KREON: And you rule the kingdom equally with her?

OEDIPUS: Everything that she wants she has from
   me.

KREON: And I am the third, equal to both of you?

65 OEDIPUS: That is why I call you a bad friend.

KREON: No. Reason it out, as I have done.
   Think of this first: would any sane man prefer
   Power, with all a king's anxieties,
   To that same power and the grace of sleep?
70   Certainly not I.
   I have never longed for the king's power — only
   his rights.
   Would any wise man differ from me in this?
   As matters stand, I have my way in everything
   With your consent, and no responsibilities.
75   If I were king, I should be a slave to policy.
   How could I desire a scepter more
   Than what is now mine — untroubled influence?
   No, I have not gone mad; I need no honors,
   Except those with the perquisites I have now.
80   I am welcome everywhere; every man salutes me,
   And those who want your favor seek my ear,
   Since I know how to manage what they ask.
   Should I exchange this ease for that anxiety?

   Besides, no sober mind is treasonable.
   I hate anarchy 85
   And never would deal with any man who likes it.
   Test what I have said. Go to the priestess
   At Delphi, ask if I quoted her correctly.
   And as for this other thing: if I am found
   Guilty of treason with Teiresias, 90
   Then sentence me to death. You have my word
   It is a sentence I should cast my vote for —
   But not without evidence!
          You do wrong
   When you take good men for bad, bad men for
   good.
   A true friend thrown aside — why, life itself 95
   Is not more precious!
            In time you will know this well:
   For time, and time alone, will show the just
   man,
   Though scoundrels are discovered in a day.

CHORAGOS: This is well said, and a prudent man
   would ponder it.
   Judgments too quickly formed are dangerous. 100

OEDIPUS: But is he not quick in his duplicity?
   And shall I not be quick to parry him?
   Would you have me stand still, hold my peace,
   and let
   This man win everything, through my inaction?

KREON: And you want — what is it, then? To
   banish me? 105

OEDIPUS: No, not exile. It is your death I want,
   So that all the world may see what treason means.

KREON: You will persist, then? You will not believe
   me?

OEDIPUS: How can I believe you?

KREON: Then you are a fool.

OEDIPUS: To save myself?

KREON: In justice, think of me. 110

OEDIPUS: You are evil incarnate.

KREON: But suppose that you are wrong?

OEDIPUS: Still I must rule.

KREON: But not if you rule badly.

OEDIPUS: O city, city!

KREON: It is my city, too!

CHORAGOS: Now, my lords, be still. I see the queen,
   Iokaste, coming from her palace chambers; 115
   And it is time she came, for the sake of you both.
   This dreadful quarrel can be resolved through her.

(*Enter Iokaste.*)

IOKASTE: Poor foolish men, what wicked din is this?
   With Thebes sick to death, is it not shameful
   That you should take some private quarrel up? 120
   (*To Oedipus.*) Come into the house.
          — And you, Kreon, go now:
   Let us have no more of this tumult over nothing.

KREON: Nothing? No, sister: what your husband
    plans for me
  Is one of two great evils: exile or death.
OEDIPUS: He is right.
125   Why, woman I have caught him squarely
  Plotting against my life.
KREON: No! Let me die
  Accurst if ever I have wished you harm!
IOKASTE: Ah, believe it, Oedipus!
  In the name of the gods, respect this oath of his
130   For my sake, for the sake of these people here!

Strophe 1

CHORAGOS: Open your mind to her, my lord. Be
    ruled by her, I beg you!
OEDIPUS: What would you have me do?
CHORAGOS: Respect Kreon's word. He has never
    spoken like a fool,
  And now he has sworn an oath.
OEDIPUS: You know what you ask?
CHORAGOS: I do.
OEDIPUS: Speak on, then.
CHORAGOS: A friend so sworn should not be baited
135   so,
  In blind malice, and without final proof.
OEDIPUS: You are aware, I hope, that what you say
  Means death for me, or exile at the least.

Strophe 2

CHORAGOS: No, I swear by Helios, first in heaven!
140   May I die friendless and accurst,
  The worst of deaths, if ever I meant that!
  It is the withering fields
    That hurt my sick heart:
  Must we bear all these ills,
145   And now your bad blood as well?
OEDIPUS: Then let him go. And let me die, if I
    must,
  Or be driven by him in shame from the land of
    Thebes.
  It is your unhappiness, and not his talk,
  That touches me.
          As for him —
150   Wherever he goes, hatred will follow him.
KREON: Ugly in yielding, as you were ugly in rage!
  Natures like yours chiefly torment themselves.
OEDIPUS: Can you not go? Can you not leave me?
KREON: I can.
  You do not know me; but the city knows me,
155   And in its eyes I am just, if not in yours.
                    (*Exit Kreon.*)

Antistrophe 1

CHORAGOS: Lady Iokaste, did you not ask the King
    to go to his chambers?
IOKASTE: First tell me what has happened.
CHORAGOS: There was suspicion without evidence;
    yet it rankled
  As even false charges will.
IOKASTE: On both sides?
CHORAGOS: On both.
IOKASTE: But what was said?   160
CHORAGOS: Oh let it rest, let it be done with!
  Have we not suffered enough?
OEDIPUS: You see to what your decency has brought
    you:
  You have made difficulties where my heart saw
    none.

Antistrophe 2

CHORAGOS: Oedipus, it is not once only I have told
    you —   165
    You must know I should count myself un-
    wise
  To the point of madness, should I now forsake
    you —
      You, under whose hand,
        In the storm of another time,
      Our dear land sailed out free.   170
      But now stand fast at the helm!
IOKASTE: In God's name, Oedipus, inform your wife
    as well:
  Why are you so set in this hard anger?
OEDIPUS: I will tell you, for none of these men
    deserves
  My confidence as you do. It is Kreon's work,   175
  His treachery, his plotting against me.
IOKASTE: Go on, if you can make this clear to me.
OEDIPUS: He charges me with the murder of Laios.
IOKASTE: Has he some knowledge? Or does he speak
    from hearsay?
OEDIPUS: He would not commit himself to such a
    charge,   180
  But he has brought in that damnable soothsayer
  To tell his story.
IOKASTE: Set your mind at rest.
  If it is a question of soothsayers, I tell you
  That you will find no man whose craft gives
    knowledge
  Of the unknowable.
          Here is my proof: 185
  An oracle was reported to Laios once
  (I will not say from Phoibos himself, but from
  His appointed ministers, at any rate)

That his doom would be death at the hands of
    his own son —
190 His son, born of his flesh and of mine!

Now, you remember the story: Laios was killed
By marauding strangers where three highways
    meet;
But his child had not been three days in this
    world
Before the king had pierced the baby's ankles
195 And left him to die on a lonely mountainside.

Thus, Apollo never caused that child
To kill his father, and it was not Laios' fate
To die at the hands of his son, as he had feared.
This is what prophets and prophecies are worth!
Have no dread of them.
200   It is God himself
Who can show us what he wills, in his own way.
OEDIPUS: How strange a shadowy memory crossed
    my mind,
Just now while you were speaking; it chilled my
    heart.
IOKASTE: What do you mean? What memory do you
    speak of?
205 OEDIPUS: If I understand you, Laios was killed
At a place where three roads meet.
IOKASTE: So it was said;
We have no later story.
OEDIPUS: Where did it happen?
IOKASTE: Phokis, it is called: at a place where the
    Theban Way
Divides into the roads toward Delphi and Daulia.
OEDIPUS: When?
IOKASTE: We had the news not long before
210   you came
And proved the right to your succession here.
OEDIPUS: Ah, what net has God been weaving for
    me?
IOKASTE: Oedipus! Why does this trouble you?
OEDIPUS: Do not ask me yet.
First, tell me how Laios looked, and tell me
How old he was.
215 IOKASTE: He was tall, his hair just touched
With white; his form was not unlike your own.
OEDIPUS: I think that I myself may be accurst
By my own ignorant edict.
IOKASTE: You speak strangely.
It makes me tremble to look at you, my king.
OEDIPUS: I am not sure that the blind man can not
220   see.
But I should know better if you were to tell me —
IOKASTE: Anything — though I dread to hear you
    ask it.
OEDIPUS: Was the king lightly escorted, or did he
    ride

With a large company, as a ruler should?
IOKASTE: There were five men with him in all: one
    was a herald;   225
And a single chariot, which he was driving.
OEDIPUS: Alas, that makes it plain enough!
                         But who —
Who told you how it happened?
IOKASTE: A household servant,
The only one to escape.
OEDIPUS: And is he still
A servant of ours?
IOKASTE: No; for when he came back at last   230
And found you enthroned in the place of the
    dead king,
He came to me, touched my hand with his, and
    begged
That I would send him away to the frontier
    district
Where only the shepherds go —
As far away from the city as I could send him.   235
I granted his prayer; for although the man was a
    slave,
He had earned more than this favor at my
    hands.
OEDIPUS: Can he be called back quickly?
IOKASTE: Easily.
But why?
OEDIPUS: I have taken too much upon myself
Without enquiry; therefore I wish to consult him.   240
IOKASTE: Then he shall come.
                 But am I not one also
To whom you might confide these fears of yours?
OEDIPUS: That is your right; it will not be denied
    you,
Now least of all; for I have reached a pitch
Of wild foreboding. Is there anyone   245
To whom I should sooner speak?

Polybos of Corinth is my father.
My mother is a Dorian: Merope.
I grew up chief among the men of Corinth
Until a strange thing happened —   250
Not worth my passion, it may be, but strange.
At a feast, a drunken man maundering in his
    cups
Cries out that I am not my father's son!
I contained myself that night, though I felt anger
And a sinking heart. The next day I visited   255
My father and mother, and questioned them.
    They stormed,
Calling it all the slanderous rant of a fool;
And this relieved me. Yet the suspicion
Remained always aching in my mind;
I knew there was talk; I could not rest;   260
And finally, saying nothing to my parents,
I went to the shrine at Delphi.

The god dismissed my question without reply;
He spoke of other things.
                         Some were clear,
265   Full of wretchedness, dreadful, unbearable:
As, that I should lie with my own mother, breed
Children from whom all men would turn their
    eyes;
And that I should be my father's murderer.

I heard all this, and fled. And from that day
270   Corinth to me was only in the stars
Descending in that quarter of the sky,
As I wandered farther and farther on my way
To a land where I should never see the evil
Sung by the oracle. And I came to this country
275   Where, so you say, King Laios was killed.

I will tell you all that happened there, my lady.
There were three highways
Coming together at a place I passed;
And there a herald came towards me, and a
    chariot
Drawn by horses, with a man such as you
280   describe
Seated in it. The groom leading the horses
Forced me off the road at his lord's command;
But as this charioteer lurched over towards me
I struck him in my rage. The old man saw me
285   And brought his double goad down upon my head
As I came abreast.
                         He was paid back, and more!
Swinging my club in this right hand I knocked
    him
Out of his car, and he rolled on the ground.
                                        I killed him.

I killed them all.
290   Now if that stranger and Laios were — kin,
Where is a man more miserable than I?
More hated by the gods? Citizen and alien
    alike
Must never shelter me or speak to me —
I must be shunned by all.
                         And I myself
295   Pronounced this malediction upon myself!

Think of it: I have touched you with these hands,
These hands that killed your husband. What
    defilement!

Am I all evil, then? It must be so,
Since I must flee from Thebes, yet never again
300   See my own countrymen, my own country,
For fear of joining my mother in marriage
And killing Polybos, my father.
                                        Ah,

If I was created so, born to this fate,
Who could deny the savagery of God?

O holy majesty of heavenly powers!   305
May I never see that day! Never!
Rather let me vanish from the race of men
Than know the abomination destined me!
CHORAGOS: We too, my lord, have felt dismay at this.
But there is hope: you have yet to hear the
    shepherd.   310
OEDIPUS: Indeed, I fear no other hope is left me.
IOKASTE: What do you hope from him when he
    comes?
OEDIPUS: This much:
If his account of the murder tallies with yours,
Then I am cleared.
IOKASTE: What was it that I said
Of such importance?
OEDIPUS: Why, "marauders," you said,   315
Killed the king, according to this man's story.
If he maintains that still, if there were several,
Clearly the guilt is not mine: I was alone.
But if he says one man, singlehanded, did it,
Then the evidence all points to me.   320
IOKASTE: You may be sure that he said there were
    several;
And can he call back that story now? He can
    not.
The whole city heard it as plainly as I.
But suppose he alters some detail of it:
He can not ever show that Laios' death   325
Fulfilled the oracle: for Apollo said
My child was doomed to kill him; and my
    child —
Poor baby! — it was my child that died first.

No. From now on, where oracles are concerned,
I would not waste a second thought on any.   330
OEDIPUS: You may be right.
                         But come: let someone go
For the shepherd at once. This matter must be
    settled.
IOKASTE: I will send for him.
I would not wish to cross you in anything,
And surely not in this. — Let us go in.   335
                         (*Exeunt into the palace.*)

ODE 2 • *Strophe 1*

CHORUS: Let me be reverent in the ways of right,
Lowly the paths I journey on;
Let all my words and actions keep
The laws of the pure universe
From highest Heaven handed down.   5
For Heaven is their bright nurse,

Those generations of the realms of light;
Ah, never of mortal kind were they begot,
Nor are they slaves of memory, lost in sleep:
Their Father is greater than Time, and ages
10   not.

Antistrophe 1

The tyrant is a child of Pride
Who drinks from his great sickening cup
Recklessness and vanity,
Until from his high crest headlong
15   He plummets to the dust of hope.
That strong man is not strong.
But let no fair ambition be denied;
May God protect the wrestler for the State
In government, in comely policy,
20   Who will fear God, and on his ordinance wait.

Strophe 2

Haughtiness and the high hand of disdain
Tempt and outrage God's holy law;
And any mortal who dares hold
No immortal Power in awe
25   Will be caught up in a net of pain:
The price for which his levity is sold.
Let each man take due earnings, then,
And keep his hands from holy things,
And from blasphemy stand apart —
30   Else the crackling blast of heaven
Blows on his head, and on his desperate heart.
Though fools will honor impious men,
In their cities no tragic poet sings.

Antistrophe 2

Shall we lose faith in Delphi's obscurities,
35   We who have heard the world's core
Discredited, and the sacred wood
Of Zeus at Elis praised no more?
The deeds and the strange prophecies
Must make a pattern yet to be understood.
40   Zeus, if indeed you are lord of all,
Throned in light over night and day,
Mirror this in your endless mind:
Our masters call the oracle
Words on the wind, and the Delphic vision
    blind!
45   Their hearts no longer know Apollo,
And reverence for the gods has died away.

SCENE 3

(*Enter Iokaste.*)

IOKASTE: Princes of Thebes, it has occurred to me
    To visit the altars of the gods, bearing
    These branches as a suppliant, and this incense.
    Our king is not himself: his noble soul
    Is overwrought with fantasies of dread,   5
    Else he would consider
    The new prophecies in the light of the old.
    He will listen to any voice that speaks disaster,
    And my advice goes for nothing. (*She approaches
    the altar, right.*)
                            To you, then, Apollo,
    Lycean lord, since you are nearest, I turn in
        prayer   10
    Receive these offerings, and grant us deliverance
    From defilement. Our hearts are heavy with fear
    When we see our leader distracted, as helpless
        sailors
    Are terrified by the confusion of their helmsman.

(*Enter Messenger.*)

MESSENGER: Friends, no doubt you can direct me: 15
    Where shall I find the house of Oedipus,
    Or, better still, where is the king himself?
CHORAGOS: It is this very place, stranger; he is
        inside.
    This is his wife and mother of his children.
MESSENGER: I wish her happiness in a happy house, 20
    Blest in all the fulfillment of her marriage.
IOKASTE: I wish as much for you: your courtesy
    Deserves a like good fortune. But now, tell me:
    Why have you come? What have you to say to us?
MESSENGER: Good news, my lady, for your house
        and your husband.   25
IOKASTE: What news? Who sent you here?
MESSENGER: I am from Corinth.
    The news I bring ought to mean joy for you,
    Though it may be you will find some grief in it.
IOKASTE: What is it? How can it touch us in both
        ways?
MESSENGER: The word is that the people of the
        Isthmus   30
    Intend to call Oedipus to be their king.
IOKASTE: But old King Polybos — is he not reigning
        still?
MESSENGER: No. Death holds him in his sepulchre.
IOKASTE: What are you saying? Polybos is dead?
MESSENGER: If I am not telling the truth, may I die
        myself.   35
IOKASTE (*to a Maidservant*): Go in, go quickly; tell
        this to your master.
    O riddlers of God's will, where are you now!

This was the man whom Oedipus, long ago,
Feared so, fled so, in dread of destroying him —
40 But it was another fate by which he died.

(*Enter Oedipus, center.*)

OEDIPUS: Dearest Iokaste, why have you sent for
me?
IOKASTE: Listen to what this man says, and then tell
me
What has become of the solemn prophecies.
OEDIPUS: Who is this man? What is his news for
me?
IOKASTE: He has come from Corinth to announce
45 your father's death!
OEDIPUS: Is it true, stranger? Tell me in your own
words.
MESSENGER: I can not say it more clearly: the king
is dead.
OEDIPUS: Was it by treason? Or by an attack of
illness?
MESSENGER: A little thing brings old men to their
rest.
OEDIPUS: It was sickness, then?
50 MESSENGER: Yes, and his many years.
OEDIPUS: Ah!
Why should a man respect the Pythian hearth,° or
Give heed to the birds that jangle above his
head?
They prophesied that I should kill Polybos,
55 Kill my own father; but he is dead and buried,
And I am here — I never touched him, never,
Unless he died of grief for my departure,
And thus, in a sense, through me. No. Polybos
Has packed the oracles off with him
underground.
They are empty words.
60 IOKASTE: Had I not told you so?
OEDIPUS: You had; it was my faint heart that
betrayed me.
IOKASTE: From now on never think of those things
again.
OEDIPUS: And yet — must I not fear my mother's
bed?
IOKASTE: Why should anyone in this world be afraid
65 Since Fate rules us and nothing can be foreseen?
A man should live only for the present day.

Have no more fear of sleeping with your mother:
How many men, in dreams, have lain with their
mothers!

52. **Pythian hearth:** Delphi.

No reasonable man is troubled by such things.
OEDIPUS: That is true, only —   70
If only my mother were not still alive!
But she is alive. I can not help my dread.
IOKASTE: Yet this news of your father's death is
wonderful.
OEDIPUS: Wonderful. But I fear the living woman.
MESSENGER: Tell me, who is this woman that you
fear?   75
OEDIPUS: It is Merope, man; the wife of King
Polybos.
MESSENGER: Merope? Why should you be afraid of
her?
OEDIPUS: An oracle of the gods, a dreadful saying.
MESSENGER: Can you tell me about it or are you
sworn to silence?
OEDIPUS: I can tell you, and I will.   80
Apollo said through his prophet that I was the
man
Who should marry his own mother, shed his
father's blood
With his own hands. And so, for all these years
I have kept clear of Corinth, and no harm has
come —
Though it would have been sweet to see my
parents again.   85
MESSENGER: And is this the fear that drove you out
of Corinth?
OEDIPUS: Would you have me kill my father?
MESSENGER: As for that
You must be reassured by the news I gave you.
OEDIPUS: If you could reassure me, I would reward
you.
MESSENGER: I had that in mind, I will confess: I
thought   90
I could count on you when you returned to
Corinth.
OEDIPUS: No: I will never go near my parents again.
MESSENGER: Ah, son, you still do not know what
you are doing —
OEDIPUS: What do you mean? In the name of God
tell me!
MESSENGER: — If these are your reasons for not
going home.   95
OEDIPUS: I tell you, I fear the oracle may come true.
MESSENGER: And guilt may come upon you through
your parents?
OEDIPUS: That is the dread that is always in my
heart.
MESSENGER: Can you not see that all your fears are
groundless?
OEDIPUS: Groundless? Am I not my parents' son?   100
MESSENGER: Polybos was not your father.
OEDIPUS: Not my father?

MESSENGER: No more your father than the man
    speaking to you.
OEDIPUS: But you are nothing to me!
MESSENGER: Neither was he.
OEDIPUS: Then why did he call me son?
MESSENGER: I will tell you:
105   Long ago he had you from my hands, as a gift.
OEDIPUS: Then how could he love me so, if I was
    not his?
MESSENGER: He had no children, and his heart
    turned to you.
OEDIPUS: What of you? Did you buy me? Did you
    find me by chance?
MESSENGER: I came upon you in the woody vales of
    Kithairon.
OEDIPUS: And what were you doing there?
110 MESSENGER: Tending my flocks.
OEDIPUS: A wandering shepherd?
MESSENGER: But your savior, son, that day.
OEDIPUS: From what did you save me?
MESSENGER: Your ankles should tell you that.
OEDIPUS: Ah, stranger, why do you speak of that
    childhood pain?
MESSENGER: I pulled the skewer that pinned your
    feet together.
OEDIPUS: I have had the mark as long as I can
115   remember.
MESSENGER: That was why you were given the
    name° you bear.
OEDIPUS: God! Was it my father or my mother who
    did it?
    Tell me!
MESSENGER: I do not know. The man who
    gave you to me
    Can tell you better than I.
OEDIPUS: It was not you that found me, but
120   another?
MESSENGER: It was another shepherd gave you to
    me.
OEDIPUS: Who was he? Can you tell me who he
    was?
MESSENGER: I think he was said to be one of Laios'
    people.
OEDIPUS: You mean the Laios who was king here
    years ago?
MESSENGER: Yes; King Laios; and the man was one
125   of his herdsmen.
OEDIPUS: Is he still alive? Can I see him?
MESSENGER: These men here
    Know best about such things.
OEDIPUS: Does anyone here
    Know this shepherd that he is talking about?
    Have you seen him in the fields, or in the town?

116. **name:** "Oedipus" literally means swollen foot.

If you have, tell me. It is time things were made
    plain.   130
CHORAGOS: I think the man he means is that same
    shepherd
    You have already asked to see. Iokaste
    perhaps
    Could tell you something.
OEDIPUS: Do you know anything
    About him, Lady? Is he the man we have
    summoned?
    Is that the man this shepherd means?
IOKASTE: Why think of him? 135
    Forget this herdsman. Forget it all.
    This talk is a waste of time.
OEDIPUS: How can you say that,
    When the clues to my true birth are in my hands?
IOKASTE: For God's love, let us have no more
    questioning!
    Is your life nothing to you?   140
    My own is pain enough for me to bear.
OEDIPUS: You need not worry. Suppose my mother a
    slave,
    And born of slaves: no baseness can touch you.
IOKASTE: Listen to me, I beg you: do not do this
    thing!
OEDIPUS: I will not listen; the truth must be made
    known.   145
IOKASTE: Everything that I say is for your own good!
OEDIPUS: My own good
    Snaps my patience, then; I want none of it.
IOKASTE: You are fatally wrong! May you never
    learn who you are!
OEDIPUS: Go, one of you, and bring the shepherd
    here.
    Let us leave this woman to brag of her royal
    name.   150
IOKASTE: Ah, miserable!
    That is the only word I have for you now.
    That is the only word I can ever have.
                           (*Exit into the palace.*)
CHORAGOS: Why has she left us, Oedipus? Why has
    she gone
    In such a passion of sorrow? I fear this silence: 155
    Something dreadful may come of it.
OEDIPUS: Let it come!
    However base my birth, I must know about it.
    The Queen, like a woman, is perhaps ashamed
    To think of my low origin. But I
    Am a child of Luck, I can not be dishonored. 160
    Luck is my mother; the passing months, my
    brothers,
    Have seen me rich and poor.
                         If this is so,
    How could I wish that I were someone else?
    How could I not be glad to know my birth?

ODE 3 • *Strophe*

CHORUS: If ever the coming time were known
    To my heart's pondering,
    Kithairon, now by Heaven I see the torches
    At the festival of the next full moon
5   And see the dance, and hear the choir sing
    A grace to your gentle shade:
    Mountain where Oedipus was found,
    O mountain guard of a noble race!
    May the god° who heals us lend his aid,
10   And let that glory come to pass
    For our king's cradling-ground.

Antistrophe

    Of the nymphs that flower beyond the years,
    Who bore you,° royal child,
    To Pan° of the hills or the timberline Apollo,
15   Cold in delight where the upland clears,
    Or Hermes° for whom Kyllene's° heights are piled?
    Or flushed as evening cloud,
    Great Dionysos,° roamer of mountains,
    He — was it he who found you there,
20   And caught you up in his own proud
    Arms from the sweet god-ravisher
    Who laughed by the Muses'° fountains?

SCENE 4

OEDIPUS. Sirs. though I do not know the man,
    I think I see him coming, this shepherd we want:
    He is old, like our friend here, and the men
    Bringing him seem to be servants of my house.
5   But you can tell, if you have ever seen him.

(*Enter Shepherd escorted by Servants.*)

CHORAGOS: I know him, he was Laios' man. You
    can trust him.
OEDIPUS: Tell me first, you from Corinth: is this the
    shepherd
    We were discussing?

9. **god:** Apollo.   13. **Who bore you:** The Chorus is asking if Oedipus is the son of an immortal nymph and a god: Pan, Apollo, Hermes, or Dionysus.   14. **Pan:** God of nature, forests, flocks, and shepherds, depicted as half-man and half-goat.   16. **Hermes:** Son of Zeus, messenger of the gods. **Kyllene:** Mountain reputed to be the birthplace of Hermes; also the center of a cult to Hermes.   18. **Dionysos:** (Dionysus) God of wine around whom wild, orgiastic rituals developed; also called Bacchus.   22. **Muses:** Nine sister goddesses who presided over poetry and music, art and sciences.

MESSENGER: This is the very man.
OEDIPUS (*to Shepherd*): Come here. No, look at me.
    You must answer
    Everything I ask. — You belonged to Laios?   10
SHEPHERD: Yes: born his slave, brought up in his
    house.
OEDIPUS: Tell me: what kind of work did you do for
    him?
SHEPHERD: I was a shepherd of his, most of my
    life.
OEDIPUS: Where mainly did you go for pasturage?
SHEPHERD: Sometimes Kithairon, sometimes the hills
    near-by.   15
OEDIPUS: Do you remember ever seeing this man out
    there?
SHEPHERD: What would he be doing there? This
    man?
OEDIPUS: This man standing here. Have you ever
    seen him before?
SHEPHERD: No. At least, not to my recollection.
MESSENGER: And that is not strange, my lord. But
    I'll refresh   20
    His memory: he must remember when we two
    Spent three whole seasons together, March to
    September,
    On Kithairon or thereabouts. He had two flocks;
    I had one. Each autumn I'd drive mine home
    And he would go back with his to Laios'
    sheepfold. —   25
    Is this not true, just as I have described it?
SHEPHERD: True, yes; but it was all so long ago.
MESSENGER: Well, then: do you remember, back in
    those days,
    That you gave me a baby boy to bring up as my
    own?
SHEPHERD: What if I did? What are you trying to
    say?   30
MESSENGER: King Oedipus was once that little child.
SHEPHERD: Damn you, hold your tongue!
OEDIPUS: No more of that!
    It is your tongue needs watching, not this man's.
SHEPHERD: My king, my master, what is it I have
    done wrong?
OEDIPUS: You have not answered his question about
    the boy.   35
SHEPHERD: He does not know . . . He is only
    making trouble . . .
OEDIPUS: Come, speak plainly, or it will go hard
    with you.
SHEPHERD: In God's name, do not torture an old
    man!
OEDIPUS: Come here, one of you; bind his arms
    behind him.
SHEPHERD: Unhappy king! What more do you wish
    to learn?   40

The Shepherd (Oliver Cliff) tells Oedipus (Kenneth Welsh) the truth about his birth in the Guthrie Theater Company's 1973 production directed by Michael Langham.

OEDIPUS: Did you give this man the child he speaks
   of?
SHEPHERD: I did.
   And I would to God I had died that very day.
OEDIPUS: You will die now unless you speak the
   truth.
SHEPHERD: Yet if I speak the truth, I am worse than
   dead.
OEDIPUS (to Attendant): He intends to draw it out,
45   apparently —
SHEPHERD: No! I have told you already that I gave
   him the boy.
OEDIPUS: Where did you get him? From your house?
   From somewhere else?
SHEPHERD: Not from mine, no. A man gave him to
   me.
OEDIPUS: Is that man here? Whose house did he
   belong to?
SHEPHERD: For God's love, my king, do not ask me
50   any more!
OEDIPUS: You are a dead man if I have to ask you
   again.
SHEPHERD: Then . . . Then the child was from the
   palace of Laios.
OEDIPUS: A slave child? or a child of his own line?
SHEPHERD: Ah, I am on the brink of dreadful
   speech!
55 OEDIPUS: And I of dreadful hearing. Yet I must hear.
SHEPHERD: If you must be told, then . . .
                          They said it was Laios' child;
   But it is your wife who can tell you about that.
OEDIPUS: My wife — Did she give it to you?
SHEPHERD: My lord, she did.
OEDIPUS: Do you know why?
SHEPHERD: I was told to get rid of it.
OEDIPUS: Oh heartless mother!
60 SHEPHERD: But in dread of prophecies . . .
OEDIPUS: Tell me.
SHEPHERD: It was said that the boy would
   kill his own father.
OEDIPUS: Then why did you give him over to this
   old man?
SHEPHERD: I pitied the baby, my king,
   And I thought that this man would take him far
   away
   To his own country.
65   He saved him — but for what a fate!
   For if you are what this man says you are,
   No man living is more wretched than Oedipus.
OEDIPUS: Ah God!
   It was true!
             All the prophecies!
                          — Now,
70 O Light, may I look on you for the last time!
   I, Oedipus,

Oedipus, damned in his birth, in his marriage
   damned,
Damned in the blood he shed with his own
   hand!
(*He rushes into the palace.*)

ODE 4 • *Strophe 1*

CHORUS: Alas for the seed of men.
   What measure shall I give these generations
   That breathe on the void and are void
   And exist and do not exist?
   Who bears more weight of joy   5
   Than mass of sunlight shifting in images,
   Or who shall make his thought stay on
   That down time drifts away?
   Your splendor is all fallen.
   O naked brow of wrath and tears,   10
   O change of Oedipus!
   I who saw your days call no man blest —
   Your great days like ghosts gone.

Antistrophe 1

   That mind was a strong bow.
   Deep, how deep you drew it then, hard archer,   15
   At a dim fearful range,
   And brought dear glory down!
   You overcame the stranger° —
   The virgin with her hooking lion claws —
   And though death sang, stood like a tower   20
   To make pale Thebes take heart.
   Fortress against our sorrow!
   True king, giver of laws,
   Majestic Oedipus!
   No prince in Thebes had ever such renown,   25
   No prince won such grace of power.

Strophe 2

   And now of all men ever known
   Most pitiful is this man's story:
   His fortunes are most changed; his state
   Fallen to a low slave's   30
   Ground under bitter fate.
   O Oedipus, most royal one!
   The great door° that expelled you to the light
   Gave at night — ah, gave night to your glory:
   As to the father, to the fathering son.   35
   All understood too late.

18. stranger: The Sphinx.   **33. door:** Iokaste's womb.

How could that queen whom Laios won,
The garden that he harrowed at his height,
Be silent when that act was done?

Antistrophe 2

40   But all eyes fail before time's eye,
All actions come to justice there.
Though never willed, though far down the deep
     past,
Your bed, your dread sirings,
Are brought to book at last.
45   Child by Laios doomed to die,
Then doomed to lose that fortunate little death,
Would God you never took breath in this air
That with my wailing lips I take to cry:
For I weep the world's outcast.
I was blind, and now I can tell why:
Asleep, for you had given ease of breath
50   To Thebes, while the false years went by.

EXODOS°

(*Enter, from the palace, Second Messenger.*)

SECOND MESSENGER: Elders of Thebes, most
          honored in this land,
What horrors are yours to see and hear, what
     weight
Of sorrow to be endured, if, true to your birth,
You venerate the line of Labdakos!
5   I think neither Istros nor Phasis, those great rivers,
Could purify this place of all the evil
It shelters now, or soon must bring to light —
Evil not done unconsciously, but willed.

The greatest griefs are those we cause ourselves.
CHORAGOS: Surely, friend, we have grief enough
10   already;
What new sorrow do you mean?
SECOND MESSENGER: The queen is dead.
CHORAGOS. O miserable queen! But at whose hand?
SECOND MESSENGER: Her own.
The full horror of what happened you can not
     know,
For you did not see it; but I, who did, will tell you
15   As clearly as I can how she met her death.

When she had left us,
In passionate silence, passing through the court,
She ran to her apartment in the house,

Exodos: Final scene.

Her hair clutched by the fingers of both hands.
She closed the doors behind her; then, by that
     bed
Where long ago the fatal son was conceived —   20
That son who should bring about his father's
     death —
We heard her call upon Laios, dead so many years,
And heard her wail for the double fruit of her
     marriage,
A husband by her husband, children by her child.   25

Exactly how she died I do not know:
For Oedipus burst in moaning and would not let
     us
Keep vigil to the end: it was by him
As he stormed about the room that our eyes
     were caught.
From one to another of us he went, begging a
     sword,   30
Hunting the wife who was not his wife, the
     mother
Whose womb had carried his own children and
     himself.
I do not know: it was none of us aided him,
But surely one of the gods was in control!
For with a dreadful cry   35
He hurled his weight, as though wrenched out of
     himself,
At the twin doors: the bolts gave, and he rushed
     in.
And there we saw her hanging, her body swaying
From the cruel cord she had noosed about her
     neck.
A great sob broke from him, heartbreaking to
     hear,   40
As he loosed the rope and lowered her to the
     ground.

I would blot out from my mind what happened
     next!
For the king ripped from her gown the golden
     brooches
That were her ornament, and raised them, and
     plunged them down
Straight into his own eyeballs, crying, "No more,   45
No more shall you look on the misery about me,
The horrors of my own doing! Too long you
     have known
The faces of those whom I should never have seen,
Too long been blind to those for whom I was
     searching!
From this hour, go in darkness!" And as he spoke, 50
He struck at his eyes — not once, but many times;
And the blood spattered his beard,
Bursting from his ruined sockets like red hail.

So from the unhappiness of two this evil has
        sprung,
55   A curse on the man and woman alike. The old
Happiness of the house of Labdakos
Was happiness enough: where is it today?
It is all wailing and ruin, disgrace, death — all
The misery of mankind that has a name —
60   And it is wholly and for ever theirs.

CHORAGOS: Is he in agony still? Is there no rest for
        him?

SECOND MESSENGER: He is calling for someone to
        open the doors wide
    So that all the children of Kadmos may look
        upon
    His father's murderer, his mother's — no,
    I can not say it!
65   And then he will leave Thebes,
    Self-exiled, in order that the curse
    Which he himself pronounced may depart from
        the house.
    He is weak, and there is none to lead him,
    So terrible is his suffering.
                       But you will see:
70   Look, the doors are opening; in a moment
    You will see a thing that would crush a heart of
        stone.

(*The central door is opened; Oedipus, blinded, is led
in.*)

CHORAGOS: Dreadful indeed for men to see.
    Never have my own eyes
    Looked on a sight so full of fear.

75   Oedipus!
    What madness came upon you, what demon
    Leaped on your life with heavier
    Punishment than a mortal man can bear?
    No: I can not even
80   Look at you, poor ruined one.
    And I would speak, question, ponder,
    If I were able. No.
    You make me shudder.

OEDIPUS: God. God.
85   Is there a sorrow greater?
    Where shall I find harbor in this world?
    My voice is hurled far on a dark wind.
    What has God done to me?

CHORAGOS: Too terrible to think of, or to see.

Strophe 1

90   OEDIPUS: O cloud of night,
    Never to be turned away: night coming on,
    I can not tell how: night like a shroud!

My fair winds brought me here.
                          O God. Again
    The pain of the spikes where I had sight,
    The flooding pain   95
    Of memory, never to be gouged out.

CHORAGOS: This is not strange.
    You suffer it all twice over, remorse in pain,
    Pain in remorse.

Antistrophe 1

OEDIPUS: Ah dear friend   100
    Are you faithful even yet, you alone?
    Are you still standing near me, will you stay
        here,
    Patient, to care for the blind?
                          The blind man!
    Yet even blind I know who it is attends me,
    By the voice's tone —   105
    Though my new darkness hide the comforter.

CHORAGOS: Oh fearful act!
    What god was it drove you to rake black
    Night across your eyes?

Strophe 2

OEDIPUS: Apollo. Apollo. Dear   110
    Children, the god was Apollo.
    He brought my sick, sick fate upon me.
    But the blinding hand was my own!
    How could I bear to see
    When all my sight was horror everywhere?   115

CHORAGOS: Everywhere; that is true.

OEDIPUS: And now what is left?
    Images? Love? A greeting even,
    Sweet to the senses? Is there anything?
    Ah, no, friends: lead me away.   120
    Lead me away from Thebes.
                      Lead the great wreck
    And hell of Oedipus, whom the gods hate.

CHORAGOS: Your misery, you are not blind to that.
    Would God you had never found it out!

Antistrophe 2

OEDIPUS: Death take the man who unbound   125
    My feet on that hillside
    And delivered me from death to life! What life?
    If only I had died,
    This weight of monstrous doom
    Could not have dragged me and my darlings
        down.   130

CHORAGOS: I would have wished the same.
OEDIPUS: Oh never to have come here
  With my father's blood upon me! Never
  To have been the man they call his mother's
    husband!
135 Oh accurst! Oh child of evil,
  To have entered that wretched bed —
                                    the selfsame one!
  More primal than sin itself, this fell to me.
CHORAGOS: I do not know what words to offer you.
  You were better dead than alive and blind.
OEDIPUS: Do not counsel me any more. This
140   punishment
  That I have laid upon myself is just.
  If I had eyes,
  I do not know how I could bear the sight
  Of my father, when I came to the house of
    Death,
  Or my mother: for I have sinned against them
145   both
  So vilely that I could not make my peace
  By strangling my own life.
                            Or do you think my children,
  Born as they were born, would be sweet to my
    eyes?
  Ah never, never! Nor this town with its high
    walls,
  Nor the holy images of the gods.
150   For I,
  Thrice miserable! — Oedipus, noblest of all the
    line
  Of Kadmos, have condemned myself to enjoy
  These things no more, by my own malediction
  Expelling that man whom the gods declared
155 To be a defilement in the house of Laios.
  After exposing the rankness of my own guilt,
  How could I look men frankly in the eyes?
  No, I swear it,
  If I could have stifled my hearing at its source,
160 I would have done it and made all this body
  A tight cell of misery, blank to light and sound:
  So I should have been safe in my dark mind
  Beyond external evil.
                          Ah Kithairon!
  Why did you shelter me? When I was cast upon
    you,
165 Why did I not die? Then I should never
  Have shown the world my execrable birth.

  Ah Polybos! Corinth, city that I believed
  The ancient seat of my ancestors: how fair
  I seemed, your child! And all the while this evil
  Was cancerous within me!
170   For I am sick
  In my own being, sick in my origin.

O three roads, dark ravine, woodland and way
Where three roads met; you, drinking my father's
  blood,
My own blood, spilled by my own hand: can
  you remember
The unspeakable things I did there, and the
  things   175
I went on from there to do?
                          O marriage, marriage!
The act that engendered me, and again the act
Performed by the son in the same bed —
                                    Ah, the net
Of incest, mingling fathers, brothers, sons,
With brides, wives, mothers: the last evil   180
That can be known by men: no tongue can say
How evil!
            No. For the love of God, conceal me
Somewhere far from Thebes; or kill me; or hurl
  me
Into the sea, away from men's eyes for ever.

Come, lead me. You need nor fear to touch me.   185
Of all men, I alone can bear this guilt.

(*Enter Kreon.*)

CHORAGOS: Kreon is here now. As to what you ask,
  He may decide the course to take. He only
  Is left to protect the city in your place.
OEDIPUS: Alas, how can I speak to him? What right
  have I   190
  To beg his courtesy whom I have deeply
    wronged?
KREON: I have not come to mock you, Oedipus,
  Or to reproach you, either.
  (*To Attendants.*)   — You, standing there:
  If you have lost all respect for man's dignity,
  At least respect the flame of Lord Helios:°   195
  Do not allow this pollution to show itself
  Openly here, an affront to the earth
  And Heaven's rain and the light of day. No, take
    him
  Into the house as quickly as you can.
  For it is proper   200
  That only the close kindred see his grief.
OEDIPUS: I pray you in God's name, since your
    courtesy
  Ignores my dark expectation, visiting
  With mercy this man of all men most execrable:
  Give me what I ask — for your good, not for
    mine.   205
KREON: And what is it that you turn to me begging
    for?

195. **Lord Helios:** The sun-god.

OEDIPUS: Drive me out of this country as quickly as
    may be
    To a place where no human voice can ever greet
    me.
KREON: I should have done that before now — only,
210   God's will had not been wholly revealed to me.
OEDIPUS: But his command is plain: the parricide
    Must be destroyed. I am that evil man.
KREON: That is the sense of it, yes; but as things are,
    We had best discover clearly what is to be done.
OEDIPUS: You would learn more about a man like
215   me?
KREON: You are ready now to listen to the god.
OEDIPUS: I will listen. But it is to you
    That I must turn for help. I beg you, hear me.

    The woman is there —
220   Give her whatever funeral you think proper:
    She is your sister.
               — But let me go, Kreon!
    Let me purge my father's Thebes of the pollution
    Of my living here, and go out to the wild hills,
    To Kithairon, that has won such fame with me,
225   The tomb my mother and father appointed for me,
    And let me die there, as they willed I should.
    And yet I know
    Death will not ever come to me through sickness
    Or in any natural way: I have been preserved
230   For some unthinkable fate. But let that be.

    As for my sons, you need not care for them.
    They are men, they will find some way to live.
    But my poor daughters, who have shared my
    table,
    Who never before have been parted from their
    father —
235   Take care of them, Kreon; do this for me.

    And will you let me touch them with my hands
    A last time, and let us weep together?
    Be kind, my lord,
    Great prince, be kind!
                  Could I but touch them,
    They would be mine again, as when I had my
240   eyes.

(*Enter Antigone and Ismene, attended.*)

    Ah, God!
    Is it my dearest children I hear weeping?
    Has Kreon pitied me and sent my daughters?
KREON: Yes, Oedipus: I knew that they were dear to
    you
    In the old days, and know you must love them
245   still.

OEDIPUS: May God bless you for this — and be a
    friendlier
    Guardian to you than he has been to me!

    Children, where are you?
    Come quickly to my hands: they are your
    brother's —
    Hands that have brought your father's once clear
    eyes   250
    To this way of seeing —
                      Ah dearest ones,
    I had neither sight nor knowledge then, your
    father
    By the woman who was the source of his own
    life!
    And I weep for you — having no strength to see
    you — ,
    I weep for you when I think of the bitterness   255
    That men will visit upon you all your lives.
    What homes, what festivals can you attend
    Without being forced to depart again in tears?
    And when you come to marriageable age,
    Where is the man, my daughters, who would
    dare   260
    Risk the bane that lies on all my children?
    Is there any evil wanting? Your father killed
    His father; sowed the womb of her who bore
    him;
    Engendered you at the fount of his own
    existence!
    That is what they will say of you.

                             Then, whom 265
    Can you ever marry? There are no bridegrooms
    for you,
    And your lives must wither away in sterile
    dreaming.

    O Kreon, son of Menoikeus!
    You are the only father my daughters have,
    Since we, their parents, are both of us gone for
    ever.   270
    They are your own blood: you will not let them
    Fall into beggary and loneliness;
    You will keep them from the miseries that are
    mine!
    Take pity on them; see, they are only children,
    Friendless except for you. Promise me this,   275
    Great prince, and give me your hand in token
    of it.

(*Kreon clasps his right hand.*)

Children:
    I could say much, if you could understand me,
    But as it is, I have only this prayer for you:

280   Live where you can, be as happy as you can —
       Happier, please God, than God has made your
           father.
    KREON: Enough. You have wept enough. Now go
       within.
    OEDIPUS: I must, but it is hard.
    KREON: Time eases all things.
    OEDIPUS: You know my mind, then?
    KREON: Say what you desire.
    OEDIPUS: Send me from Thebes!
285   KREON: God grant that I may!
    OEDIPUS: But since God hates me . . .
    KREON: No, he will grant your wish.
    OEDIPUS: You promise?
    KREON: I can not speak beyond my knowledge.
    OEDIPUS: Then lead me in.
    KREON: Come now, and leave your children.
    OEDIPUS: No! Do not take them from me!

    KREON: Think no longer
       That you are in command here, but rather think   290
       How, when you were, you served your own
           destruction.

    (*Exeunt into the house all but the Chorus; the Chor-
    agos chants directly to the audience.*)

    CHORAGOS: Men of Thebes: look upon Oedipus.

       This is the king who solved the famous riddle
       And towered up, most powerful of men.
       No mortal eyes but looked on him with envy,   295
       Yet in the end ruin swept over him.

       Let every man in mankind's frailty
       Consider his last day; and let none
       Presume on his good fortune until he find
       Life, at his death, a memory without pain.   300

ANTIGONE

Antigone was Sophocles' thirty-second play, produced in March 441 B.C., when he was in his mid-fifties. It draws a powerful response from its audience partly because it portrays the conflict between two proud, willful people: Antigone, a daughter of Oedipus and Iokaste, and Kreon, Iokaste's brother and the king of Thebes. Its original success was due in part to its portrayal of the individual's struggle against a tyrannical king. After enjoying thirty years of peace with its archrival Sparta, Athens was moving slowly toward war; and the memory of previous tyrants — both good, like Peisistratus, and bad, like his son Hippias — remained in the minds of Sophocles' audience.

It has never been easy to determine which of the two main characters is correct. Kreon's portrayal as a tyrant content to take up the state as his private property tells us that he is not to be fully trusted. At the same time, Antigone knows that the social mores of Thebes imply that a citizen must obey the ruler. Antigone's great courage makes the audience feel sympathy and admiration for her. She is a martyr to her beliefs, an ancient Joan of Arc.

The main conflict in *Antigone* centers on a distinction between law and justice, the conflict between a human law and a higher law. Kreon, the uncle of Antigone and Ismene, has made a decree: Polyneices, the brother of Antigone and Ismene, was guilty not only of killing his brother Eteocles but also of attacking the state and, like all traitors, will be denied a proper burial. When the action of the play begins, Antigone is determined to give her brother the burial that ancient tradition and her religious beliefs demand.

The opening dialogue with Ismene clarifies the important distinction between human law and the higher law on which Antigone says she must act. Ismene declares simply that she cannot go against the law of the citizens. Kreon has been willful in establishing the law, but it is nonetheless the law. Antigone, knowing full well the consequences of defying Kreon, nonetheless acts on her principles.

The complex conflict between Antigone and Kreon occurs on the level of citizen and ruler and is affected on the personal level by the relationship between Haimon, Kreon's son, and his intended bride, Antigone. The antagonism between Kreon and Haimon begins slowly, as Haimon appears to yield to the will of his father, but culminates in Haimon's ultimate rejection of his father by choosing to join Antigone in death.

When Teiresias reveals a prophecy of death and punishment and begs Kreon, for the sake of the suffering Thebes, to rescind his decree and give Polyneices a proper burial, Kreon willfully continues to heed his own declarations rather than oracular wisdom or the pleas of others.

By the time Kreon accepts Teiresias's prophecy, it is too late: He has lost his son, and his wife has killed herself. Power not only has corrupted Kreon but also has taken from him the people about whom he cared most. He emerges as an unyielding tyrant, guilty of making some of the same mistakes that haunted Oedipus.

Antigone emerges as a heroine who presses forward in the full conviction that she is right. She must honor her dead brother at all costs. Even if she must break the law of the state, she must answer to what she regards as a higher law. As she says early in the play, she has "dared the crime of piety." Yet she has within her the complexity of all humans: She in one sense acts in the knowledge that she is right but in another dares Kreon to punish her. She challenges Kreon so boldly that her every move forces the proud Kreon to harden his position and set in motion the ultimate tragedy — the loss of all he holds dear. This is yet one more tragic irony in the Theban trilogy.

Antigone in Performance

Since the eighteenth century *Antigone* has been produced in Europe and the Western Hemisphere in more or less its original form and in various adaptations and rewritings. Jean Cocteau combined his version with music by Arthur Honegger in 1930. It was rewritten and produced by Walter Hasenclever in 1917 as a protest against the First World War and then in 1944 by Jean Anouilh as a protest against Nazi occupation of Paris during World War II (see the excerpt on page 176). The Royal Shakespeare Company produced *Antigone* along with all the surviving Greek tragedies in 1980. Bertolt Brecht's production of *Antigone* in 1948 introduced a Gestapo officer and Nazi brutality. Athol Fugard's *The Island* (1973) features a remarkable production of *Antigone* as a play within a play, produced by convicts in a South African island jail as a Christmas entertainment for their jailers and specially invited white guests. Fugard found, as have so many other adapters and producers, that the political power of *Antigone* leaps out for virtually all contemporary audiences. Janusz Glowacki, a Polish playwright, produced *Antigone in New York* at the Arena Stage in Washington in March 1993. Inspired by both Sophocles and Beckett, it is set in Tompkins Square Park in New York. The action centers on a homeless Puerto Rican woman's efforts to bury a homeless man in the park. The action of the play demonstrates the durability of *Antigone*'s basic concept — that a decent burial is an essential vestige of humanity.

Sophocles (*c. 496–c. 406 B.C.*)

ANTIGONE   *441 B.C.*

TRANSLATED BY DUDLEY FITTS AND ROBERT FITZGERALD

Characters

ANTIGONE, ⎫
ISMENE,   ⎬ *daughters of Oedipus*
EURYDICE, *wife of Kreon*
KREON, *King of Thebes*
HAIMON, *son of Kreon*
TEIRESIAS, *a blind seer*
A SENTRY
A MESSENGER
CHORUS

Scene: *Before the palace of Kreon, King of Thebes. A central double door, and two lateral doors. A platform extends the length of the facade, and from this platform three steps lead down into the orchestra, or chorus-ground.*

Time: *Dawn of the day after the repulse of the Argive army from the assault on Thebes.*

PROLOGUE°

(*Antigone and Ismene enter from the central door of the palace.*)

ANTIGONE: Ismene, dear sister,
    You would think that we had already suffered
      enough
    For the curse on Oedipus.°
    I cannot imagine any grief

Prologue: Portion of the play explaining the background and current action.   **3. curse on Oedipus:** Oedipus, king of Thebes and the father of Antigone and Ismene, had been abandoned by his parents as an infant after the oracle foretold that he would one day kill his father and marry his mother. Rescued by a shepherd and raised by the king of Corinth, Oedipus returned years later to Thebes and unknowingly lived out the oracle's prophecy by killing Laios and marrying Iokaste. After his two sons, Eteocles and Polyneices, killed each other in combat, the throne went to Kreon, Iokaste's brother.

    That you and I have not gone through. And
      now —   5
    Have they told you of the new decree of our
      King Kreon?
ISMENE: I have heard nothing: I know
    That two sisters lost two brothers, a double
      death
    In a single hour; and I know that the Argive
      army
    Fled in the night; but beyond this, nothing.   10
ANTIGONE: I thought so. And that is why I wanted
    you
    To come out here with me. There is something
    we must do.
ISMENE: Why do you speak so strangely?
ANTIGONE: Listen, Ismene:
    Kreon buried our brother Eteocles   15
    With military honors, gave him a soldier's
      funeral,
    And it was right that he should; but Polyneices,
    Who fought as bravely and died as miserably, —
    They say that Kreon has sworn
    No one shall bury him, no one mourn for him,   20
    But his body must lie in the fields, a sweet
      treasure
    For carrion birds to find as they search for food.
    That is what they say, and our good Kreon is
      coming here
    To announce it publicly; and the penalty —
    Stoning to death in the public square!
                    There it is,   25
    And now you can prove what you are:
    A true sister, or a traitor to your family.
ISMENE: Antigone, you are mad! What could I
    possibly do?
ANTIGONE: You must decide whether you will help
    me or not.
ISMENE: I do not understand you. Help you in what?   30
ANTIGONE: Ismene, I am going to bury him. Will
    you come?
ISMENE: Bury him! You have just said the new law
    forbids it.
ANTIGONE: He is my brother. And he is your
    brother, too.
ISMENE: But think of the danger! Think what Kreon
    will do!

ANTIGONE: Kreon is not strong enough to stand in
35   my way.
ISMENE: Ah sister!
     Oedipus died, everyone hating him
     For what his own search brought to light, his
          eyes
     Ripped out by his own hand; and Iocaste died,
     His mother and wife at once: she twisted the
40   cords
     That strangled her life; and our two brothers died,
     Each killed by the other's sword. And we are
          left:
     But oh, Antigone,
     Think how much more terrible than these
     Our own death would be if we should go against
45   Kreon
     And do what he has forbidden! We are only
          women,
     We cannot fight with men, Antigone!
     The law is strong, we must give in to the law
     In this thing, and in worse. I beg the Dead
50   To forgive me, but I am helpless: I must yield
     To those in authority. And I think it is dangerous
          business
     To be always meddling.
ANTIGONE: If that is what you think,
     I should not want you, even if you asked to
          come.
     You have made your choice, you can be what
          you want to be.
55   But I will bury him; and if I must die,
     I say that this crime is holy: I shall lie down
     With him in death, and I shall be as dear
     To him as he to me.
                         It is the dead,
     Not the living, who make the longest demands:
     We die for ever . . .
60   You may do as you like,
     Since apparently the laws of the gods mean
          nothing to you.
ISMENE: They mean a great deal to me; but I have
          no strength
     To break laws that were made for the public good.
ANTIGONE: That must be your excuse, I suppose.
     But as for me,
     I will bury the brother I love.
65   ISMENE: Antigone,
     I am so afraid for you!
ANTIGONE: You need not be:
     You have yourself to consider, after all.
ISMENE: But no one must hear of this, you must tell
          no one!
     I will keep it a secret, I promise!
ANTIGONE: O tell it! Tell everyone!

Think how they'll hate you when it all comes out   70
If they learn that you knew about it all the time!
ISMENE: So fiery! You should be cold with fear.
ANTIGONE: Perhaps. But I am doing only what I
     must.
ISMENE: But can you do it? I say that you cannot.
ANTIGONE: Very well: when my strength gives out,   75
     I shall do no more.
ISMENE: Impossible things should not be tried at all.
ANTIGONE: Go away, Ismene:
     I shall be hating you soon, and the dead will too,
     For your words are hateful. Leave me my foolish
          plan: 80
     I am not afraid of the danger; if it means death,
     It will not be the worst of deaths — death
          without honor.
ISMENE: Go then, if you feel that you must.
     You are unwise,
     But a loyal friend indeed to those who love
          you.   85

(*Exit into the palace. Antigone goes off, left. Enter the
Chorus.*)

PARODOS° • Strophe° 1

CHORUS: Now the long blade of the sun, lying
     Level east to west, touches with glory
     Thebes of the Seven Gates. Open, unlidded
     Eye of golden day! O marching light
     Across the eddy and rush of Dirce's stream,°   5
     Striking the white shields of the enemy
     Thrown headlong backward from the blaze of
          morning!
CHORAGOS:° Polyneices their commander
     Roused them with windy phrases,
     He the wild eagle screaming   10
     Insults above our land,
     His wings their shields of snow,
     His crest their marshalled helms.

Antistrophe° 1

CHORUS: Against our seven gates in a yawning ring
     The famished spears came onward in the night;   15

Parodos: The song or ode chanted by the Chorus on their entry.   **Strophe:** Song sung by the Chorus as they danced
from stage right to stage left.   **5. Dirce's stream:** River near
Thebes.   **8. Choragos:** Leader of the Chorus.   **Antistrophe:** Song sung by the Chorus following the Strophe, as they
danced back from stage left to stage right.

Antigone (Martha Henry)
reassures Ismene in the
Repertory Theatre of Lincoln
Center production of *Antigone*
at the Vivian Beaumont
Theatre, directed by John
Hirsch in 1971.

But before his jaws were sated with our blood,
Or pinefire took the garland of our towers,
He was thrown back, and as he turned, great
    Thebes —
No tender victim for his noisy power —
20   Rose like a dragon behind him, shouting war.
CHORAGOS: For God hates utterly
    The bray of bragging tongues;
    And when he beheld their smiling,
    Their swagger of golden helms,
25   The frown of his thunder blasted
    Their first man from our walls.

Strophe 2

CHORUS: We heard his shout of triumph high in the
    air
    Turn to a scream; far out in a flaming arc
    He fell with his windy torch, and the earth
    struck him.
    And others storming in fury no less than his   30
    Found shock of death in the dusty joy of battle.
CHORAGOS: Seven captains at seven gates
    Yielded their clanging arms to the god
    That bends the battle-line and breaks it.

35 These two only, brothers in blood,
    Face to face in matchless rage,
    Mirroring each the other's death
    Clashed in long combat.

Antistrophe 2

CHORUS: But now in the beautiful morning of
              victory
40 Let Thebes of the many chariots sing for joy!
    With hearts for dancing we'll take leave of war:
    Our temples shall be sweet with hymns of praise,
    And the long nights shall echo with our chorus.

SCENE 1

CHORAGOS: But now at last our new King is
              coming:

Kreon of Thebes, Menoikeus' son.
In this auspicious dawn of his reign
What are the new complexities
That shifting Fate has woven for him?   5
What is his counsel? Why has he summoned
The old men to hear him?

(*Enter Kreon from the palace, center. He addresses
the Chorus from the top step.*)

KREON: Gentlemen: I have the honor to inform you
that our Ship of State, which recent storms have
threatened to destroy, has come safely to harbor   10
at last, guided by the merciful wisdom of
Heaven. I have summoned you here this morning
because I know that I can depend upon you:
your devotion to King Laios was absolute; you
never hesitated in your duty to our late ruler   15
Oedipus; and when Oedipus died, your loyalty
was transferred to his children. Unfortunately, as
you know, his two sons, the princes Eteocles and
Polyneices, have killed each other in battle; and I,

Kreon (Philip Bosco), Antigone, and Haimon (David Birney).

20 as the next in blood, have succeeded to the full
power of the throne.

I am aware, of course, that no Ruler can expect
complete loyalty from his subjects until he has
been tested in office. Nevertheless, I say to you at
the very outset that I have nothing but contempt
25 for the kind of Governor who is afraid, for
whatever reason, to follow the course that he
knows is best for the State; and as for the man
who sets private friendship above the public
welfare, — I have no use for him, either. I call God
30 to witness that if I saw my country headed for
ruin, I should not be afraid to speak out plainly;
and I need hardly remind you that I would never
have any dealings with an enemy of the people.
No one values friendship more highly than I; but
35 we must remember that friends made at the risk of
wrecking our Ship are not real friends at all.

These are my principles, at any rate, and that is
why I have made the following decision concerning
the sons of Oedipus: Eteocles, who died as a man
40 should die, fighting for his country, is to be buried
with full military honors, with all the ceremony
that is usual when the greatest heroes die; but his
brother Polyneices, who broke his exile to come
back with fire and sword against his native city
45 and the shrines of his fathers' gods, whose one
idea was to spill the blood of his blood and sell his
own people into slavery — Polyneices, I say, is to
have no burial: no man is to touch him or say the
least prayer for him; he shall lie on the plain,
50 unburied; and the birds and the scavenging dogs
can do with him whatever they like.

This is my command, and you can see the wisdom behind it. As long as I am King, no traitor is
going to be honored with the loyal man. But who-
55 ever shows by word and deed that he is on the
side of the State, — he shall have my respect while
he is living and my reverence when he is dead.

CHORAGOS: If that is your will, Kreon son of
Menoikeus,
You have the right to enforce it: we are yours.

KREON: That is my will. Take care that you do your
60 part.

CHORAGOS: We are old men: let the younger ones
carry it out.

KREON: I do not mean that: the sentries have been
appointed.

CHORAGOS: Then what is it that you would have us
do?

KREON: You will give no support to whoever breaks
this law.

CHORAGOS: Only a crazy man is in love with
65 death!

KREON: And death it is; yet money talks, and the
wisest

Have sometimes been known to count a few
coins too many.

(*Enter Sentry from left.*)

SENTRY: I'll not say that I'm out of breath from
running, King, because every time I stopped to
think about what I have to tell you, I felt like   70
going back. And all the time a voice kept saying,
"You fool, don't you know you're walking
straight into trouble?"; and then another voice:
"Yes, but if you let somebody else get the news
to Kreon first, it will be even worse than that for   75
you!" But good sense won out, at least I hope it
was good sense, and here I am with a story that
makes no sense at all; but I'll tell it anyhow,
because, as they say, what's going to happen's
going to happen and —

KREON: Come to the point. What have you to
say?   80

SENTRY: I did not do it. I did not see who did it.
You must not punish me for what someone
else has done.

KREON: A comprehensive defense! More effective,
perhaps,
If I knew its purpose. Come: what is it?   85

SENTRY: A dreadful thing . . . I don't know how to
put it —

KREON: Out with it!

SENTRY: Well, then;
The dead man —
                              Polyneices —

(*Pause. The Sentry is overcome, fumbles for words.
Kreon waits impassively.*)

                                              out there —
                                         someone, —
New dust on the slimy flesh!

(*Pause. No sign from Kreon.*)

Someone has given it burial that way, and   90
Gone . . .

(*Long pause. Kreon finally speaks with deadly control.*)

KREON: And the man who dared do this?

SENTRY: I swear I
Do not know! You must believe me!
                                              Listen:
The ground was dry, not a sign of digging, no,
Not a wheeltrack in the dust, no trace of anyone. 95
It was when they relieved us this morning: and
one of them,
The corporal, pointed to it.
                              There it was,
The strangest —
                      Look:

The body, just mounded over with light dust:
    you see?
100 Not buried really, but as if they'd covered it
Just enough for the ghost's peace. And no sign
Of dogs or any wild animal that had been there.

And then what a scene there was! Every man of
    us
Accusing the other: we all proved the other man
    did it.
105 We all had proof that we could not have done it.
We were ready to take hot iron in our hands,
Walk through fire, swear by all the gods,
It was not I!
I do not know who it was, but it was not I!

(*Kreon's rage has been mounting steadily, but the Sentry is too intent upon his story to notice it.*)

And then, when this came to nothing, someone
110   said
A thing that silenced us and made us stare
Down at the ground: you had to be told the
    news,
And one of us had to do it! We threw the dice,
And the bad luck fell to me. So here I am,
115 No happier to be here than you are to have me:
Nobody likes the man who brings bad news.
CHORAGOS: I have been wondering, King: can it be
    that the gods have done this?
KREON (*furiously*): Stop!
120 Must you doddering wrecks
Go out of your heads entirely? "The gods"!
Intolerable!
The gods favor this corpse? Why? How had he
    served them?
Tried to loot their temples, burn their images,
125 Yes, and the whole State, and its laws with it!
Is it your senile opinion that the gods love to
    honor bad men?
A pious thought! —
                No, from the very beginning
There have been those who have whispered
    together,
Stiff-necked anarchists, putting their heads
    together,
130 Scheming against me in alleys. These are the men,
And they have bribed my own guard to do this
    thing.
(*Sententiously.*) Money!
There's nothing in the world so demoralizing as
    money.
Down go your cities,
135 Homes gone, men gone, honest hearts corrupted,
Crookedness of all kinds, and all for money!

(*To Sentry.*)   But you —
I swear by God and by the throne of God,
The man who has done this thing shall pay for it!
Find that man, bring him here to me, or your
    death
Will be the least of your problems: I'll string you
    up   140
Alive, and there will be certain ways to make you
Discover your employer before you die;
And the process may teach you a lesson you
    seem to have missed:
The dearest profit is sometimes all too dear:
That depends on the source. Do you understand
    me?   145
A fortune won is often misfortune.
SENTRY: King, may I speak?
KREON: Your very voice distresses me.
SENTRY: Are you sure that it is my voice, and not
    your conscience?
KREON: By God, he wants to analyze me now!
SENTRY: It is not what I say, but what has been
    done, that hurts you.   150
KREON: You talk too much.
SENTRY: Maybe; but I've done nothing.
KREON: Sold your soul for some silver: that's all
    you've done.
SENTRY: How dreadful it is when the right judge
    judges wrong!
KREON: Your figures of speech
May entertain you now; but unless you bring me
    the man,   155
You will get little profit from them in the end.
            (*Exit Kreon into the palace.*)
SENTRY: "Bring me the man" — !
I'd like nothing better than bringing him the
    man!
But bring him or not, you have seen the last of
    me here.
At any rate, I am safe!   (*Exit Sentry.*)   160

ODE° 1 • *Strophe 1*

CHORUS: Numberless are the world's wonders, but
    none
More wonderful than man; the stormgray sea
Yields to his prows, the huge crests bear him
    high;
Earth, holy and inexhaustible, is graven
With shining furrows where his plows have gone   5
Year after year, the timeless labor of stallions.

Ode: Song sung by the Chorus.

Antistrophe 1

The lightboned birds and beasts that cling to
    cover,
The lithe fish lighting their reaches of dim water,
All are taken, tamed in the net of his mind;
10 The lion on the hill, the wild horse windy-maned,
Resign to him; and his blunt yoke has broken
The sultry shoulders of the mountain bull.

Strophe 2

Words also, and thought as rapid as air,
He fashions to his good use; statecraft is his
15 And his the skill that deflects the arrows of snow,
The spears of winter rain: from every wind
He has made himself secure — from all but one:
In the late wind of death he cannot stand.

Antistrophe 2

O clear intelligence, force beyond all measure!
20 O fate of man, working both good and evil!
When the laws are kept, how proudly his city
    stands!
When the laws are broken, what of his city then?
Never may the anarchic man find rest at my
    hearth,
Never be it said that my thoughts are his
    thoughts.

SCENE 2

(Reenter Sentry leading Antigone.)

CHORAGOS: What does this mean? Surely this
    captive woman
    Is the Princess, Antigone. Why should she be
    taken?
SENTRY: Here is the one who did it! We caught her
    In the very act of burying him. — Where is
    Kreon?
CHORAGOS: Just coming from the house.

(Enter Kreon, center.)

5 KREON: What has happened?
    Why have you come back so soon?
SENTRY *(expansively)*:   O King,
    A man should never be too sure of anything:
    I would have sworn

That you'd not see me here again: your anger
Frightened me so, and the things you threatened
    me with;   10
But how could I tell then
That I'd be able to solve the case so soon?
No dice-throwing this time: I was only too glad
    to come!
Here is this woman. She is the guilty one:
We found her trying to bury him.   15
Take her, then; question her; judge her as you
    will.
I am through with the whole thing now, and glad
    of it.
KREON: But this is Antigone! Why have you
    brought her here?
SENTRY: She was burying him, I tell you!
KREON *(severely)*:   Is this the truth?
SENTRY: I saw her with my own eyes. Can I say
    more?   20
KREON: The details: come, tell me quickly!
SENTRY: It was like this:
    After those terrible threats of yours, King,
    We went back and brushed the dust away from
    the body.
    The flesh was soft by now, and stinking,
    So we sat on a hill to windward and kept
    guard.   25
    No napping this time! We kept each other
    awake.
    But nothing happened until the white round
    sun
    Whirled in the center of the round sky over us:
    Then, suddenly,
    A storm of dust roared up from the earth, and
    the sky   30
    Went out, the plain vanished with all its trees
    In the stinging dark. We closed our eyes and
    endured it.
    The whirlwind lasted a long time, but it passed;
    And then we looked, and there was Antigone!
    I have seen   35
    A mother bird come back to a stripped nest,
    heard
    Her crying bitterly a broken note or two
    For the young ones stolen. Just so, when this
    girl
    Found the bare corpse, and all her love's work
    wasted,
    She wept, and cried on heaven to damn the
    hands   40
    That had done this thing.
                                And then she brought more dust
    And sprinkled wine three times for her brother's
    ghost.

We ran and took her at once. She was not afraid,
Not even when we charged her with what she
    had done.
She denied nothing.
45   And this was a comfort to me,
And some uneasiness: for it is a good thing
To escape from death, but it is no great pleasure
To bring death to a friend.
                         Yet I always say
There is nothing so comfortable as your own safe
    skin!

50 KREON (*slowly, dangerously*): And you, Antigone,
You with your head hanging, — do you confess
    this thing?
ANTIGONE: I do. I deny nothing.
KREON (*to Sentry*):   You may go.
                                    (*Exit Sentry.*)
(*To Antigone.*) Tell me, tell me briefly:
Had you heard my proclamation touching this
    matter?
55 ANTIGONE: It was public. Could I help hearing it?
KREON: And yet you dared defy the law.
ANTIGONE: I dared.
It was not God's proclamation. That final Justice
That rules the world below makes no such laws.

Your edict, King, was strong,
60 But all your strength is weakness itself against
The immortal unrecorded laws of God.
They are not merely now: they were, and shall
    be,
Operative for ever, beyond man utterly.

I knew I must die, even without your decree:
65 I am only mortal. And if I must die
Now, before it is my time to die,
Surely this is no hardship: can anyone
Living, as I live, with evil all about me,
Think Death less than a friend? This death of
    mine
70 Is of no importance; but if I had left my brother
Lying in death unburied, I should have suffered.
Now I do not.
                   You smile at me. Ah Kreon,
Think me a fool, if you like; but it may well be
That a fool convicts me of folly.
CHORAGOS: Like father, like daughter: both
75   headstrong, deaf to reason!
She has never learned to yield.
KREON: She has much to learn.
The inflexible heart breaks first, the toughest iron
Cracks first, and the wildest horses bend their
    necks
At the pull of the smallest curb.
                              Pride? In a slave?

This girl is guilty of a double insolence,   80
Breaking the given laws and boasting of it.
Who is the man here,
She or I, if this crime goes unpunished?
Sister's child, or more than sister's child,
Or closer yet in blood — she and her sister   85
Win bitter death for this!
(*To Servants.*)   Go, some of you,
Arrest Ismene. I accuse her equally.
Bring her: you will find her sniffling in the house
    there.

Her mind's a traitor: crimes kept in the dark
Cry for light, and the guardian brain shudders;   90
But how much worse than this
Is brazen boasting of barefaced anarchy!
ANTIGONE: Kreon, what more do you want than my
    death?
KREON: Nothing.
That gives me everything.
ANTIGONE: Then I beg you: kill me.
This talking is a great weariness: your words   95
Are distasteful to me, and I am sure that mine
Seem so to you. And yet they should not seem so:
I should have praise and honor for what I have
    done.
All these men here would praise me
Were their lips not frozen shut with fear of you.   100
(*Bitterly.*) Ah the good fortune of kings,
Licensed to say and do whatever they please!
KREON: You are alone here in that opinion.
ANTIGONE: No, they are with me. But they keep
    their tongues in leash.
KREON: Maybe. But you are guilty, and they are not. 105
ANTIGONE: There is no guilt in reverence for the
    dead.
KREON: But Eteocles — was he not your brother too?
ANTIGONE: My brother too.
KREON: And you insult his memory?
ANTIGONE (*softly*): The dead man would not say
    that I insult it.
KREON: He would: for you honor a traitor as much
    as him.   110
ANTIGONE: His own brother, traitor or not, and
    equal in blood.
KREON: He made war on his country. Eteocles
    defended it.
ANTIGONE: Nevertheless, there are honors due all
    the dead.
KREON: But not the same for the wicked as for the
    just.
ANTIGONE: Ah Kreon, Kreon,   115
    Which of us can say what the gods hold wicked?
KREON: An enemy is an enemy, even dead.
ANTIGONE: It is my nature to join in love, not hate.

TOP: Kreon (F. Murray
Abraham) in a scene from the
1982 New York Shakespeare
Festival production directed by
Joseph Chaikin. RIGHT:
Antigone (Lisa Banes)
steadfastly admitting her guilt.

The Chorus urges Kreon to change his decree before it is too late.

KREON (*finally losing patience*): Go join them then;
        if you must have your love,
120   Find it in hell!
CHORAGOS: But see, Ismene comes:

(*Enter Ismene, guarded.*)

        Those tears are sisterly, the cloud
        That shadows her eyes rains down gentle sorrow.
KREON: You too, Ismene,
125   Snake in my ordered house, sucking my blood
        Stealthily — and all the time I never knew
        That these two sisters were aiming at my throne!
                                                  Ismene,
        Do you confess your share in this crime, or deny
            it?
        Answer me.
130 ISMENE: Yes, if she will let me say so. I am guilty.

ANTIGONE (*coldly*): No, Ismene. You have no right
        to say so.
        You would not help me, and I will not have you
        help me.
ISMENE: But now I know what you meant; and I am
        here
        To join you, to take my share of punishment.
ANTIGONE: The dead man and the gods who rule
        the dead   135
        Know whose act this was. Words are not friends.
ISMENE: Do you refuse me, Antigone? I want to die
        with you:
        I too have a duty that I must discharge to the
        dead.
ANTIGONE: You shall not lessen my death by
        sharing it.
ISMENE: What do I care for life when you are dead?   140

ANTIGONE: Ask Kreon. You're always hanging on
    his opinions.
ISMENE: You are laughing at me. Why, Antigone?
ANTIGONE: It's a joyless laughter, Ismene.
ISMENE: But can I do nothing?
ANTIGONE: Yes. Save yourself. I shall not envy you.
    There are those who will praise you; I shall have
145   honor, too.
ISMENE: But we are equally guilty!
ANTIGONE: No more, Ismene.
    You are alive, but I belong to Death.
KREON (*to the Chorus*): Gentlemen, I beg you to
    observe these girls:
    One has just now lost her mind; the other,
150   It seems, has never had a mind at all.
ISMENE: Grief teaches the steadiest minds to waver,
    King.
KREON: Yours certainly did, when you assumed
    guilt with the guilty!
ISMENE: But how could I go on living without her?
KREON: You are.
    She is already dead.
ISMENE: But your own son's bride!
KREON: There are places enough for him to push his
155   plow.
    I want no wicked women for my sons!
ISMENE: O dearest Haimon, how your father wrongs
    you!
KREON: I've had enough of your childish talk of
    marriage!
CHORAGOS: Do you really intend to steal this girl
    from your son?
KREON: No; Death will do that for me.
160 CHORAGOS: Then she must die?
KREON (*ironically*): You dazzle me.
              — But enough of this talk!
    (*To Guards.*) You, there, take them away and
    guard them well:
    For they are but women, and even brave men run
    When they see Death coming.
           (*Exeunt° Ismene, Antigone, and Guards.*)

ODE 2 • *Strophe 1*

CHORUS: Fortunate is the man who has never tasted
    God's vengeance!
    Where once the anger of heaven has struck, that
    house is shaken
    For ever: damnation rises behind each child
    Like a wave cresting out of the black northeast,
5   When the long darkness under sea roars up

165. [S.D.] *Exeunt:* Latin for "they go out."

And bursts drumming death upon the
    windwhipped sand.

Antistrophe 1

I have seen this gathering sorrow from time long
    past
Loom upon Oedipus' children: generation from
    generation
Takes the compulsive rage of the enemy god.
So lately this last flower of Oedipus' line   10
Drank the sunlight! but now a passionate word
And a handful of dust have closed up all its
    beauty.

Strophe 2

    What mortal arrogance
    Transcends the wrath of Zeus?
Sleep cannot lull him nor the effortless long
    months   15
Of the timeless gods: but he is young for ever,
And his house is the shining day of high
    Olympos.
    All that is and shall be,
    And all the past, is his.
No pride on earth is free of the curse of
    heaven.   20

Antistrophe 2

The straying dreams of men
    May bring them ghosts of joy:
But as they drowse, the waking embers burn
    them;
Or they walk with fixed eyes, as blind men walk.
But the ancient wisdom speaks for our own
    time: 25
    Fate works most for woe
    With Folly's fairest show.
Man's little pleasure is the spring of sorrow.

SCENE 3

CHORAGOS: But here is Haimon, King, the last of all
    your sons.
    Is it grief for Antigone that brings him here,
    And bitterness at being robbed of his bride?

(*Enter Haimon.*)

KREON: We shall soon see, and no need of diviners.
                                                     — Son,
5   You have heard my final judgment on that girl:
    Have you come here hating me, or have you
        come
    With deference and with love, whatever I do?
HAIMON: I am your son, father. You are my guide.
    You make things clear for me, and I obey you.
    No marriage means more to me than your
10   continuing wisdom.
KREON: Good. That is the way to behave:
        subordinate
    Everything else, my son, to your father's will.
    This is what a man prays for, that he may get
    Sons attentive and dutiful in his house,
15 Each one hating his father's enemies,
    Honoring his father's friends. But if his sons
    Fail him, if they turn out unprofitably,
    What has he fathered but trouble for himself
    And amusement for the malicious?
                                    So you are right
20 Not to lose your head over this woman.
    Your pleasure with her would soon grow cold,
        Haimon,
    And then you'd have a hellcat in bed and
        elsewhere.
    Let her find her husband in Hell!
    Of all the people in this city, only she
25 Has had contempt for my law and broken it.

    Do you want me to show myself weak before the
        people?
    Or to break my sworn word? No, and I will not.
    The woman dies.
    I suppose she'll plead "family ties." Well, let her.
30 If I permit my own family to rebel,
    How shall I earn the world's obedience?
    Show me the man who keeps his house in hand,
    He's fit for public authority.
                                    I'll have no dealings
    With lawbreakers, critics of the government:
    Whoever is chosen to govern should be
35   obeyed —
    Must be obeyed, in all things, great and small,
    Just and unjust! O Haimon,
    The man who knows how to obey, and that man
        only,
    Knows how to give commands when the time
        comes.
40 You can depend on him, no matter how fast
    The spears come: he's a good soldier, he'll stick it
        out.
    Anarchy, anarchy! Show me a greater evil!
    This is why cities tumble and the great houses
        rain down,
    This is what scatters armies!

No, no: good lives are made so by discipline.   45
We keep the laws then, and the lawmakers,
And no woman shall seduce us. If we must lose,
Let's lose to a man, at least! Is a woman stronger
    than we?
CHORAGOS: Unless time has rusted my wits,
    What you say, King, is said with point and
        dignity.   50
HAIMON (boyishly earnest): Father:
    Reason is God's crowning gift to man, and you
        are right
    To warn me against losing mine. I cannot say —
    I hope that I shall never want to say! — that you
    Have reasoned badly. Yet there are other men   55
    Who can reason, too; and their opinions might
        be helpful.
    You are not in a position to know everything
    That people say or do, or what they feel:
    Your temper terrifies — everyone
    Will tell you only what you like to hear.   60
    But I, at any rate, can listen; and I have heard
        them
    Muttering and whispering in the dark about this
        girl.
    They say no woman has ever, so unreasonably,
    Died so shameful a death for a generous act:
    "She covered her brother's body. Is this indecent?   65
    She kept him from dogs and vultures. Is this a
        crime?
    Death? — She should have all the honor that we
        can give her!"

    This is the way they talk out there in the city.
    You must believe me:
    Nothing is closer to me than your happiness.   70
    What could be closer? Must not any son
    Value his father's fortune as his father does his?
    I beg you, do not be unchangeable:
    Do not believe that you alone can be right.
    The man who thinks that,   75
    The man who maintains that only he has the
        power
    To reason correctly, the gift to speak, the soul —
    A man like that, when you know him, turns out
        empty.
    It is not reason never to yield to reason!

    In flood time you can see how some trees bend,   80
    And because they bend, even their twigs are safe,
    While stubborn trees are torn up, roots and all.
    And the same thing happens in sailing:
    Make your sheet fast, never slacken, — and over
        you go,
    Head over heels and under: and there's your
        voyage.   85
    Forget you are angry! Let yourself be moved!

I know I am young; but please let me say this:
The ideal condition
Would be, I admit, that men should be right by
    instinct;
90 But since we are all too likely to go astray,
The reasonable thing is to learn from those who
    can teach.
CHORAGOS: You will do well to listen to him, King,
If what he says is sensible. And you, Haimon,
Must listen to your father. — Both speak well.
KREON: You consider it right for a man of my years
95   and experience
To go to school to a boy?
HAIMON: It is not right
If I am wrong. But if I am young, and right,
What does my age matter?
KREON: You think it right to stand up for an
    anarchist?
100 HAIMON: Not at all. I pay no respect to criminals.
KREON: Then she is not a criminal?
HAIMON: The City would deny it, to a man.
KREON: And the City proposes to teach me how to
    rule?
HAIMON: Ah. Who is it that's talking like a boy
    now?
KREON: My voice is the one voice giving orders in
105   this City!
HAIMON: It is no City if it takes orders from one
    voice.
KREON: The State is the King!
HAIMON: Yes, if the State is a desert.

(*Pause.*)

KREON: This boy, it seems, has sold out to a
    woman.
HAIMON: If you are a woman: my concern is only
    for you.
KREON: So? Your "concern"! In a public brawl with
110   your father!
HAIMON: How about you, in a public brawl with
    justice?
KREON: With justice, when all that I do is within
    my rights?
HAIMON: You have no right to trample on God's
    right.
KREON (*completely out of control*): Fool, adolescent
    fool! Taken in by a woman!
HAIMON: You'll never see me taken in by anything
115   vile.
KREON: Every word you say is for her!
HAIMON (*quietly, darkly*):   And for you.
And for me. And for the gods under the earth.
KREON: You'll never marry her while she lives.
HAIMON: Then she must die. — But her death will
    cause another.
120 KREON: Another?

Have you lost your senses? Is this an open threat?
HAIMON: There is no threat in speaking to
    emptiness.
KREON: I swear you'll regret this superior tone of
    yours!
You are the empty one!
HAIMON: If you were not my father,
I'd say you were perverse.   125
KREON: You girl-struck fool, don't play at words
    with me!
HAIMON: I am sorry. You prefer silence.
KREON: Now, by God —
I swear, by all the gods in heaven above us,
You'll watch it, I swear you shall!
(*To the Servants.*)   Bring her out!
Bring the woman out! Let her die before his
    eyes!   130
Here, this instant, with her bridegroom beside
    her!
HAIMON: Not here, no; she will not die here, King.
And you will never see my face again.
Go on raving as long as you've a friend to
    endure you.   (*Exit Haimon.*)
CHORAGOS: Gone, gone.   135
Kreon, a young man in a rage is dangerous!
KREON: Let him do, or dream to do, more than a
    man can.
He shall not save these girls from death.
CHORAGOS: These girls?
You have sentenced them both?
KREON: No, you are right.
I will not kill the one whose hands are clean.   140
CHORAGOS: But Antigone?
KREON (*somberly*):   I will carry her far away
Out there in the wilderness, and lock her
Living in a vault of stone. She shall have food,
As the custom is, to absolve the State of her death.
And there let her pray to the gods of hell: 145
They are her only gods:
Perhaps they will show her an escape from death,
Or she may learn,
                    though late,
That piety shown the dead is pity in vain.
                                  (*Exit Kreon.*)

ODE 3 • *Strophe*

CHORUS: Love, unconquerable
Waster of rich men, keeper
Of warm lights and all-night vigil
In the soft face of a girl:
Sea-wanderer, forest-visitor!   5
Even the pure Immortals cannot escape you,
And mortal man, in his one day's dusk,
Trembles before your glory.

Antistrophe

      Surely you swerve upon ruin
10   The just man's consenting heart,
      As here you have made bright anger
      Strike between father and son —
      And none has conquered but Love!
      A girl's glance working the will of heaven:
15   Pleasure to her alone who mocks us,
      Merciless Aphrodite.°

SCENE 4

CHORAGOS (*as Antigone enters guarded*): But I can
    no longer stand in awe of this,
  Nor, seeing what I see, keep back my tears.
  Here is Antigone, passing to that chamber
  Where all find sleep at last.

Strophe 1

5 ANTIGONE: Look upon me, friends, and pity me
      Turning back at the night's edge to say
      Good-by to the sun that shines for me no longer;
      Now sleepy Death
      Summons me down to Acheron,° that cold shore:
10 There is no bridesong there, nor any music.
  CHORUS: Yet not unpraised, not without a kind of
      honor,
      You walk at last into the underworld
      Untouched by sickness, broken by no sword.
      What woman has ever found your way to death?

Antistrophe 1

  ANTIGONE: How often I have heard the story of
15   Niobe,°
      Tantalos' wretched daughter, how the stone
      Clung fast about her, ivy-close: and they say
      The rain falls endlessly
      And sifting soft snow; her tears are never done.
20 I feel the loneliness of her death in mine.
  CHORUS: But she was born of heaven, and you
      Are woman, woman-born. If her death is yours,

16. Aphrodite: Goddess of love and beauty. **9. Acheron:**
River in Hades, domain of the dead. **15. Niobe:** When
Niobe's many children (up to twenty in some accounts) were
slain in punishment for their mother's boastfulness, Niobe
was turned into a stone on Mount Sipylus. Her tears became
the mountain's streams.

      A mortal woman's, is this not for you
      Glory in our world and in the world beyond?

Strophe 2

ANTIGONE: You laugh at me. Ah, friends, friends, 25
      Can you not wait until I am dead? O Thebes,
      O men many-charioted, in love with Fortune,
      Dear springs of Dirce, sacred Theban grove,
      Be witnesses for me, denied all pity,
      Unjustly judged! and think a word of love 30
      For her whose path turns
      Under dark earth, where there are no more tears.
CHORUS: You have passed beyond human daring
      and come at last
      Into a place of stone where Justice sits.
      I cannot tell 35
      What shape of your father's guilt appears in this.

Antistrophe 2

ANTIGONE: You have touched it at last: that bridal
      bed
      Unspeakable, horror of son and mother mingling:
      Their crime, infection of all our family!
      O Oedipus, father and brother! 40
      Your marriage strikes from the grave to murder
      mine.
      I have been a stranger here in my own land:
      All my life
      The blasphemy of my birth has followed me.
CHORUS: Reverence is a virtue, but strength 45
      Lives in established law: that must prevail.
      You have made your choice,
      Your death is the doing of your conscious hand.

Epode°

ANTIGONE: Then let me go, since all your words are
      bitter,
      And the very light of the sun is cold to me. 50
      Lead me to my vigil, where I must have
      Neither love nor lamentation; no song, but
      silence.

(*Kreon interrupts impatiently.*)

KREON: If dirges and planned lamentations could
    put off death,

Epode: Song sung by the Chorus while standing still after
singing the strophe and antistrophe.

Men would be singing for ever.
(*To the Servants.*)   Take her, go!
55 You know your orders: take her to the vault
And leave her alone there. And if she lives or
dies,
That's her affair, not ours: our hands are clean.
ANTIGONE: O tomb, vaulted bride-bed in eternal
rock,
Soon I shall be with my own again
Where Persephone° welcomes the thin ghosts
60   underground:
And I shall see my father again, and you, mother,
And dearest Polyneices —
dearest indeed
To me, since it was my hand
That washed him clean and poured the ritual
wine:
65 And my reward is death before my time!

And yet, as men's hearts know, I have done no
wrong,
I have not sinned before God. Or if I have,
I shall know the truth in death. But if the guilt
Lies upon Kreon who judged me, then, I pray,
May his punishment equal my own.
70 CHORAGOS: O passionate heart,
Unyielding, tormented still by the same winds!
KREON: Her guards shall have good cause to regret
their delaying.
ANTIGONE: Ah! That voice is like the voice of death!
KREON: I can give you no reason to think you are
mistaken.
75 ANTIGONE: Thebes, and you my fathers' gods,
And rulers of Thebes, you see me now, the last
Unhappy daughter of a line of kings,
Your kings, led away to death. You will
remember
What things I suffer, and at what men's hands,
Because I would not transgress the laws of
80   heaven.
(*To the Guards, simply.*) Come: let us wait no
longer.   (*Exit Antigone, left, guarded.*)

ODE 4 · *Strophe 1*

CHORUS: All Danae's beauty was locked away
In a brazen cell where the sunlight could not
come:
A small room still as any grave, enclosed her.
Yet she was a princess too,

60. **Persephone:** Abducted by Pluto, god of the underworld,
to be his queen.

And Zeus in a rain of gold poured love upon
her.°   5
O child, child,
No power in wealth or war
Or tough sea-blackened ships
Can prevail against untiring Destiny!

Antistrophe 1

And Dryas's son° also, that furious king,   10
Bore the god's prisoning anger for his pride:
Sealed up by Dionysos in deaf stone,
His madness died among echoes.
So at the last he learned what dreadful power
His tongue had mocked: 15
For he had profaned the revels,
And fired the wrath of the nine
Implacable Sisters° that love the sound of the
flute.

Strophe 2

And old men tell a half-remembered tale
Of horror° where a dark ledge splits the sea   20
And a double surf beats on the gray shores:
How a king's new woman, sick
With hatred for the queen he had imprisoned,
Ripped out his two sons' eyes with her bloody
hands
While grinning Ares° watched the shuttle plunge   25
Four times: four blind wounds crying for
revenge,

Antistrophe 2

Crying, tears and blood mingled. — Piteously
born,
Those sons whose mother was of heavenly birth!
Her father was the god of the North Wind

1–5. All Danae's beauty ... poured love upon her: Locked
away to prevent the fulfillment of a prophecy that she would
bear a son who would kill her father, Danae was nonetheless
impregnated by Zeus, who came to her in a shower of gold.
The prophecy was fulfilled by the son that came of their
union.   **10. Dryas's son:** King Lycurgus of Thrace, whom
Dionysus, god of wine, caused to be stricken with madness.
18. Sisters: The Muses, nine sister goddesses who presided
over poetry and music, arts and sciences.   **19–20. half-remembered tale of horror:** The second wife of King Phineas
blinded the sons of his first wife, Cleopatra, whom Phineas
had imprisoned in a cave.   **25. Ares:** God of war.

30   And she was cradled by gales,
      She raced with young colts on the glittering hills
      And walked untrammeled in the open light:
      But in her marriage deathless Fate found means
      To build a tomb like yours for all her joy.

SCENE 5

(*Enter blind Teiresias, led by a boy. The opening
speeches of Teiresias should be in singsong contrast to
the realistic lines of Kreon.*)

TEIRESIAS: This is the way the blind man comes,
      Princes, Princes,
      Lockstep, two heads lit by the eyes of one.
KREON: What new thing have you to tell us, old
      Teiresias?
TEIRESIAS: I have much to tell you: listen to the
      prophet, Kreon.
KREON: I am not aware that I have ever failed to
5   listen.
TEIRESIAS: Then you have done wisely, King, and
      ruled well.
KREON: I admit my debt to you. But what have you
      to say?
TEIRESIAS: This, Kreon: you stand once more on the
      edge of fate.
KREON: What do you mean? Your words are a kind
      of dread.
10 TEIRESIAS: Listen, Kreon:
      I was sitting in my chair of augury, at the place
      Where the birds gather about me. They were all
      a-chatter,
      As is their habit, when suddenly I heard
      A strange note in their jangling, a scream, a
15   Whirring fury; I knew that they were fighting,
      Tearing each other, dying
      In a whirlwind of wings clashing. And I was
      afraid.
      I began the rites of burnt-offering at the altar
      But Hephaistos° failed me: instead of bright
      flame,
      There was only the sputtering slime of the fat
20   thigh-flesh
      Melting: the entrails dissolved in gray smoke,
      The bare bone burst from the welter. And no
      blaze!

      This was a sign from heaven. My boy described it,
      Seeing for me as I see for others.
25   I tell you, Kreon, you yourself have brought

19. **Hephaistos:** God of fire.

This new calamity upon us. Our hearths and
      altars
Are stained with the corruption of dogs and
      carrion birds
That glut themselves on the corpse of Oedipus's
      son.
The gods are deaf when we pray to them, their
      fire
Recoils from our offering, their birds of omen   30
Have no cry of comfort, for they are gorged
With the thick blood of the dead.
                                    O my son,
These are no trifles! Think: all men make mistakes,
But a good man yields when he knows his course
      is wrong,
And repairs the evil. The only crime is pride.   35

Give in to the dead man, then: do not fight with
      a corpse —
What glory is it to kill a man who is dead?
Think, I beg you:
It is for your own good that I speak as I do.
You should be able to yield for your own good.   40
KREON: It seems that prophets have made me their
      especial province.
All my life long
I have been a kind of butt for the dull arrows
Of doddering fortune-tellers!
                        No, Teiresias:
If your birds — if the great eagles of God himself   45
Should carry him stinking bit by bit to heaven,
I would not yield. I am not afraid of pollution:
No man can defile the gods.
                        Do what you will,
Go into business, make money, speculate
In India gold or that synthetic gold from Sardis,   50
Get rich otherwise than by my consent to bury
      him.
Teiresias, it is a sorry thing when a wise man
Sells his wisdom, lets out his words for hire!
TEIRESIAS: Ah Kreon! Is there no man left in the
      world —
KREON: To do what? — Come, let's have the
      aphorism!   55
TEIRESIAS: No man who knows that wisdom
      outweighs any wealth?
KREON: As surely as bribes are baser than any
      baseness.
TEIRESIAS: You are sick, Kreon! You are deathly
      sick!
KREON: As you say: it is not my place to challenge
      a prophet.
TEIRESIAS: Yet you have said my prophecy is for
      sale.   60

KREON: The generation of prophets has always
    loved gold.
TEIRESIAS: The generation of kings has always loved
    brass.
KREON: You forget yourself! You are speaking to
    your King.
TEIRESIAS: I know it. You are a king because of me.
KREON: You have a certain skill; but you have sold
65   out.
TEIRESIAS: King, you will drive me to words that —
KREON: Say them, say them!
    Only remember: I will not pay you for them.
TEIRESIAS: No, you will find them too costly.
KREON: No doubt. Speak:
    Whatever you say, you will not change my will.
70 TEIRESIAS: Then take this, and take it to heart!
    The time is not far off when you shall pay back
    Corpse for corpse, flesh of your own flesh.
    You have thrust the child of this world into
        living night,
    You have kept from the gods below the child
        that is theirs:
75   The one in a grave before her death, the other,
    Dead, denied the grave. This is your crime:
    And the Furies° and the dark gods of Hell
    Are swift with terrible punishment for you.

    Do you want to buy me now, Kreon?

                          Not many days,
    And your house will be full of men and women
80   weeping,
    And curses will be hurled at you from far
    Cities grieving for sons unburied, left to rot
    Before the walls of Thebes.

    These are my arrows, Kreon: they are all for
    you.

85 (To Boy.) But come, child: lead me home.
    Let him waste his fine anger upon younger men.
    Maybe he will learn at last
    To control a wiser tongue in a better head.
                     (Exit Teiresias.)
CHORAGOS: The old man has gone, King, but his
    words
90   Remain to plague us. I am old, too,
    But I cannot remember that he was ever false.
KREON: That is true.... It troubles me.
    Oh it is hard to give in! but it is worse
    To risk everything for stubborn pride.

---

77. Furies: Spirits called upon to avenge crimes, especially
those against kin.

CHORAGOS: Kreon: take my advice.
KREON: What shall I do?   95
CHORAGOS: Go quickly: free Antigone from her
    vault
    And build a tomb for the body of Polyneices.
KREON: You would have me do this!
CHORAGOS: Kreon, yes!
    And it must be done at once: God moves
    Swiftly to cancel the folly of stubborn men.   100
KREON: It is hard to deny the heart! But I
    Will do it: I will not fight with destiny.
CHORAGOS: You must go yourself, you cannot leave
    it to others.
KREON: I will go.
              — Bring axes, servants:
    Come with me to the tomb. I buried her, I   105
    Will set her free.
                Oh quickly!
    My mind misgives —
    The laws of the gods are mighty, and a man
        must serve them
    To the last day of his life!   (Exit Kreon.)

PAEAN° • Strophe 1

CHORAGOS: God of many names
CHORUS: O Iacchos
                         son
    of Kadmeian Semele
                O born of the Thunder!
    Guardian of the West
                 Regent
    of Eleusis' plain
               O Prince of maenad Thebes
    and the Dragon Field by rippling Ismenos:°   5

Antistrophe 1

CHORAGOS: God of many names
CHORUS: the flame of torches
    flares on our hills
               the nymphs of Iacchos

Paean: A song of praise or prayer.   **1–5. God of many
names ... rippling Ismenos:** The following is a litany of
names for Dionysus (Iacchos): He was son of Zeus ("Thunder") and Semele; he was honored in secret rites at Eleusis;
and he was worshiped by the Maenads of Thebes. Kadmos,
Semele's father, sowed dragon's teeth in a field beside
the river Ismenos from which sprang warriors who became
the first Thebans.

dance at the spring of Castalia:°
from the vine-close mountain
                    come ah come in ivy:
Evohe evohe!° sings through the streets of
10   Thebes

Strophe 2

CHORAGOS: God of many names
CHORUS: Iacchos of Thebes
    heavenly Child
                    of Semele bride of the Thunderer!
    The shadow of plague is upon us:
                                    come
    with clement feet
                    oh come from Parnasos
    down the long slopes
15   across the lamenting water

Antistrophe 2

CHORAGOS: Io Fire! Chorister of the throbbing
        stars!
    O purest among the voices of the night!
    Thou son of God, blaze for us!
CHORUS: Come with choric rapture of circling
        Maenads
    Who cry *Io Iacche!*°
20   *God of many names!*

EXODOS°

(*Enter Messenger from left.*)

MESSENGER: Men of the line of Kadmos, you who
        live
    Near Amphion's citadel,°
                    I cannot say
    Of any condition of human life "This is fixed,
    This is clearly good, or bad." Fate raises up,
    And Fate casts down the happy and unhappy
5   alike:
    No man can foretell his Fate.
                    Take the case of Kreon:

Kreon was happy once, as I count happiness:
    Victorious in battle, sole governor of the land,
    Fortunate father of children nobly born.
    And now it has all gone from him! Who can say   10
    That a man is still alive when his life's joy fails?
    He is a walking dead man. Grant him rich,
    Let him live like a king in his great house:
    If his pleasure is gone, I would not give
    So much as the shadow of smoke for all he
        owns.   15
CHORAGOS: Your words hint at sorrow: what is
        your news for us?
MESSENGER: They are dead. The living are guilty of
        their death.
CHORAGOS: Who is guilty? Who is dead? Speak!
MESSENGER: Haimon.
    Haimon is dead; and the hand that killed him
    Is his own hand.
CHORAGOS: His father's? or his own?   20
MESSENGER: His own, driven mad by the murder his
    father had done.
CHORAGOS: Teiresias, Teiresias, how clearly you saw
        it all!
MESSENGER: This is my news: you must draw what
    conclusions you can from it.
CHORAGOS: But look: Eurydice, our Queen:
    Has she overheard us?   25

(*Enter Eurydice from the palace, center.*)

EURYDICE: I have heard something, friends:
    As I was unlocking the gate of Pallas'° shrine,
    For I needed her help today, I heard a voice
    Telling of some new sorrow. And I fainted
    There at the temple with all my maidens about
        me.   30
    But speak again: whatever it is, I can bear it:
    Grief and I are no strangers.
MESSENGER: Dearest Lady,
    I will tell you plainly all that I have seen.
    I shall not try to comfort you: what is the use,
    Since comfort could lie only in what is not true? 35
    The truth is always best.
                    I went with Kreon
    To the outer plain where Polyneices was lying,
    No friend to pity him, his body shredded by
        dogs.
    We made our prayers in that place to Hecate
    And Pluto,° that they would be merciful. And we
        bathed   40
    The corpse with holy water, and we brought

---

8. **spring of Castalia:** A spring on Mount Parnassus used by priestesses of Dionysus in rites of purification.   10. *Evohe evohe!:* Cry of the Maenads to Dionysus.   20. *Io Iacche!:* Ritual cry.   **Exodos:** Final scene.   2. **Amphion's citadel:** A name for Thebes.

27. **Pallas:** Pallas Athene, goddess of wisdom.   39–40. **Hecate and Pluto:** Goddess of witchcraft and sorcery and King of Hades, the underworld.

Fresh-broken branches to burn what was left of
   it,
And upon the urn we heaped up a towering
   barrow
Of the earth of his own land.
                        When we were done, we ran
45   To the vault where Antigone lay on her couch of
   stone.
One of the servants had gone ahead,
And while he was yet far off he heard a voice
Grieving within the chamber, and he came back
And told Kreon. And as the King went closer,
50   The air was full of wailing, the words lost,
And he begged us to make all haste. "Am I a
   prophet?"
He said, weeping, "And must I walk this road,
The saddest of all that I have gone before?
My son's voice calls me on. Oh quickly, quickly!
55   Look through the crevice there, and tell me
If it is Haimon, or some deception of the gods!"

We obeyed; and in the cavern's farthest corner
We saw her lying:
She had made a noose of her fine linen veil
60   And hanged herself. Haimon lay beside her,
His arms about her waist, lamenting her,
His love lost under ground, crying out
That his father had stolen her away from him.

When Kreon saw him the tears rushed to his eyes
65   And he called to him: "What have you done,
   child? speak to me.
What are you thinking that makes your eyes so
   strange?
O my son, my son, I come to you on my knees!"
But Haimon spat in his face. He said not a
   word,
Staring—
               And suddenly drew his sword
And lunged. Kreon shrank back, the blade
70   missed; and the boy,
Desperate against himself, drove it half its length
Into his own side, and fell. And as he died
He gathered Antigone close in his arms again,
Choking, his blood bright red on her white
   cheek.
And now he lies dead with the dead, and she is
75   his
At last, his bride in the house of the dead.
                        (*Exit Eurydice into the palace.*)
CHORAGOS: She has left us without a word. What
   can this mean?
MESSENGER: It troubles me, too; yet she knows what
   is best,
Her grief is too great for public lamentation,

And doubtless she has gone to her chamber to
   weep   80
For her dead son, leading her maidens in his
   dirge.

(*Pause.*)

CHORAGOS: It may be so: but I fear this deep
   silence.
MESSENGER: I will see what she is doing. I will go in.
                        (*Exit Messenger into the palace.*)

(*Enter Kreon with attendants, bearing Haimon's
body.*)

CHORAGOS: But here is the king himself: oh look at
   him,
Bearing his own damnation in his arms.   85
KREON: Nothing you say can touch me any more.
My own blind heart has brought me
From darkness to final darkness. Here you see
The father murdering, the murdered son—
And all my civic wisdom!   90

Haimon my son, so young, so young to die,
I was the fool, not you; and you died for me.
CHORAGOS: That is the truth; but you were late in
   learning it.
KREON: This truth is hard to bear. Surely a god
Has crushed me beneath the hugest weight of
   heaven,   95
And driven me headlong a barbaric way
To trample out the thing I held most dear.

The pains that men will take to come to pain!

(*Enter Messenger from the palace.*)

MESSENGER: The burden you carry in your hands is
   heavy,
But it is not all: you will find more in your
   house.   100
KREON: What burden worse than this shall I find
   there?
MESSENGER: The Queen is dead.
KREON: O port of death, deaf world,
Is there no pity for me? And you, Angel of
   evil,
I was dead, and your words are death again.   105
Is it true, boy? Can it be true?
Is my wife dead? Has death bred death?
MESSENGER: You can see for yourself.

(*The doors are opened and the body of Eurydice is
disclosed within.*)

KREON: Oh pity!
All true, all true, and more than I can bear!   110
O my wife, my son!

MESSENGER: She stood before the altar, and her
          heart
       Welcomed the knife her own hand guided,
       And a great cry burst from her lips for
          Megareus° dead,
       And for Haimon dead, her sons; and her last
115   breath
       Was a curse for their father, the murderer of her
          sons.
       And she fell, and the dark flowed in through her
          closing eyes.
KREON: O God, I am sick with fear.
       Are there no swords here? Has no one a blow
          for me?
MESSENGER: Her curse is upon you for the deaths of
120   both.
KREON: It is right that it should be. I alone am
          guilty.
       I know it, and I say it. Lead me in,
       Quickly, friends.
       I have neither life nor substance. Lead me in.

114. **Megareus:** Son of Kreon and brother of Haimon,
Megareus sacrificed himself in the unsuccessful attack upon
Thebes, believing that his death was necessary to save
Thebes.

CHORAGOS: You are right, if there can be right in so
          much wrong.   125
       The briefest way is best in a world of sorrow.
KREON: Let it come,
       Let death come quickly, and be kind to me.
       I would not ever see the sun again.
CHORAGOS: All that will come when it will; but we,
          meanwhile,   130
       Have much to do. Leave the future to itself.
KREON: All my heart was in that prayer!
CHORAGOS: Then do not pray any more: the sky is
          deaf.
KREON: Lead me away. I have been rash and
          foolish.
       I have killed my son and my wife.   135
       I look for comfort; my comfort lies here dead.
       Whatever my hands have touched has come to
          nothing.
       Fate has brought all my pride to a thought of dust.

(As Kreon is being led into the house, the Choragos
advances and speaks directly to the audience.)

CHORAGOS: There is no happiness where there is no
          wisdom;
       No wisdom but in submission to the gods.   140
       Big words are always punished,
       And proud men in old age learn to be wise.

COMMENTARIES

Critical comment on the plays of Sophocles has been rich and various and has spanned the centuries. We are especially fortunate to have a commentary from the great age of Greek thought a century after Sophocles himself flourished. In *Oedipus Rex* Sophocles gave the philosopher Aristotle a perfect drama on which to build a theory of tragedy, and Aristotle's observations have remained the most influential comments made on drama in the West. In some ways they have established the function, limits, and purposes of drama. In the twentieth century, for instance, when Bertolt Brecht tried to create a new theory of the drama, he specifically described his ideas as an alternative to Aristotelian notions.

Although not a critic, Sigmund Freud saw in the Oedipus myth as interpreted by Sophocles a basic psychological phenomenon experienced by all people in their infancy. This "Oedipus complex" is now well established in psychology and in the popular imagination.

The extraordinary range of commentary on the Oedipus story is demonstrated nowhere more amazingly than in Claude Lévi-Strauss's structural reading of the myth, both in Sophocles' version and in other versions. Lévi-Strauss shows that a pattern emerges when certain actions in the play are placed side by side. If he is correct, his theory offers a way to interpret myths and to see why they were valued so highly by the Greeks in their drama.

Oliver Taplin's emphasis on the audience's emotional state during the performance of a Greek tragedy brings us back to the seminal comments of Aristotle. Tragedies were noted for their capacity to invoke pity and fear in the audience. Taplin helps us understand how an audience's emotional response can clarify our critical view of tragedy. Meanwhile, George Steiner expands our understanding not only of *Antigone* but also of a generally important aspect of Greek drama by exploring the sources and nature of the conflict in that play. Steiner establishes five constants, such as confrontations of men and women and of the individual and society, that help deepen our understanding of the action in *Antigone* and other Greek tragedies.

Jean Anouilh, a major French playwright in the mid-twentieth century, wrote a version of *Antigone* during the Nazi occupation of Paris and much of France. The political content of the play takes on interesting meaning in light of his experience. The excerpt that appears here offers a modern interpretation of the struggle between Antigone and Kreon.

Aristotle (384–322 B.C.)
POETICS: COMEDY AND EPIC AND TRAGEDY   Tr. 1967

TRANSLATED BY GERALD F. ELSE

Aristotle was Plato's most brilliant student and the heir of his teaching mantle. He remained with Plato for twenty years and then began his own school, called the Lyceum. His extant work consists mainly of his lectures, which were recorded by his students and carefully preserved. Called his treatises, they have greatly influenced later thought and deal with almost every branch of philosophy, science, and the arts. His Poetics remains, more than two thousand years later, a document of immense importance for literary criticism. Although sometimes ambiguous, difficult, and unfinished, it provides insight into the theoretical basis of Greek tragedy and comedy, and it helps us see that the drama was significant enough in intellectual life to warrant an examination by the best Greek minds.

Comedy

Comedy is, as we said it was, an imitation of persons who are inferior; not, however, going all the way to full villainy, but imitating the ugly, of which the ludicrous is one part. The ludicrous, that is, is a failing or a piece of ugliness which causes no pain or destruction; thus, to go on farther, the comic mask° is something ugly and distorted but painless.

Now the stages of development of tragedy, and the men who were responsible for them, have not escaped notice but comedy did escape notice in the beginning because it was not taken seriously. (In fact it was late in its history that the presiding magistrate officially "granted a chorus" to the comic poets; until then they were volunteers.) Thus comedy already possessed certain defining characteristics when the first "comic poets," so-called, appear in the record. Who gave it masks, or prologues, or troupes of actors and all that sort of thing is not known. The composing of plots came originally from Sicily; of the Athenian poets, Crates° was the first to abandon the lampooning mode and compose arguments, that is, plots, of a general nature.

Epic and Tragedy

Well, then, epic poetry followed in the wake of tragedy up to the point of being a (1) good-sized (2) imitation (3) in verse (4) of people who are to be taken seriously; but in its having its verse unmixed with any other and being narrative in character, there they differ. Further, so far as its length is concerned, tragedy tries as hard as it can to exist during a single daylight period, or to vary but little, while the epic is not limited in its time and so differs in that respect. Yet originally they used to do this in tragedies just as much as they did in epic poems.

The constituent elements are partly identical and partly limited to tragedy.

***

the comic mask: Actors in Greek drama wore masks behind which they spoke their lines. The masks were made individually for each character.

Crates: Greek actor and playwright (fl. 470 B.C.), credited by Aristotle with developing Greek comedy into a fully plotted, credible form. Aristophanes (c. 448–c. 385 B.C.), another Greek comic playwright, says that Crates was the first to portray a drunkard onstage.

Hence anybody who knows about good and bad tragedy knows about epic also; for the elements that the epic possesses appertain to tragedy as well, but those of tragedy are not all found in the epic.

Tragedy and Its Six Constituent Elements

Our discussions of imitative poetry in hexameters,° and of comedy, will come later; at present let us deal with tragedy, recovering from what has been said so far the definition of its essential nature, as it was in development. Tragedy, then, is a process of imitating an action which has serious implications, is complete, and possesses magnitude; by means of language which has been made sensuously attractive, with each of its varieties found separately in the parts; enacted by the persons themselves and not presented through narrative; through a course of pity and fear completing the purification of tragic acts which have those emotional characteristics. By "language made sensuously attractive" I mean language that has rhythm and melody, and by "its varieties found separately" I mean the fact that certain parts of the play are carried on through spoken verses alone and others the other way around, through song.

Now first of all, since they perform the imitation through action (by acting it), the adornment of their visual appearance will perforce constitute some part of the making of tragedy; and song-composition and verbal expression also, for those are the media in which they perform the imitation. By "verbal expression" I mean the actual composition of the verses, and by "song-composition" something whose meaning is entirely clear.

Next, since it is an imitation of an action and is enacted by certain people who are performing the action, and since those people must necessarily have certain traits both of character and thought (for it is thanks to these two factors that we speak of people's actions also as having a defined character, and it is in accordance with their actions that all either succeed or fail); and since the imitation of the action is the plot, for by "plot" I mean here the structuring of the events, and by the "characters" that in accordance with which we say that the persons who are acting have a defined moral character, and by "thought" all the passages in which they attempt to prove some thesis or set forth an opinion — it follows of necessity, then, that tragedy as a whole has just six constituent elements, in relation to the essence that makes it a distinct species; and they are plot, characters, verbal expression, thought, visual adornment, and song-composition. For the elements by which they imitate are two (i.e., verbal expression and song-composition), the manner in which they imitate is one (visual adornment), the things they imitate are three (plot, characters, thought), and there is nothing more beyond these. These then are the constituent forms they use.

The Relative Importance of the Six Elements

The greatest of these elements is the structuring of the incidents. For tragedy is an imitation not of men but of a life, an action, and they have moral quality in accordance with their characters but are happy or unhappy in accordance with their actions; hence they are not active in order to imitate their characters,

---

hexameters: The first known metrical form for classical verse. Each line had six metrical feet, some of which were prescribed in advance. It is the meter used for epic poetry and for poetry designed to teach a lesson. The form has sometimes been used in comparatively modern poetry but rarely with success except in French.

but they include the characters along with the actions for the sake of the latter. Thus the structure of events, the plot, is the goal of tragedy, and the goal is the greatest thing of all.

Again: a tragedy cannot exist without a plot, but it can without characters: thus the tragedies of most of our modern poets are devoid of character, and in general many poets are like that; so also with the relationship between Zeuxis and Polygnotus,° among the painters: Polygnotus is a good portrayer of character, while Zeuxis's painting has no dimension of character at all.

Again: if one strings end to end speeches that are expressive of character and carefully worked in thought and expression, he still will not achieve the result which we said was the aim of tragedy; the job will be done much better by a tragedy that is more deficient in these other respects but has a plot, a structure of events. It is much the same case as with painting: the most beautiful pigments smeared on at random will not give as much pleasure as a black-and-white outline picture. Besides, the most powerful means tragedy has for swaying our feelings, namely the peripeties and recognitions,° are elements of plot.

Again: an indicative sign is that those who are beginning a poetic career manage to hit the mark in verbal expression and character portrayal sooner than they do in plot construction; and the same is true of practically all the earliest poets.

So plot is the basic principle, the heart and soul, as it were, of tragedy, and the characters come second: . . . it is the imitation of an action and imitates the persons primarily for the sake of their action.

Third in rank is thought. This is the ability to state the issues and appropriate points pertaining to a given topic, an ability which springs from the arts of politics and rhetoric; in fact the earlier poets made their characters talk "politically," the present-day poets rhetorically. But "character" is that kind of utterance which clearly reveals the bent of a man's moral choice (hence there is no character in that class of utterances in which there is nothing at all that the speaker is choosing or rejecting), while "thought" is the passages in which they try to prove that something is so or not so, or state some general principle.

Fourth is the verbal expression of the speeches. I mean by this the same thing that was said earlier, that the "verbal expression" is the conveyance of thought through language: a statement which has the same meaning whether one says "verses" or "speeches."

The song-composition of the remaining parts is the greatest of the sensuous attractions, and the visual adornment of the dramatic persons can have a strong emotional effect but is the least artistic element, the least connected with the poetic art; in fact the force of tragedy can be felt even without benefit of public performance and actors, while for the production of the visual effect the property man's art is even more decisive than that of the poets.

Zeuxis and Polygnotus: Zeuxis (fl. 420–390 B.C.) developed a method of painting in which the figures were rounded and apparently three-dimensional. Thus, he was an illusionistic painter, imitating life in a realistic style. Polygnotus (c. 470–440 B.C.) was famous as a painter, and his works were on the Akropolis as well as at Delphi. His draftsmanship was especially praised.

peripeties and recognitions: The turning about of fortune and the recognition on the part of the tragic hero of the truth. This is, for Aristotle, a critical moment in the drama, especially if both events happen simultaneously, as they do in *Oedipus Rex*. It is quite possible for these moments to happen apart from one another.

General Principles of the Tragic Plot

With these distinctions out of the way, let us next discuss what the structuring of the events should be like, since this is both the basic and the most important element in the tragic art. We have established, then, that tragedy is an imitation of an action which is complete and whole and has some magnitude (for there is also such a thing as a whole that has no magnitude). "Whole" is that which has beginning, middle, and end. "Beginning" is that which does not necessarily follow on something else, but after it something else naturally is or happens; "end," the other way around, is that which naturally follows on something else, either necessarily or for the most part, but nothing else after it; and "middle" that which naturally follows on something else and something else on it. So, then, well constructed plots should neither begin nor end at any chance point but follow the guidelines just laid down.

Furthermore, since the beautiful, whether a living creature or anything that is composed of parts, should not only have these in a fixed order to one another but also possess a definite size which does not depend on chance — for beauty depends on size and order; hence neither can a very tiny creature turn out to be beautiful (since our perception of it grows blurred as it approaches the period of imperceptibility) nor an excessively huge one (for then it cannot all be perceived at once and so its unity and wholeness are lost), if for example there were a creature a thousand miles long — so, just as in the case of living creatures they must have some size, but one that can be taken in a single view, so with plots: they should have length, but such that they are easy to remember. As to a limit of the length, the one is determined by the tragic competitions and the ordinary span of attention. (If they had to compete with a hundred tragedies they would compete by the water clock, as they say used to be done [?].) But the limit fixed by the very nature of the case is: the longer the plot, up to the point of still being perspicuous as a whole, the finer it is so far as size is concerned; or to put it in general terms, the length in which, with things happening in unbroken sequence, a shift takes place either probably or necessarily from bad to good fortune or from good to bad — that is an acceptable norm of length.

But a plot is not unified, as some people think, simply because it has to do with a single person. A large, indeed an indefinite number of things can happen to a given individual, some of which go to constitute no unified event; and in the same way there can be many acts of a given individual from which no single action emerges. Hence it seems clear that those poets are wrong who have composed *Heracleïds, Theseïds,* and the like. They think that since Heracles was a single person it follows that the plot will be single too. But Homer, superior as he is in all other respects, appears to have grasped this point well also, thanks either to art or nature, for in composing an *Odyssey* he did not incorporate into it everything that happened to the hero, for example how he was wounded on Mt. Parnassus° or how he feigned madness at the muster, neither of which events, by happening, made it at all necessary or probable that the other should happen. Instead, he composed the *Odyssey* — and the *Iliad* similarly — around a unified action of the kind we have been talking about.

Mt. Parnassus: A mountain in central Greece traditionally sacred to Apollo. In legend, Odysseus was wounded there, but the point Aristotle is making is that the writer of epics need not include every detail of his hero's life in a given work. Homer, in writing the *Odyssey,* was working with a hero, Odysseus, whose story had been legendary long before he began writing.

A poetic imitation, then, ought to be unified in the same way as a single imitation in any other mimetic field, by having a single object: since the plot is an imitation of an action, the latter ought to be both unified and complete, and the component events ought to be so firmly compacted that if any one of them is shifted to another place, or removed, the whole is loosened up and dislocated; for an element whose addition or subtraction makes no perceptible extra difference is not really a part of the whole.

From what has been said it is also clear that the poet's job is not to report what has happened but what is likely to happen: that is, what is capable of happening according to the rule of probability or necessity. Thus the difference between the historian and the poet is not in their utterances being in verse or prose (it would be quite possible for Herodotus's work to be translated into verse, and it would not be any the less a history with verse than it is without it); the difference lies in the fact that the historian speaks of what has happened, the poet of the kind of thing that *can* happen. Hence also poetry is a more philosophical and serious business than history; for poetry speaks more of universals, history of particulars. "Universal" in this case is what kind of person is likely to do or say certain kinds of things, according to probability or necessity; that is what poetry aims at, although it gives its persons particular names afterward; while the "particular" is what Alcibiades did or what happened to him.

In the field of comedy this point has been grasped: our comic poets construct their plots on the basis of general probabilities and then assign names to the persons quite arbitrarily, instead of dealing with individuals as the old iambic poets° did. But in tragedy they still cling to the historically given names. The reason is that what is possible is persuasive; so what has not happened we are not yet ready to believe is possible, while what has happened is, we feel, obviously possible: for it would not have happened if it were impossible. Nevertheless, it is a fact that even in our tragedies, in some cases only one or two of the names are traditional, the rest being invented, and in some others none at all. It is so, for example, in Agathon's *Antheus* — the names in it are as fictional as the events — and it gives no less pleasure because of that. Hence the poets ought not to cling at all costs to the traditional plots, around which our tragedies are constructed. And in fact it is absurd to go searching for this kind of authentication, since even the familiar names are familiar to only a few in the audience and yet give the same kind of pleasure to all.

So from these considerations it is evident that the poet should be a maker of his plots more than of his verses, insofar as he is a poet by virtue of his imitations and what he imitates is actions. Hence even if it happens that he puts something that has actually taken place into poetry, he is none the less a poet; for there is nothing to prevent some of the things that have happened from being the kind of things that can happen, and that is the sense in which he is their maker.

Simple and Complex Plots

Among simple plots and actions the episodic are the worst. By "episodic" plot I mean one in which there is no probability or necessity for the order in

---

old iambic poets: Aristotle may be referring to Archilochus (fl. 650 B.C.) and the iambic style he developed. The iamb is a metrical foot of two syllables, a short and a long syllable, and was the most popular metrical style before the time of Aristotle. "Dealing with individuals" implies using figures already known to the audience rather than figures whose names can be arbitrarily assigned because no one knows who they are.

which the episodes follow one another. Such structures are composed by the bad poets because they are bad poets, but by the good poets because of the actors: in composing contest pieces for them, and stretching out the plot beyond its capacity, they are forced frequently to dislocate the sequence.

Furthermore, since the tragic imitation is not only of a complete action but also of events that are fearful and pathetic,° and these come about best when they come about contrary to one's expectation yet logically, one following from the other; that way they will be more productive of wonder than if they happen merely at random, by chance — because even among chance occurrences the ones people consider most marvelous are those that seem to have come about as if on purpose: for example the way the statue of Mitys at Argos killed the man who had been the cause of Mitys's death, by falling on him while he was attending the festival; it stands to reason, people think, that such things don't happen by chance — so plots of that sort cannot fail to be artistically superior.

Some plots are simple, others are complex; indeed the actions of which the plots are imitations already fall into these two categories. By "simple" action I mean one the development of which being continuous and unified in the manner stated above, the reversal comes without peripety or recognition, and by "complex" action one in which the reversal is continuous but with recognition or peripety or both. And these developments must grow out of the very structure of the plot itself, in such a way that on the basis of what has happened previously this particular outcome follows either by necessity or in accordance with probability; for there is a great difference in whether these events happen because of those or merely after them.

"Peripety" is a shift of what is being undertaken to the opposite in the way previously stated, and that in accordance with probability or necessity as we have just been saying; as for example in the *Oedipus* the man who has come, thinking that he will reassure Oedipus, that is, relieve him of his fear with respect to his mother, by revealing who he once was, brings about the opposite; and in the *Lynceus*, as he (Lynceus) is being led away with every prospect of being executed, and Danaus pursuing him with every prospect of doing the executing, it comes about as a result of the other things that have happened in the play that *he* is executed and Lynceus is saved. And "recognition" is, as indeed the name indicates, a shift from ignorance to awareness, pointing in the direction either of close blood ties or of hostility, of people who have previously been in a clearly marked state of happiness or unhappiness.

The finest recognition is one that happens at the same time as a peripety, as is the case with the one in the *Oedipus*. Naturally, there are also other kinds of recognition: it is possible for one to take place in the prescribed manner in relation to inanimate objects and chance occurrences, and it is possible to recognize whether a person has acted or not acted. But the form that is most integrally a part of the plot, the action, is the one aforesaid; for that kind of recognition combined with peripety will excite either pity or fear (and these are the kinds of action of which tragedy is an imitation according to our defini-

---

fearful and pathetic: Aristotle said that tragedy should evoke two emotions: terror and pity. The terror results from our realizing that what is happening to the hero might just as easily happen to us; the pity results from our human sympathy with a fellow sufferer. Therefore, the fearful and pathetic represent significant emotions appropriate to our witnessing drama.

tion), because both good and bad fortune will also be most likely to follow that kind of event. Since, further, the recognition is a recognition of persons, some are of one person by the other one only (when it is already known who the "other one" is), but sometimes it is necessary for both persons to go through a recognition, as for example Iphigenia is recognized by her brother° through the sending of the letter, but of him by Iphigenia another recognition is required.

These then are two elements of plot: peripety and recognition; third is the *pathos*. Of these, peripety and recognition have been discussed; a *pathos* is a destructive or painful act, such as deaths on stage, paroxysms of pain, woundings, and all that sort of thing.

Sigmund Freud (1856–1939)
THE OEDIPUS COMPLEX   1900–1930°

TRANSLATED BY JAMES STRACHEY

Sigmund Freud is the most celebrated psychiatrist of the twentieth century and the father of psychoanalytic theory. His researches into the unconscious have changed the way we think about the human mind, and his explorations into the symbolic meaning of dreams have been widely regarded as a breakthrough in connecting the meaning of world myth to personal life.

In his Interpretation of Dreams *he turned to Sophocles' drama and developed his theories of the Oedipus complex: The desire to kill one parent and marry the other may be rooted in the deepest natural psychological development of the individual. The following passage provides insight not only into a psychological state that all humans may share but also into the way in which a man of Freud's temperament read and interpreted a great piece of literature. Like Sophocles himself, Freud believed that the myth underlying* Oedipus Rex *has a meaning and importance for all human beings.*

In my experience, which is already extensive, the chief part in the mental lives of all children who later become psychoneurotics is played by their parents. Being in love with the one parent and hating the other are among the essential constituents of the stock of psychical impulses which is formed at that time and which is of such importance in determining the symptoms of the later neurosis. It is not my belief, however, that psychoneurotics differ sharply in this respect from other human beings who remain normal — that they are able, that is, to create something absolutely new and peculiar to themselves. It is far more probable — and this is confirmed by occasional observations on normal children — that they are only distinguished by exhibiting on a magnified scale feelings of love and hatred to their parents which occur less obviously and less intensely in the minds of most children.

her brother: Orestes is Iphigenia's brother. Aristotle may be referring to a lost play.
1900: *Interpretation of Dreams* was first published in 1900 and updated regularly by Freud through eight editions. This passage is taken from the eighth edition, published in 1930.

This discovery is confirmed by a legend that has come down to us from classical antiquity: a legend whose profound and universal power to move can only be understood if the hypothesis I have put forward in regard to the psychology of children has an equally universal validity. What I have in mind is the legend of King Oedipus and Sophocles' drama which bears his name.

Oedipus, son of Laïus, King of Thebes, and of Jocasta, was exposed [to the elements and left to die] as an infant because an oracle had warned Laïus that the still unborn child would be his father's murderer. The child was rescued and grew up as a prince in an alien court, until, in doubts as to his origin, he too questioned the oracle and was warned to avoid his home since he was destined to murder his father and take his mother in marriage. On the road leading away from what he believed was his home, he met King Laïus and slew him in a sudden quarrel. He came next to Thebes and solved the riddle set him by the Sphinx who barred his way. Out of gratitude the Thebans made him their king and gave him Jocasta's hand in marriage. He reigned long in peace and honor, and she who, unknown to him, was his mother bore him two sons and two daughters. Then at last a plague broke out and the Thebans made inquiry once more of the oracle. It is at this point that Sophocles's tragedy opens. The messengers bring back the reply that the plague will cease when the murderer of Laïus has been driven from the land.

> But he, where is he? Where shall now be read
> The fading record of this ancient guilt?[1]

The action of the play consists in nothing other than the process of revealing, with cunning delays and ever-mounting excitement — a process that can be likened to the work of a psychoanalysis — that Oedipus himself is the murderer of Laïus, but further that he is the son of the murdered man and of Jocasta. Appalled at the abomination which he has unwittingly perpetrated, Oedipus blinds himself and forsakes his home. The oracle has been fulfilled.

Oedipus Rex is what is known as a tragedy of destiny. Its tragic effect is said to lie in the contrast between the supreme will of the gods and the vain attempts of mankind to escape the evil that threatens them. The lesson which, it is said, the deeply moved spectator should learn from the tragedy is submission to the divine will and realization of his own impotence. Modern dramatists have accordingly tried to achieve a similar tragic effect by weaving the same contrast into a plot invented by themselves. But the spectators have looked on unmoved while a curse or an oracle was fulfilled in spite of all the efforts of some innocent man: later tragedies of destiny have failed in their effect.

If *Oedipus Rex* moves a modern audience no less than it did the contemporary Greek one, the explanation can only be that its effect does not lie in the contrast between destiny and human will, but is to be looked for in the particular nature of the material on which that contrast is exemplified. There must be something which makes a voice within us ready to recognize the compelling force of destiny in the *Oedipus,* while we can dismiss as merely arbitrary such dispositions as are laid down in [Grillparzer's] *Die Ahnfrau* or other modern tragedies of destiny. And a factor of this kind is in fact involved in the story of King Oedipus. His destiny moves us only because it might have been ours — because the oracle laid the same curse upon us before our birth as upon him. It is the fate of all of us, perhaps, to direct our first sexual impulse toward our

---

[1] Lewis Campbell's translation (1883), lines 108ff [Fitts and Fitzgerald, Prologue, lines 112–13].

mother and our first hatred and our first murderous wish against our father. Our dreams convince us that that is so. King Oedipus, who slew his father Laïus and married his mother Jocasta, merely shows us the fulfillment of our own childhood wishes. But, more fortunate than he, we have meanwhile succeeded, in so far as we have not become psychoneurotics, in detaching our sexual impulses from our mothers and in forgetting our jealousy of our fathers. Here is one in whom these primeval wishes of our childhood have been fulfilled, and we shrink back from him with the whole force of the repression by which those wishes have since that time been held down within us. While the poet, as he unravels the past, brings to light the guilt of Oedipus, he is at the same time compelling us to recognize our own inner minds, in which those same impulses, though suppressed, are still to be found. The contrast with which the closing Chorus leaves us confronted —

> . . . Fix on Oedipus your eyes,
> Who resolved the dark enigma, noblest champion and most wise.
> Like a star his envied fortune mounted beaming far and wide:
> Now he sinks in seas of anguish, whelmed beneath a raging tide . . .[2]

— strikes as a warning at ourselves and our pride, at us who since our childhood have grown so wise and so mighty in our own eyes. Like Oedipus, we live in ignorance of these wishes, repugnant to morality, which have been forced upon us by Nature, and after their revelation we may all of us well seek to close our eyes to the scenes of our childhood.[3]

There is an unmistakable indication in the text of Sophocles' tragedy itself that the legend of Oedipus sprang from some primeval dream material which had as its content the distressing disturbance of a child's relation to his parents owing to the first stirrings of sexuality. At a point when Oedipus, though he is not yet enlightened, has begun to feel troubled by his recollection of the oracle, Jocasta consoles him by referring to a dream which many people dream, though, as she thinks, it has no meaning:

> Many a man ere now in dreams hath lain
> With her who bare him. He hath least annoy
> Who with such omens troubleth not his mind.[4]

Today, just as then, many men dream of having sexual relations with their mothers, and speak of the fact with indignation and astonishment. It is clearly the key to the tragedy and the complement to the dream of the dreamer's father being dead. The story of Oedipus is the reaction of the imagination to these two typical

---

[2] Lewis Campbell's translation, lines 1524ff [Fitts and Fitzgerald, Antistrophe 2, lines 292–96].

[3] [*Footnote added by Freud in 1914 edition.*] None of the findings of psychoanalytic research has provoked such embittered denials, such fierce opposition — or such amusing contortions — on the part of critics as this indication of the childhood impulses toward incest which persist in the unconscious. An attempt has even been made recently to make out, in the face of all experience, that the incest should only be taken as "symbolic." — Ferenczi (1912) has proposed an ingenious "overinterpretation" of the Oedipus myth, based on a passage in one of Schopenhauer's letters. [*Added 1919.*] Later studies have shown that the "Oedipus complex," which was touched upon for the first time in the above paragraphs in the *Interpretation of Dreams,* throws a light of undreamt-of importance on the history of the human race and the evolution of religion and morality.

[4] Lewis Campbell's translation, lines 982ff [Fitts and Fitzgerald, Scene 3, lines 67–69].

dreams. And just as these dreams, when dreamt by adults, are accompanied by feelings of repulsion, so too the legend must include horror and self-punishment. Its further modification originates once again in a misconceived secondary revision of the material, which has sought to exploit it for theological purposes. . . . The attempt to harmonize divine omnipotence with human responsibility must naturally fail in connection with this subject matter just as with any other.

Claude Lévi-Strauss (b. 1908)
FROM *THE STRUCTURAL STUDY OF MYTH*   1955

Claude Lévi-Strauss is one of a handful of modern anthropologists whose interests span the range of thought, culture, and understanding. His work has been of immense influence on French intellectual life and, by extension, on the intellectual life of our entire century. His works include Triste Tropiques *(translated as* A World on the Wane*), about his own experiences as an anthropologist;* Structural Anthropology, *about the ways in which the study of anthropology implies a study of the structure of thought; and* Mythologies, *a four-volume summation of his thought. The excerpt that follows is structuralist in scope in that it attempts to understand the myth of Oedipus by examining the patterns of repetition in the original narrative. By setting up a grid, Lévi-Strauss begins to sort out the implications of the myth and to seek a meaning that is not necessarily apparent in the chronological order of the narrative. He examines the myth diachronically — across the lines of time — and thereby sees a new range of implications, which he treats as the structural implications of the myth. His reading is complex, suggesting that the Oedipus myth is a vegetation myth explaining the origins of mankind. Lévi-Strauss gives us a new way to interpret the significance of literary myths.*

The time has come to give a concrete example of the method we propose. We will use the Oedipus myth which has the advantage of being well known to everybody and for which no preliminary explanation is therefore needed. By doing so, I am well aware that the Oedipus myth has only reached us under late forms and through literary transfigurations concerned more with esthetic and moral preoccupations than with religious or ritual ones, whatever these may have been. But as will be shown later, this apparently unsatisfactory situation will strengthen our demonstration rather than weaken it.

The myth will be treated as would be an orchestra score perversely presented as a unilinear series and where our task is to reestablish the correct disposition. As if, for instance, we were confronted with a sequence of the type: 1,2,4,7,8,2,3,4,6,8,1,4,5,7,8,1,2,5,7,3,4,5,6,8 . . . , the assignment being to put all the 1's together, all the 2's, the 3's, etc.; the result is a chart:

1	2		4			7	8
	2	3	4		6		8
1			4	5		7	8
1	2			5		7	
		3	4	5			
					6		8

We will attempt to perform the same kind of operation on the Oedipus myth, trying out several dispositions. . . . Let us suppose, for the sake of argument, that the best arrangement is the following (although it might certainly be improved by the help of a specialist in Greek mythology):

Kadmos seeks his sister Europa ravished by Zeus.		Kadmos kills the dragon.	
	The Spartoi kill each other.		Labdacos (Laios's father) = *lame* (?).
	Oedipus kills his father Laios.		Laios (Oedipus's father) = *left-sided* (?).
		Oedipus kills the Sphinx.	
Oedipus marries his mother Jocasta.	Eteocles kills his brother Polyneices.		Oedipus = *swollen-foot* (?).
Antigone buries her brother Polyneices despite prohibition.			

Thus, we find ourselves confronted with four vertical columns each of which includes several relations belonging to the same bundle. Were we to *tell* the myth, we would disregard the columns and read the rows from left to right and from top to bottom. But if we want to *understand* the myth, then we will have to disregard one half of the diachronic° dimension (top to bottom) and read from left to right, column after column, each one being considered as a unit.

All the relations belonging to the same column exhibit one common feature which it is our task to unravel. For instance, all the events grouped in the first column on the left have something to do with blood relations which are overemphasized, i.e. are subject to a more intimate treatment than they should be. Let us say, then, that the first column has as its common feature the *overrating of blood relations*. It is obvious that the second column expresses the same thing, but inverted: *underrating of blood relations*. The third column refers to monsters being slain. As to the fourth, a word of clarification is needed. The remarkable

---

diachronic: Not ordered linearly in time, but through time.

connotation of the surnames in Oedipus's father-line has often been noticed. However, linguists usually disregard it, since to them the only way to define the meaning of a term is to investigate all the contexts in which it appears, and personal names, precisely because they are used as such, are not accompanied by any context. With the method we propose to follow the objection disappears since the myth itself provides its own context. The meaningful fact is no longer to be looked for in the eventual sense of each name, but in the fact that all the names have a common feature: i.e., that they may eventually mean something and that all these hypothetical meanings (which may well remain hypothetical) exhibit a common feature, namely they refer to *difficulties to walk and to behave straight.*

What is then the relationship between the two columns on the right? Column three refers to monsters. The dragon is a chthonian° being which has to be killed in order that mankind be born from the earth; the Sphinx is a monster unwilling to permit men to live. The last unit reproduces the first one which has to do with the *autochthonous*° origin of mankind. Since the monsters are overcome by men, we may thus say that the common feature of the third column is *the denial of the autochthonous origin of man.*

This immediately helps us to understand the meaning of the fourth column. In mythology it is a universal character of men born from the earth that at the moment they emerge from the depth, they either cannot walk or do it clumsily. This is the case of the chthonian beings in the mythology of the Pueblo: Masauwu, who leads the emergence, and the chthonian Shumaikoli are lame ("bleeding-foot," "sore-foot"). The same happens to the Koskimo of the Kwakiutl after they have been swallowed by the chthonian monster, Tsiakish: when they returned to the surface of the earth "they limped forward or tripped sideways." Then the common feature of the fourth column is: *the persistence of the autochthonous origin of man.* It follows that column four is to column three as column one is to column two. The inability to connect two kinds of relationships is overcome (or rather replaced) by the positive statement that contradictory relationships are identical inasmuch as they are both self-contradictory in a similar way. Although this is still a provisional formulation of the structure of mythical thought, it is sufficient at this stage.

Turning back to the Oedipus myth, we may now see what it means. The myth has to do with the inability, for a culture which holds the belief that mankind is autochthonous . . . to find a satisfactory transition between this theory and the knowledge that human beings are actually born from the union of man and woman. Although the problem obviously cannot be solved, the Oedipus myth provides a kind of logical tool which, to phrase it coarsely, replaces the original problem: born from one or born from two? born from different or born from same? By a correlation of this type, the overrating of blood relations is to the underrating of blood relations as the attempt to escape autochthony is to the impossibility to succeed in it. Although experience contradicts theory, social life verifies the cosmology by its similarity of structure. Hence cosmology is true.

Two remarks should be made at this stage.

---

chthonian: From the underworld.
autochthonous: Native, aboriginal; in this case, born of the earth.

In order to interpret the myth, we were able to leave aside a point which has until now worried the specialists, namely, that in the earlier (Homeric) versions of the Oedipus myth, some basic elements are lacking, such as Jocasta killing herself and Oedipus piercing his own eyes. These events do not alter the substance of the myth although they can easily be integrated, the first one as a new case of autodestruction (column three) while the second is another case of crippledness (column four). At the same time there is something significant in these additions since the shift from foot to head is to be correlated with the shift from: autochthonous origin negated to: self-destruction.

Thus, our method eliminates a problem which has been so far one of the main obstacles to the progress of mythological studies, namely, the quest for the *true* version, or the *earlier* one. On the contrary, we define the myth as consisting of all its versions; to put it otherwise: a myth remains the same as long as it is felt as such. A striking example is offered by the fact that our interpretation may take into account, and is certainly applicable to, the Freudian use of the Oedipus myth. Although the Freudian problem has ceased to be that of autochthony *versus* bisexual reproduction, it is still the problem of understanding how *one* can be born from *two*: how is it that we do not have only one procreator, but a mother plus a father? Therefore, not only Sophocles, but Freud himself, should be included among the recorded versions of the Oedipus myth on a par with earlier or seemingly more "authentic" versions.

Brooks Atkinson (1894–1984)
REVIEW OF *OEDIPUS TYRANNUS*   1952

In 1952 New York audiences watched Oedipus Tyrannus (Oedipus Rex) *performed in modern Greek. Few could understand the language but probably — like* New York Times *reviewer Brooks Atkinson — they still fell under Sophocles' powerful spell.*

Despite the stubborn fact that the Sophocles tragedies are played in a language incomprehensible to most of us, the performances are illuminating and exalting on a high plane of formal art. Most of us have never had a chance to look so deep into the heart of a Greek classical drama.

In comparison with *Electra, Oedipus* is more compact, and the performance is more concise and dramatic. For the story of how Oedipus learns the awful truth about his fate is told with deliberate suspense in a style that approximates the modern manner. Again, C. Clonis has filled the stage with an imposing scene depicting the steps to a royal palace. The costumes by Antonios Phocas are formal without being severe. And the musical accompaniment, composed by Miss Paxinou, lightly underscores the dramatic episodes in the performance.

Although Mr. Minotis and Miss Paxinou are starred in the program (which, incidentally, neglects to mention the name of the author), the performance is a completely integrated work of art, as impersonal and as majestic as the drama. The acting is in the heroic style. The pace is deliberate; the groupings are planned for dramatic symmetry; the sound of the voices has the resonance of impassioned speech about terrible things. Nothing of use in the telling of a mighty fable is wasted in this articulate performance.

It is hard to imagine how the acting could be improved. Mr. Minotis's Oedipus is royal without being aloof to the personal crises of the story. Without losing regal authority, he hangs on every word that the shepherds from the hills bring unwillingly to the palace. Although Miss Paxinou's portrait of the queen is also larger than life, it is compassionate and human. N. Hadziscos's cautious Creon who does not want to face the truth; Basil Kanakis's patriarchal priest who brings news more frightening than he imagines, and the shepherd of P. Zervos — are all played with individual flavor and with respect for the unity of the whole performance.

But . . . the staging of the chorus is the most stunning contribution of the Greek National Theatre productions. It is a male chorus for *Oedipus* — bearded, gowned in subdued colors. Under the direction of Agapi Evangelidou, the chorus both judges and participates in the action, like an idealized instrument of public opinion. Although the gestures and the movements are perfectly synchronized, they are not spectacular, but spontaneous and unobtrusive. If it is possible for acting to be natural and stately at the same time, this is it.

In mastering the function of the chorus, the Greek National Theatre has mastered the art of playing Greek classical drama as a whole. Every moment of *Oedipus Tyrannus* is alive and beautiful.

Oliver Taplin (b. 1943)
EMOTION AND MEANING IN GREEK TRAGEDY   1983

Scholar Oliver Taplin focuses on one of Aristotle's concerns in his commentary on tragedy: the emotions aroused by drama. Taplin explores the argument that devalues an emotional response to tragedy, and then he considers the proposition that "tragedy is essentially the emotional experience of its audience."

It seems to me, then, that Gorgias° is right that tragedy is essentially the *emotional experience of its audience.* Whatever it tells us about the world is conveyed by means of these emotions. Plato agreed with Gorgias in this, but he disapproved of the process and regarded it as harmful. Aristotle agreed with him too, but, contrary to Plato, regarded it as beneficial and salutary. Plato's objection was that such emotions are not the province of the highest part of the soul, the intellectual part. This is the forefather of the error made by so many later critics who have not acknowledged the centrality of emotion in the communication of tragedy. They think that if tragedy is essentially an emotional experience, it must be *solely* that; and they think this because they assume that strong emotion is necessarily in opposition to thought, that the psychic activities are mutu-

---

Gorgias: Greek orator and rhetorician (c. 483–376 B.C.).

ally exclusive. But is this right? Understanding, reason, learning, moral discrimination; these things are not, in my experience, incompatible with emotion (nor presumably in the experience of Gorgias and Aristotle): What is incompatible is cold insensibility. Whether or not emotion is inimical to such intellectual processes depends on the *circumstances in which it is aroused.*

The characteristic tragic emotions — pity, horror, fascination, indignation, and so forth — are felt in many other situations besides in the theater. Above all we suffer them in the face of the misfortunes of real life, of course. What distinguishes the experience of a great tragedy? For one thing, as already remarked, we feel for the fortunes of people who have no direct personal relation to us: While this does not decrease the intensity of the emotion, it affords us some distance and perspective. We can feel and at the same time observe from outside. But does this distinguish tragedy from other "contrived" emotional experiences (most of them tending to the anti-intellectual), for example an animal hunt, a football match, an encounter group, reading a thriller, or watching a horror movie? Well, the experience of tragedy is by no means a random series of sensations. Our emotional involvement has perspective and context at the same time, and not just in retrospect. Thus the events of the tragedy are in an ordered *sequence,* a sequence which gives shape and comprehensibility to what we feel. And, most important of all, the affairs of the characters which move us are given a moral setting which is argued and explored in the play. They act and suffer within situations of moral conflict, or social, intellectual, and theological conflict. The quality of the tragedy depends *both* on its power to arouse our emotions *and* on the setting of those emotions in a sequence of moral and intellectual complications which is set out and examined. Tragedy evokes our feelings for others, like much else; but it is distinguished by the order and significance it imparts to suffering. So if the audience is not moved, then the tragedy, however intellectual, is a total failure: If its passions are aroused, but in a thoughtless, amorphous way, then it is merely a bad tragedy, sensational, melodramatic.

Thus it is that our emotions in the theater, far from driving out thought and meaning, are indivisible from them: They are simultaneous and mutually dependent. The experience of tragedy can achieve this coherence in a way that the emotional experiences of real life generally cannot because they are too close, too cluttered with detail and partiality, to be seen in perspective. Tragedy makes us feel that we understand life in its tragic aspects. We have the sense that we can better sympathize with and cope with suffering, misfortune, and waste. It is this sense of understanding (not isolated pearls of wisdom) that is the "message" of a tragedy, that the great playwright imparts. This is well put in T. S. Eliot's essay "Shakespeare and the Stoicism of Seneca," where he argues that it is the quality of the emotional expression rather than the quality of the philosophy which makes literature great, which makes it "strong, true and informative . . . useful and beneficial in the sense in which poetry is useful and beneficial." "All great poetry," Eliot° writes, "gives the illusion of a view of life . . . for every precise emotion tends towards intellectual formulation."

T. S. Eliot: Poet and critic (1888–1965).

George Steiner (b. 1929)
PRINCIPAL CONSTANTS OF CONFLICT IN *ANTIGONE*[*]   1984

George Steiner's Antigones, *a study of the history of variations on the theme of Sophocles' play, uncovers a remarkable range of interpretation, especially in the relationship of Kreon and Antigone. In his analysis, Steiner establishes five constants of conflict that he feels are responsible for much of the power of the play.*

It has, I believe, been given to only one literary text to express all the principal constants of conflict in the condition of man. These constants are fivefold: the confrontation of men and of women; of age and of youth; of society and of the individual; of the living and the dead; of men and of god(s). The conflicts which come of these five orders of confrontation are not negotiable. Men and women, old and young, the individual and the community or state, the quick and the dead, mortals and immortals, define themselves in the conflictual process of defining each other. Self-definition and the agonistic recognition of "otherness" (of *l'autre*) across the threatened boundaries of self are indissociable. The polarities of masculinity and of femininity, of aging and of youth, of private autonomy and of social collectivity, of existence and mortality, of the human and the divine, can be crystallized only in adversative terms (whatever the many shades of accommodation between them). To arrive at oneself — the primordial journey — is to come up, polemically, against "the other." The boundary-conditions of the human person are those set by gender, by age, by community, by the cut between life and death, and by the potentials of accepted or denied encounter between the existential and the transcendent.

But "collision" is, of course, a monistic and, therefore, inadequate term. Equally decisive are those categories of reciprocal perception, of grappling with "otherness," that can be defined as erotic, filial, social, ritual, and metaphysical. Men and women, old and young, individual and *communitas*, living and deceased, mortals and gods, meet and mesh in contiguities of love, of kinship, of commonality and group-communion, of caring remembrance, of worship. Sex, the honeycomb of generations and of kinship, the social unit, the presentness of the departed in the weave of the living, the practices of religion, are the modes of enactment of ultimate ontological dualities. In essence, the constants of conflict and of positive intimacy are the same. When man and woman meet, they stand against each other as they stand close. Old and young seek in each other the pain of remembrance and the matching solace of futurity. Anarchic individuation seeks interaction with the compulsions of law, of collective cohesion in the body politic. The dead inhabit the living and, in turn, await their visit. The duel between men and god(s) is the most aggressively amorous known to experience. In the physics of man's being, fission is also fusion.

It is in lines 441–581 [pp. 146–49] of Sophocles' *Antigone* that each of the five fundamental categories of man's definition and self-definition through conflict is realized, and that all five are at work in a single act of confrontation. No other moment that I know of, in either sacred or secular imagining, achieves this totality. Creon and Antigone clash as man and as woman. Creon is a mature, in-

[*][Editors' title.]

deed an aging, man; Antigone's is the virginity of youth. Their fatal debate turns on the nature of the coexistence between private vision and public need, between ego and community. The imperatives of immanence, of the living in the [*polis*], πόλις, press on Creon; in Antigone, these imperatives encounter the no less exigent night-throng of the dead. No syllable spoken, no gesture made, in the dialogue of Antigone and Creon but has within it the manifold, perhaps duplicitous, nearness of the gods. . . .

That which has in it the seed of all drama is the meeting of a man and of a woman. No experience of which we have direct knowledge is more charged with the potential of collision. Being inalienably one, by virtue of the humanity which distances them from all other life-forms, man and woman are at the same time inalienably different. The spectrum of difference is, as we know, one of most subtle continuum. There are in every human being elements of masculinity and of femininity (each encounter, each conflict is, therefore, also a civil war within the hybrid self). But at some point along the continuum, most men and women crystallize their essential manhood or womanhood. This gathering of the partly divided self to itself, this composition of identity, determines the gap across which the energies of love and of hatred meet.

Jean Anouilh (b. 1910)
FROM *ANTIGONE*   1942

TRANSLATED BY LEWIS GALANTIÈRE

> *Jean Anouilh began writing plays in 1931. Some of his best-known works, in addition to* Antigone, *are* Eurydice *(1941),* Orestes *(1942),* Medea *(1946),* Ring Round the Moon *(1947),* The Waltz of the Toreadors *(1951), and* The Lark *(1952), which is about Joan of Arc. Anouilh wrote* Antigone *in 1942 in occupied Paris and produced it with his wife in the title role in February 1944, when the Nazis controlled most of Europe. Kreon (spelled Creon in this excerpt) is more willing to compromise in Anouilh's version of the play, and for that reason some critics saw the play as pro-Nazi. But Anouilh's sympathies were with Antigone, who represented the anti-Nazi view of the Parisian Resistance. Throughout its early run, the play was an inspiration to the patriotic French.*
>
> *This excerpt begins when Ismene returns to accept some of the responsibility for Polyneices' burial and continues through the confrontation of Haimon (Haemon in this excerpt) and Kreon to the end of the play.*

(*Ismene enters through arch.*)

ISMENE (*distraught*): Antigone!
ANTIGONE (*turns to Ismene*): You, too? What do you want?
ISMENE: Oh, forgive me, Antigone. I've come back. I'll be brave. I'll go with you now.
ANTIGONE: Where will you go with me?
ISMENE (*to Creon*): Creon! If you kill her, you'll have to kill me too.

ANTIGONE: Oh, no, Ismene. Not a bit of it. I die alone. You don't think I'm going to let you die with me after what I've been through? You don't deserve it.

ISMENE: If you die, I don't want to live. I don't want to be left behind, alone.

ANTIGONE: You chose life and I chose death. Now stop blubbering. You had your chance to come with me in the black night, creeping on your hands and knees. You had your chance to claw up the earth with your nails, as I did; to get yourself caught like a thief, as I did. And you refused it.

ISMENE: Not anymore. I'll do it alone tonight.

ANTIGONE (*turns round toward Creon*): You hear that, Creon? The thing is catching! Who knows but that lots of people will catch the disease from me! What are you waiting for? Call in your guards! Come on, Creon! Show a little courage! It only hurts for a minute! Come on, cook!

CREON (*turns toward arch and calls*): Guard!

(*Guards enter through arch.*)

ANTIGONE (*in a great cry of relief*): At last, Creon!

(*Chorus enters through left arch.*)

CREON (*to the Guards*): Take her away! (*Creon goes up on top step.*)

(*Guards grasp Antigone by her arms, turn and hustle her toward the arch, right, and exeunt.° Ismene mimes horror, backs away toward the arch, left, then turns and runs out through the arch. A long pause, as Creon moves slowly downstage.*)

CHORUS (*Behind Creon. Speaks in a deliberate voice*): You are out of your mind, Creon. What have you done?

CREON (*his back to Chorus*): She had to die.

CHORUS: You must not let Antigone die. We shall carry the scar of her death for centuries.

CREON: She insisted. No man on earth was strong enough to dissuade her. Death was her purpose, whether she knew it or not. Polynices was a mere pretext. When she had to give up that pretext, she found another one — that life and happiness were tawdry things and not worth possessing. She was bent upon only one thing: to reject life and to die.

CHORUS: She is a mere child, Creon.

CREON: What do you want me to do for her? Condemn her to live?

HAEMON (*calls from offstage*): Father! (*Haemon enters through arch, right. Creon turns toward him.*)

CREON: Haemon, forget Antigone. Forget her, my dearest boy.

HAEMON: How can you talk like that?

CREON (*grasps Haemon by the hands*): I did everything I could to save her, Haemon. I used every argument. I swear I did. The girl doesn't love you. She could have gone on living for you; but she refused. She wanted it this way; she wanted to die.

HAEMON: Father! The guards are dragging Antigone away! You've got to stop them! (*He breaks away from Creon.*)

CREON (*looks away from Haemon*): I can't stop them. It's too late. Antigone has spoken. The story is all over Thebes. I cannot save her now.

CHORUS: Creon, you must find a way. Lock her up. Say that she has gone out of her mind.

CREON: Everybody will know it isn't so. The nation will say that I am making an exception of her because my son loves her. I cannot.

exeunt: Latin for "they go out."

CHORUS: You can still gain time and get her out of Thebes.

CREON: The mob already knows the truth. It is howling for her blood. I can do nothing.

HAEMON: But, Father, you are master in Thebes!

CREON: I am master under the law. Not above the law.

HAEMON: You cannot let Antigone be taken from me. I am your son!

CREON: I cannot do anything else, my poor boy. She must die and you must live.

HAEMON: Live, you say! Live a life without Antigone? A life in which I am to go on admiring you as you busy yourself about your kingdom, make your persuasive speeches, strike your attitudes? Not without Antigone. I love Antigone. I will not live without Antigone!

CREON: Haemon — you will have to resign yourself to life without Antigone. (*He moves to left of Haemon.*) Sooner or later there comes a day of sorrow in each man's life when he must cease to be a child and take up the burden of manhood. That day has come for you.

HAEMON (*backs away a step*): That giant strength, that courage. That massive god who used to pick me up in his arms and shelter me from shadows and monsters — was that you, Father? Was it of you I stood in awe? Was that man you?

CREON: For God's sake, Haemon, do not judge me! Not you, too!

HAEMON (*pleading now*): This is all a bad dream, Father. You are not yourself. It isn't true that we have been backed up against a wall, forced to surrender. We don't have to say *yes* to this terrible thing. You are still king. You are still the father I revered. You have no right to desert me, to shrink into nothingness. The world will be too bare, I shall be too alone in the world, if you force me to disown you.

CREON: The world *is* bare, Haemon, and you *are* alone. You must cease to think your father all-powerful. Look straight at me. See your father as he is. That is what it means to grow up and be a man.

HAEMON (*stares at Creon for a moment*): I tell you that I will not live without Antigone. (*Turns and goes quickly out through arch.*)

CHORUS: Creon, the boy will go mad.

CREON: Poor boy! He loves her.

CHORUS: Creon, the boy is wounded to death.

CREON: We are all wounded to death.

(*First Guard enters through arch, right, followed by Second and Third Guards pulling Antigone along with them.*)

FIRST GUARD: Sir, the people are crowding into the palace!

ANTIGONE: Creon, I don't want to see their faces. I don't want to hear them howl. You are going to kill me; let that be enough. I want to be alone until it is over.

CREON: Empty the palace! Guards at the gates!

(*Creon quickly crosses toward the arch; exit. Two Guards release Antigone; exeunt behind Creon. Chorus goes out through arch, left. The lighting dims so that only the area about the table is lighted. The cyclorama° is covered with a dark blue color. The scene is intended to suggest a prison cell, filled with shadows and dimly lit. Antigone moves to stool and sits. The First Guard stands upstage. He watches Antigone, and as she sits, he begins pacing slowly downstage, then upstage. A pause.*)

ANTIGONE (*turns and looks at the Guard*): It's you, is it?

---

cyclorama: Curved cloth or wall forming the back of many modern stage settings.

GUARD: What do you mean, me?

ANTIGONE: The last human face that I shall see. (*A pause as they look at each other, then Guard paces upstage, turns, and crosses behind table.*) Was it you that arrested me this morning?

GUARD: Yes, that was me.

ANTIGONE: You hurt me. There was no need for you to hurt me. Did I act as if I was trying to escape?

GUARD: Come on now, Miss. It was my business to bring you in. I did it. (*A pause. He paces to and fro upstage. Only the sound of his boots is heard.*)

ANTIGONE: How old are you?

GUARD: Thirty-nine.

ANTIGONE: Have you any children?

GUARD: Yes. Two.

ANTIGONE: Do you love your children?

GUARD: What's that got to do with you? (*A pause. He paces upstage and downstage.*)

ANTIGONE: How long have you been in the Guard?

GUARD: Since the war. I was in the army. Sergeant. Then I joined the Guard.

ANTIGONE: Does one have to have been an army sergeant to get into the Guard?

GUARD: Supposed to be. Either that or on special detail. But when they make you a guard, you lose your stripes.

ANTIGONE (*murmurs*): I see.

GUARD: Yes. Of course, if you're a guard, everybody knows you're something special; they know you're an old N.C.O.° Take pay, for instance. When you're a guard you get your pay, and on top of that you get six months' extra pay, to make sure you don't lose anything by not being a sergeant anymore. And of course you do better than that. You get a house, coal, rations, extras for the wife and kids. If you've got two kids, like me, you draw better than a sergeant.

ANTIGONE (*barely audible*): I see.

GUARD: That's why sergeants, now, they don't like guards. Maybe you noticed they try to make out they're better than us? Promotion, that's what it is. In the army, anybody can get promoted. All you need is good conduct. Now in the Guard, it's slow, and you have to know your business — like how to make out a report and the like of that. But when you're an N.C.O. in the Guard, you've got something that even a sergeant major ain't got. For instance —

ANTIGONE (*breaking him off*): Listen.

GUARD: Yes, Miss.

ANTIGONE: I'm going to die soon.

(*The Guard looks at her for a moment, then turns and moves away.*)

GUARD: For instance, people have a lot of respect for guards, they have. A guard may be a soldier, but he's kind of in the civil service, too.

ANTIGONE: Do you think it hurts to die?

GUARD: How would I know? Of course, if somebody sticks a saber in your guts and turns it round, it hurts.

ANTIGONE: How are they going to put me to death?

GUARD: Well, I'll tell you. I heard the proclamation all right. Wait a minute. How did it go now? (*He stares into space and recites from memory.*) "In order that our fair city shall not be pol-luted with her sinful blood, she shall be

---

N.C.O.: Noncommissioned officer, usually of a subordinate rank such as sergeant.

im-mured — immured." That means, they shove you in a cave and wall up the cave.

ANTIGONE: Alive?

GUARD: Yes. . . . (*He moves away a few steps.*)

ANTIGONE (*murmurs*): O tomb! O bridal bed! Alone! (*Antigone sits there, a tiny figure in the middle of the stage. You would say she felt a little chilly. She wraps her arms round herself.*)

GUARD: Yes! Outside the southeast gate of the town. In the Cave of Hades. In broad daylight. Some detail, eh, for them that's on the job! First they thought maybe it was a job for the army. Now it looks like it's going to be the Guard. There's an outfit for you! Nothing the Guard can't do. No wonder the army's jealous.

ANTIGONE: A pair of animals.

GUARD: What do you mean, a pair of animals?

ANTIGONE: When the winds blow cold, all they need do is to press close against one another. I am all alone.

GUARD: Is there anything you want? I can send out for it, you know.

ANTIGONE: You are very kind. (*A pause. Antigone looks up at the Guard.*) Yes, there is something I want. I want you to give someone a letter from me, when I am dead.

GUARD: How's that again? A letter?

ANTIGONE: Yes, I want to write a letter; and I want you to give it to someone for me.

GUARD (*straightens up*): Now, wait a minute. Take it easy. It's as much as my job is worth to go handing out letters from prisoners.

ANTIGONE (*removes a ring from her finger and holds it out toward him*): I'll give you this ring if you will do it.

GUARD: Is it gold? (*He takes the ring from her.*)

ANTIGONE: Yes, it is gold.

GUARD (*shakes his head*): Uh-uh. No can do. Suppose they go through my pockets. I might get six months for a thing like that. (*He stares at the ring, then glances off right to make sure that he is not being watched.*) Listen, tell you what I'll do. You tell me what you want to say, and I'll write it down in my book. Then, afterwards, I'll tear out the pages and give them to the party, see? If it's in my handwriting, it's all right.

ANTIGONE (*winces*): In your handwriting? (*She shudders slightly.*) No. That would be awful. The poor darling! In your handwriting.

GUARD (*offers back the ring*): O.K. It's no skin off my nose.

ANTIGONE (*quickly*): Of course, of course. No, keep the ring. But hurry. Time is getting short. Where is your notebook? (*The Guard pockets the ring, takes his notebook and pencil from his pocket, puts his foot up on chair, and rests the notebook on his knee, licks his pencil.*) Ready? (*He nods.*) Write, now. "My darling . . ."

GUARD (*writes as he mutters*): The boyfriend, eh?

ANTIGONE: "My darling. I wanted to die, and perhaps you will not love me anymore . . ."

GUARD (*mutters as he writes*): " . . . will not love me anymore."

ANTIGONE: "Creon was right. It is terrible to die."

GUARD (*repeats as he writes*): " . . . terrible to die."

ANTIGONE: "And I don't even know what I am dying for. I am afraid . . ."

GUARD (*looks at her*): Wait a minute! How fast do you think I can write?

ANTIGONE (*takes hold of herself*): Where are you?

GUARD (*reads from his notebook*): "And I don't even know what I am dying for."

ANTIGONE: No. Scratch that out. Nobody must know that. They have no right to know. It's as if they saw me naked and touched me, after I was dead. Scratch it all out. Just write: "Forgive me."

GUARD (*looks at Antigone*): I cut out everything you said there at the end, and I put down, "Forgive me"?

ANTIGONE: Yes. "Forgive me, my darling. You would all have been so happy except for Antigone. I love you."

GUARD (*finishes the letter*): " . . . I love you." (*He looks at her.*) Is that all?

ANTIGONE: That's all.

GUARD (*straightens up, looks at notebook*): Damn funny letter.

ANTIGONE: I know.

GUARD (*looks at her*): Who is it to? (*A sudden roll of drums begins and continues until after Antigone's exit. The First Guard pockets the notebook and shouts at Antigone.*) O.K. That's enough out of you! Come on!

(*At the sound of the drum roll, Second and Third Guards enter through the arch. Antigone rises. Guards seize her and exeunt with her. The lighting moves up to suggest late afternoon. Chorus enters.*)

CHORUS: And now it is Creon's turn.

(*Messenger runs through the arch, right.*)

MESSENGER: The Queen . . . the Queen! Where is the Queen?

CHORUS: What do you want with the Queen? What have you to tell the Queen?

MESSENGER: News to break her heart. Antigone had just been thrust into the cave. They hadn't finished heaving the last block of stone into place when Creon and the rest heard a sudden moaning from the tomb. A hush fell over us all, for it was not the voice of Antigone. It was Haemon's voice that came forth from the tomb. Everybody looked at Creon; and he howled like a man demented: "Take away the stones! Take away the stones!" The slaves leaped at the wall of stones, and Creon worked with them, sweating and tearing at the blocks with his bleeding hands. Finally a narrow opening was forced, and into it slipped the smallest guard.

Antigone had hanged herself by the cord of her robe, by the red and golden twisted cord of her robe. The cord was round her neck like a child's collar. Haemon was on his knees, holding her in his arms and moaning, his face buried in her robe. More stones were removed, and Creon went into the tomb. He tried to raise Haemon to his feet. I could hear him begging Haemon to rise to his feet. Haemon was deaf to his father's voice, till suddenly he stood up of his own accord, his eyes dark and burning. Anguish was in his face, but it was the face of a little boy. He stared at his father. Then suddenly he struck him — hard; and he drew his sword. Creon leaped out of range. Haemon went on staring at him, his eyes full of contempt — a glance that was like a knife, and that Creon couldn't escape. The King stood trembling in the far corner of the tomb, and Haemon went on staring. Then, without a word, he stabbed himself and lay down beside Antigone, embracing her in a great pool of blood.

(*A pause as Creon and Page enter through arch on the Messenger's last words. Chorus and the Messenger both turn to look at Creon; then exit the Messenger through curtain.*)

CREON: I have had them laid out side by side. They are together at last, and at peace. Two lovers on the morrow of their bridal. Their work is done.

CHORUS: But not yours, Creon. You have still one thing to learn. Eurydice, the Queen, your wife —

CREON: A good woman. Always busy with her garden, her preserves, her sweaters — those sweaters she never stopped knitting for the poor. Strange, how the poor never stop needing sweaters. One would almost think that was all they needed.

CHORUS: The poor in Thebes are going to be cold this winter, Creon. When the Queen was told of her son's death, she waited carefully until she had finished her row, then put down her knitting calmly — as she did everything. She went up to her room, her lavender-scented room, with its embroidered doilies and its pictures framed in plush; and there, Creon, she cut her throat. She is laid out now in one of those two old-fashioned twin beds, exactly where you went to her one night when she was still a maiden. Her smile is still the same, scarcely a shade more melancholy. And if it were not for that great red blot on the bed linen by her neck, one might think she was asleep.

CREON (*in a dull voice*): She, too. They are all asleep. (*Pause.*) It must be good to sleep.

CHORUS: And now you are alone, Creon.

CREON: Yes, all alone. (*To Page.*) My lad.

PAGE: Sir?

CREON: Listen to me. They don't know it, but the truth is, the work is there to be done, and a man can't fold his arms and refuse to do it. They say it's dirty work. But if we didn't do it, who would?

PAGE: I don't know, sir.

CREON: Of course you don't. You'll be lucky if you never find out. In a hurry to grow up, aren't you?

PAGE: Oh, yes, sir.

CREON: I shouldn't be if I were you. Never grow up if you can help it. (*He is lost in thought as the hour chimes.*) What time is it?

PAGE: Five o clock, sir.

CREON: What have we on at five o'clock?

PAGE: Cabinet meeting, sir.

CREON: Cabinet meeting. Then we had better go along to it.

(*Exeunt Creon and Page slowly through arch, left, and Chorus moves downstage.*)

CHORUS: And there we are. It is quite true that if it had not been for Antigone they would all have been at peace. But that is over now. And they are all at peace. All those who were meant to die have died: those who believed one thing, those who believed the contrary thing, and even those who believed nothing at all, yet were caught up in the web without knowing why. All dead: stiff, useless, rotting. And those who have survived will now begin quietly to forget the dead: they won't remember who was who or which was which. It is all over. Antigone is calm tonight, and we shall never know the name of the fever that consumed her. She has played her part.

(*Three Guards enter, resume their places on steps as at the rise of the curtain, and begin to play cards.*)

A great melancholy wave of peace now settles down upon Thebes, upon the empty palace, upon Creon, who can now begin to wait for his own death. Only the guards are left, and none of this matters to them. It's no skin off their noses. They go on playing cards.

(*Chorus walks toward the arch, left, as the curtain falls.*)

Euripides

Euripides (c. 485–c. 406 B.C.), last of the great Greek tragedians, did not enjoy the personal popularity accorded Aeschylus and Sophocles, possibly because his work criticized Athenian politics and society. Moreover, he was not highly regarded because he broke away from the formality of language and theme of his predecessors.

Euripides was raised in Salamis, the island from which the Greeks decisively defeated the Persians in 480 B.C. This victory heralded the Periclean Age (c. 460–404 B.C.), when Athens enjoyed its greatest power. During that time, however, the Athenians spent almost three decades fighting the Peloponnesian Wars (431–404 B.C.), which drained their energies and treasury. Eventually, they were forced to relinquish their dominance to Sparta. In such an environment, the officials and patriots of Athens were not happy with the work of someone who reminded them of their mistakes and questioned their values.

Euripides is especially noted for shifting the focus of dramatic events from the gods to humans. He values individual human beings and the working of their wills. Influenced by the teaching of the Sophists, wandering professors who taught argument and philosophy, he agreed with Protagoras's principle "Man is the measure of all things." The ancients sometimes referred to Euripides as the philosopher of the stage.

One aspect of his dramatic critique of Greek culture was an unusual emphasis on women. Medea is the first thoroughly developed female character in Greek drama. She is treated as an independent woman, not as Jason's wife or as someone's mother. She is herself. Athenians, intolerant of foreigners and women, felt both groups to be inferior to Greek aristocratic men. It is no wonder that of the twenty plays Euripides produced at the feasts of Dionysus only five won prizes.

Of his ninety-two plays, eighteen survive — more than twice as many as survive from any other Greek tragedian: *Alcestis* (438), *Medea* (431), *Hippolytus* (428), *Andromache* (426?), *Cyclops* (c. 423), *The Children of Heracles* (c. 430), *Heracles* (c. 417), *The Suppliants* (c. 422), *Hecuba* (c. 424), *The Trojan Women* (415), *Electra* (c. 417), *Iphigenia in Taurus* (c. 412), *Helen* (412), *Ion* (c. 411), *The Phoenician Women* (c. 412–408), *Orestes* (408), *The Bacchae* (405), and *Iphigenia in Aulis* (405). Another play, *Rhesus,* long attributed to Euripides, is now thought to have been written by an anonymous fourth-century B.C. playwright. Ten of Euripides' remaining plays place women at their center.

Euripides continued Aeschylus's innovations in his use of the *skene.* Instead of representing the front of a palace, the *skene* in Euripides' plays sometimes represented a peasant's hut, a rural shrine, or other common structure. He was interested in theatrical devices, especially machines that gave him the opportunity to achieve dramatic effects. He often used the *mekane* — a crane or derrick that lifted actors in or out of the play — to resolve his dramas when his characters found themselves in impossible situations. His choral odes, although beautiful, are sometimes considered detachable from the episodes of dramatic action. Moreover, his dialogue is more colloquial — closer to everyday speech — than is the dialogue found in other Greek tragedies. All these deviations from the dramatic norm emphasize the humanity in his plays and elevate human values over those of the gods.

Eighteen months before his death, Euripides left Athens for the court of King Archelaus in Macedon. His departure may have signaled his dissatisfaction with the politics of Athens, or it may have been prompted by the indifference of Athens to his talents. In any event, his works were performed long after his death and, ironically, his posthumous popularity dwarfed that of the other tragic playwrights.

MEDEA

Although *Medea* won only last prize at the City Dionysia festival in 431 B.C., behind works by Euphorion, son of Aeschylus, and Sophocles, the play's emotional dimension and Medea's depth of feeling have made her one of the most impressive characters in dramatic fiction.

In his first play, *The Daughters of Pelias* (454 B.C.), Euripides treated part of the well-known legend of Jason and Medea. On the order of his enemy, King Pelias of Iolcus, Jason sailed with the Argonauts to Colchis. There, with the help of Medea's witchcraft, he retrieved the Golden Fleece. Medea returned with Jason to Iolcus, where she convinced Pelias's daughters that they could restore their father's youth if they cut him into pieces and boiled the pieces with magic herbs, as she had done with a ram. When the daughters tried it, however, the treacherous Medea gave them impotent herbs and Pelias died. Jason's Argonauts captured Iolcus, and Medea and Jason escaped to Corinth.

Euripides continued the tale in *Medea*. When the play opens, Jason and Medea are in exile in Corinth. Jason has decided to marry King Creon's daughter Glauke, supposedly to guarantee the safety of the children he has had with Medea. Considering all the sacrifices she has made for Jason, Medea feels betrayed and cast aside for a younger woman.

Medea's situation is painful. The Chorus recognizes the legality of Jason's decision to put aside his wife in favor of a younger woman. His motives might be interpreted as plausible and perhaps noble. Medea is Asiatic, a foreigner. By marrying Glauke, Jason will impart noble status on his and Medea's children. By law he can maintain Medea as a concubine along with his wife. Medea knows this, but she rejects Jason's explanations. He assumes that she is merely sexually jealous of Glauke.

The themes of this tragedy are certainly accessible to modern audiences. As the critic G.M.A. Grube has pointed out, "The tragedy of *Medea* — of Love turning to hatred when betrayed, until the woman's whole soul is dominated by a lust for vengeance that overpowers even maternal love — is one which no modern reader should, in its essentials, find difficult to make his own." The modern audience, however, may take pause at Medea's revenge. She plans not only to rid Jason of his young bride but to kill Creon as well. And her vengeance does not stop there: She determines to kill those whom Jason most loves — their two sons.

Exploring Medea's feelings and her awareness of the gravity of her actions sets Euripides' work apart from that of other Greek tragedians. His sympathy for the many tragic heroines he created marks his work from beginning to end. Unlike other playwrights working with the Medea legend, Euripides saves Medea from the punishment of Jason and the people of Corinth. To do this, he uses the *mekane,* in the form of the dragon chariot that lifts her above the *skene* beyond Jason's reach at the end of the play. She leaves him in an agony of grief.

Medea in Performance

Medea has one of the longest and most active production histories in all of drama. Not only did Alexander the Great produce the play in the fourth century, but the Roman playwright Seneca wrote his own version (A.D. 60), with a much less sympathetic Medea. Seneca's Jason is a reasonable man unfairly wronged by a witch. French and English productions and adaptations began in 1553 and have continued to the present. The French playwright Corneille wrote his version in 1634, and an English version of 1756 portrays Medea as insane.

Important modern productions began early in this century. The American actress Margaret Anglin was a sensation in the 1918 production, which established her as the greatest Medea up to her time. Hans Henny Jahnne adapted *Medea* for a production in Berlin in 1926. According to a review written at the time, Medea was portrayed by an older black actress whose magic potions kept Jason young while she aged. The poisoned robe Medea gave to her young rival had the power to turn the princess into an elderly woman "who gradually [grew] older and older and [decayed] into death and decomposition."

Judith Anderson made the role hers in 1947, in a version by the American poet Robinson Jeffers that played for almost a decade. In the

1982 production with John Gielgud as Jason and Zoë Caldwell as Medea, a much older Judith Anderson played the nurse and received extraordinary reviews. In 1974 Greek actress Irene Papas starred in New York in a colloquial English version. Important productions were staged in Russia in the 1960s. Countee Cullen very successfully produced the play in 1959 with a black Medea. In 1986, an all-male Kabuki version of *Medea* was presented at the Delacorte Theater in Central Park by the Japanese Toho Company under the direction of Yukio Ninagawa. A critic from the *New York Times* described the director's intentions: "Yukio Ninagawa, known for his productions of classical theater as avant-garde spectacle, aims in his work to create a universal theater that fuses the traditions of Japanese and Western culture in an expressive style of its own" (Jennifer Dunning, *New York Times,* Aug. 31, 1986). A *Boston Globe* critic praised the power of the Kabuki production: "This was a Medea of stunning theatrical imagery. Classical Corinthian order was gradually and relentlessly replaced by savage revenge and blood-stained chaos" (Lyn Gardner, *Boston Globe,* Aug. 29, 1986). In April 1994 Diana Rigg was Medea in a production highly praised in both London and New York. She was seen as commanding and powerful in the part, played starkly and simply.

Euripides (c. 485–406 B.C.)

MEDEA   431 B.C.

TRANSLATED BY PAUL ROCHE

Characters

NURSE
TUTOR *to Medea's sons*
MEDEA, *Asiatic princess*
CHORUS *of Corinthian women*
CREON, *King of Corinth*
JASON, *husband of Medea*
AEGEUS, *King of Athens*
MESSENGER
TWO BOYS, *sons of Medea*
HANDMAIDS *of Medea*
ATTENDANTS AND GUARDS *for Creon and Aegeus*

Time and Setting: *It is midmorning outside Jason's house in Corinth. Ten years have passed since the*

Argonauts sailed home after finding the Golden Fleece. During that time, Jason and Medea [the Asian bride he brought back with him] have been living modestly in Corinth: models of an unassailable married life of devotion to each other and their children. But the news has just broken that Jason is to marry the daughter of the King of Corinth. [The exit on stage left leads to the town and royal palace, that on the right to the country.]

[Enter the Nurse from the house. She is an old woman who has looked after Medea from babyhood. Her face, the only part of her showing from the dark, heavy clothes that envelop her, is puckered with age and distress.]

PROLOGUE°

NURSE: Why did the winged oars of the Argo°
  ever weave between those gnashing blue
  fjords towards the land of Colchis?
   Why did the pines in the dells of Pelion°
5 ever fall to the axe and fill
  the rowing hands of heroes sent by Pelias°
  to fetch the Golden Fleece?
   My mistress, Medea, then
  never would have sailed to Iolcus° with its
    towers
10 or been struck to the heart with love of Jason.
   She never would have baited Pelias' daughters
  to the murder of their father°
  and be living here in Corinth° now
  with her husband and her children . . .
15 Ah, she has merited this city's good opinion,
  exile though she came,
  and was in everything Jason's perfect foil,
  being in marriage that saving thing:
  a wife who does not go against her man.

[*With a despairing glance toward the house.*]

20 Now everything has turned to hate,
  her passion to a plague.
   Jason has betrayed his sons and her,
  takes to bed a royal bride
  Creon's daughter — the king of Corinth's.
25 Medea, spurned and desolate,
  breaks out in oaths,
  invokes the solemnest vows,
  calls the gods to witness
  how Jason has rewarded her.
30 She does not eat,

lies prostrate, slumped in anguish,
wastes away in day-long tears.
  Ever since she heard of Jason's perfidy
she has not raised her eyes
or looked up from the floor.   35
  She might be a rock or wave of the sea,
for all she heeds of sympathy from friends,
except sometimes to tilt her pale head away
and moan to herself about her father —
whom she loved —   40
and her country and the home she sacrificed°
to journey here
with a man — oh — who so disdains her now.
  Yes, now she knows
at a terrible first hand   45
what it is to miss one's native land.

[*She pauses; almost whispers the next words.*]

  She hates her sons.
  Takes no pleasure in their sight.
  I dread to think
of what is hatching in her mind.   50
  She is a fierce spirit:
takes no insult lying down.
  I know her well. She frightens me:°
a dangerous woman, and
anyone who crosses her   55
will not easily sing a song of triumph.
  But here come the boys after their run:
suspecting nothing of a mother's tragedy . . .
  Oh, it is true —
unhappy thoughts and youth never go together. 60

[*Enter Tutor with Two Boys, aged about eight and
ten. Tutor is an old man, dressed loosely in an ocher-
colored cloak. The boys are squeezed into shorts and
have close-fitting woolen caps on their heads. They
hang about in the background, laughing and talking,
while the old man advances.*]

TUTOR [*with a half-teasing familiarity*]: Ah, Nurse!
  Faithful old appendage of my Lady's home,
  what are you doing here all forlorn,
  standing moaning to yourself outside the gates?
  Does Medea really want to be left alone? 65
NURSE: Ah, dogged old pedagogue of Jason's sons,

[**Prologue:** Portion of the play explaining the background
and current action. (The editor's notes are in brackets.)]
1. Argo: The ship in which Jason and his companions sailed
on the quest for the Golden Fleece. **4. Pelion:** A mountain
in northern Greece. **6. Pelias:** When Jason came to claim
the kingdom of Iolcus, from which Pelias had expelled
Jason's father, Pelias sent Jason to get the Golden Fleece.
9. Iolcus: Town from which the Argonauts sailed.
11–12. She never . . . murder of their father: Medea, a sor-
ceress by reputation, tricked Pelias's daughters into cutting
their father into pieces and boiling them, on the pretext that
this would magically restore him to youth. This was her revenge on Pelias, who had murdered Jason's father, Aeson,
during Jason's absence on the quest for the Golden Fleece,
was successful. **13. be living here in Corinth:** Expelled
from the kingdom [of Iolcus], Jason and Medea took refuge
in Corinth, a wealthy city and rival of Athens, located on the
isthmus between the Peloponnese and Attica.

41. home she sacrificed: Medea had helped Jason take the
Golden Fleece away from her own father's kingdom.
53. She frightens me: [The translator notes that he has omitted four lines bracketed by many editors as doubtful (lines
40–43 in the original Greek text).] Dramatically, they are
certainly a mistake: *"I am frightened she will slip / into the
palace unawares, / and in the nuptial bedroom / ram a sharp
knife into Jason's side, / or even kill the King as well as
bridegroom / and get herself a far worse doom."*

when a master's fortunes are struck down
the heart of a faithful slave is stricken too.
    I am plunged in such a depth of grief
70 I came out here to tell the earth and sky
    Medea's catastrophe.
TUTOR: What! Has the poor woman not stopped
        her crying yet?
NURSE: Stopped! You amaze me.
    Her ordeal, far from halfway done,
75   hardly has begun.
TUTOR: Poor innocent fool — to be quite frank
        about our mistress —
    she knows little of the latest blow.
NURSE: Latest? What's that, old man?
    Don't keep it from me.
TUTOR: Nothing, nothing . . . I'm sorry I even
80   spoke.
NURSE: Come now, we're both slaves here, are we
        not?
    By your own gray beard, do not hold it back . . .
    I can keep a secret if I must.
TUTOR: Well, I'd gone to where the old dice-players
        sit,
85 near Pirene's sacred fountain,
    and there I overheard (pretending not to listen)
    someone say:
        "Creon, this country's king,
    is making plans to drive these boys from
        Corinth —
90   their mother too" —
    I don't know if the story's true.
    I hope that it is not.
NURSE: No, surely no?
    Jason would not let his sons be treated so,
95 however far he's parted from their mother.
TUTOR [grimly]: Old loves are left behind by new.
    That man is not this house's friend.
NURSE: We're all finished, then —
    if we ship this second wave
100   before we've bailed the first.
TUTOR: Now listen —
    this is not the time to let our mistress know.
    Just keep quiet about it — not a word.
NURSE [with an anguished glance over her shoulder,
    in a whisper]: Poor little boys,
    do you hear how much your father's worth to
105   you?
    I wish he were . . .

[Checks herself.]

    no, not dead, he is my master still . . .
    but, oh, what an enemy he's proved
    to those he should have loved!
110 TUTOR: What human being is not?
    Is this news to you,

that every person's dearest neighbor is himself:
some rightly so, some out of greed and selfishness.
    This father does not love his sons, but —
    his new wedding bed.   115
NURSE: Come along, boys, into the house.
    Everything is going to be all right.

[Dropping her voice.]

    Keep them away as much as you can.
    Do not let them near their mother
    so long as she is in this deadly mood.   120
    Already I have caught her eyes on them:
    the eyes of a mad bull.
    There's something she is plotting
    and her fury won't lie down — this I know —
    until the lightning strikes and someone's felled.   125
    Let us hope it's enemies, not friends.

[A long-drawn-out sob — Medea's — is heard from
the house.]°

MEDEA: I am so unhappy — oh!
    the misery of it! I wish I were dead.
NURSE [hustling the children toward the door]:
    Listen — there . . . poor children, your mother,
    Raking her heart up, raking her rage.   130
    Quick, inside: into the house.
    Don't come anywhere near her sight.
    Don't approach. Beware, watch out
    For her savage mood, destructive spleen:
    Yes and her implacable will.   135
    Off with you now; hurry inside.
    Soon, I know, her fury will flare
    Out from the slowly gathering cloud.
    What will she perpetrate then, I fear —
    Proud, importunate willful soul —   140
        So bitterly spurned.

                                        [Exeunt° Tutor and Boys.]

[A long-suppressed shout is heard from inside:
Medea's voice.]

MEDEA: Oh, what misery! Oh, what pain!
    Cursed sons, and a mother for cursing!
    Death take you all — you and your father:
        The whole house wither.   145
NURSE [sobbing]: Oh, how it grieves me!
    Why make the sons
        share in their father's
    Guilt? Oh, why
        should they be hated?   150

126. The next 116 lines in the Greek [to the end of the
Parodos] are cast in a different meter, which [the trans-
lator] transposed into the nearest English equivalent.
[141. (S.D.) Exeunt: Latin for "they go out."]

Poor young children, your danger appals me.
Ruthless is the temper of royalty:
Often commanding, seldom commanded;
Terribly slow to forgive and forget.
155   How much better to live among equals.
I want no part of greatness and glory:
Let me decline in a safe old age.
The very name of the "middle way"
Has health in it: is best for man.
160   Good never comes from overreaching,
And when it provokes the gods, it destroys
All the more thoroughly.

PARODOS OR ENTRY SONG

[*The Chorus of Corinthian women enters, full of ap-prehension and concern for Medea.*]

CHORUS: I heard her voice, I heard her shout,
It was the most unhappy
Woman from Colchis — far from calm yet —
But tell me, old Nurse.
5   From the porch of the house, it moaned outside.
O women, I cannot delight
In the pain of Jason's house:
A house I have loved very well.
NURSE: House there is none: life of it gone.
10   The master is had . . . by a princess's bed.
The mistress in her boudoir pines.
There are no words her friends can find
To touch her disconsolate heart.
MEDEA [*in another spasm*]: Ahhh!
15   Cleave my brain with a flash from the sky.
What good is left for me in living?
Alas! Alas! Come Death, unloose
My life from a life I loathe.

[*Strophe*]°

CHORUS: Listen, O Zeus and Earth and Light
20   To the stricken tune of this plangent° wife.
And you, loveless lady,
What yearning for love on a bed of delight
Could make you hurry to death, the night?
        Pray not for that.
25   If your husband has gone to adore
A new bride in his bed, why, this
Has often happened before.

[*Strophe*: Song sung by the Chorus as they danced from stage right to stage left.]   **20. plangent**: Lamenting.

Do not harrow your soul. For Zeus
Will succor your cause. What use
To lessen your life with grief   30
For a lost lord?
MEDEA [*from inside*]: O mighty Themis,° and
        Artemis, Queen,°
For all the fine vows I bound him with,
See what my hated husband has done.
Grant me to watch him, at last, with his bride,   35
Palace and all, crumble in ruin.
How dare they do to me what they have done!
O Father, my country, the land I abandoned,
Flagrantly killing my brother.°
NURSE: Hear what she says   40
        with her cry from the heart
To Themis and Zeus:
        (goddess of rights
And he whom mankind
        makes keeper of vows.)   45
Certainly soon
        in no small way
Her fury will play itself out.

[*Antistrophe*]°

CHORUS: If she would come out and, face to face,
        Listen to what we have to say,   50
        She might let go
This rampant anger, spite of soul.
I hope I never fail my friends.
So go, Nurse, entice her to come:
Say we are *with* her: we are her friends.   55
Hurry, before she does any harm
        To those inside . . .
Grief can swell to enormity.
NURSE [*walking to the door*]: I'll do my best, but
        am afraid I   60
May *not* be able to persuade
        My Lady; and yet
I am glad to shoulder the burden;
Although she glares with a bull-mad gaze
(Or is it a lioness with her whelps)
When anyone comes or speaks or helps.   65

[*She turns at the door.*]

32. Themis: Justice.   **Artemis**: Guardian of women. Called Diana by the Romans.   **39. killing my brother**: Medea slew her brother Absyrtus when she escaped with Jason and tossed him piecemeal over the side of the ship, knowing that their pursuers would stop to pick the pieces up.   [**Antistrophe**: Song sung by the Chorus following the Strophe, as they danced back from stage left to stage right.]

Oh, botchers and blunderers! Yes,
That's what they were, those artists of old:
Makers of music for life and joy,
For grand celebrations and groaning boards;
70 But, oh, nothing for sorrow and pain:
No music or song on hand-plucked lyre
    For the thing that brings death
And terrible endings to many a home.

    Oh, what a blessing is missed
75   by having no music for this!
What a waste of it, then
    by singing in vain,
When fullness at feasts
    is its own joy and gain.
        [*Exit Nurse into the house.*]
80 CHORUS: Deep is her sobbing from depths of pain:
Shrill the news her suffering brings
Of marriage betrayed, a love gone wrong.
    Outraged, she
        importunate prays
85 To Themis, the daughter of Zeus:
Keeper of vows, who sailed her through
    Those dangerous straits and the night
To Hellas° across the salt of the sea.

FIRST EPISODE

[*Medea enters from the house, colorfully, even opu-
lently, dressed. She is wan and her eyes are red with
weeping, but she is surprisingly calm and in control.*]

MEDEA: Women of Corinth, be indulgent, please:
I have obeyed you and come out.
    The charge of aloofness — as I know too
        well —
is something often leveled
5 at both the retiring and the busy man.
    He who chooses a quiet life
has this alleged against him too:
laziness and lack of spirit.
    Yes, public opinion has most shallow eyes.
10   People hate at sight
a harmless human being,
knowing nothing of the real man.
    I agree, of course,
that a foreigner should conform,
15 adapt to his society . . .
and a citizen is censurable no less
when too self-centered or uncouth

88. Hellas: Greece.

to avoid offending his companions.
    Nevertheless, I . . .

[*She breaks off with a pang.*]

    I . . . out of a clear sky   20
have been struck a blow that breaks my heart.
    My friends, it is over.
    I want to die.
Life has lost all point.
The man who was my life   25
— and he knows it too —
has become for me beneath contempt.

[*She surveys the women.*]

    Of all the creatures that can feel and think,
we women are the worst-treated things alive.
    To begin with,   30
we bid the highest price in dowries
just to buy some man
to be dictator of our bodies . . .
    How that compounds the wrong!
Then there is the terrifying risk: 35
Shall we get a good man or a bad?
    Divorce is a disgrace
(at least for women),
to repudiate the man, not possible.
    So, plunged into habits new to her,   40
conventions she has never known at home,
she has to guess like some clairvoyant
how to handle the man who shares her bed.
    And if we learn our lesson well
in this exacting role,   45
and our husband does not kick against the
        marriage yoke,
oh, ours is an enviable life!
    Otherwise, we are better dead.
    When a man gets bored with wife and home,
he simply roams abroad,   50
relieves the tedium of his spirit:
turns to a friend or finds his cronies.
    We women, on the other hand,
turn only to a single man.
    We live safe at home, they say.   55
They do battle with the spear.
    How superficial!
I had rather stand my ground three times among
        the shields
than face a childbirth once.
    Anyway,   60
your case and mine are not the same.
    You have your city.
    You have your father's home.
Life offers you the sweet fellowship of
        friends.
    I am alone,   65

without a city, wronged by a husband,
uprooted from a foreign land.
　　I have no mother, brother, cousin;
am without a haven from this storm.
70　　　So, please, I ask you this:
if I can find a way to pay my husband back —
your silence.
　　Woman, on the whole, is a timid thing:
the din of war, the flash of steel, unnerves her;
75　but, wronged in love,
there is no heart more murderous.
LEADER: As you wish, Medea.
　　You have a score to settle with your lord.
　　I do not wonder that you smart . . .
80　　　But, look, I see Creon coming:
this country's king —
bristling, I dare say, with new decisions.

[*Enter Creon with attendants. He is a bearded man of
about sixty, royally but modestly dressed. His face
wears a look of troubled resolution.*]

CREON: Go, Medea. Remove yourself.
　　Get packing from this land.
85　　　I order you —
you with your black-faced fury
lowering against your lord.
　　And take your brace of offspring with you;
no dallying either.
90　　　I am here to see this order done,
and until I've pushed you out and over the
　　　border,
I'll not go home.
MEDEA: So.
　　I am lost — crushed utterly.
95　　My enemies let out the sail,
while I have no place to disembark from doom.
　　Nevertheless, hard-pressed as I am,
I ask you this:
　　For what reason, Creon, do you drive me
　　　out?
100 CREON: Fear:
no need to camouflage the fact;
I am afraid you'll deal my child some lethal
　　　blow . . .
and many things conspire to make me fear.
　　You are a woman of some knowledge,
105 versed in many an unsavory skill.
　　Your husband's gone:
your soul is raw with loss of love . . .
and now it is reported that you threaten me;
mean to hurt the father of the bride
110 and of course the bride and groom.
　　That is what I want to guard against —
an accident.
　　Madam, better to be hated now by you

than soften and pay later with regrets.
MEDEA [*exchanging a look with the Chorus*]:
　　Heaven help me!   115
My reputation is a curse:
This is not the only time it has done me lasting
　　　harm.
　　Oh, let the perspicacious man
keep his children from enlightenment —
above the general run.   120
　　It will earn them only
the sneer of uselessness
and the spiteful jealousy of fellow men.
　　Bring education to the dolt
and, far from being accounted wise,   125
you will yourself be cast as dolt.
　　Outshine a pundit of established fame
and you become a byword of distaste.
　　This precisely
is what I have to face.   130
　　Because I have a little knowledge,
some are filled with jealousy,
others think me secretive, and crazy.

　　In point of fact, my knowledge
does not amount to much.   135

[*She turns upon Creon eyes pathetic with innocence.*]

　　But now I frighten *you*:
do you think I'll strike some death-knell on your
　　　house?
　　No, no: I am not like that.
　　Creon, forget your fear:
I have no criminal intent against a king.   140
　　For how have *you* wronged me?
　　You simply gave your virgin child
to a suitor of your bent.
　　No, it is my husband that I hate.
　　You, I think, have acted prudently   145
and even now I don't begrudge your enterprise
　　　success.
　　Marry them both and blessings on you,
only let me go on living in this land.
　　Ill-used though I am, I shall keep quiet:
I am overruled.   150
CREON: Reassuring talk,
but it chills me to the marrow.
　　What are you really hatching in your mind?
　　I trust you, Madam,
less even than I did before.   155
　　The impassioned woman,
like the impassioned man,
is easier to watch than the crafty and the quiet.
　　So, leave, I say, at once,
and no speeches, please.   160
　　My mind's made up.

You are dangerous.
All your cleverness
shall not keep you here.
165 MEDEA: Please, I beg you — on my knees —
by your fresh young daughter-bride . . .
CREON: You waste your words.
I am adamant.
MEDEA: Will you expel me —
170 heedless of my prayers?
CREON: I will. For I love you less
than I love my home.
MEDEA: Ah, home! My own beloved country.
What memories crowd upon me now!
175 CREON: Exactly: next to my own children,
my country is *my* dearest love as well.
MEDEA: Love, did you say?
It is a mighty curse.
CREON: In my opinion . . . that depends . . .
180 MEDEA: O Zeus, remember
the author of this crime.
CREON: Go away — you poor deluded thing —
rid me of my troubles.
MEDEA: The troubles are all mine:
185 I have a glut of them.
CREON [*turning on his heel*]: I'll call the servants:
They'll put you out by force.
MEDEA [*clinging to him*]: No, not that . . . Creon,
I have something else . . .
190 CREON: You seem determined, Madam,
to make a nuisance of yourself.
MEDEA: No, I'll go into banishment . . .
That is not what I beg you now.
CREON: Then, why not *go*, and let this land be rid
of you?
195 MEDEA: Just let me stay this single day
to arrange my exodus from here
and make provision for my little sons —
whose father cannot bring himself to care.
Be kind to them.
200 You are a father too:
you know what kindly feelings are.
As for me,
it means nothing to me
whether I stay or go.
205 It's them I shed my tears for:
their lot is hard.
CREON [*after a tussle with himself*]:
My soul is not tyrannical enough.
My heart has often let me down . . .
So now, Medea,
210 though I know I take a false step:
have it your own way.
But let me warn you solemnly,
if tomorrow's holy light
sees you and your two children
215 still inside the borders of this realm,

you die.
Every word of this I mean.
Now, stay if you must; but one day only . . .
not long enough for you to perpetrate anything I
dread.
[*Exit Creon.*]
CHORUS: Ill-starred woman,   220
Oh, what a nightmare of anguish is on you!
Whom will you turn to? Where will you turn?
What country, what stranger, what home for a
haven?
Who will receive you?
God has certainly steered you —   225
Oh, my poor Medea —
Into a sea-race of sorrows.
MEDEA [*turning on them with the gleam of revenge*]:
In the center of disasters, yes,
but all is far from lost — make no mistake —
a test awaits the newlyweds,   230
no little ordeal for the happy pair.

[*With a laugh of derision.*]

Do you think I ever would have toadied to
this man
if nothing could be got from it, no gain, no
tool?
No, not one syllable,
not a touch with my little finger.   235
The fool!
He could have scotched me with one stroke,
flung me out,
instead he lets me stay one extra day,
to make three enemies three corpses: 240
ha! father, daughter, and my husband.

[*She leans toward the Chorus.*]

Friends,
I can think of several ways to bring their death
about.
Which one shall I choose?
Shall I set their house of honeymoon alight,   245
or creep into the nuptial bower
and plunge a sharp knife through their vitals?
One thing makes me pause:
if I am caught entering the palace, or red-
handed,
I die . . . and give my enemies the last laugh.   250
No, there is a surer way,
one more direct;
for which I have a natural bent:
death by poison.
Yes, that is it.   255

[*She walks, thinking.*]

Well, suppose they are dead:

will any city take me in,
will any man afford me home in a country safe
    for living
and shield me from reprisals?
260   No, there is none.
I must postpone it, therefore, for a while
until some tower of strength appears for me;
then, through trickery and stealth,
I shall proceed with death by poison.
265   What if I'm forced to go before it's done?
    Ah, then I shall seize a sword,
face certain death,
and with my own hands run them through.
    I shall not shrink from such a step,
270 by Hecate,° no: the goddess who abides
in the shrine of my inner hearth —
the one I reverence most of all the gods
and have chosen to abet me.
    Nobody breaks my heart —
275 with impunity.
    Their wedding I'll reduce
to agony and grief:
agony for having met and married,
and grief for having banished me.
280   Good!
    Use your magic to the hilt.
    Plot, Medea, devise your recipes:
advance to the deadly act that tests your
    courage.
    See your present plight:
285 laughed at by the seed of Sisyphus°
because of Jason's match?
    Never.
    Your father was a king:
his father, Helios the Sun
290 be aware of *that*.
    Besides, you are a born woman:
feeble when it comes to the sublime,
marvelously inventive over crime.

FIRST CHORAL ODE°

[*The Chorus sings an ode about the topsy-turvy changing standards of the world. Out of the turmoil*

---

270. **Hecate:** Identified with Artemis, and sometimes called Persephone (Roman name Proserpina), she was supposed to preside over magic and witchcraft.   [285. **seed of Sisyphus:** Sisyphus, a king of Corinth, was punished in the otherworld by being made to roll a boulder up a hill. As it approached the top, the boulder would roll back down, creating a neverending task. To be a descendant of Sisyphus was considered a disgrace by the ancients.]   [**Ode:** Song sung by the Chorus.]

will come a new importance for women, and a new reverence. Meanwhile, Medea is a harbinger of female independence and vitality.]

[*Strophe 1*]

Back to their fountains
    the sacred rivers are falling;
The cosmos and all morality
    turning to chaos.
The mind of a man is nothing but fraud   5
    and his faith in the gods a delusion.
One day the story will change:
    then shall the glory
    of women resound,
And reverence will come to the race of woman,   10
    Reversing at last the sad
    reputation of ladies.

[*Antistrophe 1*]

The ballads of ages gone by
    that harped on the falseness
Of women, will cease to be sung. . .   15
    If only Apollo,
Prince of the lyric, had put
    in *our* hearts the invention
Of music and songs for the lyre
Wouldn't I then have raised   20
    up a feminine paean
To answer the epic of men?
Time in the roll of the ages has much to unfold
    Of the fortunes of women no less
    than the fortunes of men.   25

[*Strophe 2*]

So you, Medea, sailing away
    from your father's house,
Threading a passage with heart on fire
    through the jowls of the Euxine
Cliffs° to inhabit a strange   30
    land where your bed is empty of man
(The lover you lost, O heartbroken lady!)
Now are chased from the realm,
    shamed and banned.

29–30. **Euxine Cliffs:** On the Black Sea.

[*Antistrophe 2*]

35   The joy of a bond is gone;
         and wide of the world of Hellas,
      All shame has flown —
         high in the sky and away.
      Bereft of a fatherly home,
40   Where can you sail for a haven against
      The storm, unfortunate woman —
         Your bed
      Royally quelled by another
         who queens it in your home?

SECOND EPISODE

[*Jason enters from the road that leads to the palace. He is a young-looking man, dressed in the swash-buckling cloak and plumed helmet of a captain in the King's Guards.*]

JASON [*embarrassed and exasperated*]:
         So ... this is not the first time
      I have seen irrevocable damage done
      by a barbarous rage.
         You could have stayed here,
5   in this land, in this house,
      had you submitted quietly to your ruler's plans.
         Instead, you ranted like a lunatic ...
      so now are banished.
         To me your tirade does not mean a thing:
10   go on declaiming what a monster Jason is.
         But when it comes to royalty,
      the princess and the king,
      count yourself lucky to be only banished.
         I have tried continuously to calm things
            down;
15   for I should like you to remain.
         But you, Madam,
      obstinate in folly,
      have continuously reviled our royalty,
      And so you are banished.
20   Yet, in spite of everything, I come, Medea,
      patient to the last with someone I am fond of,
      to do what I can to help.
         You and the children
      need not leave the country penniless
25   and unprovided for ...
      exile drags with it a chain of troubles.
         And hate me though you may,
      I cannot bring myself to wish you harm.
MEDEA: You criminal —
      an epithet too good for you ... such
30   inhumanity ...

so you come to me, do you,
you byword of aversion both in heaven and on
      earth,°
to me your own worst enemy?
      This is not courage.
      This is not being brave: 35
to look a victim in the eyes whom you've
      betrayed —
somebody you loved —
      This is a disease,
and the foulest that a man can have:
you are shameless.   40

[*With the thinnest of smiles.*]

      But you have done well to come:
I can unload some venom from my heart
and you can smart to hear it.
      To begin at the beginning,
yes, first things first: 45
      I saved your life —
as every son of Greece who stepped on board
      the *Argo* knows.
      You were sent to yoke
the fire-breathing bulls
and sow the plot of death.   50
      Yes, I saved you, lit up life for you,
when I slew the guardian of the Golden Fleece,
that giant snake which hugged it, sleepless,
coil on coil.
      I deserted my own father and my home   55
to come away with you to Iolcus by Mount
      Pelion,
full of zeal and very little sense.
      King Pelias, I killed,
a most horrid death —
perpetrated through his daughters —   60
and overturned their home.
      All this for you,
I even bore you sons — you most reprobate
      man —
just to be discarded for a new bride.
      Had you been childless,   65
this craving for another bedmate
might have been forgiven.
      But no: all faith in vows is shattered.
I am baffled:
      Do you suppose the gods of old no longer
      rule?   70
      Or is it that mankind
now has different principles —
because your every vow to me, I'm sure you
      know,
is null and void.

---

32. Editors bracket this line as doubtful.

75   Curse this right hand of mine,
so often held by yours;
and these knees of mine —
sullied to no purpose
by the grasp of a rotten man.
80   You turned my hopes to lies.
Come now, tell me frankly —
as if we were two friends,
as if you really were prepared to help
(and I hope the question makes you feel
            ashamed) —
85   where do I go from here?

[*With a bitter laugh.*]

    Home to my father, perhaps,
and my native land,
both of whom I sacrificed for *you*?
    Or to the poor deprived daughters of Pelias?
90   They would be overjoyed to entertain
their father's murderer.
    Yes: this is how things stand.
Among my own friends
I am an execrated woman.
95   There was no call for me to hurt *them*,
but now I have a death-feud on my hands —
and all for you.
    What a reward!
    What a heroine you have made me
100 among the daughters of Hellas!
    Lucky Medea, having *you*:
such a wonderful husband . . . and so loyal!
    I leave this land displaced, expelled,
deprived of friends,
105 only my children with me, and alone.
    What a charming record for our new
            bridegroom this:
"His own sons and the wife who saved him
are wayside beggars."

[*She breaks off and looks upward.*]

    O Zeus, what made you give us
110 clear signs for telling
mere glitter from true gold,
but when we need to know
the base metal of a man
no stamp upon his flesh for telling counterfeit?
115 LEADER: How frightening is resentment
            how difficult to cure,
    When lovers hurl past love
        at one another's hate.
JASON: I'll have to choose my words
120 with no uncommon skill, it seems . . .
like a good sailor riding out a storm,
if I am to sail close-sheeted, Madam,
through your lashing, dangerous tongue.

[*Folding his arms.*]

    So, you pile up what you did for me
into pinnacles of grace.   125
    Well, as far as I am concerned,
it was Aphrodite° and no one else in heaven or
        earth
who saved me on my voyage.
    Your cleverness played a part, of course,
but I could underline, if I wanted to be
        ungenerous,   130
how it was infatuation, sheer shooting passion,
that drove you to save my life.
    I shall not stress the point.
After all, your service did no harm.
    But this I shall maintain: 135
that what you gained by saving me
was far more than you gave.

[*Holds up a hand to stop Medea from interrupting.*]

    In the first place,
you have a home in Hellas
instead of some barbarian land.   140
    You have known justice:
the benefit of laws which never yield to might;
have had your talents recognized all over Greece
and won renown.
    For, were you living at the world's ends,   145
your name would not be known . . .
    Oh, to me, houses crammed with gold,
and a sweeter song than Orpheus sang,
are nothing with no name.
    But, enough discussion of my dangerous
        voyage: 150
an argument which *you* provoked.
    Now to your vindictive challenge
of my royal marriage.
    I'll show you, first, it was an act of common
        sense,
secondly, unselfish,   155
and, finally, a mark of my devotion
to you and all my family.

[*Medea gives a gasp of incredulity.*]

    No, be still.
    When I came here from the land of Iolcus,
frustrations crowding on my trail,   160
could I, a wretched fugitive,
have hit upon a greater stroke of luck
than marriage to the daughter of the king?
    It was not — which cuts you to the quick —
that I was tired of your attractions   165

---

127. Aphrodite: Goddess of love, called Venus by the Romans.

and smitten with a longing for a new wife;
still less that I was out to multiply my offspring
(I am quite satisfied with the sons we have);
no, it was simply that I wanted above all
170 to let us live in comfort, not be poor ...
     I know too well
how the pauper is avoided by his friends.
     I wanted our children to be reared
in a manner worthy of my ancestry,
175 and, begetting others, brothers for your sons,
knit them all together
into one close and happy family.
     What point was there for *you* to have more
       children?
     My intention was — and it seemed real
       gain —
180 to help the ones I have,
through those I hope to have.
     Was this such a wicked plan?
     You would not say so,
except through jealousy — that stinging jealousy
      of bed.
185   You women are all the same.
If your love life goes all right,
everything is fine;
but once crossed in bed,
the liveliest and best that life can offer
190 might as well be wormwood.
     What we poor males really need
is a way of having babies on our own —
no females, please.
     Then the world would be
195 completely trouble free.
LEADER [*sternly*]: Jason, this speech of yours is
      plausible,
But say what you like, it is not right
To sacrifice your wife.
MEDEA [*with cold disdain*]:
     My outlook must be very different, then, from
      others.
200   To my mind a hypocrite who is too glib
only multiplies the danger that it puts him in:
the more he glozes° falsehood with his tongue,
the more confident and rash he grows.
     He ends by not being very clever.
205   So, you, toward me —
you'd better drop your specious pleading.
     One simple observation
lays the whole thing flat:
were you not a coward, it was your duty
210 to convince *me*; not go sneaking off to marry.
JASON: And you would have welcomed the
      suggestion, I am sure.

202. glozes: Glosses over.

Why, even now you can't contain your blazing
     rage.
MEDEA: *That* was not what governed you:
you felt your glory tarnished by an aging
     oriental wife.
JASON: Please, please believe me: 215
it was nothing to do with women —
my desire to make this match —
but as I have already said
to safeguard you and rear young princes
to be brothers to my sons ... 220
so make our family solid.
MEDEA [*with a bitter laugh*]:
Haha! Solid happiness on the grave of love;
Prosperity with a secret sting ...
O you gods — not for me — ever.
JASON [*earnestly*]: Please change your prayer to this 225
and make it reasonable:
     "May success not seem to me sad failure,
nor good fortune ever a disaster."
MEDEA: You go on mocking me: *you* have roof
     and shelter.
I am deserted, flying for my life, alone. 230
JASON: *You* chose it. Blame no one else.
MEDEA: Did I? I was the one who wed and then
     betrayed?
JASON: No: you just swore a heap of filthy curses
     on the king.
MEDEA: Yes, and you shall find that *I* am the curse
that Fate has made to haunt you. 235
JASON: There's no point in talking any more with
     you.

[*Preparing to go.*]

Anything that you or the children want in exile,
let me know; I'd gladly furnish it,
or send letters of introduction for you
to friends abroad who will be kind. 240
     To turn this offer down, Medea,
is nothing short of madness.
     Forget your feelings of resentment:
let yourself be helped.
MEDEA [*spitting out the words*]:
Not your friends, not your things: 245
I would not touch anything of yours —
how dare you offer it!
     The presents of the wicked are pure poison.
JASON [*flinging his cloak about him*]:
In that case, heaven be my witness:
all my design to help you and your sons 250
is thwarted by your preference for evil.
     Your self-will cuts you off.
     Suffer then accordingly.

[*He begins to go.*]

MEDEA: Go then. Don't waste your passion here:
255   go to the fresh young virgin you can't wait
                 for . . .
          Have her.
                    [As Jason exits, furious and embarrassed.]
          And God grant
          the match you make, you'll long to have
                    unmade.

SECOND CHORAL ODE

[The women of the Chorus, appalled by what has
happened to Medea, speak of the dangers of love and
the sufferings of exile.]

[Strophe 1]

          Love is a dangerous thing:
          Loving without any limit.
          Discredit and loss it can bring . . .
          But, oh, if the goddess should visit
5   A love that is modest and right,
          No god is so exquisite.
          Great lady, aim not at me
          Your gold and infallibly
          Passion-tipped, poisoned delight.

[Antistrophe 1]

10   Stay me with innocent living,
          Most beautiful gift of the gods.
          Never let Cypris° the fierce
          Queen of desire propel
          My heart to a dissolute lust
15   From old to a new and another
          Bed and a dissonant longing,
          But test with a sweet eye for peace
          The love-bonds of reverent women.

[Strophe 2]

          O my country, my home, never let
20   Me lose my state and my city —
          Living that desperate loss
          so helpless and hard, without pity.
          Death: I would bargain with death,
          To die such a day to a finish.
25   For nothing is like the sorrow

12. Cypris: Aphrodite, goddess of love.

          Or supersedes the sadness
          Of losing your native land.

[Antistrophe 2]

LEADER: The thing is before my eyes.
          Learned from no rumor or lies:
          Medea without city or friends   30
          Nowhere where pity extends —
          Oh, how you must suffer! . . .
          Let a man rot in a charmless lot
          If he never unshutters his heart
          To the cleansing esteem of another.   35
          He'll not be my friend: no, never.

THIRD EPISODE

[Enter Aegeus from the country. He is a man in his
early middle years and dressed in traveling clothes.
His open features — kindly but unimaginative —
seem preoccupied. In his retinue are Noblemen and
Servants.]

AEGEUS [stretching out his hands]:
          Medea, all health and happiness . . .
          and one can say a fairer thing when greeting
                    friends?
MEDEA [wanly]: Health and happiness to you, good
                    Aegeus,
          wise Panidon's son . . . But where do you stem
                    from?
AEGEUS: I have just left Apollo's ancient oracle at
                    Delphi.   5
MEDEA: What — a pilgrim there — the nub of the
                    world of prophecy?
AEGEUS: I went to ask for progeny — for a fruitful
                    seed.
MEDEA [suddenly interested]:
          In the name of heaven! Have you been childless
          all this time?
AEGEUS: Childless, yes — by some design of
                    heaven.   10
MEDEA: But with a wife . . . or have you never
                    married?
AEGEUS: I am married. Yes, I have a wife who
                    shares my bed.
MEDEA: And what did Apollo say about your
                    having children?
AEGEUS: Something far too deep for me, a mere
                    mortal, to unravel.
MEDEA: Am I allowed to know the god's reply?   15
AEGEUS: Certainly. It would take a mind like yours

to fathom.

MEDEA: Tell me . . . what did he say . . . since you
are allowed?

AEGEUS: Why, just this:
"Do not unstopper the wine-skin till . . . "°

MEDEA: Till you've done something — been
20   somewhere — special?

AEGEUS [baffled]: Until I'm back at home again.

MEDEA: Then why did you sail in here?

AEGEUS: There is a man called Pittheus, king of
Troezen . . .

MEDEA: Yes, a son of Pelops: a very pious man,
they say.

25   AEGEUS: I want to ask his help about this oracle.

MEDEA: Yes, a clever man, and an expert in such
things.

AEGEUS: And of all my old battle cronies, my
favorite.

MEDEA: Well, I hope that all your dreams come
true.

AEGEUS: Medea, you look so pale, so sad. What is
it?

MEDEA: My husband, Aegeus: he is the world's
30   most wicked man.

AEGEUS: You don't say? . . . Come, tell me all
about your troubles.

MEDEA: He's set up a mistress to queen it in my
home.

AEGEUS: Dear me! Would he really do a thing like
that?

MEDEA: Yes, yes . . . And I am deposed — the one
he loved.

AEGEUS: Did he fall in love . . . or is he just tired of
35   you?

MEDEA: In love — Ha — head over heels . . .
flinging all fidelity to the winds.

AEGEUS: Let him get on with it . . . since he's as
wicked as you say he is.

MEDEA: But it was with royalty he fell in love:
a king's daughter.

40   AEGEUS: Eh? What king's daughter? Please go on.

MEDEA: Creon's, king of Corinth.

AEGEUS: In that case, Madam, it is serious.
You have my sympathies.

MEDEA: It is the end. What is more, I am being
banished.

AEGEUS: Banished? This is indeed a crowning
45   blow —
but by whom?

MEDEA: Creon: he wants to banish me from
Corinth.

AEGEUS: And Jason agrees? I find that monstrous.

19. "Do not . . . wine-skin": Probably "Do not have sexual
intercourse."

MEDEA [with fierce irony]: Oh, he says he
doesn't —
but he'll bear it bravely.   50

[On her knees.]

Aegeus, I beg you,
by your beard,
by these knees of yours I clasp,
pity me, pity my unhappiness.
Do not see me banished and alone,   55
let me come to Athens, shelter me,
accept me in your home.
The gods will pay you back,
give you the children you so long to have,
surround your death with happiness.   60
You do not guess how Providence has blessed
you, meeting me.
I mean to end your childlessness
and make your seed bear sons.

[Almost in a whisper.]

I promise it. I know the drugs.

AEGEUS [impressed]: Medea, many reasons make me
ready   65
to acquiesce in your request,
not least of all the gods;
then because you've given me — a promise:
promise of children . . .
oh, left to myself, I had all but given up.   70

[Gently raising her.]

My proposition, then is this:
get yourself to Athens
and there, as is incumbent on me,
I shall do my utmost to protect you.
However, I must tell you clearly,   75
I cannot take you with me out of Corinth,
but if you reach my palace on your own,
there you shall have full sanctuary
and to no one shall I give you up.
So, by your own means you must leave this
land: 80
I cannot risk offending the Corinthians —
who are also friends of mine.

MEDEA: As you say . . . but . . .
if only you could promise it on oath,
it would make it all so . . . settled between us.   85

AEGEUS: Do you not trust me? What is the matter
now?

MEDEA [glancing nervously over her shoulders]:
I do trust you . . . but . . .
but I have my enemies.
It isn't only Creon,
there is the house of Pelias too: 90
They'll want to prize me from your territories.

If you are bound by oath
you will not give me up.
But if you have only made a promise,
95   not sworn it to the gods,
there is always the chance that sheer diplomacy
will win you to their wishes.
I have no weapons on my side,
on theirs is wealth and all the weight of royalty.
100 AEGEUS: You are very provident, Medea.
However, if that is what you want,
I shall not go against it.
In point of fact,
to swear an oath protects me too:
105 I can counter those who wish you ill
with a clear excuse;
and you of course, are well secured.
So, name your deities.
MEDEA [*in crystal-cold syllables*]:
Swear by the Earth on which you tread.
110 Swear by the Sun, my father's father dread.
Swear by every god and godhead.
AEGEUS: Yes, but what to do or not to do? Please
say.
MEDEA: Never yourself to drive me from your land,
and if an enemy of mine tries to drag me off,
115 never while you live to let me go.
AEGEUS: I swear by the Earth and sacred light of
the Sun
to abide by the words you have just pronounced.
MEDEA [*relentlessly*]:
Good . . . but if you break your word — what
penalty?
AEGEUS: The penalty for sacrilege.

[*They clasp hands in silence.*]

120 MEDEA: Go now and be glad. All is well.
I shall come to Athens as quickly as I can,
but first I have some work to do, to carry out a
plan.

[*As Aegeus is leaving.*]

LEADER: We hope that Hermes, master of journeys,
Will hasten you home safely to Athens:
125 Home to the hope of your heart's desire,
For, Aegeus, you are
A most magnanimous man.
MEDEA [*wheels round and faces the Chorus*]:
O Zeus and lady daughter, Justice,
O resplendent Sun!
130 And you my friends,
At last we are on the road to vengeance
and to our song of triumph. At last there is
hope:
we shall see my enemies put down.
At the very point my plot could founder,

this man opens up a port, an anchorage.   135
So to Athens I shall go
and moor to her fast towers

[*She beckons the women closer.*]

Now I can unfold to you my whole design:
there is nothing sweet in it, as you will see.
I send a servant of my house to Jason   140
asking him to come to me.
He arrives
I tell him in the softest accents;
how I now agree;
how it all seems for the best: 145
his royal marriage, his sacrifice of me;
everything that he has planned is for the best.
But I ask him to let my children stay . . .
with no intention — you understand —
of leaving any child of mine in a hostile place 150
for those who hate me to maltreat.
No, this is just a device
for murdering the daughter of the king.
I send them there with presents in their
hands,
presents for the bride — as a kind of plea   155
against their banishment —
yes, a gown of gossamer and a diadem made of
beaten gold.
If she takes this finery and puts it on,
the girl will die in agony
and anyone who touches her;   160
so deadly are the poisons I shall steep the
presents in.
But now my whole tone changes:
a sob of pain for the next thing I must do.
I kill my sons — my own —
no one shall snatch them from me.   165
And when I have desolated Jason's house
beyond recall,
I shall escape from here:
fly from the murder of my little ones,
my mission done.
People that one hates, my friends,   170
must never have the last laugh.
Well, so be it.
What good is life to me?
I have no father, home, defense from danger.
Oh, the mistake I made was when I left his
house,   175
trusting the word of a man from Greece . . .
but he is going to pay the price.
Never again alive
shall he see the sons he had by me,
nor any child by this new bride of his —   180
poor girl, who has to die a wretched death,
poisoned by me.

Let no man think me insignificant or weak:
I am no meek martyr, no — quite the
    contrary —
185 relentless an enemy I make;
though kind enough to friends.
    Such is the genius of my life.
LEADER [*imploringly*]:
Though you have shared all this in confidence
    with us, Medea,
and though I long to be of help,
190 we must uphold the laws of life:
and so I say to you: "You must not do it."
MEDEA: There is no other way.
And though I understand your sentiments,
you have not been through my agony.
LEADER: But, my lady, to kill your own two
195   sons . . . ?
MEDEA: It is the supreme way to hurt my husband.
LEADER: And it makes you the most desolate of
    women.
MEDEA: Be that as it may.
    Argument is now superfluous.

[*She turns to the Nurse, who has entered during the
previous dialogue.*]

200   Nurse, when I need real loyalty
you are the one I always turn to.
    Go now and fetch Jason here.
    But as you are a woman
and a faithful servant of this house,
205 whisper no syllable of what I plan.
        [*Exit Nurse, dragging her feet.*]

THIRD CHORAL ODE

[*The Women of Corinth desperately try to move
Medea from her purpose. Does she imagine Athens,
that blessed land, will welcome a murderess? Surely,
she herself will flinch from the cold-blooded killing of
her sons?*]

[*Strophe 1*]

The people of Athens are blest through the ages,
    Seeds of the all-hallowed gods,
Born on a soil unravaged and holy,
    They feed on the wide
5   Bright pastures of knowledge.
Lightly they walk through the crystal air
In a land where Harmonia,
    Goldenly fair,
Once gave birth, they say, to the nine

Muses, the pure 10
    Maids of Pieria.°

[*Antistrophe 1*]

And out of the sweetly flowing currents
    Of Cephisus,° they declare,
Aphrodite sprinkles the land
    And fragrantly breathes 15
    Delicate breezes.
Forever she sheds from the stream of her hair,
    Plaited with roses,
Scented petals; and sends the Loves — the
    Erotes —
To preside with Wisdom over the heart 20
    And together prepare
    The glories of art.

[*Strophe 2*]

How then shall a glorious city,
    City of sacred rivers,
    Host of the salutary guest, 25
Kindly take to the killer of children,
Harbor among them a murderess?
Think of how you are stabbing your sons.
Think, too, of the blood you assume.
Do not, please, we beg by your knees, 30
By everything and every means —
    Murder your children.

[*Antistrophe 2*]

Where, when, will you find the mind,
    The hand or the callous heart
    Hardened enough to strike 35
These, yours — oh, heartless enough? —
How then will you see through your gaze
Swollen with tears as you sight your aim?
No, no, when your little ones kneel
Crying for mercy, you will not 40
Find the nerve, never be able,
    To bloody your hands.

7–11. where Harmonia . . . Maids of Pieria: Harmonia, the
balance of nature, and the genius of the people resulted in the
cultivation of the arts. Pieria was a holy fountain in Boetia
where the nine Muses were supposed to live. **13. Cephisus:**
An Athenian river.

FOURTH EPISODE

[*Jason enters with the Nurse behind him. On his face is written apprehension mixed with hope; on hers, despair.*]

JASON: I have come, Medea, because you asked me.
    I put myself at your disposal
even though you are against me.
    What, Madam, can I do for you?
MEDEA [*in a small, contrite voice*]:
    Jason please forgive me for all the things I
5   said.
    Bear lightly with my outbursts, will you,
if only in remembrance of our great love
        together.
    I have been arguing with myself,
have taxed myself severely.
10   "You raving fool," I said,
"To antagonize those who want to do you good,
setting yourself against your rulers and your
        husband.
    His royal marriage
and his design to bring up brothers for your
        sons
15 does you the greatest service that he could.
    Why not calm yourself?
    Are *you* suffering because the gods are good?
    Have you no children of your own?
    And are you not aware
you came as fugitive with not too many
20   friends?"
    Such reflections made me realize
I have been out of my mind, hysterical.
    Now I thank you.
    Now I am convinced
25 that in securing us this benefit
you are the wise one, *I* the fool —
I who should have been your ally
and encouraged you.
    Yes, I should have been at hand to help,
30 decked the bed, dressed the bride —
and been glad to do it . . .
    But we women —
well, we are what we are: let's leave it at that!
    Do not copy us in our perverseness
35 or try to get your own back, giving tit for tat.
    I ask your pardon.
    I admit to being wrong.
    I've thought better of it now.

[*With an upsurge of put-on happiness.*]

    Children, children, come out here,
40   out of the house.

[*The two Boys appear with their Tutor.*]

    Come greet your father, hug him, join with
        me
in loving, not resenting him.
    Your mother's rancor's over.
    There's peace between us: the fighting's done.
    Come, take his hand.   45

[*As the children run into their father's arms.*]

    O God, what a presentiment!
    What an image looming in the dark!
JASON: My sons, my sons,°
    if only you could go on living, go on loving,
with your arms stretched out like that to me
        forever . . .   50
MEDEA [*choking*]: It breaks my heart;
    I am far too prone to tears, too full of tears . . .
it is the sudden ending of my quarrel with your
        father
which makes them flow.
    A sight so touching . . .   55
    it overflows.
LEADER: My eyes, too, are stinging,
    but may this be the worst that is to come.
JASON [*gently releasing the Boys*]: I praise you now,
    Medea,
and I did not blame you then.   60
    It is natural for a woman to be enraged
when her husband goes off making second
        marriages.
    But now
you are in a better frame of mind
and, even if it took a little time,   65
realize the good points of this plan . . .
the decision is a level-headed woman's.

[*Turning to the children.*]

    As for you, my boys,
your father has been far from idle
and, heaven willing, he has made   70
good settlements for you.
    In time I shouldn't wonder
if you were not first citizens in Corinth —
along with your new brothers.

[*Laying his hands on their shoulders.*]

    Grow up now fine fellows.   75
    Your father and a kindly providence
have the rest in hand.

---

48. To my mind there is no doubt that this line and half the next (in the Greek) go to Jason, and not Medea as the manuscripts and editors have it. Otherwise, Medea's remark in 93 [930] makes no sense. The attempt to have it correspond to Jason's wish in 72 [916] does not work. [Translator's note.]

How I look toward the time
when you will be two strapping grown young
        men,
80   trampling down my enemies.

[*Medea has averted her head and is sobbing. Her feelings, though genuine, are being used by her to further
her next move.*]

        But, Medea, what is this —
these dewy eyes, these tears;
your white face turned away
as if my words struck pain, not joy?
85 MEDEA: It is nothing.
        I was just thinking of our sons.
    JASON: Well, be of good heart now:
        I shall see them through.
    MEDEA: I will do my best . . . it isn't that I don't
            believe you,
90   but you know how women weep.
    JASON: I know, but don't be sad for *them* . . . why
            should you?
    MEDEA [*watching the tender look on Jason's face*]:
        I am their mother.
        When you prayed just now
        for a long life for your sons,
95   a sudden sadness whispered: "Will this be?"
        Well, that's one item only
        of what I had to say.
        The other thing is this:
        Since the king has set his mind
100 on sending me away from Corinth,
        and since I've come to recognize that this is
            best
        (for I'd only be an obstacle to you,
        living with the royal family here —
        who think I am a menace to their house),
105 I shall take myself away, go into banishment.
        But the children, please, I should like *them*
        to grow up under your own hand.
        Persuade Creon to let them stay.
    JASON [*taken off his guard, but flattered*]:
        I — I am not certain that I can:
110 it'll take a little trying.
    MEDEA: But you could ask your wife to beg her
            father
        to let the two boys stay.
    JASON [*reflecting*]: Why not? I think I can get her
            to agree.
    MEDEA: Of course you can:
115 if she's the slightest bit like any woman.
        And here *I* can play a useful part.
        I shall send her a present
        more ravishingly beautiful, believe me,
        than anything this age has seen:

a gown of gossamer and a diadem of beaten
        gold.   120
    These the boys shall carry them to her.

[*She claps her hands and two Maids appear.*]

        Go quickly, one of you,
    and bring the gorgeous presents here.

[*One of the Maids hurries into the house.*]

        What a double delight
        What a shower of happiness for her   125
    to have you for a hero husband
    and now these treasures which were handed
            down
    by my father's father — the glorious Sun.

[*The Maid comes back with two boxes. Medea turns
to the Boys.*]

        Boys, take hold of this wedding gift.
        Carry it to the happy princess-bride.   130
        Place it in her hands.
        It is not the kind of present she'll despise.
    JASON [*as the Boys step forward*]:
        You foolish woman — why empty your
            hands?
        Do you think a royal wardrobe is in want,
    or a palace short of gold?   135
        Keep these things. Don't give them up.
        If my wife values me at all,
    my mere wish will have more weight than
            things,
    I'm sure of that.
    MEDEA [*with an onrush of conviction*]: Do not
        deny me.   140
        Even the gods, they say, succumb to gifts,
    and gold is stronger than the strongest wits.
        She is lucky, *she* is blessed, *she* increases.
        This exile I would barter for my babies
    not just with gold but with my life.   145

[*Forcing the boxes into the Boys' hands.*]

        Go, my sons, into the halls of wealth;
    down on your knees and beg her —
    this new wife of your father's, and my
            mistress —
    to let you stay in Corinth.
        Most important of all,   150
    see that she takes the precious things
    into her own hands.

[*Packing them off.*]

        Quick, now, go. Success be yours.

Come and tell me the good news.
155   Your mother waits with all ears.

[*Exeunt the Boys with their Tutor, followed by
Jason.*]

FOURTH CHORAL ODE

[*The multimurders are imminent. Woe to the victims!
Woe to the murderess!*]

[*Strophe 1*]

Now has the last hope gone of the children
     living,
Gone and forever: they walk already to murder.
The bride is taking the golden diadem,
     Is taking the poison and doom.
5   Over her yellow hair her hands are fitting
     The decorated dying.

[*Antistrophe 1*]

The gorgeousness of the gossamer gown will
     win,
And the beaten gold of the diadem embrace
     her.
The bride is decked and ready to meet the dead.
10   The trap is lethally set:
Doomed miserable woman, doomed to fall in —
     Ineluctably caught by Fate.

[*Strophe 2*]

And you who are groomed for a murder:
     Son-in-law of a king,
15   Jason unsuspecting —
Are to bring on your sons a demise, and a death
On your bride of a hideous kind.
     Unhappy man, how far
     You are falling.

[*Antistrophe 2*]

20   And you the unenviable mother,
     How I weep for your pain!
     Killer of children for
A vengeance of love that has gone, betrayed
By your man for another
25   Bride whom he sleeps beside
     In his wrong.

FIFTH EPISODE

[*The Tutor hurries in from the palace with the two
Boys.*]

TUTOR [*breathless with excitement*]: My lady, your
          boys —
they won't be banished.
     And the princess, the bride —
with her own hands —
she took your presents, oh, so gladly . . .   5
     Now the children's danger is over!

[*Baffled by Medea's grim reaction.*]

     Well I never! Isn't this good news?
     What so transfixes you?

[*Medea draws in her breath in a muffled cry of
pain.*]

TUTOR: What I hear is out of tune with what I
          say.

[*Medea sighs deeply.*]

TUTOR: I thought I brought good news.   10
     What kind of news, I wonder, have I brought?
MEDEA: What you have brought, you have brought:
     the fault is not with you.
TUTOR: Why, my Lady, these shuttered eyes:
     these tears falling?   15
MEDEA: Oh, I am pressed, old friend — hard
          pressed:
     the gods and my own evil counsels.
TUTOR: Courage, dear mistress:
     Your sons will always bring you home.
MEDEA [*in a kind of trance*]:
     Home? . . . First I must send others there . . .
          Mercy!   20
TUTOR: You are not the only mother to be severed
          from her sons.
     We have to bear our own humanity —
          humanely.
MEDEA [*pressing his hand*]:
     I shall try . . . Now go inside
     and see to what the children need today.
                                   [*Exit Tutor, worried.*]
MEDEA [*throwing out her arms toward the two
          Boys*]: My sons, my sons,   25
     you will have a city and a home
     far from me.
          I shall be left lonely,
     and you will live without your mother always.
          For I must go in exile to another land: 30
     never have my joy in you,
     or see your bright young progress;

never deck your brides, your marriage beds,
or light you radiant to your wedding day.

[*The Boys are now in her arms.*]

35   Oh, what a blight my ruthlessness has been!
        How useless, little ones,
    my nursing all your growing up!
        How useless all the cares endured:
    the wearying solicitudes,
40   the shooting agony of giving you your lives.
        And now, how miserably have dwindled
    my innumerable dreams of you:
    your loving comfort when I'm old,
    your own hands dressing me when I am dead —
45   a passing every person might desire.
        Such sweet fancy vanishes
    and, wrenched from you instead,
    I shall drag my sad life out alone.

[*She cups their faces in her hands in turn.*]

        Your own dear eyes shall miss forever
50   your poor mother's face —
    your way of life and hers utterly apart.
        Oh, children
    do you let those eyes now stare their fill,
    and your last smiles linger to the last?

[*She turns to the Chorus, panting.*]

55   O–h! What shall I do?
        My heart dissolves
    when I gaze into their bright irises . . .
        No, I cannot do it.
        Goodbye to my determination.
60   I shall take my boys away with me.
        Why damage *them* in trying to hurt their
                father,
    and only hurt myself twice over?
        No, I cannot.
        Goodbye to my decisions.

[*A pause, then she suddenly breaks away from the Boys.*]

65   What — what undermines me now?
        Do I really mean to let my enemies go,
    to laugh at me?
        Steel yourself, Medea:
    away with this cowardice, these arguments that
                melt.

[*Almost pushing them.*]

70   Go, Boys, into the house.

[*She turns to the Chorus grimly.*]

        Anyone whose conscience will not let him
                stay

let him look to it: avoid my sacrifice . . .
this hand of mine shall never falter.

[*Another spasm of emotion grips her, and she runs to the Boys as they reach the door.*]

        No, no! Stop me, my heart:
    we must not do this thing.   75
        Let them go, you stricken woman,
    spare your sons.
        Let them live with you in Athens:
    they will be your joy.

[*Throwing her arms round them again.*]

        Ah! Not by all the haunting spirits of the
                underworld,   80
    shall I leave my children for my enemies to
                trample down.
        No, never.°

[*With a sharp realization.*]

        But — they have to die —
    the whole thing is settled anyway . . .
        Yes . . . the diadem is on her head . . .   85
    the royal bride at this moment rots,
    dying in her gown — I know it.

[*She turns to the Chorus as if to explain her second impulsive embrace.*]

        You see: the path I have to tread
    is unutterably sad,
    but the one I set these children on   90
    is sadder still . . .
        Therefore I desire to speak with them.

[*Seizing their hands.*]

        Give me your right hands to kiss,   95
    each of you, my little ones —
    give them to your mother.

[*Covering their hands, their faces, their bodies, in kisses.*]

        How adorable — this hand — and this . . .
        These lips — how very much adored!
        And this face and form of childhood's
    ingenuous nobility . . . how I bless you both . . .   100
    not here — beyond . . .
    every blessing here your father has despoiled.
        So sweet . . . the mere touch of you:
    the bloom of children's skin—so soft . . .
    their breath — a perfect balm.

---

82. [Translator has followed] editors [who] omit lines 1062
and 1063 [of the Greek text] as a melodramatic interpolation: "*But they have to die, and since they must, / let it be by
the hands of her who gave them life.*"

[*Gently releasing them; then almost savagely turning her back.*]

105   Go, go . . . I cannot look at you.
       I am in an agony, and lost.

[*The two Boys, weeping, hurry into the house.*]

       The evil that I do, I understand full well,
       But a passion drives me greater than my
          will.
          Passion is the curse of man:
110   It wreaks the greatest ill.

FIFTH CHORAL ODE

[*If there can be a feminine philosophy of parenthood, is its honest judgment likely to be that children are worth it after all?*]

       So often before
       Have I gone toward concepts far too tenuous
       And come upon questions far too deep
       For the race of woman to try to unravel.
5   Nevertheless, even we women
       Have a muse of our own, that ushers us in.
       (Though, alas, not all) to the world of wisdom.
       Perhaps you might find it one in a thousand.
       It serves to inspire the talent of ladies,
10   And makes me able now to proclaim
       That people without the function of parent
       Are happier than begetters of offspring.
       The childless man has no way of telling
       Whether he misses a curse or a blessing.
15   Nevertheless, the childless person
       Certainly misses many a burden.
       I mark how the man with children growing
       Sweetly at home is worn with worrying:
       How to make sure they are properly fed,
20   How to leave them a livelihood.
       And then after all to be in the dark:
       Were all the worries worth it or not?
       Were they a worthy or worthless lot?

       But now let me tell
25   Of the worst and saddest trait of all.
       Suppose the children have quite a good life,
       Reach their teenhood honest and fine,
       What if a fate like Death the cruel
       Carries them downward body and soul?
30   What is the use if after all
       (On top of all those other ones)
       The gods let loose this grief as well . . .
       Just for the joy of having sons?

SIXTH EPISODE

[*Medea has been sitting during the Chorus. Now she leaps up as she catches sight of a man lunging breathlessly toward them from the street: the Messenger.*]

MEDEA: Somebody with news at last, my friends,
     And from the right direction.
       Yes, I see him:
     one of Jason's men — panting as he hurries —
     With some tremendous news of bad.   5

[*The Messenger — an official of the Bride's house — bursts in: hardly able to get his words out.*]

MESSENGER: Run, Medea, run!
     What — you have done . . . is . . . too
       unthinkable . . .
     too awful . . .
       Seize whatever means you can . . .
     sailing boat or chariot . . . Escape!   10
MEDEA: Run? Escape? Is it then so vital?
MESSENGER: Dead . . . They are this minute
       dead . . .
     the princess royal with her father —
     and through your poisons.
MEDEA: What a pretty word you bring —   15
     my benefactor, my friend forever!
MESSENGER [*recoiling*]: What are you saying,
       Madam?
     Are you in your right mind — not unhinged?
     A king's home a charnel house —
     and you rejoice? . . . Are you not afraid?   20
MEDEA: I have my ready answer too,
     so don't be hasty, friend,
     but tell me how they perished.
       An appalling death
     would give me double joy.   25
MESSENGER [*supports himself against a pillar as he
       begins to recollect an agonizing
       experience*]:
     We were so pleased to see your brace of boys
     come hand in hand to the bride's house with
       their father:
     for your ordeal had upset us servants greatly.
       The rumor went racing through the house
     that all was well again between your husband
       and yourself.   30
       Some of us kissed the children's hands,
     kissed their golden tops;
     and I in my enthusiasm even followed them
     to the women's wing.
       There, the mistress —   35
     I mean the one we have to honor now —
     had eyes so taken up with Jason

she did not even see at first
the two boys hand in hand.
40   But when she did,
a veil of scorn dropped over her eyes,
she turned her lovely face away,
bristling at your sons' intrusion.
Your husband then began to woo her
45 from her petulance and girlish tantrums, saying:
"You must not hate your friends.
Stop being hurt and turn your head around.
Consider yours your husband's loved ones.
Come, won't you take their presents
50 and beseech your father
to let these boys off banishment — just for me?"

[*Pauses and sits down hopelessly on a step.*]

When she saw how exquisite the presents
were,
far from holding out on him,
there was nothing she withheld:
55 but gave in completely to her groom.
And hardly had your husband and your
children
left the house
when she took the gorgeous robe and put it on,
and placed the golden circlet on her curls,
arranging the ringlets in the brightness of a
60   mirror
and smiling at her own dead image there.
Then rising from her stool
she minced off through the halls
on dainty milk white toes,
65 wildly pleased with what she had received,
over and over again
running her eyes down the clear sweep to her
heels.
But all at once
a hideous spectacle took place.
70   Her color changed. She tottered back;
shuddered in every limb; was able just in time
to fall into a chair and not upon the floor.
An old woman there, attending her,
thinking that perhaps the fierce possession of
Pan°
75 or some other power was on her,
broke into a chant of wonder,
then saw the white froth spuming at her lips,
her eyeballs bulging all askew,
her skin quite leached of blood,
80   and changed her chanting to a yelp:
a wail of horror.

74. **Pan:** The god of wild nature was supposed to be the
cause of seizures and sudden madness. Hence our word
panic.

A maid went dashing to the palace for her
father,
another went to tell the fresh-wed groom
what was happening to his bride.
The whole house rang with footsteps running.   85
It took no longer than a sprinter takes
to go the hundred yards,
before the poor girl lay unconscious with her
eyelids shut.
Then suddenly she rallied
and gave a curdling shriek,   90
fighting off a double nightmare.

[*He pauses, gulps, takes a deep breath.*]

The golden diadem that clasped her head
burst into a voracious and uncanny flow of fire,
while the robe of gossamer your children gave
her
began to eat her tender flesh away.   95
Streaming with flame,
she leapt up from her chair and fled,
tossing her mane of hair from side to side,
in a frantic bid to shake the diadem off.
But its grip was adamant   100
and the golden circlet held.
The more she tossed,
the more the flowed,
till, overwhelmed with pain,
she sank down to the floor —   105
unrecognizable to all except her father —
her calm regard grotesquely twisted,
her sweet symmetry all shattered;
and from the crown of her head in molten clots
fire and blood dripped down together.   110
The flesh curdled off her bones
like the teardrops congealing out of pines,
inexplicably dissolved by those ravening venoms.
It was curious and horrible to see.
No one dared to touch her body: 115
the warning was too obvious.
But her father, unawares, poor man,
rushed headlong through the room,
flung himself lamenting on the body,
hugged and kissed it, sobbing out: 120
"My stricken darling,
what evil power has done this to you,
who has made you dead
and left me, like some ancient tombstone,
derelict?
O gods! . . . let me die with you, my daughter." 125
But . . . but when he stopped . . .
from these outpourings —
these melancholy sobs . . .
and tried to lift his aged carcass up,
he found himself stuck fast —   130

clamped to the flimsy robe
like ivy to a laurel bole.
    A ghastly wrestling match ensued.
    He would try to raise a knee,
135 she would drag him back;
and when he took to force,
his own decrepit flesh
pulled off from the bone.
    At last, exhausted,
140 pathetically unable
to lift himself above the shambles,
he gave his spirit up.
    There they lie, corpse by corpse,
father and young daughter —
145 fit objects for our tears.

[*He rises, swaying.*]

    To you, Medea . . . from me . . .
there are no words to say.
    Retribution? You yourself will know
the best escape . . .
though in my esteem — and not just for
150   today —
the whole of life is shadow,
and I would even say:
the people who know best or seem to know,
the subtlest professors,
155 are the very ones who pay the dearest price.

[*Flinging his cloak about him.*]

    A happy human being? Ha, there's no such
        thing . . .
more prosperity, more success in one maybe:
but happier? . . . It does not make one happy.
                         [*Exit Messenger.*]

LEADER: Justice personified this day
160 has brought on Jason's head
    — oh, we have seen it! —
the richest retribution.
    But it is you we weep for,
poor blighted child of Creon,
165 walking through the gates of death
because you married Jason.

MEDEA [*in clear, cold tones*]:
    Now, friends, to complete this mission with
        dispatch:
to slay my children and hurry from this land.
I must not dawdle and betray my sons
170 to much more savage hands than mine to kill.
    There's no way out. They have to die.
    And since they must,
let me be the one to cut them down:
the very one who gave them life!

[*She begins her walk to the door, almost like a sleep-walker, talking to herself.*]

    Yes, heart, be steel.   175
    Why vacillate?
    The act is . . .
necessary as it is cruel and hard.
    Come, reluctant hand,
grip the sword — grip it, Medea: 180
cross your borderline of lifelong pain.
    Away this flinching!
    Away this longing:
consign to oblivion the love you had for them —
the children of your flesh.   185
    Even when you kill them they are dear . . .
oh, my sons! . . . I am in despair, despair.

[*Medea, with the Nurse mutely following in tears, passes into the house.*]

SIXTH CHORAL ODE

[*The women pray desperately for something to stop the imminent murder.*]

[*Strophe*]

    Come Earth, come sunshafts of the Sun,
    Behold this woman and withhold her
    From her laying scarlet fingers
    On the children of her blood.
    Gold of your gold are they begotten: 5
    Heinous is to spill this holy
    Ichor in the blood of mortals.
    Curb her, stop her, godborn Light, oh,
    Keep this house from murder! Keep it
    Never haunted by the Furies.°   10

[*Antistrophe*]

    Were those birth pangs wasted bearing:
    Children's birth pangs wasted birth?
    You, my lady, after sailing
    Safe between the dark blue clashing
    Gorges, will you hug a rankling   15
    Hatred to your heart, a loathsome
    Rage for murder and revenge?
    Those that spill the blood of family
    Stain themselves with heaven's anger,
    Haunt their homes with doom forever. 20

10. Furies: Ministers of the vengeance of the gods, employed in punishing the guilty on earth as well as in the underworld.

SEVENTH EPISODE OR DENOUEMENT

[*Cries are heard from inside the house.*]

FIRST WOMAN: A shout — listen — a shout from
    the boys.
FIRST BOY: O–h! What can we do? ...
    Our mother is on us!
SECOND BOY: Brother, brother! ... We're going to
    be killed.
SECOND WOMAN: That murderous relentless
5   woman!
THIRD WOMAN: Shall we break in, snatch them
    from death?
FIRST BOY: Yes, by heaven ... save us ... help!
SECOND BOY: We're trapped, cornered ... now ...
    by her sword.

[*As the Chorus beat on the barred doors, there are
groans and cries, and presently a trickle of blood
oozes from under the doors. The women watch it, fascinated.*]

CHORUS: Woman of stone, heart of iron,
10   Disconsolate woman, ready to kill
     The seed of your hands with the hand that
      tilled.
     One other only, one have I known
     Murderously handle the fruit of her womb:
     Ino the maniac, god-driven one,
15   Whom Zeus's wife drove out to roam —°
     Desperate woman goaded to slaughter
     The sons of her flesh, clean against nature.
     She pitched from the precipice into the sea,
     Fell where her foot fell into the ocean,
20   Dashing two infants to death with her own.
     What ghastlier thing is left to be known?

     Women, O women, in love and in pangs,
     What ruin you've brought on us human
      beings!

[*Jason, breathless, his face twisted with hatred, bursts
in with a troop of servants.*]

JASON: You women standing here outside this
    house,
25 is that she-ravager, Medea, still at home,
    or has she fled?

14–15. **Ino the maniac ... out to roam:** Ino, a daughter of
Cadmus and Harmonia, tried to destroy her two stepchildren so that her own two children might ascend the throne.
Pursued, in turn, by their father, her husband Athamas, she
leapt into the sea with her two boys. [The account given
here] is Euripides' version.

[*He waits for a reply, but the women cower before the
door.*]

    Deep down in the earth let that woman hide,
    or wing into the highest alcoves of the sky,
    before she ever saves herself from justice by this
     royal house.
    Does she think that she can kill   30
    a princess and a country's king
    and vanish with impunity?

[*He strides toward the door.*]

    But it is my sons, not her, I fear for.
    She, she shall be repaid
    through her victims.   35
    I have come to save my children's lives
    from some enormous retribution by the family of
     the dead
    for those enormities their mother did.
LEADER: Jason, you poor optimistic man,
    you still don't know the evils that have come — 40
    or you would not say what you have said.
JASON: What? Does she mean to kill me too?
LEADER: Your sons are dead: murdered by their
    mother.
JASON [*reeling*]: What — did — you — say?
    Oh, woman — my own wife — you kill me too. 45
LEADER [*as the women form an avenue to the door,
    and Jason sees for the first time the blood
    beginning to trickle down the steps*]:
    Yes. Your children.
    You cannot think of them as being alive.
JASON [*limply*]:
    Where did she kill them ... here ... outside,
    or was it in the house?
LEADER: Force these doors   50
    and you will see your children in their blood.
JASON [*drawing his sword in a frenzy*]: Servants, on
    the double,
    break these bolts,
    force the hinges: let me see
    the double homicide,   55
    the murdered dead ... and the murderess to die.

[*There is a rumbling sound, and out of a cloud above
the house Medea appears in a chariot drawn by dragons. By her side are the dead bodies of the two Boys.*]

MEDEA [*in triumphant disdain*]:
    Why this battering, this beating at the doors?
    Are you looking for their bodies —
    and for me who did this thing?
    Save yourself the trouble.   60
    If there's anything you want, then ask.
    But me you shall not lay a hand upon.
    This chariot, the Sun

— my father's father — gave me
65 to keep me safe against my enemies.
JASON [*hissing with revulsion*]:
     You miserable, mephitic° woman!
     Beyond abhorrence —
by me, the gods, the rest of men —
you could put your own sons to the sword,
70 the sons you bore,
and kill me too with childlessness . . .
Yet still look upon the sun, see the earth . . .
     Be damned! . . .
     At last I understand
75 what I never understood before,
when I took you from your foreign home to live
          in Greece,
the sheer wickedness of you,
the treachery to your father and the land that
          reared you.
     You are possessed
and the gods have unleashed the fiend in you on
80   *me*;
on your own brother, too, cut down in his home
before you came aboard the sweet ship *Argo's*
          hull.
     Your work already had begun.
     You married me, bore my sons,
85 and murdered them through jealousy of love.
     No woman in the whole of Hellas
     would have dared so much;
yet you were the one I married,
not a girl from Greece.
90   Oh, I married a tigress,
not a woman, not a wife,
and yoked myself to a hater and destroyer:
to a viciousness more fierce than any Tuscan
          Scylla.°

[*Turning away from the door in a gesture of helplessness.*]

But why go on?
95 A million accusations would not make you
          wince:
you are shameless through and through . . .
you — you bloodstained ogress, infanticide . . .
     Hell take you!
     Leave me to mourn my destiny of pain:
100 my fresh young wedding without joy,
my sons begot and reared and lost —
never to be seen alive again.

[66. **mephitic**: Foul-smelling.]   93. **Tuscan Scylla**: A monster that inhabited the straits between Italy and Sicily and snatched sailors off passing ships and devoured them.

MEDEA [*with acid imperiousness from the chariot*]:
     How tediously I could rebut you point by
          point!
     Zeus the Father knows
exactly what you got from me   105
and how you then behaved.
     I would not let you or your royal princess
set our wedded life aside,
make me cheap,
so that you could live in bliss;   110
or let that match-arranger, Creon,
dismiss me from the land without a fight.
     So, call me a tigress if you like,
or a Scylla haunting the Tyrrhenian shore,
I have done what I ought: 115
broken your own heart to the core.
JASON [*wheeling round to face her*]:
     You are in agony too:
     you share my broken life.
MEDEA: It is worth the suffering
               since *you* cannot scoff.   120
JASON: Poor children, what a monster
               fate gave you for a mother!
MEDEA: Poor sons, what a disaster
               your selfish father was!
JASON: It was not *his* right hand   125
               that killed and struck them down.
MEDEA: No, it was his pride
               the lust of his new love.
JASON: You think it right to murder
               just for a thwarted bed.   130
MEDEA: And do you think that a thwarted bed
               is trifling to a woman?
JASON: A modest woman, yes:
               to you the world's worst crime.
MEDEA [*pointing at the dead children*]:
     See, they are no more;   135
               I can hurt you too.
JASON: They'll live, I think,
               in your tormented brain.
MEDEA: The gods know who began
               this whole calamity.   140
JASON: Yes, the gods know well
               your pernicious heart.
MEDEA: Hate then: I spurn
               the wormwood from your lips.
JASON: As I do yours; so let us   145
               be rid of one another.
MEDEA: Yes, but on what terms?
               That's also what *I* want.
JASON: Let me have the boys —
               to mourn and bury them.   150
MEDEA: Never!
     My own hands shall bury them, they shall be
          carried

to the sanctuary of Hera on the Cape,
where no enemy shall ever do them harm
155 or violate their sepulchre.
    Here in Corinth, the land of Sisyphus,
I shall inaugurate a solemn festival°
with rites in perpetuity
to exorcise this murder.
    I myself shall go to Athens, land of
160   Erechtheus,
to live with Aegeus, Pandion's son . . .
you to a paltry death that fits you well:
your skull smashed by a fragment of the *Argo's*
    hull:
ironic ending to the saga of your love for me.

THE EXODUS°

[*As the Chorus begin to form for the exodos march,
the meter changes. Jason strides into the middle of the
arena.*]

JASON: Murder is punished, and you'll be destroyed
    by the avenging phantoms of your children.
MEDEA: What power or divine one is ready to hear
    you:
    perjurer, liar, treacherous guest?
5 JASON: Vile, vile, murderess of little ones!
MEDEA: Go — go and bury your bride.
JASON: Broken I go: bereft of two sons.
MEDEA: You bemoan too soon: wait till you're old.
JASON: Dearest children!
10 MEDEA: Dear to their mother.

157. **solemn festival:** Similar ceremonies were still performed
at Corinth in Euripides' time.   [**Exodus:** Final scene.]

JASON: And so she slew them.
MEDEA: To get at your heart.
JASON: You did! You did! How I long to press
    my little children's lips to mine!
MEDEA: Now you are longing, now you call;   15
    you utterly turned from them before.
JASON: For the love of the gods, allow me this:
    to stroke my children's tender skin.
MEDEA: No, you shall not: you waste your words.
JASON [*flinging out his arms*]: Zeus, do you hear
    how I'm at bay,   20
Dismissed by this ogress, odious woman,
Tigress besmirched with the blood of her young?
So I mourn and call on the gods while I may,
On the powers to witness how you have slain
My children, and now prevent my hands   25
From touching them, dead, interring their clay.
I'd rather they'd never been born to me
Than have lived to see you destroy them this
    day.

[*Before the end of these words, Medea, with a cold,
vindictive smile, has moved off in the chariot. Jason
staggers out of the arena.*]

ENVOI°

CHORUS: Wide is the range of Zeus on Olympus.
    Wide the surprise which the gods can bring:
    What was expected is never perfected,
    What was not, finds a way opened up . . .
    So ended this terrible thing.   5

[**Envoi:** Concluding remarks.]

COMMENTARY

John Simon (b. 1925)
REVIEW OF MEDEA

1994

Critic John Simon's review of Medea *focuses on the problems the play presents for modern production and how the director handled them. He is especially interested in the problem, as he views it, of the chorus, reminding us that this modern production reduced the original number from fifteen to three women. However, he also has useful commentary on the dramatic setting and the music and sounds which help us understand how the play was staged.*

"One must be absolutely modern. This is what Euripides was, as he still is," writes our premier classical scholar, Bernard Knox (with an acknowledged assist from Rimbaud), in his absorbing new book, *Backing Into the Future.* In a letter of May 17, 1948, our still undervalued poet-playwright Robinson Jeffers, who wrote his version of *Medea,* declares, "There is much in any Greek play that would seem dull or absurd to anyone but a classical scholar." Which statement is true? Both.

Any new production of *Medea* must come to grips with the fact that although Euripides speaks as one of us, much of his technique strikes us as dated, though less so than that of his fellow Greek dramatists. This *Medea,* originally produced at London's Almeida Theatre, has many features to its credit, most notably that its director, Jonathan Kent, is aware of this *aporia* (as the Greek would call it) or hot potato (as we would): Euripides today is both necessary and impossible. So Kent pawkily tries to steer a course between these internal Symplegades (or a rock and a hard place).

The first and worst problem a director of a Greek drama now faces is what to do with the chorus. In the case of *Medea,* Jeffers reduced it to three women, as Grillparzer did before him; Anouilh, in his version, eliminated it altogether. Kent, too, retains three women, but then what? How should they look? Since Paul Brown's costumes here are modern, but with classical Greek overtones, Kent picked something resembling contemporary Greek folk dress, but with distinct echoes of a Melina Mercouri movie. It doesn't look quite right, but what would? Next, how to explain the chorus's very presence? "It is hard to imagine fifteen women standing by while a mother murders her children," wrote Moses Hadas, the late, great classicist. *Three* women standing by doesn't make it much easier. For this, Kent has no solution. But by assigning the roles to three actresses of very different ages and types (the eldest coming across like a man), he achieves a nice, stylized effect – something like the Three Ages of Woman.

The Greek chorus sang and danced; so Kent lets his women do some singing and dancing. For the former, they are usually backed up by an invisible choir, which makes for a bizarre but not uninteresting effect. The dancing, such as it is, is pretty ludicrous, but one admires Kent's guts for risking it at all. And there isn't much of it.

The next problem is what kind of decor to use, other than the standard all-purpose Greek-drama set (Woolworth Hellenic), of which everyone is heartily sick. With the help of his set designer, Peter J. Davison, Kent came up with an imposingly monumental solution, which, along with the scenery for the current *Carousel,* raises the troubling possibility that British set design has way outstripped ours. What we get makes scant sense architecturally but is fiercely theatrical. Two tall, asymmetrical facades intersect at right angles; they are seemingly made of large square bronze sheets, artfully imbricated, with rivets displayed. In the lesser facade, stage right, is an empty doorway revealing some mighty girders. The main facade has, among other things, a picture window that sometimes lights up to reveal, say, Medea a shut-in in her palace, or hovering over her slain children, something the Greeks would never have shown. There is also a functioning, likewise square, onstage well. And in the end, the set does something sensational that you have to see for yourself.

Jonathan Dove's music is, in the spirit of the show, neither modern nor antiquarian, sometimes haunting and sometimes, alas, banal. More interesting sounds are produced by carefully calibrated bangings on the walls. The acting, by a low-profile British cast (save for the star, about whom more anon), is generally solid, distinguished by elocution American actors should envy. The diction of John Turner (Creon) — a tall, imposing man in a fuzzy black greatcoat for which numerous sheep must have been left shivering — is so good I felt virtually impaled by his consonants. I liked Tim Oliver Woodward's Jason, a fellow with one foot in tragedy, the other in trashiness, paltry one moment and deeply pitiable the next.

Diana Rigg's Medea is seldom absolutely right, but always hugely watchable. She, I think, suffers most from the directorial ambivalence: One moment a Mycenean lioness, she turns Mayfair hostess in a twinkling, her tigerish stalking yielding too readily to a kittenish purr. With her back frequently against the wall, her regal figure and darting eyes, she looks part caryatid, part Fury. In this she is superbly abetted by Wayne Dowdeswell's lighting, which uses horizontal and diagonal shafts of light to mesmeric or hallucinatory effect.

And yet Miss Rigg's disciplined and highly cultivated tones, and her fine sense of humor (which she has manifestly been urged to indulge), have a way of making this a thoroughly modern Medea, one eliciting too many knowingly deliberate laughs. Miss Rigg is, rightly, more sensual than her New York predecessors in the role, Judith Anderson and Zoë Caldwell, but they were, rightly, more terrifying. And for all that she looks sexy in red and marmoreal in discreetly blood-spattered white, she seems, like those others, a bit overmature for the role.

All in all, this is a production that deserves to be seen — as well as heard, in Alistair Elliot's wonderfully colloquial yet not unpoetic translation — even if its split personality militates against full impact. It is rich in ideas in its every aspect, including Miss Rigg's performance, and ideas, even intermittently misguided ones, are precious in our theater so habitually short on thought.

Aristophanes

The best known of the Greek comic playwrights, Aristophanes (c. 448–c. 385 B.C.) lived through some of the most difficult times in Athenian history. He watched Athenian democracy fade and decay as factionalism and war took their toll on the strength of the city-state. By the time he died, Athens was caught up in a fierce struggle between supporters of democracy and supporters of oligarchy, government by a small group of leaders.

Aristophanes' plays are democratic in that they appealed to sophisticated and unsophisticated theatergoers alike. Skilled at complex wordplay, he also enjoyed spirited and rowdy comedy. Since his plays were often sharply critical of Athenian policies, his ability to make people laugh was essential to conveying his message. He was a practitioner of what we now call Old Comedy, an irreverent form that ridiculed and insulted prominent people and important institutions. By Aristophanes' time, Old Comedy had become fiercely satirical, especially concerning political matters. Because Aristophanes held strong opinions, he found satire an ideal form for his talents.

Of his more than thirty known plays, only eleven survive. They come from three main periods in his life, beginning, according to legend, when he was a young man, in 427 B.C. *The Acharnians* (425 B.C.), from his first period, focuses on the theme of peace. Dicaeopolis (whose name means "honest" or "good citizen") decides to make a separate peace after the Spartans have ravaged the Acharnian vineyards. The Acharnians vow revenge, but Dicaeopolis explains that peace must begin as an individual decision. Aristophanes saw war as a corporate venture; peacemaking was easier for an individual than for a group or a nation.

The Acharnians was followed by *The Peace* in 421 B.C., just before Sparta and Athens signed a treaty, and it seems clearly to have been written in support of the Athenian peace party, whose power had been growing from the time of *The Acharnians* and whose cause had been aided by that play.

His second period was also dominated by the problems of war. Athens's ill-fated expedition to Sicily in violation of the Treaty of Nicias lies thematically beneath the surface of *The Birds* (414 B.C.), in which some citizens build Cloud-Cuckoo-Land to come between the world of humans and the world of the gods. *Lysistrata* (411 B.C.) is also from this period; its frank antiwar theme is related to the Sicilian wars and to the ultimately devastating Peloponnesian Wars. These were wars fought by Greek city-states in the areas south of Athens, the Peloponneus. The states had voluntarily contributed money to arm and support Athens against the Persians in 480 B.C. — resulting in the Athenian victory at Salamis. The states later became angry when Pericles, the Athenian leader, demanded that they continue giving contributions, much of which he used to fund the rebuilding of the Akropolis and other civic projects in Athens.

The other Greek city-states felt that Athens was becoming imperialistic and was overreaching itself. War broke out between the city-states in 431 B.C. and lasted for nearly thirty years. These struggles and the difficulties of conducting a costly, long-distance war in Sicily combined eventually to exhaust the Athenian resources of men and funds. Soundly defeated in 405 B.C., Athens surrendered to Sparta in 404. Aristophanes lived to see the Spartan ships at rest in the harbors of Athens's chief port, the Piraeus. And he saw, too, the destruction of the walls of the city, leaving it essentially defenseless.

Aristophanes' third and final period, from 393 B.C. to his death, includes *The Ecclesiazusae* (c. 392 B.C.) (translated as "The Women in Government"), in which women dress as men, find their way into parliament, and pass a new constitution. It is a highly topical play that points to the current situation in Athens and the people's general discontent and anxiety. The last part of *The Plutus,* written five years later, is an allegory about the god of wealth, who is eventually encouraged to make the just wealthy and the unjust poor.

Among the best known of Aristophanes' plays are several whose names refer to the disguises or costumes of the chorus, among them *The Knights, The Wasps,* and *The Frogs. The Frogs* (405 B.C.) is especially interesting for its focus on literary issues. It features a contest in the underworld between Aeschylus, who had been dead more than fifty years, and Euripides, who had just died at a relatively young age. Aristophanes uses the contest to make many enlightening comments about Greek tragedy and the skills of the two authors.

Even in his last period Aristophanes was an innovative force in theater. His last surviving play virtually does away with the chorus as an important character in the action. His later plays resemble modern comedies partly because the chorus does not intrude in the action. His genius helped shape later developments in comedy.

LYSISTRATA

At the time *Lysistrata* was written (411 B.C.), Athens had had a steady diet of war for more than twenty years. Political groups were actively trying to persuade Athenian leaders to discontinue the policies that had alienated Athens from the other city-states that were once its supporters in the Delian League, the group that had funded Athens's struggle against the Persian threat. Aristophanes opposed the imperialist attitudes that conflicted with the democratic spirit of only a generation earlier.

Lysistrata makes it clear that war is the central business of the nation at that time. No sooner is one campaign ended than another begins. The men encountered by the heroine Lysistrata (whose name means "disband the army") on the Akropolis — men who guard the national security and the national treasury — are old and decrepit. The young men are in the field. As Kalonike tells Lysistrata, her man has been away for five months. Such separations were common, and these women are fed up. Lysistrata has gathered the discontented women together to propose a scheme to bring peace and negotiate a treaty.

The scheme is preposterous, but, typical of Old Comedy, its very outrageousness is its source of strength. In time, the idea begins to seem almost reasonable: Lysistrata asks the women to refuse to engage in sex with their husbands until the men stop making war. The women also seize the Akropolis and hold the treasury hostage. Without the national treasury there can be no war. And because they are confident of getting the support of the larger community of women in other nations — who suffer as they do — they do not fear the consequences of their acts.

In amusing scenes generated by this situation Aristophanes pokes fun at both sexes. We hear the gossipy conversation of the women, all of whom arrive late to Lysistrata's meeting. The men are dependent, helpless, ineffectual, and cannot resist the takeover. When the truth begins to settle in, the men solicit their wives' attention with enormous erections protruding beneath their gowns, one example of the exaggerated visual humor Aristophanes counted on. The double meanings in the conversations are also a great source of humor.

The wonderful scene (3) between Myrrhine and her husband Kinesias is predicated on the agony of the husband whose wife constantly promises, and then reneges, in order to build his sexual excitement to a fever pitch. It is no wonder that Lysistrata can eventually bring the men to sign any treaties she wants.

This heterosexual hilarity is also balanced by a number of homosexual allusions. Kleisthenes, possibly a bisexual Athenian, stands ready to relieve some of the men's sexual discomfort, while Lysistrata admits that

215

if the men do not capitulate, the women will have to satisfy their own needs. Such frankness is typical of Athenian comedy.

Women dominate the action of the play, although we must remember that male actors played women's roles. The women see the stupidity and waste of the war, and devise a plan that will end it. Observing that they are the ones who suffer most from the effects of war, the women also note that they pay their taxes in babies. The suffering of women had been a major theme in the tragedies of Euripides, and everyone in Aristophanes' audience would have understood Lysistrata's motivation. The idea that a woman should keep her place is expressed by several characters. And since Athenian audiences would have agreed that women should not meddle in war or government, Aristophanes offered them a fantasy that challenged them on many levels.

Aristophanes praises Lysistrata's ingenuity and her perseverance. When the other women want to give up the plan because of their own sexual needs, she holds firm. She demands that they stand by their resolve. The picture of the strong, independent, intelligent, and capable woman obviously pleased the Athenians, because they permitted this play to be performed more than once — an unusual practice. Lysistrata became a recognizable and admirable character in Athenian life.

The following translation of *Lysistrata* has several interesting features. It is comprised of scenes, a division not made in the original Greek. The strophe and antistrophe are speeches given by the chorus, probably moving first in one direction and then in the opposite. Instead of having a chorus of elders, as in *Antigone,* Aristophanes uses two choruses — one of men and one of women — that are truly representative of the people: They are as divided and antagonistic as Sophocles' chorus is united and wise. The KORYPHAIOS (leader) of the men's chorus speaks alone, often in opposition to the koryphaios of the women's chorus.

The rhyming patterns of some of the songs are approximated in English, and the sense of dialect is maintained in the speech of Lampito, who represents a kind of country bumpkin. She is very muscular from the workouts that she and all other Spartans engaged in; Aristophanes reveals certain Athenian prejudices toward the Spartans in the scene where Lampito is taunted for her physique.

Lysistrata in Performance

Lysistrata has enjoyed and still enjoys numerous productions, both on college and commercial stages. Because it is a bawdy play, it has sometimes run into trouble. In 1932 the New York police shut down a performance and sent out a warrant for the arrest of "Arthur" Aristophanes. In 1959 Dudley Fitts's translation (used here) was performed at the Phoenix Theater in New York with "women . . . wearing simulated breasts, tipped with sequins, and the ruttish old men stripped down to union suits." Hunter College's 1968 production used rock music, hippie beads, and headbands. Less controversial productions include the first modern version, by Maurice Donnay in Paris (1892), in which Lysistrata takes a general as a lover. The Moscow Art Theater produced a highly acclaimed version in 1923 and brought it to the United States in 1925. That version, modified by Gilbert Seldes (published in book form with illustrations by Picasso), was produced throughout the 1930s. All-black versions of the play have been staged several times since 1938. *Lysistrata* ranks among the favorites of classical drama.

Aristophanes (c. 448–c. 385 B.C.)

LYSISTRATA   *411 B.C.*

TRANSLATED BY DUDLEY FITTS

Persons Represented

LYSISTRATA,
KALONIKE, } *Athenian women*
MYRRHINE,
LAMPITO, *a Spartan woman*
CHORUS
COMMISSIONER
KINESIAS, *husband of Myrrhine*
SPARTAN HERALD
SPARTAN AMBASSADOR
A SENTRY
[BABY SON OF KINESIAS
STRATYLLIS
SPARTANS
ATHENIANS]

Scene: *Athens. First, a public square; later, beneath the walls of the Akropolis;° later, a courtyard within the Akropolis.*

PROLOGUE°

(Athens; a public square; early morning; Lysistrata alone.)

LYSISTRATA: If someone had invited them to a
    festival —

Akropolis: Fortress of Athens, sacred to the goddess Athena. **Prologue:** Portion of the play explaining the background and current action.

of Bacchos,° say; or to Pan's° shrine, or to
    Aphrodite's°
over at Kolias —, you couldn't get through the
    streets,
what with the drums and the dancing. But now,
not a woman in sight!
           Except — oh, yes!   5

(Enter Kalonike.)

    Here's one of my neighbors, at last. Good
    morning, Kalonike.
KALONIKE: Good morning, Lysistrata.
                      Darling,
    don't frown so! You'll ruin your face!
LYSISTRATA: Never mind my face.
    Kalonike,
the way we women behave! Really, I don't
    blame the men   10
for what they say about us.
KALONIKE: No; I imagine they're right.
LYSISTRATA: For example: I call a meeting
to think out a most important matter   and
    what happens?
The women all stay in bed!
KALONIKE: Oh, they'll be along.
    It's hard to get away, you know: a husband, a
    cook,   15
a child . . . Home life can be *so* demanding!

---

2. Bacchos: (Bacchus) God of wine and the object of wild, orgiastic ritual and celebration; also called Dionysus. **Pan:** God of nature, forests, flocks, and shepherds, depicted as half-man and half-goat. Pan was considered playful and lecherous. **Aphrodite:** Goddess of love.

LYSISTRATA: What I have in mind is even more
   demanding.
KALONIKE: Tell me: what is it?
LYSISTRATA: It's big.
KALONIKE: Goodness! *How* big?
LYSISTRATA: Big enough for all of us.
KALONIKE: But we're not all here!
LYSISTRATA: We would be, if *that's* what was up!
20   No, Kalonike,
   this is something I've been turning over for
     nights,
   long sleepless nights.
KALONIKE: It must be getting worn down, then,
   if you've spent so much time on it.
LYSISTRATA: Worn down or not,
   it comes to this: Only we women can save
     Greece!
KALONIKE: Only we women? Poor Greece!
25 LYSISTRATA: Just the same,
   it's up to us. First, we must liquidate
   the Peloponnesians —
KALONIKE: Fun, fun!
LYSISTRATA: — and then the Boiotians.°
KALONIKE: Oh! But not those heavenly eels!
LYSISTRATA: You needn't worry.
   I'm not talking about eels. — But here's the
     point:
30   If we can get the women from those places —
   all those Boiotians and Peloponnesians —
   to join us women here, why, we can save
   all Greece!
KALONIKE: But dearest Lysistrata!
   How can women do a thing so austere, so
35   political? We belong at home. Our only armor's
   our perfumes, our saffron dresses and
   our pretty little shoes!
LYSISTRATA: Exactly. Those
   transparent dresses, the saffron, the
     perfume, those pretty shoes —
KALONIKE: Oh?
LYSISTRATA: Not a single man would lift
   his spear —
KALONIKE: I'll send my dress to the dyer's
40   tomorrow!
LYSISTRATA: — or grab a shield —
KALONIKE: The sweetest little negligee —
LYSISTRATA: — or haul out his sword.
KALONIKE: I know where
   I can buy the dreamiest sandals!
LYSISTRATA: Well, so you see. Now, shouldn't
   the women have come?
KALONIKE: Come? They should have *flown*!

27. **Boiotians:** Crude-mannered inhabitants of Boiotia,
which was noted for its seafood.

LYSISTRATA: Athenians are always late.
                But imagine!   45
   There's no one here from the South Shore, or
     from Salamis.
KALONIKE: Things are hard over in Salamis, I
     swear.
   They have to get going at dawn.
LYSISTRATA: And nobody from Acharnai.
   I thought they'd be here hours ago.
KALONIKE: Well, you'll get
   that awful Theagenes woman: she'll be   50
   a sheet or so in the wind.
              But look!
   Someone at last! Can you see who they are?

(*Enter Myrrhine and other women.*)

LYSISTRATA: They're from Anagyros.
KALONIKE: They certainly are.
   You'd know them anywhere, by the scent.
MYRRHINE: Sorry to be late, Lysistrata.
              Oh come,   55
   don't scowl so. Say something!
LYSISTRATA: My dear Myrrhine,
   what is there to say? After all,
   you've been pretty casual about the whole thing.
MYRRHINE: Couldn't find
   my girdle in the dark, that's all.
             But what *is*
   "the whole thing"?
KALONIKE: No, we've got to wait   60
   for those Boiotians and Peloponnesians.
LYSISTRATA: That's more like it. — But, look!
   Here's Lampito!

(*Enter Lampito with women from Sparta.*)

LYSISTRATA: Darling Lampito,
   how pretty you are today! What a nice color!
   Goodness, you look as though you could
     strangle a bull!   65
LAMPITO: Ah think Ah could! It's the work-out
   in the gym every day; and, of co'se that dance
     of ahs
   where y' kick yo' own tail.
KALONIKE: What an adorable figure!
LAMPITO: Lawdy, when y' touch me lahk that,
   Ah feel lahk a heifer at the altar!
LYSISTRATA: And this young lady?   70
   Where is she from?
LAMPITO: Boiotia. Social-Register type.
LYSISTRATA: Ah. "Boiotia of the fertile plain."
KALONIKE: And if you look,
   you'll find the fertile plain has just been mowed.
LYSISTRATA: And this lady?
LAMPITO: Hagh, wahd, handsome.
   She comes from Korinth.

KALONIKE: High and wide's the word for it.

LAMPITO: Which one of you
75   called this heah meeting, and why?

LYSISTRATA: I did.

LAMPITO: Well, then, tell us:
    What's up?

MYRRHINE: Yes, darling, what *is* on your
    mind, after all?

LYSISTRATA: I'll tell you. — But first, one little
    question.

MYRRHINE: Well?

LYSISTRATA: It's your husbands. Fathers of your
    children. Doesn't it bother you
    that they're always off with the Army? I'll stake
80   my life,
    not one of you has a man in the house this
    minute!

KALONIKE: Mine's been in Thrace the last five
    months, keeping an eye
    on that General.

MYRRHINE: Mine's been in Pylos for seven.

LAMPITO: And mahn,
    whenever he gets a *dis*charge, he goes raht back
85   with that li'l ole shield of his, and enlists again!

LYSISTRATA: And not the ghost of a lover to be
    found!
    From the very day the war began —
                      those Milesians!
    I could skin them alive!
            — I've not seen so much, even,
    as one of those leather consolation prizes. —
    But there! What's important is: If I've found a
90   way
    to end the war, are you with me?

MYRRHINE   I should *say* so!
    Even if I have to pawn my best dress and
    drink up the proceeds.

KALONIKE: Me, too! Even if they split me
    right up the middle, like a flounder.

LAMPITO: Ah'm shorely with you.
95   Ah'd crawl up Taygetos° on mah knees
    if that'd bring peace.

LYSISTRATA: All right, then; here it is:
    Women! Sisters!
    If we really want our men to make peace,
    we must be ready to give up —

MYRRHINE: Give up what?
    Quick, tell us!

LYSISTRATA: But *will* you?

100 MYRRHINE: We will, even if it kills us.

LYSISTRATA: Then we must give up going to bed
    with our men.

95. **Taygetos:** A mountain range.

(*Long silence.*)

    Oh? So now you're sorry? Won't look at me?
    Doubtful? Pale? All teary-eyed?
              But come: be frank with me.
    Will you do it, or not? Well? Will you do it?

MYRRHINE: I couldn't. No.
    Let the war go on.

KALONIKE: Nor I. Let the war go on.   105

LYSISTRATA: You, you little flounder,
    ready to be split up the middle?

KALONIKE: Lysistrata, no!
    I'd walk through fire for you — you *know* I
    would! — but don't
    ask us to give up *that*! Why, there's nothing like
    it!

LYSISTRATA: And you?

BOIOTIAN: No. I must say *I'd* rather walk
    through fire.   110

LYSISTRATA: What an utterly perverted sex we
    women are!
    No wonder poets write tragedies about us.
    There's only one thing we can think of.
                   But you from Sparta:
    if you stand by me, we may win yet! Will you?
    It means so much!

LAMPITO: Ah sweah, it means *too* much!   115
    By the Two Goddesses,° it does! Asking a girl
    to sleep — Heaven knows how long! — in a
    great big bed
    with nobody there but herself! But Ah'll stay
    with you!
    Peace comes first!

LYSISTRATA: Spoken like a true Spartan!

KALONIKE: But if —
            oh dear!
            — if we give up what you tell us to,   120
    will there *be* any peace?

LYSISTRATA: Why, mercy, of course there will!
    We'll just sit snug in our very thinnest gowns,
    perfumed and powdered from top to bottom,
    and those men
    simply won't stand still! And when we say No,
    they'll go out of their minds! And there's your
    peace.   125
    You can take my word for it.

LAMPITO: Ah seem to remember
    that Colonel Menelaos threw his sword away
    when he saw Helen's breast all bare.°

116. **Two Goddesses:** A woman's oath referring to Demeter, the earth goddess, and her daughter Persephone, who was associated with seasonal cycles of fertility.   **127–28. Colonel Menelaos … Helen's breast:** Helen, wife of King Menelaos of Sparta, was abducted by Paris and taken to Troy. The incident led to the Trojan War.

KALONIKE: But, goodness me!
What if they just get up and leave us?
LYSISTRATA: In that case
130   we'll have to fall back on ourselves, I suppose.
But they won't.
KALONIKE: I must say that's not much help. But
what if they drag us into the bedroom?
LYSISTRATA: Hang on to the door.
KALONIKE: What if they slap us?
LYSISTRATA: If they do, you'd better give in.
But be sulky about it. Do I have to teach you
     how?
You know there's no fun for men when they
135   have to force you.
There are millions of ways of getting them to see
     reason.
Don't you worry: a man
doesn't like it unless the girl cooperates.
KALONIKE: I suppose so. Oh, all right. We'll go
     along.
LAMPITO: Ah imagine us Spahtans can arrange a
140   peace. But you
Athenians! Why, you're just war-mongerers!
LYSISTRATA: Leave that to me.
I know how to make them listen.
LAMPITO: Ah don't see how.
After all, they've got their boats; and there's lots
     of money
piled up in the Akropolis.
LYSISTRATA: The Akropolis? Darling,
145   we're taking over the Akropolis today!
That's the older women's job. All the rest of us
are going to the Citadel to sacrifice — you
     understand me?
And once there, we're in for good!
LAMPITO: Whee! Up the rebels!
Ah can see you're a good strat*eeg*ist.
LYSISTRATA: Well, then, Lampito,
150   what we have to do now is take a solemn oath.
LAMPITO: Say it. We'll swe*ah*.
LYSISTRATA: This is it.
— But where's our Inner Guard?
               — Look. Guard: you see this shield?
Put it down here. Now bring me the victim's
     entrails.
KALONIKE: But the oath?
LYSISTRATA: You remember how in
     Aischylos' *Seven*°
they killed a sheep and swore on a shield? Well,
     then?
155

154. *Seven*: Aeschylus's *Seven Against Thebes,* which deals
with the war between the sons of Oedipus for the throne of
Thebes.

KALONIKE: But I don't see how you can swear for
     peace on a shield.
LYSISTRATA: What else do you suggest?
KALONIKE: Why not a white horse?
We could swear by that.
LYSISTRATA: And where will you get
     a white horse?
KALONIKE: I never thought of that. *What* can we
     do?
LYSISTRATA: I have it!
Let's set this big black wine-bowl on the ground   160
and pour in a gallon or so of Thasian,° and
     swear
not to add one drop of water.
LAMPITO: Ah lahk *that* oath!
LYSISTRATA: Bring the bowl and the wine-jug.
KALONIKE: Oh, what a simply *huge* one!
LYSISTRATA: Set it down. Girls, place your hands on
     the gift-offering.
O Goddess of Persuasion! And thou, O Loving-
     cup: 165
Look upon this our sacrifice, and
be gracious!
KALONIKE: See the blood spill out. How red and
     pretty it is!
LAMPITO: And Ah must say it smells good.
MYRRHINE: Let me swear first!
KALONIKE: No, by Aphrodite, we'll match for it!   170
LYSISTRATA: Lampito: all of you women: come,
     touch the bowl,
and repeat after me — remember, this is an
     oath — :
I WILL HAVE NOTHING TO DO WITH MY
     HUSBAND OR MY LOVER
KALONIKE: *I will have nothing to do with my*
     husband or my lover
LYSISTRATA: THOUGH HE COME TO ME IN
     PITIABLE CONDITION   175
KALONIKE: *Though he come to me in pitiable*
     condition
(Oh Lysistrata! This is killing me!)
LYSISTRATA: IN MY HOUSE I WILL BE
     UNTOUCHABLE
KALONIKE: *In my house I will be untouchable*
LYSISTRATA: IN MY THINNEST SAFFRON SILK   180
KALONIKE: *In my thinnest saffron silk*
LYSISTRATA: AND MAKE HIM LONG FOR ME.
KALONIKE: *And make him long for me.*
LYSISTRATA: I WILL NOT GIVE MYSELF
KALONIKE: *I will not give myself*   185
LYSISTRATA: AND IF HE CONSTRAINS ME

161. **Thasian:** Wine from Thasos.

KALONIKE: *And if he constrains me*
LYSISTRATA: I WILL BE COLD AS ICE AND
NEVER MOVE
KALONIKE: *I will be cold as ice and never move*
LYSISTRATA: I WILL NOT LIFT MY SLIPPERS
190   TOWARD THE CEILING
KALONIKE: *I will not lift my slippers toward the
ceiling*
LYSISTRATA: OR CROUCH ON ALL FOURS LIKE
THE LIONESS IN THE CARVING
KALONIKE: *Or crouch on all fours like the lioness
in the carving*
LYSISTRATA: AND IF I KEEP THIS OATH LET ME
DRINK FROM THIS BOWL
KALONIKE: *And if I keep this oath let me drink*
195   *from this bowl*
LYSISTRATA: IF NOT, LET MY OWN BOWL BE
FILLED WITH WATER.
KALONIKE: *If not, let my own bowl be filled with
water.*
LYSISTRATA: You have all sworn?
MYRRHINE: We have.
LYSISTRATA: Then thus
I sacrifice the victim.

(*Drinks largely.*)

KALONIKE: Save some for us!
200   Here's to you, darling, and to you, and to you!

(*Loud cries offstage.*)

LAMPITO: What's all *that* whoozy-goozy?
LYSISTRATA: Just what I told you.
The older women have taken the Akropolis.
Now you, Lampito,
rush back to Sparta. We'll take care of things
here. Leave
these girls here for hostages.
                                    The rest of you,
205   up to the Citadel: and mind you push in the
bolts.
KALONIKE: But the men? Won't they be after us?
LYSISTRATA: Just you leave
the men to me. There's not fire enough in the
world,
or threats either, to make me open these doors
except on my own terms.
210 KALONIKE: I hope not, by Aphrodite!
After all,
we've got a reputation for bitchiness to live up
to.   (*Exeunt.°*)

211. [S.D.] *Exeunt*: Latin for "they go out."

(*The hillside just under the Akropolis. Enter Chorus
of Old Men with burning torches and braziers; much
puffing and coughing.*)

KORYPHAIOS(man):° Forward march, Drakes, old
friend: never you mind
that damn big log banging hell down on your
back.

Strophe° 1

CHORUS(men): There's this to be said for longevity:
You see things you thought that you'd never see.
Look, Strymodoros, who would have thought
it?   5
We've caught it —
                    the New Femininity!
The wives of our bosom, our board, our bed —
Now, by the gods, they've gone ahead
And taken the Citadel (Heaven knows why!),
Profanèd the sacred statuar-y,   10
                    And barred the doors,
                    The subversive whores!
KORYPHAIOS(m): Shake a leg there, Philurgos, man:
the Akropolis or bust!
Put the kindling around here. We'll build one
almighty big
bonfire for the whole bunch of bitches, every last
one;   15
and the first we fry will be old Lykon's woman.

Antistrophe° 1

CHORUS(m): They're not going to give me the old
horse-laugh!
No, by Demeter, they won't pull this off!
Think of Kleomenes: even he
Didn't go free
                    till he brought me his stuff.   20
A good man he was, all stinking and shaggy,
Bare as an eel except for the bag he
Covered his rear with. God, what a mess!

Parodos: The song or ode chanted by the Chorus on their entry.   **Koryphaios:** Leader of the Chorus; also called *Choragos.* There are two Choruses and two Koryphaioi, one male
and one female.   **Strophe:** Song sung by the Chorus as they
danced from stage right to stage left.   **Antistrophe:** Song
sung by the Chorus following the Strophe, as they danced
back from stage left to stage right.

25   Never a bath in six years, I'd guess.
                                   Pure Sparta, man!
                                   He also ran.
       KORYPHAIOS[m]: That was a siege, friends! Seventeen
           ranks strong
       we slept at the Gate. And shall we not do as
           much
       against these women, whom God and Euripides
           hate?
       If we don't, I'll turn in my medals from
30   Marathon.

Strophe 2

CHORUS[m]: Onward and upward! A little push,
       And we're there.
       Ouch, my shoulders! I could wish
       For a pair
35   Of good strong oxen. Keep your eye
       On the fire there, it mustn't die.
                               Akh! Akh!
       The smoke would make a cadaver cough!

Antistrophe 2

       Holy Herakles, a hot spark
40   Bit my eye!
       Damn this hellfire, damn this work!
           So say I.
       Onward and upward just the same.
       (Laches, remember the Goddess: for shame!)
45   Akh! Akh!
       The smoke would make a cadaver cough!
       KORYPHAIOS[m]: At last (and let us give suitable
           thanks to God
       for his infinite mercies) I have managed to bring
       my personal flame to the common goal. It
           breathes, it lives.
50   Now, gentlemen, let us consider. Shall we insert
       the torch, say, into the brazier, and thus extract
       a kindling brand? And shall we then, do you
           think,
       push on to the gate like valiant sheep? On the
           whole yes.
       But I would have you consider this, too: if
           they —
55   I refer to the women — should refuse to open,
       what then? Do we set the doors afire
       and smoke them out? At ease, men. Meditate.
       Akh, the smoke! Woof! What we really need

is the loan of a general or two from the Samos
       Command.°
At least we've got this lumber off our backs.   60
That's something. And now let's look to our fire.

O Pot, brave Brazier, touch my torch with
       flame!
Victory, Goddess, I invoke thy name!
Strike down these paradigms of female pride
And we shall hang our trophies up inside.   65

(*Enter Chorus of Old Women on the walls of the
Akropolis, carrying jars of water.*)

KORYPHAIOS[woman]: Smoke, girls, smoke! There's
       smoke all over the place!
Probably fire, too. Hurry, girls! Fire! Fire!

Strophe 1

CHORUS[women]: Nikodike, run!
       Or Kalyke's done
       To a turn, and poor Kritylla's   70
       Smoked like a ham.
                       Damn
       These old men! Are we too late?
       I nearly died down at the place
       Where we fill our jars:
           Slaves pushing and jostling —   75
           Such a hustling
       I never saw in all my days.

Antistrophe 1

       But here's water at last.
       Haste, sisters, haste!
       Slosh it on them, slosh it down,   80
       The silly old wrecks!
                       Sex
       Almighty! What they want's
       A hot bath? Good. Send one down.
       Athena of Athens town,
           Trito-born!° Helm of Gold!   85
           Cripple the old
       Firemen! Help us help them drown!

(*The old men capture a woman, Stratyllis.*)

STRATYLLIS: Let me go! Let me go!
KORYPHAIOS[w]:   You walking corpses,
       have you no shame?

---

59. **Samos Command:** Headquarters of the Athenian military.   85. **Trito-born:** Athena, goddess of wisdom, was said
to have been born near Lake Tritonis, in Libya.

KORYPHAIOS^(m):   I wouldn't have believed it!
90   An army of women in the Akropolis!
KORYPHAIOS^(w): So we scare you, do we? Grandpa, you've seen
       only our pickets yet!
KORYPHAIOS^(m):   Hey, Phaidrias!
       Help me with the necks of these jabbering hens!
KORYPHAIOS^(w): Down with your pots, girls! We'll need both hands
       if these antiques attack us!
95 KORYPHAIOS^(m):   Want your face kicked in?
KORYPHAIOS^(w): Want your balls chewed off?
KORYPHAIOS^(m):   Look out! I've got a stick!
KORYPHAIOS^(w): You lay a half-inch of your stick on Stratyllis,
       and you'll never stick again!
KORYPHAIOS^(m): Fall apart!
KORYPHAIOS^(w):   I'll spit up your guts!
KORYPHAIOS^(m):   Euripides! Master!
       How well you knew women!
100 KORYPHAIOS^(w):   Listen to him, Rhodippe,
       up with the pots!
KORYPHAIOS^(m):   Demolition of God,
       what good are your pots?
KORYPHAIOS^(w):   You refugee from the tomb,
       what good is your fire?
KORYPHAIOS^(m):   Good enough to make a pyre
       to barbecue you!
KORYPHAIOS^(w): We'll squizzle your kindling!
KORYPHAIOS^(m): You think so?
105 KORYPHAIOS^(w):   Yah! Just hang around a while!
KORYPHAIOS^(m): Want a touch of my torch?
KORYPHAIOS^(w):   It needs a good soaping.
KORYPHAIOS^(m): How about you?
KORYPHAIOS^(w):   Soap for a senile bridegroom!
KORYPHAIOS^(m): Senile? Hold your trap
KORYPHAIOS^(w):   Just *you* try to hold it!
KORYPHAIOS^(m): The yammer of women!
KORYPHAIOS^(w):   Oh is that so?
110   You're not in the jury room now, you know.
KORYPHAIOS^(m): Gentlemen, I beg you, burn off that woman's hair!
KORYPHAIOS^(w): Let it come down!

(*They empty their pots on the men.*)

KORYPHAIOS^(m): What a way to drown!
KORYPHAIOS^(w):   Hot, hey?
KORYPHAIOS^(m):   Say,
       enough!
KORYPHAIOS^(w): Dandruff
115   needs watering. I'll make you
       nice and fresh.
KORYPHAIOS^(m):   For God's sake, you, hold off!

SCENE 1

(*Enter a Commissioner accompanied by four constables.*)

COMMISSIONER: These degenerate women! What a racket of little drums,
   what a yapping for Adonis° on every house-top!
   It's like the time in the Assembly when I was listening
   to a speech — out of order, as usual — by that fool
   Demostratos,° all about troops for Sicily,°   5
   that kind of nonsense —
                   and there was his wife
   trotting around in circles howling
   Alas for Adonis! —
                   and Demostratos insisting
   we must draft every last Zakynthian that can walk —
   and his wife up there on the roof,   10
   drunk as an owl, yowling
   Oh weep for Adonis! —
                   and that damned ox Demostratos
   mooing away through the rumpus. That's what we get
   for putting up with this wretched woman-business!
KORYPHAIOS^(m): Sir, you haven't heard the half of it.
   They laughed at us!   15
   Insulted us! They took pitchers of water
   and nearly drowned us! We're still wringing out our clothes,
   for all the world like unhousebroken brats.
COMMISSIONER: Serves you right, by Poseidon!
   Whose fault is it if these women-folk of ours   20
   get out of hand? We coddle them,
   we teach them to be wasteful and loose. You'll see a husband
   go into a jeweler's. "Look," he'll say,
   "jeweler," he'll say, "you remember that gold choker
   you made for my wife? Well, she went to a dance last night 25
   and broke the clasp. Now, I've got to go to Salamis,
   and can't be bothered. Run over to my house tonight,
   will you, and see if you can put it together for her."

2. **Adonis:** Fertility god, loved by Aphrodite.   5. **Demostratos:** Athenian orator and politician.   **Sicily:** Reference to the Sicilian Expedition (415–413 B.C.) in which Athens was decisively defeated.

Or another one
goes to a cobbler — a good strong workman,
30   too,
with an awl that was never meant for child's
    play. "Here,"
he'll tell him, "one of my wife's shoes is
    pinching
her little toe. Could you come up about noon
and stretch it out for her?"
                Well, what do you expect?
35   Look at me, for example, I'm a Public Officer,
and it's one of my duties to pay off the sailors.
And where's the money? Up there in the
    Akropolis!
And those blasted women slam the door in my
    face!
But what are we waiting for?
              — Look here, constable,
40   stop sniffing around for a tavern, and get us
some crowbars. We'll force their gates! As a
    matter of fact,
I'll do a little forcing myself.

(*Enter Lysistrata, above, with Myrrhine, Kalonike, and the Boiotian.*)

LYSISTRATA: No need of forcing.
Here I am, of my own accord. And all this talk
about locked doors — ! We don't need locked
    doors,
45   but just the least bit of common sense.
COMMISSIONER: Is that so, ma'am!
                — Where's my constable?
                — Constable,
arrest that woman, and tie her hands behind her.
LYSISTRATA: If he touches me, I swear by Artemis
there'll be one scamp dropped from the public
    pay-roll tomorrow!
COMMISSIONER: Well, constable? You're not afraid,
50   I suppose? Grab her,
two of you, around the middle!
KALONIKE: No, by Pandrosos!°
Lay a hand on her, and I'll jump on you so hard
your guts will come out the back door!
COMMISSIONER: That's what *you* think!
Where's the sergeant? — Here, you: tie up that
    trollop first,
the one with the pretty talk!
55   MYRRHINE: By the Moon-Goddess,°
just try! They'll have to scoop you up with a
    spoon!

---

51. Pandrosos: A woman's oath referring to one of the daughters of the founder of Athens.   **55. Moon-Goddess:** Artemis, goddess of the hunt and fertility, daughter of Zeus.

COMMISSIONER: Another one!
          Officer, seize that woman!
                          I swear
I'll put an end to this riot!
BOIOTIAN: By the Taurian,°
one inch closer, you'll be one screaming bald-
    head!
COMMISSIONER: Lord, what a mess! And my
    constables seem ineffective.   60
But — women get the best of us? By God, no!
                — Skythians!°
Close ranks and forward march!
LYSISTRATA: "Forward," indeed!
By the Two Goddesses, what's the sense in *that*?
They're up against four companies of women
armed from top to bottom.
COMMISSIONER: Forward, my Skythians!   65
LYSISTRATA: Forward, yourselves, dear comrades!
You grainlettucebeanseedmarket girls!
You garlicandonionbreadbakery girls!
Give it to 'em! Knock 'em down! Scratch 'em!
Tell 'em what you think of 'em!

(*General melee, the Skythians yield.*)

              — Ah, that's enough!   70
Sound a retreat: good soldiers don't rob the
    dead.
COMMISSIONER: A nice day *this* has been for the
    police!
LYSISTRATA: Well, there you are. — Did you really
    think we women
would be driven like slaves? Maybe now you'll
    admit
that a woman knows something about spirit.
COMMISSIONER: Spirit enough,   75
especially spirits in bottles! Dear Lord Apollo!
KORYPHAIOS[m]: Your Honor, there's no use talking
    to them. Words
mean nothing whatever to wild animals like
    these.
Think of the sousing they gave us! and the water
was not, I believe, of the purest.   80
KORYPHAIOS[w]: You shouldn't have come after us.
And if you try it again,
you'll be one eye short! — Although, as a matter
    of fact,
what I like best is just to stay at home and read,
like a sweet little bride: never hurting a soul, no,
never going out. But if you *must* shake hornets'
    nests,   85
look out for the hornets.

---

58. Taurian: Reference to Artemis, who was said to have been worshiped in a cult at Taurica Chersonesos.   **61. Skythians:** Athenian archers.

Strophe 1

CHORUS^(m): Of all the beasts that God hath
      wrought
        What monster's worse than woman?
      Who shall encompass with his thought
90   Their guile unending? No man.

      They've seized the Heights, the Rock, the
        Shrine —
      But to what end? I wot not.
      Sure there's some clue to their design!
      Have you the key? I thought not.
KORYPHAIOS^(m): We might question them, I suppose.
95   But I warn you, sir,
      don't believe anything you hear! It would be un-
        Athenian
      not to get to the bottom of this plot.
COMMISSIONER: Very well.
      My first question is this: Why, so help you God,
      did you bar the gates of the Akropolis?
LYSISTRATA: Why?
      To keep the money, of course. No money, no
100   war.
COMMISSIONER: You think that money's the cause
      of war?
LYSISTRATA: I do.
      Money brought about that Peisandros° business
      and all the other attacks on the State. Well and
        good!
      They'll not get another cent here!
COMMISSIONER: And what will you do?
LYSISTRATA: What a question! From now on, we
105   intend
      to control the Treasury.
COMMISSIONER: Control the Treasury!
LYSISTRATA: Why not? Does that seem strange?
      After all,
      we control our household budgets.
COMMISSIONER: But that's different!
LYSISTRATA: "Different"? What do you mean?
COMMISSIONER: I mean simply this:
110   it's the Treasury that pays for National Defense.
LYSISTRATA: Unnecessary. We propose to abolish
      war.
COMMISSIONER: Good God. — And National
      Security?
LYSISTRATA: Leave that to us.
COMMISSIONER: You?
LYSISTRATA: Us.
COMMISSIONER: We're done for, then!

---

102. Peisandros: A politician who plotted against the Athenian democracy.

LYSISTRATA: Never mind.
      We women will save you in spite of yourselves.
COMMISSIONER: What nonsense!
LYSISTRATA: If you like. But you must accept it, like
      it or not.   115
COMMISSIONER: Why, this is downright subversion!
LYSISTRATA: Maybe it is.
      But we're going to save you, Judge.
COMMISSIONER: I don't *want* to be saved.
LYSISTRATA: Tut. The death-wish. All the more
      reason.
COMMISSIONER: But the idea of women bothering
      themselves about peace and war!
LYSISTRATA: Will you listen to me?
COMMISSIONER: Yes. But be brief, or I'll —   120
LYSISTRATA: This is no time for stupid threats.
COMMISSIONER: By the gods,
      I can't stand any more!
AN OLD WOMAN: Can't stand? Well, well.
COMMISSIONER: That's enough out of you, you old
      buzzard!
      Now, Lysistrata: tell me what you're thinking.
LYSISTRATA: Glad to.
                          Ever since this war began   125
      We women have been watching you men,
        agreeing with you,
      keeping our thoughts to ourselves. That doesn't
        mean
      we were happy: we weren't, for we saw how
        things were going;
      but we'd listen to you at dinner
      arguing this way and that.
                          — Oh you, and your big   130
      Top Secrets! —
                  And then we'd grin like little patriots
      (though goodness knows we didn't feel like
        grinning) and ask you:
      "Dear, did the Armistice come up in Assembly
        today?"
      And you'd say, "None of your business! Pipe
        down!" you'd say.
      And so we would.
AN OLD WOMAN: *I* wouldn't have, by God!   135
COMMISSIONER: You'd have taken a beating, then!
                                      — Go on.
LYSISTRATA: Well, we'd be quiet. But then, you
      know, all at once
      you men would think up something worse than
        ever.
      Even *I* could see it was fatal. And, "Darling,"
      I'd say,
      "have you gone completely mad?" And my
      husband would look at me   140
      and say, "Wife, you've got your weaving to
      attend to.

Mind your tongue, if you don't want a slap.
    'War's
a man's affair!' "°
COMMISSIONER: Good words, and well pronounced.
LYSISTRATA: You're a fool if you think so.
                            It was hard enough
145   to put up with all this banquet-hall strategy.
    But then we'd hear you out in the public square:
    "Nobody left for the draft-quota here in
        Athens?"
    you'd say; and, "No," someone else would say,
        "not a man!"
    And so we women decided to rescue Greece.
    You might as well listen to us now: you'll have
150   to, later.
COMMISSIONER: *You* rescue Greece? Absurd.
LYSISTRATA: You're the absurd one.
COMMISSIONER: You expect me to take orders from
    a woman?
                 I'd die first!
LYSISTRATA: Heavens, if that's what's bothering
    you, take my veil,
    here, and wrap it around your poor head.
KALONIKE: Yes
155   and you can have my market-basket, too.
    Go home, tighten your girdle, do the washing,
        mind
    your beans! "War's
    a woman's affair!"
KORYPHAIOS[w]:   Ground pitchers! Close
    ranks!

Antistrophe

CHORUS[w]: This is a dance that I know well,
160   My knees shall never yield.
    Wobble and creak I may, but still
        I'll keep the well-fought field.
    Valor and grace march on before,
        Love prods us from behind.
165   Our slogan is EXCELSIOR,
        Our watchword SAVE MANKIND.
KORYPHAIOS[w]: Women, remember your
    grandmothers! Remember
    that little old mother of yours, what a stinger
    she was!
    On, on, never slacken. There's a strong wind
    astern!
LYSISTRATA: O Eros of delight! O Aphrodite!

Kyprian!°   170
If ever desire has drenched our breasts or
    dreamed
in our thighs, let it work so now on the men of
    Hellas°
that they shall tail us through the land, slaves,
    slaves
to Woman, Breaker of Armies!
COMMISSIONER: And if we do?
LYSISTRATA: Well, for one thing, we shan't have to
    watch you   175
going to market, a spear in one hand, and
    heaven knows
what in the other.
KALONIKE: Nicely said, by Aphrodite!
LYSISTRATA: As things stand now, you're neither
    men nor women.
Armor clanking with kitchen pans and pots —
You sound like a pack of Korybantes!°   180
COMMISSIONER: A man must do what a man must
    do.
LYSISTRATA: So I'm told.
But to see a General, complete with Gorgon-
    shield,
jingling along the dock to buy a couple of
    herrings!
KALONIKE: *I* saw a Captain the other day — lovely
    fellow he was,
nice curly hair — sitting on his horse; and —
    can you believe it? —   185
he'd just bought some soup, and was pouring it
    into his helmet!
And there was a soldier from Thrace
swishing his lance like something out of
    Euripides,
and the poor fruit-store woman got so scared
that she ran away and let him have his figs free!   190
COMMISSIONER: All this is beside the point.
                      Will you be so kind
as to tell me how you mean to save Greece?
LYSISTRATA: Of course.
Nothing could be simpler.
COMMISSIONER: I assure you, I'm all ears.
LYSISTRATA: Do you know anything about weaving?
Say the yarn gets tangled: we thread it   195
this way and that through the skein, up and
    down,
until it's free. And it's like that with war.
We'll send our envoys

142–43. **'War's a man's affair!':** Quoted from Homer's *Iliad*,
VI, 492, Hector's farewell to his wife, Andromache.

170. **Kyprian:** Reference to Aphrodite's association with
Cyprus (Kyprus), a place sacred to her and a center for her
worship.   **172. Hellas:** Greece.   **180. Korybantes:** Priestesses of Cybele, a fertility goddess, who was celebrated in
frenzied rituals accompanied by the beating of cymbals.

up and down, this way and that, all over
    Greece,
  until it's finished.

200 COMMISSIONER: Yarn? Thread? Skein?
  Are you out of your mind? I tell you,
  war is a serious business.

LYSISTRATA: So serious
  that I'd like to go on talking about weaving.

COMMISSIONER: All right. Go ahead.

LYSISTRATA: The first thing we have to do
205 is to wash our yarn, get the dirt out of it.
  You see? Isn't there too much dirt here in
    Athens?
  You must wash those men away.
                Then our spoiled wool —
  that's like your job-hunters, out for a life
  of no work and big pay. Back to the basket,
210 citizens or not, allies or not,
  or friendly immigrants.
              And your colonies?
  Hanks of wool lost in various places. Pull them
  together, weave them into one great whole,
  and our voters are clothed for ever.

COMMISSIONER: It would take a woman
  to reduce state questions to a matter of carding
215   and weaving.

LYSISTRATA: You fool! Who were the mothers
   whose sons sailed off
  to fight for Athens in Sicily?

COMMISSIONER: Enough!
  I beg you, do not call back those memories.

LYSISTRATA: And then,
  instead of the love that every woman needs,
  we have only our single beds, where we can
220   dream
  of our husbands off with the Army.
             Bad enough for wives!
  But what about our girls, getting older every
   day,
  and older, and no kisses?

COMMISSIONER: Men get older, too.

LYSISTRATA: Not in the same sense.
            A soldier's discharged,
225 and he may be bald and toothless, yet he'll find
  a pretty young thing to go to bed with.
            But a woman!
  Her beauty is gone with the first gray hair.
  She can spend her time
  consulting the oracles and the fortune-tellers,
230 but they'll never send her a husband.

COMMISSIONER: Still, if a man can rise to the
   occasion —

LYSISTRATA: Rise? Rise, yourself!

(*Furiously.*)

Go invest in a coffin!
          You've money enough.
                 I'll bake you
  a cake for the Underworld.
              And here's your funeral
  wreath!

(*She pours water upon him.*)

MYRRHINE: And here's another!

(*More water.*)

KALONIKE: And here's   235
  my contribution!

(*More water.*)

LYSISTRATA: What are you waiting for?
  All aboard Styx Ferry!
            Charon's° calling for you!
  It's sailing-time: don't disrupt the schedule!

COMMISSIONER: The insolence of women! And to
   me!
  No, by God, I'll go back to town and show   240
  the rest of the Commission what might happen
   to them.   (*Exit Commissioner.*)

LYSISTRATA: Really, I suppose we should have laid
  out his corpse
  on the doorstep, in the usual way.
               But never mind.
  We'll give him the rites of the dead tomorrow
  morning.
    (*Exit Lysistrata with Myrrhine and Kalonike.*)

PARABASIS:° CHORAL EPISODE • Ode° 1

KORYPHAIOS[(m)]: Sons of Liberty, awake! The day of
  glory is at hand.

CHORUS[(m)]: I smell tyranny afoot, I smell it rising
  from the land.
  I scent a trace of Hippias,° I sniff upon the
   breeze
  A dismal Spartan hogo that suggests King
   Kleisthenes.°
  Strip, strip for action, brothers!   5

237. **Charon:** The god who ferried the souls of the newly dead across the river Styx to Hades.   **Parabasis:** Section of the play in which the author presented his own views through the Koryphaios directly to the audience. The parabasis in *Lysistrata* is shorter than those in Aristophanes' other works and unusual in that the Koryphaios does not speak directly for the author.   **Ode:** Song sung by the Chorus.   **3. Hippias:** An Athenian tyrant.   **4. Kleisthenes:** A bisexual Athenian.

Our wives, aunts, sisters, mothers
Have sold us out: the streets are full of godless
  female rages.
Shall we stand by and let our women confiscate
  our wages?

                                              [Epirrhema° 1]
KORYPHAIOS⁽ᵐ⁾: Gentlemen, it's a disgrace to
  Athens, a disgrace
  to all that Athens stands for, if we allow these
10 grandmas
  to jabber about spears and shields and making
    friends
  with the Spartans. What's a Spartan? Give me a
    wild wolf
  any day. No. They want the Tyranny back, I
    suppose.
15 Are we going to take that? No. Let us look like
  the innocent serpent, but be the flower under it,
  as the poet sings. And just to begin with,
  I propose to poke a number of teeth
  down the gullet of that harridan over there.

Antode° 1

KORYPHAIOS⁽ʷ⁾: Oh, is that so? When you get
  home, your own mamma won't know you!
CHORUS⁽ʷ⁾: Who do you think we are, you senile
20 bravos? Well, I'll show you.
  I bore the sacred vessels in my eighth year,° and
    at ten
  I was pounding out the barley for Athena
    Goddess;° then
  They made me Little Bear
  At the Brauronian Fair;°
  I'd held the Holy Basket° by the time I was of
25 age,
  The Blessed Dry Figs had adorned my plump
    decolletage.

                                              [Antepirrhema° 1]
KORYPHAIOS⁽ʷ⁾: A "disgrace to Athens," and I, just
  at the moment

Epirrhema: A part of the parabasis spoken by the Koryphaios following an ode delivered by his or her half of the Chorus. **Antode:** Lyric song sung by half of the Chorus in response to the Ode sung by the other half.   **21. eighth year:** Young girls between the ages of seven and eleven served in the temple of Athena in the Akropolis.   **22. pounding out the barley for Athena Goddess:** At age ten a girl could be chosen to grind the sacred grain of Athena.   **24. Brauronian Fair:** A ritual in the cult of Artemis, who is associated with wild beasts, in which young girls dressed up as bears and danced for the goddess.   **25. Holy Basket:** In one ritual to Athena, young girls carried baskets of objects sacred to the goddess.   **Antepirrhema:** The speech delivered by the second Koryphaios after the second half of the Chorus had sung an ode.

I'm giving Athens the best advice she ever had?
Don't I pay taxes to the State? Yes, I pay them
in baby boys. And what do you contribute,   30
you impotent horrors? Nothing but waste: all
our Treasury,° dating back to the Persian Wars,
gone! rifled! And not a penny out of your
  pockets!
Well, then? Can you cough up an answer to
  that?
Look out for your own gullet, or you'll get a
  crack   35
from this old brogan that'll make your teeth see
  stars!

Ode 2

CHORUS⁽ᵐ⁾: Oh insolence!
  Am I unmanned?
  Incontinence!
  Shall my scarred hand   40
  Strike never a blow
  To curb this flow-
  ing female curse?

  Leipsydrion!°
  Shall I betray   45
  The laurels won
  On that great day?
  Come, shake a leg,
  Shed old age, beg
  The years reverse!   50
                                              [Epirrhema 2]
KORYPHAIOS⁽ᵐ⁾: Give them an inch, and we're done
  for! We'll have them
  launching boats next and planning naval
    strategy,
  sailing down on us like so many Artemisias.
  Or maybe they have ideas about the cavalry.
  That's fair enough, women are certainly good   55
  in the saddle. Just look at Mikon's paintings,
  all those Amazons wrestling with all those men!
  On the whole, a straitjacket's their best uniform.

Antode 2

CHORUS⁽ʷ⁾: Tangle with me,
  And you'll get cramps.   60
  Ferocity
  's no use now, Gramps!

---

32. Treasury: Athenian politicians were raiding the funds that were collected by Athens to finance a war against Persia. **44. Leipsydrion:** A place where Athenian patriots had heroically fought.

By the Two,
I'll get through
65   To you wrecks yet!

I'll scramble your eggs,
I'll burn your beans,
With my two legs.
You'll see such scenes
70   As never yet
Your two eyes met.
A curse? You bet!

[Antepirrhema 2]

KORYPHAIOS[(w)]: If Lampito stands by me, and that
       delicious Theban girl,
       Ismenia — what good are *you*? You and your
          seven
75   Resolutions! Resolutions? Rationing Boiotian eels
       and making our girls go without them at
          Hekate's° Feast!
       That was statesmanship! And we'll have to put
          up with it
       and all the rest of your decrepit legislation
       until some patriot — God give him strength! —
       grabs you by the neck and kicks you off the
80   Rock.

SCENE 2

(*Reenter Lysistrata and her lieutenants.*)

KORYPHAIOS[(w)] (*tragic tone*): Great Queen, fair
       Architect of our emprise,
       Why lookst thou on us with foreboding eyes?
LYSISTRATA: The behavior of these idiotic women!
       There's something about the female temperament
       that I can't bear!
KORYPHAIOS[(w)]:   What in the world do you
5   mean?
LYSISTRATA: Exactly what I say.
KORYPHAIOS[(w)]: What dreadful thing has happened?
       Come, tell us: we're all your friends.
LYSISTRATA: It isn't easy
       to say it; yet, God knows, we can't hush it up.
KORYPHAIOS[(w)]: Well, then? Out with it!
LYSISTRATA: To put it bluntly,
       we're dying to get laid.
10 KORYPHAIOS[(w)]:   Almighty God!
LYSISTRATA: Why bring God into it? — No, it's just
       as I say.
       I can't manage them any longer: they've gone
       man-crazy,

they're all trying to get out.
                     Why, look:
one of them was sneaking out the back door
over there by Pan's cave; another   15
was sliding down the walls with rope and tackle;
another was climbing aboard a sparrow, ready
   to take off
for the nearest brothel — I dragged *her* back by
   the hair!
They're all finding some reason to leave.
                           Look there!
There goes another one.
                     — Just a minute, you! 20
Where are you off to so fast?
FIRST WOMAN: I've got to get home.
   I've a lot of Milesian wool, and the worms are
      spoiling it.
LYSISTRATA: Oh bother you and your worms! Get
      back inside!
FIRST WOMAN: I'll be back right away, I swear I
      will.
   I just want to get it stretched out on my bed. 25
LYSISTRATA: You'll do no such thing. You'll stay
      right here.
FIRST WOMAN: And my wool?
   You want it ruined?
LYSISTRATA: Yes, for all I care.
SECOND WOMAN: Oh dear! My lovely new flax
      from Amorgos —
   I left it at home, all uncarded!
LYSISTRATA: Another one!
   And all she wants is someone to card her flax. 30
   Get back in there!
SECOND WOMAN: But I swear by the Moon
      Goddess
   the minute I get it done, I'll be back!
LYSISTRATA: I say No.
   If you, why not all the other women as well?
THIRD WOMAN: O Lady Eileithyia!° Radiant
      goddess! Thou
   intercessor for women in childbirth! Stay, I pray
      thee,   35
   oh stay this parturition. Shall I pollute
   a sacred spot?°
LYSISTRATA: And what's the matter with *you?*
THIRD WOMAN: I'm having a baby — any minute
      now.
LYSISTRATA: But you weren't pregnant yesterday.
THIRD WOMAN: Well, I am today.
   Let me go home for a midwife, Lysistrata: 40
   there's not much time.

---

76. **Hekate:** Patron of successful wars, object of a Boiotian
cult (later associated with sorcery).

34. **Eileithyia:** Goddess of childbirth. 36–37. **pollute a sacred spot:** Giving birth on the Akropolis was forbidden because it was sacred ground.

LYSISTRATA: I never heard such nonsense.
What's that bulging under your cloak?
THIRD WOMAN: A little baby boy.
LYSISTRATA: It certainly isn't. But it's something
   hollow,
   like a basin or — Why, it's the helmet of
   Athena!
   And you said you were having a baby.
45 THIRD WOMAN: Well, I am! So there!
LYSISTRATA: Then why the helmet?
THIRD WOMAN: I was afraid that my pains
   might begin here in the Akropolis; and I wanted
   to drop my chick into it, just as the dear doves
   do.
LYSISTRATA: Lies! Evasions! — But at least one
   thing's clear:
   you can't leave the place before your
50   purification.°
THIRD WOMAN: But I can't stay here in the
   Akropolis! Last night I dreamed
   of the Snake.
FIRST WOMAN: And those horrible owls, the
   noise they make!
   I can't get a bit of sleep; I'm just about dead.
LYSISTRATA: You useless girls, that's enough: Let's
   have no more lying.
   Of course you want your men. But don't you
55   imagine
   that they want you just as much? I'll give you
   my word,
   their nights must be pretty hard.
                              Just stick it out!
   A little patience, that's all, and our battle's won.
   I have heard an Oracle. Should you like to hear
   it?
FIRST WOMAN: An Oracle? Yes, tell us!
60 LYSISTRATA: Here is what it says:
   WHEN SWALLOWS SHALL THE HOOPOE
      SHUN
      AND SPURN HIS HOT DESIRE,
   ZEUS WILL PERFECT WHAT THEY'VE
      BEGUN
      AND SET THE LOWER HIGHER.
65 FIRST WOMAN: Does that mean we'll be on top?
LYSISTRATA: BUT IF THE SWALLOWS SHALL
      FALL OUT
      AND TAKE THE HOOPOE'S BAIT,
   A CURSE MUST MARK THEIR HOUR OF
      DOUBT,
      INFAMY SEAL THEIR FATE.
THIRD WOMAN: I swear, *that* Oracle's all too clear.
70 FIRST WOMAN: Oh the dear gods!

---

50. purification: A ritual cleansing of a woman after childbirth.

LYSISTRATA: Let's not be downhearted, girls. Back
   to our places!
   The god has spoken. How can we possibly fail
   him?
      (*Exit Lysistrata with the dissident women.*)

CHORAL EPISODE • *Strophe*

CHORUS(m): I know a little story that I learned way
      back in school
   Goes like this:
   Once upon a time there was a young man —
      and no fool —
   Named Melanion; and his
   One aversion was marriage. He loathed the very
      thought.   5
   So he ran off to the hills, and in a special grot
   Raised a dog, and spent his days
   Hunting rabbits. And it says
   That he never never never did come home.
   It might be called a refuge *from* the womb.   10
   All right,
            all right,
                     all right!
   We're as bright as young Melanion, and we hate
   the very sight
   Of you women!
A MAN: How about a kiss, old lady?
A WOMAN: Here's an onion for your eye!   15
A MAN: A kick in the guts, then?
A WOMAN: Try, old bristle-tail, just try!
A MAN: Yet they say Myronides
   On hands and knees
   Looked just as shaggy fore and aft as I!   20

Antistrophe

CHORUS(w): Well, *I* know a little story, and it's just
      as good as yours.
   Goes like this:
   Once there was a man named Timon — a rough
      diamond, of course,
   And that whiskery face of his
   Looked like murder in the shrubbery. By God, he
      was a son   25
   Of the Furies, let me tell you! And what did he
      do but run
   From the world and all its ways,
   Cursing mankind! And it says
   That his choicest execrations as of then
   Were leveled almost wholly at *old* men.   30
   All right,
            all right,
                     all right!

But there's one thing about Timon: he could
   always stand the sight
of us women.
A WOMAN: How about a crack in the jaw, Pop?
35 A MAN: I can take it, Ma — no fear!
A WOMAN: How about a kick in the face?
A MAN: You'd reveal your old caboose?
A WOMAN: What I'd show,
   I'll have you know,
40   Is an instrument you're too far gone to use.

SCENE 3

(*Reenter Lysistrata.*)

LYSISTRATA: Oh, quick, girls, quick! Come here!
A WOMAN: What is it?
LYSISTRATA: A man.
   A man simply bulging with love.
                                  O Kyprian Queen,°
   O Paphian, O Kythereian! Hear us and aid us!
A WOMAN: Where is this enemy?
LYSISTRATA: Over there, by Demeter's shrine.
A WOMAN: Damned if he isn't. But who *is* he?
5 MYRRHINE: My husband.
   Kinesias.
LYSISTRATA: Oh then, get busy! Tease him!
   Undermine him!
   Wreck him! Give him everything — kissing,
      tickling, nudging,
   whatever you generally torture him with — :
      give him everything
   except what we swore on the wine we would
      not give.
MYRRHINE: Trust me.
10 LYSISTRATA: I do. But I'll help you get him started.
   The rest of you women, stay back.

(*Enter Kinesias.*)

KINESIAS: Oh God! Oh my God!
   I'm stiff from lack of exercise. All I can do to
      stand up.
LYSISTRATA: Halt! Who are you, approaching our
      lines?
KINESIAS: Me? I.
LYSISTRATA: A man?
KINESIAS: You have eyes, haven't you?
LYSISTRATA: Go away.
KINESIAS: Who says so?
LYSISTRATA: Officer of the Day.

---

2. **Kyprian Queen:** Aphrodite.

KINESIAS: Officer, I beg you,   15
   by all the gods at once, bring Myrrhine out.
LYSISTRATA: Myrrhine? And who, my good sir, are
   you?
KINESIAS: Kinesias. Last name's Pennison. Her
   husband.
LYSISTRATA: Oh, of course. I beg your pardon.
      We're glad to see you.
   We've heard so much about you. Dearest
      Myrrhine   20
   is always talking about Kinesias — never nibbles
      an egg
   or an apple without saying
   "Here's to Kinesias!"
KINESIAS: Do you really mean it?
LYSISTRATA: I do.
   When we're discussing men, she always says
   "Well, after all, there's nobody like Kinesias!"   25
KINESIAS: Good God. — Well, then, please send her
      down here.
LYSISTRATA: And what do *I* get out of it?
KINESIAS: A standing promise.
LYSISTRATA: I'll take it up with her.
                              (*Exit Lysistrata.*)
KINESIAS: But be quick about it!
   Lord, what's life without a wife? Can't eat.
   Can't sleep.
   Every time I go home, the place is so empty, so   30
   insufferably sad. Love's killing me, Oh,
   hurry!

(*Enter Manes, a slave, with Kinesias's baby; the voice
of Myrrhine is heard offstage.*)

MYRRHINE: But of course I love him! Adore
      him — But no,
   he hates love. No. I won't go down.

(*Enter Myrrhine, above.*)

KINESIAS: Myrrhine!
   Darlingest Myrrhinette! Come down quick!
MYRRHINE: Certainly not.
KINESIAS: Not? But why, Myrrhine?   35
MYRRHINE: Why? You don't need me.
KINESIAS: Need you? My God, *look* at me!
MYRRHINE: So long!

(*Turns to go.*)

KINESIAS: Myrrhine, Myrrhine, Myrrhine!
   If not for my sake, for our child!

(*Pinches Baby.*)

                              — All right, you: pipe up!
BABY: Mummie! Mummie! Mummie!
KINESIAS: You hear that?
   Pitiful, I call it. Six days now   40

with never a bath; no food; enough to break
your heart!
MYRRHINE: My darlingest child! What a father *you*
acquired!
KINESIAS: At least come down for his sake.
MYRRHINE: I suppose I must.
Oh, this mother business!   (*Exit.*)
KINESIAS: How pretty she is! And younger!
The harder she treats me, the more bothered I
get.

(*Myrrhine enters, below.*)

45 MYRRHINE: Dearest child,
you're as sweet as your father's horrid. Give me
a kiss.
KINESIAS: Now don't you see how wrong it was to
get involved
in this scheming League of women? It's bad
for us both.
MYRRHINE: Keep your hands to yourself!
KINESIAS: But our house
going to rack and ruin?
MYRRHINE: I don't care.
50 KINESIAS: And your knitting
all torn to pieces by the chickens? Don't you
care?
MYRRHINE: Not at all.
KINESIAS: And our debt to Aphrodite?
Oh, *won't* you come back?
MYRRHINE: No. — At least, not until you
men
make a treaty and stop this war.
KINESIAS: Why, I suppose
that might be arranged.
55 MYRRHINE: Oh? Well, I suppose
I might come down then. But meanwhile,
I've sworn not to.
KINESIAS: Don't worry. — Now let's have fun.
MYRRHINE: No! Stop it! I said no!
                         — Although, of course,
I *do* love you.
KINESIAS: I know you do. Darling Myrrhine:
come, shall we?
MYRRHINE: Are you out of your mind? In front of
60   the child?
KINESIAS: Take him home, Manes.
                      (*Exit Manes with Baby.*)
                  There. He's gone.
                           Come on!
There's nothing to stop us now.
MYRRHINE: You devil! But where?
KINESIAS: In Pan's cave. What could be snugger
than that?
MYRRHINE: But my purification before I go back to
the Citadel?

KINESIAS: Wash in the Klepsydra.°
MYRRHINE: And my oath?
KINESIAS: Leave the oath to me. 65
After all, I'm the man.
MYRRHINE: Well . . . if you say so.
                          I'll go find a bed.
KINESIAS: Oh, bother a bed! The ground's good
enough for me.
MYRRHINE: No. You're a bad man, but you deserve
something better than dirt.   (*Exit Myrrhine.*)
KINESIAS: What a love she is! And how thoughtful!

(*Reenter Myrrhine.*)

MYRRHINE: Here's your bed.
Now let me get my clothes off.
                        But, good horrors! 70
We haven't a mattress.
KINESIAS: Oh, forget the mattress!
MYRRHINE: No.
Just lying on blankets? Too sordid.
KINESIAS: Give me a kiss.
MYRRHINE: Just a second.   (*Exit Myrrhine.*)
KINESIAS: I swear, I'll explode!

(*Reenter Myrrhine.*)

MYRRHINE: Here's your mattress.
I'll just take my dress off.
                    But look —
where's our pillow?
KINESIAS: i don't *need* a pillow!
MYRRHINE: Well. *I* do. 75
                          (*Exit Myrrhine.*)
KINESIAS: I don't suppose even Herakles°
would stand for this!

(*Reenter Myrrhine.*)

MYRRHINE: There we are. Ups-a-daisy!
KINESIAS: So we are. Well, come to bed.
MYRRHINE: But I wonder:
is everything ready now?
KINESIAS: I can swear to that. Come, darling!
MYRRHINE: Just getting out of my girdle.
                          But remember, now, 80
what you promised about the treaty.
KINESIAS: Yes, yes, yes!
MYRRHINE: But no coverlet!
KINESIAS: Damn it, I'll be
your coverlet!
MYRRHINE: Be right back.   (*Exit Myrrhine.*)

---

65. **Klepsydra:** A water clock beneath the walls of the
Akropolis. Kinesias's suggestion borders on blasphemy.
76. **Herakles:** Greek hero (Hercules) known for his Twelve
Labors.

KINESIAS: This girl and her coverlets
　　will be the death of me.

(*Reenter Myrrhine.*)

MYRRHINE: Here we are. Up you go!
KINESIAS: Up? I've been up for ages.
85　MYRRHINE: Some perfume?
KINESIAS: No, by Apollo!
MYRRHINE: Yes, by Aphrodite!
　　I don't care whether you want it or not.
　　　　　　　　　　　　　　(*Exit Myrrhine.*)

KINESIAS: For love's sake, hurry!

(*Reenter Myrrhine.*)

MYRRHINE: Here, in your hand. Rub it right in.
KINESIAS: Never cared for perfume.
90　And this is particularly strong. Still, here goes.
MYRRHINE: What a nitwit I am! I brought you the
　　　　Rhodian bottle.
KINESIAS: Forget it.
MYRRHINE: No trouble at all. You just wait here.
　　　　　　　　　　　　　(*Exit Myrrhine.*)
KINESIAS: God damn the man who invented
　　　　perfume!

(*Reenter Myrrhine.*)

MYRRHINE: At last! The right bottle!
KINESIAS: I've got the rightest
95　　bottle of all, and it's right here waiting for you.
　　Darling, forget everything else. Do come to bed.
MYRRHINE: Just let me get my shoes off.
　　　　　　　　　　— And, by the way,
　　you'll vote for the treaty?
KINESIAS: I'll think about it.
　　　　　　　　　　(*Myrrhine runs away.*)
　　There! That's done it! The damned woman,
100　she gets me all bothered, she half kills me,
　　and off she runs! What'll I do? Where
　　can I get laid?
　　　　　　　— And you, little prodding pal,
　　who's going to take care of *you*? No, you and I
　　had better get down to old Foxdog's Nursing
　　　　Clinic.
105　CHORUS[(m)]: Alas for the woes of man, alas
　　　　Specifically for you.
　　She's brought you to a pretty pass:
　　　　What are you going to do?
　　Split, heart! Sag, flesh! Proud spirit, crack!
110　　Myrrhine's got you on your back.
KINESIAS: The agony, the protraction!
KORYPHAIOS[(m)]:   Friend,
　　　　What woman's worth a damn?
　　They bitch us all, world without end.
KINESIAS: Yet they're so damned sweet, man!
115　KORYPHAIOS[(m)]: Calamitous, that's what I say.

　　You should have learned that much today.
CHORUS[(m)]: O blessed Zeus, roll womankind
　　　　Up into one great ball;
　　Blast them aloft on a high wind,
　　　　And once there, let them fall.   120
　　Down, down they'll come, the pretty dears,
　　And split themselves on our thick spears.
　　　　　　　　　　　　(*Exit Kinesias.*)

SCENE 4

(*Enter a Spartan Herald.*)

HERALD: Gentlemen, Ah beg you will be so kind
　　as to direct me to the Central Committee.
　　Ah have a communication.

(*Reenter Commissioner.*)

COMMISSIONER: Are you a man,
　　or a fertility symbol?
HERALD: Ah refuse to answer that question!
　　Ah'm a certified herald from Spahta, and Ah've
　　　　come   5
　　to talk about an ahmistice.
COMMISSIONER: Then why
　　that spear under your cloak?
HERALD: Ah have no speah!
COMMISSIONER: You don't walk naturally, with
　　　　your tunic
　　poked out so. You have a tumor, maybe,
　　or a hernia?
HERALD: You lost yo' mahnd, man?
COMMISSIONER: Well,   10
　　something's up, I can see that. And I don't like
　　　　it.
HERALD: Colonel, Ah resent this.
COMMISSIONER: So I see. But what *is* it?
HERALD: A staff
　　with a message from Spahta.
COMMISSIONER: Oh, I know about those staffs.
　　Well, then, man, speak out: How are things in
　　　　Sparta?
HERALD: Hahd, Colonel, hahd! We're at a
　　　　standstill.   15
　　Cain't seem to think of anything but women.
COMMISSIONER: How curious! Tell me, do you
　　　　Spartans think
　　that maybe Pan's to blame?
HERALD: Pan? No, Lampito and her little naked
　　　　friends.
　　They won't let a man come nigh them.   20
COMMISSIONER: How are you handling it?
HERALD: Losing our mahnds,

Scene from the 1978 production of *Lysistrata* at the Spingold Theatre, Brandeis University.

if y' want to know, and walking around
   hunched over
lahk men carrying candles in a gale.
The women have swohn they'll have nothing to
   do with us
until we get a treaty.
25 COMMISSIONER: Yes. I know.
It's a general uprising, sir, in all parts of Greece.
But as for the answer —
             Sir: go back to Sparta
and have them send us your Armistice
   Commission.
I'll arrange things in Athens.
             And I may say

that my standing is good enough to make them
   listen.   30
HERALD: A man after mah own haht! Seh, Ah
   thank you.   (*Exit Herald.*)

CHORAL EPISODE • *Strophe*

CHORUS[m]: Oh these women! Where will you
   find
A slavering beast that's more unkind?
   Where's a hotter fire?
Give me a panther, any day.

5   He's not so merciless as they,
         And panthers don't conspire.

Antistrophe

CHORUS[(w)]: We may be hard, you silly old ass,
         But who brought you to this stupid pass?
             You're the ones to blame.
10   Fighting with us, your oldest friends,
         Simply to serve your selfish ends —
             Really, you have no shame!
KORYPHAIOS[(m)]: No, I'm through with women for
             ever.
KORYPHAIOS[(w)]:   If you say so.
         Still, you might put some clothes on. You look
             too absurd
         standing around naked. Come, get into this
15   cloak.
KORYPHAIOS[(m)]: Thank you; you're right. I merely
             took it off
         because I was in such a temper.
KORYPHAIOS[(w)]:   That's much better.
         Now you resemble a man again.
                         Why have you been so horrid?
         And look: there's some sort of insect in your eye.
         Shall I take it out?
20 KORYPHAIOS[(m)]:   An insect, is it? So that's
         what's been bothering me. Lord, yes: take it out!
KORYPHAIOS[(w)]: You might be more polite.
                         — But, heavens!
         What an enormous mosquito!
KORYPHAIOS[(m)]:   You've saved my life.
         That mosquito was drilling an artesian well
         in my left eye.
25 KORYPHAIOS[(w)]:   Let me wipe
         those tears away. — And now: one little kiss?
KORYPHAIOS[(m)]: No, no kisses.
KORYPHAIOS[(w)]: You're so difficult.
KORYPHAIOS[(m)]: You impossible women! How you
             do get around us!
         The poet was right: Can't live with you, or
             without you.
30   But let's be friends.
         And to celebrate, you might join us in an Ode.

Strophe 1

CHORUS[(m and w)]: Let it never be said
         That my tongue is malicious:
         Both by word and by deed
         I would set an example that's noble and
35   gracious.

         We've had sorrow and care
         Till we're sick of the tune.
         Is there anyone here
         Who would like a small loan?
             My purse is crammed,   40
                 As you'll soon find;
         And you needn't pay me back if the Peace gets
             signed.

Strophe 2

         I've invited to lunch
         Some Karystian rips° —
         An esurient bunch,   45
         But I've ordered a menu to water their lips.
         I can still make soup
         And slaughter a pig.
         You're all coming, I hope?
         But a bath first, I beg!   50
             Walk right up
             As though you owned the place,
         And you'll get the front door slammed to in
             your face.

SCENE 5

(*Enter Spartan Ambassador, with entourage.*)

KORYPHAIOS[(m)]: The Commission has arrived from
         Sparta.
                 How oddly they're walking!
                         Gentlemen, welcome to Athens!
         How is life in Lakonia?
AMBASSADOR: Need we discuss that?
         Simply use your eyes.
CHORUS[(m)]:   The poor man's right:
                         What a sight!
AMBASSADOR: Words fail me.   5
         But come, gentlemen, call in your
             Commissioners,
         and let's get down to a Peace.
CHORAGOS[(m)]:   The state we're in! Can't bear
         a stitch below the waist. It's a kind of pelvic
         paralysis.
COMMISSIONER: Won't somebody call
             Lysistrata? — Gentlemen,
         we're no better off than you.
AMBASSADOR: So I see.   10

----

44. Karystian rips: The Karystians were allies of Athens but
were scorned for their primitive ways and loose morals.

A SPARTAN: Seh, do y'all feel a certain strain
   early in the morning?
AN ATHENIAN: I do, sir. It's worse than a strain.
   A few more days, and there's nothing for us but
      Kleisthenes,
   that broken blossom.
CHORAGOS[m]:   But you'd better get dressed again.
   You know these people going around Athens
      with chisels
15   looking for statues of Hermes.°
ATHENIAN: Sir, you are right.
SPARTAN: He certainly is! Ah'll put mah own
   clothes back on.

(*Enter Athenian Commissioners.*)

COMMISSIONER: Gentlemen from Sparta, welcome.
   This is a sorry business.
SPARTAN (*to one of his own group*): Colonel, we
      got dressed just in time. Ah sweah,
   if they'd seen us the way we were, there'd have
20   been a new wah
   between the states.
COMMISSIONER: Shall we call the meeting to order?
                                 Now, Lakonians,
   what's your proposal?
AMBASSADOR: We propose to consider peace.
COMMISSIONER: Good. That's on our minds, too.
                        — Summon Lysistrata.
   We'll never get anywhere without her.
25   AMBASSADOR: Lysistrata?
   Summon Lysis-*any*body! Only, summon!
KORYPHAIOS[m]:   No need to summon:
   here she is, herself.

(*Enter Lysistrata.*)

COMMISSIONER: Lysistrata! Lion of women!
   This is your hour to be
   hard and yielding, outspoken and shy, austere
      and
30   gentle. You see here
   the best brains of Hellas (confused, I admit,
   by your devious charming) met as one man
   to turn the future over to you.
LYSISTRATA: That's fair enough,
   unless you men take it into your heads
   to turn to each other instead of to us. But I'd
35   know
   soon enough if you did.
                     — Where is Reconciliation?

Go, some of you: bring her here.
                        (*Exeunt two women.*)
                     And now, women,
lead the Spartan delegates to me: not roughly
or insultingly, as our men handle them, but
   gently,
politely, as ladies should. Take them by the
   hand,   40
or by anything else if they won't give you their
   hands.

(*The Spartans are escorted over.*)

There. — The Athenians next, by any convenient
   handle.

(*The Athenians are escorted.*)

Stand there, please. — Now, all of you, listen to
   me.

(*During the following speech the two women reenter,
carrying an enormous statue of a naked girl; this is
Reconciliation.*)

I'm only a woman, I know; but I've a mind,
and, I think, not a bad one: I owe it to my
   father   45
and to listening to the local politicians.
So much for that.
                  Now, gentlemen,
since I have you here, I intend to give you a
   scolding.
We are all Greeks.
Must I remind you of Thermopylai,° of Olympia,   50
of Delphoi? names deep in all our hearts?
Are they not a common heritage?
                              Yet you men
go raiding through the country from both sides,
Greek killing Greek, storming down Greek
   cities —
and all the time the Barbarian across the sea   55
is waiting for his chance!
                        — That's my first point.
AN ATHENIAN: Lord! I can hardly contain myself.
LYSISTRATA: As for you Spartans:
   Was it so long ago that Perikleides°
   came here to beg our help? I can see him still,
   his gray face, his sombre gown. And what did
      he want?   60

---

16. **statues of Hermes:** The usual representation of Hermes
was with an erect phallus. Statues of Hermes were scattered
through Athens and were attacked by vandals just before the
Sicilian Expedition.

50. **Thermopylai:** A narrow pass where, in 480 B.C., an army
of three hundred Spartans held out for three days against a
superior Persian force.   58. **Perikleides:** Spartan ambassador to Athens who successfully urged Athenians to aid
Sparta in quelling a rebellion.

An army from Athens. All Messene
was hot at your heels, and the sea-god splitting
your land.
Well, Kimon and his men,
four thousand strong, marched out and saved all
Sparta.
And what thanks do we get? You come back to
65   murder us.
AN ATHENIAN: They're aggressors, Lysistrata!
A SPARTAN: Ah admit it.
When Ah look at those laigs, Ah sweah Ah'll
aggress mahself!
LYSISTRATA: And you, Athenians: do you think
you're blameless?
70   Remember that bad time when we were helpless,
and an army came from Sparta,
and that was the end of the Thessalian
menace,
the end of Hippias and his allies.
                                And that was Sparta,
and only Sparta; but for Sparta, we'd be
cringing slaves today, not free Athenians.

(*From this point, the male responses are less to Lysistrata than to the statue.*)

A SPARTAN: A well shaped speech.
75   AN ATHENIAN: Certainly it has its points.
LYSISTRATA: Why are we fighting each other? With
all this history
of favors given and taken, what stands in the
way
of making peace?
AMBASSADOR: Spahta is ready, ma'am,
so long as we get that place back.
LYSISTRATA: What place, man?
AMBASSADOR: Ah refer to Pylos.
80   COMMISSIONER: Not a chance, by God!
LYSISTRATA: Give it to them, friend.
COMMISSIONER: But — what shall we have to
bargain with?
LYSISTRATA: Demand something in exchange.
COMMISSIONER: Good idea. — Well, then:
Cockeville first, and the Happy Hills, and the
country
between the Legs of Megara.
AMBASSADOR: Mah government objects.
LYSISTRATA: Overruled. Why fuss about a pair of
85   legs?

(*General assent. The statue is removed.*)

AN ATHENIAN: I want to get out of these clothes
and start my plowing.
A SPARTAN: Ah'll fertilize mahn first, by the
Heavenly Twins!

LYSISTRATA: And so you shall,
once you've made peace. If you are serious,
go, both of you, and talk with your allies.   90
COMMISSIONER: Too much talk already. No, we'll
stand together.
We've only one end in view. All that we want
is our women; and I speak for our allies.
AMBASSADOR: Mah government concurs.
AN ATHENIAN: So does Karystos.
LYSISTRATA: Good. — But before you come inside   95
to join your wives at supper, you must perform
the usual lustration. Then we'll open
our baskets for you, and all that we have is
yours.
But you must promise upright good behavior
from this day on. Then each man home with his
woman!   100
AN ATHENIAN: Let's get it over with.
A SPARTAN: Lead on. Ah follow.
AN ATHENIAN: Quick as a cat can wink!
                  (*Exeunt all but the Choruses.*)

Antistrophe 1

CHORUS[(w)]: Embroideries and
    Twinkling ornaments and
    Pretty dresses — I hand   105
Them all over to you, and with never a qualm.
    They'll be nice for your daughters
    On festival days
    When the girls bring the Goddess
    The ritual prize.   110
    Come in, one and all:
    Take what you will.
I've nothing here so tightly corked that you can't
    make it spill.

Antistrophe 2

    You may search my house
    But you'll not find   115
    The least thing of use,
Unless your two eyes are keener than mine.
    Your numberless brats
    Are half starved? and your slaves?
    Courage, grandpa! I've lots   120
    Of grain left, and big loaves.
        I'll fill your guts,
        I'll go the whole hog;
But if you come too close to me, remember:
    'ware the dog!   (*Exeunt Choruses.*)

EXODOS°

(*A Drunken Citizen enters, approaches the gate, and is halted by a sentry.*)

CITIZEN: Open. The. Door.
SENTRY: Now, friend, just shove along!
— So you want to sit down. If it weren't such an old joke,
I'd tickle your tail with this torch. Just the sort of gag
this audience appreciates.
CITIZEN: I. Stay. Right. Here.
SENTRY: Get away from there, or I'll scalp you!
5   The gentlemen from Sparta
are just coming back from dinner.

(*Exit Citizen; the general company reenters; the two Choruses now represent Spartans and Athenians.*)

A SPARTAN: Ah must say,
Ah never tasted better grub.
AN ATHENIAN: And those Lakonians!
They're gentlemen, by the Lord! Just goes to show,
a drink to the wise is sufficient.
COMMISSIONER: And why not?
10   A sober man's an ass.
Men of Athens, mark my words: the only efficient
Ambassador's a drunk Ambassador. Is that clear?
Look: we go to Sparta,
and when we get there we're dead sober. The result?
Everyone cackling at everyone else. They make
15   speeches;
and even if we understand, we get it all wrong
when we file our reports in Athens. But today — !
Everybody's happy. Couldn't tell the difference
between *Drink to Me Only* and
The Star-Spangled Athens.
20   What's a few lies,
washed down in good strong drink?

(*Reenter the Drunken Citizen.*)

SENTRY: God almighty,
he's back again!
CITIZEN: I. Resume. My. Place.
A SPARTAN (*to an Athenian*): Ah beg yo', seh,
take yo' instrument in yo' hand and play for us.
25   Ah'm told
yo' understand the in*tric*acies of the floot?

Exodos: Final scene.

Ah'd lahk to execute a song and dance
in honor of Athens,
                    and, of cohse, of Spahta.
CITIZEN: Toot. On. Your. Flute.

(*The following song is a solo — an aria — accompanied by the flute. The Chorus of Spartans begins a slow dance.*)

A SPARTAN: O Memory,   30
Let the Muse speak once more
In my young voice. Sing glory.
Sing Artemision's shore,
Where Athens fluttered the Persians. *Alalai*,°
Sing glory, that great   35
Victory! Sing also
Our Leonidas and his men,
Those wild boars, sweat and blood
Down in a red drench. Then, then
The barbarians broke, though they had stood   40
Numberless as the sands before!

O Artemis,
Virgin Goddess, whose darts
Flash in our forests: approve
This pact of peace and join our hearts,   45
From this day on, in love.
Huntress, descend!
LYSISTRATA: All that will come in time.
                    But now, Lakonians,
take home your wives. Athenians, take yours.
Each man be kind to his woman; and you, women   50
be equally kind. Never again, pray God,
shall we lose our way in such madness.
KORYPHAIOS(Athenian):   And now
let's dance our joy.

(*From this point the dance becomes general.*)

CHORUS(Athenian): Dance, you Graces
                    Artemis, dance
Dance, Phoibos,° Lord of dancing
                    Dance,   55
In a scurry of Maenads,° Lord Dionysos
                    Dance, Zeus Thunderer
                    Dance, Lady Hera°
Queen of the sky
                    Dance, dance, all you gods
Dance witness everlasting of our pact
Evohi Evohe°   60

34. *Alalai:* War cry.   55. *Phoibos:* Apollo, god of the sun.
56. *Maenads:* Female worshipers of Bacchus (Dionysus).
57. *Hera:* Wife of Zeus.   60. *Evohi Evohe:* "Come forth! Come forth!" An orgiastic cry associated with rituals of Bacchus.

Dance for the dearest
          the Bringer of Peace
Deathless Aphrodite!
COMMISSIONER: Now let us have another song from
    Sparta.
CHORUS^(Spartan): From Taygetos, from Taygetos,
65   Lakonian Muse, come down.
  Sing to the Lord Apollo
    Who rules Amyklai Town.

  Sing Athena of the House of Brass!°
  Sing Leda's Twins,° that chivalry
70   Resplendent on the shore
  Of our Eurotas; sing the girls
    That dance along before:

68. *House of Brass:* Temple to Athena on the Akropolis of
Sparta.   69. *Leda's Twins:* Leda, raped by Zeus, bore
quadruplets, two daughters (one of whom was Helen) and
two sons.

Sparkling in dust their gleaming feet,
  Their hair a Bacchant fire,
And Leda's daughter, thyrsos° raised,   75
  Leads their triumphant choir.

CHORUS^(S and A): *Evohe!*
        Evohai!
           Evohe!
              We pass
  Dancing
         dancing
              to greet
Athena of the House of Brass.

75. *thyrsos:* A staff twined with ivy and carried by Bacchus
and his followers.

COMMENTARY

Brooks Atkinson (1894–1984)
REVIEW OF *LYSISTRATA*   1930

This 1930 review of Lysistrata *by the then-reigning* New York Times *reviewer reminds us that the play is racy enough that "members of the constabulary" needed to view it to be sure it would not offend the public's sensibilities. Atkinson's review captures the lively sense of fun manifest in producer Norman Bel Geddes's comedic romp.*

On second thought, the *Lysistrata,* which was put on at the Forty-fourth Street last evening, does not come direct from Athens. Between Aristophanes and us stands Norman Bel Geddes, scene designer extraordinary, who produced this version for the Philadelphia Theatre Association several weeks ago, and whose bountiful scenery now sweeps up toward the flies in a Broadway playhouse. He has designed a magnificent production, imaginative, free, sculptural and colorful, and the concluding bacchanal, when viewed from the rear of the auditorium, is a memorable flow of color and motion.

If *Lysistrata* were *Antigone* or *Electra,* this spacious edifice would be a masterful scene conception for the dignity of groupings and the declamation of Greek tragedy. But *Lysistrata* is horseplay, broader than a Second Avenue burlesque, full of rough-and-tumble, full of bawdry. The comic spirit could dance more freely if Mr. Geddes had spared the picture somewhat and tightened the performance. When he has experienced actors at his command — Violet Kemble Cooper, Ernest Truex, Sydney Greenstreet — Aristophanes triumphs over magnificence of scenery, for good actors know the craft of expression. But the pictorial quality of this *Lysistrata* is no unmixed dispensation for the younger actors. When the performance begins to sprawl, as it still does despite considerable cutting, you suspect that Mr. Geddes's setting is more on the side of the tragedians than the mountebanks.

But that is counsel of perfection, and *Lysistrata* is too hearty a comedy to be stared out of countenance by a promethean artist. Gilbert Seldes has written an English adaptation colloquial enough to be relished, and the sheer artlessness of the slapstick episodes makes them palatable and enjoyable even for the sciolists of Broadway. As every one must know by this time, *Lysistrata* is the story of the women of Greece who plot to conclude a tedious and ruinous interstate war by abstaining from love until their menfolk have made peace. Soldiers denied the consolations of domesticity grew less Martian and more reasonable politically....

Members of the constabulary were present last evening to safeguard the morals of Broadway art patrons. Although the police listened to some of the raciest conversation to be heard outside the marts of commerce, they will be relieved to know that it is tamer than what members of the Philadelphia Theatre Association heard when *Lysistrata* opened in that well-bred metropolis. . . .

Although *Lysistrata* is a robust comedy, it is not sophisticated. Instead of cracking jokes, it pummels and grimaces, or splashes jars of water on a parcel of feeble old men. And, although the pace of the performance is slow and uneven, and lacking rhythm, it is a tempo not unsuited to the festival quality of the humors.

Those who expect a neat, brisk show will be disappointed. But those who still like to snort over the earthy japery of elementary comedy will find that the congenial version of *Lysistrata* has laughing matter of rare quality.

Roman Drama

Indigenous Sources

Roman drama has several sources, not all of them well understood. The first and most literary is Greek drama, but among the more curious are the indigenous sources, which are especially difficult to trace. One such source might be the Etruscans, members of an old and obscure civilization in northern Italy that reached its height in the sixth century B.C. and that the Romans eventually absorbed. The Etruscans had developed an improvised song and dance that was very entertaining. The town of Atella provided another indigenous comic tradition known as the ATELLAN FARCE, a very broad and sometimes coarse popular comedy. Such entertainments may have been acted in open spaces or at fairs, probably not demanding a stage at first.

The Atellan farce is especially interesting for developments in later Roman drama and world drama. The characters in this farce seem to have been STOCK CHARACTERS, characters who are always recognizable and whose antics are predictable. The most common in the Atellan farce are Maccus the clown; Bucco the stupid, and probably fat, clown; Pappus, the foolish or stubborn old man; and the hunchbacked, wily slave Dossennus. At first these pieces of drama were improvised to a repeatable pattern, often involving a master who tries to get his slave to do his bidding but who somehow ends up being made to look the fool by the cunning slave. When the farces began to develop in Rome, they were written down and played onstage.

The concept of the stock character is associated with the masters of Roman comedy, Plautus and Terence, who often adapted Greek plays and made them their own. The braggart warrior (*miles gloriosus*), a stock character on the Roman stage, reappears in modern plays. The miser has been a mainstay in literature since Roman times and probably is best known today as Scrooge in Dickens's *A Christmas Carol* and as *The Miser* of Molière. The parasite was Roman in origin and can be seen today in numerous television situation comedies (George in *Seinfeld* is an example). Another Roman invention is the use of identical twins for comic effect. Because it permitted a wide range of comic misunderstandings this device has been used by many playwrights, including Shakespeare in *The Comedy of Errors*. The Roman use of masks made it much easier to employ than in today's productions.

The Greek Influence

According to legend, in 240 B.C., a slave, Livius Andronicus, presented performances of his Latin translations of a Greek tragedy and a Greek comedy, giving the Romans their first real taste of Greek drama and literature. Livius soon earned his freedom, and his literary career became so firmly established that his translations from the Greek were those read in Rome for more than two hundred years. His translation of the *Odyssey* was the standard text through the time of Cicero (first century B.C.).

Roman comedy derived primarily from the New Comedy of Menander, although it could, like Aristophanes' Old Comedy, sometimes be risqué. Comedy was the most well attended and the most performed of Rome's drama. That is not to say that the Romans produced no tragedies. They did, and the influence of Roman tragedy has been as long-lasting as that of comedy. Still, the Roman people preferred to laugh rather than to feel the pity and terror of tragic emotion.

Just as the Greek plays developed in connection with festivals, the Roman plays became associated with games held several times a year. During the games, performances were offered on an average of five to eleven days. The Megalesian Games took place in early April, in honor of the Great Mother, the goddess Cybele, whose temple stood on the Palatine Hill. In late April the Floral Games were held in front of the temple of Flora on the Aventine Hill. The most important were the Roman Games in September and the Plebeian Games in November.

The Greek drama competitions had no counterpart among the Romans, for whom drama was not the primary entertainment during the festivals. Roman playwrights and actors were hired to put on performances to entertain and divert the impatient audiences who could choose among a variety of spectacles, including gladiator fights, chariot races, and animal baiting. The producer had to please the audience or lose his chance to supply more entertainment.

Roman comedies were sometimes revisions or amalgamations of Greek plays. The themes and characters of Roman tragedies also derived from Greek originals. Figuring often in Roman tragedies was the Trojan War; its characters were reworked into new situations and their agonies reinterpreted.

For costumes the actors wore the Greek tunic (called a CHITON) and a long white cloak or mantle called the PALLIUM. Like the Greeks, the

Romans wore low shoes, called the SOCK, for comedy, and shoes with an elevated sole, the BUSKIN, for tragedy. For plays that had a totally Roman setting and narrative, the actors wore the Roman toga. Eventually, Roman actors used traditional Greek masks that immediately identified the characters for the audience. (The question of whether the earliest Roman actors wore masks as well has not been resolved.) The younger Roman characters wore black wigs, older characters wore white wigs, and characters representing slaves wore red wigs.

One of the most intriguing questions concerning Roman plays is the importance of music in the drama. In Greek plays the chorus took most of the responsibility for the music, but in Roman drama actors may have sung their lines, so the Roman plays may have resembled musical comedies. The dialogue in some comedies introduces an interlude of flute playing, indicating that there were times with no actor onstage, no spoken words, and no mimed action, but only a musician to entertain the audience.

The Roman Stage

In the third century B.C. the Romans began building wooden stages that could be taken down quickly and moved as necessary. Eventually, they built stone theaters following Greek plans but varying from the Greek model in a number of important respects. They were built on flat ground, rather than on the hillsides of the Greek theaters. The influence of the Romans' early wooden stage remained in the permanent buildings in several ways. The Roman stage was elevated, and since there was little or no chorus, the orchestra, in which the chorus moved from place to place, was no longer needed. The SCAENA, or background, against which the action took place, was often three stories tall and was proportionally longer than the Greek *skene*. This wide but shallow stage was exploited by the playwrights, who often set their plays on a street with various houses, temples, and other buildings along it.

The space in front of the *scaena* was known as the PROSCAENA, from which the PROSCENIUM ARCH, which frames the stage and separates the actors from the audience, developed much later in the renaissance. The action took place on the *pulpitum,* behind the *proscaena.* The potential for the proscenium arch is evident in the plan of the Theater of Marcellus (Figure 2), where the sections to the left and the right of the stage (*pulpitum*) already indicate a separation from the audience.

As in the plan of the Theater of Marcellus, the *frons scaena* (the front wall, or façade) usually had three doors (some had only two), which were ordinarily established as doors of separate buildings, sometimes a temple and the others the homes of chief characters. These doors were active "participants" in the drama; it has been said that the most common line heard in a Roman play is a statement that the door is opening and someone is coming in. The standard Roman play takes great care to

Figure 2. Theater of Marcellus

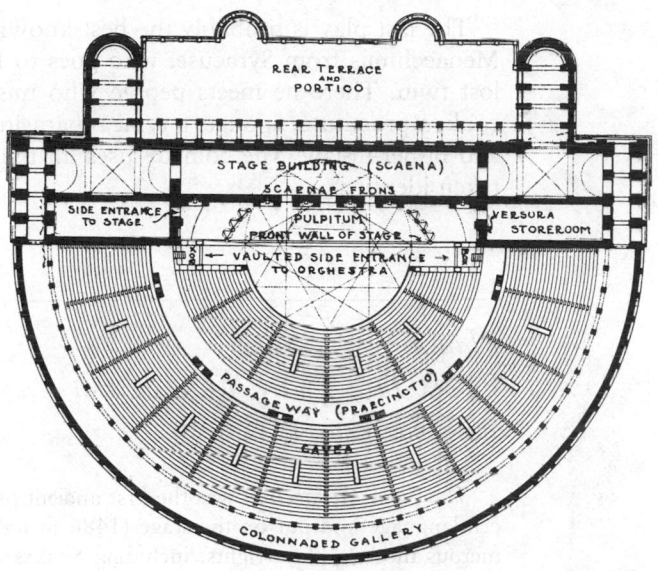

REAR TERRACE AND PORTICO

STAGE BUILDING (SCAENA)
SCAENAE FRONS
SIDE ENTRANCE TO STAGE
PULPITUM
FRONT WALL OF STAGE
VERSURA STOREROOM
VAULTED SIDE ENTRANCE TO ORCHESTRA

PASSAGE WAY (PRAECINCTIO)

CAVEA

COLONNADED GALLERY

justify the entrances and exits of its characters, which may indicate that Roman audiences expected more realism in their comedies than did their Greek counterparts.

The *scaena frons,* the front of the theater, not only was several stories high but also was much more architecturally developed than the *skene* of the Greek theater. The typical Roman architectural devices of multiple arches, columns, and pilasters decorated the *scaena,* giving it a stately appearance. Like the Greek theater, the Roman theater used machinery that permitted actors to be moved through the air and to make entrances from the heavens.

Roman Dramatists
Plautus

All surviving Roman comedy shows the influence of Greek originals. Plautus (254–184 B.C.) is among Rome's most famous playwrights and may have been a member of a troupe that performed Atellan comedy. His middle name is Maccius (a form of Maccus, the clown of the farces), possibly alluding to the role he had habitually played. Tradition has it that he was in the theater for a good while before he began writing comedies. His first plays date from 205 B.C., about thirty-five years after Livius introduced Greek drama to the Romans. No one knows how many plays he wrote, and it has been common to assign many unauthenticated titles to him. About twenty-one plays exist that are thought to be his, the most famous of which are *Amphitryon, The Pot of Gold, The Captives, Curculio, The Braggart Warrior, The Rope,* and *The Twin Menaechmi.*

The last play is probably the best-known Roman comedy. It features Menaechmus from Syracuse, who goes to Epidamnus searching for his lost twin. There he meets people who mistake him for his brother: a cook; a prostitute; Sponge, a typical parasite; and even his brother's wife and father-in-law. The comedy uses all the confusions inherent in mistaken identity.

Plautus (254–184 B.C.)

FROM *THE TWIN MENAECHMI*   C. 205–184 B.C.

TRANSLATED BY LIONEL CASSON

The Twin Menaechmi was the first ancient play to be translated into a modern language and put on the stage (1486 in Italy). It has been adapted by numerous modern playwrights, including Shakespeare in *The Comedy of Errors* and, more recently, Rodgers and Hart in *The Boys from Syracuse* (1938), a musical that ran on Broadway for 235 performances. *Boys* has been revived numerous times and is still a popular summer theater play. The following scene from the beginning of act III of *The Twin Menaechmi* shows the parasite Sponge mistaking the identity of Menaechmus of Syracuse for that of his friend Menaechmus of Epidamnus. They have a great go-around over a dress in a typical mixup of the kind that originated with Roman comedies and has been popular in farces and comedies ever since.

ACT III

SPONGE: I'm over thirty now, and never have I ever in all those years pulled a more damned fool stunt than the one I pulled today: There was this town meeting, and *I* had to dive in and come up right in the middle of it. While I'm standing there with my mouth open, Menaechmus sneaks off on me. I'll bet he's gone to his girlfriend. Perfectly willing to leave me behind, too!

(*Paces up and down a few times, shaking his head bitterly. Then, in a rage.*) Damn, damn, damn the fellow who first figured out town meetings! All they do is keep a busy man away from his business. Why don't people pick a panel of men of leisure for this kind of thing? Hold a roll call at each meeting and whoever doesn't answer gets fined on the spot. There are plenty of persons around who need only one meal a day; they don't have business hours to keep because they don't go after dinner invitations or give them out. They're the ones to fuss with town meetings and town elections. If that's how things were run, I wouldn't have lost my lunch today. He sure wanted me along, didn't he? I'll go in, anyway. There's still hope of leftovers to soothe my soul. (*He is about to go up to the door when it suddenly swings open and Menaechmus of Syracuse appears, standing on the threshold with a garland, a little askew, on his head; he is holding the dress and listening to Lovey who is chattering at him from inside. Sponge quickly backs off into a corner.*) What's this I see? Menaechmus — and he's leaving, garland and all! The table's been cleared! I sure came in time — in time to walk him home. Well, I'll watch what his game is, and then I'll go and have a word with him.

MENAECHMUS OF SYRACUSE (*to Lovey inside*): Take it easy, will you! I'll have it back to you today in plenty of time, altered and trimmed to perfection. (*Slyly.*) Believe me, you'll say it's not your dress; you won't know it any more.

SPONGE (*to the audience*): He's bringing the dress to the dressmaker. The dining's done, the drinks are down — and Sponge spent the lunch hour outside. God damn it I'm not the man I think I am if I don't get even with him for this, but really even. You just watch. I'll give it to him, I will.

MENAECHMUS OF SYRACUSE (*closing the door and walking downstage; to the audience, jubilantly*): Good god, no one ever expected less — and got more blessings from heaven in one day than me. I dined, I wined, I wenched, and (*holding up the dress*) made off with this to which, from this moment on, she hereby forfeits all right, title, and interest.

SPONGE (*straining his ears, to the audience*): I can't make out what he's saying from back here. Is that full-belly talking about me and my right title and interest?

MENAECHMUS OF SYRACUSE (*to the audience*): She said I stole it from my wife and gave it to her. I saw she was mistaking me for someone else, so I promptly played it as if she and I were having a hot and heavy affair and began to yes her; I agreed right down the line to everything she said. Well, to make a long story short, I never had it so good for so little.

SPONGE (*clenching his fists, to the audience*): I'm going up to him. I'm itching to give him the works. (*Leaves his corner and strides belligerently toward Menaechmus.*)

MENAECHMUS OF SYRACUSE (*to the audience*): Someone coming up to me. Wonder who it is?

SPONGE (*roaring*): Well! You featherweight, you filth, you slime, you disgrace to the human race, you double-crossing good-for-nothing! What did I ever do to you that you had to ruin my life? You sure gave me the slip downtown a little while ago! You killed off the day all right — and held the funeral feast without me. Me who was coheir under the will! Where do you come off to do a thing like that!

MENAECHMUS OF SYRACUSE (*too pleased with life to lose his temper*): Mister, will you please tell me what business you and I have that gives you the right to use language like that to a stranger here, someone you never saw in your life? You hand me that talk and I'll hand you something you won't like.

SPONGE (*dancing with rage*): God damn it, you already have! I know god damned well you have!

MENAECHMUS OF SYRACUSE (*amused and curious*): What's your name, mister?

SPONGE (*as before*): Still making jokes, eh? As if you don't know my name!

MENAECHMUS OF SYRACUSE: So help me, so far as I know, I never heard of you or saw you till this minute. But I know one thing for sure: whoever you are, you'd better behave yourself and stop bothering me.

SPONGE (*taken aback for a minute*): Menaechmus! Wake up!

MENAECHMUS OF SYRACUSE (*genially*): Believe me, to the best of my knowledge, I am awake.

SPONGE: You don't know me?

MENAECHMUS OF SYRACUSE (*as before*): If I did, I wouldn't say I didn't.

SPONGE (*incredulously*): You don't know your own parasite?

MENAECHMUS OF SYRACUSE: Mister, it looks to me as if you've got bats in your belfry.

SPONGE (*shaken, but not convinced*): Tell me this: Didn't you steal that dress there from your wife today and give it to Lovey?

MENAECHMUS OF SYRACUSE: Good god, no! I don't have a wife, I never gave anything to any Lovey, and I never stole any dress. Are you in your right mind?

SPONGE (*aside, groaning*): A dead loss, the whole affair. (*To Menaechmus.*) But you came out of your house wearing the dress! I saw you myself!

MENAECHMUS OF SYRACUSE (*exploding*): Damn you! You think everybody's a pervert just because you are? I was wearing this dress? Is that what you're telling me?

SPONGE: I most certainly am.

MENAECHMUS OF SYRACUSE: Now you go straight to the one place fit for you! No — get yourself to the lunatic asylum; you're stark-raving mad.

SPONGE (*venomously*): God damn it, there's one thing nobody in the world is going to stop me from doing: I'm telling the whole story, exactly what happened, to your wife this minute. All these insults are going to boomerang back on your own head. Believe you me, you'll pay for eating that whole lunch yourself. (*Dashes into the house of Menaechmus of Epidamnus.*)

MENAECHMUS OF SYRACUSE (*throwing his arms wide, to the audience*): What's going on here? Must everyone I lay eyes on play games with me this way? Wait — I hear the door.

(*The door of Lovey's house opens, and one of her maids comes out holding a bracelet. She walks over to Menaechmus and, as he looks on blankly, hands it to him.*)

MAID: Menaechmus, Lovey says would you please do her a big favor and drop this at the jeweler's on your way? She wants you to give him an ounce of gold and have him make the whole bracelet over.

MENAECHMUS OF SYRACUSE (*with alacrity*): Tell her I'll not only take care of this but anything else she wants taken care of. Anything at all. (*He takes the piece and examines it absorbedly.*)

MAID (*watching him curiously, in surprise*): Don't you know what bracelet it is?

MENAECHMUS OF SYRACUSE: Frankly no — except that it's gold.

MAID: It's the one you told us you stole from your wife's jewel box when nobody was looking.

MENAECHMUS OF SYRACUSE (*forgetting himself, in high dudgeon*): I never did anything of the kind!

MAID: You mean you don't remember it? Well, if that's the case, you give it right back!

MENAECHMUS OF SYRACUSE (*after a few seconds of highly histrionic deep thought*): Wait a second. No, I *do* remember it. Of course — this is the one I gave her. Oh, and there's something else: Where are the armlets I gave her at the same time?

MAID (*puzzled*): You never gave her any armlets.

MENAECHMUS OF SYRACUSE (*quickly*): Right you are. This was all I gave her.

MAID: Shall I tell her you'll take care of it?

MENAECHMUS OF SYRACUSE: By all means, tell her. I'll take care of it, all right. I'll see she gets it back the same time she gets the dress back.

MAID (*going up to him and stroking his cheek*): Menaechmus dear, will you do me a favor too? Will you have some earrings made for me? Drop earrings, please; ten grams of gold in each. (*Meaningfully.*) It'll make me *so* glad to see you every time you come to the house.

MENAECHMUS OF SYRACUSE: Sure. (*With elaborate carelessness.*) Just give me the gold. I'll pay for the labor myself.

MAID: Please, you pay for the gold too. I'll make it up to you afterward.

MENAECHMUS OF SYRACUSE: No, you pay for the gold. I'll make it up to *you* afterward. Double.

MAID: I don't have the money.

MENAECHMUS OF SYRACUSE (*with a great air of magnanimity*): Well, any time you get it, you just let me have it.

MAID (*turning to go*): I'm going in now. Anything I can do for you?

MENAECHMUS OF SYRACUSE: Yes. Tell her I'll see to both things — (*sotto voce, to the audience*) that they get sold as quickly as possible for whatever they'll bring. (*As the maid starts walking toward the door.*) Has she gone in yet? (*Hearing a slam.*) Ah, she's in, the door's closed. (*Jubilantly.*) The lord loves me! I've had a helping hand from heaven! (*Suddenly looks about warily.*) But why hang around when I have the time and chance to get away from this (*jerking his thumb at Lovey's house*) pimping parlor here? Menaechmus! Get a move on, hit the road, forward march! I'll take off this garland and toss it to the left here (*doing so*). Then, if anyone tries to follow me, he'll think I went that way. Now I'll go and see if I can find my servant. I want to let him know all the blessings from heaven I've had.

(*He races off, stage right. The stage is now empty.*)

Terence

Terence (c. 190–159 B.C.) is said to have been a North African slave brought to Rome, where his master realized he was unusually intelligent and gifted. After he was freed, Terence took his place in Roman literary life and produced a body of six plays, all of which still exist: *The Woman of Andros, The Self-Tormentor, The Eunuch, Phormio, The Mother-in-Law,* and *The Brothers.* Terence's plays are notable for including a subplot or secondary action — carefully — and for avoiding the technique of addressing the audience directly.

The Romans preferred Plautus's broad farcical humor to Terence's more carefully plotted, elegantly styled plays. Terence borrowed liberally from Greek sources, often more than one for each of his plays, to develop unusually complicated plots. A manager or producer worked with him on all his plays, and the musician who worked with him was a slave, Flaccus. Terence's productive life was relatively short. He died on a trip to Greece, apparently worrying over a piece of missing luggage said to have contained new plays.

Terence's situation was unusual: He had two wealthy Roman patrons who were interested in seeing the best Greek comedy brought to the Romans. Consequently, they paid for his productions and gave him more support than the average comic playwright could have expected. Terence's dramatic skills developed considerably from the beginning to the end of his work, contrasting sharply with the repetitive nature of Plautus's work. Terence was more than a translator, but he wrote at a time when Romans were interested in emulating the Greeks, and his fidelity to Greek originals was one of his strongest recommendations.

Terence (c. 190–159 B.C.)
FROM THE BROTHERS   160 B.C.

The ending of *The Brothers,* generally recognized as Terence's master-piece and certainly the most influential of his plays, has Demea planning a reversal on his brother, Micio. Micio is a good, easygoing bachelor who wishes well for others. Demea has been a stern father to one of his sons, Ctesipho, and has tried to steer him in a direction other than the one Cte-sipho wants to follow. Demea has entrusted the upbringing of his second son, Aeschinus, to his lenient brother, Micio. Both sons deceive both brothers and end up with the women they want rather than the women the brothers want for them. Meanwhile, Demea gives up and turns the ta-bles on Micio, engineering his brother's marriage to Aeschinus's mother-in-law. In the process of all this, Demea decides to adopt the gentle, easygoing ways of his brother and to forsake his former stern behavior.

This play was adapted often in the seventeenth century by Marston, Beaumont and Fletcher, and others. Molière relied on it for his *School for Wives.* At least five plays were adapted from it for the eighteenth-century English stage.

FROM ACT V

MICIO (*to Syrus, within*): My brother ordered it,° say ye! Where is he? . . . Hah, Brother, was it you who ordered this?

DEMEA: Yes, that I did! And in this and all things else I'm ready to do whatever may conduce to the uniting, serving, helping, and the joining together of both families.

AESCHINUS (*to Micio*): Pray, Sir, let it be so!

MICIO: Well, I've nothing to say against it.

DEMEA: Truth, 'tis no more than we are obliged to do. For first, she's your son's mother-in-law . . .

MICIO: What then?

DEMEA: A very virtuous and modest woman . . .

MICIO: So they say indeed.

DEMEA: Not weighed down by years . . .

MICIO: Not yet.

DEMEA: But past child-bearing: a lonesome woman whom nobody esteems . . .

MICIO (*aside*): What the Devil is he at?

DEMEA: . . . Therefore you ought to marry her; and you Aeschinus, should do what you can to bring this about.

MICIO: Who? I marry?

DEMEA: Yes, you.

MICIO: I, prithee?

DEMEA: Yes, you I say.

MICIO: Pho, you are fooling us, surely?

My brother ordered it: Demea ordered the breaking down of a wall to allow the two families to communicate. In this way Demea imitates the good-naturedness of his brother, Micio, and traps him into marrying Aeschinus's mother-in-law.

DEMEA (*to Aeschinus*): If thou hast any life in thee, persuade him to it.

AESCHINUS: Dear Father . . .

MICIO (*interrupting*): Blockhead! Dost thou take in earnest what he says?

DEMEA: 'Tis in vain to refuse; it can't be avoided.

MICIO: Pho, you are in your dotage!

AESCHINUS: Good Sir, let me win this one favor.

MICIO (*angrily*): Art out of thy wits, let me alone!

DEMEA: Come, come! Hearken for once to what your son says.

MICIO: Haven't ye played the fool enough yet? Shall I at threescore and five marry an old woman who's ready to drop into the grave? This is your wise counsel, is it?

AESCHINUS: Pray, Sir, do; I've promised you shall.

MICIO: You promised, with a mischief! Promise for thyself, thou chit!

DEMEA: Fie, fie! What if he had begged a greater favor from you?

MICIO: As if there were any greater favor than this!

DEMEA: Pray grant his request.

AESCHINUS: Good Sir, be not so hard-hearted.

DEMEA: Pho, promise him for once!

MICIO: Will ye never leave baiting me?

AESCHINUS: Not till I've prevailed, Sir.

MICIO: Truth, this is downright forcing a man.

DEMEA: Come, Micio, be good-natured and consent.

MICIO: Though this be the most damned, foolish, ridiculous whim, and the most averse to my nature that could possibly be, yet since you are so extremely set upon it, I'll humor ye for once.

AESCHINUS: That is excellent, I'm obliged to ye beyond measure.

DEMEA (*aside*): Well, what's next? . . . What shall I say next? This is as I'd have it. . . . What's more to be done?

(*To Micio.*)

Ho! There's Hegio our poor kinsman, and nearest relation; in truth, we ought in conscience to do something for him.

MICIO: What, pray?

DEMEA: There's a small plot of land in the suburbs, which you farm out — pray let's give him that to live on.

MICIO: A small one, say ye?

DEMEA: Though it were a great one, you might yet give it to him. He has been as good as a father to Pamphila; he's a very honest man, our kinsman, and you couldn't bestow it better. Besides, Brother, there's a certain proverb (none of my own, I assure you) which you so well and wisely made use of: "That age has always this ill effect of making us more worldly, as well as wiser." We should do well to avoid this scandal. 'Tis a true proverb, Brother, and ought to be held in mind.

MICIO: What's all this? . . . Well, so let it be, if he has need of it.

AESCHINUS: Brave Father, I vow!

DEMEA: Now you are my true brother, both in body and soul.

MICIO: I'm glad of it.

DEMEA (*aside, laughing*): I've stabbed him with his own weapons, i'fack!

(*Enter Syrus, with a pick-axe upon his shoulders.*)

SYRUS (*to Demea*): The job is done as ye ordered, Sir.

DEMEA: Thou art an honest lad. . . . And upon my conscience I think Syrus deserves his freedom.

MICIO: He, his freedom? For what exploit?

DEMEA: O, for a thousand.

SYRUS: O dear Mr. Demea, you are a rare gentleman, edad you are! You know

I've looked after the young gentlemen from their cradles. I taught them, advised them, and instructed them all I possibly could.

DEMEA: Nothing more evident! Nay, more than that, he catered for them, pimped for them, and in the morning took care of a debauchee for them. These are no ordinary accomplishments, I can assure ye.

SYRUS: Your worship's very merry.

DEMEA: Besides, he was prime mover in buying this music-girl. It was he who managed the whole intrigue, and 'tis no more than justice to reward him, as an encouragement to others! In short, Aeschinus desires the same thing.

MICIO (to Aeschinus): Do you desire it too?

AESCHINUS: Yes, if you please, Sir.

MICIO: Since 'tis so, come hither, Syrus! Thou art a free man.

(Syrus kneels down, Micio lays his hand on his head, and after that gives him a cuff on the ear.)

SYRUS (rising up): Generously done! A thousand thanks to ye all, and to you, Mr. Demea.

DEMEA: I'm well satisfied.

AESCHINUS: And I too.

SYRUS: I won't question it, Sir. But I wish heartily my joy were more complete, that my poor spouse Phrygia might be made as free as I am.

DEMEA: Truth, she's a mighty good woman.

SYRUS: And your grandson's first foster-mother, too.

DEMEA: Faith, in good earnest, if for that, she deserves her freedom before any woman in the world.

MICIO: What! For that simple service?

DEMEA: Yes, indeed! In fine, I'll pay for her freedom myself.

SYRUS: God's blessing light upon your worship, and grant all your wishes.

MICIO: Syrus, thou hast made a good day's work of it.

DEMEA: Besides, Brother, it would be a deed of charity to lend him a little money to set up in business that he may face the world without fear. I undertake that he'll soon repay it.

MICIO: Not a penny-piece!

AESCHINUS: He's a very honest fellow, Sir.

SYRUS: Upon my word, I'll repay you the loan. Do but trust me!

AESCHINUS: Pray do, Sir.

MICIO: I'll consider the matter with care.

DEMEA: He shall pay ye, I'll see to that.

SYRUS (to Demea): Egad, you're the best man alive.

AESCHINUS: And the pleasantest in the world.

MICIO: What's the meaning of this, Brother? How comes this sudden change of humor? Why this gallant squandering and profusion?

DEMEA: I'll tell ye, Brother. These sons of yours don't reckon you a sweet-natured and pleasant man because you live as you should and do what is just and reasonable, but because you fawn upon them, cocker them up, and give them what they'll spend. Now, son Aeschinus, if you are dissatisfied with my course of life, because I wouldn't indulge you in all things, right or wrong, then I'll not trouble my head with you any further. Be free to squander, buy mistresses, and do what you will! But if you wish me to advise ye, and set ye up, and help ye too in matters of which your youth can give ye but little understanding — matters of which you are over-fond, and don't well consider — see, here I'm ready to stand by you.

AESCHINUS: Dear Sir, we commit ourselves wholly to your charge; for you know what's fitting to be done far better than we . . . But what will ye do for my brother Ctesipho?

DEMEA: Why, let him take the music-girl; and so bid adieu to general wenching.
AESCHINUS: That's very reasonable. (*To the spectators.*) Gentlemen, your favor!
(*Exeunt° all.*)

Seneca

The surviving Roman plays come from just three hands: Plautus, Terence, and Seneca (4 B.C.–A.D. 65). The comedies of Plautus are raucous, broad, and farcical; those of Terence are polished and carefully structured. Seneca wrote tragedies that were well known to Elizabethans such as Marlowe and Shakespeare, and it is clear that the Elizabethan Age found SENECAN TRAGEDY to be peculiarly suited to its own temperament.

Senecan tragedies were based on either Greek or Roman themes and included murder, bloodthirsty actions (many of which did not occur on stage, but were only described), horror of various kinds, ghosts, and long, bombastic speeches. Signs of Senecan influence can be seen in Elizabethan drama, with its taste for many of these devices; plays like *Hamlet* are notable for ending in a pool of blood, with most of the actors lying dead onstage. The theme of revenge was also prized by Seneca and, later, by the Elizabethans.

Not a professional theater person, Seneca was wealthy and learned, a philosopher active in the government of Emperor Nero's Rome. His plays, most of which were adapted from Euripides, were probably written only to be read, as was common at his time, or perhaps recited, although there is no record of their having been performed. The Roman people thirsted for mime and farce but had much less taste for serious plays.

Ten plays attributed to Seneca exist, nine of which are surely his and one of which is only possibly his. His most famous are *Mad Hercules*, *The Phoenician Women*, *Medea*, *Phaedra*, *Agamemnon*, *Thyestes*, and *The Trojan Women*.

Seneca (4 B.C.–A.D. 65)
FROM *THYESTES*
TRANSLATED BY ELLA ISABEL HARRIS

Thyestes, probably adapted from the *Oresteia* of Aeschylus, influenced a number of Elizabethan revenge tragedies, such as Shakespeare's *Hamlet*. The story is gruesome even by modern standards. Thyestes se-

[S.D.] *Exeunt:* Latin for "they go out."

duces his brother Atreus's wife, and Atreus banishes him. When Atreus summons Thyestes to Atreus's home, he goes suspiciously, hoping to be able to see his children. The banquet Atreus holds for Thyestes seems to signal reconciliation between the brothers. But when it is over, Atreus brings in the heads of Thyestes' children, revealing that Thyestes has just eaten their bodies in the feast.

The second scene from act V — before Thyestes is told about the meal he has eaten — follows in its entirety. It shows Thyestes wrestling with himself in a passion of uncertainty. Thyestes' soliloquy is a psychological study of the effects of grief, care, uncertainty, and fear. Seneca's plays have many such soliloquies, and their revelations of complex emotional states deeply impressed the age of Shakespeare.

ACT V • Scene II

(*Thyestes sits alone at the banquet table, half overcome with wine; he tries to sing and be gay, but some premonition of evil weighs upon him.*)

THYESTES (*to himself*): By long grief dulled, put by thy cares, my heart,
Let fear and sorrow fly and bitter need,
Companion of thy timorous banishment,
And shame, hard burden of afflicted souls.
Whence thou has fallen profits more to know
Than whither; great is he who with firm step
Moves on the plain when fallen from the height;
He who, oppressed by sorrows numberless
And driven from his realm, with unbent neck
Carries his burdens, not degenerate
Or conquered, who stands firm beneath the weight
Of all his burdens, he is great indeed.
Now scatter all the clouds of bitter fate,
Put by all signs of thy unhappy days,
In happy fortunes show a happy face,
Forget the old Thyestes. Ah, this vice
Still follows misery: never to trust
In happy days; though better fortunes come,
Those who have borne afflictions find it hard
To joy in better days. What holds me back,
Forbids me celebrate the festal tide?
What cause of grief, arising causelessly,
Bids me to weep? What art thou that forbids
That I should crown my head with festal wreath?
It does forbid, forbid! Upon my head
The roses languish, and my hair that drips
With ointment rises as with sudden fear,
My face is wet with showers of tears that fall
Unwillingly, and groans break off my song.
Grief loves accustomed tears, the wretched feel
That they must weep. I would be glad to make
Most bitter lamentation, and to wail,
And rend this robe with Tyrian purple dyed.
My mind gives warning of some coming grief,

Presages future ills. The storm that smites
When all the sea is calm weighs heavily
Upon the sailor. Fool! What grief, what storm,
Dost thou conceive? Believe thy brother now.
Be what it may, thou fearest now too late,
Or causelessly. I do not wish to be
Unhappy, but vague terror smites my breast.
No cause is evident and yet my eyes
O'erflow with sudden tears. What can it be,
Or grief, or fear? Or has great pleasure tears?

The surviving Roman plays offer enough variety to give us an idea of what the drama achieved. Like so much of Roman culture, Roman drama rested in the shadow of Greek accomplishments. The Romans were responsible for maintaining the Greek texts, allowing us to see a great deal of their work. Although it may be true that much of the Roman drama that was produced no longer exists, what survives shows variety and high quality.

Medieval Drama

The Role of the Church

The medieval period in Europe (A.D. 476–1500) began with the collapse of Rome, a calamity of such magnitude that the years between then and the beginning of the Crusades in 1095 have been traditionally called the Dark Ages. Historians used this term to refer to their lack of knowledge about a time in which no great central powers organized society or established patterns of behavior and standards in the arts.

Drama, or at least records of it, all but disappeared. The major institution to profit from the fall of the Roman Empire was the church, which in the ninth and tenth centuries enjoyed considerable power and influence. Many bishops considered drama a godless activity, a distraction from the piety that the church demanded of its members. During the great age of cathedral building and the great ages of religious painting and religious music — from the seventh century to the thirteenth — drama was not officially approved. Therefore, it is a striking irony that the rebirth of drama in the Western world should have taken place in the heart of the monasteries, developing slowly and inconspicuously until it outgrew its beginnings.

The church may well have intended nothing more than the simple dramatization of its message. Or it is possible that the people may have craved drama, and the church's response could have been an attempt to answer their needs. In either event, the church could never have foreseen the outcome of adding a few moments of drama to the liturgy, the church services. LITURGICAL DRAMA began in the ninth century with TROPES, or embellishments, which were sung during parts of the Mass. The earliest known example of a trope, called the QUEM QUAERITIS ("Whom seek ye?"), grew out of the Easter Mass and was sung in a monastic settlement in Switzerland called St. Gall:

ANGEL: Whom seek ye in the sepulchre, O ye Christians?
THREE MARYS: Jesus of Nazareth, who was crucified, O ye Angels.

ANGEL: He is not here; he is risen as he has foretold.
Go, announce that he is risen from the sepulchre.

Some scholars think that in its earliest form this trope was sung by four monks in a dialogue pattern, three monks representing the three Marys at Christ's tomb and the other representing the angel. Tropes like the *Quem Quaeritis* evolved over the years to include a number of participants — monks, nuns, and choirboys in different communities — as the tropes spread from church to church throughout the Continent. These dramatic interpolations never became dramas separate from the Mass itself, although their success and popularity led to experiments with other dramatic sequences centering on moments in the Mass and in the life of Christ. The actors in these pieces did not think of themselves as specialists or professionals; they were simply monks or nuns who belonged to the church. The churchgoers obviously enjoyed the tropes, and more were created, despite the church's official position on drama.

In the tenth century a nun called Hrotswitha entertained herself and her fellow nuns with imitations of the Latin dramatist Terence. Although her own subject matter was holy in nature, she realized that Terence was an amusing comic writer with a polished style. She referred to herself as "the strong voice of Gandersheim," her community in Saxony, and said that she had "not hesitated to imitate in my writings a poet whose works are so widely read, my object being to glorify, within the limits of my poor talent, the laudable chastity of Christian virgins." Her plays are very short moral tales, often illustrating moments in the lives of Christian martyred women. As far as is known, these plays do not seem to have gone beyond the nuns' walls; therefore, they had little effect on the drama developing in the period.

In the twelfth century, for reasons that remain unclear, the church moved the liturgical drama to the churchyard (although some form of drama probably remained as part of the liturgy). It may be that the dramatic moments inside the church, which had begun to demand more elaborate equipment and settings, were too complex to remain in the spaces normally assigned them, or they may have begun to conflict with the liturgy of the Mass.

Mystery Plays

Once outside the church, the drama flourished and soon became independent, although its themes continued to be religious and its services were connected with religious festivals. In 1264 Pope Urban IV added to the religious calendar a new, important feast: Corpus Christi, celebrated beginning on the first Thursday after Trinity Sunday, about two months after Easter. The purpose of the feast was to celebrate the doctrine declaring that the body of Christ was real and present in the Host taken by the faithful in the sacrament of Communion.

At first the feast of Corpus Christi was localized in Liège, Belgium. But in the fourteenth and fifteenth centuries it spread through papal decree and became one of the chief feasts of the church. Among other things, it featured a procession and pageant in which the Host was displayed publicly through the streets of a town. Because of the importance and excitement of this feast, entire communities took part in the celebration.

The craft guilds, professional organizations of workers involved in the same trade — carpenters, wool merchants, and so on — soon began competing with each other in producing plays that could be performed during the feast of Corpus Christi. Most of their plays derived from Bible stories and the life of Christ. Religious guilds, such as the Confrerie of the Passion, produced plays in Paris and elsewhere on the Continent. Because the Bible is silent on many details of Christ's life, some plays invented new material and illuminated dark areas, thereby satisfying the intense curiosity medieval Christians had about events the Bible omitted.

The church did not ignore drama after it left the church buildings. Since the plays had religious subject matter and could be used to teach the Bible and to model Christian behavior, they remained of considerable value to the church.

First performed by the clergy, these religious plays dramatized the mystery of Christ's Passion. Later the plays were produced by members of craft guilds, and they became known as CRAFT or MYSTERY PLAYS. Beginning in the medieval period, the word *mystery* was used to describe a skill or trade known only to a few who apprenticed and mastered its special techniques; it also referred to religious mysteries.

By the fifteenth century, mystery plays and the feast of Corpus Christi were popular almost everywhere in Europe, and in England certain towns produced exceptionally elaborate cycles with unusually complex and ambitious plays. The CYCLES were groups of plays numbering from twenty-four to forty-eight. Four cycles have been preserved: the Chester, York, Towneley (Wakefield), and N-Town cycles, named for their towns of origin. N-Town plays were a generic version of plays that any town could take and use as its own, although the plays were probably written near Lincoln.

The plays were performed again and again during annual holidays and feasts, and the texts were carefully preserved. Some of the plays, such as *The Fall of Lucifer,* are very short. Others are more elaborate in length and complexity and resemble modern plays: *Noah,* from the Wakefield Cycle, which has been produced regularly in this century; *The Slaughter of Innocents*; and *The Second Shepherds' Play,* one of the most entertaining mystery plays.

The producers of the plays often had a sense of appropriateness in their choice of subjects. For example, the Water-Drawers guild sponsored *Noah's Flood,* the Butchers (because they sold "flesh") *Temptation, The Woman Taken in Adultery,* and the Shipwrights *The Building of the Ark.*

Among the best-known mystery plays is the somewhat farcical *The Second Shepherds' Play,* which is both funny and serious. It tells of a crafty shepherd named Mak who steals a lamb from his fellow shepherds and takes it home. His wife, Gill, then places it in a cradle and pretends it is her baby. Eventually the shepherds — who suspect Mak from the first — smoke out the fraud and give Mak a blanket-tossing for their trouble. But after they do so, they see a star in the heavens and turn their attention to the birth of baby Jesus, the Lamb of God. They join the Magi and come to pay homage to the Christ Child.

The easy way in which the profane elements of everyday life coexisted with the sacred in medieval times has long interested scholars. *The Second Shepherds' Play* virtually breaks into two parts, the first dedicated to the wickedness of Mak and Gill and the horseplay of the shepherds. But once Mak has had his due reward, the play alters in tone and the sense of devotion to Christian teachings becomes uppermost. The fact that the mystery plays moved away from liturgical Latin and to the vernacular (local) language made such a juxtaposition of sacred and profane much more possible.

The dominance of the guilds in producing mystery plays suggests that guilds enjoyed increasing political power and authority. The guilds grew stronger and more influential — probably at the expense of the church. Some historians have seen this development as crucial to the growing secularization of the Middle Ages.

Morality Plays

MORALITY PLAYS were never part of any cycle but developed independently as moral tales in the late fourteenth or early fifteenth century on the Continent and in England. They do not illustrate moments in the Bible, nor do they describe the life of Christ or the saints. Instead, they describe the lives of people facing the temptations of the world. The plays are careful to present a warning to the unwary that their souls are always in peril, that the devil is on constant watch, and that people must behave properly if they are to be saved.

One feature of morality plays is their reliance on ALLEGORY, a favorite medieval device. Allegory is the technique of giving abstract ideas or values a physical representation. In morality plays, abstractions such as goodness became characters in the drama. In modern times we sometimes use allegory in art, as when we represent justice as a blindfolded woman. Allegorically, justice should act impartially because she does not "see" any distinctions, such as those of rank or privilege, that characterize most people standing before a judge.

The use of allegory permitted medieval dramatists to personify abstract values such as sloth, greed, daintiness, vanity, strength, and hope by making them characters and placing them onstage in action. The dramatist specified symbols, clothing, and gestures appropriate to these abstract figures, thus helping the audience recognize the ideas the characters represented. The use of allegory was an extremely durable technique that was already established in medieval painting, printed books, and books of emblems, in which, for example, sloth would be shown as a man reclining lazily on a bed or greed would be represented as overwhelmingly fat and vanity as a figure completely absorbed in a mirror.

The central problem in the morality play was the salvation of human beings, represented by an individual's struggle to avoid sin and damnation and achieve salvation in the otherworld. As in *Everyman* (c. 1495), a late-medieval play that is the best known of the morality plays, the subjects were usually abstract battles between certain vices and specific virtues for the possession of the human soul, a theme repeated in the Elizabethan age in Marlowe's *Doctor Faustus*.

In many ways the morality play was a dramatized sermon designed to teach a moral lesson. Marked by high seriousness, it was nevertheless entertaining. Using allegory to represent abstract qualities allowed the didactic playwrights to draw clear-cut lines of moral force: Satan was always bad; angels were always good. The allegories were clear, direct, and apparent to all who witnessed the plays.

We do not have much knowledge of the origins of morality plays. Many of them are lost, but some that remain are occasionally performed: *The Pride of Life,* the earliest extant morality play; *The Castle of Perseverance; Wisdom; Mankind;* and *Everyman* are the best known. They all enjoyed a remarkable popularity in the latter part of the medieval period, all the way up to the early Renaissance.

The Medieval Stage

Relatively little commentary survives about the conventions of medieval staging, and some of it is contradictory. We know that in the earliest years — after the tropes developed into full-blown religious scenes acted inside the cathedrals — certain sections of the church were devoted to specific short plays. These areas of the church became known as MANSIONS; each mansion represented a building or physical place known to the audience. The audience moved from one mansion to another, seeing play after play, absorbing the dramatic representation of the events, characters, and locale associated with each mansion.

The tradition of moving from mansion to mansion inside the church carried over into the performances that took place later outside the church. Instead of mansions, wagons called PAGEANTS with raised stages provided the playing areas. Usually, the wagons remained stationary and the audience moved from one to another. During the guild cycles the pageants would move; the performers would give their plays at several locales so that many people could see them.

According to medieval descriptions, drawings, and reconstructions, the pageant could also be simply a flat surface drawn on wheels that had a wagon next to it; these structures touched on their long side. In some cases a figure could descend from an upper area as if from the clouds, or actors could descend from the pageants onto the audience's level to enact a descent into an underworld. The stage was, then, a raised platform visible to the audience below (Figure 3).

Figure 3. Pageant wagon

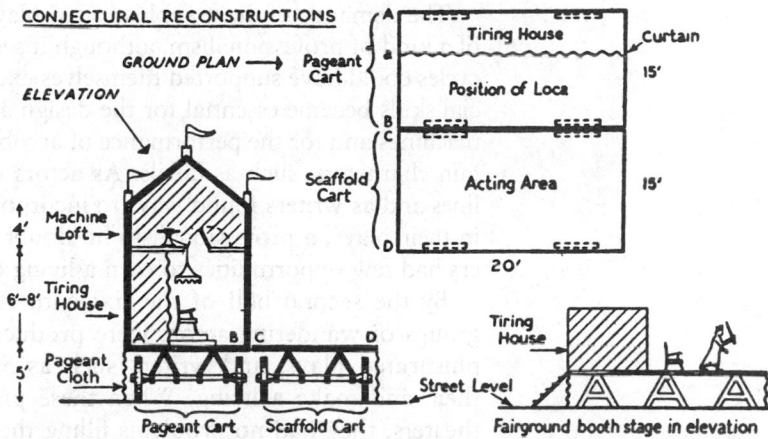

A curtain concealed a space, usually inside or below the wagon, for changing costumes. The actors used costumes and props, sometimes very elaborate and expensive, in an effort to make the drama more impressive. Indeed, between the thirteenth and the sixteenth centuries, a number of theatrical effects were developed to please a large audience. For instance, in the morality and mystery plays the devils were often portrayed as frightening, grotesque, and sometimes even comic figures. They became crowd pleasers. A sensational element was developed in some of the plays in the craft cycles, especially those about the lives of the saints and martyrs, in which there were plenty of chances to portray horrifying tortures.

The prop that seems to have pleased the most audiences was a complex machine known as the MOUTH OF HELL or "Hell mouth," usually a large fish-shaped orifice from which smoke and explosions, fueled by gunpowder, belched constantly. The devils took great delight in stuffing their victims into these maws. According to a contemporary account, one of the machines required seventeen men to operate.

The level of realism achieved by medieval plays was at times startling. In addition to visual realism, medieval plays involved a psychological level of participation on the part of both audience and actor. Sometimes they demanded that the actors suffer in accord with the characters they played. Some records attest to characters playing Christ on the cross having to be revived after their hearts stopped, and at least one Judas apparently was hanged just a little too long and had to be resuscitated.

The Actors

In the early days of liturgical drama, the actors in the tropes were monks and choirboys, and in the mystery plays they were drawn from the guilds. At first all the actors were male, but records show that eventually women took important roles.

The demands of more sophisticated plays encouraged the development of a kind of professionalism, although it seems unlikely that players in the cycles could have supported themselves exclusively on their earnings. Special skills became essential for the design and operation of complex stage machines and for the performance of acrobatics that were expected of certain characters, such as devils. As actors developed facility in delivering lines and as writers found ways to incorporate more challenging elements in their plays, a professionalism no doubt arose, even if actors and writers had few opportunities to earn a living on the stage.

By the second half of the sixteenth century, the early Renaissance, groups of wandering actors were producing highly demanding and sophisticated plays, and writers such as Shakespeare were able to join them and make a living. When these professionals secured their own theaters, they had no problems filling them with good drama, with actors, and with an audience.

Dramatic techniques developed in the medieval period were put to good use in the Renaissance theater. For example, the colorful and dramatic devil characters that stalked the mystery plays were transformed into sophisticated villains in Elizabethan drama. The devil Mephistopheles [Mephistophilis] behaves like a smooth Tudor lawyer in Marlowe's *Doctor Faustus*; Iago in *Othello* is suspected of having cloven hooves. Perhaps one important difference is that the Elizabethan devil-villains are truly frightening, since they are so recognizably human in their villainy.

EVERYMAN

This late medieval play may have origins in northern Europe. A Flemish play, *Elckerlijk* ("Everyman"), dates from c. 1495, and the question of whether the English *Everyman* was translated from it or whether it is a translation of *Everyman* has not been settled. Both plays may have had a common origin in an unknown play. The English *Everyman* was produced frequently in the early years of the sixteenth century. Its drama was largely theological; its purpose, to reform the audience. One indication that entertainment was not the primary goal of this morality play is its lack of the comic moments found in other plays, such as *The Second Shepherds' Play*.

The author of the play may have been a priest. This assumption has long been common because the play has much theological content and offers a moral message of the kind one might expect to hear from the pulpit. The theme of the play is fundamental: the inevitability of death. And for that reason, in part, the play continues to have a universal appeal. Modern productions may not give the audience a suitable medieval chill, but the message of the play is still relevant for everyone.

The medieval reliance on allegory is apparent in the naming of the characters in *Everyman*: Death, Kindred, Cousin, Goods, Knowledge, Strength, Beauty, and Everyman himself. Each character does not just stand for a specific quality; he or she *is* that quality. The allegorical way of thinking derived from the medieval faith that everything in the world had a moral meaning. Morality plays depended on this belief and always articulated setting, characters, and circumstances in terms of their moral value. This was in keeping with the medieval belief that the soul was always in jeopardy and that life was a test of one's moral condition. When Everyman meets a character, the most important information about his or her moral value is communicated instantly in the name of the character. Characters in allegorical plays also reveal themselves through their costumes and props. The character Good Deeds is simply good deeds — there is no need for psychological development because the medieval audience had a full understanding of what good deeds meant and how Good Deeds as a character would behave.

The structure of *Everyman* resembles a journey. Everyman undertakes to see who among all his acquaintances will accompany him on his most important trip: to the grave and the judgment of God Almighty. Seeing life as a journey — or as part of a journey — was especially natural for the medieval mind, which had as models the popular and costly religious pilgrimages to holy shrines and to the Holy Land itself. If life on earth is only part of the journey of the soul, then the morality play helps to put it into clear perspective. This life is not, the play tells us, the most important part of the soul's existence.

At its core, *Everyman* has a profound commercial metaphor: Everyman is called to square accounts with God. The metaphor of accounting appears early in the play, when Everyman talks about his accounts and reckonings as if they appeared in a book that should go with him to heaven. His life will be examined and if he is found wanting, he will go into the fires of hell. If he has lived profitably from a moral viewpoint, he will enjoy life everlasting. The language of the play is heavily loaded with accounting metaphors that identify it as the product of a society quite unlike that of the Greeks or the Romans. Such metaphors suggest that *Everyman* directs its message to middle-class merchants for whom accounting was a significant concept.

Like many sermons, *Everyman* imparts a lesson that its auditors were expected to heed. Hence the key points of the play are repeated at the end by the Doctor. For moderns, didactic plays are sometimes tedious. For the medieval mind, they represented delightful ways of learning important messages.

Everyman in Performance

Very little is known about early productions of *Everyman*. It was produced in Holland and England for seventy-five years beginning in the mid-fifteenth century. The play disappeared from the stage for centuries, finally resurfacing in 1901 in a production under the auspices of the Elizabethan Stage Society in London, directed by William Poel. Poel designed the costumes and set, directed, and played at first the part of Death, and then when he got older, the part of God. Poel produced *Everyman* many times over the next fifteen years.

The 1901 production was followed by a 1902 revival in New York starring Edith Wynne Matthison and produced by Ben Greet, marking the play's first American performance. Greet continued producing *Everyman* for the next thirty-five years in both England and America.

After seeing Poel's production, Max Reinhardt, the legendary German director, decided to produce *Everyman* in Germany. The Austrian poet and playwright Hugo von Hofmannsthal wrote a new German adaptation, *Jedermann,* for Reinhardt. The adaptation features Everyman as a wealthy burgher, and central to the play is an ornate banquet scene in which Death appears. Hofmannsthal's German adaptation marked a shift in emphasis from the simpler and more personal English *Everyman* to the spectacular *Jedermann* that concentrates on a wealthy man's lustful life and his attempts to get into heaven. *Jedermann* was first produced in Berlin on December 1, 1911. In 1913 Reinhardt produced the play in Salzburg, Austria, at the Salzburg Cathedral square, and except for the years of World War II, Reinhardt's version of *Jedermann* has been performed regularly at the annual Salzburg Festival. The critic Brooks Atkinson found Reinhardt's production "nothing short of miraculous."

In a review of Reinhardt's 1927 production, the critic Gilbert Gabriel found *Jedermann,* "crammed with splendors for the eye, largesse of bells and uplifting voices for the ear." A reviewer at the 1936 Salzburg Festival production of *Jedermann* wrote that the play "has everything but simplicity."

The popularity of the Reinhardt productions of *Jedermann* paved the way for numerous productions of *Everyman* over the years. In 1936, during the Great Depression in the United States, the WPA (Works Progress Administration) held special Sunday church performances of *Everyman.* Other notable productions include a 1941 *Everyman* in New York performed by refugee actors from Europe, and a 1955 tour with college casts in New England and California. In 1922 a new English adaptation of the German *Jedermann* by Sir John Martin-Harvey was presented at Stratford-on-Avon. This production toured to London and New York in 1923. In 1936 Sir John's adaptation was performed at the Hollywood Bowl in California with Peggy Wood and Lionel Braham. Long popular with college and community groups, the play continues to be performed around the world.

Anonymous

EVERYMAN

c. 1495

EDITED BY A. C. CAWLEY

Characters

GOD	KNOWLEDGE
MESSENGER	CONFESSION
DEATH	BEAUTY
EVERYMAN	STRENGTH
FELLOWSHIP	DISCRETION
KINDRED	FIVE WITS
COUSIN	ANGEL
GOODS	DOCTOR
GOOD DEEDS	

Here beginneth a treatise how the high Father of Heaven sendeth Death to summon every creature to come and give account of their lives in this world, and is in manner of a moral play.

MESSENGER: I pray you all give your audience,
    And hear this matter with reverence,
    By figure° a moral play:
    The *Summoning of Everyman* called it is,

That of our lives and ending shows
How transitory we be all day.° 5
This matter is wondrous precious,
But the intent of it is more gracious,
And sweet to bear away.
The story saith: Man, in the beginning
Look well, and take good heed to the ending, 10
Be you never so gay!
Ye think sin in the beginning full sweet,
Which in the end causeth the soul to weep,
When the body lieth in clay.
Here shall you see how Fellowship and Jollity, 15
Both Strength, Pleasure, and Beauty,
Will fade from thee as flower in May;
For ye shall hear how our Heaven King
Calleth Everyman to a general reckoning:
Give audience, and hear what he doth say. 20
    (*Exit.*)

3. By figure: In form.

6. all day: Always.

(*God speaketh.*)

GOD: I perceive, here in my majesty,
　　How that all creatures be to me unkind,°
　　Living without dread in worldly prosperity:
25　Of ghostly sight° the people be so blind,
　　Drowned in sin, they know me not for their
　　　　God;
　　In worldly riches is all their mind,
　　They fear not my righteousness, the sharp rod.
　　My law that I showed, when I for them died,
30　They forget clean, and shedding of my blood red;
　　I hanged between two, it cannot be denied;
　　To get them life I suffered to be dead;
　　I healed their feet, with thorns hurt was my head.
　　I could do no more than I did, truly;
35　And now I see the people do clean forsake me:
　　They use the seven deadly sins damnable,
　　As pride, covetise, wrath, and lechery
　　Now in the world be made commendable;
　　And thus they leave of angels the heavenly
　　　　company.
40　Every man liveth so after his own pleasure,
　　And yet of their life they be nothing sure:
　　I see the more that I them forbear
　　The worse they be from year to year.
　　All that liveth appaireth° fast;
45　Therefore I will, in all the haste,
　　Have a reckoning of every man's person;
　　For, and° I leave the people thus alone
　　In their life and wicked tempests,
　　Verily they will become much worse than beasts;
50　For now one would by envy another up eat;
　　Charity they do all clean forget.
　　I hoped well that every man
　　In my glory should make his mansion,
　　And thereto I had them all elect;
55　But now I see, like traitors deject,°
　　They thank me not for the pleasure that I to
　　　　them meant,
　　Nor yet for their being that I them have lent.
　　I proffered the people great multitude of mercy,
　　And few there be that asketh it heartily.
60　They be so cumbered with worldly riches
　　That needs on them I must do justice,
　　On every man living without fear.
　　Where art thou, Death, thou mighty messenger?

(*Enter Death.*)

DEATH: Almighty God, I am here at your will,
65　Your commandment to fulfill.
GOD: Go thou to Everyman,

And show him, in my name,
A pilgrimage he must on him take,
Which he in no wise may escape;
And that he bring with him a sure reckoning　70
Without delay or any tarrying.
　　　　　　　　　　　　(*God withdraws.*)
DEATH: Lord, I will in the world go run overall,
And cruelly outsearch both great and small;
Every man will I beset that liveth beastly
Out of God's laws, and dreadeth not folly.　75
He that loveth riches I will strike with my dart,
His sight to blind, and from heaven to depart° —
Except that alms be his good friend —
In hell for to dwell, world without end.
Lo, yonder I see Everyman walking.　80
Full little he thinketh on my coming;
His mind is on fleshly lusts and his treasure,
And great pain it shall cause him to endure
Before the Lord, Heaven King.

(*Enter Everyman.*)

Everyman, stand still! Whither art thou going　85
　　Thus gaily? Hast thou thy Maker forget?
EVERYMAN: Why askest thou?
　　Wouldest thou wit?°
DEATH: Yea, sir; I will show you:
　　In great haste I am sent to thee　90
　　From God out of his majesty.
EVERYMAN: What, sent to me?
DEATH: Yea, certainly.
　　Though thou have forget him here,
　　He thinketh on thee in the heavenly sphere,　95
　　As, ere we depart, thou shalt know.
EVERYMAN: What desireth God of me?
DEATH: That shall I show thee:
　　A reckoning he will needs have
　　Without any longer respite.　100
EVERYMAN: To give a reckoning longer leisure I
　　　　crave;
　　This blind matter troubleth my wit.
DEATH: On thee thou must take a long journey;
　　Therefore thy book of count° with thee thou
　　　　bring,
　　For turn° again thou cannot by no way.　105
　　And look thou be sure of thy reckoning,
　　For before God thou shalt answer, and show
　　Thy many bad deeds, and good but a few;
　　How thou hast spent thy life, and in what wise,
　　Before the chief Lord of paradise.　110
　　Have ado that we were in that way,°

---

23. **unkind:** Ungrateful.　25. **ghostly sight:** Spiritual vision.
44. **appaireth:** Degenerates.　47. **and:** If.　55. **deject:** Abject.

77. **depart:** Separate.　88. **wit:** Know.　104. **count:** Account.　105. **turn:** Return.　111. **Have ado . . . that way:** Let us see about making that journey.

For, wit thou well, thou shalt make none
   attorney.°
EVERYMAN: Full unready I am such reckoning to
   give.
I know thee not. What messenger art thou?
115 DEATH: I am Death, that no man dreadeth,°
For every man I rest,° and no man spareth;
For it is God's commandment
That all to me should be obedient.
EVERYMAN: O Death, thou comest when I had thee
   least in mind!
120 In thy power it lieth me to save;
Yet of my good° will I give thee, if thou will be
   kind:
Yea, a thousand pound shalt thou have,
And defer this matter till another day.
DEATH: Everyman, it may not be, by no way.
125 I set not by gold, silver, nor riches,
Ne by pope, emperor, king, duke, ne princes;
For, and I would receive gifts great,
All the world I might get;
But my custom is clean contrary.
130 I give thee no respite. Come hence, and not tarry.
EVERYMAN: Alas, shall I have no longer respite?
I may say Death giveth no warning!
To think on thee, it maketh my heart sick,
For all unready is my book of reckoning.
135 But twelve year and I might have abiding,°
My counting-book I would make so clear
That my reckoning I should not need to fear.
Wherefore, Death, I pray thee, for God's mercy,
Spare me till I be provided of remedy.
140 DEATH: Thee availeth not to cry, weep, and pray;
But haste thee lightly that thou were gone that
   journey,°
And prove thy friends if thou can;
For, wit thou well, the tide abideth no man,
And in the world each living creature
145 For Adam's sin must die of nature.°
EVERYMAN: Death, if I should this pilgrimage take,
And my reckoning surely make,
Show me, for saint charity,°
Should I not come again shortly?
150 DEATH: No, Everyman; and thou be once there,
Thou mayst never more come here,
Trust me verily.

EVERYMAN: O gracious God in the high seat
   celestial,
Have mercy on me in this most need!
Shall I have no company from this vale terrestrial   155
Of mine acquaintance, that way me to lead?
DEATH: Yea, if any be so hardy
That would go with thee and bear thee company.
Hie thee that thou were gone to God's
   magnificence,
Thy reckoning to give before his presence.   160
What, weenest° thou thy life is given thee,
And thy worldly goods also?
EVERYMAN: I had wend° so, verily.
DEATH: Nay, nay; it was but lent thee;
For as soon as thou art go,   165
Another a while shall have it, and then go
   therefro,
Even as thou has done.
Everyman, thou art mad! Thou hast thy wits five,
And here on earth will not amend thy life;
For suddenly I do come.   170
EVERYMAN: O wretched caitiff,° whither shall I flee,
That I might scape this endless sorrow?
Now, gentle Death, spare me till to-morrow,
That I may amend me
With good advisement.   175
DEATH: Nay, thereto I will not consent,
Nor no man will I respite;
But to the heart suddenly I shall smite
Without any advisement.
And now out of thy sight I will me hie;   180
See thou make thee ready shortly,
For thou mayst say this is the day
That no man living may scape away.

               (*Exit Death.*)
EVERYMAN: Alas, I may well weep with sighs deep!
Now have I no manner of company   185
To help me in my journey, and me to keep;
And also my writing is full unready,
How shall I do now for to excuse me?
I would to God I had never be get!°
To my soul a full great profit it had be;   190
For now I fear pains huge and great.
The time passeth. Lord, help, that all wrought!
For though I mourn it availeth nought.
The day passeth, and is almost ago;°
I wot not well what for to do.   195
To whom were I best my complaint to make?
What and I to Fellowship thereof spake,
And showed him of this sudden chance?
For in him is all mine affiance;°

112. **none attorney:** No one [your] advocate.   115. **no man dreadeth:** Fears no man.   116. **rest:** Arrest.   121. **good:** Goods.   135. **But twelve year ... abiding:** If I could stay for just twelve more years.   141. **But haste thee ... that journey:** But set off quickly on your journey.   145. **of nature:** In the course of nature.   148. **for saint charity:** In the name of holy charity.

161. **weenest:** Suppose.   163. **wend:** Supposed.   171. **caitiff:** Captive.   189. **be get:** Been born.   194. **ago:** Gone.   199. **affiance:** Trust.

200   We have in the world so many a day
       Be good friends in sport and play.
       I see him yonder, certainly.
       I trust that he will bear me company;
       Therefore to him will I speak to ease my sorrow.
205   Well met, good Fellowship, and good morrow!

(*Fellowship speaketh.*)

FELLOWSHIP: Everyman, good morrow, by this day!
       Sir, why lookest thou so piteously?
       If any thing be amiss, I pray thee me say,
       That I may help to remedy.
210 EVERYMAN: Yea, good Fellowship, yea;
       I am in great jeopardy.
     FELLOWSHIP: My true friend, show to me your mind;
       I will not forsake thee to my life's end,
       In the way of good company.
215 EVERYMAN: That was well spoken, and lovingly.
     FELLOWSHIP: Sir, I must needs know your heaviness;°
       I have pity to see you in any distress.
       If any have you wronged, ye shall revenged be,
       Though I on the ground be slain for thee —
220   Though that I know before that I should die.
     EVERYMAN: Verily, Fellowship, gramercy.°
     FELLOWSHIP: Tush! by thy thanks I set not a straw.
       Show me your grief, and say no more.
     EVERYMAN: If I my heart should to you break,°
225   And then you to turn your mind from me,
       And would not me comfort when ye hear me
         speak,
       Then should I ten times sorrier be.
     FELLOWSHIP: Sir, I say as I will do indeed.
     EVERYMAN: Then be you a good friend at need:
230   I have found you true herebefore.
     FELLOWSHIP: And so ye shall evermore;
       For, in faith, and thou go to hell,
       I will not forsake thee by the way.
     EVERYMAN: Ye speak like a good friend; I believe
         you well.
235   I shall deserve° it, and I may.
     FELLOWSHIP: I speak of no deserving, by this day!
       For he that will say, and nothing do,
       Is not worthy with good company to go;
       Therefore show me the grief of your mind,
240   As to your friend most loving and kind.
     EVERYMAN: I shall show you how it is:
       Commanded I am to go a journey,
       A long way, hard and dangerous,
       And give a strait count, without delay,
245   Before the high Judge, Adonai.°

       Wherefore, I pray you, bear me company,
       As ye have promised, in this journey.
     FELLOWSHIP: That is matter indeed.° Promise is
         duty;
       But, and I should take such a voyage on me,
       I know it well, it should be to my pain;   250
       Also it maketh me afeard, certain.
       But let us take counsel here as well as we can,
       For your words would fear a strong man.
     EVERYMAN: Why, ye said if I had need
       Ye would me never forsake, quick ne dead,   255
       Though it were to hell, truly.
     FELLOWSHIP: So I said, certainly,
       But such pleasures be set aside, the sooth to say;
       And also, if we took such a journey,
       When should we come again?   260
     EVERYMAN: Nay, never again, till the day of doom.
     FELLOWSHIP: In faith, then will not I come there!
       Who hath you these tidings brought?
     EVERYMAN: Indeed, Death was with me here.
     FELLOWSHIP: Now, by God that all hath bought,°   265
       If Death were the messenger,
       For no man that is living to-day
       I will not go that loath journey —
       Not for the father that begat me!
     EVERYMAN: Ye promised otherwise, pardie.°   270
     FELLOWSHIP: I wot well I said so, truly;
       And yet if thou wilt eat, and drink, and make
         good cheer,
       Or haunt to women the lusty company,°
       I would not forsake you while the day is clear,°
       Trust me verily.   275
     EVERYMAN: Yea, thereto ye would be ready!
       To go to mirth, solace, and play,
       Your mind will sooner apply,
       Than to bear me company in my long journey.
     FELLOWSHIP: Now, in good faith, I will not that
         way.   280
       But and thou will murder, or any man kill,
       In that I will help thee with a good will.
     EVERYMAN: O, that is a simple advice indeed.
       Gentle fellow, help me in my necessity!
       We have loved long, and now I need;   285
       And now, gentle Fellowship, remember me.
     FELLOWSHIP: Whether ye have loved me or no,
       By Saint John, I will not with thee go.
     EVERYMAN: Yet, I pray thee, take the labor, and do
         so much for me
       To bring me forward, for saint charity,   290

---

216. **heaviness:** Sorrow.   221. **gramercy:** Thanks.   224.
break: Open.   235. **deserve:** Repay.   245. **Adonai:** Hebrew name for God.

248. **That is matter indeed:** That is a good reason indeed [for
asking me].   265. **bought:** Redeemed.   270. **pardie:** By
God.   273. **haunt to women the lusty company:** Frequent
the lively company of women.   274. **while the day is clear:**
Until daybreak.

And comfort me till I come without the town.

FELLOWSHIP: Nay, and thou would give me a new
　　gown,
　I will not a foot with thee go;
　But, and thou had tarried, I would not have left
　　thee so.

295　And as now God speed thee in thy journey,
　For from thee I will depart as fast as I may.

EVERYMAN: Whither away, Fellowship? Will thou
　　forsake me?

FELLOWSHIP: Yea, by my fay!° To God I betake°
　　thee.

EVERYMAN: Farewell, good Fellowship; for thee my
　　heart is sore.

300　Adieu for ever! I shall see thee no more.

FELLOWSHIP: In faith, Everyman, farewell now at the
　　ending;
　For you I will remember that parting is
　　mourning.　　　　　　　　　(*Exit Fellowship.*)

EVERYMAN: Alack! shall we thus depart° indeed —
　Ah, Lady, help! — without any more comfort?

305　Lo, Fellowship forsaketh me in my most need.
　For help in this world whither shall I resort?
　Fellowship herebefore with me would merry
　　make,
　And now little sorrow for me doth he take.
　It is said, "In prosperity men friends may find,

310　Which in adversity be full unkind."
　Now whither for succor shall I flee,
　Sith° that Fellowship hath forsaken me?
　To my kinsmen I will, truly,
　Praying them to help me in my necessity;

315　I believe that they will do so,
　For kind will creep where it may not go.°
　I will go say,° for yonder I see them.
　Where be ye now, my friends and kinsmen?

(*Enter Kindred and Cousin.*)

KINDRED: Here be we now at your commandment.
320　Cousin, I pray you show us your intent
　In any wise, and do not spare.

COUSIN: Yea, Everyman, and to us declare
　If ye be disposed to go anywhither;
　For, wit you well, we will live and die together.

325　KINDRED: In wealth and woe we will with you hold,
　For over his kin a man may be bold.°

EVERYMAN: Gramercy, my friends and kinsmen kind.
　Now shall I show you the grief of my mind:

---

298. **fay:** Faith.　**betake:** Commend.　303. **depart:** Part.
312. **Sith:** Since.　316. **for kind will creep where it may not
go:** For kinship will creep where it cannot walk; i.e., blood is
thicker than water.　317. **say:** Essay, try.　326. **For over
his kin . . . may be bold:** For a man may be sure of his kins-
folk.

I was commanded by a messenger,
That is a high king's chief officer;　　　　　　　　330
He bade me go a pilgrimage, to my pain,
And I know well I shall never come again;
Also I must give a reckoning strait,
For I have a great enemy° that hath me in wait,°
Which intendeth me for to hinder.　　　　　　　335

KINDRED: What account is that which ye must
　　render?
　That would I know.

EVERYMAN: Of all my works I must show
　How I have lived and my days spent;
　Also of ill deeds that I have used　　　　　　　340
　In my time, sith life was me lent;
　And of all virtues that I have refused.
　Therefore, I pray you, go thither with me
　To help to make mine account, for saint charity.

COUSIN: What, to go thither? Is that the matter?　345
　Nay, Everyman, I had liefer fast bread and
　　water°
　All this five year and more.

EVERYMAN: Alas, that ever I was bore!
　For now shall I never be merry,
　If that you forsake me.　　　　　　　　　　　350

KINDRED: Ah, sir, what ye be a merry man!
　Take good heart to you, and make no moan.
　But one thing I warn you, by Saint Anne —
　As for me, ye shall go alone.

EVERYMAN: My Cousin, will you not with me go?　355

COUSIN: No, by our Lady! I have the cramp in my
　　toe.
　Trust not to me, for, so God me speed,
　I will deceive you in your most need.

KINDRED: It availeth not us to tice.°
　Ye shall have my maid with all my heart;　　　360
　She loveth to go to feasts, there to be nice,°
　And to dance, and abroad to start:
　I will give her leave to help you in that journey,
　If that you and she may agree.

EVERYMAN: Now show me the very effect° of your
　　mind:　　　　　　　　　　　　　　　365
　Will you go with me, or abide behind?

KINDRED: Abide behind? Yea, that will I, and I may!
　Therefore farewell till another day.
　　　　　　　　　　　　　　　(*Exit Kindred.*)

EVERYMAN: How should I be merry or glad?
　For fair promises men to me make,　　　　　　370
　But when I have most need they me forsake.
　I am deceived; that maketh me sad.

COUSIN: Cousin Everyman, farewell now,

---

334. **enemy:** Devil.　**hath me in wait:** Has me under observation.　346. **liefer fast bread and water:** Rather fast on
bread and water.　359. **tice:** Entice.　361. **nice:** Wanton.
365. **effect:** Tenor.

For verily I will not go with you.
375 Also of mine own an unready reckoning
     I have to account; therefore I make tarrying.
     Now God keep thee, for now I go.
                                          (*Exit Cousin.*)
EVERYMAN: Ah, Jesus, is all come hereto?
     Lo, fair words maketh fools fain;°
380 They promise, and nothing will do, certain.
     My kinsmen promised me faithfully
     For to abide with me steadfastly,
     And now fast away do they flee:
     Even so Fellowship promised me.
385 What friend were best me of to provide?°
     I lose my time here longer to abide.
     Yet in my mind a thing there is:
     All my life I have loved riches;
     If that my Good° now help me might,
390 He would make my heart full light.
     I will speak to him in this distress —
     Where art thou, my Goods and riches?

(*Goods speaks from a corner.*)

GOODS: Who calleth me? Everyman? What! hast
          thou haste?
     I lie here in corners, trussed and piled so high,
395 And in chests I am locked so fast,
     Also sacked in bags. Thou mayst see with shine
          eye
     I cannot stir; in packs low I lie.
     What would ye have? Lightly° me say.
EVERYMAN: Come hither, Good, in all the haste thou
          may,
400 For of counsel I must desire thee.
GOODS: Sir, and ye in the world have sorrow or
          adversity,
     That can I help you to remedy shortly.
EVERYMAN: It is another disease that grieveth me;
     In this world it is not, I tell thee so.
405 I am sent for, another way to go,
     To give a strait count general
     Before the highest Jupiter of all;
     And all my life I have had joy and pleasure in
          thee,
     Therefore, I pray thee, go with me;
     For, peradventure, thou mayst before God
410   Almighty
     My reckoning help to clean and purify;
     For it is said ever among
     That money maketh all right that is wrong.
GOODS: Nay, Everyman, I sing another song.
415 I follow no man in such voyages;

For, and I went with thee,
     Thou shouldst fare much the worse for me;
     For because on me thou did set thy mind,
     Thy reckoning I have made blotted and blind,
     That shine account thou cannot make truly;   420
     And that hast thou for the love of me.
EVERYMAN: That would grieve me full sore,
     When I should come to that fearful answer.
     Up, let us go thither together.
GOODS: Nay, not so! I am too brittle, I may not
          endure;   425
     I will follow no man one foot, be ye sure.
EVERYMAN: Alas, I have thee loved, and had great
          pleasure
     All my life-days on good and treasure.
GOODS: That is to thy damnation, without leasing,°
     For my love is contrary to the love everlasting; 430
     But if thou had me loved moderately during,
     As to the poor to give part of me,
     Then shouldst thou not in this dolor be,
     Nor in this great sorrow and care.
EVERYMAN: Lo, now was I deceived ere I was ware,   435
     And all I may wite° misspending of time.
GOODS: What, weenest thou that I am thine?
EVERYMAN: I had wend so.
GOODS: Nay, Everyman, I say no.
     As for a while I was lent thee;   440
     A season thou hast had me in prosperity.
     My condition is man's soul to kill;
     If I save one, a thousand I do spill.°
     Weenest thou that I will follow thee?
     Nay, not from this world, verily.   445
EVERYMAN: I had wend otherwise.
GOODS: Therefore to thy soul Good is a thief;
     For when thou art dead, this is my guise —
     Another to deceive in this same wise
     As I have done thee, and all to his soul's reprief.° 450
EVERYMAN: O false Good, cursed may thou be,
     Thou traitor to God, that hast deceived me
     And caught me in thy snare!
GOODS: Marry, thou brought thyself in care,
     Whereof I am glad;   455
     I must needs laugh, I cannot be sad.
EVERYMAN: Ah, Good, thou hast had long my
          heartly love;
     I gave thee that which should be the Lord's above.
     But wilt thou not go with me indeed?
     I pray thee truth to say.   460
GOODS: No, so God me speed!
     Therefore farewell, and have good day.
                                          (*Exit Goods.*)

---

379. **fain:** Glad.   385. **me of to provide:** To provide myself
with.   389. **Good:** Goods.   398. **Lightly:** Quickly.

429. **without leasing:** Without a lie, i.e., truly.   436. **wite:**
Blame.   443. **spill:** Ruin.   450. **reprief:** Shame.

EVERYMAN: O, to whom shall I make my moan
   For to go with me in that heavy journey?
465 First Fellowship said he would with me gone;
   His words were very pleasant and gay,
   But afterward he left me alone.
   Then spake I to my kinsmen, all in despair,
   And also they gave me words fair;
470 They lacked no fair speaking,
   But all forsook me in the ending.
   Then went I to my Goods, that I loved best,
   In hope to have comfort, but there had I least;
   For my Goods sharply did me tell
475 That he bringeth many into hell.
   Then of myself I was ashamed,
   And so I am worthy to be blamed;
   Thus may I well myself hate.
   Of whom shall I now counsel take?
480 I think that I shall never speed
   Till that I go to my Good Deed.
   But, alas, she is so weak
   That she can neither go nor speak;
   Yet will I venture on her now.
485 My Good Deeds, where be you?

(Good Deeds speaks from the ground.)

GOOD DEEDS: Here I lie, cold in the ground;
   Thy sins hath me sore bound,
   That I cannot stir.
EVERYMAN: O Good Deeds, I stand in fear!
490 I must you pray of counsel,
   For help now should come right well.°
GOOD DEEDS: Everyman, I have understanding
   That ye be summoned account to make
   Before Messias, of Jerusalem King;
   And you do by me,° that journey with you will I
495 take.
EVERYMAN: Therefore I come to you, my moan to
   make;
   I pray you that ye will go with me.
GOOD DEEDS: I would full fain, but I cannot stand,
   verily.
EVERYMAN: Why, is there anything on you fall?
500 GOOD DEEDS: Yea, sir, I may thank you of° all;
   If ye had perfectly cheered me,
   Your book of count full ready had be.
   Look, the books of your works and deeds eke!°
   Behold how they lie under the feet,
505 To your soul's heaviness.
EVERYMAN: Our Lord Jesus help me!
   For one letter here I cannot see.
GOOD DEEDS: There is a blind reckoning in time of
   distress.

491. **should come right well:** Would be very welcome.   495.
by me: As I advise.   500. **of:** For.   503. **eke:** Also.

EVERYMAN: Good Deeds, I pray you help me in this
   need,
   Or else I am for ever damned indeed; 510
   Therefore help me to make reckoning
   Before the Redeemer of all thing,
   That King is, and was, and ever shall.
GOOD DEEDS: Everyman, I am sorry of your fall,
   And fain would I help you, and I were able. 515
EVERYMAN: Good Deeds, your counsel I pray you
   give me.
GOOD DEEDS: That shall I do verily;
   Though that on my feet I may not go,
   I have a sister that shall with you also,
   Called Knowledge, which shall with you abide, 520
   To help you to make that dreadful reckoning.

(Enter Knowledge.)

KNOWLEDGE: Everyman, I will go with thee, and be
   thy guide,
   In thy most need to go by thy side.
EVERYMAN: In good condition I am now in every
   thing,
   And am wholly content with this good thing, 525
   Thanked be God my creator.
GOOD DEEDS: And when she hath brought you there
   Where thou shalt heal thee of thy smart,
   Then go you with your reckoning and your
     Good Deeds together,
   For to make you joyful at heart 530
   Before the blessed Trinity.
EVERYMAN: My Good Deeds, gramercy!
   I am well content, certainly,
   With your words sweet.
KNOWLEDGE: Now go we together lovingly 535
   To Confession, that cleansing river.
EVERYMAN: For joy I weep; I would we were there!
   But, I pray you, give me cognition
   Where dwelleth that holy man, Confession.
KNOWLEDGE: In the house of salvation: 540
   We shall find him in that place,
   That shall us comfort, by God's grace.

(Knowledge takes Everyman to Confession.)

   Lo, this is Confession. Kneel down and ask
   mercy,
   For he is in good conceit° with God Almighty.
EVERYMAN: O glorious fountain, that all uncleanness
   doth clarify, 545
   Wash from me the spots of vice unclean,
   That on me no sin may be seen.
   I come with Knowledge for my redemption,
   Redempt with heart° and full contrition;

544. **conceit:** Esteem.   549. **heart:** Heartfelt.

550 For I am commanded a pilgrimage to take,
And great accounts before God to make.
Now I pray you, Shrift, mother of salvation,
Help my Good Deeds for my piteous
    exclamation.
CONFESSION: I know your sorrow well, Everyman.
555 Because with Knowledge ye come to me,
I will you comfort as well as I can,
And a precious jewel I will give thee,
Called penance, voider of adversity;
Therewith shall your body chastised be,
With abstinence and perseverance in God's
560   service.
Here shall you receive that scourge of me,
Which is penance strong that ye must endure,
To remember thy Savior was scourged for thee
With sharp scourges, and suffered it patiently;
So must thou, ere thou scape that painful
565   pilgrimage.
Knowledge, keep him in this voyage,
And by that time Good Deeds will be with thee.
But in any wise be siker° of mercy,
For your time draweth fast; and° ye will saved
        be,
570 Ask God mercy, and he will grant truly.
When with the scourge of penance man doth him
        bind,
The oil of forgiveness then shall he find.
EVERYMAN: Thanked be God for his gracious work!
For now I will my penance begin;
575 This hath rejoiced and lighted my heart,
Though the knots be painful and hard within.
KNOWLEDGE: Everyman, look your penance that ye
        fulfill,
What pain that ever it to you be;
And Knowledge shall give you counsel at will
580 How your account ye shall make clearly.
EVERYMAN: O eternal God, O heavenly figure,
O way of righteousness, O goodly vision,
Which descended down in a virgin pure
Because he would every man redeem,
585 Which Adam forfeited by his disobedience:
O blessed Godhead, elect and high divine,
Forgive me my grievous offense;
Here I cry thee mercy in this presence.°
O ghostly treasure, O ransomer and redeemer,
590 Of all the world hope and conductor,
Mirror of joy, and founder of mercy,
Which enlumineth heaven and earth thereby,
Hear my clamorous complaint, though it late be;
Receive my prayers, of thy benignity;
595 Though I be a sinner most abominable,

Yet let my name be written in Moses' table.°
O Mary, pray to the Maker of all thing,
Me for to help at my ending;
And save me from the power of my enemy,
For Death assaileth me strongly.   600
And, Lady, that I may by mean of thy prayer
Of your Son's glory to be partner,
By the means of his passion, I it crave;
I beseech you help my soul to save.
Knowledge, give me the scourge of penance;   605
My flesh therewith shall give acquittance:°
I will now begin, if God give me grace.
KNOWLEDGE: Everyman, God give you time and
        space!
Thus I bequeath you in the hands of our Saviour;
Now may you make your reckoning sure.   610
EVERYMAN: In the name of the Holy Trinity,
My body sore punished shall be:
Take this, body, for the sin of the flesh!

(Scourges himself.)

Also° thou delightest to go gay and fresh,
And in the way of damnation thou did me bring, 615
Therefore suffer now strokes and punishing.
Now of penance I will wade the water clear,
To save me from purgatory, that sharp fire.

(Good Deeds rises from the ground.)

GOOD DEEDS: I thank God, now I can walk and go,
And am delivered of my sickness and woe.   620
Therefore with Everyman I will go, and not
        spare;
His good works I will help him to declare.
KNOWLEDGE: Now, Everyman, be merry and glad!
Your Good Deeds cometh now; ye may not be
        sad.
Now is your Good Deeds whole and sound,   625
Going upright upon the ground.
EVERYMAN: My heart is light, and shall be
        evermore;
Now will I smite° faster than I did before.
GOOD DEEDS: Everyman, pilgrim, my special friend,
Blessed be thou without end;   630
For thee is preparate the eternal glory.
Ye have me made whole and sound,
Therefore I will bide by thee in every stound.°

---

568. **siker:** Sure.   569. **and:** If.   588. **in this presence:** In
the presence of this company.

596. **Moses' table:** Medieval theologians regarded the two
tablets given to Moses on Mount Sinai as symbols of baptism
and penance. Thus Everyman is asking to be numbered
among those who have escaped damnation by doing penance
for their sins.   606. **acquittance:** Satisfaction (as part of the
sacrament of penance).   614. **Also:** As.   628. **smite:**
Strike.   633. **stound:** Trial.

EVERYMAN: Welcome, my Good Deeds; now I hear thy voice,
635 I weep for very sweetness of love.
KNOWLEDGE: Be no more sad, but ever rejoice;
God seeth thy living in his throne above.
Put on this garment to thy behoof,°
Which is wet with your tears,
640 Or else before God you may it miss,
When ye to your journey's end come shall.
EVERYMAN: Gentle Knowledge, what do ye it call?
KNOWLEDGE: It is a garment of sorrow:
From pain it will you borrow;°
645 Contrition it is,
That geteth forgiveness;
It pleaseth God passing well.
GOOD DEEDS: Everyman, will you wear it for your heal?°
EVERYMAN: Now blessed be Jesu, Mary's Son,
650 For now have I on true contrition.
And let us go now without tarrying;
Good Deeds, have we clear our reckoning?
GOOD DEEDS: Yea, indeed, I have it here.
EVERYMAN: Then I trust we need not fear;
655 Now, friends, let us not part in twain.
KNOWLEDGE: Nay, Everyman, that will we not, certain.
GOOD DEEDS: Yet must thou lead with thee
Three persons of great might.
EVERYMAN: Who should they be?
660 GOOD DEEDS: Discretion and Strength they hight,°
And thy Beauty may not abide behind.
KNOWLEDGE: Also ye must call to mind
Your Five Wits as for your counsellors.
GOOD DEEDS: You must have them ready at all hours.
665 EVERYMAN: How shall I get them hither?
KNOWLEDGE: You must call them all together,
And they will hear you incontinent.°
EVERYMAN: My friends, come hither and be present,
Discretion, Strength, my Five Wits, and Beauty.

(*Enter Beauty, Strength, Discretion, and Five Wits.*)

670 BEAUTY: Here at your will we be all ready.
What will ye that we should do?
GOOD DEEDS: That ye would with Everyman go,
And help him in his pilgrimage.
Advise you, will ye with him or not in that voyage?
675 STRENGTH: We will bring him all thither,
To his help and comfort, ye may believe me.

DISCRETION: So will we go with him all together.
EVERYMAN: Almighty God, lofed° may thou be!
I give thee laud that I have hither brought
Strength, Discretion, Beauty, and Five Wits. Lack I nought.   680
And my Good Deeds, with Knowledge clear,
All be in my company at my will here;
I desire no more to my business.
STRENGTH: And I, Strength, will by you stand in distress,
Though thou would in battle fight on the ground.   685
FIVE WITS: And though it were through the world round,
We will not depart for sweet ne sour.
BEAUTY: No more will I unto death's hour,
Whatsoever thereof befall.
DISCRETION: Everyman, advise you first of all;   690
Go with a good advisement and deliberation.
We all give you virtuous monition°
That all shall be well.
EVERYMAN: My friends, harken what I will tell:
I pray God reward you in his heavenly sphere.   695
Now harken, all that be here,
For I will make my testament
Here before you all present:
In alms half my good I will give with my hands twain
In the way of charity, with good intent,   700
And the other half still shall remain
In queth,° to be returned there it ought to be.°
This I do in despite of the fiend of hell,
To go quit out of his peril°
Ever after and this day.   705
KNOWLEDGE: Everyman, harken what I say:
Go to priesthood, I you advise,
And receive of him in any wise°
The holy sacrament and ointment together.
Then shortly see ye turn again hither;   710
We will all abide you here.
FIVE WITS: Yea, Everyman, hie you that ye ready were.
There is no emperor, king, duke, ne baron,
That of God hath commission
As hath the least priest in the world being;   715
For of the blessed sacraments pure and benign
He beareth the keys, and thereof hath the cure°
For man's redemption — it is ever sure —
Which God for our soul's medicine

---

638. behoof: Advantage.   644. borrow: Release.   648. heal: Salvation.   660. hight: Are called.   667. incontinent: Immediately.

678. lofed: Praised.   692. monition: Forewarning.   702. queth: Bequest.   returned there it ought to be: This line probably refers to restitution, that is, the restoration to its proper owner of unlawfully acquired property.   704. quit out of his peril: Free out of his power.   708. in any wise: Without fail.   717. cure: Charge.

Scene from the Guthrie Theatre production of *Everyman*, directed by Robert Benedetti.

720 Gave us out of his heart with great pine.°
Here in this transitory life, for thee and me,
The blessed sacraments seven there be:
Baptism, confirmation, with priesthood good,
And the sacrament of God's precious flesh and
          blood,
Marriage, the holy extreme unction, and
725   penance;
These seven be good to have in remembrance,
Gracious sacraments of high divinity.
EVERYMAN: Fain would I receive that holy body,
And meekly to my ghostly father I will go.

720. pine: Suffering.

FIVE WITS: Everyman, that is the best that ye can
          do.   730
God will you to salvation bring,
For priesthood exceedeth all other thing:
To us Holy Scripture they do teach,
And converteth man from sin heaven to reach;
God hath to them more power given   735
Than to any angel that is in heaven.
With five words° he may consecrate,
God's body in flesh and blood to make,

737. five words: *Hoc est enim Corpus meum* ("For this is My Body," the words of the consecration of the Body of Christ at Mass).

And handleth his Maker between his hands.
740 The priest bindeth and unbindeth all bands,
Both in earth and in heaven.
Thou ministers all the sacraments seven;
Though we kissed thy feet, thou were worthy;
Thou art surgeon that cureth sin deadly:
745 No remedy we find under God
But all only priesthood.°
Everyman, God gave priests that dignity,
And setteth them in his stead among us to be;
Thus be they above angels in degree.

(*Everyman goes to the priest to receive the last sacraments.*)

750 KNOWLEDGE: If priests be good, it is so, surely.
But when Jesus hanged on the cross with great smart,
There he gave out of his blessed heart
The same sacrament in great torment:
He sold them not to us, that Lord omnipotent.
755 Therefore Saint Peter the apostle doth say
That Jesu's curse hath all they
Which God their Savior do buy or sell,
Or they for any money do take or tell.°
Sinful priests giveth the sinners example bad;
Their children sitteth by other men's fires, I have
760 heard;
And some haunteth women's company
With unclean life, as lusts of lechery:
These be with sin made blind.
FIVE WITS: I trust to God no such may we find;
765 Therefore let us priesthood honor,
And follow their doctrine for our souls' succor.
We be their sheep, and they shepherds be
By whom we all be kept in surety.
Peace, for yonder I see Everyman come,
770 Which hath made true satisfaction.
GOOD DEEDS: Methink it is he indeed.

(*Reenter Everyman.*)

EVERYMAN: Now Jesu be your alder speed!°
I have received the sacrament for my redemption,
And then mine extreme unction:
775 Blessed be all they that counselled me to take it!
And now, friends, let us go without longer respite;
I thank God that ye have tarried so long.
Now set each of you on this rood° your hand,
And shortly follow me:
780 I go before there I would be; God be our guide!

STRENGTH: Everyman, we will not from you go
Till ye have done this voyage long.
DISCRETION: I, Discretion, will bide by you also.
KNOWLEDGE: And though this pilgrimage be never
so strong,°
I will never part you fro. 785
STRENGTH: Everyman, I will be as sure by thee
As ever I did by Judas Maccabee.°

(*Everyman comes to his grave.*)

EVERYMAN: Alas, I am so faint I may not stand;
My limbs under me doth fold.
Friends, let us not turn again to this land, 790
Not for all the world's gold;
For into this cave must I creep
And turn to earth, and there to sleep.
BEAUTY: What, into this grave? Alas!
EVERYMAN: Yea, there shall ye consume, more and
less. 795
BEAUTY: And what, should I smother here?
EVERYMAN: Yea, by my faith, and never more
appear.
In this world live no more we shall,
But in heaven before the highest Lord of all.
BEAUTY: I cross out all this;° adieu, by Saint John! 800
I take my cap in my lap,° and am gone.
EVERYMAN: What, Beauty, whither will ye?
BEAUTY: Peace, I am deaf; I look not behind me,
Not and thou wouldest give me all the gold in
thy chest. (*Exit Beauty.*)
EVERYMAN: Alas, whereto may I trust? 805
Beauty goeth fast away from me;
She promised with me to live and die.
STRENGTH: Everyman, I will thee also forsake and
deny;
Thy game liketh° me not at all.
EVERYMAN: Why, then, ye will forsake me all? 810
Sweet Strength, tarry a little space.
STRENGTH: Nay, sir, by the rood of grace!
I will hie me from thee fast,
Though thou weep till thy heart to-brast.°
EVERYMAN: Ye would ever bide by me, ye said. 815
STRENGTH: Yea, I have you far enough conveyed.
Ye be old enough, I understand,
Your pilgrimage to take on hand;
I repent me that I hither came.

---

746. But all only priesthood: Except only from the priesthood.   **755–58. Therefore Saint Peter . . . do take or tell:** Reference to the sin of simony, the selling of church offices or benefits.   **tell:** Count out, i.e., sell.   **772. your alder speed:** The helper of you all.   **778. rood:** Cross.

784. strong: Grievous.   **787. Judas Maccabee:** Judas Maccabeus, who overcame Syrian domination and won religious freedom for the Jews in 165 B.C., believed that his strength came not from worldly might but from heaven (1 Maccabees 3:19).   **800. I cross out all this:** I cancel all this, i.e., my promise to stay with you.   **801. I take my cap in my lap:** Doff my cap [so low that it comes] into my lap. **809. liketh:** Pleases.   **814. brast:** Break.

EVERYMAN: Strength, you to displease I am to
820   blame;
    Yet promise is debt, this ye well wot.
STRENGTH: In faith, I care not.
    Thou art but a fool to complain;
    You spend your speech and waste your brain.
825   Go thrust thee into the ground!   (*Exit Strength.*)
EVERYMAN: I had wend surer I should you have
    found.
    He that trusteth in his Strength
    She him deceiveth at the length.
    Both Strength and Beauty forsaketh me;
830   Yet they promised me fair and lovingly.
DISCRETION: Everyman, I will after Strength be
    gone;
    As for me, I will leave you alone.
EVERYMAN: Why, Discretion, will ye forsake me?
DISCRETION: Yea, in faith, I will go from thee,
835   For when Strength goeth before
    I follow after evermore.
EVERYMAN: Yet, I pray thee, for the love of the
    Trinity,
    Look in my grave once piteously.
DISCRETION: Nay, so nigh will I not come;
840   Farewell, every one!   (*Exit Discretion.*)
EVERYMAN: O, all thing faileth, save God alone —
    Beauty, Strength, and Discretion;
    For when Death bloweth his blast,
    They all run from me full fast.
845 FIVE WITS: Everyman, my leave now of thee I take;
    I will follow the other, for here I thee forsake.
EVERYMAN: Alas, then may I wail and weep,
    For I took you for my best friend.
FIVE WITS: I will no longer thee keep;
850   Now farewell, and there an end.
                        (*Exit Five Wits.*)
EVERYMAN: O Jesu, help! All hath forsaken me.
GOOD DEEDS: Nay, Everyman; I will bide with thee.
    I will not forsake thee indeed;
    Thou shalt find me a good friend at need.
EVERYMAN: Gramercy, Good Deeds! Now may I
855   true friends see.
    They have forsaken me, every one;
    I loved them better than my Good Deeds alone.
    Knowledge, will ye forsake me also?
KNOWLEDGE: Yea, Everyman, when ye to Death
    shall go;
860   But not yet, for no manner of danger.
EVERYMAN: Gramercy, Knowledge, with all my
    heart.
KNOWLEDGE: Nay, yet I will not from hence depart
    Till I see where ye shall become.
EVERYMAN: Methink, alas, that I must be gone
865   To make my reckoning and my debts pay,
    For I see my time is nigh spent away.

    Take example, all ye that this do hear or see,
    How they that I loved best do forsake me,
    Except my Good Deeds that bideth truly.
GOOD DEEDS: All earthly things is but vanity: 870
    Beauty, Strength, and Discretion do man forsake,
    Foolish friends, and kinsmen, that fair spake —
    All fleeth save Good Deeds, and that am I.
EVERYMAN: Have mercy on me, God most mighty;
    And stand by me, thou mother and maid, holy
    Mary.   875
GOOD DEEDS: Fear not; I will speak for thee.
EVERYMAN: Here I cry God mercy.
GOOD DEEDS: Short our end, and minish our pain;
    Let us go and never come again.
EVERYMAN: Into thy hands, Lord, my soul I
    commend;   880
    Receive it, Lord, that it be not lost.
    As thou me boughtest, so me defend,
    And save me from the fiend's boast,
    That I may appear with that blessed host
    That shall be saved at the day of doom.   885
    In manus tuas, of mights most
    For ever, *commendo spiritum meum.*°

(*He sinks into his grave.*)

KNOWLEDGE: Now hath he suffered that we all shall
    endure;
    The Good Deeds shall make all sure.
    Now hath he made ending;   890
    Methinketh that I hear angels sing,
    And make great joy and melody
    Where Everyman's soul received shall be.
ANGEL: Come, excellent elect spouse, to Jesu!
    Hereabove thou shalt go   895
    Because of thy singular virtue.
    Now the soul is taken the body fro,
    Thy reckoning is crystal-clear.
    Now shalt thou into the heavenly sphere,
    Unto the which all ye shall come   900
    That liveth well before the day of doom.

(*Enter Doctor.*)

DOCTOR: This moral men may have in mind.
    Ye hearers, take it of worth, old and young,
    And forsake Pride, for he deceiveth you in the
    end;
    And remember Beauty, Five Wits, Strength, and
    Discretion,   905
    They all at the last do every man forsake,
    Save his Good Deeds there doth he take.
    But beware, for and they be small
    Before God, he hath no help at all;

886–87. *In manus tuas . . . commendo spiritum meum:* Into your hands, most mighty One for ever, I commend my spirit.

910 None excuse may be there for every man.
Alas, how shall he do then?
For after death amends may no man make,
For then mercy and pity doth him forsake.
If his reckoning be not clear when he doth come,
God will say: *"Ite, maledicti, in ignem*
915 *eternum."*°

915. *Ite, maledicti, in ignem eternum*: Depart, ye cursed,
into everlasting fire.

And he that hath his account whole and sound,
High in heaven he shall be crowned;
Unto which place God bring us all thither,
That we may live body and soul together.
Thereto help the Trinity!
Amen, say ye, for saint charity. 920

Thus endeth this moral play of Everyman.

Renaissance Drama

Italian Drama

The period following the Middle Ages in Europe, from about the fourteenth to the seventeenth century, is known as the *Renaissance,* a term meaning "rebirth." In this period a shift away from medieval values and culture was motivated by a revival of classical learning; advances in physics, astronomy, and the biological sciences; the exploration of the "new world"; and political and economic developments. This shift was not abrupt, however; it was gradual, like a thaw. It began in the south, in Italy, in the late 1300s and moved northward through the activities of scholars, travelers, performers, and writers, until it reached England sometime late in the 1400s.

The Renaissance built on medieval culture and at the same time developed a secular understanding of the individual in society that eventually transformed this culture, long dominated by the Roman Catholic Church in many spheres—artistic, intellectual, and political, as well as spiritual. The transformation was influenced by the work of great writers, scholars, philosophers, and scientists such as Desiderius Erasmus (1466?–1536), Niccolò Machiavelli (1469–1527), Nicolaus Copernicus (1473–1543), Francis Bacon (1561–1626), and Galileo Galilei (1564–1642). In addition, the rise in power of the guilds and the increase in wealth of the successful Italian trading states, which produced large and influential families in cities such as Florence, Venice, Milan, and Genoa, contributed to the erosion of the church's power.

Italian scholars, following classical models, had begun in the last decades of the fourteenth century to center their studies on human achievements. Such studies, known as the humanities, became the chief concern of the most innovative thinkers of the day. Their interests were well served by the rediscovery of ancient Greek philosophical and scientific texts. Although ancient texts had been preserved in monasteries for centuries, knowledge of them was restricted. A new demand for classical texts, fed by the humanists' focus on ancient models as the source of wisdom and by their return to a liberal arts curriculum established by the Greeks, led to the wide dissemination of the works of Plato, Aristotle, Cicero, and important Greek dramatists during the Renaissance. The achievement of the ancients was an inspiration to Renaissance writers and reaffirmed their conviction that a study of the humanities was the key to transforming the old medieval attitudes into a new, dynamic worldview.

Vitruvius and the Rediscovery of Roman Design

Most medieval Italian theater depended on portable stages, but it was clear in the last decades of the fourteenth century that to present the newly rediscovered Roman or Greek plays, something more closely resembling the original Greek theater would be necessary. Fortunately, *The Ten Books of Architecture* (written c. 16–13 B.C.) of the great Roman architect Vitruvius (first century B.C.) was rediscovered in a manuscript in the monastery of St. Gall. It included detailed plans for the Greek-inspired Roman theater.

Using Vitruvius's designs, the Italians began building stages that were raised platforms with a FRONS SCAENA, the flat front wall used in the Roman theater. The earliest Italian woodcuts show the stages to be relatively simple with pillars supporting a roof or cover. Curtains stretched between the pillars permitted the actors to enter and exit. Usually, three "doors" with names over each indicated the houses of specific characters.

The study of Roman architecture eventually produced, in 1584, one of the wonders of the Renaissance, the Olympic Theater (Teatro Olimpico) in Vicenza, designed by the great Renaissance architect Andrea Palladio (1508–1580), whose interpretation of Roman architecture was so compelling that it influenced architecture all over the world (Figure 4). The Olympic Theater, which has been preserved and is still used for performances, has an orchestra, a semicircular seating area, and a multistory *frons scaena*. But it also has several vistas of streets constructed in three-dimensional forced perspective running backward from the *frons scaena*.

The Olympic Theater was built with an essentially conservative design that worked well for Roman plays but not for Renaissance plays. It did not inspire new theater designs. In newer theaters, Italian plays had begun to use scenery and painted backdrops that could be changed to suggest a change in location of the action. Carefully painted backdrops were also effective in increasing illusion—one backdrop could immediately locate an action on a city street, while another could help shift the audience imaginatively to a woodland scene. These innovations proved difficult in the Olympic Theater.

The theory of vanishing-point perspective developed by the architect Filippo Brunelleschi (1377–1446) and published by Leon Battista Alberti in *On Painting* in 1435, helped revolutionize the design of flat

ABOVE: Figure 4. Designed by
Andrea Palladio, the Teatro
Olimpico (begun 1579) in
Vicenza, Italy, was the first
indoor theater of the
Renaissance. The *scaena*'s
openings produced an illusion
of depth. RIGHT: Figure 5.
Perspective setting designed
by Baldassare Peruzzi
(1481–1536)

theatrical backdrops. Earlier Renaissance painters had had no way to establish a firm sense of perspective on a flat surface, so all three-dimensional objects appeared flat; all space in a landscape or cityscape seemed shortened and unreal. The use of a single vanishing point—in which lines were lightly drawn from the edges of the canvas (or theatrical backdrop) so that they met in a single point in the center—made it possible to show buildings, trees, and figures in their proper proportion to one another (Figure 5). For the first time, Renaissance painters could achieve lifelike illusions on a flat surface. On the other hand, three-dimensional scenery was possible in the Olympic Theater—as well as some others—at this time, and the illusion of reality was thus intensified.

The designer Sebastiano Serlio (1475–1554) used the vanishing-point technique, intensified by receding lines of tiles in the floor and on the painted backdrop. Serlio established all-purpose settings for comedy, tragedy, and satire. The rigidity of the backdrops for comedy and tragedy—both used a piazza, a small town square, ringed by stone buildings—restricted their use. But the setting for satire was rustic: trees, bushes, a couple of cottages. Until the nineteenth century, European theaters were equipped with sets of backdrops and wingpieces derived from his designs.

The most important and long-lasting development of Italian theater design in the mid-1500s was the PROSCENIUM ARCH, a "frame" that surrounds the stage, permitting the audience to look in on the scene, whether it be in a room or in a town square. The arch lent a finished touch to the theater, separating the action from the audience and distancing the actors. The proscenium arch is common in most theaters today.

Commedia dell'Arte

Renaissance Italy had two traditions of theater. *Commedia erudita* was learned, almost scholarly, in its interests in Roman staging and Roman plays. COMMEDIA DELL'ARTE was less reverent, more slapstick, and generally more popular. It is difficult, however, to say which was more influential on literature over the years. Each made its contribution.

In terms of acting and storytelling, the influence of the *commedia dell'arte* is almost unparalleled. The term means "comedy performed by professionals." The actors usually had grown up in performing families that made their living touring the countryside, performing at fairs and on feast days. From the early Renaissance through the eighteenth century, the *commedia dell'arte* entertained all of Europe and influenced comic theater in every nation.

The essence of *commedia dell'arte* was improvised scripts. A general narrative outline served as a basis, but the speeches were improvised to a degree (with some reliance on set elements and on experience with performing the same role many times). The principal characters were types who soon became familiar all over Europe: Pantalone, the often magisterial but miserly old man; Arlecchino (Harlequin), the cunning clown. Pulcinella, the Punch of Punch and Judy, and Columbina, the innocent *zanni,* began as clowns. They joined a host of other STOCK CHARACTERS such as pedantic lawyers, a braggart captain, and a serving maid. Certain versions of general characters—such as Arlecchino, who began as a simple *zanno*—became famous and were copied in many countries. When Volpone calls Mosca a "zany" near the end of Ben Jonson's *Volpone,* he reminds his audience that his characters are indebted to the *zanni* in *commedia dell'arte.* Knowing who the characters were even before the play began was a convenience that Renaissance audiences enjoyed.

The youthful lovers in the *commedia* did not require masks, but the old men, the *zanni,* and other characters all had masks that identified them and made them look, to modern eyes, rather grotesque. These masks survive today in the carnival, in Venice, where the *commedia* began. Stock characters thrive in popular comedies everywhere. Molière and, much later, Bernard Shaw depended on them. To a large extent, one of comedy's greatest sources of energy lies in the delight that audiences have always taken in stock characters. Today hardly a situation comedy on television could survive without them.

The staging of *commedia dell'arte* was simple. It often took place in open air, but sometimes indoors in a more formal theatrical setting. Sometimes performers dispensed with the stage altogether and worked in marketplaces. Their scenarios were farcical crowd pleasers filled with buffoonery. They were based on the LAZZO and the BURLA. The *burla* was the general plot for any given performance. Lazzi were comic routines something like Abbott and Costello's "Who's on First?" skit. Abbott and Costello developed their routine for burlesque, a form of comedy popular in the first half of the twentieth century centering on broad gags, routines, and running jokes. *Lazzi* were carefully planned to seem to be spontaneous interruptions of the action. Chevy Chase's trademark pratfall as he enters a scene is a descendant of the sixteenth-century *lazzo*.

Elizabethan Drama

The reign of Queen Elizabeth I, 1558–1603, is known as the Elizabethan age in England—a period of discovery and prosperity as well as a period of great achievement in the arts, especially drama. Sir Francis Drake and Sir Walter Raleigh adventured across the Atlantic Ocean to the "New World," and England secured its economic future by defeating the invasion attempt of the Spanish Armada in 1588. England had become Protestant in the 1530s—one reason Catholic Spain felt it needed to subdue the nation.

Elizabethan England, especially after the defeat of the Armada, produced one of the great ages of drama, rivaling the great age of Greece. During this period, playwrights such as Thomas Kyd (1558–1594), Christopher Marlowe (1564–1593), William Shakespeare (1564–1616), Ben Jonson (1572–1637), John Marston (1576–1634), John Fletcher (1579–1625), John Webster (1580?–1625?), Thomas Middleton (1580?–1627), and John Ford (1586–1639) were drawing crowds by the thousands.

That the Elizabethans enjoyed plays with a moral basis is plain from the fact that so much of the great drama of the late 1500s and early 1600s is moral in character. Still, early Elizabethan plays were less obviously moralistic than the then-popular morality plays. They did not aim specifically to teach a moral lesson, although it is true that there are many lessons to be learned from Shakespeare and his contemporaries.

During Shakespeare's youth wandering players put on a number of plays from REPERTORY, their stock of perhaps a dozen current plays they could perform. How many players there were or what their source of plays was, we do not know. Much of what we know comes directly from *Hamlet* and the appearance of the players who perform Hamlet's "Mouse-trap." What we learn there tells us that dramatic styles had developed in the English countryside and that theater was thriving.

The First Professional Companies

Although professional players' groups had long been licensed to perform in France and Italy, until the 1570s professional actors—those who had no other trade—did not enjoy favor in England. Such people could be arrested for vagrancy. The law, however, changed, and actors with royal patronage were permitted to perform. The history of theater changed, too. In 1576 James Burbage (father of the famous star of Shakespeare's plays, Richard Burbage) built the first building made specially for plays in England. It was called The Theatre.

Soon there were other theaters: the Swan (Figure 6), the Globe, the Rose, the Fortune, the Hope. The Globe was large enough to accommodate two to three thousand people. Because these theaters were open-air,

Figure 6. The Swan Theatre as
copied from Johannes De Witt's
sixteenth-century drawing

they could not be used in winter, but all were extraordinarily successful.
Shakespeare, who was part owner of the Globe and, later, of the second
indoor Blackfriars Theatre, received money from admission fees and from
his role as chief playwright. He became rich enough to retire in splendid
style to Stratford, his hometown. Few other Elizabethan actors and playwrights had as much of a financial stake in their work as did Shakespeare.

The Elizabethan
Theater

The design of the Elizabethan theater is a matter of some speculation.
Many of the plays popular before the theaters were built were performed in a square inn yard, with a balcony above. The audience looked
out their windows or stood in the yard. One location of the earliest Eng-

lish drama is the Inns of Court, essentially a college for law students in London, where students staged plays. The audience there would have been learned, bright, and imaginative. Indeed, the first English tragedy, *Gorboduc,* by Thomas Sackville and Thomas Norton, was played indoors at the Inner Temple, one of the Inns of Court, in 1562, before Marlowe and Shakespeare were born.

The shape of the early theaters was often octagonal or circular, like the bear pits in which bears, tied to stakes, were baited by dogs for the amusement of the audience. The stage was raised about five feet from the ground with levels of seating in several galleries. Approximately half the area over the stage was roofed and contained machinery to lower actors from the "heavens"; it was painted blue with stars to simulate the sky. Some stages were approximately twenty-five by forty feet. Doors or curtained openings at the back of the stage served for entrances and exits, and at the back of the stage was a special room for costume changes. The stage may have contained a section that was normally curtained but that opened to reveal an interior, such as a bedroom. The existence of this feature is, however, in considerable dispute.

The Elizabethan Audience

The entrance fee to the theaters was a penny, probably the equivalent of five to ten dollars in today's money. For another penny one could take a seat, probably on a bench, in one of the upper galleries. In some theaters more private spaces were available as well. A great many playgoers were satisfied to stand around the stage and were thus nicknamed "groundlings." Hamlet calls them the "understanding gentlemen of the ground." The more academic playwrights, Marlowe and Jonson, used the term to mean those who would not perfectly understand the significance of the plays.

Shakespeare and other Elizabethan playwrights expected a widely diverse audience—from coarse to extraordinarily polished. Shakespeare had the gift, as did Marlowe and even Jonson in his comedies, to appeal to them all. Shakespeare's plays were given in public playhouses open to everyone. They were also given in university theaters, as in the case of *Macbeth*; in indoor private theaters; and in royal command performances. Shakespeare's universality reveals itself in his appeal to many different kinds of people.

Female Characters on the English Stage

Because women were not allowed to act on English stages, boys and young men filled the parts of young female characters such as Juliet, Desdemona, and Ophelia. Interestingly, no contemporary commentator makes any complaint about having to put up with a boy playing the part of Juliet or any of Shakespeare's other love interests, such as Miranda in *The Tempest,* Ophelia in *Hamlet,* or even Queen Cleopatra. Older women, such as the Nurse in *Romeo and Juliet,* were played by some of the gifted male character actors of the company.

The Masque

The Elizabethan MASQUE was a special entertainment of royalty. It was a celebration that included a rudimentary plot, a great deal of singing and dancing, and magnificent costumes and lighting. Masques were performed only once, often to celebrate a royal marriage. Masque audiences participated in the dances and were usually delighted by complex machinery that lifted or lowered characters from the skies. The masque was devised in Italy in the 1570s by Count Giovanni Bardi, founder of the Florentine Camerata, a Renaissance group of theatergoers sponsored by Lorenzo de' Medici.

The geniuses of the masque are generally considered to have been Ben Jonson and Inigo Jones. Jones was the architect whose Banqueting Hall at Whitehall in London, which still stands, provided the setting for most of the great masques of the seventeenth century. Jonson and Jones worked together from 1605 to 1631 to produce a remarkable body of masques that today resemble the bones of a dinosaur: What we read on the page suggests in only the vaguest way what the presentation must have been like when the masques were mounted.

Because of the expenses of costuming and staging, masques were too costly to be produced more than once. The royal exchequer was frequently burdened in Queen Elizabeth's time; more so after King James took the throne in 1603. Masque costumes were impressive, the scenery astounding, and the effects amazing. In all of this, the words—which are, after all, at the center of Shakespeare's plays as well as other plays of the period—were of least account. As a result of the emphasis on the machinery and designs—the work of Inigo Jones—Jonson abandoned his partnership in a huff, complaining that he could not compete with the scene painters and carpenters.

The value placed on spectacle in the masques tells us something about the taste of the aristocrats, who enjoyed sumptuous foods, clothes, and amusements. Eventually, audiences of the public theaters hungered for spectacle, too. Their appetite was satisfied by masques inserted in the plays of Marston, Webster, and Shakespeare, whose masque in *The Tempest* is a delightful short tribute to the genre. An added device for achieving spectacular effects onstage was huge storm machines installed in the Globe. Some say that one reason Shakespeare wrote *The Tempest* was to take advantage of the new equipment. Foreign visitors described London theaters as gorgeous places of entertainment far surpassing their own. The quest for more intense spectacle eventually led to disaster in one theater. The Globe actually burned down in 1613 because a cannon in the roof above the stage misfired and brought the house down in real flames.

The royal demand for masques was unaffected. As Francis Bacon said in his essay "On Masques" (1625), "These things are but toys to come amongst such serious observations. But yet, since princes will have such things, it is better they should be graced with elegancy than daubed with cost. Dancing to song is a thing of great state and pleasure."

Christopher Marlowe

Christopher Marlowe (1564–1593) was born two months before William Shakespeare and in somewhat similar social circumstances. Marlowe's father was a shoemaker; Shakespeare's a glovemaker. But unlike Shakespeare, Marlowe won a scholarship to Cambridge, where he remained six years and began his career as a playwright. His first play, *Tamburlaine,* was finished before he left the university. When it was performed in London it had the benefit of Edward Alleyn, the finest actor of his time, playing the title role.

The son-in-law of Philip Henslowe, who owned the Rose, the Fortune, and the Hope theaters in London, Alleyn was a rhetorical actor with a commanding voice and gestures. His style was perfect for declaiming what Ben Jonson called Marlowe's "Mighty line": his IAMBIC PENTAMETER BLANK VERSE, which moves in stately rhythms and which dominated the Elizabethan stage. Marlowe's blank verse, especially in the emotional moments of Faustus's career — as in his invocation of the devils in act I, scene III — resonates and rolls from the tongue in mighty billows. It has a virtually incantatory effect on the listener, and in a London theater of the time, as spoken by Edward Alleyn, it must have been mesmerizing.

Marlowe also had considerable success as a poet and as a translator of the classics. His version of Ovid's *Amores* is very lively, and his long poem *Hero and Leander* is a dynamic contribution to the poetry of Renaissance humanism. It shows his affection for the classics in a form that Shakespeare also employed: the longer narrative poem.

Marlowe's university scholarship was intended for those studying for the ministry, but instead of entering the ministry, he went up to London in 1587. Some of his friends revealed that his beliefs were close to those of atheism, a charge that in his time could have resulted in death. Fortunately, when he applied for his master's degree and was on the verge of having it denied, Queen Elizabeth intervened on his behalf. Her involvement has made subsequent generations think that he must have been a spy on her behalf during at least some of the time he was in Catholic sections of France.

Partly as a result of his connection with Elizabeth, Marlowe has often been portrayed as a romantic swashbuckler in the heart of complex intrigues. He was also well known to most of the literary people of London: Shakespeare, Sir Walter Raleigh, Francis Bacon, Thomas Kyd, and Thomas Harriot (an astronomer and writer) were all close associates. They and Marlowe were also acquainted with the remarkable magician Dr. John Dee. As members of a group dubbed the School of Night, they met privately to discuss ideas of the occult, alchemy, and skeptic philosophy—subjects that could not easily be talked about in the open.

Marlowe's first play was *Tamburlaine* (1587; in two parts), followed by *The Jew of Malta* (1589) and *Edward the Second* (1592). They are all powerful plays that feature a great tragic character. *The Massacre at Paris* (1593) is based on the St. Bartholomew Day's Massacre in 1573, when some thirty thousand Huguenots — French Protestants — were killed by Catholics in Paris. Marlowe's knowledge of the details of the events seems to have been considerable, although the play itself is not as powerful as his earlier tragedies. *Dido, Queen of Carthage* (1593; with Thomas Nashe) is a typical kind of collaboration of the period. None of these plays, good as they are, come to the level of *Doctor Faustus*, which stands as one of the greatest plays of the Elizabethan age.

Apparently quick to anger, Marlowe was involved in one murder before he himself was murdered over a bar bill at the inn of the Widow Bull in Deptford. He was drinking with an acquaintance, Ingram Frizer, who worked for the great Walsingham family, a patron of Marlowe's. During an argument Marlowe grabbed Frizer from behind, but Frizer broke free and stabbed Marlowe, who died instantly. At the time of Marlowe's death Shakespeare was just beginning his career as a playwright.

DOCTOR FAUSTUS

Doctor Faustus was probably written between 1588 and 1593, shortly before Marlowe died. There is a record of its being readied for the press in 1601, but if that version was printed, no copies survive. The first printed version is from 1604; an amplified version came out in 1616. Neither had been supervised by Marlowe, and to make things more complicated, records indicate that Henslowe paid two writers a substantial sum to add to the original text. What the additions were or what the original text was, we probably will never know.

Current scholarship leads us to believe that the 1616 text, printed here, is actually closer to the original acting version than the 1604 text was. The breaking of the text into five acts and their scenes is a modern convention, as is the supplying of most of the stage directions. The five-act pattern common in classical plays is natural to Elizabethan plays as well.

The influence of the medieval stage is readily apparent in *Doctor Faustus*. The emphasis on the devils, the seven deadly sins, and the terrifying vision of hell in act V is reminiscent of the devils of the mystery plays and their reliance on frightening hell's mouth props. The allusion to medieval theater's tradition of the mansion in Mephistophilis's speech in act V also echoes the basic message of the morality plays:

> Ay, Faustus, now thou hast no hope of heaven;
> Therefore despair. Think only upon hell,
> For that must be thy mansion, there to dwell.

Doctor Faustus differs from the morality plays in one very important way, though. We are never led to think that Faustus would have lived a better or more interesting life if he had restrained his ambition. Faustus is a hero, especially of the romantic sort that strove to achieve great things and challenge the gods. The Elizabethans admired Faustus much more than they condemned him, no matter what moral tags Marlowe might have put in the play to satisfy society's official view of itself.

Among the sources of the play are a medieval folklore tradition connected with the wizard who sold his soul to the devil for greater powers and a German book called *Historia von D. Johan Fausten,* published in 1587. Marlowe may have seen the book or, more likely, may have seen an English translation in 1592 called *The History of the damnable life, and deserved death of Doctor John Faustus*. In either event, the Faust legend goes back to the early medieval period and could have reached Marlowe in any number of ways.

Doctor Faustus is one of the earliest English tragedies. Its hero is in many ways larger than life, and while not a member of the nobility, he is at ease with royalty and clearly superior in intellectual abilities. The richness of the psychological portrayal of Faustus — as well as of Wagner and Mephistophilis — elevates the play from the best earlier efforts of English and European dramatists. Faustus represents an interesting tradition: the University of Wittenberg produced the most important Protestant of the sixteenth century, Martin Luther. His daring — comparable in some ways to Faustus's overreaching — led to the Reformation, one of the most cataclysmic changes in European thought in the Renaissance. Hamlet is also a student at Wittenberg, a fact that gives us insight into the Elizabethan imagination. Wittenberg to the Elizabethans meant fierce intellectual energy and daring.

As in the case of many of Shakespeare's tragedies, *Doctor Faustus* has interludes of comic relief, with the horse coursers who are bilked by Faustus and with other clowns and mechanicals who wonder openly about the terrifying skills of the magician. This linking of magic and comic has annoyed some critics who have agreed with Aristotle that such a mixture is problematic and tends to diffuse the effect of the drama. Actually, in performance the comic scenes are in no way a dilution of effect. They tend to buoy the energy of the play and help us focus anew on the insatiable Faustus.

But *Doctor Faustus* has a modern twist that takes it out of the medieval mold. The Renaissance was a period of expansion, especially the expansion of knowledge. Astronomy was symbolic of the new age: Telescopes were beginning to give Europeans a sense of the vastness and complexity of the universe. When Faustus asks information of Mephistophilis, he begins with questions about the planets and the universe, knowledge of which had long been thought to be somehow secret. Mastering that knowledge was symbolic of mastering the knowledge of the innermost workings of science.

Faustus's quest for knowledge became for some people a Renaissance theme. The magicians referred to in the text, such as Roger Bacon and Cornelius Agrippa, were genuine. Their work was read throughout Europe, and the kinds of magic actions that Faustus aspires to were thought possible. The Elizabethans definitely believed in the presence of spirits, of ghosts, of intervention through witches of the otherworld. *Doctor Faustus* fed the contemporary interest in the occult. Faustus quests for forbidden knowledge; he must sell his soul to the devil to acquire it. His lust for knowledge — he says at the outset that he has dominated all the world of learning available to him — is without bounds.

Many of Marlowe's audience would have seen in Doctor Faustus an allusion to the magus John Dee, who cast the horoscope of Queen Elizabeth. Marlowe knew Dee, on whom the description of Faustus is based. Known throughout Europe for his almost supernormal intellectual capacity, Dee was learned in many sciences. His introduction to the first English edition of Euclid's *Geometry* made him not only respected in Europe but eventually known throughout the New World. Dee's version of Euclid was used at Harvard until the late 1700s. Because Dee was a wizard, his house at Mortlake was attacked and burned to the ground by frightened peasants while he was abroad. With his house went one of the most impressive personal libraries in Europe.

Faustus was willing to seek forbidden knowledge — in the way Adam and Eve did — at all costs, in full awareness that he risked the loss of his soul. And while Marlowe condemns Faustus to hell and does not save him at the end, we have the feeling — as did Elizabethans — that there is something grand and heroic about Faustus's risk taking. He fails, yes, but he does so in a way that makes mediocre citizens who would never have had his imagination or daring seem pallid and weak. We find ourselves involved in Faustus's struggle.

Dr. Faustus in Performance

Marlowe may not have seen *Doctor Faustus* performed. There are no performance records until 1594, when Philip Henslowe and the Royal Admiral's Men produced the play. Productions were frequent until 1598, and Henslowe's records indicate that the play was extremely popular. The great actor Edward Alleyn portrayed Faustus. Along with several reissuings of printed versions of the play, productions seem to have continued into the early part of the 1600s, when a number of writers were hired at different times to add lines to the original text. After the Restoration in 1660 and the reopening of the theaters, *Doctor Faustus* was again played frequently, with Thomas Betterton in the title role. In the eighteenth century the play was sometimes staged as a farce and in some cases reduced to a puppet show. In the nineteenth century, however, audiences were given the chance to see the play as a serious tragedy, with Sir Henry Irving, one of the greatest of the nineteenth-century actors, performing in London at the Lyceum Theatre in 1885. Twentieth-century performances included a number of amateur productions, including one during wartime by the great director Peter Brook in 1942.

Orson Welles performed the title role in a Works Progress Administration production in New York; reviews were mixed. Welles, himself a magician, emphasized the magical elements so that trapdoors and special effects became great moments of entertainment. The Phoenix Theatre's 1964 production in New York continued that tradition, with fireworks accompanying the entrance of the "hot whore." That production emphasized the blackness of the play, with dark sets and glittering dark costumes. At the end of the play, Faustus was faced with the yawning pit of hellfire. Productions of the play were also popular in Germany in the first half of the twentieth century. In his novel *Doctor Faustus*, Thomas Mann saw in the play a metaphor for Germany's having sold its soul to Hitler.

Christopher Marlowe (1564–1593)

THE TRAGICAL HISTORY OF THE LIFE AND DEATH OF DOCTOR FAUSTUS

c. 1593

The Players

THE CHORUS
DOCTOR FAUSTUS
WAGNER, *his student and servant*
VALDES
CORNELIUS
THREE SCHOLARS
AN OLD MAN

POPE ADRIAN
RAYMOND, *King of Hungary*

BRUNO, *the rival Pope*
TWO CARDINALS
THE ARCHBISHOP OF RHEIMS
CHARLES V, *Emperor of Germany*
MARTINO
FREDERICK } *Gentlemen of the Emperor's court*
BENVOLIO
BEELZEBUB
DUKE OF SAXONY
DUKE OF ANHOLT
DUCHESS OF ANHOLT
ROBIN, *the clown, a hostler*

DICK
A VINTNER
A HORSE-COURSER
A CARTER
HOSTESS

GOOD ANGEL
BAD ANGEL
LUCIFER
MEPHISTOPHILIS
PRIDE
COVETOUSNESS
ENVY
WRATH } *The Seven Deadly Sins*
GLUTTONY
SLOTH
LECHERY
ALEXANDER, THE GREAT
HIS PARAMOUR
DARIUS, *King of Persia*
HELEN OF TROY
TWO CUPIDS
DEVILS, BISHOPS, MONKS, FRIARS, SOLDIERS

The Scene: *Wittenberg, Rome, the Emperor's court at Innsbruck, court of the Duke of Anholt, and the neighboring countryside.*

PROLOGUE

(*Enter Chorus.*)

CHORUS: Not marching in the fields of Trasimene
　　Where Mars° did mate° the warlike Carthagens,°
　　Nor sporting in the dalliance of love
　　In courts of kings where state° is overturned,
5　　Nor in the pomp of proud audacious deeds
　　Intends our muse to vaunt his heavenly verse.
　　Only this, gentles: we must now perform
　　The form of Faustus' fortunes, good or bad.
　　And now to patient judgments we appeal,
10　　And speak for Faustus in his infancy.
　　Now is he born, of parents base of stock,
　　In Germany, within a town called Rhode.

Note: Material in brackets has been added by the editor.
Prologue. 1–2. Trasimene . . . Carthagens: Perhaps an allusion to a lost play about the Carthaginian Hannibal, who achieved one of his greatest victories at Lake Trasimene in 217 B.C.　**2. Mars:** Roman god of war.　**mate:** Rival, meet in battle.　**4. state:** Government.

At riper years to Wittenberg he went,
Whereas his kinsmen chiefly brought him up.
So much he profits in divinity,   15
The fruitful plot of scholarism graced,°
That shortly he was graced with doctor's name,
Excelling all whose sweet delight disputes°
In th'heavenly matters of theology,
Till swoll'n with cunning of a self-conceit,   20
His waxen wings did mount above his reach,
And melting,° heavens conspired his overthrow;
For, falling to a devilish exercise
And glutted now with learning's golden gifts,
He surfeits upon cursèd necromancy.   25
Nothing so sweet as magic is to him,
Which he prefers before his chiefest bliss;
And this the man that in his study sits.

ACT I • *Scene* I

(*Faustus in his study.*)

FAUSTUS: Settle thy studies, Faustus, and begin
　　To sound the depth of that thou wilt profess.
　　Having commenced,° be a divine in show;
　　Yet level° at the end of every art,
　　And live and die in Aristotle's works.   5
　　Sweet Analytics, 'tis thou hast ravished me!
　　Bene' disserere est finis logices.°
　　Is to dispute well logic's chiefest end?
　　Affords this art no greater miracle?
　　Then read no more; thou hast attained that end.   10
　　A greater subject fitteth Faustus' wit!
　　Bid *On cay mae on*° farewell, Galen° come.
　　Seeing *ubi desinit philosophus ibi incipit
　　　medicus,*°
　　Be a physician, Faustus; heap up gold,
　　And be eternized for some wondrous cure.   15
　　Summum bonum medicinae sanitas.°

16. fruitful plot . . . graced: Adorned the university. **18. whose sweet delight disputes:** Who takes pleasure in disputing.　**21–22. waxen wings . . . melting:** Metaphor referring to Icarus's attempt to fly with waxen wings, which melted when he ignored his father's warning and flew too near the sun.　**I, I. 3. commenced:** Taken a degree. **4. level:** Aim.　**7. *Bene' disserere est finis logices*:** The end of logic is to dispute well. A tenet of the anti-Aristotelian system introduced at Cambridge when Marlowe was a student there.　**12. *On cay mae on*:** From Aristotle, being or not being.　**Galen:** Greek physician regarded throughout the Middle Ages as a medical authority.　**13. *ubi desinit philosophus ibi incipit medicus*:** Where the philosopher stops, the doctor begins.　**16. *Summum . . . sanitas*:** Health is the highest good of the practice of medicine.

The end of physic is our body's health.
Why, Faustus, hast thou not attained that end?
Is not thy common talk sound aphorisms?
20 Are not thy bills° hung up as monuments,
Whereby whole cities have escaped the plague,
And divers desperate maladies been cured?
Yet art thou still but Faustus and a man.
Couldst thou make men to live eternally,
25 Or, being dead, raise them to life again,
Then this profession were to be esteemed.
Physic, farewell! Where is Justinian?°
Si una eademque res legatus duobus,   [*He reads.*]
Alter rem, alter valorem rei, etc.°
30 A petty case of paltry legacies!
Exhaereditare filium non potest pater nisi° —
[*He reads.*]
Such is the subject of the Institute
And universal body of the law.
This study fits a mercenary drudge
35 Who aims at nothing but external trash,
Too servile and illiberal for me.
When all is done, divinity is best.
Jeromè's Bible,° Faustus, view it well:
Stipendium peccati mors est.° Ha! *Stipendium,*
etc.   [*He reads.*]
40 The reward of sin is death. That's hard.
Si pecasse negamus, fallimur   [*He reads.*]
Et nulla est in nobis veritas.°
If we say that we have no sin,
We deceive ourselves, and there's no truth in us.
45 Why then belike we must sin,
And so consequently die.
Ay, we must die an everlasting death.
What doctrine call you this? *Che serà, serà:*
What will be, shall be! Divinity, adieu!
50 These metaphysics of magicians,
And necromantic books are heavenly.
Lines, circles, signs, letters, and characters —
Ay, these are those that Faustus most desires.
O, what a world of profit and delight,
55 Of power, of honor, of omnipotence
Is promised to the studious artisan!

All things that move between the quiet poles
Shall be at my command. Emperors and kings
Are but obeyed in their several provinces,
Nor can they raise the wind or rend the clouds,   60
But his dominion that exceeds in this
Stretcheth as far as doth the mind of man.
A sound magician is a demi-god.
Here try thy brains to get a deity!
Wagner!

(*Enter Wagner.*)

   Commend me to my dearest friends,   65
The German Valdes and Cornelius;
Request them earnestly to visit me.
WAGNER: I will sir.
                          (*Exit.*)
FAUSTUS: Their conference will be a greater help to
   me
   Than all my labors, plod I ne'er so fast.   70

(*Enter the Good Angel and the Evil Angel.*)

GOOD ANGEL: O, Faustus, lay that damnèd book
   aside,
   And gaze not on it, lest it tempt thy soul
   And heap God's heavy wrath upon thy head.
   Read, read the Scriptures. That is blasphemy.
BAD ANGEL: Go forward, Faustus, in that famous
   art   75
   Wherein all nature's treasury is contained.
   Be thou on earth as Jove is in the sky,
   Lord and commander of these elements.
                     (*Exeunt° Angels.*)
FAUSTUS: How am I glutted with conceit° of this!
   Shall I make spirits fetch me what I please,   80
   Resolve me of° all ambiguities,
   Perform what desperate enterprise I will?
   I'll have them fly to India for gold,
   Ransack the ocean for orient pearl,
   And search all corners of the new-found world   85
   For pleasant fruits and princely delicates.
   I'll have them read me strange philosophy
   And tell the secrets of all foreign kings;
   I'll have them wall all Germany with brass
   And make swift Rhine circle fair Wittenberg.°   90
   I'll have them fill the public schools with silk
   Wherewith the students shall be bravely clad.
   I'll levy soldiers with the coin they bring
   And chase the Prince of Parma from our land

---

20. **bills:** Medical prescriptions.   27. **Justinian:** Roman emperor of Constantinople (527–565), responsible for assembling the Roman law and renowned throughout the Middle Ages as a jurist.   28.–29. **Si . . . rei, etc.:** If the same object is willed to two persons, let one have the thing itself and the other its value, etc. This is an incorrect version of one of Justinian's rules.   31. **Exhaereditare . . . nisi —:** The father cannot disinherit the son except —; another of Justinian's rules roughly paraphrased.   38. **Jeromè's Bible:** St. Jerome's Vulgate [Latin] translation of the Bible.   39. **Stipendium . . . est:** Translated in line 40 (Rom. 6:23).   41–42. **Si . . . veritas:** Translated in lines 43–44 (1 John 1:8).

78. [S.D.] **Exeunt:** Latin for "they go out."   79. **conceit:** The conception of attaining.   81. **Resolve me of:** Explain to me.   90. **Rhine . . . Wittenberg:** Wittenberg is actually on the Elbe River, not the Rhine.

95   And reign sole king of all the provinces.°
       Yea, stranger engines for the brunt of war
       Than was the fiery keel at Antwerp's bridge°
       I'll make my servile spirits to invent.
       Come, German Valdes and Cornelius,
                        [*He calls within.*]
100   And make me blessed with your sage conference!

(*Enter Valdes and Cornelius.*)

       Valdes, sweet Valdes, and Cornelius,
       Know that your words have won me at the last
       To practice magic and concealed arts;
       Yet not your words only, but mine own fantasy
105   That will receive no object, for my head
       But ruminates on necromantic skill.
       Philosophy is odious and obscure;
       Both law and physic are for petty wits;
       Divinity is basest of the three,
110   Unpleasant, harsh, contemptible and vile.
       'Tis, magic, magic, that hath ravished me.
       Then, gentle friends, aid me in this attempt,
       And I, that have with subtle syllogisms
       Gravelled° the pastors of the German church,
115   And made the flowering pride of Wittenberg
       Swarm to my problems° as th'infernal spirits
       On sweet Musaeus° when he came to hell,
       Will be as cunning as Agrippa was,
       Whose shadows° made all Europe honor him.

VALDES: Faustus, these books, thy wit, and our
120   experience
       Shall make all nations to canonize us.
       As Indian Moors° obey their Spanish lords,
       So shall the spirits of every element
       Be always serviceable to us three.
125   Like lions shall they guard us when we please,
       Like Almain rutters° with their horsemen's staves
       Or Lapland giants trotting by our sides,
       Sometimes like women or unwedded maids,
       Shadowing° more beauty in their airy brows
130   Than in the white breasts of the queen of love.
       From Venice shall they drag huge argosies,
       And from America the golden fleece
       That yearly stuffs old Philip's treasury,
       If learnèd Faustus will be resolute.

FAUSTUS: Valdes, as resolute am I in this   135
       As thou to live; therefore object it not.
CORNELIUS: The miracles that magic will perform
       Will make the vow to study nothing else.
       He that is grounded in astrology,
       Enriched with tongues,° well seen in minerals,   140
       Hath all the principles magic doth require.
       Then doubt not, Faustus, but to be renowned
       And more frequented for this mystery
       Than heretofore the Delphian oracle.°
       The spirits tell me they can dry the sea   145
       And fetch the treasure of all foreign wracks,
       Yea, all the wealth that our forefathers hid
       Within the massy entrails of the earth.
       Then tell me, Faustus, what shall we three want?
FAUSTUS: Nothing, Cornelius. O, this cheers my soul!   150
       Come, show me some demonstrations magical,
       That I may conjure in some lusty grove
       And have these joys in full possession.
VALDES: Then haste thee to some solitary grove,
       And bear wise Bacon's and Abanus' works,°   155
       The Hebrew Psalter, and New Testament;
       And whatsoever else is requisite
       We will inform thee ere our conference cease.
CORNELIUS: Valdes, first let him know the words of
      art,
       And then, all other ceremonies learned,   160
       Faustus may try his cunning by himself.
VALDES: First I'll instruct thee in the rudiments,
       And then wilt thou be perfecter than I.
FAUSTUS: Then come and dine with me, and after
      meat
       We'll canvass every quiddity° thereof,   165
       For ere I sleep I'll try what I can do.
       This night I'll conjure, though I die therefore.
                         (*Exeunt.*)

Scene II

(*Enter two Scholars.*)

FIRST SCHOLAR: I wonder what's become of Faustus,
      that was wont to make our schools ring with *sic
      probo.*°

---

95. provinces: The Netherlands.   **97. fiery . . . bridge:** In April 1584 the Dutch used a fireship to destroy a bridge built across a river by the Prince of Parma in an attempt to block-ade Antwerp.   **114. Gravelled:** Puzzled and amazed.   **116. problems:** Public disputations.   **117. Musaeus:** A semi-mythical Greek poet. Following Virgil, Marlowe has him visit hell like the mythical Orpheus.   **118–119. Agrippa . . . shadows:** Cornelius Agrippa (1486?–1535), a German physi-cian and student of the occult, was said to have power to raise spirits (shadows) from the dead.   **122. Indian Moors:** American Indians.   **126. Almain rutters:** German cavalry.   **129. Shadowing:** Harboring, sheltering.

140. Enriched with tongues: Fluent in Latin, the language used for communicating with spirits.   **144. Delphian ora-cle:** The high priest of Apollo at Delphi who had power to foretell the future. [An oracle is the response of a god to a question asked by one who worships the god. The Delphic Oracle was the chief oracle of Greece, presided over by Apollo.]   **155. Bacon's . . . works:** Roger Bacon (1214?–1294) and Pietro D'Abano (1250–1316) were famous in the Middle Ages for their feats of magic.   **165. quiddity:** Es-sential element (a term from scholastic logic).   **I, II. 2. *sic probo:*** Thus I prove (used in scholastic argument).

(*Enter Wagner.*)

SECOND SCHOLAR: That shall we presently know; here
5   comes his boy.

FIRST SCHOLAR: How now sirrah! Where's thy master?

WAGNER: God in heaven knows.

SECOND SCHOLAR: Why, dost not thou know then?

10 WAGNER: Yes, I know, but that follows not.

FIRST SCHOLAR: Go to, sirrah! Leave your jesting and
tell us where he is.

WAGNER: That follows not by force of argument,
which you, being licentiates,° should stand upon;
15   therefore acknowledge your error and be attentive.

SECOND SCHOLAR: Then you will not tell us?

WAGNER: You are deceived, for I will tell you. Yet if
you were not dunces, you would never ask me
such a question. For is he not *corpus naturale*, and
20   is not that *mobile?*° Then wherefore should you
ask such a question? But that I am by nature
phlegmatic, slow to wrath, and prone to lechery —
to love, I would say — it were not for you to come
within forty foot of the place of execution, al-
25   though I do not doubt but to see you both hanged
the next sessions. Thus having triumphed over
you, I will set my countenance like a precisian° and
begin to speak thus: Truly, my dear brethren, my
master is within at dinner with Valdes and Cor-
30   nelius, as this wine, if it could speak, would inform
your worships. And so, the Lord bless you, preserve you, and keep you, my dear brethren.

(*Exit.*)

FIRST SCHOLAR: O Faustus, then I fear that which I
have long suspected.

That thou art fall'n into that damnèd art
For which they two are infamous through the
35   world.

SECOND SCHOLAR: Were he a stranger, not allied to
me,
The danger of his soul would make me mourn.
But come, let us go and inform the rector.°
It may be his grave counsel may reclaim him.

FIRST SCHOLAR: I fear me nothing will reclaim him
40   now.

SECOND SCHOLAR: Yet let us see what we can do.

(*Exeunt.*)

Scene III

(*Thunder. Enter [above] Lucifer and four Devils. Enter Faustus to conjure.*)

FAUSTUS: Now that the gloomy shadow of the night,
Longing to view Orion's drizzling look,
Leaps from th'Antarctic world unto the sky
And dims the welkin° with her pitchy breath,
Faustus begin thine incantations,   5
And try if devils will obey thy hest,
Seeing thou hast prayed and sacrificed to them.
Within this circle is Jehovah's name,
Forward and backward anagrammatized,
Th'abbreviated names of holy saints,   10
Figures of every adjunct to the heavens,
And characters of signs and erring° stars,
By which the spirits are enforced to rise.
Then fear not, Faustus, to be resolute,
And try the utmost magic can perform.   15

(*Thunder.*)

*Sint mihi Dei Acherontis propitii! Valeat numen
triplex Jehovae. Ignei, aerii, aquatani spiritus, sal-
vete! Orientis princeps, Beelzebub, inferni ardentis
monarcha, et Demogorgon, propitiamus vos, ut   20
appareat et surgat Mephistophilis. Quid tu
moraris? Per Jehovam Gehennam, et consecratam
aquam quam nunc spargo, signumque crucis quod
nunc facto, et per vota nostra, ipse nunc surgat nobis dicatus Mephistophilis.*°

(*Enter [Mephistophilis,] a Devil.*)

I charge thee to return and change thy shape;   25
Thou art too ugly to attend on me.
Go, and return an old Franciscan friar;
That holy shape becomes a devil best.

(*Exit Devil.*)

I see there's virtue in my heavenly words.
Who would not be proficient in this art?   30
How pliant is this Mephistophilis,
Full of obedience and humility.
Such is the force of magic and my spells.
Now Faustus, thou art conjurer laureate,
That canst command great Mephistophilis.   35
Quin redis Mephistophilis fratris imagine.°

I, III. **4. welkin:** Sky.   **12. erring:** Wandering.   **16–24.**
Sint . . . Mephistophilis: May the gods of Aceron be propitious to me. Let the triple name of Jehova [the trinity] be
gone. Hail spirits of fire, air, and water. Prince of the East,
Beelzebub, monarch of burning hell, and Demogorgon,
we petition you that Mephistophilis may appear and rise. Why
do you linger? By Jehova, Gehenna and the holy water which
I now sprinkle and the sign of the cross which I now make
and by our vows, let Mephistophilis himself now rise to serve
us.   **36. Quin . . . imagine:** Return, Mephistophilis, in the
shape of a friar.

---

14. licentiates: Holders of university degrees.   **19–20.** *corpus naturale . . . mobile:* The subject matter of physics, in
scholastic terms, was *corpus naturale seu mobile* (natural
body in motion).   **27. precisian:** Puritan.   **38. rector:**
Head of the university.

(*Enter Mephistophilis [dressed like a Franciscan friar].*)

MEPHISTOPHILIS: Now Faustus, what wouldst thou
    have me do?
FAUSTUS: I charge thee wait upon me whilst I live,
    To do whatever Faustus shall command,
40   Be it to make the moon drop from her sphere
    Or the ocean to overwhelm the world.
MEPHISTOPHILIS: I am a servant to great Lucifer
    And may not follow thee without his leave.
    No more than he commands must we perform.
45 FAUSTUS: Did not he charge thee to appear to me?
MEPHISTOPHILIS: No, I came hither of mine own
    accord.
FAUSTUS: Did not my conjuring speeches raise thee?
    Speak.
MEPHISTOPHILIS: That was the cause, but yet *per
    accidens,*°
    For when we hear one rack the name of God,
50   Abjure the Scriptures and his Savior Christ,
    We fly in hope to get his glorious soul;
    Nor will we come unless he use such means
    Whereby he is in danger to be damned.
    Therefore the shortest cut for conjuring
55   Is stoutly to abjure the Trinity
    And pray devoutly to the prince of hell.
FAUSTUS: So Faustus hath
    Already done, and holds this principle:
    There is no chief but only Beelzebub,
60   To whom Faustus doth dedicate himself.
    This word "damnation" terrifies not me,
    For I confound hell in Elysium.
    My ghost° be with the old philosophers!
    But leaving these vain trifles of men's souls,
65   Tell me what is that Lucifer thy lord?
MEPHISTOPHILIS: Arch-regent and commander of all
    spirits.
FAUSTUS: Was not that Lucifer an angel once?
MEPHISTOPHILIS: Yes Faustus, and most dearly loved
    of God.
FAUSTUS: How comes it then that he is prince of
    devils?
70 MEPHISTOPHILIS: O, by aspiring pride and insolence,
    For which God threw him from the face of
    heaven.
FAUSTUS: And what are you that live with Lucifer?
MEPHISTOPHILIS: Unhappy spirits that fell with
    Lucifer,
    Conspired against our God with Lucifer,
75   And are for ever damned with Lucifer.
FAUSTUS: Where are you damned?

MEPHISTOPHILIS: In hell.
FAUSTUS: How comes it then that thou art out of hell?
MEPHISTOPHILIS: Why this is hell, nor am I out of it.
    Think'st thou that I who saw the face of God
    And tasted the eternal joys of heaven   80
    Am not tormented with ten thousand hells
    In being deprived of everlasting bliss?
    O Faustus, leave these frivolous demands
    Which strike a terror to my fainting soul.
FAUSTUS: What, is great Mephistophilis so passionate 85
    For being deprivèd of the joys of heaven?
    Learn thou of Faustus' manly fortitude,
    And scorn those joys thou never shalt possess.
    Go bear these tidings to great Lucifer:
    Seeing Faustus hath incurred eternal death   90
    By desperate thoughts against Jove's deity,
    Say he surrenders up to him his soul,
    So he will spare him four and twenty years,
    Letting him live in all voluptuousness,
    Having thee ever to attend on me,   95
    To give me whatsoever I shall ask,
    To tell me whatsoever I demand,
    To slay mine enemies, and aid my friends,
    And always be obedient to my will.
    Go, and return to mighty Lucifer,   100
    And meet me in my study at midnight,
    And then resolve me of thy master's mind.
MEPHISTOPHILIS: I will, Faustus.

                        (*Exit.*)

FAUSTUS: Had I as many souls as there be stars,
    I'd give them all for Mephistophilis.   105
    By him I'll be great emperor of the world,
    And make a bridge thorough the moving air,
    To pass the ocean with a band of men.
    I'll join the hills that bind° the Afric shore,
    And make that country continent to Spain,   110
    And both contributory to my crown.
    The Emperor shall not live but by my leave,
    Nor any potentate of Germany.
    Now that I have obtained what I desire,
    I'll live in speculation of this art   115
    Till Mephistophilis return again.

                        (*Exit.*)

Scene IV

(*Enter Wagner and [Robin,] the Clown.*)

WAGNER: Come hither, sirrah boy.
ROBIN: Boy! O disgrace to my person. Zounds, boy in
    your face! You have seen many boys with such
    pickedevants,° I am sure.

---

48. cause . . . *per accidens*: The terms are from scholastic logic. **63. ghost:** Spirit.

109. bind: Enclose. **I, IV. 4. pickedevants:** Pointed beards.

5 WAGNER: Sirrah, hast thou no comings in?°
   ROBIN: Yes, and goings out too, you may see, sir.

   WAGNER: Alas, poor slave! See how poverty jests in
   his nakedness. I know the villain's out of service,
   and so hungry that I know he would give his soul
10 to the devil for a shoulder of mutton, though it
   were blood-raw.
   ROBIN: Not so neither. I had need to have it well
   roasted, and good sauce to it, if I pay so dear, I can
   tell you.
15 WAGNER: Sirrah, wilt thou be my man and wait on
   me, and I will make thee go like *Qui mihi discipulus?*°
   ROBIN: What, in verse?
   WAGNER: No slave; in beaten° silk and staves-acre.°
20 ROBIN: Staves-acre? That's good to kill vermin. Then,
   belike, if I serve you I shall be lousy.
   WAGNER: Why, so thou shalt be, whether thou dost it
   or no; for, sirrah, if thou dost not presently bind
   thyself to me for seven years, I'll turn all the lice
25 about thee into familiars° and make them tear thee
   in pieces.
   ROBIN: Nay sir, you may save yourself a labor, for
   they are as familiar with me as if they paid for
   their meat and drink, I can tell you.
30 WAGNER: Well, sirrah, leave your jesting and take
   these guilders.
   ROBIN: Yes, marry sir, and I thank you too.
   WAGNER: So, now thou art to be at an hour's warning, whensoever and wheresoever the devil shall
35 fetch thee.
   ROBIN: Here, take your guilders again. I'll none of
   'em.
   WAGNER: Not I. Thou art pressed.° Prepare thyself,
   for I will presently raise up two devils to carry thee
40 away. Banio! Belcher!
   ROBIN: Belcher? And Belcher come here, I'll belch
   him. I am not afraid of a devil.

   (*Enter two Devils.*)

   WAGNER: How now, sir? Will you serve me now?
   ROBIN: Ay, good Wagner; take away the devil then.
45 WAGNER: Spirits away! Now, sirrah, follow me.
                                        [*Exeunt Devils.*]
   ROBIN: I will sir. But hark you, master, will you teach
   me this conjuring occupation?

   WAGNER: Ay, sirrah. I'll teach thee to turn thyself to a
   dog, or a cat, or a mouse, or a rat, or any thing.
   ROBIN: A dog, or a cat, or a mouse, or a rat! O brave   50
   Wagner!
   WAGNER: Villain, call me Master Wagner, and see that
   you walk attentively, and let your right eye be always diametrally° fixed upon my left heel, that
   thou may'st *quasi vestigial nostras insistere.*°   55
   ROBIN: Well, sir, I warrant you.

                                              (*Exeunt.*)

ACT II • *Scene I*

(*Enter Faustus in his Study.*)

FAUSTUS: Now Faustus must thou needs be damned,
   And canst thou not be saved.
   What boots° it then to think on God or heaven?
   Away with such vain fancies, and despair;
   Despair in God, and trust in Beelzebub.   5
   Now go not backward; Faustus, be resolute.
   Why waver'st thou? O, something soundeth in
      mine ear:
   "Abjure this magic; turn to God again."
   Ay, and Faustus will turn to God again!
   To God? He loves thee not.   10
   The God thou serv'st is thine own appetite,
   Wherein is fixed the love of Beelzebub.
   To him I'll build an altar and a church,
   And offer lukewarm blood of new-born babes.

(*Enter the two Angels.*)

BAD ANGEL: Go forward, Faustus, in that famous
      art.   15
GOOD ANGEL: Sweet Faustus, leave that execrable
      art.
FAUSTUS: Contrition, prayer, repentance — what of
      these?
GOOD ANGEL: O, they are means to bring thee unto
      heaven.
BAD ANGEL: Rather illusions, fruits of lunacy,
      That make men foolish that do use them most.   20
GOOD ANGEL: Sweet Faustus, think of heaven and
      heavenly things.
BAD ANGEL: No Faustus, think of honor and wealth.
                                      (*Exeunt Angels.*)
FAUSTUS: Wealth? Why, the signory of Emden° shall
   be mine.

---

5. **comings in:** Earnings.   16–17. *Qui mihi discipulus*:
Who is my disciple (the opening words of a Latin poem by
William Lyly, well known to Elizabethan schoolboys).
19. **beaten:** Embroidered with metal.   **Staves-acre:** A plant
used for killing vermin.   25. **familiars:** Attendant evil spirits.   38. **pressed:** Enlisted into service in exchange for
money.

54. **diametrally:** In a straight line.   55. *quasi . . . insistere*:
As if to walk in our tracks.   II, I. 3. **boots:** Avails.
23. **Emden:** The chief city of East Friesland near the mouth
of the river Ems, which had considerable trade relations with
Elizabethan England.

When Mephistophilis shall stand by me,
25   What power can hurt me? Faustus thou art safe.
Cast no more doubts. Mephistophilis, come
And bring glad tidings from great Lucifer.
Is't not midnight? Come, Mephistophilis.
Veni,° veni, *Mephistophile.*

(*Enter Mephistophilis.*)

30   Now tell me what saith Lucifer, thy lord?
MEPHISTOPHILIS: That I shall wait on Faustus whilst
    he lives,
So he will buy my service with his soul.
FAUSTUS: Already Faustus hath hazarded that for
    thee.
MEPHISTOPHILIS: But now thou must bequeath it
    solemnly
35   And write a deed of gift with thine own blood,
For that security craves great Lucifer.
If thou deny it, I must back to hell.
FAUSTUS: Stay, Mephistophilis! Tell me what good
Will my soul do thy lord.
MEPHISTOPHILIS: Enlarge his kingdom.
40   FAUSTUS: Is that the reason why he tempts us thus?
MEPHISTOPHILIS: *Solamen miseris socios habuisse
    doloris.°*
FAUSTUS: Why, have you any pain that torture
    others?
MEPHISTOPHILIS: As great as have the human souls
    of men.
But tell me, Faustus, shall I have thy soul?
45   And I will be thy slave and wait on thee
And give thee more than thou hast wit to ask.
FAUSTUS: Ay, Mephistophilis, I'll give it him.
MEPHISTOPHILIS: Then Faustus, stab thy arm
    courageously,
And bind thy soul that at some certain day
50   Great Lucifer may claim it as his own,
And then be thou as great as Lucifer.
FAUSTUS: [*stabbing his arm*] Lo, Mephistophilis, for
    love of thee,
I cut mine arm, and with my proper° blood
Assure my soul to be great Lucifer's,
55   Chief lord and regent of perpetual night.
View here this blood that trickles from mine
    arm,
And let it be propitious for my wish.
MEPHISTOPHILIS: But Faustus,
Write it in manner of a deed of gift.
FAUSTUS: Ay, so I do. [*He writes.*] But
60   Mephistophilis,
My blood congeals, and I can write no more.

MEPHISTOPHILIS: I'll fetch thee fire to dissolve it
    straight.
                                    (*Exit.*)
FAUSTUS: What might the staying of my blood
    portend?
Is it unwilling I should write this bill?
Why streams it not that I may write afresh?   65
"Faustus gives to thee his soul." Ah, there it
    stayed.
Why shouldst thou not? Is not thy soul thine
    own?
Then write again: "Faustus gives to thee his
    soul."

(*Enter Mephistophilis with the chafer of fire.*)

MEPHISTOPHILIS: See Faustus, here is fire. Set it on.°
FAUSTUS: So. Now the blood begins to clear again.   70
Now will I make an end immediately.
                                [*He writes.*]
MEPHISTOPHILIS: [*Aside.*] What will not I do to
    obtain his soul?
FAUSTUS: *Consummatum est;°* this bill is ended,
And Faustus hath bequeathed his soul to Lucifer.
But what is this inscription on mine arm?   75
Homo fuge!° Whither should I fly?
If unto God, he'll throw me down to hell.
My senses are deceived; here's nothing writ.
O yes, I see it plain. Even here is writ
Homo fuge! Yet shall not Faustus fly.   80
MEPHISTOPHILIS: [*Aside.*] I'll fetch him somewhat to
    delight his mind.
                                    (*Exit.*)

(*Enter Devils, giving crowns and rich apparel to
Faustus. They dance and then depart. Enter
Mephistophilis.*)

FAUSTUS: What means this show? Speak
    Mephistophilis.
MEPHISTOPHILIS: Nothing, Faustus, but to delight
    thy mind
And let thee see what magic can perform.
FAUSTUS: But may I raise such spirits when I please?   85
MEPHISTOPHILIS: Ay Faustus, and do greater things
    than these.
FAUSTUS: Then, Mephistophilis, receive this scroll,
A deed of gift of body and of soul,
But yet conditionally that thou perform
All covenants and articles between us both.   90
MEPHISTOPHILIS: Faustus, I swear by hell and Lucifer
To effect all promises between us made.

---

29. *Veni:* Come.   41. *Solamen . . . doloris:* It is a consolation in misery to have a fellow sufferer.   53. **proper:** Own.

69. Set it on: Set the dish of blood on the fire.   73. *Consummatum est:* It is completed (the words of Jesus at his
Crucifixion; John 19:30).   **76. *Homo fuge:*** Fly, man.

FAUSTUS: Then hear me read it Mephistophilis.
　On these conditions following:
95　*First, that Faustus may be a spirit in form and substance;*
　Secondly, that Mephistophilis shall be his servant and be at his command;
　Thirdly, that Mephistophilis shall do for him and
100　*bring him whatsoever;*
　Fourthly, that he shall be in his chamber or house invisible;
　Lastly, that he shall appear to the said John Faustus at all times, in what form or shape soever he please:
105　*I, John Faustus, of Wittenberg, doctor, by these presents, do give both body and soul to Lucifer, Prince of the East, and his minister, Mephistophilis; and furthermore grant unto them that four and twenty years being expired, the articles above writ-*
110　*ten inviolate, full power to fetch or carry the said John Faustus, body and soul, flesh, blood, or goods, into their habitation wheresoever.*
　　　　　　　　　　By me, John Faustus.
MEPHISTOPHILIS: Speak Faustus. Do you deliver this as your deed?
FAUSTUS: Ay, take it, and the devil give thee good
115　of it.
MEPHISTOPHILIS: So now, Faustus, ask me what thou wilt.
FAUSTUS: First will I question with thee about hell.
　Tell me, where is the place that men call hell?
MEPHISTOPHILIS: Under the heavens.
120 FAUSTUS: Ay, so are all things else. But whereabouts?
MEPHISTOPHILIS: Within the bowels of these elements,
　Where we are tortured and remain for ever.
　Hell hath no limits, nor is circumscribed
　In one self place, but where we are is hell,
125　And where hell is, there must we ever be.
　And, to be short, when all the world dissolves
　And every creature shall be purified,
　All places shall be hell that is not heaven.
FAUSTUS: I think hell's a fable.
MEPHISTOPHILIS: Ay, think so still, till experience
130　change thy mind.
FAUSTUS: Why, dost thou think that Faustus shall be damned?
MEPHISTOPHILIS: Ay, of necessity, for here's the scroll
　In which thou hast given thy soul to Lucifer.
FAUSTUS: Ay, and body too. But what of that?
135　Think'st thou that Faustus is so fond° to imagine
　That after this life there is any pain?
　No, these are trifles and mere old wives' tales.
MEPHISTOPHILIS: But I am an instance to prove the contrary,

135. fond: Foolish.

　For I tell thee I am damned and now in hell.
FAUSTUS: Nay, and this be hell, I'll willingly be
　　damned.　　　　　　　　　　　　　　　140
　What? Sleeping, eating, walking and disputing?
　But, leaving off this, let me have a wife,
　The fairest maid in Germany,
　For I am wanton and lascivious,
　And cannot live without a wife.　　　　　145
MEPHISTOPHILIS: I prithee, Faustus, talk not of a wife.
FAUSTUS: Nay, sweet Mephistophilis, fetch me one, for I will have one.
MEPHISTOPHILIS: Well, Faustus, thou shalt have a wife.
　Sit there till I come.　　　　　　　*[Exit.]*

(*Enter [Mephistophilis] with a Devil dressed like a woman, with fireworks.*)

FAUSTUS: What sight is this?　　　　　　150
MEPHISTOPHILIS: Now Faustus, how dost thou like thy wife?
FAUSTUS: Here's a hot whore indeed! No, I'll no wife.
MEPHISTOPHILIS: Marriage is but a ceremonial toy,
　And if thou lovest me, think no more of it.
　I'll cull thee out the fairest courtesans　　155
　And bring them every morning to thy bed.
　She whom thine eye shall like, thy heart shall have,
　Were she as chaste as was Penelope,°
　As wise as Saba,° or as beautiful
　As was bright Lucifer before his fall.　　160
　Hold; take this book; peruse it thoroughly.
　The iterating of these lines brings gold;
　The framing of this circle on the ground
　Brings thunder, whirlwinds, storm and lightning.
　Pronounce this thrice devoutly to thyself,　165
　And men in harness° shall appear to thee,
　Ready to execute what thou command'st.
FAUSTUS: Thanks, Mephistophilis, for this sweet book.
　This will I keep as chary as my life.

　　　　　　　　　　　　(*Exeunt.*)

Scene II

(*Enter Faustus in his study and Mephistophilis.*)

FAUSTUS: When I behold the heavens, then I repent
　And curse thee, wicked Mephistophilis,
　Because thou hast deprived me of those joys.

158. Penelope: The faithful wife of Ulysses in Homer's *Odyssey.*　**159. Saba:** The Queen of Sheba.　**166. harness:** Armor.

MEPHISTOPHILIS: 'Twas thine own seeking, Faustus;
   thank thyself.
5   But think'st thou heaven is such a glorious thing?
   I tell thee, Faustus, 'tis not half so fair
   As thou, or any man that breathes on earth.
FAUSTUS: How prov'st thou that?
MEPHISTOPHILIS: 'Twas made for man; then he's
   more excellent.
FAUSTUS: If heaven was made for man, 'twas made
10   for me.
   I will renounce this magic and repent.

(*Enter the two Angels.*)

GOOD ANGEL: Faustus repent; yet God will pity
   thee.
BAD ANGEL: Thou art a spirit;° God cannot pity
   thee.
FAUSTUS: Who buzzeth in mine ears I am a spirit?
15   Be I a devil, yet God may pity me;
   Yea, God will pity me if I repent.
BAD ANGEL: Ay, but Faustus never shall repent.
                              (*Exeunt angels.*)
FAUSTUS: My heart is hardened; I cannot repent.
   Scarce can I name salvation, faith, or heaven,
20   But fearful echoes thunder in mine ears:
   "Faustus, thou art damned!" Then swords and
      knives,
   Poison, guns, halters, and envenomed steel
   Are laid before me to dispatch myself;
   And long ere this I should have done the deed,
25   Had not sweet pleasure conquered deep despair.
   Have not I made blind Homer sing to me
   Of Alexander's love and Oenone's death?°
   And hath not he, that built the walls of Thebes
   With ravishing sound of his melodious harp,°
30   Made music with my Mephistophilis?
   Why should I die then, or basely despair?
   I am resolved; Faustus shall not repent.
   Come, Mephistophilis, let us dispute again
   And reason of divine astrology.
35   Speak; are there many spheres above the moon?
   Are all celestial bodies but one globe,
   As is the substance of this centric earth?
MEPHISTOPHILIS: As are the elements, such are the
      heavens,
   Even from the moon unto the empyreal orb,
40   Mutually folded in each others' spheres,

And jointly move upon one axle-tree.
   Whose terminè° is termed the world's wide pole;
   Nor are the names of Saturn, Mars, or Jupiter
   Feigned, but are erring stars.
FAUSTUS: But have they all
   One motion, both *situ et tempore?*°   45
MEPHISTOPHILIS: All move from east to west in four
   and twenty hours upon the poles of the world, but
   differ in their motions upon the poles of the zodiac.
FAUSTUS: These slender questions Wagner can
   decide.
   Hath Mephistophilis no greater skill?   50
   Who knows not the double motion of the
      planets?
   That the first is finished in a natural day?
   The second thus? Saturn in thirty years?
   Jupiter in twelve; Mars in four; the sun, Venus and
   Mercury in a year, the moon in twenty eight days.   55
   These are freshmen's suppositions. But tell me hath
   every sphere a dominion or *intelligentia?*°
MEPHISTOPHILIS: Ay.
FAUSTUS: How many heavens or spheres are there?
MEPHISTOPHILIS: Nine — the seven planets, the firma-   60
   ment, and the empyreal heaven.
FAUSTUS: But is there not *coelum igneum, et
   crystallinum?*°
MEPHISTOPHILIS: No, Faustus, they be but fables.
FAUSTUS: Resolve me then in this one question: why   65
   are not conjunctions, oppositions, aspects, eclipses°
   all at one time, but in some years we have more, in
   some less?
MEPHISTOPHILIS: *Per inaequalem motum respectu
   totius.*°   70
FAUSTUS: Well, I am answered. Now tell me who
   made the world.
MEPHISTOPHILIS: I will not.
FAUSTUS: Sweet Mephistophilis, tell me.
MEPHISTOPHILIS: Move me not, Faustus.   75
FAUSTUS: Villain, have not I bound thee to tell me any
   thing?

II, II. **13. spirit:** Devil.   **27. Alexander's . . . death:** Paris
(also called Alexander) loved the nymph Oenone when he
lived as a shepherd on Mt. Ida. Oenone died of a broken
heart when he left her.   **28–29. he . . . harp:** Amphion, son
of Zeus and Antiope, caused stones to move and the walls of
Thebes to be built simply by playing on the lyre given to him
by Hermes.

42. terminè: Limit.   **44. erring stars:** Planets.   **45. *situ et
tempore:*** In position (direction of movement) and in the time
they take to revolve about the earth.   **57. dominion or *intelligentia:*** Governing angel.   **62–63. *coelum . . . crystallinum:*** The fiery heaven and crystalline sphere of
Ptolemaic astronomy.   **66. conjunctions:** Seeming proximi-
ties of heavenly bodies.   **oppositions:** Divergences of heavenly bodies.   **aspects:** Any other relations of such bodies to
one another.   **eclipses:** The blottings out of one heavenly
body by another.   **69–70. *Per . . . totius:*** By their unequal
movements in respect to the whole (i.e., the different speeds
of the various planets within the total cosmos).

MEPHISTOPHILIS: Ay, that is not against our
   kingdom.
   This is. Thou art damned. Think thou of hell.
FAUSTUS: Think, Faustus, upon God that made the
80   world.
MEPHISTOPHILIS: Remember this.
                                                (*Exit.*)
FAUSTUS: Ay, go accursèd spirit to ugly hell.
   'Tis thou hast damned distressèd Faustus' soul.
   Is't not too late?

(*Enter the two Angels.*)

85 BAD ANGEL: Too late.
GOOD ANGEL: Never too late, if Faustus will repent.
BAD ANGEL: If thou repent, devils will tear thee in
   pieces.
GOOD ANGEL: Repent, and they shall never raze thy
   skin.
                                       (*Exeunt Angels.*)
FAUSTUS: O Christ, my Savior, my Savior,
90   Help to save distressèd Faustus' soul.

(*Enter Lucifer, Beelzebub, and Mephistophilis.*)

LUCIFER: Christ cannot save thy soul, for he is
   just.
   There's none but I have interest in the same.
FAUSTUS: O, what art thou that look'st so terribly?
LUCIFER: I am Lucifer,
95   And this is my companion prince in hell.
FAUSTUS: O, Faustus, they are come to fetch thy
   soul.
BEELZEBUB: We are come to tell thee thou dost
   injure us.
LUCIFER: Thou call'st on Christ, contrary to thy
   promise.
BEELZEBUB: Thou shouldst not think on God.
100 LUCIFER: Think on the devil.
BEELZEBUB: And his dam too.
FAUSTUS: Nor will I henceforth. Pardon me in this,
   And Faustus vows never to look to heaven,
   Never to name God, or to pray to him,
105   To burn his Scriptures, slay his ministers,
   And make my spirits pull his churches down.
LUCIFER: So shalt thou show thyself an obedient
   servant,
   And we will highly gratify thee for it.
BEELZEBUB: Faustus, we are come from hell in person
110   to show thee some pastime. Sit down, and thou
   shalt behold the Seven Deadly Sins appear to thee
   in their own proper shapes and likeness.
FAUSTUS: That sight will be as pleasant to me as Paradise was to Adam the first day of his creation.
115 LUCIFER: Talk not of Paradise or creation, but mark
   the show. Go, Mephistophilis, fetch them in.
                                       [*Exit Mephistophilis.*]

(*Enter the Seven Deadly Sins, [with Mephistophilis,
led by a Piper].*)

BEELZEBUB: Now Faustus, question them of their
   names and dispositions.
FAUSTUS: That shall I soon. What art thou, the first?
PRIDE: I am Pride. I disdain to have any parents. I am   120
   like to Ovid's flea:° I can creep into every corner of
   a wench. Sometimes, like a periwig, I sit upon her
   brow. Next, like a necklace, I hang about her neck.
   Then, like a fan of feathers, I kiss her lips, and
   then, turning myself to a wrought smock, do what   125
   I list. But fie, what a smell is here! I'll not speak another word unless the ground be perfumed and
   covered with cloth of Arras.°
FAUSTUS: Thou art a proud knave indeed. What art
   thou, the second?   130
COVETOUSNESS: I am Covetousness, begotten of an
   old churl in a leather bag, and might I now obtain
   my wish, this house, you and all, should turn to
   gold, that I might lock you safe into my chest. O
   my sweet gold!   135
FAUSTUS: And what art thou, the third?
ENVY: I am Envy, begotten of a chimney-sweeper and
   an oyster-wife. I cannot read and therefore wish all
   books burned. I am lean with seeing others eat. O,
   that there would come a famine over all the world,   140
   that all might die, and I live alone; then thou
   shouldst see how fat I'd be. But must thou sit and
   I stand? Come down, with a vengeance.
FAUSTUS: Out envious wretch! But what are thou, the
   fourth?   145
WRATH: I am Wrath. I had neither father nor mother.
   I leaped out of a lion's mouth when I was scarce an
   hour old, and ever since have run up and down the
   world with this case of rapiers, wounding myself
   when I could get none to fight withal. I was born   150
   in hell, and look to it, for some of you shall be my
   father.
FAUSTUS: And what are you, the fifth?
GLUTTONY: I am Gluttony. My parents are all dead,
   and the devil a penny they have left me but a small   155
   pension, and that buys me thirty meals a day and
   ten bevers°—a small trifle to suffice nature. I
   come of a royal pedigree. My father was a gammon of bacon, and my mother was a hogshead of
   claret wine. My godfathers were these: Peter Pick-   160
   led-herring and Martin Martlemas-beef.° But my

---

121. Ovid's flea: The medieval poem *Carmine de Pulice*
(Poem of the Flea) was generally attributed to Ovid.
128. cloth of Arras: Flemish cloth used generally for tapestries.   **157. bevers:** Light snacks taken between regular
meals.   **161. Martlemas-beef:** Salted meat hung for the
winter on Martinmas, November 11.

Emry James (l.) as
Mephostophilis and Ian
Mckellen as Doctor Faustus
in the 1974 Royal
Shakespeare Company's
production of Marlowe's play

godmother, O, she was a jolly gentlewoman, and
well beloved in every good town and city; her
name was Mistress Margery March-beer.° Now
165   Faustus, thou hast heard all my progeny; wilt thou
bid me to a supper.

FAUSTUS: Not I. Thou wilt eat up all my victuals.

GLUTTONY: Then the devil choke thee.

FAUSTUS: Choke thyself, glutton. What art thou, the
170   sixth?

SLOTH: Heigh ho! I am Sloth. I was begotten on a
sunny bank, where I have lain ever since, and you
have done me great injury to bring me from
thence. Let me be carried thither again by Gluttony
175   and Lechery. Heigh ho! I'll not speak a word more
for a king's ransom.

FAUSTUS: And what are you Mistress Minx, the seventh and last?

LECHERY: Who, I, sir? I am one that loves an inch of
180   raw mutton° better than an ell of fried stockfish,°
and the first letter of my name begins with lechery.

LUCIFER: Away to hell! Away! On piper!

(*Exeunt the seven Sins [and the Piper].*)

---

164. March-beer: A fine ale made in the springtime and aged
for two years before being drunk.   **180. raw mutton:** Common slang for "whore";   **stockfish:** Dried codfish.

FAUSTUS: O, how this sight doth delight my soul!

LUCIFER: But Faustus, in hell is all manner of delight.   185

FAUSTUS: O, might I see hell and return again safe,
how happy were I then!

LUCIFER: Faustus, thou shalt. At midnight I will send
for thee. Meanwhile peruse this book and view it
thoroughly, and thou shalt turn thyself into what
shape thou wilt.   190

FAUSTUS: Thanks, mighty Lucifer.
This will I keep as chary as my life.

LUCIFER: Now Faustus, farewell.

FAUSTUS: Farewell, great Lucifer. Come, Mephostophilis.
(*Exeunt, several ways.*)

Scene III

(*Enter the Clown, [Robin, holding a book].*)

ROBIN: What, Dick, look to the horses there till I
come again. I have gotten one of Doctor Faustus'
conjuring books, and now we'll have such knavery
as't passes.

(*Enter Dick.*)

DICK: What, Robin, you must come away and walk   5
the horses.

ROBIN: I walk the horses? I scorn't, 'faith. I have other
matters in hand. Let the horses walk themselves

and they will. [*He reads.*] *A per se a; t, h, e, the; o*
10   *per se o; deny orgon, gorgon.* Keep further from
me, O thou illiterate and unlearned hostler.

DICK: 'Snails,° what hast thou got there? A book?
Why, thou canst not tell ne'er a word on't.

ROBIN: That thou shalt see presently. Keep out of the
15   circle, I say, lest I send you into the hostry with a
vengeance.

DICK: That's like, 'faith. You had best leave your foolery, for an my master come, he'll conjure you,
'faith.

20   ROBIN: My master conjure me? I'll tell thee what: an
my master come here, I'll clap as fair a pair of
horns° on's head as e'er thou sawest in thy life.

DICK: Thou needst not do that, for my mistress hath
done it.

25   ROBIN: Ay, there be of us here that have waded as
deep into matters as other men, if they were disposed to talk.

DICK: A plague take you! I thought you did not sneak
up and down after her for nothing. But I prithee,
30   tell me in good sadness,° Robin, is that a conjuring
book?

ROBIN: Do but speak what thou'lt have me to do, and
I'll do't. If thou'lt dance naked, put off thy clothes
and I'll conjure thee about presently. Or if thou'lt
35   go but to the tavern with me, I'll give thee white
wine, red wine, claret wine, sack, muscadine,
malmesey and whippincrust.° Hold belly, hold,
and we'll not pay one penny for it.

DICK: O brave! Prithee let's to it presently, for I am as
dry as a dog.

ROBIN: Come then, let's away.

(Exeunt.)

ACT III • *Prologue*

(Enter the Chorus.)

CHORUS: Learnèd Faustus,
   To find the secrets of astronomy
   Graven in the book of Jove's high firmament,
   Did mount him up to scale Olympus' top,
5   Where, sitting in a chariot burning bright
   Drawn by the strength of yokèd dragons' necks,
   He views the clouds, the planets, and the stars,
   The tropics, zones, and quarters of the sky,

From the bright circle of the hornèd moon
Even to the height of *Primum Mobile*.°   10
And whirling round with this circumference,
Within the concave compass of the pole,
From east to west his dragons swiftly glide
And in eight days did bring him again.
Not long he stayed within his quiet house   15
To rest his bones after his weary toil,
But new exploits do hale him out again,
And mounted then upon a dragon's back,
That with his wings did part the subtle air,
He now is gone to prove cosmography,°   20
That measures coasts and kingdoms of the earth,
And, as I guess, will first arrive at Rome
To see the Pope and manner of his court
And take some part of holy Peter's feast,
The which this day is highly solemnized.   25

(Exit.)

Scene I

(Enter Faustus and Mephistophilis.)

FAUSTUS: Having now, my good Mephistophilis,
   Passed with delight the stately town of Trier,
   Environed round with airy mountain tops,
   With walls of flint, and deep entrenchèd lakes,°
   Not to be won by any conquering prince;   5
   From Paris next, coasting the realm of France,
   We saw the river Main fall into Rhine,
   Whose banks are set with groves of fruitful vines;
   Then up to Naples, rich Campania,
   Whose buildings fair and gorgeous to the eye,   10
   The streets straight forth and paved with finest
      brick,
   Quarters the town in four equivalents.
   There saw we learnèd Maro's° golden tomb,
   The way he cut, an English mile in length,
   Through a rock of stone in one night's space.°   15
   From thence to Venice, Padua, and the rest,
   In midst of which a sumptuous temple stands,
   That threats the stars with her aspiring top,
   Whose frame is paved with sundry colored
      stones,
   And roofed aloft with curious work in gold.°   20
   Thus hitherto hath Faustus spent his time.

II, III. 12. **'Snails**: By God's nails.   22. **horns**: The common
sign of a cuckold.   30. **sadness**: Seriousness.   37. **whippincrust**: Possibly a corruption of "hippocras," a highly
spiced and sugared wine.

III, Prologue. 10. ***Primum Mobile***: In Ptolemaic astronomy
the outermost sphere of creation, which moves the other
nine spheres.   20. **prove cosmography**: Explore the universe.   III, I. 4. **entrenchèd lakes**: Castle moats.
13. **Maro**: Virgil.   14–15. **way . . . space**: A tunnel between
the bays of Naples and Baiae, through Mt. Posilipo, was said
to have been cut by Virgil (regarded as a magician in the
Middle Ages) by supernatural art.   17–20. **In midst . . .
gold**: St. Mark's cathedral in Venice.

But tell me now, what resting-place is this?
Hast thou, as erst I did command,
Conducted me within the walls of Rome?
MEPHISTOPHILIS: I have, my Faustus, and for proof
25   thereof
This is the goodly palace of the Pope;
And 'cause we are no common guests,
I choose his privy chamber for our use.
FAUSTUS: I hope his holiness will bid us welcome.
MEPHISTOPHILIS: All's one, for we'll be bold with his
30   venison.
But now, my Faustus, that thou may'st perceive
What Rome contains for to delight thine eyes,
Know that this city stands upon seven hills
That underprop the groundwork of the same.
Just through the midst runs flowing Tiber's
35   stream,
With winding banks that cut it in two parts,
Over the which four stately bridges lean,
That make safe passage to each part of Rome.
Upon the bridge called Ponte Angelo
40   Erected is a castle passing strong,
Where thou shalt see such store of ordinance
As that the double cannons, forged of brass,
Do match the number of the days contained
Within the compass of one complete year;
45   Beside the gates and high pyramidès
That Julius Caesar brought from Africa.°
FAUSTUS: Now, by the kingdoms of infernal rule,
Of Styx, of Acheron, and the fiery lake
Of ever-burning Phlegethon, I swear
50   That I do long to see the monuments
And situation of bright-splendent Rome.
Come, therefore, let's away.
MEPHISTOPHILIS: Nay, stay my Faustus. I know
        you'd see the Pope
And take some part of holy Peter's feast,
55   The which, in state and high solemnity,
This day is held through Rome and Italy
In honor of the Pope's triumphant victory.
FAUSTUS: Sweet Mephistophilis, thou pleasest me.
Whilst I am here on earth, let me be cloyed
60   With all things that delight the heart of man.
My four and twenty years of liberty
I'll spend in pleasure and in dalliance,
That Faustus' name, whilst this bright frame
        doth stand,
May be admirèd through the furthest land.
MEPHISTOPHILIS: 'Tis well said, Faustus. Come then,
65   stand by me
And thou shalt see them come immediately.

FAUSTUS: Nay, stay, my gentle Mephistophilis,
And grant me my request, and then I go.
Thou know'st within the compass of eight days
We viewed the face of heaven, of earth, and hell.   70
So high our dragons soared into the air,
That looking down, the earth appeared to me
No bigger than my hand in quantity.
There did we view the kingdoms of the world,
And what might please mine eye I there beheld.   75
Then in this show let me an actor be,
That this proud Pope may Faustus' cunning see.
MEPHISTOPHILIS: Let it be so, my Faustus. But, first
        stay
And view their triumphs° as they pass this way,
And then devise what best contents thy mind   80
By cunning in thine art to cross the Pope
Or dash the pride of this solemnity,
To make his monks and abbots stand like apes
And point like antics at his triple crown,
To beat the beads about the friars' pates   85
Or clap huge horns upon the cardinals' heads,
Or any villainy thou canst devise,
And I'll perform it, Faustus. Hark, they come.
This day shall make thee be admired in Rome.

(*Enter the Cardinals and Bishops, some bearing
crosiers, some the pillars; Monks and Friars singing
their procession. Then the Pope, and Raymond, King
of Hungary, with Bruno, led in chains.*)

POPE: Cast down our footstool.
RAYMOND: Saxon Bruno, stoop,   90
Whilst on thy back his holiness ascends
Saint Peter's chair and state pontifical.
BRUNO: Proud Lucifer, that state belongs to me,
But thus I fall to Peter, not to thee.
POPE: To me and Peter shalt thou groveling lie   95
And crouch before the papal dignity.
Sound trumpets then, for thus Saint Peter's heir
From Bruno's back ascends Saint Peter's chair.

(*A flourish while he ascends.*)

Thus, as the gods creep on with feet of wool
Long ere with iron hands they punish men,   100
So shall our sleeping vengeance now arise
And smite with death thy hated enterprise.
Lord Cardinals of France and Padua,
Go forthwith to our holy consistory,
And read amongst the Statutes Decretal°   105
What, by the holy council held at Trent,°
The sacred synod hath decreed for him

45–46. gates . . . Africa: Before the gates of St. Peter's there still stands the obelisk that was brought to Rome from Heliopolis by the Emperor Caligula in the first century A.D.

79. triumphs: Spectacular displays.   105. Statutes Decretal: Papal decrees concerning religious doctrine or ecclesiastical law.   106. council . . . Trent: The Council of Trent, held by the Church from 1545 to 1563.

That doth assume the papal government
Without election and a true consent.

110 Away, and bring us word with speed.
FIRST CARDINAL: We go my Lord.
                            (*Exeunt Cardinals.*)
POPE: Lord Raymond.   [*They talk apart.*]
FAUSTUS: Go, haste thee, gentle Mephistophilis,
Follow the cardinals to the consistory,

115 And as they turn their superstitious books,
Strike them with sloth and drowsy idleness,
And make them sleep so sound that in their
    shapes
Thyself and I may parley with this Pope,
This proud confronter of the Emperor,

120 And in despite of all his holiness
Restore this Bruno to his liberty
And bear him to the states of Germany.
MEPHISTOPHILIS: Faustus, I go.
FAUSTUS: Dispatch it soon.

125 The Pope shall curse that Faustus came to Rome.
                    (*Exeunt Faustus and Mephistophilis.*)
BRUNO: Pope Adrian,° let me have some right of
    law.
I was elected by the Emperor.
POPE: We will depose the Emperor for that deed
And curse the people that submit to him.

130 Both he and thou shalt stand excommunicate
And interdict from church's privilege
And all society of holy men.
He grows too proud in his authority,
Lifting his lofty head above the clouds,

135 And like a steeple overpeers the church.
But we'll pull down his haughty insolence,
And as Pope Alexander, our progenitor,
Trod on the neck of German Frederick,°
Adding this golden sentence to our praise,

140 "That Peter's heirs should tread on emperors
And walk upon the dreadful adder's back,
Treading the lion and the dragon down
And fearless spurn the killing basilisk,"°
So will we quell that haughty schismatic,

145 And by authority apostolical
Depose him from his regal government.

BRUNO: Pope Julius swore to princely Sigismond,°
For him and the succeeding popes of Rome,
To hold the emperors their lawful lords.
POPE: Pope Julius did abuse the church's rites,   150
And therefore none of his decrees can stand.
Is not all power on earth bestowed on us?
And therefore, though we would, we cannot err.
Behold this silver belt, whereto is fixed
Seven golden keys fast sealed with seven seals   155
In token of our sevenfold power from heaven,
To bind or loose, lock fast, condemn or judge,
Resign, or seal, or whatso pleaseth us.
Then he and thou and all the world shall stoop,
Or be assurèd of our dreadful curse   160
To light as heavy as the pains of hell.

(*Enter Faustus and Mephistophilis, like the Cardinals.*)

MEPHISTOPHILIS: Now tell me, Faustus, are we not
    fitted well?
FAUSTUS: Yes, Mephistophilis, and two such
    cardinals
Ne'er served a holy pope as we shall do.
But whilst they sleep within the consistory,   165
Let us salute his reverend fatherhood.
RAYMOND: Behold, my lord, the cardinals are
    returned.
POPE: Welcome, grave fathers. Answer presently:
What have our holy council there decreed
Concerning Bruno and the Emperor,   170
In quittance of their late conspiracy
Against our state and papal dignity?
FAUSTUS: Most sacred patron of the church of Rome,
By full consent of all the synod
Of priests and prelates it is thus decreed: 175
That Bruno and the German Emperor
Be held as Lollards° and bold schismatics
And proud disturbers of the church's peace.
And if that Bruno by his own assent,
Without enforcement of the German peers,   180
Did seek to wear the triple diadem
And by your death to climb Saint Peter's chair,
The Statutes Decretal have thus decreed:
He shall be straight condemned of heresy
And on a pile of fagots burned to death.   185

---

126. Pope Adrian: Marlowe perhaps means Pope Hadrian IV (1154–1159), who tried to assert his authority over Frederick Barbarossa, the Holy Roman Emperor. What historicity there may be in these scenes at the papal court is badly confused.   **137–138. Pope Alexander . . . Frederick:** Pope Alexander III (1159–1181), successor to Hadrian IV, continued the struggle against Barbarossa, forcing him to acknowledge the papal supremacy at Canossa.   **143. basilisk:** A mythical monster with power to kill by its looks.

147. Pope Julius . . . Sigismond: None of the three popes named Julius was contemporary with the Emperor Sigismund (1368–1437). Sigismund did, however, in 1414 summon the Council of Constance, which sought to end the Great Schism (1378–1417), during which the papacy in Rome was challenged by a line of popes in Avignon.   **177. Lollards:** Followers of John Wyclif (1320?–1384), the English reformer.

POPE: It is enough. Here, take him to your charge,
      And bear him straight to Ponte Angelo,
      And in the strongest tower enclose him fast.
      Tomorrow, sitting in our consistory
190   With all our college of grave cardinals,
      We will determine of his life or death.
      Here, take his triple crown along with you,
      And leave it in the church's treasury.
      Make haste again, my good lord cardinals,
195   And take our blessing apostolical.
MEPHISTOPHILIS: So, so. Was never devil thus blessed
      before.
FAUSTUS: Away, sweet Mephistophilis, be gone.
      The cardinals will be plagued for this anon.
                  (*Exeunt Faustus and Mephistophilis*
                              [with Bruno].)
POPE: Go presently and bring a banquet forth,
200   That we may solemnize Saint Peter's feast,
      And with Lord Raymond, King of Hungary,
      Drink to our late and happy victory.   (*Exeunt.*)

Scene II

(*A sennet [is sounded] while the banquet is brought
in; and then enter Faustus and Mephistophilis in their
own shapes.*)

MEPHISTOPHILIS: Now, Faustus, come, prepare
      thyself for mirth.
      The sleepy cardinals are hard at hand
      To censure Bruno, that is posted hence,
      And on a proud-paced steed, as swift as thought,
5   Flies o'er the Alps to fruitful Germany,
      There to salute the woeful Emperor.
FAUSTUS: The Pope will curse them for their sloth
      today,
      That slept both Bruno and his crown away.
      But now, that Faustus may delight his mind
10   And by their folly make some merriment,
      Sweet Mephistophilis, so charm me here
      That I may walk invisible to all
      And do whate'er I please unseen of any.
MEPHISTOPHILIS: Faustus, thou shalt. Then kneel
      down presently:
15   *Whilst on thy head I lay my hand*
      And charm thee with this magic wand.
      First wear this girdle; then appear
      Invisible to all are here.
      The planets seven, the gloomy air,
20   *Hell and the Furies'° forkèd hair,*
      Pluto's blue fire, and Hecate's tree,°

III, II. **20. *Furies:*** Spirits called upon to avenge crimes, especially crimes against kin.   **21. *Hecate's tree:*** Hecate is the
goddess of witchcraft.

With magic spells so compass thee
That no eye may thy body see.
      So Faustus. Now, for all their holiness,
      Do what thou wilt, thou shalt not be discerned.   25
FAUSTUS: Thanks, Mephistophilis. Now friars take
      heed
      Lest Faustus make your shaven crowns to bleed.
MEPHISTOPHILIS: Faustus, no more. See where the
      cardinals come.

(*Enter Pope and all the Lords. Enter the Cardinals
with a book.*)

POPE: Welcome, lord cardinals. Come, sit down.
      Lord Raymond, take your seat. Friars attend,   30
      And see that all things be in readiness,
      As best beseems this solemn festival.
FIRST CARDINAL: First, may it please your sacred
      holiness
      To view the sentence of the reverend synod
      Concerning Bruno and the Emperor?   35
POPE: What needs this question? Did I not tell you
      Tomorrow we would sit i' th' consistory
      And there determine of his punishment?
      You brought us word even now; it was decreed
      That Bruno and the cursèd Emperor   40
      Were by the holy council both condemned
      For loathèd Lollards and base schismatics.
      Then wherefore would you have me view that
      book?
FIRST CARDINAL: Your grace mistakes. You gave us
      no such charge.
RAYMOND: Deny it not. We all are witnesses   45
      That Bruno here was late delivered you,
      With his rich triple crown to be reserved
      And put into the church's treasury.
BOTH CARDINALS: By holy Paul, we saw them not.
POPE: By Peter, you shall die   50
      Unless you bring them forth immediately.
      Hale them to prison. Lade their limbs with
      gyves.°
      False prelates, for this hateful treachery
      Cursèd be your souls to hellish misery.
            [*Exeunt the two Cardinals with Attendants.*]
FAUSTUS: So, they are safe. Now, Faustus, to the
      feast.   55
      The Pope had never such a frolic guest.
POPE: Lord Archbishop of Rheims, sit down with
      us.
ARCHBISHOP: I thank your holiness.
FAUSTUS: Fall to. The devil choke you an you
      spare.°

---

52. Lade . . . gyves: Shackle their limbs.   **59. an you spare:**
If you hold back.

60   POPE: Who's that spoke? Friars look about.
FRIAR: Here's nobody, if it like your holiness.
POPE: Lord Raymond, pray fall to. I am beholding
    To the Bishop of Milan for this so rare a present.
FAUSTUS: I thank you, sir.   [*He snatches the dish.*]
65   POPE: How now? Who snatched the meat from me?
    Villains, why speak you not?
    My good Lord Archbishop, here's a most dainty
        dish
    Was sent me from a cardinal in France.
FAUSTUS: I'll have that too.   [*He snatches the dish.*]
70   POPE: What Lollards do attend our holiness,
    That we receive such great indignity?
    Fetch me some wine.
FAUSTUS: Ay, pray do, for Faustus is a-dry.
POPE: Lord Raymond, I drink unto your grace.
75   FAUSTUS: I pledge your grace.   [*He snatches the cup.*]
POPE: My wine gone too? Ye lubbers, look about
    And find the man that doth this villainy,
    Or by our sanctitude, you all shall die.
    I pray, my lords, have patience at this
80   Troublesome banquet.
ARCHBISHOP: Please it your holiness, I think it be
    some ghost crept out of purgatory, and now is
    come unto your holiness for his pardon.
POPE: It may be so.
85   Go then, command our priests to sing a dirge
    To lay the fury of this same troublesome ghost.
                                    [*Exit an attendant.*]
    Once again, my lord, fall to.
                                    (*The Pope crosseth himself.*)
FAUSTUS: How now?
    Must every bit be spicèd with a cross?
90   Nay then, take that.   [*He strikes the Pope.*]
POPE: O I am slain. Help me, my lords.
    O come and help to bear my body hence.
    Damned be this soul for ever for this deed.
                                    (*Exeunt the Pope and his train.*)
MEPHISTOPHILIS: Now, Faustus, what will you do
95   now? For I can tell you you'll be cursed with
    bell, book, and candle.°
FAUSTUS: Bell, book, and candle; candle, book, and
        bell,
    Forward and backward, to curse Faustus to hell.

(*Enter the Friars with bell, book, and candle for the
dirge.*)

FIRST FRIAR: Come, brethren, let's about our
100   business with good devotion.   [*They chant.*]
    *Cursed be he that stole his holiness' meat
        from the table.*

95–96. **bell, book, and candle:** Used traditionally in the rite
of excommunication.

    Maledicat Dominus!°
    *Cursed be he that struck his holiness a blow
        on the face.*
    Maledicat Dominus!
    *Cursed be he that struck Friar Sandelo a blow
        on the pate.*   105
    Maledicat Dominus!
    Cursed be he that disturbeth our holy dirge.
    Maledicat Dominus!
    *Cursed be he that took away his holiness's
        wine.*
    Maledicat Dominus! Et omnes sancti.°   110
    Amen.

([*Faustus and Mephistophilis*] *beat the Friars, fling
fireworks among them, and exeunt.*)

Scene III

(*Enter* [*Robin,*] *the clown, and Dick, with a cup.*)

DICK: Sirrah Robin, we were best look that your devil
    can answer the stealing of this same cup, for the
    vintner's boy follows us at the hard heels.
ROBIN: 'Tis no matter. Let him come. An he follow us,
    I'll so conjure him as he was never conjured in his   5
    life, I warrant him. Let me see the cup.

(*Enter Vintner.*)

DICK: Here 'tis. Yonder he comes. Now, Robin, now
    or never show thy cunning.
VINTNER: O, are you here? I am glad I have found
    you. You are a couple of fine companions. Pray,   10
    where's the cup you stole from the tavern?
ROBIN: How, how? We steal a cup? Take heed what
    you say. We look not like cup stealers, I can tell
    you.
VINTNER: Never deny's, for I know you have it, and   15
    I'll search you.
ROBIN: Search me? Ay, and spare not. Hold the cup,
    Dick. [*Aside to Dick.*] Come, come, search me,
    search me.

[*The Vintner searches Robin.*]

VINTNER: [*to Dick*] Come on, sirrah, let me search   20
    you now.
DICK: Ay, ay, do, do. Hold the cup, Robin. [*Aside to
    Robin.*] I fear not your searching. We scorn to steal
    your cups, I can tell you.

[*The Vintner searches Dick.*]

---

102. *Maledicat Dominus:* May the Lord curse him.   **110.**
Et omnes sancti: And all the saints.

25 VINTNER: Never outface me for the matter, for sure
the cup is between you two.
ROBIN: Nay, there you lie. 'Tis beyond us both.
VINTNER: A plague take you! I thought 'twas your
knavery to take it away. Come, give it me again.
30 ROBIN: Ay, much. When? Can you tell? Dick, make
me a circle, and stand close at my back, and stir
not for thy life. Vintner, you shall have your cup
anon. Say nothing, Dick, *O per se, O Demogorgon, Belcher and Mephistophilis.*

(*Enter Mephistophilis. [Exit the Vintner, in fright.*])

MEPHISTOPHILIS: Monarch of hell, under whose
35   black survey
Great potentates do kneel with awful fear,
Upon whose altars thousand souls do lie,
How am I vexèd by these villains' charms!
From Constantinople have they brought me now,
40   Only for pleasure of these damnèd slaves.
ROBIN: By Lady, sir, you have had a shrewd journey
of it. Will it please you to take a shoulder of mutton to supper and a tester° in your purse, and go
back again?
45 DICK: Ay, I pray you heartily, sir, for we called you but
in jest, I promise you.
MEPHISTOPHILIS: To purge the rashness of this
cursèd deed,
First be thou turnèd to this ugly shape,
For apish deeds transformèd to an ape.
50 ROBIN: O brave, an ape! I pray sir, let me have the
carrying of him about to show some tricks.
MEPHISTOPHILIS: And so thou shalt. Be thou transformed to a dog, and carry him upon thy back.
Away, be gone!
55 ROBIN: A dog? That's excellent. Let the maids look
well to their porridge pots, for I'll into the kitchen
presently. Come, Dick, come.
        (*Exeunt [Robin and Dick,] the two clowns.*)
MEPHISTOPHILIS: Now with the flames of
everburning fire,
I'll wing myself and forthwith fly amain
60   Unto my Faustus, to the great Turk's court.
                                      (*Exit.*)

ACT IV • *Prologue*

(*Enter Chorus.*)

CHORUS: When Faustus had with pleasure ta'en the
view
Of rarest things and royal courts of kings,
He stayed his course and so returnèd home;

III, III. **43. tester:** Sixpence.

Where such as bare his absence but with grief —
I mean his friends and nearest companions —   5
Did gratulate his safety with kind words,
And in their conference of what befell,
Touching his journey through the world and air,
They put forth questions of astrology,
Which Faustus answered with such learnèd skill   10
As they admired and wondered at his wit.
Now is his fame spread forth in every land.
Amongst the rest, the Emperor is one —
Carolus the fifth° — at whose palace now
Faustus is feasted 'mongst his noblemen.   15
What there he did in trial of his art
I leave untold, your eyes shall see performed.
                                      (*Exit.*)

Scene I

(*Enter Martino and Frederick, at several doors.*)

MARTINO: What ho, officers, gentlemen,
Hie to the presences to attend the Emperor.
Good Frederick, see the rooms be voided straight;
His majesty is coming to the hall.
Go back, and see the state° in readiness.   5
FREDERICK: But where is Bruno, our elected Pope,
That on a fury's back came post from Rome?
Will not his grace consort the Emperor?
MARTINO: O yes, and with him comes the German
conjurer,
The learnèd Faustus, fame of Wittenberg,   10
The wonder of the world for magic art;
And he intends to show great Carolus
The race of all his stout progenitors,
And bring in presence of his majesty
The royal shapes and warlike semblances   15
Of Alexander° and his beauteous paramour.
FREDERICK: Where is Benvolio?
MARTINO: Fast asleep, I warrant you.
He took his rouse with stoups° of Rhenish wine
So kindly yesternight to Bruno's health   20
That all this day the sluggard keeps his bed.
FREDERICK: See, see, his window's ope. We'll call to
him.
MARTINO: What ho, Benvolio!

(*Enter Benvolio above at a window, in his nightcap,
buttoning.*)

IV, Prologue. 14. Carolus the fifth: Charles V, King of Spain (as
Charles I from 1516 to 1556) and Holy Roman Emperor from
1519 to 1556. **IV, I. 2. presence:** Emperor's chamber.
5. state: Throne. **16. Alexander:** Alexander the Great.
19. took . . . stoups: Had a drinking bout with brimming
goblets.

BENVOLIO: What a devil ail you two?

25 MARTINO: Speak softly, sir, lest the devil hear you,
For Faustus at the court is late arrived,
And at his heels a thousand furies wait
To accomplish whatsoever the doctor please.

BENVOLIO: What of this?

MARTINO: Come, leave thy chamber first, and thou
30   shalt see
This conjurer perform such rare exploits
Before the Pope° and royal Emperor
As never yet was seen in Germany.

BENVOLIO: Has not the Pope enough of conjuring
35   yet?
He was upon the devil's back late enough,
And if he be so far in love with him,
I would he would post with him to Rome again.

FREDERICK: Speak, wilt thou come and see this
         sport?

BENVOLIO: Not I.

MARTINO: Wilt thou stand in thy window and see it
         then?

40 BENVOLIO: Ay, and I fall not asleep i' th' meantime.

MARTINO: The Emperor is at hand, who comes to
         see
What wonders by black spells may compassed
         be.

BENVOLIO: Well, go you attend the Emperor. I am
content for this once to thrust my head out at a
45   window, for they say if a man be drunk overnight
the devil cannot hurt him in the morning. If that be
true, I have a charm in my head shall control him
as well as the conjurer, I warrant you.
*(Exit [Frederick, with Martino. Benvolio remains
at the window above].)*

Scene II

*(A sennet [is sounded. Enter] Charles, the German
Emperor, Bruno, [the Duke of] Saxony, Faustus,
Mephistophilis, Frederick, Martino, and Attendants.)*

EMPEROR: Wonder of men, renowned magician,
Thrice-learnèd Faustus, welcome to our court.
This deed of thine, in setting Bruno free
From his and our professèd enemy,
5   Shall add more excellence unto thine art
Than if by powerful necromantic spells
Thou couldst command the world's obedience.
Forever be beloved of Carolus,
And if this Bruno thou hast late redeemed°
10   In peace possess the triple diadem
And sit in Peter's chair despite of chance,

Thou shalt be famous through all Italy
And honored of the German Emperor.

FAUSTUS: These gracious words, most royal Carolus,
Shall make poor Faustus to his utmost power   15
Both love and serve the German Emperor
And lay his life at holy Bruno's feet.
For proof whereof, if so your grace be pleased,
The doctor stands prepared by power of art
To cast his magic charms that shall pierce
         through   20
The ebon gates of ever-burning hell,
And hale the stubborn Furies from their caves
To compass whatsoe'er your grace commands.

BENVOLIO: *[above]* Blood, he speaks terribly, but for
all that, I do not greatly believe him. He looks as   25
like a conjurer as the Pope° to a costermonger.°

EMPEROR: Then, Faustus, as thou late did'st promise
         us,
We would behold that famous conqueror,
Great Alexander, and his paramour
In their true shapes and state majestical,   30
That we may wonder at their excellence.

FAUSTUS: Your majesty shall see them presently.
Mephistophilis, away,
And with a solemn noise of trumpets' sound
Present before this royal Emperor,   35
Great Alexander and his beauteous paramour.

MEPHISTOPHILIS: Faustus, I will.

                                        [Exit.]

BENVOLIO: Well, master doctor, an your devils come not
away quickly, you shall have me asleep presently.
Zounds, I could eat myself for anger to think I have 40
been such an ass all this while, to stand gaping after
the devil's governor and can see nothing.

FAUSTUS: I'll make you feel something anon, if my
         art fail me not
My lord, I must forewarn your majesty
That when my spirits present the royal shapes   45
Of Alexander and his paramour,
Your grace demand no questions of the king,
But in dumb silence let them come and go.

EMPEROR: Be it as Faustus please; we are content.

BENVOLIO: Ay, ay, and I am content too. And thou   50
bring Alexander and his paramour before the Emperor, I'll be Actaeon and turn myself to a stag.

FAUSTUS: And I'll play Diana and send you the
         horns presently.

*([A] sennet [is sounded]. Enter at one [door] the Em-
peror Alexander, at the other Darius.° They meet [in*

---

32. **the Pope:** Bruno.   **IV, II. 9. redeemed:** Rescued.

26. **the Pope:** Bruno.   **Costermonger:** Fruit vendor; a term
of contempt.   [S.D.] ***Darius:*** King Darius III of Persia
(336–330 B.C.), defeated at Granicus in 334 B.C. by the
Greeks under Alexander the Great.

combat]. *Darius is thrown down; Alexander kills him, takes off his crown, and, offering to go out, his paramour meets him. He embraceth her and sets Darius' crown upon her head; and coming back, both salute the Emperor, who, leaving his state, offers to embrace them, which Faustus seeing, suddenly stays him. Then trumpets cease and music sounds.*)

My gracious lord, you do forget yourself.
55   These are but shadows, not substantial.
EMPEROR: O pardon me. My thoughts are so
      ravishèd
   With sight of this renownèd emperor,
   That in mine arms I would have compassed him.
   But, Faustus, since I may not speak to them,
60   To satisfy my longing thoughts at full,
   Let me this tell thee: I have heard it said
   That this fair lady, whilst she lived on earth,
   Had on her neck a little wart or mole;
   How may I prove that saying to be true?
65   FAUSTUS: Your majesty may boldly go and see.
EMPEROR: Faustus, I see it plain,
   And in this sight thou better pleasest me
   Than if I gained another monarchy.
FAUSTUS: Away! Be gone!
                                             (*Exit show.*)
70   See, see, my gracious lord, what strange beast is yon,
      that thrusts his head out at window?
EMPEROR: O wondrous sight! See, Duke of Saxony,
   Two spreading horns most strangely fastenèd
   Upon the head of young Benvolio.
75   SAXONY: What? Is he asleep or dead?
FAUSTUS: He sleeps, my lord, but dreams not of his
      horns.
EMPEROR: This sport is excellent. We'll call and
      wake him.
   What ho, Benvolio!
BENVOLIO: A plague upon you! Let me sleep a
      while.
80   EMPEROR: I blame thee not to sleep much, having
      such a head of thine own.
SAXONY: Look up, Benvolio; 'tis the Emperor calls.
BENVOLIO: The Emperor? Where? O zounds, my
      head!
EMPEROR: Nay, and thy horns hold, 'tis no matter for
85   thy head, for that's armed sufficiently.
FAUSTUS: Why, how now, sir knight! What, hanged by
      the horns? This is most horrible. Fie, fie, pull in
      your head for shame. Let not all the world wonder
      at you.
90   BENVOLIO: Zounds, doctor, is this your villainy?
FAUSTUS: O say not so, sir. The doctor has no skill,
   No art, no cunning, to present these lords
   Or bring before this royal Emperor
   The mighty monarch, warlike Alexander.

If Faustus do it, you are straight resolved   95
   In bold Actaeon's shape to turn a stag.
   And therefore, my lord, so please your majesty,
   I'll raise a kennel of hounds shall hunt him so
   As all his footmanship shall scarce prevail
   To keep his carcass from their bloody fangs   100
   Ho, Belimote, Argiron, Asterote!
BENVOLIO: Hold, hold! Zounds, he'll raise up a ken-
   nel of devils, I think, anon. Good, my lord, entreat
   for me. 'Sblood, I am never able to endure these
   torments.   105
EMPEROR: Then, good master doctor,
   Let me entreat you to remove his horns.
   He has done penance now sufficiently.
FAUSTUS: My gracious lord, not so much for injury
   done to me, as to delight your majesty with some   110
   mirth, hath Faustus justly requited this injurious°
   knight; which being all I desire, I am content to remove his horns. Mephistophilis, transform him.
      [*Mephistophilis removes the horns.*]
   And hereafter, sir, look you speak; well of
      scholars.
BENVOLIO: [*aside.*] Speak well of ye? 'Sblood, and   115
   scholars be such cuckold makers to clap horns of
   honest men's heads o' this order, I'll ne'er trust
   smooth faces and small ruffs° more. But an I be
   not revenged for this, would I might be turned to
   a gaping oyster and drink nothing but salt   120
   water.   [*Exit Benvolio above.*]
EMPEROR: Come, Faustus. While the Emperor lives,
   In recompense of this thy high desert,
   Thou shalt command the state of Germany
   And live beloved of mighty Carolus.   125
                                             (*Exeunt.*)

Scene III

(*Enter Benvolio, Martino, Frederick, and Soldiers.*)

MARTINO: Nay, sweet Benvolio, let us sway thy
      thoughts
   From this attempt against the conjurer.
BENVOLIO: Away! You love me not to urge me thus.
   Shall I let slip so great an injury,
   When every servile groom jests at my wrongs   5
   And in their rustic gambols proudly say,
   "Benvolio's head was graced with horns today"?
   O, may these eyelids never close again
   Till with my sword I have that conjurer slain.
   If you will aid me in this enterprise,   10
   Then draw your weapons and be resolute.

---

111. injurious: Insulting.   **118. small ruffs:** Academic
gowns.

If not, depart. Here will Benvolio die,
But Faustus' death shall quit° my infamy.
FREDERICK: Nay, we will stay with thee, betide what
may,
15 And kill that doctor if he come this way.
BENVOLIO: Then, gentle Frederick, hie thee to the
grove,
And place our servants and our followers
Close in an ambush there behind the trees.
By this, I know, the conjurer is near.
20 I saw him kneel and kiss the Emperor's hand
And take his leave, laden with rich rewards.
Then, soldiers, boldly fight. If Faustus die,
Take you the wealth; leave us the victory.
FREDERICK: Come, soldiers. Follow me unto the
grove.
25 Who kills him shall have gold and endless love.
    (*Exit Frederick with the Soldiers.*)
BENVOLIO: My head is lighter than it was by
th'horns,
But yet my heart's more ponderous than my head
And pants until I see that conjurer dead.
MARTINO: Where shall we place ourselves,
Benvolio?
BENVOLIO: Here will we stay to bide the first
30   assault.
O, were that damnèd hell-hound but in place,
Thou soon shouldst see me quit my foul disgrace.

(*Enter Frederick.*)

FREDERICK: Close, close, the conjurer is at hand
And all alone comes walking in his gown.
35 Be ready then, and strike the peasant down.
BENVOLIO: Mine be that honor then. Now, sword,
strike home.
For horns he gave I'll have his head anon.

(*Enter Faustus with the false head.*)

MARTINO: See, see, he comes.
BENVOLIO: No words! This blow ends all.
Hell take his soul; his body thus must fall.
                    [*He stabs Faustus.*]
40 FAUSTUS: [*falling*] Oh!
FREDERICK: Groan you, master doctor?
BENVOLIO: Break may his heart with groans! Dear
Frederick, see,
Thus will I end his griefs immediately.
MARTINO: Strike with a willing hand. His head is off.

[*Benvolio strikes off Faustus' false head.*]

BENVOLIO: The devil's dead. The Furies now may
45   laugh.

FREDERICK: Was this that stern aspèct, that awful
frown,
Made the grim monarch of infernal spirits
Tremble and quake at his commanding charms?
MARTINO: Was this that damnèd head whose heart
conspired
Benvolio's shame before the Emperor?   50
BENVOLIO: Ay, that's the head, and here the body
lies,
Justly rewarded for his villainies.
FREDERICK: Come, let's devise how we may add
more shame
To the black scandal of his hated name.
BENVOLIO: First, on his head, in quittance of my
wrongs,   55
I'll nail huge forkèd horns and let them hang
Within the window where he yoked° me first,
That all the world may see my just revenge.
MARTINO: What use shall we put his beard to?
BENVOLIO: We'll sell it to a chimney-sweeper. It will 60
wear out ten birchen brooms, I warrant you.
FREDERICK: What shall eyes do?
BENVOLIO: We'll put out his eyes, and they shall serve
for buttons to his lips to keep his tongue from
catching cold.   65
MARTINO: An excellent policy! And now, sirs, having
divided him, what shall the body do?

[*Faustus rises.*]

BENVOLIO: Zounds, the devil's alive again.
FREDERICK: Give him his head, for God's sake.
FAUSTUS: Nay, keep it. Faustus will have heads and
hands,   70
Ay, all your hearts, to recompense this deed.
Knew you not, traitors, I was limited
For four-and-twenty years to breathe on earth?
And had you cut my body with your swords,
Or hewed this flesh and bones as small as sand, 75
Yet in a minute had my spirit returned,
And I had breathed a man made free from harm.
But wherefore do I dally my revenge?
Asteroth, Belimoth, Mephistophilis!

(*Enter Mephistophilis and other Devils.*)

Go, horse these traitors on your fiery backs,   80
And mount aloft with them as high as heaven;
Thence pitch them headlong to the lowest hell.
Yet stay. The world shall see their misery,
And hell shall after plague their treachery.
Go, Belimoth, and take this caitiff° hence   85
And hurl him in some lake of mud and dirt.

Take thou this other; drag him through the
    woods
Amongst the pricking thorns and sharpest briars,
Whilst with my gentle Mephistophilis
90 This traitor flies unto some steepy rock
That, rolling down, may break the villain's bones
As he intended to dismember me.
Fly hence. Dispatch my charge immediately.

FREDERICK: Pity us, gentle Faustus. Save our lives.

FAUSTUS: Away!

FREDERICK: He must needs go that the devil
95   drives.

          (*Exeunt Spirits with the Knights.*)

(*Enter the ambushed Soldiers.*)

FIRST SOLDIER: Come, sirs, prepare yourselves in
    readiness.
Make haste to help these noble gentlemen;
I heard them parley with the conjurer.

SECOND SOLDIER: See where he comes. Dispatch and
    kill the slave.

FAUSTUS: What's here? An ambush to betray my
100 life?
Then, Faustus, try thy skill. Base peasants, stand,
For lo, these trees remove at my command
And stand as bulwarks 'twixt yourselves and me,
To shield me from your hated treachery.
105 Yet to encounter this your weak attempt,
Behold an army comes incontinent.°

(*Faustus strikes the door, and enter a Devil playing on
a drum, after him another bearing an ensign, and
divers with weapons, Mephistophilis with fireworks.
They set upon the Soldiers and drive them out. [Exit
Faustus.]*)

Scene IV

(*Enter at several doors Benvolio, Frederick, and Martino, their heads and faces bloody and besmeared
with mud and dirt, all having horns on their heads.*)

MARTINO: What ho, Benvolio!

BENVOLIO: Here! What, Frederick, ho!

FREDERICK: O help me, gentle friend. Where is
    Martino?

MARTINO: Dear Frederick, here,
5   Half smothered in a lake of mud and dirt,
    Through which the Furies dragged me by the
    heels.

FREDERICK: Martino, see! Benvolio's horns again!

MARTINO: O misery! How now, Benvolio?

BENVOLIO: Defend me, heaven. Shall I be haunted°
    still?

MARTINO: Nay, fear not man; we have not power to
    kill.   10

BENVOLIO: My friends transformèd thus! O hellish
    spite!
Your heads are all set with horns.

FREDERICK: You hit it right.
It is your own you mean. Feel on your head.

BENVOLIO: Zounds, horns again!

MARTINO: Nay, chafe not man. We all are sped.°   15

BENVOLIO: What devil attends this damned
    magician,
That, spite of spite, our wrongs are doublèd?

FREDERICK: What may we do, that we may hide our
    shames?

BENVOLIO: If we should follow him to work
    revenge,
He'd join long asses' ears to these huge horns, 20
And make us laughing-stocks to all the world.

MARTINO: What shall we then do, dear Benvolio?

BENVOLIO: I have a castle joining near these woods,
And thither we'll repair and live obscure
Till time shall alter these our brutish shapes. 25
Sith black disgrace hath thus eclipsed our fame,
We'll rather die with grief than live with shame.

                (*Exeunt omnes.°*)

Scene V

(*Enter Faustus and Mephistophilis.*)

FAUSTUS: Now, Mephistophilis, the restless course
That time doth run with calm and silent foot,
Shortening my days and thread of vital life,
Calls for the payment of my latest years.
Therefore, sweet Mephistophilis, let us 5
Make haste to Wittenberg.

MEPHISTOPHILIS: What, will you go on horseback, or
    on foot?

FAUSTUS: Nay, till I am past this fair and pleasant
    green,
I'll walk on foot.

                [*Exit Mephistophilis.*]

(*Enter a Horse-Courser.°*)

HORSE-COURSER: I have been all this day seeking one 10
    Master Fustian.° Mass, see where he is. God save
    you, master doctor.

FAUSTUS: What, horse-courser! You are well met.

---

106. incontinent: At once.   **IV, IV. 9. haunted:** (1) Bewitched; (2) hunted, pursued (since he is a stag).

15. sped: provided (with horns).   **27.** [S.D.] *Exeunt omnes:*
Latin for "All go out."   **IV, V.** The first eleven lines of this
scene do not appear in all versions of the play, but they provide a transition to the Horse-Courser episode and remind
readers of Faustus's impending tragedy. **9.** [S.D.] *Horse-
Courser:* One who deals in horses. **11. Fustian:** The perversion of Faustus's name is a deliberate attempt at humor.

HORSE-COURSER: I beseech your worship, accept of
15   these forty dollars.
FAUSTUS: Friend, thou canst not buy so good a horse
    for so small a price. I have no great need to sell
    him, but if thou likest him for ten dollars more,
    take him, because I see thou hast a good mind to
20   him.
HORSE-COURSER: I beseech you, sir, accept of this. I
    am a very poor man and have lost very much of
    late by horse-flesh, and this bargain will set me up
    again.
25 FAUSTUS: Well, I will not stand with thee.° Give me
    the money.

[*The Horse-Courser gives Faustus money.*]

    Now, sirrah, I must tell you that you may ride him
    o'er hedge and ditch, and spare him not. But, do
    you hear? In any case, ride him not into the water.
30 HORSE-COURSER: How sir? Not into the water? Why,
    will he not drink of all waters?°
FAUSTUS: Yes, he will drink of all waters, but ride him
    not into the water — o'er hedge and ditch, or where
    thou wilt, but not into the water. Go, bid the hostler
35   deliver him unto you, and remember what I say.
HORSE-COURSER: I warrant you, sir. O joyful day!
    Now am I a man made forever.

                                           (*Exit.*)

FAUSTUS: What art thou, Faustus, but a man
    condemned to die?
    Thy fatal time draws to a final end.
40 Despair doth drive distrust into my thoughts.
    Confound these passions with a quiet sleep.
    Tush! Christ did call the thief upon the cross;
    Then rest thee, Faustus, quiet in conceit.°

(*He sits to sleep* [*in his chair*].)

(*Enter the Horse-Courser, wet.*)

HORSE-COURSER: O what a cozening doctor was this?
45   I riding my horse into the water, thinking some hid-
    den mystery° had been in the horse, I had nothing
    under me but a little straw and had much ado to es-
    cape drowning. Well, I'll go rouse him and make
    him give me my forty dollars again. Ho, sirrah doc-
50   tor, you cozening scab!° Master doctor, awake and
    rise, and give me my money again, for your horse is
    turned to a bottle° of hay. Master doctor!

(*He* [*tries to wake Faustus, and in doing so*] *pulls off
his leg.*)

Alas, I am undone! What shall I do? I have pulled
off his leg.

[*Faustus awakes.*]

FAUSTUS: O, help, help! The villain hath murdered me. 55
HORSE-COURSER: Murder or not murder, now he has
    but one leg, I'll outrun him and cast this leg into
    some ditch or other.
FAUSTUS: Stop him, stop him, stop him! Ha, ha, ha,
    Faustus hath his leg again, and the horse-courser a 60
    bundle of hay for his forty dollars.

(*Enter Wagner.*)

How now, Wagner, what news with thee?
WAGNER: If it please you, the Duke of Anholt doth
    earnestly entreat your company and hath sent
    some of his men to attend you with provision fit 65
    for your journey.
FAUSTUS: The Duke of Anholt's an honorable gentle-
    man, and one to whom I must be no niggard of my
    cunning. Come away.

                                         (*Exeunt.*)

Scene VI

(*Enter* [*Robin, the*] *Clown, Dick,* [*the*] *Horse-
Courser, and a Carter.*°)

CARTER: Come, my masters, I'll bring you to the best
    beer in Europe. What ho, hostess! Where be these
    whores?

(*Enter Hostess.*)

HOSTESS: How now, what lack you? What, my old
    guests, welcome.   5
ROBIN: Sirrah, Dick, dost thou know why I stand so
    mute?
DICK: No, Robin; why is't?
ROBIN: I am eighteen pence on the score.° But say
    nothing, see if she have forgotten me.   10
HOSTESS: Who's this that stands so solemnly by him-
    self? What, my old guest?
ROBIN: O hostess, how do you? I hope my score
    stands still.°
HOSTESS: Ay, there's no doubt of that, for methinks 15
    you make no haste to wipe it out.
DICK: Why, hostess, I say, fetch us some beer.
HOSTESS: You shall presently. Look up into th'hall
    there, ho!

                                         (*Exit.*)

DICK: Come, sirs, what shall we do now till mine 20
    hostess come?

---

25. stand with thee: Bargain.   **31. drink . . . waters:** Be ready
for anything (a common proverb of the time).   **43. conceit:**
Thoughts.   **46. mystery:** Quality.   **50. cozening scab:** Deceitful, contemptible rascal.   **52. bottle:** Bundle.

IV, VI. [S.D.] *Carter:* A person who drives a cart.   **9. on the
score:** In debt.   **13–14. stands still:** Does not go higher.

CARTER: Marry, sir, I'll tell you the bravest tale how a conjurer served me. You know Doctor Fauster?

HORSE-COURSER: Ay, a plague take him. Here's some on's have cause to know him. Did he conjure you too?

CARTER: I'll tell you how he served me. As I was going to Wittenberg t'other day with a load of hay, he met me and asked me what he should give me for as much hay as he could eat. Now, sir, I thinking that a little would serve his turn, bade him take as much as he would for three farthings. So he presently gave me my money and fell to eating; and as I am a cursen° man, he never left eating till he had eat up all my load of hay.

ALL: O monstrous! Eat a whole load of hay!

ROBIN: Yes, yes, that may be, for I have heard of one that has eat a load of logs.

HORSE-COURSER: Now, sirs, you shall hear how villainously he served me. I went to him yesterday to buy a horse of him, and he would by no means sell him under forty dollars. So, sir, because I knew him to be such a horse as would run over hedge and ditch and never tire, I gave him his money. So when I had my horse, Doctor Fauster bade me ride him night and day and spare him no time; but, quoth he, in any case ride him not into the water. Now sir, I thinking the horse had had some rare quality that he would not have me know of, what did I but rid him into a great river, and when I came just in the midst, my horse vanished away, and I sat straddling upon a bottle of hay.

ALL: O brave doctor!

HORSE-COURSER: But you shall hear how bravely I served him for it. I went me home to his house, and there I found him asleep. I kept a hallooing and whooping in his ears, but all could not wake him. I seeing that took him by the leg and never rested pulling till I had pulled me his leg quite off, and now 'tis at home in mine hostry.

ROBIN: And has the doctor but one leg then? That's excellent, for one of his devils turned me into the likeness of an ape's face.

CARTER: Some more drink, hostess.

ROBIN: Hark you, we'll into another room and drink a while, and then we'll go seek out the doctor.

(Exeunt.)

Scene VII

(Enter the Duke of Anholt, his Duchess, Faustus, and Mephistophilis, [Servants and Attendants].)

DUKE: Thanks, master doctor, for these pleasant sights.
Nor know I how sufficiently to recompense your

34. **cursen:** Christened.

great deserts° in erecting that enchanted castle in the air, the sight whereof so delighted me, as nothing in the world could please me more.

FAUSTUS: I do think myself, my good lord, highly recompensed in that it pleaseth your grace to think but well of that which Faustus hath performed. But, gracious lady, it may be that you have taken no pleasure in those sights. Therefore, I pray you, tell me what is the thing you most desire to have; be it in the world, it shall be yours. I have heard that great-bellied women do long for things are rare and dainty.

DUCHESS: True, master doctor, and since I find you so kind, I will make known unto you what my heart desires to have. And were it now summer, as it is January, a dead time of the winter, I would request no better meat than a dish of ripe grapes.

FAUSTUS: This is but a small matter. Go, Mephistophilis, away!

(Exit Mephistophilis.)

Madam I will do more than this for your content.

(Enter Mephistophilis again with the grapes.)

Here; now taste ye these. They should be good, for they come from a far country, I can tell you.

DUKE: This makes me wonder more than all the rest, that at this time of year, when every tree is barren of his fruit, from whence you had these ripe grapes.

FAUSTUS: Please it, your grace, the year is divided into two circles over the whole world, so that when it is winter with us, in the contrary circle it is likewise summer with them, as in India, Saba,° and such countries that lie far east, where they have fruit twice a year. From whence, by means of a swift spirit that I have, I had these grapes brought, as you see.

DUCHESS: And trust me, they are the sweetest grapes that e'er I tasted.

(The Clown[s, Robin, Dick, the Carter, and the Horse-Courser,] bounce at the gate within.)

DUKE: What rude disturbers have we at the gate?
Go, pacify their fury. Set it ope,
And then demand of them what they would
have.   [*Exit a Servant.*]

(They knock again and call out to talk with Faustus.)

[*Enter Servant to them.*]

SERVANT: Why, how now, masters, what a coil° is there?
What is the reason you disturb the duke.

DICK: We have no reason for it; therefore a fig for him.

IV, VII. 3. **deserts:** Good deeds. 31. **Saba:** Sheba.
41. **coil:** Disturbance.

SERVANT: What, saucy varlets,° dare you be so bold?
45 HORSE-COURSER: I hope, sir, we have wit enough to
      be more bold than welcome.
    SERVANT: It appears so. Pray be bold elsewhere,
      And trouble not the duke.
    DUKE: What would they have?
    SERVANT: They all cry out to speak with Doctor
      Faustus.
50 CARTER: Ay, and we will speak with him.
    DUKE: Will you, sir? Commit the rascals.
    DICK: Commit with us! He were as good commit with
      his father as commit with us.
    FAUSTUS: I do beseech your grace, let them come in;
55   They are good subject for a merriment.
    DUKE: Do as thou wilt, Faustus. I give thee leave.
    FAUSTUS: I thank your grace.

    (*Enter Robin, Dick, Carter, and Horse-Courser.*)

                          Why, how now, my good friends?
      'Faith you are too outrageous,° but come near;
      I have procured your pardons. Welcome all!
60 ROBIN: Nay, sir, we will be welcome for our money,
      and we will pay for what we take. What ho! Give's
      half a dozen of beer here, and be hanged.
    FAUSTUS: Nay, hark you; can you tell me where you
      are?
    CARTER: Ay, marry can I: we are under heaven.
    SERVANT: Ay, but sir sauce-box, know you in what
65   place?
    HORSE-COURSER: Ay, ay, the house is good enough to
      drink in. Zounds, fill us some beer, or we'll break
      all the barrels in the house and dash out all your
      brains with your bottles.
    FAUSTUS: Be not so furious. Come, you shall have
70   beer.
      My lord, beseech you give me leave a while:
      I'll gage my credit, 'twill content your grace.
    DUKE: With all my heart, kind doctor. Please thyself;
      Our servants and our court's at thy command.
    FAUSTUS: I humbly thank your grace. Then fetch
75   some beer.
    HORSE-COURSER: Ay, marry, there spake a doctor
      indeed, and 'faith,
      I'll drink a health to thy wooden leg for that
      word.
    FAUSTUS: My wooden leg? What dost thou mean by
      that?
    CARTER: Ha, ha, ha! Dost hear him, Dick? He has
      forgot his leg.
    HORSE-COURSER: Ay, ay, he does not stand much°
80   upon that.
    FAUSTUS: No, faith; not much upon a wooden leg.

    CARTER: Good lord, that flesh and blood should be so
      frail with your worship! Do not you remember a
      horse-courser you sold a horse to?
    FAUSTUS: Yes, I remember I sold one a horse.   85
    CARTER: And do you remember you bid he should not
      ride into the water?
    FAUSTUS: Yes, I do very well remember that.
    CARTER: And do you remember nothing of your leg?
    FAUSTUS: No, in good sooth.   90
    CARTER: Then, I pray, remember your courtesy.°
    FAUSTUS: I thank you, sir.
    CARTER: 'Tis not so much worth. I pray you, tell me
      one thing.
    FAUSTUS: What's that?   95
    CARTER: Be both your legs bedfellows every night to-
      gether?
    FAUSTUS: Wouldst thou make a Colossus° of me, that
      thou askest me such questions?
    CARTER: No, truly, sir. I would make nothing of you, 100
      but I would fain know that.

    (*Enter Hostess with drink.*)

    FAUSTUS: Then, I assure thee, certainly they are.
    CARTER: I thank you; I am fully satisfied.
    FAUSTUS: But wherefore dost thou ask?
    CARTER: For nothing, sir. But methinks you should   105
      have a wooden bedfellow of one of 'em.
    HORSE-COURSER: Why, do you hear, sir; did not I pull
      off one of your legs when you were asleep?
    FAUSTUS: But I have it again, now I am awake. Look
      you here, sir.   110
    ALL: O horrible! Had the doctor three legs?
    CARTER: Do you remember, sir, how you cozened me
      and ate up my load of —

    (*Faustus charms him dumb.*)

    DICK: Do you remember how you made me wear an
      ape's —   115

    [*Faustus charms him dumb.*]

    HORSE-COURSER: You whoreson conjuring scab, do
      you remember how you cozened me with a ho —

    [*Faustus charms him dumb.*]

    ROBIN: Ha' you forgotten me? You think to carry it
      away° with your *hey-pass* and *re-pass*; do you re-
      member the dog's fa —   120

    [*Faustus charms him dumb.*]   (*Exeunt Clowns.*)

    HOSTESS: Who pays for the ale? Hear you, master
      doctor, now you have sent away my guests, I pray
      who shall pay me for my a —

---

44. **varlets:** Knaves, rascals.   58. **outrageous:** violent.
80. **stand much:** Make much of (with a quibble).

91. **courtesy:** Curtsy, or leg.   98. **Colossus:** A giant statue
said to have stood with its legs astride at the entrance to the
ancient harbor of Rhodes.   118–119. **carry it away:** Come
off best.

[*Faustus charms her dumb.*]   (*Exit Hostess.*)

DUCHESS: My lord,
125   We are much beholding to this learnèd man.
DUKE: So are we, madam, which we will
      recompense
    With all the love and kindness that we may.
    His artful sport drives all sad thoughts away.
                              (*Exeunt.*)

ACT V • *Scene* I

(*Thunder and lightning. Enter Devils with covered dishes. Mephistophilis leads them into Faustus' study. Then enter Wagner.*)

WAGNER: I think my master means to die shortly.
    He has made his will and given me his wealth,
    His house, his goods, and store of golden plate,
    Besides two thousand ducats ready coined.
5   I wonder what he means. If death were nigh,
    He would not frolic thus. He's now at supper
    With the scholars, where there's such belly-cheer
    As Wagner in his life ne'er saw the like.
    And see where they come; belike the feast is
      done.
                              (*Exit.*)

(*Enter Faustus, Mephistophilis, and two or three Scholars.*)

10 FIRST SCHOLAR: Master Doctor Faustus, since our con-
    ference about fair ladies, which was the beautifulest
    in all the world, we have determined with ourselves
    that Helen of Greece was the admirablest lady that
    ever lived. Therefore, master doctor, if you will do
15   us so much favor as to let us see that peerless dame
    of Greece, whom all the world admires for majesty,
    we should think ourselves much beholding unto
    you.
FAUSTUS: Gentlemen,
20   For that I know your friendship is unfeigned,
    And Faustus' custom is not to deny
    The just requests of those that wish him well,
    You shall behold that peerless dame of Greece,
    No otherwise for pomp and majesty
25   Than when Sir Paris crossed the seas with her
    And brought the spoils to rich Dardania.°
    Be silent then, for danger is in words.

(*Music sounds. Mephistophilis brings in Helen; she passeth over the stage.*)

V, I. 23–26. **Peerless dame . . . Dardania:** The Greek Helen (the "peerless dame"), wife of Menelaus, was carried off to Troy (Dardania) by Paris, sparking the Trojan War.

SECOND SCHOLAR: Was this fair Helen, whose
    admirèd worth
    Made Greece with ten years' war afflict poor
      Troy?
    Too simple is my wit to tell her praise,   30
    Whom all the world admires for majesty.
THIRD SCHOLAR: No marvel though the angry
    Greeks pursued
    With ten years' war the rape of such a queen,
    Whose heavenly beauty passeth all compare.
FIRST SCHOLAR: Since we have seen the pride of
    nature's works   35
    And only paragon of excellence,
    We'll take our leaves and for this blessèd sight
    Happy and blest be Faustus evermore.
FAUSTUS: Gentlemen, farewell; the same wish I to
    you.
                     (*Exeunt Scholars.*)

(*Enter an Old Man.*)

OLD MAN: O gentle Faustus, leave this damnèd art,   40
    This magic that will charm thy soul to hell
    And quite bereave thee of salvation.
    Though thou hast now offended like a man,
    Do not persevere in it like a devil.
    Yet, yet, thou hast an amiable° soul,   45
    If sin by custom grow not into nature.
    Then, Faustus, will repentance come too late;
    Then thou art banished from the sight of heaven.
    No mortal can express the pains of hell.
    It may be this my exhortation   50
    Seems harsh and all unpleasant; let it not,
    For, gentle son, I speak it not in wrath
    Or envy of° thee, but in tender love
    And pity of thy future misery.
    And so have hope that this my kind rebuke,   55
    Checking° thy body, may amend thy soul.
FAUSTUS: Where art thou, Faustus? Wretch, what
    hast thou done?
    Damned art thou, Faustus, damned; despair and
      die!
    Hell claims his right, and with a roaring voice
    Says, "Faustus, come; thine hour is almost
      come";   60
    And Faustus now will come to do thee right.

(*Mephistophilis gives him a dagger.*)

OLD MAN: O stay, good Faustus, stay thy desperate
    steps.
    I see an angel hovers o'er thy head,
    And with a vial full of precious grace
    Offers to pour the same into thy soul.   65

45. **amiable:** Worthy of divine love or grace.   53. **envy of:** Ill will toward.   56. **Checking:** Admonishing.

Then call for mercy and avoid despair.

FAUSTUS: Ah, my sweet friend, I feel thy words
To comfort my distressèd soul.
Leave me a while to ponder on my sins.

OLD MAN: Faustus, I leave thee, but with grief of
70   heart,
Fearing the enemy of thy hapless soul.
                        (*Exit.*)

FAUSTUS: Accursèd Faustus, where is mercy now?
I do repent, and yet I do despair.
Hell strives with grace for conquest in my breast.
75 What shall I do to shun the snares of death?

MEPHISTOPHILIS: Thou traitor, Faustus, I arrest thy
    soul
For disobedience to my sovereign lord.
Revolt, or I'll in piecemeal tear thy flesh.

FAUSTUS: I do repent I e'er offended him.
80 Sweet Mephistophilis, entreat thy lord
To pardon my unjust presumption,
And with my blood again I will confirm
The former vow I made to Lucifer.

MEPHISTOPHILIS: Do it then, Faustus, with
    unfeigned° heart,
85 Lest greater dangers do attend thy drift.°

[*Faustus stabs his arm and writes on a paper with his
blood.*]

FAUSTUS: Torment, sweet friend, that base and agèd
    man
That durst dissuade me from thy Lucifer,
With greatest torment that our hell affords.

MEPHISTOPHILIS: His faith is great; I cannot touch
    his soul,
90 But what I may afflict his body with
I will attempt, which is but little worth.

FAUSTUS: One thing, good servant, let me crave of
    thee
To glut the longing of my heart's desire —
That I may have unto my paramour
95 That heavenly Helen which I saw of late,
Whose sweet embracings may extinguish clear
Those thoughts that do dissuade me from my
    vow,
And keep mine oath I made to Lucifer.

MEPHISTOPHILIS: This, or what else my Faustus shall
    desire,
100 Shall be performed in twinkling of an eye.

(*Enter Helen again, passing over [the stage] between
two Cupids.*)

FAUSTUS: Was this the face that launched a
    thousand ships

---

84. unfeignèd: Honest.   **85. drift:** Purpose.

And burnt the topless towers of Ilium?
Sweet Helen, make me immortal with a kiss.

[*She kisses him.*]

Her lips suck forth my soul. See where it flies!
Come, Helen, come, give me my soul again.   105
Here will I dwell, for heaven is in these lips,
And all is dross that is not Helena.

[*Enter the Old Man.*]

I will be Paris, and for love of thee
Instead of Troy shall Wittenberg be sacked;
And I will combat with weak Menelaus°   110
And wear thy colors on my plumèd crest.
Yea, I will wound Achilles° in the heel
And then return to Helen for a kiss.
O, thou art fairer than the evening's air,
Clad in the beauty of a thousand stars.   115
Brighter art thou than flaming Jupiter°
When he appeared to hapless Semele,°
More lovely than the monarch of the sky
In wanton Arethusa's azured arms,°
And none but thou shalt be my paramour.   120
              (*Exeunt [all but the Old Man].*)

OLD MAN: Accursèd Faustus, miserable man,
That from thy soul exclud'st the grace of heaven
And fliest the throne of his tribunal seat!

(*Enter the Devils.*)

Satan begins to sift me with his pride.
As in this furnace God shall try my faith,   125
My faith, vile hell, shall triumph over thee.
Ambitious fiends, see how the heavens smiles
At your repulse and laughs your state° to scorn.
Hence hell, for hence I fly unto my God.
                        (*Exeunt.*)

Scene II

(*Thunder. Enter [above] Lucifer, Beelzebub, and
Mephistophilis.*)

LUCIFER: Thus from infernal Dis° do we ascend
To view the subjects of our monarchy,
Those souls which sin seals the black sons of
    hell,

---

110. Menelaus: The husband of Helen of Troy.
112. Achilles: The Greek hero of the Trojan war, wounded in
the heel by Paris.   **116. Jupiter:** Zeus.   **117. Semele:** The
daughter of Cadmus and Harmonia who bore Zeus the
child, Dionysus.   **119–120. monarch . . . arms:** Arethusa
was a nymph, one of the Nereids, who governed a fountain
on the isle of Ortygia near Syracuse.   **128. state:** Royal
power.   **V, II. 1. Dis:** Hades, or hell.

5   'Mong which as chief, Faustus, we come to thee,
    Bringing with us lasting damnation
    To wait upon thy soul. The time is come
    Which makes it forfeit.
MEPHISTOPHILIS: And this gloomy night,
    Here in this room will wretched Faustus be.
BEELZEBUB: And here we'll stay
10   To mark him how he doth demean himself.
MEPHISTOPHILIS: How should he, but in desperate
      lunacy?
    Fond worldling, now his heart-blood dries with
      grief;
    His conscience kills it, and his laboring brain
    Begets a world of idle fantasies
15   To over-reach the devil. But all in vain;
    His store of pleasures must be sauced° with pain.
    He and his servant, Wagner, are at hand.
    Both come from drawing Faustus' latest will.
    See where they come.

(*Enter Faustus and Wagner.*)

20 FAUSTUS: Say, Wagner, thou has perused my will;
    How dost thou like it?
WAGNER: Sir, so wondrous well
    As in all humble duty I do yield
    My life and lasting service for your love.

(*Enter the Scholars.*)

FAUSTUS: Gramercies,° Wagner. Welcome, gentlemen.
                    [*Exit Wagner.*]
25 FIRST SCHOLAR: Now, worthy Faustus, methinks your
    looks are changed.
FAUSTUS: Ah, gentlemen!
SECOND SCHOLAR: What ails Faustus?
FAUSTUS: Ah, my sweet chamber-fellow, had I lived
30   with thee, then had I lived still, but now must die
    eternally. Look, sirs; comes he not? Comes he not?
FIRST SCHOLAR: O my dear Faustus, what imports this
    fear?
SECOND SCHOLAR: Is all our pleasure turned to melan-
35   choly?
THIRD SCHOLAR: He is not well with being over-
    solitary.
SECOND SCHOLAR: If it be so, we'll have physicians,
    and Faustus shall be cured.
THIRD SCHOLAR: 'Tis but a surfeit sir; fear nothing.
40 FAUSTUS: A surfeit of deadly sin that hath damned
    both body and soul.
SECOND SCHOLAR: Yet Faustus, look up to heaven,
    and remember mercy is infinite.
FAUSTUS: But Faustus' offence can ne'er be pardoned.
45   The serpent that tempted Eve may be saved, but
    not Faustus. Ah gentlemen, hear me with patience

16. sauced: Paid for.   24. Gramercies: Thanks.

and tremble not at my speeches. Though my heart
pants and quivers to remember that I have been a
student here these thirty years, O, would I had
never seen Wittenberg, never read book. And what 50
wonders I have done, all Germany can witness —
yea, all the world — for which Faustus hath lost
both Germany and the world, yea heaven itself,
heaven the seat of God, the throne of the blessed,
the kingdom of joy, and must remain in hell for 55
ever. Hell, ah hell for ever! Sweet friends, what
shall become of Faustus, being in hell for ever?
SECOND SCHOLAR: Yet Faustus, call on God.
FAUSTUS: On God, whom Faustus hath abjured? On
God, whom Faustus hath blasphemed? Ah, my 60
God, I would weep, but the devil draws in my
tears. Gush forth blood instead of tears, yea life
and soul. O, he stays my tongue! I would lift up
my hands, but see, they hold 'em; they hold 'em.
ALL: Who, Faustus? 65
FAUSTUS: Why, Lucifer and Mephistophilis. Ah, gentlemen, I gave them my soul for my cunning.
ALL: God forbid!
FAUSTUS: God forbade it indeed, but Faustus hath
done it. For the vain pleasure of four and twenty 70
years hath Faustus lost eternal joy and felicity. I
writ them a bill with mine own blood. The date is
expired. This is the time, and he will fetch me.
FIRST SCHOLAR: Why did not Faustus tell us of this
before, that divines might have prayed for thee? 75
FAUSTUS: Oft have I thought to have done so, but the
devil threatened to tear me in pieces if I named
God, to fetch me, body and soul, if I once gave ear
to divinity. And now 'tis too late. Gentlemen away,
lest you perish with me. 80
SECOND SCHOLAR: O, what may we do to save Faustus?
FAUSTUS: Talk not of me, but save yourselves and de-
part.
THIRD SCHOLAR: God will strengthen me; I will stay
with Faustus. 85
FIRST SCHOLAR: Tempt not God, sweet friend, but let
us into the next room and there pray for him.
FAUSTUS: Ay, pray for me, pray for me; and what
noise soever you hear, come not unto me, for noth-
ing can rescue me. 90
SECOND SCHOLAR: Pray thou, and we will pray that
God may have mercy upon thee.
FAUSTUS: Gentlemen, farewell. If I live till morning,
I'll visit you; if not, Faustus is gone to hell.
ALL: Faustus, farewell. 95

                  (*Exeunt Scholars.*)
MEPHISTOPHILIS: [*above*] Ay, Faustus, now thou hast
    no hope of heaven;
    Therefore despair. Think only upon hell,
    For that must be thy mansion, there to dwell.

FAUSTUS: O thou bewitching fiend, 'twas thy
        temptation
100   Hath robbed me of eternal happiness.
MEPHISTOPHILIS: I do confess it, Faustus, and
        rejoice.
      'Twas I, that when thou wert i' the way to
        heaven,
      Damned up thy passage. When thou took'st the
        book
      To view the Scriptures, then I turned the leaves
105   And led thine eye.
      What, weep'st thou? 'Tis too late. Despair!
        Farewell!
      Fools that will laugh on earth must weep in hell.
                                                    (*Exit.*)

(*Enter the Good Angel and the Bad Angel at several
doors.*)

GOOD ANGEL: Ah, Faustus, if thou hadst given ear
        to me,
      Innumerable joys had followed thee;
      But thou didst love the world.
110   BAD ANGEL: Gave ear to me,
      And now must taste hell's pains perpetually.
GOOD ANGEL: O what will all thy riches, pleasures,
        pomps
      Avail thee now?
      BAD ANGEL: Nothing but vex thee more,
      To want in hell, that had on earth such store.

(*Music while the throne descends.*)

115   GOOD ANGEL: O, thou hast lost celestial happiness,
      Pleasures unspeakable, bliss without end.
      Hadst thou affected sweet divinity,
      Hell or the devil had had no power on thee.
      Hadst thou kept on that way, Faustus, behold
120   In what resplendent glory thou hadst sat
      In yonder throne, like those bright shining saints,
      And triumphed over hell. That hast thou lost,
      And now, poor soul, must thy good angel leave
        thee.

[*The throne ascends.*]

      The jaws of hell are open to receive thee.
                                                    (*Exit.*)

(*Hell is discovered.*)

BAD ANGEL: Now, Faustus, let thine eyes with
125   horror stare
      Into that vast perpetual torture-house.
      There are the Furies tossing damnèd souls
      On burning forks; their bodies boil in lead.
      There are live quarters broiling on the coals,
130   That ne'er can die. This ever-burning chair
      Is for o'er-tortured souls to rest them in.

      These that are fed with sops of flaming fire
      Were gluttons and loved only delicates
      And laughed to see the poor starve at their gates.
      But yet all these are nothing; thou shalt see   135
      Ten thousand tortures that more horrid be.
FAUSTUS: O, I have seen enough to torture me.
BAD ANGEL: Nay, thou must feel them, taste the
        smart of all.
      He that loves pleasure must for pleasure fall.
      And so I leave thee, Faustus, till anon;   140
      Then wilt thou tumble in confusion.

([*Hell disappears.*] *The clock strikes eleven.*)

FAUSTUS: Ah Faustus,
      Now hast thou but one bare hour to live,
      And then thou must be damned perpetually.
      Stand still, you ever-moving spheres of heaven,   145
      That time may cease and midnight never come.
      Fair nature's eye, rise, rise again, and make
      Perpetual day; or let this hour be but
      A year, a month, a week, a natural day,
      That Faustus may repent and save his soul.   150
      O lente, lente currite noctis equi!°
      The stars move still; time runs; the clock will
        strike;
      The devil will come, and Faustus must be
        damned.
      O, I'll leap up to my God! Who pulls me down?
      See, see, where Christ's blood streams in the
        firmament!   155
      One drop would save my soul, half a drop! Ah,
        my Christ!
      Rend not my heart for naming of my Christ!
      Yet will I call on him. O, spare me, Lucifer!
      Where is it now? 'Tis gone. And see where God
      Stretcheth out his arm and bends his ireful
        brows.   160
      Mountains and hills, come, come, and fall on
        me,
      And hide me from the heavy wrath of God.
      No, no!
      Then will I headlong run into the earth.
      Earth, gape! O no, it will not harbor me!   165
      You stars that reigned at my nativity,
      Whose influence hath allotted death and hell.
      Now draw up Faustus like a foggy mist
      Into the entrails of yon laboring cloud,
      That when you vomit forth into the air,   170
      My limbs may issue from your smoky mouths,
      So that my soul may but ascend to heaven.

(*The watch strikes.*)

151. *O . . . equi*: O slowly, slowly; run you horses of night
(adapted from Ovid's *Amores*).

Ah, half the hour is past; 'twill all be past anon.
O God,
175 If thou wilt not have mercy on my soul,
Yet for Christ's sake, whose blood hath
    ransomed me,
Impose some end to my incessant pain.
Let Faustus live in hell a thousand years,
A hundred thousand, and at last be saved.
180 O, no end is limited to damnèd souls.
Why wert thou not a creature wanting soul?
Or why is this immortal that thou hast?
Ah, Pythagoras' *metempsychosis*,° were that true,
This soul should fly from me and I be changed
185 Into some brutish beast. All beasts are happy,
For, when they die
Their souls are soon dissolved in elements,
But mine must live still to be plagued in hell.
Cursed be the parents that engendered me!
190 No, Faustus, curse thyself, curse Lucifer
That hath deprived thee of the joys of heaven.

(*The clock strikes twelve.*)

O, it strikes, it strikes! Now, body, turn to air,
Or Lucifer will bear thee quick° to hell.
O soul, be changed to little water-drops,
195 And fall into the ocean, ne'er be found!

(*Thunder, and enter the Devils.*)

My God, my God, look not so fierce on me!
Adders and serpents, let me breathe a while!
Ugly hell, gape not! Come not, Lucifer!
I'll burn my books! Ah, Mephistophilis!
(*Exeunt [Faustus and Devils].*)

Scene III

(*Enter the Scholars.*)

FIRST SCHOLAR: Come, gentlemen, let us go visit
    Faustus,
For such a dreadful night was never seen

---

183. *metempsychosis*: Belief in the transmigration of souls,
associated with the Greek philosopher Pythagoras of Samos.
193. **quick**: Alive.

Since first the world's creation did begin.
Such fearful shrieks and cries were never heard.
Pray heaven the doctor have escaped the danger.   5
SECOND SCHOLAR: O help us, heaven! See, here are
    Faustus' limbs,
All torn asunder by the hand of death.
THIRD SCHOLAR: The devils whom Faustus served
    have torn him thus;
For 'twixt the hours of twelve and one,
    methought
I heard him shriek and call aloud for help,   10
At which self time the house seemed all on fire
With dreadful horror of these damnèd fiends.
SECOND SCHOLAR: Well, gentlemen, though Faustus'
    end be such
As every Christian heart laments to think on,
Yet for he was a scholar, once admired   15
For wondrous knowledge in our German schools,
We'll give his mangled limbs due burial;
And all the students clothed in mourning black,
Shall wait upon° his heavy° funeral.
(*Exeunt.*)

EPILOGUE

(*Enter Chorus.*)

CHORUS: Cut is the branch that might have grown
    full straight,
And burnèd is Apollo's laurel bough
That sometime grew within this learnèd man.
Faustus is gone. Regard his hellish fall,
Whose fiendful fortune may exhort the wise   5
Only to wonder at unlawful things,
Whose deepness doth entice such forward wits
To practice more than heavenly power permits.
[*Exit.*]

Terminat hora diem; terminat author opus.°

V, III. 19. **wait upon**: Be present at;   **heavy**: Sorrowful.
Epilogue. 9. *Terminat . . . opus*: The hour ends the day; the
author ends his work.

COMMENTARY

Ernst Honigmann (b. 1927)

FROM *TEN PROBLEMS IN DOCTOR FAUSTUS*   1991

Honigmann, a distinguished critic of Shakespeare and Renaissance drama, raises certain questions about first the "togetherness" of Faustus and Mephistophilis, then the rationality of Faustus. If Faustus is a champion of the rational, why does he behave as he does in the face of a self-confessed devil? Some of Honigmann's observations are dependent on either the A-text or the B-text, the two earliest printings of the play. But whichever text one consults, the problems he sees are intriguing.

How much genuine fellow-feeling is there in this strange relationship? Quite apart from the fact that they both enjoy the same jokes, they address each other affectionately as "my Faustus" and "my Mephostophilis," and Mephostophilis even speaks of "my Faustus" in the latter's absence.

> I'll wing myself and forthwith fly amain
> Unto my Faustus to the great Turk's court.   (B 1179)

If something close to tenderness seems at times to bind them together, let us remember that there is a connection between loving a person and thinking that you own him (or her). True, we note some dramatic irony as well, as when Faustus addresses "my good Mephostophilis" (A 822); and it suits both of them to get on together, so they call each other "sweet Mephostophilis," "sweet friend" and the like (A 696, 1342), to oil the relationship. Yet since they also rage against each other every so often it has the dynamics of a very human relationship — including deception and (on Faustus' part) some self-deception. Mephostophilis, indeed, insofar as he was once an angel and fell with Lucifer, assumes a kind of "older brother" stance in answering Faustus' questions about heaven and hell; he has been through it all himself, he understands Faustus' point of view — does that not beget fellow-feeling? And perhaps even affection? Ben Jonson remembered Faustus and Mephostophilis when he created Volpone and Mosca, including the delicious twist that the servant plans to outwit his master — yet Jonson's rogues strike me as a colder pair, their relationship as largely professional, whereas Faustus and Mephostophilis also interact unprofessionally. Mephostophilis risks losing Faustus' soul by speaking too honestly:

> FAUSTUS: And what are you that live with Lucifer?
> MEPHOST: Unhappy spirits that live with Lucifer,
>   Conspired against our God with Lucifer,
>   And are for ever damned with Lucifer.   (A 314)

We are encouraged to think of Faustus and Mephostophilis as very close — though exactly how close remains a mystery. When they play their pranks on the Pope and others they may even hug or slap each other with delight — or, alternatively, Mephostophilis may signal to us, grimacing, that he has to humour a childish master. The *togetherness* of Faustus and Mephostophilis, in short, has been an issue throughout the play, and probably one that should not be resolved until Faustus' very last utterance, the moment of truth: "ah, Mephostophilis!"

I must not pretend, however, that this central relationship is identical in the two texts — far from it. Two passages in the B text, not found in A, stress the distance between the two principals, the malignancy of Mephostophilis and his delight in destroying Faustus. These passages, both placed just before the end, suggest that in the B-text Mephostophilis savors his victim's death-agony. First the devils ascend from hell to "mark [Faustus] how he doth demean himself." How should he, exclaims Mephostophilis —

> How should he, but in desperate lunacy?
> Fond worldling, now his heart-blood dries with grief,
> His conscience kills it, and his labouring brain
> Begets a world of idle fantasies
> To overreach the devil — but all in vain.
> His store of pleasures must be sauced with pain.   (B 1906)

All fellow-feeling has vanished. And when the scholars depart, leaving Faustus to his final meditations, Mephostophilis turns on him gleefully —

> MEPHOST: Ay, Faustus, now hast thou no hope of heaven,
>   Therefore despair, think only upon hell!
>   For that must be thy mansion, there to dwell.
> FAUSTUS: O thou bewitching fiend, 'twas thy temptation
>   Hath robbed me of eternal happiness.
> MEPHOST: I do confess it, Faustus, and rejoice . . .   (B 1983)

It makes a difference, too, that in the B-text Mephostophilis remains onstage during Faustus' interview with the scholars, and that in the B-text Mephostophilis "brings in" Helen of Troy, the first time she appears — presumably like a ringmaster or auctioneer, pointing out her special attractions. (Not so in the *Faust-book,* where Faustus tells his friends that he will "bring her into your presence personally": ch. 45.) The Mephostophilis of the A-text has a subtler relationship with Faustus, less devilish, more human.

Mephostophilis, I said, risks losing Faustus' soul by speaking too honestly. Here is another "theological" problem, for which I see no easy solution. Many a rationalist has thought, before and after Marlowe, "I am aware of no convincing evidence for the existence of God, therefore I shall behave as if there is no God." Yet is it rational to go on denying God when you are talking to a self-confessed devil? And when the devil appears to be unshakeable in the conviction that God exists?

> FAUSTUS: Was not that Lucifer an angel once?
> MEPHOST: Yes, Faustus, and most dearly loved of God.   (A 309)

Put the case that *one* of the supernatural beings of the Christo-Hebraic tradition incontrovertibly exists — good angel, bad angel, Lucifer — then there is an inherent likelihood that God "exists" as well. And if a hostile witness, such as Mephostophilis, assures Faustus that God exists, how can a rational man turn his back on God? make war on the Omnipotent? and choose Hell instead? —

FAUSTUS: Come, I think hell's a fable.
MEPHOST: Ay, think so still, till experience change thy mind!   (A 574)

Could it be that Faustus is a very confused doctor of divinity? or is Marlowe a very confused dramatist? or am I guilty now of trying to "over-explain"?

Some critics have argued that Faustus deteriorates intellectually in the course of the play, like Milton's Satan, as witnessed by his childish activities in the middle scenes. Alternatively, Chorus' opening statement

So much he profits in divinity
That shortly he was graced with doctor's name,
Excelling all, and sweetly can dispute . . .   (B 16)

may refer to the past, not to Faustus as he now is —

For, falling to a devilish exercise
And glutted now with learning's golden gifts
He surfeits upon cursed necromancy.   (B 23)

Theologians sometimes talk of a "fall before the Fall" (Milton appears to allude to this in Eve's dream before the Fall). Marlowe's Faustus, perhaps, should be seen as fallen, or devil-possessed, before he signs his formal pact — therefore intellectually impaired from the play's beginning. I prefer this explanation because he behaves irrationally from the beginning, already believing in spirits, and Lucifer, but not in God. Marlowe allows us to think of Faustus as something other than the ideal theologian by inserting implicit stage directions in the speech in his study. "Bid *on kai me on* farewell; Galen, come," "Physic farewell; where is Justinian?", "divinity, adieu" — does Faustus simply pick up one book after another? or should he hurl them away, frustrated, with each sarcastic "adieu" and "farewell"? A frightening impulsiveness, breaking out during this first meditation, could help to reconcile us to Faustus' perplexing irrationality. The *Faustbook* offered this possibility: Dr. Faustus "fell into such fantasies and deep cogitations, that . . . sometime he would *throw the Scripture from him*" (Ch. I).

William Shakespeare

Despite the fact that Shakespeare wrote some thirty-seven plays, owned part of his theatrical company, acted in plays, and retired a relatively wealthy man in the city of his birth, there is much we do not know about him. His father was a glovemaker with pretensions to being a gentleman; Shakespeare himself had his coat of arms placed on his home, New Place, purchased in part because it was one of the grandest buildings in Stratford. Church records indicate that he was born in April 1564 and died in April 1616, after having been retired from the stage for two or three years. We know that he married Anne Hathaway in 1582, when he was eighteen and she twenty-six; that he had a daughter Susanna and twins, Judith and Hamnet; and that Hamnet, his only son, died at age eleven. He has no direct descendants today.

We know very little about his education. We assume that he went to the local grammar school, since as the son of a burgess he was eligible to attend for free. If he did so, he would have received a very strong education based on rhetoric, logic, and classical literature. He would have been exposed to the comedies of Plautus, the tragedies of Seneca, and the poetry of Virgil, Ovid, and a host of other, lesser writers.

A rumor has persisted that he spent some time as a Latin teacher. No evidence exists to suggest that Shakespeare went to a university, although his general learning and knowledge are so extraordinary and broad that generations of scholars have assumed that he may have also gone to the Inns of Court to study law. This cannot be proved, though; thus, some people claim that another person, with considerable university education, must have written his plays. However, no one in the Elizabethan theater had an education of the sort often proposed for Shakespeare. Marlowe and Ben Jonson were the most learned of Elizabethan playwrights, but their work is quite different in character and feeling from that of Shakespeare.

One recent theory about Shakespeare's early years suggests that before going to London to work in theater he belonged to a wandering company of actors much like those who appear in *Hamlet*. It is an ingenious theory and has much to recommend it, among which is explaining how Shakespeare could take the spotlight so quickly as to arouse the anger of more experienced London writers.

Shakespeare did not begin his career writing for the stage but, in the more conventional approach for the age, as a poet. He sought the support of an aristocratic patron, the earl of Southampton. Like many wealthy and polished young courtiers, Southampton felt it a pleasant ornament to sponsor a poet whose works would be dedicated to him. Shakespeare wrote sonnets apparently with Southampton in mind, and, hoping for preferment, the long narrative poems *Venus and Adonis, The Rape of Lucrece,* and *The Phoenix and the Turtle.* However, Southampton eventually decided to become the patron of another poet, John Florio, an Italian who had translated Michel de Montaigne's *Essays.*

Shakespeare's response was to turn to the stage. His first plays were a considerable success: *King Henry VI* in three parts — three full-length plays. Satisfying London's taste for plays that told the history of England's tangled political past, Shakespeare won considerable renown with a lengthy series of plays ranging from *Richard II* through the two parts of *King Henry IV* to *Henry V.* Audiences were delighted; competing playwrights envied him his triumphs. Francis Meres's famous book of the period, *Palladis Tamia: Wit's Treasury,* cites Shakespeare as modern Plautus and Seneca, the best in both comedy and tragedy. Meres says that by 1598 Shakespeare was known for a dozen plays. That his success was firm by this time is demonstrated by his having purchased his large house, New Place, in Stratford in 1597. He could not have done this without financial security.

In the next few years Shakespeare made a number of interesting purchases of property in Stratford; he also made deals with his own theater company to secure the rights to perform in London. These arrangements produced legal records that give us some of the clearest information we have concerning Shakespeare's activities during this period. His company was called the Lord Chamberlain's Men while Queen Elizabeth was alive but was renamed the King's Men by King James in the spring of 1603, less than two months after Elizabeth died. As the King's Men, Shakespeare's company had considerable power and success. Its audience sometimes included King James, as in the first performance of *Macbeth.*

Shakespeare was successful as a writer of histories, comedies, and tragedies. He also wrote in another genre, known as romance. These plays share elements with both comedies and tragedies, and they often depend on supernatural or improbable elements. *Cymbeline, The Winter's Tale,* and *The Tempest* are the best known of Shakespeare's romances. They are late works and have a fascinating complexity.

When Shakespeare died on April 23, 1616, he was buried as a gentleman in the church in which he had been baptized in Stratford-upon-Avon. His will left most of his money and possessions to his two daughters, Judith and Susanna.

A Midsummer Night's Dream

A *Midsummer Night's Dream* (1595–1596) is an early comedy and one of Shakespeare's most beloved works. It is also one of his most imaginative plays, introducing us to the world of fairies and the realm of dreams. Romantic painters, such as Fuseli, have long found in this play a rich store of images that stretch far beyond the limits of the real world of everyday experience.

For Shakespeare the fun of the play is in showing how the world of the fairies intersects with the world of real people, and we can interpret the play as a hint of what would happen if the world of dreams were to cross the world of real experience. The fact that these worlds are more alike than they are different gives Shakespeare the comic basis on which to work. He also finds some new and amusing ways to interpret the device of mistaken identities.

The play is set in Athens, with Duke Theseus about to wed Hippolyta, the queen of the Amazons. Helena and Hermia are young women in love with Demetrius and Lysander, respectively. Demetrius, however, wants to marry Hermia and has the blessing of Hermia's father. Hermia's refusal to follow her father's wishes drives her into the woods, where she is followed by both young men and Helena, who does not want to lose Demetrius.

The four young people find themselves in the world of the fairies, although the humans cannot see the fairies. Puck, an impish sprite, is ordered by Oberon, king of the fairies, to put the juice of a certain flower in Demetrius's eyes so that he will fall in love with Helena. When Puck puts it in Lysander's eyes instead, the plot backfires: Lysander is suddenly in love with Helena, and Hermia is confounded. Oberon has Puck place the same juice in the eyes of Titania, the queen of the fairies, causing her to fall in love with the first creature she sees when she awakes.

That creature is Bottom, the "rude mechanical" (ignorant artisan) whose head has been transformed into an ass's head. Such a trick opens up possibilities for wonderful comic elements. The richness of the illusions that operate onstage constantly draws us to the question of how we ever can know the truth of our own experiences, especially when some of them are dreams whose imaginative power is occasionally overwhelming.

Shakespeare plays here with some of the Aristotelian conventions of the drama, especially Aristotle's view that drama imitates life. One of the great comic devices in *A Midsummer Night's Dream* is the play within a play that Bottom, Quince, Snug, Flute, and Starveling are to put on before Theseus and Hippolyta. They tell the story of Pyramus and Thisby, lovers who lose each other because they misinterpret signs. It is "Merry and tragical! Tedious and brief!" But it is also a wonderful parody of what playwrights — including Shakespeare — often do when operating in the Aristotelian mode. The aim of the play is realism, yet the players are naive and inexperienced in drama; they do their best constantly to remind the audience that it is only a play.

The comic ineptness of the rude mechanicals' play needs no disclaimers of this sort, and the immediate audience — Theseus, Hippolyta, Demetrius, Helena, Lysander, and Hermia — is amused by the ardor of the players. The audience in the theater is also mightily amused at the antics of the mechanicals, which on the surface are simply funny and a wonderful pastiche of artless playacting.

Beneath the surface, something more serious is going on. Shakespeare is commenting on the entire function of drama in our lives. He constantly reminds us in this play that we are watching an illusion, even an illusion within an illusion, but he also convinces us that illusions teach us a great deal about reality. The real-world setting of *A Midsummer Night's Dream* — Athens — is quite improbable. The mechanicals all have obviously English names and are out of place in an Athenian pastoral setting. The play on the level of Athens is pure fantasy, with even more fantastic goings-on at the level of the fairy world. But fantasy nourishes us. It helps us interpret our own experiences by permitting us to distance ourselves from them and reflect on how they affect others, one of the deepest functions of drama.

As in most comedies, everything turns out exceptionally well. A multiple marriage, one of the delightful conventions of many comedies, ends the drama, and virtually everyone receives what she or he wanted. We are left with a sense of satisfaction because we, too, get our wish about how things should turn out. Puck, one of the greatest of Shakespeare's characters, turns out to be sympathetic and human in his feelings about people. And Bottom, a clown whose origins are certainly Greek and Roman, endears us to him with his generosity and caring toward others. Shakespeare promotes a remarkably warm view of humanity in this play, leaving us with a sense of delight and a glow that is rare even in comedy.

A Midsummer Night's Dream in Performance

A Midsummer Night's Dream has attracted many great directors in modern times, although in the late seventeenth and eighteenth centuries the play was adapted essentially as a vehicle for presenting the world of the fairies. It even became an opera in 1692. Ludwig Tieck engaged Mendelssohn to write incidental music for the play in Berlin in 1843; their production was for many years the most influential post-Shakespearean adaptation. Beerbohm Tree's 1900 production in London's Savoy Theatre included real rabbits and many other highly realistic details; eventually it played to more than 220,000 patrons. After numerous adaptations it was produced by Granville Barker in London from 1912 to 1914 in its original text, and in New York in 1915. The Old Vic's 1954 production was so lavish that it was staged at the Metropolitan Opera House in New York. Peter Brook played down the fairies and explored the play as a study of love. His 1970 production is well remembered for his having placed Oberon and Puck on trapezes set against a stark white background. He also used some costumes and other elements of *commedia dell'arte* to spark the comedy. (See Barnes's review of the Brook production on pages 475–76.) The American Repertory Theatre's 1986 Boston production (see photos on pages 338–39) reflects the approach to staging that the Royal Shakespeare Company has taken in recent years. The themes of love and transformation inspire the players in a way that shows off the brilliance of the play.

William Shakespeare (1564–1616)
A MIDSUMMER NIGHT'S DREAM   *c. 1596*

[Dramatis Personae

THESEUS, *Duke of Athens*
EGEUS, *father to Hermia*
LYSANDER, ⎱ *in love with Hermia*
DEMETRIUS, ⎰
PHILOSTRATE, *Master of the Revels to Theseus*

QUINCE, *a carpenter*
SNUG, *a joiner*
BOTTOM, *a weaver*
FLUTE, *a bellows-mender*
SNOUT, *a tinker*
STARVELING, *a tailor*

HIPPOLYTA, *Queen of the Amazons, betrothed to Theseus*
HERMIA, *daughter to Egeus, in love with Lysander*
HELENA, *in love with Demetrius*

OBERON, *King of the Fairies*
TITANIA, *Queen of the Fairies*
PUCK, *or Robin Goodfellow*
PEASEBLOSSOM, ⎱
COBWEB,   ⎟
MOTH,   ⎬ *fairies*
MUSTARDSEED,   ⎰
Other FAIRIES *attending their king and queen*
ATTENDANTS *on Theseus and Hippolyta*

Scene: *Athens, and a wood near it.*]

{*ACT I • Scene 1*}°

(*Enter Theseus, Hippolyta,* [*Philostrate,*] *with others.*)

THESEUS: Now, fair Hippolyta, our nuptial hour
Draws on apace. Four happy days bring in
Another moon; but, O, methinks, how slow
This old moon wanes! She lingers° my desires
Like to a step-dame° or a dowager°   5
Long withering out a young man's revenue.

Note: The text of *A Midsummer Night's Dream* has come down to us in different versions — such as the first quarto, the second quarto, and the first Folio. The copy of the text used here is largely drawn from the first quarto. Passages enclosed in square brackets are taken from one of the other versions.

I, I. Location: The palace of Theseus.   **4. lingers:** Lengthens, protects.   **5. step-dame:** Stepmother.   **dowager:** Widow with a jointure or dower [an estate or title from her deceased husband].

Cannot pursue us. If thou lovest me, then,
Steal forth thy father's house tomorrow night;
165 And in the wood, a league without the town,
Where I did meet thee once with Helena
To do observance to a morn of May,°
There will I stay for thee.
HERMIA: My good Lysander!
I swear to thee, by Cupid's strongest bow,
170 By his best arrow with the golden head,°
By the simplicity° of Venus' doves,°
By that which knitteth souls and prospers loves,
And by that fire which burn'd the Carthage
      queen,
When the false Troyan° under sail was seen,
175 By all the vows that ever men have broke,
In number more than ever women spoke,
In that same place thou hast appointed me
Tomorrow truly will I meet with thee.
LYSANDER: Keep promise, love. Look, here comes
      Helena.

(*Enter Helena.*)

180 HERMIA: God speed fair° Helena, whither away?
HELENA: Call you me fair? That fair again unsay.
      Demetrius loves your fair.° O happy fair!°
      Your eyes are lodestars,° and your tongue's sweet
         air°
      More tuneable° than lark to shepherd's ear
      When wheat is green, when hawthorn buds
185   appear.
      Sickness is catching. O, were favor° so,
      Yours would I catch, fair Hermia, ere I go;
      My ear should catch your voice, my eye your
         eye,
      My tongue should catch your tongue's sweet
         melody.
190 Were the world mine, Demetrius being bated,°
      The rest I'd give to be to you translated.°
      O, teach me how you look, and with what art
      You sway the motion° of Demetrius' heart.

HERMIA: I frown upon him, yet he loves me still.
HELENA: O that your frowns would teach my smiles
      such skill!   195
HERMIA: I give him curses, yet he gives me love.
HELENA: O that my prayers could such affection°
      move!°
HERMIA: The more I hate, the more he follows me.
HELENA: The more I love, the more he hateth me.
HERMIA: His folly, Helena, is no fault of mine.   200
HELENA: None, but your beauty. Would that fault
      were mine!
HERMIA: Take comfort. He no more shall see my
      face.
      Lysander and myself will fly this place.
      Before the time I did Lysander see,
      Seem'd Athens as a paradise to me.   205
      O, then, what graces in my love do dwell,
      That he hath turn'd a heaven unto a hell!
LYSANDER: Helen, to you our minds we will unfold.
      Tomorrow night, when Phoebe° doth behold
      Her silver visage in the wat'ry glass,°   210
      Decking with liquid pearl the bladed grass,
      A time that lovers' flights doth still° conceal,
      Through Athens' gates have we devis'd to steal.
HERMIA: And in the wood, where often you and I
      Upon faint° primrose beds were wont to lie,   215
      Emptying our bosoms of their counsel° sweet,
      There my Lysander and myself shall meet;
      And thence from Athens turn away our eyes,
      To seek new friends and stranger companies.
      Farewell, sweet playfellow. Pray thou for us,   220
      And good luck grant thee thy Demetrius!
      Keep word, Lysander. We must starve our sight
      From lovers' food till morrow deep midnight.
LYSANDER: I will, my Hermia.   (*Exit Hermia.*)
                                    Helena, adieu.
      As you on him, Demetrius dote on you!   225
                                    (*Exit Lysander.*)
HELENA: How happy some o'er other some can be!°
      Through Athens I am thought as fair as she.
      But what of that? Demetrius thinks not so;
      He will not know what all but he do know.
      And as he errs, doting on Hermia's eyes,   230
      So I, admiring of° his qualities.
      Things base and vile, holding no quantity,°
      Love can transpose to form and dignity.
      Love looks not with the eyes, but with the mind,
      And therefore is wing'd Cupid painted blind.   235

---

167. **do . . . May:** Perform the ceremonies of May Day.
170. **best arrow . . . golden head:** Cupid's best gold-pointed arrows were supposed to induce love, his blunt leaden arrows aversion.   171. **simplicity:** Innocence. **doves:** Those that drew Venus's chariot.   173–74. **by that fire . . . false Troyan:** Dido, Queen of Carthage, immolated herself on a funeral pyre after having been deserted by the Trojan hero Aeneas.   180. **fair:** Fair-complexioned (generally regarded by the Elizabethans as more beautiful than dark-complexioned).   182. **your fair:** Your beauty (even though Hermia is dark-complexioned). **happy fair:** Lucky fair one.   183. **lodestars:** Guiding stars. **air:** Music.   184. **tuneable:** Tuneful, melodious.   186. **favor:** Appearance, looks.   190. **bated:** Excepted.   191. **translated:** Transformed.   193. **motion:** Impulse.

---

197. **affection:** Passion. **move:** Arouse.   209. **Phoebe:** Diana, the moon.   210. **glass:** Mirror.   212. **still:** Always.   215. **faint:** Pale.   216. **counsel:** Secret thought.   226. **o'er . . . can be:** Can be in comparison to some others.   231. **admiring of:** Wondering at.   232. **holding no quantity:** Unsubstantial, unshapely.

Nor hath Love's mind of any judgment taste;°
Wings, and no eyes, figure° unheedy haste.
And therefore is Love said to be a child,
Because in choice he is so oft beguil'd.
240   As waggish boys in game° themselves forswear,
So the boy Love is perjur'd everywhere.
For ere Demetrius look'd on Hermia's eyne,°
He hail'd down oaths that he was only mine;
And when this hail some heat from Hermia felt,
245   So he dissolv'd, and show'rs of oaths did melt.
I will go tell him of fair Hermia's flight.
Then to the wood will he tomorrow night
Pursue her; and for this intelligence°
If I have thanks, it is a dear° expense.°
250   But herein mean I to enrich my pain,
To have his sight thither and back again.   (*Exit.*)

{*Scene II*}°

(*Enter Quince the Carpenter, and Snug the Joiner, and
Bottom the Weaver, and Flute the Bellows-Mender,
and Snout the Tinker, and Starveling the Tailor.*)

QUINCE: Is all our company here?
BOTTOM: You were best to call them generally,° man
by man, according to the scrip.°
QUINCE: Here is the scroll of every man's name which
5   is thought fit, through all Athens, to play in our interlude before the Duke and the Duchess on his
wedding-day at night.
BOTTOM: First, good Peter Quince, say what the play
treats on, then read the names of the actors, and so
10   grow to° a point.
QUINCE: Marry,° our play is "The most lamentable
comedy and most cruel death of Pyramus and
Thisby."
BOTTOM: A very good piece of work, I assure you, and
15   a merry. Now, good Peter Quince, call forth your
actors by the scroll. Masters, spread yourselves.
QUINCE: Answer as I call you. Nick Bottom, the weaver.
BOTTOM: Ready. Name what part I am for, and proceed.
QUINCE: You, Nick Bottom, are set down for Pyramus.
20   BOTTOM: What is Pyramus? A lover, or a tyrant?
QUINCE: A lover, that kills himself most gallant for
love.

BOTTOM: That will ask some tears in the true per-
forming of it. If I do it, let the audience look to
their eyes. I will move storms; I will condole° in   25
some measure. To the rest — yet my chief humor°
is for a tyrant. I could play Ercles° rarely, or a part
to tear a cat° in, to make all split.°
"The raging rocks
And shivering shocks   30
Shall break the locks
    Of prison gates;
And Phibbus' car°
Shall shine from far
And make and mar   35
    The foolish Fates."
This was lofty! Now name the rest of the players.
This is Ercles' vein, a tyrant's vein. A lover is more
condoling.
QUINCE: Francis Flute, the bellows-mender.   40
FLUTE: Here, Peter Quince.
QUINCE: Flute, you must take Thisby on you.
FLUTE: What is Thisby? A wand'ring knight?
QUINCE: It is the lady that Pyramus must love.
FLUTE: Nay, faith, let not me play a woman. I have a   45
beard coming.
QUINCE: That's all one.° You shall play it in a mask,
and you may speak as small° as you will.
BOTTOM: An° I may hide my face, let me play Thisby
too. I'll speak in a monstrous little voice, "Thisne,   50
Thisne!" "Ah Pyramus, my lover dear! Thy Thisby
dear, and lady dear!"
QUINCE: No, no; you must play Pyramus; and, Flute,
you Thisby.
BOTTOM: Well, proceed.   55
QUINCE: Robin Starveling, the tailor.
STARVELING: Here, Peter Quince.
QUINCE: Robin Starveling, you must play Thisby's
mother. Tom Snout, the tinker.
SNOUT: Here, Peter Quince.   60
QUINCE: You, Pyramus' father; myself, Thisby's fa-
ther; Snug, the joiner, you, the lion's part; and I
hope here is a play fitted.
SNUG: Have you the lion's part written? Pray you, if it
be, give it me, for I am slow of study.   65
QUINCE: You may do it extempore, for it is nothing
but roaring.
BOTTOM: Let me play the lion too. I will roar that I
will do any man's heart good to hear me. I will

---

236. Nor . . . taste: Nor has Love, which dwells in the fancy
or imagination, any *taste* or least bit of judgment or reason.
237. figure: Are a symbol of.   **240. game:** Sport, jest.
242. eyne: Eyes (old form of plural).   **248. intelligence:** Information.   **249. dear:** Costly.   **a dear expense:** A trouble
worth taking.   **I, II. Location:** Athens. Quince's house(?).
2. generally: Bottom's blunder for *individually.*   **3. scrip:**
Script, written list.   **10. grow to:** Come to.   **11. Marry:** A
mild oath, originally the name of the Virgin Mary.

25. condole: Lament, arouse pity.   **26. humor:** Inclination,
whim.   **27. Ercles:** Hercules (the tradition of ranting came
from Seneca's *Hercules Furens*).   **tear a cat:** Rant.
28. make all split: Cause a stir, bring the house down.
33. Phibbus' car: Phoebus's, the sun-god's, chariot.
47. That's all one: It makes no difference.   **48. small:**
High-pitched.   **49. An:** If.

70   roar that I will make the Duke say, "Let him roar
       again, let him roar again."
    QUINCE: An you should do it too terribly, you would
       fright the Duchess and the ladies, that they would
       shriek; and that were enough to hang us all.
75   ALL: That would hang us, every mother's son.
    BOTTOM: I grant you, friends, if you should fright the
       ladies out of their wits, they would have no more
       discretion but to hang us; but I will aggravate° my
       voice so that I will roar you° as gently as any
80   sucking dove; I will roar you an 'twere any
       nightingale.
    QUINCE: You can play no part but Pyramus; for Pyra-
       mus is a sweet-fac'd man, a proper° man as one shall
       see in a summer's day, a most lovely gentleman-like
85   man. Therefore you must needs play Pyramus.
    BOTTOM: Well, I will undertake it. What beard were I
       best to play it in?
    QUINCE: Why, what you will.
    BOTTOM: I will discharge° it in either your° straw-
90   color beard, your orange-tawny beard, your purple-
       in-grain° beard, or your French-crown-color°
       beard, your perfect yellow.
    QUINCE: Some of your French crowns° have no hair
       at all, and then you will play barefac'd. But, mas-
95   ters, here are your parts. [*He distributes parts.*]
       And I am to entreat you, request you, and desire
       you, to con° them by tomorrow night; and meet
       me in the palace wood, a mile without the town,
       by moonlight. There will we rehearse; for if we
100   meet in the city, we shall be dogg'd with company,
       and our devices° known. In the meantime I will
       draw a bill° of properties, such as our play wants.
       I pray you, fail me not.
    BOTTOM: We will meet, and there we may rehearse
105   most obscenely° and courageously. Take pains, be
       perfect;° adieu.
    QUINCE: At the Duke's oak we meet.
    BOTTOM: Enough. Hold, or cut bow-strings.°
                            (*Exeunt.*)

{ACT II • *Scene I*}°

(*Enter a Fairy at one door, and Robin Goodfellow
[Puck] at another.*)

PUCK: How now, spirit! Whither wander you?
FAIRY: Over hill, over dale,
    Thorough° bush, thorough brier,
    Over park, over pale,°
    Thorough flood, thorough fire,   5
    I do wander every where,
    Swifter than the moon's sphere;
    And I serve the Fairy Queen,
    To dew her orbs° upon the green.
    The cowslips tall her pensioners° be.   10
    In their gold coats spots you see;
    Those be rubies, fairy favors,°
    In those freckles live their savors.°
    I must go seek some dewdrops here
    And hang a pearl in every cowslip's ear.   15
    Farewell, thou lob° of spirits; I'll be gone.
    Our Queen and all her elves come here anon.°
PUCK: The King doth keep his revels here tonight.
    Take heed the Queen come not within his sight.
    For Oberon is passing fell° and wrath,°   20
    Because that she as her attendant hath
    A lovely boy, stolen from an Indian king;
    She never had so sweet a changeling.°
    And jealous Oberon would have the child
    Knight of his train, to trace° the forests wild.   25
    But she perforce° withholds the loved boy,
    Crowns him with flowers and makes him all her
       joy
    And now they never meet in grove or green,
    By fountain° clear, or spangled starlight sheen,
    But they do square,° that all their elves for fear   30
    Creep into acorn-cups and hide them there.
FAIRY: Either I mistake your shape and making
      quite,
    Or else you are that shrewd° and knavish sprite°
    Call'd Robin Goodfellow. Are not you he
    That frights the maidens of the villagery,   35
    Skim milk, and sometimes labor in the quern,°
    And bootless° make the breathless huswife churn,

---

78. aggravate: Bottom's blunder for *diminish*.   **79. roar
you:** Roar for you.   **83. proper:** Handsome.   **89. discharge:** Perform.   **your:** I.e., you know the kind I mean.
90–91. purple-in-grain: Dyed a very deep red (from *grain*,
the name applied to the dried insect used to make the dye).
91. French-crown-color: Color of a French crown, a gold
coin.   **93. crowns:** Heads bald from syphilis, the "French
disease."   **97. con:** Learn by heart.   **100. devices:** Plans.
101. bill: List.   **105. obscenely:** An unintentionally funny
blunder, whatever Bottom meant to say.   **106. perfect:** Let-
ter-perfect in memorizing your parts.   **108. Hold . . . bow-
strings:** An archer's expression not definitely explained, but
probably meaning here "keep your promises, or give up the
play."

II, 1. Location: A wood near Athens.   **3. Thorough:**
Through.   **4. pale:** Enclosure.   **9. orbs:** Circles, i.e., fairy
rings.   **10. pensioners:** Retainers, members of the royal
bodyguard.   **12. favors:** Love tokens.   **13. savors:** Sweet
smells.   **16. lob:** Country bumpkin.   **17. anon:** At once.
20. passing fell: Exceedingly angry.   **wrath:** Wrathful.
23. changeling: Child exchanged for another by the fairies.
25. trace: Range through.   **26. perforce:** Forcibly.
29. fountain: Spring.   **30. square:** Quarrel.   **33. shrewd:**
Mischievous.   **sprite:** Spirit.   **36. quern:** Handmill.
37. bootless: In vain.

And sometime make the drink to bear no barm,°
Mislead night-wanderers, laughing at their harm?
40   Those that Hobgoblin call you and sweet Puck,
You do their work, and they shall have good
         luck.
Are you not he?
PUCK: Thou speakest aright;
I am that merry wanderer of the night.
I jest to Oberon and make him smile
45   When I a fat and bean-fed horse beguile,
Neighing in likeness of a filly foal;
And sometime lurk I in a gossip's° bowl,
In very likeness of a roasted crab,°
And when she drinks, against her lips I bob
50   And on her withered dewlap° pour the ale.
The wisest aunt,° telling the saddest° tale,
Sometime for three-foot stool mistaketh me;
Then slip I from her bum, down topples she,
And "tailor"° cries, and falls into a cough;
And then the whole quire° hold their hips and
55   laugh,
And waxen° in their mirth and neeze° and swear
A merrier hour was never wasted there.
But, room, fairy! Here comes Oberon.
FAIRY: And here my mistress. Would that he were
         gone!

(Enter [Oberon] the King of Fairies at one door, with
his train; and [Titania] the Queen at another, with
hers.)

60   OBERON: Ill met by moonlight, proud Titania.
TITANIA: What, jealous Oberon? Fairies, skip hence.
I have forsworn his bed and company.
OBERON: Tarry, rash wanton.° Am not I thy lord?
TITANIA: Then I must be thy lady; but I know
65   When thou hast stolen away from fairy land,
And in the shape of Corin° sat all day,
Playing on pipes of corn° and versing love
To amorous Phillida.° Why art thou here,
Come from the farthest steep° of India,
70   But that, forsooth, the bouncing Amazon,
Your buskin'd° mistress and your warrior love,
To Theseus must be wedded, and you come
To give their bed joy and prosperity.
OBERON: How canst thou thus for shame, Titania,

Glance at my credit with Hippolyta,°   75
Knowing I know thy love to Theseus?
Didst not thou lead him through the glimmering
         night
From Perigenia,° whom he ravished?
And make him with fair Aegles° break his faith,
With Ariadne° and Antiopa?°   80
TITANIA: These are the forgeries of jealousy;
And never, since the middle summer's spring,°
Met we on hill, in dale, forest, or mead,
By paved° fountain or by rushy° brook,
Or in° the beached margent° of the sea,   85
To dance our ringlets° to the whistling wind,
But with thy brawls thou hast disturb'd our
         sport.
Therefore the winds, piping to us in vain,
As in revenge, have suck'd up from the sea
Contagious° fogs; which falling in the land   90
Hath every pelting° river made so proud
That they have overborne their continents.°
The ox hath therefore stretch'd his yoke in vain,
The ploughman lost his sweat, and the green
         corn°
Hath rotted ere his youth attain'd a beard;   95
The fold° stands empty in the drowned field,
And crows are fatted with the murrion° flock;
The nine men's morris° is fill'd up with mud,
And the quaint mazes° in the wanton° green
For lack of tread are undistinguishable.   100
The human mortals want° their winter° here;

75. Glance . . . Hippolyta: Make insinuations about my favored relationship with Hippolyta. 78. Perigenia:
Perigouna, one of Theseus's conquests. (This and the following women are named in Thomas North's translation of
Plutarch's Life of Theseus.) 79. Aegles: Aegle, for whom
Theseus deserted Ariadne according to some accounts.
80. Ariadne: The daughter of Minos, King of Crete, who
helped Theseus escape the labyrinth after killing the Mino-
taur; later she was abandoned by Theseus. Antiopa:
Queen of the Amazons and wife of Theseus; elsewhere identified with Hippolyta, but here thought of as a separate
woman. 82. middle summer's spring: Beginning of midsummer. 84. paved: With pebbled bottom. rushy: Bor-
dered with rushes. 85. in: On. margent: edge, border.
86. ringlets: Dances in a ring. (See orbs in line 9.)
90. Contagious: Noxious. 91. pelting: Paltry; or striking,
moving forcefully. 92. continents: Banks that contain
them. 94. corn: Grain of any kind. 96. fold: Pen for
sheep or cattle. 97. murrion: Having died of the murrain,
plague. 98. nine men's morris: Portion of the village green
marked out in a square for a game played with nine pebbles
or pegs. 99. quaint mazes: Intricate paths marked out
on the village green to be followed rapidly on foot as a
kind of contest. wanton: Luxuriant. 101. want: Lack.
winter: Regular winter season; or proper observances of
winter, such as the hymn or carol in the next line (?).

38. barm: Yeast, head on the ale. 47. gossip's: Old
woman's. 48. crab: Crab apple. 50. dewlap: Loose skin
on neck. 51. aunt: Old woman. saddest: Most serious.
54. tailor: Possibly because she ends up sitting cross-legged
on the floor, looking like a tailor. 55. quire: company.
56. waxen: Increase. neeze: Sneeze. 63. wanton: Headstrong creature. 66, 68. Corin, Phillida: Conventional
names of pastoral lovers. 67. corn: Here, oat stalks.
69. steep: Mountain range. 71. buskin'd: Wearing half-
boots called buskins.

No night is now with hymn or carol bless'd.
Therefore° the moon, the governess of floods,
Pale in her anger, washes all the air,
105   That rheumatic diseases° do abound.
And thorough this distemperature° we see
The seasons alter: hoary-headed frosts
Fall in the fresh lap of the crimson rose,
And on old Hiems'° thin and icy crown
110   An odorous chaplet of sweet summer buds
Is, as in mockery, set. The spring, the summer,
The childing° autumn, angry winter, change
Their wonted liveries,° and the mazed° world,
By their increase,° now knows not which is
          which.
115   And this same progeny of evils comes
From our debate,° from our dissension;
We are their parents and original.°
OBERON: Do you amend it then; it lies in you.
Why should Titania cross her Oberon?
120   I do but beg a little changeling boy,
To be my henchman.°
TITANIA: Set your heart at rest.
The fairy land buys not the child of me.
His mother was a vot'ress° of my order,
And, in the spiced Indian air, by night,
125   Full often hath she gossip'd by my side,
And sat with me on Neptune's yellow sands,
Marking th' embarked traders° on the flood,°
When we have laugh'd to see the sails conceive
And grow big-bellied with the wanton° wind;
130   Which she, with pretty and with swimming gait,
Following — her womb then rich with my young
          squire —
Would imitate, and sail upon the land
To fetch me trifles, and return again,
As from a voyage, rich with merchandise.
135   But she, being mortal, of that boy did die;
And for her sake do I rear up her boy,
And for her sake I will not part with him.
OBERON: How long within this wood intend you
          stay?
TITANIA: Perchance till after Theseus' wedding day.
140   If you will patiently dance in our round°
And see our moonlight revels, go with us;

If not, shun me, and I will spare° your haunts.
OBERON: Give me that boy, and I will go with thee.
TITANIA: Not for thy fairy kingdom. Fairies, away!
We shall chide downright, if I longer stay.   145
          (*Exeunt* [*Titania with her train*].)
OBERON: Well, go thy way. Thou shalt not from°
          this grove
Till I torment thee for this injury.
My gentle Puck, come hither. Thou rememb'rest
Since° once I sat upon a promontory,
And heard a mermaid on a dolphin's back   150
Uttering such dulcet and harmonious breath°
That the rude sea grew civil at her song
And certain stars shot madly from their spheres,
To hear the sea-maid's music.
PUCK: I remember.
OBERON: That very time I saw, but thou couldst
          not,   155
Flying between the cold moon and the earth,
Cupid all° arm'd. A certain aim he took
At a fair vestal° throned by the west,
And loos'd his love-shaft smartly from his bow,
As° it should pierce a hundred thousand hearts;   160
But I might° see young Cupid's fiery shaft
Quench'd in the chaste beams of the wat'ry
          moon,
And the imperial vot'ress passed on,
In maiden meditation, fancy-free.°
Yet mark'd I where the bolt of Cupid fell: 165
It fell upon a little western flower,
Before milk-white, now purple with love's
          wound,
And maidens call it love-in-idleness.°
Fetch me that flow'r; the herb I showed thee
          once.
The juice of it on sleeping eyelids laid   170
Will make or man or° woman madly dote
Upon the next live creature that it sees.
Fetch me this herb, and be thou here again
Ere the leviathan° can swim a league.
PUCK: I'll put a girdle round about the earth   175
In forty° minutes.   [*Exit.*]
OBERON: Having once this juice,
I'll watch Titania when she is asleep,

---

103. **Therefore:** I.e., as a result of our quarrel.
105. **rheumatic diseases:** Colds, flu, and other respiratory infections.   106. **distemperature:** Disturbance in nature.
109. **Hiems:** The winter god.   112. **childing:** Fruitful, pregnant.   113. **wonted liveries:** Usual apparel.   **mazed:** Bewildered.   114. **their increase:** Their yield, what they produce.   116. **debate:** Quarrel.   117. **original:** Origin.
121. **henchman:** Attendant, page.   123. **vot'ress:** Female votary; devotee, worshiper.   127. **traders:** Trading vessels.
flood: Flood tide.   129. **wanton:** Sportive.   140. **round:** Circular dance.

142. **spare:** Shun.   146. **from:** Go from.   149. **Since:** When.   151. **breath:** Voice, song.   157. **all:** Fully.   158. **vestal:** Vestal virgin (contains a complimentary allusion to Queen Elizabeth as a votaress of Diana and probably refers to an actual entertainment in her honor at Elvetham in 1591).   160. **As:** As if.   161. **might:** Could.   164. **fancy-free:** Free of love's spell.   168. **love-in-idleness:** Pansy, heartsease.   171. **or . . . or:** Either . . . or.   174. **leviathan:** Sea monster, whale.   176. **forty:** Used indefinitely.

And drop the liquor of it in her eyes.
The next thing then she waking looks upon,
180   Be it on lion, bear, or wolf, or bull,
On meddling monkey, or on busy ape,
She shall pursue it with the soul of love.
And ere I take this charm from off her sight,
As I can take it with another herb,
185   I'll make her render up her page to me.
But who comes here? I am invisible,
And I will overhear their conference.

(*Enter Demetrius, Helena following him.*)

DEMETRIUS: I love thee not, therefore pursue me
        not.
Where is Lysander and fair Hermia?
190   The one I'll slay, the other slayeth me.
Thou told'st me they were stol'n unto this wood;
And here am I, and wode° within this wood,
Because I cannot meet my Hermia.
Hence, get thee gone, and follow me no more.
195 HELENA: You draw me, you hard-hearted adamant;°
But yet you draw not iron, for my heart
Is true as steel. Leave° you your power to draw,
And I shall have no power to follow you.
DEMETRIUS: Do I entice you? Do I speak you fair?°
200   Or, rather, do I not in plainest truth
Tell you I do not nor I cannot love you?
HELENA: And even for that do I love you the more.
I am your spaniel; and, Demetrius,
The more you beat me, I will fawn on you.
205   Use me but as your spaniel, spurn me, strike me,
Neglect me, lose me; only give me leave,
Unworthy as I am, to follow you.
What worser place can I beg in your love —
And yet a place of high respect with me —
210   Than to be used as you use your dog?
DEMETRIUS: Tempt not too much the hatred of my
        spirit,
For I am sick when I do look on thee.
HELENA: And I am sick when I look not on you.
DEMETRIUS: You do impeach° your modesty too
        much
215   To leave the city and commit yourself
Into the hands of one that loves you not,
To trust the opportunity of night
And the ill counsel of a desert° place

With the rich worth of your virginity.
HELENA: Your virtue° is my privilege.° For that°   220
It is not night when I do see your face,
Therefore I think I am not in the night;
Nor doth this wood lack worlds of company,
For you in my respect° are all the world.
Then how can it be said I am alone,   225
When all the world is here to look on me?
DEMETRIUS: I'll run from thee and hide me in the
        brakes,°
And leave thee to the mercy of wild beasts.
HELENA: The wildest hath not such a heart as you.
Run when you will, the story shall be chang'd: 230
Apollo flies and Daphne holds the chase,°
The dove pursues the griffin,° the mild hind°
Makes speed to catch the tiger — bootless° speed,
When cowardice pursues and valor flies.
DEMETRIUS: I will not stay° thy questions. Let me
        go!   235
Or if thou follow me, do not believe
But I shall do thee mischief in the wood.
HELENA: Ay, in the temple, in the town, the field,
You do me mischief. Fie, Demetrius!
Your wrongs do set a scandal on my sex.   240
We cannot fight for love, as men may do;
We should be woo'd and were not made to woo.
        [*Exit Demetrius.*]
I'll follow thee and make a heaven of hell,
To die upon° the hand I love so well. [*Exit.*]
OBERON: Fare thee well, nymph. Ere he do leave
        this grove,   245
Thou shalt fly him and he shall seek thy love.

(*Enter Puck.*)

Hast thou the flower there? Welcome, wanderer.
PUCK: Ay, there it is.   [*Offers the flower.*]
OBERON: I pray thee, give it me.
I know a bank where the wild thyme blows,°
Where oxlips° and the nodding violet grows,   250
Quite over-canopied with luscious woodbine,°

---

192. **wode:** Mad (pronounced "wood" and often spelled so).
195. **adamant:** Lodestone, magnet (with pun on *hard-hearted,* since adamant was also thought to be the hardest of all stones and was confused with the diamond).
197. **Leave:** Give up.   199. **fair:** Courteously.   214. **impeach:** Call into question.   218. **desert:** Deserted.

220. **virtue:** Goodness or power to attract.   **privilege:** Safeguard, warrant.   **For that:** Because.   224. **in my respect:** As far as I am concerned.   227. **brakes:** Thickets. 231. **Apollo...chase:** In the ancient myth, Daphne fled from Apollo and was saved from rape by being transformed into a laurel tree; here it is the female who *holds the chase,* or pursues, instead of the male.   232. **griffin:** A fabulous monster with the head of an eagle and the body of a lion. **hind:** Female deer.   233. **bootless:** Fruitless.   235. **stay:** wait for.   **questions:** Talk or argument.   244. **upon:** By. 249. **blows:** Blooms.   250. **oxlips:** Flowers resembling cowslip and primrose.   251. **woodbine:** Honeysuckle.

With sweet musk-roses° and with eglantine.°
There sleeps Titania sometime of the night
Lull'd in these flowers with dances and delight;
255   And there the snake throws° her enamel'd skin,
Weed° wide enough to wrap a fairy in.
And with the juice of this I'll streak° her eyes,
And make her full of hateful fantasies.
Take thou some of it, and seek through this
   grove.

                [Gives some love-juice.]

260   A sweet Athenian lady is in love
With a disdainful youth. Anoint his eyes,
But do it when the next thing he espies
May be the lady. Thou shalt know the man
By the Athenian garments he hath on.
265   Effect it with some care, that he may prove
More fond on° her than she upon her love;
And look thou meet me ere the first cock crow.
PUCK: Fear not, my lord, your servant shall do so.

                (Exeunt.)

{Scene II}°

(Enter Titania, Queen of Fairies, with her train.)

TITANIA: Come, now a roundel° and a fairy song;
Then, for the third part of a minute, hence —
Some to kill cankers° in the musk-rose buds,
Some war with rere-mice° for their leathern
   wings,
5   To make my small elves coats, and some keep
   back
The clamorous owl, that nightly hoots and
   wonders
At our quaint° spirits. Sing me now asleep.
Then to your offices and let me rest.

(Fairies sing.)

FIRST FAIRY: You spotted snakes with double°
   tongue,
10   Thorny hedgehogs, be not seen;
Newts° and blindworms, do no wrong,
   Come not near our fairy queen.
   [Chorus.] Philomel,° with melody
   Sing in our sweet lullaby;

Lulla, lulla, lullaby, lulla, lulla, lullaby.   15
   Never harm,
   Nor spell nor charm,
Come our lovely lady nigh.
So, good night, with lullaby.
FIRST FAIRY: Weaving spiders, come not here;   20
   Hence, you long-legg'd spinners, hence!
Beetles black, approach not near;
   Worm nor snail, do no offense.
   [Chorus.] Philomel, with melody, etc.
SECOND FAIRY: Hence, away! Now all is well.   25
   One aloof stand sentinel.

       [Exeunt Fairies. Titania sleeps.]

*(Enter Oberon [and squeezes the flower on Titania's
eyelids].)*

OBERON: What thou seest when thou dost wake,
Do it for thy true-love take;
Love and languish for his sake.
Be it ounce,° or cat, or bear,   30
Pard,° or boar with bristled hair,
In thy eye that shall appear
When thou wak'st, it is thy dear
Wake when some vile thing is near.   *[Exit.]*

(Enter Lysander and Hermia.)

LYSANDER: Fair love, you faint with wand'ring in
   the wood;   35
   And to speak troth,° I have forgot our way.
We'll rest us, Hermia, if you think it good,
And tarry for the comfort of the day.
HERMIA: Be 't so, Lysander. Find you out a bed,
For I upon this bank will rest my head.   40
LYSANDER: One turf shall serve as pillow for us
   both,
One heart, one bed, two bosoms, and one troth.°
HERMIA: Nay, good Lysander; for my sake, my dear,
Lie further off yet, do not lie so near.
LYSANDER: O, take the sense, sweet, of my
   innocence!°   45
Love takes the meaning in love's conference.°
I mean, that my heart unto yours is knit
So that but one heart we can make of it;
Two bosoms interchained with an oath —
So then two bosoms and a single troth.   50

---

252. musk-roses: A kind of large, sweet-scented rose.
eglantine: Sweetbriar, another kind of rose.   **255. throws:**
Sloughs off, sheds.   **256. Weed:** Garment.   **257. streak:**
Anoint, touch gently.   **266. fond on:** Doting on.   **II, I.**
Location: The wood.   **1. roundel:** Dance in a ring.   **3.**
cankers: Cankerworms.   **4. rare-mice:** Bats.   **7. quaint:**
Dainty.   **9. double:** Forked.   **11. Newts:** water lizards
(considered poisonous, as were blindworms — small snakes
with tiny eyes — and spiders).

13. Philomel: The nightingale. (Philomela, daughter of King
Pandion, was transformed into a nightingale, according to
Ovid's *Metamorphoses,* after she had been raped by her
sister Procne's husband, Tereus.)   **30. ounce:** Lynx.
31. Pard: Leopard.   **36. troth:** Truth.   **42. troth:** Faith,
troth-plight.   **45. take...innocence:** Interpret my intention as innocent.   **46. Love...conference:** When lovers
confer, love teaches each lover to interpret the other's meaning lovingly.

NEAR RIGHT: Oberon instructing Puck in the power of the "little western flower."
BELOW: The young lovers in the American Repertory Theatre's 1986 production.
FAR LEFT: Oberon with Titania upon his shoulder.
FAR RIGHT: The rude mechanicals: Moonshine with Lion.

Then by your side no bed-room me deny,
For lying so, Hermia, I do not lie.°
HERMIA: Lysander riddles very prettily.
  Now much beshrew° my manners and my pride
55 If Hermia meant to say Lysander lied.
  But, gentle friend, for love and courtesy
  Lie further off, in human° modesty;
  Such separation as may well be said
  Becomes a virtuous bachelor and a maid,
60 So far be distant; and, good night, sweet friend.
  Thy love ne'er alter till thy sweet life end!
LYSANDER: Amen, amen, to that fair prayer, say I,
  And then end life when I end loyalty!
  Here is my bed. Sleep give thee all his rest!

52. **lie:** Tell a falsehood (with a riddling pun on *lie*, recline).
54. **beshrew:** Curse (but mildly meant).   57. **human:** Courteous.

HERMIA: With half that wish the wisher's eyes be
    press'd!°   65
    [*They sleep, separated by a short distance.*]

(*Enter Puck.*)

PUCK: Through the forest have I gone,
  But Athenian found I none
  On whose eyes I might approve°
  This flower's force in stirring love.
  Night and silence.— Who is here?   70
  Weeds of Athens he doth wear.
  This is he, my master said,
  Despised the Athenian maid;
  And here the maiden, sleeping sound,
  On the dank and dirty ground.   75
  Pretty soul! She durst not lie

65. **With . . . press'd:** May we share your wish, so that your eyes too are *press'd*, closed, in sleep.   68. **approve:** Test.

339

Near this lack-love, this kill-courtesy.
Churl, upon thy eyes I throw
All the power this charm doth owe.°
                    [*Applies the love-juice.*]
80   When thou wak'st, let love forbid
Sleep his seat on thy eyelid.
So awake when I am gone,
For I must now to Oberon.   (*Exit.*)

(*Enter Demetrius and Helena, running.*)

HELENA: Stay, though thou kill me, sweet
          Demetrius.
DEMETRIUS: I charge thee, hence, and do not haunt
85   me thus.
HELENA: O, wilt thou darkling° leave me? Do not
          so.
DEMETRIUS: Stay, on thy peril!° I alone will go.
                              [*Exit.*]
HELENA: O, I am out of breath in this fond° chase!
The more my prayer, the lesser is my grace.°
90   Happy is Hermia, wheresoe'er she lies,°
For she hath blessed and attractive eyes.
How came her eyes so bright? Not with salt
          tears;
If so, my eyes are oft'ner wash'd than hers.
No, no, I am as ugly as a bear;
95   For beasts that meet me run away for fear.
Therefore no marvel though Demetrius
Do, as a monster, fly my presence thus.
What wicked and dissembling glass of mine
Made me compare with Hermia's sphery eyne?°
100 But who is here? Lysander, on the ground?
Dead, or asleep? I see no blood, no wound.
Lysander, if you live, good sir, awake.
LYSANDER [*awaking*]: And run through fire I will for
          thy sweet sake.
Transparent° Helena! Nature shows art,
105 That through thy bosom makes me see thy heart.
Where is Demetrius? O, how fit a word
Is that vile name to perish on my sword!
HELENA: Do not say so, Lysander, say not so.
What though he love your Hermia? Lord, what
          though?
110 Yet Hermia still loves you. Then be content.
LYSANDER: Content with Hermia? No! I do repent
The tedious minutes I with her have spent.
Not Hermia but Helena I love.
Who will not change a raven for a dove?

The will of man is by his reason sway'd,   115
And reason says you are the worthier maid.
Things growing are not ripe until their season;
So I, being young, till now ripe not° to reason.
And touching° now the point° of human skill,°
Reason becomes the marshal to my will   120
And leads me to your eyes, where I o'erlook°
Love's stories written in love's richest book.
HELENA: Wherefore was I to this keen mockery
          born?
When at your hands did I deserve this scorn?
Is 't not enough, is 't not enough, young man,   125
That I did never, no, nor never can,
Deserve a sweet look from Demetrius' eye,
But you must flout my insufficiency?
Good troth,° you do me wrong, good sooth,° you
          do,   130
In such disdainful manner me to woo.
But fare you well. Perforce I must confess
I thought you lord of° more true gentleness.
O, that a lady, of° one man refus'd,
Should of another therefore be abus'd!°   (*Exit.*)
LYSANDER: She sees not Hermia. Hermia, sleep thou
          there,   135
And never mayst thou come Lysander near!
For as a surfeit of the sweetest things
The deepest loathing to the stomach brings,
Or as the heresies that men do leave
Are hated most of those they did deceive,   140
So thou, my surfeit and my heresy,
Of all be hated, but the most of me!
And, all my powers, address your love and might
To honor Helen and to be her knight!   (*Exit.*)
HERMIA [*awaking*]: Help me, Lysander, help me! Do
          thy best   145
To pluck this crawling serpent from my breast!
Ay me, for pity! What a dream was here!
Lysander, look how I do quake with fear.
Methought a serpent eat° my heart away,
And you sat smiling at his cruel prey.°   150
Lysander! What, remov'd? Lysander! Lord!
What, out of hearing? Gone? No sound, no
          word?
Alack, where are you? Speak, an if you hear,
Speak, of all loves!° I swoon almost with fear.
No? Then I well perceive you are not nigh.   155

---

79. **owe:** Own.   86. **darkling:** In the dark.   87. **on thy peril:** On pain of danger to you if you don't obey me and stay.   88. **fond:** Doting.   89. **my grace:** The favor I obtain.   90. **lies:** Dwells.   99. **sphery eyne:** Eyes as bright as stars in their spheres.   104. **Transparent:** (1) Radiant; (2) able to be seen through.

118. **ripe not:** (Am) not ripened.   119. **touching:** Reaching. **point:** Summit. **skill:** Judgment.   121. **o'erlook:** Read. 129. **Good troth, good sooth:** Indeed, truly.   132. **lord of:** Possessor of. **gentleness:** Courtesy.   133. **of:** By.   134. **abus'd:** Ill treated.   149. **eat:** Ate (pronounced "et"). 150. **prey:** Act of preying.   154. **of all loves:** For all love's sake.

Either death, or you, I'll find immediately.
> (*Exit.* [*Manet° Titania lying asleep.*])

{*ACT III • Scene 1*}°

(*Enter the Clowns* [*Quince, Snug, Bottom, Flute, Snout, and Starveling*].)

BOTTOM: Are we all met?

QUINCE: Pat, pat; and here's a marvailes° convenient place for our rehearsal. This green plot shall be our stage, this hawthorn brake° our tiring-house,° and
5 we will do it in action as we will do it before the Duke.

BOTTOM: Peter Quince?

QUINCE: What sayest thou, bully° Bottom?

BOTTOM: There are things in this comedy of Pyramus
10 and Thisby that will never please. First, Pyramus must draw a sword to kill himself, which the ladies cannot abide. How answer you that?

SNOUT: By 'r lakin,° a parlous° fear.

STARVELING: I believe we must leave the killing out,
15 when all is done.°

BOTTOM: Not a whit. I have a device to make all well. Write me° a prologue; and let the prologue seem to say, we will do no harm with our swords and that Pyramus is not kill'd indeed; and, for the more bet-
20 ter assurance, tell them that I Pyramus am not Pyramus, but Bottom the weaver. This will put them out of fear.

QUINCE: Well, we will have such a prologue, and it shall be written in eight and six.°

25 BOTTOM: No, make it two more; let it be written in eight and eight.

SNOUT: Will not the ladies be afeard of the lion?

STARVELING: I fear it, I promise you.

BOTTOM: Masters, you ought to consider with your-
30 selves, to bring in — God shield us! — a lion among ladies,° is a most dreadful thing. For there is not a more fearful° wild-fowl than your lion living; and we ought to look to 't.

SNOUT: Therefore another prologue must tell he is not
35 a lion.

BOTTOM: Nay, you must name his name, and half his face must be seen through the lion's neck, and he himself must speak through, saying thus, or to the same defect:° "Ladies" — or "Fair ladies — I
40 would wish you" — or "I would request you" — or "I would entreat you — not to fear, not to tremble; my life for yours.° If you think I come hither as a lion, it were pity of my life.° No, I am no such thing, I am a man as other men are." And there in-
45 deed let him name his name, and tell them plainly he is Snug the joiner.

QUINCE: Well, it shall be so. But there is two hard things: that is, to bring the moonlight into a chamber; for, you know, Pyramus and Thisby meet by
50 moonlight.

SNOUT: Doth the moon shine that night we play our play?

BOTTOM: A calendar, a calendar! Look in the almanac. Find out moonshine, find out moonshine.
> [*They consult an almanac.*]

QUINCE: Yes, it doth shine that night.   55

BOTTOM: Why then may you leave a casement of the great chamber window, where we play, open, and the moon may shine in at the casement.

QUINCE: Ay; or else one must come in with a bush of thorns° and a lantern, and say he comes to disfig-
60 ure,° or to present,° the person of Moonshine. Then there is another thing: we must have a wall in the great chamber; for Pyramus and Thisby, says the story, did talk through the chink of a wall.

SNOUT: You can never bring in a wall. What say you,
65 Bottom?

BOTTOM: Some man or other must present Wall. And let him have some plaster, or some loam, or some rough-cast° about him, to signify wall; and let him hold his fingers thus, and through that cranny shall
70 Pyramus and Thisby whisper.

QUINCE: If that may be, then all is well. Come, sit down, every mother's son, and rehearse your parts. Pyramus, you begin. When you have spoken your speech, enter into that brake, and so every one ac-
75 cording to his cue.

(*Enter Robin* [*Puck*].)

---

156. [S.D.] *Manet:* Latin for "she remains." III, I. Location: Scene continues.   2. **marvailes:** Marvelous.
4. **brake:** Thicket.   **tiring-house:** Attiring area, hence backstage.   8. **bully:** Worthy, jolly, fine fellow.   13. **By 'r lakin:** By our ladykin, the Virgin Mary.   **parlous:** Perilous.
15. **when all is done:** When all is said and done.   17. **write me:** Write at my suggestion.   24. **eight and six:** Alternate lines of eight and six syllables, a common ballad measure.
30–31. **lion among ladies:** A contemporary pamphlet tells how at the christening in 1594 of Prince Henry, eldest son of King James VI of Scotland, later James I of England, a "blackmoor" instead of a lion drew the triumphal chariot, since the lion's presence might have "brought some fear to the nearest."   32. **fearful:** Fear-inspiring.

39. **defect:** Bottom's blunder for *effect*.   42. **my life for yours:** I pledge my life to make your lives safe.   43. **it were . . . life:** My life would be endangered.   59–60. **bush of thorns:** Bundle of thornbush faggots (part of the accoutrements of the man in the moon, according to the popular notions of the time, along with his lantern and his dog).
61. **disfigure:** Quince's blunder for *prefigure*.   **present:** Represent.   69. **rough-cast:** A mixture of lime and gravel used to plaster the outside of buildings.

PUCK: What hempen° home-spuns have we
        swagg'ring here,
    So near the cradle of the Fairy Queen?
    What, a play toward?° I'll be an auditor;°
80 An actor too perhaps, if I see cause.
QUINCE: Speak, Pyramus. Thisby, stand forth.
BOTTOM: "Thisby, the flowers of odious savors
        sweet," —
QUINCE: Odors, odors.
BOTTOM: — "Odors savors sweet;
85 So hath thy breath, my dearest Thisby dear.
    But hark, a voice! Stay thou but here awhile,
    And by and by I will to thee appear."   (Exit.)
PUCK: A stranger Pyramus than e'er played here.°
                                                [Exit.]
FLUTE: Must I speak now?
90 QUINCE: Ay, marry, must you; for you must under-
        stand he goes but to see a noise that he heard, and
        is to come again.
FLUTE: "Most radiant Pyramus, most lily-white of
        hue,
    Of color like the red rose on triumphant brier,
95 Most brisky juvenal° and eke° most lovely Jew,°
    As true as truest horse that yet would never tire.
    I'll meet thee, Pyramus, at Ninny's tomb."
QUINCE: "Ninus'° tomb," man. Why, you must not
        speak that yet. That you answer to Pyramus. You
100   speak all your part at once, cues and all. Pyramus
        enter. Your cue is past; it is, "never tire."
FLUTE: O — "As true as truest horse, that yet would
        never tire."

[Enter Puck, and Bottom as Pyramus with the ass
head.]°

BOTTOM: "If I were fair,° Thisby, I were° only
        thine."
QUINCE: O monstrous! O strange! We are haunted.
105   Pray, masters! Fly, masters! Help!
                    [Exeunt Quince, Snug, Flute,
                            Snout, and Starveling.]
PUCK: I'll follow you, I'll lead you about a round,°
    Through bog, through bush, through brake,
        through brier.
    Sometime a horse I'll be, sometime a hound,

A hog, a headless bear, sometime a fire,°
And neigh, and bark, and grunt, and roar, and
    burn,   110
Like horse, hound, hog, bear, fire, at every turn.
                                                (Exit.)
BOTTOM: Why do they run away? This is a knavery of
    them to make me afeard.

(Enter Snout.)

SNOUT: O Bottom, thou art chang'd! What do I see on
    thee?   115
BOTTOM: What do you see? You see an ass-head of
    your own, do you?   [Exit Snout.]

(Enter Quince.)

QUINCE: Bless thee, Bottom, bless thee! Thou art
    translated.°   (Exit.)
BOTTOM: I see their knavery. This is to make an ass of   120
    me, to fright me, if they could. But I will not stir
    from this place, do what they can. I will walk up
    and down here, and I will sing, that they shall hear
    I am not afraid.   [Sings.]
    The woosel cock° so black of hue,   125
        With orange-tawny bill,
    The throstle° with his note so true,
        The wren with little quill°—
TITANIA [awaking]: What angel wakes me from my
    flow'ry bed?
BOTTOM [sings]: The finch, the sparrow, and the
    lark,   130
        The plain-song° cuckoo grey,
    Whose note full many a man doth mark,
        And dares not answer nay°—
    For, indeed, who would set his wit to so foolish
    a bird? Who would give a bird the lie,° though   135
    he cry "cuckoo" never so?°
TITANIA: I pray thee, gentle mortal, sing again.
    Mine ear is much enamored of thy note;
    So is mine eye enthralled to thy shape;
    And thy fair virtue's force° perforce doth move
    me   140
    On the first view to say, to swear, I love thee.
BOTTOM: Methinks, mistress, you should have little
    reason for that. And yet, to say the truth, reason
    and love keep little company together nowadays.
    The more the pity that some honest neighbors will   145

---

77. **hempen:** Made of hemp, a rough fiber.   79. **toward:**
About to take place.   **auditor:** One who listens, i.e., part of
the audience.   88. **here:** In this theater (?).   95. **brisky ju-**
venal: Brisk youth.   **eke:** Also.   **Jew:** Probably an absurd
repetition of the first syllable of *juvenal*.   98. **Ninus:** Mythical founder of Nineveh (whose wife, Semiramis, was supposed to have built the walls of Babylon where the story of
Pyramus and Thisby takes place).   102. [S.D.] *with the ass*
head: This stage direction, taken from the Folio, presumably
refers to a standard stage property.   103. **fair:** Handsome.
were: Would be.   106. **about a round:** Roundabout.

---

109. **fire:** Will-o'-the-wisp.   119. **translated:** Transformed.
125. **woosel cock:** Male ousel or ouzel, blackbird.
127. **throstle:** Song thrush.   128. **quill:** Literally, a reed
pipe; hence, the bird's piping song.   131. **plain-song:**
Singing a melody without variations.   133. **dares . . . nay:**
Cannot deny that he is a cuckold.   135. **give . . . lie:**
Call the bird a liar.   136. **never so:** Ever so much.
140. **thy . . . force:** The power of your beauty.

not make them friends. Nay, I can gleek° upon occasion.

TITANIA: Thou art as wise as thou art beautiful.

BOTTOM: Not so, neither. But if I had wit enough to
150 get out of this wood, I have enough to serve mine
own turn.°

TITANIA: Out of this wood do not desire to go.
Thou shalt remain here, whether thou wilt or no.
I am a spirit of no common rate.°
155 The summer still° doth tend upon my state;°
And I do love thee. Therefore, go with me.
I'll give thee fairies to attend on thee,
And they shall fetch thee jewels from the deep,
And sing while thou on pressed flowers dost
sleep.
160 And I will purge thy mortal grossness so
That thou shalt like an airy spirit go.
Peaseblossom, Cobweb, Moth,° and
Mustardseed!

(*Enter four Fairies [Peaseblossom, Cobweb, Moth,
and Mustardseed].*)

PEASEBLOSSOM: Ready.

COBWEB: And I.

MOTH: And I.

MUSTARDSEED: And I.

ALL: Where shall we go?

165 TITANIA: Be kind and courteous to this gentleman.
Hop in his walks and gambol in his eyes;
Feed him with apricocks and dewberries,
With purple grapes, green figs, and mulberries;
The honey-bags steal from the humble-bees,
170 And for night-tapers crop their waxen thighs
And light them at the fiery glow-worm's eyes,
To have my love to bed and to arise;
And pluck the wings from painted butterflies
To fan the moonbeams from his sleeping eyes.
175 Nod to him, elves, and do him courtesies.

PEASEBLOSSOM: Hail, mortal!

COBWEB: Hail!

MOTH: Hail!

MUSTARDSEED: Hail!

180 BOTTOM: I cry your worship's mercy, heartily. I beseech your worship's name.

COBWEB: Cobweb.

BOTTOM: I shall desire you of more acquaintance, good
Master Cobweb. If I cut my finger, I shall make bold
185 with you.° Your name, honest gentleman?

PEASEBLOSSOM: Peaseblossom.

BOTTOM: I pray you, commend me to Mistress
Squash,° your mother, and to Master Peascod,°
your father. Good Master Peaseblossom, I shall desire you of more acquaintance too. Your name, I   190
beseech you, sir?

MUSTARDSEED: Mustardseed.

BOTTOM: Good Master Mustardseed, I know your
patience° well. That same cowardly, giant-like ox-
beef hath devour'd many a gentleman of your   195
house. I promise you your kindred hath made my
eyes water ere now. I desire you of more acquaintance, good Master Mustardseed.

TITANIA: Come wait upon him; lead him to my
bower.
The moon methinks looks with a wat'ry eye;   200
And when she weeps,° weeps every little flower,
Lamenting some enforced° chastity.
Tie up my lover's tongue, bring him silently.

(*Exeunt.*)

{*Scene II*}°

(*Enter [Oberon,] King of Fairies.*)

OBERON: I wonder if Titania be awak'd;
Then, what it was that next came in her eye,
Which she must dote on in extremity.

(*[Enter] Robin Goodfellow [Puck].*)

Here comes my messenger. How now, mad spirit?
What night-rule° now about this haunted° grove? 5

PUCK: My mistress with a monster is in love.
Near to her close° and consecrated bower,
While she was in her dull° and sleeping hour,
A crew of patches,° rude mechanicals,°
That work for bread upon Athenian stalls,   10
Were met together to rehearse a play
Intended for great Theseus' nuptial day.
The shallowest thick-skin of that barren sort,°
Who Pyramus presented,° in their sport
Forsook his scene° and ent'red in a brake.   15
When I did him at this advantage take,

---

187. **Squash:** Unripe pea pod.   188. **Peascod:** Ripe pea
pod.   193–94. **your patience:** What you have endured.
201. **she weeps:** I.e., she causes dew.   202. **enforced:**
Forced, violated; or, possibly, constrained (since Titania at
this moment is hardly concerned about chastity).   **III, II.**
Location: The wood.   5. **night-rule:** Diversion for the
night.   **haunted:** Much frequented.   7. **close:** Secret, private.   8. **dull:** Drowsy.   9. **patches:** Clowns, fools.
rude mechanicals: Ignorant artisans.   13. **barren sort:** Stupid company or crew.   14. **presented:** Acted.   15. **scene:**
Playing area.

---

146. **gleek:** Scoff, jest.   150–51. **serve . . . turn:** Answer my
purpose.   154. **rate:** Rank, value.   155. **still:** Ever always.   **doth . . . state:** Waits upon me as part of my royal
retinue.   162. **Moth:** Mote, speck. (The two words *moth*
and *mote* were pronounced alike.)   184–85. **If . . . you:**
Cobwebs were used to stanch bleeding.

An ass's nole° I fixed on his head.
Anon his Thisby must be answered,
And forth my mimic° comes. When they him spy,
20   As wild geese that the creeping fowler eye,
Or russet-pared choughs,° many in sort,°
Rising and cawing at the gun's report,
Sever° themselves and madly sweep the sky,
So, at his sight, away his fellows fly;
25   And, at our stamp, here o'er and o'er one falls;
He murder cries and help from Athens calls.
Their sense thus weak, lost with their fears thus
    strong,
Made senseless things begin to do them wrong,
For briers and thorns at their apparel snatch;
Some, sleeves — some, hats; from yielders all
30   things catch.
I led them on in this distracted fear
And left sweet Pyramus translated there,
When in that moment, so it came to pass,
Titania wak'd and straightway lov'd an ass.
35 OBERON: This falls out better than I could devise.
But hast thou yet latch'd° the Athenian's eyes
With the love-juice, as I did bid thee do?
PUCK: I took him sleeping — that is finish'd too —
And the Athenian woman by his side,
40   That, when he wak'd, of force° she must be ey'd.

(Enter Demetrius and Hermia.)

OBERON: Stand close. This is the same Athenian.
PUCK: This is the woman, but not this the man.
                                    [*They stand aside.*]
DEMETRIUS: O, why rebuke you him that loves you
    so?
Lay breath so bitter on your bitter foe.
HERMIA: Now I but chide; but I should use thee
45   worse,
For thou, I fear, hast given me cause to curse.
If thou hast slain Lysander in his sleep,
Being o'er shoes in blood, plunge in the deep,
And kill me too.
50   The sun was not so true unto the day
As he to me. Would he have stolen away
From sleeping Hermia? I'll believe as soon
This whole° earth may be bor'd and that the
    moon
May through the center creep and so displease
55   Her brother's° noontide with th' Antipodes.°

It cannot be but thou has murd'red him;
So should a murderer look, so dead,° so grim.
DEMETRIUS: So should the murdered look, and so
    should I,
Pierc'd through the heart with your stern cruelty.
Yet you, the murderer, look as bright, as clear,   60
As yonder Venus in her glimmering sphere.
HERMIA: What's this to my Lysander? Where is he?
Ah, good Demetrius, wilt thou give him me?
DEMETRIUS: I had rather give his carcass to my
    hounds.   65
HERMIA: Out dog! Out cur! Thou driv'st me past
    the bounds
Of maiden's patience. Hast thou slain him, then?
Henceforth be never numb'red among men!
O, once tell true, tell true, even for my sake!
Durst thou have look'd upon him being awake,
And hast thou kill'd him sleeping? O brave
    touch!°   70
Could not a worm,° an adder, do so much?
An adder did it, for with doubler tongue
Than thine, thou serpent, never adder stung.
DEMETRIUS: You spend your passion° on a mispris'd
    mood.°
I am not guilty of Lysander's blood,   75
Nor is he dead, for aught that I can tell.
HERMIA: I pray thee, tell me then that he is well.
DEMETRIUS: An if I could, what should I get
    therefore?
HERMIA: A privilege never to see me more.
And from thy hated presence part I so.   80
See me no more, whether he be dead or no.
                                        (*Exit.*)
DEMETRIUS: There is no following her in this fierce
    vein.
Here therefore for a while I will remain.
So sorrow's heaviness doth heavier° grow
For debt that bankrupt° sleep doth sorrow owe;   85
Which now in some slight measure it will pay,
If for his tender here I make some stay.°
                            (*Lie down [and sleep].*)
OBERON: What hast thou done? Thou hast mistaken
    quite
And laid the love-juice on some true-love's sight.

---

17. **nole:** Noddle, head.   19. **mimic:** Burlesque actor.
21. **russet-paled choughs:** Gray-headed jackdaws.   **in sort:**
In a flock.   23. **Sever:** Scatter.   36. **latch'd:** Moistened,
anointed.   40. **of force:** Perforce.   53. **whole:** Solid.
55. **Her brother's:** I.e., the sun's.   **th' Antipodes:** The people on the opposite side of the earth.

57. **dead:** Deadly, or deathly pale.   70. **brave touch:** Noble
exploit (said ironically).   71. **worm:** Serpent.   74. **passion:** Violent feelings.   **mispris'd mood:** Anger based on
misconception.   84. **heavier:** (1) Harder to bear, (2)
drowsier.   85. **bankrupt:** Demetrius is saying that his
sleepiness adds to the weariness caused by sorrow.
86–87. **Which...stay:** To a small extent I will be able to
"pay back" and hence find some relief from sorrow, if I pause
here a while (*make some stay*) while sleep "tenders" or offers
itself by way of paying the debt owed to sorrow.

90 Of thy misprision° must perforce ensue
    Some true love turn'd and not a false turn'd true.
    PUCK: Then fate o'er-rules, that, one man holding
        troth,°
    A million fail, confounding oath on oath.°
    OBERON: About the wood go swifter than the wind,
95 And Helena of Athens look thou find.
    All fancy-sick° she is and pale of cheer°
    With sighs of love, that cost the fresh blood°
        dear.
    By some illusion see thou bring her here.
    I'll charm his eyes against she do appear.°
100 PUCK: I go, I go; look how I go
    Swifter than arrow from the Tartar's bow.°
                                        [*Exit.*]
    OBERON: Flower of this purple dye,
    Hit with Cupid's archery.
    Sink in angle of his eye.
        [*Applies love-juice to Demetrius' eyes.*]
105 When his love he doth espy,
    Let her shine as gloriously
    As the Venus of the sky.
    When thou wak'st, if she be by,
    Beg of her for remedy.

    (*Enter Puck.*)

110 PUCK: Captain of our fairy band,
    Helena is here at hand,
    And the youth, mistook by me,
    Pleading for a lover's fee.°
    Shall we their fond pageant° see?
115 Lord, what fools these mortals be!
    OBERON: Stand aside. The noise they make
    Will cause Demetrius to awake.
    PUCK: Then will two at once woo one;
    That must needs be sport alone;°
120 And those things do best please me
    That befall prepost'rously.°
                                [*They stand aside.*]

    (*Enter Lysander and Helena.*)

    LYSANDER: Why should you think that I should woo
        in scorn?
    Scorn and derision never come in tears.

    Look when° I vow, I weep; and vows so born,
    In their nativity all truth appears.°   125
    How can these things in me seem scorn to you,
    Bearing the badge° of faith, to prove them true?
    HELENA: You do advance° your cunning more and
        more.
    When truth kills truth,° O devilish-holy fray!
    These vows are Hermia's. Will you give her o'er? 130
    Weigh oath with oath, and you will nothing
        weigh.
    Your vows to her and me, put in two scales
    Will even weigh, and both as light as tales.°
    LYSANDER: I had no judgment when to her I swore.
    HELENA: Nor none, in my mind, now you give her
        o'er.   135
    LYSANDER: Demetrius loves her, and he loves not
        you.
    DEMETRIUS [*awaking*]: O Helen, goddess, nymph,
        perfect, divine!
    To what, my love, shall I compare thine eyne?
    Crystal is muddy. O, how ripe in show°
    Thy lips, those kissing cherries, tempting grow! 140
    That pure congealed white, high Taurus'° snow,
    Fann'd with the eastern wind, turns to a crow°
    When thou hold'st up thy hand. O, let me kiss
    This princess of pure white, this seal° of bliss!
    HELENA: O spite! O hell! I see you all are bent   145
    To set against me for your merriment.
    If you were civil and knew courtesy,
    You would not do me thus much injury.
    Can you not hate me, as I know you do,
    But you must join in souls to mock me too?   150
    If you were men, as men you are in show,
    You would not use a gentle lady so —
    To vow, and swear, and superpraise° my parts,°
    When I am sure you hate me with your hearts.
    You both are rivals, and love Hermia;   155
    And now both rivals, to mock Helena.
    A trim° exploit, a manly enterprise,
    To conjure tears up in a poor maid's eyes
    With your derision! None of noble sort
    Would so offend a virgin and extort°   160
    A poor soul's patience, all to make you sport.

---

90. **misprision:** Mistake.   92. **troth:** Faith.   93. **confounding . . . oath:** Invalidating one oath with another.
96. **fancy-sick:** Lovesick.   **cheer:** Face.   97. **sighs . . . blood:** An allusion to the physiological theory that each sigh costs the heart a drop of blood.   99. **against . . . appear:** in anticipation of her coming.   101. **Tartar's bow:** Tartars were famed for their skill with the bow.   113. **fee:** Privilege, reward.   114. **fond pageant:** Foolish exhibition.   119. **alone:** Unequaled.   121. **prepost'rously:** Out of the natural order.

124. **Look when:** Whenever.   124–25. **vows . . . appears:** Vows made by one who is weeping give evidence thereby of their sincerity.   127. **badge:** Identifying device such as that worn on servants' livery.   128. **advance:** Carry forward, display.   129. **truth kills truth:** One of Lysander's vows must invalidate the other.   133. **tales:** Lies.   139. **show:** Appearance.   141. **Taurus:** A lofty mountain range in Asia Minor.   142. **turns to a crow:** Seems black by contrast.   144. **seal:** Pledge.   153. **superpraise:** Overpraise.   **parts:** Qualities.   157. **trim:** Pretty, fine (said ironically).   160. **extort:** Twist, torture.

LYSANDER: You are unkind, Demetrius. Be not so;
　　For you love Hermia; this you know I know.
　　And here, with all good will, with all my heart,
165　In Hermia's love I yield you up my part;
　　And yours of Helena to me bequeath,
　　Whom I do love and will do till my death.
HELENA: Never did mockers waste more idle breath.
DEMETRIUS: Lysander, keep thy Hermia; I will
　　none.°
170　If e'er I lov'd her, all that love is gone.
　　My heart to her but as guest-wise sojourn'd,
　　And now to Helen is it home return'd.
　　There to remain.
LYSANDER:　　　　　Helen, it is not so.
DEMETRIUS: Disparage not the faith thou dost not
　　know,
175　Lest, to thy peril, thou aby° it dear.
　　Look where thy love comes; yonder is thy dear.

(Enter Hermia.)

HERMIA: Dark night, that from the eye his° function
　　takes,
　　The ear more quick of apprehension makes;
　　Wherein it doth impair the seeing sense,
180　It pays the hearing double recompense.
　　Thou art not by mine eye, Lysander, found;
　　Mine ear, I thank it, brought me to thy sound.
　　But why unkindly didst thou leave me so?
LYSANDER: Why should he stay, whom love doth
　　press to go?
HERMIA: What love could press Lysander from my
185　side?
LYSANDER: Lysander's love, that would not let him
　　bide,
　　Fair Helena, who more engilds the night
　　Than all yon fiery oes° and eyes of light.
　　Why seek'st thou me? Could not this make thee
　　know,
190　The hate I bear thee made me leave thee so?
HERMIA: You speak not as you think. It cannot be.
HELENA: Lo, she is one of this confederacy!
　　Now I perceive they have conjoin'd all three
　　To fashion this false sport, in spite of me.°
195　Injurious Hermia, most ungrateful maid!
　　Have you conspir'd, have you with these
　　contriv'd°
　　To bait° me with this foul derision?
　　Is all the counsel° that we two have shar'd,

The sisters' vows, the hours that we have spent,
When we have chid the hasty-footed time   200
For parting us — O, is all forgot?
All school-days friendship, childhood innocence?
We, Hermia, like two artificial° gods,
Have with our needles created both one flower,
Both on one sampler, sitting on one cushion,   205
Both warbling of one song, both in one key,
As if our hands, our sides, voices, and minds
Had been incorporate. So we grew together,
Like to a double cherry, seeming parted,
But yet an union in partition;   210
Two lovely° berries molded on one stem;
So, with two seeming bodies, but one heart;
Two of the first, like coats in heraldry,
Due but to one and crowned with one crest.°
And will you rent° our ancient love asunder,   215
To join with men in scorning your poor friend?
It is not friendly, 'tis not maidenly.
Our sex, as well as I, may chide you for it,
Though I alone do feel the injury.
HERMIA: I am amazed at your passionate words.   220
　　I scorn you not. It seems that you scorn me.
HELENA: Have you not set Lysander, as in scorn,
　　To follow me and praise my eyes and face?
　　And made your other love, Demetrius,
　　Who even but now did spurn me with his foot,   225
　　To call me goddess, nymph, divine and rare,
　　Precious, celestial? Wherefore speaks he this
　　To her he hates? And wherefore doth Lysander
　　Deny your love, so rich within his soul,
　　And tender° me, forsooth, affection,   230
　　But by your setting on, by your consent?
　　What though I be not so in grace° as you,
　　So hung upon with love, so fortunate,
　　But miserable most, to love unlov'd?
　　This you should pity rather than despise.   235
HERMIA: I understand not what you mean by this.
HELENA: Ay, do! Persever, counterfeit sad° looks,
　　Make mouths° upon° me when I turn my back,
　　Wink each at other, hold the sweet jest up.
　　This sport, well carried,° shall be chronicled. 240
　　If you have any pity, grace, or manners,
　　You would not make me such an argument.°
　　But fare ye well. 'Tis partly my own fault,
　　Which death, or absence, soon shall remedy.

---

203. **artificial:** Skilled in art or creation.　**211. lovely:** Loving.　**213–14. Two . . . crest:** We have two separate bodies, just as a coat of arms in heraldry can be represented twice on a shield but surmounted by a single crest.　**215. rent:** Rend.　**230. tender:** Offer.　**232. grace:** Favor.　**237. sad:** Grave, serious.　**238. mouths:** Maws, faces, grimaces. **upon:** At.　**240. carried:** Managed.　**242. argument:** Subject for a jest.

---

169. **will none:** Wish none of her.　**175. aby:** Pay for.
177. **his:** Its.　**188. oes:** Circles, orbs, stars.　**194. in spite of me:** To vex me.　**196. contriv'd:** Plotted.　**197. bait:** Torment, as one sets on dogs to bait a bear.　**198. counsel:** Confidential talk.

245 LYSANDER: Stay, gentle Helena; hear my excuse,
My love, my life, my soul, fair Helena!
HELENA: O excellent!
HERMIA: Sweet, do not scorn her so.
DEMETRIUS: If she cannot entreat,° I can compel.
LYSANDER: Thou canst compel no more than she
entreat.
Thy threats have no more strength than her weak
250 prayers.
Helen, I love thee, by my life, I do!
I swear by that which I will lose for thee,
To prove him false that says I love thee not.
DEMETRIUS: I say I love thee more than he can do.
LYSANDER: If thou say so, withdraw, and prove it
255 too.
DEMETRIUS: Quick, come!
HERMIA: Lysander, whereto tends all this?
LYSANDER: Away, you Ethiope!°
          [*He tries to break away from Hermia.*]
DEMETRIUS: No, no; he'll
Seem to break loose; take on as you would
follow,
But yet come not. You are a tame man, go!
LYSANDER: Hang off,° thou cat, thou burr! Vile
260 thing, let loose,
Or I will shake thee from me like a serpent!
HERMIA: Why are you grown so rude? What change
is this,
Sweet love?
LYSANDER: Thy love? Out, tawny Tartar, out!
Out, loathed med'cine!° O hated potion, hence!
HERMIA: Do you not jest?
265 HELENA: Yes, sooth,° and so do you.
LYSANDER: Demetrius, I will keep my word with
thee.
DEMETRIUS: I would I had your bond, for I perceive
A weak bond° holds you. I'll not trust your
word.
LYSANDER: What, should I hurt her, strike her, kill
her dead?
270 Although I hate her, I'll not harm her so.
HERMIA: What, can you do me greater harm than
hate?
Hate me? Wherefore? O me, what news,° my
love?
Am not I Hermia? Are not you Lysander?
I am as fair now as I was erewhile.°

Since night you lov'd me; yet since night you left
me.   275
Why, then you left me — O, the gods forbid! —
In earnest, shall I say?
LYSANDER: Ay, by my life!
And never did desire to see thee more.
Therefore be out of hope, of question, of doubt;
Be certain, nothing truer. 'Tis no jest   280
That I do hate thee and love Helena.
HERMIA: O me! You juggler! You cankerblossom!°
You thief of love! What, have you come by night
And stol'n my love's heart from him?
HELENA: Fine, i' faith!
Have you no modesty, no maiden shame,   285
No touch of bashfulness? What, will you tear
Impatient answers from my gentle tongue?
Fie, fie! You counterfeit, you puppet,° you!
HERMIA: Puppet? Why so? Ay, that way goes the
game.
Now I perceive that she hath made compare   290
Between our statures; she hath urg'd her height,
And with her personage, her tall personage,
Her height, forsooth, she hath prevail'd with
him.
And are you grown so high in his esteem,
Because I am so dwarfish and so low?   295
How low am I, thou painted maypole? Speak!
How low am I? I am not yet so low
But that my nails can reach unto thine eyes.
          [*She flails at Helena but is restrained.*]
HELENA: I pray you, though you mock me,
gentlemen,
Let her not hurt me. I was never curst;°   300
I have no gift at all in shrewishness;
I am a right° maid for my cowardice.
Let her not strike me. You perhaps may think,
Because she is something° lower than myself,
That I can match her.
HERMIA: Lower! Hark, again!   305
HELENA: Good Hermia, do not be so bitter with
me.
I evermore did love you, Hermia,
Did ever keep your counsels, never wrong'd you;
Save that, in love unto Demetrius,
I told him of your stealth° unto this wood.   310
He followed you; for love I followed him.
But he hath chid me hence and threat'ned me
To strike me, spurn me, nay, to kill me too.
And now, so° you will let me quiet go,

---

248. **entreat:** Succeed by entreaty.   257. **Ethiope:** Referring to Hermia's relatively dark hair and complexion; see also *tawny Tartar* six lines later.   260. **Hang off:** Let go. 264. **med'cine:** Poison.   265. **sooth:** Truly.   268. **weak bond:** Hermia's arm (with a pun on *bond*, oath, in the previous line).   272. **what news:** What is the matter.   274. **erewhile:** Just now.

282. **cankerblossom:** Worm that destroys the flower bud (?). 288. **puppet:** (1) Counterfeit, (2) dwarfish woman (in reference to Hermia's smaller stature).   300. **curst:** Shrewish. 302. **right:** True.   304. **something:** Somewhat.   310. **stealth:** Stealing away.   314. **so:** If only.

315 To Athens will I bear my folly back
And follow you no further. Let me go.
You see how simple and how fond° I am.
HERMIA: Why, get you gone. Who is 't that hinders
you?
HELENA: A foolish heart, that I leave here behind.
HERMIA: What, with Lysander?
320 HELENA: With Demetrius.
LYSANDER: Be not afraid; she shall not harm thee,
Helena.
DEMETRIUS: No, sir, she shall not, though you take
her part.
HELENA: O, when she is angry, she is keen and
shrewd!°
She was a vixen when she went to school;
325 And though she be but little, she is fierce.
HERMIA: "Little" again! Nothing but "low" and
"little"!
Why will you suffer her to flout me thus?
Let me come to her.
LYSANDER: Get you gone, you dwarf!
You minimus,° of hind'ring knot-grass° made!
You bead, you acorn!
330 DEMETRIUS: You are too officious
In her behalf that scorns your services.
Let her alone. Speak not of Helena;
Take not her part. For, if thou dost intend°
Never so little show of love to her,
Thou shalt aby° it.
335 LYSANDER: Now she holds me not;
Now follow, if thou dar'st, to try whose right,
Of thine or mine, is most in Helena.   [Exit.]
DEMETRIUS: Follow? Nay, I'll go with thee, cheek by
jowl.°
                    [Exit, following Lysander.]
HERMIA: You, mistress, all this coil° is 'long of° you.
Nay, go not back.°
340 HELENA: I will not trust you, I,
Nor longer stay in your curst company.
Your hands than mine are quicker for a fray;
My legs are longer, though, to run away.   [Exit.]
HERMIA: I am amaz'd, and know not what to say.
                                        (Exit.)
345 OBERON: This is thy negligence. Still thou mistak'st,
Or else committ'st thy knaveries willfully.
PUCK: Believe me, king of shadows, I mistook.
Did not you tell me I should know the man

By the Athenian garments he had on?
And so far blameless proves my enterprise   350
That I have 'nointed an Athenian's eyes;
And so far am I glad it so did sort°
As this their jangling I esteem a sport.
OBERON: Thou see'st these lovers seek a place to
fight.
Hie therefore, Robin, overcast the night;   355
The starry welkin° cover thou anon
With drooping fog as black as Acheron,°
And lead these testy rivals so astray
As° one come not within another's way.
Like to Lysander sometime frame thy tongue,   360
Then stir Demetrius up with bitter wrong;°
And sometime rail thou like Demetrius.
And from each other look thou lead them thus,
Till o'er their brows death-counterfeiting sleep
With leaden legs and batty° wings doth creep.   365
Then crush this herb° into Lysander's eye,
                              [Gives herb.]
Whose liquor hath this virtuous° property,
To take from thence all error with his° might
And make his eyeballs roll with wonted° sight.
When they next wake, all this derision°   370
Shall seem a dream and fruitless vision,
And back to Athens shall the lovers wend
With league whose date° till death shall never
end.
Whiles I in this affair do thee employ,
I'll to my queen and beg her Indian boy;   375
And then I will her charmed eye release
From monster's view, and all things shall be
peace.
PUCK: My fairy lord, this must be done with haste,
For night's swift dragons° cut the clouds full fast,
And yonder shines Aurora's harbinger,°   380
At whose approach, ghosts, wand'ring here and
there,
Troop home to churchyards. Damned spirits all,
That in crossways and floods have burial,°
Already to their wormy beds are gone.

---

317. **fond:** Foolish.   323. **shrewd:** Shrewish.   329. **minimus:** Diminutive creature.   **knot-grass:** A weed, an infusion of which was thought to stunt the growth.   333. **intend:** Give sign of.   335. **aby:** Pay for.   338. **cheek by jowl:** Side by side.   339. **coil:** Turmoil, dissension. **'long of:** On account of.   340. **go not back:** Don't retreat. (Hermia is again proposing a fight.)

352. **sort:** Turn out.   356. **welkin:** Sky.   357. **Acheron:** River of Hades (here representing Hades itself).   359. **As:** That.   361. **wrong:** Insults.   365. **batty:** Batlike.   366. **this herb:** The antidote (mentioned in II, I, 184) to love-in-idleness.   367. **virtuous:** Efficacious.   368. **his:** Its. 369. **wonted:** Accustomed.   370. **derision:** Laughable business.   373. **date:** Term of existence.   379. **dragons:** Supposed to be yoked to the car of the goddess of night.   380. **Aurora's harbinger:** The morning star, precursor of dawn. 383. **crossways . . . burial:** Those who had committed suicide were buried at crossways, with a stake driven through them; those drowned, i.e., buried in floods or great waters, were condemned to wander disconsolate for want of burial rites.

385   For fear lest day should look their shames upon,
     They willfully themselves exile from light
     And must for aye° consort with black-brow'd
     night.
OBERON: But we are spirits of another sort.
     I with the Morning's love° have oft made sport,
390   And, like a forester,° the groves may tread
     Even till the eastern gate, all fiery-red,
     Opening on Neptune with fair blessed beams,
     Turns into yellow gold his salt green streams.
     But, notwithstanding, haste; make no delay.
395   We may effect this business yet ere day.   [*Exit.*]
PUCK: Up and down, up and down,
     I will lead them up and down.
     I am fear'd in field and town.
     Goblin, lead them up and down.
400   Here comes one.

(*Enter Lysander.*)

LYSANDER: Where art thou, proud Demetrius?
     Speak thou now.
PUCK [*mimicking Demetrius*]: Here, villain, drawn°
     and ready. Where art thou?
LYSANDER: I will be with thee straight.°
PUCK: Follow me, then,
     To plainer° ground.
     [*Lysander wanders about, following the voice.*]°

(*Enter Demetrius.*)

DEMETRIUS: Lysander! Speak again!
405   Thou runaway, thou coward, art thou fled?
     Speak! In some bush? Where dost thou hide thy
     head?
PUCK [*mimicking Lysander*]: Thou coward, art thou
     bragging to the stars,
     Telling the bushes that thou look'st for wars,
     And wilt not come? Come, recreant;° come, thou
     child,
410   I'll whip thee with a rod. He is defil'd
     That draws a sword on thee.
DEMETRIUS: Yea, art thou there?
PUCK: Follow my voice. We'll try° no manhood
     here.

                         (*Exeunt.*)

---

387. **for aye:** Forever.   389. **Morning's love:** Cephalus, a
beautiful youth beloved by Aurora; or perhaps the goddess
of the dawn herself.   390. **forester:** Keeper of a royal forest.   402. **drawn:** With drawn sword.   403. **straight:** Immediately.   404. **plainer:** Smoother.   404. [S.D.] *Lysander
wanders about*: It is not clearly necessary that Lysander exit
at this point; neither exit nor reentrance is indicated in the
early texts.   409. **recreant:** Cowardly wretch.   412. **try:**
Test.

[*Lysander returns.*]

LYSANDER: He goes before me and still dares me on.
     When I come where he calls, then he is gone.
     The villain is much lighter-heel'd than I.   415
     I followed fast, but faster he did fly,
     That fallen am I in dark uneven way,
     And here will rest me. [*Lies down.*] Come, thou
     gentle day!
     For if but once thou show me thy gray light,
     I'll find Demetrius and revenge this spite. [*Sleeps.*]   420

([*Enter*] Robin [*Puck*] *and Demetrius.*)

PUCK: Ho, ho, ho! Coward, why com'st thou not?
DEMETRIUS: Abide me, if thou dar'st; for well I wot°
     Thou runn'st before me, shifting every place,
     And dar'st not stand nor look me in the face.
     Where art thou now?
PUCK: Come hither. I am here.   425
DEMETRIUS: Nay, then, thou mock'st me. Thou shalt
     buy° this dear,°
     If ever I thy face by daylight see.
     Now, go thy way. Faintness constraineth me
     To measure out my length on this cold bed.
     By day's approach look to be visited.   430
                      [*Lies down and sleeps.*]

(*Enter Helena.*)

HELENA: O weary night, O long and tedious night,
     Abate° thy hours! Shine, comforts, from the east,
     That I may back to Athens by daylight,
     From these that my poor company detest;
     And sleep, that sometimes shuts up sorrow's eye,   435
     Steal me awhile from mine own company.
                      [*Lies down and*] sleep[*s*].
PUCK: Yet but three? Come one more;
     Two of both kinds makes up four.
     Here she comes, curst and sad.
     Cupid is a knavish lad,   440
     Thus to make poor females mad.

[*Enter Hermia.*]

HERMIA: Never so weary, never so in woe,
     Bedabbled with the dew and torn with briers,
     I can no further crawl, no further go;
     My legs can keep no pace with my desires.   445
     Here will I rest me till the break of day.
     Heavens shield Lysander, if they mean a fray!
                      [*Lies down and sleeps.*]
PUCK: On the ground
     Sleep sound.
     I'll apply   450

---

422. **wot:** Know.   426. **buy:** Pay for.   **dear:** Dearly.
432. **Abate:** Lessen, shorten.

To your eye,
Gentle lover, remedy.
          [*Squeezing the juice on Lysander's eyes.*]
When thou wak'st,
Thou tak'st
455   True delight
In the sight
Of thy former lady's eye;
And the country proverb known,
That every man should take his own,
460   In your waking shall be shown:
Jack shall have Jill;
Nought shall go ill;
The man shall have his mare again, and all shall
be well.   [*Exit. Manent the four lovers.*]

{*ACT IV • Scene I*}°

(*Enter [Titania,] Queen of Fairies, and [Bottom the]
Clown, and Fairies; and [Oberon,] the King, behind
them.*)

TITANIA: Come, sit thee down upon this flow'ry bed,
          While I thy amiable° cheeks do coy,°
          And stick musk-roses in thy sleek smooth head,
          And kiss thy fair large ears, my gentle joy.
                              [*They recline.*]

BOTTOM: Where's Peaseblossom?   5
PEASEBLOSSOM: Ready.

IV, I. **Location:** Scene continues. The four lovers are still
asleep onstage.   **2. amiable:** Lovely.   **coy:** Caress.

RIGHT: Elizabeth McGovern as Helena in the 1987 New York Shakespeare festival production of *A Midsummer Night's Dream*, directed by A. J. Antoon. LEFT: F. Murray Abraham (left) as Bottom, playing Pyramus.

BOTTOM: Scratch my head, Peaseblossom. Where's Mounsieur Cobweb?

COBWEB: Ready.

10 BOTTOM: Mounsieur Cobweb, good mounsieur, get you your weapons in your hand, and kill me a red-hipp'd humble-bee on the top of a thistle; and, good mounsieur, bring me the honey-bag. Do not fret yourself too much in the action, mounsieur;

15 and, good mounsieur, have a care the honey-bag break not; I would be loath to have you overflown with a honey-bag, signior. Where's Mounsieur Mustardseed?

MUSTARDSEED: Ready.

20 BOTTOM: Give me your neaf,° Mounsieur Mustard-seed. Pray you, leave your curtsy,° good mounsieur.

MUSTARDSEED: What's your will?

BOTTOM: Nothing, good mounsieur, but to help Cav-alery° Cobweb° to scratch. I must to the barber's,

mounsieur; for methinks I am marvailes hairy 25 about the face; and I am such a tender ass, if my hair do but tickle me, I must scratch.

TITANIA: What, wilt thou hear some music, my sweet love?

BOTTOM: I have a reasonable good ear in music. Let's have the tongs and the bones.° 30

[*Music: tongs, rural music.*]°

TITANIA: Or say, sweet love, what thou desirest to eat.

BOTTOM: Truly, a peck of provender. I could munch your good dry oats. Methinks I have a great desire to a bottle° of hay. Good hay, sweet hay, hath no fellow.° 35

TITANIA: I have a venturous fairy that shall seek The squirrel's hoard, and fetch thee new nuts.

BOTTOM: I had rather have a handful or two of dried

20. **neaf:** Fist.   21. **leave your curtsy:** Put on your hat. 23–24. **Cavalery:** Cavalier. Form of address for a gentleman. 24. **Cobweb:** Seemingly an error, since Cobweb has been sent to bring honey while Peaseblossom has been asked to scratch.

30. **tongs . . . bones:** Instruments for rustic music. (The tongs were played like a triangle, whereas the bones were held be-tween the fingers and used as clappers.)   30. [S.D.] *Music . . . music:* This stage direction is added from the Folio.   34. **bottle:** Bundle.   35. **fellow:** Equal.

40 peas. But, I pray you, let none of your people stir
me. I have an exposition° of sleep come upon me.
TITANIA: Sleep thou, and I will wind thee in my
arms.
Fairies, be gone, and be all ways° away.
[Exeunt fairies.]
So doth the woodbine the sweet honeysuckle
Gently entwist; the female ivy so
45 Enrings the barky fingers of the elm.
Oh, how I love thee! How I dote on thee!
[They sleep.]

(Enter Robin Goodfellow [Puck].)

OBERON [advancing]: Welcome, good Robin. See'st
thou this sweet sight?
Her dotage now I do begin to pity.
For, meeting her of late behind the wood,
50 Seeking sweet favors° for this hateful fool,
I did upbraid her and fall out with her.
For she his hairy temples then had rounded
With coronet of fresh and fragrant flowers;
And that same dew, which sometime° on the
buds
55 Was wont to swell like round and orient pearls,°
Stood now within the pretty flouriets'° eyes
Like tears that did their own disgrace bewail.
When I had at my pleasure taunted her,
And she in mild terms begg'd my patience,
60 I then did ask of her her changeling child;
Which straight she gave me, and her fairy sent
To bear him to my bower in fairy land.
And, now I have the boy, I will undo
This hateful imperfection of her eyes.
65 And, gentle Puck, take this transformed scalp
From off the head of this Athenian swain,
That, he awaking when the other° do,
May all to Athens back again repair,
And think no more of this night's accidents
70 But as the fierce vexation of a dream.
But first I will release the Fairy Queen.
[Squeezes juice in her eyes.]
Be as thou wast wont to be;
See as thou wast wont to see.
Dian's bud° o'er Cupid's flower
75 Hath such force and blessed power.
Now, my Titania, wake you, my sweet queen.

TITANIA [waking]: My Oberon! What visions have I
seen!
Methought I was enamor'd of an ass.
OBERON: There lies your love.
TITANIA: How came these things to pass?
O, how mine eyes do loathe his visage now!   80
OBERON: Silence awhile. Robin, take off this head.
Titania, music call, and strike more dead
Than common sleep of all these five° the sense.
TITANIA: Music, ho! Music, such as charmeth sleep!
[Music.]
PUCK [removing the ass's head]: Now, when thou
wak'st, with thine own fool's eyes peep.   85
OBERON: Sound, music! Come, my queen, take
hands with me,
And rock the ground whereon these sleepers be.
[Dance.]
Now thou and I are new in amity,
And will tomorrow midnight solemnly°
Dance in Duke Theseus' house triumphantly   90
And bless it to all fair prosperity.
There shall the pairs of faithful lovers be
Wedded, with Theseus, all in jollity.
PUCK: Fairy King, attend, and mark:
I do hear the morning lark.   95
OBERON: Then, my queen, in silence sad,°
Trip we after night's shade.
We the globe can compass soon,
Swifter than the wand'ring moon.
TITANIA: Come, my lord, and in our flight   100
Tell me how it came this night
That I sleeping here was found
With these mortals on the ground.   (Exeunt.)
(Wind horn [within].)

(Enter Theseus and all his train; [Hippolyta, Egeus].)

THESEUS: Go, one of you, find out the forester,
For now our observation° is perform'd;   105
And since we have the vaward° of the day,
My love shall hear the music of my hounds.
Uncouple in the western valley; let them go.
Dispatch, I say, and find the forester.
[Exit an Attendant.]
We will, fair queen, up to the mountain's top   110
And mark the musical confusion
Of hounds and echo in conjunction.
HIPPOLYTA: I was with Hercules and Cadmus° once,
When in a wood of Crete they bay'd° the bear

40. exposition: Bottom's word for *disposition*.   42. all
ways: In all directions.   50. favors: I.e., gifts of flowers.
54. sometime: Formerly.   55. orient pearls: The most
beautiful of all pearls, those coming from the Orient.
56. flouriets': Flowerets'.   67. other: Others.   74. Dian's
bud: Perhaps the flower of the *agnus castus* or chaste-tree,
supposed to preserve chastity; or perhaps referring simply to
Oberon's herb by which he can undo the effects of "Cupid's
flower," the love-in-idleness of II, i, 166-68.

83. these five: I.e., the four lovers and Bottom.
89. solemnly: Ceremoniously.   96. sad: Sober.   105. observation: Observance to a morn of May (I, i, 167).
106. vaward: Vanguard, i.e., earliest part.   113. Cadmus:
Mythical founder of Thebes. (This story about him is unknown.)   114. bay'd: Brought to bay.

115 With hounds of Sparta.° Never did I hear
     Such gallant chiding; for, besides the groves,
     The skies, the fountains, every region near
     Seem'd all one mutual cry. I never heard
     So musical a discord, such sweet thunder.
     THESEUS: My hounds are bred out of the Spartan
120   kind,
     So flew'd,° so sanded;° and their heads are hung
     With ears that sweep away the morning dew;
     Crook-knee'd, and dewlapp'd° like Thessalian
          bulls;
     Slow in pursuit, but match'd in mouth like bells,
125 Each under each.° A cry° more tuneable°
     Was never holla'd to, nor cheer'd with horn,
     In Crete, in Sparta, nor in Thessaly.
     Judge when you hear. [*Sees the sleepers.*] But,
          soft! What nymphs are these?
     EGEUS: My lord, this' my daughter here asleep;
130 And this, Lysander; this Demetrius is;
     This Helena, old Nedar's Helena.
     I wonder of their being here together.
     THESEUS: No doubt they rose up early to observe
     The rite of May, and, hearing our intent,
135 Came here in grace of our solemnity.°
     But speak, Egeus. Is not this the day
     That Hermia should give answer of her choice?
     EGEUS: It is, my lord.
     THESEUS: Go, bid the huntsmen wake them with
          their horns.
                              [*Exit an Attendant.*]

(*Shout within. Wind horns. They all start up.*)

140 Good morrow, friends. Saint Valentine° is past.
     Begin these wood-birds but to couple now?
     LYSANDER: Pardon, my lord.   [*They kneel.*]
     THESEUS: I pray you all, stand up.
     I know you two are rival enemies;
     How comes this gentle concord in the world,
145 That hatred is so far from jealousy
     To sleep by hate and fear no enmity?
     LYSANDER: My lord, I shall reply amazedly,
     Half sleep, half waking; but as yet, I swear,
     I cannot truly say how I came here.
150 But, as I think — for truly would I speak,
     And now I do bethink me, so it is —

I came with Hermia hither. Our intent
Was to be gone from Athens, where° we might,
Without° the peril of the Athenian law —
EGEUS: Enough, enough, my lord; you have enough.   155
I beg the law, the law, upon his head.
They would have stol'n away; they would,
     Demetrius,
Thereby to have defeated you and me,
You of your wife and me of my consent,
Of my consent that she should be your wife.   160
DEMETRIUS: My lord, fair Helen told me of their
     stealth,
Of this their purpose hither to this wood,
And I in fury hither followed them,
Fair Helena in fancy following me.
But, my good lord, I wot not by what power —   165
But by some power it is — my love to Hermia,
Melted as the snow, seems to me now
As the remembrance of an idle gaud.°
Which in my childhood I did dote upon;
And all the faith, the virtue of my heart,   170
The object and the pleasure of mine eye,
Is only Helena. To her, my lord,
Was I betroth'd ere I saw Hermia,
But like a sickness did I loathe this food;
But, as in health, come to my natural taste,   175
Now I do wish it, love it, long for it,
And will for evermore be true to it.
THESEUS: Fair lovers, you are fortunately met.
Of this discourse we more will hear anon.
Egeus, I will overbear your will;   180
For in the temple, by and by, with us
These couples shall eternally be knit.
And, for° the morning now is something° worn,
Our purpos'd hunting shall be set aside.
Away with us to Athens. Three and three,   185
We'll hold a feast in great solemnity.
Come, Hippolyta.
     [*Exeunt Theseus, Hippolyta, Egeus, and train.*]
DEMETRIUS: These things seem small and
     undistinguishable,
Like far-off mountains turned into clouds.
HERMIA: Methinks I see these things with parted°
     eye,   190
When every thing seems double.
HELENA: So methinks;
And I have found Demetrius like a jewel,
Mine own, and not mine own.°

---

115. **hounds of Sparta:** Breed famous in antiquity for their hunting skill.   121. **So flew'd:** Similarly having large hanging chaps or fleshy covering of the jaw.   **sanded:** Of sandy color.   123. **dewlapp'd:** Having pendulous folds of skin under the neck.   124–25. **match'd . . . under each:** Harmoniously matched in their various cries like a set of bells, from treble down to bass.   125. **cry:** Pack of hounds.   **tuneable:** Well tuned, melodious.   135. **solemnity:** Observance of these same rites of May.   140. **Saint Valentine:** Birds were supposed to choose their mates on St. Valentine's Day.

153. **where:** Wherever; or to where.   154. **Without:** Outside of, beyond.   168. **idle gaud:** Worthless trinket.   183. **for:** Since.   **something:** Somewhat.   190. **parted:** Improperly focused.   192–93. **like . . . not mine own:** Like a jewel that one finds by chance and therefore possesses but cannot certainly consider one's own property.

DEMETRIUS: Are you sure
That we are awake? It seems to me
195   That yet we sleep, we dream. Do not you think
The Duke was here, and bid us follow him?
HERMIA: Yea, and my father.
HELENA: And Hippolyta.
LLYSANDER: And he did bid us follow to the temple.
DEMETRIUS: Why, then, we are awake. Let's follow
     him,
200   And by the way let us recount our dreams.
                             [*Exeunt.*]
BOTTOM [*awaking*]: When my cue comes, call me,
and I will answer. My next is, "Most fair Pyramus." Heigh-ho! Peter Quince! Flute, the bellows-
mender! Snout, the tinker! Starveling! God's my
205   life, stol'n hence, and left me asleep! I have had a
most rare vision. I have had a dream, past the wit
of man to say what dream it was. Man is but an
ass, if he go about° to expound this dream.
Methought I was — there is no man can tell what.
210   Methought I was — and methought I had — but
man is but a patch'd° fool, if he will offer° to say
what me-thought I had. The eye of man hath not
heard, the ear of man hath not seen, man's hand is
not able to taste, his tongue to conceive, nor his
215   heart to report, what my dream was. I will get Peter Quince to write a ballad of this dream. It shall
be call'd "Bottom's Dream," because it hath no
bottom; and I will sing it in the latter end of a play,
before the Duke. Peradventure, to make it the
220   more gracious, I shall sing it at her° death. [*Exit.*]

{*Scene II*}°

(*Enter Quince, Flute, [Snout, and Starveling].*)

QUINCE: Have you sent to Bottom's house? Is he come
home yet?
STARVELING: He cannot be heard of. Out of doubt he
is transported.°
5   FLUTE: If he come not, then the play is marr'd. It goes
not forward, doth it?
QUINCE: It is not possible. You have not a man in all
Athens able to discharge° Pyramus but he.
FLUTE: No, he hath simply the best wit of any handi-
10   craft man in Athens.
QUINCE: Yea, and the best person too; and he is a very
paramour for a sweet voice.

FLUTE: You must say "paragon." A paramour is, God
bless us, a thing of naught.

(*Enter Snug the Joiner.*)

SNUG: Masters, the Duke is coming from the temple,   15
and there is two or three lords and ladies more
married. If our sport had gone forward, we had all
been made men.
FLUTE: O sweet bully Bottom! Thus hath he lost sixpence a day° during his life; he could not have   20
scap'd sixpence a day. An the Duke had not given
him sixpence a day for playing Pyramus, I'll be
hang'd. He would have deserv'd it. Sixpence a day
in Pyramus, or nothing.

(*Enter Bottom.*)

BOTTOM: Where are these lads? Where are these hearts?°   25
QUINCE: Bottom! O most courageous day! O most
happy hour!
BOTTOM: Masters, I am to discourse wonders.° But ask
me not what; for if I tell you, I am no true Athenian. I will tell you everything, right as it fell out.   30
QUINCE: Let us hear, sweet Bottom.
BOTTOM: Not a word of° me. All that I will tell you
is, that the Duke hath din'd. Get your apparel together, good strings° to your beards, new ribands°   35
to your pumps, meet presently° at the palace, every
man look o'er his part; for the short and the long
is, our play is preferr'd.° In any case, let Thisby
have clean linen; and let not him that plays the lion
pare his nails, for they shall hang out for the lion's   40
claws. And, most dear actors, eat no onions nor
garlic, for we are to utter sweet breath; and I do
not doubt but to hear them say, it is a sweet comedy. No more words. Away! go, away!
                             [*Exeunt.*]

{*ACT V • Scene I*}°

(*Enter Theseus, Hippolyta, and Philostrate, [Lords, and Attendants].*)

HIPPOLYTA: 'Tis strange, my Theseus, that° these
     lovers speak of.
THESEUS: More strange than true. I never may°
     believe

---

208. go about: Attempt.   **211. patch'd:** Wearing motley,
i.e., a dress of various colors.   **offer:** Venture.   **220. her:**
Thisby's (?).   **IV, II. Location:** Athens, Quince's house (?).
4. transported: Carried off by fairies; or, possibly, transformed.   **8. discharge:** Perform.

19–20. sixpence a day: As a royal pension.   **25. hearts:**
Good fellows.   **28. am . . . wonders:** Have wonders to relate.   **33. of:** Out of.   **35. strings:** To attach the beards.
ribands: Ribbons.   **36. presently:** Immediately.   **38. preferr'd:** Selected for consideration.   **V, I. Location:** Athens.
The palace of Theseus.   **1. that:** That which.   **2. may:**
Can.

These antic° fables, nor these fairy toys.°
Lovers and madmen have such seething brains
5 Such shaping fantasies,° that apprehend
More than cool reason ever comprehends.
The lunatic, the lover, and the poet
Are of imagination all compact.°
One sees more devils than vast hell can hold;
10 That is the madman. The lover, all as frantic,
Sees Helen's° beauty in a brow of Egypt.°
The poet's eye, in a fine frenzy rolling,
Doth glance from heaven to earth, from earth to
    heaven;
And as imagination bodies forth
15 The forms of things unknown, the poet's pen
Turns them to shapes and gives to airy nothing
A local habitation and a name.
Such tricks hath strong imagination
That, if it would but apprehend some joy,
20 It comprehends some bringer° of that joy;
Or in the night, imagining some fear,°
How easy is a bush suppos'd a bear!
HIPPOLYTA: But all the story of the night told over,
And all their minds transfigur'd so together,
25 More witnesseth than fancy's images°
And grows to something of great constancy;°
But, howsoever,° strange and admirable.°

(*Enter lovers: Lysander, Demetrius, Hermia, and Helena.*)

THESEUS: Here come the lovers, full of joy and
    mirth.
Joy, gentle friends! Joy and fresh days of love
Accompany your hearts!
30 LYSANDER: More than to us
Wait in your royal walks, your board, your bed!
THESEUS: Come now, what masques, what dances
    shall we have,
To wear away this long age of three hours
Between our after-supper and bed-time?
35 Where is our usual manager of mirth?
What revels are in hand? Is there no play,
To ease the anguish of a torturing hour?
Call Philostrate.
PHILOSTRATE: Here, mighty Theseus.

THESEUS: Say, what abridgement° have you for this
    evening?
What masque? What music? How shall we
    beguile   40
The lazy time, if not with some delight?
PHILOSTRATE: There is a brief° how many sports are
    ripe.
Make choice of which your Highness will see
    first.
                              [*Giving a paper.*]
THESEUS [*reads*]: "The battle with the Centaurs,° to
    be sung
By an Athenian eunuch to the harp."   45
We'll none of that. That have I told my love,
In glory of my kinsman° Hercules.
[*Reads.*] "The riot of the tipsy Bacchanals,
Tearing the Thracian singer in their rage."°
That is an old device; and it was play'd   50
When I from Thebes came last a conqueror.
[*Reads.*] "The thrice three Muses mourning for
    the death
Of Learning, late deceas'd in beggary."°
That is some satire, keen and critical,
Not sorting with° a nuptial ceremony.   55
[*Reads.*] "A tedious brief scene of young
    Pyramus
And his love Thisby; very tragical mirth."
Merry and tragical? Tedious and brief?
That is, hot ice and wondrous strange° snow.
How shall we find the concord of this discord?   60
PHILOSTRATE: A play there is, my lord, some ten
    words long,
Which is as brief as I have known a play;
But by ten words, my lord, it is too long,
Which makes it tedious. For in all the play
There is not one word apt, one player fitted.   65
And tragical, my noble lord, it is,
For Pyramus therein doth kill himself.
Which, when I saw rehears'd, I must confess,

---

3. **antic:** Strange, grotesque (with additional punning sense of *antique*, ancient). **fairy toys:** Trifling stories about fairies. 5. **fantasies:** Imaginations. 8. **compact:** Formed, composed. 11. **Helen's:** Of Helen of Troy, pattern of beauty. **brow of Egypt:** Face of a gypsy. 20. **bringer:** Source. 21. **fear:** Object of fear. 25. **More...images:** Testifies to something more substantial than mere imaginings. 26. **constancy:** Certainty. 27. **howsoever:** In any case. **admirable:** A source of wonder.

39. **abridgement:** Pastime (to abridge or shorten the evening). 42. **brief:** Short written statement, list. 44. **"battle...Centaurs":** Probably refers to the battle of the Centaurs and the Lapithae, when the Centaurs attempted to carry off Hippodamia, bride of Theseus's friend Pirothous. 47. **kinsman:** Plutarch's *Life of Theseus* states that Hercules and Theseus were near-kinsmen. Theseus is referring to a version of the battle of the Centaurs in which Hercules was said to be present. 48–49. **"The riot...rage":** This was the story of the death of Orpheus, as told in *Metamorphoses*. 52–53. **"The thrice...beggary":** Possibly an allusion to Spenser's *Teares of the Muses* (1591), though "satires" deploring the neglect of learning and the creative arts were common-place. 55. **sorting with:** Befitting. 59. **strange:** Seemingly an error for some adjective that would contrast with *snow*, just as *hot* contrasts with *ice*.

Stage model of the set for Max Reinhardt's 1913 production of a *Midsummer Night's Dream* at the Deutsches Theater in Berlin. The design called for an entire forest to be built on a stage that revolved as the action shifted.

Made mine eyes water, but more merry tears
70   The passion of loud laughter never shed.
THESEUS: What are they that do play it?
PHILOSTRATE: Hard-handed men that work in Athens here,
        Which never labor'd in their minds till now,
        And now have toil'd° their unbreathed° memories
75   With this same play, against° your nuptial.
THESEUS: And we will hear it.
PHILOSTRATE: No, my noble lord,
        It is not for you. I have heard it over,
        And it is nothing, nothing in the world;
        Unless you can find sport in their intents,
80   Extremely stretch'd° and conn'd° with cruel pain,
        To do you service.
THESEUS: I will hear that play;
        For never anything can be amiss'
        When simpleness and duty tender it.
        Go, bring them in; and take your places, ladies.
                [*Philostrate goes to summon the players.*]

HIPPOLYTA: I love not to see wretchedness o'ercharg'd°
        And duty in his service° perishing.   85
THESEUS: Why, gentle sweet, you shall see no such thing.
HIPPOLYTA: He says they can do nothing in this kind.°
THESEUS: The kinder we, to give them thanks for nothing.
        Our sport shall be to take what they mistake;   90
        And what poor duty cannot do, noble respect
        Takes it in might, not merit.°
        Where I have come, great clerks° have purposed
        To greet me with premeditated welcomes;
        Where I have seen them shiver and look pale,   95
        Make periods in the midst of sentences,
        Throttle their practic'd accent° in their fears,
        And in conclusion dumbly have broke off,

74. **toil'd:** Taxed. **unbreathed:** Unexercised. 75. **against:** In preparation for. 80. **stretch'd:** Strained. **conn'd:** Memorized.

85. **wretchedness o'ercharg'd:** Incompetence over-burdened. 86. **his service:** Its attempt to serve. 88. **kind:** Kind of thing. 92. **Takes . . . merit:** Values it for the effort made rather than for the excellence achieved. 93. **clerks:** Learned men. 97. **practic'd accent:** Rehearsed speech; or usual way of speaking.

Not paying me a welcome. Trust me, sweet,
100 Out of this silence yet I pick'd a welcome;
And in the modesty of fearful duty
I read as much as from the rattling tongue
Of saucy and audacious eloquence.
Love, therefore, and tongue-tied simplicity
105 In least° speak most, to my capacity.°

[*Philostrate returns.*]

PHILOSTRATE: So please your Grace, the Prologue° is
address'd.°
THESEUS: Let him approach.   [*Flourish of trumpets.*]

(*Enter the Prologue* [*Quince*].)

PROLOGUE: If we offend, it is with our good will.
That you should think, we come not to offend,
110 But with good will. To show our simple skill,
That is the true beginning of our end.
Consider, then, we come but in despite.
We do not come, as minding° to content you,
Our true intent is. All for your delight
115 We are not here. That you should here repent
you,
The actors are at hand; and, by their show,
You shall know all that you are like to know.
THESEUS: This fellow doth not stand upon points.°
LYSANDER: He hath rid his prologue like a rough°
120 colt; he knows not the stop.° A good moral, my
lord: it is not enough to speak, but to speak true.
HIPPOLYTA: Indeed he hath play'd on his prologue like
a child on a recorder;° a sound, but not in government.°
125 THESEUS: His speech was like a tangled chain, nothing°
impair'd, but all disorder'd. Who is next?

(*Enter Pyramus and Thisby, and Wall, and Moonshine, and Lion.*)

PROLOGUE: Gentles, perchance you wonder at this
show;
But wonder on, till truth make all things plain.
This man is Pyramus, if you would know;
130 This beauteous lady Thisby is certain.
This man, with lime and rough-cast, doth present
Wall, that vile Wall which did these lovers
sunder;

And through Wall's chink, poor souls, they are
content
To whisper. At the which let no man wonder.
This man, with lantern, dog, and bush of thorn,   135
Presenteth Moonshine; for, if you will know,
By moonshine did these lovers think no scorn°
To meet at Ninus' tomb, there, there to woo.
This grisly beast, which Lion hight° by name,
The trusty Thisby, coming first by night,   140
Did scare away, or rather did affright;
And, as she fled, her mantle she did fall,°
Which Lion vile with bloody mouth did stain.
Anon comes Pyramus, sweet youth and tall,°
And finds his trusty Thisby's mantle slain;   145
Whereat, with blade, with bloody blameful blade,
He bravely broach'd° his boiling bloody breast.
And Thisby, tarrying in mulberry shade,
His dagger drew, and died. For all the rest,
Let Lion, Moonshine, Wall, and lovers twain   150
At large° discourse, while here they do remain.
     (*Exeunt Lion, Thisby, and Moonshine.*)
THESEUS: I wonder if the lion be to speak.
DEMETRIUS: No wonder, my lord. One lion may, when
many asses do.
WALL: In this same interlude it doth befall   155
That I, one Snout by name, present a wall;
And such a wall, as I would have you think,
That had in it a crannied hole or chink,
Through which the lovers, Pyramus and Thisby,
Did whisper often very secretly.   160
This loam, this rough-cast, and this stone doth
show
That I am that same wall; the truth is so.
And this the cranny is, right and sinister,°
Through which the fearful lovers are to whisper.
THESEUS: Would you desire lime and hair to speak   165
better?
DEMETRIUS: It is the wittiest partition° that ever I
heard discourse, my lord.

[*Pyramus comes forward.*]

THESEUS: Pyramus draws near the wall. Silence!
PYRAMUS: O grim-look'd° night! O night with hue
so black!   170
O night, which ever art when day is not!
O night, O night! Alack, alack, alack,
I fear my Thisby's promise is forgot.
And thou, O wall, O sweet, O lovely wall,

---

105. least: Saying least.   **to my capacity:** In my judgment
and understanding.   **106. Prologue:** Speaker of the prologue.   **address'd:** Ready.   **113. minding:** Intending.
118. stand upon points: (1) Heed niceties or small points, (2)
pay attention to punctuation in his reading. (The humor of
Quince's speech is in the blunders of its punctuation.)
119. rough: Unbroken.   **120. stop:** (1) The stopping of a
colt by reining it in, (2) punctuation mark.   **123. recorder:**
A wind instrument like a flute.   **124. government:** Control.
125. nothing: Not at all.

137. think no scorn: Think it no disgraceful matter.
139. highs: Is called.   **142. fall:** Let fall.   **144. tall:**
Courageous.   **147. broach'd:** Stabbed.   **151. At large:** In
full, at length.   **163. right and sinister:** The right side of it
and the left (sinister); or running from right to left, horizon-
tally.   **167. partition:** (1) Wall, (2) section of a learned treatise or oration.   **170. grim-look'd:** Grim-looking.

175   That stand'st between her father's ground and
      mine,
   Thou wall, O wall, O sweet and lovely wall,
   Show me thy chink, to blink through with mine
      eyne!   [*Wall holds up his fingers.*]
   Thanks, courteous wall. Jove shield thee well for
      this!
   But what see I? No Thisby do I see.
180   O wicked wall, through whom I see no bliss!
   Curs'd be thy stones for thus deceiving me!
THESEUS: The wall, methinks, being sensible,° should
   curse again.
PYRAMUS: No, in truth, sir, he should not. "Deceiving
185   me" is Thisby's cue: she is to enter now, and I am
   to spy her through the wall. You shall see, it will
   fall pat as I told you. Yonder she comes.

(*Enter Thisby.*)

THISBY: O wall, full often hast thou heard my
      moans,
   For parting my fair Pyramus and me.
190   My cherry lips have often kiss'd thy stones,
   Thy stones with lime and hair knit up in thee.
PYRAMUS: I see a voice. Now will I to the chink,
   To spy an° I can hear my Thisby's face.
   Thisby!
195 THISBY: My love! Thou art my love, I think.
PYRAMUS: Think what thou wilt, I am thy lover's
      grace;°
   And, like Limander° am I trusty still.
THISBY: And I like Helen,° till the Fates me kill.
PYRAMUS: Not Shafalus° to Procrus° was so true.
200 THISBY: As Shafalus to Procrus, I to you.
PYRAMUS: O, kiss me through the hole of this vile
      wall!
THISBY: I kiss the wall's hole, not your lips at all.
PYRAMUS: Wilt thou at Ninny's tomb meet me
      straightway?
THISBY: 'Tide° life, 'tide death, I come without delay.
      [*Exeunt Pyramus and Thisby.*]
205 WALL: Thus have I, Wall, my part discharged so;
   And, being done, thus Wall away doth go. [*Exit.*]
THESEUS: Now is the mural down between the two
   neighbors.
DEMETRIUS: No remedy, my lord, when walls are so
210   willful to hear° without warning.°

HIPPOLYTA: This is the silliest stuff that ever I heard.
THESEUS: The best in this kind° are but shadows;°
   and the worst are no worse, if imagination amend
   them.
HIPPOLYTA: It must be your imagination then, and not 215
   theirs.
THESEUS: If we imagine no worse of them than they of
   themselves, they may pass for excellent men. Here
   come two noble beasts in, a man and a lion.

(*Enter Lion and Moonshine.*)

LION: You, ladies, you, whose gentle hearts do fear 220
   The smallest monstrous mouse that creeps on
      floor,
   May now perchance both quake and tremble
      here,
   When lion rough in wildest rage doth roar.
   Then know that I, as Snug the joiner, am
   A lion fell,° nor else no lion's dam;   225
   For, if I should as lion come in strife
   Into this place, 'twere pity on my life.
THESEUS: A very gentle beast, and of a good con-
   science.
DEMETRIUS: The very best at a beast, my lord, that
   e'er I saw.   230
LYSANDER: This lion is a very fox for his valor.°
THESEUS: True; and a goose for his discretion.°
DEMETRIUS: Not so, my lord; for his valor cannot
   carry his discretion; and the fox carries the goose.
THESEUS: His discretion, I am sure, cannot carry his 235
   valor, for the goose carries not the fox. It is well.
   Leave it to his discretion, and let us listen to the
   moon.
MOON: This lanthorn° doth the horned moon pre-
   sent —
DEMETRIUS: He should have worn the horns on his 240
   head.°
THESEUS: He is no crescent, and his horns are invisible
   within the circumference.
MOON: This lanthorn doth the horned moon
      present;
   Myself the man i' th' moon do seem to be.   245

---

182. sensible: Capable of feeling.   **193. an:** If.
196. lover's grace: Gracious lover.   **197. Limander:** Blunder for *Leander.*   **198. Helen:** Blunder for *Hero.*
199. Shafalus, Procrus: Blunders for *Cephalus* and *Procris,* also famous lovers.   **204. 'Tide:** Betide, come.   **210. to hear:** As to hear.   **without warning:** Without warning the parents.

212. in this kind: Of this sort.   **shadows:** Likenesses, representations.   **225. lion fell:** Fierce lion (with a play on the idea of *lion skin*).   **231. is . . . valor:** His valor consists of craftiness and discretion.   **232. goose . . . discretion:** As discreet as a goose, that is, more foolish than discreet. **239. lanthorn:** This original spelling may suggest a play on the *horn* of which lanterns were made and also on a cuckold's horns; but the spelling *lanthorn* is not used consistently for comic effect in this play or elsewhere. In V, I, 135, for example, the word is *lantern* in the original.   **240–41. on his head:** As a sign of cuckoldry.

THESEUS: This is the greatest error of all the rest. The man should be put into the lanthorn. How is it else the man i' th' moon?

DEMETRIUS: He dares not come there for the° candle;
250　for, you see, it is already in snuff.°

HIPPOLYTA: I am aweary of this moon. Would he would change!

THESEUS: It appears, by his small light of discretion, that he is in the wane; but yet, in courtesy, in all
255　reason, we must stay the time.

LYSANDER: Proceed, Moon.

MOON: All that I have to say is to tell you that the lanthorn is the moon, I, the man in the moon, this thorn-bush my thorn-bush, and this dog my dog.

260　DEMETRIUS: Why, all these should be in the lanthorn; for all these are in the moon. But silence! Here comes Thisby.

(Enter Thisby.)

THISBY: This is old Ninny's tomb. Where is my love?

LION [*roaring*]: Oh —　　　　　　[*Thisby runs off.*]

265　DEMETRIUS: Well roar'd, Lion.

THESEUS: Well run, Thisby.

HIPPOLYTA: Well shone, Moon. Truly, the moon shines with a good grace.

　　　　[*The Lion shakes Thisby's mantle, and exit.*]

THESEUS: Well mous'd,° Lion.

270　DEMETRIUS: And then came Pyramus.

LYSANDER: And so the lion vanish'd.

(Enter Pyramus.)

PYRAMUS: Sweet Moon, I thank thee for thy sunny beams;
　　I thank thee, Moon, for shining now so bright;
　　For, by thy gracious, golden, glittering gleams,
275　I trust to take of truest Thisby sight.
　　　　But stay, O spite!
　　　　But mark, poor knight,
　　What dreadful dole° is here!
　　　　Eyes, do you see?
280　　　How can it be?
　　O dainty duck! O dear!
　　　　Thy mantle good,
　　　　What, stain'd with blood!
　　Approach, ye Furies fell!°
285　　　O Fates, come, come,
　　　　Cut thread and thrum;°
　　Quail,° crush, conclude, and quell!°

THESEUS: This passion, and the death of a dear friend, would go near to make a man look sad.°

HIPPOLYTA: Beshrew my heart, but I pity the man.　　290

PYRAMUS: O wherefore, Nature, didst thou lions frame?
　Since lion vile hath here deflow'r'd my dear,
　Which is — no, no — which was the fairest dame
　That liv'd, that lov'd, that lik'd, that look'd with cheer.°
　　　Come, tears, confound,　　　　　　　295
　　　Out, sword, and wound
　The pap of Pyramus;
　　　Ay, that left pap,
　　　Where heart doth hop.　　[*Stabs himself.*]
　Thus die I, thus, thus, thus.　　　　　300
　　　Now am I dead,
　　　Now am I fled;
　My soul is in the sky.
　　　Tongue, lose thy light;
　　　Moon, take thy flight.　[*Exit Moonshine.*]　305
　Now die, die, die, die, die.　　　[*Dies.*]

DEMETRIUS: No die, but an ace,° for him; for he is but one.°

LYSANDER: Less than an ace, man; for he is dead, he is nothing.　　　　　　　310

THESEUS: With the help of a surgeon he might yet recover, and yet prove an ass.°

HIPPOLYTA: How chance Moonshine is gone before Thisby comes back and finds her lover?

THESEUS: She will find him by starlight. Here she　315
comes; and her passion ends the play.

[*Enter Thisby.*]

HIPPOLYTA: Methinks she should not use a long one for such a Pyramus. I hope she will be brief.

DEMETRIUS: A mote will turn the balance, which Pyramus, which° Thisby, is the better: he for a man　320
God warr'nt us; she for a woman, God bless us.

LYSANDER: She hath spied him already with those sweet eyes.

DEMETRIUS: And thus she means,° videlicet:°

THISBY: Asleep, my love?　　　　　　325
　　What, dead, my dove?

288–89. This ... sad: If one had other reason to grieve, one might be sad, but not from this absurd portrayal of passion.
294. cheer: Countenance.　　**307. ace:** The side of the die featuring the single pip, or spot. (The pun is on *die* as a singular of *dice*; Bottom's performance is not worth a whole *die* but rather one single face of it, one small portion.)
308. One: (1) An individual person, (2) unique.　**312. ass:** With a pun on *ace*.　**319–20. which ... which:** Whether ... or.　**324. means:** Moans, laments.　**videlicet:** To wit.

---

249. for the: Because of the.　　**250. in snuff:** (1) Offended, (2) in need of snuffing.　**269. mous'd:** Shaken.
278. dole: Grievous event.　**284. fell:** Fierce.　**286. thread and thrum:** The warp in weaving and the loose end of the warp.　**287. Quail:** Overpower.　**quell:** Kill, destroy.

O Pyramus, arise!
   Speak, speak. Quite dumb?
Dead, dead? A tomb
330 Must cover thy sweet eyes.
   These lily lips,
   This cherry nose,
These yellow cowslip cheeks,
   Are gone, are gone!
335   Lovers, make moan.
His eyes were green as leeks.
   O Sisters Three,°
   Come, come to me,
With hands as pale as milk;
340   Lay them in gore,
   Since you have shore°
With shears his thread of silk.
   Tongue, not a word.
   Come, trusty sword,
345 Come, blade, my breast imbrue!°   [*Stabs herself.*]
   And farewell, friends.
   Thus Thisby ends.
   Adieu, adieu, adieu.   [*Dies.*]
THESEUS: Moonshine and Lion are left to bury the
350 dead.
DEMETRIUS: Ay, and Wall too.
BOTTOM [*starting up*]: No, I assure you; the wall is
  down that parted their fathers. Will it please you
  to see the epilogue, or to hear a Bergomask dance°
355 between two of our company?
THESEUS: No epilogue, I pray you; for your play needs
  no excuse. Never excuse; for when the players are
  all dead, there need none to be blam'd. Marry, if
  he that writ it had play'd Pyramus and hang'd
360 himself in Thisby's garter, it would have been a fine
  tragedy; and so it is, truly, and very notably dis-
  charg'd. But, come, your Bergomask. Let your epilogue alone.   [*A dance.*]
  The iron tongue of midnight hath told° twelve.
365 Lovers, to bed; 'tis almost fairy time.
  I fear we shall outsleep the coming morn
  As much as we this night have overwatch'd.°
  This palpable-gross° play hath well beguil'd
  The heavy° gait of night. Sweet friends, to bed.
370 A fortnight hold we this solemnity,
  In nightly revels and new jollity.   (*Exeunt.*)

(*Enter Puck*)

PUCK: Now the hungry lion roars,
   And the wolf behowls the moon;

Whilst the heavy ploughman snores,
   All with weary task fordone.°   375
Now the wasted brands° do glow,
   Whilst the screech-owl, screeching loud,
Puts the wretch that lies in woe
   In remembrance of a shroud.
Now it is the time of night   380
   That the graves, all gaping wide,
Every one lets forth his sprite,°
   In the churchway paths to glide.
And we fairies, that do run
   By the triple Hecate's° team   385
From the presence of the sun,
   Following darkness like a dream,
Now are frolic.° Not a mouse
Shall disturb this hallowed house.
I am sent with broom before,   390
To sweep the dust behind° the door.

(*Enter [Oberon and Titania,] King and Queen of
Fairies, with all their train.*)

OBERON: Through the house give glimmering light,
   By the dead and drowsy fire;
Every elf and fairy sprite
   Hop as light as bird from brier;   395
And this ditty, after me,
   Sing, and dance it trippingly.
TITANIA: First, rehearse your song by rote,
   To each word a warbling note.
Hand in hand, with fairy grace,   400
   Will we sing, and bless this place.
             [*Song and dance.*]
OBERON: Now, until the break of day,
Through this house each fairy stray.
To the best bride-bed will we,
   Which by us shall blessed be;   405
And the issue there create°
   Ever shall be fortunate.
So shall all the couples three
   Ever true in loving be;
And the blots of Nature's hand   410
   Shall not in their issue stand;
Never mole, hare lip, nor scar,
   Nor mark prodigious,° such as are
Despised in nativity,
   Shall upon their children be.   415

---

337. **Sisters Three:** The Fates.   341. **shore:** Shorn.
345. **imbrue:** Stain with blood.   354. **Bergomask dance:** A
rustic dance named for Bergamo, a province in the state
of Venice.   364. **told:** Counted, struck ("tolled").
367. **overwatch'd:** Stayed up too late.   368. **palpable-
gross:** Obviously crude.   369. **heavy:** Drowsy, dull.

375. **fordone:** Exhausted.   376. **wasted brands:** Burned-
out logs.   382. **Every . . . sprite:** Every grave lets forth its
ghost.   385. **triple Hecate's:** Hecate ruled in three capacities: as Luna or Cynthia in heaven, as Diana on earth, and as
Proserpina in hell.   388. **frolic:** Merry.   391. **behind:**
From behind. (Robin Goodfellow was a household spirit
who helped good housemaids and punished lazy ones.)
406. **create:** Created.   413. **prodigious:** Monstrous, unnatural.

With this field-dew consecrate,°
Every fairy take his gait,°
And each several° chamber bless,
Through this palace, with sweet peace;
420 And the owner of it blest
Ever shall in safety rest.
Trip away; make no stay;
Meet me all by break of day.
              (*Exeunt [Oberon, Titania, and train]*.)
Puck: If we shadows have offended,
425 Think but this, and all is mended,
That you have but slumb'red here°

While these visions did appear.
And this weak and idle theme,
No more yielding but° a dream,
Gentles, do not reprehend.   430
If you pardon, we will mend.
And, as I am an honest Puck,
If we have unearned luck
Now to scape the serpent's tongue,°
We will make amends ere long;   435
Else the Puck a liar call.
So, good night unto you all.
Give me your hands,° if we be friends,
And Robin shall restore amends.   [*Exit.*]

---

416. consecrate: Consecrated.   **417. take his gait:** Go his
way.   **418. several:** Separate.   **426. That . . . here:** That it
is a "midsummer night's dream."

429. No . . . but: Yielding no more than.   **434. serpent's
tongue:** Hissing.   **438. Give . . . hands:** Applaud.

HAMLET

Hamlet (1600–1601), Shakespeare's boldest, most profound play, is a
landmark in the poet's work. It coincides with the new century and the
uncertainties of the last years of the old regime, brought to an end by the
death of Queen Elizabeth in 1603. Until the very moment of her death,
the succession was in doubt, but at her death she indicated that her
cousin James of Scotland would take the throne. The new age was in
many ways more complicated, more ambiguous, and more democratic
than the old. It was also more dangerous because it was more uncertain.

Hamlet returns to a Denmark and a court that he hardly recognizes,
to a mother newly wed to his uncle and in many ways not the woman
he remembers, and, finally, to a ghostly father who will not rest until the
crimes against him are avenged. Like Marlowe's Faustus, Hamlet was a
scholar at the University of Wittenberg, where he presumably had studied theology and therefore had a special knowledge of the world of the
spirits. Perhaps he studied medicine and law as well. He gives evidence
of knowing literature and having a taste for theater, and he is a ready
hand with weapons when necessary.

Hamlet is also a melancholic. To the Elizabethan, *melancholic* did not
mean depressed, although Hamlet dresses in black and still mourns for his
father, even against the wishes of his uncle. The melancholic, rather, was
introspective, thoughtful, perhaps world-weary, and possibly a touch sardonic. Above all things, he was an intellectual, a person of wide-ranging
knowledge and intelligence, a reliable commentator with a probing mind.

Hamlet's broad intelligence and the penetrating introspection revealed in his soliloquies, such as his famous "To be, or not to be" meditation on suicide, make him a character with more psychological dimension, more "soul," than many people we know in life. In this sense the play is thoroughly modern; it satisfies our modern need to know the interior lives of characters who engage us onstage. Hamlet's range of feeling, his range of felt and expressed emotion, is impressive to any audience.

Hamlet is a revenge tragedy, a type of play that was especially appealing to the Elizabethans. Thomas Kyd's *The Spanish Tragedy* and John Marston's *Antonio's Revenge* are two examples of successful Elizabethan revenge tragedies. Shakespeare had written an earlier play that could be termed a revenge tragedy, *Titus Andronicus,* in 1594. Below are some characteristics of the revenge tragedy.

The revenge of a relative's murder or rape

The revenge of a father by a son or vice versa

The appearance of a ghost

The hesitancy or delay of the hero

Tricks or devices to achieve revenge

The use of real or pretended insanity

Suicide

Political intrigue in a court

An able, scheming villain or spy

Philosophical soliloquies

Sensational use of horror (murder and gore onstage)

All these elements are present in *Hamlet.* But the play has other important qualities as well. The minor characters are developed in unexpected ways. Ophelia, the innocent, loving woman, becomes a touching figure in her own right. Unable to understand the nature of evil in the Danish court and driven to insanity by Hamlet's rejection of her and by her father's murder, she permits herself to sink to a watery death in a stream. Audiences are moved by her songs, her insane ramblings, and her devotion to her father as well as to Hamlet.

Characters such as Gertrude, Hamlet's mother, reveal a richness of psychology that sometimes startles us. Polonius, Ophelia's father, is virtually a stock character — the old, foolish philosopher — but he takes on special significance when he urges Ophelia to spy for him and when he ultimately dies at the hand of Hamlet. As Hamlet says, it was an unnecessary death for a "wretched, rash, intruding fool." But Polonius's son, Laertes, loved his father, and when Laertes returns grief-stricken, he does not hesitate a moment to get his revenge.

Hamlet's hesitancy is linked with his reputation as a melancholic. Because he thinks things through so deeply, he does not act instantly, as does Laertes. Even when the ghost reveals himself as his father and tells him that he has been murdered and must be avenged, Hamlet fears that the apparition might be a dangerous fakery of the devil to lure him to murder.

But Hamlet shows that he can act swiftly — indeed, rashly. His killing of Polonius is a rash act. He thinks the man behind the tapestry in his mother's bedroom is his uncle, since no other man but her husband has any right to be there. When Hamlet is sent to England with Rosencrantz and Guildenstern, he quickly senses a plot, undoes it, leaps aboard a pirate ship, and negotiates his way home with alacrity. This is not the work of a man who cannot act. In the graveyard scene he acts just as impulsively as Laertes would when he leaps into Ophelia's grave.

Hamlet's talents exhibited in his welcoming of the players in act II show him to be an experienced theatergoer, one with some skills onstage. He is also an expert writer; his additions to *The Murder of Gonzago* convert that imaginary play into a "mousetrap" baited to catch the murderer of his father. In early Renaissance paintings the mousetrap is a symbol for Jesus Christ, who catches the devil. The allusion would not have been lost on the Elizabethan audience, who would have seen Hamlet's psychological approach as being quite reasonable.

Emotions are of great importance to Hamlet. He feels deeply and he watches others to see what their feelings are. He knows that their demeanor may not reveal them as they are, so he must learn to be a careful student of behavior. As he tells his mother, "I know not 'seems.'" What seems is only what is apparent; his procedure is always to penetrate the surfaces of things to know their reality, which is why he uses drama as an instrument to penetrate psychological surfaces.

A connection between Seneca's tragedies and the Elizabethan revenge tragedy has prompted some Shakespeare scholars to declare that Elizabethan tragedy is all-Senecan in nature. What they mean is that Seneca's preference for magic and ghosts as well as his penchant for onstage gore and murder translated well to the Elizabethan stage. Seneca has Iokaste kill herself onstage by ripping open her abdomen, and many such bloody scenes were enacted on the Elizabethan stage. Perhaps, however, the best remnant of Seneca in Elizabethan drama is the rhetorical, almost bombastic speeches of the player in act II, scene II. The lengthy nature of such speeches and their invitation to share a tragic emotion are much in the Senecan mold.

Hamlet in Performance

Richard Burbage played Hamlet in its original 1604 production and continued playing the part into advanced age. *Hamlet* was staged on an English ship off the coast of Africa in 1607. The first American production was in 1759. When one thinks of productions of the play, one thinks of the great actors who played the role. Their names read like a "Who's Who" of acting: David Garrick (1717–1779), Edmund Kean

(1789–1833), William Charles Macready (1793–1873), and Sir Henry Irving (1838–1905) were all identified with the role.

In the twentieth century the two most dominating Hamlets have been John Gielgud and Laurence Olivier, who both acted for the Old Vic Theatre. To interpret the part, Olivier studied psychoanalyst Ernest Jones's essay on Hamlet's Oedipus complex. Jones was a disciple of Freud, who discussed Hamlet in his *Interpretation of Dreams* (see Freud's commentary on pages 480–81). Paul Scofield, in Peter Brook's 1955 production, found the part so challenging that he said playing it "feels like trespassing." Christopher Plummer, Derek Jacobi, and Jonathan Pryce have played the part to acclaim from the 1950s to recent times. Richard Burton also played Hamlet in New York in 1964. Michael Pennington's version for the Royal Shakespeare Company's 1980 production (see photos on pages 400–401) was well received by both critics and audiences. Pennington felt that the part tested not only one's skill but also one's character. He said, "When things go well you could do three performances a day and still be the last to leave the party, and at other times the part shakes you like a rat."

The major productions in the 1980s alone were astonishingly numerous: Christopher Walken for the American Shakespeare Festival in Stratford, Connecticut (1982); Roger Rees for the Royal Shakespeare Company in Stratford, England (1984); Kevin Kline for the New York Shakespeare Festival (1986); Ingmar Bergman's acclaimed production in Swedish (1988) in Sweden and New York; Daniel Day-Lewis for the National Theatre in London (1989); Austin Pendleton for the Riverside Shakespeare Company in New York (1989).

Franco Zeffirelli cast Mel Gibson in his 1990 film, which presents a credible Hamlet capable of deep emotional outburst. The setting of the film is lavish, and the interaction between Hamlet and Gertrude has a special psychological valence. *Hamlet* had a banner year in 1995 when Liam Neeson played the Danish prince in London and New York to considerable acclaim. That production was marked by a careful deemphasis of the great soliloquies. Ralph Fiennes, in the wake of a film success in *Schindler's List,* played in Edwardian clothes on Broadway, using madness as "a way of acting out." Keanu Reeves, another film actor, performed the part at the Manitoba Theater Center in Winnipeg, Canada. One critic said of Reeves's performance, "His hairstyle changed with his moods." Robert Wilson, known for massive semioperatic productions, played entirely alone, in a production premiered in Houston called *Hamlet: A Monologue.* On his deathbed Hamlet relives his story in flashbacks; he provides critical speeches of other characters himself. There is no end in sight for creative interpretations of this great play.

Hamlet has been the dream role not only of great actors but of great actresses as well. Sarah Bernhardt played Hamlet in the late nineteenth century, and Eva Le Gallienne, Siobhan McKenna, and Judith Anderson took on the part in the twentieth century. *Hamlet* has also given rise to numerous spin-offs, the best of which is Tom Stoppard's *Rosencrantz and Guildenstern Are Dead* (1967). Heiner Müller's *Hamletmachine* (1977) is a respected avant-garde version of the play. Lee Blessing's *Fortinbras* (1991) is also an innovative retelling of the play from the point of view of a minor character — except that this character becomes the king. Blessing's success suggests that *Hamlet* is rich enough and inspiring enough to generate numerous further redactions and interpretations.

William Shakespeare (1564–1616)
HAMLET, PRINCE OF DENMARK   *c. 1600*

[Dramatis Personae

CLAUDIUS, *King of Denmark*
HAMLET, *son to the late King Hamlet, and nephew to the present King*
POLONIUS, *Lord Chamberlain*
HORATIO, *friend to Hamlet*
LAERTES, *son to Polonius*
VOLTIMAND,
CORNELIUS,
ROSENCRANTZ, } *courtiers*
GUILDENSTERN,
OSRIC,
GENTLEMAN,
PRIEST, OR DOCTOR OF DIVINITY
MARCELLUS, } *officers*
BERNARDO,
FRANCISCO, *a soldier*
REYNALDO, *servant to Polonius*
PLAYERS
TWO CLOWNS, *grave-diggers*
FORTINBRAS, *Prince of Norway*
CAPTAIN
ENGLISH AMBASSADORS

GERTRUDE, *Queen of Denmark, mother to Hamlet*
OPHELIA, *daughter to Polonius*

LORDS, LADIES, OFFICERS, SOLDIERS, SAILORS, MESSENGERS, AND OTHER ATTENDANTS
GHOST *of Hamlet's father*

Scene: *Denmark.*]

{ACT I • Scene 1}°

(*Enter Bernardo and Francisco, two sentinels, [meeting].*)

BERNARDO: Who's there?
FRANCISCO: Nay, answer me.° Stand and unfold
    yourself.
BERNARDO: Long live the King!
FRANCISCO: Bernardo?
BERNARDO: He.   5
FRANCISCO: You come most carefully upon your
    hour.
BERNARDO: 'Tis now struck twelve. Get thee to bed,
    Francisco.
FRANCISCO: For this relief much thanks. 'Tis bitter
    cold,
    And I am sick at heart.
BERNARDO: Have you had quiet guard?
FRANCISCO: Not a mouse stirring.   10
BERNARDO: Well, good night.
    If you do meet Horatio and Marcellus,
    The rivals° of my watch, bid them make haste.

(*Enter Horatio and Marcellus.*)

Note: The text of *Hamlet* has come down to us in different versions — such as the first quarto, the second quarto, and the first Folio. The copy of the text used here is largely drawn from the second quarto. Passages enclosed in square brackets are taken from one of the other versions, in most cases the first Folio.   **I, 1. Location:** Elsinore castle. A guard platform.   **2. me:** Francisco emphasizes that *he* is the sentry currently on watch.   **13. rivals:** Partners.

FRANCISCO: I think I hear them. Stand, ho! Who is
  there?
HORATIO: Friends to this ground.
15 MARCELLUS: And liegemen to the Dane.°
FRANCISCO: Give you° good night.
MARCELLUS: O, farewell, honest soldier.
  Who hath relieved you?
FRANCISCO: Bernardo hath my place.
  Give you good night.   (*Exit Francisco.*)
MARCELLUS: Holla, Bernardo!
BERNARDO: Say,
  What, is Horatio there?
HORATIO: A piece of him.
BERNARDO: Welcome, Horatio. Welcome, good
20   Marcellus.
HORATIO: What, has this thing appear'd again
  tonight?
BERNARDO: I have seen nothing.
MARCELLUS: Horatio says 'tis but our fantasy,
  And will not let belief take hold of him
25   Touching this dreaded sight, twice seen of us.
  Therefore I have entreated him along
  With us to watch the minutes of this night,
  That if again this apparition come
  He may approve° our eyes and speak to it.
HORATIO: Tush, tush, 'twill not appear.
30 BERNARDO: Sit down awhile,
  And let us once again assail your ears,
  That are so fortified against our story,
  What we have two nights seen.
HORATIO: Well, sit we down,
  And let us hear Bernardo speak of this.
35 BERNARDO: Last night of all,
  When yond same star that's westward from the
    pole°
  Had made his° course t' illume that part of
    heaven
  Where now it burns, Marcellus and myself,
  The bell then beating one —

(*Enter Ghost.*)

MARCELLUS: Peace, break thee off! Look where it
40   comes again!
BERNARDO: In the same figure, like the King that's
  dead.
MARCELLUS: Thou art a scholar.° Speak to it,
  Horatio.
BERNARDO: Looks 'a° not like the King? Mark it,
  Horatio.

HORATIO: Most like. It harrows me with fear and
  wonder.
BERNARDO: It would be spoke to.
MARCELLUS: Speak to it,° Horatio.   45
HORATIO: What art thou that usurp'st this time of
  night,
  Together with that fair and warlike form
  In which the majesty of buried Denmark°
  Did sometimes° march? By heaven I charge thee
    speak!
MARCELLUS: It is offended.
BERNARDO: See, it stalks away.   50
HORATIO: Stay! Speak, speak. I charge thee, speak.
                                (*Exit Ghost.*)
MARCELLUS: 'Tis gone, and will not answer.
BERNARDO: How now, Horatio? You tremble and
  look pale.
  Is not this something more than fantasy?
  What think you on 't?   55
HORATIO: Before my God, I might not this believe
  Without the sensible° and true avouch
  Of mine own eyes.
MARCELLUS: Is it not like the King?
HORATIO: As thou art to thyself.
  Such was the very armor he had on   60
  When he the ambitious Norway° combated.
  So frown'd he once when, in an angry parle,°
  He smote the sledded° Polacks° on the ice.
  'Tis strange.
MARCELLUS: Thus twice before, and jump° at this
  dead hour,   65
  With martial stalk hath he gone by our watch.
HORATIO: In what particular thought to work I
  know not,
  But, in the gross and scope° of mine opinion,
  This bodes some strange eruption to our state.
MARCELLUS: Good now,° sit down, and tell me, he
  that knows,   70
  Why this same strict and most observant watch
  So nightly toils° the subject° of the land,
  And why such daily cast° of brazen cannon,
  And foreign mart° for implements of war,
  Why such impress° of shipwrights, whose sore
    task   75

---

15. **liegemen to the Dane:** Men sworn to serve the Danish
king.   16. **Give you:** God give you.   29. **approve:** Cor-
roborate.   36. **pole:** Polestar.   37. **his:** Its.   42. **scholar:**
One learned in Latin and able to address spirits.   43. **'a:**
He.

45. **It . . . it:** A ghost could not speak until spoken to.
48. **buried Denmark:** The buried king of Denmark.
49. **sometimes:** Formerly.   57. **sensible:** Confirmed by the
senses.   61. **Norway:** King of Norway.   62. **parle:** Parley.
63. **sledded:** Traveling on sleds.   **Polacks:** Poles.
65. **jump:** Exactly.   68. **gross and scope:** General view.
70. **Good now:** An expression denoting entreaty or expostulation.   72. **toils:** Causes to toil.   **subject:** Subjects.
73. **cast:** Casting.   74. **mart:** Buying and selling.   75. **impress:** Impressment, conscription.

Does not divide the Sunday from the week.
What might be toward,° that this sweaty haste
Doth make the night joint-laborer with the day?
Who is 't that can inform me?

HORATIO: That can I,
80 At least, the whisper goes so. Our last king,
Whose image even but now appear'd to us,
Was, as you know, by Fortinbras of Norway,
Thereto prick'd on° by a most emulate° pride,
Dar'd to the combat; in which our valiant
      Hamlet —
85 For so this side of our known world esteem'd
      him —
Did slay this Fortinbras; who, by a seal'd
      compact,
Well ratified by law and heraldry,
Did forfeit, with his life, all those his lands
Which he stood seiz'd° of, to the conqueror;
90 Against the° which a moi'ty competent°
Was gaged° by our king, which had return'd
To the inheritance of Fortinbras
Had he been vanquisher, as, by the same comart°
And carriage° of the article design'd,
95 His fell to Hamlet. Now, sir, young Fortinbras,
Of unimproved° mettle hot and full,
Hath in the skirts° of Norway here and there
Shark'd up° a list of lawless resolutes°
For food and diet° to some enterprise
100 That hath a stomach° in 't, which is no other —
As it doth well appear unto our state —
But to recover of us, by strong hand
And terms compulsatory, those foresaid lands
So by his father lost. And this, I take it,
105 Is the main motive of our preparations,
The source of this our watch, and the chief head°
Of this post-haste and romage° in the land.
BERNARDO: I think it be no other but e'en so.
Well may it sort° that this portentous figure
110 Comes armed through our watch so like the King
That was and is the question of these wars.
HORATIO: A mote° it is to trouble the mind's eye.
In the most high and palmy° state of Rome,

A little ere the mightiest Julius fell,
The graves stood tenantless and the sheeted°
      dead   115
Did squeak and gibber in the Roman streets;
As° stars with trains of fire and dews of blood,
Disasters° in the sun; and the moist star°
Upon whose influence Neptune's° empire stands°
Was sick almost to doomsday° with eclipse.   120
And even the like precurse° of fear'd events,
As harbingers° preceding still° the fates
And prologue to the omen° coming on,
Have heaven and earth together demonstrated
Unto our climatures° and countrymen.   125

(*Enter Ghost.*)

But soft, behold! Lo where it comes again!
I'll cross° it, though it blast me. Stay, illusion!
If thou hast any sound, or use of voice,
Speak to me!   (*It spreads his arms.*)
If there be any good thing to be done   130
That may to thee do ease and grace to me,
Speak to me!
If thou art privy to thy country's fate,
Which, happily,° foreknowing may avoid,
O, speak!   135
Or if thou hast uphoarded in thy life
Extorted treasure in the womb of earth,
For which, they say, you spirits oft walk in
      death,
                              (*The cock crows.*)
Speak of it. Stay, and speak! Stop it, Marcellus.
MARCELLUS: Shall I strike at it with my partisan?° 140
HORATIO: Do, if it will not stand. [*They strike at
      it.*]
BERNARDO: 'Tis here!
HORATIO: 'Tis here!
MARCELLUS: 'Tis gone.   [*Exit Ghost.*]
We do it wrong, being so majestical,
To offer it the show of violence;
For it is, as the air, invulnerable,   145
And our vain blows malicious mockery.

---

77. **toward:** In preparation.   83. **prick'd on:** Incited.   **emulate:** Ambitious.   89. **seiz'd:** Possessed.   90. **Against the:** In return for. . . .   **moi'ty competent:** Sufficient portion. 91. **gaged:** Engaged, pledged.   93. **comart:** Joint bargain (?).   94. **carriage:** Import, bearing.   96. **unimproved:** Not turned to account (?) or untested (?).   97. **skirts:** Outlying regions, outskirts.   98. **Shark'd up:** Got together in haphazard fashion.   **resolutes:** Desperadoes.   99. **food and diet:** No pay but their keep.   100. **stomach:** Relish of danger.   106. **head:** Source.   107. **romage:** Bustle, commotion.   109. **sort:** Suit.   112. **mote:** Speck of dust. 113. **palmy:** Flourishing.

115. **sheeted:** Shrouded.   117. **As:** This abrupt transition suggests that matter is possibly omitted between lines 116 and 117.   118. **Disasters:** Unfavorable signs of aspects. **moist star:** Moon, governing tides.   119. **Neptune:** God of the sea.   **stands:** Depends.   120. **sick . . . doomsday:** See Matt. 24:29 and Rev. 6:12.   121. **precurse:** Heralding, foreshadowing.   122. **harbingers:** Forerunners.   **still:** Continually.   123. **omen:** Calamitous event.   125. **climatures:** Regions.   127. **cross:** Meet, face directly. 134. **happily:** Haply, perchance.   140. **partisan:** Long-handled spear.

BERNARDO: It was about to speak when the cock
    crew.
HORATIO: And then it started like a guilty thing
    Upon a fearful summons. I have heard,
150   The cock, that is the trumpet to the morn,
    Doth with his lofty and shrill-sounding throat
    Awake the god of day, and, at his warning,
    Whether in sea or fire, in earth or air,
    Th' extravagant and erring° spirit hies
155   To his confine; and of the truth herein
    This present object made probation.°
MARCELLUS: It faded on the crowing of the cock.
    Some say that ever 'gainst° that season comes
    Wherein our Savior's birth is celebrated,
160   The bird of dawning singeth all night long,
    And then, they say, no spirit dare stir abroad;
    The nights are wholesome, then no planets
      strike,°
    No fairy takes,° nor witch hath power to charm,
    So hallowed and so gracious° is that time.
165 HORATIO: So have I heard and do in part believe it.
    But, look, the morn, in russet mantle clad,
    Walks o'er the dew of yon high eastward hill.
    Break we our watch up, and by my advice
    Let us impart what we have seen tonight
170   Unto young Hamlet; for, upon my life,
    This spirit, dumb to us, will speak to him.
    Do you consent we shall acquaint him with it,
    As needful in our loves, fitting our duty?
MARCELLUS: Let's do 't, I pray, and I this morning
    know
175   Where we shall find him most conveniently.
                          (*Exeunt.*)°

{*Scene II*}°

(*Flourish. Enter Claudius, King of Denmark,
Gertrude the Queen, Councilors, Polonius and his
son Laertes, Hamlet, cum aliis*° [*including Voltimand
and Cornelius*].)

KING: Though yet of Hamlet our dear brother's
    death
    The memory be green, and that it us befitted
    To bear our hearts in grief and our whole
      kingdom
    To be contracted in one brow of woe,
5   Yet so far hath discretion fought with nature

That we with wisest sorrow think on him,
Together with remembrance of ourselves.
Therefore our sometime sister, now our queen,
Th' imperial jointress° to this warlike state,
Have we, as 'twere with a defeated joy —   10
With an auspicious and a dropping eye,
With mirth in funeral and with dirge in marriage,
In equal scale weighing delight and dole —
Taken to wife. Nor have we herein barr'd
Your better wisdoms, which have freely gone   15
With this affair along. For all, our thanks.
Now follows that you know° young Fortinbras,
Holding a weak supposal° of our worth,
Or thinking by our late dear brother's death
Our state to be disjoint and out of frame,   20
Colleagued with° this dream of his advantage,°
He hath not fail'd to pester us with message
Importing° the surrender of those lands
Lost by his father, with all bands° of law,
To our most valiant brother. So much for him.   25
Now for ourself and for this time of meeting.
Thus much the business is: we have here writ
To Norway, uncle of young Fortinbras —
Who, impotent and bed-rid, scarcely hears
Of this his nephew's purpose — to suppress   30
His° further gait° herein, in that the levies,
The lists, and full proportions are all made
Out of his subject;° and we here dispatch
You, good Cornelius, and you, Voltimand,
For bearers of this greeting to old Norway,   35
Giving to you no further personal power
To business with the King, more than the scope
Of these delated° articles allow.   [*Gives a paper.*]
Farewell, and let your haste commend your duty.
CORNELIUS, VOLTIMAND: In that, and all things, will
    we show our duty.   40
KING: We doubt it nothing. Heartily farewell.
           [*Exit Voltimand and Cornelius.*]
    And now, Laertes, what's the news with you?
    You told us of some suit; what is 't, Laertes?
    You cannot speak of reason to the Dane°
    And lose your voice.° What wouldst thou beg,
    Laertes,   45

---

154. extravagant and erring: Wandering. (The words have
similar meaning.)   **156. probation:** Proof.   **158. 'gainst:**
Just before.   **162. strike:** Exert evil influence.   **163. takes:**
Bewitches.   **164. gracious:** Full of goodness.   **175. [S.D.]**
Exeunt: Latin for "they go out"   I, II. **Location:** The castle.
[S.D.] *cum aliis:* With others.

9. jointress: Woman possessed of a joint tenancy of an estate.
17. know: Be informed (that).   **18. weak supposal:** Low es-
timate.   **21. Colleagued with:** Joined to, allied with.
dream . . . advantage: Illusory hope of success.   **23. Importing:** Pertaining to.   **24. bands:** Contracts.   **31. His:**
Fortinbras's.   **gait:** Proceeding.   **31–33. in that . . . subject:** Since the levying of troops and supplies is drawn entirely from the King of Norway's own subjects.
38. delated: Detailed. (Variant of *dilated.*)   **44. the Dane:**
The Danish king.   **45. lose your voice:** Waste your speech.

That shall not be my offer, not thy asking?
The head is not more native° to the heart,
The hand more instrumental° to the mouth,
Than is the throne of Denmark to thy father.
What wouldst thou have, Laertes?

50 LAERTES: My dread lord,
Your leave and favor to return to France,
From whence though willingly I came to Denmark
To show my duty in your coronation,
Yet now I must confess, that duty done,
55 My thoughts and wishes bend again toward France
And bow them to your gracious leave and pardon.°

KING: Have you your father's leave? What says Polonius?

POLONIUS: H'ath, my lord, wrung from me my slow leave
By laborsome petition, and at last
60 Upon his will I seal'd my hard° consent.
I do beseech you, give him leave to go.

KING: Take thy fair hour, Laertes. Time be thine,
And thy best graces spend it at thy will!
But now, my cousin° Hamlet, and my son —

HAMLET: A little more than kin, and less than
65 kind.°

KING: How is it that the clouds still hang on you?

HAMLET: Not so, my lord. I am too much in the sun.°

QUEEN: Good Hamlet, cast thy righted color off,
And let thine eye look like a friend on Denmark.
70 Do not forever with thy veiled° lids
Seek for thy noble father in the dust.
Thou know'st 'tis common,° all that lives must die,
Passing through nature to eternity.

HAMLET: Ay, madam, it is common.

QUEEN: If it be,
75 Why seems it so particular with thee?

HAMLET: Seems, madam! Nay, it is. I know not
"seems."
'Tis not alone my inky cloak, good mother,
Nor customary suits of solemn black,

Nor windy suspiration of forc'd breath,
No, nor the fruitful° river in the eye,   80
Nor the dejected havior of the visage,
Together with all forms, moods, shapes of grief,
That can denote me truly. These indeed seem,
For they are actions that a man might play.
But I have that within which passes show;   85
These but the trappings and the suits of woe.

KING: 'Tis sweet and commendable in your nature, Hamlet,
To give these mourning duties to your father.
But you must know your father lost a father,
That father lost, lost his, and the survivor bound 90
In filial obligation for some term
To do obsequious° sorrow. But to persever°
In obstinate condolement° is a course
Of impious stubbornness. 'Tis unmanly grief.
It shows a will most incorrect to heaven,   95
A heart unfortified, a mind impatient,
An understanding simple and unschool'd.
For what we know must be and is as common
As any the most vulgar thing to sense,°
Why should we in our peevish opposition   100
Take it to heart? Fie, 'tis a fault to heaven,
A fault against the dead, a fault to nature,
To reason most absurd, whose common theme
Is death of fathers, and who still hath cried,
From the first corse° till he that died today,   105
"This must be so." We pray you, throw to earth
This unprevailing° woe, and think of us
As of a father; for let the world take note,
You are the most immediate° to our throne,
And with no less nobility of love   110
Than that which dearest father bears his son
Do I impart toward you. For your intent
In going back to school in Wittenberg,°
It is most retrograde° to our desire,
And we beseech you, bend you° to remain   115
Here in the cheer and comfort of our eye,
Our chiefest courtier, cousin, and our son.

QUEEN: Let not thy mother lose her prayers, Hamlet.
I pray thee stay with us, go not to Wittenberg.

HAMLET: I shall in all my best obey you, madam.   120

KING: Why, 'tis a loving and a fair reply.
Be as ourself in Denmark. Madam, come.
This gentle and unforc'd accord of Hamlet

---

47. native: Closely connected, related.   **48. instrumental:** Serviceable.   **56. leave and pardon:** Permission to depart. **60. hard:** Reluctant.   **64. cousin:** Any kin not of the immediate family.   **65. A little ... kind:** Closer than an ordinary nephew (since I am stepson), and yet more separated in natural feeling (with pun on *kind,* meaning affectionate and natural, lawful). This line is often read as an aside, but it need not be.   **67. sun:** The sunshine of the King's royal favor (with pun on *son*).   **70. veiled:** Downcast.   **72. common:** Of universal occurrence. (But Hamlet plays on the sense of *vulgar* in line 74.)

80. fruitful: Abundant.   **92. obsequious:** Suited to obsequies or funerals.   **persever:** Persevere.   **93. condolement:** Sorrowing.   **99. As ... sense:** As the most ordinary experience.   **105. corse:** Corpse.   **107. unprevailing:** Unavailing.   **109. most immediate:** Next in succession. **113. Wittenberg:** Famous German university founded in 1502.   **114. retrograde:** Contrary.   **115. bend you:** Incline yourself.

125 Sits smiling to my heart, in grace whereof
     No jocund° health that Denmark drinks today
     But the great cannon to the clouds shall tell,
     And the King's rouse° the heaven shall bruit
         again,°
     Respeaking earthly thunder.° Come away.
                 (Flourish. Exeunt all but Hamlet.)
     HAMLET: O, that this too too sullied° flesh would
         melt,
130 Thaw, and resolve itself into a dew!
     Or that the Everlasting had not fix'd
     His canon° 'gainst self-slaughter! O God, God,
     How weary, stale, flat, and unprofitable
     Seem to me all the uses of this world!
135 Fie on 't, ah, fie! 'Tis an unweeded garden
     That grows to seed. Things rank and gross in
         nature
     Possess it merely.° That it should come to this!
     But two months dead — nay, not so much, not
         two.
     So excellent a king, that was to° this
140 Hyperion° to a satyr; so loving to my mother
     That he might not beteem° the winds of heaven
     Visit her face too roughly. Heaven and earth,
     Must I remember? Why, she would hang on him
     As if increase of appetite had grown
145 By what it fed on, and yet, within a month —
     Let me not think on 't. Frailty, thy name is
         woman! —
     A little month, or ere those shoes were old
     With which she followed my poor father's body,
     Like Niobe,° all tears, why she, even she —
150 O God, a beast, that wants discourse of reason,°
     Would have mourn'd longer — married with my
         uncle,
     My father's brother, but no more like my father
     Than I to Hercules. Within a month,
     Ere yet the salt of most unrighteous tears
155 Had left the flushing in her galled° eyes,
     She married. O, most wicked speed, to post

     With such dexterity to incestuous° sheets!
     It is not nor it cannot come to good.
     But break, my heart, for I must hold my tongue.

     (Enter Horatio, Marcellus, and Bernardo.)

     HORATIO: Hail to your lordship!
     HAMLET: I am glad to see you well. 160
         Horatio! — or I do forget myself.
     HORATIO: The same, my lord, and your poor
         servant ever.
     HAMLET: Sir, my good friend; I'll change° that name
         with you.
         And what make° you from Wittenberg, Horatio?
         Marcellus?   165
     MARCELLUS: My good lord.
     HAMLET: I am very glad to see you. [*To Bernardo.*]
         Good even, sir. —
         But what, in faith, make you from Wittenberg?
     HORATIO: A truant disposition, good my lord.
     HAMLET: I would not hear your enemy say so,   170
         Nor shall you do my ear that violence
         To make it truster of your own report
         Against yourself. I know you are no truant.
         But what is your affair in Elsinore?
         We'll teach you to drink deep ere you depart. 175
     HORATIO: My lord, I came to see your father's
         funeral.
     HAMLET: I prithee do not mock me, fellow student;
         I think it was to see my mother's wedding.
     HORATIO: Indeed, my lord, it followed hard° upon.
     HAMLET: Thrift, thrift, Horatio! The funeral bak'd
         meats   180
         Did coldly furnish forth the marriage tables.
         Would I had met my dearest° foe in heaven
         Or° ever I had seen that day, Horatio!
         My father! — Methinks I see my father.
     HORATIO: Where, my lord?
     HAMLET: In my mind's eye, Horatio. 185
     HORATIO: I saw him once. 'A° was a goodly king.
     HAMLET: 'A was a man, take him for all in all,
         I shall not look upon his like again.
     HORATIO: My lord, I think I saw him yesternight.
     HAMLET: Saw? Who?   190
     HORATIO: My lord, the King your father.
     HAMLET: The King my father?
     HORATIO: Season your admiration° for a while

---

125. jocund: Merry. **127. rouse:** Draft of liquor. **bruit again:** Loudly echo. **128. thunder:** Of trumpet and kettledrum sounded when the King drinks, see I, IV, 8–12. **129. sullied:** Defiled. (The early quartos read *sallied,* the Folio *solid.*) **132. canon:** Law. **137. merely:** Completely. **139. to:** In comparison to. **140. Hyperion:** Titan sun-god, father of Helios. **141. beteem:** Allow. **149. Niobe:** Tantalus's daughter, Queen of Thebes, who boasted that she had more sons and daughters than Leto; for this, Apollo and Artemis, children of Leto, slew her fourteen children. She was turned by Zeus into a stone that continually dropped tears. **150. wants . . . reason:** Lacks the faculty of reason. **155. galled:** Irritated, inflamed.

---

157. incestuous: In Shakespeare's day, the marriage of a man like Claudius to his deceased brother's wife was considered incestuous. **163. change:** Exchange (i.e., the name of friend). **164. make:** Do. **179. hard:** Close. **182. dearest:** Direst. **183. or:** Ere, before. **186. 'A:** He. **192. Season your admiration:** Restrain your astonishment.

With an attent° ear, till I may deliver,
Upon the witness of these gentlemen,
This marvel to you.
195 HAMLET: For God's love, let me hear!
HORATIO: Two nights together had these gentlemen,
    Marcellus and Bernardo, on their watch,
    In the dead waste and middle of the night,
    Been thus encount'red. A figure like your father,
200 Armed at point° exactly, cap-a-pe,°
    Appears before them, and with solemn march
    Goes slow and stately by them. Thrice he walk'd
    By their oppress'd and fear-surprised eyes
    Within his truncheon's° length, whilst they,
        distill'd
205 Almost to jelly with the act° of fear,
    Stand dumb and speak not to him. This to me
    In dreadful secrecy impart they did,
    And I with them the third night kept the watch,
    Where, as they had delivered, both in time,
    Form of the thing, each word made true and
210   good,
    The apparition comes. I knew your father;
    These hands are not more like.
HAMLET: But where was this?
MARCELLUS: My lord, upon the platform where we
    watch.
HAMLET: Did you not speak to it?
HORATIO: My lord, I did,
215 But answer made it none. Yet once methought
    It lifted up it° head and did address
    Itself to motion, like as it would speak;
    But even then the morning cock crew loud,
    And at the sound it shrunk in haste away,
    And vanish'd from our sight.
220 HAMLET: 'Tis very strange.
HORATIO: As I do live, my honor'd lord, 'tis true,
    And we did think it writ down in our duty
    To let you know of it.
HAMLET: Indeed, indeed, sirs. But this troubles me.
    Hold you the watch tonight?
225 ALL: We do, my lord.
HAMLET: Arm'd, say you?
ALL: Arm'd, my lord.
HAMLET: From top to toe?
ALL: My lord, from head to foot.
HAMLET: Then saw you not his face?
230 HORATIO: O, yes, my lord. He wore his beaver° up.
HAMLET: What, looked he frowningly?

HORATIO: A countenance more
    In sorrow than in anger.
HAMLET: Pale or red?
HORATIO: Nay, very pale.
HAMLET: And fix'd his eyes upon you?
HORATIO: Most constantly.
HAMLET: I would I had been there.
HORATIO: It would have much amaz'd you.   235
HAMLET: Very like, very like. Stay'd it long?
HORATIO: While one with moderate haste might
        tell° a hundred.
MARCELLUS, BERNARDO: Longer, longer.
HORATIO: Not when I saw 't.
HAMLET: His beard was grizzl'd,—no?
HORATIO: It was, as I have seen it in his life,   240
    A sable silver'd.°
HAMLET: I will watch tonight.
    Perchance 'twill walk again.
HORATIO: I warr'nt it will.
HAMLET: If it assume my noble father's person,
    I'll speak to it, though hell itself should gape
    And bid me hold my peace. I pray you all,   245
    If you have hitherto conceal'd this sight,
    Let it be tenable° in your silence still,
    And whatsomever else shall hap tonight,
    Give it an understanding, but no tongue.
    I will requite your loves. So, fare you well.   250
    Upon the platform, 'twixt eleven and twelve,
    I'll visit you.
ALL: Our duty to your honor.
HAMLET: Your loves, as mine to you. Farewell.
                    (*Exeunt* [*all but Hamlet*].)
    My father's spirit in arms! All is not well.
    I doubt° some foul play. Would the night were
        come!   255
    Till then sit still, my soul. Foul deeds will rise,
    Though all the earth o'erwhelm them, to men's
        eyes.
                                        (*Exit.*)

{*Scene III*}°

(*Enter Laertes and Ophelia, his sister.*)

LAERTES: My necessaries are embark'd. Farewell.
    And, sister, as the winds give benefit
    And convoy is assistant,° do not sleep
    But let me hear from you.
OPHELIA: Do you doubt that?
LAERTES: For Hamlet, and the trifling of his favor,   5

---

193. **attent:** Attentive. 200. **at point:** Completely. **cap-a-pe:** From head to foot. 204. **truncheon:** Officer's staff. 205. **act:** Action, operation. 216. **it:** Its. 230. **beaver:** Visor on the helmet.

237. **tell:** Count. 241. **sable silver'd:** Black mixed with white. 247. **tenable:** Held tightly. 255. **doubt:** Suspect. I, III. **Location:** Polonius's chambers. 3. **convoy is assistant:** Means of conveyance are available.

Hold it a fashion and a toy in blood,°
A violet in the youth of primy° nature,
Forward,° not permanent, sweet, not lasting,
The perfume and suppliance° of a minute —
No more.
OPHELIA: No more but so?
10 LAERTES: Think it no more.
For nature crescent° does not grow alone
In thews° and bulk, but, as this temple° waxes,
The inward service of the mind and soul
Grows wide withal.° Perhaps he loves you now,
15 And now no soil° nor cautel° doth besmirch
The virtue of his will;° but you must fear,
His greatness weigh'd,° his will is not his own.
[For he himself is subject to his birth.]
He may not, as unvalued persons do,
20 Carve° for himself; for on his choice depends
The safety and health of this whole state,
And therefore must his choice be circumscrib'd
Unto the voice and yielding° of that body
Whereof he is the head. Then if he says he loves you,
25 It fits your wisdom so far to believe it
As he in his particular act and place
May give his saying deed,° which is no further
Than the main voice of Denmark goes withal.
Then weigh what loss your honor may sustain
30 If with too credent° ear you list° his songs,
Or lose your heart, or your chaste treasure open
To his unmaster'd importunity.
Fear it, Ophelia, fear it, my dear sister,
And keep you in the rear of your affection,
35 Out of the shot° and danger of desire.
The chariest° maid is prodigal enough
If she unmask her beauty to the moon.
Virtue itself scapes not calumnious strokes.
The canker galls° the infants of the spring
40 Too oft before their buttons° be disclos'd,°
And in the morn and liquid dew° of youth
Contagious blastments° are most imminent.
Be wary then; best safety lies in fear.
Youth to itself rebels, though none else near.

OPHELIA: I shall the effect of this good lesson keep   45
As watchman to my heart. But, good my brother,
Do not, as some ungracious pastors do,
Show me the steep and thorny way to heaven,
Whiles, like a puff'd° and reckless libertine,
Himself the primrose path of dalliance treads,   50
And recks° not his own rede.°

(*Enter Polonius.*)

LAERTES: O, fear me not.
I stay too long. But here my father comes.
A double blessing is a double° grace;
Occasion° smiles upon a second leave.
POLONIUS: Yet here, Laertes? Aboard, aboard, for shame!   55
The wind sits in the shoulder of your sail,
And you are stay'd for. There — my blessing with thee!
And these few precepts in thy memory
Look thou character.° Give thy thoughts no tongue
Nor any unproportion'd thought his° act.   60
Be thou familiar,° but by no means vulgar.°
Those friends thou hast, and their adoption tried,°
Grapple them to thy soul with hoops of steel,
But do not dull thy palm with entertainment
Of each new-hatch'd, unfledg'd courage.° Beware   65
Of entrance to a quarrel, but, being in,
Bear't that° th' opposed may beware of thee.
Give every man thy ear, but few thy voice;
Take each man's censure,° but reserve thy judgment.
Costly thy habit as thy purse can buy,   70
But not express'd in fancy; rich, not gaudy,
For the apparel oft proclaims the man,
And they in France of the best rank and station
Are of a most select and generous chief° in that.
Neither a borrower nor a lender be,   75
For loan oft loses both itself and friend,
And borrowing dulleth edge of husbandry.°
This above all: to thine own self be true,
And it must follow, as the night the day,
Thou canst not then be false to any man.   80
Farewell. My blessing season° this in thee!

---

6. **toy in blood:** Passing amorous fancy.   7. **primy:** In its prime, springtime.   8. **Forward:** Precocious.   9. **suppliance:** Supply, filler.   11. **crescent:** Growing, waxing. 12. **thews:** Bodily strength.   **temple:** Body.   14. **Grows wide withal:** Grows along with it.   15. **soil:** Blemish. **cautel:** Deceit.   16. **will:** Desire.   17. **greatness weigh'd:** High position considered.   20. **carve:** Choose pleasure. 23. **voice and yielding:** Assent, approval.   27. **deed:** Effect. 30. **credent:** Credulous.   **list:** Listen to.   35. **shot:** Range. 36. **chariest:** Most scrupulously modest.   39. **canker galls:** Cankerworm destroys.   40. **buttons:** Buds.   **disclos'd:** Opened.   41. **liquid dew:** Time when dew is fresh. 42. **blastments:** Blights.

LAERTES: Most humbly do I take my leave, my lord.
POLONIUS: The time invests° you. Go, your servants
    tend.°
LAERTES: Farewell, Ophelia, and remember well
85   What I have said to you.
OPHELIA: 'Tis in my memory lock'd,
    And you yourself shall keep the key of it.
LAERTES: Farewell.   (*Exit Laertes.*)
POLONIUS: What is 't, Ophelia, he hath said to you?
OPHELIA: So please you, something touching the
90   Lord Hamlet.
POLONIUS: Marry,° well bethought.
    'Tis told me he hath very oft of late
    Given private time to you, and you yourself
    Have of your audience been most free and
        bounteous.
95   If it be so — as so 'tis put on° me,
    And that in way of caution — I must tell you
    You do not understand yourself so clearly
    As it behooves my daughter and your honor.
    What is between you? Give me up the truth.
OPHELIA: He hath, my lord, of late made many
100   tenders°
    Of his affection to me.
POLONIUS: Affection? Pooh! You speak like a green
        girl,
    Unsifted° in such perilous circumstance.
    Do you believe his tenders, as you call them?
OPHELIA: I do not know, my lord, what I should
105   think.
POLONIUS: Marry, I will teach you. Think yourself a
        baby
    That you have ta'en these tenders° for true pay,
    Which are not sterling.° Tender° yourself more
        dearly,
    Or — not to crack the wind° of the poor phrase,
110   Running it thus — you'll tender me a fool.°
OPHELIA: My lord, he hath importun'd me with love
    In honorable fashion.
POLONIUS: Ay, fashion° you may call it. Go to, go
        to.
OPHELIA: And hath given countenance° to his
    speech, my lord,

With almost all the holy vows of heaven.   115
POLONIUS: Ay, springes° to catch woodcocks.° I do
        know,
    When the blood burns, how prodigal the soul
    Lends the tongue vows. These blazes, daughter,
    Giving more light than heat, extinct in both
    Even in their promise, as it is a-making,   120
    You must not take for fire. From this time
    Be something scanter of your maiden presence.
    Set your entreatments° at a higher rate
    Than a command to parle.° For Lord Hamlet,
    Believe so much in him° that he is young,   125
    And with a larger tether may he walk
    Than may be given you. In few,° Ophelia,
    Do not believe his vows, for they are brokers,°
    Not of that dye° which their investments° show,
    But mere implorators° of unholy suits,   130
    Breathing° like sanctified and pious bawds,
    The better to beguile. This is for all:
    I would not, in plain terms, from this time forth
    Have you so slander° any moment leisure
    As to give words or talk with the Lord Hamlet.   135
    Look to 't, I charge you. Come your ways.
OPHELIA: I shall obey, my lord.   (*Exeunt.*)

{*Scene IV*}°

(*Enter Hamlet, Horatio, and Marcellus.*)

HAMLET: The air bites shrewdly; it is very cold.
HORATIO: It is a nipping and an eager air.
HAMLET: What hour now?
HORATIO: I think it lacks of twelve.
MARCELLUS: No, it is struck.
HORATIO: Indeed? I heard it not.
    It then draws near the season   5
    Wherein the spirit held his wont to walk.
        (*A flourish of trumpets, and two pieces° go off
                                [within].*)
    What does this mean, my lord?

---

83. **invests:** Besieges. . . . **tend:** Attend, wait.   **91. Marry:**
By the Virgin Mary (a mild oath).   **95. put on:** Impressed
on, told to.   **100. tenders:** Offers.   **103. Unsifted:** Un-
tried.   **107. tenders:** With added meaning here of *promises
to pay.*   **108. sterling:** Legal currency.   **Tender:** Hold.
109. crack the wind: Run it until it is broken, winded.
110. tender me a fool: (1) Show yourself to me as a fool, (2)
show me up as a fool, (3) present me with a grandchild (*fool*
was a term of endearment for a child).   **113. fashion:** Mere
form, pretense.   **114. countenance:** Credit, support.

116. springes: Snares.   **woodcocks:** Birds easily caught;
here used to connote gullibility.   **123. entreatments:** Negotiations for surrender (a military term).   **124. parle:** Discuss
terms with the enemy. (Polonius urges his daughter, in the
metaphor of military language, not to meet with Hamlet and
consider giving in to him merely because he requests an interview.)   **125. so . . . him:** This much concerning him.
127. In few: Briefly.   **128. brokers:** Go-betweens, procurers.
129. dye: Color or sort.   **investments:** Clothes (i.e., they are
not what they seem).   **130. mere implorators:** Out-and-out
solicitors.   **131. Breathing:** Speaking.   **134. slander:** Bring
disgrace or reproach upon.   **I, IV. Location:** The guard platform.   **6.** [S.D.] *pieces:* I.e., of ordnance, cannon.

HAMLET: The King doth wake° tonight and takes
   his rouse,°
   Keeps wassail,° and the swagg'ring up-spring°
     reels;
10   And as he drains his draughts of Rhenish° down,
   The kettle-drum and trumpet thus bray out
   The triumph of his pledge.°
HORATIO: Is it a custom?
HAMLET: Ay, marry, is 't,
   But to my mind, though I am native here
15   And to the manner° born, it is a custom
   More honor'd in the breach than the
     observance.°
   This heavy-headed revel east and west°
   Makes us traduc'd and tax'd of° other nations.
   They clepe° us drunkards, and with swinish
     phrase°
20   Soil our addition;° and indeed it takes
   From our achievements, though perform'd at
     height,°
   The pith and marrow of our attribute.
   So, oft it chances in particular men,
   That for some vicious mole of nature° in them,
25   As in their birth — wherein they are not guilty,
   Since nature cannot choose his° origin —
   By the o'ergrowth of some complexion,°
   Oft breaking down the pales° and forts of
     reason,
   Or by some habit that too much o'er-leavens°
30   The form of plausive° manners, that these men,
   Carrying, I say, the stamp of one defect,
   Being nature's livery,° or fortune's star,°
   Their virtues else, be they as pure as grace,
   As infinite as man may undergo,
35   Shall in the general censure take corruption
   From that particular fault. The dram of eale°

Doth all the noble substance of a doubt°
To his own scandal.°

(*Enter Ghost.*)

HORATIO: Look, my lord, it comes!
HAMLET: Angels and ministers of grace defend us! 40
   Be thou a spirit of health° or goblin damn'd,
   Bring with thee airs from heaven or blasts from
     hell,
   Be thy intents wicked or charitable,
   Thou com'st in such a questionable° shape
   That I will speak to thee. I'll call thee Hamlet,
   King, father, royal Dane. O, answer me! 45
   Let me not burst in ignorance, but tell
   Why thy canoniz'd° bones, hearsed° in death,
   Have burst their cerements;° why the sepulcher
   Wherein we saw thee quietly interr'd
   Hath op'd his ponderous and marble jaws 50
   To cast thee up again. What may this mean,
   That thou, dead corse, again in complete steel
   Revisits thus the glimpses of the moon,°
   Making night hideous, and we fools of nature°
   So horridly to shake our disposition 55
   With thoughts beyond the reaches of our souls?
   Say, why is this? Wherefore? What should we
     do?
                     ([*Ghost*] *beckons* [*Hamlet*].)
HORATIO: It beckons you to go away with it,
   As if it some impartment° did desire
   To you alone.
MARCELLUS: Look with what courteous action 60
   It waves you to a more removed ground.
   But do not go with it.
HORATIO: No, by no means.
HAMLET: It will not speak. Then I will follow it.
HORATIO: Do not, my lord.
HAMLET: Why, what should be the fear?
   I do not set my life at a pin's fee,° 65
   And for my soul, what can it do to that,
   Being a thing immortal as itself?
   It waves me forth again. I'll follow it.
HORATIO: What if it tempt you toward the flood,
   my lord
   Or to the dreadful summit of the cliff 70

---

8. wake: Stay awake and hold revel. **rouse:** Carouse, drinking bout. **9. wassail:** Carousal. **up-spring:** Wild German dance. **10. Rhenish:** Rhine wine. **12. triumph . . . pledge:** His feat in draining the wine in a single draft. **15. manner:** Custom (of drinking). **16. More . . . observance:** Better neglected than followed. **17. east and west:** I.e., everywhere. **18. tax'd of:** Censured by. **19. crepe:** Call. **with swinish phrase:** By calling us swine. **20. addition:** Reputation. **21. at height:** Outstandingly. **24. mole of nature:** Natural blemish in one's constitution. **26. his:** Its. **27. complexion:** Humor (i.e., one of the four humors or fluids thought to determine temperament). **28. pales:** Palings, fences (as of a fortification). **29. o'er-leavens:** Induces a change throughout (as yeast works in dough). **30. plausive:** Pleasing. **32. nature's livery:** Endowment from nature. **fortune's star:** Mark placed by fortune. **36. dram of eale:** Small amount of evil (?).

37. of a doubt: A famous crux, sometimes emended to *oft about* or *often dout*, i.e., often erase or do out, or to *antidote,* counteract. **38. To . . . scandal:** To the disgrace of the whole enterprise. **40. of health:** Of spiritual good. **43. questionable:** Inviting question or conversation. **47. canoniz'd:** Buried according to the canons of the church. **hearsed:** Coffined. **48. cerements:** Graveclothes. **53. glimpses of the moon:** Earth by night. **54. fools of nature:** Mere men, limited to natural knowledge. **59. impartment:** Communication. **65. fee:** Value.

That beetles o'er° his° base into the sea,
And there assume some other horrible form
Which might deprive your sovereignty of reason,°
And draw you into madness? Think of it.
75 The very place puts toys of desperation,°
Without more motive, into every brain
That looks so many fathoms to the sea
And hears it roar beneath.

HAMLET: It waves me still.
Go on, I'll follow thee.

MARCELLUS: You shall not go, my lord.

                    [*They try to stop him.*]

80 HAMLET: Hold off your hands!

HORATIO: Be rul'd, you shall not go.

HAMLET: My fate cries out,
And makes each petty artery° in this body
As hardy as the Nemean lion's° nerve.°
Still am I call'd. Unhand me, gentlemen.
By heaven, I'll make a ghost of him that lets°
85 me!
I say, away! Go on. I'll follow thee.
                    (*Exeunt Ghost and Hamlet.*)

HORATIO: He waxes desperate with imagination.

MARCELLUS: Let's follow. 'Tis not fit thus to obey
him.

HORATIO: Have after. To what issue° will this come?

MARCELLUS: Something is rotten in the state of
90 Denmark.

HORATIO: Heaven will direct it.°

MARCELLUS: Nay, let's follow him. (*Exeunt.*)

{*Scene V*}°

(*Enter Ghost and Hamlet.*)

HAMLET: Whither wilt thou lead me? Speak. I'll go
no further.

GHOST: Mark me.

HAMLET: I will.

GHOST: My hour is almost come,
When I to sulph'rous and tormenting flames
Must render up myself.

HAMLET: Alas, poor ghost!

GHOST: Pity me not, but lend thy serious hearing   5
To what I shall unfold.

HAMLET: Speak. I am bound to hear.

GHOST: So art thou to revenge, when thou shalt
hear.

HAMLET: What?

GHOST: I am thy father's spirit,   10
Doom'd for a certain term to walk the night,
And for the day confin'd to fast° in fires,
Till the foul crimes° done in my days of nature
Are burnt and purg'd away. But that° I am
forbid
To tell the secrets of my prison-house,   15
I could a tale unfold whose lightest word
Would harrow up thy soul, freeze thy young
blood,
Make thy two eyes, like stars, start from their
spheres,°
Thy knotted and combined locks° to part,
And each particular hair to stand an end,°   20
Like quills upon the fearful porpentine.°
But this eternal blazon° must not be
To ears of flesh and blood. List, list, O, list!
If thou didst ever thy dear father love —

HAMLET: O God!   25

GHOST: Revenge his foul and most unnatural
murder.

HAMLET: Murder?

GHOST: Murder most foul, as in the best it is,
But this most foul, strange, and unnatural.

HAMLET: Haste me to know 't, that I, with wings as
swift   30
As meditation or the thoughts of love,
May sweep to my revenge.

GHOST: I find thee apt;
And duller shouldst thou be than the fat weed
That roots itself in ease on Lethe° wharf,°
Wouldst thou not stir in this. Now, Hamlet, hear.   35
'Tis given out that, sleeping in my orchard,
A serpent stung me. So the whole ear of
Denmark
Is by a forged process° of my death

---

71. beetles o'er: Overhangs threateningly. **his:** Its.
73. deprive . . . reason: Take away the rule of reason over
your mind. **75. toys of desperation:** Fancies of desperate
acts, i.e., suicide. **82. artery:** Sinew. **83. Nemean lion:**
One of the monsters slain by Hercules in his twelve labors.
nerve: Sinew **85. lets:** Hinders. **89. issue:** Outcome.
91. it: The outcome.   **I, V. Location:** The battlements of
the castle.

12. fast: Do penance. **13. crimes:** Sins. **14. But that:**
Were it not that. **18. spheres:** Eye sockets, here compared
to the orbits or transparent revolving spheres in which, according to Ptolemaic astronomy, the heavenly bodies were
fixed. **19. knotted . . . locks:** Hair neatly arranged and
confined. **20. an end:** On end. **21. fearful porpentine:**
Frightened porcupine. **22. eternal blazon:** Revelation of
the secrets of eternity. **34. Lethe:** The river of forgetfulness
in Hades. **wharf:** Bank. **38. forged process:** Falsified
account.

Rankly abus'd.° But know, thou noble youth,
40 The serpent that did sting thy father's life
Now wears his crown.
HAMLET: O my prophetic soul!
My uncle!
GHOST: Ay, that incestuous, that adulterate° beast,
With witchcraft of his wits, with traitorous
      gifts —
45 O wicked wit and gifts, that have the power
So to seduce! — won to his shameful lust
The will of my most seeming-virtuous queen.
O Hamlet, what a falling-off was there!
From me, whose love was of that dignity
50 That it went hand in hand even with the vow
I made to her in marriage, and to decline
Upon a wretch whose natural gifts were poor
To those of mine!
But virtue, as it never will be moved,
55 Though lewdness court it in a shape of heaven,°
So lust, though to a radiant angel link'd,
Will sate itself in a celestial bed,
And prey on garbage.
But, soft, methinks I scent the morning air.
60 Brief let me be. Sleeping within my orchard,
My custom always of the afternoon,
Upon my secure° hour thy uncle stole,
With juice of cursed hebona° in a vial,
And in the porches of my ears did pour
65 The leprous° distillment, whose effect
Holds such an enmity with blood of man
That swift as quicksilver it courses through
The natural gates and alleys of the body,
And with a sudden vigor it doth posset°
70 And curd, like eager° droppings into milk,
The thin and wholesome blood. So did it mine,
And a most instant tetter° bark'd° about,
Most lazar-like,° with vile and loathsome crust,
All my smooth body.
75 Thus was I, sleeping, by a brother's hand
Of life, of crown, of queen, at once dispatch'd,°
Cut off even in the blossoms of my sin,
Unhous'led,° disappointed,° unanel'd,°

No reck'ning made, but sent to my account
With all my imperfections on my head.   80
O, horrible! O, horrible, most horrible!
If thou hast nature° in thee, bear it not.
Let not the royal bed of Denmark be
A couch for luxury° and damned incest.
But, howsomever thou pursues this act,   85
Taint not thy mind, nor let thy soul contrive
Against thy mother aught. Leave her to heaven
And to those thorns that in her bosom lodge,
To prick and sting her. Fare thee well at once.
The glow-worm shows the matin° to be near,   90
And 'gins to pale his uneffectual fire.°
Adieu, adieu, adieu! Remember me.   [Exit.]
HAMLET: O all you host of heaven! O earth! What
      else?
And shall I couple° hell? O fie! Hold, hold, my
      heart,
And you, my sinews, grow not instant old,   95
But bear me stiffly up. Remember thee!
Ay, thou poor ghost, whiles memory holds a seat
In this distracted globe.° Remember thee!
Yea, from the table° of my memory
I'll wipe away all trivial fond° records,   100
All saws° of books, all forms,° all pressures° past
That youth and observation copied there,
And thy commandment all alone shall live
Within the book and volume of my brain,
Unmix'd with baser matter. Yes, by heaven!   105
O most pernicious woman!
O villain, villain, smiling, damned villain!
My tables — meet it is I set it down,
That one may smile, and smile, and be a villain.
At least I am sure it may be so in Denmark.   110
                                        [Writing.]
So, uncle, there you are. Now to my word;
It is "Adieu, adieu! Remember me."
I have sworn 't.

(Enter Horatio and Marcellus.)

HORATIO: My lord, my lord!
MARCELLUS: Lord Hamlet!
HORATIO: Heavens secure him!
HAMLET: So be it!   115
MARCELLUS: Illo, ho, ho, my lord!
HAMLET: Hillo, ho, ho,° boy! Come, bird, come.

39. **abus'd:** Deceived.   43. **adulterate:** Adulterous.
55. **shape of heaven:** Heavenly form.   62. **secure:** Confident, unsuspicious.   63. **hebona:** Poison. (The word seems
to be a form of *ebony,* though it is thought perhaps to be related to *henbane,* a poison, or to *ebenus,* yew.)   65. **lep-
rous:** Causing leprosy-like disfigurement.   69. **posset:**
Coagulate, curdle.   70. **eager:** Sour, acid.   72. **tetter:**
Eruption of scabs.   **bark'd:** Covered with a rough covering, like bark on a tree.   73. **lazar-like:** Leper-like.
76. **dispatch'd:** Suddenly deprived.   78. **Unhous'led:** Without having received the sacrament [of Holy Communion].
disappointed: Unready (spiritually) for the last journey.
unanel'd: Without having received extreme unction.

82. **nature:** The promptings of a son.   84. **luxury:** Lechery.
90. **matin:** Morning.   91. **uneffectual fire:** Cold light.
94. **couple:** Add.   98. **globe:** Head.   99. **table:** Writing
tablet.   100. **fond:** Foolish.   101. **saws:** Wise sayings.
forms: Images.   **pressures:** Impressions stamped.   117.
Hillo, ho, ho: A falconer's call to a hawk in air. Hamlet is
playing upon Marcellus's *Illo,* i.e., *halloo.*

MARCELLUS: How is 't, my noble lord?
HORATIO: What news, my lord?
HAMLET: O, wonderful!
HORATIO: Good my lord, tell it.
120 HAMLET: No, you will reveal it.
HORATIO: Not I, my lord, by heaven.
MARCELLUS: Nor I, my lord.
HAMLET: How say you, then, would heart of man
    once think it?
    But you'll be secret?
HORATIO, MARCELLUS: Ay, by heaven, my
    lord.
HAMLET: There's never a villain dwelling in all
    Denmark
125 But he's an arrant° knave.
HORATIO: There needs no ghost, my lord, come
    from the grave
    To tell us this.
HAMLET: Why, right, you are in the right.
    And so, without more circumstance° at all,
    I hold it fit that we shake hands and part,
    You, as your business and desire shall point
130   you —
    For every man hath business and desire,
    Such as it is — and for my own poor part,
    Look you, I'll go pray.
HORATIO: These are but wild and whirling words,
    my lord.
135 HAMLET: I am sorry they offend you, heartily;
    Yes, faith, heartily.
HORATIO: There's no offense, my lord.
HAMLET: Yes, by Saint Patrick, but there is,
    Horatio,
    And much offense too. Touching this vision here,
    It is an honest° ghost, that let me tell you.
140   For your desire to know what is between us,
    O'ermaster 't as you may. And now, good
    friends
    As you are friends, scholars, and soldiers,
    Give me one poor request.
HORATIO: What is 't, my lord? We will.
HAMLET: Never make known what you have seen
145   tonight.
HORATIO, MARCELLUS: My lord, we will not.
HAMLET: Nay, but swear 't.
HORATIO: In faith,
    My lord, not I.
MARCELLUS: Nor I, my lord, in faith.

HAMLET: Upon my sword.°   [*Holds out his sword.*]
MARCELLUS: We have sworn, my lord, already.
HAMLET: Indeed, upon my sword, indeed.
    (*Ghost cries under the stage.*)
GHOST: Swear.   150
HAMLET: Ha, ha, boy, say'st thou so? Art thou
    there, truepenny?°
    Come on, you hear this fellow in the cellarage.
    Consent to swear.
HORATIO: Propose the oath, my lord.
HAMLET: Never to speak of this that you have seen,
    Swear by my sword.   155
GHOST [*beneath*]: Swear.
HAMLET: Hic et ubique?° Then we'll shift our
    ground.
    [*He moves to another spot.*]
    Come hither, gentlemen,
    And lay your hands again upon my sword.
    Swear by my sword   160
    Never to speak of this that you have heard.
GHOST [*beneath*]: Swear by his sword.
HAMLET: Well said, old mole! Canst work i' th'
    earth so fast?
    A worthy pioner!° Once more remove, good
    friends.
    [*Moves again.*]
HORATIO: O day and night, but this is wondrous
    strange!   165
HAMLET: And therefore as a stranger give it
    welcome.
    There are more things in heaven and earth,
    Horatio,
    Than are dreamt of in your philosophy.°
    But come;
    Here, as before, never, so help you mercy,   170
    How strange or odd soe'er I bear myself —
    As I perchance hereafter shall think meet
    To put an antic° disposition on —
    That you, at such times seeing me, never shall,
    With arms encumb'red° thus, or this headshake,   175
    Or by pronouncing of some doubtful phrase,
    As "Well, well, we know," or "We could, an if°
    we would,"
    Or "If we list° to speak," or "There be, an if
    they might,"
    Or such ambiguous giving out,° to note°

125. **arrant:** Thoroughgoing.   128. **circumstance:** Ceremony.   137. **Saint Patrick:** The keeper of purgatory and
patron saint of all blunders and confusion.   139. **honest:**
I.e., a real ghost and not an evil spirit.

148. **sword:** The hilt in the form of a cross.   **151.**
truepenny: Honest old fellow.   157. **Hic et ubique:** Here
and everywhere (Latin).   164. **pioner:** Pioneer, digger,
miner.   168. **your philosophy:** This subject called "natural
philosophy" or "science" that people talk about.   173. **an-**
tic: Fantastic.   175. **encumb'red:** Folded or entwined.
177. **an if:** If.   178. **list:** Were inclined.   179. **giving out:**
Profession of knowledge.   **note:** Give a sign, indicate.

180 That you know aught of me — this do swear,
     So grace and mercy at your most need help you.
GHOST [beneath]: Swear.   [They swear.]
HAMLET: Rest, rest, perturbed spirit! So, gentlemen,
     With all my love I do commend me to you;
185 And what so poor a man as Hamlet is
     May do, t' express his love and friending to you,
     God willing, shall not lack. Let us go in together,
     And still° your fingers on your lips, I pray.
     The time is out of joint. O cursed spite,
190 That ever I was born to set it right!
                    [They wait for him to leave first.]
     Nay, come, let's go together.   (Exeunt.)

{ACT II • Scene 1}°

(Enter old Polonius, with his man [Reynaldo].)

POLONIUS: Give him this money and these notes,
     Reynaldo.
REYNALDO: I will, my lord.
POLONIUS: You shall do marvel's° wisely, good
     Reynaldo,
     Before you visit him, to make inquire
     Of his behavior.
5 REYNALDO: My lord, I did intend it.
POLONIUS: Marry, well said, very well said. Look
     you, sir,
     Inquire me first what Danskers° are in Paris,
     And how, and who, what means,° and where
          they keep,°
     What company, at what expense; and finding
10 By this encompassment° and drift° of question
     That they do know my son, come you more
          nearer
     Than your particular demands will touch it.°
     Take° you, as 'twere, some distant knowledge of
          him,
     As thus, "I know his father and his friends,
15 And in part him." Do you mark this, Reynaldo?
REYNALDO: Ay, very well, my lord.
POLONIUS: "And in part him, but," you may say,
     "not well.
     But, if 't be he I mean, he's very wild,

Addicted so and so," and there put on° him
What forgeries° you please — marry, none so
     rank   20
As may dishonor, him take heed of that,
But, sir, such wanton,° wild, and usual slips,
As are companions noted and most known
To youth and liberty.
REYNALDO: As gaming, my lord.
POLONIUS: Ay, or drinking, fencing, swearing,   25
     Quarreling, drabbing° — you may go so far.
REYNALDO: My lord, that would dishonor him.
POLONIUS: Faith, no, as you may season° it in the
          charge.
     You must not put another scandal on him
     That he is open to incontinency;°   30
     That's not my meaning. But breathe his faults so
          quaintly°
     That they may seem the taints of liberty,°
     The flash and outbreak of a fiery mind,
     A savageness in unreclaimed° blood,
     Of general assault.°
REYNALDO: But, my good lord —   35
POLONIUS: Wherefore should you do this?
REYNALDO: Ay, my lord,
     I would know that.
POLONIUS: Marry, sir, here's my drift,
     And, I believe, it is a fetch of wit.°
     You laying these slight sullies on my son,
     As 'twere a thing a little soil'd i' th' working,° 40
     Mark you,
     Your party in converse,° him you would sound,°
     Having ever° seen in the prenominate crimes°
     The youth you breathe° of guilty, be assur'd
     He closes with you in this consequence:°   45
     "Good sir," or so, or "friend," or "gentleman,"
     According to the phrase or the addition°
     Of man and country.
REYNALDO: Very good, my lord.
POLONIUS: And then, sir, does 'a this — 'a does —
          what was I about to say?
     By the mass, I was about to say something.   50

188. still: Always. II, I. Location: Polonius's chambers.
3. marvel's: Marvelous(ly). 7. Danskers: Danes. 8.
what means: What wealth (they have). keep: Dwell.
10. encompassment: Roundabout talking. drift: Gradual
approach or course. 11–12. come . . . it: You will find out
more this way than by asking pointed questions (particular
demands). 13. Take: Assume, pretend.

19. put on: Impute to. 20. forgeries: Invented tales. 22.
wanton: Sportive, unrestrained. 26. drabbing: Whoring.
28. season: Temper, soften. 30. incontinency: Habitual
loose behavior. 31. quaintly: Delicately, ingeniously.
32. taints of liberty: Faults resulting from freedom. 34.
unreclaimed: Untamed. 35. general assault: Tendency that
assails all unrestrained youth. 38. fetch of wit: Clever
trick. 40 soil'd i' th' working: Shopworn. 42. converse:
Conversation. sound: Sound out. 43. Having ever: If
he has ever. prenominate crimes: Before-mentioned offenses. 44. breathe: Speak. 45 closes . . . consequence:
Follows your lead in some fashion as follows. 47. addition: Title.

Where did I leave?

REYNALDO: At "closes in the consequence."

POLONIUS: At "closes in the consequence," ay,
    marry.

He closes thus: "I know the gentleman;
I saw him yesterday, or th' other day,
Or then, or then, with such, or such, and, as you
55   say,
There was 'a gaming, there o'ertook in 's rouse,°
There falling out° at tennis," or perchance,
"I saw him enter such a house of sale,"
Videlicet,° a brothel, or so forth. See you now,
60 Your bait of falsehood takes this carp° of truth;
And thus do we of wisdom and of reach,°
With windlasses° and with assays of bias,°
By indirections find directions° out.
So by my former lecture and advice
65 Shall you my son. You have me, have you not?

REYNALDO: My lord, I have.

POLONIUS: God buy ye; fare ye well.

REYNALDO: Good my lord.

POLONIUS: Observe his inclination in yourself.°

REYNALDO: I shall, my lord.

POLONIUS: And let him ply° his music.

70 REYNALDO: Well, my lord.

POLONIUS: Farewell.   (*Exit Reynaldo.*)

(*Enter Ophelia.*)

How now, Ophelia, what's the matter?

OPHELIA: O, my lord, my lord, I have been so
    affrighted!

POLONIUS: With what, i' th' name of God?

OPHELIA: My lord, as I was sewing in my closet,°
75 Lord Hamlet, with his doublet° all unbrac'd,°
No hat upon his head, his stockings fouled,
Ungart'red, and down-gyved to his ankle,°
Pale as his shirt, his knees knocking each other,
And with a look so piteous in purport
80 As if he had been loosed out of hell
To speak of horrors — he comes before me.

POLONIUS: Mad for thy love?

OPHELIA: My lord, I do not know,

But truly I do fear it.

POLONIUS: What said he?

OPHELIA: He took me by the wrist and held me
    hard.
Then goes he to the length of all his arm,   85
And, with his other hand thus o'er his brow
He falls to such perusal of my face
As 'a would draw it. Long stay'd he so.
At last, a little shaking of mine arm
And thrice his head thus waving up and down,   90
He rais'd a sigh so piteous and profound
As it did seem to shatter all his bulk°
And end his being. That done, he lets me go,
And, with his head over his shoulder turn'd,
He seem'd to find his way without his eyes,   95
For out o' doors he went without their helps,
And, to the last, bended their light on me.

POLONIUS: Come, go with me. I will go seek the
    King.
This is the very ecstasy° of love
Whose violent property° fordoes° itself   100
And leads the will to desperate undertakings
As oft as any passion under heaven
That does afflict our natures. I am sorry.
What, have you given him any hard words of
    late?

OPHELIA: No, my good lord, but, as you did
    command,   105
I did repel his letters and denied
His access to me.

POLONIUS: That hath made him mad.
I am sorry that with better heed and judgment
I had not quoted° him. I fear'd he did but trifle
And meant to wrack thee; but, beshrew my
    jealousy!°   110
By heaven, it is as proper to our age°
To cast beyond° ourselves in our opinions
As it is common for the younger sort
To lack discretion. Come, go we to the King.
This must be known, which, being kept close,°
    might move   115
More grief to hide than hate to utter love.°
Come.   (*Exeunt.*)

---

56. **o'ertook in 's rouse:** Overcome by drink.   57. **falling
out:** Quarreling.   59. **Videlicet:** Namely.   60. **carp:** A
fish.   61. **reach:** Capacity, ability.   62. **windlasses:** Circuitous paths (literally, circuits made to head off the game in
hunting).   **assays of bias:** Attempts through indirection
(like the curving path of the bowling ball, which is biased or
weighted to one side).   63. **directions:** The way things
really are.   68. **in yourself:** In your own person (as well as
by asking questions).   70. **let him ply:** See that he continues to study.   74. **closet:** Private chamber.   75. **doublet:**
Close-fitting jacket.   **unbrac'd:** Unfastened.   77. **down-
gyved to his ankle:** Fallen to the ankles (like gyves or fetters).

92. **bulk:** Body.   99. **ecstasy:** Madness.   100. **property:**
Nature.   **fordoes:** Destroys.   109. **quoted:** Observed.
110. **beshrew my jealousy:** A plague upon my suspicious nature.   111. **proper . . . age:** Characteristic of us (old) men.
112. **cast beyond:** Overshoot, miscalculate.   115. **close:** Secret.   115–16. **might . . . love:** Might cause more grief (to
others) by hiding the knowledge of Hamlet's strange behavior to Ophelia than hatred by telling it.

{*Scene II*}°

(*Flourish. Enter King and Queen, Rosencrantz, and Guildenstern [with others].*)

KING: Welcome, dear Rosencrantz and Guildenstern.
Moreover that° we much did long to see you,
The need we have to use you did provoke
Our hasty sending. Something have you heard
5 Of Hamlet's transformation — so call it,
Sith° nor th' exterior nor° the inward man
Resembles that° it was. What it should be,
More than his father's death, that thus hath put
him
So much from th' understanding of himself,
10 I cannot dream of. I entreat you both
That, being of so young days° brought up with
him,
And sith so neighbor'd to his youth and havior,
That you vouchsafe your rest° here in our court
Some little time, so by your companies
15 To draw him on to pleasures, and to gather
So much as from occasion you may glean,
Whether aught to us unknown afflicts him thus,
That, open'd,° lies within our remedy.
QUEEN: Good gentlemen, he hath much talk'd of
you
20 And sure I am two men there is not living
To whom he more adheres. If it will please you
To show us so much gentry° and good will
As to expend your time with us awhile
For the supply and profit° of our hope,
25 Your visitation shall receive such thanks
As fits a king's remembrance.
ROSENCRANTZ: Both your Majesties
Might, by the sovereign power you have of us,
Put your dread pleasures more into command
Than to entreaty.
GUILDENSTERN: But we both obey,
30 And here give up ourselves in the full bent°
To lay our service freely at your feet,
To be commanded.
KING: Thanks, Rosencrantz and gentle
Guildenstern.
QUEEN: Thanks, Guildenstern and gentle
Rosencrantz.

And I beseech you instantly to visit   35
My too much changed son. Go, some of you,
And bring these gentlemen where Hamlet is.
GUILDENSTERN: Heavens make our presence and our
practices
Pleasant and helpful to him!
QUEEN: Ay, amen!
(*Exeunt Rosencrantz and Guildenstern [with
some Attendants].*)

(*Enter Polonius.*)

POLONIUS: Th' ambassadors from Norway, my good
lord,   40
Are joyfully return'd.
KING: Thou still° hast been the father of good news.
POLONIUS: Have I, my lord? I assure my good liege
I hold my duty, as I hold my soul,
Both to my God and to my gracious king;   45
And I do think, or else this brain of mine
Hunts not the trail of policy so sure
As it hath us'd to do, that I have found
The very cause of Hamlet's lunacy.
KING: O, speak of that! That do I long to hear.   50
POLONIUS: Give first admittance to th' ambassadors.
My news shall be the fruit° to that great feast.
KING: Thyself do grace to them, and bring them in.
(*Exit Polonius.*)
He tells me, my dear Gertrude, he hath found
The head and source of all your son's distemper.   55
QUEEN: I doubt° it is no other but the main,°
His father's death, and our o'erhasty marriage.

(*Enter Ambassadors [Voltimand and Cornelius, with
Polonius].*)

KING: Well, we shall sift him. — Welcome, my good
friends!
Say, Voltimand, what from our brother Norway?
VOLTIMAND: Most fair return of greetings and
desires.   60
Upon our first,° he sent out to suppress
His nephew's levies, which to him appear'd
To be a preparation 'gainst the Polack,
But, better look'd into, he truly found
It was against your Highness. Whereat griev'd   65
That so his sickness, age, and impotence
Was falsely borne in hand,° sends out arrests
On Fortinbras, which he, in brief, obeys,
Receives rebuke from Norway, and in fine°

II, II. Location: The castle.   **2. Moreover that:** Besides the
fact that.   **6. Sith:** Since.   **nor . . . nor:** Neither . . . nor.
7. that: What.   **11. of . . . days:** From such early youth.
13. vouchsafe your rest: Please to stay.   **18. open'd:** Revealed.   **22. gentry:** Courtesy.   **24. supply and profit:** Aid
and successful outcome.   **30. in . . . bent:** To the utmost degree of our capacity.

42. still: Always.   **52. fruit:** Dessert.   **56. doubt:** Fear,
suspect.   **main:** Chief point, principal concern.   **61.
Upon our first:** At our first words on the business.   **67.
borne in hand:** Deluded, taken advantage of.   **69. in fine:**
In the end.

70 Makes vow before his uncle never more
To give th' assay° of arms against your Majesty.
Whereon old Norway, overcome with joy,
Gives him three score thousand crowns in annual
    fee,
And his commission to employ those soldiers,
75 So levied as before, against the Polack,
With an entreaty, herein further shown,

                                [*Giving a paper.*]

That it might please you to give quiet pass
Through your dominions for this enterprise,
On such regards of safety and allowance°
As therein are set down.
80 KING: It likes° us well;
And at our more consider'd° time we'll read,
Answer, and think upon this business.
Meantime we thank you for your well-took
    labor.
Go to your rest; at night we'll feast together.
Most welcome home!   (*Exeunt Ambassadors.*)
85 POLONIUS: This business is well ended.
My liege, and madam, to expostulate°
What majesty should be, what duty is,
Why day is day, night night, and time is time,
Were nothing but to waste night, day, and time.
90 Therefore, since brevity is the soul of wit,°
And tediousness the limbs and outward
    flourishes,
I will be brief. Your noble son is mad.
Mad call I it, for, to define true madness,
What is 't but to be nothing else but mad?
But let that go.
95 QUEEN: More matter, with less art.
POLONIUS: Madam, I swear I use no art at all.
That he is mad, 'tis true; 'tis true 'tis pity,
And pity 'tis 'tis true — a foolish figure,°
But farewell it, for I will use no art.
100 Mad let us grant him, then, and now remains
That we find out the cause of this effect,
Or rather say, the cause of this defect,
For this effect defective comes by cause.°
Thus it remains, and the remainder thus.
105 Perpend.°
I have a daughter — have while she is mine —
Who, in her duty and obedience, mark,
Hath given me this. Now gather, and surmise.
[*Reads the letter.*] "To the celestial and my soul's
    idol,

the most beautified Ophelia" —   110
That's an ill phrase, a vile phrase; "beautified" is
    a vile
phrase. But you shall hear. Thus: [*Reads.*]
"In her excellent white bosom, these, etc."
QUEEN: Came this from Hamlet to her?
POLONIUS: Good madam, stay awhile; I will be
    faithful.   115

                                [*Reads.*]

"Doubt° thou the stars are fire,
    Doubt that the sun doth move,
Doubt truth to be a liar,
    But never doubt I love.
O dear Ophelia, I am ill at these numbers.° I have   120
not art to reckon° my groans. But that I love thee
best, O most best, believe it. Adieu.
        Thine evermore, most dear lady, whilst this
                machine° is to him, Hamlet."
This in obedience hath my daughter shown me,   125
And, more above,° hath his solicitings,
As they fell out° by time, by means, and place,
All given to mine ear.
KING: But how hath she
Receiv'd his love?
POLONIUS: What do you think of me?
KING: As of a man faithful and honorable.   130
POLONIUS: I would fain prove so. But what might
    you think,
When I had seen this hot love on the wing —
As I perceiv'd it, I must tell you that,
Before my daughter told me — what might you,
Or my dear Majesty your Queen here, think,   135
If I had play'd the desk or table-book,°
Or given my heart a winking,° mute and dumb,
Or look'd upon this love with idle sight?°
What might you think? No, I went round° to
    work,
And my young mistress thus I did bespeak:°   140
"Lord Hamlet is a prince, out of thy star;°
This must not be." And then I prescripts gave her,
That she should lock herself from his resort,
Admit no messengers, receive no tokens.
Which done, she took the fruits of my advice;   145
And he, repelled — a short tale to make —
Fell into a sadness, then into a fast,

---

71. **assay:** Trial.   79. **On . . . allowance:** With such pledges of safety and provisos.   80. **likes:** Pleases.   81. **consider'd:** Suitable for deliberation.   86. **expostulate:** Expound.   90. **wit:** Sound sense or judgment.   98. **figure:** Figure of speech.   103. **For . . . cause:** I.e., for this defective behavior, this madness has a cause.   105. **Perpend:** Consider.

116. **Doubt:** Suspect, question.   120. **ill . . . numbers:** Unskilled at writing verses.   121. **reckon:** (1) Count, (2) number metrically, scan.   124. **machine:** Body.   126. **more above:** Moreover.   127. **fell out:** Occurred.   136. **play'd . . . table-book:** Remained shut up, concealing the information.   137. **winking:** Closing of the eyes.   138. **with idle sight:** Complacently or uncomprehendingly.   139. **round:** Roundly, plainly.   140. **bespeak:** Address.   141. **out of thy star:** Above your sphere, position.

Thence to a watch,° thence into a weakness,
Thence to a lightness,° and, by this declension,°
150   Into the madness wherein now he raves,
And all we mourn for.
KING: Do you think this?
QUEEN: It may be, very like.
POLONIUS: Hath there been such a time — I would
fain know that —
That I have positively said " 'Tis so,"
When it prov'd otherwise?
155   KING: Not that I know.
POLONIUS [*pointing to his head and shoulder*]: Take
this from this, if this be otherwise.
If circumstances lead me, I will find
Where truth is hid, though it were hid indeed
Within the center.°
KING: How may we try it further?
POLONIUS: You know, sometimes he walks four
160   hours together
Here in the lobby.
QUEEN: So he does indeed.
POLONIUS: At such a time I'll loose my daughter to
him.
Be you and I behind an arras° then.
Mark the encounter. If he love her not
165   And be not from his reason fall'n thereon,°
Let me be no assistant for a state,
But keep a farm and carters.
KING: We will try it.

(*Enter Hamlet [reading on a book].*)

QUEEN: But look where sadly the poor wretch
comes reading.
POLONIUS: Away, I do beseech you both, away.
I'll board° him presently.
            (*Exeunt King and Queen [with Attendants].*)
170   O, give me leave.
How does my good Lord Hamlet?
HAMLET: Well, God-a-mercy.
POLONIUS: Do you know me, my lord?
HAMLET: Excellent well. You are a fishmonger.°
175   POLONIUS: Not I, my lord.
HAMLET: Then I would you were so honest a man.
POLONIUS: Honest, my lord?
HAMLET: Ay, sir. To be honest, as this world goes, is
to be one man pick'd out of ten thousand.
180   POLONIUS: That's very true, my lord.

HAMLET: For if the sun breed maggots in a dead dog,
being a good kissing carrion° — Have you a
daughter?
POLONIUS: I have, my lord.
HAMLET: Let her not walk i' th' sun.° Conception° is   185
a blessing, but as your daughter may conceive,
friend, look to 't.
POLONIUS [*aside*]: How say you by that? Still harping
on my daughter. Yet he knew me not at first; 'a
said I was a fishmonger. 'A is far gone. And truly   190
in my youth I suff'red much extremity for love,
very near this. I'll speak to him again. — What do
you read, my lord?
HAMLET: Words, words, words.
POLONIUS: What is the matter,° my lord?   195
HAMLET: Between who?
POLONIUS: I mean, the matter that you read, my lord.
HAMLET: Slanders, sir, for the satirical rogue says here
that old men have gray beards, that their faces are
wrinkled, their eyes purging° thick amber and   200
plum-tree gum, and that they have a plentiful lack
of wit, together with most weak hams. All which,
sir, though I most powerfully and potently believe,
yet I hold it not honesty° to have it thus set down,
for you yourself, sir, shall grow old as I am, if like   205
a crab you could go backward.
POLONIUS [*aside*]: Though this be madness, yet there
is method in 't. — Will you walk out of the air, my
lord?
HAMLET: Into my grave.   210
POLONIUS: Indeed, that's out of the air. [*Aside.*] How
pregnant° sometimes his replies are! A happiness°
that often madness hits on, which reason and sanity could not so prosperously° be deliver'd of. I
will leave him, [and suddenly contrive the means   215
of meeting between him] and my daughter. — My
honorable lord, I will most humbly take my leave
of you.
HAMLET: You cannot, sir, take from me any thing that
I will more willingly part withal — except my life,   220
except my life, except my life.

(*Enter Guildenstern and Rosencrantz.*)

POLONIUS: Fare you well, my lord.
HAMLET: These tedious old fools!°

---

148. **watch:** State of sleeplessness.   149. **lightness:** Light-
headedness.   **declension:** Decline, deterioration.   159. **center:** Middle point of the earth (which is also the center of
the Ptolemaic universe).   163. **arras:** Hanging, tapestry.
165. **thereon:** On that account.   170. **board:** Accost.
172. **God-a-mercy:** Thank you.   174. **fishmonger:** Fish
merchant (with connotation of *bawd, procurer*[?]).

182. **good kissing carrion:** A good piece of flesh for kissing,
or for the sun to kiss.   185. **i' th' sun:** With additional implication of the sunshine of princely favors.   **Conception:**
(1) Understanding, (2) pregnancy.   195. **matter:** Substance
(but Hamlet plays on the sense of *basis for a dispute*).
200. **purging:** Discharging.   204. **honesty:** Decency.
212. **pregnant:** Full of meaning.   **happiness:** Felicity of expression.   214. **prosperously:** Successfully.   223. **old
fools:** I.e., old men like Polonius.

POLONIUS: You go to seek the Lord Hamlet; there
225 he is.
ROSENCRANTZ [*to Polonius*]: God save you, sir!
                                              [*Exit Polonius.*]
GUILDENSTERN: My honor'd lord!
ROSENCRANTZ: My most dear lord!
HAMLET: My excellent good friends! How dost thou,
230 Guildenstern? Ah, Rosencrantz! Good lads, how
     do you both?
ROSENCRANTZ: As the indifferent° children of the earth.
GUILDENSTERN: Happy in that we are not over-happy.
     On Fortune's cap we are not the very button.
235 HAMLET: Nor the soles of her shoe?
ROSENCRANTZ: Neither, my lord.
HAMLET: Then you live about her waist, or in the
     middle of her favors?
GUILDENSTERN: Faith, her privates° we.
240 HAMLET: In the secret parts of Fortune? O, most true;
     she is a strumpet.° What news?
ROSENCRANTZ: None, my lord, but the world's grown
     honest.
HAMLET: Then is doomsday near. But your news is
245 not true. [Let me question more in particular.
     What have you, my good friends, deserv'd at the
     hands of Fortune that she sends you to prison
     hither?
GUILDENSTERN: Prison, my lord?
HAMLET: Denmark's a prison.
250 ROSENCRANTZ: Then is the world one.
HAMLET: A goodly one, in which there are many con-
     fines,° wards,° and dungeons, Denmark being one
     o' th' worst.
ROSENCRANTZ: We think not so, my lord.
255 HAMLET: Why then 'tis none to you, for there is noth-
     ing either good or bad but thinking makes it so. To
     me it is a prison.
ROSENCRANTZ: Why then, your ambition makes it
     one. 'Tis too narrow for your mind.
260 HAMLET: O God, I could be bounded in a nutshell
     and count myself a king of infinite space, were it
     not that I have bad dreams.
GUILDENSTERN: Which dreams indeed are ambition,
     for the very substance of the ambitious° is merely
265 the shadow of a dream.
HAMLET: A dream itself is but a shadow.
ROSENCRANTZ: Truly, and I hold ambition of so airy
     and light a quality that it is but a shadow's shadow.

HAMLET: Then are our beggars bodies,° and our mon-
     archs and outstretch'd° heroes the beggars' shad-   270
     ows. Shall we to th' court? For, by my fay,° I
     cannot reason.
ROSENCRANTZ, GUILDENSTERN: We'll wait upon° you.
HAMLET: No such matter. I will not sort° you with the
     rest of my servants, for, to speak to you like an   275
     honest man, I am most dreadfully attended.°] But,
     in the beaten way° of friendship, what make° you
     at Elsinore?
ROSENCRANTZ: To visit you, my lord, no other occasion.
HAMLET: Beggar that I am, I am even poor in thanks;   280
     but I thank you, and sure, dear friends, my thanks
     are too dear a halfpenny.° Were you not sent for?
     Is it your own inclining? Is it a free visitation?
     Come, come, deal justly with me. Come, come;
     nay, speak.   285
GUILDENSTERN: What should we say, my lord?
HAMLET: Why, anything, but to th' purpose. You
     were sent for; and there is a kind of confession in
     your looks which your modesties have not craft
     enough to color. I know the good King and Queen   290
     have sent for you.
ROSENCRANTZ: To what end, my lord?
HAMLET: That you must teach me. But let me conjure°
     you, by the rights of our fellowship, by the conso-
     nancy of our youth,° by the obligation of our ever-   295
     preserv'd love, and by what more dear a better
     proposer° could charge° you withal, be even° and
     direct with me, whether you were sent for, or no?
ROSENCRANTZ [*aside to Guildenstern*]: What say you?
HAMLET [*aside*]: Nay then, I have an eye of° you. — If   300
     you love me, hold not off.
GUILDENSTERN: My lord, we were sent for.
HAMLET: I will tell you why; so shall my anticipation
     prevent your discovery,° and your secrecy to the
     King and Queen molt no feather.° I have of late —   305
     but wherefore I know not — lost all my mirth, for-
     gone all custom of exercises; and indeed it goes so
     heavily with my disposition that this goodly frame,
     the earth, seems to me a sterile promontory; this
     most excellent canopy, the air, look you, this   310

---

232. **indifferent:** Ordinary.   239. **privates:** Close acquaintances (with sexual pun on *private parts*).   241. **strumpet:**
Prostitute (a common epithet for indiscriminate Fortune, see
line 505 p. 388).   251–52. **confines:** Places of confinement.
252. **wards:** Cells.   264. **the very . . . ambitious:** That
seemingly very substantial thing which the ambitious pursue.

269. **bodies:** Solid substances rather than shadows (since beggars are not ambitious).   270. **outstretch'd:** (1) Far-reaching
in their ambition, (2) elongated as shadows.   271. **fay:**
Faith.   273. **wait upon:** Accompany, attend.   274. **sort:**
Class, associate.   276. **dreadfully attended:** Waited upon in
slovenly fashion.   277. **beaten way:** Familiar path.   **make:**
Do.   282. **dear a halfpenny:** Expensive at the price of a halfpenny, i.e., of little worth.   293. **conjure:** Adjure, entreat.
294–95. **consonancy of our youth:** The fact that we are of the
same age.   296–97. **better proposer:** More skillful pro-
pounder.   297. **charge:** Urge.   **even:** Straight, honest.
300. **of:** On.   304. **prevent your discovery:** Forestall your
disclosure.   305. **molt no feather:** Not diminish in the least.

brave° o'erhanging firmament, this majestical roof fretted° with golden fire, why, it appeareth nothing to me but a foul and pestilent congregation of vapors. What a piece of work is a man! How noble in reason, how infinite in faculties, in form and moving how express° and admirable, in action how like an angel, in apprehension how like a god! The beauty of the world, the paragon of animals! And yet, to me, what is this quintessence° of dust? Man delights not me — no, nor woman neither, though by your smiling you seem to say so.

311. **brave:** Splendid.   312. **fretted:** Adorned (with fretwork, as in a vaulted ceiling).   316. **express:** Well-framed (?), exact (?).   319. **quintessence:** The fifth essence of ancient philosophy, beyond earth, water, air, and fire, supposed to be the substance of the heavenly bodies and to be latent in all things.

ROSENCRANTZ: My lord, there was no such stuff in my thoughts.
HAMLET: Why did you laugh then, when I said "man delights not me"?
ROSENCRANTZ: To think, my lord, if you delight not in man, what lenten entertainment° the players shall receive from you. We coted° them on the way, and hither are they coming, to offer you service.
HAMLET: He that plays the king shall be welcome; his Majesty shall have tribute of me. The adventurous knight shall use his foil and target,° the lover shall not sigh gratis, the humorous man° shall end his

327. **lenten entertainment:** Meager reception (appropriate to Lent).   328. **coted:** Overtook and passed beyond.   332. **foil and target:** Sword and shield.   333. **humorous man:** Eccentric character, dominated by one trait or "humor."

LEFT: Hamlet returns to Denmark. Left to right, Voltemand (Jeremy Geidt), Gertrude (Christine Estabrook), Claudius (Mark Metcalf), Hamlet (Mark Rylance), and Laertes (Derek Smith) in the 1991 American Repertory Theatre production of *Hamlet,* directed by Ron Daniels. RIGHT: The dumb-show sequence with Candy Buckley as the Player Queen.

part in peace, [the clown shall make those laugh
335 whose lungs are tickle o' th' sere°], and the lady
shall say her mind freely, or the blank verse shall
halt° for 't. What players are they?
ROSENCRANTZ: Even those you were wont to take
such delight in, the tragedians of the city.
340 HAMLET: How chances it they travel? Their residence,°
both in reputation and profit, was better both ways.
ROSENCRANTZ: I think their inhibition° comes by the
means of the innovation.°
HAMLET: Do they hold the same estimation they did
345 when I was in the city? Are they so follow'd?
ROSENCRANTZ: No, indeed, are they not.
[HAMLET: How comes it? Do they grow rusty?
ROSENCRANTZ: Nay, their endeavor keeps in the
wonted° pace. But there is, sir, an aery° of chil-

dren, little eyases,° that cry out on the top of ques-   350
tion,° and are most tyrannically° clapp'd for 't.
These are now the fashion, and so berattle° the
common stages° — so they call them — that many
wearing rapiers° are afraid of goose-quills° and
dare scarce come thither.   355
HAMLET: What, are they children? Who maintains 'em?
How are they escoted?° Will they pursue the quality°
no longer than they can sing?° Will they not say afterwards, if they should grow themselves to com-
mon° players — as it is most like, if their means are   360
no better — their writers do them wrong, to make
them exclaim against their own succession?°

335. **tickle o' th' sere:** Easy on the trigger, ready to laugh easily. (*Sere* is part of a gunlock.)   337. **halt:** Limp.   340. **residence:** Remaining in one place, i.e., in the city.   342. **inhibition:** Formal prohibition (from acting plays in the city).   343. **innovation:** I.e., the new fashion in satirical plays performed by boy actors in the "private" theaters; or possibly a political uprising; or the strict limitations set on the theater in London in 1600.   349. **wonted:** Usual.   **aery:** Nest.

350. **eyases:** Young hawks.   **cry . . . question:** Speak shrilly, dominating the controversy (in decrying the public theaters).   351. **tyrannically:** Outrageous.   352. **berattle:** Berate.   352–53. **common stages:** Public theaters.   353–54. **many wearing rapiers:** Many men of fashion, who were afraid to patronize the common players for fear of being satirized by the poets who wrote for the children.   354. **goose-quills:** Pens of satirists.   357. **escoted:** Maintained.   358. **quality:** (Acting) profession.   **no longer . . . sing:** Only until their voices change.   360. **common:** Regular, adult.   362. **succession:** Future careers.

ROSENCRANTZ: Faith, there has been much to do° on
both sides, and the nation holds it no sin to tarre°
365   them to controversy. There was, for a while, no
money bid for argument° unless the poet and the
player went to cuffs in the question.°
HAMLET: Is 't possible?
GUILDENSTERN: O, there has been much throwing
370   about of brains.
HAMLET: Do the boys carry it away?°
ROSENCRANTZ: Ay, that they do, my lord — Hercules
and his load° too.°]
HAMLET: It is not very strange, for my uncle is King of
375   Denmark, and those that would make mouths° at
him while my father liv'd, give twenty, forty, fifty,
a hundred ducats° apiece for his picture in little.°
'Sblood,° there is something in this more than natural, if philosophy could find it out.

(A flourish [of trumpets within].)

380 GUILDENSTERN: There are the players.
HAMLET: Gentlemen, you are welcome to Elsinore.
Your hands, come then. Th' appurtenance of welcome is fashion and ceremony. Let me comply°
with you in this garb,° lest my extent° to the play-
385   ers, which, I tell you, must show fairly outwards,°
should more appear like entertainment° than
yours. You are welcome. But my uncle-father and
aunt-mother are deceiv'd.
GUILDENSTERN: In what, my dear lord?
390 HAMLET: I am but mad north-north-west.° When the
wind is southerly I know a hawk from a handsaw.°

(Enter Polonius.)

POLONIUS: Well be with you, gentlemen!
HAMLET: Hark you, Guildenstern, and you too; at
each ear a hearer. That great baby you see there is
395   not yet out of his swaddling-clouts.°

ROSENCRANTZ: Happily° he is the second time come
to them; for they say an old man is twice a child.
HAMLET: I will prophesy he comes to tell me of the
players; mark it. — You say right, sir, o' Monday
morning, 'twas then indeed.   400
POLONIUS: My lord, I have news to tell you.
HAMLET: My lord, I have news to tell you. When
Roscius° was an actor in Rome —
POLONIUS: The actors are come hither, my lord.
HAMLET: Buzz,° buzz!   405
POLONIUS: Upon my honor —
HAMLET: Then came each actor on his ass —
POLONIUS: The best actors in the world, either for
tragedy, comedy, history, pastoral, pastoral-com-
ical, historical-pastoral, tragical-historical, tragi- 410
cal-comical-historical-pastoral, scene individable,°
or poem unlimited.° Seneca° cannot be too heavy,
nor Plautus° too light. For the law of writ and the
liberty,° these are the only men.
HAMLET: O Jephthah, judge of Israel,° what a treasure 415
hadst thou!
POLONIUS: What a treasure had he, my lord?
HAMLET: Why,
    "One fair daughter, and no more,
    The which he loved passing° well."   420
POLONIUS [aside]: Still on my daughter.
HAMLET: Am I not i' th' right, old Jephthah?
POLONIUS: If you call me Jephthah, my lord, I have a
daughter that I love passing well.
HAMLET: Nay, that follows not.   425
POLONIUS: What follows, then, my lord?
HAMLET: Why,
    "As by lot, God wot,"°
    and then, you know,
    "It came to pass, as most like° it was."   430
The first row° of the pious chanson° will show you
more, for look where my abridgement° comes.

(Enter the Players.)

---

363. **to do:** Ado.   364. **tarre:** Set on (as dogs).   366. **argument:** Plot for a play.   367. **went . . . question:** Came to
blows in the play itself.   371. **carry it away:** Win the day.
372–73. **Hercules . . . load:** Thought to be an allusion to the
sign of the Globe Theatre, which was Hercules bearing the
world on his shoulder.   347–73. **How . . . load too:** The passage, omitted from the early quartos, alludes to the so-called
War of the Theatres, 1599–1602, the rivalry between the children companies and the adult actors.   375. **mouths:** Faces.
377. **ducats:** Gold coins.   377–78. **in little:** In miniature.
378. **'Sblood:** By His (God's, Christ's) blood.   383. **comply:**
Observe the formalities of courtesy.   384. **garb:** Manner.
my extent: The extent of my showing courtesy.   385. **show
fairly outwards:** Look cordial to outward appearances.
386. **entertainment:** A (warm) reception.   390. **north-north-
west:** Only partly, at times.   391. **hawk, handsaw:** Mattock
(or *hack*) and a carpenter's cutting tool respectively; also
birds, with a play on *hernshaw* or heron.   395. **swaddling-
clouts:** Cloths in which to wrap a newborn baby.

396. **Happily:** Haply, perhaps.   403. **Roscius:** A famous
Roman actor who died in 62 B.C.   405. **Buzz:** An interjection used to denote stale news.   411. **scene individable:** A
play observing the unity of place.   412. **poem unlimited:** A
play disregarding the unities of time and place. **Seneca:**
Writer of Latin tragedies.   413. **Plautus:** Writer of Latin
comedy.   413–14. **law . . . liberty:** Dramatic composition
both according to rules and without rules, i.e., "classical"
and "romantic" dramas.   415. **Jephthah . . . Israel:** Jephthah had to sacrifice his daughter; see Judges 11. Hamlet
goes on to quote from a ballad on the theme.   420. **passing:** Surpassingly.   428. **wot:** Knows.   430. **like:** Likely,
probable.   431. **row:** Stanza. **chanson:** Ballad, song.
432. **my abridgement:** Something that cuts short my conversation; also, a diversion.

You are welcome, masters; welcome, all. I am glad to see thee well. Welcome, good friends. O, old friend! Why, thy face is valanc'd° since I saw thee last. Com'st thou to beard° me in Denmark? What, my young lady° and mistress? By 'r lady, your ladyship is nearer to heaven than when I saw you last, by the altitude of a chopine.° Pray God your voice, like a piece of uncurrent° gold, be not crack'd within the ring.° Masters, you are all welcome. We'll e'en to 't like French falconers, fly at anything we see. We'll have a speech straight.° Come, give us a taste of your quality; come, a passionate speech.

FIRST PLAYER: What speech, my good lord?

HAMLET: I heard thee speak me a speech once, but it was never acted, or, if it was, not above once, for the play, I remember, pleas'd not the million; 'twas caviary to the general.° But it was — as I receiv'd it, and others, whose judgments in such matters cried in the top of° mine — an excellent play, well digested in the scenes, set down with as much modesty as cunning.° I remember one said there were no sallets° in the lines to make the matter savory, nor no matter in the phrase that might indict° the author of affectation, but call'd it an honest method, as wholesome as sweet, and by very much more handsome than fine.° One speech in 't I chiefly lov'd: 'twas Aeneas' tale to Dido, and thereabout of it especially when he speaks of Priam's slaughter.° If it live in your memory, begin at this line: let me see, let me see —
"The rugged Pyrrhus,° like th' Hyrcanian
beast"° —
'Tis not so. It begins with Pyrrhus:
"The rugged Pyrrhus, he whose sable° arms,
Black as his purpose, did the night resemble
When he lay couched in the ominous horse,°
Hath now this dread and black complexion
smear'd
With heraldry more dismal.° Head to foot
Now is he total gules,° horridly trick'd°
With blood of fathers, mothers, daughters, sons,
Bak'd and impasted° with the parching streets,°
That lend a tyrannous and a damned light
To their lord's° murder. Roasted in wrath and
fire,
And thus o'er-sized° with coagulate gore,
With eyes like carbuncles, the hellish Pyrrhus
Old grandsire Priam seeks."
So proceed you.

POLONIUS: 'Fore God, my lord, well spoken, with good accent and good discretion.

FIRST PLAYER: "Anon he finds him
Striking too short at Greeks. His antique sword,
Rebellious to his arm, lies where it falls,
Repugnant° to command. Unequal match'd,
Pyrrhus at Priam drives, in rage strikes wide,
But with the whiff and wind of his fell° sword
Th' unnerved father falls. [Then senseless Ilium,°]
Seeming to feel this blow, with flaming top
Stoops to his° base, and with a hideous crash
Takes prisoner Pyrrhus' ear. For, lo! His sword,
Which was declining on the milky head
Of reverend Priam, seem'd i' th' air to stick.
So as a painted° tyrant Pyrrhus stood,
And, like a neutral to his will and matter,°
Did nothing.
But, as we often see, against° some storm,
A silence in the heavens, the rack° stand still,
The bold winds speechless, and the orb below
As hush as death, anon the dreadful thunder
Doth rend the region,° so, after Pyrrhus' pause,
Aroused vengeance sets him new a-work,
And never did the Cyclops'° hammers fall
On Mars's armor forg'd for proof eterne°
With less remorse than Pyrrhus' bleeding sword

435. valanc'd: Fringed (with a beard). **436. beard:** Confront (with obvious pun). **437. young lady:** Boy playing women's parts. **439. chopine:** Thick-soled shoe of Italian fashion. **440. uncurrent:** Not passable as lawful coinage. **440–41. crack'd . . . ring:** Changed from adolescent to male voice, no longer suitable for women's roles. (Coins featured rings enclosing the sovereign's head; if the coin was cracked within this ring, it was unfit for currency.) **443. straight:** At once. **449. caviary to the general:** Caviar to the multitude, i.e., a choice dish too elegant for coarse tastes. **450–51. cried in the top of:** Spoke with greater authority than. **453. cunning:** Skill. **sallets:** Salad, i.e., spicy improprieties. **455. indict:** Convict. **458. fine:** Elaborately ornamented, showy. **460. Priam's slaughter:** The slaying of the ruler of Troy, when the Greeks finally took the city. **463. Pyrrhus:** A Greek hero in the Trojan War, also known as Neoptolemus, son of Achilles. **Hyrcanian beast:** I.e., the tiger. (See Virgil, *Aeneid*, IV, 266; compare the whole speech with Marlowe's *Dido Queen of Carthage*, II, i, 214 ff.) **465. sable:** Black (for reasons of camouflage during the episode of the Trojan horse).

467. ominous horse: Trojan horse, by which the Greeks gained access to Troy. **469. dismal:** Ill-omened. **470. gules:** Red (a heraldic term). **trick'd:** Adorned, decorated. **472. impasted:** Crusted, like a thick paste. **with . . . streets:** By the parching heat of the streets (because of the fires everywhere). **474. their lord's:** Priam's. **475. o'er-sized:** Covered as with size or glue. **483. Repugnant:** Disobedient, resistant. **485. fell:** Cruel. **486. senseless Ilium:** Insensate Troy. **488. his:** Its. **492. painted:** Painted in a picture. **493. like . . . matter:** As though poised indecisively between his intention and its fulfillment. **495. against:** Just before. **496. rack:** Mass of clouds. **499. region:** Sky. **501. Cyclops:** Giant armor makers in the smithy of Vulcan. **502. proof eterne:** Eternal resistance to assault.

Now falls on Priam.

505 Out, out, thou strumpet Fortune! All you gods,
In general synod,° take away her power!
Break all the spokes and fellies° from her wheel,
And bowl the round nave° down the hill of
heaven,
As low as to the fiends!"

510 POLONIUS: This is too long.
HAMLET: It shall to the barber's with your beard. —
Prithee say on. He's for a jig° or a tale of bawdry,
or he sleeps. Say on, come to Hecuba.°
FIRST PLAYER: "But who, ah woe! had seen the
mobled° queen" —
515 HAMLET: "The mobled queen?"
POLONIUS: That's good. "Mobled queen" is good.
FIRST PLAYER: "Run barefoot up and down,
threat'ning the flames
With bisson rheum,° a clout° upon that head
Where late the diadem stood, and for a robe,
520 About her lank and all o'er-teemed° loins,
A blanket, in the alarm of fear caught up —
Who this had seen, with tongue in venom
steep'd,
'Gainst Fortune's state° would treason have
pronounc'd.°
But if the gods themselves did see her then
525 When she saw Pyrrhus make malicious sport
In mincing with his sword her husband's limbs,
The instant burst of clamor that she made,
Unless things mortal move them not at all,
Would have made milch° the burning eyes of
heaven,
530 And passion in the gods."
POLONIUS: Look whe'er° he has not turn'd his color
and has tears in 's eyes. Prithee, no more.
HAMLET: 'Tis well; I'll have thee speak out the rest of
this soon. Good my lord, will you see the players
535 well bestow'd?° Do you hear, let them be well us'd,
for they are the abstract° and brief chronicles of
the time. After your death you were better have a
bad epitaph than their ill report while you live.
POLONIUS: My lord, I will use them according to their
540 desert.
HAMLET: God's bodkin,° man, much better! Use every
man after his desert, and who shall scape whip-

ping? Use them after your own honor and dignity.
The less they deserve, the more merit is in your
bounty. Take them in.   545
POLONIUS: Come, sirs.
HAMLET: Follow him, friends. We'll hear a play to-
morrow. [As they start to leave, Hamlet detains the
First Player.] Dost thou hear me, old friend? Can
you play the Murder of Gonzago?   550
FIRST PLAYER: Ay, my lord.
HAMLET: We'll ha 't tomorrow night. You could, for
need, study a speech of some dozen or sixteen
lines, which I would set down and insert in 't,
could you not?   555
FIRST PLAYER: Ay, my lord.
HAMLET: Very well. Follow that lord, and look you
mock him not. — My good friends, I'll leave you
till night. You are welcome to Elsinore.
          (Exeunt Polonius and Players.)
ROSENCRANTZ: Good my lord!   560
          (Exeunt [Rosencrantz and Guildenstern].)
HAMLET: Ay, so, God buy you. — Now I am alone.
O, what a rogue and peasant slave am I!
Is it not monstrous that this player here,
But in a fiction, in a dream of passion,
Could force his soul so to his own conceit°   565
That from her working all his visage wann'd,°
Tears in his eyes, distraction in his aspect,
A broken voice, and his whole function suiting
With forms to his conceit?° And all for nothing!
For Hecuba!   570
What's Hecuba to him, or he to Hecuba,
That he should weep for her? What would he
do,
Had he the motive and the cue for passion
That I have? He would drown the stage with
tears
And cleave the general ear with horrid speech,   575
Make mad the guilty and appall the free,°
Confound the ignorant, and amaze indeed
The very faculties of eyes and ears. Yet I,
A dull and muddy-mettled° rascal, peak,°
Like John-a-dreams,° unpregnant of° my cause,   580
And can say nothing — no, not for a king
Upon whose property° and most dear life
A damn'd defeat was made. Am I a coward?
Who calls me villain? Breaks my pate across?
Plucks off my beard, and blows it in my face?   585

506. synod: Assembly.   507. fellies: Pieces of wood forming
the rim of a wheel.   508. nave: Hub.   512. jig: Comic song
and dance often given at the end of a play.   513. Hecuba:
Wife of Priam.   514. mobled: Muffled.   518. bisson
rheum: Blinding tears.   clout: Cloth.   520. o'er-teemed:
Worn out with bearing children.   523. state: Rule, managing.
pronounc'd: Proclaimed.   529. milch: Milky moist with
tears.   531. whe'er: Whether.   535. bestow'd: Lodged.
536. abstract: Summary account.   541. God's bodkin: By
God's (Christ's) little body, bodykin (not to be confused with
bodkin, dagger).

565. conceit: Conception.   566. wann'd: Grew pale.
568–69. his whole . . . conceit: His whole being responded
with actions to suit his thought.   576. free: Innocent.
579. muddy-mettled: Dull-spirited.   peak: Mope, pine.
580. John-a-dreams: Sleepy dreaming idler.   unpregnant
of: Not quickened by.   582. property: The crown; perhaps
also character, quality.

Tweaks me by the nose? Gives me the lie° i' th'
    throat,
As deep as to the lungs? Who does me this?
Ha, 'swounds, I should take it; for it cannot be
But I am pigeon-liver'd,° and lack gall
590 To make oppression bitter, or ere this
I should have fatted all the region kites°
With this slave's offal. Bloody, bawdy villain!
Remorseless, treacherous, lecherous, kindless°
    villain!
[O, vengeance!]
595 Why, what an ass am I! This is most brave,
That I, the son of a dear father murder'd,
Prompted to my revenge by heaven and hell,
Must, like a whore, unpack my heart with words,
And fall a-cursing, like a very drab,°
600 A stallion!° Fie upon 't, foh! About,° my brains!
Hum, I have heard
That guilty creatures sitting at a play
Have by the very cunning of the scene
Been struck so to the soul that presently°
605 They have proclaim'd their malefactions;
For murder, though it have no tongue, will speak
With most miraculous organ. I'll have these
    players
Play something like the murder of my father
Before mine uncle. I'll observe his looks;
610 I'll tent° him to the quick. If 'a do blench,°
I know my course. The spirit that I have seen
May be the devil, and the devil hath power
T' assume a pleasing shape; yea, and perhaps
Out of my weakness and my melancholy,
615 As he is very potent with such spirits,°
Abuses° me to damn me. I'll have grounds
More relative° than this. The play's the thing
Wherein I'll catch the conscience of the King.
                           (*Exit.*)

{*ACT III • Scene I*}°

(*Enter King, Queen, Polonius, Ophelia, Rosencrantz,*
Guildenstern, Lords.)

KING: And can you, by no drift of conference,°

---

586. **Gives me the lie:** Calls me a liar.   589. **pigeon-liver'd:**
The pigeon or dove was popularly supposed to be mild because it secreted no gall.   591. **region kites:** Kites (birds of
prey) of the air, from the vicinity.   593. **kindless:** Unnatural.
599. **drab:** Prostitute.   600. **stallion:** Prostitute (male or female). (Many editors follow the Folio reading of *scullion.*)
About: About it, to work.   604. **presently:** At once.
610. **tent:** Probe.   **blench:** Quail, flinch.   615. **spirits:** Humors (of melancholy).   616. **Abuses:** Deludes.   617. **relative:** Closely related, pertinent.   III, i. **Location:** The castle.
1. **drift of conference:** Direction of conversation.

Get from him why he puts on this confusion,
Grating so harshly all his days of quiet
With turbulent and dangerous lunacy?
ROSENCRANTZ: He does confess he feels himself
    distracted,   5
But from what cause 'a will by no means speak.
GUILDENSTERN: Nor do we find him forward° to be
    sounded,°
But with a crafty madness keeps aloof
When we would bring him on to some
    confession
Of his true state.
QUEEN: Did he receive you well?   10
ROSENCRANTZ: Most like a gentleman.
GUILDENSTERN: But with much forcing of his
    disposition.°
ROSENCRANTZ: Niggard of question,° but of our
    demands
Most free in his reply.
QUEEN: Did you assay° him
To any pastime?   15
ROSENCRANTZ: Madam, it so fell out that certain
    players
We o'er-raught° on the way. Of these we told
    him,
And there did seem in him a kind of joy
To hear of it. They are here about the court,
And, as I think, they have already order   20
This night to play before him.
POLONIUS: 'Tis most true,
And he beseech'd me to entreat your Majesties
To hear and see the matter.
KING: With all my heart, and it doth much content
    me
To hear him so inclin'd.   25
Good gentlemen, give him a further edge,°
And drive his purpose into these delights.
ROSENCRANTZ: We shall, my lord.
       (*Exeunt Rosencrantz and Guildenstern.*)
KING: Sweet Gertrude, leave us too,
For we have closely° sent for Hamlet hither,
That he, as 'twere by accident, may here   30
Affront° Ophelia.
Her father and myself, [lawful espials,°]
Will so bestow ourselves that seeing, unseen,
We may of their encounter frankly judge,
And gather by him, as he is behav'd,   35
If 't be th' affliction of his love or no
That thus he suffers for.
QUEEN: I shall obey you.

---

7. **forward:** Willing.   **sounded:** Tested deeply.   12. **disposition:** Inclination.   13. **question:** Conversation.   14. **assay:** Try to win.   17. **o'er-raught:** Overtook and passed.
26. **edge:** Incitement.   29. **closely:** Privately.   31. **Affront:**
Confront, meet.   32. **espials:** Spies.

And for your part, Ophelia, I do wish
That your good beauties be the happy cause
Of Hamlet's wildness. So shall I hope your
40   virtues
Will bring him to his wonted way again,
To both your honors.
OPHELIA: Madam, I wish it may.
                                    [*Exit Queen.*]
POLONIUS: Ophelia, walk you here. — Gracious,° so
        please you,
    We will bestow ourselves. [*To Ophelia.*] Read on
        this book,   [*Gives her a book.*]
45 That show of such an exercise° may color°
    Your loneliness. We are oft to blame in this —
    'Tis too much prov'd° — that with devotion's
        visage
    And pious action we do sugar o'er
    The devil himself.
50 KING [*aside*]: O, 'tis too true!
    How smart a lash that speech doth give my
        conscience!
    The harlot's cheek, beautied with plast'ring art,
    Is not more ugly to° the thing° that helps it
    Than is my deed to my most painted word.
55   O heavy burden!
POLONIUS: I hear him coming. Let's withdraw, my
    lord.   [*King and Polonius withdraw.°*]

(*Enter Hamlet. [Ophelia pretends to read a book.*])

HAMLET: To be, or not to be, that is the question:
    Whether 'tis nobler in the mind to suffer
    The slings and arrows of outrageous fortune,
60 Or to take arms against a sea of troubles,
    And by opposing end them. To die, to sleep —
    No more — and by a sleep to say we end
    The heart-ache and the thousand natural shocks
    That flesh is heir to. 'Tis a consummation
65 Devoutly to be wish'd. To die, to sleep;
    To sleep, perchance to dream. Ay, there's the
        rub,°
    For in that sleep of death what dreams may
        come
    When we have shuffled° off this mortal coil,°
    Must give us pause. There's the respect°

That makes calamity of so long life.°   70
For who would bear the whips and scorns of
    time,
Th' oppressor's wrong, the proud man's
    contumely,°
The pangs of despis'd° love, the law's delay,
The insolence of office,° and the spurns°
That patient merit of th' unworthy takes,   75
When he himself might his quietus° make
With a bare bodkin? ° Who would fardels° bear,
To grunt and sweat under a weary life,
But that the dread of something after death,
The undiscover'd country from whose bourn°   80
No traveler returns, puzzles the will,
And makes us rather bear those ills we have
Than fly to others that we know not of?
Thus conscience does make cowards of us all
And thus the native hue° of resolution   85
Is sicklied o'er with the pale cast° of thought,
And enterprises of great pitch° and moment°
With this regard° their currents° turn awry,
And lose the name of action. — Soft you now,
The fair Ophelia. Nymph, in thy orisons°   90
Be all my sins remememb'red.
OPHELIA: Good my lord,
    How does your honor for this many a day?
HAMLET: I humbly thank you; well, well, well.
OPHELIA: My lord, I have remembrances of yours,
    That I have longed long to re-deliver.   95
    I pray you, now receive them.   [*Offers tokens.*]
HAMLET: No, not I, I never gave you aught.
OPHELIA: My honor'd lord, you know right well
        you did,
    And with them words of so sweet breath
        compos'd
    As made these things more rich. Their perfume
        lost,   100
    Take these again, for to the noble mind
    Rich gifts wax poor when givers prove unkind.
    There, my lord.   [*Gives tokens.*]
HAMLET: Ha, ha! Are you honest?°
OPHELIA: My lord?   105
HAMLET: Are you fair?°
OPHELIA: What means your lordship?

---

43. **Gracious:** Your Grace (i.e., the King).   45. **exercise:**
Act of devotion. (The book she reads is one of devotion.)
color: Give a plausible appearance to.   47. **too much
prov'd:** Too often shown to be true, too often practiced.
53. **to:** Compared to.   **thing:** I.e., the cosmetic.   56. [S.D.]
withdraw: The King and Polonius may retire behind an arras. The stage directions specify that they "enter" again near
the end of the scene.   66. **rub:** Literally, an obstacle in the
game of bowls.   68. **shuffled:** Sloughed, cast.   **coil:** Turmoil.   69. **respect:** Consideration.

70. **of . . . life:** So long-lived.   72. **contumely:** Insolent
abuse.   73. **despis'd:** Rejected.   74. **office:** Officialdom.
spurns: Insults.   76. **quietus:** Acquittance; here, death.
77. **bodkin:** Dagger.   **fardels:** Burdens.   80. **bourn:**
Boundary.   85. **native hue:** Natural color, complexion.
86. **cast:** Shade of color.   87. **pitch:** Height (as of a falcon's
flight).   **moment:** Importance.   88. **regard:** Respect, consideration.   **currents:** Courses.   90. **orisons:** Prayers.
104. **honest:** (1) Truthful, (2) chaste.   106. **fair:** (1) Beautiful, (2) just, honorable.

HAMLET: That if you be honest and fair, your hon-
esty° should admit no discourse° to your beauty.
110 OPHELIA: Could beauty, my lord, have better com-
merce° than with honesty?
HAMLET: Ay, truly, for the power of beauty will sooner
transform honesty from what it is to a bawd than
the force of honesty can translate beauty into his
115 likeness. This was sometime° a paradox,° but now
the time° gives it proof. I did love you once.
OPHELIA: Indeed, my lord, you made me believe so.
HAMLET: You should not have believ'd me, for virtue
cannot so inoculate° our old stock but we shall rel-
120 ish of it.° I lov'd you not.
OPHELIA: I was the more deceiv'd.
HAMLET: Get thee to a nunn'ry.° Why wouldst thou
be a breeder of sinners? I am myself indifferent
honest;° but yet I could accuse me of such things
125 that it were better my mother had not borne me: I
am very proud, revengeful, ambitious, with more
offenses at my beck° than I have thoughts to put
them in, imagination to give them shape, or time
to act them in. What should such fellows as I do
130 crawling between earth and heaven? We are arrant
knaves, all; believe none of us. Go thy ways to a
nunn'ry. Where's your father?
OPHELIA: At home, my lord.
HAMLET: Let the doors be shut upon him, that he may
135 play the fool nowhere but in 's own house.
Farewell.
OPHELIA: O, help him, you sweet heavens!
HAMLET: If thou dost marry, I'll give thee this plague
for thy dowry: be thou as chaste as ice, as pure as
140 snow, thou shalt not escape calumny. Get thee to a
nunn'ry, farewell. Or, if thou wilt needs marry,
marry a fool, for wise men know well enough
what monsters° you° make of them. To a nunn'ry,
go, and quickly too. Farewell.
145 OPHELIA: Heavenly powers, restore him!
HAMLET: I have heard of your paintings too, well
enough. God hath given you one face, and you
make yourselves another. You jig,° and amble, and
you lisp, you nickname God's creatures, and make

your wantonness your ignorance.° Go to, I'll no   150
more on 't; it hath made me mad. I say, we will
have no moe marriage. Those that are married al-
ready — all but one — shall live. The rest shall
keep as they are. To a nunn'ry, go.   (*Exit.*)
OPHELIA: O, what a noble mind is here o'erthrown!   155
The courtier's, soldier's, scholar's, eye, tongue,
sword,
Th' expectancy and rose of the fair state,°
The glass of fashion and the mold of form,°
Th' observ'd of all observers,° quite, quite down!
And I, of ladies most deject and wretched,   160
That suck'd the honey of his music vows,
Now see that noble and most sovereign reason,
Like sweet bells jangled, out of time and harsh,
That unmatch'd form and feature of blown°
youth
Blasted with ecstasy.° O, woe is me,   165
T' have seen what I have seen, see what I see!

(*Enter King and Polonius.*)

KING: Love? His affections do not that way tend;
Nor what he spake, though it lack'd form a
little,
Was not like madness. There's something in his
soul,
O'er which his melancholy sits on brood,   170
And I do doubt° the hatch and the disclose°
Will be some danger; which for to prevent,
I have in quick determination
Thus set it down: he shall with speed to England,
For the demand of° our neglected tribute.   175
Haply the seas and countries different
With variable° objects shall expel
This something-settled° matter in his heart,
Whereon his brains still beating puts him thus
From fashion of himself.° What think you on 't?   180
POLONIUS: It shall do well. But yet do I believe
The origin and commencement of his grief
Sprung from neglected love. — How now,
Ophelia?
You need not tell us what Lord Hamlet said;
We heard it all. — My lord, do as you please,   185
But, if you hold it fit, after the play

---

108. **your honesty:** Your chastity.   109. **discourse:** Familiar
dealings.   110. **commerce:** Dealings.   115. **sometime:**
Formerly.   **paradox:** A view opposite to commonly held
opinion.   116. **the time:** The present age.   119. **inocu-
late:** Graft, be engrafted to.   119–20. **but . . . it:** That we
do not still have about us a taste of the old stock; i.e., retain
our sinfulness.   122. **nunn'ry:** (1) Convent, (2) brothel.
123–24. **indifferent honest:** Reasonably virtuous.   127. **beck:**
Command.   143. **monsters:** An allusion to the horns of a
cuckold.   **you:** You women.   148. **jig:** Dance and sing af-
fectedly and wantonly.

149–50. **make . . . ignorance:** Excuse your affection on the
grounds of your ignorance.   157. **Th' expectancy . . . state:**
The hope and ornament of the kingdom made fair (by him).
158. **The glass . . . form:** The mirror of fashion and the pattern of courtly behavior.   159. **observ'd . . . observers:** The
center of attention and honor in the court.   164. **blown:**
Blooming.   165. **ecstasy:** Madness.   171. **doubt:** Fear.
disclose: Disclosure.   175. **For . . . of:** To demand.   177.
variable: Various.   178. **something-settled:** Somewhat
settled.   180. **From . . . himself:** Out of his natural manner.

Let his queen mother all alone entreat him
To show his grief. Let her be round° with him;
And I'll be plac'd, so please you, in the ear
190 Of all their conference. If she find him not,
To England send him, or confine him where
Your wisdom best shall think.

KING: It shall be so.
Madness in great ones must not unwatch'd go.

                                            (*Exeunt.*)

{*Scene II*}°

(*Enter Hamlet and three of the Players.*)

HAMLET: Speak the speech, I pray you, as I pronounc'd it to you, trippingly on the tongue. But if
you mouth it, as many of our players° do, I had as
lief the town-crier spoke my lines. Nor do not saw
5 the air too much with your hand, thus, but use all
gently; for in the very torrent, tempest, and, as I
may say, whirlwind of your passion, you must acquire and beget a temperance that may give it
smoothness. O, it offends me to the soul to hear a
10 robustious° periwig-pated° fellow tear a passion to
tatters, to very rags, to split the ears of the
groundlings,° who for the most part are capable
of° nothing but inexplicable dumb-shows and
noise. I would have such a fellow whipp'd for o'er-
15 doing Termagant.° It out-herods Herod.° Pray
you, avoid it.

FIRST PLAYER: I warrant your honor.

HAMLET: Be not too tame neither, but let your own
discretion be your tutor. Suit the action to the
20 word, the word to the action, with this special observance, that you o'erstep not the modesty of nature. For anything so o'erdone is from° the purpose
of playing, whose end, both at the first and now,
was and is, to hold, as 't were, the mirror up to na-
25 ture, to show virtue her feature, scorn her own image, and the very age and body of the time his°
form and pressure.° Now this overdone, or come

tardy off,° though it makes the unskillful laugh,
cannot but make the judicious grieve, the censure
of which one° must in your allowance o'erweigh a 30
whole theater of others. O, there be players that I
have seen play, and heard others praise, and that
highly, not to speak it profanely, that, neither having th' accent of Christians nor the gait of Christian, pagan, nor man, have so strutted and bellow'd 35
that I have thought some of nature's journeymen°
had made men and not made them well, they imitated humanity so abominably.

FIRST PLAYER: I hope we have reform'd that indiffer-
ently° with us, sir.   40

HAMLET: O, reform it altogether. And let those that
play your clowns speak no more than is set down
for them; for there be of them° that will themselves
laugh, to set on some quantity of barren° spectators
to laugh too, though in the mean time some neces- 45
sary question of the play be then to be consider'd.
That's villainous, and shows a most pitiful ambition in the fool that uses it. Go, make you ready.

                                        [*Exeunt Players.*]

(*Enter Polonius, Guildenstern, and Rosencrantz.*)

How now, my lord? Will the King hear this piece
of work?   50

POLONIUS: And the Queen too, and that presently.°

HAMLET: Bid the players make haste.

                                        [*Exit Polonius.*]
Will you two help to hasten them?

ROSENCRANTZ: Ay, my lord.   (*Exeunt they two.*)

HAMLET: What ho, Horatio!

(*Enter Horatio.*)

HORATIO: Here, sweet lord, at your service.   55

HAMLET: Horatio, thou art e'en as just a man
As e'er my conversation cop'd withal.°

HORATIO: O, my dear lord —

HAMLET: Nay, do not think I flatter;
For what advancement may I hope from thee
That no revenue hast but thy good spirits,   60
To feed and clothe thee? Why should the poor be
flatter'd?
No, let the candied° tongue lick absurd pomp,
And crook the pregnant° hinges of the knee
Where thrift° may follow fawning. Dost thou
hear?

188. round: Blunt.   III, II. Location: The castle.   3. our
players: Indefinite use; i.e., *players nowadays.*   10. robus-
tious: Violent, boisterous.   periwig-pated: Wearing a wig.
12. groundlings: Spectators who paid least and stood in the
yard of the theater.   12–13. capable of: Susceptible of being
influenced by.   15. Termagant: A god of the Saracens; a
character in the St. Nicholas play, where one of his worshipers, leaving him in charge of goods, returns to find them
stolen; whereupon he beats the god or idol, which howls vo-
ciferously.   Herod: Herod of Jewry. (A character in *The
Slaughter of the Innocents* and other cycle plays. The part was
played with great noise and fury.)   22. from: Contrary to.
26. his: Its.   27. pressure: Stamp, impressed character.

27–28. come tardy off: Inadequately done.   29–30. the
censure . . . one: The judgment of even one of whom.
36. journeymen: Laborers not yet masters in their trade.
39–40. indifferently: Tolerably.   43. of them: Some among
them.   44. barren: I.e., of wit.   51. presently: At once.
57. my . . . withal: My contact with people provided opportunity for encounter with.   62. candied: Sugared, flattering.   63. pregnant: Compliant.   64. thrift: Profit.

65 Since my dear soul was mistress of her choice
And could of men distinguish her election,
Sh' hath seal'd thee for herself, for thou hast been
As one, in suff'ring all, that suffers nothing,
A man that Fortune's buffets and rewards
70 Hast ta'en with equal thanks; and blest are those
Whose blood° and judgment are so well
commeddled°
That they are not a pipe for Fortune's finger
To sound what stop° she please. Give me that
man
That is not passion's slave, and I will wear him
75 In my heart's core, ay, in my heart of heart,
As I do thee. — Something too much of this. —
There is a play tonight before the King.
One scene of it comes near the circumstance
Which I have told thee of my father's death.
80 I prithee, when thou seest that act afoot,
Even with the very comment of thy soul°
Observe my uncle. If his occulted° guilt
Do not itself unkennel in one speech,
It is a damned° ghost that we have seen,
85 And my imaginations are as foul
As Vulcan's stithy.° Give him heedful note,
For I mine eyes will rivet to his face,
And after we will both our judgments join
In censure of his seeming.°
HORATIO: Well, my lord.
90 If 'a steal aught the whilst this play is playing,
And scape detecting, I will pay the theft.

([*Flourish.*] *Enter trumpets and kettledrums, King,*
Queen, Polonius, Ophelia, [*Rosencrantz, Guilden-*
stern, and other Lords, with Guards carrying torches].)

HAMLET: They are coming to the play. I must be idle.
Get you a place. [*The King, Queen, and courtiers*
sit.]
KING: How fares our cousin Hamlet?
95 HAMLET: Excellent, i' faith, of the chameleon's dish:°
I eat the air, promise-cramm'd. You cannot feed
capons so.
KING: I have nothing with° this answer, Hamlet.
These words are not mine.°

HAMLET: No, nor mine now. [*To Polonius.*] My lord,   100
you played once i' th' university, you say?
POLONIUS: That did I, my lord; and was accounted a
good actor.
HAMLET: What did you enact?
POLONIUS: I did enact Julius Caesar. I was killed i' th'   105
Capitol; Brutus kill'd me.
HAMLET: It was a brute part of him to kill so capital
a calf there. Be the players ready?
ROSENCRANTZ: Ay, my lord; they stay upon your pa-
tience.   110
QUEEN: Come hither, my dear Hamlet, sit by me.
HAMLET: No, good mother, here's metal more attractive.
POLONIUS [*to the King*]: O, ho, do you mark that?
HAMLET: Lady, shall I lie in your lap?
                        [*Lying down at Ophelia's feet.*]
OPHELIA: No, my lord.   115
[HAMLET: I mean, my head upon your lap?
OPHELIA: Ay, my lord.]
HAMLET: Do you think I meant country° matters?
OPHELIA: I think nothing, my lord.
HAMLET: That's a fair thought to lie between maids'   120
legs.
OPHELIA: What is, my lord?
HAMLET: Nothing.
OPHELIA: You are merry, my lord.
HAMLET: Who, I?   125
OPHELIA: Ay, my lord.
HAMLET: O God, your only jig-maker.° What should
a man do but be merry? For look you how cheer-
fully my mother looks, and my father died within
's° two hours.   130
OPHELIA: Nay, 'tis twice two months, my lord.
HAMLET: So long? Nay then, let the devil wear black
for I'll have a suit of sables.° O heavens! Die two
months ago, and not forgotten yet? Then there's
hope a great man's memory may outlive his life   135
half a year. But, by 'r lady, 'a must build churches,
then, or else shall 'a suffer not thinking on,° with
the hobby-horse, whose epitaph is "For, O, for,
O, the hobby-horse is forgot."°

(*The trumpets sound. Dumb show follows.*)

(*Enter a King and a Queen* [*very lovingly*]; *the Queen*
embracing him, and he her. [*She kneels and makes*

---

71. **blood:** Passion.   **commeddled:** Commingled.   73. **stop:**
Hole in a wind instrument for controlling the sound.
81. **very . . . soul:** Inward and sagacious criticism.   82. **oc-**
culted: Hidden.   84. **damned:** In league with Satan.
86. **stithy:** Smithy, place of stiths (anvils).   89. **censure of**
his seeming: Judgment of his appearance or behavior.
95. **chameleon's dish:** Chameleons were supposed to feed on
air. Hamlet deliberately misinterprets the King's *fares* as
feeds. By his phrase *eat the air* he also plays on the idea of
feeding himself with the promise of succession, of being the
heir.   98. **have . . . with:** Make nothing of.   99. **are not**
mine: Do not respond to what I asked.

118. **country:** With a bawdy pun.   127. **only jig-maker:**
Very best composer of jigs (song and dance).   129. **within**
's: Within this.   133. **suit of sables:** Garments trimmed
with the fur of the sable and hence suited for a wealthy person, not a mourner (with a pun on *sable* black).   137. **suf-**
fer . . . on: Undergo oblivion.   138–39. **"For . . . forgot":**
Verse of a song occurring also in *Love's Labor's Lost*, III, i,
30. The hobby-horse was a character made up to resemble a
horse, appearing in the Morris dance and such May-game
sports. This song laments the disappearance of such customs
under pressure from the Puritans.

show of protestation unto him.] *He takes her up, and*
declines his head upon her neck. He lies him down
upon a bank of flowers. She, seeing him asleep, leaves
him. Anon comes in another man, takes off his
crown, kisses it, pours poison in the sleeper's ears,
and leaves him. The Queen returns; finds the King
dead, makes passionate action. The Poisoner, with
some three or four, come in again, seem to condole
with her. The dead body is carried away. The Poi-
soner woos the Queen with gifts; she seems harsh
awhile but in the end accepts love.)

             [*Exeunt.*]

140 OPHELIA: What means this, my lord?
  HAMLET: Marry, this' miching mallecho;° it means
   mischief.
  OPHELIA: Belike° this show imports the argument° of
   the play.

 (*Enter Prologue.*)

145 HAMLET: We shall know by this fellow. The players
   cannot keep counsel;° they'll tell all.
  OPHELIA: Will 'a tell us what this show meant?
  HAMLET: Ay, or any show that you will show him. Be
   not you° asham'd to show, he'll not shame to tell
150 you what it means.
  OPHELIA: You are naught, you are naught.° I'll mark
   the play.
  PROLOGUE: For us, and for our tragedy,
   Here stooping° to your clemency,
155 We beg your hearing patiently.   [*Exit.*]
  HAMLET: Is this a prologue, or the posy of a ring?°
  OPHELIA: 'Tis brief, my lord.
  HAMLET: As woman's love.

 (*Enter [two Players as] King and Queen.*)

  PLAYER KING: Full thirty times hath Phoebus' cart°
   gone round
160 Neptune's salt wash° and Tellus'° orbed ground,
   And thirty dozen moons with borrowed° sheen
   About the world have times twelve thirties been,
   Since love our hearts and Hymen° did our hands
   Unite commutual° in most sacred bands.
  PLAYER QUEEN: So many journeys may the sun and
165 moon

Make us again count o'er ere love be done!
But, woe is me, you are so sick of late,
So far from cheer and from your former state,
That I distrust you. Yet, though I distrust,°
Discomfort you, my lord, it nothing° must. 170
For women's fear and love hold quantity;°
In neither aught, or in extremity.
Now, what my love is, proof° hath made you
 know,
And as my love is siz'd, my fear is so.
Where love is great, the littlest doubts are fear; 175
Where little fears grow great, great love grows
 there.
PLAYER KING: Faith, I must leave thee, love, and
 shortly too;
My operant° powers their functions leave to do.°
And thou shalt live in this fair world behind,
Honor'd, belov'd; and haply one as kind 180
For husband shalt thou —
PLAYER QUEEN: O, confound the rest!
Such love must needs be treason in my breast.
In second husband let me be accurst!
None wed the second but who kill'd the first.
HAMLET: Wormwood, wormwood.   185
PLAYER QUEEN: The instances° that second marriage
 move°
Are base respects of thrift,° but none of love.
A second time I kill my husband dead,
When second husband kisses me in bed.
PLAYER KING: I do believe you think what now you
 speak, 190
But what we do determine oft we break.
Purpose is but the slave to memory,°
Of violent birth, but poor validity,°
Which now, like fruit unripe, sticks on the tree,
But fall unshaken when they mellow be. 195
Most necessary 'tis that we forget
To pay ourselves what to ourselves is debt.°
What to ourselves in passion we propose,
The passion ending, doth the purpose lose.
The violence of either grief or joy 200
Their own enactures° with themselves destroy.
Where joy most revels, grief doth most lament;
Grief joys, joy grieves, on slender accident.

---

141. this' miching mallecho: This is sneaking mischief.
143. Belike: Probably. **argument:** Plot. **146. counsel:**
Secret. **149. Be not you:** If you are not. **151. naught:**
Indecent. **154. stooping:** Bowing. **156. posy ... ring:**
Brief motto in verse inscribed in a ring. **159. Phoebus'
cart:** The sun god's chariot. **160. salt wash:** The sea.
Tellus: Goddess of the earth, of the *orbed ground.*
161. borrowed: Reflected. **163. Hymen:** God of matrimony. **164. commutual:** Mutually.

169. distrust: Am anxious about. **170. nothing:** Not at all.
171. hold quantity: Keep proportion with one another.
173. proof: Experience. **178. operant:** Active. **leave to
do:** Cease to perform. **186. instances:** Motives. **move:**
Motivate. **187. base ... thrift:** Ignoble considerations of
material prosperity. **192. Purpose ... memory:** Our good
intentions are subject to forgetfulness. **193. validity:**
Strength, durability. **196–97. Most ... debt:** It's inevitable
that in time we forget the obligations we have imposed on
ourselves. **201. enactures:** Fulfillments.

This world is not for aye,° nor 'tis not strange
That even our loves should with our fortunes
205   change;
For 'tis a question left us yet to prove,
Whether love lead fortune, or else fortune love.
The great man down, you mark his favorite flies;
The poor advanc'd makes friends of enemies.
210 And hitherto doth love on fortune tend;
For who not needs° shall never lack a friend,
And who in want° a hollow friend doth try,°
Directly seasons him° his enemy.
But, orderly to end where I begun,
215 Our wills and fates do so contrary run
That our devices still° are overthrown;
Our thoughts are ours, their ends° none of our
     own.
So think thou wilt no second husband wed,
But die thy thoughts when thy first lord is dead.
PLAYER QUEEN: Nor earth to me give food, nor
220   heaven light,
Sport and repose lock from me day and night,
To desperation turn my trust and hope,
An anchor's cheer° in prison be my scope!°
Each opposite° that blanks° the face of joy
225 Meet what I would have well and it destroy!
Both here and hence° pursue me lasting strife,
If, once a widow, ever I be wife!
HAMLET: If she should break it now!
PLAYER KING: 'Tis deeply sworn. Sweet, leave me
     here awhile;
230 My spirits grow dull, and fain I would beguile
The tedious day with sleep.   [*Sleeps.*]
PLAYER QUEEN: Sleep rock thy brain,
And never come mischance between us twain!
                     [*Exit.*]
HAMLET: Madam, how like you this play?
QUEEN: The lady doth protest too much, methinks.
235 HAMLET: O, but she'll keep her word.
KING: Have you heard the argument?° Is there no
     offense in 't?
HAMLET: No, no, they do but jest, poison in jest; no
     offense i' th' world.
240 KING: What do you call the play?
HAMLET: "The Mouse-trap." Marry, how? Tropically.°

This play is the image of a murder done in Vienna.
Gonzago is the Duke's name; his wife, Baptista. You
shall see anon. 'Tis a knavish piece of work, but
what of that? Your Majesty, and we that have free° 245
souls, it touches us not. Let the gall'd jade° winch,°
our withers° are unwrung.°

(*Enter Lucianus.*)

This is one Lucianus, nephew to the King.
OPHELIA: You are as good as a chorus,° my lord.
HAMLET: I could interpret between you and your love, 250
     if I could see the puppets dallying.°
OPHELIA: You are keen, my lord, you are keen.
HAMLET: It would cost you a groaning to take off
     mine edge.
OPHELIA: Still better, and worse.° 255
HAMLET: So° you mistake° your husbands. Begin,
     murderer, leave thy damnable faces, and begin.
     Come, the croaking raven doth bellow for revenge.
LUCIANUS: Thoughts black, hands apt, drugs fit, and
     time agreeing,
Confederate season,° else no creature seeing, 260
Thou mixture rank, of midnight weeds collected,
With Hecate's ban° thrice blasted, thrice infected,
Thy natural magic and dire property
On wholesome life usurp immediately.
         [*Pours the poison into the sleeper's ears.*]
HAMLET: 'A poisons him i' th' garden for his estate. 265
     His name's Gonzago. The story is extant, and
     written in very choice Italian. You shall see anon
     how the murderer gets the love of Gonzago's
     wife.
                 [*Claudius rises.*]
OPHELIA: The King rises.
[HAMLET: What, frighted with false fire?°] 270
QUEEN: How fares my lord?
POLONIUS: Give o'er the play.
KING: Give me some light. Away!

---

203. **aye:** Ever.   211. **who not needs:** He who is not in need (of wealth).   212. **who in want:** He who is in need.   **try:** Test (his generosity).   213. **seasons him:** Ripens him into.   216. **devices still:** Intentions continually.   217. **ends:** Results.   223. **anchor's cheer:** Anchorite's or hermit's fare. **my scope:** The extent of my happiness.   224. **opposite:** Adverse thing.   **blanks:** Causes to blanch or grow pale.   226. **hence:** In the life hereafter.   236. **argument:** Plot.   241. **Tropically:** Figuratively. (The first quarto reading, *tropically*, suggests a pun on *trap* in *Mouse-trap*.)

246. **free:** Guiltless.   **gall'd jade:** Horse whose hide is rubbed by saddle or harness.   247. **Winch:** Wince.   **withers:** The part between the horse's shoulder blades.   **unwrung:** Not rubbed sore.   249. **chorus:** In many Elizabethan plays the forthcoming action was explained by an actor known as the "chorus"; at a puppet show the actor who spoke the dialogue was known as an "interpreter," as indicated by the lines following.   251. **dallying:** With sexual suggestion, continued in *keen*, i.e., sexually aroused, *groaning*, i.e., moaning in pregnancy, and *edge*, i.e., sexual desire or impetuosity. 255. **Still . . . worse:** More keen-witted and less decorous. 256. **So:** Even thus (in marriage).   **mistake:** Mistake, take erringly, falseheartedly.   260. **Confederate season:** The time and occasion conspiring (to assist the murderer). 262. **Hecate's ban:** The curse of Hecate, the goddess of witchcraft.   270. **false fire:** The blank discharge of a gun loaded with powder but not shot.

POLONIUS: Lights, lights, lights!

    (*Exeunt all but Hamlet and Horatio.*)

275 HAMLET: "Why, let the strucken deer go weep,
    The hart ungalled° play.
For some must watch,° while some must sleep;
    Thus runs the world away."°
Would not this,° sir, and a forest of feathers° — if
280 the rest of my fortunes turn Turk with° me — with
two Provincial roses° on my raz'd° shoes, get me a
fellowship in a cry of players?°

HORATIO: Half a share.

HAMLET: A whole one, I.

285 "For thou dost know, O Damon dear,
    This realm dismantled° was
Of Jove himself, and now reigns here
    A very, very — pajock."°

HORATIO: You might have rhym'd.

290 HAMLET: O good Horatio, I'll take the ghost's word
for a thousand pound. Didst perceive?

HORATIO: Very well, my lord.

HAMLET: Upon the talk of pois'ning?

HORATIO: I did very well note him.

295 HAMLET: Ah, ha! Come, some music! Come, the
recorders!°
"For if the King like not the comedy,
Why then, belike, he likes it not, perdy"°
Come, some music!

(*Enter Rosencrantz and Guildenstern.*)

300 GUILDENSTERN: Good my lord, vouchsafe me a word
with you.

HAMLET: Sir, a whole history.

GUILDENSTERN: The King, sir —

HAMLET: Ay, sir, what of him?

305 GUILDENSTERN: Is in his retirement marvelous
distemp'red.

HAMLET: With drink, sir?

GUILDENSTERN: No, my lord, with choler.°

HAMLET: Your wisdom should show itself more richer

to signify this to the doctor, for for me to put him 310
to his purgation would perhaps plunge him into
more choler.

GUILDENSTERN: Good my lord, put your discourse into
some frame° and start not so wildly from my affair.

HAMLET: I am tame, sir. Pronounce. 315

GUILDENSTERN: The Queen, your mother, in most
great affliction of spirit, hath sent me to you.

HAMLET: You are welcome.

GUILDENSTERN: Nay, good my lord, this courtesy is
not of the right breed. If it shall please you to 320
make me a wholesome answer, I will do your
mother's commandment; if not, your pardon° and
my return shall be the end of my business.

HAMLET: Sir, I cannot.

ROSENCRANTZ: What, my lord? 325

HAMLET: Make you a wholesome answer; my wit's
diseas'd. But, sir, such answer as I can make, you
shall command, or rather, as you say, my mother.
Therefore no more, but to the matter. My mother,
you say — 330

ROSENCRANTZ: Then thus she says: your behavior
hath struck her into amazement and admiration.°

HAMLET: O wonderful son, that can so stonish a
mother! But is there no sequel at the heels of this
mother's admiration? Impart. 335

ROSENCRANTZ: She desires to speak with you in her
closet,° ere you go to bed.

HAMLET: We shall obey, were she ten times our
mother. Have you any further trade with us?

ROSENCRANTZ: My lord, you once did love me. 340

HAMLET: And do still, by these pickers and stealers.°

ROSENCRANTZ: Good my lord, what is your cause of
distemper? You do surely bar the door upon your
own liberty, if you deny your griefs to your friend.

HAMLET: Sir, I lack advancement. 345

ROSENCRANTZ: How can that be, when you have the
voice of the King himself for your succession in
Denmark?

HAMLET: Ay, sir, but "While the grass grows"° — the
proverb is something° musty. 350

(*Enter the Players with recorders.*)

O, the recorders! Let me see one. [*He takes a
recorder.*] To withdraw° with you: why do you go

---

276. **ungalled:** Unafflicted.   277. **watch:** Remain awake.
275–78. **Why . . . away:** Probably from an old ballad, with
allusion to the popular belief that a wounded deer retires to
weep and die; cf. *As You Like It*, II, I, 66.   279. **this:** The
play.   **feathers:** Allusion to the plumes that Elizabethan actors were fond of wearing.   280. **turn Turk with:** Turn
renegade against, go back on.   281. **Provincial roses:**
Rosettes of ribbon like the roses of a part of France.   **raz'd:**
With ornamental slashing.   282. **fellowship . . . players:**
Partnership in a theatrical company.   286. **dismantled:**
Stripped, divested.   288. **pajock:** Peacock, a bird with a
bad reputation (here substituted for the obvious rhyme-word
ass).   296. **recorders:** Wind instruments like the flute.
298. **perdy:** A corruption of the French *par dieu*, by God.
308. **choler:** Anger. (But Hamlet takes the word in its more
basic humors sense of *bilious disorder.*)

314. **frame:** Order.   322. **pardon:** Permission to depart.
332. **admiration:** Wonder.   337. **closet:** Private chamber.
341. **pickers and stealers:** Hands (so called from the cate-
chism, "to keep my hands from picking and stealing").
349. **While . . . grows:** The rest of the proverb is "the silly
horse starves"; Hamlet may not live long enough to succeed
to the kingdom.   350. **something:** Somewhat.   352. **withdraw:** Speak privately.

about to recover the wind° of me, as if you would
drive me into a toil?°

355 GUILDENSTERN: O, my lord, if my duty be too bold,
my love is too unmannerly.°

HAMLET: I do not well understand that. Will you play
upon this pipe?

GUILDENSTERN: My lord, I cannot.

360 HAMLET: I pray you.

GUILDENSTERN: Believe me, I cannot.

HAMLET: I do beseech you.

GUILDENSTERN: I know no touch of it, my lord.

HAMLET: It is as easy as lying. Govern these ventages°
365 with your fingers and thumb, give it breath with
your mouth, and it will discourse most eloquent
music. Look you, these are the stops.

GUILDENSTERN: But these cannot I command to any
utt'rance of harmony; I have not the skill.

370 HAMLET: Why, look you now, how unworthy a thing
you make of me! You would play upon me, you
would seem to know my stops, you would pluck
out the heart of my mystery, you would sound me
from my lowest note to the top of my compass,°
375 and there is much music, excellent voice, in this
little organ,° yet cannot you make it speak.
'Sblood, do you think I am easier to be play'd on
than a pipe? Call me what instrument you will,
though you can fret° me, you cannot play upon me.

(Enter Polonius.)

380   God bless you, sir!

POLONIUS: My lord, the Queen would speak with you,
and presently.°

HAMLET: Do you see yonder cloud that's almost in
shape of a camel?

385 POLONIUS: By th' mass, and 'tis like a camel, indeed.

HAMLET: Methinks it is like a weasel.

POLONIUS: It is back'd like a weasel.

HAMLET: Or like a whale?

POLONIUS: Very like a whale.

390 HAMLET: Then I will come to my mother by and by.°
[Aside.] They fool me° to the top of my bent.° — I
will come by and by.

POLONIUS: I will say so.   [Exit.]

HAMLET: "By and by" is easily said. Leave me,
friends.

                         [*Exeunt all but Hamlet.*]

'Tis now the very witching time° of night,   395
When churchyards yawn and hell itself breathes
out
Contagion to this world. Now could I drink hot
blood,
And do such bitter business as the day
Would quake to look on. Soft, now to my
mother.
O heart, lose not thy nature! Let not ever   400
The soul of Nero° enter this firm bosom.
Let me be cruel, not unnatural;
I will speak daggers to her, but use none.
My tongue and soul in this be hypocrites:
How in my words somever° she be shent,°   405
To give them seals° never, my soul, consent!

                                            (*Exit.*)

{*Scene III*}°

(*Enter King, Rosencrantz, and Guildenstern.*)

KING: I like him not, nor stands it safe with us
To let his madness range. Therefore prepare you.
I your commission will forthwith dispatch,°
And he to England shall along with you.
The terms° of our estate° may not endure   5
Hazard so near 's as doth hourly grow
Out of his brows.°

GUILDENSTERN: We will ourselves provide.
Most holy and religious fear it is
To keep those many many bodies safe
That live and feed upon your Majesty.   10

ROSENCRANTZ: The single and peculiar° life is bound
With all the strength and armor of the mind
To keep itself from noyance,° but much more
That spirit upon whose weal depends and rests
The lives of many. The cess° of majesty   15
Dies not alone, but like a gulf° doth draw
What's near it with it; or it is a messy wheel
Fix'd on the summit of the highest mount,
To whose huge spokes ten thousand lesser things

---

353. **recover the wind:** Get the windward side.   354. **toil:**
Snare.   355–56. **if . . . unmannerly:** If I am using an unmannerly boldness, it is my love that occasions it.
364. **ventages:** Stops of the recorder.   374. **compass:** Range
(of voice).   376. **organ:** Musical instrument.   379. **fret:**
Irritate (with a quibble on *fret* meaning the piece of wood,
gut, or metal that regulates the fingering on an instrument).
382. **presently:** At once.   390. **by and by:** Immediately.
391. **fool me:** Make me play the fool.   **top of my bent:**
Limit of my ability or endurance (literally, the extent to
which a bow may be bent).

395. **witching time:** Time when spells are cast and evil is
abroad.   401. **Nero:** Murderer of his mother, Agrippina.
405. **How . . . somever:** However much by my words.
shent: Rebuked.   406. **give them seals:** Confirm them with
deeds.   III, III. **Location:** The castle.   3. **dispatch:** Prepare, cause to be drawn up.   5. **terms:** Condition, circumstances.   **our estate:** My royal position.   7. **brows:**
Effronteries, threatening frowns (?), brain (?).   11. **single
and peculiar:** Individual and private.   13. **noyance:** Harm.
15. **cess:** Decease.   16. **gulf:** Whirlpool.

20   Are mortis'd and adjoin'd, which, when it falls,
      Each small annexment, petty consequence,
      Attends° the boist'rous ruin. Never alone
      Did the King sigh, but with a general groan.
   KING: Arm° you, I pray you, to this speedy voyage,
25   For we will fetters put about this fear,
      Which now goes too free-footed.
   ROSENCRANTZ: We will haste us.
   (Exeunt Gentlemen [Rosencrantz and Guildenstern].)

   (Enter Polonius.)

   POLONIUS: My lord, he's going to his mother's
         closet.
      Behind the arras° I'll convey myself
      To hear the process.° I'll warrant she'll tax him
         home,°
30   And, as you said, and wisely was it said,
      'Tis meet that some more audience than a
         mother,
      Since nature makes them partial, should o'erhear
      The speech, of vantage.° Fare you well, my liege.
      I'll call upon you ere you go to bed,
      And tell you what I know.
35   KING: Thanks, dear my lord.
                           (Exit [Polonius].)
      O, my offense is rank, it smells to heaven;
      It hath the primal eldest curse° upon 't,
      A brother's murder. Pray can I not,
      Though inclination be as sharp as will.°
40   My stronger guilt defeats my strong intent,
      And, like a man to double business bound,
      I stand in pause where I shall first begin,
      And both neglect. What if this cursed hand
      Were thicker than itself with brother's blood,
45   Is there not rain enough in the sweet heavens
      To wash it white as snow? Whereto serves mercy
      But to confront the visage of offense?°
      And what's in prayer but this twofold force,
      To be forestalled° ere we come to fall,
50   Or pardon'd being down? Then I'll look up;
      My fault is past. But, O, what form of prayer

Can serve my turn? "Forgive me my foul
      murder"?
That cannot be, since I am still possess'd
Of those effects for which I did the murder,
My crown, mine own ambition, and my queen.   55
May one be pardon'd and retain th' offense?
In the corrupted currents° of this world
Offense's gilded hand° may shove by justice,
And oft 'tis seen the wicked prize° itself
Buys out the law. But 'tis not so above.   60
There is no shuffling,° there the action lies°
In his° true nature, and we ourselves compell'd,
Even to the teeth and forehead° of our faults,
To give in evidence. What then? What rests?°
Try what repentance can. What can it not?   65
Yet what can it, when one cannot repent?
O wretched state! O bosom black as death!
O limed° soul, that, struggling to be free,
Art more engag'd!° Help, angels! Make assay.°
Bow, stubborn knees, and heart with strings of
      steel,   70
Be soft as sinews of the new-born babe!
All may be well.

                                    [He kneels.]

(Enter Hamlet [with sword drawn].)

HAMLET: Now might I do it pat,° now 'a is
      a-praying;
   And now I'll do 't. And so 'a goes to heaven;
   And so am I reveng'd. That would be scann'd:°   75
   A villain kills my father, and for that,
   I, his sole son, do this same villain send
   To heaven.
   Why, this is hire and salary, not revenge.
   'A took my father grossly,° full of bread,°   80
   With all his crimes broad blown,° as flush° as
      May;
   And how his audit° stands who knows save
      heaven?
   But in our circumstance and course° of thought,
   'Tis heavy with him. And am I then reveng'd,

22. Attends: Participates in.   24. Arm: Prepare.   28. arras: Screen of tapestry placed around the walls of household
apartments. (On the Elizabethan stage, the arras was presumably over a door or discovery space in the tiring-house
façade.)   29. process: Proceedings.   tax him home: Reprove him severely.   33. of vantage: From an advantageous
place.   37. primal eldest curse: The curse of Cain, the first
murderer; he killed his brother Abel.   39. Though . . . will:
Though my desire is as strong as my determination.
46–47. Whereto . . . offense: For what function does mercy
serve other than to undo the effects of sin?   49. forestalled:
Prevented (from sinning).

57. currents: Courses.   58. gilded hand: Hand offering
gold as a bribe.   59. wicked prize: Prize won by wickedness.   61. shuffling: Escape by trickery.   the action lies:
The accusation is made manifest, comes up for consideration
(a legal metaphor).   62. his: Its.   63. teeth and forehead:
Face to face, concealing nothing.   64. rests: Remains.
68. limed: Caught as with birdlime, a sticky substance used
to ensnare birds.   69. engag'd: Embedded.   assay: Trial.
73. pat: Opportunely.   75. would be scann'd: Needs to be
looked into.   80. grossly: Not spiritually prepared.   full
of bread: Enjoying his worldly pleasures. (See Ezek. 16:49.)
81. crimes broad blown: Sins in full bloom.   flush: Lusty.
82. audit: Account.   83. in . . . course: As we see it in our
mortal situation.

85 To take him in the purging of his soul,
   When he is fit and season'd for his passage?
   No!
   Up, sword, and know thou a more horrid hent.°
                          [*Puts up his sword.*]
   When he is drunk asleep, or in his rage,
90 Or in th' incestuous pleasure of his bed,
   At game a-swearing, or about some act
   That has no relish of salvation in 't —
   Then trip him, that his heels may kick at heaven,
   And that his soul may be as damn'd and black
95 As hell, whereto it goes. My mother stays.
   This physic° but prolongs thy sickly days. (*Exit.*)
   KING: My words fly up, my thoughts remain below.
   Words without thoughts never to heaven go.
                                           (*Exit.*)

{*Scene IV*}°

(*Enter [Queen] Gertrude and Polonius.*)

POLONIUS: 'A will come straight. Look you lay°
      home to him.
   Tell him his pranks have been too broad° to bear
      with,
   And that your Grace hath screen'd and stood
      between
   Much heat° and him. I'll sconce° me even here.
5 Pray you, be round° [with him.
   HAMLET (*within*): Mother, mother, mother!]
   QUEEN: I'll warrant you, fear me not.
      Withdraw, I hear him coming.
                   [*Polonius hides behind the arras.*]

(*Enter Hamlet.*)

HAMLET: Now, mother, what's the matter?
QUEEN: Hamlet, thou hast thy father° much
10   offended.
HAMLET: Mother, you have my father much
      offended.
QUEEN: Come, come, you answer with an idle°
      tongue.
HAMLET: Go, go, you question with a wicked
      tongue.
QUEEN: Why, how now, Hamlet?
HAMLET: What's the matter now?

QUEEN: Have you forgot me?
HAMLET: No, by the rood,° not so: 15
   You are the Queen, your husband's brother's wife
   And — would it were not so! — you are my
      mother.
QUEEN: Nay, then, I'll set those to you that can
      speak.
HAMLET: Come, come, and sit you down; you shall
      not budge.
   You go not till I set you up a glass   20
   Where you may see the inmost part of you.
QUEEN: What wilt thou do? Thou wilt not murder
      me?
   Help, ho!
POLONIUS [*behind*]: What, ho! Help!
HAMLET [*drawing*]: How now? A rat? Dead, for a
      ducat, dead!   25
                [*Makes a pass through the arras.*]
POLONIUS [*behind*]: O, I am slain! [*Falls and dies.*]
QUEEN: O me, what hast thou done?
HAMLET: Nay, I know not. Is it the King?
QUEEN: O, what a rash and bloody deed is this!
HAMLET: A bloody deed — almost as bad, good
      mother,
   As kill a king, and marry with his brother.   30
QUEEN: As kill a king!
HAMLET: Ay, lady, it was my word.
          [*Parts the arras and discovers Polonius.*]
   Thou wretched, rash, intruding fool, farewell!
   I took thee for thy better. Take thy fortune.
   Thou find'st to be too busy is some danger. —
   Leave wringing of your hands. Peace, sit you
      down,   35
   And let me wring your heart, for so I shall,
   If it be made of penetrable stuff,
   If damned custom° have not braz'd° it so
   That it be proof° and bulwark against sense.°
QUEEN: What have I done, that thou dar'st wag thy
      tongue   40
   In noise so rude against me?
HAMLET: Such an art
   That blurs the grace and blush of modesty,
   Calls virtue hypocrite, takes off the rose
   From the fair forehead of an innocent love
   And sets a blister° there, makes marriage-vows   45
   As false as dicers' oaths. O, such a deed
   As from the body of contraction° plucks
   The very soul, and sweet religion° makes

---

88. know ... hent: Await to be grasped by me on a more horrid occasion.   **96. physic:** Purging (by prayer).   III, IV.
Location: The queen's private chamber.   **1. lay:** Thrust (i.e., reprove him soundly).   **2. broad:** Unrestrained.
4. Much heat: The king's anger.   **sconce:** Ensconce, hide.
5. round: Blunt.   **10. thy father:** Your stepfather, Claudius.
12. idle: Foolish.

15. rood: Cross.   **38. damned custom:** Habitual wickedness.   **braz'd:** Brazened, hardened.   **39. proof:** Armor.
sense: Feeling.   **45. sets a blister:** Brands as a harlot.
47. contraction: The marriage contract.   **48. religion:** Religious vows.

FAR LEFT: Michael Pennington
as Hamlet. NEAR LEFT: A scene
from the Royal Shakespeare
Company's 1980 production.
BELOW LEFT: Gertrude watches
Laertes and Hamlet dueling.
The poisoned cup is in the
foreground. RIGHT: The grave-
digger holds up Yorick's skull
as Hamlet and Horatio (Tom
Wilkinson) look on. BELOW
RIGHT: Carol Royle as
Ophelia with Hamlet in the
nunnery scene.

A rhapsody° of words. Heaven's face does glow
50 O'er this solidity and compound mass
    With heated visage, as against the doom,
    Is thought-sick at the act.
QUEEN   Ay me, what act,
    That roars so loud and thunders in the index?°
HAMLET: Look here, upon this picture, and on this,
55 The counterfeit presentment° of two brothers.
                    [*Shows her two likenesses.*]
    See, what a grace was seated on this brow:
    Hyperion's° curls, the front° of Jove himself,
    An eye like Mars, to threaten and command,
    A station° like the herald Mercury
60 New-lighted on a heaven-kissing hill —
    A combination and a form indeed,
    Where every god did seem to set his seal,
    To give the world assurance of a man.
    This was your husband. Look you now, what
        follows:
65 Here is your husband, like a mildew'd ear,°
    Blasting his wholesome brother. Have you eyes?
    Could you on this fair mountain leave to feed,
    And batten° on this moor?° Ha, have you eyes?
    You cannot call it love, for at your age
70 The heyday° in the blood is tame, it's humble,
    And waits upon the judgment, and what
        judgment
    Would step from this to this? Sense,° sure, you
        have,
    Else could you not have motion, but sure that
        sense
    Is apoplex'd,° for madness would not err,
75 Nor sense to ecstasy was ne'er so thrall'd
    But it reserv'd some quantity of choice
    To serve in such a difference. What devil was 't
    That thus hath cozen'd° you at hoodman-blind?°
    Eyes without feeling, feeling without sight,

Ears without hands or eyes, smelling sans° all,   80
Or but a sickly part of one true sense
Could not so mope.°
O shame, where is thy blush? Rebellious hell,
If thou canst mutine° in a matron's bones,
To flaming youth let virtue be as wax,   85
And melt in her own fire. Proclaim no shame
When the compulsive ardor gives the charge,
Since frost itself as actively doth burn,
And reason panders will.°
QUEEN: O Hamlet, speak no more!   90
Thou turn'st mine eyes into my very soul,
And there I see such black and grainéd° spots
As will not leave their tinct.°
HAMLET: Nay, but to live
In the rank sweat of an enseaméd° bed,
Stew'd in corruption, honeying and making love   95
Over the nasty sty —
QUEEN: O, speak to me no more.
These words, like daggers, enter in my ears.
No more, sweet Hamlet!
HAMLET: A murderer and a villain,
A slave that is not twentieth part the tithe°   100
Of your precedent° lord, a vice° of kings,
A cutpurse of the empire and the rule,
That from a shelf the precious diadem stole,
And put it in his pocket!
QUEEN: No more!   105

(*Enter Ghost [in his nightgown].*)

HAMLET: A king of shreds and patches° —
Save me, and hover o'er me with your wings,
You heavenly guards! What would your gracious
    figure?
QUEEN: Alas, he's mad!
HAMLET: Do you not come your tardy son to
    chide,   110
That, laps'd in time and passion,° lets go by
Th' important° acting of your dread command?
O, say!
GHOST: Do not forget. This visitation

---

49. rhapsody: Senseless string.   **49–52. Heaven's . . . act:** Heaven's face flushes with anger to look down upon this solid world, this compound mass, with hot face as though the day of doom were near, and is thought-sick at the deed (i.e., Gertrude's marriage).   **53. index:** Table of contents, prelude, or preface.   **55. counterfeit presentment:** Portrayed representation.   **57. Hyperion:** The sun god. **front:** Brow.   **59. station:** Manner of standing.   **65. ear:** I.e., of grain.   **68. batten:** Gorge.   **moor:** Barren upland. **70. heyday:** State of excitement.   **72. Sense:** Perception through the five senses (the functions of the middle or sensible soul).   **74. apoplex'd:** Paralyzed. (Hamlet goes on to explain that without such a paralysis of will, mere madness would not so err, nor would the five senses so enthrall themselves to *ecstasy* or lunacy; even such deranged states of mind would be able to make the obvious choice between Hamlet Senior and Claudius.)   **78. cozen'd:** Cheated. **hoodman-blind:** Blindman's bluff.

80. sans: Without.   **82. mope:** Be dazed, act aimlessly. **84. mutine:** Mutiny.   **86–89. Proclaim . . . will:** Call it no shameful business when the compelling ardor of youth delivers the attack, i.e., commits lechery, since the frost of advanced age burns with as active a fire of lust and reason perverts itself by fomenting lust rather than restraining it. **92. grained:** Dyed in grain, indelible.   **93. tinct:** Color. **94. enseamed:** Laden with grease.   **100. tithe:** Tenth part. **101. precedent:** Former (i.e., the elder Hamlet).   **vice:** Buffoon (a reference to the vice of the morality plays). **106. shreds and patches:** Motley, the traditional costume of the clown or fool.   **111. laps'd . . . passion:** Having allowed time to lapse and passion to cool.   **112. important:** Importunate, urgent.

115 Is but to whet thy almost blunted purpose.
But, look, amazement° on thy mother sits.
O, step between her and her fighting soul!
Conceit° in weakest bodies strongest works.
Speak to her, Hamlet.
HAMLET: How is it with you, lady?
120 QUEEN: Alas, how is 't with you,
That you do bend your eye on vacancy,
And with th' incorporal° air do hold discourse?
Forth at your eyes your spirits wildly peep,
And, as the sleeping soldiers in th' alarm,
125 Your bedded° hair, like life in excrements,°
Start up and stand an° end. O gentle son,
Upon the heat and flame of thy distemper
Sprinkle cool patience. Whereon do you look?
HAMLET: On him, on him! Look you how pale he
glares!
His form and cause conjoin'd,° preaching to
130 stones,
Would make them capable.° — Do not look upon
me,
Lest with this piteous action you convert
My stern effects.° Then what I have to do
Will want true color° — tears perchance for
blood.
135 QUEEN: To whom do you speak this?
HAMLET: Do you see nothing there?
QUEEN: Nothing at all, yet all that is I see.
HAMLET: Nor did you nothing hear?
QUEEN: No, nothing but ourselves.
HAMLET: Why, look you there, look how it steals
140 away!
My father, in his habit° as he lived!
Look, where he goes, even now, out at the
portal!

                                    (*Exit Ghost.*)

QUEEN: This is the very coinage of your brain.
This bodiless creation ecstasy°
145 Is very cunning in.
HAMLET: Ecstasy?
My pulse, as yours, doth temperately keep time,
And makes as healthful music. It is not madness
That I have utter'd. Bring me to the test,
150 And I the matter will reword, which madness
Would gambol° from. Mother, for love of grace,

Lay not that flattering unction° to your soul
That not your trespass but my madness speaks.
It will but skin and film the ulcerous place,
Whiles rank corruption, mining° all within,   155
Infects unseen. Confess yourself to heaven,
Repent what's past, avoid what is to come,
And do not spread the compost° on the weeds
To make them ranker. Forgive me this my
virtue;°
For in the fatness° of these pursy° times   160
Virtue itself of vice must pardon beg,
Yea, curb° and woo for leave° to do him good.
QUEEN: O Hamlet, thou hast cleft my heart in
twain.
HAMLET: O, throw away the worser part of it,
And live the purer with the other half.   165
Good night. But go not to my uncle's bed;
Assume a virtue, if you have it not.
That monster, custom, who all sense doth eat,°
Of habits devil,° is angel yet in this,
That to the use of actions fair and good   170
He likewise gives a frock or livery°
That aptly is put on. Refrain tonight,
And that shall lend a kind of easiness
To the next abstinence; the next more easy;
For use° almost can change the stamp of nature,   175
And either°. . . the devil, or throw him out
With wondrous potency. Once more, good night;
And when you are desirous to be bless'd,°
I'll blessing beg of you. For this same lord,
                          [*Pointing to Polonius.*]
I do repent; but heaven hath pleas'd it so   180
To punish me with this, and this with me,
That I must be their scourge and minister.°
I will bestow° him, and will answer well
The death I gave him. So, again, good night.
I must be cruel only to be kind.   185
Thus bad begins and worse remains behind.°

---

116. **amazement:** Distraction.   118. **Conceit:** Imagination.   122. **incorporal:** Immaterial.   125. **bedded:** Laid in smooth layers.   **excrements:** Outgrowths.   126. **an:** On.   130. **His . . . conjoin'd:** His appearance joined to his cause for speaking.   131. **capable:** Receptive.   132–33. **convert . . . effects:** Divert me from my stern duty.   134. **want true color:** Lack plausibility so that (with a play on the normal sense of *color*) I shall shed tears instead of blood.   141. **habit:** Dress.   144. **ecstasy:** Madness.   151. **gambol:** Skip away.

152. **unction:** Ointment.   155. **mining:** Working under the surface.   158. **compost:** Manure.   159. **this my virtue:** My virtuous talk in reproving you.   160. **fatness:** Grossness.   **pursy:** Short-winded, corpulent.   162. **curb:** Bow, bend the knee.   **leave:** Permission.   168. **who . . . eat:** Who consumes all proper or natural feeling.   169. **Of habits devil:** Devil-like in prompting evil habits.   171. **livery:** An outer appearance, a customary garb (and hence a predisposition easily assumed in time of stress).   175. **use:** Habit.   176. **And either:** A defective line usually emended by inserting the word *master* after *either*, following the fourth quarto and early editors.   178. **be bless'd:** Become blessed, i.e., repentant.   182. **their scourge and minister:** Agent of heavenly retribution. (By *scourge,* Hamlet also suggests that he himself will eventually suffer punishment in the process of fulfilling heaven's will.)   183. **bestow:** Stow, dispose of.   186. **behind:** To come.

One word more, good lady.
QUEEN: What shall I do?
HAMLET: Not this, by no means, that I bid you do:
Let the bloat° king tempt you again to bed,
190 Pinch wanton on your cheek, call you his mouse,
And let him, for a pair of reechy° kisses,
Or paddling in your neck with his damn'd
    fingers,
Make you to ravel all this matter out,
That I essentially am not in madness,
But mad in craft. 'Twere good° you let him
195   know,
For who that's but a queen, fair, sober, wise,
Would from a paddock,° from a bat, a gib,°
Such dear concernings° hide? Who would do so?
No, in despite of sense and secrecy,
200 Unpeg the basket° on the house's top,
Let the birds fly, and, like the famous ape,°
To try conclusions,° in the basket creep
And break your own neck down.
QUEEN: Be thou assur'd, if words be made of breath,
205 And breath of life, I have no life to breathe
What thou hast said to me.
HAMLET: I must to England; you know that?
QUEEN: Alack,
I had forgot. 'Tis so concluded on.
HAMLET: There's letters seal'd, and my two school-
    fellows,
210 Whom I will trust as I will adders fang'd,
They bear the mandate; they must sweep my
    way,°
And marshal me to knavery. Let it work.
For 'tis the sport to have the enginer°
Hoist with° his own petar,° and 't shall go hard
215 But I will delve one yard below their mines,°
And blow them at the moon. O, 'tis most sweet,
When in one line two crafts° directly meet.
This man shall set me packing.°

189. **bloat**: Bloated. 191. **reechy**: Dirty, filthy. 195. **good**: Said ironically; also the following eight lines. 197. **paddock**: Toad. **gib**: Tomcat. 198. **dear concernings**: Important affairs. 200. **Unpeg the basket**: Open the cage, i.e., let out the secret. 201. **famous ape**: In a story now lost. 202. **conclusions**: Experiments (in which the ape apparently enters a cage from which birds have been released and then tries to fly out of the cage as they have done, falling to his death). 211. **sweep my way**: Go before me. 213. **enginer**: Constructor of military contrivances. 214. **Hoist with**: Blown up by. **petar**: Petard, an explosive used to blow in a door or make a breach. 215. **mines**: Tunnels used in warfare to undermine the enemy's emplacements; Hamlet will countermine by going under their mines. 217. **crafts**: Acts of guile, plots. 218. **set me packing**: Set me to making schemes, and set me to lugging (him) and, also, send me off in a hurry.

I'll lug the guts into the neighbor room.
Mother, good night indeed. This counselor   220
Is now most still, most secret, and most grave,
Who was in life a foolish prating knave.
Come, sir, to draw toward an end° with you.
Good night, mother.
            (Exeunt [severally, Hamlet dragging in
                            Polonius].)

{ACT IV • Scene I}°

(Enter King and Queen, with Rosencrantz and
Guildenstern.)

KING: There's matter in these sighs, these profound
    heaves
You must translate; 'tis fit we understand them.
Where is your son?
QUEEN: Bestow this place on us a little while.
            [Exeunt Rosencrantz and Guildenstern.]
Ah, mine own lord, what have I seen tonight!   5
KING: What, Gertrude? How does Hamlet?
QUEEN: Mad as the sea and wind when both
    contend
Which is the mightier. In his lawless fit,
Behind the arras hearing something stir,
Whips out his rapier, cries, "A rat, a rat!"   10
And, in this brainish apprehension,° kills
The unseen good old man.
KING: O heavy deed!
It had been so with us, had we been there.
His liberty is full of threats to all —
To you yourself, to us, to everyone.   15
Alas, how shall this bloody deed be answer'd?
It will be laid to us, whose providence°
Should have kept short,° restrain'd, and out of
    haunt°
This mad young man. But so much was our love
We would not understand what was most fit,   20
But, like the owner of a foul disease,
To keep it from divulging,° let it feed
Even on the pith of life. Where is he gone?
QUEEN: To draw apart the body he hath kill'd,
O'er whom his very madness, like some ore°   25
Among a mineral° of metals base,
Shows itself pure: 'a weeps for what is done.
KING: O Gertrude, come away!
The sun no sooner shall the mountains touch

223. **draw . . . end**: Finish up (with a pun on *draw*, pull).
IV, I. Location: The castle. 11. **brainish apprehension**: Headstrong conception. 17. **providence**: Foresight. 18. **short**: On a short tether. **out of haunt**: Secluded. 22. **divulging**: Becoming evident. 25. **ore**: Vein of gold. 26. **mineral**: Mine.

30 But we will ship him hence, and this vile deed
We must, with all our majesty and skill,
Both countenance and excuse. Ho, Guildenstern!

(*Enter Rosencrantz and Guildenstern.*)

Friends both, go join you with some further aid.
Hamlet in madness hath Polonius slain,
And from his mother's closet hath he dragg'd
35 him.
Go seek him out; speak fair, and bring the body
Into the chapel. I pray you, haste in this.
                    [*Exeunt Rosencrantz and Guildenstern.*]
Come, Gertrude, we'll call up our wisest friends
And let them know both what we mean to do
40 And what's untimely done° . . . .
Whose whisper o'er the world's diameter,°
As level° as the cannon to his blank,°
Transports his pois'ned shot, may miss our name,
And hit the woundless° air. O, come away!
45 My soul is full of discord and dismay. (*Exeunt.*)

{*Scene II*}°

(*Enter Hamlet.*)

HAMLET: Safely stow'd.
[ROSENCRANTZ, GUILDENSTERN (*within*): Hamlet!
Lord Hamlet!]
HAMLET: But soft, what noise? Who calls on Hamlet?
5 O, here they come.

(*Enter Rosencrantz and Guildenstern.*)

ROSENCRANTZ: What have you done, my lord, with
the dead body?
HAMLET: Compounded it with dust, whereto 'tis
kin.
ROSENCRANTZ: Tell us where 'tis, that we may take
it thence
And bear it to the chapel.
10 HAMLET: Do not believe it.
ROSENCRANTZ: Believe what?
HAMLET: That I can keep your counsel and not mine
own. Besides, to be demanded of° a sponge, what
replication° should be made by the son of a king?
15 ROSENCRANTZ: Take you me for a sponge, my lord?

HAMLET: Ay, sir, that soaks up the King's countenance,° his rewards, his authorities. But such officers do the King best service in the end. He keeps
them, like an ape an apple, in the corner of his jaw,
first mouth'd, to be last swallow'd. When he needs 20
what you have glean'd, it is but squeezing you,
and, sponge, you shall be dry again.
ROSENCRANTZ: I understand you not, my lord.
HAMLET: I am glad of it. A knavish speech sleeps in°
a foolish ear. 25
ROSENCRANTZ: My lord, you must tell us where the
body is, and go with us to the King.
HAMLET: The body is with the King, but the King is
not with the body.° The King is a thing —
GUILDENSTERN: A thing, my lord? 30
HAMLET: Of nothing.° Bring me to him. [Hide fox,
and all after.°]   (*Exeunt.*)

{*Scene III*}°

(*Enter King, and two or three.*)

KING: I have sent to seek him, and to find the body.
How dangerous is it that this man goes loose!
Yet must not we put the strong law on him.
He's lov'd of the distracted° multitude,
Who like not in their judgment, but their eyes, 5
And where 'tis so, th' offender's scourge° is
weigh'd,°
But never the offense. To bear° all smooth and
even,
This sudden sending him away must seem
Deliberate pause.° Diseases desperate grown
By desperate appliance are reliev'd, 10
Or not at all.

(*Enter Rosencrantz, [Guildenstern,] and all the rest.*)

                    How now? What hath befall'n?
ROSENCRANTZ: Where the dead body is bestow'd,
my lord,
We cannot get from him.
KING: But where is he?

---

16. countenance: Favor.   **24. sleeps in:** Has no meaning to.
28–29. The . . . body: Perhaps alludes to the legal commonplace of "the king's two bodies," which drew a distinction
between the sacred office of kingship and the particular mortal who possessed it at any given time.   **31. Of nothing:**
Of no account.   **31–32. Hide . . . after:** An old signal cry
in the game of hide-and-seek, suggesting that Hamlet now
runs away from them. **IV, III. Location:** The castle.
4. distracted: Fickle, unstable.   **6. scourge:** Punishment.
weigh'd: Taken into consideration.   **7. bear:** Manage.
9. Deliberate pause: Carefully considered action.

---

40. And . . . done: A defective line; conjectures as to the
missing words include *so, haply, slander* (Capell and others);
for, haply, slander (Theobald and others).   **41. diameter:**
Extent from side to side.   **42. As level:** With as direct aim.
blank: White spot in the center of a target.   **44. wound-
less:** Invulnerable.   **IV, II. Location:** The castle.   **13. demanded of:** Questioned by.   **14. replication:** Reply.

ROSENCRANTZ: Without, my lord; guarded, to know
    your pleasure.
KING: Bring him before us.
15 ROSENCRANTZ: Ho! Bring in the lord.

(*They enter* [*with Hamlet*].)

KING: Now, Hamlet, where's Polonius?
HAMLET: At supper.
KING: At supper? Where?
HAMLET: Not where he eats, but where 'a is eaten. A
20   certain convocation of politic worms° are e'en at
    him. Your worm is your only emperor for diet.°
    We fat all creatures else to fat us, and we fat our-
    selves for maggots. Your fat king and your lean
    beggar is but variable service,° two dishes, but to
25   one table — that's the end.
KING: Alas, alas!
HAMLET: A man may fish with the worm that hath
    eat° of a king, and eat of the fish that hath fed of
    that worm.
30 KING: What dost thou mean by this?
HAMLET: Nothing but to show you how a king may
    go a progress° through the guts of a beggar.
KING: Where is Polonius?
HAMLET: In heaven. Send thither to see. If your mes-
35   senger find him not there, seek him i' th' other
    place yourself. But if indeed you find him not
    within this month, you shall nose him as you go up
    the stairs into the lobby.
KING [*to some Attendants*]: Go seek him there.
40 HAMLET: 'A will stay till you come.
                         [*Exit Attendants.*]
KING: Hamlet, this deed, for thine especial safety. —
    Which we do tender,° as we dearly° grieve
    For that which thou hast done — must send thee
    hence
    [With fiery quickness.] Therefore prepare thyself.
45   The bark° is ready, and the wind at help,
    Th' associates tend,° and everything is bent°
    For England.
HAMLET: For England!
KING: Ay, Hamlet.
50 HAMLET: Good.
KING: So is it, if thou knew'st our purposes.
HAMLET: I see a cherub° that sees them. But, come,
    for England! Farewell, dear mother.

KING: Thy loving father, Hamlet.
HAMLET: My mother. Father and mother is man and 55
    wife, man and wife is one flesh, and so, my mother.
    Come, for England!   (*Exit.*)
KING: Follow him at foot;° tempt him with speed
    aboard.
    Delay it not; I'll have him hence tonight.
    Away! For everything is seal'd and done   60
    That else leans on° th' affair. Pray you, make
    haste.
                  [*Exeunt all but the King.*]
    And, England,° if my love thou hold'st at aught —
    As my great power thereof may give thee sense,
    Since yet thy cicatrice° looks raw and red
    After the Danish sword, and thy free awe°
    Pays homage to us — thou mayst not coldly set° 65
    Our sovereign process,° which imports at full,
    By letters congruing° to that effect,
    The present° death of Hamlet. Do it, England,
    For like the hectic° in my blood he rages,
    And thou must cure me. Till I know 'tis done,   70
    Howe'er my haps,° my joys were ne'er begun.
                         (*Exit.*)

{*Scene IV*}°

(*Enter Fortinbras with his Army over the stage.*)

FORTINBRAS: Go, captain, from me greet the Danish
    king.
    Tell him that, by his license,° Fortinbras
    Craves the conveyance° of a promis'd march
    Over his kingdom. You know the rendezvous.
    If that his Majesty would aught with us,   5
    We shall express our duty in his eye;°
    And let him know so.
CAPTAIN: I will do 't, my lord.
FORTINBRAS: Go softly° on.   [*Exeunt all but the
                                Captain.*]

(*Enter Hamlet, Rosencrantz, [Guildenstern,] etc.*)

HAMLET: Good sir, whose powers° are these?
CAPTAIN: They are of Norway, sir.   10
HAMLET: How purposed, sir, I pray you?
CAPTAIN: Against some part of Poland.
HAMLET: Who commands them, sir?

---

20. **politic worms:** Crafty worms (suited to a master spy like
Polonius).   21. **diet:** Food, eating (with perhaps a punning
reference to the Diet of Worms, a famous convocation held
in 1521).   24. **variable service:** Different courses of a single
meal.   28. **eat:** Eaten (pronounced "et").   32. **progress:**
Royal journey of state.   42. **tender:** Regard, hold dear.
dearly: Intensely.   45. **bark:** Sailing vessel.   46. **tend:**
Wait.   **bent:** In readiness.   52. **cherub:** Cherubim are angels of knowledge.

58. **at foot:** Close behind, at heel.   61. **leans on:** Bears upon,
is related to.   62. **England:** King of England.   64. **cicatrice:**
Scar.   65. **free awe:** Voluntary show of respect.   66. **set:**
Esteem.   67. **process:** Command.   68. **congruing:** Agreeing.   69. **present:** Immediate.   70. **hectic:** Persistent fever.
72. **haps:** Fortunes.   IV, IV. **Location:** The coast of Denmark.
2. **license:** Permission.   3. **conveyance:** Escort, convoy.
6. **eye:** Presence.   8. **softly:** Slowly.   9. **powers:** Forces.

CAPTAIN: The nephew to old Norway, Fortinbras.
15 HAMLET: Goes it against the main° of Poland, sir,
    Or for some frontier?
CAPTAIN: Truly to speak, and with no addition,°
    We go to gain a little patch of ground
    That hath in it no profit but the name.
20 To pay° five ducats, five, I would not farm it;°
    Nor will it yield to Norway or the Pole
    A ranker° rate, should it be sold in fee.°
HAMLET: Why, then the Polack never will defend it.
CAPTAIN: Yes, it is already garrison'd.
HAMLET: Two thousand souls and twenty thousand
25   ducats
    Will not debate the question of this straw.°
    This is th' imposthume° of much wealth and
        peace,
    That inward breaks, and shows no cause without
    Why the man dies. I humbly thank you, sir.
CAPTAIN: God buy you, sir.   [Exit.]
30 ROSENCRANTZ: Will 't please you go, my lord?
HAMLET: I'll be with you straight. Go a little before.
                          [Exit all except Hamlet.]
    How all occasions do inform against° me,
    And spur my dull revenge! What is a man,
    If his chief good and market of° his time
35 Be but to sleep and feed? A beast, no more.
    Sure he that made us with such large discourse,°
    Looking before and after, gave us not
    That capability and god-like reason
    To fust° in us unus'd. Now, whether it be
40 Bestial oblivion,° or some craven scruple
    Of thinking too precisely on th' event° —
    A thought which, quarter'd, hath but one part
        wisdom
    And ever three parts coward — I do not know
    Why yet I live to say "This thing's to do,"
    Sith° I have cause and will and strength and
45   means
    To do 't. Examples gross° as earth exhort me:
    Witness this army of such mass and charge°
    Led by a delicate and tender prince,
    Whose spirit, with divine ambition puff'd
50 Makes mouths° at the invisible event,
    Exposing what is mortal and unsure

To all that fortune, death, and danger dare,
Even for an egg-shell. Rightly to be great
Is not to stir without great argument,
But greatly to find quarrel in a straw   55
When honor's at the stake. How stand I then,
That have a father kill'd, a mother stain'd,
Excitements of° my reason and my blood,
And let all sleep, while, to my shame, I see
The imminent death of twenty thousand men,   60
That, for a fantasy° and trick° of fame,
Go to their graves like beds, fight for a plot°
Whereon the numbers cannot try the cause,°
Which is not tomb enough and continent°
To hide the slain? O, from this time forth,   65
My thoughts be bloody, or be nothing worth!
                                          (Exit.)

{Scene V}°

(Enter Horatio, [Queen] Gertrude, and a Gentleman.)

QUEEN: I will not speak with her.
GENTLEMAN: She is importunate, indeed distract.
    Her mood will needs be pitied.
QUEEN: What would she have?
GENTLEMAN: She speaks much of her father, says
        she hears
    There's tricks° i' th' world, and hems, and beats
        her heart,°   5
    Spurns enviously at straws,° speaks things in
        doubt°
    That carry but half sense. Her speech is nothing,
    Yet the unshaped use° of it doth move
    The hearers to collection;° they yawn° at it,
    And botch° the words up fit to their own
        thoughts,   10
    Which, as her winks and nods and gestures
        yield° them,
    Indeed would make one think there might be
        thought,°
    Though nothing sure, yet much unhappily.
HORATIO: 'Twere good she were spoken with, for
    she may strew

---

58. **Excitements of:** Promptings by.   61. **fantasy:** Fanciful
caprice.   **trick:** Trifle.   62. **plot:** I.e., of ground.   63.
Whereon . . . cause: On which there is insufficient room for the
soldiers needed to engage in a military contest.   64. **conti-**
nent: Receptacle, container.   **IV, v. Location:** The castle.
5. **tricks:** Deceptions.   **heart:** Breast.   6. **Spurns . . . straws:**
Kicks spitefully, takes offense at trifles.   **in doubt:** Obscurely.
8. **unshaped use:** Distracted manner.   9. **collection:** Inference,
a guess at some sort of meaning.   **yawn:** Wonder, grasp.
10. **botch:** Patch.   11. **yield:** Delivery, bring forth (her
words).   12. **thought:** Conjectured.

---

15. **main:** Main part.   17. **addition:** Exaggeration.   20. **To**
pay: I.e., for a yearly rental of.   **farm it:** Take a lease of it.
22. **ranker:** Higher.   **in fee:** Fee simple, outright.   26. **de-**
bate . . . straw: Settle this trifling matter.   27. **imposthume:**
Abscess.   32. **inform against:** Denounce, betray; take shape
against.   34. **market of:** Profit of compensation for.
36. **discourse:** Power of reasoning.   39. **fust:** Grow moldy.
40. **oblivion:** Forgetfulness.   41. **event:** Outcome.   45. **Sith:**
Since.   46. **gross:** Obvious.   47. **charge:** Expense.   50.
Makes mouths: Makes scornful faces.

15   Dangerous conjectures in ill-breeding° minds.
QUEEN: Let her come in.   [*Exit Gentlemen.*]
     [*Aside.*] To my sick soul, as sin's true nature is,
     Each toy° seems prologue to some great amiss.°
     So full of artless jealousy is guilt,
20   It spills itself in fearing to be spilt.°

(*Enter Ophelia [distracted].*)

OPHELIA: Where is the beauteous majesty of
          Denmark?
QUEEN: How now, Ophelia?
OPHELIA (*she sings*): "How should I your true love
          know
          From another one?
25   By his cockle hat° and staff,
          And his sandal shoon."°
QUEEN: Alas, sweet lady, what imports this song?
OPHELIA: Say you? Nay, pray you, mark.
          "He is dead and gone, lady,   (*Song.*)
30   He is dead and gone;
          At his head a grass-green turf,
          At his heels a stone."
          O, ho!
QUEEN: Nay, but Ophelia —
35 OPHELIA: Pray you mark.
          [*Sings.*] "White his shroud as the mountain
          snow" —

(*Enter King.*)

QUEEN: Alas, look here, my lord.
OPHELIA: "Larded° all with flowers   (*Song.*)
          Which bewept to the ground did not go
40   With true-love showers."
KING: How do you, pretty lady?
OPHELIA: Well, God 'ild° you! They say the owl° was
          a baker's daughter. Lord, we know what we are,
          but know not what we may be. God be at your
45   table!
KING: Conceit° upon her father.
OPHELIA: Pray let's have no words of this; but when
          they ask you what it means, say you this:
          "Tomorrow is Saint Valentine's° day.   (*Song.*)
50   All in the morning betime,

          And I a maid at your window,
          To be your Valentine.
          Then up he rose, and donn'd his clo'es,
          And dupp'd° the chamber-door,
          Let in the maid, that out a maid   55
          Never departed more."
KING: Pretty Ophelia!
OPHELIA: Indeed, la, without an oath, I'll make an
          end on 't:
          [*Sings.*] "By Gis° and by Saint Charity,   60
          Alack, and fie for shame!
          Young men will do 't, if they come to 't;
          By Cock,° they are to blame.
          Quoth she, 'Before you tumbled me,
          You promised me to wed.'"   65
He answers:
          "'So would I ha' done, by yonder sun,
          An thou hadst not come to my bed.'"
KING: How long hath she been thus?
OPHELIA: I hope all will be well. We must be patient,   70
          but I cannot choose but weep, to think they would
          lay him i' th' cold ground. My brother shall know
          of it; and so I thank you for your good counsel.
          Come, my coach! Good night, ladies; good night,
          sweet ladies; good night, good night.   75
                                                  [*Exit.*]
KING: Follow her close; give her good watch, I pray
          you.   [*Exit Horatio.*]
          O, this is the poison of deep grief; it springs
          All from her father's death — and now behold!
          O Gertrude, Gertrude,
          When sorrows come, they come not single spies,°   80
          But in battalions. First, her father slain;
          Next, your son gone, and he most violent author
          Of his own just remove; the people muddied,°
          Thick and unwholesome in their thoughts and
          whispers,
          For good Polonius' death; and we have done but
          greenly,°   85
          In hugger-mugger° to inter him; poor Ophelia
          Divided from herself and her fair judgment,
          Without the which we are pictures, or mere
          beasts;
          Last, and as much containing as all these,
          Her brother is in secret come from France,   90
          Feeds on his wonder, keeps himself in clouds,°
          And wants° not buzzers° to infect his ear
          With pestilent speeches of his father's death,

---

15. **ill-breeding:** Prone to suspect the worst. 18. **toy:** Trifle. **amiss:** Calamity. 19–20. **So . . . spilt:** Guilt is so full of suspicion that it unskillfully betrays itself in fearing betrayal. 25. **cockle hat:** Hat with cockleshell stuck in it as a sign that the wearer had been a pilgrim to the shrine of St. James of Compostella in Spain. 26. **shoon:** Shoes. 38. **Larded:** Decorated. 42. **God 'ild:** God yield or reward. **owl:** Refers to a legend about a baker's daughter who was turned into an owl for refusing Jesus bread. 46. **Conceit:** Brooding. 49. **Valentine's:** This song alludes to the belief that the first girl seen by a man on the morning of this day was his valentine or true love.

54. **dupp'd:** Opened. 60. **Gis:** Jesus. 63. **Cock:** A perversion of *God* in oaths. 80. **spies:** Scouts sent in advance of the main force. 83. **muddied:** Stirred up, confused. 85. **greenly:** Imprudently, foolishly. 86. **hugger-mugger:** Secret haste. 91. **in clouds:** I.e., of suspicion and rumor. 92. **wants:** Lacks. **buzzers:** Gossipers, informers.

Wherein necessity, of matter beggar'd,°
95 Will nothing stick our person to arraign
In ear and ear.° O my dear Gertrude, this,
Like to a murd'ring-piece,° in many places
Gives me superfluous death.   (*A noise within.*)
[QUEEN: Alack, what noise is this?]
100 KING: Attend!
Where are my Switzers?° Let them guard the
door.

(*Enter a Messenger.*)

What is the matter?
MESSENGER: Save yourself, my lord!
The ocean, overpeering of his list,°
Eats not the flats° with more impiteous° haste
105 Than young Laertes, in a riotous head,°
O'erbears your officers. The rabble call him lord,
And, as° the world were now but to begin,
Antiquity forgot, custom not known,
The ratifiers and props° of every word,°
110 They cry, "Choose we! Laertes shall be king!"
Caps, hands, and tongues applaud it to the
clouds,
"Laertes shall be king, Laertes king!"
                    (*A noise within.*)
QUEEN: How cheerfully on the false trail they cry!
O, this is counter,° you false Danish dogs!

(*Enter Laertes with others.*)

115 KING: The doors are broke.
LAERTES: Where is this King? Sirs, stand you all
without.
ALL: No, let's come in.
LAERTES: I pray you, give me leave.
ALL: We will, we will.
                    [*They retire without the door.*]
LAERTES: I thank you. Keep the door. O thou vile
king,
Give me my father!
120 QUEEN: Calmly, good Laertes.
                    [*She tries to hold him back.*]
LAERTES: That drop of blood that's calm proclaims
me bastard,

Cries cuckold to my father, brands the harlot
Even here, between the chaste unsmirched brow
Of my true mother.
KING: What is the cause, Laertes,
That thy rebellion looks so giant-like?   125
Let him go, Gertrude. Do not fear our° person.
There's such divinity doth hedge a king
That treason can but peep to what it would,°
Acts little of his will.° Tell me, Laertes,
Why thou art thus incens'd. Let him go,
Gertrude.   130
Speak, man.
LAERTES: Where is my father?
KING: Dead.
QUEEN: But not by him.
KING: Let him demand his fill.
LAERTES: How came he dead? I'll not be juggled
with.
To hell, allegiance! Vows, to the blackest devil!
Conscience and grace, to the profoundest pit!   135
I dare damnation. To this point I stand,
That both the worlds I give to negligence,°
Let come what comes, only I'll be reveng'd
Most throughly° for my father.
KING: Who shall stay you?
LAERTES: My will, not all the world's.° 140
And for my means, I'll husband them so well,
They shall go far with little.
KING: Good Laertes,
If you desire to know the certainty
Of your dear father, is 't writ in your revenge
That, swoopstake,° you will draw both friend
and foe,   145
Winner and loser?
LAERTES: None but his enemies.
KING: Will you know them then?
LAERTES: To his good friends thus wide I'll ope my
arms,
And, like the kind life-rend'ring pelican,°
Repast° them with my blood.
KING: Why, now you speak   150
Like a good child and a true gentleman.
That I am guiltless of your father's death,

---

94. **of matter beggar'd:** Unprovided with facts.   95–96.
Will . . . and ear: Will not hesitate to accuse my (royal) person in everybody's ears.   97. **murd'ring-piece:** Cannon
loaded so as to scatter its shot.   101. **Switzers:** Swiss
guards, mercenaries.   103. **overpeering of his list:**
Overflowing its shore.   104. **flats:** Flatlands near shore.
impiteous: Pitiless.   105. **head:** Armed force.   107.
as: As if.   109. **ratifiers and props:** Refer to *antiquity* and
custom. **word:** Promise.   114. **counter:** A hunting term
meaning to follow the trail in a direction opposite to that
which the game has taken.

126. **fear our:** Fear for my.   128. **can . . . would:** Can only
glance; as from far off or through a barrier, at what it would
intend.   129. **Acts . . . will:** (But) performs little of what it
intends.   137. **both . . . negligence:** Both this world and the
next are of no consequence to me.   139. **throughly:** Thoroughly.   140. **My will . . . world's:** I'll stop (*stay*) when my
will is accomplished, not for anyone else's.   145. **swoopstake:** Literally, taking all stakes on the gambling table at
once, i.e., indiscriminately; *draw* is also a gambling term.
149. **pelican:** Refers to the belief that the female pelican fed
its young with its own blood.   150. **Repast:** Feed.

And am most sensibly° in grief for it,
It shall as level° to your judgment 'pear
As day does to your eye.
155   (*A noise within:*) "Let her come in."
LAERTES: How now? What noise is that?

(*Enter Ophelia.*)

O heat, dry up my brains! Tears seven times salt
Burn out the sense and virtue° of mine eye!
By heaven, thy madness shall be paid with
        weight°
160   Till our scale turn the beam.° O rose of May!
Dear maid, kind sister, sweet Ophelia!
O heavens, is 't possible a young maid's wits
Should be as mortal as an old man's life?
[Nature is fine in° love, and where 'tis fine,
165   It sends some precious instance° of itself
After the thing it loves.°]
OPHELIA: "They bore him barefac'd on the bier;
                                            (*Song.*)
        [Hey non nonny, nonny, hey nonny,]
        And in his grave rain'd many a tear" —
170   Fare you well, my dove!
LAERTES: Hadst thou thy wits, and didst persuade°
        revenge,
        It could not move thus.
OPHELIA: You must sing "A-down a-down,
        And you call him a-down-a."
175   O, how the wheel° becomes it! It is the false steward°
        that stole his master's daughter.
LAERTES: This nothing's more than matter.°
OPHELIA: There's rosemary,° that's for remembrance;
        pray you, love, remember. And there is pansies,°
180   that's for thoughts.
LAERTES: A document° in madness, thoughts and re-
        membrance fitted.
OPHELIA: There's fennel° for you, and columbines.°
        There's rue° for you, and here's some for me; we

may call it herb of grace o' Sundays. You may   185
wear your rue with a difference.° There's a daisy. I
would give you some violets,° but they wither'd all
when my father died. They say 'e made a good
end —
[*Sings.*] "For bonny sweet Robin is all my joy."   190
LAERTES: Thought° and affliction, passion, hell itself,
        She turns to favor° and to prettiness.
OPHELIA: "And will 'a not come again? (*Song.*)
        And will 'a not come again?
        No, no, he is dead,   195
        Go to thy death-bed,
        He never will come again.

        "His beard was as white as snow,
        All flaxen was his poll.°
        He is gone, he is gone,   200
        And we cast away moan.
        God 'a' mercy on his soul!
        And of all Christians' souls, I pray God. God
        buy you.
                                            [*Exit.*]
LAERTES: Do you see this, O God?   205
KING: Laertes, I must commune with your grief,
        Or you deny me right. Go but apart,
        Make choice of whom your wisest friends you
        will,
        And they shall hear and judge 'twixt you and me.
        If by direct or by collateral° hand   210
        They find us touch'd,° we will our kingdom give,
        Our crown, our life, and all that we call ours,
        To you in satisfaction; but if not,
        Be you content to lend your patience to us,
        And we shall jointly labor with your soul   215
        To give it due content.
LAERTES: Let this be so.
        His means of death, his obscure funeral —
        No trophy,° sword, nor hatchment° o'er his
        bones,
        No noble rite nor formal ostentation° —
        Cry to be heard, as 'twere from heaven to earth, 220
        That I must call 't in question.
KING: So you shall;
        And where th' offense is, let the great ax fall.
        I pray you go with me.   (*Exeunt.*)

153. **sensibly:** Feelingly.   154. **level:** Plain.   158. **virtue:**
Faculty, power.   159. **paid with weight:** Repaid, avenged
equally or more.   160. **beam:** Crossbar of a balance.
164. **fine in:** Refined by.   165. **instance:** Token.   166. **After . . . loves:** Into the grave, along with Polonius.   171. **persuade:** Argue cogently for.   175. **wheel:** Spinning wheel as
accompaniment to the song, or refrain.   **false steward:** The
story is unknown.   177. **This . . . matter:** This seeming nonsense is more meaningful than sane utterance.   178. **rosemary:** Used as a symbol of remembrance both at weddings and
at funerals.   179. **pansies:** Emblems of love and courtship;
perhaps from French *pensées,* thoughts.   181. **document:**
Instruction, lesson.   183. **fennel:** Emblem of flattery.   **columbines:** Emblems of unchastity (?) or ingratitude (?).
184. **rue:** Emblem of repentance; when mingled with holy water, it was known as *herb of grace.*

186. **with a difference:** Suggests that Ophelia and the queen
have different causes of sorrow and repentance; perhaps
with a play on *rue* in the sense of ruth, pity.   **daisy:** Emblem of dissembling, faithlessness.   187. **violets:** Emblems
of faithfulness.   191. **Thought:** Melancholy.   192. **favor:**
Grace.   199. **poll:** Head.   210. **collateral:** Indirect.   211.
us touch'd: Me implicated.   218. **trophy:** Memorial.
hatchment: Tablet displaying the armorial bearings of a deceased person.   219. **ostentation:** Ceremony.

{*Scene VI*}°

(*Enter Horatio and others.*)

HORATIO: What are they that would speak with me?
GENTLEMAN: Seafaring men, sir. They say they have
    letters for you.
HORATIO: Let them come in.   [*Exit Gentleman.*]
5   I do not know from what part of the world
    I should be greeted, if not from lord Hamlet.

(*Enter Sailors.*)

FIRST SAILOR: God bless you sir.
HORATIO: Let him bless thee too.
FIRST SAILOR: 'A shall, sir, an 't please him. There's a
10   letter for you, sir — it came from th' ambassador
    that was bound for England — if your name be
    Horatio, as I am let to know it is.   [*Gives letter.*]
HORATIO [*reads*]: "Horatio, when thou shalt have
    over-look'd this, give these fellows some means° to
15   the King; they have letters for him. Ere we were
    two days old at sea, a pirate of very warlike ap-
    pointment° gave us chase. Finding ourselves too
    slow of sail, we put on a compell'd valor, and in the
    grapple I boarded them. On the instant they got
20   clear of our ship, so I alone became their prisoner.
    They have dealt with me like thieves of mercy,° but
    they knew what they did: I am to do a good turn
    for them. Let the King have the letters I have sent,
    and repair thou to me with as much speed as thou
25   wouldest fly death. I have words to speak in thine
    ear will make thee dumb; yet are they much too
    light for the bore° of the matter. These good fellows
    will bring thee where I am. Rosencrantz and
    Guildenstern hold their course for England. Of
30   them I have much to tell thee. Farewell.

        He that thou knowest thine, Hamlet."
Come, I will give you way for these your letters,
And do 't the speedier that you may direct me
To him from whom you brought them. (*Exeunt.*)

{*Scene VII*}°

(*Enter King and Laertes.*)

KING: Now must your conscience my acquittance
    seal,°
    And you must put me in your heart for friend,
    Sith you have heard, and with a knowing ear,

That he which hath your noble father slain
Pursued my life.
LAERTES: It well appears. But tell me   5
    Why you proceeded not against these feats°
    So criminal and so capital° in nature,
    As by your safety, greatness, wisdom, all things
        else,
    You mainly° were stirr'd up.
KING: O, for two special reasons,
    Which may to you, perhaps, seem much
        unsinew'd,°   10
    But yet to me th' are strong. The Queen his
        mother
    Lives almost by his looks, and for myself —
    My virtue or my plague, be it either which —
    She's so conjunctive° to my life and soul
    That, as the star moves not but in his sphere,°   15
    I could not but by her. The other motive,
    Why to a public count° I might not go,
    Is the great love the general gender° bear him,
    Who, dipping all his faults in their affection,
    Would, like the spring° that turneth wood to
        stone,   20
    Convert his gyves° to graces, so that my arrows,
    Too slightly timber'd° for so loud° a wind,
    Would have reverted to my bow again
    And not where I had aim'd them.
LAERTES: And so have I a noble father lost,   25
    A sister driven into desp'rate terms,°
    Whose worth, if praises may go back° again,
    Stood challenger on mount° of all the age
    For her perfections. But my revenge will come.
KING: Break not your sleeps for that. You must not
        think   30
    That we are made of stuff so flat and dull
    That we can let our beard be shook with danger
    And think it pastime. You shortly shall hear
        more.
    I lov'd your father, and we love ourself;
    And that, I hope, will teach you to imagine —   35

(*Enter a Messenger with letters.*)

6. feats: Acts.   7. capital: Punishable by death.   9. mainly: Greatly.   10. unsinew'd: Weak.   14. conjunctive: Closely united.   15. sphere: The hollow sphere in which, according to Ptolemaic astronomy, the planets moved. 17. count: Account, reckoning.   18. general gender: Common people.   20. spring: A spring with such a concentration of lime that it coats a piece of wood with limestone, in effect gilding it.   21. gyves: Fetters (which, gilded by the people's praise, would look like badges of honor). 22. slightly timber'd: Light.   loud: Strong.   26. terms: State, condition.   27. go back: Recall Ophelia's former virtues.   28. on mount: On high.

IV, VI. Location: The castle.   14. means: Means of access. 16–17. appointment: Equipage.   21. thieves of mercy: Merciful thieves.   27. bore: Caliber, i.e., importance.   IV, VII. Location: The castle.   1. my acquittance seal: Confirm or acknowledge my innocence.

[How now? What news?]

MESSENGER: [Letters, my lord, from Hamlet:]
These to your Majesty, this to the Queen.
                                [*Gives letters.*]

KING: From Hamlet? Who brought them?

MESSENGER: Sailors, my lord, they say; I saw them
    not.
    They were given me by Claudio. He receiv'd
40 them
    Of him that brought them.

KING: Laertes, you shall hear them.
    Leave us.   [*Exit Messenger.*]
[*Reads.*] "High and mighty, you shall know I am set
    naked° on your kingdom. Tomorrow shall I beg
45 leave to see your kingly eyes, when I shall, first ask-
    ing your pardon° thereunto, recount the occasion
    of my sudden and more strange return.   Hamlet."
    What should this mean? Are all the rest come
    back?
    Or is it some abuse,° and no such thing?

LAERTES: Know you the hand?

50 KING: 'Tis Hamlet's character.° "Naked!"
    And in a postscript here, he says "alone."
    Can you devise° me?

LAERTES: I am lost in it, my lord. But let him come.
    It warms the very sickness in my heart
55 That I shall live and tell him to his teeth,
    "Thus didst thou."

KING: If it be so, Laertes —
    As how should it be so? How otherwise?° —
    Will you be ruled by me?

LAERTES: Ay, my lord,
    So° you will not o'errule me to a peace.

60 KING: To thine own peace. If he be now returned,
    As checking at° his voyage, and that he means
    No more to undertake it, I will work him
    To an exploit, now ripe in my device,
    Under the which he shall not choose but fall;
    And for his death no wind of blame shall
65 breathe,
    But even his mother shall uncharge the practice°
    And call it accident.

LAERTES: My lord, I will be rul'd,
    The rather if you could devise it so
    That I might be the organ.°

KING: It falls right.
    You have been talk'd of since your travel much,   70
    And that in Hamlet's hearing, for a quality
    Wherein, they say, you shine. Your sum of parts°
    Did not together pluck such envy from him
    As did that one, and that, in my regard,
    Of the unworthiest siege.°   75

LAERTES: What part is that, my lord?

KING: A very riband in the cap of youth,
    Yet needful too, for youth no less becomes
    The light and careless livery that it wears
    Than settled age his sables° and his weeds,°   80
    Importing health° and graveness. Two months
        since
    Here was a gentleman of Normandy.
    I have seen myself, and serv'd against, the
        French,
    And they can well° on horseback, but this
        gallant
    Had witchcraft in 't; he grew unto his seat,   85
    And to such wondrous doing brought his horse
    As had he been incorps'd and demi-natured°
    With the brave beast. So far he topp'd° my
        thought
    That I, in forgery° of shapes and tricks,
    Come short of what he did.

LAERTES: A Norman was 't?   90

KING: A Norman.

LAERTES: Upon my life, Lamord.

KING: The very same.

LAERTES: I know him well. He is the brooch°
        indeed
    And gem of all the nation.

KING: He made confession° of you,   95
    And gave you such a masterly report
    For art and exercise in your defense,
    And for your rapier most especial,
    That he cried out, 'twould be a sight indeed,
    If one could match you. The scrimers° of their
        nation,   100
    He swore, had neither motion, guard, nor eye,
    If you oppos'd them. Sir, this report of his
    Did Hamlet so envenom with his envy
    That he could nothing do but wish and beg

---

44. naked: Destitute, unarmed, without following.   46. pardon: Permission.   49. abuse: Deceit.   50. character: Handwriting.   52. devise: Explain to.   57. As ... otherwise:
How can this (Hamlet's return) be true? Yet how otherwise
than true (since we have the evidence of his letter).   59. So:
Provided that.   61. checking at: Turning aside from (like a
falcon leaving the quarry to fly at a chance bird).   66. un-
charge the practice: Acquit the stratagem of being a plot.
69. organ: Agent, instrument.

72. Your ... parts: All your other virtues.   75. unworthiest
siege: Least important rank.   80. sables: Rich robes furred
with sable.   weeds: Garments.   81. Importing health: Indicating prosperity.   84. can well: Are skilled.   87. in-
corps'd and demi–natur'd: Of one body and nearly of
one nature (like the centaur).   88. topp'd: Surpassed.
89. forgery: Invention.   93. brooch: Ornament.   95. confession: Admission of superiority.   100. scrimers: Fencers.

105   Your sudden coming o'er to play° with you.
        Now, out of this —
LAERTES: What out of this, my lord?
KING: Laertes, was your father dear to you?
        Or are you like the painting of a sorrow,
        A face without a heart?
LAERTES: Why ask you this?
KING: Not that I think you did not love your
110   father,
        But that I know love is begun by time,°
        And that I see, in passages of proof,°
        Time qualifies° the spark and fire of it.
        There lives within the very flame of love
115   A kind of wick or snuff° that will abate it,
        And nothing is at a like goodness still,°
        For goodness, growing to a plurisy,°
        Dies in his own too much.° That° we would do,
        We should do when we would; for this "would"
        changes
120   And hath abatements° and delays as many
        As there are tongues, are hands, are accidents,°
        And then this "should" is like a spendthrift's
        sigh,°
        That hurts by easing.° But, to the quick o' th'
        ulcer;
        Hamlet comes back. What would you undertake
125   To show yourself your father's son in deed
        More than in words?
LAERTES: To cut his throat i' th'
        church!
KING: No place, indeed, should murder sanctuarize;°
        Revenge should have no bounds. But, good
        Laertes,
        Will you do this,° keep close within your
        chamber.
130   Hamlet return'd shall know you are come home.
        We'll put on those° shall praise your excellence
        And set a double varnish on the fame
        The Frenchman gave you, bring you in fine°
        together,

---

105. play: Fence.　**111. begun by time:** Subject to change. **112. passages of proof:** Actual instances.　**113. qualifies:** Weakens.　**115. snuff:** The charred part of a candlewick. **116. nothing . . . still:** Nothing remains at a constant level of perfection.　**117. plurisy:** Excess, plethora.　**118. in . . . much:** Of its own excess.　**That:** That which.　**120. abatements:** Diminutions.　**121. accidents:** Occurrences, incidents.　**122. spendthrift's sigh:** An allusion to the belief that each sigh cost the heart a drop of blood.　**123. hurts by easing:** Costs the heart blood even while it affords emotional relief.　**127. sanctuarize:** Protect from punishment (alludes to the right of sanctuary with which certain religious places were invested).　**129. Will you do this:** If you wish to do this.　**131. put on those:** Instigate those who.　**133. in fine:** Finally.

And wager on your heads. He, being remiss,°
    Most generous,° and free from all contriving,   135
    Will not peruse the foils, so that, with ease,
    Or with a little shuffling, you may choose
    A sword unbated,° and in a pass of practice°
    Requite him for your father.
LAERTES: I will do 't.
    And for that purpose I'll anoint my sword.   140
    I bought an unction° of a mountebank°
    So mortal that, but dip a knife in it,
    Where it draws blood no cataplasm° so rare,
    Collected from all simples° that have virtue
    Under the moon, can save the thing from death   145
    That is but scratch'd withal. I'll touch my point
    With this contagion, that, if I gall° him slightly,
    It may be death.
KING: Let's further think of this,
    Weigh what convenience both of time and means
    May fit us to our shape.° If this should fail,   150
    And that our drift look through our bad
        performance,°
    'Twere better not assay'd. Therefore this project
    Should have a back or second, that might hold
    If this did blast in proof.° Soft, let me see.
    We'll make a solemn wager on your cunnings —   155
    I ha 't!
    When in your motion you are hot and dry —
    As° make your bouts more violent to that end —
    And that he calls for drink, I'll have prepar'd
        him
    A chalice for the nonce,° whereon but sipping,   160
    If he by chance escape your venom'd stuck,°
    Our purpose may hold there. [*A cry within.*] But
        stay, what noise?

(*Enter Queen.*)

QUEEN: One woe doth tread upon another's heel,
    So fast they follow. Your sister's drowned,
        Laertes.
LAERTES: Drown'd! O, where?   165
QUEEN: There is a willow grows askant° the brook
    That shows his hoar° leaves in the glassy stream;
    Therewith fantastic garlands did she make

---

134. remiss: Negligently unsuspicious. **135. generous:** Noble-minded.　**138. unbated:** Not blunted, having no button.　**pass of practice:** Treacherous thrust.　**141. unction:** Ointment.　**mountebank:** Quack doctor.　**143. cataplasm:** Plaster or poultice.　**144. simples:** Herbs.　**147. gall:** Graze, wound.　**150. shape:** Part that we propose to act. **151. drift . . . performance:** I.e., intention be disclosed by our bungling.　**154. blast in proof:** Burst in the test (like a cannon).　**158. As:** And you should.　**160. nonce:** Occasion. **161. stuck:** Thrust (from *stoccado,* a fencing term). **166. askant:** Aslant.　**167. hoar:** White or gray.

Of crow-flowers, nettles, daisies, and long
    purples°
170 That liberal° shepherds give a grosser name,
    But our cold° maids do dead men's fingers call
        them.
    There on the pendent boughs her crownet° weeds
    Clamb'ring to hang, an envious sliver° broke,
    When down her weedy° trophies and herself
175 Fell in the weeping brook. Her clothes spread
        wide,
    And mermaid-like awhile they bore her up,
    Which time she chanted snatches of old lauds,°
    As one incapable° of her own distress,
    Or like a creature native and indued°
180 Unto that element. But long it could not be
    Till that her garments, heavy with their drink,
    Pull'd the poor wretch from her melodious lay
    To muddy death.
LAERTES: Alas, then she is drown'd?
QUEEN: Drown'd, drown'd.
LAERTES: Too much of water hast thou, poor
185   Ophelia,
    And therefore I forbid my tears. But yet
    It is our trick;° nature her custom holds,
    Let shame say what it will. [*He weeps.*] When
        these are gone,
    The woman will be out.° Adieu, my lord.
190 I have a speech of fire, that fain would blaze,
    But that this folly drowns it.   (*Exit.*)
KING: Let's follow, Gertrude.
    How much I had to do to calm his rage!
    Now fear I this will give it start again;
    Therefore let's follow.   (*Exeunt.*)

{*ACT V • Scene 1*}°

(*Enter two Clowns*° [*with spades, etc.*])

FIRST CLOWN: Is she to be buried in Christian burial
    when she willfully seeks her own salvation?
SECOND CLOWN: I tell thee she is; therefore make her
    grave straight.° The crowner° hath sat on her, and
5   finds it Christian burial.

---

169. **long purples:** Early purple orchids.   170. **liberal:** Free-spoken.   171. **cold:** Chaste.   172. **crownet:** Made into a chaplet or coronet.   173. **envious sliver:** Malicious branch. 174. **weedy:** I.e., of plants.   177. **lauds:** Hymns.   178. **incapable:** Lacking capacity to apprehend.   179. **indued:** Adapted by nature.   187. **It is our trick:** Weeping is our natural way (when sad).   188–89. **When . . . out:** When my tears are all shed, the woman in me will be expended, satisfied. V, I. **Location:** A churchyard. [S.D.] ***Clowns:*** Rustics.   4. **straight:** Straightway, immediately.   **crowner:** Coroner.

FIRST CLOWN: How can that be, unless she drown'd
    herself in her own defense?
SECOND CLOWN: Why, 'tis found so.
FIRST CLOWN: It must be "se offendendo";° it cannot
    be else. For here lies the point: if I drown myself   10
    wittingly, it argues an act, and an act hath three
    branches — it is to act, to do, and to perform.
    Argal,° she drown'd herself wittingly.
SECOND CLOWN: Nay, but hear you, goodman
    delver —   15
FIRST CLOWN: Give me leave. Here lies the water;
    good. Here stands the man; good. If the man go
    to this water, and drown himself, it is, will he,°
    nill he, he goes, mark you that. But if the water
    come to him and drown him, he drowns not him-   20
    self. Argal, he that is not guilty of his own death
    shortens not his own life.
SECOND CLOWN: But is this law?
FIRST CLOWN: Ay, marry, is 't — crowner's quest°
    law.   25
SECOND CLOWN: Will you ha' the truth on 't? If this
    had not been a gentlewoman, she should have been
    buried out o' Christian burial.
FIRST CLOWN: Why, there thou say'st.° And the more
    pity that great folk should have count'nance° in   30
    this world to drown or hang themselves, more than
    their even-Christen.° Come, my spade. There is no
    ancient gentlemen but gard'ners, ditchers, and
    grave-makers. They hold up Adam's profession.
SECOND CLOWN: Was he a gentleman?   35
FIRST CLOWN: 'A was the first that ever bore arms.
[SECOND CLOWN: Why, he had none.
FIRST CLOWN: What, art a heathen? How dost thou
    understand the Scripture? The Scripture says
    "Adam digg'd." Could he dig without arms?] I'll   40
    put another question to thee. If thou answerest me
    not to the purpose, confess thyself° —
SECOND CLOWN: Go to.
FIRST CLOWN: What is he that builds stronger than ei-
    ther the mason, the shipwright, or the carpenter?   45
SECOND CLOWN: The gallows-maker, for that frame
    outlives a thousand tenants.
FIRST CLOWN: I like thy wit well, in good faith. The
    gallows does well, but how does it well? It does
    well to those that do ill. Now thou dost ill to say   50
    the gallows is built stronger than the church. Argal,
    the gallows may do well to thee. To 't again, come.

---

9. **se offendendo:** A comic mistake for *se defendendo,* term used in verdicts of justifiable homicide.   13. **Argal:** Corruption of *ergo,* therefore.   18. **will he:** Will he not. 24. **quest:** Inquest.   29. **there you say'st:** That's right. 30. **count'nance:** Privilege.   32. **even-Christen:** Fellow Christian.   42. **confess thyself:** The saying continues, "and be hanged."

SECOND CLOWN: "Who builds stronger than a mason, a shipwright, or a carpenter?"

55 FIRST CLOWN: Ay, tell me that, and unyoke.°

SECOND CLOWN: Marry, now I can tell.

FIRST CLOWN: To 't.

SECOND CLOWN: Mass,° I cannot tell.

(Enter Hamlet and Horatio [at a distance].)

FIRST CLOWN: Cudgel thy brains no more about it, for
60 your dull ass will not mend his pace with beating; and, when you are ask'd this question next, say "a grave-maker." The houses he makes lasts till doomsday. Go, get thee in, and fetch me a stoup° of liquor.

[Exit Second Clown. First Clown digs.]
(Song.)

65 "In youth, when I did love, did love,°
    Methought it was very sweet,
    To contract — O — the time for — a — my behove,°
    O, methought there — a — was nothing — a — meet."°

HAMLET: Has this fellow no feeling of his business,
70 that 'a sings at grave-making?

HORATIO: Custom hath made it in him a property of easiness.°

HAMLET: 'Tis e'en so. The hand of little employment hath the daintier sense.°

(Song.)

75 FIRST CLOWN: "But age, with his stealing steps,
    Hath claw'd me in his clutch,
    And hath shipped me into the land,°
    As if I had never been such."

[Throws up a skull.]

HAMLET: That skull had a tongue in it, and could sing
80 once. How the knave jowls° it to the ground, as if 'twere Cain's jaw-bone, that did the first murder! This might be the pate of a politician,° which this ass now o'erreaches,° one that would circumvent God, might it not?

HORATIO: It might, my lord.   85

HAMLET: Or of a courtier, which could say "Good morrow, sweet lord! How dost thou, sweet lord?" This might be my Lord Such-a-one, that prais'd my Lord Such-a-one's horse when 'a meant to beg it, might it not?   90

HORATIO: Ay, my lord.

HAMLET: Why, e'en so, and now my Lady Worm's, chapless,° and knock'd about the mazzard° with a sexton's spade. Here's fine revolution,° an° we had the trick to see 't. Did these bones cost no more the 95
breeding,° but to play at loggats° with them? Mine ache to think on 't.

(Song.)

FIRST CLOWN: "A pick-axe, and a spade, a spade,
    For and° a shrouding sheet;
    O, a pit of clay for to be made   100
    For such a guest is meet."

[Throws up another skull.]

HAMLET: There's another. Why may not that be the skull of a lawyer? Where be his quiddities° now, his quillities,° his cases, his tenures,° and his tricks? Why does he suffer this mad knave now to knock 105
him about the sconce° with a dirty shovel, and will not tell him of his action of battery? Hum! This fellow might be in 's time a great buyer of land, with his statutes, his recognizances,° his fines, his double° vouchers,° his recoveries.° [Is this the fine of 110
his fines, and the recovery of his recoveries,] to have his fine pate full of fine dirt?° Will his vouchers vouch him no more of his purchases, and double [ones too], than the length and breadth of a pair of indentures?° The very conveyances° of his lands 115

---

55. **unyoke:** After this great effort you may unharness the team of your wits.   58. **Mass:** By the Mass.   63. **stoup:** Two-quart measure.   65. **In . . . love:** This and the two following stanzas, with nonsensical variations, are from a poem attributed to Lord Vaux and printed in *Tottel's Miscellany* (1557). The O and a (for "ah") seemingly are the grunts of the digger.   67. **To contract . . . behove:** To make a betrothal agreement for my benefit (?).   68. **meet:** Suitable, i.e., more suitable.   71–72. **property of easiness:** Something he can do easily and without thinking.   74. **daintier sense:** More delicate sense of feeling.   77. **into the land:** Toward my grave (?) (but note the lack of rhyme in *steps, land*).   80. **jowls:** Dashes.   82. **politician:** Schemer, plotter.   83. **o'erreaches:** Circumvents, gets the better of (with a quibble on the literal sense).

93. **chapless:** Having no lower jaw.   **mazzard:** Head (literally, a drinking vessel).   94. **revolution:** Change.   **an:** If.   96. **the breeding:** In the breeding, raising.   **loggats:** A game in which pieces of hardwood are thrown to lie as near as possible to a stake.   99. **For and:** And moreover.   103. **quiddities:** Subtleties, quibbles (from Latin *quid*, a thing).   104. **quillities:** Verbal niceties, subtle distinctions (variation of *quiddities*).   **tenures:** The holding of a piece of property or office, or the conditions or period of such holding.   106. **sconce:** Head.   109. **statutes, recognizances:** Legal documents guaranteeing a debt by attaching land and property.   109–10. **fines, recoveries:** Ways of converting entailed estates into "fee simple" or freehold.   110. **double:** Signed by two signatories.   **vouchers:** Guarantees of the legality of a title to real estate.   110–12. **fine of his fines . . . fine pate . . . fine dirt:** End of his legal maneuvers . . . elegant head . . . minutely sifted dirt.   114–15. **pair of indentures:** Legal document drawn up in duplicate on a single sheet and then cut apart on a zigzag line so that each pair was uniquely matched. (Hamlet may refer to two rows of teeth, or dentures.)   115. **conveyances:** Deeds.

will scarcely lie in this box,° and must th' inheritor° himself have no more, ha?

HORATIO: Not a jot more, my lord.

HAMLET: Is not parchment made of sheep-skins?

120 HORATIO: Ay, my lord, and of calf-skins too.

HAMLET: They are sheep and calves which seek out assurance in that.° I will speak to this fellow. — Whose grave's this, sirrah?°

FIRST CLOWN: Mine, sir.

125 [*Sings.*] "O, a pit of clay for to be made [For such a guest is meet]."

HAMLET: I think it be thine, indeed, for thou liest in 't.

FIRST CLOWN: You lie out on 't, sir, and therefore 'tis

130 not yours. For my part, I do not lie in 't, yet it is mine.

HAMLET: Thou dost lie in 't, to be in 't and say it is thine. 'Tis for the dead, not for the quick;° therefore thou liest.

135 FIRST CLOWN: 'Tis a quick lie, sir; 'twill away again from me to you.

HAMLET: What man dost thou dig it for?

FIRST CLOWN: For no man, sir.

HAMLET: What woman, then?

140 FIRST CLOWN: For none, neither.

HAMLET: Who is to be buried in 't?

FIRST CLOWN: One that was a woman, sir, but, rest her soul, she's dead.

HAMLET: How absolute° the knave is! We must speak

145 by the card,° or equivocation° will undo us. By the Lord, Horatio, this three years I have taken note of it: the age is grown so pick'd° that the toe of the peasant comes so near the heel of the courtier, he galls his kibe.° How long hast thou been a grave-

150 maker?

FIRST CLOWN: Of all the days i' th' year, I came to 't that day that our last king Hamlet overcame Fortinbras.

HAMLET: How long is that since?

155 FIRST CLOWN: Cannot you tell that? Every fool can tell that. It was that very day that young Hamlet was born — he that is mad, and sent into England.

HAMLET: Ay, marry, why was he sent into England?

FIRST CLOWN: Why, because 'a was mad. 'A shall re-

160 cover his wits there, or, if 'a do not, 'tis no great matter there.

HAMLET: Why?

FIRST CLOWN: 'Twill not be seen in him there. There the men are as mad as he.

HAMLET: How came he mad? 165

FIRST CLOWN: Very strangely, they say.

HAMLET: How strangely?

FIRST CLOWN: Faith, e'en with losing his wits.

HAMLET: Upon what ground?

FIRST CLOWN: Why, here in Denmark. I have been 170 sexton here, man and boy, thirty years.

HAMLET: How long will a man lie i' th' earth ere he rot?

FIRST CLOWN: Faith, if 'a be not rotten before 'a die — as we have many pocky° corses [now-a- 175 days], that will scarce hold the laying in — 'a will last you some eight year or nine year. A tanner will last you nine year.

HAMLET: Why he more than another?

FIRST CLOWN: Why, sir, his hide is so tann'd with his 180 trade that 'a will keep out water a great while, and your water is a sore decayer of your whoreson dead body. [*Picks up a skull*] Here's a skull now hath lain you° i' th' earth three and twenty years.

HAMLET: Whose was it? 185

FIRST CLOWN: A whoreson mad fellow's it was. Whose do you think it was?

HAMLET: Nay, I know not.

FIRST CLOWN: A pestilence on him for a mad rogue! 'A pour'd a flagon of Rhenish° on my head once. This 190 same skull, sir, was Yorick's skull, the King's jester.

HAMLET: This?

FIRST CLOWN: E'en that.

HAMLET: [Let me see.] [*Takes the skull.*] Alas, poor 195 Yorick! I knew him, Horatio, a fellow of infinite jest, of most excellent fancy. He hath borne me on his back a thousand times; and now, how abhorr'd in my imagination it is! My gorge rises at it. Here hung those lips that I have kiss'd I know not how 200 oft. Where be your gibes now? Your gambols, your songs, your flashes of merriment that were wont to set the table on a roar? Not one now, to mock your own grinning? Quite chap-fall'n?° Now get you to my lady's chamber, and tell her, let 205 her paint an inch thick, to this favor° she must come; make her laugh at that. Prithee, Horatio, tell me one thing.

HORATIO: What's that, my lord?

HAMLET: Dost thou think Alexander look'd o' this 210 fashion i' th' earth?

---

116. this box: The skull.   **inheritor:** Possessor, owner.
122. assurance in that: Safety in legal parchments.
123. sirrah: Term of address to inferiors.   **133. quick:** Living.   **144. absolute:** Positive, decided.   **145. by the card:** By the mariner's card on which the points of the compass were marked, i.e., with precision.   **equivocation:** Ambiguity in the use of terms.   **147. pick'd:** Refined, fastidious.
149. galls his kibe: Chafes the courtier's chilblain (a swelling or sore caused by cold).

175. pocky: Rotten, diseased (literally, with the pox, or syphilis).   **184. lain you:** Lain.   **190. Rhenish:** Rhine wine.   **204. chap-fall'n:** (1) Lacking the lower jaw, (2) dejected.   **206. favor:** Aspect, appearance.

HORATIO: E'en so.

HAMLET: And smelt so? Pah! [*Puts down the skull.*]

HORATIO: E'en so, my lord.

215 HAMLET: To what base uses we may return, Horatio!
    Why may not imagination trace the noble dust of
    Alexander, till 'a find it stopping a bung-hole?

HORATIO: 'Twere to consider too curiously,° to con-
    sider so.

220 HAMLET: No, faith, not a jot, but to follow him thither
    with modesty° enough, and likelihood to lead it. [As
    thus]: Alexander died, Alexander was buried, Alexan-
    der returneth to dust; the dust is earth; of earth we
    make loam;° and why of that loam, whereto he was
225 converted, might they not stop a beer-barrel?
    Imperious° Caesar, dead and turn'd to clay,
    Might stop a hole to keep the wind away.
    O, that that earth which kept the world in awe
    Should patch a wall t' expel the winter's flaw!°
230 But soft, but soft awhile! Here comes the King.

(*Enter King, Queen, Laertes, and the Corse* [*of Ophelia, in procession, with Priest, Lords etc.*].)

    The Queen, the courtiers. Who is this they
        follow?
    And with such maimed rites? This doth betoken
    The corse they follow did with desp'rate hand
    Fordo it° own life. 'Twas of some estate.°
235 Couch° we awhile, and mark.
                        [*He and Horatio conceal themselves.*
                        Ophelia's body is taken to the grave.]

LAERTES: What ceremony else?

HAMLET [*to Horatio*]: That is Laertes, a very noble
    youth. Mark.

LAERTES: What ceremony else?

PRIEST: Her obsequies have been as far enlarg'd
240 As we have warranty. Her death was doubtful,
    And, but that great command o'ersways the
        order,
    She should in ground unsanctified been lodg'd
    Till the last trumpet. For° charitable prayers,
    Shards,° flints, and pebbles should be thrown on
        her.
245 Yet here she is allow'd her virgin crants,°
    Her maiden strewments,° and the bringing home
    Of bell and burial.°

LAERTES: Must there no more be done?

PRIEST: No more be done.
    We should profane the service of the dead
    To sing a requiem and such rest to her   250
    As to peace-parted souls.

LAERTES: Lay her i' th' earth,
    And from her fair and unpolluted flesh
    May violets° spring! I tell thee, churlish priest,
    A minist'ring angel shall my sister be
    When thou liest howling!

HAMLET [*to Horatio*]:   What, the fair Ophelia!   255

QUEEN [*scattering flowers*]: Sweets to the sweet!
        Farewell.
    I hoped thou shouldst have been my Hamlet's
        wife.
    I thought thy bride-bed to have deck'd, sweet
        maid,
    And not have strew'd thy grave.

LAERTES: O, treble woe
    Fall ten times treble on that cursed head   260
    Whose wicked deed thy most ingenious sense°
    Depriv'd thee of! Hold off the earth awhile,
    Till I have caught her once more in mine arms.
        [*Leaps into the grave and embraces Ophelia.*]
    Now pile your dust upon the quick and dead,
    Till of this flat a mountain you have made   265
    T 'o'ertop old Pelion,° or the skyish head
    Of blue Olympus.°

HAMLET [*coming forward*]: What is he whose grief
    Bears such an emphasis, whose phrase of sorrow
    Conjures the wand'ring stars,° and makes them
        stand   270
    Like wonder-wounded hearers? This is I,
    Hamlet the Dane.°

LAERTES: The devil take thy soul!
                            [*Grappling with him.*]

HAMLET: Thou pray'st not well.
    I prithee, take thy fingers from my throat;
    For, though I am not splenitive° and rash,   275
    Yet have I in me something dangerous,
    Which let thy wisdom fear. Hold off thy hand.

KING: Pluck them asunder.

QUEEN: Hamlet, Hamlet!

ALL: Gentlemen!

HORATIO: Good my lord, be quiet.
                        [*Hamlet and Horatio are parted.*]

HAMLET: Why, I will fight with him upon this theme 280
    Until my eyelids will no longer wag.

---

218. curiously: Minutely. **221. modesty:** Moderation.
224. loam: Clay mixture for brickmaking or other clay use.
226. Imperious: Imperial. **229. flaw:** Gust of wind.
234. Fordo it: Destroy its. **estate:** Rank. **235. Couch:**
Hide, lurk. **243. For:** In place of. **244. Shards:** Broken
bits of pottery. **245. crants:** Garland. **246. strewments:**
Traditional strewing of flowers. **246–47. bringing . . .
burial:** Laying to rest of the body in consecrated ground, to
the sound of the bell.

253. violets: See IV, v, 187 and note. **261. ingenious
sense:** Mind endowed with finest qualities. **266, 267. Pelion, Olympus:** Mountains in the north of Thessaly; see also
Ossa at line 297. **270. wand'ring stars:** Planets.
272. the Dane: This title normally signifies the king, see I, i,
15 and note. **275. splenitive:** Quick-tempered.

QUEEN: O my son, what theme?

HAMLET: I lov'd Ophelia. Forty thousand brothers
Could not with all their quantity of love
285 Make up my sum. What wilt thou do for her?

KING: O, he is mad, Laertes.

QUEEN: For love of God, forbear him.

HAMLET: 'Swounds,° show me what thou' do.
Woo 't° weep? Woo 't fight? Woo 't fast? Woo 't
tear thyself?
290 Woo 't drink up eisel?° Eat a crocodile?
I'll do 't. Dost thou come here to whine?
To outface me with leaping in her grave?
Be buried quick° with her, and so will I.
And, if thou prate of mountains, let them throw
295 Millions of acres on us, till our ground,
Singeing his pate° against the burning zone,°
Make Ossa° like a wart! Nay, an thou 'lt
mouth,°
I'll rant as well as thou.

QUEEN: This is mere° madness,
And thus a while the fit will work on him;
300 Anon, as patient as the female dove
When that her golden couplets° are disclos'd,°
His silence will sit drooping.

HAMLET: Hear you, sir.
What is the reason that you use me thus?
I lov'd you ever. But it is no matter.
305 Let Hercules himself do what he may,
The cat will mew, and dog will have his day.°

KING: I pray thee, good Horatio, wait upon him.
                        (*Exit Hamlet and Horatio.*)
[*To Laertes.*] Strengthen your patience in° our
last night's speech;
We'll put the matter to the present push.° —
Good Gertrude, set some watch over your
310 son. —
This grave shall have a living° monument.
An hour of quiet shortly shall we see;
Till then, in patience our proceeding be. (*Exeunt.*)

288. 'Swounds: By His (Christ's) wounds.   289. Woo 't:
Wilt thou.   290. eisel: Vinegar.   293. quick: Alive.
296. his pate: Its head, i.e., top.   burning zone: Sun's orbit.
297. Ossa: Another mountain in Thessaly. (In their war
against the Olympian gods, the giants attempted to heap
Ossa, Pelion, and Olympus on one another to scale heaven.)
mouth: Rant.   298. mere: Utter.   301. golden couplets:
Two baby pigeons, covered with yellow down.   disclos'd:
Hatched.   305–6. Let . . . day: Despite any blustering attempts at interference every person will sooner or later do
what he must do.   308. in: By recalling.   309. present
push: Immediate test.   311. living: Lasting; also refers (for
Laertes' benefit) to the plot against Hamlet.

{*Scene II*}°

(*Enter Hamlet and Horatio.*)

HAMLET: So much for this, sir; now shall you see
the other.°
You do remember all the circumstance?

HORATIO: Remember it, my lord!

HAMLET: Sir, in my heart there was a kind of
fighting
That would not let me sleep. Methought I lay   5
Worse than the mutines° in the bilboes.° Rashly,°
And prais'd be rashness for it — let us know,°
Our indiscretion sometime serves us well
When our deep plots do pall,° and that should
learn° us
There's a divinity that shapes our ends,   10
Rough-hew° them how we will —

HORATIO: That is most certain.

HAMLET: Up from my cabin,
My sea-gown scarf'd about me, in the dark
Grop'd I to find out them, had my desire,
Finger'd° their packet, and in fine° withdrew   15
To mine own room again, making so bold,
My fears forgetting manners, to unseal
Their grand commission; where I found,
Horatio —
Ah, royal knavery! — an exact command,
Larded° with many several sorts of reasons   20
Importing° Denmark's health and England's too,
With, ho, such bugs° and goblins in my life,°
That, on the supervise,° no leisure bated,°
No, not to stay the grinding of the axe,
My head should be struck off.

HORATIO: Is 't possible?   25

HAMLET: Here's the commission; read it at more
leisure.   [*Gives document.*]
But wilt thou hear now how I did proceed?

HORATIO: I beseech you.

HAMLET: Being thus benetted round with villainies,
Or I could make a prologue to my brains,   30
They had begun the play.° I sat me down,

V, II. Location: The castle.   1. see the other: Hear the
other news.   6. mutines: Mutineers.   bilboes: Shackles.
Rashly: On impulse (this adverb goes with lines 12ff.).
7. know: Acknowledge.   9. pall: Fail.   learn: Teach.
11. Rough-hew: Shape roughly.   15. Finger'd: Pilfered,
pinched.   in fine: Finally, in conclusion.   20. Larded: Enriched.   21. Importing: Relating to.   22. bugs: Bugbears,
hobgoblins.   in my life: To be feared if I were allowed to
live.   23. supervise: Reading.   leisure bated: Delay allowed.   30–31. Or . . . play: Before I could consciously
turn my brain to the matter, it had started working on a
plan. (Or means ere.)

Devis'd a new commission, wrote it fair.°
I once did hold it, as our statists° do,
A baseness° to write fair, and labor'd much
35 How to forget that learning, but, sir, now
It did me yeoman's° service. Wilt thou know
Th' effect° of what I wrote?
HORATIO: Ay, good my lord.
HAMLET: An earnest conjuration from the King,
As England was his faithful tributary,
As love between them like the palm might
40   flourish,
As peace should still her wheaten garland° wear
And stand a comma° 'tween their amities,
And many such-like as's° of great charge,°
That, on the view and knowing of these
        contents,
45 Without debasement further, more or less,
He should those bearers put to sudden death,
Not shriving time° allow'd.
HORATIO: How was this seal'd?
HAMLET: Why, even in that was heaven ordinant.°
I had my father's signet° in my purse,
50 Which was the model of that Danish seal;
Folded the writ up in the form of th' other,
Subscrib'd° it, gave 't th' impression,° plac'd it
        safely,
The changeling° never known. Now, the next day
Was our sea-fight, and what to this was sequent
55 Thou knowest already.
HORATIO: So Guildenstern and Rosencrantz go
        to 't.
HAMLET: [Why, man, they did make love to this
        employment.]
They are not near my conscience. Their defeat
Does by their own insinuation° grow.
60 'Tis dangerous when the baser nature comes
Between the pass° and fell° incensed points
Of mighty opposites.
HORATIO: Why, what a king is this!

HAMLET: Does it not, think thee, stand° me now
        upon —
He that hath killed my king and whor'd my
        mother,
Popp'd in between th' election° and my hopes,   65
Thrown out his angle° for my proper° life,
And with such coz'nage° — is 't not perfect
        conscience
[To quit° him with this arm? And is 't not to be
        damn'd
To let this canker° of our nature come
In further evil?   70
HORATIO: It must be shortly known to him from
        England
What is the issue of the business there.
HAMLET: It will be short. The interim is mine,
And a man's life 's no more than to say "One."°
But I am very sorry, good Horatio,   75
That to Laertes I forgot myself,
For by the image of my cause I see
The portraiture of his. I'll court his favors.
But, sure, the bravery° of his grief did put me
Into a tow'ring passion.
HORATIO: Peace, who comes here?] 80

(*Enter a Courtier* [*Osric*].)

OSRIC: Your lordship is right welcome back to
        Denmark.
HAMLET: I humbly thank you, sir. [*To Horatio.*] Dost
        know this water-fly?
HORATIO: No, my good lord.   85
HAMLET: Thy state is the more gracious, for 'tis a vice
        to know him. He hath much land, and fertile. Let
        a beast be lord of beasts, and his crib shall stand at
        the King's mess.° 'Tis a chough,° but, as I say, spa-
        cious in the possession of dirt.   90
OSRIC: Sweet lord, if your lordship were at leisure, I
        should impart a thing to you from his Majesty.
HAMLET: I will receive it, sir, with all diligence of
        spirit. Put your bonnet to his right use; 'tis for the
        head.   95
OSRIC: I thank your lordship, it is very hot.

---

32. **fair:** In a clear hand.   33. **statists:** Statesmen.
34. **baseness:** Lower-class trait.   36. **yeoman's:** Substantial,
workmanlike.   37. **effect:** Purport.   41. **wheaten garland:**
Symbolic of fruitful agriculture, of peace.   42. **comma:** Indicating continuity, link.   43. **as's:** (1) The "whereases" of
formal document, (2) asses.   **charge:** (1) Import, (2) burden.   47. **shriving time:** Time for confession and absolu-
tion.   48. **ordinant:** Directing.   49. **signet:** Small seal.
52. **Subscrib'd:** Signed.   **impression:** With a wax seal.
53. **changeling:** The substituted letter (literally, a fairy child
substituted for a human one).   59. **insinuation:** Interference.   61. **pass:** Thrust.   **fell:** Fierce.

63. **stand:** Become incumbent.   65. **election:** The Danish
monarch was "elected" by a small number of high-
ranking electors.   66. **angle:** Fishing line.   **proper:** Very.
67. **coz'nage:** Trickery.   68. **quit:** Repay.   69. **canker:** Ulcer.   74. **a man's...."One":** To take a man's life requires
no more than to count to one as one duels.   79. **bravery:**
Bravado.   87–89. **Let . . . mess:** If a man, no matter how
beastlike, is as rich in possessions as Osric, he may eat at the
king's table.   89. **chough:** Chattering jackdaw.

HAMLET: No, believe me, 'tis very cold; the wind is northerly.

OSRIC: It is indifferent° cold, my lord, indeed.

100 HAMLET: But yet methinks it is very sultry and hot for my complexion.°

OSRIC: Exceedingly, my lord; it is very sultry, as 'twere — I cannot tell how. My lord, his Majesty bade me signify to you that 'a has laid a great wa-
105 ger on your head. Sir, this is the matter —

HAMLET: I beseech you, remember —

[*Hamlet moves him to put on his hat.*]

OSRIC: Nay, good my lord; for my ease,° in good faith. Sir, here is newly come to court Laertes — believe me, an absolute gentleman, full of most excellent
110 differences,° of very soft society° and great show-ing.° Indeed, to speak feelingly° of him, he is the card° or calendar° of gentry,° for you shall find in him the continent of what part° a gentleman would see.

115 HAMLET: Sir, his definement° suffers no perdition° in you, though, I know, to divide him inventorially° would dozy° th' arithmetic of memory, and yet but yaw° neither° in respect of° his quick sail. But, in the verity of extolment,° I take him to be a soul of
120 great article,° and his infusion° of such dearth and rareness,° as, to make true diction° of him, his semblable° is his mirror, and who else would trace° him, his umbrage,° nothing more.

OSRIC: Your lordship speaks most infallibly of him.

125 HAMLET: The concernancy,° sir? Why do we wrap the gentleman in our more rawer breath?°

OSRIC: Sir?

HORATIO: Is 't not possible to understand in another tongue?° You will do 't,° sir, really.

HAMLET: What imports the nomination° of this 130 gentleman?

OSRIC: Of Laertes?

HORATIO [*to Hamlet*]: His purse is empty already; all 's golden words are spent.

HAMLET: Of him, sir.   135

OSRIC: I know you are not ignorant —

HAMLET: I would you did, sir; yet, in faith, if you did, it would not much approve° me. Well, sir?

OSRIC: You are not ignorant of what excellence Laertes is —   140

HAMLET: I dare not confess that, lest I should com-pare° with him in excellence; but to know a man well were to know himself.°

OSRIC: I mean, sir, for his weapon; but in the imputation laid on him by them,° in his meed° he's unfellow'd.° 145

HAMLET: What's his weapon?

OSRIC: Rapier and dagger.

HAMLET: That's two of his weapons — but well.

OSRIC: The King, sir, hath wager'd with him six Bar-bary horses, against the which he has impawn'd,° 150 as I take it, six French rapiers and poniards, with their assigns,° as girdle, hangers,° and so. Three of the carriages,° in faith, are very dear to fancy,° very responsive° to the hilts, most delicate° car-riages, and of very liberal conceit.°   155

HAMLET: What call you the carriages?

HORATIO [*to Hamlet*]: I knew you must be edified by the margent° ere you had done.

OSRIC: The carriages, sir, are the hangers.

HAMLET: The phrase would be more germane to the 160 matter if we could carry a cannon by our sides; I would it might be hangers till then. But, on: six Barb'ry horses against six French swords, their as-

---

99. indifferent: Somewhat.   **101. complexion:** Tempera-ment.   **107. for my ease:** A conventional reply declining the invitation to put his hat back on.   **110. differences:** Special qualities.   **soft society:** Agreeable manners.   **110–11. great showing:** Distinguished appearance.   **111. feelingly:** With just perception.   **112. card:** Chart, map.   **calendar:** Guide.   **gentry:** Good breeding.   **113. the continent . . . part:** One who contains in him all the qualities (a *continent* is that which contains).   **115. definement:** Definition. (Hamlet proceeds to mock Osric by using his lofty diction back at him.)   **perdition:** Loss, diminution.   **116. divide him inventorially:** Enumerate his graces.   **117. dozy:** Dizzy.   **118. yaw:** To move unsteadily (said of a ship).   **neither:** For all that.   **in respect of:** In comparison with.   **118–19. in . . . extolment:** In true praise (of him).   **120. article:** Moment or importance.   **infusion:** Essence, character im-parted by nature.   **120–21. dearth and rareness:** Rarity.   **121. make true diction:** Speak truly.   **122. semblable:** Only true likeness.   **who . . . trace:** Any other person who would wish to follow.   **123. umbrage:** Shadow.   **125. concer-nancy:** Import, relevance.   **126. breath:** Speech.

128–29. to understand . . . tongue: For Osric to understand when someone else speaks in his manner. (Horatio twits Os-ric for not being able to understand the kind of flowery speech he himself uses when Hamlet speaks in such a vein.)   **129. You will do't:** You can if you try.   **130. nomination:** Naming.   **138. approve:** Commend.   **141. compare:** Seem to compete.   **142–43. but . . . himself:** For, to recognize excellence in another man, one must know oneself.   **144–45. imputation . . . them:** Reputation given him by others.   **145. meed:** Merit.   **unfellow'd:** Unmatched.   **150. impawn'd:** Staked, wagered.   **152. assigns:** Appurte-nances.   **hangers:** Straps on the sword belt (*girdle*) from which the sword hung.   **153. carriages:** An affected way of saying *hangers;* literally, gun-carriages.   **dear to fancy:** Fancifully designed, tasteful.   **154. responsive:** Correspond-ing closely, matching.   **delicate:** I.e., in workmanship.   **155. liberal conceit:** Elaborate design.   **158. margent:** Mar-gin of a book, place for explanatory notes.

165 signs, and three liberal-conceited carriages; that's the French bet against the Danish. Why is this im-pawn'd, as you call it?

OSRIC: The King, sir, hath laid,° sir, that in a dozen passes° between yourself and him, he shall not ex-ceed you three hits. He hath laid on twelve for
170 nine, and it would come to immediate trial, if your lordship would vouchsafe the answer.

HAMLET: How if I answer no?

OSRIC: I mean, my lord, the opposition of your person in trial.

175 HAMLET: Sir, I will walk here in the hall. If it please his Majesty, it is the breathing time° of day with me. Let the foils be brought, the gentleman willing, and the King hold his purpose, I will win for him an I can; if not, I will gain nothing but my shame
180 and the odd hits.

OSRIC: Shall I deliver you so?

HAMLET: To this effect, sir — after what flourish your nature will.

OSRIC: I commend my duty to your lordship.

185 HAMLET: Yours, yours. [*Exit Osric.*] He does well to commend it himself; there are no tongues else for 's turn.

HORATIO: This lapwing° runs away with the shell on his head.

190 HAMLET: 'A did comply, sir, with his dug,° before 'a suck'd it. Thus has he — and many more of the same breed that I know the drossy° age dotes on — only got the tune° of the time and, out of an habit of encounter,° a kind of yesty° collection,°
195 which carries them through and through the most fann'd and winnow'd° opinions; and do but blow them to their trial, the bubbles are out.°

(*Enter a Lord.*)

LORD: My lord, his Majesty commended him to you by young Osric, who brings back to him that you
200 attend him in the hall. He sends to know if your

pleasure hold to play with Laertes, or that you will take longer time.

HAMLET: I am constant to my purposes; they follow the King's pleasure. If his fitness speaks,° mine is ready; now or whensoever, provided I be so able 205 as now.

LORD: The King and Queen and all are coming down.

HAMLET: In happy time.°

LORD: The Queen desires you to use some gentle en-tertainment° to Laertes before you fall to play. 210

HAMLET: She well instructs me.   [*Exit Lord.*]

HORATIO: You will lose, my lord.

HAMLET: I do not think so. Since he went into France, I have been in continual practice; I shall win at the odds. But thou wouldst not think how ill all's here 215 about my heart; but it is no matter.

HORATIO: Nay, good my lord —

HAMLET: It is but foolery, but it is such a kind of gain-giving,° as would perhaps trouble a woman.

HORATIO: If your mind dislike anything, obey it. I 220 will forestall their repair hither, and say you are not fit.

HAMLET: Not a whit, we defy augury. There is special providence in the fall of a sparrow. If it be now, 'tis not to come; if it be not to come, it will be now, if 225 it be not now, yet it will come. The readiness is all. Since no man of aught he leaves knows what is 't to leave betimes,° let be.

(*A table prepar'd. [Enter] trumpets, drums, and Offi-cers with cushions; King, Queen, [Osric,] and all the State; foils, daggers, [and wine borne in;] and Laertes.*)

KING: Come, Hamlet, come, and take this hand from me.
          [*The King puts Laertes' hand into Hamlet's.*]

HAMLET: Give me your pardon, sir. I have done you wrong,   230
But pardon 't, as you are a gentleman.
This presence° knows,
And you must needs have heard, how I am punish'd
With a sore distraction. What I have done
That might your nature, honor, and exception°   235
Roughly awake, I here proclaim was madness.
Was 't Hamlet wrong'd Laertes? Never Hamlet.
If Hamlet from himself be ta'en away,
And when he's not himself does wrong Laertes,

---

167. **laid:** Wagered.   168. **passes:** Bouts. (The odds of the betting are hard to explain. Possibly the king bets that Ham-let will win at least five out of twelve, at which point Laertes raises the odds against himself by betting he will win nine.) 176. **breathing time:** Exercise period.   188. **lapwing:** A bird that draws intruders away from its nest and was thought to run about when newly hatched with its head in the shell; a seeming reference to Osric's hat.   190. **com-ply . . . dug:** Observe ceremonious formality toward his mother's teat.   192. **drossy:** Frivolous.   193. **tune:** Tem-per, mood, manner of speech.   194. **habit of encounter:** Demeanor of social intercourse.   **yesty:** Yeasty, frothy. **collection:** I.e., of current phrases.   196. **fann'd and win-now'd:** Select and refined.   196–97. **blow . . . out:** Put them to the test, and their ignorance is exposed.

---

204. **If . . . speaks:** If his readiness answers to the time. 208. **In happy time:** A phrase of courtesy indicating ac-ceptance.   209–10. **entertainment:** Greeting.   219. **gain-giving:** Misgiving.   227–28. **what . . . betimes:** What is the best time to leave it.   232. **presence:** Royal assembly. 235. **exception:** Disapproval.

240 Then Hamlet does it not, Hamlet denies it.
Who does it, then? His madness. If 't be so,
Hamlet is of the faction that is wrong'd;
His madness is poor Hamlet's enemy.
[Sir, in this audience,]
245 Let my disclaiming from a purpos'd evil
Free me so far in your most generous thoughts
That I have shot my arrow o'er the house
And hurt my brother.
LAERTES: I am satisfied in nature,°
Whose motive in this case should stir me most
250 To my revenge. But in my terms of honor
I stand aloof, and will no reconcilement
Till by some elder masters of known honor
I have a voice° and precedent of peace
To keep my name ungor'd. But till that time,
255 I do receive your offer'd love like love,
And will not wrong it.
HAMLET: I embrace it freely,
And will this brothers' wager frankly play.
Give us the foils. Come on.
LAERTES: Come, one for me.
HAMLET: I'll be your foil,° Laertes. In mine
ignorance
260 Your skill shall, like a star i' th' darkest night,
Stick fiery off° indeed
LAERTES: You mock me, sir.
HAMLET: No, by this hand.
KING: Give them the foils, young Osric. Cousin
Hamlet,
You know the wager?
HAMLET: Very well, my lord.
265 Your Grace has laid the odds o' th' weaker side.
KING: I do not fear it; I have seen you both.
But since he is better'd,° we have therefore odds.
LAERTES: This is too heavy, let me see another.
                    [Exchanges his foil for another.]
HAMLET: This likes me well. These foils have all a
length?
                    [They prepare to play.]
270 OSRIC: Ay, my good lord.
KING: Set me the stoups of wine upon that table.
If Hamlet give the first or second hit,
Or quit° in answer of the third exchange,
Let all the battlements their ordnance fire.
275 The King shall drink to Hamlet's better breath,

And in the cup an union° shall he throw,
Richer than that which four successive kings
In Denmark's crown have worn. Give me the
cups,
And let the kettle° to the trumpet speak,
The trumpet to the cannoneer without,   280
The cannons to the heavens, the heaven to earth,
"Now the King drinks to Hamlet." Come, begin.
                    (Trumpets the while.)
And you, the judges, bear a wary eye.
HAMLET: Come on sir.
LAERTES: Come, my lord. [They play. Hamlet scores   285
                    a hit.]
HAMLET: One.
LAERTES: No.
HAMLET: Judgment.
OSRIC: A hit, a very palpable hit.
                    (Drum, trumpets, and shot. Flourish.
                    A piece goes off.)
LAERTES: Well, again.
KING: Stay, give me drink. Hamlet, this pearl is
thine.   290
                    [He throws a pearl in Hamlet's cup and drinks.]
Here's to thy health. Give him the cup.
HAMLET: I'll play this bout first set it by awhile.
Come. [They play.] Another hit; what say you?
LAERTES: A touch, a touch. I do confess 't.
KING: Our son shall win.
QUEEN: He's fat,° and scant of breath.   295
Here, Hamlet, take my napkin,° rub thy brows.
The Queen carouses° to thy fortune, Hamlet.
HAMLET: Good madam!
KING: Gertrude, do not drink.
QUEEN: I will, my lord; I pray you pardon me.   300
                    [Drinks.]
KING [aside]: It is the pois'ned cup. It is too late.
HAMLET: I dare not drink yet, madam; by and by.
QUEEN: Come, let me wipe thy face.
LAERTES [to King]: My lord, I'll hit him now.
KING: I do not think 't.
LAERTES [aside]: And yet it is almost against my
conscience.   305
HAMLET: Come, for the third Laertes. You do but
dally.
I pray you, pass with your best violence;
I am afeard you make a wanton of me.°
LAERTES: Say you so? Come on.   [They play.]
OSRIC: Nothing, neither way.   310

---

248. **in nature:** As to my personal feelings.   253. **voice:**
Authoritative pronouncement.   259. **foil:** Thin metal background which sets a jewel off (with pun on the blunted
rapier for fencing).   261. **Stick fiery off:** Stand out brilliantly.   267. **is better'd:** Has improved; is the odds-on favorite.   273. **quit:** Repay (with a hit).

276. **union:** Pearl (so called, according to Pliny's *Natural
History*, IX, because pearls are *unique*, never identical).
279. **kettle:** Kettledrum.   295. **fat:** Not physically fit, out
of training.   296. **napkin:** Handkerchief.   297. **carouses:**
Drinks a toast.   308. **make . . . me:** Treat me like a spoiled
child, holding back to give me an advantage.

LAERTES: Have at you now!
　　　[*Laertes wounds Hamlet; then, in scuffling,*
　　　they change rapiers,° and Hamlet wounds Laertes.]
KING:　　　　　　　Part them! They are incens'd.
HAMLET: Nay, come, again.　　　[*The Queen falls.*]
OSRIC:　　　　　　　Look to the Queen there, ho!
HORATIO: They bleed on both sides. How is it, my
　　　lord?
OSRIC: How is 't, Laertes?
LAERTES: Why, as a woodcock° to mine own
315　　　springe,° Osric;
　　　I am justly kill'd with mine own treachery.
HAMLET: How does the Queen?
KING:　　　　　　　She swoons to see them bleed.
QUEEN: No, no, the drink, the drink — O my dear
　　　Hamlet —
　　　The drink, the drink! I am pois'ned.　　[*Dies.*]
320 HAMLET: O villainy! Ho, let the door be lock'd!
　　　Treachery! Seek it out.　　　[*Laertes falls.*]
LAERTES: It is here, Hamlet. Hamlet, thou art slain.
　　　No med'cine in the world can do thee good;
　　　In thee there is not half an hour's life.
325　　The treacherous instrument is in thy hand,
　　　Unbated° and envenom'd. The foul practice
　　　Hath turn'd itself on me. Lo, here I lie,
　　　Never to rise again. Thy mother's pois'ned.
　　　I can no more. The King, the King's to blame.
330 HAMLET: The point envenom'd too? Then, venom,
　　　to thy work.　　　[*Stabs the King.*]
ALL: Treason! Treason!
KING: O, yet defend me, friends; I am but hurt.
HAMLET: Here, thou incestuous, murd'rous, damned
　　　Dane,
　　　　　[*He forces the King to drink*
　　　　　the poisoned cup.]
　　　Drink off this potion. Is thy union° here?
　　　Follow my mother.　　　[*King dies.*]
335 LAERTES:　　　　　He is justly serv'd.
　　　It is a poison temper'd° by himself.
　　　Exchange forgiveness with me, noble Hamlet.
　　　Mine and my father's death come not upon thee,
　　　Nor thine on me!　　　[*Dies.*]
340 HAMLET: Heaven make thee free of it! I follow thee.
　　　I am dead, Horatio. Wretched Queen, adieu!

You that look pale and tremble at this chance,
That are but mutes° or audience to this act,
Had I but time — as this fell° sergeant,° Death,
Is strict in his arrest — O, I could tell you —　　345
But let it be. Horatio, I am dead;
Thou livest. Report me and my cause aright
To the unsatisfied.
HORATIO:　　　　Never believe it.
I am more an antique Roman° than a Dane.
Here's yet some liquor left.
　　　[*He attempts to drink from the poisoned cup.*
　　　　　Hamlet prevents him.]
HAMLET:　　　　As th' art a man,　　345
Give me the cup! Let go! By heaven, I'll ha 't.
O God, Horatio, what a wounded name,
Things standing thus unknown, shall I leave
　　behind me!
If thou didst ever hold me in thy heart,
Absent thee from felicity awhile,　　355
And in this harsh world draw thy breath in pain
To tell my story.
　　　(*A march afar off* [*and a volley within*].)
　　　What warlike noise is this?
OSRIC: Young Fortinbras, with conquest come from
　　Poland,
To the ambassadors of England gives
This warlike volley.
HAMLET:　　　　　O, I die, Horatio!　　360
The potent poison quite o'ercrows° my spirit.
I cannot live to hear the news from England,
But I do prophesy th' election lights
On Fortinbras. He has my dying voice.°
So tell him, with th' occurrents° more and less　　365
Which have solicited° — the rest is silence. [*Dies.*]
HORATIO: Now cracks a noble heart. Good night,
　　sweet prince;
And flights of angels sing thee to thy rest!
　　　[*March within.*]
Why does the drum come hither?

(*Enter Fortinbras, with the* [*English*] *Ambassadors*
[*with drum, colors, and attendants*].)

FORTINBRAS: Where is this sight?
HORATIO:　　　　What is it you would see?　　370
If aught of woe or wonder, cease your search.
FORTINBRAS: This quarry° cries on havoc.° O proud
　　Death.

---

311. [S.D.] *in scuffling, they change rapiers:* This stage direction occurs in the Folio. According to a widespread stage tradition, Hamlet receives a scratch, realizes that Laertes' sword is unbated, and accordingly forces an exchange. **315. woodcock:** A bird, a type of stupidity or as a decoy. **springe:** Trap, snare. **326. Unbated:** Not blunted with a button. **334. union:** Pearl (see line 276; with grim puns on the word's other meanings: marriage, shared death[?]). **336. temper'd:** Mixed.

343. mutes: Silent observers. **344. fell:** Cruel. **sergeant:** Sheriff's officer. **349. Roman:** It was the Roman custom to follow masters in death. **361. o'ercrows:** Triumphs over. **364. voice:** Vote. **365. occurrents:** Events, incidents. **366. solicited:** Moved, urged. **372. quarry:** Heap of dead. **cries on havoc:** Proclaims a general slaughter.

What feast is toward° in thine eternal cell,
That thou so many princes at a shot
So bloodily hast struck?
375 FIRST AMBASSADOR: The sight is dismal;
And our affairs from England come too late.
The ears are senseless that should give us
     hearing,
To tell him his commandment is fulfill'd,
That Rosencrantz and Guildenstern are dead.
Where should we have our thanks?
380 HORATIO: Not from his° mouth,
Had it th' ability of life to thank you.
He never gave commandment for their death.
But since, so jump° upon this bloody question,°
You from the Polack wars, and you from
     England,
385 Are here arriv'd, give order that these bodies
High on a stage° be placed to the view,
And let me speak to th' yet unknowing world
How these things came about. So shall you hear
Of carnal, bloody, and unnatural acts,
390 Of accidental judgments,° casual° slaughters,
Of deaths put on° by cunning and forc'd cause,
And, in this upshot, purposes mistook
Fall'n on th' inventors' heads. All this can I
Truly deliver.

373. **toward:** In preparation.   380. **his:** Claudius's.
383. **jump:** Precisely.   **question:** Dispute.   386. **stage:**
Platform.   390. **judgments:** Retributions.   **casual:** Occurring by chance.   391. **put on:** Instigated.

FORTINBRAS: Let us haste to hear it,
And call the noblest to the audience.   395
For me, with sorrow I embrace my fortune.
I have some rights of memory° in this kingdom,
Which now to claim my vantage° doth invite me.
HORATIO: Of that I shall have also cause to speak,
And from his mouth whose voice will draw on
     more.°   400
But let this same be presently° perform'd,
Even while men's minds are wild, lest more
     mischance
On° plots and errors happen.
FORTINBRAS: Let four captains
Bear Hamlet, like a soldier, to the stage,
For he was likely, had he been put on,°   405
To have prov'd most royal; and, for his passage,°
The soldiers' music and the rite of war
Speak loudly for him.
Take up the bodies. Such a sight as this
Becomes the field,° but here shows much amiss.   410
Go, bid the soldiers shoot.
     (*Exeunt* [*marching, bearing off the dead bodies;*
                    a peal of ordnance is shot off].)

397. **of memory:** Traditional, remembered.   398. **vantage:**
Presence at this opportune moment.   400. **voice . . . more:**
Vote will influence still others.   401. **presently:** Immediately.   403. **On:** On the basis of.   405. **put on:** Invested
in royal office and so put to the test.   406. **passage:** Death.
410. **field:** I.e., of battle.

THE TEMPEST

    One of Shakespeare's most thought-provoking plays, *The Tempest*
links Renaissance Italy, Elizabethan England, and the discoveries of the
New World. Shakespeare had an interest in the Virginia Company, an
investment group that sent a flotilla of ships to Virginia in 1609. Its flag-
ship, carrying the governor-to-be of Virginia, Sir Thomas Gates, was
lost in a July storm and washed up on Bermuda, then reputed to be the
Isle of Devils. Admiral Sir George Somers built new boats and, with
Gates and the rest of the crew, continued the journey, arriving
in Jamestown in May 1610. All this news was reported in England on
the eve of Shakespeare's preparation to write a new play for the Globe

Theatre. With the "still-vexed Bermudas" of *The Tempest* (not to mention its opening storm), drama now touches on current events in the Elizabethan world of politics and adventure.

There is also a connection between Prospero, the philosopher-magician of *The Tempest*, and the most celebrated Elizabethan magician of the time, John Dee (1527–1608). This learned mathematician was also an astrologer, whom Queen Elizabeth consulted when she wanted to have her horoscope cast. His fame as a necromancer — one who called the spirits to do his bidding — took him as far as Poland to perform magic. While he was there in 1583 an English mob, certain Dee was a dangerous wizard, destroyed his library, furnishings, and laboratories. He was known by reputation to the audiences of the original productions of *The Tempest*, which occurred in November 1611 and again in 1612–1613.

King James I, who was almost surely at its first performances, took a special interest in magic. The play was performed at courtly festivities celebrating the marriage of James's daughter Elizabeth. The marriage of Miranda and Ferdinand paralleled this real-life marriage. Moreover, the masque that the spirits perform for Miranda and Ferdinand (act IV, scene I) served as a special wedding celebration, since masques were dedicated to Hymen, the god of marriage.

Apart from relying on current events, *The Tempest* is notable in that it is one of the few plays for which Shakespeare did not use an earlier source from fiction, drama, or history. The plot — the good duke and his daughter being cast adrift by his evil brother and then ending on an island that the duke controls through his magic — seems entirely original. Early critics saw the play as a moral excursion in which the power of good, after great trial, eventually overcomes evil. However, Shakespeare leaves a loose end at the conclusion of the play. While most of those who colluded to remove Prospero from his dukedom are contrite and ashamed — and express honest regret at their earlier actions — Prospero's brother Antonio remains unrepentant at the end. Prospero, whose magic controls everyone on the island, forsakes magic when he declares that he will return to Milan. Thus he leaves himself potentially defenseless against a possible repetition of his brother's crimes. This detail emphasizes the island as a magical place, while reminding us of the existence of evil in the world of Renaissance politics.

The political aspect of the play hints at governmental negligence. Antonio is hungry for power, but Prospero is neglectful of it. Some critics have suggested that Niccoló Machiavelli (1469–1527) may have provided some thematic underpinning for the play in his political treatise *The Prince,* which insists that a prince (or duke) should hold on to power by any means possible. By spending his time cultivating magic, Prospero neglects his political duties, leaving the way open to his usurping brother.

Early Shakespeare critics would have been surprised by late twentieth-century interpretations of *The Tempest* that posit colonialism as one of the primary themes of the play. Connected as the play is with the colonizing efforts of the Virginia Company, such a reading is plausible. In these interpretations Prospero is not seen primarily as a benevolent father of Miranda or as a magnanimous and forgiving ruler who restores his uninvited guests to their previously "wrecked" ship. Instead, taking Caliban's island from him, putting Caliban into slavery, and demanding his obeisance cast Prospero as a representative of the Europeans who usurped the land of Native Americans and enslaved them.

Modern-day Shakespeareans find that the play's richness of characterization, impressive theatricality, and complex range of themes definitely support a multiple critical perspective.

The Tempest in Performance

Modern productions of the play are often based on their interpretations of Prospero's role. Late nineteenth-century actors did not especially enjoy playing Prospero. When Beerbohm Tree, an important Shakespearean actor, produced *The Tempest* in the early 1900s, he took the part of Caliban. He enjoyed the ambiguity of that role, which he played sympathetically.

John Gielgud has been the most durable Prospero of the twentieth century, first at the Old Vic in 1930 and, more recently, in Peter Greenaway's 1991 film *Prospero's Books*. In 1957 he played Prospero in Peter Brook's first production, which emphasized the theme of revenge. After his second production (1963) Brook said that *The Tempest* "includes all the themes from [Shakespeare's] earlier work — kingship, inheritance, treachery, conscience, identity, love, music, God; he draws them together as if to find the key to it all, but there is no such key. There is no grand order and Prospero returns to Milan not bathed in tranquility, but a wreck."

Peter Hall's 1974 production at London's National Theatre presented Gielgud in makeup that made him resemble John Dee, the Elizabethan magus. The emphasis on magic was clear and powerful. As Prospero, Patrick Stewart began what was supposed to be a limited run in a 1995 New York Shakespeare in the Park production directed by George Wolfe. The play proved to be so popular, however, that it moved on to become a Broadway hit. Stewart was known to the public from the television sci-fi series *Star Trek*, but his training with the Royal Shakespeare Company was evident in his powerful Prospero. This production also brought out a post-colonial issue — the tension between Ariel and Caliban as two members of the oppressed tribe. The numerous productions in Europe and the Americas in the last three decades of this century demonstrate the increasing power of the play. *The Tempest* seems to grow in our imagination rather than diminish.

William Shakespeare *(1564–1616)*
THE TEMPEST

1611

Names of the Actors

ALONSO, *King of Naples*
SEBASTIAN, *his brother*
PROSPERO, *the right Duke of Milan*
ANTONIO, *his brother, the usurping Duke of Milan*
FERDINAND, *son to the King of Naples*
GONZALO, *an honest old councillor*
ADRIAN,
FRANCISCO, } *lords*
CALIBAN, *a savage and deformed slave*
TRINCULO, *a jester*
STEPHANO, *a drunken butler*
MASTER, *of a ship*
BOATSWAIN
MARINERS

MIRANDA, *daughter to Prospero*

ARIEL, *an airy Spirit*
IRIS,
CERES,
JUNO, } *[presented by] Spirits*
NYMPHS,
REAPERS,

[Other Spirits attending Prospero]

Scene: *An uninhabited island*

ACT I • Scene I°

(*A tempestuous noise of thunder and lightning heard. Enter a Shipmaster and a Boatswain.*)

MASTER: Boatswain!
BOATSWAIN: Here, Master. What cheer?
MASTER: Good,° speak to the mariners. Fall to 't yarely,° or we run ourselves aground. Bestir, bestir!   (*Exit.*)

(*Enter Mariners.*)

BOATSWAIN: Heigh, my hearts! Cheerly,° cheerly, my hearts! Yare, yare! Take in the topsail. Tend° to the

I, I. **Location:** On board ship, off the island's coast.
3. **Good:** I.e., it's good you've come; or, my good fellow. 4. **yarely:** Nimbly. 6. **Cheerly:** Cheerily. 7. **Tend:** Attend.

Master's whistle. — Blow° till thou burst thy wind, if room enough!°

(*Enter Alonso, Sebastian, Antonio, Ferdinand, Gonzalo, and others.*)

ALONSO: Good Boatswain, have care. Where's the Master? Play the men.°   10
BOATSWAIN: I pray now, keep° below.
ANTONIO: Where is the Master, Boatswain?
BOATSWAIN: Do you not hear him? You mar our labor. Keep° your cabins! You do assist the storm.   15
GONZALO: Nay, good,° be patient.
BOATSWAIN: When the sea is. Hence!° What cares these roarers° for the name of king? To cabin! Silence! Trouble us not.
GONZALO: Good, yet remember whom thou hast   20 aboard.
BOATSWAIN: None that I more love than myself. You are a councillor; if you can command these elements to silence and work the peace of the present,° we will not hand° a rope more. Use your authority. If   25 you cannot, give thanks you have lived so long and make yourself ready in your cabin for the mischance° of the hour, if it so hap.° — Cheerly, good hearts! — Out of our way, I say.   (*Exit.*)
GONZALO: I have great comfort from this fellow.   30 Methinks he hath no drowning mark upon him; his complexion is perfect gallows.° Stand fast, good Fate, to his hanging! Make the rope of his destiny our cable, for our own doth little advantage.° If he be not born to be hanged, our case is   35 miserable.°   (*Exeunt.*)°

8. **Blow:** Addressed to the wind.   9. **if room enough:** As long as we have sea room enough.   11. **Play the men:** Act like men (?) ply, urge the men to exert themselves (?). 12. **keep:** Stay.   15. **Keep:** Remain in.   16. **good:** Good fellow.   17. **Hence:** Get away.   18. **roarers:** Waves or winds, or both; spoken to as though they were "bullies" or "blusterers."   24. **work . . . present:** Bring calm to our present circumstances.   25. **hand:** Handle.   28. **mischance:** Misfortune.   **hap:** Happen.   32. **complexion . . . gallows:** Appearance shows he was born to be hanged (and therefore, according to the proverb, in no danger of drowning). 34. **our . . . advantage:** I.e., our own cable is of little benefit. 35–36. **case is miserable:** Circumstances are desperate. 36. [S.D.] **Exeunt:** Latin for "they go out."

(*Enter Boatswain.*)

BOATSWAIN: Down with the topmast! Yare! Lower, lower! Bring her to try wi' the main course.° (*A cry within.*) A plague upon this howling! They are
40   louder than the weather or our office.°

(*Enter Sebastian, Antonio, and Gonzalo.*)

  Yet again? What do you here? Shall we give o'er° and drown? Have you a mind to sink?
SEBASTIAN: A pox o' your throat, you bawling, blasphemous, incharitable dog!
45 BOATSWAIN: Work you, then.
ANTONIO: Hang, cur! Hang, you whoreson, insolent noisemaker! We are less afraid to be drowned than thou art.
GONZALO: I'll warrant him for drowning,° though the
50   ship were no stronger than a nutshell and as leaky as an unstanched° wench.
BOATSWAIN: Lay her ahold,° ahold! Set her two courses.° Off to sea again! Lay her off!

(*Enter Mariners, wet.*)

MARINERS: All lost! To prayers, to prayers! All lost!
                    [*Exeunt Mariners.*]
55 BOATSWAIN: What, must our mouths be cold?°
GONZALO: The King and Prince at prayers! Let's assist them,
  For our case is as theirs.
SEBASTIAN: I am out of patience.
ANTONIO: We are merely° cheated of our lives by drunkards.
  This wide-chapped° rascal! Would thou mightst lie drowning
60   The washing of ten tides!°
GONZALO: He'll be hanged yet,
  Though every drop of water swear against it
  And gape at wid'st° to glut° him.
  (*A confused noise within.*)   "Mercy on us!" —
  "We split,° we split!" — "Farewell my wife and children!" —

"Farewell, brother!" — "We split, we split, we split!"
                    [*Exit Boatswain.*]
ANTONIO: Let's all sink wi' the King.   65
SEBASTIAN: Let's take leave of him.
               (*Exit* [*with Antonio*].)
GONZALO: Now would I give a thousand furlongs of sea for an acre of barren ground: long heath,° brown furze,° anything. The wills above be done! But I would fain° die a dry death.   (*Exit.*) 70

Scene II°

(*Enter Prospero* [*in his magic cloak*] *and Miranda.*)

MIRANDA: If by your art,° my dearest father, you have
  Put the wild waters in this roar,° allay° them.
  The sky, it seems, would pour down stinking pitch,°
  But that the sea, mounting to th' welkin's cheek,°
  Dashes the fire out. O, I have suffered   5
  With those that I saw suffer! A brave° vessel,
  Who had, no doubt, some noble creature in her,
  Dashed all to pieces. O, the cry did knock
  Against my very heart! Poor souls, they perished.
  Had I been any god of power, I would   10
  Have sunk the sea within the earth or ere°
  It should the good ship so have swallowed and
  The freighting° souls within her.
PROSPERO: Be collected.°
  No more amazement.° Tell your piteous° heart
  There's no harm done.
MIRANDA: O, woe the day!
PROSPERO: No harm.   15
  I have done nothing but° in care of thee,
  Of thee, my dear one, thee, my daughter, who
  Art ignorant of what thou art, naught knowing
  Of whence I am, nor that I am more better°
  Than Prospero, master of a full° poor cell,   20

---

38. **Bring . . . course:** Sail her close to the wind by means of the mainsail. **40. our office:** I.e., the noise we make at our work. **41. give o'er:** Give up. **49. warrant him for drowning:** Guarantee that he will never be drowned. **51. unstanched:** Insatiable, loose, unrestrained. **52. ahold:** Ahull, close to the wind. **53. courses:** Sails, i.e., foresail as well as mainsail, set in an attempt to get the ship back out into open water. **55. must . . . cold:** I.e., must we drown in the cold sea, or, let us heat up our mouths with liquor. **58. merely:** Utterly. **59. wide-chapped:** With mouth wide open. **59–60. lie . . . tides:** Pirates were hanged on the shore and left until three tides had come in. **62. at wid'st:** Wide. **glut:** Swallow. **63. split:** Break apart.

68. heath: Heather. **69. furze:** Gorse, a weed growing on wasteland. **70. fain:** Rather. **I, II. Location:** The island. Prospero's cell is visible, and on the Elizabethan stage it presumably remains so throughout the play, although in some scenes the convention of flexible distance allows us to imagine characters in other parts of the island. **1. art:** Magic. **2. roar:** Uproar. **allay:** Pacify. **3. pitch:** A thick, viscous substance produced by boiling down tar or turpentine. **4. welkin's cheek:** Sky's face. **6. brave:** Gallant, splendid. **11. or ere:** Before. **13. freighting:** Forming the cargo. **collected:** Calm, composed. **14. amazement:** Consternation. **piteous:** Pitying. **16. but:** Except. **19. more better:** Of higher rank. **20. full:** Very.

And thy no greater father.

MIRANDA: More to know
Did never meddle° with my thoughts.

PROSPERO: 'Tis time
I should inform thee farther. Lend thy hand
And pluck my magic garment from me. So,
            [*Laying down his magic cloak and staff.*]
Lie there, my art. — Wipe thou thine eyes. Have
25 comfort.
The direful spectacle of the wreck,° which
    touched
The very virtue° of compassion in thee,
I have with such provision° in mine art
So safely ordered that there is no soul —
30 No, not so much perdition° as an hair
Betid° to any creature in the vessel
Which° thou heardst cry, which thou sawst sink.
    Sit down,
For thou must now know farther.

MIRANDA [*sitting*]:   You have often
Begun to tell me what I am, but stopped
35 And left me to a bootless inquisition,°
Concluding, "Stay, not yet."

PROSPERO: The hour's now come;
The very minute bids thee ope° thine ear.
Obey, and be attentive. Canst thou remember
A time before we came unto this cell?
I do not think thou canst, for then thou wast
40 not
Out° three years old.

MIRANDA: Certainly, sir, I can.

PROSPERO: By what? By any other house or person?
Of anything the image, tell me, that
Hath kept with thy remembrance.

MIRANDA: 'Tis far off,
45 And rather like a dream than an assurance
That my remembrance warrants.° Had I not
Four or five women once that tended° me?

PROSPERO: Thou hadst, and more, Miranda. But
    how is it
That this lives in thy mind? What seest thou else
50 In the dark backward and abysm of time?°
If thou rememberest aught° ere thou cam'st here,
How thou cam'st here thou mayst.

MIRANDA: But that I do not.

PROSPERO: Twelve year since, Miranda, twelve year
    since,

Thy father was the Duke of Milan and
A prince of power.

MIRANDA: Sir, are not you my father? 55

PROSPERO: Thy mother was a piece° of virtue, and
She said thou wast my daughter; and thy father
Was Duke of Milan, and his only heir
And princess no worse issued.°

MIRANDA: O the heavens!
What foul play had we, that we came from
    thence?   60
Or Blessèd was 't we did?

PROSPERO: Both, both, my girl.
By foul play, as thou sayst, were we heaved
    thence,
But blessedly holp° hither.

MIRANDA: O, my heart bleeds
To think o' the teen that I have turned you to,°
Which is from° my remembrance! Please you,
    farther.   65

PROSPERO: My brother and thy uncle, called
    Antonio —
I pray thee, mark me, that a brother should
Be so perfidious! — he whom next° thyself
Of all the world I loved, and to him put
The manage° of my state, as at that time   70
Through all the seigniories° it was the first,
And Prospero the prime° duke, being so reputed
In dignity, and for the liberal arts
Without a parallel; those being all my study,
The government I cast upon my brother   75
And to my state grew stranger,° being
    transported°
And rapt in secret studies. Thy false uncle —
Dost thou attend me?

MIRANDA: Sir, most heedfully.

PROSPERO: Being once perfected° how to grant suits,
How to deny them, who t' advance and who   80
To trash° for overtopping,° new created
The creatures° that were mine, I say, or changed
    'em,
Or else new formed 'em;° having both the key°

---

22. **meddle:** Mingle.   26. **wreck:** Shipwreck.   27. **virtue:**
Essence.   28. **provision:** Foresight.   30. **perdition:** Loss.
31. **Betid:** Happened.   32. **Which:** Whom.   35. **bootless**
inquisition: Profitless inquiry.   37. **ope:** Open.   41. **Out:**
Fully.   45–46. **assurance . . . warrants:** Certainty that my
memory guarantees.   47. **tended:** Attended, waited
upon.   50. **backward . . . time:** Abyss of the past.   51. **aught:**
Anything.

56. **piece:** Masterpiece, exemplar.   59. **no worse issued:**
No less nobly born, descended.   63. **holp:** Helped.   64.
teen . . . to: Trouble I've caused you to remember or put you
to.   65. **from:** Out of.   68. **next:** Next to.   70. **manage:**
Management, administration.   71. **seigniories:** City-states of
northern Italy.   72. **prime:** Of highest rank.   76. **to . . .**
stranger: Withdrew from my responsibilities as duke.   **trans-**
ported: Carried away.   79. **perfected:** Grown skillful.
81. **trash:** Check a hound by tying a cord or weight to its
neck.   **overtopping:** Running too far ahead of the pack; sur-
mounting, exceeding one's authority.   82. **creatures:** Dependents.   82–83. **or changed . . . formed 'em:** Either changed
their loyalties and duties or else created new ones.   83. **key:**
(1) Key for unlocking, (2) tool for tuning stringed instruments.

Of officer and office, set all hearts i' the state
85   To what tune pleased his ear, that° now he was
The ivy which had hid my princely trunk
And sucked my verdure° out on 't.° Thou
    attend'st not.
MIRANDA: O, good sir, I do.
PROSPERO: I pray thee, mark me.
I, thus neglecting worldly ends, all dedicated
90   To closeness° and the bettering of my mind
With that which, but by being so retired,
O'erprized all popular rate,° in my false brother
Awaked an evil nature; and my trust,
Like a good parent,° did beget of° him
95   A falsehood in its contrary as great
As my trust was, which had indeed no limit,
A confidence sans° bound. He being thus lorded°
Not only with what my revenue yielded
But what my power might else° exact, like one
100   Who, having into° truth by telling of it,
Made such a sinner of his memory
To° credit his own lie,° he did believe
He was indeed the Duke, out o'° the substitution
And executing th' outward face of royalty°
With all prerogative. Hence his ambition
105   growing —
Dost thou hear?
MIRANDA: Your tale, sir, would cure deafness.
PROSPERO: To have no screen between this part he
    played
And him he played it for,° he needs° will be
Absolute Milan.° Me, poor man, my library
Was dukedom large enough. Of temporal
110   royalties°
He thinks me now incapable; confederates° —

85. **that:** So that.   87. **verdure:** Vitality.   **on 't:** Of it.
90. **closeness:** Retirement, seclusion.   **91–92. but . . . rate:**
Simply because it was done in such seclusion, had a value
not appreciated by popular opinion.   94. **good parent:** Alludes to the proverb that good parents often bear bad children; see also line 120.   **of:** In.   97. **sans:** Without.
lorded: Raised to lordship, with power and wealth.
99. **else:** Otherwise, additionally.   100–102. **Who . . . lie:**
Who, by repeatedly telling the lie (that he was indeed Duke
of Milan), made his memory such a confirmed sinner against
truth that he began to believe his own lie.   **into:** Unto,
against.   **To:** So as to.   103. **out o':** As a result of.
104. **And . . . royalty:** And (as a result of) his carrying out all
the ceremonial functions of royalty.   107–8. **To have . . . it
for:** To have no separation or barrier between his role and
himself. (Antonio wanted to act in his own person, not as
substitute.)   108. **needs:** Necessarily.   109. **Absolute Milan:** Unconditional duke of Milan.   110. **temporal royalties:** Practical prerogatives and responsibilities of a
sovereign.   111. **confederates:** Conspires, allies himself.

So dry° he was for sway° — wi' the King of
    Naples
To give him° annual tribute, do him homage,
Subject his coronet to his° crown, and bend°
The dukedom yet° unbowed — alas, poor
    Milan! —   115
To most ignoble stooping.
MIRANDA: O the heavens!
PROSPERO: Mark his condition° and th' event,° then
    tell me
If this might be a brother.
MIRANDA: I should sin
To think but° nobly of my grandmother.
Good wombs have borne bad sons.
PROSPERO: Now the condition.   120
This King of Naples, being an enemy
To me inveterate, hearkens° my brother's suit,
Which was that he, in lieu o' the premises°
Of homage and I know not how much tribute,
Should presently extirpate° me and mine   125
Out of the dukedom and confer fair Milan,
With all the honors, on my brother. Whereon
A treacherous army levied, one midnight
Fated to th' purpose did Antonio open
The gates of Milan, and, i' the dead of darkness,   130
The ministers for the purpose° hurried thence°
Me and thy crying self.
MIRANDA: Alack, for pity!
I, not remembering how I cried out then,
Will cry it o'er again. It is a hint°
That wrings° mine eyes to 't.
PROSPERO: Hear a little further,   135
And then I'll bring thee to the present business
Which now's upon 's, without the which this
    story
Were most impertinent.°
MIRANDA: Wherefore° did they not
That hour destroy us?
PROSPERO: Well demanded,° wench.°
My tale provokes that question. Dear, they durst
    not,   140
So dear the love my people bore me, nor set

112. **dry:** Thirsty.   **sway:** Power.   113. **him:** The King of
Naples.   114. **his . . . his:** Antonio's . . . the King of
Naples's.   **bend:** Make bow down.   115. **yet:** Hitherto.
117. **condition:** Pact.   **event:** Outcome.   119. **but:** Other
than.   122. **hearkens:** Listens to.   123. **in . . . premises:**
In return for the stipulation.   125. **presently extirpate:** At
once remove.   131. **ministers . . . purpose:** Agents employed to do this.   **thence:** From there.   134. **hint:** Occasion.   135. **wrings:** (1) Constraints, (2) wrings tears from.
138. **impertinent:** Irrelevant.   **Wherefore:** Why.   139. **demanded:** Asked.   **wench:** Here a term of endearment.

A mark so bloody° on the business, but
With colors fairer° painted their foul ends.
In few,° they hurried us aboard a bark,°
Bore us some leagues to sea, where they
145   prepared
A rotten carcass of a butt,° not rigged,
Nor tackle,° sail, nor mast; the very rats
Instinctively have quit° it. There they hoist us
To cry to th' sea that roared to us, to sigh
150   To th' winds whose pity, sighing back again,
Did us but loving wrong.°
MIRANDA: Alack, what trouble
Was I then to you!
PROSPERO: O, a cherubin°
Thou wast that did preserve me. Thou didst
    smile,
Infusèd with a fortitude from heaven,
155   When I have decked° the sea with drops full salt,
Under my burden groaned, which° raised in me
An undergoing stomach,° to bear up
Against what should ensue.
MIRANDA: How came we ashore?
160   PROSPERO: By Providence divine.
Some food we had, and some fresh water, that
A noble Neapolitan, Gonzalo,
Out of his charity, who being then appointed
Master of this design, did give us, with
165   Rich garments, linens, stuffs,° and necessaries,
Which since have steaded much.° So, of his
    gentleness,
Knowing I loved my books, he furnished me
From mine own library with volumes that
I prize above my dukedom.
MIRANDA: Would° I might
But ever° see that man!
170   PROSPERO: Now I arise.
                  [*He puts on his magic cloak.*]
Sit still and hear the last of our sea sorrow.°
Here in this island we arrived; and here
Have I, thy schoolmaster, made thee more profit°

141–42. set . . . bloody: Make obvious their murderous intent. (From the practice of marking with the blood of the
prey those who have participated in a successful hunt.)
143. fairer: Apparently more attractive.   **144. few:** Few
words. **bark:** Ship.   **146. butt:** Cask, tub.   **147. Nor
tackle:** Neither rigging (i.e., the pulleys and ropes designed
for hoisting sails).   **148. quit:** Abandoned.   **151. loving
wrong:** I.e., the winds pitied Prospero and Miranda though
of necessity they blew them from shore.   **152. cherubin:**
Angel.   **155. decked:** Covered (with salt tears); adorned.
156. which: I.e., the smile.   **157. undergoing stomach:**
Courage to go on.   **165. stuffs:** Supplies.   **166. steaded
much:** Been of much use.   **169. Would:** I wish.   **170. But
ever:** Someday.   **171. sea sorrow:** Sorrowful adventure at
sea.   **173. more profit:** Profit more.

Than other princess'° can, that have more time
For vainer° hours and tutors not so careful.   175
MIRANDA: Heavens thank you for 't! And now, I
    pray you, sir —
For still 'tis beating in my mind — your reason
For raising this sea storm?
PROSPERO: Know thus far forth:
By accident most strange, bountiful Fortune,
Now my dear lady, hath mine enemies   180
Brought to this shore; and by my prescience
I find my zenith° doth depend upon
A most auspicious star, whose influence°
If now I court not, but omit,° my fortunes
Will ever after droop. Here cease more
    questions.   185
Thou art inclined to sleep. 'Tis a good dullness,°
And give it way.° I know thou canst not choose.
                  [*Miranda sleeps.*]
Come away,° servant, come! I am ready now.
Approach, my Ariel, come.

(*Enter Ariel.*)

ARIEL: All hail, great master, grave sir, hail! I come   190
To answer thy best pleasure; be 't to fly,
To swim, to dive into the fire, to ride
On the curled clouds, to thy strong bidding task°
Ariel and all his quality.°
PROSPERO: Hast thou, spirit,
Performed to point° the tempest that I bade thee?   195
ARIEL: To every article.
I boarded the King's ship. Now on the beak,°
Now in the waist,° the deck,° in every cabin,
I flamed amazement.° Sometimes I'd divide
And burn in many places; on the topmast,   200
The yards, and the bowsprit would I flame
    distinctly,°
Then meet and join. Jove's lightning, the
    precursors
O' the dreadful thunderclaps, more momentary
And sight-outrunning° were not. The fire and
    cracks

---

174. princess': Princesses. (Or the word may be *princes,* referring to royal children both male and female.)
175. vainer: More foolishly spent.   **182. zenith:** Height of
fortune (astrological term).   **183. influence:** Astrological
power.   **184. omit:** Ignore.   **186. dullness:** Drowsiness.
187. give it way: Let it happen (i.e., don't fight it).
188. Come away: Come.   **193. task:** Make demands
upon.   **194. quality:** (1) Fellow spirits, (2) abilities.
195. to point: To the smallest detail.   **197. beak:** Prow.
198. waist: Midships. **deck:** Poop deck at the stern.
199. flamed amazement: Struck terror in the guise of fire,
i.e., Saint Elmo's fire.   **201. distinctly:** In different places.
204. sight-outrunning: Swifter than sight.

205 Of sulfurous roaring the most mighty Neptune°
    Seem to besiege and make his bold waves
        tremble,
    Yea, his dread trident shake.
PROSPERO: My brave spirit!
    Who was so firm, so constant, that this coil°
    Would not infect his reason?
ARIEL: Not a soul
210 But felt a fever of the mad° and played
    Some tricks of desperation. All but mariners
    Plunged in the foaming brine and quit the vessel,
    Then all afire with me. The King's son,
        Ferdinand,
    With hair up-staring° — then like reeds, not
        hair —
    Was the first man that leapt; cried, "Hell is
215   empty,
    And all the devils are here!"
PROSPERO: Why, that's my spirit!
    But was not this nigh shore?
ARIEL: Close by, my master.
PROSPERO: But are they, Ariel, safe?
ARIEL: Not a hair perished.
    On their sustaining garments° not a blemish,
220 But fresher than before; and, as thou bad'st° me,
    In troops° I have dispersed them 'bout the isle.
    The King's son have I landed by himself,
    Whom I left cooling of° the air with sighs
    In an odd angle° of the isle, and sitting,
    His arms in this sad knot.°   [He folds his arms.]
225 PROSPERO: Of the King's ship,
    The mariners, say how thou hast disposed,
    And all the rest o' the fleet.
ARIEL: Safely in harbor
    Is the King's ship; in the deep nook,° where once
    Thou calledst me up at midnight to fetch dew
230 From the still-vexed Bermudas,° there she's hid;
    The mariners all under hatches stowed,
    Who, with a charm joined to their suffered
        labor,°
    I have left asleep. And for the rest o' the fleet,
    Which I dispersed, they all have met again
235 And are upon the Mediterranean float°

Bound sadly home for Naples,
    Supposing that they saw the King's ship wrecked
    And his great person perish.
PROSPERO: Ariel, thy charge
    Exactly is performed. But there's more work.
    What is the time o' the day?
ARIEL: Past the mid season.° 240
PROSPERO: At least two glasses.° The time twixt six
        and now
    Must by us both be spent most preciously.
ARIEL: Is there more toil? Since thou dost give me
        pains,°
    Let me remember° thee what thou hast promised,
    Which is not yet performed me.
PROSPERO: How now? Moody? 245
    What is 't thou canst demand?
ARIEL: My liberty.
PROSPERO: Before the time be out? No more!
ARIEL: I prithee,
    Remember I have done thee worthy service,
    Told thee no lies, made thee no mistakings,
        served
    Without or grudge or rumblings. Thou did
        promise   250
    To bate° me a full year.
PROSPERO: Dost thou forget
    From what a torment I did free thee?
ARIEL: No.
PROSPERO: Thou dost, and think'st it much to tread
        the ooze
    Of the salt deep,
    To run upon the sharp wind of the north,   255
    To do me° business in the veins° o' the earth
    When it is baked° with frost.
ARIEL: I do not, sir.
PROSPERO: Thou liest, malignant thing! Hast thou
        forgot
    The foul witch Sycorax, who with age and envy°
    Was grown into a hoop?° Hast thou forgot her? 260
ARIEL: No, sir.
PROSPERO: Thou hast. Where was she born? Speak.
        Tell me.
ARIEL: Sir, in Algiers.
PROSPERO: O, was she so? I must
    Once in a month recount what thou hast been,

---

205. **Neptune:** Roman god of the sea.   208. **coil:** Tumult.
210. **of the mad:** I.e., such as madmen feel.   214. **up-
staring:** Standing on end.   219. **sustaining garments:** Garments that buoyed them up in the sea.   220. **bad'st:** Ordered.   221. **troops:** Groups.   223. **cooling of:** Cooling.
224. **angle:** Corner.   225. **sad knot:** Folded arms are indicative of melancholy.   228. **nook:** Bay.   230. **still-vexed
Bermudas:** Ever-stormy Bermudas. (Perhaps refers to the
then-recent Bermuda shipwreck [see page 424]. The Folio
text reads "Bermoothes.")   232. **with . . . labor:** By means
of a spell added to all the labor they have undergone.
235. **float:** Sea.

240. **mid season:** Noon.   241. **glasses:** Hourglasses.   243.
pains: Labors.   244. **remember:** Remind.   251. **bate:** Re-
mit, deduct.   256. **do me:** Do for me.   **veins:** Veins of
minerals, or underground streams thought to be analogous
to the veins of the human body.   257. **baked:** Hardened.
259. **envy:** Malice.   260. **grown into a hoop:** I.e., so bent
over with age as to resemble a hoop.

Which thou forgett'st. This damned witch
265   Sycorax,
For mischiefs manifold and sorceries terrible
To enter human hearing, from Algiers,
Thou know'st, was banished. For one thing she
   did°
They would not take her life. Is not this true?
270 ARIEL: Ay, sir.
PROSPERO: This blue-eyed° hag was hither brought
   with child°
And here was left by the sailors. Thou, my slave,
As thou report'st thyself, was then her servant;
And, for° thou wast a spirit too delicate
275 To act her earthy and abhorred commands,
Refusing her grand hests,° she did confine thee,
By help of her more potent ministers
And in her most unmitigable rage,
Into a cloven pine, within which rift
280 Imprisoned thou didst painfully remain
A dozen years; within which space she died
And left thee there, where thou didst vent thy
   groans
As fast as mill wheels strike.° Then was this
   island —
Save° for the son that she did litter° here,
A freckled whelp,° hag-born° — not honored
285   with
A human shape.
ARIEL: Yes, Caliban her son.
PROSPERO: Dull thing, I say so:° he, that Caliban
Whom now I keep in service. Thou best know'st
What torment I did find thee in. Thy groans
290 Did make wolves howl, and penetrate the breasts
Of ever-angry bears. It was a torment
To lay upon the damned, which Sycorax
Could not again undo. It was mine art,
When I arrived and heard thee, that made gape°
The pine and let thee out.
295 ARIEL: I thank thee, master.
PROSPERO: If thou more murmur'st, I will rend an
   oak
And peg thee in his° knotty entrails till
Thou hast howled away twelve winters.

ARIEL: Pardon, master.
I will be correspondent° to command
And do my spriting° gently.°   300
PROSPERO: Do so, and after two days
I will discharge thee.
ARIEL: That's my noble master!
What shall I do? Say what? What shall I do?
PROSPERO: Go make thyself like a nymph o' the sea.
   Be subject
To no sight but thine and mine, invisible   305
To every eyeball else. Go take this shape
And hither come in 't. Go, hence with diligence!
              (Exit [Ariel].)
Awake, dear heart, awake! Thou hast slept well.
Awake!
MIRANDA: The strangeness of your story put
Heaviness° in me.
PROSPERO: Shake it off. Come on,   310
We'll visit Caliban, my slave, who never
Yields us kind answer.
MIRANDA: 'Tis a villain, sir,
I do not love to look on.
PROSPERO: But, as 'tis,
We cannot miss° him. He does make our fire,
Fetch in our wood, and serves in offices°   315
That profit us. — What ho! Slave! Caliban!
Thou earth, thou! Speak.
CALIBAN (*within*):   There's wood enough within.
PROSPERO: Come forth, I say! There's other business
   for thee.
Come, thou tortoise! When?°

(Enter Ariel like a water nymph.)

Fine apparition! My quaint° Ariel,   320
Hark in thine ear.   [*He whispers.*]
ARIEL: My lord, it shall be done. (*Exit.*)
PROSPERO: Thou poisonous slave, got° by the devil
   himself
Upon thy wicked dam,° come forth!

(Enter Caliban.)

CALIBAN: As wicked° dew as e'er my mother
   brushed
With raven's feather from unwholesome fen°   325
Drop on you both! A southwest° blow on ye
And blister you all o'er!

---

268. one...did: Perhaps a reference to her pregnancy, for which her life would be spared.   **271. blue-eyed:** With dark circles under the eyes or with blue eyelids, implying pregnancy. **with child:** Pregnant.   **274. for:** Because. **276. hests:** Commands.   **283. as mill wheels strike:** As the blades of a mill wheel strike the water.   **284. Save:** Except. **litter:** Give birth to.   **285. whelp:** Offspring (used of animals). **hag-born:** Born of a female demon.   **287. Dull... so:** I.e., exactly, that's what I said, you dullard.   **294. gape:** Open wide.   **297. his:** Its.

299. correspondent: Responsive, submissive.   **300. spriting:** Duties as a spirit. **gently:** Willingly, ungrudgingly. **310. Heaviness:** Drowsiness.   **314. miss:** Do without. **315. offices:** Functions, duties.   **319. When:** An exclamation of impatience.   **320. quaint:** Ingenious.   **322. got:** Begotten, sired.   **323. dam:** Mother (used of animals). **324. wicked:** Mischievous, harmful.   **325. fen:** Marsh, bog.   **326. southwest:** I.e., wind thought to bring disease.

PROSPERO: For this, be sure, tonight thou shalt have
    cramps,
    Side-stitches that shall pen thy breath up. Urchins°
330 Shall forth at vast° of night that they may work
    All exercise on thee. Thou shalt be pinched
    As thick as honeycomb,° each pinch more
      stinging
    Than bees that made 'em.°
CALIBAN: I must eat my dinner.
    This island's mine, by Sycorax my mother,
    Which thou tak'st from me. When thou cam'st
335   first,
    Thou strok'st me and made much of me, wouldst
      give me
    Water with berries in 't, and teach me how
    To name the bigger light, and how the less,°
    That burn by day and night. And then I loved
      thee
340 And showed thee all the qualities o' th' isle,
    The fresh springs, brine pits, barren place and
      fertile.
    Cursed be I that did so! All the charms°
    Of Sycorax, toads, beetles, bats, light on you!
    For I am all the subjects that you have,
    Which first was mine own king; and here you
345   sty° me
    In this hard rock, whiles you do keep from me
    The rest o' th' island.
PROSPERO: Thou most lying slave,
    Whom stripes° may move, not kindness! I have
      used thee,
    Filth as thou art, with humane° care, and lodged
      thee
350 In mine own cell, till thou didst seek to violate
    The honor of my child.
CALIBAN: Oho, Oho! Would 't had been done!
    Thou didst prevent me; I had peopled else°
    This isle with Calibans.
MIRANDA: Abhorrèd slave,°

Which any print° of goodness wilt not take,   355
    Being capable of all ill! I pitied thee,
    Took pains to make thee speak, taught thee each
      hour
    One thing or other. When thou didst not, savage,
    Know thine own meaning, but wouldst gabble
      like
    A thing most brutish, I endowed thy purposes°   360
    With words that made them known. But thy vile
      race,°
    Though thou didst learn, had that in 't which
      good natures
    Could not abide to be with; therefore wast thou
    Deservedly confined into this rock,
    Who hadst deserved more than a prison.   365
CALIBAN: You taught me language, and my profit on 't
    Is I know how to curse. The red plague° rid° you
    For learning° me your language!
PROSPERO: Hagseed,° hence!
    Fetch us in fuel, and be quick, thou'rt best,°
    To answer other business.° Shrugg'st thou,
      malice?   370
    If thou neglect'st or dost unwillingly
    What I command, I'll rack thee with old°
      cramps,
    Fill all thy bones with aches,° make thee roar
    That beasts shall tremble at thy din.
CALIBAN: No, pray thee.
    [Aside.] I must obey. His art is of such power   375
    It would control my dam's god, Setebos,°
    And make a vassal of him.
PROSPERO: So, slave, hence!
                         (Exit Caliban.)

(Enter Ferdinand; and Ariel, invisible,° playing and
singing. [Ferdinand does not see Prospero and Miranda.])

                         (Ariel's Song.)
ARIEL: Come unto these yellow sands,
    And then take hands;

---

329. **Urchins:** Hedgehogs; here, suggesting goblins in the guise of hedgehogs.   330. **vast:** Lengthy, desolate time. (Malignant spirits were thought to be restricted to the hours of darkness.)   332. **As thick as honeycomb:** I.e., all over, with as many pinches as a honeycomb has cells.   333. **'em:** I.e., the honeycomb.   338. **the bigger ... less:** I.e., the sun and the moon. (See Genesis 1:16: "God then made two great lights: the greater light to rule the day, and the less light to rule the night.")   342. **charms:** Spells.   345. **sty:** Confine as in a sty.   348. **stripes:** Lashes.   349. **humane:** Not distinguished as a word from *human.*   353. **peopled else:** Otherwise populated.   354–65. **Abhorrèd ... prison:** These lines are sometimes assigned by editors to Prospero.

355. **print:** Imprint, impression.   360. **purposes:** Meanings, desires.   361. **race:** Natural disposition; species, nature. 367. **red plague:** Plague characterized by red sores and evacuation of blood. **rid:** Destroy.   368. **learning:** Teaching. **Hagseed:** Offspring of a female demon.   369. **thou'rt best:** You'd be well advised.   370. **answer other business:** Perform other tasks.   372. **old:** Such as old people suffer, or, plenty of.   373. **aches:** Pronounced "aitches."   376. **Setebos:** A god of the Patagonians, named in Robert Eden's *History of Travel* (1577).   377. [S.D.] *Ariel, invisible:* Ariel wears a garment that by convention indicates he is invisible to the other characters.

380 Curtsied when you have,° and kissed
        The wild waves whist,°
    Foot it featly° here and there,
        And, sweet sprites,° bear
    The burden.° Hark, hark!
385   (*Burden, dispersedly°* [*within*].) Bow-wow.
        The watchdogs bark.
            [*Burden, dispersedly within*]. Bow-wow.
    Hark, hark! I hear
    The strain of strutting chanticleer
390   Cry Cock-a-diddle-dow.
FERDINAND: Where should this music be? I' th' air
    or th' earth?
    It sounds no more and sure it waits upon°
    Some god o' th' island. Sitting on a bank,°
    Weeping again the King my father's wreck,
395 This music crept by me upon the waters,
    Allaying both their fury and my passion°
    With its sweet air. Thence° I have followed it,
    Or it hath drawn me rather. But 'tis gone.
    No, it begins again.
                                    (*Ariel's Song.*)
400 ARIEL: Full fathom five thy father lies.
        Of his bones are coral made.
        Those are pearls that were his eyes.
        Nothing of him that doth fade
        But doth suffer a sea change
405   Into something rich and strange.
        Sea nymphs hourly ring his knell.°
                    (*Burden* [*within*].) Ding dong.
        Hark, now I hear them, ding dong bell.
FERDINAND: The ditty does remember° my drowned
    father.
410 This is no mortal business, nor no sound
    That the earth owes.° I hear it now above me.
PROSPERO [*to Miranda*]: The fringed curtains of
    thine eye advance°
    And say what thou seest yond.
MIRANDA: What is 't? A spirit?
    Lord, how it looks about! Believe me, sir,
415 It carries a brave° form. But 'tis a spirit.

PROSPERO: No, wench, it eats and sleeps and hath
    such senses
    As we have, such. This gallant which thou seest
    Was in the wreck; and, but° he's something
    stained°
    With grief, that's beauty's canker,° thou mightst
    call him
    A goodly person. He hath lost his fellows   420
    And strays about to find 'em.
MIRANDA: I might call him
    A thing divine, for nothing natural
    I ever saw so noble.
PROSPERO [*aside*]:   It goes on,° I see,
    As my soul prompts it. — Spirit, fine spirit, I'll
    free thee
    Within two days for this.
FERDINAND [*seeing Miranda*]: Most sure, the
    goddess   425
    On whom these airs° attend! — Vouchsafe° my
    prayer
    May know° if you remain° upon this island,
    And that you will some good instruction give
    How I may bear me° here. My prime° request,
    Which I do last pronounce, is — O you
    wonder!° —   430
    If you be maid or no?°
MIRANDA: No wonder, sir,
    But certainly a maid.
FERDINAND: My language? Heavens!
    I am the best° of them that speak this speech,
    Were I but where 'tis spoken.
PROSPERO [*coming forward*]:   How? The best?
    What wert thou if the King of Naples heard
    thee?   435
FERDINAND: A single thing, as I am now, that
    wonders
    To hear thee speak of Naples.° He does hear
    me,°
    And that he does I weep.° Myself am Naples,

---

380. Curtsied...have: When you have curtsied.
380–81. kissed...whist: Kissed the waves into silence, or kissed while the waves are being hushed. **382. Foot it featly:** Dance nimbly. **383. sprites:** Spirits. **384. burden:** Refrain, undersong. **385.** [S.D.] *dispersedly*: From all directions, not in unison. **392. waits upon:** Serves, attends. **393. bank:** Sandbank. **396. passion:** Grief. **397. Thence:** From the bank on which he sat. **406. knell:** Announcement of a death by the tolling of a bell. **409. remember:** Commemorate. **411. owes:** Owns. **412. advance:** Raise. **415. brave:** Excellent.

418. but: Except that.   **something stained:** Somewhat disfigured.   **419. canker:** Cankerworm (feeding on buds and leaves).   **423. It goes on:** I.e., my plan works.   **426. airs:** Songs.   **Vouchsafe:** Grant.   **427. May know:** I.e., that I may know.   **remain:** Dwell.   **429. bear me:** Conduct myself.   **prime:** Chief.   **430. wonder:** Miranda's name means "to be wondered at."   **431. maid or no:** I.e., a human maiden as opposed to a goddess or married woman.   **433. best:** I.e., in birth.   **436. single:** (1) Solitary, being at once King of Naples and myself, (2) feeble.   **437, 438. Naples:** The King of Naples.   **437. He does hear me:** I.e., the King of Naples does hear my words, for I am King of Naples.   **438. And...weep:** I.e., and I weep at this reminder that my father is seemingly dead, leaving me heir.

Who with mine eyes, never since at ebb,° beheld
The King my father wrecked.
440 MIRANDA: Alack, for mercy!
FERDINAND: Yes, faith, and all his lords, the Duke
     of Milan
And his brave son° being twain.
PROSPERO [*aside*]:   The Duke of Milan
And his more braver° daughter could control
     thee,
If now 'twere fit to do 't. At the first sight
445 They have changed eyes.° — Delicate Ariel,
I'll set thee free for this. [*To Ferdinand.*] A word,
     good sir.
I fear you have done yourself some wrong.° A
     word!
MIRANDA [*aside*]: Why speaks my father so
     ungently? This
Is the third man that e'er I saw, the first
450 That e'er I sighed for. Pity move my father
To be inclined my way!

FERDINAND: O, if a virgin,
And your affection not gone forth, I'll make you
The Queen of Naples.
PROSPERO: Soft, sir! One word more.
[*Aside.*] They are both in either's° powers; but
     this swift business
I must uneasy° make, lest too light winning   455
Make the prize light.° [*To Ferdinand.*] One word
     more: I charge thee
That thou attend° me. Thou dost here usurp
The name thou ow'st° not, and hast put thyself
Upon this island as a spy, to win it
From me, the lord on 't.°
FERDINAND: No, as I am a man.   460
MIRANDA: There's nothing ill can dwell in such a
     temple.
If the ill spirit have so fair a house,
Good things will strive to dwell with 't.°
PROSPERO: Follow me. —
Speak not you for him, he's a traitor. — Come,

439. **at ebb:** I.e., dry, not weeping.   442. **son:** The only reference in the play to a son of Antonio.   443. **more braver:** More splendid.   **control:** Refute.   445. **changed eyes:** Exchanged amorous glances.   447. **done . . . wrong:** I.e., spoken falsely.

454. **both in either's:** Each in the other's.   455. **uneasy:** Difficult.   455–56. **light . . . light:** Easy . . . cheap.   457. **attend:** follow, obey.   458. **ow'st:** Ownest.   460. **on 't:** Of it.   463. **strive . . . with 't:** I.e., expel the evil and occupy the *temple*, the body.

LEFT: Raul Julia as Prospero (right) and Rick Elice as Ariel in the 1981 New York Shakespeare Festival production of *The Tempest*, directed by Lee Breuer with Ruth Maleczech at the Delacorte Theatre. RIGHT: Aunjanue Ellis (foreground) as Ariel and Patrick Stewart (background) as Prospero in the New York Shakespeare Festival/Public Theatre's (1995) production of *The Tempest* directed by George C. Wolfe at the Broadhurst Theatre. Photo by Michal Daniel.

465   I'll manacle thy neck and feet together.
Seawater shalt thou drink; thy food shall be
The fresh-brook mussels, withered roots, and
    husks
Wherein the acorn cradled. Follow.
FERDINAND: No!
  I will resist such entertainment° till
Mine enemy has more power.
        (*He draws and is charmed° from moving.*)
470 MIRANDA: O dear father,

Make not too rash° a trial of him, for
He's gentle,° and not fearful.°
PROSPERO: What, I say,
My foot° my tutor? — Put thy sword up, traitor,
Who mak'st a show but dar'st not strike, thy
    conscience
Is so possessed with guilt. Come from thy ward,°   475
For I can here disarm thee with this stick
And make thy weapon drop.
                [*He brandishes his staff.*]

---

469. entertainment: Treatment.   **470. [S.D.]** *charmed:* Magically prevented.

471. rash: Harsh.   **472. gentle:** Well-born.   **fearful:** frightening, dangerous; or, perhaps, cowardly.   **473. foot:** Subordinate. (Miranda, the foot, presumes to instruct Prospero, the head.)   **475. ward:** Defensive posture (in fencing).

MIRANDA [*trying to hinder him*]: Beseech you,
    father!
PROSPERO: Hence! Hang not on my garments.
MIRANDA: Sir, have pity!
    I'll be his surety.°
PROSPERO: Silence! One word more
    Shall make me chide thee, if not hate thee.
480   What,
    An advocate for an impostor? Hush!
    Thou think'st there is no more such shapes as he,
    Having seen but him and Caliban. Foolish
      wench,
    To° the most of men this is a Caliban,
    And they to him are angels.
485 MIRANDA: My affections
    Are then most humble; I have no ambition
    To see a goodlier man.
PROSPERO [*to Ferdinand*]: Come on, obey.
    Thy nerves° are in their infancy again
    And have no vigor in them.
FERDINAND: So they are.
490   My spirits,° as in a dream, are all bound up.
    My father's loss, the weakness which I feel,
    The wreck of all my friends, nor this man's
      threats
    To whom I am subdued, are but light° to me
    Might I but through my prison once a day
495   Behold this maid. All corners else° o' th' earth
    Let liberty make use of; space enough
    Have I in such a prison.
PROSPERO [*aside*]: It works. [*To Ferdinand.*] Come
    on. — Thou hast done well, fine Ariel! [*To
    Ferdinand.*] Follow me.
    [*To Ariel.*] Hark what thou else shalt do me.°
MIRANDA [*to Ferdinand*]:   Be of comfort.
500   My father's of a better nature, sir,
    Than he appears by speech. This is unwonted°
    Which now came from him.
PROSPERO [*to Ariel*]:   Thou shalt be as free
    As mountain winds; but then° exactly do
    All points of my command.
ARIEL: To th' syllable.
PROSPERO [*to Ferdinand*]: Come, follow. [*To
505   Miranda.*] Speak not for him.

                            (*Exeunt.*)

479. **surety:** Guarantee.   484. **To:** Compared to.   488.
nerves: Sinews.   490. **spirits:** Vital powers.   493. **light:**
Unimportant.   495. **corners else:** Other corners, regions.
499. **me:** For me.   501. **unwonted:** Unusual.   503. **then:**
Until then; or, if that is to be so.

ACT II • *Scene 1*°

(*Enter Alonso, Sebastian, Antonio, Gonzalo, Adrian,
Francisco, and others.*)

GONZALO [*to Alonso*]: Beseech you, sir, be merry.
    You have cause,
    So have we all, of joy, for our escape
    Is much beyond° our loss. Our hint of° woe
    Is common; every day some sailor's wife,
    The masters of some merchant, and the
      merchant°   5
    Have just° our theme of woe. But for the miracle,
    I mean our preservation, few in millions
    Can speak like us. Then wisely, good sir, weigh
    Our sorrow with° our comfort.
ALONSO: Prithee, peace.
SEBASTIAN [*to Antonio*]: He receives comfort like cold   10
    porridge.°
ANTONIO [*to Sebastian*]: The visitor° will not give him
    o'er° so.
SEBASTIAN: Look, he's winding up the watch of his
    wit; by and by it will strike.   15
GONZALO [*to Alonso*]: Sir —
SEBASTIAN [*to Antonio*]: One. Tell.°
GONZALO: When every grief is entertained
    That's offered, comes to th' entertainer° —
SEBASTIAN: A dollar.°   20
GONZALO: Dolor comes to him, indeed. You have
    spoken truer than you purposed.
SEBASTIAN: You have taken it wiselier than I meant
    you should.
GONZALO [*to Alonso*]: Therefore, my lord —   25
ANTONIO: Fie, what a spendthrift is he of his tongue!
ALONSO [*to Gonzalo*]: I prithee, spare.°
GONZALO: Well, I have done. But yet —
SEBASTIAN: He will be talking.

II, I. **Location:** Another part of the island.   3. **much beyond:** More remarkable than.   **hint of:** Occasion for.
5. **masters . . . the merchant:** Officers of some merchant vessel and the merchant himself, the owner (or else the ship itself).   6. **just:** Exactly.   9. **with:** Against.   11. **porridge:**
With a pun on *peace* (line 9) and *peas* or *pease*, a common
ingredient of porridge.   12. **visitor:** One taking nourishment and comfort to the sick, i.e., Gonzalo.   12–13. **give
him o'er:** Abandon him.   17. **Tell:** Keep count.   18–
19. **When . . . entertainer:** When every sorrow that presents
itself is accepted without resistance, there comes to the re-
cipient.   20. **dollar:** Widely circulated coin, the German
thaler and the Spanish piece of eight. (Sebastian puns on *entertainer* in the sense of innkeeper; to Gonzalo, *dollar* suggests *dolor*, grief.)   27. **spare:** Forbear, cease.

30 ANTONIO: Which, of he or Adrian, for a good wager,
    first begins to crow?°
  SEBASTIAN: The old cock.°
  ANTONIO: The cockerel.°
  SEBASTIAN: Done. The wager?
35 ANTONIO: A laughter.°
  SEBASTIAN: A match!°
  ADRIAN: Though this island seem to be desert° —
  ANTONIO: Ha, ha, ha!
  SEBASTIAN: So, you're paid.°
40 ADRIAN: Uninhabitable and almost inaccessible —
  SEBASTIAN: Yet —
  ADRIAN: Yet —
  ANTONIO: He could not miss 't.°
  ADRIAN: It must needs be° of subtle, tender, and deli-
45   cate temperance.°
  ANTONIO: Temperance° was a delicate° wench.
  SEBASTIAN: Ay, and a subtle,° as he most learnedly de-
  livered.°
  ADRIAN: The air breathes upon us here most sweetly.
50 SEBASTIAN: As if it had lungs, and rotten ones.
  ANTONIO: Or as 'twere perfumed by a fen.
  GONZALO: Here is everything advantageous to life.
  ANTONIO: True, save° means to live.
  SEBASTIAN: Of that there's none, or little.
55 GONZALO: How lush and lusty° the grass looks! How
  green!
  ANTONIO: The ground indeed is tawny.°

SEBASTIAN: With an eye° of green in 't.
ANTONIO: He misses not much.
SEBASTIAN: No. He doth but° mistake the truth totally. 60
GONZALO: But the rarity of it is — which is indeed al-
  most beyond credit —
SEBASTIAN: As many vouched° rarities are.
GONZALO: That our garments, being, as they were,
  drenched in the sea, hold notwithstanding their 65
  freshness and glosses, being rather new-dyed than
  stained with salt water.
ANTONIO: If but one of his pockets° could speak,
  would it not say he lies?
SEBASTIAN: Ay, or very falsely pocket up° his report.° 70
GONZALO: Methinks our garments are now as fresh
  as when we put them on first in Afric, at the marriage of the King's fair daughter Claribel to the
  King of Tunis.
SEBASTIAN: 'Twas a sweet marriage, and we prosper 75
  well in our return.
ADRIAN: Tunis was never graced before with such a
  paragon to° their queen.
GONZALO: Not since widow Dido's° time.
ANTONIO: Widow! A pox o' that! How came that 80
  "widow" in? Widow Dido!
SEBASTIAN: What if he had said "widower Aeneas"
  too? Good Lord, how you take° it!
ADRIAN: "Widow Dido" said you? You make me
  study of° that. She was of Carthage, not of Tunis. 85
GONZALO: This Tunis, sir, was Carthage.
ADRIAN: Carthage?
GONZALO: I assure you, Carthage.
ANTONIO: His word is more than the miraculous
  harp.° 90
SEBASTIAN: He hath raised the wall, and houses too.
ANTONIO: What impossible matter will he make easy
  next?

30–31. Which . . . crow: Which of the two, Gonzalo or
Adrian, do you bet will speak (crow) first?   **32. old cock:**
I.e., Gonzalo.   **33. cockerel:** I.e., Adrian.   **35. laughter:**
(1) Burst of laughter, (2) sitting of eggs. (When Adrian, the
cockerel, begins to speak two lines later, Sebastian loses the
bet. The Folio speech prefixes in lines 38–39 are here reversed
so that Antonio enjoys his laugh as the prize for winning, as
in the proverb "He who laughs last laughs best" or "He
laughs that wins." The Folio assignment can work in the theater, however, if Sebastian pays for losing with a sardonic
laugh of concession.)   **36. A match:** A bargain; agreed.
37. desert: Uninhabited.   **39. you're paid:** I.e. you've had
your laugh.   **43. miss 't:** (1) Avoid saying "Yet," (2) miss
the island.   **44. must needs be:** Has to be.   **45. temperance:** Mildness of climate.   **46. Temperance:** A girl's name.
delicate: Here it means "given to pleasure, voluptuous"; in
line 44, "pleasant." (Antonio is evidently suggesting that *tender, and delicate temperance* sounds like a Puritan phrase,
which Antonio then mocks by applying the words to a
woman rather than an island. He began this bawdy comparison with a double entendre on *inaccessible*, line
40.)   **47. subtle:** Here it means "tricky, sexually crafty"; in
line 44, "delicate."   **48. delivered:** Uttered. (Sebastian joins
Antonio in baiting the Puritans with his use of the pious cant
phrase *learnedly delivered*.)   **53. save:** Except.   **55. lusty:**
Healthy.   **57. tawny:** Dull brown, yellowish.

58. eye: Tinge, or spot (perhaps with reference to Gonzalo's
eye or judgment).   **60. but:** Merely.   **63. vouched:** Certified.   **68. pockets:** I.e., because they are muddy.
70. pocket up: I.e., conceal, suppress; often used in the sense
of "receive unprotestingly, fail to respond to a challenge."
his report: Sebastian's jest is that the evidence of Gonzalo's
soggy and sea-stained pockets would confute Gonzalo's
speech and his reputation for truth telling.   **78. to:** For.
79. widow Dido: Queen of Carthage, deserted by Aeneas.
(She was in fact a widow when Aeneas, a widower, met her,
but Antonio may be amused at Gonzalo's prudish use of the
term *widow* to describe a woman deserted by her lover.)
83. take: Understand, respond to, interpret.   **85. study of:**
Think about.   **89–90. miraculous harp:** Alludes to Amphion's harp, with which he raised the walls of Thebes; Gonzalo has exceeded that deed by creating a modern
Carthage — walls *and houses* — mistakenly on the site of
Tunis.

SEBASTIAN: I think he will carry this island home in his
95   pocket and give it his son for an apple.
ANTONIO: And, sowing the kernels° of it in the sea,
      bring forth more islands.
GONZALO: Ay.°
ANTONIO: Why, in good time.
100 GONZALO [to Alonso]: Sir, we were talking° that our
      garments seem now as fresh as when we were at
      Tunis at the marriage of your daughter, who is
      now queen.
ANTONIO: And the rarest° that e'er came there.
105 SEBASTIAN: Bate,° I beseech you, widow Dido.
ANTONIO: O, widow Dido? Ay, widow Dido.
GONZALO: Is not, sir, my doublet° as fresh as the first
      day I wore it? I mean, in a sort.°
ANTONIO: That "sort"° was well fished for.
110 GONZALO: When I wore it at your daughter's
      marriage.
ALONSO: You cram these words into mine ears against
      The stomach° of my sense.° Would I had never
      Married° my daughter there! For, coming thence,
115 My son is lost and, in my rate,° she too,
      Who is so far from Italy removed
      I ne'er again shall see her. O thou mine heir
      Of Naples and of Milan, what strange fish
      Hath made his meal° on thee?
FRANCISCO: Sir, he may live.
120 I saw him beat the surges° under him
      And ride upon their backs. He trod the water,
      Whose enmity he flung aside, and breasted
      The surge most swoll'n that met him. His bold
         head
      'Bove the contentious waves he kept, and oared
125 Himself with his good arms in lusty° stroke
      To th' shore, that o'er his wave-worn basis
         bowed,°
      As° stooping to relieve him. I not° doubt

He came alive to land.°
ALONSO: No, no, he's gone.
SEBASTIAN [to Alonso]: Sir, you may thank yourself
      for this great loss,
      That° would not bless our Europe with your
         daughter,   130
      But rather° loose° her to an African,
      Where she at least is banished from your eye,°
      Who hath cause to wet the grief on 't.°
ALONSO: Prithee, peace.
SEBASTIAN: You were kneeled to and importuned°
      otherwise
      By all of us, and the fair soul herself   135
      Weighed between loathness and obedience at
      Which end o' the beam should bow.° We have
         lost your son,
      I fear, forever. Milan and Naples have
      More widows in them of this business' making°
      Than we bring men to comfort them.   140
      The fault's your own.
ALONSO: So is the dear'st° o' the loss.
GONZALO: My lord Sebastian,
      The truth you speak doth lack some gentleness
      And time° to speak it in. You rub the sore   145
      When you should bring the plaster.°
SEBASTIAN: Very well.
ANTONIO: And most chirugeonly.°
GONZALO [to Alonso]:
      It is foul weather in us all, good sir,
      When you are cloudy.
SEBASTIAN [to Antonio]: Fowl° weather?
ANTONIO [to Sebastian]:   Very foul.   150
GONZALO: Had I plantation° of this isle, my lord —
ANTONIO [to Sebastian]:
      He'd sow 't with nettle seed.
SEBASTIAN: Or docks, or mallows.°

96. kernels: Seeds.   98. Ay: Gonzalo may be reasserting his
point about Carthage, or he may be responding ironically to
Antonio, who in turn answers sarcastically.   99. in good
time: An expression of ironical acquiescence or amazement; i.e., "sure, right away."   100. talking: Saying.
104. rarest: Most remarkable, beautiful.   105. Bate:
Abate, except, leave out. (Sebastian says, "Don't forget
Dido," or "Let's have no more talk of Dido.")   107. doublet: Close-fitting jacket.   108. in a sort: In a way.
109. "sort": Antonio plays on the idea of drawing lots.
112–13. against . . . sense: I.e., against my will.   stomach:
Appetite.   114. Married: Given in marriage.   115. rate:
Estimation, opinion.   119. made his meal: Fed himself.
120. surges: Waves.   125. lusty: Vigorous.   126. that . . .
bowed: I.e., that projected out over the base of the cliff that
had been eroded by the surf, thus seeming to bend down toward the sea.   127. As: As if.   I not: I do not.

128. came . . . land: Reached land alive.   130. That: You
who.   131. rather: Would rather.   loose: (1) Release, let
loose, (2) lose.   132. is banished from your eye: Is not constantly before your eye to serve as a reproachful reminder of
what you have done.   133. Who . . . on 't: I.e., your eye
which has good reason to weep because of this; or Claribel,
who has good reason to weep for it.   134. importuned:
Urged, implored.   135–37. the fair . . . bow: I.e., Claribel
herself was poised uncertainly between unwillingness to
marry and obedience to her father as to which end of the
scale should sink, which should prevail.   139. of . . . making: On account of this marriage.   142. dear'st: Heaviest,
most costly.   145. time: Appropriate time.   146. plaster:
A medical application.   147. chirugeonly: Like a skilled
surgeon. (Antonio mocks Gonzalo's medical analogy of a
plaster applied curatively to a wound.)   150. Fowl: With a
pun on foul, returning to the imagery of lines 30–35.
151. plantation: Colonization (with subsequent wordplay on
the literal meaning).   152. docks, mallows: Weeds used as
antidotes for nettle stings.

GONZALO: And were the king on 't, what would I
　　do?
SEBASTIAN: Scape° being drunk for want° of wine.
GONZALO: I' the commonwealth I would by
155　　contraries°
　　Execute all things; for no kind of traffic°
　　Would I admit; no name of magistrate;
　　Letters° should not be known; riches, poverty,
　　And use of service,° none; contract, succession,°
160　　Bourn,° bound of land,° tilth,° vineyard, none;
　　No use of metal, corn,° or wine, or oil;
　　No occupation; all men idle, all,
　　And women too, but innocent and pure;
　　No sovereignty —
SEBASTIAN:　　　　　　Yet he would be king on 't.
165 ANTONIO: The latter end of his commonwealth for-
　　gets the beginning.
GONZALO: All things in common nature should
　　produce
　　Without sweat or endeavor. Treason, felony,
　　Sword, pike,° knife, gun, or need of any engine°
170　　Would I not have; but nature should bring forth,
　　Of its own kind, all foison,° all abundance,
　　To feed my innocent people.
SEBASTIAN: No marrying 'mong his subjects?
ANTONIO: None, man, all idle — whores and
　　knaves.
175 GONZALO: I would with such perfection govern, sir,
　　T' excel the Golden Age.°
SEBASTIAN:　　　　　　Save° His Majesty!
ANTONIO: Long live Gonzalo!
GONZALO:　　　　　And — do you mark me, sir?
ALONSO: Prithee, no more. Thou dost talk nothing
　　to me.
GONZALO: I do well believe Your Highness, and did it
180　　to minister occasion° to these gentlemen, who are
　　of such sensible° and nimble lungs that they al-
　　ways use° to laugh at nothing.
ANTONIO: 'Twas you we laughed at.
GONZALO: Who in this kind of merry fooling am

nothing to you; so you may continue, and laugh at 185
　nothing still.
ANTONIO: What a blow was there given!
SEBASTIAN: An° it had not fallen flat-long.°
GONZALO: You are gentlemen of brave mettle:° you
　would lift the moon out of her sphere° if she 190
　would continue in it five weeks without changing.

(*Enter Ariel* [*invisible*] *playing solemn music.*)

SEBASTIAN: We would so, and then go a-batfowling.°
ANTONIO: Nay, good my lord, be not angry.
GONZALO: No, I warrant you, I will not adventure my
　discretion so weakly.° Will you laugh me asleep? 195
　For I am very heavy.°
ANTONIO: Go sleep, and hear us.°
　　　　　[*All sleep except Alonso, Sebastian, and
　　　　　　　　　　　　　　　　　Antonio.*]
ALONSO: What, all so soon asleep? I wish mine eyes
　Would, with themselves, shut up my thoughts.° I
　find
　They are inclined to do so.
SEBASTIAN:　　　　　　　Please you, sir, 200
　Do not omit° the heavy° offer of it.
　It seldom visits sorrow; when it doth,
　It is a comforter.
ANTONIO:　　　　　We two, my lord,
　Will guard your person while you take your rest,
　And watch your safety.
ALONSO:　　　　　Thank you. Wondrous heavy. 205
　　　　　　　　[*Alonso sleeps. Exit Ariel.*]
SEBASTIAN: What a strange drowsiness possesses
　them!
ANTONIO: It is the quality o' the climate.
SEBASTIAN:　　　　　　　　　　Why
　Doth it not then our eyelids sink? I find not
　Myself disposed to sleep.
ANTONIO:　　　　　　Nor I. My spirits are nimble.

---

154. Scape: Escape. **want:** Lack. (Sebastian jokes sarcastically that this hypothetical ruler would be saved from dissipation only by the barrenness of the island.) **155. by contraries:** By what is directly opposite to usual custom. **156. traffic:** Trade. **158. Letters:** Learning. **159. use of service:** Custom of employing servants. **succession:** Holding of property by right of inheritance. **160. Bourn:** Boundaries. **bound of land:** Landmarks. **tilth:** Tillage of soil. **161. corn:** Grain. **169. pike:** Lance. **engine:** Instrument of warfare. **171. foison:** Plenty. **176. the Golden Age:** The age, according to Hesiod, when Cronus, or Saturn, ruled the world; an age of innocence and abundance. **Save:** God save. **180. minister occasion:** Furnish opportunity. **181. sensible:** Sensitive. **182. use:** Are accustomed.

188. An: If **flat-long:** With the flat of the sword, i.e., ineffectually. (Compare "fallen flat.") **189. mettle:** Temperament, courage. (The sense of *metal*, indistinguishable as a form from *mettle*, continues the metaphor of the sword.) **190. sphere:** Orbit. (Literally, one of the concentric zones occupied by planets in the Ptolemaic astronomy.) **192. a-batfowling:** Hunting birds at night with lantern and *bat* or stick; also, gulling a simpleton. (Gonzalo is the simpleton, or fowl, and Sebastian will use the moon as his lantern.) **194–95. adventure . . . weakly:** Risk my reputation for discretion for so trivial a cause (by getting angry at these sarcastic fellows). **196. heavy:** Sleepy. **197. Go . . . us:** Let our laughing send you to sleep, or go to sleep and hear us laugh at you. **199. Would . . . thoughts:** Would shut off my melancholy brooding when they close themselves in sleep. **201. omit:** Neglect. **heavy:** Drowsy.

210 They fell together all, as by consent,°
    They dropped, as by a thunderstroke. What
        might,
    Worthy Sebastian, O, what might — ? No more.
    And yet methinks I see it in thy face,
    What thou shouldst be. Th' occasion° speaks
        thee,° and
215 My strong imagination sees a crown
    Dropping upon thy head.
SEBASTIAN: What, art thou waking?
ANTONIO: Do you not hear me speak?
SEBASTIAN: I do, and surely
    It is a sleepy language, and thou speak'st
    Out of thy sleep. What is it thou didst say?
220 This is a strange repose, to be asleep
    With eyes wide open — standing, speaking,
        moving —
    And yet so fast asleep.
ANTONIO: Noble Sebastian,
    Thou lett'st thy fortune sleep — die, rather;
        wink'st°
    Whiles thou art waking.
SEBASTIAN: Thou dost snore distinctly;°
225 There's meaning in thy snores.
ANTONIO: I am more serious than my custom. You
    Must be so too, if heed° me; which to do
    Trebles thee o'er.°
SEBASTIAN: Well, I am standing water.°
ANTONIO: I'll teach you how to flow.
SEBASTIAN: Do so. To ebb°
    Hereditary sloth° instructs me.
230 ANTONIO: O,
    If you but knew how you the purpose cherish
    Whiles thus you mock it!° How, in stripping it,
    You more invest° it! Ebbing men, indeed,
    Most often do so near the bottom° run

                    By their own fear or sloth.
SEBASTIAN: Prithee, say on.   235
    The setting° of thine eye and cheek proclaim
    A matter° from thee, and a birth indeed
    Which throes° thee much to yield.°
ANTONIO: Thus, sir:
    Although this lord° of weak remembrance,° this
    Who shall be of as little memory   240
    When he is earthed,° hath here almost
        persuaded —
    For he's a spirit of persuasion, only
    Professes to persuade° — the King his son's alive,
    'Tis as impossible that he's uncrowned
    As he that sleeps here swims.
SEBASTIAN: I have no hope   245
    That he's undrowned.
ANTONIO: O, out of that "no hope"
    What great hope have you! No hope that way° is
    Another way so high a hope that even
    Ambition cannot pierce a wink° beyond,
    But doubt discovery there.° Will you grant with
        me   250
    That Ferdinand is drowned?
SEBASTIAN: He's gone.
ANTONIO: Then tell me,
    Who's the next heir of Naples?
SEBASTIAN: Claribel.
ANTONIO: She that is Queen of Tunis, she that
        dwells
    Ten leagues beyond man's life;° she that from
        Naples
    Can have no note,° unless the sun were post° —   255
    The man i' the moon's too slow — till newborn
        chins
    Be rough and razorable,° she that from° whom
    We all were sea-swallowed, though some cast°
        again,

---

210. **consent:** Common agreement.   214. **occasion:** Opportunity of the moment.   **speaks thee:** I.e., calls upon you, proclaims you usurper of Alonso's crown.   223. **wink'st:** (You) shut your eyes.   224. **distinctly:** Articulately.   227. **if heed:** If you heed.   228. **Trebles thee o'er:** Makes you three times as great and rich.   **standing water:** Water that neither ebbs nor flows, at a standstill.   229. **ebb:** Recede, decline.   230. **Hereditary sloth:** Natural laziness and the position of younger brother, one who cannot inherit. 231–32. **If . . . mock it:** I.e., if you only knew how much you really enhance the value of ambition even while your words mock your purpose.   232–33. **How . . . invest it:** I.e., how the more you speak flippantly of ambition, the more you in effect affirm it.   233. **invest:** Clothe. (Antonio's paradox is that by skeptically stripping away illusions Sebastian can see the essence of a situation and the opportunity it presents, or that by disclaiming and deriding his purpose Sebastian shows how he values it.)   234. **the bottom:** I.e., on which unadventurous men may go aground and miss the tide of fortune.

236. **setting:** Set expression (of earnestness).   237. **matter:** Matter of importance.   238. **throes:** Causes pain, as in giving birth.   **yield:** Give forth, speak about.   239. **this lord:** I.e., Gonzalo.   **remembrance:** (1) Power of remembering, (2) being remembered after his death.   241. **earthed:** Buried.   242–43. **only . . . persuade:** I.e., whose whole function (as a privy councilor) is to persuade.   247. **that way:** I.e., in regard to Ferdinand's being saved.   249–50. **Ambition . . . there:** Ambition itself cannot see any further than that hope (of the crown), but is unsure of itself in seeing even so far, is dazzled by daring to think so high. 249. **wink:** Glimpse.   254. **Ten . . . life:** I.e., it would take more than a lifetime to get there.   255. **note:** News, intimation.   **post:** Messenger.   257. **razorable:** Ready for shaving.   **from:** On our voyage from.   258. **cast:** Were disgorged (with a pun on *casting* of parts for a play).

And by that destiny to perform an act
260   Whereof what's past is prologue, what to come
      In yours and my discharge.°
   SEBASTIAN: What stuff is this? How say you?
      'Tis true my brother's daughter's Queen of Tunis,
      So is she heir of Naples, twixt which regions
      There is some space.
265 ANTONIO: A space whose every cubit°
      Seems to cry out, "How shall that Claribel
      Measure us° back to Naples? Keep° in Tunis,
      And let Sebastian wake."° Say this were death
      That now hath seized them, why, they were no
         worse
      Than now they are. There be° that can rule
270   Naples
      As well as he that sleeps, lords that can prate°
      As amply and unnecessarily
      As this Gonzalo. I myself could make
      A chough of as deep chat.° O, that you bore
275   The mind that I do! What a sleep were this
      For your advancement! Do you understand me?
   SEBASTIAN: Methinks I do.
   ANTONIO: And how does your content°
      Tender° your own good fortune?
   SEBASTIAN: I remember
      You did supplant your brother Prospero.
   ANTONIO: True.
280   And look how well my garments sit upon me,
      Much feater° than before. My brother's servants
      Were then my fellows. Now they are my men.
   SEBASTIAN: But, for your conscience?
   ANTONIO: Ay, sir, where lies that? If 'twere a kibe,°
285   'Twould put me to° my slipper; but I feel not
      This deity in my bosom. Twenty consciences
      That stand twixt me and Milan,° candied° be
         they°
      And melt ere they molest!° Here lies your
         brother,
      No better than the earth he lies upon,
      If he were that which now he's like — that's
290   dead,

Whom I, with this obedient steel, three inches of
      it,
      Can lay to bed forever; whiles you, doing thus,°
      To the perpetual wink° for aye° might put
      This ancient morsel, this Sir Prudence, who
      Should not° upbraid our course. For all the rest,   295
      They'll take suggestion° as a cat laps milk;
      They'll tell the clock° to any business that
      We say befits the hour.
   SEBASTIAN: Thy case, dear friend,
      Shall be my precedent. As thou gott'st Milan,
      I'll come by Naples. Draw thy sword. One
         stroke   300
      Shall free thee from the tribute° which thou
         payest,
      And I the king shall love thee.
   ANTONIO: Draw together;
      And when I rear my hand, do you the like
      To fall it° on Gonzalo.   [They draw.]
   SEBASTIAN: O, but one word.
                                        [They talk apart.]

(Enter Ariel [invisible], with music and song.)

   ARIEL: My master through his art foresees the
         danger   305
      That you, his friend, are in, and sends me
         forth —
      For else his project dies — to keep them living.
                                 (Sings in Gonzalo's ear.)
      While you here do snoring lie,
      Open-eyed conspiracy
         His time° doth take.   310
      If of life you keep a care,
      Shake off slumber, and beware.
         Awake, awake!
   ANTONIO: Then let us both be sudden.°
   GONZALO [waking]: Now, good angels preserve the
         King!   315
                                        [The others wake.]
   ALONSO: Why, how now, ho, awake? Why are you
         drawn?
      Wherefore this ghastly looking?
   GONZALO: What's the matter?
   SEBASTIAN: Whiles we stood here securing° your
      repose,

---

261. **discharge:** Performance.   265. **cubit:** Ancient measure
of length, about twenty inches.   267. **Measure us:** I.e.,
traverse the cubits, find her way.   **Keep:** Stay (addressed
to Claribel).   268. **wake:** I.e., to his good fortune.   270.
There be: There are those.   271. **prate:** Speak foolishly.
273–74. **I . . . chat:** I could teach a jackdaw to talk as wisely,
or, be such a garrulous talker myself.   277. **content:** Desire, inclination.   278. **Tender:** Regard, look after.   281.
feater: More becomingly, fittingly.   284. **kibe:** Chilblain,
here a sore on the heel.   285. **put me to:** Oblige me to
wear.   287. **Milan:** The dukedom of Milan.   **candied:**
Frozen, congealed in crystalline form.   **be they:** May they
be.   288. **molest:** Interfere.

292. **thus:** The actor makes a stabbing gesture.   293. **wink:**
Sleep, closing of eyes.   **aye:** Ever.   295. **Should not:**
Would not then be able to.   296. **take suggestion:** Respond
to prompting.   297. **tell the clock:** I.e., agree, answer
appropriately, chime.   301. **tribute:** See I, II, 113–24.
304. **fall it:** Let it fall.   310. **time:** Opportunity.   314.
sudden: Quick.   318. **securing:** Standing guard over.

Even now, we heard a hollow burst of bellowing
320   Like bulls, or rather lions. Did 't not wake you?
It struck mine ear most terribly.
ALONSO: I heard nothing.
ANTONIO: O, 'twas a din to fright a monster's ear,
To make an earthquake! Sure it was the roar
Of a whole herd of lions.
325 ALONSO: Heard you this, Gonzalo?
GONZALO: Upon mine honor, sir, I heard a
humming,
And that a strange one too, which did awake
me.
I shaked you, sir, and cried.° As mine eyes
opened,
I saw their weapons drawn. There was a noise,
330   That's verily.° 'Tis best we stand upon our guard,
Or that we quit this place. Let's draw our
weapons.
ALONSO: Lead off this ground, and let's make
further search
For my poor son.
GONZALO: Heavens keep him from these
beasts!
For he is, sure, i' th' island.
ALONSO: Lead away.
ARIEL [aside]: Prospero my lord shall know what I
335   have done.
So, King, go safely on to seek thy son.
                              (Exeunt [separately].)

Scene II°

(Enter Caliban with a burden of wood. A noise of
thunder heard.)

CALIBAN: All the infections that the sun sucks up
From bogs, fens, flats,° on Prosper fall, and make
him
By inchmeal° a disease! His spirits hear me,
And yet I needs must° curse. But they'll nor°
pinch,
Fright me with urchin shows,° pitch me i' the
5   mire,
Nor lead me, like a firebrand,° in the dark
Out of my way, unless he bid 'em. But
For every trifle are they set upon me,
Sometimes like apes, that mow° and chatter at
me

And after bite me; then like hedgehogs, which   10
Lie tumbling in my barefoot way and mount
Their pricks at my footfall. Sometimes am I
All wound with° adders, who with cloven
tongues
Do hiss me into madness.

(Enter Trinculo.)

                              Lo, now, lo!
Here comes a spirit of his, and to torment me   15
For bringing wood in slowly. I'll fall flat.
Perchance he will not mind° me. [He lies down.]
TRINCULO: Here's neither bush nor shrub to bear off°
any weather at all. And another storm brewing; I
hear it sing i' the wind. Yond same black cloud,   20
yond huge one, looks like a foul bombard° that
would shed his° liquor. If it should thunder as it
did before, I know not where to hide my head.
Yond same cloud cannot choose but fall by pailfuls.
[Seeing Caliban.] What have we here, a man or a   25
fish? Dead or alive? A fish, he smells like a fish; a
very ancient and fishlike smell; a kind of not-of-
the-newest Poor John.° A strange fish! Were I in
England now, as once I was, and had but this fish
painted,° not a holiday fool there but would give   30
a piece of silver. There would this monster make
a man.° Any strange beast there makes a man.
When they will not give a doit° to relieve a lame
beggar, they will lay out ten to see a dead Indian.
Legged like a man, and his fins like arms! Warm,   35
o' my troth!° I do now let loose my opinion, hold
it° no longer: this is no fish, but an islander, that
hath lately suffered° by a thunderbolt. [Thunder.]
Alas, the storm is come again! My best way is to
creep under his gaberdine.° There is no other shelter   40
hereabout. Misery acquaints a man with strange
bedfellows. I will here shroud° till the dregs° of the
storm be past.
                    [He creeps under Caliban's garment.]

(Enter Stephano, singing, [a bottle in his hand].)

STEPHANO: "I shall no more to sea, to sea,
      Here shall I die ashore —"   45
This is a very scurvy tune to sing at a man's funeral.

328. cried: Called out.   **330. verily:** True.   **II, II. Location:** Another part of the island.   **2. flats:** Swamps.   **3. By
inchmeal:** Inch by inch.   **4. needs must:** Have to.   **nor:**
neither.   **5. urchin shows:** Elvish apparitions shaped like
hedgehogs.   **6. like a firebrand:** In the guise of a will-o'-
the-wisp.   **9. mow:** Make faces.

13. wound with: Entwined by.   **17. mind:** Notice.   **18.
bear off:** Keep off.   **21. foul bombard:** Dirty leather jug.
22. his: Its.   **28. Poor John:** Salted fish, type of poor fare.
30. painted: I.e., painted on a sign set up outside a booth or
tent at a fair.   **31–32. make a man:** (1) Make one's fortune,
(2) be indistinguishable from an Englishman.   **33. doit:**
Small coin.   **36. o' my troth:** By my faith.   **36–37. hold
it:** Hold it in.   **38. suffered:** I.e., died.   **40. gaberdine:**
Cloak, loose upper garment.   **42. shroud:** Take shelter.
dregs: Last remains (as in a *bombard* or jug, line 21).

Well, here's my comfort.   (*Drinks.*)
(*Sings.*)
"The master, the swabber,° the boatswain, and I,
    The gunner and his mate,
50 Loved Mall, Meg, and Marian, and Margery,
    But none of us cared for Kate.
        For she had a tongue with a tang,°
        Would cry to a sailor, 'Go hang!'
She loved not the savor of tar nor of pitch,
55 Yet a tailor might scratch her where'er she did itch.°
    Then to sea, boys, and let her go hang!"

This is a scurvy tune too. But here's my comfort.
                                            (*Drinks.*)
CALIBAN: Do not torment me!° O!
STEPHANO: What's the matter?° Have we devils here?
60 Do you put tricks upon 's° with savages and men
of Ind,° ha? I have not scaped drowning to be
afeard now of your four legs. For it hath been said,
"As proper° a man as ever went on four legs° cannot make him give ground"; and it shall be said so
65 again while Stephano breathes at'° nostrils.
CALIBAN: This spirit torments me! O!
STEPHANO: This is some monster of the isle with four
legs, who hath got, as I take it, an ague.° Where
the devil should he learn° our language? I will give
70 him some relief, if it be but for that.° If I can re-
cover° him and keep him tame and get to Naples
with him, he's a present for any emperor that ever
trod on neat's leather.°
CALIBAN: Do not torment me, prithee. I'll bring my
75 wood home faster.
STEPHANO: He's in his fit now and does not talk after
the wisest.° He shall taste of my bottle. If he have
never drunk wine afore,° it will go near to° remove
his fit. If I can recover° him and keep him tame, I
80 will not take too much° for him. He shall pay for
him that hath° him,° and that soundly.

48. **swabber:** Crew member whose job is to wash the decks.
52. **tang:** Sting.   55. **tailor ... itch:** A dig at tailors for their
supposed effeminacy and a bawdy suggestion of satisfying a
sexual craving.   58. **Do ... me:** Caliban assumes that one
of Prospero's spirits has come to punish him.   59. **What's
the matter:** What's going on here?   60. **put tricks upon 's:**
Trick us with conjuring shows.   61. **Ind:** India.   **proper:**
Handsome.   **four legs:** The conventional phrase would
supply *two legs*.   65. **at':** At the.   68. **ague:** Fever. (Probably both Caliban and Trinculo are quaking; see lines 58
and 83.)   69. **should he learn:** Could he have learned.
70. **for that:** I.e., for knowing our language.   71. **recover:**
Restore.   73. **neat's leather:** Cowhide.   76–77. **after the
wisest:** In the wisest fashion.   78. **afore:** Before.   **go near
to:** Nearly.   79. **recover:** Restore.   79–80. **I will ...
much:** I.e., no sum can be too much.   80–81. **He shall ...
hath him:** I.e., anyone who wants him will have to pay
dearly for him.   81. **hath:** Possesses, receives.

CALIBAN: Thou does me yet but little hurt; thou wilt
anon,° I know it by thy trembling. Now Prosper
works upon thee.
STEPHANO: Come on your ways. Open your mouth. 85
Here is that which will give language to you, cat.
Open your mouth.° This will shake your shaking, I
can tell you, and that soundly. [*Giving Caliban a
drink.*] You cannot tell who's your friend. Open
your chaps° again.   90
TRINCULO: I should know that voice. It should be —
but he is drowned, and these are devils. O, defend
me!
STEPHANO: Four legs and two voices — a most deli-
cate° monster! His forward voice now is to speak 95
well of his friend, his backward voice° is to utter
foul speeches and to detract. If all the wine in my
bottle will recover him,° I will help° his ague.
Come. [*Giving a drink.*] Amen! I will pour some in
thy other mouth.   100
TRINCULO: Stephano!
STEPHANO: Doth thy other mouth call me?° Mercy,
mercy! This is a devil, and no monster. I will leave
him. I have no long spoon.°
TRINCULO: Stephano! If thou beest Stephano, touch 105
me and speak to me, for I am Trinculo — be not
afeard — thy good friend Trinculo.
STEPHANO: If thou beest Trinculo, come forth. I'll pull
thee by the lesser legs. If any be Trinculo's legs,
these are they. [*Pulling him out.*] Thou art very 110
Trinculo indeed! How cam'st thou to be the siege°
of this mooncalf?° Can he vent° Trinculos?
TRINCULO: I took him to be killed with a thunder-
stroke. But art thou not drowned, Stephano? I hope
now thou art not drowned. Is the storm over- 115
blown?° I hid me under the dead mooncalf's gaberdine for fear of the storm. And art thou living,
Stephano? O Stephano, two Neapolitans scaped!
                        [*He capers with Stephano.*]
STEPHANO: Prithee, do not turn me about. My stom-
ach is not constant.°   120

83. **anon:** Presently.   86–87. **cat ... mouth:** Allusion to the
proverb "Good liquor will make a cat speak." 90. **chaps:**
Jaws.   94–95. **delicate:** Ingenious.   96. **backward voice:**
Trinculo and Caliban are facing in opposite directions.
Stephano supposes the monster to have a rear end that can
emit *foul speeches* or foul-smelling wind at the monster's
other mouth, line 100.   97–98. **If ... him:** Even if it takes
all the wine in my bottle to cure him.   98. **help:** Cure.
102. **call me:** I.e., call me by name, know supernaturally who
I am.   104. **long spoon:** Allusion to the proverb "He that
sups with the devil has need of a long spoon." 111. **siege:**
Excrement.   112. **mooncalf:** Monstrous or misshapen creature (whose deformity is caused by the malignant influence of
the moon).   **vent:** Excrete, defecate.   115–16. **overblown:**
Blown over.   120. **not constant:** Unsteady.

BELOW: Caliban (Avery Brooks), Stephano (Ernest Perry, Jr.), and Trinculo (Kelly Walters) in the 1987 Theatre for a New Audience production of *The Tempest,* directed by Julie Taymor. RIGHT: Avery Brooks as Caliban.

CALIBAN: These be fine things, an if° they be not
    spirits.
  That's a brave° god, and bears° celestial liquor.
  I will kneel to him.
STEPHANO: How didst thou scape? How cam'st thou
125   hither? Swear by this bottle how thou cam'st
   hither. I escaped upon a butt of sack° which the
   sailors heaved o'erboard — by this bottle,° which I
   made of the bark of a tree with mine own hands
   since° I was cast ashore.
130 CALIBAN [kneeling]: I'll swear upon that bottle to be
   thy true subject, for the liquor is not earthly.
STEPHANO: Here. Swear then how thou escapedst.
TRINCULO: Swum ashore, man, like a duck. I can
   swim like a duck, I'll be sworn.
135 STEPHANO: Here, kiss the book.° Though thou canst
   swim like a duck, thou art made like a goose.
                       [Giving him a drink.]
TRINCULO: O Stephano, hast any more of this?
STEPHANO: The whole butt, man. My cellar is in a
   rock by the seaside, where my wine is hid. — How
140 now, mooncalf? How does thine ague?
CALIBAN: Hast thou not dropped from heaven?
STEPHANO: Out o' the moon, I do assure thee. I was
   the man i' the moon when time was.°
CALIBAN: I have seen thee in her, and I do adore
   thee.
  My mistress showed me thee, and thy dog, and
145   thy bush.°
STEPHANO: Come, swear to that. Kiss the book. I will
   furnish it anon with new contents. Swear.
                       [Giving him a drink.]
TRINCULO: By this good light,° this is a very shallow
   monster! I afeard of him? A very weak monster!
150 The man i' the moon? A most poor credulous
   monster! Well drawn,° monster, in good sooth!°
CALIBAN [to Stephano]: I'll show thee every fertile
   inch o'th'island,
  And I will kiss thy foot. I prithee, be my god.
TRINCULO: By this light, a most perfidious and
155 drunken monster! When 's god's asleep, he'll rob
   his bottle.°

CALIBAN: I'll kiss thy foot. I'll swear myself thy sub-
   ject.
STEPHANO: Come on then. Down, and swear.
                     [Caliban kneels.]
TRINCULO: I shall laugh myself to death at this puppy-   160
   headed monster. A most scurvy monster! I could
   find in my heart to beat him —
STEPHANO: Come, kiss.
TRINCULO: But that the poor monster's in drink.° An
   abominable monster!   165
CALIBAN: I'll show thee the best springs. I'll pluck
   thee berries.
  I'll fish for thee and get thee wood enough.
  A plague upon the tyrant that I serve!
  I'll bear him no more sticks, but follow thee,
  Thou wondrous man.   170
TRINCULO: A most ridiculous monster, to make a
   wonder of a poor drunkard!
CALIBAN: I prithee, let me bring thee where crabs°
   grow;
  And I with my long nails will dig thee pignuts,°
  Show thee a jay's nest, and instruct thee how   175
  To snare the nimble marmoset.° I'll bring thee
  To clustering filberts, and sometimes I'll get thee
  Young scamels° from the rock. Wilt thou go with
   me?
STEPHANO: I prithee now, lead the way without any
   more talking. — Trinculo, the King and all our   180
   company else° being drowned, we will inherit°
   here. — Here, bear my bottle. — Fellow Trinculo,
   we'll fill him by and by again.
CALIBAN (sings drunkenly): Farewell, master, farewell,
   farewell!   185
TRINCULO: A howling monster; a drunken monster!
CALIBAN: No more dams I'll make for fish,
   Nor fetch in firing°
    At requiring,
  Nor scrape trenchering,° nor wash dish.   190
   'Ban, 'Ban, Ca-Caliban
   Has a new master. Get a new man!°
  Freedom, high-day!° High-day, freedom!
  Freedom, high-day, freedom!
STEPHANO: O brave monster! Lead the way.   195
                     (Exeunt.)

---

121. an if: If.   **122. brave:** Fine, magnificent.   **bears:** He
carries.   **126. butt of sack:** barrel of Canary wine.   **127.
by this bottle:** I.e., I swear by this bottle.   **128. since:** After.
135. book: I.e., bottle (but with ironic reference to the practice of kissing the Bible in swearing an oath; see *I'll be sworn*
in line 134).   **143. when time was:** Once upon a time.
145. dog . . . bush: The man in the moon was popularly
imagined to have with him a dog and a bush of thorn.
148. By . . . light: By God's light, by this good light from
heaven.   **151. Well drawn:** Well pulled (on the bottle).
in good sooth: Truly, indeed.   **155–56. When . . . bottle:**
I.e., Caliban wouldn't even stop at robbing his god of his
bottle if he could catch him asleep.

164. in drink: Drunk.   **173. crabs:** Crab apples, or perhaps
crabs.   **174. pignuts:** earthnuts, edible tuberous roots.
176. marmoset: Small monkey.   **178. scamels:** Possibly
seamews, mentioned in Strachey's letter, or shellfish; or perhaps from *squamelle*, furnished with little scales. Contemporary French and Italian travel accounts report that the natives
of Patagonia in South America ate small fish described as *fort
scameux* and *squame*.   **181. else:** In addition, besides ourselves.   **inherit:** Take possession.   **188. firing:** Firewood.
190. trenchering: Trenchers, wooden plates.   **192. Get a
new man:** Addressed to Prospero.   **193. high-day:** Holiday.

ACT III • Scene 1°

(*Enter Ferdinand, bearing a log.*)

FERDINAND: There be some sports° are painful,° and their labor
　Delight in them sets off.° Some kinds of baseness°
　Are nobly undergone,° and most poor° matters
　Point to rich ends. This my mean° task
5　Would be as heavy to me as odious, but°
　The mistress which I serve quickens° what's dead
　And makes my labors pleasures. O, she is
　Ten times more gentle than her father's crabbèd,
　And he's composed of harshness. I must remove
10　Some thousands of these logs and pile them up,
　Upon a sore injunction.° My sweet mistress
　Weeps when she sees me work and says such baseness
　Had never like executor.° I forget;°
　But these sweet thoughts do even refresh my labors,
　Most busy lest when I do it.°

(*Enter Miranda; and Prospero [at a distance, unseen].*)

15 MIRANDA:　　　　　　　　Alas now, pray you,
　Work not so hard. I would the lightning had
　Burnt up those logs that you are enjoined° to pile!
　Pray, set it down and rest you. When this° burns,
　'Twill weep° for having wearied you. My father
20　Is hard at study. Pray now, rest yourself.
　He's safe for these° three hours.
FERDINAND:　　　　　　　O most dear mistress,
　The sun will set before I shall discharge°
　What I must strive to do.
MIRANDA:　　　　　　　If you'll sit down,
　I'll bear your logs the while. Pray, give me that.
　I'll carry it to the pile.

FERDINAND:　　　　　　No, precious creature,　25
　I had rather crack my sinews, break my back,
　Than you should such dishonor undergo
　While I sit lazy by.
MIRANDA:　　　　　　It would become me
　As well as it does you; and I should do it
　With much more ease, for my good will is to it,　30
　And yours it is against.
PROSPERO [*aside*]:　　　Poor worm, thou art infected!
　This visitation° shows it.
MIRANDA:　　　　　　You look wearily.
FERDINAND: No, noble mistress, 'tis fresh morning with me
　When you are by° at night. I do beseech you —
　Chiefly that I might set it in my prayers —　35
　What is your name?
MIRANDA:　　　　　Miranda. — O my father,
　I have broke your hest° to say so.
FERDINAND:　　　　　　　Admired Miranda!°
　Indeed the top of admiration, worth
　What's dearest° to the world! Full many a lady
　I have eyed with best regard,° and many a time　40
　The harmony of their tongues hath into bondage
　Brought my too diligent° ear. For several° virtues
　Have I liked several women, never any
　With so full soul but some defect in her
　Did quarrel with the noblest grace she owed°　45
　And put it to the foil.° But you, O you,
　So perfect and so peerless, are created
　Of° every creature's best!
MIRANDA:　　　　　　I do not know
　One of my sex; no woman's face remember,
　Save, from my glass, mine own. Nor have I seen　50
　More that I may call men than you, good friend,
　And my dear father. How features are abroad°
　I am skilless° of; but, by my modesty,°
　The jewel in my dower, I would not wish
　Any companion in the world but you;　55
　Nor can imagination form a shape,
　Besides yourself, to like of.° But I prattle
　Something° too wildly, and my father's precepts
　I therein do forget.
FERDINAND:　　　　　I am in my condition°

60 A prince, Miranda; I do think, a king —
    I would, not so! — and would° no more endure
    This wooden slavery° than to suffer
    The flesh-fly° blow° my mouth. Hear my soul
        speak:
    The very instant that I saw you did
65 My heart fly to your service; there resides
    To make me slave to it, and for your sake
    Am I this patient log-man.
MIRANDA: Do you love me?
FERDINAND. O heaven, O earth, bear witness to this
        sound,
    And crown what I profess with kind event°
70 If I speak true! If hollowly,° invert°
    What best is boded° me to mischief!° I
    Beyond all limit of what° else i' the world
    Do love, prize, honor you.
MIRANDA [*weeping*]:   I am a fool
    I weep at what I am glad of.
PROSPERO [*aside*]:   Fair encounter
75 Of two most rare affections! Heavens rain grace
    On that which breeds between 'em!
FERDINAND: Wherefore weep you?
MIRANDA: At mine unworthiness, that dare not
        offer
    What I desire to give, and much less take
    What I shall die° to want.° But this is trifling,
80 And all the more it seeks to hide itself
    The bigger bulk it shows. Hence, bashful
        cunning,°
    And prompt me, plain and holy innocence!
    I am your wife, if you will marry me;
    If not, I'll die your maid.° To be your fellow°
85 You may deny me, but I'll be your servant
    Whether you will° or no.
FERDINAND: My mistress, dearest,
    And I thus humble ever.
MIRANDA: My husband, then?
FERDINAND: Ay, with a heart as willing°
90 As bondage e'er of freedom. Here's my hand.
MIRANDA [*clasping his hand*]: And mine, with my
        heart in 't. And now farewell
    Till half an hour hence.

FERDINAND: A thousand thousand!°
    (*Exeunt [Ferdinand and Miranda, separately]*.)
PROSPERO: So glad of this as they I cannot be,
    Who are surprised with all;° but my rejoicing
    At nothing can be more. I'll to my book,   95
    For yet ere suppertime must I perform
    Much business appertaining.°   (*Exit.*)

Scene II°

(*Enter Caliban, Stephano, and Trinculo.*)

STEPHANO: Tell not me. When the butt is out,° we will
    drink water, not a drop before. Therefore bear up
    and board 'em.° Servant monster, drink to me.
TRINCULO: Servant monster? The folly of° this island!
    They say there's but five upon this isle. We are   5
    three of them; if th' other two be brained° like us,
    the state totters.
STEPHANO: Drink, servant monster, when I bid thee.
    Thy eyes are almost set° in thy head.
            [*Giving a drink.*]
TRINCULO: Where should they be set° else? He were a   10
    brave° monster indeed if they were set in his tail.
STEPHANO: My man-monster hath drowned his
    tongue in sack. For my part, the sea cannot drown
    me. I swam, ere I could recover° the shore, five and
    thirty leagues° off and on.° By this light,° thou   15
    shalt be my lieutenant, monster, or my standard.°
TRINCULO: Your lieutenant, if you list.° He's no
    standard.°
STEPHANO: We'll not run,° Monsieur Monster.
TRINCULO: Nor go° neither, but you'll lie° like dogs   20
    and yet say nothing neither.
STEPHANO: Mooncalf, speak once in thy life, if thou
    beest a good mooncalf.

92. A thousand thousand: I.e., a thousand thousand
farewells.   **94. with all:** By everything that has happened;
or *withal*, with it.   **97. appertaining:** Related to this.   **III,
II. Location:** Another part of the island.   **1. out:** Empty.
2–3. bear . . . 'em: Stephano uses the terminology of maneuvering at sea and boarding a vessel under attack as a way of
urging an assault on the liquor supply.   **4. folly of:** I.e.
stupidity found on.   **6. be brained:** Are endowed with intelligence.   **9. set:** Fixed in a drunken state; or sunk, like
the sun.   **10. set:** Placed.   **11. brave:** Fine, splendid.
14. recover: Gain, reach.   **15. leagues:** Units of distance
each equaling about three miles.   **off and on:** Intermittently.   **By this light:** An oath by the light of the sun.
16. standard: Standard-bearer, ensign (as distinguished from
lieutenant, lines 15–17).   **17. list:** Prefer.   **17–18. no
standard:** I.e., not able to stand up.   **19. run:** (1) Retreat,
(2) urinate (taking Trinculo's *standard*, line 17, in the old
sense of "conduit").   **20. go:** Walk.   **lie:** (1) Tell lies, (2)
lie prostrate, (3) excrete.

61. would: Wish (it were).   **62. wooden slavery:** Being
compelled to carry wood.   **63. flesh-fly:** Insect that deposits its eggs in dead flesh.   **blow:** Befoul with fly eggs.
69. kind event: Favorable outcome.   **70. hollowly:** Insincerely, falsely.   **invert:** Turn.   **71. boded:** Destined for.
mischief: Evil.   **72. what:** Whatever.   **79. die:** Probably
with an unconscious sexual meaning that underlies all of
lines 77–81.   **want:** Lack.   **81. bashful cunning:** Coyness.
84. maid: Handmaiden, servant.   **fellow:** Mate, equal.
86. will: Desire it.   **My mistress:** I.e., the woman I adore
and serve (not an illicit sexual partner).   **89. willing:**
Desirous.

CALIBAN: How does thy honor? Let me lick thy
    shoe.
25   I'll not serve him. He is not valiant.
TRINCULO: Thou liest, most ignorant monster, I am in
    case to jostle a constable.° Why, thou debauched
    fish, thou, was there ever man a coward that hath
    drunk so much sack° as I today? Wilt thou tell a
30   monstrous lie, being but half a fish and half a
    monster?
CALIBAN: Lo, how he mocks me! Wilt thou let him,
    my lord?
TRINCULO: "Lord," quoth he? That a monster should
    be such a natural!°
35 CALIBAN: Lo, lo, again! Bite him to death, I prithee.
STEPHANO: Trinculo, keep a good tongue in your
    head. If you prove a mutineer — the next tree!°
    The poor monster's my subject, and he shall not
    suffer indignity.
CALIBAN: I thank my noble lord. Wilt thou be
40   pleased
    To hearken once again to the suit I made to
    thee?
STEPHANO: Marry,° will I. Kneel and repeat it. I will
    stand, and so shall Trinculo. [*Caliban kneels.*]

(*Enter Ariel, invisible.°*)

CALIBAN: As I told thee before, I am subject to a
    tyrant,
45   A sorcerer, that by his cunning hath
    Cheated me of the island.
ARIEL [*mimicking Trinculo*]: Thou liest.
CALIBAN: Thou liest, thou jesting monkey, thou!
    I would my valiant master would destroy thee.
    I do not lie.
50 STEPHANO: Trinculo, if you trouble him any more in 's
    tale, by this hand, I will supplant° some of your
    teeth.
TRINCULO: Why, I said nothing.
STEPHANO: Mum, then, and no more. — Proceed.
55 CALIBAN: I say by sorcery he got this isle;
    From me he got it. If thy greatness will
    Revenge it on him — for I know thou dar'st,
    But this thing° dare not —
STEPHANO: That's most certain.
CALIBAN: Thou shalt be lord of it, and I'll serve
60   thee.

STEPHANO: How now shall this be compassed?°
    Canst thou bring me to the party?
CALIBAN: Yea, yea, my lord. I'll yield him thee
    asleep,
    Where thou mayst knock a nail into his head.
ARIEL: Thou liest; thou canst not.   65
CALIBAN: What a pied ninny's° this! Thou scurvy
    patch!° —
    I do beseech thy greatness, give him blows
    And take his bottle from him. When that's gone
    He shall drink naught but brine, for I'll not show
    him
    Where the quick freshes° are.   70
STEPHANO: Trinculo, run into no further danger. In-
    terrupt the monster one word further° and, by this
    hand, I'll turn my mercy out o' doors° and make a
    stockfish° of thee.
TRINCULO: Why, what did I? I did nothing. I'll go far- 75
    ther off.°
STEPHANO: Didst thou not say he lied?
ARIEL: Thou liest.
STEPHANO: Do I so? Take thou that. [*He beats Trin-*
    culo.] As you like this, give me the lie° another 80
    time.
TRINCULO: I did not give the lie. Out o' your wits and
    hearing too? A pox o' your bottle! This can sack
    and drinking do. A murrain° on your monster, and
    the devil take your fingers!   85
CALIBAN: Ha, ha, ha!
STEPHANO: Now, forward with your tale. [*To*
    Trinculo.] Prithee, stand further off.
CALIBAN: Beat him enough. After a little time
    I'll beat him too.
STEPHANO: Stand farther. — Come, proceed.   90
CALIBAN: Why, as I told thee, tis a custom with him
    I' th' afternoon to sleep. There thou mayst brain
    him,
    Having first seized his books; or with a log
    Batter his skull, or paunch° him with a stake,
    Or cut his weasand° with thy knife. Remember   95
    First to possess his books, for without them
    He's but a sot,° as I am, nor hath not
    One spirit to command. They all do hate him
    As rootedly as I. Burn but his books.
    He has brave utensils° — for so he calls them —   100

---

27. **in case . . . constable:** I.e., in fit condition, made valiant
by drink, to taunt or challenge the police.   **29. sack:** Spanish white wine.   **34. natural:** (1) Idiot, (2) natural as opposed to unnatural, monsterlike.   **37. the next tree:** I.e.,
you'll hang.   **42. Marry:** I.e., indeed. (Originally an oath:
by the Virgin Mary.)   **43.** [S.D.] *invisible*: I.e., wearing a
garment to connote invisibility, as at I, II, 377.   **51. supplant:** Uproot, displace.   **58. this thing:** I.e., Trinculo.

61. **compassed:** Achieved.   **66. pied ninny:** Fool in motley.
patch: Fool.   **70. quick freshes:** Running springs.
72. one word further: I.e., one more time.   **73. turn . . .
doors:** I.e., forget about being merciful.   **74. stockfish:**
Dried cod beaten before cooking.   **76. off:** Away.
80. give me the lie: Call me a liar to my face.   **84. murrain:**
Plague (literally, a cattle disease).   **94. paunch:** Stab in
the belly.   **95. weasand:** Windpipe.   **97. sot:** Fool.   **100.
brave utensils:** Fine furnishings.

Which, when he has a house, he'll deck withal.°
And that most deeply to consider is
The beauty of his daughter. He himself
Calls her a nonpareil. I never saw a woman
105 But only Sycorax my dam and she;
But she as far surpasseth Sycorax
As great'st does least.
STEPHANO: Is it so brave° a lass?
CALIBAN: Ay, lord. She will become° thy bed, I
warrant,
110 And bring thee forth brave brood.
STEPHANO: Monster, I will kill this man. His daughter
and I will be king and queen — save Our
Graces! — and Trinculo and thyself shall be
viceroys. Dost thou like the plot, Trinculo?
115 TRINCULO: Excellent.
STEPHANO: Give me thy hand. I am sorry I beat thee;
but, while thou liv'st, keep a good tongue in thy
head.
CALIBAN: Within this half hour will he be asleep. Wilt
120 thou destroy him then?
STEPHANO: Ay, on mine honor.
ARIEL [aside]: This will I tell my master.
CALIBAN: Thou mak'st me merry; I am full of
pleasure.
Let us be jocund.° Will you troll the catch°
125 You taught me but whilere?°
STEPHANO: At thy request, monster, I will do reason,
any reason.° Come on, Trinculo, let us sing.
(Sings.)
"Flout° 'em and scout° 'em
And scout 'em and flout 'em!
130   Thought is free."
CALIBAN: That's not the tune.
(Ariel plays the tune on a tabor° and pipe.)
STEPHANO: What is this same?
TRINCULO: This is the tune of our catch, played by the
picture of Nobody.°
135 STEPHANO: If thou beest a man, show thyself in thy
likeness. If thou beest a devil, take 't as thou list.°
TRINCULO: O, forgive me my sins!
STEPHANO: He that dies pays all debts. I defy thee.
Mercy upon us!
140 CALIBAN: Art thou afeard?
STEPHANO: No, monster, not I.

CALIBAN: Be not afeard. The isle is full of noises,
Sounds, and sweet airs, that give delight and hurt
not.
Sometimes a thousand twangling instruments
Will hum about mine ears, and sometimes voices 145
That, if I then had waked after long sleep,
Will make me sleep again; and then, in dreaming,
The clouds methought would open and show
riches
Ready to drop upon me, that when I waked
I cried to dream° again.   150
STEPHANO: This will prove a brave kingdom to me,
where I shall have my music for nothing.
CALIBAN: When Prospero is destroyed.
STEPHANO: That shall be by and by.° I remember the
story.   155
TRINCULO: The sound is going away. Let's follow it,
and after do our work.
STEPHANO: Lead, monster; we'll follow. I would I
could see this laborer! He lays it on.°
TRINCULO: Wilt come? I'll follow Stephano.   160
(Exeunt [following Ariel's music].)

Scene III°

(Enter Alonso, Sebastian, Antonio, Gonzalo, Adrian,
Francisco, etc.)

GONZALO: By 'r lakin,° I can go no further, sir.
My old bones aches. Here's a maze trod indeed
Through forthrights and meanders!° By your
patience,
I needs must° rest me.
ALONSO: Old lord, I cannot blame thee,
Who am myself attached° with weariness,   5
To the dulling of my spirits.° Sit down and rest.
Even here I will put off my hope, and keep it
No longer for° my flatterer. He is drowned
Whom thus we stray to find, and the sea mocks
Our frustrate° search on land. Well, let him go. 10
[Alonso and Gonzalo sit.]
ANTONIO [aside to Sebastian]: I am right° glad that
he's so out of hope.°
Do not, for° one repulse, forgo the purpose

101. deck withal: Furnish it with.   108. brave: Splendid,
attractive.   109. become: Suit.   124. jocund: Jovial,
merry.   troll the catch: Sing the round.   125. but whilere:
Only a short time ago.   126–27. reason, any reason: Anything reasonable.   128. Flout: Scoff at.   scout: Deride.
131. [S.D.] tabor: Small drum.   134. picture of Nobody:
Refers to a familiar figure with head, arms, and legs but no
trunk.   136. take 't . . . list: I.e., take my defiance as you
please, as best you can.

150. to dream: Desirous of dreaming.   154. by and by:
Very soon.   159. lays it on: I.e., plays the drum skillfully
and energetically.   III, III. Location: Another part of the island.   1. By 'r lakin: By our Ladykin, by our Lady.
3. forthrights and meanders: Paths straight and crooked.
4. needs must: Have to.   5. attached: Seized.   6. To . . .
spirits: To the point of being dull-spirited.   8. for: As.
10. frustrate: Frustrated.   11. right: Very.   out of hope:
Despairing, discouraged.   12. for: Because of.

That you resolved t' effect.
SEBASTIAN [*to Antonio*]:   The next advantage
  Will we take throughly.°
ANTONIO [*to Sebastian*]: Let it be tonight,
15 For, now° they are oppressed with travel,° they
  Will not, nor cannot, use° such vigilance
  As when they are fresh.
SEBASTIAN [*to Antonio*]:   I say tonight. No more.
              (*Solemn and strange music; and
              Prospero on the top,° invisible.*)
ALONSO: What harmony is this? My good friends,
  hark!
GONZALO: Marvelous sweet music!

(*Enter several strange shapes, bringing in a banquet,
and dance about it with gentle actions of salutations;
and, inviting the King, etc., to eat, they depart.*)

ALONSO: Give us kind keepers,° heavens! What were
20 these?
SEBASTIAN: A living° drollery.° Now I will believe
  That there are unicorns; that in Arabia
  There is one tree, the phoenix'° throne, one
    phoenix
  At this hour reigning there.
ANTONIO: I'll believe both;
25 And what does else want credit,° come to me
  And I'll be sworn 'tis true. Travelers ne'er did lie,
  Thou fools at home condemn 'em.
GONZALO: If in Naples
  I should report this now, would they believe me
  If I should say I saw such islanders?
30 For, certes,° these are people of the island,
  Who though they are of monstrous shape, yet
    note,
  Their manners are more gentle, kind, than of
  Our human generation you shall find
  Many, nay, almost any.
PROSPERO [*aside*]:   Honest lord,
  Thou hast said well, for some of you there
35   present
  Are worse than devils.
ALONSO: I cannot too much muse°
  Such shapes, such gesture, and such sound,
    expressing —

Although they want° the use of tongue — a kind
  Of excellent dumb discourse.
PROSPERO [*aside*]:   Praise in departing.°
FRANCISCO: They vanished strangely.
SEBASTIAN: No matter, since   40
  They have left their viands° behind, for we have
    stomachs.°
  Will 't please you taste of what is here?
ALONSO: Not I.
GONZALO: Faith, sir, you need not fear. When we
  were boys,
  Who would believe that there were
    mountaineers°
  Dewlapped° like bulls, whose throats had
    hanging et 'em   45
  Wallets° of flesh? Or that there were such men
  Whose heads stood in their breasts?° Which now
    we find
  Each putter-out of five for one° will bring us
  Good warrant° of.
ALONSO: I will stand to° and feed,
  Although my last° — no matter, since I feel   50
  The best° is past. Brother, my lord the Duke,
  Stand to, and do as we.
              [*They approach the table.*]

(*Thunder and lightning. Enter Ariel, like a harpy,°
claps his wings upon the table, and with a quaint de-
vice° the banquet vanishes.°*)

ARIEL: You are three men of sin, whom Destiny —
  That hath to° instrument this lower world
  And what is in 't — the never-surfeited sea   55
  Hath caused to belch up you, and on this island
  Where man doth not inhabit, you 'mongst men
  Being most unfit to live. I have made you mad;
  And even with suchlike valor° men hang and
    drown

---

14. **throughly:** Thoroughly.   15. **now:** Now that.   **travel:**
Spelled *trauaile* in the Folio and carrying the sense of labor as
well as traveling.   16. **use:** Apply.   17. [S.D.] **on the top:** At
some high point of the tiring-house or the theater, on a third
level above the gallery.   20. **kind keepers:** Guardian angels.
21. **living:** With live actors.   **drollery:** Comic entertainment,
caricature, puppet show.   23. **phoenix:** Mythical bird consumed to ashes every five to six hundred years only to be renewed into another cycle.   25. **want credit:** Lack credence.
30. **certes:** Certainly.   36. **muse:** Wonder at.

38. **want:** Lack.   39. **Praise in departing:** I.e., save your
praise until the end of the performance (proverbial).
41. **viands:** Provisions.   **stomachs:** Appetites.   44. **moun-
taineers:** Mountain dwellers.   45. **Dewlapped:** Having a
dewlap, or fold of skin hanging from the neck, like cattle.
46. **Wallets:** Pendent folds of skin, wattles.   47. **in their
breasts:** I.e., like the Anthropophagi described in *Othello*, I,
III, 146.   48. **putter-out . . . one:** One who invests money or
gambles on the risks of travel on the condition that, if he returns safely, he is to receive five times the amount deposited;
hence, any traveler.   49. **Good warrant:** Assurance.
stand to: Fall to; take the risk.   50. **Although my last:** Even
if this were to be my last meal.   51. **best:** Best part of life.
52. [S.D.] **harpy:** A fabulous monster with a woman's face
and breasts and a vulture's body, supposed to be a minister
of divine vengeance.   **quaint device:** Ingenious stage contrivance.   **the banquet vanishes:** I.e., the food vanishes, the
table remains until line 82.   54. **to:** I.e., as its.   59. **such-
like valor:** I.e., the reckless valor derived from madness.

Their proper° selves.

[*Alonso, Sebastian, and Antonio draw their swords.*]

60   You fools! I and my fellows
Are ministers of Fate. The elements
Of whom° your swords are tempered° may as
   well
Wound the loud winds, or with bemocked-at°
   stabs
Kill the still-closing° waters, as diminish
65 One dowl° that's in my plume. My fellow
   ministers
Are like° invulnerable. If° you could hurt,
Your swords are now too massy° for your
   strengths
And will not be uplifted. But remember —
For that's my business to you — that you three
70 From Milan did supplant good Prospero;
Exposed unto the sea, which hath requit° it,
Him and his innocent child; for which foul deed
The powers, delaying, not forgetting, have
Incensed the seas and shores, yea, all the
   creatures,
75 Against your peace. Thee of thy son, Alonso,
They have bereft; and do pronounce by me
Lingering perdition,° worse than any death
Can be at once, shall step by step attend
You and your ways; whose° wraths to guard you
   from —
80 Which here, in this most desolate isle, else° falls
Upon your heads — is nothing° but heart's
   sorrow
And a clear° life ensuing.

(*He vanishes in thunder; then, to soft music, enter the shapes again, and dance, with mocks and mows,° and carrying out the table.*)

PROSPERO: Bravely° the figure of this harpy hast
   thou
Performed, my Ariel; a grace it had devouring.°

Of my instruction hast thou nothing bated°   85
In what thou hadst to say. So,° with good life°
And observation strange,° my meaner° ministers
Their several kinds° have done. My high charms
   work,
And these mine enemies are all knit up
In their distractions. They now are in my power;   90
And in these fits I leave them, while I visit
Young Ferdinand, whom they suppose is
   drowned,
And his and mine loved darling.   [*Exit above.*]
GONZALO: I' the name of something holy, sir, why°
   stand you
In this strange stare?
ALONSO: O, it° is monstrous, monstrous!   95
Methought the billows° spoke and told me of it;
The winds did sing it to me, and the thunder,
That deep and dreadful organ pipe, pronounced
The name of Prosper; it did bass my trespass.°
Therfor° my son i' th' ooze is bedded; and   100
I'll seek him deeper than e'er plummet sounded,°
And with him there lie mudded.   (*Exit.*)
SEBASTIAN: But one fiend at a time,
I'll fight their legions o'er.°
ANTONIO: I'll be thy second.
(*Exeunt* [*Sebastian and Antonio*].)
GONZALO: All three of them are desperate.° Their
   great guilt,   105
Like poison given to work a great time after,
Now 'gins to bite the spirits.° I do beseech you
That are of suppler joints, follow them swiftly
And hinder them from what this ecstasy°
May now provoke them to.
ADRIAN: Follow, I pray you.   110
(*Exeunt omnes.°*)

---

60. proper: Own.   **62. whom:** Which.   **tempered:** Composed and hardened.   **63. bemocked-at:** Scorned.   **64. still-closing:** Always closing again when parted.   **65. dowl:** Soft, fine feather.   **66. like:** Likewise, similarly.   **If:** Even if.   **67. massy:** Heavy.   **71. requit:** Requited, avenged.   **77. perdition:** Ruin, destruction.   **79. whose:** Refers to the heavenly powers.   **80. else:** Otherwise.   **81. is nothing:** There is no way.   **82. clear:** Unspotted, innocent.   [S.D.] *mocks and mows:* Mocking gestures and grimaces. **83. Bravely:** Finely, dashingly.   **84. a grace . . . devouring:** I.e., you gracefully caused the banquet to disappear as if you had consumed it (with puns on *grace* meaning "gracefulness" and "a blessing on the meal" and on *devouring* meaning "a literal eating" and "an all-consuming or ravishing grace").

85. bated: Abated, omitted.   **86. So:** In the same fashion. **good life:** Faithful reproduction.   **87. observation strange:** Exceptional attention to detail.   **meaner:** I.e., subordinate to Ariel.   **88. several kinds:** Individual parts.   **94. why:** Gonzalo was not addressed in Ariel's speech to the *three men of sin,* (line 53) and is not, as they are, in a maddened state; see lines 105–7.   **95. it:** I.e., my sin (also in line 96). **96. billows:** Waves.   **99. bass my trespass:** Proclaim my trespass like a bass note in music.   **100. Therefor:** In consequence of that.   **101. plummet:** A lead weight attached to a line for testing depth.   **sounded:** Probed, tested the depth of.   **104. o'er:** One after another.   **105. desperate:** Despairing and reckless.   **107. bite the spirits:** Sap their vital powers through anguish.   **109. ecstasy:** mad frenzy. **110.** [S.D.] *omnes:* Latin for "all."

ACT IV • *Scene I*°

(*Enter Prospero, Ferdinand, and Miranda.*)

PROSPERO: If I have too austerely° punished you,
   Your compensation makes amends, for I
   Have given you here a third° of mine own life,
   Or that for which I live; who once again
5 I tender to thy hand. All thy vexations°
   Were but my trials of thy love, and thou
   Hast strangely° stood the test. Here, afore
     Heaven,
   I ratify this my rich gift. O Ferdinand,
   Do not smile at me that I boast her off,°
10 For thou shalt find she will outstrip all praise
   And make it halt° behind her.
FERDINAND: I do believe it
   Against an oracle.°
PROSPERO: Then, as my gift and thine own
     acquisition
   Worthily purchased, take my daughter. But
15 If thou dost break her virgin-knot before
   All sanctimonious° ceremonies may
   With full and holy rite be ministered,
   No sweet aspersion° shall the heavens let fall
   To make this contract grow; but barren hate
20 Sour-eyed disdain, and discord shall bestrew
   The union of your bed with weeds° so loathly
   That you shall hate it both. Therefore take heed,
   As Hymen's lamps shall light you.°
FERDINAND: As I hope
   For quiet days, fair issue,° and long life,
25 With such love as 'tis now, the murkiest den,
   The most opportune place, the strong'st
     suggestion°
   Our worser genius° can,° shall never melt
   Mine honor into lust, to° take away

The edge° of that day's celebration
When I shall think or° Phoebus' steeds are
   foundered°   30
Or Night kept chained below.
PROSPERO: Fairly spoke.
Sit then and talk with her. She is thine own.
   [*Ferdinand and Miranda sit and talk together.*]
What,° Ariel! My industrious servant, Ariel!

(*Enter Ariel.*)

ARIEL: What would my potent master? Here I am.
PROSPERO: Thou and thy meaner fellows° your last
   service   35
   Did worthily perform, and I must use you
   In such another trick.° Go bring the rabble,°
   O'er whom I give thee power, here to this place.
   Incite them to quick motion, for I must
   Bestow upon the eyes of this young couple   40
   Some vanity° of mine art. It is my promise,
   And they expect it from me.
ARIEL: Presently?°
PROSPERO: Ay, with a twink.°
ARIEL: Before you can say "Come" and "Go,"
   And breathe twice, and cry "So, so,"   45
   Each one, tripping on his toe,
   Will be here with mop and mow.°
   Do you love me, master? No?
PROSPERO: Dearly, my delicate Ariel. Do not
     approach
   Till thou dost hear me call.
ARIEL: Well, I conceive.°   50
                          (*Exit.*)
PROSPERO: Look thou be true;° do not give dalliance
   Too much the rein. The strongest oaths are straw
   To the fire i' the blood. Be more abstemious,
   Or else good night° your vow!
FERDINAND: I warrant° you, sir,
   The white cold virgin snow upon my heart°   55
   Abates the ardor of my liver.°

IV, I. **Location:** Before Prospero's cell. **1. austerely:** Severely. **3. a third:** I.e., Miranda, into whose education Prospero has put a third of his life (?) or who represents a large part of what he cares about, along with his dukedom and his learned study (?). **5. vexations:** Torments. **7. strangely:** Extraordinarily. **9. boast her off:** I.e., praise her so; or perhaps an error for "boast of her"; the Folio reads "boast her of." **11. halt:** Limp. **12. Against an oracle:** I.e., even if an oracle should declare otherwise. **16. sanctimonious:** Sacred. **18. aspersion:** Dew, shower. **21. weeds:** In place of the flowers customarily strewn on the marriage bed. **23. As . . . you:** I.e., as you long for happiness and concord in your marriage. (Hymen was the Greek and Roman god of marriage; his symbolic torches, the wedding torches, were supposed to burn brightly for a happy marriage, smokily for a troubled one.) **24. issue:** Offspring. **26. suggestion:** Temptation. **27. worser genius:** Evil genius, or evil attendant spirit. **can:** Is capable of. **28. to:** So as to.

29. edge: Keen enjoyment, sexual ardor. **30. or:** either. **foundered:** Broken down, made lame. (Ferdinand will wait impatiently for the bridal night.) **33. What:** Now then. **35. meaner fellows:** Subordinates. **37. trick:** Device. **rabble:** Band, i.e., the *meaner fellows* of line 35. **41. vanity:** (1) Illusion, (2) trifle, (3) desire for admiration, conceit. **42. Presently:** Immediately. **43. with a twink:** In the twinkling of an eye, in an instant. **47. mop and mow:** Gestures and grimaces. **50. conceive:** Understand. **51. true:** True to your promise. **54. good night:** I.e., say good-bye to. **warrant:** Guarantee. **55. The white . . . heart:** I.e., the ideal of chastity and consciousness of Miranda's chaste innocence enshrined in my heart. **56. liver:** As the presumed seat of the passions.

PROSPERO: Well.
    Now come, my Ariel! Bring a corollary,°
    Rather than want° a spirit. Appear, and
       pertly!° —
    No tongue!° All eyes! Be silent.   (*Soft music.*)

(*Enter Iris.*°)

60 IRIS: Ceres,° most bounteous lady, thy rich leas°
    Of wheat, rye, barley, vetches,° oats, and peas;
    Thy turfy mountains, where live nibbling sheep,
    And flat meads° thatched with stover,° them to
      keep;
    Thy banks with pionèd and twillèd° brims,
65   Which spongy° April at thy hest betrims
    To make cold nymphs chaste crowns; and thy
      broom groves,°
    Whose shadow the dismissèd bachelor° loves
    Being lass-lorn; thy poll-clipped° vineyard;
    And thy sea marge,° sterile and rocky hard,
    Where thou thyself dost air: the queen o' the
70   sky,°
    Whose watery arch° and messenger am I,
    Bids thee leave these, and with her sovereign
      grace,
         (*Juno descends*° [*slowly in her car*].)
    Here on this grass plot, in this very place,
    To come and sport. Her peacocks° fly amain.°
75   Approach, rich Ceres, her to entertain.°

(*Enter Ceres.*)

CERES: Hail, many-colored messenger, that ne'er
    Dost disobey the wife of Jupiter,
    Who with thy saffron° wings upon my flowers
    Diffusest honeydrops, refreshing showers,
80   And with each end of thy blue bow° dost crown
    My bosky° acres and my unshrubbed down,°

Rich scarf to my proud earth. Why hath thy
    queen
Summoned me hither to this short-grassed green?
IRIS: A contract of true love to celebrate,
    And some donation freely to estate°   85
    On the blest lovers.
CERES: Tell me, heavenly bow,
    If Venus or her son,° as° thou dost know,
    Do now attend the Queen? Since they did plot
    The means that dusky° Dis my daughter got,°
    Her° and her blind boy's scandaled° company   90
    I have forsworn.
IRIS: Of her society°
    Be not afraid. I met her deity°
    Cutting the clouds towards Paphos,° and her son
    Dove-drawn° with her. Here thought they to
      have done°
    Some wanton charm° upon this man and maid,   95
    Whose vows are that no bed-right shall be paid
    Till Hymen's torch be lighted, but in vain.
    Mars's hot minion° is returned° again;
    Her waspish-headed° son has broke his arrows,
    Swears he will shoot no more, but play with
      sparrows°   100
    And be a boy right out.°

[*Juno alights.*]

CERES: Highest Queen of state,°
    Great Juno, comes; I know her by her gait.°
JUNO: How does my bounteous sister? Go with me
    To bless this twain, that they may prosperous be
    And honored in their issue.°   (*They sing.*)   105
JUNO: Honor, riches, marriage blessing,
    Long continuance, and increasing,
    Hourly joys be still° upon you!
    Juno sings her blessings on you.
CERES: Earth's increase, foison plenty,°   110
    Barns and garners° never empty,

---

57. corollary: Surplus, extra supply.   **58. want:** Lack.
pertly: Briskly.   **59. No tongue:** All the beholders are to be
silent (lest the spirits vanish).   [S.D.] *Iris:* Goddess of the
rainbow and Juno's messenger.   **60. Ceres:** Goddess of
the generative power of nature.   **leas:** Meadows.   **61.
vetches:** Plants for forage, fodder.   **63. meads:** Meadows.
stover: Winter fodder for cattle.   **64. pionèd and twillèd:**
Undercut by the swift current and protected by roots and
branches that tangle to form a barricade.   **65. spongy:**
Wet.   **66. broom groves:** Clumps of broom, gorse, yellow-
flowered shrub.   **67. dismissèd bachelor:** Rejected male
lover.   **68. poll-clipped:** Pruned, looped at the top, or *pole-
clipped*, hedged in with poles.   **69. sea marge:** Shore.
70. queen o' the sky: I.e., Juno.   **71. watery arch:** Rainbow.   **72.** [S.D.] *Juno descends:* I.e., starts her descent from
the "heavens" above the stage (?).   **74. peacocks:** Birds sacred to Juno and used to pull her chariot.   **amain:** With
full speed.   **75. entertain:** Receive.   **78. saffron:** Yellow.
80. bow: I.e., rainbow.   **81. bosky:** Wooded.   **down:** Upland.

85. estate: Bestow.   **87. son:** I.e., Cupid.   **as:** As far as.
89. dusky: Dark.   **Dis . . . got:** Pluto, or *Dis,* god of the infernal regions, carried off Persephone, daughter of Ceres, to
be his bride in Hades.   **90. Her:** I.e., Venus's.   **scandaled:**
Scandalous.   **91. society:** Company.   **92. her deity:** I.e.,
Her highness.   **93. Paphos:** Place on the island of
Cyprus sacred to Venus.   **94. Dove-drawn:** Venus's chariot
was drawn by doves.   **done:** Placed.   **95. wanton
charm:** Lustful spell.   **98. Mars's hot minion:** I.e., Venus,
the beloved of Mars.   **returned:** I.e., returned to Paphos.
99. waspish-headed: Fiery, hotheaded, peevish.   **100. spar-
rows:** Supposed lustful, and sacred to Venus.   **101. right
out:** Outright.   **Highest . . . state:** Most majestic Queen.
102. gait: I.e., majestic bearing.   **105. issue:** Offspring.
108. still: Always.   **110. foison plenty:** Plentiful harvest.
111. garners: Granaries.

Vines with clustering bunches growing,
Plants with goodly burden bowing;

Spring come to you at the farthest
115   In the very end of harvest!°
Scarcity and want shall shun you;
Ceres' blessing so is on you.
FERDINAND: This is a most majestic vision, and
Harmonious charmingly.° May I be bold
To think these spirits?
120   PROSPERO: Spirits, which by mine art
I have from their confines called to enact
My present fancies.
FERDINAND: Let me live here ever!
So rare a wondered° father and a wife
Makes this place Paradise.
          (*Juno and Ceres whisper, and send Iris on
                                        employment.*)
PROSPERO: Sweet now, silence!
125   Juno and Ceres whisper seriously;
There's something else to do. Hush and be mute.
Or else our spell is marred.
IRIS: You nymphs, called naiads,° of the windring°
          brooks,
With your sedged° crowns and ever-harmless°
          looks,
Leave your crisp° channels, and on this green
130   land
Answer your summons; Juno does command.
Come, temperate° nymphs, and help to celebrate
A contract of true love. Be not too late.

(*Enter certain nymphs.*)

You sunburnt sicklemen,° of August weary,°
135   Come hither from the furrow° and be merry.
Make holiday; your rye-straw hats put on,
And these fresh nymphs encounter° every one
In country footing.°

(*Enter certain reapers, properly° habited. They join
with the nymphs in a graceful dance, toward the end
whereof Prospero starts suddenly, and speaks; after
which, to a strange, hollow, and confused noise, they
heavily° vanish.*)

PROSPERO [*aside*]: I had forgot that foul conspiracy
Of the beast Caliban and his confederates   140
Against my life. The minute of their plot
Is almost come. [*To the Spirits.*] Well done!
          Avoid;° no more!
FERDINAND [*to Miranda*]: This is strange. Your
          father's in some passion
That works° him strongly.
MIRANDA: Never till this day
Saw I him touched with anger so distempered.   145
PROSPERO: You do look, my son, in a moved sort,°
As if you were dismayed. Be cheerful, sir.
Our revels° now are ended. These our actors,
As I foretold you, were all spirits and
Are melted into air, into thin air;   150
And, like the baseless° fabric of this vision,
The cloud-capped towers, the gorgeous palaces,
The solemn temples, the great globe° itself,
Yea, all which it inherit,° shall dissolve,
And, like this insubstantial pageant faded,   155
Leave not a rack° behind. We are such stuff
As dreams are made on,° and our little life
Is rounded° with a sleep. Sir, I am vexed.
Bear with° my weakness. My old brain is
          troubled.
Be not disturbed with my infirmity.   160
If you be pleased, retire° into my cell
And there repose. A turn or two I'll walk
To still my beating° mind.
FERDINAND, MIRANDA: We wish your peace.
          (*Exeunt [Ferdinand and Miranda].*)
PROSPERO: Come with a thought!° I thank thee,
          Ariel. Come.

(*Enter Ariel.*)

ARIEL: Thy thoughts I cleave° to. What's thy
          pleasure?
PROSPERO: Spirit,   165
We must prepare to meet with Caliban.
ARIEL: Ay, my commander. When I presented° Ceres,
I thought to have told thee of it, but I feared
Lest I might anger thee.

---

115. **In...harvest:** I.e., with no winter in between.
119. **charmingly:** Enchantingly. 123. **wondered:** Wonder-performing, wondrous. 128. **naiads:** Nymphs of springs, rivers, or lakes. **windring:** wandering, winding (?). 129. **sedged:** Made of reeds. **ever-harmless:** Ever-innocent. 130. **crisp:** Curled, rippled. 132. **temperate:** Chaste. 134. **sicklemen:** Harvesters, field workers who cut down grain and grass. **weary:** I.e., weary of the hard work of the harvest. 135. **furrow:** I.e., plowed fields. 137. **encounter:** Join. 138. **country footing:** Country dancing. [S.D.] *properly:* Suitably. *heavily:* Slowly, dejectedly.

142. **Avoid:** Depart, withdraw. 144. **works:** Affects, agitates. 146. **moved sort:** Troubled state, condition. 148. **revels:** Entertainment, pageant. 151. **baseless:** Without substance. 153. **great globe:** With a glance at the Globe Theatre. 154. **which it inherit:** Who subsequently occupy it. 156. **rack:** Wisp of cloud. 157. **on:** Of. 158. **rounded:** Surrounded, or crowned, rounded off. 159. **with:** By. 161. **retire:** Withdraw, go. 163. **beating:** Agitated. 164. **with a thought:** I.e., on the instant, or summoned by my thought, no sooner thought of than here. 165. **cleave:** Cling, adhere. 167. **presented:** Acted the part of, or introduced.

PROSPERO: Say again, where didst thou leave these
170   varlets?
ARIEL: I told you, sir, they were red-hot with
     drinking,
     So full of valor that they smote the air
     For breathing in their faces, beat the ground
     For kissing of their feet, yet always bending°
175   Towards their project. Then I beat my tabor,
     At which, like unbacked° colts, they pricked their
       ears,
     Advanced° their eyelids, lifted up their noses
     As° they smelt music. So I charmed their ears
     That calflike they my lowing° followed through
     Toothed briers, sharp furzes, pricking gorse,° and
180   thorns,
     Which entered their frail shins. At last I left them
     I' the filthy-mantled° pool beyond your cell,
     There dancing up to the chins, that the foul lake
     O'erstunk° their feet.
PROSPERO: This was well done, my bird.
185   Thy shape invisible retain thou still.
     The trumpery° in my house, go bring it hither,
     For stale° to catch these thieves
ARIEL: I go. I go.   (*Exit.*)
PROSPERO: A devil, a born devil, on whose nature
     Nurture can never stick; on whom my pains,
190   Humanely taken, all, all lost, quite lost!
     And as with age his body uglier grows,
     So his mind cankers.° I will plague them all,
     Even to roaring.

(*Enter Ariel, loaden with glistering apparel, etc.*)

          Come, hang them on this line.°

([*Ariel hangs up the showy finery; Prospero and Ariel remain,° invisible.*] *Enter Caliban, Stephano, and Trinculo, all wet.*)

CALIBAN: Pray you, tread softly, that the blind mole
     may
195   Not hear a footfall. We now are near his cell.

STEPHANO: Monster, your fairy, which you say is a
     harmless fairy, has done little better than played
     the jack° with us.
TRINCULO: Monster, I do smell all horse piss, at which
     my nose is in great indignation.   200
STEPHANO: So is mine. Do you hear, monster? If I
     should take a displeasure against you, look
     you —
TRINCULO: Thou wert but a lost monster.
CALIBAN: Good my lord, give me thy favor still.
     Be patient, for the prize I'll bring thee to   205
     Shall hoodwink° this mischance.° Therefore
     speak softly.
     All's hushed as midnight yet.
TRINCULO: Ay, but to lose our bottles in the pool —
STEPHANO: There is not only disgrace and dishonor in
     that, monster, but an infinite loss.   210
TRINCULO: That's more to me than my wetting. Yet
     this is your harmless fairy, monster!
STEPHANO: I will fetch off my bottle, though I be o'er
     ears° for my labor.
CALIBAN: Prithee, my king, be quiet. Seest thou here, 215
     This is the mouth o' the cell. No noise, and
     enter.
     Do that good mischief which may make this
     island
     Thine own forever, and I thy Caliban
     For aye thy footlicker.
STEPHANO: Give me thy hand. I do begin to have 220
     bloody thoughts.
TRINCULO [*seeing the finery*]: O King Stephano! O
     peer!° O worthy Stephano! Look what a wardrobe
     here is for thee!
CALIBAN: Let it alone, thou fool, it is but trash.   225
TRINCULO: Oho, monster! We know what belongs to
     a frippery.° O King Stephano! [*He takes a gown.*]
STEPHANO: Put off° that gown, Trinculo. By this hand,
     I'll have that gown.
TRINCULO: Thy Grace shall have it.   230
CALIBAN: The dropsy° drown this fool! What do
     you mean
     To dote thus on such luggage?° Let 't alone
     And do the murder first. If he awake,
     From toe to crown° he'll fill our skins with
     pinches,

---

174. bending: Aiming.   **176. unbacked:** Unbroken, unridden.   **177. Advanced:** Lifted up.   **178. As:** As if.   **179. lowing:** Mooing.   **180. furzes . . . gorse:** Prickly shrubs.   **182. filthy-mantled:** Covered with a slimy coating.   **184. O'erstunk:** Smelled worse than, or caused to stink terribly.   **186. trumpery:** Cheap goods, the *glistering apparel* mentioned in the following stage direction.   **187. stale:** (1) Decoy, (2) out-of-fashion garments (with possible further suggestions of *fit for a stale* or prostitute, *stale* meaning "horse piss," line 199, and *steal*, pronounced like *stale*).   **192. cankers:** Festers, grows malignant.   **193. line:** Lime tree or linden.   [S.D.] ***Prospero and Ariel remain:*** The staging is uncertain. They may instead exit here and return with the spirits at line 256.

198. jack: (1) Knave, (2) will-o'-the wisp.   **206. hoodwink:** Cover up, make you not see (a hawking term).   **mischance:** Mishap, misfortune.   **213–14. o'er ears:** I.e., totally submerged and perhaps drowned.   **222–23. King . . . peer:** Alludes to the old ballad beginning "King Stephen was a worthy peer."   **227. frippery:** Place where cast-off clothes are sold.   **228. Put off:** Put down, or take off.   **231. dropsy:** Disease characterized by the accumulation of fluid in the connective tissue of the body.   **232. luggage:** Cumbersome trash.   **234. crown:** Head.

235 Make us strange stuff.

STEPHANO: Be you quiet, monster. — Mistress line,° is not this my jerkin?° [*He takes it down.*] Now is the jerkin under the line.° Now, jerkin, you are like° to lose your hair and prove a bald° jerkin.

236. **Mistress line:** Addressed to the linden or lime tree upon which, at line 193, Ariel hung the *glistering apparel*. 237. **jerkin:** Jacket made of leather. 238. **under the line:** Under the lime tree (with punning sense of being south of the equinoctial line or equator; sailors on long voyages to the southern regions were popularly supposed to lose their hair from scurvy or other diseases. Stephano also quibbles handily on losing hair through syphilis, and in *Mistress* and *jerkin*). 239. **like:** Likely. **bald:** (1) Hairless, napless, (2) meager.

TRINCULO: Do, do!° We steal by line and level,° an 't like° Your Grace. 240

STEPHANO: I thank thee for that jest. Here's a garment for 't. [*He gives a garment.*] Wit shall not go unrewarded while I am king of this country. "Steal by line and level" is an excellent pass of pate.° There's another garment for 't. 245

240. **Do, do:** I.e., bravo. (Said in response to the jesting or to the taking of the jerkin, or both.) **by line and level:** I.e., by means of plumb line and carpenter's level, methodically (with pun on *line*, "lime tree," line 238, and *steal*, pronounced like *stale*, i.e., prostitute, continuing Stephano's bawdy quibble). 240–41. **an 't like:** If it please. 245. **pass of pate:** Sally of wit. (The metaphor is from fencing.)

RIGHT: Ferdinand (Boyd Gaines) and Miranda (Frances Conroy) in the 1981 Guthrie Theater production of *The Tempest*, directed by Liviu Ciulei. FAR RIGHT: Prospero, right front, reflects on his handiwork in the masque scene from *The Tempest*.

TRINCULO: Monster, come, put some lime° upon your
    fingers, and away with the rest.
CALIBAN: I will have none on 't. We shall lose our
    time,
250   And all be turned to barnacles,° or to apes
    With foreheads villainous° low.
STEPHANO: Monster, lay to° your fingers. Help to bear

247. lime: Birdlime, sticky substance (to give Caliban sticky
fingers).   **250. barnacles:** Barnacle geese, formerly supposed to be hatched from seashells attached to trees and
to fall thence into the water, here evidently used, like *apes*,
as types of simpletons.   **251. villainous:** Miserably.   **252. l
ay to:** Start using.

this° away where my hogshead° of wine is, or I'll
    turn you out of my kingdom. Go to,° carry this.
TRINCULO: And this.   255
STEPHANO: Ay, and this.
    [*They load Caliban with more and more garments.*]

(*A noise of hunters heard. Enter divers spirits, in
shape of dogs and hounds, hunting them about, Prospero and Ariel setting them on.*)

PROSPERO: Hey, Mountain, hey!
ARIEL: Silver! There it goes, Silver!

253. this: I.e., the *glistering apparel.*   **hogshead:** Large
cask.   **254. Go to:** An expression of exhortation or remonstrance.

PROSPERO: Fury, Fury! There, Tyrant, there! Hark!
Hark!
[*Caliban, Stephano, and Trinculo are driven out.*]
Go, charge my goblins that they grind their
260 joints
With dry° convulsions,° shorten up their sinews
With agèd° cramps, and more pinch-spotted
make them
Than pard° or cat o' mountain.°
ARIEL: Hark, they roar!
PROSPERO: Let them be hunted soundly.° At this
hour
265 Lies at my mercy all mine enemies.
Shortly shall all my labors end, and thou
Shalt have the air at freedom. For a little°
Follow, and do me service. (*Exeunt.*)

ACT V • Scene 1°

(*Enter Prospero in his magic robes, [with his staff,]
and Ariel.*)

PROSPERO: Now does my project gather to a head.
My charms crack° not, my spirits obey, and Time
Goes upright with his carriage.° How's the day?
ARIEL: On° the sixth hour, at which time, my lord,
You said our work should cease.
5 PROSPERO: I did say so,
When first I raised the tempest. Say, my spirit,
How fares the King and 's followers?
ARIEL: Confined together
In the same fashion as you gave in charge,
Just as you left them; all prisoners, sir,
10 In the line grove° which weather-fends° your cell.
They cannot budge till your release.° The King,
His brother, and yours abide all three distracted,°
And the remainder mourning over them,
Brim full of sorrow and dismay; but chiefly
Him that you termed, sir, the good old lord,
15 Gonzalo.

His tears runs down his beard like winter's drops
From eaves of reeds.° Your charm so strongly
works 'em
That if you now beheld them your affections°
Would become tender.
PROSPERO: Dost thou think so, spirit?
ARIEL: Mine would, sir, were I human.
PROSPERO: And mine shall. 20
Hast thou, which art but air, a touch° a feeling
Of their afflictions, and shall not myself,
One of their kind, that relish all as sharply
Passion as they,° be kindlier° moved than thou
art?
Though with their high wrongs I am struck to
the quick, 25
Yet with my nobler reason 'gainst my fury
Do I take part. The rarer° action is
In virtue than in vengeance. They being penitent,
The sole drift of my purpose doth extend
Not a frown further. Go release them, Ariel. 30
My charms I'll break, their senses I'll restore,
And they shall be themselves.
ARIEL: I'll fetch them, sir.
(*Exit.*)
[*Prospero traces a charmed circle with his staff.*]
PROSPERO: Ye elves of hills, brooks, standing lakes,
and groves,°
And ye that on the sands with printless foot
Do chase the ebbing Neptune, and do fly him 35
When he comes back; you demi-puppets° that
By moonshine do the green sour ringlets° make,
Whereof the ewe not bites; and you whose
pastime
Is to make midnight mushrooms,° that rejoice
To hear the solemn curfew,° by whose aid, 40
Weak masters though ye be, I have bedimmed
The noontide sun, called forth the mutinous
winds,
And twixt the green sea and the azured vault°

---

261. **dry:** Associated with age, arthritic (?). **convulsions:** Cramps. 262. **agèd:** Characteristic of old age. 263. **pard:** Panther or leopard. **cat o' mountain:** Wildcat. 264. **soundly:** Thoroughly. 267. **little:** little while longer. V, I. **Location:** Before Prospero's cell. 2. **crack:** Collapse, fail. (The metaphor is probably alchemical, as in *project* and *gather to a head*, line 1.) 3. **his carriage:** Its burden. (Time is no longer heavily burdened and so can go upright, standing straight and unimpeded.) 4. **On:** Approaching. 10. **line grove:** Grove of lime trees. **weather-fends:** Protects from the weather. 11. **your release:** You release them. 12. **distracted:** Out of their wits.

17. **eaves of reeds:** Thatched roofs. 18. **affections:** Feelings. 21. **touch:** Sense, feeling. 23–24. **that . . . they:** I.e., I who am just as sensitive to suffering as they. 24. **kindlier:** (1) More sympathetically, (2) more naturally, humanly. 27. **rarer:** Nobler. 33–50. **Ye . . . art:** This famous passage is an embellished paraphrase of Golding's translation of Ovid's *Metamorphoses*, 7. 197–219. 36. **demi-puppets:** Puppets of half size, i.e., elves and fairies. 37. **green sour ringlets:** Fairy rings, circles in grass (actually produced by mushrooms). 39. **midnight mushrooms:** Mushrooms appearing overnight. 40. **curfew:** Evening bell, usually rung at nine o'clock, ushering in the time when spirits are abroad. 43. **the azured vault:** I.e., the sky.

Set roaring war; to the dread rattling thunder
45 Have I given fire,° and rifted,° Jove's stout oak
With his own bolt;° the strong-based promontory
Have I made shake, and by the spurs° plucked
    up
The pine and cedar; graves at my command
Have waked their sleepers, oped, and let 'em
    forth
50 By my so potent art. But this rough° magic
I here abjure, and when I have required°
Some heavenly music — which even now I do —
To work mine end upon their senses that°
This airy charm° is for, I'll break my staff,
55 Bury it certain fathoms in the earth,
And deeper than did ever plummet sound
I'll drown my book.   (*Solemn music.*)

(*Here enters Ariel before; then Alonso, with a frantic
gesture, attended by Gonzalo; Sebastian and Antonio
in like manner, attended by Adrian and Francisco.
They all enter the circle which Prospero had made,
and there stand charmed; which Prospero observing,
speaks.*)

    [*To Alonso.*] A solemn air,° and° the best
        comforter
    To an unsettled fancy,° cure thy brains,
60 Now useless, boiled within thy skull! [*To
        Sebastian and Antonio.*] There stand,
    For you are spell-stopped. —
    Holy Gonzalo, honorable man,
    Mine eyes, e'en sociable° to the show° of thine,
    Fall° fellowly drops. [*Aside.*] The charm dissolves
        apace,
65 And as the morning steals upon the night,
    Melting the darkness, so their rising senses
    Begin to chase the ignorant fumes° that mantle°
    Their clearer° reason. — O good Gonzalo,
    My true preserver, and a loyal sir
70 To him thou follow'st! I will pay thy graces°
    Home° both in word and deed. — Most cruelly
    Didst thou, Alonso, use me and my daughter.
    Thy brother was a furtherer° in the act. —

Thou art pinched° for 't now, Sebastian. [*To
    Antonio.*] Flesh and blood,
You, brother mine, that entertained ambition, 75
Expelled remorse° and nature,° whom,° with
    Sebastian,
Whose inward pinches therefore are most strong,
Would here have killed your king, I do forgive
    thee,
Unnatural though thou art. — Their
    understanding
Begins to swell, and the approaching tide 80
Will shortly fill the reasonable shore°
That now lies foul and muddy. Not one of them
That yet looks on me, or would know me. —
    Ariel,
Fetch me the hat and rapier in my cell.
    [*Ariel goes to the cell and returns immediately.*]
I will discase° me and myself present 85
As I was sometime Milan.° Quickly, spirit!
Thou shalt ere long be free.
        (*Ariel sings and helps to attire him.*)
ARIEL: Where the bee sucks, there suck I.
    In a cowslip's bell I lie;
    There I couch° when owls do cry. 90
    On the bat's back I do fly
    After° summer merrily.
Merrily, merrily shall I live now
Under the blossom that hangs on the bough.
PROSPERO: Why, that's my dainty Ariel! I shall miss
    thee, 95
But yet thou shalt have freedom. So, so, so.°
To the King's ship, invisible as thou art!
There shalt thou find the mariners asleep
Under the hatches. The Master and the Boatswain
Being awake, enforce them to this place, 100
And presently,° I prithee.
ARIEL: I drink the air before me and return
Or ere° your pulse twice beat.   (*Exit.*)
GONZALO: All torment, trouble, wonder, and
    amazement
Inhabits here. Some heavenly power guide us 105
Out of this fearful° country!
PROSPERO: Behold, sir King,
    The wrongèd Duke of Milan, Prospero.
    For more assurance that a living prince

44–45. to . . . fire: I have discharged the dread rattling thunderbolt. **45. rifted:** Riven, split. **46. bolt:** Lightning bolt. **47. spurs:** Roots. **50. rough:** Violent. **51. required:** Requested. **53. their senses that:** The senses of those whom. **54. airy charm:** I.e., music. **58. air:** Song. **and:** I.e., which is. **59. fancy:** Imagination. **63. sociable:** Sympathetic. **show:** Appearance. **64. Fall:** Let fall. **67. ignorant fumes:** Fumes that render them incapable of comprehension. **mantle:** Envelop. **68. clearer:** Growing clearer. **70. pay thy graces:** Reward your favors. **71. Home:** Fully. **73. furtherer:** Accomplice.

74. pinched: Punished, afflicted. **76. remorse:** Pity. **nature:** Natural feeling. **whom:** I.e., who. **81. reasonable shore:** Shores of reason, i.e., minds. (Their reason returns like the incoming tide.) **85. discase:** Disrobe. **86. As . . . Milan:** In my former appearance as Duke of Milan. **90. couch:** Lie. **92. After:** I.e., pursuing. **96. So, so, so:** Expresses approval of Ariel's help as valet. **101. presently:** Immediately. **103. Or ere:** Before. **106. fearful:** Frightening.

Does now speak to thee, I embrace thy body;
110 And to thee and thy company I bid
A hearty welcome.   [*Embracing him.*]
ALONSO: Whe'er thou be'st he or no,
Or some enchanted trifle° to abuse° me,
As late° I have been, I not know. Thy pulse
Beats as of flesh and blood; and, since I saw
    thee,
115 Th' affliction of my mind amends, with which
I fear a madness held me. This must crave° —
An if this be at all° — a most strange story.°
Thy dukedom I resign,° and do entreat
Thou pardon me my wrongs.° But how should
    Prospero
Be living, and be here?
120 PROSPERO [*to Gonzalo*]:   First, noble friend,
Let me embrace thine age,° whose honor cannot
Be measured or confined.   [*Embracing him.*]
GONZALO: Whether this be
Or be not, I'll not swear.
PROSPERO: You do yet taste
Some subtleties° o' th' isle, that will not let you
125 Believe things certain. Welcome, my friends all!
[*Aside to Sebastian and Antonio.*] But you, my
    brace° of lords, were I so minded,
I here could pluck His Highness' frown upon
    you
And justify you° traitors. At this time
I will tell no tales.
SEBASTIAN: The devil speaks in him.
PROSPERO: No.
[*To Antonio.*] For you, most wicked sir, whom to
130   call brother
Would even infect my mouth, I do forgive
Thy rankest fault — all of them; and require
My dukedom of thee, which perforce° I know
Thou must restore.
ALONSO: If thou be'st Prospero,
135 Give us particulars of thy preservation,
How thou hast met us here, whom° three hours
    since
Were wrecked upon this shore; where I have
    lost —
How sharp the point of this remembrance is! —
My dear son Ferdinand.

PROSPERO: I am woe° for 't, sir.
ALONSO: Irreparable is the loss, and Patience   140
Says it is past her cure.
PROSPERO: I rather think
You have not sought her help, of whose soft
    grace°
For the like loss I have her sovereign° aid
And rest myself content.
ALONSO: You the like loss?
PROSPERO: As great to me as late,° and supportable   145
To make the dear loss, have I° means much
    weaker
Than you may call to comfort you; for I
Have lost my daughter.
ALONSO: A daughter?
O heavens, that they were living both in Naples,   150
The king and queen there! That° they were, I
    wish
Myself were mudded° in that oozy bed
Where my son lies. When did you lose your
    daughter?
PROSPERO: In this last tempest. I perceive these lords
At this encounter do so much admire°   155
That they devour their reason° and scarce think
Their eyes do offices of truth, their words
Are natural breath.° But, howsoever you have
Been jostled from your senses, know for certain
That I am Prospero and that very duke   160
Which was thrust forth of° Milan, who most
    strangely
Upon this shore, where you were wrecked, was
    landed
To be the lord on 't. No more yet of this,
For 'tis a chronicle of day by day,°
Not a relation for a breakfast nor   165
Befitting this first meeting. Welcome, sir.
This cell's my court. Here have I few attendants,
And subjects none abroad.° Pray you, look in.
My dukedom since you have given me again,
I will requite° you with as good a thing,   170
At least bring forth a wonder to content ye
As much as me my dukedom.

---

112. **trifle**: Trick of magic.   **abuse**: Deceive.   113. **late**: Lately.   116. **crave**: Require.   117. **An . . . all**: If this is actually happening.   **story**: I.e., explanation.   118. **Thy . . . resign**: Alonso made an arrangement with Antonio at the time of Prospero's banishment for Milan to pay tribute to Naples; see I, II, 113–27.   119. **wrongs**: Wrongdoings.   121. **thine age**: Your venerable self.   124. **subtleties**: Illusions, magical powers.   126. **brace**: Pair.   128. **justify you**: Prove you to be.   133. **perforce**: Necessarily.   136. **whom**: I.e., who.

139. **woe**: Sorry.   142. **of . . . grace**: By whose mercy.   143. **sovereign**: Efficacious.   145. **late**: Recent.   145–46. **supportable . . . have I**: To make the deeply felt loss bearable, I have.   151. **That**: So that.   152. **mudded**: Buried in the mud.   155. **admire**: Wonder.   156. **devour their reason**: I.e., are dumbfounded.   156–58. **scarce . . . breath**: Scarcely believe that their eyes inform them accurately what they see or that their words are naturally spoken.   161. **of**: From.   164. **of day by day**: Requiring days to tell.   168. **abroad**: Away from here, anywhere else.   170. **requite**: Repay.

(*Here Prospero discovers° Ferdinand and Miranda playing at chess.*)

MIRANDA: Sweet lord, you play me false.

FERDINAND: No, my dearest love,

175   I would not for the world.

MIRANDA: Yes, for a score of kingdoms you should
              wrangle,
      And I would call it fair play.°

ALONSO: If this prove
      A vision° of the island, one dear son
      Shall I twice lose.

SEBASTIAN: A most high miracle!

FERDINAND [*approaching his father*]:

180   Though the seas threaten, they are merciful;
      I have cursed them without cause.   [*He kneels.*]

ALONSO: Now all the blessings
      Of a glad father compass° thee about!
      Arise, and say how thou cam'st here.
                                  [*Ferdinand rises.*]

MIRANDA: O, wonder!
      How many goodly creatures are there here!
      How beauteous mankind is! O, brave° new
              world,

185   That has such people in 't!

PROSPERO: 'Tis new to thee.

ALONSO: What is this maid with whom thou wast
              at play?
      Your eld'st° acquaintance cannot be three hours.
      Is she the goddess that hath severed us
      And brought us thus together?

190 FERDINAND: Sir, she is mortal;
      But by immortal Providence she's mine.
      I chose her when I could not ask my father
      For his advice, nor thought I had one. She
      Is daughter to this famous Duke of Milan,

195   Of whom so often I have heard renown
      But never saw before, of whom I have
      Received a second life; and second father
      This lady makes him to me.

ALONSO: I am hers.
      But O, how oddly will it sound that I
      Must ask my child forgiveness!

200 PROSPERO: There, sir, stop.

Let us not burden our remembrances with
      A heaviness° that's gone.

GONZALO: I have inly° wept,
      Or should have spoke ere this. Look down, you
              gods,
      And on this couple drop a blessèd crown!
      For it is you that have chalked forth the way°   205
      Which brought us hither.

ALONSO: I say amen, Gonzalo!

GONZALO: Was Milan° thrust from Milan that his
              issue
      Should become kings of Naples? O, rejoice
      Beyond a common joy, and set it down
      With gold on lasting pillars: In one voyage   210
      Did Claribel her husband find at Tunis,
      And Ferdinand, her brother, found a wife
      Where he himself was lost; Prospero his
              dukedom
      In a poor isle; and all of us ourselves
      When no man was his own.°

ALONSO [*to Ferdinand and Miranda*]: Give me your
              hands.   215
      Let grief and sorrow still° embrace his° heart
      That° doth not wish you joy!

GONZALO: Be it so! Amen!

(*Enter Ariel, with the Master and Boatswain amazedly following.*)

      O, look, sir, look, sir! Here is more of us.
      I prophesied, if a gallows were on land,
      This fellow could not drown. — Now,
              blasphemy,°   220
      That swear'st grace o'erboard,° not an oath° on
              shore?
      Hast thou no mouth by land? What is the news?

BOATSWAIN: The best news is that we have safely
              found
      Our King and company; the next, our ship —
      Which, but three glasses° since, we gave out°
              split —   225
      Is tight and yare° and bravely° rigged as when
      We first put out to sea.

ARIEL [*aside to Prospero*]: Sir, all this service
      Have I done since I went.

---

172. [S.D.] *discovers*: I.e., by opening a curtain, presumably rear stage.   176–77. Yes . . . play: I.e., yes, even if we were playing for twenty kingdoms, something less than the whole world, you would still contend mightily against me and play me false, and I would let you do it as though it were fair play; or, if you were to play not just for stakes but literally for kingdoms, my accusation of false play would be out of order in that your "wrangling" would be proper.   178. vision: Illusion.   182. compass: Encompass, embrace.   185. brave: Splendid, gorgeously appareled, handsome.   188. eld'st: Longest.

202. heaviness: Sadness.   inly: Inwardly.   205. chalked . . . way: Marked as with a piece of chalk the pathway. 207. Was Milan: Was the Duke of Milan.   214–15. all . . . own: All of us have found ourselves and our sanity when we all had lost our senses.   216. still: Always.   his: That person's.   217. That: Who.   220. blasphemy: I.e., blasphemer.   221. That . . . o'erboard: I.e., you who banish heavenly grace from the ship by your blasphemies.   not an oath: Aren't you going to swear an oath.   225. glasses: I.e., hours.   gave out: Reported, professed to be.   226. yare: Ready.   bravely: Splendidly.

PROSPERO [*aside to Ariel*]: My tricksy° spirit!
ALONSO: These are not natural events; they strengthen°
   From strange to stranger. Say, how came you
230   hither?
BOATSWAIN: If I did think, sir, I were well awake,
   I'd strive to tell you. We were dead of sleep,°
   And — how we know not — all clapped under hatches,
   Where but even now, with strange and several°
      noises
235 Of roaring, shrieking, howling, jingling chains,
   And more diversity of sounds, all horrible,
   We were awaked; straightway at liberty;
   Where we, in all her trim, freshly beheld
   Our royal, good, and gallant ship, our Master
240 Cap'ring to eye° her. On a trice,° so please you,
   Even in a dream, were we divided from them°
   And were brought moping° hither.
ARIEL [*aside to Prospero*]:   Was 't well done?
PROSPERO [*aside to Ariel*]: Bravely, my diligence.
   Thou shalt be free.
ALONSO: This is as strange a maze as e'er men trod,
245   And there is in this business more than nature
   Was ever conduct° of. Some oracle
   Must rectify our knowledge.
PROSPERO: Sir, my liege,
   Do not infest° your mind with beating on°
   The strangeness of this business. At picked°
      leisure,
250 Which shall be shortly, single° I'll resolve° you,
   Which to you shall seem probable,° of every
   These° happened accidents,° till when, be
      cheerful
   And think of each thing well.° [*Aside to Ariel.*]
      Come hither, spirit.
   Set Caliban and his companions free.
   Untie the spell. [*Exit Ariel.*] How fares my
255   gracious sir?
   There are yet missing of your company
   Some few odd° lads that you remember not.

(*Enter Ariel, driving in Caliban, Stephano, and Trinculo in their stolen apparel.*)

STEPHANO: Every man shift° for all the rest,° and let
   no man take care for himself; for all is but fortune.
   Coraggio,° bully monster,° coraggio!   260
TRINCULO: If these be true spies° which I wear in my
   head, here's a goodly sight.
CALIBAN: O Setebos, these be brave° spirits indeed!
   How fine° my master is! I am afraid
   He will chastise me.   265
SEBASTIAN: Ha, ha!
   What things are these, my lord Antonio?
   Will money buy 'em?
ANTONIO: Very like. One of them
   Is a plain fish, and no doubt marketable.
PROSPERO: Mark but the badges° of these men, my
      lords,   270
   Then say if they be true.° This misshapen knave,
   His mother was a witch, and one so strong
   That could control the moon, make flows and
      ebbs,
   And deal in her command without her power.°
   These three have robbed me, and this
      demidevil —   275
   For he's a bastard° one — had plotted with them
   To take my life. Two of these fellows you
   Must know and own.° This thing of darkness I
   Acknowledge mine.
CALIBAN: I shall be pinched to death.
ALONSO: Is not this Stephano, my drunken butler?   280
SEBASTIAN: He is drunk now. Where had he wine?
ALONSO: And Trinculo is reeling ripe.° Where
      should they
   Find this grand liquor that hath gilded° 'em?
   [*To Trinculo.*] How cam'st thou in this pickle?°
TRINCULO: I have been in such a pickle since I saw   285
   you last that, I fear me, will never out of my bones.
   I shall not fear flyblowing.°

---

228. **tricksy:** Ingenious, sportive.   229. **strengthen:** Increase.   232. **dead of sleep:** Deep in sleep.   234. **several:** Different, diverse.   240. **Cap'ring to eye:** Dancing for joy to see.   **On a trice:** In an instant.   241. **them:** I.e., the other crew members.   242. **moping:** In a daze.   246. **conduct:** Guide, leader.   248. **infest:** Harass, disturb.   **beating on:** Worrying about.   249. **picked:** Chosen, convenient.   250. **single:** I.e., by my own human powers.   **resolve:** Satisfy, explain to.   251. **probable:** Explicable, plausible.   251–52. **of every These:** About every one of these.   252. **accidents:** Occurrences.   253. **well:** Favorably.   257. **odd:** Unaccounted for.

258. **shift:** Provide.   **for all the rest:** Stephano drunkenly gets wrong the saying "Every man for himself."   260. **Coraggio:** Courage.   **bully monster:** Gallant monster. (Ironical.)   261. **true spies:** Accurate observers (i.e., sharp eyes).   263. **brave:** Handsome.   264. **fine:** Splendidly attired.   270. **badges:** Emblems of cloth or silver worn on the arms of retainers. (Prospero refers here to the stolen clothes as emblems of their villainy.)   271. **true:** Honest.   274. **deal . . . power:** Wield the moon's power, either without her authority or beyond her influence.   276. **bastard:** Counterfeit.   278. **own:** Recognize, admit as belonging to you.   282. **reeling ripe:** Stumblingly drunk.   283. **gilded:** (1) Flushed, made drunk, (2) covered with gilt (suggesting the horse urine).   284. **pickle:** (1) Fix, predicament, (2) pickling brine (in this case, horse urine).   287. **flyblowing:** I.e., being fouled by fly eggs (from which he is saved by being pickled).

SEBASTIAN: Why, how now, Stephano?

STEPHANO: O, touch me not! I am not Stephano, but
290 a cramp.

PROSPERO: You'd be king o' the isle, sirrah?°

STEPHANO: I should have been a sore° one, then.

ALONSO [*pointing to Caliban*]: This is a strange thing
as e'er I looked on.

PROSPERO: He is as disproportioned in his manners
295 As in his shape. — Go, sirrah, to my cell.
Take with you your companions. As you look
To have my pardon, trim° it handsomely.

CALIBAN: Ay, that I will; and I'll be wise hereafter
And seek for grace. What a thrice-double ass
300 Was I to take this drunkard for a god
And worship this dull fool!

PROSPERO: Go to. Away!

ALONSO: Hence, and bestow your luggage where
you found it.

SEBASTIAN: Or stole it rather.

> [*Exeunt Caliban, Stephano, and Trinculo.*]

PROSPERO: Sir, I invite Your Highness and your train
305 To my poor cell, where you shall take your rest
For this one night; which, part of it, I'll waste°
With such discourse as, I not doubt, shall make
it
Go quick away: the story of my life,
And the particular accidents° gone by
310 Since I came to this isle. And in the morn
I'll bring you to your ship, and so to Naples,
Where I have hope to see the nuptial
Of these our dear-belovèd solemnized;
And thence retire me° to my Milan, where
Every third thought shall be my grave.

315 ALONSO: I long
To hear the story of your life, which must
Take° the ear strangely.

PROSPERO: I'll deliver° all;

And promise you calm seas, auspicious gales,
And sail so expeditious that shall catch
Your royal fleet far off. [*Aside to Ariel.*] My
Ariel, chick,   320
That is thy charge. Then to the elements
Be free, and fare thou well! — Please you, draw
near.°

> (*Exeunt omnes.*)

EPILOGUE

(*Spoken by Prospero.*)

Now my charms are all o'erthrown,
And what strength I have 's mine own,
Which is most faint. Now, 'tis true,
I must be here confined by you
Or sent to Naples. Let me not,   5
Since I have my dukedom got
And pardoned the deceiver, dwell
In this bare island by your spell,
But release me from my bands°
With the help of your good hands.°   10
Gentle breath° of yours my sails
Must fill, or else my project fails,
Which was to please. Now I want°
Spirits to enforce,° art to enchant,
And my ending is despair   15
Unless I be relieved by prayer,°
Which pierces so that it assaults°
Mercy itself, and frees° all faults.
As you from crimes° would pardoned be,
Let your indulgence° set me free.   (*Exit.*) 20

---

322. **draw near:** I.e., enter my cell.   9. **bands:** Bonds.
10. **hands:** I.e., applause (the noise of which would break the
spell of silence).   11. **Gentle breath:** Favorable breeze (produced by hands clapping or favorable comment).
13. **want:** Lack.   14. **enforce:** Control.   16. **prayer:** I.e.,
Prospero's petition to the audience.   17. **assaults:** Right-
fully gains the attention of.   18. **frees:** Obtains forgiveness
for.   19. **crimes:** Sins.   20. **indulgence:** (1) Humoring, lenient approval, (2) remission of punishment for sin.

---

291. **sirrah:** Standard form of address to an inferior, here
expressing reprimand.   292. **sore:** (1) Tyrannical, (2) sorry,
inept, (3) wracked by pain.   297. **trim:** Prepare, decorate.
306. **waste:** Spend.   309. **accidents:** Occurrences.   314.
retire me: Return.   317. **Take:** Take effect upon, enchant.
deliver: Declare, relate.

COMMENTARIES

Some of the finest critical commentary ever written has been devoted to the works of Shakespeare. From the seventeenth century to the present, critics have taken a considerable interest in the nuances of his work.

In the commentary on *A Midsummer Night's Dream* we find a wide range of responses to the work. Enid Welsford's comments are in a special context, that of the court masque, the rich entertainments that were designed to please royalty. As Welsford explains, *A Midsummer Night's Dream* has many elements of the masque.

In more specifically feminist observations, the critics Carol Thomas Neely and Linda Bamber show how assumptions regarding power in a male-female relationship affect our interpretation of the play. Their readings are fresh, exciting, and provocative.

Peter Brook, one of the most notable contemporary directors of Shakespeare and the producer of a landmark production of *A Midsummer Night's Dream* (1970), gives us a director's view of the play. He centers the discussion on love, which in many forms is at the heart of the play. See the review of his production on pp. 475–76.

The modern era of Shakespeare criticism probably begins with Samuel Taylor Coleridge, whose lectures on Shakespeare were instrumental in helping a generation of early-nineteenth-century theatergoers take the playwright seriously. Coleridge, adapting the ideas of the German romantic critic Friedrich Schlegel, reached a wide and generally popular audience. His work centers on the character of Hamlet and his problems in the play, examining how Hamlet reveals himself both to us and to himself.

Sigmund Freud sees in *Hamlet* the seeds of the Oedipus complex that he had already identified in Sophocles' *Oedipus Rex*. The question of how one psychoanalyzes a literary character is perhaps best raised in Freud's essay. Later, a follower of Freud, Ernest Jones, wrote an entire book on Hamlet, analyzing him from the psychoanalytic perspective.

T. S. Eliot, speaking as a careful and noted student of Elizabethan and Jacobean drama, begins to point out some of the difficulties he sees with *Hamlet*. It is fascinating to see how great poets such as Coleridge and Eliot can approach the same play from such diverse points of view.

Clive Barnes's review gives us a clear sense of the visual and kinetic details that made Peter Brook's *A Midsummer Night's Dream* one of the most memorable modern stagings of Shakespeare. The use of juggling, acrobats, and trapezes energized the production and underscored the youthful vitality of the characters.

Contemporary reviews of *Hamlet, A Midsummer Night's Dream,* and

The Tempest take a very different approach to the plays than do studies such as those of Coleridge. The reviewers are concerned first with the actors and their interpretation of the drama. They are then concerned with the director's insights and sense of pacing. John Lahr, for example, comments that Jonathan Kent cuts an hour off the length of *Hamlet,* thus making it, as he says, more of a "people's *Hamlet.*" In addition to focusing on the title roles, critics also aim to communicate a sense of the dynamics of the production as a whole. Peter Brook's production of *A Midsummer Night's Dream,* for example, was perhaps most startling for its all-white set and backdrop, and for the marvelous scenes staged with principal actors lolling on simple white swings. Critics can give us insight into the staging of the work and the ways in which the staging imparts meaning to the drama.

Stephen J. Greenblatt comments on the theme of colonialism in *The Tempest.* On the island before Prospero arrived, Caliban complains that Prospero robbed him of what was his own. Shakespeare seems to have been well informed about the original inhabitants of the New World, and while many critics resist Greenblatt's interpretation, his questions are worth considering.

Enid Welsford (1892–1981)
MASQUE ELEMENTS IN *A MIDSUMMER NIGHT'S DREAM*   1927

Enid Welsford examines A Midsummer Night's Dream *from the point of view of its masquelike qualities. Shakespeare's* The Tempest *includes a masque and has certain scenic qualities that link it to that tradition, and so does* A Midsummer Night's Dream. *Its fantastic costumes and remarkable fairy population could be considered part of the antimasque, a parody of the masque itself. The antimasque often involved masquers dressed in grotesque animal costumes, making a loud racket, and dancing in erratic and fantastic gestures. Meant originally as a contrast to the magnificence of the masque, the antimasque became a favorite of the less conservative masquers.*

The only character study in *A Midsummer Night's Dream* is to be found in the portrayal of Bottom, Theseus, and perhaps Hippolyta. Even in drawing these characters Shakespeare was evidently influenced by the memory of pageants, complimentary speeches, and entertainments addressed by townspeople and humble folk to the Queen or to the nobility. A glance through Nichols's *Public Progresses* shows what innumerable lengthy speeches, what innumerable disguisings and shows, Elizabeth was obliged to bear with gracious demeanor. Her experiences were similar to those of Theseus:

> Where I have come, great clerks have purposed
> To greet me with premeditated welcomes;

> Where I have seen them shiver and look pale,
> Make periods in the midst of sentences,
> Throttle their practic'd accent in their fears,
> And, in conclusion, dumbly have broke off,
> Not paying me a welcome.

One Sunday afternoon, at Kenilworth Castle, Elizabeth and her court whiled away the time by watching the countrypeople at a Brideale and Morris Dance. Their amused kindly tolerance is just that of Theseus and the lovers toward the Athenian workmen. So that even in the most solid and dramatic parts of his play Shakespeare is only giving an idealized version of courtly and country revels and of the people that played a part in them.

In *A Midsummer Night's Dream* Bottom and his companions serve the same purpose as the antimasque in the courtly revels. It is true that Shakespeare's play was written before Ben Jonson had elaborated and defined the antimasque, but from the first grotesque dances were popular, and the principle of contrast was always latent in the masque. There is, however, a great difference between Jonson's and Shakespeare's management of foil and relief. In the antimasque the transition is sudden and the contrast complete, a method of composition effective enough in spectacle and ballet. But in a play, as Shakespeare well knew, the greatest beauty is gained through contrast when the difference is not obvious and striking, but rises out of a deep though unobtrusive resemblance. This could not be better illustrated than by the picture of Titania winding the ass-headed Bottom in her arms. Why is it that this is a pleasing picture, why is it that the rude mechanicals do not, as a matter of fact, disturb or sully Titania's "close and consecrated bower"? Malvolio° in Bottom's place would be repellent, yet Malvolio, regarded superficially, is less violently contrasted to the Fairy Queen than is Nick Bottom. Bottom with his ass's head is grotesquely hideous, and in ordinary life he is crude, raw, and very stupid. We have no reason to suppose that Malvolio was anything but a well-set-up, proper-looking man, spruce, well dressed, the perfect family butler. His mentality too is of a distinctly higher order than Bottom's. He fills a responsible position with credit, he follows a reasoned line of conduct, he thinks nobly of the soul. Two things alone he lacks (and that is why no self-respecting fey could ever kiss him)—humor and imagination. Malvolio is, therefore, the only character who cannot be included in the final harmony of *Twelfth Night*. Bottom and his fellows did perhaps lack humor (though the interview with the fairies suggests that Bottom had a smack of it), but in its place they possessed unreason. Imagination they did have, of the most simple, primal, childlike kind. It is their artistic ambition that lifts them out of the humdrum world and turns them into Midsummer Dreamers, and we have seen how cunningly Shakespeare extracts from their very stupidity romance and moonshine. But, indeed, grotesqueness and stupidity (of a certain kind) have a kinship with beauty. For these qualities usually imply a measure of spiritual freedom, they lead to at least a temporary relief from the tyranny of reason and from the pressure of the external world. In *A Midsummer Night's Dream* the dominance of the Lord of Misrule is not marked by coarse parody, but by the

---

Malvolio: A character in Shakespeare's *Twelfth Night*.

partial repeal of the laws of cause and effect. By delicate beauty, gentle mockery, and simple romantic foolishness our freedom is gained.

Carol Thomas Neely (b. 1939)
BROKEN NUPTIALS   1985

Carol Thomas Neely is interested in the problem of marriage in A Midsummer Night's Dream, *examining it not from the traditional point of view — which essentially accepted the status quo of the play and then ignored it — but from a modernist point of view that brings into question the institution of marriage and how it functions in the play. She is interested in the relationships of Titania and Oberon, who "make up" during the play, and of Theseus and Hippolyta, whose own nuptials have been postponed for the while it takes the action of the play to unfold. Neely reminds us how much "coupling" there is in the play.*

In *Midsummer Night's Dream* desire, symbolized by the operations of the fairy juice, is urgent, promiscuous, and threatening to women as well as to men. Its effects mock the protestations of constancy by Lysander and Demetrius and exaggerate the patriarchal possessiveness of Theseus and Oberon: "every man should take his own.... The man shall have his mare again, and all shall be well" (III, II). All is made well in part because the erratic or aggressive desires of the controlling men are "linger[ed]" (I, I) by the chaste constancy of Hermia and Helena and the poised detachment of Hippolyta, or tempered by the inconstancy of Titania with Bottom. Oberon, engineering this union, imagines it as an ugly, bestial coupling "with lion, bear, or wolf, or bull" (II, I), an apt punishment for Titania's multiple desires and intimacies. But from Titania's perspective (and ours) it is a comically fulfilling alternate nuptial — and was staged as such by Peter Brook,° complete with streamers, the wedding march, a plumed bower of bliss, and a waving phallus. The union is a respite for Titania from the conflicts of her hierarchical marriage. She and Bottom experience not animal lust but a blissful, sensual, symbiotic union, characterized, like that of mother and child, by mutual affection and a shared sense of effortless omnipotence. Their eroticism, the opposite of Oberon's bestial fantasies or Theseus's phallic wooing, is tenderly gynocentric:° "So doth the woodbine the sweet honeysuckle / Gently entwist; the female ivy so / Enrings the barky fingers of the elm" (IV, I). Although Titania disavows her "enamored" visions (IV, I), and Oberon misconstrues them, the couple's "amity" (IV, I) depends on that prior union: freed by it to relinquish her other love object, the Indian boy, to Oberon, Titania's submission generates in him the tenderness she craves.

While Theseus and Hippolyta await their nuptials, marital harmony is reestablished by Titania and Oberon, and the chaotic desires of the young lovers are sorted out. During the last-act interval between the weddings and their con-

---

Peter Brook: Innovative British film and theater director (b. 1925). His *Midsummer Night's Dream* was produced in 1970.
Gynocentric: Women-centered.

summations, the violent potentials in love, sex, and marriage are comically incorporated in the rejected and enacted entertainments. "The battle with the centaurs" interrupted the wedding of Theseus's friend Pirithous when the drunken centaurs attacked the Lapiths to capture the bride; during "the riot of the tipsy Bacchanals," the Bacchantes tore Orpheus to pieces, enraged by his devotion to Eurydice and his scorn of other women. The Pyramus and Thisby play dramatizes a lovers' union aborted by parental obstructions, devouring lion, and the lovers' deaths. The play within the play's joining of parodic romance with bawdy innuendo brings into the festive conclusion the two dimensions of love — conventional romanticism and uncontrollable desire — which, converging, threatened but did not harm the couples in the forest and which facilitated the union of Titania and Bottom.

Linda Bamber (b. 1945)
ON *A MIDSUMMER NIGHT'S DREAM* 1982

The question of masculine and feminine is central to A Midsummer Night's Dream. *Much of the action is precipitated by a power struggle between Titania and Oberon, and the young Athenians who rush off to the woods are there because a father has decided to oppose the will of his daughter regarding her marriage. Linda Bamber is a feminist critic interested in examining the centers of power in the play, particularly with an eye for what we accept as the natural order of relationships. She shows that the action of the comedy is essentially tied into questions of gender, which begin to become questions of genre.*

The best example [in Shakespeare] of the relationship between male dominance and the status quo comes in *A Midsummer Night's Dream,* which begins with a rebellion of the feminine against the power of masculine authority. Hermia refuses the man both Aegeus and Theseus order her to marry; her refusal sends us off into the forest, beyond the power of the father and the masculine state. Once in the forest, of course, we find the social situation metaphorically repeated in this world of imagination and nature. The fairy king, Oberon, rules the forest. His rule, too, is troubled by the rebellion of the feminine. Titania has refused to give him her page, the child of a human friend who died in childbirth. But by the end of the story Titania is conquered, the child relinquished, and order restored. Even here the comic upheavals, whether we see them as May games or bad dreams, are associated with an uprising of women. David P. Young has pointed out how firmly this play connects order with masculine dominance and the disruption of order with the rebellion of the feminine:

> It is appropriate that Theseus, as representative of daylight and right reason, should have subdued his bride-to-be to the rule of his masculine will. That is the natural order of things. It is equally appropriate that Oberon, as king of darkness and fantasy, should have lost control of his wife, and that the corresponding natural disorder described by Titania should ensue.[1]

---

[1]David P. Young, *Something of Great Constancy* (New Haven, CT: Yale UP, 1966), 183.

The natural order, the status quo, is for men to rule women. When they fail to do so, we have the exceptional situation, the festive, disruptive, disorderly moment of comedy.

A Midsummer Night's Dream is actually an anomaly among the festive comedies. It is unusual for the forces of the green world to be directed, as they are here, by a masculine figure. Because the green world here is a partial reproduction of the social world, the feminine is reduced to a kind of first cause of the action while a masculine power directs it. In the other festive comedies the feminine Other presides. She does not *command* the forces of the alternative world, as Oberon does, but since she acts in harmony with these forces her will and desire often prevail.

Where are we to bestow our sympathies? On the forces that make for the disruption of the status quo and therefore for the plot? Or on the force that asserts itself against the disruption and reestablishes a workable social order? Of course we cannot choose. We can only say that in comedy we owe our holiday to such forces as the tendency of the feminine to rebel, whereas to the successful reassertion of masculine power we owe our everyday order. Shakespearean comedy endorses both sides. Holiday is, of course, the subject and the analogue of each play; but the plays always end in a return to everyday life. The optimistic reading of Shakespearean comedy says that everyday life is clarified and enriched by our holiday from it; according to the pessimistic reading the temporary subversion of the social order has revealed how much that order excludes, how high a price we pay for it. But whether our return to everyday life is a comfortable one or not, the return itself is the inevitable conclusion to the journey out.

Does this make the comedies sexist? Is the association of women with the disruption of the social order an unconscious and insulting projection? It seems to begin as such; but as the form of Shakespearean comedy develops, the Otherness of the feminine develops into as powerful a force in the drama as the social authority of the masculine Self. For the feminine in Shakespearean comedy begins as a shrew but develops into a comic heroine. The shrew's rebellion directly challenges masculine authority, whereas the comic heroine merely presides over areas of experience to which masculine authority is irrelevant. But the shrew is essentially powerless against the social system, whereas the comic heroine is in alliance with forces that can never be finally overcome. The shrew is defeated by the superior strength, physical and social, of a man, or by women who support the status quo. She provokes a battle of the sexes, and the outcome of this battle, from Shakespeare's point of view, is inevitable. The comic heroine, on the other hand, does not fight the system but merely surfaces, again and again, when and where the social system is temporarily subverted. The comic heroine does not actively resist the social and political hegemony° of the men, but as an irresistible version of the Other she successfully competes for our favor with the (masculine) representatives of the social Self. The development of the feminine from the shrew to the comic heroine indicates a certain consciousness on the author's part of sexual politics; and it indicates a desire, at least, to create conditions of sexual equality within the drama even while reflecting the unequal conditions of men and women in the society at large.

hegemony: Overriding authority.

Peter Brook (b. 1925)
THE PLAY IS THE MESSAGE . . .   1987

When a distinguished director becomes a critic, we have the opportunity to
understand a play from the point of view of one who has to make the play work
in front of an audience. Brook's production of A Midsummer Night's Dream
was a sensation in England and the United States in 1970. It featured absolutely
white lighting, white sets, and actors in swings. Brook had analyzed the play in
such a fashion that he saw love as its constant concern, "constantly repeated."
He concluded that to present the play, the players must embody the concept of
love. They must bring to the play their own realization of the play's themes —
even to the point of seeing theater anew, like the mechanicals "who are touch-
ing an extraordinary world with the tips of their fingers, a world which tran-
scends their daily experience and which fills them with wonder" — the effect of
the love they bring to their task.

People have often asked me: "What is the theme of *A Midsummer Night's
Dream*?" There is only one answer to that question, the same as one would give
regarding a cup. The quality of a cup is its cupness. I say this by way of introduction, to show that if I lay so much stress on the dangers involved in trying to
define the themes of the *Dream* it is because too many productions, too many
attempts at visual interpretation are based on preconceived ideas, as if these had
to be illustrated in some way. In my opinion we should first of all try to redis-
cover the play as a living thing; then we shall be able to analyze our discoveries.
Once I have finished working on the play, I can begin to produce my theories. It
was fortunate that I did not attempt to do so earlier because the play would not
have yielded up its secrets.

At the center of the *Dream,* constantly repeated, we find the word "love."
Everything comes back to this, even the structure of the play, even its music. The
quality the play demands from its performers is to build up an atmosphere of
love during the performance itself, so that this abstract idea — for the word
"love" is in itself a complete abstraction — may become palpable. The play presents us with forms of love which become less and less blurred as it goes on.
"Love" soon begins to resound like a musical scale and little by little we are introduced to its various modes and tones.

Love is, of course, a theme which touches all men. No one, not even the most
hardened, the coldest, or the most despairing, is insensitive to it, even if he does
not know what love is. Either his practical experience confirms its existence or
he suffers from its absence, which is another way of recognizing that it exists. At
every moment the play touches something which concerns everyone.

As this is theater, there must be conflicts, so this play about love is also a play
about the opposite of love, love and its opposite force. We are brought to realize that love, liberty, and imagination are closely connected. Right at the beginning of the play, for example, the father in a long speech tries to obstruct his
daughter's love and we are surprised that such a character, apparently a secondary role, should have so long a speech — until we discover the real importance of his words. What he says not only reflects a generation gap (a father

opposing his daughter's love because he had intended her for someone else), it also explains the reasons for his feeling of suspicion toward the young man whom his daughter loves. He describes him as an individual prone to fantasy, led by his imagination — an unpardonable weakness in the father's eyes.

From this starting point we see, as in any of Shakespeare's plays, a confrontation. Here it is between love and its opposing qualities, between fantasy and solid common sense — caught in an endless series of mirrors. As usual, Shakespeare confuses the issue. If we asked someone's opinion on the father's point of view, he might say, for example, that "The father is in the wrong because he is against freedom of the imagination," a very widespread attitude today.

In this way, for most present-day audiences, the girl's father comes over as the classical father figure who misunderstands young people and their flights of fancy. But later on, we discover surprisingly that he is right, because the imaginative world in which this lover lives causes him to behave in a quite disgusting way toward the very same daughter: as soon as a drop of liquid falls into his eyes, acting as a drug which liberates natural tendencies, he not only jilts her but his love is transformed into violent hate. He uses words which might well be borrowed from *Measure for Measure,* denouncing the girl with the kind of vehemence that, in the Middle Ages, led people to burn one another at the stake. Yet at the end of the play we are once more in agreement with the Duke, who rejects the father in the name of love. The young man has now been transformed.

So we observe this game of love in a psychological and metaphysical context; we hear Titania's assertion that the opposition between herself and Oberon is fundamental, primordial. But Oberon's acts deny this, for he perceives that within their opposition a reconciliation is possible.

The play covers an extraordinarily broad range of universal forces and feelings in a mythical world, which suddenly changes, in the last part, into high society. We find ourselves back in the very real palace: and the same Shakespeare who, a few pages earlier, offered us a scene of pure fantasy between Titania and Oberon, where it would be absurd to ask prosaic questions like "Where does Oberon live?" or "When describing a queen like Titania did Shakespeare wish to express political ideas?," now takes us into a precise social environment. We are present at the meeting point of two worlds, that of the workmen and the court, the world of wealth and elegance, and alleged sensitivity, the world of people who have had the leisure to cultivate fine sentiments and are now shown as insensitive and even disgusting in their superior attitude toward the poor.

At the beginning of the court scene we see our former heroes, who have spent the entire play involved in the theme of love, and would no doubt be quite capable of giving academic lectures on the subject, suddenly finding themselves plunged into a context which has apparently nothing to do with love (with their own love, since all their problems have been solved). Now they are in the context of a relationship with each other and with another social class, and they are at a loss. They do not realize that here too scorn eliminates love.

We see how well Shakespeare has situated everything. Athens in the *Dream* resembles our Athens in the sixties: the workmen, as they state in the first scene, are very much afraid of the authorities; if they commit the slightest error they will be hanged, and there is nothing comical about that. Indeed, they risk hanging as soon as they shed their anonymity. At the same time they are irresistibly attracted by the carrot of "sixpence a day" which will enable them to escape poverty. Yet their real motive is neither glory nor adventure nor money (that is made very clear and should guide the actors who perform this scene). Those simple men who have only ever worked with their hands apply to the use of the imagination exactly the same quality of love which traditionally underlies the relationship between a craftsman and his tools. That is what gives these scenes both their strength and their comic quality. These craftsmen make efforts which are grotesque in one sense because they push awkwardness to its limit, but at another level they set themselves to their task with such love that the meaning of their clumsy efforts changes before our eyes.

The spectators can easily decide to adopt the same attitude as the courtiers: to find all this quite simply ridiculous; to laugh with the complacency of people who quite confidently mock the efforts of others. Yet the audience is invited to take a step back: to feel it cannot quite identify with the court, with people who are too grand and too unkind. Little by little, we come to see that the craftsmen, who behave with little understanding but who approach their new job with love, are discovering theater — an imaginary world for them, toward which they instinctively feel great respect. In fact, the "mechanicals" scene is often misinterpreted because the actors forget to look at theater through innocent eyes, they take a professional actor's views of good or bad acting, and in so doing they diminish the mystery and the sense of magic felt by these amateurs, who are touching an extraordinary world with the tips of their fingers, a world which transcends their daily experience and which fills them with wonder.

We see this quite clearly in the part of the boy who plays the girl, Thisby. At first sight this tough lad is irresistibly absurd, but by degrees, through his love for what he is doing, we discover what more is involved. In our production, the actor playing the part is a professional plumber, who only took to acting a short while ago. He well understands what is involved, what it means to feel this nameless and shapeless kind of love. This boy, himself new to theater, acts the part of someone who is new to theater. Through his conviction and his identification we discover that these awkward craftsmen, without knowing it, are teaching us a lesson — or it might be preferable to say that a lesson is being taught us through them. These craftsmen are able to make the connection between love for their trade and for a completely different task, whereas the courtiers are not capable of linking the love about which they talk so well with their simple role as spectators.

Nonetheless, little by little the courtiers become involved, even touched by the play within the play, and if one follows very closely what is there in the text we see that for a moment the situation is completely transformed. One of the central images of the play is a wall, which, at a given moment, vanishes. Its disappearance, to which Bottom draws our attention, is caused by an act of love. Shakespeare is showing us how love can pervade a situation and act as a transforming force.

The *Dream* touches lightly on the fundamental question of the transformations which may occur if certain things are better understood. It requires us to reflect on the nature of love. All the landscapes of love are thrown into relief, and we are given a particular social context through which the other situations can be measured. Through the subtlety of its language the play removes all kinds of barriers. It is therefore not a play which provokes resistance, or creates disturbance in the usual sense. Rival politicians could sit side by side at a performance of *A Midsummer Night's Dream* and each leave with the impression that the play fits his point of view perfectly. But if they give it a fine, sensitive attention they cannot fail to perceive a world just like their own, more and more riddled with contradictions and, like their own, waiting for that mysterious force, love, without which harmony will never return.

Clive Barnes (b. 1927)
REVIEW OF *A MIDSUMMER NIGHT'S DREAM*   1970

Clive Barnes's review credits the Peter Brook production of A Midsummer Night's Dream *as a landmark. Audiences in Stratford, London, New York, and elsewhere agreed. Brook (b. 1925) emphasized the dramatic spectacle — the sets, costumes, and action — in such a way as to reveal new depths of emotion. The playfulness of the jugglers, acrobats, and those on the trapezes emphasized the joy and youth of the main characters.*

Once in a while, once in a very rare while, a theatrical production arrives that is going to be talked about as long as there is a theater, a production that, for good or ill, is going to exert a major influence on the contemporary stage. Such a production is Peter Brook's staging of Shakespeare's *A Midsummer Night's Dream,* which the Royal Shakespeare Company introduced here tonight.

It is a magnificent production, the most important work yet of the world's most imaginative and inventive director. If Peter Brook had done nothing else but this "Dream" he would have deserved a place in theater history,

Brook has approached the play with a radiant innocence. He has treated the script as if it had just been written and sent to him through the mail. He has staged it with no reference to the past, no reverence for tradition.

He has stripped the play down, asked exactly what it is about. He has forgotten gossamer fairies, sequined eyelids, gauzy veils and whole forests of Beerbohm-trees.

He sees the play for what it is — an allegory of sensual love, and a magic playground of lost innocence and hidden fears. Love in Shakespeare comes as suddenly as death, and when Shakespeare's people love they are all but consumed with sexual passion.

Brook's first concern is to enchant us — to reveal this magic playground. He has conceived the production as a box of theatrical miracles. It takes place in a pure-white setting. The stage is walled in on three sides and the floor is also white. Ladders lead up the walls and on the top are scaffolds and rostrums from which actors can look down on the playing area like spectators at a bullfight.

The fairy characters — Oberon, Titania and Puck — are made into acrobats and jugglers. They swing in on trapezes, they amaze us with juggling tricks, Tarzan-like swings across the stage, all the sad deftness of clowns.

Shakespeare's quartet of mingled lovers, now mod kids humming love songs to loosely strummed guitars, are lost in the Venetian woods. The trees are vast metal coils thrown down from the walls on fishing rods, and moving in on unwary lovers like spiraling metallic tendrils. And in this wood of animal desire the noises are not the friendly warblings of fairyland, but the grunts and groans of some primeval jungle.

Sex and sexuality are vital in the play. Oberon and Titania, even when quarreling, kiss with hasty, hungry passion — no shining moon for them — and the lovers seem to be journeying through some inner landscape of their own desires toward maturity.

The sexual relationships — with the wittiest use of phallic symbolism the stage can have ever seen — is stressed between Titania and her Bottom. Yet the carnality of the piece is seen with affectionate tolerance rather than the bitterness the playwright shows in *Troilus and Cressida,* and this tolerance, even playfulness, suffuses the production.

Brook is a magician and he gives us new eyes. Here, for reasons admirably supported by the text, he has Theseus and Hippolyta (that previously rather dull royal couple whose wedding provides the framework for the play) played by the same actors as play Oberon and Titania. At once the play takes on a new and personal dimension. The fairies take on a new humanity, and these human princelings, once so uninteresting, are now endowed with a different mystery, and the gentle, almost sad note on which the play ends has a feeling of human comprehension and godlike compassion to it. It is most moving

Two other characters take on dual assignments. Philostrate, that court master of ceremonies for Theseus, is also, naturally enough, Puck, and, rather more puzzlingly, Egeus, the angry father of Hermia, whose opposition to her marriage sets off the action, is also Peter Quince, one of the mechanicals. Presumably the purpose is to bring the play within the play more closely into the main structure, for just as Egeus initiates the real action, so Quince initiates the inner play. But it savors of a literary rather than dramatic device.

Puck is the key figure in this version. Looking like a more than usually perky Picasso clown, he bounces through the action with happy amiability, the model of toleration. John Kane plays him delightfully, performing his tricks with a true circus expertise and acting with unaffected delight.

The Theseus/Oberon and Hippolyta/Titania of Alan Howard and Sara Kestelman are special pleasures, and the mechanicals with the terrible tragedy of *Pyramus and Thisbe* are the best I have ever seen, with David Waller's virile Bottom particularly splendid.

But the star of this dream is Peter Brook himself, with his ideas, his theories and above all his practices. Of course he is helped — first by the samite-white pleasure palace devised by his Los Angeles-based designer, Sally Jacobs, and the richly evocative music and sound score provided by Richard Peaslee. But Mr. Brook is the genius architect of our most substantial pleasure.

He makes it all so fresh and so much fun. After a riotously funny and bawdy courtship of Titania by Bottom, the two leave the stage to, of all wonderful things, Mendelssohn's Wedding March, and all hell breaks loose, with confetti, paper streamers and Oberon himself flying in urbane mockery across the stage.

And Brook uses everything to hand — he is defiantly eclectic. It is as though he is challenging the world, by saying that there is no such thing as Shakespearean style. If it suits his purpose he will use a little kathakali, a pop song, sparklers borrowed from a toyshop, dramatic candles borrowed from Grotowski. It is all splendid grist to his splendid mill. Shakespeare can be fun, Shakespeare can be immediate, Shakespeare can most richly live.

Samuel Taylor Coleridge (1772–1834)
On Hamlet   1812

Samuel Taylor Coleridge was the first modern English critic of Shakespeare to develop influential readings of the great plays. He visited atheneums and lyceums (institutions promoting learning) on both sides of the Atlantic delivering his lectures on Shakespeare, and his interpretations stimulated a new age of thoughtful criticism. His lecture on Hamlet includes a careful reading of difficult lines, but it also centers on questions of the relationship of Shakespeare to his creation. Further, the mental state of Hamlet becomes of central interest to Coleridge and a basis of much of his observation.

The seeming inconsistencies in the conduct and character of Hamlet have long exercised the conjectural ingenuity of critics; and, as we are always loath to suppose that the cause of defective apprehension is in ourselves, the mystery has been too commonly explained by the very easy process of setting it down as in fact inexplicable, and by resolving the phenomenon into a misgrowth or *lusus* of the capricious and irregular genius of Shakespeare. The shallow and stupid arrogance of these vulgar and indolent decisions I would fain do my best to expose. I believe the character of Hamlet may be traced to Shakespeare's deep and accurate science in mental philosophy. Indeed, that this character must have some connection with the common fundamental laws of our nature may be assumed from the fact that Hamlet has been the darling of every country in which the literature of England has been fostered. In order to understand him, it is essential that we should reflect on the constitution of our own minds. Man is distinguished from the brute animals in proportion as thought prevails over sense: but in the healthy processes of the mind, a balance is constantly maintained between the impressions from outward objects and the inward operations of the intellect: — for if there be an overbalance in the contemplative faculty, man thereby becomes the creature of mere meditation, and loses his natural power of action. Now one of Shakespeare's modes of creating characters is to conceive any one intellectual or moral faculty in morbid excess, and then to place himself, Shakespeare, thus mutilated or diseased, under given circumstances. In Hamlet he seems to have wished to exemplify the moral necessity of a due balance between our attention to the objects of our senses, and our meditation on the workings of our minds, — an *equilibrium* between the real and the imaginary worlds. In Hamlet this balance is disturbed: his thoughts, and the images of his fancy, are far more vivid than his actual perceptions, and his very perceptions, instantly passing through the *medium* of his contemplations, acquire, as they pass, a form and a color not naturally their own. Hence we see a great, an almost enormous, intellectual activity, and a proportionate aversion to real action, consequent upon it, with all its symptoms and accompanying qualities. This character Shakespeare places in circumstances, under which it is obliged to act on the spur of the moment: — Hamlet is brave and careless of death; but he vacillates from sensibility, and procrastinates from thought, and loses the power of action in the energy of resolve. Thus it is that this tragedy presents a direct contrast to that of Macbeth; the one proceeds with the utmost slowness, the other with a crowded and breathless rapidity.

The effect of this overbalance of the imaginative power is beautifully illustrated in the everlasting broodings and superfluous activities of Hamlet's mind, which, unseated from its healthy relation, is constantly occupied with the world within, and abstracted from the world without, — giving substance to shadows, and throwing a mist over all commonplace actualities. It is the nature of thought to be indefinite; — definiteness belongs to external imagery alone. Hence it is that the sense of sublimity arises, not from the sight of an outward object, but from the beholder's reflection upon it; — not from the sensuous impression, but from the imaginative reflex. Few have seen a celebrated waterfall without feeling something akin to disappointment: it is only subsequently that the image comes back full into the mind, and brings with it a train of grand or beautiful associations. Hamlet feels this; his senses are in a state of trance, and he looks upon external things as hieroglyphics. His soliloquy —

Oh! that this too, too solid flesh would melt, &c.

springs from that craving after the indefinite—for that which is not — which most easily besets men of genius; and the self-delusion common to this temper of mind is finely exemplified in the character which Hamlet gives of himself: —

— It can not be
But I am pigeon-livered, and lack gall
To make oppression bitter.

He mistakes the seeing his chains for the breaking of them, delays action till action is of no use, and dies the victim of mere circumstance and accident. . . .

Act I, scene IV. The unimportant conversation with which this scene opens is a proof of Shakespeare's minute knowledge of human nature. It is a well-established fact, that on the brink of any serious enterprise, or event of moment, men almost invariably endeavor to elude the pressure of their own thoughts by turning aside to trivial objects and familiar circumstances: thus this dialogue on the platform begins with remarks on the coldness of the air, and inquiries, obliquely connected, indeed, with the expected hour of the visitation, but thrown out in a seeming vacuity of topics, as to the striking of the clock and so forth. The same desire to escape from the impending thought is carried on in Hamlet's account of, and moralizing on, the Danish custom of wassailing: he runs off from the particular to the universal, and in his repugnance to personal and individual concerns, escapes, as it were, from himself in generalizations, and smothers the impatience and uneasy feelings of the moment in abstract reasoning. Besides this, another purpose is answered; — for by thus entangling the attention of the audience in the nice distinctions and parenthetical sentences of this speech of Hamlet's, Shakespeare takes them completely by surprise on the appearance of the Ghost, which comes upon them in all the suddenness of its visionary character. Indeed, no modern writer would have dared, like Shakespeare, to have preceded this last visitation by two distinct appearances, — or could have contrived that the third should rise upon the former two in impressiveness and solemnity of interest.

But in addition to all the other excellences of Hamlet's speech concerning the wassail-music — so finely revealing the predominant idealism, the ratiocinative°

ratiocinative: Reasoned.

meditativeness, of his character — it has the advantage of giving nature and probability to the impassioned continuity of the speech instantly directed to the Ghost. The *momentum* had been given to his mental activity; the full current of the thoughts and words had set in, and the very forgetfulness, in the fervor of his augmentation, of the purpose for which he was there, aided in preventing the appearance from benumbing the mind. Consequently, it acted as a new impulse, — a sudden stroke which increased the velocity of the body already in motion, whilst it altered the direction. The copresence of Horatio, Marcellus, and Bernardo is most judiciously contrived; for it renders the courage of Hamlet and his impetuous eloquence perfectly intelligible. The knowledge, — the unthought of consciousness, — the sensation, — of human auditors — of flesh and blood sympathists — acts as a support and a stimulation of *a tergo*, while the front of the mind, the whole consciousness of the speaker, is filed, yea, absorbed, by the apparition. Add too, that the apparition itself has by its previous appearances been brought nearer to a thing of this world. This accrescence° of objectivity in a Ghost that yet retains all its ghostly attributes and fearful subjectivity, is truly wonderful.

Act I, scene v. Hamlet's speech: —

O all you host of heaven! O earth! What else?
And shall I couple hell? —

I remember nothing equal to this burst unless it be the first speech of Prometheus in the Greek drama, after the exit of Vulcan and the two Afrites. But Shakespeare alone could have produced the vow of Hamlet to make his memory a blank of all maxims and generalized truths, that "observation had copied there," — followed immediately by the speaker noting down the generalized fact,

That one may smile, and smile, and be a villain!

MARCELLUS: Hillo, ho, ho, my lord!
HAMLET: Hillo, ho, ho, boy! come bird, come, &c.

This part of the scene after Hamlet's interview with the Ghost has been charged with an improbable eccentricity. But the truth is that after the mind has been stretched beyond its usual pitch and tone, it must either sink into exhaustion and inanity, or seek relief by change. It is thus well known, that persons conversant in deeds of cruelty contrive to escape from conscience by connecting something of the ludicrous with them, and by inventing grotesque terms and a certain technical phraseology to disguise the horror of their practices. Indeed, paradoxical as it may appear, the terrible by a law of the human mind always touches on the verge of the ludicrous. Both arise from the perception of something out of the common order of things — something, in fact, out of its place; and if from this we can abstract danger, the uncommonness will alone remain, and the sense of the ridiculous be excited. The close alliance of these opposites — they are not contraries — appears from the circumstance, that laughter is equally the expression of extreme anguish and horror as of joy: as there are tears of sorrow and tears of joy, so is there a laugh of terror and a laugh of merriment. These complex causes will naturally have produced in Hamlet the disposition to escape from his own feelings of the overwhelming and supernatural by a wild transition

accrescence: Accumulation or concentration.

to the ludicrous, — a sort of cunning bravado, bordering on the flights of delirium. For you may, perhaps, observe that Hamlet's wildness is but half false; he plays that subtle trick of pretending to act only when he is very near really being what he acts.

Sigmund Freud (1856–1939)
HAMLET'S SCRUPLES   1900–1930°

Sigmund Freud is the most celebrated psychiatrist of the twentieth century. He was especially interested in Greek myth, as his comments on Oedipus Rex *suggest.* Hamlet *was another play that took on mythic proportions for him, in part because Freud saw in Hamlet the operation of his famous theory of the Oedipus complex. In the following excerpt Freud examines the events of the play that bear on his theory.*

Another of the great creations of tragic poetry, Shakespeare's *Hamlet,* has its roots in the same soil as *Oedipus Rex.* But the changed treatment of the same material reveals the whole difference in the mental life of these two widely separated epochs of civilization: the secular advance of repression in the emotional life of mankind. In the *Oedipus* the child's wishful fantasy that underlies it is brought into the open and realized as it would be in a dream. In *Hamlet* it remains repressed; and — just as in the case of a neurosis — we only learn of its existence from its inhibiting consequences. Strangely enough, the overwhelming effect produced by the more modern tragedy has turned out to be compatible with the fact that people have remained completely in the dark as to the hero's character. The play is built up on Hamlet's hesitations over fulfilling the task of revenge that is assigned to him; but its text offers no reasons or motives for these hesitations and an immense variety of attempts at interpreting them have failed to produce a result. According to the view which was originated by Goethe and is still the prevailing one today, Hamlet represents the type of man whose power of direct action is paralyzed by an excessive development of his intellect. (He is "sicklied o'er with the pale cast of thought.") According to another view, the dramatist has tried to portray a pathologically irresolute character which might be classed as neurasthenic. The plot of the drama shows us, however, that Hamlet is far from being represented as a person incapable of taking any action. We see him doing so on two occasions: first in a sudden outburst of temper, when he runs his sword through the eavesdropper behind the arras, and secondly in a premeditated and even crafty fashion, when, with all the callousness of a Renaissance prince, he sends the two courtiers to the death that had been planned for himself. What is it, then, that inhibits him in fulfilling the task set him by his father's ghost? The answer, once again, is that it is the peculiar nature of the task. Hamlet is able to do anything — except take vengeance on the man who did away with his father and took that father's place with his

1900–1930: Freud's *Interpretation of Dreams,* from which this excerpt is taken, was first published in 1900 and updated regularly by Freud through eight editions. This passage is taken from the eighth edition, published in 1930.

mother, the man who shows him the repressed wishes of his own childhood re-alized. Thus the loathing which should drive him on to revenge is replaced in him by self-reproaches, by scruples of conscience, which remind him that he himself is literally no better than the sinner whom he is to punish. Here I have translated into conscious terms what was bound to remain unconscious in Ham-let's mind; and if anyone is inclined to call him a hysteric, I can only accept the fact as one that is implied by my interpretation. The distaste for sexuality ex-pressed by Hamlet in his conversation with Ophelia fits in very well with this: the same distaste which was destined to take possession of the poet's mind more and more during the years that followed, and which reached its extreme expres-sion in *Timon of Athens*. For it can of course only be the poet's own mind which confronts us in Hamlet. I observe in a book on Shakespeare by Georg Brandes (1896) a statement that *Hamlet* was written immediately after the death of Shakespeare's father (in 1601), that is, under the immediate impact of his be-reavement and, as we may well assume, while his childhood feelings about his father had been freshly revived. It is known, too, that Shakespeare's own son who died at an early age bore the name of "Hamnet," which is identical with "Hamlet." Just as *Hamlet* deals with the relation of a son to his parents, so *Macbeth* (written at approximately the same period) is concerned with the sub-ject of childlessness. But just as all neurotic symptoms, and, for that matter, dreams, are capable of being "overinterpreted" and indeed need to be if they are to be fully understood, so all genuinely creative writings are the product of more than a single motive and more than a single impulse in the poet's mind, and are open to more than a single interpretation. In what I have written I have only at-tempted to interpret the deepest layer of impulses in the mind of the creative writer.

T. S. Eliot (1888–1965)
Hamlet and His Problems   *1934*

Not only a leading poet of the twentieth-century modernist period, T. S. Eliot also produced extremely interesting criticism of Elizabethan literature. His sev-eral collections of essays have in some cases defined important critical terms that later readers have used to gain insight into great writers. One of those terms is developed here: the objective correlative, which Eliot feels is missing in Hamlet. *His argument is provocative and revealing.*

Few critics have ever admitted that *Hamlet* the play is the primary problem, and Hamlet the character only secondary. And Hamlet the character has had an especial temptation for that most dangerous type of critic: the critic with a mind which is naturally of the creative order, but which through some weakness in cre-ative power exercises itself in criticism instead. These minds often find in Hamlet a vicarious existence for their own artistic realization. Such a mind had Goethe, who made of Hamlet a Werther; and such had Coleridge who made of Hamlet a Coleridge; and probably neither of these men in writing about Hamlet remem-bered that his first business was to study a work of art. The kind of criticism that

Goethe and Coleridge produced, in writing of Hamlet, is the most misleading kind possible. For they both possessed unquestionable critical insight, and both make their critical aberrations the more plausible by the substitution — of their own Hamlet for Shakespeare's — which their creative gift effects. We should be thankful that Walter Pater° did not fix his attention on this play.

Two writers of our time, Mr. J. M. Robertson and Professor Stoll of the University of Minnesota, have issued small books which can be praised for moving in the other direction. Mr. Stoll performs a service in recalling to our attention the labors of the critics of the seventeenth and eighteenth centuries, observing that

> they knew less about psychology than more recent Hamlet critics, but they were nearer in spirit to Shakespeare's art; and as they insisted on the importance of the effect of the whole rather than on the importance of the leading character, they were nearer, in their old-fashioned way, to the secret of dramatic art in general.

Qua work of art, the work of art cannot be interpreted; there is nothing to interpret; we can only criticize it according to standards, in comparison to other works of art; and for "interpretation" the chief task is the presentation of relevant historical facts which the reader is not assumed to know. Mr. Robertson points out, very pertinently, how critics have failed in their "interpretation" of *Hamlet* by ignoring what ought to be very obvious: that *Hamlet* is a stratification, that it represents the efforts of a series of men, each making what he could out of the work of his predecessors. The *Hamlet* of Shakespeare will appear to us very differently if, instead of treating the whole action of the play as due to Shakespeare's design, we perceive his *Hamlet* to be superposed upon much cruder material which persists even in the final form.

We know that there was an older play by Thomas Kyd, that extraordinary dramatic (if not poetic) genius who was in all probability the author of two plays so dissimilar as the *Spanish Tragedy* and *Arden of Feversham;* and what this play was like we can guess from three clues: from the *Spanish Tragedy* itself, from the tale of Belleforest upon which Kyd's *Hamlet* must have been based, and from a version acted in Germany in Shakespeare's lifetime which bears strong evidence of having been adapted from the earlier, not from the later, play. From these three sources it is clear that in the earlier play the motive was a revenge motive simply; that the action or delay is caused, as in the *Spanish Tragedy,* solely by the difficulty of assassinating a monarch surrounded by guards; and that the "madness" of Hamlet was feigned in order to escape suspicion, and successfully. In the final play of Shakespeare, on the other hand, there is a motive which is more important than that of revenge, and which explicitly "blunts" the latter; the delay in revenge is unexplained on grounds of necessity or expediency; and the effect of the "madness" is not to lull but to arouse the king's suspicion. The alteration is not complete enough, however, to be convincing. Furthermore, there are verbal parallels so close to the *Spanish Tragedy* as to leave no doubt that in places Shakespeare was merely *revising* the text of Kyd. And finally there are unexplained scenes — the Polonius-Laertes and the Polonius-Reynaldo scenes — for which there is little excuse; these scenes are not in the verse style of Kyd, and not beyond doubt in the style of Shakespeare.

Walter Pater: English writer and critic (1839–1894). His writings were often over-elaborate.

These Mr. Robertson believes to be scenes in the original play of Kyd reworked by a third hand, perhaps Chapman,° before Shakespeare touched the play. And he concludes, with very strong show of reason, that the original play of Kyd was, like certain other revenge plays, in two parts of five acts. The upshot of Mr. Robertson's examination is, we believe, irrefragable: that Shakespeare's *Hamlet,* so far as it is Shakespeare's, is a play dealing with the effect of a mother's guilt upon her son, and that Shakespeare was unable to impose this motive successfully upon the "intractable" material of the old play.

Of the intractability there can be no doubt. So far from being Shakespeare's masterpiece, the play is most certainly an artistic failure. In several ways the play is puzzling, and disquieting as is none of the others. Of all the plays it is the longest and is possibly the one on which Shakespeare spent most pains; and yet he has left in it superfluous and inconsistent scenes which even hasty revision should have noticed. The versification is variable. Lines like

> Look, the morn, in russet mantle clad,
> Walks o'er the dew of yon high eastern hill,

are of the Shakespeare of *Romeo and Juliet.* The lines in act V. scene II,

> Sir, in my heart there was a kind of fighting
> That would not let me sleep . . .
> Up from my cabin,
> My sea-grown scarf'd about me, in the dark
> Grop'd I to find out them: had my desire;
> Finger'd their packet;

are of his quite mature. Both workmanship and thought are in an unstable position. We are surely justified in attributing the play, with that other profoundly interesting play of "intractable" material and astonishing versification, *Measure for Measure,* to a period of crisis, after which follow the tragic successes which culminate in *Coriolanus. Coriolanus* may be not as "interesting" as *Hamlet,* but it is, with *Antony and Cleopatra,* Shakespeare's most assured artistic success. And probably more people have thought *Hamlet* a work of art because they found it interesting, than have found it interesting because it is a work of art. It is the *Mona Lisa* of literature.

The grounds of *Hamlet*'s failure are not immediately obvious. Mr. Robertson is undoubtedly correct in concluding that the essential emotion of the play is the feeling of a son toward a guilty mother:

> [Hamlet's] tone is that of one who has suffered tortures on the score of his mother's degradation. . . . The guilt of a mother is an almost intolerable motive for drama, but it had to be maintained and emphasized to supply a psychological solution, or rather a hint of one.

This, however, is by no means the whole story. It is not merely the "guilt of a mother" that cannot be handled as Shakespeare handled the suspicion of Othello, the infatuation of Antony, or the pride of Coriolanus. The subject might conceivably have expanded into a tragedy like these, intelligible, self-complete, in the sunlight. *Hamlet,* like the sonnets, is full of some stuff that the writer could not drag to light, contemplate, or manipulate into art. And when we search for this feeling, we find it, as in the sonnets, very difficult to localize.

Chapman: George Chapman (1559?–1634), Elizabethan poet and playwright.

You cannot point to it in the speeches; indeed, if you examine the two famous soliloquies you see the versification of Shakespeare, but a content which might be claimed by another, perhaps by the author of the *Revenge of Bussy d'Am-bois*,° act V, scene I. We find Shakespeare's Hamlet not in the action, not in any quotations that we might select, so much as in an unmistakable tone which is unmistakably not in the earlier play.

The only way of expressing emotion in the form of art is by finding an "objective correlative"; in other words, a set of objects, a situation, a chain of events which shall be the formula of that *particular* emotion; such that when the external facts, which must terminate in sensory experience, are given, the emotion is immediately evoked. If you examine any of Shakespeare's more successful tragedies, you will find this exact equivalence; you will find that the state of mind of Lady Macbeth walking in her sleep has been communicated to you by a skillful accumulation of imagined sensory impressions; the words of Macbeth on hearing of his wife's death strike us as if, given the sequence of events, these words were automatically released by the last event in the series. The artistic "inevitability" lies in this complete adequacy of the external to the emotion; and this is precisely what is deficient in *Hamlet*. Hamlet (the man) is dominated by an emotion which is inexpressible, because it is in *excess* of the facts as they appear. And the supposed identity of Hamlet with his author is genuine to this point: that Hamlet's bafflement at the absence of objective equivalent to his feelings is a prolongation of the bafflement of his creator in the face of his artistic problem. Hamlet is up against the difficulty that his disgust is occasioned by his mother, but that his mother is not an adequate equivalent for it; his disgust envelops and exceeds her. It is thus a feeling which he cannot understand; he cannot objectify it, and it therefore remains to poison life and obstruct action. None of the possible actions can satisfy it; and nothing that Shakespeare can do with the plot can express Hamlet for him. And it must be noticed that the very nature of the *données* of the problem precludes objective equivalence. To have heightened the criminality of Gertrude would have been to provide the formula for a totally different emotion in Hamlet; it is just *because* her character is so negative and insignificant that she arouses in Hamlet the feeling which she is incapable of representing.

The "madness" of Hamlet lay to Shakespeare's hand; in the earlier play a simple ruse, and to the end, we may presume, understood as a ruse by the audience. For Shakespeare it is less than madness and more than feigned. The levity of Hamlet, his repetition of phrase, his puns, are not part of a deliberate plan of dissimulation, but a form of emotional relief. In the character Hamlet it is the buffoonery of an emotion which can find no outlet in action; in the dramatist it is the buffoonery of an emotion which he cannot express in art. The intense feeling, ecstatic or terrible, without an object or exceeding its object, is something which every person of sensibility has known; it is doubtless a subject of study for pathologists. It often occurs in adolescence: the ordinary person puts these feelings to sleep, or trims down his feelings to fit the business world; the artist keeps them alive by his ability to intensify the world to his emotions. The Hamlet of Laforgue° is an adolescent; the Hamlet of Shakespeare is not, he has not

Revenge of Bussy d'Ambois: Tragedy (1610–1611) by George Chapman, dealing with the reluctance of Clement d'Ambois to avenge his brother's death.
Laforgue: Jules Laforgue (1860–1887), French poet who was an important influence on Eliot.

that explanation and excuse. We must simply admit that here Shakespeare tackled a problem which proved too much for him. Why he attempted it at all is an insoluble puzzle; under compulsion of what experience he attempted to express the inexpressibly horrible, we cannot ever know. We need a great many facts in his biography; and we should like to know whether, and when, and after or at the same time as what personal experience, he read Montaigne's *Apologie de Raimond Sebond*. We should have, finally, to know something which is by hypothesis unknowable, for we assume it to be an experience which, in the manner indicated, exceeded the facts. We should have to understand things which Shakespeare did not understand himself.

John Lahr (b. 1941)
REVIEW OF *HAMLET*   *1994*

As John Lahr reminds us, any review of Hamlet *always discusses the lead actor. All past productions are identified in terms of the actor who played the part. Lahr, like most reviewers, centers first on Ralph Fiennes's performance in the title role. He then goes on, focusing on elements such as costumes and stage settings as a way of describing the overall production.*

Hamlet is a play that tests the best actors of each generation, and also each generation's sense of itself. Over the last thirty years, in England, no fewer than three *Hamlet*s have served as such cultural bellwethers. In 1965, during the Vietnam War, David Warner gave us an untidy undergraduate Hamlet who was frustrated by Denmark's military-industrial complex. In 1980, as Britain's economy went into a weird free fall, Jonathan Pryce's *Hamlet* was possessed by the ghost of his father, who spoke through him in a frightening supernatural flirtation with madness. And now, in the neutral, post-Thatcher nineties, Ralph Fiennes has pitched his drop-dead matinee-idol profile and the modesty of his sensitive soul into a postmodern *Hamlet* whose refusal to risk interpretation reflects Britain's current bland and winded times.

Fiennes, an intelligent, reticent player, seems almost as unwilling to enter the vortex of Hamlet's torment as Hamlet himself is to take action. Fiennes radiates an elegance of spirit that rivets the audience with its sense of unspoken mystery. His performance is a stylish event, much more the "mould of form" than the "glass of fashion." He has a mellow, reedy voice that filters Shakespeare's gorgeous complexity and gives the language an accessible colloquial ring. Fiennes is not one for grand histrionic gestures. His personality doesn't take up a lot of space. He compels attention by his decency, not by his declaiming. Fiennes, who has limpid green eyes and tousled chestnut hair, and who is a laid-back, brooding, romantic star, is catnip to the public and oxygen at the box office. (The Almeida Theatre Company's production, which began its much ballyhooed life at the Hackney Empire, the wonderful old music-hall venue in London's East End, has arrived at the Belasco for a fourteen-week Broadway engagement.) This *Hamlet* has been designed to be a people's *Hamlet*, which is to say a *Hamlet* in which the plot, not the psychology, is complicated, and in which the cast works the room instead of working for meaning. Inevitably, therefore, Fiennes's Hamlet is not a navel-gazing scholar or an alienated adolescent or a demented psychological case study. His Hamlet turns out to be the guy Horatio always said he was: a "sweet prince," a sort of rogue and *pleasant* slave.

The director, Jonathan Kent, who last year transferred the Almeida's *Medea,* with Diana Rigg, to Broadway with great success, has set the play in Edwardian England and has lopped an hour off the playing time. The speed favors breadth over depth; the streamlining suits the cut of Fiennes's jib, and he wears James Acheson's period clothes well. What we have here is a ripping Shakespearean yarn that shows off the thrills and chills of the story's melodramatic elements: the ghost of a murdered king, a mother's hasty marriage to her husband's murderer, a prince driven to near-madness and revenge, a lovelorn suicide, a lot of ghoulish high jinks around graves, a terrific sword fight, and a quadruple poisoning. The result is lucid without being moving: a kind of aerobic *Hamlet,* which works hard to keep up the pace while going nowhere.

The lights come up on a bare, raked stage, and the sound of crashing waves fills the auditorium. In the background, the environs of Elsinore are suggested by faint, blurred beams of light projected through a murky scrim on which the outlines of rocks are just visible. A sentinel climbs up through a trapdoor — more for effect than for sense, it seems, like many things in this production. "Who's there?" he calls. That's the play; the whole existential ball of wax. Hamlet's entire dramatic journey is foreshadowed in these first words. He, too, must penetrate the surrounding darkness and tease out the reality of his parents, of the corrupt court, and of himself. By finally taking action — which means accepting loss, including the loss of his own life, Hamlet sees clear into the heart of things and achieves his adulthood. In this sense, *Hamlet* is both a detective story and a metaphysical investigation. The practical and the philosophical aspects of the tale need time to build properly, as the saying goes, "No delay, no play." But here, with the proceedings speeded up, the text is not so much examined as *done.* It's significant that Fiennes attacks the "To be, or not to be" soliloquy, which sets out Hamlet's spiritual quandary, by coming toward us in manic stutter steps and turning the famous meditation into yapping thought. He skirts the issue of interpretation by turning talk into behavior. The image is novel but little nuance comes across the footlights. In this ranting mode, dissembling a madness that is really giddy grief, the barefoot Fiennes grabs Ophelia's crotch and insolently shoves Claudius's shoulder. But Fiennes can't really get up a convincingly antic head of steam. He is slow to kindle and never really burns. He's not so much tormented as pissed off.

Fiennes has his best moment with the Gravedigger (the excellent grizzled Terence Rigby, who also plays Hamlet's father's ghost and the Player King). Listening to the Gravedigger expound matter-of-factly on how a body decomposes, and learning that a skull he has unearthed belonged to Yorick, the former King's jester, Hamlet gently takes this relic of his old acquaintance from the Gravedigger. "This?" Fiennes says, uttering the word with a huge sense of recognition, wonder, and sadness. His sensitivity and the mournfulness of the moment coalesce. "Where be your gibes now? your gambols? your songs? your flashes of merriment, that were wont to set the table on a roar?" Fiennes says, with a delicacy that delivers Shakespeare's observations about mortality like a punch to the heart.

The production's obsession with surface has its most effective expression in Peter J. Davison's sets. He creates a dark, lugubrious officialdom of behemoth ceilings, heavy brown-stained doors, and large shuttered windows that turn the actors into scuttling Lilliputians. Hamlet is first seen framed by one of these gigantic windows, standing upstage with his back turned away from the bustle of power, whose aggrandizement is reflected in the monumentality that surrounds it. Still, Davison, too, succumbs to the production's impulse to startle rather than compel. The ghost is conjured up on a high platform behind the scrim. There, lit from above by the white glare of a halogen lamp and announced by a jolt of electronic sound, Hamlet's dead father appears twice, in his carapace of armor: a "Star Wars" effect that is a projection of commercial instincts more than of Hamlet's unconscious. Similarly, Jonathan Kent's eye for business is sometimes shrewder than his eye for detail. When Laertes and Hamlet take turns leaping into Ophelia's grave and embracing her body, each trying to outdo the remorse of the other, the poor dead girl bobs up and down like a hand puppet. And at the finale, when Fortinbras (Rupert Penry-Jones, who is also Fiennes's understudy) arrives to take over the kingdom that Hamlet has died to save, his Aryan good looks and the gray capes of his lieutenants make it seem as if the Luftwaffe had invaded Denmark.

In American theatrical circles, the definition of a genius is anybody from England. But the prestige of this production can't hide the unevenness of its seasoned supporting cast, who prove the adage that British actors are either tours de force or forced to tour. Besides Terence Rigby, only the lanky, bearded Peter Eyre, as Polonius, breathes distinctive life into his role. Eyre plays the meddling bureaucrat as a long drink of cold water: cleaning his pince-nez as he counsels his hotheaded son to "neither a borrower, nor a lender be," and withholding his hand from Laertes when he goes, Eyre misses no opportunity to have fun with the old blowhard's pedantry. Polonius rushes to the Queen with a letter that Hamlet has sent his daughter, and reads it to her as a presenting symptom of Hamlet's lunacy. Reciting "To the celestial and my soul's idol, the most beautified Ophelia," Eyre's Polonius bristles with dopey patrician disdain. "That's an ill phrase, a vile phrase, 'beautified' is a vile phrase," he says, and gets one of the evening's best laughs.

Others are not so much at home in Shakespeare's climate of delirium. Tara FitzGerald, a talented young actress with a bright future, flounders as Ophelia. There is nothing fractured or vulnerable about her, and when Ophelia goes mad FitzGerald won't let her rip. FitzGerald's behavior — the compulsive walking back and forth, the sexual taunts directed at Claudius — feels tame and glib: a trick of the mind, not a journey of the heart. Often, when English actors are nowhere near the center of their parts they rely on the power of their articulate voices; James Laurenson's Claudius falls into the trap of such posturing. Claudius is John Gotti with a pedigree — carnal, vicious, powerhungry, ruthless — but Laurenson gives us chicanery on the half shell. He does a lot of Urgent Shakespeare Acting. A few wheeling turns upstage, some nips at the top of his hand, a little booming oratory, and — presto! — you have a villain. This stock rep stuff is also dished up by the beautiful Francesca Annis, as a Gertrude who can't manage much grief at the sight of Ophelia's dementia but does manage a long, lingering kiss with Hamlet. It's a bit of business that has become the theatrical baggage of the role in this century, but the incestuous overtone seems inappropriate, especially in such an unanalytic production.

A word about Hamlet's duel. Jonathan Kent and the fight director, William Hobbs, have built up this face-off between idealism and treachery into a scintillating contest that takes excellent advantage of the story's melodrama. A cream-colored tarp is rolled downstage for the match, and the court sits watching upstage right, in gray upholstered chairs. Hamlet fights with graceful, playful enthusiasm, unaware that he's up against the double whammy of Laertes' poisoned sword and Claudius's poisoned chalice. Hamlet gets the first couple of touches; then Laertes' temper flares, and he cuts Hamlet. They scuffle, and in the hurly-burly their swords get mixed up. Hamlet chases Laertes around the room, sending chairs flying and courtiers scurrying for safety. It's exciting and well-staged hokom, in which Laertes ends up hoist with his own petard. At that point, the Queen, who has drunk from the chalice, collapses; then the Grand Guignol of Shakespeare's ending quickly plays itself out. At the finale, Fortinbras's men lift Hamlet's corpse on their shoulders and, swaying, carry him slowly upstage and toward the light beyond. Fiennes's head falls back, giving the audience one last glimpse of the star. Even backward, upside down, and dead, Fiennes exits looking good.

Stephen J. Greenblatt (b. 1943)
THE TEMPEST AND THE NEW WORLD   1990

One current question regarding The Tempest *centers on colonialism and its significance in the play. Greenblatt, in studying the history of the setting of the New World, raises interesting points when he describes the dramatist as a colonist. By pointing to Shakespeare's own ambivalence on the matter, he reminds us how difficult the question of colonialism was even in the seventeenth century.*

The link between *The Tempest* and the New World has often been noted, as, for example, by Terence Hawkes who suggests, in his book *Shakespeare's Talking Animals,* that in creating Prospero, the playwright's imagination was fired by the resemblance he perceived between himself and a colonist. "A colonist," writes Hawkes,

> acts essentially as a dramatist. He imposes the "shape" of his own culture, *embodied in his speech,* on the new world, and makes that world recognizable, habitable, "natural," able to speak his language.

Conversely,

> the dramatist is metaphorically a colonist. His art penetrates new areas of experience, his language expands the boundaries of our culture, and makes the new territory over in its own image. His "raids on the inarticulate" open up new worlds for the imagination.

The problem for critics has been to accommodate this perceived resemblance between dramatist and colonist with a revulsion that reaches from the political critiques of colonialism in our own century back to the moral outrage of Las Casas° and Montaigne.° Moreover, there are many aspects of the play itself that make colonialism a problematical model for the theatrical imagination: If *The*

Las Casas: Bartolomé de Las Casas (1474–1566), bishop of Chiapa in Mexico, who became known as "the protector of the Indians."
Montaigne: Michel de Montaigne (1533–1592), author of one of the first works of anthropology, "Apology of Raymond Sebonde," to which Shakespeare alludes in *The Tempest.*

Tempest holds up a mirror to empire, Shakespeare would appear deeply ambivalent about using the reflected image as a representation of his own practice.

Caliban enters in act I, cursing Prospero and protesting bitterly: "This island's mine, by Sycorax my mother, / Which thou tak'st from me" (I, II, 334–35). When he first arrived, Prospero made much of Caliban, and Caliban, in turn, showed Prospero "all the qualities o'th'isle." But now, Caliban complains, "I am all the subjects that you have, / Which first was mine own King." Prospero replies angrily that he had treated Caliban "with human care" until he tried to rape Miranda, a charge Caliban does not deny. At this point, Miranda herself chimes in, with a speech Dryden and others have found disturbingly indelicate:

> Abhorrèd slave,
> Which any print of goodness wilt not take,
> Being capable of all ill! I pitied thee,
> Took pains to make thee speak, taught thee each hour
> One thing or other: when thou didst not, savage,
> Know thine own meaning, but wouldst gabble like
> A thing most brutish, I endow'd thy purposes
> With words that made them known. But thy vile race,
> Though thou didst learn, had that in 't which good natures
> Could not abide to be with; therefore wast thou
> Deservedly confin'd into this rock,
> Who hadst deserv'd more than a prison. (I, II, 354–65)

To this, Caliban replies:

> You taught me language, and my profit on 't
> Is I know how to curse. The red plague rid you
> For learning me your language! (I, II, 366–68)

Caliban's retort might be taken as self-indictment: Even with the gift of language, his nature is so debased that he can only learn to curse. But the lines refuse to mean this; what we experience instead is a sense of their devastating justness. Ugly, rude, savage, Caliban nevertheless achieves for an instant an absolute if intolerably bitter moral victory. There is no reply; only Prospero's command: "Hayseed, hence! / Fetch us in fuel," coupled with an ugly threat:

> If thou neglect'st, or dost unwillingly
> What I command, I'll rack thee with old cramps,
> Fill all thy bones with aches, make thee roar
> That beasts shall tremble at thy din. (I, II, 371–74)

What makes this exchange so powerful, I think, is that Caliban is anything but a Noble Savage. Shakespeare does not shrink from the darkest European fantasies about the Wild Man; indeed he exaggerates them: Caliban is deformed, lecherous, evil-smelling, idle, treacherous, naive, drunken, rebellious, violent, and devil-worshipping. According to Prospero, he is not even human: a "born devil," "got by the devil himself / Upon thy wicked dam" (I, II, 322–23). *The Tempest* utterly rejects the uniformitarian view of the human race, the view that would later triumph in the Enlightenment and prevail in the West to this day. All men, the play seems to suggest, are *not* alike; strip away the adornments of culture and you will *not* reach a single human essence. If anything, *The Tempest* seems closer in spirit to the attitude of the present-day inhabitants of Java who, according to Clifford Geertz, quite flatly say, "To be human is to be Javanese."

And yet out of the midst of this attitude Caliban wins a momentary victory that is, quite simply, an assertion of inconsolable human pain and bitterness. And out of the midst of this attitude Prospero comes, at the end of the play, to say of Caliban, "this thing of darkness I / Acknowledge mine" (V, I, 275–76). Like Caliban's earlier reply, Prospero's words are ambiguous; they might be taken as a bare statement that the strange "demi-devil" is one of Prospero's party as opposed to Alonso's, or even that Caliban is Prospero's slave. But again the lines refuse to mean this: They acknowledge a deep, if entirely unsentimental, bond. By no means is Caliban accepted into the family of man; rather, he is claimed as Philoctetes° might claim his own festering wound. Perhaps, too, the word "acknowledge" implies some moral responsibility, as when the Lord, in the King James translation of Jeremiah, exhorts men to "acknowledge thine iniquity, that thou hast transgressed against the Lord thy God" (3:13). Certainly the Caliban of act V is in a very real sense Prospero's creature, and the bitter justness of his retort early in the play still casts a shadow at its close. With Prospero restored to his dukedom, the match of Ferdinand and Miranda blessed, Ariel freed to the elements, and even the wind and tides of the return voyage settled, Shakespeare leaves Caliban's fate naggingly unclear. Prospero has acknowledged a bond; that is all.

Ben Brantley (b. 1954)
REVIEW OF *THE TEMPEST*   1995

One of the most successful of recent productions of The Tempest *starred Patrick Stewart, familiar to many in the audience from the television series* Star Trek: The Next Generation. *Stewart, originally with the Royal Shakespeare Company, combined with director George C. Wolfe of New York's Public Theater to create a Prospero driven by revenge and the conflicting desires for control and freedom. Brantley describes in this review a powerful production strengthened by an emphasis on themes of colonialism and innovative uses of puppetry.*

The philosophizing wizard known as Prospero is a very angry man these days. As portrayed by Patrick Stewart, in George C. Wolfe's blazingly vital, vastly enjoyable production of *The Tempest* at the Delacorte Theater in Central Park, the dispossessed Duke of Milan seems white-hot with a fury that gives new punch to his phrase "rough magic."

Unlike most Prosperos of recent years, who have been presented as practitioners of an ordering art that parallels the playwright's and director's crafts, Mr. Stewart's fascinating, combustible performance suggests that the real squall of the title is within the character himself.

Anger is what gives this *Tempest* its momentum. Nearly all of the characters portrayed here, from the captive sprites of the enchanted island to the scheming Italian courtiers who are shipwrecked there, are propelled by violent, deeply familiar impulses for power, revenge, freedom and control.

Philoctetes: Minor Greek hero and famous archer who was bitten by a snake and made lame.

This is no contemplative pipe dream of a production, but an invigorating series of emotional and moral battles between the instincts to dominate and to forgive. And for once, Prospero seems less a magisterial moral instructor, who manipulates his enemies into submission with Jovean detachment, than a mirror of our own frailties: a potentially tragic hero who, unlike the Macbeths and the Lears, veers away from self-destruction, if only provisionally.

The much traveled road to redemption of Shakespeare's last completed play has seldom been as viscerally exciting as it is here. Underscored with a sharp visual sense of menace as well as comic enchantment, and a musical score by Dan Moses Schreir that has room for the urgency of tribal drumbeats as well as ethereal chimes, this fiercely intelligent production finds universal human immediacy beneath the work's cosmic magic.

This is not to say that it lacks the sense of theatrical wonder that audiences demand of *The Tempest*. Mr. Wolfe, the New York Shakespeare Festival's producer, who is making an important debut here as a director of Shakespeare, is already well-known as a magician of stage-craft, and he doesn't disappoint.

Working with an exceptional technical team, the director and his set and lighting designers, Riccardo Hernandez and Paul Gallo, turn a stage that is basically a simple circle of sand into a forum for illusions that evoke both the mysteries of a universe beyond rational understanding, and the poignant human urge to represent them.

From the crucial opening scene of the shipwreck (achieved with undulating bolts of cloth and a configuration of actors as the physical body of the ship) to the transfiguration of the sprite Ariel (Aunjanue Ellis) into a towering, ferocious harpie, the production creates an exotic landscape that seems to spring less from the abstractly supernatural than the animism of civilizations alien to Western Europeans.

Brazilian stilt walkers, Kabuki-style masks, Indonesian shadow players and otherworldly puppets (the work of the gifted Barbara Pollitt) are all ingeniously deployed in an alternately threatening and celebratory backdrop before which the plotting of the shipwrecked courtiers seems to shrink into pathetic pettiness.

Mr. Wolfe is making a point here about the clash of cultures in the burgeoning age of colonialism. (Shakespeare's portrait of Prospero's Island was apparently inspired by accounts of English explorers in Bermuda.) That point has been made before, for example in Jonathan's Miller's version at the Old Vic in 1988. And there is no question that Ariel and the monstrous Caliban (Teagle F. Bougere), both played by dark-skinned young actors, are meant to reflect the experience of African slaves.

The fact that this *Tempest* never seems to suffer from political reductionism has everything to do with Mr. Wolfe's inspired handling of his actors. He is less interested in making an abstract statement about the immorality of slavery than in examining its emotional consequences for both master and servant.

The hostile sarcasm with which Ms. Ellis and Mr. Bougere (whose character's "monstrousness" is indicated only by his near nakedness and a red-capped skull) intone the word "master" is perhaps overdone. But there is no denying the disquieting impact of the scene in which Prospero threatens to return Ariel to the imprisonment of a tree trunk, as an ensemble of actors in black advance menacingly with tall bamboo poles that encage the hauntingly terrified sprite.

The ambivalence that infuses Prospero's dealings with these creatures extends to every aspect of Mr. Stewart's performance, including what are clearly conflicted relationships with his daughter, Miranda, and with Ariel, who is very much a woman here. Mr. Stewart seesaws carefully between rage and heroic restraint, using pauses that are perhaps on occasion too pregnant.

But he brings deeply felt readings to his lines that force you to consider them anew. Even Prospero's early account to Miranda (Carrie Preston) of how they came to the island becomes, in Mr. Stewart's anguished recollection of past griefs, more a definition of a divided soul than the usual leaden piece of exposition.

Mr. Stewart is not alone in finding fresh, vital life in a well-worn character. Ms. Preston's wonderful Miranda, androgynously dressed in her father's hand-me-downs (part of Toni-Leslie James's well-thought-out costume scheme), is a fiery, impetuous hoyden, bursting with a sense of newly discovered womanhood, who has little in common with the usual sleeping-beauty portrayals.

Larry Bryggman's grief-frayed Alonso; John Pankow's posturing butler, in love with his own delusional, drunken grandiloquence, and Liev Schreiber's slimy, regicidal courtier are all first-rate. And if the great clown Bill Irwin, in a classic comic turn as the jester Trinculo, seems to belong to another planet, this at least accords with W. H. Auden's description of the character as a man "whose head is in the clouds and can never get down."

One occasionally misses the sheer poetry of Ariel's speeches. Here, ritualistic rhythm takes precedence over the meanings of words. And not every actor is equally at ease with the language. But all the cast members (who include the dashing, if thick-tongued, Kamar de los Reyes as the smitten Ferdinand) have obviously been encouraged to find a comfortable point of emotional connection with their characters.

As a consequence, Mr. Wolfe's *Tempest* engages us on levels that transcend the work's status as a lovely philosophical pageant. Beneath the play's symmetrical patterns of providence, there is a clearly limned sense that paradise can never be more than a myth.

The fourth act's blissful celebration of the rites of marriage, here presented as a jubilant Brazilian carnival replete with campy, stilt-walking goddesses and a boogieing Prospero, inevitably dissolves before the specter of would-be murderers in skeleton masks. By the play's last act, Prospero is still warring with his demons. And when he lays down his magician's staff, in Mr. Stewart's splendid rendition of the character's farewell to magic, it seems to be only a temporary truce.

Miranda's much quoted exclamation, "O brave new world that has such people in 't!" is of course answered by Prospero's admonition, "'Tis new to thee." Mr. Wolfe's particular triumph is that he has given equally stirring due to the girl's wonder and the man's melancholy.

Late Seventeenth- and Eighteenth-Century Drama

The Restoration: Rebirth of Drama

Theater in England continued to thrive after Shakespeare's death, with a host of successful playwrights, including John Webster (1580?–1638?), Francis Beaumont (c. 1584–1616) and his collaborator John Fletcher (1579–1625), Philip Massinger (1583–1640), Thomas Middleton (1580–1627), John Ford (1586–c. 1655), and James Shirley (1596–1666). All these playwrights were busy working independently or in collaboration. Fletcher, chosen successor to Shakespeare at the Globe, furnished the theater with as many as four plays a year. But in 1642 long-standing religious and political conflicts between King Charles I and Parliament finally erupted into civil war, with the Parliament, under the influence of Puritanism, eventually winning.

The Puritans were religious extremists with narrow, specific values. They were essentially an emerging merchant class of well-to-do citizens who viewed the aristocracy as wastrels. Theater for them was associated with both the aristocracy and the low life. Theatergoing was synonymous with wasting time; the theaters were often a focus for immoral activity and the neighborhoods around the theaters were as unsavory as any in England. Under the Puritan government, all theaters in England were closed for almost twenty years. When the new king, Charles II, was crowned in 1660, those that had not been converted to other uses had become completely outmoded.

As a young prince, Charles, with his mother and brother, had been sent to the Continent in the early stages of the civil war. When his father, Charles I, was beheaded, the future king and his family were in France, where they were in a position to see the remarkable achievements of French comedy and French classical tragedy. Charles II developed a taste for theater that accompanied him back to England. And when he returned in triumph to usher in the exciting and swashbuckling period known as the Restoration, he permitted favorites to build new theaters.

Theater on the Continent: Neoclassicism

Interaction among the leading European countries — England, Spain, and France — was sporadic at best in the seventeenth century because of intermittent wars among the nations, yet the development of theater in all three countries took similar turns throughout the early 1600s.

The Spanish developed, independently, a corral, or open theatrical space, resembling the Elizabethan inn yard, in which they produced plays. This development may have been an accident of architecture — because of the widespread need for inns and for places to store horses — that permitted the symmetry of growth of the English Elizabethan and the Spanish Golden Age theaters.

The most important playwright of the Spanish theater was Lope de Vega (1562–1635), who is said to have written twelve hundred plays (seven hundred fifty survive). Many of them are relatively brief, and some resemble the scenarios for the *commedia dell'arte*. A good number, though, are full-length and impressive works, such as *Fuente Ovejuna* (*The Sheep Well*), *The King, The Greatest Alcalde,* and *The Gardener's Dog.* Calderón (Pedro Calderón de la Barca, 1600–1681) became, on Lope de Vega's death, the reigning Spanish playwright. His *Life Is a Dream* is performed regularly throughout the world. Calderón became a priest in 1651 and wrote religious plays that on rare occasions got him into trouble with the Inquisition, an agency of the church that searched out and punished heresy. He was especially imaginative in his use of stage machinery and especially gifted in producing philosophical and poetic dialogue.

By the 1630s, the French were aware of Spanish achievements in the theater and Pierre Corneille (1606–1684), who emerged as France's leading playwright of the time, adapted a Spanish story by de Castro that became one of his most important plays, *Le Cid.*

By the time Charles II took up residence in France in the 1640s, the French had developed a suave, polished, and intellectually demanding approach to drama. Corneille and the neoclassicists were part of a large movement in European culture and the arts that tried to codify and emulate the achievement of the ancients. Qualities such as harmony, symmetry, balance in everything structural, and clear moral themes were most in evidence. Because NEOCLASSICISM valued thought over feeling, the thematic material in neoclassical drama was very important. That material was sometimes political, reflecting the values of Augustan Rome — 27 B.C. to A.D. 17 — when Caesar Augustus lived and when it was appropriate to think in terms of subordinating the self to the interests of the state. Neoclassical dramatists focused on honor, moral integrity, self-sacrifice, and heroic political subjects.

One school of critics held playwrights strictly to the Aristotelian concepts of the unities of time, place, character, and action. These "rules critics" demanded a perfect observance of the unities, that is, they wanted a play to have one plot, a single action that takes place in one day, and a single setting. In most cases the plays that satisfied them are now often thought of as static, cold, limited, and dull. Their perfection is seen today as rigid and emotionally icy.

Corneille's work did not please such critics, and they turned to a much younger competitor, Jean Racine (1639–1699), who brought the tradition of French tragedy to its fullest. Most of his plays are on classical subjects, beginning in 1667 with *Andromache,* continuing with *Britannicus* (1669), *Iphigenia* (1674), and *Mithridate* (1673), and ending in 1677 with his most famous and possibly best play, *Phaedra.*

Phaedra is a deeply passionate, moral play centering on the love of Phaedra for her stepson, Hippolytus. Venus is responsible for her incestuous love — which is the playwright's way of saying that Phaedra is impelled by the gods or by destiny, almost against her will.

The French stage, unlike the English, never substituted boys for female roles, and so plays such as *Phaedra* were opportunities for brilliant actresses. Phaedra, in particular, dominates the stage — she is a commanding and infinitely complex figure. It is no wonder that this play was a favorite of Sarah Bernhardt (1844–1923), one of France's greatest actresses.

French Comedy: Molière

At the same time that Racine commanded the tragic stage, Jean Baptiste Poquelin (1622–1673), known as Molière, began his dominance of the comic stage. He was aware of Racine's achievements and applauded them strongly. His career started with a small theater company that spent most of its time touring the countryside beyond Paris. When the company settled in Paris, its plays were influenced by some of the stock characters and situations of the *commedia dell'arte,* but they also began to reflect Molière's own genius for composition.

Seeing the company in 1658, King Louis XIV found it so much to his liking that he installed it in a theater and demanded to see more of its work. From that time on, Molière wrote, produced, and acted in one comedy after another, most of which have become part of the permanent repertoire of the French stage. Plays such as *The Misanthrope* (1666), *The Miser* (1669), *The Bourgeois Gentleman* (1670), *The Imaginary Invalid* (1673), and his satire on the theme of religious hypocrisy, *Tartuffe* (1669), are also staged all over the world.

Theater in England: Restoration Comedy of Manners

When the theaters reopened in England in the 1660s, they needed new plays. Times and tastes had changed, England had suffered enormous upheaval, and the Puritan-dominated, theater-darkened past was quickly undone. The new age wanted glitter, excitement, sensuality, and dramatic dazzle. Audiences wanted upbeat comedies that poked fun at the stuffed shirts of society and at old-fashioned institutions and fashions.

Several important physical changes took effect immediately. The new stages were in indoor theaters using artificial light. They could be operated year-round, and the price for seats varied according to location. The middle-priced seats were in the pit before the proscenium-arched stage (Figure 7). The first-level boxes against the walls were most expensive, while the lowest-priced seats were in the upper ranges of the balconies.

Figure 7. Conjectural reconstruction of an early Restoration theater. By Peter Kahn, Cornell University.

The new indoor theaters were generally adapted from spaces designed for courtly events. They were rectangular, often twice as long as they were wide, and usually lighted by candles in chandeliers. The proscenium frame around the stage appeared in the new theaters. Eventually, movable scenery and changeable painted backdrops helped the playwrights create their illusions, although some plays of the period could easily be performed on a bare stage.

Once English women were permitted to take part in theater, actresses appeared who commanded the stage immediately. The actresses of the period were bright, witty, and charming and were often the most important draw for seventeenth-century audiences. Nell Gwynne (1650–1687), one of the most famous actresses of her day and mistress to Charles II, became a legend of the English stage.

Among England's notable playwrights from 1660 through the eighteenth century were Aphra Behn (1640–1689), the first professional woman playwright on the English stage and author of *The Rover*, one of the most frequently performed plays of the period; William Wycherley (1640–1716), whose *The Plain Dealer*, indebted to Molière, and *The Country Wife* are regarded as his best work; William Congreve (1670–1729), whose *The Way of the World* is justly famous; and Richard Brinsley Sheridan (1751–1816), whose *School for Scandal* is still bright, lively, and engaging for modern audiences. Other important playwrights whose work is still performed are George Farquhar (1678–1707), especially known for *The Beaux Stratagem* (1707), John Gay (1685–1732), whose *Beggar's Opera* has been revived constantly since its first performance in 1728, and Oliver Goldsmith (1730–1774), author of *She Stoops to Conquer* (1773).

John Dryden (1631–1700), perhaps the most highly regarded English playwright from 1664 to 1677, collaborated in adaptations of Shakespeare's plays, but he became popular for his heroic dramas in rhymed verse: *The Indian Queen* (1664), its sequel *The Indian Emperor* (1665), *Tyrannick Love* (1669), and the two-part, ten-act *The Conquest of Granada* (1670). Montezuma is at the center of the first two plays; *Tyrannick Love* concerns the martyrdom of St. Catherine by the Roman emperor, Maximin. *The Conquest of Granada* focuses on internal conflicts among the Moors fighting for survival in Spain. Almanzor, the main character, is considered one of Dryden's most accomplished creations. *Aureng-Zebe* (1675), his last effort in heroic rhymed drama, focuses on Aureng-Zebe, emperor of India and among the most rational and moral of his characters. Its plot and love complications are extremely dense and its mood somewhat melancholy. Today the heroic plays of the 1660s resemble high-style melodramas, but they were enormously popular in their time.

Dryden was also successful writing comedies such as *The Wild Gallant* (1663) and *The Rival Ladies* (1664). His tragicomedies were popular in his time and represent some of his most imaginative dramatic efforts. *Marriage à-la-Mode* (1672) is still highly regarded, especially for Dryden's songs. Among his experiments in opera is a version of Milton's *Paradise Lost* which he called *The State of Innocence and the Fall of Man* (1677) in which he rhymed some of Milton's blank verse. This work was never performed, although it remains a curiosity of the age. Dryden is also to be noted for his critical writing on drama, such as his famous *Of Dramatick Poesie* (1668) and *Of Heroick Plays* (1672) which laid down the theory behind his dramas and opened the questions of dramatic practice for examination.

The English playwrights produced a wide range of comedy, drawing on their understanding of the audience's desire for bright, gay, and witty entertainment. The comedies of the period came to be known in the twentieth century as COMEDIES OF MANNERS because they reveal the foibles of the society that watched them. Society enjoyed laughing at itself. Although some of the English drama of the eighteenth century developed a moralistic tone and was often heavily classical, the earlier RESTORATION COMEDIES were less interested in reforming the society than in capitalizing on its faults.

Eighteenth-Century Drama

Eighteenth-century Europe absorbed much of the spirit of France and the French neoclassicists. England, like other European countries, began to see the effects of neoclassicism in the arts and literature. Emulation of classical art and classical values was common throughout Europe, and critics established standards of excellence in the arts to guarantee quality.

The most famous name in eighteenth-century English drama is David Garrick (1717–1779), the legendary actor and manager of the Drury Lane Theatre. The theaters, including his own, often reworked French drama and earlier English and Italian drama, but they began to develop a new SENTIMENTAL COMEDY to balance the neoclassical heroic tragedies of the period. It was a comedy in which the emotions of the audience were played on, manipulated, and exploited to arouse sympathy for the characters in the play.

Sentimental comedy flourished after 1720, but Colley Cibber (1671–1757) is sometimes credited with beginning the sentimental comedy with his *Love's Last Shift* (1696). The play centers on Loveless, who wanders from his marriage only to find that his wife has disguised herself as a prostitute to win him back. As in all sentimental comedies, what the audience most wants is what it gets: a certain amount of tears, a contrasting amount of laughter, and a happy ending. Cibber was especially well known as an actor for his portrayal of fops, his way of poking satiric fun at his own society and its pretensions.

Sir Richard Steele (1672–1729) wrote one of the best-known sentimental comedies, *The Conscious Lovers* (1722). Steele's coauthor of *The Spectator,* Joseph Addison (1672–1719), also distinguished himself with his contribution to the heroic tragedy of the age, the long neoclassical *Cato* (1713). It was considered to be the finest example of the moral heroic style. Today it is not a playable drama because the action is too slow, the speeches too long, and the theme too obscure, although it is a perfect model of what the age preferred in heroic tragedy. George Lillo (1693–1739) in *The London Merchant* (1731) produced a bourgeois tragedy in which the main character was from the middle class. It was one of the most frequently produced plays of its time.

The audiences at the time enjoyed bright, amusing comedies that often criticized wayward youth, overprotective parents, dishonest financial dealings, and social expectations. Their taste in tragedies veered toward a moralizing heroism that extolled the ideals of dedication to the values of the community and self-sacrifice on the part of the hero.

Molière

Molière (1622–1673, born Jean Baptiste Poquelin) came from a family attached to the glittering court of King Louis XIV, the Sun King. His father had purchased an appointment to the king, and as a result the family was familiar with the exciting court life of Paris. That is not to say that they were on intimate terms with the courtiers who surrounded the king. Molière's father was a furnisher and upholsterer to the king; the family, while well-to-do and enjoying some power, was still apart from royalty and the privileged aristocracy.

Molière's education was exceptional. He went to Jesuit schools and spent more than five years at Collège de Clermont, which he left in 1641 having studied both the humanities and philosophy. His knowledge of philosophy was unusually deep, and his background in the classics was exceptionally strong. He also took a law degree in 1641 at Orléans, but never practiced. His father's dream was that his son should inherit his appointment as furnisher to the king, thereby guaranteeing himself a comfortable future.

That, however, was not to be. Instead of following the law, Molière decided at the last minute to abandon his secure future, change his name so as not to scandalize his family, and take up a career in the theater. He began by joining a company of actors run by the Béjart family. They established a theater based in Paris called the Illustre Théâtre. It was run by Madeleine Béjart, with whom Molière had a professional and personal relationship until she died in 1672. Eventually, Molière began writing plays but only after he had worked extensively as an actor.

The famed *commedia dell'arte* actor Tiberio Fiorillo, known as Scaramouche, was a close friend of Molière and perhaps responsible for Molière's choice of a career in theater. Scaramouche may have been part of the Illustre Théâtre, or he may have acted in it on occasion. Unfortunately, the Illustre Théâtre lasted only a year. It was one of several Parisian theatrical groups, and none of them prospered.

The company went bankrupt in 1644, and Molière, forced to leave Paris for about thirteen years, played in the provinces and remote towns. Before leaving Paris he had to be bailed out of debtors' prison. What was left of the Béjart group merged with another company on tour, and Molière became director of that company. During this time he suffered most of the indignities typical of the traveling life, including impoverishment.

In October 1658 Louis XIV saw Molière's troupe acting in one of his comedies at the Louvre. The royal court was so impressed with what it saw that the king gave him the use of a theater. Molière's work remained immensely popular and controversial. He acted in his own plays, produced his own plays, and wrote a succession of major works that are still favorites.

Because other companies envied his success and favor with the king, a number of "scandals" arose around some of his plays. The first play to invite controversy was *The School for Wives* (1662), in which Arnolphe reacts in horror to the infidelities he sees in the wives all around him. He decides that his wife-to-be must be raised far from the world, where she will be ignorant of the wayward lives of the Parisians. A man who intends to seduce her tells Arnolphe (not knowing who he is) how he will get her out of Arnolphe's grasp. The play is highly comic, but groups of theatergoers protested that it was immoral and scandalous. In response Molière wrote *Criticism of the School for Wives* (1663), in which the debate over the play is enacted.

One of Molière's most popular plays, *Tartuffe* (written in 1664), concerns a religious hypocrite who weasels his way into a noble household and then goes about trying to seduce its mistress. Molière envisioned the religious con man as his target in this play, and the name *Tartuffe* became shorthand for a religious hypocrite. The name still implies hypocrisy in France.

A French church group, the Society of the Holy Sacrament, thought it was being portrayed in the title role and protested that the play was immoral and offensive. The society's condemnation of the play effectively prevented it from being performed. Molière tried rewriting *Tartuffe,* but the society would not approve its production.

In 1669 the Society of the Holy Sacrament was dissolved in a restructuring of the French church, and *Tartuffe* was finally permitted to be played to large audiences. Theatergoers loved the play and found great amusement in the sly, lecherous rogue who completely beguiles Orgon, the man who thinks Tartuffe is a great saint and who introduces him into his household. In most modern productions Tartuffe is played broadly, almost as a caricature or a clown. Audiences find him amusing, scabrous, and irresistible. They usually find the play irresistible as well, because it involves crafty maneuvering onstage and complicated deceptions.

Among Molière's other successes are *The Miser* (1668), *The Bourgeois Gentleman* (1670), and his final play, *The Imaginary Invalid* (1673). Molière had a bad cough for most of the last decade of his life, which onstage he often made to seem the cough of the character he was playing. But Molière was genuinely ill; he died on stage, playing the title role of *The Imaginary Invalid.*

THE MISANTHROPE

The Misanthrope (1666) in its own age was not the most successful of Molière's plays, but it has certainly been one of the most produced of all the plays in his canon. Typical of his work, it derives from a close and careful observation of French life and manners. Recently, English-language audiences have been able to savor this play in Richard Wilbur's superb translation, which catches the sharpness of the French wit and the elegance of the verse — both hallmarks of French seventeenth-century drama.

In one sense the play is based on the type of improbability that marks Greek New Comedy. It portrays the romance of two very different people, Alceste, the misanthrope who speaks his mind and brashly tells people what he thinks of them, and Célimène, the coquette who rarely says what she thinks but who enjoys the attention of many suitors. She enjoys society and her capacity to dominate it. Alceste cannot abide society and its superficialities. At the end of the play he resolves to leave it.

A revelation in the play is that while Alceste and Célimène are different on the surface, beneath the surface they are similar. They are both extreme types who behave extremely. Célimène carries coquetry to great lengths, leading on as many men as possible. Alceste is the epitome of a misanthrope, refusing to flatter people just to make them feel good. He says that he must tell the truth, and he does — even when it hurts, perhaps especially when it hurts. For him to fall in love with a coquette who must deceive those around her to keep herself at the center of attention is a wonderful comic irony. But beneath that irony lies the thought that Alceste himself may have flaws that are the opposite of Célimène's.

The ending of *The Misanthrope,* which avoids the marriage of the protagonists (a more typical ending of comedies), may have contributed to the disappointment of its initial audiences. Another comic playwright would have brought the two lovers together. But Molière chose a more complex and, for some, a less satisfying ending. While two secondary characters marry, the main characters — Alceste and Célimène — agree to disagree and decide to live separately after all. Molière leaves his audience simply hoping that the two will change their minds. But as the play ends, the audience has no real reason to expect that they will.

This is a very French drama. The society is elegant, formal, and mannered. Molière knows every character and reveals each one totally. The surface elegance of the verse is such that the manners of the society seem polished, artificial, and ritualistic without being especially deceptive. The deception in this play is not at the center of things nor does the play depend on mix-ups and misapprehensions for its success. This in itself gives us a rather intriguing hint about Molière's intentions. The theme of honesty is at the play's center, but it is no simple thing to decide, in a social situation such as these characters enjoy, exactly how honest honesty should be or when honesty is the best policy. Alceste has one view and Célimène has another.

Molière enjoys pitting the values of Célimène and Alceste against one another, but it is clear that he does not want to offer sweeping or simple solutions to their conflict. Instead, he is content to leave his audience thinking and wondering.

The Misanthrope in Performance

The first full production of *The Misanthrope* was on June 4, 1666, with Molière as Alceste and his wife as Célimène. Most of the players who joined them were aware that Alceste was modeled after Molière himself and that Molière was poking fun at himself and his marriage. Molière made the part more comical than serious. The French national theater, Comédie-Française, records some fifteen hundred performances of the play between 1680 and 1960, making it one of the most performed of all French comedies. Late in the eighteenth century, actors began playing Alceste as a serious character, as he is played today.

The first important American production in English was by Richard Mansfield, who acted the part of Alceste in New York in 1905. The reviews noted that "his embodiment of Alceste is vibrant with pain. . . . He smiles, but it is always the smile of bitterness." Richard Wilbur's verse translation played in the tiny Theatre East in New York in 1956 while the original rhymed French version with a French company played simultaneously at the Winter Garden on Broadway. Both productions were very successful. Wilbur's version has since played virtually all over America, with several productions in New York in the 1960s, 70s, and 80s. The West Side Repertory Theater performed it in modern black tie and tails in 1991, with James Jacobus as Alceste. *The Misanthrope* has also had innumerable college productions since Wilbur's translation, which has, at least in the United States, become the standard version.

Tony Harrison also translated the play for the British National Theatre in 1975 with Alec McCowan as Alceste and Diana Rigg as Célimène. Reviews were mixed, but the play was said to have "the brilliance of a tiara of diamonds."

Molière [*Jean Baptiste Poquelin*] *(1622–1673)*

THE MISANTHROPE   *1666*

TRANSLATED BY RICHARD WILBUR

Characters

ALCESTE, *in love with Célimène*
PHILINTE, *Alceste's friend*
ORONTE, *in love with Célimène*
CÉLIMÈNE, *Alceste's beloved*
ÉLIANTE, *Célimène's cousin*
ARSINOÉ, *a friend of Célimène's*
ACASTE ⎫
CLITANDRE ⎬ *Marquesses*
BASQUE, *Célimène's servant*
A GUARD *of the Marshalsea*
DUBOIS, *Alceste's valet*

The scene throughout is in Célimène's house at Paris.

ACT I • Scene 1   [*Philinte, Alceste.*]

PHILINTE: Now, what's got into you?
ALCESTE (*seated*):   Kindly leave me alone.
PHILINTE: Come, come, what is it? This lugubrious
    tone . . .
ALCESTE: Leave me, I said; you spoil my solitude.
PHILINTE: Oh, listen to me, now, and don't be rude.
ALCESTE: I choose to be rude, Sir, and to be hard of
5   hearing.
PHILINTE: These ugly moods of yours are not
    endearing;
    Friends though we are, I really must insist . . .
ALCESTE (*abruptly rising*): Friends? Friends, you say?
    Well, cross me off your list.
    I've been your friend till now, as you well know;
10   But after what I saw a moment ago
    I tell you flatly that our ways must part.
    I wish no place in a dishonest heart.
PHILINTE: Why, what have I done, Alceste? Is this
    quite just?
ALCESTE: My God, you ought to die of self-disgust.
15   I call your conduct inexcusable, Sir,
    And every man of honor will concur.
    I see you almost hug a man to death,
    Exclaim for joy until you're out of breath,
    And supplement these loving demonstrations
20   With endless offers, vows, and protestations;

Then when I ask you "Who was that?" I find
That you can barely bring his name to mind!
Once the man's back is turned, you cease to love
    him,
And speak with absolute indifference of him!
By God, I say it's base and scandalous   25
To falsify the heart's affections thus;
If I caught myself behaving in such a way,
I'd hang myself for shame, without delay.
PHILINTE: It hardly seems a hanging matter to me;
    I hope that you will take it graciously   30
    If I extend myself a slight reprieve,
    And live a little longer, by your leave.
ALCESTE: How dare you joke about a crime so grave?
PHILINTE: What crime? How else are people to
    behave?
ALCESTE: I'd have them be sincere, and never part   35
    With any word that isn't from the heart.
PHILINTE: When someone greets us with a show of
    pleasure,
    It's but polite to give him equal measure,
    Return his love the best that we know how,
    And trade him offer for offer, vow for vow.   40
ALCESTE: No, no, this formula you'd have me
    follow,
    However fashionable, is false and hollow,
    And I despise the frenzied operations
    Of all these barterers of protestations,
    These lavishers of meaningless embraces   45
    These utterers of obliging commonplaces,
    Who court and flatter everyone on earth
    And praise the fool no less than the man of
    worth.
    Should you rejoice that someone fondles you,
    Offers his love and service, swears to be true,   50
    And fills your ears with praises of your name,
    When to the first damned fop he'll say the same?
    No, no: no self-respecting heart would dream
    Of prizing so promiscuous an esteem;
    However high the praise, there's nothing worse   55
    Than sharing honors with the universe.
    Esteem is founded on comparison:
    To honor all men is to honor none.
    Since you embrace this indiscriminate vice
    Your friendship comes at far too cheap a price;   60

I spurn the easy tribute of a heart
Which will not set the worthy man apart:
I choose, Sir, to be chosen; and in fine,
The friend of mankind is no friend of mine.
65 PHILINTE: But in polite society, custom decrees
That we show certain outward courtesies . . . .
ALCESTE: Ah, no! we should condemn with all our
force
Such false and artificial intercourse.
Let men behave like men; let them display
70 Their inmost hearts in everything they say;
Let the heart speak, and let our sentiments
Not mask themselves in silly compliments.
PHILINTE: In certain cases it would be uncouth
And most absurd to speak the naked truth;
75 With all respect for your exalted notions,
It's often best to veil one's true emotions.
Wouldn't the social fabric come undone
If we were wholly frank with everyone?
Suppose you met with someone you couldn't
bear;
80 Would you inform him of it then and there?
ALCESTE: Yes.
PHILINTE: Then you'd tell old Emilie it's pathetic
The way she daubs her features with cosmetic
And plays the gay coquette at sixty-four?
ALCESTE: I would.
PHILINTE: And you'd call Dorilas a bore,
85 And tell him every ear at court is lame
From hearing him brag about his noble name?
ALCESTE: Precisely.
PHILINTE: Ah, you're joking.
ALCESTE: *Au contraire.°*
In this regard there's none I'd choose to spare.
All are corrupt; there's nothing to be seen
90 In court or town but aggravates my spleen.°
I fall into deep gloom and melancholy
When I survey the scene of human folly,
Finding on every hand base flattery,
Injustice, fraud, self-interest, treachery. . . .
95 Ah, it's too much; mankind has grown so base,
I mean to break with the whole human race.
PHILINTE: This philosophic rage is a bit extreme;
You've no idea how comical you seem;
Indeed, we're like those brothers in the play
Called *School for Husbands,°* one of whom was
100   prey . . .

87. *Au contraire*: On the contrary.   90. spleen: A body organ thought to be the seat of melancholy, one of the four humors of medieval physiology.   100. *School for Husbands*: A
play by Molière (1661) in which two brothers, Sganarelle and
Ariste, are guardians of two orphan girls. Sganarelle hopes to
marry one of the girls, Isabelle, but she frees herself by trickery from his domineering ways and marries someone else.

ALCESTE: Enough, now! None of your stupid
similes.
PHILINTE: Then let's have no more tirades, if you
please.
The world won't change, whatever you say
or do;
And since plain speaking means so much to you,
I'll tell you plainly that by being frank   105
You've earned the reputation of a crank,
And that you're thought ridiculous when you
rage
And rant against the manners of the age.
ALCESTE: So much the better; just what I wish to
hear.
No news could be more grateful to my ear.   110
All men are so detestable in my eyes,
I should be sorry if they thought me wise.
PHILINTE: Your hatred's very sweeping, is it not?
ALCESTE: Quite right: I hate the whole degraded
lot.
PHILINTE: Must all poor human creatures be
embraced,   115
Without distinction, by your vast distaste?
Even in these bad times, there are surely a
few . . .
ALCESTE: No, I include all men in one dim view:
Some men I hate for being rogues: the others
I hate because they treat the rogues like
brothers,   120
And, lacking a virtuous scorn for what is vile,
Receive the villain with a complaisant smile.
Notice how tolerant people choose to be
Toward that bold rascal who's at law with me.
His social polish can't conceal his nature;   125
One sees at once that he's a treacherous creature;
No one could possibly be taken in
By those soft speeches and that sugary grin.
The whole world knows the shady means by
which
The low-brow's grown so powerful and rich,   130
And risen to a rank so bright and high
That virtue can but blush, and merit sigh.
Whenever his name comes up in conversation,
None will defend his wretched reputation;
Call him knave, liar, scoundrel, and all the rest,   135
Each head will nod, and no one will protest.
And yet his smirk is seen in every house,
He's greeted everywhere with smiles and bows,
And when there's any honor that can be got
By pulling strings, he'll get it, like as not.   140
My God! It chills my heart to see the ways
Men come to terms with evil nowadays
Sometimes, I swear, I'm moved to flee and find
Some desert land unfouled by humankind.
PHILINTE: Come, let's forget the follies of the times   145

And pardon mankind for its petty crimes;
Let's have an end of rantings and of railings,
And show some leniency toward human failings.
This world requires a pliant rectitude;
150   Too stern a virtue makes one stiff and rude;
Good sense views all extremes with detestation,
And bids us to be noble in moderation.
The rigid virtues of the ancient days
Are not for us; they jar with all our ways
155   And ask of us too lofty a perfection.
Wise men accept their times without objection,
And there's no greater folly, if you ask me,
Than trying to reform society.
Like you, I see each day a hundred and one
160   Unhandsome deeds that might be better done,
But still, for all the faults that meet my view,
I'm never known to storm and rave like you.
I take men as they are, or let them be,
And teach my soul to bear their frailty;
And whether in court or town, whatever the
165   scene,
My phlegm's° as philosophic as your spleen.
ALCESTE: This phlegm which you so eloquently
            commend,
Does nothing ever rile it up, my friend?
Suppose some man you trust should
            treacherously
170   Conspire to rob you of your property,
And do his best to wreck your reputation?
Wouldn't you feel a certain indignation?
PHILINTE: Why, no. These faults of which you so
            complain
Are part of human nature, I maintain,
175   And it's no more a matter for disgust
That men are knavish, selfish and unjust,
Than that the vulture dines upon the dead,
And wolves are furious, and apes ill-bred.
ALCESTE: Shall I see myself betrayed, robbed, torn
            to bits,
180   And not . . . Oh, let's be still and rest our wits.
Enough of reasoning, now. I've had my fill.
PHILINTE: Indeed, you would do well, Sir, to be still.
Rage less at your opponent, and give some
            thought
To how you'll win this lawsuit that he's brought.
185   ALCESTE: I assure you I'll do nothing of the sort.
PHILINTE: Then who will plead your case before the
            court?
ALCESTE: Reason and right and justice will plead
            for me.

166. **phlegm:** In medieval physiology, the humor thought to
be cold and moist and to cause sluggishness.

PHILINTE: Oh, Lord. What judges do you plan to
            see?
ALCESTE: Why, none. The justice of my cause is
            clear.
PHILINTE: Of course, man; but there's politics to
            fear. . . .   190
ALCESTE: No, I refuse to lift a hand. That's flat.
I'm either right, or wrong.
PHILINTE: Don't count on that.
ALCESTE: No, I'll do nothing.
PHILINTE: Your enemy's influence
Is great, you know . . .
ALCESTE: That makes no difference.
PHILINTE: It will; you'll see.
ALCESTE: Must honor bow to guile?   195
If so, I shall be proud to lose the trial.
PHILINTE: Oh, really . . .
ALCESTE: I'll discover by this case
Whether or not men are sufficiently base
And impudent and villainous and perverse
To do me wrong before the universe.   200
PHILINTE: What a man!
ALCESTE: Oh, I could wish, whatever the cost,
Just for the beauty of it, that my trial were lost.
PHILINTE: If people heard you talking so, Alceste,
They'd split their sides. Your name would be a
            jest.
ALCESTE: So much the worse for jesters.
PHILINTE: May I enquire   205
Whether this rectitude you so admire,
And these hard virtues you're enamored of
Are qualities of the lady whom you love?
It much surprises me that you, who seem
To view mankind with furious disesteem,   210
Have yet found something to enchant your eyes
Amidst a species which you so despise.
And what is more amazing, I'm afraid,
Is the most curious choice your heart has made.
The honest Éliante is fond of you,   215
Arsinoé, the prude, admires you too;
And yet your spirit's been perversely led
To choose the flighty Célimène instead,
Whose brittle malice and coquettish ways
So typify the manners of our days.   220
How is it that the traits you most abhor
Are bearable in this lady you adore?
Are you so blind with love that you can't find
            them?
Or do you contrive, in her case, not to mind
            them?
ALCESTE: My love for that young widow's not the
            kind   225
That can't perceive defects; no, I'm not blind.
I see her faults, despite my ardent love,
And all I see I fervently reprove.

And yet I'm weak; for all her falsity,
230 That woman knows the art of pleasing me,
And though I never cease complaining of her,
I swear I cannot manage not to love her.
Her charm outweighs her faults; I can but aim
To cleanse her spirit in my love's pure flame.
PHILINTE: That's no small task; I wish you all
235   success.
You think then that she loves you?
ALCESTE: Heavens, yes!
I wouldn't love her did she not love me.
PHILINTE: Well, if her taste for you is plain to see,
Why do these rivals cause you such despair?
ALCESTE: True love, Sir, is possessive, and cannot
240   bear
To share with all the world. I'm here today
To tell her she must send that mob away.
PHILINTE: If I were you, and had your choice to
      make,
Éliante, her cousin, would be the one I'd take;
245 That honest heart, which cares for you alone,
Would harmonize far better with your own.
ALCESTE: True, true: each day my reason tells me
      so;
But reason doesn't rule in love, you know.
PHILINTE: I fear some bitter sorrow is in store;
250 This love . . .

Scene II [*Oronte, Alceste, Philinte.*]

ORONTE (*to Alceste*): The servants told me at the
      door
That Éliante and Célimène were out,
But when I heard, dear Sir, that you were about,
I came to say, without exaggeration,
5 That I hold you in the vastest admiration,
And that it's always been my dearest desire
To be the friend of one I so admire.
I hope to see my love of merit recuited,
And you and I in friendship's bond united.
I'm sure you won't refuse — if I may be
10   frank —
A friend of my devotedness—and rank.

(*During this speech of Oronte's Alceste is abstracted
and seems unaware that he is being spoken to. He
only breaks off his reverie when Oronte says:*)

It was for you, if you please, that my words were
      intended.
ALCESTE: For me, Sir?
ORONTE: Yes, for you. You're not offended?
ALCESTE: By no means. But this much surprises
      me. . . .

The honor comes most unexpectedly. . . .   15
ORONTE: My high regard should not astonish you;
The whole world feels the same. It is your due.
ALCESTE: Sir . . .
ORONTE: Why, in all the State there isn't one
Can match your merits; they shine, Sir, like the
      sun.
ALCESTE: Sir . . .
ORONTE: You are higher in my estimation   20
Than all that's most illustrious in the nation.
ALCESTE: Sir . . .
ORONTE: If I lie, may heaven strike me dead!
To show you that I mean what I have said,
Permit me, Sir, to embrace you most sincerely,
And swear that I will prize our friendship dearly.   25
Give me your hand. And now, Sir, if you
      choose,
We'll make our vows.
ALCESTE: Sir . . .
ORONTE: What! You refuse?
ALCESTE: Sir, it's a very great honor you extend:
But friendship is a sacred thing, my friend;
It would be profanation to bestow   30
The name of friend on one you hardly know.
All parts are better played when well-rehearsed
Let's put off friendship, and get acquainted first.
We may discover it would be unwise
To try to make our natures harmonize.   35
ORONTE: By heaven! You're sagacious to the core;
This speech has made me admire you even more.
Let time, then, bring us closer day by day;
Meanwhile, I shall be yours in every way.
If, for example, there should be anything   40
You wish at court, I'll mention it to the King.
I have his ear, of course; it's quite well known
That I am much in favor with the throne.
In short, I am your servant. And now, dear
      friend,
Since you have such fine judgment, I intend   45
To please you, if I can, with a small sonnet
I wrote not long ago. Please comment on it,
And tell me whether I ought to publish it.
ALCESTE: You must excuse me, Sir; I'm hardly fit
To judge such matters.
ORONTE: Why not?
ALCESTE: I am. I fear,   50
Inclined to be unfashionably sincere.
ORONTE: Just what I ask; I'd take no satisfaction
In anything but your sincere reaction.
I beg you not to dream of being kind.
ALCESTE: Since you desire it, Sir, I'll speak my
      mind.   55
ORONTE: *Sonnet*. It's a sonnet. . . . *Hope* . . . The
      poem's addressed
To a lady who wakened hopes within my breast.

Hope . . . this is not the pompous sort of thing,
Just modest little verses, with a tender ring.
ALCESTE: Well, we shall see.

60 ORONTE: _Hope_ . . . I'm anxious to hear
Whether the style seems properly smooth and
    clear,
And whether the choice of words is good or bad.
ALCESTE: We'll see, we'll see.
ORONTE: Perhaps I ought to add
That it took me only a quarter-hour to write it.

65 ALCESTE: The time's irrelevant, Sir: kindly recite it.
ORONTE (_reading_): Hope comforts us awhile, 'tis
    true,
Lulling our cares with careless laughter,
And yet such joy is full of rue,
My Phyllis, if nothing follows after.
PHILINTE: I'm charmed by this already; the style's

70   delightful.
ALCESTE (_sotto voce,° to Philinte_): How can you say
    that? Why, the thing is frightful.
ORONTE: Your fair face smiled on me awhile,
But was it kindness so to enchant me?
'Twould have been fairer not to smile,

75   If hope was all you meant to grant me.
PHILINTE: What a clever thought! How handsomely
    you phrase it!
ALCESTE (_sotto voce, to Philinte_): You know the
    thing is trash. How dare you praise it?
ORONTE: If it's to be my passion's fate
Thus everlastingly to wait,

80 Then death will come to set me free:

For death is fairer than the fair;
Phyllis, to hope is to despair
When one must hope eternally.
PHILINTE: The close is exquisite—full of feeling and
    grace.
ALCESTE (_sotto voce, aside_): Oh, blast the close;

85   you'd better close your face
Before you send your lying soul to hell.
PHILINTE: I can't remember a poem I've liked so
    well.
ALCESTE (_sotto voce, aside_): Good Lord!
ORONTE (_to Philinte_):   I fear you're flattering
    me a bit.
PHILINTE: Oh, no!
ALCESTE (_sotto voce, aside_):   What else d'you
    call it, you hypocrite?
ORONTE (_to Alceste_): But you, Sir, keep your

90   promise now: don't shrink
From telling me sincerely what you think.

71. [S.D.] **_sotto voce_**: In a soft voice or stage whisper.

ALCESTE: Sir, these are delicate matters; we all
    desire
To be told that we've the true poetic fire.
But once, to one whose name I shall not mention
I said, regarding some verse of his invention,   95
That gentlemen should rigorously control
That itch to write which often afflicts the soul;
That one should curb the heady inclination
To publicize one's little avocation
And that in showing off one's works of art   100
One often plays a very clownish part.
ORONTE: Are you suggesting in a devious way
That I ought not . . .
ALCESTE: Oh, that I do not say.
Further, I told him that no fault is worse
Than that of writing frigid, lifeless verse,   105
And that the merest whisper of such a shame
Suffices to destroy a man's good name.
ORONTE: D'you mean to say my sonnet's dull and
    trite?
ALCESTE: I don't say that. But I went on to cite
Numerous cases of once-respected men   110
Who came to grief by taking up the pen.
ORONTE: And am I like them? Do I write so
    poorly?
ALCESTE: I don't say that. But I told this person,
    "Surely
You're under no necessity to compose;
Why you should wish to publish, heaven knows.   115
There's no excuse for printing tedious rot
Unless one writes for bread, as you do not.
Resist temptation, then, I beg of you;
Conceal your pastimes from the public view;
And don't give up, on any provocation,   120
Your present high and courtly reputation,
To purchase at a greedy printer's shop
The name of silly author and scribbling fop."
These were the points I tried to make him see.
ORONTE: I sense that they are also aimed at me,   125
But now — about my sonnet — I'd like to be
    told . . .
ALCESTE: Frankly, that sonnet should be
    pigeonholed.
You've chosen the worst models to imitate.
The style's unnatural. Let me illustrate:
For example, Your fair face smiled on me awhile,   130
Followed by, 'Twould have been fairer not to
    smile!
Or this: such joy is full of rue;
Or this: For death is fairer than the fair;
Or, Phyllis, to hope is to despair
When one must hope eternally!   135
This artificial style, that's all the fashion,
Has neither taste, nor honesty, nor passion;
It's nothing but a sort of wordy play,

And nature never spoke in such a way.
140 What, in this shallow age, is not debased?
Our fathers, though less refined, had better taste;
I'd barter all that men admire today
For one old love song I shall try to say:
If the King had given me for my own
145 Paris, his citadel,
And I for that must leave alone
Her whom I love so well,
I'd say then to the Crown,
Take back your glittering town;
150 My darling is more fair, I swear,
My darling is more fair.
The rhyme's not rich, the style is rough and old,
But don't you see that it's the purest gold
Beside the tinsel nonsense now preferred,
155 And that there's passion in its every word?
If the King had given me for my own
Paris, his citadel,
And I for that must leave alone
Her whom I love so well,
160 I'd say then to the Crown,
Take back your glittering town;
My darling is more fair, I swear,
My darling is more fair.
There speaks a loving heart. (*To Philinte.*) You're
laughing, eh?
165 Laugh on, my precious wit. Whatever you say,
I hold that song's worth all the bibelots°
That people hail today with ah's and oh's.
ORONTE: And I maintain my sonnet's very good.
ALCESTE: It's not at all surprising that you should.
170 You have your reasons; permit me to have mine
For thinking that you cannot write a line.
ORONTE: Others have praised my sonnet to the
skies.
ALCESTE: I lack their art of telling pleasant lies.
ORONTE: You seem to think you've got no end of
wit.
175 ALCESTE: To praise your verse, I'd need still more of
it.
ORONTE: I'm not in need of your approval, Sir.
ALCESTE: That's good; you couldn't have it if you
were.
ORONTE: Come now, I'll lend you the subject of my
sonnet;
I'd like to see you try to improve upon it.
ALCESTE: I might, by chance, write something just as
180 shoddy;
But then I wouldn't show it to everybody.
ORONTE: You're most opinionated and conceited.

166. bibelots: Trinkets.

ALCESTE: Go find your flatterers, and be better
treated.
ORONTE: Look here, my little fellow, pray watch
your tone.
ALCESTE: My great big fellow, you'd better watch
your own.   185
PHILINTE (*stepping between them*): Oh, please,
please, gentlemen! This will never do.
ORONTE: The fault is mine, and I leave the field to
you.
I am your servant, Sir, in every way.
ALCESTE: And I, Sir, am your most abject valet.

Scene III   [*Philinte, Alceste.*]

PHILINTE: Well, as you see, sincerity in excess
Can get you into a very pretty mess;
Oronte was hungry for appreciation . . .
ALCESTE: Don't speak to me.
PHILINTE: What?
ALCESTE: No more conversation.
PHILINTE: Really, now . . .
ALCESTE: Leave me alone.
PHILINTE: If I . . .
ALCESTE: Out of my sight!   5
PHILINTE: But what . . .
ALCESTE: I won't listen.
PHILINTE: But . . .
ALCESTE: Silence!
PHILINTE: Now, it is polite . . .
ALCESTE: By heaven, I've had enough. Don't follow
me.
PHILINTE: Ah, you're just joking. I'll keep you
company.

ACT II • Scene I   [*Alceste, Célimène.*]

ALCESTE: Shall I speak plainly, Madam? I confess
Your conduct gives me infinite distress,
And my resentment's grown too hot to smother.
Soon, I foresee, we'll break with one another.
If I said otherwise, I should deceive you;   5
Sooner or later, I shall be forced to leave you,
And if I swore that we shall never part
I should misread the omens of my heart.
CÉLIMÈNE: You kindly saw me home, it would
appear,
So as to pour invectives in my ear.   10
ALCESTE: I've no desire to quarrel. But I deplore
Your inability to shut the door
On all these suitors who beset you so.
There's what annoys me, if you care to know.

CÉLIMÈNE: Is it my fault that all these men pursue
15   me?
    Am I to blame if they're attracted to me?
    And when they gently beg an audience,
    Ought I to take a stick and drive them hence?
ALCESTE: Madam, there's no necessity for a stick;
20   A less responsive heart would do the trick.
    Of your attractiveness I don't complain;
    But those your charms attract, you then detain
    By a most melting and receptive manner,
    And so enlist their hearts beneath your banner.
25   It's the agreeable hopes which you excite
    That keep these lovers round you day and night;
    Were they less liberally smiled upon,
    That sighing troop would very soon be gone.
    But tell me, Madam, why it is that lately
30   This man Clitandre interests you so greatly?
    Because of what high merits do you deem
    Him worthy of the honor of your esteem?
    Is it that your admiring glances linger
    On the splendidly long nail of his little finger?
35   Or do you share the general deep respect
    For the blond wig he chooses to affect?
    Are you in love with his embroidered hose?
    Do you adore his ribbons and his bows?
    Or is it that this paragon bewitches
40   Your tasteful eye with his vast German breeches?
    Perhaps his giggle, or his falsetto voice,
    Makes him the latest gallant of your choice?
CÉLIMÈNE: You're much mistaken to resent him so.
    Why I put up with him you surely know:
45   My lawsuit's very shortly to be tried,
    And I must have his influence on my side.
ALCESTE: Then lose your lawsuit, Madam, or let it
      drop;
    Don't torture me by humoring such a fop.
CÉLIMÈNE: You're jealous of the whole world, Sir.
ALCESTE: That's true,
50   Since the whole world is well-received by you.
CÉLIMÈNE: That my good nature is so unconfined
    Should serve to pacify your jealous mind;
    Were I to smile on one, and scorn the rest,
    Then you might have some cause to be
      distressed.
55 ALCESTE: Well, if I mustn't be jealous, tell me, then,
    Just how I'm better treated than other men.
CÉLIMÈNE: You know you have my love. Will that
      not do?
ALCESTE: What proof have I that what you say is
      true?
CÉLIMÈNE: I would expect, Sir, that my having said
      it
60   Might give the statement a sufficient credit.
ALCESTE: But how can I be sure that you don't tell
    The selfsame thing to other men as well?

CÉLIMÈNE: What a gallant speech! How flattering to
      me!
    What a sweet creature you make me out to be!
    Well then, to save you from the pangs of doubt,   65
    All that I've said I hereby cancel out;
    Now, none but yourself shall make a monkey of
      you:
    Are you content?
ALCESTE: Why, why am I doomed to love you?
    I swear that I shall bless the blissful hour
    When this poor heart's no longer in your power!   70
    I make no secret of it: I've done my best
    To exorcise this passion from my breast
    But thus far all in vain; it will not go;
    It's for my sins that I must love you so.
CÉLIMÈNE: Your love for me is matchless, Sir; that's
      clear.   75
ALCESTE: Indeed, in all the world it has no peer;
    Words can't describe the nature of my passion,
    And no man ever loved in such a fashion.
CÉLIMÈNE: Yes, it's a brand-new fashion, I agree:
    You show your love by castigating me,   80
    And all your speeches are enraged and rude.
    I've never been so furiously wooed.
ALCESTE: Yet you could calm that fury, if you
      chose.
    Come, shall we bring our quarrels to a close?
    Let's speak with open hearts, then, and
    begin . . .   85

Scene II   [*Célimène, Alceste, Basque.*]

CÉLIMÈNE: What is it?
BASQUE: Acaste is here.
CÉLIMÈNE: Well, send him in.

Scene III   [*Célimène, Alceste.*]

ALCESTE: What! Shall we never be alone at all?
    You're always ready to receive a call,
    And you can't bear, for ten ticks of the clock,
    Not to keep open house for all who knock.
CÉLIMÈNE: I couldn't refuse him: he'd be most put
      out.   5
ALCESTE: Surely that's not worth worrying about.
CÉLIMÈNE: Acaste would never forgive me if he
      guessed
    That I consider him a dreadful pest.
ALCESTE: If he's a pest, why bother with him then?
CÉLIMÈNE: Heavens! One can't antagonize such
      men;   10
    Why, they're the chartered gossips of the court,
    And have a say in things of every sort.

One must receive them, and be full of charm;
They're no great help, but they can do you harm,
15 And though your influence be ever so great,
They're hardly the best people to alienate.
ALCESTE: I see, dear lady, that you could make a case
For putting up with the whole human race;
These friendships that you calculate so nicely . . .

Scene IV   [*Alceste, Célimène, Basque.*]

BASQUE: Madam, Clitandre is here as well.
ALCESTE: Precisely.
CÉLIMÈNE: Where are you going?
ALCESTE: Elsewhere.
CÉLIMÈNE: Stay.
ALCESTE: No, no.
CÉLIMÈNE: Stay, Sir.
ALCESTE: I can't.
CÉLIMÈNE: I wish it.
ALCESTE: No, I must go.
I beg you, Madam, not to press the matter;
5   You know I have no taste for idle chatter.
CÉLIMÈNE: Stay. I command you.
ALCESTE: No, I cannot stay.
CÉLIMÈNE: Very well; you have my leave to go
away.

Scene V   [*Éliante, Philinte, Acaste, Clitandre, Alceste, Célimène, Basque.*]

ÉLIANTE (*to Célimène*): The Marquesses have kindly
come to call.
Were they announced?
CÉLIMÈNE: Yes. Basque, bring chairs for all.

(*Basque provides the chairs and exits.*)

(*To Alceste.*) You haven't gone?
ALCESTE: No; and I shan't depart
Till you decide who's foremost in your heart.
CÉLIMÈNE: Oh, hush.
5   ALCESTE: It's time to choose; take them, or me.
CÉLIMÈNE: You're mad.
ALCESTE: I'm not, as you shall shortly see.
CÉLIMÈNE: Oh?
ALCESTE: You'll decide.
CÉLIMÈNE: You're joking now, dear friend.
ALCESTE: No, no; you'll choose; my patience is at an
end.
CLITANDRE: Madam, I come from court, where poor
Cléonte
10 Behaved like a perfect fool, as is his wont.

Has he no friend to counsel him, I wonder,
And teach him less unerringly to blunder?
CÉLIMÈNE: It's true, the man's a most accomplished
dunce;
His gauche behavior charms the eye at once;
And every time one sees him, on my word,   15
His manner's grown a trifle more absurd.
ACASTE: Speaking of dunces, I've just now
conversed
With old Damon, who's one of the very worst;
I stood a lifetime in the broiling sun
Before his dreary monologue was done.   20
CÉLIMÈNE: Oh, he's a wondrous talker, and has the
power
To tell you nothing hour after hour:
If, by mistake, he ever came to the point,
The shock would put his jawbone out of joint.
ÉLIANTE (*to Philinte*): The conversation takes its
usual turn,   25
And all our dear friends' ears will shortly burn.
CLITANDRE: Timante's a character, Madam.
CÉLIMÈNE: Isn't he, though?
A man of mystery from top to toe,
Who moves about in a romantic mist
On secret missions which do not exist.   30
His talk is full of eyebrows and grimaces;
How tired one gets of his momentous faces;
He's always whispering something confidential
Which turns out to be quite inconsequential;
Nothing's too slight for him to mystify;   35
He even whispers when he says "good-by."
ACASTE: Tell us about Géralde.
CÉLIMÈNE: That tiresome ass.
He mixes only with the titled class,
And fawns on dukes and princes, and is bored
With anyone who's not at least a lord.   40
The man's obsessed with rank, and his
discourses
Are all of hounds and carriages and horses;
He uses Christian names with all the great,
And the word Milord, with him, is out of date.
CLITANDRE: He's very taken with Bélise, I hear.   45
CÉLIMÈNE: She is the dreariest company, poor dear.
Whenever she comes to call, I grope about
To find some topic which will draw her out,
But, owing to her dry and faint replies,
The conversation wilts, and droops, and dies.   50
In vain one hopes to animate her face
By mentioning the ultimate commonplace;
But sun or shower, even hail or frost
Are matters she can instantly exhaust.
Meanwhile her visit, painful though it is,   55
Drags on and on through mute eternities,
And though you ask the time, and yawn, and
yawn,

She sits there like a stone and won't be gone.
ACASTE: Now for Adraste.
CÉLIMÈNE: Oh, that conceited elf
60   Has a gigantic passion for himself;
He rails against the court, and cannot bear it
That none will recognize his hidden merit;
All honors given to others give offense
To his imaginary excellence.
CLITANDRE: What about young Cléon? His house,
65   they say,
Is full of the best society, night and day.
CÉLIMÈNE: His cook has made him popular, not he:
It's Cléon's table that people come to see.
ÉLIANTE: He gives a splendid dinner, you must
admit.
70   CÉLIMÈNE: But must he serve himself along with it?
For my taste, he's a most insipid dish
Whose presence sours the wine and spoils the
fish.
PHILINTE: Damis, his uncle is admired no end.
What's your opinion, Madam?
CÉLIMÈNE: Why, he's my friend.
PHILINTE: He seems a decent fellow, and rather
75   clever.
CÉLIMÈNE: He works too hard at cleverness,
however.
I hate to see him sweat and struggle so
To fill his conversation with *bons mots.*°
Since he's decided to become a wit
80   His taste's so pure that nothing pleases it;
He scolds at all the latest books and plays,
Thinking that wit must never stoop to praise,
That finding fault's a sign of intellect,
That all appreciation is abject,
85   And that by damning everything in sight
One shows oneself in a distinguished light.
He's scornful even of our conversations:
Their trivial nature sorely tries his patience;
He folds his arms, and stands above the battle,
90   And listens sadly to our childish prattle.
ACASTE: Wonderful, Madam! You've hit him off
precisely.
CLITANDRE: No one can sketch a character so nicely.
ALCESTE: How bravely, Sirs, you cut and thrust at
all
These absent fools, till one by one they fall:
95   But let one come in sight, and you'll at once
Embrace the man you lately called a dunce,
Telling him in a tone sincere and fervent
How proud you are to be his humble servant.
CLITANDRE: Why pick on us? *Madame's* been
speaking, Sir.

And you should quarrel, if you must, with her.   100
ALCESTE: No, no, by God, the fault is yours,
because
You lead her on with laughter and applause,
And make her think that she's the more
delightful
The more her talk is scandalous and spiteful.
Oh, she would stoop to malice far, far less   105
If no such claque approved her cleverness.
It's flatterers like you whose foolish praise
Nourishes all the vices of these days.
PHILINTE: But why protest when someone ridicules
Those you'd condemn, yourself, as knaves or
fools?   110
CÉLIMÈNE: Why, Sir? Because he loves to make a
fuss.
You don't expect him to agree with us,
When there's an opportunity to express
His heaven-sent spirit of contrariness?
What other people think, he can't abide;   115
Whatever they say, he's on the other side;
He lives in deadly terror of agreeing;
'Twould make him seem an ordinary being.
Indeed, he's so in love with contradiction,
He'll turn against his most profound conviction   120
And with a furious eloquence deplore it,
If only someone else is speaking for it.
ALCESTE: Go on, dear lady, mock me as you please;
You have your audience in ecstasies.
PHILINTE: But what she says is true: you have a
way   125
Of bridling at whatever people say;
Whether they praise or blame, your angry spirit
Is equally unsatisfied to hear it.
ALCESTE: Men, Sir, are always wrong, and that's the
reason
That righteous anger's never out of season;   130
All that I hear in all their conversation
Is flattering praise or reckless condemnation.
CÉLIMÈNE: But . . .
ALCESTE: No, no, Madam, I am forced to state
That you have pleasures which I deprecate,
And that these others, here, are much to blame   135
For nourishing the faults which are your shame.
CLITANDRE: I shan't defend myself, Sir; but I vow
I'd thought this lady faultless until now.
ACASTE: I see her charms and graces, which are
many;   140
But as for faults, I've never noticed any.
ALCESTE: I see them, Sir; and rather than ignore
them,
I strenuously criticize her for them.
The more one loves, the more one should object
To every blemish, every least defect.
Were I this lady, I would soon get rid   145

78. *bons mots*: Clever remarks, witticisms.

Of lovers who approved of all I did,
And by their slack indulgence and applause
Endorsed my follies and excused my flaws.
CÉLIMÈNE: If all hearts beat according to your
measure,
150   The dawn of love would be the end of pleasure;
And love would find its perfect consummation
In ecstasies of rage and reprobation.
ÉLIANTE: Love, as a rule, affects men otherwise
And lovers rarely love to criticize.
155   They see their lady as a charming blur,
And find all things commendable in her.
If she has any blemish, fault, or shame,
They will redeem it by a pleasing name.
The pale-faced lady's lily-white, perforce;
160   The swarthy one's a sweet brunette, of course;
The spindly lady has a slender grace;
The fat one has a most majestic pace;
The plain one, with her dress in disarray
They classify as *beauté négligée*;°
165   The hulking one's a goddess in their eyes,
The dwarf, a concentrate of Paradise;
The haughty lady has a noble mind;
The mean one's witty, and the dull one's kind;
The chatterbox has liveliness and verve,
170   The mute one has a virtuous reserve.
So lovers manage, in their passion's cause,
To love their ladies even for their flaws.
ALCESTE: But I still say . . .
CÉLIMÈNE   I think it would be nice
To stroll around the gallery once or twice.
What! You're not going, Sirs?
175   CLITANDRE AND ACASTE: No, Madam, no.
ALCESTE: You seem to be in terror lest they go.
Do what you will, Sirs; leave, or linger on,
But I shan't go till after you are gone.
ACASTE: I'm free to linger, unless I should perceive
180   *Madame* is tired, and wishes me to leave.
CLITANDRE: And as for me, I needn't go today
Until the hour of the King's *coucher*.°
CÉLIMÈNE (*to Alceste*): You're joking, surely?
ALCESTE: Not in the least; we'll see
Whether you'd rather part with them, or me.

Scene VI   [*Alceste, Célimène, Éliante, Acaste,
Philinte, Clitandre, Basque.*]

BASQUE (*to Alceste*): Sir, there's a fellow here who
bids me state
That he must see you, and that it can't wait.

164. *beauté négligée*: Slovenly beauty.   182. the King's
coucher: The King's bedtime, a ceremonial occasion.

ALCESTE: Tell him that I have no such pressing
affairs.
BASQUE: It's a long tailcoat that this fellow wears,
With gold all over.
CÉLIMÈNE (*to Alceste*):   You'd best go down
and see.   5
Or — have him enter.

Scene VII   [*Alceste, Célimène, Éliante, Acaste,
Philinte, Clitandre, Guard.*]

ALCESTE (*confronting the Guard*):   Well, what
do you want with me?
Come in, Sir.
GUARD: I've a word, Sir, for your ear.
ALCESTE: Speak it aloud, Sir; I shall strive to hear.
GUARD: The Marshals have instructed me to say
You must report to them without delay.   5
ALCESTE: Who? Me, Sir?
GUARD: Yes, Sir; you.
ALCESTE: But what do they want?
PHILINTE (*to Alceste*): To scotch your silly quarrel
with Oronte.
CÉLIMÈNE (*to Philinte*): What quarrel?
PHILINTE: Oronte and he have fallen out
Over some verse he spoke his mind about;
The Marshals wish to arbitrate the matter.   10
ALCESTE: Never shall I equivocate or flatter!
PHILINTE: You'd best obey their summons; come,
let's go.
ALCESTE: How can they mend our quarrel, I'd like
to know?
Am I to make a cowardly retraction,
And praise those jingles to his satisfaction?   15
I'll not recant; I've judged that sonnet rightly.
It's bad.
PHILINTE: But you might say so more politely. . . .
ALCESTE: I'll not back down; his verses make me
sick.
PHILINTE: If only you could be more politic!
But come, let's go.
ALCESTE: I'll go, but I won't unsay   20
A single word.
PHILINTE: Well, let's be on our way.
ALCESTE: Till I am ordered by my lord the King
To praise that poem, I shall say the thing
Is scandalous, by God, and that the poet
Ought to be hanged for having the nerve to
show it.   25

(*To Clitandre and Acaste, who are laughing.*)

By heaven, Sirs, I really didn't know
That I was being humorous.

Scene from the Williamstown Theatre Festival's 1973 production of *The Misanthrope*, directed by Austin Pendleton.

CÉLIMÈNE: Go, Sir, go;
  Settle your business.
ALCESTE: I shall, and when I'm through,
  I shall return to settle things with you.

ACT III • Scene I   [*Clitandre, Acaste.*]

CLITANDRE: Dear Marquess, how contented you
    appear;
  All things delight you, nothing mars your cheer.
  Can you, in perfect honesty, declare
  That you've a right to be so debonair?
5 ACASTE: By Jove, when I survey myself, I find
  No cause whatever for distress of mind.
  I'm young and rich; I can in modesty
  Lay claim to an exalted pedigree;
  And owing to my name and my condition
10   I shall not want for honors and position.
  Then as to courage, that most precious trait,
  I seem to have it, as was proved of late

Upon the field of honor, where my bearing,
They say, was very cool and rather daring.
I've wit, of course; and taste in such perfection   15
That I can judge without the least reflection,
And at the theater, which is my delight,
Can make or break a play on opening night,
And lead the crowd in hisses or bravos,
And generally be known as one who knows.   20
I'm clever, handsome, gracefully polite;
My waist is small, my teeth are strong and white;
As for my dress, the world's astonished eyes
Assure me that I bear away the prize.
I find myself in favor everywhere,   25
Honored by men, and worshiped by the fair;
And since these things are so, it seems to me
I'm justified in my complacency.
CLITANDRE: Well, if so many ladies hold you dear,
  Why do you press a hopeless courtship here?   30
ACASTE: Hopeless, you say? I'm not the sort of fool
  That likes his ladies difficult and cool.
  Men who are awkward, shy, and peasantish
  May pine for heartless beauties, if they wish,

35   Grovel before them, bear their cruelties,
     Woo them with tears and sighs and bended
          knees,
     And hope by dogged faithfulness to gain
     What their poor merits never could obtain.
     For men like me, however, it makes no sense
40   To love on trust, and foot the whole expense.
     Whatever any lady's merits be,
     I think, thank God, that I'm as choice as she;
     That if my heart is kind enough to burn
     For her, she owes me something in return;
45   And that in any proper love affair
     The partners must invest an equal share.
CLITANDRE: You think, then, that our hostess favors
          you?
ACASTE: I've reason to believe that that is true.
CLITANDRE: How did you come to such a mad
          conclusion?
50   You're blind, dear fellow. This is sheer delusion.
ACASTE: All right, then: I'm deluded and I'm blind.
CLITANDRE: Whatever put the notion in your mind?
ACASTE: Delusion.
CLITANDRE: What persuades you that you're
          right?
ACASTE: I'm blind.
CLITANDRE: But have you any proofs to cite?
ACASTE: I tell you I'm deluded.
55   CLITANDRE: Have you, then,
     Received some secret pledge from Célimène?
ACASTE: Oh, no: she scorns me.
CLITANDRE: Tell me the truth, I beg.
ACASTE: She just can't bear me.
CLITANDRE: Ah, don't pull my leg.
     Tell me what hope she's given you, I pray.
ACASTE: I'm hopeless, and it's you who win the
60   day.
     She hates me thoroughly, and I'm so vexed
     I mean to hang myself on Tuesday next.
CLITANDRE: Dear Marquess, let us have an armistice
     And make a treaty. What do you say to this?
65   If ever one of us can plainly prove
     That Célimène encourages his love,
     The other must abandon hope, and yield,
     And leave him in possession of the field.
ACASTE: Now, there's a bargain that appeals to me;
70   With all my heart, dear Marquess, I agree.
     But hush.

Scene II   [*Célimène, Acaste, Clitandre.*]

CÉLIMÈNE: Still here?
CLITANDRE: 'Twas love that stayed our feet.
CÉLIMÈNE: I think I heard a carriage in the street.
     Whose is it? D'you know?

Scene III   [*Célimène, Acaste, Clitandre, Basque.*]

BASQUE: Arsinoé is here,
     Madame.
CÉLIMÈNE: Arsinoé, you say? Oh, dear.
BASQUE: Éliante is entertaining her below.
CÉLIMÈNE: What brings the creature here, I'd like to
          know?
ACASTE: They say she's dreadfully prudish, but in
          fact   5
     I think her piety . . .
CÉLIMÈNE: It's all an act.
     At heart she's worldly, and her poor success
     In snaring men explains her prudishness.
     It breaks her heart to see the beaux and gallants
     Engrossed by other women's charms and talents,   10
     And so she's always in a jealous rage
     Against the faulty standards of the age.
     She lets the world believe that she's a prude
     To justify her loveless solitude,
     And strives to put a brand of moral shame   15
     On all the graces that she cannot claim.
     But still she'd love a lover; and Alceste
     Appears to be the one she'd love the best.
     His visits here are poison to her pride;
     She seems to think I've lured him from her side   20
     And everywhere, at court or in the town,
     The spiteful, envious woman runs me down.
     In short, she's just as stupid as can be,
     Vicious and arrogant in the last degree,
     And . .   25

Scene IV   [*Arsinoé, Célimène, Clitandre, Acaste.*]

CÉLIMÈNE: Ah! What happy chance has brought you
          here?
     I've thought about you ever so much, my dear.
ARSINOÉ I've come to tell you something you
          should know.
CÉLIMÈNE: How good of you to think of doing so!

(*Clitandre and Acaste go out, laughing.*)

Scene V   [*Arsinoé, Célimène.*]

ARSINOÉ: It's just as well those gentlemen didn't
          tarry.
CÉLIMÈNE: Shall we sit down?
ARSINOÉ: That won't be necessary.
     Madam, the flame of friendship ought to burn
     Brightest in matters of the most concern,
     And as there's nothing which concerns us more   5
     Than honor, I have hastened to your door

To bring you, as your friend, some information
About the status of your reputation.
I visited, last night, some virtuous folk,
10   And, quite by chance, it was of you they spoke;
There was, I fear, no tendency to praise
Your light behavior and your dashing ways.
The quantity of gentlemen you see
And your by now notorious coquetry
15   Were both so vehemently criticized
By everyone, that I was much surprised.
Of course, I needn't tell you where I stood;
I came to your defense as best I could,
Assured them you were harmless, and declared
20   Your soul was absolutely unimpaired.
But there are some things, you must realize,
One can't excuse, however hard one tries,
And I was forced at last into conceding
That your behavior, Madam, is misleading,
25   That it makes a bad impression, giving rise
To ugly gossip and obscene surmise,
And that if you were more *overtly* good,
You wouldn't be so much misunderstood.
Not that I think you've been unchaste — no! no!
30   The saints preserve me from a thought so low!
But mere good conscience never did suffice:
One must avoid the outward show of vice.
Madam, you're too intelligent, I'm sure,
To think my motives anything but pure
35   In offering you this counsel — which I do
Out of a zealous interest in you.
CÉLIMÈNE: Madam, I haven't taken you amiss;
I'm very much obliged to you for this;
And I'll at once discharge the obligation
40   By telling you about *your* reputation.
You've been so friendly as to let me know
What certain people say of me, and so
I mean to follow your benign example
By offering you a somewhat similar sample.
45   The other day, I went to an affair
And found some most distinguished people
        there
Discussing piety, both false and true.
The conversation soon came round to you.
Alas! Your prudery and bustling zeal
50   Appeared to have a very slight appeal.
Your affectation of a grave demeanor,
Your endless talk of virtue and of honor,
The aptitude of your suspicious mind
For finding sin where there is none to find,
55   Your towering self-esteem, that pitying face
With which you contemplate the human race,
Your sermonizings and your sharp aspersions
On people's pure and innocent diversions —
All these were mentioned, Madam, and, in fact,
60   Were roundly and concertedly attacked.

"What good," they said, "are all these outward
        shows,
When everything belies her pious pose?
She prays incessantly, but then, they say,
She beats her maids and cheats them of their
        pay;
She shows her zeal in every holy place,   65
But still she's vain enough to paint her face;
She holds that naked statues are immoral,
But with a naked *man* she'd have no quarrel."
Of course, I said to everybody there
That they were being viciously unfair;   70
But still they were disposed to criticize you,
And all agreed that someone should advise you
To leave the morals of the world alone,
And worry rather more about your own.
They felt that one's self-knowledge should be
        great   75
Before one thinks of setting others straight;
That one should learn the art of living well
Before one threatens other men with hell,
And that the Church is best equipped, no doubt,
To guide our souls and root our vices out.   80
Madam, you're too intelligent, I'm sure,
To think my motives anything but pure
In offering you this counsel — which I do
Out of a zealous interest in you.
ARSINOÉ: I dared not hope for gratitude, but I   85
Did not expect so acid a reply;
I judge, since you've been so extremely tart,
That my good counsel pierced you to the heart.
CÉLIMÈNE: Far from it, Madam. Indeed, it seems to
        me
We ought to trade advice more frequently.   90
One's vision of oneself is so defective
That it would be an excellent corrective.
If you are willing, Madam, let's arrange
Shortly to have another frank exchange
In which we'll tell each other, *entre nous,*°   95
What you've heard tell of me, and I of you.
ARSINOÉ: Oh, people never censure you, my dear;
It's me they criticize. Or so I hear.
CÉLIMÈNE: Madam, I think we either blame or
        praise
According to our taste and length of days.   100
There is a time of life for coquetry,
And there's a season, too, for prudery.
When all one's charms are gone, it is, I'm sure,
Good strategy to be devout and pure:
It makes one seem a little less forsaken.   105
Some day, perhaps, I'll take the road you've
        taken:
Time brings all things. But I have time aplenty,

95. *entre nous:* Between ourselves.

And see no cause to be a prude at twenty.
ARSINOÉ: You give your age in such a gloating tone
110   That one would think I was an ancient crone;
   We're not so far apart, in sober truth,
   That you can mock me with a boast of youth!
   Madam, you baffle me. I wish I knew
   What moves you to provoke me as you do.
CÉLIMÈNE: For my part, Madam, I should like to
115   know
   Why you abuse me everywhere you go.
   Is it my fault, dear lady, that your hand
   Is not, alas, in very great demand?
   If men admire me, if they pay me court
120   And daily make me offers of the sort
   You'd dearly love to have them make to you,
   How can I help it? What would you have me
   do?
   If what you want is lovers, please feel free
   To take as many as you can from me.
ARSINOÉ: Oh, come. D'you think the world is losing
125   sleep
   Over the flock of lovers which you keep,
   Or that we find it difficult to guess
   What price you pay for their devotedness?
   Surely you don't expect us to suppose
130   Mere merit could attract so many beaux?
   It's not your virtue that they're dazzled by;
   Nor is it virtuous love for which they sigh.
   You're fooling no one, Madam; the world's not
   blind;
   There's many a lady heaven has designed
135   To call men's noblest, tenderest feelings out,
   Who has no lovers dogging her about;
   From which it's plain that lovers nowadays
   Must be acquired in bold and shameless ways,
   And only pay one court for such reward
140   As modesty and virtue can't afford.
   Then don't be quite so puffed up, if you please,
   About your tawdry little victories;
   Try, if you can, to be a shade less vain,
   And treat the world with somewhat less disdain.
145   If one were envious of your amours,
   One soon could have a following like yours;
   Lovers are no great trouble to collect
   If one prefers them to one's self-respect.
CÉLIMÈNE: Collect them then, my dear; I'd love to
   see
150   You demonstrate that charming theory;
   Who knows, you might . . .
ARSINOÉ: Now, Madam, that will do;
   It's time to end this trying interview.
   My coach is late in coming to your door,
   Or I'd have taken leave of you before.
CÉLIMÈNE: Oh, please don't feel that you must rush
155   away;

I'd be delighted, Madam, if you'd stay.
However, lest my conversation bore you,
Let me provide some better company for you;
This gentleman, who comes most apropos,
Will please you more than I could do, I know.   160

Scene VI [*Alceste, Célimène, Arsinoé.*]

CÉLIMÈNE: Alceste, I have a little note to write
   Which simply must go out before tonight;
   Please entertain *Madame;* I'm sure that she
   Will overlook my incivility.

Scene VII [*Alceste, Arsinoé.*]

ARSINOÉ: Well, Sir, our hostess graciously contrives
   For us to chat until my coach arrives;
   And I shall be forever in her debt
   For granting me this little *tête-à-tête.*°
   We women very rightly give our hearts   5
   To men of noble character and parts,
   And your especial merits, dear Alceste
   Have roused the deepest sympathy in my breast.
   Oh, how I wish they had sufficient sense
   At court, to recognize your excellence!   10
   They wrong you greatly, Sir. How it must hurt
   you
   Never to be rewarded for your virtue!
ALCESTE: Why, Madam, what cause have I to feel
   aggrieved?
   What great and brilliant thing have I achieved?
   What service have I rendered to the King   15
   That I should look to him for anything?
ARSINOÉ: Not everyone who's honored by the State
   Has done great services. A man must wait
   Till time and fortune offer him the chance.
   Your merit, Sir, is obvious at a glance,   20
   And . . .
ALCESTE: Ah, forget my merit; I am not neglected.
   The court, I think, can hardly be expected
   To mine men's souls for merit, and unearth
   Our hidden virtues and our secret worth.
ARSINOÉ: *Some* virtues, though, are far too bright to
   hide;   25
   Yours are acknowledged, Sir, on every side.
   Indeed, I've heard you warmly praised of late
   By persons of considerable weight.
ALCESTE: This fawning age has praise for everyone,
   And all distinctions, Madam, are undone.   30

4. *tête-à-tête*: French for "head-to-head," in private conversation.

All things have equal honor nowadays,
And no one should be gratified by praise.
To be admired, one only need exist,
And every lackey's on the honors list.

35 ARSINOÉ: I only wish, Sir, that you had your eye
On some position at court, however high;
You'd only have to hint at such a notion
For me to set the proper wheels in motion
I've certain friendships I'd be glad to use
40 To get you any office you might choose.

ALCESTE: Madam, I fear that any such ambition
Is wholly foreign to my disposition.
The soul God gave me isn't of the sort
That prospers in the weather of a court.
45 It's all too obvious that I don't possess
The virtues necessary for success.
My one great talent is for speaking plain;
I've never learned to flatter or to feign;
And anyone so stupidly sincere
50 Had best not seek a courtier's career.
Outside the court, I know, one must dispense
With honors, privilege, and influence;
But still one gains the right, foregoing these,
Not to be tortured by the wish to please.
55 One needn't live in dread of snubs and slights,
Nor praise the verse that every idiot writes,
Nor humor silly Marquesses, nor bestow
Politic sighs on Madam So-and-So.

ARSINOÉ: Forget the court, then; let the matter
rest.
60 But I've another cause to be distressed
About your present situation, Sir.
It's to your love affair that I refer.
She whom you love, and who pretends to love
you,
Is, I regret to say, unworthy of you.

65 ALCESTE: Why, Madam? Can you seriously intend
To make so grave a charge against your friend?

ARSINOÉ: Alas, I must. I've stood aside too long
And let that lady do you grievous wrong;
But now my debt to conscience shall be paid:
70 I tell you that your love has been betrayed.

ALCESTE: I thank you, Madam; you're extremely
kind.
Such words are soothing to a lover's mind.

ARSINOÉ: Yes, though she *is* my friend, I say again
You're very much too good for Célimène.
75 She's wantonly misled you from the start.

ALCESTE: You may be right; who knows another's
heart?
But ask yourself if it's the part of charity
To shake my soul with doubts of her sincerity.

ARSINOÉ: Well, if you'd rather be a dupe than doubt
her,
80 That's your affair. I'll say no more about her.

ALCESTE: Madam, you know that doubt and vague
suspicion
Are painful to a man in my position;
It's most unkind to worry me this way
Unless you've some real proof of what you say.

ARSINOÉ: Sir, say no more: all doubts shall be
removed, 85
And all that I've been saying shall be proved.
You've only to escort me home, and there
We'll look into the heart of this affair.
I've ocular evidence which will persuade you
Beyond a doubt, that Célimène's betrayed you. 90
Then, if you're saddened by that revelation,
Perhaps I can provide some consolation.

ACT IV • *Scene I* [*Éliante, Philinte.*]

PHILINTE: Madam, he acted like a stubborn child
I thought they never would be reconciled;
In vain we reasoned, threatened, and appealed;
He stood his ground and simply would not yield.
The Marshals, I feel sure have never heard 5
An argument so splendidly absurd.
"No, gentlemen," said he, "I'll not retract.
His verse is bad: extremely bad, in fact.
Surely it does the man no harm to know it.
Does it disgrace him, not to be a poet? 10
A gentleman may be respected still,
Whether he writes a sonnet well or ill.
That I dislike his verse should not offend him;
In all that touches honor, I commend him;
He's noble, brave, and virtuous — but I fear 15
He can't in truth be called a sonneteer.
I'll gladly praise his wardrobe; I'll endorse
His dancing, or the way he sits a horse;
But, gentlemen, I cannot praise his rhyme.
In fact, it ought to be a capital crime 20
For anyone so sadly unendowed
To write a sonnet, and read the thing aloud."
At length he fell into a gentler mood
And, striking a concessive attitude,
He paid Oronte the following courtesies: 25
"Sir, I regret that I'm so hard to please,
And I'm profoundly sorry that your lyric
Failed to provoke me to a panegyric."°
After these curious words, the two embraced
And then the hearing was adjourned — in haste. 30

ÉLIANTE: His conduct has been very singular lately;
Still, I confess that I respect him greatly.
The honesty in which he takes such pride
Has — to my mind — its noble, heroic side.

28. panegyric: Elaborate praise.

35 In this false age, such candor seems outrageous;
But I could wish that it were more contagious.
PHILINTE: What most intrigues me in our friend
    Alceste
Is the grand passion that rages in his breast.
The sullen humors he's compounded of
40 Should not, I think, dispose his heart to love;
But since they do, it puzzles me still more
That he should choose your cousin to adore.
ÉLIANTE: It does, indeed, belie the theory
That love is born of gentle sympathy,
45 And that the tender passion must be based
On sweet accords of temper and of taste.
PHILINTE: Does she return his love, do you suppose?
ÉLIANTE: Ah, that's a difficult question, Sir. Who
    knows?
How can we judge the truth of her devotion?
50 Her heart's a stranger to its own emotion.
Sometimes it thinks it loves, when no love's
    there;
At other times it loves quite unaware.
PHILINTE: I rather think Alceste is in for more
Distress and sorrow than he's bargained for;
55 Were he of my mind, Madam, his affection
Would turn in quite a different direction,
And we would see him more responsive to
The kind regard which he receives from you.
ÉLIANTE: Sir, I believe in frankness, and I'm
    inclined
60 In matters of the heart, to speak my mind.
I don't oppose his love for her; indeed,
I hope with all my heart that he'll succeed,
And were it in my power, I'd rejoice
In giving him the lady of his choice.
65 But if, as happens frequently enough
In love affairs, he meets with a rebuff —
If Célimène should grant some rival's suit —
I'd gladly play the role of substitute;
Nor would his tender speeches please me less
70 Because they'd once been made without success.
PHILINTE: Well, Madam, as for me, I don't oppose
Your hopes in this affair; and heaven knows
That in my conversations with the man
I plead your cause as often as I can.
75 But if those two should marry, and so remove
All chance that he will offer you his love,
Then I'll declare my own, and hope to see
Your gracious favor pass from him to me.
In short, should you be cheated of Alceste,
80 I'd be most happy to be second best.
ÉLIANTE: Philinte, you're teasing.
PHILINTE: Ah, Madam, never fear;
No words of mine were ever so sincere
And I shall live in fretful expectation
Till I can make a fuller declaration.

Scene II   *[Alceste, Éliante, Philinte.]*

ALCESTE: Avenge me, Madam! I must have
    satisfaction,
Or this great wrong will drive me to distraction!
ÉLIANTE: Why, what's the matter? What's upset you
    so?
ALCESTE: Madam, I've had a mortal, mortal blow.
If Chaos repossessed the universe,   5
I swear I'd not be shaken any worse.
I'm ruined.... I can say no more.... My
    soul ...
ÉLIANTE: Do try, Sir, to regain your self-control.
ALCESTE: Just heaven! Why were so much beauty
    and grace
Bestowed on one so vicious and so base?   10
ÉLIANTE: Once more, Sir, tell us
ALCESTE: My world has gone to wrack:
I'm — I'm betrayed; she's stabbed me in the
    back:
Yes, Célimène (who would have thought it of
    her?)
Is false to me, and has another lover.
ÉLIANTE: Are you quite certain? Can you prove
    these things?   15
PHILINTE: Lovers are prey to wild imaginings
And jealous fancies. No doubt there's some
    mistake. ...
ALCESTE: Mind your own business, Sir, for heaven's
    sake.
    (To Éliante.) Madam, I have the proof that you
    demand
Here in my pocket, penned by her own hand.   20
Yes, all the shameful evidence one could want
Lies in this letter written to Oronte —
Oronte! whom I felt sure she couldn't love,
And hardly bothered to be jealous of.
PHILINTE: Still, in a letter, appearances may deceive;   25
This may not be so bad as you believe.
ALCESTE: Once more I beg you, Sir, to let me be;
Tend to your own affairs; leave mine to me.
ÉLIANTE: Compose yourself; this anguish that you
    feel ...
ALCESTE: Is something, Madam, you alone can heal.   30
My outraged heart, beside itself with grief,
Appeals to you for comfort and relief.
Avenge me on your cousin, whose unjust
And faithless nature has deceived my trust;
Avenge a crime your pure soul must detest.   35
ÉLIANTE: But how, Sir?
ALCESTE: Madam, this heart within my breast
Is yours; pray take it; redeem my heart from her,
And so avenge me on my torturer.
Let her be punished by the fond emotion,
The ardent love, the bottomless devotion,   40

The faithful worship which this heart of mine
Will offer up to yours as to a shrine.
ÉLIANTE: You have my sympathy, Sir, in all you
    suffer;
Nor do I scorn the noble heart you offer;
45   But I suspect you'll soon be mollified
And this desire for vengeance will subside.
When some belovèd hand has done us wrong
We thirst for retribution — but not for long;
However dark the deed that she's committed,
50   A lovely culprit's very soon acquitted.
Nothing's so stormy as an injured lover,
And yet no storm so quickly passes over.
ALCESTE: No, Madam, no — this is no lovers' spat;
I'll not forgive her, it's gone too far for that;
55   My mind's made up; I'll kill myself before
I waste my hopes upon her any more.
Ah, here she is. My wrath intensifies.
I shall confront her with her tricks and lies,
And crush her utterly, and bring you then
60   A heart no longer slave to Célimène.

Scene III   [*Célimène, Alceste.*]

ALCESTE (*aside*): Sweet heaven, help me to control
    my passion.
CÉLIMÈNE (*aside*): Oh, Lord. (*To Alceste.*) Why
    stand there staring in that fashion?
And what d'you mean by those dramatic sighs,
And that malignant glitter in your eyes?
ALCESTE: I mean that sins which cause the blood to
5   freeze
Look innocent beside your treacheries;
That nothing Hell's or Heaven's wrath could do
Ever produced so bad a thing as you.
CÉLIMÈNE: Your compliments were always sweet
    and pretty.
10 ALCESTE: Madam, it's not the moment to be witty.
No, blush and hang your head; you've ample
    reason,
Since I've the fullest evidence of your treason.
Ah, this is what my sad heart prophesied;
Now all my anxious fears are verified;
15   My dark suspicion and my gloomy doubt
Divined the truth, and now the truth is out.
For all your trickery, I was not deceived;
It was my bitter stars that I believed.
But don't imagine that you'll go scot-free;
20   You shan't misuse me with impunity.
I know that love's irrational and blind;
I know the heart's not subject to the mind,
And can't be reasoned into beating faster;
I know each soul is free to choose its master;
25   Therefore had you but spoken from the heart,

Rejecting my attention from the start,
I'd have no grievance, or at any rate
I could complain of nothing but my fate.
Ah, but so falsely to encourage me —
That was a treason and a treachery   30
For which you cannot suffer too severely,
And you shall pay for that behavior dearly.
Yes, now I have no pity, not a shred;
My temper's out of hand, I've lost my head
Shocked by the knowledge of your double-
    dealings,   35
My reason can't restrain my savage feelings;
A righteous wrath deprives me of my senses,
And I won't answer for the consequences.
CÉLIMÈNE: What does this outburst mean? Will you
    please explain?
Have you, by any chance, gone quite insane?   40
ALCESTE: Yes, yes, I went insane the day I fell
A victim to your black and fatal spell,
Thinking to meet with some sincerity
Among the treacherous charms that beckoned
    me.
CÉLIMÈNE: Pooh. Of what treachery can you
    complain?   45
ALCESTE: How sly you are, how cleverly you feign!
But you'll not victimize me any more.
Look: here's a document you've seen before.
This evidence, which I acquired today,
Leaves you, I think, without a thing to say.   50
CÉLIMÈNE: Is this what sent you into such a fit?
ALCESTE: You should be blushing at the sight of it.
CÉLIMÈNE: Ought I to blush? I truly don't see why.
ALCESTE: Ah, now you're being bold as well as sly;
Since there's no signature, perhaps you'll
    claim . . .   55
CÉLIMÈNE: I wrote it, whether or not it bears my
    name.
ALCESTE: And you can view with equanimity
his proof of your disloyalty to me!
CÉLIMÈNE: Oh, don't be so outrageous and extreme.
ALCESTE: You take this matter lightly, it would
    seem.   60
Was it no wrong to me, no shame to you,
That you should send Oronte this *billet-doux*?°
CÉLIMÈNE: Oronte! Who said it was for him?
ALCESTE: Why, those
Who brought me this example of your prose.
But what's the difference? If you wrote the letter   65
To someone else, it pleases me no better.
My grievance and your guilt remain the same.
CÉLIMÈNE: But need you rage, and need I blush for
    shame,
If this was written to a *woman* friend?

62. *billet-doux*: Love letter.

ALCESTE: Ah! Most ingenious. I'm impressed no
70 end;
And after that incredible evasion
Your guilt is clear. I need no more persuasion.
How dare you try so clumsy a deception?
D'you think I'm wholly wanting in perception?
75 Come, come, let's see how brazenly you'll try
To bolster up so palpable a lie:
Kindly construe this ardent closing section
As nothing more than sisterly affection!
Here, let me read it. Tell me, if you dare to,
That this is for a woman . . .
80 CÉLIMÈNE: I don't dare to.
What right have you to badger and berate me,
And so high-handedly interrogate me?
ALCESTE: Now, don't be angry; all I ask of you
Is that you justify a phrase or two . . .
85 CÉLIMÈNE: No, I shall not. I utterly refuse,
And you may take those phrases as you choose.
ALCESTE: Just show me how this letter could be
meant
For a woman's eyes, and I shall be content.
CÉLIMÈNE: No, no, it's for Oronte; you're perfectly
right.
90 I welcome his attentions with delight,
I prize his character and his intellect
And everything is just as you suspect.
Come, do your worst now; give your rage free
rein;
But kindly cease to bicker and complain.
ALCESTE (aside): Good God! Could anything be
95 more inhuman?
Was ever a heart so mangled by a woman?
When I complain of how she has betrayed me,
She bridles, and commences to upbraid me!
She tries my tortured patience to the limit;
100 She won't deny her guilt; she glories in it!
And yet my heart's too faint and cowardly
To break these chains of passion, and be free,
To scorn her as it should, and rise above
This unrewarded, mad, and bitter love.
(To Célimène.) Ah, traitress, in how confident a
105 fashion
You take advantage of my helpless passion,
And use my weakness for your faithless charms
To make me once again throw down my arms!
But do at least deny this black transgression;
110 Take back that mocking and perverse confession;
Defend this letter and your innocence,
And I, poor fool, will aid in your defense.
Pretend, pretend, that you are just and true,
And I shall make myself believe in you.
CÉLIMÈNE: Oh, stop it. Don't be such a jealous
115 dunce,
Or I shall leave off loving you at once.

Just why should I *pretend*? What could impel me
To stoop so low as that? And kindly tell me
Why, if I loved another, I shouldn't merely
Inform you of it, simply and sincerely!   120
I've told you where you stand, and that
admission
Should altogether clear me of suspicion;
After so generous a guarantee
What right have you to harbor doubts of me?
Since women are (from natural reticence)   125
Reluctant to declare their sentiments,
And since the honor of our sex requires
That we conceal our amorous desires,
Ought any man for whom such laws are broken
To question what the oracle has spoken?   130
Should he not rather feel an obligation
To trust that most obliging declaration?
Enough, now. Your suspicions quite disgust me;
Why should I love a man who doesn't trust me?
I cannot understand why I continue,   135
Fool that I am, to take an interest in you.
I ought to choose a man less prone to doubt,
And give you something to be vexed about.
ALCESTE: Ah, what a poor enchanted fool I am;
These gentle words, no doubt, were all a sham,   140
But destiny requires me to entrust
My happiness to you, and so I must.
I'll love you to the bitter end, and see
How false and treacherous you dare to be.
CÉLIMÈNE: No, you don't really love me as you
ought.   145
ALCESTE: I love you more than can be said or
thought;
Indeed, I wish you were in such distress
That I might show my deep devotedness.
Yes, I could wish that you were wretchedly poor,
Unloved, uncherished, utterly obscure;   150
That fate had set you down upon the earth
Without possessions, rank, or gentle birth;
Then, by the offer of my heart, I might
Repair the great injustice of your plight;
I'd raise you from the dust, and proudly prove   155
The purity and vastness of my love.
CÉLIMÈNE: This is a strange benevolence indeed!
God grant that I may never be in need. . . .
Ah, here's Monsieur Dubois in quaint disguise.

Scene IV [*Célimène, Alceste, Dubois.*]

ALCESTE: Well, why this costume? Why those
frightened eyes?
What ails you?
DUBOIS: Well, Sir, things are most mysterious.
ALCESTE: What do you mean?

DUBOIS: I fear they're very serious.
ALCESTE: What?
DUBOIS: Shall I speak more loudly?
ALCESTE: Yes; speak out.
DUBOIS: Isn't there someone here, Sir?
5   ALCESTE: Speak, you lout!
    Stop wasting time.
DUBOIS: Sir, we must slip away.
ALCESTE: How's that?
DUBOIS: We must decamp without delay.
ALCESTE: Explain yourself.
DUBOIS: I tell you we must fly.
ALCESTE: What for?
DUBOIS: We mustn't pause to say good-by.
ALCESTE: Now what d'you mean by all of this, you
10   clown?
DUBOIS: I mean, Sir, that we've got to leave this
    town.
ALCESTE: I'll tear you limb from limb and joint from
    joint
    If you don't come more quickly to the point.
DUBOIS: Well, Sir, today a man in a black suit,
15   Who wore a black and ugly scowl to boot,
    Left us a document scrawled in such a hand
    As even Satan couldn't understand.
    It bears upon your lawsuit, I don't doubt;
    But all hell's devils couldn't make it out.
20   ALCESTE: Well, well, go on. What then? I fail to see
    How this event obliges us to flee.
DUBOIS: Well, Sir, an hour later, hardly more,
    A gentleman who's often called before
    Came looking for you in an anxious way.
25   Not finding you, he asked me to convey
    (Knowing I could be trusted with the same)
    The following message.... Now, what *was* his
    name?
ALCESTE: Forget his name, you idiot. What did he
    say?
DUBOIS: Well, it was one of your friends, Sir,
    anyway.
30   He warned you to begone, and he suggested
    That if you stay, you may well be arrested.
ALCESTE: What? Nothing more specific? Think,
    man, think!
DUBOIS: No, Sir. He had me bring him pen and ink,
    And dashed you off a letter which, I'm sure,
35   Will render things distinctly less obscure.
ALCESTE: Well — let me have it!
CÉLIMÈNE: What *is* this all about?
ALCESTE: God knows; but I have hopes of finding
    out.
    How long am I to wait, you blitherer?
DUBOIS: (*after a protracted search for the letter*): I
    must have left it on your table, Sir.
ALCESTE: I ought to . . .

CÉLIMÈNE: No, no, keep your self-control;   40
    Go find out what's behind his rigmarole.
ALCESTE: It seems that fate, no matter what I do,
    Has sworn that I may not converse with you;
    But, Madam, pray permit your faithful lover
    To try once more before the day is over.   45

ACT V • *Scene 1*   [*Alceste, Philinte.*]

ALCESTE: No, it's too much. My mind's made up, I
    tell you.
PHILINTE: Why should this blow, however hard,
    compel you . . .
ALCESTE: No, no, don't waste your breath in
    argument;
    Nothing you say will alter my intent;
    This age is vile, and I've made up my mind   5
    To have no further commerce with mankind.
    Did not truth, honor, decency, and the laws
    Oppose my enemy and approve my cause?
    My claims were justified in all men's sight;
    I put my trust in equity and right;   10
    Yet, to my horror and the world's disgrace,
    Justice is mocked, and I have lost my case!
    A scoundrel whose dishonesty is notorious
    Emerges from another lie victorious!
    Honor and right condone his brazen fraud,   15
    While rectitude and decency applaud!
    Before his smirking face, the truth stands
    charmed,
    And virtue conquered, and the law disarmed!
    His crime is sanctioned by a court decree!
    And not content with what he's done to me,   20
    The dog now seeks to ruin me by stating
    That I composed a book now circulating,
    A book so wholly criminal and vicious
    That even to speak its title is seditious!
    Meanwhile Oronte, my rival, lends his credit   25
    To the same libelous tale, and helps to spread it!
    Oronte! a man of honor and of rank,
    With whom I've been entirely fair and frank;
    Who sought me out and forced me, willy-nilly,
    To judge some verse I found extremely silly;   30
    And who, because I properly refused
    To flatter him, or see the truth abused,
    Abets my enemy in a rotten slander!
    There's the reward of honesty and candor!
    The man will hate me to the end of time   35
    For failing to commend his wretched rhyme!
    And not this man alone, but all humanity
    Do what they do from interest and vanity;
    They prate of honor, truth, and righteousness,
    But lie, betray, and swindle nonetheless.   40

Come then: man's villainy is too much to bear;
Let's leave this jungle and this jackal's lair.
Yes! treacherous and savage race of men,
You shall not look upon my face again.

45 PHILINTE: Oh, don't rush into exile prematurely;
Things aren't as dreadful as you make them,
   surely.
It's rather obvious, since you're still at large,
That people don't believe your enemy's charge.
Indeed, his tale's so patently untrue

50 That it may do more harm to him than you.
ALCESTE: Nothing could do that scoundrel any
   harm:
His frank corruption is his greatest charm,
And, far from hurting him, a further shame
Would only serve to magnify his name.

55 PHILINTE: In any case, his bald prevarication
Has done no injury to your reputation,
And you may feel secure in that regard.
As for your lawsuit, it should not be hard
To have the case reopened, and contest
This judgment . . .

60 ALCESTE: No, no, let the verdict rest.
Whatever cruel penalty it may bring,
I wouldn't have it changed for anything.
It shows the times' injustice with such clarity
That I shall pass it down to our posterity

65 As a great proof and signal demonstration
Of the black wickedness of this generation.
It may cost twenty thousand francs; but I
Shall pay their twenty thousand, and gain thereby
The right to storm and rage at human evil,

70 And send the race of mankind to the devil.
PHILINTE: Listen to me . . .
ALCESTE: Why? What can you possibly say?
Don't argue, Sir; your labor's thrown away.
Do you propose to offer lame excuses
For men's behavior and the times' abuses?

75 PHILINTE: No, all you say I'll readily concede:
This is a low, conniving age, indeed;
Nothing but trickery prospers nowadays,
And people ought to mend their shabby ways.
Yes, man's a beastly creature; but must we then

80 Abandon the society of men?
Here in the world, each human frailty
Provides occasion for philosophy,
And that is virtue's noblest exercise;
If honesty shone forth from all men's eyes,

85 If every heart were frank and kind and just,
What could our virtues do but gather dust
(Since their employment is to help us bear
The villainies of men without despair)?
A heart well-armed with virtue can endure. . . .

90 ALCESTE: Sir, you're a matchless reasoner, to be sure;
Your words are fine and full of cogency;

But don't waste time and eloquence on me.
My reason bids me go, for my own good.
My tongue won't lie and flatter as it should;
God knows what frankness it might next
   commit,   95
And what I'd suffer on account of it.
Pray let me wait for Célimène's return
In peace and quiet. I shall shortly learn,
By her response to what I have in view,
Whether her love for me is feigned or true.   100
PHILINTE: Till then, let's visit Éliante upstairs.
ALCESTE: No, I am too weighed down with somber
   cares.
Go to her, do; and leave me with my gloom
Here in the darkened corner of this room.
PHILINTE: Why, that's no sort of company, my
   friend;   105
I'll see if Éliante will not descend.

Scene II   [*Célimène, Oronte, Alceste.*]

ORONTE: Yes, Madam, if you wish me to remain
Your true and ardent lover, you must deign
To give me some more positive assurance.
All this suspense is quite beyond endurance.
If your heart shares the sweet desires of mine,   5
Show me as much by some convincing sign;
And here's the sign I urgently suggest:
That you no longer tolerate Alceste,
But sacrifice him to my love, and sever
All your relations with the man forever.   10
CÉLIMÈNE: Why do you suddenly dislike him so?
You praised him to the skies not long ago.
ORONTE: Madam, that's not the point. I'm here to
   find
Which way your tender feelings are inclined.
Choose, if you please, between Alceste and me,   15
And I shall stay or go accordingly.
ALCESTE (*emerging from the corner*): Yes, Madam,
   choose; this gentleman's demand
Is wholly just, and I support his stand.
I too am true and ardent; I too am here
To ask you that you make your feelings clear.   20
No more delays, now; no equivocation;
The time has come to make your declaration.
ORONTE: Sir, I've no wish in any way to be
An obstacle to your felicity.
ALCESTE: Sir, I've no wish to share her heart with
   you;   25
That may sound jealous, but at least it's true.
ORONTE: If, weighing us, she leans in your
   direction . . .
ALCESTE: If she regards you with the least
   affection . . .

ORONTE: I swear I'll yield her to you there and
    then.
30 ALCESTE: I swear I'll never see her face again.
ORONTE: Now, Madam, tell us what we've come to
    hear.
ALCESTE: Madam, speak openly and have no fear.
ORONTE: Just say which one is to remain your lover.
ALCESTE: Just name one name, and it will all be
    over.
35 ORONTE: What! Is it possible that you're undecided?
ALCESTE: What! Can your feelings possibly be
    divided?
CÉLIMÈNE: Enough: this inquisition's gone too far:
    How utterly unreasonable you are!
    Not that I couldn't make the choice with ease;
40   My heart has no conflicting sympathies
    I know full well which one of you I favor,
    And you'd not see me hesitate or waver.
    But how can you expect me to reveal
    So cruelly and bluntly what I feel?
45 I think it altogether too unpleasant
    To choose between two men when both are
      present;
    One's heart has means more subtle and more kind
    Of letting its affections be divined,
    Nor need one be uncharitably plain
50   To let a lover know he loves in vain.
ORONTE: No, no, speak plainly; I for one can stand
    it.
    I beg you to be frank.
ALCESTE: And I demand it.
    The simple truth is what I wish to know,
    And there's no need for softening the blow.
55   You've made an art of pleasing everyone,
    But now your days of coquetry are done:
    You have no choice now, Madam, but to choose,
    For I'll know what to think if you refuse;
    I'll take your silence for a clear admission
60   That I'm entitled to my worst suspicion.
ORONTE: I thank you for this ultimatum, Sir.
    And I may say I heartily concur.
CÉLIMÈNE: Really, this foolishness is very wearing:
    Must you be so unjust and overbearing?
65   Haven't I told you why I must demur?
    Ah, here's Éliante; I'll put the case to her.

Scene III   [*Éliante, Philinte, Célimène, Oronte,
Alceste.*]

CÉLIMÈNE: Cousin, I'm being persecuted here
    By these two persons, who, it would appear,
    Will not be satisfied till I confess
    Which one I love the more, and which the less,
5   And tell the latter to his face that he

    Is henceforth banished from my company.
    Tell me, has ever such a thing been done?
ÉLIANTE: You'd best not turn to me; I'm not the one
    To back you in a matter of this kind:
    I'm all for those who frankly speak their mind.   10
ORONTE: Madam, you'll search in vain for a
    defender.
ALCESTE: You're beaten, Madam, and may as well
    surrender.
ORONTE: Speak, speak, you must; and end this
    awful strain.
ALCESTE: Or don't, and your position will be plain.
ORONTE: A single word will close this painful scene.   15
ALCESTE: But if you're silent, I'll know what you
    mean.

Scene IV   [*Arsinoé, Célimène, Éliante, Alceste,
Philinte, Acaste, Clitandre, Oronte.*]

ACASTE (*to Célimène*): Madam, with all due
    deference, we two
    Have come to pick a little bone with you.
CLITANDRE (*to Oronte and Alceste*): I'm glad you're
    present, Sirs, as you'll soon learn,
    Our business here is also your concern.
ARSINOÉ (*to Célimène*): Madam, I visit you so soon
    again   5
    Only because of these two gentlemen,
    Who came to me indignant and aggrieved
    About a crime too base to be believed.
    Knowing your virtue, having such confidence in
      it,
    I couldn't think you guilty for a minute,   10
    In spite of all their telling evidence;
    And, rising above our little difference
    I've hastened here in friendship's name to see
    You clear yourself of this great calumny.
ACASTE: Yes, Madam, let us see with what
    composure   15
    You'll manage to respond to this disclosure.
    You lately sent Clitandre this tender note.
CLITANDRE: And this one, for Acaste, you also
    wrote.
ACASTE (*to Oronte and Alceste*): You'll recognize
    this writing, Sirs, I think;
    The lady is so free with pen and ink   20
    That you must know it all too well, I fear.
    But listen: this is something you should hear.

    "How absurd you are to condemn my light-
heartedness in society, and to accuse me of being
happiest in the company of others. Nothing could   25
be more unjust; and if you do not come to me instantly and beg pardon for saying such a thing, I

shall never forgive you as long as I live. Our big
bumbling friend the Viscount . . ."

30   What a shame that he's not here.

"Our big bumbling friend the Viscount, whose
name stands first in your complaint, is hardly a
man to my taste; and ever since the day I watched
him spend three-quarters of an hour spitting into a
35   well, so as to make circles in the water, I have been
unable to think highly of him. As for the little
Marquess . . ."

In all modesty, gentlemen, that is I.

"As for the little Marquess, who sat squeezing
40   my hand for such a long while yesterday, I find him
in all respects the most trifling creature alive; and the
only things of value about him are his cape and his
sword. As for the man with the green ribbons . . ."

(*To Alceste.*) It's your turn now, Sir.

45   "As for the man with the green ribbons, he
amuses me now and then with his bluntness and
his bearish ill-humor; but there are many times indeed when I think him the greatest bore in the
world. And as for the sonneteer . . ."

50   (*To Oronte.*) Here's your helping.

"And as for the sonneteer, who has taken it into
his head to be witty, and insists on being an author
in the teeth of opinion, I simply cannot be bothered
to listen to him, and his prose wearies me quite as
55   much as his poetry. Be assured that I am not always
so well-entertained as you suppose; that I long for
your company, more than I dare to say, at all these
entertainments to which people drag me; and that
the presence of those one loves is the true and per-
60   fect seasoning to all one's pleasures."

CLITANDRE: And now for me.

"Clitandre, whom you mention, and who so
pesters me with his saccharine speeches, is the last
man on earth for whom I could feel any affection.
65   He is quite mad to suppose that I love him, and so
are you, to doubt that you are loved. Do come to
your senses; exchange your suppositions for his;
and visit me as often as possible, to help me bear
the annoyance of his unwelcome attentions."

70   It's sweet character that these letters show,
And what to call it, Madam, you well know.

Enough. We're off to make the world acquainted
With this sublime self-portrait that you've painted.
ACASTE: Madam, I'll make you no farewell oration;
No, you're not worthy of my indignation.   75
Far choicer hearts than yours, as you'll discover,
Would like this little Marquess for a lover.

Scene V [*Célimène, Éliante, Arsinoé, Alceste,
Oronte, Philinte.*]

ORONTE: So! After all those loving letters you wrote,
You turn on me like this, and cut my throat!
And your dissembling, faithless heart, I find,
Has pledged itself by turns to all mankind!
How blind I've been! But now I clearly see;   5
I thank you, Madam, for enlightening me.
My heart is mine once more, and I'm content;
The loss of it shall be your punishment.
(*To Alceste.*) Sir, she is yours; I'll seek no more
to stand
Between your wishes and this lady's hand.   10

Scene VI [*Célimène, Éliante, Arsinoé, Alceste,
Philinte.*]

ARSINOÉ: (to Célimène): Madam, I'm forced to
speak. I'm far too stirred
To keep my counsel, after what I've heard.
I'm shocked and staggered by your want of morals.
It's not my way to mix in others' quarrels;
But really, when this fine and noble spirit,   5
This man of honor and surpassing merit,
Laid down the offering of his heart before you,
How *could* you . . .
ALCESTE: Madam, permit me, I implore you,
To represent myself in this debate.
Don't bother, please, to be my advocate.   10
My heart, in any case, could not afford
To give your services their due reward;
And if I chose, for consolation's sake,
Some other lady, 'twould not be you I'd take.
ARSINOÉ: What makes you think you could, Sir?
And how dare you   15
Imply that I've been trying to ensnare you?
If you can for a moment entertain
Such flattering fancies, you're extremely vain.
I'm not so interested as you suppose
In Célimène's discarded gigolos.   20
Get rid of that absurd illusion, do.
Women like me are not for such as you.
Stay with this creature, to whom you're so
attached;
I've never seen two people better matched.

Scene VII [*Célimène, Éliante, Alceste, Philinte.*]

ALCESTE (*to Célimène*): Well, I've been still
    throughout this exposé,
Till everyone but me has said his say.
Come, have I shown sufficient self-restraint?
And may I now . . .
  CÉLIMÈNE: Yes, make your just complaint.
5   Reproach me freely, call me what you will;
You've every right to say I've used you ill.
I've wronged you, I confess it; and in my shame
I'll make no effort to escape the blame.
The anger of those others I could despise;
10   My guilt toward you I sadly recognize.
Your wrath is wholly justified, I fear
I know how culpable I must appear,
I know all things bespeak my treachery,
And that, in short, you've grounds for hating me.
Do so; I give you leave.
15   ALCESTE: Ah, traitress — how,
How should I cease to love you, even now?
Though mind and will were passionately bent
On hating you, my heart would not consent.
(*To Éliante and Philinte.*) Be witness to my
    madness, both of you;
20   See what infatuation drives one to;
But wait; my folly's only just begun,
And I shall prove to you before I'm done
How strange the human heart is, and how far
From rational we sorry creatures are.
(*To Célimène.*) Woman, I'm willing to forget
    your shame,
25   And clothe your treacheries in a sweeter name;
I'll call them youthful errors, instead of crimes,
And lay the blame on these corrupting times.
My one condition is that you agree
30   To share my chosen fate, and fly with me
To that wild, trackless, solitary place
In which I shall forget the human race.
Only by such a course can you atone
For those atrocious letters; by that alone
35   Can you remove my present horror of you,
And make it possible for me to love you.
CÉLIMÈNE: What! *I* renounce the world at my young
    age,
And die of boredom in some hermitage?
ALCESTE: Ah, if you really loved me as you ought,
40   You wouldn't give the world a moment's thought;

Must you have me, and all the world beside?
CÉLIMÈNE: Alas, at twenty one is terrified
Of solitude. I fear I lack the force
And depth of soul to take so stern a course.
But if my hand in marriage will content you,   45
Why, there's a plan which I might well consent
    to,
And . . .
ALCESTE: No, I detest you now. I could excuse
Everything else, but since you thus refuse
To love me wholly, as a wife should do,   50
And see the world in me, as I in you,
Go! I reject your hand, and disenthrall
My heart from your enchantments, once for all.

Scene VIII   [*Éliante, Alceste, Philinte.*]

ALCESTE (*to Éliante*): Madam, your virtuous beauty
    has no peer;
Of all this world you only are sincere;
I've long esteemed you highly, as you know;
Permit me ever to esteem you so,
And if I do not now request your hand,   5
Forgive me, Madam, and try to understand.
I feel unworthy of it; I sense that fate
Does not intend me for the married state,
That I should do you wrong by offering you
My shattered heart's unhappy residue,   10
And that in short . . .
ÉLIANTE: Your argument's well taken:
Nor need you fear that I shall feel forsaken.
Were I to offer him this hand of mine,
Your friend Philinte, I think, would not decline.
PHILINTE: Ah, Madam, that's my heart's most
    cherished goal,   15
For which I'd gladly give my life and soul.
ALCESTE (*to Éliante and Philinte*): May you be true
    to all you now profess,
And so deserve unending happiness.
Meanwhile, betrayed and wronged in
    everything,
I'll flee this bitter world where vice is king,   20
And seek some spot unpeopled and apart
Where I'll be free to have an honest heart.
PHILINTE: Come, Madam, let's do everything we can
To change the mind of this unhappy man.

COMMENTARY

Lionel Gossman (b. 1929)

ALCESTE'S LOVE FOR CÉLIMÈNE

1963

What underlies Alceste's unlikely infatuation with Célimène? Gossman suggests that Alceste is playing to the very people of fashion whom he affects to look down upon; consequently, he must conceal the real reasons for his love.

In reality, Alceste's love for Célimène is neither super-rational (above all reason and all explanation) nor irrational (below all reason and explanation). It is quite simply a peculiar and contradictory fascination which goes by the name of love in the vocabulary of the Alcestes of the world. It *can* be explained, and the explanation reveals that far from being the sincere and spontaneous being he says he is, Alceste is as calculating as anyone else.

It is precisely because Célimène is the most sought after and *worldly* of women (to all *appearances* the most unsuitable for Alceste) that he falls in love with her. It is not Célimène that Alceste loves or desires. She is irrelevant *as a person* to his "love." It is the world that he seeks to reach and possess through her. To have at his feet this woman whom all the world admires and courts would be to win the recognition of the world for himself. Alceste's love is entirely mediated by those very "gens à la mode"° for whom he so loudly protests his contempt. He "loves" Célimène because she has what he wants — the admiration of the world — and cannot admit he wants, without at the same time admitting that he is not the free, frank, and independent person he wants to be admired as. The object of his desire is thus also his unavowed rival, and this *for the very same reason* that she is the object of his desire. While he protests his love for Célimène, Alceste must therefore conceal the real reason for this love by affecting to deplore her participation in the "false" society of the *gens à la mode* and to despise her charms and her popularity. The final break with Célimène strikingly illustrates the ambiguity that characterizes Alceste's entire relationship with her from the beginning. Alceste calls on witnesses to observe how superior and disinterested his love is compared to the love of the elegant suitors who have abandoned Célimène, while at the same time he affirms before them his own contempt for it as unworthy of him:

> *Vous voyez* ce que peut une indigne tendresse,
> Et je vous fais tous deux *témoins* de ma foiblesse.
> Mais, à vous dire vrai, ce n'est pas encor tout,
> Et *vous allez me voir* la pousser jusqu'au bout,
> *Montrer* que c'est à tort que sages on nous nomme,
> Et que dans tous les coeurs il est toujours de l'homme.
> [V, VI, 19–24][1]

"gens à la mode": Fashionable people.
[1] V, IV, 1751–56 of original text; italics added by Gossman.

Having once proved how different his love is from that of Célimène's frivolous and calculating suitors, however, Alceste is only too quick to use her unwillingness to follow him to his desert as an excuse to drop her. Célimène without her suitors can have no attraction for Alceste.

Those who fall for Alceste's argument about the irrationality of passion are his dupes. Alceste cannot accept in the front rank of his own consciousness, or admit to others, that his whole life is pure posturing before others, that he who claims to be sincere and spontaneous is as preoccupied with the public as anybody and as mediated by it as those whom he charges with acting parts for others. Is he not, after all, the only person in the world who does not posture, whose emotions spring directly from the heart and who speaks nothing but what he really thinks and feels? Alceste uses the myth of the irrationality of passion to hide from others and from himself a character that is every bit as cold and ungenerous as the characters of those he criticizes for their coldness and lack of generosity. . . .

Alceste's life is in an important sense a life not of participation but of demonstration. This is one way in which he differs from the tragic heroes of Racine. The scandalous contradiction between the ideal and the real, between being and appearance, between the world of absolute values and the world of contingent opportunities is at the heart of seventeenth-century tragedy. There is never any danger, however, that Alceste will share in the somber destinies of Racine's heroes. His world is far removed from theirs. He does not stake his destiny, as Junie or Andromaque or Monime° does, on living an authentic life in a world of inauthenticity. The inauthenticity of the world is not a menace to him; on the contrary, it is the very source of all his satisfactions. It provides the basis for his own superiority and he spends his time not in a real struggle to reach authenticity, but in endless efforts to have his superiority recognized by the very world of inauthenticity which he affects to detest. The absence of value in the world becomes, with Alceste, a matter for personal self-congratulation. Far from threatening his existence, the world of lies and deceit founds it. He exhausts himself in theatrical gestures, because all his wrestling with the ideal and the real, all his disgust with the world's falseness, however painfully experienced subjectively, is, objectively viewed, nothing but vain, ineffectual, and deeply inauthentic posturing. He does not really suffer because life is full of pretense and selfishness, because men have made their lives so vain and stupid. He suffers because he cannot bear to be like others and because others refuse him the adulation which he wants from them. . . .

Alceste acts the part of an absolute, but no one accepts his absoluteness: He loses his lawsuit, he fails to make Célimène submit to him, and he is laughed at by the world at large. He is an absolute in the world of his own conceptualizing alone, and thither he withdraws to decide for himself the fate of all his battles. The desert to which Alceste has always thought of withdrawing and to which he makes as if to withdraw at the end of the comedy is the world of his own mind. In it there is nothing to contradict his absoluteness, but there is unfortunately nothing to confirm it either. Alceste's difficulty is that his absoluteness can be experienced as real only with reference to others. Withdrawal to the desert cannot therefore be a final solution. It can only be an *act,* just as his rejection of Philinte

Junie . . . Andromaque . . . Monime: Characters in plays by Racine.

at the beginning of the play was an act. This withdrawal requires an audience to watch it; and this hermit seeks not to escape but to be pursued. Alceste's withdrawal is simply a pose. And this is the very marrow of Molière's play. Alceste literally *joue la comédie*.° He is perpetually play-acting, whether we think of his passion for Célimène or of his passion for justice, and in this respect he resembles Molière's other comic heroes.

joue la comédie: Play a sham part; play-act.

Aphra Behn

Although not technically the first English woman playwright, or the first woman to earn a living by her pen, Aphra Behn (c. 1640–1689) was the first notably successful woman playwright. She wrote twenty plays, several novels, among them *Oroonoko* (c. 1688), and *Poems on Several Occasions* (1684). She also published translations and edited volumes of poetry.

Behn grew up in an England governed by the Puritan Commonwealth. Throughout the 1650s Cromwell was Protector, and the theaters were closed. The Puritans were, in her eyes, dull, hypocritical, and repressive. Her allegiance was with the Stuarts, whose King Charles I was beheaded by order of Parliament in 1649. His sons, Charles and James, were forced into exile on the Continent, along with many Stuart courtiers, such as the gallants who appear in *The Rover*. When Charles II was restored to the throne in 1660, the period known as the Restoration began. Behn was twenty years old.

Very little is known of her, and much of that is guesswork based on her writing. For example, *Oroonoko* is a novel set in Surinam, which was a British colony when she visited there with members of her family in 1663–1664. Her father, who had been appointed lieutenant-general of Surinam, died, and she returned to London. She married Mr. Behn, possibly a Dutch merchant in England, who died two years later. She seems to have been persuaded by the writer and theater manager Thomas Killigrew to become an English spy in Antwerp. She was residing there when the great fire of 1666 destroyed most of London. Her services were so little valued that she was not paid and ended up for a brief time in debtors' prison when she returned to England.

Once out of prison, she took advantage of her friendship with Thomas Betterton, who belonged to a theater company at Lincoln's Inn Fields. He played the lead in her first play, *The Forced Marriage* (1670), which ran successfully for six nights. The record for the first run of a play was thirteen nights. In 1670 Behn reached a mostly courtly audience, those politically aligned with Charles II or somehow involved in court politics.

Behn succeeded again with *The Amorous Prince* following *The Forced Marriage* in 1671. Those first two plays were wholly original, but she quickly resorted to the Shakespearean device of adapting the work of others. Like Shakespeare, she made considerable changes and constantly improved the material she borrowed. After the success of *The*

Rover (1677), she was accused of plagiarism and answered the charge in the Postscript to the play. She did borrow some characters and details from Thomas Killigrew's *Thomaso; or, The Wanderer,* a closet drama, or play intended to be read, not staged (1654; published 1664); but, as she says in her Postscript, no one would have taken notice if her play were not so successful — and written by a woman. Playwrights commonly adapted earlier material because they had to produce many plays in a short time to earn a meager living.

The theme of her first play, loveless and unhappy marriages arranged by families, recurs throughout Behn's work. All we know about her own marriage is that it was brief; she did not remarry despite having long-term relationships. But she concerned herself with the fate of women in her society. A young woman could not hope to marry if she were not a virgin. Once she was married, a woman's property became her husband's and her legal identity was melded with his. Consequently, she was at her husband's mercy since she had no recourse in law against any of his excesses.

However, the alternative to marriage was considered worse. If a woman was seduced, and people found out, she could expect to lose her status and forsake marriage. As a result, she would be forced to earn her own living, a harsh prospect since women were not given the same education as men and could not take part in any of the professions. One fate of many such women was to become prostitutes. In the meantime men pursued their goal of seduction, as they do in *The Rover* and other Behn plays, with no thought given to the welfare of the women they seduced. Furthermore, they frequently threatened women with rape if the women were uncompliant. The theme of rape echoes through Behn's plays. By necessity Behn had to appeal to a predominantly male audience, but even so she expresses some of her deeper concerns for the welfare of her sex. She exposes the unfairness and pain of arranged marriages and portrays women as complex and intelligent. Her work seems to bear the influence of Shakespeare's female characters, such as Helena and Hermia in *A Midsummer Night's Dream* and Beatrice in *Much Ado About Nothing.*

Behn's plays include *Abdelazer* (1676), *The Town Fop* (1676), *The Lucky Chance* (1686), and *The Emperor of the Moon* (1687). Her last play, *The Widow Ranter* (1689), produced posthumously, was a failure. But it is an interesting portrait of the settlement of the Virginias, based on her experience in the New World. The prefaces to Behn's plays treat important issues, such as the unequal education of women. She points out, however, that in playwriting the lack of education in Greek and Latin is no handicap. She reminds her readers that Shakespeare and Jonson did very well with limited education, and that "gownmen" (scholars) talked incessantly and to little account. What was needed for the stage was experience and a good ear, and Aphra Behn had both.

THE ROVER; OR, THE BANISHED CAVALIERS

The English rakes who swagger through this play are displaced Royalist cavaliers who lived perilously in exile during the Puritan Interregnum of the 1650s as they awaited the restoration of Charles II to the throne. Their concerns in Naples are warlike and lusty. Their frequent dueling delighted the audiences of 1677 and caused *The Rover* to be one of Behn's best-received plays. Beneath the brawling, however, is a more serious struggle between the sexes.

It is pre-Lenten carnival time in Naples, when all the people dress in masquerade. The players in *The Rover* disguise themselves — Hellena as a gypsy or a page, Belvile as Antonio, the others in costumes that make them unrecognizable — from the first act to the last. Such masquerading permits the young men and women to meet and talk without supervision. Among the characters, the most stable are Florinda and Belvile, who love each other from the beginning and who end up married despite the objections of Florinda's brother Pedro and their father, who has promised Florinda to Don Vincentio, a wealthy old man.

Behn's favorite theme of arranged or forced marriage thus surfaces quickly in this play, and much of the action involves its circumvention. A related theme also develops quickly: forcible rape. The Cavaliers, or rakes, treat women of lower social class as if they were whores. In this play Florinda faces rape not once, but twice. First Willmore, the Rover, treats her as "an errant harlot" and forces her to scream rape (III, v). When Frederick and Belvile intervene, he explains that he was drunk and not to blame. Florinda's second close call comes with Blunt. When she runs into his apartment to escape discovery on the street, Blunt decides to avenge his disgrace at the hands of Lucetta by raping Florinda — thus punishing the entire sex for his mishandling. This time Frederick, without knowing who Florinda is, decides both to help Blunt and to rape her as well. When she gives them a ring that reveals her to be an aristocrat, a woman of quality, Frederick says, "'twould anger us vilely to be trussed up for a rape upon a maid of quality, when we only believe we ruffle a harlot" (IV, v, 157–60).

These scenes are painful from our modern perspective and must have been even more so to women in Behn's audience. Part of her purpose, though, is to point out that men treated women differently according to class. Aristocrats such as these cavaliers were sometimes willfully brutal toward women in a lower class. Behn builds sympathy for Florinda and, by extension, for all women who are treated viciously by men. It is conceivable that some men in the audiences of Behn's day might not have been conscious of her purpose, since they may have approved of behavior such as Blunt's and Frederick's.

Like Florinda, the other female characters in *The Rover* face obstacles with wit and resourcefulness, but not all the women are successful. Behn's portrait of the courtesan Angellica is laced with irony. Against her will and better judgment, Angellica finds herself falling in love with Willmore. When she takes Willmore as a lover without demanding from him the usual thousand crowns, her handmaid Moretta watches in horror, realizing that her mistress is giving away something she would normally sell at a dear price. Angellica is smitten by Willmore — just as Hellena is smitten by the same rover — but once Willmore enjoys Angellica's pleasures, he dismisses her from his mind. Angellica the courtesan knows that this is the way men relate to women. But Angellica the woman, who gave Willmore her "virgin heart," is as deceived as any woman could be.

Hellena, promised to the church as a nun by her father, begins the play revealing her plans to avoid the convent at all costs. Her brother Pedro does not say so, but he seems to expect that when she is in the convent he will have access to the three hundred thousand crowns her uncle has bequeathed her. Pedro attempts to force Hellena to "marry" the church in the same way that he attempts to force Florinda to marry a man she does not love. Neither sister will have any of it.

The play centers more on the success of Florinda and Hellena than it does on Belvile or Willmore. Hellena, by virtue of her wit — which is equal to Willmore's — and her understanding of social realities, forces Willmore to submit to her will. He is all for making love, but she demands that Hymen, the god of marriage, be invoked before their lovemaking. When he tells her that she should be content with love and not demand marriage, she replies, "What shall I get? A cradle full of noise and mischief, with a pack of repentance at my back?" She is more than his match. The play ends with Florinda, Hellena, and Valeria all winning the husbands of their choice on their own terms.

The Rover; or, The Banished Cavaliers in Performance

King Charles II attended the March 24, 1677, production of *The Rover*, and successive royal performances were commanded before different monarchs in 1724 and 1729. Some seventy performances of the play took place between 1700 and 1725, and even more were recorded between 1726 and 1760. However, after 1790 the play was not produced for many decades.

Today's productions indicate a modern understanding of the play's feminist themes and its subtle wit-play between the sexes. The Folger Theater Group in Washington, D.C., produced the work in 1982, playing it broadly for its humor. Critics praised the play for its vitality but complained that the production overdid the "business" — stage gestures, movement, and action — and did not clearly deliver the lines. Christopher Reeve played Willmore in the Williamstown Theater production in 1987, with Kate Burton as Florinda. The director, John Rubinstein, moved the setting from Naples to the West Indies. One of the most interesting, although not wholly satisfying, productions was in 1986 by the Royal Shakespeare Company. Jeremy Irons played Willmore and Imogen Stubbs played Hellena. The director, John Barton, adapted the text using the earlier source play *Thomaso; or, The Wanderer* by Thomas Killigrew. Critics of the Royal Shakespeare production were struck by the modernity of Behn's play.

Aphra Behn (1640–1689)

THE ROVER; OR, THE BANISHED CAVALIERS   *1677*

PROLOGUE

Wits, like physicians, never can agree,
When of a different society.
And Rabel's drops° were never more cried down
By all the learned doctors of the town,
5   Than a new play whose author is unknown.
Nor can those doctors with more malice sue
(And powerful purses) the dissenting few,
Than those, with an insulting pride, do rail
At all who are not of their own cabal.°
10   If a young poet hit your humor right,
You judge him then out of revenge and spite.
So amongst men there are ridiculous elves,
Who monkeys hate for being too like themselves.
So that the reason of the grand debate
15   Why wit so oft is damned when good plays take,
Is that you censure as you love, or hate.
      Thus like a learned conclave poets sit,
Catholic° judges both of sense and wit,
And damn or save as they themselves think fit.
20   Yet those who to others' faults are so severe,
Are not so perfect but themselves may err.
Some write correct, indeed, but then the whole
(Bating° their own dull stuff i'th' play) is stole:

As bees do suck from flowers their honeydew,
So they rob others striving to please you.   25
      Some write their characters genteel and fine,
But then they do so toil for every line,
That what to you does easy seem, and plain,
Is the hard issue of their laboring brain.
And some th' effects of all their pains, we see,   30
Is but to mimic good extempore.°
Others, by long converse about the town,
Have wit enough to write a lewd lampoon,
But their chief skill lies in a bawdy song.
In short, the only wit that's now in fashion,   35
Is but the gleanings of good conversation.
As for the author of this coming play,
I asked him what he thought fit I should say
In thanks for your good company today:
He called me fool, and said it was well known   40
You came not here for our sakes, but your own.
New plays are stuffed with wits, and with
      deboches,°
That crowd and sweat like cits° in May-Day°
      coaches.°

WRITTEN BY A PERSON OF QUALITY

---

3. **Rabel's drops:** A patent medicine.   9. **cabal:** A small, secret political group.   18. **Catholic:** Having broad tastes or interests.   23. **Bating:** Leaving out.

31. **extempore:** A performance given without a script or rehearsal.   42. **deboches:** Orgies, debauches.   43. **cits:** Residents of cities.   **May-Day:** May 1, celebrated as a spring festival.   **coaches:** Carriages on parade during a May Day celebration.

The Actors' Names

[Men]
DON ANTONIO, *the Viceroy's son*
DON PEDRO, *a noble Spaniard, his friend*
BELVILE, *an English colonel in love with Florinda*
WILLMORE, *the Rover*
FREDERICK, *an English gentleman, and friend to Belvile and Blunt*
BLUNT, *an English country gentleman*
STEPHANO, *servant to Don Pedro*
PHILIPPO, *Lucetta's gallant*
SANCHO, *pimp to Lucetta*
BISKEY *and* SEBASTIAN, *two bravos° to Angellica*
OFFICER *and* SOLDIERS
[DIEGO,] *Page to Don Antonio*

[Women]
FLORINDA, *sister to Don Pedro*
HELLENA, *a gay young woman designed for a nun, and sister to Florinda*
VALERIA, *a kinswoman to Florinda*
ANGELLICA BIANCA, *a famous courtesan*
MORETTA, *her woman*
CALLIS, *governess to Florinda and Hellena*
LUCETTA, *a jilting wench*
SERVANTS, *other* MASQUERADERS, MEN *and* WOMEN

The Scene: *Naples, in Carnival time.*

ACT I • *Scene I*

(*A Chamber. Enter Florinda and Hellena.*)

FLORINDA: What an impertinent thing is a young girl bred in a nunnery! How full of questions! Prithee no more, Hellena; I have told thee more than thou understand'st already.

5 HELLENA: The more's my grief. I would fain know as much as you, which makes me so inquisitive; nor is't enough I know you're a lover, unless you tell me too who 'tis you sigh for.

FLORINDA: When you're a lover I'll think you fit for a
10 secret of that nature.

HELLENA: 'Tis true, I never was a lover yet, but I begin to have a shrewd guess what 'tis to be so, and fancy it very pretty to sigh, and sing, and blush, and wish, and dream and wish, and long and wish
15 to see the man, and when I do, look pale and tremble, just as you did when my brother brought

home the fine English colonel to see you. What do you call him? Don Belvile?

FLORINDA: Fie, Hellena.

HELLENA: That blush betrays you. I am sure 'tis so. Or 20 is it Don Antonio the Viceroy's son? Or perhaps the rich old Don Vincentio, whom my father designs you for a husband? Why do you blush again?

FLORINDA: With indignation; and how near soever my father thinks I am to marrying that hated object, I 25 shall let him see I understand better what's due to my beauty, birth, and fortune, and more to my soul, than to obey those unjust commands.

HELLENA: Now hang me, if I don't love thee for that dear disobedience. I love mischief strangely, as 30 most of our sex do who are come to love nothing else. But tell me, dear Florinda, don't you love that fine *Anglese?°* For I vow, next to loving him myself, 'twill please me most that you do so, for he is so gay and so handsome. 35

FLORINDA: Hellena, a maid designed for a nun ought not to be so curious in a discourse of love.

HELLENA: And dost thou think that ever I'll be a nun? Or at least till I'm so old I'm fit for nothing else? Faith no, sister; and that which makes me long to 40 know whether you love Belvile, is because I hope he has some mad companion or other that will spoil my devotion. Nay, I'm resolved to provide myself this Carnival, if there be e'er a handsome proper fellow of my humor above ground,° though I 45 ask first.

FLORINDA: Prithee be not so wild.

HELLENA: Now you have provided yourself of a man you take no care of poor me. Prithee tell me, what dost thou see about me that is unfit for love? Have 50 I not a world of youth? A humor gay? A beauty passable? A vigor desirable? Well shaped? Clean limbed? Sweet breathed? And sense enough to know how all these ought to be employed to the best advantage? Yes, I do and will; therefore lay 55 aside your hopes of my fortune by my being a devote,° and tell me how you came acquainted with this Belvile. For I perceive you knew him before he came to Naples.

FLORINDA: Yes, I knew him at the siege of Pamplona; 60 he was then a colonel of French horse,° who when the town was ransacked, nobly treated my brother and myself, preserving us from all insolences. And I must own, besides great obligations, I have I know not what that pleads kindly for him about 65 my heart, and will suffer no other to enter. But see, my brother.

33. *Anglese*: The English colonel Belvile.   45. **above ground:** In the real world (i.e., outside the convent).   57. **devote:** Nun.   61. **of French horse:** In the French cavalry.

[The Actors' Names] bravos: Villains, adventurers.

(*Enter Don Pedro, Stephano with a masking habit,°
and Callis.*)

PEDRO: Good morrow, sister. Pray when saw you your
lover Don Vincentio?

70 FLORINDA: I know not, sir. Callis, when was he here?
For I consider it so little I know not when it was.

PEDRO: I have a command from my father here to tell
you you ought not to despise him, a man of so vast
a fortune, and such a passion for you. —
75 Stephano, my things.

(*Puts on his masking habit.*)

FLORINDA: A passion for me? 'Tis more than e'er I
saw, or he had a desire should be known. I hate
Vincentio, sir, and I would not have a man so dear
to me as my brother follow the ill customs of our
80 country and make a slave of his sister. And, sir, my
father's will I'm sure you may divert.

PEDRO: I know not how dear I am to you, but I wish
only to be ranked in your esteem equal with the
English colonel Belvile. Why do you frown and
85 blush? Is there any guilt belongs to the name of
that cavalier?

FLORINDA: I'll not deny I value Belvile. When I was
exposed to such dangers as the licensed lust of
common soldiers threatened when rage and con-
90 quest flew through the city, then Belvile, this criminal for my sake, threw himself into all dangers to
save my honor. And will you not allow him my esteem?

PEDRO: Yes, pay him what you will in honor, but you
95 must consider Don Vincentio's fortune, and the
jointure° he'll make you.

FLORINDA: Let him consider my youth, beauty, and
fortune, which ought not to be thrown away on
his age and jointure.

100 PEDRO: 'Tis true, he's not so young and fine a gentleman as that Belvile. But what jewels will that cavalier present you with? Those of his eyes and heart?

HELLENA: And are not those better than any Don Vincentio has brought from the Indies?

105 PEDRO: Why, how now! Has your nunnery breeding
taught you to understand the value of hearts and
eyes?

HELLENA: Better than to believe Vincentio's deserve
value from any woman. He may perhaps increase
110 her bags, but not her family.°

PEDRO: This is fine! Go! Up to your devotion! You are
not designed for the conversation of lovers.

HELLENA (*aside*): Nor saints yet a while, I hope. — Is't
not enough you make a nun of me, but you must
cast my sister away too, exposing her to a worse 115
confinement than a religious life?

PEDRO: The girl's mad! It is a confinement to be carried into the country to an ancient villa belonging
to the family of the Vincentios these five hundred
years, and have no other prospect than that pleas- 120
ing one of seeing all her own that meets her eyes: a
fine air, large fields, and gardens where she may
walk and gather flowers?

HELLENA: When, by moonlight? For I am sure she
dares not encounter with the heat of the sun; that 125
were a task only for Don Vincentio and his Indian
breeding, who loves it in the dog days.° And if
these be her daily divertissements,° what are those
of the night? To lie in a wide moth-eaten bed-
chamber with furniture in fashion in the reign of 130
King Sancho the First;° the bed, that which his
forefathers lived and died in.

PEDRO: Very well.

HELLENA: This apartment, new furbrushed° and fitted
out for the young wife, he out of freedom makes 135
his dressing room; and being a frugal and a jealous
coxcomb,° instead of a valet to uncase° his feeble
carcass, he desires you to do that office. Signs of
favor, I'll assure you, and such as you must not
hope for unless your woman be out of the way. 140

PEDRO: Have you done yet?

HELLENA: That honor being past, the giant stretches
itself, yawns and sighs a belch or two loud as a
musket, throws himself into bed, and expects you
in his foul sheets; and ere you can get yourself un- 145
dressed, calls you with a snore or two. And are not
these fine blessings to a young lady?

PEDRO: Have you done yet?

HELLENA: And this man you must kiss, nay you must
kiss none but him too, and nuzzle through his beard 150
to find his lips. And this you must submit to for
threescore years, and all for a jointure.

PEDRO: For all your character of Don Vincentio, she is
as like to marry him as she was before.

HELLENA: Marry Don Vincentio! Hang me, such a 155
wedlock would be worse than adultery with another man. I had rather see her in the *Hostel de
Dieu,°* to waste her youth there in vows, and be a
handmaid to lazars° and cripples, than to lose it in
such a marriage. 160

---

67. [S.D.] *masking habit*: Costume for the Carnival mas-
querades.   96. jointure: An estate given by a husband to a
wife in lieu of her dowry.   109–110. increase her bags . . .
family: Give her material goods but not enhance her family's
standing.

127. dog days: The hot days of summer.   128. divertissements: Amusements.   131. King Sancho the First: King of
Spain, probably Sancho I of Castile (970–1035).   134. new
furbrushed: Refurbished.   137. coxcomb: Conceited person, fop.   uncase: Disrobe.   157–58. *Hostel de Dieu*:
Hospital operated by a group of nuns.   159. lazars: Lepers.

PEDRO: You have considered, sister, that Belvile has no fortune to bring you to; banished his country, despised at home, and pitied abroad.

HELLENA: What then? The Viceroy's son is better than
165   that old Sir Fifty. Don Vincentio! Don Indian! He thinks he's trading to Gambo° still, and would barter himself — that bell and bauble — for your youth and fortune.

PEDRO: Callis, take her hence and lock her up all this
170   Carnival, and at Lent she shall begin her everlasting penance in a monastery.

HELLENA: I care not; I had rather be a nun than be obliged to marry as you would have me if I were designed for't.

175 PEDRO: Do not fear the blessing of that choice. You shall be a nun.

HELLENA (aside): Shall I so? You may chance to be mistaken in my way of devotion. A nun! Yes, I am like to make a fine nun! I have an excellent humor
180   for a grate!° No, I'll have a saint of my own to pray to shortly, if I like any that dares venture on me.

PEDRO: Callis, make it your business to watch this wildcat. — As for you, Florinda, I've only tried
185   you all this while and urged my father's will; but mine is that you would love Antonio: He is brave and young, and all that can complete the happiness of a gallant maid. This absence of my father will give us opportunity to free you from Vincentio by
190   marrying here, which you must do tomorrow.

FLORINDA: Tomorrow!

PEDRO: Tomorrow, or 'twill be too late. 'Tis not my friendship to Antonio which makes me urge this, but love to thee and hatred to Vincentio; therefore
195   resolve upon tomorrow.

FLORINDA: Sir, I shall strive to do as shall become your sister.

PEDRO: I'll both believe and trust you. Adieu.
                        (Exeunt° Pedro and Stephano.)

HELLENA: As becomes his sister! That is to be as re-
200   solved your way as he is his.
                        (Hellena goes to Callis.)

FLORINDA: I ne'er till now perceived my ruin near. I've no defense against Antonio's love, For he has all the advantages of nature, The moving arguments of youth and fortune.

205 HELLENA: But hark you, Callis, you will not be so cruel to lock me up indeed, will you?

CALLIS: I must obey the commands I have. Besides, do you consider what a life you are going to lead?

HELLENA: Yes, Callis, that of a nun; and till then I'll

be indebted a world of prayers to you if you'll let 210 me now see what I never did, the divertissements of a Carnival.

CALLIS: What, go in masquerade? 'Twill be a fine farewell to the world, I take it. Pray what would you do there? 215

HELLENA: That which all the world does, as I am told: Be as mad as the rest and take all innocent freedoms. Sister, you'll go too, will you not? Come, prithee be not sad. We'll outwit twenty brothers if you'll be ruled by me. Come, put off this dull hu- 220 mor with your clothes, and assume one as gay and as fantastic as the dress my cousin Valeria and I have provided, and let's ramble.

FLORINDA: Callis, will you give us leave to go?

CALLIS (aside): I have a youthful itch of going 225 myself. — Madam, if I thought your brother might not know it, and I might wait on you; for by my troth I'll not trust young girls alone.

FLORINDA: Thou seest my brother's gone already, and thou shalt attend and watch us. 230

(Enter Stephano.)

STEPHANO: Madam, the habits are come, and your cousin Valeria is dressed and stays for you.

FLORINDA (aside): 'Tis well. I'll write a note, and if I chance to see Belvile and want an opportunity to speak to him, that shall let him know what I've re- 235 solved in favor of him.

HELLENA: Come, let's in and dress us.   (Exeunt.)

Scene II

(*A long street. Enter Belvile, melancholy; Blunt and Frederick.*)

FREDERICK: Why, what the devil ails the colonel, in a time when all the world is gay to look like mere Lent thus? Hadst thou been long enough in Naples to have been in love, I should have sworn some such judgment had befallen thee. 5

BELVILE: No, I have made no new amours since I came to Naples.

FREDERICK: You have left none behind you in Paris?

BELVILE: Neither.

FREDERICK: I cannot divine the cause then, unless the 10 old cause, the want of money.

BLUNT: And another old cause, the want of a wench. Would not that revive you?

BELVILE: You are mistaken, Ned.

BLUNT: Nay, 'adsheartlikins,° then thou'rt past cure. 15

---

166. **Gambo:** British colony in West Africa.   **180. grate:** The grille covering the windows in a convent (i.e., the convent).   **198.** [S.D.] *Exeunt:* Latin for "they go out."

15. **'adsheartlikins:** Expostulation equivalent to "As God loves us."

FREDERICK: I have found it out: Thou hast renewed thy
acquaintance with the lady that cost thee so many
sighs at the siege of Pamplona — pox on't, what
d'ye call her — her brother's a noble Spaniard,
nephew to the dead general. Florinda. Ay, Florinda.
And will nothing serve thy turn but that damned
virtuous woman, whom on my conscience thou
lov'st in spite too, because thou seest little or no
possibility of gaining her.

BELVILE: Thou art mistaken; I have int'rest enough in
that lovely virgin's heart to make me proud and
vain, were it not abated by the severity of a
brother, who, perceiving my happiness —

FREDERICK: Has civilly forbid thee the house?

BELVILE: 'Tis so, to make way for a powerful rival, the
Viceroy's son, who has the advantage of me in being a man of fortune, a Spaniard, and her brother's
friend; which gives him liberty to make his court,
whilst I have recourse only to letters and distant
looks from her window, which are as soft and kind
as those which heaven sends down on penitents.

BLUNT: Heyday! 'Adsheartlikins, simile! By this light
the man is quite spoiled. Fred, what the devil are
we made of that we cannot be thus concerned for
a wench? 'Adsheartlikins, our Cupids are like the
cooks of the camp: They can roast or boil a
woman, but they have none of the fine tricks to set
'em off; no hogoes° to make the sauce pleasant and
the stomach sharp.

FREDERICK: I dare swear I have had a hundred as
young, kind, and handsome as this Florinda; and
dogs eat me if they were not as troublesome to me
i'th' morning as they were welcome o'er night.

BLUNT: And yet I warrant he would not touch another
woman if he might have her for nothing.

BELVILE: That's thy joy, a cheap whore.

BLUNT: Why, 'adsheartlikins, I love a frank soul.
When did you ever hear of an honest woman that
took a man's money? I warrant 'em good ones. But
gentlemen, you may be free; you have been kept so
poor with parliaments and protectors that the little
stock you have is not worth preserving. But I
thank my stars I had more grace than to forfeit my
estate by cavaliering.

BELVILE: Methinks only following the court should be
sufficient to entitle 'em to that.

BLUNT: 'Adsheartlikins, they know I follow it to do it
no good, unless they pick a hole in my coat for
lending you money now and then, which is a
greater crime to my conscience, gentlemen, than to
the commonwealth.

(*Enter Willmore.*)

WILLMORE: Ha! Dear Belvile! Noble colonel!

BELVILE: Willmore! Welcome ashore, my dear rover!
What happy wind blew us this good fortune?

WILLMORE: Let me salute my dear Fred, and then
command me. — How is't, honest lad?

FREDERICK: Fair, sir, the old compliment, infinitely the
better to see my dear mad Willmore again. Prithee,
why camest thou ashore? And where's the Prince?°

WILLMORE: He's well, and reigns still lord of the
wat'ry element. I must aboard again within a day
or two, and my business ashore was only to enjoy
myself a little this Carnival.

BELVILE: Pray know our new friend, sir; he's but bashful, a raw traveler, but honest, stout, and one of us.
(*Embraces Blunt.*)

WILLMORE: That you esteem him gives him an int'rest
here.

BLUNT: Your servant, sir.

WILLMORE: But well, faith, I'm glad to meet you again
in a warm climate, where the kind sun has its godlike power still over the wine and women. Love
and mirth are my business in Naples, and if I mistake not the place, here's an excellent market for
chapmen° of my humor.

BELVILE: See, here be those kind merchants of love
you look for.

(*Enter several men in masking habits, some playing
on music, others dancing after; women dressed like
courtesans, with papers pinned on their breasts, and
baskets of flowers in their hands.*)

BLUNT: 'Adsheartlikins, what have we here?

FREDERICK: Now the game begins.

WILLMORE: Fine pretty creatures! May a stranger
have leave to look and love? What's here? "Roses
for every month"?   (*Reads the papers.*)

BLUNT: Roses for every month? What means that?

BELVILE: They are, or would have you think they're
courtesans, who here in Naples are to be hired by
the month.

WILLMORE: Kind and obliging to inform us, pray
where do these roses grow? I would fain plant
some of 'em in a bed of mine.

WOMAN: Beware such roses, sir.

WILLMORE: A pox of fear: I'll be baked with thee between a pair of sheets, and that's thy proper still; so
I might but strew such roses over me and under me.
Fair one, would you would give me leave to gather
at your bush this idle month; I would go near to
make somebody smell of it all the year after.

___

44. **hogoes:** Relishes.

75. **Prince:** Charles II, in exile on the Continent during the
reign of Cromwell.   91. **chapmen:** Merchants, in this case
merchants of love.

BELVILE: And thou hast need of such a remedy, for
115 thou stink'st of tar and ropes' ends like a dock or
pesthouse.
(The Woman puts herself into the hands of a
man and exeunt.)
WILLMORE: Nay, nay, you shall not leave me so.
BELVILE: By all means use no violence here.
WILLMORE: Death! Just as I was going to be
120 damnably in love, to have her led off! I could
pluck that rose out of his hand, and even kiss the
bed the bush grew in.
FREDERICK: No friend to love like a long voyage at
sea.
125 BLUNT: Except a nunnery, Fred.
WILLMORE: Death! But will they not be kind? Quickly
be kind? Thou know'st I'm no tame sigher, but a
rampant lion of the forest.

(Advances from the farther end of the scenes two men
dressed all over with horns° of several sorts, making
grimaces at one another, with papers pinned on their
backs.)

BELVILE: Oh the fantastical rogues, how they're
130 dressed! 'Tis a satire against the whole sex.
WILLMORE: Is this a fruit that grows in this warm
country?
BELVILE: Yes, 'tis pretty to see these Italians start,
swell, and stab at the word cuckold, and yet stum-
135 ble at horns on every threshold.
WILLMORE: See what's on their back. *(Reads.)* "Flowers of every night." Ah, rogue! And more sweet
than roses of every month! This is a gardener of
Adam's own breeding.
(They dance.)
140 BELVILE: What think you of these grave people? Is a
wake in Essex half so mad or extravagant?
WILLMORE: I like their sober grave way; 'tis a kind of
legal authorized fornication, where the men are
not chid° for't, nor the women despised, as
145 amongst our dull English. Even the monsieurs°
want that part of good manners.
BELVILE: But here in Italy, a monsieur is the humblest
best-bred gentleman: Duels are so baffled by
bravos that an age shows not one but between a
150 Frenchman and a hangman, who is as much too
hard for him on the Piazza as they are for a Dutchman on the New Bridge. But see, another crew.

(Enter Florinda, Hellena, and Valeria, dressed like
gypsies; Callis and Stephano, Lucetta, Philippo, and
Sancho in masquerade.)

HELLENA: Sister, there's your Englishman, and with
him a handsome proper fellow. I'll to him, and instead of telling him his fortune, try my own.   155
WILLMORE: Gypsies, on my life. Sure these will prattle
if a man cross their hands.° *(Goes to Hellena.)* —
Dear, pretty, and, I hope, young devil, will you tell
an amorous stranger what luck he's like to have?
HELLENA: Have a care how you venture with me, sir,   160
lest I pick your pocket, which will more vex your
English humor than an Italian fortune will please
you.
WILLMORE: How the devil cam'st thou to know my
country and humor?   165
HELLENA: The first I guess by a certain forward impudence, which does not displease me at this time;
and the loss of your money will vex you because I
hope you have but very little to lose.
WILLMORE: Egad, child, thou'rt i'th' right; it is so little   170
I dare not offer it thee for a kindness. But cannot
you divine what other things of more value I have
about me that I would more willingly part with?
HELLENA: Indeed no, that's the business of a witch,   175
and I am but a gypsy yet. Yet without looking in
your hand, I have a parlous° guess 'tis some foolish heart you mean, an inconstant English heart, as
little worth stealing as your purse.
WILLMORE: Nay, then thou dost deal with the devil,   180
that's certain. Thou hast guessed as right as if thou
hadst been one of that number it has languished
for. I find you'll be better acquainted with it, nor
can you take it in a better time; for I am come
from sea, child, and Venus not being propitious to   185
me in her own element,° I have a world of love in
store. Would you would be good-natured and take
some on't° off my hands.
HELLENA: Why, I could be inclined that way, but for a
foolish vow I am going to make to die a maid.   190
WILLMORE: Then thou art damned without redemption, and as I am a good Christian, I ought in charity to divert so wicked a design. Therefore prithee,
dear creature, let me know quickly when and
where I shall begin to set a helping hand to so   195
good a work.
HELLENA: If you should prevail with my tender heart,
as I begin to fear you will, for you have horrible
loving eyes, there will be difficulty in't that you'll
hardly undergo for my sake.   200

---

128. [S.D.] *horns:* Emblem of the cuckold, a man whose wife
is unfaithful.   144. *chid:* Chided, reproached.   145.
monsieurs: Frenchmen.

157. **cross their hands:** cross their hands with silver: pay
them to tell his fortune.   177. **parlous:** Dangerously cunning, clever (from *perilous*).   185–86. **Venus . . . element:**
Venus, the goddess of love, was supposedly born from the
foam of the sea.   188. **on't:** Of it.

WILLMORE: Faith, child, I have been bred in dangers, and wear a sword that has been employed in a worse cause than for a handsome kind woman. Name the danger; let it be anything but a long
205   siege, and I'll undertake it.
HELLENA: Can you storm?
WILLMORE: Oh, most furiously.
HELLENA: What think you of a nunnery wall? For he that wins me must gain that first.
210   WILLMORE: A nun! Oh, now I love thee for't! There's no sinner like a young saint. Nay, now there's no denying me; the old law had no curse to a woman like dying a maid: Witness Jeptha's daughter.°
HELLENA: A very good text this, if well handled; and
215   I perceive, Father Captain, you would impose no severe penance on her who were inclined to console herself before she took orders.°
WILLMORE: If she be young and handsome.
HELLENA: Ay, there's it. But if she be not —
220   WILLMORE: By this hand, child, I have an implicit faith, and dare venture on thee with all faults. Besides, 'tis more meritorious to leave the world when thou hast tasted and proved the pleasure on't. Then 'twill be a virtue in thee, which now
225   will be pure ignorance.
HELLENA: I perceive, good Father Captain, you design only to make me fit for heaven. But if, on the contrary, you should quite divert me from it, and bring me back to the world again, I should have a
230   new man to seek, I find. And what a grief that will be; for when I begin, I fancy I shall love like anything; I never tried yet.
WILLMORE: Egad, and that's kind! Prithee, dear creature, give me credit for a heart, for faith, I'm a very
235   honest fellow. Oh, I long to come first to the banquet of love! And such a swinging appetite I bring. Oh, I'm impatient. Thy lodging, sweetheart, thy lodging, or I'm a dead man!
HELLENA: Why must we be either guilty of fornication
240   or murder if we converse with you men? And is there no difference between leave to love me, and leave to lie with me?
WILLMORE: Faith, child, they were made to go together.
245   LUCETTA (pointing to Blunt): Are you sure this is the man?

213. **Jeptha's daughter:** To fulfill a vow, Jeptha sacrificed his only child, a virgin daughter, whom he allowed to go off to the mountains for two months to "bewail" her virginity before he killed her. "And it became a custom in Israel that the daughters of Israel went year by year to lament the daughter of Jeptha . . . four days in the year" (Judges 11:39–40). 217. **took orders:** Entered the convent.

SANCHO: When did I mistake your game?
LUCETTA: This is a stranger, I know by his gazing; if he be brisk he'll venture to follow me, and then, if I understand my trade, he's mine. He's English, 250 too, and they say that's a sort of good-natured loving people, and have generally so kind an opinion of themselves that a woman with any wit may flatter 'em into any sort of fool she pleases.

(She often passes by Blunt and gazes on him; he struts and cocks, and walks and gazes on her.)

BLUNT: 'Tis so, she is taken; I have beauties which my 255 false glass° at home did not discover.
FLORINDA (aside): This woman watches me so, I shall get no opportunity to discover myself to him, and so miss the intent of my coming. — [To Belvile.] But as I was saying, sir, by this line you should be 260 a lover.   (Looking in his hand.)
BELVILE: I thought how right you guessed: All men are in love, or pretend to be so. Come, let me go; I'm weary of this fooling.   (Walks away.)
FLORINDA: I will not, sir, till you have confessed 265 whether the passion that you have vowed Florinda be true or false.
(She holds him; he strives to get from her.)
BELVILE: Florinda!   (Turns quick toward her.)
FLORINDA: Softly.
BELVILE: Thou hast nam'd one will fix me here forever. 270
FLORINDA: She'll be disappointed then, who expects you this night at the garden gate. And if you fail not, as — (Looks on Callis, who observes 'em.) Let me see the other hand — you will go near to do, she vows to die or make you happy. 275
BELVILE: What canst thou mean?
FLORINDA: That which I say. Farewell.
                    (Offers to go.)
BELVILE: O charming sibyl,° stay; complete that joy which as it is will turn into distraction! Where must I be? At the garden gate? I know it. At night, 280 you say? I'll sooner forfeit heaven than disobey.

(Enter Don Pedro and other maskers, and pass over the stage.)

CALLIS: Madam, your brother's here.
FLORINDA: Take this to instruct you farther.
                    (Gives him a letter, and goes off.)
FREDERICK: Have a care, sir, what you promise; this may be a trap laid by her brother to ruin you. 285
BELVILE: Do not disturb my happiness with doubts.
                    (Opens the letter.)

256. **false glass:** Lying mirror.   278. **sibyl:** A female prophet; fortune-teller.

WILLMORE: My dear pretty creature, a thousand blessings on thee! Still in this habit, you say? And after dinner at this place?

290 HELLENA: Yes, if you will swear to keep your heart and not bestow it between this and that.

WILLMORE: By all the little gods of love, I swear; I'll leave it with you, and if you run away with it, those deities of justice will revenge me.

(*Exeunt all the women [except Lucetta].*)

295 FREDERICK: Do you know the hand?

BELVILE: 'Tis Florinda's.
All blessings fall upon the virtuous maid.

FREDERICK: Nay, no idolatry; a sober sacrifice I'll allow you.

300 BELVILE: Oh friends, the welcom'st news! The softest letter! Nay, you shall all see it. And could you now be serious, I might be made the happiest man the sun shines on!

WILLMORE: The reason of this mighty joy?

305 BELVILE: See how kindly she invites me to deliver her from the threatened violence of her brother. Will you not assist me?

WILLMORE: I know not what thou mean'st, but I'll make one at any mischief where a woman's con-
310 cerned. But she'll be grateful to us for the favor, will she not?

BELVILE: How mean you?

WILLMORE: How should I mean? Thou know'st there's but one way for a woman to oblige me.

315 BELVILE: Do not profane; the maid is nicely virtuous.

WILLMORE: Who, pox, then she's fit for nothing but a husband. Let her e'en go, colonel.

FREDERICK: Peace, she's the colonel's mistress, sir.

WILLMORE: Let her be the devil; if she be thy mistress,
320 I'll serve her. Name the way.

BELVILE: Read here this postscript.

(*Gives him a letter.*)

WILLMORE (*reads*): "At ten at night, at the garden gate, of which, if I cannot get the key, I will contrive a way over the wall. Come attended with a friend or
325 two." — Kind heart, if we three cannot weave a string to let her down a garden wall, 'twere pity but the hangman wove one for us all.

FREDERICK: Let her alone for that; your woman's wit, your fair kind woman, will outtrick a broker
330 or a Jew, and contrive like a Jesuit° in chains. But see, Ned Blunt is stolen out after the lure of a damsel.

(*Exeunt Blunt and Lucetta.*)

BELVILE: So, he'll scarce find his way home again unless we get him cried by the bellman in the market

place. And 'twould sound prettily: "A lost English 335 boy of thirty."

FREDERICK: I hope 'tis some common crafty sinner, one that will fit him. It may be she'll sell him for Peru:° The rogue's sturdy, and would work well in a mine. At least I hope she'll dress him for our 340 mirth, cheat him of all, then have him well-favoredly banged, and turned out at midnight.

WILLMORE: Prithee what humor is he of, that you wish him so well?

BELVILE: Why, of an English elder brother's humor: 345 educated in a nursery, with a maid to tend him till fifteen, and lies with his grandmother till he's of age; one that knows no pleasure beyond riding to the next fair, or going up to London with his right worshipful father in parliament time, wearing gay 350 clothes, or making honorable love to his lady mother's laundry maid; gets drunk at a hunting match, and ten to one then gives some proofs of his prowess. A pox upon him, he's our banker, and has all our cash about him; and if he fail, we are all broke. 355

FREDERICK: Oh, let him alone for that matter; he's of a damned stingy quality that will secure our stock. I know not in what danger it were indeed if the jilt should pretend she's in love with him, for 'tis a kind believing coxcomb; otherwise, if he part with 360 more than a piece of eight,° geld° him — for which offer he may chance to be beaten if she be a whore of the first rank.

BELVILE: Nay, the rogue will not be easily beaten; he's stout enough. Perhaps if they talk beyond his ca- 365 pacity he may chance to exercise his courage upon some of them, else I'm sure they'll find it as diffi-cult to beat as to please him.

WILLMORE: 'Tis a lucky devil to light upon so kind a wench! 370

FREDERICK: Thou hadst a great deal of talk with thy little gypsy; couldst thou do no good upon her? For mine was hardhearted.

WILLMORE: Hang her, she was some damned honest person of quality, I'm sure, she was so very free and 375 witty. If her face be but answerable to her wit and humor, I would be bound to constancy this month to gain her. In the meantime, have you made no kind acquaintance since you came to town? You do not use to be honest° so long, gentlemen. 380

FREDERICK: Faith, love has kept us honest: We have been all fir'd with a beauty newly come to town, the famous Paduana° Angellica Bianca.

---

330. **Jew . . . Jesuit:** Anti-Semitic and anti-Catholic attitudes of the time portrayed Jews and Jesuits as cunning and not worthy of trust.

338–39. **sell him for Peru:** Sell him as a slave.   361. **piece of eight:** Spanish money.   **geld:** Castrate.   380. **honest:** Sexually inactive.   383. **Paduana:** Angellica was born in Padua, Italy.

WILLMORE: What, the mistress of the dead Spanish
385   general?
BELVILE: Yes, she's now the only ador'd beauty of all
      the youth in Naples, who put on all their charms
      to appear lovely in her sight: Their coaches, liver-
      ies, and themselves all gay as on a monarch's birth-
390   day to attract the eyes of this fair charmer, while
      she has the pleasure to behold all languish for her
      that see her.
FREDERICK: 'Tis pretty to see with how much love the
      men regard her, and how much envy the women.
395   WILLMORE: What gallant has she?
BELVILE: None; she's exposed to sale, and four days in
      the week she's yours, for so much a month.
WILLMORE: The very thought of it quenches all man-
      ner of fire in me. Yet prithee, let's see her.
400   BELVILE: Let's first to dinner, and after that we'll pass
      the day as you please. But at night ye must all be
      at my devotion.
WILLMORE: I will not fail you.   [Exeunt.]

ACT II • Scene I

(*The long street. Enter Belvile and Frederick in masking habits, and Willmore in his own clothes, with a
vizard° in his hand.*)

WILLMORE: But why thus disguised and muzzled?
BELVILE: Because whatever extravagances we commit
      in these faces, our own may not be obliged to an-
      swer 'em.
5   WILLMORE: I should have changed my eternal buff,°
      too; but no matter, my little gypsy would not have
      found me out then. For if she should change hers,
      it is impossible I should know her unless I should
      hear her prattle. A pox on't, I cannot get her out of
10   my head. Pray heaven, if ever I do see her again,
      she prove damnably ugly, that I may fortify myself
      against her tongue.
BELVILE: Have a care of love, for o' my conscience she
      was not of a quality to give thee any hopes.
15   WILLMORE: Pox on 'em, why do they draw a man in
      then? She has played with my heart so, that 'twill
      never lie still till I have met with some kind wench
      that will play the game out with me. Oh, for my
      arms full of soft, white, kind woman — such as I
20   fancy Angellica.
BELVILE: This is her house, if you were but in stock to

get admittance. They have not dined yet; I perceive
the picture is not out.°

(*Enter Blunt.*)

WILLMORE: I long to see the shadow of the fair sub-
      stance; a man may gaze on that for nothing.   25
BLUNT: Colonel, thy hand. And thine, Fred. I have
      been an ass, a deluded fool, a very coxcomb from
      my birth till this hour, and heartily repent my little
      faith.
BELVILE: What the devil's the matter with thee, Ned?   30
BLUNT: Oh, such a mistress, Fred! Such a girl!
WILLMORE: Ha! Where?
FREDERICK: Ay, where?
BLUNT: So fond, so amorous, so toying, and so fine!
      And all for sheer love, ye rogue! Oh, how she   35
      looked and kissed! And soothed my heart from my
      bosom! I cannot think I was awake, and yet me-
      thinks I see and feel her charms still. Fred, try if
      she have not left the taste of her balmy kisses upon
      my lips.   (*Kisses him.*)   40
BELVILE: Ha! Ha! Ha!
WILLMORE: Death, man, where is she?
BLUNT: What a dog was I to stay in dull England so
      long! How have I laughed at the colonel when he
      sighed for love! But now the little archer° has re-   45
      venged him! And by this one dart I can guess at all
      his joys, which then I took for fancies, mere
      dreams and fables. Well, I'm resolved to sell all in
      Essex and plant here forever.
BELVILE: What a blessing 'tis, thou hast a mistress thou   50
      dar'st boast of; for I know thy humor is rather to
      have a proclaimed clap than a secret amour.
WILLMORE: Dost know her name?
BLUNT: Her name? No, 'adsheartlikins. What care I
      for names? She's fair, young, brisk and kind, even   55
      to ravishment! And what a pox care I for knowing
      her by any other title?
WILLMORE: Didst give her anything?
BLUNT: Give her? Ha! Ha! Ha! Why, she's a person of
      quality. That's a good one! Give her? 'Adsheart-   60
      likins, dost think such creatures are to be bought?
      Or are we provided for such a purchase? Give her,
      quoth ye? Why, she presented me with this bracelet
      for the toy of a diamond I used to wear. No, gen-
      tlemen, Ned Blunt is not everybody. She expects   65
      me again tonight.
WILLMORE: Egad, that's well; we'll all go.
BLUNT: Not a soul! No, gentlemen, you are wits; I am
      a dull country rogue, I.

II, I. [S.D.] *vizard*: Face mask.   **5. buff:** Military coat made
of buff (leather).

23. picture is not out: Hanging her picture outside the house
is a sign that she is open for business. (See lines 117–18 later
in the scene.)   **45. little archer:** Cupid.

70   FREDERICK: Well, sir, for all your person of quality, I
        shall be very glad to understand your purse be se-
        cure; 'tis our whole estate at present, which we are
        loath to hazard in one bottom.° Come sir, unlade.
75   BLUNT: Take the necessary trifle useless now to me,
        that am beloved by such a gentlewoman. 'Ads-
        heartlikins, money! Here, take mine too.
      FREDERICK: No, keep that to be cozened,° that we
        may laugh.
80   WILLMORE: Cozened? Death! Would I could meet
        with one that would cozen me of all the love I
        could spare tonight.
      FREDERICK: Pox, 'tis some common whore, upon my
        life.
85   BLUNT: A whore? Yes, with such clothes, such jewels,
        such a house, such furniture, and so attended! A
        whore!
      BELVILE: Why yes, sir, they are whores, though they'll
        neither entertain you with drinking, swearing, or
90   bawdry; are whores in all those gay clothes and
        right° jewels; are whores with those great houses
        richly furnished with velvet beds, store of plate,°
        handsome attendance, and fine coaches; are
        whores, and errant° ones.
95   WILLMORE: Pox on't, where do these fine whores live?
      BELVILE: Where no rogues in office, ycleped° consta-
        bles, dare give 'em laws, nor the wine-inspired bul-
        lies of the town break their windows; yet they are
        whores though this Essex calf° believe 'em persons
100   of quality.
      BLUNT: 'Adsheartlikins, y'are all fools. There are
        things about this Essex calf that shall take with the
        ladies, beyond all your wit and parts. This shape
        and size, gentlemen, are not to be despised; my
105   waist, too, tolerably long, with other inviting signs
        that shall be nameless.
      WILLMORE: Egad, I believe he may have met with
        some person of quality that may be kind to him.
      BELVILE: Dost thou perceive any such tempting things
110   about him that should make a fine woman, and of
        quality, pick him out from all mankind to throw
        away her youth and beauty upon; nay, and her
        dear heart, too? No, no, Angellica has raised the
        price too high.
115   WILLMORE: May she languish for mankind till she die,
        and be damned for that one sin alone.

(*Enter two Bravos and hang up a great picture of Angellica's against the balcony, and two little ones at
each side of the door.*)

---

73. **hazard in one bottom:** Keep in one place, as in the hold
(bottom) of a ship.   78. **cozened:** Cheated.   91. **right:**
Real.   92. **plate:** Silverware.   94. **errant:** Unmitigated.
96. **ycleped:** Past participle of *clepe:* called.   99. **Essex calf:**
Derogatory term meaning "fool," referring to Essex, Eng-
land, Blunt's home.

      BELVILE: See there the fair sign to the inn where a man
        may lodge that's fool enough to give her price.
                        (*Willmore gazes on the picture.*)
      BLUNT: 'Adsheartlikins, gentlemen, what's this?
      BELVILE: A famous courtesan, that's to be sold.   120
      BLUNT: How? To be sold? Nay, then I have nothing to
        say to her. Sold? What impudence is practiced in
        this country; with what order and decency whor-
        ing's established here by virtue of the Inquisition!°
        Come, let's be gone; I'm sure we're no chapmen   125
        for this commodity.
      FREDERICK: Thou art none, I'm sure, unless thou
        couldst have her in thy bed at a price of a coach in
        the street.
      WILLMORE: How wondrous fair she is! A thousand   130
        crowns a month? By heaven, as many kingdoms
        were too little! A plague of this poverty, of which I
        ne'er complain but when it hinders my approach
        to beauty which virtue ne'er could purchase.
                        (*Turns from the picture.*)
      BLUNT: What's this? (*Reads.*) "A thousand crowns a   135
        month"! 'Adsheartlikins, here's a sum! Sure 'tis a
        mistake. — [*To one of the Bravos.*] Hark you,
        friend, does she take or give so much by the month?
      FREDERICK: A thousand crowns! Why, 'tis a portion
        for the Infanta!°   140
      BLUNT: Hark ye, friends, won't she trust?°
      BRAVO: This is a trade, sir, that cannot live by credit.

(*Enter Don Pedro in masquerade, followed by
Stephano.*)

      BELVILE: See, here's more company; let's walk off a
        while.
                        (*Exeunt English,° Pedro reads.*)
      PEDRO: Fetch me a thousand crowns; I never wished   145
        to buy this beauty at an easier rate. (*Passes off.*)

(*Enter Angellica and Moretta in the balcony, and
draw a silk curtain.*)

      ANGELLICA: Prithee, what said those fellows to thee?
      BRAVO: Madam, the first were admirers of beauty
        only, but no purchasers; they were merry with
        your price and picture, laughed at the sum, and so   150
        passed off.
      ANGELLICA: No matter, I'm not displeased with their
        rallying; their wonder feeds my vanity, and he that
        wishes but to buy gives me more pride than he that
        gives my price can make my pleasure.   155

---

124. **Inquisition:** The Spanish Inquisition (1478–1834)
forced prostitutes out of Spain and into neighboring countries.   139–40. **portion for the Infanta:** Dowry for the
Spanish princess.   141. **trust:** Extend credit for payment.
144. [S.D.] *English:* All the English characters.

Ann Reinking and Ed
Herrmann in the Williamstown
Theatre Festival's 1987
production of *The Rover*,
directed by John Rubinstein.

BRAVO: Madam, the last I knew through all his disguises to be Don Pedro, nephew to the general,
and who was with him in Pamplona.

ANGELLICA: Don Pedro? My old gallant's nephew?
When his uncle died he left him a vast sum of
money; it is he who was so in love with me at
Padua, and who used to make the general so jealous.

MORETTA: Is this he that used to prance before our
window, and take such care to show himself an
amorous ass? If I am not mistaken, he is the likeli-
est man to give your price.

ANGELLICA: The man is brave and generous, but of a
humor so uneasy and inconstant that the victory
over his heart is as soon lost as won; a slave that
can add little to the triumph of the conqueror. But
inconstancy's the sin of all mankind, therefore I'm
resolved that nothing but gold shall charm my
heart.

MORETTA: I'm glad on't; 'tis only interest that women
of our profession ought to consider, though I wonder what has kept you from that general disease of
our sex so long; I mean, that of being in love.

ANGELLICA: A kind but sullen star under which I had
the happiness to be born. Yet I have had no time
for love; the bravest and noblest of mankind have
purchased my favors at so dear a rate, as if no coin
but gold were current with our trade. But here's

185   Don Pedro again; fetch me my lute, for 'tis for him
    or Don Antonio the Viceroy's son that I have
    spread my nets.

(*Enter at one door Don Pedro, Stephano; Don Antonio and Diego [his page] at the other door, with people following him in masquerade, antically attired, some with music. They both go up to the picture.*)

ANTONIO: A thousand crowns! Had not the painter
    flattered her, I should not think it dear.

PEDRO: Flattered her? By heaven, he cannot. I have
190   seen the original, nor is there one charm here more
    than adorns her face and eyes; all this soft and
    sweet, with a certain languishing air that no artist
    can represent.

ANTONIO: What I heard of her beauty before had
195   fired my soul, but this confirmation of it has blown
    it to a flame.

PEDRO: Ha!

PAGE: Sir, I have known you throw away a thousand
    crowns on a worse face, and though y'are near
200   your marriage, you may venture a little love here;
    Florinda will not miss it.

PEDRO (*aside*): Ha! Florinda! Sure 'tis Antonio.

ANTONIO: Florinda! Name not those distant joys;
    there's not one thought of her will check my pas-
205   sion here.

PEDRO [*aside*]: Florinda scorned! (*A noise of a lute above.*) And all my hopes defeated of the posses-
    sion of Angellica! (*Antonio gazes up.*) Her injuries,
    by heaven, he shall not boast of!
                   (*Song to a lute above.*)

SONG
[*I*]
210   *When Damon first began to love*
    He languished in a soft desire,
    And knew not how the gods to move,
    To lessen or increase his fire.
    For Caelia in her charming eyes
215 *Wore all love's sweets, and all his cruelties.*

    II
    But as beneath a shade he lay,
    Weaving of flowers for Caelia's hair,
    She chanced to lead her flock that way,
    And saw the am'rous shepherd there.
220 *She gazed around upon the place,*
    And saw the grove, resembling night,
    To all the joys of love invite,
    Whilst guilty smiles and blushes dressed her face.
    At this the bashful youth all transport grew,
225 *And with kind force he taught the virgin how*
    To yield what all his sighs could never do.

(*Angellica throws open the curtains and bows to Antonio, who pulls off his vizard and bows and blows up kisses. Pedro, unseen, looks in's face. [The curtains close.]*)

ANTONIO: By heaven, she's charming fair!

PEDRO (*aside*): 'Tis he, the false Antonio!

ANTONIO (*to the Bravo*): Friend, where must I pay
    my off'ring of love?
    My thousand crowns I mean.   230

PEDRO: That off'ring I have designed to make,
    And yours will come too late.

ANTONIO: Prithee begone; I shall grow angry else,
    And then thou art not safe.

PEDRO: My anger may be fatal, sir, as yours,   235
    And he that enters here may prove this truth.

ANTONIO: I know not who thou art, but I am sure
    thou'rt worth my killing, for aiming at Angellica.
                   (*They draw and fight.*)

(*Enter Willmore and Blunt, who draw and part 'em.*)

BLUNT: 'Adsheartlikins, here's fine doings.

WILLMORE: Tilting for the wench, I'm sure. Nay, gad,   240
    if that would win her I have as good a sword as
    the best of ye. Put up, put up, and take another
    time and place, for this is designed for lovers only.
                   (*They all put up.*)

PEDRO: We are prevented; dare you meet me
    tomorrow on the Molo?°   245
    For I've a title to a better quarrel,
    That of Florinda, in whose credulous heart
    Thou'st made an int'rest, and destroyed my
    hopes.

ANTONIO: Dare!
    I'll meet thee there as early as the day.   250

PEDRO: We will come thus disguised, that whosoever
    chance to get the better, he may escape unknown.

ANTONIO: It shall be so.
              (*Exeunt Pedro and Stephano.*)
    — Who should this rival be? Unless the English
    colonel, of whom I've often heard Don Pedro   255
    speak. It must be he, and time he were removed
    who lays a claim to all my happiness.

(*Willmore, having gazed all this while on the picture[s], pulls down a little one.*)

WILLMORE: This posture's loose and negligent;
    The sight on't would beget a warm desire
    In souls whom impotence and age had chilled.   260
    This must along with me.

BRAVO: What means this rudeness, sir? Restore the
    picture.

ANTONIO: Ha! Rudeness committed to the fair Angel-
    lica! — Restore the picture, sir.   265

WILLMORE: Indeed I will not, sir.

---

245. Molo: Wharf.

ANTONIO: By heaven, but you shall.

WILLMORE: Nay, do not show your sword; if you do, by this dear beauty, I will show mine too.

270 ANTONIO: What right can you pretend to't?

WILLMORE: That of possession, which I will maintain. You, perhaps, have a thousand crowns to give for the original.

ANTONIO: No matter, sir, you shall restore the picture.

([The curtains open.] Angellica and Moretta above.)

275 ANGELLICA: Oh, Moretta, what's the matter?

ANTONIO: Or leave your life behind.

WILLMORE: Death! You lie; I will do neither.

(They fight. The Spaniards join with Antonio, Blunt laying on like mad.)

ANGELLICA: Hold, I command you, if for me you fight.

(They leave off and bow.)

WILLMORE [*aside*]: How heavenly fair she is! Ah,
280   plague of her price!

ANGELLICA: You sir, in buff, you that appear a soldier, that first began this insolence —

WILLMORE: 'Tis true, I did so, if you call it insolence for a man to preserve himself. I saw your charming
285   picture and was wounded; quite through my soul each pointed beauty ran; and wanting a thousand crowns to procure my remedy, I laid this little picture to my bosom, which, if you cannot allow me, I'll resign.

290 ANGELLICA: No, you may keep the trifle.

ANTONIO: You shall first ask me leave, and this.

(Fight again as before.)

(Enter Belvile and Frederick, who join with the English.)

ANGELLICA: Hold! Will you ruin me? — Biskey! Sebastian! Part 'em!

(The Spaniards are beaten off.)

MORETTA: Oh, madam, we're undone. A pox upon
295   that rude fellow; he's set on to ruin us. We shall never see good days again till all these fighting poor rogues are sent to the galleys.

(Enter Belvile, Blunt, Frederick, and Willmore with's shirt bloody.)

BLUNT: 'Adsheartlikins, beat me at this sport and I'll ne'er wear sword more.

300 BELVILE (*to Willmore*): The devil's in thee for a mad fellow; thou art always one at an unlucky adventure. Come, let's be gone whilst we're safe, and remember these are Spaniards, a sort of people that know how to revenge an affront.

FREDERICK: You bleed! I hope you are not wounded.   305

WILLMORE: Not much. A plague on your dons; if they fight no better they'll ne'er recover Flanders.° What the devil was't to them that I took down the picture?

BLUNT: Took it! 'Adsheartlikins, we'll have the great   310
one too; 'tis ours by conquest. Prithee help me up and I'll pull it down.

ANGELLICA [*to Willmore*]: Stay, sir, and ere you affront me farther let me know how you durst commit this outrage. To you I speak, sir, for you appear a   315
gentleman.

WILLMORE: To me, madam? — Gentlemen, your servant.

(Belvile stays him.°)

BELVILE: Is the devil in thee? Dost know the danger of ent'ring the house of an incensed courtesan?   320

WILLMORE: I thank you for your care, but there are other matters in hand, there are, though we have no great temptation. Death! Let me go!

FREDERICK: Yes, to your lodging if you will, but not in here. Damn these gay harlots; by this hand I'll   325
have as sound and handsome a whore for a patacoon.° Death, man, she'll murder thee!

WILLMORE: Oh, fear me not. Shall I not venture where a beauty calls? A lovely charming beauty! For fear of danger? When, by heaven, there's none   330
so great as to long for her whilst I want money to purchase her.

FREDERICK: Therefore 'tis loss of time unless you had the thousand crowns to pay.

WILLMORE: It may be she may give a favor; at least I   335
shall have the pleasure of saluting her when I enter and when I depart.

BELVILE: Pox, she'll as soon lie with thee as kiss thee, and sooner stab than do either. You shall not go.

ANGELLICA: Fear not, sir, all I have to wound with is   340
my eyes.

BLUNT: Let him go. 'Adsheartlikins, I believe the gentlewoman means well.

BELVILE: Well, take thy fortune; we'll expect you in the next street. Farewell, fool, farewell.   345

WILLMORE: Bye, colonel.   *(Goes in.)*

FREDERICK: The rogue's stark mad for a wench.

(Exeunt.)

---

307. ne'er recover Flanders: In 1659 the Spanish gave Flanders, which had been part of the Spanish Netherlands, to France as settlement to end a war.   **318.** [S.D.] *stays him:* Keeps him from leaving.   **326–27. patacoon:** Portuguese or Spanish coin of small denomination.

Scene II

(*A fine chamber. Enter Willmore, Angellica, and Moretta.*)

ANGELLICA: Insolent sir, how durst you pull down my picture?

WILLMORE: Rather, how durst you set it up to tempt poor am'rous mortals with so much excellence, which I find you have but too well consulted by the unmerciful price you set upon't. Is all this heaven of beauty shown to move despair in those that cannot buy? And can you think th'effects of that despair should be less extravagant than I have shown?

ANGELLICA: I sent for you to ask my pardon, sir, not to aggravate your crime. I thought I should have seen you at my feet imploring it.

WILLMORE: You are deceived. I came to rail at you, and rail such truths too, as shall let you see the vanity of that pride which taught you how to set such price on sin.
For such it is whilst that which is love's due
Is meanly bartered for.

ANGELLICA: Ha! Ha! Ha! Alas, good captain, what pity 'tis your edifying doctrine will do no good upon me. Moretta, fetch the gentleman a glass,° and let him survey himself to see what charms he has. — (*Aside, in a soft tone.*) And guess my business.

MORETTA: He knows himself of old: I believe those breeches and he have been acquainted ever since he was beaten at Worcester.°

ANGELLICA: Nay, do not abuse the poor creature.

MORETTA: Good weather-beaten corporal, will you march off? We have no need of your doctrine, though you have of our charity. But at present we have no scraps; we can afford no kindness for God's sake. In fine, sirrah, the price is too high i'th' mouth° for you, therefore troop, I say.

WILLMORE: Here, good forewoman of the shop, serve me and I'll be gone.

MORETTA: Keep it to pay your laundress; your linen stinks of the gun room. For here's no selling by retail.

WILLMORE: Thou hast sold plenty of thy stale ware at a cheap rate.

MORETTA: Ay, the more silly kind heart I, but this is an age wherein beauty is at higher rates. In fine, you know the price of this.

WILLMORE: I grant you 'tis here set down, a thousand crowns a month. Pray, how much may come to my share for a pistole?° Bawd, take your black lead° and sum it up, that I may have a pistole's worth of this vain gay thing, and I'll trouble you no more.

MORETTA: Pox on him, he'll fret me to death! Abominable fellow, I tell thee we only sell by the whole piece.

WILLMORE: 'Tis very hard, the whole cargo or nothing. Faith, madam, my stock will not reach it; I cannot be your chapman. Yet I have countrymen in town, merchants of love like me; I'll see if they'll put in for a share. We cannot lose much by it, and what we have no use for, we'll sell upon the Friday's mart at "Who gives more?" — I am studying, madam, how to purchase you, though at present I am unprovided of money.

ANGELLICA (*aside*): Sure this from any other man would anger me; nor shall he know the conquest he has made. — Poor angry man, how I despise this railing.

WILLMORE: Yes, I am poor. But I'm a gentleman,
And one that scorns this baseness which you practice.
Poor as I am I would not sell myself,
No, not to gain your charming high-prized person.
Though I admire you strangely for your beauty,
Yet I contemn your mind.
And yet I would at any rate enjoy you;
At your own rate; but cannot. See here
The only sum I can command on earth:
I know not where to eat when this is gone.
Yet such a slave I am to love and beauty
This last reserve I'll sacrifice to enjoy you.
Nay, do not frown, I know you're to be bought,
And would be bought by me. By me,
For a meaning trifling sum, if I could pay it down.
Which happy knowledge I will still repeat,
And lay it to my heart: It has a virtue in't,
And soon will cure those wounds your eyes have made.
And yet, there's something so divinely powerful there —

---

22. glass: Mirror.   **28. Worcester:** Charles II was routed by Cromwell at Worcester in 1651 and was forced into exile on the Continent.   **34–35. high i'th' mouth:** High.

47–48. how much . . . pistole: How much will my pistole (a Spanish coin) buy?   **48–49. black lead:** Pencil.

Nay, I will gaze, to let you see my strength.

(*Holds her, looks on her, and pauses and sighs.*)

By heav'n, bright creature, I would not for the
   world
Thy fame were half so fair as is thy face.
                     (*Turns her away from him.*)

ANGELLICA (*aside*): His words go through me to the
90   very soul. —
If you have nothing else to say to me —
WILLMORE: Yes, you shall hear how infamous you
   are —
For which I do not hate thee —
But that secures my heart, and all the flames it
   feels
95   Are but so many lusts:
I know it by their sudden bold intrusion.
The fire's impatient and betrays; 'tis false.
For had it been the purer flame of love,
I should have pined and languished at your feet,
100   Ere found the impudence to have discovered it.
I now dare stand your scorn and your denial.
MORETTA: Sure she's bewitched, that she can stand
   thus tamely and hear his saucy railing. — Sirrah,
   will you be gone?
105 ANGELLICA (*to Moretta*): How dare you take this liberty! Withdraw! — Pray tell me, sir, are not you
   guilty of the same mercenary crime? When a lady
   is proposed to you for a wife, you never ask how
   fair, discreet, or virtuous she is, but what's her for-
110   tune; which, if but small, you cry "She will not do
   my business," and basely leave her, though she languish for you. Say, is not this as poor?
WILLMORE: It is a barbarous custom, which I will
   scorn to defend in our sex, and do despise in yours.
ANGELLICA: Thou'rt a brave fellow! Put up thy gold,
115   and know,
That were thy fortune as large as is thy soul,
Thou shouldst not buy my love
Couldst thou forget those mean effects of vanity
Which set me out to sale,
120 And as a lover prize my yielding joys.
Canst thou believe they'll be entirely thine,
Without considering they were mercenary?
WILLMORE: I cannot tell, I must bethink me first.
   (*Aside.*) Ha! Death, I'm going to believe her.
ANGELLICA: Prithee confirm that faith, or if thou
125   canst not,
Flatter me a little: 'Twill please me from thy
   mouth.
WILLMORE (*aside*): Curse on thy charming tongue!
   Dost thou return
My feigned contempt with so much subtlety? —
Thou'st found the easiest way into my heart,

Though I yet know that all thou say'st is false.   130
              (*Turning from her in rage.*)
ANGELLICA: By all that's good, 'tis real;
I never loved before, though oft a mistress.
Shall my first vows be slighted?
WILLMORE (*aside*): What can she mean?
ANGELLICA (*in an angry tone*): I find you cannot
   credit me.   135
WILLMORE: I know you take me for an errant ass,
An ass that may be soothed into belief,
And then be used at pleasure;
But, madam, I have been so often cheated
By perjured, soft, deluding hypocrites,   140
That I've no faith left for the cozening sex,
Especially for women of your trade.
ANGELLICA: The low esteem you have of me perhaps
May bring my heart again:
For I have pride that yet surmounts my love.   145
       (*She turns with pride; he holds her.*)
WILLMORE: Throw off this pride, this enemy to
   bliss,
And show the power of love: 'Tis with those
   arms
I can be only vanquished, made a slave.
ANGELLICA: Is all my mighty expectation vanished?
No, I will not hear thee talk; thou hast a charm   150
In every word that draws my heart away,
And all the thousand trophies I designed
Thou hast undone. Why art thou soft?
Thy looks are bravely rough, and meant for war.
Couldst thou not storm on still?   155
I then perhaps had been as free as thou.
WILLMORE (*aside*): Death, how she throws her fire
   about my soul!
Take heed, fair creature, how you raise my
   hopes,
Which once assumed pretends to all dominion:
There's not a joy thou hast in store   160
I shall not then command.
For which I'll pay you back my soul, my life!
Come, let's begin th'account this happy minute!
ANGELLICA: And will you pay me then the price I
   ask?
WILLMORE: Oh, why dost thou draw me from an
   awful worship,   165
By showing thou art no divinity.
Conceal the fiend, and show me all the angel!
Keep me but ignorant, and I'll be devout
And pay my vows forever at this shrine.
           (*Kneels and kisses her hand.*)
ANGELLICA: The pay I mean is but thy love for
   mine.   170
Can you give that?
WILLMORE: Entirely. Come, let's withdraw where I'll

renew my vows, and breathe 'em with such ardor
thou shalt not doubt my zeal.

175   ANGELICA: Thou hast a power too strong to be resisted.

(Exeunt Willmore and Angellica.)

MORETTA: Now my curse go with you! Is all our project fallen to this? To love the only enemy to our
trade? Nay, to love such a shameroon;° a very beg-
180   gar; nay, a pirate beggar, whose business is to rifle
and be gone; a no-purchase, no-pay tatterdemalion,° and English picaroon;° a rogue that fights
for daily drink, and takes a pride in being loyally
lousy? Oh, I could curse now, if I durst. This is
185   the fate of most whores.

Trophies, which from believing fops we win,
Are spoils to those who cozen us again. [*Exit.*]

ACT III • *Scene I*

(*A street. Enter Florinda, Valeria, Hellena, in antic°*
different dresses from what they were in before; Cal-
lis attending.)

FLORINDA: I wonder what should make my brother in
so ill a humor? I hope he has not found out our
ramble this morning.

HELLENA: No, if he had, we should have heard on't at
5   both ears, and have been mewed up° this afternoon, which I would not for the world should have
happened. Hey ho, I'm as sad as a lover's lute.

VALERIA: Well, methinks we have learnt this trade of
gypsies as readily as if we had been bred upon the
10   road to Loretto;° and yet I did so fumble when I
told the stranger his fortune that I was afraid I
should have told my own and yours by mistake.
But methinks Hellena has been very serious ever
since.

15   FLORINDA: I would give my garters she were in love,
to be revenged upon her for abusing me. How is't,
Hellena?

HELLENA: Ah, would I had never seen my mad monsieur. And yet, for all your laughing, I am not in
20   love. And yet this small acquaintance, o' my conscience, will never out of my head.

VALERIA: Ha! Ha! Ha! I laugh to think how thou art

fitted with a lover, a fellow that I warrant loves
every new face he sees.

HELLENA: Hum, he has not kept his word with me   25
here, and may be taken up. That thought is not
very pleasant to me. What the deuce should this be
now that I feel?

VALERIA: What is't like?

HELLENA: Nay, the Lord knows, but if I should be   30
hanged I cannot choose but be angry and afraid
when I think that mad fellow should be in love
with anybody but me. What to think of myself I
know not: Would I could meet with some true
damned gypsy, that I might know my fortune.   35

VALERIA: Know it! Why there's nothing so easy: Thou
wilt love this wand'ring inconstant till thou find'st
thyself hanged about his neck, and then be as mad
to get free again.

FLORINDA: Yes, Valeria, we shall see her bestride his   40
baggage horse and follow him to the campaign.

HELLENA: So, so, now you are provided for there's no
care taken of poor me. But since you have set my
heart a-wishing, I am resolved to know for what, I
will not die of the pip,° so I will not.   45

FLORINDA: Art thou mad to talk so? Who will like
thee well enough to have thee, that hears what a
mad wench thou art?

HELLENA: Like me? I don't intend every he that likes
me shall have me, but he that I like. I should have   50
stayed in the nunnery still if I had liked my lady
abbess as well as she liked me. No, I came thence
not, as my wise brother imagines, to take an eternal farewell of the world, but to love and to be
beloved; and I will be beloved, or I'll get one of   55
your men, so I will.

VALERIA: Am I put into° the number of lovers?

HELLENA: You? Why, coz, I know thou'rt too good-
natured to leave us in any design; thou wouldst
venture a cast° though thou comest off a loser, es-   60
pecially with such a gamester. I observed your
man, and your willing ear incline that way; and if
you are not a lover, 'tis an art soon learnt — that I
find.   (*Sighs.*)

FLORINDA: I wonder how you learnt to love so easily.   65
I had a thousand charms to meet my eyes and ears
ere I could yield, and 'twas the knowledge of
Belvile's merit, not the surprising person, took my
soul. Thou art too rash, to give a heart at first
sight.   70

HELLENA: Hang your considering lover! I never

---

179. **shameroon:** Shameful person.   181–82. **tatterdemalion:** Ragamuffin.   182. **picaroon:** Wandering rogue.   **III,
I.** [**S.D.**] *antic:* Absurd, ludicrous, strange.   5. **mewed up:**
Shut in, imprisoned.   10. **Loretto:** Loreto is an Italian
town on the Adriatic coast, a destination for pilgrims visiting
the cottage of the Virgin Mary.

45. **pip:** A disease of poultry and birds, applied vaguely, usually humorously, to various ailments in humans.   57. **Am I
put into:** Do you include me among?   60. **venture a cast:**
Throw the dice.

thought beyond the fancy that 'twas a very pretty, idle, silly kind of pleasure to pass one's time with: to write little soft nonsensical billets,° and with
75 great difficulty and danger receive answers in which I shall have my beauty praised, my wit admired, though little or none, and have the vanity and power to know I am desirable. Then I have the more inclination that way because I am to be a
80 nun, and so shall not be suspected to have any such earthly thoughts about me; but when I walk thus — and sigh thus — they'll think my mind's upon my monastery, and cry, "How happy 'tis she's so resolved." But not a word of man.
85 FLORINDA: What a mad creature's this!
HELLENA: I'll warrant, if my brother hears either of you sigh, he cries gravely, "I fear you have the indiscretion to be in love, but take heed of the honor of our house, and your own unspotted fame"; and
90 so he conjures on till he has laid the soft winged god in your hearts, or broke the bird's nest.° But see, here comes your lover, but where's my inconstant? Let's step aside, and we may learn something.

                                                          (Go aside.)

(Enter Belvile, Frederick, and Blunt.)

95 BELVILE: What means this! The picture's taken in.
BLUNT: It may be the wench is good-natured, and will be kind gratis.° Your friend's a proper handsome fellow.
BELVILE: I rather think she has cut his throat and is
100 fled; I am mad he should throw himself into dangers. Pox on't, I shall want him, too, at night. Let's knock and ask for him.
HELLENA: My heart goes a-pit, a-pat, for fear 'tis my man they talk of.

                                       (Knock; Moretta above.)

105 MORETTA: What would you have?
BELVILE: Tell the stranger that entered here about two hours ago that his friends stay here for him.
MORETTA: A curse upon him for Moretta: Would he were at the devil! But he's coming to you.

(Enter Willmore.)

110 HELLENA: Ay, ay 'tis he. Oh, how this vexes me!
BELVILE: And how and how, dear lad, has fortune smiled? Are we to break her windows, or raise up altars to her, hah?

WILLMORE: Does not my fortune sit triumphant on my brow? Dost not see the little wanton god there 115 all gay and smiling? Have I not an air about my face and eyes that distinguish me from the crowd of common lovers? By heaven, Cupid's quiver has not half so many darts as her eyes! Oh, such a bona roba!° To sleep in her arms is lying in fresco,° 120 all perfumed air about me.
HELLENA (aside): Here's fine encouragement for me to fool on!
WILLMORE: Hark'ee, where didst thou purchase that rich Canary° we drank today? Tell me, that I may 125 adore the spigot and sacrifice to the butt.° The juice was divine; into which I must dip my rosary, and then bless all things that I would have bold or fortunate.
BELVILE: Well, sir, let's go take a bottle and hear the 130 story of your success.
FREDERICK: Would not French wine do better?
WILLMORE: Damn the hungry balderdash!° Cheerful sack° has a generous virtue in't inspiring a successful confidence, gives eloquence to the tongue and 135 vigor to the soul, and has in a few hours completed all my hopes and wishes! There's nothing left to raise a new desire in me. Come, let's be gay and wanton. And, gentlemen, study; study what you want, for here are friends that will supply gentle- 140 men. [Jingles gold.] Hark what a charming sound they make! 'Tis he and she gold whilst here, and shall beget new pleasures every moment.
BLUNT: But hark'ee, sir, you are not married, are you?
WILLMORE: All the honey of matrimony but none of 145 the sting, friend.
BLUNT: 'Adsheartlikins, thou'rt a fortunate rogue!
WILLMORE: I am so, sir: let these inform you! Ha, how sweetly they chime! Pox of poverty: It makes a man a slave, makes wit and honor sneak. My 150 soul grew lean and rusty for want of credit.
BLUNT: 'Adsheartlikins, this I like well; it looks like my lucky bargain! Oh, how I long for the approach of my squire, that is to conduct me to her house again. Why, here's two provided for! 155
FREDERICK: By this light, y'are happy men.
BLUNT: Fortune is pleased to smile on us, gentlemen, to smile on us.

---

74. billets: Brief letters, notes.   90–92. laid . . . bird's nest: Ruined your chances.   97. gratis: Free of charge.

120. bona robe: A courtesan.   in fresco: In the fresh air out of doors.   125. Canary: A light sweet wine from the Canary Islands.   126. butt: Large wine cask.   133. hungry balderdash: Cheap mixture of liquor.   134. sack: Dry white Spanish wine.

(*Enter Sancho and pulls down Blunt by the sleeve; they go aside.*)

SANCHO: Sir, my lady expects you. She has removed
    all that might oppose your will and pleasure, and
    is impatient till you come.

BLUNT: Sir, I'll attend you. — Oh the happiest rogue!
    I'll take no leave, lest they either dog me or stay
    me.   (*Exit with Sancho.*)

BELVILE: But then the little gypsy is forgot?

WILLMORE: A mischief on thee for putting her into my
    thoughts! I had quite forgot her else, and this
    night's debauch had drunk her quite down.

HELLENA: Had it so, good captain!
                    (*Claps him on the back.*)

WILLMORE (*aside*): Ha! I hope she did not hear me!

HELLENA: What, afraid of such a champion?

WILLMORE: Oh, you're a fine lady of your word, are
    you not? To make a man languish a whole day —

HELLENA: In tedious search of me.

WILLMORE: Egad, child, thou'rt in the right. Hadst
    thou seen what a melancholy dog I have been ever
    since I was a lover, how I have walked the streets
    like a Capuchin,° with my hands in my sleeves —
    faith, sweetheart, thou wouldst pity me.

HELLENA [*aside*]: Now if I should be hanged I can't be
    angry with him, he dissembles so heartily. — Alas,
    good captain, what pains you have taken; now
    were I ungrateful not to reward so true a servant.

WILLMORE: Poor soul, that's kindly said; I see thou
    barest a conscience. Come then, for a beginning
    show me thy dear face.

HELLENA: I'm afraid, my small acquaintance, you
    have been staying that swinging stomach you
    boasted of this morning. I then remember my little
    collation° would have gone down with you with-
    out the sauce of a handsome face. Is your stomach
    so queasy now?

WILLMORE: Faith, long fasting, child, spoils a man's
    appetite. Yet if you durst treat, I could so lay about
    me still —

HELLENA: And would you fall to before a priest says
    grace?

WILLMORE: O fie, fie, what an old out-of-fashioned
    thing hast thou named? Thou couldst not dash me
    more out of countenance shouldst thou show me
    an ugly face.

(*Whilst he is seemingly courting Hellena, enter Angel-*)

160

165

170

175

180

185

190

195

200

178. Capuchin: Franciscan monk. **190–91. collation:**
Snack.

*lica, Moretta, Biskey, and Sebastian, all in masquer-
ade. Angellica sees Willmore and stares.*)

ANGELLICA: Heavens, 'tis he! And passionately fond
    to see another woman!

MORETTA: What could you less expect from such a
    swaggerer?

ANGELLICA: Expect? As much as I paid him: a heart
    entire,
    Which I had pride enough to think when'er I
      gave,
    It would have raised the man above the vulgar,
    Made him all soul, and that all soft and
    constant.

HELLENA: You see, captain, how willing I am to be
    friends with you, till time and ill luck make us
    lovers; and ask you the question first rather than
    put your modesty to the blush by asking me. For
    alas, I know you captains are such strict men, and
    such severe observers of your vows to chastity, that
    'twill be hard to prevail with your tender con-
    science to marry a young willing maid.

WILLMORE: Do not abuse me, for fear I should take
    thee at thy word and marry thee indeed, which I'm
    sure will be revenge sufficient.

HELLENA: O' my conscience, that will be our destiny,
    because we are both of one humor: I am as in-
    constant as you, for I have considered, captain,
    that a handsome woman has a great deal to do
    whilst her face is good. For then is our harvest-
    time to gather friends, and should I in these days
    of my youth catch a fit of foolish constancy, I
    were undone: 'tis loitering by daylight in our
    great journey. Therefore, I declare I'll allow but
    one year for love, one year for indifference, and
    one year for hate; and then go hang yourself, for
    I profess myself the gay, the kind, and the incon-
    stant. The devil's in't if this won't please you!

WILLMORE: Oh, most damnably. I have a heart with a
    hole quite through it too; no prison mine, to keep
    a mistress in.

ANGELLICA (*aside*): Perjured man! How I believe thee
    now!

HELLENA: Well, I see our business as well as humors
    are alike: yours to cozen as many maids as will
    trust you, and I as many men as have faith. See if I
    have not as desperate a lying look as you can have
    for the heart of you. (*Pulls off her vizard; he
    starts.*) How do you like it, captain?

WILLMORE: Like it! By heaven, I never saw so much
    beauty! Oh, the charms of those sprightly black
    eyes! That strangely fair face, full of smiles and
    dimples! Those soft round melting cherry lips and
    small even white teeth! Not to be expressed, but

205

210

215

220

225

230

235

240

245

250

silently adored! [*She replaces her mask.*] Oh, one look more, and strike me dumb, or I shall repeat nothing else till I'm mad.

(*He seems to court her to pull off her vizard; she refuses.*)

255 ANGELLICA: I can endure no more. Nor is it fit to interrupt him, for if I do, my jealousy has so destroyed my reason I shall undo him. Therefore I'll retire, and you, Sebastian (*to one of her Bravos*), follow that woman and learn who 'tis; while you (*to the other Bravo*) tell the fugitive I would speak
260 to him instantly.   (*Exit.*)

(*This while Florinda is talking to Belvile, who stands sullenly; Frederick courting Valeria.*)

VALERIA [*to Belvile*]: Prithee, dear stranger, be not so sullen, for though you have lost your love you see my friend frankly offers you hers to play with in the meantime.
265 BELVILE: Faith, madam, I am sorry I can't play at her game.
FREDERICK [*to Valeria*]: Pray leave your intercession and mind your own affair. They'll better agree apart: He's a modest sigher in company, but alone
270 no woman 'scapes him.
FLORINDA [*aside*]: Sure he does but rally. Yet, if it should be true? I'll tempt him farther. — Believe me, noble stranger, I'm no common mistress. And for a little proof on't, wear this jewel.° Nay, take
275 it, sir, 'tis right, and bills of exchange may sometimes miscarry.
BELVILE: Madam, why am I chose out of all mankind to be the object of your bounty?
VALERIA: There's another civil question asked.
280 FREDERICK [*aside*]: Pox of's modesty; it spoils his own markets and hinders mine.
FLORINDA: Sir, from my window I have often seen you, and women of my quality have so few opportunities for love that we ought to lose none.
285 FREDERICK [*to Valeria*]: Ay, this is something! Here's a woman! When shall I be blest with so much kindness from your fair mouth? — (*Aside to Belvile.*) Take the jewel, fool!
BELVILE: You tempt me strangely, madam, every
290 way —
FLORINDA (*aside*): So, if I find him false, my whole repose is gone.
BELVILE: And but for a vow I've made to a very fair lady, this goodness had subdued me.

274. jewel: A locket with her picture in it.

FREDERICK [*aside to Belvile*]: Pox on't, be kind, in pity 295
to me be kind. For I am to thrive here but as you treat her friend.
HELLENA: Tell me what you did in yonder house, and I'll unmask.
WILLMORE: Yonder house? Oh, I went to a — to — 300
why, there's a friend of mine lives there.
HELLENA: What, a she or a he friend?
WILLMORE: A man, upon honor, a man. A she friend? No, no, madam, you have done my business, I thank you. 305
HELLENA: And was't your man friend that had more darts in's eyes than Cupid carries in's whole budget of arrows?
WILLMORE: So —
HELLENA: "Ah, such a *bona roba*! To be in her arms 310
is lying *in fresco*, all perfumed air about me." Was this your man friend too?
WILLMORE: So —
HELLENA: That gave you the he and the she gold, that begets young pleasures? 315
WILLMORE: Well, well, madam, then you can see there are ladies in the world that will not be cruel. There are, madam, there are.
HELLENA: And there be men, too, as fine, wild, inconstant fellows as yourself. There be, captain, there 320
be, if you go to that now. Therefore, I'm resolved —
WILLMORE: Oh!
HELLENA: To see your face no more —
WILLMORE: Oh! 325
HELLENA: Till tomorrow.
WILLMORE: Egad, you frighted me.
HELLENA: Nor then neither, unless you'll swear never to see that lady more.
WILLMORE: See her! Why, never to think of wom- 330
ankind again.
HELLENA: Kneel and swear.
              (*Kneels, she gives him her hand.*)
WILLMORE: I do, never to think, to see, to love, nor lie, with any but thyself.
HELLENA: Kiss the book. 335
WILLMORE: Oh, most religiously.   (*Kisses her hand.*)
HELLENA: Now what a wicked creature am I, to damn a proper fellow.
CALLIS (*to Florinda*): Madam, I'll stay no longer: 'tis e'en dark. 340
FLORINDA [*to Belvile*]: However, sir, I'll leave this with you, that when I'm gone you may repent the opportunity you have lost by your modesty.
(*Gives him the jewel, which is her picture, and exit. He gazes after her.*)
WILLMORE [*to Hellena*]: 'Twill be an age till tomor-

345   row, and till then I will most impatiently expect
    you. Adieu, my dear pretty angel.
                          (*Exeunt all the women.*)

BELVILE: Ha! Florinda's picture! 'Twas she herself.
    What a dull dog was I! I would have given the
    world for one minute's discourse with her.

350 FREDERICK: This comes of your modesty. Ah, pox o'
    your vow; 'twas ten to one but we had lost the
    jewel by't.

BELVILE: Willmore, the blessed'st opportunity lost!
    Florinda, friends, Florinda!

355 WILLMORE: Ah, rogue! Such black eyes! Such a face!
    Such a mouth! Such teeth! And so much wit!

BELVILE: All, all, and a thousand charms besides.

WILLMORE: Why, dost thou know her?

BELVILE: Know her! Ay, ay, and a pox take me with all
360   my heart for being so modest.

WILLMORE: But hark'ee, friend of mine, are you my
    rival? And have I been only beating the bush all
    this while?

BELVILE: I understand thee not. I'm mad! See here —
                          (*Shows the picture.*)

365 WILLMORE: Ha! Whose picture's this? 'Tis a fine
    wench!

FREDERICK: The colonel's mistress, sir.

WILLMORE: Oh, oh, here. (*Gives the picture back.*) I
    thought't had been another prize. Come, come, a
370   bottle will set thee right again.

BELVILE: I am content to try, and by that time 'twill be
    late enough for our design.

WILLMORE: Agreed.
    Love does all day the soul's great empire keep,
375   *But wine at night lulls the soft god asleep.*
                          (*Exeunt.*)

Scene II

(*Lucetta's house. Enter Blunt and Lucetta with a
light.*)

LUCETTA: Now we are safe and free: no fears of the
    coming home of my old jealous husband, which
    made me a little thoughtful when you came in first.
    But now love is all the business of my soul.

5 BLUNT: I am transported! — (*Aside.*) Pox on't, that I
    had but some fine things to say to her, such as
    lovers use. I was a fool not to learn of Fred a little
    by heart before I came. Something I must say. —
    'Adsheartlikins, sweet soul, I am not used to com-
10   pliment, but I'm an honest gentleman, and thy
    humble servant.

LUCETTA: I have nothing to pay for so great a favor,

but such a love as cannot but be great, since at first
sight of that sweet face and shape it made me your
absolute captive.   15

BLUNT (*aside*): Kind heart, how prettily she talks!
    Egad, I'll show her husband a Spanish trick: Send
    him out of the world and marry her; she's
    damnably in love with me, and will ne'er mind set-
    tlements,° and so there's that saved.   20

LUCETTA: Well, sir, I'll go and undress me, and be with
    you instantly.

BLUNT: Make haste then, for 'adsheartlikins, dear
    soul, thou canst not guess at the pain of a longing
    lover when his joys are drawn within the compass   25
    of a few minutes.

LUCETTA: You speak my sense, and I'll make haste to
    prove it.   (*Exit.*)

BLUNT: 'Tis a rare girl, and this one night's enjoyment
    with her will be worth all the days I ever passed in   30
    Essex. Would she would go with me into England,
    though to say truth, there's plenty of whores al-
    ready. Put a pox on 'em, they are such mercenary
    prodigal whores that they want such a one as this,
    that's free and generous, to give 'em good exam-   35
    ples. Why, what a house she has, how rich and
    fine!

(*Enter Sancho.*)

SANCHO: Sir, my lady has sent me to conduct you to
    her chamber.

BLUNT: Sir, I shall be proud to follow. — (*Aside.*)   40
    Here's one of her servants too; 'adsheartlikins, by
    this garb and gravity he might be a justice of peace
    in Essex, and is but a pimp here.

                                  (*Exeunt.*)

Scene III

(*The scene changes to a chamber with an alcove bed
in't, a table, etc.; Lucetta in bed. Enter Sancho
and Blunt, who takes the candle of Sancho at the
door.*)

SANCHO: Sir, my commission reaches no farther.

BLUNT: Sir, I'll excuse your compliment.
                             [*Exit Sancho.*]
    — What, in bed, my sweet mistress?

LUCETTA: You see, I still outdo you in kindness.

19–20. will ne'er mind settlements: Won't require the gifts of
property usually settled on a wife after marriage.

5 BLUNT: And thou shalt see what haste I'll make to
quit scores. Oh, the luckiest rogue!
                              (*He undresses himself.*)
LUCETTA: Should you be false or cruel now —
BLUNT: False! 'Adsheartlikins, what dost thou take me
for, a Jew? An insensible heathen? A pox of thy old
10 jealous husband: An° he were dead, egad, sweet
soul, it should be none of my fault if I did not
marry thee.
LUCETTA: It never should be mine.
BLUNT: Good soul! I'm the fortunatest dog!
15 LUCETTA: Are you not undressed yet?
BLUNT: As much as my impatience will permit.
        (*Goes toward the bed in his shirt, drawers, etc.*)
LUCETTA: Hold, sir, put out the light; it may betray us
else.
BLUNT: Anything; I need no other light but that of
20 thine eyes. — (*Aside.*) 'Adsheartlikins, there I think
I had it.
            (*Puts out the candle; the bed descends; he
                      gropes about to find it.*)
Why, why, where am I got? What, not yet? Where
are you, sweetest? — Ah, the rogue's silent now. A
pretty love-trick this; how she'll laugh at me
25 anon! — You need not, my dear rogue, you need
not! I'm all on fire already; come, come, now call
me, in pity. — Sure I'm enchanted! I have been
round the chamber, and can find neither woman
nor bed. I locked the door; I'm sure she cannot go
30 that way, or if she could, the bed could not. —
Enough, enough, my pretty wanton; do not carry
the jest too far! (*Lights on a trap, and is let
down.*) — Ha! Betrayed! Dogs! Rogues! Pimps!
Help! Help!

(*Enter Lucetta, Philippo, and Sancho with a light.*)

35 PHILIPPO: Ha! Ha! Ha! He's dispatched finely.
LUCETTA: Now, sir, had I been coy, we had missed of
this booty.
PHILIPPO: Nay, when I saw 'twas a substantial fool, I
was mollified. But when you dote upon a serenad-
40 ing coxcomb, upon a face, fine clothes, and a lute,
it makes me rage.
LUCETTA: You know I was never guilty of that folly,
my dear Philippo, but with yourself. But come,
let's see what we have got by this.
45 PHILIPPO: A rich coat; sword and hat; these breeches,
too, are well lined! See here, a gold watch! A
purse — Ha! Gold! At least two hundred pistoles!
A bunch of diamond rings, and one with the fam-

ily arms! A gold box, with a medal of his king, and
his lady mother's picture! These were sacred relics, 50
believe me. See, the waistband of his breeches have
a mine of gold — old queen Bess's!° We have a
quarrel to her ever since eighty-eight,° and may
therefore justify the theft: The Inquisition might
have committed it.   55
LUCETTA: See, a bracelet of bowed gold! These his sisters tied about his arm at parting. But well, for all
this, I fear his being a stranger may make a noise
and hinder our trade with them hereafter.
PHILIPPO: That's our security: He is not only a stranger 60
to us, but to the country too. The common shore°
into which he is descended, thou know'st, conducts
him into another street, which this light will hinder
him from ever finding again. He knows neither
your name, nor that of the street where your house 65
is; nay, nor the way to his own lodgings.
LUCETTA: And art thou not an unmerciful rogue, not
to afford him one night for all this? I should not
have been such a Jew.
PHILIPPO: Blame me not, Lucetta, to keep as much of 70
thee as I can to myself. Come, that thought makes
me wanton; let's to bed. — Sancho, lock up these.
        This is the fleece which fools do bear,
        Designed for witty men to shear.   (*Exeunt.*)

Scene IV

(*The scene changes, and discovers Blunt creeping out
of a common shore; his face, etc., all dirty.*)

BLUNT (*climbing up*): Oh, Lord, I am got out at last,
and, which is a miracle, without a clue. And now
to damning and cursing! But if that would ease me,
where shall I begin? With my fortune, myself, or
the quean° that cozened me? What a dog was I to   5
believe in woman! Oh, coxcomb! Ignorant conceited coxcomb! To fancy she could be enamored
with my person! At first sight enamored! Oh, I'm a
cursed puppy! 'Tis plain, fool was writ upon my
forehead! She perceived it; saw the Essex calf   10
there. For what allurements could there be in this
countenance, which I can endure because I'm acquainted with it. Oh dull, silly dog, to be thus
soothed into a cozening! Had I been drunk, I
might fondly have credited the young quean; but   15
as I was in my right wits to be thus cheated, con-

---

10. An: If.

52. old queen Bess's: Queen Elizabeth I (reigned
1558–1603).   53. eighty-eight: The year the Spanish Armada was defeated by the English (1588).   61. common
shore: Sewer.   5. quean: Harlot, tramp.

firms it: I am a dull believing English country fop. But my comrades! Death and the devil, there's the worst of all! Then a ballad will be sung tomorrow
20 on the Prado,° to a lousy tune of the enchanted squire and the annihilated damsel. But Fred — that rogue — and the colonel will abuse me beyond all Christian patience. Had she left me my clothes, I have a bill of exchange at home would have saved
25 my credit. But now all hope is taken from me. Well, I'll home, if I can find the way, with this consolation: that I am not the first kind believing coxcomb; but there are, gallants, many such good natures amongst ye.

> *And though you've better arts to hide your*
>   *follies,*
30 *'Adsheartlikins, y'are all as errant cullies.°*

(*Exit.*)

Scene V

(*Scene: the garden in the night. Enter Florinda in an undress,° with a key and a little box.*)

FLORINDA: Well, thus far I'm in my way to happiness. I have got myself free from Callis; my brother too, I find by yonder light, is got into his cabinet,° and thinks not of me; I have by good fortune got the
5 key of the garden back door. I'll open it to prevent Belvile's knocking: A little noise will now alarm my brother. Now am I as fearful as a young thief. (*Unlocks the door.*) Hark! What noise is that? Oh, 'twas the wind that played amongst the boughs.
10 Belvile stays long, methinks; it's time. Stay, for fear of a surprise, I'll hide these jewels in yonder jasmine.   (*She goes to lay down the box.*)

(*Enter Willmore, drunk.*)

WILLMORE: What the devil is become of these fellows Belvile and Frederick? They promised to stay at the
15 next corner for me, but who the devil knows the corner of a full moon? Now, whereabouts am I? Ha, what have we here? A garden! A very convenient place to sleep in. Ha! What has God sent us here? A female! By this light, a woman! I'm a dog
20 if it be not a very wench!

FLORINDA: He's come! Ha! Who's there?

WILLMORE: Sweet soul, let me salute thy shoestring.

FLORINDA [*aside*]: 'Tis not my Belvile. Good heavens,

I know him not! — Who are you, and from whence come you?   25

WILLMORE: Prithee, prithee, child, not so many hard questions! Let it suffice I am here, child. Come, come kiss me.

FLORINDA: Good gods! What luck is mine?

WILLMORE: Only good luck, child, parlous° good   30 luck. Come hither. — 'Tis a delicate shining wench. By this hand, she's perfumed, and smells like any nosegay. — Prithee, dear soul, let's not play the fool and lose time — precious time. For as Gad shall save me, I'm as honest a fellow as breathes,   35 though I'm a little disguised° at present. Come, I say. Why, thou mayst be free with me: I'll be very secret. I'll not boast who 'twas obliged me, not I; for hang me if I know thy name.

FLORINDA: Heavens! What a filthy beast is this!   40

WILLMORE: I am so, and thou ought'st the sooner to lie with me for that reason. For look you, child, there will be no sin in't, because 'twas neither designed nor premeditated: 'Tis pure accident on both sides. That's a certain thing now. Indeed,   45 should I make love to you, and you vow fidelity, and swear and lie till you believed and yielded — that were to make it willful fornication, the crying sin of the nation. Thou art, therefore, as thou art a good Christian, obliged in conscience to deny me   50 nothing. Now, come be kind without any more idle prating.

FLORINDA: Oh, I am ruined! Wicked man, unhand me!

WILLMORE: Wicked? Egad, child, a judge, were he   55 young and vigorous, and saw those eyes of thine, would know 'twas they gave the first blow, the first provocation. Come, prithee let's lose no time, I say. This is a fine convenient place.

FLORINDA: Sir, let me go, I conjure° you, or I'll call   60 out.

WILLMORE: Ay, ay, you were best to call witness to see how finely you treat me. Do!

FLORINDA: I'll cry murder, rape, or anything, if you do not instantly let me go!   65

WILLMORE: A rape? Come, come, you lie, you baggage, you lie. What! I'll warrant you would fain have the world believe now that you are not so forward as I. No, not you. Why at this time of night was your cobweb door set open, dear spider,   70 but to catch flies? Ha! Come, or I shall be damnably angry. Why, what a coil° is here!

FLORINDA: Sir, can you think —

WILLMORE: That you would do't for nothing? Oh, oh,

19–20. ballad . . . Prado: A song satirizing him will be sung on the Prado, a fashionable promenade in Madrid, for common amusement.   **30. cullies:** A cully is one easily fooled: a simpleton.   **III, v. [S.D.] undress:** Undergarment.   **3. cabinet:** Private room.

30. parlous: Excessively, with pun on *perilous*.   **36. disguised:** I.e., by liquor.   **60. conjure:** Entreat, implore.   **72. coil:** Noisy disturbance.

75 I find what you would be at. Look here, here's a
pistole for you. Here's a work indeed! Here, take
it, I say!

FLORINDA: For heaven's sake, sir, as you're a gentleman —

80 WILLMORE: So now, now, she would be wheedling me
for more! What, you will not take it then? You are
resolved you will not? Come, come, take it or I'll
put it up again, for look ye, I never give more.
Why, how now, mistress, are you so high i'th'
85 mouth a pistole won't down with you? Ha! Why,
what a work's here! In good time! Come, no struggling to be gone. But an y'are good at a dumb
wrestle, I'm for ye. Look ye, I'm for ye.
                                (She struggles with him.)

(Enter Belvile and Frederick.)

BELVILE: The door is open. A pox of this mad fellow!
90 I'm angry that we've lost him; I durst have sworn
he had followed us.
FREDERICK: But you were so hasty, colonel, to be
gone.
FLORINDA: Help! Help! Murder! Help! Oh, I am ruined!
95 BELVILE: Ha! Sure that's Florinda's voice! (Comes up
to them.) A man! — Villain, let go that lady!

(A noise; Willmore turns and draws; Frederick interposes.)

FLORINDA: Belvile! Heavens! My brother too is coming, and 'twill be impossible to escape. Belvile, I
conjure you to walk under my chamber window,
100 from whence I'll give you some instructions what
to do. This rude man has undone us.   (Exit.)
WILLMORE: Belvile!

(Enter Pedro, Stephano, and other servants, with
lights.)

PEDRO: I'm betrayed! Run, Stephano, and see if
Florinda be safe.
                                (Exit Stephano.)

(They fight, and Pedro's party beats 'em out.)

105 — So, whoe'er they be, all is not well. I'll to
Florinda's chamber. (Going out, meets Stephano.)
STEPHANO: You need not, sir: The poor lady's fast
asleep, and thinks no harm. I would not awake
her, sir, for fear of frighting her with your danger.
110 PEDRO: I'm glad she's there. — Rascals, how came the
garden door open?
STEPHANO: That question comes too late, sir. Some of
my fellow servants masquerading, I'll warrant.
PEDRO: Masquerading! A lewd custom to debauch
115 our youth! There's something more in this than I
imagine.   (Exeunt.)

Scene VI

(Scene changes to the street. Enter Belvile in rage,
Frederick holding him, Willmore melancholy.)

WILLMORE: Why, how the devil should I know
Florinda?
BELVILE: Ah, plague of your ignorance! If it had not
been Florinda, must you be a beast? A brute? A
senseless swine?   5
WILLMORE: Well, sir, you see I am endued° with patience: I can bear. Though egad, y'are very free
with me, methinks. I was in good hopes the quarrel would have been on my side, for so uncivilly interrupting me.   10
BELVILE: Peace, brute, whilst thou'rt safe. Oh, I'm distracted!
WILLMORE: Nay, nay, I'm an unlucky dog, that's certain.
BELVILE: Ah, curse upon the star that ruled my birth, 15
or whatsoever other influence that makes me still
so wretched.
WILLMORE: Thou break'st my heart with these complaints. There is no star in fault, no influence but
sack, the cursed sack I drunk.   20
FREDERICK: Why, how the devil came you so drunk?
WILLMORE: Why, how the devil came you so sober?
BELVILE: A curse upon his thin skull, he was always
beforehand that way.
FREDERICK: Prithee, dear colonel, forgive him; he's   25
sorry for his fault.
BELVILE: He's always so after he has done a mischief.
A plague on all such brutes!
WILLMORE: By this light, I took her for an errant harlot.   30
BELVILE: Damn your debauched opinion! Tell me, sot,
hadst thou so much sense and light about thee to
distinguish her woman, and couldst not see some-
thing about her face and person to strike an awful
reverence into thy soul?   35
WILLMORE: Faith no, I considered her as mere a
woman as I could wish.
BELVILE: 'Sdeath, I have no patience. Draw, or I'll kill
you!
WILLMORE: Let that alone till tomorrow, and if I set   40
not all right again, use your pleasure.
BELVILE: Tomorrow! Damn it,
The spiteful light will lead me to no happiness.
Tomorrow is Antonio's, and perhaps
Guides him to my undoing. Oh, that I could
        meet   45
This rival, this powerful fortunate!

6. endued: Endowed.

WILLMORE: What then?

BELVILE: Let thy own reason, or my rage, instruct thee.

WILLMORE: I shall be finely informed then, no doubt.
50 Hear me, colonel, hear me; show me the man and I'll do his business.

BELVILE: I know him no more than thou, or if I did I should not need thy aid.

WILLMORE: This you say is Angellica's house; I prom-
55 ised the kind baggage to lie with her tonight.
                              (*Offers to go in.*)

(*Enter Antonio and his Page. Antonio knocks on the hilt of's sword.*)

ANTONIO: You paid the thousand crowns I directed?

PAGE: To the lady's old woman, sir, I did.

WILLMORE: Who the devil have we here?

BELVILE: I'll now plant myself under Florinda's win-
60 dow, and if I find no comfort there, I'll die.
                      (*Exeunt Belvile and Frederick.*)

(*Enter Moretta.*)

MORETTA: Page?

PAGE: Here's my lord.

WILLMORE: How is this? A picaroon going to board my frigate? — Here's one chase gun for you!

(*Drawing his sword, justles Antonio, who turns and draws. They fight; Antonio falls.*)

65 MORETTA: Oh, bless us! We're all undone!
                      (*Runs in and shuts the door.*)

PAGE: Help! Murder!

(*Belvile returns at the noise of fighting.*)

BELVILE: Ha! The mad rogue's engaged in some un-lucky adventure again.

(*Enter two or three Masqueraders.*)

MASQUERADER: Ha! A man killed!

70 WILLMORE: How, a man killed? Then I'll go home to sleep.
          (*Puts up and reels out. Exeunt Masqueraders another way.*)

BELVILE: Who should it be? Pray heaven the rogue is safe, for all my quarrel to him.

(*As Belvile is groping about, enter an Officer and six Soldiers.*)

SOLDIER: Who's there?

75 OFFICER: So, here's one dispatched. Secure the mur-derer.

BELVILE: Do not mistake my charity for murder! I came to his assistance! (*Soldiers sieze on Belvile.*)

OFFICER: That shall be tried, sir. St. Jago! Swords
80 drawn in the Carnival time!   (*Goes to Antonio.*)

ANTONIO: Thy hand, prithee.

OFFICER: Ha! Don Antonio! Look well to the villain there. — How is it, sir?

ANTONIO: I'm hurt.

BELVILE: Has my humanity made me a criminal?   85

OFFICER: Away with him!

BELVILE: What a curst chance is this!
                      (*Exeunt soldiers with Belvile.*)

ANTONIO [*aside*]: This is the man that has set upon me twice. — (*To the officer.*) Carry him to my
apartment till you have further orders from me.   90
                          (*Exit Antonio, led.*)

ACT IV • *Scene 1*

(*A fine room. Discovers Belvile as by dark alone.*)

BELVILE: When shall I be weary of railing on fortune, who is resolved never to turn with smiles upon me? Two such defeats in one night none but the devil and that mad rogue could have contrived to have plagued me with. I am here a prisoner. But   5
where, heaven knows. And if there be murder done, I can soon decide the fate of a stranger in a nation without mercy. Yet this is nothing to the torture my soul bows with when I think of losing my fair, my dear Florinda. Hark, my door opens. A   10
light! A man, and seems of quality. Armed, too! Now shall I die like a dog, without defense.

(*Enter Antonio in a nightgown, with a light; his arm in a scarf, and a sword under his arm. He sets the candle on the table.*)

ANTONIO: Sir, I come to know what injuries I have done you, that could provoke you to so mean an action as to attack me basely without allowing   15
time for my defense?

BELVILE: Sir, for a man in my circumstances to plead innocence would look like fear. But view me well, and you will find no marks of coward on me, nor anything that betrays that brutality you accuse me   20
with.

ANTONIO: In vain, sir, you impose upon my sense. You are not only he who drew on me last night, but yesterday before the same house, that of An-gellica. Yet there is something in your face and   25
mien° that makes me wish I were mistaken.

BELVILE: I own I fought today in the defense of a friend of mine with whom you, if you're the same, and your party were first engaged. Perhaps you

26. mien: Demeanor, appearance.

30   think this crime enough to kill me; but if you do, I
      cannot fear you'll do it basely.
ANTONIO: No sir, I'll make you fit for a defense with
      this.   (Gives him the sword.)
BELVILE: This gallantry surprises me, nor know I how
35   to use this present, sir, against a man so brave.
ANTONIO: You shall not need. For know, I come to
      snatch you from a danger that is decreed against
      you: perhaps your life, or long imprisonment. And
      'twas with so much courage you offended, I cannot
40   see you punished.
BELVILE: How shall I pay this generosity?
ANTONIO: It had been safer to have killed another
      than have attempted me. To show your danger, sir,
      I'll let you know my quality: And 'tis the Viceroy's
45   son whom you have wounded.
BELVILE: The Viceroy's son! — (Aside.) Death and
      confusion! Was this plague reserved to complete all
      the rest? Obliged by° him, the man of all the world
      I would destroy!
50   ANTONIO: You seem disordered, sir.
BELVILE: Yes, trust me, I am, and 'tis with pain that
      man receives such bounties who wants the power
      to pay 'em back again.
ANTONIO: To gallant spirits 'tis indeed uneasy, but
55   you may quickly overpay me, sir.
BELVILE (aside): Then I am well. Kind heaven, but set
      us even, that I may fight with him and keep my
      honor safe. — Oh, I'm impatient, sir, to be dis-
      counting the mighty debt I owe you. Command me
60   quickly.
ANTONIO: I have a quarrel with a rival, sir, about the
      maid we love.
BELVILE (aside): Death, 'tis Florinda he means! That
      thought destroys my reason, and I shall kill him.
65   ANTONIO: My rival, sir, is one has all the virtues man
      can boast of —
BELVILE (aside): Death, who should this be?
ANTONIO: He challenged me to meet him on the Molo
      as soon as day appeared, but last night's quarrel
70   has made my arm unfit to guide a sword.
BELVILE: I apprehend you, sir. You'd have me kill the
      man that lays a claim to the maid you speak of. I'll
      do't. I'll fly to do't!
ANTONIO: Sir, do you know her?
75   BELVILE: No, sir, but 'tis enough she is admired by
      you.
ANTONIO: Sir, I shall rob you of the glory on't, for
      you must fight under my name and dress.
BELVILE: That opinion must be strangely obliging that
80   makes you think I can personate the brave Anto-
      nio, whom I can but strive to imitate.

---

48. Obliged by: Favored by.

ANTONIO: You say too much to my advantage. Come,
      sir, the day appears that calls you forth. Within, sir,
      is the habit.°   (Exit Antonio.)
BELVILE: Fantastic fortune, thou deceitful light,   85
      That cheats the wearied traveler by night,
      Though on a precipice each step you tread,
      I am resolved to follow where you lead.   (Exit.)

Scene II

(The Molo. Enter Florinda and Callis in masks, with
Stephano.)

FLORINDA (aside): I'm dying with my fears: Belvile's
      not coming as I expected under my window makes
      me believe that all those fears are true. — Canst
      thou not tell with whom my brother fights?
STEPHANO: No, madam, they were both in masquer-   5
      ade. I was by when they challenged one another,
      and they had decided the quarrel then, but were
      prevented by some cavaliers; which made 'em put
      it off till now. But I am sure 'tis about you they
      fight.   10
FLORINDA (aside): Nay, then, 'tis with Belvile, for
      what other lover have I that dares fight for me ex-
      cept Antonio, and he is too much in favor with my
      brother. If it be he, for whom shall I direct my
      prayers to heaven?   15
STEPHANO: Madam, I must leave you, for if my mas-
      ter see me, I shall be hanged for being your con-
      ductor. I escaped narrowly for the excuse I made
      for you last night i'th' garden.
FLORINDA: I'll reward thee for't. Prithee, no more.   20
                                        (Exit Stephano.)

(Enter Don Pedro in his masking habit.)

PEDRO: Antonio's late today; the place will fill, and we
      may be prevented.   (Walks about.)
FLORINDA (aside): Antonio? Sure I heard amiss.
PEDRO: But who will not excuse a happy lover
      When soft fair arms confine the yielding neck,   25
      And the kind whisper languishingly breathes
      "Must you be gone so soon?"
      Sure I had dwelt forever on her bosom —
      But stay, he's here.

(Enter Belvile dressed in Antonio's clothes.)

FLORINDA [aside]: 'Tis not Belvile; half my fears are   30
      vanished.
PEDRO: Antonio!
BELVILE (aside): This must be he. — You're early, sir; I
      do not use to be outdone this way.

---

84. habit: Antonio's clothing.

35 PEDRO: The wretched, sir, are watchful, and 'tis
         enough you've the advantage of me in Angellica.
    BELVILE (*aside*): Angellica! Or° I've mistook my man,
         or else Antonio! Can he forget his interest in
         Florinda and fight for common prize?
40 PEDRO: Come, sir, you know our terms.
    BELVILE (*aside*): By heaven, not I. — No talking; I am
         ready, sir.
                    (*Offers to fight; Florinda runs in.*)
    FLORINDA (*to Belvile*): Oh, hold! Whoever you be, I
         do conjure you hold! If you strike here, I die!
45 PEDRO: Florinda!
    BELVILE: Florinda imploring for my rival!
    PEDRO: Away; this kindness is unseasonable.
       (*Puts her by; they fight; she runs in just as Belvile
                                  disarms Pedro.*)
    FLORINDA: Who are you, sir, that dares deny my
         prayers?
50 BELVILE: Thy prayers destroy him; if thou wouldst
         preserve him, do that thou'rt unacquainted with,
         and curse him.
                              (*She holds him.*)
    FLORINDA: By all you hold most dear, by her you
         love,
         I do conjure you, touch him not.
55 BELVILE: By her I love?
         See, I obey, and at your feet resign
         The useless trophy of my victory.
                         (*Lays his sword at her feet.*)
    PEDRO: Antonio, you've done enough to prove you
         love Florinda.
60 BELVILE: Love Florinda! Does heaven love adoration,
         prayer, or penitence? Love her? Here, sir, your
         sword again.
              (*Snatches up the sword and gives it to him.*)
         Upon this truth I'll fight my life away.
    PEDRO: No, you've redeemed my sister, and my
65   friendship.

    (*He gives him Florinda, and pulls off his vizard to
    show his face, and puts it on again.*)

    BELVILE: Don Pedro!
    PEDRO: Can you resign your claims to other women,
         and give your heart entirely to Florinda?
    BELVILE: Entire, as dying saints' confessions are!
70   I can delay my happiness no longer:
         This minute let me make Florinda mine.
    PEDRO: This minute let it be. No time so proper: This
         night my father will arrive from Rome, and possi-
         bly may hinder what we purpose.
75 FLORINDA: O, heavens! This minute?

    (*Enter Masqueraders and pass over.*)

    37. Or: Either.

    BELVILE: Oh, do not ruin me!
    PEDRO: The place begins to fill, and that we may not
         be observed, do you walk off to St. Peter's church,
         where I will meet you and conclude your happiness.
    BELVILE: I'll meet you there. — (*Aside.*) If there be no   80
         more saints' churches in Naples.
    FLORINDA: Oh, stay, sir, and recall your hasty
         doom!
         Alas, I have not yet prepared my heart
         To entertain so strange a guest.
    PEDRO: Away; this silly modesty is assumed too late.   85
    BELVILE: Heaven, madam, what do you do?
    FLORINDA: Do? Despise the man that lays a tyrant's
         claim
         To what he ought to conquer by submission.
    BELVILE: You do not know me. Move a little this way.
                              (*Draws her aside.*)
    FLORINDA: Yes, you may force me even to the altar,   90
         But not the holy man that offers there
         Shall force me to be thine.
                    (*Pedro talks to Callis this while.*)
    BELVILE: Oh, do not lose so blest an opportunity!
                         (*Pulls off his vizard.*)
         See, 'tis your Belvile, not Antonio,
         Whom your mistaken scorn and anger ruins.   95
    FLORINDA: Belvile!
         Where was my soul it could not meet thy voice,
         And take this knowledge in.

    (*As they are talking, enter Willmore, finely dressed,
    and Frederick.*)

    WILLMORE: No intelligence? No news of Belvile yet?
         Well, I am the most unlucky rascal in nature. Ha!   100
         Am I deceived, or is it he? Look, Fred! 'Tis he, my
         dear Belvile!
              (*Runs and embraces him; Belvile's vizard falls
                                       out on's hand.*)
    BELVILE: Hell and confusion seize thee!
    PEDRO: Ha! Belvile! I beg your pardon, sir.
                    (*Takes Florinda from him.*)
    BELVILE: Nay, touch her not. She's mine by
         conquest, sir;   105
         I won her by my sword.
    WILLMORE: Didst thou so? And egad, child, we'll
         keep her by the sword.
                 (*Draws on Pedro; Belvile goes between.*)
    BELVILE: Stand off!
         Thou'rt so profanely lewd, so curst by heaven,
         All quarrels thou espousest must be fatal.   110
    WILLMORE: Nay, an you be so hot, my valor's coy,
         And shall be courted when you want it next.
                         (*Puts up his sword.*)
    BELVILE (*to Pedro*): You know I ought to claim a
         victor's right,
         But you're the brother to divine Florinda,

115 To whom I'm such a slave. To purchase her
I durst not hurt the man she holds so dear.
PEDRO: 'Twas by Antonio's, not by Belvile's sword
This question should have been decided, sir.
I must confess much to your bravery's due,
120 Both now and when I met you last in arms;
But I am nicely punctual in my word,
As men of honor ought, and beg your pardon:
For this mistake another time shall clear.
(*Aside to Florinda as they are going out.*)
— This was some plot between you and Belvile,
125 But I'll prevent you.
[*Exeunt Pedro and Florinda.*]

(*Belvile looks after her and begins to walk up and down in rage.*)

WILLMORE: Do not be modest now and lose the
woman. But if we shall fetch her back so —
BELVILE: Do not speak to me!
WILLMORE: Not speak to you? Egad, I'll speak to you,
130 and will be answered, too.
BELVILE: Will you, sir?
WILLMORE: I know I've done some mischief, but
I'm so dull a puppy that I'm the son of a whore
if I know how or where. Prithee inform my
135 understanding.
BELVILE: Leave me, I say, and leave me instantly!
WILLMORE: I will not leave you in this humor, nor till
I know my crime.
BELVILE: Death, I'll tell you, sir —
(*Draws and runs at Willmore; he runs out, Belvile
after him; Frederick interposes.*)

(*Enter Angellica, Moretta, and Sebastian.*)

140 ANGELLICA: Ha! Sebastian, is that not Willmore?
Haste! haste and bring him back.
[*Exit Sebastian.*]
FREDERICK [*aside*]: The colonel's mad: I never saw
him thus before. I'll after 'em lest he do some mis-
chief, for I am sure Willmore will not draw on
145 him.   (*Exit.*)
ANGELLICA: I am all rage! My first desires defeated!
For one for aught he knows that has no
Other merit than her quality,
Her being Don Pedro's sister. He loves her!
150 I know 'tis so. Dull, dull, insensible,
He will not see me now, though oft invited,
And broke his word last night. False perjured man!
He that but yesterday fought for my favors,
And would have made his life a sacrifice
155 To've gained one night with me,
Must now be hired and courted to my arms.
MORETTA: I told you what would come on't, but
Moretta's an old doting fool. Why did you give
him five hundred crowns, but to set himself out for

other lovers? You should have kept him poor if
160 you had meant to have had any good from him.
ANGELLICA: Oh, name not such mean trifles! Had I
given
Him all my youth has earned from sin,
I had not lost a thought nor sigh upon't.
But I have given him my eternal rest,
165 My whole repose, my future joys, my heart!
My virgin heart, Moretta! Oh, 'tis gone!
MORETTA: Curse on him, here he comes. How fine she
has made him, too.

(*Enter Willmore and Sebastian; Angellica turns and
walks away.*)

WILLMORE: How now, turned shadow?
170 Fly when I pursue, and follow when I fly? (*Sings.*)
Stay, gentle shadow of my dove,
And tell me ere I go,
Whether the substance may not prove
A fleeting thing like you.
175 (*As she turns she looks on him.*)
There's a soft kind look remaining yet.
ANGELLICA: Well, sir, you may be gay: All happiness,
all joys pursue you still. Fortune's your slave, and
gives you every hour choice of new hearts and
beauties, till you are cloyed° with the repeated
180 bliss which others vainly languish for. But know,
false man, that I shall be revenged.
(*Turns away in rage.*)
WILLMORE: So, gad, there are of those faint-hearted
lovers, whom such a sharp lesson next their hearts
185 would make as impotent as fourscore.° Pox o' this
whining; my business is to laugh and love. A pox
on't, I hate your sullen lover: A man shall lose as
much time to put you in humor now as would
serve to gain a new woman.
190 ANGELLICA: I scorn to cool that fire I cannot raise,
Or do the drudgery of your virtuous mistress.
WILLMORE: A virtuous mistress? Death, what a thing
thou hast found out for me! Why, what the devil
should I do with a virtuous woman, a sort of ill-
195 natured creatures that take a pride to torment a
lover. Virtue is but an infirmity in woman, a disease that renders even the handsome ungrateful;
whilst the ill-favored, for want of solicitations and
address, only fancy themselves so. I have lain with
200 a woman of quality who has all the while been
railing at whores.
ANGELLICA: I will not answer for your mistress's
virtue,
Though she be young enough to know no guilt;
And I could wish you would persuade my heart

---

180. **cloyed:** Full to bursting.   185. **as fourscore:** As an
eighty-year-old.

'Twas the two hundred thousand crowns you
205   courted.
WILLMORE: Two hundred thousand crowns! What
        story's this? What trick? What woman, ha?
ANGELLICA: How strange you make it. Have you for-
        got the creature you entertained on the Piazzo last
210   night?
WILLMORE (*aside*): Ha! My gypsy worth two hundred
        thousand crowns! Oh, how I long to be with her!
        Pox, I knew she was of quality.
ANGELLICA: False man! I see my ruin in thy face.
215   How many vows you breathed upon my bosom
        Never to be unjust. Have you forgot so soon?
WILLMORE: Faith, no; I was just coming to repeat 'em.
        But here's a humor indeed would make a man a
        saint. — (*Aside.*) Would she would be angry
220   enough to leave me, and command me not to wait
        on her.

(*Enter Hellena dressed in man's clothes.*)

HELLENA: This must be Angellica: I know it by her
        mumping° matron here. Ay, ay, 'tis she. My mad
        captain's with her, too, for all his swearing. How
225   this unconstant humor makes me love him! — Pray,
        good grave gentlewoman, is not this Angellica?
MORETTA: My too young sir, it is. — [*Aside.*] I hope
        'tis one from Don Antonio.   (*Goes to Angellica.*)
HELLENA (*aside*): Well, something I'll do to vex him
230   for this.
ANGELLICA: I will not speak with him. Am I in humor
        to receive a lover?
WILLMORE: Not speak with him? Why, I'll be gone,
        and wait your idler minutes. Can I show less obe-
235   dience to the thing I love so fondly?
                                            (*Offers to go.*)
ANGELLICA: A fine excuse this! Stay —
WILLMORE: And hinder your advantage? Should I re-
        pay your bounties so ungratefully?
ANGELLICA [*to Hellena*]: Come hither, boy. — [*To
        Willmore.*] That I may let you see
240   How much above the advantages you name
        I prize one minute's joy with you.
WILLMORE (*impatient to be gone*): Oh, you destroy
        me with this endearment. — [*Aside.*] Death, how
        shall I get away? — Madam, 'twill not be fit I
245   should be seen with you. Besides, it will not be
        convenient. And I've a friend — that's dangerously
        sick.
ANGELLICA: I see you're impatient. Yet you shall stay.
WILLMORE (*aside*): And miss my assignation with my
250   gypsy.

(*Walks about impatiently; Moretta brings Hellena,
who addresses herself to Angellica.*)

223. mumping: Moping.

HELLENA: Madam,
        You'll hardly pardon my intrusion
        When you shall know my business,
        And I'm too young to tell my tale with art;
        But there must be a wondrous store of goodness   255
        Where so much beauty dwells.
ANGELLICA: A pretty advocate, whoever sent thee.
        Prithee proceed.
                    (*To Willmore, who is stealing off.*)
                — Nay, sir, you shall not go.
WILLMORE (*aside*): Then I shall lose my dear gypsy
        forever. Pox on't, she stays me out of spite.   260
HELLENA: I am related to a lady, madam,
        Young, rich, and nobly born, but has the fate
        To be in love with a young English gentleman.
        Strangely she loves him, at first sight she loved
            him,
        But did adore him when she heard him speak;   265
        For he, she said, had charms in every word
        That failed not to surprise, to wound and
        conquer.
WILLMORE (*aside*): Ha! Egad, I hope this concerns me.
ANGELLICA (*aside*): 'Tis my false man he means.
        Would he were gone:
        This praise will raise his pride, and ruin me.
                            (*To Willmore.*) — Well,   270
        Since you are so impatient to be gone,
        I will release you, sir.
WILLMORE (*aside*): Nay, then I'm sure 'twas me he
        spoke of: This cannot be the effects of kindness in
        her. — No, Madam, I've considered better on't,   275
        and will not give you cause of jealousy.
ANGELLICA: But sir, I've business that —
WILLMORE: This shall not do; I know 'tis but to try
        me.
ANGELLICA: Well, to your story, boy. — (*Aside*).   280
        Though 'twill undo me.
HELLENA: With this addition to his other beauties,
        He won her unresisting tender heart.
        He vowed, and sighed, and swore he loved her
            dearly;
        And she believed the cunning flatterer,   285
        And thought herself the happiest maid alive.
        Today was the appointed time by both
        To consummate their bliss:
        The virgin, altar, and the priest were dressed;
        And whilst she languished for th'expected
            bridegroom,
        She heard he paid his broken vows to you.   290
WILLMORE (*aside*): So, this is some dear rogue that's
        in love with me, and this way lets me know it. Or,
        if it be not me, he means someone whose place I
        may supply.   295
ANGELLICA: Now I perceive
        The cause of thy impatience to be gone,

And all the business of this glorious dress.
WILLMORE: Damn the young prater; I know not what
300   he means.
HELLENA: Madam,
    In your fair eyes I read too much concern
    To tell my further business.
ANGELLICA: Prithee, sweet youth, talk on: Thou
        mayst perhaps
305   Raise here a storm that may undo my passion,
    And then I'll grant thee anything.
HELLENA: Madam, 'tis to entreat you (oh
        unreasonable)
    You would not see this stranger.
    For if you do, she vows you are undone;
310   Though nature never made a man so excellent,
    And sure he 'ad been a god, but for inconstancy.
WILLMORE (aside): Ah, rogue, how finely he's in-
    structed! 'Tis plain, some woman that has seen me
    en passant.°
315 ANGELLICA: Oh, I shall burst with jealousy! Do you
    know the man you speak of?
HELLENA: Yes, madam, he used to be in buff and scar-
    let.
ANGELLICA (to Willmore): Thou false as hell, what
320   canst thou say to this?
WILLMORE: By heaven —
ANGELLICA: Hold, do not damn thyself —
HELLENA: Nor hope to be believed.
            (He walks about; they follow.)
ANGELLICA: Oh perjured man!
325   Is't thus you pay my generous passion back?
HELLENA: Why would you, sir, abuse my lady's faith?
ANGELLICA: And use me so unhumanely.
HELLENA: A maid so young, so innocent —
WILLMORE: Ah, young devil!
330 ANGELLICA: Dost thou not know thy life is in my
    power?
HELLENA: Or think my lady cannot be revenged?
WILLMORE (aside): So, so, the storm comes finely on.
ANGELLICA: Now thou art silent: Guilt has struck
    thee dumb.
335   Oh, hadst thou still been so, I'd lived in safety.
            (She turns away and weeps.)
WILLMORE (aside to Hellena): Sweetheart, the lady's
    name and house — quickly! I'm impatient to be
    with her.

(Looks toward Angellica to watch her turning, and as
she comes towards them he meets her.)

HELLENA (aside): So, now is he for another woman.
340 WILLMORE: The impudent'st young thing in nature:
    I cannot persuade him out of his error, madam.

314. en passant: In passing.

ANGELLICA: I know he's in the right; yet thou'st a
    tongue
    That would persuade him to deny his faith.
                (In rage walks away.)
WILLMORE (said softly to Hellena): Her name, her
    name, dear boy!   345
HELLENA: Have you forgot it, sir?
WILLMORE (aside): Oh, I perceive he's not to know I
    am a stranger to his lady. — Yes, yes, I do know,
    but I have forgot the — (Angellica turns.) — By
    heaven, such early confidence I never saw.   350
ANGELLICA: Did I not charge you with this mistress,
        sir?
    Which you denied, though I beheld your perjury.
    This little generosity of thine has rendered back
        my heart.   (Walks away.)
WILLMORE (to Hellena): So, you have made sweet
    work here, my little mischief. Look your lady be   355
    kind and good-natured now, or I shall have but a
    cursed bargain on't. (Angellica turns toward
    them.) — The rogue's bred up to mischief; art thou
    so great a fool to credit him?
ANGELLICA: Yes, I do, and you in vain impose upon   360
    me. Come hither, boy. Is not this he you spake of?
HELLENA: I think it is. I cannot swear, but I vow he
    has just such another lying lover's look.

(Hellena looks in his face; he gazes on her.)

WILLMORE (aside): Ha! Do I not know that face? By
    heaven, my little gypsy! What a dull dog was I: 365
    Had I but looked that way I'd known her. Are all
    my hopes of a new woman banished? — Egad, if I
    do not fit thee for this, hang me. — [To Angellica.]
    Madam, I have found out the plot.
HELLENA [aside]: Oh lord, what does he say? Am I   370
    discovered now?
WILLMORE: Do you see this young spark here?
HELLENA [aside]: He'll tell her who I am.
WILLMORE: Who do you think this is?
HELLENA [aside]: Ay, ay, he does know me. — Nay,   375
    dear captain, I am undone if you discover me.
WILLMORE: Nay, nay, no cogging;° she shall know
    what a precious mistress I have.
HELLENA: Will you be such a devil?
WILLMORE: Nay, nay, I'll teach you to spoil sport you   380
    will not make. — This small ambassador comes
    not from a person of quality, as you imagine and he
    says, but from a very errant gypsy: the talking'st,
    prating'st, canting'st little animal thou ever saw'st.
ANGELLICA: What news you tell me, that's the thing I   385
    mean.

377. cogging: Fawning, coaxing.

HELLENA (*aside*): Would I were well off the place! If ever I go a-captain-hunting again —

WILLMORE: Mean that thing? That gypsy thing? Thou
390 mayst as well be jealous of thy monkey or parrot as of her. A German motion° were worth a dozen of her, and a dream were a better enjoyment — a creature of a constitution fitter for heaven than man.

395 HELLENA (*aside*): Though I'm sure he lies, yet this vexes me.

ANGELLICA: You are mistaken: she's a Spanish woman made up of no such dull materials.

WILLMORE: Materials? Egad, an she be made of any
400 that will either dispense or admit of love, I'll be bound to continence.

HELLENA (*aside to him*): Unreasonable man, do you think so?

WILLMORE: You may return, my little brazen head,
405 and tell your lady, that till she be handsome enough to be beloved, or I dull enough to be religious, there will be small hopes of me.

ANGELLICA: Did you not promise, then, to marry her?

WILLMORE: Not I, by heaven.

410 ANGELLICA: You cannot undeceive my fears and torments, till you have vowed you will not marry her.

HELLENA (*aside*): If he swears that, he'll be revenged on me indeed for all my rogueries.

ANGELLICA: I know what arguments you'll bring
415 against me: fortune and honor.

WILLMORE: Honor! I tell you, I hate it in your sex; and those that fancy themselves possessed of that foppery are the most impertinently troublesome of all womankind, and will transgress nine com-
420 mandments to keep one. And to satisfy your jealousy, I swear —

HELLENA (*aside to him*): Oh, no swearing, dear captain.

WILLMORE: If it were possible I should ever be in-
425 clined to marry, it should be some kind young sinner: one that has generosity enough to give a favor handsomely to one that can ask it discreetly, one that has wit enough to manage an intrigue of love. Oh, how civil such a wench is to a man that does
430 her the honor to marry her.

ANGELLICA: By heaven, there's no faith in anything he says.

(*Enter Sebastian.*)

SEBASTIAN: Madam, Don Antonio —

ANGELLICA: Come hither.

435 HELLENA [*aside*]: Ha! Antonio! He may be coming hither, and he'll certainly discover me. I'll therefore retire without a ceremony.   (*Exit Hellena.*)

391. **motion:** Puppet show.

ANGELLICA: I'll see him. Get my coach ready.

SEBASTIAN: It waits you, madam.

WILLMORE [*aside*]: This is lucky. — What, madam,   440
now I may be gone and leave you to the enjoyment of my rival?

ANGELLICA: Dull man, that canst not see how ill, how poor,
That false dissimulation looks. Be gone,
And never let me see thy cozening face again,   445
Lest I relapse and kill thee.

WILLMORE: Yes, you can spare me now. Farewell, till you're in better humor. — [*Aside.*] I'm glad of this release. Now for my gypsy:
For though to worse we change, yet still we find   450
New joys, new charms, in a new miss that's kind.   (*Exit Willmore.*)

ANGELLICA: He's gone, and in this ague° of my soul
The shivering fit returns.
Oh, with what willing haste he took his leave,
As if the longed-for minute were arrived   455
Of some blest assignation.
In vain I have consulted all my charms,
In vain this beauty prized, in vain believed
My eyes could kindle any lasting fires;
I had forgot my name, my infamy,   460
And the reproach that honor lays on those
That dare pretend a sober passion here.
Nice reputation, though it leave behind
More virtues than inhabit where that dwells,
Yet that once gone, those virtues shine no more.   465
Then since I am not fit to be beloved,
I am resolved to think on a revenge
On him that soothed° me thus to my undoing.
(*Exeunt.*)

Scene III

(*A street. Enter Florinda and Valeria in habits different from what they have been seen in.*)

FLORINDA: We're happily escaped, and yet I tremble still.

VALERIA: A lover, and fear? Why, I am but half an one, and yet I have courage for any attempt. Would Hellena were here: I would fain have had   5
her as deep in this mischief as we; she'll fare but ill else, I doubt.

FLORINDA: She pretended a visit to the Augustine nuns; but I believe some other design carried her out; pray heaven we light on her. Prithee, what   10
didst do with Callis?

452. **ague:** Fever, accompanied by shivering.   468. **soothed:** Advised.

VALERIA: When I saw no reason would do good on
her, I followed her into the wardrobe, and as she
was looking for something in a great chest, I top-
pled her in by the heels, snatched the key of the
apartment where you were confined, locked her in,
and left her bawling for help.

FLORINDA: 'Tis well you resolve to follow my fortunes, for thou darest never appear at home again
after such an action.

VALERIA: That's according as the young stranger and I
shall agree. But to our business. I delivered your
note to Belvile when I got out under pretense of
going to mass. I found him at his lodging, and believe me it came seasonably, for never was man in
so desperate a condition. I told him of your resolution of making your escape today if your brother
would be absent long enough to permit you; if not,
to die rather than be Antonio's.

FLORINDA: Thou should'st have told him I was confined to my chamber upon my brother's suspicion
that the business on the Molo was a plot laid between him and I.

VALERIA: I said all this, and told him your brother
was now gone to his devotion; and he resolves to
visit every church till he find him, and not only
undeceive him in that, but caress him so as shall
delay his return home.

FLORINDA: Oh heavens! He's here, and Belvile with
him, too.

(They put on their vizards.)

(Enter Don Pedro, Belvile, Willmore; Belvile and Don
Pedro seeming in serious discourse.)

VALERIA: Walk boldly by them, and I'll come at a distance, lest he suspect us.

(She walks by them and looks back on them.)

WILLMORE: Ha! A woman, and of excellent mien!

PEDRO: She throws a kind look back on you.

WILLMORE: Death, 'tis a likely wench and that kind
look shall not be cast away. I'll follow her.

BELVILE: Prithee do not.

WILLMORE: Do not? By heavens, to the antipodies,°
with such an invitation.

(She goes out, and Willmore follows her.)

BELVILE: 'Tis a mad fellow for a wench.

(Enter Frederick.)

FREDERICK: Oh, colonel, such news!

BELVILE: Prithee what?

FREDERICK: News that will make you laugh in spite of
fortune.

BELVILE: What, Blunt has had some damned trick put
upon him? Cheated, banged, or clapped?°

FREDERICK: Cheated, sir, rarely cheated of all but his
shirt and drawers; the unconscionable whore too
turned him out before consummation, so that, tra-
versing the streets at midnight, the watch found
him in this *fresco* and conducted him home. By
heaven, 'tis such a sight, and yet I durst as well
been hanged as laughed at him or pity him: He
beats all that do but ask him a question, and is in
such an humor.

PEDRO: Who is't has met with this ill usage, sir?

BELVILE: A friend of ours whom you must see for
mirth's sake. — (Aside.) I'll employ him to give
Florinda time for an escape.

PEDRO: What is he?

BELVILE: A young countryman of ours, one that has
been educated at so plentiful a rate he yet ne'er
knew the want of money; and 'twill be a great jest
to see how simply he'll look without it. For my
part, I'll lend him none: And the rogue know not
how to put on a borrowing face and ask first, I'll
let him see how good 'tis to play our parts whilst I
play his. Prithee, Fred, do you go home and keep
him in that posture till we come.   (Exeunt.)

(Enter Florinda from the farther end of the scene,
looking behind her.)

FLORINDA: I am followed still. Ha! My brother too
advancing this way! Good heavens defend me
from being seen by him!   (She goes off.)

(Enter Willmore, and after him Valeria, at a little distance.)

WILLMORE: Ah, there she sails! She looks back as she
were willing to be boarded; I'll warrant her prize.°
(He goes out, Valeria following.)

(Enter Hellena, just as he goes out, with a page.)

HELLENA: Ha, is not that my captain that has a
woman in chase? 'Tis not Angellica. — Boy, follow
those people at a distance, and bring me an account where they go in.   (Exit Page.)
— I'll find his haunts, and plague him
everywhere.
Ha! My brother!
(Belvile, Willmore, Pedro cross the stage;
Hellena runs off.)

Scene IV

(Scene changes to another street. Enter Florinda.)

FLORINDA: What shall I do? My brother now pursues
me. Will no kind power protect me from his

---

48. antipodies: Antipodes; parts of the earth diametrically
opposite.   **56. clapped:** Given gonorrhea.

83. warrant her prize: Consider her worthy of pursuing.

tyranny? Ha! Here's a door open; I'll venture in, since nothing can be worse than to fall into his hands. My life and honor are at stake, and my necessity has no choice.   (*She goes in.*)

(*Enter Valeria, Hellena's Page peeping after Florinda.*)

PAGE: Here she went in; I shall remember this house.
                                                    (*Exit Boy.*)

VALERIA: This is Belvile's lodging, she's gone in as readily as if she knew it. Ha! Here's that mad fellow again; I dare not venture in. I'll watch my opportunity.   (*Goes aside.*)

(*Enter Willmore, gazing about him.*)

WILLMORE: I have lost her hereabouts. Pox on't, she must not 'scape me so.   (*Goes out.*)

Scene V

(*Scene changes to Blunt's chamber, discovers him sitting on a couch in his shirt and drawers, reading.*)

BLUNT: So, now my mind's a little at peace, since I have resolved revenge. A pox on this tailor, though, for not bringing home the clothes I bespoke. And a pox of all poor cavaliers: A man can never keep a spare suit for 'em, and I shall have these rogues come in and find me naked, and then I'm undone. But I'm resolved to arm myself: The rascals shall not insult over me too much. (*Puts on an old rusty sword and buff belt.*) Now, how like a morris dancer° I am equipped! A fine ladylike whore to cheat me thus without affording me a kindness for my money! A pox light on her, I shall never be reconciled to the sex more; she has made me as faithless as a physician, as uncharitable as a churchman, and as ill-natured as a poet. Oh, how I'll use all womankind hereafter! What would I give to have one of 'em within my reach now! Any mortal thing in petticoats, kind fortune, send me, and I'll forgive thy last night's malice. — Here's a cursed book, too — a warning to all young travelers — that can instruct me how to prevent such mischiefs now 'tis too late. Well, 'tis a rare convenient thing to read a little now and then, as well as hawk and hunt.
                              (*Sits down again and reads.*)

(*Enter to him Florinda.*)

FLORINDA: This house is haunted, sure: 'Tis well furnished, and no living thing inhabits it. Ha! A man! Heavens, how he's attired! Sure 'tis some rope

9–10. morris dancer: The morris dance is a lively dance performed by men wearing costumes and bells.

dancer, or fencing master. I tremble now for fear, and yet I must venture now to speak to him. — Sir, if I may not interrupt your meditations —
                              (*He starts up and gazes.*)

BLUNT: Ha, what's here? Are my wishes granted? And is not that a she creature? 'Adsheartlikins, 'tis. — What wretched thing art thou, ha?

FLORINDA: Charitable sir, you've told yourself already what I am: a very wretched maid, forced by a strange unlucky accident to seek a safety here, and must be ruined if you do not grant it.

BLUNT: Ruined! Is there any ruin so inevitable as that which now threatens thee? Dost thou know, miserable woman, into what den of mischiefs thou art fallen; what abyss of confusion, ha? Dost not see something in my looks that frights thy guilty soul, and makes thee wish to change that shape of woman for any humble animal, or devil? For those were safer for thee, and less mischievous.

FLORINDA: Alas, what mean you, sir? I must confess, your looks have something in 'em makes me fear, but I beseech you, as you seem a gentleman, pity a harmless virgin that takes your house for sanctuary.

BLUNT: Talk on, talk on; and weep, too, till my faith so return. Do, flatter me out of my senses again. A harmless virgin with a pox; as much one as t'other, 'adsheartlikins. Why, what the devil, can I not be safe in my house for you, not in my chamber? Nay, not even being naked too cannot secure me? This is an impudence greater than has invaded me yet. Come, no resistance.   (*Pulls her rudely.*)

FLORINDA: Dare you be so cruel?

BLUNT: Cruel? 'Adsheartlikins, as a galley slave, or a Spanish whore. Cruel? Yes, I will kiss and beat thee all over, kiss and see thee all over; thou shalt lie with me too, not that I care for the enjoyment, but to let thee see I have ta'en deliberated malice to thee, and will be revenged on one whore for the sins of another. I will smile and deceive thee; flatter thee, and beat thee; embrace thee and rob thee, as she did me; fawn on thee, and strip thee stark naked; then hang thee out at my window by the heels, with a paper of scurvy verses fastened to thy breast in praise of damnable women. Come, come, along.

FLORINDA: Alas, sir, must I be sacrificed for the crimes of the most infamous of my sex? I never understood the sins you name.

BLUNT: Do, persuade the fool you love him, or that one of you can be just or honest; tell me I was not an easy coxcomb, or any strange impossible tale: It will be believed sooner than thy false showers or protestations. A generation of damned hypocrites! To flatter my very clothes from my back! Dissembling witches! Are these the returns you make an honest gentleman that trusts, believes, and loves you? But if I be not even with you — Come along, or I shall —   (*Pulls her again.*)

(*Enter Frederick.*)

85   FREDERICK: Ha, what's here to do?

BLUNT: 'Adsheartlikins, Fred, I am glad thou art come, to be a witness of my dire revenge.

FREDERICK: What's this, a person of quality too, who is upon the ramble° to supply the defects of some

90   grave impotent husband?

BLUNT: No, this has another pretense: Some very unfortunate accident brought her hither, to save a life pursued by I know not who or why, and forced to take sanctuary here at fool's haven. 'Adsheart-

95   likins, to me of all mankind for protection? Is the ass to be cajoled again, think ye? No, young one, no prayers or tears shall mitigate my rage; therefore prepare for both my pleasures of enjoyment and revenge. For I am resolved to make up my loss

100   here on thy body: I'll take it out in kindness and in beating.

FREDERICK: Now, mistress of mine, what do you think of this?

FLORINDA: I think he will not, dares not be so

105   barbarous.

FREDERICK: Have a care, Blunt, she fetched a deep sigh; she is enamored with thy shirt and drawers. She'll strip thee even of that; there are of her calling such unconscionable baggages and such dex-

110   terous thieves, they'll flea° a man and he shall ne'er miss his skin till he feels the cold. There was a countryman of ours robbed of a row of teeth whilst he was a-sleeping, which the jilt made him buy again when he waked. You see, lady, how lit-

115   tle reason we have to trust you.

BLUNT: 'Adsheartlikins, why this is most abominable!

FLORINDA: Some such devils there may be, but by all that's holy, I am none such. I entered here to save a life in danger.

120   BLUNT: For no goodness, I'll warrant her.

FREDERICK: Faith, damsel, you had e'en confessed the plain truth, for we are fellows not to be caught twice in the same trap. Look on that wreck: a tight vessel when he set out of haven, well trimmed and

125   laden. And see how a female picaroon of this island of rogues has shattered him, and canst thou hope for any mercy?

BLUNT: No, no, gentlewoman, come along; 'adsheartlikins, we must be better acquainted. — We'll both

130   lie with her, and then let me alone to bang her.

FREDERICK: I'm ready to serve you in matters of revenge that has a double pleasure in't.

BLUNT: Well said. — You hear, little one, how you are condemned by public vote to the bed within; there's no resisting your destiny, sweetheart.   135

(*Pulls her.*)

FLORINDA: Stay, sir. I have seen you with Belvile, an English cavalier. For his sake, use me kindly. You know him, sir.

BLUNT: Belvile? Why yes, sweeting, we do know Belvile, and wish he were with us now. He's a cor-   140 morant at whore and bacon:° He'd have a limb or two of thee, my virgin pullet. But 'tis no matter; we'll leave him the bones to pick.

FLORINDA: Sir, if you have any esteem for that Belvile, I conjure you to treat me with more gentleness;   145 he'll thank you for the justice.

FREDERICK: Hark'ee, Blunt, I doubt we are mistaken in this matter.

FLORINDA: Sir, if you find me not worth Belvile's care, use me as you please. And that you may think I   150 merit better treatment than you threaten, pray take this present.

(*Gives him a ring; he looks on it.*)

BLUNT: Hum, a diamond! Why, 'tis a wonderful virtue now that lies in this ring, a mollifying virtue. 'Adsheartlikins, there's more persuasive rhetoric   155 in't than all her sex can utter.

FREDERICK: I begin to suspect something, and 'twould anger us vilely to be trussed up for a rape upon a maid of quality, when we only believe we ruffle a harlot.   160

BLUNT: Thou art a credulous fellow, but 'adsheartlikins, I have no faith yet. Why, my saint prattled as parlously as this does; she gave me a bracelet, too, a devil on her! But I sent my man to sell it today for necessaries, and it proved as counterfeit as   165 her vows of love.

FREDERICK: However, let it reprieve her till we see Belvile.

BLUNT: That's hard, yet I will grant it.

(*Enter a Servant.*)

SERVANT: Oh, sir, the colonel is just come in with his   170 new friend and a Spaniard of quality, and talks of having you to dinner with 'em.

BLUNT: 'Adsheartlikins, I'm undone! I would not see 'em for the world. Hark'ee, Fred, lock up the wench in your chamber.   175

FREDERICK: Fear nothing, madam: Whate'er he threatens, you are safe whilst in my hands.

(*Exeunt Frederick and Florinda.*)

---

89. **upon the ramble:** Rambling, wandering.   110. **flea:** Strip off the skin (flay).

140–41. **cormorant . . . bacon:** Glutton for sex.

BLUNT: And sirrah, upon your life, say I am not at
180   home, or that I'm asleep, or — or — anything.
Away; I'll prevent their coming this way.
                (*Locks the door, and exeunt.*)

ACT V

(*Blunt's chamber. After a great knocking as at his
chamber door, enter Blunt softly crossing the stage, in
his shirt and drawers as before.*)

[VOICES] (*call within*): Ned! Ned Blunt! Ned Blunt!
BLUNT: The rogues are up in arms. 'Adsheartlikins,
    this villainous Frederick has betrayed me: They
    have heard of my blessed fortune.
5 [VOICES] (*and knocking within*): Ned Blunt! Ned!
    Ned!
BELVILE [*within*]: Why, he's dead, sir, without dispute
    dead; he has not been seen today. Let's break open
    the door. Here, boy —
10 BLUNT: Ha, break open the door? 'Adsheartlikins,
    that mad fellow will be as good as his word.
BELVILE [*within*]: Boy, bring something to force the
    door.
          (*A great noise within, at the door again.*)
BLUNT: So, now must I speak in my own defense, I'll
15 try what rhetoric will do. — Hold, hold! What do
    you mean, gentlemen, what do you mean?
BELVILE (*within*): Oh, rogue, art alive? Prithee open
    the door and convince us.
BLUNT: Yes, I am alive, gentlemen, but at present a lit-
20 tle busy.
BELVILE (*within*): How, Blunt grown a man of busi-
    ness? Come, come, open and let's see this miracle.
BLUNT: No, no, no, no, gentlemen, 'tis no great busi-
    ness. But — I am — at — my devotion. 'Adsheart-
25 likins, will you not allow a man time to pray?
BELVILE (*within*): Turned religious? A greater wonder
    than the first! Therefore open quickly, or we shall
    unhinge, we shall.
BLUNT [*aside*]: This won't do. — Why hark'ee,
30 colonel, to tell you the truth, I am about a neces-
    sary affair of life: I have a wench with me. You ap-
    prehend me? — The devil's in't if they be so uncivil
    as to disturb me now.
WILLMORE [*within*]: How, a wench? Nay then, we
35 must enter and partake. No resistance. Unless it be
    your lady of quality, and then we'll keep our dis-
    tance.
BLUNT: So, the business is out.
WILLMORE [*within*]: Come, come, lend's more hands
40 to the door. Now heave, all together. (*Breaks open
    the door.*) So, well done, my boys.

(*Enter Belvile [and his Page], Willmore, Frederick,
and Pedro. Blunt looks simply, they all laugh at him;
he lays his hand on his sword, and comes up to Willmore.*)

BLUNT: Hark'ee, sir, laugh out your laugh quickly,
    d'ye hear, and be gone. I shall spoil your sport
    else, 'adsheartlikins, sir. I shall. The jest has been
    carried on too long. — (*Aside.*) A plague upon my 45
    tailor!
WILLMORE: 'Sdeath, how the whore has dressed him!
    Faith, sir, I'm sorry.
BLUNT: Are you so, sir? Keep't to yourself then, sir, I
    advise you, d'ye hear, for I can as little endure 50
    your pity as his mirth.
              (*Lays his hand on's sword.*)
BELVILE: Indeed, Willmore, thou wert a little too
    rough with Ned Blunt's mistress. Call a person of
    quality whore, and one so young, so handsome,
    and so eloquent? Ha, ha, he. 55
BLUNT: Hark'ee, sir, you know me, and know I can be
    angry. Have a care, for 'adsheartlikins, I can fight,
    too, I can, sir. Do you mark me? No more.
BELVILE: Why so peevish, good Ned? Some disap-
    pointments, I'll warrant. What, did the jealous 60
    count, her husband, return just in the nick?
BLUNT: Or the devil, sir. (*They laugh.*) D'ye laugh?
    Look ye settle me a good sober countenance, and
    that quickly, too, or you shall know Ned Blunt is
    not — 65
BELVILE: Not everybody, we know that.
BLUNT: Not an ass to be laughed at, sir.
WILLMORE: Unconscionable sinner! To bring a lover
    so near his happiness — a vigorous passionate
    lover — and then not only cheat him of his mov- 70
    ables, but his very desires, too.
BELVILE: Ah, sir, a mistress is a trifle with Blunt; he'll
    have a dozen the next time he looks abroad. His
    eyes have charms not to be resisted; there needs no
    more than to expose that taking person to the view 75
    of the fair, and he leads 'em all in triumph.
PEDRO: Sir, though I'm a stranger to you, I am
    ashamed at the rudeness of my nation; and could
    you learn who did it, would assist you to make an
    example of 'em. 80
BLUNT: Why ay, there's one speaks sense now, and
    handsomely. And let me tell you, gentlemen, I
    should not have showed myself like a jack pud-
    ding° thus to have made you mirth, but that I have
    revenge within my power. For know, I have got 85
    into my possession a female, who had better have
    fallen under any curse than the ruin I design her.
    'Adsheartlikins, she assaulted me here in my own

83. **jack pudding:** Clown.

lodgings, and had doubtless committed a rape
90 upon me, had not this sword defended me.
FREDERICK: I know not that, but o' my conscience
thou had ravished her, had she not redeemed herself with a ring. Let's see't, Blunt.
                              (*Blunt shows the ring.*)
BELVILE [*aside*]: Ha! The ring I gave Florinda when we
95 exchanged our vows! — Hark'ee, Blunt —
                              (*Goes to whisper to him.*)
WILLMORE: No whispering, good colonel, there's a
woman in the case. No whispering.
BELVILE [*aside to Blunt*]: Hark'ee, fool, be advised,
and conceal both the ring and the story for your
100 reputation's sake. Do not let people know what
despised cullies we English are; to be cheated and
abused by one whore, and another rather bribe
thee than be kind to thee, is an infamy to our nation.
105 WILLMORE: Come, come, where's the wench? We'll
see her; let her be what she will, we'll see her.
PEDRO: Ay, ay, let us see her. I can soon discover
whether she be of quality, or for your diversion.
BLUNT: She's in Fred's custody.
110 WILLMORE: Come, come, the key —
                              (*To Frederick, who gives him the key; they are
                              going.*)
BELVILE [*aside*]: Death, what shall I do? — Stay, gentlemen. — [*Aside.*] Yet if I hinder 'em, I shall discover all. — Hold, let's go one at once.° Give me
the key.
115 WILLMORE: Nay, hold there, colonel, I'll go first.
FREDERICK: Nay, no dispute, Ned and I have the propriety of her.
WILLMORE: Damn propriety! Then we'll draw cuts.
                              (*Belvile goes to whisper [to] Willmore.*) Nay, no
120 corruption, good colonel. Come, the longest sword
carries her.

(*They all draw, forgetting Don Pedro, being a
Spaniard, had the longest.*)

BLUNT: I yield up my interest to you, gentlemen, and
that will be revenge sufficient.
WILLMORE (*to Pedro*): The wench is yours. — [*Aside.*]
125 Pox of his Toledo,° I had forgot that.
FREDERICK: Come, sir, I'll conduct you to the lady.
                              (*Exeunt Frederick and Pedro.*)
BELVILE (*aside*): To hinder him will certainly discover
her. — Dost know, dull beast, what mischief thou
hast done?
                              (*Willmore walking up and down, out of humor.*)

113. **one at once:** One after the other.   125. **Toledo:** His
sword, which won the draw, was made in Toledo, Spain.

WILLMORE: Ay, ay, to trust our fortune to lots! A devil   130
on't, 'twas madness, that's the truth on't.
BELVILE: Oh, intolerable sot —

(*Enter Florinda running, masked, Pedro after her;
Willmore gazing round her.*)

FLORINDA (*aside*): Good heaven defend me from discovery!
PEDRO: 'Tis but in vain to fly me; you're fallen to my   135
lot.
BELVILE [*aside*]: Sure she's undiscovered yet, but now I
fear there is no way to bring her off.
WILLMORE [*aside*]: Why, what a pox, is not this my
woman, the same I followed but now?   140
                              (*Pedro talking to Florinda, who walks up
                              and down.*)
PEDRO: As if I did not know ye, and your business
here.
FLORINDA (*aside*): Good heaven, I fear he does indeed!
PEDRO: Come, pray be kind; I know you meant to be
so when you entered here, for these are proper   145
gentlemen.
WILLMORE: But sir, perhaps the lady will not be imposed upon: She'll choose her man.
PEDRO: I am better bred than not to leave her choice
free.   150

(*Enter Valeria, and is surprised at sight of Don Pedro.*)

VALERIA (*aside*): Don Pedro here! There's no avoiding
him.
FLORINDA (*aside*): Valeria! Then I'm undone.
VALERIA (*to Pedro, running to him*): Oh, I have found
you, sir! The strangest accident — if I had   155
breath — to tell it.
PEDRO: Speak! Is Florinda safe? Hellena well?
VALERIA: Ay, ay, sir. Florinda is safe. — [*Aside.*] From
any fears of you.
PEDRO: Why, where's Florinda? Speak!   160
VALERIA: Ay, where indeed, sir; I wish I could inform
you. But to hold you no longer in doubt —
FLORINDA (*aside*): Oh, what will she say?
VALERIA: She's fled away in the habit — of one of her
pages, sir. But Callis thinks you may retrieve her   165
yet, if you make haste away. She'll tell you, sir, the
rest. — (*Aside.*) If you can find her out.
PEDRO: Dishonorable girl, she has undone my aim. —
[*To Belvile.*] Sir, you see my necessity of leaving
you, and I hope you'll pardon it. My sister, I know,   170
will make her flight to you, and if she do, I shall
expect she should be rendered back.
BELVILE: I shall consult my love and honor, sir.
                              (*Exit Pedro.*)
FLORINDA (*to Valeria*): My dear preserver, let me embrace thee.   175
WILLMORE: What the devil's all this?

BLUNT: Mystery, by this light.

VALERIA: Come, come, make haste and get yourselves married quickly, for your brother will return again.

180 BELVILE: I'm so surprised with fears and joys, so amazed to find you here in safety, I can scarce persuade my heart into a faith of what I see.

WILLMORE: Hark'ee, colonel, is this that mistress who has cost you so many sighs, and me so many quar-

185 rels with you?

BELVILE: It is. — [*To Florinda.*] Pray give him the honor of your hand.

WILLMORE: Thus it must be received, then. (*Kneels and kisses her hand.*) And with it give your par-

190 don, too.

FLORINDA: The friend to Belvile may command me anything.

WILLMORE (*aside*): Death, would I might; 'tis a surprising beauty.

195 BELVILE: Boy, run and fetch a father instantly.

(*Exit Boy.*)

FREDERICK: So, now do I stand like a dog, and have not a syllable to plead my own cause with. By this hand, madam, I was never thoroughly confounded before, nor shall I ever more dare look up with

200 confidence, till you are pleased to pardon me.

FLORINDA: Sir, I'll be reconciled to you on one condition: that you'll follow the example of your friend in marrying a maid that does not hate you, and whose fortune, I believe, will not be unwelcome to

205 you.

FREDERICK: Madam, had I no inclinations that way, I should obey your kind commands.

BELVILE: Who, Fred marry? He has so few inclinations for womankind that had he been possessed of par-

210 adise he might have continued there to this day, if no crime but love could have disinherited him.

FREDERICK: Oh, I do not use to boast of my intrigues.

BELVILE: Boast! Why, thou cost nothing but boast. And I dare swear, wert thou as innocent from the

215 sin of the grape as thou art from the apple, thou might'st yet claim that right in Eden which our first parents lost by too much loving.

FREDERICK: I wish this lady would think me so modest a man.

220 VALERIA: She would be sorry then, and not like you half so well. And I should be loath to break my word with you, which was, that if your friend and mine agreed, it should be a match between you and I.   (*She gives him her hand.*)

225 FREDERICK: Bear witness, colonel, 'tis a bargain.

(*Kisses her hand.*)

BLUNT (*to Florinda*): I have a pardon to beg, too; but 'adsheartlikins, I am so out of countenance that I'm a dog if I can say anything to purpose.

FLORINDA: Sir, I heartily forgive you all.

BLUNT: That's nobly said, sweet lady. — Belvile, 230
prithee present her her ring again, for I find I have not courage to approach her myself.

(*Gives him the ring; he gives it to Florinda.*)

(*Enter Boy.*)

BOY: Sir, I have brought the father that you sent for.

[*Exit Boy.*]

BELVILE: 'Tis well. And now, my dear Florinda, let's fly to complete that mighty joy we have so long wished 235
and sighed for. — Come, Fred, you'll follow?

FREDERICK: Your example, sir, 'twas ever my ambition in war, and must be so in love.

WILLMORE: And must not I see this juggling° knot 240
tied?

BELVILE: No, thou shalt do us better service and be our guard, lest Don Pedro's sudden return interrupt the ceremony.

WILLMORE: Content; I'll secure this pass. 245

(*Exeunt Belvile, Florinda, Frederick, and Valeria.*)

(*Enter Boy.*)

BOY (*to Willmore*): Sir, there's a lady without would speak to you.

WILLMORE: Conduct her in; I dare not quit my post.

BOY [*to Blunt*]: And sir, your tailor waits you in your chamber. 250

BLUNT: Some comfort yet: I shall not dance naked at the wedding.

(*Exeunt Blunt and Boy.*)

(*Enter again the Boy, conducting in Angelica in a masking habit and a vizard. Willmore runs to her.*)

WILLMORE [*aside*]: This can be none but my pretty gypsy. — Oh, I see you can follow as well as fly. Come, confess thyself the most malicious devil in 255
nature; you think you have done my business with Angellica —

ANGELLICA: Stand off, base villain!

(*She draws a pistol and holds it to his breast.*)

WILLMORE: Ha, 'tis not she! Who art thou, and what's thy business? 260

ANGELLICA: One thou hast injured, and who comes to kill thee for't.

WILLMORE: What the devil canst thou mean?

ANGELLICA: By all my hopes to kill thee —

(*Holds still the pistol to his breast; he going back, she following still.*)

WILLMORE: Prithee, on what acquaintance? For I 265
know thee not.

---

240. **juggling**: Based on trickery or deception.

ANGELLICA: Behold this face so lost to thy remembrance,   (*Pulls off her vizard.*)
And then call all thy sins about thy soul
270 And let 'em die with thee.
WILLMORE: Angellica!
ANGELLICA: Yes, traitor! Does not thy guilty blood
run shivering through thy veins? Hast thou no horror at this sight, that tells thee thou hast not long
275 to boast thy shameful conquest?
WILLMORE: Faith, no, child. My blood keeps its old
ebbs and flows still, and that usual heat too, that
could oblige thee with a kindness, had I but opportunity.
280 ANGELLICA: Devil! Dost wanton with my pain? Have
at thy heart!
WILLMORE: Hold, dear virago!° Hold thy hand a little; I am not now at leisure to be killed. Hold and
hear me. — (*Aside.*) Death, I think she's in earnest.
285 ANGELLICA (*aside, turning from him*): Oh, if I take
not heed, my coward heart will leave me to his
mercy. — What have you, sir, to say? — But should
I hear thee, thoud'st talk away all that is brave
about me, and I have vowed thy death by all that's
290 sacred.
        (*Follows him with the pistol to his breast.*)
WILLMORE: Why then, there's an end of a proper
handsome fellow, that might 'a lived to have done
good service yet. That's all I can say to't.
ANGELLICA (*pausingly*): Yet — I would give thee time
295 for — penitence.
WILLMORE: Faith, child, I thank God I have ever took
care to lead a good, sober, hopeful life, and am of
a religion that teaches me to believe I shall depart
in peace.
300 ANGELLICA: So will the devil! Tell me,
How many poor believing fools thou hast
        undone?
How many hearts thou hast betrayed to ruin?
Yet these are little mischiefs to the ills
Thou'st taught mine to commit: Thou'st taught it
        love.
305 WILLMORE: Egad, 'twas shrewdly hurt the while.
ANGELLICA: Love, that has robbed it of its
        unconcern,
Of all that pride that taught me how to value it.
And in its room
A mean submissive passion was conveyed,
310 That made me humbly bow, which I ne'er did
To anything but heaven.

282. **virago:** A woman of great stature, strength, and
courage.

Thou, perjured man, didst this; and with thy
        oaths,
Which on thy knees thou didst devoutly make,
Softened my yielding heart, and then I was a
        slave.
Yet still had been content to've worn my chains,   315
Worn 'em with vanity and joy forever,
Hadst thou not broke those vows that put them
        on.
'Twas then I was undone.
        (*All this while follows him with the pistol
                                        to his breast.*)
WILLMORE: Broke my vows? Why, where hast thou   320
lived? Amongst the gods? For I never heard of
mortal man that has not broke a thousand vows.
ANGELLICA: Oh, impudence!
WILLMORE: Angellica, that beauty has been too long
tempting, not to have made a thousand lovers languish; who, in the amorous fever, no doubt have   325
sworn like me. Did they all die in that faith, still
adoring? I do not think they did.
ANGELLICA: No, faithless man; had I repaid their
vows, as I did shine, I would have killed the in-
grateful that had abandoned me.   330
WILLMORE: This old general has quite spoiled thee:
Nothing makes a woman so vain as being flattered. Your old lover ever supplies the defects of
age with intolerable dotage, vast charge, and that
which you call constancy; and attributing all this
to your own merits, you domineer, and throw   335
your favors in's teeth, upbraiding him still with
the defects of age, and cuckold him as often as he
deceives your expectations. But the gay, young,
brisk lover, that brings his equal fires, and can give
you dart for dart, you'll find will be as nice as you 340
sometimes.
ANGELLICA: All this thou'st made me know, for
        which I hate thee.
Had I remained in innocent security,
I should have thought all men were born my
        slaves,
And worn my power like lightning in my eyes,   345
To have destroyed at pleasure when offended.
But when love held the mirror, the undeceiving
        glass
Reflected all the weakness of my soul, and made
        me know
My richest treasure being lost, my honor,
All the remaining spoil could not be worth   350
The conqueror's care or value.
Oh, how I fell, like a long-worshiped idol,
Discovering all the cheat.
Would not the incense and rich sacrifice
Which blind devotion offered at my altars   355
Have fallen to thee?

Why wouldst thou then destroy my fancied
    power?
WILLMORE: By heaven, thou'rt brave, and I admire
    thee strangely.
I wish I were that dull, that constant thing
Which thou wouldst have, and nature never
360   meant me.
I must, like cheerful birds, sing in all groves,
And perch on every bough,
Billing the next kind she that flies to meet me;
Yet, after all, could build my nest with thee,
365 Thither repairing when I'd loved my round,
And still reserve a tributary flame.
To gain your credit, I'll pay you back your
    charity,
And be obliged for nothing but for love.
                  (Offers her a purse of gold.)
ANGELLICA: Oh, that thou wert in earnest!
370 So mean a thought of me
Would turn my rage to scorn, and I should pity
    thee,
And give thee leave to live;
Which for the public safety of our sex,
And my own private injuries, I dare not do.
375 Prepare —   (Follows still, as before.)
I will no more be tempted with replies.
WILLMORE: Sure —
ANGELLICA: Another word will damn thee! I've heard
    thee talk too long.

(She follows him with the pistol ready to shoot; he retires, still amazed. Enter Don Antonio, his arm in a
scarf, and lays hold on the pistol.)

380 ANTONIO: Ha! Angellica!
ANGELLICA: Antonio! What devil brought thee hither?
ANTONIO: Love and curiosity, seeing your coach at
    door. Let me disarm you of this unbecoming in-
    strument of death.   (Takes away the pistol.)
385 Amongst the number of your slaves was there not
    one worthy the honor to have fought your quar-
    rel? — [To Willmore.] Who are you, sir, that are so
    very wretched to merit death from her?
WILLMORE: One, sir, that could have made a better
390   end of an amorous quarrel without you, than with
    you.
ANTONIO: Sure 'tis some rival. Ha! The very man
    took down her picture yesterday; the very same
    that set on me last night! Blessed opportunity —
                    (Offers to shoot him.)
395 ANGELLICA: Hold, you're mistaken, sir.
ANTONIO: By heaven, the very same! — Sir, what pre-
    tensions have you to this lady?
WILLMORE: Sir, I do not use to be examined, and am
    ill at all disputes but this —

            (Draws; Antonio offers to shoot.)
ANGELLICA (to Willmore): Oh, hold! You see he's
    armed with certain death.   400
    — And you, Antonio, I command you hold,
By all the passion you've so lately vowed me.

(Enter Don Pedro, sees Antonio, and stays.)

PEDRO (aside): Ha! Antonio! And Angellica!
ANTONIO: When I refuse obedience to your will,
    May you destroy me with your mortal hate.   405
By all that's holy, I adore you so,
That even my rival, who has charms enough
To make him fall a victim to my jealousy,
Shall live; nay, and have leave to love on still.
PEDRO (aside): What's this I hear?   410
ANGELLICA (pointing to Willmore): Ah thus, 'twas
    thus he talked, and I believed.
Antonio, yesterday
I'd not have sold my interest in his heart
For all the sword has won and lost in battle.
    — But now, to show my utmost of contempt,   415
I give thee life; which, if thou wouldst preserve,
Live where my eyes may never see thee more.
Live to undo someone whose soul may prove
So bravely constant to revenge my love.
         (Goes out. Antonio follows, but Pedro
                    pulls him back.)
PEDRO: Antonio, stay.   420
ANTONIO: Don Pedro!
PEDRO: What coward fear was that prevented thee
    from meeting me this morning on the Molo?
ANTONIO: Meet thee?
PEDRO: Yes, me; I was the man that dared thee to't.   425
ANTONIO: Hast thou so often seen me fight in war, to
    find no better cause to excuse my absence? I sent
    my sword and one to do thee right, finding myself
    uncapable to use a sword.
PEDRO: But 'twas Florinda's quarrel that we fought,   430
    and you, to show how little you esteemed her, sent
    me your rival, giving him your interest. But I have
    found the cause of this affront, and when I meet
    you fit for the dispute, I'll tell you my resentment.
ANTONIO: I shall be ready, sir, ere long, to do you rea-   435
    son.   (Exit Antonio.)
PEDRO: If I could find Florinda, now whilst my anger's
    high, I think I should be kind, and give her to
    Belvile in revenge.
WILLMORE: Faith, sir, I know not what you would do,   440
    but I believe the priest within has been so kind.
PEDRO: How? My sister married?
WILLMORE: I hope by this time he is, and bedded too,
    or he has not my longings about him.
PEDRO: Dares he do this? Does he not fear my power?   445
WILLMORE: Faith, not at all; if you will go in and

thank him for the favor he has done your sister, so;
if not, sir, my power's greater in this house than
yours: I have a damned surly crew here that will
keep you till the next tide, and then clap you on
450 board for prize. My ship lies but a league off the
Molo, and we shall show your donship a damned
Tramontana° rover's trick.

(*Enter Belvile.*)

BELVILE: This rogue's in some new mischief. Ha! Pe-
455 dro returned!
PEDRO: Colonel Belvile, I hear you have married my
sister.
BELVILE: You have heard truth then, sir.
PEDRO: Have I so? Then, sir, I wish you joy.
460 BELVILE: How?
PEDRO: By this embrace I do, and I am glad on't.
BELVILE: Are you in earnest?
PEDRO: By our long friendship and my obligations to
thee, I am; the sudden change I'll give you reasons
465 for anon. Come, lead me to my sister, that she may
know I now approve her choice.

(*Exit Belvile with Pedro.*)

(*Willmore goes to follow them. Enter Hellena, as before in boy's clothes, and pulls him back.*)

WILLMORE: Ha! My gypsy! Now a thousand blessings
on thee for this kindness. Egad, child, I was e'en in
despair of ever seeing thee again; my friends are all
470 provided for within, each man his kind woman.
HELLENA: Ha! I thought they had served me some
such trick!
WILLMORE: And I was e'en resolved to go aboard, and
condemn myself to my lone cabin, and the
475 thoughts of thee.
HELLENA: And could you have left me behind? Would
you have been so ill natured?
WILLMORE: Why, 'twould have broke my heart, child.
But since we are met again, I defy foul weather to
480 part us.
HELLENA: And would you be a faithful friend now, if
a maid should trust you?
WILLMORE: For a friend I cannot promise: Thou art of
a form so excellent, a face and humor too good for
485 cold dull friendship. I am parlously afraid of being
in love, child; and you have not forgotten how severely you have used me?
HELLENA: That's all one; such usage you must still
look for: to find out all your haunts, to rail at you
490 to all that love you, till I have made you love only
me in your own defense, because nobody else will
love you.

WILLMORE: But hast thou no better quality to recommend thyself by?
HELLENA: Faith, none, captain. Why, 'twill be the   495
greater charity to take me for thy mistress. I am a
lone child, a kind of orphan lover, and why I
should die a maid, and in a captain's hands too, I
do not understand.
WILLMORE: Egad, I was never clawed away with   500
broadsides from any female before. Thou hast one
virtue I adore — good nature. I hate a coy demure
mistress, she's as troublesome as a colt, I'll break
none. No, give me a mad mistress when mewed,
and in flying, one I dare trust upon the wing, that   505
whilst she's kind will come to the lure.°
HELLENA: Nay, as kind as you will, good captain,
whilst it lasts. But let's lose no time.
WILLMORE: My time's as precious to me as thine can
be. Therefore, dear creature, since we are so well   510
agreed, let's retire to my chamber; and if ever thou
wert treated with such savory love! Come, my
bed's prepared for such a guest all clean and sweet
as thy fair self. I love to steal a dish and a bottle
with a friend, and hate long graces. Come, let's re-   515
tire and fall to.
HELLENA: 'Tis but getting my consent, and the business is soon done. Let but old gaffer Hymen° and
his priest say amen to's, and I dare lay my mother's
daughter by as proper a fellow as your father's   520
son, without fear or blushing.
WILLMORE: Hold, hold, no bug words,° child. Priest
and Hymen? Prithee add a hangman to 'em to
make up the consort. No, no, we'll have no vows
but love, child, nor witness but the lover: The kind   525
deity enjoins naught but love and enjoy. Hymen
and priest wait still upon portion and jointure;
love and beauty have their own ceremonies. Marriage is as certain a bane to love as lending money
is to friendship. I'll neither ask nor give a vow,   530
though I could be content to turn gypsy and become a left-handed bridegroom to have the pleasure of working that great miracle of making a
maid a mother, if you durst venture. 'Tis upse
gypsy° that, and if I miss I'll lose my labor.   535
HELLENA: And if you do not lose, what shall I get? A
cradle full of noise and mischief, with a pack of repentance at my back? Can you teach me to weave
incle° to pass my time with? 'Tis upse gypsy that,
too.   540

---

453. **Tramontana:** Region of Italy north of the Alps.

505–6. **flying . . . lure:** I.e., one who will be faithful as long
as that doesn't interfere with her wishes.   518. **Hymen:**
God of marriage.   522. **bug words:** Words that inspire fear.
534. **upse gypsy:** Gypsy fashion.   539. **incle:** Linen yarn or
tape.

WILLMORE: I can teach thee to weave a true love's knot better.

HELLENA: So can my dog.

WILLMORE: Well, I see we are both upon our guards,
545   and I see there's no way to conquer good nature
but by yielding. Here, give me thy hand: One kiss,
and I am thine.

HELLENA: One kiss! How like my page he speaks! I
am resolved you shall have none, for asking such a
550   sneaking sum. He that will be satisfied with one
kiss will never die of that longing. Good friend
single-kiss, is all your talking come to this? A kiss,
a caudle!° Farewell, captain single-kiss.

(*Going out; he stays her.*)

WILLMORE: Nay, if we part so, let me die like a bird
555   upon a bough, at the sheriff's charge. By heaven,
both the Indies shall not buy thee from me. I adore
thy humor and will marry thee, and we are so of
one humor it must be a bargain. Give me thy hand.
(*Kisses her hand.*) And now let the blind ones, love
560   and fortune, do their worst.

HELLENA: Why, god-a-mercy, captain!

WILLMORE: But hark'ee: the bargain is now made, but
is it not fit we should know each other's names,
that when we have reason to curse one another
565   hereafter, and people ask me who 'tis I give to the
devil, I may at least be able to tell what family you
came of?

HELLENA: Good reason, captain, and where I have
cause, as I doubt not but I shall have plentiful, that
570   I may know at whom to throw my — blessings, I
beseech ye your name.

WILLMORE: I am called Robert the Constant.

HELLENA: A very fine name! Pray was it your
faulkner° or butler that christened you? Do they
575   not use to whistle when they call you?

WILLMORE: I hope you have a better, that a man may
name without crossing himself — you are so merry
with mine.

HELLENA: I am called Hellena the Inconstant.

(*Enter Pedro, Belvile, Florinda, Frederick, Valeria.*)

580 PEDRO: Ha! Hellena!

FLORINDA: Hellena!

HELLENA: The very same. Ha! My brother! Now, captain, show your love and courage; stand to your
arms and defend me bravely, or I am lost forever.

585 PEDRO: What's this I hear? False girl, how came you
hither, and what's your business? Speak!

(*Goes roughly to her.*)

---

553. **caudle:** A warm drink made of gruel and wine or ale,
sweetened and spiced, given to the sick.   573. **faulkner:**
Falconer, trainer of hawks.

WILLMORE: Hold off, sir; you have leave to parley°
only.   (*Puts himself between.*)

HELLENA: I had e'en as good tell it, as you guess it.
Faith, brother, my business is the same with all liv- 590
ing creatures of my age: to love and be beloved —
and here's the man.

PEDRO: Perfidious maid, hast thou deceived me too;
deceived thyself and heaven?

HELLENA: 'Tis time enough to make my peace with
that;   595
Be you but kind, let me alone with heaven.

PEDRO: Belvile, I did not expect this false play from
you. Was't not enough you'd gain Florinda, which
I pardoned, but your lewd friends too must be enriched with the spoils of a noble family?   600

BELVILE: Faith, sir, I am as much surprised at this as
you can be. Yet, sir, my friends are gentlemen, and
ought to be esteemed for their misfortunes, since
they have the glory to suffer with the best of men
and kings. 'Tis true, he's a rover of fortune, yet a 605
prince aboard his little wooden world.

PEDRO: What's this to the maintenance of a woman of
her birth and quality?

WILLMORE: Faith, sir, I can boast of nothing but a
sword which does me right where'er I come, and 610
has defended a worse cause than a woman's, and
since I loved her before I either knew her birth or
name, I must pursue my resolution and marry her.

PEDRO: And is all your holy intent of becoming a nun
debauched into a desire of man?   615

HELLENA: Why, I have considered the matter, brother,
and find the three hundred thousand crowns my
uncle left me, and you cannot keep from me, will
be better laid out in love than in religion, and turn
to as good an account. Let most voices carry it: for 620
heaven or the captain?

ALL CRY: A captain! A captain!

HELLENA: Look ye, sir, 'tis a clear case.

PEDRO: Oh, I am mad! — (*Aside.*) If I refuse, my life's
in danger. — Come, there's one motive induces me. 625
Take her; I shall now be free from fears of her
honor. Guard it you now, if you can; I have been a
slave to't long enough.   (*Gives her to him.*)

WILLMORE: Faith, sir, I am of a nation that are of
opinion a woman's honor is not worth guarding 630
when she has a mind to part with it.

HELLENA: Well said, captain.

PEDRO (*to Valeria*): This was your plot, mistress, but I
hope you have married one that will revenge my
quarrel to you.   635

VALERIA: There's no altering destiny, sir.

---

587. **parley:** Speak or discuss.

PEDRO: Sooner than a woman's will; therefore I forgive you all, and wish you may get my father's
pardon as easily, which I fear.

(*Enter Blunt dressed in a Spanish habit, looking very
ridiculous; his Man adjusting his band.*)

640   MAN: 'Tis very well, sir.
BLUNT: Well, sir! 'Adsheartlikins, I tell you 'tis damnable ill, sir. A Spanish habit! Good Lord! Could the
devil and my tailor devise no other punishment for
me but the mode of a nation I abominate?
645   BELVILE: What's the matter, Ned?
BLUNT: Pray view me round, and judge.
                                            (*Turns round.*)
BELVILE: I must confess thou art a kind of an odd figure.
BLUNT: In a Spanish habit with a vengeance! I had
650   rather be in the Inquisition for Judaism° than in
this doublet and breeches; a pillory were an easy
collar to this, three handfuls high; and these shoes,
too, are worse than the stocks, with the sole an
inch shorter than my foot. In fine, gentlemen, me-
655   thinks I look like a bag of bays° stuffed full of
fool's flesh.
BELVILE: Methinks 'tis well, and makes thee look e'en
cavalier. Come, sir, settle your face and salute our
friends. Lady —
660   BLUNT (*to Hellena*): Ha! Sayst thou so, my little
rover? Lady, if you be one, give me leave to kiss
your hand, and tell you, 'adsheartlikins, for all I
look so, I am your humble servant. A pox of my
Spanish habit!   (*Music is heard to play.*)
665   WILLMORE: Hark! What's this?

(*Enter Boy.*)

BOY: Sir, as the custom is, the gay people in masquerade, who make every man's house their own, are
coming up.

(*Enter several men and women in masking habits,
with music; they put themselves in order and dance.*)

670   BLUNT: 'Adsheartlikins, would 'twere lawful to pull
off their false faces, that I might see if my doxy°
were not amongst 'em.
BELVILE (*to the maskers*): Ladies and gentlemen, since
you are come so *a propos,*° you must take a small
collation with us.
675   WILLMORE (*to Hellena*): Whilst we'll to the good man
within, who stays to give us a cast of his office.°

Have you no trembling at the near approach?
HELLENA: No more than you have in an engagement
or a tempest.
WILLMORE: Egad, thou'rt a brave girl, and I admire   680
thy love and courage.
        Lead on; no other dangers they can dread,
        Who venture in the storms o'th' marriage bed.
                                            (*Exeunt.*)

EPILOGUE

The banished cavaliers! A roving blade!
A popish carnival! A masquerade!
The devil's in't if this will please the nation
In these our blessed times of reformation,
When conventickling° is so much in fashion.   5
And yet —
That mutinous tribe less factions do beget,
Than your continual differing in wit.
Your judgment's, as your passion's, a disease:
Nor muse nor miss your appetite can please;   10
You're grown as nice as queasy consciences,
Whose each convulsion, when the spirit moves,
Damns everything that maggot° disapproves.
    With canting° rule you would the stage refine,
And to dull method all our sense confine.   15
With th'insolence of commonwealths you rule,
Where each gay fop and politic grave fool
On monarch wit impose, without control.
As for the last, who seldom sees a play,
Unless it be the old Blackfriars° way;   20
Shaking his empty noddle o'er bamboo,°
He cries, "Good faith, these plays will never do!
Ah, sir, in my young days, what lofty wit,
What high-strained scenes of fighting there were
        writ.   25
These are slight airy toys. But tell me, pray,
What has the House of Commons done today?"
Then shows his politics, to let you see
Of state affairs he'll judge as notably
As he can do of wit and poetry.
The younger sparks, who hither do resort,   30
Cry,
"Pox o' your genteel things! Give us more sport'!
Damn me, I'm sure 'twill never please the court."
    Such fops are never pleased, unless the play
Be stuffed with fools as brisk and dull as they.   35

---

650. Inquisition for Judaism: The Spanish Inquisition, which
persecuted heretics, Jews, and Muslims.   **655. bag of bays:**
Spices wrapped in cloth and used for flavoring in cooking.
670. doxy: Mistress, prostitute.   **673. *a propos*:** In a timely
fashion; appropriately.   **676. stays . . . office:** The priest
waits to perform his office, i.e., to marry them.

5. conventickling: A pun. A conventicle was a secret meeting
of religious dissenters (those who were not members of the
Church of England).   **13. maggot:** Conscience.   **14. canting:** Hypocritical.   **20. Blackfriars:** The Blackfriars Theatre
(1576–1655), considered old-fashioned in Behn's time.   **21.
o'er bamboo:** Over a cane, implying old age.

Such might the half-crown spare, and in a glass
At home behold a more accomplished ass.
Where they may set their cravats, wigs, and faces,
And practice all their buffoonry grimaces:
40 See how this huff becomes, this damny,° stare,
Which they at home may act because they dare,
But must with prudent caution do elsewhere.
Oh that our Nokes, or Tony Lee,° could show
A fop but half so much to th' life as you.

POSTSCRIPT

This play had been sooner in print, but for a report about the town (made by some either very
malicious or very ignorant) that 'twas *Thomaso*°
altered; which made the booksellers fear some
5   trouble from the proprietor of that admirable play,
which indeed has wit enough to stock a poet, and
is not to be pieced or mended by any but the excellent author himself. That I have stolen some
hints from it, may be a proof that I valued it more
than to pretend to alter it, had I the dexterity of   10
some poets, who are not more expert in stealing
than in the art of concealing, and who even that
way outdo the Spartan boys.° I might have appropriated all to myself; but I, vainly proud of my
judgment, hang out the sign of Angellica (the only   15
stolen object) to give notice where a great part of
the wit dwelt; though if the *Play of the Novella*°
were as well worth remembering as *Thomaso*, they
might (bating° the name) have as well said I took
it from thence. I will only say the plot and business   20
(not to boast on't) is my own; as for the words and
characters, I leave the reader to judge and compare
'em with *Thomaso*, to whom I recommend the
great entertainment of reading it. Though had this
succeeded ill, I should have had no need of im-   25
ploring that justice from the critics, who are naturally so kind to any that pretend to usurp their
dominion, especially of our sex: They would
doubtless have given me the whole honor on't.
Therefore I will only say in English what the fa-   30
mous Vergil does in Latin: I make verses, and others have the fame.

---

40. damny: Damn me.   **43. Nokes . . . Lee:** The best low
comedians of the day. James Nokes performed in Thomas
Betterton's company.   **3. *Thomaso*:** Thomas Killigrew's
Thomaso; or, The Wanderer (1654; published 1664).

12. Spartan boys: Those who hid in the Trojan horse.   **16.**
Play of the Novella: *The Novella* (1632) by Richard Brome,
from which Behn borrowed several ideas.   **17–18. bating:**
Excepting.

COMMENTARIES

Virginia Woolf (1882–1941)
ON APHRA BEHN   1929

*Virginia Woolf was a leading experimental writer of fiction in the first half of
the twentieth century. She is known for the novels* Mrs. Dalloway (1925), To the
Lighthouse (1927), *and* Orlando (1928) *and for her essays, including* A Room
of One's Own (1929), *from which this excerpt comes. Woolf was one of the first
modern commentators to call attention to the extraordinary achievement of
Aphra Behn.*

With Mrs. Behn we turn a very important corner on the road. We leave behind, shut up in their parks among their folios, those solitary great ladies who

wrote without audience or criticism, for their own delight alone. We come to town and rub shoulders with ordinary people in the streets. Mrs. Behn was a middle-class woman with all the plebeian virtues of humor, vitality, and courage; a woman forced by the death of her husband and some unfortunate adventures of her own to make her living by her wits. She had to work on equal terms with men. She made, by working very hard, enough to live on. The importance of that fact outweighs anything that she actually wrote, even the splendid "A Thousand Martyrs I Have Made," or "Love in Fantastic Triumph Sat," for here begins the freedom of the mind, or rather the possibility that in the course of time the mind will be free to write what it likes. For now that Aphra Behn had done it, girls could go to their parents and say, You need not give me an allowance; I can make money by my pen. Of course the answer for many years to come was, Yes, by living the life of Aphra Behn! Death would be better! and the door was slammed faster than ever. That profoundly interesting subject, the value that men set upon women's chastity and its effect upon their education, here suggests itself for discussion, and might provide an interesting book if any student at Girton or Newnham cared to go into the matter. Lady Dudley, sitting in diamonds among the midges of a Scottish moor, might serve for frontispiece. Lord Dudley, *The Times* said when Lady Dudley died the other day, "a man of cultivated taste and many accomplishments, was benevolent and bountiful, but whimsically despotic. He insisted upon his wife's wearing full dress, even at the remotest shooting-lodge in the Highlands; he loaded her with gorgeous jewels," and so on, "he gave her everything — always excepting any measure of responsibility." Then Lord Dudley had a stroke and she nursed him and ruled his estates with supreme competence for ever after. That whimsical despotism was in the nineteenth century too.

But to return. Aphra Behn proved that money could be made by writing at the sacrifice, perhaps, of certain agreeable qualities; and so by degrees writing became not merely a sign of folly and a distracted mind, but was of practical importance. A husband might die, or some disaster overtake the family. Hundreds of women began as the eighteenth century drew on to add to their pin money, or to come to the rescue of their families by making translations or writing the innumerable bad novels which have ceased to be recorded even in textbooks, but are to be picked up in the fourpenny boxes in the Charing Cross Road. The extreme activity of mind which showed itself in the later eighteenth century among women — the talking, and the meeting, the writing of essays on Shakespeare, the translating of the classics — was founded on the solid fact that women could make money by writing. Money dignifies what is frivolous if unpaid for. It might still be well to sneer at "blue stockings with an itch for scribbling," but it could not be denied that they could put money in their purses. Thus, towards the end of the eighteenth century a change came about which, if I were rewriting history, I should describe more fully and think of greater importance than the Crusades or the Wars of the Roses. The middle-class woman began to write. For if *Pride and Prejudice* matters, and *Middlemarch* and *Vilette* and *Wuthering Heights* matter, then it matters far more than I can prove in an hour's discourse that women generally, and not merely the lonely aristocrat shut up in her country house among her folios and her flatterers, took to writing. Without those forerunners, Jane Austen and the Brontës and George Eliot could no more have written than Shakespeare could have written without Marlowe, or Marlowe without Chaucer, or Chaucer without those forgotten poets who paved the ways and tamed the natural savagery of the tongue. For masterpieces are not single and solitary births; they are the outcome of many years of thinking in common, of thinking by the body of the people, so that the experience of the mass is behind the single voice. Jane Austen should have laid a wreath upon the grave of Fanny Burney, and George Eliot done homage to the robust shade of Eliza Carter — the valiant old woman who tied a bell to her bedstead in order that she might wake early and learn Greek. All women together ought to let flowers fall upon the tomb of Aphra Behn, which is, most scandalously but rather appropriately, in Westminster Abbey,° for it was she who earned them the right to speak their minds. It is she — shady and amorous as she was — who makes it not quite fantastic for me to say to you tonight: Earn five hundred a year by your wits.

Westminster Abbey: The burial place in London of British royalty as well as distinguished citizens, including, in the Poets' Corner, famous writers.

Elaine Hobby (b. 1956)
COURTSHIP AND MARRIAGE IN *THE ROVER*   1989

Elaine Hobby closely examines The Rover *to help us understand the conventions of romantic love in Aphra Behn's work. Her essay is especially enlightening on the questions of marriage and rape and on the differences in the viewpoints of men and women characters in the play. Hobby notes the complexities implied in the characterization of Angellica, the courtesan.*

Commonly, Behn's plays feature at least two pairs of young lovers, whose attitudes to love and marriage serve as contrasting strategies in courtship. A common pattern is that of the "constant couple," who remain true to one another, and finally marry, despite parental opposition and, usually, confusions over one another's true identity and conduct. These lovers are not, however, idyllically well matched or perfectly happy. In *The Rover,* Florinda and Belvile are just such a constant couple. From the beginning they are in love with one another, and resolved to accept no other partner. Except for her stubbornness on this one issue, Florinda is all quiet obedience, failing to argue her case against an arranged marriage. Her passivity is no ideal. Twice in the course of the play she narrowly escapes being raped by the friends of her beloved, and on each occasion is only saved because her obvious high social class causes her attackers to hesitate, fearing retribution from her relatives. The second of these incidents is a nightmare scene where, seeking refuge in Blunt's house, she is regarded by him as the perfect target for his revenge against all women (and Lucetta in particular) for making fun of him. When Frederick, the play's great upholder of patriarchal morality, arrives, the two men agree to rape her.

> BLUNT: We'll both lie with her, and then let me alone to bang her.
> FREDERICK: I'm ready to serve you in matters of revenge that has a double pleasure in't.
>   (IV, v, 129–32)

In a world where men can choose to rape a woman, any woman, for spite, there is no safety for the romantic heroine. In Behn's plays, as in her novels, rape or the threat of it is shown to be an almost routine masculine strategy to bully and manipulate women. In *The Amorous Prince,* Frederick threatens to rape Laura at knifepoint to humble her for scorning him, and in the same play Silvio threatens to rape his "sister" Cleonte. Sir Timothy Tawdrey in *The Town-Fopp,* when threatening to rape Phillis, tells her that old patriarchal lie: that all women want to be forcibly taken. Phillis's fate is the most terrible of all. Having no economic choices (like Philadelphia in Behn's novel *The Unfortunate Happy Lady*), she has no option but to marry her would-be rapist.

Setting out with a theme of courtship and marriage, Behn writes about rape and prostitution, constructing scenarios that show how closely connected these fates are for women. Where Florinda's reliance on "true love" for her salvation twice brings her to the brink of being raped, the courtesan Angellica Bianca in the same play is betrayed by her final inability to escape from the tempting lies of romance. Early in the play, she makes a cool assessment of women's position, explaining that she had opted to sell her body for the solid return of financial reward, rather than trusting to illusory male fidelity: "Nothing but gold shall charm my heart" (II, I, 173–74). She knows, too, that marriage for money is a no less mercenary affair than prostitution. Disaster arrives, however, because she has seriously misjudged the power structure of her society. She arrives in town hoping to captivate either the viceroy's son Don Antonio, or Don Pedro, the nephew of her deceased "protector." Had she been married to her old lover, Don Pedro would have been her kin, and had some social duty to support her. As it is, she is left to live on her wits and her transitory physical charms. When Willmore, the "rover" of the title, finally rejects her in favor of the wealthy virgin Hellena, she is forced to recognize that her chosen independence was illusory. In a world where men make the rules, her only salable item is her virginity. Having sold that in the wrong market, she is damned.

When Angellica falls hopelessly for the feckless Willmore, she wants to believe that love and romance can be dissociated from social and economic structures, that "true love" in her world can be above financial considerations. She calls on him to see things her way and, blinded by this desire, does not recognize that he is using her for his pleasure.

> ANGELLICA: Thou'rt a brave fellow! Put up thy gold, and know,
> That were thy fortune large as is thy soul,
> Thou shouldst not buy my love
> Couldst thou forget these mean effects of vanity
> Which set me out to sale,
> And as a lover prize my yielding joys.
> Canst thou believe they'll be entirely thine,
> Without considering they were mercenary?   (II, II, 115–22)

In the course of the play, Willmore's repeated answer to this is a resounding "No." Having worshiped her beauty, tasted the pleasures of her body, and spent her money to attract a wealthier woman, he leaves her for a better catch.

Angellica is a troubling and uncomfortable figure in the play, disrupting the wit and airiness of scenes between Hellena and Willmore and undercutting the conventional "happy ending" of true lovers united. Realizing she has been betrayed by Willmore despite giving him "My virgin heart . . . Oh! 'tis gone!" (IV, II, 167) she plots her revenge "for the public safety of our sex" (V, 373). Trapping him at gunpoint she decides, however, to let him live: he is not worth the trouble of an execution: "But now, to show my utmost of contempt, / I give thee life" (V, 415–16). Through Willmore, she has learned that male protestations of devotion, and all their courtly love rhetoric, are for them just a game. There is no true power, no safety, for women. . . .

In many of Behn's plays, men's obsessions with their courtship conventions prevent them from understanding the women they address. Romance is a male invention, and women are jeopardized and often betrayed if they believe such declarations of undying passion. The task for the witty heroine who is at the center of many of Behn's plays, as Hellena is in *The Rover,* is to discover as much as possible about her man's true intentions, beneath his courtly facade. Willmore refers to both Angellica and to Hellena as his "angel" in high-flown rhetoric, but where Angellica is briefly fooled by this worship, Hellena is quite clear-sighted about the limit of his commitment. As far as possible, she takes control of her situation, disguising herself and playing parts, testing out and then capturing the man she has chosen Disguised, she watches him court and promise fidelity to Angellica, and in a bitter but witty scene mocks him, throwing back at him the overblown promises she has heard him make (III, i). She has no interest in traditional courtship rituals, thinking them "a very pretty, idle, silly kind of pleasure to pass one's time with" (III, i, 72–73), but she is not deceived by Willmore's forthright arguments in favor of unfettered sensuality. She knows already what Angellica shows the audience: Marriage is a necessity for women, otherwise, as she challenges Willmore, "What shall I get? A cradle full of noise and mischief, with a pack of repentance at my back?" (V, 536–38).

She gets her man, but it is a tawdry victory and the audience knows it, with Angellica there to remind them. Willmore has shown himself to be insensitive, capricious, and dangerous to women, and there is no reason to imagine that he will be faithful to Hellena for longer than the month that he originally resolves to sacrifice to gain her. In *The Second Part of the Rover,* where Willmore again chooses between two women (and this time chooses the prostitute), it is revealed in passing that Hellena had died at sea within three months of the marriage.

The world of courtship and marriage depicted by Behn in these plays is a bleak one. Bright, witty women like Hellena use daring and imagination in a desperate attempt to evade the arranged marriages or confinements to nunneries destined them by their families. They race against time, trying their best to negotiate when all power lies in others' hands. None of the dashing young blades they choose and test out are admirable characters, but they seem preferable to a fool like Haunce van Ezel (in *The Dutch Lover*) or an odious tyrant like Octavio (in *The Feign'd Curtizans*). Woven in with the wit and humor, music and spectacle, are hard, sober women's truths about the debauchery of the Restoration court and its acolytes. Armed with wit and driven by necessity, like her heroines, Aphra Behn succeeded in dramatizing in marketable form the dilemmas that faced her and her sisters.

William Congreve

Although born in England, William Congreve (1670–1729) was educated in Ireland, first at Kilkenny School and then at Trinity College, Dublin. Jonathan Swift, whose poetry praised Congreve, was also at Kilkenny and Trinity during part of this time. They were lifelong friends and central figures in literary London. Later, Congreve read law at the Middle Temple in London and was able to make good use of his legal training in several of his plays.

Congreve's literary career began with a novel, *Incognita* (1691), which he wrote in his teens. John Dryden praised the novel and, later, his plays. After Congreve's first play was produced, the poet Thomas Southerne named Congreve the likely inheritor of Dryden's crown as poet laureate.

His first play, *The Old Bachelor* (1693) was an immediate success, establishing him as an important playwright. Later in 1693 he produced his second play, *The Double Dealer,* which had a mixed reception. Dryden, in a letter, said, "The women thinke he has exposed their Bitchery too much and the Gentlemen are offended with him; for the discovery of their follyes: & the way of their Intrigues, under the notion of Friendship to their Ladyes Husbands." Maskwell, the double dealer, is a classic manipulator who forwards his own interests while damaging those of other characters. Congreve defended the play as a moral fable, and it was not until Queen Mary requested a command performance that the play was restored in the eyes of the public. *Love for Love* (1695) was for many years Congreve's most popular and best-liked play. It is the story of the worthy Valentine, who is about to lose an inheritance to a younger brother. In the end Valentine's intelligence wins out, and by pretending madness he secures his beloved, the wealthy heiress Angelica, as well as his own estate. Thomas Betterton, the acclaimed Restoration actor, played Valentine in the first performances; his theater company at Lincoln's Inn Fields produced all of Congreve's work. John Gielgud played Valentine in London, opening on April 8, 1943, to considerable acclaim and continuing for 471 performances through World War II. Laurence Olivier and Lynn Redgrave played in the 1965 revival, also a success. Congreve's one tragedy, *The Mourning Bride* (1697), was very successful although it has not been revived in the twentieth century.

Congreve's career as a playwright lasted only seven years. He left the stage after the production of *The Way of the World* (1700), ostensibly because of its cool reception. Although not technically a failure, the play was not received with the enthusiasm Congreve thought it deserved. He was stung by the criticism of Jeremy Collier in *A Short View of The Immorality and Profaneness of the English Stage* (1698). Congreve was also annoyed by the rise of the new sentimental middle-class drama. He spent the rest of his life writing occasional poetry, such as *A Pindarique Ode on the Victorious Progress of Her Majesties Arms* (1706), and libretti for several operas: *The Judgment of Paris* (1701), *A Hymn to Harmony* (1703), and *The Tears of Amarylis* (1703). He spent much of his later years as a retiring gentleman in the company of the duchess of Marlborough, with whom he probably had a child, Lady Mary Godolphin, who inherited his estate.

Congreve was buried in the Poet's Corner of Westminster Abbey, near the grave of Aphra Behn, who is buried at the entrance to the cloisters. Critics in his time and in succeeding generations have regarded his plays as among the purest examples of the English comic style of the late seventeenth century. *The Way of the World* has been especially singled out for praise because while it is witty, brisk, and amusing, it is pungent and serious at the core, with characters whose intelligence and essential worth help animate a drama that vies with the achievement of Molière.

THE WAY OF THE WORLD

The Way of the World (1700), Congreve's fifth and last play, has been his most enduring and — taking the long view — his most successful. It is an intellectual romp, with plot twists, disguises, and numerous complications. The names of the characters — Fainall, Mirabell, Wilfull, Witwoud, Waitwell, and Petulant — indicate Congreve's use of stock or TYPE CHARACTERS, characters immediately recognizable for their stereotypical behavior and traits. However, he always moves beneath the surfaces of types and reveals a satisfying complexity. Type characters have been used to advantage in all ages of comic drama but especially so in the English Restoration.

Congreve's genius shows up in his witty use of REPARTEE, or quick replies. He is a master of the one-liner and the RIPOSTE, a sharp return in speech. Wit was a rapier in the late seventeenth century, to be used for the amusement of those intelligent enough to follow the exchanges. Early on, Witwoud says, "A wit should no more be sincere than a woman constant; one argues a decay of parts, as t'other of beauty."

Mirabell tells Mrs. Fainall, "You should have just so much disgust for your husband as may be sufficient to make you relish your lover." Such witty comment on early eighteenth-century marriage, once we get to know Fainall and his essential viciousness, takes on a serious cast.

The plot of *The Way of the World* centers on marriage, adultery, and family fortunes. Man-about-town Mirabell wishes to marry Mrs. Millamant, who has inherited six thousand pounds and will receive another six thousand pounds if she marries in accord with the wishes of her aunt, Lady Wishfort (an older woman "full of the vigor of fifty-five"). Lady Wishfort, however, feels betrayed by Mirabell, who pretended to love her to get close to Millamant. Lady Wishfort wants Millamant to marry Sir Wilfull Witwoud, and Mirabell's efforts to make Lady Wishfort relent in this wish are carried forth on a wave of deception, disguise, and comic mixups. Mirabell and Millamant resemble traditional Shakespearean lovers such as Petruchio and Katharine in *The Taming of the Shrew* and Benedick and Beatrice in *Much Ado About Nothing*. They also resemble Aphra Behn's Willmore and Hellena and Molière's Alceste and Célimène. Millamant is every bit a match for Mirabell, and, as a result, their comic scenes are intense and engaging even as they reveal the limits of Congreve's society.

The "contract" scene in act IV, in which Millamant and Mirabell discuss their intentions to marry, is both funny and very serious. Their use of legal language in what is ostensibly a romantic situation is pointedly ironic. Millamant is no starry-eyed bride. She knows that once she is married all her possessions will belong to her husband; she will be like his chattel, to do with as he pleases. Having had the advantage of studying the marriages around her, she covenants in this scene for her independence.

The villain in the play is Fainall. While having an affair with Mrs. Marwood, he discovers that she is seriously attracted to Mirabell. No longer interested in Mrs. Marwood, he cannot turn away from her because she can expose him to his wife as an adulterer. Fainall's wife is Lady Wishfort's daughter, once married to a Mr. Languish, who has died. Before becoming involved with Fainall, Mrs. Fainall was Mirabell's mistress, but when she feared she was pregnant, Mirabell arranged the hasty marriage to Fainall, knowing that Fainall needed the widow's money and that Mrs. Fainall needed the respectability of marriage. It turned out that Mrs. Fainall was not pregnant and now regrets her marriage. In act II when she asks Mirabell why she married, he responds: "Why do we daily commit disagreeable and dangerous actions? To save that idol, reputation." Of her husband Fainall, he says, "When you are weary of him, you know your remedy." (The epigraph at the beginning of the play warns us that adultery is the subject of the drama.) These circumstances demonstrate that Fainall, for all his villainy, is being used by the Wishfort family for their ends almost as much as he is using them for his own.

Mirabell, like Fainall, is a manipulator but is not a villain at heart. He respects Millamant and manages ultimately to find a way to undo Fainall's schemes to control Millamant's fortune. The play does not end with everyone happy, but with Mirabell and Millamant possessing the advantage and looking forward to marriage and children. Eventually, all deceptions are revealed, the proper lovers are joined, and the complications are smoothed out. Because of its careful examination of the relationship between the sexes and of the impediments a sophisticated society can throw between them, *The Way of the World* is virtually a timeless comedy.

The Way of the World in Performance

After the play's initial poor reception, Alexander Pope praised *The Way of the World* as having "so much bullion in it as would serve to lace fifty modern comedies." It was revived relatively soon after 1701 in London and, according to theater historian Emmet Avery, it played 285 times in the eighteenth century. It was one of the first plays at the new Covent Garden Theatre on December 7, 1732, and is said to be the most produced English comedy ever since. It is manifestly a vehicle for female stars. The great actress Dame Peggy Ashcroft, along with Dame Edith Evans, starred in the London production of 1942. The play has been done steadily in the United States since the 1920s. The Tyrone Guthrie Theater in Minneapolis produced it in 1965 to rave notices; Jessica Tandy as Lady Wishfort essentially stole the show. Britain's Actor's Company brought it to the Brooklyn Academy of Music in 1974, with the characters wearing cutaway formal clothes, top hats, and tails instead of eighteenth-century garb. The production used telephones and other modern conveniences to demonstrate that the play is not a museum piece. Robin Phillips's 1976 Stratford, Ontario, production was described as "nothing short of brilliant." Maggie Smith played Millamant several times in the 1980s, joining Jessica Tandy in her role as Lady Wishfort. Smith's performance in the January 1985 London production underscored the fact that the role is ideal for a great comic actress. She made the play her own.

William Congreve (1670–1729)

THE WAY OF THE WORLD   1700

Audire est operae pretium, procedere recte
Qui moechis non vultis.   — HORACE, *Satires*°

— Metuat doti deprensa.°

PROLOGUE

(*Spoken by Mr. Fainall.*)

Of those few fools who with ill stars are curst,
Sure scribbling fools, call'd poets, fare the worst;
For they're a sort of fools which Fortune makes,
And after she has made 'em fools, forsakes.
5 With Nature's oafs 'tis quite a different case,
For Fortune favors all her idiot-race;
In her° own nest the cuckoo-eggs we find,
O'er which she broods to hatch the changeling-kind.°
No portion for her own she has to spare,
10 So much she dotes on her adopted care.
    Poets are bubbles,° by the town drawn in,
Suffer'd at first some trifling stakes to win;
But what unequal hazards do they run!
Each time they write, they venture all they've won;
15 The squire that's buttered° still, is sure to be undone.
This author, heretofore, has found your favor,
But pleads no merit from his past behavior.
To build on that might prove a vain presumption,
Should grants to poets made admit resumption;
20 And in Parnassus° he must lose his seat,
If that be found a forfeited estate.
    He owns, with toil he wrought the following
      scenes,
But, if they're naught, ne'er spare him for his pains;
Damn him the more; have no commiseration

For dullness on mature deliberation.   25
He swears he'll not resent one hiss'd-off scene,
Nor, like those peevish wits, his play maintain,
Who, to assert their sense, your taste arraign.
Some plot we think he has, and some new thought;
Some humor too, no farce; but that's a fault.   30
Satire, he thinks, you ought not to expect;
For so reform'd a town who dares correct?
To please, this time, has been his sole pretense;
He'll not instruct, lest it should give offense.
Should he by chance a knave or fool expose,   35
That hurts none here, sure here are none of those.
In short, our play shall (with your leave to show it)
Give you one instance of a passive poet,
Who to your judgments yields all resignation;
So save or damn, after your own discretion.   40

Dramatis Personae

Men

FAINALL, *in love with Mrs. Marwood*
MIRABELL, *in love with Mrs. Millamant*
WITWOUD, ⎫
PETULANT, ⎭ *followers of Mrs. Millamant*
SIR WILFULL WITWOUD, *half brother to Witwoud, and*
   nephew to Lady Wishfort
WAITWELL, *servant to Mirabell*

Women

LADY WISHFORT, *enemy to Mirabell, for having falsely*
   pretended love to her
MRS. MILLAMANT, *a fine lady, niece to Lady Wish-*
   fort, and loves Mirabell
MRS. MARWOOD, *friend to Mr. Fainall, and likes Mira-*
   bell
MRS. FAINALL, *daughter to Lady Wishfort, and wife*
   to Fainall, formerly friend to Mirabell
FOIBLE, *woman to Lady Wishfort*
MINCING, *woman to Mrs. Millamant*
BETTY, *waiting-maid at a chocolate-house*
PEG, *maid to Lady Wishfort*
DANCERS, FOOTMEN, *and* ATTENDANTS

[Epigraphs] *Audire . . . vultis*: Horace, *Satires* I.2.37–38. "Ye that do not wish well to the proceedings of adulterers, it is worth your while to hear how they are hampered on all sides" (trans. Christopher Smart). *Metuat doti deprensa*: Ibid., line 131. The context of the lines in which the epigraph appears is "Nor am I apprehensive, while I am in her company, . . . lest the maid . . . should be in apprehension for her limbs, *the detected wife for her portion* [dowry], I for myself" (trans. Smart). **7. her**: Fortune's. **8. O'er which . . . changeling-kind**: The cuckoo lays its eggs in the nests of other birds to whom they are left to be hatched. The implication is that Fortune is favorable to fools. **11. bubbles**: Dupes. **15. buttered**: Abundantly flattered. **20. Parnassus**: The Greek mountain sacred to Apollo and the Muses.

Scene: *London. The time equal to that of the presentation.*

ACT I

(*A Chocolate-House. Mirabell and Fainall, rising from cards; Betty waiting.*)

MIRABELL: You are a fortunate man, Mr. Fainall.

FAINALL: Have we done?

MIRABELL: What you please. I'll play on to entertain you.

5 FAINALL: No, I'll give you your revenge another time, when you are not so indifferent; you are thinking of something else now, and play too negligently. The coldness of a losing gamester lessens the pleasure of the winner. I'd no more play with a man

10 that slighted his ill fortune than I'd make love to a woman who undervalued the loss of her reputation.

MIRABELL: You have a taste extremely delicate and are for refining on your pleasures.

15 FAINALL: Prithee, why so reserved? Something has put you out of humor.

MIRABELL: Not at all. I happen to be grave today, and you are gay; that's all.

FAINALL: Confess, Millamant and you quarreled last

20 night, after I left you; my fair cousin has some humors° that would tempt the patience of a Stoic.° What, some coxcomb° came in, and was well received by her, while you were by.

MIRABELL: Witwoud and Petulant, and what was

25 worse, her aunt, your wife's mother, my evil genius; or to sum up all in her own name, my old Lady Wishfort came in.

FAINALL: Oh, there it is then! She has a lasting passion for you, and with reason. What, then my wife was

30 there?

MIRABELL: Yes, and Mrs. Marwood, and three or four more, whom I never saw before. Seeing me, they all put on their grave faces, whispered one another; then complained aloud of the vapors,° and after

35 fell into a profound silence.

FAINALL: They had a mind to be rid of you.

MIRABELL: For which reason I resolved not to stir. At last the good old lady broke through her painful taciturnity with an invective against long visits. I

40 would not have understood her, but Millamant

joining in the argument, I rose. and, with a constrained smile, told her, I thought nothing was so easy as to know when a visit began to be troublesome. She reddened, and I withdrew, without ex-
pecting° her reply.   45

FAINALL: You were to blame to resent what she spoke only in compliance with her aunt.

MIRABELL: She is more mistress of herself than to be under the necessity of such a resignation.

FAINALL: What? though half her fortune depends   50
upon her marrying with my lady's approbation?

MIRABELL: I was then in such a humor that I should have been better pleased if she had been less discreet.

FAINALL: Now I remember, I wonder not they were   55
weary of you. Last night was one of their cabal nights; they have 'em three times a week, and meet by turns at one another's apartments, where they come together like the coroner's inquest, to sit upon the murdered reputations of the week. You   60
and I are excluded; and it was once proposed that all the male sex should be excepted. But somebody moved that, to avoid scandal, there might be one man of the community; upon which motion Witwoud and Petulant were enrolled members.°   65

MIRABELL: And who may have been the foundress of this sect? My Lady Wishfort, I warrant, who publishes her detestation of mankind, and full of the vigor of fifty-five, declares for a friend° and ratafia,° and let posterity shift for itself, she'll   70
breed no more.

FAINALL: The discovery of your sham addresses to her, to conceal your love to her niece, has provoked this separation; had you dissembled better, things might have continued in the state of nature.   75

MIRABELL: I did as much as man could, with any reasonable conscience; I proceeded to the very last act of flattery with her, and was guilty of a song in her commendation. Nay, I got a friend to put her into a lampoon, and compliment her with the imputa-   80
tion of an affair with a young fellow, which I carried so far that I told her the malicious town took notice that she was grown fat of a sudden; and when she lay in of a dropsy,° persuaded her she was reported to be in labor. The devil's in't, if an   85
old woman is to be flattered further, unless a man should endeavor downright personally to debauch° her; and that my virtue forbade me. But for

---

21. **humors:** Moods.   **Stoic:** One who subscribes to the Stoic school of philosophy, which teaches freedom from passion and indifference to pleasure and pain.   22. **coxcomb:** Conceited person, fop.   34. **vapors:** Boredom.

45. **expecting:** Awaiting.   64–65. **Witwoud . . . members:** The implication is that Witwoud and Petulant are but half-men. 69. **friend:** Lover. When applied to a lady, the word carries the meaning of "mistress."   **ratafia:** Fruit-flavored liqueur. 84. **dropsy:** An excessive accumulation of fluid in the body. 88. **debauch:** Seduce.

90   the discovery of this amour I am indebted to your
     friend, or your wife's friend, Mrs. Marwood.
FAINALL: What should provoke her to be your enemy,
     unless she has made you advances which you have
     slighted? Women do not easily forgive omissions of
     that nature.
95   MIRABELL: She was always civil to me till of late. I
     confess I am not one of those coxcombs who are
     apt to interpret a woman's good manners to her
     prejudice, and think that she who does not refuse
     'em everything can refuse 'em nothing.
100 FAINALL: You are a gallant man, Mirabell; and though
     you may have cruelty enough not to satisfy a lady's
     longing, you have too much generosity not to be
     tender of her honor. Yet you speak with an indif-
     ference which seems to be affected, and confesses
105 you are conscious of a negligence.
MIRABELL: You pursue the argument with a distrust
     that seems to be unaffected, and confesses you are
     conscious of a concern for which the lady is more
     indebted to you than is your wife.
110 FAINALL: Fie, fie, friend! If you grow censorious, I
     must leave you. I'll look upon the gamesters in the
     next room.
MIRABELL: Who are they?
FAINALL: Petulant and Witwoud. (*To Betty*.) Bring me
115 some chocolate.   (*Exit*.)
MIRABELL: Betty, what says your clock?
BETTY: Turned of the last canonical hour,° sir.
                                                      (*Exit*.)
MIRABELL: How pertinently the jade° answers me!
     (*Looking on his watch*.) Ha? almost one o'clock!
120 O, y'are come!

(*Enter a Footman*.)

     Well, is the grand affair over? You have been
     something tedious.
FOOTMAN: Sir, there's such coupling at Pancras° that
     they stand behind one another, as 'twere in a coun-
125 try dance. Ours was the last couple to lead up, and
     no hopes appearing of dispatch, besides the parson
     growing hoarse, we were afraid his lungs would
     have failed before it came to our turn, so we drove
     round to Duke's place,° and there they were riv-
130 eted in a trice.°
MIRABELL: So, so, you are sure they are married.
FOOTMAN: Married and bedded, sir; I am witness.
MIRABELL: Have you the certificate?

---

117. **canonical hour:** It was only during the canonical hours
(eight in the morning to twelve noon) that marriages could be
legally performed.   118. **jade:** Derogatory term for a
woman.   123. **Pancras:** St. Pancras Church, where marriages were performed without license and outside the canonical hours.   129. **Duke's place:** St. James's Church, Aldgate.
129–30. **riveted in a trice:** Married quickly.

FOOTMAN: Here it is, sir.
MIRABELL: Has the tailor brought Waitwell's clothes   135
     home, and the new liveries?
FOOTMAN: Yes, sir.
MIRABELL: That's well. Do you go home again, d'ye
     hear, and adjourn the consummation till further
     order; bid Waitwell shake his ears, and Dame Part-   140
     let° rustle up her feathers, and meet me at one
     o'clock by Rosamond's Pond,° that I may see her
     before she returns to her lady; and as you tender
     your ears, be secret.

                                        (*Exit Footman*.)

(*Reenter Fainall and Betty*.)

FAINALL: Joy of your success, Mirabell; you look   145
     pleased.
MIRABELL: Aye, I have been engaged in a matter of
     some sort of mirth, which is not yet ripe for dis-
     covery. I am glad this is not a cabal night. I won-
     der, Fainall, that you who are married, and of   150
     consequence should be discreet, will suffer your
     wife to be of such a party.
FAINALL: Faith, I am not jealous. Besides, most who
     are engaged are women and relations; and for the
     men, they are of a kind too contemptible to give   155
     scandal.
MIRABELL: I am of another opinion. The greater the
     coxcomb, always the more the scandal; for a
     woman who is not a fool can have but one reason
     for associating with a man who is one.   160
FAINALL: Are you jealous as often as you see Witwoud
     entertained by Millamant?
MIRABELL: Of her understanding I am, if not of her
     person.
FAINALL: You do her wrong; for, to give her her due,   165
     she has wit.
MIRABELL: She has beauty enough to make any man
     think so, and complaisance enough not to contra-
     dict him who shall tell her so.
FAINALL: For a passionate lover, methinks you are a   170
     man somewhat too discerning in the failings of
     your mistress.
MIRABELL: And for a discerning man, somewhat too
     passionate a lover; for I like her with all her faults,
     nay, like her for her faults. Her follies are so nat-   175
     ural, or so artful, that they become her, and those
     affectations which in another woman would be
     odious, serve but to make her more agreeable. I'll
     tell thee, Fainall, she once used me with that inso-
     lence, that in revenge I took her to pieces, sifted°   180

140–41. **Dame Partlet:** Refers to Foible, who has just been
married to Waitwell. "Partlet" derives from Pertelote, the hen
in Chaucer's "Nun's Priest's Tale."   142. **Rosamond's Pond:**
A lake in St. James's Park.   180. **sifted:** Examined closely.

her, and separated her failings, I studied 'em, and
got 'em by rote.° The catalogue was so large that I
was not without hopes one day or other to hate
her heartily: To which end I so used° myself to
185 think of 'em that at length, contrary to my design
and expectation, they gave me every hour less and
less disturbance, till in a few days it became habitual to me to remember 'em without being displeased. They are now grown as familiar to me as
190 my own frailties; and in all probability, in a little
time longer I shall like 'em as well.

FAINALL: Marry her, marry her! Be half as well acquainted with her charms as you are with her defects, and my life on't, you are your own man
195 again.

MIRABELL: Say you so?

FAINALL: Aye, aye, I have experience; I have a wife,
and so forth.

(Enter a Messenger.)

MESSENGER: Is one Squire Witwoud here?

200 BETTY: Yes; what's your business?

MESSENGER: I have a letter for him, from his brother
Sir Wilfull, which I am charged to deliver into his
own hands.

BETTY: He's in the next room, friend; that way.

(Exit Messenger.)

205 MIRABELL: What, is the chief of that noble family in
town, Sir Wilfull Witwoud?

FAINALL: He is expected today. Do you know him?

MIRABELL: I have seen him. He promises to be an ex-
traordinary° person; I think you have the honor to
210 be related to him.

FAINALL: Yes, he is half brother to this Witwoud by a
former wife, who was sister to my Lady Wishfort,
my wife's mother. If you marry Millamant, you
must call cousins too.

215 MIRABELL: I had rather be his relation than his acquaintance.

FAINALL: He comes to town in order to equip himself
for travel.

MIRABELL: For travel! Why the man that I mean is
220 above forty.°

FAINALL: No matter for that; 'tis for the honor of England that all Europe should know we have block-
heads of all ages.

MIRABELL: I wonder there is not an act of parliament
225 to save the credit of the nation, and prohibit the
exportation of fools.

182. **by rote:** In a mechanical way.   184. **used:** Accustomed.   209. **extraordinary:** Somewhat eccentric.   220.
above forty: It was customary for a gentleman of quality
to make a "grand tour" of continental capitals in his early
twenties.

FAINALL: By no means; 'tis better as 'tis. 'Tis better to
trade with a little loss than to be quite eaten up
with being overstocked.

MIRABELL: Pray, are the follies of this knight-errant 230
and those of the squire his brother anything related?

FAINALL: Not at all; Witwoud grows by the knight,
like a medlar grafted on a crab.° One will melt in
your mouth, and t'other set your teeth on edge; 235
one is all pulp, and the other all core.

MIRABELL: So one will be rotten before he be ripe, and
the other will be rotten without ever being ripe at
all.

FAINALL: Sir Wilfull is an odd mixture of bashfulness 240
and obstinacy. But when he's drunk, he's as loving
as the monster in *The Tempest,*° and much after
the same manner. To give t'other his due, he has
something of good nature and does not always
want wit. 245

MIRABELL: Not always; but as often as his memory
fails him, and his commonplace° of comparisons.
He is a fool with a good memory and some few
scraps of other folks' wit. He is one whose conversation can never be approved, yet it is now and 250
then to be endured. He has indeed one good quality, he is not exceptious;° for he so passionately
affects the reputation of understanding raillery°
that he will construe an affront into a jest and call
downright rudeness and ill language, satire and fire. 255

FAINALL: If you have a mind to finish his picture, you
have an opportunity to do it at full length. Behold
the original!

(Enter Witwoud.)

WITWOUD: Afford me your compassion, my dears!
Pity me, Fainall! Mirabell, pity me! 260

MIRABELL: I do from my soul.

FAINALL: Why, what's the matter?

WITWOUD: No letters for me, Betty?

BETTY: Did not a messenger bring you one but now,
sir? 265

WITWOUD: Aye, but no other?

BETTY: No, sir.

WITWOUD: That's hard, that's very hard. A messenger,
a mule, a beast of burden! He has brought me a

234. **medlar grafted on a crab:** The medlar is like a crab apple
and is edible only when it begins to decay. The crab apple is
always sour.   242. **the monster in *The Tempest*:** Caliban (or
Sycorax) in the adaptation of Shakespeare's play by John
Dryden and Sir William Davenant (1667).   247. **commonplace:** Commonplace book; scrapbook.   252. **exceptious:**
Inclined to take exceptions.   253. **raillery:** Good-humored
ridicule; banter.

270   letter from the fool my brother, as heavy as a pan-
egyric° in a funeral sermon, or a copy of com-
mendatory verses from one poet to another. And
what's worse, 'tis as sure a forerunner of the author as an epistle dedicatory.

275   MIRABELL: A fool, and your brother, Witwoud!

WITWOUD: Aye, aye, my half brother. My half brother
he is, no nearer upon honor.

MIRABELL: Then 'tis possible he may be but half a
fool.

280   WITWOUD: Good, good, Mirabell, *le drôle!*° Good,
good; hang him, don't let's talk of him. Fainall,
how does your lady? Gad, I say anything in the
world to get this fellow out of my head. I beg pardon that I should ask a man of pleasure and the

285   town a question at once so foreign and domestic.°
But I talk like an old maid at a marriage, I don't
know what I say; but she's the best woman in the
world.°

FAINALL: 'Tis well you don't know what you say, or

290   else your commendation would go near to make
me either vain or jealous.

WITWOUD: No man in town lives well with a wife but
Fainall. Your judgment, Mirabell?

MIRABELL: You had better step and ask his wife, if

295   you would be credibly informed.

WITWOUD: Mirabell.

MIRABELL: Aye.

WITWOUD: My dear, I ask ten thousand pardons; gad,
I have forgot what I was going to say to you!

300   MIRABELL: I thank you heartily, heartily.

WITWOUD: No, but prithee excuse me; my memory is
such a memory.

MIRABELL: Have a care of such apologies, Witwoud;
for I never knew a fool but he affected to com-

305   plain, either of the spleen° or his memory.

FAINALL: What have you done with Petulant?

WITWOUD: He's reckoning his money — my money it
was. I have no luck today.

FAINALL: You may allow him to win of you at play, for

310   you are sure to be too hard for him at repartee;°
since you monopolize the wit that is between you,
the fortune must be his, of course.

MIRABELL: I don't find that Petulant confesses the superiority of wit to be your talent, Witwoud.

WITWOUD: Come, come, you are malicious now, and   315
would breed debates. Petulant's my friend, and a
very honest fellow, and a very pretty fellow, and
has a smattering — faith and troth,° a pretty deal
of an odd sort of a small wit; nay, I'll do him justice. I'm his friend, I won't wrong him. And if he   320
had any judgment in the world, he would not be
altogether contemptible. Come, come, don't detract from the merits of my friend.

FAINALL: You don't take your friend to be over-nicely
bred?   325

WITWOUD: No, no, hang him, the rogue has no manners at all, that I must own. No more breeding
than a bum-baily,° that I grant you. 'Tis pity, faith;
the fellow has fire and life.

MIRABELL: What, courage?   330

WITWOUD: Hum, faith I don't know as to that; I can't
say as to that. Yes, faith, in a controversy he'll contradict anybody.

MIRABELL: Though 'twere a man whom he feared, or
a woman whom he loved.   335

WITWOUD: Well, well, he does not always think before he speaks; we have all our failings. You are
too hard upon him, you are, faith. Let me excuse
him. I can defend most of his faults, except one or
two. One he has, that's the truth on't; if he were   340
my brother, I could not acquit him. That indeed I
could wish were otherwise.

MIRABELL: Aye, marry, what's that, Witwoud?

WITWOUD: Oh, pardon me! Expose the infirmities of
my friend? No, my dear, excuse me there.   345

FAINALL: What, I warrant he's unsincere, or 'tis some
such trifle.

WITWOUD: No, no, what if he be? 'Tis no matter for
that; his wit will excuse that. A wit should no
more be sincere than a woman constant; one ar-   350
gues a decay of parts,° as t'other of beauty.

MIRABELL: Maybe you think him too positive?

WITWOUD: No, no, his being positive is an incentive
to argument, and keeps up conversation.

FAINALL: Too illiterate?   355

WITWOUD: That! that's his happiness; his want of
learning gives him the more opportunities to show
his natural parts.

MIRABELL: He wants words?

WITWOUD: Aye, but I like him for that now; for his   360
want of words gives me the pleasure very often to
explain his meaning.

FAINALL: He's impudent?

WITWOUD: No, that's not it.

MIRABELL: Vain?   365

---

271. **panegyric:** Eulogy, especially involving elaborate praise.
280. *le drôle*: The wag.   285–86. **foreign and domestic:**
Since he knows (by gossip) that the Fainall marriage is not
working out very well, Witwoud plays on the words "foreign
and domestic."   287–88. **best woman in the world:** I.e.,
Mrs. Fainall. Witwoud realizes that he has blundered into a
rather delicate situation.   305. **spleen:** Ill humor; peevish-
ness.   310. **repartee:** Adroitness and cleverness in making
replies in conversation.

318. **troth:** Loyalty, faithfulness.   328. **bum-baily:** An under-
bailiff, a minor court officer.   351. **parts:** Personal endowments.

WITWOUD: No.

MIRABELL: What! he speaks unseasonable truths sometimes, because he has not wit enough to invent an evasion?

370 WITWOUD: Truths! ha! ha! ha! No, no; since you will have it, I mean he never speaks truth at all, that's all. He will lie like a chambermaid, or a woman of quality's porter. Now that is a fault.

(Enter a Coachman.)

COACHMAN: Is Master Petulant here, mistress?

375 BETTY: Yes.

COACHMAN: Three gentlewomen in a coach would speak with him.

FAINALL: O brave Petulant! Three!

BETTY: I'll tell him.

380 COACHMAN: You must bring two dishes of chocolate and a glass of cinnamon-water.°

(Exeunt° Betty and Coachman.)

WITWOUD: That should be for two fasting strumpets,° and a bawd troubled with wind.° Now you may know what the three are.

385 MIRABELL: You are very free with your friend's acquaintance.

WITWOUD: Aye, aye, friendship without freedom is as dull as love without enjoyment, or wine without toasting. But to tell you a secret, these are trulls° whom he allows coach-hire, and something more, by the week, to call on him once a day at public places.

MIRABELL: How!

WITWOUD: You shall see how he won't go to 'em, because there's no more company here to take notice of him. Why, this is nothing to what he used to do; before he found out this way, I have known him call for himself.

FAINALL: Call for himself? What dost thou mean?

400 WITWOUD: Mean! Why, he would slip you out° of this chocolate-house, just when you had been talking to him; as soon as your back was turned, whip, he was gone! Then trip to his lodging, clap on a hood and scarf, and a mask, slap into a hackney-coach, and drive hither to the door again in a trice, where he would send in for himself; that I mean, call for himself, wait for himself. Nay, and what's more, not finding himself, sometimes leave a letter for himself.

410 MIRABELL: I confess this is something extraordinary. I

believe he waits for himself now, he is so long a-coming. Oh! I ask his pardon.

(Enter Petulant and Betty.)

BETTY: Sir, the coach stays.

PETULANT: Well, well, I come. 'Sbud,° a man had as good be a professed midwife as a professed whoremaster, at this rate! To be knocked up and raised at all hours, and in all places! Pox on 'em, I won't come! D'ye hear, tell 'em I won't come. Let 'em snivel and cry their hearts out.

420 FAINALL: You are very cruel, Petulant.

PETULANT: All's one, let it pass. I have a humor to be cruel.

MIRABELL: I hope they are not persons of condition° that you use at this rate.

425 PETULANT: Condition! Condition's a dried fig, if I am not in humor! By this hand, if they were your — a — a — your what-d'ye-call-'ems themselves, they must wait or rub off,° if I want appetite.°

MIRABELL: What-d'ye-call-'ems! What are they, Witwoud?

430 WITWOUD: Empresses, my dear; by your what-d'ye-call-'ems he means sultana queens.

PETULANT: Aye, Roxolanas.°

MIRABELL: Cry you mercy!

FAINALL: Witwoud says they are —

PETULANT: What does he say th'are?

WITWOUD: I? Fine ladies, I say.

PETULANT: Pass on, Witwoud. Harkee, by this light his relations: two co-heiresses his cousins, and an old aunt, who loves caterwauling° better than a conventicle.°

WITWOUD: Ha! ha! ha! I had a mind to see how the rogue would come off. Ha! ha! ha! Gad, I can't be angry with him, if he had said they were my mother and my sisters.

MIRABELL: No!

WITWOUD: No; the rogue's wit and readiness of invention charm me. Dear Petulant!

BETTY: They are gone, sir, in great anger.

450 PETULANT: Enough, let 'em trundle. Anger helps complexion, saves paint.°

FAINALL: This continence is all dissembled; this is in order to have something to brag of the next time

---

381. **cinnamon-water:** A cordial of spirits, cinnamon, and hot water, prescribed to aid digestion.   [S.D.] *Exeunt:* Latin for "they go out." 382. **strumpets:** Prostitutes. 383. **wind:** Air in the stomach or bowels.   389. **trulls:** Women of easy virtue.   400. **slip you out:** Slip out.

414. **'Sbud:** "God's blood," a mild oath.   423. **condition:** Social distinction.   428. **rub off:** Go away.   **want appetite:** Lack desire for them.   433. **Roxolanas:** Roxolana is the name of the Turkish sultana in Davenant's *The Siege of Rhodes* (1656), one of the first "heroic plays."   440. **caterwauling:** Noisy quarreling.   441. **conventicle:** A meeting-house of nonconformist religious sects, especially Presbyterians.   451. **paint:** Makeup.

he makes court to Millamant, and swear he has
455   abandoned the whole sex for her sake.
MIRABELL: Have you not left off your impudent pretensions there yet? I shall cut your throat some
time or other, Petulant, about that business.
PETULANT: Aye, aye, let that pass. There are other
460   throats to be cut.
MIRABELL: Meaning mine, sir?
PETULANT: Not I. I mean nobody; I know nothing.
But there are uncles and nephews in the world,
and they may be rivals. What then? All's one for
465   that.
MIRABELL: How! harkee Petulant, come hither. Explain, or I shall call your interpreter.°
PETULANT: Explain! I know nothing. Why, you have
an uncle, have you not, lately come to town, and
470   lodges by my Lady Wishfort's?
MIRABELL: True.
PETULANT: Why, that's enough. You and he are not
friends; and if he should marry and have a child,
you may be disinherited, ha?
475   MIRABELL: Where hast thou stumbled upon all this
truth?
PETULANT: All's one for that; why, then say I know
something.
MIRABELL: Come, thou art an honest fellow, Petulant,
480   and shalt make love to my mistress, thou sha't,°
faith. What hast thou heard of my uncle?
PETULANT: I? Nothing I. If throats are to be cut, let
swords clash! Snug's the word;° I shrug and am
silent.
485   MIRABELL: Oh, raillery, raillery! Come, I know thou
art in the women's secrets. What, you're a cabalist;
I know you stayed at Millamant's last night, after I
went. Was there any mention made of my uncle or
me? Tell me. If thou hadst but good nature equal
490   to thy wit, Petulant, Tony Witwoud, who is now
thy competitor in fame, would show as dim by
thee as a dead whiting's° eye by a pearl of orient;°
he would no more be seen by thee than Mercury is
by the sun.° Come, I'm sure thou wo't° tell me.
495   PETULANT: If I do, will you grant me common sense
then for the future?
MIRABELL: Faith, I'll do what I can for thee, and I'll
pray that Heaven may grant it thee in the meantime.
500   PETULANT: Well, harkee.

(Mirabell and Petulant talk apart.)

FAINALL: Petulant and you both will find Mirabell as
warm a rival as a lover.
WITWOUD: Pshaw! pshaw! That she laughs at Petulant is plain. And for my part, but that it is almost
a fashion to admire her, I should — Harkee, to tell   505
you a secret, but let it go no further; between
friends, I shall never break my heart for her.
FAINALL: How!
WITWOUD: She's handsome; but she's a sort of an uncertain woman.   510
FAINALL: I thought you had died for her.
WITWOUD: Umh — no —
FAINALL: She has wit.
WITWOUD: 'Tis what she will hardly allow anybody
else. Now, demme,° I should hate that, if she were   515
as handsome as Cleopatra. Mirabell is not so sure
of her as he thinks for.
FAINALL: Why do you think so?
WITWOUD: We stayed pretty late there last night, and
heard something of an uncle to Mirabell, who is   520
lately come to town, and is between him and the
best part of his estate. Mirabell and he are at some
distance, as my Lady Wishfort has been told; and
you know she hates Mirabell worse than a Quaker
hates a parrot,° or than a fishmonger hates a hard   525
frost.° Whether this uncle has seen Mrs. Millamant
or not, I cannot say; but there were items of such a
treaty being in embryo, and if it should come to
life, poor Mirabell would be in some sort unfortunately fobbed,° i'faith.   530
FAINALL: 'Tis impossible Millamant should hearken to
it.
WITWOUD: Faith, my dear, I can't tell; she's a woman,
and a kind of a humorist.°
MIRABELL: And this° is the sum of what you could   535
collect last night?
PETULANT: The quintessence. Maybe Witwoud knows
more; he stayed longer. Besides, they never mind
him; they say anything before him.
MIRABELL: I thought you had been the greatest fa-   540
vorite.
PETULANT: Aye, *tête à tête*,° but not in public, because
I make remarks.
MIRABELL: You do?
PETULANT: Aye, aye, pox, I'm malicious, man! Now   545

---

467. interpreter: Possibly a second, as in a duel.   480. sha't:
Slangy contraction for "shalt."   483. Snug's the word: In
modern slang, "Mum's the word."   492. whiting: A kind
of codfish.   pearl of orient: Said to be particularly brilliant.
493–94. than Mercury is by the sun: The planet nearest the
sun and of very low magnitude.   494. wo't: Wilt.

515. demme: Contraction of "damn me."   524–25.
Quaker . . . parrot: Parrots are proverbially known to swear.
525–26. fishmonger . . . frost: Fishmongers peddled fish and
consequently hated very cold weather.   530. fobbed:
Cheated.   534. humorist: A moody or capricious person,
hence unreliable.   535. And this: During the dialogue of
Fainall and Witwoud, Mirabell and Petulant have been talking "apart." They now reenter the general dialogue.
542. tête à tête: Head to head.

Scene from an updated version of *The Way of the World* directed by Sharon Ott in 1992 at the Huntington Theatre in Boston.

he's soft, you know; they are not in awe of him. The fellow's well bred; he's what you call a what-d'ye-call-'em, a fine gentleman; but he's silly withal.

MIRABELL: I thank you. I know as much as my cu-
550   riosity requires. Fainall, are you for the Mall?°

FAINALL: Aye, I'll take a turn before dinner.

WITWOUD: Aye, we'll walk in the Park; the ladies talked of being there.

MIRABELL: I thought you were obliged to watch for
555   your brother Sir Wilfull's arrival.

WITWOUD: No, no, he comes to his aunt's, my Lady Wishfort. Pox on him! I shall be troubled with him too; what shall I do with the fool?

PETULANT: Beg him for his estate, that I may beg you
560   afterwards; and so have but one trouble with you both.

WITWOUD: O rare Petulant! Thou art as quick as fire in a frosty morning; thou shalt to the Mall with us, and we'll be very severe.

PETULANT: Enough, I'm in a humor to be severe.   565

MIRABELL: Are you? Pray then walk by yourselves: Let us not be accessory to your putting the ladies out of countenance with your senseless ribaldry,° which you roar out aloud as often as they pass by you; and when you have made a handsome woman   570 blush, then you think you have been severe.

PETULANT: What, what? Then let 'em either show their innocence by not understanding what they hear, or else show their discretion by not hearing what they would not be thought to understand.   575

MIRABELL: But hast not thou then sense enough to know that thou oughtest to be most ashamed thy-

---

550. Mall: A fashionable walk in St. James's Park.

568. ribaldry: Coarse behavior or language.

self, when thou hast put another out of countenance?

580 PETULANT: Not I, by this hand! I always take blushing
either for a sign of guilt or ill breeding.

MIRABELL: I confess you ought to think so. You are in
the right, that you may plead the error of your
judgment in defense of your practice.

585   Where modesty's ill manners, 'tis but fit
That impudence and malice pass for wit.

(*Exeunt.*)

ACT II

(*St. James's Park. Enter Mrs. Fainall and Mrs. Marwood.*)

MRS. FAINALL: Aye, aye, dear Marwood, if we will be
happy, we must find the means in ourselves, and
among ourselves. Men are ever in extremes, either
doting or averse. While they are lovers, if
5   they have fire and sense, their jealousies are insupportable. And when they cease to love (we
ought to think at least) they loathe; they look upon
us with horror and distaste; they meet us like the
ghosts of what we were, and as from such, fly from
10   us.

MRS. MARWOOD: True, 'tis an unhappy circumstance
of life that love should ever die before us; and that
the man so often should outlive the lover. But say
what you will, 'tis better to be left than never to
15   have been loved. To pass our youth in dull indifference, to refuse the sweets of life because they
once must leave us, is as preposterous as to wish to
have been born old, because we one day must be
old. For my part, my youth may wear and waste,
20   but it shall never rust in my possession.

MRS. FAINALL: Then it seems you dissemble an aversion to mankind, only in compliance to my mother's
humor?

MRS. MARWOOD: Certainly. To be free,° I have no taste
25   of those insipid dry discourses with which our sex
of force must entertain themselves, apart from men.
We may affect endearments to each other, profess
eternal friendships, and seem to dote like lovers; but
'tis not in our natures long to persevere. Love will
30   resume his empire in our breasts; and every heart,
or soon or late, receive and readmit him as its lawful tyrant.

MRS. FAINALL: Bless me, how have I been deceived!
Why, you profess a libertine!°

35 MRS. MARWOOD: You see my friendship by my free-

dom. Come, be as sincere, acknowledge that your
sentiments agree with mine.

MRS. FAINALL: Never!

MRS. MARWOOD: You hate mankind?

MRS. FAINALL: Heartily, inveterately.   40

MRS. MARWOOD: Your husband?

MRS. FAINALL: Most transcendently; aye, though I say
it, meritoriously.

MRS. MARWOOD: Give me your hand upon it.

MRS. FAINALL: There.   45

MRS. MARWOOD: I join with you; what I have said
has been to try you.

MRS. FAINALL: Is it possible? Dost thou hate those
vipers, men?

MRS. MARWOOD: I have done hating 'em; and am   50
now come to despise 'em; the next thing I have to
do, is eternally to forget 'em.

MRS. FAINALL: There spoke the spirit of an Amazon,
a Penthesilea!°

MRS. MARWOOD: And yet I am thinking sometimes to   55
carry my aversion further.

MRS. FAINALL: How?

MRS. MARWOOD: Faith, by marrying; if I could but
find one that loved me very well and would be
thoroughly sensible of ill usage, I think I should do   60
myself the violence of undergoing the ceremony.

MRS. FAINALL: You would not make him a cuckold?

MRS. MARWOOD: No, but I'd make him believe I did,
and that's as bad.

MRS. FAINALL: Why had not you as good do it?   65

MRS. MARWOOD: Oh, if he should ever discover it, he
would then know the worst, and be out of his
pain; but I would have him ever to continue upon
the rack of fear and jealousy.

MRS. FAINALL: Ingenious mischief! Would thou wert   70
married to Mirabell.

MRS. MARWOOD: Would I were!

MRS. FAINALL: You change color.

MRS. MARWOOD: Because I hate him.

MRS. FAINALL: So do I; but I can hear him named. But 75
what reason have you to hate him in particular?

MRS. MARWOOD: I never loved him; he is, and always
was, insufferably proud.

MRS. FAINALL: By the reason you give for your aversion, one would think it dissembled; for you have   80
laid a fault to his charge of which his enemies must
acquit him.

MRS. MARWOOD: Oh, then it seems you are one of his
favorable enemies. Methinks you look a little pale,
and now you flush again.   85

---

24. **free:** Frank.   34. **profess a libertine:** Speak as one who
leads a loose, unconventional life.

54. Penthesilea: Queen of the Amazons, the mythical race of
women warriors. After befriending Priam following the
death of Hector, she was killed by Achilles, who fell in love
with her as she lay dying.

MRS. FAINALL: Do I? I think I am a little sick o' the
sudden.
MRS. MARWOOD: What ails you?
MRS. FAINALL: My husband. Don't you see him? He
90 turned short upon me unawares, and has almost
overcome me.

(*Enter Fainall and Mirabell.*)

MRS. MARWOOD: Ha! ha! ha! He comes opportunely
for you.
MRS. FAINALL: For you, for he has brought Mirabell
95 with him.
FAINALL: My dear!
MRS. FAINALL: My soul!
FAINALL: You don't look well today, child.
MRS. FAINALL: D'ye think so?
100 MIRABELL: He is the only man that does, madam.
MRS. FAINALL: The only man that would tell me so at
least; and the only man from whom I could hear it
without mortification.
FAINALL: O my dear, I am satisfied of your tenderness;
105 I know you cannot resent anything from me, especially what is in effect of my concern.
MRS. FAINALL: Mr. Mirabell, my mother interrupted
you in a pleasant relation last night; I would fain
hear it out.
110 MIRABELL: The persons concerned in that affair have
yet a tolerable reputation. I am afraid Mr. Fainall
will be censorious.
MRS. FAINALL: He has a humor more prevailing than
his curiosity and will willingly dispense with the
115 hearing of one scandalous story, to avoid giving an
occasion to make another by being seen to walk
with his wife. This way, Mr. Mirabell, and I dare
promise you will oblige us both.
                    (*Exeunt Mrs. Fainall and Mirabell.*)
FAINALL: Excellent creature! Well, sure if I should live
120 to be rid of my wife, I should be a miserable man.
MRS. MARWOOD: Aye!
FAINALL: For having only that one hope, the accomplishment of it, of consequence, must put an end to
all my hopes; and what a wretch is he who must
125 survive his hopes! Nothing remains when that day
comes, but to sit down and weep like Alexander,°
when he wanted other worlds to conquer.
MRS. MARWOOD: Will you not follow 'em?
FAINALL: Faith, I think not.
130 MRS. MARWOOD: Pray let us; I have a reason.
FAINALL: You are not jealous?
MRS. MARWOOD: Of whom?
FAINALL: Of Mirabell.

MRS. MARWOOD: If I am, is it inconsistent with my
love to you that I am tender of your honor?   135
FAINALL: You would intimate, then, as if there were a
fellow-feeling between my wife and him.
MRS. MARWOOD: I think she does not hate him to
that degree she would be thought.
FAINALL: But he, I fear, is too insensible.   140
MRS. MARWOOD: It may be you are deceived.
FAINALL: It may be so. I do now begin to apprehend
it.
MRS. MARWOOD: What?
FAINALL: That I have been deceived, madam, and you 145
are false.
MRS. MARWOOD: That I am false! What mean you?
FAINALL: To let you know I see through all your little
arts. Come, you both love him; and both have
equally dissembled your aversion. Your mutual   150
jealousies of one another have made you clash till
you have both struck fire. I have seen the warm
confession reddening on your cheeks and sparkling
from your eyes.
MRS. MARWOOD: You do me wrong.   155
FAINALL: I do not. 'Twas for my ease to oversee° and
willfully neglect the gross advances made him by
my wife; that by permitting her to be engaged, I
might continue unsuspected in my pleasures, and
take you oftener to my arms in full security. But   160
could you think, because the nodding husband
would not awake, that e'er the watchful lover
slept?
MRS. MARWOOD: And wherewithal can you reproach
me?   165
FAINALL: With infidelity, with loving another, with
love of Mirabell.
MRS. MARWOOD: 'Tis false! I challenge you to show
an instance that can confirm your groundless accusation. I hate him.   170
FAINALL: And wherefore do you hate him? He is insensible, and your resentment follows his neglect.
An instance? The injuries you have done him are a
proof, your interposing in his love. What cause
had you to make discoveries of his pretended passion? to undeceive the credulous aunt, and be the 175
officious obstacle of his match with Millamant?
MRS. MARWOOD: My obligations to my lady urged
me; I had professed a friendship to her, and
could not see her easy nature so abused by that
dissembler.   180
FAINALL: What, was it conscience then? Professed a
friendship! Oh, the pious friendships of the female
sex!
MRS. MARWOOD: More tender, more sincere, and

126. **Alexander:** Alexander the Great (356–323 B.C.), the
powerful ruler and conqueror.

156. **oversee:** Overlook.

185 more enduring, than all the vain and empty vows
of men, whether professing love to us, or mutual
faith to one another.

FAINALL: Ha! ha! ha! You are my wife's friend too.

MRS. MARWOOD: Shame and ingratitude! Do you re-
190 proach me? You, you upbraid me? Have I been
false to her, through strict fidelity to you, and sacrificed my friendship to keep my love inviolate?
And have you the baseness to charge me with the
guilt, unmindful of the merit? To you it should be
195 meritorious, that I have been vicious, and do you
reflect that guilt upon me, which should lie buried
in your bosom?

FAINALL: You misinterpret my reproof. I meant but to
remind you of the slight account you once could
200 make of strictest ties, when set in competition with
your love to me.

MRS. MARWOOD: 'Tis false; you urged it with deliberate malice! 'Twas spoke in scorn, and I never will
forgive it.

205 FAINALL: Your guilt, not your resentment, begets your
rage. If yet you loved, you could forgive a jealousy;
but you are stung to find that you are discovered.

MRS. MARWOOD: It shall be all discovered. You too
shall be discovered, be sure you shall. I can but be
210 exposed. If I do it myself, I shall prevent° your
baseness.

FAINALL: Why, what will you do?

MRS. MARWOOD: Disclose it to your wife; own what
has passed between us.

215 FAINALL: Frenzy!

MRS. MARWOOD: By all my wrongs I'll do't! I'll publish to the world the injuries you have done me,
both in my fame and fortune! With both I trusted
you, you bankrupt in honor, as indigent of wealth.

220 FAINALL: Your fame I have preserved. Your fortune
has been bestowed as the prodigality of your love
would have it, in pleasures which we both have
shared. Yet, had not you been false, I had ere this
repaid it. 'Tis true, had you permitted Mirabell
225 with Millamant to have stolen their marriage, my
lady had been incensed beyond all means of reconcilement, Millamant had forfeited the moiety° of
her fortune, which then would have descended to
my wife. And wherefore did I marry, but to make
230 lawful prize of a rich widow's wealth, and squander it on love and you?

MRS. MARWOOD: Deceit and frivolous pretense!

FAINALL: Death, am I not married! What's pretense?
Am I not imprisoned, fettered? Have I not a wife?
235 nay a wife that was a widow, a young widow, a
handsome widow; and would be again a widow,

but that I have a heart of proof,° and something of
a constitution to bustle through the ways of wedlock and this world! Will you yet be reconciled to
truth and me?   240

MRS. MARWOOD: Impossible. Truth and you are inconsistent. I hate you, and shall for ever.

FAINALL: For loving you?

MRS. MARWOOD: I loathe the name of love after such
usage; and next to the guilt with which you would   245
asperse me, I scorn you most. Farewell!

FAINALL: Nay, we must not part thus.

MRS. MARWOOD: Let me go.

FAINALL: Come, I'm sorry.

MRS. MARWOOD: I care not, let me go, break my   250
hands, do! I'd leave 'em to get loose.

FAINALL: I would not hurt you for the world. Have I
no other hold to keep you here?

MRS. MARWOOD: Well, I have deserved it all.

FAINALL: You know I love you.   255

MRS. MARWOOD: Poor dissembling! Oh, that — well,
It is not yet —

FAINALL: What? what is it not? what is it not yet? It is
not yet too late —

MRS. MARWOOD: No, it is not yet too late; I have that   260
comfort.

FAINALL: It is, to love another.

MRS. MARWOOD: But not to loathe, detest, abhor
mankind, myself, and the whole treacherous world.

FAINALL: Nay, this is extravagance. Come, I ask your   265
pardon. No tears. I was to blame; I could not love
you and be easy in my doubts. Pray, forbear. I believe you. I'm convinced I've done you wrong; and
any way, every way will make amends. I'll hate my
wife yet more, damn her! I'll part with her, rob her   270
of all she's worth, and we'll retire somewhere, anywhere, to another world. I'll marry thee; be paci-
fied. 'Sdeath,° they come; hide your face, your
tears. You have a mask;° wear it a moment. This
way, this way. Be persuaded.   275

(Exeunt.)

(Reenter Mirabell and Mrs. Fainall.)

MRS. FAINALL: They are here yet.

MIRABELL: They are turning into the other walk.

MRS. FAINALL: While I only hated my husband, I
could bear to see him; but since I have despised
him, he's too offensive.   280

MIRABELL: Oh, you should hate with prudence.

MRS. FAINALL: Yes, for I have loved with indiscretion.

---

237. heart of proof: A heart that is proof against such wishes.
273. 'Sdeath: "God's death," an oath.   274. mask: Ladies'
masks were fashionable and reputable except when worn at
the theater, where they were construed as the mark of a loose
woman.

---

210. prevent: Anticipate.   227. moiety: Half.

MIRABELL: You should have just so much disgust for your husband as may be sufficient to make you rel-
285   ish your lover.

MRS. FAINALL: You have been the cause that I have loved without bounds, and would you set limits to that aversion of which you have been the occasion? Why did you make me marry this man?

290 MIRABELL: Why do we daily commit disagreeable and dangerous actions? To save that idol, reputation. If the familiarities of our loves had produced that consequence of which you were apprehensive, where could you have fixed a father's name with
295   credit, but on a husband?° I knew Fainall to be a man lavish of his morals, an interested and professing° friend, a false and a designing lover; yet one whose wit and outward fair behavior have gained a reputation with the town enough to make that
300   woman stand excused who has suffered herself to be won by his addresses. A better man ought not to have been sacrificed to the occasion; a worse had not answered to the purpose. When you are weary of him, you know your remedy.

305 MRS. FAINALL: I ought to stand in some degree of credit with you, Mirabell.

MIRABELL: In justice to you, I have made you privy to my whole design, and put it in your power to ruin or advance my fortune.

310 MRS. FAINALL: Whom have you instructed to represent your pretended uncle?

MIRABELL: Waitwell, my servant.

MRS. FAINALL: He is an humble servant° to Foible, my mother's woman, and may win her to your
315   interest.

MIRABELL: Care is taken for that. She is won and worn by this time. They were married this morning.

MRS. FAINALL: Who?

MIRABELL: Waitwell and Foible. I would not tempt
320   my servant to betray me by trusting him too far. If your mother, in hopes to ruin me, should consent to marry my pretended uncle, he might, like Mosca in *The Fox*,° stand upon terms;° so I made him sure beforehand.

325 MRS. FAINALL: So if my poor mother is caught in a contract, you will discover the imposture betimes,

and release her by producing a certificate of her gallant's former marriage?

MIRABELL: Yes, upon condition that she consent to my marriage with her niece, and surrender the 330 moiety of her fortune in her possession.°

MRS. FAINALL: She talked last night of endeavoring at a match between Millamant and your uncle.

MIRABELL: That was by Foible's direction, and my instruction, that she might seem to carry it more pri- 335 vately.°

MRS. FAINALL: Well, I have an opinion of your success for I believe my lady will do anything to get a husband; and when she has this, which you have provided for her, I suppose she will submit to anything 340 to get rid of him.

MIRABELL: Yes, I think the good lady would marry anything that resembled a man, though 'twere no more than what a butler could pinch out of a napkin.° 345

MRS. FAINALL: Female frailty! We must all come to it, if we live to be old and feel the craving of a false appetite when the true is decayed.

MIRABELL: An old woman's appetite is depraved like that of a girl. 'Tis the green sickness° of a second 350 childhood; and, like the faint offer of a latter spring, serves but to usher in the fall, and withers in an affected bloom.

MRS. FAINALL: Here's your mistress.

(Enter Mrs. Millamant, Witwoud, and Mincing.)

MIRABELL: Here she comes, i'faith, full sail, with her 355 fan spread and streamers out, and a shoal of fools for tenders.° Ha, no, I cry her mercy!

MRS. FAINALL: I see but one poor empty sculler,° and he tows her woman after him.

MIRABELL (*to Mrs. Millamant*): You seem to be unat- 360 tended, madam. You used to have the *beau monde*° throng after you, and a flock of gay, fine perukes° hovering round you.

329–31. condition that she . . . possession: Lady Wishfort has control of half of Mrs. Millamant's (her niece's) fortune, which Millamant will acquire upon her marriage, provided Lady Wishfort approves of the match; should Millamant marry without her aunt's approval, she forfeits the half of her fortune in trust.   335–36. she might . . . privately: I.e., to allay any suspicions Lady Wishfort might have about the validity of Mirabell's "uncle."   344–45. pinch out of a napkin: It was fashionable to pinch table napkins into curious and fancy shapes.   350. green sickness: An anemia prevalent in adolescent girls, marked by a sallow yellow-green complexion. 357. tenders: Small boats that attend larger ships. 358. sculler: A man operating a rowboat; i.e., Witwoud. 361–62. *beau monde*: People of fashion.   363. perukes: Suitors, referring to the wigs worn by gentlemen of the period.

292–95. If the familiarities . . . husband: Mirabell refers to his affair with Mrs. Fainall, after the death of her first husband, Mr. Languish, and prior to her marriage to Fainall. She feared that she was pregnant by Mirabell, and as a result Mirabell urged her marriage to Fainall.   296–97. professing: Self-interested and dissembling.   313. servant: Suitor. 322–23. Mosca . . . Fox: Mosca, the crafty servant in Ben Jonson's play *Volpone; or, The Fox* (1606).   323. stand upon terms: Insist upon the proper terms of a binding contract, as Mosca does in the denouement of the Jonson play.

WITWOUD: Like moths about a candle. I had like to have lost my comparison for want of breath.

MRS. MILLAMANT: Oh, I have denied myself airs today. I have walked as fast through the crowd —

WITWOUD: As a favorite just disgraced, and with as few followers.

MRS. MILLAMANT: Dear Mr. Witwoud, truce with your similitudes;° for I'm as sick of 'em —

WITWOUD: As a physician of a good air. I cannot help it, madam, though 'tis against myself.

MRS. MILLAMANT: Yet again! Mincing, stand between me and his wit.

WITWOUD: Do, Mrs. Mincing, like a screen before a great fire. I confess I do blaze today; I am too bright.

MRS. FAINALL: But, dear Millamant, why were you so long?

MRS. MILLAMANT: Long! Lord, have I not made violent haste? I have asked every living thing I met for you; I have inquired after you, as after a new fashion.

WITWOUD: Madam, truce with your similitudes. No, you met her husband, and did not ask him for her.

MIRABELL: By your leave, Witwoud, that were like inquiring after an old fashion, to ask a husband for his wife.

WITWOUD: Hum, a hit! a hit! a palpable hit!° I confess it.

MRS. FAINALL: You were dressed before I came abroad.

MRS. MILLAMANT: Aye, that's true. Oh, but then I had — Mincing, what had I? Why was I so long?

MINCING: O mem,° your laship° stayed to peruse a pecket° of letters.

MRS. MILLAMANT: Oh, aye, letters; I had letters. I am persecuted with letters. I hate letters. Nobody knows how to write letters, and yet one has 'em, one does not know why. They serve one to pin up one's hair.

WITWOUD: Is that the way? Pray, madam, do you pin up your hair with all your letters? I find I must keep copies.

MRS. MILLAMANT: Only with those in verse, Mr. Witwoud. I never pin up my hair with prose, I think I tried once, Mincing.

MINCING: O mem, I shall never forget it.

MRS. MILLAMANT: Aye, poor Mincing tiffed° and tiffed all the morning.

MINCING: Till I had the cremp in my fingers, I'll vow, mem. And all to no purpose. But when your laship pins it up with poetry, it sits so pleasant the next day as anything, and is so pure and so crips.°

WITWOUD: Indeed, so crips?

MINCING: You're such a critic, Mr. Witwoud.

MRS. MILLAMANT: Mirabell, did you take exceptions last night? Oh, aye, and went away. Now I think on't, I'm angry. No, now I think on't, I'm pleased; for I believe I gave you some pain.

MIRABELL: Does that please you?

MRS. MILLAMANT: Infinitely; I love to give pain.

MIRABELL: You would affect a cruelty which is not in your nature; your true vanity is in the power of pleasing.

MRS. MILLAMANT: Oh, I ask your pardon for that. One's cruelty is one's power; and when one parts with one's cruelty, one parts with one's power; and when one has parted with that, I fancy one's old and ugly.

MIRABELL: Aye, aye, suffer your cruelty to ruin the object of your power, to destroy your lover, and then how vain, how lost a thing you'll be! Nay, 'tis true: You are no longer handsome when you've lost your lover; your beauty dies upon the instant. For beauty is the lover's gift; 'tis he bestows your charms, your glass is all a cheat. The ugly and the old, whom the looking-glass mortifies, yet after commendation° can be flattered by it, and discover beauties in it; for that reflects our praises, rather than your face.

MRS. MILLAMANT: Oh, the vanity of these men! Fainall, d'ye hear him? If they did not commend us, we were not handsome! Now, you must know they could not commend one, if one was not handsome. Beauty the lover's gift! Lord, what is a lover, that it can give? Why, one makes lovers as fast as one pleases, and they live as long as one pleases, and they die as soon as one pleases; and then, if one pleases, one makes more.

WITWOUD: Very pretty. Why, you make no more of making of lovers, madam, than of making so many card matches.°

MRS. MILLAMANT: One no more owes one's beauty to a lover than one's wit to an echo. They can but reflect what we look and say; vain empty things if we are silent or unseen, and want a being.

MIRABELL: Yet to those two vain empty things you owe two° the greatest pleasures of your life.

MRS. MILLAMANT: How so?

MIRABELL: To your lover you owe the pleasure of

---

371. **similitudes:** Witwoud is a tireless (and tiresome) maker of comparisons, or similes. See "his commonplace [book] of comparisons" in act I.   390. **a palpable hit:** See Osric in *Hamlet,* V, II: "A hit, a very palpable hit."   396. **mem:** Madam.   **laship:** Ladyship.   397. **pecket:** Packet.   410. **tiffed:** Arranged.

415. **crips:** Crisp.   440. **commendation:** Praise.   454. **card matches:** Matches made from pieces of heavy paper tipped with sulfur.   460. **two:** Two of.

hearing yourselves praised; and to an echo the pleasure of hearing yourselves talk.

465 WITWOUD: But I know a lady that loves talking so incessantly, she won't give an echo fair play; she has that everlasting rotation of tongue, that an echo must wait till she dies, before it can catch her last words.

470 MRS. MILLAMANT: Oh, fiction! Fainall, let us leave these men.

MIRABELL (*aside to Mrs. Fainall*): Draw off Witwoud.

MRS. FAINALL: Immediately. I have a word or two for Mr. Witwoud.

(*Exeunt Witwoud and Mrs. Fainall.*)

475 MIRABELL: I would beg a little private audience too. You had the tyranny to deny me last night, though you knew I came to impart a secret to you that concerned my love.

MRS. MILLAMANT: You saw I was engaged.

480 MIRABELL: Unkind! You had the leisure to entertain a herd of fools; things who visit you from their excessive idleness, bestowing on your easiness that time which is the encumbrance of their lives. How can you find delight in such society? It is impossible
485 they should admire you; they are not capable. Or if they were, it should be to you as a mortification, for sure to please a fool is some degree of folly.

MRS. MILLAMANT: I please myself. Besides, sometimes to converse with fools is for my health.

490 MIRABELL: Your health! Is there a worse disease than the conversation of fools?

MRS. MILLAMANT: Yes, the vapors; fools are physic° for it, next to assafetida.°

MIRABELL: You are not in a course of fools?°

495 MRS. MILLAMANT: Mirabell, if you persist in this offensive freedom, you'll displease me. I think I must resolve, after all, not to have you; we shan't agree.

MIRABELL: Not in our physic, it may be.

MRS. MILLAMANT: And yet our distemper°, in all like-
500 lihood, will be the same; for we shall be sick of one another. I shan't endure to be reprimanded nor instructed; 'tis so dull to act always by advice, and so tedious to be told of one's faults — I can't bear it. Well, I won't have you, Mirabell. I'm resolved — I
505 think — you may go. Ha! ha! ha! What would you give that you could help loving me?

MIRABELL: I would give something that you did not know I could not help it.

MRS. MILLAMANT: Come, don't look grave then.
510 Well, what do you say to me?

MIRABELL: I say that a man may as soon make a friend by his wit, or a fortune by his honesty, as win a woman with plain dealing° and sincerity.

MRS. MILLAMANT: Sententious Mirabell! Prithee, don't look with that violent and inflexible wise 515 face, like Solomon at the dividing of the child° in an old tapestry hanging.

MIRABELL: You are merry, madam, but I would persuade you for a moment to be serious.

MRS. MILLAMANT: What, with that face? No, if you 520 keep your countenance, 'tis impossible I should hold mine. Well, after all, there is something very moving in a lovesick face. Ha! ha! ha! Well, I won't laugh; don't be peevish. Heigho! now I'll be melancholy, as melancholy as a watchlight.° Well, 525 Mirabell, if ever you will win me, woo me now. Nay, if you are so tedious, fare you well; I see they are walking away.

MIRABELL: Can you not find in the variety of your disposition one moment —   530

MRS. MILLAMANT: To hear you tell me Foible's married, and your plot like to speed? No.

MIRABELL: But how you came to know it —

MRS. MILLAMANT: Without the help of the devil, you can't imagine; unless she should tell me herself. 535 Which of the two it may have been, I will leave you to consider; and when you have done thinking of that, think of me.

(*Exeunt Mrs. Millamant with Mincing.*)

MIRABELL: I have something more — Gone! Think of you! To think of a whirlwind, though 'twere in a 540 whirlwind, were a case of more steady contemplation; a very tranquility of mind and mansion. A fellow that lives in a windmill has not a more whimsical dwelling than the heart of a man that is lodged in a woman. There is no point of the com- 545 pass to which they cannot turn, and by which they are not turned; and by one as well as another; for motion, not method, is their occupation. To know this, and yet continue to be in love, is to be made wise from the dictates of reason, and yet 550 persevere to play the fool by the force of instinct. Oh, here come my pair of turtles!° What, billing so sweetly? Is not Valentine's Day over with you yet?

---

492. **physic:** Medicine.   493. **assafetida:** A gum resin prescribed by doctors as an antidote to "the vapors." 494. **course of fools:** Series of treatments.   499. **distemper:** Illness.

513. **plain dealing:** Honesty, frankness.   516. **Solomon . . . child:** The Old Testament Solomon, king of Israel, was known for his wisdom. When confronted with two women both claiming to be the mother of a newborn baby, Solomon said he would divide the baby in two and give one half to each woman. When one of the women told the king not to slay the baby but to let it live and give it whole to the other woman, Solomon declared the first woman the baby's true mother (I Kings 3:16–28).   525. **watchlight:** A small night candle.   552. **pair of turtles:** Turtle doves; lovers.

(*Enter Waitwell and Foible.*)

555   Sirrah, Waitwell, why, sure you think you were
      married for your own recreation, and not for my
      conveniency.

WAITWELL: Your pardon, sir. With submission, we
      have indeed been solacing° in lawful delights; but
560   still with an eye to business, sir. I have instructed
      her as well as I could. If she can take your direc-
      tions as readily as my instructions, sir, your affairs
      are in a prosperous way.

MIRABELL: Give you joy, Mrs. Foible.

565   FOIBLE: O las, sir, I'm so ashamed! I'm afraid my lady
      has been in a thousand inquietudes for me. But I
      protest, sir, I made as much haste as I could.

WAITWELL: That she did indeed, sir. It was my fault
      that she did not make more.

570   MIRABELL: That I believe.

FOIBLE: But I told my lady as you instructed me, sir
      that I had a prospect of seeing Sir Rowland, your
      uncle; and that I would put her ladyship's picture
      in my pocket to show him, which I'll be sure to say
575   has made him so enamored of her beauty, that he
      burns with impatience to lie at her ladyship's feet
      and worship the original.

MIRABELL: Excellent Foible! Matrimony has made
      you eloquent in love.

580   WAITWELL: I think she has profited, sir. I think so.

FOIBLE: You have seen Madam Millamant, sir?

MIRABELL: Yes.

FOIBLE: I told her, sir, because I did not know that you
      might find an opportunity; she had so much com-
585   pany last night.

MIRABELL: Your diligence will merit more. In the
      meantime —   (*Gives money.*)

FOIBLE: O dear sir, your humble servant!

WAITWELL: Spouse.

590   MIRABELL: Stand off, sir, not a penny! Go on and
      prosper, Foible; the lease shall be made good and
      the farm stocked, if we succeed.°

FOIBLE: I don't question your generosity, sir; and you
      need not doubt of success. If you have no more
595   commands, sir, I'll be gone, I'm sure my lady is at
      her toilet and can't dress till I come. Oh, dear, I'm
      sure that (*looking out*) was Mrs. Marwood that
      went by in a mask; if she has seen me with you,
      I'm sure she'll tell my lady. I'll make haste home
600   and prevent her. Your servant, sir. B'w'y,° Wait-
      well.   (*Exit.*)

WAITWELL: Sir Rowland, if you please. The jade's so
      pert upon her preferment° she forgets herself.

---

559. **solacing:** Taking pleasure.   591–92. **the lease . . . succeed:** I.e., "If our little plot succeeds, I'll be even more generous."   600. **B'w'y:** A slurred form of "God be with you."
603. **preferment:** Her advancement in the world; her new status as a wife.

MIRABELL: Come, sir, will you endeavor to forget
      yourself, and transform into Sir Rowland?   605

WAITWELL: Why, sir, it will be impossible I should re-
      member myself. Married, knighted, and attended°
      all in one day! 'Tis enough to make any forget
      himself. The difficulty will be how to recover my
      acquaintance and familiarity with my former self, 610
      and fall from my transformation to a reformation
      into Waitwell. Nay, I shan't be quite the same
      Waitwell neither; for, now I remember me, I'm
      married and can't be my own man again.

      Aye, there's my grief; that's the sad change of
      life,   615
      To lose my title, and yet keep my wife.
                                       (*Exeunt.*)

ACT III

(*A room in Lady Wishfort's house. Lady Wishfort at
her toilet, Peg waiting.*)

LADY WISHFORT: Merciful! no news of Foible yet?

PEG: No, madam.

LADY WISHFORT: I have no more patience. If I have
      not fretted myself till I am pale again, there's no
      veracity in me! Fetch me the red; the red, do you   5
      hear, sweetheart? An arrant ash-color, as I'm a per-
      son! Look you how this wench stirs! Why dost
      thou not fetch me a little red? Didst thou not hear
      me, mopus?°

PEG: The red ratafia° does your ladyship mean, or the   10
      cherry-brandy?

LADY WISHFORT: Ratafia, fool! No, fool! Not the
      ratafia, fool. Grant me patience! I mean the Span-
      ish paper,° idiot; complexion, darling. Paint, paint,
      paint; dost thou understand that, changeling,° dan- 15
      gling thy hands like bobbins° before thee? Why
      dost thou not stir, puppet? thou wooden thing
      upon wires!

PEG: Lord, madam, your ladyship is so impatient! I
      cannot come at the paint, madam; Mrs. Foible has   20
      locked it up and carried the key with her.

LADY WISHFORT: A pox take you both! Fetch me the
      cherry-brandy then. (*Exit Peg.*) I'm as pale and as
      faint, I look like Mrs. Qualmsick, the curate's wife,
      that's always breeding. Wench, come, come, wench, 25
      what art thou doing? sipping? tasting? Save thee,
      dost thou not know the bottle?

(*Reenter Peg with a bottle and china cup.*)

607–8. **attended:** Waited upon.   9. **mopus:** Idiot; dull-
witted girl.   10. **ratafia:** Fruit-flavored brandy.   13–14.
Spanish paper: Cosmetic rouge.   15. **changeling:** Simpleton.   16. **bobbins:** Spools of yarn.

PEG: Madam, I was looking for a cup.

LADY WISHFORT: A cup, save thee! and what a cup
30   hast thou brought! Does thou take me for a fairy,
to drink out of an acorn? Why didst thou not
bring thy thimble? Hast thou ne'er a brass thimble
clinking in thy pocket with a bit of nutmeg? I warrant thee. Come, fill, fill! So; again. (*One knocks.*)
35   See who that is. Set down the bottle first. Here,
here under the table. What, wouldst thou go with
the bottle in thy hand, like a tapster?° As I'm a
person, this wench has lived in an inn upon the
road, before she came to me, like Maritornes the
40   Asturian in *Don Quixote*!° No Foible yet?

PEG: No, madam; Mrs. Marwood.

LADY WISHFORT: Oh, Marwood; let her come in.
Come in, good Marwood.

(*Enter Mrs. Marwood.*)

MRS. MARWOOD: I'm surprised to find your ladyship
45   in *déshabillé*° at this time of day.

LADY WISHFORT: Foible's a lost thing; has been
abroad since morning, and never heard of since.

MRS. MARWOOD: I saw her but now, as I came masked
through the park, in conference with Mirabell.

50   LADY WISHFORT: With Mirabell! You call my blood
into my face, with mentioning that traitor. She
durst not have the confidence! I sent her to negotiate an affair in which, if I'm detected, I'm undone. If that wheedling villain has wrought upon
55   Foible to detect me, I'm ruined. O my dear friend,
I'm a wretch of wretches if I'm detected.

MRS. MARWOOD: O madam, you cannot suspect Mrs.
Foible's integrity.

LADY WISHFORT: Oh, he carries poison in his tongue
60   that would corrupt integrity itself! If she has given
him an opportunity, she has as good as put her integrity into his hands. Ah, dear Marwood, what's
integrity to an opportunity? Hark! I hear her! Go,
you thing, and send her in. (*Exit Peg.*) Dear friend,
65   retire into my closet,° that I may examine her with
more freedom. You'll pardon me, dear friend; I can
make bold with you. There are books over the
chimney, Quarles° and Prynne,° and the *Short*

View of the Stage,° with Bunyan's works,° to entertain you.   (*Exit Mrs. Marwood.*)   70

(*Enter Foible.*)

O Foible, where hast thou been? What hast thou
been doing?

FOIBLE: Madam, I have seen the party.

LADY WISHFORT: But what hast thou done?

FOIBLE: Nay, 'tis your ladyship has done, and are to   75
do; I have only promised. But a man so enamored,
so transported! Well, if worshiping of pictures be a
sin, poor Sir Rowland, I say.

LADY WISHFORT: The miniature has been counted
like. But hast thou not betrayed me, Foible? Hast   80
thou not detected me to that faithless Mirabell?
What hadst thou to do with him in the Park? Answer me, has he got nothing out of thee?

FOIBLE (*aside*): So the devil has been beforehand with
me. What shall I say? (*Aloud.*) Alas, madam, could   85
I help it, if I met that confident thing? Was I in
fault? If you had heard how he used me, and all
upon your ladyship's account, I'm sure you would
not suspect my fidelity. Nay, if that had been the
worst, I could have borne; but he had a fling at   90
your ladyship too. And then I could not hold; but
i'faith I gave him his own.

LADY WISHFORT: Me? what did the filthy fellow say?

FOIBLE: O madam! 'tis a shame to say what he said,
with his taunts and his fleers, tossing up his nose.   95
"Humh!" says he. "What, you are a-hatching
some plot," says he, "you are so early abroad, or
catering," says he. "Ferreting for some disbanded°
officer, I warrant. Half-pay is but thin subsistence," says he. "Well, what pension does your   100
lady propose? Let me see," says he. "What, she
must come down pretty deep now, she's superannuated,"° says he, "and —"

LADY WISHFORT: Ods° my life, I'll have him, I'll have
him murdered! I'll have him poisoned! Where does   105
he eat? I'll marry a drawer° to have him poisoned
in his wine! I'll send for Robin° from Locket's° immediately.

FOIBLE: Poison him? Poisoning's too good for him.
Starve him, madam, starve him; marry Sir Row-   110

---

37. **tapster:** A person who taps beer in a tavern.   **39–40.**
Maritornes . . . *Don Quixote*: In Cervantes's *Don Quixote*
(part 1, chapter 16), Maritornes is an Austrian chambermaid
with whom the Don fancies himself in love.   **45. *déshabillé*:**
Casual attire.   **65. closet:** Private sitting room.   **68. Quar-**
les: Francis Quarles, devotional poet, author of *Emblems, Di-*
vine and Moral (1635).   **Prynne:** William Prynne, Puritan
author of *Histrio-Mastix* (1633), an attack on the immorality
of the stage.

68–69. *Short View of the Stage*: By Jeremy Collier an attack on
"the Immorality and Profaneness of the English Stage" (1698),
directly aimed at the earlier plays of Congreve. Dryden answered the censures of Collier in his Preface to the *Fables*
(1700).   **69. Bunyan's works:** John Bunyan, the great Puritan writer and preacher. A one-volume edition of the *Works of*
That Eminent Servant of Christ, Mr. John Bunyan had appeared in 1692.   **98. disbanded:** Discharged.   **102–3. su-**
perannuated: Old and infirm.   **104. Ods:** "God's."
106. drawer: One who draws wine or ale; a waiter.
107. Robin: Common name for a waiter.   **Locket's:** A fashionable restaurant in Charing Cross.

land, and get him disinherited. Oh, you would bless yourself to hear what he said!

LADY WISHFORT: A villain! "superannuated"!

FOIBLE: "Humh," says he. "I hear you are laying designs against me too," says he, "and Mrs. Millamant is to marry my uncle" (he does not suspect a word of your ladyship); "but," says he, "I'll fit you for that." "I warrant you," says he. "I'll hamper you for that," says he. "You and your old frippery° too," says he. "I'll handle you —"

LADY WISHFORT: Audacious villain! "handle" me; would he durst! "Frippery! old frippery!" Was there ever such a foul-mouthed fellow? I'll be married tomorrow; I'll be contracted tonight.

FOIBLE: The sooner the better, madam.

LADY WISHFORT: Will Sir Rowland be here, sayest thou? When, Foible?

FOIBLE: Incontinently,° madam. No new sheriff's wife expects the return of her husband after knighthood with that impatience in which Sir Rowland burns for the dear hour of kissing your ladyship's hands after dinner.

LADY WISHFORT: "Frippery! superannuated! frippery!" I'll frippery the villain; I'll reduce him to frippery and rags! A tatterdemalion!° I hope to see him hung with tatters, like a Long Lane penthouse° or a gibbet thief. A slander-mouthed railer! I warrant the spendthrift prodigal's in debt as much as the million lottery,° or the whole court upon a birthday.° I'll spoil his credit with his tailor. Yes, he shall have my niece with her fortune, he shall!

FOIBLE: He! I hope to see him lodge in Ludgate° first, and angle into Blackfriars° for brass farthings with an old mitten.°

LADY WISHFORT: Aye, dear Foible; thank thee for that, dear Foible. He has put me out of all patience. I shall never recompose my features to receive Sir Rowland with any economy of face.° This wretch has fretted me that I am absolutely decayed. Look, Foible.

FOIBLE: Your ladyship has frowned a little too rashly, indeed, madam. There are some cracks discernible in the white varnish.

LADY WISHFORT: Let me see the glass. "Cracks," sayest thou? Why I am arrantly fleaed;° I look like an old peeled wall. Thou must repair me, Foible, before Sir Rowland comes, or I shall never keep up to my picture.°

FOIBLE: I warrant you, madam, a little art once made your picture like you; and now a little of the same art must make you like your picture. Your picture must sit for you, madam.

LADY WISHFORT: But art thou sure Sir Rowland will not fail to come? Or will 'a not fail when he does come? Will he be importunate, Foible, and push? For if he should not be importunate, I shall never break decorums. I shall die with confusion, if I am forced to advance. Oh no, I can never advance! I shall swoon if he should expect advances. No, I hope Sir Rowland is better bred than to put a lady to the necessity of breaking her forms. I won't be too coy neither. I won't give him despair; but a little disdain is not amiss, a little scorn is alluring.

FOIBLE: A little scorn becomes your ladyship.

LADY WISHFORT: Yes, but tenderness becomes me best, a sort of dyingness. You see that picture has a sort of a — ha, Foible? a swimmingness in the eyes. Yes, I'll look so. My niece affects it; but she wants features. Is Sir Rowland handsome? Let my toilet be removed. I'll dress above. I'll receive Sir Rowland here. Is he handsome? Don't answer me. I won't know; I'll be surprised, I'll be taken by surprise.

FOIBLE: By storm, madam. Sir Rowland's a brisk man.

LADY WISHFORT: Is he! Oh, then he'll importune, if he's a brisk man. I shall save decorums if Sir Rowland importunes. I have a mortal terror at the apprehension of offending against decorums. Oh, I'm glad he's a brisk man. Let my things be removed, good Foible.   (Exit.)

(Enter Mrs. Fainall.)

MRS. FAINALL: O Foible, I have been in a fright, lest I should come too late! That devil Marwood saw

---

119–20. old frippery: Old clothes, as applied to Lady Wishfort, "old clotheshorse."   128. Incontinently: Immediately, and with the added suggestion of passionate impatience.   135. tatterdemalion: Ragamuffin.   136. Long Lane penthouse: A shed with a sloping roof in Long Lane, a district famous for its shops of old and secondhand clothes.   139. million lottery: A wild scheme to raise a million pounds by the sale of lottery tickets.   139–40. the whole . . . birthday: Since custom demanded gifts on such an occasion, a royal birthday was an expensive event.   142. Ludgate: The debtors' prison.   143. angle into Blackfriars: Ludgate Prison abutted on the precinct of Blackfriars, the area of London between Ludgate Hill and the river.   144. old mitten: It was the practice of Ludgate prisoners to beg money from passersby, probably by lowering an old mitten on a string from a high window.

148. economy of face: The sense is that Lady Wishfort has been so distressed by Foible's account of Mirabell's words that her makeup has been ruined, and the cosmetics necessary to make her face presentable to Sir Rowland will be very expensive.   155. fleaed: Flayed; skinned.   157–58. keep . . . picture: I.e., "look as lovely as I do in my picture."

Chris Christman and Tag Tanalski in the 1986 production of *Way of the World* at the Spingold Theater, Brandeis University.

you in the Park with Mirabell, and I'm afraid will discover it to my lady.

195 FOIBLE: Discover what, madam?

MRS. FAINALL: Nay, nay, put not on that strange face. I am privy to the whole design, and know that Waitwell, to whom thou wert this morning married, is to personate Mirabell's uncle, and as such,

200 winning my lady, to involve her in those difficulties from which Mirabell only must release her, by his making his conditions to have my cousin and her fortune left to her own disposal.

FOIBLE: O dear madam, I beg your pardon. It was not

205 my confidence in your ladyship that was deficient; but I thought the former good correspondence between your ladyship and Mr. Mirabell might have hindered his communicating this secret.

MRS. FAINALL: Dear Foible, forget that.

210 FOIBLE: O dear madam, Mr. Mirabell is such a sweet, winning gentleman, but your ladyship is the pattern of generosity. Sweet lady, to be so good! Mr. Mirabell cannot choose but be grateful. I find your ladyship has his heart still. Now, madam, I can

215 safely tell your ladyship our success. Mrs. Mar-

wood had told my lady, but I warrant I managed myself. I turned it all for the better. I told my lady that Mr. Mirabell railed at her. I laid horrid things to his charge, I'll vow; and my lady is so incensed that she'll be contracted to Sir Rowland tonight, 220 she says. I warrant I worked her up, that he may have her for asking for, as they say of a Welsh maidenhead.

MRS. FAINALL: O rare Foible!

FOIBLE: I beg your ladyship to acquaint Mr. Mirabell 225 of his success. I would be seen as little as possible to speak to him; besides, I believe Madam Marwood watches me. She has a month's mind;° but I know Mr. Mirabell can't abide her. (*Calls.*) John! Remove my lady's toilet. Madam, your servant. 230 My lady is so impatient, I fear she'll come for me if I stay.

MRS. FAINALL: I'll go with you up the back stairs, lest I should meet her.   (*Exeunt.*)

(*Reenter Mrs. Marwood alone.*)

---

228. month's mind: A longing, desire.

235 MRS. MARWOOD: Indeed, Mrs. Engine,° is it thus with you? Are you become a go-between of this importance? Yes, I shall watch you. Why, this wench is the *passe-partout,* a very master-key to everybody's strong-box. My friend Fainall,° have you

240 carried it so swimmingly? I thought there was something in it; but it seems it's over with you.° Your loathing is not from a want of appetite then, but from a surfeit. Else you could never be so cool to fall from a principal to be an assistant; to pro-

245 cure for him! "A pattern of generosity," that I confess. Well, Mr. Fainall, you have met with your match. O man, man! woman, woman! the devil's an ass; if I were a painter, I would draw him like an idiot, a driveller with a bib and bells. Man

250 should have his head and horns,° and woman the rest of him. Poor simple fiend! "Madam Marwood has a month's mind, but he can't abide her." 'Twere better for him you had not been his confessor in that affair, without° you could have kept

255 his counsel closer. I shall not prove another "pattern of generosity." He has not obliged me to that with those excesses of himself; and now I'll have none of him. Here comes the good lady, panting ripe; with a heart full of hope, and a head full of

260 care, like any chemist upon the day of projection.°

(Reenter Lady Wishfort.)

LADY WISHFORT: O dear Marwood, what shall I say for this rude forgetfulness? But my dear friend is all goodness.

MRS. MARWOOD: No apologies, dear madam. I have

265 been very well entertained.

LADY WISHFORT: As I'm a person, I am in a very chaos to think I should so forget myself, but I have such an olio of affairs,° really I know not what to do. *(Calls.)* Foible! I expect my nephew, Sir Wilfull,

270 every moment too. *(Calls.)* Why, Foible! He means to travel for improvement.

MRS. MARWOOD: Methinks Sir Wilfull should rather think of marrying than travelling at his years. I hear he is turned of forty.

LADY WISHFORT: Oh, he's in less danger of being 275 spoiled by his travels. I am against my nephew's marrying too young. It will be time enough when he comes back and has acquired discretion to choose for himself.

MRS. MARWOOD: Methinks Mrs. Millamant and he 280 would make a very fit match. He may travel afterwards. 'Tis a thing very usual with young gentlemen.

LADY WISHFORT: I promise you I have thought on't; and since 'tis your judgment, I'll think on't again. I 285 assure you I will; I value your judgment extremely. On my word, I'll propose it.

(Reenter Foible.)

Come, come, Foible, I had forgot my nephew will be here before dinner. I must make haste.

FOIBLE: Mr. Witwoud and Mr. Petulant are come to 290 dine with your ladyship.

LADY WISHFORT: Oh, dear, I can't appear till I am dressed. Dear Marwood, shall I be free with you again, and beg you to entertain 'em? I'll make all imaginable haste. Dear friend, excuse me. 295

(Exeunt Lady Wishfort and Foible.)

(Enter Mrs. Millamant and Mincing.)

MRS. MILLAMANT: Sure never anything was so unbred as that odious man! Marwood, your servant.

MRS. MARWOOD: You have a color; what's the matter?

MRS. MILLAMANT: That horrid fellow, Petulant, has provoked me into a flame. I have broke my fan. 300 Mincing, lend me yours; is not all the powder out of my hair?

MRS. MARWOOD: No. What has he done?

MRS. MILLAMANT: Nay, he has done nothing; he has only talked. Nay, he has said nothing neither; but 305 he has contradicted everything that has been said. For my part, I thought Witwoud and he would have quarreled.

MINCING: I vow, mem, I thought once they would have fit.° 310

MRS. MILLAMANT: Well, 'tis a lamentable thing, I swear, that one has not the liberty of choosing one's acquaintance as one does one's clothes.

MRS. MARWOOD: If we had that liberty, we should be as weary of one set of acquaintance, though never 315 so good, as we are of one suit, though never so fine. A fool and a doily stuff° would now and then find days of grace, and be worn for variety.

MRS. MILLAMANT: I could consent to wear 'em, if they would wear alike; but fools never wear out, 320

235. **Mrs. Engine:** I.e., Foible, the agent of the plot, which Mrs. Marwood has discovered by eavesdropping on the discourse between Foible and Mrs. Fainall.   239. **Fainall:** Mrs. Fainall.   241. **it seems . . . you:** Among other things, Mrs. Marwood has learned of Mrs. Fainall's affair with Mirabell before her marriage to Fainall.   250. **horns:** The traditional sign of the cuckold, a man whose wife is unfaithful.   254. **without:** Unless.   260. **like any chemist . . . projection:** The comparison refers to the attempts of the alchemists to transmute base metals into gold. The "day of projection" is the last day of the experiment, when success or failure will be known.   268. **such an olio of affairs:** I.e., "such a number of things on my mind."

310. **fit:** Fought.   317. **doily stuff:** A coarse woolen material.

they are such *drap-de-Berry°* things! without one could give 'em to one's chambermaid after a day or two.

MRS. MARWOOD: 'Twere better so indeed. Or what
325 think you of the playhouse? A fine, gay, glossy fool should be given there, like a new masking habit, after the masquerade is over, and we have done with the disguise. For a fool's visit is always a disguise, and never admitted by a woman of wit, but
330 to blind° her affair with a lover of sense. If you would but appear barefaced now, and own Mirabell, you might as easily put off Petulant and Witwoud as your hood and scarf. And indeed 'tis time, for the town has found it; the secret is grown
335 too big for the pretense. 'Tis like Mrs. Primly's great belly, she may lace it down before, but it burnishes° on her hips. Indeed, Millamant, you can no more conceal it than my Lady Strammel can her face, that goodly face, which, in defiance of her
340 Rhenish-wine tea,° will not be comprehended in a mask.°

MRS. MILLAMANT: I'll take my death, Marwood, you are more censorious than a decayed beauty, or a discarded toast. Mincing, tell the men they may
345 come up. My aunt is not dressing here; their folly is less provoking than your malice. (*Exit Mincing.*) "The town has found it!" What has it found? That Mirabell loves me is no more a secret than it is a secret that you discovered it to my aunt, or than
350 the reason why you discovered it is a secret.

MRS. MARWOOD: You are nettled.°

MRS. MILLAMANT: You're mistaken. Ridiculous!

MRS. MARWOOD: Indeed, my dear, you'll tear another fan, if you don't mitigate those violent airs.

355 MRS. MILLAMANT: O silly! ha! ha! ha! I could laugh immoderately. Poor Mirabell! His constancy to me has quite destroyed his complaisance for all the world beside. I swear I never enjoined it him to be so coy. If I had the vanity to think he would obey
360 me, I would command him to show more gallantry. 'Tis hardly well-bred to be so particular° on one hand, and so insensible on the other. But I despair to prevail, and so let him follow his own way, ha! ha! ha! Pardon me, dear creature, I must laugh,
365 ha! ha! ha! though I grant you 'tis a little barbarous, ha! ha! ha!

MRS. MARWOOD: What pity 'tis, so much fine raillery,

and delivered with so significant gesture, should be so unhappily directed to miscarry!

MRS. MILLAMANT: Ha? Dear creature, I ask your par- 370 don. I swear I did not mind you.°

MRS. MARWOOD: Mr. Mirabell and you both may think it a thing impossible, when I shall tell him by telling you —

MRS. MILLAMANT: Oh, dear, what? For it is the same 375 thing if I hear it, ha! ha! ha!

MRS. MARWOOD: That I detest him, hate him, madam.

MRS. MILLAMANT: O madam, why so do I. And yet the creature loves me, ha! ha! ha! How can one forbear laughing to think of it! I am a sibyl° if I am 380 not amazed to think what he can see in me. I'll take my death, I think you are handsomer and, within a year or two as young; if you could but stay for me, I should overtake you, but that cannot be. Well, that thought makes me melancholic. 385 Now, I'll be sad.

MRS. MARWOOD: Your merry note may be changed sooner than you think.

MRS. MILLAMANT: D'ye say so? Then I'm resolved I'll have a song to keep up my spirits. 390

(*Reenter Mincing.*)

MINCING: The gentlemen stay but to comb,° madam, and will wait on you.

MRS. MILLAMANT: Desire Mrs. —, that is in the next room, to sing the song I would have learnt yester- day. You shall hear it, madam, not that there's any 395 great matter in it, but 'tis agreeable to my humor.

(*Song.*)

[*Set by Mr. John Eccles.*]

I
Love's but the frailty of the mind,
When 'tis not with ambition join'd;
A sickly flame, which, if not fed, expires,
And feeding, wastes in self-consuming fires. 400

II
'Tis not to wound a wanton boy
Or am'rous youth, that gives the joy;
But 'tis the glory to have pierc'd a swain,
For whom inferior beauties sigh'd in vain.

III
Then I alone the conquest prize, 405
When I insult a rival's eyes;
If there's delight in love, 'tis when I see
That heart, which others bleed for, bleed for me.

---

321. *drap-de-Berry*: Wooler cloth, probably coarse, from the French province of Berry.   330. blind: Camouflage. 337. burnishes: Is all the more evident.   340. Rhenish-wine tea: Rhenish white wine was supposed to reduce corpulence. 340–41. will not . . . mask: The sense is that the lady's face was so fat that no mask would fit it.   351. nettled: Annoyed. 361. particular: Attentive to one lady (i.e., Millamant).

371. I did not mind you: "I did not have you in mind." 380. sibyl: A female prophet or seer.   391. comb: I.e., comb their wigs.

(*Enter Petulant and Witwoud.*)

MRS. MILLAMANT: Is your animosity composed, gen-
410   tlemen?
WITWOUD: Raillery, raillery, madam; we have no ani-
       mosity. We hit off a little wit now and then, but no
       animosity. The falling-out of wits is like the falling-
       out of lovers; we agree in the main, like treble and
415   bass. Ha, Petulant?
PETULANT: Aye, in the main, but when I have a humor
       to contradict.
WITWOUD: Aye, when he has a humor to contradict,
       then I contradict too. What, I know my cue. Then
420   we contradict one another like two battledores; for
       contradictions beget one another like Jews.
PETULANT: If he says black's black, if I have a humor
       to say 'tis blue, let that pass; all's one for that. If I
       have a humor to prove it, it must be granted.
425   WITWOUD: Not positively must, but it may, it may.
PETULANT: Yes, it positively must, upon proof posi-
       tive.
WITWOUD: Aye, upon proof positive it must; but upon
       proof presumptive it only may. That's a logical dis-
430   tinction now, madam.
MRS. MARWOOD: I perceive your debates are of im-
       portance and very learnedly handled.
PETULANT: Importance is one thing, and learning's an-
       other; but a debate's a debate, that I assert.
435   WITWOUD: Petulant's an enemy to learning; he relies
       altogether on his parts.
PETULANT: No, I'm no enemy to learning; it hurts not
       me.
MRS. MARWOOD: That's a sign indeed it's no enemy to
440   you.
PETULANT: No, no, it's no enemy to anybody but
       them that have it.
MRS. MILLAMANT: Well, an illiterate man's my aver-
       sion; I wonder at the impudence of any illiterate
445   man to offer to make love.
WITWOUD: That I confess I wonder at too.
MRS. MILLAMANT: Ah! to marry an ignorant that can
       hardly read or write!
PETULANT: Why should a man be any further from be-
450   ing married, though he can't read, than he is from
       being hanged? The ordinary's° paid for setting the
       psalm, and the parish priest for reading the cere-
       mony. And for the rest which is to follow in both
       cases, a man may do it without book; so all's one
455   for that.
MRS. MILLAMANT: D'ye hear the creature? Lord,
       here's company; I'll be gone.
              (*Exeunt Mrs. Millamant and Mincing.*)

451. **ordinary's:** The ordinary was the chaplain of a prison,
who prepared criminals for death.

(*Enter Sir Wilfull Witwoud in a riding dress, and a
Footman to Lady Wishfort.*)

WITWOUD: In the name of Bartlemew and his fair,°
       what have we here?
MRS. MARWOOD: 'Tis your brother, I fancy. Don't you   460
       know him?
WITWOUD: Not I. Yes, I think it is he. I've almost for-
       got him; I have not seen him since the Revolution.°
FOOTMAN (*to Sir Wilfull*): Sir, my lady's dressing.   465
       Here's company; if you please to walk in, in the
       meantime.
SIR WILFULL: Dressing! What, it's but morning here, I
       warrant, with you in London; we should count it
       towards afternoon in our parts, down in Shrop-   470
       shire. Why then, belike my aunt han't dined yet,
       ha, friend?
FOOTMAN: Your aunt, sir?
SIR WILFULL: My aunt, sir! Yes, my aunt, sir, and your
       lady, sir; your lady is my aunt, sir. Why, what, dost   475
       thou not know me, friend? Why, then send some-
       body hither that does. How long hast thou lived
       with thy lady, fellow, ha?
FOOTMAN: A week, sir; longer than anybody else in
       the house, except my lady's woman.   480
SIR WILFULL: Why then, belike thou dost not know
       thy lady, if thou seest her, ha, friend?
FOOTMAN: Why truly, sir, I cannot safely swear to her
       face in a morning, before she is dressed. 'Tis like I
       may give a shrewd guess at her by this time.   485
SIR WILFULL: Well, prithee try what thou canst do; if
       thou canst not guess, inquire her out, dost hear,
       fellow? And tell her, her nephew, Sir Wilfull Wit-
       woud, is in the house.
FOOTMAN: I shall, sir.   490
SIR WILFULL: Hold ye, hear me, friend; a word with
       you in your ear. Prithee who are these gallants?
FOOTMAN: Really, sir, I can't tell; here come so many
       here, 'tis hard to know 'em all.   (*Exit.*)
SIR WILFULL: Oons,° this fellow knows less than a   495
       starling;° I don't think 'a knows his own name.
MRS. MARWOOD: Mr. Witwoud, your brother is not
       behind-hand in forgetfulness; I fancy he has forgot
       you too.

458. **Bartlemew and his fair:** Bartholomew Fair was held in
August of each year at Smithfield. Since it was specially
renowned for its sale of country cloths, Witwoud may here
be referring to the inappropriateness of his brother's riding
habit in a London drawing room.   464. **Revolution:** The
bloodless Revolution of 1688, which marked the defeat of
James II and the accession to the throne of William and
Mary.   495. **Oons:** "God's wounds," an oath.   496. **star-
ling:** Proverbially a stupid bird.

500 WITWOUD: I hope so. The devil take him that remembers first, I say.

SIR WILFULL: Save you, gentlemen and lady!

MRS. MARWOOD: For shame, Mr. Witwoud; why won't you speak to him? And you, sir.

505 WITWOUD: Petulant, speak.

PETULANT: And you, sir.

SIR WILFULL: No offense, I hope.

(*Salutes Mrs. Marwood.*)

MRS. MARWOOD: No sure, sir.

WITWOUD: This is a vile dog; I see that already. No of-
510 fense! Ha! ha! ha! to him; to him, Petulant, smoke° him.

PETULANT: It seems as if you had come a journey, sir; hem, hem.   (*Surveying him round.*)

SIR WILFULL: Very likely, sir, that it may seem so.

515 PETULANT: No offense, I hope, sir.

WITWOUD: Smoke the boots, the boots; Petulant, the boots, ha! ha! ha!

SIR WILFULL: Maybe not, sir; thereafter as 'tis meant,° sir.

520 PETULANT: Sir, I presume upon the information of your boots.

SIR WILFULL: Why, 'tis like you may, sir. If you are not satisfied with the information of my boots, sir, if you will step to the stable, you may inquire further
525 of my horse, sir.

PETULANT: Your horse, sir! Your horse is an ass, sir!

SIR WILFULL: Do you speak by way of offense, sir?

MRS. MARWOOD: The gentleman's merry, that's all, sir. (*Aside.*) 'Slife,° we shall have a quarrel betwixt
530 an horse and an ass, before they find one another out. (*Aloud.*) You must not take anything amiss from your friends, sir. You are among your friends here, though it may be you don't know it. If I am not mistaken, you are Sir Wilfull Witwoud.

535 SIR WILFULL: Right, lady; I am Sir Wilfull Witwoud, so I write myself; no offense to anybody, I hope; and nephew to the Lady Wishfort of this mansion.

MRS. MARWOOD: Don't you know this gentleman, sir?

SIR WILFULL: Hum! What, sure 'tis not — yea by'r
540 Lady, but 'tis. 'Sheart° I know not whether 'tis or no. Yea, but 'tis, by the Wrekin.° Brother Antony! What, Tony, i'faith! What, dost thou not know me? By'r Lady, nor I thee, thou art so becravated° and so beperiwigged.° 'Sheart, why dost not
545 speak? Art thou o'erjoyed?

WITWOUD: Odso, brother, is it you? Your servant, brother.

SIR WILFULL: Your servant! Why, yours, sir. Your servant again, 'sheart, and your friend and servant to that, and a — (*puff*) and a flapdragon for your 550 service,° sir! and a hare's foot, and a hare's scut° for your service, sir, an you be so cold and so courtly!

WITWOUD: No offense, I hope, brother.

SIR WILFULL: 'Sheart, sir, but there is, and much of- 555 fense! A pox, is this your Inns o' Court° breeding, not to know your friends and your relations, your elders and your betters?

WITWOUD: Why, brother Wilfull of Salop,° you may be as short as a Shrewsbury° cake, if you please. 560 But I tell you 'tis not modish to know relations in town. You think you're in the country, where great lubberly° brothers slabber° and kiss one another when they meet, like a call of serjeants.° 'Tis not the fashion here, 'tis not indeed, dear brother. 565

SIR WILFULL: The fashion's a fool; and you're a fop, dear brother. 'Sheart, I've suspected this. By'r Lady, I conjectured you were a fop, since you began to change the style of your letters, and write in a scrap of paper, gilt round the edges, no broader than a 570 *subpoena.*° I might expect this when you left off, "Honored brother," and "hoping you are in good health," and so forth, to begin with a "Rat me,° knight, I'm so sick of a last night's debauch," ods heart, and then tell a familiar tale of a cock and a 575 bull,° and a whore and a bottle, and so conclude. You could write news before you were out of your time,° when you lived with honest Pumple Nose, the attorney of Furnival's Inn,° you could entreat to be remembered then to your friends round the 580 Wrekin. We could have gazettes, then, and *Dawks's Letter,*° and the *Weekly Bill,*° till of late days.

---

510. **smoke:** "To affront a stranger at his coming in" (Summers, *Dictionary of the Canting Crew*).   518. **as 'tis meant:** "According to the way it is meant."   529. **'Slife:** "God's life."   540. **'Sheart:** "God's heart."   541. **Wrekin:** A hill in his native Shropshire.   543. **becravated:** Wearing a cravat, or tie.   544. **beperiwigged:** Wearing a wig.

550–51. **flapdragon . . . service:** Derived from the game of catching raisins out of burning brandy; meaning "a fig for your service."   551. **scut:** Tail.   556. **Inns o' Court:** The center of the legal world of London, used for the city itself. Sir Wilfull, the country squire, simply asks if Witwoud's rudeness is a mark of city manners.   559. **Salop:** Another name for Shropshire.   560. **Shrewsbury:** The capital of Shropshire.   563. **lubberly:** Loutish.   **slabber:** Slobber   564. **serjeants:** When sergeants-at-law are admitted to the bar.   571. ***subpoena:*** A legal summons.   573. **"Rat me":** Contraction of the oath "May God rot me."   575–78. **tale . . . bull:** A wildly exaggerated tale.   577–78. **out of your time:** I.e., before he had finished his legal apprenticeship.   579. **Furnival's Inn:** One of the Inns of Court (Chancery) attached to Lincoln's Inn.   581–82. ***Dawks's Letter:*** A newsletter with a wide circulation in the provinces.   582. ***Weekly Bill:*** It reported all deaths in and around London.

PETULANT: 'Slife, Witwoud, were you ever an attorney's clerk? of the family of the Furnivals? Ha! ha!
585 ha!

WITWOUD: Aye, aye, but that was but for a while, not long, not long. Pshaw! I was not in my own power then; an orphan, and this fellow was my guardian. Aye, aye, I was glad to consent to that
590 man to come to London. He had the disposal of me then. If I had not agreed to that, I might have been bound prentice to a felt maker in Shrewsbury; this fellow would have bound me to a maker of felts.

595 SIR WILFULL: 'Sheart, and better than to be bound to a maker of fops, where, I suppose, you have served your time; and now you may set up for yourself.

MRS. MARWOOD: You intend to travel, sir, as I'm informed.

600 SIR WILFULL: Belike I may, madam. I may chance to sail upon the salt seas, if my mind hold.

PETULANT: And the wind serve.

SIR WILFULL: Serve or not serve, I shan't ask license of you, sir; nor the weathercock your companion. I
605 direct my discourse to the lady, sir. 'Tis like my aunt may have told you, madam. Yes, I have settled my concerns, I may say now, and am minded to see foreign parts. If an how that the peace° holds, whereby, that is, taxes abate.

610 MRS. MARWOOD: I thought you had designed for France at all adventures.°

SIR WILFULL: I can't tell that; 'tis like I may, and 'tis like I may not. I am somewhat dainty in making a resolution, because when I make it, I keep it. I
615 don't stand shill I, shall I,° then; if I say't, I'll do't. But I have thoughts to tarry a small matter in town, to learn somewhat of your lingo first, before I cross the seas. I'd gladly have a spice of your French, as they say, whereby to hold discourse in foreign
620 countries.

MRS. MARWOOD: Here's an academy in town for that use.

SIR WILFULL: There is? 'Tis like there may.

MRS. MARWOOD: No doubt you will return very
625 much improved.

WITWOUD: Yes, refined, like a Dutch skipper from a whale-fishing.

(*Reenter Lady Wishfort with Fainall.*)

LADY WISHFORT: Nephew, you are welcome.

SIR WILFULL: Aunt, your servant.

FAINALL: Sir Wilfull, your most faithful servant.   630

SIR WILFULL: Cousin Fainall, give me your hand.

LADY WISHFORT: Cousin Witwoud, your servant; Mr. Petulant, your servant. Nephew, you are welcome again. Will you drink anything after your journey, nephew, before you eat? Dinner's almost ready.   635

SIR WILFULL: I'm very well, I thank you, aunt; however, I thank you for your courteous offer. 'Sheart I was afraid you would have been in the fashion too, and have remembered to have forgot your relations. Here's your cousin Tony; belike I mayn't   640 call him brother for fear of offense.

LADY WISHFORT: O, he's a rallier,° nephew. My cousin's a wit; and your great wits always rally their best friends to choose.° When you have been abroad, nephew, you'll understand raillery better.   645
(*Fainall and Mrs. Marwood talk apart.*)

SIR WILFULL: Why then, let him hold his tongue in the meantime, and rail when that day comes.

(*Reenter Mincing.*)

MINCING: Mem, I come to acquaint your laship that dinner is impatient.

SIR WILFULL: Impatient? Why then, belike it won't   650 stay till I pull off my boots. Sweetheart, can you help me to a pair of slippers? My man's with the horses, I warrant.

LADY WISHFORT: Fie, fie, nephew, you would not pull off your boots here. Go down into the hall; dinner   655 shall stay for you. My nephew's a little unbred; you'll pardon him, madam. Gentlemen, will you walk? Marwood?

MRS. MARWOOD: I'll follow you, madam, before Sir Wilfull is ready.   660
(*Exeunt all but Mrs. Marwood and Fainall.*)

FAINALL: Why then, Foible's a bawd, an arrant, rank, match-making bawd. And I, it seems, am a husband, a rank husband; and my wife a very arrant, rank wife, all in the way of the world. 'Sdeath, to be a cuckold by anticipation, a cuckold in embryo!°   665 Sure I was born with budding antlers, like a young satyr, or a citizen's child.° 'Sdeath! to be outwitted, to be outjilted, outmatrimonied! If I had kept my speed like a stag, 'twere somewhat; but to crawl after, with my horns, like a snail, and be out-stripped   670 by my wife, 'tis scurvy wedlock.

MRS. MARWOOD: Then shake it off. You have often

---

608. peace: The Treaty of Ryswick (1697), which temporarily terminated the war between France on the one hand and England and her Continental allies on the other.   611. at all adventures: In any case.   615. shill I, shall I: Shilly-shally. Sir Wilfull is saying that he is not an indecisive man.

642. rallier: A railer; one who delights in raillery, gentle mockery.   644. to choose: As they like.   664–65. to be . . . embryo: In their "talk apart," Mrs. Marwood has told Mr. Fainall what she has learned of his wife's affair with Mirabell before her marriage to Fainall.   667. citizen's child: I.e., a cuckold's child. Many a child of an honest citizen was fathered by a gentleman of the town.

wished for an opportunity to part; and now you
have it. But first prevent their plot; the half of Mil-
675   lamant's fortune is too considerable to be parted
with, to a foe, to Mirabell.

FAINALL: Damn him! that had been mine, had you
not made that fond° discovery. That had been forfeited, had they been married. My wife had added
680   luster to my horns by that increase of fortune, I
could have worn 'em tipped with gold, though my
forehead had been furnished like a deputy lieutenant's hall.°

MRS. MARWOOD: They may prove a cap of mainte-
685   nance° to you still, if you can away with° your
wife. And she's no worse than when you had her. I
dare swear she had given up her game before she
was married.

FAINALL: Hum! that may be.

690   MRS. MARWOOD: You married her to keep you; and if
you can contrive to have her keep you better than
you expected, why should you keep her longer than
you intended?

FAINALL: The means, the means.

695   MRS. MARWOOD: Discover to my lady your wife's
conduct; threaten to part with her. My lady loves
her, and will come to any composition° to save her
reputation. Take the opportunity of breaking it,
just upon the discovery of this imposture. My lady
700   will be enraged beyond bounds, and sacrifice niece
and fortune and all, at that conjuncture. And let
me alone to keep her warm; if she should flag in
her part, I will not fail to prompt her.

FAINALL: Faith, this has an appearance.°

705   MRS. MARWOOD: I'm sorry I hinted to my lady to endeavor a match between Millamant and Sir Wilfull; that may be an obstacle.

FAINALL: Oh, for that matter leave me to manage him;
I'll disable him for that. He will drink like a Dane;°
710   after dinner, I'll set his hand in.°

MRS. MARWOOD: Well, how do you stand affected towards your lady?

FAINALL: Why, faith, I'm thinking of it. Let me see. I
am married already, so that's over. My wife has
played the jade with me; well, that's over too. I   715
never loved her, or if I had, why, that would have
been over too by this time. Jealous of her I cannot
be, for I am certain; so there's an end of jealousy.
Weary of her I am, and shall be. No, there's no end
of that; no, no, that were too much to hope. Thus   720
far concerning my repose; now for my reputation.
As to my own, I married not for it, so that's out of
the question. And as to my part in my wife's, why,
she had parted with hers before; so bringing none
to me, she can take none from me. 'Tis against all   725
rule of play that I should lose to one who has not
wherewithal to stake.

MRS. MARWOOD: Besides, you forget marriage is honorable.

FAINALL: Hum! Faith, and that's well thought on.   730
Marriage is honorable, as you say; and if so,
wherefore should cuckoldom be a discredit, being
derived from so honorable a root?

MRS. MARWOOD: Nay, I know not; if the root be honorable, why not the branches?°   735

FAINALL: So, so; why, this point's clear. Well, how do
we proceed?

MRS. MARWOOD: I will contrive a letter which shall
be delivered to my lady at the time when that rascal who is to act Sir Rowland is with her. It shall   740
come as from an unknown hand, for the less I appear to know of the truth, the better I can play the
incendiary. Besides, I would not have Foible provoked if I could help it, because you know she
knows some passages.° Nay, I expect all will come   745
out; but let the mine be sprung first, and then I
care not if I am discovered.

FAINALL: If the worst come to the worst, I'll turn my
wife to grass,° I have already a deed of settlement
of the best part of her estate, which I wheedled out   750
of her; and that you shall partake at least.

MRS. MARWOOD: I hope you are convinced that I hate
Mirabell now; you'll be no more jealous?

FAINALL: Jealous! No, by this kiss. Let husbands be
jealous; but let the lover still believe. Or if he doubt,   755
let it be only to endear his pleasure, and prepare
the joy that follows, when he proves his mistress
true. But let husbands' doubts convert to endless
jealousy; or if they have belief, let it corrupt to
superstition and blind credulity. I am single, and   760
will herd no more with 'em. True, I wear the badge,

---

678. **fond:** Foolish.   682–83. **forehead . . . hall:** I.e., though
he had been cuckolded as many times as there are antlers of
stags and deer decorating the country mansion of a deputy
lieutenant.   684–85. **cap of maintenance:** A term in heraldry. The coat of arms of a royal bastard sometimes included a cap with two points behind, like the horns of a
cuckold. Mrs. Marwood puns on the word *maintenance*
since she is insinuating that, armed with this new information
concerning his wife, Fainall may be in a better position to
blackmail Lady Wishfort to the amount of Millamant's fortune that she controls.   635. **away with:** Continue to tolerate.   697. **come to any composition:** Agree to anything.
704. **an appearance:** Possibilities.   709. **drink like a Dane:**
The Danes were known as heavy drinkers.   710. **I'll set . . .
in:** I.e., "I'll involve him in the plot."

735. **branches:** I.e., the cuckold's horns.   744–45. **she
knows some passages:** I.e., Foible knows of Mrs. Marwood's
affair with Mr. Fainall and may divulge it. Indeed, she does,
in the denouement of act V.   748–49. **turn . . . grass:** Turn
her out, as he would an animal to graze.

but I'll disown the order. And since I take my leave
of 'em, I care not if I leave 'em a common motto
to their common crest.

765   All husbands must or pain or shame endure
           The wise too jealous are, fools too secure.
                                                        (*Exeunt.*)

ACT IV

([*Scene continues.*] *Enter Lady Wishfort and Foible.*)

LADY WISHFORT: Is Sir Rowland coming, sayest thou,
Foible? and are things in order?

FOIBLE: Yes, madam, I have put wax-lights in the
sconces, and placed the footmen in a row in the
5   hall, in their best liveries, with the coachman and
postillion to fill up the equipage.

LADY WISHFORT: Have you pulvilled° the coachman
and postillion, that they may not stink of the stable when Sir Rowland comes by?

10   FOIBLE: Yes, madam.

LADY WISHFORT: And are the dancers and the music
ready, that he may be entertained in all points with
correspondence to his passion?

FOIBLE: All is ready, madam.

15   LADY WISHFORT: And — well, and how do I look,
Foible?

FOIBLE: Most killing well, madam.

LADY WISHFORT: Well, and how shall I receive him? In
what figure shall I give his heart the first impres-
20   sion? There is a great deal in the first impression.
Shall I sit? No, I won't sit, I'll walk; aye, I'll walk
from the door upon his entrance; and then turn
full upon him. No, that will be too sudden. I'll
lie, aye, I'll lie down. I'll receive him in my little
25   dressing-room; there's a couch. Yes, yes, I'll
give the first impression on a couch. I won't lie
neither, but loll and lean upon one elbow; with
one foot a little dangling off, jogging in a thoughtful way. Yes, and then as soon as he appears, start,
30   aye, start and be surprised, and rise to meet him
in a pretty disorder. Yes, oh, nothing is more alluring than a levee° from a couch, in some confusion;
it shows the foot to advantage, and furnishes with blushes and recomposing airs beyond
35   comparison. Hark! there's a coach.

FOIBLE: 'Tis he, madam.

LADY WISHFORT: Oh dear, has my nephew made his
addresses to Millamant? I ordered him.

FOIBLE: Sir Wilfull is set in to drinking, madam, in the
parlor.   40

LADY WISHFORT: Ods my life, I'll send him to her.
Call her down, Foible; bring her hither. I'll send
him as I go. When they are together, then come to
me, Foible, that I may not be too long alone with
Sir Rowland.   (*Exit.*)   45

(*Enter Mrs. Millamant and Mrs. Fainall.*)

FOIBLE: Madam, I stayed here to tell your ladyship
that Mr. Mirabell has waited this half hour for an
opportunity to talk with you, though my lady's orders were to leave you and Sir Wilfull together.
Shall I tell Mr. Mirabell that you are at leisure?   50

MRS. MILLAMANT: No, what would the dear man
have? I am thoughtful, and would amuse myself;
bid him come another time.
           "There never yet was woman made,
              Nor shall, but to be curs'd."°   55
                          (*Repeating and walking about.*)
That's hard!

MRS. FAINALL: You are very fond of Sir John Suckling
today, Millamant, and the poets.

MRS. MILLAMANT: He? Aye, and filthy verses; so I am.   60

FOIBLE: Sir Wilfull is coming, madam. Shall I send Mr.
Mirabell away?

MRS. MILLAMANT: Aye, if you please, Foible, send
him away, or send him hither; just as you will, dear
Foible. I think I'll see him; shall I? Aye, let the   65
wretch come.
                                        (*Exit Foible.*)
        "Thyrsis, a youth of the inspired train."°
                                            (*Repeating.*)
Dear Fainall, entertain° Sir Wilfull. Thou hast philosophy to undergo° a fool; thou art married and
hast patience. I would confer with my own   70
thoughts.

MRS. FAINALL: I am obliged to you, that you would
make me your proxy in this affair; but I have business of my own.

(*Enter Sir Wilfull.*)

O Sir Wilfull, you are come at the critical instant.   75
There's your mistress up to the ears in love and
contemplation; pursue your point, now or never.

SIR WILFULL: Yes; my aunt will have it so. I would
gladly have been encouraged with a bottle or two,

---

7. **pulvilled:** Scented with a sweet-smelling powder.   **32.
levee:** Rising.

54–55. **"There never ... curs'd":** The opening lines of a
poem by Sir John Suckling (1609–1642).   **67. "Thyrsis ...
train":** The first line of *The Story of Phoebus and Daphne,
Applied,* a poem by Edmund Waller (1606–1687), a poet
much admired by Dryden and renowned for the "sweetness"
of his verse.   **69. undergo:** Put up with.

80　because I'm somewhat wary at first, before I am
acquainted. (*This while Millamant walks about repeating to herself.*) But I hope, after a time, I shall
break my mind; that is, upon further acquaintance.
So for the present, cousin, I'll take my leave. If so
85　be you'll be so kind to make my excuse, I'll return
to my company.

Mrs. Fainall: Oh, fie, Sir Wilfull! What, you must
not be daunted.

Sir Wilfull: Daunted! No, that's not it. It is not so
90　much for that; for if so be that I set on't, I'll do't.
But only for the present; 'tis sufficient till further
acquaintance, that's all. Your servant.

Mrs. Fainall: Nay, I'll swear you shall never lose so
favorable an opportunity, if I can help it. I'll leave
95　you together and lock the door.　　　　(*Exit.*)

Sir Wilfull: Nay, nay, cousin. I have forgot my
gloves. What d'ye do? 'Sheart, 'a has locked the
door indeed, I think. Nay, Cousin Fainall, open
the door! Pshaw, what a vixen trick is this? Nay,
100　now 'a has seen me too. Cousin, I made bold to
pass through as it were. I think this door's enchanted!

Mrs. Millamant (*repeating*):
　　"I prithee spare me, gentle boy,
　　Press me no more for that slight toy —"°

105　Sir Wilfull: Anan?° Cousin, your servant.

Mrs. Millamant (*repeating*):
　　"That foolish trifle of a heart —"
　　Sir Wilfull!

Sir Wilfull: Yes. Your servant. No offense, I hope,
cousin.

Mrs. Millamant (*repeating*):
110　　"I swear it will not do its part,
　　Though thou dost shine, employ'st thy pow'r
　　　　and art."
　　Natural, easy Suckling!

Sir Wilfull: Anan? Suckling? No such suckling neither, cousin, nor stripling! I thank Heaven, I'm no
115　minor.

Mrs. Millamant: Ah, rustic! ruder than Gothic.°

Sir Wilfull: Well, well, I shall understand your lingo
one of these days, cousin; in the meanwhile I must
answer in plain English.

120　Mrs. Millamant: Have you any business with me,
Sir Wilfull?

Sir Wilfull: Not at present, cousin. Yes, I made bold
to see, to come and know if that how you were

disposed to fetch a walk this evening; if so be that
I might not be troublesome, I would have fought°　125
a walk with you.

Mrs. Millamant: A walk! What then?

Sir Wilfull: Nay, nothing. Only for the walk's sake,
that's all.

Mrs. Millamant: I nauseate walking; 'tis a country　130
diversion. I loathe the country and everything that
relates to it.

Sir Wilfull: Indeed! hah! Look ye, look ye, you do?
Nay, 'tis like you may. Here are choice of pastimes
here in town, as plays and the like: that must be　135
confessed indeed.

Mrs. Millamant: *Ah, l'étourdi!*° I hate the town too.

Sir Wilfull: Dear heart, that's much. Hah! that you
should hate 'em both! Hah! 'tis like you may; there　140
are some can't relish the town, and others can't
away with the country. 'Tis like you may be one of
those, cousin.

Mrs. Millamant: Ha! ha! ha! Yes, 'tis like I may.
You have nothing further to say to me?　　　145

Sir Wilfull: Not at present, cousin. 'Tis like when I
have an opportunity to be more private, I may
break my mind in some measure. I conjecture you
partly guess — however, that's as time shall try;
but spare to speak and spare to speed,° as they say.　150

Mrs. Millamant: If it is of no great importance, Sir
Wilfull, you will oblige me to leave me; I have just
now a little business —

Sir Wilfull: Enough, enough, cousin, yes, yes, all a
case;° when you're disposed, when you're disposed.　155
Now's as well as another time; and another time as
well as now. All's one for that. Yes, yes, if your concerns call you, there's no haste; it will keep cold, as
they say. Cousin, your servant. I think this door's
locked.　　　　　　　　　　　　　　　160

Mrs. Millamant: You may go this way, sir.

Sir Wilfull: Your servant; then with your leave I'll
return to my company.

Mrs. Millamant: Aye, aye; ha! ha! ha!
　　"Like Phoebus sung the no less am'rous boy."°　165

(*Enter Mirabell.*)

Mirabell: "Like Daphne, she, as lovely and as coy."°

103–4. **"I prithee . . . toy":** The first two lines of a "Song" by
Suckling. The three lines quoted by Millamant in her next
two speeches complete the first stanza of the poem.
105. Anan: "I beg your pardon." **116. Gothic:** The
Restoration and early eighteenth century considered the civilization of the Goths and "Gothic" art rude and barbarous.

125. fought: A provincial form of "fetched." **137. l'é-
tourdi:** The silly fellow. **150. spare to speak . . . speed:**
Proverb meaning "If you hold your tongue, you won't get
along in the world." **154–55. all a case:** Idiomatic for "It's
all the same." **165. "Like Phoebus . . . boy":** The third line
of Waller's *Story of Phoebus and Daphne, Applied.*
166. "Like Daphne . . . coy": The fourth line of Waller's
poem. Mirabell completes the couplet begun by Millamant.

Do you lock yourself up from me, to make my search more curious?° Or is this pretty artifice contrived, to signify that here the chase must end and
170 my pursuit be crowned, for you can fly no further?

Mrs. Millamant: Vanity! No. I'll fly and be followed to the last moment. Though I am upon the very verge of matrimony, I expect you should solicit me as much as if I were wavering at the grate of a
175 monastery, with one foot over the threshold. I'll be solicited to the very last, nay, and afterwards.

Mirabell: What, after the last?

Mrs. Millamant: Oh, I should think I was poor and had nothing to bestow, if I were reduced to an in-
180 glorious ease and freed from the agreeable fatigues of solicitation.

Mirabell: But do not you know that when favors are conferred upon instant and tedious solicitation, that they diminish in their value, and that both the
185 giver loses the grace, and the receiver lessens his pleasure?

Mrs. Millamant: It may be in things of common application; but never sure in love. Oh, I hate a lover that can dare to think he draws a moment's air in-
190 dependent on the bounty of his mistress. There is not so impudent a thing in nature as the saucy look of an assured man, confident of success. The pedantic arrogance of a very husband has not so pragmatical° an air. Ah! I'll never marry, unless I
195 am first made sure of my will and pleasure.

Mirabell: Would you have 'em both before marriage? Or will you be contented with the first now, and stay for the other till after grace?

Mrs. Millamant: Ah! don't be impertinent. My dear
200 liberty, shall I leave thee? My faithful solitude, my darling contemplation, must I bid you then adieu? Ay-h adieu, my morning thoughts, agreeable wakings, indolent slumbers, all ye *douceurs,*° ye *sommeils du matin,*° adieu. I can't do't, 'tis more than
205 impossible. Positively, Mirabell, I'll lie abed in a morning as long as I please.

Mirabell: Then I'll get up in a morning as early as I please.

Mrs. Millamant: Ah! idle creature, get up when you
210 will. And d'ye hear, I won't be called names after I'm married; positively I won't be called names.

Mirabell: Names!

Mrs. Millamant: Aye, as wife, spouse, my dear, joy, jewel, love, sweetheart, and the rest of that nau-
215 seous cant, in which men and their wives are so fulsomely familiar; I shall never bear that. Good Mirabell, don't let us be familiar or fond, nor kiss

before folks, like my Lady Fadler and Sir Francis; nor go to Hyde Park together the first Sunday in a new chariot, to provoke eyes and whispers, and 220 then never be seen there together again, as if we were proud of one another the first week, and ashamed of one another ever after. Let us never visit together, nor go to a play together. But let us be very strange and well-bred; let us be as strange 225 as if we had been married a great while, and as well-bred as if we were not married at all.

Mirabell: Have you any more conditions to offer? Hitherto your demands are pretty reasonable.

Mrs. Millamant: Trifles! As liberty to pay and re- 230 ceive visits to and from whom I please; to write and receive letters, without interrogatories° or wry faces on your part; to wear what I please, and choose conversation with regard only to my own taste; to have no obligation upon me to converse 235 with wits that I don't like, because they are your acquaintance, or to be intimate with fools, because they may be your relations. Come to dinner when I please; dine in my dressing-room when I'm out of humor, without giving a reason. To have my closet 240 inviolate; to be sole empress of my tea-table, which you must never presume to approach without first asking leave. And lastly, wherever I am, you shall always knock at the door before you come in. These articles subscribed, if I continue to endure 245 you a little longer, I may by degrees dwindle into a wife.

Mirabell: Your bill of fare is something advanced in this latter account. Well, have I liberty to offer conditions, that when you are dwindled into a 250 wife, I may not be beyond measure enlarged into a husband?

Mrs. Millamant: You have free leave. Propose your utmost; speak and spare not.

Mirabell: I thank you. *Imprimis*° then, I covenant° 255 that your acquaintance be general; that you admit no sworn confidante, or intimate of your own sex; no she-friend to screen her affairs under your countenance, and tempt you to make trial of a mutual secrecy. No decoy-duck to wheedle° you a fop, 260 scrambling° to the play in a mask; then bring you home in a pretended fright, when you think you shall be found out, and rail at me for missing the play, and disappointing the frolic which you had to pick me up and prove my constancy. 265

Mrs. Millamant: Detestable *imprimis*! I go to the play in a mask!

---

168. curious: Difficult.   194. pragmatical: Officious.
203. *douceurs:* Sweet pleasures.   203–4. *sommeils du matin:* Morning sleep.

232. interrogatories: Prying questions.   255. *Imprimis:* First.
covenant: Decree.   260. wheedle: Procure.   261. scrambling: Going without suitable dignity.

MIRABELL: *Item,*° I article that you continue to like your own face, as long as I shall; and while it passes current with me, that you endeavor not to new-coin it. To which end, together with all vizards for the day, I prohibit all masks for the night, made of oiled skins and I know not what: hog's bones, hare's gall, pig water, and the marrow of a roasted cat.° In short, I forbid all commerce with the gentle-woman in What-d'ye-call-it Court. *Item,* I shut my doors against all bawds with baskets, and pennyworths of muslin, china, fans, atlases,° etc. *Item,* when you shall be breeding —

MRS. MILLAMANT: Ah! name it not.

MIRABELL: Which may be presumed, with a blessing on our endeavors —

MRS. MILLAMANT: Odious endeavors!

MIRABELL: I denounce against all strait-lacing, squeezing for a shape, till you mold my boy's head like a sugar-loaf, and instead of a man child, make me father to a crooked billet.° Lastly, to the dominion of the tea-table I submit, but with *proviso* that you exceed not in your province, but restrain yourself to native and simple tea-table drinks, as tea, chocolate, and coffee, as likewise to genuine and authorized tea-table talk, such as mending of fashions, spoiling reputations, railing at absent friends, and so forth; but that on no account you encroach upon the men's prerogative, and presume to drink healths, or toast fellows; for prevention of which, I banish all foreign forces, all auxiliaries to the tea-table, as orange brandy, all aniseed, cinnamon, citron, and Barbados waters, together with ratafia and the most noble spirit of clary.° But for cowslip wine, poppy water, and all dormitives,° those I allow. These *provisos* admitted, in other things I may prove a tractable and complying husband.

MRS. MILLAMANT: O horrid *provisos!* filthy strong-waters! I toast fellows, odious men! I hate your odious *provisos.*

MIRABELL: Then we're agreed. Shall I kiss your hand upon the contract? And here comes one to be a witness to the sealing of the deed.

(*Reenter Mrs. Fainall.*)

MRS. MILLAMANT: Fainall, what shall I do? Shall I have him? I think I must have him.

MRS. FAINALL: Aye, aye, take him, take him; what should you do?

MRS. MILLAMANT: Well then — I'll take my death I'm in a horrid fright. Fainall, I shall never say it. Well — I think — I'll endure you.

MRS. FAINALL: Fie! fie! have him, have him, and tell him so in plain terms; for I am sure you have a mind to him.

MRS. MILLAMANT: Are you? I think I have; and the horrid man looks as if he thought so too. Well, you ridiculous thing you, I'll have you; I won't be kissed, nor I won't be thanked. Here, kiss my hand though. So, hold your tongue now; don't say a word.

MRS. FAINALL Mirabell, there's a necessity for your obedience; you have neither time to talk nor stay. My mother is coming; and in my conscience, if she should see you, would fall into fits and maybe not recover, time enough to return to Sir Rowland, who, as Foible tells me, is in a fair way to succeed. Therefore spare your ecstacies for another occasion, and slip down the back stairs, where Foible waits to consult you.

MRS. MILLAMANT: Aye, go, go. In the meantime I suppose you have said something to please me.

MIRABELL: I am all obedience.   (*Exit.*)

MRS. FAINALL: Yonder Sir Wilfull's drunk, and so noisy that my mother has been forced to leave Sir Rowland to appease him; but he answers her only with singing and drinking. What they may have done by this time I know not; but Petulant and he were upon quarreling as I came by.

MRS. MILLAMANT: Well, if Mirabell should not make a good husband, I am a lost thing; for I find I love him violently.

MRS. FAINALL: So it seems; for you mind not what's said to you. If you doubt him, you had best take up with Sir Wilfull.

MRS. MILLAMANT: How can you name that superannuated lubber? Foh!

(*Enter Witwoud, from drinking.*)

MRS. FAINALL: So, is the fray made up, that you have left 'em?

WITWOUD: Left 'em? I could stay no longer. I have laughed like ten christenings; I am tipsy with laughing. If I had stayed any longer I should have burst; I must have been let out and pieced in the sides like an unsized camlet.° Yes, yes, the fray is composed; my lady came in like a *noli prosequi*° and stopped the proceedings.

MRS. MILLAMANT: What was the dispute?

WITWOUD: That's the jest; there was no dispute. They

---

268. *Item:* In addition.   273–75. hog's bones . . . cat: All were ingredients in cosmetics.   278. atlases: A kind of satin.   287. billet: Stick.   298–300. orange brandy . . . clary: All these "auxiliaries" were cordials made of brandy and variously flavored.   301. dormitives: Sedatives.

353. unsized camlet: I.e., like a piece of unstiffened satin. 359. *noli prosequi:* A legal term meaning that the plaintiff does not wish to continue the prosecution.

could neither of 'em speak for rage, and so fell
asputtering at one another like two roasting apples.

(*Enter Petulant, drunk.*)

365 Now, Petulant? All's over, all's well? Gad, my head
begins to whim° it about. Why dost thou not speak?
Thou art both as drunk and as mute as a fish.

PETULANT: Look you, Mrs. Millamant, if you can love
me, dear nymph, say it, and that's the conclusion.
370 Pass on, or pass off; that's all.

WITWOUD: Thou hast uttered volumes, folios, in less
than *decimo sexto*,° my dear Lacedemonian.° Sirrah, Petulant, thou art an epitomizer of words.°

PETULANT: Witwoud, you are an annihilator of sense.

375 WITWOUD: Thou art a retailer of phrases and dost
deal in remnants of remnants, like a maker of pin-
cushions; thou art in truth (metaphorically speaking) a speaker of shorthand.

PETULANT: Thou art (without a figure) just one half of
380 an ass, and Baldwin° yonder, thy half brother, is
the rest. A Gemini° of asses split would make just
four of you.

WITWOUD: Thou dost bite, my dear mustard seed; kiss
me for that.

385 PETULANT: Stand off! I'll kiss no more males. I have
kissed your twin yonder in a humor of reconciliation, till he (*hiccup*) rises upon my stomach like a
radish.

MRS. MILLAMANT: Eh! filthy creature! What was the
390 quarrel?

PETULANT: There was no quarrel; there might have
been a quarrel.

WITWOUD: If there had been words enow between 'em
to have expressed provocation, they had gone to-
395 gether by the ears like a pair of castanets.

PETULANT: You were the quarrel.

MRS. MILLAMANT: Me!

PETULANT: If I have a humor to quarrel, I can make
less matters conclude premises. If you are not
400 handsome, what then, if I have a humor to prove
it? If I shall have my reward, say so; if not, fight
for your face the next time yourself. I'll go sleep.

WITWOUD: Do, wrap thyself up like a wood louse,
and dream revenge; and hear me, if thou canst
405 learn to write by tomorrow morning, pen me a
challenge. I'll carry it for thee.

---

366. **whim:** Spin.   372. *decimo sexto*: A very tiny book.
Lacedemonian: Spartan. (The Spartans were known to be
very laconic people, that is, terse in their speech.)
373. **thou art . . . words:** I.e., "You say much in few words."
380. **Baldwin:** The name of the ass in the medieval tale *Rey-
nard the Fox.*   381. **Gemini:** Matched pair of twins. The
constellation Gemini derives its name from the twin stars
Castor and Pollux.

PETULANT: Carry your mistress's monkey a spider! Go
flea dogs, and read romances! I'll go to bed to my
maid.   (*Exit.*)

MRS. FAINALL: He's horridly drunk. How came you 410
all in this pickle?

WITWOUD: A plot! a plot! to get rid of the knight.
Your husband's advice; but he sneaked off.

(*Reenter Sir Wilfull drunk, and Lady Wishfort.*)

LADY WISHFORT: Out upon't, out upon't! At years of
discretion, and comport yourself at this rantipole° 415
rate!

SIR WILFULL: No offense, aunt.

LADY WISHFORT: Offense? As I'm a person, I'm
ashamed of you. Fogh! how you stink of wine!
D'ye think my niece will ever endure such a bora- 420
chio!° you're an absolute borachio.

SIR WILFULL: Borachio!

LADY WISHFORT: At a time when you should commence an amour, and put your best foot
foremost —   425

SIR WILFULL: 'Sheart, an you grutch° me your liquor,
make a bill. Give me more drink, and take my
purse.

(*Sings.*) "Prithee fill me the glass
        Till it laugh in my face,   430
With ale that is potent and mellow;
        He that whines for a lass
        Is an ignorant ass,
For a bumper has not its fellow."

But if you would have me marry my cousin, say   435
the word, and I'll do't. Wilfull will do't; that's the
word. Wilfull will do't; that's my crest. My motto
I have forgot.

LADY WISHFORT: My nephew's a little overtaken,°
cousin, but 'tis with drinking your health. O' my 440
word you are obliged to him.

SIR WILFULL: *In vino veritas*,° aunt. If I drunk your
health today, cousin, I am a borachio. But if you
have a mind to be married, say the word, and send
for the piper; Wilfull will do't. If not, dust it away, 445
and let's have t'other round. Tony! Ods-heart,
where's Tony? Tony's an honest fellow; but he spits
after a bumper, and that's a fault.

(*Sings.*) "We'll drink, and we'll never ha' done,
        boys,
        Put the glass then around with the sun, boys; 450

---

415. **rantipole:** Wild.   420–21. **borachio:** Spanish for
"wine bag," a drunkard. Shakespeare has a character named
Borachio in *Much Ado About Nothing.*   426. **grutch:**
Grudge.   439. **overtaken:** Overcome by drink.   442. *In
vino veritas*: "In wine (there is) truth."

Let Apollo's example invite us;
  For he's drunk every night,
  And that makes him so bright,
That he's able next morning to light us."

455 The sun's a good pimple,° an honest soaker, he has
a cellar at your Antipodes.° If I travel, aunt, I
touch at your Antipodes; your Antipodes are a
good, rascally sort of topsy-turvy fellows. If I had
a bumper, I'd stand upon my head and drink a
460 health to 'em. A match or no match, cousin, with
the hard name. Aunt, Wilfull will do't. If she has
her maidenhead, let her look to't, if she has not, let
her keep her own counsel in the meantime, and cry
out at the nine months' end.
465 MRS. MILLAMANT: Your pardon, madam, I can stay
no longer. Sir Wilfull grows very powerful. Egh!
how he smells! I shall be overcome if I stay. Come,
cousin.

    (*Exeunt Mrs. Millamant and Mrs. Fainall.*)

LADY WISHFORT: Smells! he would poison a tallow-
470 chandler° and his family! Beastly creature, I know
not what to do with him. Travel, quotha! aye,
travel, travel, get thee gone, get thee but far
enough, to the Saracens, or the Tartars, or the
Turks, for thou art not fit to live in a Christian
475 commonwealth, thou beastly pagan!
SIR WILFULL: Turks, no; no Turks, aunt; your Turks
are infidels, and believe not in the grape. Your Ma-
hometan, your Mussulman, is a dry stinkard.° No
offense, aunt. My map says that your Turk is not
480 so honest a man as your Christian. I cannot find by
the map that your mufti° is orthodox; whereby it is
a plain case that orthodox is a hard word, aunt,
and (*hiccup*) Greek for claret.

  (*Sings.*) "To drink is a Christian diversion,
485   Unknown to the Turk or the Persian
    Let Mahometan fools
    Live by heathenish rules,
  And be damn'd over teacups and coffee!
    But let British lads sing,
490   Crown a health to the king,
  And a fig for your sultan and sophy!"°

Ah, Tony!

(*Enter Foible, and whispers* [*to*] *Lady Wishfort.*)

LADY WISHFORT (*aside to Foible*): Sir Rowland impatient? Good lack! what shall I do with this beastly

tumbril?° (*Aloud.*) Go lie down and sleep, you sot! 495
or, as I'm a person, I'll have you bastinadoed° with
broomsticks. Call up the wenches with broomsticks.   (*Exit Foible.*)
SIR WILFULL: Ahey! Wenches, where are the wenches?
LADY WISHFORT: Dear Cousin Witwoud, get him 500
away, and you will bind me to you inviolably. I
have an affair of moment that invades me with
some precipitation. You will oblige me to all futu-
rity.
WITWOUD: Come, knight. Pox on him. I don't know 505
what to say to him. Will you go to a cock match?
SIR WILFULL: With a wench, Tony? Is she a shakebag,°
Sirrah? Let me bite your cheek° for that.
WITWOUD: Horrible! he has a breath like a bagpipe!
Aye, aye, come, will you march, my Salopian?° 510
SIR WILFULL: Lead on, little Tony, I'll follow thee, my
Anthony, my Tantony. Sirrah, thou shalt be my
Tantony, and I'll be thy pig.°
  "And a fig for your sultan and sophy."

    (*Exit singing with Witwoud.*)

LADY WISHFORT: This will never do. It will never 515
make a match; at least before he has been abroad.

(*Enter Waitwell, disguised as Sir Rowland.*)

Dear Sir Rowland, I am confounded with confusion at the retrospection of my own rudeness! I
have more pardons to ask than the Pope distributes in the Year of Jubilee.° But I hope, where 520
there is likely to be so near an alliance, we may unbend the severity of decorum, and dispense with a
little ceremony.
WAITWELL: My impatience, madam, is the effect of
my transport; and till I have the possession of your 525
adorable person, I am tantalized on the rack, and
do but hang, madam, on the tenter° of expectation.
LADY WISHFORT: You have excess of gallantry, Sir
Rowland, and press things to a conclusion with a
most prevailing vehemence. But a day or two for 530
decency of marriage —
WAITWELL: For decency of funeral, madam! The delay
will break my heart; or, if that should fail, I shall
be poisoned. My nephew will get an inkling of my
designs, and poison me — and I would willingly 535

---

455. **pimple:** Drinking companion.   456. **Antipodes:** The
opposite end of the world, or its inhabitants. 469–70.
tallow-chandler: Candle maker. 478. **dry stinkard:** A miserable nondrinker. Mohammedans drink neither wine nor
spirits. 481. **mufti:** An expert in Mohammedan religious
law. 491. **sophy:** A former title of the Persian shah.

495. **tumbril:** Dump-cart. 496. **bastinadoed:** Beaten.
507. **shake-bag:** A term in cock fighting for a very game or
sporting cock. 508. **bite your cheek:** I.e., "give you a big
kiss." 510. **Salopian:** Shropshireman. 513. **pig:** In art
and legend, the pig is associated with St. Anthony the Great.
520. **Year of Jubilee:** The year (approximately every twenty-
fifth) in which the pope grants general remission from the
consequences of sin. 527. **tenter:** A tenterhook.

starve him before I die; I would gladly go out of
the world with that satisfaction. That would be
some comfort to me, if I could but live so long as
to be revenged on that unnatural viper.

540   LADY WISHFORT: Is he so unnatural, say you? Truly I
would contribute much both to the saving of your
life, and the accomplishment of your revenge. Not
that I respect myself, though he has been a perfidious wretch to me.

545   WAITWELL: Perfidious to you!

LADY WISHFORT: O Sir Rowland, the hours that he
has died away at my feet, the tears that he has
shed, the oaths that he has sworn, the palpitations
that he has felt, the trances and the tremblings, the

550   ardors and the ecstasies, the kneelings and the risings, the heart-heavings and the hand-gripings, the
pangs and the pathetic regards of his protesting
eyes! Oh, no memory can register!

WAITWELL: What, my rival! Is the rebel my rival! 'A
555   dies.

LADY WISHFORT: No, don't kill him at once, Sir Rowland; starve him gradually, inch by inch.

WAITWELL: I'll do't. In three weeks he shall be barefoot; in a month out at knees with begging an

560   alms. He shall starve upward and upward, till he
has nothing living but his head, and then go out in
a stink like a candle's end upon a save-all.°

LADY WISHFORT: Well, Sir Rowland, you have the
way. You are no novice in the labyrinth of love;

565   you have the clue. But as I am a person, Sir Rowland, you must not attribute my yielding to any
sinister appetite, or indigestion of widowhood; nor
impute my complacency to any lethargy of continence. I hope you do not think me prone to any

570   iteration° of nuptials.

WAITWELL: Far be it from me —

LADY WISHFORT: If you do, I protest I must recede,
or think that I have made a prostitution of decorums; but in the vehemence of compassion, and

575   to save the life of a person of so much importance —

WAITWELL: I esteem it so.

LADY WISHFORT: Or else you wrong my condescension.

580   WAITWELL: I do not, I do not!

LADY WISHFORT: Indeed you do.

WAITWELL: I do not, fair shrine of virtue!

LADY WISHFORT: If you think the least scruple of
carnality° was an ingredient —

WAITWELL: Dear madam, no. You are all camphire°   585
and frankincense, all chastity and odor.

LADY WISHFORT: Or that —

(*Reenter Foible.*)

FOIBLE: Madam, the dancers are ready; and there's
one with a letter, who must deliver it into your
own hands.   590

LADY WISHFORT: Sir Rowland, will you give me
leave? Think favorably, judge candidly, and conclude you have found a person who would suffer
racks in honor's cause, dear Sir Rowland, and will
wait on you incessantly.°   (*Exit.*)   595

WAITWELL: Fie, fie! What a slavery have I undergone!
Spouse, hast thou any cordial? I want spirits.

FOIBLE: What a washy° rogue art thou, to pant thus
for a quarter of an hour's lying and swearing to a
fine lady!   600

WAITWELL: Oh, she is the antidote to desire! Spouse,
thou wilt fare the worse for't. I shall have no
appetite to "iteration of nuptials" this eight-and-
forty hours. By this hand I'd rather be a chair-
man° in the dog days° than act Sir Rowland till   605
this time tomorrow!

(*Reenter Lady Wishfort, with a letter.*)

LADY WISHFORT: Call in the dancers. Sir Rowland,
we'll sit, if you please, and see the entertainment.
(*Dance.*) Now, with your permission, Sir Rowland,
I will peruse my letter. I would open it in your   610
presence, because I would not make you uneasy. If
it should make you uneasy, I would burn it —
speak if it does — but you may see, the superscrip-
tion is like a woman's hand.

FOIBLE (*aside to Waitwell*): By Heaven! Mrs. Mar-   615
wood's; I know it. My heart aches. Get it from
her.

WAITWELL: A woman's hand? No, madam, that's no
woman's hand; I see that already. That's somebody
whose throat must be cut.   620

LADY WISHFORT: Nay, Sir Rowland, since you give me
a proof of your passion by your jealousy, I promise
you I'll make a return, by a frank communication.
You shall see it; we'll open it together. Look you
here. (*Reads.*) "Madam, though unknown to you."   625
Look you there; 'tis from nobody that I know. "I
have that honor for your character, that I think
myself obliged to let you know you are abused. He

---

562. **save-all:** A device in a candlestick to ensure that the candle will be completely burned.   570. **iteration:** Repetition.
The sense seems to be that Lady Wishfort hopes Sir Rowland
will not suspect her of a willingness to marry just any man.
584. **carnality:** Sensuality, lust.

585. **camphire:** Camphor was believed to reduce sexual desire.   595. **incessantly:** Immediately.   598. **washy:** Weak.
604–5. **chair-man:** A sedan-chair carrier.   605. **dog days:**
The sultriest days of the summer, a period of about six weeks
beginning in early July.

who pretends to be Sir Rowland is a cheat and a
630   rascal." Oh, heavens! what's this?

FOIBLE (*aside*): Unfortunate! all's ruined!

WAITWELL: How, how, let me see, let me see! (*Reading.*) "A rascal, and disguised and suborned° for
       that imposture." O villainy! O villainy! "by the
635   contrivance of —"

LADY WISHFORT: I shall faint, I shall die, oh!

FOIBLE (*aside to Waitwell*): Say 'tis your nephew's
       hand. Quickly, his plot, swear, swear it!

WAITWELL: Here's a villain! Madam, don't you per-
640   ceive it? don't you see it?

LADY WISHFORT: Too well, too well! I have seen too
       much.

WAITWELL: I told you at first I knew the hand. A
       woman's hand? The rascal writes a sort of a large
645   hand, your Roman hand. I saw there was a throat
       to be cut presently. If he were my son, as he is my
       nephew, I'd pistol him!

FOIBLE: Oh, treachery! But are you sure, Sir Rowland,
       it is his writing?

650   WAITWELL: Sure? Am I here? Do I live? Do I love this
       pearl of India? I have twenty letters in my pocket
       from him in the same character.°

LADY WISHFORT: How!

FOIBLE: Oh, what luck it is, Sir Rowland, that you
655   were present at this juncture! This was the business
       that brought Mr. Mirabell disguised to Madam
       Millamant this afternoon. I thought something
       was contriving, when he stole by me and would
       have hid his face.

660   LADY WISHFORT: How, how! I heard the villain was in
       the house indeed; and now I remember, my niece
       went away abruptly, when Sir Wilfull was to have
       made his addresses.

FOIBLE: Then, then, madam, Mr. Mirabell waited for
665   her in her chamber, but I would not tell your lady-
       ship to discompose° you when you were to receive
       Sir Rowland.

WAITWELL: Enough, his date is short.

FOIBLE: No, good Sir Rowland, don't incur the law.

670   WAITWELL: Law? I care not for law. I can but die,
       and 'tis in a good cause. My lady shall be satisfied
       of my truth and innocence, though it cost me my
       life.

LADY WISHFORT: No, dear Sir Rowland, don't fight; if
675   you should be killed, I must never show my face;
       or hanged! Oh, consider my reputation, Sir Row-
       land! No, you shan't fight. I'll go in and examine
       my niece; I'll make her confess. I conjure you, Sir
       Rowland, by all your love, not to fight.

680   WAITWELL: I am charmed, madam; I obey. But some

---

633. **suborned:** Bribed.   652. **character:** Handwriting.
666. **discompose:** Distress, upset.

---

proof you must let me give you; I'll go for a black
box, which contains the writings of my whole estate, and deliver that into your hands.

LADY WISHFORT: Aye, dear Sir Rowland, that will be
some comfort; bring the black box.   685

WAITWELL: And may I presume to bring a contract to
be signed this night? May I hope so far?

LADY WISHFORT: Bring what you will; but come alive,
pray come alive. Oh, this is a happy discovery!

WAITWELL: Dead or alive I'll come, and married we   690
will be in spite of treachery; aye, and get an heir
that shall defeat the last remaining glimpse of hope
in my abandoned nephew. Come, my buxom
widow.

      Ere long you shall substantial proof receive,   695
   That I'm an arrant knight —°

FOIBLE (*aside*):   Or arrant° knave.
                                    (*Exeunt.*)

ACT V

([*Scene continues.*] *Enter Lady Wishfort and Foible.*)

LADY WISHFORT: Out of my house, out of my house,
thou viper! thou serpent, that I have fostered! thou
bosom traitress, that I raised from nothing! Begone! begone! begone! go! go! That I took from
washing of old gauze and weaving of dead hair,   5
with a bleak blue nose, over a chafing-dish of
starved embers, and dining behind a traverse rag,°
in a shop no bigger than a birdcage! Go, go! starve
again, do, do!

FOIBLE: Dear madam, I'll beg your pardon on my   10
knees.

LADY WISHFORT: Away! out! out! Go set up for yourself again! Do, drive a trade, do, with your three-
pennyworth of small ware flaunting upon a
pack-thread under a brandy-seller's bulk,° or   15
against a dead wall by a ballad-monger! Go, hang
out an old frisoneer-gorget,° with a yard of yellow
colberteen° again. Do; an old gnawed mask, two
rows of pins, and a child's fiddle; a glass necklace
with the beads broken, and a quilted nightcap with 20
one ear. Go, go, drive a trade! These were your
commodities, you treacherous trull! this was the
merchandise you dealt in, when I took you into my
house, placed you next myself, and made you gov-

---

696. **arrant knight:** I.e., a true knight-errant.   **arrant:**
Downright.   7. **traverse rag:** A curtain or hanging that
serves as a screen.   15. **bulk:** A booth where brandy is sold.
17. **frisoneer-gorget:** A kind of wimple, or head covering,
made of coarse woolen cloth.   18. **colberteen:** A French
lace of inferior quality.

25 ernante of my whole family! You have forgot this, have you, now you have feathered your nest?

FOIBLE: No, no, dear madam. Do but hear me; have but a moment's patience. I'll confess all. Mr. Mirabell seduced me; I am not the first that he has
30 wheedled with his dissembling tongue. Your ladyship's own wisdom has been deluded by him, then how should I, a poor ignorant, defend myself? O madam, if you knew but what he promised me, and how he assured me your ladyship should come
35 to no damage! Or else the wealth of the Indies should not have bribed me to conspire against so good, so sweet, so kind a lady as you have been to me.

LADY WISHFORT: No damage? What, to betray me, to
40 marry me to a cast-servingman?° To make me a receptacle, a hospital for a decayed pimp? "No damage"? O thou frontless° impudence, more than a big-bellied actress!

FOIBLE: Pray do but hear me, madam; he could not
45 marry your ladyship, madam. No indeed; his marriage was to have been void in law, for he was married to me first, to secure your ladyship. He could not have bedded your ladyship; for if he had consummated with your ladyship, he must have
50 run the risk of the law and been put upon his clergy.° Yes indeed, I inquired of the law in that case before I would meddle or make.°

LADY WISHFORT: What, then I have been your property, have I? I have been convenient to you, it
55 seems! While you were catering for Mirabell, I have been broker° for you? What, have you made a passive bawd of me? This exceeds all precedent; I am brought to fine uses, to become a botcher° of second-hand marriages between Abigails° and An-
60 drews!° I'll couple you! Yes, I'll baste you together, you and your Philander!° I'll Duke's-Place you, as I'm a person! Your turtle is in custody already; you shall coo in the same cage, if there be constable or warrant in the parish.   (*Exit.*)

65 FOIBLE: Oh, that ever I was born! Oh, that I was ever married! A bride! aye, I shall be a Bridewell-bride.° Oh!

---

40. **cast-servingman:** A discharged servant.   42. **frontless:** Shameless.   50–51. **put upon his clergy:** Forced to plead benefit of clergy. Clergy (and, later, people who could read or write) could claim exemption from punishment imposed by a secular court.   52. **meddle or make:** A colloquialism for "get mixed up in this business."   56. **broker:** Marriage broker.   58. **botcher:** A maker or mender.   59. **Abigails:** A maidservant in Beaumont and Fletcher's play *The Scornful Lady.*   59–60. **Andrews:** A manservant in Fletcher and Massinger's *The Elder Brother.*   61. **Philander:** The lover in Beaumont and Fletcher's *The Laws of Candy.*   66. **Bridewell-bride:** Bridewell was a house of correction.

(*Enter Mrs. Fainall.*)

MRS. FAINALL: Poor Foible, what's the matter?

FOIBLE: O madam, my lady's gone for a constable. I shall be had to a justice, and put to Bridewell to 70 beat hemp. Poor Waitwell's gone to prison already.

MRS. FAINALL: Have a good heart, Foible; Mirabell's gone to give security for him. This is all Marwood's and my husband's doing.

FOIBLE: Yes, yes, I know it, madam; she was in my 75 lady's closet, and overheard all that you said to me before dinner. She sent the letter to my lady; and that missing effect, Mr. Fainall laid this plot to arrest Waitwell, when he pretended to go for the papers; and in the meantime Mrs. Marwood declared 80 all to my lady.

MRS. FAINALL: Was there no mention made of me in the letter? My mother does not suspect my being in the confederacy? I fancy Marwood has not told her, though she has told my husband. 85

FOIBLE: Yes, madam; but my lady did not see that part. We stifled the letter before she read so far. Has that mischievous devil told Mr. Fainall of your ladyship then?

MRS. FAINALL: Aye, all's out, my affair with Mirabell, 90 everything discovered. This is the last day of our living together; that's my comfort.

FOIBLE: Indeed, madam, and so 'tis a comfort if you knew all. He has been even with your ladyship; which I could have told you long enough since, but 95 I love to keep peace and quietness by my good will. I had rather bring friends together than set 'em at distance. But Mrs. Marwood and he are nearer related than ever their parents thought for.

MRS. FAINALL: Sayest thou so, Foible? Canst thou 100 prove this?

FOIBLE: I can take my oath of it, madam; so can Mrs. Mincing. We have had many a fair word from Madam Marwood, to conceal something that passed in our chamber one evening when you were 105 at Hyde Park and we were thought to have gone awalking; but we went up unawares, though we were sworn to secrecy too. Madam Marwood took a book and swore us upon it, but it was but a book of poems. So long as it was not a Bible oath, 110 we may break it with a safe conscience.

MRS. FAINALL: This discovery is the most opportune thing I could wish. Now, Mincing?

(*Enter Mincing.*)

MINCING: My lady° would speak with Mrs. Foible, mem. Mr. Mirabell is with her; he has set your 115 spouse at liberty, Mrs. Foible, and would have you hide yourself in my lady's closet till my old lady's

---

114. **My lady:** I.e., Millamant.

anger is abated. Oh, my old lady is in a perilous
passion at something Mr. Fainall has said, he
120 swears, and my old lady cries. There's a fearful
hurricane, I vow. He says, mem, how that he'll
have my lady's fortune made over to him, or he'll
be divorced.

MRS. FAINALL: Does your lady or Mirabell know that?

125 MINCING: Yes, mem, they have sent me to see if Sir
Wilfull be sober and to bring him to them. My
lady is resolved to have him, I think, rather than
lose such a vast sum as six thousand pound. Oh,
come, Mrs. Foible, I hear my old lady.

130 MRS. FAINALL: Foible, you must tell Mincing that she
must prepare to vouch° when I call her.

FOIBLE: Yes, yes, madam.

MINCING: O yes, mem, I'll vouch anything for your
ladyship's service, be what it will.

(*Exeunt Mincing and Foible.*)

(*Reenter Lady Wishfort, with, Mrs. Marwood.*)

135 LADY WISHFORT: O my dear friend, how can I enumerate the benefits that I have received from your
goodness? To you I owe the timely discovery of the
false vows of Mirabell, to you I owe the detection
of the impostor, Sir Rowland. And now you are
140 become an intercessor with my son-in-law, to save
the honor of my house, and compound for the
frailties of my daughter. Well, friend, you are
enough to reconcile me to the bad world, or else I
would retire to deserts and solitudes, and feed
145 harmless sheep by groves and purling streams.
Dear Marwood, let us leave the world, and retire
by ourselves and be shepherdesses.

MRS. MARWOOD: Let us first dispatch the affair in
hand, madam. We shall have leisure to think of re-
150 tirement afterwards. Here is one who is concerned
in the treaty.

LADY WISHFORT: O daughter, daughter, is it possible
thou shouldst be my child, bone of my bone, and
flesh of my flesh, and, as I may say, another me,
155 and yet transgress the most minute particle of severe virtue? Is it possible you should lean aside to
iniquity, who have been cast in the direct mold of
virtue? I have not only been a mold but a pattern
for you, and a model for you, after you were
160 brought into the world.

MRS. FAINALL: I don't understand your ladyship.

LADY WISHFORT: Not understand? Why, have you not
been naught?° Have you not been sophisticated?°
Not understand? Here I am ruined to compound°

for your caprices and your cuckoldoms. I must   165
pawn my plate and my jewels, and ruin my niece,
and all little enough.

MRS. FAINALL: I am wronged and abused, and so are
you. 'Tis a false accusation, as false as hell, as false
as your friend there, aye, or your friend's friend,   170
my false husband.

MRS. MARWOOD: My friend, Mrs. Fainall? Your husband my friend? What do you mean?

MRS. FAINALL: I know what I mean, madam, and so
do you; and so shall the world at a time convenient.   175

MRS. MARWOOD: I am sorry to see you so passionate,
madam. More temper° would look more like innocence. But I have done. I am sorry my zeal to serve
your ladyship and family should admit of miscon-
struction, or make me liable to affronts. You will   180
pardon me, madam, if I meddle no more with an
affair in which I am not personally concerned.

LADY WISHFORT: O dear friend, I am so ashamed that
you should meet with such returns! (*To Mrs.
Fainall.*) You ought to ask pardon on your knees,   185
ungrateful creature; she deserves more from you
than all your life can accomplish. (*To Mrs. Marwood.*) Oh, don't leave me destitute in this per-
plexity! No, stick to me, my good genius.

MRS. FAINALL: I tell you, madam, you're abused. Stick   190
to you? Aye, like a leech, to suck your best blood;
she'll drop off when she's full. Madam, you shan't
pawn a bodkin,° nor part with a brass counter,° in
composition for me. I defy 'em all. Let 'em prove
their aspersions; I know my own innocence, and   195
dare stand a trial.   (*Exit.*)

LADY WISHFORT: Why, if she should be innocent, if she
should be wronged after all, ha? I don't know what
to think; and, I promise you, her education has
been unexceptionable.° I may say it; for I chiefly   200
made it my own care to initiate her very infancy in
the rudiments of virtue, and to impress upon her
tender years a young odium° and aversion to the
very sight of men. Aye, friend, she would ha'
shrieked if she had but seen a man, till she was in   205
her teens. As I'm a person 'tis true. She was never
suffered to play with a male child, though but in
coats; nay, her very babies° were of the feminine
gender. Oh, she never looked a man in the face but
her own father, or the chaplain, and him we made a   210
shift° to put upon her for a woman, by the help of
his long garments and his sleek face, till she was going in her fifteen.°

---

131. vouch: Testify.   163. naught: Naughty, wicked.   sophisticated: Corrupted, debauched.   164. compound:
Compensate. Lady Wishfort refers to Mr. Fainall's blackmail-
ing tactics.

177. temper: Temperateness.   193. bodkin: Needle or hairpin.   brass counter: A farthing (a quarter of a penny).
200. unexceptionable: Exemplary.   203. odium: Dislike.
208. babies: Dolls.   211. made a shift: Devised a plan.
213. in her fifteen: Into her fifteenth year.

MRS. MARWOOD: 'Twas much she should be deceived
so long.

LADY WISHFORT: I warrant you, or she would never
have borne to have been catechized by him; and
have heard his long lectures against singing and
dancing, and such debaucheries, and going to filthy
plays and profane music meetings, where the lewd
trebles squeak nothing but bawdy, and the basses
roar blasphemy. Oh, she would have swooned at
the sight or name of an obscene playbook! And
can I think, after all this, that my daughter can be
naught? What, a whore? and thought it excommunication to set her foot within the door of a
playhouse! O dear friend, I can't believe it, no, no!
As she says, let him prove it, let him prove it.

MRS. MARWOOD: Prove it, madam? What, and have
your name prostituted in a public court? yours and
your daughter's reputation worried at the bar by a
pack of bawling lawyers? To be ushered in with an
Oyez° of scandal, and have your case opened by
an old fumbling lecher in a quoif° like a man-
midwife; to bring your daughter's infamy to light;
to be a theme for legal punsters and quibblers by
the statute, and become a jest against a rule of
court, where there is no precedent for a jest in
any record, not even in Doomsday Book;° to discompose the gravity of the bench, and provoke
naughty interrogatories in more naughty law
Latin, while the good judge, tickled with the proceeding, simpers under a gray beard, and fidges°
off and on his cushion as if he had swallowed
cantharides,° or sat upon cow-itch!°

LADY WISHFORT: Oh, 'tis very hard!

MRS. MARWOOD: And then to have my young revelers of the Temple° take notes, like prentices at a
conventicle;° and after, talk it over again in
Commons,° or before drawers in an eating-house.

LADY WISHFORT: Worse and worse!

MRS. MARWOOD: Nay, this is nothing; if it would end
here, 'twere well. But it must, after this, be con-
signed by the shorthand writers to the public press;
and from thence be transferred to the hands, nay
into the throats and lungs of hawkers,° with voices
more licentious than the loud flounder-man's.°
And this you must hear till you are stunned; nay,
you must hear nothing else for some days.

LADY WISHFORT: Oh, 'tis insupportable! No, no,
dear friend; make it up, make it up; aye, aye, I'll
compound. I'll give up all, myself and my all, my
niece and her all, anything, everything for composition.

MRS. MARWOOD: Nay, madam, I advise nothing; I
only lay before you, as a friend, the inconvenien-
cies which perhaps you have overseen. Here comes
Mr. Fainall; if he will be satisfied to huddle up all
in silence, I shall be glad. You must think I would
rather congratulate than condole with you.

(Enter Fainall.)

LADY WISHFORT: Aye, aye, I do not doubt it, dear
Marwood; no, no, I do not doubt it.

FAINALL: Well, madam, I have suffered myself to be
overcome by the importunity of this lady, your
friend, and am content you shall enjoy your own
proper estate during life, on condition you oblige
yourself never to marry, under such penalty as I
think convenient.

LADY WISHFORT: Never to marry?

FAINALL: No more Sir Rowlands; the next imposture
may not be so timely detected.

MRS. MARWOOD: That condition, I dare answer, my
lady will consent to, without difficulty; she has already but too much experienced the perfidiousness
of men. Besides, madam, when we retire to our
pastoral solitude, we shall bid adieu to all other
thoughts.

LADY WISHFORT: Aye, that's true; but in case of necessity, as of health, or some such emergency —

FAINALL: Oh, if you are prescribed marriage, you shall
be considered; I will only reserve to myself the
power to choose for you. If your physic be wholesome, it matters not who is your apothecary. Next,
my wife shall settle on me the remainder of her
fortune, not made over already; and for her maintenance depend entirely on my discretion.

LADY WISHFORT: This is most inhumanly savage, exceeding the barbarity of a Muscovite° husband.

FAINALL: I learned it from his Czarish majesty's retinue,° in a winter evening's conference over brandy
and pepper, amongst other secrets of matrimony
and policy, as they are at present practiced in the
northern hemisphere. But this must be agreed

---

233. *Oyez:* The court crier's call for silence.   234. quoif:
Coif, the lawyer's white cap.   239. **Doomsday Book:** A
record of a survey of the lands of England made by order of
William the Conqueror.   243. **fidges:** Fidgets.   244. cantharides:** A powder made from dried beetles and used medic-
inally as a skin irritant.   245. **cow-itch:** Cowage, a plant
that causes intense itching.   248. **Temple:** The courts of
law.   248–49. **prentices at a conventicle:** It was customary
for a Puritan master to require his apprentice to take notes on
the Sunday sermon in the meetinghouse (conventicle).
249. **Commons:** The dining hall.   256. **hawkers:** Peddlers.

257. **flounder-man:** An actual flounder seller, well known to
the Londoners of the day and noted for his "loud, but not un-
musical" voice.   298. **Muscovite:** Russian.   299–300.
Czarish majesty's retinue: Referring to Peter the Great's visit
to England in 1697.

305   unto, and that positively. Lastly, I will be endowed, in right of my wife, with that six thousand pound, which is the moiety of Mrs. Millamant's fortune in your possession; and which she has forfeited (as will appear by the last will and testament of your deceased husband, Sir Jonathan Wishfort) by her

310   disobedience in contracting herself against your consent or knowledge, and by refusing the offered match with Sir Wilfull Witwoud, which you, like a careful aunt, had provided for her.

LADY WISHFORT: My nephew was *non compos*,° and

315   could not make his addresses.

FAINALL: I come to make demands. I'll hear no objections.

LADY WISHFORT: You will grant me time to consider?

FAINALL: Yes, while the instrument° is drawing, to

320   which you must set your hand till more sufficient deeds can be perfected; which I will take care shall be done with all possible speed. In the meanwhile I will go for the said instrument, and till my return you may balance this matter in your own

325   discretion.   (*Exit.*)

LADY WISHFORT: This insolence is beyond all precedent, all parallel; must I be subject to this merciless villain?

MRS. MARWOOD: 'Tis severe indeed, madam, that you

330   should smart for your daughter's wantonness.

LADY WISHFORT: 'Twas against my consent that she married this barbarian, but she would have him, though her year° was not out. Ah! her first husband, my son Languish, would not have carried it

335   thus. Well, that was my choice, this is hers; she is matched now with a witness.° I shall be mad! Dear friend, is there no comfort for me? Must I live to be confiscated at this rebel-rate?° Here come two more of my Egyptian plagues° too.

(*Enter Mrs. Millamant and Sir Wilfull Witwoud.*)

340   SIR WILFULL: Aunt, your servant.

LADY WISHFORT: Out, caterpillar, call not me aunt! I know thee not!

SIR WILFULL: I confess I have been a little in disguise,° as they say. 'Sheart! and I'm sorry for't. What

345   would you have? I hope I committed no offense, aunt, and if I did, I am willing to make satisfaction; and what can a man say fairer? If I have broke any-

thing, I'll pay for't, an it cost a pound. And so let that content for what's past, and make no more words. For what's to come, to pleasure you I'm   350   willing to marry my cousin. So pray let's all be friends; she and I are agreed upon the matter before a witness.

LADY WISHFORT: How's this, dear niece? Have I any comfort? Can this be true?   355

MRS. MILLAMANT: I am content to be a sacrifice to your repose, madam; and to convince you that I had no hand in the plot, as you were misinformed, I have laid my commands on Mirabell to come in person, and be a witness that I give my hand to   360   this flower of knighthood; and for the contract that passed between Mirabell and me, I have obliged him to make a resignation of it in your ladyship's presence. He is without, and waits your leave for admittance.   365

LADY WISHFORT: Well, I'll swear I am something revived at this testimony of your obedience; but I cannot admit that traitor. I fear I cannot fortify myself to support his appearance. He is as terrible to me as a Gorgon;° if I see him, I fear I shall turn   370   to stone, petrify incessantly.

MRS. MILLAMANT: If you disoblige him, he may resent your refusal, and insist upon the contract still. Then 'tis the last time he will be offensive to you.

LADY WISHFORT: Are you sure it will be the last time?   375   If I were sure of that! Shall I never see him again?

MRS. MILLAMANT: Sir Wilfull, you and he are to travel together, are you not?

SIR WILFULL: 'Sheart, the gentleman's a civil gentleman, aunt; let him come in. Why, we are sworn   380   brothers and fellow travelers. We are to be Pylades and Orestes,° he and I. He is to be my interpreter in foreign parts. He has been overseas once already; and with *proviso* that I marry my cousin, will cross 'em once again, only to bear me company. 'Sheart, I'll call him in. An I set on't once, he   385   shall come in; and see who'll hinder him.

(*Goes to the door and hems.*)

MRS. MARWOOD: This is precious fooling, if it would pass; but I'll know the bottom of it.

LADY WISHFORT: O dear Marwood, you are not going?   390

MRS. MARWOOD: Not far, madam; I'll return immediately.   (*Exit.*)

---

314. *non compos*: I.e., *non compos mentis,* not in his right mind.   **319. instrument** Formal agreement.   **333. her year**: Period of mourning for her first husband.   **336. with a witness**: Colloquialism meaning "with a vengeance." **337–38. must I live . . . rebel-rate**: The sense is "Must I live to see my property and fortune confiscated in this piratical fashion?"   **339. Egyptian plagues**: Referring to the plagues of Egypt recorded in Exodus 7ff.   **343. disguise:** Drunk.

370. Gorgon: Any one of the three sisters in Greek legend (Medusa was one) whose hair was wreathed with snakes and whose glance turned the beholder to stone.   **381–82. Pylades and Orestes:** In Greek legend Pylades was the loyal and trusted friend of Orestes, son of Agamemnon and brother of Elektra.

(*Reenter Sir Wilfull with Mirabell.*)

SIR WILFULL: Look up, man, I'll stand by you; 'sbud
and she do frown, she can't kill you, besides, harkee, she dare not frown desperately, because her
face is none of her own. 'Sheart, an she should, her
forehead would wrinkle like the coat of a cream
cheese; but mum for that, fellow traveler.

MIRABELL: If a deep sense of the many injuries I have
offered to so good a lady, with a sincere remorse
and a hearty contrition, can but obtain the least
glance of compassion, I am too happy. Ah,
madam, there was a time! But let it be forgotten. I
confess I have deservedly forfeited the high place I
once held, of sighing at your feet. Nay, kill me not,
by turning from me in disdain. I come not to plead
for favor; nay, not for pardon. I am a suppliant
only for pity. I am going where I shall never behold
you more.

SIR WILFULL: How, fellow traveler! You shall go by
yourself then.

MIRABELL: Let me be pitied first, and afterwards forgotten. I ask no more.

SIR WILFULL: By'r lady, a very reasonable request, and
will cost you nothing, aunt. Come, come, forgive
and forget, aunt; why, you must, an you are a
Christian.

MIRABELL: Consider, madam, in reality you could not
receive much prejudice; it was an innocent device,
though I confess it had a face of guiltiness. It was
at most an artifice which love contrived, and errors
which love produces have ever been accounted ve-
nial. At least think it is punishment enough that I
have lost what in my heart I hold most dear, that
to your cruel indignation I have offered up this
beauty, and with her my peace and quiet; nay, all
my hopes of future comfort.

SIR WILFULL: An he does not move me, would I may
never be o' the quorum!° An it were not as good a
deed as to drink, to give her to him again, I would
I might never take shipping! Aunt, if you don't forgive quickly, I shall melt, I can tell you that. My
contract went no farther than a little mouth-glue,
and that's hardly dry; one doleful sigh more from
my fellow traveler, and 'tis dissolved.

LADY WISHFORT: Well, nephew, upon your account —
ah, he has a false insinuating tongue! Well, sir, I
will stifle my just resentment at my nephew's request. I will endeavor what I can to forget, but on
proviso that you resign the contract with my niece
immediately.

MIRABELL: It is in writing, and with papers of concern;
but I have sent my servant for it, and will deliver it
to you, with all acknowledgments for your transcendent goodness.

LADY WISHFORT (*aside*): Oh, he has witchcraft in his
eyes and tongue! When I did not see him, I could
have bribed a villain to his assassination; but his
appearance rakes the embers which have so long
lain smothered in my breast.

(*Reenter Fainall and Mrs. Marwood.*)

FAINALL: Your date of deliberation, madam, is expired. Here is the instrument; are you prepared to
sign?

LADY WISHFORT: If I were prepared, I am not empowered. My niece exerts a lawful claim, having
matched herself by my direction to Sir Wilfull.

FAINALL: That sham is too gross to pass on me,
though 'tis imposed on you, madam.

MRS. MILLAMANT: Sir, I have given my consent.

MIRABELL: And, sir, I have resigned my pretensions.

SIR WILFULL: And, sir, I assert my right; and will
maintain it in defiance of you, sir, and of your instrument. 'Sheart, an you talk of an instrument, sir,
I have an old fox° by my thigh shall hack your instrument of ram vellum° to shreds, sir! It shall not
be sufficient for a *mittimus*° or a tailor's measure.°
Therefore withdraw your instrument, sir, or, by'r
lady, I shall draw mine.

LADY WISHFORT: Hold, nephew, hold!

MRS. MILLAMANT: Good Sir Wilfull, respite° your
valor.

FAINALL: Indeed? Are you provided of your guard,
with your single beefeater° there? But I'm prepared
for you, and insist upon my first proposal. You
shall submit your own estate to my management
and absolutely make over my wife's to my sole use,
as pursuant to the purpose and tenor of this other
covenant. (*To Mrs. Millamant.*) I suppose, madam,
your consent is not requisite in this case; nor, Mr.
Mirabell, your resignation; nor, Sir Wilfull, your
right. You may draw your fox if you please, sir,
and make a Bear Garden° flourish somewhere else;
for here it will not avail. — This, my Lady Wishfort, must be subscribed, or your darling daughter's turned adrift, like a leaky hulk, to sink or
swim, as she and the current of this lewd town can
agree.

LADY WISHFORT: Is there no means, no remedy to

---

430. **quorum:** An indispensable member of the legal bench.

465. **fox:** Sword.   466. **ram vellum:** Parchment (made from
sheepskin).   467. *mittimus*: Legal term for a warrant of
commitment to prison.   **tailor's measure:** Tailors' measurements were recorded on parchment.   471. **respite:** Control.
474. **beefeater:** A guard of the Tower of London.   483. **Bear
Garden:** Bear baiting was a popular amusement in the London
of the day, and the gardens in which it took place were notorious for brawls and rowdy behavior.

490 stop my ruin? Ungrateful wretch! dost thou not
owe thy being, thy subsistence, to my daughter's
fortune?

FAINALL: I'll answer you when I have the rest of it in
my possession.

495 MIRABELL (*to Lady Wishfort*): But that you would not
accept of a remedy from my hands — I own I have
not deserved you should owe any obligation to me;
or else perhaps I could advise —

LADY WISHFORT: Oh, what? what? to save me and my
500 child from ruin, from want, I'll forgive all that's
past; nay, I'll consent to anything to come, to be
delivered from this tyranny.

MIRABELL: Aye, madam, but that is too late; my reward
is intercepted. You have disposed of her who only
505 could have made me a compensation for all my services. But be it as it may, I am resolved I'll serve you;
you shall not be wronged in this savage manner.

LADY WISHFORT: How! Dear Mr. Mirabell, can you
510 be so generous at last? But it is not possible. Harkee, I'll break my nephew's match; you shall have
my niece yet, and all her fortune, if you can but
save me from this imminent danger.

MIRABELL: Will you? I take you at your word. I ask
515 no more. I must have leave for two criminals to
appear.

LADY WISHFORT: Aye, aye; anybody, anybody!

MIRABELL: Foible is one, and a penitent.

(*Reenter Mrs. Fainall, Foible, and Mincing.*)

MRS. MARWOOD (*to Fainall*): O my shame! (*Mirabell*
520 *and Lady Wishfort go to Mrs. Fainall and Foible.*)
These corrupt things are brought hither to expose me.

FAINALL: If it must all come out, why let 'em know it;
'tis but the way of the world. That shall not urge
me to relinquish or abate one tittle of my terms;
525 no, I will insist the more.

FOIBLE: Yes indeed, madam; I'll take my Bible oath of
it.

MINCING: And so will I, mem.

LADY WISHFORT: O Marwood. Marwood, art thou
530 false? my friend deceive me? Hast thou been a
wicked accomplice with that profligate man?

MRS. MARWOOD: Have you so much ingratitude and
injustice, to give credit against your friend to the
aspersions of two such mercenary trulls?

535 MINCING: "Mercenary," mem? I scorn your words.
'Tis true we found you and Mr. Fainall in the blue
garret; by the same token, you swore us to secrecy
upon Messalina's poems.° "Mercenary?" No, if we

would have been mercenary, we should have held
our tongues; you would have bribed us sufficiently.   540

FAINALL: Go, you are an insignificant thing! Well,
what are you the better for this? Is this Mr.
Mirabell's expedient? I'll be put off no longer. You
thing, that was a wife, shall smart for this! I will
not leave thee wherewithal to hide thy shame; your   545
body shall be naked as your reputation.

MRS. FAINALL: I despise you, and defy your malice!
You have aspersed me wrongfully. I have proved
your falsehood. Go, you and your treacherous — I
will not name it, but starve together, perish!   550

FAINALL: Not while you are worth a groat,° indeed,
my dear. Madam, I'll be fooled no longer.

LADY WISHFORT: Ah, Mr. Mirabell, this is small comfort, the detection of this affair.

MIRABELL: Oh, in good time. Your leave for the other   555
offender and penitent to appear, madam.

(*Enter Waitwell, with a box of writings.*)

LADY WISHFORT: O Sir Rowland! Well, rascal?

WAITWELL: What your ladyship pleases. I have
brought the black box at last, madam.

MIRABELL: Give it me. Madam, you remember your   560
promise.

LADY WISHFORT: Aye, dear sir.

MIRABELL: Where are the gentlemen?

WAITWELL: At hand, sir, rubbing their eyes; just risen
from sleep.   565

FAINALL: 'Sdeath, what's this to me? I'll not wait your
private concerns.

(*Enter Petulant and Witwoud.*)

PETULANT: How now? What's the matter? Whose
hand's out?°

WITWOUD: Heyday! what, are you all got together,   570
like players at the end of the last act?

MIRABELL: You may remember, gentlemen, I once requested your hands as witnesses to a certain parchment.

WITWOUD: Aye, I do; my hand I remember. Petulant   575
set his mark.

MIRABELL: You wrong him, his name is fairly written,
as shall appear. You do not remember, gentlemen,
anything of what that parchment contained?
                              (*Undoing the box.*)

WITWOUD: No.   580

PETULANT: Not I. I writ. I read nothing.

MIRABELL: Very well; now you shall know. Madam,
your promise.

LADY WISHFORT: Aye, aye, sir, upon my honor.

MIRABELL: Mr. Fainall, it is now time that you should   585
know that your lady, while she was at her own dis-

---

538. **Messalina's poems:** Mincing means a volume of "miscellaneous" poems. Her mistake presents an amusing irony,
since Messalina, the wife of the Roman Emperor Claudius,
was notorious for her avarice, treachery, and dissoluteness.

551. **groat:** An old silver coin worth about fourpence.
568–69. **Whose hand's out:** "What is the trouble?"

posal, and before you had by your insinuations wheedled her out of a pretended settlement of the greatest part of her fortune —

590 FAINALL: Sir! pretended!

MIRABELL: Yes, sir. I say that this lady, while a widow, having it seems received some cautions respecting your inconstancy and tyranny of temper, which from her own partial opinion and fondness of you

595 she could never have suspected — she did, I say, by the wholesome advice of friends and of sages learned in the laws of this land, deliver this same as her act and deed to me in trust, and to the uses within mentioned. You may read if you please

600 (*holding out the parchment*), though perhaps what is written on the back may serve your occasions.

FAINALL: Very likely, sir. What's here? Damnation! (*Reads.*) "A deed of conveyance of the whole estate real of Arabella Languish, widow, in trust to

605 Edward Mirabell." Confusion!

MIRABELL: Even so, sir; 'tis the way of the world, sir, of the widows of the world. I suppose this deed may bear an elder° date than what you have obtained from your lady?

610 FAINALL: Perfidious fiend! Then thus I'll be revenged.
(*Offers to run at Mrs. Fainall.*)

SIR WILFULL: Hold, sir! Now you may make your Bear Garden flourish somewhere else, sir.

FAINALL: Mirabell, you shall hear of this, sir; be sure you shall. (*To Sir Wilfull.*) Let me pass, oaf!
(*Exit.*)

615 MRS. FAINALL (*to Mrs. Marwood*): Madam, you seem to stifle your resentment; you had better give it vent.

MRS. MARWOOD: Yes, it shall have vent, and to your confusion; or I'll perish in the attempt.   (*Exit.*)

620 LADY WISHFORT: O daughter, daughter, 'tis plain thou hast inherited thy mother's prudence.

MRS. FAINALL: Thank Mr. Mirabell, a cautious friend, to whose advice all is owing.

LADY WISHFORT: Well, Mr. Mirabell, you have kept

625 your promise, and I must perform mine. First, I pardon, for your sake, Sir Rowland there, and Foible. The next thing is to break the matter to my nephew, and how to do that —

MIRABELL: For that, madam, give yourself no trouble;

630 let me have your consent. Sir Wilfull is my friend; he has had compassion upon lovers, and generously engaged a volunteer° in this action, for our service, and now designs to prosecute his travels.

SIR WILFULL: 'Sheart, aunt, I have no mind to marry.

635 My cousin's a fine lady, and the gentleman loves her, and she loves him, and they deserve one another; my resolution is to see foreign parts. I have set on't, and when I'm set on't, I must do't. And if

these two gentlemen would travel too, I think they may be spared.   640

PETULANT: For my part, I say little; I think things are best off or on.°

WITWOUD: Egad, I understand nothing of the matter; I'm in a maze yet, like a dog in a dancing school.

LADY WISHFORT: Well, sir, take her, and with her all 645
the joy I can give you.

MRS. MILLAMANT: Why does not the man take me? Would you have me give myself to you over again?

MIRABELL: Aye, and over and over again; (*kisses her hand*) for I would have you as often as possibly I 650
can. Well, Heaven grant I love you not too well; that's all my fear.

SIR WILFULL: 'Sheart, you'll have time enough to toy° after you're married; or if you will toy now, let us have a dance in the meantime, that we who are not 655
lovers may have some other employment besides looking on.

MIRABELL: With all my heart, dear Sir Wilfull. What shall we do for music?

FOIBLE: Oh, sir, some that were provided for Sir Row- 660
land's entertainment are yet within call.

(*A dance.*)

LADY WISHFORT: As I am a person, I can hold out no longer. I have wasted my spirits so today already that I am ready to sink under the fatigue; and I cannot but have some fears upon me yet that my 665
son Fainall will pursue some desperate course.

MIRABELL: Madam, disquiet not yourself on that account; to my knowledge his circumstances are such, he must of force° comply. For my part, I will contribute all that in me lies to a reunion; in the 670
meantime, madam (*to Mrs. Fainall*), let me before these witnesses restore to you this deed of trust; it may be a means, well-managed, to make you live easily together.

From hence let those be warn'd, who mean to 675
    wed,
Lest mutual falsehood stain the bridal bed;
For each deceiver to his cost may find
That marriage frauds too oft are paid in kind.
(*Exeunt omnes.*)°

EPILOGUE

(*Spoken by Mrs. Millamant.*)

After our Epilogue this crowd dismisses,
I'm thinking how this play'll be pull'd to pieces.
But pray consider, ere you doom its fall,

---

608. **elder**: Earlier.   632. **a volunteer**: As a volunteer.

641. **off or on**: One way or the other.   653. **toy**: Play.
669. **of force**: Of necessity.   679. [S.D.] *omnes*: Latin for "all."

How hard a thing 'twould be to please you all.
5   There are some critics so with spleen diseas'd,
They scarcely come inclining to be pleas'd;
And sure he must have more than mortal skill,
Who pleases any one against his will.
Then, all bad poets we are sure are foes,
And how their number's swell'd the town well
10   knows;
In shoals I've mark'd 'em judging in the pit;
Though they're on no pretense for judgment fit,
But that they have been damn'd for want of wit.
Since when they, by their own offenses taught,
15 Set up for spies on plays, and finding fault.
Others there are whose malice we'd prevent;
Such who watch plays with scurrilous intent
To mark out who by characters are meant.
And though no perfect likeness they can trace,
20 Yet each pretends to know the copy'd face.
These with false glosses° feed their own ill nature,

21. glosses: Marginal notes.

And turn to libel what was meant a satire.°
May such malicious fops this fortune find,
To think themselves alone the fools design'd;
If any are so arrogantly vain,   25
To think they singly can support a scene,
And furnish fool enough to entertain.
For well the learn'd and the judicious know
That satire scorns to stoop so meanly low
As any one abstracted° fop to show.   30
For, as when painters form a matchless face
They from each fair one catch some diff'rent grace;
And shining features in one portrait blend,
To which no single beauty must pretend;
So poets oft do in one piece expose   35
Whole *belles assemblées*° of coquettes and beaux.

21–22. nature . . . satire: According to seventeenth-century pronunciation, "nature" and "satire" were good rhymes. **30. abstracted:** Particular. **36. *belles assemblées*:** Fine gatherings.

COMMENTARY

Howard Taubman (1907–1996)
REVIEW OF *THE WAY OF THE WORLD*   1965

Howard Taubman reviewed one of the notable modern productions of The Way of the World, starring Zoe Caldwell, a British actress who went on to win numerous awards. The question of accents, which Taubman discusses, is important for any audience, since the lines are often rapid-fire and the wit razor-sharp. Caldwell's authenticity and style charmed Taubman, who was pleased enough with the production to forgive its minor flaws.

There are many good reasons to justify going out of one's way for the Minnesota Theater Company's *The Way of the World,* and hardly the least of them is Congreve himself. But an excellent one is to enjoy the impeccable high-comedy playing of Zoe Caldwell as Millamant.

Jessica Tandy brings a raffish gusto to Lady Wishfort, Nancy Wickwire is a cool, suave intriguer as Marwood, Robert Pastene is all showy manners and hard bargainer as Fainall, Robert Milli conveys the shrewd charm of Mirabell. But it is Miss Caldwell who is unfaltering in every velvet thrust.

Not an inflection or a gesture is out of place in this handsomely composed portrait of a wise and witty young woman of the London world of 1700. In Tanya Moiseiwitch's modish clothes, with their headdresses and trains, Miss Caldwell moves with the poised self-knowledge of one who has stepped out of a Restoration drawing room.

Her face with its pale make-up, obviously the careful concern of a young woman of breeding who will not look vulgarly outdoorsy, rarely betrays an emotion. The eyes are detached but brighten occasionally with mischief. The voice is silken, but what humor there is in the phrasing — not catchpenny humor but the sense of fun that sparkles in a civilized mind.

When Miss Caldwell talks of being persecuted by letters, there is amusement in the weariness of her tone. When she reads the poems of Sir John Suckling to confuse addle-brained Sir Wilfull, it is as if only she and we were privy to the dry jesting.

When she sets forth the conditions on which she will agree to marry Mirabell, she does so with a mingling of seriousness and laughter that suits perfectly Congreve's milieu and style. And Mr. Milli's response in kind gives the necessary fillip to a scene that has not lost its edge in 265 years.

Douglas Campbell has directed *The Way of the World* with a relish of its manners and mannerisms. Miss Moiseiwitch's designs with their suggestion of colorful elegancies turn the open stage of the Tyrone Guthrie Theater into a garden or boudoir with equal felicity.

The over-all tone of the production, with its occasional background of Purcell music and with its ingratiating concluding dance, is admirable. But the Minnesota Theater Company would be deluding itself if it thought that it had met all the challenges implicit in a Congreve revival.

The balance of the performance is not always right. One or two players handle the Restoration extravagances self-consciously, making their points too obviously. Several others lack the flexibility of movement and diction needed for this kind of work.

And what is to be done about the mélange of accents with which Congreve's glittering English is spoken?

Consider Miss Tandy, Miss Wickwire and Miss Caldwell, all of whom know their business and speak well. Miss Wickwire's speech has the flatness of the American timbre. Miss Tandy's seems now to be an accommodation between her native English and the American approach. Miss Caldwell's enunciation and rhythm have the ring of authenticity. As for some of the company's younger members, they are struggling in deep, unfamiliar waters.

But if we are going to wait for perfection, we will never attempt revivals of the classics. It is better to do a Congreve with forces not equal in all parts than not to do him at all, provided, of course, you have such delightful exemplars as Miss Caldwell to show the irresistible way.

Nineteenth-Century Drama Through the Turn of the Century

Technical Innovations

Technically, theaters changed more during the period between 1800 and 1900 than in any comparable earlier period. The introduction of gas jets early in the century had a major effect. Now, light could be dimmed or raised as needed; the house could be gradually and entirely darkened. With gaslight onstage, selective lighting contributed to the emotional effect of plays and allowed actors to move deeper into the stage instead of playing important scenes on the apron. With the advent of elaborate scenery, as in the Drottningholm Theater in Sweden, lighting devices were often placed behind the proscenium pillars and scenery so that actors were more visible when they stood within the proscenium. The changes did not take place overnight, but as new theaters were built in the early nineteenth century (and as older theaters were refurbished) the apron shrank and the front doors leading to it disappeared. That change reinforced the nineteenth-century practice of treating the proscenium opening as the imaginary "fourth wall" of a room.

Numerous other technical innovations were introduced into the new theaters, such as London's Drury Lane Theatre, which was rebuilt in 1812. Highly sophisticated machinery lifted actors from below the stage, and flies or fly galleries above the stage permitted scene changes and other dramatic alterations and effects. The technical resources of the modern theaters in Europe were extraordinary by midcentury.

Romantic Drama

The architectural and lighting changes were complex and uneven, but they accompanied changes in styles of acting, styles of plays, and the content of plays. Early nineteenth-century English Romantic poets produced a variety of plays espousing a new philosophy of the individual, a philosophy of democracy, and a cry for personal liberation, but unfortunately their plays failed to capture the popular stage. William Wordsworth's *The Borderers* (1796–1797), concerning political struggles on the border between England and Scotland, was a failure. A recent production (1989) at Yale University revealed its static, declamatory nature. Even a play with an inherently dramatic subject such as *The Fall of Robespierre* (1794) by Robert Southey and Samuel Taylor Coleridge — concerning the violent excesses of the French Revolution of 1789 — could not stir popular audiences. John Keats wrote *Otho the Great* (1819) about a tenth-century dispute between brothers and a father and son. He hoped that the great actor and producer Edmund Kean would want to produce the play, but Kean declined. Percy Bysshe Shelley wrote *The Cenci* (1819) when he was in Italy, hoping it would be produced on the English stage, but it was banned by the censors. The style of Shelley's play has been compared with John Webster's *The Dutchess of Malfi* (1613); its themes include violent death and insanity. George Gordon, Lord Byron, wrote several plays that had admirers but were not successful. *Manfred* (1817) is a CLOSET DRAMA — a play meant to be read, not produced. It presents a powerful portrait of a brooding intellect that could, in some ways, be compared with Hamlet. Allardyce Nicoll, the British drama historian and critic, has said of this and other Romantic plays that "audiences and readers familiar with *Lear* and *Macbeth* and *Othello* could not be expected to feel a thrill of wonder and delight in the contemplation of works so closely akin to these in general aim and yet so far removed from them in freshness of imaginative power."

French and German Romantic dramatists were more successful than their English counterparts. Johann Wolfgang von Goethe (1749–1832), one of Germany's most important playwrights, produced a number of successful plays in the late eighteenth century. Then came his masterpiece, *Faust* (1808, 1832), in two parts, with a scope and grandeur of concept that challenged the theaters of his day. The play opens in heaven, with Mephistopheles presenting his plan for tempting Faust; Faust signs over his soul to Mephistopheles in return for one moment of perfect joy. Faust was willing to risk all in his efforts to live life to its fullest, and despite his sins he was admired as a hero. Faust's self-analytic individualism, marked by a love of excess and a capacity for deep feeling and frightening intensity, has fascinated the German mind ever since Goethe rediscovered him. His development of Faust as a psychologically complex character contrasts with Marlowe's version in *Doctor Faustus*.

Another important force in German theater was Johann Cristoph Friedrich von Schiller (1759–1805), whose early play *The Robbers* (1781) was written when he was twenty-two. This still-popular (and still-produced) play reminds English audiences of the legend of Robin Hood since its hero, Karl von Moor, is a robber admirable for his generosity and seriousness. His adversary is his evil brother, who dominates the castle, the emblem of local repressive political power. Schiller was a highly successful playwright throughout the late eighteenth century. In the early nineteenth century he produced several popular historical plays such as *Maria Stuart* (1800) on Scotland's Queen Mary, the ill-fated cousin of Queen Elizabeth I. *The Maid of Orleans* (1801) told the story of Joan of Arc, the French heroine who led her army to victory only to be burned at the stake to satisfy political and religious exigencies. Both plays evoke deep sympathy for their heroines and both have been noted for their sentimentality. His last play, *William Tell* (1804), like *The Robbers,* tells the story of a heroic individual's fight against the oppressive forces of an evil baron. Schiller made the story of William Tell universal, and his theatrical successes were soon known throughout Europe and the Americas.

In France, the romantic tragedy held sway for some time in the 1830s. Victor Hugo (1802–1885) had a great success in *Hernani* (1830), although critics and writers who insisted on classical rules were so disturbed by its innovation that they made disturbances in the theater. They attended only to jeer the pardon of Hernani, an outlaw, by Don Carlos, king of Spain. At the end Hernani and Donna Sol, his loved one, drink a poison so as to die together because they could not live together. Alexandre Dumas (1802–1879), soon to be famous as a novelist, produced a number of successful, influential plays, among them *Henry III and His Court* (1829) and *The Tower of Nesle* (1832).

Melodrama

MELODRAMA developed in Germany and France in the mid- and late eighteenth century. The *melo* in *melodrama* means "song"; incidental music was a hallmark of melodrama. In England certain regulations separated Covent Garden, Drury Lane, and the Haymarket — the three "major" theaters with exclusive licences to produce spoken drama — from the "minor" theaters, which had to produce musical plays such as burlettas, which resembled our comic operettas. Eventually, the minor theaters began to produce plays with spoken dialogue and accompanying music, heralding a new, popular style. Melodrama proved to be one of the most durable innovations of the late eighteenth century.

In Germany, August Friedrich Ferdinand von Kotzebue (1761–1819) and in France Guilbert de Pixérécourt (1773–1844), who coined the term *melodrama,* began developing the melodramatic play. Many of these dramas used background music that altered according to the mood of the scene, a tradition that continues in films and on television. Nineteenth-century melodramas featured familiar crises: the virtuous maiden fallen into the hands of an unscrupulous landlord; the father who, lamenting over a portrait of his dead wife, discovers that he is speaking to his — until then — lost daughter. Nineteenth-century melodramas had well-defined heroes, heroines, and villains. The plots were filled with surprises and unlikely twists designed to amaze and delight the audience. Most of the plays were explicitly sentimental, depending on a strong emotional appeal with clear-cut and relatively decisive endings.

Though not popular later on, the plays of Kotzebue and Pixérécourt pleased their contemporary audiences and helped establish melodrama as a dominant style for the first six decades of the nineteenth century. Kotzebue published thirty-six plays (twenty-two were produced) and enjoyed an immense popularity in England and the United States. Translated into several languages, his works influenced later popular playwrights, who admired his ability to invent and resolve complex plot situations. An example of the ending of *La-Peyrouse* (1798) may provide a taste of the mode. The hero, cast ashore on a desert island, falls in love with the "savage" Malvina. When he rejoins his wife, Adelaide, he is presented with the problem of what to do with Malvina. Here is the women's solution:

> MALVINA (*turning affectionately, yet with trembling to Adelaide*): I have prayed for thee, and for myself — let us be sisters!
> ADELAIDE: Sisters! (*She remains some moments lost in thought.*) Sisters! Sweet girl, you have awakened a consoling idea in my bosom! Yes, we will be sisters, and this man shall be our brother! Share him we cannot, nor can either possess him singly. (*With enthusiasm.*) We, the sisters, will inhabit one hut, he shall dwell in another. We will educate our children, he shall assist us both — by day we will make but one family, at night we will separate — how say you? will you consent? . . . (*Extending her arms to La-Peyrouse.*) A sisterly embrace!

In France Pixérécourt produced a similar and highly successful drama that pleased his audiences. Not everyone was pleased, however. Goethe resigned his office from the Weimar Court Theatre when Pixérécourt's *The Dog of Montargis* was produced in 1816 because he did not want to be associated with any play that had a dog as its hero.

Not all these plays have been forgotten. Alexandre Dumas's *La Dame aux camélias* (Camille) was a theatrical hit in 1852 and has remained popular ever since, inspiring the Verdi opera *La Traviata* (1853) and revivals and adaptations up to the present, including the British playwright Pam Gems's recent feminist version (1987), starring Kathleen Turner. Based on a woman Dumas knew in Paris, it is the story of a wealthy young man who falls in love with a courtesan, Marguerite Gauthier. Like Angellica in *The Rover,* she has manipulated men throughout her life, but now she is truly in love with Armand. The young man's father opposes the match, but even he is moved by the majesty of their love. Eventually, the father faces Marguerite and convinces her that if she really loves his son, she will let him go since their union can bring nothing but harm to Armand. She then fabricates a contempt for Armand and dismisses him, broken-hearted. Later, after they have been separated and she has fallen deathly ill, Armand learns the truth and rushes to her. On her deathbed Armand professes his love as she dies in his arms.

In the United States, George Aiken produced another long-lasting and influential drama, *Uncle Tom's Cabin* (1852), based on Harriet Beecher Stowe's novel. Stowe, a prominent northern abolitionist, poured all her anger at slavery into her novel. Aiken's stage version played for three hundred nights in its first production and across the nation more than a quarter of a million times. Some of its characters — Uncle Tom, Little Eva, Sambo, Topsy, and Simon Legree — live on in the popular imagination, but despite the contemporary interest in Stowe and in this play, the paternalistic subtitle, "Life Among the Lowly," marks its era.

The Well-Made Play

Early in the nineteenth century, a Frenchman with an unusual theatrical gift for pleasing popular audiences began a career that spanned fifty successful years. Eugène Scribe (1791–1861) may have produced as many as four or five hundred plays. He employed collaborators and mined novels and stories for his plots, producing tragedies, comedies, opera libretti, and vaudeville one-act pieces. He quickly determined that the plot held the attention of the audience and that rambling character studies were of lesser interest. Consequently, he developed a formula for dramatic action and made sure that all his works fit into it. The result was the creation of a "factory" for making plays. Among the elements of Scribe's formula were the following:

1. A careful exposition telling the audience what the situation is, usually including one or more secrets to be revealed later.
2. Surprises, such as letters to be opened at a critical moment and identities to be revealed later.
3. Suspense that builds steadily throughout the play, usually sustained by cliff-hanging situations and characters who miss each other by way of carefully timed entrances and exits. At critical moments, characters lose important papers or misplace identifying jewelry, for instance.
4. A CLIMAX late in the play when the secrets are revealed and the hero confronts his antagonists and succeeds.
5. A DENOUEMENT, the resolution of the drama when all the loose ends are drawn together and explanations are made that render all the action plausible.

It should be evident from this description that the WELL-MADE PLAY still thrives, not only on the stage but also in films and on television. Scribe's emphasis on plot was sensational for his time, and his success was unrivaled; however, none of his plays has survived in contemporary performance. Only one, *Adrienne Lecouvreur* (1849), the story of a famous actress poisoned by a rival, is mentioned by critics as interesting because of its depth of characterization. Scribe was superficial and brilliant — a winning combination in theater at the time. He had numerous imitators and prepared the way for later developments in theater.

The Rise of Realism

Technical changes in theaters during the latter part of the nineteenth century continued at a rapid pace. When limelight was added to gas, the result was bright, intense lighting onstage; in the last decades of the century electric light heralded a new era in lighting design. Good lighting generally demanded detailed and authentic scenery; the dreamy light produced by gas often hid imperfections that were now impossible to disguise. The new Madison Square Theater (1879) in New York was built with elevators that allowed its stage, complete with detailed and realistic scenery as well as actors, to be raised into position. European theaters had developed similar capacities.

In the 1840s accurate period costumes began to be the norm for historical plays. In the Elizabethan theater, contemporary clothing had been worn onstage, but by the mid-1800s costume designers were researching historical periods and producing costumes that aimed at historical accuracy.

In addition to offering lifelike scenery, lighting, and costumes, the theaters of the latter part of the century also featured plays whose circumstances and language were recognizable, contemporary, and believable. Even the sentimental melodramas seemed more realistic than productions of *King Lear* or *Macbeth,* plays that were still popular. The work of Scribe, including his historical plays, used a relatively prosaic everyday language. The situations may not seem absolutely lifelike to our eyes, but in their day they prepared the way for realism.

Changes in philosophy also contributed to the development of a realistic drama. Émile Zola (1840–1902) preached a doctrine of NATURALISM, demanding that drama avoid the artificiality of convoluted plot and urging a drama of natural, lifelike action. He intended his work to help change social conditions in France. His naturalistic novel *Nana* (1880) focused on a courtesan whose life came to a terrifying end. The play *Thérèse Raquin* (1873), based on Zola's novel of the same name, told the story of a woman and her lover who murder her husband and then commit suicide out of a sense of mutual guilt. There are no twists, surprises, or even much suspense in the play. Zola's subjects seem to have been uniformly grim, and naturalism became associated with the darker side of life.

REALISM, which avoided mechanical "clockwork" plots with their artificially contrived conclusions, began in the later years of the eighteenth century (some scholars claim to see evidence of it even earlier, in the work of Middleton) and progressed steadily to the end of the nineteenth century. In the realistic plays of Henrik Ibsen (1828–1906) and August Strindberg (1849–1912), the details of the setting, the costuming, and the circumstances of the action were so fully realized as to convince au-

Figure 8. Realistic setting in a 1941 production of Anton Chekhov's *The Cherry Orchard*.

diences that they were listening in on life itself. (See Figure 8 for an example of a realistic stage setting.)

In England, Oscar Wilde (1854–1900), poet, novelist, and playwright, offered an alternative to both melodrama and realistic drama near the end of the century. Wilde had spent much of his literary life promoting the philosophy of art for art's sake. He asserted that the pleasure of poetry was in its sounds, images, and thoughts. Poetry and drama did not serve religious, political, social, or even personal goals. For Wilde, art served itself. He was such a brilliant conversationalist that the Irish poet-playwright W. B. Yeats declared him the only person he ever heard who spoke complete, rounded sentences that sounded as if he had written and polished them the night before. His witticisms were often barbed and vicious but always incisive and perceptive. He became famous for his bright, witty comedies. *The Importance of Being Earnest* (1895), sometimes wrongly accused of being about nothing, is the most performed. It is an unsentimental, witty, and sometimes brittle comedy that dissects English upper-class attitudes that most of his audience would have taken for granted.

Wilde competed with numerous comic playwrights in England and abroad, such as the enormously successful Arthur Wing Pinero

(1855–1934) and W. S. Gilbert (1836–1911) in England and Georges Feydeau (1862–1921) in France. None, though, could manage the unusual combination of wit and seriousness that marks Wilde's achievement. Another important competitor was also an Irish playwright, Bernard Shaw (1856–1950), whose plays were also comic and serious, such as *Arms and the Man* (1894), *You Never Can Tell* (1898), and *Pygmalion* (1913). But Shaw is probably best known for his plays of ideas — plays in which an underlying idea or principle drives the action — such as *Mrs. Warren's Profession* (1898), *Man and Superman* (1903), and *Major Barbara* (1905).

After a disappointing beginning as a playwright, Anton Chekhov (1860–1904) worked with the Moscow Arts Theatre under the directorship of Konstantin Stanislavski (1865–1938), one of the most influential figures in modern western drama. Stanislavski emphasized "inner realism" by having the actor become the character even in situations off stage by developing improvisational experiences to let the actor explore the character in situations other than those within the play. The Stanislavski Method helped the actor become the part, rather than just play the part. Chekhov and Stanislavski worked together to produce Chekhov's plays at a time when Chekhov felt himself a failure as a dramatist.

The first production of Chekhov's *The Seagull* (1896), his sixth major staged play, was a failure. Stanislavski convinced Chekhov to give it to his company to produce, resulting in an important triumph. Chekhov then reworked an earlier play into *Uncle Vanya* (1899) for Stanislavski and it, too, was a hit. *Three Sisters* (1901) was not successful in its first performances, but it later became known as one of Chekhov's finest works. His last play, *The Cherry Orchard* (1904), was put on by Stanislavski's company and has become one of the most important works of twentieth-century drama. Chekhov died of a heart attack soon after the play's first production. Today Chekhov's legacy continues, with all his major plays staged throughout the world in the latter half of the twentieth century. Thus one of the most important nineteenth-century writers led the way to new developments in twentieth-century drama that are evident on the stage as well as in films and on television. Modern treatments of Chekhov's plays include Michael Picardie's adaptation of *The Cherry Orchard* to South Africa and Brian Friel's adaptation to Ireland. Mustapha Matura's *Trinidad Sisters* (1988) moves *Three Sisters* to Trinidad, demonstrating in part the universal appeal of Chekhov's plays.

Henrik Ibsen

Using the new style of realism, Henrik Ibsen (1828–1906) slowly and painfully became the most influential modern dramatist. Subjects that had been ignored on the stage became the center of his work. But his rise to fame was anything but direct. His family was extremely poor, and as a youth he worked in a drugstore in Grimstad, a seaport town in Norway. At seventeen he had an illegitimate child with a servant girl. At twenty-one he wrote his first play, in verse. In 1850, at the age of twenty-two, he left Grimstad for Oslo (then called Christiana) to become a student, but within a year he joined the new National Theater and stayed for six years, writing and directing.

In the 1850s he wrote numerous plays that did not bring him recognition: *St. John's Eve* (1853), *Lady Inger of Østraat* (1855), *Olaf Liljekrans* (1857), and *The Vikings at Helgeland* (1857). In the early 1860s, with a wife and daughter to support, he went through a period of serious self-doubt and despair, and his first play in five years, *Love's Comedy* (1862), was turned down for performance. Eventually, he got a job with the Christiana Theater and had a rare success with *The Pretenders* (1864), a historical play about thirteenth-century warriors vying for the vacant throne of Norway.

His breakthrough came with the publication in 1866 of the verse play *Brand*, which was written to be read and not performed. (It was first produced in 1885.) It is the portrait of a clergyman who takes the strictures of religion so seriously that he rejects the New Testament doctrine of love and accepts the Old Testament doctrine of the will of God. He destroys himself in the process and ends the play on a mountaintop in the Ice Church, facing an avalanche about to kill him. Out of the clouds comes the answer to his questions of whether love or will achieves salvation: "He is the God of Love." *Brand* made Ibsen famous. He followed it with another successful closet drama, *Peer Gynt* (1867), about a character, quite unlike Brand, who avoids the rigors of morality and ends up unable to know if he has been saved or condemned.

Despite these successes, Ibsen still struggled for recognition. It was not until 1877 that he had his first success in a play that experimented with the new realistic style of drama: *The Pillars of Society*, which probed behind the hypocrisies of Karsten Bernick, a merchant who prospers by all manner of double-dealing and betrayal of his relatives. Eventually, he admits his crimes but, instead of being punished, is welcomed back into society and is more successful than ever. This play gave Ibsen a reputation in Germany, where it was frequently performed, and prepared him for his great successes. *A Doll House* (1879), which he wrote in Italy, came two years later. It was more fully realistic in style than *The Pillars of Society* and, while immensely successful in Scandinavia, did not become widely known elsewhere for another ten years.

His next play, *Ghosts* (1881), was denounced violently because it dared to treat a subject that had been taboo on the stage: syphilis. *Ghosts* introduced a respectable family, the Alvings, who harbor the secret that the late father contracted the disease and passed it on to Oswald, his son. In addition, the theme of incest is suggested in the presence of Alving's illegitimate daughter, Regina, who falls in love with Oswald. This kind of material was so foreign to the late nineteenth-century stage that Ibsen was vilified and isolated by the literary community in Norway. He chose exile for a time in Rome, Amalfi, and Munich.

Ibsen's last years were filled with activity. He wrote some of his best-known plays in rapid succession: *An Enemy of the People* (1882), *The Wild Duck* (1884), *Hedda Gabler* (1890), *The Master Builder* (1892), and *John Gabriel Borkman* (1896). In 1891 he returned to live in Norway, where he died fifteen years later.

The most influential European dramatist in the late nineteenth century, Ibsen inspired emerging writers in the United States, Ireland, and many other nations. But his full influence was not felt until the early decades of the twentieth century, when other writers were able to spread the revolutionary doctrine that was implied in realism as practiced by Ibsen and Strindberg. Being direct, honest, and unsparing in treating character and theme became the normal mode of serious drama after Ibsen.

A DOLL HOUSE

Once Henrik Ibsen found his voice as a realist playwright, he began to develop plays centering on social problems and the problems of the individual struggling against the demands of society. In *A Doll House* (1879) he focused on the repression of women. It was a subject that deeply offended conservatives and was very much on the minds of progressive and liberal Scandinavians. It was therefore a rather daring theme. The play opens with the dutiful, eager wife Nora Helmer twittering like a lark and pattering like a squirrel pleasing her husband,

Torvald. Helmer is consumed with propriety. As far as he is concerned, Nora is only a woman, an empty-headed ornament in a house designed to keep his life functioning smoothly.

Nora is portrayed as a macaroon-eating, sweet-toothed creature looking for ways to please her husband. When she reveals that she borrowed the money that took them to Italy for a year to save her husband's life, she shows us that she is made of much stronger stuff than anyone has given her credit for. Yet the manner in which she borrowed the money is technically criminal because she had to forge her father's signature, and she now finds herself at the mercy of the lender, Nils Krogstad.

From a modern perspective, Nora's action seems daring and imaginative rather than merely illegal and surreptitious. Torvald Helmer's moralistic position is to us essentially stifling. He condemns Nora's father for a similar failure to secure proper signatures, just as he condemns Nils Krogstad for doing the same. He condemns people for their crimes without considering their circumstances or motives. He is moralistic rather than moral.

The atmosphere of the Helmer household is oppressive. Everything is set up to amuse Torvald, and he lacks any awareness that other people might be his equal. Early in the play Ibsen establishes Nora's longings: She explains that to pay back her loan she has had to take in copying work; and, rather than resent her labor, she observes that it made her feel wonderful, the way a man must feel. Ibsen said that his intention in the play was not primarily to promote the emancipation of women; it was to establish, as Ibsen's biographer Michael Meyer says, "that the primary duty of anyone was to find out who he or she really was and to become that person."

However, the play from the first was seen as addressing the problems of women, especially married women who were treated as their husbands' property. When the play was first performed, the slam of the door at Nora's leaving was much louder than it is today. It was shocking to late nineteenth-century society, which took Torvald Helmer's attitudes for granted. The first audiences probably were split in their opinions about Nora's actions. As Meyer reminds us, "No play had ever before contributed so momentously to the social debate, or been so widely and furiously discussed among people who were not normally interested in theatrical or even artistic matters." Although the critics in Copenhagen and England were very negative, the audiences were filled with curiosity and flocked to the theaters to see the play.

What the audiences saw was that once Nora is awakened, the kind of life Torvald imagines for her is death to Nora. Torvald cannot see how his self-absorbed concern and fear for his own social standing reveal his limitations and selfishness. Nora sees immediately the limits of his concern, and her only choice is to leave him so that she can grow morally and spiritually.

BELOW: For this 1906 production of Ibsen's *The Wild Duck*, the director, André Antoine had the set constructed of Norwegian pine to achieve a high degree of realism. RIGHT: Edvard Munch's 1906 stage design for Max Reinhardt's production of Ibsen's *Ghosts* at the Kammerspiele in Berlin. Although *Ghosts* (1881) was written in Ibsen's realistic style, Munch's expressionistic lines and shadows seem to reflect the tendencies in Ibsen's late plays to move beyond realism to a more dreamlike structure.

What she does and where she goes have been a matter of speculation since the play was first performed. Ibsen refused to encourage any specific conjecture. It is enough that she has the courage to leave. But the ending of the play bothered audiences as well as critics, and it was performed in Germany in 1880 with a happy ending that Ibsen himself wrote to forestall anyone else from doing so. The first German actress to play the part insisted that she would personally never leave her children and therefore would not do the play as written. In the revised version, instead of leaving, Nora is led to the door of her children's room and falls weeping as the curtain goes down. The so-called happy-ending version was played for a while in England and elsewhere. No one was satisfied with this ending, and eventually the play reverted to its original form.

Through the proscenium arch of the theater in Ibsen's day audiences were permitted to eavesdrop on themselves, since Ibsen clearly was analyzing their own mores. In a way the audience was looking at a dollhouse; but instead of containing miniature furniture and miniature people, it contained replicas of those watching. That very sense of intimacy, made possible by the late nineteenth-century theater, heightened the intensity of the play.

A Doll House in Performance

A Doll House was first produced in the Royal Theatre, Copenhagen, in December 1879. Despite its immediate success in Scandinavia and Germany, two years passed before the play appeared elsewhere and ten years before it appeared in England and America in a complete and accurate text. Further, the early German version (February 1880), with Hedwig Niemann-Raabe as Nora, had to be revised with a happy ending because the actress refused to play the original ending. Fortunately, the "happy ending," in which Nora does not leave home, was not successful and Niemann-Raabe eventually played the part as written. An adaptation, also with the happy ending, titled *The Child Wife,* was produced in Milwaukee in 1882. While the first professional London production of the play in 1889 found favor with the public, it was attacked in the press for being "unnatural, immoral and, in its concluding scene, essentially undramatic." Among other things, Ibsen was being condemned for not providing a vibrant plot.

Among the play's memorable performances was Ethel Barrymore's version in New York in 1905. Barrymore was praised for a brilliant interpretation of "the child wife." Ruth Gordon played the part to acclaim in 1937, as did Claire Bloom in 1971 on the stage and in 1973 in film. Jane Fonda played in Joseph Losey's film version of 1973. The Norwegian actress Liv Ullmann performed the role in Lincoln Center in 1975 and was praised as "the most enchanting," the "most honest" Nora that the critic Walter Kerr had seen. Other critics were less kind, but it was a successful run. The play is performed regularly in college and regional theaters in the United States and elsewhere.

Henrik Ibsen (1828–1906)

A DOLL HOUSE   1879

TRANSLATED BY ROLF FJELDE

The Characters

TORVALD HELMER, *a lawyer*
NORA, *his wife*
DR. RANK
MRS. LINDE
NILS KROGSTAD, *a bank clerk*
THE HELMERS' THREE SMALL CHILDREN
ANNE-MARIE, *their nurse*
HELENE, *a maid*
A DELIVERY BOY

The action takes place in Helmer's residence.

ACT I

(*A comfortable room, tastefully but not expensively furnished. A door to the right in the back wall leads to the entryway; another to the left leads to Helmer's study. Between these doors, a piano. Midway in the left-hand wall a door, and further back a window. Near the window a round table with an armchair and a small sofa. In the right-hand wall, toward the rear, a door, and nearer the foreground a porcelain stove with two armchairs and a rocking chair beside it. Between the stove and the side door, a small table. Engravings on the walls. An étagère° with china figures and other small art objects; a small bookcase with richly bound books; the floor carpeted; a fire burning in the stove. It is a winter day.*)

(*A bell rings in the entryway; shortly after we hear the door being unlocked. Nora comes into the room, humming happily to herself; she is wearing street clothes and carries an armload of packages, which she*

As Fjelde explains in his forward to the translation, he does not use the possessive "A Doll's House" because "the house is not Nora's, as the possessive implies." Fjelde believes that Ibsen includes Torvald with Nora in the original title, "for the two of them at the play's opening are still posing like the little marzipan bride and groom atop the wedding cake."

[S.D.] **étagère:** Cabinet with shelves.

puts down on the table to the right. She has left the hall door open, and through it a Delivery Boy is seen holding a Christmas tree and a basket, which he gives to the Maid who let them in.)

NORA: Hide the tree well, Helene. The children mustn't get a glimpse of it till this evening, after it's trimmed. (*To the Delivery Boy, taking out her purse.*) How much?
DELIVERY BOY: Fifty, ma'am.
NORA: There's a crown. No, keep the change. (*The Boy thanks her and leaves. Nora shuts the door. She laughs softly to herself while taking off her street things. Drawing a bag of macaroons from her pocket, she eats a couple, then steals over and listens at her husband's study door.*) Yes, he's home. (*Hums again as she moves to the table right.*)
HELMER (*from the study*): Is that my little lark twittering out there?
NORA (*busy opening some packages*): Yes, it is.
HELMER: Is that my squirrel rummaging around?
NORA: Yes!
HELMER: When did my squirrel get in?
NORA: Just now. (*Putting the macaroon bag in her pocket and wiping her mouth.*) Do come in, Torvald, and see what I've bought.
HELMER: Can't be disturbed. (*After a moment he opens the door and peers in, pen in hand.*) Bought, you say? All that there? Has the little spendthrift been out throwing money around again?
NORA: Oh, but Torvald, this year we really should let ourselves go a bit. It's the first Christmas we haven't had to economize.
HELMER: But you know we can't go squandering.
NORA: Oh yes, Torvald, we can squander a little now. Can't we? Just a tiny, wee bit. Now that you've got a big salary and are going to make piles and piles of money.
HELMER: Yes — starting New Year's. But then it's a full three months till the raise comes through.
NORA: Pooh! We can borrow that long.
HELMER: Nora! (*Goes over and playfully takes her by the ear.*) Are your scatterbrains off again? What if today I borrowed a thousand crowns, and you squandered them over Christmas week, and then

on New Year's Eve a roof tile fell on my head, and
I lay there —

NORA (*putting her hand on his mouth*): Oh! Don't
say such things!

HELMER: Yes, but what if it happened — then what?

NORA: If anything so awful happened, then it just
wouldn't matter if I had debts or not.

HELMER: Well, but the people I'd borrowed from?

NORA: Them? Who cares about them! They're
strangers.

HELMER: Nora, Nora, how like a woman! No, but seriously, Nora, you know what I think about that.
No debts! Never borrow! Something of freedom's
lost — and something of beauty, too — from a
home that's founded on borrowing and debt.
We've made a brave stand up to now, the two of
us; and we'll go right on like that the little while
we have to.

NORA (*going toward the stove*): Yes, whatever you
say, Torvald.

HELMER (*following her*): Now, now, the little lark's
wings mustn't droop. Come on, don't be a sulky
squirrel. (*Taking out his wallet.*) Nora, guess what
I have here.

NORA (*turning quickly*): Money!

HELMER: There, see. (*Hands her some notes.*) Good
grief, I know how costs go up in a house at Christ-
mastime.

NORA: Ten — twenty — thirty — forty. Oh, thank
you, Torvald; I can manage no end on this.

HELMER: You really will have to.

NORA: Oh yes, I promise I will! But come here so I
can show you everything I bought. And so cheap!
Look, new clothes for Ivar here — and a sword.
Here a horse and a trumpet for Bob. And a doll
and a doll's bed here for Emmy; they're nothing
much, but she'll tear them to bits in no time anyway. And here I have dress material and handkerchiefs for the maids. Old Anne-Marie really
deserves something more.

HELMER: And what's in that package there?

NORA (*with a cry*): Torvald, no! You can't see that till
tonight!

HELMER: I see. But tell me now, you little prodigal,
what have you thought of for yourself?

NORA: For myself? Oh, I don't want anything at all.

HELMER: Of course you do. Tell me just what —
within reason — you'd most like to have.

NORA: I honestly don't know. Oh, listen, Torvald —

HELMER: Well?

NORA (*fumbling at his coat buttons, without looking
at him*): If you want to give me something, then
maybe you could — you could —

HELMER: Come on, out with it.

NORA (*hurriedly*): You could give me money, Torvald.

No more than you think you can spare; then one
of these days I'll buy something with it.

HELMER: But Nora —

NORA: Oh, please, Torvald darling, do that! I beg you,
please. Then I could hang the bills in pretty gilt paper on the Christmas tree. Wouldn't that be fun?

HELMER: What are those little birds called that always
fly through their fortunes?

NORA: Oh yes, spendthrifts; I know all that. But let's
do as I say, Torvald; then I'll have time to decide
what I really need most. That's very sensible, isn't
it?

HELMER (*smiling*): Yes, very — that is, if you actually
hung onto the money I give you, and you actually
used it to buy yourself something. But it goes for
the house and for all sorts of foolish things, and
then I only have to lay out some more.

NORA: Oh, but Torvald —

HELMER: Don't deny it, my dear little Nora. (*Putting
his arm around her waist.*) Spendthrifts are sweet,
but they use up a frightful amount of money. It's
incredible what it costs a man to feed such birds.

NORA: Oh, how can you say that! Really, I save everything I can.

HELMER (*laughing*): Yes, that's the truth. Everything
you can. But that's nothing at all.

NORA (*humming, with a smile of quiet satisfaction*):
Hm, if you only knew what expenses we larks and
squirrels have, Torvald.

HELMER: You're an odd little one. Exactly the way
your father was. You're never at a loss for scaring
up money; but the moment you have it, it runs
right out through your fingers; you never know
what you've done with it. Well, one takes you as
you are. It's deep in your blood. Yes, these things
are hereditary, Nora.

NORA: Ah, I could wish I'd inherited many of Papa's
qualities.

HELMER: And I couldn't wish you anything but just
what you are, my sweet little lark. But wait; it
seems to me you have a very — what should I call
it? — a very suspicious look today —

NORA: I do?

HELMER: You certainly do. Look me straight in the
eye.

NORA (*looking at him*): Well?

HELMER (*shaking an admonitory finger*): Surely my
sweet tooth hasn't been running riot in town today, has she?

NORA: No. Why do you imagine that?

HELMER: My sweet tooth really didn't make a little
detour through the confectioner's?

NORA: No, I assure you, Torvald —

HELMER: Hasn't nibbled some pastry?

NORA: No, not at all.

HELMER: Not even munched a macaroon or two?

NORA: No, Torvald, I assure you, really —

HELMER: There, there now. Of course I'm only joking.

NORA (*going to the table, right*): You know I could never think of going against you.

HELMER: No, I understand that; and you *have* given me your word. (*Going over to her.*) Well, you keep your little Christmas secrets to yourself, Nora darling. I expect they'll come to light this evening, when the tree is lit.

NORA: Did you remember to ask Dr. Rank?

HELMER: No. But there's no need for that, it's assumed he'll be dining with us. All the same, I'll ask him when he stops by here this morning. I've ordered some fine wine. Nora, you can't imagine how I'm looking forward to this evening.

NORA: So am I. And what fun for the children, Torvald!

HELMER: Ah, it's so gratifying to know that one's gotten a safe, secure job, and with a comfortable salary. It's a great satisfaction, isn't it?

NORA: Oh, it's wonderful!

HELMER: Remember last Christmas? Three whole weeks before, you shut yourself in every evening till long after midnight, making flowers for the Christmas tree, and all the other decorations to surprise us. Ugh, that was the dullest time I've ever lived through.

NORA: It wasn't at all dull for me.

HELMER (*smiling*): But the outcome *was* pretty sorry, Nora.

NORA: Oh, don't tease me with that again. How could I help it that the cat came in and tore everything to shreds.

HELMER: No, poor thing, you certainly couldn't. You wanted so much to please us all, and that's what counts. But it's just as well that the hard times are past.

NORA: Yes, it's really wonderful.

HELMER: Now I don't have to sit here alone, boring myself, and you don't have to tire your precious eyes and your fair little delicate hands —

NORA (*clapping her hands*): No, is it really true, Torvald, I don't have to? Oh, how wonderfully lovely to hear! (*Taking his arm.*) Now I'll tell you just how I've thought we should plan things. Right after Christmas — (*The doorbell rings.*) Oh, the bell. (*Straightening the room up a bit.*) Somebody would have to come. What a bore!

HELMER: I'm not at home to visitors, don't forget.

MAID (*from the hall doorway*): Ma'am, a lady to see you —

NORA: All right, let her come in.

MAID (*to Helmer*): And the doctor's just come too.

HELMER: Did he go right to my study?

MAID: Yes, he did.

(*Helmer goes into his room. The Maid shows in Mrs. Linde, dressed in traveling clothes, and shuts the door after her.*)

MRS. LINDE (*in a dispirited and somewhat hesitant voice*): Hello, Nora.

NORA (*uncertain*): Hello —

MRS. LINDE: You don't recognize me.

NORA: No, I don't know — but wait, I think — (*Exclaiming.*) What! Kristine! Is it really you?

MRS. LINDE: Yes, it's me.

NORA: Kristine! To think I didn't recognize you. But then, how could I? (*More quietly.*) How you've changed, Kristine!

MRS. LINDE: Yes, no doubt I have. In nine — ten long years.

NORA: Is it so long since we met! Yes, it's all of that. Oh, these last eight years have been a happy time, believe me. And so now you've come in to town, too. Made the long trip in the winter. That took courage.

MRS. LINDE: I just got here by ship this morning.

NORA: To enjoy yourself over Christmas, of course. Oh, how lovely! Yes, enjoy ourselves, we'll do that. But take your coat off. You're not still cold? (*Helping her.*) There now, let's get cozy here by the stove. No, the easy chair there! I'll take the rocker here. (*Seizing her hands.*) Yes, now you have your old look again; it was only in that first moment. You're a bit more pale, Kristine — and maybe a bit thinner.

MRS. LINDE: And much, much older, Nora.

NORA: Yes, perhaps a bit older; a tiny, tiny bit; not much at all. (*Stopping short; suddenly serious.*) Oh, but thoughtless me, to sit here, chattering away. Sweet, good Kristine, can you forgive me?

MRS. LINDE: What do you mean, Nora?

NORA (*softly*): Poor Kristine, you've become a widow.

MRS. LINDE: Yes, three years ago.

NORA: Oh, I knew it, of course; I read it in the papers. Oh, Kristine, you must believe me; I often thought of writing you then, but I kept postponing it, and something always interfered.

MRS. LINDE: Nora dear, I understand completely.

NORA: No, it was awful of me, Kristine. You poor thing, how much you must have gone through. And he left you nothing?

MRS. LINDE: No.

NORA: And no children?

MRS. LINDE: No.

NORA: Nothing at all, then?

MRS. LINDE: Not even a sense of loss to feed on.

NORA (*looking incredulously at her.*): But Kristine, how could that be?

MRS. LINDE (*smiling wearily and smoothing her hair*): Oh, sometimes it happens, Nora.

NORA: So completely alone. How terribly hard that must be for you. I have three lovely children. You can't see them now; they're out with the maid. But now you must tell me everything —

MRS. LINDE: No, no, no, tell me about yourself.

NORA: No, you begin. Today I don't want to be selfish. I want to think only of you today. But there is something I must tell you. Did you hear of the wonderful luck we had recently?

MRS. LINDE: No, what's that?

NORA: My husband's been made manager in the bank, just think!

MRS. LINDE: Your husband? How marvelous!

NORA: Isn't it? Being a lawyer is such an uncertain living, you know, especially if one won't touch any cases that aren't clean and decent. And of course Torvald would never do that, and I'm with him completely there. Oh, we're simply delighted, believe me! He'll join the bank right after New Year's and start getting a huge salary and lots of commissions. From now on we can live quite differently — just as we want. Oh, Kristine, I feel so light and happy! Won't it be lovely to have stacks of money and not a care in the world?

MRS. LINDE: Well, anyway, it would be lovely to have enough for necessities.

NORA: No, not just for necessities, but stacks and stacks of money!

MRS. LINDE (*smiling*): Nora, Nora, aren't you sensible yet? Back in school you were such a free spender.

NORA (*with a quiet laugh*): Yes, that's what Torvald still says. (*Shaking her finger.*) But "Nora, Nora" isn't as silly as you all think. Really, we've been in no position for me to go squandering. We've had to work, both of us.

MRS. LINDE: You too?

NORA: Yes, at odd jobs — needlework, crocheting, embroidery, and such — (*casually*) and other things too. You remember that Torvald left the department when we were married? There was no chance of promotion in his office, and of course he needed to earn more money. But that first year he drove himself terribly. He took on all kinds of extra work that kept him going morning and night. It wore him down, and then he fell deathly ill. The doctors said it was essential for him to travel south.

MRS. LINDE: Yes, didn't you spend a whole year in Italy?

NORA: That's right. It wasn't easy to get away, you know. Ivar had just been born. But of course we had to go. Oh, that was a beautiful trip, and it saved Torvald's life. But it cost a frightful sum, Kristine.

MRS. LINDE: I can well imagine.

NORA: Four thousand, eight hundred crowns it cost. That's really a lot of money.

MRS. LINDE: But it's lucky you had it when you needed it.

NORA: Well, as it was, we got it from Papa.

MRS. LINDE: I see. It was just about the time your father died.

NORA: Yes, just about then. And, you know, I couldn't make that trip out to nurse him. I had to stay here, expecting Ivar any moment, and with my poor sick Torvald to care for. Dearest Papa, I never saw him again, Kristine. Oh, that was the worst time I've known in all my marriage.

MRS. LINDE: I know how you loved him. And then you went off to Italy?

NORA: Yes. We had the means now, and the doctors urged us. So we left a month after.

MRS. LINDE: And your husband came back completely cured?

NORA: Sound as a drum!

MRS. LINDE: But — the doctor?

NORA: Who?

MRS. LINDE: I thought the maid said he was a doctor, the man who came in with me.

NORA: Yes, that was Dr. Rank — but he's not making a sick call. He's our closest friend, and he stops by at least once a day. No, Torvald hasn't had a sick moment since, and the children are fit and strong, and I am, too. (*Jumping up and clapping her hands.*) Oh, dear God, Kristine, what a lovely thing to live and be happy! But how disgusting of me — I'm talking of nothing but my own affairs. (*Sits on a stool close by Kristine, arms resting across her knees.*) Oh, don't be angry with me! Tell me, is it really true that you weren't in love with your husband? Why did you marry him, then?

MRS. LINDE: My mother was still alive, but bedridden and helpless — and I had my two younger brothers to look after. In all conscience, I didn't think I could turn him down.

NORA: No, you were right there. But was he rich at the time?

MRS. LINDE: He was very well off, I'd say. But the business was shaky, Nora. When he died, it all fell apart, and nothing was left.

NORA: And then — ?

MRS. LINDE: Yes, so I had to scrape up a living with a little shop and a little teaching and whatever else I could find. The last three years have been like one endless workday without a rest for me. Now, it's over, Nora. My poor mother doesn't need me, for she's passed on. Nor the boys, either; they're working now and can take care of themselves —

NORA: How free you must feel —

MRS. LINDE: No — only unspeakably empty. Nothing to live for now. (*Standing up anxiously.*) That's why I couldn't take it any longer out in that desolate hole. Maybe here it'll be easier to find something to do and keep my mind occupied. If I could only be lucky enough to get a steady job, some office work —

NORA: Oh, but Kristine, that's so dreadfully tiring, and you already look so tired. It would be much better for you if you could go off to a bathing resort.

MRS. LINDE (*going toward the window*): I have no father to give me travel money, Nora.

NORA (*rising*): Oh, don't be angry with me.

MRS. LINDE (*going to her*): Nora dear, don't you be angry with me. The worst of my kind of situation is all the bitterness that's stored away. No one to work for, and yet you're always having to snap up your opportunities. You have to live; and so you grow selfish. When you told me the happy change in your lot, do you know I was delighted less for your sakes than for mine?

NORA: How so? Oh, I see. You think maybe Torvald could do something for you.

MRS. LINDE: Yes, that's what I thought.

NORA: And he will, Kristine! Just leave it to me; I'll bring it up so delicately — find something attractive to humor him with. Oh, I'm so eager to help you.

MRS. LINDE: How very kind of you, Nora, to be so concerned over me — doubly kind, considering you really know so little of life's burdens yourself.

NORA: I — ? I know so little — ?

MRS. LINDE (*smiling*): Well, my heavens — a little needlework and such — Nora, you're just a child.

NORA (*tossing her head and pacing the floor*): You don't have to act so superior.

MRS. LINDE: Oh?

NORA: You're just like the others. You all think I'm incapable of anything serious —

MRS. LINDE: Come now —

NORA: That I've never had to face the raw world.

MRS. LINDE: Nora dear, you've just been telling me all your troubles.

NORA: Hm! Trivial! (*Quietly.*) I haven't told you the big thing.

MRS. LINDE: Big thing? What do you mean?

NORA: You look down on me so, Kristine, but you shouldn't. You're proud that you worked so long and hard for your mother.

MRS. LINDE: I don't look down on a soul. But it is

true: I'm proud — and happy, too — to think it was given to me to make my mother's last days almost free of care.

NORA: And you're also proud thinking of what you've done for your brothers.

MRS. LINDE: I feel I've a right to be.

NORA: I agree. But listen to this, Kristine — I've also got something to be proud and happy for.

MRS. LINDE: I don't doubt it. But whatever do you mean?

NORA: Not so loud. What if Torvald heard! He mustn't, not for anything in the world. Nobody must know, Kristine. No one but you.

MRS. LINDE: But what is it, then?

NORA: Come here. (*Drawing her down beside her on the sofa.*) It's true — I've also got something to be proud and happy for. I'm the one who saved Torvald's life.

MRS. LINDE: Saved — ? Saved how?

NORA: I told you about the trip to Italy. Torvald never would have lived if he hadn't gone south —

MRS. LINDE: Of course; your father gave you the means —

NORA (*smiling*): That's what Torvald and all the rest think, but —

MRS. LINDE: But — ?

NORA: Papa didn't give us a pin. I was the one who raised the money.

MRS. LINDE: You? That whole amount?

NORA: Four thousand, eight hundred crowns. What do you say to that?

MRS. LINDE: But Nora, how was it possible? Did you win the lottery?

NORA (*disdainfully*): The lottery? Pooh! No art to that.

MRS. LINDE: But where did you get it from then?

NORA (*humming, with a mysterious smile*): Hmm, tra-la-la-la.

MRS. LINDE: Because you couldn't have borrowed it.

NORA: No? Why not?

MRS. LINDE: A wife can't borrow without her husband's consent.

NORA (*tossing her head*): Oh, but a wife with a little business sense, a wife who knows how to manage —

MRS. LINDE: Nora, I simply don't understand —

NORA: You don't have to. Whoever said I *borrowed* the money? I could have gotten it other ways. (*Throwing herself back on the sofa.*) I could have gotten it from some admirer or other. After all, a girl with my ravishing appeal —

MRS. LINDE: You lunatic.

NORA: I'll bet you're eaten up with curiosity, Kristine.

MRS. LINDE: Now listen here, Nora — you haven't done something indiscreet?

NORA (*sitting up again*): Is it indiscreet to save your husband's life?

MRS. LINDE: I think it's indiscreet that without his knowledge you —

NORA: But that's the point: He mustn't know! My Lord, can't you understand? He mustn't ever know the close call he had. It was to *me* the doctors came to say his life was in danger — that nothing could save him but a stay in the south. Didn't I try strategy then! I began talking about how lovely it would be for me to travel abroad like other young wives; I begged and I cried; I told him please to remember my condition, to be kind and indulge me; and then I dropped a hint that he could easily take out a loan. But at that, Kristine, he nearly exploded. He said I was frivolous, and it was his duty as man of the house not to indulge me in whims and fancies — as I think he called them. Aha, I thought, now you'll just have to be saved — and that's when I saw my chance.

MRS. LINDE: And your father never told Torvald the money wasn't from him?

NORA: No, never. Papa died right about then. I'd considered bringing him into my secret and begging him never to tell. But he was too sick at the time — and then, sadly, it didn't matter.

MRS. LINDE: And you've never confided in your husband since?

NORA: For heaven's sake, no! Are you serious? He's so strict on that subject. Besides — Torvald, with all his masculine pride — how painfully humiliating for him if he ever found out he was in debt to me. That would just ruin our relationship. Our beautiful, happy home would never be the same.

MRS. LINDE: Won't you ever tell him?

NORA (*thoughtfully, half smiling*): Yes — maybe sometime years from now, when I'm no longer so attractive. Don't laugh! I only mean when Torvald loves me less than now, when he stops enjoying my dancing and dressing up and reciting for him. Then it might be wise to have something in reserve — (*Breaking off.*) How ridiculous! That'll never happen — Well, Kristine, what do you think of my big secret? I'm capable of something too, hm? You can imagine, of course, how this thing hangs over me. It really hasn't been easy meeting the payments on time. In the business world there's what they call quarterly interest and what they call amortization, and these are always so terribly hard to manage. I've had to skimp a little here and there, wherever I could, you know. I could hardly spare anything from my house allowance, because Torvald has to live well. I couldn't let the children go poorly dressed; whatever I got for them, I felt I had to use up completely — the darlings!

MRS. LINDE: Poor Nora, so it had to come out of your own budget, then?

NORA: Yes, of course. But I was the one most responsible, too. Every time Torvald gave me money for new clothes and such, I never used more than half; always bought the simplest, cheapest outfits. It was a godsend that everything looks so well on me that Torvald never noticed. But it did weigh me down at times, Kristine. It *is* such a joy to wear fine things. You understand.

MRS. LINDE: Oh, of course.

NORA: And then I found other ways of making money. Last winter I was lucky enough to get a lot of copying to do. I locked myself in and sat writing every evening till late in the night. Ah, I was tired so often, dead tired. But still it was wonderful fun, sitting and working like that, earning money. It was almost like being a man.

MRS. LINDE: But how much have you paid off this way so far?

NORA: That's hard to say, exactly. These accounts, you know, aren't easy to figure. I only know that I've paid out all I could scrape together. Time and again I haven't known where to turn. (*Smiling.*) Then I'd sit here dreaming of a rich old gentleman who had fallen in love with me —

MRS. LINDE: What! Who is he?

NORA: Oh, really! And that he'd died, and when his will was opened, there in big letters it said, "All my fortune shall be paid over in cash, immediately, to that enchanting Mrs. Nora Helmer."

MRS. LINDE: But Nora dear — who *was* this gentleman?

NORA: Good grief, can't you understand? The old man never existed; that was only something I'd dream up time and again whenever I was at my wits' end for money. But it makes no difference now; the old fossil can go where he pleases for all I care; I don't need him or his will — because now I'm free. (*Jumping up.*) Oh, how lovely to think of that, Kristine! Carefree! To know you're carefree, utterly carefree; to be able to romp and play with the children, and to keep up a beautiful, charming home — everything just the way Torvald likes it! And think, spring is coming, with big blue skies. Maybe we can travel a little then. Maybe I'll see the ocean again. Oh yes, it *is* so marvelous to live and be happy!

(*The front doorbell rings.*)

MRS. LINDE (*rising*): There's the bell. It's probably best that I go.

NORA: No, stay. No one's expected. It must be for Torvald.

MAID (*from the hall doorway*): Excuse me, ma'am —

there's a gentleman here to see Mr. Helmer, but I didn't know — since the doctor's with him —

NORA: Who is the gentleman?

KROGSTAD (*from the doorway*): It's me, Mrs. Helmer.

(*Mrs. Linde starts and turns away toward the window.*)

NORA (*stepping toward him, tense, her voice a whisper*): You? What is it? Why do you want to speak to my husband?

KROGSTAD: Bank business — after a fashion. I have a small job in the investment bank, and I hear now your husband is going to be our chief —

NORA: In other words, it's —

KROGSTAD: Just dry business, Mrs. Helmer. Nothing but that.

NORA: Yes, then please be good enough to step into the study. (*She nods indifferently as she sees him out by the hall door, then returns and begins stirring up the stove.*)

MRS. LINDE: Nora — who was that man?

NORA: That was a Mr. Krogstad — a lawyer.

MRS. LINDE: Then it really was him.

NORA: Do you know that person?

MRS. LINDE: I did once — many years ago. For a time he was a law clerk in our town.

NORA: Yes, he's been that.

MRS. LINDE: How he's changed.

NORA: I understand he had a very unhappy marriage.

MRS. LINDE: He's a widower now.

NORA: With a number of children. There now, it's burning. (*She closes the stove door and moves the rocker a bit to one side.*)

MRS. LINDE: They say he has a hand in all kinds of business.

NORA: Oh? That may be true; I wouldn't know. But let's not think about business. It's so dull.

(*Dr. Rank enters from Helmer's study.*)

RANK (*still in the doorway*): No, no, really — I don't want to intrude, I'd just as soon talk a little while with your wife. (*Shuts the door, then notices Mrs. Linde.*) Oh, beg pardon. I'm intruding here too.

NORA: No, not at all. (*Introducing him.*) Dr. Rank, Mrs. Linde.

RANK: Well now, that's a name much heard in this house. I believe I passed the lady on the stairs as I came.

MRS. LINDE: Yes, I take the stairs very slowly. They're rather hard on me.

RANK: Uh-hm, some touch of internal weakness?

MRS. LINDE: More overexertion, I'd say.

RANK: Nothing else? Then you're probably here in town to rest up in a round of parties?

MRS. LINDE: I'm here to look for work.

RANK: Is that the best cure for overexertion?

MRS. LINDE: One has to live, Doctor.

RANK: Yes, there's a common prejudice to that effect.

NORA: Oh, come on, Dr. Rank — you really do want to live yourself.

RANK: Yes, I really do. Wretched as I am, I'll gladly prolong my torment indefinitely. All my patients feel like that. And it's quite the same, too, with the morally sick. Right at this moment there's one of those moral invalids in there with Helmer —

MRS. LINDE (*softly*): Ah!

NORA: Who do you mean?

RANK: Oh, it's a lawyer, Krogstad, a type you wouldn't know. His character is rotten to the root — but even he began chattering all-importantly about how he had to *live*.

NORA: Oh? What did he want to talk to Torvald about?

RANK: I really don't know. I only heard something about the bank.

NORA: I didn't know that Krog — that this man Krogstad had anything to do with the bank.

RANK: Yes, he's gotten some kind of berth down there. (*To Mrs. Linde.*) I don't know if you also have, in your neck of the woods, a type of person who scuttles about breathlessly, sniffing out hints of moral corruption, and then maneuvers his victim into some sort of key position where he can keep an eye on him. It's the healthy these days that are out in the cold.

MRS. LINDE: All the same, it's the sick who most need to be taken in.

RANK (*with a shrug*): Yes, there we have it. That's the concept that's turning society into a sanatorium.

(*Nora, lost in her thoughts, breaks out into quiet laughter and claps her hands.*)

RANK: Why do you laugh at that? Do you have any real idea of what society is?

NORA: What do I care about dreary old society? I was laughing at something quite different — something terribly funny. Tell me, Doctor — is everyone who works in the bank dependent now on Torvald?

RANK: Is that what you find so terribly funny?

NORA (*smiling and humming*): Never mind, never mind! (*Pacing the floor.*) Yes, that's really immensely amusing: that we — that Torvald has so much power now over all those people. (*Taking the bag out of her pocket.*) Dr. Rank, a little macaroon on that?

RANK: See here, macaroons! I thought they were contraband here.

NORA: Yes, but these are some that Kristine gave me.

MRS. LINDE: What? I — ?

NORA: Now, now, don't be afraid. You couldn't possibly know that Torvald had forbidden them. You see, he's worried they'll ruin my teeth. But hmp! Just this once! Isn't that so, Dr. Rank? Help yourself! (*Puts a macaroon in his mouth.*) And you too, Kristine. And I'll also have one, only a little one — or two, at the most. (*Walking about again.*) Now I'm really tremendously happy. Now's there's just one last thing in the world that I have an enormous desire to do.

RANK: Well! And what's that?

NORA: It's something I have such a consuming desire to say so Torvald could hear.

RANK: And why can't you say it?

NORA: I don't dare. It's quite shocking.

MRS. LINDE: Shocking?

RANK: Well, then it isn't advisable. But in front of us you certainly can. What do you have such a desire to say so Torvald could hear?

NORA: I have such a huge desire to say — to hell and be damned!

RANK: Are you crazy?

MRS. LINDE: My goodness, Nora!

RANK: Go on, say it. Here he is.

NORA (*hiding the macaroon bag*): Shh, shh, shh!

(*Helmer comes in from his study, hat in hand, overcoat over his arm.*)

NORA (*going toward him*): Well, Torvald dear, are you through with him?

HELMER: Yes, he just left.

NORA: Let me introduce you — this is Kristine, who's arrived here in town.

HELMER: Kristine — ? I'm sorry, but I don't know —

NORA: Mrs. Linde, Torvald dear. Mrs. Kristine Linde.

HELMER: Of course. A childhood friend of my wife's, no doubt?

MRS. LINDE: Yes, we knew each other in those days.

NORA: And just think, she made the long trip down here in order to talk with you.

HELMER: What's this?

MRS. LINDE: Well, not exactly —

NORA: You see, Kristine is remarkably clever in office work, and so she's terribly eager to come under a capable man's supervision and add more to what she already knows —

HELMER: Very wise, Mrs. Linde.

NORA: And then when she heard that you'd become a bank manager — the story was wired out to the papers — then she came in as fast as she could and — Really, Torvald, for my sake you can do a little something for Kristine, can't you?

HELMER: Yes, it's not at all impossible. Mrs. Linde, I suppose you're a widow?

MRS. LINDE: Yes.

HELMER: Any experience in office work?

MRS. LINDE: Yes, a good deal.

HELMER: Well, it's quite likely that I can make an opening for you —

NORA (*clapping her hands*): You see, you see!

HELMER: You've come at a lucky moment, Mrs. Linde.

MRS. LINDE: Oh, how can I thank you?

HELMER: Not necessary. (*Putting his overcoat on.*) But today you'll have to excuse me —

RANK: Wait, I'll go with you. (*He fetches his coat from the hall and warms it at the stove.*)

NORA: Don't stay out long, dear.

HELMER: An hour; no more.

NORA: Are you going too, Kristine?

MRS. LINDE (*putting on her winter garments*): Yes, I have to see about a room now.

HELMER: Then perhaps we can all walk together.

NORA (*helping her*): What a shame we're so cramped here, but it's quite impossible for us to —

MRS. LINDE: Oh, don't even think of it! Good-bye, Nora dear, and thanks for everything.

NORA: Good-bye for now. Of course you'll be back this evening. And you too, Dr. Rank. What? If you're well enough? Oh, you've got to be! Wrap up tight now.

(*In a ripple of small talk the company moves out into the hall; children's voices are heard outside on the steps.*)

NORA: There they are! There they are! (*She runs to open the door. The children come in with their nurse, Anne-Marie.*) Come in, come in! (*Bends down and kisses them.*) Oh, you darlings — ! Look at them, Kristine. Aren't they lovely!

RANK: No loitering in the draft here.

HELMER: Come, Mrs. Linde — this place is unbearable now for anyone but mothers.

(*Dr. Rank, Helmer, and Mrs. Linde go down the stairs. Anne-Marie goes into the living room with the children. Nora follows, after closing the hall door.*)

NORA: How fresh and strong you look. Oh, such red cheeks you have! Like apples and roses. (*The children interrupt her throughout the following.*) And it was so much fun? That's wonderful. Really? You pulled both Emmy and Bob on the sled? Imagine, all together! Yes, you're a clever boy, Ivar. Oh, let me hold her a bit, Anne-Marie. My sweet little doll baby! (*Takes the smallest from the nurse and dances with her.*) Yes, yes, Mama will dance with Bob as well. What? Did you throw snowballs? Oh, if I'd only been there! No, don't bother, Anne-Marie — I'll undress them myself. Oh yes, let me. It's such fun. Go in and rest; you look half frozen. There's hot coffee waiting for you on the stove.

(*The nurse goes into the room to the left. Nora takes the children's winter things off, throwing them about, while the children talk to her all at once.*) Is that so? A big dog chased you? But it didn't bite? No, dogs never bite little, lovely doll babies. Don't peek in the packages, Ivar! What is it? Yes, wouldn't you like to know. No, no, it's an ugly something. Well? Shall we play? What shall we play? Hide-and-seek? Yes, let's play hide-and-seek. Bob must hide first. I must? Yes, let me hide first. (*Laughing and shouting, she and the children play in and out of the living room and the adjoining room to the right. At last Nora hides under the table. The children come storming in, search, but cannot find her, then hear her muffled laughter, dash over to the table, lift the cloth up and find her. Wild shouting. She creeps forward as if to scare them. More shouts. Meanwhile, a knock at the hall door; no one has noticed it. Now the door half opens, and Krogstad appears. He waits a moment; the game goes on.*)

KROGSTAD: Beg pardon, Mrs. Helmer —

NORA (*with a strangled cry, turning and scrambling to her knees*): Oh! What do you want?

KROGSTAD: Excuse me. The outer door was ajar; it must be someone forgot to shut it —

NORA (*rising*): My husband isn't home, Mr. Krogstad.

KROGSTAD: I know that.

NORA: Yes — then what do you want here?

KROGSTAD: A word with you.

NORA: With — ? (*To the children, quietly.*) Go in to Anne-Marie. What? No, the strange man won't hurt Mama. When he's gone, we'll play some more. (*She leads the children into the room to the left and shuts the door after them. Then, tense and nervous:*) You want to speak to me?

KROGSTAD: Yes, I want to.

NORA: Today? But it's not yet the first of the month —

KROGSTAD: No, it's Christmas Eve. It's going to be up to you how merry a Christmas you have.

NORA: What is it you want? Today I absolutely can't —

KROGSTAD: We won't talk about that till later. This is something else. You do have a moment to spare, I suppose?

NORA: Oh yes, of course — I do, except —

KROGSTAD: Good. I was sitting over at Olsen's Restaurant when I saw your husband go down the street —

NORA: Yes?

KROGSTAD: With a lady.

NORA: Yes. So?

KROGSTAD: If you'll pardon my asking: Wasn't that lady a Mrs. Linde?

NORA: Yes.

KROGSTAD: Just now come into town?

NORA: Yes, today.

KROGSTAD: She's a good friend of yours?

NORA: Yes, she is. But I don't see —

KROGSTAD: I also knew her once.

NORA: I'm aware of that.

KROGSTAD: Oh? You know all about it. I thought so. Well, then let me ask you short and sweet: Is Mrs. Linde getting a job in the bank?

NORA: What makes you think you can cross-examine me, Mr. Krogstad — you, one of my husband's employees? But since you ask, you might as well know — yes, Mrs. Linde's going to be taken on at the bank. And I'm the one who spoke for her Mr. Krogstad. Now you know.

KROGSTAD: So I guessed right.

NORA (*pacing up and down*): Oh, one does have a tiny bit of influence, I should hope. Just because I am a woman, don't think it means that — When one has a subordinate position, Mr. Krogstad, one really ought to be careful about pushing somebody who — hm —

KROGSTAD: Who has influence?

NORA: That's right.

KROGSTAD (*in a different tone*): Mrs. Helmer, would you be good enough to use your influence on my behalf?

NORA: What? What do you mean?

KROGSTAD: Would you please make sure that I keep my subordinate position in the bank?

NORA: What does that mean? Who's thinking of taking away your position?

KROGSTAD: Oh, don't play the innocent with me. I'm quite aware that your friend would hardly relish the chance of running into me again; and I'm also aware now whom I can thank for being turned out.

NORA: But I promise you —

KROGSTAD: Yes, yes, yes, to the point: There's still time, and I'm advising you to use your influence to prevent it.

NORA: But Mr. Krogstad, I have absolutely no influence.

KROGSTAD: You haven't? I thought you were just saying —

NORA: You shouldn't take me so literally. I! How can you believe that I have any such influence over my husband?

KROGSTAD: Oh, I've known your husband from our student days. I don't think the great bank manager's more steadfast than any other married man.

NORA: You speak insolently about my husband, and I'll show you the door.

KROGSTAD: The lady has spirit.

NORA: I'm not afraid of you any longer. After New Year's, I'll soon be done with the whole business.

KROGSTAD: (*restraining himself*): Now listen to me, Mrs. Helmer. If necessary, I'll fight for my little job in the bank as if it were life itself.

NORA: Yes, so it seems.

KROGSTAD: It's not just a matter of income; that's the least of it. It's something else — All right, out with it! Look, this is the thing. You know, just like all the others, of course, that once, a good many years ago, I did something rather rash.

NORA: I've heard rumors to that effect.

KROGSTAD: The case never got into court; but all the same, every door was closed in my face from then on. So I took up those various activities you know about. I had to grab hold somewhere; and I dare say I haven't been among the worst. But now I want to drop all that. My boys are growing up. For their sakes, I'll have to win back as much respect as possible here in town. That job in the bank was like the first rung in my ladder. And now your husband wants to kick me right back down in the mud again.

NORA: But for heaven's sake, Mr. Krogstad, it's simply not in my power to help you.

KROGSTAD: That's because you haven't the will to — but I have the means to make you.

NORA: You certainly won't tell my husband that I owe you money?

KROGSTAD: Hm — what if I told him that?

NORA: That would be shameful of you. (*Nearly in tears.*) This secret — my joy and my pride — that he should learn it in such a crude and disgusting way — learn it from you. You'd expose me to the most horrible unpleasantness —

KROGSTAD: Only unpleasantness?

NORA (*vehemently*): But go on and try. It'll turn out the worse for you, because then my husband will really see what a crook you are, and then you'll never be able to hold your job.

KROGSTAD: I asked if it was just domestic unpleasantness you were afraid of?

NORA: If my husband finds out, then of course he'll pay what I owe at once, and then we'd be through with you for good.

KROGSTAD (*a step closer*): Listen, Mrs. Helmer — you've either got a very bad memory, or else no head at all for business. I'd better put you a little more in touch with the facts.

NORA: What do you mean?

KROGSTAD: When your husband was sick, you came to me for a loan of four thousand, eight hundred crowns.

NORA: Where else could I go?

KROGSTAD: I promised to get you that sum —

NORA: And you got it.

KROGSTAD: I promised to get you that sum, on certain conditions. You were so involved in your husband's illness, and so eager to finance your trip, that I guess you didn't think out all the details. It might just be a good idea to remind you. I promised you the money on the strength of a note I drew up.

NORA: Yes, and that I signed.

KROGSTAD: Right. But at the bottom I added some lines for your father to guarantee the loan. He was supposed to sign down there.

NORA: Supposed to? He did sign.

KROGSTAD: I left the date blank. In other words, your father would have dated his signature himself. Do you remember that?

NORA: Yes, I think —

KROGSTAD: Then I gave you the note for you to mail to your father. Isn't that so?

NORA: Yes.

KROGSTAD: And naturally you sent it at once — because only some five, six days later you brought me the note, properly signed. And with that, the money was yours.

NORA: Well, then; I've made my payments regularly, haven't I?

KROGSTAD: More or less. But — getting back to the point — those were hard times for you then, Mrs. Helmer.

NORA: Yes, they were.

KROGSTAD: Your father was very ill, I believe.

NORA: He was near the end.

KROGSTAD: He died soon after?

NORA: Yes.

KROGSTAD: Tell me, Mrs. Helmer, do you happen to recall the date of your father's death? The day of the month, I mean.

NORA: Papa died the twenty-ninth of September.

KROGSTAD: That's quite correct; I've already looked into that. And now we come to a curious thing — (*taking out a paper*) which I simply cannot comprehend.

NORA: Curious thing? I don't know —

KROGSTAD: This is the curious thing: that your father co-signed the note for your loan three days after his death.

NORA: How — ? I don't understand.

KROGSTAD: Your father died the twenty-ninth of September. But look. Here your father dated his signature October second. Isn't that curious, Mrs. Helmer? (*Nora is silent.*) Can you explain it to me? (*Nora remains silent.*) It's also remarkable that the words "October second" and the year aren't written in your father's hand, but rather in one that I think I know. Well, it's easy to understand. Your father forgot perhaps to date his signature, and then someone or other added it, a bit sloppily, before anyone knew of his death. There's nothing wrong in that. It all comes down to the signature. And there's no question about *that*, Mrs. Helmer. It really *was* your father who signed his own name here, wasn't it?

NORA (*after a short silence, throwing her head back and looking squarely at him*): No, it wasn't. *I* signed Papa's name.

KROGSTAD: Wait, now — are you fully aware that this is a dangerous confession?

NORA: Why? You'll soon get your money.

KROGSTAD: Let me ask you a question — why didn't you send the paper to your father?

NORA: That was impossible. Papa was so sick. If I'd asked him for his signature, I also would have had to tell him what the money was for. But I couldn't tell him, sick as he was, that my husband's life was in danger. That was just impossible.

KROGSTAD: Then it would have been better if you'd given up the trip abroad.

NORA: I couldn't possibly. The trip was to save my husband's life. I couldn't give that up.

KROGSTAD: But didn't you ever consider that this was a fraud against me?

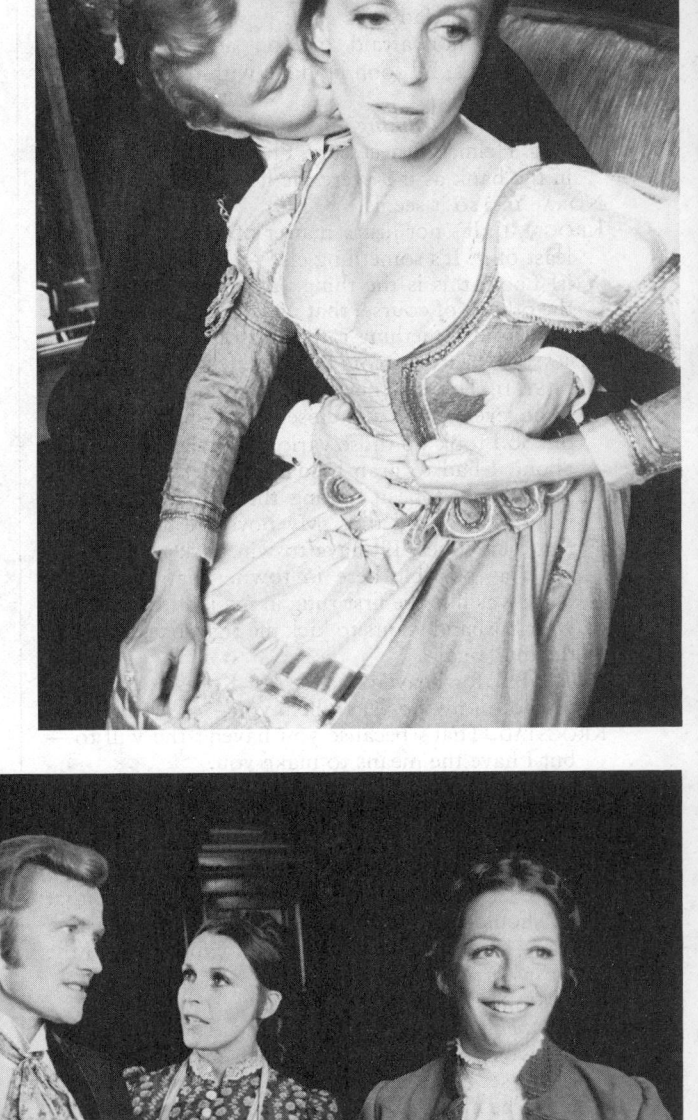

ABOVE: Nora (Claire Bloom) is troubled as Helmer (Donald Madden) kisses her in Patrick Garland's 1971 production.
BELOW: Helmer, Nora, and Mrs. Linde (Patricia Elliott) discuss the possibility of finding a suitable job for Mrs. Linde in the bank.
FAR RIGHT: Krogstad (Robert Gerringer) explains the seriousness of her actions to Nora.

NORA: I couldn't let myself be bothered by that. You weren't any concern of mine. I couldn't stand you, with all those cold complications you made, even though you knew how badly off my husband was.

KROGSTAD: Mrs. Helmer, obviously you haven't the vaguest idea of what you've involved yourself in. But I can tell you this: It was nothing more and nothing worse that I once did — and it wrecked my whole reputation.

NORA: You? Do you expect me to believe that you ever acted bravely to save your wife's life?

KROGSTAD: Laws don't inquire into motives.

NORA: Then they must be very poor laws.

KROGSTAD: Poor or not — if I introduce this paper in court, you'll be judged according to law.

NORA: This I refuse to believe. A daughter hasn't a right to protect her dying father from anxiety and care? A wife hasn't a right to save her husband's life? I don't know much about laws, but I'm sure that somewhere in the books these things are allowed. And you don't know anything about it — you who practice the law? You must be an awful lawyer, Mr. Krogstad.

KROGSTAD: Could be. But business — the kind of business we two are mixed up in — don't you think I know about that? All right. Do what you want now. But I'm telling you *this:* If I get shoved down a second time, you're going to keep me company. (*He bows and goes out through the hall.*)

NORA (*pensive for a moment, then tossing her head*): Oh, really! Trying to frighten me! I'm not so silly as all that. (*Begins gathering up the children's clothes, but soon stops.*) But — ? No, but that's impossible! I did it out of love.

THE CHILDREN (*in the doorway, left*): Mama, that strange man's gone out the door.

NORA: Yes, yes, I know it. But don't tell anyone about the strange man. Do you hear? Not even Papa!

THE CHILDREN: No, Mama. But now will you play again?

NORA: No, not now.

THE CHILDREN: Oh, but Mama, you promised.

NORA: Yes, but I can't now. Go inside; I have too much to do. Go in, go in, my sweet darlings. (*She herds them gently back in the room and shuts the door after them. Settling on the sofa, she takes up a piece of embroidery and makes some stitches, but soon stops abruptly.*) No! (*Throws the work aside, rises, goes to the hall door and calls out.*) Helene! Let me have the tree in here. (*Goes to the table, left, opens the table drawer, and stops again.*) No, but that's utterly impossible!

MAID (*with the Christmas tree*): Where should I put it, ma'am?

NORA: There. The middle of the floor.

MAID: Should I bring anything else?

NORA: No, thanks. I have what I need.

(*The Maid, who has set the tree down, goes out.*)

NORA (*absorbed in trimming the tree*): Candles here — and flowers here. That terrible creature! Talk, talk, talk! There's nothing to it at all. The tree's going to be lovely. I'll do anything to please you Torvald. I'll sing for you, dance for you —

(*Helmer comes in from the hall, with a sheaf of papers under his arm.*)

NORA: Oh! You're back so soon?

HELMER: Yes. Has anyone been here?

NORA: Here? No.

HELMER: That's odd. I saw Krogstad leaving the front door.

NORA: So? Oh yes, that's true. Krogstad was here a moment.

HELMER: Nora, I can see by your face that he's been here, begging you to put in a good word for him.

NORA: Yes.

HELMER: And it was supposed to seem like your own idea? You were to hide it from me that he'd been here. He asked you that, too, didn't he?

NORA: Yes, Torvald, but —

HELMER: Nora, Nora, and you could fall for that? Talk with that sort of person and promise him anything? And then in the bargain, tell me an untruth.

NORA: An untruth — ?

HELMER: Didn't you say that no one had been here? (*Wagging his finger.*) My little songbird must never do that again. A songbird needs a clean beak to warble with. No false notes. (*Putting his arm about her waist.*) That's the way it should be, isn't it? Yes, I'm sure of it. (*Releasing her.*) And so, enough of that. (*Sitting by the stove.*) Ah, how snug and cozy it is here. (*Leafing among his papers.*)

NORA (*busy with the tree, after a short pause*): Torvald!

HELMER: Yes.

NORA: I'm so much looking forward to the Stenborgs' costume party, day after tomorrow.

HELMER: And I can't wait to see what you'll surprise me with.

NORA: Oh, that stupid business!

HELMER: What?

NORA: I can't find anything that's right. Everything seems so ridiculous, so inane.

HELMER: So my little Nora's come to *that* recognition?

NORA (*going behind his chair, her arms resting on its back*): Are you very busy, Torvald?

HELMER: Oh —

NORA: What papers are those?

HELMER: Bank matters.

NORA: Already?

HELMER: I've gotten full authority from the retiring management to make all necessary changes in personnel and procedure. I'll need Christmas week for that. I want to have everything in order by New Year's.

NORA: So that was the reason this poor Krogstad —

HELMER: Hm.

NORA (*still leaning on the chair and slowly stroking the nape of his neck*): If you weren't so very busy, I would have asked you an enormous favor, Torvald.

HELMER: Let's hear. What is it?

NORA: You know, there isn't anyone who has your good taste — and I want so much to look well at the costume party. Torvald, couldn't you take over and decide what I should be and plan my costume?

HELMER: Ah, is my stubborn little creature calling for a lifeguard?

NORA: Yes, Torvald, I can't get anywhere without your help.

HELMER: All right — I'll think it over. We'll hit on something.

NORA: Oh, how sweet of you. (*Goes to the tree again. Pause.*) Aren't the red flowers pretty — ? But tell me, was it really such a crime that this Krogstad committed?

HELMER: Forgery. Do you have any idea what that means?

NORA: Couldn't he have done it out of need?

HELMER: Yes, or thoughtlessness, like so many others. I'm not so heartless that I'd condemn a man categorically for just one mistake.

NORA: No, of course not, Torvald!

HELMER: Plenty of men have redeemed themselves by openly confessing their crimes and taking their punishment.

NORA: Punishment — ?

HELMER: But now Krogstad didn't go that way. He got himself out by sharp practices, and that's the real cause of his moral breakdown.

NORA: Do you really think that would — ?

HELMER: Just imagine how a man with that sort of guilt in him has to lie and cheat and deceive on all sides, has to wear a mask even with the nearest and dearest he has, even with his own wife and children. And with the children, Nora — that's where it's most horrible.

NORA: Why?

HELMER: Because that kind of atmosphere of lies infects the whole life of a home. Every breath the children take in is filled with the germs of something degenerate.

NORA (*coming closer behind him*): Are you sure of that?

HELMER: Oh, I've seen it often enough as a lawyer. Almost everyone who goes bad early in life has a mother who's a chronic liar.

NORA: Why just — the mother?

HELMER: It's usually the mother's influence that's dominant, but the father's works in the same way, of course. Every lawyer is quite familiar with it. And still this Krogstad's been going home year in, year out, poisoning his own children with lies and pretense; that's why I call him morally lost. (*Reaching his hands out toward her.*) So my sweet little Nora must promise me never to plead his cause. Your hand on it. Come, come, what's this? Give me your hand. There, now. All settled. I can tell you it'd be impossible for me to work alongside of him. I literally feel physically revolted when I'm anywhere near such a person.

NORA (*withdraws her hand and goes to the other side of the Christmas tree*): How hot it is here! And I've got so much to do.

HELMER (*getting up and gathering his papers*): Yes, and I have to think about getting some of these read through before dinner. I'll think about your costume, too. And something to hang on the tree in gilt paper, I may even see about that. (*Putting his hand on her head.*) Oh you, my darling little songbird. (*He goes into his study and closes the door after him.*)

NORA (*softly, after a silence*): Oh, really! It isn't so. It's impossible. It must be impossible.

ANNE-MARIE (*in the doorway left*): The children are begging so hard to come in to Mama.

NORA: No, no, no, don't let them in to me! You stay with them, Anne-Marie.

ANNE-MARIE: Of course, ma'am. (*Closes the door.*)

NORA (*pale with terror*): Hurt my children — ! Poison my home? (*A moment's pause; then she tosses her head.*) That's not true. Never. Never in all the world.

ACT II

(*Same room. Beside the piano the Christmas tree now stands stripped of ornament, burned-down candle stubs on its ragged branches. Nora's street clothes lie on the sofa. Nora, alone in the room, moves restlessly about; at last she stops at the sofa and picks up her coat.*)

NORA (*dropping the coat again*): Someone's coming! (*Goes toward the door, listens.*) No — there's no one. Of course — nobody's coming today, Christmas Day — or tomorrow, either. But maybe — (*Opens the door and looks out.*) No, nothing in the mailbox. Quite empty. (*Coming forward.*) What nonsense! He won't do anything serious. Nothing terrible could happen. It's impossible. Why, I have three small children.

(*Anne-Marie, with a large carton, comes in from the room to the left.*)

ANNE-MARIE: Well, at last I found the box with the masquerade clothes.

NORA: Thanks. Put it on the table.

ANNE-MARIE (*does so*): But they're all pretty much of a mess.

NORA: Ahh! I'd love to rip them in a million pieces!

ANNE-MARIE: Oh, mercy, they can be fixed right up. Just a little patience.

NORA: Yes, I'll go get Mrs. Linde to help me.

ANNE-MARIE: Out again now? In this nasty weather? Miss Nora will catch cold — get sick.

NORA: Oh, worse things could happen — How are the children?

ANNE-MARIE: The poor mites are playing with their Christmas presents, but —

NORA: Do they ask for me much?

ANNE-MARIE: They're so used to having Mama around, you know.

NORA: Yes, but Anne-Marie, I *can't* be together with them as much as I was.

ANNE-MARIE: Well, small children get used to anything.

NORA: You think so? Do you think they'd forget their mother if she was gone for good?

ANNE-MARIE: Oh, mercy — gone for good!

NORA: Wait, tell me. Anne-Marie — I've wondered so often — how could you ever have the heart to give your child over to strangers?

ANNE-MARIE: But I had to, you know, to become little Nora's nurse.

NORA: Yes, but how could you *do* it?

ANNE-MARIE: When I could get such a good place? A girl who's poor and who's gotten in trouble is glad enough for that. Because that slippery fish, he didn't do a thing for me, you know.

NORA: But your daughter's surely forgotten you.

ANNE-MARIE: Oh, she certainly has not. She's written to me, both when she was confirmed and when she was married.

NORA (*clasping her about the neck*): You old Anne-Marie, you were a good mother for me when I was little.

ANNE-MARIE: Poor little Nora, with no other mother but me.

NORA: And if the babies didn't have one, then I know that you'd — What silly talk! (*Opening the carton.*) Go in to them. Now I'll have to — Tomorrow you can see how lovely I'll look.

ANNE-MARIE: Oh, there won't be anyone at the party as lovely as Miss Nora. (*She goes off into the room, left.*)

NORA (*begins unpacking the box, but soon throws it aside*): Oh, if I dared to go out. If only nobody would come. If only nothing would happen here while I'm out. What craziness — nobody's coming. Just don't think. This muff — needs a brushing. Beautiful gloves, beautiful gloves. Let it go. Let it go! One, two, three, four, five, six — (*With a cry.*) Oh, there they are! (*Poises to move toward the door, but remains irresolutely standing. Mrs. Linde enters from the hall, where she has removed her street clothes.*)

NORA: Oh, it's you, Kristine. There's no one else out there? How good that you've come.

MRS. LINDE: I hear you were up asking for me.

NORA: Yes, I just stopped by. There's something you really can help me with. Let's get settled on the sofa. Look, there's going to be a costume party tomorrow evening at the Stenborgs' right above us, and now Torvald wants me to go as a Neapolitan peasant girl and dance the tarantella that I learned in Capri.

MRS. LINDE: Really, are you giving a whole performance?

NORA: Torvald says yes, I should. See, here's the dress. Torvald had it made for me down there; but now it's all so tattered that I just don't know —

MRS. LINDE: Oh, we'll fix that up in no time. It's nothing more than the trimmings — they're a bit loose here and there. Needle and thread? Good, now we have what we need.

NORA: Oh, how sweet of you!

MRS. LINDE (*sewing*): So you'll be in disguise tomorrow, Nora. You know what? I'll stop by then for a moment and have a look at you all dressed up. But listen, I've absolutely forgotten to thank you for that pleasant evening yesterday.

NORA (*getting up and walking about*): I don't think it was as pleasant as usual yesterday. You should have come to town a bit sooner, Kristine — Yes, Torvald really knows how to give a home elegance and charm.

MRS. LINDE: And you do, too, if you ask me. You're not your father's daughter for nothing. But tell me, is Dr. Rank always so down in the mouth as yesterday?

NORA: No, that was quite an exception. But he goes around critically ill all the time — tuberculosis of the spine, poor man. You know, his father was a disgusting thing who kept mistresses and so on — and that's why the son's been sickly from birth.

MRS. LINDE (*lets her sewing fall to her lap*): But my dearest Nora, how do you know about such things?

NORA (*walking more jauntily*): Hmp! When you've had three children, then you've had a few visits from — from women who know something of medicine, and they tell you this and that.

MRS. LINDE (*resumes sewing; a short pause*): Does Dr. Rank come here every day?

NORA: Every blessed day. He's Torvald's best friend from childhood, and *my* good friend, too. Dr. Rank almost belongs to this house.

MRS. LINDE: But tell me — is he quite sincere? I mean, doesn't he rather enjoy flattering people?

NORA: Just the opposite. Why do you think that?

MRS. LINDE: When you introduced us yesterday, he was proclaiming that he'd often heard my name in this house; but later I noticed that your husband hadn't the slightest idea who I really was. So how could Dr. Rank — ?

NORA: But it's all true, Kristine. You see, Torvald loves me beyond words, and, as he puts it, he'd like to keep me all to himself. For a long time he'd almost be jealous if I even mentioned any of my old friends back home. So of course I dropped that. But with Dr. Rank I talk a lot about such things because he likes hearing about them.

MRS. LINDE: Now listen, Nora; in many ways you're still like a child. I'm a good deal older than you, with a little more experience. I'll tell you something: You ought to put an end to all this with Dr. Rank.

NORA: What should I put an end to?

MRS. LINDE: Both parts of it, I think. Yesterday you said something about a rich admirer who'd provide you with money —

NORA: Yes, one who doesn't exist — worse luck. So?

MRS. LINDE: Is Dr. Rank well off?

NORA: Yes, he is.

MRS. LINDE: With no dependents?

NORA: No, no one. But —

MRS. LINDE: And he's over here every day?

NORA: Yes, I told you that.

MRS. LINDE: How can a man of such refinement be so grasping?

NORA: I don't follow you at all.

MRS. LINDE: Now don't try to hide it, Nora. You think I can't guess who loaned you the forty-eight hundred crowns?

NORA: Are you out of your mind? How could you think such a thing! A friend of ours, who comes here every single day. What an intolerable situation that would have been!

MRS. LINDE: Then it really wasn't him.

NORA: No, absolutely not. It never even crossed my mind for a moment — And he had nothing to lend in those days; his inheritance came later.

MRS. LINDE: Well, I think that was a stroke of luck for you, Nora dear.

NORA: No, it never would have occurred to me to ask Dr. Rank — Still, I'm quite sure that if I had asked him —

MRS. LINDE: Which you won't, of course.

NORA: No, of course not. I can't see that I'd ever need to. But I'm quite positive that if I talked to Dr. Rank —

MRS. LINDE: Behind your husband's back?

NORA: I've got to clear up this other thing; *that's* also behind his back. I've *got* to clear it all up.

MRS. LINDE: Yes, I was saying that yesterday, but —

NORA (*pacing up and down*): A man handles these problems so much better than a woman —

MRS. LINDE: One's husband does, yes.

NORA: Nonsense. (*Stopping.*) When you pay everything you owe, then you get your note back, right?

MRS. LINDE: Yes, naturally.

NORA: And can rip it into a million pieces and burn it up — that filthy scrap of paper!

MRS. LINDE (*looking hard at her, laying her sewing aside, and rising slowly*): Nora, you're hiding something from me.

NORA: You can see it in my face?

MRS. LINDE: Something's happened to you since yesterday morning. Nora, what is it?

NORA (*hurrying toward her*): Kristine! (*Listening.*) Shh! Torvald's home. Look, go in with the children a while. Torvald can't bear all this snipping and stitching. Let Anne-Marie help you.

MRS. LINDE (*gathering up some of the things*): All right, but I'm not leaving here until we've talked this out. (*She disappears into the room, left, as Torvald enters from the hall.*)

NORA: Oh, how I've been waiting for you, Torvald dear.

HELMER: Was that the dressmaker?

NORA: No, that was Kristine. She's helping me fix up my costume. You know, it's going to be quite attractive.

HELMER: Yes, wasn't that a bright idea I had?

NORA: Brilliant! But then wasn't I good as well to give in to you?

HELMER: Good — because you give in to your husband's judgment? All right, you little goose, I know you didn't mean it like that. But I won't disturb you. You'll want to have a fitting, I suppose.

NORA: And you'll be working?

HELMER: Yes. (*Indicating a bundle of papers.*) See. I've been down to the bank. (*Starts toward his study.*)

NORA: Torvald.

HELMER (*stops*): Yes.

NORA: If your little squirrel begged you, with all her heart and soul, for something — ?

HELMER: What's that?

NORA: Then would you do it?

HELMER: First, naturally, I'd have to know what it was.

NORA: Your squirrel would scamper about and do tricks, if you'd only be sweet and give in.

HELMER: Out with it.

NORA: Your lark would be singing high and low in every room —

HELMER: Come on, she does that anyway.

NORA: I'd be a wood nymph and dance for you in the moonlight.

HELMER: Nora — don't tell me it's that same business from this morning?

NORA (*coming closer*): Yes, Torvald, I beg you, please!

HELMER: And you actually have the nerve to drag that up again?

NORA: Yes, yes, you've got to give in to me; you *have* to let Krogstad keep his job in the bank.

HELMER: My dear Nora, I've slated his job for Mrs. Linde.

NORA: That's awfully kind of you. But you could just fire another clerk instead of Krogstad.

HELMER: This is the most incredible stubbornness! Because you go and give an impulsive promise to speak up for him, I'm expected to —

NORA: That's not the reason, Torvald. It's for your own sake. That man does writing for the worst papers; you said it yourself. He could do you any amount of harm. I'm scared to death of him —

HELMER: Ah, I understand. It's the old memories haunting you.

NORA: What do you mean by that?

HELMER: Of course, you're thinking about your father.

NORA: Yes, all right. Just remember how those nasty gossips wrote in the papers about Papa and slandered him so cruelly. I think they'd have had him dismissed if the department hadn't sent you up to investigate, and if you hadn't been so kind and open-minded toward him.

HELMER: My dear Nora, there's a notable difference between your father and me. Your father's official career was hardly above reproach. But mine is; and I hope it'll stay that way as long as I hold my position.

NORA: Oh, who can ever tell what vicious minds can invent? We could be so snug and happy now in our quiet, carefree home — you and I and the children, Torvald! That's why I'm pleading with you so —

HELMER: And just by pleading for him you make it impossible for me to keep him on. It's already known at the bank that I'm firing Krogstad. What if it's rumored around now that the new bank manager was vetoed by his wife —

NORA: Yes, what then — ?

HELMER: Oh yes — as long as our little bundle of stubbornness gets her way — ! I should go and make myself ridiculous in front of the whole office — give people the idea I can be swayed by all kinds of outside pressure. Oh, you can bet I'd feel the effects of that soon enough! Besides — there's something that rules Krogstad right out at the bank as long as I'm the manager.

NORA: What's that?

HELMER: His moral failings I could maybe overlook if I had to —

NORA: Yes, Torvald, why not?

HELMER: And I hear he's quite efficient on the job. But he was a crony of mine back in my teens — one of those rash friendships that crop up again and again to embarrass you later in life. Well, I might as well say it straight out: We're on a first-name basis. And that tactless fool makes no effort at all to hide it in front of others. Quite the contrary — he thinks that entitles him to take a familiar air around me, and so every other second he comes booming out with his, "Yes, Torvald!" and "Sure thing, Torvald!" I tell you, it's been excruciating for me. He's out to make my place in the bank unbearable.

NORA: Torvald, you can't be serious about all this.

HELMER: Oh no? Why not?

NORA: Because these are such petty considerations.

HELMER: What are you saying? Petty? You think I'm petty!

NORA: No, just the opposite, Torvald dear. That's exactly why —

HELMER: Never mind. You call my motives petty; then I might as well be just that. Petty! All right! We'll put a stop to this for good. (Goes to the hall door and calls.) Helene!

NORA: What do you want?

HELMER (searching among his papers): A decision. (The Maid comes in.) Look here; take this letter; go out with it at once. Get hold of a messenger and have him deliver it. Quick now. It's already addressed. Wait, here's some money.

MAID: Yes, sir. (She leaves with the letter.)

HELMER (straightening his papers): There, now, little Miss Willful.

NORA (breathlessly): Torvald, what was that letter?

HELMER: Krogstad's notice.

NORA: Call it back, Torvald! There's still time. Oh, Torvald, call it back! Do it for my sake — for your sake, for the children's sake! Do you hear, Torvald; do it! You don't know how this can harm us.

HELMER: Too late.

NORA: Yes, too late.

HELMER: Nora, dear, I can forgive you this panic, even though basically you're insulting me. Yes, you are! Or isn't it an insult to think that I should be afraid of a courtroom hack's revenge? But I forgive you anyway, because this shows so beautifully how much you love me. (Takes her in his arms.) This is the way it should be, my darling Nora. Whatever comes, you'll see: When it really counts, I have strength and courage enough as a man to take on the whole weight myself.

NORA (terrified): What do you mean by that?

HELMER: The whole weight, I said.

NORA (resolutely): No, never in all the world.

HELMER: Good. So we'll share it, Nora, as man and wife. That's as it should be. (Fondling her.) Are you happy now? There, there, there — not these frightened dove's eyes. It's nothing at all but empty fantasies — Now you should run through your tarantella and practice your tambourine. I'll go to the inner office, and shut both doors, so I won't hear a thing; you can make all the noise you like. (Turning in the doorway.) And when Rank comes, just tell him where he can find me. (He nods to her and goes with his papers into the study, closing the door.)

NORA (standing as though rooted, dazed with fright, in a whisper): He really could do it. He will do it. He'll do it in spite of everything. No, not that, never, never! Anything but that! Escape! A way out — (The doorbell rings.) Dr. Rank! Anything but that! Anything, whatever it is! (Her hands pass over her face, smoothing it; she pulls herself together, goes over and opens the hall door. Dr. Rank stands outside, hanging his fur coat up. During the following scene, it begins getting dark.)

NORA: Hello, Dr. Rank. I recognized your ring. But you mustn't go in to Torvald yet; I believe he's working.

RANK: And you?

NORA: For you, I always have an hour to spare — you know that. (He has entered, and she shuts the door after him.)

RANK: Many thanks. I'll make use of these hours while I can.

NORA: What do you mean by that? While you can?

RANK: Does that disturb you?

NORA: Well, it's such an odd phrase. Is anything going to happen?

RANK: What's going to happen is what I've been expecting so long — but I honestly didn't think it would come so soon.

NORA (gripping his arm): What is it you've found out? Dr. Rank, you have to tell me!

RANK (sitting by the stove): It's all over with me. There's nothing to be done about it.

NORA (breathing easier): Is it you — then — ?

RANK: Who else? There's no point in lying to one's self. I'm the most miserable of all my patients, Mrs. Helmer. These past few days I've been auditing my internal accounts. Bankrupt! Within a month I'll probably be laid out and rotting in the churchyard.

NORA: Oh, what a horrible thing to say.

RANK: The thing itself is horrible. But the worst of it is all the other horror before it's over. There's only one final examination left; when I'm finished with that, I'll know about when my disintegration will begin. There's something I want to say. Helmer with his sensitivity has such a sharp distaste for anything ugly. I don't want him near my sickroom.

NORA: Oh, but Dr. Rank —

RANK: I won't have him in there. Under no condition. I'll lock my door to him — As soon as I'm completely sure of the worst, I'll send you my calling card marked with a black cross, and you'll know then the wreck has started to come apart.

NORA: No, today you're completely unreasonable. And I wanted you so much to be in a really good humor.

RANK: With death up my sleeve? And then to suffer this way for somebody else's sins. Is there any justice in that? And in every single family, in some way or another, this inevitable retribution of nature goes on —

NORA (*her hands pressed over her ears*): Oh, stuff! Cheer up! Please — be gay!

RANK: Yes, I'd just as soon laugh at it all. My poor, innocent spine, serving time for my father's gay army days.

NORA (*by the table, left*): He was so infatuated with asparagus tips and pâté de foie gras, wasn't that it?

RANK: Yes — and with truffles.

NORA: Truffles, yes. And then with oysters, I suppose?

RANK: Yes, tons of oysters, naturally.

NORA: And then the port and champagne to go with it. It's so sad that all these delectable things have to strike at our bones.

RANK: Especially when they strike at the unhappy bones that never shared in the fun.

NORA: Ah, that's the saddest of all.

RANK (*looks searchingly at her*): Hm.

NORA (*after a moment*): Why did you smile?

RANK: No, it was you who laughed.

NORA: No, it was you who smiled, Dr. Rank!

RANK (*getting up*): You're even a bigger tease than I'd thought.

NORA: I'm full of wild ideas today.

RANK: That's obvious.

NORA (*putting both hands on his shoulders*): Dear, dear Dr. Rank, you'll never die for Torvald and me.

RANK: Oh, that loss you'll easily get over. Those who go away are soon forgotten.

NORA (*looks fearfully at him*): You believe that?

RANK: One makes new connections, and then —

NORA: Who makes new connections?

RANK: Both you and Torvald will when I'm gone. I'd say you're well under way already. What was that Mrs. Linde doing here last evening?

NORA: Oh, come — you can't be jealous of poor Kristine?

RANK: Oh yes, I am. She'll be my successor here in the house. When I'm down under, that woman will probably —

NORA: Shh! Not so loud. She's right in there.

RANK: Today as well. So you see.

NORA: Only to sew on my dress. Good gracious, how unreasonable you are. (*Sitting on the sofa.*) Be nice now, Dr. Rank. Tomorrow you'll see how beautifully I'll dance; and you can imagine then that I'm dancing only for you — yes, and of course for Torvald, too — that's understood. (*Takes various items out of the carton.*) Dr. Rank, sit over here and I'll show you something.

RANK (*sitting*): What's that?

NORA: Look here. Look.

RANK: Silk stockings.

NORA: Flesh-colored. Aren't they lovely? Now it's so dark here, but tomorrow — No, no, no, just look at the feet. Oh well, you might as well look at the rest.

RANK: Hm —

NORA: Why do you look so critical? Don't you believe they'll fit?

RANK: I've never had any chance to form an opinion on that.

NORA (*glancing at him a moment*): Shame on you. (*Hits him lightly on the ear with the stockings.*) That's for you. (*Puts them away again.*)

RANK: And what other splendors am I going to see now?

NORA: Not the least bit more, because you've been naughty. (*She hunts a little and rummages among her things.*)

RANK (*after a short silence*): When I sit here together with you like this, completely easy and open, then I don't know — I simply can't imagine — whatever would have become of me if I'd never come into this house.

NORA (*smiling*): Yes, I really think you feel completely at ease with us.

RANK (*more quietly, staring straight ahead*): And then to have to go away from it all —

NORA: Nonsense, you're not going away.

RANK (*his voice unchanged*): — and not even be able to leave some poor show of gratitude behind, scarcely a fleeting regret — no more than a vacant place that anyone can fill.

NORA: And if I asked you now for — No —

RANK: For what?

NORA: For a great proof of your friendship —

RANK: Yes, yes?

NORA: No, I mean — for an exceptionally big favor —

RANK: Would you really, for once, make me so happy?

NORA: Oh, you haven't the vaguest idea what it is.

RANK: All right, then tell me.

NORA: No, but I can't, Dr. Rank — it's all out of reason. It's advice and help, too — and a favor —

RIGHT: Cheryl Campbell as
Nora in the 1981–1982 Royal
Shakespeare Company
production of *A Doll House*.
FAR RIGHT: Nora and Torvald
(Stephen Moore).

RANK: So much the better. I can't fathom what you're
hinting at. Just speak out. Don't you trust me?

NORA: Of course. More than anyone else. You're my
best and truest friend, I'm sure. That's why I want
to talk to you. All right, then, Dr. Rank: There's
something you can help me prevent. You know
how deeply, how inexpressibly dearly Torvald
loves me; he'd never hesitate a second to give up
his life for me.

RANK (*leaning close to her*): Nora — do you think
he's the only one —

NORA (*with a slight start*): Who — ?

RANK: Who'd gladly give up his life for you.

NORA (*heavily*): I see.

RANK: I swore to myself you should know this before
I'm gone. I'll never find a better chance. Yes, Nora,
now you know. And also you know now that you
can trust me beyond anyone else.

NORA (*rising, natural and calm*): Let me by.

RANK (*making room for her, but still sitting*): Nora —

NORA (*in the hall doorway*): Helene, bring the lamp
in. (*Goes over to the stove.*) Ah, dear Dr. Rank,
that was really mean of you.

RANK (*getting up*): That I've loved you just as deeply
as somebody else? Was *that* mean?

NORA: No, but that you came out and told me. That
was quite unnecessary —

RANK: What do you mean? Have you known — ?

(*The Maid comes in with the lamp, sets it on the
table, and goes out again.*)

RANK: Nora — Mrs. Helmer — I'm asking you: Have
you known about it?

NORA: Oh, how can I tell what I know or don't
know? Really, I don't know what to say — Why
did you have to be so clumsy, Dr. Rank! Everything was so good.

RANK: Well, in any case, you now have the knowledge
that my body and soul are at your command. So
won't you speak out?

NORA (*looking at him*): After that?

RANK: Please, just let me know what it is.

NORA: You can't know anything now.

RANK: I have to. You mustn't punish me like this.
Give me the chance to do whatever is humanly
possible for you.

NORA: Now there's nothing you can do for me. Besides, actually. I don't need any help. You'll see — it's only my fantasies. That's what it is. Of course! (*Sits in the rocker, looks at him, and smiles.*) What a nice one you are, Dr. Rank. Aren't you a little bit ashamed, now that the lamp is here?

RANK: No, not exactly. But perhaps I'd better go — for good?

NORA: No, you certainly can't do that. You must come here just as you always have. You know Torvald can't do without you.

RANK: Yes, but *you*?

NORA: You know how much I enjoy it when you're here.

RANK: That's precisely what threw me off. You're a mystery to me. So many times I've felt you'd almost rather be with me than with Helmer.

NORA: Yes — you see, there are some people that one loves most and other people that one would almost prefer being with.

RANK: Yes, there's something to that.

NORA: When I was back home, of course I loved Papa most. But I always thought it was so much fun when I could sneak down to the maids' quarters, because they never tried to improve me, and it was always so amusing, the way they talked to each other.

RANK: Aha, so it's their place that I've filled.

NORA (*jumping up and going to him*): Oh, dear, sweet Dr. Rank, that's not what I meant at all. But you can understand that with Torvald it's just the same as with Papa —

(*The Maid enters from the hall.*)

MAID: Ma'am — please! (*She whispers to Nora and hands her a calling card.*)

NORA (*glancing at the card*): Ah! (*Slips it into her pocket.*)

RANK: Anything wrong?

NORA: No, no, not at all. It's only some — it's my new dress —

RANK: Really? But — there's your dress.

NORA: Oh, that. But this is another one — I ordered it — Torvald mustn't know —

RANK: Ah, now we have the big secret.

NORA: That's right. Just go in with him — he's back in the inner study. Keep him there as long as —

RANK: Don't worry. He won't get away. (*Goes into the study.*)

NORA (*to the Maid*): And he's standing waiting in the kitchen?

MAID: Yes, he came up by the back stairs.

NORA: But didn't you tell him somebody was here?

MAID: Yes, but that didn't do any good.

NORA: He won't leave?

MAID: No, he won't go till he's talked with you, ma'am.

NORA: Let him come in, then — but quietly. Helene, don't breathe a word about this. It's a surprise for my husband.

MAID: Yes, yes, I understand — (*Goes out.*)

NORA: This horror — it's going to happen. No, no, no, it can't happen, it mustn't. (*She goes and bolts Helmer's door. The Maid opens the hall door for Krogstad and shuts it behind him. He is dressed for travel in a fur coat, boots, and a fur cap.*)

NORA (*going toward him*): Talk softly. My husband's home.

KROGSTAD: Well, good for him.

NORA: What do you want?

KROGSTAD: Some information.

NORA: Hurry up, then. What is it?

KROGSTAD: You know, of course, that I got my notice.

NORA: I couldn't prevent it, Mr. Krogstad. I fought for you to the bitter end, but nothing worked.

KROGSTAD: Does your husband's love for you run so thin? He knows everything I can expose you to, and all the same he dares to —

NORA: How can you imagine he knows anything about this?

KROGSTAD: Ah, no — I can't imagine it either, now. It's not at all like my fine Torvald Helmer to have so much guts —

NORA: Mr. Krogstad, I demand respect for my husband!

KROGSTAD: Why, of course — all due respect. But since the lady's keeping it so carefully hidden, may I presume to ask if you're also a bit better informed than yesterday about what you've actually done?

NORA: More than you ever could teach me.

KROGSTAD: Yes, I *am* such an awful lawyer.

NORA: What is it you want from me?

KROGSTAD: Just a glimpse of how you are, Mrs. Helmer. I've been thinking about you all day long. A cashier, a night-court scribbler, a — well, a type like me also has a little of what they call a heart, you know.

NORA: Then show it. Think of my children.

KROGSTAD: Did you or your husband ever think of mine? But never mind. I simply wanted to tell you that you don't need to take this thing too seriously. For the present, I'm not proceeding with any action.

NORA: Oh no, really! Well — I knew that.

KROGSTAD: Everything can be settled in a friendly spirit. It doesn't have to get around town at all; it can stay just among us three.

NORA: My husband must never know anything of this.

KROGSTAD: How can you manage that? Perhaps you can pay me the balance?

NORA: No, not right now.

KROGSTAD: Or you know some way of raising the money in a day or two?

NORA: No way that I'm willing to use.

KROGSTAD: Well, it wouldn't have done you any good, anyway. If you stood in front of me with a fistful of bills, you still couldn't buy your signature back.

NORA: Then tell me what you're going to do with it.

KROGSTAD: I'll just hold onto it — keep it on file. There's no outsider who'll even get wind of it. So if you've been thinking of taking some desperate step —

NORA: I have.

KROGSTAD: Been thinking of running away from home —

NORA: I have!

KROGSTAD: Or even of something worse —

NORA: How could you guess that?

KROGSTAD: You can drop those thoughts.

NORA: How could you guess I was thinking of *that*?

KROGSTAD: Most of us think about *that* at first. I thought about it too, but I discovered I hadn't the courage —

NORA (*lifelessly*): I don't either.

KROGSTAD (*relieved*): That's true, you haven't the courage? You too?

NORA: I don't have it — I don't have it.

KROGSTAD: It would be terribly stupid, anyway. After that first storm at home blows out, why, then — I have here in my pocket a letter for your husband —

NORA: Telling everything?

KROGSTAD: As charitably as possible.

NORA (*quickly*): He mustn't ever get that letter. Tear it up. I'll find some way to get money.

KROGSTAD: Beg pardon, Mrs. Helmer, but I think I just told you —

NORA: Oh, I don't mean the money I owe you. Let me know how much you want from my husband, and I'll manage it.

KROGSTAD: I don't want any money from your husband.

NORA: What do you want, then?

KROGSTAD: I'll tell you what. I want to recoup, Mrs. Helmer; I want to get on in the world — and there's where your husband can help me. For a year and a half I've kept myself clean of anything disreputable — all that time struggling with the worst conditions; but I was satisfied, working my way up step by step. Now I've been written right off, and I'm just not in the mood to come crawling back. I tell you, I want to move on. I want to get back in the bank — in a better position. Your husband can set up a job for me —

NORA: He'll never do that!

KROGSTAD: He'll do it. I know him. He won't dare breathe a word of protest. And once I'm in there together with him, you just wait and see! Inside of a year, I'll be the manager's right-hand man. It'll be Nils Krogstad, not Torvald Helmer, who runs the bank.

NORA: You'll never see the day!

KROGSTAD: Maybe you think you can —

NORA: I have the courage now — for *that*.

KROGSTAD: Oh, you don't scare me. A smart, spoiled lady like you —

NORA: You'll see; you'll see!

KROGSTAD: Under the ice, maybe? Down in the freezing, coal-black water? There, till you float up in the spring, ugly unrecognizable, with your hair falling out —

NORA: You don't frighten me.

KROGSTAD: Nor do you frighten me. One doesn't do these things, Mrs. Helmer. Besides what good would it be? I'd still have him safe in my pocket.

NORA: Afterwards? When I'm no longer — ?

KROGSTAD: Are you forgetting that *I'll* be in control then over your final reputation? (*Nora stands speechless, staring at him.*) Good; now I've warned you. Don't do anything stupid. When Helmer's read my letter, I'll be waiting for his reply. And bear in mind that it's your husband himself who's forced me back to my old ways. I'll never forgive him for that. Good-bye, Mrs. Helmer. (*He goes out through the hall.*)

NORA (*goes to the hall door, opens it a crack, and listens*): He's gone. Didn't leave the letter. Oh no, no, that's impossible too! (*Opening the door more and more.*) What's that? He's standing outside — not going downstairs. He's thinking it over? Maybe he'll — ? (*A letter falls in the mailbox; then Krogstad's footsteps are heard, dying away down a flight of stairs. Nora gives a muffled cry and runs over toward the sofa table. A short pause.*) In the mailbox. (*Slips warily over to the hall door.*) It's lying there. Torvald, Torvald — now we're lost!

MRS. LINDE (*entering with the costume from the room, left*): There now, I can't see anything else to mend. Perhaps you'd like to try —

NORA (*in a hoarse whisper*): Kristine, come here.

MRS. LINDE (*tossing the dress on the sofa*): What's wrong? You look upset.

NORA: Come here. See that letter? There! Look — through the glass in the mailbox.

MRS. LINDE: Yes, yes, I see it.

NORA: That letter's from Krogstad —

MRS. LINDE: Nora — it's Krogstad who loaned you the money!

NORA: Yes, and now Torvald will find out everything.

MRS. LINDE: Believe me, Nora, it's best for both of you.

NORA: There's more you don't know. I forged a name.

MRS. LINDE: But for heaven's sake —?

NORA: I only want to tell you that, Kristine, so that you can be my witness.

MRS. LINDE: Witness? Why should I — ?

NORA: If I should go out of my mind — it could easily happen —

MRS. LINDE: Nora!

NORA: Or anything else occurred — so I couldn't be present here —

MRS. LINDE: Nora, Nora, you aren't yourself at all!

NORA: And someone should try to take on the whole weight, all of the guilt, you follow me —

MRS. LINDE: Yes, of course, but why do you think — ?

NORA: Then you're the witness that it isn't true, Kristine. I'm very much myself; my mind right now is perfectly clear; and I'm telling you: Nobody else has known about this; I alone did everything. Remember that.

MRS. LINDE: I will. But I don't understand all this.

NORA: Oh, how could you ever understand it? It's the miracle now that's going to take place.

MRS. LINDE: The miracle?

NORA: Yes, the miracle. But it's so awful, Kristine. It mustn't take place, not for anything in the world.

MRS. LINDE: I'm going right over and talk with Krogstad.

NORA: Don't go near him; he'll do you some terrible harm!

MRS. LINDE: There was a time once when he'd gladly have done anything for me.

NORA: He?

MRS. LINDE: Where does he live?

NORA: Oh, how do I know? Yes. (*Searches in her pocket.*) Here's his card. But the letter, the letter — !

HELMER (*from the study, knocking on the door*): Nora!

NORA (*with a cry of fear*): Oh! What is it? What do you want?

HELMER: Now, now, don't be so frightened. We're not coming in. You locked the door — are you trying on the dress?

NORA: Yes, I'm trying it. I'll look just beautiful, Torvald.

MRS. LINDE (*who has read the card*): He's living right around the corner.

NORA: Yes, but what's the use? We're lost. The letter's in the box.

MRS. LINDE: And your husband has the key?

NORA: Yes, always.

MRS. LINDE: Krogstad can ask for his letter back unread; he can find some excuse —

NORA: But it's just this time that Torvald usually —

MRS. LINDE: Stall him. Keep him in there. I'll be back as quick as I can. (*She hurries out through the hall entrance.*)

NORA (*goes to Helmer's door, opens it, and peers in*): Torvald!

HELMER (*from the inner study*): Well — does one dare set foot in one's own living room at last? Come on, Rank, now we'll get a look — (*In the doorway.*) But what's this?

NORA: What, Torvald dear?

HELMER: Rank had me expecting some grand masquerade.

RANK (*in the doorway*): That was my impression, but I must have been wrong.

NORA: No one can admire me in my splendor — not till tomorrow.

HELMER: But Nora dear, you look so exhausted. Have you practiced too hard?

NORA: No, I haven't practiced at all yet.

HELMER: You know, it's necessary —

NORA: Oh, it's absolutely necessary, Torvald. But I can't get anywhere without your help. I've forgotten the whole thing completely.

HELMER: Ah, we'll soon take care of that.

NORA: Yes, take care of me, Torvald, please! Promise me that? Oh, I'm so nervous. That big party — You must give up everything this evening for me. No business — don't even touch your pen. Yes? Dear Torvald, promise?

HELMER: It's a promise. Tonight I'm totally at your service — you little helpless thing. Hm — but first there's one thing I want to — (*Goes toward the hall door.*)

NORA: What are you looking for?

HELMER: Just to see if there's any mail.

NORA: No, no, don't do that, Torvald!

HELMER: Now what?

NORA: Torvald, please. There isn't any.

HELMER: Let me look, though. (*Starts out. Nora, at the piano, strikes the first notes of the tarantella. Helmer, at the door, stops.*) Aha!

NORA: I can't dance tomorrow if I don't practice with you.

HELMER (*going over to her*): Nora dear, are you really so frightened?

NORA: Yes, so terribly frightened. Let me practice right now; there's still time before dinner. Oh, sit down and play for me, Torvald. Direct me. Teach me, the way you always have.

HELMER: Gladly, if it's what you want. (*Sits at the piano.*)

NORA (*snatches the tambourine up from the box, then a long, varicolored shawl, which she throws around herself, whereupon she springs forward and cries out*): Play for me now! Now I'll dance!

(*Helmer plays and Nora dances. Rank stands behind Helmer at the piano and looks on.*)

HELMER (*as he plays*): Slower. Slow down.

NORA: Can't change it.

HELMER: Not so violent, Nora!

NORA: Has to be just like this.

HELMER (*stopping*): No, no, that won't do at all.

NORA (*laughing and swinging her tambourine*): Isn't that what I told you?

RANK: Let me play for her.

HELMER (*getting up*): Yes, go on. I can teach her more easily then.

(*Rank sits at the piano and plays, Nora dances more and more wildly. Helmer has stationed himself by the stove and repeatedly gives her directions; she seems not to hear them; her hair loosens and falls over her shoulders; she does not notice, but goes on dancing. Mrs. Linde enters.*)

MRS. LINDE (*standing dumbfounded at the door*): Ah — !

NORA (*still dancing*): See what fun, Kristine!

HELMER: But Nora darling, you dance as if your life were at stake.

NORA: And it is.

HELMER: Rank, stop! This is pure madness. Stop it, I say!

(*Rank breaks off playing, and Nora halts abruptly*).

HELMER (*going over to her*): I never would have believed it. You've forgotten everything I taught you.

NORA (*throwing away the tambourine*): You see for yourself.

HELMER: Well, there's certainly room for instruction here.

NORA: Yes, you see how important it is. You've got to teach me to the very last minute. Promise me that, Torvald?

HELMER: You can bet on it.

NORA: You mustn't, either today or tomorrow, think about anything else but me; you mustn't open any letters — or the mailbox —

HELMER: Ah, it's still the fear of that man —

NORA: Oh yes, yes, that too.

HELMER: Nora, it's written all over you — there's already a letter from him out there.

NORA: I don't know. I guess so. But you mustn't read such things now; there mustn't be anything ugly between us before it's all over.

RANK (*quietly to Helmer*): You shouldn't deny her.

HELMER (*putting his arm around her*): The child can have her way. But tomorrow night, after you've danced —

NORA: Then you'll be free.

MAID (*in the doorway, right*): Ma'am, dinner is served.

NORA: We'll be wanting champagne, Helene.

MAID: Very good, ma'am. (*Goes out.*)

HELMER: So — a regular banquet, hm?

NORA: Yes, a banquet — champagne till daybreak! (*Calling out.*) And some macaroons, Helene. Heaps of them — just this once.

HELMER (*taking her hands*): Now, now, now — no hysterics. Be my own little lark again.

NORA: Oh, I will soon enough. But go on in — and you, Dr. Rank. Kristine, help me put up my hair.

RANK (*whispering, as they go*): There's nothing wrong — really wrong, is there?

HELMER: Oh, of course not. It's nothing more than this childish anxiety I was telling you about. (*They go out, right.*)

NORA: Well?

MRS. LINDE: Left town.

NORA: I could see by your face.

MRS. LINDE: He'll be home tomorrow evening. I wrote him a note.

NORA: You shouldn't have. Don't try to stop anything now. After all, it's a wonderful joy, this waiting here for the miracle.

MRS. LINDE: What is it you're waiting for?

NORA: Oh, you can't understand that. Go in to them; I'll be along in a moment.

(*Mrs. Linde goes into the dining room. Nora stands a short while as if composing herself; then she looks at her watch.*)

NORA: Five. Seven hours to midnight. Twenty-four hours to the midnight after, and then the tarantella's done. Seven and twenty-four? Thirty-one hours to live.

HELMER (*in the doorway, right*): What's become of the little lark?

NORA (*going toward him with open arms*): Here's your lark!

ACT III

(*Same scene. The table, with chairs around it, has been moved to the center of the room. A lamp on the table is lit. The hall door stands open. Dance music drifts down from the floor above. Mrs. Linde sits at the table, absently paging through a book, trying to read, but apparently unable to focus her thoughts.*)

Once or twice she pauses, tensely listening for a sound at the outer entrance.)

MRS. LINDE (*glancing at her watch*): Not yet — and there's hardly any time left. If only he's not — (*Listening again.*) Ah, there it is. (*She goes out in the hall and cautiously opens the outer door. Quiet footsteps are heard on the stairs. She whispers.*) Come in. Nobody's here.

KROGSTAD (*in the doorway*): I found a note from you at home. What's back of all this?

MRS. LINDE: I just *had* to talk to you.

KROGSTAD: Oh? And it just *had* to be here in this house?

MRS. LINDE: At my place it was impossible; my room hasn't a private entrance. Come in, we're all alone. The maid's asleep, and the Helmers are at the dance upstairs.

KROGSTAD (*entering the room*): Well, well, the Helmers are dancing tonight? Really?

MRS. LINDE: Yes, why not?

KROGSTAD: How true — why not?

MRS. LINDE: All right, Krogstad, let's talk.

KROGSTAD: Do we two have anything more to talk about?

MRS. LINDE: We have a great deal to talk about.

KROGSTAD: I wouldn't have thought so.

MRS. LINDE: No, because you've never understood me, really.

KROGSTAD: Was there anything more to understand — except what's all too common in life? A calculating woman throws over a man the moment a better catch comes by.

MRS. LINDE: You think I'm so thoroughly calculating? You think I broke it off lightly?

KROGSTAD: Didn't you?

MRS. LINDE: Nils — is that what you really thought?

KROGSTAD: If you cared, then why did you write me the way you did?

MRS. LINDE: What else could I do? If I had to break off with you, then it was my job as well to root out everything you felt for me.

KROGSTAD (*wringing his hands*): So that was it. And this — all this, simply for money!

MRS. LINDE: Don't forget I had a helpless mother and two small brothers. We couldn't wait for you, Nils; you had such a long road ahead of you then.

KROGSTAD: That may be; but you still hadn't the right to abandon me for somebody else's sake.

MRS. LINDE: Yes — I don't know. So many, many times I've asked myself if I did have that right.

KROGSTAD (*more softly*): When I lost you, it was as if all the solid ground dissolved from under my feet. Look at me; I'm a half-drowned man now, hanging onto a wreck.

MRS. LINDE: Help may be near.

KROGSTAD: It was near — but then you came and blocked it off.

MRS. LINDE: Without my knowing it, Nils. Today for the first time I learned that it's you I'm replacing at the bank.

KROGSTAD: All right — I believe you. But now that you know, will you step aside?

MRS. LINDE: No, because that wouldn't benefit you in the slightest.

KROGSTAD: Not "benefit" me, hm! I'd step aside anyway.

MRS. LINDE: I've learned to be realistic. Life and hard, bitter necessity have taught me that.

KROGSTAD: And life's taught me never to trust fine phrases.

MRS. LINDE: Then life's taught you a very sound thing. But you do have to trust in actions, don't you?

KROGSTAD: What does that mean?

MRS. LINDE: You said you were hanging on like a half-drowned man to a wreck.

KROGSTAD: I've good reason to say that.

MRS. LINDE: I'm also like a half-drowned woman on a wreck. No one to suffer with; no one to care for.

KROGSTAD: You made your choice.

MRS. LINDE: There wasn't any choice then.

KROGSTAD: So — what of it?

MRS. LINDE: Nils, if only we two shipwrecked people could reach across to each other.

KROGSTAD: What are you saying?

MRS. LINDE: Two on one wreck are at least better off than each on his own.

KROGSTAD: Kristine!

MRS. LINDE: Why do you think I came into town?

KROGSTAD: Did you really have some thought of me?

MRS. LINDE: I have to work to go on living. All my born days, as long as I can remember, I've worked, and it's been my best and my only joy. But now I'm completely alone in the world; it frightens me to be so empty and lost. To work for yourself — there's no joy in that. Nils, give me something — someone to work for.

KROGSTAD: I don't believe all this. It's just some hysterical feminine urge to go out and make a noble sacrifice.

MRS. LINDE: Have you ever found me to be hysterical?

KROGSTAD: Can you honestly mean this? Tell me — do you know everything about my past?

MRS. LINDE: Yes.

KROGSTAD: And you know what they think I'm worth around here.

MRS. LINDE: From what you were saying before, it would seem that with me you could have been another person.

KROGSTAD: I'm positive of that.

MRS. LINDE: Couldn't it happen still?

KROGSTAD: Kristine — you're saying this in all seriousness? Yes, you are! I can see it in you. And do you really have the courage, then — ?

MRS. LINDE: I need to have someone to care for, and your children need a mother. We both need each other. Nils, I have faith that you're good at heart — I'll risk everything together with you.

KROGSTAD (gripping her hands): Kristine, thank you, thank you — Now I know I can win back a place in their eyes. Yes — but I forgot —

MRS. LINDE (listening): Shh! The tarantella. Go now! Go on!

KROGSTAD: Why? What is it?

MRS. LINDE: Hear the dance up there? When that's over, they'll be coming down.

KROGSTAD: Oh, then I'll go. But — it's all pointless. Of course, you don't know the move I made against the Helmers.

MRS. LINDE: Yes, Nils, I know.

KROGSTAD: And all the same, you have the courage to — ?

MRS. LINDE: I know how far despair can drive a man like you.

KROGSTAD: Oh, if I only could take it all back.

MRS. LINDE: You easily could — your letter's still lying in the mailbox.

KROGSTAD: Are you sure of that?

MRS. LINDE: Positive. But —

KROGSTAD (looks at her searchingly): Is that the meaning of it, then? You'll save your friend at any price. Tell me straight out. Is that it?

MRS. LINDE: Nils — anyone who's sold herself for somebody else once isn't going to do it again.

KROGSTAD: I'll demand my letter back.

MRS. LINDE: No, no.

KROGSTAD: Yes, of course. I'll stay here till Helmer comes down; I'll tell him to give me my letter again — that it only involves my dismissal — that he shouldn't read it —

MRS. LINDE: No, Nils, don't call the letter back.

KROGSTAD: But wasn't that exactly why you wrote me to come here?

MRS. LINDE: Yes, in that first panic. But it's been a whole day and night since then, and in that time I've seen such incredible things in this house. Helmer's got to learn everything; this dreadful secret has to be aired; those two have to come to a full understanding; all these lies and evasions can't go on.

KROGSTAD: Well, then, if you want to chance it. But at least there's one thing I can do, and do right away —

MRS. LINDE (listening): Go now, go, quick! The dance is over. We're not safe another second.

KROGSTAD: I'll wait for you downstairs.

MRS. LINDE: Yes, please do; take me home.

KROGSTAD: I can't believe it; I've never been so happy. (*He leaves by way of the outer door; the door between the room and the hall stays open.*)

MRS. LINDE (*straightening up a bit and getting together her street clothes*): How different now! How different! Someone to work for, to live for — a home to build. Well, it is worth the try! Oh, if they'd only come! (*Listening.*) Ah, there they are. Bundle up. (*She picks up her hat and coat. Nora's and Helmer's voices can be heard outside; a key turns in the lock, and Helmer brings Nora into the hall almost by force. She is wearing the Italian costume with a large black shawl about her; he has on evening dress, with a black domino open over it.*)

NORA (*struggling in the doorway*): No, no, no, not inside! I'm going up again. I don't want to leave so soon.

HELMER: But Nora dear —

NORA: Oh, I beg you, please, Torvald. From the bottom of my heart, *please* — only an hour more!

HELMER: Not a single minute, Nora darling. You know our agreement. Come on, in we go; you'll catch cold out here. (*In spite of her resistance, he gently draws her into the room.*)

MRS. LINDE: Good evening.

NORA: Kristine!

HELMER: Why, Mrs. Linde — are you here so late?

MRS. LINDE: Yes, I'm sorry, but I did want to see Nora in costume.

NORA: Have you been sitting here, waiting for me?

MRS. LINDE: Yes. I didn't come early enough; you were all upstairs; and then I thought I really couldn't leave without seeing you.

HELMER (*removing Nora's shawl*): Yes, take a good look. She's worth looking at. I can tell you that, Mrs. Linde. Isn't she lovely?

MRS. LINDE: Yes, I should say —

HELMER: A dream of loveliness, isn't she? That's what everyone thought at the party, too. But she's horribly stubborn — this sweet little thing. What's to be done with her? Can you imagine, I almost had to use force to pry her away.

NORA: Oh, Torvald, you're going to regret you didn't indulge me, even for just a half hour more.

HELMER: There, you see. She danced her tarantella and got a tumultuous hand — which was well earned, although the performance may have been a bit too naturalistic — I mean it rather overstepped the proprieties of art. But never mind — what's important is, she made a success, an overwhelming success. You think I could let her stay on after that and spoil the effect? Oh no; I took my lovely little Capri girl — my capricious little Capri girl, I should say — took her under my arm; one quick tour of the ballroom, a curtsy to every side, and then — as they say in novels — the beautiful vision disappeared. An exit should always be effective, Mrs. Linde, but that's what I can't get Nora to grasp. Phew, It's hot in here. (*Flings the domino on a chair and opens the door to his room.*) Why's it dark in here? Oh yes, of course. Excuse me. (*He goes in and lights a couple of candles.*)

NORA (*in a sharp, breathless whisper*): So?

MRS. LINDE (*quietly*): I talked with him.

NORA: And — ?

MRS. LINDE: Nora — you must tell your husband everything.

NORA (*dully*): I knew it.

MRS. LINDE: You've got nothing to fear from Krogstad, but you have to speak out.

NORA: I won't tell.

MRS. LINDE: Then the letter will.

NORA: Thanks, Kristine. I know now what's to be done. Shh!

HELMER (*reentering*): Well, then, Mrs. Linde — have you admired her?

MRS. LINDE: Yes, and now I'll say good night.

HELMER: Oh, come, so soon? Is this yours, this knitting?

MRS. LINDE: Yes, thanks. I nearly forgot it.

HELMER: Do you knit, then?

MRS. LINDE: Oh yes.

HELMER: You know what? You should embroider instead.

MRS. LINDE: Really? Why?

HELMER: Yes, because it's a lot prettier. See here, one holds the embroidery so, in the left hand, and then one guides the needle with the right — so — in an easy, sweeping curve — right?

MRS. LINDE: Yes, I guess that's —

HELMER: But, on the other hand, knitting — it can never be anything but ugly. Look, see here, the arms tucked in, the knitting needles going up and down — there's something Chinese about it. Ah, that was really a glorious champagne they served.

MRS. LINDE: Yes, good night, Nora, and don't be stubborn anymore.

HELMER: Well put, Mrs. Linde!

MRS. LINDE: Good night, Mr. Helmer.

HELMER (*accompanying her to the door*): Good night, good night. I hope you get home all right. I'd be very happy to — but you don't have far to go. Good night, good night. (*She leaves. He shuts the door after her and returns.*) There, now, at last we got her out the door. She's a deadly bore, that creature.

NORA: Aren't you pretty tired, Torvald?

HELMER: No, not a bit.

NORA: You're not sleepy?

HELMER: Not at all. On the contrary, I'm feeling quite exhilarated. But you? Yes, you really look tired and sleepy.

NORA: Yes, I'm very tired. Soon now I'll sleep.

HELMER: See! You see! I was right all along that we shouldn't stay longer.

NORA: Whatever you do is always right.

HELMER (*kissing her brow*): Now my little lark talks sense. Say, did you notice what a time Rank was having tonight?

NORA: Oh, was he? I didn't get to speak with him.

HELMER: I scarcely did either, but it's a long time since I've seen him in such high spirits. (*Gazes at her a moment, then comes nearer her.*) Hm — it's marvelous, though, to be back home again — to be completely alone with you. Oh, you bewitchingly lovely young woman!

NORA: Torvald, don't look at me like that!

HELMER: Can't I look at my richest treasure? At all that beauty that's mine, mine alone — completely and utterly.

NORA (*moving around to the other side of the table*): You mustn't talk to me that way tonight.

HELMER (*following her*): The tarantella is still in your blood. I can see — and it makes you even more enticing. Listen. The guests are beginning to go. (*Dropping his voice.*) Nora — it'll soon be quiet through this whole house.

NORA: Yes, I hope so.

HELMER: You do, don't you, my love? Do you realize — when I'm out at a party like this with you — do you know why I talk to you so little, and keep such a distance away; just send you a stolen look now and then — you know why I do it? It's because I'm imagining then that you're my secret darling, my secret young bride-to-be, and that no one suspects there's anything between us.

NORA: Yes, yes; oh, yes, I know you're always thinking of me.

HELMER: And then when we leave and I place the shawl over those fine young rounded shoulders — over that wonderful curving neck — then I pretend that you're my young bride, that we're just coming from the wedding, that for the first time I'm bringing you into my house — that for the first time I'm alone with you — completely alone with you, your trembling young beauty! All this evening I've longed for nothing but you. When I saw you turn and sway in the tarantella — my blood was pounding till I couldn't stand it — that's why I brought you down here so early —

NORA: Go away, Torvald! Leave me alone. I don't want all this.

HELMER: What do you mean? Nora, you're teasing me. You will, won't you? Aren't I your husband — ?

(*A knock at the outside door.*)

NORA (*startled*): What's that?

HELMER (*going toward the hall*): Who is it?

RANK (*outside*): It's me. May I come in a moment?

HELMER (*with quiet irritation*): Oh, what does he want now? (*Aloud.*) Hold on. (*Goes and opens the door.*) Oh, how nice that you didn't just pass us by!

RANK: I thought I heard your voice, and then I wanted so badly to have a look in. (*Lightly glancing about.*) Ah, me, these old familiar haunts. You have it snug and cozy in here, you two.

HELMER: You seemed to be having it pretty cozy upstairs, too.

RANK: Absolutely. Why shouldn't I? Why not take in everything in life? As much as you can, anyway, and as long as you can. The wine was superb —

HELMER: The champagne especially.

RANK: You noticed that too? It's amazing how much I could guzzle down.

NORA: Torvald also drank a lot of champagne this evening.

RANK: Oh?

NORA: Yes, and that always makes him so entertaining.

RANK: Well, why shouldn't one have a pleasant evening after a well-spent day?

HELMER: Well spent? I'm afraid I can't claim that.

RANK (*slapping him on the back*): But I can, you see!

NORA: Dr. Rank, you must have done some scientific research today.

RANK: Quite so.

HELMER: Come now — little Nora talking about scientific research!

NORA: And can I congratulate you on the results?

RANK: Indeed you may.

NORA: Then they were good?

RANK: The best possible for both doctor and patient — certainty.

NORA (*quickly and searchingly*): Certainty?

RANK: Complete certainty. So don't I owe myself a gay evening afterwards?

NORA: Yes, you're right, Dr. Rank.

HELMER: I'm with you — just so long as you don't have to suffer for it in the morning.

RANK: Well, one never gets something for nothing in life.

NORA: Dr. Rank — are you very fond of masquerade parties?

RANK: Yes, if there's a good array of odd disguises —

NORA: Tell me, what should we two go as at the next masquerade?

HELMER: You little featherhead — already thinking of the next!

RANK: We two? I'll tell you what: You must go as Charmed Life —

HELMER: Yes, but find a costume for that!

RANK: Your wife can appear just as she looks every day.

HELMER: That was nicely put. But don't you know what you're going to be?

RANK: Yes, Helmer, I've made up my mind.

HELMER: Well?

RANK: At the next masquerade I'm going to be invisible.

HELMER: That's a funny idea.

RANK: They say there's a hat — black, huge — have you never heard of the hat that makes you invisible? You put it on, and then no one on earth can see you.

HELMER (*suppressing a smile*): Ah, of course.

RANK: But I'm quite forgetting what I came for. Helmer, give me a cigar, one of the dark Havanas.

HELMER: With the greatest pleasure. (*Holds out his case.*)

RANK: Thanks. (*Takes one and cuts off the tip.*)

NORA (*striking a match*): Let me give you a light.

RANK: Thank you. (*She holds the match for him; he lights the cigar.*) And now good-bye.

HELMER: Good-bye, good-bye, old friend.

NORA: Sleep well, Doctor.

RANK: Thanks for that wish.

NORA: Wish me the same.

RANK: You? All right, if you like — Sleep well. And thanks for the light. (*He nods to them both and leaves.*)

HELMER (*his voice subdued*): He's been drinking heavily.

NORA (*absently*): Could be. (*Helmer takes his keys from his pocket and goes out in the hall.*) Torvald — what are you after?

HELMER: Got to empty the mailbox; it's nearly full. There won't be room for the morning papers.

NORA: Are you working tonight?

HELMER: You know I'm not. Why — what's this? Someone's been at the lock.

NORA: At the lock — ?

HELMER: Yes, I'm positive. What do you suppose — ? I can't imagine one of the maids — ? Here's a broken hairpin. Nora, it's yours —

NORA (*quickly*): Then it must be the children —

HELMER: You'd better break them of that. Hm, hm — well, opened it after all. (*Takes the contents out and calls into the kitchen.*) Helene! Helene, would you put out the lamp in the hall. (*He returns to the room, shutting the hall door, then displays the handful of mail.*) Look how it's piled up. (*Sorting through them.*) Now what's this?

NORA (*at the window*): The letter! Oh, Torvald, no!

HELMER: Two calling cards — from Rank.

NORA: From Dr. Rank?

HELMER (*examining them*): "Dr. Rank, Consulting Physician." They were on top. He must have dropped them in as he left.

NORA: Is there anything on them?

HELMER: There's a black cross over the name. See? That's a gruesome notion. He could almost be announcing his own death.

NORA: That's just what he's doing.

HELMER: What! You've heard something? Something he's told you?

NORA: Yes. That when those cards came, he'd be taking his leave of us. He'll shut himself in now and die.

HELMER: Ah, my poor friend! Of course I knew he wouldn't be here much longer. But so soon — And then to hide himself away like a wounded animal.

NORA: If it has to happen, then it's best it happens in silence — don't you think so, Torvald?

HELMER (*pacing up and down*): He's grown right into our lives. I simply can't imagine him gone. He with his suffering and loneliness — like a dark cloud setting off our sunlit happiness. Well, maybe it's best this way. For him, at least. (*Standing still.*) And maybe for us too, Nora. Now we're thrown back on each other, completely. (*Embracing her.*) Oh you, my darling wife, how can I hold you close enough? You know what, Nora — time and again I've wished you were in some terrible danger, just so I could stake my life and soul and everything, for your sake.

NORA (*tearing herself away, her voice firm and decisive*): Now you must read your mail, Torvald.

HELMER: No, no, not tonight. I want to stay with you, dearest

NORA: With a dying friend on your mind?

HELMER: You're right. We've both had a shock. There's ugliness between us — these thoughts of death and corruption. We'll have to get free of them first. Until then — we'll stay apart.

NORA (*clinging about his neck*): Torvald — good night! Good night!

HELMER (*kissing her on the cheek*): Good night, little songbird. Sleep well, Nora. I'll be reading my mail now. (*He takes the letters into his room and shuts the door after him.*)

NORA (*with bewildered glances, groping about, seizing Helmer's domino, throwing it around her, and speaking in short, hoarse, broken whispers*): Never see him again. Never, never. (*Putting her shawl over her head.*) Never see the children either — them, too. Never, never. Oh, the freezing black water! The depths — down — Oh, I wish it were over — He has it now; he's reading it — now. Oh no, no, not yet. Torvald, good-bye, you and the children — (*She starts for the hall; as she does, Helmer throws open his door and stands with an open letter in his hand.*)

HELMER: Nora!

NORA (*screams*): Oh — !

HELMER: What is this? You know what's in this letter?

NORA: Yes, I know. Let me go! Let me out!

HELMER (*holding her back*): Where are you going?

NORA (*struggling to break loose*): You can't save me, Torvald!

HELMER (*slumping back*): True! Then it's true what he writes? How horrible! No, no, it's impossible — it can't be true.

NORA: It *is* true. I've loved you more than all this world.

HELMER: Ah, none of your slippery tricks.

NORA (*taking one step toward him*): Torvald — !

HELMER: What *is* this you've blundered into!

NORA: Just let me loose. You're not going to suffer for my sake. You're not going to take on my guilt.

HELMER: No more playacting. (*Locks the hall door.*) You stay right here and give me a reckoning. You understand what you've done? Answer! You understand?

NORA (*looking squarely at him, her face hardening*): Yes. I'm beginning to understand everything now.

HELMER (*striding about*): Oh, what an awful awakening! In all these eight years — she who was my pride and joy — a hypocrite, a liar — worse, worse — a criminal! How infinitely disgusting it all is! The shame! (*Nora says nothing and goes on looking straight at him. He stops in front of her.*) I should have suspected something of the kind. I should have known. All your father's flimsy values — Be still! All your father's flimsy values have come out in you. No religion, no morals, no sense of duty — Oh, how I'm punished for letting him off! I did it for your sake, and you repay me like this.

NORA: Yes, like this.

HELMER: Now you've wrecked all my happiness — ruined my whole future. Oh, it's awful to think of. I'm in a cheap little grafter's hands; he can do anything he wants with me, ask for anything, play with me like a puppet — and I can't breathe a word. I'll be swept down miserably into the depths on account of a featherbrained woman.

NORA: When I'm gone from this world, you'll be free.

HELMER: Oh, quit posing. Your father had a mess of those speeches too. What good would that ever do me if you were gone from this world, as you say? Not the slightest. He can still make the whole thing known; and if he does, I could be falsely suspected as your accomplice. They might even think that I was behind it — that I put you up to it. And all that I can thank you for — you that I've coddled the whole of our marriage. Can you see now what you've done to me?

NORA (*icily calm*): Yes.

HELMER: It's so incredible, I just can't grasp it. But we'll have to patch up whatever we can. Take off the shawl. I said, take it off! I've got to appease him somehow or other. The thing has to be hushed up at any cost. And as for you and me, it's got to seem like everything between us is just as it was — to the

outside world, that is. You'll go right on living in this house, of course. But you can't be allowed to bring up the children; I don't dare trust you with them — Oh, to have to say this to someone I've loved so much! Well, that's done with. From now on happiness doesn't matter; all that matters is saving the bits and pieces, the appearance — (*The doorbell rings. Helmer starts.*) What's that? And so late. Maybe the worst — ? You think he'd — ? Hide, Nora! Say you're sick. (*Nora remains standing motionless. Helmer goes and opens the door.*)

MAID (*half dressed, in the hall*): A letter for Mrs. Helmer.

HELMER: I'll take it. (*Snatches the letter and shuts the door.*) Yes, it's from him. You don't get it; I'm reading it myself.

NORA: Then read it.

HELMER (*by the lamp*): I hardly dare. We may be ruined, you and I. But — I've got to know. (*Rips open the letter, skims through a few lines, glances at an enclosure, then cries out joyfully.*) Nora! (*Nora looks inquiringly at him.*) Nora! Wait — better check it again — Yes, yes, it's true. I'm saved. Nora, I'm saved!

NORA: And I?

HELMER: You too, of course. We're both saved, both of us. Look. He's sent back your note. He says he's sorry and ashamed — that a happy development in his life — oh, who cares what he says! Nora, we're saved! No one can hurt you. Oh, Nora, Nora — but first, this ugliness all has to go. Let me see — (*Takes a look at the note.*) No, I don't want to see it; I want the whole thing to fade like a dream. (*Tears the note and both letters to pieces, throws them into the stove and watches them burn.*) There — now there's nothing left — He wrote that since Christmas Eve you — Oh, they must have been three terrible days for you, Nora.

NORA: I fought a hard fight.

HELMER: And suffered pain and saw no escape but — No, we're not going to dwell on anything unpleasant. We'll just be grateful and keep on repeating: It's over now, it's over! You hear me, Nora? You don't seem to realize — it's over. What's it mean — that frozen look? Oh, poor little Nora, I understand. You can't believe I've forgiven you. But I have, Nora; I swear I have. I know that what you did, you did out of love for me.

NORA: That's true.

HELMER: You loved me the way a wife ought to love her husband. It's simply the means that you couldn't judge. But you think I love you any the less for not knowing how to handle your affairs? No, no — just lean on me; I'll guide you and teach you. I wouldn't be a man if this feminine helplessness didn't make you twice as attractive to me.

You mustn't mind those sharp words I said — that was all in the first confusion of thinking my world had collapsed. I've forgiven you, Nora; I swear I've forgiven you.

NORA: My thanks for your forgiveness. (*She goes out through the door, right.*)

HELMER: No, wait — (*Peers in.*) What are you doing in there?

NORA (*inside*): Getting out of my costume.

HELMER (*by the open door*): Yes, do that. Try to calm yourself and collect your thoughts again, my frightened little songbird. You can rest easy now; I've got wide wings to shelter you with. (*Walking about close by the door.*) How snug and nice our home is, Nora. You're safe here; I'll keep you like a hunted dove I've rescued out of a hawk's claws. I'll bring peace to your poor, shuddering heart. Gradually it'll happen, Nora; you'll see. Tomorrow all this will look different to you; then everything will be as it was. I won't have to go on repeating I forgive you; you'll feel it for yourself. How can you imagine I'd ever conceivably want to disown you — or even blame you in any way? Ah, you don't know a man's heart, Nora. For a man there's something indescribably sweet and satisfying in knowing he's forgiven his wife — and forgiven her out of a full and open heart. It's as if she belongs to him in two ways now: In a sense he's given her fresh into the world again, and she's become his wife and his child as well. From now on that's what you'll be to me — you little, bewildered, helpless thing. Don't be afraid of anything, Nora; just open your heart to me, and I'll be conscience and will to you both — (*Nora enters in her regular clothes.*) What's this? Not in bed? You've changed your dress?

NORA: Yes, Torvald, I've changed my dress.

HELMER: But why now, so late?

NORA: Tonight I'm not sleeping.

HELMER: But Nora dear —

NORA (*looking at her watch*): It's still not so very late. Sit down, Torvald; we have a lot to talk over. (*She sits at one side of the table.*)

HELMER: Nora — what is this? That hard expression —

NORA: Sit down. This'll take some time. I have a lot to say.

HELMER (*sitting at the table directly opposite her*): You worry me, Nora. And I don't understand you.

NORA: No, that's exactly it. You don't understand me. And I've never understood you either — until tonight. No, don't interrupt. You can just listen to what I say. We're closing out accounts, Torvald.

HELMER: How do you mean that?

NORA (*after a short pause*): Doesn't anything strike you about our sitting here like this?

HELMER: What's that?

NORA: We've been married now eight years. Doesn't it occur to you that this is the first time we two, you and I, man and wife, have ever talked seriously together?

HELMER: What do you mean — seriously?

NORA: In eight whole years — longer even — right from our first acquaintance, we've never exchanged a serious word on any serious thing.

HELMER: You mean I should constantly go and involve you in problems you couldn't possibly help me with?

NORA: I'm not talking of problems. I'm saying that we've never sat down seriously together and tried to get to the bottom of anything.

HELMER: But dearest, what good would that ever do you?

NORA: That's the point right there: You've never understood me. I've been wronged greatly, Torvald — first by Papa, and then by you.

HELMER: What! By us — the two people who've loved you more than anyone else?

NORA (*shaking her head*): You never loved me. You've thought it fun to be in love with me, that's all.

HELMER: Nora, what a thing to say!

NORA: Yes, it's true now, Torvald. When I lived at home with Papa, he told me all his opinions, so I had the same ones too; or if they were different I hid them, since he wouldn't have cared for that. He used to call me his doll-child, and he played with me the way I played with my dolls. Then I came into your house —

HELMER: How can you speak of our marriage like that?

NORA (*unperturbed*): I mean, then I went from Papa's hands into yours. You arranged everything to your own taste, and so I got the same taste as you — or I pretended to; I can't remember. I guess a little of both, first one, then the other. Now when I look back, it seems as if I'd lived here like a beggar — just from hand to mouth. I've lived by doing tricks for you, Torvald. But that's the way you wanted it. It's a great sin what you and Papa did to me. You're to blame that nothing's become of me.

HELMER: Nora, how unfair and ungrateful you are! Haven't you been happy here?

NORA: No, never. I thought so — but I never have.

HELMER: Not — not happy!

NORA: No, only lighthearted. And you've always been so kind to me. But our home's been nothing but a playpen. I've been your doll-wife here, just as at home I was Papa's doll-child. And in turn the children have been my dolls. I thought it was fun when you played with me, just as they thought it fun when I played with them. That's been our marriage, Torvald.

HELMER: There's some truth in what you're saying —

under all the raving exaggeration. But it'll all be different after this. Playtime's over; now for the schooling.

NORA: Whose schooling — mine or the children's?

HELMER: Both yours and the children's, dearest.

NORA: Oh, Torvald, you're not the man to teach me to be a good wife to you.

HELMER: And you can say that?

NORA: And I — how am I equipped to bring up children?

HELMER: Nora!

NORA: Didn't you say a moment ago that that was no job to trust me with?

HELMER: In a flare of temper! Why fasten on that?

NORA: Yes, but you were so very right. I'm not up to the job. There's another job I have to do first. I have to try to educate myself. You can't help me with that. I've got to do it alone. And that's why I'm leaving you now.

HELMER (*jumping up*): What's that?

NORA: I have to stand completely alone, if I'm ever going to discover myself and the world out there. So I can't go on living with you.

HELMER: Nora, Nora!

NORA: I want to leave right away. Kristine should put me up for the night —

HELMER: You're insane! You've no right! I forbid you!

NORA: From here on, there's no use forbidding me anything. I'll take with me whatever is mine. I don't want a thing from you, either now or later.

HELMER: What kind of madness is this!

NORA: Tomorrow I'm going home — I mean, home where I came from. It'll be easier up there to find something to do.

HELMER: Oh, you blind, incompetent child!

NORA: I must learn to be competent, Torvald.

HELMER: Abandon your home, your husband, your children! And you're not even thinking what people will say.

NORA: I can't be concerned about that. I only know how essential this is.

HELMER: Oh, it's outrageous. So you'll run out like this on your most sacred vows.

NORA: What do you think are my most sacred vows?

HELMER: And I have to tell you that! Aren't they your duties to your husband and children?

NORA: I have other duties equally sacred.

HELMER: That isn't true. What duties are they?

NORA: Duties to myself.

HELMER: Before all else, you're a wife and a mother.

NORA: I don't believe in that anymore. I believe that before all else, I'm a human being, no less than you — or anyway, I ought to try to become one. I know the majority thinks you're right, Torvald, and plenty of books agree with you, too. But I can't go on believing what the majority says, or what's written in books. I have to think over these things myself and try to understand them.

HELMER: Why can't you understand your place in your own home? On a point like that, isn't there one everlasting guide you can turn to? Where's your religion?

NORA: Oh, Torvald, I'm really not sure what religion is.

HELMER: What — ?

NORA: I only know what the minister said when I was confirmed. He told me religion was this thing and that. When I get clear and away by myself, I'll go into that problem too. I'll see if what the minister said was right, or, in any case, if it's right for me.

HELMER: A young woman your age shouldn't talk like that. If religion can't move you, I can try to rouse your conscience. You do have some moral feeling? Or, tell me — has that gone too?

NORA: It's not easy to answer that, Torvald. I simply don't know. I'm all confused about these things. I just know I see them so differently from you. I find out for one thing, that the law's not at all what I'd thought — but I can't get it through my head that the law is fair. A woman hasn't a right to protect her dying father or save her husband's life! I can't believe that.

HELMER: You talk like a child. You don't know anything of the world you live in.

NORA: No, I don't. But now I'll begin to learn for myself. I'll try to discover who's right, the world or I.

HELMER: Nora, you're sick; you've got a fever. I almost think you're out of your head.

NORA: I've never felt more clearheaded and sure in my life.

HELMER: And — clearheaded and sure — you're leaving your husband and children?

NORA: Yes.

HELMER: Then there's only one possible reason.

NORA: What?

HELMER: You no longer love me.

NORA: No. That's exactly it.

HELMER: Nora! You can't be serious!

NORA: Oh, this is so hard, Torvald — you've been so kind to me always. But I can't help it. I don't love you anymore.

HELMER (*struggling for composure*): Are you also clearheaded and sure about that?

NORA: Yes, completely. That's why I can't go on staying here.

HELMER: Can you tell me what I did to lose your love?

NORA: Yes, I can tell you. It was this evening when the miraculous thing didn't come — then I knew you weren't the man I'd imagined.

HELMER: Be more explicit; I don't follow you.

NORA: I've waited now so patiently eight long years — for, my Lord, I know miracles don't come every day. Then this crisis broke over me, and such a certainty filled me: *Now* the miraculous event would occur. While Krogstad's letter was lying out there, I never for an instant dreamed that you could give in to his terms. I was so utterly sure you'd say to him: Go on, tell your tale to the whole wide world. And when he'd done that —

HELMER: Yes, what then? When I'd delivered my own wife into shame and disgrace — !

NORA: When he'd done that, I was so utterly sure that you'd step forward, take the blame on yourself and say: I am the guilty one.

HELMER: Nora !

NORA: You're thinking I'd never accept such a sacrifice from you? No, of course not. But what good would my protests be against you? That was the miracle I was waiting for, in terror and hope. And to stave that off, I would have taken my life.

HELMER: I'd gladly work for you day and night, Nora — and take on pain and deprivation. But there's no one who gives up honor for love.

NORA: Millions of women have done just that.

HELMER: Oh, you think and talk like a silly child.

NORA: Perhaps. But you neither think nor talk like the man I could join myself to. When your big fright was over — and it wasn't from any threat against me, only for what might damage you — when all the danger was past, for you it was just as if nothing had happened. I was exactly the same, your little lark, your doll, that you'd have to handle with double care now that I'd turned out so brittle and frail. (*Gets up.*) Torvald — in that instant it dawned on me that for eight years I've been living here with a stranger, and that I'd even conceived three children — oh, I can't stand the thought of it! I could tear myself to bits.

HELMER (*heavily*): I see. There's a gulf that's opened between us — that's clear. Oh, but Nora, can't we bridge it somehow?

NORA: The way I am now, I'm no wife for you.

HELMER: I have the strength to make myself over.

NORA: Maybe — if your doll gets taken away.

HELMER: But to part! To part from you! No, Nora, no — I can't imagine it.

NORA (*going out, right*): All the more reason why it has to be. (*She reenters with her coat and a small overnight bag, which she puts on a chair by the table.*)

HELMER: Nora, Nora, not now! Wait till tomorrow.

NORA: I can't spend the night in a strange man's room.

HELMER: But couldn't we live here like brother and sister —

NORA: You know very well how long that would last. (*Throws her shawl about her.*) Good-bye, Torvald. I won't look in on the children. I know they're in better hands than mine. The way I am now, I'm no use to them.

HELMER: But someday, Nora — someday — ?

NORA: How can I tell? I haven't the least idea what'll become of me.

HELMER: But you're my wife, now and wherever you go.

NORA: Listen, Torvald — I've heard that when a wife deserts her husband's house just as I'm doing, then the law frees him from all responsibility. In any case, I'm freeing you from being responsible. Don't feel yourself bound, any more than I will. There has to be absolute freedom for us both. Here, take your ring back. Give me mine.

HELMER: That too?

NORA: That too.

HELMER: There it is.

NORA: Good. Well, now it's all over. I'm putting the keys here. The maids know all about keeping up the house — better than I do. Tomorrow, after I've left town, Kristine will stop by to pack up everything that's mine from home. I'd like those things shipped up to me.

HELMER: Over! All over! Nora, won't you ever think about me?

NORA: I'm sure I'll think of you often, and about the children and the house here.

HELMER: May I write you?

NORA: No — never. You're not to do that.

HELMER: Oh, but let me send you —

NORA: Nothing. Nothing.

HELMER: Or help you if you need it.

NORA: No. I accept nothing from strangers.

HELMER: Nora — can I never be more than a stranger to you?

NORA (*picking up the overnight bag*): Ah, Torvald — it would take the greatest miracle of all —

HELMER: Tell me the greatest miracle!

NORA: You and I both would have to transform ourselves to the point that — Oh, Torvald, I've stopped believing in miracles.

HELMER: But I'll believe. Tell me! Transform ourselves to the point that — ?

NORA: That our living together could be a true marriage. (*She goes out down the hall.*)

HELMER (*sinks down on a chair by the door, face buried in his hands*): Nora! Nora! (*Looking about and rising.*) Empty. She's gone. (*A sudden hope leaps in him.*) The greatest miracle — ?

(*From below, the sound of a door slamming shut.*)

HEDDA GABLER

Hedda Gabler (1890) is today Ibsen's most produced and perhaps his most respected play, but at first it provoked a more uniformly negative response than did any of his other plays. Critics were alarmed at the depressing environment that Ibsen created, and some Scandinavians were especially annoyed by the sense that Ibsen was condemning their entire society. The critics denounced the play "as a base escape of moral sewage gas" and Hedda herself as "acrawl with the foulest passions of humanity."

Hedda Gabler is an intense, powerful woman living in a world totally dominated by men. She is herself dominated by her memory of her father, General Gabler, a man of action whose pistols she now uses to amuse herself. What she enjoys is something of the general's prerogative: the shaping of the destiny of men, especially the manner of their death. Her rejection of anything she deems bourgeois, including sex, which seems to repulse her, drives her to reject the baby she is about to have and to lure Eilert Løvborg to her only to destroy him.

She wants to be an independent woman just as her father was independent and free. She chooses marriage not because she wants to give herself to George Tesman but because she anticipates, on the strength of his expectations of a professorship, a life of comfort and influence. The play opens on Hedda's return from her wedding trip abroad, with the question of whether or not she is pregnant, but Hedda is not interested in children or domesticity. We realize that Hedda and Tesman's marriage is bound for failure, and that Tesman cannot see the truth about her.

Eilert Løvborg, Hedda's friend before she married, is also Tesman's professional rival. Løvborg has the fire and genius needed to be truly distinguished — unlike Tesman, who is most comfortable gathering material for other people's books. But Løvborg is intemperate, doing everything to excess, including drinking. Hedda drives Løvborg to drink after he has been "renovated" by her friend Mrs. Elvsted. This is only one way in which Hedda's cruelty is revealed. She abuses the innocent Aunt Julia and actually burns Løvborg's book because it was created in part by Mrs. Elvsted and is therefore their "baby."

Hedda is a frustrated woman who cannot satisfy herself in the stifling society she hoped to dominate. To ensure that Løvborg commits suicide in an elegant, romantic way, she gives him one of General Gabler's pistols, but her dreams for a romantic shot in the temple are shattered when Judge Brack reveals that Løvborg actually died miserably in a brothel from a pistol that discharged into his "stomach — more or less."

Hedda watches on as Mrs. Elvsted and Tesman team up to rewrite Løvborg's lost book, and when she turns from them she discovers that she has lost all her independence. Judge Brack knows about the pistol, and it is clear that the price of silence is her becoming his mistress.

Hedda's fate has been variously interpreted. Is she a worthwhile character? Is her behavior excusable because she is a woman in a society that will value her not for what she can do but only for who she is? Is her fate determined by the fact that as a woman she cannot live the life she knows she should? Hedda does some frightful things in the play, but how are we to take her? She is clearly larger than anyone else in the play, and certainly more interesting. The men are all weak: Tesman is tied to his aunt's apron strings; Løvborg cannot control himself; and Brack is corrupt. Mrs. Elvsted is a sympathetic character, but her ambition is to be nothing more than a helpmate. None of these fates would satisfy Hedda; her action at the end of the play is almost inevitable.

The sense in which this is a realistic play is qualified by Ibsen's adherence to most of the standards of classical theater. The characters, plot, and setting are established according to the Scribean principles of the well-made play, and the effort to maintain a sense that the play is a "slice of life" seems minimal. The play is structured in four acts, and its rhythms resemble those of a tragedy. There is no attempt to raise issues that are especially shocking to the society or the audiences, as Ibsen had done, for instance, in dealing with syphilis in his play *Ghosts*.

The way we are to interpret Hedda is complicated by some facts that we know about the composition of the play. When Ibsen was writing it, he was himself an unfulfilled husband, with a profoundly repressed sex life. But he was also famous and as a result attracted a great many young women who were interested in him sexually. One of these, Emilie Bardach, age eighteen, fell in love with him, and he with her. They agreed to go off together, but soon Ibsen had second thoughts. He was afraid to take the chance of happiness when it was finally offered.

Ibsen's biographer, Michael Meyer, in a commentary on the play refers to Hedda Gabler as "a merciless self-portrait of Ibsen in skirts." The psychologist Arne Duve has argued that Hedda is a portrait of Ibsen's "repressed and crippled emotional life." Whether this biographical interpretation is fully warranted is difficult to say, but if it is true, then the character of Hedda and our interpretation of the play are intensely complicated.

Hedda Gabler in Performance

In January 1891 *Hedda Gabler* debuted in Munich and that year played elsewhere in Germany, as well as in Scandinavia and England. It was not well received. Feeling Hedda to be evil, the public and the press called the play incoherent and unpleasant. French audiences even jeered the first performances in Paris. The play withstood its unfavorable reception, though, and was eventually a worldwide success. In February 1899 the great theorist of acting, Konstantin Stanislavsky, played the part of Løvborg in the Moscow Arts Theatre's first production of an Ibsen play.

Blanche Bates first played Hedda Gabler in the United States in Philadelphia in 1904, and the reviews read as if they deplored a real woman when they spoke about Hedda's "degeneracy." Its performance in New York in 1918 met with critical attacks and the accusation that it was essentially meaningless. Critical taste changed, however, and by 1948 it was praised because it proved itself resistant to being dated or old-fashioned.

Ingmar Bergman's 1968 Stockholm production moved to England in 1970 with Maggie Smith as an "icily aware" Hedda. Bergman, an eminent filmmaker, divided the stage in two so that characters, especially Hedda, could exit from a scene but linger at a doorway to eavesdrop on the other characters' conversations. One critic said, "At times the drama seems to be taking place in different levels of the mind."

Trevor Nunn's production at the National Theater in Washington, D.C., in 1975 relied on Glenda Jackson as Hedda, but critics complained that she played the part as if it were comedic. No such complaints were raised, however, when Nunn's production was made into a film (1976), which won Jackson a nomination for an Academy Award.

Henrik Ibsen (1828–1906)

HEDDA GABLER   *1890*

TRANSLATED BY ROLF FJELDE

The Characters

GEORGE TESMAN, *research fellow in cultural history*
HEDDA TESMAN, *his wife*
MISS JULIANA TESMAN, *his aunt*
MRS. ELVSTED
JUDGE BRACK
EILERT LØVBORG
BERTA, *the Tesmans' maid*

The action takes place in Tesman's residence in the fashionable part of town.

ACT I

(*A large, attractively furnished drawing room, decorated in dark colors. In the rear wall, a wide doorway with curtains drawn back. The doorway opens into a smaller room in the same style as the drawing room.* In the right wall of the front room, a folding door that leads to the hall. In the left wall opposite, a glass door, with curtains similarly drawn back. Through the panes one can see part of an overhanging veranda and trees in autumn colors. In the foreground is an oval table, with tablecloth and chairs around it. By the right wall, a wide, dark porcelain stove, a high-backed armchair, a cushioned footstool, and two taborets.° In the right-hand corner, a settee with a small round table in front. Nearer, on the left and slightly out from the wall, a piano. On either side of the doorway in back, étagères° with terra cotta and majolica ornaments. Against the back wall of the inner room, a sofa, a table, and a couple of chairs can be seen. Above this sofa hangs a portrait of a handsome, elderly man in a general's uniform. Over the table, a hanging lamp with an opalescent glass shade. A num-*

[S.D.] **taborets**: Stools without back or arms.
[S.D.] *étagères*: Cabinets with shelves.

ber of bouquets of flowers are placed about the drawing room in vases and glasses. Others lie on the tables. The floors in both rooms are covered with thick
carpets. Morning light. The sun shines in through the
glass door.)

(Miss Juliana Tesman, wearing a hat and carrying
a parasol, comes in from the hall, followed by Berta,
who holds a bouquet wrapped in paper. Miss Tesman
is a lady around sixty-five with a kind and good-
natured look, nicely but simply dressed in a gray tailored suit. Berta is a maid somewhat past middle age,
with a plain and rather provincial appearance.)

MISS TESMAN (stops close by the door, listens, and says
softly): Goodness, I don't think they're even up yet!
BERTA (also softly): That's just what I said, Miss Juliana. Remember how late the steamer got in last
night. Yes, and afterward! My gracious, how much
the young bride had to unpack before she could
get to bed.
MISS TESMAN: Well, then — let them enjoy a good
rest. But they must have some of this fresh morning air when they do come down. (She goes to the
glass door and opens it wide.)
BERTA (by the table, perplexed, with the bouquet in
her hand): I swear there isn't a bit of space left. I
think I'll have to put it here, miss. (Places the bouquet on the piano.)
MISS TESMAN: So now you have a new mistress, Berta
dear. Lord knows it was misery for me to give you
up.
BERTA (on the verge of tears): And for me, miss! What
can I say? All those many blessed years I've been in
your service, you and Miss Rina.
MISS TESMAN: We must take it calmly, Berta. There's
really nothing else to do. George needs you here in
this house, you know that. You've looked after
him since he was a little boy.
BERTA: Yes, but miss, I'm all the time thinking of her
lying at home. Poor thing — completely helpless.
And with that new maid! She'll never take proper
care of an invalid, that one.
MISS TESMAN: Oh, I'll manage to teach her. And most
of it, you know, I'll do myself. So you mustn't be
worrying over my poor sister.
BERTA: Well, but there's something else too, miss. I'm
really so afraid I won't please the young mistress.
MISS TESMAN: Oh, well — there might be something
or other at first —
BERTA: Because she's so very particular.
MISS TESMAN: Well of course. General Gabler's
daughter. What a life she had in the general's day!
Remember seeing her out with her father — how
she'd go galloping past in that long black riding
outfit, with a feather in her hat?
BERTA: Oh yes — I remember! But I never would have

dreamed then that she and George Tesman would
make a match of it.
MISS TESMAN: Nor I either. But now, Berta — before I
forget: From now on, you mustn't say George Tesman. You must call him Doctor Tesman.
BERTA: Yes, the young mistress said the same thing —
last night, right after they came in the door. Is that
true then, miss?
MISS TESMAN: Yes, absolutely. Think of it, Berta —
they gave him his doctor's degree. Abroad,
that is — on this trip you know. I hadn't heard
one word about it, till he told me down on the
pier.
BERTA: Well, he's clever enough to be anything. But I
never thought he'd go in for curing people.
MISS TESMAN: No, he wasn't made that kind of doctor. (Nods significantly.) But as a matter of fact,
you may soon now have something still greater to
call him.
BERTA: Oh, really! What's that, miss?
MISS TESMAN (smiling): Hm, wouldn't you like to
know! (Moved.) Ah, dear God — if only my poor
brother could look up from his grave and see what
his little boy has become! (Glancing about.) But
what's this, Berta? Why, you've taken all the slip-
covers off the furniture —?
BERTA: Madam told me to. She doesn't like covers on
chairs, she said.
MISS TESMAN: Are they going to make this their regular living room, then?
BERTA: It seems so — with her. For his part — the
doctor — he said nothing.

(George Tesman enters the inner room from the right,
singing to himself and carrying an empty, unstrapped
suitcase. He is a youngish-looking man of thirty-
three, medium sized, with an open, round, cheerful
face, blond hair and beard. He is somewhat carelessly
dressed in comfortable lounging clothes.)

MISS TESMAN: Good morning, good morning,
George!
TESMAN (in the doorway): Aunt Julie! Dear Aunt
Julie! (Goes over and warmly shakes her hand.)
Way out here — so early in the day — uh?
MISS TESMAN: Yes, you know I simply had to look in
on you a moment.
TESMAN: And that without a decent night's sleep.
MISS TESMAN: Oh, that's nothing at all to me.
TESMAN: Well, then you did get home all right from
the pier? Uh?
MISS TESMAN: Why, of course I did — thank good-
ness. Judge Brack was good enough to see me right
to my door.
TESMAN: We were sorry we couldn't drive you up. But
you saw for yourself — Hedda had all those boxes
to bring along.

MISS TESMAN: Yes, that was quite something, the number of boxes she had.

BERTA (*to Tesman*): Should I go in and ask Mrs. Tesman if there's anything I can help her with?

TESMAN: No, thanks, Berta — don't bother. She said she'd ring if she needed anything.

BERTA (*going off toward the right*): All right.

TESMAN: But wait now — you can take this suitcase with you.

BERTA (*taking it*): I'll put it away in the attic. (*She goes out by the hall door.*)

TESMAN: Just think, Aunt Julie — I had that whole suitcase stuffed full of notes. You just can't imagine all I've managed to find, rummaging through archives. Marvelous old documents that nobody knew existed —

MISS TESMAN: Yes, you've really not wasted any time on your wedding trip, George.

TESMAN: I certainly haven't. But do take your hat off, Auntie. Here — let me help you — uh?

MISS TESMAN (*as he does so*): Goodness — this is exactly as if you were still back at home with us.

TESMAN (*turning the hat in his hand and studying it from all sides*): My — what elegant hats you go in for!

MISS TESMAN: I bought that for Hedda's sake.

TESMAN: For Hedda's sake? Uh?

MISS TESMAN: Yes, so Hedda wouldn't feel ashamed of me if we walked down the street together.

TESMAN (*patting her cheek*): You think of everything, Aunt Julie! (*Laying the hat on a chair by the table.*) So — look, suppose we sit down on the sofa and have a little chat till Hedda comes. (*They settle themselves. She puts her parasol on the corner of the sofa.*)

MISS TESMAN (*takes both of his hands and gazes at him*): How wonderful it is having you here, right before my eyes again, George! You — dear Jochum's own boy!

TESMAN: And for me too, to see you again, Aunt Julie! You, who've been father and mother to me both.

MISS TESMAN: Yes, I'm sure you'll always keep a place in your heart for your old aunts.

TESMAN: But Auntie Rina — hm? Isn't she any better?

MISS TESMAN: Oh no — we can hardly expect that she'll ever be better, poor thing. She lies there, just as she has all these years. May God let me keep her a little while longer! Because otherwise, George, I don't know what I'd do with my life. The more so now, when I don't have you to look after.

TESMAN (*patting her on the back*): There, there, there —

MISS TESMAN (*suddenly changing her tone*): No, but to think of it, that now you're a married man! And that it was *you* who carried off Hedda Gabler. The beautiful Hedda Gabler! Imagine! She, who always had so many admirers!

TESMAN (*hums a little and smiles complacently*): Yes, I rather suspect I have several friends who'd like to trade places with me.

MISS TESMAN: And then to have such a wedding trip! Five — almost six months —

TESMAN: Well, remember, I used it for research, too. All those libraries I had to check — and so many books to read!

MISS TESMAN: Yes, no doubt. (*More confidentially; lowering her voice.*) But now listen, George — isn't there something — something special you have to tell me?

TESMAN: From the trip?

MISS TESMAN: Yes.

TESMAN: No, I can't think of anything beyond what I wrote in my letters. I got my doctor's degree down there — but I told you that yesterday.

MISS TESMAN: Yes, of course. But I mean — whether you have any kind of — expectations —?

TESMAN: Expectations?

MISS TESMAN: My goodness, George — I'm your old aunt!

TESMAN: Why, naturally I have expectations.

MISS TESMAN: Ah!

TESMAN: I have every expectation in the world of becoming a professor shortly.

MISS TESMAN: Oh, a professor, yes —

TESMAN: Or I might as well say, I'm sure of it. But, Aunt Julie — you know that perfectly well yourself.

MISS TESMAN (*with a little laugh*): That's right, so I do. (*Changing the subject.*) But we were talking about your trip. It must have cost a terrible amount of money.

TESMAN: Well, that big fellowship, you know — it took us a good part of the way.

MISS TESMAN: But I don't see how you could stretch it enough for two.

TESMAN: No, that's not so easy to see — uh?

MISS TESMAN: And especially traveling with a lady. For I hear tell that's much more expensive.

TESMAN: Yes, of course — it's a bit more expensive. But Hedda just had to have that trip. She *had* to. There was nothing else to be done.

MISS TESMAN: No, no, I guess not. A honeymoon abroad seems to be the thing nowadays. But tell me — have you had a good look around your house?

TESMAN: You can bet I have! I've been up since daybreak.

MISS TESMAN: And how does it strike you, all in all?

TESMAN: First-rate! Absolutely first-rate! Only I don't know what we'll do with the two empty rooms between the back parlor and Hedda's bedroom.

MISS TESMAN (*laughing again*): Oh, my dear George, I think you can use them — as time goes on.

TESMAN: Yes, you're quite right about that, Aunt Julie! In time, as I build up my library — uh?

MISS TESMAN: Of course, my dear boy. It was your library I meant.

TESMAN: I'm happiest now for Hedda's sake. Before we were engaged, she used to say so many times there was no place she'd rather live than here, in Secretary Falk's town house.

MISS TESMAN: Yes, and then to have it come on the market just after you'd sailed.

TESMAN: We really have had luck, haven't we?

MISS TESMAN: But expensive, George dear! You'll find it expensive, all this here.

TESMAN (*looks at her, somewhat crestfallen*): Yes, I suppose I will.

MISS TESMAN: Oh, Lord, yes!

TESMAN: How much do you think? Approximately? Hm?

MISS TESMAN: It's impossible to say till the bills are all in.

TESMAN: Well, fortunately Judge Brack has gotten me quite easy terms. That's what he wrote Hedda.

MISS TESMAN: Don't worry yourself about that, dear. I've also put up security to cover the carpets and furniture.

TESMAN: Security? Aunt Julie, dear — you? What kind of security could *you* give?

MISS TESMAN: I took out a mortgage on our pension.

TESMAN (*jumping up*): What! On your — and Auntie Rina's pension!

MISS TESMAN: I saw nothing else to do.

TESMAN (*standing in front of her*): But you're out of your mind, Aunt Julie! That pension — it's all Aunt Rina and you have to live on.

MISS TESMAN: Now, now — don't make so much of it. It's only a formality; Judge Brack said so. He was good enough to arrange the whole thing for me. Just a formality, he said.

TESMAN: That's all well enough. But still —

MISS TESMAN: You'll be drawing your own salary now. And good gracious, if we have to lay out a bit, just now at the start — why, it's no more than a pleasure for us.

TESMAN: Oh, Aunt Julie — you never get tired of making sacrifices for me!

MISS TESMAN (*rises and places her hands on his shoulders*): What other joy do I have in this world than smoothing the path for you, my dear boy? You, without father or mother to turn to. And now we've come to the goal, George! Things may have looked black at times; but now, thank heaven, you've made it.

TESMAN: Yes, it's remarkable, really, how everything's turned out for the best.

MISS TESMAN: Yes — and those who stood against you — who wanted to bar your way — they've gone down. They've fallen, George. The one most dangerous to you — he fell farthest. And he's lying there now, in the bed he made — poor, misguided creature.

TESMAN: Have you heard any news of Eilert? I mean, since I went away.

MISS TESMAN: Only that he's supposed to have brought out a new book.

TESMAN: What's that? Eilert Løvborg? Just recently, uh?

MISS TESMAN: So they say. But considering everything, it can hardly amount to much. Ah, but when *your* new book comes out — it'll be a different story, George! What will it be about?

TESMAN: It's going to treat the domestic handicrafts of Brabant in the Middle Ages.

MISS TESMAN: Just imagine — that you can write about things like that!

TESMAN: Actually, the book may take quite a while yet. I have this tremendous collection of material to put in order, you know.

MISS TESMAN: Yes, collecting and ordering — you do that so well. You're not my brother's son for nothing.

TESMAN: I look forward so much to getting started. Especially now, with a comfortable home of my own to work in.

MISS TESMAN: And most of all, dear, now that you've won her, the wife of your heart.

TESMAN (*embracing her*): Yes, yes, Aunt Julie! Hedda — that's the most beautiful part of it all! (*Glancing toward the doorway.*) But I think she's coming — uh?

(*Hedda enters from the left through the inner room. She is a woman of twenty-nine. Her face and figure show breeding and distinction; her complexion is pallid and opaque. Her steel gray eyes express a cool, unruffled calm. Her hair is an attractive medium brown, but not particularly abundant. She wears a tasteful, rather loose-fitting gown.*)

MISS TESMAN (*going to meet Hedda*): Good morning, Hedda dear — how good to see you!

HEDDA (*holding out her hand*): Good morning, my dear Miss Tesman! Calling so early? This *is* kind of you.

MISS TESMAN (*slightly embarrassed*): Well — did the bride sleep well in her new home?

HEDDA: Oh yes, thanks. Quite adequately.

TESMAN: Adequately! Oh, I like that, Hedda! You were sleeping like a stone when I got up.

HEDDA: Fortunately. But of course one has to grow accustomed to anything new, Miss Tesman — little by little. (*Looking toward the left.*) Oh! That maid has left the door open — and the sunlight's just flooding in.

MISS TESMAN (*going toward the door*): Well, we can close it.

HEDDA: No, no — don't! (*To Tesman.*) There, dear, draw the curtains. It gives a softer light.

TESMAN (*by the glass door*): All right — all right. Look, Hedda — now you have shade and fresh air both.

HEDDA: Yes, we really need some fresh air here, with all these piles of flowers — But — won't you sit down, Miss Tesman?

MISS TESMAN: Oh no, thank you. Now that I know that everything's fine — thank goodness — I will have to run along home. My sister's lying there waiting, poor thing.

TESMAN: Give her my very, very best, won't you? And say I'll be looking in on her later today.

MISS TESMAN: Oh, you can be sure I will. But what do you know, George — (*Searching in her bag.*) — I nearly forgot. I have something here for you.

TESMAN: What's that, Aunt Julie? Hm?

MISS TESMAN (*brings out a flat package wrapped in newspaper and hands it to him*): There, dear. Look.

TESMAN (*opening it*): Oh, my — you kept them for me, Aunt Julie! Hedda! That's really touching! Uh!

HEDDA (*by the étagère on the right*): Yes, dear, what is it?

TESMAN: My old bedroom slippers! My slippers!

HEDDA: Oh yes. I remember how often you spoke of them during the trip.

TESMAN: Yes, I missed them terribly. (*Going over to her.*) Now you can see them, Hedda!

HEDDA (*moves toward the stove*): Thanks, but I really don't care to.

TESMAN (*following her*): Imagine — Auntie Rina lay and embroidered them, sick as she was. Oh, you couldn't believe how many memories are bound up in them.

HEDDA (*at the table*): But not for me.

MISS TESMAN: I think Hedda is right, George.

TESMAN: Yes, but I only thought, now that she's part of the family —

HEDDA (*interrupting*): We're never going to manage with this maid, Tesman.

MISS TESMAN: Not manage with Berta?

TESMAN: But dear — why do you say that? Uh?

HEDDA (*pointing*): See there! She's left her old hat lying out on a chair.

TESMAN (*shocked; dropping the slippers*): But Hedda —!

HEDDA: Suppose someone came in and saw it.

TESMAN: Hedda — that's Aunt Julie's hat!

HEDDA: Really?

MISS TESMAN (*picking it up*): That's right, it's mine. And what's more, it certainly is not old — Mrs. Tesman.

HEDDA: I really hadn't looked closely at it, Miss Tesman.

MISS TESMAN (*putting on the hat*): It's actually the first time I've had it on. The very first time.

TESMAN: And it's lovely, too. Most attractive!

MISS TESMAN: Oh, it's hardly all that, George. (*Looks about.*) My parasol —? Ah, here. (*Takes it.*) For that's mine too. (*Murmurs.*) Not Berta's.

TESMAN: New hat and new parasol! Just imagine, Hedda!

HEDDA: Quite charming, really.

TESMAN: Yes, aren't they, huh? But Auntie, take a good look at Hedda before you leave. See how charming *she* is!

MISS TESMAN: But George dear, there's nothing new in that. Hedda's been lovely all her life. (*She nods and starts out, right.*)

TESMAN (*following her*): But have you noticed how plump and buxom she's grown? How much she's filled out on the trip?

HEDDA (*crossing the room*): Oh, do be quiet —!

MISS TESMAN (*who has stopped and turned*): Filled out?

TESMAN: Of course, you can't see it so well when she has that dressing gown on. But I, who have the opportunity to —

HEDDA (*by the glass door, impatiently*): Oh, you have no opportunity for anything!

TESMAN: It must have been the mountain air, down in the Tyrol —

HEDDA (*brusquely interrupting*): I'm exactly as I was when I left.

TESMAN: Yes, that's your claim. But you certainly are not. Auntie, don't you agree?

MISS TESMAN (*gazing at her with folded hands*): Hedda is lovely — lovely — lovely. (*Goes up to her, takes her head in both hands, bends it down and kisses her hair.*) God bless and keep Hedda Tesman — for George's sake.

HEDDA (*gently freeing herself*): Oh —! Let me go.

MISS TESMAN (*with quiet feeling*): I won't let a day go by without looking in on you two.

TESMAN: Yes, please do that, Aunt Julie! Uh?

MISS TESMAN: Good-bye — good-bye!

(*She goes out by the hall door. Tesman accompanies her, leaving the door half open. He can be heard reiterating his greetings to Aunt Rina and his thanks for the slippers. At the same time, Hedda moves about the room, raising her arms and clenching her fists as if in a frenzy. Then she flings back the curtains from the glass door and stands there, looking out. A moment later Tesman comes back, closing the door after him.)*

TESMAN (*retrieving the slippers from the floor*): What are you standing and looking at, Hedda?

HEDDA (*again calm and controlled*): I'm just looking at the leaves — they're so yellow — and so withered.

TESMAN (*wraps up the slippers and puts them on the table*): Yes, well, we're into September now.

HEDDA (*once more restless*): Yes, to think — that already we're in — in September.

TESMAN: Didn't Aunt Julie seem a bit strange? A little — almost formal? What do you suppose was bothering her? Hm?

HEDDA: I hardly know her at all. Isn't that how she usually is?

TESMAN: No, not like this, today.

HEDDA (*leaving the glass door*): Do you think this thing with the hat upset her?

TESMAN: Oh, not very much. A little, just at the moment, perhaps —

HEDDA: But really, what kind of manners has she — to go throwing her hat about in a drawing room! It's just not proper.

TESMAN: Well, you can be sure Aunt Julie won't do it again.

HEDDA: Anyhow, I'll manage to smooth it over with her.

TESMAN: Yes, Hedda dear, I wish you would!

HEDDA: When you go in to see them later on, you might ask her out for the evening.

TESMAN: Yes, I'll do that. And there's something else you could do that would make her terribly happy.

HEDDA: Oh?

TESMAN: If only you could bring yourself to speak to her warmly, by her first name. For my sake, Hedda? Uh?

HEDDA: No, no — don't ask me to do that. I told you this once before. I'll try to call her "Aunt." That should be enough.

TESMAN: Oh, all right. I was only thinking, now that you belong to the family —

HEDDA: Hm — I really don't know — (*She crosses the room to the doorway.*)

TESMAN (*after a pause*): Is something the matter, Hedda? Uh?

HEDDA: I'm just looking at my old piano. It doesn't really fit in with all these other things.

TESMAN: With the first salary I draw, we can see about trading it in on a new one.

HEDDA: No, not traded in. I don't want to part with it. We can put it there, in the inner room, and get another here in its place. When there's a chance, I mean.

TESMAN (*slightly cast down*): Yes, we could do that, of course.

HEDDA (*picks up the bouquet from the piano*): These flowers weren't here when we got in last night.

TESMAN: Aunt Julie must have brought them for you.

HEDDA (*examining the bouquet*): A visiting card. (*Takes it out and reads it.*) "Will stop back later today." Can you guess who this is from?

TESMAN: No. Who? Hm?

HEDDA: It says, Mrs. Elvsted.

TESMAN: No, really? Sheriff Elvsted's wife. Miss Rysing, she used to be.

HEDDA: Exactly. The one with the irritating hair that she was always showing off. An old flame of yours, I've heard.

TESMAN (*laughing*): Oh, that wasn't for long. And it was before I knew you, Hedda. But imagine — that she's here in town.

HEDDA: It's odd that she calls on us. I've hardly seen her since we were in school.

TESMAN: Yes, I haven't seen her either — since God knows when. I wonder how she can stand living in such an out-of-the-way place. Hm?

HEDDA (*thinks a moment, then bursts out*): But wait — isn't it somewhere up in those parts that he — that Eilert Løvborg lives?

TESMAN: Yes, it's someplace right around there. (*Berta enters by the hall door.*)

BERTA: She's back again, ma'am — that lady who stopped by and left the flowers an hour ago. (*Pointing.*) The ones you have in your hand, ma'am.

HEDDA: Oh, is she? Good. Would you ask her to come in.

(*Berta opens the door for Mrs. Elvsted and goes out. Mrs. Elvsted is a slender woman with soft, pretty features. Her eyes are light blue, large, round, and somewhat prominent, with a startled, questioning look. Her hair is remarkably light, almost a white-gold, and unusually abundant and wavy. She is a couple of years younger than Hedda. She wears a dark visiting dress, tasteful, but not quite in the latest fashion.*)

HEDDA (*going to greet her warmly*): Good morning, my dear Mrs. Elvsted. How delightful to see you again!

MRS. ELVSTED (*nervously; struggling to control herself*): Yes, it's a very long time since we last met.

TESMAN (*gives her his hand*): Or since *we* met, uh?

HEDDA: Thank you for your beautiful flowers —

MRS. ELVSTED: Oh, that's nothing — I would have come straight out here yesterday afternoon, but then I heard you weren't at home —

TESMAN: Have you just now come to town? Uh?

MRS. ELVSTED: I got in yesterday toward noon. Oh, I was in desperation when I heard that you weren't at home.

HEDDA: Desperation! Why?

TESMAN: But my dear Mrs. Rysing — Mrs. Elvsted, I mean —

HEDDA: You're not in some kind of trouble?

MRS. ELVSTED: Yes, I am. And I don't know another living soul down here I can turn to.

HEDDA (*putting the bouquet down on the table*): Come, then — let's sit here on the sofa —

MRS. ELVSTED: Oh, I can't sit down. I'm really too much on edge!

HEDDA: Why, of course you can. Come here.

(*She draws Mrs. Elvsted down on the sofa and sits beside her.*)

TESMAN: Well? What is it, Mrs. Elvsted?

HEDDA: Has anything particular happened at home?

MRS. ELVSTED: Yes, that's both it — and not it. Oh, I do want so much that you don't misunderstand me —

HEDDA: But then the best thing, Mrs. Elvsted, is simply to speak your mind.

TESMAN: Because I suppose that's why you've come. Hm?

MRS. ELVSTED: Oh yes, that's why. Well, then, I have to tell you — if you don't already know — that Eilert Løvborg's also in town.

HEDDA: Løvborg —!

TESMAN: What! Is Eilert Løvborg back! Just think, Hedda!

HEDDA: Good Lord, I can hear.

MRS. ELVSTED: He's been back all of a week's time now. A whole week — in this dangerous town! Alone! With all the bad company that's around.

HEDDA: But my dear Mrs. Elvsted, what does *he* have to do with you?

MRS. ELVSTED (*glances anxiously at her and says quickly*): He was the children's tutor.

HEDDA: Your children's?

MRS. ELVSTED: My husband's. I have none.

HEDDA: Your stepchildren's, then.

MRS. ELVSTED: Yes.

TESMAN (*somewhat hesitantly*): But was he — I don't know quite how to put it — was he sufficiently — responsible in his habits for such a job? Uh?

MRS. ELVSTED: In these last two years, there wasn't a word to be said against him.

TESMAN: Not a word? Just think of that, Hedda!

HEDDA: I heard it.

MRS. ELVSTED: Not even a murmur, I can assure you! Nothing. But anyway — now that I know he's here — in this big city — and with so much money in his hands — then I'm just frightened to death for him.

TESMAN: But why didn't he stay up there where he was? With you and your husband? Uh?

MRS. ELVSTED: After the book came out, he just couldn't rest content with us.

TESMAN: Yes, that's right — Aunt Julie was saying he'd published a new book.

MRS. ELVSTED: Yes, a great new book, on the course of civilization — in all its stages. It's been out two weeks. And now it's been bought and read so much — and it's made a tremendous stir —

TESMAN: Has it really? It must be something he's had lying around from his better days.

MRS. ELVSTED: Years back, you mean?

TESMAN: I suppose.

MRS. ELVSTED: No, he's written it all up there with us. Now — in this last year.

TESMAN: That's marvelous to hear. Hedda! Just imagine!

MRS. ELVSTED: Yes, if only it can go on like this!

HEDDA: Have you seen him here in town?

MRS. ELVSTED: No, not yet. I had such trouble finding out his address. But this morning I got it at last.

HEDDA (*looks searchingly at her*): I must say it seems rather odd of your husband —

MRS. ELVSTED (*with a nervous start*): Of my husband —! What?

HEDDA: To send you to town on this sort of errand. Not to come and look after his friend himself.

MRS. ELVSTED: No, no, my husband hasn't the time for that. And then I had — some shopping to do.

HEDDA (*with a slight smile*): Oh, that's different.

MRS. ELVSTED (*getting up quickly and uneasily*): I beg you, please, Mr. Tesman — be good to Eilert Løvborg if he comes to you. And he will, I'm sure. You know — you were such good friends in the old days. And you're both doing the same kind of work. The same type of research — from what I can gather.

TESMAN: We were once, at any rate.

MRS. ELVSTED: Yes, and that's why I'm asking you, please — you too — to keep an eye on him. Oh, you will do that, Mr. Tesman — promise me that?

TESMAN: I'll be only too glad to, Mrs. Rysing —

HEDDA: Elvsted.

TESMAN: I'll certainly do everything in my power for Eilert. You can depend on that.

MRS. ELVSTED: Oh, how terribly kind of you! (*Pressing his hands.*) Many, many thanks! (*Frightened.*) He means so much to my husband, you know.

HEDDA (*rising*): You ought to write him, dear. He might not come by on his own.

TESMAN: Yes, that probably would be the best, Hedda? Hm?

HEDDA: And the sooner the better. Right now, I'd say.

MRS. ELVSTED (*imploringly*): Oh yes, if you could!

TESMAN: I'll write him this very moment. Have you got his address, Mrs. — Mrs. Elvsted?

MRS. ELVSTED: Yes. (*Takes a slip of paper from her pocket and hands it to him.*) Here it is.

TESMAN: Good, good. Then I'll go in — (*Looking about.*) But wait — my slippers? Ah! Here. (*Takes the package and starts to leave.*)

HEDDA: Write him a really warm, friendly letter. Nice and long, too.

TESMAN: Don't worry, I will.

MRS. ELVSTED: But please, not a word that I asked you to!

TESMAN: No, that goes without saying. Uh? (*Leaves by the inner room, to the right.*)

HEDDA (*goes over to Mrs. Elvsted, smiles, and speaks softly*): How's that! Now we've killed two birds with one stone.

MRS. ELVSTED: What do you mean?

HEDDA: Didn't you see that I wanted him out of the room?

MRS. ELVSTED: Yes, to write the letter —

HEDDA: But also to talk with you alone.

MRS. ELVSTED (*confused*): About this same thing?

HEDDA: Precisely.

MRS. ELVSTED (*upset*): But Mrs. Tesman, there's nothing more to say! Nothing!

HEDDA: Oh yes, but there is. There's a great deal more — I can see that. Come, sit here — and let's speak openly now, the two of us. (*She forces Mrs. Elvsted down into the armchair by the stove and sits on one of the taborets.*)

MRS. ELVSTED (*anxiously glancing at her watch*): But Mrs. Tesman, dear — I was just planning to leave.

HEDDA: Oh, you can't be in such a rush — Now! Tell me a little about how things are going at home.

MRS. ELVSTED: Oh, that's the last thing I'd ever want to discuss.

HEDDA: But with me, dear —? After all, we were in school together.

MRS. ELVSTED: Yes, but you were a class ahead of me. Oh, I was terribly afraid of you then!

HEDDA: Afraid of me?

MRS. ELVSTED: Yes, terribly. Because whenever we met on the stairs, you'd always pull my hair.

HEDDA: Did I really?

MRS. ELVSTED: Yes, and once you said you would burn it off.

HEDDA: Oh, that was just foolish talk, you know.

MRS. ELVSTED: Yes, but I was so stupid then. And, anyway, since then — we've drifted so far — far apart from each other. We've moved in such different circles.

HEDDA: Well, let's try now to come closer again. Listen, at school we were quite good friends, and we called each other by our first names —

MRS. ELVSTED: No, I'm sure you're mistaken.

HEDDA: Oh, I couldn't be! I remember it clearly. And

that's why we have to be perfectly open, just as we were. (*Moves the stool nearer Mrs. Elvsted.*) There now! (*Kissing her cheek.*) You have to call me Hedda.

MRS. ELVSTED (*pressing and patting her hands*): Oh, you're so good and kind —! It's not at all what I'm used to.

HEDDA: There, there! And I'm going to call you my own dear Thora.

MRS. ELVSTED: My name is Thea.

HEDDA: Oh yes, of course. I meant Thea. (*Looks at her compassionately.*) So you're not much used to goodness or kindness, Thea? In your own home?

MRS. ELVSTED: If only I had a home! But I don't. I never have.

HEDDA (*glances quickly at her*): I thought it had to be something like that.

MRS. ELVSTED (*gazing helplessly into space*): Yes — yes — yes.

HEDDA: I can't quite remember now — but wasn't it as a housekeeper that you first came up to the Elvsteds?

MRS. ELVSTED: Actually as a governess. But his wife — his first wife — she was an invalid and mostly kept to her bed. So I had to take care of the house too.

HEDDA: But finally you became mistress of the house yourself.

MRS. ELVSTED (*heavily*): Yes, I did.

HEDDA: Let me see — about how long ago was that?

MRS. ELVSTED: That I was married?

HEDDA: Yes.

MRS. ELVSTED: It's five years now.

HEDDA: That's right. It must be.

MRS. ELVSTED: Oh, these five years —! Or the last two or three, anyway. Oh, if you only knew, Mrs. Tesman —

HEDDA (*gives her hand a little slap*): Mrs. Tesman! Now, Thea!

MRS. ELVSTED: I'm sorry; I'll try — Yes, if you could only understand — Hedda —

HEDDA (*casually*): Eilert Løvborg has lived up there about three years too, hasn't he?

MRS. ELVSTED (*looks at her doubtfully*): Eilert Løvborg? Yes — he has.

HEDDA: Had you already known him here in town?

MRS. ELVSTED: Hardly at all. Well, I mean — by name, of course.

HEDDA: But up there — I suppose he'd visit you both?

MRS. ELVSTED: Yes, he came to see us every day. He was tutoring the children, you know. Because, in the long run, I couldn't do it all myself.

HEDDA: No, that's obvious. And your husband —? I suppose he often has to be away?

MRS. ELVSTED: Yes, you can imagine, as sheriff, how much traveling he does around in the district.

HEDDA (*leaning against the chair arm*): Thea — my poor, sweet Thea — now you must tell me everything — just as it is.

MRS. ELVSTED: Well, then you have to ask the questions.

HEDDA: What sort of man is your husband, Thea? I mean — you know — to be with. Is he good to you?

MRS. ELVSTED (*evasively*): He believes he does everything for the best.

HEDDA: I only think he must be much too old for you. More than twenty years older, isn't he?

MRS. ELVSTED (*irritated*): That's true. Along with everything else. I just can't stand him! We haven't a single thought in common. Nothing at all — he and I.

HEDDA: But doesn't he care for you all the same — in his own way?

MRS. ELVSTED: Oh, I don't know what he feels. I'm no more than useful to him. And then it doesn't cost much to keep me. I'm inexpensive.

HEDDA: That's stupid of you.

MRS. ELVSTED (*shaking her head*): It can't be otherwise. Not with him. He really doesn't care for anyone but himself — and maybe a little for the children.

HEDDA: And for Eilert Løvborg, Thea.

MRS. ELVSTED (*looking at her*): Eilert Løvborg! Why do you think so?

HEDDA: But my dear — it seems to me, when he sends you all the way into town to look after him — (*Smiles almost imperceptibly.*) Besides, it's what you told my husband.

MRS. ELVSTED (*with a little nervous shudder*): Really? Yes, I suppose I did. (*In a quiet outburst.*) No — I might as well tell you here and now! It's bound to come out in time.

HEDDA: But my dear Thea —?

MRS. ELVSTED: All right, then! My husband never knew I was coming here.

HEDDA: What! Your husband never knew —

MRS. ELVSTED: Of course not. Anyway, he wasn't at home. Off traveling somewhere. Oh, I couldn't bear it any longer, Hedda. It was impossible! I would have been so alone up there now.

HEDDA: Well? What then?

MRS. ELVSTED: So I packed a few of my things together — the barest necessities — without saying a word. And I slipped away from the house.

HEDDA: Right then and there?

MRS. ELVSTED: Yes, and took the train straight into town.

HEDDA: But my dearest girl — that you could dare to do such a thing!

MRS. ELVSTED (*rising and walking about the room*): What else could I possibly do!

HEDDA: But what do you think your husband will say when you go back home?

MRS. ELVSTED (*by the table, looking at her*): Back to him?

HEDDA: Yes, of course.

MRS. ELVSTED: I'll never go back to him.

HEDDA (*rising and approaching her*): You mean you've left, in dead earnest, for good?

MRS. ELVSTED: Yes. There didn't seem anything else to do.

HEDDA: But — to go away so openly.

MRS. ELVSTED: Oh, you can't keep a thing like that secret.

HEDDA: But what do you think people will say about you, Thea?

MRS. ELVSTED: God knows they'll say what they please. (*Sitting wearily and sadly on the sofa.*) I only did what I had to do.

HEDDA (*after a short silence*): What do you plan on now? What kind of work?

MRS. ELVSTED: I don't know yet. I only know I have to live here, where Eilert Løvborg is — if I'm going to live at all.

HEDDA (*moves a chair over from the table, sits beside her, and strokes her hands*): Thea dear — how did this — this friendship — between you and Eilert Løvborg come about?

MRS. ELVSTED: Oh, it happened little by little. I got some kind of power, almost, over him.

HEDDA: Really?

MRS. ELVSTED: He gave up his old habits. Not because I'd asked him to. I never dared do that. But he could tell they upset me, and so he dropped them.

HEDDA (*hiding an involuntary, scornful smile*): My dear little Thea — just as they say — you rehabilitated him.

MRS. ELVSTED: Well, he says so, at any rate. And he — on his part — he's made a real human being out of me. Taught me to think — and understand so many things.

HEDDA: You mean he tutored you also?

MRS. ELVSTED: No, not exactly. But he'd talk to me — talk endlessly on about one thing after another. And then came the wonderful, happy time when I could share in his work! When I could help him!

HEDDA: Could you really?

MRS. ELVSTED: Yes! Whenever he wrote anything, we'd always work on it together.

HEDDA: Like two true companions.

MRS. ELVSTED (*eagerly*): Companions! You know, Hedda — that's what he said too! Oh, I ought to feel so happy — but I can't. I just don't know if it's going to last.

HEDDA: You're no more sure of him than that?

MRS. ELVSTED (*despondently*): There's a woman's shadow between Eilert Løvborg and me.

HEDDA (*looks at her intently*): Who could that be?

MRS. ELVSTED: I don't know. Someone out of his — his past. Someone he's really never forgotten.

HEDDA: What has he said — about this!

MRS. ELVSTED: It's only once — and just vaguely — that he touched on it.

HEDDA: Well! And what did he say!

MRS. ELVSTED: He said that when they broke off she was going to shoot him with a pistol.

HEDDA (*with cold constraint*): That's nonsense! Nobody behaves that way around here.

MRS. ELVSTED: No. And that's why I think it must have been that redheaded singer that at one time he —

HEDDA: Yes, quite likely.

MRS. ELVSTED: I remember they used to say about her that she carried loaded weapons.

HEDDA: Ah — then of course it must have been her.

MRS. ELVSTED (*wringing her hands*): But you know what, Hedda — I've heard that this singer — that she's in town again! Oh, it has me out of my mind —

HEDDA (*glancing toward the inner room*): Shh! Tesman's coming. (*Gets up and whispers.*) Thea — keep all this just between us.

MRS. ELVSTED (*jumping up*): Oh yes! In heaven's name —!

(*George Tesman, with a letter in his hand, enters from the right through the inner room.*)

TESMAN: There, now — the letter's signed and sealed.

HEDDA: That's fine. I think Mrs. Elvsted was just leaving. Wait a minute. I'll go with you to the garden gate.

TESMAN: Hedda, dear — could Berta maybe look after this?

HEDDA (*taking the letter*): I'll tell her to.

(*Berta enters from the hall.*)

BERTA: Judge Brack is here and says he'd like to greet you and the Doctor, ma'am.

HEDDA: Yes, ask Judge Brack to come in. And, here — put this letter in the mail.

BERTA (*takes the letter*): Yes, ma'am.

(*She opens the door for Judge Brack and goes out. Brack is a man of forty-five, thickset, yet well built, with supple movements. His face is roundish, with a distinguished profile. His hair is short, still mostly black, and carefully groomed. His eyes are bright and lively. Thick eyebrows; a mustache to match, with neatly clipped ends. He wears a trimly tailored walking suit, a bit too youthful for his age. Uses a monocle, which he now and then lets fall.*)

JUDGE BRACK (*hat in hand, bowing*): May one dare to call so early?

HEDDA: Of course one may.

TESMAN (*shakes his hand*): You're always welcome here. (*Introducing him.*) Judge Brack — Miss Rysing —

HEDDA: Ah —!

BRACK (*bowing*): I'm delighted.

HEDDA (*looks at him and laughs*): It's really a treat to see you by daylight, Judge!

BRACK: You find me — changed?

HEDDA: Yes. A bit younger, I think.

BRACK: Thank you, most kindly.

TESMAN: But what do you say for Hedda, uh? Doesn't she look flourishing? She's actually —

HEDDA: Oh, leave me out of it! You might thank Judge Brack for all the trouble he's gone to —

BRACK: Nonsense — it was a pleasure —

HEDDA: Yes, you're a true friend. But here's Thea, standing here, aching to get away. Excuse me, Judge; I'll be right back.

(*Mutual good-byes. Mrs. Elvsted and Hedda go out by the hall door.*)

BRACK: So — is your wife fairly well satisfied, then —?

TESMAN: Yes, we can't thank you enough. Of course — I gather there's some rearrangement called for here and there. And one or two things are lacking. We still have to buy a few minor items.

BRACK: Really?

TESMAN: But that's nothing for you to worry about. Hedda said she'd pick up those things herself. Why don't we sit down, hm?

BRACK: Thanks. Just for a moment. (*Sits by the table.*) There's something I'd like to discuss with you, Tesman.

TESMAN: What? Oh, I understand! (*Sitting.*) It's the serious part of the banquet we're coming to, uh?

BRACK: Oh, as far as money matters go, there's no great rush — though I must say I wish we'd managed things a bit more economically.

TESMAN: But that was completely impossible! Think about Hedda, Judge! You, who know her so well — I simply couldn't have her live like a grocer's wife.

BRACK: No, no — that's the trouble, exactly.

TESMAN: And then — fortunately — it can't be long before I get my appointment.

BRACK: Well, you know — these things can often hang fire.

TESMAN: Have you heard something further? Hm?

BRACK: Nothing really definite — (*Changing the subject.*) But incidentally — I do have one piece of news for you.

TESMAN: Well?

BRACK: Your old friend Eilert Løvborg is back in town.

TESMAN: I already know.

BRACK: Oh? How did you hear?

TESMAN: She told me. The lady that left with Hedda.

BRACK: I see. What was her name again? I didn't quite catch it —

TESMAN: Mrs. Elvsted.

BRACK: Aha — Sheriff Elvsted's wife. Yes — it's up near them he's been staying.

TESMAN: And, just think — what a pleasure to hear that he's completely stable again!

BRACK: Yes, that's what they claim.

TESMAN: And that he's published a new book, uh?

BRACK: Oh yes!

TESMAN: And it's created quite a sensation.

BRACK: An extraordinary sensation.

TESMAN: Just imagine — isn't that marvelous? He, with his remarkable talents — I was so very afraid that he'd really gone down for good.

BRACK: That's what everyone thought.

TESMAN: But I've no idea what he'll find to do now. How on earth can he ever make a living? Hm?

(*During the last words, Hedda comes in by the hall door.*)

HEDDA (*to Brack, laughing, with a touch of scorn*): Tesman always goes around worrying about how people are going to make a living.

TESMAN: My Lord — it's poor Eilert Løvborg we're talking of, dear.

HEDDA (*glancing quickly at him*): Oh, really? (*Sits in the armchair by the stove and asks casually.*) What's the matter with him?

TESMAN: Well — he must have run through his inheritance long ago. And he can't write a new book every year. Uh? So I was asking, really, what's going to become of him.

BRACK: Perhaps I can shed some light on that.

TESMAN: Oh?

BRACK: You must remember that he does have relatives with a great deal of influence.

TESMAN: Yes, but they've washed their hands of him altogether.

BRACK: They used to call him the family's white hope.

TESMAN: They used to, yes! But he spoiled all that himself.

HEDDA: Who knows? (*With a slight smile.*) He's been rehabilitated up at the Elvsteds —

BRACK: And then this book that he's published —

TESMAN: Oh, well, let's hope they really help him some way or other. I just now wrote to him. Hedda dear, I asked him out here this evening.

BRACK: But my dear fellow, you're coming to my stag party this evening. You promised down on the pier last night.

HEDDA: Had you forgotten, Tesman?

TESMAN: Yes, I absolutely had.

BRACK: For that matter, you can rest assured that he'd never come.

TESMAN: What makes you say that, hm?

BRACK (*hesitating, rising and leaning on the back of the chair*): My dear Tesman — and you too, Mrs. Tesman — I can't, in all conscience, let you go on without knowing something that — that —

TESMAN: Something involving Eilert —?

BRACK: Both you and him.

TESMAN: But my dear Judge, then tell us!

BRACK: You must be prepared that your appointment may not come through as quickly as you've wished or expected.

TESMAN (*jumping up nervously*): Has something gone wrong? Uh?

BRACK: It may turn out that there'll have to be a competition for the post —

TESMAN: A competition! Imagine, Hedda!

HEDDA (*leaning further back in the chair*): Ah, there — you see!

TESMAN: But with whom! You can't mean —?

BRACK: Yes, exactly. With Eilert Løvborg.

TESMAN (*striking his hands together*): No, no — that's completely unthinkable! It's impossible! Uh?

BRACK: Hm — but it may come about, all the same.

TESMAN: No, but, Judge Brack — that would just be incredibly inconsiderate toward me! (*Waving his arms.*) Yes, because — you know — I'm a married man! We married on my prospects, Hedda and I. We went into debt. And even borrowed money from Aunt Julie. Because that job — my Lord, it was as good as promised to me, uh?

BRACK: Easy now — I'm sure you'll get the appointment. But you will have to compete for it.

HEDDA (*motionless in the armchair*): Just think, Tesman — it will be like a kind of championship match.

TESMAN: But Hedda dearest, how can you take it so calmly!

HEDDA (*as before*): I'm not the least bit calm. I can't wait to see how it turns out.

BRACK: In any case, Mrs. Tesman, it's well that you know now how things stand. I mean — with respect to those little purchases I hear you've been threatening to make.

HEDDA: This business can't change anything.

BRACK: I see! Well, that's another matter. Good-bye. (*To Tesman.*) When I take my afternoon walk, I'll stop by and fetch you.

TESMAN: Oh yes, please do — I don't know where I'm at.

HEDDA (*leaning back and reaching out her hand*): Good-bye, Judge. And come again soon.

BRACK: Many thanks. Good-bye now.

TESMAN (*accompanying him to the door*): Good-bye, Judge! You really must excuse me —

(*Brack goes out by the hall door.*)

TESMAN (*pacing about the room*): Oh, Hedda — one should never go off and lose oneself in dreams, uh?

HEDDA (*looks at him and smiles*): Do *you* do that?

TESMAN: No use denying it. It was living in dreams to go and get married and set up house on nothing but expectations.

HEDDA: Perhaps you're right about that.

TESMAN: Well, at least we have our comfortable home, Hedda! The home that we always wanted. That we both fell in love with, I could almost say. Hm?

HEDDA (*rising slowly and wearily*): It was part of our bargain that we'd live in society — that we'd keep a great house —

TESMAN: Yes, of course — how I'd looked forward to that! Imagine — seeing you as a hostess — in our own select circle of friends! Yes, yes — well for a while, we two will just have to get on by ourselves, Hedda. Perhaps have Aunt Julie here now and then. Oh, you — for you I wanted to have things so — so utterly different —!

HEDDA: Naturally this means I can't have a butler now.

TESMAN: Oh no — I'm sorry, a butler — we can't even talk about that, you know.

HEDDA: And the riding horse I was going to have —

TESMAN (*appalled*): Riding horse!

HEDDA: I suppose I can't think of that anymore.

TESMAN: Good Lord, no — that's obvious!

HEDDA (*crossing the room*): Well, at least I have one thing left to amuse myself with.

TESMAN (*beaming*): Ah, thank heaven for that! What is it, Hedda? Uh?

HEDDA (*in the center doorway, looking at him with veiled scorn*): My pistols, George.

TESMAN (*in fright*): Your pistols!

HEDDA (*her eyes cold*): General Gabler's pistols. (*She goes through the inner room and out to the left.*)

TESMAN (*runs to the center doorway and calls after her*): No, for heaven's sake, Hedda darling — don't touch those dangerous things! For my sake, Hedda! Uh?

ACT II

(*The rooms at the Tesmans', same as in the first act, except that the piano has been moved out and an elegant little writing table with a bookcase put in its place. A smaller table stands by the sofa to the left. Most of the flowers have been removed. Mrs. Elvsted's bouquet stands on the large table in the foreground. It is afternoon.*)

(*Hedda, dressed to receive callers, is alone in the room. She stands by the open glass door, loading a revolver. The match to it lies in an open pistol case on the writing table.*)

HEDDA (*looking down into the garden and calling*): Good to see you again, Judge!

BRACK (*heard from below, at a distance*): Likewise, Mrs. Tesman!

HEDDA (*raises the pistol and aims*): And now, Judge, I'm going to shoot you!

BRACK (*shouting from below*): No — no — no! Don't point that thing at me!

HEDDA: That's what comes of sneaking in the back way. (*She fires.*)

BRACK (*nearer*): Are you out of your mind —!

HEDDA: Oh dear — I didn't hit you, did I?

BRACK (*still outside*): Just stop this nonsense!

HEDDA: All right, you can come in, Judge.

(*Judge Brack, dressed for a stag party, enters through the glass door. He carries a light overcoat on his arm.*)

BRACK: Good God! Are you still playing such games? What are you shooting at?

HEDDA: Oh, I was just shooting into the sky.

BRACK (*gently taking the pistol out of her hand*): Permit me. (*Looks at it.*) Ah, this one — I know it well. (*Glancing around.*) Where's the case? Ah, here. (*Puts the pistol away and shuts the case.*) We'll have no more of that kind of fun today.

HEDDA: Well, what in heaven's name do you want me to do with myself?

BRACK: You haven't had any visitors?

HEDDA (*closing the glass door*): Not a single one. All of our set are still in the country, I guess.

BRACK: And Tesman isn't home either?

HEDDA (*at the writing table, putting the pistol case away in a drawer*): No. Right after lunch he ran over to his aunts. He didn't expect you so soon.

BRACK: Hm — I should have realized. That was stupid of me.

HEDDA (*turning her head and looking at him*): Why stupid?

BRACK: Because in that case I would have stopped by a little bit — earlier.

HEDDA (*crossing the room*): Well, you'd have found no one here then at all. I've been up in my room dressing since lunch.

BRACK: And there's not the least little crack in the door we could have conferred through.

HEDDA: You forgot to arrange it.

BRACK: Also stupid of me.

HEDDA: Well, we'll just have to settle down here — and wait. Tesman won't be back for a while.

BRACK: Don't worry, I can be patient.

(*Hedda sits in the corner of the sofa. Brack lays his coat over the back of the nearest chair and sits down, keeping his hat in his hand. A short pause. They look at each other.*)

HEDDA: Well?

BRACK (*in the same tone*): Well?

HEDDA: I spoke first.

BRACK (*leaning slightly forward*): Then let's have a nice little cozy chat, Mrs. Hedda.

HEDDA (*leaning further back on the sofa*): Doesn't it seem like a whole eternity since the last time we talked together? Oh, a few words last night and this morning — but they don't count.

BRACK: You mean, like this — between ourselves? Just the two of us?

HEDDA: Well, more or less.

BRACK: There wasn't a day that I didn't wish you were home again.

HEDDA: And I was wishing exactly the same.

BRACK: You? Really, Mrs. Hedda? And I thought you were having such a marvelous time on this trip.

HEDDA: Oh, you can imagine!

BRACK: But that's what Tesman always wrote.

HEDDA: Oh, him! There's nothing he likes better than grubbing around in libraries and copying out old parchments, or whatever you call them.

BRACK (*with a touch of malice*): But after all, it's his calling in life. In good part, anyway.

HEDDA: Yes, that's true. So there's nothing wrong with it — But what about *me*! Oh, Judge, you don't know — I've been so dreadfully bored.

BRACK (*sympathetically*): You really mean that? In all seriousness?

HEDDA: Well, you can understand —! To go for a whole six months without meeting a soul who knew the least bit about our circle. No one that one could talk to about our kind of things.

BRACK: Ah, yes — I think that would bother me too.

HEDDA: But then the most unbearable thing of all —

BRACK: What?

HEDDA: To be everlastingly together with — with one and the same person —

BRACK (*nodding in agreement*): Morning, noon, and night — yes. At every conceivable hour.

HEDDA: I said "everlastingly."

BRACK: All right. But with our good friend Tesman I really should have thought —

HEDDA: My dear Judge, Tesman is — a specialist.

BRACK: Undeniably.

HEDDA: And specialists aren't at all amusing to travel with. Not in the long run, anyway.

BRACK: Not even — the specialist that one *loves*.

HEDDA: Ugh — don't use that syrupy word!

BRACK (*startled*): What's that, Mrs. Hedda!

HEDDA (*half laughing, half annoyed*): Well, just try it yourself! Try listening to the history of civilization morning, noon, and —

BRACK: Everlastingly.

HEDDA: Yes! Yes! And then all this business about domestic crafts in the Middle Ages —! That really is just too revolting!

BRACK (*looks searchingly at her*): But tell me — I can't see how it ever came about that —? Hm —

HEDDA: That George Tesman and I could make a match?

BRACK: All right, let's put it that way.

HEDDA: Good Lord, does it seem so remarkable?

BRACK: Well, yes — and no, Mrs. Hedda.

HEDDA: I really had danced myself out, Judge. My time was up. (*With a slight shudder.*) Ugh! No, I don't want to say that. Or think it, either.

BRACK: You certainly have no reason to.

HEDDA: Oh — reasons — (*Watching him carefully.*) And George Tesman — he is, after all, a thoroughly acceptable choice.

BRACK: Acceptable and dependable, beyond a doubt.

HEDDA: And I don't find anything especially ridiculous about him. Do you?

BRACK: Ridiculous? No-o-o, I wouldn't say that.

HEDDA: Hm. Anyway, he works incredibly hard on his research! There's every chance that, in time, he could still make a name for himself.

BRACK (*looking at her with some uncertainty*): I thought you believed, like everyone else, that he was going to be quite famous some day.

HEDDA (*wearily*): Yes, so I did. And then when he kept pressing and pleading to be allowed to take care of me — I didn't see why I ought to resist.

BRACK: No. From that point of view, of course not —

HEDDA: It was certainly more than my other admirers were willing to do for me, Judge.

BRACK (*laughing*): Well, I can't exactly answer for all the others. But as far as I'm concerned, you know that I've always cherished a — a certain respect for the marriage bond. Generally speaking, that is.

HEDDA (*bantering*): Oh, I never really held out any hopes for *you*.

BRACK: All I want is to have a warm circle of intimate friends, where I can be of use one way or another, with the freedom to come and go as — as a trusted friend —

HEDDA: Of the man of the house, you mean?

BRACK (*with a bow*): Frankly — I prefer the lady. But the man, too, of course, in his place. That kind of — let's say, triangular arrangement — you can't imagine how satisfying it can be all around.

HEDDA: Yes, I must say I longed for some third person so many times on that trip. Oh — those endless tête-à-têtes° in railway compartments —!

BRACK: Fortunately the wedding trip's over now.

HEDDA (*shaking her head*): The trip will go on — and on. I've only come to one stop on the line.

BRACK: Well, then what you do is jump out — and stretch yourself a little, Mrs. Hedda.

HEDDA: I'll never jump out.

BRACK: Never?

HEDDA: No. Because there's always someone on the platform who —

BRACK (*with a laugh*): Who looks at your legs, is that it?

HEDDA: Precisely.

BRACK: Yes, but after all —

HEDDA (*with a disdainful gesture*): I'm not interested. I'd rather keep my seat — right here, where I am. Tête à tête.

BRACK: Well, but suppose a third person came on board and joined the couple.

HEDDA: Ah! That's entirely different.

BRACK: A trusted friend, who understands —

HEDDA: And can talk about all kinds of lively things —

BRACK: Who's not in the least a specialist.

HEDDA (*with an audible sigh*): Yes, that would be a relief.

BRACK (*hearing the front door open and glancing toward it*): The triangle is complete.

HEDDA (*lowering her voice*): And the train goes on.

(*George Tesman, in a gray walking suit and a soft felt hat, enters from the hall. He has a good number of unbound books under his arm and in his pockets.*)

TESMAN (*going up to the table by the corner settee*): Phew! Let me tell you, that's hot work — carrying all these. (*Setting the books down.*) I'm actually sweating, Hedda. And what's this — you're already here, Judge? Hm? Berta didn't tell me.

BRACK (*rising*): I came in through the garden.

HEDDA: What are all these books you've gotten?

TESMAN (*stands leafing through them*): They're new publications in my special field. I absolutely need them.

HEDDA: Your special field?

BRACK: Of course. Books in his special field, Mrs. Tesman.

(*Brack and Hedda exchange a knowing smile.*)

HEDDA: You need still more books in your special field?

TESMAN: Hedda, my dear, it's impossible ever to have too many. You have to keep up with what's written and published.

HEDDA: Oh, I suppose so.

TESMAN (*searching among the books*): And look — I picked up Eilert Løvborg's new book too. (*Offering it to her.*) Maybe you'd like to have a look at it? Uh?

HEDDA: No, thank you. Or — well, perhaps later.

TESMAN: I skimmed through some of it on the way home.

HEDDA: Well, what do you think of it — as a specialist?

TESMAN: I think it's amazing how well it holds up. He's never written like this before. (*Gathers up the books.*) But I'll take these into the study now. I can't wait to cut the pages° —! And then I better dress up a bit. (*To Brack.*) We don't have to rush right off, do we? Hm?

BRACK: No, not at all. There's ample time.

TESMAN: Ah, then I'll be at my leisure. (*Starts out with the books, but pauses and turns in the doorway.*) Oh, incidentally, Hedda — Aunt Julie won't be by to see you this evening.

HEDDA: She won't? I suppose it's that business with the hat?

TESMAN: Don't be silly. How can you think that of Aunt Julie? Imagine —! No, it's Auntie Rina — she's very ill.

HEDDA: She always is.

TESMAN: Yes, but today she really took a turn for the worse.

HEDDA: Well, then it's only right for her sister to stay with her. I'll have to bear with it.

TESMAN: But you can't imagine how delighted Aunt Julie was all the same — because you'd filled out so nicely on the trip!

HEDDA (*under her breath; rising*): Oh, these eternal aunts!

TESMAN: What?

HEDDA (*going over to the glass door*): Nothing.

TESMAN: All right, then. (*He goes through the inner room and out, right.*)

BRACK: What were you saying about a hat?

---

cut the pages: Book pages were printed on large sheets of paper that were folded and bound in groups of four. Readers had to trim the edges to separate the pages.

tête-à-têtes: Face-to-face conversations.

HEDDA: Oh, it's something that happened with Miss Tesman this morning. She'd put her hat down over there on the chair. (*Looks at him and smiles.*) And I pretended I thought it was the maid's.

BRACK (*shaking his head*): But my dear Mrs. Hedda, how could you do that! Hurt that fine old lady!

HEDDA (*nervously, pacing the room*): Well, it's — these things come over me, just like that, suddenly. And I can't hold back. (*Throws herself down in the armchair by the stove.*) Oh, I don't know myself how to explain it.

BRACK (*behind the armchair*): You're not really happy — that's the heart of it.

HEDDA (*gazing straight ahead*): And I don't know why I ought to be — happy. Or maybe you can tell me why?

BRACK: Yes — among other things, because you've gotten just the home you've always wanted.

HEDDA (*looks up at him and laughs*): You believe that story too?

BRACK: You mean there's nothing to it?

HEDDA: Oh, yes — there's something to it.

BRACK: Well?

HEDDA: There's this much to it, that I used Tesman as my escort home from parties last summer —

BRACK: Unfortunately — I was going in another direction then.

HEDDA: How true. Yes, you had other directions to go last summer.

BRACK (*laughing*): For shame, Mrs. Hedda! Well — so you and Tesman —?

HEDDA: Yes, so one evening we walked by this place. And Tesman, poor thing, was writhing in torment, because he couldn't find anything to say. And I felt sorry for a man of such learning —

BRACK (*smiling skeptically*): Did you? Hm —

HEDDA: No, I honestly did. And so — just to help him off the hook — I came out with some rash remark about this lovely house being where I'd always wanted to live.

BRACK: No more than that?

HEDDA: No more that evening.

BRACK: But afterward?

HEDDA: Yes, my rashness had its consequences, Judge.

BRACK: I'm afraid our rashness all too often does Mrs. Hedda.

HEDDA: Thanks! But don't you see, it was this passion for the old Falk mansion that drew George Tesman and me together! It was nothing more than that, that brought on our engagement and the marriage and the wedding trip and everything else. Oh yes,

Marit Gronhaug as Hedda in the 1986 Rogaland Teater (Norway) production of *Hedda Gabler* in London.

Judge — I was going to say, you make your bed and then you lie in it.

BRACK: But that's priceless! So actually you couldn't care less about all this?

HEDDA: God knows, not in the least.

BRACK: But even now? Now that we've made it somewhat comfortable for you here?

HEDDA: Ugh — all the rooms seem to smell of lavender and dried roses. But maybe that scent was brought in by Aunt Julie.

BRACK (*laughing*): No, I think it's a bequest from the late Mrs. Falk.

HEDDA: Yes, there's something in it of the odor of death. It's like a corsage — the day after the dance. (*Folds her hands behind her neck, leans back in her chair, and looks at him.*) Oh, my dear Judge — you can't imagine how horribly I'm going to bore myself here.

BRACK: But couldn't you find some goal in life to work toward? Others do, Mrs. Hedda.

HEDDA: A goal — that would really absorb me?

BRACK: Yes, preferably.

HEDDA: God only knows what that could be. I often wonder if — (*Breaks off.*) But that's impossible too.

BRACK: Who knows? Tell me.

HEDDA: I was thinking — if I could get Tesman to go into politics.

BRACK (*laughing*): Tesman! No, I can promise you — politics is absolutely out of his line.

HEDDA: No, I can believe you. But even so, I wonder if I could get him into it?

BRACK: Well, what satisfaction would you have in that, if he can't succeed? Why push him in that direction?

HEDDA: Because, I've told you, I'm bored! (*After a pause.*) Then you think it's really out of the question that he could ever be a cabinet minister?

BRACK: Hm — you see, Mrs. Hedda — to be anything like that, he'd have to be fairly wealthy to start with.

HEDDA (*rising impatiently*): Yes, there it is! It's this tight little world I've stumbled into — (*Crossing the room.*) That's what makes life so miserable! So utterly ludicrous! Because that's what it *is*.

BRACK: I'd say the fault lies elsewhere.

HEDDA: Where?

BRACK: You've never experienced anything that's really stirred you.

HEDDA: Anything serious, you mean.

BRACK: Well, you can call it that, if you like. But now perhaps it's on the way.

HEDDA (*tossing her head*): Oh, you mean all the fuss over that wretched professorship! But that's Tes-

man's problem. I'm not going to give it a single thought.

BRACK: No, that isn't — ah, never mind. But suppose you were to be confronted now by what — in rather elegant language — is called your most solemn responsibility. (*Smiling.*) A new responsibility, Mrs. Hedda.

HEDDA (*angrily*): Be quiet! You'll never see me like that!

BRACK (*delicately*): We'll discuss it again in a year's time — at the latest.

HEDDA (*curtly*): I have no talent for such things, Judge. I won't have responsibilities!

BRACK: Don't you think you've a talent for what almost every woman finds the most meaningful —

HEDDA (*over by the glass door*): Oh, I told you, be quiet! I often think I have talent for only one thing in life.

BRACK (*moving closer*): And what, may I ask, is that?

HEDDA (*stands looking out*): Boring myself to death. And that's the truth. (*Turns, looks toward the inner room, and laughs.*) See what I mean! Here comes the professor.

BRACK (*in a low tone of warning*): Ah-ah-ah, Mrs. Hedda!

(*George Tesman, dressed for the party, with hat and gloves in hand, enters from the right through the inner room.*)

TESMAN: Hedda — there's been no word from Eilert Løvborg, has there? Hm?

HEDDA: No.

TESMAN: Well, he's bound to be here soon then. You'll see.

BRACK: You really believe he'll come?

TESMAN: Yes, I'm almost positive of it. Because I'm sure they're nothing but rumors, what you told us this morning.

BRACK: Oh?

TESMAN: Yes. At least Aunt Julie said she couldn't for the world believe that he'd stand in my way again. Can you imagine that!

BRACK: So, then everything's well and good.

TESMAN (*putting his hat with the gloves inside on a chair to the right*): Yes, but I really would like to wait for him as long as possible.

BRACK: We have plenty of time for that. There's no one due at my place till seven or half past.

TESMAN: Why, then we can keep Hedda company for a while. And see what turns up. Uh?

HEDDA (*taking Brack's hat and coat over to the settee*): And if worst comes to worst, Mr. Løvborg can sit and talk with me.

BRACK (*trying to take his things himself*): Ah, please,

Mrs. Tesman —! What do you mean by "worst," in this case?

HEDDA: If he won't go with you and Tesman.

TESMAN (*looks doubtfully at her*): But Hedda dear — is it quite right that he stays with you here? Uh? Remember that Aunt Julie isn't coming.

HEDDA: No, but Mrs. Elvsted is. The three of us can have tea together.

TESMAN: Oh, well, that's all right.

BRACK (*smiling*): And that might be the soundest plan for him too.

HEDDA: Why?

BRACK: Well, really, Mrs. Tesman, you've made enough pointed remarks about my little bachelor parties. You've always said they're only fit for men of the strictest principles.

HEDDA: But Mr. Løvborg is surely a man of principle now. After all, a reformed sinner —

(*Berta appears at the hall door.*)

BERTA: Ma'am, there's a gentleman here who'd like to see you —

HEDDA: Yes, show him in.

TESMAN (*softly*): I'm sure it's him! Just think!

(*Eilert Løvborg enters from the hall. He is lean and gaunt, the same age as Tesman, but looks older and rather exhausted. His hair and beard are dark brown, his face long and pale, but with reddish patches over the cheekbones. He is dressed in a trim black suit, quite new, and holds dark gloves and a top hat in his hand. He hesitates by the door and bows abruptly. He seems somewhat embarrassed.*)

TESMAN (*crosses over and shakes his hand*): Ah, my dear Eilert — so at last we meet again!

EILERT LØVBORG (*speaking in a hushed voice*): Thanks for your letter, George! (*Approaching Hedda.*) May I shake hands with you too, Mrs. Tesman?

HEDDA (*taking his hand*): So glad to see you, Mr. Løvborg. (*Gesturing with her hand.*) I don't know if you two gentlemen —?

LØVBORG (*bowing slightly*): Judge Brack, I believe.

BRACK (*reciprocating*): Of course. It's been some years —

TESMAN (*to Løvborg, with his hands on his shoulders*): And now, Eilert, make yourself at home, completely! Right, Hedda? I hear you'll be settling down here in town again? Uh?

LØVBORG: I plan to.

TESMAN: Well, that makes sense. Listen — I just got hold of your new book. But I really haven't had time to read it yet.

LØVBORG: You can save yourself the bother.

TESMAN: Why? What do you mean?

LØVBORG: There's very little to it.

TESMAN: Imagine — you can say that!

BRACK: But it's won such high praise, I hear.

LØVBORG: That's exactly what I wanted. So I wrote a book that everyone could agree with.

BRACK: Very sound.

TESMAN: Yes, but my dear Eilert —!

LØVBORG: Because now I want to build up my position again — and try to make a fresh start.

TESMAN (*somewhat distressed*): Yes, that is what you want, I suppose. Uh?

LØVBORG (*smiling, puts down his hat and takes a thick manila envelope out of his pocket*): But when this comes out — George Tesman — you'll have to read it. Because this is the real book — the one that speaks for my true self.

TESMAN: Oh, really? What sort of book is that?

LØVBORG: It's the sequel.

TESMAN: Sequel? To what?

LØVBORG: To the book.

TESMAN: The one just out?

LØVBORG: Of course.

TESMAN: Yes, but my dear Eilert — that comes right down to our own time!

LØVBORG: Yes, it does. And this one deals with the future.

TESMAN: The future! But good Lord, there's nothing we know about that!

LØVBORG: True. But there are one or two things worth saying about it all the same. (*Opens the envelope.*) Here, take a look —

TESMAN: But that's not your handwriting.

LØVBORG: I dictated it. (*Paging through the manuscript.*) It's divided into two sections. The first is about the forces shaping the civilization of the future. And the second part, here — (*paging further on*) suggests what lines of development it's likely to take.

TESMAN: How extraordinary! It never would have occurred to me to write about anything like that.

HEDDA (*at the glass door, drumming on the pane*): Hm — no, of course not.

LØVBORG (*puts the manuscript back in the envelope and lays it on the table*): I brought it along because I thought I might read you a bit of it this evening.

TESMAN: Ah, that's very good of you, Eilert; but this evening — (*Glancing at Brack.*) I'm really not sure that it's possible —

LØVBORG: Well, some other time, then. There's no hurry.

BRACK: I should explain, Mr. Løvborg — there's a little party at my place tonight. Mostly for Tesman, you understand.

LØVBORG (*looking for his hat*): Ah — then I won't stay —

BRACK: No, listen — won't you give me the pleasure of having you join us?

LØVBORG (*sharply and decisively*): No, I can't. Thanks very much.

BRACK: Oh, nonsense! Do that. We'll be a small, select group. And you can bet we'll have it "lively," as Mrs. Hed — Mrs. Tesman says.

LØVBORG: I don't doubt it. But nevertheless —

BRACK: You could bring your manuscript with you and read it to Tesman there, at my place. I have a spare room you could use.

TESMAN: Why, of course, Eilert — you could do that, couldn't you? Uh?

HEDDA (*intervening*): But dear, if Mr. Løvborg simply doesn't want to! I'm sure Mr. Løvborg would much prefer to settle down here and have supper with me.

LØVBORG (*looking at her*): With you, Mrs. Tesman!

HEDDA: And with Mrs. Elvsted.

LØVBORG: Ah. (*Casually.*) I saw her a moment this afternoon.

HEDDA: Oh, did you? Well, she'll be here soon. So it's almost essential for you to stay, Mr. Løvborg. Otherwise, she'll have no one to see her home.

LØVBORG: That's true. Yes, thank you, Mrs. Tesman — I'll be staying, then.

HEDDA: Then let me just tell the maid —

(*She goes to the hall door and rings. Berta enters. Hedda talks to her quietly and points toward the inner room. Berta nods and goes out again.*)

TESMAN (*at the same time, to Løvborg*): Tell me, Eilert — is it this new material — about the future — that you're going to be lecturing on?

LØVBORG: Yes.

TESMAN: Because I heard at the bookstore that you'll be giving a lecture series here this autumn.

LØVBORG: I intend to. I hope you won't be offended, Tesman.

TESMAN: Why, of course not! But —?

LØVBORG: I can easily understand that it makes things rather difficult for you.

TESMAN (*dispiritedly*): Oh, I could hardly expect that for my sake you'd —

LØVBORG: But I'm going to wait till you have your appointment.

TESMAN: You'll wait! Yes, but — but — you're not competing for it, then? Uh?

LØVBORG: No. I only want to win in the eyes of the world.

TESMAN: But, my Lord — then Aunt Julie was right after all! Oh yes — I knew it all along! Hedda! Can you imagine — Eilert Løvborg won't stand in our way!

HEDDA (*brusquely*): Our way? Leave me out of it.

(*She goes up toward the inner room where Berta is putting a tray with decanters and glasses on the table.*

Hedda nods her approval and comes back again. Berta goes out.)

TESMAN (*at the same time*): But you, Judge — what do you say to all this? Uh?

BRACK: Well, I'd say that victory and honor — hm — after all, they're very sweet —

TESMAN: Yes, of course. But still —

HEDDA (*regarding Tesman with a cold smile*): You look as if you'd been struck by lightning.

TESMAN: Yes — something like it — I guess —

BRACK: That's because a thunderstorm just passed over us, Mrs. Tesman.

HEDDA (*pointing toward the inner room*): Won't you gentlemen please help yourselves to a glass of cold punch?

BRACK (*looking at his watch*): A parting cup? That's not such a bad idea.

TESMAN: Marvelous, Hedda! Simply marvelous! The way I feel now, with this weight off my mind —

HEDDA: Please, Mr. Løvborg, you too.

LØVBORG (*with a gesture of refusal*): No, thank you. Not for me.

BRACK: Good Lord, cold punch — it isn't poison, you know.

LØVBORG: Perhaps not for everyone.

HEDDA: I'll keep Mr. Løvborg company a while.

TESMAN: All right, Hedda dear, you do that.

(*He and Brack go into the inner room, sit down, drink punch, smoke cigarettes, and talk animatedly during the following. Løvborg remains standing by the stove. Hedda goes to the writing table.*)

HEDDA (*slightly raising her voice*): I can show you some photographs, if you like. Tesman and I traveled through the Tyrol on our way home.

(*She brings over an album and lays it on the table by the sofa, seating herself in the farthest corner. Eilert Løvborg comes closer, stops and looks at her. Then he takes a chair and sits down on her left, his back toward the inner room.*)

HEDDA (*opening the album*): You see this view of the mountains, Mr. Løvborg. That's the Ortler group. Tesman's labeled them underneath. Here it is: "The Ortler group, near Meran."

LØVBORG (*whose eyes have never left her, speaking in a low, soft voice*): Hedda — Gabler!

HEDDA (*with a quick glance at him*): Ah! Shh!

LØVBORG (*repeating softly*): Hedda Gabler!

HEDDA (*looks at the album*): Yes, I used to be called that. In those days — when we two knew each other.

LØVBORG: And from now on — for the rest of my life — I have to teach myself not to say Hedda Gabler.

HEDDA (*turning the pages*): Yes, you have to. And I think you ought to start practicing it. The sooner the better, I'd say.

LØVBORG (*resentment in his voice*): Hedda Gabler married? And to George Tesman!

HEDDA: Yes — that's how it goes.

LØVBORG: Oh, Hedda, Hedda — how could you throw yourself away like that!

HEDDA (*looks at him sharply*): All right — no more of that!

LØVBORG: What do you mean?

(*Tesman comes in and over to the sofa.*)

HEDDA (*hears him coming and says casually*): And this one, Mr. Løvborg, was taken from the Val d'Ampezzo. Just look at the peaks of those mountains. (*Looks warmly up at Tesman.*) Now what were those marvelous mountains called, dear?

TESMAN: Let me see. Oh, those are the Dolomites.

HEDDA: Why, of course! Those are the Dolomites, Mr. Løvborg.

TESMAN: Hedda dear — I only wanted to ask if we shouldn't bring in some punch anyway. At least for you, hm?

HEDDA: Yes, thank you. And a couple of *petits fours,* please.

TESMAN: No cigarettes?

HEDDA: No.

TESMAN: Right.

(*He goes through the inner room and out to the right. Brack remains sitting inside, keeping his eye from time to time on Hedda and Løvborg.*)

LØVBORG (*softly, as before*): Answer me, Hedda — how could you go and do such a thing?

HEDDA (*apparently immersed in the album*): If you keep on saying Hedda like that to me, I won't talk to you.

LØVBORG: Can't I say Hedda even when we're alone?

HEDDA: No. You can think it, but you mustn't say it like that.

LØVBORG: Ah, I understand. It offends your — love for George Tesman.

HEDDA (*glances at him and smiles*): Love? You *are* absurd!

LØVBORG: Then you don't love him!

HEDDA: I don't expect to be unfaithful, either. I'm not having any of that!

LØVBORG: Hedda, just answer me one thing —

HEDDA: Shh!

(*Tesman, carrying a tray, enters from the inner room.*)

TESMAN: Look out! Here come the goodies. (*He sets the tray on the table.*)

HEDDA: Why do you do the serving?

TESMAN (*filling the glasses*): Because I think it's such fun to wait on you, Hedda.

HEDDA: But now you've poured out two glasses. And you know Mr. Løvborg doesn't want —

TESMAN: Well, but Mrs. Elvsted will be along soon.

HEDDA: Yes, that's right — Mrs. Elvsted —

TESMAN: Had you forgotten her? Uh?

HEDDA: We've been so caught up in these. (*Showing him a picture.*) Do you remember this little village?

TESMAN: Oh, that's the one just below the Brenner Pass! It was there that we stayed overnight —

HEDDA: And met all those lively summer people.

TESMAN: Yes, that's the place. Just think — if we could have had you with us, Eilert! My! (*He goes back and sits beside Brack.*)

LØVBORG: Answer me just one thing, Hedda —

HEDDA: Yes?

LØVBORG: Was there no love with respect to me, either? Not a spark — not one glimmer of love at all?

HEDDA: I wonder, really, was there? To me it was as if we were two true companions — two very close friends. (*Smiling.*) You, especially, were so open with me.

LØVBORG: You wanted it that way.

HEDDA: When I look back on it now, there was really something beautiful and fascinating — and daring, it seems to me, about — about our secret closeness — our companionship that no one, not a soul, suspected.

LØVBORG: Yes, Hedda, that's true! Wasn't there? When I'd come over to your father's in the afternoon — and the general sat by the window reading his papers — with his back to us —

HEDDA: And we'd sit on the corner sofa —

LØVBORG: Always with the same illustrated magazine in front of us —

HEDDA: Yes, for the lack of an album.

LØVBORG: Yes, Hedda — and the confessions I used to make — telling you things about myself that no one else knew of then. About the way I'd go out, the drinking, the madness that went on day and night, for days at a time. Ah, what power was it in you, Hedda, that made me tell you such things?

HEDDA: You think it was some kind of power in me?

LØVBORG: How else can I explain it? And all those — those devious questions you asked me —

HEDDA: That you understood so remarkably well —

LØVBORG: To think you could sit there and ask such questions! So boldly.

HEDDA: Deviously, please.

LØVBORG: Yes, but boldly, all the same. Interrogating me about — all that kind of thing!

HEDDA: And to think that you could answer, Mr. Løvborg.

LØVBORG: Yes, that's exactly what I don't understand — now, looking back. But tell me, Hedda — the root of that bond between us, wasn't it love? Didn't you feel, on your part, as if you wanted to cleanse and absolve me — when I brought those confessions to you? Wasn't that it?

HEDDA: No, not quite.

LØVBORG: What was your power, then?

HEDDA: Do you find it so very surprising that a young girl — if there's no chance of anyone knowing —

LØVBORG: Yes?

HEDDA: That she'd like some glimpse of a world that —

LØVBORG: That —?

HEDDA: That she's forbidden to know anything about.

LØVBORG: So that was it?

HEDDA: Partly. Partly that, I guess.

LØVBORG: Companionship in a thirst for life. But why, then, couldn't it have gone on?

HEDDA: But that was your fault.

LØVBORG: You broke it off.

HEDDA: Yes, when that closeness of ours threatened to grow more serious. Shame on you, Eilert Løvborg! How could you violate my trust when I'd been so — so bold with my friendship?

LØVBORG (clenching his fists): Oh, why didn't you do what you said! Why didn't you shoot me down!

HEDDA: I'm — much too afraid of scandal.

LØVBORG: Yes, Hedda, you're a coward at heart.

HEDDA: A terrible coward. (Changing her tone.) But that was lucky for you. And now you're so nicely consoled at the Elvsteds'.

LØVBORG: I know what Thea's been telling you.

HEDDA: And perhaps you've been telling her all about us?

LØVBORG: Not a word. She's too stupid for that sort of thing.

HEDDA: Stupid?

LØVBORG: When it comes to those things, she's stupid.

HEDDA: And I'm a coward. (Leans closer, without looking him in the eyes, and speaks softly.) But there is something now that I can tell you.

LØVBORG (intently): What?

HEDDA: When I didn't dare shoot you —

LØVBORG: Yes?

HEDDA: That wasn't my worst cowardice — that night.

LØVBORG (looks at her a moment, understands, and whispers passionately): Oh, Hedda! Hedda Gabler! Now I begin to see it, the hidden reason why we've been so close! You and I —! . . . It was the hunger for life in you —

HEDDA (quietly, with a sharp glance): Careful! That's no way to think!

(It has begun to grow dark. The hall door is opened from without by Berta.)

HEDDA (clapping the album shut and calling out with a smile): Well, at last! Thea dear — please come in!

(Mrs. Elvsted enters from the hall. She is in evening dress. The door is closed behind her.)

HEDDA (on the sofa, stretching her arms out toward her): Thea, my sweet — I thought you were never coming!

(In passing, Mrs. Elvsted exchanges light greetings with the gentlemen in the inner room, then comes over to the table and extends her hand to Hedda. Løvborg has gotten up. He and Mrs. Elvsted greet each other with a silent nod.)

MRS. ELVSTED: Perhaps I ought to go in and talk a bit with your husband?

HEDDA: Oh, nonsense. Let them be. They're leaving soon.

MRS. ELVSTED: They're leaving?

HEDDA: Yes, for a drinking party.

MRS. ELVSTED (quickly, to Løvborg): But you're not?

LØVBORG: No.

HEDDA: Mr. Løvborg — is staying with us.

MRS. ELVSTED (taking a chair, about to sit down beside him): Oh, it's so good to be here!

HEDDA: No, no, Thea dear! Not there! You have to come over here by me. I want to be in the middle.

MRS. ELVSTED: Any way you please.

(She goes around the table and sits on the sofa to Hedda's right. Løvborg resumes his seat.)

LØVBORG (after a brief pause, to Hedda): Isn't she lovely to look at?

HEDDA (lightly stroking her hair): Only to look at?

LØVBORG: Yes. Because we two — she and I — we really are true companions. We trust each other completely. We can talk things out together without any reservations —

HEDDA: Never anything devious, Mr. Løvborg?

LØVBORG: Well —

MRS. ELVSTED (quietly, leaning close to Hedda): Oh, Hedda, you don't know how happy I am! Just think — he says that I've inspired him!

HEDDA (regarding her with a smile): Really, dear; did he say that?

LØVBORG: And then the courage she has, Mrs. Tesman, when it's put to the test.

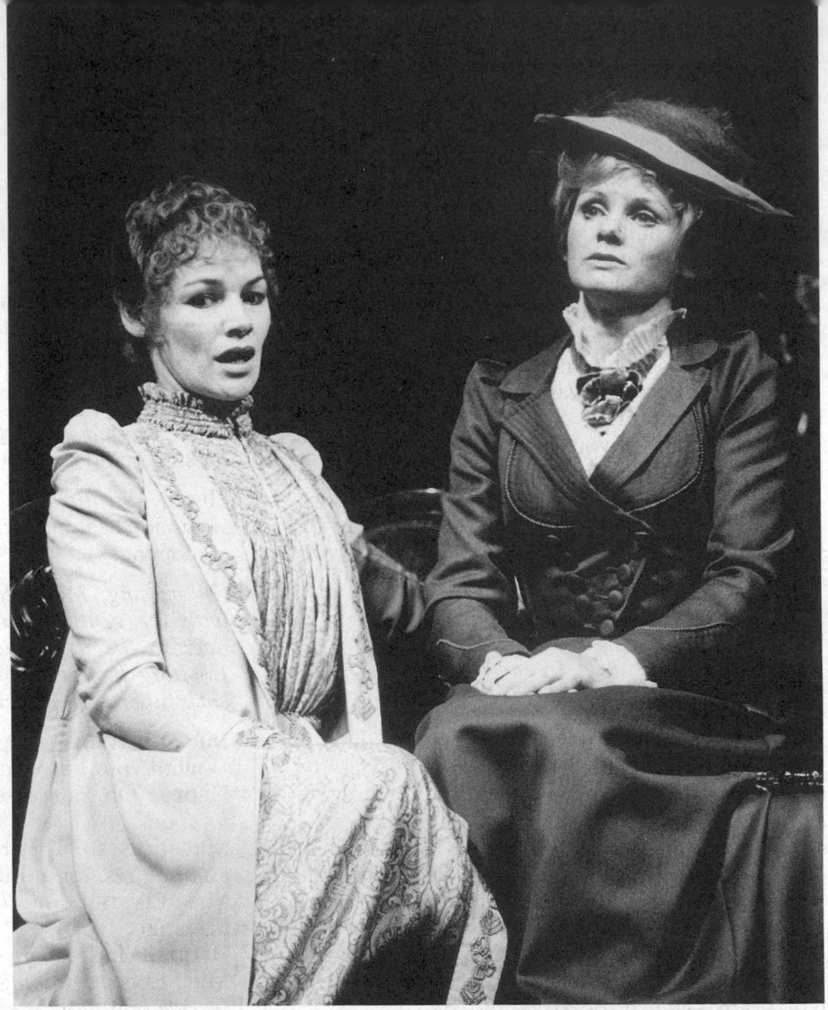

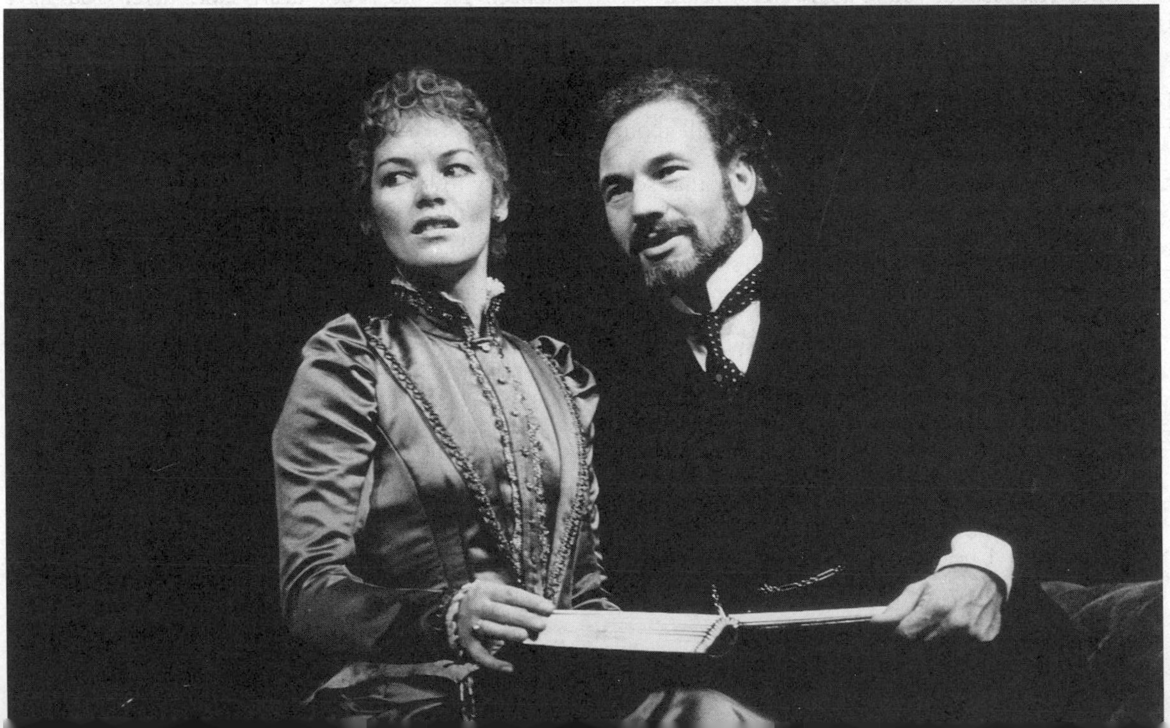

ABOVE LEFT: Hedda (Glenda Jackson) and Mrs. Elvsted (Jennie Linden) in the 1975 Royal Shakespeare Company production of *Hedda Gabler* at the Aldwych. BELOW LEFT: Hedda and Eilert Løvborg (Patrick Stewart). RIGHT: Mrs. Elvsted and Hedda.

MRS. ELVSTED: Good heavens, me! Courage!

LØVBORG: Enormous courage — where I'm concerned.

HEDDA: Yes, courage — yes! If one only had that.

LØVBORG: Then what?

HEDDA: Then life might still be bearable. (*Suddenly changing her tone.*) But now, Thea dearest — you really must have a nice cold glass of punch.

MRS. ELVSTED: No, thank you. I never drink that sort of thing.

HEDDA: Well, then you, Mr. Løvborg.

LØVBORG: Thanks, not for me either.

MRS. ELVSTED: No, not for him either!

HEDDA (*looking intently at him*): But if I insist?

LØVBORG: Makes no difference.

HEDDA (*with a laugh*): Poor me, then I have no power over you at all?

LØVBORG: Not in that area.

HEDDA: But seriously, I think you ought to, all the same. For your own sake.

MRS. ELVSTED: But Hedda — !

LØVBORG: Why do you think so?

HEDDA: Or, to be more exact, for others' sakes.

LØVBORG: Oh?

HEDDA: Otherwise, people might get the idea that you're not very bold at heart. That you're not really sure of yourself at all.

MRS. ELVSTED (*softly*): Oh, Hedda, don't — !

LØVBORG: People can think whatever they like, for all I care.

MRS. ELVSTED (*happily*): Yes, that's right!

HEDDA: I saw it so clearly in Judge Brack a moment ago.

LØVBORG: What did you see?

HEDDA: The contempt in his smile when you didn't dare join them for a drink.

LØVBORG: Didn't dare! Obviously I'd rather stay here and talk with you.

MRS. ELVSTED: That's only reasonable, Hedda.

HEDDA: But how could the judge know that? And besides, I noticed him smile and glance at Tesman when you couldn't bring yourself to go to their wretched little party.

LØVBORG: Couldn't! Are you saying I couldn't?

HEDDA: *I'm* not. But that's the way Judge Brack sees it.

LØVBORG: All right, let him.

HEDDA: Then you won't go along?

LØVBORG: I'm staying here with you and Thea.

MRS. ELVSTED: Yes, Hedda — you can be sure he is!

HEDDA (*smiles and nods approvingly at Løvborg*): I see. Firm as a rock. True to principle, to the end of time. There, that's what a man ought to be! (*Turning to Mrs. Elvsted and patting her.*) Well, now, didn't I tell you that, when you came here so distraught this morning —

LØVBORG (*surprised*): Distraught?

MRS. ELVSTED (*terrified*): Hedda —! But Hedda —!

HEDDA: Can't you see for yourself? There's no need at all for your going around so deathly afraid that — (*Changing her tone.*) There! Now we can all enjoy ourselves!

LØVBORG (*shaken*): What is all this, Mrs. Tesman?

MRS. ELVSTED: Oh, God, oh, God, Hedda! What are you saying! What are you doing!

HEDDA: Not so loud. That disgusting judge is watching you.

LØVBORG: So deathly afraid? For my sake?

MRS. ELVSTED (*in a low moan*): Oh, Hedda, you've made me so miserable!

LØVBORG (*looks intently at her a moment, his face drawn*): So that's how completely you trusted me.

MRS. ELVSTED (*imploringly*): Oh, my dearest — if you'll only listen —!

LØVBORG (*takes one of the glasses of punch, raises it, and says in a low, hoarse voice*): Your health, Thea! (*He empties the glass, puts it down, and takes the other.*)

MRS. ELVSTED (*softly*): Oh, Hedda, Hedda — how could you want such a thing!

HEDDA: Want it? I? Are you crazy?

LØVBORG: And your health too, Mrs. Tesman. Thanks for the truth. Long live truth! (*Drains the glass and starts to refill it.*)

HEDDA (*laying her hand on his arm*): All right — no more for now. Remember, you're going to a party.

MRS. ELVSTED: No, no, no!

HEDDA: Shh! They're watching you.

LØVBORG (*putting down his glass*): Now, Thea — tell me honestly —

MRS. ELVSTED: Yes!

LØVBORG: Did your husband know that you followed me?

MRS. ELVSTED (*wringing her hands*): Oh, Hedda — listen to him!

LØVBORG: Did you have it arranged, you and he, that you should come down into town and spy on me? Or maybe he got you to do it himself? Ah, yes — I'm sure he needed me back in the office! Or maybe he missed my hand at cards?

MRS. ELVSTED (*softly, in anguish*): Oh, Eilert, Eilert —!

LØVBORG (*seizing his glass to fill it*): Skoal to the old sheriff, too!

HEDDA (*stopping him*): That's enough. Don't forget, you're giving a reading for Tesman.

LØVBORG (*calmly, setting down his glass*): That was stupid of me, Thea. I mean, taking it like this. Don't be angry at me, my dearest. You'll see — you and all the others — that if I stumbled and fell — I'm back on my feet again now! With your help, Thea.

MRS. ELVSTED (*radiant with joy*): Oh, thank God —!

(*Brack, in the meantime, has looked at his watch. He and Tesman stand up and enter the drawing room.*)

BRACK (*takes his hat and overcoat*): Well, Mrs. Tesman, our time is up.

HEDDA: I suppose it is.

LØVBORG (*rising*): Mine too, Judge.

MRS. ELVSTED (*softly pleading*): Oh, Eilert — don't!

HEDDA (*pinching her arm*): They can hear you!

MRS. ELVSTED (*with a small cry*): Ow!

LØVBORG (*to Brack*): You were kind enough to ask me along.

BRACK: Oh, then you *are* coming, after all?

LØVBORG: Yes, thank you.

BRACK: I'm delighted —

LØVBORG (*putting the manila envelope in his pocket, to Tesman*): I'd like to show you one or two things before I turn this in.

TESMAN: Just think — how exciting! But Hedda dear, how will Mrs. Elvsted get home? Uh?

HEDDA: Oh, we'll hit on something.

LØVBORG (*glancing toward the ladies*): Mrs. Elvsted? Don't worry, I'll stop back and fetch her. (*Coming nearer.*) Say about ten o'clock, Mrs. Tesman? Will that do?

HEDDA: Yes. That will do very nicely.

TESMAN: Well, then everything's all set. But you mustn't expect *me* that early, Hedda.

HEDDA: Dear, you stay as long — just as long as you like.

MRS. ELVSTED (*with suppressed anxiety*): Mr. Løvborg — I'll be waiting here till you come.

LØVBORG (*his hat in hand*): Yes, I understand.

BRACK: So, gentlemen — the excursion train is leaving! I hope it's going to be lively, as a certain fair lady puts it.

HEDDA: Ah, if only that fair lady could be there, invisible —!

BRACK: Why invisible?

HEDDA: To hear a little of your unadulterated liveliness, Judge.

BRACK (*laughs*): I wouldn't advise the fair lady to try.

TESMAN (*also laughing*): Hedda, you are the limit! What an idea!

BRACK: Well, good night. Good night, ladies.

LØVBORG (*bowing*): About ten o'clock, then.

(*Brack, Løvborg, and Tesman go out the hall door. At the same time, Berta enters from the inner room with a lighted lamp, which she sets on the drawing room table, then goes out the same way.*)

MRS. ELVSTED (*having risen, moving restlessly about the room*): Hedda — Hedda — what's going to come of all this?

HEDDA: At ten o'clock — he'll be here. I can see him now — with vine leaves in his hair — fiery and bold —

MRS. ELVSTED: Oh, how good that would be!

HEDDA: And then, you'll see — he'll be back in control of himself. He'll be a free man, then, for the rest of his days.

MRS. ELVSTED: Oh, God — if only he comes as you see him now!

HEDDA: He'll come back like that, and no other way! (*Gets up and goes closer.*) Go on and doubt him as much as you like. I believe in him. And now we'll find out —

MRS. ELVSTED: There's something behind what you're doing, Hedda.

HEDDA: Yes, there is. For once in my life, I want to have power over a human being.

MRS. ELVSTED: But don't you have that?

HEDDA: I don't have it. I've never had it.

MRS. ELVSTED: Not with your husband?

HEDDA: Yes, what a bargain *that* was! Oh, if you only could understand how poor I am. And you're allowed to be so rich! (*Passionately throws her arms about her.*) I think I'll burn your hair off, after all!

MRS. ELVSTED: Let go! Let me go! I'm afraid of you, Hedda!

BERTA (*in the doorway to the inner room*): Supper's waiting in the dining room, ma'am.

HEDDA: All right, we're coming.

MRS. ELVSTED: No, no, no! I'd rather go home alone! Right away — now!

HEDDA: Nonsense! First you're going to have tea, you little fool. And then — ten o'clock — Eilert Løvborg comes — with vine leaves in his hair.

(*She drags Mrs. Elvsted, almost by force, toward the doorway.*)

ACT III

(*The same rooms at the Tesmans'. The curtains are down across the doorway to the inner room, and also across the glass door. The lamp, shaded and turned down low, is burning on the table. The door to the stove stands open; the fire has nearly gone out.*)

(*Mrs. Elvsted, wrapped in a large shawl, with her feet up on a footstool, lies back in the armchair close by the stove. Hedda, fully dressed, is asleep on the sofa, with a blanket over her. After a pause, Mrs. Elvsted suddenly sits straight up in the chair, listening tensely. Then she sinks wearily back again.*)

MRS. ELVSTED (*in a low moan*): Not yet — oh, God — oh, God — not yet!

(*Berta slips in cautiously by the hall door. She holds a letter in her hand.*)

MRS. ELVSTED (*turns and whispers anxiously*): Yes? Has anyone come?

BERTA (*softly*): Yes, a girl just now stopped by with this letter.

MRS. ELVSTED (*quickly, reaching out her hand*): A letter! Give it to me!

BERTA: No, it's for the Doctor, ma'am.

MRS. ELVSTED: Oh.

BERTA: It was Miss Tesman's maid that brought it. I'll leave it here on the table.

MRS. ELVSTED: Yes, do.

BERTA (*putting the letter down*): I think I'd best put out the lamp. It's smoking.

MRS. ELVSTED: Yes, put it out. It'll be daylight soon.

BERTA (*does so*): It's broad daylight already, ma'am.

MRS. ELVSTED: It's daylight! And still no one's come —!

BERTA: Oh, mercy — I knew it would go like this.

MRS. ELVSTED: You knew?

BERTA: Yes, when I saw that a certain gentleman was back here in town — and that he went off with them. We've heard plenty about that gentleman over the years.

MRS. ELVSTED: Don't talk so loud. You'll wake Mrs. Tesman.

BERTA (*looks toward the sofa and sighs*): Goodness me — yes, let her sleep, poor thing. Should I put a bit more on the fire?

MRS. ELVSTED: Thanks, not for me.

BERTA: All right. (*She goes quietly out the hall door.*)

HEDDA (*wakes as the door shuts and looks up*): What's that?

MRS. ELVSTED: It was just the maid —

HEDDA (*glancing about*): In here —? Oh yes, I remember now. (*Sits up on the sofa, stretches, and rubs her eyes.*) What time is it, Thea?

MRS. ELVSTED (*looking at her watch*): It's after seven.

HEDDA: When did Tesman get in?

MRS. ELVSTED: He isn't back.

HEDDA: Not back yet?

MRS. ELVSTED (*getting up*): No one's come in.

HEDDA: And we sat here and waited up for them till four o'clock —

MRS. ELVSTED (*wringing her hands*): And *how* I've waited for him!

HEDDA (*yawns, and speaks with her hand in front of her mouth*): Oh, dear — we could have saved ourselves the trouble.

MRS. ELVSTED: Did you get any sleep?

HEDDA: Oh yes. I slept quite well, I think. Didn't you?

MRS. ELVSTED: No, not at all. I couldn't, Hedda! It was just impossible.

HEDDA (*rising and going toward her*): There, there, now! There's nothing to worry about. It's not hard to guess what happened.

MRS. ELVSTED: Oh, what? Tell me!

HEDDA: Well, it's clear that the party must have gone on till all hours —

MRS. ELVSTED: Oh, Lord, yes — it must have. But even so —

HEDDA: And then, of course, Tesman didn't want to come home and make a commotion in the middle of the night. (*Laughs.*) Probably didn't care to show himself, either — so full of his party spirits.

MRS. ELVSTED: But where else could he have gone?

HEDDA: He must have gone up to his aunts' to sleep. They keep his old room ready.

MRS. ELVSTED: No, he can't be with them. Because he just now got a letter from Miss Tesman. It's over there.

HEDDA: Oh? (*Looking at the address.*) Yes, that's Aunt Julie's handwriting, all right. Well, then he must have stayed over at Judge Brack's. And Eilert Løvborg — he's sitting with vine leaves in his hair, reading away.

MRS. ELVSTED: Oh, Hedda, you say these things, and you really don't believe them at all.

HEDDA: You're such a little fool, Thea.

MRS. ELVSTED: That's true; I guess I am.

HEDDA: And you really look dead tired.

MRS. ELVSTED: Yes, I feel dead tired.

HEDDA: Well, you just do as I say, then. Go in my room and stretch out on the bed for a while.

MRS. ELVSTED: No, no — I still wouldn't get any sleep.

HEDDA: Why, of course you would.

MRS. ELVSTED: Well, but your husband's sure to be home now soon. And I've got to know right away —

HEDDA: I'll call you the moment he comes.

MRS. ELVSTED: Yes? Promise me, Hedda?

HEDDA: You can count on it. Just go and get some sleep.

MRS. ELVSTED: Thanks. I'll try. (*She goes out through the inner room.*)

(*Hedda goes over to the glass door and draws the curtains back. Bright daylight streams into the room. She goes over to the writing table, takes out a small hand mirror, regards herself and arranges her hair. She then goes to the hall door and presses the bell. After a moment, Berta enters.*)

BERTA: Did you want something, ma'am?

HEDDA: Yes, you can build up the fire. I'm freezing in here.

BERTA: Why, my goodness — we'll have it warm in no time. (*She rakes the embers together and puts some wood on, then stops and listens.*) There's the front doorbell, ma'am.

HEDDA: Go see who it is. I'll take care of the stove.

BERTA: It'll be burning soon. (*She goes out the hall door.*)

(*Hedda kneels on the footstool and lays more wood on the fire. After a moment, George Tesman comes in from the hall. He looks tired and rather serious. He tiptoes toward the doorway to the inner room and is about to slip through the curtains.*)

HEDDA (*at the stove, without looking up*): Good morning.

TESMAN (*turns*): Hedda! (*Approaching her.*) But what on earth —! You're up so early? Uh?

HEDDA: Yes, I'm up quite early today.

TESMAN: And I was so sure you were still in bed sleeping. Isn't that something, Hedda!

HEDDA: Not so loud. Mrs. Elvsted's resting in my room.

TESMAN: Was Mrs. Elvsted here all night?

HEDDA: Well, no one returned to take her home.

TESMAN: No, I guess that's right.

HEDDA (*shuts the door to the stove and gets up*): So — did you enjoy your party?

TESMAN: Were you worried about me? Hm?

HEDDA: No, that never occurred to me. I just asked if you'd had a good time.

TESMAN: Oh yes, I really did, for once. But more at the beginning, I'd say — when Eilert read to me out of his book. We got there more than an hour too soon — imagine! And Brack had so much to get ready. But then Eilert read to me.

HEDDA (*sitting at the right-hand side of the table*): Well? Tell me about it —

TESMAN (*sitting on a footstool by the stove*): Really, Hedda — you can't imagine what a book that's going to be! I do believe it's one of the most remarkable things ever written. Just think!

HEDDA: Yes, I don't mean the book —

TESMAN: But I have to make a confession, Hedda. When he'd finished reading — I had such a nasty feeling —

HEDDA: Nasty?

TESMAN: I found myself envying Eilert, that he was able to write such a book. Can you imagine, Hedda!

HEDDA: Oh yes, I can imagine!

TESMAN: And then how sad to see — that with all his gifts — he's still quite irreclaimable.

HEDDA: Don't you mean that he has more courage to live than the others?

TESMAN: Good Lord, no — I mean, he simply can't take his pleasures in moderation.

HEDDA: Well, what happened then — at the end?

TESMAN: I suppose I'd have to say it turned into an orgy, Hedda.

HEDDA: Were there vine leaves in his hair?

TESMAN: Vine leaves? Not that I noticed. But he gave a long, muddled speech in honor of the woman who'd inspired his work. Yes, that was his phrase for it.

HEDDA: Did he give her name?

TESMAN: No, he didn't. But it seems to me it has to be Mrs. Elvsted. Wait and see!

HEDDA: Oh? Where did you leave him?

TESMAN: On the way here. We broke up — the last of us — all together. And Brack came along with us too, to get a little fresh air. And then we did want to make sure that Eilert got home safe. Because he really had a load on, you know.

HEDDA: He must have.

TESMAN: But here's the curious part of it, Hedda. Or perhaps I should say, the distressing part. Oh, I'm almost ashamed to speak of it — for Eilert's sake —

HEDDA: Yes, go on —

TESMAN: Well, as we were walking toward town, you see, I happened to drop back a little behind the others. Only for a minute or two — you follow me?

HEDDA: Yes, yes, so —?

TESMAN: And then when I was catching up with the rest of them, what do you think I found on the sidewalk? Uh?

HEDDA: Oh, how should I know!

TESMAN: You mustn't breathe a word to anyone, Hedda — you hear me? Promise me that, for Eilert's sake. (*Takes a manila envelope out of his coat pocket.*) Just think — I found this.

HEDDA: Isn't that what he had with him yesterday?

TESMAN: That's right. It's the whole of his precious, irreplaceable manuscript. And he went and lost it — without even noticing. Can you imagine, Hedda! How distressing —

HEDDA: But why didn't you give it right back to him?

TESMAN: No, I didn't dare do that — in the state he was in —

HEDDA: And you didn't tell any of the others you'd found it?

TESMAN: Of course not. I'd never do that, you know — for Eilert's sake.

HEDDA: Then there's no one who knows you have Eilert Løvborg's manuscript?

TESMAN: No. And no one must ever know, either.

HEDDA: What did you say to him afterwards?

TESMAN: I had no chance at all to speak with him. As soon as we reached the edge of town, he and a couple of others got away from us and disappeared. Imagine!

HEDDA: Oh? I expect they saw him home.

TESMAN: Yes, they probably did, I suppose. And also Brack went home.

HEDDA: And where've you been carrying on since then?

TESMAN: Well, I and some of the others — we were invited up by one of the fellows and had morning coffee at his place. Or a post-midnight snack, maybe — uh? But as soon as I've had a little rest — and given poor Eilert time to sleep it off, then I've got to take this back to him.

HEDDA (*reaching out for the envelope*): No — don't give it back! Not yet, I mean. Let me read it first.

TESMAN: Hedda dearest, no. My Lord, I can't do that.

HEDDA: You can't?

TESMAN: No. Why, you can just imagine the anguish he'll feel when he wakes up and misses the manuscript. He hasn't any copy of it, you know. He told me that himself.

HEDDA (*looks searchingly at him*): Can't such a work be rewritten? I mean, over again?

TESMAN: Oh, I don't see how it could. Because the inspiration, you know —

HEDDA: Yes, yes — that's the thing, I suppose. (*Casually.*) Oh, by the way — there's a letter for you.

TESMAN: No, really —?

HEDDA (*handing it to him*): It came early this morning.

TESMAN: Dear, from Aunt Julie! What could that be? (*Sets the envelope on the other taboret, opens the letter, skims through it, and springs to his feet.*) Oh, Hedda — she says poor Auntie Rina's dying!

HEDDA: It's no more than we've been expecting.

TESMAN: And if I want to see her one last time, I've got to hurry. I'll have to hop right over.

HEDDA (*suppressing a smile*): Hop?

TESMAN: Oh, Hedda dearest, if you could only bring yourself to come with me! Think of it!

HEDDA (*rises and dismisses the thought wearily*): No no, don't ask me to do such things. I don't want to look on sickness and death. I want to be free of everything ugly.

TESMAN: Yes, all right, then — (*Dashing about.*) My hat —? My overcoat —? Oh, in the hall — I do hope I'm not there too late, Hedda! Hm?

HEDDA: Oh, if you hurry —

(*Berta appears at the hall door.*)

BERTA: Judge Brack's outside, asking if he might stop in.

TESMAN: At a time like this! No, I can't possibly see him now.

HEDDA: But I can. (*To Berta.*) Ask the judge to come in.

(*Berta goes out.*)

HEDDA (*quickly, in a whisper*): Tesman, the manuscript! (*She snatches it from the taboret.*)

TESMAN: Yes, give it here!

HEDDA: No, no, I'll keep it till you're back.

(*She moves over to the writing table and slips it in the bookcase. Tesman stands flustered, unable to get his gloves on. Brack enters from the hall.*)

HEDDA: Well, aren't you the early bird.

BRACK: Yes, wouldn't you say so? (*To Tesman.*) Are you off and away too?

TESMAN: Yes, I absolutely have to get over to my aunts'. Just think — the invalid one, she's dying.

BRACK: Good Lord, she is? But then you mustn't let me detain you. Not at a moment like this —

TESMAN: Yes, I really must run — Good-bye! Good-bye! (*He goes hurriedly out the hall door.*)

HEDDA: It would seem you had quite a time of it last night, Judge.

BRACK: I've not been out of my clothes yet, Mrs. Hedda.

HEDDA: Not you, either?

BRACK: No, as you can see. But what's Tesman been telling you about our night's adventures?

HEDDA: Oh, some tedious tale. Something about stopping up somewhere for coffee.

BRACK: Yes, I know all about the coffee party. Eilert Løvborg wasn't with them, I expect?

HEDDA: No, they'd already taken him home.

BRACK: Tesman, as well.

HEDDA: No, but he said some others had.

BRACK (*smiles*): George Tesman is really a simple soul, Mrs. Hedda.

HEDDA: God knows he's that. But was there something else that went on?

BRACK: Oh, you might say so.

HEDDA: Well, now! Let's sit down, Judge; you'll talk more easily then.

(*She sits at the left-hand side of the table, with Brack at the long side, near her.*)

HEDDA: So?

BRACK: I had particular reasons for keeping track of my guests — or, I should say, certain of my guests, last night.

HEDDA: And among them Eilert Løvborg, perhaps?

BRACK: To be frank — yes.

HEDDA: Now you really have me curious —

BRACK: You know where he and a couple of the others spent the rest of the night, Mrs. Hedda?

HEDDA: Tell me — if it's fit to be told.

BRACK: Oh, it's very much fit to be told. Well, it seems they showed up at a quite animated soiree.

HEDDA: Of the lively sort.

BRACK: Of the liveliest.

HEDDA: Do go on, Judge —

BRACK: Løvborg, and the others also, had advance invitations. I knew all about it. But Løvborg had begged off, because now, of course, he was supposed to have become a new man, as you know.

HEDDA: Up at the Elvsteds', yes. But he went anyway?

BRACK: Well, you see, Mrs. Hedda — unfortunately the spirit moved him up at my place last evening —

HEDDA: Yes, I hear that he *was* inspired there.

BRACK: To a very powerful degree, I'd say. Well, so his mind turned to other things, that's clear. We males, sad to say — we're not always so true to principle as we ought to be.

HEDDA: Oh, I'm sure you're an exception, Judge. But what about Løvborg —?

BRACK: Well, to cut it short — the result was that he wound up in Mademoiselle Diana's parlors.

HEDDA: Mademoiselle Diana's?

BRACK: It was Mademoiselle Diana who was holding the soiree. For a select circle of lady friends and admirers.

HEDDA: Is she a red-haired woman?

BRACK: Precisely.

HEDDA: Sort of a — singer?

BRACK: Oh yes — she's that too. And also a mighty huntress — of men, Mrs. Hedda. You've undoubtedly heard about her. Løvborg was one of her ruling favorites — back there in his palmy° days.

HEDDA: And how did all this end?

BRACK: Less amicably, it seems. She gave him a most tender welcoming, with open arms, but before long she'd taken to fists.

HEDDA: Against Løvborg?

BRACK: That's right. He accused her or her friends of having robbed him. He claimed that his wallet was missing — along with some other things. In short, he must have made a frightful scene.

HEDDA: And what did it come to?

palmy: Prosperous.

BRACK: It came to a regular free-for-all, the men and the women both. Luckily the police finally got there.

HEDDA: The police too?

BRACK: Yes. But it's likely to prove an expensive little romp for Eilert Løvborg. That crazy fool.

HEDDA: So?

BRACK: He apparently made violent resistance. Struck one of the officers on the side of the head and ripped his coat. So they took him along to the station house.

HEDDA: Where did you hear all this?

BRACK: From the police themselves.

HEDDA (*gazing straight ahead*): So that's how it went. Then he had no vine leaves in his hair.

BRACK: Vine leaves, Mrs. Hedda?

HEDDA (*changing her tone*): But tell me, Judge — just why do you go around like this, spying on Eilert Løvborg?

BRACK: In the first place, it's hardly a matter of no concern to me, if it's brought out during the investigation that he'd come direct from my house.

HEDDA: There'll be an investigation —?

BRACK: Naturally. Anyway, that takes care of itself. But I felt that as a friend of the family I owed you and Tesman a full account of his nocturnal exploits.

HEDDA: Why, exactly?

BRACK: Well, because I have a strong suspicion that he'll try to use you as a kind of screen.

HEDDA: Oh, how could you ever think such a thing!

BRACK: Good Lord — we're really not blind, Mrs. Hedda. You'll see! This Mrs. Elvsted, she won't be going home now so quickly.

HEDDA: Well, even supposing there were something between them, there are plenty of other places where they could meet.

BRACK: Not one single home. From now on, every decent house will be closed to Eilert Løvborg.

HEDDA: So mine ought to be too, is that what you mean?

BRACK: Yes. I'll admit I'd find it more than annoying if that gentleman were to have free access here. If he came like an intruder, an irrelevancy, forcing his way into —

HEDDA: Into the triangle?

BRACK: Precisely. It would almost be like turning me out of my home.

HEDDA (*looks at him with a smile*): I see. The one cock of the walk — that's what you want to be.

BRACK (*nodding slowly and lowering his voice*): Yes, that's what I want to be. And that's what I'll fight for — with every means at my disposal.

HEDDA (*her smile vanishing*): You can be a dangerous person, can't you — in a tight corner.

BRACK: Do you think so?

HEDDA: Yes, now I'm beginning to think so. And I'm thoroughly grateful — that you have no kind of hold over me.

BRACK (*with an ambiguous laugh*): Ah, yes, Mrs. Hedda — perhaps you're right about that. If I had, then who knows just what I might do?

HEDDA: Now you listen here, Judge! That sounds too much like a threat.

BRACK (*rising*): Oh, nothing of the kind! A triangle, after all — is best fortified and defended by volunteers.

HEDDA: There we're agreed.

BRACK: Well, now that I've said all I have to say, I'd better get back to town. Good-bye, Mrs. Hedda. (*He goes toward the glass door.*)

HEDDA (*rising*): Are you going through the garden?

BRACK: Yes, I find it's shorter.

HEDDA: Yes, and then it's the back way, too.

BRACK: How true. I have nothing against back ways. At certain times they can be rather piquant.

HEDDA: You mean, when somebody's sharpshooting?

BRACK (*in the doorway, laughing*): Oh, people don't shoot their tame roosters!

HEDDA (*also laughing*): I guess not. Not when there's only one —

(*Still laughing, they nod good-bye to each other. He goes. She shuts the door after him, then stands for a moment, quite serious, looking out. She then goes over and glances through the curtains to the inner room. Moves to the writing table, takes Løvborg's envelope from the bookcase, and is about to page through it, when Berta's voice is heard loudly in the hall. Hedda turns and listens. She hurriedly locks the envelope in the drawer and lays the key on the inkstand. Eilert Løvborg, with his overcoat on and his hat in his hand, throws open the hall door. He looks confused and excited.*)

LØVBORG (*turned toward the hall*): And I'm telling you, I have to go in! I will, you hear me! (*He shuts the door, turns, sees Hedda, immediately gains control of himself and bows.*)

HEDDA (*at the writing table*): Well, Mr. Løvborg, it's late to call for Thea.

LØVBORG: Or rather early to call on you. You must forgive me.

HEDDA: How did you know she was still with me?

LØVBORG: They said at her lodgings that she'd been out all night.

HEDDA (*goes to the center table*): Did you notice anything in their faces when they said that?

LØVBORG (*looking at her inquiringly*): Notice anything?

HEDDA: I mean, did it look like they had their own thoughts on the matter?

LØVBORG (*suddenly understanding*): Oh yes, that's true? I'm dragging her down with me! Actually, I didn't notice anything. Tesman — I don't suppose he's up yet?

HEDDA: No, I don't think so.

LØVBORG: When did he get in?

HEDDA: Very late.

LØVBORG: Did he tell you anything?

HEDDA: Well, I heard you'd had a high time of it out at Judge Brack's.

LØVBORG: Anything else?

HEDDA: No, I don't think so. As a matter of fact, I was terribly sleepy —

(*Mrs. Elvsted comes in through the curtains to the inner room.*)

MRS. ELVSTED (*running toward him*): Oh, Eilert! At last —!

LØVBORG: Yes, at last. And too late.

MRS. ELVSTED (*looking anxiously at him*): What's too late?

LØVBORG: Everything's too late now. It's over with me.

MRS. ELVSTED: Oh no, no — don't say that!

LØVBORG: You'll say the same thing when you've heard —

MRS. ELVSTED: I won't hear anything!

HEDDA: Maybe you'd prefer to talk with her alone. I can leave.

LØVBORG: No, stay — you too. Please.

MRS. ELVSTED: But I tell you, I don't want to hear anything!

700

FAR LEFT: Hedda silhouetted near a portrait of her father, the General, in the Hartford Stage Company's 1988 production. NEAR LEFT: Tesman (Scott Wentworth), Løvborg (Richard Bekins), and Hedda (Mary Layne) discuss Løvborg's manuscript. RIGHT: Tesman and Mrs. Elvsted (Elisabeth Berridge) plan to rewrite Løvborg's lost manuscript. BELOW RIGHT: Judge Brack (William Duff-Griffin) examines Hedda's father's pistol.

LØVBORG: It's nothing about last night.

MRS. ELVSTED: What is it, then —

LØVBORG: It's simply this, that from now on, we separate.

MRS. ELVSTED: Separate!

HEDDA (*involuntarily*): I knew it!

LØVBORG: Because I have no more use for you, Thea.

MRS. ELVSTED: And you can stand there and say that! No more use for me! Then I'm not going to help you now, as I have? We're not going to go on working together?

LØVBORG: I have no plans for any more work.

MRS. ELVSTED (*in desperation*): Then what will I do with my life?

LØVBORG: You must try to go on living as if you'd never known me.

MRS. ELVSTED: But I can't do that!

LØVBORG: You must try to, Thea. You'll have to go home again —

MRS. ELVSTED (*in a fury of protest*): Never! No! Where you are, that's where I want to be! I won't be driven away like this! I'm going to stay right here — and be together with you when the book comes out.

HEDDA (*in a tense whisper*): Ah, yes — the book!

LØVBORG (*looks at her*): My book and Thea's — for that's what it is.

MRS. ELVSTED: Yes, that's what I feel it is. And that's why I have the right, as well, to be with you when it comes out. I want to see you covered with honor and respect again. And the joy — I want to share the joy of it with you too.

LØVBORG: Thea — our book's never coming out.

HEDDA: Ah!

MRS. ELVSTED: Never coming out!

LØVBORG: *Can* never come out.

MRS. ELVSTED (*with anguished foreboding*): Eilert — what have you done with the manuscript?

HEDDA (*watching him intently*): Yes, the manuscript —?

MRS. ELVSTED: Where is it!

LØVBORG: Oh, Thea — don't ask me that.

MRS. ELVSTED: Yes, yes, I have to know. I've got a right to know, this minute!

LØVBORG: The manuscript — well, you see — I tore the manuscript into a thousand pieces.

MRS. ELVSTED (*screams*): Oh no, no —!

HEDDA (*involuntarily*): But that just isn't —!

LØVBORG (*looks at her*): Isn't so, you think?

HEDDA (*composing herself*): All right. Of course; if you say it yourself. But it sounds so incredible —

LØVBORG: It's true, all the same.

MRS. ELVSTED (*wringing her hands*): Oh, God — oh, God, Hedda — to tear his own work to bits!

LØVBORG: I've torn my own life to bits. So why not tear up my life's work as well —

MRS. ELVSTED: And you did this thing last night!

LØVBORG: Yes, you heard me. In a thousand pieces. And scattered them into the fjord. Far out. At least there, there's clean salt water. Let them drift out to sea — drift with the tide and the wind. And after a while, they'll sink. Deeper and deeper. As I will, Thea.

MRS. ELVSTED: Do you know, Eilert, this thing you've done with the book — for the rest of my life it will seem to me as if you'd killed a little child.

LØVBORG: You're right. It was like murdering a child.

MRS. ELVSTED: But how could you do it —! It was my child too.

HEDDA (*almost inaudible*): Ah, the child —

MRS. ELVSTED (*breathes heavily*): Then it *is* all over. Yes, yes, I'm going now, Hedda.

HEDDA: But you're not leaving town, are you?

MRS. ELVSTED: Oh, I don't know myself what I'll do. Everything's dark for me now. (*She goes out the hall door.*)

HEDDA (*stands waiting a moment*): You're not going to take her home, then, Mr. Løvborg?

LØVBORG: I? Through the streets? So people could see that she'd been with me?

HEDDA: I don't know what else may have happened last night. But is it so completely irredeemable?

LØVBORG: It won't just end with last night — I know that well enough. But the thing is, I've lost all desire for that kind of life. I don't want to start it again, not now. It's the courage and daring for life — that's what she's broken in me.

HEDDA (*staring straight ahead*): To think that pretty little fool could have a man's fate in her hands. (*Looks at him.*) But still, how could you treat her so heartlessly?

LØVBORG: Oh, don't say it was heartless!

HEDDA: To go ahead and destroy what's filled her whole being for months and years! That's not heartless?

LØVBORG: To you, Hedda — I can tell the truth.

HEDDA: The truth?

LØVBORG: Promise me first — give me your word that what I tell you now, you'll never let Thea know.

HEDDA: You have my word.

LØVBORG: Good. I can tell you, then, that what I said here just now isn't true.

HEDDA: About the manuscript?

LØVBORG: Yes. I didn't tear it up — or throw it in the fjord.

HEDDA: No, but — where is it, then?

LØVBORG: I've destroyed it all the same, Hedda. Utterly destroyed it.

HEDDA: I don't understand.

LØVBORG: Thea said that what I've done, for her was like killing a child.

HEDDA: Yes — that's what she said.

LØVBORG: But killing his child — that's not the worst thing a father can do.

HEDDA: *That's* not the worst?

LØVBORG: No. I wanted to spare Thea the worst.

HEDDA: And what's that — the worst?

LØVBORG: Suppose now, Hedda, that a man — in the early morning hours, say — after a wild, drunken night, comes home to his child's mother and says: "Listen — I've been out to this place and that — here and there. And I had our child with me. In this place and that. And I lost the child. Just lost it. God only knows what hands it's come into. Or who's got hold of it."

HEDDA: Well — but when all's said and done — it was only a book —

LØVBORG: Thea's pure soul was in that book.

HEDDA: Yes, I understand.

LØVBORG: Well, then you can understand that for her and me there's no future possible any more.

HEDDA: What do you intend to do?

LØVBORG: Nothing. Just put an end to it all. The sooner the better.

HEDDA (*coming a step closer*): Eilert Løvborg — listen to me. Couldn't you arrange that — that it's done beautifully?

LØVBORG: Beautifully? (*Smiles.*) With vine leaves in my hair, as you used to dream in the old days —

HEDDA: No. I don't believe in vine leaves anymore. But beautifully, all the same. For this once —! Good-bye! You must go now — and never come here again.

LØVBORG: Good-bye, then. And give my best to George Tesman. (*He turns to leave.*)

HEDDA: No, wait. I want you to have a souvenir from me.

(*She goes to the writing desk and opens the drawer and the pistol case, then comes back to Løvborg with one of the pistols.*)

LØVBORG (*looks at her*): That? Is that the souvenir?

HEDDA (*nods slowly*): Do you recognize it? It was aimed at you once.

LØVBORG: You should have used it then.

HEDDA: Here! Use it now.

LØVBORG (*puts the pistol in his breast pocket*): Thanks.

HEDDA: And beautifully, Eilert Løvborg. Promise me that!

LØVBORG: Good-bye, Hedda Gabler.

(*He goes out the hall door. Hedda listens a moment at the door. Then she goes over to the writing table,* takes out the envelope with the manuscript, glances inside, pulls some of the sheets half out and looks at them. She then goes over to the armchair by the stove and sits, with the envelope in her lap. After a moment, she opens the stove door, then brings out the manuscript.)

HEDDA (*throwing some of the sheets into the fire and whispering to herself*): Now I'm burning your child, Thea! You, with your curly hair! (*Throwing another sheaf in the stove.*) Your child and Eilert Løvborg's. (*Throwing in the rest.*) Now I'm burning — I'm burning the child.

ACT IV

(*The same rooms at the Tesmans'. It is evening. The drawing room is in darkness. The inner room is lit by the hanging lamp over the table. The curtains are drawn across the glass door. Hedda, dressed in black, is pacing back and forth in the dark room. She then enters the inner room, moving out of sight toward the left. Several chords are heard on the piano. She comes in view again, returning into the drawing room. Berta enters from the right through the inner room with a lighted lamp, which she puts on the table in front of the settee in the drawing room. Her eyes are red from crying, and she has black ribbons on her cap. She goes quietly and discreetly out to the right. Hedda moves to the glass door, lifts the curtains aside slightly, and gazes out into the darkness.*)

(*Shortly after, Miss Tesman, in mourning, with a hat and veil, comes in from the hall. Hedda goes toward her, extending her hand.*)

MISS TESMAN: Well, Hedda, here I am, all dressed in mourning. My poor sister's ordeal is finally over.

HEDDA: As you see, I've already heard. Tesman sent me a note.

MISS TESMAN: Yes, he promised he would. But all the same I thought that, to Hedda — here in the house of life — I ought to bear the news of death myself.

HEDDA: That was very kind of you.

MISS TESMAN: Ah, Rina ought not to have passed on just now. This is no time for grief in Hedda's house.

HEDDA (*changing the subject*): She had a peaceful death, then, Miss Tesman?

MISS TESMAN: Oh, she went so calmly, so beautifully. And so inexpressibly happy that she could see George once again. And say good-bye to him properly. Is it possible that he's still not home?

HEDDA: No, he wrote that I shouldn't expect him too early. But won't you sit down?

MISS TESMAN: No, thank you, my dear — blessed Hedda. I'd love to, but I have so little time. I want to see her dressed and made ready as best as I can. She should go to her grave looking her finest.

HEDDA: Can't I help you with something?

MISS TESMAN: Oh, you mustn't think of it. This is nothing for Hedda Tesman to put her hands to. Or let her thoughts dwell on, either. Not at a time like this, no.

HEDDA: Ah, thoughts — they're not so easy to control —

MISS TESMAN (*continuing*): Well, there's life for you. At my house now we'll be sewing a shroud for Rina. And here, too, there'll be sewing soon, I imagine. But a far different kind, praise God!

(*George Tesman enters from the hall.*)

HEDDA: Well, at last! It's about time.

TESMAN: Are you here, Aunt Julie? With Hedda? Think of that!

MISS TESMAN: I was just this minute leaving, dear boy. Well, did you get done all you promised you would?

TESMAN: No, I'm really afraid I've forgotten half. I'll have to run over and see you tomorrow. My brain's completely in a whirl today. I can't keep my thoughts together.

MISS TESMAN: But George dear, you mustn't take it that way.

TESMAN: Oh? Well, how should I, then?

MISS TESMAN: You should rejoice in your grief. Rejoice in everything that's happened, as I do.

TESMAN: Oh yes, of course. You're thinking of Auntie Rina.

HEDDA: It's going to be lonely for you, Miss Tesman.

MISS TESMAN: For the first few days, yes. But it won't be for long, I hope. I won't let dear Rina's little room stand empty.

TESMAN: No? Who would you want to have in it? Hm?

MISS TESMAN: Oh, there's always some poor invalid in need of care and attention.

HEDDA: Would you really take another burden like that on yourself?

MISS TESMAN: Burden! Mercy on you, child — it's been no burden for me.

HEDDA: But now, with a stranger —

MISS TESMAN: Oh, you soon make friends with an invalid. And I do so much need someone to live for — I, too. Well, thank God, in this house as well, there soon ought to be work that an old aunt can turn her hand to.

HEDDA: Oh, forget about us —

TESMAN: Yes, think how pleasant it could be for the three of us if —

HEDDA: If —?

TESMAN (*uneasily*): Oh, nothing. It'll all take care of itself. Let's hope so. Uh?

MISS TESMAN: Ah, yes. Well, I expect you two have things to talk about. (*Smiles.*) And perhaps Hedda has something to tell you, George. Good-bye. I'll have to get home now to Rina. (*Turning at the door.*) Goodness me, how strange! Now Rina's both with me and with poor dear Jochum as well.

TESMAN: Yes, imagine that, Aunt Julie! Hm?

(*Miss Tesman goes out the hall door.*)

HEDDA (*follows Tesman with a cold, probing look*): I almost think you feel this death more than she.

TESMAN: Oh, it's not just Auntie Rina's death. It's Eilert who has me worried.

HEDDA (*quickly*): Any news about him?

TESMAN: I stopped up at his place this afternoon, thinking to tell him that the manuscript was safe.

HEDDA: Well? Didn't you see him then?

TESMAN: No, he wasn't home. But afterward I met Mrs. Elvsted, and she said he'd been here early this morning.

HEDDA: Yes, right after you left.

TESMAN: And apparently he said he'd torn his manuscript up. Uh?

HEDDA: Yes, he claimed that he had.

TESMAN: But good Lord, then he must have been completely demented! Well, then I guess you didn't dare give it back to him, Hedda, did you?

HEDDA: No, he didn't get it.

TESMAN: But you did tell him we had it, I suppose?

HEDDA: No. (*Quickly.*) Did you tell Mrs. Elvsted anything?

TESMAN: No, I thought I'd better not. But you should have said something to him. Just think, if he goes off in desperation and does himself some harm! Give me the manuscript, Hedda! I'm taking it back to him right away. Where do you have it?

HEDDA (*cold and impassive, leaning against the armchair*): I don't have it anymore.

TESMAN: You don't have it! What on earth do you mean by that?

HEDDA: I burned it — the whole thing.

TESMAN (*with a start of terror*): Burned it! Burned Eilert Løvborg's manuscript!

HEDDA: Stop shouting. The maid could hear you.

TESMAN: Burned it! But my God in heaven —! No, no, no — that's impossible!

HEDDA: Yes, but it's true, all the same.

TESMAN: But do you realize what you've done, Hedda! It's illegal disposition of lost property. Just think! Yes, you can ask Judge Brack; he'll tell you.

HEDDA: It would be wiser not mentioning this — either to the judge or to anyone else.

TESMAN: But how could you go and do such an incredible thing! Whatever put it into your head? What got into you, anyway? Answer me! Well?

HEDDA (*suppressing an almost imperceptible smile*): I did it for your sake, George.

TESMAN: For my sake!

HEDDA: When you came home this morning and told about how he'd read to you —

TESMAN: Yes, yes, then what?

HEDDA: Then you confessed that you envied him this book.

TESMAN: Good Lord, I didn't mean it literally.

HEDDA: Never mind. I still couldn't bear the thought that anyone should eclipse you.

TESMAN (*in an outburst of mingled doubt and joy*): Hedda — is this true, what you say! Yes, but — but — I never dreamed you could show your love like this. Imagine!

HEDDA: Well, then it's best you know that — that I'm going to — (*Impatiently, breaking off.*) No, no — you ask your Aunt Julie. She's the one who can tell you.

TESMAN: Oh, I'm beginning to understand you, Hedda! (*Claps his hands together.*) Good heavens, no! Is it actually *that*! Can it be? Uh?

HEDDA: Don't shout so. The maid can hear you.

TESMAN: The maid! Oh, Hedda, you're priceless, really! The maid — but that's Berta! Why, I'll go out and tell her myself.

HEDDA (*clenching her fists in despair*): Oh, I'll die — I'll die of all this!

TESMAN: Of what, Hedda? Uh?

HEDDA: Of all these — absurdities — George.

TESMAN: Absurdities? What's absurd about my being so happy? Well, all right — I guess there's no point in my saying anything to Berta.

HEDDA: Oh, go ahead — why not that, too?

TESMAN: No, no, not yet. But Aunt Julie will have to hear. And then, that you've started to call me George, too! Imagine! Oh, Aunt Julie will be so glad — so glad!

HEDDA: When she hears that I burned Eilert Løvborg's book — for your sake?

TESMAN: Well, as far as that goes — this thing with the book — of course, no one's to know about that. But that you have a love that burns for me Hedda — Aunt Julie can certainly share in that! You know, I wonder, really, if things such as this are common among young wives? Hm?

HEDDA: I think you should ask Aunt Julie about that, too.

TESMAN: Yes, I definitely will, when I have the chance.

(*Mrs. Elvsted, dressed as on her first visit, with hat and coat, comes in the hall door.*)

MRS. ELVSTED (*greets them hurriedly and speaks in agitation*): Oh, Hedda dear, don't be annoyed that I'm back again.

HEDDA: Has something happened, Thea?

TESMAN: Something with Eilert Løvborg? Uh?

MRS. ELVSTED: Yes, I'm so terribly afraid he's met with an accident.

HEDDA (*seizing her arm*): Ah — you think so!

TESMAN: But, Mrs. Elvsted, where did you get that idea?

MRS. ELVSTED: Well, because I heard them speaking of him at the boardinghouse, just as I came in. Oh, there are the most incredible rumors about him in town today.

TESMAN: Yes, you know, I heard them too! And yet I could swear that he went right home to bed last night. Imagine!

HEDDA: Well — what did they say at the boardinghouse?

MRS. ELVSTED: Oh, I couldn't get anything clearly. They either didn't know much themselves, or else — They stopped talking when they saw me. And I didn't dare to ask.

TESMAN (*restlessly moving about*): Let's hope — let's hope you misunderstood them, Mrs. Elvsted!

MRS. ELVSTED: No, no, I'm sure they were talking of him. And then I heard them say something or other about the hospital, or —

TESMAN: The hospital!

HEDDA: No — but that's impossible!

MRS. ELVSTED: Oh, I'm so deathly afraid for him now. And later I went up to his lodging to ask about him.

HEDDA: But was that very wise to do, Thea?

MRS. ELVSTED: What else could I do? I couldn't bear the uncertainty any longer.

TESMAN: But didn't you find him there either? Hm?

MRS. ELVSTED: No. And no one had any word of him. He hadn't been in since yesterday afternoon, they said.

TESMAN: Yesterday! Imagine them saying that!

MRS. ELVSTED: I think there can only be one reason — something terrible must have happened to him!

TESMAN: Hedda dear — suppose I went over and made a few inquiries —?

HEDDA: No, no — don't you get mixed up in this business.

(*Judge Brack, with hat in hand, enters from the hall, Berta letting him in and shutting the door after him. He looks grave and bows silently.*)

TESMAN: Oh, is that you, Judge? Uh?

BRACK: Yes, it's imperative that I see you this evening.

TESMAN: I can see that you've heard the news from Aunt Julie.

BRACK: Among other things, yes.

TESMAN: It's sad, isn't it? Uh?

BRACK: Well, my dear Tesman, that depends on how you look at it.

TESMAN (*eyes him doubtfully*): Has anything else happened?

BRACK: Yes, as a matter of fact.

HEDDA (*intently*): Something distressing, Judge?

BRACK: Again, that depends on how you look at it, Mrs. Tesman.

MRS. ELVSTED (*in an uncontrollable outburst*): Oh, it's something about Eilert Løvborg!

BRACK (*glancing at her*): Now how did you hit upon that, Mrs. Elvsted? Have you, perhaps, heard something already —?

MRS. ELVSTED (*in confusion*): No, no, nothing like that — but —

TESMAN: Oh, for heaven's sake, tell us!

BRACK (*with a shrug*): Well — I'm sorry, but — Eilert Løvborg's been taken to the hospital. He's dying.

MRS. ELVSTED (*crying out*): Oh, God, oh, God —!

TESMAN: To the hospital! And dying!

HEDDA (*involuntarily*): All so soon —!

MRS. ELVSTED (*wailing*): And we parted in anger, Hedda!

HEDDA (*in a whisper*): Thea — be careful, Thea!

MRS. ELVSTED (*ignoring her*): I have to see him! I have to see him alive!

BRACK: No use, Mrs. Elvsted. No one's allowed in to see him.

MRS. ELVSTED: Oh, but tell me, at least, what happened to him! What is it?

TESMAN: Don't tell me he tried to —! Uh?

HEDDA: Yes, he did, I'm sure of it.

TESMAN: Hedda — how can you say —!

BRACK (*his eyes steadily on her*): Unhappily, you've guessed exactly right, Mrs. Tesman.

MRS. ELVSTED: Oh, how horrible!

TESMAN: Did it himself! Imagine!

HEDDA: Shot himself!

BRACK: Again, exactly right, Mrs. Tesman.

MRS. ELVSTED (*trying to control herself*): When did it happen, Mr. Brack?

BRACK: This afternoon. Between three and four.

TESMAN: But good Lord — where did he do it, then? Hm?

BRACK (*hesitating slightly*): Where? Why — in his room, I suppose.

MRS. ELVSTED: No, that can't be right. I was there between six and seven.

BRACK: Well, somewhere else, then. I don't know exactly. I only know he was found like that. Shot — in the chest.

MRS. ELVSTED: What a horrible thought! That he should end that way!

HEDDA (*to Brack*): In the chest, you say.

BRACK: Yes — I told you.

HEDDA: Not the temple?

BRACK: In the chest, Mrs. Tesman.

HEDDA: Well — well, the chest is just as good.

BRACK: Why, Mrs. Tesman?

HEDDA (*evasively*): Oh, nothing — never mind.

TESMAN: And the wound is critical, you say? Uh?

BRACK: The wound is absolutely fatal. Most likely, it's over already.

MRS. ELVSTED: Yes, yes, I can feel that it is! It's over! All over! Oh, Hedda —!

TESMAN: But tell me now — how did you learn about this?

BRACK (*brusquely*): One of the police. Someone I talked to.

HEDDA (*in a clear, bold voice*): At last, something truly done!

TESMAN (*shocked*): My God, what are you saying, Hedda!

HEDDA: I'm saying there's beauty in all this.

BRACK: Hm, Mrs. Tesman —

TESMAN: Beauty! What an idea!

MRS. ELVSTED: Oh, Hedda, how can you talk about beauty in such a thing?

HEDDA: Eilert Løvborg's settled accounts with himself. He's had the courage to do what — what had to be done.

MRS. ELVSTED: Don't you believe it! It never happened like that. When he did this, he was in a delirium!

TESMAN: In despair, you mean.

HEDDA: No, he wasn't. I'm certain of that.

MRS. ELVSTED: But he was! In delirium! The way he was when he tore up our book.

BRACK (*startled*): The book? His manuscript, you mean? He tore it up?

MRS. ELVSTED: Yes. Last night.

TESMAN (*in a low whisper*): Oh, Hedda, we'll never come clear of all this.

BRACK: Hm, that's very strange.

TESMAN (*walking about the room*): To think Eilert could be gone like that! And then not to have left behind the one thing that could have made his name live on.

MRS. ELVSTED: Oh, if it could only be put together again!

TESMAN: Yes, imagine if that were possible! I don't know what I wouldn't give —

MRS. ELVSTED: Perhaps it can, Mr. Tesman.

TESMAN: What do you mean?

MRS. ELVSTED (*searching in the pockets of her dress*): Look here. I've kept all these notes that he used to dictate from.

HEDDA (*coming a step closer*): Ah —!

TESMAN: You've kept them, Mrs. Elvsted! Uh?

MRS. ELVSTED: Yes, here they are. I took them along

when I left home. And they've stayed right here in my pocket —

TESMAN: Oh, let me look!

MRS. ELVSTED (*hands him a sheaf of small papers*): But they're in such a mess. All mixed up.

TESMAN: But just think, if we could decipher them, even so! Maybe the two of us could help each other —

MRS. ELVSTED: Oh yes! At least, we could try —

TESMAN: We can do it! We *must*! I'll give my whole life to this!

HEDDA: You, George. Your life?

TESMAN: Yes. Or, let's say, all the time I can spare. My own research will have to wait. You can understand, Hedda. Hm! It's something I owe to Eilert's memory.

HEDDA: Perhaps.

TESMAN: And so, my dear Mrs. Elvsted, let's see if we can't join forces. Good Lord, there's no use brooding over what's gone by. Uh? We must try to compose our thoughts as much as we can, in order that —

MRS. ELVSTED: Yes, yes, Mr. Tesman, I'll do the best I can.

TESMAN: Come on, then. Let's look over these notes right away. Where shall we sit? Here? No, in there, in the back room. Excuse us, Judge. You come with me, Mrs. Elvsted.

MRS. ELVSTED: Dear God — if only we can do this!

(*Tesman and Mrs. Elvsted go into the inner room. She takes off her hat and coat. They both sit at the table under the hanging lamp and become totally immersed in examining the papers. Hedda goes toward the stove and sits in the armchair. After a moment Brack goes over by her.*)

HEDDA (*her voice lowered*): Ah, Judge — what a liberation it is, this act of Eilert Løvborg's.

BRACK: Liberation, Mrs. Hedda? Well, yes, for him; you could certainly say he's been liberated —

HEDDA: I mean for me. It's liberating to know that there can still actually be a free and courageous action in this world. Something that shimmers with spontaneous beauty.

BRACK (*smiling*): Hm — my dear Mrs. Hedda —

HEDDA: Oh, I already know what you're going to say. Because you're a kind of specialist too, you know, just like — Oh, well!

BRACK (*looking fixedly at her*): Eilert Løvborg meant more to you than you're willing to admit, perhaps even to yourself. Or am I wrong about that?

HEDDA: I won't answer that sort of question. I simply know that Eilert Løvborg's had the courage to live life after his own mind. And now — this last great act, filled with beauty! That he had the strength

and the will to break away from the banquet of life — so young.

BRACK: It grieves me, Mrs. Hedda — but I'm afraid I have to disburden you of this beautiful illusion.

HEDDA: Illusion?

BRACK: One that, in any case, you'd soon be deprived of.

HEDDA: And what's that?

BRACK: He didn't shoot himself — of his own free will.

HEDDA: He didn't —!

BRACK: No. This whole affair didn't go off quite the way I described it.

HEDDA (*in suspense*): You've hidden something? What is it?

BRACK: For poor Mrs. Elvsted's sake, I did a little editing here and there.

HEDDA: Where?

BRACK: First, the fact that he's already dead.

HEDDA: In the hospital?

BRACK: Yes. Without regaining consciousness.

HEDDA: What else did you hide?

BRACK: That the incident didn't occur in his room.

HEDDA: Well, that's rather unimportant.

BRACK: Not entirely. Suppose I were to tell you that Eilert Løvborg was found shot in — in Mademoiselle Diana's boudoir.

HEDDA (*half rises, then sinks back again*): That's impossible, Judge! He wouldn't have gone there again today!

BRACK: He was there this afternoon. He went there, demanding something he said they'd stolen from him. Kept raving about a lost child —

HEDDA: Ah — so that was it —

BRACK: I thought perhaps that might be his manuscript. But, I hear now, he destroyed that himself. So it must have been his wallet.

HEDDA: I suppose so. Then, there — that's where they found him.

BRACK: Yes, there. With a discharged pistol in his breast pocket. The bullet had wounded him fatally.

HEDDA: In the chest — yes.

BRACK: No — in the stomach — more or less.

HEDDA (*stares up at him with a look of revulsion*): That too! What is it, this — this curse — that everything I touch turns ridiculous and vile?

BRACK: There's something else, Mrs. Hedda. Another ugly aspect to the case.

HEDDA: What's that?

BRACK: The pistol he was carrying —

HEDDA (*breathlessly*): Well! What about it!

BRACK: He must have stolen it.

HEDDA (*springs up*): Stolen! That's not true! He didn't!

BRACK: It seems impossible otherwise. He must have stolen it — shh!

(*Tesman and Mrs. Elvsted have gotten up from the table in the inner room and come into the drawing room.*)

TESMAN (*with both hands full of papers*): Hedda dear — it's nearly impossible to see in there under that overhead lamp. You know?

HEDDA: Yes, I know.

TESMAN: Do you think it would be all right if we used your table for a while? Hm?

HEDDA: Yes, I don't mind. (*Quickly.*) Wait! No, let me clear it off first.

TESMAN: Oh, don't bother, Hedda. There's plenty of room.

HEDDA: No, no, let me just clear it off, can't you? I'll put all this in by the piano. There!

(*She has pulled out an object covered with sheet music from under the bookcase, adds more music to it, and carries the whole thing into the inner room and off left. Tesman puts the scraps of paper on the writing table and moves the lamp over from the corner table. He and Mrs. Elvsted sit down and go on with their work. Hedda comes back.*)

HEDDA (*behind Mrs. Elvsted's chair, gently ruffling her hair*): Well, my sweet little Thea — how is it going with Eilert Løvborg's monument?

MRS. ELVSTED (*looking despondently up at her*): Oh, dear — it's going to be terribly hard to set these in order.

TESMAN: It's got to be done. There's just no alternative. Besides, setting other people's papers in order — it's exactly what I can do best.

(*Hedda goes over by the stove and sits on one of the taborets. Brack stands over her, leaning on the armchair.*)

HEDDA (*whispering*): What did you say about the pistol?

BRACK (*softly*): That he must have stolen it.

HEDDA: Why, necessarily, that?

BRACK: Because every other explanation would seem impossible, Mrs. Hedda.

HEDDA: I see.

BRACK (*glancing at her*): Of course, Eilert Løvborg was here this morning. Wasn't he?

HEDDA: Yes.

BRACK: Were you alone with him?

HEDDA: Yes, briefly.

BRACK: Did you leave the room while he was here?

HEDDA: No.

BRACK: Consider. You didn't leave, even for a moment.

HEDDA: Well, yes, perhaps, just for a moment — into the hall.

BRACK: And where did you have your pistol case?

HEDDA: I had it put away in —

BRACK: Yes, Mrs. Hedda?

HEDDA: It was lying over there, on the writing table.

BRACK: Have you looked since to see if both pistols are there?

HEDDA: No.

BRACK: No need to. I saw the pistol. Løvborg had it on him. I knew it immediately, from yesterday. And other days too.

HEDDA: Do you have it, maybe?

BRACK: No, the police have it.

HEDDA: What will they do with it?

BRACK: Try to trace it to the owner.

HEDDA: Do you think they'll succeed?

BRACK (*bending over her and whispering*): No, Hedda Gabler — as long as I keep quiet.

HEDDA (*looking at him anxiously*): And if you don't keep quiet — then what?

BRACK (*with a shrug*): Counsel could always claim that the pistol was stolen.

HEDDA (*decisively*): I'd rather die!

BRACK (*smiling*): People *say* such things. But they don't *do* them.

HEDDA (*without answering*): And what, then, if the pistol wasn't stolen. And they found the owner. What would happen?

BRACK: Well, Hedda — there'd be a scandal.

HEDDA: A scandal!

BRACK: A scandal, yes — the kind you're so deathly afraid of. Naturally, you'd appear in court — you and Mademoiselle Diana. She'd have to explain how the whole thing occurred. Whether it was an accident or homicide. Was he trying to pull the pistol out of his pocket to threaten her? Is that why it went off? Or had she torn the pistol out of his hand, shot him, and slipped it back in his pocket again? It's rather like her to do that, you know. She's a powerful woman, this Mademoiselle Diana.

HEDDA: But all that sordid business is no concern of mine.

BRACK: No. But you'll have to answer the question: Why did you give Eilert Løvborg the pistol? And what conclusions will people draw from the fact that you did give it to him?

HEDDA (*her head sinking*): That's true. I hadn't thought of that.

BRACK: Well, luckily there's no danger, as long as I keep quiet.

HEDDA: So I'm in your power, Judge. You have your hold over me from now on.

BRACK (*whispers more softly*): My dearest Hedda — believe me — I won't abuse my position.

HEDDA: All the same, I'm in your power. Tied to your will and desire. Not free. Not free, then! (*Rises impetuously.*) No — I can't bear the thought of it. Never!

BRACK (*looks at her half mockingly*): One usually manages to adjust to the inevitable.

HEDDA (*returning his look*): Yes, perhaps so. (*She goes over to the writing table. Suppressing an involuntary smile, she imitates Tesman's intonation.*) Well? Getting on with it, George? Uh?

TESMAN: Goodness knows, dear. It's going to mean months and months of work, in any case.

HEDDA (*as before*): Imagine that! (*Runs her hand lightly through Mrs. Elvsted's hair.*) Don't you find it strange, Thea? Here you are, sitting now beside Tesman — just as you used to sit with Eilert Løvborg.

MRS. ELVSTED: Oh, if I could only inspire your husband in the same way.

HEDDA: Oh, that will surely come — in time.

TESMAN: Yes, you know what, Hedda — I really think I'm beginning to feel something of the kind. But you go back and sit with Judge Brack.

HEDDA: Is there nothing the two of you need from me now?

TESMAN: No, nothing in the world. (*Turning his head.*) From now on, Judge, you'll have to be good enough to keep Hedda company.

BRACK (*with a glance at Hedda*): I'll take the greatest pleasure in that.

HEDDA: Thanks. But I'm tired this evening. I want to rest a while in there on the sofa.

TESMAN: Yes, do that, dear. Uh?

(*Hedda goes into the inner room, pulling the curtains closed after her. Short pause. Suddenly she is heard playing a wild dance melody on the piano.*)

MRS. ELVSTED (*starting up from her chair*): Oh — what's that?

TESMAN (*running to the center doorway*): But Hedda dearest — don't go playing dance music tonight! Think of Auntie Rina! And Eilert, too!

HEDDA (*putting her head out between the curtains*): And Auntie Julie. And all the rest of them. From now on I'll be quiet. (*She closes the curtains again.*)

TESMAN (*at the writing table*): She can't feel very happy seeing us do this melancholy work. You know what, Mrs. Elvsted — you must move in with Aunt Julie. Then I can come over evenings. And then we can sit and work *there*. Uh?

MRS. ELVSTED: Yes, perhaps that would be best —

HEDDA: I can hear everything you say, Tesman. But what will I do evenings over here?

TESMAN (*leafing through the notes*): Oh, I'm sure Judge Brack will be good enough to stop by and see you.

BRACK (*in the armchair, calling out gaily*): I couldn't miss an evening, Mrs. Tesman! We'll have great times here together, the two of us!

HEDDA (*in a clear, ringing voice*): Yes, you can hope so, Judge, can't you? You, the one cock of the walk —

(*A shot is heard within. Tesman, Mrs. Elvsted, and Brack start from their chairs.*)

TESMAN: Oh, now she's fooling with those pistols again.

(*He throws the curtains back and runs in. Mrs. Elvsted follows. Hedda lies, lifeless, stretched out on the sofa. Confusion and cries. Berta comes in, bewildered, from the right.*)

TESMAN (*shrieking to Brack*): Shot herself! Shot herself in the temple! Can you imagine!

BRACK (*in the armchair, prostrated*): But good God! People don't *do* such things!

COMMENTARIES

Ibsen wrote about his own work, both in his letters to producers and actors and in his notes describing the development of his plays. Such notes reveal his concern, his insights as he wrote the plays, and his motives. Sometimes what he says about the plays does not completely square with modern interpretations. On the other hand, he explains in his notes that the circumstances of women in modern society were much on his mind when he was working on *A Doll House*.

Ibsen's "Notes for the Modern Tragedy" is remarkable for suggesting a separate sensibility (spiritual law) for men and for women. His observations about the society in which women live — and in which Nora is confounded — sound as if they could have been written a century later than they were. When Bernard Shaw wrote his comments on *A Doll House,* the play was a popular shocker; Shaw's observations were designed to help audiences interpret the play's actions more carefully. He is one of the earliest critics of the play, and one must remember while reading Shaw that some productions of the play changed the ending to make it happy. Muriel Bradbrook's discussion of *A Doll House* focuses on the moral bankruptcy of Nora's situation, which is to say the situation of all wives of the period.

Ibsen's notes to *Hedda Gabler* show us what a complex process he went through to conceive the character and to put her in action. One sees his method of sketching out the action of the play, then commenting to himself on what the action implies. Caroline Mayerson's extensive commentary gives us insight into the symbolic levels of meaning in the play. Since the play has been considered a masterpiece of realism, some critics have assumed that it has no symbolic texture. Mayerson counters that view with a detailed analysis. Jan Kott's interpretation of Hedda's pistols, which he sees as explicit sexual symbols, helps to expand Mayerson's claim that the drama, while realistic, does not ignore the deeper significance of its own imagery.

Henrik Ibsen (1828–1906)
NOTES FOR THE MODERN TRAGEDY   1878

TRANSLATED BY A. G. CHATER

Ibsen's first notes for A Doll House *were jotted down on October 19, 1878. They show that his thinking on the relations between men and women was considerably sophisticated and that the material for the play had been gestating. His comments indicate that the essentially male society he knew was one of his central concerns in the play.*

There are two kinds of spiritual law, two kinds of conscience, one in man and another, altogether different, in woman. They do not understand each other; but in practical life the woman is judged by man's law, as though she were not a woman but a man.

The wife in the play ends by having no idea of what is right or wrong; natural feeling on the one hand and belief in authority on the other have altogether bewildered her.

A woman cannot be herself in the society of the present day, which is an exclusively masculine society, with laws framed by men and with a judicial system that judges feminine conduct from a masculine point of view.

She has committed forgery, and she is proud of it; for she did it out of love for her husband, to save his life. But this husband with his commonplace principles of honor is on the side of the law and looks at the question from the masculine point of view.

Spiritual conflicts. Oppressed and bewildered by the belief in authority, she loses faith in her moral right and ability to bring up her children. Bitterness. A mother in modern society, like certain insects who go away and die when she has done her duty in the propagation of the race. Love of life, of home, of husband and children and family. Now and then a womanly shaking off of her thoughts. Sudden return of anxiety and terror. She must bear it all alone. The catastrophe approaches, inexorably, inevitably. Despair, conflict, and destruction.

(Krogstad has acted dishonorably and thereby become well-to-do; now his prosperity does not help him, he cannot recover his honor.)

Bernard Shaw (1856–1950)
A DOLL'S HOUSE

1891

One of the first English men of letters to pay close attention to Ibsen's work was Bernard Shaw. While beginning to write his own plays, Shaw also spent time in the theater as a critic. His landmark book The Quintessence of Ibsenism *(1891; rev. ed. 1913), in which this comment on* A Doll House *appears, is a thorough discussion not only of the individual plays that Ibsen had produced but also of their implication for future literature. Shaw saw the significance of the new realism and its implications for the audiences of the later nineteenth century. He saw, too, that Ibsen's brand of realism would have an effect on the beliefs of his audiences, that Ibsen's drama was a drama of important ideas. In the following excerpt Shaw is especially sensitive to the feminist issues that are at the heart of the play, and he pays close attention to Nora's character development.*

Unfortunately, *Pillars of Society,* as a propagandist play, is disabled by the circumstance that the hero, being a fraudulent hypocrite in the ordinary police-court sense of the phrase, would hardly be accepted as a typical pillar of society by the class he represents. Accordingly, Ibsen took care next time to make his idealist irreproachable from the standpoint of the ordinary idealist morality. In the famous *Doll's House,* the pillar of society who owns the doll is a model husband, father, and citizen. In his little household, with the three darling children and the affectionate little wife, all on the most loving terms with one another, we have the sweet home, the womanly woman, the happy family life of the idealist's dream. Mrs. Nora Helmer is happy in the belief that she has attained a valid realization of all these illusions; that she is an ideal wife and mother; and that Helmer is an ideal husband who would, if the necessity arose, give his life to save her reputation. A few simply contrived incidents disabuse her effectually on all these points. One of her earliest acts of devotion to her husband has been the secret raising of a sum of money to enable him to make a tour which was necessary to restore his health. As he would have broken down sooner than go into debt, she has had to persuade him that the money was a gift from her father. It was really obtained from a moneylender, who refused to make her the loan unless she induced her father to endorse the promissory note. This being impossible, as her father was dying at the time, she took the shortest way out of the difficulty by writing the name herself, to the entire satisfaction of the moneylender, who, though not at all duped, knew that forged bills are often the surest to be paid. Since then she has slaved in secret at scrivener's work until she has nearly paid off the debt.

At this point Helmer is made manager of the bank in which he is employed; and the moneylender, wishing to obtain a post there, uses the forged bill to force Nora to exert her influence with Helmer on his behalf. But she, having a hearty contempt for the man, cannot be persuaded by him that there was any harm in putting her father's name on the bill, and ridicules the suggestion that the law would not recognize that she was right under the circumstances. It is her husband's own contemptuous denunciation of a forgery formerly committed by the moneylender himself that destroys her self-satisfaction and opens her eyes to her ignorance of the serious business of the world to which her husband belongs: the world outside the home he shares with her. When he goes on to tell her that commercial dishonesty is generally to be traced to the influence of bad mothers, she begins to perceive that the happy way in which she plays with the children, and the care she takes to dress them nicely, are not sufficient to constitute her a fit person to train them. To redeem the forged bill, she resolves to borrow the balance due upon it from an intimate friend of the family. She has learnt to coax her husband into giving her what she asks by appealing to his affection for her: that is, by playing all sorts of pretty tricks until he is wheedled into an amorous humor. This plan she has adopted without thinking about it, instinctively taking the line of least resistance with him. And now she naturally takes the same line with her husband's friend. An unexpected declaration of love from him is the result; and it at once explains to her the real nature of the domestic influence she has been so proud of.

All her illusions about herself are now shattered. She sees herself as an ignorant and silly woman, a dangerous mother, and a wife kept for her husband's pleasure merely; but she clings all the harder to her illusion about him: He is still the ideal husband who would make any sacrifice to rescue her from ruin. She resolves to kill herself rather than allow him to destroy his own career by taking the forgery on himself to save her reputation. The final disillusion comes when he, instead of at once proposing to pursue this ideal line of conduct when he hears of the forgery, naturally enough flies into a vulgar rage and heaps invective on her for disgracing him. Then she sees that their whole family life has been a fiction: their home a mere doll's house in which they have been playing at ideal husband and father, wife and mother. So she leaves him then and there and goes out into the real world to find out its reality for herself, and to gain some position not fundamentally false, refusing to see her children again until she is fit to be in charge of them, or to live with him until she and he become capable of a more honorable relation to one another. He at first cannot understand what has happened, and flourishes the shattered ideals over her as if they were as potent as ever. He presents the course most agreeable to him — that of her staying at home and avoiding a scandal — as her duty to her husband, to her children, and to her religion; but the magic of these disguises is gone; and at last even he understands what has really happened, and sits down alone to wonder whether that more honorable relation can ever come to pass between them.

Muriel C. Bradbrook (1909–1993)
A DOLL'S HOUSE: Ibsen the Moralist   *1948*

In her important study of Ibsen, Ibsen: The Norwegian, *Muriel Bradbrook discusses all the important plays, but she reserves a special place for* A Doll House. *In her analysis she suggests that Nora slowly discovers the fundamental bankruptcy of her marriage. Bradbrook calls it "eight years' prostitution." She also shows the true extent of Torvald's possessiveness and immaturity. As Bradbrook says, the true moment of recognition — in the Greek tragic sense — occurs when Nora sees both herself and Torvald in their true nature. Bradbrook also helps us see the full implication of Nora's leaving her home. She can never hope again for the comforts she has enjoyed as Torvald's wife.*

Poor Nora, living by playing her tricks like a little pet animal, sensing how to manage Torvald by those pettinesses in his character she does not know she knows of, is too vulnerably sympathetic to find her life-work in reading John Stuart Mill. At the end she still does not understand the strange world in which she has done wrong by forging a signature. She does understand that she has lived by what Virginia Woolf called "the slow waterlogged sinking of her will into his." And this picture is built up for her and for us by the power of structural implication, a form of writing particularly suited to drama, where the latent possibilities of a long stretch of past time can be thrown into relief by a crisis. In *A Doll's House,* the past is not only lighted up by the present, as a transparency might be lit up with a lamp; the past is changed by the present so that it becomes a different thing. Nora's marriage becomes eight years' prostitution, as she gradually learns the true nature of her relations with Torvald and the true nature of Torvald's feelings for her.

In Act I, no less than six different episodes bring out the war that is secretly waged between his masculine dictatorship and her feminine wiles:

Her wheedling him for money with a simple transference: "Let us do as *you* suggest. . . ."

Her promise to Christine: "Just leave it to me: I will broach the matter very cleverly." She is evidently habituated to and aware of her own technique.

Her description of how she tried to coax Torvald into taking the holiday and how she was saving up the story of the bond "for when I am no longer as good-looking as I am now." She knows the precarious nature of her hold.

Her method of asking work for Christine by putting Christine also into a (completely bogus) position of worshiping subservience to Torvald.

Her boast to Krogstad about her influence. Whilst this may be a justifiable triumph over her tormentor, it is an unconscious betrayal of Torvald (witness his fury in Act II at the idea of being thought uxorious).

After this faceted exposition, the treatment grows much broader. Nora admits Torvald's jealousy: Yet she flirts with Rank, aware but not acknowledging the grounds of her control. The pressure of implication remains constant throughout: It is comparable with the effect of a dialect, coloring all that is said. To take a few lines at random from the dialogue of Nora and Rank in Act II:

> NORA (*putting her hand on his shoulder*): Dear, dear Dr. Rank! Death mustn't take you away from Torvald and me. [Nora is getting demonstrative as she senses Rank's

responsiveness, and her hopes of obtaining a loan from him rise. Hence her warmth
of feeling, purely seductive.]

RANK: It is a loss you will easily recover from. Those who are gone away are soon forgotten. [Poor Rank is reminded by that "Torvald and me" how little he really
counts to Nora.]

NORA (*anxiously*): Do you believe that? [Rank has awakened her thoughts of what
may happen if *she* has to go away.]

Her methods grow more desperate — the open appeal to Torvald to keep
Krogstad and the frantic expedient of the tarantella. In the last act her fate is
upon her; yet in spite of all her terror and Torvald's tipsy amorousness, she still
believes in his chivalry and devotion. This extraordinary self-deception is perhaps the subtlest and most telling implication of all. Practice had left her theory
unshaken: So when the crash comes, she cries, "I have been living with a strange
man," yet it was but the kind of man her actions had always implied him to be.
Her vanity had completely prevented her from recognizing what she was doing,
even though she had become such an expert at doing it.

Torvald is more gradually revealed. In the first act he appears indulgent, perhaps a trifle inclined to nag about the macaroons and to preach, but virtually a
more efficient David Copperfield curbing a rather better-trained Dora. In the
second act, his resentment and his pleasure alike uncover the deeper bases of his
dominance. His anger at the prospect of being thought under his wife's influence
and his fury at the imputation of narrow-mindedness show that it is really based
on his own cowardice, the need for something weaker to bully: This is confirmed when he gloats over Nora's panic as evidence of her love for him, and
over her agitation in the tarantella ("you little helpless thing!"). His love of order and his fastidiousness, when joined to such qualities, betray a set personality; and the last act shows that he has neither control nor sympathy on the
physical level. But he is no fool, and his integrity is not all cowardice. Doubtless,
debt or forgery really was abhorrent to him.

The climax of the play comes when Nora sees Torvald and sees herself: It is
an *anagnorisis,* a recognition. Her life is cored like an apple. For she has had no
life apart from this. Behind the irrelevant program for self-education there
stands a woman, pitifully inexperienced, numbed by emotional shock, but with
a newfound will to face what has happened, to accept her bankruptcy, as, in a
very different way, Peer Gynt had at last accepted his.

"Yes, I am beginning to understand. . . ." she says. "What you did," observes
the now magnanimous Torvald, "you did out of love for me." "That is true,"
says Nora: And she calls him to a "settling of accounts," not in any spirit of hostility but in an attempt to organize vacancy. "I have made nothing of my life. . . .
I must stand quite alone . . . it is necessary to me . . ." That is really the program.
Ainsi tout leur a craqué dans les mains.°

The spare and laminated speech gains its effect by inference and riddle. But
these are the characteristic virtues of Norse. Irony is its natural weapon. Ibsen
was working with the grain of the language. It was no accident that it fell to a
Norwegian to take that most finely tooled art, the drama, and bring it to a
point and precision so nice that literally not a phrase is without its direct con-

---

Ainsi . . . mains: Thus everything has shattered in their hands.

tribution to the structure. The unrelenting cohesion of *A Doll's House* is per-haps, like that of the *Oedipus the King,* too hard on the playgoer; he is al-lowed no relief. Nora cannot coo to her baby without saying: "My sweet little *baby doll!*" or play with her children without choosing, significantly, *Hide and Seek.* Ibsen will not allow the smallest action to escape from the psy-chopathology of everyday life. However, a play cannot be acted so that every moment is tense with significance, and, in practice, an actor, for the sake of light and shade, will probably slur some of Ibsen's points, deliberately or un-consciously. The tension between the characters is such that the slightest movement of one sets all the others quivering. But this is partly because they are seen with such detachment, like a clear-cut intaglio. The play is, above all, articulated.

That is not to say that it is the mere dissection of a problem. Perhaps Rank and Mrs. Linde would have been more subtly wrought into the action at a later date; but the tight control kept over Nora and Torvald does not mean that they can be exhausted by analysis or staled by custom. They are so far in advance of the characters of *Pillars of Society* that they are capable of the surprising yet in-evitable development that marks the character conceived "in the round," the character that is, in Ibsen's phrase, fully "seen."

Consider, for example, Torvald's soliloquy whilst Nora is taking off her mas-querade dress. It recalls at one moment Dickens's most unctuous hypocrites — "Here I will protect you like a hunted dove that I have saved from the claws of the hawk!" — at another Meredith's Willoughby Patterne° — "Only be frank and open with me and I will be both will and conscience to you" — yet from broadest caricature to sharpest analysis, it remains the self-glorified strut of the one character, the bank clerk in his pride, cousin to Peer Gynt, that typical Nor-wegian, and to Hjalmer Ekdal, the toiling breadwinner of the studio.

Whilst the Ibsenites might have conceded that Torvald is Art, they would probably have contended that Nora is Truth. Nora, however, is much more than a Revolting Wife. She is not a sour misanthropist or a fighting suffragette, but a lovely young woman who knows that she still holds her husband firmly infatu-ated after eight years of marriage. . . .

In leaving her husband Nora is seeking a fuller life as a human being. She is emancipating herself. Yet the seeking itself is also a renunciation, a kind of death — "I must stand alone." No less than Falk, or the hero of *On the Vidda,* she gives up something that has been her whole life. She is as broken as Torvald in the end: But she is a strong character and he is a weak one. In the "happy ending" which Ibsen reluctantly allowed to be used, it was the sight of the chil-dren that persuaded her to stay, and unless it is remembered that leaving Torvald means leaving the children, the full measure of Nora's decision cannot be taken. An actress gets her chance to make this point in the reply to Torvald's plea that Nora should stay for the children's sake.

It should be remembered, too, that the seriousness of the step she takes is lost on the present generation. She was putting herself outside society, inviting insult, destitution, and loneliness. She went out into a very dark night.

Willoughby Patterne: The protagonist in George Meredith's novel *The Egoist* (1879), an arrogant aristocrat who lacks awareness of the needs and desires of the women in his life.

Henrik Ibsen (1828–1906)
Notes for Hedda Gabler   1890

TRANSLATED BY EVERT SPRINCHORN

Like most playwrights, Ibsen kept a notebook into which he jotted ideas as he was writing his plays. The notes that follow are some of those he gathered as he was writing Hedda Gabler. *They show how his mind worked on the material, how he considered alternatives to what he was doing, and how he permitted his material to grow and develop.*

¶ One talks about building railways and highways for the cause of progress. But no, no, that is not what is needed. Space must be cleared so that the spirit of man can make its great turnabout. For it has gone astray. The spirit of man has gone astray. . . .

¶ *Notes:* One evening as Hedda and Tesman, together with some others, were on their way home from a party, Hedda remarked as they walked by a charming house that was where she would like to live. She meant it, but she said it only to keep the conversation with Tesman going. "He simply cannot carry on a conversation."

The house was actually for rent or sale. Tesman had been pointed out as the coming young man. And later when he proposed, and let slip that he too had dreamed of living there, she accepted.

He too had liked the house very much.

They get married. And they rent the house.[1]

But when Hedda returns as a young wife, with a vague sense of responsibility, the whole thing seems distasteful to her. She conceives a kind of hatred for the house just because it has become her home. She confides this to Brack. She evades the question with Tesman.

¶ The play shall deal with "the impossible," that is, to aspire to and strive for something which is against all the conventions, against that which is acceptable to conscious minds — Hedda's included.

¶ The episode of the hat makes Aunt Rising° lose her composure. She leaves — That it could be taken for the maid's hat — no, that's going too far!

That my hat, which I've had for over nine years, could be taken for the maid's — no, that's really too much! . . .

¶ Very few true parents are to be found in the world. Most people grow up under the influence of aunts or uncles — either neglected and misunderstood or else spoiled. . . .

---

[1]Both of them, each in his and her own way, have seen in their common love for this house a sign of their mutual understanding. As if they sought and were drawn to a common home.

Then he rents the house. They get married and go abroad. He orders the house bought and his aunt furnishes it at his expense. Now it is their home. It is theirs and yet it is not, because it is not paid for. Everything depends on his getting the professorship. [Ibsen's note.]

Aunt Rising: Ibsen also spelled it *Rysing*. She became Aunt Juliana Tesman in the final version of the play.

¶ Hedda feels herself demoniacally attracted by the tendencies of the times. But she lacks courage. Her thoughts remain theories, ineffective dreams.

¶ The feminine imagination is not active and independently creative like the masculine. It needs a bit of reality as a help.

¶ Løvborg has had inclinations toward "the bohemian life." Hedda is attracted in the same direction, but she does not dare to take the leap.

¶ Buried deep within Hedda there is a level of poetry. But the environment frightens her. Suppose she were to make herself ridiculous!

¶ Hedda realizes that she, much more than Thea, has abandoned her husband.

¶ The newly wedded couple return home in September — as the summer is dying. In the second act they sit in the garden — but with their coats on.

¶ Being frightened by one's own voice. Something strange, foreign.

¶ NEWEST PLAN: The festivities in Tesman's garden — and Løvborg's defeat — already prepared for in the 1st act. Second act: the party —

¶ Hedda energetically refuses to serve as hostess. She will not celebrate their marriage because (in her opinion, it isn't a marriage) . . .

¶ Hedda is the type of woman in her position and with her character. She marries Tesman but she devotes her imagination to Eilert Løvborg. She leans back in her chair, closes her eyes, and dreams of his adventures. . . . This is the enormous difference: Mrs. Elvsted "works for his moral improvement." But for Hedda he is the object of cowardly, tempting daydreams. In reality she does not have the courage to be a part of anything like that. Then she realizes her condition. Caught! Can't comprehend it. Ridiculous! Ridiculous!

¶ The traditional delusion that one man and one woman are made for each other. Hedda has her roots in the conventional. She marries Tesman but she dreams of Eilert Løvborg. . . . She is disgusted by the latter's flight from life. He believes that this has raised him in her estimation. . . . Thea Elvsted is the conventional, sentimental, hysterical Philistine.

¶ Those Philistines, Mrs. E. and Tesman, explain my behavior by saying first I drink myself drunk and that the rest is done in insanity. It's a flight from reality which is an absolute necessity to me.

¶ E. L.: Give me something — a flower — at our parting. Hedda hands him the revolver.

Then Tesman arrives: Has he gone? "Yes." Do you think he will still compete against me? No, I don't think so. You can set your mind at rest.

¶ Tesman relates that when they were in Gratz she did not want to visit her relatives —

He misunderstands her real motives.

¶ In the last act as Tesman, Mrs. Elvsted, and Miss Rysing are consulting, Hedda plays in the small room at the back. She stops. The conversation continues. She appears in the doorway — Good night — I'm going now. Do you need me for anything? Tesman: No, nothing at all. Good night, my dear! . . . The shot is fired —

¶ CONCLUSION: All rush into the back room. Brack sinks as if paralyzed into a chair near the stove: But God have mercy — people don't *do* such things!

¶ When Hedda hints at her ideas to Brack, he says: Yes, yes, that's extraordinarily amusing — Ha ha ha! He does not understand that she is quite serious.

¶ Hedda is right in this: There is no love on Tesman's part. Nor on the aunt's part. However full of love she may be.

Eilert Løvborg has a double nature. It is a fiction that one loves only one person. He loves two — or many — alternately (to put it frivolously). But how can he explain his position? Mrs. Elvsted, who forces him to behave correctly, runs away from her husband. Hedda, who drives him beyond all limits, draws back at the thought of a scandal.

¶ Neither he nor Mrs. Elvsted understands the point. Tesman reads in the manuscript that was left behind about "the two ideals." Mrs. Elvsted can't explain to him what E. L. meant. Then comes the burlesque note: Both T. and Mrs. E. are going to devote their future lives to interpreting the mystery.

¶ Tesman thinks that Hedda hates E. L.

Mrs. Elvsted thinks so too.

Hedda sees their delusion but dares not disabuse them of it. There is something beautiful about having an aim in life. Even if it is a delusion —

She cannot do it. Take part in someone else's.

That is when she shoots herself.

The destroyed manuscript is entitled "The ~~Philosophy~~ Ethics of Future Society."

¶ Tesman is on the verge of losing his head. All this work meaningless. New thoughts! New visions! A whole new world! Then the two of them sit there, trying to find the meaning in it. Can't make any sense of it. . . .

¶ The greatest misery in this world is that so many have nothing to do but pursue happiness without being able to find it. . . .

¶ The simile: The journey of life = the journey on a train.

H.: One doesn't usually jump out of the compartment.

No, not when the train is moving.

Nor stand still when it is stationary. There's always someone on the platform, staring in.

¶ *Hedda*: Dream of a scandal — yes, I understand that well enough. But commit one — no, no, no.

¶ *Løvborg*: Now I understand. My ideal was an illusion. You aren't a bit better than I. Now I have nothing left to live for. Except pleasure — dissipation — as you call it . . . Wait, here's a present (The pistol)

¶ Tesman is nearsighted. Wears glasses. My, what a beautiful rose! Then he stuck his nose in the cactus. Ever since then —!

¶ NB: The mutual hatred of women. Women have no influence on external matters of government. Therefore they want to have an influence on souls. And then so many of them have no aim in life (the lack thereof is inherited) —

¶ Men and women don't belong to the same century. . . . What a great prejudice that one should love only *one*! . . .

¶ The demoniacal element in Hedda is this: She wants to exert her influence on someone — But once she has done so, she despises him. . . . The manuscript?

¶ In the third act Hedda questions Mrs. Elvsted. But if he's like that, why is he worth holding on to. . . . Yes, yes, I know — . . .

¶ NB!! The reversal in the play occurs during the big scene between Hedda and E. L. *He*: What a wretched business it is to conform to the existing morals. It would be ideal if a man of the present could live the life of the future. What a miserable business it is to fight over a professorship!

Hedda — that lovely girl! *H.*: No! *E. L.*: Yes, I'm going to say it. That lovely, cold girl — cold as marble.

I'm not dissipated fundamentally. But the life of reality isn't livable — . . .

¶ Life becomes for Hedda a ridiculous affair that isn't "worth seeing through to the end."

¶ The happiest mission in life is to place the people of today in the conditions of the future.

L.: Never put a child in this world, H.!

¶ When Brack speaks of a "triangular affair," Hedda thinks about what is going to happen and refers ambiguously to it. Brack doesn't understand.

¶ Brack cannot bear to be in a house where there are small children. "Children shouldn't be allowed to exist until they are fourteen or fifteen. That is, girls. What about boys? Shouldn't be allowed to exist at all — or else they should be raised outside the house."

¶ H. admits that children have always been a horror to her too.

¶ Hedda is strongly but imprecisely opposed to the idea that one should love "the family." The aunts mean nothing to her.

¶ It liberated Hedda's spirit to serve as a confessor to E. L. Her sympathy has secretly been on his side — But it became ugly when the public found out everything. Then she backed out.

¶ MAIN POINTS: (1) They are not all made to be mothers. (2) They are passionate but they are afraid of scandal. (3) They perceive that the times are full of missions worth devoting one's life to, but they cannot discover them.

¶ And besides Tesman is not exactly a professional, but he is a specialist. The Middle Ages are dead —

¶ T.: Now there you see also the great advantages to my studies. I can lose manuscripts and rewrite them — no inspiration needed —

¶ Hedda is completely taken up by the child that is to come, but when it is born she dreads what is to follow —

¶ Hedda must say somewhere in the play that she did not like to get out of her compartment while on the trip. Why not? I don't like to show my legs. . . . Ah, Mrs. H., but they do indeed show themselves. Nevertheless, I don't.

¶ Shot herself! Shot herself!

Brack (collapsing in the easy chair): But great God — people don't *do* such things!

¶ NB!! Eilert Løvborg believes that a comradeship must be formed between man and woman out of which the truly spiritual human being can arise. Whatever else the two of them do is of no concern. This is what the people around him do not understand. To them he is dissolute. Inwardly he is not.

¶ If a man can have several male friends, why can't he have several lady friends?

¶ It is precisely the sensual feelings that are aroused while in the company of his female "friends" or "comrades" that seek release in his excesses.

¶ Now I'm going. Don't you have some little remembrance to give me —? You have flowers — and so many other things — (The story of the pistol from before) — But you won't use it anyhow —

¶ In the fourth act when Hedda finds out that he has shot himself, she is jubilant. . . . He had courage.

Here is the rest of the manuscript.

¶ CONCLUSION: Life isn't tragic. . . . Life is ridiculous. . . . And that's what I can't bear.

¶ Do you know what happens in novels? All those who kill themselves — through the head   not in the stomach. . . . How ridiculous — how baroque — . . .

Caroline W. Mayerson (b. 1907)
THEMATIC SYMBOLS IN *HEDDA GABLER*   1965

Sometimes the designation of realism has been applied to Ibsen in such a way as to suggest that all we get in his plays is a slice of life, with details that are meaningless except that they are there. The fact is that, like Gustave Flaubert, James Joyce, August Strindberg, and other realistic writers of his time, Ibsen was a craftsman who tried to make every detail in his plays add up to something. Caroline Mayerson shows us how loaded with significance certain otherwise innocent-looking objects are in Hedda Gabler. *She begins with Thea's hair, the manuscript that Løvborg loses, and General Gabler's pistols. In analyzing them, she shows us just how rich the surfaces of Ibsen's plays can be.*

During the course of the play, Ibsen places considerable emphasis upon Thea's hair, upon the manuscript as her "child," and upon General Gabler's pistols, and his treatment of these items suggests that he intended them to have symbolic significance. We shall be concerned in this essay with determining this significance and its effect upon the total meaning of the play. My analysis of the three symbols in their relationship to the theme, the characters, and the action will be based upon several broad assumptions which reflect views of Ibsen's concepts and methods implied or expressed by a number of previous commentators: (1) In *Hedda Gabler,* Ibsen examines the possibility of attaining freedom and fulfillment in modern society. (2) Hedda is a woman, not a monster; neurotic, but not psychotic. Thus, she may be held accountable for her behavior. But she is spiritually sterile. Her yearning for self-realization through exercise of her natural endowments is in conflict with her enslavement to a narrow standard of conduct. This conflict is complicated by her incomplete understanding of what freedom and fulfillment mean and how they may be achieved. She fails to realize that one must earn his inheritance in order to possess it, and she romanticizes the destructive and sensational aspects of Dionysiac ecstasy without perceiving that its true end is regeneration through sublimation of the ego in a larger unity. (3) Ibsen, as an experienced artist, was aware of the impact of minutiae and the need for integrating these with the general impression to be projected; therefore we may regard his descriptions, his stage directions, and his properties, no less than his dialogue, as means whereby intention and significance are conveyed.

While all the other characters in *Hedda Gabler* are implicitly compared to Hedda and serve, in one way or another, to throw light upon her personality, Thea Elvsted is the one with whom she is most obviously contrasted. Furthermore, their contest for the control of Loevborg is the most prominent external conflict in the play. The sterility-fertility antithesis from which central action proceeds is chiefly realized through the opposition of these two. Hedda is pregnant, and Thea is physically barren. But in emotionally repudiating her unborn child, Hedda rejects what Ibsen considered woman's opportunity to advance the march of progress.[1] The many other symptoms of her psychic sterility need little

---

[1] Cf. Ibsen's speech to the Norwegian Women's Rights League (1898): "It is women who are to solve the social problems. As mothers they are to do it. And only as such can they do it. Here lies a great task for woman" (*Speeches and New Letters of Henrik Ibsen,* trans. Arne Kildal [Boston, 1901], 66).

enlargement. Unwilling to give or even share herself, she maintains her independence at the price of complete frustration. Ibsen uses Thea, on the other hand, to indicate a way to freedom which Hedda never apprehends. Through her ability to extend herself in comradeship with Loevborg, Thea not only brings about the rebirth of his creative powers, but merges her own best self with his to produce a prophecy of the future, conceivably of the "Third Kingdom," in which Ibsen believed that the ideals of the past would coalesce in a new and more perfect unity. Having lost herself to find herself, she almost instinctively breaks with the mores of her culture in order to ensure continuance of function. Despite her palpitating femininity, she is the most truly emancipated person in the play. And it is she who wins at least a limited victory in the end. Although Loevborg has failed her, her fecundity is indefatigable; as Hedda kills herself, Thea is busily preparing to recreate her "child" with Tesman, thereby at once enabling him to realize his own little talents and weakening even further the tenuous bond which ties him to Hedda.

The contrast outlined above is reinforced by the procreative imagery of the play. The manuscript is Loevborg's and Thea's "child," the idea of progress born of a union between individuals who have freed themselves from the preconceptions of their environment.[2] This manuscript the sterile Hedda throws into the fire at the climax of her vindictive passion. Her impulse to annihilate by burning is directed both toward Thea's "child" and toward Thea's hair and calls attention to the relationship between them. Even without other indications that Ibsen was using hair as a symbol of fertility, such an inference might be made from the words which accompany the destruction of the manuscript:

> Now I am burning your child, Thea! Burning it, curly-locks! Your child and Eilert Loevborg's. I am burning — I am burning your child.

There is, however, considerable evidence, both before and after this scene, that Thea's hair is a sign of that potency which Hedda envies even while she ridicules and bullies its possessor. Ibsen, of course, had ample precedent for employing hair as a symbol of fertility. Perhaps the best support for the argument that he made a literary adaptation of this well-known, ancient idea in *Hedda Gabler* is a summary of the instances in which the hair is mentioned.

Although Ibsen's unobtrusive description of the hair of each of these women at her initial entrance may seem at the time only a casual stroke in the sketch, it assumes importance in retrospect. Hedda's hair is "not particularly abundant," whereas Thea's is "unusually abundant and wavy." Hedda's strongest impression of Thea is of that abundance: She recalls her as "the girl with the irritating hair, that she was always showing off." Moreover, Thea fearfully recollects Hedda's schoolgirl reaction to it: ". . . When we met on the stairs you used always to pull my hair. . . . Yes, and once you said you would burn it off my head." When Thea and Loevborg first meet in the play, Hedda seats herself, significantly, between them; the brief exchange of questions and answers which ensues is notable for its overtones: "Is not she [Thea] lovely to look at?" Loevborg asks. Hedda, lightly stroking Thea's hair, answers, "Only to look at?" Loevborg understands the innuendo, for he replies, "Yes. For we two — she and I — we two are real comrades." Later, when the women are alone, Hedda, now fully in-

---

[2] Cf. Ibsen's statement: "I firmly believe in the capacity for procreation and development of ideals" (*Speeches and New Letters*, 57).

formed of the extent to which Thea has realized her generative powers, laments her own meager endowment and renews her threat in its adolescent terms:

> Oh, if you could only understand how poor I am, and fate has made you so rich! (Clasps her passionately in her arms.) I think I must burn your hair off after all.

Hedda's violent gesture and Thea's almost hysterical reaction ("Let me go! Let me go! I am afraid of you, Hedda!") indicate the dangerous seriousness of words which otherwise might be mistaken for a joke; the threat prepares us for the burning of the manuscript, which follows in Act III. In the last tense scene of the play Hedda twice handles Thea's hair. The reader's imagination readily constructs the expressions and gestures whereby an actress could show Hedda's true attitude toward the hair which Ibsen directs her to ruffle "gently" and to pass her hands "softly through." The first gesture follows immediately upon an important action — Hedda has just removed the pistol to the inner room. The second accompanies dialogue which for the last time emphasizes Hedda's association of the hair with Thea's fertility and which brings home to Hedda her own predicament:

> HEDDA (*passes her hands softly through Mrs. Elvsted's hair*): Doesn't it seem strange to you, Thea? Here you are sitting with Tesman — just as you used to sit with Eilert Loevborg?
> MRS. ELVSTED: Ah, if I could only inspire your husband in the same way!
> HEDDA: Oh, that will come too — in time.
> TESMAN: Yes, do you know, Hedda — I really think I begin to feel something of the sort. But won't you go to sit with Brack again?
> HEDDA: Is there nothing I can do to help you two?
> TESMAN: No, nothing in the world.

These scenes in which the hair plays a part not only call attention to Hedda's limitations but show her reaction to her partial apprehension of them. In adapting a primitive symbol, Ibsen slightly altered its conventional meaning, substituting psychic for physical potency. Its primitivistic associations nevertheless pervade the fundamental relationships between the two women. The weapons Hedda uses against Thea are her hands and fire. The shock of the climactic scene results chiefly from seeing the savage emerge from behind her veneer of sophistication — the Hedda who feeds the manuscript to the flames is a naked woman engaged in a barbaric act. In contrast, the Hedda who handles her father's pistols is self-consciously cloaked in illusions of her hereditary participation in a chivalric tradition.

The pistols, like many other symbols used by Ibsen, quite obviously are not merely symbols, but have important plot function as well. Moreover, their symbolic significance cannot be reduced to a simple formula, but must be thought of in the light of the complex of associations which they carry as Hedda's legacy from General Gabler. Through Hedda's attitude toward and uses of the pistols, Ibsen constantly reminds us that Hedda "is to be regarded rather as her father's daughter than as her husband's wife."[3] Clearly the pistols are linked with certain values in her background which Hedda cherishes. Complete definition of these values is difficult without a more thorough knowledge of Ibsen's conception of a Norwegian general than the play or contemporary comment on it allows. Per-

[3] *The Correspondence of Henrik Ibsen*, trans. & ed. Mary Morison (London, 1905), 435.

haps, as Brandes said, nineteenth-century audiences recognized that Hedda's pretensions to dignity and grandeur as a general's daughter were falsely based, "that a Norwegian general is a cavalry officer, who as a rule, has never smelt powder, and whose pistols are innocent of bloodshed."[4] Such a realization, however, by no means nullifies the *theoretical* attributes and privileges of generalship to which Hedda aspires. Possibly Ibsen intended us to understand that Hedda is a member of a second generation of "ham actors" who betray their proud tradition by their melodramatic posturings. But it is this tradition, however ignoble its carrier, to which the pistols and Hedda (in her own mind) belong, and it is, after all, the general only as glimpsed through his daughter's ambitions and conceptions of worth that is of real importance in the play. These conceptions, as embodied in Hedda's romantic ideal of manhood, may be synthesized from the action and dialogue. The aristocrat possesses, above all, courage and self-control. He expresses himself through direct and independent action, living to capacity and scorning security and public opinion. Danger only piques big appetite, and death with honor is the victory to be plucked from defeat. But the recklessness of this Hotspur is tempered by a disciplined will, by means of which he "beautifully" orders both his own actions and those of others on whom his power is imposed. Such a one uses his pistols with deliberation, with calculated aim. He shoots straight — to defend his life or his honor, and to maintain his authority. Pistols, however, have no intrinsic glamor. Of the several possible accoutrements of a general, his pistols are those least likely to evoke thoughts of chivalric principles and most likely to recall the menace of the power vested in him. And such power, as *Hedda Gabler* shows us, delivered into the hands of a confused and irresponsible egotist, brings only meaningless destruction to all who come within its range.

The manipulation of the pistols throughout the play is a mockery of their traditional role. Except at target practice, Hedda does not even shoot straight until her suicide. Her potential danger is recognized by both men whom she threatens, but both understand (Brack, immediately; Loevborg, in Act II) that her threat is a theatrical gesture and that she has no real intention of acting directly, in defiance of the conventions which bid her "go roundabout." Her crass dishonesty in her sexual encounters is highlighted by this gun play. She uses the pistols, to be sure, to ward off or warn off encroachments upon her "honor." This honor, however, is rooted in social expedience rather than in a moral code. Having indirectly encouraged Loevborg by a succession of intimate *tête-à-têtes*, she poses as an outraged maiden when he makes amorous advances, thereby, as she later hints, thwarting her own emotional needs. Subsequently she sells her body to Tesman as cynically as (and far less honestly than) Madame Diana sells hers, then deliberately participates in the form, if not the substance, of marital infidelity with Brack in order to relieve her boredom. Both Hedda and Brack become aware of the cold ruthlessness of the other and the consequent danger to the loser if the delicate equilibrium of their relationship should be disturbed. But until the end Brack is so complacently convinced that Hedda is his female counterpart that he has no fear she will do more than shoot over his head; even as she lies dead, he can hardly believe that she has resorted to direct action — "People don't do such things."

The part the pistols play in Loevborg's death makes a central contribution to

[4]Georg Brandes, *Henrik Ibsen. Björnstjerne Björnson: Critical Studies* (New York, 1899), 94.

our understanding of the degree to which the ideals they represent are distorted by the clouded perspective from which Hedda views them. She has no real comprehension of, nor interest in, the vital creative powers Thea helps Loevborg to realize. Instead, she glorifies his weaknesses, mistaking bravado for courage, the indulgence of physical appetites for godlike participation in "the banquet of life," a flight from reality for a heroic quest for totality of experience. Even more important is the fact that as she inhibits her own instinctive urge for fulfillment, she romanticizes its converse. Thus, having instigated his ruin, she incites Loevborg to commit suicide with her pistol. This radical denial of the will to live she arbitrarily invests with the heroism and beauty one associates with a sacrificial death; Hedda is incapable of making the distinction between an exhibitionistic gesture which inflates the ego and the tragic death, in which the ego is sublimated in order that the values of life may be extended and reborn.

Her inability to perceive the difference between melodrama and tragedy accounts for the disparity between Hedda's presumptive view of her own suicide and our evaluation of its significance. Ibsen with diabolical irony arranged a situation which bears close superficial resemblance to the traditional tragic end. Symbolically withdrawing herself from the bourgeois environment into the inner chamber which contains the relics of her earlier life, Hedda plays a "wild dance" upon her piano and, beneath her father's portrait, shoots herself "beautifully" through the temple with her father's pistol. She dies to vindicate her heritage of independence; with disciplined and direct aim she at last defeats the Bogy, which hitherto she has unsuccessfully attempted to circumvent. So Hedda would see her death, we are led to believe, could she be both principal and spectator; and no doubt she would find high-sounding phrases with which to memorialize it. But of course it is Brack and Tesman who have the curtain lines, and these lines show how little of her intent Hedda has conveyed to her world. And we, having the opportunity to judge the act with relation to its full context, may properly interpret it as the final self-dramatization of the consistently sterile protagonist. Hedda gains no insight; her death affirms nothing of importance. She never understands why, at her touch, everything becomes "ludicrous and mean." She dies to escape a sordid situation that is largely of her own making; she will not face reality nor assume responsibility for the consequences of her acts. The pistols, having descended to a coward and a cheat, bring only death without honor.

It would appear, then, that the symbols, while they do not carry the whole thematic burden of *Hedda Gabler,* illuminate the meaning of the characters and the action with which they are associated. As Eric Bentley has suggested, the characters, like those in the other plays of Ibsen's last period, are the living dead who dwell in a waste-land that resembles T. S. Eliot's. And, like Eliot later, Ibsen emphasized the aridity of the present by contrasting it with the heroic past. Indeed, *Hedda Gabler* may be thought of as a mock-tragedy, a sardonically contrived travesty of tragic action, which Ibsen shows us is no longer possible in the world of the play. This world is sick with a disease less curable than that of Oedipus's Thebes or Hamlet's Denmark. For its hereditary leaders are shrunken in stature, maimed and paralyzed by their enslavement to the ideals of the dominant middle class. With the other hollow men, they despise but nonetheless worship the false gods of respectability and security, paying only lip service to their ancestral principles. Such geniuses as this society produces are, when left to themselves, too weak to do more than batter their own heads against constricting barriers. They dissipate their talents and so fail in their mission as prophets and disseminators of Western culture; its interpretation is left to the unimaginative pedant, picking over the dry bones of the past. Women, the natural seminal vesicles of that culture, the mothers of the future, are those most cruelly inhibited by the sterilizing atmosphere of their environment. At one extreme is Aunt Julia, the genteel spinster, overcompensating for her starved emotions with obsessive self-dedication. At the other is Diana, the harlot. Even Thea, the progenitive spirit, the girl with the abundant hair, is a frail and colorless repository for the seeds of generation. Her break with convention when it threatens her maternity is shown to be the one mode of escape from the fate that overtakes the others. But Ibsen gives her triumph, too, a ludicrous twist. Hardly having begun the mourning song for her Adonis, she brings forth her embryonic offspring from her pocket and proceeds to mold it into shape with the aid of a Tesman — an echo of the classic death and rebirth, to be sure, but one not likely to produce the glorious Third Kingdom of which Ibsen dreamed. And appropriately holding the center of the stage throughout is Hedda, in whom the shadows of the past still struggle in a losing battle with the sterile specter of the present. Her pistols are engraved with insignia which the others understand not at all and which she only dimly comprehends. Her colossal egotism, her lack of self-knowledge, her cowardice, render her search for fulfillment but a succession of futile blunders which culminate in the supreme futility of death. Like Peer Gynt, she is fit only for the ladle of the button-molder;° she fails to realize a capacity either for great good or for great evil. Her mirror-image wears the mask of tragedy, but Ibsen makes certain that we see the horns and pointed ears of the satyr protruding from behind it.

Jan Kott (b. 1914)
ON HEDDA GABLER

1984

Jan Kott's sexual analysis of Hedda's pistols introduces important levels of metaphor into a play that is already laden with sexual imagery.

Chekhov wrote: "If in the first act a gun hangs on the wall, in the last act it must go off." In laying down this dramatic precept, he must surely have had *Hedda Gabler* in mind. Hedda inherits two pistols from her father. She fires the first one over Judge Brack's head when he approaches the house from the garden; and again at the end, when she shoots herself. The other pistol is fired offstage. It kills Eilert Loevborg. But the two pistols in *Hedda Gabler* are not only props exploited by Ibsen with iron-clad dramatic logic and preordained consequences; they also have sexual undertones. A Scandinavian Madame Bovary, well read in romantic novels, gives Loevborg a pistol: "use it now . . . and beautifully." But the fatal shot wounds him "in the stomach — more or less," and is fired in the parlor of the red-haired Mademoiselle Diana.

---

button-molder: At the end of Ibsen's play *Peer Gynt*, the Button Molder tries to melt Peer in his ladle, an action that symbolizes loss of identity.

Ibsen's setting for *Hedda Gabler* is striking. The action takes place in a spacious salon with French windows which open out on a veranda and a garden in the "fashionable part of town," not a fjord. The windows are curtained; the theater had already learned the advantages of gaslight.

In the first scene, Hedda orders the curtains drawn. She can't stand sunlight. This is our first glimpse of her character. The salon is spacious and the furniture arrangement makes it possible for two separate conversations to be carried on at the same time. The old-fashioned *a parte*° is no longer necessary. Chekhov borrowed this "contrapuntal" dialogue from Ibsen and masterfully refined it.

The crucial part of the stage design is the room in the background, with a huge portrait of "a handsome, elderly man in a general's uniform" hanging on the wall behind the sofa. In the last scene Hedda will enter this room, draw the curtains, and shoot herself in front of her father's portrait. Hedda Tesman, two months pregnant, kills Hedda Gabler. The inner room, whose only exit leads to the salon in the foreground, is at once the concrete and the symbolic setting of the conflict between the Father/superego and the id. By shooting herself, Hedda kills the shadow of her Father and the child she never wanted. The "shadow" of the father kills the daughter. In contrast to the earlier dramas [by Ibsen], *Lady from the Sea* and *Rosmersholm,* where the prehistory of the conflicts, traumas, and sexual complexes festers beneath the surface, and though continuing to grow they are never seen, in *Hedda Gabler* nothing remains unspoken.

In this case study of a neurosis, the mother's place is left empty. Hedda was raised by her father, who would have preferred a son. She rode horses and learned to shoot guns. In school, like a tomboy, she pulled her girlfriends' hair. She can barely resist pulling Thea's blond locks in Act II. In the last *Hedda Gabler* I saw, in Bochum in 1977, Peter Zadek directed the scene of Hedda's and Thea's drinking bout with distinct lesbian undertones. It is an extreme though not arbitrary reading of the text. In this record of sexual neurosis, the inversion and displacement of libido are intended. Thirty-year-old Hedda Gabler is frigid.

General Gabler's daughter not only wants to rule in a man's world. Unable to assume her female sexual role, she escapes by playing out the male one in her imagination. She demands that Loevborg initiate her into masculine rites and describe his visits to the red-haired Diana. Imaginary sex is vicarious. Hedda, rejecting the traditional roles of wife and mother, is condemned to live vicariously, full of the frustration and sense of emptiness which she calls deadly boredom. Madame Bovary's love affairs with shallow men were substitutions for the romantic ecstasies she read about in contemporary novels. For General Gabler's daughter these flights and escapes are ruled out. She has only her inner room "with its heavy curtains and her father's portrait."

It is not only sexual fulfillment that Hedda strives for through imagination. Until the very last scene, all her passions and hatreds are realized only by acts of substitution. The manuscript of Loevborg's new book is twice called his and Thea's "child"; Hedda commits a substitute "infanticide" by burning it in the fireplace. The pistol shot above Judge Brack's head was a substitute murder and a substitute sexual act. Fear paralyzed her twice before: once when she was afraid to shoot Loevborg for his aggressive advances, and then a second time when she was afraid to sleep with him. Handing the pistol to Loevborg is mur-

---

a parte: Keeping different conversations separate from one another as if in different spaces.

der by intent: The shot that kills him, in keeping with the logic of the dramaturgy, symbolically castrates him as well.

In coded messages, myths, dreams, and unconscious acts, opposite terms are interchangeable: They assume the guise of their antitheses. As in Racine and Chekhov (although in Chekhov it is deeply hidden), the appeal of death in Ibsen disguises itself as the pulse of life, the instinct toward self-destruction is masked as libido. *Hedda Gabler* appears to return to the realistic technique of the earlier dramas, but along with *Rosmersholm,* it marks the beginning of Ibsen's last cycle of plays, from *Little Eyolf* to *When We Dead Awaken,* each of which repeats the theme of sexual frustration leading to self-destruction. With the exception of his final masterpiece, *John Gabriel Borkman,* in all these plays the balance between the realistic world and its symbolic projection is broken.

In his biography of Ibsen (1957), Michael Meyer entitled his chapter on *Hedda Gabler* "Portrait of the Dramatist as a Young Woman." "*Madame Bovary — c'est moi,*" Flaubert once wrote, and Hedda Gabler is in some sense Ibsen's alter ego. The psychoanalysis of Hedda would no doubt become the merciless psychoanalysis of her author. But in psychoanalytic interpretations of the author or of his work Ibsen's invention and artistic discoveries are usually neglected, and what is even more important, the historical context, the customs and atmospheric realism of the *fin de siècle,*° are altogether lost.

Ibsen never read a page of Freud. Neither did Strindberg. In the early 1890s Freud began his first methodical studies of hysteria; in 1895 he announced his first analysis of dreams; and he used the term "psychoanalysis" for the first time in 1896. The Scandinavian Miss Julies and Heddas were finding their dramatists in Strindberg and Ibsen while the Viennese Julies and Heddas were finding their analyst in Freud.

T. E. Kalem (1919–1985)
REVIEW OF *A DOLL HOUSE*   *1971*

T. E. Kalem's review begins with a discussion of Clare Bloom's memorable performance, but moves quickly to a consideration of the ideas in A Doll House, particularly its feminist issues. Kalem implies that Ibsen was a social rebel on a par with James Joyce, but Kalem takes issue with Ibsen's philosophical perspective. Kalem's view is that Nora may have been "selfishly irresponsible."

A strong, scrupulous and thoroughly rewarding revival of Ibsen's *A Doll's House* now graces off-Broadway. Matching the exquisite delicacy of her features, Claire Bloom moves with emotional assurance from the early phase of the wife as kept puppet to the later phase of the woman who issues an emancipation proclamation to her husband. The larky girlishness of the early Nora is always a bit of a problem, but Miss Bloom manages to be a trifle giddy without appearing inane. As the later Nora, her performance is informed with a grave clarity.

---

fin de siècle: Turn of the century.

As Nora's husband, Torvald Helmer, Donald Madden is an excellent foil. His blond Scandinavian looks, his slightly mannered stuffiness, arrogance and condescension all contribute to a solid and coherent character. He conveys just the inflexible sense of property and propriety that is so necessary to the role. There is no falling off in the rest of the cast — in Nora's worldly wise friend (Patricia Elliott) or in the doctor (Roy Shuman), who is paying mortally for the sins of his father, or in the unscrupulous moneylender (Robert Gerringer), who is trying to keep a slippery foot on the frayed bottom rung of the social ladder. All do the right things rightly.

As everyone probably knows, Nora Helmer has saved her husband's life with a convalescent trip financed by an indiscreet secret loan from the moneylender, who writes a letter exposing her to her husband. Torvald plays a cravenly abusive blame game with Nora, then, when the threat lifts wants to go on together as if nothing had happened. But Nora sees her idealistic love shattered. She feels that she has been treated like a doll-child in her father's house and a doll-woman in her husband's. She opts to leave him and her three children in order to forge an independent soul and consciousness in the outer world. The children are inexplicably reduced to two in this production, perhaps as a sign of the faltering G.N.P.° or as propaganda for Z.P.G.°

Without violating the text, which has been rendered into fluently idiomatic English by Christopher Hampton, the sure and subtle inflection of Patrick Garland's direction makes Ibsen appear as the godfather of Women's Lib. If it counts as an imprimatur, Betty Friedan° was in the opening-night audience. Since Ibsen is a seductively powerful dramatist and the evening's didactic thrust is something like "Go thou and do likewise," it is important to examine Ibsen's intent and Nora's behavior.

The world's view of Ibsen has too often been filtered through the bristling eyebrows of Bernard Shaw, who foisted upon Ibsen all of his own social-reformist instincts and his penchant for exposing economically motivated hypocrisy in all of man's social institutions. But Ibsen was not like that. He was Lucifer's child, a moral rebel with a lone eagle complex who believed that the master spirit soars above the common herd of slaves, who mill about in their social bondage of marriages, families, businesses, religions, political parties and national allegiances. A friend who heard Ibsen fulminating at the playwright Bjørnson's home in 1883 said of him: "He is an absolute anarchist, wants to make a *tabula rasa,* put a torpedo under the whole Ark; mankind must begin again at the beginning of the world . . . the great task of our time is to blow up all existing institutions — to destroy."

Ibsen's teen-age disciple, James Joyce, understood him much better than Shaw. As Ibsen had slammed the door on a claustrophobic Norway, Joyce slammed the door on Ireland and uttered his *non serviam:* "I will not serve that in which I no longer believe." Nora's door slam is a crisis of belief, her *non serviam.* But is she saving herself or indulging herself? To judge her act, one must imagine the alternatives. In that final scene in which Nora accuses Torvald of never having talked to her seriously about serious things, man and wife are,

G.N.P.: Gross national product.
Z.P.G.: Zero Population Growth.
Betty Friedan: One of the leaders of the feminist movement and author of *The Feminine Mystique* (1963).

in fact, doing just that. Torvald is changing, seeing his wife as a person in her own right, and forgiving her. If she were really maturing, as Ibsen claims, she would forgive him and try to make a wiser go of things. Instead, she abdicates in the way that a child leaves a game in which he cannot dictate the rules.

In a different ending, Torvald might say, "O.K., Nora. I agree it's been a bad marriage. I'm leaving, too. Let the children fend for themselves." Viewed in that light, the cost Nora is inflicting on others by her abandonment is clearer. She is being selfishly irresponsible. The logic of her act is that one no longer honors a commitment as soon as it displeases one to do so.

There are several glaring fallacies in Ibsen's reasoning. One is that a woman who has been married for eight years and borne three children knows absolutely nothing about life. On the contrary, she has learned an enormous amount, precisely about life.

A more serious fallacy is Ibsen's assumption that doing one's own thing takes priority over everything else. True, in his own day he was battling the late 19th century's cant about honor, duty, the family, patriotism and God. Into a stiflingly confining atmosphere, he brought the courageous spirit of free inquiry. Still, in any era, society is a web of which the family forms the central strands. Children must be safeguarded and reared, and a continuity of values preserved. This is what society is about, and it provides order and sustenance for the vast community of men and women who cannot fly, breathe, or even live in the ego-rarefied air of the master artists and the lone eagles. Daedalus flew but Icarus fell — so it is with Ibsen and his Nora.

Clive Barnes (b. 1927)
REVIEW OF *HEDDA GABLER*   *1975*

Barnes appreciates the originality of interpretation in this Royal Shakespeare production of Hedda Gabler. *He admires the way the production reveals Ibsen's "satirical malevolent humor" and his contempt for the "shabby way life was lived." In keeping with this focus, director Trevor Nunn and actress Glenda Jackson create a Hedda who is the "vicious mistress of her own fate" — a Hedda "to chill the mind."*

We all knew that Washington was rapidly becoming an important theater town, but the idea that a major imported production, from Britain's Royal Shakespeare Company, no less, and starring Glenda Jackson, should bypass New York and play Washington may seem outlandish. Yet that is precisely what is happening to Trevor Nunn's new staging of Ibsen's *Hedda Gabler,* which began life in Australia this season, appeared in Los Angeles and last night opened at the National Theater here, on its way home to its London premiere.

Washington's gain is very pointedly New York's loss, for this production — which I caught at today's matinee — is an adornment even to the Royal Shakespeare Company repertory. It is a beautiful and provoking rethinking of this modern classic and could be a landmark for English-speaking versions of Ibsen.

Everyone is aware of the humor in Ibsen, and most productions try to steer clear of laughs. The freshness of this new staging is [that] it on the contrary tries to steer into them. Mr Nunn most persuasively takes literally Hedda's remark, twice-repeated, incidentally, that her life is a "grotesque farce," and he seizes every opportunity to point up Ibsen's satirical, malevolent humor, until the final stroke of tragic irony comes with Hedda's death.

The entire production is a dusty window on shallow, silly and selfish people caught frozen in a cold, monochromatic provincial landscape. This Hedda is no wilful child of circumstances but the vicious mistress of her own fate, an impartial force of evil leading an almost whimsical danse macabre.

In this view of Ibsen everyone is flayed. We see Ibsen's cynical view of bourgeois parochialism most clearly perhaps in plays such as *An Enemy of the People,* but this staging of *Hedda* helps to show that the playwright's contempt for the shabby way life was lived runs throughout all his work.

The production's bitter and emphatic insistence upon Ibsen's sardonic mockery of convention is not its only claim to originality. Mr. Nunn — and in this he treads a path not unlike that earlier taken by Ingmar Bergman in the same play — focuses on the smallness of Hedda's world. This is a petty story, full of small-scale lies, defections, vanities and betrayals. Here only Hedda is larger than the life of the play, and she is monstrous, a female Machiavel.

Part of the enclosed atmosphere of this complacent microcosm is provided by the repetitiveness of Ibsen's convoluted but commonplace use of language. We are accustomed to the repetition of Tesman's monotonous "What about that!" which he tags onto sentences like a catch phrase. Mr. Nunn, who has produced his own English adaptation of the original, stresses elsewhere the flatness of the language, with his constant repeating of simple words such as "beautiful." The verbal result is a kind of mad, comic oppressiveness.

At the storm center of any *Hedda* must stand Hedda herself, and in Mr. Nunn's conception and Miss Jackson's portrayal, she is an unforgettable, all but unforgivable, harpy. But if to understand is to forgive, then this Hedda must be forgiven, for few portrayals of the role can have been so dense, complex and yet, at last, comprehensible.

This Hedda has a wonderful snub-nosed arrogance, a remarkable way of flapping her hands in affectation. She is as cold as the submerged part of the iceberg, and she exhibits all the hugging charm of a boa constrictor. This is a merciless yet beautiful performance, reaching its terrible and great climax in its paroxysms of pure triumph when Hedda sends Eilert to his death, and then with calculated hatred burns his manuscript. This is a Hedda to chill the mind.

The rest of the cast offers Miss Jackson the perfect ensemble for her performance. Peter Eyre's Tesman, her husband, makes an interestingly irresolute spider figure, with thinning hair and hardening arteries, old out of his time. Timothy West, totally unctuous, sniffing superciliously and smiling pithily under raised eyebrows, is a splendidly menacing Judge Brack, while Patrick Stewart as a gruff, withdrawn Eilert Luvborg and Jennie Linden as a terrified victim of a Mrs. Elvsted are equally part of Mr. Nunn's picture.

And picture it is, for one of the abiding impressions of this fine *Hedda* is left by the lighting of Andy Phillips and the designs of John Napier, all in browns and grays (even the flowers are brown) and conceived all in 19th century Scandinavian-modern, with stuffed sofas and art-nouveau stained glass. It is the ridiculous common-place world of sudden death.

August Strindberg

The Swedish playwright August Strindberg (1849–1912) wrote fifty-eight plays, more than a dozen novels, and more than a hundred short stories, all collected now in fifty-five volumes. Much of the time he was producing this astonishing body of work, he was the victim of persistent paranoia, suffered the destruction of three marriages, and lived through a major nervous breakdown.

He was a man of enormous complexity whose work has traditionally been broken into two parts: The first comprises the work he wrote up to 1894, which includes *The Father* (1877), *Miss Julie* (1888), *The Creditors* (1889), and other naturalistic plays; the second comprises work he wrote after 1897, including *To Damascus* (1898–1901), *There Are Crimes and Crimes* (1899), *Easter,* and *The Dance of Death* (both 1901), *A Dream Play* (1902), and *Ghost Sonata* (1907). These are largely expressionist plays. EXPRESSIONISM disregarded the strict demands of naturalism to present a "slice of life" without artistic shaping of plot and resolution. Instead, expressionist drama used materials that resembled dreams — or nightmares — and focused on symbolic actions and a subjective interpretation of the world. Strindberg's later drama is often symbolic, taut, and psychological. His novel *Inferno* (1897) not only marks the transition between his early and late work; it gives this period of his life its name. Strindberg's Inferno period was a time of madness and paranoic behavior that virtually redirected his life for more than three years. During this time he was convinced that the secrets of life were wrapped in the occult, and his energies went into alchemical experiments and studies of cabalistic lore.

The first period of his dramatic career began with *Master Olof* (1872), a historical drama that he chose to write in prose, which he felt was a more natural medium than verse, the convention for such plays at the time. The play was turned down and he rewrote it in verse in 1876. It was rejected for a second time by the Royal Dramatic Theater but was finally produced the following year. At that time, Strindberg recorded: "In 1877 Antoine opened his Théâtre Libre in Paris, and *Thérèse Raquin,* although nothing but an adapted novel, became the dominant model. It was the powerful theme and the concentrated form that showed innovation, although the unity of time was not yet observed, and curtain falls were retained. It was then I wrote my dramas: *Lady Julie, The Father,* and *Creditors.*" *Thérèse Raquin,* Émile Zola's naturalistic play, inspired Strindberg to move further toward his own interpretation of naturalism, which is perhaps most evident in *Miss Julie*. Strindberg was more subjective in his approach to naturalism, less scientific and deterministic, than Zola. Whereas Zola's approach might be described as "photographic" realism, Strindberg's was more selective and impressionistic, but no less honest and true. He saw his characters operating out of "a whole series of deeply buried motives." They were not necessarily the product of their biology or their social circumstances, as the naturalists of Zola's stripe sometimes implied. Yet Strindberg saw clearly that class distinctions helped determine the behavior of many people. He seemed to accept the view that people were not created by their class but rather belonged to their class because of the kind of people they were. Strindberg probed deeply into the psychology of his characters, whose emotional lives, rather than outward social qualities, determined their actions.

Strindberg is often described as a woman-hater, a misogynist. For periods of his life he seems to have been misogynistic, but he was nonetheless extremely contradictory in both behavior and belief. There is no simple way to talk about Strindberg's attitude toward women. On the one hand, he is conventional in his thinking that women belong in the home. On the other hand, he married a highly successful actress, Siri von Essen. As he said in a letter in 1895, "Woman is to me the earth and all its glory, the bond that binds, and of all the evil the worst evil I have seen is the female sex." A decade later in *A Blue Book*, he wrote, "When I approach a woman as a lover, I look up to her, I see something of the mother in her, and this I respect. I assume a subordinate position, become childish and puerile and actually am subordinate, like most men. . . . I put her on a pedestal." As in many things, including his attitude toward dramatic techniques and style, Strindberg is a mass of contradictions and complexities of the sort sometimes associated with genius.

MISS JULIE

Miss Julie, the daughter of a count, and Jean, the count's valet, come from strikingly different social backgrounds. In ordinary circumstances, they might not have been on friendly terms, much less have become lovers, as they do. But the count is away, and Miss Julie and Jean are drawn into a sexual liaison marked by a struggle for dominance and control. Miss Julie's fiancé has been disposed of before the play begins because he refused to debase himself slavishly to her will. She is a free spirit, but her breeding is suspect because her mother, like her, took a lover and defied the count. Miss Julie's mother rebelled against her husband and punished him by burning their house down after the insurance expired. As further punishment and abasement, she humiliated the count by arranging to have her lover loan him the money to rebuild the house. Thus, Miss Julie's heritage is one of independence, rebellion, and unorthodoxy.

Under her mother's tutelage, Miss Julie was raised to manipulate men, but she cannot accept them totally. She also seems to feel a mixture of contempt for herself as a woman along with her contempt for men. In his preface to the play, Strindberg says that Julie is a modern "half-woman" "man-hater" who sells herself for honors of various kinds. (See the commentary on pages 751–52.)

The play has a mysterious quality. It takes place on Midsummer Eve, when lovers reveal themselves to one another and when almost anything can happen. In primitive fertility rites it was a time associated with sexual awakening. Kristine mentions that it is the feast of St. John and alludes to his beheading for spurning Salome's advances. Jean (French for John) in one tense moment of the play beheads Julie's pet bird as a sign of the violence pent up in him. This incident also foreshadows Miss Julie's death.

The fairy-tale quality that creeps into the play — as in *A Midsummer Night's Dream,* set on the same day — may seem out of place in a realistic drama, but it is profoundly compelling. It is also typical of Strindberg, who often uses symbolism to suggest a dream quality and deepen the significance of the action. (Dreams are a part of reality that modern playwrights have taken great pains to explore.)

The count himself, Julie's father, never appears in the play, but his presence is always ominous and intense, again much as in a fairy tale. Jean tells Miss Julie that he would willingly kill himself if the count were to order it. The cook, Kristine, like a witch, demands retribution because she was spurned by Jean, who once was her lover. Near the end of the play she prevents Julie and Jean from running away from the count by impounding the horses in the stable, thus wreaking her revenge on both of them.

Although Julie may be seen as the princess, Jean has very little claim to being Prince Charming of the play, especially since he has little strength of character. He feels superior to his station as a valet, and Strindberg in his preface refers to him as a nobleman. However, like Kristine, he is coarse beneath his outwardly polished appearance. His highest ambition is to be the proprietor of a first-class hotel, a prospect he wants to share with Julie.

One of the most striking passages in the play is the story Jean tells Julie almost reluctantly. He tries to explain to her what it feels like to be "down below," where she has never been. When he was a boy, he thought of the apple trees in her father's garden as part of the "Garden of Eden, guarded by angry angels." He entered this enchanted place with his mother to weed onions and wandered into the outhouse — a building like a Turkish pavilion whose function he could not guess. While he was exploring it, he heard someone coming and had to exit beneath the outhouse and hide himself under a pile of weeds and "wet dirt that stank." From his hiding place he saw Julie in a pink dress and white stockings. He rushed to the millpond and jumped in to wash the filth off himself. Ironically, only a few moments after he tells her this story he calls her a whore, and she, in response, says, "Oh, God in heaven, end my wretched life! Take me away from the filth I'm sinking into! Save me! Save me!"

Miss Julie falls under the power of her lover and cannot redirect her life; she sinks deeper and deeper into "filth." She has few choices at the end of the play, and the conclusion to *Miss Julie* is swift. The contrast between the willfulness of Julie and the caution of Jean makes their situation especially desperate. When Julie leaves at the end of the play to seal her fate, we sense the terrible weight of their society's values. Those values are symbolized by the return of the count and the expectations he had of Julie's behavior while he was gone.

Miss Julie in Performance

The first planned professional production of *Miss Julie* was canceled at the last minute by censors in Copenhagen on March 1, 1889. Although the play was performed privately on March 14, 1889, in Copenhagen University's Students' Union, it was not performed professionally in Stockholm until 1906. Some important early productions of the play were in Paris in Antoine's distinguished Théâtre Libre in 1893 and in Berlin in Max Reinhardt's Kleine Theater in 1904. Reinhardt produced seventeen of Strindberg's plays and was one of his great champions. In 1907 Strindberg produced the play in his own Intimate Theatre in Stockholm, where it ran intermittently for 134 showings. He even arranged a special performance for Bernard Shaw. The first London production was in 1912, but since the 1930s it has been revived many times, with many distinguished actors in all three major roles.

Among the notable modern productions is the Old Vic's 1966 version directed by Michael Elliott, with Maggie Smith and Albert Finney starring. The Baxter Theatre of Johannesburg, South Africa, produced the play in 1985 with the black actor John Kani as Jean and the white Afrikaner actress Sandra Prinsloo as Julie. Some white audiences considered that casting as outrageous. The sensational Ingmar Bergman production at the Brooklyn Academy of Music in 1991 stretched the play to two hours and made it more of a domestic tragedy — as John Simon said, "more like us, more believable, and, therefore, more terrifying."

Filmed at least five times, *Miss Julie* has been televised as well. It is one of the most produced of modern plays.

August Strindberg (1849–1912)

MISS JULIE

TRANSLATED BY HARRY G. CARLSON

1888

Characters

MISS JULIE, *25 years old*
JEAN, *her father's valet, 30 years old*
KRISTINE, *her father's cook, 35 years old*

(*The action takes place in the Count's kitchen on midsummer eve.*)

Setting: (*A large kitchen, the ceiling and side walls of which are hidden by draperies. The rear wall runs diagonally from down left to up right. On the wall down left are two shelves with copper, iron, and pewter utensils; the shelves are lined with scalloped paper. Visible to the right is most of a set of large, arched glass doors, through which can be seen a fountain with a statue of Cupid, lilac bushes in bloom, and the tops of some Lombardy poplars. At down left is the corner of a large tiled stove; a portion of its hood is showing. At right, one end of the servants' white pine dining table juts out; several chairs stand around it. The stove is decorated with birch branches; juniper twigs are strewn on the floor. On the end of the table stands a large Japanese spice jar, filled with lilac blossoms. An ice box, a sink, and a washstand. Above the door is an old-fashioned bell on a spring; to the left of the door, the mouthpiece of a speaking tube is visible.*)

(*Kristine is frying something on the stove. She is wearing a light-colored cotton dress and an apron. Jean enters. He is wearing livery and carries a pair of high riding boots with spurs, which he puts down on the floor where they can be seen by the audience.*)

JEAN: Miss Julie's crazy again tonight; absolutely crazy!

KRISTINE: So you finally came back?

JEAN: I took the Count to the station and when I returned past the barn I stopped in for a dance. Who do I see but Miss Julie leading off the dance with the gamekeeper! But as soon as she saw me she rushed over to ask me for the next waltz. And she's been waltzing ever since — I've never seen anything like it. She's crazy!

KRISTINE: She always has been, but never as bad as the last two weeks since her engagement was broken off.

JEAN: Yes, I wonder what the real story was there. He was a gentleman, even if he wasn't rich. Ah! These people have such romantic ideas. (*Sits at the end of the table.*) Still, it's strange, isn't it? I mean that she'd rather stay home with the servants on midsummer eve instead of going with her father to visit relatives?

KRISTINE: She's probably embarrassed after that row with her fiancé.

JEAN: Probably! He gave a good account of himself, though. Do you know how it happened, Kristine? I saw it, you know, though I didn't let on I had.

KRISTINE: No! You saw it?

JEAN: Yes, I did. ——— That evening they were out near the stable, and she was "training" him — as she called it. Do you know what she did? She made him jump over her riding crop, the way you'd teach a dog to jump. He jumped twice and she hit him each time. But the third time he grabbed the crop out of her hand, hit her with it across the cheek, and broke it in pieces. Then he left.

KRISTINE: So, that's what happened! I can't believe it!

JEAN: Yes, that's the way it went! —— What have you got for me that's tasty, Kristine?

KRISTINE (*serving him from the pan*): Oh, it's only a piece of kidney I cut from the veal roast.

JEAN (*smelling the food*): Beautiful! That's my favorite *délice.*° (*Feeling the plate.*) But you could have warmed the plate!

KRISTINE: You're fussier than the Count himself, once you start! (*She pulls his hair affectionately.*)

JEAN (*angry*): Stop it, leave my hair alone! You know I'm touchy about that.

KRISTINE: Now, now, it's only love, you know that. (*Jean eats. Kristine opens a bottle of beer.*)

JEAN: Beer? On midsummer eve? No thank you! I can do better than that. (*Opens a drawer in the table and takes out a bottle of red wine with yellow sealing wax.*) See that? Yellow seal! Give me a glass! A wine glass! I'm drinking this *pur.*°

KRISTINE (*returns to the stove and puts on a small saucepan*): God help the woman who gets you for a husband! What a fussbudget.

JEAN: Nonsense! You'd be damned lucky to get a man like me. It certainly hasn't done you any harm to have people call me your sweetheart. (*Tastes the wine.*) Good! Very good! Just needs a little warming. (*Warms the glass between his hands.*) We bought this in Dijon. Four francs a liter, not counting the cost of the bottle, or the customs duty. —— What are you cooking now? It stinks like hell!

KRISTINE: Oh, some slop Miss Julie wants to give Diana.

JEAN: Watch your language, Kristine. But why should you have to cook for that damn mutt on midsummer eve? Is she sick?

KRISTINE: Yes, she's sick! She sneaked out with the gatekeeper's dog — and now there's hell to pay. Miss Julie won't have it!

JEAN: Miss Julie has too much pride about some things and not enough about others, just like her mother was. The Countess was most at home in the kitchen and the cowsheds, but a *one*-horse carriage wasn't elegant enough for her. The cuffs of her blouse were dirty, but she had to have her coat of arms on her cufflinks. —— And Miss Julie won't take proper care of herself either. If you ask me, she just isn't refined. Just now, when she was dancing in the barn, she pulled the gamekeeper

away from Anna and made him dance with her. *We* wouldn't behave like that, but that's what happens when aristocrats pretend they're common people — they get *common!* —— But she is quite a woman! Magnificent! What shoulders, and what — et cetera!

KRISTINE: Oh, don't overdo it! I've heard what Clara says, and she dresses her.

JEAN: Ha, Clara! You're all jealous of each other! I've been out riding with her. . . . And the way she dances!

KRISTINE: Listen, Jean! You're going to dance with me, when I'm finished here, aren't you?

JEAN: Of course I will.

KRISTINE: Promise?

JEAN: Promise? When I say I'll do something, I do it! By the way, the kidney was very good. (*Corks the bottle.*)

JULIE (*in the doorway to someone outside*): I'll be right back! You go ahead for now! (*Jean sneaks the bottle back into the table drawer and gets up respectfully. Miss Julie enters and crosses to Kristine by the stove.*) Well? Is it ready? (*Kristine indicates that Jean is present.*)

JEAN (*gallantly*): Are you ladies up to something secret?

JULIE (*flicking her handkerchief in his face*): None of your business!

JEAN: Hmm! I like the smell of violets!

JULIE (*coquettishly*): Shame on you! So you know about perfumes, too? You certainly know how to dance. Ah, ah! No peeking! Go away.

JEAN (*boldly but respectfully*): Are you brewing up a magic potion for midsummer eve? Something to prophesy by under a lucky star, so you'll catch a glimpse of your future husband!

JULIE (*caustically*): You'd need sharp eyes to see him! (*To Kristine.*) Pour out half a bottle and cork it well. —— Come and dance a schottische° with me, Jean . . .

JEAN (*hesitating*): I don't want to be impolite to anyone, and I've already promised this dance to Kristine . . .

JULIE: Oh, she can have another one — can't you, Kristine? Won't you lend me Jean?

KRISTINE: It's not up to me, ma'am. (*To Jean.*) If the mistress is so generous, it wouldn't do for you to say no. Go on, Jean, and thank her for the honor.

JEAN: To be honest, and no offense intended, I wonder whether it's wise for you to dance twice running with the same partner, especially since these people are quick to jump to conclusions . . .

---

délice: Delight.
pur: Pure; the first drink from the bottle.

schottische: A Scottish round dance resembling a polka.

JULIE (*flaring up*): What's that? What sort of conclusions? What do you mean?

JEAN (*submissively*): If you don't understand, ma'am, I must speak more plainly. It doesn't look good to play favorites with your servants. . . .

JULIE: Play favorites! What an idea! I'm astonished! As mistress of the house, I honor your dance with my presence. And when I dance, I want to dance with someone who can lead, so I won't look ridiculous.

JEAN: As you order, ma'am! I'm at your service!

JULIE (*gently*): Don't take it as an order! On a night like this we're all just ordinary people having fun, so we'll forget about rank. Now, take my arm! —— Don't worry, Kristine! I won't steal your sweetheart! (*Jean offers his arm and leads Miss Julie out.*)

Mime

(*The following should be played as if the actress playing Kristine were really alone. When she has to, she turns her back to the audience. She does not look toward them, nor does she hurry as if she were afraid they would grow impatient. Schottische music played on a fiddle sounds in the distance. Kristine hums along with the music. She clears the table, washes the dishes, dries them, and puts them away. She takes off her apron. From a table drawer she removes a small mirror and leans it against the bowl of lilacs on the table. She lights a candle, heats a hairpin over the flame, and uses it to set a curl on her forehead. She crosses to the door and listens, then returns to the table. She finds the handkerchief Miss Julie left behind, picks it up, and smells it. Then, preoccupied, she spreads it out, stretches it, smoothes out the wrinkles, and folds it into quarters, and so forth.*)

JEAN (*enters alone*): God, she really *is* crazy! What a way to dance! Everybody's laughing at her behind her back. What do you make of it, Kristine?

KRISTINE: Ah! It's that time of the month for her, and she always gets peculiar like that. Are you going to dance with me now?

JEAN: You're not mad at me, are you, for leaving . . . ?

KRISTINE: Of course not! —— Why should I be, for a little thing like that? Besides, I know my place . . .

JEAN (*puts his arm around her waist*): You're a sensible girl, Kristine, and you'd make a good wife . . .

JULIE (*entering; uncomfortably surprised; with forced good humor*): What a charming escort — running away from his partner.

JEAN: On the contrary, Miss Julie. Don't you see how I rushed back to the partner I abandoned!

JULIE (*changing her tone*): You know, you're a superb dancer! —— But why are you wearing livery on a holiday? Take it off at once!

JEAN: Then I must ask you to go outside for a moment. You see, my black coat is hanging over here . . . (*Gestures and crosses right.*)

JULIE: Are you embarrassed about changing your coat in front of me? Well, go in your room then. Either that or stay and I'll turn my back.

JEAN: With your permission, ma'am! (*He crosses right. His arm is visible as he changes his jacket.*)

JULIE (*to Kristine*): Tell me, Kristine — you two are so close —. Is Jean your fiancé?

KRISTINE: Fiancé? Yes, if you wish. We can call him that.

JULIE: What do you mean?

KRISTINE: You had a fiancé yourself, didn't you? So . . .

JULIE: Well, we were properly engaged . . .

KRISTINE: But nothing came of it, did it? (*Jean returns dressed in a frock coat and bowler hat.*)

JULIE: *Très gentil, monsieur Jean! Très gentil!*

JEAN: *Vous voulez plaisanter, madame!*

JULIE: *Et vous voulez parler français!*° Where did you learn that?

JEAN: In Switzerland, when I was wine steward in one of the biggest hotels in Lucerne!

JULIE: You look like a real gentleman in that coat! *Charmant!*° (*Sits at the table.*)

JEAN: Oh, you're flattering me!

JULIE (*offended*): Flattering you?

JEAN: My natural modesty forbids me to believe that you would really compliment someone like me, and so I took the liberty of assuming that you were exaggerating, which polite people call flattering.

JULIE: Where did you learn to talk like that? You must have been to the theater often.

JEAN: Of course. And I've done a lot of traveling.

JULIE: But you come from here, don't you?

JEAN: My father was a farmhand on the district attorney's estate nearby. I used to see you when you were little, but you never noticed me.

JULIE: No! Really?

JEAN: Sure. I remember one time especially . . . but I can't talk about that.

JULIE: Oh, come now! Why not? Just this once!

JEAN: No, I really couldn't, not now. Some other time, perhaps.

JULIE: Why some other time? What's so dangerous about now?

Très gentil . . . français!: Very pleasing, Mr. Jean! Very pleasing. You would trifle with me, madam! And you want to speak French!
Charmant: Charming.

JEAN: It's not dangerous, but there are obstacles. —— Her, for example. (*Indicating Kristine, who has fallen asleep in a chair by the stove.*)

JULIE: What a pleasant wife she'll make! She probably snores, too.

JEAN: No, she doesn't, but she talks in her sleep.

JULIE (*cynically*): How do *you* know?

JEAN (*audaciously*): I've heard her! (*Pause, during which they stare at each other.*)

JULIE: Why don't you sit down?

JEAN: I couldn't do that in your presence.

JULIE: But if I order you to?

JEAN: Then I'd obey.

JULIE: Sit down, then. —— No, wait. Can you get me something to drink first?

JEAN: I don't know what we have in the ice box. I think there's only beer.

JULIE: Why do you say "only"? My tastes are so simple I prefer beer to wine. (*Jean takes a bottle of beer from the ice box and opens it. He looks for a glass and a plate in the cupboard and serves her.*)

JEAN: Here you are, ma'am.

JULIE: Thank you. Won't you have something yourself?

JEAN: I'm not partial to beer, but if it's an order . . .

JULIE: An order? —— Surely a gentleman can keep his lady company.

JEAN: You're right, of course. (*Opens a bottle and gets a glass.*)

JULIE: Now, drink to my health! (*He hesitates.*) What? A man of the world — and shy?

JEAN (*in mock romantic fashion, he kneels and raises his glass*): *Skål* to my mistress!

JULIE: Bravo! —— Now kiss my shoe, to finish it properly. (*Jean hesitates, then boldly seizes her foot and kisses it lightly.*) Perfect! You should have been an actor.

JEAN (*rising*): That's enough now, Miss Julie! Someone might come in and see us.

JULIE: What of it?

JEAN: People talk, that's what! If you knew how their tongues were wagging just now at the dance, you'd . . .

JULIE: What were they saying? Tell me! —— Sit down!

JEAN (*sits*): I don't want to hurt you, but they were saying things —— suggestive things, that, that . . . well, you can figure it out for yourself! You're not a child. If a woman is seen drinking alone with a man — let alone a servant — at night — then . . .

JULIE: Then what? Besides, we're not alone. Kristine is here.

JEAN: Asleep!

JULIE: Then I'll wake her up. (*Rising.*) Kristine! Are you asleep? (*Kristine mumbles in her sleep.*)

JULIE: Kristine! —— She certainly can sleep!

KRISTINE (*in her sleep*): The Count's boots are brushed — put the coffee on — right away, right away — uh, huh — oh!

JULIE (*grabbing Kristine's nose*): Will you wake up!

JEAN (*severely*): Leave her alone — let her sleep!

JULIE (*sharply*): What?

JEAN: Someone who's been standing over a stove all day has a right to be tired by now. Sleep should be respected . . .

JULIE (*changing her tone*): What a considerate thought — it does you credit — thank you! (*Offering her hand.*) Come outside and pick some lilacs for me! (*During the following, Kristine awakens and shambles sleepily off right to bed.*)

JEAN: Go with you?

JULIE: With me!

JEAN: We couldn't do that! Absolutely not!

JULIE: I don't understand. Surely you don't imagine . . .

JEAN: No, I don't, but the others might.

JULIE: What? That I've fallen in love with a servant?

JEAN: I'm not a conceited man, but such things happen — and for these people, nothing is sacred.

JULIE: I do believe you're an aristocrat!

JEAN: Yes, I am.

JULIE: And I'm stepping down . . .

JEAN: Don't step down, Miss Julie, take my advice. No one'll believe you stepped down voluntarily. People will always say you fell.

JULIE: I have a higher opinion of people than you. Come and see! —— Come! (*She stares at him broodingly.*)

JEAN: You're very strange, do you know that?

JULIE: Perhaps! But so are you! —— For that matter, everything is strange. Life, people, everything. Like floating scum, drifting on and on across the water, until it sinks down and down! That reminds me of a dream I have now and then. I've climbed up on top of a pillar. I sit there and see no way of getting down. I get dizzy when I look down, and I must get down, but I don't have the courage to jump. I can't hold on firmly, and I long to be able to fall, but I don't fall. And yet I'll have no peace until I get down, no rest unless I get down, down on the ground! And if I did get down to the ground, I'd want to be under the earth . . . Have you ever felt anything like that?

JEAN: No. I dream that I'm lying under a high tree in a dark forest. I want to get up, up on top, and look out over the bright landscape, where the sun is shining, and plunder the bird's nest up there, where the golden eggs lie. And I climb and climb, but the trunk's so thick and smooth, and it's so far to the first branch. But I know if I just reached that first branch, I'd go right to the top, like up a ladder. I haven't reached it yet, but I will, even if it's only in a dream!

JULIE: Here I am chattering with you about dreams. Come, let's go out! Just into the park! (*She offers him her arm, and they start to leave.*)

JEAN: We'll have to sleep on nine midsummer flowers, Miss Julie, to make our dreams come true! (*They turn at the door. Jean puts his hand to his eye.*)

JULIE: Did you get something in your eye?

JEAN: It's nothing — just a speck — it'll be gone in a minute.

JULIE: My sleeve must have brushed against you. Sit down and let me help you. (*She takes him by the arm and seats him. She tilts his head back and with the tip of a handkerchief tries to remove the speck.*) Sit still, absolutely still! (*She slaps his hand.*) Didn't you hear me? —— Why, you're trembling; the big, strong man is trembling! (*Feels his biceps.*) What muscles you have!

JEAN (*warning*): Miss Julie!

JULIE: Yes, *monsieur* Jean.

JEAN: *Attention! Je ne suis qu'un homme!*°

JULIE Will you sit still! —— There! Now it's gone! Kiss my hand and thank me.

JEAN (*rising*): Miss Julie, listen to me! —— Kristine has gone to bed! —— Will you listen to me!

JULIE: Kiss my hand first!

JEAN: Listen to me!

JULIE: Kiss my hand first!

JEAN: All right, but you've only yourself to blame!

JULIE: For what?

JEAN: For what? Are you still a child at twenty-five? Don't you know that it's dangerous to play with fire?

JULIE: Not for me. I'm insured.

JEAN (*boldly*): No, you're not! But even if you were, there's combustible material close by.

JULIE: Meaning you?

JEAN: Yes! Not because it's me, but because I'm young ——

JULIE: And handsome — what incredible conceit! A Don Juan perhaps! Or a Joseph!° Yes, that's it, I do believe you're a Joseph!

JEAN: Do you?

JULIE: I'm almost afraid so. (*Jean boldly tries to put his arm around her waist and kiss her. She slaps his face.*) How dare you?

JEAN: Are you serious or joking?

JULIE: Serious.

Attention! Je ne suis qu'un homme!: Watch out! I am only a man!

Don Juan . . . Joseph: Don Juan in Spanish legend is a seducer of women; in Genesis, Joseph resists the advances of Potiphar's wife.

JEAN: Then so was what just happened. You play games too seriously, and that's dangerous. Well, I'm tired of games. You'll excuse me if I get back to work. I haven't done the Count's boots yet and it's long past midnight.

JULIE: Put the boots down!

JEAN: No! It's the work I have to do. I never agreed to be your playmate, and never will. It's beneath me.

JULIE: You're proud.

JEAN: In certain ways, but not in others.

JULIE: Have you ever been in love?

JEAN: We don't use that word, but I've been fond of many girls, and once I was sick because I couldn't have the one I wanted. That's right, sick, like those princes in the Arabian Nights — who couldn't eat or drink because of love.

JULIE: Who was she? (*Jean is silent.*) Who was she?

JEAN: You can't force me to tell you that.

JULIE: But if I ask you as an equal, as a — friend! Who was she?

JEAN: You!

JULIE (*sits*): How amusing . . .

JEAN: Yes, if you like! It was ridiculous! —— You see, that was the story I didn't want to tell you earlier. Maybe I will now. Do you know how the world looks from down below? —— Of course you don't. Neither do hawks and falcons, whose backs we can't see because they're usually soaring up there above us. I grew up in a shack with seven brothers and sisters and a pig, in the middle of a wasteland, where there wasn't a single tree. But from our window I could see the tops of apple trees above the wall of your father's garden. That was the Garden of Eden, guarded by angry angels with flaming swords. All the same, the other boys and I managed to find our way to the Tree of Life. —— Now you think I'm contemptible, I suppose.

JULIE: Oh, all boys steal apples.

JEAN: You say that, but you think I'm contemptible anyway. Oh well! One day I went into the Garden of Eden with my mother, to weed the onion beds. Near the vegetable garden was a small Turkish pavilion in the shadow of jasmine bushes and overgrown with honeysuckle. I had no idea what it was used for, but I'd never seen such a beautiful building. People went in and came out again, and one day the door was left open. I sneaked close and saw walls covered with pictures of kings and emperors, and red curtains with fringes at the windows — now you know the place I mean. I —— (*Breaks off a sprig of lilac and holds it in front of Miss Julie's nose.*) —— I'd never been inside the manor house, never seen anything except the church—but this was more beautiful. From then on, no matter where my thoughts wandered, they returned — there. And gradually I got a longing to experience, just once, the full pleasure of — *enfin,*° I sneaked in, saw, and marveled! But then I heard someone coming! There was only one exit for ladies and gentlemen, but for me there was another, and I had no choice but to take it! (*Miss Julie, who has taken the lilac sprig, lets it fall on the table.*) Afterwards, I started running. I crashed through a raspberry bush, flew over a strawberry patch, and came up onto the rose terrace. There I caught sight of a pink dress and a pair of white stockings — it was you. I crawled under a pile of weeds, and I mean under — under thistles that pricked me and wet dirt that stank. And I looked at you as you walked among the roses, and I thought: If it's true that a thief can enter heaven and be with the angels, then why can't a farmhand's son here on God's earth enter the manor house garden and play with the Count's daughter?

JULIE (*romantically*): Do you think all poor children would have thought the way you did?

JEAN (*at first hesitant, then with conviction*): If *all* poor — yes — of course. Of course!

JULIE: It must be terrible to be poor!

JEAN (*with exaggerated suffering*): Oh, Miss Julie! Oh! ——— A dog can lie on the Countess's sofa, a horse can have his nose patted by a young lady's hand, but a servant ——— (*Changing his tone.*) ——— oh, I know — now and then you find one with enough stuff in him to get ahead in the world, but how often? ——— Anyhow, do you know what I did then? ——— I jumped in the millstream with my clothes on, was pulled out, and got a beating. But the following Sunday, when my father and all the others went to my grandmother's, I arranged to stay home. I scrubbed myself with soap and water, put on my best clothes, and went to church so that I could see you! I saw you and returned home, determined to die. But I wanted to die beautifully and pleasantly, without pain. And then I remembered that it was dangerous to sleep under an elder bush. We had a big one, and it was in full flower. I plundered its treasures and bedded down under them in the oat bin. Have you ever noticed how smooth oats are? — and soft to the touch, like human skin . . . ! Well, I shut the lid and closed my eyes. I fell asleep and woke up feeling very sick. But I didn't die, as you can see. What was I after? ——— I don't know. There was no hope of winning you, of course. ——— You were a symbol of the hopelessness of ever rising out of the class in which I was born.

JULIE: You're a charming storyteller. Did you ever go to school?

JEAN: A bit, but I've read lots of novels and been to the theater often. And then I've listened to people like you talk — that's where I learned most.

JULIE: Do you listen to what we say?

JEAN: Naturally! And I've heard plenty, too, driving the carriage or rowing the boat. Once I heard you and a friend . . .

JULIE: Oh? ——— What did you hear?

JEAN: I'd better not say. But I was surprised a little. I couldn't imagine where you learned such words. Maybe at bottom there isn't such a great difference between people as we think.

JULIE: Shame on you! We don't act like you when we're engaged.

JEAN (*staring at her*): Is that true? ——— You don't have to play innocent with me, Miss . . .

JULIE: The man I gave my love to was a swine.

JEAN: That's what you all say — afterwards.

JULIE: All?

JEAN: I think so. I know I've heard that phrase before, on similar occasions.

JULIE: What occasions?

JEAN: Like the one I'm talking about. The last time . . .

JULIE (*rising*): Quiet! I don't want to hear any more!

JEAN: That's interesting — that's what *she* said, too. Well, if you'll excuse me, I'm going to bed.

JULIE (*gently*): To bed? On midsummer eve?

JEAN: Yes! Dancing with the rabble out there doesn't amuse me much.

JULIE: Get the key to the boat and row me out on the lake. I want to see the sun come up.

JEAN: Is that wise?

JULIE: Are you worried about your reputation?

JEAN: Why not? Why should I risk looking ridiculous and getting fired without a reference, just when I'm trying to establish myself. Besides, I think I owe something to Kristine.

JULIE: So, now it's Kristine . . .

JEAN: Yes, but you, too. ——— Take my advice, go up and go to bed!

JULIE: Am I to obey you?

JEAN: Just this once — for your own good! Please! It's very late. Drowsiness makes people giddy and liable to lose their heads! Go to bed! Besides — unless I'm mistaken — I hear the others coming to look for me. And if they find us together, you'll be lost!

(*The Chorus approaches, singing.*)

The swineherd found his true love
a pretty girl so fair,
The swineherd found his true love
but let the girl beware.

---

enfin: Finally.

For then he saw the princess
the princess on the golden hill,
but then saw the princess,
so much fairer still.

So the swineherd and the princess
they danced the whole night through,
and he forgot his first love,
to her he was untrue.

And when the long night ended,
and in the light of day, of day,
the dancing too was ended,
and the princess could not stay.

Then the swineherd lost his true love,
and the princess grieves him still,
and never more she'll wander
from atop the golden hill.

JULIE: I know all these people and I love them, just as they love me. Let them come in and you'll see.

JEAN: No, Miss Julie, they don't love you. They take your food, but they spit on it! Believe me! Listen to them, listen to what they're singing! ——— No. don't listen to them!

JULIE (*listening*): What are they singing?

JEAN: It's a dirty song! About you and me!

JULIE: Disgusting! Oh! How deceitful! ———

JEAN: The rabble is always cowardly! And in a battle like this, you don't fight; you can only run away!

JULIE: Run away? But where? We can't go out — or into Kristine's room.

JEAN: True. But there's my room. Necessity knows no rules. Besides, you can trust me. I'm your friend and I respect you.

JULIE: But suppose — suppose they look for you in there?

JEAN: I'll bolt the door, and if anyone tries to break in, I'll shoot! ——— Come! (*On his knees.*) Come!

JULIE (*urgently*): Promise me . . . ?

JEAN: I swear! (*Miss Julie runs off right. Jean hastens after her.*)

Ballet

(*Led by a fiddler, the servants and farm people enter, dressed festively, with flowers in their hats. On the table they place a small barrel of beer and a keg of schnapps, both garlanded. Glasses are brought out, and the drinking starts. A dance circle is formed and "The Swineherd and the Princess" is sung. When the dance is finished, everyone leaves, singing.*)

(*Miss Julie enters alone. She notices the mess in the kitchen, wrings her hands, then takes out her powder puff and powders her nose.*)

JEAN (*enters, agitated*): There, you see? And you heard them. We can't possibly stay here now, you know that.

JULIE: Yes, I know. But what can we do?

JEAN: Leave, travel, far away from here.

JULIE: Travel? Yes, but where?

JEAN: To Switzerland, to the Italian lakes. Have you ever been there?

JULIE: No. Is it beautiful?

JEAN: Oh, an eternal summer — oranges growing everywhere, laurel trees, always green . . .

JULIE: But what'll we do there?

JEAN: I'll open a hotel — with first-class service for first-class people.

JULIE: Hotel?

JEAN: That's the life, you know. Always new faces, new languages. No time to worry or be nervous. No hunting for something to do — there's always work to be done: bells ringing night and day, train whistles blowing, carriages coming and going, and all the while gold rolling into the till! That's the life!

JULIE: Yes, it sounds wonderful. But what'll I do?

JEAN: You'll be mistress of the house: the jewel in our crown! With your looks . . . and your manner — oh — success is guaranteed! It'll be wonderful! You'll sit in your office like a queen and push an electric button to set your slaves in motion. The guests will file past your throne and timidly lay their treasures before you. ——— You have no idea how people tremble when they get their bill. ——— I'll salt the bills° and you'll sweeten them with your prettiest smile. ——— Let's get away from here ——— (*Takes a timetable out of his pocket.*) ——— Right away, on the next train! ——— We'll be in Malmö six-thirty tomorrow morning, Hamburg at eight-forty; from Frankfort to Basel will take a day, then on to Como by way of the St. Gotthard Tunnel, in, let's see, three days. Three days!

JULIE: That's all very well! But Jean — you must give me courage! ——— Tell me you love me! Put your arms around me!

JEAN (*hesitating*): I want to — but I don't dare. Not in this house, not again. I love you — never doubt that — you don't doubt it, do you, Miss Julie?

JULIE (*shy; very feminine*): "Miss!" ——— Call me Julie! There are no barriers between us anymore. Call me Julie!

JEAN (*tormented*): I can't! There'll always be barriers between us as long as we stay in this house. ——— There's the past and there's the Count. I've never

---

salt the bills: Inflate or pad the bills.

Helen Mirren as Miss Julie in a 1971 production of Strindberg's play.

mania and be decorated. I could — mind you I said *could* — end up a count!

JULIE: Wonderful, wonderful!

JEAN: Ah, in Rumania you just buy your title, and so you'll be a countess after all. My countess!

JULIE: But I don't care about that — that's what I'm putting behind me! Show me you love me, otherwise — otherwise, what am I?

JEAN: I'll show you a thousand times — afterwards! Not here! And whatever you do, no emotional outbursts, or we'll both be lost! We must think this through coolly, like sensible people. (*He takes out a cigar, snips the end, and lights it.*) You sit there, and I'll sit here. We'll talk as if nothing happened.

JULIE (*desperately*): Oh, my God! Have you no feelings?

JEAN: Me? No one has more feelings than I do, but I know how to control them.

JULIE: A little while ago you could kiss my shoe — and now!

JEAN (*harshly*): Yes, but that was before. Now we have other things to think about.

JULIE: Don't speak harshly to me!

JEAN: I'm not — just sensibly! We've already done one foolish thing, let's not have any more. The Count could return any minute, and by then we've got to decide what to do with our lives. What do you think of my plans for the future? Do you approve?

JULIE: They sound reasonable enough. I have only one question: For such a big undertaking you need capital — do you have it?

JEAN (*chewing on the cigar*): Me? Certainly! I have my professional expertise, my wide experience, and my knowledge of languages. That's capital enough, I should think!

JULIE: But all that won't even buy a train ticket.

JEAN: That's true. That's why I'm looking for a partner to advance me the money.

JULIE: Where will you find one quickly enough?

JEAN: That's up to you, if you want to come with me.

JULIE: But I can't; I have no money of my own. (*Pause.*)

JEAN: Then it's all off . . .

JULIE: And . . .

JEAN: Things stay as they are.

JULIE: Do you think I'm going to stay in this house as your lover? With all the servants pointing their fingers at me? Do you imagine I can face my father after this? No! Take me away from here, away from shame and dishonor — Oh, what have I done! My God, my God! (*She cries.*)

JEAN: Now, don't start that old song! — What have you done? The same as many others before you.

met anyone I had such respect for. — When I see his gloves lying on a chair, I feel small. — When I hear that bell up there ring, I jump like a skittish horse. — And when I look at his boots standing there so stiff and proud, I feel like bowing! (*Kicking the boots.*) Superstitions and prejudices we learned as children — but they can easily be forgotten. If I can just get to another country, a republic, people will bow and scrape when they see my livery — *they'll* bow and scrape, you hear, not me! I wasn't born to cringe. I've got stuff in me, I've got character, and if I can only grab onto that first branch, you watch me climb! I'm a servant today, but next year I'll own my own hotel. In ten years I'll have enough to retire. Then I'll go to Ru-

JULIE (*screaming convulsively*): And now you think I'm contemptible!———I'm falling, I'm falling!

JEAN: Fall down to my level and I'll lift you up again.

JULIE: What terrible power drew me to you? The attraction of the weak to the strong? The falling to the rising? Or was it love? Was this love? Do you know what love is?

JEAN: Me? What do you take me for? You don't think this was my first time, do you?

JULIE: The things you say, the thoughts you think!

JEAN: That's the way I was taught, and that's the way I am! Now don't get excited and don't play the grand lady, because we're in the same boat now!———Come on, Julie, I'll pour you a glass of something special! (*He opens a drawer in the table, takes out a wine bottle, and fills two glasses already used.*)

JULIE: Where did you get that wine?

JEAN: From the cellar.

JULIE: My father's burgundy!

JEAN: That'll do for his son-in-law, won't it?

JULIE: And I drink beer! Beer!

JEAN: That only shows I have better taste.

JULIE: Thief!

JEAN: Planning to tell?

JULIE: Oh, oh! Accomplice of a common thief! Was I drunk? Have I been walking in a dream the whole evening? Midsummer eve! A time of innocent fun!

JEAN: Innocent, eh?

JULIE (*pacing back and forth*): Is there anyone on earth more miserable than I am at this moment?

JEAN: Why should you be? After such a conquest? Think of Kristine in there. Don't you think she has feelings, too?

JULIE: I thought so awhile ago, but not any more. No, a servant is a servant . . .

JEAN: And a whore is a whore!

JULIE (*on her knees, her hands clasped*): Oh, God in heaven, end my wretched life! Take me away from the filth I'm sinking into! Save me! Save me!

JEAN: I can't deny I feel sorry for you. When I lay in that onion bed and saw you in the rose garden, well . . . I'll be frank . . . I had the same dirty thoughts all boys have.

JULIE: And you wanted to die for me!

JEAN: In the oat bin? That was just talk.

JULIE: A lie, in other words!

JEAN (*beginning to feel sleepy*): More or less! I got the idea from a newspaper story about a chimney sweep who curled up in a firewood bin full of lilacs because he got a summons for not supporting his illegitimate child . . .

JULIE: So, that's what you're like . . .

JEAN: I had to think of something. And that's the kind of story women always go for.

JULIE: Swine!

JEAN: *Merde!*

JULIE: And now you've seen the hawk's back . . .

JEAN: Not exactly its *back* . . .

JULIE: And I was to be the first branch . . .

JEAN: But the branch was rotten . . .

JULIE: I was to be the sign on the hotel . . .

JEAN: And I the hotel . . .

JULIE: Sit at your desk, entice your customers, pad their bills . . .

JEAN: That I'd do myself . . .

JULIE: How can anyone be so thoroughly filthy?

JEAN: Better clean up then!

JULIE: You lackey, you menial, stand up, when I speak to you!

JEAN: Menial's strumpet, lackey's whore, shut up and get out of here! Who are you to lecture me on coarseness? None of my kind is ever as coarse as you were tonight. Do you think one of your maids would throw herself at a man the way you did? Have you ever seen any girl of my class offer herself like that? I've only seen it among animals and streetwalkers.

JULIE (*crushed*): You're right. Hit me, trample on me. I don't deserve any better. I'm worthless. But help me! If you see any way out of this, help me, Jean, please!

JEAN (*more gently*): I'd be lying if I didn't admit to a sense of triumph in all this, but do you think that a person like me would have dared even to look at someone like you if you hadn't invited it? I'm still amazed . . .

JULIE: And proud . . .

JEAN: Why not? Though I must say it was too easy to be really exciting.

JULIE: Go on, hit me, hit me harder!

JEAN (*rising*): No! Forgive me for what I've said! I don't hit a man when he's down, let alone a woman. I can't deny though, that I'm pleased to find out that what looked so dazzling to us from below was only tinsel, that the hawk's back was only gray, after all, that the lovely complexion was only powder, that those polished fingernails had black edges, and that a dirty handkerchief is still dirty, even if it smells of perfume . . . ! On the other hand, it hurts me to find out that what I was striving for wasn't finer, more substantial. It hurts me to see you sunk so low that you're inferior to your own cook. It hurts like watching flowers beaten down by autumn rains and turned into mud.

JULIE: You talk as if you were already above me.

JEAN: I am. You see, I could make you a countess, but you could never make me a count.

JULIE: But I'm the child of a count — something you could never be!

JEAN: That's true. But I could be the father of counts — if . . .

JULIE: But you're a thief. I'm not.

JEAN: There are worse things than being a thief! Besides, when I'm working in a house, I consider myself sort of a member of the family, like one of the children. And you don't call it stealing when a child snatches a berry off a full bush. (*His passion is aroused again.*) Miss Julie, you're a glorious woman, much too good for someone like me! You were drinking and you lost your head. Now you want to cover up your mistake by telling yourself that you love me! You don't. Maybe there was a physical attraction — but then your love is no better than mine. ———— I could never be satisfied to be no more than an animal to you, and I could never arouse real love in you.

JULIE: Are you sure of that?

JEAN: You're suggesting it's possible ———— Oh, I could fall in love with you, no doubt about it. You're beautiful, you're refined ———— (*approaching and taking her hand*) ———— cultured, lovable when you want to be, and once you start a fire in a man, it never goes out. (*Putting his arm around her waist.*) You're like hot, spicy wine, and one kiss from you . . . (*He tries to lead her out, but she slowly frees herself.*)

JULIE: Let me go!? ———— You'll never win me like that.

JEAN: *How* then? ———— Not like that? Not with caresses and pretty speeches. Not with plans about the future or rescue from disgrace! *How* then?

JULIE: How? How? I don't know! ———— I have no idea! ———— I detest you as I detest rats, but I can't escape from you.

JEAN: Escape with me!

JULIE (*pulling herself together*): Escape? Yes, we must escape! ———— But I'm so tired. Give me a glass of wine? (*Jean pours the wine. She looks at her watch.*) But we must talk first. We still have a little time. (*She drains the glass, then holds it out for more.*)

JEAN: Don't drink so fast. It'll go to your head.

JULIE: What does it matter?

JEAN: What does it matter? It's vulgar to get drunk! What did you want to tell me?

JULIE: We must escape! But first we must talk, I mean I must talk. You've done all the talking up to now. You told about your life, now I want to tell about mine, so we'll know all about each other before we go off together.

JEAN: Just a minute! Forgive me! If you don't want to regret it afterwards, you'd better think twice before revealing any secrets about yourself.

JULIE: Aren't you my friend?

JEAN: Yes, sometimes! But don't rely on me.

JULIE: You're only saying that. ———— Besides, every-one already knows my secrets. ———— You see, my mother was a commoner — very humble background. She was brought up believing in social equality, women's rights, and all that. The idea of marriage repelled her. So, when my father proposed, she replied that she would never become his wife, but he could be her lover. He insisted that he didn't want the woman he loved to be less respected than he. But his passion ruled him, and when she explained that the world's respect meant nothing to her, he accepted her conditions.

But now his friends avoided him and his life was restricted to taking care of the estate, which couldn't satisfy him. I came into the world — against my mother's wishes, as far as I can understand. She wanted to bring me up as a child of nature, and, what's more, to learn everything a boy had to learn, so that I might be an example of how a woman can be as good as a man. I had to wear boy's clothes and learn to take care of horses, but I was never allowed in the cowshed. I had to groom and harness the horses and go hunting — and even had to watch them slaughter animals — that was disgusting! On the estate men were put on women's jobs and women on men's jobs — with the result that the property became run down and we became the laughingstock of the district. Finally, my father must have awakened from his trance because he rebelled and changed everything his way. My parents were then married quietly. Mother became ill — I don't know what illness it was — but she often had convulsions, hid in the attic and in the garden, and sometimes stayed out all night. Then came the great fire, which you've heard about. The house, the stables, and the cowshed all burned down, under very curious circumstances, suggesting arson, because the accident happened the day after the insurance had expired. The quarterly premium my father sent in was delayed because of a messenger's carelessness and didn't arrive in time. (*She fills her glass and drinks.*)

JEAN: Don't drink any more!

JULIE: Oh, what does it matter. ———— We were left penniless and had to sleep in the carriages. My father had no idea where to find money to rebuild the house because he had so slighted his old friends that they had forgotten him. Then my mother suggested that he borrow from a childhood friend of hers, a brick manufacturer who lived nearby. Father got the loan without having to pay interest, which surprised him. And that's how the estate was rebuilt. ———— (*Drinks again.*) Do you know who started the fire?

JEAN: The Countess, your mother.

JULIE: Do you know who the brick manufacturer was?

JEAN: Your mother's lover?

JULIE: Do you know whose money it was?

JEAN: Wait a moment — no, I don't.

JULIE: It was my mother's.

JEAN: You mean the Count's, unless they didn't sign an agreement when they were married.

JULIE: They didn't. ——— My mother had a small inheritance which she didn't want under my father's control, so she entrusted it to her — friend.

JEAN: Who stole it!

JULIE: Exactly! He kept it. ——— All this my father found out, but he couldn't bring it to court, couldn't repay his wife's lover, couldn't prove it was his wife's money! It was my mother's revenge for being forced into marriage against her will. It nearly drove him to suicide — there was a rumor that he tried with a pistol, but failed. So, he managed to live through it and my mother had to suffer for what she'd done. You can imagine that those were a terrible five years for me. I loved my father, but I sided with my mother because I didn't know the circumstances. I learned from her to hate men — you've heard how she hated the whole male sex — and I swore to her I'd never be a slave to any man.

JEAN: But you got engaged to that lawyer.

JULIE: In order to make him my slave.

JEAN: And he wasn't willing?

JULIE: He was willing, all right, but I wouldn't let him. I got tired of him.

JEAN: I saw it — out near the stable.

JULIE: What did you see?

JEAN: I saw — how he broke off the engagement.

JULIE: That's a lie! I was the one who broke it off. Has he said that he did? That swine . . .

JEAN: He was no swine, I'm sure. So, you hate men, Miss Julie?

JULIE: Yes! ——— Most of the time! But sometimes — when the weakness comes, when passion burns! Oh, God, will the fire never die out?

JEAN: Do you hate me, too?

JULIE: Immeasurably! I'd like to have you put to death, like an animal . . .

JEAN: I see — the penalty for bestiality — the woman gets two years at hard labor and the animal is put to death. Right?

JULIE: Exactly!

JEAN: But there's no prosecutor here — and no animal. So, what'll we do?

JULIE: Go away!

JEAN: To torment each other to death?

JULIE: No! To be happy for — two days, a week, as long as we can be happy, and then — die . . .

JEAN: Die? That's stupid! It's better to open a hotel!

JULIE (without listening): ——— on the shore of Lake Como, where the sun always shines, where the laurels are green at Christmas and the oranges glow.

JEAN: Lake Como is a rainy hole, and I never saw any oranges outside the stores. But tourists are attracted there because there are plenty of villas to be rented out to lovers, and that's a profitable business. ——— Do you know why? Because they sign a lease for six months — and then leave after three weeks!

JULIE (naively): Why after three weeks?

JEAN: They quarrel, of course! But they still have to pay the rent in full! And so you rent the villas out again. And that's the way it goes, time after time. There's never a shortage of love — even if it doesn't last long!

JULIE: You don't want to die with me?

JEAN: I don't want to die at all! For one thing, I like living, and for another, I think suicide is a crime against the Providence which gave us life.

JULIE: You believe in God? You?

JEAN: Of course I do. And I go to church every other Sunday. ——— To be honest, I'm tired of all this, and I'm going to bed.

JULIE: Are you? And do you think I can let it go at that? A man owes something to the woman he's shamed.

JEAN (taking out his purse and throwing a silver coin on the table): Here! I don't like owing anything to anybody.

JULIE (pretending not to notice the insult): Do you know what the law states . . .

JEAN: Unfortunately the law doesn't state any punishment for the woman who seduces a man!

JULIE (as before): Do you see any way out but to leave, get married, and then separate?

JEAN: Suppose I refuse such a mésalliance?°

JULIE: Mésalliance . . .

JEAN: Yes, for me! You see, I come from better stock than you. There's no arsonist in my family.

JULIE: How do you know?

JEAN: You can't prove otherwise. We don't keep charts on our ancestors — there's just the police records! But I've read about your family. Do you know who the founder was? He was a miller who let the king sleep with his wife one night during the Danish War. I don't have any noble ancestors like that. I don't have any noble ancestors at all, but I could become one myself.

JULIE: This is what I get for opening my heart to someone unworthy, for giving my family's honor . . .

JEAN: Dishonor! ——— Well, I told you so: When people drink, they talk, and talk is dangerous!

JULIE: Oh, how I regret it! ——— How I regret it! ——— If you at least loved me.

JEAN: For the last time ——— what do you want? Shall I cry; shall I jump over your riding crop? Shall I kiss you and lure you off to Lake Como for three weeks,

---

mésalliance: Misalliance or mismatch, especially regarding relative social status.

and then God knows what . . . ? What shall I do? What do you want? This is getting painfully embarrassing! But that's what happens when you stick your nose in women's business. Miss Julie! I see that you're unhappy. I know you're suffering, but I can't understand you. We don't have such romantic ideas; there's not this kind of hate between us. Love is a game we play when we get time off from work, but we don't have all day and night, like you. I think you're sick, really sick. Your mother was crazy, and her ideas have poisoned your life.

JULIE: Be kind to me. At least now you're talking like a human being.

JEAN: Be human yourself, then. You spit on me, and you won't let me wipe myself off ———

JULIE: Help me! Help me! Just tell me what to do, where to go!

JEAN: In God's name, if I only knew myself!

JULIE: I've been crazy, out of my mind, but isn't there any way out?

JEAN: Stay here and keep calm! No one knows anything!

JULIE: Impossible! The others know and Kristine knows.

JEAN: No they don't, and they'd never believe a thing like that!

JULIE (*hesitantly*): But — it could happen again!

JEAN: That's true!

JULIE: And then?

JEAN (*frightened*): Then? ——— Why didn't I think about that? Yes, there is only one thing to do — get away from here! Right away! I can't come with you, then we'd be finished, so you'll have to go alone — away — anywhere!

JULIE: Alone? ——— Where? ——— I can't do that!

JEAN: You must! And before the Count gets back! If you stay, you know what'll happen. Once you make a mistake like this, you want to continue because the damage has already been done. . . . Then you get bolder and bolder — until finally you're caught! So leave! Later you can write to the Count and confess everything — except that it was me! He'll never guess who it was, and he's not going to be eager to find out, anyway.

JULIE: I'll go if you come with me.

JEAN: Are you out of your head? Miss Julie runs away with her servant! In two days it would be in the newspapers, and that's something your father would never live through.

JULIE: I can't go and I can't stay! Help me! I'm so tired, so terribly tired. ——— Order me! Set me in motion — I can't think or act on my own . . .

JEAN: What miserable creatures you people are! You strut around with your noses in the air as if you were the lords of creation! All right, I'll order

you. Go upstairs and get dressed! Get some money for the trip, and then come back down!

JULIE (*in a half-whisper*): Come up with me!

JEAN: To your room? ——— Now you're crazy again! (*Hesitates for a moment.*) No! Go, at once! (*Takes her hand to lead her out.*)

JULIE (*as she leaves*): Speak kindly to me, Jean!

JEAN: An order always sounds unkind — now you know how it feels. (*Jean, alone, sighs with relief. He sits at the table, takes out a notebook and pencil, and begins adding up figures, counting aloud as he works. He continues in dumb show until Kristine enters, dressed for church. She is carrying a white tie and shirt front.*)

KRISTINE: Lord Jesus, what a mess! What have you been up to?

JEAN: Oh, Miss Julie dragged everybody in here. You mean you didn't hear anything? You must have been sleeping soundly.

KRISTINE: Like a log.

JEAN: And dressed for church already?

KRISTINE: Of course! You remember you promised to come with me to communion today!

JEAN: Oh, yes, that's right. ——— And you brought my things. Come on, then! (*He sits down. Kristine starts to put on his shirt front and tie. Pause. Jean begins sleepily.*) What's the gospel text for today?

KRISTINE: On St. John's Day? — the beheading of John the Baptist, I should think!

JEAN: Ah, that'll be a long one, for sure. ——— Hey, you're choking me! ——— Oh, I'm sleepy, so sleepy!

KRISTINE: Yes, what have you been doing, up all night? Your face is absolutely green.

JEAN: I've been sitting here gabbing with Miss Julie.

KRISTINE: She has no idea what's proper, that one! (*Pause.*)

JEAN: You know, Kristine . . .

KRISTINE: What?

JEAN: It's really strange when you think about it. ——— Her!

KRISTINE: What's so strange?

JEAN: Everything! (*Pause.*)

KRISTINE (*looking at the half-empty glasses standing on the table*): Have you been drinking together, too?

JEAN: Yes.

KRISTINE: Shame on you! ——— Look me in the eye!

JEAN: Well?

KRISTINE: Is it possible? Is it possible?

JEAN (*thinking it over for a moment*): Yes, it is.

KRISTINE: Ugh! I never would have believed it! No, shame on you, shame!

JEAN: You're not jealous of her, are you?

KRISTINE: No, not of her! If it had been Clara or Sofie I'd have scratched your eyes out! ——— I don't know why, but that's the way I feel. —— Oh, it's disgusting!

JEAN: Are you angry at her, then?

KRISTINE: No, at you! That was an awful thing to do, awful! Poor girl! —— No, I don't care who knows it — I won't stay in a house where we can't respect the people we work for.

JEAN: Why should we respect them?

KRISTINE: You're so clever, you tell me! Do you want to wait on people who can't behave decently? Do you? You disgrace yourself that way, if you ask me.

JEAN: But it's a comfort to know they aren't any better than us.

KRISTINE: Not for me. If they're no better, what do we have to strive for to better ourselves. —— And think of the Count! Think of him! As if he hasn't had enough misery in his life! Lord Jesus! No, I won't stay in this house any longer! —— And it had to be with someone like you! If it had been that lawyer, if it had been a real gentleman . . .

JEAN: What do you mean?

KRISTINE: Oh, you're all right for what you are, but there are men and gentlemen, after all! —— No, this business with Miss Julie I can never forget. She was so proud, so arrogant with men, you wouldn't have believed she could just go and give herself — and to someone like you! And she was going to have poor Diana shot for running after the gate-keepers' mutt! —— Yes, I'm giving my notice, I mean it — I won't stay here any longer. On the twenty-fourth of October, I leave!

JEAN: And then?

KRISTINE: Well, since the subject has come up, it's about time you looked around for something since we're going to get married, in any case.

JEAN: Where am I going to look? I couldn't find a job like this if I was married.

KRISTINE: No, that's true. But you can find work as a porter or as a caretaker in some government office. The state doesn't pay much, I know, but it's secure, and there's a pension for the wife and children . . .

JEAN (grimacing): That's all very well, but it's a bit early for me to think about dying for a wife and children. My ambitions are a little higher than that.

KRISTINE: Your ambitions, yes! Well, you have obligations, too! Think about them!

JEAN: Don't start nagging me about obligations. I know what I have to do! (Listening for something outside.) Besides, this is something we have plenty of time to think over. Go and get ready for church.

KRISTINE: Who's that walking around up there?

JEAN: I don't know, unless it's Clara.

KRISTINE (going): You don't suppose it's the Count, who came home without us hearing him?

JEAN (frightened): The Count? No, I don't think so. He'd have rung.

KRISTINE (going): Well, God help us! I've never seen anything like this before. (The sun has risen and shines through the treetops in the park. The light shifts gradually until it slants in through the windows. Jean goes to the door and signals. Miss Julie enters, dressed in travel clothes and carrying a small bird cage, covered with a cloth, which she places on a chair.)

JULIE: I'm ready now.

JEAN: Shh! Kristine is awake.

JULIE (very nervous during the following): Does she suspect something?

JEAN: She doesn't know anything. But my God, you look awful!

JULIE: Why? How do I look?

JEAN: You're pale as a ghost and — excuse me, but your face is dirty.

JULIE: Let me wash up then. —— (She goes to the basin and washes her hands and face.) Give me a towel! —— Oh —— the sun's coming up.

JEAN: Then the goblins will disappear.

JULIE: Yes, there must have been goblins out last night! —— Jean, listen, come with me! I have some money now.

JEAN (hesitantly): Enough?

JULIE: Enough to start with. Come with me! I just can't travel alone on a day like this — midsummer day on a stuffy train — jammed in among crowds of people staring at me. Eternal delays at every station, while I'd wish I had wings. No, I can't, I can't! And then there'll be memories, memories of midsummer days when I was little. The church — decorated with birch leaves and lilacs; dinner at the big table with relatives and friends, the afternoons in the park, dancing, music, flowers, and games. Oh, no matter how far we travel, the memories will follow in the baggage car, with remorse and guilt!

JEAN: I'll go with you — but right away, before it's too late. Right this minute!

JULIE: Get dressed, then! (Picking up the bird cage.)

JEAN: But no baggage! It would give us away!

JULIE: No, nothing! Only what we can have in the compartment with us.

JEAN (has taken his hat): What've you got there? What is it?

JULIE: It's only my greenfinch. I couldn't leave her behind.

JEAN: What? Bring a bird cage with us? You're out of your head! Put it down!

JULIE: It's the only thing I'm taking from my home — the only living being that loves me, since Diana was unfaithful. Don't be cruel! Let me take her!

JEAN: Put the cage down, I said! ——— And don't talk so loudly — Kristine will hear us!

JULIE: No, I won't leave her in the hands of strangers! I'd rather you killed her.

JEAN: Bring the thing here, then, I'll cut its head off!

JULIE: Oh! But don't hurt her! Don't . . . no, I can't.

JEAN: Bring it here! I can!

JULIE (*taking the bird out of the cage and kissing it*): Oh, my little Serena, must you die and leave your mistress?

JEAN: Please don't make a scene! Your whole future is at stake! Hurry up! (*He snatches the bird from her, carries it over to the chopping block, and picks up a meat cleaver. Miss Julie turns away.*) You should have learned how to slaughter chickens instead of how to fire pistols. (*He chops off the bird's head.*) Then you wouldn't feel faint at the sight of blood.

JULIE (*screaming*): Kill me, too! Kill me! You, who can slaughter an innocent animal without blinking an eye! Oh, how I hate, how I detest you! There's blood between us now! I curse the moment I set eyes on you! I curse the moment I was conceived in my mother's womb!

JEAN: What good does cursing do? Let's go!

JULIE (*approaching the chopping block, as if drawn against her will*): No, I don't want to go yet. I can't . . . until I see . . . Shh! I hear a carriage ——— — (*She listens, but her eyes never leave the cleaver and the chopping block.*) Do you think I can't stand the sight of blood? You think I'm so weak . . . Oh — I'd like to see your blood and your brains on a chopping block! ——— I'd like to see your whole sex swimming in a sea of blood, like my little bird . . . I think I could drink from your skull! I'd like to bathe my feet in your open chest and eat your heart roasted whole! ——— You think I'm weak. You think I love you because my womb craved your seed. You think I want to carry your spawn under my heart and nourish it with my blood — bear your child and take your name! By the way, what is your family name? I've never heard it. ——— Do you have one? I was to be Mrs. Bootblack — or Madame Pigsty. ——— You dog, who wears my collar, you lackey, who bears my coat of arms on your buttons — do I have to share you with my cook, compete with my own servant? Oh! Oh! Oh! ——— You think I'm a coward who wants to run away! No, now I'm staying — and let the storm break! My father will come home . . . to find his desk broken open . . . and his money gone! Then he'll ring — that bell . . . twice for his valet — and then he'll send for the police . . . and then I'll tell everything! Everything! Oh, what a relief it'll be to have it all end — if only it will end! ——— And then he'll have a stroke and die . . . That'll be the end of all of us — and there'll be peace . . . quiet . . . eternal rest! ——— And then our coat of arms will be broken against his coffin — the family title extinct — but the valet's line will go on in an orphanage . . . win laurels in the gutter, and end in jail!

JEAN: There's the blue blood talking! Very good, Miss Julie! Just don't let that miller out of the closet! (*Kristine enters, dressed for church, with a psalmbook in her hand.*)

JULIE (*rushing to Kristine and falling into her arms, as if seeking protection*): Help me, Kristine! Help me against this man!

KRISTINE (*unmoved and cold*): What a fine way to behave on a Sunday morning! (*Sees the chopping block.*) And look at this mess! ——— What does all this mean? Why all this screaming and carrying on?

JULIE: Kristine! You're a woman and my friend! Beware of this swine!

JEAN (*uncomfortable*): While you ladies discuss this, I'll go in and shave. (*Slips off right.*)

JULIE: You must listen to me so you'll understand!

KRISTINE: No, I could never understand such disgusting behavior! Where are you off to in your traveling clothes? ——— And he had his hat on. ——— Well? ——— Well? ———

JULIE: Listen to me, Kristine! Listen, and I'll tell you everything ———

KRISTINE: I don't want to hear it . . .

JULIE: But you must listen to me . . .

KRISTINE: What about? If it's about this silliness with Jean, I'm not interested, because it's none of my business. But if you're thinking of tricking him into running out, we'll soon put a stop to that!

JULIE (*extremely nervous*): Try to be calm now, Kristine, and listen to me! I can't stay here, and neither can Jean — so we must go away . . .

KRISTINE: Hm, hm!

JULIE (*brightening*): You see, I just had an idea ——— What if all three of us go — abroad — to Switzerland and start a hotel together? ——— I have money, you see — and Jean and I could run it — and I thought you, you could take care of the kitchen . . . Wouldn't that be wonderful? ——— Say yes! And come with us, and then everything will be settled! ——— Oh, do say yes! (*Embracing Kristine and patting her warmly.*)

KRISTINE (*coolly, thoughtfully*): Hm, hm!

JULIE (*presto tempo*):° You've never traveled, Kristine. ——— You must get out and see the world. You can't imagine how much fun it is to travel by train — always new faces — new countries. ——— And when we get to Hamburg, we'll stop off at the zoo — you'll like that. ——— and

---

presto tempo: At a rapid pace.

then we'll go to the theater and the opera — and when we get to Munich, dear, there we have museums, with Rubens and Raphael, the great painters, as you know. —— You've heard of Munich, where King Ludwig lived — the king who went mad. —— And then we'll see his castles — they're still there and they're like castles in fairy tales. —— And from there it isn't far to Switzerland — and the Alps. —— Imagine — the Alps have snow on them even in the middle of summer! —— And oranges grow there and laurel trees that are green all year round —— (*Jean can be seen in the wings right, sharpening his razor on a strop which he holds with his teeth and his left hand. He listens to the conversation with satisfaction, nodding now and then in approval. Miss Julie continues tempo prestissimo.*)° And then we'll start a hotel — and I'll be at the desk, while Jean greets the guests . . . does the shopping . . . writes letters. —— You have no idea what a life it'll be — the train whistles blowing and the carriages arriving and the bells ringing in the rooms and down in the restaurant. —— And I'll make out the bills — and I know how to salt them! . . . You'll never believe how timid travelers are when they have to pay their bills! —— And you — you'll be in charge of the kitchen. —— Naturally, you won't have to stand over the stove yourself. —— And since you're going to be seen by people, you'll have to wear beautiful clothes. —— And you, with your looks — no, I'm not flattering you — one fine day you'll grab yourself a husband! —— You'll see! —— A rich Englishman — they're so easy to —— (*Slowing down.*) —— catch — and then we'll get rich — and build ourselves a villa on Lake Como. —— It's true it rains there a little now and then, but —— (*Dully.*) —— the sun has to shine sometimes — although it looks dark — and then . . . of course we could always come back home again —— (*Pause.*) —— here — or somewhere else ——

KRISTINE: Listen, Miss Julie, do you believe all this?

JULIE (*crushed*): Do I believe it?

KRISTINE: Yes!

JULIE (*wearily*): I don't know. I don't believe in anything anymore. (*She sinks down on the bench and cradles her head in her arms on the table.*) Nothing! Nothing at all!

KRISTINE (*turning right to where Jean is standing*): So, you thought you'd run out!

JEAN (*embarrassed; puts the razor on the table*): Run out? That's no way to put it. You hear Miss Julie's plan, and even if she is tired after being up all night, it's still a practical plan.

tempo prestissimo: At a very rapid pace.

KRISTINE: Now you listen to me! Did you think I'd work as a cook for that . . .

JEAN (*sharply*): You watch what you say in front of your mistress! Do you understand?

KRISTINE: Mistress!

JEAN: Yes!

KRISTINE: Listen to him! Listen to him!

JEAN: Yes, you listen! It'd do you good to listen more and talk less! Miss Julie is your mistress. If you despise her, you have to despise yourself for the same reason!

KRISTINE: I've always had enough self-respect ——

JEAN: —— to be able to despise other people!

KRISTINE: —— to stop me from doing anything that's beneath me. You can't say that the Count's cook has been up to something with the groom or the swineherd! Can you?

JEAN: No, you were lucky enough to get hold of a gentleman!

KRISTINE: Yes, a gentleman who sells the Count's oats from the stable.

JEAN: You should talk — taking a commission from the grocer and bribes from the butcher.

KRISTINE: What?

JEAN: And you say you can't respect your employers any longer. You, you, you!

KRISTINE: Are you coming to church with me, now? You could use a good sermon after your fine deed!

JEAN: No, I'm not going to church today. You'll have to go alone and confess what you've been up to.

KRISTINE: Yes, I'll do that, and I'll bring back enough forgiveness for you, too. The Savior suffered and died on the Cross for all our sins, and if we go to Him with faith and a penitent heart, He takes all our sins on Himself.

JEAN: Even grocery sins?

JULIE: And do you believe that, Kristine?

KRISTINE: It's my living faith, as sure as I stand here. It's the faith I learned as a child, Miss Julie, and kept ever since. "Where sin abounded, grace did much more abound!"

JULIE: Oh, if I only had your faith. If only . . .

KRISTINE: Well, you see, we can't have it without God's special grace, and that isn't given to everyone ——

JULIE: Who is it given to then?

KRISTINE: That's the great secret of the workings of grace, Miss Julie, and God is no respecter of persons, for the last shall be the first . . .

JULIE: Then He does respect the last.

KRISTINE (*continuing*): . . . and it is easier for a camel to go through the eye of a needle, than for a rich man to enter the Kingdom of God. That's how it is, Miss Julie! Anyhow, I'm going now — alone, and on the way I'm going to tell the groom not to let any horses out, in case anyone wants to leave before the Count gets back! —— Goodbye! (*Leaves.*)

JEAN: What a witch! —— And all this because of a greenfinch! ——

JULIE (*dully*): Never mind the greenfinch! —— Can you see any way out of this? Any end to it?

JEAN (*thinking*): No!

JULIE: What would you do in my place?

JEAN: In your place? Let's see — as a person of position, as a woman who had — fallen. I don't know — wait, now I know.

JULIE (*taking the razor and making a gesture*): You mean like this?

JEAN: Yes! But — understand — *I* wouldn't do it! That's the difference between us!

JULIE: Because you're a man and I'm a woman? What sort of difference is that?

JEAN: The usual difference — between a man and a woman.

JULIE (*with the razor in her hand*): I want to, but I can't! —— My father couldn't either, the time he should have done it.

JEAN: No, he shouldn't have! He had to revenge himself first.

JULIE: And now my mother is revenged again, through me.

JEAN: Didn't you ever love your father, Miss Julie?

JULIE: Oh yes, deeply, but I've hated him, too. I must have done so without realizing it! It was he who brought me up to despise my own sex, making me half woman, half man. Whose fault is what's happened? My father's, my mother's, my own? My own? I don't have anything that's my own. I don't have a single thought that I didn't get from my father, not an emotion that I didn't get from my mother, and this last idea — that all people are equal — I got that from my fiancé. —— That's why I called him a swine! How can it be my fault? Shall I let Jesus take on the blame, the way Kristine does? —— No, I'm too proud to do that and too sensible — thanks to my father's teachings. —— And as for someone rich not going to heaven, that's a lie. But Kristine won't get in — how will she explain the money she has in the savings bank? Whose fault is it? —— What does it matter whose fault it is? I'm still the one who has to bear the blame, face the consequences . . .

JEAN: Yes, but . . . (*The bell rings sharply twice. Miss Julie jumps up. Jean changes his coat.*) The Count is back! Do you suppose Kristine — (*He goes to the speaking tube, taps the lid, and listens.*)

JULIE: He's been to his desk!

JEAN: It's Jean, sir! (*Listening; the audience cannot hear the Count's voice.*) Yes, sir! (*Listening.*) Yes, sir! Right away! (*Listening.*) At once, sir! (*Listening.*) I see, in half an hour!

JULIE (*desperately frightened*): What did he say? Dear Lord, what did he say?

JEAN: He wants his boots and his coffee in half an hour.

JULIE: So, in half an hour! Oh, I'm so tired. I'm not able to do anything. I can't repent, can't run away, can't stay, can't live — can't die! Help me now! Order me, and I'll obey like a dog! Do me this last service, save my honor, save his name! You know what I *should* do, but don't have the will to . . . You will it, you order me to do it!

JEAN: I don't know why —— but now I can't either —— I don't understand. —— It's as if this coat made it impossible for me to order you to do anything. —— And now, since the Count spoke to me — I — I can't really explain it — but — ah, it's the damn lackey in me! —— I think if the Count came down here now — and ordered me to cut my throat, I'd do it on the spot.

JULIE: Then pretend you're he, and I'm you! —— You gave such a good performance before when you knelt at my feet. —— You were a real nobleman. —— Or — have you ever seen a hypnotist in the theater? (*Jean nods.*) He says to his subject: "Take the broom," and he takes it. He says: "Sweep," and he sweeps ——

JEAN: But the subject has to be asleep.

JULIE (*ecstatically*): I'm already asleep.——The whole room is like smoke around me . . . and you look like an iron stove . . . shaped like a man in black, with a tall hat — and your eyes glow like coals when the fire is dying — and your face is a white patch, like ashes —— (*The sunlight has reached the floor and now shines on Jean.*) —— it's so warm and good —— (*She rubs her hands as if warming them before a fire.*) —— and bright — and so peaceful!

JEAN (*taking the razor and putting it in her hand*): Here's the broom! Go now while it's bright — out to the barn — and . . . (*Whispers in her ear.*)

JULIE (*awake*): Thank you. I'm going now to rest! But just tell me — that those who are first can also receive the gift of grace. Say it, even if you don't believe it.

JEAN: The first? No, I can't —— But wait — Miss Julie — now I know! You're no longer among the first — you're now among — the last!

JULIE: That's true. —— I'm among the very last. I'm the last one of all! Oh! —— But now I can't go! —— Tell me once more to go!

JEAN: No, now I can't either! I can't!

JULIE: And the first shall be the last!

JEAN: Don't think, don't think! You're taking all my strength from me, making me a coward. —— What was that? I thought the bell moved! —— No! Shall we stuff paper in it? —— To be so afraid of a bell! ———— But it isn't just a bell. ———— — There's someone behind it — a hand sets it in motion — and something else sets the hand in motion. ———— Maybe if you cover your ears — cover your ears! But then it rings even louder! rings until someone answers. ———— And then it's too late!

And then the police come — and — then ———— (*The bell rings twice loudly. Jean flinches, then straightens up.*) It's horrible! But there's no other way! ——Go! (*Miss Julie walks firmly out through the door.*)

COMMENTARY

August Strindberg (1849–1912)

FROM THE PREFACE TO *MISS JULIE*   *1888*

TRANSLATED BY HARRY G. CARLSON

Strindberg's preface sets out his intentions in writing Miss Julie, *a play concerned with the problem of "social climbing or falling, of higher or lower, better or worse, man or woman." He discusses the struggle for dominance between Miss Julie and Jean, and characterizes Miss Julie as a woman forced to "wreak vengeance" upon herself.*

Miss Julie is a modern character. Not that the man-hating half-woman has not existed in all ages but because now that she has been discovered, she has come out in the open to make herself heard. The half-woman is a type who pushes her way ahead, selling herself nowadays for power, decorations, honors, and diplomas, as formerly she used to do for money. The type implies a retrogressive step in evolution, an inferior species who cannot endure. Unfortunately, they are able to pass on their wretchedness; degenerate men seem unconsciously to choose their mates from among them. And so they breed, producing an indeterminate sex for whom life is a torture. Fortunately, the offspring go under either because they are out of harmony with reality or because their repressed instincts break out uncontrollably or because their hopes of achieving equality with men are crushed. The type is tragic, revealing the drama of a desperate struggle against Nature, tragic as the romantic heritage now being dissipated by naturalism, which has a contrary aim: happiness, and happiness belongs only to the strong and skillful species.

But Miss Julie is also a relic of the old warrior nobility now giving way to a new nobility of nerve and intellect, a victim of her own flawed constitution, a victim of the discord caused in a family by a mother's "crime," a victim of the delusions and conditions of her age — and together these are the equivalent of the concept of Destiny, or Universal Law, of antiquity. Guilt has been abolished by the naturalist, along with God, but the consequences of an action — punishment, imprisonment or the fear of it — that he cannot erase, for the simple reason that they remain, whether he pronounces acquittal or not. Those who have been injured are not as kind and understanding as an unscathed outsider can afford to be. Even if her father felt constrained not to seek revenge, his daughter would wreak vengeance upon herself, as she does here, out of an innate or acquired sense of honor, which the upper classes inherit — from where? From barbarism, from the ancient Aryan home of the race, from medieval chivalry. It is a beautiful thing, but nowadays a hindrance to the survival of the race. It is the nobleman's harikari, which compels him to slit open his own stomach when someone insults him and which survives in a modified form in the duel, that privilege of the nobility. That is why Jean, the servant, lives, while Miss Julie cannot live without honor. The slave's advantage over the nobleman is that he lacks this fatal preoccupation with honor. But in all of us Aryans there is something of the nobleman, or a Don Quixote. And so we sympathize with the suicide, whose act means a loss of honor. We are noblemen enough to be pained when we see the mighty fallen and as superfluous as a corpse, yes, even if the fallen should rise again and make amends through an honorable act. The servant Jean is a race-founder, someone in whom the process of differentiation can be detected. Born the son of a tenant farmer, he has educated himself in the things a gentleman should know. He has been quick to learn, has finely developed senses (smell, taste, sight) and a feeling for what is beautiful. He is already moving up in the world and is not embarrassed about using other people's help. He is alienated from his fellow servants, despising them as parts of a past he has already put behind him. He fears and flees them because they know his secrets, pry into his intentions, envy his rise, and look forward eagerly to his fall. Hence his dual, indecisive nature, vacillating between sympathy for people in high social positions and hatred for those who currently occupy those positions. He is an aristocrat, as he himself says, has learned the secrets of good society, is polished on the surface but coarse beneath, wears a frock coat tastefully but without any guarantee that his body is clean.

He has respect for Miss Julie, but is afraid of Kristine because she knows his dangerous secrets. He is sufficiently callous not to let the night's events disturb his plans for the future. With both a slave's brutality and a master's lack of squeamishness, he can see blood without fainting and shake off misfortune easily. Consequently, he comes through the struggle unscathed and will probably end up an innkeeper. And even if *he* does not become a Rumanian count, his son will become a university student and possibly a county police commissioner. . . .

Apart from the fact that Jean is rising in the world, he is superior to Miss Julie because he is a man. Sexually, he is an aristocrat because of his masculine strength, his more keenly developed senses, and his capacity for taking the initiative. His sense of inferiority is mostly due to the social circumstances in which he happens to be living, and he can probably shed it along with his valet's jacket.

His slave mentality expresses itself in the fearful respect he has for the Count (the boots) and his religious superstition; but he respects the Count mainly as the occupant of the kind of high position to which he himself aspires; and the respect remains even after he has conquered the daughter of the house and seen how empty the lovely shell was.

I do not believe that love in any "higher" sense can exist between two people of such different natures, and so I have Miss Julie's love as something she fabricates in order to protect and excuse herself; and I have Jean suppose himself capable of loving her under other social circumstances. I think it is the same with love as with the hyacinth, which must take root in darkness *before* it can produce a sturdy flower. Here a flower shoots up, blooms, and goes to seed all at once, and that is why it dies so quickly.

Oscar Wilde

Oscar Fingal O'Flahertie Wills Wilde (1854–1900) was born to a famous eye surgeon who maintained a home in Dublin's most exclusive neighborhood. Wilde's mother, known by her literary name as Speranza, was noted for collecting Irish folk stories in the western hills in the late 1870s. Her work was important to later literature, but it was especially important for its timing, since most of the storytellers in Ireland were gone by the turn of the century.

Wilde was a brilliant classics scholar at Trinity College, Dublin, where his tutor was the legendary Mahaffy, who later traveled with him in France. After Trinity, he went to Magdalen College, Oxford, where he took a distinguished degree. Among his influences in Oxford was Slade Professor of Art John Ruskin, with whom Wilde had long walks and talks. Ruskin had published important books on northern Gothic art and on Italian art, especially the art of Venice. Art was one of Wilde's primary passions, especially decoration and the decorative arts. He agreed with Walter Pater, a contemporary art critic, that art must best serve the needs of art. He felt, for example, that poetry did not serve religious, political, social, or biographical goals. Its ends were aesthetic and its pleasures were in its sounds, images, and thoughts.

Partly because of his brilliance and partly because he was one of the age's greatest conversationalists, he was soon in the company of the famous and amusing people of his generation. Some of his conversational gift is apparent in his plays.

By his own admission, his life was marked by an overindulgence in sensuality: "What paradox was to me in the sphere of thought, perversity became to me in the sphere of passion." He married Constance Lloyd in 1884 and soon had two sons. But by 1891 he had already had several homosexual liaisons, one of which was to bring him to ruin. His relationship with the much younger Lord Alfred Douglas ended with Douglas's father, the marquis of Queensberry, publicly denouncing Wilde as a sodomite. Wilde sued for libel but lost. As a result, in 1895 he was tried for sodomy, convicted, and sentenced to two years' hard labor. Wilde's actions have been seen as self-destructive, but they are also consistent with his efforts to force society to examine its own hypocrisy. Unfortunately, his efforts in court and prison ruined him and he died in exile in Paris three years after his release.

His best-known novel, *The Picture of Dorian Gray* (1890; expanded 1891), is the story of a young man whose sensual life eats away at him and eventually destroys him. The novel's failure led Wilde to try the stage, where he was a signal success. Remarkably, all his plays were written in the period between 1891 and his imprisonment in 1895. Most of his plays — *Salomé* (1891), *Lady Windermere's Fan* (1892), *A Woman of No Importance* (1893), *An Ideal Husband* (1895), and *The Importance of Being Earnest* (1895) — rank as witty, insightful, and sharp commentaries on the upper-class British society he knew best. They owe a great deal to eighteenth-century comedies, such as William Congreve's *The Way of the World*. But they also owe a great deal to English and European farces and comedies of his own time, many of which he seems to have studied closely. Unlike those plays — many have never been published and no longer exist — Wilde's are still funny and still seem pertinent even though the class he criticized has long vanished.

The Importance of Being Earnest was a remarkable success when it opened at St. James's Theatre on Valentine's Day 1895, but it closed in two months after fewer than one hundred performances when the scandal of Wilde's conviction became public. Wilde's reputation as playwright was made and broken in a matter of a few years, and it was not restored until after his death.

THE IMPORTANCE OF BEING EARNEST

The play was originally written in four acts, but because the producer requested it be cut, Wilde reworked it into three acts, agreeing that the excisions made the play stronger. Its subtitle, *A Trivial Comedy for Serious People,* has prompted commentators to think of the play as farcical fluff, a play about little or nothing that is nonetheless profoundly amusing. The *New York Times* commented after its first U.S. opening, "The thing is as slight in structure and as devoid of purpose as a paper balloon, but it is extraordinarily funny." Recent critics have challenged this view on the grounds that its subject matter centers on the questions of identity and reality. One current view is that its surfaces are slight but that beneath the surface is a commentary on a society that judges things only by appearance.

The primary characters are Algernon Moncrieff and Jack Worthing, young gentlemen of marriageable age. Among the women are Algernon's cousin Gwendolen Fairfax, who adores the name Ernest and is in love with Jack; Lady Bracknell, her mother; and Cecily Cardew, Jack's ward. Bunbury, referred to by Algernon, seems to be a character, but is instead an invention. He is a convenience for Algernon, a country friend whose illnesses Algernon uses to avoid social events he dislikes, such as Lady Bracknell's dinners. Jack, who lives in the country, has created a similar figure to help him escape to town — an imaginary brother Ernest. In town, Jack pretends to be Ernest; and all his town acquaintances, including Algernon and Gwendolen, know Jack by that name.

The similarities with Congreve's *The Way of the World* are striking. The question of marriage is central in both plays, and attitudes toward marriage in Wilde's social class are among the targets of his satire. When Lady Bracknell probes into Jack Worthing's background, she discovers the distressing news about his family "line": Jack is a foundling who had been left in a handbag in Victoria Station. His family "line" is the Brighton Line. Gwendolen could also have stepped from a Congreve comedy. She is determined to have Jack Worthing, and when he seems sluggish about proposing she prompts him, offering a critique of his proposal by telling him he seems inexperienced at it.

The play owes perhaps even more to the farces of the 1880s and 1890s and a great deal to the well-made play of Eugène Scribe and his successors. Critics often compare Wilde to Alexandre Dumas, the author of *La Dame aux camélias* (*Camille*), because both writers fashioned their plays with a considerable degree of artificiality, planting information in the first act that would prove the solution to problems in the last act. They also play with questions of identity, disguise, and revelation at the last minute in much the way Wilde does here when he reveals the identity of Ernest.

In melodramas and well-made plays, the revelation at the end was not that the potential husband had the right name so much as that he had the right background: He was an aristocrat and not the commoner he seemed to be. Wilde has fun with this convention and many others. In an instant, he ridicules the trick of revealing the hero to be "marriageable" because of his birth by emphasizing the triviality of a name. Yet names are of great importance (as Shakespeare tells us in *Romeo and Juliet*), and the earnestness implied in Ernest is one ingredient that helps Jack Worthing succeed.

Kerry Powell has demonstrated that almost every device in *The Importance of Being Earnest* was drawn from a contemporary farce or comedy. The device of the child lost in a piece of luggage was used in *The Lost Child* (1863), and *The Foundling* (1894) actually takes place in Brighton. The name Bunbury and the concept of "Bunburying" come from *The Godpapa* (1891). Even the device of baptism was used in *Crimes and Christening* (1891). Wilde was adept at taking the theater conventions his audience was most familiar with and using them to his own ends — to entertain his audience, but at the same time to help him put an extra edge on his satire.

The Importance of Being Earnest in Performance

After the first production closed down in 1895, the play was revived in London in 1898 and 1902, but an even more successful production in 1909 saw 324 performances. The benchmark for a truly successful play in those days seems to have been one hundred performances, and Wilde would have felt vindicated by the 1909 production, had he lived to see it. *The Importance of Being Earnest* has been produced so often in England and the United States that only a few productions can be taken into account here. The first New York production was in 1902. John Gielgud and Edith Evans played in the 1939 London production, then again in 1942. In 1947 Gielgud played in New York with Clifton Webb and Estelle Winwood. The reviews were especially strong, calling the play "as insolently monocled in manner and as killingly high-toned in language as mischievous tomfoolery can make it."

The play inspired at least five musicals between 1927 and 1984. The 1979 production at Stratford, Ontario, was called "a perfect play in a perfect production." An unsuccessful production by the Berlin Play Actors in 1987 used all men and relied on insights drawn from transvestite performers, but it was badly received. University productions of the play are fairly common, although, like the Yale Repertory production in 1986, they are not always able to pull off the comic demands of the play's exacting language. The original four-act version of the play, discovered in 1977 in the New York Public Library, was produced in Ohio in the John Carroll University's Marinello Theater in 1985. It was more a curiosity than a triumph. The 1993 production at the Aldwych in London received great praise for its dazzling sets that "matched Wilde's word pictures with bold stage pictures." Maggie Smith played Lady Bracknell.

The play is a witty tour de force of language. Its surfaces gleam, and the best productions play it straight.

Oscar Wilde *(1854–1900)*

THE IMPORTANCE OF BEING EARNEST   *1895*
A TRIVIAL COMEDY FOR SERIOUS PEOPLE

The Persons of the Play

JOHN WORTHING, J.P., *of the Manor House, Woolton, Hertfordshire*
ALGERNON MONCRIEFF, *his friend*
REV. CANON CHASUBLE, D.D., *rector of Woolton*
MERRIMAN, *butler to Mr. Worthing*
LANE, *Mr. Moncrieff's manservant*
LADY BRACKNELL
HON. GWENDOLEN FAIRFAX, *her daughter*
CECILY CARDEW, *John Worthing's ward*
MISS PRISM, *her governess*

The Scenes of the Play

Act I: *Algernon Moncrieff's Flat in Half Moon Street, W.*
Act II: *The Garden at the Manor House, Woolton*
Act III: *Morning Room at the Manor House, Woolton*

ACT I

(*Scene: Morning room in Algernon's flat in Half Moon Street. The room is luxuriously and artistically furnished. The sound of a piano is heard in the adjoining room. Lane is arranging afternoon tea on the table, and after the music has ceased, Algernon enters.*)

ALGERNON: Did you hear what I was playing, Lane?
LANE: I didn't think it polite to listen, sir.

ALGERNON: I'm sorry for that, for your sake. I don't play accurately — anyone can play accurately — but I play with wonderful expression. As far as the piano is concerned, sentiment is my forte. I keep science for Life.
LANE: Yes, sir.
ALGERNON: And, speaking of the science of Life, have you got the cucumber sandwiches cut for Lady Bracknell?
LANE: Yes, sir.   (*Hands them on a salver.*)
ALGERNON (*inspects them, takes two, and sits down on the sofa*): Oh! — by the way, Lane, I see from your book that on Thursday night, when Lord Shoreham and Mr. Worthing were dining with me, eight bottles of champagne are entered as having been consumed.
LANE: Yes, sir; eight bottles and a pint.
ALGERNON: Why is it that at a bachelor's establishment the servants invariably drink the champagne? I ask merely for information.
LANE: I attribute it to the superior quality of the wine, sir. I have often observed that in married households the champagne is rarely of a first-rate brand.
ALGERNON: Good heavens! Is marriage so demoralizing as that?
LANE: I believe it *is* a very pleasant state, sir. I have had very little experience of it myself up to the present. I have only been married once. That was in consequence of a misunderstanding between myself and a young person.
ALGERNON (*languidly*): I don't know that I am much interested in your family life, Lane.

LANE: No, sir; it is not a very interesting subject. I never think of it myself.

ALGERNON: Very natural, I am sure. That will do, Lane, thank you.

LANE: Thank you, sir.   (*Lane goes out.*)

ALGERNON: Lane's views on marriage seem somewhat lax. Really, if the lower orders don't set us a good example, what on earth is the use of them? They seem, as a class, to have absolutely no sense of moral responsibility.

(*Enter Lane.*)

LANE: Mr. Ernest Worthing.

(*Enter Jack. Lane goes out.*)

ALGERNON: How are you, my dear Ernest? What brings you up to town?

JACK: Oh, pleasure, pleasure! What else should bring one anywhere? Eating as usual, I see, Algy!

ALGERNON (*stiffly*): I believe it is customary in good society to take some slight refreshment at five o'clock. Where have you been since last Thursday?

JACK (*sitting down on the sofa*): In the country.

ALGERNON: What on earth do you do there?

JACK (*pulling off his gloves*): When one is in town one amuses oneself. When one is in the country one amuses other people. It is excessively boring.

ALGERNON: And who are the people you amuse?

JACK (*airily*): Oh, neighbors, neighbors.

ALGERNON: Got nice neighbors in your part of Shropshire?

JACK: Perfectly horrid! Never speak to one of them.

ALGERNON: How immensely you must amuse them! (*Goes over and takes sandwich.*) By the way, Shropshire is your county, is it not?

JACK: Eh? Shropshire? Yes, of course. Hallo! Why all these cups? Why cucumber sandwiches? Why such reckless extravagance in one so young? Who is coming to tea?

ALGERNON: Oh! merely Aunt Augusta and Gwendolen.

JACK: How perfectly delightful!

ALGERNON: Yes, that is all very well; but I am afraid Aunt Augusta won't quite approve of your being here.

JACK: May I ask why?

ALGERNON: My dear fellow, the way you flirt with Gwendolen is perfectly disgraceful. It is almost as bad as the way Gwendolen flirts with you.

JACK: I am in love with Gwendolen. I have come up to town expressly to propose to her.

ALGERNON: I thought you had come up for pleasure? — I call that business.

JACK: How utterly unromantic you are!

ALGERNON: I really don't see anything romantic in proposing. It is very romantic to be in love. But there is nothing romantic about a definite proposal. Why, one may be accepted. One usually is, I believe. Then the excitement is all over. The very essence of romance is uncertainty. If ever I get married, I'll certainly try to forget the fact.

JACK: I have no doubt about that, dear Algy. The Divorce Court was specially invented for people whose memories are so curiously constituted.

ALGERNON: Oh! there is no use speculating on that subject. Divorces are made in heaven — (*Jack puts out his hand to take a sandwich. Algernon at once interferes.*) Please don't touch the cucumber sandwiches. They are ordered specially for Aunt Augusta.   (*Takes one and eats it.*)

JACK: Well, you have been eating them all the time.

ALGERNON: That is quite a different matter. She is my aunt. (*Takes plate from below.*) Have some bread and butter. The bread and butter is for Gwendolen. Gwendolen is devoted to bread and butter.

JACK (*advancing to table and helping himself*): And very good bread and butter it is too.

ALGERNON: Well, my dear fellow, you need not eat as if you were going to eat it all. You behave as if you were married to her already. You are not married to her already, and I don't think you ever will be.

JACK: Why on earth do you say that?

ALGERNON: Well, in the first place, girls never marry the men they flirt with. Girls don't think it right.

JACK: Oh, that is nonsense!

ALGERNON: It isn't. It is a great truth. It accounts for the extraordinary number of bachelors that one sees all over the place. In the second place, I don't give my consent.

JACK: Your consent!

ALGERNON: My dear fellow, Gwendolen is my first cousin. And before I allow you to marry her, you will have to clear up the whole question of Cecily.   (*Rings bell.*)

JACK: Cecily! What on earth do you mean? What do you mean, Algy, by Cecily? I don't know anyone of the name of Cecily.

(*Enter Lane.*)

ALGERNON: Bring me that cigarette case Mr. Worthing left in the smoking room the last time he dined here.

LANE: Yes, sir.   (*Lane goes out.*)

JACK: Do you mean to say you have had my cigarette case all this time? I wish to goodness you had let me know. I have been writing frantic letters to Scotland Yard about it. I was very nearly offering a large reward.

ALGERNON: Well, I wish you would offer one. I happen to be more than usually hard up.

JACK: There is no good offering a large reward now that the thing is found.

(*Enter Lane with the cigarette case on a salver. Algernon takes it at once. Lane goes out.*)

ALGERNON: I think that is rather mean of you, Ernest, I must say. (*Opens case and examines it.*) However, it makes no matter, for, now that I look at the inscription inside, I find that the thing isn't yours after all.

JACK: Of course it's mine. (*Moving to him.*) You have seen me with it a hundred times, and you have no right whatsoever to read what is written inside. It is a very ungentlemanly thing to read a private cigarette case.

ALGERNON: Oh! it is absurd to have a hard-and-fast rule about what one should read and what one shouldn't. More than half of modern culture depends on what one shouldn't read.

JACK: I am quite aware of the fact, and I don't propose to discuss modern culture. It isn't the sort of thing one should talk of in private. I simply want my cigarette case back.

ALGERNON: Yes; but this isn't your cigarette case. This cigarette case is a present from someone of the name of Cecily, and you said you didn't know anyone of that name.

JACK: Well, if you want to know, Cecily happens to be my aunt.

ALGERNON: Your aunt!

JACK: Yes. Charming old lady she is, too. Lives at Tunbridge Wells. Just give it back to me, Algy.

ALGERNON (*retreating to back of sofa*): But why does she call herself little Cecily if she is your aunt and lives at Tunbridge Wells? (*Reading.*) "From little Cecily with her fondest love."

JACK (*moving to sofa and kneeling upon it*): My dear fellow, what on earth is there in that? Some aunts are tall, some aunts are not tall. That is a matter that surely an aunt may be allowed to decide for herself. You seem to think that every aunt should be exactly like your aunt! That is absurd! For heaven's sake give me back my cigarette case.

(*Follows Algernon round the room.*)

ALGERNON: Yes. But why does your aunt call you her uncle? "From little Cecily, with her fondest love to her dear Uncle Jack." There is no objection, I admit, to an aunt being a small aunt, but why an aunt, no matter what her size may be, should call her own nephew her uncle, I can't quite make out. Besides, your name isn't Jack at all; it is Ernest.

JACK: It isn't Ernest; it's Jack.

ALGERNON: You have always told me it was Ernest. I have introduced you to everyone as Ernest. You answer to the name of Ernest. You look as if your name was Ernest. You are the most earnest looking person I ever saw in my life. It is perfectly absurd your saying that your name isn't Ernest. It's on your cards. Here is one of them (*taking it from case*) "Mr. Ernest Worthing, B.4, The Albany." I'll keep this as a proof that your name is Ernest if ever you attempt to deny it to me, or to Gwendolen, or to anyone else.

(*Puts the card in his pocket.*)

JACK: Well, my name is Ernest in town and Jack in the country, and the cigarette case was given to me in the country.

ALGERNON: Yes, but that does not account for the fact that your small Aunt Cecily, who lives at Tunbridge Wells, calls you her dear uncle. Come, old boy, you had much better have the thing out at once.

JACK: My dear Algy, you talk exactly as if you were a dentist. It is very vulgar to talk like a dentist when one isn't a dentist. It produces a false impression.

ALGERNON: Well, that is exactly what dentists always do. Now, go on! Tell me the whole thing. I may mention that I have always suspected you of being a confirmed and secret Bunburyist; and I am quite sure of it now.

JACK: Bunburyist? What on earth do you mean by a Bunburyist?

ALGERNON: I'll reveal to you the meaning of that incomparable expression as soon as you are kind enough to inform me why you are Ernest in town and Jack in the country.

JACK: Well, produce my cigarette case first.

ALGERNON: Here it is. (*Hands cigarette case.*) Now produce your explanation, and pray make it improbable. (*Sits on sofa.*)

JACK: My dear fellow, there is nothing improbable about my explanation at all. In fact it's perfectly ordinary. Old Mr. Thomas Cardew, who adopted me when I was a little boy, made me in his will guardian to his granddaughter, Miss Cecily Cardew. Cecily, who addresses me as her uncle from motives of respect that you could not possibly appreciate, lives at my place in the country under the charge of her admirable governess, Miss Prism.

ALGERNON: Where is that place in the country, by the way?

JACK: That is nothing to you, dear boy. You are not going to be invited — I may tell you candidly that the place is not in Shropshire.

ALGERNON: I suspected that, my dear fellow! I have Bunburyed all over Shropshire on two separate occasions. Now, go on. Why are you Ernest in town and Jack in the country?

JACK: My dear Algy, I don't know whether you will be

able to understand my real motives. You are
hardly serious enough. When one is placed in the
position of guardian, one has to adopt a very high
moral tone on all subjects. It's one's duty to do so.
And as a high moral tone can hardly be said to
conduce very much to either one's health or one's
happiness, in order to get up to town I have always
pretended to have a younger brother of the name
of Ernest, who lives in the Albany, and gets into
the most dreadful scrapes. That, my dear Algy, is
the whole truth pure and simple.

ALGERNON: The truth is rarely pure and never simple.
Modern life would be very tedious if it were either
and modern literature a complete impossibility!

JACK: That wouldn't be at all a bad thing.

ALGERNON: Literary criticism is not your forte, my
dear fellow. Don't try it. You should leave that to
people who haven't been at a university. They do it
so well in the daily papers. What you really are is
a Bunburyist. I was quite right in saying you were
a Bunburyist. You are one of the most advanced
Bunburyists I know.

JACK: What on earth do you mean?

ALGERNON: You have invented a very useful younger
brother called Ernest, in order that you may be
able to come up to town as often as you like. I
have invented an invaluable permanent invalid
called Bunbury, in order that I may be able to go
down into the country whenever I choose. Bunbury is perfectly invaluable. If it wasn't for Bunbury's extraordinary bad health, for instance, I
wouldn't be able to dine with you at Willis's
tonight, for I have been really engaged to Aunt
Augusta for more than a week.

JACK: I haven't asked you to dine with me anywhere
tonight.

ALGERNON: I know. You are absurdly careless about
sending out invitations. It is very foolish of you.
Nothing annoys people so much as not receiving
invitations.

JACK: You had much better dine with your Aunt Augusta.

ALGERNON: I haven't the smallest intention of doing
anything of the kind. To begin with, I dined there
on Monday, and once a week is quite enough to
dine with one's own relations. In the second place,
whenever I do dine there I am always treated as a
member of the family, and sent down with° either
no woman at all, or two. In the third place, I know
perfectly well whom she will place me next to,
tonight. She will place me next Mary Farquhar,
who always flirts with her own husband across the
dinner table. That is not very pleasant. Indeed, it is
not even decent — and that sort of thing is enormously on the increase. The amount of women in
London who flirt with their own husbands is perfectly scandalous. It looks so bad. It is simply
washing one's clean linen in public. Besides, now
that I know you to be a confirmed Bunburyist I
naturally want to talk to you about Bunburying. I
want to tell you the rules.

JACK: I'm not a Bunburyist at all. If Gwendolen accepts me, I am going to kill my brother, indeed I
think I'll kill him in any case. Cecily is a little too
much interested in him. It is rather a bore. So I am
going to get rid of Ernest. And I strongly advise
you to do the same with Mr. — with your invalid
friend who has the absurd name.

ALGERNON: Nothing will induce me to part with Bunbury, and if you ever get married, which seems to
me extremely problematic, you will be very glad to
know Bunbury. A man who marries without
knowing Bunbury has a very tedious time of it.

JACK: That is nonsense. If I marry a charming girl like
Gwendolen, and she is the only girl I ever saw in
my life that I would marry, I certainly won't want
to know Bunbury.

ALGERNON: Then your wife will. You don't seem to
realize, that in married life three is company and
two is none.

JACK (sententiously): That, my dear young friend, is
the theory that the corrupt French drama has been
propounding for the last fifty years.

ALGERNON: Yes; and that the happy English home has
proved in half the time.

JACK: For heaven's sake, don't try to be cynical. It's
perfectly easy to be cynical.

ALGERNON: My dear fellow, it isn't easy to be anything nowadays. There's such a lot of beastly competition about. (The sound of an electric bell is
heard.) Ah! that must be Aunt Augusta. Only relatives, or creditors, ever ring in that Wagnerian°
manner. Now, if I get her out of the way for ten
minutes, so that you can have an opportunity for
proposing to Gwendolen, may I dine with you
tonight at Willis's?

JACK: I suppose so, if you want to.

ALGERNON: Yes, but you must be serious about it. I
hate people who are not serious about meals. It is
so shallow of them.

(Enter Lane.)

LANE: Lady Bracknell and Miss Fairfax.

---

sent down with: Assigned a woman to escort into the dining
room for dinner.

Wagnerian: Referring to the operas of Richard Wagner
(1813–1883), whose music was popularly thought to be
loud.

(*Algernon goes forward to meet them. Enter Lady Bracknell and Gwendolen.*)

LADY BRACKNELL: Good afternoon, dear Algernon, I hope you are behaving very well.

ALGERNON: I'm feeling very well, Aunt Augusta.

LADY BRACKNELL: That s not quite the same thing. In fact the two things rarely go together.
    (*Sees Jack and bows to him with icy coldness.*)

ALGERNON (*to Gwendolen*): Dear me, you are smart!

GWENDOLEN: I am always smart! Aren't I, Mr. Worthing?

JACK: You're quite perfect, Miss Fairfax.

GWENDOLEN: Oh! I hope I am not that. It would leave no room for developments, and I intend to develop in many directions.

(*Gwendolen and Jack sit down together in the corner.*)

LADY BRACKNELL: I'm sorry if we are a little late Algernon, but I was obliged to call on dear Lady Harbury. I hadn't been there since her poor husband's death. I never saw a woman so altered; she looks quite twenty years younger. And now I'll have a cup of tea, and one of those nice cucumber sandwiches you promised me.

ALGERNON: Certainly, Aunt Augusta.
                    (*Goes over to tea table.*)

LADY BRACKNELL: Won't you come and sit here, Gwendolen?

GWENDOLEN: Thanks, Mama, I'm quite comfortable where I am.

ALGERNON (*picking up empty plate in horror*): Good heavens! Lane! Why are there no cucumber sandwiches? I ordered them specially.

LANE (*gravely*): There were no cucumbers in the market this morning, sir. I went down twice.

ALGERNON: No cucumbers!

LANE: No, sir. Not even for ready money.

ALGERNON: That will do, Lane, thank you.

LANE: Thank you, sir.   (*Goes out.*)

ALGERNON: I am greatly distressed, Aunt Augusta, about there being no cucumbers, not even for ready money.

LADY BRACKNELL: It really makes no matter, Algernon. I had some crumpets with Lady Harbury, who seems to me to be living entirely for pleasure now.

ALGERNON: I hear her hair has turned quite gold from grief.

LADY BRACKNELL: It certainly has changed its color. From what cause I, of course, cannot say. (*Algernon crosses and hands tea.*) Thank you. I've quite a treat for you tonight, Algernon. I am going to send you down with Mary Farquhar. She is such a nice woman, and so attentive to her husband. It's delightful to watch them.

ALGERNON: I am afraid, Aunt Augusta, I shall have to give up the pleasure of dining with you tonight after all.

LADY BRACKNELL (*frowning*): I hope not, Algernon. It would put my table completely out. Your uncle would have to dine upstairs. Fortunately he is accustomed to that.

ALGERNON: It is a great bore, and, I need hardly say, a terrible disappointment to me, but the fact is I have just had a telegram to say that my poor friend Bunbury is very ill again. (*Exchanges glances with Jack.*) They seem to think I should be with him.

LADY BRACKNELL: It is very strange. This Mr. Bunbury seems to suffer from curiously bad health.

ALGERNON: Yes; poor Bunbury is a dreadful invalid.

LADY BRACKNELL: Well, I must say, Algernon, that I think it is high time that Mr. Bunbury made up his mind whether he was going to live or to die. This shilly-shallying with the question is absurd. Nor do I in any way approve of the modern sympathy with invalids. I consider it morbid. Illness of any kind is hardly a thing to be encouraged in others. Health is the primary duty of life. I am always telling that to your poor uncle, but he never seems to take much notice — as far as any improvement in his ailments goes. I should be much obliged if you would ask Mr. Bunbury, from me, to be kind enough not to have a relapse on Saturday, for I rely on you to arrange my music for me. It is my last reception, and one wants something that will encourage conversation, particularly at the end of the season when everyone has practically said whatever they had to say, which, in most cases, was probably not much.

ALGERNON: I'll speak to Bunbury, Aunt Augusta, if he is still conscious, and I think I can promise you he'll be all right by Saturday. Of course the music is a great difficulty. You see, if one plays good music, people don't listen, and if one plays bad music people don't talk. But I'll run over the program I've drawn out, if you will kindly come into the next room for a moment.

LADY BRACKNELL: Thank you, Algernon. It is very thoughtful of you. (*Rising, and following Algernon.*) I'm sure the program will be delightful, after a few expurgations. French songs I cannot possibly allow. People always seem to think that they are improper, and either look shocked, which is vulgar, or laugh, which is worse. But German sounds a thoroughly respectable language, and indeed, I believe is so. Gwendolen, you will accompany me.

GWENDOLEN: Certainly, Mama.

(*Lady Bracknell and Algernon go into the music room. Gwendolen remains behind.*)

JACK: Charming day it has been, Miss Fairfax.

GWENDOLEN: Pray don't talk to me about the weather Mr. Worthing. Whenever people talk to me about the weather, I always feel quite certain that they mean something else. And that makes me so nervous.

JACK: I do mean something else.

GWENDOLEN: I thought so. In fact, I am never wrong.

JACK: And I would like to be allowed to take advantage of Lady Bracknell's temporary absence —

GWENDOLEN: I would certainly advise you to do so. Mama has a way of coming back suddenly into a room that I have often had to speak to her about.

JACK (*nervously*): Miss Fairfax, ever since I met you I have admired you more than any girl — I have ever met since — I met you.

GWENDOLEN: Yes, I am quite aware of the fact. And I often wish that in public, at any rate, you had been more demonstrative. For me you have always had an irresistible fascination. Even before I met you I was far from indifferent to you. (*Jack looks at her in amazement.*) We live, as I hope you know Mr. Worthing, in an age of ideals. The fact is constantly mentioned in the more expensive monthly magazines, and has reached the provincial pulpits I am told: And my ideal has always been to love someone of the name of Ernest. There is something in that name that inspires absolute confidence. The moment Algernon first mentioned to me that he had a friend called Ernest, I knew I was destined to love you.

JACK: You really love me, Gwendolen?

GWENDOLEN: Passionately!

JACK: Darling! You don't know how happy you've made me.

GWENDOLEN: My own Ernest!

JACK: But you don't mean to say that you couldn't love me if my name wasn't Ernest?

GWENDOLEN: But your name is Ernest.

JACK: Yes, I know it is. But supposing it was something else? Do you mean to say you couldn't love me then?

GWENDOLEN (*glibly*): Ah! that is clearly a metaphysical speculation, and like most metaphysical speculations has very little reference at all to the actual facts of real life, as we know them.

JACK: Personally, darling, to speak quite candidly, I don't much care about the name of Ernest — I don't think the name suits me at all.

GWENDOLEN: It suits you perfectly. It is a divine name. It has a music of its own. It produces vibrations.

JACK: Well, really, Gwendolen, I must say that I think there are lots of other much nicer names. I think Jack, for instance, a charming name.

GWENDOLEN: Jack? — No, there is very little music in the name Jack, if any at all, indeed. It does not thrill. It produces absolutely no vibrations — I have known several Jacks, and they all, without exception, were more than usually plain. Besides, Jack is a notorious domesticity for John! And I pity any woman who is married to a man called John. She would probably never be allowed to know the entrancing pleasure of a single moment's solitude. The only really safe name is Ernest.

JACK: Gwendolen, I must get christened at once — I mean we must get married at once. There is no time to be lost.

GWENDOLEN: Married, Mr. Worthing?

JACK (*astounded*): Well — surely. You know that I love you, and you led me to believe, Miss Fairfax that you were not absolutely indifferent to me.

GWENDOLEN: I adore you. But you haven't proposed to me yet. Nothing has been said at all about marriage. The subject has not even been touched on.

JACK: Well — may I propose to you now?

GWENDOLEN: I think it would be an admirable opportunity. And to spare you any possible disappointment, Mr. Worthing, I think it only fair to tell you quite frankly beforehand that I am fully determined to accept you.

JACK: Gwendolen!

GWENDOLEN: Yes, Mr. Worthing, what have you got to say to me?

JACK: You know what I have got to say to you.

GWENDOLEN: Yes, but you don't say it.

JACK: Gwendolen, will you marry me?

(*Goes on his knees.*)

GWENDOLEN: Of course I will, darling. How long you have been about it! I am afraid you have had very little experience in how to propose.

JACK: My own one, I have never loved anyone in the world but you.

GWENDOLEN: Yes, but men often propose for practice. I know my brother Gerald does. All my girlfriends tell me so. What wonderfully blue eyes you have, Ernest! They are quite, quite blue. I hope you will always look at me just like that, especially when there are other people present.

(*Enter Lady Bracknell.*)

LADY BRACKNELL: Mr. Worthing! Rise, sir, from this semirecumbent posture. It is most indecorous.

GWENDOLEN: Mama! (*He tries to rise; she restrains him.*) I must beg you to retire. This is no place for you. Besides, Mr. Worthing has not quite finished yet.

LADY BRACKNELL: Finished what, may I ask?

GWENDOLEN: I am engaged to Mr. Worthing, Mama.

(*They rise together.*)

LADY BRACKNELL: Pardon me, you are not engaged to anyone. When you do become engaged to someone, I, or your father, should his health permit him, will inform you of the fact. An engagement should come on a young girl as a surprise, pleasant or unpleasant, as the case may be. It is hardly a matter that she could be allowed to arrange for herself — And now I have a few questions to put to you, Mr. Worthing. While I am making these inquiries, you, Gwendolen, will wait for me below in the carriage.

GWENDOLEN (*reproachfully*): Mama!

LADY BRACKNELL: In the carriage, Gwendolen! (*Gwendolen goes to the door. She and Jack blow kisses to each other behind Lady Bracknell's back. Lady Bracknell looks vaguely about as if she could not understand what the noise was. Finally turns round.*) Gwendolen, the carriage!

GWENDOLEN: Yes, Mama.

(*Goes out, looking back at Jack.*)

LADY BRACKNELL (*sitting down*): You can take a seat, Mr. Worthing.

(*Looks in her pocket for notebook and pencil.*)

JACK: Thank you, Lady Bracknell, I prefer standing.

LADY BRACKNELL (*pencil and notebook in hand*): I feel bound to tell you that you are not down on my list of eligible young men, although I have the same list as the dear Duchess of Bolton has. We work together, in fact. However, I am quite ready to enter your name, should your answers be what a really affectionate mother requires. Do you smoke?

JACK: Well, yes, I must admit I smoke.

LADY BRACKNELL: I am glad to hear it. A man should always have an occupation of some kind. There are far too many idle men in London as it is. How old are you?

JACK: Twenty-nine.

LADY BRACKNELL: A very good age to be married at. I have always been of opinion that a man who desires to get married should know either everything or nothing. Which do you know?

JACK (*after some hesitation*): I know nothing, Lady Bracknell.

LADY BRACKNELL: I am pleased to hear it. I do not approve of anything that tampers with natural ignorance. Ignorance is like a delicate exotic fruit; touch it and the bloom is gone. The whole theory of modern education is radically unsound. Fortunately in England, at any rate, education produces no effect whatsoever. If it did, it would prove a serious danger to the upper classes, and probably lead to acts of violence in Grosvenor Square. What is your income?

JACK: Between seven and eight thousand a year.

LADY BRACKNELL (*makes a note in her book*): In land, or in investments?

JACK: In investments, chiefly.

LADY BRACKNELL: That is satisfactory. What between the duties expected of one during one's lifetime, and the duties exacted from one after one's death, land has ceased to be either a profit or a pleasure. It gives one position, and prevents one from keeping it up. That's all that can be said about land.

JACK: I have a country house with some land, of course, attached to it, about fifteen hundred acres, I believe; but I don't depend on that for my real income. In fact, as far as I can make out, the poachers are the only people who make anything out of it.

LADY BRACKNELL: A country house! How many bedrooms? Well, that point can be cleared up afterwards. You have a town house, I hope? A girl with a simple, unspoiled nature, like Gwendolen, could hardly be expected to reside in the country.

JACK: Well, I own a house in Belgrave Square, but it is let by the year to Lady Bloxham. Of course, I can get it back whenever I like, at six months' notice.

LADY BRACKNELL: Lady Bloxham? I don't know her.

JACK: Oh, she goes about very little. She is a lady considerably advanced in years.

LADY BRACKNELL: Ah, nowadays that is no guarantee of respectability of character. What number in Belgrave Square?

JACK: 149.

LADY BRACKNELL (*shaking her head*): The unfashionable side. I thought there was something. However, that could easily be altered.

JACK: Do you mean the fashion, or the side?

LADY BRACKNELL (*sternly*): Both, if necessary, I presume. What are your politics?

JACK: Well, I am afraid I really have none. I am a Liberal Unionist.

LADY BRACKNELL: Oh, they count as Tories. They dine with us. Or come in the evening, at any rate. Now to minor matters. Are your parents living?

JACK: I have lost both my parents.

LADY BRACKNELL: Both? To lose one parent may be regarded as a misfortune — to lose *both* seems like carelessness. Who was your father? He was evidently a man of some wealth. Was he born in what the Radical papers call the purple of commerce, or did he rise from the ranks of the aristocracy?

JACK: I am afraid I really don't know. The fact is, Lady Bracknell, I said I had lost my parents. It would be nearer the truth to say that my parents seem to have lost me — I don't actually know who I am by birth. I was — well, I was found.

LADY BRACKNELL: Found!

JACK: The late Mr. Thomas Cardew, an old gentleman of a very charitable and kindly disposition, found me, and gave me the name of Worthing, because he happened to have a first-class ticket for Worthing in his pocket at the time. Worthing is a place in Sussex. It is a seaside resort.

LADY BRACKNELL: Where did the charitable gentleman who had a first-class ticket for this seaside resort find you?

JACK (*gravely*): In a handbag.

LADY BRACKNELL: A handbag?

JACK (*very seriously*): Yes, Lady Bracknell. I was in a handbag — a somewhat large, black leather handbag, with handles to it — an ordinary handbag in fact.

LADY BRACKNELL: In what locality did this Mr. James, or Thomas, Cardew come across this ordinary handbag?

JACK: In the cloakroom at Victoria Station. It was given to him in mistake for his own.

LADY BRACKNELL: The cloakroom at Victoria Station?

JACK: Yes. The Brighton line.

LADY BRACKNELL: The line is immaterial. Mr. Worthing, I confess I feel somewhat bewildered by what you have just told me. To be born, or at any rate bred, in a handbag, whether it had handles or not, seems to me to display a contempt for the ordinary decencies of family life that reminds one of the worst excesses of the French Revolution. And I presume you know what that unfortunate movement led to? As for the particular locality in which the handbag was found, a cloakroom at a railway station might serve to conceal a social indiscretion — has probably, indeed, been used for that purpose before now — but it could hardly be regarded as an assured basis for a recognized position in good society.

JACK: May I ask you then what you would advise me to do? I need hardly say I would do anything in the world to ensure Gwendolen's happiness.

LADY BRACKNELL: I would strongly advise you, Mr. Worthing, to try and acquire some relations as soon as possible, and to make a definite effort to produce at any rate one parent of either sex, before the season is quite over.

JACK: Well, I don't see how I could possibly manage to do that. I can produce the handbag at any moment. It is in my dressing room at home. I really think that should satisfy you, Lady Bracknell.

LADY BRACKNELL: Me, sir! What has it to do with me? You can hardly imagine that I and Lord Bracknell would dream of allowing our only daughter — a girl brought up with the utmost care — to marry into a cloakroom, and form an alliance with a parcel? Good morning, Mr. Worthing!

(*Lady Bracknell sweeps out in majestic indignation.*)

JACK: Good morning! (*Algernon, from the other room, strikes up the Wedding March. Jack looks perfectly furious, and goes to the door.*) For goodness' sake don't play that ghastly tune, Algy! How idiotic you are!

(*The music stops, and Algernon enters cheerily.*)

ALGERNON: Didn't it go off all right, old boy? You don't mean to say Gwendolen refused you? I know it is a way she has. She is always refusing people. I think it is most ill-natured of her.

JACK: Oh, Gwendolen is as right as a trivet. As far as she is concerned, we are engaged. Her mother is perfectly unbearable. Never met such a Gorgon° — I don't really know what a Gorgon is like, but I am quite sure that Lady Bracknell is one. In any case, she is a monster, without being a myth, which is rather unfair. I beg your pardon, Algy, I suppose I shouldn't talk about your own aunt in that way before you.

ALGERNON: My dear boy, I love hearing my relations abused. It is the only thing that makes me put up with them at all. Relations are simply a tedious pack of people, who haven't got the remotest knowledge of how to live, nor the smallest instinct about when to die.

JACK: Oh, that is nonsense!

ALGERNON: It isn't!

JACK: Well, I won't argue about the matter. You always want to argue about things.

ALGERNON: That is exactly what things were originally made for.

JACK: Upon my word, if I thought that, I'd shoot myself — (*A pause.*) You don't think there is any chance of Gwendolen becoming like her mother in about a hundred and fifty years, do you Algy?

ALGERNON: All women become like their mothers. That is their tragedy. No man does. That's his.

JACK: Is that clever?

ALGERNON: It is perfectly phrased! and quite as true as any observation in civilized life should be.

JACK: I am sick to death of cleverness. Everybody is clever nowadays. You can't go anywhere without meeting clever people. The thing has become an absolute public nuisance. I wish to goodness we had a few fools left.

ALGERNON: We have.

JACK: I should extremely like to meet them. What do they talk about?

ALGERNON: The fools? Oh! about the clever people, of course.

Gorgon: In Greek myth, one of three very ugly sisters who had, among other characteristics, serpents for hair.

JACK: What fools!

ALGERNON: By the way, did you tell Gwendolen the truth about your being Ernest in town, and Jack in the country?

JACK (*in a very patronizing manner*): My dear fellow, the truth isn't quite the sort of thing one tells to a nice sweet refined girl. What extraordinary ideas you have about the way to behave to a woman!

ALGERNON: The only way to behave to a woman is to make love to her if she is pretty, and to someone else if she is plain.

JACK: Oh, that is nonsense.

ALGERNON: What about your brother? What about the profligate Ernest?

JACK: Oh, before the end of the week I shall have got rid of him. I'll say he died in Paris of apoplexy. Lots of people die of apoplexy, quite suddenly, don't they?

ALGERNON: Yes, but it's hereditary, my dear fellow. It's a sort of thing that runs in families. You had much better say a severe chill.

JACK: You are sure a severe chill isn't hereditary, or anything of that kind?

ALGERNON: Of course it isn't!

JACK: Very well, then. My poor brother Ernest is carried off suddenly in Paris, by a severe chill. That gets rid of him.

ALGERNON: But I thought you said that — Miss Cardew was a little too much interested in your poor brother Ernest? Won't she feel his loss a good deal?

JACK: Oh, that is all right. Cecily is not a silly romantic girl, I am glad to say. She has got a capital appetite, goes long walks, and pays no attention at all to her lessons.

ALGERNON: I would rather like to see Cecily.

JACK: I will take very good care you never do. She is excessively pretty, and she is only just eighteen.

ALGERNON: Have you told Gwendolen yet that you have an excessively pretty ward who is only just eighteen?

JACK: Oh! one doesn't blurt these things out to people. Cecily and Gwendolen are perfectly certain to be extremely great friends. I'll bet you anything you like that half an hour after they have met, they will be calling each other sister.

ALGERNON: Women only do that when they have called each other a lot of other things first. Now, my dear boy, if we want to get a good table at Willis's, we really must go and dress. Do you know it is nearly seven?

JACK (*irritably*): Oh! it always is nearly seven.

ALGERNON: Well, I'm hungry.

JACK: I never knew you when you weren't —

ALGERNON: What shall we do after dinner? Go to a theater?

JACK: Oh, no! I loathe listening.

ALGERNON: Well, let us go to the Club?

JACK: Oh, no! I hate talking.

ALGERNON: Well, we might trot round to the Empire° at ten?

JACK: Oh, no! I can't bear looking at things. It is so silly.

ALGERNON: Well, what shall we do?

JACK: Nothing!

ALGERNON: It is awfully hard work doing nothing. However, I don't mind hard work where there is no definite object of any kind.

(*Enter Lane.*)

LANE: Miss Fairfax.

(*Enter Gwendolen. Lane goes out.*)

ALGERNON: Gwendolen, upon my word!

GWENDOLEN: Algy, kindly turn your back. I have something very particular to say to Mr. Worthing.

ALGERNON: Really, Gwendolen, I don't think I can allow this at all.

GWENDOLEN: Algy, you always adopt a strictly immoral attitude towards life. You are not quite old enough to do that.

(*Algernon retires to the fireplace.*)

JACK: My own darling!

GWENDOLEN: Ernest, we may never be married. From the expression on Mama's face I fear we never shall. Few parents nowadays pay any regard to what their children say to them. The old-fashioned respect for the young is fast dying out. Whatever influence I ever had over Mama, I lost at the age of three. But although she may prevent us from becoming man and wife, and I may marry someone else, and marry often, nothing that she can possibly do can alter my eternal devotion to you.

JACK: Dear Gwendolen!

GWENDOLEN: The story of your romantic origin, as related to me by Mama, with unpleasing comments, has naturally stirred the deeper fibers of my nature. Your Christian name has an irresistible fascination. The simplicity of your character makes you exquisitely incomprehensible to me. Your town address at the Albany I have. What is your address in the country?

JACK: The Manor House, Woolton, Hertfordshire.

(*Algernon, who has been carefully listening, smiles to himself, and writes the address on his shirt cuff. Then picks up the Railway Guide.*)

GWENDOLEN: There is a good postal service, I suppose? It may be necessary to do something desperate. That

---

Empire: Empire Theatre, a London music hall that was also a rendezvous for prostitutes.

Scene from the Huntington Theatre Company's production of *The Importance of Being Earnest.*

of course will require serious consideration. I will communicate with you daily.

JACK: My own one!

GWENDOLEN: How long do you remain in town?

JACK: Till Monday.

GWENDOLEN: Good! Algy, you may turn round now.

ALGERNON: Thanks, I've turned round already.

GWENDOLEN: You may also ring the bell.

JACK: You will let me see you to your carriage, my own darling?

GWENDOLEN: Certainly.

JACK (*to Lane, who now enters*): I will see Miss Fairfax out.

LANE: Yes, sir.   (*Jack and Gwendolen go off.*)

(*Lane presents several letters on a salver to Algernon. It is to be surmised that they are bills, as Algernon, after looking at the envelopes, tears them up.*)

ALGERNON: A glass of sherry, Lane.

LANE: Yes, sir.

ALGERNON: Tomorrow, Lane, I'm going Bunburying.

LANE: Yes, sir.

ALGERNON: I shall probably not be back till Monday. You can put up my dress clothes, my smoking jacket, and all the Bunbury suits —

LANE: Yes, sir.   (*Handing sherry.*)

ALGERNON: I hope tomorrow will be a fine day, Lane.

LANE: It never is, sir.

ALGERNON: Lane, you're a perfect pessimist.

LANE: I do my best to give satisfaction, sir.

(*Enter Jack. Lane goes off.*)

JACK: There's a sensible, intellectual girl! the only girl I ever cared for in my life. (*Algernon is laughing immoderately.*) What on earth are you so amused at?

ALGERNON: Oh, I'm a little anxious about poor Bunbury, that is all.

JACK: If you don't take care, your friend Bunbury will get you into a serious scrape some day.

ALGERNON: I love scrapes. They are the only things that are never serious.

JACK: Oh, that's nonsense, Algy. You never talk anything but nonsense.

ALGERNON: Nobody ever does.

(*Jack looks indignantly at him, and leaves the room. Algernon lights a cigarette, reads his shirt cuff, and smiles.*)

ACT II

(*Scene: Garden at the Manor House. A flight of gray stone steps leads up to the house. The garden, an old-fashioned one, full of roses. Time of year, July. Basket chairs, and a table covered with books, are set under a large yew tree. Miss Prism discovered seated at the table. Cecily is at the back watering flowers.*)

MISS PRISM (*calling*): Cecily, Cecily! Surely such a utilitarian occupation as the watering of flowers is rather Moulton's duty than yours? Especially at a moment when intellectual pleasures await you. Your German grammar is on the table. Pray open it at page fifteen. We will repeat yesterday's lesson.

CECILY (*coming over very slowly*): But I don't like German. It isn't at all a becoming language. I know perfectly well that I look quite plain after my German lesson.

MISS PRISM: Child, you know how anxious your guardian is that you should improve yourself in every way. He laid particular stress on your German, as he was leaving for town yesterday. Indeed, he always lays stress on your German when he is leaving for town.

CECILY: Dear Uncle Jack is so very serious! Sometimes he is so serious that I think he cannot be quite well.

MISS PRISM (*drawing herself up*): Your guardian enjoys the best of health, and his gravity of demeanor is especially to be commended in one so comparatively young as he is. I know no one who has a higher sense of duty and responsibility.

CECILY: I suppose that is why he often looks a little bored when we three are together.

MISS PRISM: Cecily! I am surprised at you. Mr. Worthing has many troubles in his life. Idle merriment and triviality would be out of place in his conversation. You must remember his constant anxiety about that unfortunate young man his brother.

CECILY: I wish Uncle Jack would allow that unfortunate young man, his brother, to come down here sometimes. We might have a good influence over him, Miss Prism. I am sure you certainly would. You know German, and geology, and things of that kind influence a man very much.
> (*Cecily begins to write in her diary.*)

MISS PRISM (*shaking her head*): I do not think that even I could produce any effect on a character that according to his own brother's admission is irretrievably weak and vacillating. Indeed I am not sure that I would desire to reclaim him. I am not in favor of this modern mania for turning bad people into good people at a moment's notice. As a man sows so let him reap. You must put away your diary, Cecily. I really don't see why you should keep a diary at all.

CECILY: I keep a diary in order to enter the wonderful secrets of my life. If I didn't write them down I should probably forget all about them.

MISS PRISM: Memory, my dear Cecily, is the diary that we all carry about with us.

CECILY: Yes, but it usually chronicles the things that have never happened, and couldn't possibly have happened. I believe that Memory is responsible for nearly all the three-volume novels that Mudie sends us.

MISS PRISM: Do not speak slightingly of the three-volume novel, Cecily. I wrote one myself in earlier days.

CECILY: Did you really, Miss Prism? How wonderfully clever you are! I hope it did not end happily? I don't like novels that end happily. They depress me so much.

MISS PRISM: The good ended happily, and the bad unhappily. That is what Fiction means.

CECILY: I suppose so. But it seems very unfair. And was your novel ever published?

MISS PRISM: Alas! no. The manuscript unfortunately was abandoned. I use the word in the sense of lost or mislaid. To your work, child, these speculations are profitless.

CECILY (*smiling*): But I see dear Dr. Chasuble coming up through the garden.

MISS PRISM (*rising and advancing*): Dr. Chasuble! This is indeed a pleasure.

(*Enter Canon Chasuble.*)

CHASUBLE: And how are we this morning? Miss Prism, you are, I trust, well?

CECILY: Miss Prism has just been complaining of a slight headache. I think it would do her so much good to have a short stroll with you in the park, Dr. Chasuble.

MISS PRISM: Cecily, I have not mentioned anything about a headache.

CECILY: No, dear Miss Prism, I know that, but I felt instinctively that you had a headache. Indeed I was thinking about that, and not about my German lesson, when the Rector came in.

CHASUBLE: I hope, Cecily, you are not inattentive.

CECILY: Oh, I am afraid I am.

CHASUBLE: That is strange. Were I fortunate enough to be Miss Prism's pupil, I would hang upon her lips. (*Miss Prism glares.*) I spoke metaphorically. — My metaphor was drawn from bees. Ahem! Mr. Worthing, I suppose, has not returned from town yet?

MISS PRISM: We do not expect him till Monday afternoon.

CHASUBLE: Ah yes, he usually likes to spend his Sunday in London. He is not one of those whose sole aim is enjoyment, as, by all accounts, that unfortunate young man his brother seems to be. But I must not disturb Egeria° and her pupil any longer.

MISS PRISM: Egeria? My name is Laetitia, Doctor.

CHASUBLE (*bowing*): A classical allusion merely, drawn from the Pagan authors. I shall see you both no doubt at Evensong.

MISS PRISM: I think, dear Doctor, I will have a stroll with you. I find I have a headache after all, and a walk might do it good.

CHASUBLE: With pleasure, Miss Prism, with pleasure. We might go as far as the schools and back.

MISS PRISM: That would be delightful. Cecily, you will read your Political Economy in my absence. The chapter on the Fall of the Rupee° you may omit. It is somewhat too sensational. Even these metallic problems have their melodramatic side.

(*Goes down the garden with Dr. Chasuble.*)

CECILY (*picks up books and throws them back on table*): Horrid Political Economy! Horrid Geography! Horrid, horrid German!

(*Enter Merriman with a card on a salver.*)

MERRIMAN: Mr. Ernest Worthing has just driven over from the station. He has brought his luggage with him.

CECILY (*takes the card and reads it*): "Mr. Ernest Worthing, B.4, The Albany, W." Uncle Jack's brother! Did you tell him Mr. Worthing was in town?

MERRIMAN: Yes, Miss. He seemed very much disappointed. I mentioned that you and Miss Prism were in the garden. He said he was anxious to speak to you privately for a moment.

CECILY: Ask Mr. Ernest Worthing to come here. I suppose you had better talk to the housekeeper about a room for him.

MERRIMAN: Yes, Miss.   (*Merriman goes off.*)

CECILY: I have never met any really wicked person before. I feel rather frightened. I am so afraid he will look just like everyone else.

(*Enter Algernon, very gay and debonair.*)

He does!

ALGERNON (*raising his hat*): You are my little cousin Cecily, I'm sure.

Egeria: Roman goddess of water.
Fall of the Rupee: Reference to the Indian rupee, whose steady deflation between 1873 and 1893 caused the Indian governments finally to close the mints.

CECILY: You are under some strange mistake. I am not little. In fact, I believe I am more than usually tall for my age (*Algernon is rather taken aback*). But I am your cousin Cecily. You, I see from your card, are Uncle Jack's brother, my cousin Ernest, my wicked cousin Ernest.

ALGERNON: Oh! I am not really wicked at all, Cousin Cecily. You mustn't think that I am wicked.

CECILY: If you are not, then you have certainly been deceiving us all in a very inexcusable manner. I hope you have not been leading a double life, pretending to be wicked and being really good all the time. That would be hypocrisy.

ALGERNON (*looks at her in amazement*): Oh! Of course I have been rather reckless.

CECILY: I am glad to hear it.

ALGERNON: In fact, now you mention the subject, I have been very bad in my own small way.

CECILY: I don't think you should be so proud of that, though I am sure it must have been very pleasant.

ALGERNON: It is much pleasanter being here with you.

CECILY: I can't understand how you are here at all. Uncle Jack won't be back till Monday afternoon.

ALGERNON: That is a great disappointment. I am obliged to go up by the first train on Monday morning. I have a business appointment that I am anxious — to miss.

CECILY: Couldn't you miss it anywhere but in London?

ALGERNON: No: the appointment is in London.

CECILY: Well, I know, of course, how important it is not to keep a business engagement, if one wants to retain any sense of the beauty of life, but still I think you had better wait till Uncle Jack arrives. I know he wants to speak to you about your emigrating.

ALGERNON: About my what?

CECILY: Your emigrating. He has gone up to buy your outfit.

ALGERNON: I certainly wouldn't let Jack buy my outfit. He has no taste in neckties at all.

CECILY: I don't think you will require neckties. Uncle Jack is sending you to Australia.

ALGERNON: Australia! I'd sooner die.

CECILY: Well, he said at dinner on Wednesday night, that you would have to choose between this world, the next world, and Australia.

ALGERNON: Oh, well! The accounts I have received of Australia and the next world are not particularly encouraging. This world is good enough for me, Cousin Cecily.

CECILY: Yes, but are you good enough for it?

ALGERNON: I'm afraid I'm not that. That is why I want you to reform me. You might make that your mission, if you don't mind, Cousin Cecily.

CECILY: I'm afraid I've no time, this afternoon.

ALGERNON: Well, would you mind my reforming myself this afternoon?

CECILY: It is rather quixotic° of you. But I think you should try.

ALGERNON: I will. I feel better already.

CECILY: You are looking a little worse.

ALGERNON: That is because I am hungry.

CECILY: How thoughtless of me. I should have remembered that when one is going to lead an entirely new life, one requires regular and wholesome meals. Won't you come in?

ALGERNON: Thank you. Might I have a buttonhole° first? I never have any appetite unless I have a buttonhole first.

CECILY: A Maréchal Niel?°

ALGERNON: No, I'd sooner have a pink rose.

CECILY: Why?   (Cuts a flower.)

ALGERNON: Because you are like a pink rose, Cousin Cecily.

CECILY: I don't think it can be right for you to talk to me like that. Miss Prism never says such things to me.

ALGERNON: Then Miss Prism is a shortsighted old lady. (Cecily puts the rose in his buttonhole.) You are the prettiest girl I ever saw.

CECILY: Miss Prism says that all good looks are a snare.

ALGERNON: They are a snare that every sensible man would like to be caught in.

CECILY: Oh! I don't think I would care to catch a sensible man. I shouldn't know what to talk to him about.

(They pass into the house. Miss Prism and Dr. Chasuble return.)

MISS PRISM: You are too much alone, dear Dr. Chasuble. You should get married. A misanthrope I can understand — a womanthrope, never!

CHASUBLE (with a scholar's shudder): Believe me, I do not deserve so neologistic a phrase. The precept as well as the practice of the Primitive Church was distinctly against matrimony.

MISS PRISM (sententiously): That is obviously the reason why the Primitive Church has not lasted up to the present day. And you do not seem to realize, dear Doctor, that by persistently remaining single, a man converts himself into a permanent public temptation. Men should be more careful; this very celibacy leads weaker vessels astray.

CHASUBLE: But is a man not equally attractive when married?

MISS PRISM: No married man is ever attractive except to his wife.

CHASUBLE: And often, I've been told, not even to her.

---

quixotic: Foolishly impractical, from the idealistic hero of Cervantes' *Don Quixote*.
buttonhole: Boutonniere.
Maréchal Niel: A yellow rose.

MISS PRISM: That depends on the intellectual sympathies of the woman. Maturity can always be depended on. Ripeness can be trusted. Young women are green. (Dr. Chasuble starts.) I spoke horticulturally. My metaphor was drawn from fruits. But where is Cecily?

CHASUBLE: Perhaps she followed us to the schools.

(Enter Jack slowly from the back of the garden. He is dressed in the deepest mourning, with crepe hatband and black gloves.)

MISS PRISM: Mr. Worthing!

CHASUBLE: Mr. Worthing?

MISS PRISM: This is indeed a surprise. We did not look for you till Monday afternoon.

JACK (shakes Miss Prism's hand in a tragic manner): I have returned sooner than I expected. Dr. Chasuble, I hope you are well?

CHASUBLE: Dear Mr. Worthing, I trust this garb of woe does not betoken some terrible calamity?

JACK: My brother.

MISS PRISM: More shameful debts and extravagance?

CHASUBLE: Still leading his life of pleasure?

JACK (shaking his head): Dead!

CHASUBLE: Your brother Ernest dead?

JACK: Quite dead.

MISS PRISM: What a lesson for him! I trust he will profit by it.

CHASUBLE: Mr. Worthing, I offer you my sincere condolence. You have at least the consolation of knowing that you were always the most generous and forgiving of brothers.

JACK: Poor Ernest! He had many faults, but it is a sad, sad blow.

CHASUBLE: Very sad indeed. Were you with him at the end?

JACK: No. He died abroad, in Paris, in fact. I had a telegram last night from the manager of the Grand Hotel.

CHASUBLE: Was the cause of death mentioned?

JACK: A severe chill, it seems.

MISS PRISM: As a man sows, so shall he reap.

CHASUBLE (raising his hand): Charity, dear Miss Prism, charity! None of us are perfect. I myself am peculiarly susceptible to drafts. Will the interment take place here?

JACK: No. He seemed to have expressed a desire to be buried in Paris.

CHASUBLE: In Paris! (Shakes his head.) I fear that hardly points to any very serious state of mind at the last. You would no doubt wish me to make some slight allusion to this tragic domestic affliction next Sunday. (Jack presses his hand convulsively.) My sermon on the meaning of the manna in the wilderness can be adapted to almost any occasion, joyful, or, as in the present case, distressing. (All *sigh.*) I have preached it at harvest celebrations, christenings, confirmations, on days of humiliation and festal days. The last time I delivered it was in the Cathedral, as a charity sermon on behalf of the Society for the Prevention of Discontent among the Upper Orders. The Bishop, who was present, was much struck by some of the analogies I drew.

JACK: Ah! that reminds me, you mentioned christenings I think, Dr. Chasuble? I suppose you know how to christen all right? (*Dr. Chasuble looks astounded.*) I mean, of course, you are continually christening, aren't you?

MISS PRISM: It is, I regret to say, one of the Rector's most constant duties in this parish. I have often spoken to the poorer classes on the subject. But they don't seem to know what thrift is.

CHASUBLE: But is there any particular infant in whom you are interested, Mr. Worthing? Your brother was, I believe, unmarried, was he not?

JACK: Oh yes.

MISS PRISM (*bitterly*): People who live entirely for pleasure usually are.

JACK: But it is not for any child, dear Doctor. I am very fond of children. No! the fact is, I would like to be christened myself, this afternoon, if you have nothing better to do.

CHASUBLE: But surely, Mr. Worthing, you have been christened already?

JACK: I don't remember anything about it.

CHASUBLE: But have you any grave doubts on the subject?

JACK: I certainly intend to have. Of course I don't know if the thing would bother you in any way, or if you think I am a little too old now.

CHASUBLE: Not at all. The sprinkling, and, indeed, the immersion of adults is a perfectly canonical practice.

JACK: Immersion!

CHASUBLE: You need have no apprehensions. Sprinkling is all that is necessary, or indeed I think advisable. Our weather is so changeable. At what hour would you wish the ceremony performed?

JACK: Oh, I might trot round about five if that would suit you.

CHASUBLE: Perfectly, perfectly! In fact I have two similar ceremonies to perform at that time. A case of twins that occurred recently in one of the outlying cottages on your own estate. Poor Jenkins the carter, a most hardworking man.

JACK: Oh! I don't see much fun in being christened along with other babies. It would be childish. Would half-past five do?

CHASUBLE: Admirably! Admirably! (*Takes out watch.*) And now, dear Mr. Worthing, I will not intrude any longer into a house of sorrow. I would merely beg you not to be too much bowed down by grief.

What seem to us bitter trials are often blessings in disguise.

MISS PRISM: This seems to me a blessing of an extremely obvious kind.

(*Enter Cecily from the house.*)

CECILY: Uncle Jack! Oh, I am pleased to see you back. But what horrid clothes you have got on! Do go and change them.

MISS PRISM: Cecily!

CHASUBLE: My child! my child!

(*Cecily goes towards Jack; he kisses her brow in a melancholy manner.*)

CECILY: What is the matter, Uncle Jack? Do look happy! You look as if you had toothache, and I have got such a surprise for you. Who do you think is in the dining room? Your brother!

JACK: Who?

CECILY: Your brother Ernest. He arrived about half an hour ago.

JACK: What nonsense! I haven't got a brother.

CECILY: Oh, don't say that. However badly he may have behaved to you in the past he is still your brother. You couldn't be so heartless as to disown him. I'll tell him to come out. And you will shake hands with him, won't you, Uncle Jack?
             (*Runs back into the house.*)

CHASUBLE: These are very joyful tidings.

MISS PRISM: After we had all been resigned to his loss, his sudden return seems to me peculiarly distressing.

JACK: My brother is in the dining room? I don't know what it all means. I think it is perfectly absurd.

(*Enter Algernon and Cecily hand in hand. They come slowly up to Jack.*)

JACK: Good heavens!   (*Motions Algernon away.*)

ALGERNON: Brother John, I have come down from town to tell you that I am very sorry for all the trouble I have given you, and that I intend to lead a better life in the future.
             (*Jack glares at him and does not take his hand.*)

CECILY: Uncle Jack, you are not going to refuse your own brother's hand?

JACK: Nothing will induce me to take his hand. I think his coming down here disgraceful. He knows perfectly well why.

CECILY: Uncle Jack, do be nice. There is some good in everyone. Ernest has just been telling me about his poor invalid friend Mr. Bunbury whom he goes to visit so often. And surely there must be much good in one who is kind to an invalid, and leaves the pleasures of London to sit by a bed of pain.

JACK Oh! he has been talking about Bunbury has he?

CECILY: Yes, he has told me all about poor Mr. Bunbury, and his terrible state of health.

JACK: Bunbury! Well, I won't have him talk to you about Bunbury or about anything else. It is enough to drive one perfectly frantic.

ALGERNON: Of course I admit that the faults were all on my side. But I must say that I think that Brother John's coldness to me is peculiarly painful. I expected a more enthusiastic welcome, especially considering it is the first time I have come here.

CECILY: Uncle Jack, if you don't shake hands with Ernest I will never forgive you.

JACK: Never forgive me?

CECILY: Never, never, never!

JACK: Well, this is the last time I shall ever do it.
            (*Shakes hands with Algernon and glares.*)

CHASUBLE: It's pleasant, is it not, to see so perfect a reconciliation? I think we might leave the two brothers together.

MISS PRISM: Cecily, you will come with us.

CECILY: Certainly, Miss Prism. My little task of reconciliation is over.

CHASUBLE: You have done a beautiful action today, dear child.

MISS PRISM: We must not be premature in our judgments.

CECILY: I feel very happy.   (*They all go off.*)

JACK: You young scoundrel, Algy, you must get out of this place as soon as possible. I don't allow any Bunburying here.

(*Enter Merriman.*)

MERRIMAN: I have put Mr. Ernest's things in the room next to yours, sir. I suppose that is all right?

JACK: What?

MERRIMAN: Mr. Ernest's luggage, sir. I have unpacked it and put it in the room next to your own.

JACK: His luggage?

MERRIMAN: Yes, sir. Three portmanteaus, a dressing case, two hatboxes, and a large luncheon basket.

ALGERNON: I am afraid I can't stay more than a week this time.

JACK: Merriman, order the dog cart at once. Mr. Ernest has been suddenly called back to town.

MERRIMAN: Yes, sir.   (*Goes back into the house.*)

ALGERNON: What a fearful liar you are, Jack. I have not been called back to town at all.

JACK: Yes, you have.

ALGERNON: I haven't heard anyone call me.

JACK: Your duty as a gentleman calls you back.

ALGERNON: My duty as a gentleman has never interfered with my pleasures in the smallest degree.

JACK: I can quite understand that.

ALGERNON: Well, Cecily is a darling.

JACK: You are not to talk of Miss Cardew like that. I don't like it.

ALGERNON: Well, I don't like your clothes. You look perfectly ridiculous in them. Why on earth don't you go up and change? It is perfectly childish to be in deep mourning for a man who is actually staying for a whole week in your house as a guest. I call it grotesque.

JACK: You are certainly not staying with me for a whole week as a guest or anything else. You have got to leave — by the four-five train.

ALGERNON: I certainly won't leave you so long as you are in mourning. It would be most unfriendly. If I were in mourning you would stay with me, I suppose. I should think it very unkind if you didn't.

JACK: Well, will you go if I change my clothes?

ALGERNON: Yes, if you are not too long. I never saw anybody take so long to dress, and with such little result.

JACK: Well, at any rate, that is better than being always overdressed as you are.

ALGERNON: If I am occasionally a little overdressed, I make up for it by being always immensely overeducated.

JACK: Your vanity is ridiculous, your conduct an outrage, and your presence in my garden utterly absurd. However, you have got to catch the four-five, and I hope you will have a pleasant journey back to town. This Bunburying, as you call it, has not been a great success for you.
            (*Goes into the house.*)

ALGERNON: I think it has been a great success. I'm in love with Cecily, and that is everything.

(*Enter Cecily at the back of the garden. She picks up the can and begins to water the flowers.*)

But I must see her before I go, and make arrangements for another Bunbury. Ah, there she is.

CECILY: Oh, I merely came back to water the roses. I thought you were with Uncle Jack.

ALGERNON: He's gone to order the dog cart for me.

CECILY: Oh, is he going to take you for a nice drive?

ALGERNON: He's going to send me away.

CECILY: Then have we got to part?

ALGERNON: I am afraid so. It's a very painful parting.

CECILY: It is always painful to part from people whom one has known for a very brief space of time. The absence of old friends one can endure with equanimity. But even a momentary separation from anyone to whom one has just been introduced is almost unbearable.

ALGERNON: Thank you.

(*Enter Merriman.*)

MERRIMAN: The dog cart is at the door, sir.
            (*Algernon looks appealingly at Cecily.*)

CECILY: It can wait, Merriman — for — five minutes.

MERRIMAN: Yes, miss.   (*Exit Merriman.*)

ALGERNON: I hope, Cecily, I shall not offend you if I state quite frankly and openly that you seem to me to be in every way the visible personification of absolute perfection.

CECILY: I think your frankness does you great credit, Ernest. If you will allow me I will copy your remarks into my diary.

(*Goes over to table and begins writing in diary.*)

ALGERNON: Do you really keep a diary? I'd give anything to look at it. May I?

CECILY: Oh no. (*Puts her hand over it.*) You see, it is simply a very young girl's record of her own thoughts and impressions, and consequently meant for publication. When it appears in volume form I hope you will order a copy. But pray, Ernest, don't stop. I delight in taking down from dictation. I have reached "absolute perfection." You can go on. I am quite ready for more.

ALGERNON (*somewhat taken aback*): Ahem! Ahem!

CECILY: Oh, don't cough, Ernest. When one is dictating one should speak fluently and not cough. Besides, I don't know how to spell a cough.

(*Writes as Algernon speaks.*)

ALGERNON (*speaking very rapidly*): Cecily, ever since I first looked upon your wonderful and incomparable beauty, I have dared to love you wildly, passionately, devotedly, hopelessly.

CECILY: I don't think that you should tell me that you love me wildly, passionately, devotedly, hopelessly. Hopelessly doesn't seem to make much sense, does it?

ALGERNON: Cecily!

(*Enter Merriman.*)

MERRIMAN: The dog cart is waiting, sir.

ALGERNON: Tell it to come round next week, at the same hour.

MERRIMAN (*looks at Cecily, who makes no sign*): Yes, sir.   (*Merriman retires.*)

CECILY: Uncle Jack would be very much annoyed if he knew you were staying on till next week, at the same hour.

ALGERNON: Oh, I don't care about Jack. I don't care for anybody in the whole world but you. I love you, Cecily. You will marry me, won't you?

CECILY: You silly boy! Of course. Why, we have been engaged for the last three months.

ALGERNON: For the last three months?

CECILY: Yes, it will be exactly three months on Thursday.

ALGERNON: But how did we become engaged?

CECILY: Well, ever since dear Uncle Jack first confessed to us that he had a younger brother who was very wicked and bad, you of course have formed the chief topic of conversation between myself and Miss Prism. And of course a man who is much talked about is always very attractive. One

feels there must be something in him after all. I daresay it was foolish of me, but I fell in love with you, Ernest.

ALGERNON: Darling! And when was the engagement actually settled?

CECILY: On the 14th of February last. Worn out by your entire ignorance of my existence, I determined to end the matter one way or the other, and after a long struggle with myself I accepted you under this dear old tree here. The next day I bought this little ring in your name, and this is the little bangle with the true lovers' knot I promised you always to wear.

ALGERNON: Did I give you this? It's very pretty, isn't it?

CECILY: Yes, you've wonderfully good taste, Ernest. It's the excuse I've always given for your leading such a bad life. And this is the box in which I keep all your dear letters.

(*Kneels at table, opens box, and produces letters tied up with blue ribbon.*)

ALGERNON: My letters! But my own sweet Cecily, I have never written you any letters.

CECILY: You need hardly remind me of that, Ernest. I remember only too well that I was forced to write your letters for you. I wrote always three times a week, and sometimes oftener.

ALGERNON: Oh, do let me read them, Cecily!

CECILY: Oh, I couldn't possibly. They would make you far too conceited. (*Replaces box.*) The three you wrote me after I had broken off the engagement are so beautiful, and so badly spelled, that even now I can hardly read them without crying a little.

ALGERNON: But was our engagement ever broken off?

CECILY: Of course it was. On the 22nd of last March. You can see the entry if you like. (*Shows diary.*) "Today I broke off my engagement with Ernest. I feel it is better to do so. The weather still continues charming."

ALGERNON: But why on earth did you break it off? What had I done? I had done nothing at all. Cecily, I am very much hurt indeed to hear you broke it off. Particularly when the weather was so charming.

CECILY: It would hardly have been a really serious engagement if it hadn't been broken off at least once. But I forgave you before the week was out.

ALGERNON (*crossing to her, and kneeling*): What a perfect angel you are, Cecily.

CECILY: You dear romantic boy. (*He kisses her; she puts her fingers through his hair.*) I hope your hair curls naturally, does it?

ALGERNON: Yes, darling, with a little help from others.

CECILY: I am so glad.

ALGERNON: You'll never break off our engagement again, Cecily?

CECILY: I don't think I could break it off now that I have actually met you. Besides, of course, there is the question of your name.

ALGERNON (*nervously*): Yes, of course.

CECILY: You must not laugh at me, darling, but it had always been a girlish dream of mine to love someone whose name was Ernest. (*Algernon rises, Cecily also.*) There is something in that name that seems to inspire absolute confidence. I pity any poor married woman whose husband is not called Ernest.

ALGERNON: But, my dear child, do you mean to say you could not love me if I had some other name?

CECILY: But what name?

ALGERNON: Oh, any name you like — Algernon — for instance —

CECILY: But I don't like the name of Algernon.

ALGERNON: Well, my own dear, sweet, loving little darling, I really can't see why you should object to the name of Algernon. It is not at all a bad name. In fact, it is rather an aristocratic name. Half of the chaps who get into the Bankruptcy Court are called Algernon. But seriously, Cecily — (*moving to her*) — if my name was Algy, couldn't you love me?

CECILY (*rising*): I might respect you, Ernest, I might admire your character, but I fear that I should not be able to give you my undivided attention.

ALGERNON: Ahem! Cecily! (*Picking up hat.*) Your Rector here is, I suppose, thoroughly experienced in the practice of all the rites and ceremonials of the Church?

CECILY: Oh yes. Dr. Chasuble is a most learned man. He has never written a single book, so you can imagine how much he knows.

ALGERNON: I must see him at once on a most important christening — I mean on most important business.

CECILY: Oh!

ALGERNON: I shan't be away more than half an hour.

CECILY: Considering that we have been engaged since February the 14th, and that I only met you today for the first time, I think it is rather hard that you should leave me for so long a period as half an hour. Couldn't you make it twenty minutes?

ALGERNON: I'll be back in no time.

(*Kisses her and rushes down the garden.*)

CECILY: What an impetuous boy he is! I like his hair so much. I must enter his proposal in my diary.

(*Enter Merriman.*)

MERRIMAN: A Miss Fairfax has just called to see Mr. Worthing. On very important business Miss Fairfax states.

CECILY: Isn't Mr. Worthing in his library?

MERRIMAN: Mr. Worthing went over in the direction of the Rectory some time ago.

CECILY: Pray ask the lady to come out here; Mr. Worthing is sure to be back soon. And you can bring tea.

MERRIMAN: Yes, miss.   (*Goes out.*)

CECILY: Miss Fairfax! I suppose one of the many good elderly women who are associated with Uncle Jack in some of his philanthropic work in London. I don't quite like women who are interested in philanthropic work. I think it is so forward of them.

(*Enter Merriman.*)

MERRIMAN: Miss Fairfax.

(*Enter Gwendolen. Exit Merriman.*)

CECILY (*advancing to meet her*): Pray let me introduce myself to you. My name is Cecily Cardew.

GWENDOLEN: Cecily Cardew? (*Moving to her and shaking hands.*) What a very sweet name! Something tells me that we are going to be great friends. I like you already more than I can say. My first impressions of people are never wrong.

CECILY: How nice of you to like me so much after we have known each other such a comparatively short time. Pray sit down.

GWENDOLEN (*still standing up*): I may call you Cecily, may I not?

CECILY: With pleasure!

GWENDOLEN: And you will always call me Gwendolen, won't you?

CECILY: If you wish.

GWENDOLEN: Then that is all quite settled, is it not?

CECILY: I hope so.

(*A pause. They both sit down together.*)

GWENDOLEN: Perhaps this might be a favorable opportunity for my mentioning who I am. My father is Lord Bracknell. You have never heard of Papa, I suppose?

CECILY: I don't think so.

GWENDOLEN: Outside the family circle, Papa, I am glad to say, is entirely unknown. I think that is quite as it should be. The home seems to me to be the proper sphere for the man. And certainly once a man begins to neglect his domestic duties he becomes painfully effeminate, does he not? And I don't like that. It makes men so very attractive. Cecily, Mama, whose views on education are remarkably strict, has brought me up to be extremely shortsighted; it is part of her system, so do you mind my looking at you through my glasses?

CECILY: Oh! not at all, Gwendolen. I am very fond of being looked at.

GWENDOLEN (*after examining Cecily carefully through a lorgnette*): You are here on a short visit I suppose?

CECILY: Oh no! I live here.

GWENDOLEN (*severely*): Really? Your mother, no doubt, or some female relative of advanced years, resides here also?

CECILY: Oh no! I have no mother, nor, in fact, any relations.

GWENDOLEN: Indeed?

CECILY: My dear guardian, with the assistance of Miss Prism, has the arduous task of looking after me.

GWENDOLEN: Your guardian?

CECILY: Yes, I am Mr. Worthing's ward.

GWENDOLEN: Oh! It is strange he never mentioned to me that he had a ward. How secretive of him! He grows more interesting hourly. I am not sure, however, that the news inspires me with feelings of unmixed delight. (*Rising and going to her.*) I am very fond of you, Cecily; I have liked you ever since I met you! But I am bound to state that now that I know that you are Mr. Worthing's ward, I cannot help expressing a wish you were — well just a little older than you seem to be — and not quite so very alluring in appearance. In fact, if I may speak candidly —

CECILY: Pray do! I think that whenever one has anything unpleasant to say, one should always be quite candid.

GWENDOLEN: Well, to speak with perfect candor, Cecily, I wish that you were fully forty-two, and more than usually plain for your age. Ernest has a strong upright nature. He is the very soul of truth and honor. Disloyalty would be as impossible to him as deception. But even men of the noblest possible moral character are extremely susceptible to the influence of the physical charms of others. Modern, no less than Ancient History, supplies us with many most painful examples of what I refer to. If it were not so, indeed, History would be quite unreadable.

CECILY: I beg your pardon, Gwendolen, did you say Ernest?

GWENDOLEN: Yes.

CECILY: Oh, but it is not Mr. Ernest Worthing who is my guardian. It is his brother — his elder brother.

GWENDOLEN (*sitting down again*): Ernest never mentioned to me that he had a brother.

CECILY: I am sorry to say they have not been on good terms for a long time.

GWENDOLEN: Ah! that accounts for it. And now that I think of it I have never heard any man mention his brother. The subject seems distasteful to most men. Cecily, you have lifted a load from my mind. I was growing almost anxious. It would have been terrible if any cloud had come across a friendship like ours, would it not? Of course you are quite, quite sure that it is not Mr. Ernest Worthing who is your guardian?

CECILY: Quite sure. (*A pause.*) In fact, I am going to be his.

GWENDOLEN (*inquiringly*): I beg your pardon?

CECILY (*rather shy and confidingly*): Dearest Gwendolen, there is no reason why I should make a secret of it to you. Our little county newspaper is sure to chronicle the fact next week. Mr. Ernest Worthing and I are engaged to be married.

GWENDOLEN (*quite politely, rising*): My darling Cecily, I think there must be some slight error. Mr. Ernest Worthing is engaged to me. The announcement will appear in the *Morning Post* on Saturday at the latest.

CECILY (*very politely, rising*): I am afraid you must be under some misconception. Ernest proposed to me exactly ten minutes ago.   (*Shows diary.*)

GWENDOLEN (*examines diary through her lorgnette carefully*): It is certainly very curious, for he asked me to be his wife yesterday afternoon at 5:30. If you would care to verify the incident, pray do so. (*Produces diary of her own.*) I never travel without my diary. One should always have something sensational to read in the train. I am so sorry, dear Cecily, if it is any disappointment to you, but I am afraid *I* have the prior claim.

CECILY: It would distress me more than I can tell you, dear Gwendolen, if it caused you any mental or physical anguish, but I feel bound to point out that since Ernest proposed to you he clearly has changed his mind.

GWENDOLEN (*meditatively*): If the poor fellow has been entrapped into any foolish promise I shall consider it my duty to rescue him at once, and with a firm hand.

CECILY (*thoughtfully and sadly*): Whatever unfortunate entanglement my dear boy may have got into, I will never reproach him with it after we are married.

GWENDOLEN: Do you allude to me, Miss Cardew, as an entanglement? You are presumptuous. On an occasion of this kind it becomes more than a moral duty to speak one's mind. It becomes a pleasure.

CECILY: Do you suggest, Miss Fairfax, that I entrapped Ernest into an engagement? How dare you? This is no time for wearing the shallow mask of manners. When I see a spade I call it a spade.

GWENDOLEN (*satirically*): I am glad to say that I have never seen a spade. It is obvious that our social spheres have been widely different.

(*Enter Merriman, followed by the Footman. He car-*

ries a salver, tablecloth, and plate stand. Cecily is
about to retort. The presence of the servants exercises
a restraining influence, under which both girls chafe.)

MERRIMAN: Shall I lay tea here as usual, miss?
CECILY (sternly, in a calm voice): Yes, as usual.

(Merriman begins to clear table and lay cloth. A long
pause. Cecily and Gwendolen glare at each other.)

GWENDOLEN: Are there many interesting walks in the
vicinity, Miss Cardew?
CECILY: Oh! Yes! a great many. From the top of one
of the hills quite close one can see five counties.
GWENDOLEN: Five counties! I don't think I should like
that. I hate crowds.
CECILY (sweetly): I suppose that is why you live in
town?

(Gwendolen bites her lip, and beats her foot nervously with her parasol.)

GWENDOLEN (looking round): Quite a well-kept garden this is, Miss Cardew.
CECILY: So glad you like it, Miss Fairfax.
GWENDOLEN: I had no idea there were any flowers in
the country.
CECILY: Oh, flowers are as common here, Miss Fairfax, as people are in London.
GWENDOLEN: Personally I cannot understand how
anybody manages to exist in the country, if anybody who is anybody does. The country always
bores me to death.
CECILY: Ah! This is what the newspapers call agricultural depression, is it not? I believe the aristocracy
are suffering very much from it just at present. It is
almost an epidemic amongst them, I have been
told. May I offer you some tea, Miss Fairfax?
GWENDOLEN (with elaborate politeness): Thank you.
(Aside.) Detestable girl! But I require tea!
CECILY (sweetly): Sugar?
GWENDOLEN (superciliously): No, thank you. Sugar is
not fashionable anymore.

(Cecily looks angrily at her, takes up the tongs, and
puts four lumps of sugar into the cup.)

CECILY (severely): Cake or bread and butter?
GWENDOLEN (in a bored manner): Bread and butter,
please. Cake is rarely seen at the best houses nowadays.
CECILY (cuts a very large slice of cake, and puts it on
the tray): Hand that to Miss Fairfax.

(Merriman does so, and goes out with Footman.
Gwendolen drinks the tea and makes a grimace. Puts
down cup at once, reaches out her hand to the bread
and butter, looks at it, and finds it is cake. Rises in indignation.)

GWENDOLEN: You have filled my tea with lumps of
sugar, and though I asked most distinctly for bread
and butter, you have given me cake. I am known
for the gentleness of my disposition, and the extraordinary sweetness of my nature, but I warn you,
Miss Cardew, you may go too far.
CECILY (rising): To save my poor, innocent, trusting
boy from the machinations of any other girl there
are no lengths to which I would not go.
GWENDOLEN: From the moment I saw you I distrusted
you. I felt that you were false and deceitful. I am
never deceived in such matters. My first impressions of people are invariably right.
CECILY: It seems to me, Miss Fairfax, that I am trespassing on your valuable time. No doubt you have
many other calls of a similar character to make in
the neighborhood.

(Enter Jack.)

GWENDOLEN (catching sight of him): Ernest! My own
Ernest!
JACK: Gwendolen! Darling!   (Offers to kiss her.)
GWENDOLEN (drawing back): A moment! May I ask if
you are engaged to be married to this young lady?
(Points to Cecily.)
JACK (laughing): To dear little Cecily! Of course not!
What could have put such an idea into your pretty
little head?
GWENDOLEN: Thank you. You may!
(Offers her cheek.)
CECILY (very sweetly): I knew there must be some mis-
understanding, Miss Fairfax. The gentleman whose
arm is at present round your waist is my dear
guardian, Mr. John Worthing.
GWENDOLEN: I beg your pardon?
CECILY: This is Uncle Jack.
GWENDOLEN (receding): Jack! Oh!

(Enter Algernon.)

CECILY: Here is Ernest.
ALGERNON (goes straight over to Cecily without
noticing anyone else): My own love!
(Offers to kiss her.)
CECILY (drawing back): A moment, Ernest! May I ask
you — are you engaged to be married to this
young lady?
ALGERNON (looking round): To what young lady?
Good heavens! Gwendolen!
CECILY: Yes! to good heavens, Gwendolen, I mean to
Gwendolen.
ALGERNON (laughing): Of course not! What could
have put such an idea into your pretty little head?
CECILY: Thank you. (Presenting her cheek to be
kissed.) You may.   (Algernon kisses her.)
GWENDOLEN: I felt there was some slight error, Miss

Cardew. The gentleman who is now embracing you is my cousin, Mr. Algernon Moncrieff.

CECILY (*breaking away from Algernon*): Algernon Moncrieff! Oh!

(*The two girls move towards each other and put their arms round each other's waists as if for protection.*)

CECILY: Are you called Algernon?

ALGERNON: I cannot deny it.

CECILY: Oh!

GWENDOLEN: Is your name really John?

JACK (*standing rather proudly*): I could deny it if I liked. I could deny anything if I liked. But my name certainly is John. It has been John for years.

CECILY (*to Gwendolen*): A gross deception has been practiced on both of us.

GWENDOLEN: My poor wounded Cecily!

CECILY: My sweet wronged Gwendolen!

GWENDOLEN (*slowly and seriously*): You will call me sister, will you not?

(*They embrace. Jack and Algernon groan and walk up and down.*)

CECILY (*rather brightly*): There is just one question I would like to be allowed to ask my guardian.

GWENDOLEN: An admirable idea! Mr. Worthing, there is just one question I would like to be permitted to put to you. Where is your brother Ernest? We are both engaged to be married to your brother Ernest, so it is a matter of some importance to us to know where your brother Ernest is at present.

JACK (*slowly and hesitatingly*): Gwendolen — Cecily — it is very painful for me to be forced to speak the truth. It is the first time in my life that I have ever been reduced to such a painful position, and I am really quite inexperienced in doing anything of the kind. However I will tell you quite frankly that I have no brother Ernest. I have no brother at all. I never had a brother in my life, and I certainly have not the smallest intention of ever having one in the future.

CECILY (*surprised*): No brother at all?

JACK (*cheerily*): None!

GWENDOLEN (*severely*): Had you never a brother of any kind?

JACK (*pleasantly*): Never. Not even of any kind.

GWENDOLEN: I am afraid it is quite clear, Cecily, that neither of us is engaged to be married to anyone.

CECILY: It is not a very pleasant position for a young girl suddenly to find herself in. Is it?

GWENDOLEN: Let us go into the house. They will hardly venture to come after us there.

CECILY: No, men are so cowardly, aren't they?

(*They retire into the house with scornful looks.*)

JACK: This ghastly state of things is what you call Bunburying, I suppose?

ALGERNON: Yes, and a perfectly wonderful Bunbury it is. The most wonderful Bunbury I have ever had in my life.

JACK: Well, you've no right whatsoever to Bunbury here.

ALGERNON: That is absurd. One has a right to Bunbury anywhere one chooses. Every serious Bunburyist knows that.

JACK: Serious Bunburyist! Good heavens!

ALGERNON: Well, one must be serious about something, if one wants to have any amusement in life. I happen to be serious about Bunburying. What on earth you are serious about I haven't got the remotest idea. About everything, I should fancy. You have such an absolutely trivial nature.

JACK: Well, the only small satisfaction I have in the whole of this wretched business is that your friend Bunbury is quite exploded. You won't be able to run down to the country quite so often as you used to do, dear Algy. And a very good thing too.

ALGERNON: Your brother is a little off color, isn't he, dear Jack? You won't be able to disappear to London quite so frequently as your wicked custom was. And not a bad thing either.

JACK: As for your conduct towards Miss Cardew, I must say that your taking in a sweet, simple, innocent girl like that is quite inexcusable. To say nothing of the fact that she is my ward.

ALGERNON: I can see no possible defense at all for your deceiving a brilliant, clever, thoroughly experienced young lady like Miss Fairfax. To say nothing of the fact that she is my cousin.

JACK: I wanted to be engaged to Gwendolen, that is all. I love her.

ALGERNON: Well, I simply wanted to be engaged to Cecily. I adore her.

JACK: There is certainly no chance of your marrying Miss Cardew.

ALGERNON: I don't think there is much likelihood, Jack, of you and Miss Fairfax being united.

JACK: Well, that is no business of yours.

ALGERNON: If it was my business, I wouldn't talk about it. (*Begins to eat muffins.*) It is very vulgar to talk about one's business. Only people like stockbrokers do that, and then merely at dinner parties.

JACK: How you can sit there, calmly eating muffins when we are in this horrible trouble. I can't make out. You seem to me to be perfectly heartless.

ALGERNON: Well, I can't eat muffins in an agitated manner. The butter would probably get on my cuffs. One should always eat muffins quite calmly. It is the only way to eat them.

JACK: I say it's perfectly heartless your eating muffins at all, under the circumstances.

ALGERNON: When I am in trouble, eating is the only thing that consoles me. Indeed, when I am in really great trouble, as anyone who knows me intimately will tell you, I refuse everything except food and drink. At the present moment I am eating muffins because I am unhappy. Besides, I am particularly fond of muffins. *(Rising.)*

JACK *(rising)*: Well, that is no reason why you should eat them all in that greedy way.
(Takes muffins from Algernon.)

ALGERNON *(offering tea cake)*: I wish you would have tea cake instead. I don't like tea cake.

JACK: Good heavens! I suppose a man may eat his own muffins in his own garden.

ALGERNON: But you have just said it was perfectly heartless to eat muffins.

JACK: I said it was perfectly heartless of you, under the circumstances. That is a very different thing.

ALGERNON: That may be, but the muffins are the same.   *(He seizes the muffin dish from Jack.)*

JACK: Algy, I wish to goodness you would go.

ALGERNON: You can't possibly ask me to go without having some dinner. It's absurd. I never go without my dinner. No one ever does, except vegetarians and people like that. Besides I have just made arrangements with Dr. Chasuble to be christened at a quarter to six under the name of Ernest.

JACK: My dear fellow, the sooner you give up that nonsense the better. I made arrangements this morning with Dr. Chasuble to be christened myself at 5:30, and I naturally will take the name of Ernest. Gwendolen would wish it. We can't both be christened Ernest. It's absurd. Besides, I have a perfect right to be christened if I like. There is no evidence at all that I ever have been christened by anybody. I should think it extremely probable I never was, and so does Dr. Chasuble. It is entirely different in your case. You have been christened already.

ALGERNON: Yes, but I have not been christened for years.

JACK: Yes, but you have been christened. That is the important thing.

ALGERNON: Quite so. So I know my constitution can stand it. If you are not quite sure about your ever having been christened, I must say I think it rather dangerous your venturing on it now. It might make you very unwell. You can hardly have forgotten that someone very closely connected with you was very nearly carried off this week in Paris by a severe chill.

JACK: Yes, but you said yourself that a severe chill was not hereditary.

ALGERNON: It usen't to be, I know — but I daresay it is now. Science is always making wonderful improvements in things.

JACK *(picking up the muffin dish)*: Oh, that is nonsense; you are always talking nonsense.

ALGERNON: Jack, you are at the muffins again! I wish you wouldn't. There are only two left. *(Takes them.)* I told you I was particularly fond of muffins.

JACK: But I hate tea cake.

ALGERNON: Why on earth then do you allow tea cake to be served up for your guests? What ideas you have of hospitality!

JACK: Algernon! I have already told you to go. I don't want you here. Why don't you go!

ALGERNON: I haven't quite finished my tea yet! and there is still one muffin left.

(Jack groans, and sinks into a chair. Algernon still continues eating.)

ACT III

(Scene: Morning room at the Manor House. Gwendolen and Cecily are at the window, looking out into the garden.)

GWENDOLEN: The fact that they did not follow us at once into the house, as anyone else would have done, seems to me to show that they have some sense of shame left.

CECILY: They have been eating muffins. That looks like repentance.

GWENDOLEN *(after a pause)*: They don't seem to notice us at all. Couldn't you cough?

CECILY: But I haven't got a cough.

GWENDOLEN: They're looking at us. What effrontery!

CECILY: They're approaching. That's very forward of them.

GWENDOLEN: Let us preserve a dignified silence.

CECILY: Certainly. It's the only thing to do now.

(Enter Jack followed by Algernon. They whistle some dreadful popular air from a British opera.)

GWENDOLEN: This dignified silence seems to produce an unpleasant effect.

CECILY: A most distasteful one.

GWENDOLEN: But we will not be the first to speak.

CECILY: Certainly not.

GWENDOLEN: Mr. Worthing, I have something very particular to ask you. Much depends on your reply.

CECILY: Gwendolen, your common sense is invaluable. Mr. Moncrieff, kindly answer me the following question. Why did you pretend to be my guardian's brother?

ALGERNON: In order that I might have an opportunity of meeting you.

CECILY *(to Gwendolen)*: That certainly seems a satisfactory explanation, does it not?

GWENDOLEN: Yes, dear, if you can believe him.

CECILY: I don't. But that does not affect the wonderful beauty of his answer.

GWENDOLEN: True. In matters of grave importance,

style, not sincerity is the vital thing. Mr. Worthing, what explanation can you offer to me for pretending to have a brother? Was it in order that you might have an opportunity of coming up to town to see me as often as possible?

JACK: Can you doubt it, Miss Fairfax?

GWENDOLEN: I have the gravest doubts upon the subject. But I intend to crush them. This is not the moment for German skepticism. (*Moving to Cecily.*) Their explanations appear to be quite satisfactory, especially Mr. Worthing's. That seems to me to have the stamp of truth upon it.

CECILY: I am more than content with what Mr. Moncrieff said. His voice alone inspires one with absolute credulity.

GWENDOLEN: Then you think we should forgive them?

CECILY: Yes. I mean no.

GWENDOLEN: True! I had forgotten. There are principles at stake that one cannot surrender. Which of us should tell them? The task is not a pleasant one.

CECILY: Could we not both speak at the same time?

GWENDOLEN: An excellent idea! I nearly always speak at the same time as other people. Will you take the time from me?

CECILY: Certainly.

(*Gwendolyn beats time with uplifted finger.*)

GWENDOLEN and CECILY (*speaking together*): Your Christian names are still an insuperable barrier. That is all!

JACK and ALGERNON (*speaking together*): Our Christian names! Is that all? But we are going to be christened this afternoon.

GWENDOLEN (*to Jack*): For my sake you are prepared to do this terrible thing?

JACK: I am!

CECILY (*to Algernon*): To please me you are ready to face this fearful ordeal?

ALGERNON: I am!

GWENDOLEN: How absurd to talk of the equality of the sexes! Where questions of self-sacrifice are concerned, men are infinitely beyond us.

JACK: We are! (*Clasps hands with Algernon.*)

CECILY: They have moments of physical courage of which we women know absolutely nothing.

GWENDOLEN (*to Jack*): Darling!

ALGERNON (*to Cecily*): Darling!

(*They fall into each other's arms.*)

(*Enter Merriman. When he enters he coughs loudly, seeing the situation.*)

MERRIMAN: Ahem! Ahem! Lady Bracknell!

JACK: Good heavens!

(*Enter Lady Bracknell. The couples separate, in alarm. Exit Merriman.*)

LADY BRACKNELL: Gwendolen! What does this mean?

GWENDOLEN: Merely that I am engaged to be married to Mr. Worthing, Mama.

LADY BRACKNELL: Come here. Sit down. Sit down immediately. Hesitation of any kind is a sign of mental decay in the young, of physical weakness in the old. (*Turns to Jack.*) Apprised, sir, of my daughter's sudden flight by her trusty maid, whose confidence I purchased by means of a small coin, I followed her at once by a luggage train. Her unhappy father is, I am glad to say, under the impression that she is attending a more than usually lengthy lecture by the University Extension Scheme on the influence of a permanent income on thought. I do not propose to undeceive him. Indeed I have never undeceived him on any question. I would consider it wrong. But of course, you will clearly understand that all communication between yourself and my daughter must cease immediately from this moment. On this point, as indeed on all points, I am firm.

JACK: I am engaged to be married to Gwendolen, Lady Bracknell!

LADY BRACKNELL: You are nothing of the kind, sir. And now, as regards Algernon! — Algernon!

ALGERNON: Yes, Aunt Augusta.

LADY BRACKNELL: May I ask if it is in this house that your invalid friend Mr. Bunbury resides?

ALGERNON (*stammering*): Oh! No! Bunbury doesn't live here. Bunbury is somewhere else at present. In fact, Bunbury is dead.

LADY BRACKNELL: Dead! When did Mr. Bunbury die? His death must have been extremely sudden.

ALGERNON (*airily*): Oh! I killed Bunbury this afternoon. I mean poor Bunbury died this afternoon.

LADY BRACKNELL: What did he die of?

ALGERNON: Bunbury? Oh, he was quite exploded.

LADY BRACKNELL: Exploded! Was he the victim of a revolutionary outrage? I was not aware that Mr. Bunbury was interested in social legislation. If so, he is well punished for his morbidity.

ALGERNON: My dear Aunt Augusta, I mean he was found out! The doctors found out that Bunbury could not live, that is what I mean — so Bunbury died.

LADY BRACKNELL: He seems to have had great confidence in the opinion of his physicians. I am glad, however, that he made up his mind at the last to some definite course of action, and acted under proper medical advice. And now that we have finally got rid of this Mr. Bunbury, may I ask, Mr. Worthing, who is that young person whose hand my nephew Algernon is now holding in what seems to me a peculiarly unnecessary manner?

JACK: That lady is Miss Cecily Cardew, my ward.

(*Lady Bracknell bows coldly to Cecily.*)

ALGERNON: I am engaged to be married to Cecily, Aunt Augusta.

LADY BRACKNELL: I beg your pardon?

CECILY: Mr. Moncrieff and I are engaged to be married, Lady Bracknell.

LADY BRACKNELL (*with a shiver, crossing to the sofa and sitting down*): I do not know whether there is anything peculiarly exciting in the air of this particular part of Hertfordshire, but the number of engagements that go on seems to me considerably above the proper average that statistics have laid down for our guidance. I think some preliminary inquiry on my part would not be out of place. Mr. Worthing, is Miss Cardew at all connected with any of the larger railway stations in London? I merely desire information. Until yesterday I had no idea that there were any families or persons whose origin was a Terminus.

(*Jack looks perfectly furious, but restrains himself.*)

JACK (*in a clear, cold voice*): Miss Cardew is the granddaughter of the late Mr. Thomas Cardew of 149, Belgrave Square, S.W.; Gervase Park, Dorking, Surrey; and the Sporran, Fifeshire, N.B.

LADY BRACKNELL: That sounds not unsatisfactory. Three addresses always inspire confidence, even in tradesmen. But what proof have I of their authenticity?

JACK: I have carefully preserved the Court Guides of the period. They are open to your inspection, Lady Bracknell.

LADY BRACKNELL (*grimly*): I have known strange errors in that publication.

JACK: Miss Cardew's family solicitors are Messrs. Markby, Markby, and Markby.

LADY BRACKNELL: Markby, Markby, and Markby? A firm of the very highest position in their profession. Indeed I am told that one of the Mr. Markbys is occasionally to be seen at dinner parties. So far I am satisfied.

JACK (*very irritably*): How extremely kind of you, Lady Bracknell! I have also in my possession, you will be pleased to hear, certificates of Miss Cardew's birth, baptism, whooping cough, registration, vaccination, confirmation, and the measles; both the German and the English variety.

LADY BRACKNELL: Ah! A life crowded with incident I see; though perhaps somewhat too exciting for a young girl. I am not myself in favor of premature experiences. (*Rises, looks at her watch.*) Gwendolen! the time approaches for our departure. We have not a moment to lose. As a matter of form, Mr. Worthing, I had better ask you if Miss Cardew has any little fortune?

JACK: Oh! about a hundred and thirty thousand pounds in the Funds. That is all. Good-bye, Lady Bracknell. So pleased to have seen you.

LADY BRACKNELL (*sitting down again*): A moment, Mr. Worthing. A hundred and thirty thousand pounds! And in the Funds! Miss Cardew seems to me a most attractive young lady, now that I look at her. Few girls of the present day have any really solid qualities, any of the qualities that last, and improve with time. We live, I regret to say, in an age of surfaces. (*To Cecily.*) Come over here, dear. (*Cecily goes across.*) Pretty child! your dress is sadly simple, and your hair seems almost as Nature might have left it. But we can soon alter all that. A thoroughly experienced French maid produces a really marvelous result in a very brief space of time. I remember recommending one to young Lady Lancing, and after three months her own husband did not know her.

JACK (*aside*): And after six months nobody knew her.

LADY BRACKNELL (*glares at Jack for a few moments. Then bends, with a practiced smile, to Cecily*): Kindly turn round, sweet child. (*Cecily turns completely round.*) No, the side view is what I want. (*Cecily presents her profile.*) Yes, quite as I expected. There are distinct social possibilities in your profile. The two weak points in our age are its want of principle and its want of profile. The chin a little higher, dear. Style largely depends on the way the chin is worn. They are worn very high, just at present. Algernon!

ALGERNON: Yes, Aunt Augusta!

LADY BRACKNELL: There are distinct social possibilities in Miss Cardew's profile.

ALGERNON: Cecily is the sweetest, dearest, prettiest girl in the whole world. And I don't care twopence about social possibilities.

LADY BRACKNELL: Never speak disrespectfully of Society, Algernon. Only people who can't get into it do that. (*To Cecily.*) Dear child, of course you know that Algernon has nothing but his debts to depend upon. But I do not approve of mercenary marriages. When I married Lord Bracknell I had no fortune of any kind. But I never dreamed for a moment of allowing that to stand in my way. Well, I suppose I must give my consent.

ALGERNON: Thank you, Aunt Augusta.

LADY BRACKNELL: Cecily, you may kiss me!

CECILY (*kisses her*): Thank you, Lady Bracknell.

LADY BRACKNELL: You may also address me as Aunt Augusta for the future.

CECILY: Thank you, Aunt Augusta.

LADY BRACKNELL: The marriage, I think, had better take place quite soon.

ALGERNON: Thank you, Aunt Augusta.

CECILY: Thank you, Aunt Augusta.

LADY BRACKNELL: To speak frankly, I am not in favor of long engagements. They give people the opportunity of finding out each other's character before marriage, which I think is never advisable.

JACK: I beg your pardon for interrupting you, Lady Bracknell, but this engagement is quite out of the question. I am Miss Cardew's guardian, and she cannot marry without my consent until she comes of age. That consent I absolutely decline to give.

LADY BRACKNELL: Upon what grounds may I ask? Algernon is an extremely, I may almost say an ostentatiously, eligible young man. He has nothing, but he looks everything. What more can one desire?

JACK: It pains me very much to have to speak frankly to you, Lady Bracknell, about your nephew, but the fact is that I do not approve at all of his moral character. I suspect him of being untruthful.

(*Algernon and Cecily look at him in indignant amazement.*)

LADY BRACKNELL: Untruthful! My nephew Algernon? Impossible! He is an Oxonian.°

JACK: I fear there can be no possible doubt about the matter. This afternoon, during my temporary absence in London on an important question of romance, he obtained admission to my house by means of the false pretense of being my brother. Under an assumed name he drank, I've just been informed by my butler, an entire pint bottle of my Perrier-Jouêt, Brut, '89; a wine I was specially reserving for myself. Continuing his disgraceful deception, he succeeded in the course of the afternoon in alienating the affections of my only ward. He subsequently stayed to tea, and devoured every single muffin. And what makes his conduct all the more heartless is, that he was perfectly well aware from the first that I have no brother, that I never had a brother, and that I don't intend to have a brother, not even of any kind. I distinctly told him so myself yesterday afternoon.

LADY BRACKNELL: Ahem! Mr. Worthing, after careful consideration I have decided entirely to overlook my nephew's conduct to you.

JACK: That is very generous of you, Lady Bracknell. My own decision, however, is unalterable. I decline to give my consent.

LADY BRACKNELL (*to Cecily*): Come here, sweet child. (*Cecily goes over.*) How old are you, dear?

CECILY: Well, I am really only eighteen, but I always admit to twenty when I go to evening parties.

LADY BRACKNELL: You are perfectly right in making some slight alteration. Indeed, no woman should ever be quite accurate about her age. It looks so

calculating — (*In a meditative manner.*) Eighteen but admitting to twenty at evening parties. Well, it will not be very long before you are of age and free from the restraints of tutelage. So I don't think your guardian's consent is, after all, a matter of any importance.

JACK: Pray excuse me, Lady Bracknell, for interrupting you again, but it is only fair to tell you that according to the terms of her grandfather's will Miss Cardew does not come legally of age till she is thirty-five.

LADY BRACKNELL: That does not seem to me to be a grave objection. Thirty-five is a very attractive age. London society is full of women of the very highest birth who have, of their own free choice, remained thirty-five for years. Lady Dumbleton is an instance in point. To my own knowledge she has been thirty-five ever since she arrived at the age of forty, which was many years ago now. I see no reason why our dear Cecily should not be even still more attractive at the age you mention than she is at present. There will be a large accumulation of property.

CECILY: Algy, could you wait for me till I was thirty-five?

ALGERNON: Of course I could, Cecily. You know I could.

CECILY: Yes, I felt it instinctively, but I couldn't wait all that time. I hate waiting even five minutes for anybody. It always makes me rather cross. I am not punctual myself, I know, but I do like punctuality in others, and waiting, even to be married, is quite out of the question.

ALGERNON: Then what is to be done, Cecily?

CECILY: I don't know, Mr. Moncrieff.

LADY BRACKNELL: My dear Mr. Worthing, as Miss Cardew states positively that she cannot wait till she is thirty-five — a remark which I am bound to say seems to me to show a somewhat impatient nature — I would beg of you to reconsider your decision.

JACK: But my dear Lady Bracknell, the matter is entirely in your own hands. The moment you consent to my marriage with Gwendolen, I will most gladly allow your nephew to form an alliance with my ward.

LADY BRACKNELL (*rising and drawing herself up*): You must be quite aware that what you propose is out of the question.

JACK: Then a passionate celibacy is all that any of us can look forward to.

LADY BRACKNELL: That is not the destiny I propose for Gwendolen. Algernon, of course, can choose for himself. (*Pulls out her watch.*) Come, dear; (*Gwendolen rises*) we have already missed five, if

Oxonian: Educated at Oxford university.

not six, trains. To miss any more might expose us to comment on the platform.

(*Enter Dr. Chasuble.*)

CHASUBLE: Everything is quite ready for the christenings.

LADY BRACKNELL: The christenings, sir! Is not that somewhat premature?

CHASUBLE (*looking rather puzzled, and pointing to Jack and Algernon*): Both these gentlemen have expressed a desire for immediate baptism.

LADY BRACKNELL: At their age? The idea is grotesque and irreligious! Algernon, I forbid you to be baptized. I will not hear of such excesses. Lord Bracknell would be highly displeased if he learned that that was the way in which you wasted your time and money.

CHASUBLE: Am I to understand then that there are to be no christenings at all this afternoon?

JACK: I don't think that, as things are now, it would be of much practical value to either of us, Dr. Chasuble.

CHASUBLE: I am grieved to hear such sentiments from you, Mr. Worthing. They savor of the heretical views of the Anabaptists,° views that I have completely refuted in four of my unpublished sermons. However, as your present mood seems to be one peculiarly secular, I will return to the church at once. Indeed, I have just been informed by the pew opener that for the last hour and a half Miss Prism has been waiting for me in the vestry.

LADY BRACKNELL (*starting*): Miss Prism! Did I hear you mention a Miss Prism?

CHASUBLE: Yes, Lady Bracknell I am on my way to join her.

LADY BRACKNELL: Pray allow me to detain you for a moment. This matter may prove to be one of vital importance to Lord Bracknell and myself. Is this Miss Prism a female of repellent aspect, remotely connected with education?

CHASUBLE (*somewhat indignantly*): She is the most cultivated of ladies, and the very picture of respectability.

LADY BRACKNELL: It is obviously the same person. May I ask what position she holds in your household?

CHASUBLE (*severely*): I am a celibate, madam.

JACK (*interposing*): Miss Prism, Lady Bracknell, has been for the last three years Miss Cardew's esteemed governess and valued companion.

Anabaptists: A religious sect beginning in the sixteenth century and advocating adult baptism and church membership by adults only.

LADY BRACKNELL: In spite of what I hear of her, I must see her at once. Let her be sent for.

CHASUBLE (*looking off*): She approaches; she is nigh.

(*Enter Miss Prism hurriedly.*)

MISS PRISM: I was told you expected me in the vestry, dear Canon. I have been waiting for you there for an hour and three-quarters.

(*Catches sight of Lady Bracknell who has fixed her with a stony glare. Miss Prism grows pale and quails. She looks anxiously round as if desirous to escape.*)

LADY BRACKNELL (*in a severe, judicial voice*): Prism! (*Miss Prism bows her head in shame.*) Come here, Prism! (*Miss Prism approaches in a humble manner.*) Prism! Where is that baby? (*General consternation. The Canon starts back in horror. Algernon and Jack pretend to be anxious to shield Cecily and Gwendolen from hearing the details of a terrible public scandal.*) Twenty-eight years ago, Prism, you left Lord Bracknell's house, Number 104, Upper Grosvenor Street, in charge of a perambulator that contained a baby, of the male sex. You never returned. A few weeks later, through the elaborate investigations of the Metropolitan police, the perambulator was discovered at midnight, standing by itself in a remote corner of Bayswater. It contained the manuscript of a three-volume novel of more than usually revolting sentimentality. (*Miss Prism starts in involuntary indignation.*) But the baby was not there! (*Everyone looks at Miss Prism.*) Prism! Where is that baby?   (*A pause.*)

MISS PRISM: Lady Bracknell, I admit with shame that I do not know. I only wish I did. The plain facts of the case are these. On the morning of the day you mention, a day that is forever branded on my memory, I prepared as usual to take the baby out in its perambulator. I had also with me a somewhat old, but capacious handbag in which I had intended to place the manuscript of a work of fiction that I had written during my few unoccupied hours. In a moment of mental abstraction, for which I never can forgive myself, I deposited the manuscript in the bassinette, and placed the baby in the handbag.

JACK (*who has been listening attentively*): But where did you deposit the handbag?

MISS PRISM: Do not ask me, Mr. Worthing.

JACK: Miss Prism, this is a matter of no small importance to me. I insist on knowing where you deposited the handbag that contained that infant.

MISS PRISM: I left it in the cloakroom of one of the larger railway stations in London.

JACK: What railway station?

MISS PRISM (*quite crushed*): Victoria. The Brighton line.   (*Sinks into a chair.*)

JACK: I must retire to my room for a moment. Gwendolen, wait here for me.

GWENDOLEN: If you are not too long, I will wait here for you all my life.

(*Exit Jack in great excitement.*)

CHASUBLE: What do you think this means, Lady Bracknell?

LADY BRACKNELL: I dare not even suspect, Dr. Chasuble. I need hardly tell you that in families of high position strange coincidences are not supposed to occur. They are hardly considered the thing.

(*Noises heard overhead as if someone was throwing trunks about. Everyone looks up.*)

CECILY: Uncle Jack seems strangely agitated.

CHASUBLE: Your guardian has a very emotional nature.

LADY BRACKNELL: This noise is extremely unpleasant. It sounds as if he was having an argument. I dislike arguments of any kind. They are always vulgar, and often convincing.

CHASUBLE (*looking up*): It has stopped now.

(*The noise is redoubled.*)

LADY BRACKNELL: I wish he would arrive at some conclusion.

GWENDOLEN: This suspense is terrible. I hope it will last.

(*Enter Jack with a handbag of black leather in his hand.*)

JACK (*rushing over to Miss Prism*): Is this the handbag, Miss Prism? Examine it carefully before you speak. The happiness of more than one life depends on your answer.

MISS PRISM (*calmly*): It seems to be mine. Yes, here is the injury it received through the upsetting of a Gower Street omnibus in younger and happier days. Here is the stain on the lining caused by the explosion of a temperance beverage, an incident that occurred at Leamington. And here, on the lock, are my initials. I had forgotten that in an extravagant mood I had had them placed there. The bag is undoubtedly mine. I am delighted to have it so unexpectedly restored to me. It has been a great inconvenience being without it all these years.

JACK (*in a pathetic voice*): Miss Prism, more is restored to you than this handbag. I was the baby you placed in it.

MISS PRISM (*amazed*): You?

JACK (*embracing her*): Yes — mother!

MISS PRISM (*recoiling in indignant astonishment*): Mr. Worthing! I am unmarried!

JACK: Unmarried! I do not deny that is a serious blow. But after all, who has the right to cast a stone against one who has suffered? Cannot repentance wipe out an act of folly? Why should there be one law for men, and another for women? Mother, I forgive you. (*Tries to embrace her again.*)

MISS PRISM (*still more indignant*): Mr. Worthing, there is some error. (*Pointing to Lady Bracknell.*) There is the lady who can tell you who you really are.

JACK (*after a pause*): Lady Bracknell, I hate to seem inquisitive, but would you kindly inform me who I am?

LADY BRACKNELL: I am afraid that the news I have to give you will not altogether please you. You are the son of my poor sister, Mrs. Moncrieff, and consequently Algernon's elder brother.

JACK: Algy's elder brother! Then I have a brother after all. I knew I had a brother! I always said I had a brother! Cecily, — how could you have ever doubted that I had a brother. (*Seizes hold of Algernon.*) Dr. Chasuble, my unfortunate brother. Miss Prism, my unfortunate brother. Gwendolen, my unfortunate brother. Algy, you young scoundrel, you will have to treat me with more respect in the future. You have never behaved to me like a brother in all your life.

ALGERNON: Well, not till today, old boy, I admit. I did my best, however, though I was out of practice. (*Shakes hands.*)

GWENDOLEN (*to Jack*): My own! But what own are you? What is your Christian name, now that you have become someone else?

JACK: Good heavens! — I had quite forgotten that point. Your decision on the subject of my name is irrevocable, I suppose?

GWENDOLEN: I never change, except in my affections.

CECILY: What a noble nature you have, Gwendolen!

JACK: Then the question had better be cleared up at once. Aunt Augusta, a moment. At the time when Miss Prism left me in the handbag, had I been christened already?

LADY BRACKNELL: Every luxury that money could buy, including christening, had been lavished upon you by your fond and doting parents.

JACK: Then I was christened! That is settled. Now, what name was I given? Let me know the worst.

LADY BRACKNELL: Being the eldest son you were naturally christened after your father.

JACK (*irritably*): Yes, but what was my father's Christian name?

LADY BRACKNELL (*meditatively*): I cannot at the present moment recall what the General's Christian name was. But I have no doubt he had one. He was eccentric, I admit. But only in later years. And that was the result of the Indian climate, and marriage, and indigestion, and other things of that kind.

JACK: Algy! Can't you recollect what our father's Christian name was?

ALGERNON: My dear boy, we were never even on speaking terms. He died before I was a year old.

JACK: His name would appear in the Army Lists of the period, I suppose, Aunt Augusta?

LADY BRACKNELL: The General was essentially a man of peace, except in his domestic life. But I have no doubt his name would appear in any military directory.

JACK: The Army Lists of the last forty years are here. These delightful records should have been my constant study. (*Rushes to bookcase and tears the books out.*) M. Generals — Mallam, Maxbohm, Magley, what ghastly names they have — Markby, Migsby, Mobbs, Moncrieff! Lieutenant 1840, Captain, Lieutenant-Colonel, Colonel, General 1869, Christian names, Ernest John. (*Puts book very quietly down and speaks quite calmly.*) I always told you, Gwendolen, my name was Ernest, didn't I? Well, it is Ernest after all. I mean it naturally is Ernest.

LADY BRACKNELL: Yes, I remember now that the General was called Ernest. I knew I had some particular reason for disliking the name.

GWENDOLEN: Ernest! My own Ernest! I felt from the first that you could have no other name!

JACK: Gwendolen, it is a terrible thing for a man to find out suddenly that all his life he has been speaking nothing but the truth. Can you forgive me?

GWENDOLEN: I can. For I feel that you are sure to change.

JACK: My own one!

CHASUBLE (*to Miss Prism*): Laetitia! (*Embraces her.*)

MISS PRISM (*enthusiastically*): Frederick! At last!

ALGERNON: Cecily! (*Embraces her.*) At last!

JACK: Gwendolen! (*Embraces her.*) At last!

LADY BRACKNELL: My nephew, you seem to be displaying signs of triviality.

JACK: On the contrary, Aunt Augusta, I've now realized for the first time in my life the vital Importance of Being Earnest.

COMMENTARY

Peter Raby

AN UNPUBLISHED LETTER FROM OSCAR WILDE
ON *THE IMPORTANCE OF BEING EARNEST*   1991

Peter Raby introduces an 1894 letter from Oscar Wilde describing the plot of the play to his friend George Alexander. Wilde was under enormous financial pressure at the time and was eager to have his play produced. What we see in this letter is the human, vulnerable side of a witty, ironic comic playwright.

The full text of Oscar Wilde's first version of *The Importance of Being Earnest* has been lost for many years. Wilde sent it to George Alexander in July 1894, before leaving for a two-month holiday with his family in Worthing. He was desperate for money. Every encounter with Lord Alfred Douglas cost him more: he was overdrawn at the bank, and, so he claims in the letter, he had to bear the expenses of his mother's household as well as his own

Wilde's output during 1894 was astonishing: he completed *An Ideal Husband,* wrote the contrasting *A Florentine Tragedy* and most of *La Sainte Courtisane,* and embarked on an entirely new genre in *Earnest.* The more tumultuous and complex his private life, the more productive he became. He was in frequent correspondence with a number of producers and managers during the course of the year: with John Hare and Lewis Waller over *An Ideal Husband,* with Charles Frohman and Albert Palmer in New York in connection with a number of properties, both existing and unwritten, and with Dion Boucicault, who was producing *Lady Windermere's Fan* in Australia. Frohman, who controlled the American rights to *Lady Windermere's Fan,* was negotiating for *An Ideal Husband.* The year before, he had invited Wilde to write him a new play, perhaps a "modern 'School for Scandal' style of play"; Wilde's American agent, the "brilliant delightful" Elizabeth Marbury, wrote to Wilde in July from Paris with details of Frohman's latest offer, which included an option on his next modern comedy. Albert Palmer was also angling for a comedy "with no real serious interest".

Completed plays and royalties were no longer enough to keep Wilde's finances buoyant. He turned his gift for story-telling to advantage in the form of the scenario. Alexander, generous and approachable, and the producer of Wilde's first great theatrical success, *Lady Windermere's Fan,* had expressed an interest in the new comedy. Wilde seems to have dashed off the *Earnest* scenario more to secure a £150 advance than because he thought the play right for a romantic actor of modern and costume pieces. (In fact, having received the advance, he rapidly backpedalled, suggesting the piece was too farcical, and sending Alexander a more suitable scenario from Worthing, something "strong" and serious, which Frank Harris eventually turned into *Mr and Mrs Daventry.*)

There are many stages between the outline of *Earnest* and the script which was played at the St James's Theatre on February 14, 1895, while the Marquess of Queensberry prowled around the building, unable to gain admission, and when Wilde's world was on the point of disintegration. There are some manuscript pages in a notebook in the Clark Library, at the University of California in Los Angeles, containing notes and scraps of dialogue, for example:

> Beautiful name — Ernest, I couldn't love anybody who wasn't called Ernest —
> Oh! don't say that Gwendolen. It sounds perfectly heartless of you — why should love be dependent on the action of an irresponsible godfather. Is a man's whole fortune to depend on the font. I am told that there was a moment when my father contemplated calling me John —

Another fragment seems to encapsulate a sharply visualized image:

> Gwen: Leave the room, Mamma. This is no place for you.
> Duchess: Mr Worthing rise from this semi-recumbent posture — it is most unbefitting.

The future Lady Bracknell springs fully armed from that one phrase. Indeed, the women characters — Prism, Gwendolen, Duchess — are throughout more vividly delineated in these early phases.

From these fragments, the play grew into a four-act version, with a brace of butlers named after Wilde's publishers, a gardener, and an ominous solicitor. There followed a collection of names with geographical or personal associations: Lancing, Shoreham, Bracknell, Blaxam, Bunbury, Maxbohm, Cardew. (Cicely Cardew, daughter of friends of Wilde, was born in 1893; her uncle was a director of the London and South East Railway, and the Cardew engine hauled the evening boat-train to Newhaven.) By Christmas, the new play had been promised to Charles Wyndham. When Alexander found he had a failure on his hands in Henry James's *Guy Domville,* Wyndham agreed to concede his rights in *Earnest,* provided Wilde wrote him an original play before completing yet another for Alexander. Alexander persuaded Wilde to compress *Earnest* into three acts (which was the form of the original scenario he had been shown). Wilde resisted for a little, but trusted Alexander's judgment; the play, he told Ada Leverson, "must go like a pistol shot". Wilde wanted to attend rehearsals, as he had for his previous London openings, but Douglas, "so beautiful is his nature," declined. Instead, Wilde accompanied Douglas on a final Bunbury to Algeria, returning alone for the final rehearsals of this play.

The following letter was described in Sotheby's Sale Catalogue for July 1933, under item 608, one of a number of Wilde's letters to her husband sold by Lady Alexander. The catalogue provided a synopsis, and reproduced one section. The text is taken from papers at the Clark Library. These are typewritten copies of letters from Wilde to Alexander, marked for inclusion in A.E.W. Mason' s study, *Sir George Alexander and the St James's Theatre,* which was published in 1935. Mason wrote to Vyvyan Holland's solicitors, asking for permission to print excerpts, and bracketing those passages he wished to include: these papers are, most probably, Mason's originals. Mason printed only brief extracts from the opening and the last two paragraphs, and his book is the source for the extract printed in Sir Rupen Hart-Davis's edition of Wilde's *Letters.* So far as I am aware, the full letter has not been published before. It is reproduced here by permission of Mr Merlin Holland and the Clark Library (the letter is © Merlin Holland):

16, Tite Street,
S.W.

My dear Aleck,

Thanks for your letter. There really is nothing more to tell you about the comedy beyond what I said already. I mean that the real charm of the play, if it is to have charm, must be in the dialogue. The plot is slight, but, I think, adequate.

Act I. Evening party. 10 p.m.

Lord Alfred Rufford's rooms in Mayfair. Arrives from country Bertram Ashton his friend: a man of 25 or 30 years of age: his great friend.

Rufford asks him about his life. He tells him that he has a ward, etc. very young and pretty. That in the country he has to be serious, etc. that he comes to town to enjoy himself, and has invented a fictitious younger brother of the name of George — to whom all his misdeeds are put down. Rufford is deeply interested about the ward.

Guests arrive: the Duchess of Selby and her daughter, Lady Maud Rufford, with whom the guardian is in love — fin-de-siècle talk, a lot of guests — the guardian proposes to Lady Maud on his knees — enter Duchess —

Lady Maud. "Mamma, this is no place for you."

Scene: Duchess enquires for *her son Lord Alfred Rufford*: servant comes in with note to say that Lord Alfred has been suddenly called away to the country. Lady Maud vows eternal fidelity to the guardian whom she only knows under the name of *George* Ashton.

(P.S. The disclosure of the guardian of his double life is occasioned by Lord Alfred saying to him "You left your handkerchief here the last time you were up" (or cigarette case). The guardian takes it — the Lord A. says but "why, dear George, is it marked Bertram — who is Bertram Ashton?" Guardian discloses plot.)

Act II

The guardian's home — pretty cottage. Mabel Harbord, his ward, and her governess, Miss Prism, Governess of course dragon of propriety. Talk about the profligate George: maid comes in to say "Mr. George Ashton". — governess protests against his admission. Mabel insists. Enter Lord Alfred. Falls in love with ward at once. He is reproached with his bad life, etc. Expressed great repentance. They go to garden.

Enter guardian: Mabel comes in: "I have a great surprise for you — your brother is here" — Guardian, of course, denies having a brother. Mabel says "You cannot disown your own brother, whatever he has done." — and brings in Lord Alfred. Scene: also scene between two men alone. Finally Lord Alfred arrested for debt contracted by guardian: guardian delighted. Mabel, however, makes him forgive his brother and pay up. Guardian looks over bills and scolds Lord Alfred for profligacy.

Miss Prism backs the guardian up. Guardian then orders his brother out of the house. Mabel intercedes, and brother remains. Miss Prism has designs on the guardian — matrimonial — she is 40 at least — she believes he is proposing to her and accepts him — his consternation.

Act III. Mabel and the false brother. He proposes, and is accepted.

When Mabel is alone, Lady Maud, who only knows the guardian under the name of George, arrives alone. She tells Mabel she is engaged to George — scene naturally. Mabel retires: enter George, he kisses his sister naturally. Enter Mabel and sees them. Explanations, of course. Mabel breaks off the match on the ground that there is nothing to reform in George: she only consented to marry him because she thought he was bad and wanted guidance — He promises to be a bad husband — so as to give her an opportunity of making him a better man; she is a little mollified.

Enter guardian: he is reproached also by Lady Maud for his respectable life in the country: a J.P.: a county-councillor: a churchwarden: a philanthropist: a good example. He appeals to his life in London: she is mollified, on condition that he never lives in the country: the country is demoralising: it makes you respectable. "The simple fare at the Savoy: the quiet life in Piccadilly: the solitude of Mayfair is what you need, etc."

Enter Duchess in pursuit of her daughter — objects to both matches. Miss Prism, who had in early days been governess to the Duchess, sets it all right, without intending to do so — everything ends happily.

Result   Curtain

Author called.

Cigarette called.

Manager called.

Royalties for a year for author.

Manager credited with writing the play. He consoles himself for the slander with bag of red gold.

Fireworks

Of course this scenario is open to alterations: the third act, after entrance of Duchess, will have to be elaborated: also, the local doctor, or clergyman, must be brought in, in the play, for Prism.

Well, I think an amusing thing with lots of fun and wit might be made. If you think so, too, and care to have the refusal of it — do let me know — and send me £150. If, when the play is finished, you think it too slight — not serious enough — of course you have the £150 back — I want to go away and write it — and it could be ready in October — as I have nothing else to do — and Palmer is anxious to have a play from me for the States "with no real serious interest" — just a comedy.

In the meanwhile, my dear Aleck, I am so pressed for money, that I don't know what to do. Of course I am extravagant, but a great deal of my worries comes from the fact that I have had for three years to keep up two establishments — my dear Mother's as well as my own — like many Irish ladies she never gets her jointure° paid — small though it is — and naturally it falls on me — this is of course *quite private* but for these years I have had two houses on my shoulders — and of course, am extravagant besides — you have always been a good wise friend to me — so think what you can do.

Kind regards to Mrs. Aleck.

Ever,

OSCAR

---

jointure: A widow's portion of her husband's estate.

Anton Chekhov

Anton Chekhov (1860–1904) spent most of his childhood in relative poverty. His family managed to set up its household in Moscow after years spent in remote Taganrog, six hundred miles to the south. He studied medicine in Moscow and eventually took his degree. Though he practiced medicine most of his life, he said that if medicine was his wife, literature was his mistress. His earliest literary efforts were for the purpose of relieving his family's poverty, but it was not long before he earned more from writing than from medicine. By 1896 he had written more than three hundred short stories, most of them published in newspapers. Many of them are classics.

His first theatrical works, apart from his short farces, were not successful. *Ivanov* (1887–1889), rushed to production, was a failure, but its revised 1889 version, reflecting much of his personal life, was successful. *The Wood Demon* (1889), also a failure, helped Chekhov eventually produce his great plays: *The Seagull* (1896); *Uncle Vanya* (1897); *Three Sisters* (1901); and his last, *The Cherry Orchard* (1903). These plays essentially reshaped modern drama, creating a style that critic Richard Peace describes as a "subtle blend of naturalism and symbolism."

The Seagull attracted the attention of the Moscow Art Theatre. The play was not a success in its production in 1896, but two years later it became one of the theater's triumphs. Konstantin Stanislavsky, the great Russian director and actor, played Trigorin, the lead character, but Chekhov felt that he was overacting. They often had disagreements about the playwright's work, but the Moscow Art Theatre supported Chekhov fully.

The surfaces of Chekhov's plays are so lifelike that at times one feels his dramatic purposes are submerged, and to an extent that is true. Chekhov is the master of the SUBTEXT, a technique in which the surface of the dialogue seems innocuous or meandering, but deeper meanings are implied. Madame Ranevskaya's musings about her childhood in act I of *The Cherry Orchard* contrast with the purposeful dialogue of Lopakhin. Her long speeches in act III talking about the "millstone" she loves in Paris are also meanderings, but they reveal an idealistic character doomed to suffer at the hands of a new generation of realists who have no time for her ramblings and sentimentalism.

Because Chekhov's subtexts are always present, to read his work requires close attention. One must constantly probe, analyze, ask what is implied by what is being said. Chekhov resists "explaining" his plays by having key characters give key thematic speeches. Instead, the meaning builds slowly. Our understanding of what a situation or circumstance finally means will change as we read and as we gather more understanding of the subtleties veiled by surfaces.

Chekhov's style is remarkable for its clarity; its surface is direct, simple, and effective. Even his short stories have a clear dramatic center, and the characters he chose to observe are exceptionally modern in that they are not heroes, not villains. The dramatic concept of a larger-than-life Oedipus or of *Hamlet*'s devilish Claudius is nowhere to be seen in his work. Chekhov's characters are limited, recognizable, and in many ways completely ordinary.

Chekhov's genius was in showing such characters' ambitions, pain, and successes. He was quite aware of important social changes taking place in Russia; the old aristocratic classes, who once owned serfs, were being reduced to a genteel impoverishment, while the children of former slaves were beginning to succeed in business and real estate ventures. Since Chekhov's grandfather had been a serf who bought his freedom in 1841, it is likely that Chekhov was especially supportive of such social change; we see evidence of that in his best plays.

THE CHERRY ORCHARD

The Cherry Orchard (1903), premiered on Chekhov's birthday, January 17, in 1904. The Moscow Art Theatre performance was directed by Konstantin Stanislavsky, an actor-director who pioneered a new method of realistic acting. (Stanislavsky is still read and admired the world over. His techniques were modified in the United States and form the basis of METHOD ACTING.) For the subtle effects that Chekhov wanted, however, he found Stanislavsky too stagey, flamboyant, and melodramatic. They argued hotly over what should happen in his plays, and often Stanislavsky prevailed.

One argument was over whether *The Cherry Orchard* was a tragedy. Chekhov steadfastly called it a comedy, but Stanislavsky saw the ruin of Madame Ranevskaya and the destruction of the cherry orchard as tragic. Chekhov perhaps saw it the same way, but he also considered its potential as the beginning of a new, more realistic life for Madame Ranevskaya and her brother Gayev. Their impracticality was an important cause of their having lost their wealth and estate.

How audiences interpret Lopakhin depends on how they view the ambition of the new class of businessmen whose zeal, work, and cleverness earn them the estates that previously they could have hoped only to work on. Social change is fueled by money, which replaces an inherited aristocracy with ambitious moneymakers who earn the power to force changes on the old, less flexible aristocrats. In Russia massive social change was eventually effected by revolution and the institution of communism. But *The Cherry Orchard* shows that change would have come to Russia in any event.

Perhaps Chekhov's peasant blood helped him see the play as more of a comedy than a tragedy, even though he portrays the characters with greater complexity than we might expect in comedy. Lopakhin is not a simple, unsympathetic character; Trofimov is not a simple dreamer. We need to look closely at what they do and why they do it. For example, when thinking about preserving the beauties of the cherry orchard, Trofimov reminds people that all of Russia is an orchard, that the world is filled with beautiful places. Such a view makes it difficult for him to feel nostalgia for aristocratic privilege.

Trofimov sounds a striking note about the practice of slavery in Russia. He tells Madame Ranevskaya and Gayev that they are living on credit, that they must repay debts to the Russian people. The cherry orchard is beautiful because each tree represents the soul of a serf. The beautiful class of people to which the impractical Madame Ranevskaya belongs owes its beauty and grace to the institution of slavery, and soon the note will be presented for payment. The sound of the breaking string in act I, repeated at the end of the play, is Chekhov's way of symbolizing the losses and changes represented in the play.

Madame Ranevskaya, however, cannot change. Her habits of mind are fully formed before the play begins; nothing that Lopakhin can say will help change her. Even though she knows she is dangerously in debt, she gives a gold coin to a beggar. *Noblesse oblige* — the duty of the upper class to help the poor — is still part of her ethos, even if it also involves her own ruin.

A sense of tragedy is apparent in Madame Ranevskaya's feelings and her helplessness. She seems incapable of transforming herself, no matter how much she may wish to change. We see her as a victim of fate, a fate that is formed by her expectations and training. But the play also contains comic and nonsensical moments, as, for example, in the byplay of Varya, Yasha, and Yepikhodov over a game of billiards in act III. In his letters Chekhov mentions that the play is happy and frivolous, "in places even a farce."

The Cherry Orchard in Performance

Since its first production in 1904, *The Cherry Orchard* has played to responsive audiences in Europe and abroad. It was produced in London in 1911, Berlin in 1919, and New York in 1923 (in Russian). Eva Le Gallienne produced it in New York in her English version in 1928. In 1968 she directed the play with Uta Hagen as Madame Ranevskaya. Tyrone Guthrie directed it at the Old Vic in 1933 and again in 1941. John Gielgud, Peggy Ashcroft, Judy Dench, and Dorothy Tutin performed in a powerful and well-reviewed version in London in 1961. When an all-black *Cherry Orchard* was produced by Joseph Papp in 1973, James Earl Jones was praised as a powerful Lopakhin.

Andrei Serban's 1977 production for Joseph Papp at Lincoln Center in New York was praised for its extraordinary stage effects. According to the reviewer at *Time* magazine,

> Serban's best images effectively magnify the play's conflict between the old order and the bright new world that is its doom: a frieze of peasants laboring beneath modern telegraph wires, a group of aristocrats watching the setting sun silhouette a factory on the horizon.

The American playwright Jean Claude van Italie has revised the text for contemporary audiences. His version, produced at the John Drew Theater of Guild Hall in East Hampton in July 1985, was directed by Elinor Renfield. Amanda Plummer played Anya and Joanna Merlin played Madame Ranevskaya. Peter Brook's 1987 New York production, with Brian Dennehy as a notable Lopakhin, had little scenery beyond a great number of Oriental rugs. It was played without intermissions at breakneck speed. *New York Times* critic Frank Rich said of it, "On this director's magic carpets, *The Cherry Orchard* flies."

Anton Chekhov (1860–1904)

THE CHERRY ORCHARD   *1903*

TRANSLATED BY ANN DUNNIGAN

Characters

RANEVSKAYA, LYUBOV ANDREYEVNA, *a landowner*
ANYA, *her daughter, seventeen years old*
VARYA, *her adopted daughter, twenty-four years old*
GAYEV, LEONID ANDREYEVICH, *Madame Ranevskaya's brother*
LOPAKHIN, YERMOLAI ALEKSEYEVICH, *a merchant*
TROFIMOV, PYOTR SERGEYEVICH, *a student*
SEMYONOV-PISHCHIK, BORIS BORISOVICH, *a landowner*
CHARLOTTA IVANOVNA, *a governess*
YEPIKHODOV, SEMYON PANTELEYEVICH, *a clerk*
DUNYASHA, *a maid*
FIRS, *an old valet, eighty-seven years old*
YASHA, *a young footman*
A STRANGER
THE STATIONMASTER
A POST OFFICE CLERK
GUESTS, SERVANTS

The action takes place on Madame Ranevskaya's estate.

ACT I

(*A room that is still called the nursery. One of the doors leads into Anya's room. Dawn; the sun will soon rise. It is May, the cherry trees are in bloom, but it is cold in the orchard; there is a morning frost. The windows in the room are closed. Enter Dunyasha with a candle, and Lopakhin with a book in his hand.*)

LOPAKHIN: The train is in, thank God. What time is it?
DUNYASHA: Nearly two. (*Blows out the candle.*) It's already light.
LOPAKHIN: How late is the train, anyway? A couple of hours at least. (*Yawns and stretches.*) I'm a fine one! What a fool I've made of myself! Came here on purpose to meet them at the station, and then overslept.... Fell asleep in the chair. It's annoying.... You might have waked me.
DUNYASHA: I thought you had gone. (*Listens.*) They're coming now, I think!

LOPAKHIN (*listens*): No... they've got to get the luggage and one thing and another. (*Pause.*) Lyubov Andreyevna has lived abroad for five years, I don't know what she's like now.... She's a fine person. Sweet-tempered, simple. I remember when I was a boy of fifteen, my late father — he had a shop in the village then — gave me a punch in the face and made my nose bleed.... We had come into the yard here for some reason or other, and he'd had a drop too much. Lyubov Andreyevna — I remember as if it were yesterday — still young, and so slender, led me to the washstand in this very room, the nursery. "Don't cry, little peasant," she said, "it will heal in time for your wedding...." (*Pause.*) Little peasant... my father was a peasant, it's true, and here I am in a white waistcoat and tan shoes. Like a pig in a pastry shop.... I may be rich, I've made a lot of money, but if you think about it, analyze it, I'm a peasant through and through. (*Turning pages of the book.*) Here I've been reading this book, and I didn't understand a thing. Fell asleep over it. (*Pause.*)
DUNYASHA: The dogs didn't sleep all night: They can tell that their masters are coming.
LOPAKHIN: What's the matter with you, Dunyasha, you're so...
DUNYASHA: My hands are trembling. I'm going to faint.
LOPAKHIN: You're much too delicate, Dunyasha. You dress like a lady, and do your hair like one, too. It's not right. You should know your place.

(*Enter Yepikhodov with a bouquet, he wears a jacket and highly polished boots that squeak loudly. He drops the flowers as he comes in.*)

YEPIKHODOV (*picking up the flowers*): Here, the gardener sent these. He says you're to put them in the dining room. (*Hands the bouquet to Dunyasha.*)
LOPAKHIN: And bring me some kvas.°
DUNYASHA: Yes, sir. (*Goes out.*)
YEPIKHODOV: There's a frost this morning — three degrees — and the cherry trees are in bloom. I cannot approve of our climate. (*Sighs.*) I cannot. Our cli-

---

kvas: A Russian beer.

mate is not exactly conducive. And now, Yermolai Alekseyevich, permit me to append: The day before yesterday I bought myself a pair of boots, which, I venture to assure you, squeak so that it's quite infeasible. What should I grease them with?

LOPAKHIN: Leave me alone. You make me tired.

YEPIKHODOV: Every day some misfortune happens to me. But I don't complain, I'm used to it, I even smile.

(*Dunyasha enters, serves Lopakhin the kvas.*)

YEPIKHODOV: I'm going. (*Stumbles over a chair and upsets it.*) There! (*As if in triumph.*) Now you see, excuse the expression . . . the sort of circumstance, incidentally. . . . It's really quite remarkable! (*Goes out.*)

DUNYASHA: You know, Yermolai Alekseyich, I have to confess that Yepikhodov has proposed to me.

LOPAKHIN: Ah!

DUNYASHA: And I simply don't know. . . . He's a quiet man, but sometimes, when he starts talking, you can't understand a thing he says. It's nice, and full of feeling, only it doesn't make sense. I sort of like him. He's madly in love with me. But he's an unlucky fellow: Every day something happens to him. They tease him about it around here; they call him Two-and-twenty Troubles.

LOPAKHIN (*listening*): I think I hear them coming . . .

DUNYASHA: They're coming! What's the matter with me? I'm cold all over.

LOPAKHIN: They're really coming. Let's go and meet them. Will she recognize me? It's five years since we've seen each other.

DUNYASHA (*agitated*): I'll faint this very minute . . . oh, I'm going to faint!

(*Two carriages are heard driving up to the house. Lopakhin and Dunyasha go out quickly. The stage is empty. There is a hubbub in the adjoining rooms. Firs hurriedly crosses the stage leaning on a stick. He has been to meet Lyubov Andreyevna and wears old fashioned livery and a high hat. He mutters something to himself, not a word of which can be understood. The noise offstage grows louder and louder. A voice: "Let's go through here. . . ." Enter Lyubov Andreyevna, Anya, Charlotta Ivanovna with a little dog on a chain, all in traveling dress; Varya wearing a coat and kerchief; Gayev, Semyonov-Pishchik, Lopakhin, Dunyasha with a bundle and parasol; servants with luggage — all walk through the room.*)

ANYA: Let's go this way. Do you remember, Mama, what room this is?

LYUBOV ANDREYEVNA: (*joyfully, through tears*): The nursery!

VARYA: How cold it is! My hands are numb. (*To Lyubov Andreyevna.*) Your rooms, both the white one and the violet one, are just as you left them, Mama.

LYUBOV ANDREYEVNA: The nursery . . . my dear, lovely nursery. . . . I used to sleep here when I was little. . . . (*Weeps.*) And now, like a child, I . . . (*Kisses her brother, Varya, then her brother again.*) Varya hasn't changed; she still looks like a nun. And I recognized Dunyasha. . . . (*Kisses Dunyasha.*)

GAYEV: The train was two hours late. How's that? What kind of management is that?

CHARLOTTA (*to Pishchik*): My dog even eats nuts.

PISHCHIK (*amazed*): Think of that now!

(*They all go out except Anya and Dunyasha.*)

DUNYASHA: We've been waiting and waiting for you. . . . (*Takes off Anya's coat and hat.*)

ANYA: I didn't sleep for four nights on the road . . . now I feel cold.

DUNYASHA: It was Lent when you went away, there was snow and frost then, but now? My darling! (*Laughs and kisses her.*) I've waited so long for you, my joy, my precious . . . I must tell you at once, I can't wait another minute. . . .

ANYA (*listlessly*): What now?

DUNYASHA: The clerk, Yepikhodov, proposed to me just after Easter.

ANYA: You always talk about the same thing. . . . (*Straightening her hair.*) I've lost all my hairpins. . . . (*She is so exhausted she can hardly stand.*)

DUNYASHA: I really don't know what to think. He loves me — he loves me so!

ANYA (*looking through the door into her room, tenderly*): My room, my windows . . . it's just as though I'd never been away. I am home! Tomorrow morning I'll get up and run into the orchard. . . . Oh, if I could only sleep! I didn't sleep during the entire journey, I was so tormented by anxiety.

DUNYASHA: Pyotr Sergeich arrived the day before yesterday.

ANYA (*joyfully*): Petya!

DUNYASHA: He's asleep in the bathhouse, he's staying there. "I'm afraid of being in the way," he said. (*Looks at her pocket watch.*) I ought to wake him up, but Varvara Mikhailovna told me not to. "Don't you wake him," she said.

(*Enter Varya with a bunch of keys at her waist.*)

VARYA: Dunyasha, coffee, quickly . . . Mama's asking for coffee.

DUNYASHA: This very minute. (*Goes out.*)

VARYA: Thank God, you've come! You're home again.

(*Caressing her.*) My little darling has come back! My pretty one is here!

ANYA: I've been through so much.

VARYA: I can imagine!

ANYA: I left in Holy Week, it was cold then. Charlotta never stopped talking and doing her conjuring tricks the entire journey. Why did you saddle me with Charlotta?

VARYA: You couldn't have traveled alone, darling. At seventeen!

ANYA: When we arrived in Paris, it was cold, snowing. My French is awful. . . . Mama was living on the fifth floor, and when I got there, she had all sorts of Frenchmen and ladies with her, and an old priest with a little book, and it was full of smoke, dismal. Suddenly I felt sorry for Mama, so sorry. I took her head in my arms and held her close and couldn't let her go. Afterward she kept hugging me and crying. . . .

VARYA (*through her tears*): Don't talk about it, don't talk about it. . . .

ANYA: She had already sold her villa near Mentone, and she had nothing left, nothing. And I hadn't so much as a kopeck left, we barely managed to get there. But Mama doesn't understand! When we had dinner in a station restaurant, she always ordered the most expensive dishes and tipped each of the waiters a ruble. Charlotta is the same. And Yasha also ordered a dinner, it was simply awful. You know, Yasha is Mama's footman; we brought him with us.

VARYA: I saw the rogue.

ANYA: Well, how are things? Have you paid the interest?

VARYA: How could we?

ANYA: Oh, my God, my God!

VARYA: In August the estate will be put up for sale.

ANYA: My God!

(*Lopakhin peeps in at the door and moos like a cow.*)

LOPAKHIN: Moo-o-o! (*Disappears.*)

VARYA (*through her tears*): What I couldn't do to him! (*Shakes her fist.*)

ANYA (*embracing Varya, softly*): Varya, has he proposed to you? (*Varya shakes her head.*) But he loves you. . . . Why don't you come to an understanding, what are you waiting for?

VARYA: I don't think anything will ever come of it. He's too busy, he has no time for me . . . he doesn't even notice me. I've washed my hands of him, it makes me miserable to see him. . . . Everyone talks of our wedding, they all congratulate me, and actually there's nothing to it — it's all like a dream. . . . (*In a different tone.*) You have a brooch like a bee.

ANYA (*sadly*): Mama bought it. (*Goes into her own room; speaks gaily, like a child.*) In Paris I went up in a balloon!

VARYA: My darling is home! My pretty one has come back!

(*Dunyasha has come in with the coffeepot and prepares coffee.*)

VARYA (*stands at the door of Anya's room*): You know, darling, all day long I'm busy looking after the house, but I keep dreaming. If we could marry you to a rich man I'd be at peace. I could go into a hermitage, then to Kiev, to Moscow, and from one holy place to another. . . . I'd go on and on. What a blessing!

ANYA: The birds are singing in the orchard. What time is it?

VARYA: It must be after two. Time you were asleep, darling. (*Goes into Anya's room.*) What a blessing!

(*Yasha enters with a lap robe and a traveling bag.*)

YASHA (*crosses the stage mincingly*): May one go through here?

DUNYASHA: A person would hardly recognize you, Yasha. Your stay abroad has done wonders for you.

YASHA: Hm. . . . And who are you?

DUNYASHA: When you left here I was only that high — (*indicating with her hand*). I'm Dunyasha, Fyodor Kozoyedov's daughter. You don't remember?

YASHA: Hm. . . . A little cucumber! (*Looks around, then embraces her; she cries out and drops a saucer. He quickly goes out.*)

VARYA (*in a tone of annoyance, from the doorway*): What's going on here?

DUNYASHA (*tearfully*): I broke a saucer.

VARYA: That's good luck.

ANYA: We ought to prepare Mama: Petya is here. . . .

VARYA: I gave orders not to wake him.

ANYA (*pensively*): Six years ago Father died, and a month later brother Grisha drowned in the river . . . a pretty little seven-year-old boy. Mama couldn't bear it and went away . . . went without looking back. . . . (*Shudders.*) How I understand her, if she only knew! (*Pause.*) And Petya Trofimov was Grisha's tutor, he may remind her. . . .

(*Enter Firs wearing a jacket and a white waistcoat.*)

FIRS (*goes to the coffeepot, anxiously*): The mistress will have her coffee here. (*Puts on white gloves.*) Is the coffee ready? (*To Dunyasha, sternly.*) You! Where's the cream?

DUNYASHA: Oh, my goodness! (*Quickly goes out.*)

FIRS (*fussing over the coffeepot*): Ah, what an addlepate! (*Mutters to himself.*) They've come back from Paris. . . . The master used to go to Paris . . . by carriage. . . . (*Laughs.*)

VARYA: What is it, Firs?

FIRS: If you please? (*Joyfully.*) My mistress has come home! At last! Now I can die. . . . (*Weeps with joy.*)

(*Enter Lyubov Andreyevna, Gayev, and Semyonov-Pishchik, the last wearing a sleeveless peasant coat of fine cloth and full trousers. Gayev, as he comes in, goes through the motions of playing billiards.*)

LYUBOV ANDREYEVNA: How does it go? Let's see if I can remember . . . cue ball into the corner! Double the rail to center table.

GAYEV: Cut shot into the corner! There was a time, sister, when you and I used to sleep here in this very room, and now I'm fifty-one, strange as it may seem. . . .

LOPAKHIN: Yes, time passes.

GAYEV: How's that?

LOPAKHIN: Time, I say, passes.

GAYEV: It smells of patchouli here.

ANYA: I'm going to bed. Good night, Mama. (*Kisses her mother.*)

LYUBOV ANDREYEVNA: My precious child. (*Kisses her hands.*) Are you glad to be home? I still feel dazed.

ANYA: Good night, Uncle.

GAYEV (*kisses her face and hands*): God bless you. How like your mother you are! (*To his sister.*) At her age you were exactly like her, Lyuba.

(*Anya shakes hands with Lopakhin and Pishchik and goes out, closing the door after her.*)

LYUBOV ANDREYEVNA: She's exhausted.

PISHCHIK: Must have been a long journey.

VARYA: Well, gentlemen? It's after two, high time you were going.

LYUBOV ANDREYEVNA (*laughs*): You haven't changed, Varya. (*Draws Varya to her and kisses her.*) I'll just drink my coffee and then we'll all go. (*Firs places a cushion under her feet.*) Thank you, my dear. I've got used to coffee. I drink it day and night. Thanks, dear old man. (*Kisses him.*)

VARYA: I'd better see if all the luggage has been brought in.

LYUBOV ANDREYEVNA: Is this really me sitting here? (*Laughs.*) I feel like jumping about and waving my arms. (*Buries her face in her hands.*) What if it's only a dream! God knows I love my country, love it dearly. I couldn't look out the train window, I was crying so! (*Through tears.*) But I must drink my coffee. Thank you, Firs, thank you, my dear old friend. I'm so glad you're still alive.

FIRS: The day before yesterday.

GAYEV: He's hard of hearing.

LOPAKHIN: I must go now, I'm leaving for Kharkov

about five o'clock. It's so annoying! I wanted to have a good look at you, and have a talk. You're as splendid as ever.

PISHCHIK (*breathing heavily*): Even more beautiful. . . . Dressed like a Parisienne. . . . There goes my wagon, all four wheels!

LOPAKHIN: Your brother here, Leonid Andreich, says I'm a boor, a moneygrubber, but I don't mind. Let him talk. All I want is that you should trust me as you used to, and that your wonderful, touching eyes should look at me as they did then. Merciful God! My father was one of your father's serfs, and your grandfather's, but you yourself did so much for me once, that I've forgotten all that and love you as if you were my own kin — more than my kin.

LYUBOV ANDREYEVNA: I can't sit still, I simply cannot. (*Jumps up and walks about the room in great excitement.*) I cannot bear this joy. . . . Laugh at me, I'm silly. . . . My dear little bookcase . . . (*kisses bookcase*) my little table . . .

GAYEV: Nurse died while you were away.

LYUBOV ANDREYEVNA (*sits down and drinks coffee*): Yes, God rest her soul. They wrote me.

GAYEV: And Anastasy is dead. Petrushka Kosoi left me and is now with the police inspector in town. (*Takes a box of hard candies from his pocket and begins to suck one.*)

PISHCHIK: My daughter, Dashenka . . . sends her regards . . .

LOPAKHIN: I wish I could tell you something very pleasant and cheering. (*Glances at his watch.*) I must go directly, there's no time to talk, but . . . well, I'll say it in a couple of words. As you know, the cherry orchard is to be sold to pay your debts. The auction is set for August twenty-second, but you need not worry, my dear, you can sleep in peace, there is a way out. This is my plan. Now, please listen! Your estate is only twenty versts° from town, the railway runs close by, and if the cherry orchard and the land along the river were cut up into lots and leased for summer cottages, you'd have, at the very least, an income of twenty-five thousand a year.

GAYEV: Excuse me, what nonsense!

LYUBOV ANDREYEVNA: I don't quite understand you, Yermolai Alekseich.

LOPAKHIN: You will get, at the very least, twenty-five rubles a year for a two-and-a-half-acre lot, and if you advertise now, I guarantee you won't have a single plot of ground left by autumn, everything will be snapped up. In short, I congratulate you,

---

versts: A verst is approximately equal to a kilometer, a little more than half a mile.

you are saved. The site is splendid, the river is deep. Only, of course, the ground must be cleared . . . you must tear down all the old out-buildings, for instance, and this house, which is worthless, cut down the old cherry orchard —

LYUBOV ANDREYEVNA: Cut it down? Forgive me, my dear, but you don't know what you are talking about. If there is one thing in the whole province that is interesting, not to say remarkable, it's our cherry orchard.

LOPAKHIN: The only remarkable thing about this orchard is that it is very big. There's a crop of cherries every other year, and then you can't get rid of them, nobody buys them.

GAYEV: This orchard is even mentioned in the *Encyclopedia*.

LOPAKHIN (*glancing at his watch*): If we don't think of something and come to a decision, on the twenty-second of August the cherry orchard, and the entire estate, will be sold at auction. Make up your minds! There is no other way out, I swear to you. None whatsoever.

FIRS: In the old days, forty or fifty years ago, the cherries were dried, soaked, marinated, and made into jam, and they used to —

GAYEV: Be quiet, Firs.

FIRS: And they used to send cartloads of dried cherries to Moscow and Kharkov. And that brought in money! The dried cherries were soft and juicy in those days, sweet, fragrant. . . . They had a method then . . .

LYUBOV ANDREYEVNA: And what has become of that method now?

FIRS: Forgotten. Nobody remembers. . . .

PISHCHIK: How was it in Paris? What's it like there? Did you eat frogs?

LYUBOV ANDREYEVNA: I ate crocodiles.

PISHCHIK: Think of that now!

LOPAKHIN: There used to be only the gentry and the peasants living in the country, but now these summer people have appeared. All the towns, even the smallest ones, are surrounded by summer cottages. And it is safe to say that in another twenty years these people will multiply enormously. Now the summer resident only drinks tea on his porch, but it may well be that he'll take to cultivating his acre and then your cherry orchard will be a happy, rich, luxuriant —

GAYEV (*indignantly*): What nonsense!

(*Enter Varya and Yasha.*)

VARYA: There are two telegrams for you, Mama. (*Picks out a key and with a jingling sound opens an old-fashioned bookcase.*) Here they are.

LYUBOV ANDREYEVNA: From Paris. (*Tears up the telegrams without reading them.*) That's all over. . . .

GAYEV: Do you know, Lyuba, how old this bookcase is? A week ago I pulled out the bottom drawer, and what do I see? Some figures burnt into it. The bookcase was made exactly a hundred years ago. What do you think of that? Eh? We could have celebrated its jubilee. It's an inanimate object, but nevertheless, for all that, it's a bookcase.

PISHCHIK: A hundred years . . . think of that now!

GAYEV: Yes . . . that is something. . . . (*Feeling the bookcase.*) Dear, honored bookcase. I salute thy existence, which for over one hundred years has served the glorious ideals of goodness and justice; thy silent appeal to fruitful endeavor, unflagging in the course of a hundred years, tearfully sustaining through generations of our family, courage and faith in a better future, and fostering in us ideals of goodness and social consciousness. . . .

(*A pause.*)

LOPAKHIN: Yes . . .

LYUBOV ANDREYEVNA: You are the same as ever, Lyonya.

GAYEV (*somewhat embarrassed*): Carom into the corner, cut shot to center table.

LOPAKHIN (*looks at his watch*): Well, time for me to go.

YASHA (*hands medicine to Lyubov Andreyevna*): Perhaps you will take your pills now.

PISHCHIK: Don't take medicaments, dearest lady, they do neither harm nor good. Let me have them, honored lady. (*Takes the pillbox, shakes the pills into his hand, blows on them, puts them into his mouth and washes them down with kvas.*) There!

LYUBOV ANDREYEVNA (*alarmed*): Why, you must be mad!

PISHCHIK: I've taken all the pills.

LOPAKHIN: What a glutton!

(*Everyone laughs.*)

FIRS: The gentleman stayed with us during Holy Week . . . ate half a bucket of pickles. . . . (*Mumbles.*)

LYUBOV ANDREYEVNA: What is he saying?

VARYA: He's been muttering like that for three years now. We've grown used to it.

YASHA: He's in his dotage.

(*Charlotta Ivanovna, very thin, tightly laced, in a white dress with a lorgnette at her belt, crosses the stage.*)

LOPAKHIN: Forgive me, Charlotta Ivanovna, I haven't had a chance to say how do you do to you. (*Tries to kiss her hand.*)

CHARLOTTA (*pulls her hand away*): If I permit you to kiss my hand you'll be wanting to kiss my elbow next, then my shoulder.

LOPAKHIN: I have no luck today. (*Everyone laughs.*) Charlotta Ivanovna, show us a trick!

LYUBOV ANDREYEVNA: Charlotta, show us a trick!

CHARLOTTA: No. I want to sleep. (*Goes out.*)

LOPAKHIN: In three weeks we'll meet again. (*Kisses Lyubov Andreyevna's hand.*) Good-bye till then. Time to go. (*To Gayev.*) Good-bye. (*Kisses Pishchik.*) Good-bye. (*Shakes hands with Varya, then with Firs and Yasha.*) I don't feel like going. (*To Lyubov Andreyevna.*) If you make up your mind about the summer cottages and come to a decision, let me know; I'll get you a loan of fifty thousand or so. Think it over seriously.

VARYA (*angrily*): Oh, why don't you go!

LOPAKHIN: I'm going, I'm going. (*Goes out.*)

GAYEV: Boor. Oh, pardon. Varya's going to marry him, he's Varya's young man.

VARYA: Uncle dear, you talk too much.

LYUBOV ANDREYEVNA: Well, Varya, I shall be very glad. He's a good man.

PISHCHIK: A man, I must truly say . . . most worthy. . . . And my Dashenka . . . says, too, that . . . says all sorts of things. (*Snores but wakes up at once.*) In any case, honored lady, oblige me . . . a loan of two hundred and forty rubles . . . tomorrow the interest on my mortgage is due. . . .

VARYA (*in alarm*): We have nothing, nothing at all!

LYUBOV ANDREYEVNA: I really haven't any money.

PISHCHIK: It'll turn up. (*Laughs.*) I never lose hope. Just when I thought everything was lost, that I was done for, lo and behold — the railway line ran through my land . . . and they paid me for it. And before you know it, something else will turn up, if not today — tomorrow. . . . Dashenka will win two hundred thousand . . . she's got a lottery ticket.

LYUBOV ANDREYEVNA: The coffee is finished, we can go to bed.

FIRS (*brushing Gayev's clothes, admonishingly*): You've put on the wrong trousers again. What am I to do with you?

VARYA (*softly*): Anya's asleep. (*Quietly opens the window.*) The sun has risen, it's no longer cold. Look, Mama dear, what wonderful trees! Oh, Lord, the air! The starlings are singing!

GAYEV (*opens another window*): The orchard is all white. You haven't forgotten, Lyuba? That long avenue there that runs straight — straight as a stretched-out strap; it gleams on moonlight nights. Remember? You've not forgotten?

LYUBOV ANDREYEVNA (*looking out the window at the orchard*): Oh, my childhood, my innocence! I used to sleep in this nursery, I looked out from here into the orchard, happiness awoke with me each morning, it was just as it is now, nothing has changed. (*Laughing with joy.*) All, all white! Oh, my orchard! After the dark, rainy autumn and the cold winter, you are young again, full of happiness, the heavenly angels have not forsaken you. . . . If I could cast off this heavy stone weighing on my breast and shoulders, if I could forget my past!

GAYEV: Yes, and the orchard will be sold for our debts, strange as it may seem. . . .

LYUBOV ANDREYEVNA: Look, our dead mother walks in the orchard . . . in a white dress! (*Laughs with joy.*) It is she!

GAYEV: Where?

VARYA: God be with you, Mama dear.

LYUBOV ANDREYEVNA: There's no one there, I just imagined it. To the right, as you turn to the summerhouse, a slender white sapling is bent over . . . it looks like a woman.

(*Enter Trofimov wearing a shabby student's uniform and spectacles.*)

LYUBOV ANDREYEVNA: What a wonderful orchard! The white masses of blossoms, the blue sky —

TROFIMOV: Lyubov Andreyevna! (*She looks around at him.*) I only want to pay my respects, then I'll go at once. (*Kisses her hand ardently.*) I was told to wait until morning, but I hadn't the patience.

(*Lyubov Andreyevna looks at him, puzzled.*)

VARYA (*through tears*): This is Petya Trofimov.

TROFIMOV: Petya Trofimov, I was Grisha's tutor. . . . Can I have changed so much?

(*Lyubov Andreyevna embraces him, quietly weeping.*)

GAYEV (*embarrassed*): There, there, Lyuba.

VARYA (*crying*): Didn't I tell you, Petya, to wait till tomorrow?

LYUBOV ANDREYEVNA: My Grisha . . . my little boy . . . Grisha . . . my son. . . .

VARYA: What can we do, Mama dear? It's God's will.

TROFIMOV (*gently, through tears*): Don't, don't. . . .

LYUBOV ANDREYEVNA (*quietly weeping*): My little boy dead, drowned. . . . Why? Why, my friend? (*In a lower voice.*) Anya is sleeping in there, and I'm talking loudly . . . making all this noise. . . . But Petya, why do you look so bad? Why have you grown so old?

TROFIMOV: A peasant woman in the train called me a mangy gentleman.

LYUBOV ANDREYEVNA: You were just a boy then, a charming little student, and now your hair is thin — and spectacles! Is it possible you are still a student? (*Goes toward the door.*)

TROFIMOV: I shall probably be an eternal student.

LYUBOV ANDREYEVNA (*kisses her brother, then Varya*): Now, go to bed. . . . You've grown older too, Leonid.

PISHCHIK (*follows her*): Well, seems to be time to sleep. . . . Oh, my gout! I'm staying the night.

Lyubov Andreyevna, my soul, tomorrow morning . . . two hundred and forty rubles. . . .

GAYEV: He keeps at it.

PISHCHIK: Two hundred and forty rubles . . . to pay the interest on my mortgage.

LYUBOV ANDREYEVNA: I have no money, my friend.

PISHCHIK: My dear, I'll pay it back. . . . It's a trifling sum.

LYUBOV ANDREYEVNA: Well, all right, Leonid will give it to you. . . . Give it to him, Leonid.

GAYEV: Me give it to him! . . . Hold out your pocket!

LYUBOV ANDREYEVNA: It can't be helped, give it to him. . . . He needs it. . . . He'll pay it back.

(*Lyubov Andreyevna, Trofimov, Pishchik, and Firs go out. Gayev, Varya, and Yasha remain.*)

GAYEV: My sister hasn't yet lost her habit of squandering money. (*To Yasha.*) Go away, my good fellow, you smell of the henhouse.

YASHA (*with a smirk*): And you, Leonid Andreyevich, are just the same as ever.

GAYEV: How's that? (*To Varya.*) What did he say?

VARYA: Your mother has come from the village; she's been sitting in the servants' room since yesterday, waiting to see you. . . .

YASHA: Let her wait, for God's sake!

VARYA: Aren't you ashamed?

YASHA: A lot I need her! She could have come tomorrow. (*Goes out.*)

VARYA: Mama's the same as ever, she hasn't changed a bit. She'd give away everything, if she could.

GAYEV: Yes. . . . (*A pause.*) If a great many remedies are suggested for a disease, it means that the disease is incurable. I keep thinking, racking my brains, I have many remedies, a great many, and that means in effect, that I have none. It would be good to receive a legacy from someone, good to marry our Anya to a very rich man, good to go to Yaroslav and try our luck with our aunt, the Countess. She is very, very rich, you know.

VARYA (*crying*): If only God would help us!

GAYEV: Stop bawling. Auntie's very rich, but she doesn't like us. In the first place, sister married a lawyer, not a nobleman . . . (*Anya appears in the doorway.*) She married beneath her, and it cannot be said that she has conducted herself very virtuously. She is good, kind, charming, and I love her dearly, but no matter how much you allow for extenuating circumstances, you must admit she leads a sinful life. You feel it in her slightest movement.

VARYA (*in a whisper*): Anya is standing in the doorway.

GAYEV: What? (*Pause.*) Funny, something got into my right eye . . . I can't see very well. And Thursday, when I was in the district court . . .

(*Anya enters.*)

VARYA: Why aren't you asleep, Anya?

ANYA: I can't get to sleep. I just can't.

GAYEV: My little one! (*Kisses Anya's face and hands.*) My child. . . . (*Through tears.*) You are not my niece, you are my angel, you are everything to me. Believe me, believe . . .

ANYA: I believe you, Uncle. Everyone loves you and respects you, but, Uncle dear, you must keep quiet, just keep quiet. What were you saying just now about my mother, about your own sister? What made you say that?

GAYEV: Yes, yes. . . . (*Covers his face with her hand.*) Really, it's awful! My God! God help me! And today I made a speech to the bookcase . . . so stupid! And it was only when I had finished that I realized it was stupid.

VARYA: It's true, Uncle dear, you ought to keep quiet. Just don't talk, that's all.

ANYA: If you could keep from talking, it would make things easier for you, too.

GAYEV: I'll be quiet. (*Kisses Anya's and Varya's hands.*) I'll be quiet. Only this is about business. On Thursday I was in the district court, well, a group of us gathered together and began talking about one thing and another, this and that, and it seems it might be possible to arrange a loan on a promissory note to pay the interest at the bank.

VARYA: If only God would help us!

GAYEV: On Tuesday I'll go and talk it over again. (*To Varya.*) Stop bawling. (*To Anya.*) Your mama will talk to Lopakhin; he, of course, will not refuse her. . . . And as soon as you've rested, you will go to Yaroslav to the Countess, your great-aunt. In that way we shall be working from three directions — and our business is in the hat. We'll pay the interest, I'm certain of it. . . . (*Puts a candy in his mouth.*) On my honor, I'll swear by anything you like, the estate shall not be sold. (*Excitedly.*) By my happiness, I swear it! Here's my hand on it, call me a worthless, dishonorable man if I let it come to auction! I swear by my whole being!

ANYA (*a calm mood returns to her, she is happy*): How good you are, Uncle, how clever! (*Embraces him.*) Now I am at peace! I'm at peace! I'm happy!

(*Enter Firs.*)

FIRS (*reproachfully*): Leonid Andreich, have you no fear of God? When are you going to bed?

GAYEV: Presently, presently. Go away, Firs. I'll . . . all right, I'll undress myself. Well, children, bye-bye. . . . Details tomorrow, and now go to sleep. (*Kisses Anya and Varya.*) I am a man of the eighties. . . . They don't think much of that period today, nevertheless, I can say that in the course of my life I have suffered not a little for my convictions. It is not for nothing that the peasant loves me. You have to know the peasant! You have to know from what —

ANYA: There you go again, Uncle!

VARYA: Uncle dear, do be quiet.

FIRS (*angrily*): Leonid Andreich!

GAYEV: I'm coming, I'm coming.... Go to bed. A clean double rail shot to center table.... (*Goes out; Firs hobbles after him.*)

ANYA: I'm at peace now. I would rather not go to Yaroslav, I don't like my great-aunt, but still, I'm at peace, thanks to Uncle. (*She sits down.*)

VARYA: We must get some sleep. I'm going now. Oh, something unpleasant happened while you were away. In the old servants' quarters, as you know, there are only the old people: Yefimushka, Polya, Yevstignei, and, of course, Karp. They began letting in all sorts of rogues to spend the night — I didn't say anything. But then I heard they'd been spreading a rumor that I'd given an order for them to be fed nothing but dried peas. Out of stinginess, you see.... It was all Yevstignei's doing.... Very well, I think, if that's how it is, you just wait. I send for Yevstignei ... (*yawning*) he comes.... "How is it, Yevstignei," I say, "that you could be such a fool...." (*Looks at Anya.*) She's fallen asleep. (*Takes her by the arm.*) Come to your little bed.... Come along. (*Leading her.*) My little darling fell asleep. Come.... (*They go.*)

(*In the distance, beyond the orchard, a shepherd is playing on a reed pipe. Trofimov crosses the stage and, seeing Varya and Anya, stops.*)

VARYA: Sh! She's asleep ... asleep.... Come along, darling.

ANYA (*softly, half-asleep*): I'm so tired.... Those bells ... Uncle ... dear ... Mama and Uncle ...

VARYA: Come, darling, come along. (*They go into Anya's room.*)

TROFIMOV (*deeply moved*): My sunshine! My spring!

ACT II

(*A meadow. An old, lopsided, long-abandoned little chapel; near it a well, large stones that apparently were once tombstones, and an old bench. A road to the Gayev manor house can be seen. On one side, where the cherry orchard begins, tall poplars loom. In the distance a row of telegraph poles, and far, far away, on the horizon, the faint outline of a large town, which is visible only in very fine, clear weather.*

The sun will soon set. Charlotta, Yasha, and Dunyasha are sitting on the bench; Yepikhodov stands near playing something sad on the guitar. They are all lost in thought. Charlotta wears an old forage cap; she has taken a gun from her shoulder and is adjusting the buckle on the sling.)

CHARLOTTA (*reflectively*): I haven't got a real passport, I don't know how old I am, but it always seems to me that I'm quite young. When I was a little girl, my father and mother used to travel from one fair to another giving performances — very good ones. And I did the *salto mortale*° and all sorts of tricks. Then when Papa and Mama died, a German lady took me to live with her and began teaching me. Good. I grew up and became a governess. But where I come from and who I am — I do not know.... Who my parents were — perhaps they weren't even married — I don't know. (*Takes a cucumber out of her pocket and eats it.*) I don't know anything. (*Pause.*) One wants so much to talk, but there isn't anyone to talk to ... I have no one.

YEPIKHODOV (*plays the guitar and sings*): "What care I for the clamorous world, what's friend or foe to me?" ... How pleasant it is to play a mandolin!

DUNYASHA: That's a guitar, not a mandolin. (*Looks at herself in a hand mirror and powders her face.*)

YEPIKHODOV: To a madman, in love, it is a mandolin.... (*Sings.*) "Would that the heart were warmed by the flame of requited love ... "

(*Yasha joins in.*)

CHARLOTTA: How horribly these people sing! ... Pfui! Like jackals!

DUNYASHA (*to Yasha*): Really, how fortunate to have been abroad!

YASHA: Yes, to be sure. I cannot but agree with you there. (*Yawns, then lights a cigar.*)

YEPIKHODOV: It stands to reason. Abroad everything has long since been fully constituted.

YASHA: Obviously.

YEPIKHODOV: I am a cultivated man, I read all sorts of remarkable books, but I am in no way able to make out my own inclinations, what it is I really want, whether, strictly speaking, to live or to shoot myself; nevertheless, I always carry a revolver on me. Here it is. (*Shows revolver.*)

CHARLOTTA: Finished. Now I'm going. (*Slings the gun over her shoulder.*) You're a very clever man, Yepikhodov, and quite terrifying; women must be mad about you. Brrr! (*Starts to go.*) These clever people are all so stupid, there's no one for me to

---

salto mortale: Somersault.

talk to.... Alone, always alone, I have no one ... and who I am, and why I am, nobody knows.... (*Goes out unhurriedly.*)

YEPIKHODOV: Strictly speaking, all else aside, I must state regarding myself, that fate treats me unmercifully, as a storm does a small ship. If, let us assume, I am mistaken, then why, to mention a single instance, do I wake up this morning, and there on my chest see a spider of terrifying magnitude? ... Like that. (*Indicates with both hands.*) And likewise, I take up some kvas to quench my thirst, and there see something in the highest degree unseemly, like a cockroach. (*Pause.*) Have you read Buckle?° (*Pause.*) If I may trouble you, Avdotya Fedorovna, I should like to have a word or two with you.

DUNYASHA: Go ahead.

YEPIKHODOV: I prefer to speak with you alone.... (*Sighs.*)

DUNYASHA (*embarrassed*): Very well ... only first bring me my little cape ... you'll find it by the cupboard.... It's rather damp here....

YEPIKHODOV: Certainly, ma'am ... I'll fetch it, ma'am.... Now I know what to do with my revolver.... (*Takes the guitar and goes off playing it.*)

YASHA: Two-and-twenty Troubles! Between ourselves, a stupid fellow. (*Yawns.*)

DUNYASHA: God forbid that he should shoot himself. (*Pause.*) I've grown so anxious, I'm always worried. I was only a little girl when I was taken into the master's house, and now I'm quite unused to the simple life, and my hands are white as can be, just like a lady's. I've become so delicate, so tender and ladylike, I'm afraid of everything.... Frightfully so. And, Yasha, if you deceive me, I just don't know what will become of my nerves.

YASHA (*kisses her*): You little cucumber! Of course, a girl should never forget herself. What I dislike above everything is when a girl doesn't conduct herself properly.

DUNYASHA: I'm passionately in love with you, you're educated, you can discuss anything. (*Pause.*)

YASHA (*yawns*): Yes.... As I see it, it's like this: If a girl loves somebody, that means she's immoral. (*Pause.*) Very pleasant smoking a cigar in the open air.... (*Listens.*) Someone's coming this way.... It's the masters. (*Dunyasha impulsively embraces him.*) You go home, as if you'd been to the river to bathe; take that path, otherwise they'll see you and suspect me of having a ren-

dezvous with you. I can't endure that sort of thing.

DUNYASHA (*with a little cough*): My head is beginning to ache from your cigar.... (*Goes out.*)

(*Yasha remains, sitting near the chapel. Lyubov Andreyevna, Gayev, and Lopakhin enter.*)

LOPAKHIN: You must make up your mind once and for all — time won't stand still. The question, after all, is quite simple. Do you agree to lease the land for summer cottages or not? Answer in one word: Yes or no? Only one word!

LYUBOV ANDREYEVNA: Who is it that smokes those disgusting cigars out here? (*Sits down.*)

GAYEV: Now that the railway line is so near, it's made things convenient. (*Sits down.*) We went to town and had lunch ... cue ball to the center! I feel like going to the house first and playing a game.

LYUBOV ANDREYEVNA: Later.

LOPAKHIN: Just one word! (*Imploringly.*) Do give me an answer!

GAYEV (*yawning*): How's that?

LYUBOV ANDREYEVNA (*looks into her purse*): Yesterday I had a lot of money, and today there's hardly any left. My poor Varya tries to economize by feeding everyone milk soup, and in the kitchen the old people get nothing but dried peas, while I squander money foolishly.... (*Drops the purse, scattering gold coins.*) There they go.... (*Vexed.*)

YASHA: Allow me, I'll pick them up in an instant. (*Picks up the money.*)

LYUBOV ANDREYEVNA: Please do, Yasha. And why did I go to town for lunch? ... That miserable restaurant of yours with its music, and tablecloths smelling of soap.... Why drink so much, Lyonya? Why eat so much? Why talk so much? Today in the restaurant again you talked too much, and it was all so pointless. About the seventies, about the decadents. And to whom? Talking to waiters about the decadents!

LOPAKHIN: Yes.

GAYEV (*waving his hand*): I'm incorrigible, that's evident.... (*Irritably to Yasha.*) Why do you keep twirling about in front of me?

YASHA (*laughs*): I can't help laughing when I hear your voice.

GAYEV (*to his sister*): Either he or I —

LYUBOV ANDREYEVNA: Go away, Yasha, run along.

YASHA (*hands Lyubov Andreyevna her purse*): I'm going, right away. (*Hardly able to contain his laughter.*) This very instant.... (*Goes out.*)

LOPAKHIN: That rich man, Deriganov, is prepared to buy the estate. They say he's coming to the auction himself.

LYUBOV ANDREYEVNA: Where did you hear that?

Buckle: Thomas Henry Buckle (1821–1862) was a radical historian who formulated a scientific basis for history emphasizing the interrelationship of climate, food production, population, and wealth.

LOPAKHIN: That's what they're saying in town.

LYUBOV ANDREYEVNA: Our aunt in Yaroslav promised to send us something, but when and how much, no one knows.

LOPAKHIN: How much do you think she'll send? A hundred thousand? Two hundred?

LYUBOV ANDREYEVNA: Oh . . . ten or fifteen thousand, and we'll be thankful for that.

LOPAKHIN: Forgive me, but I have never seen such frivolous, such queer, unbusinesslike people as you, my friends. You are told in plain language that your estate is to be sold, and it's as though you don't understand it.

LYUBOV ANDREYEVNA: But what are we to do? Tell us what to do.

LOPAKHIN: I tell you every day. Every day I say the same thing. Both the cherry orchard and the land must be leased for summer cottages, and it must be done now, as quickly as possible — the auction is close at hand. Try to understand! Once you defi-

ABOVE: The spare set in Ron Daniel's 1993 production of *The Cherry Orchard* at the American Repertory Theatre highlights the characters' emotional isolation. RIGHT: Claire Bloom as Madame Ranevskaya.

nitely decide on the cottages, you can raise as much money as you like, and then you are saved.

LYUBOV ANDREYEVNA: Cottages, summer people — forgive me, but it's so vulgar.

GAYEV: I agree with you, absolutely.

LOPAKHIN: I'll either burst into tears, start shouting, or fall into a faint! I can't stand it! You've worn me out! (*To Gayev.*) You're an old woman!

GAYEV: How's that?

LOPAKHIN: An old woman! (*Starts to go.*)

LYUBOV ANDREYEVNA (*alarmed*): No, don't go, stay, my dear. I beg you. Perhaps we'll think of something!

LOPAKHIN: What is there to think of?

LYUBOV ANDREYEVNA: Don't go away, please. With you here it's more cheerful somehow. . . . (*Pause.*) I keep expecting something to happen, like the house caving in on us.

GAYEV (*in deep thought*): Double rail shot into the corner. . . . Cross table to the center. . . .

LYUBOV ANDREYEVNA: We have sinned so much. . . .

LOPAKHIN: What sins could you have —

GAYEV (*puts a candy into his mouth*): They say I've eaten up my entire fortune in candies. . . . (*Laughs.*)

LYUBOV ANDREYEVNA: Oh, my sins. . . . I've always squandered money recklessly, like a madwoman, and I married a man who did nothing but amass debts. My husband died from champagne — he drank terribly — then, to my sorrow, I fell in love with another man, lived with him, and just at that time — that was my first punishment, a blow on the head — my little boy was drowned . . . here in the river. And I went abroad, went away for good, never to return, never to see this river. . . . I closed my eyes and ran, beside myself, and *he* after me . . . callously, without pity. I bought a villa near Mentone, because he fell ill there, and for three years I had no rest, day or night. The sick man wore me out, my soul dried up. Then last year, when the villa was sold to pay my debts, I went to Paris, and there he stripped me of everything, and left me for another woman; I tried to poison myself. . . . So stupid, so shameful. . . . And suddenly I felt a longing for Russia, for my own country, for my little girl. . . . (*Wipes away her tears.*) Lord, Lord, be merciful, forgive my sins! Don't punish me anymore! (*Takes a telegram out of her pocket.*) This came today from Paris. . . . He asks my forgiveness, begs me to return. . . . (*Tears up telegram.*) Do I hear music? (*Listens.*)

GAYEV: That's our famous Jewish band. You remember, four violins, a flute, and double bass.

LYUBOV ANDREYEVNA: It's still in existence? We ought to send for them sometime and give a party.

LOPAKHIN (*listens*): I don't hear anything. . . . (*Sings softly.*) "The Germans, for pay, will turn Russians into Frenchmen, they say." (*Laughs.*) What a play I saw yesterday at the theater — very funny!

LYUBOV ANDREYEVNA: There was probably nothing funny about it. Instead of going to see plays you ought to look at yourselves a little more often. How drab your lives are, how full of futile talk!

LOPAKHIN: That's true. I must say, this life of ours is stupid. . . . (*Pause.*) My father was a peasant, an idiot; he understood nothing, taught me nothing; all he did was beat me when he was drunk, and always with a stick. As a matter of fact, I'm as big a blockhead and idiot as he was. I never learned anything, my handwriting's disgusting, I write like a pig — I'm ashamed to have people see it.

LYUBOV ANDREYEVNA: You ought to get married, my friend.

LOPAKHIN: Yes . . . that's true.

LYUBOV ANDREYEVNA: To our Varya. She's a nice girl.

LOPAKHIN: Yes.

LYUBOV ANDREYEVNA: She's a girl who comes from simple people, works all day long, but the main thing is she loves you. Besides, you've liked her for a long time now.

LOPAKHIN: Well? I've nothing against it. . . . She's a good girl. (*Pause.*)

GAYEV: I've been offered a place in the bank. Six thousand a year. . . . Have you heard?

LYUBOV ANDREYEVNA: How could you! You stay where you are. . . .

(*Firs enters carrying an overcoat.*)

FIRS (*to Gayev*): If you please, sir, put this on, it's damp.

GAYEV (*puts on the overcoat*): You're a pest, old man.

FIRS: Never mind. . . . You went off this morning without telling me. (*Looks him over.*)

LYUBOV ANDREYEVNA: How you have aged, Firs!

FIRS: What do you wish, madam?

LOPAKHIN: She says you've grown very old!

FIRS: I've lived a long time. They were arranging a marriage for me before your papa was born. . . . (*Laughs.*) I was already head footman when the emancipation came. At that time I wouldn't consent to my freedom, I stayed with the masters. . . . (*Pause.*) I remember, everyone was happy, but what they were happy about, they themselves didn't know.

LOPAKHIN: It was better in the old days. At least they flogged them.

FIRS (*not hearing*): Of course. The peasants kept to the masters, the masters kept to the peasants; but now they have all gone their own ways, you can't tell about anything.

GAYEV: Be quiet, Firs. Tomorrow I must go to town.

I've been promised an introduction to a certain general who might let us have a loan.

LOPAKHIN: Nothing will come of it. And you can rest assured, you won't even pay the interest.

LYUBOV ANDREYEVNA: He's raving. There is no such general.

(*Enter Trofimov, Anya, and Varya.*)

GAYEV: Here come our young people.

ANYA: There's Mama.

LYUBOV ANDREYEVNA (*tenderly*): Come, come along, my darlings. (*Embraces Anya and Varya.*) If you only knew how I love you both! Sit here beside me — there, like that.

(*They all sit down.*)

LOPAKHIN: Our eternal student is always with the young ladies.

TROFIMOV: That's none of your business.

LOPAKHIN: He'll soon be fifty, but he's still a student.

TROFIMOV: Drop your stupid jokes.

LOPAKHIN: What are you so angry about, you queer fellow?

TROFIMOV: Just leave me alone.

LOPAKHIN (*laughs*): Let me ask you something: What do you make of me?

TROFIMOV: My idea of you, Yermolai Alekseich, is this: You're a rich man, you will soon be a millionaire. Just as the beast of prey, which devours everything that crosses its path, is necessary in the metabolic process, so are you necessary.

(*Everyone laughs.*)

VARYA: Petya, you'd better tell us something about the planets.

LYUBOV ANDREYEVNA: No, let's go on with yesterday's conversation.

TROFIMOV: What was it about?

GAYEV: About the proud man.

TROFIMOV: We talked a long time yesterday, but we didn't get anywhere. In the proud man, in your sense of the word, there's something mystical. And you may be right from your point of view, but if you look at it simply, without being abstruse, why even talk about pride? Is there any sense in it if, physiologically, man is poorly constructed, if, in the vast majority of cases, he is coarse, ignorant, and profoundly unhappy? We should stop admiring ourselves. We should just work, and that's all.

GAYEV: You die, anyway.

TROFIMOV: Who knows? And what does it mean — to die? It may be that man has a hundred senses, and at his death only the five that are known to us perish, and the other ninety-five go on living.

LYUBOV ANDREYEVNA: How clever you are, Petya!

LOPAKHIN (*ironically*): Terribly clever!

TROFIMOV: Mankind goes forward, perfecting its powers. Everything that is now unattainable will some day be comprehensible and within our grasp, only we must work, and help with all our might those who are seeking the truth. So far, among us here in Russia, only a very few work. The great majority of the intelligentsia that I know seek nothing, do nothing, and as yet are incapable of work. They call themselves the intelligentsia, yet they belittle their servants, treat the peasants like animals, are wretched students, never read anything serious, and do absolutely nothing; they only talk about science and know very little about art. They all look serious, have grim expressions, speak of weighty matters, and philosophize; and meanwhile anyone can see that the workers eat abominably, sleep without pillows, thirty or forty to a room, and everywhere there are bedbugs, stench, dampness, and immorality. . . . It's obvious that all our fine talk is merely to delude ourselves and others. Show me the day nurseries they are always talking about — and where are the reading rooms? They only write about them in novels, but in reality they don't exist. There is nothing but filth, vulgarity, asiaticism.° . . . I'm afraid of those very serious countenances, I don't like them, I'm afraid of serious conversations. We'd do better to remain silent.

LOPAKHIN: You know, I get up before five in the morning, and I work from morning to night; now, I'm always handling money, my own and other people's, and I see what people around me are like. You have only to start doing something to find out how few honest, decent people there are. Sometimes, when I can't sleep, I think: "Lord, Thou gavest us vast forests, boundless fields, broad horizons, and living in their midst we ourselves ought truly to be giants. . . ."

LYUBOV ANDREYEVNA: Now you want giants! They're good only in fairy tales, otherwise they're frightening.

(*Yepikhodov crosses at the rear of the stage, playing the guitar.*)

LYUBOV ANDREYEVNA (*pensively*): There goes Yepikhodov . . .

ANYA (*pensively*): There goes Yepikhodov . . .

GAYEV: The sun has set, ladies and gentlemen.

TROFIMOV: Yes.

GAYEV (*in a low voice, as though reciting*): Oh, Nature, wondrous Nature, you shine with eternal radiance, beautiful and indifferent; you, whom we

---

asiaticism: Trofimov, expressing a common prejudice of the time, refers to Asian apathy.

call mother, unite within yourself both life and death, giving life and taking it away. . . .

VARYA (*beseechingly*): Uncle dear!

ANYA: Uncle, you're doing it again!

TROFIMOV: You'd better cue ball into the center.

GAYEV: I'll be silent, silent.

(*All sit lost in thought. The silence is broken only by the subdued muttering of Firs. Suddenly a distant sound is heard, as if from the sky, like the sound of a snapped string mournfully dying away.*)

LYUBOV ANDREYEVNA: What was that?

LOPAKHIN: I don't know. Somewhere far off in a mine shaft a bucket's broken loose. But somewhere very far away.

GAYEV: It might be a bird of some sort . . . like a heron.

TROFIMOV: Or an owl . . .

LYUBOV ANDREYEVNA (*shudders*): It's unpleasant somehow. . . . (*Pause.*)

FIRS: The same thing happened before the troubles: An owl hooted and the samovar hissed continually.

GAYEV: Before what troubles?

FIRS: Before the emancipation.

LYUBOV ANDREYEVNA: Come along, my friends, let us go, evening is falling. (*To Anya.*) There are tears in your eyes — what is it, my little one?

(*Embraces her.*)

ANYA: It's all right, Mama. It's nothing.

TROFIMOV: Someone is coming.

(*A Stranger appears wearing a shabby white forage cap and an overcoat. He is slightly drunk.*)

STRANGER: Permit me to inquire, can I go straight through here to the station?

GAYEV: You can. Follow the road.

STRANGER: I am deeply grateful to you. (*Coughs.*) Splendid weather. . . . (*Reciting.*) "My brother, my suffering brother . . . come to the Volga, whose groans" . . . (*To Varya.*) Mademoiselle, will you oblige a hungry Russian with thirty kopecks?

(*Varya, frightened, cries out.*)

LOPAKHIN (*angrily*): There's a limit to everything.

LYUBOV ANDREYEVNA (*panic-stricken*): Here you are — take this. . . . (*Fumbles in her purse.*) I have no silver. . . . Never mind, here's a gold piece for you. . . .

STRANGER: I am deeply grateful to you. (*Goes off.*)

(*Laughter.*)

VARYA (*frightened*): I'm leaving . . . I'm leaving. . . . Oh, Mama, dear, there's nothing in the house for the servants to eat, and you give him a gold piece!

LYUBOV ANDREYEVNA: What's to be done with such a silly creature? When we get home I'll give you all I've got. Yermolai Alekseyevich, you'll lend me some more!

LOPAKHIN: At your service.

LYUBOV ANDREYEVNA: Come, my friends, it's time to go. Oh, Varya, we have definitely made a match for you. Congratulations!

VARYA (*through tears*): Mama, that's not something to joke about.

LOPAKHIN: "Aurelia, get thee to a nunnery . . . "°

GAYEV: Look, my hands are trembling: It's a long time since I've played a game of billiards.

LOPAKHIN: "Aurelia, O Nymph, in thy orisons, be all my sins remember'd!"

LYUBOV ANDREYEVNA: Let us go, my friends, it will soon be suppertime.

VARYA: He frightened me. My heart is simply pounding.

LOPAKHIN: Let me remind you, ladies and gentlemen: On the twenty-second of August the cherry orchard is to be sold. Think about that! — Think!

(*All go out except Trofimov and Anya.*)

ANYA (*laughs*): My thanks to the stranger for frightening Varya, now we are alone.

TROFIMOV: Varya is so afraid we might suddenly fall in love with each other that she hasn't left us alone for days. With her narrow mind she can't understand that we are above love. To avoid the petty and the illusory, which prevent our being free and happy — that is the aim and meaning of life. Forward! We are moving irresistibly toward the bright star that burns in the distance! Forward! Do not fall behind, friends!

ANYA (*clasping her hands*): How well you talk! (*Pause.*) It's marvelous here today!

TROFIMOV: Yes, the weather is wonderful.

ANYA: What have you done to me, Petya, that I no longer love the cherry orchard as I used to? I loved it so tenderly, it seemed to me there was no better place on earth than our orchard.

TROFIMOV: All Russia is our orchard. It is a great and beautiful land, and there are many wonderful places in it. (*Pause.*) Just think, Anya: Your grandfather, your great-grandfather, and all your ancestors were serf-owners, possessors of living souls. Don't you see that from every cherry tree, from every leaf and trunk, human beings are peering out at you? Don't you hear their voices? To possess living souls — that has corrupted all of you, those

---

"**Aurelia . . . nunnery**": From Hamlet's famous line rejecting Ophelia (Lopakhin's next line is also from Shakespeare's *Hamlet*).

who lived before and you who are living now, so that your mother, you, your uncle, no longer perceive that you are living in debt, at someone else's expense, at the expense of those whom you wouldn't allow to cross your threshold.... We are at least two hundred years behind the times, we have as yet absolutely nothing, we have no definite attitude toward the past, we only philosophize, complain of boredom, or drink vodka. Yet it's quite clear that to begin to live we must first atone for the past, be done with it, and we can atone for it only by suffering, only by extraordinary, unceasing labor. Understand this, Anya.

ANYA: The house we live in hasn't really been ours for a long time, and I shall leave it, I give you my word.

TROFIMOV: If you have the keys of the household, throw them into the well and go. Be as free as the wind.

ANYA (*in ecstasy*): How well you put that!

TROFIMOV: Believe me, Anya, believe me! I am not yet thirty, I am young, still a student, but I have already been through so much! As soon as winter comes, I am hungry, sick, worried, poor as a beggar, and — where has not fate driven me! Where have I not been? And yet always, every minute of the day and night, my soul was filled with inexplicable premonitions. I have a premonition of happiness, Anya, I can see it...

ANYA: The moon is rising.

(*Yepikhodov is heard playing the same melancholy song on the guitar. The moon rises. Somewhere near the poplars Varya is looking for Anya and calling: "Anya, where are you?"*)

TROFIMOV: Yes, the moon is rising. (*Pause.*) There it is — happiness ... it's coming, nearer and nearer, I can hear its footsteps. And if we do not see it, if we do not recognize it, what does it matter? Others will see it.

VARYA'S VOICE: Anya! Where are you?

TROFIMOV: That Varya again! (*Angrily.*) It's revolting!

ANYA: Well? Let's go down to the river. It's lovely there.

TROFIMOV: Come on. (*They go.*)

VARYA'S VOICE: Anya! Anya!

ACT III

(*The drawing room, separated by an arch from the ballroom. The chandelier is lighted. The Jewish band that was mentioned in act II is heard playing in the hall. It is evening. In the ballroom they are dancing a*

grand rond. The voice of Semyonov-Pishchik: "Promenade à une paire!"° They all enter the drawing room: Pishchik and Charlotta Ivanovna are the first couple, Trofimov and Lyubov Andreyevna the second, Anya and the Post-Office Clerk the third, Varya and the Stationmaster the fourth, etc. Varya, quietly weeping, dries her tears as she dances. Dunyasha is in the last couple. As they cross the drawing room Pishchik calls: "Grand rond, balancez!" and "Les cavaliers à genoux et remercier vos dames!"° Firs, wearing a dress coat, brings in a tray with seltzer water. Pishchik and Trofimov come into the drawing room.*)

PISHCHIK: I'm a full-blooded man, I've already had two strokes, and dancing's hard work for me, but as they say, "If you run with the pack, you can bark or not, but at least wag your tail." At that, I'm as strong as a horse. My late father — quite a joker he was, God rest his soul — used to say, talking about our origins, that the ancient line of Semyonov-Pishchik was descended from the very horse that Caligula had seated in the Senate.° ... (*Sits down.*) But the trouble is — no money! A hungry dog believes in nothing but meat.... (*Snores but wakes up at once.*) It's the same with me — I can think of nothing but money....

TROFIMOV: You know, there really is something equine about your figure.

PISHCHIK: Well, a horse is a fine animal.... You can sell a horse.

(*There is the sound of a billiard game in the next room. Varya appears in the archway.*)

TROFIMOV (*teasing her*): Madame Lopakhina! Madame Lopakhina!

VARYA (*angrily*): Mangy gentleman!

TROFIMOV: Yes, I am a mangy gentleman, and proud of it!

VARYA (*reflecting bitterly*): Here we've hired musicians, and what are we going to pay them with? (*Goes out.*)

TROFIMOV (*to Pishchik*): If the energy you have expended in the course of your life trying to find money to pay interest had gone into something else, ultimately, you might very well have turned the world upside down.

PISHCHIK: Nietzsche ... the philosopher ... the greatest, most renowned ... a man of tremendous intel-

---

"Promenade à une paire!": French for "Walk in pairs."
"Grand rond ... dames!": Instructions in the dance: "Large circle!" and "Gentlemen, kneel down and thank your ladies!"
Caligula ... Senate: Caligula (A.D. 12–41), a cavalry soldier, was Roman emperor (A.D. 37–41).

lect . . . says in his works that it is possible to forge banknotes.

TROFIMOV: And have you read Nietzsche?

PISHCHIK: Well . . . Dashenka told me. I'm in such a state now that I'm just about ready for forging. . . . The day after tomorrow I have to pay three hundred and ten rubles . . . I've got a hundred and thirty. . . . (*Feels in his pocket, grows alarmed.*) The money is gone! I've lost the money! (*Tearfully.*) Where is my money? (*Joyfully.*) Here it is, inside the lining. . . . I'm all in a sweat. . . .

(*Lyubov Andreyevna and Charlotta Ivanovna come in.*)

LYUBOV ANDREYEVNA (*humming a* Lezginka):° Why does Leonid take so long? What is he doing in town? (*To Dunyasha.*) Dunyasha, offer the musicians some tea.

TROFIMOV: In all probability, the auction didn't take place.

LYUBOV ANDREYEVNA: It was the wrong time to have the musicians, the wrong time to give a dance. . . . Well, never mind. . . . (*Sits down and hums softly.*)

CHARLOTTA (*gives Pishchik a deck of cards*): Here's a deck of cards for you. Think of a card.

PISHCHIK: I've thought of one.

CHARLOTTA: Now shuffle the pack. Very good. And now, my dear Mr. Pishchik, hand it to me. *Ein, zwei, drei!*° Now look for it — it's in your side pocket.

PISHCHIK (*takes the card out of his side pocket*): The eight of spades — absolutely right! (*Amazed.*) Think of that, now!

CHARLOTTA (*holding the deck of cards in the palm of her hand, to Trofimov*): Quickly, tell me, which card is on top?

TROFIMOV: What? Well, the queen of spades.

CHARLOTTA: Right! (*To Pishchik.*) Now which card is on top?

PISHCHIK: The ace of hearts.

CHARLOTTA: Right! (*Claps her hands and the deck of cards disappears.*) What lovely weather we're having today! (*A mysterious feminine voice, which seems to come from under the floor, answers her:* "Oh, yes, splendid weather, madam.") You are so nice, you're my ideal. . . . (*The voice:* "And I'm very fond of you, too, madam.")

STATIONMASTER (*applauding*): Bravo, Madame Ventriloquist!

PISHCHIK (*amazed*): Think of that, now! Most enchanting Charlotta Ivanovna . . . I am simply in love with you. . . .

CHARLOTTA: In love? (*Shrugs her shoulders.*) Is it possible that you can love? *Guter Mensch, aber schlechter Musikant.*°

TROFIMOV (*claps Pishchik on the shoulder*): You old horse, you!

CHARLOTTA: Attention, please! One more trick. (*Takes a lap robe from a chair.*) Here's a very fine lap robe; I should like to sell it. (*Shakes it out.*) Doesn't anyone want to buy it?

PISHCHIK (*amazed*): Think of that, now!

CHARLOTTA: *Ein, zwei, drei!* (*Quickly raises the lap robe, behind it stands Anya, who curtsies, runs to her mother, embraces her, and runs back into the ballroom amid the general enthusiasm.*)

LYUBOV ANDREYEVNA (*applauding*): Bravo, bravo!

CHARLOTTA: Once again! *Ein, zwei, drei.* (*Raises the lap robe; behind it stands Varya, who bows.*)

PISHCHIK (*amazed*): Think of that, now!

CHARLOTTA: The end! (*Throws the robe at Pishchik, makes a curtsy, and runs out of the room.*)

PISHCHIK (*hurries after her*): The minx! . . . What a woman! What a woman! (*Goes out.*)

LYUBOV ANDREYEVNA: And Leonid still not here. What he is doing in town so long, I do not understand! It must be all over by now. Either the estate is sold, or the auction didn't take place — but why keep us in suspense so long!

VARYA (*trying to comfort her*): Uncle has bought it, I am certain of that.

TROFIMOV (*mockingly*): Yes.

VARYA: Great-aunt sent him power of attorney to buy it in her name and transfer the debt. She's doing it for Anya's sake. And I am sure, with God's help, Uncle will buy it.

LYUBOV ANDREYEVNA: Our great-aunt in Yaroslav sent fifteen thousand to buy the estate in her name — she doesn't trust us — but that's not even enough to pay the interest. (*Covers her face with her hands.*) Today my fate will be decided, my fate . . .

TROFIMOV (*teasing Varya*): Madame Lopakhina!

VARYA (*angrily*): Eternal student! Twice already you've been expelled from the university.

LYUBOV ANDREYEVNA: Why are you so cross, Varya? If he teases you about Lopakhin, what of it? Go ahead and marry Lopakhin if you want to. He's a nice man, he's interesting. And if you don't want to, don't. Nobody's forcing you, my pet.

VARYA: To be frank, Mama dear, I regard this matter seriously. He is a good man, I like him.

LYUBOV ANDREYEVNA: Then marry him. I don't know what you're waiting for!

Lezginka: A lively Russian tune for a dance.
Ein, zwei, drei!: "One, two, three" (German).

Guter Mensch, aber schlechter Musikant: "Good man, but poor musician" (German).

VARYA: Mama, I can't propose to him myself. For the last two years everyone's been talking to me about him; everyone talks, but he is either silent or he jokes. I understand. He's getting rich, he's absorbed in business, he has no time for me. If I had some money, no matter how little, if it were only a hundred rubles, I'd drop everything and go far away. I'd go into a nunnery.

TROFIMOV: A blessing!

VARYA (to Trofimov): A student ought to be intelligent! (In a gentle tone, tearfully.) How homely you have grown, Petya, how old! (To Lyubov Andreyevna, no longer crying.) It's just that I cannot live without work, Mama. I must be doing something every minute.

(Yasha enters.)

YASHA (barely able to suppress his laughter): Yepikhodov has broken a billiard cue! (Goes out.)

VARYA: But why is Yepikhodov here? Who gave him permission to play billiards? I don't understand these people.... (Goes out.)

LYUBOV ANDREYEVNA: Don't tease her, Petya. You can see she's unhappy enough without that.

TROFIMOV: She's much too zealous, always meddling in other people's affairs. All summer long she's given Anya and me no peace — afraid a romance might develop. What business is it of hers? Besides, I've given no occasion for it, I am far removed from such banality. We are above love!

LYUBOV ANDREYEVNA: And I suppose I am beneath love. (In great agitation.) Why isn't Leonid here? If only I knew whether the estate had been sold or not! The disaster seems to me so incredible that I don't even know what to think, I'm lost.... I could scream this very instant ... I could do something foolish. Save me, Petya. Talk to me, say something....

TROFIMOV: Whether or not the estate is sold today — does it really matter? That's all done with long ago; there's no turning back, the path is overgrown. Be calm, my dear. One must not deceive oneself; at least once in one's life one ought to look the truth straight in the eye.

LYUBOV ANDREYEVNA: What truth? You can see where there is truth and where there isn't, but I seem to have lost my sight, I see nothing. You boldly settle all the important problems, but tell me, my dear boy, isn't it because you are young and have not yet had to suffer for a single one of your problems? You boldly look ahead, but isn't it because you neither see nor expect anything dreadful, since life is still hidden from your young eyes? You're bolder, more honest, deeper than we are, but think about it, be just a little bit magnanimous,

and spare me. You see, I was born here, my mother and father lived here, and my grandfather. I love this house, without the cherry orchard my life has no meaning for me, and if it must be sold, then sell me with the orchard.... (Embraces Trofimov and kisses him on the forehead.) And my son was drowned here.... (Weeps.) Have pity on me, you good, kind man.

TROFIMOV: You know I feel for you with all my heart.

LYUBOV ANDREYEVNA: But that should have been said differently, quite differently.... (Takes out her handkerchief and a telegram falls to the floor.) My heart is heavy today, you can't imagine. It's so noisy here, my soul quivers at every sound, I tremble all over, and yet I can't go to my room. When I am alone the silence frightens me. Don't condemn me, Petya ... I love you as if you were my own. I would gladly let you marry Anya, I swear it, only you must study, my dear, you must get your degree. You do nothing, fate simply tosses you from place to place — it's so strange.... Isn't that true? Isn't it? And you must do something about your beard, to make it grow somehow.... (Laughs.) You're so funny!

TROFIMOV (picks up the telegram): I have no desire to be an Adonis.°

LYUBOV ANDREYEVNA: That's a telegram from Paris. I get them every day. One yesterday, one today. That wild man has fallen ill again, he's in trouble again.... He begs my forgiveness, implores me to come, and really, I ought to go to Paris to be near him. Your face is stern, Petya, but what can one do, my dear? What am I to do? He is ill, he's alone and unhappy, and who will look after him there, who will keep him from making mistakes, who will give him his medicine on time? And why hide it or keep silent, I love him, that's clear. I love him, love him.... It's a millstone round my neck, I'm sinking to the bottom with it, but I love that stone, I cannot live without it. (Presses Trofimov's hand.) Don't think badly of me, Petya, and don't say anything to me, don't say anything....

TROFIMOV (through tears): For God's sake, forgive my frankness: You know that he robbed you!

LYUBOV ANDREYEVNA: No, no, no, you mustn't say such things! (Covers her ears.)

TROFIMOV: But he's a scoundrel! You're the only one who doesn't know it! He's a petty scoundrel, a nonentity —

LYUBOV ANDREYEVNA (angry, but controlling herself): You are twenty-six or twenty-seven years old, but you're still a schoolboy!

TROFIMOV: That may be!

Adonis: From Greek myth, a beautiful young man.

LYUBOV ANDREYEVNA: You should be a man, at your age you ought to understand those who love. And you ought to be in love yourself. (*Angrily.*) Yes, yes! It's not purity with you, it's simply prudery, you're a ridiculous crank, a freak —
TROFIMOV (*horrified*): What is she saying!
LYUBOV ANDREYEVNA: I am above love! You're not above love, you're just an addlepate, as Firs would say. Not to have a mistress at your age!
TROFIMOV (*in horror*): This is awful! What is she saying! . . . (*Goes quickly toward the ballroom.*) This is awful . . . I can't . . . I won't stay here. . . . (*Goes out, but immediately returns.*) All is over between us! (*Goes out to the hall.*)
LYUBOV ANDREYEVNA (*calls after him*): Petya, wait! You absurd creature, I was joking! Petya!

(*In the hall there is the sound of someone running quickly downstairs and suddenly falling with a crash. Anya and Varya scream, but a moment later laughter is heard.*)

LYUBOV ANDREYEVNA: What was that?

(*Anya runs in.*)

ANYA (*laughing*): Petya fell down the stairs! (*Runs out.*)
LYUBOV ANDREYEVNA: What a funny boy that Petya is!

(*The Stationmaster stands in the middle of the ballroom and recites A. Tolstoy's° "The Sinner." Everyone listens to him, but he has no sooner spoken a few lines than the sound of a waltz is heard from the hall and the recitation is broken off. They all dance. Trofimov, Anya, Varya, and Lyubov Andreyevna come in from the hall.*)

LYUBOV ANDREYEVNA: Come, Petya . . . come, you pure soul . . . please, forgive me. . . . Let's dance. . . . (*They dance.*)

(*Anya and Varya dance. Firs comes in, puts his stick by the side door. Yasha also comes into the drawing room and watches the dancers.*)

YASHA: What is it, grandpa?
FIRS: I don't feel well. In the old days, we used to have generals, barons, admirals, dancing at our balls, but now we send for the post office clerk and the stationmaster, and even they are none too eager to come. Somehow I've grown weak. The late master, their grandfather, dosed everyone with sealing wax, no matter what ailed them. I've been taking

A. *Tolstoy:* Aleksey Konstantinovich Tolstoy (1817–1875), Russian novelist, dramatist, and poet.

sealing wax every day for twenty years or more, maybe that's what's kept me alive.
YASHA: You bore me, grandpa. (*Yawns.*) High time you croaked.
FIRS: Ah, you . . . addlepate! (*Mumbles.*)

(*Trofimov and Lyubov Andreyevna dance from the ballroom into the drawing room.*)

LYUBOV ANDREYEVNA: *Merci.* I'll sit down a while. (*Sits.*) I'm tired.

(*Anya comes in.*)

ANYA (*excitedly*): There was a man in the kitchen just now saying that the cherry orchard was sold today.
LYUBOV ANDREYEVNA: Sold to whom?
ANYA: He didn't say. He's gone. (*Dances with Trofimov; they go into the ballroom.*)
YASHA: That was just some old man babbling. A stranger.
FIRS: Leonid Andreich is not back yet, still hasn't come. And he's wearing the light, between-seasons overcoat; like enough he'll catch cold. Ah, when they're young they're green.
LYUBOV ANDREYEVNA: This is killing me. Yasha, go and find out who it was sold to.
YASHA: But that old man left long ago. (*Laughs.*)
LYUBOV ANDREYEVNA (*slightly annoyed*): Well, what are you laughing at? What are you so happy about?
YASHA: That Yepikhodov is very funny! Hopeless! Two-and-twenty Troubles.
LYUBOV ANDREYEVNA: Firs, if the estate is sold, where will you go?
FIRS: Wherever you tell me to go, I'll go.
LYUBOV ANDREYEVNA: Why do you look like that? Aren't you well? You ought to go to bed.
FIRS: Yes. . . . (*With a smirk.*) Go to bed, and without me who will serve, who will see to things? I'm the only one in the whole house.
YASHA (*to Lyubov Andreyevna*): Lyubov Andreyevna! Permit me to make a request, be so kind! If you go back to Paris again, do me the favor of taking me with you. It is positively impossible for me to stay here. (*Looking around, then in a low voice.*) There's no need to say it, you can see for yourself, it's an uncivilized country, the people have no morals, and the boredom! The food they give us in the kitchen is unmentionable, and besides, there's this Firs who keeps walking about mumbling all sorts of inappropriate things. Take me with you, be so kind!

(*Enter Pishchik.*)

PISHCHIK: May I have the pleasure of a waltz with you, fairest lady? (*Lyubov Andreyevna goes with him*.) I really must borrow a hundred and eighty rubles from you, my charmer . . . I really must. . . . (*Dancing*.) Just a hundred and eighty rubles. . . . (*They pass into the ballroom*.)

YASHA (*softly sings*): "Wilt thou know my soul's unrest . . . "

(*In the ballroom a figure in a gray top hat and checked trousers is jumping about, waving its arms; there are shouts of "Bravo, Charlotta Ivanovna!"*)

DUNYASHA (*stopping to powder her face*): The young mistress told me to dance — there are lots of gentlemen and not enough ladies — but dancing makes me dizzy, and my heart begins to thump. Firs Nikolayevich, the post office clerk just said something to me that took my breath away.

(*The music grows more subdued*.)

FIRS: What did he say to you?
DUNYASHA: "You," he said, "are like a flower."
YASHA (*yawns*): What ignorance. . . . (*Goes out*.)
DUNYASHA: Like a flower. . . . I'm such a delicate girl, I just adore tender words.
FIRS: You'll get your head turned.

(*Enter Yepikhodov*.)

YEPIKHODOV: Avdotya Fyodorovna, you are not desirous of seeing me. . . . I might almost be some sort of insect. (*Sighs*.) Ah, life!
DUNYASHA: What is it you want?
YEPIKHODOV: Indubitably, you may be right. (*Sighs*.) But, of course, if one looks at it from a point of view, then, if I may so express myself, and you will forgive my frankness, you have completely reduced me to a state of mind. I know my fate, every day some misfortune befalls me, but I have long since grown accustomed to that; I look upon my fate with a smile. But you gave me your word, and although I —
DUNYASHA: Please, we'll talk about it later, but leave me in peace now. Just now I'm dreaming. . . . (*Plays with her fan*.)
YEPIKHODOV: Every day a misfortune, and yet, if I may so express myself, I merely smile, I even laugh.

(*Varya enters from the ballroom*.)

VARYA: Are you still here, Semyon? What a disrespectful man you are, really! (*To Dunyasha*.) Run along, Dunyasha. (*To Yepikhodov*.) First you play billiards and break a cue, then you wander about the drawing room as though you were a guest.
YEPIKHODOV: You cannot, if I may so express myself, penalize me.
VARYA: I am not penalizing you, I'm telling you. You do nothing but wander from one place to another,

and you don't do your work. We keep a clerk, but for what, I don't know.
YEPIKHODOV (*offended*): Whether I work, or wander about, or eat, or play billiards, these are matters to be discussed only by persons of discernment, and my elders.
VARYA: You dare say that to me! (*Flaring up*.) You dare? You mean to say I have no discernment? Get out of here! This instant!
YEPIKHODOV (*intimidated*): I beg you to express yourself in a more delicate manner.
VARYA (*beside herself*): Get out, this very instant! Get out! (*He goes to the door, she follows him*.) Two-and-twenty Troubles! Don't let me set eyes on you again!
YEPIKHODOV (*goes out, his voice is heard behind the door*): I shall lodge a complaint against you!
VARYA: Oh, you're coming back? (*Seizes the stick left near the door by Firs*.) Come, come on. . . . Come, I'll show you. . . . Ah, so you're coming, are you? Then take that — (*Swings the stick just as Lopakhin enters*.)
LOPAKHIN: Thank you kindly.
VARYA (*angrily and mockingly*): I beg your pardon.
LOPAKHIN: Not at all. I humbly thank you for your charming reception.
VARYA: Don't mention it. (*Walks away, then looks back and gently asks*.) I didn't hurt you, did I?
LOPAKHIN: No, it's nothing. A huge bump coming up, that's all.

(*Voices in the ballroom: "Lopakhin has come! Yermolai Alekseich!" Pishchik enters*.)

PISHCHIK: As I live and breathe! (*Kisses Lopakhin*.) There is a whiff of cognac about you, dear soul. And we've been making merry here, too.

(*Enter Lyubov Andreyevna*.)

LYUBOV ANDREYEVNA: Is that you, Yermolai Alekseich? What kept you so long? Where's Leonid?
LOPAKHIN: Leonid Andreich arrived with me, he's coming . . .
LYUBOV ANDREYEVNA (*agitated*): Well, what happened? Did the sale take place? Tell me!
LOPAKHIN (*embarrassed, fearing to reveal his joy*): The auction was over by four o'clock. . . . We missed the train, had to wait till half past nine. (*Sighing heavily*.) Ugh! My head is swimming. . . .

(*Enter Gayev; he carries his purchases in one hand and wipes away his tears with the other*.)

LYUBOV ANDREYEVNA: Lyonya, what happened? Well, Lyonya? (*Impatiently, through tears*.) Be quick, for God's sake!
GAYEV (*not answering her, simply waves his hand. To*

Firs, weeping): Here, take these.... There's an-
chovies, Kerch herrings.... I haven't eaten anything all day.... What I have been through! (*The
click of billiard balls is heard through the open
door to the billiard room, and Yasha's voice:
"Seven and eighteen!" Gayev's expression changes,
he is no longer weeping.*) I'm terribly tired. Firs,
help me change. (*Goes through the ballroom to his
own room, followed by Firs.*)

PISHCHIK: What happened at the auction? Come on,
tell us!

LYUBOV ANDREYEVNA: Is the cherry orchard sold?

LOPAKHIN: It's sold.

LYUBOV ANDREYEVNA: Who bought it?

LOPAKHIN: I bought it. (*Pause.*)

(*Lyubov Andreyevna is overcome; she would fall to
the floor if it were not for the chair and table near
which she stands. Varya takes the keys from her belt
and throws them on the floor in the middle of the
drawing room and goes out.*)

LOPAKHIN: I bought it! Kindly wait a moment, ladies
and gentlemen, my head is swimming. I can't
talk.... (*Laughs.*) We arrived at the auction, Deriganov was already there. Leonid Andreich had
only fifteen thousand, and straight off Deriganov
bid thirty thousand over and above the mortgage. I
saw how the land lay, so I got into the fight and bid
forty. He bid forty-five. I bid fifty-five. In other
words, he kept raising it by five thousand, and I by
ten. Well, it finally came to an end. I bid ninety
thousand above the mortgage, and it was knocked
down to me. The cherry orchard is now mine!
Mine! (*Laughs uproariously.*) Lord! God in
heaven! The cherry orchard is mine! Tell me I'm
drunk, out of my mind, that I imagine it....
(*Stamps his feet.*) Don't laugh at me! If my father
and my grandfather could only rise from their
graves and see all that has happened, how their
Yermolai, their beaten, half-literate Yermolai, who
used to run about barefoot in winter, how that
same Yermolai has bought an estate, the most
beautiful estate in the whole world! I bought the estate where my father and grandfather were slaves,
where they weren't even allowed in the kitchen. I'm
asleep, this is just some dream of mine, it only
seems to be.... It's the fruit of your imagination,
hidden in the darkness of uncertainty.... (*Picks up
the keys, smiling tenderly.*) She threw down the
keys, wants to show that she's not mistress here
anymore.... (*Jingles the keys.*) Well, no matter.
(*The orchestra is heard tuning up.*) Hey, musicians,
play, I want to hear you! Come on, everybody, and
see how Yermolai Lopakhin will lay the ax to the
cherry orchard, how the trees will fall to the
ground! We're going to build summer cottages and
our grandsons and great-grandsons will see a new
life here.... Music! Strike up!

(*The orchestra plays. Lyubov Andreyevna sinks into a
chair and weeps bitterly.*)

LOPAKHIN (*reproachfully*): Why didn't you listen to
me, why? My poor friend, there's no turning back
now. (*With tears.*) Oh, if only all this could be over
quickly, if somehow our discordant, unhappy life
could be changed!

PISHCHIK (*takes him by the arm; speaks in an under-
tone*): She's crying. Let's go into the ballroom, let
her be alone.... Come on.... (*Leads him into the
ballroom.*)

LOPAKHIN: What's happened? Musicians, play so I can
hear you! Let everything be as I want it! (*Ironically.*) Here comes the new master, owner of the
cherry orchard! (*Accidentally bumps into a little
table, almost upsetting the candelabrum.*) I can
pay for everything! (*Goes out with Pishchik.*)

(*There is no one left in either the drawing room or the
ballroom except Lyubov Andreyevna, who sits huddled up and weeping bitterly. The music plays softly.
Anya and Trofimov enter hurriedly. Anya goes to her
mother and kneels before her. Trofimov remains in the
doorway of the ballroom.*)

ANYA: Mama!... Mama, you're crying! Dear, kind,
good Mama, my beautiful one, I love you... I
bless you. The cherry orchard is sold, it's gone,
that's true, true, but don't cry, Mama, life is still
before you, you still have your good, pure soul....
Come with me, come, darling, we'll go away from
here!... We'll plant a new orchard, more luxuriant than this one. You will see it and understand;
and joy, quiet, deep joy, will sink into your soul,
like the evening sun, and you will smile, Mama!
Come, darling, let us go....

ACT IV

(*The scene is the same as act I. There are neither curtains on the windows nor pictures on the walls, and
only a little furniture piled up in one corner, as if for
sale. There is a sense of emptiness. Near the outer
door, at the rear of the stage, suitcases, traveling
bags, etc., are piled up. Through the open door on
the left the voices of Varya and Anya can be heard.
Lopakhin stands waiting. Yasha is holding a tray
with little glasses of champagne. In the hall,
Yepikhodov is tying up a box. Offstage, at the rear,
there is a hum of voices. It is the peasants who have*

come to say good-bye. *Gayev's voice: "Thanks, brothers, thank you."*)

YASHA: The peasants have come to say good-bye. In my opinion, Yermolai Alekseich, peasants are good-natured, but they don't know much.

(*The hum subsides. Lyubov Andreyevna enters from the hall with Gayev. She is not crying, but she is pale, her face twitches, and she cannot speak.*)

GAYEV: You gave them your purse, Lyuba. That won't do! That won't do!

LYUBOV ANDREYEVNA: I couldn't help it! I couldn't help it! (*They both go out.*)

LOPAKHIN (*in the doorway, calls after them*): Please, do me the honor of having a little glass at parting. I didn't think of bringing champagne from town, and at the station I found only one bottle. Please! What's the matter, friends, don't you want any? (*Walks away from the door.*) If I'd known that, I wouldn't have bought it. Well, then I won't drink any either. (*Yasha carefully sets the tray down on a chair.*) At least you have a glass, Yasha.

YASHA: To those who are departing! Good luck! (*Drinks.*) This champagne is not the real stuff, I can assure you.

LOPAKHIN: Eight rubles a bottle. (*Pause.*) It's devilish cold in here.

YASHA: They didn't light the stoves today; it doesn't matter, since we're leaving. (*Laughs.*)

LOPAKHIN: Why are you laughing?

YASHA: Because I'm pleased.

LOPAKHIN: It's October, yet it's sunny and still outside, like summer. Good for building. (*Looks at his watch, then calls through the door.*) Bear in mind, ladies and gentlemen, only forty-six minutes till train time! That means leaving for the station in twenty minutes. Better hurry up!

(*Trofimov enters from outside wearing an overcoat.*)

TROFIMOV: Seems to me it's time to start. The carriages are at the door. What the devil has become of my rubbers? They're lost. (*Calls through the door.*) Anya, my rubbers are not here. I can't find them.

LOPAKHIN: I've got to go to Kharkov. I'm taking the same train you are. I'm going to spend the winter in Kharkov. I've been hanging around here with you, and I'm sick and tired of loafing. I can't live without work, I don't know what to do with my hands; they dangle in some strange way, as if they didn't belong to me.

TROFIMOV: We'll soon be gone, then you can take up your useful labors again.

LOPAKHIN: Here, have a little drink.

TROFIMOV: No, I don't want any.

LOPAKHIN: So you're off for Moscow?

TROFIMOV: Yes, I'll see them into town, and tomorrow I'll go to Moscow.

LOPAKHIN: Yes.... Well, I expect the professors haven't been giving any lectures: They're waiting for you to come!

TROFIMOV: That's none of your business.

LOPAKHIN: How many years is it you've been studying at the university?

TROFIMOV: Can't you think of something new? That's stale and flat. (*Looks for his rubbers.*) You know we'll probably never see each other again, so allow me to give you one piece of advice at parting: Don't wave your arms about! Get out of that habit — of arm-waving. And another thing, building cottages and counting on the summer residents in time becoming independent farmers — that's just another form of arm-waving. Well, when all's said and done, I'm fond of you anyway. You have fine, delicate fingers, like an artist; you have a fine delicate soul.

LOPAKHIN (*embraces him*): Good-bye, my dear fellow. Thank you for everything. Let me give you some money for the journey, if you need it.

TROFIMOV: What for? I don't need it.

LOPAKHIN: But you haven't any!

TROFIMOV: I have. Thank you. I got some money for a translation. Here it is in my pocket. (*Anxiously.*) But where are my rubbers?

VARYA (*from the next room*): Here, take the nasty things! (*Flings a pair of rubbers onto the stage.*)

TROFIMOV: What are you so cross about, Varya? Hm.... But these are not my rubbers.

LOPAKHIN: In the spring I sowed three thousand acres of poppies, and now I've made forty thousand rubles clear. And when my poppies were in bloom, what a picture it was! So, I'm telling you, I've made forty thousand, which means I'm offering you a loan because I can afford to. Why turn up your nose? I'm a peasant — I speak bluntly.

TROFIMOV: Your father was a peasant, mine was a pharmacist — which proves absolutely nothing. (*Lopakhin takes out his wallet.*) No, don't — even if you gave me two hundred thousand I wouldn't take it. I'm a free man. And everything that is valued so highly and held so dear by all of you, rich and poor alike, has not the slightest power over me — it's like a feather floating in the air. I can get along without you, I can pass you by, I'm strong and proud. Mankind is advancing toward the highest truth, the highest happiness attainable on earth, and I am in the front ranks!

LOPAKHIN: Will you get there?

TROFIMOV: I'll get there. (*Pause.*) I'll either get there or I'll show others the way to get there.

(*The sound of axes chopping down trees is heard in the distance.*)

LOPAKHIN: Well, good-bye, my dear fellow. It's time to go. We turn up our noses at one another, but life goes on just the same. When I work for a long time without stopping, my mind is easier, and it seems to me that I, too, know why I exist. But how many there are in Russia, brother, who exist nobody knows why. Well, it doesn't matter, that's not what makes the wheels go round. They say Leonid Andreich has taken a position in the bank, six thousand a year. . . . Only, of course, he won't stick it out, he's too lazy. . . .

ANYA (*in the doorway*): Mama asks you not to start cutting down the cherry orchard until she's gone.

TROFIMOV: Yes, really, not to have had the tact . . . (*Goes out through the hall.*)

LOPAKHIN: Right away, right away. . . . Ach, what people. . . . (*Follows Trofimov out.*)

ANYA: Has Firs been taken to the hospital?

YASHA: I told them this morning. They must have taken him.

ANYA (*to Yepikhodov, who is crossing the room*): Semyon Panteleich, please find out if Firs has been taken to the hospital.

YASHA (*offended*): I told Yegor this morning. Why ask a dozen times?

YEPIKHODOV: It is my conclusive opinion that the venerable Firs is beyond repair; it's time he was gathered to his fathers. And I can only envy him. (*Puts a suitcase down on a hatbox and crushes it.*) There you are! Of course! I knew it! (*Goes out.*)

YASHA (*mockingly*): Two-and-twenty Troubles!

VARYA (*through the door*): Has Firs been taken to the hospital?

ANYA: Yes, he has.

VARYA: Then why didn't they take the letter to the doctor?

ANYA: We must send it on after them. . . . (*Goes out.*)

VARYA (*from the adjoining room*): Where is Yasha? Tell him his mother has come to say good-bye to him.

YASHA (*waves his hand*): They really try my patience.

(*Dunyasha has been fussing with the luggage; now that Yasha is alone she goes up to him.*)

DUNYASHA: You might give me one little look, Yasha. You're going away . . . leaving me. . . . (*Cries and throws herself on his neck.*)

YASHA: What's there to cry about? (*Drinks champagne.*) In six days I'll be in Paris again. Tomorrow we'll take the express, off we go, and that's the last you'll see of us. I can hardly believe it. *Vive la France!* This place is not for me, I can't live

here. . . . It can't be helped. I've had enough of this ignorance — I'm fed up with it. (*Drinks champagne.*) What are you crying for? Behave yourself properly, then you won't cry.

DUNYASHA (*looks into a small mirror and powders her face*): Send me a letter from Paris. You know, I loved you, Yasha, how I loved you! I'm such a tender creature, Yasha!

YASHA: Here they come. (*Busies himself with the luggage, humming softly.*)

(*Enter Lyubov Andreyevna, Gayev, Charlotta Ivanovna.*)

GAYEV: We ought to be leaving. There's not much time now. (*Looks at Yasha.*) Who smells of herring?

LYUBOV ANDREYEVNA: In about ten minutes we should be getting into the carriages. (*Glances around the room.*) Good-bye, dear house, old grandfather. Winter will pass, spring will come, and you will no longer be here, they will tear you down. How much these walls have seen! (*Kisses her daughter warmly.*) My treasure, you are radiant, your eyes are sparkling like two diamonds. Are you glad? Very?

ANYA: Very! A new life is beginning, Mama!

GAYEV (*cheerfully*): Yes, indeed, everything is all right now. Before the cherry orchard was sold we were all worried and miserable, but afterward, when the question was finally settled once and for all, everybody calmed down and felt quite cheerful. . . . I'm in a bank now, a financier . . . cue ball into the center . . . and you, Lyuba, say what you like, you look better, no doubt about it.

LYUBOV ANDREYEVNA: Yes. My nerves are better, that's true. (*Her hat and coat are handed to her.*) I sleep well. Carry out my things, Yasha, it's time. (*To Anya.*) My little girl, we shall see each other soon. . . . I shall go to Paris and live there on the money your great-aunt sent to buy the estate — long live Auntie! — but that money won't last long.

ANYA: You'll come back soon, Mama, soon . . . won't you? I'll study hard and pass my high school examinations, and then I can work and help you. We'll read all sorts of books together, Mama. . . . Won't we? (*Kisses her mother's hand.*) We'll read in the autumn evenings, we'll read lots of books, and a new and wonderful world will open up before us. . . . (*Dreaming.*) Mama, come back. . . .

LYUBOV ANDREYEVNA: I'll come, my precious. (*Embraces her.*)

(*Enter Lopakhin, Charlotta Ivanovna is softly humming a song.*)

GAYEV: Happy Charlotta: She's singing!

CHARLOTTA (*picks up a bundle and holds it like a baby in swaddling clothes*): Bye, baby, bye. . . . (*A baby's crying is heard, "Wah! Wah!"*) Be quiet, my darling, my dear little boy. (*"Wah! Wah!"*) I'm so sorry for you! (*Throws the bundle down.*) You will find me a position, won't you? I can't go on like this.

LOPAKHIN: We'll find something, Charlotta Ivanovna, don't worry.

GAYEV: Everyone is leaving us, Varya's going away . . . all of a sudden nobody needs us.

CHARLOTTA: I have nowhere to go in town. I must go away. (*Hums.*) It doesn't matter . . .

(*Enter Pishchik.*)

LOPAKHIN: Nature's wonder!

PISHCHIK (*panting*): Ugh! Let me catch my breath. . . . I'm exhausted. . . . My esteemed friends. . . . Give me some water. . . .

GAYEV: After money, I suppose? Excuse me, I'm fleeing from temptation. . . . (*Goes out.*)

PISHCHIK: It's a long time since I've been to see you . . . fairest lady. . . . (*To Lopakhin*) So you're here. . . . Glad to see you, you intellectual giant. . . . Here . . . take it . . . four hundred rubles . . . I still owe you eight hundred and forty . . .

LOPAKHIN (*shrugs his shoulders in bewilderment*): I must be dreaming. . . . Where did you get it?

PISHCHIK: Wait . . . I'm hot. . . . A most extraordinary event. Some Englishmen came to my place and discovered some kind of white clay on my land. (*To Lyubov Andreyevna*) And four hundred for you . . . fairest, most wonderful lady. . . . (*Hands her the money.*) The rest later. (*Takes a drink of water.*) Just now a young man in the train was saying that a certain . . . great philosopher recommends jumping off roofs. . . . "Jump!" he says, and therein lies the whole problem. (*In amazement.*) Think of that, now! . . . Water!

LOPAKHIN: Who were those Englishmen?

PISHCHIK: I leased them the tract of land with the clay on it for twenty-four years. . . . And now, excuse me, I have no time . . . I must be trotting along . . . I'm going to Znoikov's . . . to Kardamanov's . . . I owe everybody. (*Drinks.*) Keep well . . . I'll drop in on Thursday . . .

LYUBOV ANDREYEVNA: We're just moving into town, and tomorrow I go abroad . . .

PISHCHIK: What? (*Alarmed.*) Why into town? That's why I see the furniture . . . suitcases. . . . Well, never mind. . . . (*Through tears.*) Never mind. . . . Men of the greatest intellect, those Englishmen. . . . Never mind. . . . Be happy . . . God will help you. . . . Never mind. . . . Everything in this world comes to an end. . . . (*Kisses Lyubov Andreyevna's hand.*)

And should the news reach you that my end has come, just remember this old horse, and say: "There once lived a certain Semyonov-Pishchik, God rest his soul." . . . Splendid weather. . . . Yes. . . . (*Goes out greatly disconcerted, but immediately returns and speaks from the doorway.*) Dashenka sends her regards. (*Goes out.*)

LYUBOV ANDREYEVNA: Now we can go. I am leaving with two things on my mind. First — that Firs is sick. (*Looks at her watch.*) We still have about five minutes. . . .

ANYA: Mama, Firs has already been taken to the hospital. Yasha sent him there this morning.

LYUBOV ANDREYEVNA: My second concern is Varya. She's used to getting up early and working, and now, with no work to do, she's like a fish out of water. She's grown pale and thin, and cries all the time, poor girl. . . . (*Pauses.*) You know very well, Yermolai Alekseich, that I dreamed of marrying her to you, and everything pointed to your getting married. (*Whispers to Anya, who nods to Charlotta, and they both go out.*) She loves you, you are fond of her, and I don't know — I don't know why it is you seem to avoid each other. I can't understand it!

LOPAKHIN: To tell you the truth, I don't understand it myself. The whole thing is strange, somehow. . . . If there's still time, I'm ready right now. . . . Let's finish it up — and *basta,*° but without you I feel I'll never be able to propose to her.

LYUBOV ANDREYEVNA: Splendid! After all, it only takes a minute. I'll call her in at once. . . .

LOPAKHIN: And we even have the champagne. (*Looks at the glasses.*) Empty! Somebody's already drunk it. (*Yasha coughs.*) That's what you call lapping it up.

LYUBOV ANDREYEVNA (*animatedly*): Splendid! We'll leave you. . . . Yasha, *allez!*° I'll call her. . . . (*At the door.*) Varya, leave everything and come here. Come! (*Goes out with Yasha.*)

LOPAKHIN (*looking at his watch*): Yes. . . . (*Pause.*)

(*Behind the door there is smothered laughter and whispering; finally Varya enters.*)

VARYA (*looking over the luggage for a long time*): Strange, I can't seem to find it . . .

LOPAKHIN: What are you looking for?

VARYA: I packed it myself, and I can't remember . . . (*Pause.*)

LOPAKHIN: Where are you going now, Varya Mikhailovna?

VARYA: I? To the Ragulins'. . . . I've agreed to go there

basta: Italian for "enough."
allez: French for "go."

to look after the house . . . as a sort of house-keeper.

LOPAKHIN: At Yashnevo? That would be about seventy versts from here. (*Pause.*) Well, life in this house has come to an end. . . .

VARYA (*examining the luggage*): Where can it be? . . . Perhaps I put it in the trunk. . . . Yes, life in this house has come to an end . . . there'll be no more . . .

LOPAKHIN: And I'm off for Kharkov . . . by the next train. I have a lot to do. I'm leaving Yepikhodov here . . . I've taken him on.

VARYA: Really!

LOPAKHIN: Last year at this time it was already snowing, if you remember, but now it's still and sunny. It's cold though. . . . About three degrees of frost.

VARYA: I haven't looked. (*Pause.*) And besides, our thermometer's broken. (*Pause.*)

(*A voice from the yard calls: "Yermolai Alekseich!"*)

LOPAKHIN (*as if he had been waiting for a long time for the call*): Coming! (*Goes out quickly.*)

(*Varya sits on the floor, lays her head on a bundle of clothes, and quietly sobs. The door opens and Lyubov Andreyevna enters cautiously.*)

LYUBOV ANDREYEVNA: Well? (*Pause.*) We must be going.

VARYA (*no longer crying, dries her eyes*): Yes, it's time, Mama dear. I can get to the Ragulins' today, if only we don't miss the train.

LYUBOV ANDREYEVNA (*in the doorway*): Anya, put your things on!

(*Enter Anya, then Gayev and Charlotta Ivanovna. Gayev wears a warm overcoat with a hood. The servants and coachmen come in. Yepikhodov bustles about the luggage.*)

LYUBOV ANDREYEVNA: Now we can be on our way.

ANYA (*joyfully*): On our way!

GAYEV: My friends, my dear, cherished friends! Leaving this house forever, can I pass over in silence, can I refrain from giving utterance, as we say farewell, to those feelings that now fill my whole being —

ANYA (*imploringly*): Uncle!

VARYA: Uncle dear, don't!

GAYEV (*forlornly*): Double the rail off the white to center table . . . yellow into the side pocket. . . . I'll be quiet. . . .

(*Enter Trofimov, then Lopakhin.*)

TROFIMOV: Well, ladies and gentlemen, it's time to go!

LOPAKHIN: Yepikhodov, my coat!

LYUBOV ANDREYEVNA: I'll sit here just one more minute. It's as though I had never before seen what the walls of this house were like, what the ceilings were like, and now I look at them hungrily, with such tender love . . .

GAYEV: I remember when I was six years old, sitting on this windowsill on Whitsunday, watching my father going to church . . .

LYUBOV ANDREYEVNA: Have they taken all the things?

LOPAKHIN: Everything, I think. (*Puts on his overcoat.*) Yepikhodov, see that everything is in order.

YEPIKHODOV (*in a hoarse voice*): Rest assured, Yermolai Alekseich!

LOPAKHIN: What's the matter with your voice?

YEPIKHODOV: Just drank some water . . . must have swallowed something.

YASHA (*contemptuously*): What ignorance!

LYUBOV ANDREYEVNA: When we go — there won't be a soul left here. . . .

LOPAKHIN: Till spring.

VARYA (*pulls an umbrella out of a bundle as though she were going to hit someone; Lopakhin pretends to be frightened*): Why are you — I never thought of such a thing!

TROFIMOV: Ladies and gentlemen, let's get into the carriages — it's time now! The train will soon be in!

VARYA: Petya, there they are — your rubbers, by the suitcase. (*Tearfully.*) And what dirty old things they are!

TROFIMOV (*putting on his rubbers*): Let's go, ladies and gentlemen!

GAYEV (*extremely upset, afraid of bursting into tears*): The train . . . the station. . . . Cross table to the center, double the rail . . . on the white into the corner.

LYUBOV ANDREYEVNA: Let us go!

GAYEV: Are we all here? No one in there? (*Locks the side door on the left.*) There are some things stored in there, we must lock up. Let's go!

ANYA: Good-bye, house! Good-bye, old life!

TROFIMOV: Hail to the new life! (*Goes out with Anya.*)

(*Varya looks around the room and slowly goes out. Yasha and Charlotta with her dog go out.*)

LOPAKHIN: And so, till spring. Come along, my friends. . . . Till we meet! (*Goes out.*)

(*Lyubov Andreyevna and Gayev are left alone. As though they had been waiting for this, they fall onto each other's necks and break into quiet, restrained sobs, afraid of being heard.*)

GAYEV (*in despair*): My sister, my sister. . . .

LYUBOV ANDREYEVNA: Oh, my dear, sweet, lovely orchard! . . . My life, my youth, my happiness, good-bye! . . . Good-bye!

ANYA'S VOICE (*gaily calling*): Mama!

TROFIMOV'S VOICE (*gay and excited*): Aa-oo!

LYUBOV ANDREYEVNA: One last look at these walls, these windows. . . . Mother loved to walk about in this room. . . .

GAYEV: My sister, my sister!

ANYA'S VOICE: Mama!

TROFIMOV'S VOICE: Aa-oo!

LYUBOV ANDREYEVNA: We're coming! (*They go out.*)

(*The stage is empty. There is the sound of doors being locked, then of the carriages driving away. It grows quiet. In the stillness there is the dull thud of an ax on a tree, a forlorn, melancholy sound. Footsteps are heard. From the door on the right Firs appears. He is dressed as always in a jacket and white waistcoat, and wears slippers. He is ill.*)

FIRS (*goes to the door and tries the handle*): Locked. They have gone. . . . (*Sits down on the sofa.*) They've forgotten me. . . . Never mind. . . . I'll sit here awhile. . . . I expect Leonid Andreich hasn't put on his fur coat and has gone off in his overcoat. (*Sighs anxiously.*) And I didn't see to it. . . . When they're young, they're green! (*Mumbles something which cannot be understood.*) I'll lie down awhile. . . . There's no strength left in you, nothing's left, nothing. . . . Ach, you . . . addlepate! (*Lies motionless.*)

(*A distant sound is heard that seems to come from the sky, the sound of a snapped string mournfully dying away. A stillness falls, and nothing is heard but the thud of the ax on a tree far away in the orchard.*)

COMMENTARIES

Anton Chekhov (1860–1904)

FROM *LETTERS OF ANTON CHEKOV*   *(1888–1903)*

TRANSLATED BY MICHAEL HENRY HEIM WITH SIMON KARLINSKY

Chekhov, like Ibsen, was an inveterate letter writer. In letters to family members and colleagues, he spoke quite frankly about his hopes, expectations, and difficulties regarding his work. Chekhov's letters concerning his purpose as an artist and his play The Cherry Orchard *give us some insight into the anxieties and hopes that Chekhov had for his work. His awareness of the difficulties he faced in his writing helps us understand how his plays developed into complex and demanding works.*

October 4, 1888

The people I fear are those who look for tendentiousness between the lines and are determined to see me as either liberal or conservative. I am neither liberal, nor conservative, nor gradualist, nor monk, nor indifferentist. I should like to be a free artist and nothing else. That is why I cultivate no particular predilection for policemen, butchers, scientists, writers, or the younger generation. I look upon tags and labels as prejudices. My holy of holies is the human body, health, intelligence, talent, inspiration, love and the most absolute freedom imaginable, freedom from violence and lies.

November 25, 1892

Keep in mind that the writers we call eternal or simply good, the writers who intoxicate us, have one highly important trait in common: They are moving towards something definite and beckon you to follow, and you feel with your entire being, not only with your mind, that they have a certain goal, like the ghost of Hamlet's father, which had a motive for coming and stirring Hamlet's imagination. Depending on their caliber, some have immediate goals — the abolition of serfdom, the liberation of one's country, politics, beauty, or simply vodka . . . — while the goals of others are more remote — God, life after death, the happiness of mankind, etc. The best of them are realistic and describe life as it is, but because each line is saturated with the consciousness of its goal, you feel life as it should be in addition to life as it is, and you are captivated by it. But what about us? Us! We describe life as it is and stop dead right there. We wouldn't lift a hoof if you lit into us with a whip. We have neither immediate nor remote goals, and there is an emptiness in our souls. We have no politics, we don't believe in revolution, there is no God, we're not afraid of ghosts, and I personally am not even afraid of death or blindness. If you want nothing, hope for nothing, and fear nothing, you cannot be an artist.

To K.S. Stanislavsky°
Yalta. Oct. 30, 1903

When I was writing Lopakhin, I thought of it as a part for you. If for any reason you don't care for it, take the part of Gayev. Lopakhin is a merchant, of course, but he is a very decent person in every sense. He must behave with perfect decorum, like an educated man, with no petty ways or tricks of any sort, and it seemed to me this part, the central one of the play, would come out brilliantly in your hands. . . . In choosing an actor for the part you must remember that Varya, a serious and religious girl, is in love with Lopakhin; she wouldn't be in love with a mere moneygrubber. . . .

To Vl. I. Nemirovich-Danchenko°
Yalta. Nov. 2, 1903

. . . Pishchik is a Russian, an old man, worn out by the gout, age, and satiety; stout, dressed in a sleeveless undercoat (à la Simov [an actor in the Moscow Art Theatre]), boots without heels. Lopakhin — a white waistcoat, yellow shoes; when walking, swings his arms, a broad stride, thinks deeply while walking, walks as if on a straight line. Hair not short, and therefore often throws back his head; while in thought he passes his hand through his beard, combing it from the back forward, i.e., from the neck toward the mouth. Trofimov, I think, is clear. Varya — black dress, wide belt.

Three years I spent writing "The Cherry Orchard," and for three years I have been telling you that it is necessary to invite an actress for the role of Lyubov Andreyevna. And now you see you are trying to solve a puzzle that won't work out.

K.S. Stanislavsky: Konstantin Stanislavsky (1863–1938), director with the Moscow Art Theatre, which produced most of Chekhov's plays.
Vl. I. Nemirovich-Danchenko: Vladimir Ivanovich Nemirovich-Danchenko, novelist and codirector of the Moscow Art Theatre.

To K.S. Alekseyev (Stanislavsky)
Yalta. Nov. 5, 1903

The house in the play is two-storied, a large one. But in the third act does it not speak of a stairway leading down? Nevertheless, this third act worries me.... N. has it that the third act takes place in "some kind of hotel"; ... evidently I made an error in the play. The action does not pass in "some kind of hotel," but in a *drawing-room.* If I mention a hotel in the play, which I cannot now doubt, after Vl. Iv.'s [Nemirovich-Danchenko] letter, please telegraph me. We must correct it; we cannot issue it thus, with grave errors distorting its meaning.

The house must be large, solid; wooden (like Aksakov's, which, I think, S.T. Morozov has seen) or stone, it is all the same. It is very old and imposing; country residents do not take such houses; such houses are usually wrecked and the material employed for the construction of a country house. The furniture is ancient, stylish, solid; ruin and debt have not affected the surroundings.

When they buy such a house, they reason thus: it is cheaper and easier to build a new and smaller one than to repair this old one.

Your shepherd played well. That was most essential.

Maxim Gorky (1868–1936)
FROM *RECOLLECTIONS*

Alexei Maximovitch Pyeshkov changed his name to Maxim Gorky, which in Russian means "Maxim the Bitter." His childhood and early years gave him great reason for bitterness, because he was raised by a brutal grandfather who regularly beat Maxim and his mother. Once, when Maxim was eight, he attacked his grandfather with a bread knife for beating his frail and sick mother. Gorky spent many years tramping through Russia and became a writer of the common people. He was introduced to the Moscow Art Theatre by Chekhov, and his first play, The Lower Depths (1902), *starred Chekhov's wife, Olga Knipper. It was a mercilessly realistic portrait of the homeless, impoverished castaways of Russian life. It established Gorky as a major dramatist, and after the Russian revolution he became the most revered of Soviet writers.*

Reading Anton Chekhov's stories, one feels oneself in a melancholy day of late autumn, when the air is transparent and the outline of naked trees, narrow houses, grayish people, is sharp. Everything is strange, lonely, motionless, helpless. The horizon, blue and empty, melts into the pale sky, and its breath is terribly cold upon the earth, which is covered with frozen mud. The author's mind, like the autumn sun, shows up in hard outline the monotonous roads, the crooked streets, the little squalid houses in which tiny, miserable people are stifled by boredom and laziness and fill the houses with an unintelligible, drowsy bustle....

Here is the lachrymose Ranevskaya and the other owners of *The Cherry Orchard,* egotistical like children, with the flabbiness of senility. They missed the right moment for dying; they whine, seeing nothing of what is going on around them, understanding nothing, parasites without the power of again taking root in life. The wretched little student, Trofimov, speaks eloquently of the necessity of working — and does nothing but amuse himself, out of sheer boredom, with stupid mockery of Varya, who works ceaselessly for the good of idlers. . . .

There passes before one a long file of men and women, slaves of their love, of their stupidity and idleness, of their greed for the good things of life; there walk the slaves of the dark fear of life; they straggle anxiously along, filling life with incoherent words about the future, feeling that in the present there is no place for them.

At moments out of the gray mass of them one hears the sound of a shot: Ivanov [in *Ivanov*] or Treplev [in *The Seagull*] has guessed what he ought to do and has died.

Many of them have nice dreams of how pleasant life will be in three hundred years, but it occurs to none of them to ask themselves who will make life pleasant if we only dream.

In front of that dreary, gray crowd of helpless people there passed a great, wise, and observant man; he looked at all these dreary inhabitants of his country, and, with a sad smile, with a tone of gentle but deep reproach, with anguish in his face and in his heart, in a beautiful and sincere voice, he said to them:

"You live badly, my friends. It is shameful to live like that."

Virginia Woolf (1882–1941)
ON *THE CHERRY ORCHARD* (1920)

Virginia Woolf was one of the most important experimental writers of fiction in the first half of the twentieth century. Her best-known works include Mrs. Dalloway *(1925),* To the Lighthouse *(1927),* Orlando *(1928),* A Room of One's Own *(1930), and* The Waves *(1931). But in addition to these landmark works, she wrote a huge number of essays and commentaries, not to mention letters that have now been gathered into five large volumes. Her insight into literature is always keen and original. Her approach, for instance, to a 1920 production of* The Cherry Orchard *is through language. She is naturally sensitive to careful use of language, and it is therefore important for her to observe that out of the apparently disjointed use of sentences comes extraordinary drama. She ends her commentary with an interesting comparison that delves into the realm of music — or, more properly, into an imaginative realm in which the theatergoers themselves are musical instruments.*

It is, as a rule, when a critic does not wish to commit himself or to trouble himself, that he refers to atmosphere. And, given time, something might be said in greater detail of the causes which produced this atmosphere — the strange dislocated sentences, each so erratic and yet cutting out the shape so firmly, of the realism, of the humor, of the artistic unity. But let the word atmosphere be taken literally to mean that Chekhov has contrived to shed over us a luminous vapor in which life appears as it is, without veils, transparent and visible to the depths. Long before the play was over, we seemed to have sunk below the surface of things and to be feeling our way among submerged but recognizable emotions. "I have no proper passport. I don't know how old I am; I always feel I am still young" — how the words go sounding on in one's mind — how the whole play resounds with such sentences, which reverberate, melt into each other, and pass far away out beyond everything! In short, if it is permissible to use such vague language, I do not know how better to describe the sensation at the end of *The Cherry Orchard*, than by saying that it sends one into the street feeling like a piano played upon at last, not in the middle only but all over the keyboard and with the lid left open so that the sound goes on.

John Corbin (1870–1959)
REVIEW OF *THE CHERRY ORCHARD*   1923

After brief praise for the Russian language production of the Moscow Play-ers, John Corbin's review centers itself entirely on an analysis of the play. Clearly, he sees the main characters as feckless and wasteful and has little sym-pathy for them. On the other hand, he sees in Lopakhin a man of industry and progress. His interpretation may well depend on the emphasis of the post-revolutionary Russian players, whose sympathies would certainly not have aligned with aristocrats.

The Moscow players proceeded last night from the lower depths of Gorky to the high comedy of Tchekhoff, revealing new artistic resources. Stanislavsky, Olga Knipper-Tchekhova, Moskvin, Leonidoff and half a dozen others entered with consummate ease into a rich variety of new characterizations. The stage management was less signal in its effects, but no less perfect. Yet for some rea-son *The Cherry Orchard* failed to stir the audience, even the Russian portion of it, as did *The Lower Depths* and even *Tsar Fyodor*.

This is a play of comedy values both high and light. The milleu is that of the ancient landed aristocracy, beautifully symbolized by an orchard of cherry trees in full bloom which surrounds the crumbling manor house. Quite obviously, these amiable folks have fallen away from the pristine vigor of their race.

The middle-aged brother and sister who live together are unconscious, ir-reclaimable spendthrifts, both of their shrinking purses and of their waning lives. With a little effort, one is made to feel, even with a modicum of mental concentration, calamity could be averted. But that is utterly beyond their vacu-ous and futile amiability; so their estate is sold over their heads and the leagues of gay cherry trees are felled to make way for suburban villas.

Beneath the graceful, easy-going surface of the play one feels rather than per-ceives a criticism on the Russia of two decades ago. Here is a woman of truly Slavic instability, passing with a single gesture from heartbreak to the gayety of a moment, from acutely maternal grief for an only child long dead to weak dot-ing on a Parisian lover who is faithless to her and yet has power to hold her and batten on her bounty. Here is a man whose sentiment for the home of his an-cestors breaks forth in fluent declaiming, quasi-poetic and quasi-philosophic, yet who cannot lift a finger to avert financial disaster.

In the entire cast only one person has normal human sense. Lopakhin is the son of a serf who has prospered in freedom. He is loyal enough to the old masters, dogging their footsteps with good advice. But in the end it is he who buys the estate and fells the cherry trees for the villas of an industrial population. It is as if Tchekhoff saw in the new middle class the hope of a disenchanted yet sounder and more progressive Russia. The war has halted that movement, but indications are not lacking that it is already resuming.

With such a theme developed by the subtly masterful act of Tchekhoff there is scope for comedy acting of the highest quality. It is more than likely that the company seized every opportunity and improved upon it. But to any one who does not understand Russian, judgment in such a matter is quite impossible. Where effects are to be achieved only by the subtlest intonation, the most delicate phrasing, it fares ill with those whose entire vocabulary is da, da.

As an example of the art of the most distinguished company that has visited our shores in modern memory, this production of *The Cherry Orchard* is abundantly worth seeing. The play in itself is of interest as the masterpiece of the man who, with Gorky, has touched the pinnacle of modern Russian comedy. But if some Moscovite should rise up and tell us that in any season our own stage produces casts as perfect and ensembles as finely studied in detail, it would be quite possible to believe him.

Peter Brook (b. 1925)
ON CHEKHOV   (1987)

Peter Brook has established himself as one of the most distinguished modern directors. He was educated at Oxford University and has been a director of the Royal Shakespeare Company in England. In 1987 he directed The Cherry Orchard *at the Brooklyn Academy of Music. Some of his thoughts as he prepared to direct the play are presented here, showing his awareness of Chekhov's "film sense" in a play that was written just as film was emerging as a popular form. He is also aware of Chekhov's personal vision of death and sees it expressed in the circumstances of the play.*

Chekhov always looked for what's natural; he wanted performances and productions to be as limpid as life itself. Chekhov's writing is extremely concentrated, employing a minimum of words; in a way, it is similar to Pinter or Beckett. As with them, it is construction that counts, rhythm, the purely theatrical poetry that comes not from beautiful words but from the right word at the right moment. In the theater, someone can say "yes" in such a way that the "yes" is no longer ordinary — it can become a beautiful word, because it is the perfect expression of what cannot be expressed in any other way. With Chekhov, periods, commas, points of suspension are all of a fundamental importance, as fundamental as the "pauses" precisely indicated by Beckett. If one fails to observe them, one loses the rhythm and tensions of the play. In Chekhov's work, the punctuation represents a series of coded messages which record characters' relationships and emotions, the moments at which ideas come together or follow their own course. The punctuation enables us to grasp what the words conceal.

Chekhov is like a perfect filmmaker. Instead of cutting from one image to another — perhaps from one place to another — he switches from one emotion to another just before it gets too heavy. At the precise moment when the spectator risks becoming too involved in a character, an unexpected situation cuts across: Nothing is stable. Chekhov portrays individuals and a society in a state of perpetual change, he is the dramatist of life's movement, simultaneously smiling and serious, amusing and bitter — completely free from the "music," the Slav "nostalgia" that Paris nightclubs still preserve. He often stated that his plays were comedies — this was the central issue of his conflict with Stanislavsky.

But it's wrong to conclude that *The Cherry Orchard* should be performed as a vaudeville. Chekhov is an infinitely detailed observer of the human comedy. As a doctor, he knew the meaning of certain kinds of behavior, how to discern what was essential, to expose what he diagnosed. Although he shows tenderness and an attentive sympathy, he never sentimentalizes. One doesn't imagine a doctor shedding tears over the illnesses of his patients. He learns how to balance compassion with distance.

In Chekhov's work, death is omnipresent — he knew it well — but there is nothing negative or unsavory in its presence. The awareness of death is balanced with a desire to live. His characters possess a sense of the present moment, and the need to taste it fully. As in great tragedies, one finds a harmony between life and death.

Chekhov died young, having traveled, written, and loved enormously, having taken part in the events of his day, in great schemes of social reform. He died shortly after asking for some champagne, and his coffin was transported in a wagon bearing the inscription "Fresh Oysters." His awareness of death, and of the precious moments that could be lived, endow his work with a sense of the relative: in other words, a viewpoint from which the tragic is always a bit absurd.

In Chekhov's work, each character has its own existence: not one of them resembles another, particularly in *The Cherry Orchard,* which presents a microcosm of the political tendencies of the time. There are those who believe in social transformations, others attached to a disappearing past. None of them can achieve satisfaction or plenitude, and seen from outside, their existences might well appear empty, senseless. But they all burn with intense desires. They are not disillusioned, quite the contrary: In their own ways, they are all searching for a better quality of life, emotionally and socially. Their drama is that society — the outside world — blocks their energy. The complexity of their behavior is not indicated in the words, it emerges from the mosaic construction of an infinite number of details. What is essential is to see that these are not plays about lethargic people. They are hypervital people in a lethargic world, forced to dramatize the minutest happening out of a passionate desire to live. They have not given up.

Bernard Shaw

The Irish playwright Bernard Shaw (1856–1950) was astonishing not only for the range of his writing but also for the length and vigor of his life. He was a public figure for most of his days, with an especially keen ability to catch public attention and to make his presence felt. His early work was devoted to criticism in newspapers, then to a series of fairly successful novels. He began writing plays in his late thirties; once he began, he realized that he had discovered his vocation, and he went on to write more than fifty. Some of them, such as *Arms and the Man* (1894), *Candida* (1897), *Mrs. Warren's Profession* (1898), *Man and Superman* (1901–1903), *Pygmalion* (1913), *Heartbreak House* (1919), and *St. Joan* (1923), are among the most performed plays by any English-language writer of his time.

Shaw's gift of analysis and philosophical reflection created in his works a new kind of drama that has sometimes been named for him — Shavian. The term implies a deep interest in ideas rather than in character and a propensity for elaborate discourse between characters who represent different points of view. Shaw assumed that drama should amuse and entertain, but of much greater importance was his didactic motive. Drama should teach a lesson about something of great moral importance.

This is not to say that Shaw was unable to be entertaining. Some of his comedies, still played today, are bright and witty. *You Never Can Tell* (1898), a comedy about male-female relationships whose main character is a dentist, and *Pygmalion,* a comedy in which a man teaches a cockney girl how to speak with an upper-class accent with unexpected results, are both funny plays. *Pygmalion* was redone as a musical, *My Fair Lady,* and has been Shaw's most financially successful play.

Still, Shaw was basically a philosophical writer. His plays can usually be seen as having a specific theme on which the characters constantly discourse. Whether it is on the relation of England to Ireland, on the state of the medical profession, on genetics and propagation, or on poverty, Shaw always focused on an issue and even commented that Shakespeare's shortcoming was that his plays have no message.

Shaw frequently wrote elaborate and lengthy prefaces to his published plays. The preface to *Pygmalion* (see pages 871–74) is Shaw's opportunity to comment directly on phonetics, shorthand, and pronunciation — some of his favorite subjects. In his other prefaces, Shaw takes time to explain — and fully explore — the messages of his plays. He discusses the questions of genetic planning and the improvement of the race in his preface to *Man and Superman;* in the preface to *Candida* he discusses the relationship of pity to love.

Shaw's lifelong socialism affected his work and his thinking, and he himself was a socialist politician for a short period. Consequently, it is not uncommon to see political concerns expressed and debated in his plays.

Shaw's political ideas were shaped by his concern for economics as a discipline, beginning in 1882. In 1884 he joined the Fabian Society, established a year earlier as a group to study and promote socialism, and remained active until 1911. Fabianism, unlike Marxism or communism, believed that society need not be destroyed by revolution but could become an instrument of socialist reform. For this reason Fabianism was known as evolutionary socialism. *Fabian Essays* (1889), which Shaw edited, was used by study groups that sprouted up throughout England to spread Fabian socialist ideas through politics, religion, and society. The result of the movement was the organization of a new political party, the Labor Party (1893), which still exists. The socialist government of England in the 1960s and 1970s was a direct outgrowth of Fabian theories.

While Shaw studied economics, he grew to believe that all social values were built on an economic base. He developed this idea in his Fabian essays and maintained it throughout his plays. He also maintained a presence as a critic of theater and accepted Ibsen as a major playwright when most London critics found his work unacceptable. Shaw's *Quintessence of Ibsenism* (1891; revised after Ibsen's death in 1913) is still a useful commentary on that playwright's work. (See an excerpt from *Quintessence of Ibsenism* on pages 711–12.)

PYGMALION

Written in 1912 and first performed in 1913, *Pygmalion* is said to be Shaw's most popular play. As Shaw implies in his preface (see pages 871–74), its development is connected to his strong language. In making his male protagonist a phonetician, Shaw demonstrates how language reveals not only character but station and class values as well. Shaw wrote elsewhere about a simplified system of the spelling of English, and he took a strong interest in shorthand, which respects the phonetic structure of words. But the concern for the science of language, emphasized in the first act, gives way rapidly to a larger concern for the consequences of a society in which the way people talk and write establishes the limits of their social status.

Shaw tells us plainly that a person's accent instantly encourages delight or disdain on the part of the listener. It identifies social class, social opportunity, birth, and education. In Great Britain even today much the same could be said, and in the United States concern for "proper" use of the language is a constant in schools and colleges. Shaw calls *Pygmalion* a didactic play, a play that teaches a lesson. But it is didactic in another way in that it concerns the question of teaching and its effects on those who are taught. Henry Higgins is a professor who is "engaged" to teach Eliza Doolittle to speak like a duchess. He takes upon himself the further task of instructing her to behave like — and, to an extent, think like — an aristocrat. In other words, he takes as his responsibilty the "elevation" of a street urchin to the level of the aristocracy.

Shaw wants us to consider all the ramifications of Higgins's actions. For one thing, the language of scientific experimentation is used often in describing Higgins's work with Eliza. It implies that Eliza is a kind of experiment and that Higgins is the detached scientist whose feelings are cool and remote. It also implies that the scientist does not take into account the consequences of his actions. In Eliza's case, she is a willing subject who sees an opportunity to change herself and to qualify herself for a better job — as a clerk in a flower shop. But she, like Higgins, is unaware of how she will feel when the experiment is over.

Eliza's father, Alfred Doolittle, is, on the other hand, not interested in changing himself. He describes himself as one of the "undeserving poor," a man who will take five pounds and put it to good use by drinking it up. His straightforwardness, however, earns him an unexpected recommendation by Higgins. Before the play ends, Doolittle is thrust into the middle class and thus adheres to middle-class morals. This part of the play is satire and an opportunity to examine the attitudes of the well-off toward those who have little or nothing. Shaw's social concerns come to the fore in his development of Alfred Doolittle.

The question of emotion, affection, even love is present in the play. Ovid's *Metamorphoses,* from which the original story of Pygmalion comes, gives us a portrait of a sculptor who was helped by the goddess Venus to fashion a perfect woman, Galatea. She was created for Pygmalion to fall in love with and marry. Viewers of Shaw's play expect that Higgins will fall in love with Eliza — or at least that she will fall in love with him. But Shaw is exact in making this love difficult for us to contemplate. Higgins's emotional limitations seem more intense at the end of the play than at its beginning. Essentially unsure what the outcome of his experiment is or ought to be, he is not planning to marry Eliza or to consider her an irresistible product of his own fashioning. In 1914 the then-reigning leading man in London, Beerbohm Tree, played the part of Higgins in a subtle way and by innuendo implied at the end of the play that he and Eliza would certainly marry. Shaw was angry enough to protest (it did no good) and to ensure that the final printed version of the play made clear that Eliza would eventually marry Freddy, a ne'er-do-well aristocratic boy who needed her. In his "Sequel," or afterword, to the play, Shaw goes virtually overboard in clarifying what will happen after the play's ending. Besides telling us that Eliza and Freddy will marry, he even maps out their future employment.

Some of the issues raised in the play concern the entire role of class and birth in an individual's life. After all, the way one speaks is an accident of birth. That it should "classify" a person for life and limit economic opportunity is perhaps pitiful. That the way one speaks can be changed by education is interesting and important, but should it be a requirement for a successful and happy life? To some extent the question is whether society ought to change or the individual ought to change. Higgins is obviously satisfied with his Oxonian accent and with the social status quo. Eliza sees an opportunity in changing the way she speaks, but she does not anticipate the changes that are produced by her being treated with kindness — especially by Pickering and Mrs. Higgins. She finds that she cannot go back to being a flower girl on the corner. Something in her has changed forever.

Pygmalion in Performance

By 1912 Shaw had been established as one of the most important living playwrights; not surprisingly, the early performances of this play were successful. The first production was in German at the Hofburg Theatre in Vienna. In April 1914 it was produced in London by Beerbohm Tree, with Tree as Higgins and Mrs. Patrick Campbell, one of Shaw's favorite actresses, as Eliza. Shaw's use of the word *bloody* in this play caused minor scandal and the threat of censorship. The play has been performed constantly since 1914 and was made into a film (1938) with Leslie Howard as Henry Higgins and Wendy Hiller as Eliza. Shaw won an Academy Award for the screenplay. Perhaps more famously, it took on a new life as a musical, *My Fair Lady* (1956) by Alan Jay

Lerner and Frederick Lowe with Rex Harrison as Higgins and Julie Andrews as Eliza. It was one of the most successful of all productions on Broadway, with 2,717 performances in six years, and it ran for five years at the Drury Lane Theatre in London. When filmed in 1964, Rex Harrison and Audrey Hepburn had the leading roles. *Pygmalion* in all its forms has produced an enormous amount of royalties for the Shaw estate and serves to fund some of his favorite charities, such as the Irish National Museum in Dublin. The life-size bronze statue of Shaw on its lawn was paid for by royalties from the musical version of *Pygmalion*.

Bernard Shaw (1856–1950)

PYGMALION   *1912*

Characters

CLARA EYNSFORD-HILL, *daughter of Mrs Eynsford-Hill*
MRS EYNSFORD-HILL, *a lady*
FREDDY EYNSFORD-HILL, *son of Mrs Eynsford Hill*
ELIZA DOOLITTLE, *a flower girl*
COLONEL PICKERING, *British officer, amateur phonetician*
PROFESSOR HENRY HIGGINS, *a phonetician*
MRS PEARCE, *Professor Higgins's housekeeper*
ALFRED DOOLITTLE, *Eliza's father*
MRS HIGGINS, *Professor Higgins's mother*
HOSTESS
HOST
NEPOMMUCK, *Professor Higgins's former student*

ACT 1

(*London at 11:15 p.m. Torrents of heavy summer rain. Cab whistles blowing frantically in all directions. Pedestrians running for shelter into the portico of St Paul's church (not Wren's cathedral but Inigo Jones's church in Covent Garden vegetable market), among them a lady and her daughter in evening dress. All are peering out gloomily at the rain, except one*

Note: Peculiarities of punctuation and spelling follow Shaw's instructions.

man with his back turned to the rest, wholly preoccupied with a notebook in which he is writing. The church clock strikes the first quarter.)

THE DAUGHTER (*in the space between the central pillars, close to the one on her left*): I'm getting chilled to the bone. What can Freddy be doing all this time? He's been gone twenty minutes.
THE MOTHER (*on her daughter's right*): Not so long. But he ought to have got us a cab by this.
A BYSTANDER (*on the lady's right*): He wont get no cab not until half-past eleven, missus, when they come back after dropping their theatre fares.
THE MOTHER: But we must have a cab. We cant stand here until half-past eleven. It's too bad.
THE BYSTANDER: Well it aint my fault, missus.
THE DAUGHTER: If Freddy had a bit of gumption, he would have got one at the theatre door.
THE MOTHER: What could he have done, poor boy?
THE DAUGHTER: Other people get cabs. Why couldnt he?

(*Freddy rushes in out of the rain from the Southampton Street side, and comes between them closing a dripping umbrella. He is a young man of twenty, in evening dress, very wet round the ankles.*)

THE DAUGHTER: Well, havnt you got a cab?
FREDDY: Theres not one to be had for love or money.
THE MOTHER: Oh, Freddy, there must be one. You cant have tried.

THE DAUGHTER: It's too tiresome. Do you expect us to go and get one ourselves?

FREDDY: I tell you theyre all engaged. The rain was so sudden: nobody was prepared; and everybody had to take a cab. Ive been to Charing Cross one way and nearly to Ludgate Circus the other; and they were all engaged.

THE MOTHER: Did you try Trafalgar Square?

FREDDY: There wasnt one at Trafalgar Square.

THE DAUGHTER: Did you try?

FREDDY: I tried as far as Charing Cross Station. Did you expect me to walk to Hammersmith?

THE DAUGHTER: You havnt tried at all.

THE MOTHER: You really are very helpless, Freddy. Go again; and dont come back until you have found a cab.

FREDDY: I shall simply get soaked for nothing.

THE DAUGHTER: And what about us? Are we to stay here all night in this draught, with next to nothing on? You selfish pig —

FREDDY: Oh, very well: I'll go, I'll go. (*He opens his umbrella and dashes off Strandwards, but comes into collision with a flower girl who is hurrying in for shelter, knocking her basket out of her hands. A blinding flash of lightning, followed instantly by a rattling peal of thunder, orchestrates the incident.*)

THE FLOWER GIRL: Nah then, Freddy: look wh' y' gowin, deah.

FREDDY: Sorry (*he rushes off*).

THE FLOWER GIRL (*picking up her scattered flowers and replacing them in the basket*): Theres menners f' yer! Tə-oo banches o voylets trod into the mad. (*She sits down on the plinth of the column, sorting her flowers, on the lady's right. She is not at all a romantic figure. She is perhaps eighteen, perhaps twenty, hardly older. She wears a little sailor hat of black straw that has long been exposed to the dust and soot of London and has seldom if ever been brushed. Her hair needs washing rather badly: its mousy color can hardly be natural. She wears a shoddy black coat that reaches nearly to her knees and is shaped to her waist. She has a brown skirt with a coarse apron. Her boots are much the worse for wear. She is no doubt as clean as she can afford to be; but compared to the ladies she is very dirty. Her features are no worse than theirs; but their condition leaves something to be desired; and she needs the services of a dentist.*)

THE MOTHER: How do you know that my son's name is Freddy, pray?

THE FLOWER GIRL: Ow, eez, yə-ooa san, is e? Wal, fewd dan y' d-ooty bawmz a mather should, eed now bettern to spawl a pore gel's flahrzn than ran awy athaht pyin. Will yə-oo py me f'them?

(*Here, with apologies, this desperate attempt to represent her dialect without a phonetic alphabet must be abandoned as unintelligible outside London.*)

THE DAUGHTER: Do nothing of the sort, mother. The idea!

THE MOTHER: Please allow me, Clara. Have you any pennies?

THE DAUGHTER: No. Ive nothing smaller than sixpence.

THE FLOWER GIRL (*hopefully*): I can give you change for a tanner, kind lady.

THE MOTHER (*to Clara*): Give it to me. (*Clara parts reluctantly.*) Now (*to the girl*) this is for your flowers.

THE FLOWER GIRL: Thank you kindly, lady.

THE DAUGHTER: Make her give you the change. These things are only a penny a bunch.

THE MOTHER: Do hold your tongue, Clara. (*To the girl.*) You can keep the change.

THE FLOWER GIRL: Oh, thank you, lady.

THE MOTHER: Now tell me how you know that young gentleman's name.

THE FLOWER GIRL: I didnt.

THE MOTHER: I heard you call him by it. Dont try to deceive me.

THE FLOWER GIRL (*protesting*): Who's trying to deceive you? I called him Freddy or Charlie same as you might yourself if you was talking to a stranger and wished to be pleasant.

THE DAUGHTER: Sixpence thrown away! Really, mamma, you might have spared Freddy that. (*She retreats in disgust behind the pillar.*)

(*An elderly gentleman of the amiable military type rushes into the shelter, and closes a dripping umbrella. He is in the same plight as Freddy, very wet about the ankles. He is in evening dress, with a light overcoat. He takes the place left vacant by the daughter.*)

THE GENTLEMAN: Phew!

THE MOTHER (*to the gentleman*): Oh, sir, is there any sign of its stopping?

THE GENTLEMAN: I'm afraid not. It started worse than ever about two minutes ago. (*He goes to the plinth beside the flower girl; puts up his foot on it; and stoops to turn down his trouser ends.*)

THE MOTHER: Oh dear! (*She retires sadly and joins her daughter.*)

THE FLOWER GIRL (*taking advantage of the military gentleman's proximity to establish friendly relations with him*): If it's worse, it's a sign it's nearly over. So cheer up, Captain; and buy a flower off a poor girl.

THE GENTLEMAN: I'm sorry. I havnt any change.

THE FLOWER GIRL: I can give you change, Captain.

THE GENTLEMAN: For a sovereign? Ive nothing less.

THE FLOWER GIRL: Garn! Oh do buy a flower off me, Captain. I can change half-a-crown. Take this for tuppence.

THE GENTLEMAN: Now dont be troublesome: theres a good girl. (*Trying his pockets.*) I really havnt any change — Stop: heres three hapence, if thats any use to you. (*He retreats to the other pillar.*)

THE FLOWER GIRL (*disappointed, but thinking three halfpence better than nothing*): Thank you, sir.

THE BYSTANDER (*to the girl*): You be careful: give him a flower for it. Theres a bloke here behind taking down every blessed word youre saying. (*All turn to the man who is taking notes.*)

THE FLOWER GIRL (*springing up terrified*): I aint done nothing wrong by speaking to the gentleman. Ive a right to sell flowers if I keep off the kerb. (*Hysterically.*) I'm a respectable girl: so help me, I never spoke to him except to ask him to buy a flower off me.

(*General hubbub, mostly sympathetic to the flower girl, but deprecating her excessive sensibility. Cries of Dont start hollerin. Who's hurting you? Nobody's going to touch you. Whats the good of fussing? Steady on. Easy easy, etc., come from the elderly staid spectators, who pat her comfortingly. Less patient ones bid her shut her head, or ask her roughly what is wrong with her. A remoter group, not knowing what the matter is, crowd in and increase the noise with question and answer: Whats the row? What-she-do? Where is he? A tec taking her down. What! him? Yes: him over there: Took money off the gentleman, etc.*)

THE FLOWER GIRL (*breaking through them to the gentleman, crying wildly*): Oh, sir, dont let him charge me. You dunno what it means to me. Theyll take away my character and drive me on the streets for speaking to gentlemen. They —

THE NOTE TAKER (*coming forward on her right, the rest crowding after him*): There! there! there! there! who's hurting you, you silly girl? What do you take me for?

THE BYSTANDER: It's aw rawt: e's a genleman: look at his bɘ-oots. (*Explaining to the note taker.*) She thought you was a copper's nark, sir.

THE NOTE TAKER (*with quick interest*): Whats a copper's nark?

THE BYSTANDER (*inapt at definition*): it's a — well, it's a copper's nark, as you might say. What else would you call it? A sort of informer.

THE FLOWER GIRL (*still hysterical*): I take my Bible oath I never said a word —

THE NOTE TAKER (*overbearing but good-humored*): Oh, shut up, shut up. Do I look like a policeman?

THE FLOWER GIRL (*far from reassured*): Then what did you take down my words for? How do I know whether you took me down right? You just shew me what youve wrote about me. (*The note taker opens his book and holds it steadily under her nose, though the pressure of the mob trying to read it over his shoulders would upset a weaker man.*) Whats that? That aint proper writing. I cant read that.

THE NOTE TAKER: I can. (*Reads, reproducing her pronunciation exactly*): "Cheer ap, Keptin; n' baw ya flahr orf a pore gel."

THE FLOWER GIRL (*much distressed*): It's because I called him Captain. I meant no harm. (*To the gentleman.*) Oh, sir, dont let him lay a charge agen me for a word like that. You —

THE GENTLEMAN: Charge! I make no charge. (*To the note taker.*) Really, sir, if you are a detective, you need not begin protecting me against molestation by young women until I ask you. Anybody could see that the girl meant no harm.

THE BYSTANDERS GENERALLY (*demonstrating against police espionage*): Course they could. What business is it of yours? You mind your own affairs. He wants promotion, he does. Taking down people's words! Girl never said a word to him. What harm if she did? Nice thing a girl cant shelter from the rain without being insulted, etc., etc., etc. (*She is conducted by the more sympathetic demonstrators back to her plinth, where she resumes her seat and struggles with her emotion.*)

THE BYSTANDER: He aint a tec. He's a blooming busybody: thats what he is. I tell you, look at his bɘ-oots.

THE NOTE TAKER (*turning on him genially*): And how are all your people down at Selsey?

THE BYSTANDER (*suspiciously*): Who told you my people come from Selsey?

THE NOTE TAKER: Never you mind. They did. (*To the girl.*) How do you come to be up so far east? You were born in Lisson Grove.

THE FLOWER GIRL (*appalled*): Oh, what harm is there in my leaving Lisson Grove? It wasnt fit for a pig to live in; and I had to pay four-and-six a week. (*In tears.*) Oh, boo — hoo — oo —

THE NOTE TAKER: Live where you like; but stop that noise.

THE GENTLEMAN (*to the girl*): Come, come! he cant touch you: you have a right to live where you please.

A SARCASTIC BYSTANDER (*thrusting himself between the note taker and the gentleman*): Park Lane, for instance. I'd like to go into the Housing Question with you, I would.

THE FLOWER GIRL (*subsiding into a brooding melancholy over her basket, and talking very low-spiritedly to herself*): I'm a good girl, I am.

THE SARCASTIC BYSTANDER (*not attending to her*): Do you know where *I* come from?

THE NOTETAKER (*promptly*): Hoxton.

(*Titterings. Popular interest in the note taker's performance increases.*)

THE SARCASTIC ONE (*amazed*): Well, who said I didnt? Bly me! you know everything, you do.

THE FLOWER GIRL (*still nursing her sense of injury*): Aint no call to meddle with me, he aint.

THE BYSTANDER (*to her*): Of course he aint. Dont you stand it from him. (*To the note taker.*) See here: what call have you to know about people what never offered to meddle with you?

THE FLOWER GIRL: Let him say what he likes. I dont want to have no truck with him.

THE BYSTANDER: You take us for dirt under your feet, dont you? Catch you taking liberties with a gentleman!

THE SARCASTIC BYSTANDER: Yes: tell him where he come from if you want to go fortune-telling.

THE NOTE TAKER: Cheltenham, Harrow, Cambridge, and India.

THE GENTLEMAN: Quite right.

(*Great laughter. Reaction in the note taker's favor. Exclamations of* He knows all about it. Told him proper. Hear him tell the toff where he come from? *etc.*)

THE GENTLEMAN: May I ask, sir, do you do this for your living at a music hall?

THE NOTE TAKER: I've thought of that. Perhaps I shall some day.

(*The rain has stopped; and the persons on the outside of the crowd begin to drop off.*)

THE FLOWER GIRL (*resenting the reaction*): He's no gentleman, he aint, to interfere with a poor girl.

THE DAUGHTER (*out of patience, pushing her way rudely to the front and displacing the gentleman, who politely retires to the other side of the pillar*): What on earth is Freddy doing? I shall get pneumownia if I stay in this draught any longer.

THE NOTE TAKER (*to himself, hastily making a note of her pronunciation of "monia"*): Earlscourt.

THE DAUGHTER (*violently*): Will you please keep your impertinent remarks to yourself.

THE NOTE TAKER: Did I say that out loud? I didnt mean to. I beg your pardon. Your mother's Epsom, unmistakeably.

THE MOTHER (*advancing between the daughter and the note taker*): How very curious! I was brought up in Largelady Park, near Epsom.

THE NOTE TAKER (*uproariously amused*): Ha! ha! what a devil of a name! Excuse me. (*To the daughter.*) You want a cab, do you?

THE DAUGHTER: Dont dare speak to me.

THE MOTHER: Oh, please, please, Clara. (*Her daughter repudiates her with an angry shrug and retires haughtily.*) We should be so grateful to you, sir, if you found us a cab. (*The note taker produces a whistle.*) Oh, thank you. (*She joins her daughter.*)

(*The note taker blows a piercing blast.*)

THE SARCASTIC BYSTANDER: There! I knowed he was a plain-clothes copper.

THE BYSTANDER: That aint a police whistle: thats a sporting whistle.

THE FLOWER GIRL (*still preoccupied with her wounded feelings*): He's no right to take away my character. My character is the same to me as any lady's.

THE NOTE TAKER: I dont know whether youve noticed it; but the rain stopped about two minutes ago.

THE BYSTANDER: So it has. Why didnt you say so before? and us losing our time listening to your silliness! (*He walks off towards the Strand.*)

THE SARCASTIC BYSTANDER: I can tell where you come from. You come from Anwell. Go back there.

THE NOTE TAKER (*helpfully*): Hanwell.

THE SARCASTIC BYSTANDER (*affecting great distinction of speech*): Thenk you, teacher. Haw haw! So long. (*He touches his hat with mock respect and strolls off.*)

THE FLOWER GIRL: Frightening people like that! How would he like it himself?

THE MOTHER: It's quite fine now, Clara. We can walk to a motor bus. Come. (*She gathers her skirts above her ankles and hurries off towards the Strand.*)

THE DAUGHTER: But the cab — (*her mother is out of hearing.*) Oh, how tiresome! (*She follows angrily.*)

(*All the rest have gone except the note taker, the gentleman, and the flower girl, who sits arranging her basket, and still pitying herself in murmurs.*)

THE FLOWER GIRL: Poor girl! Hard enough for her to live without being worried and chivied.

THE GENTLEMAN (*returning to his former place on the note taker's left*): How do you do it, if I may ask?

THE NOTE TAKER: Simply phonetics. The science of speech. Thats my profession: also my hobby. Happy is the man who can make a living by his hobby! You can spot an Irishman or a Yorkshireman by his brogue. *I* can place any man within six miles. I can place him within two miles in London. Sometimes within two streets.

THE FLOWER GIRL: Ought to be ashamed of himself, unmanly coward!

THE GENTLEMAN: But is there a living in that?

THE NOTE TAKER: Oh, yes. Quite a fat one. This is an age of upstarts. Men begin in Kentish Town with

£80 a year, and end in Park Lane with a hundred thousand. They want to drop Kentish Town; but they give themselves away every time they open their mouths. Now I can teach them —

THE FLOWER GIRL: Let him mind his own business and leave a poor girl —

THE NOTE TAKER (*explosively*): Woman: cease this detestable boohooing instantly; or else seek the shelter of some other place of worship.

THE FLOWER GIRL (*with feeble defiance*): Ive a right to be here if I like, same as you.

THE NOTE TAKER: A woman who utters such depressing and disgusting sounds has no right to be anywhere — no right to live. Remember that you are a human being with a soul and the divine gift of articulate speech: that your native language is the language of Shakespear and Milton and The Bible; and dont sit there crooning like a bilious pigeon.

THE FLOWER GIRL (*quite overwhelmed, looking up at him in mingled wonder and deprecation without daring to raise her head*): Ah-ah-ah-ow-ow-ow-oo!

THE NOTE TAKER (*whipping out his book*): Heavens! what a sound! (*He writes; then holds out the book and reads, reproducing her vowels exactly*). Ah-ah-ah-ow-ow-ow-oo!

THE FLOWER GIRL (*tickled by the performance, and laughing in spite of herself*): Garn!

THE NOTE TAKER: You see this creature with her kerbstone English: the English that will keep her in the gutter to the end of her days. Well, sir, in three months I could pass that girl off as a duchess at an ambassador's garden party. I could even get her a place as lady's maid or shop assistant, which requires better English.

THE FLOWER GIRL: What's that you say?

THE NOTE TAKER: Yes, you squashed cabbage leaf, you disgrace to the noble architecture of these columns, you incarnate insult to the English language: I could pass you off as the Queen of Sheba. (*To the Gentleman.*) Can you believe that?

THE GENTLEMAN: Of course I can. I am myself a student of Indian dialects; and —

THE NOTE TAKER (*eagerly*): Are you? Do you know Colonel Pickering, the author of Spoken Sanscrit?

THE GENTLEMAN: I am Colonel Pickering. Who are you?

THE NOTE TAKER: Henry Higgins, author of Higgins's Universal Alphabet.

PICKERING (*with enthusiasm*): I came from India to meet you.

HIGGINS: I was going to India to meet you.

PICKERING: Where do you live?

HIGGINS: 27A Wimpole Street. Come and see me tomorrow.

PICKERING: I'm at the Carlton. Come with me now and lets have a jaw over some supper.

HIGGINS: Right you are.

THE FLOWER GIRL (*to Pickering, as he passes her*): Buy a flower, kind gentleman. I'm short for my lodging.

PICKERING: I really havnt any change. I'm sorry. (*He goes away.*)

HIGGINS (*shocked at the girl's mendacity*): Liar. You said you could change half-a-crown.

THE FLOWERGIRL (*rising in desperation*): You ought to be stuffed with nails, you ought. (*Flinging the basket at his feet.*) Take the whole blooming basket for sixpence.

(*The church clock strikes the second quarter.*)

HIGGINS (*hearing in it the voice of God, rebuking him for his Pharisaic want of charity to the poor girl*): A reminder. (*He raises his hat solemnly; then throws a handful of money into the basket and follows Pickering.*)

THE FLOWER GIRL (*picking up a half-crown*): Ah-ow-ooh! (*Picking up a couple of florins.*) Aaah-ow-ooh! (*Picking up several coins*): Aaaaah-ow-ooh! (*Picking up a half-sovereign.*) Aaaaaaaaaaaah-ow-ooh!!!

FREDDY (*springing out of a taxicab*): Got one at last. Hallo! (*To the girl.*) Where are the two ladies that were here?

THE FLOWER GIRL: They walked to the bus when the rain stopped.

FREDDY: And left me with a cab on my hands! Damnation!

THE FLOWER GIRL (*with grandeur*): Never mind, young man. I'm going home in a taxi. (*She sails off to the cab. The driver puts his hand behind him and holds the door firmly shut against her. Quite understanding his mistrust, she shews him her handful of money.*) A taxi fare aint no object to me, Charlie. (*He grins and opens the door.*) Here. What about the basket?

THE TAXIMAN: Give it here. Tuppence extra.

LIZA: No. I dont want nobody to see it. (*She crushes it into the cab and gets in, continuing the conversation through the window.*) Goodbye, Freddy.

FREDDY (*dazedly raising his hat*): Goodbye.

TAXIMAN: Where to?

LIZA: Bucknam Pellis (Buckingham Palace).

TAXIMAN: What d'ye mean — Bucknam Pellis?

LIZA: Dont you know where it is? In the Green Park, where the King lives. Goodbye, Freddy. Dont let me keep you standing there. Goodbye.

FREDDY: Goodbye. (*He goes.*)

TAXIMAN: Here? Whats this about Bucknam Pellis? What business have you at Bucknam Pellis?

LIZA: Of course I havnt none. But I wasnt going to let him know that. You drive me home.

TAXIMAN: And wheres home?

LIZA: Angel Court, Drury Lane, next Meiklejohn's oil shop.

TAXIMAN: That sounds more like it, Judy. (*He drives off.*)

(*Let us follow the taxi to the entrance to Angel Court, a narrow little archway between two shops, one of them Meiklejohn's oil shop. When it stops there, Eliza gets out, dragging her basket with her.*)

LIZA: How much?

TAXIMAN (*indicating the taximeter*): Cant you read? A shilling.

LIZA: A shilling for two minutes!!

TAXIMAN: Two minutes or ten: it's all the same.

LIZA: Well, I dont call it right.

TAXIMAN: Ever been in a taxi before?

LIZA (*with dignity*): Hundreds and thousands of times, young man.

TAXIMAN (*laughing at her*): Good for you, Judy. Keep the shilling, darling, with best love from all at home. Good luck! (*He drives off.*)

LIZA (*humiliated*): Impidence!

(*She picks up the basket and trudges up the alley with it to her lodging: a small room with very old wall paper hanging loose in the damp places. A broken pane in the window is mended with paper. A portrait of a popular actor and a fashion plate of ladies' dresses, all wildly beyond poor Eliza's means, both torn from newspapers, are pinned up on the wall. A birdcage hangs in the window; but its tenant died long ago: it remains as a memorial only.*

These are the only visible luxuries: the rest is the irreducible minimum of poverty's needs: a wretched bed heaped with all sorts of coverings that have any warmth in them, a draped packing case with a basin and jug on it and a little looking glass over it, a chair and table, the refuse of some suburban kitchen, and an American alarum clock on the shelf above the unused fireplace: the whole lighted with a gas lamp with a penny in the slot meter. Rent: four shillings a week.

Here Eliza, chronically weary, but too excited to go to bed, sits, counting her new riches and dreaming and planning what to do with them, until the gas goes out, when she enjoys for the first time the sensation of being able to put in another penny without grudging it. This prodigal mood does not extinguish her gnawing sense of the need for economy sufficiently to prevent her from calculating that she can dream and plan in bed more cheaply and warmly than sitting up without a fire. So she takes off her shawl and skirt and adds them to the miscellaneous bedclothes. Then she kicks off her shoes and gets into bed without any further change.)

ACT 2

(*Next day at 11 a.m. Higgins's laboratory in Wimpole Street. It is a room on the first floor, looking on the street, and was meant for the drawing room. The double doors are in the middle of the back wall; and persons entering find in the corner to their right two tall file cabinets at right angles to one another against the wall. In this corner stands a flat writing-table, on which are a phonograph, a laryngoscope, a row of tiny organ pipes with a bellows, a set of lamp chimneys for singing flames with burners attached to a gas plug in the wall by an indiarubber tube, several tuning-forks of different sizes, a life-size image of half a human head, shewing in section the vocal organs, and a box containing a supply of wax cylinders for the phonograph.*

Further down the room, on the same side, is a fireplace, with a comfortable leather-covered easy-chair at the side of the hearth nearest the door, and a coalscuttle. There is a clock on the mantelpiece. Between the fireplace and the phonograph table is a stand for newspapers.

On the other side of the central door, to the left of the visitor, is a cabinet of shallow drawers. On it is a telephone and the telephone directory. The corner beyond, and most of the side wall, is occupied by a grand piano, with the keyboard at the end furthest from the door, and a bench for the player extending the full length of the keyboard. On the piano is a dessert dish heaped with fruit and sweets, mostly chocolates.

The middle of the room is clear. Besides the easy-chair, the piano bench, and two chairs at the phonograph table, there is one stray chair. It stands near the fireplace. On the walls, engravings: mostly Piranesis and mezzotint portraits. No paintings.

Pickering is seated at the table, putting down some cards and a tuning-fork which he has been using. Higgins is standing up near him, closing two or three file drawers which are hanging out. He appears in the morning light as a robust, vital, appetizing sort of man of forty or thereabouts, dressed in a professional-looking black frock-coat with a white linen collar and black silk tie. He is of the energetic scientific type, heartily, even violently interested in everything that can be studied as a scientific subject, and careless about himself and other people, including their feelings. He is, in fact, but for his years and size, rather like a wry impetuous baby "taking notice" eagerly and loudly, and requiring almost as much watching to keep him out of unintended mischief. His manner varies from genial bullying when he is in a good humor to stormy petulance when anything goes wrong; but he is so entirely frank and void of malice that he remains likeable even in his least reasonable moments.)

HIGGINS (*as he shuts the last drawer*): Well, I think thats the whole show.

PICKERING: It's really amazing. I havnt taken half of it in, you know.

HIGGINS: Would you like to go over any of it again?

PICKERING (*rising and coming to the fireplace, where he plants himself with his back to the fire*): No, thank you: not now. I'm quite done up for this morning.

HIGGINS (*following him, and standing beside him on his left*): Tired of listening to sounds?

PICKERING: Yes. It's a fearful strain. I rather fancied myself because I can pronounce twenty-four distinct vowel sounds; but your hundred and thirty beat me. I cant hear a bit of difference between most of them.

HIGGINS (*chuckling and going over to the piano to eat sweets*): Oh, that comes with practice. You hear no difference at first; but you keep on listening, and presently you find theyre all as different as A from B. (*Mrs Pearce looks in: she is Higgins's housekeeper.*) Whats the matter?

MRS PEARCE (*hesitating, evidently perplexed*): A young woman asks to see you, sir.

HIGGINS: A young woman! What does she want?

MRS PEARCE: Well, sir, she says youll be glad to see her when you know what she's come about. She's quite a common girl, sir. Very common indeed. I should have sent her away, only I thought perhaps you wanted her to talk into your machines. I hope Ive not done wrong: but really you see such queer people sometimes — youll excuse me, I'm sure, sir —

HIGGINS: Oh, thats all right, Mrs Pearce. Has she an interesting accent?

MRS PEARCE: Oh, something dreadful, sir, really. I dont know how you can take an interest in it.

HIGGINS (*to Pickering*): Lets have her up. Shew her up, Mrs Pearce. (*He rushes across to his working table and picks out a cylinder to use on the phonograph.*)

MRS PEARCE (*only half resigned to it*): Very well, sir. It's for you to say. (*She goes downstairs.*)

HIGGINS: This is rather a bit of luck. I'll shew you how I make records. We'll set her talking; and I'll take it down first in Bell's Visible Speech; then in broad Romic; and then we'll get her on the phonograph so that you can turn her on as often as you like with the written transcript before you.

MRS PEARCE (*returning*): This is the young woman, sir.

(*The flower girl enters in state. She has a hat with three ostrich feathers, orange, sky-blue, and red. She has a nearly clean apron and the shoddy coat has been tidied a little. The pathos of this deplorable figure, with its innocent vanity and consequential air, touches Pickering, who has already straightened himself in the presence of Mrs Pearce. But as to Higgins, the only distinction he makes between men and women is that when he is neither bullying nor exclaiming to the heavens against some featherweight cross, he coaxes women as a child coaxes its nurse when it wants to get anything out of her.*)

HIGGINS (*brusquely, recognizing her with unconcealed disappointment, and at once, babylike, making an intolerable grievance of it*): Why, this is the girl I jotted down last night. She's no use: Ive got all the records I want of the Lisson Grove lingo; and I'm not going to waste another cylinder on it. (*To the girl.*) Be off with you: I dont want you.

THE FLOWER GIRL: Dont you be so saucy. You aint heard what I come for yet. (*To Mrs Pearce, who is waiting at the door for further instructions.*) Did you tell him I come in a taxi?

MRS PEARCE: Nonsense, girl! what do you think a gentleman like Mr Higgins cares what you came in?

THE FLOWER GIRL: Oh, we are proud! He aint above giving lessons, not him: I heard him say so. Well, I aint come here to ask for any compliment; and if my money's not good enough I can go elsewhere.

HIGGINS: Good enough for what?

THE FLOWER GIRL: Good enough for yə-oo. Now you know, dont you? I'm coming to have lessons, I am. And to pay for em tə-oo: make no mistake.

HIGGINS (*stupent*): Well!!! (*Recovering his breath with a gasp.*) What do you expect me to say to you?

THE FLOWER GIRL: Well, if you was a gentleman, you might ask me to sit down, I think. Dont I tell you I'm bringing you business?

HIGGINS: Pickering: shall we ask this baggage to sit down, or shall we throw her out of the window?

THE FLOWER GIRL (*running away in terror to the piano, where she turns at bay*): Ah-ah-oh-ow-ow-ow-oo! (*Wounded and whimpering.*) I wont be called a baggage when Ive offered to pay like any lady.

(*Motionless, the two men stare at her from the other side of the room, amazed.*)

PICKERING (*gently*): But what is it you want?

THE FLOWER GIRL: I want to be a lady in a flower

Jackie Smith-Wood as Eliza and Peter O'Toole as Higgins in the 1984 Shaftesbury Theatre production of *Pygmalion*.

shop stead of sellin at the corner of Tottenham Court Road. But they wont take me unless I can talk more genteel. He said he could teach me. Well, here I am ready to pay him — not asking any favor — and he treats me zif I was dirt.

MRS PEARCE: How can you be such a foolish ignorant girl as to think you could afford to pay Mr Higgins?

THE FLOWER GIRL: Why shouldnt I? I know what lessons cost as well as you do; and I'm ready to pay.

HIGGINS: How much?

THE FLOWER GIRL (*coming back to him, triumphant*): Now youre talking! I thought youd come off it when you saw a chance of getting back a bit of what you chucked at me last night. (*Confidentially.*) Youd had a drop in, hadnt you?

HIGGINS (*peremptorily*): Sit down.

THE FLOWER GIRL: Oh, if youre going to make a compliment of it —

HIGGINS (*thundering at her*): Sit down.

MRS PEARCE (*severely*): Sit down, girl. Do as youre told.

THE FLOWER GIRL: Ah-ah-ah-ow-ow-oo! (*She stands, half rebellious, half bewildered.*)

PICKERING (*very courteous*): Wont you sit down? (*He places the stray chair near the hearthrug between himself and Higgins.*)

LIZA (*coyly*): Dont mind if I do. (*She sits down. Pickering returns to the hearthrug.*)

HIGGINS: Whats your name?

THE FLOWER GIRL: Liza Doolittle.

HIGGINS (*declaiming gravely*):
Eliza, Elizabeth, Betsy and Bess,
They went to the woods to get a bird's nes':

PICKERING: They found a nest with four eggs in it:

HIGGINS: They took one apiece, and left three in it.

(*They laugh heartily at their own fun.*)

LIZA: Oh, dont be silly.

MRS PEARCE (*placing herself behind Eliza's chair*): You mustnt speak to the gentleman like that.

LIZA: Well, why wont he speak sensible to me?

HIGGINS: Come back to business. How much do you propose to pay me for the lessons?

LIZA: Oh, I know whats right. A lady friend of mine gets French lessons for eighteenpence an hour from a real French gentleman. Well, you wouldnt have the face to ask me the same for teaching me my own language as you would for French; so I wont give more than a shilling. Take it or leave it.

HIGGINS (*walking up and down the room, rattling his keys and his cash in his pockets*): You know, Pickering, if you consider a shilling, not as a simple shilling, but as a percentage of this girl's income, it works out as fully equivalent to sixty or seventy guineas from a millionaire.

PICKERING: How so?

HIGGINS: Figure it out. A millionaire has about £150 a day. She earns about half-a-crown.

LIZA (*haughtily*): Who told you I only —

HIGGINS (*continuing*): She offers me two-fifths of her day's income for a lesson. Two-fifths of a millionaire's income for a day would be somewhere about £60. It's handsome. By George. It's enormous! it's the biggest offer I ever had.

LIZA (*rising, terrified*): Sixty pounds! What are you talking about? I never offered you sixty pounds. Where would I get —

HIGGINS: Hold your tongue.

LIZA (*weeping*): But I aint got sixty pounds. Oh —

MRS PEARCE: Dont cry, you silly girl. Sit down. Nobody is going to touch your money.

HIGGINS: Somebody is going to touch you, with a broomstick, if you dont stop snivelling. Sit down.

LIZA (*obeying slowly*): Ah-ah-ah-ow-o! One would think you was my father.

HIGGINS: If I decide to teach you, I'll be worse than two fathers to you. Here! (*He offers her his silk handkerchief.*)

LIZA: Whats this for?

HIGGINS: To wipe your eyes. To wipe any part of your face that feels moist. Remember: thats your handkerchief; and thats your sleeve. Dont mistake the one for the other if you wish to become a lady in a shop.

(*Liza, utterly bewildered, stares helplessly at him.*)

MRS PEARCE: It's no use talking to her like that, Mr Higgins: she doesnt understand you. Besides, youre quite wrong: she doesnt do it that way at all. (*She takes the handkerchief.*)

LIZA (*snatching it*): Here! You give me that handkerchief. He gev it to me, not to you.

PICKERING (*laughing*): He did. I think it must be regarded as her property, Mrs Pearce.

MRS PEARCE (*resigning herself*): Serve you right, Mr Higgins.

PICKERING: Higgins: I'm interested. What about the ambassador's garden party? I'll say youre the greatest teacher alive if you make that good. I'll bet you all the expenses of the experiment you cant do it. And I'll pay for the lessons.

LIZA: Oh, you are real good. Thank you, Captain.

HIGGINS (*tempted, looking at her*): It's almost irresistible. She's so deliciously low — so horribly dirty —

LIZA (*protesting extremely*): Ah-ah-ah-ah-ow-ow-oo!!! I aint dirty: I washed my face and hands afore I come, I did.

PICKERING: Youre certainly not going to turn her head with flattery, Higgins.

MRS PEARCE (*uneasy*): Oh, dont say that, sir: theres more ways than one of turning a girl's head; and nobody can do it better than Mr Higgins, though

he may not always mean it. I do hope, sir, you wont encourage him to do anything foolish.

HIGGINS (*becoming excited as the idea grows on him*): What is life but a series of inspired follies? The difficulty is to find them to do. Never lose a chance: it doesnt come every day. I shall make a duchess of this draggletailed guttersnipe.

LIZA (*strongly deprecating this view of her*): Ah-ah-ah-ow-ow-oo!

HIGGINS (*carried away*): Yes: in six months — in three if she has a good ear and a quick tongue — I'll take her anywhere and pass her off as anything. We'll start today: now! this moment! Take her away and clean her, Mrs Pearce. Monkey Brand, if it wont come off any other way. Is there a good fire in the kitchen?

MRS PEARCE (*protesting*): Yes; but —

HIGGINS (*storming on*): Take all her clothes off and burn them. Ring up Whiteley or somebody for new ones. Wrap her up in brown paper til they come.

LIZA: Youre no gentleman, youre not, to talk of such things. I'm a good girl, I am; and I know what the like of you are, I do!

HIGGINS: We want none of your Lisson Grove prudery here, young woman. Youve got to learn to behave like a duchess. Take her away, Mrs Pearce. If she gives you any trouble, wallop her.

LIZA (*springing up and running between Pickering and Mrs Pearce for protection*): No! I'll call the police, I will.

MRS PEARCE: But Ive no place to put her.

HIGGINS: Put her in the dustbin.

LIZA: Ah-ah-ah-ow-ow-oo!

PICKERING: Oh come, Higgins! be reasonable.

MRS PEARCE (*resolutely*): You must be reasonable, Mr Higgins: really you must. You cant walk over everybody like this.

(*Higgins, thus scolded, subsides. The hurricane is succeeded by a zephyr of amiable surprise.*)

HIGGINS (*with professional exquisiteness of modulation*): I walk over everybody! My dear Mrs Pearce, my dear Pickering, I never had the slightest intention of walking over anyone. All I propose is that we should be kind to this poor girl. We must help her to prepare and fit herself for her new station in life. If I did not express myself clearly it was because I did not wish to hurt her delicacy, or yours.

(*Liza, reassured, steals back to her chair.*)

MRS PEARCE (*to Pickering*): Well, did you ever hear anything like that, sir?

PICKERING (*laughing heartily*): Never, Mrs Pearce: never.

HIGGINS (*patiently*): Whats the matter?

MRS PEARCE: Well, the matter is, sir, that you cant take a girl up like that as if you were picking up a pebble on the beach.

HIGGINS: Why not?

MRS PEARCE: Why not! But you dont know anything about her. What about her parents? She may be married.

LIZA: Garn!

HIGGINS: There! As the girl very properly says, Garn! Married indeed! Dont you know that a woman of that class looks a worn out drudge of fifty a year after she's married?

LIZA: Whood marry me?

HIGGINS (*suddenly resorting to the most thrillingly beautiful low tones in his best elocutionary style*): By George, Eliza, the streets will be strewn with the bodies of men shooting themselves for your sake before Ive done with you.

MRS PEARCE: Nonsense, sir. You mustnt talk like that to her.

LIZA (*rising and squaring herself determinedly*): I'm going away. He's off his chump, he is. I dont want no balmies teaching me.

HIGGINS (*wounded in his tenderest point by her insensibility to his elocution*): Oh, indeed! I'm mad, am I? Very well, Mrs Pearce: you neednt order the new clothes for her. Throw her out.

LIZA (*whimpering*): Nah-ow. You got no right to touch me.

MRS PEARCE: You see now what comes of being saucy. (*Indicating the door.*) This way, please.

LIZA (*almost in tears*): I didnt want no clothes. I wouldnt have taken them. (*She throws away the handkerchief.*) I can buy my own clothes.

HIGGINS (*deftly retrieving the handkerchief and intercepting her on her reluctant way to the door*): Youre an ungrateful wicked girl. This is my return for offering to take you out of the gutter and dress you beautifully and make a lady of you.

MRS PEARCE: Stop, Mr Higgins. I wont allow it. It's you that are wicked. Go home to your parents, girl; and tell them to take better care of you.

LIZA: I aint got no parents. They told me I was big enough to earn my own living and turned me out.

MRS PEARCE: Wheres your mother?

LIZA: I aint got no mother. Her that turned me out was my sixth stepmother. But I done without them. And I'm a good girl, I am.

HIGGINS: Very well, then, what on earth is all this fuss about? The girl doesnt belong to anybody — is no use to anybody but me. (*He goes to Mrs Pearce and begins coaxing.*) You can adopt her, Mrs Pearce: I'm sure a daughter would be a great amusement to you. Now dont make any more fuss. Take her downstairs; and —

MRS PEARCE: But whats to become of her? Is she to be paid anything? Do be sensible, sir.

HIGGINS: Oh, pay her whatever is necessary: put it down in the housekeeping book. (*Impatiently.*) What on earth will she want with money? She'll have her food and her clothes. She'll only drink if you give her money.

LIZA (*turning, on him*): Oh you are a brute. It's a lie: nobody ever saw the sign of liquor on me. (*To Pickering.*) Oh, sir: youre a gentleman: dont let him speak to me like that.

PICKERING (*in good-humored remonstrance*): Does it occur to you, Higgins, that the girl has some feelings?

HIGGINS (*looking critically at her*): Oh no, I dont think so. Not any feelings that we need bother about. (*Cheerily.*) Have you, Eliza?

LIZA: I got my feelings same as anyone else.

HIGGINS (*to Pickering, reflectively*): You see the difficulty?

PICKERING: Eh? What difficulty?

HIGGINS: To get her to talk grammar. The mere pronunciation is easy enough.

LIZA: I dont want to talk grammar. I want to talk like a lady in a flower-shop.

MRS PEARCE: Will you please keep to the point, Mr Higgins. I want to know on what terms the girl is to be here. Is she to have any wages? And what is to become of her when youve finished your teaching? You must look ahead a little.

HIGGINS (*impatiently*): Whats to become of her if I leave her in the gutter? Tell me that, Mrs Pearce.

MRS PEARCE: Thats her own business, not yours, Mr Higgins.

HIGGINS: Well, when Ive done with her, we can throw her back into the gutter; and then it will be her own business again; so thats all right.

LIZA: Oh, youve no feeling heart in you: you dont care for nothing but yourself. (*She rises and takes the floor resolutely.*) Here! Ive had enough of this. I'm going (*making for the door*). You ought to be ashamed of yourself, you ought.

HIGGINS (*snatching a chocolate cream from the piano, his eyes suddenly beginning to twinkle with mischief*): Have some chocolates, Eliza.

LIZA (*halting, tempted*): How do I know what might be in them? Ive heard of girls being drugged by the like of you.

(*Higgins whips out his penknife; cuts a chocolate in two; puts one half into his mouth and bolts it; and offers her the other half.*)

HIGGINS: Pledge of good faith, Eliza. I eat one half: you eat the other. (*Liza opens her mouth to retort: he pops the half chocolate into it.*) You shall have boxes of them, barrels of them, every day. You shall live on them. Eh?

LIZA (*who has disposed of the chocolate after being nearly choked by it*): I wouldnt have ate it, only I'm too ladylike to take it out of my mouth.

HIGGINS: Listen, Eliza. I think you said you came in a taxi.

LIZA: Well, what if I did? Ive as good a right to take a taxi as anyone else.

HIGGINS: You have, Eliza: and in future you shall have as many taxis as you want. You shall go up and down and round the town in a taxi every day. Think of that, Eliza.

MRS PEARCE: Mr Higgins: youre tempting the girl. It's not right. She should think of the future.

HIGGINS: At her age! Nonsense! Time enough to think of the future when you havnt any future to think of. No, Eliza: do as this lady does: think of other people's futures; but never think of your own. Think of chocolates, and taxis, and gold, and diamonds.

LIZA: No: I dont want no gold and no diamonds. I'm a good girl, I am. (*She sits down again, with an attempt at dignity.*)

HIGGINS: You shall remain so, Eliza, under the care of Mrs Pearce. And you shall marry an officer in the Guards, with a beautiful moustache: the son of a marquis, who will disinherit him for marrying you, but will relent when he sees your beauty and goodness —

PICKERING: Excuse me, Higgins; but I really must interfere. Mrs Pearce is quite right. If this girl is to put herself in your hands for six months for an experiment in teaching, she must understand thoroughly what she's doing.

HIGGINS: How can she? She's incapable of understanding anything. Besides, do any of us understand what we are doing? If we did, would we ever do it?

PICKERING: Very clever, Higgins; but not to the present point. (*To Eliza.*) Miss Doolittle —

LIZA (*overwhelmed*): Ah-ah-ow-oo!

HIGGINS: There! Thats all youll get out of Eliza. Ah-ah-ow-oo! No use explaining. As a military man you ought to know that. Give her her orders: thats enough for her. Eliza: you are to live here for the next six months, learning how to speak beautifully, like a lady in a florist's shop. If youre good and do whatever youre told, you shall sleep in a proper bedroom, and have lots to eat, and money to buy chocolates and take rides in taxis. If youre naughty and idle you will sleep in the back kitchen among the black beetles, and be walloped by Mrs Pearce with a broomstick. At the end of six months you shall go to Buckingham Palace in a carriage, beau-

tifully dressed. If the King finds out youre not a lady, you will be taken by the police to the Tower of London, where your head will be cut off as a warning to other presumptuous flower girls. If you are not found out, you shall have a present of seven-and-sixpence to start life with as a lady in a shop. If you refuse this offer you will be a most ungrateful wicked girl; and the angels will weep for you. (*To Pickering.*) Now are you satisfied, Pickering? (*To Mrs Pearce.*) Can I put it more plainly and fairly, Mrs Pearce?

MRS PEARCE (*patiently*): I think youd better let me speak to the girl properly in private. I dont know that I can take charge of her or consent to the arrangement at all. Of course I know you dont mean her any harm; but when you get what you call interested in people's accents, you never think or care what may happen to them or you. Come with me, Eliza.

HIGGINS: Thats all right. Thank you, Mrs Pearce. Bundle her off to the bathroom.

LIZA (*rising reluctantly and suspiciously*): Youre a great bully, you are. I wont stay here if I dont like. I wont let nobody wallop me. I never asked to go to Bucknam Palace, I didnt. I was never in trouble with the police, not me. I'm a good girl —

MRS PEARCE: Dont answer back, girl. You dont understand the gentleman. Come with me. (*She leads the way to the door, and holds it open for Eliza.*)

LIZA (*as she goes out*): Well, what I say is right. I wont go near the King, not if I'm going to have my head cut off. If I'd known what I was letting myself in for, I wouldnt have come here. I always been a good girl; and I never offered to say a word to him; and I dont owe him nothing; and I dont care; and I wont be put upon; and I have my feelings the same as anyone else —

(*Mrs Pearce shuts the door; and Eliza's plaints are no longer audible.*)

(*Eliza is taken upstairs to the third floor greatly to her surprise; for she expected to be taken down to the scullery. There Mrs Pearce opens a door and takes her into a spare bedroom.*)

MRS PEARCE: I will have to put you here. This will be your bedroom.

LIZA: O-h, I couldnt sleep here, missus. It's too good for the likes of me. I should be afraid to touch anything. I aint a duchess yet, you know.

MRS PEARCE: You have got to make yourself as clean as the room: then you wont be afraid of it. And you must call me Mrs Pearce, not missus. (*She throws open the door of the dressing-room, now modernized as a bathroom.*)

LIZA: Gawd! whats this? Is this where you wash clothes? Funny sort of copper I call it.

MRS PEARCE: It is not a copper. This is where we wash ourselves, Eliza, and where I am going to wash you.

LIZA: You expect me to get into that and wet myself all over! Not me. I should catch my death. I knew a woman did it every Saturday night; and she died of it.

MRS PEARCE: Mr Higgins has the gentlemen's bathroom downstairs; and he has a bath every morning, in cold water.

LIZA: Ugh! He's made of iron, that man.

MRS PEARCE: If you are to sit with him and the Colonel and be taught you will have to do the same. They wont like the smell of you if you dont. But you can have the water as hot as you like. There are two taps: hot and cold.

LIZA (weeping): I couldnt. I dursnt. Its not natural: it would kill me. Ive never had a bath in my life: not what youd call a proper one.

MRS PEARCE: Well, dont you want to be clean and sweet and decent, like a lady? You know you cant be a nice girl inside if youre a dirty slut outside.

LIZA: Boohoo!!!!

MRS PEARCE: Now stop crying and go back into your room and take off all your clothes. Then wrap yourself in this (taking down a gown from its peg and handing it to her) and come back to me. I will get the bath ready.

LIZA (all tears): I cant. I wont. I'm not used to it. Ive never took off all my clothes before. It's not right: it's not decent.

MRS PEARCE: Nonsense, child. Dont you take off all your clothes every night when you go to bed?

LIZA (amazed): No. Why should I? I should catch my death. Of course I take off my skirt.

MRS PEARCE: Do you mean that you sleep in the underclothes you wear in the daytime?

LIZA: What else have I to sleep in?

MRS PEARCE: You will never do that again as long as you live here. I will get you a proper nightdress.

LIZA: Do you mean change into cold things and lie awake shivering half the night? You want to kill me, you do.

MRS PEARCE: I want to change you from a frowzy slut to a clean respectable girl fit to sit with the gentlemen in the study. Are you going to trust me and do what I tell you or be thrown out and sent back to your flower basket?

LIZA: But you dont know what the cold is to me. You dont know how I dread it.

MRS PEARCE: Your bed wont be cold here: I will put a hot water bottle in it. (Pushing her into the bedroom.) Off with you and undress.

LIZA: Oh, if only I'd a known what a dreadful thing it is to be clean I'd never have come. I didnt know when I was well off. I — (Mrs Pearce pushes her through the door, but leaves it partly open lest her prisoner should take to flight.)

(Mrs Pearce puts on a pair of white rubber sleeves, and fills the bath, mixing hot and cold, and testing the result with the bath thermometer. She perfumes it with a handful of bath salts and adds a palmful of mustard. She then takes a formidable looking long handled scrubbing brush and soaps it profusely with a ball of scented soap.

Eliza comes back with nothing on but the bath gown huddled tightly round her, a piteous spectacle of abject terror.)

MRS PEARCE: Now come along. Take that thing off.

LIZA: Oh I couldnt, Mrs Pearce: I reely couldnt. I never done such a thing.

MRS PEARCE: Nonsense. Here: step in and tell me whether it's hot enough for you.

LIZA: Ah-oo! Ah-oo! It's too hot.

MRS PEARCE (deftly snatching the gown away and throwing Eliza down on her back): It wont hurt you. (She sets to work with the scrubbing brush.)

(Eliza's screams are heartrending.)

(Meanwhile the Colonel has been having it out with Higgins about Eliza. Pickering has come from the hearth to the chair and seated himself astride of it with his arms on the back to cross-examine him.)

PICKERING: Excuse the straight question, Higgins. Are you a man of good character where women are concerned?

HIGGINS (moodily): Have you ever met a man of good character where women are concerned?

PICKERING: Yes: very frequently.

HIGGINS (dogmatically, lifting himself on his hands to the level of the piano, and sitting on it with a bounce): Well, I havnt. I find that the moment I let a woman make friends with me, she becomes jealous, exacting, suspicious, and a damned nuisance. I find that the moment I let myself make friends with a woman, I become selfish and tyrannical. Women upset everything. When you let them into your life, you find that the woman is driving at one thing and youre driving at another.

PICKERING: At what, for example?

HIGGINS (coming off the piano restlessly): Oh, Lord knows! I suppose the woman wants to live her own life; and the man wants to live his; and each tries to drag the other on to the wrong track. One wants to go north and the other south; and the result is that both have to go east, though they both hate the east wind. (*He sits down on the bench at the keyboard.*) So here I am, a confirmed old bachelor, and likely to remain so.

PICKERING (*rising and standing over him gravely*): Come, Higgins! You know what I mean. If I'm to be in this business I shall feel responsible for that girl. I hope it's understood that no advantage is to be taken of her position.

HIGGINS: What! That thing! Sacred, I assure you. (*Rising to explain.*) You see, she'll be a pupil; and teaching would be impossible unless pupils were sacred. Ive taught scores of American millionairesses how to speak English: the best looking women in the world. I'm seasoned. They might as well be blocks of wood. *I* might as well be a block of wood. It's —

(*Mrs Pearce opens the door. She has Eliza's hat in her hand. Pickering retires to the easy-chair at the hearth and sits down.*)

HIGGINS (*eagerly*): Well, Mrs Pearce: is it all right?

MRS PEARCE (*at the door*): I just wish to trouble you with a word, if I may, Mr Higgins.

HIGGINS: Yes, certainly. Come in. (*She comes forward.*) Dont burn that, Mrs Pearce. I'll keep it as a curiosity. (*He takes the hat.*)

MRS PEARCE: Handle it carefully, sir, please. I had to promise her not to burn it; but I had better put it in the oven for a while.

HIGGINS (*putting it down hastily on the piano*): Oh! thank you. Well, what have you to say to me?

PICKERING: Am I in the way?

MRS PEARCE: Not at all, sir. Mr Higgins: will you please be very particular what you say before the girl?

HIGGINS (*sternly*): Of course. I'm always particular about what I say. Why do you say this to me?

MRS PEARCE (*unmoved*): No sir: youre not at all particular when youve mislaid anything or when you get a little impatient. Now it doesnt matter before me: I'm used to it. But you really must not swear before the girl.

HIGGINS (*indignantly*): I swear! (*Most emphatically.*) I never swear. I detest the habit. What the devil do you mean?

MRS PEARCE (*stolidly*): Thats what I mean, sir. You swear a great deal too much. I dont mind your damning and blasting, and what the devil and where the devil and who the devil —

HIGGINS: Mrs Pearce: this language from your lips! Really!

MRS PEARCE (*not to be put off*): — but there is a certain word I must ask you not to use. The girl used it herself when she began to enjoy the bath. It begins with the same letter as bath. She knows no

better: she learnt it at her mother's knee. But she must not hear it from your lips.

HIGGINS (*loftily*): I cannot charge myself with having ever uttered it, Mrs Pearce. (*She looks at him steadfastly. He adds, hiding an uneasy conscience with a judicial air.*) Except perhaps in a moment of extreme and justifiable excitement.

MRS PEARCE: Only this morning, sir, you applied it to your boots, to the butter, and to the brown bread.

HIGGINS: Oh, that! Mere alliteration, Mrs Pearce, natural to a poet.

MRS PEARCE: Well, sir, whatever you choose to call it, I beg you not to let the girl hear you repeat it.

HIGGINS: Oh, very well, very well. Is that all?

MRS PEARCE: No, sir. We shall have to be very particular with this girl as to personal cleanliness.

HIGGINS: Certainly. Quite right. Most important.

MRS PEARCE: I mean not to be slovenly about her dress or untidy in leaving things about.

HIGGINS (*going to her solemnly*): Just so. I intended to call your attention to that. (*He passes on to Pickering, who is enjoying the conversation immensely.*) It is these little things that matter, Pickering. Take care of the pence and the pounds will take care of themselves is as true of personal habits as of money. (*He comes to anchor on the hearthrug, with the air of a man in an unassailable position.*)

MRS PEARCE: Yes, sir. Then might I ask you not to come down to breakfast in your dressing-gown, or at any rate not to use it as a napkin to the extent you do, sir. And if you would be so good as not to eat everything off the same plate, and to remember not to put the porridge saucepan out of your hand on the clean tablecloth, it would be a better example to the girl. You know you nearly choked yourself with a fishbone in the jam only last week.

HIGGINS (*routed from the hearthrug and drifting back to the piano*): I may do these things sometimes in absence of mind; but surely I dont do them habitually. (*Angrily.*) By the way: my dressing-gown smells most damnably of benzine.

MRS PEARCE: No doubt it does, Mr Higgins. But if you will wipe your fingers —

HIGGINS (*yelling*): Oh very well, very well: I'll wipe them in my hair in future.

MRS PEARCE: I hope youre not offended, Mr Higgins.

HIGGINS (*shocked at finding himself thought capable of an unamiable sentiment*): Not at all, not at all. Youre quite right, Mrs Pearce: I shall be particularly careful before the girl. Is that all?

MRS PEARCE: No, sir. Might she use some of those Japanese dresses you brought from abroad? I really cant put her back into her old things.

HIGGINS: Certainly. Anything you like. Is that all?

MRS PEARCE: Thank you, sir. Thats all. (*She goes out.*)

HIGGINS: You know, Pickering, that woman has the most extraordinary ideas about me. Here I am, a shy, diffident sort of man. Ive never been able to feel really grown-up and tremendous, like other chaps. And yet she's firmly persuaded that I'm an arbitrary overbearing bossing kind of person. I cant account for it.

(*Mrs Pearce returns.*)

MRS PEARCE: If you please, sir, the trouble's beginning already. Theres a dustman downstairs, Alfred Doolittle, wants to see you. He says you have his daughter here.

PICKERING (*rising*): Phew! I say!

HIGGINS (*promptly*): Send the blackguard up.

MRS PEARCE: Oh, very well, sir. (*She goes out.*)

PICKERING: He may not be a blackguard, Higgins.

HIGGINS: Nonsense. Of course he's a blackguard.

PICKERING: Whether he is or not, I'm afraid we shall have some trouble with him.

HIGGINS (*confidently*): Oh no: I think not. If theres any trouble he shall have it with me, not I with him. And we are sure to get something interesting out of him.

PICKERING: About the girl?

HIGGINS: No. I mean his dialect.

PICKERING: Oh!

MRS PEARCE (*at the door*): Doolittle, sir. (*She admits Doolittle and retires.*)

(*Alfred Doolittle is an elderly but vigorous dustman, clad in the costume of his profession, including a hat with a back brim covering his neck and shoulders. He has well marked and rather interesting features, and seems equally free from fear and conscience. He has a remarkably expressive voice, the result of a habit of giving vent to his feelings without reserve. His present pose is that of wounded honor and stern resolution.*)

DOOLITTLE (*at the door, uncertain which of the two gentlemen is his man*): Professor Iggins?

HIGGINS: Here. Good morning. Sit down.

DOOLITTLE: Morning, Governor. (*He sits down magisterially.*) I come about a very serious matter, Governor.

HIGGINS (*to Pickering*): Brought up in Hounslow. Mother Welsh, I should think. (*Doolittle opens his mouth, amazed. Higgins continues.*) What do you want, Doolittle?

DOOLITTLE (*menacingly*): I went my daughter: thats what I want. See?

HIGGINS: Of course you do. Youre her father, arnt you? You dont suppose anyone else wants her, do you? I'm glad to see you have some spark of family feeling left. She's upstairs. Take her away at once.

DOOLITTLE (*rising, fearfully taken aback*): What!

HIGGINS: Take her away. Do you suppose I'm going to keep your daughter for you?

DOOLITTLE (*remonstrating*): Now, now, look here, Governor. Is this reasonable? Is it fairty to take advantage of a man like this? The girl belongs to me. You got her. Where do I come in? (*He sits down again.*)

HIGGINS: Your daughter had the audacity to come to my house and ask me to teach her how to speak properly so that she could get a place in a flowershop. This gentleman and my housekeeper have been here all the time. (*Bullying him.*) How dare you come here and attempt to blackmail me? You sent her here on purpose.

DOOLITTLE (*protesting*): No, Governor.

HIGGINS: You must have. How else could you possibly know that she is here?

DOOLITTLE: Dont take a man up like that, Governor.

HIGGINS: The police shall take you up. This is a plant — a plot to extort money by threats. I shall telephone for the police. (*He goes resolutely to the telephone and opens the directory.*)

DOOLITTLE: Have I asked you for a brass farthing? I leave it to the gentleman here: have I said a word about money?

HIGGINS (*throwing the book aside and marching down on Doolittle with a poser*): What else did you come for?

DOOLITTLE (*sweetly*): Well, what would a man come for? Be human, Governor.

HIGGINS (*disarmed*): Alfred: did you put her up to it?

DOOLITTLE: So help me, Governor, I never did. I take my Bible oath I aint seen the girl these two months past.

HIGGINS: Then how did you know she was here?

DOOLITTLE (*"most musical, most melancholy"*): I'll tell you, Governor, if youll only let me get a word in. I'm willing to tell you. I'm wanting to tell you. I'm waiting to tell you.

HIGGINS: Pickering: this chap has a certain natural gift of rhetoric. Observe the rhythm of his native woodnotes wild. "I'm willing to tell you: I'm wanting to tell you: I'm waiting to tell you." Sentimental rhetoric! thats the Welsh strain in him. It also accounts for his mendacity and dishonesty.

PICKERING: Oh, please, Higgins: I'm west country myself. (*To Doolittle.*) How did you know the girl was here if you didnt send her?

DOOLITTLE: It was like this, Governor. The girl took a boy in the taxi to give him a jaunt. Son of her landlady, he is. He hung about on the chance of her giving him another ride home. Well, she sent him back for her luggage when she heard you was willing for her to stop here. I met the boy at the corner of Long Acre and Endell Street.

HIGGINS: Public house. Yes?

DOOLITTLE: The poor man's club. Governor: why shouldnt I?

PICKERING: Do let him tell his story, Higgins.

DOOLITTLE: He told me what was up. And I ask you, what was my feelings and my duty as a father? I said to the boy, "You bring me the luggage," I says —

PICKERING: Why didnt you go for it yourself?

DOOLITTLE: Landlady wouldnt have trusted me with it, Governor. She's that kind of woman: you know. I had to give the boy a penny afore he trusted me with it, the little swine. I brought it to her just to oblige you like, and make myself agreeable. Thats all.

HIGGINS: How much luggage?

DOOLITTLE: Musical instrument, Governor. A few pictures, a trifle of jewelry, and a bird-cage. She said she didn't want no clothes. What was I to think from that, Governor? I ask you as a parent what was I to think?

HIGGINS: So you came to rescue her from worse than death eh?

DOOLITTLE (appreciatively: relieved at being so well understood): Just so, Governor. Thats right.

PICKERING: But why did you bring your luggage if you intended to take her away?

DOOLITTLE: Have I said a word about taking her away? Have I now?

HIGGINS (determinedly): Youre going to take her away, double quick. (He crosses to the hearth and rings the bell.)

DOOLITTLE (rising): No, Governor. Dont say that. I'm not the man to stand in my girl's light. Heres a career opening for her as you might say; and —

(Mrs Pearce opens the door and awaits orders.)

HIGGINS: Mrs Pearce: this is Eliza's father. He has come to take her away. Give her to him. (He goes back to the piano, with an air of washing his hands of the whole affair.)

DOOLITTLE: No. This is a misunderstanding. Listen here —

MRS PEARCE: He cant take her away. Mr Higgins: how can he? You told me to burn her clothes.

DOOLITTLE: Thats right. I cant carry the girl through the streets like a blooming monkey, can I? I put it to you.

HIGGINS: You have put it to me that you want your daughter. Take your daughter. If she has no clothes go out and buy her some.

DOOLITTLE (desperate): Wheres the clothes she come in? Did I burn them or did your missus here?

MRS PEARCE: I am the housekeeper, if you please. I have sent for some clothes for the girl. When they come you can take her away. You can wait in the kitchen. This way, please.

(Doolittle, much troubled, accompanies her to the door; then hesitates: finally turns confidentially to Higgins.)

DOOLITTLE: Listen here, Governor. You and me is men of the world, aint we?

HIGGINS: Oh! Men of the world, are we? Youd better go, Mrs Pearce.

MRS PEARCE: I think so, indeed, sir. (She goes, with dignity.)

PICKERING: The floor is yours, Mr Doolittle.

DOOLITTLE (to Pickering): I thank you, Governor. (To Higgins, who takes refuge on the piano bench, a little overwhelmed by the proximity of his visitor; for Doolittle has a professional flavor of dust about him.) Well, the truth is, Ive taken a sort of fancy to you, Governor; and if you want the girl, I'm not so set on having her back home again but what I might be open to an arrangement. Regarded in the light of a young woman, she's a fine handsome girl. As a daughter she's not worth her keep; and so I tell you straight. All I ask is my rights as a father; and youre the last man alive to expect me to let her go for nothing; for I can see youre one of the straight sort, Governor. Well, whats a five-pound note to you? and whats Eliza to me? (He turns to his chair and sits down judicially.)

PICKERING: I think you ought to know, Doolittle, that Mr Higgins's intentions are entirely honorable.

DOOLITTLE: Course they are, Governor. If I thought they wasn't, I'd ask fifty.

HIGGINS (revolted): Do you mean to say that you would sell your daughter for £50?

DOOLITTLE: Not in a general way I wouldnt; but to oblige a gentleman like you I'd do a good deal, I do assure you.

PICKERING: Have you no morals, man?

DOOLITTLE (unabashed): Cant afford them, Governor. Neither could you if you was as poor as me. Not that I mean any harm, you know. But if Liza is going to have a bit out of this, why not me too?

HIGGINS (troubled): I dont know what to do, Pickering. There can be no question that as a matter of morals it's a positive crime to give this chap a farthing. And yet I feel a sort of rough justice in his claim.

DOOLITTLE: Thats it, Governor. Thats all I say. A father's heart, as it were.

PICKERING: Well, I know the feeling; but really it seems hardly right —

DOOLITTLE: Dont say that, Governor. Dont look at it

that way. What am I, Governors both? I ask you, what am I? I'm one of the undeserving poor: thats what I am. Think of what that means to a man. It means that he's up agen middle class morality all the time. If theres anything going, and I put in for a bit of it, it's always the same story: "Youre undeserving; so you cant have it." But my needs is as great as the most deserving widow's that ever got money out of six different charities in one week for the death of the same husband. I dont need less than a deserving man: I need more. I dont eat less hearty than him; and I drink a lot more. I want a bit of amusement, cause I'm a thinking man. I want cheerfulness and a song and a band when I feel low. Well, they charge me just the same for everything as they charge the deserving. What is middle class morality? Just an excuse for never giving me anything. Therefore, I ask you, as two gentlemen, not to play that game on me. I'm playing straight with you. I aint pretending to be deserving. I'm undeserving; and I mean to go on being undeserving. I like it; and thats the truth. Will you take advantage of a man's nature to do him out of the price of his own daughter what he's brought up and fed and clothed by the sweat of his brow until she's growed big enough to be interesting to you two gentlemen? Is five pounds unreasonable? I put it to you; and I leave it to you.

HIGGINS (*rising, and going over to Pickering*): Pickering: if we were to take this man in hand for three months, he could choose between a seat in the Cabinet and a popular pulpit in Wales.

PICKERING: What do you say to that, Doolittle?

DOOLITTLE: Not me. Governor, thank you kindly. Ive heard all the preachers and all the prime ministers — for I'm a thinking man and game for politics or religion or social reform same as all the other amusements — and I tell you it's a dog's life any way you look at it. Undeserving poverty is my line. Taking one station in society with another, it's — it's — well, it's the only one that has any ginger in it, to my taste.

HIGGINS: I suppose we must give him a fiver.

PICKERING: He'll make a bad use of it, I'm afraid.

DOOLITTLE: Not me, Governor, so help me I wont. Dont you be afraid that I'll save it and spare it and live idle on it. There wont be a penny of it left by Monday: I'll have to go to work same as if I'd never had it. It wont pauperize me, you bet. Just one good spree for myself and the missus, giving pleasure to ourselves and employment to others, and satisfaction to you to think it's not been throwed away. You couldnt spend it better.

HIGGINS (*taking out his pocket book and coming between Doolittle and the piano*): This is irresistible.

Lets give him ten. (*He offers two notes to the dustman.*)

DOOLITTLE: No, Governor. She wouldnt have the heart to spend ten; and perhaps I shouldnt neither. Ten pounds is a lot of money: it makes a man feel prudent like; and then goodbye to happiness. You give me what I ask you, Governor: not a penny more, and not a penny less.

PICKERING: Why dont you marry that missus of yours? I rather draw the line at encouraging that sort of immorality.

DOOLITTLE: Tell her so, Governor: tell her so. *I'm* willing. It's me that suffers by it. Ive no hold on her. I got to be agreeable to her. I got to give her presents. I got to buy her clothes something sinful. I'm a slave to that woman, Governor, just because I'm not her lawful husband. And she knows it too. Catch her marrying me! Take my advice, Governor — marry Eliza while she's young and dont know no better. If you dont youll be sorry for it after. If you do, she'll be sorry for it after; but better her than you, because youre a man, and she's only a woman and dont know how to be happy anyhow.

HIGGINS: Pickering: If we listen to this man another minute, we shall have no convictions left. (*To Doolittle.*) Five pounds I think you said.

DOOLITTLE: Thank you kindly, Governor.

HIGGINS: Youre sure you wont take ten?

DOOLITTLE: Not now. Another time, Governor.

HIGGINS (*handing him a five-pound note*): Here you are.

DOOLITTLE: Thank you, Governor. Good morning. (*He hurries to the door, anxious to get away with his booty. When he opens it he is confronted with a dainty and exquisitely clean young Japanese lady in a simple blue cotton kimono printed cunningly with small white jasmine blossoms. Mrs Pearce is with her. He gets out of her way deferentially and apologizes.*) Beg pardon, miss.

THE JAPANESE LADY: Garn! Dont you know your own daughter?

DOOLITTLE	⎰ *exclaiming* ⎱	Bly me! it's Eliza!
HIGGINS	*simul-*	Whats that? This!
PICKERING	⎱ *taneously* ⎰	By Jove!

LIZA: Dont I look silly?

HIGGINS: Silly?

MRS PEARCE (*at the door*): Now, Mr Higgins, please dont say anything to make the girl conceited about herself.

HIGGINS (*conscientiously*): Oh! Quite right, Mrs Pearce. (*To Eliza.*) Yes: damned silly.

MRS PEARCE: Please, sir.

HIGGINS (*correcting himself*): I mean extremely silly.

LIZA: I should look all right with my hat on. (*She*

takes up her hat; puts it on; and walks across the room to the fireplace with a fashionable air.)

HIGGINS: A new fashion, by George! And it ought to look horrible!

DOOLITTLE (*with fatherly pride*): Well, I never thought she'd clean up as good looking as that, Governor. She's a credit to me, aint she?

LIZA: I tell you, it's easy to clean up here. Hot and cold water on tap, just as much as you like, there is. Woolly towels, there is; and a towel horse so hot, it burns your fingers. Soft brushes to scrub yourself, and a wooden bowl of soap smelling like primroses. Now I know why ladies is so clean. Washing's a treat for them. Wish they could see what it is for the like of me!

HIGGINS: I'm glad the bathroom met with your approval.

LIZA: It didnt: not all of it; and I dont care who hears me say it. Mrs Pearce knows.

HIGGINS: What was wrong, Mrs Pearce?

MRS PEARCE (*blandly*): Oh, nothing, sir. It doesnt matter.

LIZA: I had a good mind to break it. I didn't know which way to look. But I hung a towel over it, I did.

HIGGINS: Over what?

MRS PEARCE: Over the looking-glass sir.

HIGGINS: Doolittle: you have brought your daughter up too strictly.

DOOLITTLE: Me! I never brought her up at all, except to give her a lick of a strap now and again. Dont put it on me, Governor. She aint accustomed to it, you see: thats all. But she'll soon pick up your free-and-easy ways.

LIZA: I'm a good girl, I am; and I wont pick up no free-and-easy ways.

HIGGINS: Eliza: if you say again that youre a good girl, your father shall take you home.

LIZA: Not him. You dont know my father. All he come here for was to touch you for some money to get drunk on.

DOOLITTLE: Well, what else would I want money for? To put into the plate in church, I suppose. (*She puts out her tongue at him. He is so incensed by this that Pickering presently finds it necessary to step between them.*) Dont you give me none of your lip; and dont let me hear you giving this gentleman any of it neither, or youll hear from me about it. See?

HIGGINS: Have you any further advice to give her before you go, Doolittle? Your blessing, for instance.

DOOLITTLE: No, Governor: I aint such a mug as to put up my children to all I know myself. Hard enough to hold them in without that. If you want Eliza's mind improved, Governor, you do it your-self with a strap. So long, gentlemen. (*He turns to go.*)

HIGGINS (*impressively*): Stop. Youll come regularly to see your daughter. It's your duty, you know. My brother is a clergyman; and he could help you in your talks with her.

DOOLITTLE (*evasively*): Certainly, I'll come, Governor. Not just this week, because I have a job at a distance. But later on you may depend on me. Afternoon, gentlemen. Afternoon, maam. (*He touches his hat to Mrs Pearce, who disdains the salutation and goes out. He winks at Higgins, thinking him probably a fellow-sufferer from Mrs Pearce's difficult disposition, and follows her.*)

LIZA: Dont you believe the old liar. He'd as soon set a bulldog on him as a clergyman. You wont see him again in a hurry.

HIGGINS: I dont want to, Eliza. Do you?

LIZA: Not me. I dont want never to see him again, I dont. He's a disgrace to me, he is, collecting dust, instead of working at his trade.

PICKERING: What is his trade, Eliza?

LIZA: Talking money out of other people's pockets into his own. His proper trade's a navvy; and he works at it sometimes too — for exercise — and earns good money at it. Aint you going to call me Miss Doolittle any more?

PICKERING: I beg your pardon, Miss Doolittle. It was a slip of the tongue.

LIZA: Oh, I dont mind; only it sounded so genteel. I should just like to take a taxi to the corner of Tottenham Court Road and get out there and tell it to wait for me, just to put the girls in their place a bit. I wouldnt speak to them, you know.

PICKERING: Better wait til we get you something really fashionable.

HIGGINS: Besides, you shouldnt cut your old friends now that you have risen in the world. Thats what we call snobbery.

LIZA: You dont call the like of them my friends now, I should hope. Theyve took it out of me often enough with their ridicule when they had the chance; and now I mean to get a bit of my own back. But if I'm to have fashionable clothes, I'll wait. I should like to have some. Mrs Pearce says youre going to give me some to wear in bed at night different to what I wear in the daytime; but it do seem a waste of money when you could get something to shew. Besides, I never could fancy changing into cold things on a winter night.

MRS PEARCE (*coming back*): Now, Eliza. The new things have come for you to try on.

LIZA: Ah-ow-oo-ooh! (*She rushes out.*)

MRS PEARCE (*following her*): Oh, dont rush about like that, girl. (*She shuts the door behind her.*)

HIGGINS: Pickering: we have taken on a stiff job.

PICKERING (*with conviction*): Higgins: we have.

(*There seems to be some curiosity as to what Higgins's lessons to Eliza were like. Well, here is a sample: the first one.*

Picture Eliza, in her new clothes, and feeling her inside put out of step by a lunch, dinner, and breakfast of a kind to which it is unaccustomed, seated with Higgins and the Colonel in the study, feeling like a hospital out-patient at a first encounter with the doctors.

Higgins, constitutionally unable to sit still, discomposes her still more by striding restlessly about. But for the reassuring presence and quietude of her friend the Colonel she would run for her life, even back to Drury Lane.)

HIGGINS: Say your alphabet.

LIZA: I know my alphabet. Do you think I know nothing? I dont need to be taught like a child.

HIGGINS (*thundering*): Say your alphabet.

PICKERING: Say it, Miss Doolittle. You will understand presently. Do what he tells you; and let him teach you in his own way.

LIZA: Oh well, if you put it like that — Ahyee, bəyee, cəyee, dəyee —

HIGGINS (*with the roar of a wounded lion*): Stop. Listen to this, Pickering. This is what we pay for as elementary education. This unfortunate animal has been locked up for nine years in school at our expense to teach her to speak and read the language of Shakespear and Milton. And the result is Ahyee, Bə-yee, Cə-yee, Də-yee. (*To Eliza.*) Say A, B, C, D.

LIZA (*almost in tears*): But I'm saying it. Ahyee, Bə yee, Cəyee —

HIGGINS: Stop. Say a cup of tea.

LIZA: A cappətə-ee.

HIGGINS: Put your tongue forward until it squeezes against the top of your lower teeth. Now say cup.

LIZA: C-c-c — I cant. C-Cup.

PICKERING: Good. Splendid, Miss Doolittle.

HIGGINS: By Jupiter, she's done it at the first shot. Pickering: we shall make a duchess of her. (*To Eliza.*) Now do you think you could possibly say tea? Not tə-yee, mind: if you ever say bə-yee cə-yee də-yee again you shall be dragged round the room three times by the hair of your head. (*Fortissimo.*) T, T, T, T.

LIZA (*weeping*): I cant hear no difference cep that it sounds more genteel-like when you say it.

HIGGINS: Well, if you can hear that difference, what the devil are you crying for? Pickering: give her a chocolate.

PICKERING: No, no. Never mind crying a little. Miss

Doolittle: you are doing very well; and the lessons wont hurt. I promise you I wont let him drag you round the room by your hair.

HIGGINS: Be off with you to Mrs Pearce and tell her about it. Think about it. Try to do it by yourself: and keep your tongue well forward in your mouth instead of trying to roll it up and swallow it. Another lesson at half-past four this afternoon. Away with you.

(*Eliza, still sobbing, rushes from the room.*)

(*And that is the sort of ordeal poor Eliza has to go through for months before we meet her again on her first appearance in London society of the professional class.*)

ACT 3

(*It is Mrs Higgins's at-home day. Nobody has yet arrived. Her drawing room, in a flat on Chelsea Embankment, has three windows looking on the river; and the ceiling is not so lofty as it would be in an older house of the same pretension. The windows are open, giving access to a balcony with flowers in pots. If you stand with your face to the windows, you have the fireplace on your left and the door in the right-hand wall close to the corner nearest the windows.*

Mrs Higgins was brought up on Morris and Burne Jones; and her room, which is very unlike her son's room in Wimpole Street, is not crowded with furniture and little tables and nicknacks. In the middle of the room there is a big ottoman; and this, with the carpet, the Morris wallpapers, and the Morris chintz window curtains and brocade covers of the ottoman and its cushions, supply all the ornament, and are much too handsome to be hidden by odds and ends of useless things. A few good oil-paintings from the exhibitions in the Grosvenor Gallery thirty years ago (the Burne Jones, not the Whistler side of them) are on the walls. The only landscape is a Cecil Lawson on the scale of a Rubens. There is a portrait of Mrs Higgins as she was when she defied the fashion in her youth in one of the beautiful Rossettian costumes which, when caricatured by people who did not understand, led to the absurdities of popular estheticism in the eighteen-seventies.

In the corner diagonally opposite the door Mrs Higgins, now over sixty and long past taking the trouble to dress out of the fashion, sits writing at an elegantly simple writing-table with a bell button within reach of her hand. There is a Chippendale chair further back in the room between her and the window nearest her side. At the other side of the room, further forward, is an Elizabethan chair roughly carved in the taste of Inigo Jones. On the same side a piano in a decorated case. The corner between the fireplace and the window is occupied by a divan cushioned in Morris chintz.

It is between four and five in the afternoon.

The door is opened violently; and Higgins enters with his hat on.)

MRS HIGGINS (*dismayed*): Henry! (*Scolding him.*) What are you doing here today? It is my at-home day: you promised not to come. (*As he bends to kiss her, she takes his hat off, and presents it to him.*)

HIGGINS: Oh bother! (*He throws the hat down on the table.*)

MRS HIGGINS: Go home at once.

HIGGINS (*kissing her*): I know, mother. I came on purpose.

MRS HIGGINS: But you mustnt. I'm serious, Henry. You offend all my friends: they stop coming whenever they meet you.

HIGGINS: Nonsense! I know I have no small talk; but people dont mind. (*He sits on the settee.*)

MRS HIGGINS: Oh! dont they? Small talk indeed! What about your large talk? Really, dear, you mustnt stay.

HIGGINS: I must. Ive a job for you. A phonetic job.

MRS HIGGINS: No use, dear. I'm sorry; but I cant get round your vowels; and though I like to get pretty postcards in your patent shorthand, I always have to read the copies in ordinary writing you so thoughtfully send me.

HIGGINS: Well, this isnt a phonetic job.

MRS HIGGINS: You said it was.

HIGGINS: Not your part of it. Ive picked up a girl.

MRS HIGGINS: Does that mean that some girl has picked you up?

HIGGINS: Not at all. I dont mean a love affair.

MRS HIGGINS: What a pity!

HIGGINS: Why?

MRS HIGGINS: Well, you never fall in love with anyone under forty-five. When will you discover that there are some rather nice-looking young women about?

HIGGINS: Oh, I cant be bothered with young women. My idea of a lovable woman is somebody as like you as possible. I shall never get into the way of seriously liking young women: some habits lie too deep to be changed. (*Rising abruptly and walking about, jingling his money and his keys in his trouser pockets.*) Besides, theyre all idiots.

MRS HIGGINS: Do you know what you would do if you really loved me, Henry?

HIGGINS: Oh bother! What? Marry, I suppose.

MRS HIGGINS: No. Stop fidgeting and take your hands out of your pockets. (*With a gesture of despair, he*

obeys and sits down again.) Thats a good boy. Now tell me about the girl.

HIGGINS: She's coming to see you.

MRS HIGGINS: I dont remember asking her.

HIGGINS: You didnt. *I* asked her. If youd known her you wouldnt have asked her.

MRS HIGGINS: Indeed! Why?

HIGGINS: Well, it's like this. She's a common flower girl. I picked her off the kerbstone.

MRS HIGGINS: And invited her to my at-home!

HIGGINS (*rising and coming to her to coax her*): Oh, thatll be all right. Ive taught her to speak properly; and she has strict orders as to her behavior. She's to keep to two subjects: the weather and everybody's health — Fine day and How do you do, you know — and not to let herself go on things in general. That will be safe.

MRS HIGGINS: Safe! To talk about our health! about our insides! perhaps about our outsides! How could you be so silly, Henry?

HIGGINS (*impatiently*): Well, she must talk about something. (*He controls himself and sits down again.*) Oh, she'll be all right: dont you fuss. Pickering is in it with me. Ive a sort of bet on that I'll pass her off as a duchess in six months. I started on her some months ago; and she's getting on like a house on fire. I shall win my bet. She has a quick ear; and she's been easier to teach than my middle-class pupils because she's had to learn a complete new language. She talks English almost as you talk French.

MRS HIGGINS: Thats satisfactory, at all events.

HIGGINS: Well, it is and it isnt.

MRS HIGGINS: What does that mean?

HIGGINS: You see, Ive got her pronunciation all right; but you have to consider not only how a girl pronounces, but what she pronounces; and thats where —

(*They are interrupted by the parlormaid, announcing guests.*)

THE PARLORMAID: Mrs and Miss Eynsford Hill. (*She withdraws.*)

HIGGINS: Oh Lord! (*He rises: snatches his hat from the table; and makes for the door; but before he reaches it his mother introduces him.*)

(*Mrs and Miss Eynsford Hill are the mother and daughter who sheltered from the rain in Covent Garden. The mother is well bred, quiet, and has the habitual anxiety of straitened means. The daughter has acquired a gay air of being very much at home in society: the bravado of genteel poverty.*)

MRS EYNSFORD HILL (*to Mrs Higgins*): How do you do? (*They shake hands.*)

MISS EYNSFORD HILL: How d'you do? (*She shakes.*)

MRS HIGGINS (*introducing*): My son Henry.

MRS EYNSFORD HILL: Your celebrated son! I have so longed to meet you, Professor Higgins.

HIGGINS: (*glumly, making no movement in her direction.*): Delighted. (*He backs against the piano and bows brusquely.*)

MISS EYNSFORD HILL (*going to him with confident familiarity*): How do you do?

HIGGINS (*staring at her*): Ive seen you before somewhere. I havnt the ghost of a notion where; but Ive heard your voice. (*Drearily.*) It doesnt matter. Youd better sit down.

MRS HIGGINS: I'm sorry to say that my celebrated son has no manners. You mustnt mind him.

MISS EYNSFORD HILL (*gaily*): I dont. (*She sits in the Elizabethan chair.*)

MRS EYNSFORD HILL (*a little bewildered*): Not at all. (*She sits on the ottoman between her daughter and Mrs Higgins, who has turned her chair away from the writing-table.*)

HIGGINS: Oh, have I been rude? I didnt mean to be.

(*He goes to the central window, through which, with his back to the company, he contemplates the river and the flowers in Battersea Park on the opposite bank as if they were a frozen desert.*

The parlormaid returns, ushering in Pickering.)

THE PARLORMAID: Colonel Pickering. (*She withdraws.*)

PICKERING: How do you do, Mrs Higgins?

MRS HIGGINS: So glad youve come. Do you know Mrs Eynsford Hill — Miss Eynsford Hill? (*Exchange of bows. The Colonel brings the Chippendale chair a little forward between Mrs Hill and Mrs Higgins, and sits down.*)

PICKERING: Has Henry told you what weve come for?

HIGGINS (*over his shoulder*): We were interrupted: damn it!

MRS HIGGINS: Oh Henry, Henry, really!

MRS EYNSFORD HILL (*half rising*): Are we in the way?

MRS HIGGINS (*rising and making her sit down again*): No, no. You couldnt have come more fortunately: we want you to meet a friend of ours.

HIGGINS (*turning hopefully*): Yes, by George! We want two or three people. Youll do as well as anybody else.

(*The parlor maid returns, ushering Freddy.*)

THE PARLORMAID: Mr Eynsford Hill.

HIGGINS (*almost audibly, past endurance*): God of Heaven! another of them.

FREDDY (*shaking hands with Mrs Higgins*): Ahdedo?

MRS HIGGINS: Very good of you to come. (*Introducing.*) Colonel Pickering.

FREDDY (*bowing*): Ahdedo?

MRS HIGGINS: I dont think you know my son, Professor Higgins.

FREDDY (*going to Higgins*): Ahdedo?

HIGGINS (*looking at him much as if he were a pickpocket*): I'll take my oath Ive met you before somewhere. Where was it?

FREDDY: I dont think so.

HIGGINS (*resignedly*): It dont matter, anyhow. Sit down.

(*He shakes Freddy's hand and almost slings him on to the ottoman with his face to the window; then comes round to the other side of it.*)

HIGGINS: Well, here we are, anyhow! (*He sits down on the ottoman next Mrs Eynsford Hill, on her left.*) And now, what the devil are we going to talk about until Eliza comes?

MRS HIGGINS: Henry: you are the life and soul of the Royal Society's soirées: but really youre rather trying on more commonplace occasions.

HIGGINS: Am I? Very sorry. (*Beaming suddenly.*) I suppose I am, you know. (*Uproariously.*) Ha, ha!

MISS EYNSFORD HILL (*who considers Higgins quite eligible matrimonially*): I sympathize. I havnt any small talk. If people would only be frank and say what they really think!

HIGGINS (*relapsing into gloom*): Lord forbid!

MRS EYNSFORD HILL (*taking up her daughter's cue*): But why?

HIGGINS: What they think they ought to think is bad enough, Lord knows; but what they really think would break up the whole show. Do you suppose it would be really agreeable if I were to come out now with what I really think?

MISS EYNSFORD HILL (*gaily*): Is it so very cynical?

HIGGINS: Cynical! Who the dickens said it was cynical? I mean it wouldnt be decent.

MRS EYNSFORD HILL (*seriously*): Oh! I'm sure you dont mean that, Mr Higgins.

HIGGINS: You see, we're all savages, more or less. We're supposed to be civilized and cultured — to know all about poetry and philosophy and art and science, and so on; but how many of us know even the meanings of these names? (*To Miss Hill.*) What do you know of poetry? (*To Mrs Hill.*) What do you know of science? (*Indicating Freddy.*) What does he know of art or science or anything else? What the devil do you imagine I know of philosophy?

MRS HIGGINS: (*warningly*): Or of manners, Henry?

THE PARLORMAID: (*opening the door*): Miss Doolittle. (*She withdraws.*)

HIGGINS (*rising hastily and running to Mrs Higgins*): Here she is, mother. (*He stands on tiptoe and makes signs over his mother's head to Eliza to indicate to her which lady is her hostess.)*

(*Eliza, who is exquisitely dressed, produces an impression of such remarkable distinction and beauty as she enters that they all rise, quite fluttered. Guided by Higgins's signals, she comes to Mrs Higgins with studied grace.*)

LIZA: (*speaking with pedantic correctness of pronunciation and great beauty of tone*): How do you do, Mrs Higgins? (*She gasps slightly in making sure of the H in Higgins, but is quite successful.*) Mr Higgins told me I might come.

MRS HIGGINS (*cordially*): Quite right: I'm very glad indeed to see you.

PICKERING: How do you do, Miss Doolittle?

LIZA (*shaking hands with him*): Colonel Pickering, is it not?

MRS EYNSFORD HILL: I feel sure we have met before, Miss Doolittle. I remember your eyes.

LIZA: How do you do? (*She sits down on the ottoman gracefully in the place just left vacant by Higgins.*)

MRS EYNSFORD HILL (*introducing*): My daughter Clara.

LIZA: How do you do?

CLARA (*impulsively*): How do you do? (*She sits down on the ottoman beside Eliza, devouring her with her eyes.*)

FREDDY (*coming to their side of the ottoman*): Ive certainly had the pleasure.

MRS EYNSFORD HILL (*introducing*): My son Freddy.

LIZA: How do you do?

(*Freddy bows and sits down in the Elizabethan chair, infatuated.*)

HIGGINS (*suddenly*): By George, yes: it all comes back to me! (*They stare at him.*) Covent Garden! (*Lamentably.*) What a damned thing!

MRS HIGGINS: Henry, please! (*He is about to sit on the edge of the table.*) Dont sit on my writing-table: youll break it.

HIGGINS (*sulkily*): Sorry.

(*He goes to the divan, stumbling into the fender and over the fire-irons on his way; extricating himself with muttered imprecations; and finishing his disastrous journey by throwing himself so impatiently on the divan that he almost breaks it. Mrs Higgins looks at him, but controls herself and says nothing.*

A long and painful pause ensues.)

MRS HIGGINS (*at last, conversationally*): Will it rain, do you think?

LIZA: The shallow depression in the west of these islands is likely to move slowly in an easterly direc-

tion. There are no indications of any great change in the barometrical situation.

FREDDY: Ha! ha! how awfully funny!

LIZA: What is wrong with that, young man? I bet I got it right.

FREDDY: Killing!

MRS EYNSFORD HILL: I'm sure I hope it wont turn cold. Theres so much influenza about. It runs right through our whole family regularly every spring.

LIZA (*darkly*): My aunt died of influenza: so they said.

MRS EYNSFORD HILL (*clicks her tongue sympathetically*): !!!

LIZA (*in the same tragic tone*): But it's my belief they done the old woman in.

MRS HIGGINS (*puzzled*): Done her in?

LIZA: Y-e-e-e-es, Lord love you! Why should she die of influenza? She come through diphtheria right enough the year before. I saw her with my own eyes. Fairly blue with it, she was. They all thought she was dead; but my father he kept ladling gin down her throat til she came to so sudden that she bit the bowl off the spoon.

MRS EYNSFORD HILL (*startled*): Dear me!

LIZA (*piling up the indictment*): What call would a woman with that strength in her have to die of influenza? What become of her new straw hat that should have come to me? Somebody pinched it; and what I say is, them as pinched it done her in.

MRS EYNSFORD HILL: What does doing her in mean?

HIGGINS (*hastily*): Oh, thats the new small talk. To do a person in means to kill them.

MRS EYNSFORD HILL (*to Eliza, horrified*): You surely dont believe that your aunt was killed?

LIZA: Do I not! Them she lived with would have killed her for a hat-pin, let alone a hat.

MRS EYNSFORD HILL: But it cant have been right for your father to pour spirits down her throat like that. It might have killed her.

LIZA: Not her. Gin was mother's milk to her. Besides, he'd poured so much down his own throat that he knew the good of it.

MRS EYNSFORD HILL: Do you mean that he drank?

LIZA: Drank! My word! Something chronic.

MRS EYNSFORD HILL: How dreadful for you!

LIZA: Not a bit. It never did him no harm what I could see. But then he did not keep it up regular. (*Cheerfully.*) On the burst, as you might say, from time to time. And always more agreeable when he had a drop in. When he was out of work, my mother used to give him fourpence and tell him to go out and not come back until he'd drunk himself cheerful and loving-like. Theres lots of women has to make their husbands drunk to make them fit to live with. (*Now quite at her ease.*) You see, it's like this. If a man has a bit of a conscience, it always takes him when he's sober; and then it makes him low-spirited. A drop of booze just takes that off and makes him happy. (*To Freddy, who is in convulsions of suppressed laughter.*) Here! what are you sniggering at?

FREDDY: The new small talk. You do it so awfully well.

LIZA: If I was doing it proper, what was you laughing at? (*To Higgins.*) Have I said anything I oughtnt?

MRS HIGGINS (*interposing*): Not at all, Miss Doolittle.

LIZA: Well, thats a mercy, anyhow. (*Expansively.*) What I always say is —

HIGGINS (*rising and looking at his watch*): Ahem!

LIZA (*looking round at him; taking the hint; and rising*): Well: I must go. (*They all rise. Freddy goes to the door.*) So pleased to have met you. Goodbye. (*She shakes hands with Mrs Higgins.*)

MRS HIGGINS: Goodbye.

LIZA: Goodbye, Colonel Pickering.

PICKERING: Goodbye, Miss Doolittle. (*They shake hands.*)

LIZA (*nodding to the others*): Goodbye, all.

FREDDY (*opening the door for her*): Are you walking across the Park, Miss Doolittle? If so —

LIZA (*perfectly elegant diction*): Walk! Not bloody likely. (*Sensation.*) I am going in a taxi. (*She goes out.*)

(*Pickering gasps and sits down. Freddy goes out on the balcony to catch another glimpse of Eliza.*)

MRS EYNSFORD HILL (*suffering from shock*): Well, I really cant get used to the new ways.

CLARA (*throwing herself discontentedly into the Elizabethan chair*): Oh, it's all right, mamma, quite right. People will think we never go anywhere or see anybody if you are so old-fashioned.

MRS EYNSFORD HILL: I daresay I am very old-fashioned; but I do hope you wont begin using that expression, Clara. I have got accustomed to hear you talking about men as rotters, and calling everything filthy and beastly, though I do think it horrible and unladylike. But this last is really too much. Dont you think so, Colonel Pickering?

PICKERING: Dont ask me. Ive been away in India for several years; and manners have changed so much that I sometimes dont know whether I'm at a respectable dinner-table or in a ship's forecastle.

CLARA: It's all a matter of habit. Theres no right or wrong in it. Nobody means anything by it. And it's so quaint, and gives such a smart emphasis to things that are not in themselves very witty. I find the new small talk delightful and quite innocent.

MRS EYNSFORD HILL (*rising*): Well, after that, I think it's time for us to go.

(*Pickering and Higgins rise.*)

CLARA (*rising*): Oh yes: we have three at-homes to go to still. Goodbye, Mrs Higgins. Goodbye, Colonel Pickering. Goodbye, Professor Higgins.

HIGGINS (*coming grimly at her from the divan, and accompanying her to the door*): Goodbye. Be sure you try on that small talk at the three at-homes. Dont be nervous about it. Pitch it in strong.

CLARA (*all smiles*): I will. Goodbye. Such nonsense, all this early Victorian prudery!

HIGGINS (*tempting her*): Such damned nonsense!

CLARA: Such bloody nonsense!

MRS EYNSFORD HILL (*convulsively*): Clara!

CLARA: Ha! ha! (*She goes out radiant, conscious of being thoroughly up to date, and is heard descending the stairs in a stream of silvery laughter.*)

FREDDY (*to the heavens at large*): Well, I ask you — (*He gives it up, and comes to Mrs Higgins.*) Goodbye.

MRS HIGGINS (*shaking hands*): Goodbye. Would you like to meet Miss Doolittle again?

FREDDY (*eagerly*): Yes, I should, most awfully.

MRS HIGGINS: Well, you know my days.

FREDDY: Yes. Thanks awfully. Goodbye. (*He goes out.*)

MRS EYNSFORD HILL: Goodbye, Mr Higgins.

HIGGINS: Goodbye. Goodbye.

MRS EYNSFORD HILL (*to Pickering*): It's no use. I shall never be able to bring myself to use that word.

PICKERING: Dont. It's not compulsory, you know. Youll get on quite well without it.

MRS EYNSFORD HILL: Only, Clara is so down on me if I am not positively reeking with the latest slang. Goodbye.

PICKERING: Goodbye. (*They shake hands.*)

MRS EYNSFORD HILL (*to Mrs Higgins*): You mustnt mind Clara. (*Pickering, catching from her lowered tone that this is not meant for him to hear, discreetly joins Higgins at the window.*) We're so poor! and she gets so few parties, poor child! She doesnt quite know. (*Mrs Higgins, seeing that her eyes are moist, takes her hand sympathetically and goes with her to the door.*) But the boy is nice. Dont you think so?

MRS HIGGINS: Oh, quite nice. I shall always be delighted to see him.

MRS EYNSFORD HILL: Thank you, dear. Goodbye. (*She goes out.*)

HIGGINS (*eagerly*): Well? Is Eliza presentable? (*He swoops on his mother and drags her to the ottoman, where she sits down in Eliza's place with her son on her left.*)

(*Pickering returns to his chair on her right.*)

MRS HIGGINS: You silly boy, of course she's not presentable. She's a triumph of your art and of her dressmaker's; but if you suppose for a moment that she doesnt give herself away in every sentence she utters, you must be perfectly cracked about her.

PICKERING: But dont you think something might be done? I mean something to eliminate the sanguinary element from her conversation.

MRS HIGGINS: Not as long as she is in Henry's hands.

HIGGINS (*aggrieved*): Do you mean that my language is improper?

MRS HIGGINS: No, dearest: it would be quite proper — say on a canal barge; but it would not be proper for her at a garden party.

HIGGINS (*deeply injured*): Well I must say —

PICKERING (*interrupting him*): Come, Higgins: you must learn to know yourself. I havnt heard such language as yours since we used to review the volunteers in Hyde Park twenty years ago.

HIGGINS (*sulkily*): Oh, well, if you say so. I suppose I dont always talk like a bishop.

MRS HIGGINS (*quieting Henry with a touch*): Colonel Pickering: will you tell me what is the exact state of things in Wimpole Street?

PICKERING (*cheerfully: as if this completely changed the subject*): Well, I have come to live there with Henry. We work together at my Indian Dialects; and we think it more convenient —

MRS HIGGINS: Quite so. I know all about that: it's an excellent arrangement. But where does this girl live?

HIGGINS: With us, of course. Where should she live?

MRS HIGGINS: But on what terms? Is she a servant? If not, what is she?

PICKERING (*slowly*): I think I know what you mean, Mrs Higgins.

HIGGINS: Well, dash me if *I* do! Ive had to work at the girl every day for months to get her to her present pitch. Besides, she's useful. She knows where my things are, and remembers my appointments and so forth.

MRS HIGGINS: How does your housekeeper get on with her?

HIGGINS: Mrs Pearce? Oh, she's jolly glad to get so much taken off her hands; for before Eliza came, she used to have to find things and remind me of my appointments. But she's got some silly bee in her bonnet about Eliza. She keeps saying "You dont think, sir": doesnt she, Pick?

PICKERING: Yes: thats the formula. "You dont think, sir." Thats the end of every conversation about Eliza.

HIGGINS: As if I ever stop thinking about the girl and her confounded vowels and consonants. I'm worn out, thinking about her, and watching her lips and her teeth and her tongue, not to mention her soul, which is the quaintest of the lot.

MRS HIGGINS: You certainly are a pretty pair of babies, playing with your live doll.

HIGGINS: Playing! The hardest job I ever tackled: make no mistake about that, mother. But you have no idea how frightfully interesting it is to take a human being and change her into a quite different human being by creating a new speech for her. It's filling up the deepest gulf that separates class from class and soul from soul.

PICKERING (*drawing his chair closer to Mrs Higgins and bending over to her eagerly*): Yes: it's enormously interesting. I assure you, Mrs Higgins, we take Eliza very seriously. Every week — every day almost — there is some new change. (*Closer again.*) We keep records of every stage — dozens of gramophone disks and photographs —

HIGGINS (*assailing her at the other ear*): Yes, by George: it's the most absorbing experiment I ever tackled. She regularly fills our lives up: doesnt she, Pick?

PICKERING: We're always talking Eliza.

HIGGINS: Teaching Eliza.

PICKERING: Dressing Eliza.

MRS HIGGINS: What!

HIGGINS: Inventing new Elizas.

HIGGINS:	(*speaking together*)	You know she has the most extraordinary quickness of ear:
PICKERING:		I assure you, my dear Mrs Higgins, that girl
HIGGINS:		just like a parrot. Ive tried her with every
PICKERING:		is a genius. She can play the piano quite beautifully.
HIGGINS:		possible sort of sound that a human being can make —
PICKERING:		We have taken her to classical concerts and to music
HIGGINS:		Continental dialects, African dialects, Hottentot
PICKERING:		halls; and it's all the same to her: she plays everything
HIGGINS:		clicks, things it took me years to get hold of; and
PICKERING:		she hears right off when she comes home, whether it's
HIGGINS:		she picks them up like a shot, right away, as if she had
PICKERING:		Beethoven and Brahms or Lehar and Lionel Monckton;
HIGGINS:		been at it all her life.
PICKERING:		though six months ago, she'd never as much as touched a piano —

MRS HIGGINS (*putting her fingers in her ears, as they are by this time shouting one another down with an intolerable noise*): Sh-sh-sh — sh!

(*They stop.*)

PICKERING: I beg your pardon. (*He draws his chair back apologetically.*)

HIGGINS: Sorry. When Pickering starts shouting nobody can get a word in edgeways.

MRS HIGGINS: Be quiet, Henry. Colonel Pickering: dont you realize that when Eliza walked into Wimpole Street, something walked in with her?

PICKERING: Her father did. But Henry soon got rid of him.

MRS HIGGINS: It would have been more to the point if her mother had. But as her mother didnt something else did.

PICKERING: But what?

MRS HIGGINS (*unconsciously dating herself by the word.*): A problem.

PICKERING: Oh I see. The problem of how to pass her off as a lady.

HIGGINS: I'll solve that problem. Ive half solved it already.

MRS HIGGINS: No, you two infinitely stupid male creatures: the problem of what is to be done with her afterwards.

HIGGINS: I dont see anything in that. She can go her own way, with all the advantages I have given her.

MRS HIGGINS: The advantages of that poor woman who was here just now! The manners and habits that disqualify a fine lady from earning her own living without giving her a fine lady's income! Is that what you mean?

PICKERING (*indulgently, being rather bored*): Oh, that will be all right, Mrs Higgins. (*He rises to go.*)

HIGGINS (*rising also*): We'll find her some light employment.

PICKERING: She's happy enough. Dont you worry about her. Goodbye. (*He shakes hands as if he were consoling a frightened child, and makes for the door.*)

HIGGINS: Anyhow, theres no good bothering now. The thing's done. Goodbye, mother. (*He kisses her, and follows Pickering.*)

PICKERING (*turning for a final consolation*): There are plenty of openings. We'll do whats right. Goodbye.

HIGGINS (*to Pickering as they go out together*): Lets take her to the Shakespear exhibition at Earls Court.

PICKERING: Yes: lets. Her remarks will be delicious.

HIGGINS: She'll mimic all the people for us when we get home.

PICKERING: Ripping. (*Both are heard laughing as they go downstairs.*)

MRS HIGGINS (*rises with an impatient bounce, and returns to her work at the writing-table. She sweeps a litter of disarranged papers out of the*

way; snatches a sheet of paper from her stationery case; and tries resolutely to write. At the third time she gives it up; flings down her pen; grips the table angrily and exclaims): Oh, men! men!! men!!!

(*Clearly Eliza will not pass as a duchess yet; and Higgins's bet remains unwon. But the six months are not yet exhausted; and just in time Eliza does actually pass as a princess. For a glimpse of how she did it imagine an Embassy in London one summer evening after dark. The hall door has an awning and a carpet across the sidewalk to the kerb, because a grand reception is in progress. A small crowd is lined up to see the guests arrive.*

A Rolls-Royce car drives up. Pickering in evening dress, with medals and orders, alights, and hands out Eliza, in opera cloak, evening dress, diamonds, fan, flowers and all accessories. Higgins follows. The car drives off; and the three go up the steps and into the house, the door opening for them as they approach.

Inside the house they find themselves in a spacious hall from which the grand staircase rises. On the left are the arrangements for the gentlemen's cloaks. The male guests are depositing their hats and wraps there.

On the right is a door leading to the ladies' cloakroom. Ladies are going in cloaked and coming out in splendor. Pickering whispers to Eliza and points out the ladies' room. She goes into it. Higgins and Pickering take off their overcoats and take tickets for them from the attendant.

One of the guests, occupied in the same way, has his back turned. Having taken his ticket, he turns round and reveals himself as an important looking young man with an astonishingly hairy face. He has an enormous moustache, flowing out into luxuriant whiskers. Waves of hair cluster on his brow. His hair is cropped closely at the back, and glows with oil. Otherwise he is very smart. He wears several worthless orders. He is evidently a foreigner, guessable as a whiskered Pandour from Hungary; but in spite of the ferocity of his moustache he is amiable and genially voluble.

Recognizing Higgins, he flings his arms wide apart and approaches him enthusiastically.)

WHISKERS: Maestro, maestro. (*He embraces Higgins and kisses him on both cheeks.*) You remember me?

HIGGINS: No I dont. Who the devil are you?

WHISKERS: I am your pupil: your first pupil, your best and greatest pupil. I am little Nepommuck, the marvellous boy. I have made your name famous throughout Europe. You teach me phonetic. You cannot forget ME.

HIGGINS: Why dont you shave?

NEPOMMUCK: I have not your imposing appearance, your chin, your brow. Nobody notices me when I shave. Now I am famous: they call me Hairy Faced Dick.

HIGGINS: And what are you doing here among all these swells?

NEPOMMUCK: I am interpreter. I speak 32 languages. I am indispensable at these international parties. You are great cockney specialist: you place a man anywhere in London the moment he open his mouth. I place any man in Europe.

(*A footman hurries down the grand staircase and comes to Nepommuck.*)

FOOTMAN: You are wanted upstairs. Her Excellency cannot understand the Greek gentleman.

NEPOMMUCK: Thank you, yes, immediately.

(*The footman goes and is lost in the crowd.*)

NEPOMMUCK (*to Higgins*): This Greek diplomatist pretends he cannot speak nor understand English. He cannot deceive me. He is the son of a Clerkenwell watchmaker. He speaks English so villainously that he dare not utter a word of it without betraying his origin. I help him to pretend; but I make him pay through the nose. I make them all pay. Ha ha! (*He hurries upstairs.*)

PICKERING: Is this fellow really an expert? Can he find out Eliza and blackmail her?

HIGGINS: We shall see. If he finds her out I lose my bet.

(*Eliza comes from the cloakroom and joins them.*)

PICKERING: Well, Eliza, now for it. Are you ready?

LIZA: Are you nervous, Colonel?

PICKERING: Frightfully. I feel exactly as I felt before my first battle. It's the first time that frightens.

LIZA: It is not the first time for me, Colonel. I have done this fifty times — hundreds of times — in my little piggery in Angel Court in my day-dreams. I am in a dream now. Promise me not to let Professor Higgins wake me; for if he does I shall forget everything and talk as I used to in Drury Lane.

PICKERING: Not a word, Higgins. (*To Eliza.*) Now ready?

LIZA: Ready.

PICKERING: Go.

(*They mount the stairs, Higgins last. Pickering whispers to the footman on the first landing.*)

FIRST LANDING FOOTMAN: Miss Doolittle, Colonel Pickering, Professor Higgins.

SECOND LANDING FOOTMAN: Miss Doolittle, Colonel Pickering, Professor Higgins.

(*At the top of the staircase the Ambassador and his wife, with Nepommuck at her elbow, are receiving.*)

HOSTESS (*taking Eliza's hand*): How d'ye do?

HOST (*same play*): How d'ye do? How d'ye do, Pickering?

LIZA (*with a beautiful gravity that awes her hostess*): How do you do? (*She passes on to the drawing room.*)

HOSTESS: Is that your adopted daughter, Colonel Pickering? She will make a sensation.

PICKERING: Most kind of you to invite her for me. (*He passes on.*)

HOSTESS (*to Nepommuck*): Find out all about her.

NEPOMMUCK (*bowing*): Excellency — (*He goes into the crowd.*)

HOST: How d'ye do, Higgins? You have a rival here tonight. He introduced himself as your pupil. Is he any good?

HIGGINS: He can learn a language in a fortnight — knows dozens of them. A sure mark of a fool. As a phonetician, no good whatever.

HOSTESS. How d'ye do, Professor?

HIGGINS: How do you do? Fearful bore for you this sort of thing. Forgive my part in it. (*He passes on.*)

(*In the drawing room and its suite of salons the reception is in full swing. Eliza passes through. She is so intent on her ordeal that she walks like a somnambulist in a desert instead of a débutante in a fashionable crowd. They stop talking to look at her, admiring her dress, her jewels, and her strangely attractive self. Some of the younger ones at the back stand on their chairs to see.*

The Host and Hostess come in from the staircase and mingle with their guests. Higgins, gloomy and contemptuous of the whole business, comes into the group where they are chatting.)

HOSTESS: Ah, here is Professor Higgins: he will tell us. Tell us all about the wonderful young lady, Professor.

HIGGINS (*almost morosely*): What wonderful young lady?

HOSTESS: You know very well. They tell me there has been nothing like her in London since people stood on their chairs to look at Mrs Langtry.

(*Nepommuck joins the group, full of news.*)

HOSTESS: Ah, here you are at last, Nepommuck. Have you found out all about the Doolittle lady?

NEPOMMUCK: I have found out all about her. She is a fraud.

HOSTESS: A fraud! Oh no.

NEPOMMUCK: YES, yes. She cannot deceive me. Her name cannot be Doolittle.

HIGGINS: Why?

NEPOMMUCK: Because Doolittle is an English name. And she is not English.

HOSTESS: Oh, nonsense! She speaks English perfectly.

NEPOMMUCK: Too perfectly. Can you shew me any English woman who speaks English as it should be spoken? Only foreigners who have been taught to speak it speak it well.

HOSTESS: Certainly she terrified me by the way she said How d'ye do. I had a schoolmistress who talked like that; and I was mortally afraid of her. But if she is not English what is she?

NEPOMMUCK: Hungarian.

ALL THE REST: Hungarian!

NEPOMMUCK: Hungarian. And of royal blood. I am Hungarian. My blood is royal.

HIGGINS: Did you speak to her in Hungarian?

NEPOMMUCK: I did. She was very clever. She said "Please speak to me in English: I do not understand French." French! She pretends not to know the difference between Hungarian and French. Impossible: she knows both.

HIGGINS: And the blood royal? How did you find that out?

NEPOMMUCK: Instinct, maestro, instinct. Only the Magyar races can produce that air of the divine right, those resolute eyes. She is a princess.

HOST: What do you say, Professor?

HIGGINS: I say an ordinary London girl out of the gutter and taught to speak by an expert. I place her in Drury Lane.

NEPOMMUCK: Ha ha ha! Oh, maestro, maestro, you are mad on the subject of cockney dialects. The London gutter is the whole world for you.

HIGGINS (to the Hostess): What does your Excellency say?

HOSTESS: Oh, of course I agree with Nepommuck. She must be a princess at least.

HOST: Not necessarily legitimate, of course. Morganatic perhaps. But that is undoubtedly her class.

HIGGINS: I stick to my opinion.

HOSTESS: Oh, you are incorrigible.

(The group breaks up, leaving Higgins isolated. Pickering joins him.)

PICKERING: Where is Eliza? We must keep an eye on her.

(Eliza joins them.)

LIZA: I dont think I can bear much more. The people all stare so at me. An old lady has just told me that I speak exactly like Queen Victoria. I am sorry if I have lost your bet. I have done my best; but nothing can make me the same as these people.

PICKERING: You have not lost it, my dear. You have won it ten times over.

HIGGINS: Let us get out of this. I have had enough of chattering to these fools.

PICKERING: Eliza is tired; and I am hungry. Let us clear out and have supper somewhere.

ACT 4

(The Wimpole Street laboratory. Midnight. Nobody in the room. The clock on the mantelpiece strikes twelve. The fire is not alight: it is a summer night.

Presently Higgins and Pickering are heard on the stairs.)

HIGGINS (calling down to Pickering): I say, Pick: lock up, will you? I shant be going out again.

PICKERING: Right. Can Mrs Pearce go to bed? We dont want anything more, do we?

HIGGINS: Lord, no!

(Eliza opens the door and is seen on the lighted landing in all the finery in which she has just won Higgins's bet for him. She comes to the hearth, and switches on the electric lights there. She is tired: her pallor contrasts strongly with her dark eyes and hair; and her expression is almost tragic. She takes off her cloak; puts her fan and gloves on the piano; and sits down on the bench, brooding and silent. Higgins, in evening dress, with overcoat and hat, comes in, carrying a smoking jacket which he has picked up downstairs. He takes off the hat and overcoat; throws them carelessly on the newspaper stand; disposes of his coat in the same way; puts on the smoking jacket; and throws himself wearily into the easy-chair at the hearth. Pickering, similarly attired, comes in. He also takes off his hat and overcoat, and is about to throw them on Higgins's when he hesitates.)

PICKERING: I say: Mrs Pearce will row if we leave these things lying about in the drawing room.

HIGGINS: Oh, chuck them over the bannisters into the hall. She'll find them there in the morning and put them away all right. She'll think we were drunk.

PICKERING: We are, slightly. Are there any letters?

HIGGINS: I didnt look. (Pickering takes the overcoats and hats and goes downstairs. Higgins begins half singing half yawning an air from La Fanciulla del Golden West. Suddenly he stops and exclaims.) I wonder where the devil my slippers are!

(Eliza looks at him darkly; then rises suddenly and leaves the room.

Higgins yawns again, and resumes his song.

Pickering returns, with the contents of the letter-box in his hand.)

PICKERING: Only circulars, and this coroneted billet-doux for you. (*He throws the circulars into the fender, and posts himself on the hearthrug, with his back to the grate.*)

HIGGINS (*glancing at the billet-doux*): Money-lender. (*He throws the letter after the circulars.*)

(*Eliza returns with a pair of large down-at-heel slippers. She places them on the carpet before Higgins, and sits as before without a word.*)

HIGGINS (*yawning again*): Oh Lord! What an evening! What a crew! What a silly tomfoolery! (*He raises his shoe to unlace it, and catches sight of the slippers. He stops unlacing and looks at them as if they had appeared there of their own accord.*) Oh! theyre there, are they?

PICKERING (*stretching himself*): Well, I feel a bit tired. It's been a long day. The garden party, a dinner party, and the reception! Rather too much of a good thing. But youve won your bet, Higgins. Eliza did the trick, and something to spare, eh?

HIGGINS (*fervently*): Thank God it's over!

(*Eliza flinches violently; but they take no notice of her; and she recovers herself and sits stonily as before.*)

PICKERING: Were you nervous at the garden party? *I* was. Eliza didnt seem a bit nervous.

HIGGINS: Oh, she wasnt nervous. I knew she'd be all right. No: it's the strain of putting the job through all these months that has told on me. It was interesting enough at first, while we were at the phonetics; but after that I got deadly sick of it. If I hadnt backed myself to do it I should have chucked the whole thing up two months ago. It was a silly notion: the whole thing has been a bore.

PICKERING: Oh come! the garden party was frightfully exciting. My heart began beating like anything.

HIGGINS: Yes, for the first three minutes. But when I saw we were going to win hands down, I felt like a bear in a cage, hanging about doing nothing. The dinner was worse: sitting gorging there for over an hour, with nobody but a damned fool of a fashionable woman to talk to! I tell you, Pickering, never again for me. No more artificial duchesses. The whole thing has been simple purgatory.

PICKERING: Youve never been broken in properly to the social routine. (*Strolling over to the piano.*) I rather enjoy dipping into it occasionally myself: it makes me feel young again. Anyhow, it was a great success: an immense success. I was quite frightened once or twice because Eliza was doing it so well. You see, lots of the real people cant do it at all: theyre such fools that they think style comes by nature to people in their position; and so they never

learn. Theres always something professional about doing a thing superlatively well.

HIGGINS: Yes: thats what drives me mad: the silly people dont know their own silly business. (*Rising.*) However, it's over and done with; and now I can go to bed at last without dreading tomorrow.

(*Eliza's beauty becomes murderous.*)

PICKERING: I think I shall turn in too. Still, it's been a great occasion: a triumph for you. Goodnight. (*He goes.*)

HIGGINS (*following him*): Goodnight. (*Over his shoulder, at the door.*) Put out the lights, Eliza; and tell Mrs Pearce not to make coffee for me in the morning: I'll take tea. (*He goes out.*)

(*Eliza tries to control herself and feel indifferent as she rises and walks across to the hearth to switch off the lights. By the time she gets there she is on the point of screaming. She sits down in Higgins's chair and holds on hard to the arms. Finally she gives way and flings herself furiously on the floor, raging.*)

HIGGINS (*in despairing wrath outside*): What the devil have I done with my slippers? (*He appears at the door.*)

LIZA (*snatching up the slippers, and hurling them at him one after the other with all her force*): There are your slippers. And there. Take your slippers; and may you never have a day's luck with them!

HIGGINS (*astounded*): What on earth — ! (*He comes to her.*) Whats the matter? Get up. (*He pulls her up.*) Anything wrong?

LIZA (*breathless*): Nothing wrong — with you. Ive won your bet for you, havnt I? Thats enough for you. *I* dont matter, I suppose.

HIGGINS: You won my bet! You! Presumptuous insect! *I* won it. What did you throw those slippers at me for?

LIZA: Because I wanted to smash your face. I'd like to kill you, you selfish brute. Why didnt you leave me where you picked me out of — in the gutter? You thank God it's all over, and that now you can throw me back again there, do you? (*She crisps her fingers frantically.*)

HIGGINS (*looking at her in cool wonder*): The creature is nervous, after all.

LIZA (*gives a suffocated scream of fury, and instinctively darts her nails at his face*): !!

HIGGINS (*catching her wrists*): Ah! would you? Claws in, you cat. How dare you shew your temper to me? Sit down and be quiet. (*He throws her roughly into the easy-chair.*)

LIZA (*crushed by superior strength and weight*): Whats to become of me? Whats to become of me?

HIGGINS: How the devil do I know whats to become
of you? What does it matter what becomes of you?

LIZA: You dont care. I know you dont care. You
wouldnt care if I was dead. I'm nothing to you —
not so much as them slippers.

HIGGINS (*thundering*): Those slippers.

LIZA (*with bitter submission*): Those slippers. I didnt
think it made any difference now.

(*A pause. Eliza hopeless and crushed. Higgins a little
uneasy.*)

HIGGINS (*in his loftiest manner*): Why have you begun
going on like this? May I ask whether you complain of your treatment here?

LIZA: No.

HIGGINS: Has anybody behaved badly to you? Colonel
Pickering? Mrs Pearce? Any of the servants?

LIZA: No.

HIGGINS: I presume you dont pretend that *I* have
treated you badly?

LIZA: No.

HIGGINS: I am glad to hear it. (*He moderates his
tone.*) Perhaps youre tired after the strain of the
day. Will you have a glass of champagne? (*He
moves towards the door.*)

LIZA: No. (*Recollecting her manners.*) Thank you.

HIGGINS (*good-humored again*): This has been coming on you for some days. I suppose it was natural
for you to be anxious about the garden party. But
thats all over now. (*He pats her kindly on the
shoulder. She writhes.*) Theres nothing more to
worry about.

LIZA: No. Nothing more for you to worry about. (*She
suddenly rises and gets away from him by going to
the piano bench, where she sits and hides her face.*)
Oh God! I wish I was dead.

HIGGINS (*staring after her in sincere surprise*): Why?
In heaven's name, why? (*Reasonably, going to her.*)
Listen to me, Eliza. All this irritation is purely sub-
jective.

LIZA: I dont understand. I'm too ignorant.

HIGGINS: It's only imagination. Low spirits and nothing else. Nobody's hurting you. Nothing's wrong.
You go to bed like a good girl and sleep it off.
Have a little cry and say your prayers: that will
make you comfortable.

LIZA: I heard your prayers. "Thank God it's all over!"

HIGGINS (*impatiently*): Well, dont you thank God it's
all over? Now you are free and can do what you
like.

LIZA (*pulling herself together in desperation*): What
am I fit for? What have you left me fit for? Where
am I to go? What am I to do? Whats to become of
me?

HIGGINS (*enlightened, but not at all impressed*): Oh,
thats whats worrying you, is it? (*He thrusts his
hands into his pockets, and walks about in his
usual manner, rattling the contents of his pockets,
as if condescending to a trivial subject out of pure
kindness.*) I shouldnt bother about it if I were you.
I should imagine you wont have much difficulty in
settling yourself somewhere or other, though I
hadnt quite realized that you were going away.
(*She looks quickly at him: he does not look at her,
but examines the dessert stand on the piano and
decides that he will eat an apple.*) You might
marry, you know. (*He bites a large piece out of the
apple and munches it noisily.*) You see, Eliza, all
men are not confirmed old bachelors like me and
the Colonel. Most men are the marrying sort (poor
devils!); and youre not bad-looking: it's quite a
pleasure to look at you sometimes — not now, of
course, because youre crying and looking as ugly
as the very devil; but when youre all right and
quite yourself, youre what I should call attractive.
That is, to the people in the marrying line, you understand. You go to bed and have a good nice rest;
and then get up and look at yourself in the glass;
and you wont feel so cheap.

(*Eliza again looks at him, speechless, and does not
stir.*

*The look is quite lost on him: he eats his apple
with a dreamy expression of happiness, as it is quite a
good one.*)

HIGGINS (*a genial afterthought occurring to him*): I
daresay my mother could find some chap or other
who would do very well.

LIZA: We were above that at the corner of Tottenham
Court Road.

HIGGINS (*waking up*): What do you mean?

LIZA: I sold flowers. I didnt sell myself. Now youve
made a lady of me I'm not fit to sell anything else.
I wish youd left me where you found me.

HIGGINS (*slinging the core of the apple decisively into
the grate*): Tosh, Eliza. Dont you insult human relations by dragging all this cant about buying and
selling into it. You neednt marry the fellow if you
dont like him.

LIZA: What else am I to do?

HIGGINS: Oh, lots of things. What about your old idea
of a florist's shop? Pickering could set you up in
one: he has lots of money. (*Chuckling.*) He'll have
to pay for all those togs you have been wearing today; and that, with the hire of the jewellery, will
make a big hole in two hundred pounds. Why, six
months ago you would have thought it the millennium to have a flower shop of your own. Come!

youll be all right. I must clear off to bed: I'm devilish sleepy. By the way, I came down for something: I forget what it was.

LIZA: Your slippers.

HIGGINS: Oh yes, of course. You shied them at me.
(*He picks them up, and is going out when she rises
and speaks to him.*)

LIZA: Before you go, sir —

HIGGINS (*dropping the slippers in his surprise at her
calling him Sir*): Eh?

LIZA: Do my clothes belong to me or to Colonel Pickering?

HIGGINS (*coming back into the room as if her question were the very climax of unreason*): What the
devil use would they be to Pickering?

LIZA: He might want them for the next girl you pick
up to experiment on.

HIGGINS (*shocked and hurt*): Is that the way you feel
towards us?

LIZA: I dont want to hear anything more about that.
All I want to know is whether anything belongs to
me. My own clothes were burnt.

HIGGINS: But what does it matter? Why need you
start bothering about that in the middle of the
night?

LIZA: I want to know what I may take away with me.
I dont want to be accused of stealing.

HIGGINS (*now deeply wounded*): Stealing! You shouldnt
have said that, Eliza. That shews a want of feeling.

LIZA: I'm sorry. I'm only a common ignorant girl; and
in my station I have to be careful. There cant be
any feelings between the like of you and the like of
me. Please will you tell me what belongs to me and
what doesnt?

HIGGINS (*very sulky*): You may take the whole
damned houseful if you like. Except the jewels.
Theyre hired. Will that satisfy you? (*He turns on
his heel and is about to go in extreme dudgeon.*)

LIZA (*drinking in his emotion like nectar, and nagging
him to provoke a further supply*): Stop, please.
(*She takes off her jewels.*) Will you take these to
your room and keep them safe? I dont want to run
the risk of their being missing.

HIGGINS (*furious*): Hand them over. (*She puts them
into his hands.*) If these belonged to me instead of
to the jeweller, I'd ram them down your ungrateful
throat. (*He perfunctorily thrusts them into his
pockets, unconsciously decorating himself with the
protruding ends of the chains.*)

LIZA (*taking a ring off*): This ring isnt the jeweller's:
it's the one you bought me in Brighton. I dont
want it now. (*Higgins dashes the ring violently into
the fireplace, and turns on her so threateningly that
she crouches over the piano with her hands over
her face, and exclaims*) Dont you hit me.

HIGGINS: Hit you! You infamous creature, how dare
you accuse me of such a thing? It is you who have
hit me. You have wounded me to the heart.

LIZA (*thrilling with hidden joy*): I'm glad. Ive got a little of my own back, anyhow.

HIGGINS (*with dignity, in his finest professional style*):
You have caused me to lose my temper: a thing
that has hardly ever happened to me before. I prefer to say nothing more tonight. I am going to bed.

LIZA (*pertly*): Youd better leave a note for Mrs Pearce
about the coffee; for she wont be told by me.

HIGGINS (*formally*): Damn Mrs Pearce; and damn the
coffee; and damn you; and (*wildly*) damn my own
folly in having lavished my hard-earned knowledge
and the treasure of my regard and intimacy on a
heartless guttersnipe. (*He goes out with impressive
decorum, and spoils it by slamming the door savagely.*)

(*Eliza goes down on her knees on the hearthrug to
look for the ring. When she finds it she considers for
a moment what to do with it. Finally she flings it
down on the dessert stand and goes upstairs in a tearing rage.*)

(*The furniture of Eliza's room has been increased by
a big wardrobe and a sumptuous dressing-table. She
comes in and switches on the electric light. She goes
to the wardrobe; opens it; and pulls out a walking
dress, a hat, and a pair of shoes, which she throws
on the bed. She takes off her evening dress and
shoes; then takes a padded hanger from the wardrobe; adjusts it carefully in the evening dress; and
hangs it in the wardrobe, which she shuts with a
slam. She puts on her walking shoes, her walking
dress, and hat. She takes her wrist watch from the
dressing-table and fastens it on. She pulls on her
gloves; takes her vanity bag; and looks into it to see
that her purse is there before hanging it on her wrist.
She makes for the door. Every movement expresses
her furious resolution.*

She takes a last look at herself in the glass.

*She suddenly puts out her tongue at herself; then
leaves the room, switching off the electric light at the
door.*

*Meanwhile, in the street outside, Freddy Eynsford
Hill, lovelorn, is gazing up at the second floor, in
which one of the windows is still lighted.*

The light goes out.)

FREDDY: Goodnight, darling, darling, darling.

(*Eliza comes out, giving the door a considerable bang
behind her.*)

LIZA: Whatever are you doing here?

FREDDY: Nothing. I spend most of my nights here. It's

the only place where I'm happy. Dont laugh at me, Miss Doolittle.

LIZA: Dont you call me Miss Doolittle, do you hear? Liza's good enough for me. (*She breaks down and grabs him by the shoulders.*) Freddy: you dont think I'm a heartless guttersnipe, do you?

FREDDY: Oh no, no, darling: how can you imagine such a thing? You are the loveliest, dearest —

(*He loses all self-control and smothers her with kisses. She, hungry for comfort, responds. They stand there in one another's arms.*

An elderly police constable arrives.)

CONSTABLE (*scandalized*): Now then! Now then!! Now then!!!

(*They release one another hastily.*)

FREDDY: Sorry, constable. Weve only just become engaged.

(*They run away.*)

(*The constable shakes his head, reflecting on his own courtship and on the vanity of human hopes. He moves off in the opposite direction with slow professional steps.*

The flight of the lovers takes them to Cavendish Square. There they halt to consider their next move.)

LIZA (*out of breath*): He didnt half give me a fright, that copper. But you answered him proper.

FREDDY: I hope I havnt taken you out of your way. Where were you going?

LIZA: To the river.

FREDDY: What for?

LIZA: To make a hole in it.

FREDDY (*horrified*): Eliza, darling. What do you mean? What's the matter?

LIZA: Never mind. It doesnt matter now. Theres nobody in the world now but you and me, is there?

FREDDY: Not a soul.

(*They indulge in another embrace, and are again surprised by a much younger constable.*)

SECOND CONSTABLE: Now then, you two! What's this? Where do you think you are? Move along here, double quick.

FREDDY: As you say, sir, double quick.

(*They run away again, and are in Hanover Square before they stop for another conference.*)

FREDDY: I had no idea the police were so devilishly prudish.

LIZA: It's their business to hunt girls off the streets.

FREDDY: We must go somewhere. We cant wander about the streets all night.

LIZA: Cant we? I think it'd be lovely to wander about for ever.

FREDDY: Oh, darling.

(*They embrace again, oblivious of the arrival of a crawling taxi. It stops.*)

TAXIMAN: Can I drive you and the lady anywhere, sir?

(*They start asunder.*)

LIZA: Oh, Freddy, a taxi. The very thing.

FREDDY: But, damn it, Ive no money.

LIZA: I have plenty. The Colonel thinks you should never go out without ten pounds in your pocket. Listen. We'll drive about all night; and in the morning I'll call on old Mrs Higgins and ask her what I ought to do. I'll tell you all about it in the cab. And the police wont touch us there.

FREDDY: Righto! Ripping. (*To the Taximan.*) Wimbledon Common. (*They drive off.*)

ACT 5

(*Mrs Higgins's drawing room. She is at her writing-table as before. The parlormaid comes in.*)

THE PARLORMAID (*at the door*): Mr Henry, maam, is downstairs with Colonel Pickering.

MRS HIGGINS: Well, shew them up.

THE PARLORMAID: Theyre using the telephone, maam. Telephoning to the police, I think.

MRS HIGGINS: What!

THE PARLORMAID (*coming further in and lowering her voice*): Mr Henry is in a state, maam. I thought I'd better tell you.

MRS HIGGINS: If you had told me that Mr Henry was not in a state it would have been more surprising. Tell them to come up when theyve finished with the police. I suppose he's lost something.

THE PARLORMAID: Yes, maam. (*Going.*)

MRS HIGGINS: Go upstairs and tell Miss Doolittle that Mr Henry and the Colonel are here. Ask her not to come down til I send for her.

THE PARLORMAID: Yes, maam.

(*Higgins bursts in. He is, as the parlormaid has said, in a state.*)

HIGGINS: Look here, mother: heres a confounded thing!

MRS HIGGINS: Yes, dear. Good morning. (*He checks his impatience and kisses her, whilst the parlormaid goes out.*) What is it?

HIGGINS: Eliza's bolted.

MRS HIGGINS (*calmly continuing her writing*): You must have frightened her.

HIGGINS: Frightened her! nonsense! She was left last night, as usual, to turn out the lights and all that; and instead of going to bed she changed her clothes and went right off: her bed wasnt slept in. She came in a cab for her things before seven this morning, and that fool Mrs Pearce let her have them without telling me a word about it. What am I to do?

MRS HIGGINS: Do without, I'm afraid, Henry. The girl has a perfect right to leave if she chooses.

HIGGINS (wandering distractedly across the room): But I cant find anything. I dont know what appointments Ive got. I'm — (Pickering comes in. Mrs Higgins puts down her pen and turns away from the writing-table.)

PICKERING (shaking hands): Good morning, Mrs Higgins. Has Henry told you? (He sits down on the ottoman.)

HIGGINS: What does that ass of an inspector say? Have you offered a reward?

MRS HIGGINS (rising in indignant amazement): You dont mean to say you have set the police after Eliza?

HIGGINS: Of course. What are the police for? What else could we do? (He sits in the Elizabethan chair.)

PICKERING: The inspector made a lot of difficulties. I really think he suspected us of some improper purpose.

MRS HIGGINS: Well, of course he did. What right have you to go to the police and give the girl's name as if she were a thief, or a lost umbrella, or something? Really! (She sits down again, deeply vexed.)

HIGGINS: But we want to find her.

PICKERING: We cant let her go like this, you know, Mrs Higgins. What were we to do?

MRS HIGGINS: You have no more sense, either of you, than two children. Why —

(The parlormaid comes in and breaks off the conversation.)

THE PARLORMAID: Mr Henry: a gentleman wants to see you very particular. He's been sent on from Wimpole Street.

HIGGINS: Oh, bother! I cant see anyone now. Who is it?

THE PARLORMAID: A Mr Doolittle, sir.

PICKERING: Doolittle! Do you mean the dustman?

THE PARLORMAID: Dustman! Oh no, sir: a gentleman.

HIGGINS (springing up excitedly): By George, Pick, it's some relative of hers that she's gone to. Somebody we know nothing about. (To the parlormaid.) Send him up, quick.

THE PARLORMAID: Yes, sir. (She goes.)

HIGGINS (eagerly, going to his mother): Genteel relatives! now we shall hear something. (He sits down in the Chippendale chair.)

MRS HIGGINS: Do you know any of her people?

PICKERING: Only her father: the fellow we told you about.

THE PARLORMAID (announcing): Mr Doolittle. (She withdraws.)

(Doolittle enters. He is resplendently dressed as for a fashionable wedding, and might, in fact, be the bridegroom. A flower in his buttonhole, a dazzling silk hat, and patent leather shoes complete the effect. He is too concerned with the business he has come on to notice Mrs Higgins. He walks straight to Higgins, and accosts him with vehement reproach.)

DOOLITTLE (indicating his own person): See here! Do you see this? You done this.

HIGGINS: Done what, man?

DOOLITTLE: This, I tell you. Look at it. Look at this hat. Look at this coat.

PICKERING: Has Eliza been buying you clothes?

DOOLITTLE: Eliza! not she. Why would she buy me clothes?

MRS HIGGINS: Good morning, Mr Doolittle. Wont you sit down?

DOOLITTLE (taken aback as he becomes conscious that he has forgotten his hostess): Asking your pardon, maam. (He approaches her and shakes her proffered hand.) Thank you. (He sits down on the ottoman, on Pickering's right.) I am that full of what has happened to me that I cant think of anything else.

HIGGINS: What the dickens has happened to you?

DOOLITTLE: I shouldnt mind if it had only happened to me: anything might happen to anybody and nobody to blame but Providence, as you might say. But this is something that you done to me: yes, you, Enry Iggins.

HIGGINS: Have you found Eliza?

DOOLITTLE: Have you lost her?

HIGGINS: Yes.

DOOLITTLE: You have all the luck, you have. I aint found her; but she'll find me quick enough now after what you done to me.

MRS HIGGINS: But what has my son done to you, Mr Doolittle?

DOOLITTLE: Done to me! Ruined me. Destroyed my happiness. Tied me up and delivered me into the hands of middle class morality.

HIGGINS (rising intolerantly and standing over Doolittle): Youre raving. Youre drunk. Youre mad. I gave you five pounds. After that I had two conversations with you, at half-a-crown an hour. Ive never seen you since.

DOOLITTLE: Oh! Drunk am I? Mad am I? Tell me this.

Did you or did you not write a letter to an old blighter in America that was giving five millions to found Moral Reform Societies all over the world, and that wanted you to invent a universal language for him?

HIGGINS: What! Ezra D. Wannafeller! He's dead. (*He sits down again carelessly.*)

DOOLITTLE: Yes: he's dead; and I'm done for. Now did you or did you not write a letter to him to say that the most original moralist at present in England, to the best of your knowledge, was Alfred Doolittle, a common dustman?

HIGGINS: Oh, after your first visit I remember making some silly joke of the kind.

DOOLITTLE: Ah! You may well call it a silly joke. It put the lid on me right enough. Just give him the chance he wanted to shew that Americans is not like us: that they reckonize and respect merit in every class of life, however humble. Them words is in his blooming will, in which, Henry Higgins, thanks to your silly joking, he leaves me a share in his Pre-digested Cheese Trust worth three thousand a year on condition that I lecture for his Wannafeller Moral Reform World League as often as they ask me up to six times a year.

HIGGINS: The devil he does! Whew! (*Brightening suddenly.*) What a lark!

PICKERING: A safe thing for you, Doolittle. They wont ask you twice.

DOOLITTLE: It aint the lecturing I mind. I'll lecture them blue in the face, I will, and not turn a hair. It's making a gentleman of me that I object to. Who asked him to make a gentleman of me? I was happy. I was free. I touched pretty nigh everybody for money when I wanted it, same as I touched you, Enry Iggins. Now I am worrited; tied neck and heels; and everybody touches me for money. It's a fine thing for you, says my solicitor. Is it? says I. You mean it's a good thing for you, I says. When I was a poor man and had a solicitor once when they found a pram in the dust cart, he got me off, and got shut of me and got me shut of him as quick as he could. Same with the doctors: used to shove me out of the hospital before I could hardly stand on my legs, and nothing to pay. Now they finds out that I'm not a healthy man and cant live unless they looks after me twice a day. In the house I'm not let do a hand's turn for myself: somebody else must do it and touch me for it. A year ago I hadnt a relative in the world except two or three that wouldnt speak to me. Now Ive fifty, and not a decent week's wages among the lot of them. I have to live for others and not for myself: thats middle class morality. You talk of losing Eliza. Dont you be anxious: I bet she's on my doorstep by this: she

that could support herself easy by selling flowers if I wasnt respectable. And the next one to touch me will be you, Enry Iggins. I'll have to learn to speak middle class language from you, instead of speaking proper English. Thats where youll come in; and I daresay thats what you done it for.

MRS HIGGINS: But, my dear Mr Doolittle, you need not suffer all this if you are really in earnest. Nobody can force you to accept this bequest. You can repudiate it. Isnt that so, Colonel Pickering?

PICKERING: I believe so.

DOOLITTLE (*softening his manner in deference to her sex*): Thats the tragedy of it, maam. It's easy to say chuck it; but I havnt the nerve. Which of us has? We're all intimidated. Intimidated, maam: thats what we are. What is there for me if I chuck it but the workhouse in my old age? I have to dye my hair already to keep my job as a dustman. If I was one of the deserving poor, and had put by a bit, I could chuck it; but then why should I, acause the deserving poor might as well be millionaires for all the happiness they ever has. They dont know what happiness is. But I, as one of the undeserving poor, have nothing between me and the pauper's uniform but this here blasted three thousand a year that shoves me into the middle class. (Excuse the expression, maam; youd use it yourself if you had my provocation.) Theyve got you every way you turn: it's a choice between the Skilly of the workhouse and the Char By dis of the middle class; and I havnt the nerve for the workhouse. Intimidated: thats what I am. Broke. Bought up. Happier men than me will call for my dust, and touch me for their tip; and I'll look on helpless, and envy them. And thats what your son has brought me to. (*He is overcome by emotion.*)

MRS HIGGINS: Well, I'm very glad youre not going to do anything foolish, Mr Doolittle. For this solves the problem of Eliza's future. You can provide for her now.

DOOLITTLE (*with melancholy resignation*): Yes, maam: I'm expected to provide for everyone now, out of three thousand a year.

HIGGINS (*jumping up*): Nonsense! he cant provide for her. He shant provide for her. She doesnt belong to him. I paid him five pounds for her. Doolittle: either youre an honest man or a rogue.

DOOLITTLE (*tolerantly*): A little of both, Henry, like the rest of us: a little of both.

HIGGINS: Well, you took that money for the girl; and you have no right to take her as well.

MRS HIGGINS: Henry: dont be absurd. If you want to know where Eliza is, she is upstairs.

HIGGINS (*amazed*): Upstairs!!! Then I shall jolly soon fetch her downstairs. (*He makes resolutely for the door.*)

MRS HIGGINS (*rising and following him*): Be quiet, Henry. Sit down.
HIGGINS: I —
MRS HIGGINS: Sit down, dear; and listen to me.
HIGGINS: Oh very well, very well, very well. (*He throws himself ungraciously on the ottoman, with his face towards the windows.*) But I think you might have told us this half an hour ago.
MRS HIGGINS: Eliza came to me this morning. She told me of the brutal way you two treated her.
HIGGINS (*bouncing up again*): What!
PICKERING (*rising also*): My dear Mrs Higgins, she's been telling you stories. We didnt treat her brutally. We hardly said a word to her; and we parted on particularly good terms. (*Turning on Higgins.*) Higgins: did you bully her after I went to bed?
HIGGINS: Just the other way about. She threw my slippers in my face. She behaved in the most outrageous way. I never gave her the slightest provocation. The slippers came bang into my face the moment I entered the room — before I had uttered a word. And used perfectly awful language.
PICKERING (*astonished*): But why? What did we do to her?
MRS HIGGINS: I think I know pretty well what you did. The girl is naturally rather affectionate, I think. Isnt she, Mr Doolittle?
DOOLITTLE: Very tender-hearted, maam. Takes after me.
MRS HIGGINS: Just so. She had become attached to you both. She worked very hard for you, Henry. I dont think you quite realize what anything in the nature of brain work means to a girl of her class. Well, it seems that when the great day of trial came, and she did this wonderful thing for you without making a single mistake, you two sat there and never said a word to her, but talked together of how glad you were that it was all over and how you had been bored with the whole thing. And then you were surprised because she threw your slippers at you! *I* should have thrown the fire-irons at you.
HIGGINS: We said nothing except that we were tired and wanted to go to bed. Did we, Pick?
PICKERING (*shrugging his shoulders*): That was all.
MRS HIGGINS (*ironically*): Quite sure?
PICKERING: Absolutely. Really, that was all.
MRS HIGGINS: You didnt thank her, or pet her, or admire her or tell her how splendid she'd been.
HIGGINS (*impatiently*): But she knew all about that. We didnt make speeches to her, if thats what you mean.
PICKERING (*conscience stricken*): Perhaps we were a little inconsiderate. Is she very angry?
MRS HIGGINS (*returning to her place at the writing-table*): Well, I'm afraid she wont go back to Wim-

pole Street, especially now that Mr Doolittle is able to keep up the position you have thrust on her; but she says she is quite willing to meet you on friendly terms and to let bygones be bygones.
HIGGINS (*furious*): Is she, by George? Ho!
MRS HIGGINS: If you promise to behave yourself, Henry, I'll ask her to come down. If not, go home: for you have taken up quite enough of my time.
HIGGINS: Oh, all right. Very well. Pick: you behave yourself. Let us put on our best Sunday manners for this creature that we picked out of the mud. (*He flings himself sulkily into the Elizabethan chair.*)
DOOLITTLE (*remonstrating*): Now, now, Enry Iggins! Have some consideration for my feelings as a middle class man.
MRS HIGGINS: Remember your promise, Henry. (*She presses the bell-button on the writing-table.*) Mr Doolittle: will you be so good as to step out on the balcony for a moment. I dont want Eliza to have the shock of your news until she has made it up with these two gentlemen. Would you mind?
DOOLITTLE: As you wish, lady. Anything to help Henry to keep her off my hands. (*He disappears through the window.*)

(*The parlormaid answers the bell. Pickering sits down in Doolittle's place.*)

MRS HIGGINS: Ask Miss Doolittle to come down, please.
THE PARLORMAID: Yes, maam. (*She goes out.*)
MRS HIGGINS: Now, Henry: be good.
HIGGINS: I am behaving myself perfectly.
PICKERING: He is doing his best, Mrs Higgins.

(*A pause. Higgins throws back his head; stretches out his legs; and begins to whistle.*)

MRS HIGGINS: Henry, dearest, you dont look at all nice in that attitude.
HIGGINS (*pulling himself together*): I was not trying to look nice, mother.
MRS HIGGINS: It doesnt matter, dear. I only wanted to make you speak.
HIGGINS: Why?
MRS HIGGINS: Because you cant speak and whistle at the same time.

(*Higgins groans. Another very trying pause.*)

HIGGINS (*springing up, out of patience*): Where the devil is that girl? Are we to wait here all day?

(*Eliza enters, sunny, self-possessed, and giving a staggeringly convincing exhibition of ease of manner. She carries a little work-basket, and is very much at home. Pickering is too much taken aback to rise.*)

LIZA: How do you do, Professor Higgins? Are you quite well?

HIGGINS (*choking*): Am I — (*He can say no more.*)

LIZA: But of course you are: you are never ill. So glad to see you again, Colonel Pickering. (*He rises hastily; and they shake hands.*) Quite chilly this morning, isnt it? (*She sits down on his left. He sits beside her.*)

HIGGINS: Dont you dare try this game on me. I taught it to you; and it doesnt take me in. Get up and come home; and dont be a fool.

(*Eliza takes a piece of needlework from her basket, and begins to stitch at it, without taking the least notice of this outburst.*)

MRS HIGGINS: Very nicely put, indeed, Henry. No woman could resist such an invitation.

HIGGINS: You let her alone, mother. Let her speak for herself. You will jolly soon see whether she has an idea that I havnt put into her head or a word that I havnt put into her mouth. I tell you I have created this thing out of the squashed cabbage leaves of Covent Garden; and now she pretends to play the fine lady with me.

MRS HIGGINS (*placidly*): Yes, dear; but youll sit down, wont you? (*Higgins sits down again, savagely.*)

LIZA (*to Pickering, taking no apparent notice of Higgins, and working away deftly*): Will you drop me altogether now that the experiment is over, Colonel Pickering?

PICKERING: Oh dont. You mustnt think of it as an experiment. It shocks me, somehow.

LIZA: Oh, I'm only a squashed cabbage leaf —

PICKERING (*impulsively*): No.

LIZA (*continuing quietly*): — but I owe so much to you that I should be very unhappy if you forgot me.

PICKERING: It's very kind of you to say so, Miss Doolittle.

LIZA: It's not because you paid for my dresses. I know you are generous to everybody with money. But it was from you that I learnt really nice manners; and that is what makes one a lady, isnt it? You see it was so very difficult for me with the example of Professor Higgins always before me. I was brought up to be just like him, unable to control myself, and using bad language on the slightest provocation. And I should never have known that ladies and gentlemen didnt behave like that if you hadnt been there.

HIGGINS: Well!!

PICKERING: Oh, thats only his way, you know. He doesnt mean it.

LIZA: Oh, *I* didnt mean it either, when I was a flower girl. It was only my way. But you see I did it; and thats what makes the difference after all.

PICKERING: No doubt. Still, he taught you to speak; and I couldnt have done that, you know.

LIZA (*trivially*): Of course: that is his profession.

HIGGINS: Damnation!

LIZA (*continuing*): It was just like learning to dance in the fashionable way: there was nothing more than that in it. But do you know what began my real education?

PICKERING: What?

LIZA (*stopping her work for a moment*): Your calling me Miss Doolittle that day when I first came to Wimpole Street. That was the beginning of self-respect for me. (*She resumes her stitching.*) And there were a hundred little things you never noticed, because they came naturally to you. Things about standing up and taking off your hat and opening doors —

PICKERING: Oh, that was nothing.

LIZA: Yes: things that shewed you thought and felt about me as if I were something better than a scullery-maid; though of course I know you would have been just the same to a scullery-maid if she had been let into the drawing room. You never took off your boots in the dining room when I was there.

PICKERING: You mustnt mind that. Higgins takes off his boots all over the place.

LIZA: I know. I am not blaming him. It is his way, isnt it? But it made such a difference to me that you didnt do it. You see, really and truly, apart from the things anyone can pick up (the dressing and the proper way of speaking, and so on), the difference between a lady and a flower girl is not how she behaves, but how she's treated. I shall always be a flower girl to Professor Higgins, because he always treats me as a flower girl, and always will; but I know I can be a lady to you, because you always treat me as a lady, and always will.

MRS HIGGINS: Please dont grind your teeth, Henry.

PICKERING: Well, this is really very nice of you, Miss Doolittle.

LIZA: I should like you to call me Eliza, now, if you would.

PICKERING: Thank you. Eliza, of course.

LIZA: And I should like Professor Higgins to call me Miss Doolittle.

HIGGINS: I'll see you damned first.

MRS HIGGINS: Henry! Henry!

PICKERING: (*laughing*): Why dont you slang back at him? Dont stand it. It would do him a lot of good.

LIZA: I cant. I could have done it once but now I cant go back to it. You told me, you know, that when a child is brought to a foreign country, it picks up the language in a few weeks, and forgets its own. Well, I am a child in your country. I have forgotten my own language, and can speak nothing but yours. Thats the real break-off with the corner of Tottenham Court Road. Leaving Wimpole Street finishes it.

PICKERING (*much alarmed*): Oh! but youre coming back to Wimpole Street, arnt you? Youll forgive Higgins?

HIGGINS (*rising*): Forgive! Will she, by George! Let her go. Let her find out how she can get on without us. She will relapse into the gutter in three weeks without me at her elbow.

(*Doolittle appears at the centre window. With a look of dignified reproach at Higgins, he comes slowly and silently to his daughter, who, with her back to the window, is unconscious of his approach.*)

PICKERING: He's incorrigible, Eliza. You wont relapse, will you?

LIZA: No: not now. Never again. I have learnt my lesson. I dont believe I could utter one of the old sounds if I tried. (*Doolittle touches her on her left shoulder. She drops her work, losing her self-possession utterly at the spectacle of her father's splendor.*) A-a-a-a-a-ah-ow-ooh!

HIGGINS (*with a crow of triumph*): Aha! Just so. A-a-a-a-ahowooh! A-a-a-a-ahowooh! A-a-a-a-ahowooh! Victory! Victory! (*He throws himself on the divan, folding his arms, and spraddling arrogantly.*)

DOOLITTLE: Can you blame the girl? Dont look at me like that, Eliza. It aint my fault. Ive come into some money.

LIZA: You must have touched a millionaire this time, dad.

DOOLITTLE: I have. But I'm dressed something special today. I'm going to St George's, Hanover Square. Your stepmother is going to marry me.

LIZA (*angrily*): Youre going to let yourself down to marry that low common woman!

PICKERING (*quietly*): He ought to, Eliza. (*To Doolittle.*) Why has she changed her mind?

DOOLITTLE (*sadly*): Intimidated, Governor. Intimidated. Middle class morality claims its victim. Wont you put on your hat, Liza, and come and see me turned off?

LIZA: If the Colonel says I must, I — I'll (*almost sobbing*) I'll demean myself. And get insulted for my pains, like enough.

DOOLITTLE: Dont be afraid: she never comes to words with anyone now, poor woman! respectability has broke all the spirit out of her.

PICKERING (*squeezing Eliza's elbow gently*): Be kind to them, Eliza. Make the best of it.

LIZA (*forcing a little smile for him through her vexa-*

tion): Oh well, just to shew theres no ill feeling. I'll be back in a moment. (*She goes out.*)

DOOLITTLE (*sitting down beside Pickering*): I feel uncommon nervous about the ceremony, Colonel. I wish youd come and see me through it.

PICKERING: But youve been through it before, man. You were married to Eliza's mother.

DOOLITTLE: Who told you that, Colonel?

PICKERING: Well, nobody told me. But I concluded naturally —

DOOLITTLE: No: that aint the natural way, Colonel: it's only the middle class way. My way was always the undeserving way. But dont say nothing to Eliza. She dont know: I always had a delicacy about telling her.

PICKERING: Quite right. We'll leave it so, if you dont mind.

DOOLITTLE: And youll come to the church, Colonel, and put me through straight?

PICKERING: With pleasure. As far as a bachelor can.

MRS HIGGINS: May I come, Mr Doolittle? I should be very sorry to miss your wedding.

DOOLITTLE: I should indeed be honored by your condescension, maam; and my poor old woman would take it as a tremenjous compliment. She's been very low, thinking of the happy days that are no more.

MRS HIGGINS (*rising*): I'll order the carriage and get ready. (*The men rise, except Higgins.*) I shant be more than fifteen minutes. (*As she goes to the door Eliza comes in, hatted and buttoning her gloves.*) I'm going to the church to see your father married, Eliza. You had better come in the brougham with me. Colonel Pickering can go on with the bridegroom.

(*Mrs Higgins goes out. Eliza comes to the middle of the room between the centre window and the ottoman. Pickering joins her.*)

DOOLITTLE: Bridegroom! What a word! It makes a man realize his position, somehow. (*He takes up his hat and goes towards the door.*)

PICKERING: Before I go, Eliza, do forgive Higgins and come back to us.

LIZA: I dont think dad would allow me. Would you, dad?

DOOLITTLE (*sad but magnanimous*): They played you off very cunning, Eliza, them two sportsmen. If it had been only one of them, you could have nailed him. But you see, there was two; and one of them chaperoned the other, as you might say. (*To Pickering.*) It was artful of you, Colonel; but I bear no malice: I should have done the same myself. I been the victim of one woman after another all my life, and I dont grudge you two getting the better of Liza. I shant interfere. It's time for us to go,

Colonel. So long, Henry. See you in St George's, Eliza. (*He goes out.*)

PICKERING (*coaxing*): Do stay with us, Eliza. (*He follows Doolittle.*)

(*Eliza goes out on the balcony to avoid being alone with Higgins. He rises and joins her there. She immediately comes back into the room and makes for the door; but he goes along the balcony quickly and gets his back to the door before she reaches it.*)

HIGGINS: Well, Eliza, youve had a bit of your own back, as you call it. Have you had enough? and are you going to be reasonable? Or do you want any more?

LIZA: You want me back only to pick up your slippers and put up with your tempers and fetch and carry for you.

HIGGINS: I havnt said I wanted you back at all.

LIZA: Oh, indeed. Then what are we talking about?

HIGGINS: About you, not about me. If you come back I shall treat you just as I have always treated you. I cant change my nature; and I dont intend to change my manners. My manners are exactly the same as Colonel Pickering's.

LIZA: Thats not true. He treats a flower girl as if she was a duchess.

HIGGINS: And I treat a duchess as if she was a flower girl.

LIZA: I see. (*She turns away composedly, and sits on the ottoman, facing the window.*) The same to everybody.

HIGGINS: Just so.

LIZA: Like father.

HIGGINS (*grinning, a little taken down*): Without accepting the comparison at all points, Eliza, it's quite true that your father is not a snob, and that he will be quite at home in any station of life to which his eccentric destiny may call him. (*Seriously.*) The great secret, Eliza, is not having bad manners or good manners or any other particular sort of manners, but having the same manner for all human souls: in short, behaving as if you were in Heaven, where there are no third-class carriages, and one soul is as good as another.

LIZA: Amen. You are a born preacher.

HIGGINS (*irritated*): The question is not whether I treat you rudely, but whether you ever heard me treat anyone else better.

LIZA (*with sudden sincerity*): I dont care how you treat me. I dont mind your swearing at me. I shouldnt mind a black eye: Ive had one before this. But (*standing up and facing him*) I wont be passed over.

HIGGINS: Then get out of my way; for I wont stop for you. You talk about me as if I were a motor bus.

LIZA: So you are a motor bus: all bounce and go, and no consideration for anyone. But I can do without you: dont think I cant.

HIGGINS: I know you can. I told you you could.

LIZA (*wounded, getting away from him to the other side of the ottoman with her face to the hearth*): I know you did, you brute. You wanted to get rid of me.

HIGGINS: Liar.

LIZA: Thank you. (*She sits down with dignity.*)

HIGGINS: You never asked yourself, I suppose, whether I could do without you.

LIZA (*earnestly*): Dont you try to get round me. Youll have to do without me.

HIGGINS (*arrogant*): I can do without anybody. I have my own soul: my own spark of divine fire. But (*with sudden humility*) I shall miss you, Eliza. (*He sits down near her on the ottoman.*) I have learnt something from your idiotic notions: I confess that humbly and gratefully. And I have grown accustomed to your voice and appearance. I like them, rather.

LIZA: Well, you have both of them on your gramophone and in your book of photographs. When you feel lonely without me, you can turn the machine on. It's got no feelings to hurt.

HIGGINS: I cant turn your soul on. Leave me those feelings; and you can take away the voice and the face. They are not you.

LIZA: Oh, you are a devil. You can twist the heart in a girl as easy as some could twist her arms to hurt her. Mrs Pearce warned me. Time and again she has wanted to leave you; and you always got round her at the last minute. And you dont care a bit for her. And you dont care a bit for me.

HIGGINS: I care for life, for humanity; and you are a part of it that has come my way and been built into my house. What more can you or anyone ask?

LIZA: I wont care for anybody that doesnt care for me.

HIGGINS: Commercial principles, Eliza. Like (*reproducing her Covent Garden pronunciation with professional exactness*) s'yollin voylets (*selling violets*), isnt it?

LIZA: Dont sneer at me. It's mean to sneer at me.

HIGGINS: I have never sneered in my life. Sneering doesnt become either the human face or the human soul. I am expressing my righteous contempt for Commercialism. I dont and wont trade in affection. You call me a brute because you couldnt buy a claim on me by fetching my slippers and finding my spectacles. You were a fool: I think a woman fetching a man's slippers is a disgusting sight: did I ever fetch your slippers? I think a good deal more of you for throwing them in my face. No use slaving for me and then saying you want to be cared for: who cares for a slave? If you come back, come back for the sake of good fellowship; for youll get nothing else. Youve had a thousand times as much out of me as I have out of you; and if you dare to set up your little dog's tricks of fetching and carrying slippers against my creation of a Duchess Eliza, I'll slam the door in your silly face.

LIZA: What did you do it for if you didnt care for me?

HIGGINS (*heartily*): Why, because it was my job.

LIZA: You never thought of the trouble it would make for me.

HIGGINS: Would the world ever have been made if its maker had been afraid of making trouble? Making life means making trouble. Theres only one way of escaping trouble; and thats killing things. Cowards, you notice, are always shrieking to have troublesome people killed.

LIZA: I'm no preacher: I dont notice things like that. I notice that you dont notice me.

HIGGINS (*jumping up and walking about intolerantly*): Eliza: youre an idiot. I waste the treasures of my Miltonic mind by spreading them before you. Once for all, understand that I go my way and do my work without caring twopence what happens to either of us. I am not intimidated, like your father and your stepmother. So you can come back or go to the devil: which you please.

LIZA: What am I to come back for?

HIGGINS (*bouncing up on his knees on the ottoman and leaning over it to her*): For the fun of it. Thats why I took you on.

LIZA (*with averted face*): And you may throw me out tomorrow if I dont do everything you want me to?

HIGGINS: Yes; and you may walk out tomorrow if I dont do everything you want me to.

LIZA: And live with my stepmother?

HIGGINS: Yes, or sell flowers.

LIZA: Oh! If I only could go back to my flower basket! I should be independent of both you and father and all the world! Why did you take my independence from me? Why did I give it up? I'm a slave now, for all my fine clothes.

HIGGINS: Not a bit. I'll adopt you as my daughter and settle money on you if you like. Or would you rather marry Pickering?

LIZA (*looking fiercely round at him*): I wouldnt marry you if you asked me; and youre nearer my age than what he is.

HIGGINS (*gently*): Than he is: not "than what he is".

LIZA (*losing her temper and rising*): I'll talk as I like. Youre not my teacher now.

HIGGINS (*reflectively*): I dont suppose Pickering would, though. He's as confirmed an old bachelor as I am.

LIZA: Thats not what I want; and dont you think it.

Ive always had chaps enough wanting me that way. Freddy Hill writes to me twice and three times a day, sheets and sheets.

HIGGINS (*disagreeably surprised*): Damn his impudence! (*He recoils and finds himself sitting on his heels.*)

LIZA: He has a right to if he likes, poor lad. And he does love me.

HIGGINS (*getting off the ottoman*): You have no right to encourage him.

LIZA: Every girl has a right to be loved.

HIGGINS: What! By fools like that?

LIZA: Freddy's not a fool. And if he's weak and poor and wants me, may be he'd make me happier than my betters that bully me and dont want me.

HIGGINS: Can he make anything of you? Thats the point.

LIZA: Perhaps I could make something of him. But I never thought of us making anything of one another; and you never think of anything else. I only want to be natural.

HIGGINS: In short, you want me to be as infatuated about you as Freddy? Is that it?

LIZA: No I dont. Thats not the sort of feeling I want from you. And dont you be too sure of yourself or of me. I could have been a bad girl if I'd liked. Ive seen more of some things than you, for all your learning. Girls like me can drag gentlemen down to make love to them easy enough. And they wish each other dead the next minute.

HIGGINS: Of course they do. Then what in thunder are we quarrelling about?

LIZA (*much troubled*): I want a little kindness. I know I'm a common ignorant girl, and you a book-learned gentleman; but I'm not dirt under your feet. What I done (*correcting herself*) what I did was not for the dresses and the taxis: I did it because we were pleasant together and I come — came — to care for you; not to want you to make love to me, and not forgetting the difference between us, but more friendly like.

HIGGINS: Well, of course. Thats just how I feel. And how Pickering feels. Eliza: youre a fool.

LIZA: Thats not a proper answer to give me. (*She sinks on the chair at the writing-table in tears.*)

HIGGINS: It's all youll get until you stop being a common idiot. If youre going to be a lady, youll have to give up feeling neglected if the men you know dont spend half their time snivelling over you and the other half giving you black eyes. If you cant stand the coldness of my sort of life, and the strain of it, go back to the gutter. Work til youre more a brute than a human being; and then cuddle and squabble and drink til you fall asleep. Oh, it's a fine life, the life of the gutter. It's real: it's warm: it's violent: you can feel it through the thickest skin: you can taste it and smell it without any training or any work. Not like Science and Literature and Classical Music and Philosophy and Art. You find me cold, unfeeling, selfish, dont you? Very well: be off with you to the sort of people you like. Marry some sentimental hog or other with lots of money, and a thick pair of lips to kiss you with and a thick pair of boots to kick you with. If you cant appreciate what youve got, youd better get what you can appreciate.

LIZA (*desperate*): Oh, you are a cruel tyrant. I cant talk to you: you turn everything against me: I'm always in the wrong. But you know very well all the time that youre nothing but a bully. You know I cant go back to the gutter, as you call it, and that I have no real friends in the world but you and the Colonel. You know well I couldnt bear to live with a low common man after you two; and it's wicked and cruel of you to insult me by pretending I could. You think I must go back to Wimpole Street because I have nowhere else to go but father's. But dont you be too sure that you have me under your feet to be trampled on and talked down. I'll marry Freddy, I will, as soon as I'm able to support him.

HIGGINS (*thunderstruck*): Freddy!!! that young fool! That poor devil who couldnt get a job as an errand boy even if he had the guts to try for it! Woman: do you not understand that I have made you a consort for a king?

LIZA: Freddy loves me: that makes him king enough for me. I dont want him to work: he wasnt brought up to it as I was. I'll go and be a teacher.

HIGGINS: Whatll you teach, in heaven's name?

LIZA: What you taught me. I'll teach phonetics.

HIGGINS: Ha! ha! ha!

LIZA: I'll offer myself as an assistant to that hairy-faced Hungarian.

HIGGINS (*rising in a fury*): What! That impostor! that humbug! that toadying ignoramus! Teach him my methods! my discoveries! You take one step in his direction and I'll wring your neck. (*He lays hands on her.*) Do you hear?

LIZA (*defiantly non-resistant*): Wring away. What do I care? I knew youd strike me some day. (*He lets her go, stamping, with rage at having forgotten himself, and recoils so hastily that he stumbles back into his seat on the ottoman.*) Aha! Now I know how to deal with you. What a fool I was not to think of it before! You cant take away the knowledge you gave me. You said I had a finer ear than you. And I can be civil and kind to people, which is more than you can. Aha! (*Purposely dropping her aitches to annoy him.*) Thats done you, Enry Iggins, it az. Now I dont care that (*snapping her fingers*) for your bullying and your big talk. I'll ad-

vertize it in the papers that your duchess is only a flower girl that you taught, and that she'll teach anybody to be a duchess just the same in six months for a thousand guineas. Oh, when I think of myself crawling under your feet and being trampled on and called names, when all the time I had only to lift up my finger to be as good as you, I could just kick myself.

HIGGINS (*wondering at her*): You damned impudent slut, you! But it's better than snivelling; better than fetching slippers and finding spectacles, isnt it? (*Rising.*) By George, Eliza, I said I'd make a woman of you; and I have. I like you like this.

LIZA: Yes: you can turn round and make up to me now that I'm not afraid of you, and can do without you.

HIGGINS: Of course I do, you little fool. Five minutes ago you were like a millstone round my neck. Now youre a tower of strength: a consort battleship. You and I and Pickering will be three old bachelors instead of only two men and a silly girl.

(*Mrs Higgins returns, dressed for the wedding. Eliza instantly becomes cool and elegant.*)

MRS HIGGINS: The carriage is waiting, Eliza. Are you ready?

LIZA: Quite. Is the Professor coming?

MRS HIGGINS: Certainly not. He cant behave himself in church. He makes remarks out loud all the time on the clergyman's pronunciation.

LIZA: Then I shall not see you again, Professor. Goodbye. (*She goes to the door.*)

MRS HIGGINS (*coming to Higgins*): Goodbye, dear.

HIGGINS: Goodbye, mother. (*He is about to kiss her, when he recollects something.*) Oh, by the way, Eliza, order a ham and a Stilton cheese, will you? And buy me a pair of reindeer gloves, number eights, and a tie to match that new suit of mine. You can choose the color. (*His cheerful, careless, vigorous voice shews that he is incorrigible.*)

LIZA (*disdainfully*): Number eights are too small for you if you want them lined with lamb's wool. You have three new ties that you have forgotten in the drawer of your washstand. Colonel Pickering prefers double Gloucester to Stilton; and you dont notice the difference. I telephoned Mrs Pearce this morning not to forget the ham. What you are to do without me I cannot imagine. (*She sweeps out.*)

MRS HIGGINS: I'm afraid youve spoilt that girl, Henry. I should be uneasy about you and her if she were less fond of Colonel Pickering.

HIGGINS: Pickering! Nonsense: she's going to marry Freddy. Ha ha! Freddy! Freddy!! Ha ha ha ha ha!!!!!

(*He roars with laughter as the play ends.*)

SEQUEL

The rest of the story need not be shewn in action, and indeed, would hardly need telling if our imaginations were not so enfeebled by their lazy dependence on the ready-mades and reach-me-downs of the ragshop in which Romance keeps its stock of "happy endings" to misfit all stories. Now, the history of Eliza Doolittle, though called a romance because the transfiguration it records seems exceedingly improbable, is common enough. Such transfigurations have been achieved by hundreds of resolutely ambitious young women since Nell Gwynne set them the example by playing queens and fascinating kings in the theatre in which she began by selling oranges. Nevertheless, people in all directions have assumed, for no other reason than that she became the heroine of a romance, that she must have married the hero of it. This is unbearable, not only because her little drama, if acted on such a thoughtless assumption, must be spoiled, but because the true sequel is patent to anyone with a sense of human nature in general, and of feminine instinct in particular.

Eliza, in telling Higgins she would not marry him if he asked, was not coquetting: she was announcing a well-considered decision. When a bachelor interests, and dominates, and teaches, and becomes important to a spinster, as Higgins with Eliza, she always, if she has character enough to be capable of it, considers very seriously indeed whether she will play for becoming that bachelor's wife, especially if he is so little interested in marriage that a determined and devoted woman might capture him if she set herself resolutely to do it. Her decision will depend a good deal on whether she is really free to choose; and that, again, will depend on her age and income. If she is at the end of her youth, and has no security for her livelihood, she will marry him because she must marry anybody who will provide for her. But at Eliza's age a good-looking girl does not feel that pressure: she feels free to pick and choose. She is therefore guided by her instinct in the matter. Eliza's instinct tells her not to marry Higgins. It does not tell her to give him up. It is not in the slightest doubt as to his remaining one of the strongest personal interests in her life. It would be very sorely strained if there was another woman likely to supplant her with him. But as she feels sure of him on that last point, she has no doubt at all as to her course, and would not have any, even if the difference of twenty years in age, which seems so great to youth, did not exist between them.

As our own instincts are not appealed to by her conclusion, let us see whether we cannot discover some reason in it. When Higgins excused his indifference to young women on the ground that they had an irresistible rival in his mother, he gave the clue to his inveterate old-bachelordom. The case is uncommon only to the extent that remarkable mothers are uncommon. If an imaginative boy has a sufficiently rich mother who has intelligence, personal grace, dignity of character without harshness, and a cultivated sense of the best art of her time to enable her to make her house beautiful, she sets a standard for him against which very few women can struggle, besides effecting for him a disengagement of his affections, his sense of beauty, and his idealism from his specifically sexual impulses. This makes him a standing puzzle to the huge number of uncultivated people who have been brought up in tasteless homes by commonplace or disagreeable parents, and to whom, consequently, literature, painting, sculpture, music, and affectionate personal relations come as modes of sex if they come at all. The word passion means nothing else to them; and that

Higgins could have a passion for phonetics and idealize his mother instead of Eliza, would seem to them absurd and unnatural. Nevertheless, when we look round and see that hardly anyone is too ugly or disagreeable to find a wife or a husband if he or she wants one, whilst many old maids and bachelors are above the average in quality and culture, we cannot help suspecting that the disentanglement of sex from the associations with which it is commonly confused, a disentanglement which persons of genius achieve by sheer intellectual analysis, is sometimes produced or aided by parental fascination.

Now, though Eliza was incapable of thus explaining to herself Higgins's formidable powers of resistance to the charm that prostrated Freddy at the first glance, she was instinctively aware that she could never obtain a complete grip of him, or come between him and his mother (the first necessity of the married woman). To put it shortly, she knew that for some mysterious reason he had not the makings of a married man in him, according to her conception of a husband as one to whom she would be his nearest and fondest and warmest interest. Even had there been no mother rival, she would still have refused to accept an interest in herself that was secondary to philosophic interests. Had Mrs Higgins died, there would still have been Milton and the Universal Alphabet. Landor's remark that to those who have the greatest power of loving, love is a secondary affair, would not have recommended Landor to Eliza. Put that along with her resentment of Higgins's domineering superiority, and her mistrust of his coaxing cleverness in getting round her and evading her wrath when he had gone too far with his impetuous bullying, and you will see that Eliza's instinct had good grounds for warning her not to marry her Pygmalion.

And now, whom did Eliza marry? For if Higgins was a predestinate old bachelor, she was most certainly not a predestinate old maid. Well, that can be told very shortly to those who have not guessed it from the indications she has herself given them.

Almost immediately after Eliza is stung into proclaiming her considered determination not to marry Higgins, she mentions the fact that young Mr Frederick Eynsford Hill is pouring out his love for her daily through the post. Now Freddy is young, practically twenty years younger than Higgins: he is a gentleman (or, as Eliza would qualify him, a toff), and speaks like one. He is nicely dressed, is treated by the Colonel as an equal, loves her unaffectedly, and is not her master, nor ever likely to dominate her in spite of his advantage of social standing. Eliza has no use for the foolish romantic tradition that all women love to be mastered, if not actually bullied and beaten. "When you go to women" says Nietzsche "take your whip with you." Sensible despots have never confined that precaution to women: they have taken their whips with them when they have dealt with men, and been slavishly idealized by the men over whom they have flourished the whip much more than by women. No doubt there are slavish women as well as slavish men; and women, like men, admire those that are stronger than themselves. But to admire a strong person and to live under that strong person's thumb are two different things. The weak may not be admired and hero-worshipped; but they are by no means disliked or shunned; and they never seem to have the least difficulty in marrying people who are too good for them. They may fail in emergencies; but life is not one long emergency: it is mostly a string of situations for which no exceptional strength is needed, and with which even rather weak people can cope if they have a stronger partner to help them out. Accordingly, it is a truth everywhere in evidence that strong people, masculine or feminine, not only do not marry stronger people, but do not shew any preference for them in selecting their friends. When a lion meets another with a louder roar "the first lion thinks the last a bore". The man or woman who feels strong enough for two, seeks for every other quality in a partner than strength.

The converse is also true. Weak people want to marry strong people who do not frighten them too much; and this often leads them to make the mistake we describe metaphorically as "biting off more than they can chew". They want too much for too little; and when the bargain is unreasonable beyond all bearing, the union becomes impossible: it ends in the weaker party being either discarded or borne as a cross, which is worse. People who are not only weak, but silly or obtuse as well, are often in these difficulties.

This being the state of human affairs, what is Eliza fairly sure to do when she is placed between Freddy and Higgins? Will she look forward to a lifetime of fetching Higgins's slippers or to a lifetime of Freddy fetching hers? There can be no doubt about the answer. Unless Freddy is biologically repulsive to her, and Higgins biologically attractive to a degree that overwhelms all her other instincts, she will, if she marries either of them, marry Freddy.

And that is just what Eliza did.

Complications ensued; but they were economic, not romantic. Freddy had no money and no occupation. His mother's jointure, a last relic of the opulence of Largelady Park, had enabled her to struggle along in Earlscourt with an air of gentility, but not to procure any serious secondary education for her children, much less give the boy a profession. A clerkship at thirty shillings a week was beneath Freddy's dignity, and extremely distasteful to him besides. His prospects consisted of a hope that if he kept up appearances somebody would do something for him. The something appeared vaguely to his imagination as a private secretaryship or a sinecure of some sort. To his mother it perhaps appeared as a marriage to some lady of means who could not resist her boy's niceness. Fancy her feelings when he married a flower girl who had become disclassed under extraordinary circumstances which were now notorious!

It is true that Eliza's situation did not seem wholly ineligible. Her father, though formerly a dustman, and now fantastically disclassed, had become extremely popular in the smartest society by a social talent which triumphed over every prejudice and every disadvantage. Rejected by the middle class, which he loathed, he had shot up at once into the highest circles by his wit, his dustmanship (which he carried like a banner), and his Nietzschean transcendence of good and evil. At intimate ducal dinners he sat on the right hand of the Duchess; and in country houses he smoked in the pantry and was made much of by the butler when he was not feeding in the dining room and being consulted by cabinet ministers. But he found it almost as hard to do all this on four thousand a year as Mrs Eynsford Hill to live in Earlscourt on an income so pitiably smaller that I have not the heart to disclose its exact figure. He absolutely refused to add the last straw to his burden by contributing to Eliza's support.

Thus Freddy and Eliza, now Mr and Mrs Eynsford Hill, would have spent a penniless honeymoon but for a wedding present of £500 from the Colonel to Eliza. It lasted a long time because Freddy did not know how to spend money, never having had any to spend, and Eliza, socially trained by a pair of old bachelors, wore her clothes as long as they held together and looked pretty, without the least regard to their being many months out of fashion. Still, £500 will not last two young people for ever; and they both knew, and Eliza felt as well, that they must shift themselves in the end. She could quarter herself on Wimpole Street because it had come to be her home; but she was quite aware that she ought not to quarter Freddy there, and that it would not be good for his character if she did.

Not that the Wimpole Street bachelors objected. When she consulted them, Higgins declined to be bothered about her housing problem when that solution was so simple. Eliza's desire to have Freddy in the house with her seemed of no more importance than if she had wanted an extra piece of bedroom furniture. Pleas as to Freddy's character, and the moral obligation on him to earn his own living, were lost on Higgins. He denied that Freddy had any character, and declared that if he tried to do any useful work some competent person would have the trouble of undoing it: a procedure involving a net loss to the community, and great unhappiness to Freddy himself, who was obviously intended by Nature for such light work as amusing Eliza, which, Higgins declared, was a much more useful and honorable occupation than working in the city. When Eliza referred again to her project of teaching phonetics, Higgins abated not a jot of his violent opposition to it. He said she was not within ten years of being qualified to meddle with his pet subject; and as it was evident that the Colonel agreed with him, she felt she could not go against them in this grave matter, and that she had no right, without Higgins's consent, to exploit the knowledge he had given her; for his knowledge seemed to her as much his private property as his watch: Eliza was no communist. Besides, she was superstitiously devoted to them both, more entirely and frankly after her marriage than before it.

It was the Colonel who finally solved the problem, which had cost him much perplexed cogitation. He one day asked Eliza, rather shyly, whether she had quite given up her notion of keeping a flower shop. She replied that she had thought of it, but had put it out of her head, because the Colonel had said, that day at Mrs Higgins's, that it would never do. The Colonel confessed that when he said that, he had not quite recovered from the dazzling impression of the day before. They broke the matter to Higgins that evening. The sole comment vouchsafed by him very nearly led to a serious quarrel with Eliza. It was to the effect that she would have in Freddy an ideal errand boy.

Freddy himself was next sounded on the subject. He said he had been thinking of a shop himself; though it had presented itself to his pennilessness as a small place in which Eliza should sell tobacco at one counter whilst he sold newspapers at the opposite one. But he agreed that it would be extraordinarily jolly to go early every morning with Eliza to Covent Garden and buy flowers on the scene of their first meeting: a sentiment which earned him many kisses from his wife. He added that he had always been afraid to propose anything of the sort, because Clara would make an awful row about a step that must damage her matrimonial chances, and his mother could not be expected to like it after clinging for so many years to that step of the social ladder on which retail trade is impossible.

This difficulty was removed by an event highly unexpected by Freddy's mother. Clara, in the course of her incursions into those artistic circles which were the highest within her reach, discovered that her conversational qualifications were expected to include a grounding in the novels of Mr H. G. Wells. She borrowed them in various directions so energetically that she swallowed them all within two months. The result was a conversion of a kind quite common today. A modern Acts of the Apostles would fill fifty whole Bibles if anyone were capable of writing it.

Poor Clara, who appeared to Higgins and his mother as a disagreeable and ridiculous person, and to her own mother as in some inexplicable way a social failure, had never seen herself in either light; for, though to some extent ridiculed and mimicked in West Kensington like everybody else there, she was accepted as a rational and normal — or shall we say inevitable? — sort of human being. At worst they called her The Pusher; but to them no more than to herself had it ever occurred that she was pushing the air, and pushing it in a wrong direction. Still, she was not happy. She was growing desperate. Her one asset, the fact that her mother was what the Epsom greengrocer called a carriage lady, had no exchange value, apparently. It had prevented her from getting educated, because the only education she could have afforded was education with the Earlscourt greengrocer's daughter. It had led her to seek the society of her mother's class; and that class simply would not have her, because she was much poorer than the greengrocer, and, far from being able to afford a maid, could not afford even a housemaid, and had to scrape along at home with an illiberally treated general servant. Under such circumstances nothing could give her an air of being a genuine product of Largelady Park. And yet its tradition made her regard a marriage with anyone within her reach as an unbearable humiliation. Commercial people and professional people in a small way were odious to her. She ran after painters and novelists; but she did not charm them; and her bold attempts to pick up and practice artistic and literary talk irritated them. She was, in short, an utter failure, an ignorant, incompetent, pretentious, unwelcome, penniless, useless little snob; and though she did not admit these disqualifications (for nobody ever faces unpleasant truths of this kind until the possibility of a way out dawns on them) she felt their effects too keenly to be satisfied with her position.

Clara had a startling eyeopener when, on being suddenly wakened to enthusiasm by a girl of her own age who dazzled her and produced in her a gushing desire to take her for a model, and gain her friendship, she discovered that this exquisite apparition had graduated from the gutter in a few months time. It shook her so violently, that when Mr H. G. Wells lifted her on the point of his puissant pen, and placed her at the angle of view from which the life she was leading and the society to which she clung appeared in its true relation to real human needs and worthy social structure, he effected a conversion and a conviction of sin comparable to the most sensational feats of General Booth or Gypsy Smith. Clara's snobbery went bang. Life suddenly began to move with her. Without knowing how or why, she began to make friends and enemies. Some of the acquaintances to whom she had been a tedious or indifferent or ridiculous affliction, dropped her: others became cordial. To her amazement she found that some "quite nice" people were saturated with Wells, and that this accessibility to ideas was the secret of their niceness. People she had thought deeply religious and had tried to conciliate on that tack with disastrous results, suddenly took an interest in her, and revealed a hostility to conventional religion which she had never conceived possible except among the most desperate characters. They made her read Galsworthy; and Galsworthy exposed the vanity of Largelady Park and finished her. It exasperated her to think that the dungeon in which she had languished for so many unhappy years had been unlocked all the time, and that the impulses she had so carefully struggled with and stifled for the sake of keeping well with society, were precisely those by which alone she could have come into any sort of sincere human contact. In the radiance of these discoveries, and the tumult of their reaction, she made a fool of herself as freely and conspicuously as when she so rashly adopted Eliza's expletive in Mrs Higgins's drawing room; for the new-born Wellsian had to find her bearings almost as ridiculously as a baby; but nobody hates a baby for its ineptitudes, or thinks the worse of it for trying to eat the matches; and Clara lost no friends by her follies. They laughed at her to her face this time; and she had to defend herself and fight it out as best she could.

When Freddy paid a visit to Earlscourt (which he never did when he could possibly help it) to make the desolating announcement that he and his Eliza were thinking of blackening the Largelady scutcheon by opening a shop, he found the little household already convulsed by a prior announcement from Clara that she also was going to work in an old furniture shop in Dover Street, which had been started by a fellow Wellsian. This appointment Clara owed, after all, to her old social accomplishment of Push. She had made up her mind that, cost what it might, she would see Mr Wells in the flesh; and she had achieved her end at a garden party. She had better luck than so rash an enterprise deserved. Mr Wells came up to her expectations. Age had not withered him, nor could custom stale his infinite variety in half an hour. His pleasant neatness and compactness, his small hands and feet, his teeming ready brain, his unaffected accessibility, and a certain fine apprehensiveness which stamped him as susceptible from his topmost hair to his upmost toe, proved irresistible. Clara talked of nothing else for weeks and weeks afterwards. And as she happened to talk to the lady of the furniture shop, and that lady also desired above all things to know Mr Wells and sell pretty things to him, she offered Clara a job on the chance of achieving that end through her.

And so it came about that Eliza's luck held, and the expected opposition to the flower shop melted away. The shop is in the arcade of a railway station not very far from the Victoria and Albert Museum; and if you live in that neighborhood you may go there any day and buy a buttonhole from Eliza.

Now here is a last opportunity for romance. Would you not like to be assured that the shop was an immense success, thanks to Eliza's charms and her early business experience in Covent Garden? Alas! the truth is the truth: the shop did not pay for a long time, simply because Eliza and her Freddy did not know how to keep it. True, Eliza had not to begin at the very beginning: she knew the names and prices of the cheaper flowers; and her elation was unbounded when she found that Freddy, like all youths educated at cheap, pretentious, and thoroughly inefficient schools, knew a little Latin. It was very little, but enough to make him appear to her a Porson or Bentley, and to put him at his ease with botanical nomenclature. Unfortunately he knew nothing else; and Eliza, though she could count money up to eighteen shillings or so, and had acquired a certain familiarity with the language of Milton from her struggles to qualify herself for winning Higgins's bet, could not write out a bill without utterly disgracing the establishment. Freddy's power of stating in Latin that Balbus built a wall and that Gaul was divided into three parts did not carry with it the slightest knowledge of accounts or business: Colonel Pickering had to explain to him what a cheque book and a bank account meant. And the pair were by no means easily teachable. Freddy backed up Eliza in her obstinate refusal to believe that they could save money by engaging a bookkeeper with some knowledge of the business. How, they argued, could you possibly save money by going to extra expense when you already could not make both ends meet? But the Colonel, after making the ends meet over and over again, at last gently insisted; and Eliza, humbled to the dust by having to beg from him so often, and stung by the uproarious derision of Higgins, to whom the notion of Freddy succeeding at anything was a joke that never palled, grasped the fact that business, like phonetics, has to be learned.

On the piteous spectacle of the pair spending their evenings in shorthand schools and polytechnic classes, learning bookkeeping and typewriting with incipient junior clerks, male and female, from the elementary schools, let me not dwell. There were even classes at the London School of Economics, and a humble personal appeal to the director of that institution to recommend a course bearing on the flower business. He, being a humorist, explained to them the method of the celebrated Dickensian essay on Chinese Metaphysics by the gentleman who read an article on China and an article on Metaphysics and combined the information. He suggested that they should combine the London School with Kew Gardens. Eliza, to whom the procedure of the Dickensian gentleman seemed perfectly correct (as in fact it was) and not in the least funny (which was only her ignorance), took the advice with entire gravity. But the effort that cost her the deepest humiliation was a request to Higgins, whose pet artistic fancy, next to Milton's verse, was calligraphy, and who himself wrote a most beautiful Italian hand, that he would teach her to write. He declared that she was congenitally incapable of forming a single letter worthy of the least of Milton's words; but she persisted; and again he suddenly threw himself into the task of teaching her with a combination of stormy intensity, concentrated patience, and occasional bursts of interesting disquisition on the beauty and nobility, the august mission and destiny, of human handwriting. Eliza ended by acquiring an extremely uncommercial script which was a positive extension of her personal beauty, and spending three times as much on stationery as anyone else because certain qualities and shapes of paper became indispensable to her. She could not even address an envelope in the usual way because it made the margins all wrong.

Their commercial schooldays were a period of disgrace and despair for the young couple. They seemed to be learning nothing about flower shops. At last they gave it up as hopeless, and shook the dust of the shorthand schools, and the polytechnics, and the London School of Economics from their feet for ever. Besides, the business was in some mysterious way beginning to take care of itself. They had somehow forgotten their objections to employing other people. They came to the conclusion that their own way was the best, and that they had really a remarkable talent for business. The Colonel, who had been compelled for some years to keep a sufficient sum on current account at his bankers to make up their deficits, found that the provision was unnecessary: the young people were prospering. It is true that there was not quite fair play between them and their competitors in trade. Their week-ends in the country cost them nothing, and saved them the price of their Sunday dinners; for the motor car was the Colonel's; and he and Higgins paid the hotel bills. Mr F. Hill, florist and greengrocer (they soon discovered that there was money in asparagus; and asparagus led to other vegetables), had an air which stamped the business as classy; and in private life he was still Frederick Eynsford Hill, Esquire. Not that there was any swank about him: nobody but Eliza knew that he had been christened Frederick Challoner. Eliza herself swanked like anything.

That is all. That is how it has turned out. It is astonishing how much Eliza still manages to meddle in the housekeeping at Wimpole Street in spite of the shop and her own family. And it is notable that though she never nags her husband, and frankly loves the Colonel as if she were his favorite daughter, she has never got out of the habit of nagging Higgins that was established on the fatal night when she won his bet for him. She snaps his head off on the faintest provocation, or on none. He no longer dares to tease her by assuming an abysmal inferiority of Freddy's mind to his own. He stones and bullies and derides; but she stands up to him so ruthlessly that the Colonel has to ask her from time to time to be kinder to Higgins; and it is the only request of his that brings a mulish expression into her face. Nothing but some emergency or calamity great enough to break down all likes and dislikes, and throw them both back on their common humanity — and may they be spared any such trial! — will ever alter this. She knows that Higgins does not need her, just as her father did not need her. The very scrupulousness with which he told her that day that he had become used to having her there, and dependent on her for all sorts of little services, and that he should miss her if she went away (it would never have occurred to Freddy or the Colonel to say anything of the sort) deepens her inner certainty that she is "no more to him than them slippers"; yet she has a sense, too, that his indifference is deeper than the infatuation of commoner souls. She is immensely interested in him. She has even secret mischievous moments in which she wishes she could get him alone, on a desert island, away from all ties and with nobody else in the world to consider, and just drag him off his pedestal and see him making love like any common man. We all have private imaginations of that sort. But when it comes to business, to the life that she really leads as distinguished from the life of dreams and fancies, she likes Freddy and she likes the Colonel; and she does not like Higgins and Mr Doolittle. Galatea never does quite like Pygmalion: his relation to her is too godlike to be altogether agreeable.

COMMENTARIES

Bernard Shaw (1856–1950)
PREFACE TO *PYGMALION*   *1916*

A PROFESSOR OF PHONETICS

As will be seen later on, Pygmalion needs, not a preface, but a sequel, which I have supplied in its due place.

The English have no respect for their language, and will not teach their children to speak it. They spell it so abominably that no man can teach himself what it sounds like. It is impossible for an Englishman to open his mouth without making some other Englishman hate or despise him. German and Spanish are accessible to foreigners: English is not accessible even to Englishmen. The reformer England needs today is an energetic phonetic enthusiast: that is why I have made such a one the hero of a popular play. There have been heroes of that kind crying in the wilderness for many years past. When I became interested in the subject towards the end of the eighteen-seventies, Melville Bell was dead; but Alexander J. Ellis was still a living patriarch, with an impressive head always covered by a velvet skull cap, for which he would apologize to public meetings in a very courtly manner. He and Tito Pagliardini, another phonetic veteran, were men whom it was impossible to dislike. Henry Sweet, then a young man, lacked their sweetness of character: he was about as conciliatory to conventional mortals as Ibsen or Samuel Butler. His great ability as a phonetician (he was, I think, the best of them all at his job) would have entitled him to high official recognition, and perhaps enabled him to popularize his subject, but for his Satanic contempt for all academic dignitaries and persons in general who thought more of Greek than of phonetics. Once, in the days when the Imperial Institute rose in South Kensington, and Joseph Chamberlain was booming the Empire, I induced the editor of a leading monthly review to commission an article from Sweet on the imperial importance of his subject. When it arrived, it contained nothing but a savagely derisive attack on a professor of language and literature whose chair Sweet regarded as proper to a phonetic expert only. The article, being libellous, had to be returned as impossible; and I had to renounce my dream of dragging its author into the limelight. When I met him afterwards, for the first time in many years, I found to my astonishment that he, who had been a quite tolerably presentable young man, had actually managed by sheer scorn to alter his personal appearance until he had become a sort of walking repudiation of Oxford and all its traditions. It must have been largely in his own despite that he was squeezed into something called a Readership of phonetics there. The future of phonetics rests probably with his pupils, who all swore by him; but nothing could bring the man himself into any sort of compliance with the university to which he nevertheless clung by divine right in an intensely Oxonian way. I daresay his papers, if he has left any, include some satires that may be published without too destructive results fifty years hence. He was, I believe, not in the least an illnatured man: very much the opposite, I should say; but he would not suffer fools gladly.

Those who knew him will recognize in my third act the allusion to the patent shorthand in which he used to write postcards, and which may be acquired from a four and sixpenny manual published by the Clarendon Press. The postcards which Mrs Higgins describes are such as I have received from Sweet. I would decipher a sound which a cockney would represent by *zerr,* and a Frenchman by *seu,* and then write demanding with some heat what on earth it meant. Sweet, with boundless contempt for my stupidity, would reply that it not only meant but obviously was the word *Result,* as no other word containing that sound, and capable of making sense with the context, existed in any language spoken on earth. That less expert mortals should require fuller indications was beyond Sweet's patience. Therefore, though the whole point of his "Current Shorthand" is that it can express every sound in the language perfectly, vowels as well as consonants, and that your hand has to make no stroke except the easy and current ones with which you write *m, n,* and *u, l, p,* and *q,* scribbling them at whatever angle comes easiest to you, his unfortunate determination to make this remarkable and quite legible script serve also as a shorthand reduced it in his own practice to the most inscrutable of cryptograms. His true objective was the provision of a full, accurate, legible script for our noble but ill-dressed language; but he was led past that by his contempt for the popular Pitman system of shorthand, which he called the Pitfall system. The triumph of Pitman was a triumph of business organization: there was a weekly paper to persuade you to learn Pitman: there were cheap textbooks and exercise books and transcripts of speeches for you to copy, and schools where experienced teachers coached you up to the necessary proficiency. Sweet could not organize his market in that fashion. He might as well have been the Sybil who tore up the leaves of prophecy that nobody would attend to. The four and sixpenny manual, mostly in his lithographed handwriting, that was never vulgarly advertised, may perhaps some day be taken up by a syndicate and pushed upon the public as The Times pushed the Encyclopædia Britannica; but until then it will certainly not prevail against Pitman. I have bought three copies of it during my lifetime; and I am informed by the publishers that its cloistered existence is still a steady and healthy one. I actually learned the system two several times; and yet the shorthand in which I am writing these lines is Pitman's. And the reason is, that my secretary cannot transcribe Sweet, having been perforce taught in the schools of Pitman. Therefore, Sweet railed at Pitman as vainly as Thersites railed at Ajax: his raillery, however it may have eased his soul, gave no popular vogue to Current Shorthand.

Pygmalion Higgins is not a portrait of Sweet, to whom the adventure of Eliza Doolittle would have been impossible; still, as will be seen, there are touches of Sweet in the play. With Higgins's physique and temperament Sweet might have set the Thames on fire. As it was, he impressed himself professionally on Europe to an extent that made his comparative personal obscurity, and the failure of Oxford to do justice to his eminence, a puzzle to foreign specialists in his subject. I do not blame Oxford, because I think Oxford is quite right in demanding a certain social amenity from its nurslings (heaven knows it is not exorbitant in its requirements!); for although I well know how hard it is for a man of genius with a seriously underrated subject to maintain serene and kindly relations with the men who underrate it, and who keep all the best places for less important subjects which they profess without originality and sometimes without much capacity for them, still, if he overwhelms them with wrath and disdain, he cannot expect them to heap honors on him.

Of the later generations of phoneticians I know little. Among them towers the Poet Laureate, to whom perhaps Higgins may owe his Miltonic sympathies, though here again I must disclaim all portraiture. But if the play makes the public aware that there are such people as phoneticians, and that they are among the most important people in England at present, it will serve its turn.

I wish to boast that Pygmalion has been an extremely successful play over all Europe and North America as well as at home. It is so intensely and deliberately didactic, and its subject is esteemed so dry, that I delight in throwing it at the heads of the wiseacres who repeat the parrot cry that art should never be didactic. It goes to prove my contention that art should never be anything else.

Finally, and for the encouragement of people troubled with accents that cut them off from all high employment, I may add that the change wrought by Professor Higgins in the flower-girl is neither impossible nor uncommon. The modern concierge's daughter who fulfills her ambition by playing the Queen of Spain in Ruy Blas at the Théâtre Français is only one of many thousands of men and women who have sloughed off their native dialects and acquired a new tongue. But the thing has to be done scientifically, or the last state of the aspirant may be worse than the first. An honest and natural slum dialect is more tolerable than the attempt of a phonetically untaught person to imitate the vulgar dialect of the golf club; and I am sorry to say that in spite of the efforts of our Academy of Dramatic Art, there is still too much sham golfing English on our stage, and too little of the noble English of Forbes Robertson.

Arnold Silver
HIGGINS AND SHAW   *1982*

The artist always has a special relationship with the thing created, but when the creation is a person, such as Galatea or Eliza, that relationship is complex. Silver examines the connections between sculpture and playwrighting while also noting the ways in which Higgins is like Shaw himself.

Higgins as a scientist will require some further comment after we broaden our knowledge of his character, but now we must note some of the ways in which he is, not professionally different from Shaw, but surprisingly like him. As the play's title intimates, Higgins is something of an artist, a role compatible with his scientific pursuits since the experiment with Eliza will supposedly confirm his theories even as it provides him with a creative way of displaying his skills. But what type of artist is he? Here the sculptural reference in the title is suggestive rather than definitive, for Higgins as an artist most clearly resembles none other than a playwright-director. He creates a role for Eliza, supplies her with lines and polishes her delivery, plots for her a climactic scene, and then tests her out beforehand in a dress rehearsal at his mother's house; but ironically he treats her throughout as if she were a slab of stone.

In thus making the protagonist into a sort of playwright-director tempted by a sculptor's attitude toward his material, Shaw offers a profounder consideration of his own art than can be found anywhere else in his dramatic writings, and this underlying professional similarity undoubtedly accounts for his greater sureness of touch with Higgins than with such other artists as the painter Dubedat or the poet Marchbanks.[1] The struggle between Higgins and Eliza, as he prepares her for her debut, duplicates the struggle for ascendancy between the director and his leading lady, as Shaw himself knew from having directed many of his own plays; and as much as Higgins would like to credit himself with Eliza's achievement, hers is clearly the greater contribution. This struggle represents as well the initial one between the writer and the creatures of his imagination, who may guide his pen in ways he neither anticipated nor even desired, and who somehow take on independent lives. Shaw in the prefaces often

---

[1] It will of course be understood that the phrase "sculptor's attitude toward his material" is used with deliberate looseness in order to emphasize the title's implied irony that this modern Pygmalion, unlike his legendary prototype, is a fatally flawed artist. True sculptors, in contrast to Henry Higgins, cherish their material and seek to awaken the form that lies sleeping in the stone, as Rodin once put it.

claimed that this or that character had been consciously designed to prove some particular point, and as the world came to accept these claims it drew the reasonable inference that the author's characters were merely his talkative dolls. But in *Pygmalion,* to the very degree that it satirizes a would-be dollmaker, Shaw honors those unconscious forces within himself that gave the soul of life to his more successful creations. And Shaw's muse, returning the compliment, gave this play's doll and its dollmaker their immortal souls.

This mystery of the creative process seems to have been on Shaw's mind even as he wrote the play, or perhaps as the play wrote itself, since it appears to propel itself forward with the rapid inevitability of a happy dream. Shaw acknowledged not long after finishing the work that actors often stimulated his imagination: "If Forbes Robertson had not been there to play Caesar, I should not have written Caesar and Cleopatra. If Ellen Terry had never been born, Captain Brassbound's conversion would never have been effected." And of course, had Mrs. Patrick Campbell not lived, *Pygmalion* would never have been written, for the part of Eliza was written expressly for her and had been directly inspired by her. Fifteen years earlier, in 1897, even while Shaw was in the midst of conceiving *Caesar and Cleopatra,* he informed a friend that the historical play had been nearly driven out of his mind by another one he had hit upon after watching Mrs. Campbell and Forbes Robertson working together. It was to be the story of a flower girl and a West End gentleman. This is the only remark available on the play before its actual composition in 1912, but it indicates that the gestation period had been unusually lengthy; and when Shaw finally came to write the play he no doubt found his control facilitated by a prior unconscious integration of the material. The question of who had really created Eliza, Mrs. Campbell or himself, is in the play transposed into the question of who created the independent Eliza of the last two acts, Higgins or Eliza herself? The obvious answer in both cases is that the creation was collaborative, though Higgins resists acknowledging it. "*You* won my bet! You! Presumptuous insect! *I* won it.*" "*I said I'd make a woman of you, and I have," he still boasts to Eliza, and Shaw smiles and would have us smile too at this misplaced assertion of artistic vanity.

J. Ellen Gainor
PATRIARCHY IN *PYGMALION*   *1991*

Gainor sees Eliza Doolittle as a victim of a patriarchal culture. The three older men in Eliza's life, Higgins, Pickering, and Doolittle, stand in a fatherly relation to her. Doolittle wants her off his hands; Higgins wants her to win his bet; Pickering wants only to be kind. The question of how much Eliza has been created in the image of a man is central to Gainor's interests.

Higgins, of course, is actually one of three fathers for Eliza, the other two being Colonel Pickering — another teacher from whom she "learnt really nice manners" — and "the regulation natural chap," Alfred Doolittle. These three men represent the social spectrum of patriarchy, each with his own mode of keeping Eliza "in her place." Doolittle, who knows nothing of the didactic arrangement under which Eliza will stay at Wimpole Street, arrives at the house to arrange the "sale" of his daughter for five pounds, acting out the exchange of women in patriarchal culture. He makes the Victorian assumption that Higgins's job, as the prospective husband in this burlesqued exchange, will be to "improve Eliza's mind" and suggests that the most efficacious method will be "with a strap."

Unbeknownst to Doolittle, of course, Higgins manipulates their conversation so that the member of "the undeserving poor" will reveal his class differences and prejudices. Eliza, from the same class origins, is a victim of both class and sex discrimination, and Shaw draws parallels between these two forms of injustice in the play. Although Eliza repeatedly asserts her essential similarity to the upper classes, with whom she shares self-respect and human feelings, Higgins maintains a stance in opposition to her beliefs.

> PICKERING (*in good-humored remonstrance*): Does it occur to you, Higgins, that the girl has some feelings?
> HIGGINS (*looking critically at her*): Oh no, I dont think so. Not any feelings that we need bother about. (*Cheerily*) Have you, Eliza?
> LIZA: I got my feelings same as anyone else.

Through Higgins's infantilization of Eliza, treating her as a child and talking about her as if she weren't present or able to understand, Shaw creates a parallel between issues of class and sex: discrimination toward the poor and toward women (who are tantamount to children) appear very similar. By erasing detectable class difference in Eliza through speech education, Higgins believes he will be endowing her with the humanity she lacks. The issue of Eliza's sex, however, does not enter into Higgins's equation in any considered way. Speech training and gender programming go hand in hand with Higgins's method, and thus as Eliza learns Henry's speech, she also absorbs the masculine context from which it evolved.

Late in the play, Henry delivers the first of his "creation" speeches, fulfilling his Pygmalion image: "I have created this thing out of the squashed cabbage leaves of Covent Garden." Eliza clarifies this creative, educational process, highlighting the masculine nature of his precepts: "I was brought up to be just like him, unable to control myself, and using bad language on the slightest provocation." In other words, Higgins has reared Eliza in his own image, a male image. Significantly, language, the instrument of male paternity, is the medium through which Eliza assumes her resemblance to Higgins.

Drama in the Early and Mid-Twentieth Century

The realist tradition in drama had certain EXPRESSIONIST qualities evident in the symbolic actions in Strindberg's *Miss Julie* and the romantic fantasies of Hedda in *Hedda Gabler*. But the surfaces of the plays appear realistic, consisting of a sequence of events that we might imagine happening in real life. The subject matter is also in the tradition of naturalism because it is drawn from life and not beautified or toned down for the middle-class audience.

But in the early to mid-twentieth century realistic drama took a new turn, incorporating distortions of reality that border on the unreal or *surreal*. From the time of Anton Chekhov in 1903 to Samuel Beckett in the 1950s, drama exploited the possibilities of realism, antirealism, and the poetic expansion of expressionism.

The Heritage of Realism

In the late nineteenth century realism was often perceived as too severe for an audience that had loved melodrama. Realistic plays forced comfortable audiences to observe psychological and physical problems that their status as members of the middle class usually allowed them to avoid. Audiences often protested loudly at this painful experience.

The technique of realism could, however, be adapted for many different purposes, and eventually realism was reshaped to satisfy middle-class sensibilities by commercial playwrights, who produced popular, pleasant plays. By the 1920s in Europe and the 1930s in America, theatergoing audiences expected plays to be realistic. Even the light comedies dominating the commercial stage were in a more or less realistic mode. Anything that disturbed the illusion of realism was thought to be a flaw.

Reactions to the comfortable use of realistic techniques were numerous, especially after the First World War. One extreme reaction was that of the Dadaists. Through the group's chief propagandist, Tristan Tzara

(1896–1963), Dadaists promoted an art that was essentially enigmatic and incoherent to the average person. That was its point. The Dadaists blamed World War I on sensible, middle-class people who were logical and well intentioned. The brief plays that were performed in many Dadaist clubs in Europe often featured actors speaking simultaneously so that nothing they said could be understood. The purpose was to confound the normal expectations of theatergoers.

Other developments were also making it possible for playwrights to experiment and move away from a strict reliance on "comfortable" realism. By World War I motion pictures began to make melodramatic entertainment available to most people in the world. Even when films were silent, they relied on techniques that had been common on the nineteenth-century stage. Their growing domination of popular dramatic entertainment provided an outlet for the expectations of middle-class audiences and freed more imaginative playwrights to experiment and develop in different directions.

Realism and Myth

The incorporation of myth in drama offered new opportunities to expand the limits of realism. Sigmund Freud's theories of psychoanalysis at the turn of the century stimulated a new interest in myth and dreams as a psychological link between people. Freud studied Greek myths for clues to the psychic state of his patients, and he published a number of commentaries on Greek plays and on *Hamlet*. (See excerpts on pp. 166–69 and pp. 480–81.) The psychologist Carl Jung, a follower of Freud who eventually split with him, helped give a powerful impetus to the interest in dreams and the symbolism of myth by suggesting that all members of a culture share an inborn knowledge of the basic myths of the culture. Jung postulated a collective unconscious, a repository of mythic material in the mind that all humans inherit as part of their birthright. This theory gave credence to the power of myth in everyday life; along with Freud's theories, it is one of the most important ideas empowering drama and other art forms in this century. Playwrights who used elements of myth in their plays produced a poetic form of realism that deals with a level of truth common to all humans.

Poetic Realism

The Abbey Theatre in Dublin, which functioned with distinction from the turn of the century, produced major works by John Millington Synge, W. B. Yeats, Sean O'Casey, and Lady Gregory. Lady Gregory's peasant plays concentrated on the charming, the amusing, and occasionally the grotesque. She tried to represent the dialect she heard in the west of Ireland, a dialect that was distinctive, poetic, and colorful. She also took advantage of local Irish myths and used some of them for her most powerful plays, such as *Dervorgilla* and *Grania,* both portraits of passionate women from Irish legend and myth.

John Millington Synge, like Lady Gregory, was interested in the twin forces of myth and peasant dialects. His plays are difficult to fit into a realist mold, although their surfaces are sometimes naturalistic. Some audiences reacted violently to his realistic portrayals of peasant life because they were unflattering. Synge's plays were sometimes directly connected with ancient Irish myth, as in *Deirdre of the Sorrows* (1910), which concerns a willful Irish princess who runs off with a young warrior and his brothers on the eve of her wedding to an old king. The story ends sadly for Deirdre, and she is regarded as a fated heroine, almost a Greek figure. Synge's great short tragedy *Riders to the Sea* may also have derived from an anecdote or legend; it is an expressionist play in its use of unreal moments, such as Maurya's encounter with the ghost of her son Michael and her vision of her dead son Bartley.

In the United States, Eugene O'Neill, influenced by Strindberg, experimented with realism, first by presenting stark, powerful plays that disturbed his audiences. *The Hairy Ape* (1922) portrayed a primitive coal stoker on a passenger liner who awakened base emotions in the more refined passengers. In *The Emperor Jones* (1921) O'Neill produced the first important American expressionist play. The shifting scenery, created by lighting, was dreamlike and at times frightening. The experience of the play reflected the frightening psychic experiences of the main character, Brutus Jones.

O'Neill also experimented with more poetic forms of realism. In *Desire Under the Elms* (1924), he explores the myth of Phaedra — centering on her incestuous love for her husband's son — but sets it in rural New England on a rock-hard farm. In the tradition of realism, the play treats unpleasant themes: sons' distrust of their father and their dishonoring him; lust between a son and his stepmother; and the murder of a baby to "prove" love. But it is not simply realistic. Without its underpinning of myth, the play would be only sordid, but the myth helps us see things much more clearly: Fate operates even today, but not in terms of messages from the gods. Rather, it works in terms of messages from our hearts and bodies. Lust is a force in nature that drives and destroys.

Meanwhile, in Fascist Spain, Federico García Lorca, also a poetic realist, was uncovering dark emotional centers of the psyche in his *House of Bernarda Alba* (1936), which explores erotic forces repressed and then set loose. Lorca was opposed to fascism and was murdered by a Fascist agent. His plays reveal a bleakness of spirit that helps us imagine the darkness — moral and psychological — that enveloped Europe in the 1940s.

Social Realism

Ten years after *Desire Under the Elms* enjoyed popularity, a taste for plays based on social realism developed. This was realism with a political conscience. Because the world was in the throes of a depression that reduced many people to destitution and homelessness, drama began to aim at awakening governments to the consequences of unbridled capitalism and the depressions that freewheeling economies produced.

Plays like Jack Kirkland's *Tobacco Road* (1933), adapted from Erskine Caldwell's novel, presented a grim portrait of rural poverty in America. Sidney Kingsley's *Dead End* (1935) portrayed the life of virtually homeless boys on the Lower East Side of Manhattan. In the same year Maxwell Anderson produced a verse tragedy, *Winterset,* with gangsters and gangsterism at its core. Also in 1935 Clifford Odets produced *Waiting for Lefty,* an openly leftist labor drama. These plays' realist credentials lay primarily in their effort to show audiences portraits of life that might shock their middle-class sensibilities.

Realism and Expressionism

After Eugene O'Neill's experiments in combining myth and realism, later American dramatists looked for new ways to expand the resources of realism while retaining its power. The use of expressionism — often poetic in language and effect — was one solution that appealed to both Tennessee Williams and Arthur Miller. Expressionism developed in the first and second decades of the twentieth century. The movement began in Germany, and was influenced by some of Strindberg's work. Because expressionism takes many forms, there is no simple way to define the term except to see it as an alternative to realistic drama. Instead of having realistic sets, the stage may sometimes be barren or flooded with light or draped. Characters sometimes become symbolic; dialogue is often sharp, abrupt, enigmatic. The German theater saw its earliest developments in Frank Wedekind, whose first play, *Spring Awakening,* which explored sexual repression, abandoned a naturalistic style. His work influenced later German playwrights such as George Kaiser, Ernst Toller, Erwin Piscator, and Bertolt Brecht, whose *Three-Penny Opera* (1928) incorporated some of the hallmarks of expressionism, such as a music-hall atmosphere and broadly drawn characters.

Later American playwrights modified the characteristics of expressionism; they melded expressionist elements, such as fantastic sets and highly poetic diction, with a relatively realistic style. Tennessee Williams's *The Glass Menagerie* (1944) and Arthur Miller's *Death of a Salesman* (1949) both use expressionist techniques. Williams's poetic stage directions make clear that he is drawing on non-realistic dramatic devices. He describes the scene as "memory and . . . therefore nonrealistic." He calls for an interior "rather dim and poetic," and he uses a character who also steps outside the staged action to serve as a narrator — one who "takes whatever license with dramatic convention as is convenient to his purposes." As the narrator tells his story, the walls of the building seem to melt away, revealing the inside of a house and the lives and fantasies of his mother and sister, both caught in their own distorted visions of life.

Arthur Miller's original image for *Death of a Salesman* was the inside

Figure 9. Expressionistic
setting in Arthur Miller's
Death of a Salesman

of Willy Loman's mind; Jo Mielziner's expressionist set represented his
idea as a cross-section of Loman's house. As the action in one room concluded, lights went up to begin action in another (Figure 9). This evocative staging influenced the production of numerous plays by later
writers. In the original set, a scrim, or gauze screen, was painted with
branches and leaves. When this scrim was lit from the front for memory
scenes, the set was transformed to evoke an earlier time when the sons
were boys.

Miller used expressionist techniques to create the hallucinatory sequences when Willy talks with Ben, the man who walked into the jungle poor and walked out a millionaire, and when Biff recalls seeing
Willy with the woman in Boston.

While expressionism made some inroads in American theater, the
techniques of realism persisted and developed. Lorraine Hansberry's *A*

Raisin in the Sun (1959) uses basically realistic staging and dialogue to portray the difficulties of the members of one family in reaching for opportunity to overcome poverty. For Williams and Miller, expressionism offered a way to bring other worlds to bear on the staged action — the worlds of dream and fantasy. Hansberry does not use the expressionist techniques of Miller. Her only exotic touch is the visit of the African young man, Asagai, who offers a moment of cultural counterpoint. Hansberry's realism is essentially conservative.

Antirealism

SURREALISM (literally, "beyond realism") in the early twentieth century was based originally on an interpretation of experience not through the lucid mind of the waking person but though the mind of the dreamer, the unconscious mind that Freud described. Surrealism augmented or, for some playwrights, supplanted realism and became a means of distorting reality for emotional purposes.

When Pirandello's six characters come onstage looking for their author in *Six Characters in Search of an Author* (1921), no one believes that they are characters rather than actors. Pirandello's play is an examination of the realities we take for granted in drama. He turns the world of expectation in drama upside down. He reminds us that what we assume to be real is always questionable — we cannot be sure of anything; we must presume that things are true, and in some cases we must take them on faith.

Pirandello's philosophy dominated his stories, plays, and novels. His questioning of the certainty of human knowledge was designed to undermine his audience's faith in an absolute reality. Modern physicists have concurred with philosophers, ancient and modern, who question everyday reality. Pirandello was influenced by the modern theories of relativity that physicists were developing, and he found in them validation of his own attack on certainty.

Epic Theater

Bertolt Brecht (1898–1956) began writing plays just after World War I. He was a political dramatist who rejected the theater of his day, which valued the realistic "well-made play," in which all the parts fit perfectly together and function like a machine. His feeling was that such plays were too mechanical, like a "clockwork mouse."

Exploring the style of his predecessor Irwin Piscator, Brecht developed EPIC THEATER. The term implies a sequence of actions or episodes of the kind found in Homer's *Iliad*. In epic theater the sense of dramatic illusion is constantly voided by reminders from the stage that one is watching a play. Stark, harsh lighting, blank stages, placards announcing changes of scenes, bands playing music onstage, and long, discomfiting pauses make it impossible for an audience to become totally immersed in a realistic illusion. Brecht, offering a genuine alternative to realistic drama, wanted the audience to analyze the play's thematic content rather than to sit back and be entertained. He believed that realistic drama convinced audiences that the play's vision of reality described not just things as they are, but things as they must be. Such drama, Brecht asserted, helped maintain the social problems that they portrayed by reinforcing, rather than challenging, their realities.

Brecht's *Mother Courage* (1941) is an antiwar drama written early in World War II. The use of song, an unreal setting, and an unusual historical perspective (the Thirty Years' War in the seventeenth century) help to achieve the "defamiliarization" that Brecht thought drama ought to produce in its audiences. The techniques of epic theater in *Galileo* and *The Good Woman of Setzuan* (1943) — a study of the immoralities that prosper under capitalism — were imitated by playwrights in the 1950s. Hardly a major play in that period is free of Brecht's influence.

Absurdist Drama

The critic Martin Esslin coined the term THEATER OF THE ABSURD when describing the work of Samuel Beckett (1906–1989), the Irish playwright whose dramas often dispense with almost everything that makes the well-made play well made. Some of his plays have no actors onstage — amplified breathing is the only hint of human presence in one case. Some have little or no plot; others have no words. His theater is minimalist, offering a stage reality that seems cut to the bone, without the usual realistic devices of plot, character development, and intricate setting.

The theater of the absurd assumes that the world is meaningless, that meaning is a human concept, and that individuals must create significance and not rely on institutions or traditions to provide it. The absurdist movement grew out of existentialism, a postwar French philosophy demanding that the individual face the emptiness of the universe and create meaning in a life that has no essential meaning within itself. *Waiting for Godot* (1952) captured the modern imagination and established a landmark in absurdist drama.

In *Waiting for Godot* two tramps, Vladimir and Estragon, meet near a tree where they expect Godot to arrive to talk with them. The play has two acts that both end with a small boy explaining that Godot cannot come today but will come tomorrow. Godot is not coming, and the tramps who wait for Godot will wait forever. While they wait they entertain themselves with vaudeville routines and eventually are met by a rich man, Pozzo, and his slave, Lucky. Lucky, on the command "Think, pig," speaks in a stream of garbled phrases that evoke Western philosophy and religion but that remain meaningless. Pozzo and Lucky have no interest in joining Vladimir and Estragon in waiting for Godot. They leave the two alone, waiting — afraid to leave for fear of missing Godot, but uncertain that Godot will ever arrive.

Beckett seems to be saying that in an absurd world such gestures are necessary to create the sense of significance that people need to live. His characters' awareness of an audience and his refusal to create a drama in which an audience can "lose" itself in a comfortable surface of realistic illusion are all, in their own way, indebted to Brecht.

Beckett's *Krapp's Last Tape* (1958) places some extraordinary limitations on performance. Krapp is the only person onstage throughout the play, and his dialogues are with tapes of himself made many years before. The situation is absurd, but as Beckett reveals to us, the absurd has its own complexities, and situations such as Krapp's can sustain complex interpretations. Beckett expects his audience to analyze the drama, not merely be entertained.

The illusion of reality is shed almost entirely in *Endgame*. Hamm cannot move. His parents, both legless, are in trashcans onstage. Clov performs all the play's movement on a barren, cellarlike stage.

The great plays of this period reflect the values of the cultures from which they spring. They make comments on life in the modern world and question the values that the culture takes for granted. The drama of this part of the twentieth century is a drama of examination.

John Millington Synge

John Millington Synge (1871–1909) was one of the brilliant discoveries of the Irish Literary Renaissance, which was largely the product of Lady Gregory and William Butler Yeats, the codirectors of the Abbey Theatre in Dublin. The Abbey ranks as one of the most influential and successful national theaters in European history. From 1904 to the present, it has been devoted to producing plays by Irish writers, some of whom have gone on to be ranked among the greatest of their age. Besides Synge, Bernard Shaw, Lady Gregory, Yeats, Sean O'Casey, and Brian Friel are among the many whose names still loom impressively as having contributed to the reputation of the Abbey.

Synge was gifted in languages, with a degree in German from Trinity College, Dublin. Also a violinist, he went to Paris to study music and live the bohemian life of the artist. It was there in 1896 that Yeats and Lady Gregory met him, persuading him to return to Ireland and write plays for what was to become the Abbey. They convinced him to spend time in the Aran Islands, the wildest part of Ireland. It is there that he set his play *Riders to the Sea*. Yeats felt the Arans were an important source of the literary energy of the nation because the Islanders' colorful language sounded like English filtered through Irish Gaelic.

Synge wrote a number of important plays within less than ten years. Most of them remain in the repertory of modern drama: *In the Shadow of the Glen* (1903); *Riders to the Sea* (1904); *The Well of the Saints* (1905); *The Tinker's Wedding* (1907); *The Playboy of the Western World* (1907); and *Deirdre of the Sorrows* (1910). With the exception of *The Tinker's Wedding*, which is so anticlerical that it has never been given a production at the Abbey, they are all still regularly produced there.

Synge was not always a popular playwright in Ireland. He felt that he faithfully represented peasant ways, but his Dublin audiences often protested that he insulted the Irish. Synge's kind of realism, while not especially harsh or critical, was an unvarnished view of the west of Ireland. The Abbey audiences wanted an idealized portrait of their countrymen and countrywomen, not straightforward and sometimes embarrassing portraits such as the one Synge offered them in *The Playboy of the Western World*. That play caused riots in the Abbey Theatre when first performed.

The Playboy of the Western World is about a young man who, thinking he has killed his father, arrives at a shebeen — a kind of tavern — in Mayo, where the townfolk make a hero of him rather than turning him in to the police. He joins in their games and wins all the prizes; he woos and almost wins Pegeen Mike, the local beauty. The subject matter — Irish people lionizing a presumed murderer — and the frank language were departures from previous Irish drama, but neither the playwright nor his producers at the Abbey Theatre were prepared for the audience's reaction. At its first performance when Christy, the Playboy, actually hit his father (who was not really dead) late in the play, the audience could sit still no longer. Such an act was perceived as an offense against all the Irish.

But vocal protest finally erupted at a line that describes women standing in their slips in front of the hero. At that point the crowd was so noisy that no one could hear what was said onstage. For subsequent performances Lady Gregory advised the actors to move their lips when the crowd roared, but not to waste their voices unless the crowd noise died down. Eventually, the police were called in to throw out troublemakers and to keep the audience noise down. When the Abbey company toured the United States in 1909 and performed the play in Boston, riots ensued again, with the local chapter of the nationalist Irish organization Sinn Féin enlisted to make a deafening racket during the performances.

Synge was shocked at the uproar; he had never expected his play to stimulate such a response. The question of realism was probably not on Synge's mind at all. *Playboy* is less a realistic play than is *Riders to the Sea,* and both are rooted not in any effort to force the audience to look at life as it is really lived but rather in the mythic and symbolic forces that underlie everyone's experiences of heroism, life, and death. The deep roots of both plays are in Irish myth and the Christian religion. Synge was amazed to think that audiences ignored those important aspects and that they focused on other, less significant issues.

Synge's early death robbed world drama of a figure who certainly would have been among the greatest writers of the century. As it is, his work is remarkable; but in his last play, *Deirdre of the Sorrows,* which he never finished, we can see the promise of a body of work that would have taken its place with the best plays of our time.

RIDERS TO THE SEA

Riders to the Sea (1904) was the first success that Synge produced for the Abbey Theatre. In some ways it is still one of the most impressive plays to come out of the Irish Literary Renaissance. It is a one-act play, which the Abbey found congenial for its early programs, but its brevity in no way diminishes its power.

The play is set in the west of Ireland, the part least touched by English influence. Aran Islanders speak both Gaelic and English, but their English is marked with a very expressive and idiosyncratic flavor, which Synge tries to replicate in this play. The syntax of Synge's peasants benefits from his musician's ear as well as from his having lived in an inn in Wicklow, where he eavesdropped on the local Irish kitchen girls speaking naturally and unaffectedly.

Riders to the Sea owes much of its power to the local speech and the local way of life portrayed faithfully in the play. In his preface to *The Playboy of the Western World,* Synge credits Irish writers with the advantage of listening "for a few years more" to a language that is "rich as a nut." Maurya's long speeches at the end of *Riders to the Sea* are filled with the rhythms of the sea and the agony of someone who has suffered as much as the world can demand. Even the speeches of the lesser characters have an extraordinarily expressive flavor.

The drama depicts the sufferings of a superstitious peasant woman, yet it contains the same kinds of intensity of dramatic action found in Greek tragedies. It maintains a unity of time, place, character, and action, as well as an intense sense of fate and impending doom. Synge may well have begun developing a new genre of folk tragedy, just as Arthur Miller later began developing a genre of middle-class tragedy in *Death of a Salesman. Riders to the Sea* is permeated by a sense of fate; and Maurya, whose name is remarkably close in sound to *moira,* the Greek word for "fate," senses the inevitability of the premature death of her last son on the sea. The feeling of inevitability is heightened by the discussion between the daughters about the son Michael, who has been feared lost at sea, by their identification of his sock that was recovered from the sea, and by the willful insistence of the last son, Bartley, to ride the mares across the sea to the mainland, knowingly risking his life. (In fact, men did swim their animals from the islands to the mainland, and they often went out to meet the large boats that came near. Even today those waters are difficult, and Aran Islanders still use the same black curraghs their ancestors used to ferry themselves, their goods, and their livestock between the mainland and their homes.) Maurya's horrifying vision of Michael and Bartley on the mares confirms her premonitions and fears. It also provides an element of supernatural intensity.

Perhaps because of its tragic Greek pattern, *Riders to the Sea* has a mythic force. The sense of destiny that Maurya feels is built into her life. Her sense of resignation and deep faith help her grow in our imagination and give her a heroic dimension. Synge's approach to realism is much different from Ibsen's or Chekhov's. It is more elemental, based on the spiritual life of the folk as expressed in the eloquence of their language.

Riders to the Sea in Performance

All of Synge's plays were written for the early Abbey Theatre, founded in 1904 by Lady Gregory and William Butler Yeats to perform Irish plays. At that time all performances were in Molesworth Hall, leased facilities. Synge's *In the Shadow of the Glen* was one of the first plays to be performed by the company, then known as the Irish National Theatre. The play opened in October 1903, coinciding with an Irish holiday, Samhain. Although controversial, it was a success. *Riders to the Sea* was Synge's second play, produced in Molesworth Hall in February 1904. At this time the Abbey had already attracted some excellent actors. Bartley was played by W. G. Fay, who was instrumental in shaping the Abbey. Sarah Allgood, destined to become a standard player in American films in the 1930s and 1940s, played Cathleen. The production was well received by press and public.

Riders to the Sea has usually been paired with other Irish plays in production. The Abbey Theatre Company still produces the play regularly and often takes it on tour. One of the most memorable tours was in 1957 when the Abbey brought the play to the tiny Theatre East in New York. Despite the theater's small size, the effect of the play, which had not been seen in an Abbey performance in the United States since 1911, was electrifying. The finest Irish actress of the age, Siobhan McKenna, played Maurya.

Riders to the Sea enjoys frequent production both by high school and college students. Its brevity and power make it a strong vehicle for amateur productions.

John Millington Synge (1871–1909)
RIDERS TO THE SEA

1904

Persons in the Play

MAURYA (*an old woman*)
BARTLEY (*her son*)
CATHLEEN (*her daughter*)
NORA (*a younger daughter*)
MEN *and* WOMEN

Scene: *An Island off the West of Ireland.*

(*Cottage kitchen, with nets, oilskins, spinning wheel, some new boards standing by the wall, etc. Cathleen, a girl of about twenty, finishes kneading cake, and puts it down in the pot-oven by the fire; then wipes* her hands, and begins to spin at the wheel. Nora, a young girl, puts her head in at the door.)

NORA (*in a low voice*): Where is she?

CATHLEEN: She's lying down, God help her, and may be sleeping, if she's able.

(*Nora comes in softly and takes a bundle from under her shawl.*)

CATHLEEN (*spinning the wheel rapidly*): What is it you have?

NORA: The young priest is after bringing them. It's a shirt and a plain stocking were got off a drowned man in Donegal.

(*Cathleen stops her wheel with a sudden movement, and leans out to listen.*)

NORA: We're to find out if it's Michael's they are, some time herself will be down looking by the sea.

CATHLEEN: How would they be Michael's, Nora. How would he go the length of that way to the far north?

NORA: The young priest says he's known the like of it. "If it's Michael's they are," says he, "you can tell herself he's got a clean burial by the grace of God, and if they're not his, let no one say a word about them, for she'll be getting her death," says he, "with crying and lamenting."

(*The door which Nora half closed is blown open by a gust of wind.*)

CATHLEEN (*looking out anxiously*): Did you ask him would he stop Bartley going this day with the horses to the Galway fair?

NORA: "I won't stop him," says he, "but let you not be afraid. Herself does be saying prayers half through the night, and the Almighty God won't leave her destitute," says he, "with no son living."

CATHLEEN: Is the sea bad by the white rocks, Nora?

NORA: Middling bad, God help us. There's a great roaring in the west, and it's worse it'll be getting when the tide's turned to the wind. (*She goes over to the table with the bundle.*) Shall I open it now?

CATHLEEN: Maybe she'd wake up on us, and come in before we'd done. (*Coming to the table.*) It's a long time we'll be, and the two of us crying.

NORA (*goes to the inner door and listens*): She's moving about on the bed. She'll be coming in a minute.

CATHLEEN: Give me the ladder, and I'll put them up in the turf-loft, the way she won't know of them at all, and maybe when the tide turns she'll be going down to see would he be floating from the east.

(*They put the ladder against the gable of the chimney;*

Cathleen goes up a few steps and hides the bundle in the turf-loft. Maurya comes from the inner room.)

MAURYA (*looking up at Cathleen and speaking querulously*): Isn't it turf enough you have for this day and evening?

CATHLEEN: There's a cake baking at the fire for a short space (*throwing down the turf*) and Bartley will want it when the tide turns if he goes to Connemara.

(*Nora picks up the turf and puts it round the pot-oven.*)

MAURYA (*sitting down on a stool at the fire*): He won't go this day with the wind rising from the south and west. He won't go this day, for the young priest will stop him surely.

NORA: He'll not stop him, mother, and I heard Eamon Simon and Stephen Pheety and Colum Shawn saying he would go.

MAURYA: Where is he itself?

NORA: He went down to see would there be another boat sailing in the week, and I'm thinking it won't be long till he's here now, for the tide's turning at the green head, and the hooker's tacking from the east.

CATHLEEN: I hear some one passing the big stones.

NORA (*looking out*): He's coming now, and he in a hurry.

BARTLEY (*comes in and looks round the room. Speaking sadly and quietly*): Where is the bit of new rope, Cathleen, was bought in Connemara?

CATHLEEN (*coming down*): Give it to him, Nora; it's on a nail by the white boards. I hung it up this morning, for the pig with the black feet was eating it.

NORA (*giving him a rope*): Is that it, Bartley?

MAURYA: You'd do right to leave that rope, Bartley, hanging by the boards. (*Bartley takes the rope.*) It will be wanting in this place, I'm telling you, if Michael is washed up tomorrow morning, or the next morning, or any morning in the week, for it's a deep grave we'll make him by the grace of God.

BARTLEY (*beginning to work with the rope*): I've no halter the way I can ride down on the mare, and I must go now quickly. This is the one boat going for two weeks or beyond it, and the fair will be a good fair for horses I heard them saying below.

MAURYA: It's a hard thing they'll be saying below if the body is washed up and there's no man in it to make the coffin, and I after giving a big price for the finest white boards you'd find in Connemara.

(*She looks round at the boards.*)

BARTLEY: How would it be washed up, and we after

looking each day for nine days, and a strong wind blowing a while back from the west and south?

MAURYA: If it wasn't found itself, that wind is raising the sea, and there was a star up against the moon, and it rising in the night. If it was a hundred horses, or a thousand horses you had itself, what is the price of a thousand horses against a son where there is one son only?

BARTLEY (*working at the halter, to Cathleen*): Let you go down each day, and see the sheep aren't jumping in on the rye, and if the jobber comes you can sell the pig with the black feet if there is a good price going.

MAURYA: How would the like of her get a good price for a pig?

BARTLEY (*to Cathleen*): If the west wind holds with the last bit of the moon let you and Nora get up weed enough for another cock for the kelp. It's hard set we'll be from this day with no one in it but one man to work.

MAURYA: It's hard set we'll be surely the day you're drownd'd with the rest. What way will I live and the girls with me, and I an old woman looking for the grave?

(*Bartley lays down the halter, takes off his old coat, and puts on a newer one of the same flannel.*)

BARTLEY (*to Nora*): Is she coming to the pier?

NORA (*looking out*): She's passing the green head and letting fall her sails.

BARTLEY (*getting his purse and tobacco*): I'll have half an hour to go down, and you'll see me coming again in two days, or in three days, or maybe in four days if the wind is bad.

MAURYA (*turning round to the fire, and putting her shawl over her head*): Isn't it a hard and cruel man won't hear a word from an old woman, and she holding him from the sea?

CATHLEEN: It's the life of a young man to be going on the sea, and who would listen to an old woman with one thing and she saying it over?

BARTLEY (*taking the halter*): I must go now quickly. I'll ride down on the red mare, and the gray pony 'll run behind me.... The blessing of God on you.

(*He goes out.*)

MAURYA (*crying out as he is in the door*): He's gone now, God spare us, and we'll not see him again. He's gone now, and when the black night is falling I'll have no son left me in the world.

CATHLEEN: Why wouldn't you give him your blessing and he looking round in the door? Isn't it sorrow enough is on every one in this house without your sending him out with an unlucky word behind him, and a hard word in his ear?

(*Maurya takes up the tongs and begins raking the fire aimlessly without looking round.*)

NORA (*turning toward her*): You're taking away the turf from the cake.

CATHLEEN (*crying out*): The Son of God forgive us, Nora, we're after forgetting his bit of bread.

(*She comes over to the fire.*)

NORA: And it's destroyed he'll be going till dark night, and he after eating nothing since the sun went up.

CATHLEEN (*turning the cake out of the oven*): It's destroyed he'll be, surely. There's no sense left on any person in a house where an old woman will be talking forever.

(*Maurya sways herself on her stool.*)

CATHLEEN (*cutting off some of the bread and rolling it in a cloth; to Maurya*): Let you go down now to the spring well and give him this and he passing. You'll see him then and the dark word will be broken, and you can say "God speed you," the way he'll be easy in his mind.

MAURYA (*taking the bread*): Will I be in it as soon as himself?

CATHLEEN: If you go now quickly.

MAURYA (*standing up unsteadily*): It's hard set I am to walk.

CATHLEEN (*looking at her anxiously*): Give her the stick, Nora, or maybe she'll slip on the big stones.

NORA: What stick?

CATHLEEN: The stick Michael brought from Connemara.

MAURYA (*taking a stick Nora gives her*): In the big world the old people do be leaving things after them for their sons and children, but in this place it is the young men do be leaving things behind for them that do be old.

(*She goes out slowly. Nora goes over to the ladder.*)

CATHLEEN: Wait, Nora, maybe she'd turn back quickly. She's that sorry, God help her, you wouldn't know the thing she'd do.

NORA: Is she gone round by the bush?

CATHLEEN (*looking out*): She's gone now. Throw it down quickly, for the Lord knows when she'll be out of it again.

NORA (*getting the bundle from the loft*): The young priest said he'd be passing tomorrow, and we might go down and speak to him below if it's Michael's they are surely.

CATHLEEN (*taking the bundle*): Did he say what way they were found?

NORA (*coming down*): "There were two men," says he, "and they rowing round with poteen before the cocks crowed, and the oar of one of them caught the body, and they passing the black cliffs of the north."

CATHLEEN (*trying to open the bundle*): Give me a knife, Nora, the string's perished with the salt water, and there's a black knot on it you wouldn't loosen in a week.

NORA (*giving her a knife*): I've heard tell it was a long way to Donegal.

CATHLEEN (*cutting the string*): It is surely. There was a man in here a while ago — the man sold us that knife — and he said if you set off walking from the rocks beyond, it would be seven days you'd be in Donegal.

NORA: And what time would a man take, and he floating?

(*Cathleen opens the bundle and takes out a bit of a stocking. They look at them eagerly.*)

CATHLEEN (*in a low voice*): The Lord spare us, Nora! isn't it a queer hard thing to say if it's his they are surely?

NORA: I'll get his shirt off the hook the way we can put the one flannel on the other. (*She looks through some clothes hanging in the corner.*) It's not with them, Cathleen, and where will it be?

CATHLEEN: I'm thinking Bartley put it on him in the morning, for his own shirt was heavy with the salt in it (*pointing to the corner*). There's a bit of a sleeve was of the same stuff. Give me that and it will do.

(*Nora brings it to her and they compare the flannel.*)

CATHLEEN: It's the same stuff, Nora; but if it is itself aren't there great rolls of it in the shops of Galway, and isn't it many another man may have a shirt of it as well as Michael himself?

NORA (*who has taken up the stocking and counted the stitches, crying out*): It's Michael, Cathleen, it's Michael; God spare his soul, and what will herself say when she hears this story, and Bartley on the sea?

CATHLEEN (*taking the stocking*): It's a plain stocking.

NORA: It's the second one of the third pair I knitted, and I put up three score stitches, and I dropped four of them.

CATHLEEN (*counts the stitches*): It's that number is in it. (*Crying out.*) Ah, Nora, isn't it a bitter thing to think of him floating that way to the far north, and no one to keen him but the black hags that do be flying on the sea?

NORA (*swinging herself round, and throwing out her arms on the clothes*): And isn't it a pitiful thing when there is nothing left of a man who was a great rower and fisher, but a bit of an old shirt and a plain stocking?

CATHLEEN (*after an instant*): Tell me is herself coming, Nora? I hear a little sound on the path.

NORA (*looking out*): She is, Cathleen. She's coming up to the door.

CATHLEEN: Put these things away before she'll come in. Maybe it's easier she'll be after giving her blessing to Bartley, and we won't let on we've heard anything the time he's on the sea.

NORA (*helping Cathleen to close the bundle*): We'll put them here in the corner.

(*They put them into a hole in the chimney corner. Cathleen goes back to the spinning wheel.*)

NORA: Will she see it was crying I was?

CATHLEEN: Keep your back to the door the way the light'll not be on you.

(*Nora sits down at the chimney corner, with her back to the door. Maurya comes in very slowly, without looking at the girls, and goes over to her stool at the other side of the fire. The cloth with the bread is still in her hand. The girls look at each other, and Nora points to the bundle of bread.*)

CATHLEEN (*after spinning for a moment*): You didn't give him his bit of bread?

(*Maurya begins to keen softly, without turning round.*)

CATHLEEN: Did you see him riding down?

(*Maurya goes on keening.*)

CATHLEEN (*a little impatiently*): God forgive you; isn't it a better thing to raise your voice and tell what you seen, than to be making lamentation for a thing that's done? Did you see Bartley, I'm saying to you.

MAURYA (*with a weak voice*): My heart's broken from this day.

CATHLEEN (*as before*): Did you see Bartley?

MAURYA: I seen the fearfulest thing.

CATHLEEN (*leaves her wheel and looks out*): God forgive you; he's riding the mare now over the green head, and the gray pony behind him.

MAURYA (*starts, so that her shawl falls back from her head and shows her white tossed hair. With a frightened voice*): The gray pony behind him.

CATHLEEN (*coming to the fire*): What is it ails you, at all?

MAURYA (*speaking very slowly*): I've seen the fearfulest thing any person has seen, since the day

Bride Dara seen the dead man with the child in his arms.

CATHLEEN AND NORA: Uah.

(*They crouch down in front of the old woman at the fire.*)

NORA: Tell us what it is you seen.

MAURYA: I went down to the spring well, and I stood there saying a prayer to myself. Then Bartley came along, and he riding on the red mare with the gray pony behind him. (*She puts up her hands, as if to hide something from her eyes.*) The Son of God spare us, Nora!

CATHLEEN: What is it you seen.

MAURYA: I seen Michael himself.

CATHLEEN (*speaking softly*): You did not, mother. It wasn't Michael you seen, for his body is after being found in the far north, and he's got a clean burial by the grace of God.

MAURYA (*a little defiantly*): I'm after seeing him this day, and he riding and galloping. Bartley came first on the red mare; and I tried to say "God speed you," but something choked the words in my throat. He went by quickly; and "the blessing of God on you," says he, and I could say nothing. I looked up then, and I crying, at the gray pony, and there was Michael upon it — with fine clothes on him, and new shoes on his feet.

CATHLEEN (*begins to keen*): It's destroyed we are from this day. It's destroyed, surely.

NORA: Didn't the young priest say the Almighty God wouldn't leave her destitute with no son living?

MAURYA (*in a low voice, but clearly*): It's little the like of him knows of the sea.... Bartley will be lost now, and let you call in Eamon and make me a good coffin out of the white boards, for I won't live after them. I've had a husband, and a husband's father, and six sons in this house — six fine men, though it was a hard birth I had with every one of them and they coming to the world — and some of them were found and some of them were not found, but they're gone now the lot of them.... There were Stephen, and Shawn, were lost in the great wind, and found after in the Bay of Gregory of the Golden Mouth, and carried up the two of them on the one plank, and in by that door.

(*She pauses for a moment, the girls start as if they heard something through the door that is half open behind them.*)

NORA (*in a whisper*): Did you hear that, Cathleen? Did you hear a noise in the northeast?

CATHLEEN (*in a whisper*): There's some one after crying out by the seashore.

MAURYA (*continues without hearing anything*): There was Sheamus and his father, and his own father again, were lost in a dark night, and not a stick or sign was seen of them when the sun went up. There was Patch after was drowned out of a curagh° that turned over. I was sitting here with Bartley, and he a baby, lying on my two knees, and I seen two women, and three women, and four women coming in, and they crossing themselves, and not saying a word. I looked out then, and there were men coming after them, and they holding a thing in the half of a red sail, and water dripping out of it — it was a dry day, Nora — and leaving a track to the door.

(*She pauses again with her hand stretched out toward the door. It opens softly and old women begin to come in, crossing themselves on the threshold, and kneeling down in front of the stage with red petticoats over their heads.*)

MAURYA (*half in a dream, to Cathleen*): Is it Patch or Michael, or what is it at all?

CATHLEEN: Michael is after being found in the far north, and when he is found there how could he be here in this place?

MAURYA: There does be a power of young men floating round in the sea, and what way would they know if it was Michael they had, or another man like him, for when a man is nine days in the sea, and the wind blowing, it's hard set his own mother would be to say what man was it.

CATHLEEN: It's Michael, God spare him, for they're after sending us a bit of his clothes from the far north.

(*She reaches out and hands Maurya the clothes that belonged to Michael. Maurya stands up slowly and takes them in her hands. Nora looks out.*)

NORA: They're carrying a thing among them and there's water dripping out of it and leaving a track by the big stones.

CATHLEEN (*in a whisper to the women who have come in*): Is it Bartley it is?

ONE OF THE WOMEN: It is surely, God rest his soul.

(*Two younger women come in and pull out the table. Then men carry in the body of Bartley, laid on a plank, with a bit of a sail over it, and lay it on the table.*)

CATHLEEN (*to the women, as they are doing so*): What way was he drowned?

ONE OF THE WOMEN: The gray pony knocked him into the sea, and he was washed out where there is a great surf on the white rocks.

---

curagh: A small boat with a hide- or tarpaulin-covered frame.

(*Maurya has gone over and knelt down at the head of the table. The women are keening softly and swaying themselves with a slow movement. Cathleen and Nora kneel at the other end of the table. The men kneel near the door.*)

MAURYA (*raising her head and speaking as if she did not see the people around her*): They're all gone now, and there isn't anything more the sea can do to me. . . . I'll have no call now to be up crying and praying when the wind breaks from the south, and you can hear the surf is in the east, and the surf is in the west, making a great stir with the two noises, and they hitting one on the other. I'll have no call now to be going down and getting Holy Water in the dark nights after Samhain,° and I won't care what way the sea is when the other women will be keening. (*To Nora.*) Give me the Holy Water, Nora, there's a small sup still on the dresser.

(*Nora gives it to her.*)

MAURYA (*drops Michael's clothes across Bartley's feet, and sprinkles the Holy Water over him*): It isn't that I haven't prayed for you, Bartley, to the Almighty God. It isn't that I haven't said prayers in the dark night till you wouldn't know what I'll be saying; but it's a great rest I'll have now, and it's time surely. It's a great rest I'll have now, and great sleeping in the long nights after Samhain, if it's only a bit of wet flour we do have to eat, and maybe a fish that would be stinking.

(*She kneels down again, crossing herself, and saying prayers under her breath.*)

CATHLEEN (*to an old man*): Maybe yourself and Eamon would make a coffin when the sun rises. We have fine white boards herself bought, God help her, thinking Michael would be found, and I have a new cake you can eat while you'll be working.

Samhain: Feast of All Saints, November 1.

THE OLD MAN (*looking at the boards*): Are there nails with them?

CATHLEEN: There are not, Colum; we didn't think of the nails.

ANOTHER MAN: It's a great wonder she wouldn't think of the nails, and all the coffins she's seen made already.

CATHLEEN: It's getting old she is, and broken.

(*Maurya stands up again very slowly and spreads out the pieces of Michael's clothes beside the body, sprinkling them with the last of the Holy Water.*)

NORA (*in a whisper to Cathleen*): She's quiet now and easy; but the day Michael was drowned you could hear her crying out from this to the spring well. It's fonder she was of Michael, and would any one have thought that?

CATHLEEN (*slowly and clearly*): An old woman will be soon tired with anything she will do, and isn't it nine days herself is after crying and keening, and making great sorrow in the house?

MAURYA (*puts the empty cup mouth downward on the table, and lays her hands together on Bartley's feet*): They're all together this time, and the end is come. May the Almighty God have mercy on Bartley's soul, and on Michael's soul, and on the souls of Sheamus and Patch, and Stephen and Shawn (*bending her head*); and may He have mercy on my soul, Nora, and on the soul of every one is left living in the world.

(*She pauses, and the keen rises a little more loudly from the women, then sinks away.*)

MAURYA (*continuing*): Michael has a clean burial in the far north, by the grace of the Almighty God. Bartley will have a fine coffin out of the white boards, and a deep grave surely. What more can we want than that? No man at all can be living forever, and we must be satisfied.

(*She kneels down again and the curtain falls slowly.*)

Susan Glaspell

Susan Glaspell (1876–1948) is an important figure in early twentieth-century American drama. Through her influence, serious theater began to thrive in an environment used to musicals, sentimental comedies, and fashionable revivals. She was born in Davenport, Iowa, to Irish immigrant parents and grew up writing. After graduating from Drake University, she took a job as a reporter and by 1901 had become a full-time writer. Her first novel, *The Glory of the Conquered: The Story of a Great Love,* published in 1909, earned her enough to spend a year in Paris. *The Visioning,* which followed in 1911, was set on an army base and presented a less sentimentalized world than did her first book. She published her first collection of stories, *Lifted Masks,* in 1912. Her best novel, *Fidelity,* was published in 1915, after she had returned to the United States.

In 1908 Glaspell first met her future husband, George Cram (Jig) Cook, a traveled intellectual and Harvard graduate who was teaching at Iowa University. After the initial meeting, Cook eventually married someone else, but five years later was divorced. Following Glaspell's return from Europe in 1913, they were reintroduced by mutual friends; they now felt that they had been fated for each other. They settled on Cape Cod and, with Mary Heaton Vorse, founded the Provincetown Players. The theater company became a highly influential platform for a number of important American writers, such as Djuna Barnes, Edna Ferber, and Edna St. Vincent Millay. Eugene O'Neill, a prominent member of the Provincetown Players, played roles in Glaspell's works, including *Trifles* (1916). Her earliest play — first produced in her living room then moved to the Provincetown Playhouse — was *Suppressed Desires* (1915), a spoof on the rage for using Freudian theories to explain everyday life. In a letter to the New York *Times* (February 13, 1920) she said that the play "is having fun with the people who went off their heads about psychoanalysis — went 'bugs' — when this subject reached the first circle in New York to know of it."

Glaspell's one-act plays, including *Close the Book* (1917), *A Woman's Honor* (1918), and *Tickless Time* (1919), were collected in 1920. Her first full-length play, *Bernice* (1919), centered on interpreting the character of a dead woman. Its success led to another full-length play, *The Verge* (1921), about a woman who tries to make a new reality around herself and begins with creating new kinds of plants. Some critics saw the protagonist as an admirable new woman; others saw her as neurotic. *The Inheritors* (1921), also a full-length drama, focuses on the third-generation inheritors of a Midwestern college who clash because one family has liberal views and one has conservative views. Her last play, winner of the Pulitzer Prize, was *Alison's House* (1930), based on the life of Emily Dickinson. The latter part of Glaspell's life was spent writing fiction, concentrating on four novels set in the Midwest about the struggles of women to maintain their ideals and values.

Jig Cook, a writer himself, and a partner in many of Glaspell's ventures, spent the last two years of his life living in Delphi, Greece, in the manner of the peasants living on Mount Parnassus near the temple of Apollo. He died in 1924, and when Glaspell returned to the United States she wrote a memoir of their life together called *The Road to the Temple*. In 1925 she broke with the Provincetown Players, who had moved in directions she did not approve of under the directorship of Eugene O'Neill. O'Neill tried to mollify Glaspell, but she never accepted his use of the theater company she and her husband had cofounded. When she died in 1948, she and O'Neill were essentially unreconciled.

TRIFLES

Trifles (1916) was apparently written as a companion piece for Eugene O'Neill's first produced play, the one-act *Bound East for Cardiff*. The two were put together to make a complete evening presentation. In one sense *Trifles* is a murder mystery, but in another it is a critique of the gender-rigid attitudes of the officials whose responsibility it is to investigate the death of John Wright. Its main character, Minnie Foster Wright, is never presented, only described as a sweet woman who loved to sing when she was young, but who married a man who slowly stifled her joy in living.

The setting of the play is a kitchen where the women, Mrs. Peters and Mrs. Hale, remain throughout the action. They examine the condition of the room and by extension, the condition of Minnie Foster Wright. The men, examining the crime scene, the upstairs bedroom, spend much of the time offstage. They feel that they are examining the important evidence; yet when they return with their findings, they are unable to understand what led to the death of John Wright, who to them seems quite a normal farmer.

The women, however, by examining the messy condition of the kitchen, the state of Minnie's preserves, and the quilt she was working on, begin to understand the motive behind Wright's murder. When they get to the dead body of the songbird Minnie had valued, they understand things in a way that the men cannot. The men observe that women are concerned with trifles, things of no importance. But the truth is that the women understand the fate of Minnie Foster Wright and John Wright in a way that would be almost impossible for the men, given their sense of what is significant and what is a trifle.

In many ways the play is a study of gender differences and the way men's expectations and their sense of reality can distort the truth and deform a woman's life. In 1917 Glaspell wrote a short story, using all the same material, called "A Jury of Her Peers," implying that the only peers of Minnie Foster Wright would be women like Mrs. Hale and Mrs. Peters. In 1917, however, women could not vote and in most states could not serve on juries.

Trifles in Performance

The original production included Eugene O'Neill among its cast members and received a positive response, but after Glaspell's death most of her work fell out of fashion. *Trifles* was neglected until the early 1960s, when feminist interest helped revive her plays. Teacher and writer Sylvan Barnet included the play in his drama anthology, helping to bring it to the attention of contemporary viewers. Now produced most often by school and college groups, the play enjoys considerable popularity.

Susan Glaspell (1882–1948)
Trifles

1916

Characters

GEORGE HENDERSON, *county attorney*
HENRY PETERS, *sheriff*
LEWIS HALE, *a neighboring farmer*
MRS. PETERS
MRS. HALE

Scene: *The kitchen in the now abandoned farmhouse of John Wright, a gloomy kitchen, and left without having been put in order — the walls covered with a faded wall paper. Down right is a door leading to the parlor. On the right wall above this door is a built-in kitchen cupboard with shelves in the upper portion and drawers below. In the rear wall at right, up two steps is a door opening onto stairs leading to the second floor. In the rear wall at left is a door to the shed and from there to the outside. Between these two doors is an old-fashioned black iron stove. Running along the left wall from the shed door is an old iron sink and sink shelf, in which is set a hand pump. Downstage of the sink is an uncurtained window. Near the window is an old wooden rocker. Center stage is an unpainted wooden kitchen table with straight chairs on either side. There is a small chair down right. Unwashed pans under the sink, a loaf of bread outside the breadbox, a dish towel on the table — other signs of incompleted work. At the rear the shed door opens and the Sheriff comes in followed by the County Attorney and Hale. The Sheriff and Hale are men in middle life, the County Attorney is a young man; all are much bundled up and go at once to the stove. They are followed by the two women — the Sheriff's wife, Mrs. Peters, first: she is a slight wiry woman, a thin nervous face. Mrs. Hale is larger and would ordinarily be called more comfortable looking, but she is disturbed now and looks fearfully about as she enters. The women have come in slowly, and stand close together near the door.*

COUNTY ATTORNEY (*at stove rubbing his hands*): This feels good. Come up to the fire, ladies.

MRS. PETERS (*after taking a step forward*): I'm not — cold.

SHERIFF (*unbuttoning his overcoat and stepping away from the stove to right of table as if to mark the beginning of official business*): Now, Mr. Hale, be-fore we move things about, you explain to Mr. Henderson just what you saw when you came here yesterday morning.

COUNTY ATTORNEY (*crossing down to left of the table*): By the way, has anything been moved? Are things just as you left them yesterday?

SHERIFF (*looking about*): It's just about the same. When it dropped below zero last night I thought I'd better send Frank out this morning to make a fire for us — (*sits right of center table*) no use getting pneumonia with a big case on, but I told him not to touch anything except the stove — and you know Frank.

COUNTY ATTORNEY: Somebody should have been left here yesterday.

SHERIFF: Oh — yesterday. When I had to send Frank to Morris Center for that man who went crazy — I want you to know I had my hands full yesterday. I knew you could get back from Omaha by today and as long as I went over everything here my-self ——

COUNTY ATTORNEY: Well, Mr. Hale, tell just what happened when you came here yesterday morning.

HALE (*crossing down to above table*): Harry and I had started to town with a load of potatoes. We came along the road from my place and as I got here I said, "I'm going to see if I can't get John Wright to go in with me on a party telephone." I spoke to Wright about it once before and he put me off, saying folks talked too much anyway, and all he asked was peace and quiet — I guess you know about how much he talked himself; but I thought maybe if I went to the house and talked about it before his wife, though I said to Harry that I didn't know as what his wife wanted made much difference to John ——

COUNTY ATTORNEY: Let's talk about that later, Mr. Hale. I do want to talk about that, but tell now just what happened when you got to the house.

HALE: I didn't hear or see anything; I knocked at the door, and still it was all quiet inside. I knew they must be up, it was past eight o'clock. So I knocked again, and I thought I heard someone say, "Come in." I wasn't sure, I'm not sure yet, but I opened the door — this door (*indicating the door by which the two women are still standing*) and there in that rocker — (*pointing to it*) sat Mrs. Wright. (*They all look at the rocker down left.*)

COUNTY ATTORNEY: What — was she doing?

HALE: She was rockin' back and forth. She had her apron in her hand and was kind of — pleating it.

COUNTY ATTORNEY: And how did she — look?

HALE: Well, she looked queer.

COUNTY ATTORNEY: How do you mean — queer?

HALE: Well, as if she didn't know what she was going to do next. And kind of done up.

COUNTY ATTORNEY (*takes out notebook and pencil and sits left of center table*): How did she seem to feel about your coming?

HALE: Why, I don't think she minded — one way or other. She didn't pay much attention. I said, "How do, Mrs. Wright, it's cold, ain't it?" And she said, "Is it?" — and went on kind of pleating at her apron. Well, I was surprised: she didn't ask me to come up to the stove, or to set down, but just sat there, not even looking at me, so I said, "I want to see John." And then she — laughed. I guess you would call it a laugh. I thought of Harry and the team outside, so I said a little sharp: "Can't I see John?" "No," she says, kind o' dull like. "Ain't he home?" says I. "Yes," says she, "he's home." "Then why can't I see him?" I asked her, out of patience. "'Cause he's dead," says she. "*Dead?*" says I. She just nodded her head, not getting a bit excited, but rockin' back and forth. "Why — where is he?" says I, not knowing what to say. She just pointed upstairs — like that. (*Himself pointing to the room above.*) I started for the stairs, with the idea of going up there. I walked from there to here — then I says, "Why, what did he die of?" "He died of a rope round his neck," says she, and just went on pleatin' at her apron. Well, I went out and called Harry. I thought I might — need help. We went upstairs and there he was lyin'———

COUNTY ATTORNEY: I think I'd rather have you go into that upstairs, where you can point it all out. Just go on now with the rest of the story.

HALE: Well, my first thought was to get that rope off. It looked . . . (*stops: his face twitches*) . . . but Harry, he went up to him, and he said, "No, he's dead all right, and we'd better not touch anything." So we went right back downstairs. She was still sitting that same way. "Has anybody been notified?" I asked. "No," says she, unconcerned. "Who did this, Mrs. Wright?" said Harry. He said it businesslike — and she stopped pleatin' of her apron. "I don't know," she says. "You don't *know?*" says Harry. "No," says she. "Weren't you sleepin' in the bed with him?" says Harry. "Yes," says she, "but I was on the inside." "Somebody

slipped a rope round his head and strangled him and you didn't wake up?" says Harry. "I didn't wake up," she said after him. We must 'a' looked as if we didn't see how that could be, for after a minute she said, "I sleep sound." Harry was going to ask her more questions but I said maybe we ought to let her tell her story first to the coroner, or the sheriff, so Harry went fast as he could to Rivers' place, where there's a telephone.

COUNTY ATTORNEY: And what did Mrs. Wright do when she knew that you had gone for the coroner?

HALE: She moved from the rocker to that chair over there (*pointing to a small chair in the down right corner*) and just sat there with her hands held together and looking down. I got a feeling that I ought to make some conversation, so I said I had come in to see if John wanted to put in a telephone, and at that she started to laugh, and then she stopped and looked at me — scared. (*The County Attorney, who has had his notebook out, makes a note.*) I dunno, maybe it wasn't scared. I wouldn't like to say it was. Soon Harry got back, and then Dr. Lloyd came and you, Mr. Peters, and so I guess that's all I know that you don't.

COUNTY ATTORNEY (*rising and looking around*): I guess we'll go upstairs first — and then out to the barn and around there. (*To the Sheriff.*) You're convinced that there was nothing important here — nothing that would point to any motive?

SHERIFF: Nothing here but kitchen things. (*The County Attorney, after again looking around the kitchen, opens the door of a cupboard closet in right wall. He brings a small chair from right — gets on it and looks on a shelf. Pulls his hand away, sticky.*)

COUNTY ATTORNEY: Here's a nice mess. (*The women draw nearer up to center.*)

MRS. PETERS (*to the other woman*): Oh, her fruit; it did freeze. (*To the Lawyer.*) She worried about that when it turned so cold. She said the fire'd go out and her jars would break.

SHERIFF (*rises*): Well, can you beat the woman! Held for murder and worryin' about her preserves.

COUNTY ATTORNEY (*getting down from chair*): I guess before we're through she may have something more serious than preserves to worry about. (*Crosses down right center.*)

HALE: Well, women are used to worrying over trifles. (*The two women move a little closer together.*)

COUNTY ATTORNEY (*with the gallantry of a young politician*): And yet, for all their worries, what would we do without the ladies? (*The women do not unbend. He goes below the center table to the sink, takes a dipperful of water from the pail, and *pouring it into a basin, washes his hands. While he is doing this the Sheriff and Hale cross to cupboard, which they inspect. The County Attorney starts to wipe his hands on the roller towel, turns it for a cleaner place.) Dirty towels! (Kicks his foot against the pans under the sink.) Not much of a housekeeper, would you say, ladies?*

MRS. HALE (*stiffly*): There's a great deal of work to be done on a farm.

COUNTY ATTORNEY: To be sure. And yet (*with a little bow to her*) I know there are some Dickson County farmhouses which do not have such roller towels. (*He gives it a pull to expose its full-length again.*)

MRS. HALE: Those towels get dirty awful quick. Men's hands aren't always clean as they might be.

COUNTY ATTORNEY: Ah, loyal to your sex, I see. But you and Mrs. Wright were neighbors. I suppose you were friends, too.

MRS. HALE (*shaking her head*): I've not seen much of her of late years. I've not been in this house — it's more than a year.

COUNTY ATTORNEY (*crossing to women up center*): And why was that? You didn't like her?

MRS. HALE: I liked her all well enough. Farmer's wives have their hands full, Mr. Henderson. And then ——

COUNTY ATTORNEY: Yes —— ?

MRS. HALE (*looking about*): It never seemed a very cheerful place.

COUNTY ATTORNEY: No — it's not cheerful. I shouldn't say she had the homemaking instinct.

MRS. HALE: Well, I don't know as Wright had, either.

COUNTY ATTORNEY: You mean that they didn't get on very well?

MRS. HALE: No, I don't mean anything. But I don't think a place'd be any cheerfuller for John Wright's being in it.

COUNTY ATTORNEY: I'd like to talk more of that a little later. I want to get the lay of things upstairs now. (*He goes past the women to up right where the steps lead to a stair door.*)

SHERIFF: I suppose anything Mrs. Peters does'll be all right. She was to take in some clothes for her, you know, and a few little things. We left in such a hurry yesterday.

COUNTY ATTORNEY: Yes, but I would like to see what you take, Mrs. Peters, and keep an eye out for anything that might be of use to us.

MRS. PETERS: Yes, Mr. Henderson. (*The men leave by up right door to stairs. The women listen to the men's steps on the stairs, then look about the kitchen.*)

MRS. HALE (*crossing left to sink*): I'd hate to have men coming into my kitchen, snooping around and criticizing. (*She arranges the pans under sink which the lawyer had shoved out of place.*)

MRS. PETERS: Of course it's no more than their duty. (*Crosses to cupboard up right.*)

MRS. HALE: Duty's all right, but I guess that deputy sheriff that came out to make the fire might have got a little of this on. (*Gives the roller towel a pull.*) Wish I'd though of that sooner. Seems mean to talk about her for not having things slicked up when she had to come away in such a hurry. (*Crosses right to Mrs. Peters at cupboard.*)

MRS. PETERS (*who has been looking through cupboard, lifts one end of towel that covers a pan*): She had bread set. (*Stands still.*)

MRS. HALE (*eyes fixed on a loaf of bread beside the breadbox, which is on a low shelf of the cupboard*): She was going to put this in there. (*Picks up loaf, abruptly drops it. In a manner of returning to familiar things.*) It's a shame about her fruit. I wonder if it's all gone. (*Gets up on chair and looks.*) I think there's some here that's all right, Mrs. Peters. Yes — here; (*holding it toward the window*) this is cherries, too. (*Looking again.*) I declare I believe that's the only one. (*Gets down, jar in hand. Goes to the sink and wipes it off on the outside.*) She'll feel awful bad after all her hard work in the hot weather. I remember the afternoon I put up my cherries last summer. (*She puts the jar on the big kitchen table, center of the room. With a sigh, is about to sit down in the rocking chair. Before she is seated realizes what chair it is; with a slow look at it, steps back. The chair which she has touched rocks back and forth. Mrs. Peters moves to center table and they both watch the chair rock for a moment or two.*)

MRS. PETERS (*shaking off the mood which the empty rocking chair has evoked. Now in a businesslike manner she speaks*): Well I must get those things from the front room closet. (*She goes to the door at the right but, after looking into the other room, steps back.*) You coming with me, Mrs. Hale? You could help me carry them. (*They go in the other room; reappear, Mrs. Peters carrying a dress, petticoat, and skirt, Mrs. Hale following with a pair of shoes.*) My, it's cold in there. (*She puts the clothes on the big table and hurries to the stove.*)

MRS. HALE (*right of center table examining the skirt*): Wright was close. I think maybe that's why she kept so much to herself. She didn't even belong to the Ladies' Aid. I suppose she felt she couldn't do her part, and then you don't enjoy things when you feel shabby. I heard she used to wear pretty clothes and be lively, when she was Minnie Foster, one of the town girls singing in the choir. But that — oh, that was thirty years ago. This all you want to take in?

MRS. PETERS: She said she wanted an apron. Funny thing to want, for there isn't much to get you dirty in jail, goodness knows. But I suppose just to make her feel more natural. (*Crosses to cupboard.*) She said they was in the top drawer in this cupboard. Yes, here. And then her little shawl that always hung behind the door. (*Opens stair door and looks.*) Yes, here it is. (*Quickly shuts door leading upstairs.*)

MRS. HALE (*abruptly moving toward her*): Mrs. Peters?

MRS. PETERS: Yes, Mrs. Hale? (*At up right door.*)

MRS. HALE: Do you think she did it?

MRS. PETERS (*in a frightened voice*): Oh, I don't know.

MRS. HALE: Well, I don't think she did. Asking for an apron and her little shawl. Worrying about her fruit.

MRS. PETERS (*starts to speak, glances up, where footsteps are heard in the room above. In a low voice*): Mr. Peters says it looks bad for her. Mr. Henderson is awful sarcastic in a speech and he'll make fun of her sayin' she didn't wake up.

MRS. HALE: Well, I guess John Wright didn't wake when they was slipping that rope under his neck.

MRS. PETERS (*crossing slowly to table and placing shawl and apron on table with other clothing*): No, it's strange. It must have been done awful crafty and still. They say it was such a — funny way to kill a man, rigging it all up like that.

MRS. HALE (*crossing to left of Mrs. Peters at table*): That's just what Mr. Hale said. There was a gun in the house. He says that's what he can't understand.

MRS. PETERS: Mr. Henderson said coming out that what was needed for the case was a motive: something to show anger, or — sudden feeling.

MRS. HALE (*who is standing by the table*): Well, I don't see any signs of anger around here. (*She puts her hand on the dish towel, which lies on the table, stands looking down at table, one-half of which is clean, the other half messy.*) It's wiped to here. (*Makes a move as if to finish work, then turns and looks at loaf of bread outside the breadbox. Drops towel. In that voice of coming back to familiar things.*) Wonder how they are finding things upstairs. (*Crossing below table to down right.*) I hope she had it a little more red-up° up there. You know, it seems kind of *sneaking.* Locking her up in town and then coming out here and trying to get her own house to turn against her!

red-up: (slang) Ready for company.

MRS. PETERS: But, Mrs. Hale, the law is the law.

MRS. HALE: I s'pose 'tis. (*Unbuttoning her coat.*) Better loosen up your things, Mrs. Peters. You won't feel them when you go out. (*Mrs. Peters takes off her fur tippet, goes to hang it on chair back left of table, stands looking at the work basket on floor near down left window.*)

MRS. PETERS: She was piecing a quilt. (*She brings the large sewing basket to the center table and they look at the bright pieces, Mrs. Hale above the table and Mrs. Peters left of it.*)

MRS. HALE: It's a log cabin pattern. Pretty, isn't it? I wonder if she was goin' to quilt it or just knot it? (*Footsteps have been heard coming down the stairs. The Sheriff enters followed by Hale and the County Attorney.*)

SHERIFF: They wonder if she was going to quilt it or just knot it! (*The men laugh, the women look abashed.*)

COUNTY ATTORNEY (*rubbing his hands over the stove*): Frank's fire didn't do much up there, did it? Well, let's go out to the barn and get that cleared up. (*The men go outside by up left door.*)

MRS. HALE (*resentfully*): I don't know as there's anything so strange, our takin' up our time with little things while we're waiting for them to get the evidence. (*She sits in chair right of table smoothing out a block with decision.*) I don't see as it's anything to laugh about.

MRS. PETERS (*apologetically*): Of course they've got awful important things on their minds. (*Pulls up a chair and joins Mrs. Hale at the left of the table.*)

MRS. HALE (*examining another block*): Mrs. Peters, look at this one. Here, this is the one she was working on, and look at the sewing! All the rest of it has been so nice and even. And look at this! It's all over the place! Why, it looks as if she didn't know what she was about! (*After she has said this they look at each other, then start to glance back at the door. After an instant Mrs. Hale has pulled at a knot and ripped the sewing.*)

MRS. PETERS: Oh, what are you doing, Mrs. Hale?

MRS. HALE (*mildly*): Just pulling out a stitch or two that's not sewed very good. (*Threading a needle.*) Bad sewing always made me fidgety.

MRS. PETERS (*with a glance at the door, nervously*): I don't think we ought to touch things.

MRS. HALE: I'll just finish up this end. (*Suddenly stopping and leaning forward.*) Mrs. Peters?

MRS. PETERS: Yes, Mrs. Hale?

MRS. HALE: What do you suppose she was so nervous about?

MRS. PETERS: Oh — I don't know. I don't know as she was nervous. I sometimes sew awful queer when I'm just tired. (*Mrs. Hale starts to say something, looks at Mrs. Peters, then goes on sewing.*) Well, I must get these things wrapped up. They may be through sooner than we think. (*Putting apron and other things together.*) I wonder where I can find a piece of paper, and string. (*Rises.*)

MRS. HALE: In that cupboard, maybe.

MRS. PETERS (*crosses right looking in cupboard*): Why, here's a bird-cage. (*Holds it up.*) Did she have a bird, Mrs. Hale?

MRS. HALE: Why, I don't know whether she did or not — I've not been here for so long. There was a man around last year selling canaries cheap, but I don't know as she took one; maybe she did. She used to sing real pretty herself.

MRS. PETERS (*glancing around*): Seems funny to think of a bird here. But she must have had one, or why would she have a cage? I wonder what happened to it?

MRS. HALE: I s'pose maybe the cat got it.

MRS. PETERS: No, she didn't have a cat. She's got that feeling some people have about cats — being afraid of them. My cat got in her room and she was real upset and asked me to take it out.

MRS. HALE: My sister Bessie was like that. Queer, ain't it?

MRS. PETERS (*examining the cage*): Why, look at this door. It's broke. One hinge is pulled apart. (*Takes a step down to Mrs. Hale's right.*)

MRS. HALE (*looking too*): Looks as if someone must have been rough with it.

MRS. PETERS Why, yes. (*She brings the cage forward and puts it on the table.*)

MRS. HALE (*glancing toward up left door*): I wish if they're going to find any evidence they'd be about it. I don't like this place.

MRS. PETERS: But I'm awful glad you came with me, Mrs. Hale. It would be lonesome for me sitting here alone.

MRS. HALE: It would, wouldn't it? (*Dropping her sewing.*) But I tell you what I do wish, Mrs. Peters. I wish I had come over sometimes when *she* was here. I — (*looking around the room*) — wish I had.

MRS. PETERS: But of course you were awful busy, Mrs. Hale — your house and your children.

MRS. HALE (*rises and crosses left*): I could've come. I stayed away because it weren't cheerful — and that's why I ought to have come. I — (*looking out left window*) — I've never liked this place. Maybe it's because it's down in a hollow and you don't see the road. I dunno what it is, but it's a lonesome place and always was. I wish I had come over to see Minnie Foster sometimes. I can see now — (*Shakes her head.*)

MRS. PETERS (*left of table and above it*): Well, you mustn't reproach yourself, Mrs. Hale. Somehow we just don't see how it is with other folks until — something turns up.

MRS. HALE: Not having children makes less work — but it makes a quiet house, and Wright out to work all day, and no company when he did come in. (*Turning from window.*) Did you know John Wright, Mrs. Peters?

MRS. PETERS: Not to know him; I've seen him in town. They say he was a good man.

MRS. HALE: Yes — good; he didn't drink, and kept his word as well as most, I guess, and paid his debts. But he was a hard man, Mrs. Peters. Just to pass the time of day with him — (*Shivers.*) Like a raw wind that gets to the bone. (*Pauses, her eye falling on the cage.*) I should think she would 'a' wanted a bird. But what do you suppose went with it?

MRS. PETERS: I don't know, unless it got sick and died. (*She reaches over and swings the broken door, swings it again, both women watch it.*)

MRS. HALE: You weren't raised round here, were you? (*Mrs. Peters shakes her head.*) You didn't know — her?

MRS. PETERS: Not till they brought her yesterday.

MRS. HALE: She — come to think of it, she was kind of like a bird herself — real sweet and pretty, but kind of timid and — fluttery. How — she — did change. (*Silence: then as if struck by a happy thought and relieved to get back to everyday things. Crosses right above Mrs. Peters to cupboard, replaces small chair used to stand on to its original place down right.*) Tell you what, Mrs. Peters, why don't you take the quilt in with you? It might take up her mind.

MRS. PETERS: Why, I think that's a real nice idea, Mrs. Hale. There couldn't possibly be any objection to it could there? Now, just what would I take? I wonder if her patches are in here — and her things. (*They look in the sewing basket.*)

MRS. HALE (*crosses to right of table*): Here's some red. I expect this has got sewing things in it. (*Brings out a fancy box.*) What a pretty box. Looks like something somebody would give you. Maybe her scissors are in here. (*Opens box. Suddenly puts her hand to her nose.*) Why —— (*Mrs. Peters bends nearer, then turns her face away.*) There's something wrapped up in this piece of silk.

MRS. PETERS: Why, this isn't her scissors.

MRS. HALE (*lifting the silk*): Oh, Mrs. Peters — it's —— (*Mrs. Peters bends closer.*)

MRS. PETERS: It's the bird.

MRS. HALE: But, Mrs. Peters — look at it! Its neck! Look at its neck! It's all — other side to.

MRS. PETERS: Somebody — wrung — its — neck. (*Their eyes meet. A look of growing comprehen-*

sion, of horror. Steps are heard outside. Mrs. Hale slips box under quilt pieces, and sinks into her chair. Enter Sheriff and County Attorney. Mrs. Peters steps down left and stands looking out of window.)

COUNTY ATTORNEY (*as one turning from serious things to little pleasantries*): Well, ladies, have you decided whether she was going to quilt it or knot it? (*Crosses to center above table.*)

MRS. PETERS: We think she was going to — knot it. (*Sheriff crosses to right of stove, lifts stove lid, and glances at fire, then stands warming hands at stove.*)

COUNTY ATTORNEY: Well, that's interesting, I'm sure. (*Seeing the bird-cage.*) Has the bird flown?

MRS. HALE (*putting more quilt pieces over the box*): We think the — cat got it.

COUNTY ATTORNEY (*preoccupied*): Is there a cat? (*Mrs. Hale glances in a quick covert way at Mrs. Peters.*)

MRS. PETERS (*turning from window takes a step in*): Well, not *now*. They're superstitious, you know. They leave.

COUNTY ATTORNEY (*to Sheriff Peters, continuing an interrupted conversation*): No sign at all of anyone having come from the outside. Their own rope. Now let's go up again and go over it piece by piece. (*They start upstairs.*) It would have to have been someone who knew just the ——— (*Mrs. Peters sits down left of table. The two women sit there not looking at one another, but as if peering into something and at the same time holding back. When they talk now it is in the manner of feeling their way over strange ground, as if afraid of what they are saying, but as if they cannot help saying it.*)

MRS. HALE (*hesistatively and in hushed voice*): She liked the bird. She was going to bury it in that pretty box.

MRS. PETERS (*in a whisper*): When I was a girl — my kitten — there was a boy took a hatchet, and before my eyes — and before I could get there ——— (*Covers her face an instant.*) If they hadn't held me back I would have — (*catches herself, looks upstairs where steps are heard, falters weakly*) — hurt him.

MRS. HALE (*with a slow look around her*): I wonder how it would seem never to have had any children around. (*Pause.*) No, Wright wouldn't like the bird — a thing that sang. She used to sing. He killed that, too.

MRS. PETERS (*moving uneasily*): We don't know who killed the bird.

MRS. HALE: I knew John Wright.

MRS. PETERS: It was an awful thing was done in this house that night, Mrs. Hale. Killing a man while he slept, slipping a rope around his neck that choked the life out of him.

MRS. HALE: His neck. Choked the life out of him. (*Her hand goes out and rests on the bird-cage.*)

MRS. PETERS (*with rising voice*): We don't know who killed him. We don't *know*.

MRS. HALE (*her own feelings not interrupted*): If there'd been years and years of nothing, then a bird to sing to you, it would be awful — still, after the bird was still.

MRS. PETERS (*something within her speaking*): I know what stillness is. When we homesteaded in Dakota, and my first baby died — after he was two years old, and me with no other then ———

MRS. HALE (*moving*): How soon do you suppose they'll be through looking for the evidence?

MRS. PETERS: I know what stillness is. (*Pulling herself back.*) The law has got to punish crimes, Mrs. Hale.

MRS. HALE (*not as if answering that*): I wish you'd seen Minnie Foster when she wore a white dress with blue ribbons and stood up there in the choir and sang. (*A look around the room.*) Oh, I wish I'd come over here once in a while! That was a crime! That was a crime! Who's going to punish that?

MRS. PETERS (*looking upstairs*): We mustn't — take on.

MRS. HALE: I might have known she needed help! I know how things can be — for women. I tell you, it's queer, Mrs. Peters. We live close together and we live far apart. We all go through the same things — it's all just a different kind of the same thing. (*Brushes her eyes, noticing the jar of fruit, reaches out for it.*) If I was you I wouldn't tell her her fruit was gone. Tell her it *ain't*. Tell her it's all right. Take this in to prove it to her. She — she may never know whether it was broke or not.

MRS. PETERS (*takes the jar, looks about for something to wrap it in; takes petticoat from the clothes brought from the other room, very nervously begins winding this around the jar. In a false voice*): My, it's a good thing the men couldn't hear us. Wouldn't they just laugh! Getting all stirred up over a little thing like a — dead canary. As if they could have anything to do with — with — wouldn't they *laugh*! (*The men are heard coming downstairs.*)

MRS. HALE (*under her breath*): Maybe they would — maybe they wouldn't.

COUNTY ATTORNEY: No, Peters, it's all perfectly clear except a reason for doing it. But you know juries when it comes to women. If there was some definite thing. (*Crosses slowly to above table. Sheriff crosses down right. Mrs. Hale and Mrs. Peters remain seated at either side of table.*) Something to show — something to make a story about — a thing that would connect up with this strange way of doing it ——— (*The women's eyes meet for an instant. Enter Hale from outer door.*)

HALE (*remaining by door*): Well, I've got the team around. Pretty cold out there.

COUNTRY ATTORNEY: I'm going to stay awhile by myself. (*To the Sheriff.*) You can send Frank out for me, can't you? I want to go over everything. I'm not satisfied that we can't do better.

SHERIFF: Do you want to see what Mrs. Peters is going to take in? (*The Lawyer picks up the apron, laughs.*)

COUNTY ATTORNEY: Oh, I guess they're not very dangerous things the ladies have picked out. (*Moves a few things about, disturbing the quilt pieces which cover the box. Steps back.*) No, Mrs. Peters doesn't need supervising. For that matter a sheriff's wife is married to the law. Ever think of it that way, Mrs. Peters?

MRS. PETERS: Not — just that way.

SHERIFF (*chuckling*): Married to the law. (*Moves to down right door to the other room.*) I just want you to come in here a minute, George. We ought to take a look at these windows.

COUNTY ATTORNEY (*scoffingly*): Oh, windows!

SHERIFF: We'll be right out, Mr. Hale. (*Hale goes outside. The Sheriff follows the County Attorney into the room. Then Mrs. Hale rises, hands tight together, looking intensely at Mrs. Peters, whose eyes make a slow turn, finally meeting Mrs. Hale's. A moment Mrs. Hale holds her, then her own eyes point the way to where the box is concealed. Suddenly Mrs. Peters throws back quilt pieces and tries to put the box in the bag she is carrying. It is too big. She opens box, starts to take bird out, cannot touch it, goes to pieces, stands there helpless. Sound of a knob turning in the other room. Mrs. Hale snatches the box and puts it in the pocket of her big coat. Enter County Attorney and Sheriff, who remains down right.*)

COUNTY ATTORNEY (*crosses to up left door facetiously*): Well, Henry, at least we found out that she was not going to quilt it. She was going to — what is it you call it, ladies?

MRS. HALE (*standing center below table facing front, her hand against her pocket*): We call it — knot it, Mr. Henderson.

Luigi Pirandello

Luigi Pirandello (1867–1936) was an Italian short-story writer and novelist, a secondary school teacher, and finally a playwright. His life was complicated by business failures that wiped out his personal income and threw his wife into a psychological depression that Pirandello quite bluntly described as madness. Out of his acquaintance with madness — he remained with his wife for fourteen years after she lost touch with reality — Pirandello claimed to have developed much of his attitude toward the shifting surfaces of appearances.

Pirandello's short stories and novels show the consistent pattern of his plays: a deep examination of what we know to be real and a questioning of our confidence in our beliefs. His novel *Shoot* (1915) questions the surfaces of cinema reality, to which contemporary Italy had yielded with great enthusiasm. His relentless examination of the paradoxes of experience has given him a reputation for pessimism. He himself said, "I think of life as a very sad piece of buffoonery," and he insisted that people bear within them a deep need to deceive themselves "by creating a reality . . . which . . . is discovered to be vain and illusory."

As Pirandello was not a popular writer in Italy, much of his dramatic work was first performed abroad. But he did win the Nobel Prize for literature in 1934, an indication that his particular brand of modernism was indeed influential. At that time Pirandello was a member of the Fascist party in Italy, although his participation was limited primarily to his work in the state-supported Art Theater of Rome, which he founded.

Pirandello's influence in modern theater resulted from his experimentation with the concept of realism that dominated drama from the time of Strindberg and Ibsen. The concept of the imaginary "fourth wall" of the stage through which the audience observed the action of characters in their living rooms had become the norm in theater. Pirandello, however, questioned all thought of norms by bringing the very idea of reality under philosophical scrutiny. His questioning helped playwrights around the world expand their approaches to theater in the early part of the twentieth century. Pirandello was one of the first, and one of the best, experimentalists.

SIX CHARACTERS IN SEARCH OF AN AUTHOR

Pirandello's play is part of a trilogy: *Six Characters in Search of an Author* (1921); *Each in His Own Way* (1924); and *Tonight We Improvise* (1930). These plays all examine the impossibility of knowing reality. There is no objective truth to know, Pirandello tells us, and what we think of as reality is totally subjective, something that each of us maintains independently of other people and that none of us can communicate. We are, in other words, apart, sealed into our own limited world.

These ideas were hardly novel. Playwrights had dealt with them before, even during the Elizabethan age, at a time when — because of the Protestant Reformation — the absolute systems of reality promoted by the Roman Catholic church had crumbled. Pirandello's plays were also produced during a period — the 1920s — when his culture was uncertain, frightened, and still reeling in shock from the destruction of World War I. In this depressed time, Pirandello's audience saw in his work a reflection of their own dispirited, fearful selves.

In a sense, *Six Characters in Search of an Author* is about the relationship between art and life, and especially about the relationship between drama and life. The premise of the play is absurd. In the middle of a rehearsal of a Pirandello play, several characters appear and request that an author be present to cobble them into a play. The stage manager assumes that they are presenting themselves as actors to be in a play, but they explain that they are not actors. They are real characters. This implies a paradox that characters are independent of the actors who play them (we are used to the characters being only on paper). When they demand actors to represent them, we know that one limit of impossibility has been reached.

The characters who appear are, in a sense, types: a father, a mother, a stepdaughter, a son, two silent figures — the boy and the child — and, finally, a milliner, Madame Pace. They share the stage with the actors of the company who are rehearsing the Pirandello play *Mixing It Up*. The six characters have been abandoned by their creator, the author who has absconded, leaving them in search of a substitute. The stepdaughter, late in the play, surmises that their author abandoned them "in a fit of depression, of disgust for the ordinary theater as the public knows it and likes it."

Pirandello uses his characters and their situation to comment on the life of the theater in the 1920s, and he also uses them to begin a series of speculations on the relationship of a public to the actors they see in plays, the characters the actors play, and the authors who create them. To an extent, the relationship between an author and his or her characters always implies a metaphor for the relationship between a creator and all creation. It is tempting to think of Samuel Beckett years later in his *Waiting for Godot* imagining an "author" having abandoned his creations because they failed to satisfy him. The six characters — or creations — who invade the stage in Pirandello's play have a firm sense of themselves and their actions. They bring with them a story — as all characters in plays do — and they invite the manager to participate in their stories, just as characters invite audiences to become one with their narratives.

One of the more amusing scenes depicts the characters' reactions to seeing actors play their parts. Since they are "real" characters, they have the utmost authority in knowing how their parts should be played, and they end up laughing at the inept efforts of the actors in act II. When the manager disputes with them, wondering why they protest so vigorously, they explain that they want to make sure the truth is told. The truth. The concept seems so simple on the surface, but in the situation that Pirandello has conceived, it is loaded with complexities that the stage manager cannot fathom.

By the time the question of the truth has been raised, the manager has begun to get a sense of the poignancy of the story that these characters have to tell. He has also begun to see that he must let them continue to tell their story — except that they are not telling it, they are living it. When the climax of their story is reached in the last moments of the play, the line between what is acted and what is lived onstage has become almost completely blurred. When the play ends, it is difficult to know what has truly occurred and what has truly been acted out.

Six Characters in Search of an Author has endured because it still rings true in its examination of the relationship between art and life, illusion and reality. The very word *illusion* is rejected by the characters — as characters they are part of the illusion of reality. They reject the thought that they are literature, asserting, "This is Life, this is passion!"

Six Characters in Search of an Author in Performance

The 1916 Italian production of *Six Characters in Search of an Author* established Pirandello as a dramatist of major importance. The first London production was in the Kingsway Theatre in March 1922. The reviews were positive, and the audiences, although at times puzzled, were responsive to what the *Christian Science Monitor* called "one of the freshest and most original productions seen for a long time." The first production in New York was directed by Brock Pemberton at the Princess Theater in October 1922 with the distinguished American actress Florence Eldridge as the stepdaughter. One newspaper critic said,

"Pirandello turns a powerful microscope on the dramatist's mental workshop — the modus operandi of play production — and after having destroyed our illusion, like a prestidigitator who shows us how a trick is done, expects us to believe in him."

Pirandello directed the play in Italian in London in 1925, and despite the audience's general inability to understand the language, the New Oxford Theatre was filled for every night of its run. He brought the company to the United States after the British censor determined that the play was "unsuitable for English audiences" and closed the play in London. It was not officially licensed for performance in England again until 1928.

Revivals of the play have been numerous. Three productions in New York in the 1930s preceded revivals in 1948 and 1955. London saw productions in February 1932 and November 1950. By the 1930s audience confusion had simmered down, and in 1932 one London critic declared, "Repetition cannot dull the brilliance of the play's attack on theatrical shams." Sir Ralph Richardson performed in London's West End in 1963. In 1955, Tyrone Guthrie's Phoenix Theater used a translation and adaptation by Guthrie and Michael Wager. The production was not successful, although critics liked the translation. Robert Brustein received extraordinary praise for his American Repertory Theatre (ART) production in 1985. Instead of having the six characters interrupt a Pirandello play, they interrupt the rehearsal of a Molière play, *Sganarelle,* which has roots in Italian *commedia dell'arte,* and which had been a highly successful ART production. This self-reference — in Pirandellian fashion — helped to blur the line between the realities on and off the stage. Boston critic Kevin Kelly said of the performance, "Brustein immediately links the paradox in Pirandello's theme about reality in illusion / illusion in reality to . . . the pragmatic fantasy of theater itself."

Luigi Pirandello (1867–1936)

SIX CHARACTERS IN SEARCH OF AN AUTHOR   1921

A COMEDY IN THE MAKING

TRANSLATED BY EDWARD STORER

Characters of the Comedy in the Making

THE FATHER	THE BOY ⎫
THE MOTHER	THE CHILD ⎬ *do not speak*
THE STEPDAUGHTER	MADAME PACE
THE SON	

Actors of the Company

THE MANAGER	L'INGÉNUE
LEADING LADY	JUVENILE LEAD
LEADING MAN	OTHER ACTORS
SECOND LADY LEAD	AND ACTRESSES

PROPERTY MAN   MANAGER'S SECRETARY
PROMPTER   DOOR-KEEPER
MACHINIST   SCENE SHIFTERS

Scene: *Daytime. The stage of a theater.*

(**N.B.:** *The Comedy is without acts or scenes. The performance is interrupted once, without the curtain being lowered, when the Manager and the chief characters withdraw to arrange a scenario. A second interruption of the action takes place when, by mistake, the stage hands let the curtain down.*)

ACT I

(*The spectators will find the curtain raised and the stage as it usually is during the daytime. It will be half dark, and empty, so that from the beginning the public may have the impression of an impromptu performance.*)

(*Prompter's box and a small table and chair for the Manager.*)

(*Two other small tables and several chairs scattered about as during rehearsals.*)

(*The Actors and Actresses of the company enter from the back of the stage: first one, then another, then two together; nine or ten in all. They are about to rehearse a Pirandello play:* Mixing It Up. *Some of the company move off toward their dressing rooms. The Prompter, who has the "book" under his arm, is waiting for the Manager in order to begin the rehearsal.*)

(*The Actors and Actresses, some standing, some sitting, chat and smoke. One perhaps reads a paper; another cons his part.*)

(*Finally, the Manager enters and goes to the table prepared for him. His Secretary brings him his mail, through which he glances. The Prompter takes his seat, turns on a light, and opens the "book."*)

THE MANAGER (*throwing a letter down on the table*): I can't see. (*To Property Man.*) Let's have a little light, please!

PROPERTY MAN: Yes, sir, yes, at once. (*A light comes down on to the stage.*)

THE MANAGER (*clapping his hands*): Come along! Come along! Second act of "Mixing It Up." (*Sits down.*)

(*The Actors and Actresses go from the front of the stage to the wings, all except the three who are to begin the rehearsal.*)

THE PROMPTER (*reading the "book"*): "Leo Gala's house. A curious room serving as dining-room and study."

THE MANAGER (*to Property Man*): Fix up the old red room.

PROPERTY MAN (*noting it down*): Red set. All right!

THE PROMPTER (*continuing to read from the "book"*): "Table already laid and writing desk with books and papers. Bookshelves. Exit rear to Leo's bedroom. Exit left to kitchen. Principal exit to right."

THE MANAGER (*energetically*): Well, you understand: The principal exit over there; here, the kitchen. (*Turning to actor who is to play the part of Socrates.*) You make your entrances and exits here. (*To Property Man.*) The baize doors at the rear, and curtains.

PROPERTY MAN (*noting it down*): Right!

PROMPTER (*reading as before*): "When the curtain rises, Leo Gala, dressed in cook's cap and apron, is busy beating an egg in a cup. Philip, also dressed as a cook, is beating another egg. Guidi Venanzi is seated and listening."

LEADING MAN (*to Manager*): Excuse me, but must I absolutely wear a cook's cap?

THE MANAGER (*annoyed*): I imagine so. It says so there anyway. (*Pointing to the "book."*)

LEADING MAN: But it's ridiculous!

THE MANAGER (*jumping up in a rage*): Ridiculous? Ridiculous? Is it my fault if France won't send us any more good comedies, and we are reduced to putting on Pirandello's works, where nobody understands anything, and where the author plays the fool with us all? (*The Actors grin. The Manager goes to Leading Man and shouts.*) Yes sir, you put on the cook's cap and beat eggs. Do you suppose that with all this egg-beating business you are on an ordinary stage? Get that out of your head. You represent the shell of the eggs you are beating! (*Laughter and comments among the Actors.*) Silence! and listen to my explanations, please! (*To Leading Man.*) "The empty form of reason without the fullness of instinct, which is blind." — You stand for reason, your wife is instinct. It's a mixing up of the parts, according to which you who act your own part become the puppet of yourself. Do you understand?

LEADING MAN: I'm hanged if I do.

THE MANAGER: Neither do I. But let's get on with it. It's sure to be a glorious failure anyway. (*Confidentially.*) But I say, please face three-quarters. Otherwise, what with the abstruseness of the dialogue, and the public that won't be able to hear you, the whole thing will go to hell. Come on! come on!

PROMPTER: Pardon sir, may I get into my box? There's a bit of a draft.

THE MANAGER: Yes, yes, of course!

(*At this point, the Door-Keeper has entered from the*

stage door and advances toward the Manager's table, taking off his braided cap. During this maneuver, the Six Characters enter, and stop by the door at back of stage, so that when the Door-Keeper is about to announce their coming to the Manager, they are already on the stage. A tenuous light surrounds them, almost as if irradiated by them — the faint breath of their fantastic reality.)

(This light will disappear when they come forward toward the actors. They preserve, however, something of the dream lightness in which they seem almost suspended; but this does not detract from the essential reality of their forms and expressions.)

(He who is known as the Father is a man of about 50: hair, reddish in color, thin at the temples; he is not bald, however, thick mustaches, falling over his still fresh mouth, which often opens in an empty and uncertain smile. He is fattish, pale; with an especially wide forehead. He has blue, oval-shaped eyes, very clear and piercing. Wears light trousers and a dark jacket. He is alternatively mellifluous and violent in his manner.)

(The Mother seems crushed and terrified as if by an intolerable weight of shame and abasement. She is dressed in modest black and wears a thick widow's veil of crepe. When she lifts this, she reveals a waxlike face. She always keeps her eyes downcast.)

(The Stepdaughter is dashing, almost impudent, beautiful. She wears mourning too, but with great elegance. She shows contempt for the timid half-frightened manner of the wretched Boy (14 years old, and also dressed in black); on the other hand, she displays a lively tenderness for her little sister, the Child (about four), who is dressed in white, with a black silk sash at the waist.)

(The Son (22) is tall, severe in his attitude of contempt for the Father, supercilious and indifferent to the Mother. He looks as if he had come on the stage against his will.)

DOOR-KEEPER *(cap in hand)*: Excuse me, sir . . .

THE MANAGER *(rudely)*: Eh? What is it?

DOOR-KEEPER *(timidly)*: These people are asking for you, sir.

THE MANAGER *(furious)*: I am rehearsing, and you know perfectly well no one's allowed to come in during rehearsals! *(Turning to the Characters.)* Who are you, please? What do you want?

THE FATHER *(coming forward a little, followed by the others who seem embarrassed)*: As a matter of fact . . . we have come here in search of an author . . .

THE MANAGER *(half angry, half amazed)*: An author? What author?

THE FATHER: Any author, sir.

THE MANAGER: But there's no author here. We are not rehearsing a new piece.

THE STEPDAUGHTER *(vivaciously)*: So much the better, so much the better! We can be your new piece.

AN ACTOR *(coming forward from the others)*: Oh, do you hear that?

THE FATHER *(to Stepdaughter)*: Yes, but if the author isn't here . . . *(To Manager.)* unless you would be willing . . .

THE MANAGER: You are trying to be funny.

THE FATHER: No, for Heaven's sake, what are you saying? We bring you a drama, sir.

THE STEPDAUGHTER: We may be your fortune.

THE MANAGER: Will you oblige me by going away? We haven't time to waste with mad people.

THE FATHER *(mellifluously)*: Oh sir, you know well that life is full of infinite absurdities, which, strangely enough, do not even need to appear plausible, since they are true.

THE MANAGER: What the devil is he talking about?

THE FATHER: I say that to reverse the ordinary process may well be considered a madness: that is, to create credible situations, in order that they may appear true. But permit me to observe that if this be madness, it is the sole *raison d'être*° of your profession, gentlemen. *(The Actors look hurt and perplexed.)*

THE MANAGER *(getting up and looking at him)*: So our profession seems to you one worthy of madmen then?

THE FATHER: Well, to make seem true that which isn't true . . . without any need . . . for a joke as it were . . . Isn't that your mission, gentlemen: to give life to fantastic characters on the stage?

THE MANAGER *(interpreting the rising anger of the Company)*: But I would beg you to believe, my dear sir, that the profession of the comedian is a noble one. If today, as things go, the playwrights give us stupid comedies to play and puppets to represent instead of men, remember we are proud to have given life to immortal works here on these very boards! *(The Actors, satisfied, applaud their Manager.)*

THE FATHER *(interrupting furiously)*: Exactly, perfectly, to living beings more alive than those who breathe and wear clothes: beings less real perhaps, but truer! I agree with you entirely. *(The Actors look at one another in amazement.)*

THE MANAGER: But what do you mean? Before, you said . . .

THE FATHER: No, excuse me, I meant it for you, sir, who were crying out that you had no time to lose with madmen, while no one better than yourself knows that nature uses the instrument of human

raison d'être: French for "reason to exist."

fantasy in order to pursue her high creative purpose.

THE MANAGER: Very well, — but where does all this take us?

THE FATHER: Nowhere! It is merely to show you that one is born to life in many forms, in many shapes, as tree, or as stone, as water, as butterfly, or as woman. So one may also be born a character in a play.

THE MANAGER (*with feigned comic dismay*): So you and these other friends of yours have been born characters?

THE FATHER: Exactly, and alive as you see! (*Manager and Actors burst out laughing.*)

THE FATHER (*hurt*): I am sorry you laugh, because we carry in us a drama, as you can guess from this woman here veiled in black.

THE MANAGER (*losing patience at last and almost indignant*): Oh, chuck it! Get away please! Clear out of here! (*To Property Man.*) For Heaven's sake, turn them out!

THE FATHER (*resisting*): No, no, look here, we . . .

THE MANAGER (*roaring*): We come here to work, you know.

LEADING ACTOR: One cannot let oneself be made such a fool of.

THE FATHER (*determined, coming forward*): I marvel at your incredulity, gentlemen. Are you not accustomed to see the characters created by an author spring to life in yourselves and face each other? Just because there is no "book" (*pointing to the Prompter's box*) which contains us, you refuse to believe . . .

THE STEPDAUGHTER (*advances toward Manager, smiling and coquettish*): Believe me, we are really six most interesting characters, sir; sidetracked however.

THE FATHER: Yes, that is the word! (*To Manager all at once.*) In the sense, that is, that the author who created us alive no longer wished, or was no longer able, materially to put us into a work of art. And this was a real crime, sir, because he who has had the luck to be born a character can laugh even at death. He cannot die. The man, the writer, the instrument of the creation will die, but his creation does not die. And to live for ever, it does not need to have extraordinary gifts or to be able to work wonders. Who was Sancho Panza? Who was Don Abbondio?° Yet they live eternally because — live germs as they were — they had the fortune to find a fecundating matrix, a fantasy which could raise and nourish them: make them live for ever!

Sancho Panza . . . Don Abbondio: Memorable characters in novels: the squire in Cervantes's *Don Quixote* and the priest in Manzoni's *I Promessi Sposi* (*The Betrothed*), respectively.

THE MANAGER: That is quite all right. But what do you want here, all of you?

THE FATHER: We want to live.

THE MANAGER (*ironically*): For Eternity?

THE FATHER: No, sir, only for a moment . . . in you.

AN ACTOR: Just listen to him!

LEADING LADY: They want to live, in us . . . !

JUVENILE LEAD (*pointing to the Stepdaughter*): I've no objection, as far as that one is concerned!

THE FATHER: Look here! look here! The comedy has to be made. (*To the Manager.*) But if you and your actors are willing, we can soon concert it among ourselves.

THE MANAGER (*annoyed*): But what do you want to concert? We don't go in for concerts here. Here we play dramas and comedies!

THE FATHER: Exactly! That is just why we have come to you.

THE MANAGER: And where is the "book"?

THE FATHER: It is in us! (*The Actors laugh.*) The drama is in us, and we are the drama. We are impatient to play it. Our inner passion drives us on to this.

THE STEPDAUGHTER (*disdainful, alluring, treacherous full of impudence*): My passion, sir! Ah, if you only knew! My passion for him! (*Points to the Father and makes a pretense of embracing him. Then she breaks out into a loud laugh.*)

THE FATHER (*angrily*): Behave yourself! And please don't laugh in that fashion.

THE STEPDAUGHTER: With your permission, gentlemen, I, who am a two months orphan, will show you how I can dance and sing. (*Sings and then dances Prenez garde à Tchou-Tchin-Tchou.*)

Les chinois sont un peuple malin,
De Shangaî à Pékin,
Ils ont mis des écriteaux partout:
Prenez garde à Tchou-Tchin-Tchou.°

ACTORS AND ACTRESSES: Bravo! Well done! Tip-top!

THE MANAGER: Silence! This isn't a café concert, you know! (*Turning to the Father in consternation.*) Is she mad?

THE FATHER: Mad? No, she's worse than mad.

THE STEPDAUGHTER (*to Manager*): Worse? Worse? Listen! Stage this drama for us at once! Then you will see that at a certain moment I . . . when this little darling here. . . . (*Takes the Child by the hand and leads her to the Manager.*) Isn't she a dear?

Prenez . . . Tchou: This French popular song is an adaptation of "Chu-Chin-Chow," an old Broadway show tune. "The Chinese are a sly people; / From Shanghai to Peking, / They've stuck up warning signs: / Beware of Tchou-Tchin-Tchou." (The words are funnier in French because *chou* means "cabbage.")

(*Takes her up and kisses her.*) Darling! Darling! (*Puts her down again and adds feelingly.*) Well, when God suddenly takes this dear little child away from that poor mother there; and this imbecile here (*seizing hold of the Boy roughly and pushing him forward*) does the stupidest things, like the fool he is, you will see me run away. Yes, gentlemen, I shall be off. But the moment hasn't arrived yet. After what has taken place between him and me (*indicates the Father with a horrible wink*) I can't remain any longer in this society, to have to witness the anguish of this mother here for that fool. . . . (*Indicates the Son.*) Look at him! Look at him! See how indifferent, how frigid he is, because he is the legitimate son. He despises me, despises him (*pointing to the Boy*), despises this baby here; because . . . we are bastards. (*Goes to the Mother and embraces her.*) And he doesn't want to recognize her as his mother — she who is the common mother of us all. He looks down upon her as if she were only the mother of us three bastards. Wretch! (*She says all this very rapidly, excitedly. At the word "bastards" she raises her voice, and almost spits out the final "Wretch!"*)

THE MOTHER (*to the Manager, in anguish*): In the name of these two little children, I beg you. . . . (*She grows faint and is about to fall.*) Oh God!

THE FATHER (*coming forward to support her as do some of the Actors*): Quick, a chair, a chair for this poor widow!

THE ACTORS: Is it true? Has she really fainted?

THE MANAGER: Quick, a chair! Here!

(*One of the Actors brings a chair, the others proffer assistance. The Mother tries to prevent the Father from lifting the veil which covers her face.*)

THE FATHER: Look at her! Look at her!

THE MOTHER: No, no; stop it please!

THE FATHER (*raising her veil*): Let them see you!

THE MOTHER (*rising and covering her face with her hands, in desperation*): I beg you, sir, to prevent this man from carrying out his plan which is loathsome to me.

THE MANAGER (*dumbfounded*): I don't understand at all. What is the situation? (*To the Father.*) Is this lady your wife?

THE FATHER: Yes, gentlemen: my wife!

THE MANAGER: But how can she be a widow if you are alive? (*The Actors find relief for their astonishment in a loud laugh.*)

THE FATHER: Don't laugh! Don't laugh like that, for Heaven's sake. Her drama lies just here in this: she has had a lover, a man who ought to be here.

THE MOTHER (*with a cry*): No! No!

THE STEPDAUGHTER: Fortunately for her, he is dead.

Two months ago as I said. We are in mourning, as you see.

THE FATHER: He isn't here, you see, not because he is dead. He isn't here — look at her a moment and you will understand — because her drama isn't a drama of the love of two men for whom she was incapable of feeling anything except possibly a little gratitude — gratitude not for me but for the other. She isn't a woman, she is a mother, and her drama — powerful, sir, I assure you — lies, as a matter of fact, all in these four children she has had by two men.

THE MOTHER: I had them? Have you got the courage to say that I wanted them? (*To the Company.*) It was his doing. It was he who gave me that other man, who forced me to go away with him.

THE STEPDAUGHTER: It isn't true.

THE MOTHER (*startled*): Not true, isn't it?

THE STEPDAUGHTER: No, it isn't true, it just isn't true.

THE MOTHER: And what can you know about it?

THE STEPDAUGHTER: It isn't true. Don't believe it. (*To Manager.*) Do you know why she says so? For that fellow there. (*Indicates the Son.*) She tortures herself, destroys herself on account of the neglect of that son there, and she wants him to believe that if she abandoned him when he was only two years old, it was because he (*indicates the Father*) made her do so.

THE MOTHER (*vigorously*): He forced me to it, and I call God to witness. (*To the Manager.*) Ask him (*indicates Husband*) if it isn't true. Let him speak. You (*to Daughter*) are not in a position to know anything about it.

THE STEPDAUGHTER: I know you lived in peace and happiness with my father while he lived. Can you deny it?

THE MOTHER: No, I don't deny it. . . .

THE STEPDAUGHTER: He was always full of affection and kindness for you. (*To the Boy, angrily.*) It's true, isn't it? Tell them! Why don't you speak, you little fool?

THE MOTHER: Leave the poor boy alone. Why do you want to make me appear ungrateful, daughter? I don't want to offend your father. I have answered him that I didn't abandon my house and my son through any fault of mine, nor from any wilful passion.

THE FATHER: It is true. It was my doing.

LEADING MAN (*to the Company*): What a spectacle!

LEADING LADY: We are the audience this time.

JUVENILE LEAD: For once, in a way.

THE MANAGER (*beginning to get really interested*): Let's hear them out. Listen!

THE SON: Oh yes, you're going to hear a fine bit now. He will talk to you of the Demon of Experiment.

THE FATHER: You are a cynical imbecile. I've told you so already a hundred times. (*To the Manager.*) He tries to make fun of me on account of this expression which I have found to excuse myself with.

THE SON (*with disgust*): Yes, phrases! phrases!

THE FATHER: Phrases! Isn't everyone consoled when faced with a trouble or fact he doesn't understand, by a word, some simple word, which tells us nothing and yet calms us?

THE STEPDAUGHTER: Even in the case of remorse. In fact, especially then.

THE FATHER: Remorse? No, that isn't true. I've done more than use words to quiet the remorse in me.

THE STEPDAUGHTER: Yes, there was a bit of money too. Yes, yes, a bit of money. There were the hundred lire he was about to offer me in payment, gentlemen.... (*Sensation of horror among the Actors.*)

THE SON (*to the Stepdaughter*): This is vile.

THE STEPDAUGHTER: Vile? There they were in a pale blue envelope on a little mahogany table in the back of Madame Pace's shop. You know Madame Pace — one of those ladies who attract poor girls of good family into their ateliers, under the pretext of their selling *robes et manteaux.*°

THE SON: And he thinks he has bought the right to tyrannize over us all with those hundred lire he was going to pay; but which, fortunately — note this, gentlemen — he had no chance of paying.

THE STEPDAUGHTER: It was a near thing, though, you know! (*Laughs ironically.*)

THE MOTHER (*protesting*): Shame, my daughter, shame!

THE STEPDAUGHTER: Shame indeed! This is my revenge! I am dying to live that scene ... The room ... I see it ... Here is the window with the mantles exposed, there the divan, the looking-glass, a screen, there in front of the window the little mahogany table with the blue envelope containing one hundred fire. I see it. I see it. I could take hold of it.... But you, gentlemen, you ought to turn your backs now: I am almost nude, you know. But I don't blush: I leave that to him. (*Indicating Father.*)

THE MANAGER: I don't understand this at all.

THE FATHER: Naturally enough. I would ask you, sir, to exercise your authority a little here, and let me speak before you believe all she is trying to blame me with. Let me explain.

THE STEPDAUGHTER: Ah yes, explain it in your own way.

THE FATHER: But don't you see that the whole trouble lies here? In words, words. Each one of us has

robes et manteaux: French for "dresses and capes."

within him a whole world of things, each man of us his own special world. And how can we ever come to an understanding if I put in the words I utter the sense and value of things as I see them; while you who listen to me must inevitably translate them according to the conception of things each one of you has within himself. We think we understand each other, but we never really do. Look here! This woman (*indicating the Mother*) takes all my pity for her as a specially ferocious form of cruelty.

THE MOTHER: But you drove me away.

THE FATHER: Do you hear her? I drove her away! She believes I really sent her away.

THE MOTHER: You know how to talk, and I don't but, believe me, sir (*to Manager*), after he had married me ... who knows why? ... I was a poor insignificant woman....

THE FATHER: But, good Heavens! it was just for your humility that I married you. I loved this simplicity in you. (*He stops when he sees she makes signs to contradict him, opens his arms wide in sign of desperation, seeing how hopeless it is to make himself understood.*) You see she denies it. Her mental deafness, believe me, is phenomenal, the limit: (*touches his forehead*) deaf, deaf, mentally deaf! She has plenty of feeling. Oh yes, a good heart for the children; but the brain — deaf, to the point of desperation — !

THE STEPDAUGHTER: Yes, but ask him how his intelligence has helped us.

THE FATHER: If we could see all the evil that may spring from good, what should we do? (*At this point the Leading Lady, who is biting her lips with rage at seeing the Leading Man flirting with the Stepdaughter, comes forward and speaks to the Manager.*)

LEADING LADY: Excuse me, but are we going to rehearse today?

MANAGER: Of course, of course; but let's hear them out.

JUVENILE LEAD: This is something quite new.

L'INGÉNUE: Most interesting!

LEADING LADY: Yes, for the people who like that kind of thing. (*Casts a glance at Leading Man.*)

THE MANAGER (*to Father*): You must please explain yourself quite clearly. (*Sits down.*)

THE FATHER: Very well then: listen! I had in my service a poor man, a clerk, a secretary of mine, full of devotion, who became friends with her. (*Indicating the Mother.*) They understood one another, were kindred souls in fact, without, however, the least suspicion of any evil existing. They were incapable even of thinking of it.

THE STEPDAUGHTER: So he thought of it — for them!

THE FATHER: That's not true. I meant to do good to them — and to myself, I confess, at the same time. Things had come to the point that I could not say a word to either of them without their making a mute appeal, one to the other, with their eyes. I could see them silently asking each other how I was to be kept in countenance, how I was to be kept quiet. And this, believe me, was just about enough of itself to keep me in a constant rage, to exasperate me beyond measure.

THE MANAGER: And why didn't you send him away then — this secretary of yours?

THE FATHER: Precisely what I did, sir. And then I had to watch this poor woman drifting forlornly about the house like an animal without a master, like an animal one has taken in out of pity.

THE MOTHER: Ah yes . . . !

THE FATHER (*suddenly turning to the Mother*): It's true about the son anyway, isn't it?

THE MOTHER: He took my son away from me first of all.

THE FATHER: But not from cruelty. I did it so that he should grow up healthy and strong by living in the country.

THE STEPDAUGHTER (*pointing to him ironically*): As one can see.

THE FATHER (*quickly*): Is it my fault if he has grown up like this? I sent him to a wet nurse in the country, a peasant, as *she* did not seem to me strong enough, though she is of humble origin. That was, anyway, the reason I married her. Unpleasant all this may be, but how can it be helped? My mistake possibly, but there we are! All my life I have had these confounded aspirations towards a certain moral sanity. (*At this point the Stepdaughter bursts into a noisy laugh.*) Oh, stop it! Stop it! I can't stand it.

THE MANAGER: Yes, please stop it, for Heaven's sake.

THE STEPDAUGHTER: But imagine moral sanity from him, if you please — the client of certain ateliers like that of Madame Pace!

THE FATHER: Fool! That is the proof that I am a man! This seeming contradiction, gentlemen, is the strongest proof that I stand here a live man before you. Why, it is just for this very incongruity in my nature that I have had to suffer what I have. I could not live by the side of that woman (*indicating the Mother*) any longer; but not so much for the boredom she inspired me with as for the pity I felt for her.

THE MOTHER: And so he turned me out — .

THE FATHER: — well provided for! Yes, I sent her to that man, gentlemen . . . to let her go free of me.

THE MOTHER: And to free himself.

THE FATHER: Yes, I admit it. It was also a liberation for me. But great evil has come of it. I meant well

when I did it, and I did it more for her sake than mine. I swear it. (*Crosses his arms on his chest; then turns suddenly to the Mother.*) Did I ever lose sight of you until that other man carried you off to another town, like the angry fool he was? And on account of my pure interest in you . . . my pure interest, I repeat, that had no base motive in it . . . I watched with the tenderest concern the new family that grew up around her. She can bear witness to this. (*Points to the Stepdaughter.*)

THE STEPDAUGHTER: Oh yes, that's true enough. When I was a kiddie so so high, you know, with plaits over my shoulders and knickers longer than my skirts, I used to see him waiting outside the school for me to come out. He came to see how I was growing up.

THE FATHER: This is infamous, shameful!

THE STEPDAUGHTER: No. Why?

THE FATHER: Infamous! infamous! (*Then excitedly to Manager, explaining.*) After she (*indicating the Mother*) went away, my house seemed suddenly empty. She was my incubus, but she filled my house. I was like a dazed fly alone in the empty rooms. This boy here (*indicating the Son*) was educated away from home, and when he came back, he seemed to me to be no more mine. With no mother to stand between him and me, he grew up entirely for himself, on his own, apart, with no tie of intellect or affection binding him to me. And then — strange but true — I was driven, by curiosity at first and then by some tender sentiment, towards her family, which had come into being through my will. The thought of her began gradually to fill up the emptiness I felt all around me. I wanted to know if she were happy in living out the simple daily duties of life. I wanted to think of her as fortunate and happy because far away from the complicated torments of my spirit. And so, to have proof of this, I used to watch that child coming out of school.

THE STEPDAUGHTER: Yes, yes. True. He used to follow me in the street and smiled at me, waved his hand, like this. I would look at him with interest, wondering who he might be. I told my mother, who guessed at once. (*The Mother agrees with a nod.*) Then she didn't want to send me to school for some days; and when I finally went back, there he was again — looking so ridiculous — with a paper parcel in his hands. He came close to me, caressed me, and drew out a fine straw hat from the parcel, with a bouquet of flowers — all for me!

THE MANAGER: A bit discursive this, you know!

THE SON (*contemptuously*): Literature! Literature!

THE FATHER: Literature indeed! This is life, this is passion!

THE MANAGER: It may be, but it won't act.

THE FATHER: I agree. This is only the part leading up. I don't suggest this should be staged. She (*pointing to the Stepdaughter*), as you see, is no longer the flapper with plaits down her back —

THE STEPDAUGHTER: — and knickers showing below the skirt!

THE FATHER: The drama is coming now, sir; something new, complex, most interesting.

THE STEPDAUGHTER: As soon as my father died . . .

THE FATHER: — there was absolute misery for them. They came back here, unknown to me. Through her stupidity! (*Pointing to the Mother.*) It is true she can barely write her own name; but she could anyhow have got her daughter to write to me that they were in need . . .

THE MOTHER: And how was I to divine all this sentiment in him?

THE FATHER: That is exactly your mistake, never to have guessed any of my sentiments.

THE MOTHER: After so many years apart, and all that had happened . . .

THE FATHER: Was it my fault if that fellow carried you away? It happened quite suddenly, for after he had obtained some job or other, I could find no trace of them; and so, not unnaturally, my interest in them dwindled. But the drama culminated unforeseen and violent on their return, when I was impelled by my miserable flesh that still lives. . . . Ah! what misery, what wretchedness is that of the man who is alone and disdains debasing *liaisons!* Not old enough to do without women, and not young enough to go and look for one without shame. Misery? It's worse than misery; it's a horror; for no woman can any longer give him love; and when a man feels this. . . . One ought to do without, you say? Yes, yes, I know. Each of us when he appears before his fellows is clothed in a certain dignity. But every man knows what unconfessable things pass within the secrecy of his own heart. One gives way to the temptation, only to rise from it again, afterwards, with a great eagerness to reestablish one's dignity, as if it were a tombstone to place on the grave of one's shame, and a monument to hide and sign the memory of our weaknesses. Everybody's in the same case. Some folks haven't the courage to say certain things, that's all!

THE STEPDAUGHTER: All appear to have the courage to do them though.

THE FATHER: Yes, but in secret. Therefore, you want more courage to say these things. Let a man but speak these things out, and folks at once label him a cynic. But it isn't true. He is like all the others, better indeed, because he isn't afraid to reveal with the light of the intelligence the red shame of human bestiality on which most men close their eyes so as not to see it.

Woman — for example, look at her case! She turns tantalizing inviting glances on you. You seize her. No sooner does she feel herself in your grasp than she closes her eyes. It is the sign of her mission, the sign by which she says to man: "Blind yourself, for I am blind."

THE STEPDAUGHTER: Sometimes she can close them no more: when she no longer feels the need of hiding her shame to herself, but dry-eyed and dispassionately, sees only that of the man who has blinded himself without love. Oh, all these intellectual complications make me sick, disgust me — all this philosophy that uncovers the beast in man, and then seeks to save him, excuse him . . . I can't stand it, sir. When a man seeks to "simplify" life bestially, throwing aside every relic of humanity, every chaste aspiration, every pure feeling, all sense of ideality, duty, modesty, shame . . . then nothing is more revolting and nauseous than a certain kind of remorse — crocodiles' tears, that's what it is.

THE MANAGER: Let's come to the point. This is only discussion.

THE FATHER: Very good, sir! But a fact is like a sack which won't stand up when it's empty. In order that it may stand up, one has to put into it the reason and sentiment which have caused it to exist. I couldn't possibly know that after the death of that man, they had decided to return here, that they were in misery, and that she (*pointing to the Mother*) had gone to work as a modiste,° and at a shop of the type of that of Madame Pace.

THE STEPDAUGHTER: A real high-class modiste, you must know, gentlemen. In appearance, she works for the leaders of the best society; but she arranges matters so that these elegant ladies serve her purpose . . . without prejudice to other ladies who are . . . well . . . only so so.

THE MOTHER: You will believe me, gentlemen, that it never entered my mind that the old hag offered me work because she had her eye on my daughter.

THE STEPDAUGHTER: Poor mamma! Do you know, sir, what that woman did when I brought her back the work my mother had finished? She would point out to me that I had torn one of my frocks, and she would give it back to my mother to mend. It was I who paid for it, always I; while this poor creature here believed she was sacrificing herself for me and these two children here, sitting up at night sewing Madame Pace's robes.

THE MANAGER: And one day you met there . . .

---

modiste: A person who makes fashionable clothing for women.

Scene from the 1984
American Repertory Theatre
production of *Six Characters
in Search of an Author,*
directed by Robert Brustein.

THE STEPDAUGHTER: Him, him. Yes sir, an old client. There's a scene for you to play! Superb!

THE FATHER: She, the Mother arrived just then ...

THE STEPDAUGHTER (*treacherously*): Almost in time!

THE FATHER (*crying out*): No, in time! in time! Fortunately I recognized her ... in time. And I took them back home with me to my house. You can imagine now her position and mine; she, as you see her; and I who cannot look her in the face.

THE STEPDAUGHTER: Absurd! How can I possibly be expected — after that — to be a modest young miss, a fit person to go with his confounded aspirations for "a solid moral sanity"?

THE FATHER: For the drama lies all in this — in the conscience that I have, that each one of us has. We believe this conscience to be a single thing, but it is many-sided. There is one for this person, and another for that. Diverse consciences. So we have this illusion of being one person for all, of having a personality that is unique in all our acts. But it isn't true. We perceive this when, tragically perhaps, in something we do, we are as it were, suspended, caught up in the air on a kind of hook. Then we perceive that all of us was not in that act, and that it would be an atrocious injustice to judge us by that action alone, as if all our existence were summed up in that one deed. Now do you understand the perfidy of this girl? She surprised me in a place, where she ought not to have known me, just as I could not exist for her; and she now seeks to attach to me a reality such as I could never suppose I should have to assume for her in a shameful and fleeting moment of my life. I feel this above all else. And the drama, you will see, acquires a tremendous value from this point. Then there is the position of the others ... his. ... (*Indicating the Son.*)

THE SON (*shrugging his shoulders scornfully*): Leave me alone! I don't come into this.

THE FATHER: What? You don't come into this?

THE SON: I've got nothing to do with it, and don't want to have; because you know well enough I wasn't made to be mixed up in all this with the rest of you.

THE STEPDAUGHTER: We are only vulgar folk! He is the fine gentleman. You may have noticed, Mr. Manager, that I fix him now and again with a look of scorn while he lowers his eyes — for he knows the evil he has done me.

THE SON (*scarcely looking at her*): I?

THE STEPDAUGHTER: You! you! I owe my life on the streets to you. Did you or did you not deny us, with your behavior, I won't say the intimacy of home, but even that mere hospitality which makes guests feel at their ease? We were intruders who had come to disturb the kingdom of your legitimacy. I should like to have you witness, Mr. Manager, certain scenes between him and me. He says I have tyrannized over everyone. But it was just his behavior which made me insist on the reason for which I had come into the house, — this reason he calls "vile" — into his house, with my mother who is his mother too. And I came as mistress of the house.

THE SON: It's easy for them to put me always in the wrong. But imagine, gentlemen, the position of a son, whose fate it is to see arrive one day at his home a young woman of impudent bearing, a young woman who inquires for his father, with whom who knows what business she has. This young man has then to witness her return bolder than ever, accompanied by that child there. He is obliged to watch her treat his father in an equivocal and confidential manner. She asks for money of him in a way that lets one suppose he must give it to her, *must*, do you understand, because he has every obligation to do so.

THE FATHER: But I have, as a matter of fact, this obligation. I owe it to your mother.

THE SON: How should I know? When had I ever seen or heard of her? One day there arrive with her (*indicating Stepdaughter*) that lad and this baby here. I am told: "This is *your* mother too, you know." I divine from her manner (*indicating Stepdaughter again*) why it is they have come home. I had rather not say what I feel and think about it. I shouldn't even care to confess to myself. No action can therefore be hoped for from me in this affair. Believe me, Mr. Manager, I am an "unrealized" character, dramatically speaking; and I find myself not at all at ease in their company. Leave me out of it, I beg you.

THE FATHER: What? It is just because you are so that . . .

THE SON: How do you know what I am like? When did you ever bother your head about me?

THE FATHER: I admit it. I admit it. But isn't that a situation in itself? This aloofness of yours which is so cruel to me and to your mother, who returns home and sees you almost for the first time grown up, who doesn't recognize you but knows you are her son. . . . (*Pointing out the Mother to the Manager.*) See, she's crying!

THE STEPDAUGHTER (*angrily, stamping her foot*): Like a fool!

THE FATHER (*indicating Stepdaughter*): She can't stand him, you know. (*Then referring again to the Son.*) He says he doesn't come into the affair, whereas he is really the hinge of the whole action. Look at that lad who is always clinging to his mother, frightened and humiliated. It is on account of this fellow here. Possibly his situation is the

most painful of all. He feels himself a stranger more than the others. The poor little chap feels mortified, humiliated at being brought into a home out of charity as it were. (*In confidence.*) He is the image of his father. Hardly talks at all. Humble and quiet.

THE MANAGER: Oh, we'll cut him out. You've no notion what a nuisance boys are on the stage. . . .

THE FATHER: He disappears soon, you know. And the baby too. She is the first to vanish from the scene. The drama consists finally in this: when that mother reenters my house, her family born outside of it, and shall we say superimposed on the original, ends with the death of the little girl, the tragedy of the boy and the flight of the elder daughter. It cannot go on, because it is foreign to its surroundings. So after much torment, we three remain: I, the mother, that son. Then, owing to the disappearance of that extraneous family, we too find ourselves strange to one another. We find we are living in an atmosphere of mortal desolation which is the revenge, as he (*indicating Son*) scornfully said of the Demon of Experiment, that unfortunately hides in me. Thus, sir, you see when faith is lacking, it becomes impossible to create certain states of happiness, for we lack the necessary humility. Vaingloriously, we try to substitute ourselves for this faith, creating thus for the rest of the world a reality which we believe after their fashion, while, actually, it doesn't exist. For each one of us has his own reality to be respected before God, even when it is harmful to one's very self.

THE MANAGER: There is something in what you say. I assure you all this interests me very much. I begin to think there's the stuff for a drama in all this, and not a bad drama either.

THE STEPDAUGHTER (*coming forward*): When you've got a character like me . . .

THE FATHER (*shutting her up, all excited to learn the decision of the Manager*): You be quiet!

THE MANAGER (*reflecting, heedless of interruption*): It's new . . . hem . . . yes. . . .

THE FATHER: Absolutely new!

THE MANAGER: You've got a nerve though, I must say, to come here and fling it at me like this . . .

THE FATHER: You will understand, sir, born as we are for the stage . . .

THE MANAGER: Are you amateur actors then?

THE FATHER: No, I say born for the stage, because . . .

THE MANAGER: Oh, nonsense. You're an old hand, you know.

THE FATHER: No sir, no. We act that role for which we have been cast, that role which we are given in life. And in my own case, passion itself, as usually happens, becomes a trifle theatrical when it is exalted.

THE MANAGER: Well, well, that will do. But you see, without an author. . . . I could give you the address of an author if you like . . .

THE FATHER: No, no. Look here! You must be the author.

THE MANAGER: I? What are you talking about?

THE FATHER: Yes, you, you! Why not?

THE MANAGER: Because I have never been an author: that's why.

THE FATHER: Then why not turn author now? Everybody does it. You don't want any special qualities. Your task is made much easier by the fact that we are all here alive before you. . . .

THE MANAGER: It won't do.

THE FATHER: What? When you see us live our drama. . . .

THE MANAGER: Yes, that's all right. But you want someone to write it.

THE FATHER: No, no. Someone to take it down, possibly, while we play it, scene by scene! It will be enough to sketch it out at first, and then try it over.

THE MANAGER: Well . . . I am almost tempted. It's a bit of an idea. One might have a shot at it.

THE FATHER: Of course. You'll see what scenes will come out of it. I can give you one, at once . . .

THE MANAGER: By Jove, it tempts me. I'd like to have a go at it. Let's try it out. Come with me to my office. (Turning to the Actors.) You are at liberty for a bit, but don't step out of the theater for long. In a quarter of an hour, twenty minutes, all back here again! (To the Father.) We'll see what can be done. Who knows if we don't get something really extraordinary out of it?

THE FATHER: There's no doubt about it. They (indicating the Characters) had better come with us too, hadn't they?

THE MANAGER: Yes, yes. Come on! come on! (Moves away and then turning to the Actors.) Be punctual, please! (Manager and the Six Characters cross the stage and go off. The other Actors remain, looking at one another in astonishment.)

LEADING MAN: Is he serious? What the devil does he want to do?

JUVENILE LEAD: This is rank madness.

THIRD ACTOR: Does he expect to knock up a drama in five minutes?

JUVENILE LEAD: Like the improvisers!

LEADING LADY: If he thinks I'm going to take part in a joke like this. . . .

JUVENILE LEAD: I'm out of it anyway.

FOUTH ACTOR: I should like to know who they are. (Alludes to Characters.)

THIRD ACTOR: What do you suppose? Madmen or rascals!

JUVENILE LEAD: And he takes them seriously!

L'INGÉNUE: Vanity! He fancies himself as an author now.

LEADING MAN: It's absolutely unheard of. If the stage has come to this . . . well I'm . . .

FIFTH ACTOR: It's rather a joke.

THIRD ACTOR: Well, we'll see what's going to happen next.

(Thus talking, the Actors leave the stage, some going out by the little door at the back, others retiring to their dressing rooms.)
(The curtain remains up.)
(The action of the play is suspended for twenty minutes.)

ACT II

(The stage call-bells ring to warn the company that the play is about to begin again.)
(The Stepdaughter comes out of the Manager's office along with the Child and the Boy. As she comes out of the office, she cries: —)

Nonsense! nonsense! Do it yourselves! I'm not going to mix myself up in this mess. (Turning to the Child and coming quickly with her on to the stage.) Come on, Rosetta, let's run!

(The Boy follows them slowly, remaining a little behind and seeming perplexed.)

THE STEPDAUGHTER (stops, bends over the Child and takes the latter's face between her hands): My little darling! You're frightened, aren't you? You don't know where we are, do you? (Pretending to reply to a question of the Child.) What is the stage? It's a place, baby, you know, where people play at being serious, a place where they act comedies. We've got to act a comedy now, dead serious, you know; and you're in it also, little one. (Embraces her, pressing the little head to her breast, and rocking the Child for a moment.) Oh darling, darling, what a horrid comedy you've got to play! What a wretched part they've found for you! A garden . . . a fountain . . . look . . . just suppose, kiddie, it's here. Where, you say? Why, right here in the middle. It's all pretense you know. That's the trouble, my pet: it's all make-believe here. It's better to imagine it though, because if they fix it up for you, it'll only be painted cardboard, painted cardboard for the rockery, the water, the plants. . . . Ah, but I think a baby like this one would sooner have a make-believe fountain than a real one, so she could play with it. What a joke it'll be for the others! But for you, alas! not quite such a joke: you who are real, baby dear, and really play by a real fountain that is big and green and beautiful, with ever so many bamboos around it that are reflected in the water, and a whole lot of little ducks swimming about. . . . No, Rosetta, no, your mother doesn't bother about you on account of that wretch of a son there. I'm in the devil of a temper, and as for that lad. . . . (*Seizes Boy by the arm to force him to take one of his hands out of his pockets.*) What have you got there? What are you hiding? (*Pulls his hand out of his pocket, looks into it, and catches the glint of a revolver.*) Ah! where did you get this? (*The Boy, very pale in the face, looks at her, but does not answer.*) Idiot! If I'd been in your place, instead of killing myself, I'd have shot one of those two, or both of them: father and son.

(*The Father enters from the office, all excited from his work. The Manager follows him.*)

THE FATHER: Come on, come on dear! Come here for a minute! We've arranged everything. It's all fixed up.
THE MANAGER (*also excited*): If you please, young lady, there are one or two points to settle still. Will you come along?
THE STEPDAUGHTER (*following him toward the office*): Ouff! what's the good, if you've arranged everything.

(*The Father, Manager, and Stepdaughter go back into the office again [off] for a moment. At the same time, the Son, followed by the Mother, comes out.*)

THE SON (*looking at the three entering office*): Oh this is fine, fine! And to think I can't even get away!

(*The Mother attempts to look at him, but lowers her eyes immediately when he turns away from her. She then sits down. The Boy and the Child approach her. She casts a glance again at the Son, and speaks with humble tones, trying to draw him into conversation.*)

THE MOTHER: And isn't my punishment the worst of all? (*Then seeing from the Son's manner that he will not bother himself about her.*) My God! Why are you so cruel? Isn't it enough for one person to support all this torment? Must you then insist on others seeing it also?
THE SON (*half to himself, meaning the Mother to hear, however*): And they want to put it on the stage! If there was at least a reason for it! He thinks he has got at the meaning of it all. Just as if each one of us in every circumstance of life couldn't find his own explanation of it! (*Pauses.*) He complains he was discovered in a place where he ought not to have been seen, in a moment of his life which ought to

have remained hidden and kept out of the reach of that convention which he has to maintain for other people. And what about my case? Haven't I had to reveal what no son ought ever to reveal: how father and mother live and are man and wife for themselves quite apart from that idea of father and mother which we give them? When this idea is revealed, our life is then linked at one point only to that man and that woman; and as such it should shame them, shouldn't it?

(*The Mother hides her face in her hands. From the dressing rooms and the little door at the back of the stage the Actors and Stage Manager return, followed by the Property Man and the Prompter. At the same moment, the Manager comes out of his office, accompanied by the Father and the Stepdaughter.*)

THE MANAGER: Come on, come on, ladies and gentlemen! Heh! you there, machinist!
MACHINIST: Yes sir?
THE MANAGER: Fix up the parlor with the floral decorations. Two wings and a drop with a door will do. Hurry up!

(*The Machinist runs off at once to prepare the scene and arranges it while the Manager talks with the Stage Manager, the Property Man, and the Prompter on matters of detail.*)

THE MANAGER (*to Property Man*): Just have a look, and see if there isn't a sofa or a divan in the wardrobe . . .
PROPERTY MAN: There's the green one.
THE STEPDAUGHTER: No no! Green won't do. It was yellow, ornamented with flowers — very large! and most comfortable!
PROPERTY MAN: There isn't one like that.
THE MANAGER: It doesn't matter. Use the one we've got.
THE STEPDAUGHTER: Doesn't matter? It's most important!
THE MANAGER: We're only trying it now. Please don't interfere. (*To Property Man.*) See if we've got a shop window — long and narrowish.
THE STEPDAUGHTER: And the little table! The little mahogany table for the pale blue envelope!
PROPERTY MAN (*to Manager*): There's that little gilt one.
THE MANAGER: That'll do fine.
THE FATHER: A mirror.
THE STEPDAUGHTER: And the screen! We must have a screen. Otherwise how can I manage?
PROPERTY MAN: That's all right, Miss. We've got any amount of them.
THE MANAGER (*to the Stepdaughter*): We want some clothes pegs too, don't we?

THE STEPDAUGHTER: Yes, several, several!

THE MANAGER: See how many we've got and bring them all.

PROPERTY MAN: All right!

(*The Property Man hurries off to obey his orders. While he is putting the things in their places, the Manager talks to the Prompter and then with the Characters and the Actors.*)

THE MANAGER (*to Prompter*): Take your seat. Look here: this is the outline of the scenes, act by act. (*Hands him some sheets of paper.*) And now I'm going to ask you to do something out of the ordinary.

PROMPTER: Take it down in shorthand?

THE MANAGER (*pleasantly surprised*): Exactly! Can you do shorthand?

PROMPTER: Yes, a little.

THE MANAGER: Good! (*Turning to a Stage Hand.*) Go and get some paper from my office, plenty, as much as you can find.

(*The Stage Hand goes off and soon returns with a handful of paper which he gives to the Prompter.*)

THE MANAGER (*to Prompter*): You follow the scenes as we play them, and try and get the points down, at any rate the most important ones. (*Then addressing the Actors.*) Clear the stage, ladies and gentlemen! Come over here (*pointing to the left*) and listen attentively.

LEADING LADY: But, excuse me, we . . .

THE MANAGER (*guessing her thought*): Don't worry! You won't have to improvise.

LEADING MAN: What have we to do then?

THE MANAGER: Nothing. For the moment you just watch and listen. Everybody will get his part written out afterwards. At present we're going to try the thing as best we can. They're going to act now.

THE FATHER (*as if fallen from the clouds into the confusion of the stage*): We? What do you mean, if you please, by a rehearsal?

THE MANAGER: A rehearsal for them. (*Points to the Actors.*)

THE FATHER: But since we are the characters . . .

THE MANAGER: All right: "characters" then, if you insist on calling yourselves such. But here, my dear sir, the characters don't act. Here the actors do the acting. The characters are there, in the "book" (*pointing toward Prompter's box*) — when there is a "book"!

THE FATHER: I won't contradict you; but excuse me, the actors aren't the characters. They want to be, they pretend to be, don't they? Now if these gentlemen here are fortunate enough to have us alive before them . . .

THE MANAGER: Oh, this is grand! You want to come before the public yourselves then?

THE FATHER: As we are. . . .

THE MANAGER: I can assure you it would be a magnificent spectacle!

LEADING MAN: What's the use of us here anyway then?

THE MANAGER: You're not going to pretend that you can act? It makes me laugh! (*The Actors laugh.*) There, you see, they are laughing at the notion. But, by the way, I must cast the parts. That won't be difficult. They cast themselves. (*To the Second Lady Lead.*) You play the Mother. (*To the Father.*) We must find her a name.

THE FATHER: Amalia, sir.

THE MANAGER: But that is the real name of your wife. We don't want to call her by her real name.

THE FATHER: Why ever not, if it is her name? . . . Still, perhaps, if that lady must . . . (*Makes a slight motion of the hand to indicate the Second Lady Lead.*) I see this woman here (*means the Mother*) as Amalia. But do as you like. (*Gets more and more confused.*) I don't know what to say to you. Already, I begin to hear my own words ring false, as if they had another sound . . .

THE MANAGER: Don't you worry about it. It'll be our job to find the right tones. And as for her name, if you want her Amalia, Amalia it shall be; and if you don't like it, we'll find another! For the moment though, we'll call the characters in this way: (*To Juvenile Lead.*) You are the Son. (*To the Leading Lady.*) You naturally are the Stepdaughter. . . .

THE STEPDAUGHTER (*excitedly*): What? what? I, that woman there? (*Bursts out laughing.*)

THE MANAGER (*angry*): What is there to laugh at?

LEADING LADY (*indignant*): Nobody has ever dared to laugh at me. I insist on being treated with respect; otherwise I go away.

THE STEPDAUGHTER: No, no, excuse me . . . I am not laughing at you. . . .

THE MANAGER (*to Stepdaughter*): You ought to feel honored to be played by . . .

LEADING LADY (*at once, contemptuously*): "That woman there" . . .

THE STEPDAUGHTER: But I wasn't speaking of you, you know. I was speaking of myself — whom I can't see at all in you! That is all. I don't know . . . but . . . you . . . aren't in the least like me. . . .

THE FATHER: True. Here's the point. Look here, sir, our temperaments, our souls. . . .

THE MANAGER: Temperament, soul, be hanged! Do you suppose the spirit of the piece is in you? Nothing of the kind!

THE FATHER: What, haven't we our own temperaments, our own souls?

THE MANAGER: Not at all. Your soul or whatever you like to call it takes shape here. The actors give body and form to it, voice and gesture. And my actors — I may tell you — have given expression to much more lofty material than this little drama of yours, which may or may not hold up on the stage. But if it does, the merit of it, believe me, will be due to my actors.

THE FATHER: I don't dare contradict you, sir, but, believe me, it is a terrible suffering for us who are as we are, with these bodies of ours, these features to see. . . .

THE MANAGER (*cutting him short and out of patience*): Good heavens! The make-up will remedy all that, man, the make-up. . . .

THE FATHER: Maybe. But the voice, the gestures . . .

THE MANAGER: Now, look here! On the stage, you as yourself, cannot exist. The actor here acts you, and that's an end to it!

THE FATHER: I understand. And now I think I see why our author who conceived us as we are, all alive, didn't want to put us on the stage after all. I haven't the least desire to offend your actors. Far from it! But when I think that I am to be acted by . . . I don't know by whom. . . .

LEADING MAN (*on his dignity*): By me, if you've no objection!

THE FATHER (*humbly, mellifluously*): Honored, I assure you, sir. (*Bows.*) Still, I must say that try as this gentleman may, with all his good will and wonderful art, to absorb me into himself. . . .

LEADING MAN: Oh chuck it! "Wonderful art!" Withdraw that, please!

THE FATHER: The performance he will give, even doing his best with make-up to look like me. . . .

LEADING MAN: It will certainly be a bit difficult! (*The Actors laugh.*)

THE FATHER: Exactly! It will be difficult to act me as I really am. The effect will be rather — apart from the make-up — according as to how he supposes I am, as he senses me — if he does sense me — and not as I inside of myself feel myself to be. It seems to me then that account should be taken of this by everyone whose duty it may become to criticize us. . . .

THE MANAGER: Heavens! The man's starting to think about the critics now! Let them say what they like. It's up to us to put on the play if we can. (*Looking around.*) Come on! come on! Is the stage set? (*To the Actors and Characters.*) Stand back — stand back! Let me see, and don't let's lose any more time! (*To the Stepdaughter.*) Is it all right as it is now?

THE STEPDAUGHTER: Well, to tell the truth, I don't recognize the scene.

THE MANAGER: My dear lady, you can't possibly suppose that we can construct that shop of Madame Pace piece by piece here? (*To the Father.*) You said a white room with flowered wallpaper, didn't you?

THE FATHER: Yes.

THE MANAGER: Well then. We've got the furniture right more or less. Bring that little table a bit further forward. (*The Stage Hands obey the order. To Property Man.*) You go and find an envelope, if possible, a pale blue one; and give it to that gentleman. (*Indicates Father.*)

PROPERTY MAN: An ordinary envelope?

MANAGER AND FATHER: Yes, yes, an ordinary envelope.

PROPERTY MAN: At once, sir. (*Exit.*)

THE MANAGER: Ready, everyone! First scene — the Young Lady. (*The Leading Lady comes forward.*) No, no, you must wait. I meant her. (*Indicating the Stepdaughter.*) You just watch —

THE STEPDAUGHTER (*adding at once*): How I shall play it, how I shall live it! . . .

LEADING LADY (*offended*): I shall live it also, you may be sure, as soon as I begin!

THE MANAGER (*with his hands to his head*): Ladies and gentlemen, if you please! No more useless discussions! Scene I: the Young Lady with Madame Pace: Oh! (*Looks around as if lost.*) And this Madame Pace, where is she?

THE FATHER: She isn't with us, sir.

THE MANAGER: Then what the devil's to be done?

THE FATHER: But she is alive too.

THE MANAGER: Yes, but where is she?

THE FATHER: One minute. Let me speak! (*Turning to the Actresses.*) If these ladies would be so good as to give me their hats for a moment. . . .

THE ACTRESSES (*half surprised, half laughing, in chorus*): What? Why? Our hats? What does he say?

THE MANAGER: What are you going to do with the ladies' hats? (*The Actors laugh.*)

THE FATHER: Oh nothing. I just want to put them on these pegs for a moment. And one of the ladies will be so kind as to take off her mantle. . . .

THE ACTORS: Oh, what d'you think of that? Only the mantle? He must be mad.

SOME ACTRESSES: But why? Mantles as well?

THE FATHER: To hang them up here for a moment. Please be so kind, will you?

THE ACTRESSES (*taking off their hats, one or two also their cloaks, and going to hang them on the racks*): After all, why not? There you are! This is really funny. We've got to put them on show.

THE FATHER: Exactly; just like that, on show.

THE MANAGER: May we know why?

THE FATHER: I'll tell you. Who knows if, by arranging the stage for her, she does not come here herself, attracted by the very articles of her trade? (*Inviting the Actors to look toward the exit at back of stage.*) Look! Look!

(*The door at the back of stage opens and Madame Pace enters and takes a few steps forward. She is a fat, oldish woman with puffy oxygenated hair. She is rouged and powdered, dressed with a comical elegance in black silk. Round her waist is a long silver chain from which hangs a pair of scissors. The Stepdaughter runs over to her at once amid the stupor of the Actors.*)

THE STEPDAUGHTER (*turning toward her*): There she is! There she is!

THE FATHER (*radiant*): It's she! I said so, didn't I! There she is!

THE MANAGER (*conquering his surprise, and then becoming indignant*): What sort of a trick is this?

LEADING MAN (*almost at the same time*): What's going to happen next?

JUVENILE LEAD: Where does she come from?

L'INGÉNUE: They've been holding her in reserve, I guess.

LEADING LADY: A vulgar trick!

THE FATHER (*dominating the protests*): Excuse me, all of you! Why are you so anxious to destroy in the name of a vulgar, commonplace sense of truth, this reality which comes to birth attracted and formed by the magic of the stage itself, which has indeed more right to live here than you, since it is much truer than you — if you don't mind my saying so? Which is the actress among you who is to play Madame Pace? Well, here is Madame Pace herself. And you will allow, I fancy, that the actress who acts her will be less true than this woman here, who is herself in person. You see my daughter recognized her and went over to her at once. Now you're going to witness the scene!

(*But the scene between the Stepdaughter and Madame Pace has already begun despite the protest of the Actors and the reply of the Father. It has begun quietly, naturally, in a manner impossible for the stage. So when the Actors, called to attention by the Father, turn round and see Madame Pace, who has placed one hand under the Stepdaughter's chin to raise her head, they observe her at first with great attention, but hearing her speak in an unintelligible manner their interest begins to wane.*)

THE MANAGER: Well? well?

LEADING MAN: What does she say?

LEADING LADY: One can't hear a word.

JUVENILE LEAD: Louder! Louder please!

THE STEPDAUGHTER (*leaving Madame Pace, who smiles a Sphinx-like smile, and advancing toward the Actors*): Louder? Louder? What are you talking about? These aren't matters which can be shouted at the top of one's voice. If I have spoken them out loud, it was to shame him and have my revenge. (*Indicates Father.*) But for Madame it's quite a different matter.

THE MANAGER: Indeed? indeed? But here, you know people have got to make themselves heard, my dear. Even we who are on the stage can't hear you. What will it be when the public's in the theater? And anyway, you can very well speak up now among yourselves, since we shan't be present to listen to you as we are now. You've got to pretend to be alone in a room at the back of a shop where no one can hear you.

(*The Stepdaughter coquettishly and with a touch of malice makes a sign of disagreement two or three times with her finger.*)

THE MANAGER: What do you mean by no?

THE STEPDAUGHTER (*sotto voce,° mysteriously*): There's someone who will hear us if she (*indicating Madame Pace*) speaks out loud.

THE MANAGER (*in consternation*): What? Have you got someone else to spring on us now? (*The Actors burst out laughing.*)

THE FATHER: No, no sir. She is alluding to me. I've got to be here — there behind that door, in waiting; and Madame Pace knows it. In fact, if you will allow me, I'll go there at once, so I can be quite ready. (*Moves away.*)

THE MANAGER (*stopping him*): No! wait! wait! We must observe the conventions of the theater. Before you are ready . . .

THE STEPDAUGHTER (*interrupting him*): No, get on with it at once! I'm just dying, I tell you, to act this scene. If he's ready, I'm more than ready.

THE MANAGER (*shouting*): But, my dear young lady, first of all, we must have the scene between you and this lady. . . . (*Indicates Madame Pace.*) Do you understand?

THE STEPDAUGHTER: Good Heavens! She's been telling me what you know already: that mama's work is badly done again, that the material's ruined; and that if I want her to continue to help us in our misery I must be patient. . . .

MADAME PACE (*coming forward with an air of great importance*): Yes indeed, sir, I no wanta take advantage of her, I no wanta be hard. . . .

(*Note: Madame Pace is supposed to talk in a jargon half Italian, half English.*)

THE MANAGER (*alarmed*): What? What? She talks like that? (*The Actors burst out laughing again.*)

THE STEPDAUGHTER (*also laughing*): Yes yes, that's the

° *sotto voce*: In a soft voice or stage whisper.

way she talks, half English, half Italian! Most comical it is!

MADAME PACE: Itta seem not verra polite gentlemen laugha atta me eeff I trya best speaka English.

THE MANAGER: *Diamine!°* Of course! Of course! Let her talk like that! Just what we want. Talk just like that, Madame, if you please! The effect will be certain. Exactly what was wanted to put a little comic relief into the crudity of the situation. Of course she talks like that! Magnificent!

THE STEPDAUGHTER: Magnificent? Certainly! When certain suggestions are made to one in language of that kind, the effect is certain, since it seems almost a joke. One feels inclined to laugh when one hears her talk about an "old signore" "who wanta talka nicely with you." Nice old signore, eh, Madame?

MADAME PACE: Not so old my dear, not so old! And even if you no like him, he won't make any scandal!

THE MOTHER (*jumping up amid the amazement and consternation of the Actors, who had not been noticing her. They move to restrain her*): You old devil! You murderess!

THE STEPDAUGHTER (*running over to calm her Mother*): Calm yourself, Mother, calm yourself! Please don't. . . .

THE FATHER (*going to her also at the same time*): Calm yourself! Don't get excited! Sit down now!

THE MOTHER: Well then, take that woman away out of my sight!

THE STEPDAUGHTER (*to Manager*): It is impossible for my mother to remain here.

THE FATHER (*to Manager*): They can't be here together. And for this reason, you see: that woman there was not with us when we came. . . . If they are on together, the whole thing is given away inevitably, as you see.

THE MANAGER: It doesn't matter. This is only a first rough sketch — just to get an idea of the various points of the scene, even confusedly. . . . (*Turning to the Mother and leading her to her chair.*) Come along, my dear lady, sit down now, and let's get on with the scene. . . .

(*Meanwhile, the Stepdaughter, coming forward again, turns to Madame Pace.*)

THE STEPDAUGHTER: Come on, Madame, come on!

MADAME PACE (*offended*): No, no, *grazie.* I do not do anything witha your mother present.

THE STEPDAUGHTER: Nonsense! Introduce this "old signore" who wants to talk nicely to me. (*Addressing the Company imperiously.*) We've got to do this scene one way or another, haven't we? Come on! (*To Madame Pace.*) You can go!

Diamine!: Italian for "Well, I'll be damned!"

MADAME PACE: Ah yes! I go'way! I go'way! Certainly! (*Exits furious.*)

THE STEPDAUGHTER (*to the Father*): Now you make your entry. No, you needn't go over there. Come here. Let's suppose you've already come in. Like that, yes! I'm here with bowed head, modest like. Come on! Out with your voice! Say "Good morning, Miss" in that peculiar tone, that special tone. . . .

THE MANAGER: Excuse me, but are you the Manager, or am I? (*To the Father, who looks undecided and perplexed.*) Get on with it, man! Go down there to the back of the stage. You needn't go off. Then come right forward here.

(*The Father does as he is told, looking troubled and perplexed at first. But as soon as he begins to move, the reality of the action affects him, and he begins to smile and to be more natural. The Actors watch intently.*)

THE MANAGER (*sotto voce, quickly to the Prompter in his box*): Ready! ready! Get ready to write now.

THE FATHER (*coming forward and speaking in a different tone*): Good afternoon, Miss!

THE STEPDAUGHTER (*head bowed down slightly, with restrained disgust*): Good afternoon!

THE FATHER (*looks under her hat which partly covers her face. Perceiving she is very young, he makes an exclamation, partly of surprise, partly of fear lest he compromise himself in a risky adventure*): Ah . . . but . . . ah . . . I say . . . this is not the first time that you have come here, is it?

THE STEPDAUGHTER (*modestly*): No sir.

THE FATHER: You've been here before, eh? (*Then seeing her nod agreement.*) More than once? (*Waits for her to answer, looks under her hat, smiles, and then says:*) Well then, there's no need to be so shy, is there? May I take off your hat?

THE STEPDAUGHTER (*anticipating him and with veiled disgust*): No sir . . . I'll do it myself. (*Takes it off quickly.*)

(*The Mother, who watches the progress of the scene with the Son and the other two children who cling to her, is on thorns; and follows with varying expressions of sorrow, indignation, anxiety, and horror the words and actions of the other two. From time to time she hides her face in her hands and sobs.*)

THE MOTHER: Oh, my God, my God!

THE FATHER (*playing his part with a touch of gallantry*): Give it to me! I'll put it down. (*Takes hat from her hands.*) But a dear little head like yours ought to have a smarter hat. Come and help me choose one from the stock, won't you?

L'INGÉNUE (*interrupting*): I say . . . those are our hats you know.

THE MANAGER (*furious*): Silence! silence! Don't try and be funny, if you please.... We're playing the scene now, I'd have you notice (*To the Stepdaughter.*) Begin again, please!

THE STEPDAUGHTER (*continuing*): No thank you, sir.

THE FATHER: Oh, come now. Don't talk like that. You must take it. I shall be upset if you don't. There are some lovely little hats here; and then — Madame will be pleased. She expects it, anyway, you know.

THE STEPDAUGHTER: No, no! I couldn't wear it!

THE FATHER: Oh, you're thinking about what they'd say at home if they saw you come in with a new hat? My dear girl, there's always a way round these little matters, you know.

THE STEPDAUGHTER (*all keyed up*): No, it's not that. I couldn't wear it because I am...as you see... you might have noticed...

(*Showing her black dress.*)

THE FATHER: ... in mourning! Of course: I beg your pardon: I'm frightfully sorry....

THE STEPDAUGHTER (*forcing herself to conquer her indignation and nausea*): Stop! Stop! It's I who must thank you. There's no need for you to feel mortified or specially sorry. Don't think any more of what I've said. (*Tries to smile.*) I must forget that I am dressed so....

THE MANAGER (*interrupting and turning to the Prompter*): Stop a minute! Stop! Don't write that down. Cut out that last bit. (*Then to the Father and Stepdaughter.*) Fine! it's going fine! (*To the Father only.*) And now you can go on as we arranged. (*To the Actors.*) Pretty good that scene, where he offers her the hat, eh?

THE STEPDAUGHTER: The best's coming now. Why can't we go on?

THE MANAGER: Have a little patience! (*To the Actors.*) Of course, it must be treated rather lightly.

LEADING MAN: Still, with a bit of go in it!

LEADING LADY: Of course! It's easy enough! (*To Leading Man.*) Shall you and I try it now?

LEADING MAN: Why, yes! I'll prepare my entrance. (*Exit in order to make his entrance.*)

THE MANAGER (*to Leading Lady*): See here! The scene between you and Madame Pace is finished. I'll have it written out properly after. You remain here ... oh, where are you going?

LEADING LADY: One minute. I want to put my hat on again. (*Goes over to hatrack and puts her hat on her head.*)

THE MANAGER: Good! You stay here with your head bowed down a bit.

THE STEPDAUGHTER: But she isn't dressed in black.

LEADING LADY: But I shall be, and much more effectively than you.

THE MANAGER (*to Stepdaughter*): Be quiet please, and watch! You'll be able to learn something (*Clapping his hands.*) Come on! come on! Entrance, please!

(*The door at rear of stage opens, and the Leading Man enters with the lively manner of an old gallant. The rendering of the scene by the Actors from the very first words is seen to be quite a different thing, though it has not in any way the air of a parody. Naturally, the Stepdaughter and the Father, not being able to recognize themselves in the Leading Lady and the Leading Man, who deliver their words in different tones and with a different psychology, express, sometimes with smiles, sometimes with gestures, the impression they receive.*)

LEADING MAN: Good afternoon, Miss ...

THE FATHER (*at once unable to contain himself*): No! no!

(*The Stepdaughter, noticing the way the Leading Man enters, bursts out laughing.*)

THE MANAGER (*furious*): Silence! And you, please, just stop that laughing. If we go on like this, we shall never finish.

THE STEPDAUGHTER: Forgive me, sir but it's natural enough. This lady (*indicating Leading Lady*) stands there still; but if she is supposed to be me, I can assure you that if I heard anyone say "Good afternoon" in that manner and in that tone, I should burst out laughing as I did.

THE FATHER: Yes, yes, the manner, the tone ...

THE MANAGER: Nonsense! Rubbish! Stand aside and let me see the action.

LEADING MAN: If I've got to represent an old fellow who's coming into a house of an equivocal character ...

THE MANAGER: Don't listen to them, for Heaven's sake! Do it again! It goes fine. (*Waiting for the Actors to begin again.*) Well?

LEADING MAN: Good afternoon, Miss.

LEADING LADY: Good afternoon.

LEADING MAN (*imitating the gesture of the Father when he looked under the hat, and then expressing quite clearly first satisfaction and then fear*): Ah, but...I say...this is not the first time that you have come here, is it?

THE MANAGER: Good, but not quite so heavily. Like this. (*Acts himself.*) "This isn't the first time that you have come here" ... (*To Leading Lady.*) And you say: "No, sir."

LEADING LADY: No, sir.

LEADING MAN: You've been here before, more than once.

THE MANAGER: No, no, stop! Let her nod "yes" first.

"You've been here before, eh?" (*The Leading Lady lifts up her head slightly and closes her eyes as though in disgust. Then she inclines her head twice.*)

THE STEPDAUGHTER (*unable to contain herself*): Oh my God! (*Puts a hand to her mouth to prevent herself from laughing.*)

THE MANAGER (*turning round*): What's the matter?

THE STEPDAUGHTER: Nothing, nothing!

THE MANAGER (*to Leading Man*): Go on!

LEADING MAN: You've been here before, eh? Well then, there's no need to be so shy, is there? May I take off your hat?

(*The Leading Man says this last speech in such a tone and with such gestures that the Stepdaughter, though she has her hand to her mouth, cannot keep from laughing.*)

LEADING LADY (*indignant*): I'm not going to stop here to be made a fool of by that woman there.

LEADING MAN: Neither am I! I'm through with it!

THE MANAGER (*shouting to Stepdaughter*): Silence! for once and all, I tell you!

THE STEPDAUGHTER: Forgive me! forgive me!

THE MANAGER: You haven't any manners: that's what it is! You go too far.

THE FATHER (*endeavoring to intervene*): Yes, it's true, but excuse her . . .

THE MANAGER: Excuse what? It's absolutely disgusting.

THE FATHER: Yes, sir, but believe me, it has such a strange effect when . . .

THE MANAGER: Strange? Why strange? Where is it strange?

THE FATHER: No, sir; I admire your actors — this gentleman here, this lady; but they are certainly not us!

THE MANAGER: I should hope not. Evidently they cannot be you, if they are actors.

THE FATHER: Just so: actors! Both of them act our parts exceedingly well. But, believe me, it produces quite a different effect on us. They want to be us, but they aren't, all the same.

THE MANAGER: What is it then anyway?

THE FATHER: Something that is . . . that is theirs — and no longer ours . . .

THE MANAGER: But naturally, inevitably, I've told you so already.

THE FATHER: Yes, I understand . . . I understand . . .

THE MANAGER: Well then, let's have no more of it! (*Turning to the Actors.*) We'll have the rehearsals by ourselves, afterwards, in the ordinary way. I never could stand rehearsing with the author present. He's never satisfied! (*Turning to Father and Stepdaughter.*) Come on! Let's get on with it again; and try and see if you can't keep from laughing.

THE STEPDAUGHTER: Oh, I shan't laugh any more. There's a nice little bit coming from me now: you'll see.

THE MANAGER: Well then: when she says "Don't think any more of what I've said, I must forget, etc.," you (*addressing the Father*) come in sharp with "I understand"; and then you ask her . . .

THE STEPDAUGHTER (*interrupting*): What?

THE MANAGER: Why she is in mourning.

THE STEPDAUGHTER: Not at all! See here: when I told him that it was useless for me to be thinking about my wearing mourning, do you know how he answered me? "Ah well," he said, "then let's take off this little frock."

THE MANAGER: Great! Just what we want, to make a riot in the theater!

THE STEPDAUGHTER: But it's the truth!

THE MANAGER: What does that matter? Acting is our business here. Truth up to a certain point, but no further.

THE STEPDAUGHTER: What do you want to do then?

THE MANAGER: You'll see, you'll see! Leave it to me.

THE STEPDAUGHTER: No sir! What you want to do is to piece together a little romantic sentimental scene out of my disgust, out of all the reasons, each more cruel and viler than the other, why I am what I am. He is to ask me why I'm in mourning; and I'm to answer with tears in my eyes, that it is just two months since papa died. No sir, no! He's got to say to me, as he did say, "Well, let's take off this little dress at once." And I, with my two months' mourning in my heart, went there behind that screen, and with these fingers tingling with shame . . .

THE MANAGER (*running his hands through his hair*): For Heaven's sake! What are you saying?

THE STEPDAUGHTER (*crying out excitedly*): The truth! The truth!

THE MANAGER: It may be. I don't deny it, and I can understand all your horror; but you must surely see that you can't have this kind of thing on the stage. It won't go.

THE STEPDAUGHTER: Not possible, eh? Very well! I'm much obliged to you — but I'm off.

THE MANAGER: Now be reasonable! Don't lose your temper!

THE STEPDAUGHTER: I won't stop here! I won't! I can see you fixed it all up with him in your office. All this talk about what is possible for the stage . . . I understand! He wants to get at his complicated "cerebral drama," to have his famous remorses and torments acted; but I want to act my part, *my part!*

THE MANAGER: (*annoyed, shaking his shoulders*): Ah! Just *your* part! But, if you will pardon me, there are other parts than yours: His (*indicating the Fa-*

ther) and hers (*indicating the Mother*)! On the stage you can't have a character becoming too prominent and overshadowing all the others. The thing is to pack them all into a neat little framework and then act what is actable. I am aware of the fact that everyone has his own interior life which he wants very much to put forward. But the difficulty lies in this fact: to set out just so much as is necessary for the stage, taking the other characters into consideration, and at the same time hint at the unrevealed interior life of each. I am willing to admit, my dear young lady, that from your point of view it would be a fine idea if each character could tell the public all his troubles in a nice monologue or a regular one hour lecture. (*Good humoredly.*) You must restrain yourself, my dear, and in your own interest, too; because this fury of yours, this exaggerated disgust you show, may make a bad impression, you know. After you have confessed to me that there were others before him at Madame Pace's and more than once . . .

THE STEPDAUGHTER (*bowing her head, impressed*): It's true. But remember those others mean him for me all the same.

THE MANAGER (*not understanding*): What? The others? What do you mean?

THE STEPDAUGHTER: For one who has gone wrong, sir, he who was responsible for the first fault is responsible for all that follow. He is responsible for my faults, was, even before I was born. Look at him, and see if it isn't true!

THE MANAGER: Well, well! And does the weight of so much responsibility seem nothing to you? Give him a chance to act it, to get it over!

THE STEPDAUGHTER: How? How can he act all his "noble remorses," all his "moral torments," if you want to spare him the horror of being discovered one day — after he had asked her what he did ask her — in the arms of her, that already fallen woman, that child, sir, that child he used to watch come out of school? (*She is moved.*)

(*The Mother at this point is overcome with emotion and breaks out into a fit of crying. All are touched. A long pause.*)

THE STEPDAUGHTER (*as soon as the Mother becomes a little quieter, adds resolutely and gravely*): At present, we are unknown to the public. Tomorrow, you will act us as you wish, treating us in your own manner. But do you really want to see drama, do you want to see it flash out as it really did?

THE MANAGER: Of course! That's just what I do want, so I can use as much of it as is possible.

THE STEPDAUGHTER: Well then, ask that Mother there to leave us.

THE MOTHER (*changing her low plaint into a sharp cry*): No! No! Don't permit it, sir, don't permit it!

THE MANAGER: But it's only to try . . .

THE MOTHER: I can't bear it. I can't.

THE MANAGER: But since it has happened already . . . I don't understand!

THE MOTHER: It's taking place now. It happens all the time. My torment isn't a pretended one. I live and feel every minute of my torture. Those two children there — have you heard them speak? They can't speak anymore. They cling to me to keep my torment actual and vivid for me. But for themselves, they do not exist, they aren't anymore. And she (*indicating the Stepdaughter*) has run away, she has left me, and is lost. If I now see her here before me, it is only to renew for me the tortures I have suffered for her too.

THE FATHER: The eternal moment! She (*indicating the Stepdaughter*) is here to catch me, fix me, and hold me eternally in the stocks for that one fleeting and shameful moment of my life. She can't give it up! And you, sir, cannot either fairly spare me . . .

THE MANAGER: I never said I didn't want to act it. It will form, as a matter of fact, the nucleus of the whole first act right up to her surprise. (*Indicates the Mother.*)

THE FATHER: Just so! This is my punishment: the passion in all of us that must culminate in her final cry.

THE STEPDAUGHTER: I can hear it still in my ears. It's driven me mad, that cry! — You can put me on as you like; it doesn't matter. Fully dressed, if you like — provided I have at least the arm bare; because, standing like this (*she goes close to the Father and leans her head on his breast*) with my head so, and my arms round his neck, I saw a vein pulsing in my arm here; and then, as if that live vein had awakened disgust in me, I closed my eyes like this, and let my head sink on his breast. (*Turning to the Mother.*) Cry out, mother! Cry out! (*Buries head in Father's breast, and with her shoulders raised as if to prevent her hearing the cry, adds in tones of intense emotion.*) Cry out as you did then!

THE MOTHER (*coming forward to separate them*): No! My daughter, my daughter! (*And after having pulled her away from him.*) You brute! you brute! She is my daughter! Don't you see she's my daughter?

THE MANAGER (*walking backward toward footlights*): Fine! fine! Damned good! And then, of course — curtain!

THE FATHER (*going toward him excitedly*): Yes, of course, because that's the way it really happened.

THE MANAGER (*convinced and pleased*): Oh, yes, no doubt about it. Curtain here, curtain!

(*At the reiterated cry of the Manager, the Machinist lets the curtain down, leaving the Manager and the Father in front of it before the footlights.*)

THE MANAGER: The darned idiot! I said "curtain" to show the act should end there, and he goes and lets it down in earnest. (*To the Father, while he pulls the curtain back to go on to the stage again.*) Yes, yes, it's all right. Effect certain! That's the right ending. I'll guarantee the first act at any rate.

ACT III

(*When the curtain goes up again, it is seen that the stage hands have shifted the bit of scenery used in the last part and have rigged up instead at the back of the stage a drop, with some trees, and one or two wings. A portion of a fountain basin is visible. The Mother is sitting on the right with the two children by her side. The Son is on the same side, but away from the others. He seems bored, angry, and full of shame. The Father and the Stepdaughter are also seated toward the right front. On the other side (left) are the Actors, much in the positions they occupied before the curtain was lowered. Only the Manager is standing up in the middle of the stage, with his hand closed over his mouth, in the act of meditating.*)

THE MANAGER (*shaking his shoulders after a brief pause*): Ah yes: the second act! Leave it to me, leave it all to me as we arranged, and you'll see! It'll go fine!

THE STEPDAUGHTER: Our entry into his house (*indicates Father*) in spite of him . . . (*Indicates the Son.*)

THE MANAGER (*out of patience*): Leave it to me, I tell you!

THE STEPDAUGHTER: Do let it be clear, at any rate, that it is in spite of my wishes.

THE MOTHER (*from her corner, shaking her head*): For all the good that's come of it . . .

THE STEPDAUGHTER (*turning toward her quickly*): It doesn't matter. The more harm done us, the more remorse for him.

THE MANAGER (*impatiently*): I understand! Good Heavens! I understand! I'm taking it into account.

THE MOTHER (*supplicatingly*): I beg you, sir, to let it appear quite plain that for conscience' sake I did try in every way . . .

THE STEPDAUGHTER (*interrupting indignantly and continuing for the Mother*): . . . to pacify me, to dissuade me from spiting him. (*To Manager.*) Do as she wants: satisfy her, because it is true! I enjoy it immensely. Anyhow, as you can see, the meeker she is, the more she tries to get at his heart, the more distant and aloof does he become.

THE MANAGER: Are we going to begin this second act or not?

THE STEPDAUGHTER: I'm not going to talk any more now. But I must tell you this: you can't have the whole action take place in the garden, as you suggest. It isn't possible!

THE MANAGER: Why not?

THE STEPDAUGHTER: Because he (*indicates the Son again*) is always shut up alone in his room. And then there's all the part of that poor dazed-looking boy there which takes place indoors.

THE MANAGER: Maybe! On the other hand, you will understand — we can't change scenes three or four times in one act.

LEADING MAN: They used to once.

THE MANAGER: Yes, when the public was up to the level of that child there.

LEADING LADY: It makes the illusion easier.

THE FATHER (*irritated*): The illusion! For Heaven's sake, don't say illusion. Please don't use that word, which is particularly painful for . . .

THE MANAGER (*astounded*): And why, if you please?

THE FATHER: It's painful, cruel, really cruel; and you ought to understand that.

THE MANAGER: But why? What ought we to say then? The illusion, I tell you, sir, which we've got to create for the audience. . . .

THE LEADING MAN: With our acting.

THE MANAGER: The illusion of a reality.

THE FATHER: I understand; but you, perhaps, do not understand us. Forgive me! You see . . . here for you and your actors, the thing is only — and rightly so . . . a kind of game. . . .

THE LEADING LADY (*interrupting indignantly*): A game! We're not children here, if you please! We are serious actors.

THE FATHER: I don't deny it. What I mean is the game, or play, of your art, which has to give, as the gentleman says, a perfect illusion of reality.

THE MANAGER: Precisely — !

THE FATHER: Now, if you consider the fact that we (*indicates himself and the other five Characters*), as we are, have no other reality outside of this illusion. . . .

THE MANAGER (*astonished, looking at his Actors, who are also amazed*): And what does that mean?

THE FATHER (*after watching them for a moment with a wan smile*): As I say, sir, that which is a game of art for you is our sole reality. (*Brief pause. He goes a step or two nearer the Manager and adds.*) But not only for us, you know, by the way. Just you think it over well. (*Looks him in the eyes.*) Can you tell me who you are?

THE MANAGER (*perplexed, half-smiling*): What? Who am I? I am myself.

THE FATHER: And if I were to tell you that that isn't true, because you and I . . . ?

THE MANAGER: I should say you were mad — ! (*The Actors laugh.*)

THE FATHER: You're quite right to laugh: because we are all making believe here. (*To Manager.*) And you can therefore object that it's only for a joke that that gentleman there (*indicates the Leading Man*), who naturally is himself, has to be me, who am on the contrary myself — this thing you see here. You see I've caught you in a trap! (*The Actors laugh.*)

THE MANAGER (*annoyed*): But we've had all this over once before. Do you want to begin again?

THE FATHER: No, no! That wasn't my meaning! In fact, I should like to request you to abandon this game of art (*looking at the Leading Lady as if anticipating her*) which you are accustomed to play here with your actors, and to ask you seriously once again: who are you?

THE MANAGER (*astonished and irritated, turning to his Actors*): If this fellow here hasn't got a nerve! A man who calls himself a character comes and asks me who I am!

THE FATHER (*with dignity, but not offended*): A character, sir, may always ask a man who he is. Because a character has really a life of his own, marked with his especial characteristics; for which reason he is always "somebody." But a man — I'm not speaking of you now — may very well be "nobody."

THE MANAGER: Yes, but you are asking these questions of me, the boss, the manager! Do you understand?

THE FATHER: But only in order to know if you, as you really are now, see yourself as you once were with all the illusions that were yours then, with all the things both inside and outside of you as they seemed to you — as they were then indeed for you. Well, sir, if you think of all those illusions that mean nothing to you now, of all those things which don't even *seem* to you to exist anymore, while once they *were* for you, don't you feel that — I won't say these boards — but the very earth under your feet is sinking away from you when you reflect that in the same way this *you* as you feel it today — all this present reality of yours — is fated to seem a mere illusion to you tomorrow?

THE MANAGER (*without having understood much, but astonished by the specious argument*): Well, well! And where does all this take us anyway?

THE FATHER: Oh, nowhere! It's only to show you that if we (*indicating the Characters*) have no other re-

ality beyond the illusion, you too must not count overmuch on your reality as you feel it today, since, like that of yesterday, it may prove an illusion for you tomorrow.

THE MANAGER (*determining to make fun of him*): Ah, excellent! Then you'll be saying next that you, with this comedy of yours that you brought here to act, are truer and more real than I am.

THE FATHER (*with the greatest seriousness*): But of course, without doubt!

THE MANAGER: Ah, really?

THE FATHER: Why, I thought you'd understand that from the beginning.

THE MANAGER: More real than I?

THE FATHER: If your reality can change from one day to another. . . .

THE MANAGER: But everyone knows it can change. It is always changing, the same as anyone else's.

THE FATHER (*with a cry*): No, sir, not ours! Look here! That is the very difference! Our reality doesn't change: it can't change! It can't be other than what it is, because it is already fixed for ever. It's terrible. Ours is an immutable reality which should make you shudder when you approach us if you are really conscious of the fact that your reality is a mere transitory and fleeting illusion, taking this form today and that tomorrow, according to the conditions, according to your will, your sentiments, which in turn are controlled by an intellect that shows them to you today in one manner and tomorrow . . . who knows how? . . . Illusions of reality represented in this fatuous comedy of life that never ends, nor can ever end! Because if tomorrow it were to end . . . then why, all would be finished.

THE MANAGER: Oh for God's sake, will you *at least* finish with this philosophizing and let us try and shape this comedy which you yourself have brought me here? You argue and philosophize a bit too much, my dear sir. You know you seem to me almost, almost . . . (*Stops and looks him over from head to foot.*) Ah, by the way, I think you introduced yourself to me as a — what shall . . . we say — a "character," created by an author who did not afterward care to make a drama of his own creations.

THE FATHER: It is the simple truth, sir.

THE MANAGER: Nonsense! Cut that out, please! None of us believes it, because it isn't a thing, as you must recognize yourself, which one can believe seriously. If you want to know, it seems to me you are trying to imitate the manner of a certain author whom I heartily detest — I warn you — although I have unfortunately bound myself to put on one of his works. As a matter of fact, I was just starting to rehearse it, when you arrived. (*Turning to the*

Actors.) And this is what we've gained — out of the frying-pan into the fire!

THE FATHER: I don't know to what author you may be alluding, but believe me I feel what I think; and I seem to be philosophizing only for those who do not think what they feel, because they blind themselves with their own sentiment. I know that for many people this self-blinding seems much more "human"; but the contrary is really true. For man never reasons so much and becomes so introspective as when he suffers, since he is anxious to get at the cause of his sufferings, to learn who has produced them, and whether it is just or unjust that he should have to bear them. On the other hand, when he is happy, he takes his happiness as it comes and doesn't analyze it, just as if happiness were his right. The animals suffer without reasoning about their sufferings. But take the case of a man who suffers and begins to reason about it. Oh no! it can't be allowed! Let him suffer like an animal, and then — ah yes, he is "human"!

THE MANAGER: Look here! Look here! You're off again, philosophizing worse than ever.

THE FATHER: Because I suffer, sir! I'm not philosophizing: I'm crying aloud the reason of my sufferings.

THE MANAGER (*makes brusque movement as he is taken with a new idea*): I should like to know if anyone has ever heard of a character who gets right out of his part and perorates and speechifies as you do. Have you ever heard of a case? I haven't.

THE FATHER: You have never met such a case, sir, because authors, as a rule, hide the labor of their creations. When the characters are really alive before their author, the latter does nothing but follow them in their action, in other words, in the situations which they suggest to him; and he has to will them the way they will themselves — for there's trouble if he doesn't. When a character is born, he acquires at once such an independence, even of his own author, that he can be imagined by everybody even in many other situations where the author never dreamed of placing him; and so he acquires for himself a meaning which the author never thought of giving him.

THE MANAGER: Yes, yes, I know this.

THE FATHER: What is there then to marvel at in us? Imagine such a misfortune for characters as I have described to you: to be born of an author's fantasy, and be denied life by him; and then answer me if these characters left alive, and yet without life, weren't right in doing what they did do and are doing now, after they have attempted everything in their power to persuade him to give them their stage life. We've all tried him in turn, I, she (*indi-cating the Stepdaughter*) and she (*indicating the Mother*).

THE STEPDAUGHTER: It's true. I too have sought to tempt him, many, many times, when he has been sitting at his writing table, feeling a bit melancholy, at the twilight hour. He would sit in his armchair too lazy to switch on the light, and all the shadows that crept into his room were full of our presence coming to tempt him. (*As if she saw herself still there by the writing table, and was annoyed by the presence of the Actors.*) Oh, if you would only go away, go away and leave us alone — mother here with that son of hers — I with that child — that boy there always alone — and then I with him (*just hints at the Father*) — and then I alone, alone . . . in those shadows! (*Makes a sudden movement as if in the vision she has of herself illuminating those shadows she wanted to seize hold of herself.*) Ah! my life! my life! Oh, what scenes we proposed to him — and I tempted him more than any of the others!

THE FATHER: Maybe. But perhaps it was your fault that he refused to give us life: because you were too insistent, too troublesome.

THE STEPDAUGHTER: Nonsense! Didn't he make me so himself? (*Goes close to the Manager to tell him as if in confidence.*) In my opinion he abandoned us in a fit of depression, of disgust for the ordinary theater as the public knows it and likes it.

THE SON: Exactly what it was, sir; exactly that!

THE FATHER: Not at all! Don't believe it for a minute. Listen to me! You'll be doing quite right to modify, as you suggest, the excesses both of this girl here, who wants to do too much, and of this young man, who won't do anything at all.

THE SON: No, nothing!

THE MANAGER: You too get over the mark occasionally, my dear sir, if I may say so.

THE FATHER: I? When? Where?

THE MANAGER: Always! Continuously! Then there's this insistence of yours in trying to make us believe you are a character. And then too, you must really argue and philosophize less, you know, much less.

THE FATHER: Well, if you want to take away from me the possibility of representing the torment of my spirit which never gives me peace, you will be suppressing me: that's all. Every true man, sir, who is a little above the level of the beasts and plants does not live for the sake of living, without knowing how to live; but he lives so as to give a meaning and a value of his own to life. For me this is *every-thing*. I cannot give up this, just to represent a mere fact as she (*indicating the Stepdaughter*) wants. it's all very well for her, since her "vendetta" lies in the "fact." I'm not going to do it. It destroys my *raison d'être*.

THE MANAGER: Your *raison d'être!* Oh, we're going ahead fine! First she starts off, and then you jump in. At this rate, we'll never finish.

THE FATHER: Now, don't be offended! Have it your own way — provided, however, that within the limits of the parts you assign us each one's sacrifice isn't too great.

THE MANAGER: You've got to understand that you can't go on arguing at your own pleasure. Drama is action, sir, action and not confounded philosophy.

THE FATHER: All right. I'll do just as much arguing and philosophizing as everybody does when he is considering his own torments.

THE MANAGER: If the drama permits! But for Heaven's sake, man, let's get along and come to the scene.

THE STEPDAUGHTER: It seems to me we've got too much action with our coming into his house. (*Indicating Father.*) You said, before, you couldn't change the scene every five minutes.

THE MANAGER: Of course not. What we've got to do is to combine and group up all the facts in one simultaneous, close-knit action. We can't have it as you want, with your little brother wandering like a ghost from room to room, hiding behind doors and meditating a project which — what did you say it did to him?

THE STEPDAUGHTER: Consumes him, sir, wastes him away!

THE MANAGER: Well, it may be. And then at the same time, you want the little girl there to be playing in the garden . . . one in the house, and the other in the garden; isn't that it?

THE STEPDAUGHTER: Yes, in the sun, in the sun! That is my only pleasure: to see her happy and careless in the garden after the misery and squalor of the horrible room where we all four slept together. And I had to sleep with her — I, do you understand? — with my vile contaminated body next to hers; with her holding me fast in her loving little arms. In the garden, whenever she spied me, she would run to take me by the hand. She didn't care for the big flowers, only the little ones; and she loved to show me them and pet me.

THE MANAGER: Well then, we'll have it in the garden. Everything shall happen in the garden; and we'll group the other scenes there. (*Calls a Stage Hand.*) Here, a backcloth with trees and something to do as a fountain basin. (*Turning round to look at the back of the stage.*) Ah, you've fixed it up. Good! (*To Stepdaughter.*) This is just to give an idea, of course. The Boy, instead of hiding behind the doors, will wander about here in the garden, hiding behind the trees. But it's going to be rather dif-

ficult to find a child to do that scene with you where she shows you the flowers. (*Turning to the Boy.*) Come forward a little, will you please? Let's try it now! Come along! come along! (*Then seeing him come shyly forward, full of fear and looking lost.*) It's a nice business, this lad here. What's the matter with him? We'll have to give him a word or two to say. (*Goes close to him, puts a hand on his shoulders, and leads him behind one of the trees.*) Come on! come on! Let me see you a little! Hide here . . . yes, like that. Try and show your head just a little as if you were looking for someone. . . . (*Goes back to observe the effect, when the Boy at once goes through the action.*) Excellent! fine! (*Turning to Stepdaughter.*) Suppose the little girl there were to surprise him as he looks round, and run over to him, so we could give him a word or two to say?

THE STEPDAUGHTER: It's useless to hope he will speak, as long as that fellow there is here. . . . (*Indicates the Son.*) You must send him away first.

THE SON (*jumping up*): Delighted! Delighted! I don't ask for anything better. (*Begins to move away.*)

THE MANAGER (*at once stopping him*): No! No! Where are you going? Wait a bit!

(*The Mother gets up alarmed and terrified at the thought that he is really about to go away. Instinctively she lifts her arms to prevent him, without, however, leaving her seat.*)

THE SON (*to Manager, who stops him*): I've got nothing to do with this affair. Let me go, please! Let me go!

THE MANAGER: What do you mean by saying you've got nothing to do with this?

THE STEPDAUGHTER (*calmly, with irony*): Don't bother to stop him: he won't go away.

THE FATHER: He has to act the terrible scene in the garden with his mother.

THE SON (*suddenly resolute and with dignity*): I shall act nothing at all. I've said so from the very beginning. (*To the Manager.*) Let me go!

THE STEPDAUGHTER (*going over to the Manager*): Allow me? (*Puts down the Manager's arm which is restraining the Son.*) Well, go away then, if you want to! (*The Son looks at her with contempt and hatred. She laughs and says,*) You see, he can't, he can't go away! He is obliged to stay here, indissolubly bound to the chain. If I, who fly off when that happens which has to happen because I can't bear him — if I am still here and support that face and expression of his, you can well imagine that he is unable to move. He has to remain here, has to stop with that nice father of his, and that mother whose only son he is. (*Turning to the Mother.*) Come on, mother, come along! (*Turning to Manager to indicate her.*) You see, she was getting up to keep him back. (*To the Mother, beckoning her with her hand.*) Come on, come on! (*Then to Manager.*) You can imagine how little she wants to show these actors of yours what she really feels; but so eager is she to get near him that. . . . There, you see? She is willing to act her part. (*And in fact, the Mother approaches him; and as soon as the Stepdaughter has finished speaking, opens her arms to signify that she consents.*)

THE SON (*suddenly*): No! no! If I can't go away, then I'll stop here; but I repeat: I act nothing!

THE FATHER (*to Manager excitedly*): You can force him, sir.

THE SON: Nobody can force me.

THE FATHER: I can.

THE STEPDAUGHTER: Wait a minute, wait . . . First of all, the baby has to go to the fountain. . . . (*Runs to take the Child and leads her to the fountain.*)

THE MANAGER: Yes, yes of course; that's it. Both at the same time.

(*The Second Lady Lead and the Juvenile Lead at this point separate themselves from the group of Actors. One watches the Mother attentively; the other moves about studying the movements and manner of the Son whom he will have to act.*)

THE SON (*to Manager*): What do you mean by both at the same time? It isn't right. There was no scene between me and her. (*Indicates the Mother.*) Ask her how it was!

THE MOTHER: Yes, it's true. I had come into his room. . . .

THE SON: Into my room, do you understand? Nothing to do with the garden.

THE MANAGER: It doesn't matter. Haven't I told you we've got to group the action?

THE SON (*observing the Juvenile Lead studying him*): What do you want?

THE JUVENILE LEAD: Nothing! I was just looking at you.

THE SON (*turning toward the Second Lady Lead*): Ah! she's at it too: to re-act her part! (*Indicating the Mother.*)

THE MANAGER: Exactly! And it seems to me that you ought to be grateful to them for their interest.

THE SON: Yes, but haven't you yet perceived that it isn't possible to live in front of a mirror which not only freezes us with the image of ourselves, but throws our likeness back at us with a horrible grimace?

THE FATHER: That is true, absolutely true. You must see that.

THE MANAGER (*to Second Lady Lead and Juvenile Lead*): He's right! Move away from them!

THE SON: Do as you like. I'm out of this!

THE MANAGER: Be quiet, you, will you? And let me hear your mother! (*To Mother.*) You were saying you had entered. . . .

THE MOTHER: Yes, into his room, because I couldn't stand it any longer. I went to empty my heart to him of all the anguish that tortures me. . . . But as soon as he saw me come in. . . .

THE SON: Nothing happened! There was no scene. I went away, that's all! I don't care for scenes!

THE MOTHER: It's true, true. That's how it was.

THE MANAGER: Well now, we've got to do this bit between you and him. It's indispensable.

THE MOTHER: I'm ready . . . when you are ready. If you could only find a chance for me to tell him what I feel here in my heart.

THE FATHER (*going to Son in a great rage*): You'll do this for your mother, for your mother, do you understand?

THE SON (*quite determined*): I do nothing!

THE FATHER (*taking hold of him and shaking him*): For God's sake, do as I tell you! Don't you hear your mother asking you for a favor? Haven't you even got the guts to be a son?

THE SON (*taking hold of the Father*): No! No! And for God's sake stop it, or else. . . . (*General agitation. The Mother, frightened, tries to separate them.*)

THE MOTHER (*pleading*): Please! please!

THE FATHER (*not leaving hold of the Son*): You've got to obey, do you hear?

THE SON (*almost crying from rage*): What does it mean, this madness you've got? (*They separate.*) Have you no decency, that you insist on showing everyone our shame? I won't do it! I won't! And I stand for the will of our author in this. He didn't want to put us on the stage, after all!

THE MANAGER: Man alive! You came here . . .

THE SON (*indicating Father*): He did! I didn't!

THE MANAGER: Aren't you here now?

THE SON: It was his wish, and he dragged us along with him. He's told you not only the things that did happen, but also things that have never happened at all.

THE MANAGER: Well, tell me then what did happen. You went out of your room without saying a word?

THE SON: Without a word, so as to avoid a scene!

THE MANAGER: And then what did you do?

THE SON: Nothing . . . walking in the garden. . . . (*Hesitates for a moment with expression of gloom.*)

THE MANAGER (*coming closer to him, interested by his extraordinary reserve*): Well, well . . . walking in the garden. . . .

THE SON (*exasperated*): Why on earth do you insist? It's horrible!

(*The Mother trembles, sobs, and looks toward the fountain.*)

THE MANAGER (*slowly observing the glance and turning toward the Son with increasing apprehension*): The baby?

THE SON: There in the fountain. . . .

THE FATHER (*pointing with tender pity to the Mother*): She was following him at the moment. . . .

THE MANAGER (*to the Son anxiously*): And then you. . . .

THE SON: I ran over to her; I was jumping in to drag her out when I saw something that froze my blood . . . the boy standing stock still, with eyes like a madman's, watching his little drowned sister, in the fountain! (*The Stepdaughter bends over the fountain to hide the Child. She sobs.*) Then. . . . (*A revolver shot rings out behind the trees where the Boy is hidden.*)

THE MOTHER (*with a cry of terror runs over in that direction together with several of the Actors amid general confusion*): My son! My son! (*Then amid the cries and exclamations one hears her voice.*) Help! Help!

THE MANAGER (*pushing the Actors aside while they lift up the Boy and carry him off*): Is he really wounded?

SOME ACTORS: He's dead! dead!

OTHER ACTORS: No, no, it's only make-believe, it's only pretense!

THE FATHER (*with a terrible cry*): Pretense? Reality, sir, reality!

THE MANAGER: Pretense? Reality? To hell with it all! Never in my life has such a thing happened to me. I've lost a whole day over these people, a whole day!

COMMENTARY

John Corbin (1870–1959)
REVIEW OF *SIX CHARACTERS IN SEARCH OF AN AUTHOR*   *1922*

> *Corbin's review of the distinguished 1922 production of* Six Characters in Search of an Author *reminds us how much the audiences loved the play. They stood clapping long after the last curtain. Florence Eldridge, who became famous for her role, is given relatively little attention here. Corbin instead focused his comments on the complexity of the play's comic premise.*

Philosophical fooling and shrewd criticism on the art of the theatre mingle in the Italian play which Brock Pemberton is presenting in translation at the Princess. Imagine a playwright whose creative mind is haunted by six characters, the persons of a harrowing family drama, all urging insistently that they be given full and subtly shaded representation in the theatre. That is the normal condition of authentic creation; but as art consists in rigid elimination as well as in delicate emphasis, many of the aspirations of the six for self-expression have to be denied. Imagine next that the subject of their suffering is not sympathetic to the public, and that the only true and significant outcome is undramatic — not moving and inspiring, but static. That very often happens when a dramatist takes his real inspiration from life as it is actually lived, and in the supreme court of the manager's office he is nonsuited. There is no play.

But there are characters more live and vital than most of those that see the footlights. Imagine, finally, that these characters, still longing to live out their lives on the scene, go out in search of a more obliging author — and find a stage manager who has a company but no new play, only the stock stuff of a world somewhat deficient in new inspiration. Recognizing raw materials of interest and power, the enterprising business man undertakes to supply the place of the author. It seems to him a positive windfall to be relieved of that insistent and obnoxious incident of production. He will allow the six characters to live out their own lives while a secretary takes down the dialogue and his company stands by preparing to assume the parts. Magnificent!

Those who look upon ordinary rehearsals as a madhouse will receive illumination. Instead of a single author, long subdued in misery, the manager has his six orphans to contend with. The actors of his company, accustomed to have parts ruthlessly adapted to their personalities, are confronted each with a fury of unreason, demanding the absolute. For these characters, though the shadows of a dream, are "real" in the sense of being raw vitality unshaped to the necessities of art and the practical ends of the theatre. In the turmoil that ensues there is much satire on the foibles of player folk and managers and no little philosophy of dramatic art and dramatic criticism.

Margaret Wycherly is Mother in the roving dramatis personae and lends to the character genuine imagination and emotional power. Moffat Johnston is the garrulous father, eagerly philosophic and disquisitional. Florence Eldridge is the stepdaughter, overflowing with eager youth and charm. Throughout the production is able and highly competent. The audience last night, largely composed of folk of the theatre, rose to the novelty and humor of the idea and lingered long in applause after the brief three acts were over.

What the public will say to this rather slender and technical satire remains to be seen, but already it may be said that the season is indebted to Mr. Pemberton for one more exploration of strange fields and pastures new.

Eugene O'Neill

Eugene O'Neill (1888–1953) is a major figure in American drama. His enormous output is in the tradition of realism established by Strindberg and Ibsen; and his early plays, such as *Anna Christie* (1921), introduced Americans to the techniques of the great European realists. Realism for Americans was a move away from the sentimental comedies, the pathetic dramas, and the melodrama that dominated the American stage from before the Civil War to World War I. Some of O'Neill's plays, such as *Strange Interlude* (1928) and *Dynamo* (1929), were expressionist in style, demonstrating a considerable range. O'Neill rejected the kind of theater in which his father had thrived. James O'Neill had long been a stage star, traveling across the country in his production of *The Count of Monte Cristo,* which had made him rich but had also made him a prisoner of a single role.

Eugene O'Neill won the Pulitzer Prize for drama three times in the 1920s and the Nobel Prize for literature in 1936. Although not popular successes in his own day, his plays — including those published posthumously — are now mainstays of the American theater. Some of America's finest actors have taken a strong interest in his work, both producing his plays and acting in them on the stage and on television. From the 1950s to the 1990s, the late Colleen Dewhurst and Jason Robards, Jr., in particular, gave some magnificent performances and interpretations of O'Neill's work.

The young O'Neill was a romantic in the popular sense of the word. After a year at Princeton University, he began to travel on the sea. His jaunts took him to South America, and he once wound up virtually broke and without resources in Buenos Aires. When he returned to America, he studied for a year with George Pierce Baker, the most famous drama teacher of his day. Eventually, he took up residence in Provincetown, Massachusetts, where a group of people dedicated to theater — including the playwright Susan Glaspell — began to put on plays in their living rooms. When their audiences spilled over, the group created the Provincetown Playhouse, the theater in which many of O'Neill's earliest pieces were first performed.

The subjects of many of O'Neill's plays were not especially appealing to general theater audiences. Those who hoped for light comedy and a good laugh or light melodrama and a good cry found the intensity of his dark vision of the world to be overwhelming. They came for mere entertainment, and he was providing them with frightening visions of the soul's interior. The glum and painful surroundings of *Anna Christie*

(1921) and the brutality of the lower-class coal stoker in *The Hairy Ape* (1922) were foreign to the comfortable middle-class audiences who supported commercial theater in America. They found O'Neill's characters to be haunted by family agonies, affections never given, ambitions never realized, pains never assuaged. Despite his remarkable abilities and the power of his drama, audiences often did not know what to make of him. To a large extent, his acceptance came on waves of shock, as had the acceptance of the Scandinavian realists.

O'Neill's early work is marked by a variety of experiments with theatrical effects and moods. He tried to use the primary influences of Greek drama in such plays as *Desire Under the Elms* (1924), which has been described by critics as Greek tragedy, and *Mourning Becomes Electra* (1931), based on the *Oresteia,* which took three days to perform. But many of his early plays now seem dated and strange. His most impressive plays are his later work, such as *Ah, Wilderness!* (1933), *The Iceman Cometh* (1939), *Long Day's Journey into Night* (1939–1941), *A Moon for the Misbegotten* (1943), and *A Touch of the Poet* (1935–1942), which was performed posthumously in 1957.

DESIRE UNDER THE ELMS

Desire Under the Elms (1924) is Eugene O'Neill's first effort at writing in the style of Greek tragedy. He did not follow the Greek tradition and choose a great figure of noble birth about whom the fates would unravel their mystery. Rather, he was deliberately democratic and American, choosing a New England farmer and his family as the protagonists of his drama. The powers of fate that would animate a Greek tragedy are expressed in the emotional forces of jealousy, resentment, lust, and incestuous love.

O'Neill set his play on a typically rocky New England soil, which in many ways bears a striking resemblance to the rocky soil of Athens and the Greek coastline. The unyielding toughness of life on that land contrasts with the easy life to be made from gold mining in California. Ephraim Cabot, the seventy-five-year-old father, has been made hard and physically powerful by his work. He has just taken a young and scheming wife, Abbie. Eben Cabot, one of Ephraim's sons, has decided to stay on the farm while his two brothers go to California and try to put New England behind them.

The sense of having been dispossessed of his farm drives Eben to hate his new mother, who married the elder Cabot merely to inherit his farm. Abbie knows that Cabot is not a satisfying sexual partner, but she sees Eben as a reasonable substitute. At first the sparring between Abbie and Eben is based on calculating self-interest, but eventually their feelings for each other become overpowering. Lust turns to love, and the desires and emotions they thought they could control are quite out of control. The son they produce is passed off as old Cabot's, although the townspeople have no illusion about whose child it is.

The farm itself is a powerful presence in the play. Whenever old Cabot thinks he should give up and follow the promise of easy money in California, he feels God's presence urging him to stay. God operates for Ephraim as the oracle in *Oedipus Rex* does, giving him a message that is painful but must be obeyed. The rocks on the farm are unforgiving, and so is the fate that Abbie and Eben face. Theirs is an impossible love; everything they do to prove their love condemns them even more. The forces of fate center on the farm. When the play opens, Eben says of it, "God! Purty!" When the play ends, the sheriff praises the farm and says he surely would like to own it, striking a clear note of irony: The agony of the play is rooted in lust — lust for the farm that parallels the lust between Abbie and Eben.

The play is haunted by the ghost of Eben's mother, whom Ephraim married primarily for her farm. Her ghost is exorcised only after the cycle of retribution has begun. Old Cabot has committed a crime against her, and now he must become the victim.

The language of the dialogue is that of New England in the mid-nineteenth century. Living in New England, O'Neill understood the ways and the language of its people. He seems to have imagined the "down-east" flavor of Maine in the language, and he has been careful to build the proper pronunciation into the dialogue. This folksy way of speaking helps emphasize the peasantlike qualities in these New England farmers. O'Neill's careful use of language is reminiscent of Synge's masterful representation of the Irish-English speech of the Aran Islanders in *Riders to the Sea,* a play that is also a kind of folk tragedy.

The language of O'Neill's characters has a rocky toughness at times. Characters are laconic — they often answer in a single word: "Ay-eh." Faithful to his vision of the simple speech of country folk, O'Neill avoids giving them elaborate poetic soliloquies. Instead, he shows how, despite their limited language, rural people feel profound emotions and act on them.

O'Neill carefully links Abbie with Queen Phaedra, who in Euripides' play *Hippolytus* and in Racine's seventeenth-century play *Phèdre* finds herself uncontrollably desiring her husband's son as a lover. Racine and Racine's audience could easily imagine such intense emotions overwhelming a noblewoman because they thought that nobility felt more intensely and lived more intensely than ordinary people. But O'Neill is trying to make his audience see that even unlettered farm people can feel as deeply as tragic heroes of any age do. The Cabots are victims of passion. They share their fate with the great families of the Greek tragedies.

Desire Under the Elms in Performance

Desire Under the Elms was first performed in Greenwich Village in 1924 under the auspices of the Provincetown Players. A year later it appeared on Broadway for thirty-six weeks, a long run for a tragedy. Its first reviewers were courteous but puzzled. They compared the play with earlier O'Neill works, remarking on its "tragic gloom and irony" and praising its language. At the Los Angeles production in 1926, the cast was arrested for "giving an obscene play." The sexual themes offended theatergoers in California, and even those who defended the play admitted that the text would be offensive to some members of the audience.

Because the English censor banned the play until 1938, its first European production was in Prague's National Theatre in 1925. Its Czech title translated as "The Farm Under the Elms." The director used a highly stylized set influenced by the Moscow Art Theatre and later described as "a sort of two-storied wooded edifice . . . rather like a log cabin multiplied by four."

Other earlier European productions followed in Moscow in 1932, in Stockholm in 1933, and finally in London in 1940. The 1952 New York revival was not successful. The 1963 revival at the Circle in the Square in New York starred George C. Scott and his wife, Colleen Dewhurst. Jose Quintero, a notable interpreter of O'Neill, directed. Critics complained about "awkward" echoes of Greek tragedy while admitting that the play had an uncanny power despite its flaws. It ran for 380 performances.

The play has often been revived: in Boston in 1967; at the Berkshire Theater Festival in 1974; at the Roundabout Theater in New York, directed by Terry Schrieber, in 1984; and by numerous local theater groups. In 1978 Edward Thomas staged it at Connecticut College in New London as an opera. A creditable production, it emphasized the play's American folk qualities.

Eugene O'Neill (1888–1953)
DESIRE UNDER THE ELMS
1924

Characters

EPHRAIM CABOT
SIMEON ⎫
PETER ⎬ *his sons*
EBEN   ⎭
ABBIE PUTNAM
YOUNG GIRL, TWO FARMERS, *the* FIDDLER, *a* SHERIFF, *and other folk from the neighboring farms.*

The action of the entire play takes place in, and immediately outside of, the Cabot farmhouse in New England, in the year 1850. The south end of the house faces front to a stone wall with a wooden gate at center opening on a country road. The house is in good condition but in need of paint. Its walls are a sickly grayish, the green of the shutters faded. Two enormous elms are on each side of the house. They bend their trailing branches down over the roof. They appear to protect and at the same time subdue. There is a sinister maternity in their aspect, a crushing, jealous absorption. They have developed from their intimate contact with the life of man in the house an appalling humaneness. They brood oppressively over the house. They are like exhausted women resting their sagging breasts and hands and hair on its roof, and when it rains their tears trickle down monotonously and rot on the shingles.

There is a path running from the gate around the right corner of the house to the front door. A narrow porch is on this side. The end wall facing us has two windows in its upper story, two larger ones on the floor below. The two upper are those of the father's bedroom and that of the brothers. On the left, ground floor, is the kitchen — on the right, the parlor, the shades of which are always drawn down.*

PART I • *Scene* 1

(Exterior of the farmhouse. It is sunset of a day at the beginning of summer in the year 1850. There is no wind and everything is still. The sky above the roof is suffused with deep colors, the green of the elms glows, but the house is in shadow, seeming pale and washed out by contrast.)

(A door opens and Eben Cabot comes to the end of the porch and stands looking down the road to the right. He has a large bell in his hand and this he swings mechanically, awakening a deafening clangor. Then he puts his hands on his hips and stares up at the sky. He sighs with a puzzled awe and blurts out with halting appreciation.)

EBEN: God! Purty! (*His eyes fall and he stares about him frowningly. He is twenty-five, tall and sinewy. His face is well formed, good-looking, but its expression is resentful and defensive. His defiant, dark eyes remind one of a wild animal's in captivity. Each day is a cage in which he finds himself trapped but inwardly unsubdued. There is a fierce repressed vitality about him. He has black hair, mustache, a thin curly trace of beard. He is dressed in rough farm clothes.)*

(He spits on the ground with intense disgust, turns, and goes back into the house.)

(Simeon and Peter come in from their work in the fields. They are tall men, much older than their half-brother [Simeon is thirty-nine and Peter thirty-seven], built on a squarer, simpler model, fleshier in body, more bovine and homelier in face, shrewder and more practical. Their shoulders stoop a bit from years of farm work. They clump heavily along in their clumsy thick-soled boots caked with earth. Their clothes, their faces, hands, bare arms, and throats are earth-stained. They smell of earth. They stand together for a moment in front of the house and, as if with the one impulse, stare dumbly up at the sky, leaning on their hoes. Their faces have a compressed, unresigned expression. As they look upward, this softens.)

SIMEON *(grudgingly)*: Purty.
PETER: Ay-eh.
SIMEON *(suddenly)*: Eighteen year ago.
PETER: What?
SIMEON: Jenn. My woman. She died.
PETER: I'd fergot.
SIMEON: I rec'lect — now an' agin. Makes it lonesome. She'd hair long's a hoss' tail — an' yeller like gold!
PETER: Waal — she's gone. *(This with indifferent finality — then after a pause.)* They's gold in the West, Sim.
SIMEON *(still under the influence of sunset — vaguely)*: In the sky?
PETER: Waal — in a manner o' speakin' — that's the promise. *(Growing excited.)* Gold in the sky — in the West — Golden Gate — Californi-a! — Goldest West! — fields o' gold!
SIMEON *(excited in his turn)*: Fortunes layin' just atop o' the ground waitin' t' be picked! Solomon's mines, they says! *(For a moment they continue looking up at the sky — then their eyes drop.)*
PETER *(with sardonic bitterness)*: Here — it's stones atop o' the ground — stones atop o' stones — makin' stone walls — year atop o' year — him 'n' yew 'n' me 'n' then Eben — makin' stone walls fur him to fence us in!
SIMEON: We've wuked. Give our strength. Give our years. Plowed 'em under in the ground — *(He stamps rebelliously.)* — rottin' — makin' soil for his crops! *(A pause.)* Waal — the farm pays good for hereabouts.
PETER: If we plowed in Californi-a, they'd be lumps o' gold in the furrow!
SIMEON: Californi-a's t'other side o' earth, a'most. We got t' calc'late —
PETER *(after a pause)*: 'Twould be hard fur me, too, to give up what we've 'arned here by our sweat. *(A pause. Eben sticks his head out of the dining room window, listening.)*
SIMEON: Ay-eh. *(A pause.)* Mebbe — he'll die soon.
PETER *(doubtfully)*: Mebbe.
SIMEON: Mebbe — fur all we knows — he's dead now.
PETER: Ye'd need proof.
SIMEON: He's been gone two months — with no word.
PETER: Left us in the fields an evenin' like this. Hitched up an' druv off into the West. That's plum onnateral. He hadn't never been off this farm 'ceptin' t' the village in thirty year or more, not since he married Eben's maw. *(A pause. Shrewdly.)* I calc'late we might git him declared crazy by the court.
SIMEON: He skinned 'em too slick. He got the best o' all on 'em. They'd never b'lieve him crazy. *(A pause.)* We got t' wait — till he's underground.
EBEN *(with a sardonic chuckle)*: Honor thy father! *(They turn startled, and stare at him. He grins, then scowls.)* I pray he's died. *(They stare at him. He continues matter-of-factly.)* Supper's ready.
SIMEON AND PETER *(together)*: Ay-eh.
EBEN *(gazing up at the sky)*: Sun's downin' purty.
SIMEON AND PETER *(together)*: Ay-eh. They's gold in the West.
EBEN: Ay-eh. *(Pointing.)* Yonder atop o' the hill pasture, ye mean?
SIMEON AND PETER *(together)*: In Californi-a!
EBEN: Hunh? *(Stares at them indifferently for a second, then drawls.)* Waal — supper's gittin' cold. *(He turns back into kitchen.)*
SIMEON *(startled — smacks his lips)*: I air hungry!
PETER *(sniffing)*: I smells bacon!
SIMEON *(with hungry appreciation)*: Bacon's good!
PETER *(in same tone)*: Bacon's bacon! *(They turn, shouldering each other, their bodies bumping and rubbing together as they hurry clumsily to their food, like two friendly oxen toward their evening meal. They disappear around the right corner of house and can be heard entering the door.)*

Scene II

(The color fades from the sky. Twilight begins. The interior of the kitchen is now visible. A pine table is at center, a cook-stove in the right rear corner, four rough wooden chairs, a tallow candle on the table. In the middle of the rear wall is fastened a big advertising poster with a ship in full sail and the word "California" in big letters. Kitchen utensils hang from nails. Everything is neat and in order but the atmosphere is of a men's camp kitchen rather than that of a home.)

(Places for three are laid. Eben takes boiled potatoes and bacon from the stove and puts them on the

table, also a loaf of bread and a crock of water. Simeon and Peter shoulder in, slump down in their chairs without a word. Eben joins them. The three eat in silence for a moment, the two elder as naturally unrestrained as beasts of the field, Eben picking at his food without appetite, glancing at them with a tolerant dislike.)

SIMEON (*suddenly turns to Eben*): Looky here! Ye'd oughtn't t' said that, Eben.

PETER: 'Twa'n't righteous.

EBEN: What?

SIMEON: Ye prayed he'd died.

EBEN: Waal — don't yew pray it? (*A pause.*)

PETER: He's our Paw.

EBEN (*violently*): Not mine!

SIMEON (*dryly*): Ye'd not let no one else say that about yer Maw! Ha! (*He gives one abrupt sardonic guffaw. Peter grins.*)

EBEN (*very pale*): I meant — I hain't his'n — I hain't like him — he hain't me!

PETER (*dryly*): Wait till ye've growed his age!

EBEN (*intensely*): I'm Maw — every drop o' blood! (*A pause. They stare at him with indifferent curiosity.*)

PETER (*reminiscently*): She was good t' Sim 'n' me. A good Stepmaw's scurse.

SIMEON: She was good t' everyone.

EBEN (*greatly moved, gets to his feet and makes an awkward bow to each of them — stammering*): I be thankful t' ye. I'm her — her heir. (*He sits down in confusion.*)

PETER (*after a pause — judicially*): She was good even t' him.

EBEN (*fiercely*): An' fur thanks he killed her!

SIMEON (*after a pause*): No one never kills nobody. It's allus somethin'. That's the murderer.

EBEN: Didn't he slave Maw t' death?

PETER: He's slaved himself t' death. He's slaved Sim 'n' me 'n' yew t' death — on'y none o' us hain't died — yit.

SIMEON: It's somethin' — drivin' him — t' drive us!

EBEN (*vengefully*): Waal — I hold him t' jedgment! (*Then scornfully.*) Somethin'! What's somethin'?

SIMEON: Dunno.

EBEN (*sardonically*): What's drivin' yew to California, mebbe? (*They look at him in surprise.*) Oh, I've heerd ye! (*Then, after a pause.*) But ye'll never go t' the gold fields!

PETER (*assertively*): Mebbe!

EBEN: Whar'll ye git the money?

PETER: We kin walk. It's an a'mighty ways — California — but if yew was t' put all the steps we've walked on this farm end t' end we'd be in the moon!

EBEN: The Injuns'll skulp ye on the plains.

SIMEON (*with grim humor*): We'll mebbe make 'em pay a hair fur a hair!

EBEN (*decisively*): But t'aint that. Ye won't never go because ye'll wait here fur yer share o' the farm, thinkin' allus he'll die soon.

SIMEON (*after a pause*): We've a right.

PETER: Two-thirds belongs t'us.

EBEN (*jumping to his feet*): Ye've no right! She wa'n't yewr Maw! It was her farm! Didn't he steal it from her? She's dead. It's my farm.

SIMEON (*sardonically*): Tell that t' Paw — when he comes! I'll bet ye a dollar he'll laugh — fur once in his life. Ha! (*He laughs himself in one single mirthless bark.*)

PETER (*amused in turn, echoes his brother*): Ha!

SIMEON (*after a pause*): What've ye got held agin us, Eben? Year arter year it's skulked in yer eye — somethin'.

PETER: Ay eh.

EBEN: Ay-eh. They's somethin'. (*Suddenly exploding.*) Why didn't ye never stand between him 'n' my Maw when he was slavin' her to her grave — t' pay her back fur the kindness she done t' yew? (*There is a long pause. They stare at him in surprise.*)

SIMEON: Waal — the stock'd got t' be watered.

PETER: 'R they was woodin' t' do.

SIMEON: 'R plowin'.

PETER: 'R hayin'.

SIMEON: 'R spreadin' manure.

PETER: 'R weedin'.

SIMEON: 'R prunin'.

PETER: 'R milkin'.

EBEN (*breaking in harshly*): An' makin' walls — stone atop o' stone — makin' walls till yer heart's a stone ye heft up out o' the way o' growth onto a stone wall t' wall in yer heart!

SIMEON (*matter-of-factly*): We never had no time t' meddle.

PETER (*to Eben*): Yew was fifteen afore yer Maw died — an' big fur yer age. Why didn't ye never do nothin'?

EBEN (*harshly*): They was chores t' do, wasn't they? (*A pause — then slowly.*) It was on'y arter she died I come to think o' it. Me cookin' — doin' her work — that made me know her, suffer her sufferin' — she'd come back t' help — come back t' bile potatoes — come back t' fry bacon — come back t' bake biscuits — come back all cramped up t' shake the fire, an' carry ashes, her eyes weepin' an' bloody with smoke an' cinders same's they used t' be. She still comes back — stands by the stove thar in the evenin' — she can't find it nateral sleepin' an' restin' in peace. She can't git used t' bein' free — even in her grave.

SIMEON: She never complained none.

EBEN: She'd got too tired. She'd got too used t' bein' too tired. That was what he done. (*With vengeful* passion.) An' sooner'r later, I'll meddle. I'll say the thin's I didn't say then t' him! I'll yell 'em at the top o' my lungs. I'll see t' it my Maw gits some rest an' sleep in her grave! (*He sits down again, relapsing into a brooding silence. They look at him with a queer indifferent curiosity.*)

PETER (*after a pause*): Whar in tarnation d'ye s'pose he went, Sim?

SIMEON: Dunno. He druv off in the buggy, all spick an' span, with the mare all breshed an' shiny, druv off clackin' his tongue an' wavin' his whip. I remember it right well. I was finishin' plowin', it was spring an' May an' sunset, an' gold in the West, an' he druv off into it. I yells "Whar ye goin', Paw?" an' he hauls up by the stone wall a jiffy. His old snake's eyes was glitterin' in the sun like he'd been drinkin' a jugful an' he says with a mule's grin: "Don't ye run away till I come back!"

PETER: Wonder if he knowed we was wantin' fur Californi-a?

SIMEON: Mebbe. I didn't say nothin' and he says, lookin' kinder queer an' sick: "I been hearin' the hens cluckin' an' the roosters crowin' all the durn day. I been listenin't' the cows lowin' an' everythin' else kickin' up till I can't stand it no more. It's spring an' I'm feelin' damned," he says. "Damned like an old bare hickory tree fit on'y fur burnin'," he says. An' then I calc'late I must've looked a mite hopeful, fur he adds real spry and vicious: "But don't git no fool idee I'm dead. I've sworn t' live a hundred an' I'll do it, if on'y t' spite yer sinful greed! An' now I'm ridin' out t' learn God's message t' me in the spring, like the prophets done. An' yew git back t' yer plowin'," he says. An' he druv off singin' a hymn. I thought he was drunk — 'r I'd stopped him goin'.

EBEN (*scornfully*): No, ye wouldn't! Ye're scared o' him. He's stronger — inside — than both o' ye put together!

PETER (*sardonically*): An' yew — be yew Samson?°

EBEN: I'm gittin' stronger. I kin feel it growin' in me — growin' an' growin' — till it'll bust out — ! (*He gets up and puts on his coat and a hat. They watch him, gradually breaking into grins. Eben avoids their eyes sheepishly.*) I'm goin' out fur a spell — up the road.

PETER: T' the village.

SIMEON: T' see Minnie?

EBEN (*defiantly*): Ay-eh!

PETER (*jeeringly*): The Scarlet Woman!

SIMEON: Lust — that's what's growin' in ye!

EBEN: Waal — she's purty!

Samson: A biblical hero known for his great physical strength.

PETER: She's been purty fur twenty year.

SIMEON: A new coat o' paint'll make a heifer out of forty.

EBEN: She hain't forty!

PETER: If she hain't, she's teeterin' on the edge.

EBEN (*desperately*): What d'yew know —

PETER: All they is . . . Sim knew her — an' then me arter —

SIMEON: An' Paw kin tell yew somethin' too! He was fust!

EBEN: D'ye mean t' say he . . . ?

SIMEON (*with a grin*): Ay-eh! We air his heirs in everythin'!

EBEN (*intensely*): That's more to it! That grows on it! It'll bust soon! (*Then violently.*) I'll go smash my fist in her face! (*He pulls open the door in rear violently.*)

SIMEON (*with a wink at Peter — drawlingly*): Mebbe — but the night's wa'm — purty — by the time ye git thar mebbe ye'll kiss her instead!

PETER: Sart'n he will! (*They both roar with coarse laughter. Eben rushes out and slams the door — then the outside front door — comes around the corner of the house and stands still by the gate, staring up at the sky.*)

SIMEON (*looking after him*): Like his Paw.

PETER: Dead spit an' image!

SIMEON: Dog'll eat dog!

PETER: Ay-eh. (*Pause. With yearning.*) Mebbe a year from now we'll be in Californi-a.

SIMEON: Ay-eh. (*A pause. Both yawn.*) Let's git t'bed. (*He blows out the candle. They go out door in rear. Eben stretches his arms up to the sky — rebelliously.*)

EBEN: Waal — thar's a star, an' somewhar's they's him, an' here's me, an' thar's Min up the road — in the same night. What if I does kiss her? She's like t'night, she's soft 'n' wa'm, her eyes kin wink like a star, her mouth's wa'm, her arms're wa'm, she smells like a wa'm plowed field, she's purty . . . Ay-eh! By God A'mighty she's purty, an' I don't give a damn how many sins she's sinned afore mine or who she's sinned 'em with, my sin's as purty as any one on 'em! (*He strides off down the road to the left.*)

Scene III

(*It is the pitch darkness just before dawn. Eben comes in from the left and goes around to the porch, feeling his way, chuckling bitterly and cursing half-aloud to himself.*)

EBEN: The cussed old miser! (*He can be heard going in the front door. There is a pause as he goes up-*

stairs, then a loud knock on the bedroom door of the brothers.) Wake up!

SIMEON *(startledly)*: Who's thar?

EBEN *(Pushing open the door and coming in, a lighted candle in his hand. The bedroom of the brothers is revealed. Its ceiling is the sloping roof. They can stand upright only close to the center dividing wall of the upstairs. Simeon and Peter are in a double bed, front. Eben's cot is to the rear. Eben has a mixture of silly grin and vicious scowl on his face.)*: I be!

PETER *(angrily)*: What in hell's-fire . . . ?

EBEN: I got news fur ye! Ha! *(He gives one abrupt sardonic guffaw.)*

SIMEON *(angrily)*: Couldn't ye hold it 'til we'd got our sleep?

EBEN: It's nigh sunup. *(Then explosively.)* He's gone an' married agen!

SIMEON AND PETER *(explosively)*: Paw?

EBEN: Got himself hitched to a female 'bout thirty-five — an' purty, they says . . .

SIMEON *(aghast)*: It's a durn lie!

PETER: Who says?

SIMEON: They been stringin' ye!

EBEN: Think I'm a dunce, do ye? The hull village says. The preacher from New Dover, he brung the news — told it t'our preacher — New Dover, that's whar the old loon got himself hitched — that's whar the woman lived —

PETER *(no longer doubting — stunned)*: Waal . . . !

SIMEON *(the same)*: Waal . . . !

EBEN *(sitting down on a bed — with vicious hatred)*: Ain't he a devil out o' hell? It's jest t' spite us — the damned old mule!

PETER *(after a pause)*: Everythin'll go t'her now.

SIMEON: Ay-eh. *(A pause — dully.)* Waal — if it's done —

PETER: It's done us. *(Pause — then persuasively.)* They's gold in the fields o' Californi-a, Sim. No good a-stayin' here now.

SIMEON: Jest what I was a-thinkin'. *(Then with decision.)* S'well fust's last! Let's light out and git this mornin'.

PETER: Suits me.

EBEN: Ye must like walkin'.

SIMEON *(sardonically)*: If ye'd grow wings on us we'd fly thar!

EBEN: Ye'd like ridin' better — on a boat, wouldn't ye? *(Fumbles in his pocket and takes out a crumpled sheet of foolscap.)* Waal, if ye sign this ye kin ride on a boat. I've had it writ out an' ready in case ye'd ever go. It says fur three hundred dollars t' each ye agree yewr shares o' the farm is sold t' me. *(They look suspiciously at the paper. A pause.)*

SIMEON *(wonderingly)*: But if he's hitched agen —

PETER: An' whar'd yew git that sum o' money, anyways?

EBEN *(cunningly)*: I know whar it's hid. I been waitin' — Maw told me. She knew whar it lay fur years, but she was waitin' . . . It's her'n — the money he hoarded from her farm an' hid from Maw. It's my money by rights now.

PETER: Whar's it hid?

EBEN *(cunningly)*: Whar yew won't never find it without me. Maw spied on him — 'r she'd never knowed. *(A pause. They look at him suspiciously, and he at them.)* Waal, is it fa'r trade?

SIMEON: Dunno.

PETER: Dunno.

SIMEON *(looking at window)*: Sky's grayin'.

PETER: Ye better start the fire, Eben.

SIMEON: An' fix some vittles.

EBEN: Ay-eh. *(Then with a forced jocular heartiness.)* I'll git ye a good one. If ye're startin' t' hoof it t' Californi-a ye'll need somethin' that'll stick t' yer ribs. *(He turns to the door, adding meaningly.)* But ye kin ride on a boat if ye'll swap. *(He stops at the door and pauses. They stare at him.)*

SIMEON *(suspiciously)*: Whar was ye all night?

EBEN *(defiantly)*: Up t' Min's. *(Then slowly.)* Walkin' thar, fust I felt 's if I'd kiss her; then I got a-thinkin' o' what ye'd said o' him an' her an' I says, I'll bust her nose fur that! Then I got t' the village an' heerd the news an' I got madder'n hell an' run all the way t' Min's not knowin' what I'd do — *(He pauses — then sheepishly but more defiantly.)* Waal — when I seen her, I didn't hit her — nor I didn't kiss her nuther — I begun t' beller like a calf an' cuss at the same time, I was so durn mad — an' she got scared — an' I jest grabbed holt an' tuk her! *(Proudly.)* Yes, sirree! I tuk her. She may've been his'n — an' your'n, too — but she's mine now!

SIMEON *(dryly)*: In love, air yew?

EBEN *(with lofty scorn)*: Love! I don't take no stock in sech slop!

PETER *(winking at Simeon)*: Mebbe Eben's aimin' t' marry, too.

SIMEON: Min'd make a true faithful he'pmeet! *(They snicker.)*

EBEN: What do I care fur her — 'ceptin' she's round an' wa'm? The p'int is she was his'n — an' now she b'longs t' me! *(He goes to the door — then turns — rebelliously.)* An' Min hain't sech a bad un. They's worse'n Min in the world, I'll bet ye! Wait'll we see this cow the Old Man's hitched t'! She'll beat Min, I got a notion! *(He starts to go out.)*

SIMEON *(suddenly)*: Mebbe ye'll try t' make her your'n, too?

PETER: Ha! *(He gives a sardonic laugh of relish at this idea.)*

EBEN (*spitting with disgust*): Her — here — sleepin' with him — stealin' my Maw's farm! I'd as soon pet a skunk 'r kiss a snake! (*He goes out. The two stare after him suspiciously. A pause. They listen to his steps receding.*)

PETER: He's startin' the fire.

SIMEON: I'd like t' ride t' Californi-a — but —

PETER: Min might o' put some scheme in his head.

SIMEON: Mebbe it's all a lie 'bout Paw marryin'. We'd best wait an' see the bride.

PETER: An' don't sign nothin' till we does!

SIMEON: Nor till we've tested it's good money! (*Then with a grin.*) But if Paw's hitched we'd be sellin' Eben somethin' we'd never git nohow!

PETER: We'll wait an' see. (*Then with sudden vindictive anger.*) An' till he comes, let's yew 'n' me not wuk a lick, let Eben tend to thin's if he's a mind t', let's us jest sleep an' eat an' drink likker, an' let the hull damned farm go t' blazes!

SIMEON (*excitedly*): By God, we've 'arned a rest! We'll play rich fur a change. I hain't a-going to stir outa bed till breakfast's ready.

PETER: An' on the table!

SIMEON (*after a pause — thoughtfully*): What d'ye calc'late she'll be like — our new Maw? Like Eben thinks?

PETER: More'n' likely.

SIMEON (*vindictively*): Waal — I hope she's a she-devil that'll make him wish he was dead an' livin' in the pit o' hell fur comfort!

PETER (*fervently*): Amen!

SIMEON (*imitating his father's voice*): "I'm ridin' out t' learn God's message t' me in the spring like the prophets done," he says. I'll bet right then an' thar he knew plumb well he was goin' whorin', the stinkin' old hypocrite!

Scene IV

(*Same as scene II — shows the interior of the kitchen with a lighted candle on table. It is gray dawn outside. Simeon and Peter are just finishing their breakfast. Eben sits before his plate of untouched food, brooding frowningly.*)

PETER (*glancing at him rather irritably*): Lookin' glum don't help none.

SIMEON (*sarcastically*): Sorrowin' over his lust o' the flesh!

PETER (*with a grin*): Was she yer fust?

EBEN (*angrily*): None o'yer business. (*A pause.*) I was thinkin' o' him. I got a notion he's gittin' near — I kin feel him comin' on like yew kin feel malaria chill afore it takes ye.

PETER: It's too early yet.

SIMEON: Dunno. He'd like t' catch us nappin' — jest t' have somethin' t' hoss us 'round over.

PETER (*Mechanically gets to his feet. Simeon does the same.*): Waal — let's git t'wuk. (*They both plod mechanically toward the door before they realize. Then they stop short.*)

SIMEON (*grinning*): Ye're a cussed fool, Pete — and I be wuss! Let him see we hain't wukin'! We don't give a durn!

PETER (*as they go back to the table*): Not a damned durn! It'll serve t' show him we're done with him. (*They sit down again. Eben stares from one to the other with surprise.*)

SIMEON (*grins at him*): We're aimin' t' start bein' lilies o' the field.

PETER: Nary a toil 'r spin 'r lick o' wuk do we put in!

SIMEON: Ye're sole owner — till he comes — that's what ye wanted. Waal, ye got t' be sole hand, too.

PETER: The cows air bellerin'. Ye better hustle at the milkin'.

EBEN (*with excited joy*): Ye mean ye'll sign the paper?

SIMEON (*dryly*): Mebbe.

PETER: Mebbe.

SIMEON: We're considerin'. (*Peremptorily.*) Ye better git t' wuk.

EBEN (*with queer excitement*): It's Maw's farm agen! It's my farm! Them's my cows! I'll milk my durn fingers off fur cows o' mine! (*He goes out door in rear, they stare after him indifferently.*)

SIMEON: Like his Paw.

PETER: Dead spit 'n' image!

SIMEON: Waal — let dog eat dog! (*Eben comes out of front door and around the corner of the house. The sky is beginning to grow flushed with sunrise. Eben stops by the gate and stares around him with glowing, possessive eyes. He takes in the whole farm with his embracing glance of desire.*)

EBEN: It's purty! It's damned purty! It's mine! (*He suddenly throws his head back boldly and glares with hard, defiant eyes at the sky.*) Mine, d'ye hear? Mine! (*He turns and walks quickly off left, rear, toward the barn. The two brothers light their pipes.*)

SIMEON (*putting his muddy boots up on the table, tilting back his chair, and puffing defiantly*): Waal — this air solid comfort — fur once.

PETER: Ay-eh. (*He follows suit. A pause. Unconsciously they both sigh.*)

SIMEON (*suddenly*): He never was much o' a hand at milkin', Eben wa'n't.

PETER (*with a snort*): His hands air like hoofs! (*A pause.*)

SIMEON: Reach down the jug thar! Let's take a swaller. I'm feelin' kind o' low.

PETER: Good idee! (*He does so — gets two glasses —*

they pour out drinks of whisky.) Here's t' the gold in Californi-a!

SIMEON: An' luck t' find it! (*They drink — puff resolutely — sigh — take their feet down from the table.*)

PETER: Likker don't pear t' sot right.

SIMEON: We hain't used t' it this early. (*A pause. They become very restless.*)

PETER: Gittin' close in this kitchen.

SIMEON (*with immense relief*): Let's git a breath o' air. (*They arise briskly and go out rear — appear around house and stop by the gate. They stare up at the sky with a numbed appreciation.*)

PETER: Purty!

SIMEON: Ay-eh. Gold's t' the East now.

PETER: Sun's startin' with us fur the Golden West.

SIMEON (*staring around the farm, his compressed face tightened, unable to conceal his emotion*): Waal — it's our last mornin' — mebbe.

PETER (*the same*): Ay-eh.

SIMEON (*stamps his foot on the earth and addresses it desperately*): Waal — ye've thirty year o' me buried in ye — spread out over ye — blood an' bone an' sweat — rotted away — fertilizin' ye — richin' yer soul — prime manure, by God, that's what I been t' ye!

PETER: Ay-eh! An' me.

SIMEON: An' yew, Peter. (*He sighs — then spits.*) Waal — no use'n cryin' over spilt milk.

PETER: They's gold in the West — an' freedom, mebbe. We been slaves t' stone walls here.

SIMEON (*defiantly*): We hain't nobody's slaves from this out — nor nothin's slaves nuther. (*A pause — restlessly.*) Speaking o' milk, wonder how Eben's managin'?

PETER: I s'pose he's managin'.

SIMEON: Mebbe we'd ought t' help — this once.

PETER: Mebbe. The cows knows us.

SIMEON: An' likes us. They don't know him much.

PETER: An' the hosses, an' pigs, an' chickens. They don't know him much.

SIMEON: They knows us like brothers — an' likes us! (*Proudly.*) Hain't we raised 'em t' be fust-rate, number one prize stock?

PETER: We hain't — not no more.

SIMEON (*dully*): I was fergittin'. (*Then resignedly.*) Waal, let's go help Eben a spell an' git waked up.

PETER: Suits me. (*They are starting off down left, rear, for the barn when Eben appears from there hurrying toward them, his face excited.*)

EBEN (*breathlessly*): Waal — har they be! The old mule an' the bride! I seen 'em from the barn down below at the turnin'.

PETER: How could ye tell that far?

EBEN: Hain't I as far-sight as he's near-sight? Don't I

know the mare 'n' buggy, an' two people settin' in it? Who else . . . ? An' I tell ye I kin feel 'em a-comin', too! (*He squirms as if he had the itch.*)

PETER (*beginning to be angry*): Waal — let him do his own unhitchin'!

SIMEON (*angry in his turn*): Let's hustle in an' git our bundles an' be a-goin' as he's a-comin'. I don't want never t' step inside the door agen arter he's back. (*They both start back around the corner of the house. Eben follows them.*)

EBEN (*anxiously*): Will ye sign it afore ye go?

PETER: Let's see the color o' the old skinflint's money an' we'll sign. (*They disappear left. The two brothers clump upstairs to get their bundles. Eben appears in the kitchen, runs to window, peers out, comes back and pulls up a strip of flooring in under stove, takes out a canvas bag and puts it on table, then sets the floorboard back in place. The two brothers appear a moment after. They carry old carpetbags.*)

EBEN (*puts his hand on bag guardingly*): Have ye signed?

SIMEON (*shows paper in his hand*): Ay-eh. (*Greedily.*) Be that the money?

EBEN (*opens bag and pours out pile of twenty-dollar gold pieces*): Twenty-dollar pieces — thirty on 'em. Count 'em. (*Peter does so, arranging them in stacks of five, biting one or two to test them.*)

PETER: Six hundred. (*He puts them in bag and puts it inside his shirt carefully.*)

SIMEON (*handing paper to Eben*): Har ye be.

EBEN (*after a glance, folds it carefully and hides it under his shirt — gratefully*): Thank yew.

PETER: Thank yew fur the ride.

SIMEON: We'll send ye a lump o' gold fur Christmas. (*A pause. Eben stares at them and they at him.*)

PETER (*awkwardly*): Waal — we're a-goin'.

SIMEON: Comin' out t' the yard?

EBEN: No. I'm waitin' in here a spell. (*Another silence. The brothers edge awkwardly to door in rear — then turn and stand.*)

SIMEON: Waal — good-by.

PETER: Good-by.

EBEN: Good-by. (*They go out. He sits down at the table, faces the stove and pulls out the paper. He looks from it to the stove. His face, lighted up by the shaft of sunlight from the window, has an expression of trance. His lips move. The two brothers come out to the gate.*)

PETER (*looking off toward barn*): Thar he be — unhitchin'.

SIMEON (*with a chuckle*): I'll bet ye he's riled!

PETER: An thar she be.

SIMEON: Let's wait 'n' see what our new Maw looks like.

PETER (*with a grin*): An' give him our partin' cuss!

SIMEON (*grinning*): I feel like raisin' fun. I feel light in my head an' feet.

PETER: Me, too. I feel like laffin' till I'd split up the middle.

SIMEON: Reckon it's the likker?

PETER: No. My feet feel itchin' t' walk an' walk — an' jump high over thin's — an'. . . .

SIMEON: Dance? (*A pause.*)

PETER (*puzzled*): It's plumb onnateral.

SIMEON (*a light coming over his face*): I calc'late it's 'cause school's out. It's holiday. Fur once we're free!

PETER (*dazedly*): Free?

SIMEON: The halter's broke — the harness is busted — the fence bars is down — the stone walls air crumblin' an' tumblin'! We'll be kickin' up an' tearin' away down the road!

PETER (*drawing a deep breath — oratorically*): Anybody that wants this stinkin' old rock-pile of a farm kin hev it. T'ain't our'n, no sirree!

SIMEON (*takes the gate off its hinges and puts it under his arm*): We harby 'bolishes shet gates, an' open gates, an' all gates, by thunder!

PETER: We'll take it with us fur luck an' let 'er sail free down some river.

SIMEON (*as a sound of voices comes from left, rear*): Har they comes! (*The two brothers congeal into two stiff, grim-visaged statues. Ephraim Cabot and Abbie Putnam come in. Cabot is seventy-five, tall and gaunt, with great, wiry, concentrated power, but stoop-shouldered from toil. His face is as hard as if it were hewn out of a boulder, yet there is a weakness in it, a petty pride in its own narrow strength. His eyes are small, close together, and extremely near-sighted, blinking continually in the effort to focus on objects, their stare having a straining, ingrowing quality. He is dressed in his dismal black Sunday suit. Abbie is thirty-five, buxom, full of vitality. Her round face is pretty but marred by its rather gross sensuality. There is strength and obstinacy in her jaw, a hard determination in her eyes, and about her whole personality the same unsettled, untamed, desperate quality which is so apparent in Eben.*)

CABOT (*as they enter — a queer strangled emotion in his dry cracking voice*): Har we be t' hum, Abbie.

ABBIE (*with lust for the word*): Hum! (*Her eyes gloating on the house without seeming to see the two stiff figures at the gate.*) It's purty — purty! I can't b'lieve it's r'ally mine.

CABOT (*sharply*): Yewr'n? Mine! (*He stares at her penetratingly. She stares back. He adds relentingly.*) Our'n — mebbe! It was lonesome too long. I was growin' old in the spring. A hum's got t' hev a woman.

ABBIE (*her voice taking possession*): A woman's got t' hev a hum!

CABOT (*nodding uncertainly*): Ay-eh. (*Then irritably.*) Whar be they? Ain't thar nobody about — 'r wukin' — 'r nothin'?

ABBIE (*Sees the brothers. She returns their stare of cold appraising contempt with interest — slowly.*): Thar's two men loafin' at the gate an' starin' at me like a couple o' strayed hogs.

CABOT (*straining his eyes*): I kin see 'em — but I can't make out. . . .

SIMEON: It's Simeon.

PETER: It's Peter.

CABOT (*exploding*): Why hain't ye wukin'?

SIMEON (*dryly*): We're waitin' t' welcome ye hum — yew an' the bride!

CABOT (*confusedly*): Huh? Waal — this be yer new Maw, boys. (*She stares at them and they at her.*)

SIMEON (*turns away and spits contemptuously*): I see her!

PETER (*spits also*): An' I see her!

ABBIE (*with the conqueror's conscious superiority*): I'll go in an' look at *my* house. (*She goes slowly around to porch.*)

SIMEON (*with a snort*): Her house!

PETER (*calls after her*): Ye'll find Eben inside. Ye better not tell him it's yewr house.

ABBIE (*mouthing the name*): Eben. (*Then quietly.*) I'll tell Eben.

CABOT (*with a contemptuous sneer*): Ye needn't heed Eben. Eben's a dumb fool — like his Maw — soft an' simple!

SIMEON (*with his sardonic burst of laughter*): Ha! Eben's a chip o' yew — spit 'n' image — hard 'n' bitter's a hickory tree! Dog'll eat dog. He'll eat ye yet, old man!

CABOT (*commandingly*): Ye git t' wuk.

SIMEON (*as Abbie disappears in house — winks at Peter and says tauntingly*): So that thar's our new Maw, be it? Whar in hell did ye dig her up? (*He and Peter laugh.*)

PETER: Ha! Ye'd better turn her in the pen with the other sows. (*They laugh uproariously, slapping their thighs.*)

CABOT (*so amazed at their effrontery that he stutters in confusion*): Simeon! Peter! What's come over ye? Air ye drunk?

SIMEON: We're free, old man — free o' yew an' the hull damned farm! (*They grow more and more hilarious and excited.*)

PETER: An' we're startin' out fur the gold fields o' Californi-a!

SIMEON: Ye kin take this place an' burn it!

PETER: An' bury it — fur all we cares!

SIMEON: We're free, old man! (*He cuts a caper.*)

PETER: Free! (*He gives a kick in the air.*)

SIMEON (*in a frenzy*): Whoop!

PETER: Whoop! (*They do an absurd Indian war dance about the old man who is petrified between rage and the fear that they are insane.*)

SIMEON: We're free as Injuns! Lucky we don't skulp ye!

PETER: An' burn yer barn an' kill the stock!

SIMEON: An' rape yer new woman! Whoop! (*He and Peter stop their dance, holding their sides, rocking with wild laughter.*)

CABOT (*edging away*): Lust fur gold — fur the sinful, easy gold o' Californi-a! It's made ye mad!

SIMEON (*tauntingly*): Wouldn't ye like us to send ye back some sinful gold, ye old sinner?

PETER: They's gold besides what's in Californi-a! (*He retreats back beyond the vision of the old man and takes the bag of money and flaunts it in the air above his head, laughing.*)

SIMEON: And sinfuller, too!

PETER: We'll be voyagin' on the sea! Whoop! (*He leaps up and down.*)

SIMEON: Livin' free! Whoop! (*He leaps in turn.*)

CABOT (*suddenly roaring with rage*): My cuss on ye!

SIMEON: Take our'n in trade fur it! Whoop!

CABOT: I'll hev ye both chained up in the asylum!

PETER: Ye old skinflint! Good-by!

SIMEON: Ye old blood sucker! Good-by!

CABOT: Go afore I . . . !

PETER: Whoop! (*He picks a stone from the road. Simeon does the same.*)

SIMEON: Maw'll be in the parlor.

PETER: Ay-eh! One! Two!

CABOT (*frightened*): What air ye . . . ?

PETER: Three! (*They both throw, the stones hitting the parlor window with a crash of glass, tearing the shade.*)

SIMEON: Whoop!

PETER: Whoop!

CABOT (*in a fury now, rushing toward them*): If I kin lay hands on ye — I'll break yer bones fur ye! (*But they beat a capering retreat before him, Simeon with the gate still under his arm. Cabot comes back, panting with impotent rage. Their voices as they go off take up the song of the gold-seekers to the old tune of "Oh, Susannah!"*)

"I jumped aboard the Liza ship,
And traveled on the sea,
And every time I thought of home
I wished it wasn't me!
Oh! Californi-a,
That's the land fur me!
I'm off to Californi-a!
With my wash bowl on my knee."

(*In the meantime, the window of the upper bedroom on right is raised and Abbie sticks her head out. She looks down at Cabot — with a sigh of relief.*)

ABBIE: Waal — that's the last o' them two, hain't it? (*He doesn't answer. Then in possessive tones.*) This here's a nice bedroom, Ephraim. It's a r'al nice bed. Is it my room, Ephraim?

CABOT (*grimly — without looking up*): Our'n! (*She cannot control a grimace of aversion and pulls back her head slowly and shuts the window. A sudden horrible thought seems to enter Cabot's head.*) They been up to somethin'! Mebbe — mebbe they've pizened the stock — 'r somethin'! (*He almost runs off down toward the barn. A moment later the kitchen door is slowly pushed open and Abbie enters. For a moment she stands looking at Eben. He does not notice her at first. Her eyes take him in penetratingly with a calculating appraisal of his strength as against hers. But under this her desire is dimly awakened by his youth and good looks. Suddenly he becomes conscious of her presence and looks up. Their eyes meet. He leaps to his feet, glowering at her speechlessly.*)

ABBIE (*in her most seductive tones which she uses all through this scene*): Be you — Eben? I'm Abbie — (*She laughs.*) I mean, I'm yer new Maw.

EBEN (*viciously*): No, damn ye!

ABBIE (*as if she hain't heard — with a queer smile*): Yer Paw's spoke a lot o' yew. . . .

EBEN: Ha!

ABBIE: Ye mustn't mind him. He's an old man. (*A long pause. They stare at each other.*) I don't want t' pretend playin' Maw t' ye, Eben. (*Admiringly.*) Ye're too big an' too strong fur that. I want t' be frens with ye. Mebbe with me fur a fren ye'd find ye'd like livin' here better. I kin make it easy fur ye with him, mebbe. (*With a scornful sense of power.*) I calc'late I kin git him t' do most anythin' fur me.

EBEN (*with bitter scorn*): Ha! (*They stare again, Eben obscurely moved, physically attracted to her — in forced stilted tones.*) Yew kin go t' the devil!

ABBIE (*calmly*): If cussin' me does ye good, cuss all ye've a mind t'. I'm all prepared t' have ye agin me — at fust. I don't blame ye nuther. I'd feel the same at any stranger comin' t' take my Maw's place. (*He shudders. She is watching him carefully.*) Yew must've cared a lot fur yewr Maw, didn't ye? My Maw died afore I'd growed. I don't remember her none. (*A pause.*) But yew won't hate me long, Eben. I'm not the wust in the world — an' yew an' me've got a lot in common. I kin tell that by lookin' at ye. Waal — I've had a hard life, too — oceans o' trouble an' nuthin' but wuk fur reward. I was a orphan early an' had t' wuk fur others in other folks' hums. Then I married an' he turned out a drunken spreer an' so he had to wuk fur others an' me too agen in other folks' hums, an' the baby died, an' my husband got sick an' died too, an' I was glad sayin' now I'm free fur once, on'y I diskivered right away all I was free fur was t'wuk agen in other folks' hums, doin' other folks' wuk till I'd most give up hope o' ever doin' my own wuk in my own hum, an' then your Paw come . . . (*Cabot appears returning from the barn. He comes to the gate and looks down the road the brothers have gone. A faint strain of their retreating voices is heard: "Oh, Californi-a! That's the place for me." He stands glowering, his fist clenched, his face grim with rage.*)

EBEN (*fighting against his growing attraction and sympathy — harshly*): An' bought yew — like a harlot! (*She is stung and flushes angrily. She has been sincerely moved by the recital of her troubles. He adds furiously.*) An' the price he's payin' ye — this farm — was my Maw's, damn ye! — an' mine now!

ABBIE (*with a cool laugh of confidence*): Yewr'n? We'll see 'bout that! (*Then strongly.*) Waal — what if I did need a hum? What else'd I marry an old man like him fur?

EBEN (*maliciously*): I'll tell him ye said that!

ABBIE (*smiling*): I'll say ye're lyin' a-purpose — an' he'll drive ye off the place!

EBEN: Ye devil!

ABBIE (*defying him*): This be my farm — this be my hum — this be my kitchen — !

EBEN (*furiously, as if he were going to attack her*): Shut up, damn ye!

ABBIE (*walks up to him — a queer coarse expression of desire in her face and body — slowly*): An' upstairs — that be my bedroom — an' my bed! (*He stares into her eyes, terribly confused and torn. She adds softly.*) I hain't bad nor mean — 'ceptin' fur an enemy — but I got t' fight fur what's due me out o' life, if I ever 'spect t' git it. (*Then putting her hand on his arm — seductively.*) Let's yew 'n' me be frens, Eben.

EBEN (*stupidly — as if hypnotized*): Ay-eh. (*Then furiously flinging off her arm.*) No, ye durned old witch! I hate ye! (*He rushes out the door.*)

ABBIE (*looks after him smiling satisfiedly — then half to herself, mouthing the word*): Eben's nice. (*She looks at the table, proudly.*) I'll wash up *my* dishes now. (*Eben appears outside, slamming the door behind him. He comes around corner, stops on seeing his father, and stands staring at him with hate.*)

CABOT (*raising his arms to heaven in the fury he can no longer control*): Lord God o' Hosts, smite the undutiful sons with Thy wust cuss!

EBEN (*breaking in violently*): Yew 'n' yewr God! Allus cussin' folks — allus naggin' 'em!

CABOT (*oblivious to him — summoningly*): God o' the old! God o' the lonesome!

EBEN (*mockingly*): Naggin' His sheep t' sin! T' hell with yewr God! (*Cabot turns. He and Eben glower at each other.*)

CABOT (*harshly*): So it's yew. I might've knowed it. (*Shaking his finger threateningly at him.*) Blasphemin' fool! (*Then quickly.*) Why hain't ye t' wuk?

EBEN: Why hain't yew? They've went. I can't wuk it all alone.

CABOT (*contemptuously*): Nor noways! I'm wuth ten o' ye yit, old's I be! Ye'll never be more'n half a man! (*Then, matter-of-factly.*) Waal — let's git t' the barn. (*They go. A last faint note of the "Californi-a" song is heard from the distance. Abbie is washing her dishes.*)

PART II • Scene 1

(*The exterior of the farmhouse, as in part I — a hot Sunday afternoon two months later. Abbie, dressed in her best, is discovered sitting in a rocker at the end of the porch. She rocks listlessly, enervated by the heat, staring in front of her with bored, half-closed eyes.*)

(*Eben sticks his head out of his bedroom window. He looks around furtively and tries to see — or hear — if anyone is on the porch, but although he has been careful to make no noise, Abbie has sensed his movement. She stops rocking, her face grows animated and eager, she waits attentively. Eben seems to feel her presence, he scowls back his thoughts of her and spits with exaggerated disdain — then withdraws back into the room. Abbie waits, holding her breath as she listens with passionate eagerness for every sound within the house.*)

(*Eben comes out. Their eyes meet; his falter. He is confused, he turns away and slams the door resentfully. At this gesture, Abbie laughs tantalizingly, amused but at the same time piqued and irritated. He scowls, strides off the porch to the path and starts to walk past her to the road with a grand swagger of ignoring her existence. He is dressed in his store suit, spruced up, his face shines from soap and water. Abbie leans forward on her chair, her eyes hard and angry now, and, as he passes her, gives a sneering, taunting chuckle.*)

EBEN (*stung — turns on her furiously*): What air yew cacklin' 'bout?

ABBIE (*triumphant*): Yew!

EBEN: What about me?

ABBIE: Ye look all slicked up like a prize bull.

EBEN (*with a sneer*): Waal — ye hain't so durned purty yerself, be ye? (*They stare into each other's eyes, his held by hers in spite of himself, hers glow-*

ingly possessive. Their physical attraction becomes a palpable force quivering in the hot air.)

ABBIE (*softly*): Ye don't mean that, Eben. Ye may think ye mean it, mebbe, but ye don't. Ye can't. It's agin nature, Eben. Ye been fightin' yer nature ever since the day I come — tryin' t' tell yerself I hain't purty t'ye. (*She laughs a low humid laugh without taking her eyes from his. A pause — her body squirms desirously — she murmurs languorously.*) Hain't the sun strong an' hot? Ye kin feel it burnin' into the earth — Nature — makin' thin's grow — bigger 'n' bigger — burnin' inside ye — makin' ye want t' grow — into somethin' else — till ye're jined with it — an' it's your'n — but it owns ye, too — ant makes ye grow bigger — like a tree — like them elums — (*She laughs again softly, holding his eyes. He takes a step toward her, compelled against his will.*) Nature'll beat ye, Eben. Ye might's well own up t' it fust 's last.

EBEN (*trying to break from her spell — confusedly*): If Paw'd hear ye goin' on. . . . (*Resentfully.*) But ye've made such a damned idjit out o' the old devil . . . ! (*Abbie laughs.*)

ABBIE: Waal — hain't it easier fur yew with him changed softer?

EBEN (*defiantly*): No. I'm fightin' him — fightin' yew — fightin' fur Maw's rights t' her hum! (*This breaks her spell for him. He glowers at her.*) An' I'm onto ye. Ye hain't foolin' me a mite. Ye're aimin' t' swaller up everythin' an' make it your'n. Waal, you'll find I'm a heap sight bigger hunk nor yew kin chew! (*He turns from her with a sneer.*)

ABBIE (*trying to regain her ascendancy — seductively*): Eben!

EBEN: Leave me be! (*He starts to walk away.*)

ABBIE (*more commandingly*): Eben!

EBEN (*stops — resentfully*): What d'ye want?

ABBIE (*trying to conceal a growing excitement*): Whar air ye goin'?

EBEN (*with malicious nonchalance*): Oh — up the road a spell.

ABBIE: T' the village?

EBEN (*airily*): Mebbe.

ABBIE (*excitedly*): T' see that Min, I s'pose?

EBEN: Mebbe.

ABBIE (*weakly*): What d'ye want t' waste time on her fur?

EBEN (*revenging himself now — grinning at her*): Ye can't beat Nature, didn't ye say? (*He laughs and again starts to walk away.*)

ABBIE (*bursting out*): An ugly old hake!

EBEN (*with a tantalizing sneer*): She's purtier'n yew be!

ABBIE: That every wuthless drunk in the country has. . . .

EBEN (*tauntingly*): Mebbe — but she's better'n yew. She owns up fa'r 'n' squar' t' her doin's.

ABBIE (*furiously*): Don't ye dare compare. . . .

EBEN: She don't go sneakin' an' stealin' — what's mine.

ABBIE (*savagely seizing on his weak point*): Your'n? Yew mean — my farm?

EBEN: I mean the farm yew sold yerself fur like any other old whore — my farm!

ABBIE (*stung — fiercely*): Ye'll never live t' see the day when even a stinkin' weed on it'll belong t' ye! (*Then in a scream.*) Git out o' my sight! Go on t' yer slut — disgracin' yer Paw 'n' me! I'll git yer Paw t' horsewhip ye off the place if I want t'! Ye're only livin' here 'cause I tolerate ye! Git along! I hate the sight o' ye! (*She stops, panting and glaring at him.*)

EBEN (*returning her glance in kind*): An' I hate the sight o' yew! (*He turns and strides off up the road. She follows his retreating figure with concentrated hate. Old Cabot appears coming up from the barn. The hard, grim expression of his face has changed. He seems in some queer way softened, mellowed. His eyes have taken on a strange, incongruous dreamy quality. Yet there is no hint of physical weakness about him — rather he looks more robust and younger. Abbie sees him and turns away quickly with unconcealed aversion. He comes slowly up to her.*)

CABOT (*mildly*): War yew an' Eben quarrelin' agen?

ABBIE (*shortly*): No.

CABOT: Ye was talkie' a'mighty loud. (*He sits down on the edge of porch.*)

ABBIE (*snappishly*): If ye heerd us they hain't no need askin' questions.

CABOT: I didn't hear what ye said.

ABBIE (*relieved*): Waal — it wa'n't nothin' t' speak on.

CABOT (*after a pause*): Eben's queer.

ABBIE (*bitterly*): He's the dead spit 'n' image o' yew!

CABOT (*queerly interested*): D'ye think so, Abbie? (*After a pause, ruminatingly.*) Me 'n' Eben's allus fit 'n' fit. I never could b'ar him noways. He's so thunderin' soft — like his Maw.

ABBIE (*scornfully*): Ay-eh! 'Bout as soft as yew be!

CABOT (*as if he hadn't heard*): Mebbe I been too hard on him.

ABBIE (*jeeringly*): Waal — ye're gittin' soft now — soft as slop! That's what Eben was sayin'.

CABOT (*his face instantly grim and ominous*): Eben was sayin'? Waal, he'd best not do nothin' t' try me 'r he'll soon diskiver. . . . (*A pause. She keeps her face turned away. His gradually softens. He stares up at the sky.*) Purty, hain't it?

ABBIE (*crossly*): I don't see nothin' purty.

CABOT: The sky. Feels like a wa'm field up thar.

ABBIE (*sarcastically*): Air yew aimin' t' buy up over the farm too? (*She snickers contemptuously.*)

CABOT (*strangely*): I'd like t' own my place up thar. (*A pause.*) I'm gittin' old, Abbie. I'm gittin' ripe on the bough. (*A pause. She stares at him mystified. He goes on.*) It's allus lonesome cold in the house — even when it's bilin' hot outside. Hain't yew noticed?

ABBIE: No.

CABOT: It's wa'm down t' the barn — nice smellin' an' warm — with the cows. (*A pause.*) Cows is queer.

ABBIE: Like yew?

CABOT: Like Eben. (*A pause.*) I'm gittin' t' feel resigned t' Eben — jest as I got t' feel 'bout his Maw. I'm gittin' t' learn to b'ar his softness — jest like her'n. I calc'late I c'd a'most take t' him — if he wa'n't sech a dumb fool! (*A pause.*) I s'pose it's old age a-creepin' in my bones.

ABBIE (*indifferently*): Waal — ye hain't dead yet.

CABOT (*roused*): No, I hain't, yew bet — not by a hell of a sight — I'm sound 'n' tough as hickory! (*Then moodily.*) But arter three score and ten the Lord warns ye t' prepare. (*A pause.*) That's why Eben's come in my head. Now that his cussed sinful brothers is gone their path t' hell, they's no one left but Eben.

ABBIE (*resentfully*): They's me, hain't they? (*Agitatedly.*) What's all this sudden likin' ye've tuk to Eben? Why don't ye say nothin' 'bout me? Hain't I yer lawful wife?

CABOT (*simply*): Ay-eh. Ye be. (*A pause — he stares at her desirously — his eyes grow avid — then with a sudden movement he seizes her hands and squeezes them, declaiming in a queer camp meeting preacher's tempo.*) Yew air my Rose o' Sharon! Behold, yew air fair; yer eyes air doves; yer lips air like scarlet; yer two breasts air like two fawns; yer navel be like a round goblet; yer belly be like a heap o' wheat.... (*He covers her hand with kisses. She does not seem to notice. She stares before her with hard angry eyes.*)

ABBIE (*jerking her hands away — harshly*): So ye're plannin' t' leave the farm t' Eben, air ye?

CABOT (*dazedly*): Leave ... ? (*Then with resentful obstinacy.*) I hain't a-givin' it t' no one!

ABBIE (*remorselessly*): Ye can't take it with ye.

CABOT (*thinks a moment — then reluctantly*): No, I calc'late not. (*After a pause — with a strange passion.*) But if I could, I would, by the Eternal! 'R if I could, in my dyin' hour, I'd set it afire an' watch it burn — this house an' every ear o' corn an' every tree down t' the last blade o' hay! I'd sit an' know it was all a-dying with me an' no one else'd ever own what was mine, what I'd made out o' nothin' with my own sweat 'n' blood! (*A pause — then he adds with a queer affection.*) 'Ceptin' the cows. Them I'd turn free.

ABBIE (*harshly*): An' me?

CABOT (*with a queer smile*): Ye'd be turned free, too.

ABBIE (*furiously*): So that's the thanks I git fur marryin' ye — t' have ye change kind to Eben who hates ye, an' talk o' turnin' me out in the road.

CABOT (*hastily*): Abbie! Ye know I wa'n't. . . .

ABBIE (*vengefully*): Just let me tell ye a thing or two 'bout Eben! Whar's he gone? T' see that harlot, Min! I tried fur t' stop him. Disgracin' yew an' me — on the Sabbath, too!

CABOT (*rather guiltily*): He's a sinner — nateral-born. It's lust eatin' his heart.

ABBIE (*enraged beyond endurance — wildly vindictive*): An' his lust fur me! Kin ye find excuses fur that?

CABOT (*stares at her — after a dead pause*): Lust — fur yew?

ABBIE (*defiantly*): He was tryin' t' make love t' me — when ye heerd us quarrelin'.

CABOT (*stares at her — then a terrible expression of rage comes over his face — he springs to his feet shaking all over*): By the A'mighty God — I'll end him!

ABBIE (*frightened now for Eben*): No! Don't ye!

CABOT (*violently*): I'll git the shotgun an' blow his soft brains t' the top o' them elums!

ABBIE (*throwing her arms around him*): No, Ephraim!

CABOT (*pushing her away violently*): I will, by God!

ABBIE (*in a quieting tone*): Listen, Ephraim. 'Twa'n't nothin' bad — on'y a boy's foolin' — 'twa'n't meant serious — jest jokin' an' teasin'. . . .

CABOT: Then why did ye say — lust?

ABBIE: It must hev sounded wusser'n I meant. An' I was mad at thinkin' — ye'd leave him the farm.

CABOT (*quieter but still grim and cruel*): Waal then, I'll horsewhip him off the place if that much'll content ye.

ABBIE (*reaching out and taking his hand*): No. Don't think o' me! Ye mustn't drive him off. 'Tain't sensible. Who'll ye get to help ye on the farm? They's no one hereabouts.

CABOT (*considers this — then nodding his appreciation*): Ye got a head on ye. (*Then irritably.*) Waal, let him stay. (*He sits down on the edge of the porch. She sits beside him. He murmurs contemptuously.*) I oughtn't t' git riled so — at that 'ere fool calf. (*A pause.*) But har's the p'int. What son o' mine'll keep on here t' the farm — when the Lord does call me? Simeon an' Peter air gone t' hell — an' Eben's follerin' 'em.

ABBIE: They's me.

CABOT: Ye're on'y a woman.

ABBIE: I'm yewr wife.

CABOT: That hain't me. A son is me — my blood —

minc. Mine ought t' git mine. An' then it's still mine — even though I be six foot under. D'ye see?

ABBIE (*giving him a look of hatred*): Ay-eh. I see. (*She becomes very thoughtful, her face growing shrewd, her eyes studying Cabot craftily.*)

CABOT: I'm gittin' old — ripe on the bough. (*Then with a sudden forced reassurance.*) Not but what I hain't a hard nut t' crack even yet — an' fur many a year t' come! By the Etarnal, I kin break most o' the young fellers' backs at any kind o' work any day o' the year!

ABBIE (*suddenly*): Mebbe the Lord'll give *us* a son.

CABOT (*turns and stares at her eagerly*): Ye mean — a son — t' me 'n' yew?

ABBIE (*with a cajoling smile*): Ye're a strong man yet, hain't ye? 'Tain't noways impossible, be it? We know that. Why d'ye stare so? Hain't ye never thought o' that afore? I been thinkin' o' it all along. Ay-eh — an' I been prayin' it'd happen, too.

CABOT (*his face growing full of joyous pride and a sort of religious ecstasy*): Ye been prayin', Abbie? — fur a son? — t' us?

ABBIE: Ay-eh. (*With a grim resolution.*) I want a son now.

CABOT (*excitedly clutching both of her hands in his*): It'd be the blessin' o' God, Abbie — the blessin' o' God A'mighty on me — in my old age — in my lonesomeness! They hain't nothin' I wouldn't do fur ye then, Abbie. Ye'd hev on'y t' ask it — anythin' ye'd a mind t'!

ABBIE (*interrupting*): Would ye will the farm t' me then — t' me an' it . . . ?

CABOT (*vehemently*): I'd do anythin' ye axed, I tell ye! I swar it! May I be everlastin' damned t' hell if I wouldn't! (*He sinks to his knees pulling her down with him. He trembles all over with the fervor of his hopes.*) Pray t' the Lord agen, Abbie. It's the Sabbath! I'll jine ye! Two prayers air better nor one. "An' God hearkened unto Rachel"! An' God hearkened unto Abbie! Pray, Abbie! Pray fur him to hearken! (*He bows his head, mumbling. She pretends to do likewise but gives him a side glance of scorn and triumph.*)

Scene II

(*About eight in the evening. The interior of the two bedrooms on the top floor is shown. Eben is sitting on the side of his bed in the room on the left. On account of the heat he has taken off everything but his undershirt and pants. His feet are bare. He faces front, brooding moodily, his chin propped on his hands, a desperate expression on his face.*)

(*In the other room Cabot and Abbie are sitting side by side on the edge of their bed, an old four-poster with feather mattress. He is in his nightshirt, she in her nightdress. He is still in the queer, excited mood into which the notion of a son has thrown him. Both rooms are lighted dimly and flickeringly by tallow candles.*)

CABOT: The farm needs a son.

ABBIE: I need a son.

CABOT: Ay-eh. Sometimes ye air the farm an' sometimes the farm be yew. That's why I clove t'ye in my lonesomeness. (*A pause. He pounds his knee with his fist.*) Me an' the farm has got t' beget a son!

ABBIE: Ye'd best go t' sleep. Ye're gittin' thin's all mixed.

CABOT (*with an impatient gesture*): No, I hain't. My mind's clear's a well. Ye don't know me, that's it. (*He stares hopelessly at the floor.*)

ABBIE (*indifferently*): Mebbe. (*In the next room Eben gets up and paces up and down distractedly. Abbie hears him. Her eyes fasten on the intervening wall with concentrated attention. Eben stops and stares. Their hot glances seem to meet through the wall. Unconsciously he stretches out his arms for her and she half rises. Then aware, he mutters a curse at himself and flings himself face downward on the bed, his clenched fists above his head, his face buried in the pillow. Abbie relaxes with a faint sigh but her eyes remain fixed on the wall; she listens with all her attention for some movement from Eben.*)

CABOT (*suddenly raises his head and looks at her — scornfully*): Will ye ever know me — 'r will any man 'r woman? (*Shaking his head.*) No. I calc'late wa'n't t' be. (*He turns away. Abbie looks at the wall. Then, evidently unable to keep silent about his thoughts, without looking at his wife, he puts out his hand and clutches her knee. She starts violently, looks at him, sees he is not watching her, concentrates again on the wall, and pays no attention to what he says.*) Listen, Abbie. When I come here fifty odd year ago — I was jest twenty an' the strongest an' hardest ye ever seen — ten times as strong an' fifty times as hard as Eben. Waal — this place was nothin' but fields o' stones. Folks laughed when I tuk it. They couldn't know what I knowed. When ye kin make corn sprout out o' stones, God's livin' in yew! They wa'n't strong enuf fur that! They reckoned God was easy. They laughed. They don't laugh no more. Some died hereabouts. Some went West an' died. They're all underground — fur follerin' arter an easy God. God hain't easy. (*He shakes his head slowly.*) An' I growed hard. Folks kept allus sayin' he's a hard man like 'twas sinful t' be hard, so's at last I said back at 'em: Waal then, by thunder, ye'll git me hard an' see how ye like it! (*Then suddenly.*) But I give in t' weakness once. 'Twas arter I'd been here two year. I got weak — despairful — they was so many stones. They was a party leavin', givin' up, goin' West. I jined 'em. We tracked on 'n' on. We come t' broad medders, plains, whar the soil was black an' rich as gold. Nary a stone. Easy. Ye'd on'y to plow an' sow an' then set an' smoke yer pipe an' watch thin's grow. I could o' been a rich man — but somethin' in me fit me an' fit me — the voice o' God sayin': "This hain't wuth nothin' t' Me. Git ye back t' hum!" I got afeerd o' that voice an' I lit out back t' hum here, leavin' my claim an' crops t' whoever'd a mind t' take 'em. Ay-eh. I ac-toolly give up what was rightful mine! God's hard, not easy! God's in the stones! Build my church on a rock — out o' stones an' I'll be in them! That's what He meant t' Peter! (*He sighs heavily — a pause.*) Stones. I picked 'em up an' piled 'em into walls. Ye kin read the years of my life in them walls, every day a hefted stone, climbin' over the hills up and down, fencin' in the fields that was mine, whar I'd made thin's grow out o' nothin' — like the will o' God, like the servant o' His hand. It wa'n't easy. It was hard an' He made me hard fur it. (*He pauses.*) All the time I kept gittin' lone-somer. I tuk a wife. She bore Simeon an' Peter. She was a good woman. She wuked hard. We was married twenty year. She never knowed me. She helped but she never knowed what she was helpin'. I was allus lonesome. She died. After that it wa'n't so lonesome fur a spell. (*A pause.*) I lost count o' the years. I had no time t' fool away countin' 'em. Sim an' Peter helped. The farm growed. It was all mine! When I thought o' that I didn't feel lonesome. (*A pause.*) But ye can't hitch yer mind t' one thin' day an' night. I tuk another wife — Eben's Maw. Her folks was contestin' me at law over my deeds t' the farm — my farm! That's why Eben keeps a-talkin' his fool talk o' this bein' his Maw's farm. She bore Eben. She was purty — but soft. She tried t' be hard. She could-n't. She never knowed me nor nothin'. It was lone-somer 'n hell with her. After a matter o' sixteen odd years, she died. (*A pause.*) I lived with the boys. They hated me 'cause I was hard. I hated them 'cause they was soft. They coveted the farm without knowin' what it meant. It made me bitter 'n wormwood. It aged me — them covetin' what I'd made fur mine. Then this spring the call come — the voice o' God cryin' in my wilderness, in my lonesomeness — t' go out an' seek an' find! (*Turning to her with strange passion.*) I sought ye an' I found ye! Yew air my Rose o' Sharon! Yer eyes air like.... (*She has turned a blank face, re-sentful eyes to his. He stares at her for a*

moment — then harshly.) Air ye any the wiser fur all I've told ye?

ABBIE (*confusedly*): Mebbe.

CABOT (*pushing her away from him — angrily*): Ye don't know nothin' — nor never will. If ye don't hev a son t' redeem ye.... (*This in a tone of cold threat.*)

ABBIE (*resentfully*): I've prayed, hain't I?

CABOT (*bitterly*): Pray agen — fur understandin'!

ABBIE (*a veiled threat in her tone*): Ye'll have a son out o' me, I promise ye.

CABOT: How kin ye promise?

ABBIE: I got second-sight mebbe. I kin foretell. (*She gives a queer smile.*)

CABOT: I believe ye have. Ye give me the chills some-times. (*He shivers.*) It's cold in this house. It's oneasy. They's thin's pokin' about in the dark — in the corners. (*He pulls on his trousers, tucking in his nightshirt, and pulls on his boots.*)

ABBIE (*surprised*): Whar air ye goin'?

CABOT (*queerly*): Down whar it's restful — whar it's warm — down t' the barn. (*Bitterly.*) I kin talk t' the cows. They know. They know the farm an' me. They'll give me peace. (*He turns to go out the door.*)

ABBIE (*a bit frightenedly*): Air ye ailin' tonight, Ephraim?

CABOT: Growin'. Growin' ripe on the bough. (*He turns and goes, his boots clumping down the stairs. Eben sits up with a start, listening. Abbie is conscious of his movement and stares at the wall. Cabot comes out of the house around the corner and stands by the gate, blinking at the sky. He stretches up his hands in a tortured gesture.*) God A'mighty, call from the dark! (*He listens as if ex-pecting an answer. Then his arms drop, he shakes his head and plods off toward the barn. Eben and Abbie stare at each other through the wall. Eben sighs heavily and Abbie echoes it. Both become terribly nervous, uneasy. Finally Abbie gets up and listens, her ear to the wall. He acts as if he saw every move she was making, he becomes res-olutely still. She seems driven into a decision — goes out the door in rear determinedly. His eyes follow her. Then as the door of his room is opened softly, he turns away, waits in an attitude of strained fixity. Abbie stands for a second staring at him, her eyes burning with desire. Then with a lit-tle cry she runs over and throws her arms about his neck, she pulls his head back and covers his mouth with kisses. At first, he submits dumbly; then he puts his arms about her neck and returns her kisses, but finally, suddenly aware of his ha-tred, he hurls her away from him, springing to his feet. They stand speechless and breathless, panting like two animals.*)

ABBIE (*at last — painfully*): Ye shouldn't, Eben — ye shouldn't — I'd make ye happy!

EBEN (*harshly*): I don't want t' be happy — from yew!

ABBIE (*helplessly*): Ye do, Eben! Ye do! Why d'ye lie?

EBEN (*viciously*): I don't take t'ye, I tell ye! I hate the sight o' ye!

ABBIE (*with an uncertain troubled laugh*): Waal, I kissed ye anyways — an' ye kissed back — yer lips was burnin' — ye can't lie 'bout that! (*Intensely.*) If ye don't care, why did ye kiss me back — why was yer lips burnin'?

EBEN (*wiping his mouth*): It was like pizen on 'em. (*Then tauntingly.*) When I kissed ye back, mebbe I thought 'twas someone else.

ABBIE (*wildly*): Min?

EBEN: Mebbe.

ABBIE (*torturedly*): Did ye go t' see her? Did ye r'ally go? I thought ye mightn't. Is that why ye throwed me off jest now?

EBEN (*sneeringly*): What if it be?

ABBIE (*raging*): Then ye're a dog, Eben Cabot!

EBEN (*threateningly*): Ye can't talk that way t' me!

ABBIE (*with a shrill laugh*): Can't I? Did ye think I was in love with ye — a weak thin' like yew? Not much! I on'y wanted ye fur a purpose o' my own — an' I'll hev ye fur it yet 'cause I'm stronger'n yew be!

EBEN (*resentfully*): I knowed well it was on'y part o' yer plan t' swaller everythin'!

ABBIE (*tauntingly*): Mebbe!

EBEN (*furious*): Git out o' my room!

ABBIE: This air my room an' ye're on'y hired help!

EBEN (*threateningly*): Git out afore I murder ye!

ABBIE (*quite confident now*): I hain't a mite afeerd. Ye want me, don't ye? Yes, ye do! An' yer Paw's son'll never kill what he wants! Look at yer eyes! They's lust fur me in 'em, burnin' 'em up! Look at yer lips now! They're tremblin' an' longin' t' kiss me, an' yer teeth t' bite! (*He is watching her now with a horrible fascination. She laughs a crazy triumphant laugh.*) I'm a-goin' t' make all o' this hum my hum! They's one room hain't mine yet, but it's a-goin' t' be tonight. I'm a-goin' down now an' light up! (*She makes him a mocking bow.*) Won't ye come courtin' me in the best parlor, Mister Cabot?

EBEN (*staring at her — horribly confused — dully*): Don't ye dare! It hain't been opened since Maw died an' was laid out thar! Don't ye . . . ! (*But her eyes are fixed on his so burningly that his will seems to wither before hers. He stands swaying toward her helplessly.*)

ABBIE (*holding his eyes and putting all her will into her words as she backs out the door*): I'll expect ye afore long, Eben.

EBEN (*Stares after her for a while, walking toward the door. A light appears in the parlor window. He murmurs.*): In the parlor? (*This seems to arouse connotations, for he comes back and puts on his white shirt, collar, half ties the tie mechanically, puts on coat, takes his hat, stands barefooted looking about him in bewilderment, mutters wonderingly.*) Maw! Whar air yew? (*Then goes slowly toward the door in rear.*)

Scene III

(*A few minutes later. The interior of the parlor is shown. A grim, repressed room like a tomb in which the family has been interred alive. Abbie sits on the edge of the horsehair sofa. She has lighted all the candles and the room is revealed in all its preserved ugliness. A change has come over the woman. She looks awed and frightened now, ready to run away.*)

(*The door is opened and Eben appears. His face wears an expression of obsessed confusion. He stands staring at her, his arms hanging disjointedly from his shoulders, his feet bare, his hat in his hand.*)

ABBIE (*after a pause — with a nervous, formal politeness*): Won't ye set?

EBEN (*dully*): Ay-eh. (*Mechanically he places his hat carefully on the floor near the door and sits stiffly beside her on the edge of the sofa. A pause. They both remain rigid, looking straight ahead with eyes full of fear.*)

ABBIE: When I fust come in — in the dark — they seemed somethin' here.

EBEN (*simply*): Maw.

ABBIE: I kin still feel — somethin'. . . .

EBEN: It's Maw.

ABBIE: At fust I was feered o' it. I wanted t' yell an' run. Now — since yew come — seems like it's growin' soft an' kind t' me. (*Addressing the air — queerly.*) Thank yew.

EBEN: Maw allus loved me.

ABBIE: Mebbe it knows I love yew, too. Mebbe that makes it kind t' me.

EBEN (*dully*): I dunno. I should think she'd hate ye.

ABBIE (*with certainty*): No. I kin feel it don't — not no more.

EBEN: Hate ye fur stealin' her place — here in her hum — settin' in her parlor whar she was laid — (*He suddenly stops, staring stupidly before him.*)

ABBIE: What is it, Eben?

EBEN (*in a whisper*): Seems like Maw didn't want me t' remind ye.

ABBIE (*excitedly*): I knowed, Eben! It's kind t' me! It don't b'ar me no grudges fur what I never knowed an' couldn't help!

EBEN: Maw b'ars him a grudge.

Abbie in the 1988 Pushkin Theatre (Moscow) production of *Desire Under the Elms,* directed by Mark Lamos of the Hartford Stage Company.

ABBIE: Waal, so does all o' us.

EBEN: Ay-eh. (*With passion.*) I does, by God!

ABBIE (*taking one of his hands in hers and patting it*): Thar! Don't git riled thinkin' o' him. Think o' yer Maw who's kind t' us. Tell me about yer Maw, Eben.

EBEN: They hain't nothin' much. She was kind. She was good.

ABBIE (*Putting one arm over his shoulder. He does not seem to notice — passionately.*): I'll be kind an' good t' ye!

EBEN: Sometimes she used t' sing fur me.

ABBIE: I'll sing fur ye!

EBEN: This was her hum. This was her farm.

ABBIE: This is my hum! This is my farm!

EBEN: He married her t' steal 'em. She was soft an' easy. He couldn't 'preciate her.

ABBIE: He can't 'preciate me!

EBEN: He murdered her with his hardness.

ABBIE: He's murderin' me!

EBEN: She died. (*A pause.*) Sometimes she used to sing fur me. (*He bursts into a fit of sobbing.*)

ABBIE (*both her arms around him — with wild pas-*sion): I'll sing fur ye! I'll die fur ye! (*In spite of her overwhelming desire for him, there is a sincere maternal love in her manner and voice — a horribly frank mixture of lust and mother love.*) Don't cry, Eben! I'll take yer Maw's place! I'll be everythin' she was t' ye! Let me kiss ye, Eben! (*She pulls his head around. He makes a bewildered pretense of resistance. She is tender.*) Don't be afeered! I'll kiss ye pure, Eben — same 's if I was a Maw t' ye — an' ye kin kiss me back 's if yew was my son — my boy — sayin' good-night t' me! Kiss me, Eben. (*They kiss in restrained fashion. Then suddenly wild passion overcomes her. She kisses him lustfully again and again and he flings his arms about her and returns her kisses. Suddenly, as in the bedroom, he frees himself from her violently and springs to his feet. He is trembling all over, in a strange state of terror. Abbie strains her arms toward him with fierce pleading.*) Don't ye leave me, Eben! Can't ye see it hain't enuf — lovin' ye like a Maw — can't ye see it's got t' be that an' more — much more — a hundred times more — fur me t' be happy — fur yew t' be happy?

EBEN (*to the presence he feels in the room*): Maw! Maw! What d'ye want? What air ye tellin' me?

ABBIE: She's tellin' ye t' love me. She knows I love ye an' I'll be good t' ye. Can't ye feel it? Don't ye know? She's tellin' ye t' love me, Eben!

EBEN: Ay-eh. I feel — mebbe she — but — I can't figger out — why — when ye've stole her place — here in her hum — in the parlor whar she was —

ABBIE (*fiercely*): She knows I love ye!

EBEN (*his face' suddenly lighting up with a fierce, triumphant grin*): I see it! I sees why. It's her vengeance on him — so's she kin rest quiet in her grave!

ABBIE (*wildly*): Vengeance o' God on the hull o' us! What d'we give a durn? I love ye, Eben! God knows I love ye! (*She stretches out her arms for him.*)

EBEN (*throws himself on his knees beside the sofa and grabs her in his arms — releasing all his pent-up passion*): An' I love ye, Abbie! — now I kin say it! I been dyin' fur want o' ye — every hour since ye come! I love ye! (*Their lips meet in a fierce, bruising kiss.*)

Scene IV

(*Exterior of the farmhouse. It is just dawn. The front door at right is opened and Eben comes out and walks around to the gate. He is dressed in his working clothes. He seems changed. His face wears a bold and confident expression, he is grinning to himself with evident satisfaction. As he gets near the gate, the window of the parlor is heard opening and the shutters are flung back and Abbie sticks her head out. Her hair tumbles over her shoulders in disarray, her face is flushed, she looks at Eben with tender, languorous eyes and calls softly.*)

ABBIE: Eben. (*As he turns — playfully.*) Jest one more kiss afore ye go. I'm goin' to miss ye fearful all day.

EBEN: An' me yew, ye kin bet! (*He goes to her. They kiss several times. He draws away, laughingly.*) Thar. That's enuf, hain't it? Ye won't hev none left fur next time.

ABBIE: I got a million o' 'em left fur yew! (*Then a bit anxiously.*) D'ye r'ally love me, Eben?

EBEN (*emphatically*): I like ye better'n any gal I ever knowed! That's gospel!

ABBIE: Likin' hain't lovin'.

EBEN: Waal then — I love ye. Now air yew satisfied?

ABBIE: Ay-eh, I be. (*She smiles at him adoringly.*)

EBEN: I better git t' the barn. The old critter's liable t' suspicion an' come sneakin' up.

ABBIE (*with a confident laugh*): Let him! I kin allus pull the wool over his eyes. I'm goin' t' leave the shutters open and let in the sun 'n' air. This room's been dead long enuf. Now it's goin' t' be my room!

EBEN (*frowning*): Ay-eh.

ABBIE (*hastily*): I meant — our room.

EBEN: Ay-eh.

ABBIE: We made it our'n last night, didn't we? We give it life — our lovin' did. (*A pause.*)

EBEN (*with a strange look*): Maw's gone back t' her grave. She kin sleep now.

ABBIE: May she rest in peace! (*Then tenderly rebuking.*) Ye oughtn't t' talk o' sad thin's — this mornin'.

EBEN: It jest come up in my mind o' itself.

ABBIE: Don't let it. (*He doesn't answer. She yawns.*) Waal, I'm a-goin' t' steal a wink o' sleep. I'll tell the Old Man I hain't feelin' pert. Let him git his own vittles.

EBEN: I see him comin' from the barn. Ye better look smart an' git upstairs.

ABBIE: Ay-eh. Good-by. Don't ferget me. (*She throws him a kiss. He grins — then squares his shoulders and awaits his father confidently. Cabot walks slowly up from the left, staring up at the sky with a vague face.*)

EBEN (*jovially*): Mornin', Paw. Star-gazin' in daylight?

CABOT: Purty, hain't it?

EBEN (*looking around him possessively*): It's a durned purty farm.

CABOT: I mean the sky.

EBEN (*grinning*): How d'ye know? Them eyes o' your'n can't see that fur. (*This tickles his humor and he slaps his thigh and laughs.*) Ho-ho! That's a good un!

CABOT (*grimly sarcastic*): Ye're feelin' right chipper, hain't ye? Whar'd ye steal the likker?

EBEN (*good-naturedly*): 'Tain't likker. Jest life. (*Suddenly holding out his hand — soberly.*) Yew 'n' me is quits. Let's shake hands.

CABOT (*suspiciously*): What's come over ye?

EBEN: Then don't. Mebbe it's jest as well. (*A moment's pause.*) What's come over me? (*Queerly.*) Didn't ye feel her passin' — goin' back t' her grave?

CABOT (*dully*): Who?

EBEN: Maw. She kin rest now an' sleep content. She's quit with ye.

CABOT (*confusedly*): I rested. I slept good — down with the cows. They know how t' sleep. They're teachin' me.

EBEN (*suddenly jovial again*): Good fur the cows! Waal — ye better git t' work.

CABOT (*grimly amused*): Air yew bossin' me, ye calf?

EBEN (*beginning to laugh*): Ay-eh! I'm bossin' yew! Ha-ha-ha! See how ye like it! Ha-ha-ha! I'm the prize rooster o' this roost. Ha-ha-ha! (*He goes off toward the barn laughing.*)

CABOT (*looks after him with scornful pity*): Soft-headed. Like his Maw. Dead spit 'n' image. No hope in him! (*He spits with contemptuous dis-*

gust.) A born fool! (*Then matter-of-factly.*) Waal — I'm gittin' peckish. (*He goes toward door.*)

PART III • *Scene* I

(*A night in late spring the following year. The kitchen and the two bedrooms upstairs are shown. The two bedrooms are dimly lighted by a tallow candle in each. Eben is sitting on the side of the bed in his room, his chin propped on his fists, his face a study of the struggle he is making to understand his conflicting emotions. The noisy laughter and music from below where a kitchen dance is in progress annoy and distract him. He scowls at the floor.*)

(*In the next room a cradle stands beside the double bed.*)

(*In the kitchen all is festivity. The stove has been taken down to give more room to the dancers. The chairs, with wooden benches added, have been pushed back against the walls. On these are seated, squeezed in tight against one another, farmers and their wives and their young folks of both sexes from the neighboring farms. They are all chattering and laughing loudly. They evidently have some secret joke in common. There is no end of winking, of nudging, of meaning nods of the head toward Cabot who, in a state of extreme hilarious excitement increased by the amount he has drunk, is standing near the rear door where there is a small keg of whisky and serving drinks to all the men. In the left corner, front, dividing the attention with her husband, Abbie is sitting in a rocking chair, a shawl wrapped about her shoulders. She is very pale, her face is thin and drawn, her eyes are fixed anxiously on the open door in rear as if waiting for someone.*)

(*The musician is tuning up his fiddle, seated in the far right corner. He is a lanky young fellow with a long, weak face. His pale eyes blink incessantly and he grins about him slyly with a greedy malice.*)

ABBIE (*suddenly turning to a young girl on her right*): Whar's Eben?

YOUNG GIRL (*eyeing her scornfully*): I dunno, Mrs. Cabot. I hain't seen Eben in ages. (*Meaningly.*) Seems like he's spent most o' his time t' hum since yew come.

ABBIE (*vaguely*): I tuk his Maw's place.

YOUNG GIRL: Ay-eh. So I've heerd. (*She turns away to retail this bit of gossip to her mother sitting next to her. Abbie turns to her left to a big stoutish middle-aged man whose flushed face and starting eyes show the amount of "likker" he has consumed.*)

ABBIE: Ye hain't seen Eben, hev ye?

MAN: No, I hain't. (*Then he adds with a wink.*) If yew hain't, who would?

ABBIE: He's the best dancer in the county. He'd ought t' come an' dance.

MAN (*with a wink*): Mebbe he's doin' the dutiful an' walkin' the kid t' sleep. It's a boy, hain't it?

ABBIE (*nodding vaguely*): Ay-eh — born two weeks back — purty's a picter.

MAN: They all is — t' their Maws. (*Then in a whisper, with a nudge and a leer.*) Listen, Abbie — if ye ever git tired o' Eben, remember me! Don't fergit now! (*He looks at her uncomprehending face for a second — then grunts disgustedly.*) Waal — guess I'll likker agin. (*He goes over and joins Cabot who is arguing noisily with an old farmer over cows. They all drink.*)

ABBIE (*this time appealing to nobody in particular*): Wonder what Eben's a-doin'? (*Her remark is repeated down the line with many a guffaw and titter until it reaches the fiddler. He fastens his blinking eyes on Abbie.*)

FIDDLER (*raising his voice*): Bet I kin tell ye, Abbie, what Eben's doin'! He's down t' the church offerin' up prayers o' thanksgivin'. (*They all titter expectantly.*)

A MAN: What fur? (*Another titter.*)

FIDDLER: 'Cause unto him a — (*He hesitates just long enough.*) brother is born! (*A roar of laughter. They all look from Abbie to Cabot. She is oblivious, staring at the door. Cabot, although he hasn't heard the words, is irritated by the laughter and steps forward, glaring about him. There is an immediate silence.*)

CABOT: What're ye all bleatin' about — like a flock o' goats? Why don't ye dance, damn ye? I axed ye here t' dance — t' eat, drink an' be merry — an' thar ye set cacklin' like a lot o' wet hens with the pip! Ye've swilled my likker an' guzzled my vittles like hogs, hain't ye? Then dance fur me, can't ye? That's fa'r an' squar', hain't it? (*A grumble of resentment goes around but they are all evidently in too much awe of him to express it openly.*)

FIDDLER (*slyly*): We're waitin' fur Eben. (*A suppressed laugh.*)

CABOT (*with a fierce exultation*): T'hell with Eben! Eben's done fur now! I got a new son! (*His mood switching with drunken suddenness.*) But ye needn't t' laugh at Eben, none o' ye! He's my blood, if he be a dumb fool. He's better nor any o' yew! He kin do a day's work a'most up t' what I kin — an' that'd put any o' yew pore critters t' shame!

FIDDLER: An' he kin do a good night's work, too! (*A roar of laughter.*)

CABOT: Laugh, ye damn fools! Ye're right jist the same, Fiddler. He kin work day an' night too, like I kin, if need be!

OLD FARMER (*from behind the keg where he is weav-*

ing drunkenly back and forth — with great simplicity): They hain't many t' touch ye, Ephraim — a son at seventy-six. That's a hard man fur ye! I be on'y sixty-eight an' I couldn't do it. (*A roar of laughter in which Cabot joins uproariously.*)

CABOT (*slapping him on the back*): I'm sorry fur ye, Hi. I'd never suspicion sech weakness from a boy like yew!

OLD FARMER: An' I never reckoned yew had it in ye nuther, Ephraim. (*There is another laugh.*)

CABOT (*suddenly grim*): I got a lot in me — a hell of a lot — folks don't know on. (*Turning to the fiddler.*) Fiddle 'er up, durn ye! Give 'em somethin' t' dance t'! What air ye, an ornament? Hain't this a celebration? Then grease yer elbow an' go it!

FIDDLER (*seizes a drink which the Old Farmer holds out to him and downs it*): Here goes! (*He starts to fiddle "Lady of the Lake." Four young fellows and four girls form in two lines and dance a square dance. The Fiddler shouts directions for the different movements, keeping his words in the rhythm of the music and interspersing them with jocular personal remarks to the dancers themselves. The people seated along the walls stamp their feet and clap their hands in unison. Cabot is especially active in this respect. Only Abbie remains apathetic, staring at the door as if she were alone in a silent room.*)

FIDDLER: Swing your partner t' the right! That's it, Jim! Give her a b'ar hug. Her Maw hain't lookin'. (*Laughter.*) Change partners! That suits ye, don't it, Essie, now ye got Reub afore ye? Look at her redden up, will ye? Waal, life is short an' so's love, as the feller says. (*Laughter.*)

CABOT (*excitedly, stamping his foot*): Go it, boys! Go it, gals!

FIDDLER (*with a wink at the others*): Ye're the spryest seventy-six ever I sees, Ephraim! Now if ye'd on'y good eyesight . . . ! (*Suppressed laughter. He gives Cabot no chance to retort but roars.*) Promenade! Ye're walkin' like a bride down the aisle, Sarah! Waal, while they's life they's allus hope, I've heerd tell. Swing your partner to the left! Gosh A'mighty, look at Johnny Cook high-steppin'! They hain't goin' t' be much strength left fur howin' in the corn lot t'morrow. (*Laughter.*)

CABOT: Go it! Go it! (*Then suddenly, unable to restrain himself any longer, he prances into the midst of the dancers, scattering them, waving his arms about wildly.*) Ye're all hoofs! Git out o' my road! Give me room! I'll show ye dancin'. Ye're all too soft! (*He pushes them roughly away. They crowd back toward the walls, muttering, looking at him resentfully.*)

FIDDLER (*jeeringly*): Go it, Ephraim! Go it! (*He starts*

"Pop, Goes the Weasel," *increasing the tempo with every verse until at the end he is fiddling crazily as fast as he can go.*)

CABOT (*Starts to dance, which he does very well and with tremendous vigor. Then he begins to improvise, cuts incredibly grotesque capers, leaping up and cracking his heels together, prancing around in a circle with body bent in an Indian war dance, then suddenly straightening up and kicking as high as he can with both legs. He is like a monkey on a string. And all the while he intersperses his antics with shouts and derisive comments.*): Whoop! Here's dancin' fur ye! Whoop! See that! Seventy-six, if I'm a day! Hard as iron yet! Beatin' the young 'uns like I allus done! Look at me! I'd invite ye t' dance on my hundredth birthday on'y ye'll all be dead by then. Ye're a sickly generation! Yer hearts air pink, not red! Yer veins is full o' mud an' water! I be the on'y man in the county! Whoop! See that! I'm a Injun! I've killed Injuns in the West afore ye was born — an' skulped 'em too! They's a arrer wound on my backside I c'd show ye! The hull tribe chased me. I outrun 'em all — with the arrer stuck in me! An' I tuk vengeance on 'em. Ten eyes fur an eye, that was my motter! Whoop! Look at me! I kin kick the ceilin' off the room! Whoop!

FIDDLER (*stops playing — exhaustedly*): God A'mighty, I got enuf. Ye got the devil's strength in ye.

CABOT (*delightedly*): Did I beat yew, too? Waal, ye played smart. Hev a swig. (*He pours whisky for himself and Fiddler. They drink. The others watch Cabot silently with cold, hostile eyes. There is a dead pause. The Fiddler rests. Cabot leans against the keg, panting, glaring around him confusedly. In the room above, Eben gets to his feet and tiptoes out the door in rear, appearing a moment later in the other bedroom. He moves silently, even frightenedly, toward the cradle and stands there looking down at the baby. His face is as vague as his reactions are confused, but there is a trace of tenderness, of interested discovery. At the same moment that he reaches the cradle, Abbie seems to sense something. She gets up weakly and goes to Cabot.*)

ABBIE: I'm goin' up t' the baby.

CABOT (*with real solicitation*): Air ye able fur the stairs? D'ye want me t' help ye, Abbie?

ABBIE: No. I'm able. I'll be down agen soon.

CABOT: Don't ye git wore out! He needs ye, remember — our son does! (*He grins affectionately, patting her on the back. She shrinks from his touch.*)

ABBIE (*dully*): Don't — tech me. I'm goin' — up. (*She goes. Cabot looks after her. A whisper goes around the room. Cabot turns. It ceases. He wipes his forehead streaming with sweat. He is breathing pantingly.*)

CABOT: I'm a-goin' out t' git fresh air. I'm feelin' a mite dizzy. Fiddle up thar! Dance, all o' ye! Here's likker fur them as wants it. Enjoy yerselves. I'll be back. (*He goes, closing the door behind him.*)

FIDDLER (*sarcastically*): Don't hurry none on our account! (*A suppressed laugh. He imitates Abbie.*) Whar's Eben? (*More laughter.*)

A WOMAN (*loudly*): What's happened in this house is plain as the nose on yer face! (*Abbie appears in the doorway upstairs and stands looking in surprise and adoration at Eben who does not see her.*)

A MAN: Ssshh! He's li'ble t' be listenin' at the door. That'd be like him. (*Their voices die to an intensive whispering. Their faces are concentrated on this gossip. A noise as of dead leaves in the wind comes from the room. Cabot has come out from the porch and stands by the gate, leaning on it, staring at the sky blinkingly. Abbie comes across the room silently. Eben does not notice her until quite near.*)

EBEN (*starting*): Abbie!

ABBIE: Ssshh! (*She throws her arms around him. They kiss — then bend over the cradle together.*) Ain't he purty? — dead spit 'n' image o' yew!

EBEN (*pleased*): Air he? I can't tell none.

ABBIE: E-zactly like!

EBEN (*frowningly*): I don't like this. I don't like lettin' on what's mine's his'n. I been doin' that all my life. I'm gittin' t' the end o' b'arin' it!

ABBIE (*putting her finger on his lips*): We're doin' the best we kin. We got t' wait. Somethin's bound t' happen. (*She puts her arms around him.*) I got t' go back.

EBEN: I'm goin' out. I can't b'ar it with the fiddle playin' an' the laughin'.

ABBIE: Don't git feelin' low. I love ye, Eben. Kiss me. (*He kisses her. They remain in each other's arms.*)

CABOT (*at the gate, confusedly*): Even the music can't drive it out — somethin'. Ye kin feel it droppin' off the elums, climbin' up the roof, sneakin' down the chimney, pokin' in the corners! They's no peace in houses, they's no rest livin' with folks. Somethin's always livin' with ye. (*With a deep sigh.*) I'll go t' the barn an' rest a spell. (*He goes wearily toward the barn.*)

FIDDLER (*tuning up*): Let's celebrate the old skunk gittin' fooled! We kin have some fun now he's went. (*He starts to fiddle "Turkey in the Straw." There is real merriment now. The young folks get up to dance.*)

Scene II

(*A half hour later — exterior — Eben is standing by the gate looking up at the sky, an expression of dumb pain bewildered by itself on his face. Cabot appears,* returning from the barn, walking wearily, his eyes on the ground. He sees Eben and his whole mood immediately changes. He becomes excited, a cruel, triumphant grin comes to his lips, he strides up and slaps Eben on the back. From within comes the whining of the fiddle and the noise of stamping feet and laughing voices.*)

CABOT: So har ye be!

EBEN (*startled, stares at him with hatred for a moment — then dully*): Ay-eh.

CABOT (*surveying him jeeringly*): Why hain't ye been in t' dance? They was all axin' fur ye.

EBEN: Let 'em ax.

CABOT: They's a hull passel o' purty gals.

EBEN: T' hell with 'em!

CABOT: Ye'd ought t' be marryin' one o' 'em soon.

EBEN: I hain't marryin' no one.

CABOT: Ye might 'arn a share o' a farm that way.

EBEN (*with a sneer*): Like yew did, ye mean? I hain't that kind.

CABOT (*stung*): Ye lie! 'Twas yer Maw's folks aimed t' steal my farm from me.

EBEN: Other folks don't say so. (*After a pause — defiantly.*) An' I got a farm, anyways!

CABOT (*derisively*): Whar?

EBEN (*stamps a foot on the ground*): Har!

CABOT (*throws his head back and laughs coarsely*): Ho-ho! Ye hev, hev ye? Waal, that's a good un!

EBEN (*controlling himself — grimly*): Ye'll see!

CABOT (*stares at him suspiciously, trying to make him out — a pause — then with scornful confidence*): Ay-eh. I'll see. So'll ye. It's ye that's blind — blind as a mole underground. (*Eben suddenly laughs, one short sardonic bark: "Ha." A pause. Cabot peers at him with renewed suspicion.*) What air ye hawin' 'bout? (*Eben turns away without answering. Cabot grows angry.*) God A'mighty, yew air a dumb dunce! They's nothin' in that thick skull o' your'n but noise — like a empty keg it be! (*Eben doesn't seem to hear. Cabot's rage grows.*) Yewr farm! God A'mighty! If ye wa'n't a born donkey ye'd know ye'll never own stick nor stone on it, specially now arter him bein' born. It's his'n, I tell ye — his'n arter I die — but I'll live a hundred jest t' fool ye all — an' he'll be growed then — yewr age a'most! (*Eben laughs again his sardonic "Ha." This drives Cabot into a fury.*) Ha? Ye think ye kin git 'round that someways, do ye? Waal, it'll be her'n, too — Abbie's — ye won't git 'round her — she knows yer tricks — she'll be too much fur ye — she wants the farm her'n — she was afeerd o' ye — she told me ye was sneakin' 'round tryin' t' make love t' her t' git her on yer side . . . ye . . . ye mad fool, ye! (*He raises his clenched fists threateningly.*)

EBEN (*is confronting him, choking with rage*): Ye lic, ye old skunk! Abbie never said no sech thing!

CABOT (*suddenly triumphant when he sees how shaken Eben is*): She did. An' I says, I'll blow his brains t' the top o' them elums — an' she says no that hain't sense, who'll ye git t'help ye on the farm in his place — an' then she says yew'n me ought t' have a son — I know we kin, she says — an' I says, if we do, ye kin have anythin' I've got ye've a mind t'. An' she says, I wants Eben cut off so's this farm'll be mine when ye die! (*With terrible gloating.*) An' that's what's happened, hain't it? An' the farm's her'n! An' the dust o' the road — that's you'rn! Ha! Now who's hawin'?

EBEN (*has been listening, petrified with grief and rage — suddenly laughs wildly and brokenly*): Ha-ha-ha! So that's her sneakin' game — all along! — like I suspicioned at fust — t' swaller it all — an' me, too . . . ! (*Madly.*) I'll murder her! (*He springs toward the porch but Cabot is quicker and gets in between.*)

CABOT: No, ye don't!

EBEN: Git out o' my road! (*He tries to throw Cabot aside. They grapple in what becomes immediately a murderous struggle. The old man's concentrated strength is too much for Eben. Cabot gets one hand on his throat and presses him back across the stone wall. At the same moment, Abbie comes out on the porch. With a stifled cry she runs toward them.*)

ABBIE: Eben! Ephraim! (*She tugs at the hand on Eben's throat.*) Let go, Ephraim! Ye're chokin' him!

CABOT (*Removes his hand and flings Eben sideways full length on the grass, gasping and choking. With a cry, Abbie kneels beside him, trying to take his head on her lap, but he pushes her away. Cabot stands looking down with fierce triumph.*): Ye needn't t've fret, Abbie, I wa'n't aimin' t' kill him. He hain't wuth hangin' fur — not by a hell of a sight! (*More and more triumphantly.*) Seventy-six an' him not thirty yit — an' look whar he be fur thinkin' his Paw was easy! No, by God, I hain't easy! An' him upstairs, I'll raise him t' be like me! (*He turns to leave them.*) I'm goin' in an' dance! — sing an' celebrate! (*He walks to the porch — then turns with a great grin.*) I don't calc'late it's left in him, but if he gits pesky, Abbie, ye jest sing out. I'll come a-runnin' an' by the Etarnal, I'll put him across my knee an' birch him! Ha-ha-ha! (*He goes into the house laughing. A moment later his loud "whoop" is heard.*)

ABBIE (*tenderly*): Eben. Air ye hurt? (*She tries to kiss him but he pushes her violently away and struggles to a sitting position.*)

EBEN (*gaspingly*): T'hell — with ye!

ABBIE (*not believing her ears*): It's me, Eben — Abbie — don't ye know me?

EBEN (*glowering at her with hatred*): Ay-eh — I know ye — now! (*He suddenly breaks down, sobbing weakly.*)

ABBIE (*fearfully*): Eben — what's happened t' ye — why did ye look at me 's if ye hated me?

EBEN (*violently, between sobs and gasps*): I do hate ye! Ye're a whore — a damn trickin' whore!

ABBIE (*shrinking back horrified*): Eben! Ye don't know what ye're sayin'!

EBEN (*scrambling to his feet and following her — accusingly*): Ye're nothin' but a stinkin' passel o' lies! Ye've been lyin' t' me every word ye spoke, day an' night, since we fust — done it. Ye've kept sayin' ye loved me. . . .

ABBIE (*frantically*): I do love ye! (*She takes his hand but he flings hers away.*)

EBEN (*unheeding*): Ye've made a fool o' me — a sick, dumb fool — a-purpose! Ye've been on'y playin' yer sneakin', stealin' game all along — gittin' me t' lie with ye so's ye'd hev a son he'd think was his'n, an' makin' him promise he'd give ye the farm and let me eat dust, if ye did git him a son! (*Staring at her with anguished, bewildered eyes.*) They must be a devil livin' in ye! T'ain't human t' be as bad as that be!

ABBIE (*stunned — dully*): He told yew . . . ?

EBEN: Hain't it true? It hain't no good in yew lyin'.

ABBIE (*pleadingly*): Eben, listen — ye must listen — it was long ago — afore we done nothin' — yew was scornin' me — goin' t' see Min — when I was lovin' ye — an' I said it t' him t' git vengeance on ye!

EBEN (*Unheedingly. With tortured passion.*): I wish ye was dead! I wish I was dead along with ye afore this come! (*Ragingly.*) But I'll git my vengeance too! I'll pray Maw t' come back t' help me — t' put her cuss on yew an' him!

ABBIE (*brokenly*): Don't ye, Eben! Don't ye! (*She throws herself on her knees before him, weeping.*) I didn't mean t' do bad t'ye! Fergive me, won't ye?

EBEN (*not seeming to hear her — fiercely*): I'll git squar' with the old skunk — an' yew! I'll tell him the truth 'bout the son he's so proud o'! Then I'll leave ye here t' pizen each other — with Maw comin' out o' her grave at nights — an' I'll go t' the gold fields o' Californi-a whar Sim an' Peter be!

ABBIE (*terrified*): Ye won't — leave me? Ye can't!

EBEN (*with fierce determination*): I'm a-goin', I tell ye! I'll git rich thar an' come back an' fight him fur the farm he stole — an' I'll kick ye both out in the road — t' beg an' sleep in the woods — an' yer son along with ye — t' starve an' die! (*He is hysterical at the end.*)

ABBIE (*with a shudder — humbly*): He's yewr son, too, Eben.

EBEN (*torturedly*): I wish he never was born! I wish he'd die this minit! I wish I'd never sot eyes on him! It's him — yew havin' him — a-purpose t' steal — that's changed everythin'!

ABBIE (*gently*): Did ye believe I loved ye — afore he come?

EBEN: Aye-eh — like a dumb ox!

ABBIE: An' ye don't believe no more?

EBEN: B'lieve a lyin' thief! Ha!

ABBIE (*shudders — then humbly*): An' did ye r'ally love me afore?

EBEN (*brokenly*): Ay-eh — an' ye was trickin' me!

ABBIE: An' ye don't love me now!

EBEN (*violently*): I hate ye, I tell ye!

ABBIE: An' ye're truly goin' West — goin' t' leave me — all account o' him being born?

EBEN: I'm a-goin' in the mornin' — or may God strike me t' hell!

ABBIE (*after a pause — with a dreadful cold intensity — slowly*): If that's what his comin's done t' me — killin' yewr love — takin' yew away — my on'y joy — the on'y joy I ever knowed — like heaven t' me — purtier'n heaven — then I hate him, too, even if I be his Maw!

EBEN (*bitterly*): Lies! Ye love him! He'll steal the farm fur ye! (*Brokenly.*) But t'ain't the farm so much — not no more — it's yew foolin' me — gittin' me t' love ye — lyin' yew loved me — jest t' git a son t' steal!

ABBIE (*distractedly*): He won't steal! I'd kill him fust! I do love ye! I'll prove t' ye . . . !

EBEN (*harshly*): T'ain't no use lyin' no more. I'm deaf t' ye! (*He turns away.*) I hain't seein' ye agen. Good-by!

ABBIE (*pale with anguish*): Hain't ye even goin' t' kiss me — not once — arter all we loved?

EBEN (*in a hard voice*): I hain't wantin' t' kiss ye never agen! I'm wantin' t' forget I ever sot eyes on ye!

ABBIE: Eben! — ye mustn't — wait a spell — I want t' tell ye. . . .

EBEN: I'm a-goin' in t' git drunk. I'm a-goin' t' dance.

ABBIE (*clinging to his arm — with passionate earnestness*): If I could make it — 's if he'd never come up between us — if I could prove t' ye I wa'n't schemin' t' steal from ye — so's everythin' could be jest the same with us, lovin' each other jest the same, kissin' an' happy the same's we've been happy afore he come — if I could do it — ye'd love me agen, wouldn't ye? Ye'd kiss me agen? Ye wouldn't never leave me, would ye?

EBEN (*moved*): I calc'late not. (*Then shaking her hand off his arm — with a bitter smile.*) But ye hain't God, be ye?

ABBIE (*exultantly*): Remember ye've promised! (*Then with strange intensity.*) Mebbe I kin take back one thin' God does!

EBEN (*peering at her*): Ye're gittin' cracked, hain't ye? (*Then going toward door.*) I'm a-goin' t' dance.

ABBIE (*calls after him intensely*): I'll prove t' ye! I'll prove I love ye better'n. . . . (*He goes in the door, not seeming to hear. She remains standing where she is, looking after him — then she finishes desperately.*) Better'n everythin' else in the world!

Scene III

(*Just before dawn in the morning — shows the kitchen and Cabot's bedroom. In the kitchen, by the light of a tallow candle on the table, Eben is sitting, his chin propped on his hands, his drawn face blank and expressionless. His carpetbag is on the floor beside him. In the bedroom, dimly lighted by a small whale-oil lamp, Cabot lies asleep. Abbie is bending over the cradle, listening, her face full of terror yet with an undercurrent of desperate triumph. Suddenly, she breaks down and sobs, appears about to throw herself on her knees beside the cradle, but the old man turns restlessly, groaning in his sleep, and she controls herself, and, shrinking away from the cradle with a gesture of horror, backs swiftly toward the door in rear and goes out. A moment later she comes into the kitchen, and, running to Eben, flings her arms about his neck and kisses him wildly. He hardens himself, he remains unmoved and cold, he keeps his eyes straight ahead.*)

ABBIE (*hysterically*): I done it, Eben! I told ye I'd do it! I've proved I love ye — better'n everythin' — so's ye can't never doubt me no more!

EBEN (*dully*): Whatever ye done, it hain't no good now.

ABBIE (*wildly*): Don't ye say that! Kiss me, Eben, won't ye? I need ye t' kiss me arter what I done! I need ye t' say ye love me!

EBEN (*kisses her without emotion — dully*): That's fur good-by. I'm a-goin' soon.

ABBIE: No! No! Ye won't go — not now!

EBEN (*going on with his own thoughts*): I been a-thinkin' — an' I hain't goin' t' tell Paw nothin'. I'll leave Maw t' take vengeance on ye. If I told him, the old skunk'd jest be stinkin' mean enuf to take it out on that baby. (*His voice showing emotion in spite of him.*) An' I don't want nothin' bad t' happen t' him. He hain't t' blame fur yew. (*He adds with a certain queer pride.*) An' he looks like me! An' by God, he's mine! An' some day I'll be a-comin' back an' . . . !

ABBIE (*too absorbed in her own thoughts to listen to him — pleadingly*): They's no cause fur ye t' go now — they's no sense — it's all the same's it was — they's nothin' come b'tween us now — arter what I done!

EBEN (*Something in her voice arouses him. He stares at her a bit frightenedly.*): Ye look mad, Abbie. What did ye do?

ABBIE: I — I killed him, Eben.

EBEN (*amazed*): Ye killed him?

ABBIE (*dully*): Ay-eh.

EBEN (*recovering from his astonishment — savagely*): An' serves him right! But we got t' do somethin' quick t' make it look s'if the old skunk'd killed himself when he was drunk. We kin prove by 'em all how drunk he got.

ABBIE (*wildly*): No! No! Not him! (*Laughing distractedly.*) But that's what I ought t' done, hain't it? I oughter killed him instead! Why didn't ye tell me?

EBEN (*appalled*): Instead? What d'ye mean?

ABBIE: Not him.

EBEN (*his face grown ghastly*): Not — not that baby!

ABBIE (*dully*): Ay-eh.

EBEN (*falls to his knees as if he'd been struck — his voice trembling with horror*): Oh, God A'mighty! A'mighty God! Maw, whar was ye, why didn't ye stop her?

ABBIE (*simply*): She went back t' her grave that night we fust done it, remember? I hain't felt her about since. (*A pause. Eben hides his head in his hands, trembling all over as if he had the ague. She goes on dully.*) I left the piller over his little face. Then he killed himself. He stopped breathin'. (*She begins to weep softly.*)

EBEN (*rage beginning to mingle with grief*): He looked like me. He was mine, damn ye!

ABBIE (*slowly and brokenly*): I didn't want t' do it. I hated myself fur doin' it. I loved him. He was so purty — dead spit 'n' image o' yew. But I loved yew more — an' yew was goin' away — far off whar I'd never see ye agen, never kiss ye, never feel ye pressed agin me agen — an' ye said ye hated me fur havin' him — ye said ye hated him an' wished he was dead — ye said if it hain't been fur him comin' it'd be the same's afore between us.

EBEN (*unable to endure this, springs to his feet in a fury, threatening her, his twitching fingers seeming to reach out for her throat*): Ye lie! I never said — I never dreamed ye'd — I'd cut off my head afore I'd hurt his finger!

ABBIE (*piteously, sinking on her knees*): Eben, don't ye look at me like that — hatin' me — not after what I done fur ye — fur us — so's we could be happy agen —

EBEN (*furiously now*): Shut up, or I'll kill ye! I see yer game now — the same old sneakin' trick — ye're aimin' t' blame me fur the murder ye done!

ABBIE (*moaning — putting her hands over her ears*): Don't ye, Eben! Don't ye! (*She grasps his legs.*)

EBEN (*his mood suddenly changing to horror, shrinks away from her*): Don't ye tech me! Ye're pizen! How could ye — t' murder a pore little critter — Ye must've swapped yer soul t' hell! (*Suddenly raging.*) Ha! I kin see why ye done it! Not the lies ye jest told — but 'cause ye wanted t' steal agen — steal the last thin' ye'd left me — my part o' him — no, the hull o' him — ye saw he looked like me — ye knowed he was all mine — an' ye couldn't b'ar it — I know ye! Ye killed him fur bein' mine! (*All this has driven him almost insane. He makes a rush past her for the door — then turns — shaking both fists at her, violently.*) But I'll take vengeance now! I'll git the Sheriff! I'll tell him everythin'! Then I'll sing "I'm off to Californi-a!" an' go — gold — Golden Gate — gold sun — fields o' gold in the West! (*This last he half shouts, half croons incoherently, suddenly breaking off passionately.*) I'm a-goin' fur the Sheriff t' come an' git ye! I want ye tuk away, locked up from me! I can't stand t' luk at ye! Murderer an' thief 'r not, ye still tempt me! I'll give ye up t' the Sheriff! (*He turns and runs out, around the corner of house, panting and sobbing, and breaks into a swerving sprint down the road.*)

ABBIE (*struggling to her feet, runs to the door, calling after him*): I love ye, Eben! I love ye! (*She stops at the door weakly, swaying, about to fall.*) I don't care what ye do — if ye'll on'y love me agen — (*She falls limply to the floor in a faint.*)

Scene IV

(*About an hour later. Same as scene III. Shows the kitchen and Cabot's bedroom. It is after dawn. The sky is brilliant with the sunrise. In the kitchen, Abbie sits at the table, her body limp and exhausted, her head bowed down over her arms, her face hidden. Upstairs, Cabot is still asleep but awakens with a start. He looks toward the window and gives a snort of surprise and irritation — throws back the covers and begins hurriedly pulling on his clothes. Without looking behind him, he begins talking to Abbie whom he supposes beside him.*)

CABOT: Thunder 'n' lightin', Abbie! I hain't slept this late in fifty year! Looks 's if the sun was full riz a'-most. Must've been the dancin' an' likker. Must be gittin' old. I hope Eben's t' wuk. Ye might've tuk the trouble t' rouse me, Abbie. (*He turns — sees no one there — surprised.*) Waal — whar air she? Gittin' vittles, I calc'late. (*He tiptoes to the cradle and peers down — proudly.*) Mornin', sonny. Purty's a picter! Sleepin' sound. He don't beller all night like most o' 'em. (*He goes quietly out the door in rear — a few moments later enters kitchen — sees Abbie — with satisfaction.*) So thar ye be. Ye got any vittles cooked?

ABBIE (*without moving*): No.

CABOT (*coming to her, almost sympathetically*): Ye feelin' sick?

ABBIE: No.

CABOT (*Pats her on shoulder. She shudders.*): Ye'd best lie down a spell. (*Half jocularly.*) Yer son'll be needin' ye soon. He'd ought t' wake up with a gnashin' appetite, the sound way he's sleepin'.

ABBIE (*shudders — then in a dead voice*): He hain't never goin' t' wake up.

CABOT (*jokingly*): Takes after me this mornin'. I hain't slept so late in . . .

ABBIE: He's dead.

CABOT (*stares at her — bewilderedly*): What. . . .

ABBIE: I killed him.

CABOT (*stepping back from her — aghast*): Air ye drunk — 'r crazy — 'r . . . ?

ABBIE (*suddenly lifts her head and turns on him — wildly*): I killed him, I tell ye! I smothered him. Go up an' see if ye don't b'lieve me!

(*Cabot stares at her a second, then bolts out the rear door, can be heard bounding up the stairs, and rushes into the bedroom and over to the cradle. Abbie has sunk back lifelessly into her former position. Cabot puts his hand down on the body in the crib. An expression of fear and horror comes over his face.*)

CABOT (*shrinking away — tremblingly*): God A'mighty! God A'mighty. (*He stumbles out the door — in a short while returns to the kitchen — comes to Abbie, the stunned expression still on his face — hoarsely.*) Why did ye do it? Why? (*As she doesn't answer, he grabs her violently by the shoulder and shakes her.*) I ax ye why ye done it! Ye'd better tell me 'r . . . !

ABBIE (*gives him a furious push which sends him staggering back and springs to her feet — with wild rage and hatred*): Don't ye dare tech me! What right hev ye t' question me 'bout him? He wa'n't yewr son! Think I'd have a son by yew? I'd die fust! I hate the sight o' ye an' allus did! It's yew I should've murdered, if I'd had good sense! I hate ye! I love Eben. I did from the fust. An' he was Eben's son — mine an' Eben's — not your'n!

CABOT (*stands looking at her dazedly — a pause — finding his words with an effort — dully*): That was it — what I felt — pokin' round the corners —

while ye lied — holdin' yerself from me — sayin' ye'd already conceived — (*He lapses into crushed silence — then with a strange emotion.*) He's dead, sart'n. I felt his heart. Pore little critter! (*He blinks back one tear, wiping his sleeve across his nose.*)

ABBIE (*hysterically*): Don't ye! Don't ye! (*She sobs unrestrainedly.*)

CABOT (*with a concentrated effort that stiffens his body into a rigid line and hardens his face into a stony mask — through his teeth to himself*): I got t' be — like a stone — a rock o' jedgment! (*A pause. He gets complete control over himself — harshly.*) If he was Eben's, I be glad he air gone! An' mebbe I suspicioned it all along. I felt they was somethin' onnateral — somewhars — the house got so lonesome — an' cold — drivin' me down t' the barn — t' the beasts o' the field. . . . Ay-eh. I must've suspicioned — somethin'. Ye didn't fool me — not altogether, leastways — I'm too old a bird — growin' ripe on the bough. . . . (*He becomes aware he is wandering, straightens again, looks at Abbie with a cruel grin.*) So ye'd liked t' hev murdered me 'steed o' him, would ye? Waal, I'll live to a hundred! I'll live t' see ye hung! I'll deliver ye up t' the jedgment o' God an' the law! I'll git the Sheriff now. (*Starts for the door.*)

ABBIE (*dully*): Ye needn't. Eben's gone fur him.

CABOT (*amazed*): Eben — gone fur the Sheriff?

ABBIE: Ay-eh.

CABOT: T' inform agen ye?

ABBIE: Ay-eh.

CABOT (*considers this — a pause — then in a hard voice*): Waal, I'm thankful fur him savin' me the trouble. I'll git t' wuk. (*He goes to the door — then turns — in a voice full of strange emotion.*) He'd ought t' been my son, Abbie. Ye'd ought t' loved me. I'm a man. If ye'd loved me, I'd never told no Sheriff on ye no matter what ye did, if they was t' brile me alive!

ABBIE (*defensively*): They's more to it nor yew know, makes him tell.

CABOT (*dryly*): Fur yewr sake, I hope they be. (*He goes out — comes around to the gate — stares up at the sky. His control relaxes. For a moment he is old and weary. He murmurs despairingly.*) God A'mighty, I be lonesomer'n ever! (*He hears running footsteps from the left, immediately is himself again. Eben runs in, panting exhaustedly, wild-eyed and mad looking. He lurches through the gate. Cabot grabs him by the shoulder. Eben stares at him dumbly.*) Did ye tell the Sheriff?

EBEN (*nodding stupidly*): Ay-eh.

CABOT (*gives him a push away that sends him sprawling — laughing with withering contempt*): Good fur ye! A prime chip o' yer Maw ye be! (*He goes toward the barn, laughing harshly. Eben scrambles to his feet. Suddenly Cabot turns — grimly threatening.*) Git off this farm when the Sheriff takes her — or, by God, he'll have t' come back an' git me fur murder, too! (*He stalks off. Eben does not appear to have heard him. He runs to the door and comes into the kitchen. Abbie looks up with a cry of anguished joy. Eben stumbles over and throws himself on his knees beside her sobbing brokenly.*)

EBEN: Fergive me!

ABBIE (*happily*): Eben! (*She kisses him and pulls his head over against her breast.*)

EBEN: I love ye! Fergive me!

ABBIE (*ecstatically*): I'd fergive ye all the sins in hell fur sayin' that! (*She kisses his head, pressing it to her with a fierce passion of possession.*)

EBEN (*brokenly*): But I told the Sheriff. He's comin' fur ye!

ABBIE: I kin b'ar what happens t' me — now!

EBEN: I woke him up. I told him. He says, wait 'til I git dressed. I was waiting. I got to thinkin' o' yew. I got to thinkin' how I'd loved ye. It hurt like somethin' was bustin' in my chest an' head. I got t' cryin'. I knowed sudden I loved ye yet, an' allus would love ye!

ABBIE (*caressing his hair — tenderly*): My boy, hain't ye?

EBEN: I begun t' run back. I cut across the fields an' through the woods. I thought ye might have time t' run away — with me — an' . . .

ABBIE (*shaking her head*): I got t' take my punishment — t' pay fur my sin.

EBEN: Then I want t' share it with ye.

ABBIE: Ye didn't do nothin'.

EBEN: I put it in yer head. I wisht he was dead! I as much as urged ye t' do it!

ABBIE: No. It was me alone!

EBEN: I'm as guilty as yew be! He was the child o' our sin.

ABBIE (*lifting her head as if defying God*): I don't repent that sin! I hain't askin' God t' fergive that!

EBEN: Nor me — but it led up t' the other — an' the murder ye did, ye did 'count o' me — an' it's my murder, too, I'll tell the Sheriff — an' if ye deny it, I'll say we planned it t'gether — an' they'll all b'lieve me, fur they suspicion everythin' we've done, an' it'll seem likely an' true to 'em. An' it is true — way down. I did help ye — somehow.

ABBIE (*laying her head on his — sobbing*): No! I don't want yew t' suffer!

EBEN: I got t' pay fur my part o' the sin! An' I'd suffer wuss leavin' ye, goin' West, thinkin' o' ye day an' night, bein' out when yew was in — (*lowering his voice*) 'r bein' alive when yew was dead. (*A pause.*) I want t' share with ye, Abbie — prison 'r

death 'r hell 'r anythin'! (*He looks into her eyes and forces a trembling smile.*) If I'm sharin' with ye, I won't feel lonesome, leastways.

ABBIE (*weakly*): Eben! I won't let ye! I can't let ye!

EBEN (*kissing her — tenderly*): Ye can't he'p yerself. I got ye beat fur once!

ABBIE (*forcing a smile — adoringly*): I hain't beat — s'long's I got ye!

EBEN (*hears the sound of feet outside*): Ssshh! Listen! They've come t' take us!

ABBIE: No, it's him. Don't give him no chance to fight ye, Eben. Don't say nothin' — no matter what he says. An' I won't neither. (*It is Cabot. He comes up from the barn in a great state of excitement and strides into the house and then into the kitchen. Eben is kneeling beside Abbie, his arm around her, hers around him. They stare straight ahead.*)

CABOT (*Stares at them, his face hard. A long pause — vindictively.*): Ye make a slick pair o' murderin' turtle doves! Ye'd ought t' be both hung on the same limb an' left thar t' swing in the breeze an' rot — a warnin' t' old fools like me t' b'ar their lonesomeness alone — an' fur young fools like ye t' hobble their lust. (*A pause. The excitement returns to his face, his eyes snap, he looks a bit crazy.*) I couldn't work today. I couldn't take no interest. T' hell with the farm! I'm leavin' it! I've turned the cows an' other stock loose! I've druv 'em into the woods whar they kin be free! By freein' 'em, I'm freein' myself! I'm quittin' here today! I'll set fire t' house an' barn an' watch 'em burn, an' I'll leave yer Maw t' haunt the ashes, an' I'll will the fields back t' God, so that nothin' human kin never touch 'em! I'll be a-goin' to Californi-a — t' jine Simeon an' Peter — true sons o' mine if they be dumb fools — an' the Cabots'll find Solomon's Mines t'gether! (*He suddenly cuts a mad caper.*) Whoop! What was the song they sung? "Oh, Californi-a! That's the land fur me." (*He sings this — then gets on his knees by the floorboard under which the money was hid.*) An' I'll sail thar on one o' the finest clippers I kin find! I've got the money! Pity ye didn't know whar this was hidden so's ye could steal. . . . (*He has pulled up the board. He stares — feels — stares again. A pause of dead silence. He slowly turns, slumping into a sitting position on the floor, his eyes like those of a dead fish, his face the sickly green of an attack of nausea. He swallows painfully several times — forces a weak smile at last.*) So — ye did steal it!

EBEN (*emotionlessly*): I swapped it t' Sim an' Peter fur their share o' the farm — t' pay their passage t' Californi-a.

CABOT (*with one sardonic*): Ha! (*He begins to recover. Gets slowly to his feet — strangely.*) I calc'late God give it to 'em — not yew! God's hard, not easy! Mebbe they's easy gold in the West but it hain't God's gold. It hain't fur me. I kin hear His voice warnin' me agen t' be hard an' stay on my farm. I kin see his hand usin' Eben t' steal t' keep me from weakness. I kin feel I be in the palm o' His hand, His fingers guidin' me. (*A pause — then he mutters sadly.*) It's a-goin' t' be lonesomer now than ever it war afore — an' I'm gittin' old, Lord — ripe on the bough.... (*Then stiffening.*) Waal — what d'ye want? God's lonesome, hain't He? God's hard an' lonesome! (*A pause. The Sheriff with two men comes up the road from the left. They move cautiously to the door. The Sheriff knocks on it with the butt of his pistol.*)

SHERIFF: Open in the name o' the law! (*They start.*)

CABOT: They've come fur ye. (*He goes to the rear door.*) Come in, Jim! (*The three men enter. Cabot meets them in doorway.*) Jest a minit, Jim. I got 'em safe here. (*The Sheriff nods. He and his companions remain in the doorway.*)

EBEN (*suddenly calls*): I lied this mornin', Jim. I helped her to do it. Ye kin take me, too.

ABBIE (*brokenly*): No!

CABOT: Take 'em both. (*He comes forward — stares at Eben with a trace of grudging admiration.*) Purty good — fur yew! Waal, I got t' round up the stock. Good-by.

EBEN: Good-by.

ABBIE: Good-by. (*Cabot turns and strides past the men — comes out and around the corner of the house, his shoulders squared, his face stony, and stalks grimly toward the barn. In the meantime the Sheriff and men have come into the room.*)

SHERIFF (*embarrassedly*): Waal — we'd best start.

ABBIE: Wait. (*Turns to Eben.*) I love ye, Eben.

EBEN: I love ye, Abbie. (*They kiss. The three men grin and shuffle embarrassedly. Eben takes Abbie's hand. They go out the door in rear, the men following, and come from the house, walking hand in hand to the gate. Eben stops there and points to the sunrise sky.*) Sun's a-rizin'. Purty, hain't it?

ABBIE: Ay-eh. (*They both stand for a moment looking up raptly in attitudes strangely aloof and devout.*)

SHERIFF (*looking around at the farm enviously — to his companions*): It's a jim-dandy farm, no denyin'. Wished I owned it!

COMMENTARY

Stark Young (1881–1963)
REVIEW OF *DESIRE UNDER THE ELMS*   1924

Stark Young's sensitive review of this play contrasted with other reviewers. He saw the work as a significant advance for O'Neill and extensively discusses the drama in terms that reveal its importance. Young also gives particular praise to Walter Huston's performance and to the work's farmhouse setting. His final comments praise the writing in a specific scene "written with such poetry and terrible beauty as we rarely see in theatre."

Desire Under the Elms, the first play by Eugene O'Neill to be produced since *Welded*, was presented last night at the Greenwich Village Theatre and proved to be as unlike that drama as it was unlike *The Hairy Ape* or *The Emperor Jones*. *Desire Under the Elms* reverts in character to the earlier *Beyond the Horizon*, though it exhibits by comparison a fine progress in solidity and finish.

It has less sentiment that this older piece and more passion; it is better written throughout; it has much tragic gloom and irony but a more mature conception and a more imaginative austerity.

Desire Under the Elms is essentially a story of solitude, physical solitude, the solitude of the land, of men's dreams, of love, of life. The God behind the existence created on this New England farm is a harsh God, who is alone and is not understood. The minds of the people in this story are shaken and tinged with loneliness, with thwarted passion, with the trivial, the intense, the drab exaltation and denial of life. Underneath this solitude desire works, the redemption through love.

The children of old Cabot hate him. The youngest, the son of the second wife, remembers his dead mother, worked to death, and sees her about the place, risen from her grave. The father brings home a third wife. The two older sons go away to California; the younger stays and thinks to avenge his mother. In time he and the young wife come to love each other.

A son is born, which old Cabot thinks is to be heir to the farm, leaving the second wife's son adrift in the world. While a dance in honor of the newborn child goes on in the kitchen, the father and son quarrel outside; the son believes his father when he hears that the woman wanted a son only to cheat him out of the farm. He reviles her. To prove to him that it was the love of him and not the desire for the farm that had driven her to him, she kills the child. He runs off for the sheriff. The father turns the live stock loose in the woods and plans to go away, but when he finds the money gone from its hiding place, he believes that God another time has willed that he stand by the farm. The son returns from the sheriff's, he falls at the knees of the woman, takes part of the blame on himself, and they go away together to prison.

Robert Edmond Jones's setting for *Desire Under the Elms* was profoundly dramatic. The end of a New England farmhouse with its overhanging elms was for all practical purposes built there on stage, with a wall of actual stone coming down to the footlights; a scene that was realistic but at the same time strangely and powerfully heightened in effect.

The general performance of the play was unusually adequate though not often on a level with the writing. Mary Morris, however, whose career as the fair Gertrude in *Fashion* last year was one of the flowers of the season's acting, played the wife in *Desire Under the Elms* with a new and suppressed method that deepened at times into an admirable poignancy and a kind of grim, thin poetry that seemed the exact truth of her lines. Charles Ellis, though his work in earlier scenes was less successful or convincing, played with real poetry the passage where the boy is possessed with love for the woman and for his child. Walter Huston as the old man was everywhere trenchant, gaunt, fervid, harsh, as he should be in the part. In his ability to cover his gradations, to express the natural and convincing emotion, and to convey the harsh, inarticulate life embodied in this extraordinary portrait that Eugene O'Neill has drawn. Mr. Huston showed his talent and proved to be the best choice possible for the role.

The scene of *Desire Under the Elms* that best illustrates the highest quality of the play is that in which we see the dance going on, the father outside the house, the young wife and her lover in the upstairs room in each other's arms beside the child's cradle, a scene written with such poetry and terrible beauty as we rarely see in the theatre, a scene that for these qualities of poetry, terror and at the same time unflinching realism rises above anything that Mr. O'Neill has written.

Federico García Lorca

Lorca (1898–1936) lived through some of the most troubling times of modern Spain. He was born in the countryside near Granada, Spain, and maintained a lifelong love of the Spanish village and country people. His father was a wealthy farmer, and his mother was a teacher who encouraged his early love of literature, art, and music. Lorca's talents were extraordinary. A fine pianist, he counted among his friends some of Spain's greatest musicians, including Manuel de Falla. Lorca painted throughout his life and maintained a close friendship with Salvador Dalí. His career in the university was not especially distinguished, but as a student he became famous for readings of his own poetry. He produced an early play, *The Butterfly's Evil Spell,* in 1920, the year before he published his first book of poems. His political leanings throughout his life were liberal and reformist, but his early years were spent living under a Spanish dictatorship. General elections ended Spain's monarchy and established the Second Spanish Republic in 1931, but Fascist leaders, notably Francisco Franco, began agitating for control. Standing for a free republic and prominent as a leftist, Lorca was killed suddenly and without explanation by Franco's forces in 1936, just two days before the start of the Spanish Civil War.

Lorca's dramatic work had developed steadily. His second play, *The Girl Who Waters the Sweet Basil Flower and the Inquisitive Prince* (1923), was a puppet show. Lorca, who especially enjoyed this form of drama, had bought his own puppet theater when he was fifteen. He designed the sets, and Manuel de Falla provided the music. Unfortunately, the manuscript for this play has been lost. Text for another puppet play of the same period, *The Billy-Club Puppets,* does exist, as do copies of some later dramatic sketches: *Buster Keaton's Promenade* (1926), which takes off on Buster Keaton's film character, and *The Public* (1933), one of several experimental surrealist plays. His first real success was *Mariana Pineda* (1927), produced in Granada. After suffering a personal crisis, perhaps connected to his growing awareness of his homosexuality, Lorca spent a year in New York, from which experience he wrote *The Poet in New York,* published — much later — in 1940.

Lorca returned to Spain and produced a number of plays in the early 1930s, such as *The Shoemaker's Prodigious Wife* (1930), *The Love of*

Don Perlimplin with Belisa in the Garden (1933), and *Doña Rosita, the Spinster* (1935), the last of his plays to be produced during his lifetime. His three most important plays are generally referred to as folk tragedies: *Blood Wedding* (1933) and *Yerma* (1934) were produced in Madrid, and *The House of Bernarda Alba* was produced in Buenos Aires in 1945. These three plays were influenced by a great Spanish actress and producer, Margarita Xirgu, for whom the title role of Yerma was created.

Lorca's reputation flourished after the end of World War II, but because Spain's Fascist government continued until Franco's death in 1975, Lorca's work could not be produced in his native country until the 1980s. His gift was in combining poetry, music, original set designs, and a sense of the language of the country people who inspired his work. He had a feel for the pagan forces that informed the country people and aimed to show their creative power in everyday life. He celebrated instinctive, primitive religious feeling, the joy of living, the sexual energy of the universe, and the fullness of life.

THE HOUSE OF
BERNARDA ALBA

Lorca diverged from his earlier poetic style when he created this play, subtitled "a drama about women in the villages of Spain." He is on record as having said, "Not a drop of poetry! Reality! Realism!" Supposed to be as realistic and detailed as a "photographic document," the play pointed to some of the harsher realities of life for women in rural Spain. Indeed, there are only women in the play. Pepe el Romano, a young handsome man, betrothed to Angustias, Bernarda's eldest daughter (apparently for her money), is mentioned often but never appears. In the beginning of the third act, a stallion making loud sounds in his stall represents the symbolic force of sex in nature. Interestingly, Bernarda Alba demands that the stallion be freed before it brings the walls down. But at the same time she determines to keep her daughters hidden away in her house and under her thumb. The focus of the play is on Bernarda Alba's determination to preserve her dignity in her village. She wants to make sure that no one talks about her family disparagingly; she must keep up appearances even at the risk of smothering the sexual energies of her five daughters.

When the play opens, Bernarda's husband has just died and she declares that the household shall mourn for eight years. Her daughters would be shut in and not see a man for any of that time. However, since Angustias has her own money from her father, Bernarda's first husband, she is courted by Pepe el Romano. At the same time Pepe secretly expresses his true affection to Augustia's sister Adela, who is much closer to him in age and who would be a more suitable wife. Bernarda, however, is adamant about the period of mourning and eventually chases Pepe off with a shotgun after discovering that he has given in to his desires.

This is a play about the tyranny of Bernarda over her daughters. It portrays her desire to be respected in the community at all costs, even the cost of living a lie. It is also a play about "Women without men." Some critics have seen in the prisonlike atmosphere (note the constant reference to bars) a suggestion of the religious convent and the sexual repression it implies. The Cistercians, known as Bernardas, are an order of nuns familiar to Lorca. But Lorca is exploring a number of powerful forces in life: the power of the family and tradition; the power of religion and its structures of moral behavior; the power of economic necessity and the way it distorts lives; and the power of a political force that maintains itself through absolute authority. Most of these forces were evident in the Spain Lorca knew throughout his life. From 1932 much of his time was spent traveling with, and writing for, a government-sponsored touring company, La Barraca, that put on classic Spanish plays in the remote towns around the nation. He had plenty of opportunity to observe everyday life in rural Spain. This play reveals some of its nature.

The House of Bernarda Alba in Performance

The first production of the play was in Buenos Aires in 1945 because Lorca had visited Argentina shortly before he died and impressed those he met with his genius. South America has long found his work important; Lorca's play was produced in various South American countries long before it appeared in Spain. Eric Bentley staged a minimalist production of the play at the Abbey Theatre in 1950, with Peggy Hayes as Bernarda and Angela Newmann as Adela. He describes this production in his *In Search of Theater* (1953) saying, "Ireland and Spain are two of the remaining vestiges of Catholic-peasant civilization. Lorca's play springs from this civilization, gives it amazingly full expression, and is a bitter rejection of it."

The play was given a limited production in Paris in the Studio des Champs-Élysées, in 1946, employing a very fine set with stark white walls and black wrought-iron bars across the windows. A New York production at the ANTA Playhouse lasted for seventeen performances in January 1951. Bentley had earlier speculated that the play would be very difficult to communicate to 1950s London or New York audiences, and he seems to have been correct. It was produced in New York again by Teatro Hispano, directed by Max Ferra, in early 1972. Bernarda was played by the Cuban actress Ofelia Gonzalez. Numerous productions in Europe followed; one of the most powerful was in 1986 at the Lyric Theatre in Hammersmith, London, directed by Nuria Espert. The sets and the lighting served to intensify the sense of overwhelming heat from the Andalusian sun. Paul Preston, in his review in the *Times Literary Supplement,* said, "Glenda Jackson's Bernarda is as stiff-backed as the most humourless prison governor or mother superior, dominating her brood with snarling sarcasm and fulminating looks." Joan Plowright played a powerful Poncia, but Patricia Hayes, as Bernarda's mother, was singled out for a stunning performance: "wearing muslin rags over white flesh like a feverish and ecstatic moth" (Michael Ratcliffe in the *Observer*). The play moved into the West End (London's Broadway) to the Globe Theatre in 1987 with the same cast. Among the most recent productions is the 1993 production in Northern Ireland at the adventurous women's company, the Charabanc Theatre Company. Lynne Parker adapted and directed the play to exceptional reviews, and the production toured twenty towns throughout Ireland and Northern Ireland before settling in at the Project Arts Centre in Dublin. The reviews of the production celebrated its excellence and explored the women's issues in the drama.

Federico García Lorca *(1898–1936)*

THE HOUSE OF BERNARDA ALBA   *1936*
A DRAMA ABOUT WOMEN IN THE VILLAGES OF SPAIN

TRANSLATED BY JAMES GRAHAM-LUJÁN AND RICHARD L. O'CONNELL

Characters

BERNARDA *(age 60)*
MARIA JOSEFA, *Bernarda's Mother (age 80)*
ANGUSTIAS, *Bernarda's Daughter (age 39)*
MAGDALENA, *Bernarda's Daughter (age 30)*
AMELIA, *Bernarda's Daughter (age 27)*
MARTIRIO, *Bernarda's Daughter (age 24)*
ADELA, *Bernarda's Daughter (age 20)*
A MAID *(age 50)*
LA PONCIA, *A Maid (age 60)*
PRUDENCIA *(age 50)*
WOMEN IN MOURNING

The writer states that these Three Acts are intended as a photographic document.

ACT 1

(A very white room in Bernarda Alba's house. The walls are white. There are arched doorways with jute curtains tied back with tassels and ruffles. Wicker chairs. On the walls, pictures of unlikely landscapes full of nymphs or legendary kings.

It is summer. A great brooding silence fills the stage. It is empty when the curtain rises. Bells can be heard tolling outside.)

FIRST SERVANT *(entering)*: The tolling of those bells hits me right between the eyes.

PONCIA *(she enters, eating bread and sausage)*: More than two hours of mumbo jumbo. Priests are here from all the towns. The church looks beautiful. At the first responsory for the dead, Magdalena fainted.

FIRST SERVANT: She's the one who's left most alone.

PONCIA: She's the only one who loved her father. Ay! Thank God we're alone for a little. I came over to eat.

FIRST SERVANT: If Bernarda sees you . . . !

PONCIA: She's not eating today so she'd just as soon we'd all die of hunger! Domineering old tyrant! But she'll be fooled! I opened the sausage crock.

FIRST SERVANT *(with an anxious sadness)*: Couldn't you give me some for my little girl, Poncia?

PONCIA: Go ahead! And take a fistful of peas too. She won't know the difference today.

VOICE *(within)*: Bernarda!

PONCIA: There's the grandmother! Isn't she locked up tight?

FIRST SERVANT: Two turns of the key.

PONCIA: You'd better put the cross-bar up too. She's got the fingers of a lock-picker!

VOICE *(within)*: Bernarda!

PONCIA *(shouting)*: She's coming! *(to the servant)* Clean everything up good. If Bernarda doesn't find things shining, she'll pull out the few hairs I have left.

SERVANT: What a woman!

PONCIA: Tyrant over everyone around her. She's perfectly capable of sitting on your heart and watching you die for a whole year without turning off that cold little smile she wears on her wicked face. Scrub, scrub those dishes!

SERVANT: I've got blood on my hands from so much polishing of everything.

PONCIA: She's the cleanest, she's the decentest, she's the highest everything! A good rest her poor husband's earned!

(The bells stop.)

SERVANT: Did all the relatives come?

PONCIA: Just hers. His people hate her. They came to see him dead and make the sign of the cross over him; that's all.

SERVANT: Are there enough chairs?

PONCIA: More than enough. Let them sit on the floor. When Bernarda's father died people stopped coming under this roof. She doesn't want them to see her in her "domain." Curse her!

SERVANT: She's been good to you.

PONCIA: Thirty years washing her sheets. Thirty years eating her leftovers. Nights of watching when she had a cough. Whole days peeking through a crack in the shutters to spy on the neighbors and carry her the tale. Life without secrets one from the other. But in spite of that —

curse her! May the "pain of the piercing nail" strike her in the eyes.

SERVANT: Poncia!

PONCIA: But I'm a good watchdog! I bark when I'm told and bite beggars' heels when she sics me on 'em. My sons work in her fields — both of them already married, but one of these days I'll have enough.

SERVANT: And then . . . ?

PONCIA: Then I'll lock myself up in a room with her and spit in her face — a whole year. "Bernarda, here's for this, that and the other!" Till I leave her — just like a lizard the boys have squashed. For that's what she is — she and her whole family! Not that I envy her her life. Five girls are left her, five ugly daughters — not counting Angustias the eldest, by her first husband, who has money — the rest of them, plenty of eyelets to embroider, plenty of linen petticoats, but bread and grapes when it comes to inheritance.

SERVANT: Well, *I'd* like to have what they've got!

PONCIA: All we have is our hands and a hole in God's earth.

SERVANT: And that's the only earth they'll ever leave to us — to us who have nothing!

PONCIA (*at the cupboard*): This glass has some specks.

SERVANT: Neither soap nor rag will take them off.

(*The bells toll.*)

PONCIA: The last prayer! I'm going over and listen. I certainly like the way our priest sings. In the Pater Noster his voice went up, and up — like a pitcher filling with water little by little. Of course, at the end his voice cracked, but it's glorious to hear it. No, there never was anybody like the old Sacristan — Tronchapinos. At my mother's Mass, may she rest in peace, he sang. The walls shook — and when he said "Amen," it was as if a wolf had come into the church.

(*Imitating him.*)

A-a-a-a-men!

(*She starts coughing.*)

SERVANT: Watch out — you'll strain your windpipe!

PONCIA: I'd rather strain something else!

(*Goes out laughing.*)

(*The servant scrubs. The bells toll.*)

SERVANT (*imitating the bells*): Dong, dong, dong. Dong, dong, dong. May God forgive him!

BEGGAR WOMAN (*at the door, with a little girl*): Blesséd be God!

SERVANT: Dong, dong, dong. I hope he waits many years for us! Dong, dong, dong.

BEGGAR (*loudly, a little annoyed*): Blesséd be God!

SERVANT (*annoyed*): Forever and ever!

BEGGAR: I came for the scraps.

(*The bells stop tolling.*)

SERVANT: You can go right out the way you came in. Today's scraps are for me.

BEGGAR: But you have somebody to take care of you — and my little girl and I are all alone!

SERVANT: Dogs are alone too, and they live.

BEGGAR: They always give them to me.

SERVANT: Get out of here! Who let you in anyway? You've already tracked up the place.

(*The beggar woman and little girl leave. The servant goes on scrubbing.*)

Floors finished with oil, cupboards, pedestals, iron beds — but us servants, we can suffer in silence — and live in mud huts with a plate and a spoon. I hope someday not a one will be left to tell it.

(*The bells sound again.*)

Yes, yes — ring away. Let them pelt you in a coffin with gold inlay and brocade to carry it on — you're no less dead than I'll be, so take what's coming to you, Antonio María Benavides — stiff in your broadcloth suit and your high boots — take what's coming to you! You'll never again lift my skirts behind the corral door!

(*From the rear door, two by two, women in mourning with large shawls and black skirts and fans, begin to enter. They come in slowly until the stage is full.*)

SERVANT (*breaking into a wail*): Oh, Antonio María Benavides, now you'll never see these walls, nor break bread in this house again! I'm the one who loved you most of all your servants.

(*Pulling her hair.*)

Must I love on after you've gone? Must I go on living?

(*The two hundred women finish coming in, and Bernarda and her five daughters enter. Bernarda leans on a cane.*)

BERNARDA (*to the servant*): Silence!

SERVANT (*weeping*): Bernarda!

BERNARDA: Less shrieking and more work. You should have had all this cleaner for the wake. Get out. This isn't your place.

(*The servant goes off crying.*)

The poor are like animals — they seem to be made of different stuff.

FIRST WOMAN: The poor feel their sorrows too.

BERNARDA: But they forget them in front of a plateful of peas.

FIRST GIRL (timidly): Eating is necessary for living.

BERNARDA: At your age one doesn't talk in front of older people.

WOMAN: Be quiet, child.

BERNARDA: I've never taken lessons from anyone. Sit down.

(They sit down. Pause. Loudly.)

Magdalena, don't cry. If you want to cry, get under your bed. Do you hear me?

SECOND WOMAN (to Bernarda): Have you started to work the fields?

BERNARDA: Yesterday.

THIRD WOMAN: The sun comes down like lead.

FIRST WOMAN: I haven't known heat like this for years.

(Pause. They all fan themselves.)

BERNARDA: Is the lemonade ready?

PONCIA: Yes, Bernarda.

(She brings in a large tray full of little white jars which she distributes.)

BERNARDA: Give the men some.

PONCIA: They're already drinking in the patio.

BERNARDA: Let them get out the way they came in. I don't want them walking through here.

A GIRL (to Angustias): Pepe el Romano was with the men during the service.

ANGUSTIAS: There he was.

BERNARDA: His mother was there. She saw his mother. Neither she nor I saw Pepe . . .

GIRL: I thought . . .

BERNARDA: The one who was there was Darajalí, the widower. Very close to your Aunt. We all of us saw him.

SECOND WOMAN (aside, in a low voice): Wicked, worse than wicked woman!

THIRD WOMAN: A tongue like a knife!

BERNARDA: Women in church shouldn't look at any man but the priest — and him only because he wears skirts. To turn your head is to be looking for the warmth of corduroy.

FIRST WOMAN: Sanctimonious old snake!

PONCIA (between her teeth): Itching for a man's warmth.

BERNARDA (beating with her cane on the floor): Blessèd be God!

ALL (crossing themselves): Forever blessèd and praised.

BERNARDA: Rest in peace with holy company at your head.

ALL: Rest in peace!

BERNARDA: With the Angel Saint Michael, and his sword of justice.

ALL: Rest in peace!

BERNARDA: With the key that opens, and the hand that locks.

ALL: Rest in peace!

BERNARDA: With the most blessèd, and the little lights of the field.

ALL: Rest in peace!

BERNARDA: With our holy charity, and all souls on land and sea.

ALL: Rest in peace!

BERNARDA: Grant rest to your servant, Antonio María Benavides, and give him the crown of your blessèd glory.

ALL: Amen.

BERNARDA (she rises and chants): Requiem aeternam donat eis domine.

ALL (standing and chanting in the Gregorian fashion): Et lux perpetua luce ab eis.°

(They cross themselves.)

FIRST WOMAN: May you have health to pray for his soul. (They start filing out.)

THIRD WOMAN: You won't lack loaves of hot bread.

SECOND WOMAN: Nor a roof for your daughters.

(They are all filing in front of Bernarda and going out. Angustias leaves by the door to the patio.)

FOURTH WOMAN: May you go on enjoying your wedding wheat.

PONCIA (she enters, carrying a money bag): From the men — this bag of money for Masses.

BERNARDA: Thank them — and let them have a glass of brandy.

GIRL (to Magdalena): Magdalena . . .

BERNARDA (to Magdalena, who is starting to cry): Sh-h-h-h!

(She beats with her cane on the floor.)
(All the women have gone out.)

BERNARDA (to the women who have just left): Go back to your houses and criticize everything you've seen! I hope it'll be many years before you pass under the archway of my door again.

PONCIA: You've nothing to complain about. The whole town came.

BERNARDA: Yes, to fill my house with the sweat from their wraps and the poison of their tongues.

AMELIA: Mother, don't talk like that.

BERNARDA: What other way is there to talk about this

Requiem aeternam . . . ab eis: Eternal rest grant to him, O Lord. And let perpetual light shine on him. (Latin) cursèd village with no river — this village full of wells where you drink water always fearful it's been poisoned?

PONCIA: Look what they've done to the floor!

BERNARDA: As though a herd of goats had passed through.

(*Poncia cleans the floor.*)

Adela, give me a fan.

ADELA: Take this one.

(*She gives her a round fan with green and red flowers.*)

BERNARDA (*throwing the fan on the floor*): Is that the fan to give to a widow? Give me a black one and learn to respect your father's memory.

MARTIRIO: Take mine.

BERNARDA: And you?

MARTIRIO: I'm not hot.

BERNARDA: Well, look for another, because you'll need it. For the eight years of mourning, not a breath of air will get in this house from the street. We'll act as if we'd sealed up doors and windows with bricks. That's what happened in my father's house — and in my grandfather's house. Meantime, you can all start embroidering your hope-chest linens. I have twenty bolts of linen in the chest from which to cut sheets and coverlets. Magdalena can embroider them.

MAGDALENA: It's all the same to me.

ADELA (*sourly*): If you don't want to embroider them — they can go without. That way yours will look better.

MAGDALENA: Neither mine nor yours. I know I'm not going to marry. I'd rather carry sacks to the mill. Anything except sit here day after day in this dark room.

BERNARDA: That's what a woman is for.

MAGDALENA: Cursed be all women.

BERNARDA: In this house you'll do what I order. You can't run with the story to your father any more. Needle and thread for women. Whiplash and mules for men. That's the way it has to be for people who have certain obligations.

(*Adela goes out.*)

VOICE: Bernarda! Let me out!

BERNARDA (*calling*): Let her out now!

(*The first servant enters.*)

FIRST SERVANT: I had a hard time holding her. In spite of her eighty years, your mother's strong as an oak.

BERNARDA: It runs in the family. My grandfather was the same way.

SERVANT: Several times during the wake I had to cover her mouth with an empty sack because she wanted to shout out to you to give her dishwater to drink at least, and some dogmeat, which is what she says you feed her.

MARTIRIO: She's mean!

BERNARDA (*to servant*): Let her get some fresh air in the patio.

SERVANT: She took her rings and the amethyst earrings out of the box, put them on, and told me she wants to get married.

(*The daughters laugh.*)

BERNARDA: Go with her and be careful she doesn't get near the well.

SERVANT: You don't need to be afraid she'll jump in.

BERNARDA: It's not that — but the neighbors can see her there from their windows.

(*The servant leaves.*)

MARTIRIO: We'll go change our clothes.

BERNARDA: Yes, but don't take the kerchiefs from your heads.

(*Adela enters.*)

And Angustias?

ADELA (*meaningfully*): I saw her looking out through the cracks of the back door. The men had just gone.

BERNARDA: And you, what were *you* doing at the door?

ADELA: I went there to see if the hens had laid.

BERNARDA: But the men had already gone!

ADELA (*meaningfully*): A group of them were still standing outside.

BERNARDA (*furiously*): Angustias! Angustias!

ANGUSTIAS (*entering*): Did you want something?

BERNARDA: For what — and at whom — were you looking?

ANGUSTIAS: Nobody.

BERNARDA: Is it decent for a woman of your class to be running after a man the day of her father's funeral? Answer me! Whom were you looking at?

(*Pause*)

ANGUSTIAS: I . . .

BERNARDA: Yes, you!

ANGUSTIAS: Nobody.

BERNARDA: Soft! Honeytongue!

(*She strikes her.*)

PONCIA (*running to her*): Bernarda, calm down!

(*She holds her. Angustias weeps.*)

BERNARDA: Get out of here, all of you!

(*They all go out.*)

PONCIA: She did it not realizing what she was doing — although it's bad, of course. It really disgusted me to see her sneak along to the patio. Then she stood at the window listening to the men's talk, which, as usual, was not the sort one should listen to.

BERNARDA: That's what they come to funerals for. (*With curiosity.*) What were they talking about?

PONCIA: They were talking about Paca la Roseta. Last night they tied her husband up in a stall, stuck her on a horse behind the saddle, and carried her away to the depths of the olive grove.

BERNARDA: And what did she do?

PONCIA: She? She was just as happy — they say her breasts were exposed and Maximiliano held on to her as if he were playing a guitar. Terrible!

BERNARDA: And what happened?

PONCIA: What had to happen. They came back almost at daybreak. Paca la Roseta with her hair loose and a wreath of flowers on her head.

BERNARDA: She's the only bad woman we have in the village.

PONCIA: Because she's not from here. She's from far away. And those who went with her are the sons of outsiders too. The men from here aren't up to a thing like that.

BERNARDA: No, but they like to see it, and talk about it, and suck their fingers over it.

PONCIA: They were saying a lot more things.

BERNARDA (*looking from side to side with a certain fear*): What things?

PONCIA: I'm ashamed to talk about them.

BERNARDA: And my daughter heard them?

PONCIA: Of course!

BERNARDA: That one takes after her Aunts: white and mealy-mouthed and casting sheep's eyes at any little barber's compliment. Oh, what one has to go through and put up with so people will be decent and not too wild!

PONCIA: It's just that your daughters are of an age when they ought to have husbands. Mighty little trouble they give you. Angustias must be much more than thirty now.

BERNARDA: Exactly thirty-nine.

PONCIA: Imagine. And she's never had a beau . . .

BERNARDA (*furiously*): None of them has ever had a beau and they've never needed one! They get along very well.

PONCIA: I didn't mean to offend you.

BERNARDA: For a hundred miles around there's no one good enough to come near them. The men in this town are not of their class. Do you want me to turn them over to the first shepherd?

PONCIA: You should have moved to another town.

BERNARDA: That's it. To sell them!

PONCIA: No, Bernarda, to change. . . . Of course, any place else, they'd be the poor ones.

BERNARDA: Hold your tormenting tongue!

PONCIA: One can't even talk to you. Do we, or do we not share secrets?

BERNARDA: We do not. You're a servant and I pay you. Nothing more.

PONCIA: But . . .

FIRST SERVANT (*entering*): Don Arturo's here. He's come to see about dividing the inheritance.

BERNARDA: Let's go. (*to the servant*) You start whitewashing the patio. (*to La Poncia*) And you start putting all the dead man's clothes away in the chest.

PONCIA: We could give away some of the things.

BERNARDA: Nothing — not a button even! Not even the cloth we covered his face with.

(*She goes out slowly, leaning on her cane. At the door she turns to look at the two servants. They go out. She leaves.*)
(*Amelia and Martirio enter.*)

AMELIA: Did you take the medicine?

MARTIRIO: For all the good it'll do me.

AMELIA: But you took it?

MARTIRIO: I do things without any faith, but like clockwork.

AMELIA: Since the new doctor came you look livelier.

MARTIRIO: I feel the same.

AMELIA: Did you notice? Adelaida wasn't at the funeral.

MARTIRIO: I know. Her sweetheart doesn't let her go out even to the front doorstep. Before, she was gay. Now, not even powder on her face.

AMELIA: These days a girl doesn't know whether to have a beau or not.

MARTIRIO: It's all the same.

AMELIA: The whole trouble is all these wagging tongues that won't let us live. Adelaida has probably had a bad time.

MARTIRIO: She's afraid of our mother. Mother is the only one who knows the story of Adelaida's father and where he got his lands. Everytime she comes here, Mother twists the knife in the wound. Her father killed his first wife's husband in Cuba so he could marry her himself. Then he left her there and went off with another woman who already had one daughter, and then he took up with this other girl, Adelaida's mother, and married her after his second wife died insane.

AMELIA: But why isn't a man like that put in jail?

MARTIRIO: Because men help each other cover up things like that and no one's able to tell on them.

AMELIA: But Adelaida's not to blame for any of that.

MARTIRIO: No. But history repeats itself. I can see that everything is a terrible repetition. And she'll

have the same fate as her mother and grandmother — both of them wife to the man who fathered her.

AMELIA: What an awful thing!

MARTIRIO: It's better never to look at a man. I've been
afraid of them since I was a little girl. I'd see them
in the yard, yoking the oxen and lifting grain
sacks, shouting and stamping, and I was always
afraid to grow up for fear one of them would suddenly take me in his arms. God has made me weak
and ugly and has definitely put such things away
from me.

AMELIA: Don't say that! Enrique Humanas was after
you and he liked you.

MARTIRIO: That was just people's ideas! One time I
stood in my nightgown at the window until daybreak because he let me know through his shepherd's little girl that he was going to come, and he
didn't. It was all just talk. Then he married someone else who had more money than I.

AMELIA: And ugly as the devil.

MARTIRIO: What do men care about ugliness? All they
care about is lands, yokes of oxen, and a submissive bitch who'll feed them.

AMELIA: Ay!

(*Magdalena enters.*)

MAGDALENA: What are you doing?

MARTIRIO: Just here.

AMELIA: And you?

MAGDALENA: I've been going through all the rooms.
Just to walk a little, and look at Grandmother's
needlepoint pictures — the little woolen dog, and
the black man wrestling with the lion — which we
liked so much when we were children. Those were
happier times. A wedding lasted ten days and evil
tongues weren't in style. Today people are more refined. Brides wear white veils, just as in the cities,
and we drink bottled wine, but we rot inside because of what people might say.

MARTIRIO: Lord knows what went on then!

AMELIA (*to Magdalena*): One of your shoelaces has
come untied.

MAGDALENA: What of it?

AMELIA: You'll step on it and fall.

MAGDALENA: One less!

MARTIRIO: And Adela?

MAGDALENA: Ah! She put on the green dress she
made to wear for her birthday, went out to the
yard, and began shouting: "Chickens! Chickens,
look at me!" I had to laugh.

AMELIA: If Mother had only seen her!

MAGDALENA: Poor little thing! She's the youngest one
of us and still has her illusions. I'd give something
to see her happy.

(*Pause. Angustias crosses the stage, carrying some
towels.*)

ANGUSTIAS: What time is it?

MAGDALENA: It must be twelve.

ANGUSTIAS: So late?

AMELIA: It's about to strike.

(*Angustias goes out.*)

MAGDALENA (*meaningfully*): Do you know what?

(*Pointing after Angustias.*)

AMELIA: No.

MAGDALENA: Come on!

MARTIRIO: I don't know what you're talking about!

MAGDALENA: Both of you know it better than I do, always with your heads together, like two little
sheep, but not letting anybody else in on it. I mean
about Pepe el Romano!

MARTIRIO: Ah!

MAGDALENA (*mocking her*): Ah! The whole town's
talking about it. Pepe el Romano is coming to
marry Angustias. Last night he was walking
around the house and I think he's going to send a
declaration soon.

MARTIRIO: I'm glad. He's a good man.

AMELIA: Me too. Angustias is well off.

MAGDALENA: Neither one of you is glad.

MARTIRIO: Magdalena! What do you mean?

MAGDALENA: If he were coming because of Angustias'
looks, for Angustias as a woman, I'd be glad too,
but he's coming for her money. Even though Angustias is our sister, we're her family here and we
know she's old and sickly, and always has been the
least attractive one of us! Because if she looked like
a dressed-up stick at twenty, what can she look
like now, now that she's forty?

MARTIRIO: Don't talk like that. Luck comes to the one
who least expects it.

AMELIA: But Magdalena's right after all! Angustias
has all her father's money; she's the only rich one
in the house and that's why, now that Father's
dead and the money will be divided, they're coming for her.

MAGDALENA: Pepe el Romano is twenty-five years old
and the best looking man around here. The natural
thing would be for him to be after you, Amelia, or
our Adela, who's twenty — not looking for the
least likely one in this house, a woman who, like
her father, talks through her nose.

MARTIRIO: Maybe he likes that!

MAGDALENA: I've never been able to bear your
hypocrisy.

MARTIRIO: Heavens!

(*Adela enters.*)

MAGDALENA: Did the chickens see you?

ADELA: What did you want me to do?

AMELIA: If Mother sees you, she'll drag you by your hair!

ADELA: I had a lot of illusions about this dress. I'd planned to put it on the day we were going to eat watermelons at the well. There wouldn't have been another like it.

MARTIRIO: It's a lovely dress.

ADELA: And one that looks very good on me. It's the best thing Magdalena's ever cut.

MAGDALENA: And the chickens, what did they say to you?

ADELA: They presented me with a few fleas that riddled my legs.

(*They laugh.*)

MARTIRIO: What you can do is dye it black.

MAGDALENA: The best thing you can do is give it to Angustias for her wedding with Pepe el Romano.

ADELA (*with hidden emotion*): But Pepe el Romano . . .

AMELIA: Haven't you heard about it?

ADELA: No.

MAGDALENA: Well, now you know!

ADELA: But it can't be!

MAGDALENA: Money can do anything.

ADELA: Is that why she went out after the funeral and stood looking through the door?

(*Pause.*)

And that man would . . .

MAGDALENA: Would do anything.

(*Pause.*)

MARTIRIO: What are you thinking, Adela?

ADELA: I'm thinking that this mourning has caught me at the worst moment of my life for me to bear it.

MAGDALENA: You'll get used to it.

ADELA (*bursting out, crying with rage*): I will not get used to it! I can't be locked up. I don't want my skin to look like yours. I don't want my skin's whiteness lost in these rooms. Tomorrow I'm going to put on my green dress and go walking in the streets. I want to go out!

(*The first servant enters.*)

MAGDALENA (*in a tone of authority*): Adela!

SERVANT: The poor thing! How she misses her father. . . .

(*She goes out.*)

MARTIRIO: Hush!

AMELIA: What happens to one will happen to all of us.

(*Adela grows calm.*)

MAGDALENA: The servant almost heard you.

SERVANT (*entering*): Pepe el Romano is coming along at the end of the street.

(*Amelia, Martirio and Magdalena run hurriedly.*)

MAGDALENA: Let's go see him!

(*They leave rapidly.*)

SERVANT (*to Adela*): Aren't you going?

ADELA: It's nothing to me.

SERVANT: Since he has to turn the corner, you'll see him better from the window of your room.

(*The servant goes out. Adela is left on the stage, standing doubtfully; after a moment, she also leaves rapidly, going toward her room. Bernarda and La Poncia come in.*)

BERNARDA: Damned portions and shares.

PONCIA: What a lot of money is left to Angustias!

BERNARDA: Yes.

PONCIA: And for the others, considerably less.

BERNARDA: You've told me that three times now, when you know I don't want it mentioned! Considerably less; a lot less! Don't remind me any more.

(*Angustias comes in, her face heavily made up.*)

Angustias!

ANGUSTIAS: Mother.

BERNARDA: Have you dared to powder your face? Have you dared to wash your face on the day of your father's death?

ANGUSTIAS: He wasn't my father. Mine died a long time ago. Have you forgotten that already?

BERNARDA: You owe more to this man, father of your sisters, than to your own. Thanks to him, your fortune is intact.

ANGUSTIAS: We'll have to see about that first!

BERNARDA: Even out of decency! Out of respect!

ANGUSTIAS: Let me go out, mother!

BERNARDA: Let you go out? After I've taken that powder off your face, I will. Spineless! Painted hussy! Just like your aunts!

(*She removes the powder violently with her handkerchief.*)

Now get out!

PONCIA: Bernarda, don't he so hateful!

BERNARDA: Even though my mother is crazy, I still have my five senses and I know what I'm doing.

(*They all enter.*)

MAGDALENA: What's going on here?

BERNARDA: Nothing's "going on here"!

MAGDALENA (*to Angustias*): If you're fighting over the inheritance, you're the richest one and can hang on to it all.

ANGUSTIAS: Keep your tongue in your pocketbook!

BERNARDA (*beating on the floor*): Don't fool yourselves into thinking you'll sway me. Until I go out of this house feet first I'll give the orders for myself and for you!

(*Voices are heard and María Josefa, Bernarda's mother, enters. She is very old and has decked out her head and breast with flowers.*)

MARIA JOSEFA: Bernarda, where is my mantilla? Nothing, nothing of what I own will be for any of you. Not my rings nor my black moiré dress. Because not a one of you is going to marry — not a one. Bernarda, give me my necklace of pearls.

BERNARDA (*to the servant*): Why did you let her get in here?

SERVANT (*trembling*): She got away from me!

MARIA JOSEFA: I ran away because I want to marry — I want to get married to a beautiful manly man from the shore of the sea. Because here the men run from women.

BERNARDA: Hush, hush, Mother!

MARIA JOSEFA: No, no — I won't hush. I don't want to see these single women, longing for marriage, turning their hearts to dust; and I want to go to my home town. Bernarda, I want a man to get married to and be happy with!

BERNARDA: Lock her up!

MARIA JOSEFA: Let me go out, Bernarda!

(*The servant seizes María Josefa.*)

BERNARDA: Help her, all of you!

(*They all grab the old woman.*)

MARIA JOSEFA: I want to get away from here! Bernarda! To get married by the shore of the sea — by the shore of the sea!

(*Quick curtain.*)

ACT 2

(*A white room in Bernarda's house. The doors on the left lead to the bedrooms. Bernarda's daughters are seated on low chairs, sewing. Magdalena is embroidering. La Poncia is with them.*)

ANGUSTIAS: I've cut the third sheet.

MARTIRIO: That one goes to Amelia.

MAGDALENA: Angustias, shall I put Pepe's initials here too?

ANGUSTIAS (*dryly*): No.

MAGDALENA (*calling, from off stage to Adela*): Adela, aren't you coming?

AMELIA: She's probably stretched out on the bed.

PONCIA: Something's wrong with that one. I find her restless, trembling, frightened — as if a lizard were between her breasts.

MARTIRIO: There's nothing, more or less, wrong with her than there is with all of us.

MAGDALENA: All of us except Angustias.

ANGUSTIAS: I feel fine, and anybody who doesn't like it can pop.

MAGDALENA: We all have to admit the nicest things about you are your figure and your tact.

ANGUSTIAS: Fortunately, I'll soon be out of this hell.

MAGDALENA: Maybe you won't get out!

MARTIRIO: Stop this talk!

ANGUSTIAS: Besides, a good dowry is better than dark eyes in one's face!

MAGDALENA: All you say just goes in one ear and out the other.

AMELIA (*to La Poncia*): Open the patio door and see if we can get a bit of a breeze.

(*La Poncia opens the door.*)

MARTIRIO: Last night I couldn't sleep because of the heat.

AMELIA: Neither could I.

MAGDALENA: I got up for a bit of air. There was a black storm cloud and a few drops even fell.

PONCIA: It was one in the morning and the earth seemed to give off fire. I got up too. Angustias was still at the window with Pepe.

MAGDALENA (*with irony*): That late? What time did he leave?

ANGUSTIAS: Why do you ask, if you saw him?

AMELIA: He must have left about one-thirty.

ANGUSTIAS: Yes. How did you know?

AMELIA: I heard him cough and heard his mare's hoofbeats.

PONCIA: But I heard him leave around four.

ANGUSTIAS: It must have been someone else!

PONCIA: No, I'm sure of it!

AMELIA: That's what it seemed to me, too.

MAGDALENA: That's very strange!

(*Pause.*)

PONCIA: Listen, Angustias, what did he say to you the first time he came by your window?

ANGUSTIAS: Nothing. What should he say? Just talked.

MARTIRIO: It's certainly strange that two people who never knew each other should suddenly meet at a window and be engaged.

ANGUSTIAS: Well, I didn't mind.

The women stand as witnesses in a scene from *The House of Bernarda Alba* directed by Julia Robinson at the *AlbaTomi* Theatre in New York in 1987.

AMELIA: I'd have felt very strange about it.

ANGUSTIAS: No, because when a man comes to a window he knows, from all the busybodies who come and go and fetch and carry, that he's going to be told "yes."

MARTIRIO: All right, but he'd have to ask you.

ANGUSTIAS: Of course!

AMELIA (*inquisitively*): And how did he ask you?

ANGUSTIAS: Why, no way: — "You know I'm after you. I need a good, well brought up woman, and that's you — if it's agreeable."

AMELIA: These things embarrass me!

ANGUSTIAS: They embarrass me too, but one has to go through it!

PONCIA: And did he say anything more?

ANGUSTIAS: Yes, he did all the talking.

MARTIRIO: And you?

ANGUSTIAS: I couldn't have said a word. My heart was almost coming out of my mouth. It was the first time I'd ever been alone at night with a man.

MAGDALENA: And such a handsome man.

ANGUSTIAS: He's not bad looking!

PONCIA: Those things happen among people who have an idea how to do things, who talk and say and move their hand. The first time my husband, Evaristo the Short-tailed, came to my window . . . Ha! Ha! Ha!

AMELIA: What happened?

PONCIA: It was very dark. I saw him coming along and as he went by he said, "Good evening." "Good evening," I said. Then we were both silent for more than half an hour. The sweat poured down my body. Then Evaristo got nearer and nearer as if he wanted to squeeze in through the bars and said in a very low voice — "Come here and let me feel you!"

(*They all laugh. Amelia gets up, runs, and looks through the door.*)

AMELIA: Ay, I thought mother was coming!

MAGDALENA: What she'd have done to us!

(*They go on laughing.*)

AMELIA: Sh-h-h! She'll hear us.

PONCIA: Then he acted very decently. Instead of getting some other idea, he went to raising birds, until he died. You aren't married but it's good for you to know, anyway, that two weeks after the wedding a man gives up the bed for the table, then the table for the tavern, and the woman who doesn't like it can just rot, weeping in a corner.

AMELIA: You liked it.

PONCIA: I learned how to handle him!

MARTIRIO: Is it true that you sometimes hit him?

PONCIA: Yes, and once I almost poked out one of his eyes!

MAGDALENA: All women ought to be like that!

PONCIA: I'm one of your mother's school. One time I don't know what he said to me, and then I killed all his birds — with the pestle!

(*They laugh.*)

MAGDALENA: Adela, child! Don't miss this.

AMELIA: Adela!

(*Pause.*)

MAGDALENA: I'll go see!

(*She goes out.*)

PONCIA: That child is sick!

MARTIRIO: Of course. She hardly sleeps!

PONCIA: What *does* she do, then?

MARTIRIO: How do I know what she does?

PONCIA: You probably know better than we do, since you sleep with just a wall between you.

ANGUSTIAS: Envy gnaws on people.

AMELIA: Don't exaggerate.

ANGUSTIAS: I can tell it in her eyes. She's getting the look of a crazy woman.

MARTIRIO: Don't talk about crazy women. This is one place you're not allowed to say that word.

(*Magdalena and Adela enter.*)

MAGDALENA: Didn't you say she was asleep?

ADELA: My body aches.

MARTIRIO (*with a hidden meaning*): Didn't you sleep well last night?

ADELA: Yes.

MARTIRIO: Then?

ADELA (*loudly*): Leave me alone. Awake or asleep, it's no affair of yours. I'll do whatever I want to with my body.

MARTIRIO: I was just concerned about you!

ADELA: Concerned? — curious! Weren't you sewing? Well, continue! I wish I were invisible so I could pass through a room without being asked where I was going!

SERVANT (*entering*): Bernarda is calling you. The man with the laces is here.

(*All but Adela and La Poncia go out, and as Martirio leaves, she looks fixedly at Adela.*)

ADELA: Don't look at me like that! If you want, I'll give you my eyes, for they're younger, and my back to improve that hump you have, but look the other way when I go by.

PONCIA: Adela, she's your sister, and the one who most loves you besides!

ADELA: She follows me everywhere. Sometimes she looks in my room to see if I'm sleeping. She won't let me breathe, and always, "Too bad about that face!" "Too bad about that body! It's going to waste!" But I won't let that happen. My body will be for whomever I choose.

PONCIA (*insinuatingly, in a low voice*): For Pepe el Romano, no?

ADELA (*frightened*): What do you mean?

PONCIA: What I said, Adela!

ADELA: Shut up!

PONCIA (*loudly*): Don't you think I've noticed?

ADELA: Lower your voice!

PONCIA: Then forget what you're thinking about!

ADELA: What do you know?

PONCIA: We old ones can see through walls. Where do you go when you get up at night?

ADELA: I wish you were blind!

PONCIA: But my head and hands are full of eyes, where something like this is concerned. I couldn't possibly guess your intentions. Why did you sit almost naked at your window, and with the light on and the window open, when Pepe passed by the second night he came to talk with your sister?

ADELA: That's not true!

PONCIA: Don't be a child! Leave your sister alone. And if you like Pepe el Romano, keep it to yourself.

(*Adela weeps.*)

Besides, who says you can't marry him? Your sister Angustias is sickly. She'll die with her first child. Narrow waisted, old — and out of my experience I can tell you she'll die. Then Pepe will do what all widowers do in these parts: he'll marry the youngest and most beautiful, and that's you. Live on that hope, forget him, anything; but don't go against God's law.

ADELA: Hush!

PONCIA: I won't hush!

ADELA: Mind your own business. Snooper, traitor!

PONCIA: I'm going to stick to you like a shadow!

ADELA: Instead of cleaning the house and then going to bed and praying for the dead, you root around like an old sow about goings on between men and women — so you can drool over them.

PONCIA: I keep watch; so people won't spit when they pass our door.

ADELA: What a tremendous affection you've suddenly conceived for my sister.

PONCIA: I don't have any affection for any of you. I want to live in a decent house. I don't want to be dirtied in my old age!

ADELA: Save your advice. It's already too late. For I'd leap not over you, just a servant, but over my mother to put out this fire I feel in my legs and my mouth. What can you possibly say about me? That I lock myself in my room and will not open the door? That I don't sleep? I'm smarter than you! See if you can catch the hare with your hands.

PONCIA: Don't defy me, Adela, don't defy me! Because I can shout, light lamps, and make bells ring.

ADELA: Bring four thousand yellow flares and set them about the walls of the yard. No one can stop what has to happen.

PONCIA: You like him that much?

ADELA: That much! Looking in his eyes I seem to drink his blood in slowly.

PONCIA: I won't listen to you.

ADELA: Well, you'll have to. I've been afraid of you. But now I'm stronger than you!

(Angustias enters.)

ANGUSTIAS: Always arguing!

PONCIA: Certainly. She insists that in all this heat I have to go bring her I don't know what from the store.

ANGUSTIAS: Did you buy me the bottle of perfume?

PONCIA: The most expensive one. And the face powder. I put them on the table in your room.

(Angustias goes out.)

ADELA: And be quiet!

PONCIA: We'll see!

(Martirio and Amelia enter.)

MARTIRIO (*to Adela*): Did you see the laces?

AMELIA: Angustias', for her wedding sheets, are beautiful.

ADELA (*to Martirio, who is carrying some lace*): And these?

MARTIRIO: They're for me. For a nightgown.

ADELA (*with sarcasm*): One needs a sense of humor around here!

MARTIRIO (*meaningfully*): But only for me to look at. I don't have to exhibit myself before anybody.

PONCIA: No one ever sees us in our nightgowns.

MARTIRIO (*meaningfully, looking at Adela*): Sometimes they don't! But I love nice underwear. If I were rich, I'd have it made of Holland Cloth. It's one of the few tastes I've left.

PONCIA: These laces are beautiful for babies caps and christening gowns. I could never afford them for my own. Now let's see if Angustias will use them for hers. Once she starts having children, they'll keep her running night and day.

MAGDALENA: I don't intend to sew a stitch on them.

AMELIA: And much less bring up some stranger's children. Look how our neighbors across the road are — making sacrifices for four brats.

PONCIA: They're better off than you. There at least they laugh and you can hear them fight.

MARTIRIO: Well, you go work for them, then.

PONCIA: No, fate has sent me to this nunnery!

(Tiny bells are heard distantly as though through several thicknesses of wall.)

MAGDALENA: It's the men going back to work.

PONCIA: It was three o'clock a minute ago.

MARTIRIO: With this sun!

ADELA (*sitting down*): Ay! If only we could go out in the fields too!

MAGDALENA (*sitting down*): Each class does what it has to!

MARTIRIO (*sitting down*): That's it!

AMELIA (*sitting down*): Ay!

PONCIA: There's no happiness like that in the fields right at this time of year. Yesterday morning the reapers arrived. Forty or fifty handsome young men.

MAGDALENA: Where are they from this year?

PONCIA: From far, far away. They came from the mountains! Happy! Like weathered trees! Shouting and throwing stones! Last night a woman who dresses in sequins and dances, with an accordion, arrived, and fifteen of them made a deal with her to take her to the olive grove. I saw them from far away. The one who talked with her was a boy with green eyes — tight knit as a sheaf of wheat.

AMELIA: Really?

ADELA: Are you sure?

PONCIA: Years ago another one of those women came here, and I myself gave my eldest son some money so he could go. Men need things like that.

ADELA: Everything's forgiven *them*.

AMELIA: To be born a woman's the worst possible punishment.

MAGDALENA: Even our eyes aren't our own.

(A distant song is heard, coming nearer.)

PONCIA: There they are. They have a beautiful song.

AMELIA: They're going out to reap now.

CHORUS:

> *The reapers have set out*
> *Looking for ripe wheat;*
> *They'll carry off the hearts*
> *Of any girls they meet.*

(Tambourines and carrañacas are heard. Pause. They all listen in the silence cut by the sun.)

AMELIA: And they don't mind the sun!

MARTIRIO: They reap through flames.

ADELA: How I'd like to be a reaper so I could come and go as I pleased. Then we could forget what's eating us all.

MARTIRIO: What do you have to forget?
ADELA: Each one of us has something.
MARTIRIO (*intensely*): Each one!
PONCIA: Quiet! Quiet!
CHORUS (*very distantly*):
> Throw wide your doors and windows,
> You girls who live in the town
> The reaper asks you for roses
> With which to deck his crown.

PONCIA: What a song!
MARTIRIO (*with nostalgia*):
> Throw wide your doors and windows,
> You girls who live in the town.

ADELA (*passionately*):
> The reaper asks you for roses
> With which to deck his crown.

(*The song grows more distant.*)

PONCIA: Now they're turning the corner.
ADELA: Let's watch them from the window of my room.
PONCIA: Be careful not to open the shutters too much because they're likely to give them a push to see who's looking.

(*The three leave. Martirio is left sitting on the low chair with her head between her hands.*)

AMELIA (*drawing near her*): What's wrong with you?
MARTIRIO: The heat makes me feel ill.
AMELIA: And it's no more than that?
MARTIRIO: I was wishing it were November, the rainy days, the frost — anything except this unending summertime.
AMELIA: It'll pass and come again.
MARTIRIO: Naturally.

(*Pause.*)

What time did you go to sleep last night?
AMELIA: I don't know. I sleep like a log. Why?
MARTIRIO: Nothing. Only I thought I heard someone in the yard.
AMELIA: Yes?
MARTIRIO: Very late.
AMELIA: And weren't you afraid?
MARTIRIO: No. I've heard it other nights.
AMELIA: We'd better watch out! Couldn't it have been the shepherds?
MARTIRIO: The shepherds come at six.
AMELIA: Maybe a young, unbroken mule?
MARTIRIO (*to herself, with double meaning*): That's it! That's it. An unbroken little mule.
AMELIA: We'll have to set a watch.
MARTIRIO: No. No. Don't say anything. It may be I've just imagined it.
AMELIA: Maybe.

(*Pause. Amelia starts to go.*)

MARTIRIO: Amelia!
AMELIA (*at the door*): What?

(*Pause.*)

MARTIRIO: Nothing.

(*Pause.*)

AMELIA: Why did you call me?

(*Pause.*)

MARTIRIO: It just came out. I didn't mean to.

(*Pause.*)

AMELIA: Lie down for a little.
ANGUSTIAS (*she bursts in furiously, in a manner that makes a great contrast with previous silence*): Where's that picture of Pepe I had under my pillow? Which one of you has it?
MARTIRIO: No one.
AMELIA: You'd think he was a silver St. Bartholomew.°
ANGUSTIAS: Where's the picture?

(*Poncia, Magdalena and Adela enter.*)

ADELA: What picture?
ANGUSTIAS: One of you has hidden it from me.
MAGDALENA: Do you have the effrontery to say that?
ANGUSTIAS: I had it in my room, and now it isn't there.
MARTIRIO: But couldn't it have jumped out into the yard at midnight? Pepe likes to walk around in the moonlight.
ANGUSTIAS: Don't joke with me! When he comes I'll tell him.
PONCIA: Don't do that! Because it'll turn up.

(*Looking at Adela.*)

ANGUSTIAS: I'd like to know which one of you has it.
ADELA (*looking at Martirio*): Somebody has it! But not me!
MARTIRIO (*with meaning*): Of course not you!
BERNARDA (*entering with her cane*): What scandal is this in my house in the heat's heavy silence? The neighbors must have their ears glued to the walls.
ANGUSTIAS: They've stolen my sweetheart's picture!
BERNARDA (*fiercely*): Who? Who?
ANGUSTIAS: They have!
BERNARDA: Which one of you?

(*Silence.*)

Answer me!

(*Silence.*) (*To La Poncia.*)

---

silver St. Bartholomew: A medallion used for good fortune.

Search their rooms! Look in their beds. This comes of not tying you up with shorter leashes. But I'll teach you now! (*to Angustias*) Are you sure?

ANGUSTIAS: Yes.

BERNARDA: Did you look everywhere?

ANGUSTIAS: Yes, Mother.

(*They all stand in an embarrassed silence.*)

BERNARDA: At the end of my life — to make me drink the bitterest poison a mother knows. (*to Poncia*) Did you find it?

PONCIA: Here it is.

BERNARDA: Where did you find it?

PONCIA: It was . . .

BERNARDA: Say it! Don't be afraid.

PONCIA (*wonderingly*): Between the sheets in Martirio's bed.

BERNARDA (*to Martirio*): Is that true?

MARTIRIO: It's true.

BERNARDA (*advancing on her, beating her with her cane*): You'll come to a bad end yet, you hypocrite! Trouble maker!

MARTIRIO (*fiercely*): Don't hit me, Mother!

BERNARDA: All I want to!

MARTIRIO: If I let you! You hear me? Get back!

PONCIA: Don't be disrespectful to your mother!

ANGUSTIAS (*holding Bernarda*): Let her go, please!

BERNARDA: Not even tears in your eyes.

MARTIRIO: I'm not going to cry just to please you.

BERNARDA: Why did you take the picture?

MARTIRIO: Can't I play a joke on my sister? What else would I want it for?

ADELA (*leaping forward, full of jealousy*): It wasn't a joke! You never liked to play jokes. It was something else bursting in her breast — trying to come out. Admit it openly now.

MARTIRIO: Hush, and don't make me speak; for if I should speak the walls would close together one against the other with shame.

ADELA: An evil tongue never stops inventing lies.

BERNARDA: Adela!

MAGDALENA: You're crazy.

AMELIA: And you stone us all with your evil suspicions.

MARTIRIO: But some others do things more wicked!

ADELA: Until all at once they stand forth stark naked and the river carries them along.

BERNARDA: Spiteful!

ANGUSTIAS: It's not my fault Pepe el Romano chose me!

ADELA: For your money.

ANGUSTIAS: Mother!

BERNARDA: Silence!

MARTIRIO: For your fields and your orchards.

MAGDALENA: That's only fair.

BERNARDA: Silence, I say! I saw the storm coming but I didn't think it'd burst so soon. Oh, what an avalanche of hate you've thrown on my heart! But I'm not old yet — I have five chains for you, and this house my father built, so not even the weeds will know of my desolation. Out of here!

(*They go out. Bernarda sits down desolately. La Poncia is standing close to the wall. Bernarda recovers herself, and beats on the floor.*)

I'll have to let them feel the weight of my hand! Bernarda, remember your duty!

PONCIA: May I speak?

BERNARDA: Speak. I'm sorry you heard. A stranger is always out of place in a family.

PONCIA: What I've seen, I've seen.

BERNARDA: Angustias must get married right away.

PONCIA: Certainly. We'll have to get her away from here.

BERNARDA: Not her, him!

PONCIA: Of course. He's the one to get away from here. You've thought it all out.

BERNARDA: I'm not thinking. These are things that shouldn't and can't be thought out. I give orders.

PONCIA: And you think he'll be satisfied to go away?

BERNARDA (*rising*): What are you imagining now?

PONCIA: He will, of course, marry Angustias.

BERNARDA: Speak up! I know you well enough to see that your knife's out for me.

PONCIA: I never knew a warning could be called murder.

BERNARDA: Have you some "warning" for me?

PONCIA: I'm not making any accusations, Bernarda. I'm only telling you to open your eyes and you'll see.

BERNARDA: See what?

PONCIA: You've always been smart, Bernarda. You've seen other people's sins a hundred miles away. Many times I've thought you could read minds. But, your children are your children, and now you're blind.

BERNARDA: Are you talking about Martirio?

PONCIA: Well, yes — about Martirio . . .

(*With curiosity.*)

I wonder why she hid the picture?

BERNARDA (*shielding her daughter*): After all, she says it was a joke. What else could it be?

PONCIA (*scornfully*): Do you believe that?

BERNARDA (*sternly*): I don't merely believe it. It's so!

PONCIA: Enough of this. We're talking about your family. But if we were talking about your neighbor across the way, what would it be?

BERNARDA: Now you're beginning to pull the point of the knife out.

PONCIA (*always cruelly*): No, Bernarda. Something very grave is happening here. I don't want to put the blame on your shoulders, but you've never given your daughters any freedom. Martirio is lovesick. I don't care what you say. Why didn't you let her marry Enrique Humanas? Why, on the very day he was coming to her window did you send him a message not to come?

BERNARDA (*loudly*): I'd do it a thousand times over! My blood won't mingle with the Humanas' while I live! His father was a shepherd.

PONCIA: And you see now what's happening to you with these airs!

BERNARDA: I have them because I can afford to. And you don't have them because you know where you came from!

PONCIA (*with hate*): Don't remind me! I'm old now. I've always been grateful for your protection.

BERNARDA (*emboldened*): You don't seem so!

PONCIA (*with hate, behind softness*): Martirio will forget this.

BERNARDA: And if she doesn't — the worse for her. I don't believe this is that "very grave thing" that's happening here. Nothing's happening here. It's just that you wish it would! And if it should happen one day, you can be sure it won't go beyond these walls.

PONCIA: I'm not so sure of that! There are people in town who can also read hidden thoughts, from afar.

BERNARDA: How you'd like to see me and my daughters on our way to a whorehouse!

PONCIA: No one knows her own destiny!

BERNARDA: I know my destiny! And my daughters! The whorehouse was for a certain woman, already dead. . . .

PONCIA (*fiercely*): Bernarda, respect the memory of my mother!

BERNARDA: Then don't plague me with your evil thoughts!

(*Pause.*)

PONCIA: I'd better stay out of everything.

BERNARDA: That's what you ought to do. Work and keep your mouth shut. The duty of all who work for a living.

PONCIA: But we can't do that. Don't you think it'd be better for Pepe to marry Martirio or . . . yes! . . . Adela?

BERNARDA: No, I *don't* think so.

PONCIA (*with meaning*): Adela! She's Romano's real sweetheart!

BERNARDA: Things are never the way we want them!

PONCIA: But it's hard work to turn them from their destined course. For Pepe to be with Angustias

seems wrong to me — and to other people — and even to the wind. Who knows if they'll get what they want?

BERNARDA: There you go again! Sneaking up on me — giving me bad dreams. But I won't listen to you, because if all you say should come to pass — I'd scratch your face.

PONCIA: Frighten someone else with that.

BERNARDA: Fortunately, my daughters respect me and have never gone against my will!

PONCIA: That's right! But, as soon as they break loose they'll fly to the rooftops!

BERNARDA: And I'll bring them down with stones!

PONCIA: Oh, yes! You were always the bravest one!

BERNARDA: I've always enjoyed a good fight!

PONCIA: But aren't people strange. You should see Angustias' enthusiasm for her lover, at her age! And he seems very smitten too. Yesterday my oldest son told me that when he passed by with the oxen at four-thirty in the morning they were still talking.

BERNARDA: At four-thirty?

ANGUSTIAS (*entering*): That's a lie!

PONCIA: That's what he told me.

BERNARDA (*to Angustias*): Speak up!

ANGUSTIAS: For more than a week Pepe has been leaving at one. May God strike me dead if I'm lying.

MARTIRIO (*entering*): I heard him leave at four too.

BERNARDA: But did you see him with your eyes?

MARTIRIO: I didn't want to look out. Don't you talk now through the side window?

ANGUSTIAS: We talk through my bedroom window.

(*Adela appears at the door.*)

MARTIRIO: Then . . .

BERNARDA: What's going on here?

PONCIA: If you're not careful, you'll find out! At least Pepe was at *one* of your windows — and at four in the morning too!

BERNARDA: Are you sure of that?

PONCIA: You can't be sure of anything in this life!

ADELA: Mother, don't listen to someone who wants us to lose everything we have.

BERNARDA: I know how to take care of myself! If the townspeople want to come bearing false witness against me, they'll run into a stone wall! Don't any of you talk about this! Sometimes other people try to stir up a wave of filth to drown us.

MARTIRIO: I don't like to lie.

PONCIA: So there must be something.

BERNARDA: There won't be anything. I was born to have my eyes always open. Now I'll watch without closing them 'til I die.

ANGUSTIAS: I have the right to know.

BERNARDA: You don't have any right except to obey.

No one's going to fetch and carry for me. (*to La Poncia*) And don't meddle in our affairs. No one will take a step without my knowing it.

SERVANT (*entering*): There's a big crowd at the top of the street, and all the neighbors are at their doors!

BERNARDA (*to Poncia*): Run see what's happening!

(*The girls are about to run out.*)

Where are you going? I always knew you for window-watching women and breakers of your mourning. All of you, to the patio!

(*They go out. Bernarda leaves. Distant shouts are heard.*)

(*Martirio and Adela enter and listen, not daring to step farther than the front door.*)

MARTIRIO: You can be thankful I didn't happen to open my mouth.

ADELA: I would have spoken too.

MARTIRIO: And what were you going to say? Wanting isn't doing!

ADELA: I do what I can and what happens to suit me. You've wanted to, but haven't been able.

MARTIRIO: You won't go on very long.

ADELA: I'll have everything!

MARTIRIO: I'll tear you out of his arms!

ADELA (*pleadingly*): Martirio, let me be!

MARTIRIO: None of us will have him!

ADELA: He wants me for his house!

MARTIRIO: I saw how he embraced you!

ADELA: I didn't want him to. It's as if I were dragged by a rope.

MARTIRIO: I'll see you dead first!

(*Magdalena and Angustias look in. The tumult is increasing. A servant enters with Bernarda. Poncia also enters from another door.*)

PONCIA: Bernarda!

BERNARDA: What's happening?

PONCIA: Librada's daughter, the unmarried one, had a child and no one knows whose it is!

ADELA: A child?

PONCIA: And to hide her shame she killed it and hid it under the rocks, but the dogs, with more heart than most Christians, dug it out and, as though directed by the hand of God, left it at her door. Now they want to kill her. They're dragging her through the streets — and down the paths and across the olive groves the men are coming, shouting so the fields shake.

BERNARDA: Yes, let them all come with olive whips and hoe handles — let them all come and kill her!

ADELA: No, not to kill her!

MARTIRIO: Yes — and let us go out too!

BERNARDA: And let whoever loses her decency pay for it!

(*Outside a woman's shriek and a great clamor is heard.*)

ADELA: Let her escape! Don't you go out!

MARTIRIO (*looking at Adela*): Let her pay what she owes!

BERNARDA (*at the archway*): Finish her before the guards come! Hot coals in the place where she sinned!

ADELA (*holding her belly*): No! No!

BERNARDA: Kill her! Kill her!

(*Curtain.*)

ACT 3

(*Four white walls, lightly washed in blue, of the interior patio of Bernarda Alba's house. The doorways, illumined by the lights inside the rooms, give a tenuous glow to the stage. At the center there is a table with a shaded oil lamp about which Bernarda and her daughters are eating. La Poncia serves them. Prudencia sits apart. When the curtain rises, there is a great silence interrupted only by the noise of plates and silverware.*)

PRUDENCIA: I'm going. I've made you a long visit.

(*She rises.*)

BERNARDA: But wait, Prudencia. We never see one another.

PRUDENCIA: Have they sounded the last call to rosary?

PONCIA: Not yet.

(*Prudencia sits down again.*)

BERNARDA: And your husband, how's he getting on?

PRUDENCIA: The same.

BERNARDA: We never see him either.

PRUDENCIA: You know how he is. Since he quarrelled with his brothers over the inheritance, he hasn't used the front door. He takes a ladder and climbs over the back wall.

BERNARDA: He's a real man! And your daughter?

PRUDENCIA: He's never forgiven her.

BERNARDA: He's right.

PRUDENCIA: I don't know what he told you. I suffer because of it.

BERNARDA: A daughter who's disobedient stops being a daughter and becomes an enemy.

PRUDENCIA: I let water run. The only consolation I've left is to take refuge in the church, but, since I'm losing my sight, I'll have to stop coming so the children won't make fun of me.

(*A heavy blow is heard against the walls.*)

What's that?

BERNARDA: The stallion. He's locked in the stall and he kicks against the wall of the house.

(*Shouting.*)

Tether him and take him out in the yard!

(*In a lower voice.*)

He must be too hot.

PRUDENCIA: Are you going to put the new mares to him?

BERNARDA: At daybreak.

PRUDENCIA: You've known how to increase your stock.

BERNARDA: By dint of money and struggling.

PONCIA (*interrupting*): And she has the best herd in these parts. It's a shame that prices are low.

BERNARDA: Do you want a little cheese and honey?

PRUDENCIA: I have no appetite.

(*The blow is heard again.*)

PONCIA: My God!

PRUDENCIA: It quivered in my chest.

BERNARDA (*rising, furiously*): Do I have to say things twice? Let him out to roll on the straw.

(*Pause. Then, as though speaking to the stableman.*)

Well then, lock the mares in the corral, but let him run free or he may kick down the walls.

(*She returns to the table and sits again.*)

Ay, what a life!

PRUDENCIA: You have to fight like a man.

BERNARDA: That's it.

(*Adela gets up from the table.*)

Where are you going?

ADELA: For a drink of water.

BERNARDA (*raising her voice*): Bring a pitcher of cool water. (*to Adela*) You can sit down. (*Adela sits down.*)

PRUDENCIA: And Angustias, when will she get married?

BERNARDA: They're coming to ask for her within three days.

PRUDENCIA: You must be happy.

ANGUSTIAS: Naturally!

AMELIA (*to Magdalena*): You've spilled the salt!

MAGDALENA: You can't possibly have worse luck than you're having.

AMELIA: It always brings bad luck.

BERNARDA: That's enough!

PRUDENCIA (*to Angustias*): Has he given you the ring yet?

ANGUSTIAS: Look at it.

(*She holds it out.*)

PRUDENCIA: It's beautiful. Three pearls. In my day, pearls signified tears.

ANGUSTIAS: But things have changed now.

ADELA: I don't think so. Things go on meaning the same. Engagement rings should be diamonds.

PONCIA: The most appropriate.

BERNARDA: With pearls or without them, things are as one proposes.

MARTIRIO: Or as God disposes.

PRUDENCIA: I've been told your furniture is beautiful.

BERNARDA: It cost sixteen thousand *reales*.°

PONCIA (*interrupting*): The best is the wardrobe with the mirror.

PRUDENCIA: I never saw a piece like that.

BERNARDA: We had chests.

PRUDENCIA: The important thing is that everything be for the best.

ADELA: And that you never know.

BERNARDA: There's no reason why it shouldn't be.

(*Bells are heard very distantly.*)

PRUDENCIA: The last call. (*to Angustias*) I'll be coming back to have you show me your clothes.

ANGUSTIAS: Whenever you like.

PRUDENCIA: Good evening — God bless you!

BERNARDA: Good-bye, Prudencia.

ALL FIVE DAUGHTERS (*at the same time*): God go with you!

(*Pause. Prudencia goes out.*)

BERNARDA: Well, we've eaten.

(*They rise.*)

ADELA: I'm going to walk as far as the gate to stretch my legs and get a bit of fresh air.

(*Magdalena sits down in a low chair and leans against the wall.*)

AMELIA: I'll go with you.

MARTIRIO: I too.

ADELA (*with contained hate*): I'm not going to get lost!

AMELIA: One needs company at night.

(*They go out. Bernarda sits down. Angustias is clearing the table.*)

BERNARDA: I've told you once already! I want you to talk to your sister Martirio. What happened about the picture was a joke and you must forget it.

ANGUSTIAS: You know she doesn't like me.

BERNARDA: Each one knows what she thinks inside. I don't pry into anyone's heart, but I want to put up

---

reales: Spanish silver coin. Sixteen thousand would have been a great sum.

a good front and have family harmony. You understand?

ANGUSTIAS: Yes.

BERNARDA: Then that's settled.

MAGDALENA (*she is almost asleep*): Besides, you'll be gone in no time.

(*She falls asleep.*)

ANGUSTIAS: Not soon enough for me.

BERNARDA: What time did you stop talking last night?

ANGUSTIAS: Twelve-thirty.

BERNARDA: What does Pepe talk about?

ANGUSTIAS: I find him absent-minded. He always talks to me as though he were thinking of something else. If I ask him what's the matter, he answers — "We men have our worries."

BERNARDA: You shouldn't ask him. And when you're married, even less. Speak if he speaks, and look at him when he looks at you. That way you'll get along.

ANGUSTIAS: But, Mother, I think he's hiding things from me.

BERNARDA: Don't try to find out. Don't ask him, and above all, never let him see you cry.

ANGUSTIAS: I should be happy, but I'm not.

BERNARDA: It's all the same.

ANGUSTIAS: Many nights I watch Pepe very closely through the window bars and he seems to fade away — as though he were hidden in a cloud of dust like those raised by the flocks.

BERNARDA: That's just because you're not strong.

ANGUSTIAS: I hope so!

BERNARDA: Is he coming tonight?

ANGUSTIAS: No, he went into town with his mother.

BERNARDA: Good, we'll get to bed early. Magdalena!

ANGUSTIAS: She's asleep.

(*Adela, Martirio and Amelia enter.*)

AMELIA: What a dark night!

ADELA: You can't see two steps in front of you.

MARTIRIO: A good night for robbers, for anyone who needs to hide.

ADELA: The stallion was in the middle of the corral. White. Twice as large. Filling all the darkness.

AMELIA: It's true. It was frightening. Like a ghost.

ADELA: The sky has stars as big as fists.

MARTIRIO: This one stared at them till she almost cracked her neck.

ADELA: Don't you like them up there?

MARTIRIO: What goes on over the roof doesn't mean a thing to me. I have my hands full with what happens under it.

ADELA: Well, that's the way it goes with you!

BERNARDA: And it goes the same for you as for her.

ANGUSTIAS: Good night.

ADELA: Are you going to bed now?

ANGUSTIAS: Yes, Pepe isn't coming tonight.

(*She goes out.*)

ADELA: Mother, why, when a stars falls or lightning flashes, does one say:
Holy Barbara, blessed on high
May your name be in the sky
With holy water written high?

BERNARDA: The old people know many things we've forgotten.

AMELIA: I close my eyes so I won't see them.

ADELA: Not I. I like to see what's quiet and been quiet for years on end, running with fire.

MARTIRIO: But all that has nothing to do with us.

BERNARDA: And it's better not to think about it.

ADELA: What a beautiful night! I'd like to stay up till very late and enjoy the breeze from the fields.

BERNARDA: But we have to go to bed. Magdalena!

AMELIA: She's just dropped off.

BERNARDA: Magdalena!

MAGDALENA (*annoyed*): Leave me alone!

BERNARDA: To bed!

MAGDALENA (*rising, in a bad humor*): You don't give anyone a moment's peace!

(*She goes off grumbling.*)

AMELIA: Good night!

(*She goes out.*)

BERNARDA: You two get along, too.

MARTIRIO: How is it Angustias' sweetheart isn't coming tonight?

BERNARDA: He went on a trip.

MARTIRIO (*looking at Adela*): Ah!

ADELA: I'll see you in the morning!

(*She goes out. Martirio drinks some water and goes out slowly, looking at the door to the yard. La Poncia enters.*)

PONCIA: Are you still here?

BERNARDA: Enjoying this quiet and not seeing anywhere the "very grave thing" that's happening here — according to you.

PONCIA: Bernarda, let's not go any further with this.

BERNARDA: In this house there's no question of a yes or a no. My watchfulness can take care of anything.

PONCIA: Nothing's happening outside. That's true, all right. Your daughters act and are as though stuck in a cupboard. But neither you nor anyone else can keep watch inside a person's heart.

BERNARDA: My daughters breathe calmly enough.

PONCIA: That's your business, since you're their mother. I have enough to do just with serving you.

BERNARDA: Yes, you've turned quiet now.

PONCIA: I keep my place — that's all.

BERNARDA: The trouble is you've nothing to talk about. If there were grass in this house, you'd make it your business to put the neighbors' sheep to pasture here.

PONCIA: I hide more than you think.

BERNARDA: Do your sons still see Pepe at four in the morning? Are they still repeating this house's evil litany?

PONCIA: They say nothing.

BERNARDA: Because they can't. Because there's nothing for them to sink their teeth in. And all because my eyes keep constant watch!

PONCIA: Bernarda, I don't want to talk about this because I'm afraid of what you'll do. But don't you feel so safe.

BERNARDA: Very safe!

PONCIA: Who knows, lightning might strike suddenly. Who knows but what all of a sudden, in a rush of blood, your heart might stop.

BERNARDA: Nothing will happen here. I'm on guard now against all your suspicions.

PONCIA: All the better for you.

BERNARDA: Certainly, all the better!

SERVANT (*entering*): I've just finished with the dishes. Is there anything else, Bernarda?

BERNARDA (*rising*): Nothing. I'm going to get some rest.

PONCIA: What time do you want me to call you?

BERNARDA: No time. Tonight I intend to sleep well.

(*She goes out.*)

PONCIA: When you're powerless against the sea, it's easier to turn your back on it and not look at it.

SERVANT: She's so proud! She herself pulls the blindfold over her eyes.

PONCIA: I can do nothing. I tried to head things off, but now they frighten me too much. You feel this silence? — in each room there's a thunderstorm and the day it breaks, it'll sweep all of us along with it. But I've said what I had to say.

SERVANT: Bernarda thinks nothing can stand against her, yet she doesn't know the strength a man has among women alone.

PONCIA: It's not all the fault of Pepe el Romano. It's true last year he was running after Adela; and she was crazy about him — but she ought to keep her place and not lead him on. A man's a man.

SERVANT: And some there are who believe he didn't have to talk many times with Adela.

PONCIA: That's true.

(*In a low voice.*)

And some other things.

SERVANT: I don't know what's going to happen here.

PONCIA: How I'd like to sail across the sea and leave this house, this battleground, behind!

SERVANT: Bernarda's hurrying the wedding and it's possible nothing will happen.

PONCIA: Things have gone much too far already. Adela is set no matter what comes, and the rest of them watch without rest.

SERVANT: Martirio too . . . ?

PONCIA: That one's the worst. She's a pool of poison. She sees El Romano is not for her, and she'd sink the world if it were in her hand to do so.

SERVANT: How bad they all are!

PONCIA: They're women without men, that's all. And in such matters even blood is forgotten. Sh-h-h-h!

(*She listens.*)

SERVANT: What's the matter?

PONCIA (*she rises*): The dogs are barking.

SERVANT: Someone must have passed by the back door.

(*Adela enters wearing a white petticoat and corselet.*)

PONCIA: Aren't you in bed yet?

ADELA: I want a drink of water.

(*She drinks from a glass on the table.*)

PONCIA: I imagined you were asleep.

ADELA: I got thirsty and woke up. Aren't you two going to get some rest?

SERVANT: Soon now.

(*Adela goes out.*)

PONCIA: Let's go.

SERVANT: We've certainly earned some sleep. Bernarda doesn't let me rest the whole day.

PONCIA: Take the light.

SERVANT: The dogs are going mad.

PONCIA: They're not going to let us sleep.

(*They go out. The stage is left almost dark. María Josefa enters with a lamb in her arms.*)

MARIA JOSEFA (*singing*):
> Little lamb, child of mine,
> Let's go to the shore of the sea,
> The tiny ant will be at his doorway,
> I'll nurse you and give you your bread.
> Bernarda, old leopard-face,
> And Magdalena, hyena-face,
> Little lamb . . .
> Rock, rock a bye,
> Let's go to the palms at Bethlehem's gate.

(*She laughs.*)

> Neither you nor I would want to sleep
> The door will open by itself
> And on the beach we'll go and hide
> In a little coral cabin.
> Bernarda, old leopard face,

And Magdalena, hyena-face,
Little lamb . . .
Rock, rock-a-bye,
Let's go to the palms at Bethlehem's gate.

(*She goes off singing.*)
(*Adela enters. She looks about cautiously and disappears out the door leading to the corral. Martirio enters by another door and stands in anguished watchfulness near the center of the stage. She also is in petticoats. She covers herself with a small black scarf. María Josefa crosses before her.*)

MARTIRIO: Grandmother, where are you going?

MARIA JOSEFA: You are going to open the door for me? Who are you?

MARTIRIO: How did you get out here?

MARIA JOSEFA: I escaped. You, who are you?

MARTIRIO: Go back to bed.

MARIA JOSEFA: You're Martirio. Now I see you. Martirio, face of a martyr. And when are you going to have a baby? I've had this one.

MARTIRIO: Where did you get that lamb?

MARIA JOSEFA: I know it's a lamb. But can't a lamb be a baby? It's better to have a lamb than to have anything. Old Bernarda, leopard-face, and Magdalena, hyena-face!

MARTIRIO: Don't shout.

MARIA JOSEFA: It's true. Everything's very dark. Just because I have white hair you think I can't have babies, but I can — babies and babies and babies. This baby will have white hair, and I'd have *this* baby, and another, and this *one* other; and with all of us with snow white hair we'll be like the waves — one, then another, and another. Then we'll all sit down and all of us will have white heads, and we'll be seafoam. Why isn't there any seafoam here? Nothing but mourning shrouds here.

MARTIRIO: Hush, hush.

MARIA JOSEFA: When my neighbor had a baby, I'd carry her some chocolate and later she'd bring me some, and so on — always and always and always. You'll have white hair, but your neighbors won't come. Now I have to go away, but I'm afraid the dogs will bite me. Won't you come with me as far as the fields? I don't like fields. I like houses, but open houses, and the neighbor women asleep in their beds with their little tiny tots, and the men outside sitting in their chairs. Pepe el Romano is a giant. All of you love him. But he's going to devour you because you're grains of wheat. No, not grains of wheat. Frogs with no tongues!

MARTIRIO (*angrily*): Come, off to bed with you.

(*She pushes her.*)

MARIA JOSEFA: Yes, but then you'll open the door for me, won't you?

MARTIRIO: Of course.

MARIA JOSEFA (*weeping*):
Little lamb, child of mine,
Let's go to the shore of the sea,
The tiny ant will be at his doorway,
I'll nurse you and give you your bread.

(*Martirio locks the door through which María Josefa came out and goes to the yard door. There she hesitates, but goes two steps farther.*)

MARTIRIO (*in a low voice*): Adela! (*Pause. She advances to the door. Then, calling.*) Adela!

(*Adela enters. Her hair is disarranged.*)

ADELA: And what are you looking for me for?

MARTIRIO: Keep away from him.

ADELA: Who are you to tell me that?

MARTIRIO: That's no place for a decent woman.

ADELA: How you wish *you'd* been there!

MARTIRIO (*shouting*): This is the moment for me to speak. This can't go on.

ADELA: This is just the beginning. I've had strength enough to push myself forward — the spirit and looks you lack. I've seen death under this roof, and gone out to look for what was mine, what belonged to me.

MARTIRIO: That soulless man came for another woman. You pushed yourself in front of him.

ADELA: He came for the money, but his eyes were always on me.

MARTIRIO: I won't allow you to snatch him away. He'll marry Angustias.

ADELA: You know better than I he doesn't love her.

MARTIRIO: I know.

ADELA: You know because you've seen — he loves me, me!

MARTIRIO (*desperately*): Yes.

ADELA (*close before her*): He loves me, *me!* He loves me, *me!*

MARTIRIO: Stick me with a knife if you like, but don't tell me that again.

ADELA: That's why you're trying to fix it so I won't go away with him. It makes no difference to you if he puts his arms around a woman he doesn't love. Nor does it to me. He could be a hundred years with Angustias, but for him to have his arms around me seems terrible to you — because you too love him! You love him!

MARTIRIO (*dramatically*) Yes! Let me say it without hiding my head. Yes! my breast's bitter, bursting like a pomegranate. I love him!

ADELA (*impulsively, hugging her*): Martirio, Martirio, I'm not to blame!

MARTIRIO: Don't put your arms around me! Don't try to smooth it over. My blood's no longer yours, and even though I try to think of you as a sister, I see you as just another woman.

(*She pushes her away.*)

ADELA: There's no way out here. Whoever has to drown — let her drown. Pepe is mine. He'll carry me to the rushes along the river bank. . . .

MARTIRIO: He won't!

ADELA: I can't stand this horrible house after the taste of his mouth. I'll be what he wants me to be. Everybody in the village against me, burning me with their fiery fingers; pursued by those who claim they're decent, and I'll wear, before them all, the crown of thorns that belongs to the mistress of a married man.

MARTIRIO: Hush!

ADELA: Yes, yes. (*In a low voice.*) Let's go to bed. Let's let him marry Angustias. I don't care any more, but I'll go off alone to a little house where he'll come to see me whenever he wants, whenever he feels like it.

MARTIRIO: That'll never happen! Not while I have a drop of blood left in my body.

ADELA: Not just weak you, but a wild horse I could force to his knees with just the strength of my little finger.

MARTIRIO: Don't raise that voice of yours to me. It irritates me. I have a heart full of a force so evil that, without my wanting to be, I'm drowned by it.

ADELA: You show us the way to love our sisters. God must have meant to leave me alone in the midst of darkness because I can see you as I've never seen you before.

(*A whistle is heard and Adela runs toward the door, but Martirio gets in front of her.*)

MARTIRIO: Where are you going?

ADELA: Get away from that door!

MARTIRIO: Get by me if you can!

ADELA: Get away!

(*They struggle.*)

MARTIRIO (*shouts*): Mother! Mother!

ADELA: Let me go!

(*Bernarda enters. She wears petticoats and a black shawl.*)

BERNARDA: Quiet! Quiet! How poor I am without even a man to help me!

MARTIRIO (*pointing to Adela*): She was with him. Look at those skirts covered with straw!

BERNARDA (*going furiously toward Adela*): That's the bed of a bad woman!

ADELA (*facing her*): There'll be an end to prison voices here! (*Adela snatches away her mother's cane and breaks it in two.*) This is what I do with the tyrant's cane. Not another step. No one but Pepe commands me!

(*Magdalena enters.*)

MAGDALENA: Adela!

(*La Poncia and Angustias enter.*)

ADELA: I'm his. (*to Angustias*) Know that — and go out in the yard and tell him. He'll be master in this house.

ANGUSTIAS: My God!

BERNARDA: The gun! Where's the gun?

(*She rushes out. La Poncia runs ahead of her. Amelia enters and looks on frightened, leaning her head against the wall. Behind her comes Martirio.*)

ADELA: No one can hold me back!

(*She tries to go out.*)

ANGUSTIAS (*holding her*): You're not getting out of here with your body's triumph! Thief! Disgrace of this house!

MAGDALENA: Let her go where we'll never see her again!

(*A shot is heard.*)

BERNARDA (*entering*): Just try looking for him now!

MARTIRIO (*entering*): That does away with Pepe el Romano.

ADELA: Pepe! My God! Pepe!

(*She runs out.*)

PONCIA: Did you kill him?

MARTIRIO: No. He raced away on his mare!

BERNARDA: It was my fault. A woman can't aim.

MAGDALENA: Then, why did you say . . . ?

MARTIRIO: For her! I'd like to pour a river of blood over her head!

PONCIA: Curse you!

MAGDALENA: Devil!

BERNARDA: Although it's better this way!

(*A thud is heard.*)

Adela! Adela!

PONCIA (*at her door*): Open this door!

BERNARDA: Open! Don't think the walls will hide your shame!

SERVANT (*entering*): All the neighbors are up!

BERNARDA (*in a low voice, but like a roar*): Open! Or I'll knock the door down!

(*Pause. Everything is silent.*)

Adela!

(*She walks away from the door.*)

A hammer!

(*La Poncia throws herself against the door. It opens and she goes in. As she enters, she screams and backs out.*)

What is it?

PONCIA (*she puts her hands to her throat*): May we never die like that!

(*The sisters fall back. The servant crosses herself. Bernarda screams and goes forward.*)

Don't go in!

BERNARDA: No, not I! Pepe, you're running now, alive in the darkness, under the trees, but another day you'll fall. Cut her down! My daughter died a vir-gin. Take her to another room and dress her as though she were a virgin. No one will say anything about this! She died a virgin. Tell them, so that at dawn, the bells will ring twice.

MARTIRIO: A thousand times happy she, who had him.

BERNARDA: And I want no weeping. Death must be looked at face to face. Silence!

(*To one daughter.*)

Be still, I said!

(*To another daughter.*)

Tears when you're alone! We'll drown ourselves in a sea of mourning. She, the youngest daughter of Bernarda Alba, died a virgin. Did you hear me? Silence, silence, I said. Silence!

COMMENTARY

John Gilmour (*b. 1939*)
RELIGION IN *THE HOUSE OF BERNARDA ALBA*   1992

In this commentary Gilmour examines the function of Christian faith in the play. He sees a profound contrast between a true Christian regime and the supposedly Christian regime that Bernarda imposes on her daughters. Gilmour also sees that the hypocrisy in the play is connected to Spain's social conditions at the time of Lorca's writing.

Bernarda may be very scrupulous about the way in which her family should show respect for the dead, and very familiar with Catholic ritual, but that is as far as her Christianity extends. Religion for her seems to mean blind, unquestioning adherence to an established set of rules which are there to be observed solely for the purpose of keeping up appearances. Her daughter Magdalena's sad comment, "nos pudrimos por el qué dirán" [we rot inside because of what people might say], is an indication of the destructive effect which this code of behaviour has on her family's well-being. Nowhere is there room in this scheme of things for the more positive and fundamental aspects of the Christian faith, notably love and charity towards others. Ronaldo Cueto, in a recent article in which he investigates the religious significance of the character Bernarda Alba, makes the interesting point that Bernardas are the name commonly given in Spain to nuns of the Cistercian order whose main tenet of faith is "God is love."

Yet it is surely hard to find a character as far removed from the true Bernardine spirit of love as Lorca's protagonist. A life of rigid conformity has corrupted her entire being, destroyed her soul and poisoned her home and social environment. Angustia describes the atmosphere inside their home as "un infierno" [a hell] — a damning indictment indeed of Bernarda's supposedly Christian regime. Bernarda shows no sign of being a loving mother. She is not prepared to trust her daughters with any kind of freedom (La Poncia tells her, "Tú no has dejado a tus hijas libres" [you never gave your daughters any freedom]). She keeps them prisoner in their own house (Magdelena complains of being "sentada días y días dentro de esta sala oscura" [sitting day after day in this dark room]). Like Yerma's sisters-in-law, she considers it her duty to stand guard over the family's honour; she blindly assures La Poncia, "Mi vigilancia lo puede todo . . . aquí no pasa nada" [My eyes kept constant watch . . . nothing gets by me]. She happily ruins the few chances which her daughters have to fall in love, either through snobbery ("Su padre fue gañán" [His father was a shepherd] is her explanation of why Martirio could not marry Enrique Humanas) or through social convention (Angustias's rich inheritance puts paid to Adela's relationship with Pepe el Romano). She thinks nothing of resorting to physical violence against her children. Angustias and Martirio are beaten to the ground amid a barrage of expletives which show the intensity of her fury. Not even the loss of Adela can release any emotion from her. Her "no quiero llantos" (I want no weeping) is the cold reaction of a mother whose only care appears to be that her daughter must be laid out "como una doncella" (like a virgin). Her stoicism in the face of tragedy is so remarkable as to be unnatural. . . .

In their painful search for individual fulfillment, Lorca's tragic heroines in the rural plays reflect this bitter struggle to throw off the shackles of an ideologically dominant social institution which, in the eyes of the reformist Republicans of the 1930s, had for so long been synonymous with intolerance, immobilism, obscurantism and repression. Lorca may not have claimed allegiance to any particular left-wing political movement or party, but his depiction of a rural society, pious and ritualistic yet lacking the most basic Christian virtues, casts him as an outspoken opponent of conservative, bourgeois values. In short it is possibly his social conscience that makes him present religion in this negative manner.

Bertolt Brecht

Among the most inventive and influential of modern playwrights, Bertolt Brecht (1898–1956) has left a legacy of important plays and theories about how those plays should be produced. Throughout most of his career he felt that drama should inform and awaken sensibilities, not just entertain or anesthetize an audience. Most of his plays concern philosophical and political issues, and some of them so threatened the Nazi regime that his works were burned publicly in Germany during the Third Reich.

At nineteen, Brecht was an orderly in a hospital during the last months of World War I. Seeing so much carnage and misery in the medical wards made him a lifelong pacifist. After the war he began writing plays while a student in Munich. His first successes in the Munich theater took the form of commentary on returned war veterans, on the questions of duty and heroism — which he treated negatively. His materialistic attitude (his rejection of spiritual concepts) was influenced by his readings of Hegel and the doctrines of Marx's dialectical materialism. Marx's theories predicted class struggles and based most social values in economic realities. Brecht eventually moved to Berlin, the theatrical center of Germany, and by 1926 was on his way to becoming a Communist.

Finding the political pressures in early Nazi Germany too frightening and dangerous for his writing, Brecht went into exile in 1933. He lived for a time in Scandinavia and later in the United States. After World War II Brecht and his wife returned to Berlin where, in 1949, he founded the Berliner Ensemble, which produced most of his later work. Brecht chose East Berlin as his home, in part because he felt his work could best be understood in a Communist setting. One irony is that his work has been even more widely appreciated and accepted in the West than in the former Communist eastern bloc.

Brecht wrote his most popular play in 1928, a musical in collaboration with the German composer Kurt Weill: *The Threepenny Opera*. The model for this play, the English writer John Gay's 1728 ballad opera *The Beggar's Opera*, provided Brecht with a perfect platform on which to comment satirically on the political and economic circumstances in Germany two hundred years after Gay wrote. The success of the Brecht-Weill collaboration — the work is still performed regularly — is due in part to Brecht's capacity to create appealing underworld characters such as Polly Peachum and Macheath, known as Mack the Knife.

Brecht's wife, Helene Weigel, played Mrs. Peachum, the madam of the brothel in which the action takes place. Kurt Weill's second wife, Lotte Lenya, was an overnight sensation in the part of Jenny. She had a reprise in New York almost twenty-five years later when she was as highly acclaimed as in the original Berlin production.

Brecht's most successful plays are *Galileo* (1938–1939); *Mother Courage* (1939); *The Good Woman of Setzuan* (1943); *The Private Lives of the Master Race* (1945); and *The Caucasian Chalk Circle* (1948). But these represent only a tiny fraction of a mass of work, including plays, poetry, criticism, and fiction. His output is extraordinary in volume and quality. It includes plays borrowed not only from Gay but also from Sophocles, Molière, Gorky, Shakespeare, and John Webster, among others.

Brecht developed a number of theories regarding drama. He defined the concept of epic theater as an alternative to the traditional Aristotelian theory. Brecht wanted his audience to be in a dialectical and sometimes alienated relationship to the drama. He expected his audience to observe, but to observe critically, to draw conclusions and to participate in an intellectual argument with the work at hand. The confrontational relationship he intended was designed to engage the audience in analyzing what they saw rather than in identifying with the main characters or in enjoying a wash of sentimentality or emotion.

One of the ways Brecht achieved his ends was by making the theatricality of the production's props, lights, sets, and equipment visible, thereby reminding the audience that they were seeing a play. He hoped that by alienating his audience from the drama he would keep them emotionally detached and intellectually alert. He used the term ALIENATION to define the effect he wanted his theater to have on an audience. Brecht's theater was political. He saw a connection between a critical theater audience and an audience able to analyze reality critically and see that social, political, and economic conditions were not "natural," or fixed immutably, but could (and should) be changed.

Brecht's theories produced interesting results and helped stimulate audiences that expected to be entertained by realistic or sentimental plays. His style spread rapidly throughout the world of theater, and it is still being used and developed by contemporary playwrights such as Heiner Müller and performers such as Pina Bausch.

MOTHER COURAGE

Since *Mother Courage* was first produced in 1941 in Zurich, it has become a true classic of modern theater, performed successfully in the United States, most Western theaters, and Germany. Brecht conceived of the drama as a powerful antiwar play. He set it in Germany during the Thirty Years' War, in which the German Protestants, supported by countries such as France, Denmark, and England, fought against the Hapsburg empire, which was allied with the Holy Roman Empire and the German Catholic princes. Actually a combination of many wars fought during the period of thirty years, the "War" was bloody and seemingly interminable, devastating Germany's towns and citizenry as well as its agriculture and commerce. Though the armies fought to control territory and economic markets, the religious differences between the German Lutherans and the Roman Catholics provided further reason for conflict.

Brecht was not interested in the immediate causes underlying the Thirty Years' War. He was making a case against war entirely, regardless of its cause. To do this, he deliberately avoided making his play realistic. The stage setting is essentially barren; and the play is structured in scenes that are very intense but that avoid any sense of continuity of action. Audiences cannot become involved in unfolding action; they must always remain conscious of themselves as audience. Moreover, the lighting is high intensity, almost cruel at times, spotlighting the action in a way that is completely unnatural. In the early productions, Brecht included slide projections of the headings that accompany each of the twelve scenes so that the audience was always reminded of the presence of the playwright and the fact that they were seeing a play. These headings provided yet another break in the continuity of the action.

Although the printed text does not convey it, the play in production employs long silences, some of which can be unsettling to the audience. When Swiss Cheese, Mother Courage's "honest" son, has a moment of rest in scene 3, he is in an intense ring of stage light as he comments on sitting in the sun in his shirtsleeves. He is relaxing for the last time, and the intensity of the light becomes an ironic device: It exposes him as a thief and he is dragged off to his death as a result of having stolen the cash box from the regiment. Swiss Cheese has been corrupted by the war, just as virtually everyone is corrupted.

Mother Courage herself lives off the war by selling goods to the soldiers. She and her children haul their wagon across the battlefields with no concern for who is winning, who is losing, or even where they are. Her only ambition is to stock her wagon, sell her goods, and make sure she does not get stuck with any useless inventory. When the chaplain tells her that peace has broken out, she laments their condition because without war the family has no livelihood.

As Mother Courage continues to pull her wagon across field after field, she learns how to survive. But she also loses her children, one by one, to the war. Eilif, seduced into joining the army by a recruitment officer, is led into battle thinking that war is a heroic adventure. Swiss Cheese thinks he found a good deal in a paymaster's uniform. Both are wrong: There is no security in war, and they eventually perish.

Kattrin, the daughter, is likewise a victim of the violence of war. Having been violated by a Swedish soldier, she becomes mute. Near the end of the play she is treated violently again, and the terrible scar on her face leaves her unmarriageable. At the end Kattrin dies while sounding an alarm to give the sleeping town warning of an imminent attack.

Finally, Mother Courage is left alone. She picks up her wagon and finds that she can maneuver it herself. The play ends as she circles the stage, with everything around her consumed by war.

Brecht's stated intentions were somewhat thwarted by the reactions of the play's first audiences. They were struck by the power of Brecht's characterization of Mother Courage and treated her with immense sympathy. They saw her as an indomitable woman whose strength in the face of adversity was so great that she could not be overwhelmed. But Brecht intended the audience to analyze Mother Courage further and to see in her a reflection of society's wrong values. She conducts business on the field of battle, paying no attention to the moral question of war itself. She makes her living from the war but cannot see that it is the war that causes her anguish.

In response to the audiences' sympathetic reactions, Brecht revised the play, adding new lines to help audiences see the venality of Mother Courage's motives. But subsequent audiences have continued to treat her as a survivor — almost a biblical figure. Brecht's German critics saw her as a model for one who endures all the terrors of war, and yet remains a testament for the resilience of humankind. No matter how one decides to interpret her, Mother Courage remains one of the most unusual and haunting characters in modern drama.

Mother Courage in Performance

Brecht wrote *Mother Courage* in three months, beginning in September 1939, while he and Helene Weigel were in Sweden, in exile from Nazi Germany. It's first production was on April 19, 1941, in Zurich, Switzerland, while Brecht waited in Sweden for entry papers to the United States. Brecht and Weigel returned to Europe after the war; in 1948 they went to East Berlin to work with a new theater group explicitly to produce *Mother Courage* with Helene Weigel in the title role in January 1949. In October 1950 Brecht directed Thérèsa Giehse as Courage in Munich. Other productions were staged in provincial

German towns and in other European cities, such as Rotterdam and Paris, both in 1951.

Brecht's productions are sometimes regarded as "canonical," although contemporary directors often modify his original plans. He usually began the performance with a half-curtain and a four-person orchestra playing an overture. Next, an unseen record player played a song associated with Courage; as Courage came on stage, she sang the second verse of her song herself. The stage had only a cyclorama, a large curved curtain used as a backdrop, and a circle marked on the floor. This defined the space that was Mother Courage's world, and various sets were placed on the circle to accommodate successive scenes. The circle itself was a turntable on which the wagon moved, going essentially nowhere. Brecht used placards to indicate changes in time and place as well as to indicate events in the life of Mother Courage and her children. The lighting was generally bright, and the effect was lively and colorful.

Brecht was not widely produced in the West during the cold war, but Leon Epp directed *Mother Courage* at the Volkstheater in Vienna in 1963. In the same year Jerome Robbins produced the play at the Martin Beck Theatre on Broadway, with sets by Ming Cho Lee. Anne Bancroft played Mother Courage, and Zohra Lampert was Kattrin. The reviews praised Bancroft for achieving a "lonely magnificence" at the end of the play and maintained that Brecht produced a considerable emotional intensity despite his theoretical distaste for such effects.

The next year Joseph Slowik produced the play in the Goodman Theater in Chicago with a partial student cast and the distinguished Eugenie Leontovich as Mother Courage. In England *Mother Courage* was produced twice in the 1950s in London. In 1961 and 1965 it was produced by the Old Vic. Numerous local theaters put on the play in the late 1960s and 1970s. In 1980 Ntozake Shange adapted it for its second New York production and reset it in the period after the American Civil War; Gloria Foster and Morgan Freeman had the major roles. Frank Rich praised the acting and the energy of the play but feared that Brecht's original vision was altered almost beyond recognition: Mother Courage becomes "an innocent victim of an entire system," which is exactly what Brecht argued against.

The Royal Shakespeare Company produced the play in London in 1984 with Judi Dench as Courage and Zoë Wanamaker as Kattrin. Both received fine reviews, as did the production itself. Diana Rigg was Mother Courage in the production at the Olivier Theatre in London (November 1995–January 1996), which featured a new colloquial translation by the playwright David Hare and which reset the play in the period of World War I. Like all these productions, it maintained the circular set that Brecht had originally used and experimented with Brecht's theories of alienation and distancing. The success of these productions indicates the play's appeal for our time.

Bertolt Brecht (1898–1956)

MOTHER COURAGE AND HER CHILDREN   *1939*
A CHRONICLE OF THE THIRTY YEARS' WAR

TRANSLATED BY JOHN WILLETT

Characters

MOTHER COURAGE
KATTRIN, *her dumb daughter*
EILIF, *the elder son*
SWISS CHEESE, *the younger son*
THE RECRUITER
THE SERGEANT
THE COOK
THE GENERAL
THE CHAPLAIN
THE ARMOURER
YVETTE POTTIER
THE MAN WITH THE PATCH
ANOTHER SERGEANT
THE ANCIENT COLONEL
A CLERK
A YOUNG SOLDIER
AN OLDER SOLDIER
A PEASANT
THE PEASANT'S WIFE
THE YOUNG MAN
THE OLD WOMAN
ANOTHER PEASANT
HIS WIFE
THE YOUNG PEASANT
THE ENSIGN
SOLDIERS
A VOICE

SCENE 1

(*Spring 1624. The Swedish Commander-in-Chief Count Oxenstierna is raising troops in Dalecarlia for the Polish campaign. The canteen woman Anna Fierling, known under the name of Mother Courage, loses one son.*)
(*Country road near a town.*)
(*A sergeant and a recruiter stand shivering.*)

RECRUITER: How can you muster a unit in a place like this? I've been thinking about suicide, sergeant. Here am I, got to find our commander four com-

panies before the twelfth of the month, and people round here are so nasty I can't sleep nights. S'pose I get hold of some bloke and shut my eye to his pigeon chest and varicose veins, I get him proper drunk, he signs on the line, I'm just settling up, he goes for a piss, I follow him to the door because I smell a rat; bob's your uncle, he's off like a flea with the itch. No notion of word of honour, loyalty, faith, sense of duty. This place has shattered my confidence in the human race, sergeant.

SERGEANT: It's too long since they had a war here; stands to reason. Where's their sense of morality to come from? Peace — that's just a mess; takes a war to restore order. Peacetime, the human race runs wild. People and cattle get buggered about, who cares? Everyone eats just as he feels inclined, a hunk of cheese on top of his nice white bread, and a slice of fat on top of the cheese. How many young blokes and good horses in that town there, nobody knows; they never thought of counting. I been in places ain't seen a war for nigh seventy years: folks hadn't got names to them, couldn't tell one another apart. Takes a war to get proper nominal rolls and inventories — shoes in bundles and corn in bags, and man and beast properly numbered and carted off, cause it stands to reason: no order, no war.

RECRUITER: Too true.

SERGEANT: Same with all good things, it's a job to get a war going. But once it's blossomed out there's no holding it; folk start fighting shy of peace like punters what can't stop for fear of having to tot up what they lost. Before that it's war they're fighting shy of. It's something new to them.

RECRUITER: Hey, here's a cart coming. Two tarts with two young fellows. Stop her, sergeant. If this one's a flop I'm not standing around in your spring winds any longer, I can tell you.

(*Sound of a jew's-harp. Drawn by two young fellows, a covered cart rolls in. On it sit Mother Courage and her dumb daughter Kattrin.*)

MOTHER COURAGE: Morning, sergeant.

SERGEANT (*blocking the way*): Morning, all. And who are you?

MOTHER COURAGE: Business folk. (*Sings.*)

> You captains, tell the drums to slacken
> And give your infanteers a break:
> It's Mother Courage with her waggon
> Full of the finest boots they make.
> With crawling lice and looted cattle
> With lumbering guns and straggling kit —
> How can you flog them into battle
> Unless you get them boots that fit?
>> The new year's come. The watchmen shout.
>> The thaw sets in. The dead remain.
>> Whatever life has not died out
>> It staggers to its feet again.
>
> Captains, how can you make them face it —
> Marching to death without a brew?
> Courage has rum with which to lace it
> And boil their souls and bodies through.
> Their musket primed, their stomach hollow —
> Captains, your men don't look so well.
> So feed them up and let them follow
> While you command them into hell.
>> The new year's come. The watchmen shout.
>> The thaw sets in. The dead remain.
>> Wherever life has not died out
>> It staggers to its feet again.

SERGEANT: Halt! Who are you with, you trash?

THE ELDER SON: Second Finnish Regiment.

SERGEANT: Where's your papers?

MOTHER COURAGE: Papers?

THE YOUNGER SON: What, mean to say you don't know Mother Courage?

SERGEANT: Never heard of her. What's she called Courage for?

MOTHER COURAGE: Courage is the name they gave me because I was scared of going broke, sergeant, so I drove me cart right through the bombardment of Riga with fifty loaves of bread aboard. They were going mouldy, it was high time, hadn't any choice really.

SERGEANT: Don't be funny with me. Your papers.

MOTHER COURAGE (*pulling a bundle of papers from a tin box and climbing down off the cart*): That's all my papers, sergeant. You'll find a whole big missal from Altötting in Bavaria for wrapping gherkins in, and a road map of Moravia, the Lord knows when I'll ever get there, might as well chuck it away, and here's a stamped certificate that my horse hasn't got foot-and-mouth, only he's dead worse luck, cost fifteen florins he did — not me luckily. That enough paper for you?

SERGEANT: You pulling my leg? I'll knock that sauce out of you. S'pose you know you got to have a licence.

MOTHER COURAGE: Talk proper to me, do you mind, and don't you dare say I'm pulling your leg in front of my unsullied children, 'tain't decent, I got no time for you. My honest face, that's me licence with the Second Regiment, and if it's too difficult for you to read there's nowt I can do about it. Nobody's putting a stamp on that.

RECRUITER: Sergeant, methinks I smell insubordination in this individual. What's needed in our camp is obedience.

MOTHER COURAGE: Sausage, if you ask me.

SERGEANT: Name.

MOTHER COURAGE: Anna Fierling.

SERGEANT: You all called Fierling then?

MOTHER COURAGE: What'd you mean? It's me's called Fierling, not them.

SERGEANT: Aren't all this lot your children?

MOTHER COURAGE: You bet they are, but why should they all have to be called the same, eh? (*Pointing to her elder son.*) For instance, that one's called Eilif Nojocki — Why? his father always claimed he was called Kojocki or Mojocki or something. The boy remembers him clearly, except that the one he remembers was someone else, a Frenchie with a little beard. Aside from that he's got his father's wits; that man knew how to snitch a peasant's pants off his bum without him noticing. This way each of us has his own name, see.

SERGEANT: What, each one different?

MOTHER COURAGE: Don't tell me you ain't never come across that.

SERGEANT: So I s'pose he's a Chinaman? (*Pointing to the younger son.*)

MOTHER COURAGE: Wrong. Swiss.

SERGEANT: After the Frenchman?

MOTHER COURAGE: What Frenchman? I never heard tell of no Frenchman. You keep muddling things up, we'll be hanging around here till dark. A Swiss, but called Fejos, and the name has nowt to do with his father. He was called something quite different and was a fortifications engineer, only drunk all the time.

(*Swiss Cheese beams and nods; dumb Kattrin too is amused.*)

SERGEANT: How in hell can he be called Fejos?

MOTHER COURAGE: I don't like to be rude, sergeant, but you ain't got much imagination, have you? Course he's called Fejos, because when he arrived I was with a Hungarian, very decent fellow, had terrible kidney trouble though he never touched a drop. The boy takes after him.

SERGEANT: But he wasn't his father . . .

MOTHER COURAGE: Took after him just the same. I call him Swiss Cheese. (*Pointing to her daughter.*) And that's Kattrin Haupt, she's half German.

SERGEANT: Nice family, I must say.

MOTHER COURAGE: Aye, me cart and me have seen the world.

SERGEANT: I'm writing all this down. (*He writes.*) And you're from Bamberg in Bavaria; how d'you come to be here?

MOTHER COURAGE: Can't wait till war chooses to visit Bamberg, can I?

RECRUITER (*to Eilif*): You two should be called Jacob Ox and Esau Ox, pulling the cart like that. I s'pose you never get out of harness?

EILIF: Ma, can I clobber him onc? I wouldn't half like to.

MOTHER COURAGE: And I says you can't; just you stop where you are. And now two fine officers like you, I bet you could use a good pistol, or a belt buckle, yours is on its last legs, sergeant.

SERGEANT: I could use something else. Those boys are healthy as young birch trees, I observe: chests like barrels, solid leg muscles. So why are they dodging their military service, may I ask?

MOTHER COURAGE (*quickly*): Nowt doing, sergeant. Yours is no trade for my kids.

RECRUITER: But why not? There's good money in it, glory too. Flogging boots is women's work. (*To Eilif.*) Come here, let's see if you've muscles in you or if you're a chicken.

MOTHER COURAGE: He's a chicken. Give him a fierce look, he'll fall over.

RECRUITER: Killing a young bull that happens to be in his way. (*Wants to lead him off.*)

MOTHER COURAGE: Let him alone, will you? He's nowt for you folk.

RECRUITER: He was crudely offensive and talked about clobbering me. The two of us are going to step into that field and settle it man to man.

EILIF: Don't you worry, mum, I'll fix him.

MOTHER COURAGE: Stop there! You varmint! I know you, nowt but fights. There's a knife down his boot. A slasher, that's what he is.

RECRUITER: I'll draw it out of him like a milk-tooth. Come along, sonny.

MOTHER COURAGE: Sergeant, I'll tell the colonel. He'll have you both in irons. The lieutenant's going out with my daughter.

SERGEANT: No rough stuff, chum. (*To Mother Courage.*) What you got against military service? Wasn't his own father a soldier? Died a soldier's death, too? Said it yourself.

MOTHER COURAGE: He's nowt but a child. You want to take him off to slaughterhouse, I know you lot. They'll give you five florins for him.

RECRUITER: First he's going to get a smart cap and boots, eh?

EILIF: Not from you.

MOTHER COURAGE: Let's both go fishing, said angler to worm. (*To Swiss Cheese.*) Run off, call out

they're trying to kidnap your brother. (*She pulls a knife.*) Go on, you kidnap him, just try. I'll slit you open, trash. I'll teach you to make war with him. We're doing an honest trade in ham and linen, and we're peaceable folk.

SERGEANT: Peaceable I don't think; look at your knife. You should be ashamed of yourself; put that knife away, you old harridan. A minute back you were admitting you live off the war, how else should you live, what from? But how's anyone to have war without soldiers?

MOTHER COURAGE: No need for it to be my kids.

SERGEANT: Oh, you'd like war to eat the pips but spit out the apple? It's to fatten up your kids, but you won't invest in it. Got to look after itself, eh? And you called Courage, fancy that. Scared of the war that keeps you going? Your sons aren't scared of it, I can see that.

EILIF: Take more than a war to scare me.

SERGEANT: And why? Look at me: has army life done all that badly by me? Joined up at seventeen.

MOTHER COURAGE: Still got to reach seventy.

SERGEANT: I don't mind waiting.

MOTHER COURAGE: Under the sod, eh?

SERGEANT: You trying to insult me, saying I'll die?

MOTHER COURAGE: S'pose it's true? S'pose I can see the mark's on you? S'pose you look like a corpse on leave to me? Eh?

SWISS CHEESE: She's got second sight, Mother has.

RECRUITER: Go ahead, tell the sergeant's fortune, might amuse him.

MOTHER COURAGE: Gimme helmet. (*He gives it to her.*)

SERGEANT: It don't mean a bloody sausage. Anything for a laugh though.

MOTHER COURAGE (*taking out a sheet of parchment and tearing it up*): Eilif, Swiss Cheese and Kattrin, may all of us be torn apart like this if we lets ourselves get too mixed up in the war. (*To the sergeant.*) Just for you I'm doing it for free. Black's for death. I'm putting a big black cross on this slip of paper.

SWISS CHEESE: Leaving the other one blank, see?

MOTHER COURAGE: Then I fold them across and shake them. All of us is jumbled together like this from our mother's womb, and now draw a slip and you'll know. (*The sergeant hesitates.*)

RECRUITER (*to Eilif*): I don't take just anybody, they all know I'm choosey, but you got the kind of fire I like to see.

SERGEANT (*fishing in the helmet*): Too silly. Load of eyewash.

SWISS CHEESE: Drawn a black cross, he has. Write him off.

RECRUITER: They're having you on; not everybody's name's on a bullet.

SERGEANT (*hoarsely*): You've put me in the shit.

MOTHER COURAGE: Did that yourself the day you became a soldier. Come along, let's move on now. 'Tain't every day we have a war, I got to get stirring.

SERGEANT: God damn it, you can't kid me. We're taking that bastard of yours for a soldier.

EILIF: Swiss Cheese'd like to be a soldier too.

MOTHER COURAGE: First I've heard of that. You'll have to draw too, all three of you. (*She goes to the rear to mark crosses on further slips.*)

RECRUITER (*to Eilif*): One of the things they say against us is that it's all holy-holy in the Swedish camp; but that's a malicious rumour to do us down. There's no hymn-singing but Sundays, just a single verse, and then only for those got voices.

MOTHER COURAGE (*coming back with the slips, which she drops into the sergeant's helmet*): Trying to get away from their ma, the devils, off to war like calves to salt-lick. But I'm making you draw lots, and that'll show you the world is no vale of joys with "Come along, son, we need a few more generals." Sergeant, I'm so scared they won't get through the war. Such dreadful characters, all three of them. (*She hands the helmet to Eilif.*) Hey, come on, fish out your slip. (*He fishes one out, unfolds it. She snatches it from him.*) There you are, it's a cross. Oh, wretched mother that I am, o pain-racked giver of birth! Shall he die? Aye, in the springtime of life he is doomed. If he becomes a soldier he shall bite the dust, it's plain to see. He is too foolhardy, like his dad was. And if he ain't sensible he'll go the way of all flesh, his slip proves it. (*Shouts at him.*) You going to be sensible?

EILIF: Why not?

MOTHER COURAGE: Sensible thing is stay with your mother, never mind if they poke fun at you and call you chicken, just you laugh.

RECRUITER: If you're pissing in your pants I'll make do with your brother.

MOTHER COURAGE: I told you laugh. Go on, laugh. Now you draw, Swiss Cheese. I'm not so scared on account you're honest. (*He fishes in the helmet.*) Oh, why look at your slip in that strange way? It's got to be a blank. There can't be any cross on it. Surely I'm not going to lose *you*. (*She takes the slip.*) A cross? What, you too? Is that because you're so simple, perhaps? O Swiss Cheese, you too will be sunk if you don't stay utterly honest all the while, like I taught you from childhood when you brought the change back from the baker's. Else you can't save yourself. Look, sergeant, that's a black cross, ain't it?

SERGEANT: A cross, that's right. Can't think how I come to get one. I always stay in the rear. (*To the recruiter.*) There's no catch. Her own family get it too.

SWISS CHEESE: I get it too. But I listen to what I'm told.

MOTHER COURAGE (*to Kattrin*): And now you're the only one I know's all right, you're a cross yourself; got a kind heart you have. (*Holds the helmet up to her on the cart, but takes the slip out herself.*) No, that's too much. That can't be right; must have made a mistake shuffling. Don't be too kind-hearted, Kattrin, you'll have to give it up, there's a cross above your path too. Lie doggo, girl, it can't be that hard once you're born dumb. Right, all of you know now. Look out for yourselves, you'll need to. And now we up we get and on we go. (*She climbs on to the cart.*)

RECRUITER (*to the sergeant*): Do something.

SERGEANT: I don't feel very well.

RECRUITER: Must of caught a chill taking your helmet off in that wind. Involve her in a deal. (*Aloud.*) Might as well have a look at that belt-buckle, sergeant. After all, our friends here have to live by their business. Hey, you people, the sergeant wants to buy that belt-buckle.

MOTHER COURAGE: Half a florin. Two florins is what a belt like that's worth. (*Climbs down again.*)

SERGEANT: 'Tain't new. Let me get out of this damned wind and have a proper look at it. (*Goes behind the cart with the buckle.*)

MOTHER COURAGE: Ain't what I call windy.

SERGEANT: I s'pose it might be worth half a florin, it's silver.

MOTHER COURAGE (*joining him behind the cart*): It's six solid ounces.

RECRUITER (*to Eilif*): And then we men'll have one together. Got your bounty money here, come along. (*Eilif stands undecided.*)

MOTHER COURAGE: Half a florin it is.

SERGEANT: It beats me. I'm always at the rear. Sergeant's the safest job there is. You can send the others up front, cover themselves with glory. Me dinner hour's properly spoiled. Shan't be able to hold nowt down, I know.

MOTHER COURAGE: Mustn't let it prey on you so's you can't eat. Just stay at the rear. Here, take a swig of brandy, man. (*Gives him a drink.*)

RECRUITER (*has taken Eilif by the arm and is leading him away up stage*): Ten florins bounty money, then you're a gallant fellow fighting for the king and women'll be after you like flies. And you can clobber me for free for insulting you.

(*Exeunt both.°*)
(*Dumb Kattrin leans down from the cart and makes hoarse noises.*)

Exeunt both: They both leave.

MOTHER COURAGE: All right, Kattrin, all right. Sergeant's just paying. (*Bites the half-florin.*) I got no faith in any kind of money. Burnt child, that's me, sergeant. This coin's good, though. And now let's get moving. Where's Eilif?

SWISS CHEESE: Went off with the recruiter.

MOTHER COURAGE (*stands quite still, then*): You simpleton. (*To Kattrin.*) 'Tain't your fault, you can't speak, I know.

SERGEANT: Could do with a swig yourself, ma. That's life. Plenty worse thing's than being a soldier. Want to live off war, but keep yourself and family out of it, eh?

MOTHER COURAGE: You'll have to help your brother pull now, Kattrin.

(*Brother and sister hitch themselves to the cart and start pulling. Mother Courage walks alongside. The cart rolls on.*)

SERGEANT (*looking after them*):
Like the war to nourish you?
Have to feed it something too.

SCENE 2

(*In the years 1625 and 1626 Mother Courage crosses Poland in the train of the Swedish armies. Before the fortress of Wallhof she meets her son again. Successful sale of a capon and heyday of her dashing son.*)
(*The general's tent.*)
(*Beside it, his kitchen. Thunder of cannon. The cook is arguing with Mother Courage, who wants to sell him a capon.*)

THE COOK: Sixty hellers for a miserable bird like that?

MOTHER COURAGE: Miserable bird? This fat brute? Mean to say some greedy old general — and watch your step if you got nowt for his dinner — can't afford sixty hellers for him?

THE COOK: I can get a dozen like that for ten hellers just down the road.

MOTHER COURAGE: What, a capon like this you can get just down the road? In time of siege, which means hunger that tears your guts. A rat you might get: "might" I say because they're all being gobbled up, five men spending best part of day chasing one hungry rat. Fifty hellers for a giant capon in time of siege!

THE COOK: But it ain't us having the siege, it's t'other side. We're conducting the siege, can't you get that in your head?

MOTHER COURAGE: But we got nowt to eat too, even worse than them in the town. Took it with them,

didn't they? They're having a high old time, everyone says. And look at us! I been to the peasants, there's nowt there.

THE COOK: There's plenty. They're sitting on it.

MOTHER COURAGE (*triumphantly*): They ain't. They're bust, that's what they are. Just about starving. I saw some, were grubbing up roots from sheer hunger, licking their fingers after they boiled some old leather strap. That's way it is. And me got a capon here and supposed to take forty hellers for it.

THE COOK: Thirty, not forty. I said thirty.

MOTHER COURAGE: Here, this ain't just any old capon. It was such a gifted beast, I been told, it could only eat to music, had a military march of its own. It could count, it was that intelligent. And you say forty hellers is too much? General will make mincemeat of you if there's nowt on his table.

THE COOK: See what I'm doing? (*He takes a piece of beef and puts his knife to it.*) Here I got a bit of beef, I'm going to roast it. Make up your mind quick.

MOTHER COURAGE: Go on, roast it. It's last year's.

THE COOK: Last night's. That animal was still alive and kicking, I saw him myself.

MOTHER COURAGE: Alive and stinking, you mean.

THE COOK: I'll cook him five hours if need be. I'll just see if he's still tough. (*He cuts into it.*)

MOTHER COURAGE: Put plenty of pepper on it so his lordship the general don't smell the pong.

(*The general, a chaplain and Eilif enter the tent.*)

THE GENERAL (*slapping Eilif on the shoulder*): Now then, Eilif my son, into your general's tent with you and sit thou at my right hand. For you accomplished a deed of heroism, like a pious cavalier; and doing what you did for God, and in a war of religion at that, is something I commend in you most highly, you shall have a gold bracelet as soon as we've taken this town. Here we are, come to save their souls for them, and what do those insolent dung-encrusted yokels go and do? Drive their beef away from us. They stuff it into those priests of theirs all right, back and front, but you taught 'em manners, ha! So here's a pot of red wine for you, the two of us'll knock it back at one gulp. (*They do so.*) Piss all for the chaplain, the old bigot. And now, what would you like for dinner, my darling?

EILIF: A bit of meat, why not?

THE GENERAL: Cook! Meat!

THE COOK: And then he goes and brings guests when there's nowt there.

(*Mother Courage silences him so she can listen.*)

EILIF: Hungry job cutting down peasants.

MOTHER COURAGE: Jesus Christ, it's my Eilif.

Lotte Lenya as Mother Courage pulling her wagon in Brecht's 1979 Berliner Ensemble production of his play.

THE COOK: Your what?

MOTHER COURAGE: My eldest boy. It's two years since I lost sight of him, they pinched him from me on the road, must think well of him if the general's asking him to dinner, and what kind of a dinner can you offer? Nowt. You heard what the visitor wishes to eat: meat. Take my tip, you settle for the capon, it'll be a florin.

THE GENERAL (*has sat down with Eilif, and bellows*): Food, Lamb, you foul cook, or I'll have your hide.

THE COOK: Give it over, dammit, this is blackmail.

MOTHER COURAGE: Didn't someone say it was a miserable bird?

THE COOK: Miserable; give it over, and a criminal price, fifty hellers.

MOTHER COURAGE: A florin, I said. For my eldest boy, the general's guest, no expense is too great for me.

THE COOK (*gives her the money*): You might at least pluck it while I see to the fire.

MOTHER COURAGE (*sits down to pluck the fowl*): He won't half be surprised to see me. He's my dashing clever son. Then I got a stupid one too, he's honest though. The girl's nowt. One good thing, she don't talk.

THE GENERAL: Drink up, my son, this is my best Falernian; only got a barrel or two left, but that's nothing to pay for a sign that there's still true faith to be found in my army. As for that shepherd of souls he can just look on, because all he does is preach, without the least idea how it's to be carried out. And now, my son Eilif, tell us more about the neat way you smashed those yokels and captured the twenty oxen. Let's hope they get here soon.

EILIF: A day or two at most.

MOTHER COURAGE: Thoughtful of our Eilif not to bring the oxen in till tomorrow, else you lot wouldn't have looked twice at my capon.

EILIF: Well, it was like this, see. I'd heard peasants had been driving the oxen they'd hidden, out of the forest into one particular wood, on the sly and mostly by night. That's where people from the town were s'posed to come and pick them up. So I holds off and lets them drive their oxen together, reckoning they'd be better than me at finding 'em. I had my blokes slavering after the meat, cut their emergency rations even further for a couple of days till their mouths was watering at the least sound of any word beginning with "me-," like "measles" say.

THE GENERAL: Very clever of you.

EILIF: Possibly. The rest was a piece of cake. Except that the peasants had cudgels and outnumbered us three to one and made a murderous attack on us. Four of 'em shoved me into a thicket, knocked my sword from my hand and bawled out "Surrender!" What's the answer, I wondered; they're going to make mincemeat of me.

THE GENERAL: What did you do?

EILIF: I laughed.

THE GENERAL: You did what?

EILIF: Laughed. So we got talking. I put it on a business footing from the start, told them "Twenty florins a head's too much. I'll give you fifteen." As if I was meaning to pay. That threw them, and they began scratching their heads. In a flash I'd picked up my sword and was hacking 'em to pieces. Necessity's the mother of invention, eh, sir?

THE GENERAL: What is your view, pastor of souls?

THE CHAPLAIN: That phrase is not strictly speaking in

the Bible, but when Our Lord turned the five loaves into five hundred there was no war on and he could tell people to love their neighbours as they'd had enough to eat. Today it's another story.

THE GENERAL (*laughs*): Quite another story. You can have a swig after all for that, you old Pharisee.° (*To Eilif.*) Hacked 'em to pieces, did you, so my gallant lads can get a proper bite to eat? What do the Scriptures say? "Whatsoever thou doest for the least of my brethren, thou doest for me." And what did you do for them? Got them a good square meal of beef, because they're not accustomed to mouldy bread, the old way was to fix a cold meal of rolls and wine in your helmet before you went out to fight for God.

EILIF: Aye, in a flash I'd picked up my sword and was hacking them to pieces.

THE GENERAL: You've the makings of a young Caesar. You ought to see the King.

EILIF: I have from a distance. He kind of glows. I'd like to model myself on him.

THE GENERAL: You've got something in common already. I appreciate soldiers like you, Eilif, men of courage. Somebody like that I treat as I would my own sort. (*He leads him over to the map.*) Have a look at the situation, Eilif; it's a long haul still.

MOTHER COURAGE (*who has been listening and now angrily plucks the fowl*): That must be a rotten general.

THE COOK: He's ravenous all right, but why rotten?

MOTHER COURAGE: Because he's got to have men of courage, that's why. If he knew how to plan a proper campaign what would he be needing men of courage for? Ordinary ones would do. It's always the same; whenever there's a load of special virtues around it means something stinks.

THE COOK: I thought it meant things is all right.

MOTHER COURAGE: No, that they stink. Look, s'pose some general or king is bone stupid and leads his men up shit creek, then those men've got to be fearless, there's another virtue for you. S'pose he's stingy and hires too few soldiers, then they got to be a crowd of Hercules's. And s'pose he's slapdash and don't give a bugger, then they got to be clever as monkeys else their number's up. Same way they got to show exceptional loyalty each time he gives them impossible jobs. Nowt but virtues no proper country and no decent king or general would ever need. In decent countries folk don't have to have virtues, the whole lot can be perfectly ordinary, average intelligence, and for all I know cowards.

Pharisee: A member of a Jewish sect current in biblical days; the term is now commonly used to refer to a hypocritical, self-righteous person.

THE GENERAL: I'll wager your father was a soldier.

EILIF: A great soldier, I been told. My mother warned me about it. There's a song I know.

THE GENERAL: Sing it to us. (*Roars.*) When's that dinner coming?

EILIF: It's called The Song of the Girl and the Soldier. (*He sings it, dancing a war dance with his sabre.*)

The guns blaze away, and the bay'nit'll slay
And the water can't hardly be colder.
What's the answer to ice? Keep off's my advice!
That's what the girl told the soldier.
Next thing the soldier, wiv' a round up the spout
Hears the band playing and gives a great shout:
Why, it's marching what makes you a soldier!
So it's down to the south and then northwards once more:
See him catching that bay'nit in his naked paw!
That's what his comrades done told her.

Oh, do not despise the advice of the wise
Learn wisdom from those that are older
And don't try for things that are out of your reach —
That's what the girl told the soldier.
Next thing the soldier, his bay'nit in place
Wades into the river and laughs in her face
Though the water comes up to his shoulder.
When the shingle roof glints in the light o' the moon
We'll be wiv' you again, not a moment too soon!
That's what his comrades done told her.

MOTHER COURAGE (*takes up the song in the kitchen, beating on a pot with her spoon*):

You'll go out like a light! And the sun'll take flight
For your courage just makes us feel colder.
Oh, that vanishing light! May God see that it's right! —
That's what the girl told the soldier.

EILIF: What's that?

MOTHER COURAGE (*continues singing*):

Next thing the soldier, his bay'nit in place
Was caught by the current and went down without trace
And the water couldn't hardly be colder.
Then the shingle roof froze in the light o' the moon
As both soldier and ice drifted down to their doom —
And d'you know what his comrades done told her?

He went out like a light. And the sunshine took flight
For his courage just made 'em feel colder.
Oh, do not despise the advice of the wise!
That's what the girl told the soldier.

THE GENERAL: The things they get up to in my kitchen these days.

EILIF (*Has gone into the kitchen. He flings his arms round his mother.*): Fancy seeing you again, ma! Where's the others?

MOTHER COURAGE (*in his arms*): Snug as a bug in a rug. They made Swiss Cheese paymaster of the Second Finnish; any road he'll stay out of fighting that way, I couldn't keep him out altogether.

EILIF: How's the old feet?

MOTHER COURAGE: Bit tricky getting me shoes on of a morning.

THE GENERAL (*has joined them*): So you're his mother, I hope you've got plenty more sons for me like this one.

EILIF: Ain't it my lucky day? You sitting out there in the kitchen, ma, hearing your son commended . . .

MOTHER COURAGE: You bet I heard. (*Slaps his face.*)

EILIF (*holding his cheek*): What's that for? Taking the oxen?

MOTHER COURAGE: No. Not surrendering when those four went for you and wanted to make mincemeat of you. Didn't I say you should look after yourself? You Finnish devil!

(*The general and the chaplain stand in the doorway laughing.*)

SCENE 3

(*Three years later Mother Courage is taken prisoner along with elements of a Finnish regiment. She manages to save her daughter, likewise her covered cart, but her honest son is killed.*)

(*Military camp.*)

(*Afternoon. A flagpole with the regimental pay. From her cart, festooned now with all kinds of goods, Mother Courage has stretched a washing line to a large cannon, across which she and Kattrin are folding the washing. She is bargaining at the same time with an armourer over a sack of shot. Swiss Cheese, now wearing a paymaster's uniform, is looking on. A comely person, Yvette Pottier, is sewing a gaily coloured hat, a glass of brandy before her. She is in her stockinged feet, having laid aside her red high-heeled boots.*)

THE ARMOURER: I'll let you have that shot for a couple of florins. It's cheap at the price, I got to have the money because the colonel's been boozing with his officers since two days back, and the drink's run out.

MOTHER COURAGE: That's troops' munitions. They catch me with that, I'm for court-martial. You crooks flog the shot, and troops got nowt to fire at enemy.

THE ARMOURER: Have a heart, can't you; you scratch my back and I'll scratch yours.

MOTHER COURAGE: I'm not taking army property. Not at that price.

THE ARMOURER: You can sell it on the q.t. tonight to the Fourth Regiment's armourer for five florins, eight even, if you let him have a receipt for twelve. He's right out of ammunition.

MOTHER COURAGE: Why not you do it?

THE ARMOURER: I don't trust him, he's a pal of mine.

MOTHER COURAGE (*takes the sack*): Gimme. (*To Kattrin.*) Take it away and pay him a florin and a half. (*The armourer protests.*) I said a florin and a half. (*Kattrin drags the sack upstage, the armourer following her. Mother Courage addresses Swiss Cheese.*) Here's your woollies, now look after them, it's October and autumn may set in any time. I ain't saying it's got to, cause I've learned nowt's got to come when you think it will, not even seasons of the year. But your regimental accounts got to add up right, come what may. Do they add up right?

SWISS CHEESE: Yes, mother.

MOTHER COURAGE: Don't you forget they made you paymaster cause you was honest, not dashing like your brother, and above all so stupid I bet you ain't even thought of clearing off with it, no not you. That's a big consolation to me. And don't lose those woollies.

SWISS CHEESE: No, mother, I'll put them under my mattress. (*Begins to go.*)

THE ARMOURER: I'll go along with you, paymaster.

MOTHER COURAGE: And don't you start learning him none of your tricks.

(*The armourer leaves with Swiss Cheese without any farewell gesture.*)

YVETTE (*waving to him*): No reason not to say goodbye, armourer.

MOTHER COURAGE (*to Yvette*): I don't like to see them together. He's wrong company for our Swiss Cheese. Oh well, war's off to a good start. Easily take four, five years before all countries are in. A bit of foresight, don't do nothing silly, and business'll flourish. Don't you know you ain't s'posed to drink before midday with your complaint?

YVETTE: Complaint, who says so, it's a libel.

MOTHER COURAGE: They all say so.

YVETTE: Because they're all telling lies, Mother Courage, and me at my wits' end cause they're all avoiding me like something the cat brought in thanks to those lies, what the hell am I remodelling my hat for? (*She throws it away.*) That's why I drink before midday. Never used to, gives you crows' feet, but now what the hell? All the Second Finnish know me. Ought to have stayed at home when my first fellow did me wrong. No good our sort being proud. Eat shit, that's what you got to do, or down you go.

MOTHER COURAGE: Now don't you start up again about that Pieter of yours and how it all happened, in front of my innocent daughter too.

YVETTE: She's the one should hear it, put her off love.

MOTHER COURAGE: Nobody can put 'em off that.

YVETTE: Then I'll go on, get it off my chest. It all starts with yours truly growing up in lovely Flanders, else I'd never of seen him and wouldn't be stuck here now in Poland, cause he was an army cook, fair-haired, a Dutchman but thin for once. Kattrin, watch out for the thin ones, only in those days I didn't know that, or that he'd got a girl already, or that they all called him Puffing Piet cause he never took his pipe out of his mouth when he was on the job, it meant that little to him. (*She sings the Song of Fraternisation.*)

When I was only sixteen
The foe came into our land.
He laid aside his sabre
And with a smile he took my hand.
After the May parade
The May light starts to fade.
The regiment dressed by the right
The drums were beaten, that's the drill.
The foe took us behind the hill
And fraternised all night.

There were so many foes then
But mille worked in the mess.
I loathed him in the daytime.
At night I loved him none the less.
After the May parade
The May light starts to fade.
The regiment dressed by the right
The drums were beaten, that's the drill.
The foe took us behind the hill
And fraternised all night.

The love which came upon me
Was wished on me by fate.
My friends could never grasp why
I found it hard to share their hate.
The fields were wet with dew
When sorrow first I knew.
The regiment dressed by the right
The drums were beaten, that's the drill.
And then the foe, my lover still
Went marching out of sight.

I followed him, fool that I was, but I never found him, and that was five years back. (*She walks unsteadily behind the cart.*)

MOTHER COURAGE: You left your hat here.

YVETTE: Anyone wants it can have it.

MOTHER COURAGE: Let that be a lesson, Kattrin. Don't you start anything with them soldiers. Love makes the world go round, I'm warning you. Even with fellows not in the army it's no bed of roses. He says he'd like to kiss the ground your feet walk on — reminds me, did you wash them yesterday? — and after that you're his skivvy. Be thankful you're dumb, then you can't contradict yourself and won't be wanting to bite your tongue off for speaking the truth; it's a godsend, being dumb is. And here comes the general's cook, now what's he after?

(*Enter the cook and the chaplain.*)

THE CHAPLAIN: I have a message for you from your son Eilif, and the cook has come along because you made such a profound impression on him.

THE COOK: I just came along to get a bit of air.

MOTHER COURAGE: That you can always do here if you behave yourself, and if you don't I can deal with you. What does he want? I got no spare cash.

THE CHAPLAIN: Actually I had a message for his brother the paymaster.

MOTHER COURAGE: He ain't here now nor anywhere else neither. He ain't his brother's paymaster. He's not to lead him into temptation nor be clever at his expense. (*Giving him money from the purse slung round her.*) Give him this, it's a sin, he's banking on mother's love and ought to be ashamed of himself.

THE COOK: Not for long, he'll have to be moving off with the regiment, might be to his death. Give him a bit extra, you'll be sorry later. You women are tough, then later on you're sorry. A little glass of brandy wouldn't have been a problem, but it wasn't offered and, who knows, a bloke may lie beneath the green sod and none of you people will ever be able to dig him up again.

THE CHAPLAIN: Don't give way to your feelings, cook. To fall in battle is a blessing, not an inconvenience, and why? It is a war of faith. None of your common wars but a special one, fought for the faith and therefore pleasing to God.

THE COOK: Very true. It's a war all right in one sense, what with requisitioning, murder and looting and the odd bit of rape thrown in, but different from all the other wars because it's a war of faith; stands to reason. But it's thirsty work at that, you must admit.

THE CHAPLAIN (*to Mother Courage, indicating the cook*): I tried to stop him, but he says he's taken a shine to you, you figure in his dreams.

THE COOK (*lighting a stumpy pipe*): Just want a glass of brandy from a fair hand, what harm in that? Only I'm groggy already cause the chaplain here's been telling such jokes all the way along you bet I'm still blushing.

MOTHER COURAGE: Him a clergyman too. I'd best give the pair of you a drink or you'll start making me immoral suggestions cause you've nowt else to do.

THE CHAPLAIN: Behold a temptation, said the court preacher, and fell. (*Turning back to look at Kattrin as he leaves.*) And who is this entrancing young person?

MOTHER COURAGE: That ain't an entrancing but a decent young person. (*The chaplain and the cook go behind the cart with Mother Courage. Kattrin looks after them, then walks away from her washing towards the hat. She picks it up and sits down, pulling the red boots towards her. Mother Courage can be heard in the background talking politics with the chaplain and the cook.*)

MOTHER COURAGE: Those Poles here in Poland had no business sticking their noses in. Right, our king moved in on them, horse and foot, but did they keep the peace? no, went and stuck their noses into their own affairs, they did, and fell on king just as he was quietly clearing off. They committed a breach of peace, that's what, so blood's on their own head.

THE CHAPLAIN: All our king minded about was freedom. The emperor had made slaves of them all, Poles and Germans alike, and the king had to liberate them.

THE COOK: Just what I say, your brandy's first rate, I weren't mistaken in your face, but talk of the king, it cost the king dear trying to give freedom to Germany, what with giving Sweden the salt tax, what cost the poor folk a bit, so I've heard, on top of which he had to have the Germans locked up and drawn and quartered cause they wanted to carry on slaving for the emperor. Course the king took a serious view when anybody didn't want to be free. He set out by just trying to protect Poland against bad people, particularly the emperor, then it started to become a habit till he ended up protecting the whole of Germany. They didn't half kick. So the poor old king's had nowt but trouble for all his kindness and expenses, and that's something he had to make up for by taxes of course, which caused bad blood, not that he'd let a little matter like that depress him. One thing he had on his side, God's word, that was a help. Because otherwise folk would of been saying he done it all for himself and to make a bit on the side. So he's always had a good conscience, which was the main point.

MOTHER COURAGE: Anyone can see you're no Swede or you wouldn't be talking that way about the Hero King.

THE CHAPLAIN: After all he provides the bread you eat.

THE COOK: I don't eat it, I bake it.

MOTHER COURAGE: They'll never beat him, and why, his men got faith in him. (*Seriously.*) To go by what the big shots say, they're waging war for almighty God and in the name of everything that's good and lovely. But look closer, they ain't so silly, they're waging it for what they can get. Else little folk like me wouldn't be in it at all.

THE COOK: That's the way it is.

THE CHAPLAIN: As a Dutchman you'd do better to glance at the flag above your head before venting your opinions here in Poland.

MOTHER COURAGE: All good Lutherans here. Prosit!°

(*Kattrin has put on Yvette's hat and begun strutting around in imitation of her way of walking.*)
(*Suddenly there is a noise of cannon fire and shooting. Drums. Mother Courage, the cook and the chaplain rush out from behind the cart, the two last-named still carrying their glasses. The armourer and another soldier run up to the cannon and try to push it away.*)

MOTHER COURAGE: What's happening? Wait till I've taken my washing down, you louts! (*She tries to rescue her washing.*)

THE ARMOURER: The Catholics! Broken through. Don't know if we'll get out of here. (*To the soldier.*) Get that gun shifted! (*Runs on.*)

THE COOK: God, I must find the general. Courage, I'll drop by in a day or two for another talk.

MOTHER COURAGE: Wait, you forgot your pipe.

THE COOK (*in the distance*): Keep it for me. I'll be needing it.

MOTHER COURAGE: Would happen just as we're making a bit of money.

THE CHAPLAIN: Ah well, I'll be going too. Indeed, if the enemy is so close as that it might be dangerous. Blesséd are the peacemakers is the motto in wartime. If only I had a cloak to cover me.

MOTHER COURAGE: I ain't lending no cloaks, not on your life. I been had too often.

THE CHAPLAIN: But my faith makes it particularly dangerous for me.

MOTHER COURAGE (*gets him a cloak*): Goes against my conscience, this does. Now you run along.

THE CHAPLAIN: Thank you, dear lady, that's very generous of you, but I think it might be wiser for me to remain seated here; it could arouse suspicion

Prosit: Cheers!

and bring the enemy down on me if I were seen to run.

MOTHER COURAGE (*to the soldier*): Leave it, you fool, who's going to pay you for that? I'll look after it for you, you're risking your neck.

THE SOLDIER (*running away*): You can tell 'em I tried.

MOTHER COURAGE: Cross my heart. (*Sees her daughter with the hat.*) What you doing with that strumpet's hat? Take that lid off, you gone crazy? And the enemy arriving any minute! (*Pulls the hat off Kattrin's head.*) Want 'em to pick you up and make a prostitute of you? And she's gone and put those boots on, whore of Babylon! Off with those boots! (*Tries to tug them off her.*) Jesus Christ, chaplain, gimme a hand, get those boots off her, I'll be right back. (*Runs to the cart.*)

YVETTE (*arrives, powdering her face*): Fancy that, the Catholics are coming. Where's my hat? Who's been kicking it around? I can't go about looking like this if the Catholics are coming. What'll they think of me? No mirror either. (*To the chaplain.*) How do I look? Too much powder?

THE CHAPLAIN: Exactly right.

YVETTE: And where are them red boots? (*Fails to find them as Kattrin hides her feet under her skirt.*) I left them here all right. Now I'll have to get to me tent barefoot. It's an outrage.

(*Exit.*)
(*Swiss Cheese runs in carrying in a small box.*)

MOTHER COURAGE (*Arrives with her hands full of ashes. To Kattrin.*): Here some ashes. (*To Swiss Cheese.*) What's that you're carrying?

SWISS CHEESE: Regimental cash box.

MOTHER COURAGE: Chuck it away. No more paymastering for you.

SWISS CHEESE: I'm responsible. (*He goes to the rear.*)

MOTHER COURAGE (*to the chaplain*): Take your clerical togs off, padre, or they'll spot you under that cloak. (*She rubs Kattrin's face with ash.*) Keep still, will you? There you are, a bit of muck and you'll be safe. What a disaster. Sentries were drunk. Hide your light under a bushel, it says. Take a soldier, specially a Catholic one, add a clean face, and there's your instant whore. For weeks they get nowt to eat, then soon as they manage to get it by looting they're falling on anything in skirts. That ought to do. Let's have a look. Not bad. Looks like you been grubbing in muckheap. Stop trembling. Nothing'll happen to you like that. (*To Swiss Cheese.*) Where d'you leave cash box?

SWISS CHEESE: Thought I'd put it in cart.

MOTHER COURAGE (*horrified*): What, my cart? Sheer criminal idiocy. Only take me eyes off you one instant. Hang us all three, they will.

SWISS CHEESE: I'll put it somewhere else then, or clear out with it.

MOTHER COURAGE: You sit on it, it's too late now.

THE CHAPLAIN (*who is changing his clothes downstage*): For heaven's sake, the flag!

MOTHER COURAGE (*hauls down the regimental flag*): Bozhe moi! I'd given up noticing it were there. Twenty-five years I've had it.

(*The thunder of cannon intensifies.*)

(*A morning three days later. The cannon has gone. Mother Courage, Kattrin, the chaplain and Swiss Cheese are sitting gloomily over a meal.*)

SWISS CHEESE: That's three days I been sitting around with nowt to do, and sergeant's always been kind to me but any moment now he'll start asking where's Swiss Cheese with the pay box?

MOTHER COURAGE: You thank your stars they ain't after you.

THE CHAPLAIN: What can I say? I can't even hold a service here, it might make trouble for me. Whosoever hath a full heart, his tongue runneth over, it says, but heaven help me if mine starts running over.

MOTHER COURAGE: That's how it goes. Here they sit, one with his faith and the other with his cash box. Dunno which is more dangerous.

THE CHAPLAIN: We are all of us in God's hands.

MOTHER COURAGE: Oh, I don't think it's as bad as that yet, though I must say I can't sleep nights. If it weren't for you, Swiss Cheese, things'd be easier. I think I got meself cleared. I told 'em I didn't hold with Antichrist, the Swedish one with horns on, and I'd observed left horn was a bit unserviceable. Half way through their interrogation I asked where I could get church candles not too dear. I knows the lingo cause Swiss Cheese's dad were Catholic, often used to make jokes about it, he did. They didn't believe me all that much, but they ain't got no regimental canteen lady. So they're winking an eye. Could turn out for the best, you know. We're prisoners, but same like fleas on dog.

THE CHAPLAIN: That's good milk. But we'll need to cut down our Swedish appetites a bit. After all, we've been defeated.

MOTHER COURAGE: Who's been defeated? Look, victory and defeat ain't bound to be same for the big shots up top as for them below, not by no means. Can be times the bottom lot find a defeat really pays them. Honour's lost, nowt else. I remember once up in Livonia our general took such a beating from enemy I got a horse off our baggage train in the confusion, pulled me cart seven months, he did, before we won and they checked up. As a rule you can say victory and defeat both come expensive to us ordinary folk. Best thing for us is when politics get bogged down solid. (*To Swiss Cheese.*) Eat up.

SWISS CHEESE: Got no appetite for it. What's sergeant to do when pay day comes round?

MOTHER COURAGE: They don't have pay days on a retreat.

SWISS CHEESE: It's their right, though. They needn't retreat if they don't get paid. Needn't stir a foot.

MOTHER COURAGE: Swiss Cheese, you're that conscientious it makes me quite nervous. I brought you up to be honest, you not being clever, but you got to know where to stop. Chaplain and me, we're off now to buy Catholic flag and some meat. Dunno anyone so good at sniffing meat, like sleepwalking it is, straight to target. I'd say he can pick out a good piece by the way his mouth starts watering. Well, thank goodness they're letting me go on trading. You don't ask tradespeople their faith but their prices. And Lutheran trousers keep cold out too.

THE CHAPLAIN: What did the mendicant say when he heard the Lutherans were going to turn everything in town and country topsy-turvy? "They'll always need beggars." (*Mother Courage disappears into the cart.*) So she's still worried about the cash box. So far they've taken us all for granted as part of the cart, but how long for?

SWISS CHEESE: I can get rid of it.

THE CHAPLAIN: That's almost more dangerous. Suppose you're seen. They have spies. Yesterday a fellow popped up out of the ditch in front of me just as I was relieving myself first thing. I was so scared I only just suppressed an ejaculatory prayer. That would have given me away all right. I think what they'd like best is to go sniffing people's excrement to see if they're Protestants. The spy was a little runt with a patch over one eye.

MOTHER COURAGE (*clambering out of the cart with a basket*): What have I found, you shameless creature? (*She holds up the red boots in triumph.*) Yvette's red high-heeled boots! Coolly went and pinched them, she did. Cause you put it in her head she was an enchanting young person. (*She lays them in the basket.*) I'm giving them back. Stealing Yvette's boots! She's wrecking herself for money. That's understandable. But you'd do it for nothing, for pleasure. What did I tell you: you're to wait till it's peace. No soldiers for you. You're not to start exhibiting yourself till it's peacetime.

THE CHAPLAIN: I don't find she exhibits herself.

MOTHER COURAGE: Too much for my liking. Let her be like a stone in Dalecarlia, where there's nowt else, so folk say "Can't see that cripple," that's how I'd lief have her. Then nowt'll happen to her.

(*To Swiss Cheese.*) You leave that box where it is, d'you hear? And keep an eye on your sister, she needs it. The pair of you'll have me in grave yet. Sooner be minding a bagful of fleas.

(*She leaves with the chaplain. Kattrin clears away the dishes.*)

SWISS CHEESE: Won't be able to sit out in the sun in shirt-sleeves much longer. (*Kattrin points at a tree.*) Aye, leaves turning yellow. (*Kattrin asks by gestures if he wants a drink.*) Don't want no drink. I'm thinking. (*Pause.*) Said she can't sleep. Best if I got rid of that box, found a good place for it. All right, let's have a glass. (*Kattrin goes behind the cart.*) I'll stuff it down the rat-hole by the river for the time being. Probably pick it up tonight before first light and take it to Regiment. How far can they have retreated in three days? Bet sergeant's surprised. I'm agreeably disappointed in you, Swiss Cheese, he'll say. I make you responsible for the cash, and you go and bring it back.

(*As Kattrin emerges from behind the cart with a full glass in her hand, two men confront her. One is a sergeant, the other doffs his hat to her. He has a patch over one eye.*)

THE MAN WITH THE PATCH: God be with you, mistress. Have you seen anyone round here from Second Finnish Regimental Headquarters?

(*Kattrin, badly frightened, runs downstage, spilling the brandy. The two men look at one another, then withdraw on seeing Swiss Cheese sitting there.*)

SWISS CHEESE (*interrupted in his thoughts*): You spilt half of it. What are those faces for? Jabbed yourself in eye? I don't get it. And I'll have to be off, I've thought it over, it's the only way. (*He gets up. She does everything possible to make him realise the danger. He only shrugs her off.*) Wish I knew what you're trying to say. Sure you mean well, poor creature, just can't get words out. What's it matter your spilling my brandy, I'll drink plenty more glasses yet, what's one more or less? (*He gets the box from the cart and takes it under his tunic.*) Be back in a moment. Don't hold me up now, or I'll be angry. I know you mean well. Too bad you can't speak.

(*As she tries to hold him back he kisses her and tears himself away. Exit. She is desperate, running hither and thither uttering little noises. The chaplain and Mother Courage return. Kattrin rushes to her mother.*)

MOTHER COURAGE: What's all this? Pull yourself together, love. They done something to you?

Where's Swiss Cheese? Tell it me step by step,
Kattrin. Mother understands you. What, so that
bastard did take the box? I'll wrap it round his
ears, the little hypocrite. Take your time and
don't gabble, use your hands, I don't like it when
you howl like a dog, what'll his reverence say?
Makes him uncomfortable. What, a one-eyed
man came along?

THE CHAPLAIN: That one-eyed man is a spy. Have
they arrested Swiss Cheese? (*Kattrin shakes her
head, shrugs her shoulders.*) We're done for.

MOTHER COURAGE (*fishes in her basket and brings
out a Catholic flag, which the chaplain fixes to the
mast*): Better hoist new flag.

THE CHAPLAIN (*bitterly*): All good Catholics here.

(*Voices are heard from the rear. The two men bring in
Swiss Cheese.*)

SWISS CHEESE: Let me go, I got nowt. Don't twist my
shoulder, I'm innocent.

SERGEANT: Here's where he came from. You know
each other.

MOTHER COURAGE: Us? How?

SWISS CHEESE: I don't know her. Got no idea who she
is, had nowt to do with them. I bought me dinner
here, ten hellers it cost. You might have seen me
sitting here, it was too salty.

SERGEANT: Who are you people, eh?

MOTHER COURAGE: We're law-abiding folk. That's
right, he bought a dinner. Said it was too salty.

SERGEANT: Trying to pretend you don't know each
other, that it?

MOTHER COURAGE: Why should I know him? Can't
know everyone. I don't go asking 'em what they're
called and are they a heretic; if he pays he ain't a
heretic. You a heretic?

SWISS CHEESE: Go on.

THE CHAPLAIN: He sat there very properly, never
opening his mouth except when eating. Then he
had to.

SERGEANT: And who are you?

MOTHER COURAGE: He's just my potboy. Now I expect you gentlemen are thirsty, I'll get you a glass
of brandy, you must be hot and tired with running.

SERGEANT: No brandy on duty. (*To Swiss Cheese.*)
You were carrying something. Must have hidden it
by the river. Was a bulge in your tunic when you
left here.

MOTHER COURAGE: You sure it was him?

SWISS CHEESE: You must be thinking of someone else.
I saw someone bounding off with a bulge in his tunic. I'm the wrong man.

MOTHER COURAGE: I'd say it was a misunderstanding
too, such things happen. I'm a good judge of peo-

ple, I'm Courage, you heard of me, everyone knows
me, and I tell you that's an honest face he has.

SERGEANT: We're on the track of the Second Finnish
Regiment's cash box. We got the description of the
fellow responsible for it. Been trailing him two
days. It's you.

SWISS CHEESE: It's not me.

SERGEANT: And you better cough it up, or you're a
goner, you know. Where is it?

MOTHER COURAGE (*urgently*): Of course he'd give it
over rather than be a goner. Right out he'd say: I
got it, here it is, you're too strong. He ain't all that
stupid. Speak up, stupid idiot, here's the sergeant
giving you a chance.

SWISS CHEESE: S'pose I ain't got it.

SERGEANT: Then come along. We'll get it out of you.
(*They lead him off.*)

MOTHER COURAGE (*calls after them*): He'd tell you.
He's not that stupid. And don't you twist his
shoulder! (*Runs after them.*)

(*Evening of the same day. The chaplain and dumb
Kattrin are cleaning glasses and polishing knives.*)

THE CHAPLAIN: Cases like that, where somebody gets
caught, are not unknown in religious history. It reminds me of the Passion of Our Lord and Saviour.
There's an old song about that. (*He sings the Song
of the Hours.°*)

> In the first hour Jesus mild
> Who had prayed since even
> Was betrayed and led before
> Pontius the heathen.
>
> Pilate found him innocent
> Free from fault and error
> Therefore, having washed his hands
> Sent him to King Herod.
>
> In the third hour he was scourged
> Stripped and clad in scarlet
> And a plaited crown of thorns
> Set upon his forehead.
>
> On the Son of Man they spat
> Mocked him and made merry.
> Then the cross of death was brought
> Given him to carry.
>
> At the sixth hour with two thieves
> To the cross they nailed him
> And the people and the thieves
> Mocked him and reviled him.
>
> This is Jesus King of Jews
> Cried they in derision

Song of Hours: Translated by Ralph Manheim.

Till the sun withdrew its light
From that awful vision.

At the ninth hour Jesus wailed
Why hast thou me forsaken?
Soldiers brought him vinegar
Which he left untaken.

Then he yielded up the ghost
And the earth was shaken.
Rended was the temple's veil
And the saints were wakened.

Soldiers broke the two thieves' legs
As the night descended.
Thrust a spear in Jesus' side
When his life had ended.

Still they mocked, as from his wound
Flowed the blood and water
And blasphemed the Son of Man
With their cruel laughter.

MOTHER COURAGE (*entering excitedly*): It's touch and go. They say sergeant's open to reason though. Only we mustn't let on it's Swiss Cheese else they'll say we helped him. It's a matter of money, that's all. But where's money to come from? Hasn't Yvette been round? I ran into her, she's got her hooks on some colonel, maybe he'd buy her a canteen business.

THE CHAPLAIN: Do you really wish to sell?

MOTHER COURAGE: Where's money for sergeant to come from?

THE CHAPLAIN: What'll you live on, then?

MOTHER COURAGE: That's just it.

(*Yvette Pottier arrives with an extremely ancient colonel.*)

YVETTE (*embracing Mother Courage*): My dear Courage, fancy seeing you so soon. (*Whispers.*) He's not unwilling. (*Aloud.*) This is my good friend who advises me in business matters. I happened to hear you wanted to sell your cart on account of circumstances. I'll think it over.

MOTHER COURAGE: Pledge it, not sell, just not too much hurry, tain't every day you find a cart like this in wartime.

YVETTE (*disappointed*): Oh, pledge. I thought it was for sale. I'm not so sure I'm interested. (*To the colonel.*) How do you feel about it?

THE COLONEL: Just as you feel, pet.

MOTHER COURAGE: I'm only pledging it.

YVETTE: I thought you'd got to have the money.

MOTHER COURAGE (*firmly*): I got to have it, but sooner run myself ragged looking for a bidder than sell outright. And why? The cart's our livelihood. It's a chance for you, Yvette; who knows when you'll get another like it and have a special friend to advise you, am I right?

YVETTE: Yes, my friend thinks I should clinch it, but I'm not sure. If it's only a pledge . . . so you agree we ought to buy outright?

THE COLONEL: I agree, pet.

MOTHER COURAGE: Best look and see if you can find anything for sale then; maybe you will if you don't rush it, take your friend along with you, say a week or fortnight, might find something suits you.

YVETTE: Then let's go looking. I adore going around looking for things, I adore going around with you, Poldi, it's such fun, isn't it? No matter if it takes a fortnight. How soon would you pay the money back if you got it?

MOTHER COURAGE: I'd pay back in two weeks, maybe one.

YVETTE: I can't make up my mind, Poldi chéri, you advise me. (*Takes the colonel aside.*) She's got to sell, I know, no problem there. And there's that ensign, you know, the fair-haired one, he'd be glad to lend me the money. He's crazy about me, says there's someone I remind him of. What do you advise?

THE COLONEL: You steer clear of him. He's no good. He's only making use of you. I said I'd buy you something, didn't I, pussykins?

YVETTE: I oughtn't to let you. Of course if you think the ensign might try to take advantage . . . Poldi, I'll accept it from you.

THE COLONEL: That's how I feel too.

YVETTE: Is that your advice?

THE COLONEL: That is my advice.

YVETTE (*to Courage once more*): My friend's advice would be to accept. Make me out a receipt saying the cart's mine once two weeks are up, with all its contents, we'll check it now, I'll bring the two hundred florins later. (*To the colonel.*) You go back to the camp, I'll follow, I got to check it all and see there's nothing missing from my cart. (*She kisses him. He leaves. She climbs up on the cart.*) Not all that many boots, are there?

MOTHER COURAGE: Yvette, it's no time for checking your cart, s'posing it is yours. You promised you'd talk to sergeant about Swiss Cheese, there ain't a minute to lose, they say in an hour he'll be court-martialled.

YVETTE: Just let me count the shirts.

MOTHER COURAGE (*pulling her down by the skirt*): You bloody vampire. Swiss Cheese's life's at stake. And not a word about who's making the offer, for God's sake, pretend it's your friend, else we're all done for cause we looked after him.

YVETTE: I fixed to meet that one-eyed fellow in the copse, he should be there by now.

THE CHAPLAIN: It doesn't have to be the whole two hundred either, I'd go up to a hundred and fifty, that may be enough.

MOTHER COURAGE: Since when has it been your money? You kindly keep out of this. You'll get your hotpot all right, don't worry. Hurry up and don't haggle, it's life or death. (*Pushes Yvette off.*)

THE CHAPLAIN: Far be it from me to interfere, but what are we going to live on? You're saddled with a daughter who can't earn her keep.

MOTHER COURAGE: I'm counting on regimental cash box, Mr. Clever. They'll allow it as his expenses.

THE CHAPLAIN: But will she get the message right?

MOTHER COURAGE: It's her interest I should spend her two hundred so she gets the cart. She's set on that, God knows how long that colonel of hers'll last. Kattrin, polish the knives, there's the pumice. And you, stop hanging round like Jesus on Mount of Olives,° get moving, wash them glasses, we'll have fifty or more of cavalry in tonight and I don't want to hear a lot of "I'm not accustomed to having to run about, oh my poor feet, we never ran in church." Thank the Lord they're corruptible. After all, they ain't wolves, just humans out for money. Corruption in humans is same as compassion in God. Corruption's our only hope. Long as we have it there'll be lenient sentences and even an innocent man'll have a chance of being let off.

YVETTE (*comes in panting*): They'll do it for two hundred. But it's got to be quick. Soon be out of their hands. Best thing is I go right away to my colonel with the one-eyed man. He's admitted he had the box, they put the thumbscrews on him. But he chucked it in the river soon as he saw they were on his track. The box is a write-off. I'll go and get the money from my colonel, shall I?

MOTHER COURAGE: Box is a write-off? How'm I to pay back two hundred then?

YVETTE: Oh, you thought you'd get it from the box, did you? And I was to be Joe Soap I suppose? Better not count on that. You'll have to pay up if you want Swiss Cheese back, or would you sooner I dropped the whole thing so's you can keep your cart?

MOTHER COURAGE: That's something I didn't allow for. Don't worry, you'll get your cart, I've said goodbye to it, had it seventeen years, I have. I just need a moment to think, it's bit sudden, what'm I

Jesus on Mount of Olives: The bible shows Jesus on the Mount of Olives when he preaches the Sermon on the Mount and when he prays in anguish before his betrayal by Peter.

to do, two hundred's too much for me, pity you didn't beat 'em down. Must keep a bit back, else any Tom, Dick and Harry'll be able to shove me in ditch. Go and tell them I'll pay hundred and twenty florins, else it's all off, either way I'm losing me cart.

YVETTE: They won't do it. That one-eyed man's impatient already, keeps looking over his shoulder, he's so worked up. Hadn't I best pay them the whole two hundred?

MOTHER COURAGE (*in despair*): I can't pay that. Thirty years I been working. She's twenty-five already, and no husband. I got her to think of too. Don't push me, I know what I'm doing. Say a hundred and twenty, or it's off.

YVETTE: It's up to you. (*Rushes off.*)

(*Without looking at either the chaplain or her daughter, Mother Courage sits down to help Kattrin polish knives.*)

MOTHER COURAGE: Don't smash them glasses, they ain't ours now. Watch what you're doing, you'll cut yourself. Swiss Cheese'll be back, I'll pay two hundred if it comes to the pinch. You'll get your brother, love. For eighty florins we could fill a pack with goods and start again. Plenty of folk has to make do.

THE CHAPLAIN: The Lord will provide, it says.

MOTHER COURAGE: See they're properly dry. (*She cleans knives in silence. Kattrin suddenly runs behind the cart, sobbing.*)

YVETTE (*comes running in*): They won't do it. I told you so. The one-eyed man wanted to leave right away, said there was no point. He says he's just waiting for the drum-roll; that means sentence has been pronounced. I offered a hundred and fifty. He didn't even blink. I had to convince him to stay there so's I could have another word with you.

MOTHER COURAGE: Tell him I'll pay the two hundred. Hurry! (*Yvette runs off. They sit in silence. The chaplain has stopped polishing the glasses.*) I reckon I bargained too long.

(*In the distance drumming is heard. The chaplain gets up and goes to the rear. Mother Courage remains seated. It grows dark. The drumming stops. It grows light once more. Mother Courage is sitting exactly as before.*)

YVETTE (*arrives, very pale*): Well, you got what you asked for, with your haggling and trying to keep your cart. Eleven bullets they gave him, that's all. You don't deserve I should bother any more about you. But I did hear they don't believe the box really is in the river. They've an idea it's here and anyhow that you're connected with him. They're going to bring him here, see if you gives yourself away when you sees him. Thought I'd better warn you so's you don't recognise him, else you'll all be for it. They're right on my heels, best tell you quick. Shall I keep Kattrin away? (*Mother Courage shakes her head.*) Does she know? She mayn't have heard the drumming or know what it meant.

MOTHER COURAGE: She knows. Get her.

(*Yvette fetches Kattrin, who goes to her mother and stands beside her. Mother Courage takes her hand. Two lansequenets come carrying a stretcher with something lying on it covered by a sheet. The sergeant marches beside them. They set down the stretcher.*)

SERGEANT: Here's somebody we dunno the name of. It's got to be listed, though, so everything's shipshape. He had a meal here. Have a look, see if you know him. (*He removes the sheet.*) Know him? (*Mother Courage shakes her head.*) What, never see him before he had that meal here? (*Mother Courage shakes her head.*) Pick him up. Chuck him in the pit. He's got nobody knows him. (*They carry him away.*)

SCENE 4

(*Mother Courage sings the Song of the Grand Capitulation.*)
(*Outside an officer's tent.*)
(*Mother Courage is waiting. A clerk looks out of the tent.*)

THE CLERK: I know you. You had a paymaster from the Lutherans with you, what was in hiding. I'd not complain if I were you.

MOTHER COURAGE: But I got a complaint to make. I'm innocent, would look as how I'd a bad conscience if I let this pass. Slashed everything in me cart to pieces with their sabres, they did, then wanted I should pay five taler fine for nowt, I tell you, nowt.

CLERK: Take my tip, better shut up. We're short of canteens, so we let you go on trading, specially if you got a bad conscience and pay a fine now and then.

MOTHER COURAGE: I got a complaint.

CLERK: Have it your own way. Then you must wait till the captain's free. (*Withdraws inside the tent.*)

YOUNG SOLDIER (*enters aggressively*): Bouque la Madonne! Where's that bleeding pig of a captain what's took my reward money to swig with his tarts? I'll do him.

OLDER SOLDIER (*running after him*): Shut up. They'll put you in irons.

YOUNG SOLDIER: Out of there, you thief! I'll slice you into pork chops, I will. Pocketing my prize money after I'd swum the river, only one in the whole squadron, and now I can't even buy meself a beer. I'm not standing for that. Come on out there so I can cut you up!

OLDER SOLDIER: Blessed Mother of God, he's asking for trouble.

MOTHER COURAGE: Is it some reward he weren't paid?

YOUNG SOLDIER: Lemme go, I'll slash you too while I'm at it.

OLDER SOLDIER: He rescued the colonel's horse and got no reward for it. He's young yet, still wet behind the ears.

MOTHER COURAGE: Let him go, he ain't a dog you got to chain up. Wanting your reward is good sound sense. Why be a hero otherwise?

YOUNG SOLDIER: So's he can sit in there and booze. You're shit-scared, the lot of you. I done something special and I want my reward.

MOTHER COURAGE: Don't you shout at me, young fellow. Got me own worries, I have; any road you should spare your voice, be needing it when captain comes, else there'll be and you too hoarse to make a sound, which'll make it hard for him to clap you in irons till you turn blue. People what shouts like that can't keep it up ever; half an hour, and they have to be rocked to sleep, they're so tired.

YOUNG SOLDIER: I ain't tired and to hell with sleep. I'm hungry. They make our bread from acorns and hemp-seed, and they even skimp on that. He's whoring away my reward and I'm hungry. I'll do him.

MOTHER COURAGE: Oh I see, you're hungry. Last year that general of yours ordered you all off roads and across fields so corn should be trampled flat; I could've got ten florins for a pair of boots s'pose I'd had boots and s'pose anyone'd been able to pay ten florins. Thought he'd be well away from that area this year, he did, but here he is, still there, and hunger is great. I see what you're angry about.

YOUNG SOLDIER: I won't have it, don't talk to me, it ain't fair and I'm not standing for that.

MOTHER COURAGE: And you're right; but how long? How long you not standing for unfairness? One hour, two hours? Didn't ask yourself that, did you, but it's the whole point, and why, once you're in irons it's too bad if you suddenly finds you can put up with unfairness after all.

YOUNG SOLDIER: What am I listening to you for, I'd like to know? Bouque la Madonne, where's that captain?

MOTHER COURAGE: You been listening to me because you knows it's like what I say, your anger has gone up in smoke already, it was just a short one and you needed a long one, but where you going to get it from?

YOUNG SOLDIER: Are you trying to tell me asking for my reward is wrong?

MOTHER COURAGE: Not a bit. I'm just telling you your anger ain't long enough, it's good for nowt, pity. If you'd a long one I'd be trying to prod you on. Cut him up, the swine, would be my advice to you in that case; but how about if you don't cut him up cause you feels your tail going between your legs? Then I'd look silly and captain'd take it out on me.

OLDER SOLDIER: You're perfectly right, he's just a bit crazy.

YOUNG SOLDIER: Very well, let's see if I don't cut him up. (*Draws his sword.*) When he arrives I'm going to cut him up.

CLERK (*looks out*): The captain'll be here in one minute. Sit down.

(*The young soldier sits down.*)

MOTHER COURAGE: He's sitting now. See, what did I say? You're sitting now. Ah, how well they know us, no one need tell 'em how to go about it. Sit down! and, bingo, we're sitting. And sitting and sedition don't mix. Don't try to stand up, you won't stand the way you was standing before. I shouldn't worry about what I think; I'm no better, not one moment. Bought up all our fighting spirit, they have. Eh? S'pose I kick back, might be bad for business. Let me tell you a thing or two about the Grand Capitulation. (*She sings the Song of the Grand Capitulation.*)

Back when I was young, I was brought to realise
What a very special person I must be
(Not just any old cottager's daughter, what with
    my looks and my talents and my urge towards
    Higher Things)
And insisted that my soup should have no hairs
    in it.
No one makes a sucker out of me!
(All or nothing, only the best is good enough, each
    man for himself, nobody's telling *me* what
    to do.)
Then I heard a tit
Chirp: Wait a bit!
    And you'll be marching with the band
    In step, responding to command
    And striking up your little dance:
    Now we advance.
    And now: parade, form square!

Then men swear God's there —
Not the faintest chance!

In no time at all anyone who looked could see
That I'd learned to take my medicine with good
    grace.
(Two kids on my hands and look at the price of
    bread, and things they expect of you!)
When they finally came to feel that they were
    through with me
They'd got me grovelling on my face.
(Takes all sorts to make a world, you scratch my
    back and I'll scratch yours, no good banging
    your head against a brick wall.)
Then I heard that tit
Chirp: Wait a bit!
    And you'll be marching with the band
    In step, responding to command
    And striking up your little dance:
    Now they advance.
    And now: parade, form square!
Then men swear God's there —
Not the faintest chance!

I've known people tried to storm the summits:
There's no star too bright or seems too far away.
(Dogged does it, where there's a will there's a way,
    by hook or by crook.)
As each peak disclosed fresh peaks to come, it's
Strange how much a plain straw hat could weigh.
(You have to cut your coat according to your
    cloth.)
Then I hear the tit
Chirp: Wait a bit!
    And they'll be marching with the band
    In step, responding to command
    And striking up their little dance:
    Now they advance.
    And now: parade, form square!
Then men swear God's there —
Not the faintest chance!

MOTHER COURAGE (*to the young soldier*): That's why I reckon you should stay there with your sword drawn if you're truly set on it and your anger's big enough, because you got grounds, I agree, but if your anger's a short one best leave right away.

YOUNG SOLDIER: Oh stuff it. (*He staggers off with the older soldier following.*)

CLERK (*sticks his head out*): Captain's here now. You can make your complaint.

MOTHER COURAGE: I changed me mind. I ain't complaining.

(*Exit.*)

SCENE 5

(*Two years have gone by. The war is spreading to new areas. Ceaselessly on the move, Courage's little cart crosses Poland, Moravia, Bavaria, Italy then Bavaria again. 1631. Tilly's victory at Magdeburg costs Mother Courage four officers' shirts.*)

(*Mother Courage's cart has stopped in a badly shot-up village. Thin military music in the distance. Two soldiers at the bar being served by Kattrin and Mother Courage. One of them has a lady's fur coat over his shoulders.*)

MOTHER COURAGE: Can't pay, that it? No money, no schnapps. They give us victory parades, but catch them giving men their pay.

SOLDIER: I want my schnapps. I missed the looting. That double-crossing general only allowed an hour's looting in the town. He ain't an inhuman monster, he said. Town must of paid him.

THE CHAPLAIN (*stumbles in*): There are people still lying in that yard. The peasant's family. Somebody give me a hand. I need linen.

(*The second soldier goes off with him. Kattrin becomes very excited and tries to make her mother produce linen.*)

MOTHER COURAGE: I got none. All my bandages was sold to regiment. I ain't tearing up my officer's shirts for that lot.

CHAPLAIN (*calling back*): I need linen, I tell you.

MOTHER COURAGE (*blocking Kattrin's way into the cart by sitting on the step*): I'm giving nowt. They'll never pay, and why, nowt to pay with.

CHAPLAIN (*bending over a woman he has carried in*): Why d'you stay around during the gunfire?

PEASANT WOMAN (*feebly*): Farm.

MOTHER COURAGE: Catch them abandoning anything. But now I'm s'posed to foot the bill. I won't do it.

FIRST SOLDIER: Those are Protestants. What they have to be Protestants for?

MOTHER COURAGE: They ain't bothering about faith. They lost their farm.

SECOND SOLDIER: They're no Protestants. They're Catholics like us.

FIRST SOLDIER: No way of sorting 'em out in a bombardment.

A PEASANT (*brought in by the chaplain*): My arm's gone.

THE CHAPLAIN: Where's that linen?

MOTHER COURAGE: I can't give nowt. What with expenses, taxes, loan interest and bribes. (*Making guttural noises, Kattrin raises a plank and threatens her mother with it.*) You gone plain crazy? Put that plank away or I'll paste you one, you cow. I'm giving nowt, don't want to, got to think of meself. (*The chaplain lifts her off the steps and sets her on the ground, then starts pulling out shirts and tearing them into strips.*) My officers' shirts! Half a florin apiece! I'm ruined. (*From the house comes the cry of a child in pain.*)

THE PEASANT: The baby's in there still. (*Kattrin dashes in.*)

THE CHAPLAIN (*to the woman*): Don't move. They'll get it out.

MOTHER COURAGE: Stop her, roof may fall in.

THE CHAPLAIN: I'm not going back in there.

MOTHER COURAGE (*torn both ways*): Don't waste my precious linen.

(*Kattrin brings a baby out of the ruins.*)

MOTHER COURAGE: How nice, found another baby to cart around? Give it to its ma this instant, unless you'd have me fighting for hours to get it off you, like last time, d'you hear? (*To the second soldier.*) Don't stand there gawping, you go back and tell them cut out that music, we can see it's a victory with our own eyes. All your victories mean to me is losses.

THE CHAPLAIN (*tying a bandage*): Blood's coming through.

(*Kattrin is rocking the baby and making lullaby noises.*)

MOTHER COURAGE: Look at her, happy as a queen in all this misery; give it back at once, its mother's coming round. (*She catches the first soldier, who has been attacking the drinks and is trying to make off with one of the bottles.*) Psia krew! Thought you'd score another victory, you animal? Now pay.

FIRST SOLDIER: I got nowt.

MOTHER COURAGE (*pulling the fur coat off his back*): Then leave that coat, it's stolen any road.

THE CHAPLAIN: There's still someone under there.

SCENE 6

(*Outside the Bavarian town of Ingolstadt Courage participates in the funeral of the late Imperial commander Tilly. Discussions are held about war heroes and the war's duration. The chaplain complains that his talents are lying fallow, and dumb Kattrin gets the red boots. The year is 1632.*)

(*Inside a canteen tent.*)

(*It has a bar towards the rear. Rain. Sound of drums and Funeral music. The chaplain and the regimental clerk are playing a board game. Mother Courage and her daughter are stocktaking.*)

THE CHAPLAIN: Now the funeral procession will be moving off.

MOTHER COURAGE: Too bad about commander in chief — twenty-two pairs those socks — he fell by accident, they say. Mist over fields, that was the trouble. General had just been haranguing a regiment saying they must fight to last man and last round, he was riding back when mist made him lose direction so he was up front and a bullet got him in midst of battle — only four hurricane lamps left. (*A whistle from the rear. She goes to the bar.*) You scrimshankers, dodging your commander in chief's funeral, scandal I call it. (*Pours drinks.*)

THE CLERK: They should never of paid troops out before the funeral. Instead of going now they're all getting pissed.

THE CHAPLAIN (*to the clerk*): Aren't you supposed to go to the funeral?

THE CLERK: Dodged it cause of the rain.

MOTHER COURAGE: It's different with you, your uniform might get wet. I heard they wanted to toll bells for funeral as usual, except it turned out all churches had been blown to smithereens by his orders, so poor old commander in chief won't be hearing no bells as they let the coffin down. They're going to let off three salvoes instead to cheer things up — seventeen belts.

SHOUTS (*from the bar*): Hey, Missis, a brandy!

MOTHER COURAGE: Let's see your money. No, I ain't having you in my tent with your disgusting boots. You can drink outside, rain or no rain. (*To the clerk.*) I'm only letting in sergeants and up. Commander in chief had been having his worries, they say. S'posed to have been trouble with Second Regiment cause he stopped their pay, said it was a war of faith and they should do it for free. (*Funeral march. All look to the rear.*)

THE CHAPLAIN: Now they'll be filing past the noble corpse.

MOTHER COURAGE: Can't help feeling sorry for those generals and emperors, there they are maybe thinking they're doing something extra special what folk'll talk about in years to come, and earning a public monument, like conquering the world for instance, that's a fine ambition for a general, how's he to know any better? I mean, he plagues hisself to death, then it all breaks down on account of ordinary folk what just wants their beer and bit of a chat, nowt higher. Finest plans get bollocksed up by the pettiness of them as should be carrying them out, because emperors can't do nowt themselves, they just counts on soldiers and people to back 'em up whatever happens, am I right?

THE CHAPLAIN (*laughs*): Courage, you're right, aside from the soldiers. They do their best. Give me that lot outside there, for instance, drinking their brandy in the rain, and I'd guarantee to make you one war after another for a hundred years if need be, and I'm no trained general.

MOTHER COURAGE: You don't think war might end, then?

THE CHAPLAIN: What, because the commander in chief's gone? Don't be childish. They're two a penny, no shortage of heroes.

MOTHER COURAGE: Ee, I'm not asking for fun of it, but because I'm thinking whether to stock up, prices are low now, but if war's going to end it's money down the drain.

THE CHAPLAIN: I realise it's a serious question. There've always been people going round saying "the war can't go on for ever." I tell you there's nothing to stop it going on for ever. Of course there can be a bit of a breathing space. The war may need to get its second wind, it may even have an accident so to speak. There's no guarantee against that; nothing's perfect on this earth of ours. A perfect war, the sort you might say couldn't be improved on, that's something we shall probably never see. It can suddenly come to a standstill for some quite unforeseen reason, you can't allow for everything. A slight case of negligence, and it's bogged down up to the axles. And then it's a matter of hauling the war out of the mud again. But emperor and kings and popes will come to its rescue. So on the whole it has nothing serious to worry about, and will live to a ripe old age.

A SOLDIER (*sings at the bar*):

A schnapps, landlord, you're late!
A soldier cannot wait
To do his emperor's orders.

Make it a double, this is a holiday.

MOTHER COURAGE: S'pose I went by what you say . . .

THE CHAPLAIN: Think it out for yourself. What's to compete with the war?

THE SOLDIER (*at the rear*):

Your breast, my girl, you're late!
A soldier cannot wait
To ride across the borders.

THE CLERK (*unexpectedly*): And what about peace? I'm from Bohemia and I'd like to go home some day.

THE CHAPLAIN: Would you indeed? Ah, peace. Where is the hole once the cheese has been eaten?

THE SOLDIER (*at the rear*):

Lead trumps, my friend, you're late!
A soldier cannot wait.
His emperor needs him badly.

Your blessing, priest, you're late!
A soldier cannot wait.
Must lay his life down gladly.

THE CLERK: In the long run lifes impossible if there's no peace.
THE CHAPLAIN: I'd say there's peace in war too; it has its peaceful moments. Because war satisfies all requirements, peaceable ones included, they're catered for, and it would simply fizzle out if they weren't. In war you can do a crap like in the depths of peacetime, then between one battle and the next you can have a beer, then even when you're moving up you can lay your head on your arms and have a bit of shuteye in the ditch, it's entirely possible. During a charge you can't play cards maybe, but nor can you in the depths of peacetime when you're ploughing, and after a victory there are various openings. You may get a leg blown off, then you start by making a lot of fuss as though it were serious, but afterwards you calm down or get given a schnapps, and you end up hopping around and the war's no worse off than before. And what's to stop you being fruitful and multiplying in the middle of all the butchery, behind a barn or something, in the long run you can't be held back from it, and then the war will have your progeny and can use them to carry on with. No, the war will always find an outlet, mark my words. Why should it ever stop?

(*Kattrin has ceased working and is staring at the chaplain.*)

MOTHER COURAGE: I'll buy fresh stock then. If you say so. (*Kattrin suddenly flings a basket full of bottles to the ground and runs off.*) Kattrin! (*Laughs.*) Damn me if she weren't waiting for peace. I promised her she'd get a husband soon as peace came. (*Hurries after her.*)
THE CLERK (*standing up*): I won. You been talking too much. Pay up.
MOTHER COURAGE (*returning with Kattrin*): Don't be silly, war'll go on a bit longer, and we'll make a bit more money, and peacetime'll be all the nicer for it. Now you go into town, that's ten minutes' walk at most, fetch things from Golden Lion, the expensive ones, we can fetch rest in cart later, it's all arranged, regimental clerk here will go with you. Nearly everybody's attending commander in chief's funeral, nowt can happen to you. Careful now, don't let them steal nowt, think of your dowry.

(*Kattrin puts a cloth over her head and leaves with the clerk.*)

THE CHAPLAIN: Is that all right to let her go with the clerk?
MOTHER COURAGE: She's not that pretty they'd want to ruin her.
THE CHAPLAIN: I admire the way you run your business and always win through. I see why they called you Courage.
MOTHER COURAGE: Poor folk got to have courage. Why, they're lost. Simply getting up in morning takes some doing in their situation. Or ploughing a field, and in a war at that. Mere fact they bring kids into world shows they got courage, cause there's no hope for them. They have to hang one another and slaughter one another, so just looking each other in face must call for courage. Being able to put up with emperor and pope shows supernatural courage, cause those two cost 'em their lives. (*She sits down, takes a little pipe from her purse and smokes.*) You might chop us a bit of kindling.
THE CHAPLAIN (*reluctantly removing his coat and preparing to chop up sticks*): I happen to be a pastor of souls, not a woodcutter.
MOTHER COURAGE: I got no soul, you see. Need firewood, though.
THE CHAPLAIN: Where's that stumpy pipe from?
MOTHER COURAGE: Just a pipe.
THE CHAPLAIN: What d'you mean, "just," it's a quite particular pipe, that.
MOTHER COURAGE: Aha?
THE CHAPLAIN: That stumpy pipe belongs to the Oxenstierna Regiment's cook.
MOTHER COURAGE: If you know that already why ask, Mr. Clever?
THE CHAPLAIN: Because I didn't know if you were aware what you're smoking. You might just have been rummaging around in your things, come across some old pipe or other, and used it out of sheer absence of mind.
MOTHER COURAGE: And why not?
THE CHAPLAIN: Because you didn't. You're smoking that deliberately.
MOTHER COURAGE: And why shouldn't I?
THE CHAPLAIN: Courage, I'm warning you. It's my duty. Probably you'll never clap eyes on the gentleman again, and that's no loss but your good fortune. He didn't make at all a reliable impression on me. Quite the opposite.
MOTHER COURAGE: Really? Nice fellow that.
THE CHAPLAIN: So he's what you would call a nice fellow? I wouldn't. Far be it from me to bear him the least ill-will, but nice is not what I would call him.

More like one of those Don Juans, a slippery one. Have a look at that pipe if you don't believe me. You must admit it tells you a good deal about his character.

MOTHER COURAGE: Nowt that I can see. Worn out, I'd call it.

THE CHAPLAIN: Practically bitten through, you mean. A man of wrath. That is the pipe of an unscrupulous man of wrath; you must see that if you have any discrimination left.

MOTHER COURAGE: Don't chop my chopping block in two.

THE CHAPLAIN: I told you I'm not a woodcutter by trade. I studied to be a pastor of souls. My talent and abilities are being abused in this place, by manual labour. My God-given endowments are denied expression. It's a sin. You have never heard me preach. One sermon of mine can put a regiment in such a frame of mind it'll treat the enemy like a flock of sheep. Life to them is a smelly old foot cloth which they fling away in a vision of final victory. God has given me the gift of speech. I can preach so you'll lose all sense of sight and hearing.

MOTHER COURAGE: I don't wish to lose my sense of sight and hearing. Where'd that leave me?

THE CHAPLAIN: Courage, I have often thought that your dry way of talking conceals more than just a warm heart. You too are human and need warmth.

MOTHER COURAGE: Best way for us to get this tent warm is have plenty of firewood.

THE CHAPLAIN: Don't change the subject. Seriously, Courage, I sometimes ask myself what it would be like if our relationship were to become somewhat closer. I mean, given that the whirlwind of war has so strangely whirled us together.

MOTHER COURAGE: I'd say it was close enough. I cook meals for you and you run around and chop firewood for instance.

THE CHAPLAIN (coming closer): You know what I mean by closer; it's not a relationship founded on meals and wood-chopping and other such base necessities. Let your head speak, harden thyself not.

MOTHER COURAGE: Don't you come at me with that axe. That'd be too close a relationship.

THE CHAPLAIN: You shouldn't make a joke of it. I'm a serious person and I've thought about what I'm saying.

MOTHER COURAGE: Be sensible, padre. I like you. I don't want to row you. All I'm after is get myself and children through all this with my cart. I don't see it as mine, and I ain't in the mood for private affairs. Right now I'm taking a gamble, buying stores just when commander in chief's fallen and all the talk's of peace. Where d'you reckon you'd turn if I'm ruined? Don't know, do you? You chop us some

kindling wood, then we can keep warm at night, that's quite something these times. What's this? (She gets up. Enter Kattrin, out of breath, with a wound above her eye. She is carrying a variety of stuff: parcels, leather goods, a drum and so on.)

MOTHER COURAGE: What happened, someone assault you? On way back? She was assaulted on her way back. Bet it was that trooper was getting drunk here. I shouldn't have let you go, love. Drop that stuff. Not too bad, just a flesh wound you got. I'll bandage it and in a week it'll be all right. Worse than wild beasts, they are. (She ties up the wound.)

THE CHAPLAIN: It's not them I blame. They never went raping back home. The fault lies with those that start wars, it brings humanity's lowest instincts to the surface.

MOTHER COURAGE: Calm down. Didn't clerk come back with you? That's because you're respectable, they don't bother. Wound ain't a deep one, won't leave no mark. There you are, all bandaged up. You'll get something, love, keep calm. Something I put aside for you, wait till you see. (She delves into a sack and brings out Yvette's red high-heeled boots.) Made you open your eyes, eh? Something you always wanted. They're yours. Put 'em on quick, before I change me mind. Won't leave no mark, and what if it does? Ones I'm really sorry for's the ones they fancy. Drag them around till they're worn out, they do. Those they don't care for they leaves alive. I seen girls before now had pretty faces, then in no time looking fit to frighten a hyaena. Can't even go behind a bush without risking trouble, horrible life they lead. Same like with trees, straight well-shaped ones get chopped down to make beams for houses and crooked ones live happily ever after. So it's a stroke of luck for you really. Them boots'll be all right, I greased them before putting them away.

(Kattrin leaves the boots where they are and crawls into the cart.)

THE CHAPLAIN: Let's hope she's not disfigured.

MOTHER COURAGE: She'll have a scar. No use her waiting for peacetime now.

THE CHAPLAIN: She didn't let them steal the things.

MOTHER COURAGE: Maybe I shouldn't have dinned that into her so. Wish I knew what went on in that head of hers. Just once she stayed out all night, once in all those years. Afterwards she went around like before, except she worked harder. Couldn't get her to tell what had happened. Worried me quite a while, that did. (She collects the articles brought by Kattrin, and sorts them angrily.) That's war for you. Nice way to get a living!

(*Sound of cannon fire.*)

THE CHAPLAIN: Now they'll be burying the commander in chief. This is a historic moment.

MOTHER COURAGE: What I call a historic moment is them bashing my daughter over the eye. She's half wrecked already, won't get no husband now, and her so crazy about kids; anyway, she's only dumb from war, soldier stuffed something in her mouth when she was little. As for Swiss Cheese I'll never see him again, and where Eilif is God alone knows. War be damned.

SCENE 7

(*Mother Courage at the peak of her business career.*)
(*High road.*)
(*The chaplain, Mother Courage, and Kattrin are pulling the cart, which is hung with new wares. Mother Courage is wearing a necklace of silver coins.*)

MOTHER COURAGE: I won't have you folk spoiling my war for me. I'm told it kills off the weak, but they're write-off in peacetime too. And war gives its people a better deal. (*She sings.*)

> And if you feel your forces fading
> You won't be there to share the fruits.
> But what is war but private trading
> That deals in blood instead of boots?

And what's the use of settling down? Them as does are first to go. (*Sings.*)

> Some people think to live by looting
> The goods some others haven't got.
> You think it's just a line they're shooting
> Until you hear they have been shot.

> And some I saw dig six feet under
> In haste to lie down and pass out.
> Now they're at rest perhaps they wonder
> Just what was all their haste about.

(*They pull it further.*)

SCENE 8

(*The same year sees the death of the Swedish king Gustavus Adolphus at the battle of Lützen. Peace threatens to ruin Mother Courage's business. Courage's dashing son performs one heroic deed too many and comes to a sticky end.*)
(*Camp.*)

(*A summer morning. In front of the cart stand an old woman and her son. The son carries a large sack of bedding.*)

MOTHER COURAGE'S VOICE (*from inside the cart*): Does it need to be this ungodly hour?

THE YOUNG MAN: We walked twenty miles in the night and got to be back today.

MOTHER COURAGE'S VOICE: What am I to do with bedding? Folk've got no houses.

THE YOUNG MAN: Best have a look first.

THE OLD WOMAN: This place is no good either. Come on.

THE YOUNG MAN: What, and have them sell the roof over our head for taxes? She might pay three florins if you throw in the bracelet. (*Bells start ringing.*) Listen, mother.

VOICES (*from the rear*): Peace! Swedish king's been killed.

MOTHER COURAGE (*Sticks her head out of the cart. She has not yet done her hair.*): What's that bell-ringing about in mid-week?

THE CHAPLAIN (*crawling out from under the cart*): What are they shouting? Peace?

MOTHER COURAGE: Don't tell me peace has broken out just after I laid in new stock.

THE CHAPLAIN (*calling to the rear*): That true? Peace?

VOICES: Three weeks ago, they say, only no one told us.

THE CHAPLAIN (*to Courage*): What else would they be ringing the bells for?

VOICES: A whole lot of Lutherans have driven into town, they brought the news.

THE YOUNG MAN: Mother, it's peace. What's the matter?

(*The old woman has collapsed.*)

MOTHER COURAGE (*speaking into the cart*): Holy cow! Kattrin, peace! Put your black dress on, we're going to church. Least we can do for Swiss Cheese. Is it true, though?

THE YOUNG MAN: The people here say so. They've made peace. Can you get up? (*The old woman stands up dumbfounded.*) I'll get the saddlery going again. I promise. It'll all work out. Father will get his bedding back. Can you walk? (*To the chaplain.*) She came over queer. It's the news. She never thought there'd be peace again. Father always said so. We're going straight home. (*They go off.*)

MOTHER COURAGE'S VOICE: Give her a schnapps.

THE CHAPLAIN: They've already gone.

MOTHER COURAGE'S VOICE: What's up in camp?

THE CHAPLAIN: They're assembling. I'll go on over. Shouldn't I put on my clerical garb?

MOTHER COURAGE'S VOICE: Best check up before parading yourself as heretic. I'm glad about peace, never mind if I'm ruined. Any road I'll have got two of me children through the war. Be seeing Eilif again now.

THE CHAPLAIN: And who's that walking down the lines? Bless me, the army commander's cook.

THE COOK (*somewhat bedraggled and carrying a bundle*): What do I behold? The padre!

THE CHAPLAIN: Courage, we've got company.

(*Mother Courage clambers out.*)

THE COOK: I promised I'd drop over for a little talk soon as I had the time. I've not forgotten your brandy, Mrs. Fierling.

MOTHER COURAGE: Good grief, the general's cook! After all these years! Where's my eldest boy Eilif?

THE COOK: Hasn't he got here? He left before me, he was on his way to see you too.

THE CHAPLAIN: I shall don my clerical garb, just a moment.

(*Goes off behind the cart.*)

MOTHER COURAGE: Then he may be here any minute. (*Calls into the cart.*) Kattrin, Eilif's on his way. Get cook a glass of brandy, Kattrin! (*Kattrin does not appear.*) Drag your hair down over it, that's all right. Mr. Lamb's no stranger. (*Fetches the brandy herself.*) She don't like to come out, peace means nowt to her. Took too long coming, it did. They gave her a crack over one eye, you barely notice it now but she thinks folks are staring at her.

THE COOK: Ah yes. War. (*He and Mother Courage sit down.*)

MOTHER COURAGE: Cooky, you caught me at bad moment. I'm ruined.

THE COOK: What? That's hard.

MOTHER COURAGE: Peace'll wring my neck. I went and took chaplain's advice, laid in fresh stocks only t'other day. And now they're going to demobilise and I'll be left sitting on me wares.

THE COOK: What'd you want to go and listen to padre for? If I hadn't been in such a hurry that time, the Catholics arriving so quickly and all, I'd warned you against that man. All piss and wind, he is. So he's the authority around here, eh?

MOTHER COURAGE: He's been doing washing-up for me and helping pull.

THE COOK: Him pull! I bet he told you some of those jokes of his too, I know him, got a very unhealthy view of women, he has, all my good influence on him went for nowt. He ain't steady.

MOTHER COURAGE: You steady then?

THE COOK: Whatever else I ain't, I'm steady. Mud in your eye!

MOTHER COURAGE: Steady, that's nowt. I only had one steady fellow, thank God. Hardest I ever had to work in me life; he flogged the kids' blankets soon as autumn came, and he called me mouth-organ an unchristian instrument. Ask me, you ain't saying much for yourself admitting you're steady.

THE COOK: Still tough as nails, I see; but that's what I like about you.

MOTHER COURAGE: Now don't tell me you been dreaming of me nails.

THE COOK: Well, well, here we are, along with armistice bells and your brandy like what nobody else ever serves, it's famous, that is.

MOTHER COURAGE: I don't give two pins for your armistice bells just now. Can't see 'em handing out all the back pay what's owing, so where does that leave me with my famous brandy? Had your pay yet?

THE COOK (*hesitantly*): Not exactly. That's why we all shoved off. If that's how it is, I thought, I'll go and visit friends. So here I am sitting with you.

MOTHER COURAGE: Other words you got nowt.

THE COOK: High time they stopped that bloody clanging. Wouldn't mind getting into some sort of trade. I'm fed up being cook to that lot. I'm s'posed to rustle them up meals out of tree roots and old bootsoles, then they fling the hot soup in my face. Cook these days is a dog's life. Sooner do war service, only of course it's peacetime now. (*He sees the chaplain reappearing in his old garments.*) More about that later.

THE CHAPLAIN: It's still all right, only had a few moths in it.

THE COOK: Can't see why you bother. You won't get your old job back, who are you to inspire now to earn his pay honourably and lay down his life? What's more I got a bone to pick with you, cause you advised this lady to buy a lot of unnecessary goods saying war would go on for ever.

THE CHAPLAIN (*heatedly*): I'd like to know what concern that is of yours.

THE COOK: Because it's unscrupulous, that sort of thing is. How dare you meddle in other folks' business arrangements with your unwanted advice?

THE CHAPLAIN: Who's meddling? (*To Courage.*) I never knew this gentleman was such an intimate you had to account to him for everything.

MOTHER COURAGE: Keep your hair on, cook's only giving his personal opinion and you can't deny your war was a flop.

THE CHAPLAIN: You should not blaspheme against peace, Courage. You are a hyaena of the battlefield.

MOTHER COURAGE: I'm what?

THE COOK: If you're going to insult this lady you'll have to settle with me.

THE CHAPLAIN: It's not you I'm talking to. Your intentions are only too transparent. (*To Courage.*) But when I see you picking up peace betwixt your finger and your thumb like some dirty old snot-rag, then my humanity feels outraged; for then I see that you don't want peace but war, because you profit from it; in which case you shouldn't forget the ancient saying that whosoever sups with the devil needs a long spoon.

MOTHER COURAGE: I got no use for war, and war ain't got much use for me. But I'm not being called no hyaena, you and me's through.

THE CHAPLAIN: Then why grumble about peace when everybody's breathing sighs of relief? Because of some old junk in your cart?

MOTHER COURAGE: My goods ain't old junk but what I lives by, and you too up to now.

THE CHAPLAIN: Off war, in other words. Aha.

THE COOK (*to the chaplain*): You're old enough to know it's always a mistake offering advice. (*To Courage.*) Way things are, your best bet's to get rid of certain goods quick as you can before prices hit rock-bottom. Dress yourself and get moving, not a moment to lose.

MOTHER COURAGE: That ain't bad advice. I'll do that, I guess.

THE CHAPLAIN: Because cooky says it.

MOTHER COURAGE: Why couldn't you say it? He's right, I'd best go off to market. (*Goes inside the cart.*)

THE COOK: That's one to me, padre. You got no presence of mind. What you should of said was: what, me offer advice, all I done was discuss politics. Better not take me on. Cockfighting don't suit that get-up.

THE CHAPLAIN: If you don't stop your gob I'll murder you, get-up or no get-up.

THE COOK (*pulling off his boots and unwrapping his footcloths*): Pity the war made such a godless shit of you, else you'd easily get another parsonage now it's peacetime. Cooks won't be needed, there's nowt to cook, but faith goes on just the same, nowt changed in that direction.

THE CHAPLAIN: Mr. Lamb, I'm asking you not to elbow me out. Since I came down in the world I've become a better person. I couldn't preach to anyone now.

(*Enter Yvette Pottier in black, dressed up to the nines, carrying a cane. She is much older and fatter, and heavily powdered. She is followed by a manservant.*)

YVETTE: Hullo there, everybody. Is this Mother Courage's establishment?

THE CHAPLAIN: It is. And with whom have we the honour . . . ?

YVETTE: With the Countess Starhemberg, my good man. Where's Courage?

THE CHAPLAIN (*calls into the cart*): The Countess Starhemberg wishes to speak to you.

MOTHER COURAGE'S VOICE: Just coming.

YVETTE: It's Yvette.

MOTHER COURAGE'S VOICE: Oh, Yvette!

YVETTE: Come to see how you are. (*Sees the cook turn round aghast.*) Pieter!

THE COOK: Yvette!

YVETTE: Well I never! How d'you come to be here?

THE COOK: Got a lift.

THE CHAPLAIN: You know each other then? Intimately?

YVETTE: I should think so. (*She looks the cook over.*) Fat.

THE COOK: Not all that skinny yourself.

YVETTE: All the same I'm glad to see you, you shit. Gives me a chance to say what I think of you.

THE CHAPLAIN: You say it, in full; but don't start till Courage is out here.

MOTHER COURAGE (*coming out with all kinds of goods*): Yvette! (*They embrace.*) But what are you in mourning for?

YVETTE: Suits me, don't it? My husband the colonel died a few years back.

MOTHER COURAGE: That old fellow what nearly bought the cart?

YVETTE: His elder brother.

MOTHER COURAGE: Then you're sitting pretty. Nice to find somebody what's made it in this war.

YVETTE: Up and down and up again, that's the way it went.

MOTHER COURAGE: I'm not hearing a word against colonels, they make a mint of money.

THE CHAPLAIN: I would put my boots back on if I were you. (*To Yvette.*) You promised you would say what you think of the gentleman.

THE COOK: Don't kick up a stink here, Yvette.

MOTHER COURAGE: Yvette, this is a friend of mine.

YVETTE: That's old Puffing Piet.

THE COOK: Let's drop the nicknames. I'm called Lamb.

MOTHER COURAGE (*laughs*): Puffing Piet! Him as made all the women crazy! Here, I been looking after your pipe for you.

THE CHAPLAIN: Smoking it, too.

YVETTE: What luck I can warn you against him. Worst of the lot, he was, rampaging along the whole Flanders coastline. Got more girls in trouble than he has fingers.

THE COOK: That's all a long while ago. Tain't true anyhow.

YVETTE: Stand up when a lady brings you into the conversation! How I loved this man! All the time he had a little dark girl with bandy legs, got her in trouble too of course.

THE COOK: Got you into high society more like, far as I can see.

YVETTE: Shut your trap, you pathetic remnant! Better watch out for him, though; fellows like that are still dangerous even when on their last legs.

MOTHER COURAGE (*to Yvette*): Come along, got to get rid of my stuff afore prices start dropping. You might be able to put a word in for me at regiment, with your connections. (*Calls into the cart.*) Kattrin, church is off, I'm going to market instead. When Eilif turns up, one of you give him a drink. (*Exit with Yvette.*)

YVETTE (*as she leaves*): Fancy a creature like that ever making me leave the straight and narrow path. Thank my lucky stars I managed to reach the top all the same. But I've cooked your goose, Puffing Piet, and that's something that'll be credited to me one day in the world to come.

THE CHAPLAIN: I would like to take as a text for our little talk "The mills of God grind slowly." Weren't you complaining about my jokes?

THE COOK: Dead out of luck, I am. It's like this, you see: I thought I might get a hot meal. Here am I starving, and now they'll be talking about me and she'll get quite a wrong picture. I think I'll clear out before she's back.

THE CHAPLAIN: I think so too.

THE COOK: Padre, I'm fed up already with this bloody peace. Human race has to go through fire and sword cause it's sinful from the cradle up. I wish I could be roasting a fat capon once again for the general, wherever he's got to, in mustard sauce with a carrot or two.

THE CHAPLAIN: Red cabbage. Red cabbage for a capon.

THE COOK: You're right, but carrots was what he had to have.

THE CHAPLAIN: No sense of what's fitting.

THE COOK: Not that it stopped you guzzling your share.

THE CHAPLAIN: With misgivings.

THE COOK: Anyway you must admit those were the days.

THE CHAPLAIN: I might admit it if pressed.

THE COOK: Now you've called her a hyaena your days here are finished. What you staring at?

THE CHAPLAIN: Eilif! (*Eilif arrives, followed by soldiers with pikes. His hands are fettered. His face is chalky-white.*) What's wrong?

EILIF: Where's mother?

THE CHAPLAIN: Gone into town.

EILIF: I heard she was around. They've allowed me to come and see her.

THE COOK (*to the soldiers*): What you doing with him?

A SOLDIER: Something not nice.

THE CHAPLAIN: What's he been up to?

THE SOLDIER: Broke into a peasant's place. The wife's dead.

THE CHAPLAIN: How could you do a thing like that?

EILIF: It's what I did last time, ain't it?

THE COOK: Aye, but it's peace now.

EILIF: Shut up! All right if I sit down till she comes?

THE SOLDIER: We've no time.

THE CHAPLAIN: In wartime they recommended him for that, sat him at the general's right hand. Dashing, it was, in those days. Any chance of a word with the provost-marshal?

THE SOLDIER: Wouldn't do no good. Taking some peasant's cattle, what's dashing about that?

THE COOK: Dumb, I call it.

EILIF: If I'd been dumb you'd of starved, clever bugger.

THE COOK: But as you were clever you're going to be shot.

THE CHAPLAIN: We'd better fetch Kattrin out anyhow.

EILIF: Sooner have a glass of schnapps, could do with that.

THE SOLDIER: No time, come along.

THE CHAPLAIN: And what shall we tell your mother?

EILIF: Tell her it wasn't any different, tell her it was the same thing. Or tell her nowt. (*The soldiers propel him away.*)

THE CHAPLAIN: I'll accompany you on your grievous journey.

EILIF: Don't need any bloody parsons.

THE CHAPLAIN: Wait and see. (*Follows him.*)

THE COOK (*calls after them*): I'll have to tell her, she'll want to see him.

THE CHAPLAIN: I wouldn't tell her anything. At most that he was here and will come again, maybe tomorrow. By then I'll be back and can break it to her. (*Hurries off.*)

(*The cook looks after him, shaking his head, then walks restlessly around. Finally he comes up to the cart.*)

THE COOK: Hoy! Don't you want to come out? I can understand you hiding away from peace. Like to do the same myself. Remember me, I'm general's cook? I was wondering if you'd a bit of something to eat while I wait for your mum. I don't half feel like a bit of pork, or bread even, just to fill the time. (*Peers inside.*) Head under blanket. (*Sound of gunfire off.*)

MOTHER COURAGE (*runs in, out of breath and with all her goods still*): Cooky, peacetime's over. War's been on again three days now. Heard news before selling me stuff, thank God. They're having a shooting match with Lutherans in town. We must get cart away at once. Kattrin, pack up! What you in the dumps for? What's wrong?

THE COOK: Nowt.

MOTHER COURAGE: Something is. I see it way you look.

THE COOK: Cause war's starting up again, I s'pose.

Looks as if it'll be tomorrow night before I get next hot food inside me.

MOTHER COURAGE: You're lying, cooky.

THE COOK: Eilif was here. Had to leave almost at once, though.

MOTHER COURAGE: Was he now? Then we'll be seeing him on the march. I'm joining our side this time. How's he look?

THE COOK: Same as usual.

MOTHER COURAGE: Oh, he'll never change. Take more than war to steal him from me. Clever, he is. You going to help me get packed? (*Begins to pack up.*) What's his news? Still in general's good books? Say anything about his deeds of valour?

THE COOK (*glumly*): Repeated one of them, I'm told.

MOTHER COURAGE: Tell it me later, we got to move off. (*Kattrin appears.*) Kattrin, peacetime's finished now. We're moving on. (*To the cook.*) How about you?

THE COOK: Have to join up again.

MOTHER COURAGE: Why don't you . . . Where's padre?

THE COOK: Went into town with Eilif.

MOTHER COURAGE: Then you come along with us a way. Need somebody to help me.

THE COOK: That business with Yvette, you know . . .

MOTHER COURAGE: Done you no harm in my eyes. Opposite. Where there's smoke there's fire, they say. You coming along?

THE COOK: I won't say no.

MOTHER COURAGE: The Twelfth moved off already. Take the shaft. Here's a bit of bread. We must get round behind to Lutherans. Might even be seeing Eilif tonight. He's my favourite one. Short peace, wasn't it? Now we're off again. (*She sings as the cook and Kattrin harness themselves up.*)

> From Ulm to Metz, from Metz to Munich
> Courage will see the war gets fed.
> The war will show a well-filled tunic
> Given its daily shot of lead.
> But lead alone can hardly nourish
> It must have soldiers to subsist.
> It's you it needs to make it flourish.
> The war's still hungry. So enlist!

SCENE 9

(*It is the seventeenth year of the great war of faith. Germany has lost more than half her inhabitants. Those who survive the bloodbath are killed off by terrible epidemics. Once fertile areas are ravaged by famine, wolves roam the burnt-out towns. In autumn 1634 we find Courage in the Fichtelgebirge, off the main axis of the Swedish armies. The winter this year is early and harsh. Business is bad, so that there is nothing to do but beg. The cook gets a letter from Utrecht and is sent packing.*)

(*Outside a semi-dilapidated parsonage.*)

(*Grey morning in early winter. Gusts of wind. Mother Courage and the cook in shabby sheepskins, drawing the cart.*)

THE COOK: It's all dark, nobody up yet.

MOTHER COURAGE: Except it's parson's house. Have to crawl out of bed to ring bells. Then he'll have hot soup.

THE COOK: What from, when the whole village is burnt? We seen it.

MOTHER COURAGE: It's lived in, though, dog was barking.

THE COOK: S'pose parson's got, he'll give nowt.

MOTHER COURAGE: Maybe if we sing. . . .

THE COOK: I've had enough. (*Abruptly.*) Got a letter from Utrecht saying mother died of cholera and inn's mine. Here's letter if you don't believe me. No business of yours the way aunty goes on about my mode of existence, but have a look.

MOTHER COURAGE: (*Reads the letter.*) Lamb, I'm tired too of always being on the go. I feel like butcher's dog, dragging meat round customers and getting nowt off it. I got nowt left to sell, and folk got nowt left to buy nowt with. Saxony a fellow in rags tried landing me a stack of old books for two eggs, Württemberg they wanted to swap their plough for a titchy bag of salt. What's to plough for? Nowt growing no more, just brambles. In Pomerania villages are s'posed to have started in eating the younger kids, and nuns have been caught sticking folk up.

THE COOK: World's dying out.

MOTHER COURAGE: Sometimes I sees meself driving through hell with me cart selling brimstone, or across heaven with packed lunches for hungry souls. Give me my kids what's left, let's find some place they ain't shooting, and I'd like a few more years undisturbed.

THE COOK: You and me could get that inn going, Courage, think it over. Made up me mind in the night, I did: back to Utrecht with or without you, and starting today.

MOTHER COURAGE: Have to talk to Kattrin. That's a bit quick for me; I'm against making decisions all freezing cold and nowt inside you. Kattrin! (*Kattrin climbs out of the cart.*) Kattrin, got something to tell you. Cook and I want to go to Utrecht. He's been

left an inn there. That'd be a settled place for you,
let you meet a few people. Lots of 'em respect somebody mature, looks ain't everything. I'd like it too. I
get on with cook. Say one thing for him, got a head
for business. We'd have our meals for sure, not bad,
eh? And your own bed too; like that, wouldn't you?
Road's no life really. God knows how you might finish up. Lousy already, you are. Have to make up
our minds, see, we could move with the Swedes, up
north, they're somewhere up that way. (*She points
to the left.*) Reckon that's fixed, Kattrin.

THE COOK: Anna, I got something private to say to
you.

MOTHER COURAGE: Get back in cart, Kattrin.

(*Kattrin climbs back.*)

THE COOK: I had to interrupt, cause you don't understand, far as I can see. I didn't think there was need
to say it, sticks out a mile. But if it don't, then let
me tell you straight, no question of taking her
along, not on your life. You get me, eh.

(*Kattrin sticks her head out of the cart behind them
and listens.*)

MOTHER COURAGE: You mean I'm to leave Kattrin
back here?

THE COOK: Use your imagination. Inn's got no room.
It ain't one of the sort got three bar parlours. Put
our backs in it we two'll get a living, but not three,
no chance of that. She can keep cart.

MOTHER COURAGE: Thought she might find husband
in Utrecht.

THE COOK: Go on, make me laugh. Find a husband,
how? Dumb and that scar on top of it. And at her
age?

MOTHER COURAGE: Don't talk so loud.

THE COOK: Loud or soft, no getting over facts. And
that's another reason why I can't have her in the
inn. Customers don't want to be looking at that all
the time. Can't blame them.

MOTHER COURAGE: Shut your big mouth. I said not
so loud.

THE COOK: Light's on in parson's house. We can try
singing.

MOTHER COURAGE: Cooky, how's she to pull the cart
on her own? War scares her. She'll never stand it.
The dreams she must have . . . I hear her nights
groaning. Mostly after a battle. What's she seeing
in those dreams, I'd like to know. She's got a soft
heart. Lately I found she'd got another hedgehog
tucked away what we'd run over.

THE COOK: Inn's too small. (*Calls out.*) Ladies and
gentlemen, domestic staff and other residents! We
are now going to give you a song concerning

Solomon, Julius Caesar and other famous person-
ages what had bad luck. So's you can see we're respectable folk, which makes it difficult to carry on,
particularly in winter. (*They sing.*)

> You saw sagacious Solomon
> You know what came of him.
> To him complexities seemed plain.
> He cursed the hour that gave birth to him
> And saw that everything was vain.
> How great and wise was Solomon!
> The world however didn't wait
> But soon observed what followed on.
> It's wisdom that had brought him to this
>   state —
> How fortunate the man with none!

Yes, the virtues are dangerous stuff in this world,
as this fine song proves, better not to have them
and have a pleasant life and breakfast instead, hot
soup for instance. Look at me: I haven't any but
I'd like some. I'm a serving soldier but what good
did my courage do me in all them battles, nowt,
here I am starving and better have been shit-scared
and stayed at home. For why?

> You saw courageous Caesar next
> You know what he became.
> They deified him in his life
> Then had him murdered just the same.
> And as they raised the fatal knife
> How loud he cried: You too, my son!
> The world however didn't wait
> But soon observed what followed on.
> It's courage that had brought him to that state.
> How fortunate the man with none!

(*Sotto voce.*) Don't even look out. (*Aloud.*) Ladies
and gentlemen, domestic staff and other inmates!
All right, you may say, gallantry never cooked a
man's dinner, what about trying honesty? You can
eat all you want then, or anyhow not stay sober.
How about it?

> You heard of honest Socrates
> The man who never lied:
> They weren't so grateful as you'd think
> Instead the rulers fixed to have him tried
> And handed him the poisoned drink.
> How honest was the people's noble son!
> The world however didn't wait
> But soon observed what followed on.
> It's honesty that brought him to that state.
> How fortunate the man with none!

Ah yes, they say, be unselfish and share what
you've got, but how about if you got nowt? It's all

very well to say the do-gooders have a hard time, but you still got to have something. Aye, unselfishness is a rare virtue, cause it just don't pay.

> Saint Martin couldn't bear to see
> His fellows in distress.
> He met a poor man in the snow
> And shared his cloak with him, we know.
> Both of them therefore froze to death.
> His place in Heaven was surely won!
> The world however didn't wait
> But soon observed what followed on.
> Unselfishness had brought him to that state.
> How fortunate the man with none!

That's how it is with us. We're respectable folk, stick together, don't steal, don't murder, don't burn places down And all the time you might say we're sinking lower and lower, and it's true what the song says, and soup is few and far between, and if we weren't like this but thieves and murderers I dare say we'd be eating our fill. For virtues aren't their own reward, only wickednesses are, that's how the world goes and it didn't ought to.

> Here you can see respectable folk
> Keeping to God's own laws.
> So far he hasn't taken heed.
> You who sit safe and warm indoors
> Help to relieve our bitter need!
> How virtuously we had begun!
> The world however didn't wait
> But soon observed what followed on.
> It's fear of God that brought us to that state.
> How fortunate the man with none!

VOICE (*from above*): Hey, you there! Come on up! There's hot soup if you want.
MOTHER COURAGE: Lamb, me stomach won't stand nowt. 'Tain't that it ain't sensible, what you say, but is that your last word? We got on all right.
THE COOK: Last word. Think it over.
MOTHER COURAGE: I've nowt to think. I'm not leaving her here.
THE COOK: That's proper senseless, nothing I can do about it though. I'm not a brute, just the inn's a small one. So now we better get on up, or there'll be nowt here either and wasted time singing in the cold.
MOTHER COURAGE: I'll get Kattrin.
THE COOK: Better bring a bit back for her. Scare them if they sees three of us coming. (*Exeunt both.*)

(*Kattrin climbs out of the cart with a bundle. She looks around to see if the other two have gone. Then she takes an old pair of trousers of the cook's and a skirt of her mother's, and lays them side by side on one of the wheels, so that they are easily seen. She has finished and is picking up her bundle to go, when Mother Courage comes back from the house.*)

MOTHER COURAGE (*with a plate of soup*): Kattrin! Will you stop there? Kattrin! Where you off to with that bundle? Has devil himself taken you over? (*She examines the bundle.*) She's packed her things. You been listening? I told him nowt doing, Utrecht, his rotten inn, what'd we be up to there? You and me, inn's no place for us. Still plenty to be got out of war. (*She sees the trousers and the skirt.*) You're plain stupid. S'pose I'd seen that, and you gone away? (*She holds Kattrin back as she tries to break away.*) Don't you start thinking it's on your account I given him the push. It was cart, that's it. Catch me leaving my cart I'm used to, it ain't you, it's for cart. We'll go off in t'other direction, and we'll throw cook's stuff out so he finds it, silly man. (*She climbs in and throws out a few other articles in the direction of the trousers.*) There, he's out of our business now, and I ain't having nobody else in, ever. You and me'll carry on now. This winter will pass, same as all the others. Get hitched up, it looks like snow.

(*They both harness themselves to the cart, then wheel it round and drag it off. When the cook arrives he looks blankly at his kit.*)

SCENE 10

(*During the whole of 1635 Mother Courage and her daughter Kattrin travel over the highroads of central Germany, in the wake of the increasingly bedraggled armies.*)
(*High road.*)
(*Mother Courage and Kattrin are pulling the cart. They pass a peasant's house inside which there is a voice singing.*)

THE VOICE:

> The roses in our arbour
> Delight us with their show:
> They have such lovely flowers
> Repaying all our labour
> After the summer showers.
> Happy are those with gardens now:
> They have such lovely flowers.
>
> When winter winds are freezing
> As through the woods they blow

Our home is warm and pleasing.
We fixed the thatch above it
With straw and moss we wove it.
Happy are those with shelter now
When winter winds are freezing.

(*Mother Courage and Kattrin pause to listen, then continue pulling.*)

SCENE 11

(*January 1636. The emperor's troops are threatening the Protestant town of Halle. The stone begins to speak. Mother Courage loses her daughter and trudges on alone. The war is a long way from being over.*)
(*The cart is standing, much the worse for wear, alongside a peasant's house with a huge thatched roof, backing on a wall of rock. It is night.*)
(*An ensign and three soldiers in heavy armour step out of the wood.*)

THE ENSIGN: I want no noise now. Anyone shouts, shove your pike into him.

FIRST SOLDIER: Have to knock them up, though, if we're to find a guide.

THE ENSIGN: Knocking sounds natural. Could be a cow bumping the stable wall.

(*The soldiers knock on the door of the house. The peasant's wife opens it. They stop her mouth. Two soldiers go in.*)

MAN'S VOICE (*within*): What is it?

(*The soldiers bring out the peasant and his son.*)

THE ENSIGN (*pointing at the cart, where Kattrin's head has appeared*): There's another one. (*A Soldier drags her out.*) Anyone else live here beside you lot?

THE PEASANTS: This is our son. And she's dumb. Her mother's gone into town to buy stuff. For their business, cause so many people's getting out and selling things cheap. They're just passing through. Canteen folk.

THE ENSIGN: I'm warning you, keep quiet, or if there's the least noise you get a pike across your nut. Now I want someone to come with us and show us the path to the town. (*Points to the young peasant.*) Here, you.

THE YOUNG PEASANT: I don't know no path.

SECOND SOLDIER (*grinning*): He don't know no path.

THE YOUNG PEASANT: I ain't helping Catholics.

THE ENSIGN (*to the second soldier*): Stick your pike in his ribs.

THE YOUNG PEASANT (*forced to his knees, with the pike threatening him*): I won't do it, not to save my life.

FIRST SOLDIER: I know what'll change his mind. (*Goes towards the stable.*) Two cows and an ox. Listen, you: if you're not reasonable I'll chop up your cattle.

THE YOUNG PEASANT: No, not that!

THE PEASANT'S WIFE (*weeps*): Please spare our cattle, captain, it'd be starving us to death.

THE ENSIGN: They're dead if he goes on being obstinate.

FIRST SOLDIER: I'm taking the ox first.

THE YOUNG PEASANT (*to his father*): Have I got to? (*The wife nods.*) Right.

THE PEASANT'S WIFE: And thank you kindly, captain, for sparing us, for ever and ever, Amen.

(*The peasant stops his wife from further expressions of gratitude.*)

FIRST SOLDIER: I knew the ox was what they minded about most, was I right?

(*Guided by the young peasant, the ensign and his men continue on their way.*)

THE PEASANT: What are they up to, I'd like to know. Nowt good.

THE PEASANT'S WIFE: Perhaps they're just scouting. What you doing?

THE PEASANT (*putting a ladder against the roof and climbing up it*): Seeing if they're on their own. (*From the top.*) Something moving in the wood. Can see something down by the quarry. And there are men in armour in the clearing. And a gun. That's at least a regiment. God's mercy on the town and everyone in it!

THE PEASANT'S WIFE: Any lights in the town?

THE PEASANT: No. They'll all be asleep. (*Climbs down.*) If those people get in they'll butcher the lot.

THE PEASANT'S WIFE: Sentries're bound to spot them first.

THE PEASANT: Sentry in the tower up the hill must have been killed, or he'd have blown his bugle.

THE PEASANT'S WIFE: If only there were more of us.

THE PEASANT: Just you and me and that cripple.

THE PEASANT'S WIFE: Nowt we can do, you'd say. . . .

THE PEASANT: Nowt.

THE PEASANT'S WIFE: Can't possibly run down there in the blackness.

THE PEASANT: Whole hillside's crawling with 'em. We could give a signal.

THE PEASANT'S WIFE: What, and have them butcher us too?

THE PEASANT: You're right, nowt we can do.

THE PEASANT'S WIFE (*to Kattrin*): Pray, poor creature, pray! Nowt we can do to stop bloodshed. You can't talk, maybe, but at least you can pray. He'll hear you if no one else can. I'll help you. (*All kneel, Kattrin behind the two peasants.*) Our Father, which art in Heaven, hear Thou our prayer, let not the town be destroyed with all what's in it sound asleep and suspecting nowt. Arouse Thou them that they may get up and go to the walls and see how the enemy approacheth with picks and guns in the blackness across fields below the slope. (*Turning to Kattrin.*) Guard Thou our mother and ensure that the watchman sleepeth not but wakes up, or it will be too late. Succour our brother-in-law also, he is inside there with his four children, spare Thou them, they are innocent and know nowt. (*To Kattrin, who gives a groan.*) One of them's not two yet, the eldest's seven. (*Kattrin stands up distractedly.*) Our Father, hear us, for only Thou canst help; we look to be doomed, for why, we are weak and have no pike and nowt and can risk nowt and are in Thy hand along with our cattle and all the farm, and same with the town, it too is in Thy hand and the enemy is before the walls in great strength.

(*Unobserved, Kattrin has slipped away to the cart and taken from it something which she hides beneath her apron; then she climbs up the ladder on to the stable roof.*)

THE PEASANT'S WIFE: Forget not the children, what are in danger, the littlest ones especially, the old folk what can't move, and every living creature.
THE PEASANT: And forgive us our trespasses as we forgive them that trespass against us. Amen.

(*Sitting on the roof, Kattrin begins to beat the drum which she has pulled out from under her apron.*)

THE PEASANT'S WIFE: Jesus Christ, what's she doing?
THE PEASANT: She's out of her mind.
THE PEASANT'S WIFE: Quick, get her down.

(*The peasant hurries to the ladder, but Kattrin pulls it up on to the roof.*)

THE PEASANT'S WIFE: She'll do us in.
THE PEASANT: Stop drumming at once, you cripple!
THE PEASANT'S WIFE: Bringing the Catholics down on us!
THE PEASANT (*looking for stones to throw*): I'll stone you.
THE PEASANT'S WIFE: Where's your feelings? Where's your heart? We're done for if they come down on us. Slit our throats, they will.

(*Kattrin stares into the distance towards the town and carries on drumming.*)

THE PEASANT'S WIFE (*to her husband*): I told you we shouldn't have allowed those vagabonds on to farm. What do they care if our last cows are taken?
THE ENSIGN (*runs in with his soldiers and the young peasant*): I'll cut you to ribbons, all of you!
THE PEASANT'S WIFE: Please, sir, it's not our fault, we couldn't help it. It was her sneaked up there. A foreigner.
THE ENSIGN: Where's the ladder?
THE PEASANT: There.
THE ENSIGN (*calls up*): I order you, throw that drum down.

(*Kattrin goes on drumming.*)

THE ENSIGN: You're all in this together. It'll be the end of you.
THE PEASANT: They been cutting pine trees in that wood. How about if we got one of the trunks and poked her off. . . .
FIRST SOLDIER (*to the ensign*): Permission to make a suggestion, sir! (*He whispers something in the ensign's ear.*) Listen, we got a suggestion could help you. Get down off there and come into town with us right away. Show us which your mother is and we'll see she ain't harmed.

(*Kattrin goes on drumming.*)

THE ENSIGN (*pushes him roughly aside*): She doesn't trust you; with a mug like yours it's not surprising. (*Calls up.*) Suppose I gave you my word? I can give my word of honour as an officer.

(*Kattrin drums harder.*)

THE ENSIGN: Is nothing sacred to her?
THE YOUNG PEASANT: There's more than her mother involved, sir.
FIRST SOLDIER: This can't go on much longer. They're bound to hear in the town.
THE ENSIGN: We'll have somehow to make a noise that's louder than her drumming. What can we make a noise with?
FIRST SOLDIER: Thought we weren't s'posed to make no noise.
THE ENSIGN: A harmless one, you fool. A peaceful one.
THE PEASANT: I could chop wood with my axe.
THE ENSIGN: Good: you chop. (*The peasant fetches his axe and attacks a tree-trunk.*) Chop harder! Harder! You're chopping for your life.

(*Kattrin has been listening, drumming less loudly the while. She now looks wildly round, and goes on drumming.*)

THE ENSIGN: Not loud enough. (*To the first soldier.*) You chop too.

THE PEASANT: Only got the one axe. (*Stops chopping.*)

THE ENSIGN: We'll have to set the farm on fire. Smoke her out, that's it.

THE PEASANT: It wouldn't help, captain. If the townspeople see a fire here they'll know what's up.

(*Kattrin has again been listening as she drums. At this point she laughs.*)

THE ENSIGN: Look at her laughing at us. I'm not having that. I'll shoot her down, and damn the consequences. Fetch the harquebus.

(*Three soldiers hurry off. Kattrin goes on drumming.*)

THE PEASANT'S WIFE: I got it, captain. That's their cart. If we smash it up she'll stop. Cart's all they got.

THE ENSIGN (*to the young peasant*): Smash it up. (*Calls up.*) We're going to smash up your cart if you don't stop drumming. (*The young peasant gives the cart a few feeble blows.*)

THE PEASANT'S WIFE: Stop it, you animal!

(*Desperately looking towards the cart, Kattrin emits pitiful noises. But she goes on drumming.*)

THE ENSIGN: Where are those clodhoppers with the harquebus?

FIRST SOLDIER: Can't have heard nowt in town yet, else we'd be hearing their guns.

THE ENSIGN (*calls up*): They can't hear you at all. And now we're going to shoot you down. For the last time: throw down that drum!

THE YOUNG PEASANT (*suddenly flings away his plank*): Go on drumming! Or they'll all be killed! Go on, go on. . . .

(*The soldier knocks him down and beats him with his pike. Kattrin starts to cry, but she goes on drumming.*)

THE PEASANT'S WIFE: Don't strike his back! For God's sake, you're beating him to death!

(*The soldiers hurry in with the harquebus.*)

SECOND SOLDIER: Colonel's frothing at the mouth, sir. We're all for court martial.

THE ENSIGN: Set it up! Set it up! (*Calls up while the gun is being erected.*) For the very last time: stop drumming! (*Kattrin, in tears, drums as loud as she can.*) Fire! (*The soldiers fire. Kattrin is hit, gives a few more drumbeats and then slowly crumples.*)

THE ENSIGN: That's the end of that.

(*But Kattrin's last drumbeats are taken up by the town's cannon. In the distance can be heard a confused noise of tocsins and gunfire.*)

FIRST SOLDIER: She's made it.

SCENE 12

(*Before first light. Sound of the fifes and drums of troops marching off into the distance.*)

(*In front of the cart Mother Courage is squatting by her daughter. The peasant family are standing near her.*)

THE PEASANTS (*with hostility*): You must go, missis. There's only one more regiment behind that one. You can't go on your own.

MOTHER COURAGE: I think she's going to sleep. (*She sings.*)

> Lullaby baby
> What's that in the hay?
> Neighbours' kids grizzle
> But my kids are gay.
> Neighbours' are in tatters
> And you're dressed in lawn
> Cut down from the raiment an
> Angel has worn.
> Neighbours' kids go hungry
> And you shall eat cake
> Suppose it's too crumbly
> You've only to speak.
> Lullaby baby
> What's that in the hay?
> The one lies in Poland
> The other — who can say?

Better if you'd not told her nowt about your brother-in-law's kids.

THE PEASANT: If you'd not gone into town to get your cut it might never of happened.

MOTHER COURAGE: Now she's asleep.

THE PEASANT'S WIFE: She ain't asleep. Can't you see she's passed over?

THE PEASANT: And it's high time you got away yourself. There are wolves around and, what's worse, marauders.

MOTHER COURAGE: Aye.

(*She goes and gets a tarpaulin to cover the dead girl with.*)

THE PEASANT'S WIFE: Ain't you got nobody else? What you could go to?

MOTHER COURAGE: Aye, one left. Eilif.

THE PEASANT (*as Mother Courage covers the dead girl*): Best look for him, then. We'll mind her, see she gets proper burial. Don't you worry about that.

MOTHER COURAGE: Here's money for expenses.

(*She counts out coins into the peasant's hands. The peasant and his son shake hands with her and carry Kattrin away.*)

THE PEASANT'S WIFE (*as she leaves*): I'd hurry.
MOTHER COURAGE (*harnessing herself to the cart*):
    Hope I can pull cart all right by meself. Be all
    right, nowt much inside it. Got to get back in busi-
    ness again.

(*Another regiment with its fifes and drums marches
past in the background.*)

MOTHER COURAGE (*tugging the cart*): Take me along!
(*Singing is heard from offstage.*)

    With all its luck and all its danger

The war is dragging on a bit
Another hundred years or longer
The common man won't benefit.
Filthy his food, no soap to shave him
The regiment steals half his pay.
But still a miracle may save him:
Tomorrow is another day!
    The new year's come. The watchmen shout.
    The thaw sets in. The dead remain.
    Wherever life has not died out
    It staggers to its feet again.

Tennessee Williams

Tennessee Williams (1911–1983) was one of a handful of post-World War II American playwrights to achieve an international reputation. He was born Thomas Lanier Williams in Columbus, Mississippi, the son of a traveling shoe salesman who eventually moved the family to a dark and dreary tenement in St. Louis. A precocious child, Williams was given a typewriter by his mother when he was eleven years old. The instrument helped him create fantasy worlds that seemed more real, more important to him than the dark and sometimes threatening world in which he lived. His parents, expecting a third child, bought a house whose gloominess depressed virtually everyone in it. His mother and father found themselves arguing, and his sister, Rose, took refuge from the real world by closeting herself with a collection of glass animals.

Both Rose and Tennessee responded badly to their environment, and both had breakdowns. Tennessee was so ill that he suffered a partial paralysis of his legs, a disorder that made him a victim of bullies at school and a disappointment to his father at home. He could never participate in sports and was always somewhat frail; however, he was very advanced intellectually and published his first story when he was sixteen.

His education was sporadic. He attended the University of Missouri but, failing ROTC because of his physical limitations, soon dropped out to work in a shoe company. He then went to Washington University in St. Louis but dropped out again. Finally, he earned a bachelor's degree in playwriting at the State University of Iowa when he was twenty-four. During this time he was writing plays, some of which were produced at Washington University. Two years after he graduated, the Theatre Guild produced his first commercial play, *Battle of Angels* (1940), in Boston. It was such a distinct failure that he feared his fledgling career was stunted, but he kept writing and managed to live for a few years on foundation grants. It was not until the production of *The Glass Menagerie* (1944 in Chicago, 1945 in New York) that he achieved the kind of notice he knew he deserved. His first real success, the play was given the New York Drama Critics' Circle Award, the sign of his having achieved a measure of professional recognition and financial independence.

After trying several jobs, including an unsuccessful attempt at screenwriting, he had no more worries about work after *The Glass Menagerie* ran on Broadway for 561 performances. In 1947 his second success, *A Streetcar Named Desire*, starring the then unknown Marlon Brando, was an even bigger box-office smash. It ran for 855 performances and won the Pulitzer Prize. By the time Tennessee Williams was thirty-six, he was regarded as one of the most important playwrights in America.

Williams followed these successes with a number of plays that were not all as well received as his first works. *Summer and Smoke* (1948), *The Rose Tattoo* (1951), and *Camino Real* (1953) were met with measured enthusiasm from the public, although the critics thought highly of Williams's work. These plays were followed by the saga of a southern family, *Cat on a Hot Tin Roof,* which won all the major drama prizes in 1955, including the Pulitzer.

Williams's energy was unfailing in the next several years. He authored a screenplay, *Baby Doll,* with the legendary director Elia Kazan, in 1956. In 1958 he wrote a one-act play, *Suddenly Last Summer,* and in 1959 *Sweet Bird of Youth.* Some of his later plays are *The Night of the Iguana* (1961), *The Milk Train Doesn't Stop Here Anymore* (1963), and *Small Craft Warnings* (1972). He also wrote a novel and several volumes of short stories, establishing himself as an important writer in many genres. His sudden death in 1983 shocked the theater world.

THE GLASS MENAGERIE

Tennessee Williams has often been accused of exorcising his family demons in his plays and of therefore sometimes cloaking events in a personal symbolism that is impossible for an audience to penetrate totally. *The Glass Menagerie* (1944) certainly derives from his personal experience growing up in St. Louis in a tenement, the setting for the play. The characters are drawn from his own family, particularly the character Laura, who is based on his sister. But the symbolism in the play is not so obscure as to give an audience special difficulty.

In a way Williams thought of the play as a tribute to his sister, Rose. Rose's depressions were so severe that eventually she received a lobotomy, which rendered her more passive and more hopeless than before. The operation did not achieve anything positive, and Williams felt somewhat responsible because he had not urged the family to refuse the treatment.

In the play Amanda Wingfield is obsessed with finding gentlemen callers and a suitable career for her daughter, Laura, who is partially lame and exceedingly shy. Amanda lives in a world of imagination, inventing stories about a glorious past she never lived and about all the suitors she could have had before she married. Amanda bullies Laura, whose only defense is to bury herself in her own fantasy world of spunglass animals. Tom, the son and narrator of the play, is also a victim of Amanda's bullying, but he is more independent and better able to withstand her assaults.

Both children are great disappointments to Amanda. Tom is aloof, indolent, something like his father who is present only in his picture on the wall. Laura calls herself a cripple and has no self-esteem or hope for a future such as the one her mother conceives for her. Laura's shyness is almost uncontrollable. It has ruined any hope of a business career, to Amanda's intense distress. When Tom brings home Jim, the one boy Laura remembers from high school, Laura is nearly too shy to come to the dinner table. And when it becomes clear that Jim is not the gentleman caller of Amanda's dreams, Amanda and Laura are left to face reality or to continue living in their fantasy worlds.

Amanda confronts Tom at the end of the play and asserts that he "live[s] in a dream" and "manufacture[s] illusions." She could be speaking about any character in the play, including Jim, who lives according to popular illusions about self-fulfillment. But the Wingfields in particular pay dearly for their illusions, perhaps Laura more than anyone because of her mother's inability to relinquish intense but unrealistic hopes for her daughter.

Williams's written presentation of the play provides more insights than usual for a reading audience. His stage directions are elaborate, poetic, and exceptionally evocative. Through Tom, as narrator, he says that the play is not realistic but rather is a memory play, an enactment of moments in Tom's memory.

Williams specifies a setting that is almost dreamlike, using Brechtian devices such as the visual images and screen legends flashed at appropriate moments. He uses music to establish a mood or stimulate an association. Because modern productions rarely follow Williams's directions, the dreamlike quality is sometimes lost. In fact, ironically, modern productions of this play are often realistic rather than symbolic, although they usually maintain the mood that Williams hoped to achieve.

The Glass Menagerie in Performance

The first production of *The Glass Menagerie* opened in Chicago on December 26, 1944, during World War II. Audiences were not drawn to it at first, but the critics' positive reviews began to attract people to the theater. In March 1945, when it was playing to full houses, the play transferred to New York and began a run of 561 performances. It won the Drama Critics' Circle Award as the best American play of the 1944–1945 season. Two road companies then toured the play around the country. The first London performance, in the large and distinguished Theatre Royal in Haymarket in July 1948, was directed by John Gielgud and starred Helen Hayes as Amanda Wingfield. A film version followed in 1950.

Revivals of the play have been both numerous and successful. Laurette Taylor, who played Amanda in the original New York production, set a standard with her interpretation of Williams's poetic language. Maureen Stapleton, whose more vigorous approach contrasted sharply with Taylor's, took the role in the 1965 production in the Brooks Atkinson Theater in New York. The critic Howard Taubman said, "Maureen Stapleton does not cause one to forget Miss Taylor. . . . Through the magic of her own sensitivity, she gives Amanda a strong, binding thread of sadness and tenderness." Katharine Hepburn's first television performance was as Amanda in 1973. "She gives a brilliant, multifaceted performance that is surely the acting tour de force of the year," said Percy Shain. Jessica Tandy performed the role in 1983 at the Eugene O'Neill Theater in New York, with Amanda Plummer as Laura. *New York Times* critic Frank Rich declared, "This Amanda is tough, and even her most comic badgerings leave a bitter aftertaste." Interestingly, the British director of that production, John Dexter, used some of the flash cards that Williams specified in the original published version but that had been omitted from previous productions. They flashed important speeches on the scrim during the performance.

Joanne Woodward played Amanda in the 1986 revival at the Long

Wharf Theater in New Haven in a version that had been performed at the Williamstown Theatre Festival in 1982. Treat Williams was the son, James Naughton was the suitor, and the Long Wharf production was impressively dreamlike and powerful. Woodward's husband, Paul Newman, directed this version in the 1987 film of the play.

Tennessee Williams (1911–1983)
THE GLASS MENAGERIE

1944

nobody, not even the rain, has such small hands — E. E. CUMMINGS

Production Notes by Tennessee Williams

Being a "memory play," *The Glass Menagerie* can be presented with unusual freedom of convention. Because of its considerably delicate or tenuous material, atmospheric touches and subtleties of direction play a particularly important part. Expressionism and all other unconventional techniques in drama have only one valid aim, and this is a closer approach to truth. When a play employs unconventional techniques, it is not, or certainly shouldn't be, trying to escape its responsibility of dealing with reality, or interpreting experience, but is actually or should be attempting to find a closer approach, or more penetrating and vivid expression of things as they are. The straight realistic play with its genuine frigidaire and authentic ice cubes, its characters that speak exactly as its audience speaks, corresponds to the academic landscape and has the same virtue of a photographic likeness. Everyone should know nowadays the unimportance of the photographic in art: that truth, life, or reality is an organic thing which the poetic imagination can represent or suggest, in essence, only through transformation, through changing into other forms than those which were merely present in appearance.

These remarks are not meant as a preface only to this particular play. They have to do with a conception of a new, plastic theatre which must take the place of the exhausted theatre of realistic conventions if the theatre is to resume vitality as a part of our culture.

The Screen Device. There is *only one important difference between the original and acting version of the play* and that is the *omission* in the latter of the device which I tentatively included in my *original* script. This device was the use of a screen on which were projected magic-lantern slides bearing images or titles. I do not regret the omission of this device from the present Broadway production. The extraordinary power of Miss Taylor's performance made it suitable to have the utmost simplicity in the physical production. But I think it may be interesting to some readers to see how this device was conceived. So I am putting it into the published manuscript. These images and legends, projected from behind, were cast on a section of wall between the front-room and dining-room areas, which should be indistinguishable from the rest when not in use.

The purpose of this will probably be apparent. It is to give accent to certain values in each scene. Each scene contains a particular point (or several) which is structurally the most important. In an episodic play, such as this, the basic structure or narrative line may be obscured from the audience; the effect may seem fragmentary rather than architectural. This may not be the fault of the play so much as a lack of attention in the audience. The legend or image upon the screen will strengthen the effect of what is merely allusion in the writing and allow the primary point to be made more simply and lightly than if the entire responsibility were on the spoken lines. Aside from this structural value, I think the screen will have a definite emotional appeal, less definable but just as important. An imaginative producer or director may invent many other uses for this device than those indicated in the present script. In fact the possibilities of the device seem much larger to me than the instance of this play can possibly utilize.

The Music. Another extra-literary accent in this play is provided by the use of music. A single recurring tune, "The Glass Menagerie," is used to give emotional emphasis to suitable passages. This tune is like circus music, not when you are on the grounds or in the immediate vicinity of the parade, but when you are at some distance and very likely thinking of something else. It seems under those circumstances to continue almost interminably and it weaves in and out of your preoccupied consciousness; then it is the lightest, most delicate music in the world and perhaps the saddest. It expresses the surface vivacity of life with the underlying strain of immutable and inexpressible sorrow. When you look at a piece of delicately spun glass you think of two things: how beautiful it is and how easily it can be broken. Both of those ideas should be woven into the recurring tune, which dips in and out of the play as if it were carried on a wind that changes. It serves as a thread of connection and allusion between the narrator with his separate point in time and space and the subject of his story. Between each episode it returns as reference to the emotion, nostalgia, which is the first condition of the play. It is primarily Laura's music and therefore comes out most clearly when the play focuses upon her and the lovely fragility of glass which is her image.

The Lighting. The lighting in the play is not realistic. In keeping with the atmosphere of memory, the stage is dim. Shafts of light are focused on selected areas or actors, sometimes in con-

tradistinction to what is the apparent center. For instance, in the quarrel scene between Tom and Amanda, in which Laura has no active part, the clearest pool of light is on her figure. This is also true of the supper scene, when her silent figure on the sofa should remain the visual center. The light upon Laura should be distinct from the others, having a peculiar pristine clarity such as light used in early religious portraits of female saints or madonnas. A certain correspondence to light in religious paintings, such as El Greco's, where the figures are radiant in atmosphere that is relatively dusky, could be effectively used throughout the play. (It will also permit a more effective use of the screen.) A free, imaginative use of light can be of enormous value in giving a mobile, plastic quality to plays of a more or less static nature.

Characters

AMANDA WINGFIELD, *the mother. A little woman of great but confused vitality clinging frantically to another time and place. Her characterization must be carefully created, not copied from type. She is not paranoiac, but her life is paranoia. There is much to admire in Amanda, and as much to love and pity as there is to laugh at. Certainly she has endurance and a kind of heroism, and though her foolishness makes her unwittingly cruel at times, there is tenderness in her slight person.*

LAURA WINGFIELD, *her daughter. Amanda, having failed to establish contact with reality, continues to live vitally in her illusions, but Laura's situation is even graver. A childhood illness has left her crippled, one leg slightly shorter than the other, and held in a brace. This defect need not be more than suggested on the stage. Stemming from this, Laura's separation increases till she is like a piece of her own glass collection, too exquisitely fragile to move from the shelf.*

TOM WINGFIELD, *her son. And the narrator of the play. A poet with a job in a warehouse. His nature is not remorseless, but to escape from a trap he has to act without pity.*

JIM O'CONNOR, *the gentleman caller. A nice, ordinary, young man.*

Scene: *An alley in St. Louis.*
Part I: *Preparation for a Gentleman Caller.*
Part II: *The Gentleman Calls.*
Time: *Now and the Past.*

SCENE 1

(The Wingfield apartment is in the rear of the building, one of those vast hive-like conglomerations of cellular living-units that flower as warty growths in overcrowded urban centers of lower middle-class population and are symptomatic of the impulse of this largest and fundamentally enslaved section of American society to avoid fluidity and differentiation and to exist and function as one interfused mass of automatism.)

(The apartment faces an alley and is entered by a fire escape, a structure whose name is a touch of accidental poetic truth, for all of these huge buildings are always burning with the slow and implacable fires of human desperation. The fire escape is included in the set — that is, the landing of it and steps descending from it.)

(The scene is memory and is therefore nonrealistic. Memory takes a lot of poetic license. It omits some details; others are exaggerated, according to the emotional value of the articles it touches, for memory is seated predominantly in the heart. The interior is therefore rather dim and poetic.)

(At the rise of the curtain, the audience is faced with the dark, grim rear wall of the Wingfield tenement. This building, which runs parallel to the footlights, is flanked on both sides by dark, narrow alleys which run into murky canyons of tangled clotheslines, garbage cans, and the sinister latticework of neighboring fire escapes. It is up and down these side alleys that exterior entrances and exits are made, during the play. At the end of Tom's opening commentary, the dark tenement wall slowly reveals (by means of a transparency) the interior of the ground floor Wingfield apartment.)

(Downstage is the living room, which also serves as a sleeping room for Laura, the sofa unfolding to make her bed. Upstage, center, and divided by a wide arch or second proscenium with transparent faded portieres (or second curtain), is the dining room. In an old-fashioned what-not in the living room are seen scores of transparent glass animals. A blown-up photograph of the father hangs on the wall of the living room, facing the audience, to the left of the archway. It is the face of a very handsome young man in a doughboy's First World War cap. He is gallantly smiling, ineluctably smiling, as if to say, "I will be smiling forever.")

(The audience hears and sees the opening scene in the dining room through both the transparent fourth wall of the building and the transparent gauze portieres of the dining-room arch. It is during this revealing scene that the fourth wall slowly ascends, out of sight. This transparent exterior wall is not brought down again until the very end of the play, during Tom's final speech.)

(The narrator is an undisguised convention of the play. He takes whatever license with dramatic convention as is convenient to his purposes.)

(Tom enters dressed as a merchant sailor from alley, stage left, and strolls across the front of the stage to the fire escape. There he stops and lights a cigarette. He addresses the audience.)

TOM: Yes, I have tricks in my pocket, I have things up my sleeve. But I am the opposite of a stage magician. He gives you illusion that has the appearance of truth. I give you truth in the pleasant disguise of illusion. To begin with, I turn back time. I reverse it to that quaint period, the thirties, when the huge middle class of America was matriculating in a school for the blind. Their eyes had failed them, or they had failed their eyes, and so they were having their fingers pressed forcibly down on the fiery Braille alphabet of a dissolving economy. In Spain there was revolution. Here there was only shouting and confusion. In Spain there was Guernica. Here there were disturbances of labor, sometimes pretty violent, in otherwise peaceful cities such as Chicago, Cleveland, Saint Louis. . . . This is the social background of the play.

(Music.)

The play is memory. Being a memory play, it is dimly lighted, it is sentimental, it is not realistic. In memory everything seems to happen to music. That explains the fiddle in the wings. I am the narrator of the play, and also a character in it. The other characters are my mother, Amanda, my sister, Laura, and a gentleman caller who appears in the final scenes. He is the most realistic character in the play, being an emissary from a world of reality that we were somehow set apart from. But since I have a poet's weakness for symbols, I am using this character also as a symbol; he is the long delayed but always expected something that we live for. There is a fifth character in the play who doesn't appear except in this larger-than-life photograph over the mantel. This is our father who left us a long time ago. He was a telephone man who fell in love with long distances; he gave up his job with the telephone company and skipped the light fantastic out of town . . . The last we heard of him was a picture postcard from Mazatlan, on the Pacific coast of Mexico, containing a message of two words — "Hello — Good-bye!" and no address. I think the rest of the play will explain itself. . . .

(Amanda's voice becomes audible through the portieres.)

(Legend on Screen: "Où Sont les Neiges.")°

Où Sont les Neiges: Where are the snows [of yesteryear].

(*He divides the portieres and enters the upstage area.*)

(*Amanda and Laura are seated at a drop-leaf table. Eating is indicated by gestures without food or utensils. Amanda faces the audience. Tom and Laura are seated in profile.*)

(*The interior has lit up softly and through the scrim we see Amanda and Laura seated at the table in the upstage area.*)

AMANDA (*calling*): Tom?

TOM: Yes, Mother.

AMANDA: We can't say grace until you come to the table!

TOM: Coming, Mother. (*He bows slightly and withdraws, reappearing a few moments later in his place at the table.*)

AMANDA (*to her son*): Honey, don't *push* with your fingers. If you have to push with something, the thing to push with is a crust of bread. And chew — chew! Animals have sections in their stomachs which enable them to digest food without mastication, but human beings are supposed to chew their food before they swallow it down. Eat food leisurely, son, and really enjoy it. A well-cooked meal has lots of delicate flavors that have to be held in the mouth for appreciation. So chew your food and give your salivary glands a chance to function!

(*Tom deliberately lays his imaginary fork down and pushes his chair back from the table.*)

TOM: I haven't enjoyed one bite of this dinner because of your constant directions on how to eat it. It's you that makes me rush through meals with your hawk-like attention to every bite I take. Sickening — spoils my appetite — all this discussion of animals' secretion — salivary glands — mastication!

AMANDA (*lightly*): Temperament like a Metropolitan° star! (*He rises and crosses downstage.*) You're not excused from the table.

TOM: I'm getting a cigarette.

AMANDA: You smoke too much.

(*Laura rises.*)

LAURA: I'll bring in the blancmange.

(*He remains standing with his cigarette by the portieres during the following.*)

AMANDA (*rising*): No, sister, no, sister — you be the lady this time and I'll be the darky.

LAURA: I'm already up.

AMANDA: Resume your seat, little sister — I want you to stay fresh and pretty — for gentlemen callers!

LAURA: I'm not expecting any gentlemen callers.

AMANDA (*crossing out to kitchenette. Airily*): Some-

Metropolitan: The Metropolitan Opera in New York City.

times they come when they are least expected! Why, I remember one Sunday afternoon in Blue Mountain — (*Enters kitchenette.*)

TOM: I know what's coming!

LAURA: Yes. But let her tell it.

TOM: Again?

LAURA: She loves to tell it.

(*Amanda returns with bowl of dessert.*)

AMANDA: One Sunday afternoon in Blue Mountain — your mother received — *seventeen!* — gentlemen callers! Why, sometimes there weren't chairs enough to accommodate them all. We had to send the nigger over to bring in folding chairs from the parish house.

TOM (*remaining at portieres*): How did you entertain those gentlemen callers?

AMANDA: I understood the art of conversation!

TOM: I bet you could talk.

AMANDA: Girls in those days *knew* how to talk, I can tell you.

TOM: Yes?

(*Image: Amanda as a girl on a porch greeting callers.*)

AMANDA: They knew how to entertain their gentlemen callers. It wasn't enough for a girl to be possessed of a pretty face and a graceful figure — although I wasn't slighted in either respect. She also needed to have a nimble wit and a tongue to meet all occasions.

TOM: What did you talk about?

AMANDA: Things of importance going on in the world! Never anything coarse or common or vulgar. (*She addresses Tom as though he were seated in the vacant chair at the table though he remains by portieres. He plays this scene as though he held the book.*) My callers were gentlemen — all! Among my callers were some of the most prominent young planters of the Mississippi Delta — planters and sons of planters!

(*Tom motions for music and a spot of light on Amanda.*)

(*Her eyes lift, her face glows, her voice becomes rich and elegiac.*)

(*Screen legend: "Où Sont les Neiges."*)

There was young Champ Laughlin who later became vice-president of the Delta Planters Bank. Hadley Stevenson who was drowned in Moon Lake and left his widow one hundred and fifty thousand in Government bonds. There were the Cutrere brothers, Wesley and Bates. Bates was one of my bright particular beaux! He got in a quarrel with that wild Wainright boy. They shot it out on the floor of Moon Lake Casino. Bates was shot through the stomach. Died in the ambulance on his way to Memphis. His widow was also well-provided for, came into eight or ten thousand acres, that's all. She married him on the rebound — never loved her — carried my picture on him the night he died! And there was that boy that every girl in the Delta had set her cap for! That beautiful, brilliant young Fitzhugh boy from Greene County!

TOM: What did he leave his widow?

AMANDA: He never married! Gracious, you talk as though all of my old admirers had turned up their toes to the daisies!

TOM: Isn't this the first you mentioned that still survives?

AMANDA: That Fitzhugh boy went North and made a fortune — came to be known as the Wolf of Wall Street! He had the Midas touch, whatever he touched turned to gold! And I could have been Mrs. Duncan J. Fitzhugh, mind you! But — I picked your *father!*

LAURA (*rising*): Mother, let me clear the table.

AMANDA: No, dear, you go in front and study your typewriter chart. Or practice your shorthand a little. Stay fresh and pretty! — It's almost time for our gentlemen callers to start arriving. (*She flounces girlishly toward the kitchenette.*) How many do you suppose we're going to entertain this afternoon?

(*Tom throws down the paper and jumps up with a groan.*)

LAURA (*alone in the dining room*): I don't believe we're going to receive any, Mother.

AMANDA (*reappearing, airily*): What? No one — not one? You must be joking! (*Laura nervously echoes her laugh. She slips in a fugitive manner through the half-open portieres and draws them gently behind her. A shaft of very clear light is thrown on her face against the faded tapestry of the curtains. Music: "The Glass Menagerie" under faintly. Lightly.*) Not one gentleman caller? It can't be true! There must be a flood, there must have been a tornado!

LAURA: It isn't a flood, it's not a tornado, Mother. I'm just not popular like you were in Blue Mountain. . . . (*Tom utters another groan. Laura glances at him with a faint, apologetic smile. Her voice catching a little.*) Mother's afraid I'm going to be an old maid.

(*The scene dims out with "Glass Menagerie" music.*)

SCENE 2

(*"Laura, Haven't You Ever Liked Some Boy?"*)

(*On the dark stage the screen is lighted with the image of blue roses.*)

(*Gradually Laura's figure becomes apparent and the screen goes out.*)

(*The music subsides.*)

(*Laura is seated in the delicate ivory chair at the small clawfoot table.*)

(*She wears a dress of soft violet material for a kimono — her hair tied back from her forehead with a ribbon.*)

(*She is washing and polishing her collection of glass.*)

(*Amanda appears on the fire escape steps. At the sound of her ascent, Laura catches her breath, thrusts the bowl of ornaments away and seats herself stiffly before the diagram of the typewriter keyboard as though it held her spellbound. Something has happened to Amanda. It is written in her face as she climbs to the landing: a look that is grim and hopeless and a little absurd.*)

(*She has on one of those cheap or imitation velvety-looking cloth coats with imitation fur collar. Her hat is five or six years old, one of those dreadful cloche hats that were worn in the late twenties, and she is clasping an enormous black patent-leather pocketbook with nickel clasp and initials. This is her full-dress outfit, the one she usually wears to the D.A.R.°*)

(*Before entering she looks through the door.*)

(*She purses her lips, opens her eyes wide, rolls them upward and shakes her head.*)

(*Then she slowly lets herself in the door. Seeing her mother's expression Laura touches her lips with a nervous gesture.*)

LAURA: Hello, Mother, I was — (*She makes a nervous gesture toward the chart on the wall. Amanda leans against the shut door and stares at Laura with a martyred look.*)

AMANDA: Deception? Deception? (*She slowly removes her hat and gloves, continuing the swift suffering stare. She lets the hat and gloves fall on the floor — a bit of acting.*)

LAURA (*shakily*): How was the D.A.R. meeting? (*Amanda slowly opens her purse and removes a dainty white handkerchief which she shakes out delicately and delicately touches to her lips and nostrils.*) Didn't you go to the D.A.R. meeting, Mother?

AMANDA (*faintly, almost inaudibly*): — No. — No. (*Then more forcibly*). I did not have the strength — to go to the D.A.R. In fact, I did not have the courage! I wanted to find a hole in the ground and hide myself in it forever! (*She crosses slowly to the wall and removes the diagram of the typewriter keyboard. She holds it in front of her for a second,*

D.A.R.: Daughters of the American Revolution, a conservative, patriotic organization for women whose ancestors were involved in the American Revolutionary War.

staring at it sweetly and sorrowfully — then bites her lips and tears it in two pieces.)

LAURA (*faintly*): Why did you do that, Mother? (*Amanda repeats the same procedure with the chart of the Gregg Alphabet.*) Why are you —

AMANDA: Why? Why? How old are you, Laura?

LAURA: Mother, you know my age.

AMANDA: I thought that you were an adult; it seems that I was mistaken. (*She crosses slowly to the sofa and sinks down and stares at Laura.*)

LAURA: Please don't stare at me, Mother.

(*Amanda closes her eyes and lowers her head. Count ten.*)

AMANDA: What are we going to do, what is going to become of us, what is the future?

(*Count ten.*)

LAURA: Has something happened, Mother? (*Amanda draws a long breath and takes out the handkerchief again. Dabbing process.*) Mother, has — something happened?

AMANDA: I'll be all right in a minute. I'm just bewildered — (*Count five.*) — by life. . . .

LAURA: Mother, I wish that you would tell me what's happened.

AMANDA: As you know, I was supposed to be inducted into my office at the D.A.R. this afternoon. (*Image: a swarm of typewriters.*) But I stopped off at Rubicam's Business College to speak to your teachers about your having a cold and ask them what progress they thought you were making down there.

LAURA: Oh. . . .

AMANDA: I went to the typing instructor and introduced myself as your mother. She didn't know who you were. Wingfield, she said. We don't have any such student enrolled at the school! I assured her she did, that you had been going to classes since early in January. "I wonder," she said, "if you could be talking about that terribly shy little girl who dropped out of school after only a few days' attendance?" "No," I said, "Laura, my daughter, has been going to school every day for the past six weeks!" "Excuse me," she said. She took the attendance book out and there was your name, unmistakably printed, and all the dates you were absent until they decided that you had dropped out of school. I still said, "No, there must have been some mistake! There must have been some mix-up in the records!" And she said, "No — I remember her perfectly now. Her hands shook so that she couldn't hit the right keys! The first time we gave a speed test, she broke down completely — was sick at the stomach and almost had to be carried into the wash-room! After that morning she never showed up any more. We phoned the house but never got any answer" — while I was working at Famous and Barr, I suppose, demonstrating those — Oh! I felt so weak I could barely keep on my feet. I had to sit down while they got me a glass of water! Fifty dollars' tuition, all of our plans — my hopes and ambitions for you — just gone up the spout, just gone up the spout like that. (*Laura draws a long breath and gets awkwardly to her feet. She crosses to the victrola and winds it up.*) What are you doing?

LAURA: Oh! (*She releases the handle and returns to her seat.*)

AMANDA: Laura, where have you been going when you've gone out pretending that you were going to business college?

LAURA: I've just been going out walking.

AMANDA: That's not true.

LAURA: It is. I just went walking.

AMANDA: Walking? Walking? In winter? Deliberately courting pneumonia in that light coat? Where did you walk to, Laura?

LAURA: All sorts of places — mostly in the park.

AMANDA: Even after you'd started catching that cold?

LAURA: It was the lesser of two evils, Mother. (*Image: winter scene in park.*) I couldn't go back up. I — threw up — on the floor!

AMANDA: From half past seven till after five every day you mean to tell me you walked around in the park, because you wanted to make me think that you were still going to Rubicam's Business College?

LAURA: It wasn't as bad as it sounds. I went inside places to get warmed up.

AMANDA: Inside where?

LAURA: I went in the art museum and the bird houses at the Zoo. I visited the penguins every day! Sometimes I did without lunch and went to the movies. Lately I've been spending most of my afternoons in the Jewel-box, that big glass house where they raise the tropical flowers.

AMANDA: You did all this to deceive me, just for the deception? (*Laura looks down.*) Why?

LAURA: Mother, when you're disappointed, you get that awful suffering look on your face, like the picture of Jesus' mother in the museum!

AMANDA: Hush!

LAURA: I couldn't face it.

(*Pause. A whisper of strings.*)
(*Legend: "The Crust of Humility."*)

AMANDA (*hopelessly fingering the huge pocketbook*): So what are we going to do the rest of our lives? Stay home and watch the parades go by? Amuse ourselves with the glass menagerie, darling? Eternally play those worn-out phonograph records your father left as a painful reminder of him? We won't have a business career — we've given that up because it gave us nervous indigestion! (*Laughs wearily.*) What is there left but dependency all our lives? I know so well what becomes of unmarried women who aren't prepared to occupy a position. I've seen such pitiful cases in the South — barely tolerated spinsters living upon the grudging patronage of sister's husband or brother's wife! — stuck away in some little mousetrap of a room — encouraged by one in-law to visit another — little birdlike women without any nest — eating the crust of humility all their life! Is that the future that we've mapped out for ourselves? I swear it's the only alternative I can think of! It isn't a very pleasant alternative, is it? Of course — some girls do *marry.* (*Laura twists her hands nervously.*) Haven't you ever liked some boy?

LAURA: Yes. I liked one once. (*Rises.*) I came across his picture a while ago.

AMANDA (*with some interest*): He gave you his picture?

LAURA: No, it's in the yearbook.

AMANDA (*disappointed*): Oh — a high-school boy.

(*Screen image: Jim as high school hero bearing a silver cup.*)

LAURA: Yes. His name was Jim. (*Laura lifts the heavy annual from the clawfoot table.*) Here he is in *The Pirates of Penzance.*

AMANDA (*absently*): The what?

LAURA: The operetta the senior class put on. He had a wonderful voice and we sat across the aisle from each other Mondays, Wednesdays, and Fridays in the Aud. Here he is with the silver cup for debating! See his grin?

AMANDA (*absently*): He must have had a jolly disposition.

LAURA: He used to call me — Blue Roses.

(*Image: blue roses.*)

AMANDA: Why did he call you such a name as that?

LAURA: When I had that attack of pleurosis — he asked me what was the matter when I came back. I said pleurosis — he thought that I said Blue Roses! So that's what he always called me after that. Whenever he saw me, he'd holler, "Hello, Blue Roses!" I didn't care for the girl that he went out with. Emily Meisenbach. Emily was the best-dressed girl at Soldan. She never struck me, though, as being sincere . . . It says in the Personal Section — they're engaged. That's — six years ago! They must be married by now.

AMANDA: Girls that aren't cut out for business careers usually wind up married to some nice man. (*Gets up with a spark of revival.*) Sister, that's what you'll do!

(*Laura utters a startled, doubtful laugh. She reaches quickly for a piece of glass.*)

LAURA: But, Mother —

AMANDA: Yes? (*Crossing to photograph.*)

LAURA (*in a tone of frightened apology*): I'm — crippled!

(*Image: screen.*)

AMANDA: Nonsense! Laura, I've told you never, never to use that word. Why, you're not crippled, you just have a little defect — hardly noticeable, even! When people have some slight disadvantage like that, they cultivate other things to make up for it — develop charm — and vivacity — and — *charm!* That's all you have to do! (*She turns again to the photograph.*) One thing your father had *plenty* of — was *charm!*

(*Tom motions to the fiddle in the wings.*)
(*The scene fades out with music.*)

SCENE 3

(*Legend on screen: "After the Fiasco — "*)
(*Tom speaks from the fire escape landing.*)

TOM: After the fiasco at Rubicam's Business College, the idea of getting a gentleman caller for Laura began to play a more important part in Mother's calculations. It became an obsession. Like some archetype of the universal unconscious, the image of the gentleman caller haunted our small apartment. . . . (*Image: young man at door with flowers.*) An evening at home rarely passed without some allusion to this image, this specter, this hope. . . . Even when he wasn't mentioned, his presence hung in Mother's preoccupied look and in my sister's frightened, apologetic manner — hung like a sentence passed upon the Wingfields! Mother was a woman of action as well as words. She began to take logical steps in the planned direction. Late that winter and in the early spring — realizing that extra money would be needed to properly feather the nest and plume the bird — she conducted a vigorous campaign on the telephone, roping in subscribers to one of those magazines for matrons called *The Home-maker's Companion,* the type of journal that features the serialized sublimations of ladies of letters who think in terms of delicate cup-like breasts, slim, tapering waists, rich, creamy thighs, eyes like wood smoke in autumn, fingers that soothe and caress like strains of music, bodies as powerful as Etruscan sculpture.

(*Screen image: glamor magazine cover.*)

(*Amanda enters with phone on long extension cord. She is spotted in the dim stage.*)

AMANDA: Ida Scott? This is Amanda Wingfield! We *missed* you at the D.A.R. last Monday! I said to myself: She's probably suffering with that sinus condition! How is that sinus condition? Horrors! Heaven have mercy! — You're a Christian martyr, yes, that's what you are, a Christian martyr! Well I just now happened to notice that your subscription to the *Companion*'s about to expire! Yes, it expires with the next issue, honey! — just when that wonderful new serial by Bessie Mae Hopper is getting off to such an exciting start. Oh, honey, it's something that you can't miss! You remember how *Gone With the Wind* took everybody by storm? You simply couldn't go out if you hadn't read it. All everybody *talked* was Scarlett O'Hara. Well, this is a book that critics already compare to *Gone With the Wind*. It's the *Gone With the Wind* of the post–World War generation! — What? — Burning? — Oh, honey, don't let them burn, go take a look in the oven and I'll hold the wire! Heavens — I think she's hung up!

(*Dim out.*)

(*Legend on screen: "You Think I'm in Love with Continental Shoemakers?"*)

(*Before the stage is lighted, the violent voices of Tom and Amanda are heard.*)

(*They are quarreling behind the portieres. In front of them stands Laura with clenched hands and panicky expression.*)

(*A clear pool of light on her figure throughout this scene.*)

TOM: What in Christ's name am I —
AMANDA (*shrilly*): Don't you use that —
TOM: Supposed to do!
AMANDA: Expression! Not in my —
TOM: Ohhh!
AMANDA: Presence! Have you gone out of your senses?
TOM: I have, that's true, *driven* out!
AMANDA: What is the matter with you, you — big — big — IDIOT!
TOM: Look — I've got *no thing*, no single thing —
AMANDA: Lower your voice!
TOM: In my life here that I can call my OWN! Everything is —
AMANDA: Stop that shouting!
TOM: Yesterday you confiscated my books! You had the nerve to —
AMANDA: I took that horrible novel back to the li-

brary — yes! That hideous book by that insane Mr. Lawrence. (*Tom laughs wildly.*) I cannot control the output of diseased minds or people who cater to them — (*Tom laughs still more wildly.*) BUT I WON'T ALLOW SUCH FILTH BROUGHT INTO MY HOUSE! No, no, no, no, no!
TOM: House, house! Who pays rent on it, who makes a slave of himself to —
AMANDA (*fairly screeching*): Don't you DARE to —
TOM: No, no, *I* mustn't say things! *I've* got to just —
AMANDA: Let me tell you —
TOM: I don't want to hear any more! (*He tears the portieres open. The upstage area is lit with a turgid smoky red glow.*)

(*Amanda's hair is in metal curlers and she wears a very old bathrobe, much too large for her slight figure, a relic of the faithless Mr. Wingfield.*)

(*An upright typewriter and a wild disarray of manuscripts are on the dropleaf table. The quarrel was probably precipitated by Amanda's interruption of his creative labor. A chair lying overthrown on the floor.*)

(*Their gesticulating shadows are cast on the ceiling by the fiery glow.*)

AMANDA: You *will* hear more, you —
TOM: No, I won't hear more, I'm going out!
AMANDA: You come right back in —
TOM: Out, out out! Because I'm —
AMANDA: Come back here, Tom Wingfield! I'm not through talking to you!
TOM: Oh, go —
LAURA (*desperately*): Tom!
AMANDA: You're going to listen, and no more insolence from you! I'm at the end of my patience! (*He comes back toward her.*)
TOM: What do you think I'm at? Aren't I supposed to have any patience to reach the end of, Mother? I know, I know. It seems unimportant to you, what I'm *doing* — what I *want* to do — having a little *difference* between them! You don't think that —
AMANDA: I think you've been doing things that you're ashamed of. That's why you act like this. I don't believe that you go every night to the movies. Nobody goes to the movies night after night. Nobody in their right minds goes to the movies as often as you pretend to. People don't go to the movies at nearly midnight, and movies don't let out at two A.M. Come in stumbling. Muttering to yourself like a maniac! You get three hours' sleep and then go to work. Oh, I can picture the way you're doing down there. Moping, doping, because you're in no condition!
TOM (*wildly*): No, I'm in no condition!
AMANDA: What right have you got to jeopardize your job? Jeopardize the security of us all? How do you think we'd manage if you were —

TOM: Listen! You think I'm crazy *about the warehouse?* (*He bends fiercely toward her slight figure.*) You think I'm in love with the Continental Shoemakers? You think I want to spend fifty-five *years* down there in that — *celotex interior!* with — *fluorescent — tubes!* Look! I'd rather somebody picked up a crowbar and battered out my brains — than go back mornings! I *go!* Every time you come in yelling that God damn *"Rise and Shine!" "Rise and Shine!"* I say to myself, *"How lucky dead* people are!" But I get up. I *go!* For sixty-five dollars a month I give up all that I dream of doing and being *ever!* And you say self — *self's* all I ever think of. Why, listen, if self is what I thought of, Mother, I'd be where he is — GONE! (*Pointing to father's picture.*) As far as the system of transportation reaches! (*He starts past her. She grabs his arm.*) Don't grab at me, Mother!

AMANDA: Where are you going?

TOM: I'm going to the *movies!*

AMANDA: I don't believe that lie!

TOM (*Crouching toward her, overtowering her tiny figure. She backs away, gasping.*): I'm going to opium dens! Yes, opium dens, dens of vice and criminals' hangouts, Mother. I've joined the Hogan gang, I'm a hired assassin, I carry a tommy-gun in a violin case! I run a string of cathouses in the Valley! They call me Killer, Killer Wingfield, I'm leading a double life, a simple, honest warehouse worker by day, by night, a dynamic *czar* of the *underworld,* Mother. I go to gambling casinos, I spin away fortunes on the roulette table! I wear a patch over one eye and a false mustache, sometimes I put on green whiskers. On those occasions they call me — *El Diablo!* Oh, I could tell you things to make you sleepless! My enemies plan to dynamite this place. They're going to blow us all skyhigh some night! I'll be glad, very happy, and so will you! You'll go up, up on a broomstick, over Blue Mountain with seventeen gentlemen callers! You ugly — babbling old — *witch.* . . . (*He goes through a series of violent, clumsy movements, seizing his overcoat, lunging to the door, pulling it fiercely open. The women watch him, aghast. His arm catches in the sleeve of the coat as he struggles to pull it on. For a moment he is pinioned by the bulky garment. With an outraged groan he tears the coat off again, splitting the shoulders of it, and hurls it across the room. It strikes against the shelf of Laura's glass collection, there is a tinkle of shattering glass. Laura cries out as if wounded.*)

(*Music legend: "The Glass Menagerie."*)

LAURA (*shrilly*): My glass! — menagerie. . . . (*She covers her face and turns away.*)

(*But Amanda is still stunned and stupefied by the "ugly witch" so that she barely notices this occurrence. Now she recovers her speech.*)

AMANDA (*in an awful voice*): I won't speak to you — until you apologize! (*She crosses through portieres and draws them together behind her. Tom is left with Laura. Laura clings weakly to the mantel with her face averted. Tom stares at her stupidly for a moment. Then he crosses to shelf. Drops awkwardly to his knees to collect the fallen glass, glancing at Laura as if he would speak but couldn't.*)

(*"The Glass Menagerie" steals in as the scene dims out.*)

SCENE 4

(*The interior is dark. Faint light in the alley.*)

(*A deep-voiced bell in a church is tolling the hour of five as the scene commences.*)

(*Tom appears at the top of the alley. After each solemn boom of the bell in the tower, he shakes a little noisemaker or rattle as if to express the tiny spasm of man in contrast to the sustained power and dignity of the Almighty. This and the unsteadiness of his advance make it evident that he has been drinking.*)

(*As he climbs the few steps to the fire escape landing light steals up inside. Laura appears in nightdress, observing Tom's empty bed in the front room.*)

(*Tom fishes in his pockets for the door key, removing a motley assortment of articles in the search, including a perfect shower of movie ticket stubs and an empty bottle. At last he finds the key, but just as he is about to insert it, it slips from his fingers. He strikes a match and crouches below the door.*)

TOM (*bitterly*): One crack — and it falls through!

(*Laura opens the door.*)

LAURA: Tom! Tom, what are you doing?

TOM: Looking for a door key.

LAURA: Where have you been all this time?

TOM: I have been to the movies.

LAURA: All this time at the movies?

TOM: There was a very long program. There was a Garbo picture and a Mickey Mouse and a travelogue and a newsreel and a preview of coming attractions. And there was an organ solo and a collection for the milk fund — simultaneously — which ended up in a terrible fight between a fat lady and an usher!

LAURA (*innocently*): Did you have to stay through everything?

TOM: Of course! And, oh, I forgot! There was a big

stage show! The headliner on this stage show was
Malvolio the Magician. He performed wonderful
tricks, many of them, such as pouring water back
and forth between pitchers. First it turned to wine
and then it turned to beer and then it turned to
whiskey. I know it was whiskey it finally turned
into because he needed somebody to come up out
of the audience to help him, and I came up — both
shows! It was Kentucky Straight Bourbon. A very
generous fellow, he gave souvenirs. (*He pulls from
his back pocket a shimmering rainbow-colored
scarf.*) He gave me this. This is his magic scarf. You
can have it, Laura. You wave it over a canary cage
and you get a bowl of goldfish. You wave it over
the goldfish bowl and they fly away canaries. . . .
But the wonderfullest trick of all was the coffin
trick. We nailed him into a coffin and he got out of
the coffin without removing one nail. (*He has come
inside.*) There is a trick that would come in handy
for me — get me out of this 2 by 4 situation! (*Flops
onto bed and starts removing shoes.*)

LAURA: Tom — Shhh!

TOM: What you shushing me for?

LAURA: You'll wake up Mother.

TOM: Goody, goody! Pay 'er back for all those "Rise
an' Shines." (*Lies down, groaning.*) You know it
don't take much intelligence to get yourself into a
nailed-up coffin, Laura. But who in hell ever got
himself out of one without removing one nail?

(*As if in answer, the father's grinning photograph
lights up.*)

(*Scene dims out.*)

(*Immediately following: The church bell is heard
striking six. At the sixth stroke the alarm clock goes
off in Amanda's room, and after a few moments we
hear her calling: "Rise and Shine! Rise and Shine!
Laura, go tell your brother to rise and shine!"*)

TOM (*sitting up slowly*): I'll rise — but I won't shine.

(*The light increases.*)

AMANDA: Laura, tell your brother his coffee is ready.

(*Laura slips into front room.*)

LAURA: Tom! it's nearly seven. Don't make Mother
nervous. (*He stares at her stupidly. Beseechingly.*)
Tom, speak to Mother this morning. Make up
with her, apologize, speak to her!

TOM: She won't to me. It's her that started not speaking.

LAURA: If you just say you're sorry she'll start speaking.

TOM: Her not speaking — is that such a tragedy?

LAURA: Please — please!

AMANDA (*calling from kitchenette*): Laura, are you

going to do what I asked you to do, or do I have
to get dressed and go out myself?

LAURA: Going, going — soon as I get on my coat!
(*She pulls on a shapeless felt hat with nervous,
jerky movement, pleadingly glancing at Tom.
Rushes awkwardly for coat. The coat is one of
Amanda's, inaccurately made over, the sleeves too
short for Laura.*) Butter and what else?

AMANDA (*entering upstage*): Just butter. Tell them to
charge it.

LAURA: Mother, they make such faces when I do that.

AMANDA: Sticks and stones may break my bones, but
the expression on Mr. Garfinkel's face won't harm
us! Tell your brother his coffee is getting cold.

LAURA (*at door*): Do what I asked you, will you, will
you, Tom?

(*He looks sullenly away.*)

AMANDA: Laura, go now or just don't go at all!

LAURA (*rushing out*): Going — going! (*A second later
she cries out. Tom springs up and crosses to the
door. Amanda rushes anxiously in. Tom opens the
door.*)

TOM: Laura?

LAURA: I'm all right. I slipped, but I'm all right.

FAR LEFT: Laurette Taylor as
Amanda in the original 1944
production of *The Glass
Menagerie*. LEFT: Julie
Haydon as Laura. ABOVE: Joe
Mielziner's drawing of the set
for the original production of
The Glass Menagerie.

AMANDA (*peering anxiously after her*): If anyone breaks a leg on those fire escape steps, the landlord ought to be sued for every cent he possesses! (*She shuts door. Remembers she isn't speaking and returns to other room.*)

(*As Tom enters listlessly for his coffee, she turns her back to him and stands rigidly facing the window on the gloomy gray vault of the areaway. Its light on her face with its aged but childish features is cruelly sharp, satirical as a Daumier print.*)

(*Music under: "Ave Maria."*)

(*Tom glances sheepishly but sullenly at her averted figure and slumps at the table. The coffee is scalding hot; he sips it and gasps and spits it back in the cup. At his gasp, Amanda catches her breath and half turns. Then catches herself and turns back to window.*)

(*Tom blows on his coffee, glancing sidewise at his mother. She clears her throat. Tom clears his. He starts to rise. Sinks back down again, scratches his head, clears his throat again. Amanda coughs. Tom raises his cup in both hands to blow on it, his eyes staring over the rim of it at his mother for several moments. Then he slowly sets the cup down and awkwardly and hesitantly rises from the chair.*)

TOM (*hoarsely*): Mother. I — I apologize. Mother. (*Amanda draws a quick, shuddering breath. Her face works grotesquely. She breaks into childlike tears.*) I'm sorry for what I said, for everything that I said, I didn't mean it.

AMANDA (*sobbingly*): My devotion has made me a witch and so I make myself hateful to my children!

TOM: *No, you don't.*

AMANDA: I worry so much, don't sleep, it makes me nervous!

TOM (*gently*): I understand that.

AMANDA: I've had to put up a solitary battle all these years. But you're my right-hand bower! Don't fall down, don't fail!

TOM (*gently*): I try, Mother.

AMANDA (*with great enthusiasm*): Try and you will SUCCEED! (*The notion makes her breathless.*) Why, you — you're just *full* of natural endowments! Both of my children — they're *unusual* children! Don't you think I know it? I'm so — *proud!* Happy and — feel I've — so much to be thankful for but — Promise me one thing, son!

TOM: What, Mother?

AMANDA: Promise, son, you'll — never be a drunkard!

TOM (*turns to her grinning*): I will never be a drunkard, Mother.

AMANDA: That's what frightened me so, that you'd be drinking! Eat a bowl of Purina!

TOM: Just coffee, Mother.

AMANDA: Shredded wheat biscuit?

TOM: No, no, Mother, just coffee.

AMANDA: You can't put in a day's work on an empty stomach. You've got ten minutes — don't gulp! Drinking too-hot liquids makes cancer of the stomach. . . . Put cream in.

TOM: No, thank you.

AMANDA: To cool it.

TOM: No! No, thank you, I want it black.

AMANDA: I know, but it's not good for you. We have to do all that we can to build ourselves up. In these trying times we live in, all that we have to cling to is — each other. . . . That's why it's so important to — Tom, I — I sent out your sister so I could discuss something with you. If you hadn't spoken I would have spoken to you. (*Sits down.*)

TOM (*gently*): What is it, Mother, that you want to discuss?

AMANDA: *Laura!*

(*Tom puts his cup down slowly.*)

(*Legend on screen: "Laura."*)

(*Music: "The Glass Menagerie."*)

TOM: — Oh. — Laura . . .

AMANDA (*touching his sleeve*): You know how Laura is. So quiet but — still water runs deep! She notices things and I think she — broods about them. (*Tom looks up.*) A few days ago I came in and she was crying.

TOM: What about?

AMANDA: You.

TOM: Me?

AMANDA: She has an idea that you're not happy here.

TOM: What gave her that idea?

AMANDA: What gives her any idea? However, you do act strangely. I — I'm not criticizing, understand *that!* I know your ambitions do not lie in the warehouse, that like everybody in the whole wide world — you've had to — make sacrifices, but — Tom — Tom — life's not easy, it calls for — Spartan endurance! There's so many things in my heart that I cannot describe to you! I've never told you but I — *loved your father.* . . .

TOM (*gently*): I know that, Mother.

AMANDA: And you — when I see you taking after his ways! Staying out late — and — well, you *had* been drinking the night you were in that — terrifying condition! Laura says that you hate the apartment and that you go out nights to get away from it! Is that true, Tom?

TOM: No. You say there's so much in your heart that you can't describe to me. That's true of me, too. There's so much in my heart that I can't describe to *you!* So let's respect each other's —

AMANDA: But, why — *why,* Tom — are you always so *restless?* Where do you go to, nights?

TOM: I — go to the movies.

AMANDA: Why do you go to the movies so much, Tom?

TOM: I go to the movies because — I like adventure. Adventure is something I don't have much of at work, so I go to the movies.

AMANDA: But, Tom, you go to the movies *entirely* too *much!*

TOM: I like a lot of adventure.

(*Amanda looks baffled, then hurt. As the familiar inquisition resumes he becomes hard and impatient again. Amanda slips back into her querulous attitude toward him.*)

(*Image on screen: sailing vessel with Jolly Roger.°*)

AMANDA: Most young men find adventure in their careers.

TOM: Then most young men are not employed in a warehouse.

AMANDA: The world is full of young men employed in warehouses and offices and factories.

TOM: Do all of them find adventure in their careers?

AMANDA: They do or they do without it! Not everybody has a craze for adventure.

TOM: Man is by instinct a lover, a hunter, a fighter, and none of those instincts are given much play at the warehouse!

AMANDA: Man is by instinct! Don't quote instinct to me! Instinct is something that people have got away from! It belongs to animals! Christian adults don't want it!

TOM: What do Christian adults want, then, Mother?

AMANDA: Superior things! Things of the mind and the spirit! Only animals have to satisfy instincts! Surely your aims are somewhat higher than theirs! Than monkeys — pigs —

TOM: I reckon they're not.

AMANDA: You're joking. However, that isn't what I wanted to discuss.

TOM (*rising*): I haven't much time.

AMANDA (*pushing his shoulders*): Sit down.

TOM: You want me to punch in red at the warehouse, Mother?

AMANDA: You have five minutes. I want to talk about Laura.

(*Legend: "Plans and Provisions."*)

TOM: All right! What about Laura?

AMANDA: We have to be making plans and provisions for her. She's older than you, two years, and nothing has happened. She just drifts along doing nothing. It frightens me terribly how she just drifts along.

Jolly Roger: The black flag with white skull and crossbones used by pirates.

TOM: I guess she's the type that people call home girls.

AMANDA: There's no such type, and if there is, it's a pity! That is unless the home is hers, with a husband!

TOM: What?

AMANDA: Oh, I can see the handwriting on the wall as plain as I see the nose in front of my face! It's terrifying! More and more you remind me of your father! He was out all hours without explanation — Then *left!* Good-bye! And me with a bag to hold. I saw that letter you got from the Merchant Marine. I know what you're dreaming of. I'm not standing here blindfolded. Very well, then. Then *do* it! But not till there's somebody to take your place.

TOM: What do you mean?

AMANDA: I mean that as soon as Laura has got somebody to take care of her, married, a home of her own, independent — why, then you'll be free to go wherever you please, on land, on sea, whichever way the wind blows you! But until that time you've got to look out for your sister. I don't say me because I'm old and don't matter! I say for your sister because she's young and dependent. I put her in business college — a dismal failure! Frightened her so it made her sick to her stomach. I took her over to the Young People's League at the church. Another fiasco. She spoke to nobody, nobody spoke to her. Now all she does is fool with those pieces of glass and play those worn-out records. What kind of a life is that for a girl to lead!

TOM: What can I do about it?

AMANDA: Overcome selfishness! Self, self, self is all that you ever think of! (*Tom springs up and crosses to get his coat. It is ugly and bulky. He pulls on a cap with earmuffs.*) Where is your muffler? Put your wool muffler on! (*He snatches it angrily from the closet and tosses it around his neck and pulls both ends tight.*) Tom! I haven't said what I had in mind to ask you.

TOM: I'm too late to —

AMANDA (*Catching his arms — very importunately. Then shyly*): Down at the warehouse, aren't there some — nice young men?

TOM: No!

AMANDA: There *must* be — some . . .

TOM: Mother —

(*Gesture.*)

AMANDA: Find out one that's clean-living — doesn't drink and — ask him out for sister!

TOM: What?

AMANDA: For *sister!* To *meet!* Get *acquainted!*

TOM (*stamping to door*): Oh, my go-osh!

AMANDA: Will you? (*He opens door. Imploringly.*) Will you? (*He starts down.*) Will you? *Will* you, dear?

TOM (*calling back*): YES!

(*Amanda closes the door hesitantly and with a troubled but faintly hopeful expression.*)
   (*Screen image: glamor magazine cover.*)
   (*Spot° Amanda at phone.*)

AMANDA: Ella Cartwright? This is Amanda Wingfield! How are you, honey? How is that kidney condition? (*Count five.*) Horrors! (*Count five.*) You're a Christian martyr, yes, honey, that's what you are, a Christian martyr! Well, I just happened to notice in my little red book that your subscription to the *Companion* has just run out! I knew that you wouldn't want to miss out on the wonderful serial starting in this new issue. It's by Bessie Mae Hopper, the first thing she's written since *Honeymoon for Three*. Wasn't that a strange and interesting story? Well, this one is even lovelier, I believe. It has a sophisticated society background. It's all about the horsey set on Long Island!

(*Fade out.*)

SCENE 5

(*Legend on screen "Annunciation." Fade with music.*)
   (*It is early dusk of a spring evening. Supper has just been finished in the Wingfield apartment. Amanda and Laura in light colored dresses are removing dishes from the table, in the upstage area, which is shadowy, their movements formalized almost as a dance or ritual, their moving forms as pale and silent as moths.*)
   (*Tom, in white shirt and trousers, rises from the table and crosses toward the fire escape.*)

AMANDA (*as he passes her*): Son, will you do me a favor?
TOM: What?
AMANDA: Comb your hair! You look so pretty when your hair is combed! (*Tom slouches on sofa with evening paper. Enormous caption "Franco Triumphs."*) There is only one respect in which I would like you to emulate your father.
TOM: What respect is that?
AMANDA: The care he always took of his appearance. He never allowed himself to look untidy. (*He throws down the paper and crosses to fire escape.*) Where are you going?
TOM: I'm going out to smoke.
AMANDA: You smoke too much. A pack a day at fifteen cents a pack. How much would that amount to in a month? Thirty times fifteen is how much, Tom? Figure it out and you will be astounded at

Spot: Spotlight.

what you could save. Enough to give you a night school course in accounting at Washington U! Just think what a wonderful thing that would be for you, son!

(*Tom is unmoved by the thought.*)

TOM: I'd rather smoke. (*He steps out on landing, letting the screen door slam.*)
AMANDA (*sharply*): I know! That's the tragedy of it.... (*Alone, she turns to look at her husband's picture.*)

(*Dance music: "All the World is Waiting for the Sunrise!"*)

TOM (*to the audience*): Across the alley from us was the Paradise Dance Hall. On evenings in spring the windows and doors were open and the music came outdoors. Sometimes the lights were turned out except for a large glass sphere that hung from the ceiling. It would turn slowly about and filter the dusk with delicate rainbow colors. Then the orchestra played a waltz or a tango, something that had a slow and sensuous rhythm. Couples would come outside, to the relative privacy of the alley. You could see them kissing behind ash-pits and telephone poles. This was the compensation for lives that passed like mine, without any change or adventure. Adventure and change were imminent in this year. They were waiting around the corner for all these kids. Suspended in the mist over Berchtesgaden, caught in the folds of Chamberlain's umbrella — In Spain there was Guernica!° But here there was only hot swing music and liquor, dance halls, bars, and movies, and sex that hung in the gloom like a chandelier and flooded the world with brief, deceptive rainbows.... All the world was waiting for bombardments!

(*Amanda turns from the picture and comes outside.*)

AMANDA (*sighing*): A fire escape landing's a poor excuse for a porch. (*She spreads a newspaper on a step and sits down, gracefully and demurely as if she were settling into a swing on a Mississippi veranda.*) What are you looking at?
TOM: The moon.
AMANDA: Is there a moon this evening?
TOM: It's rising over Garfinkel's Delicatessen.
AMANDA: So it is! A little silver slipper of a moon. Have you made a wish on it yet?
TOM: Um-hum.

Berchtesgaden ... Chamberlain ... Guernica: All references to the approach of World War II in Europe. Berchtesgaden was Hitler's summer home; Neville Chamberlain was the prime minister of England who signed the Munich Pact, which was regarded as a capitulation to Hitler; and the Spanish town Guernica was destroyed by German bombs during the Spanish Civil War in the late 1930s.

AMANDA: What did you wish for?

TOM: That's a secret.

AMANDA: A secret, huh? Well, I won't tell mine either. I will be just as mysterious as you.

TOM: I bet I can guess what yours is.

AMANDA: Is my head so transparent?

TOM: You're not a sphinx.

AMANDA: No, I don't have secrets. I'll tell you what I wished for on the moon. Success and happiness for my precious children! I wish for that whenever there's a moon, and when there isn't a moon, I wish for it, too.

TOM: I thought perhaps you wished for a gentleman caller.

AMANDA: Why do you say that?

TOM: Don't you remember asking me to fetch one?

AMANDA: I remember suggesting that it would be nice for your sister if you brought home some nice young man from the warehouse. I think I've made that suggestion more than once.

TOM: Yes, you have made it repeatedly.

AMANDA: Well?

TOM: We are going to have one.

AMANDA: *What?*

TOM: A gentleman caller!

(*The annunciation is celebrated with music.*)
    (*Amanda rises.*)
    (*Image on screen: caller with bouquet.*)

AMANDA: You mean you have asked some nice young man to come over?

TOM: Yep. I've asked him to dinner.

AMANDA: You really did?

TOM: I did!

AMANDA: You did, and did he — *accept?*

TOM: He did!

AMANDA: Well, well — well, well! That's — lovely!

TOM: I thought that you would be pleased.

AMANDA: It's definite, then?

TOM: Very definite.

AMANDA: Soon?

TOM: Very soon.

AMANDA: For heaven's sake, stop putting on and tell me some things, will you?

TOM: What things do you want me to tell you?

AMANDA: *Naturally* I would like to know when he's *coming!*

TOM: He's coming tomorrow.

AMANDA: *Tomorrow?*

TOM: Yep. Tomorrow.

AMANDA: But, Tom!

TOM: Yes, Mother?

AMANDA: Tomorrow gives me no time!

TOM: Time for what?

AMANDA: Preparations! Why didn't you phone me at once, as soon as you asked him, the minute that he accepted? Then, don't you see, I could have been getting ready!

TOM: You don't have to make any fuss.

AMANDA: Oh, Tom, Tom, Tom, of course I have to make a fuss! I want things nice, not sloppy! Not thrown together. I'll certainly have to do some fast thinking, won't I?

TOM: I don't see why you have to think at all.

AMANDA: You just don't know. We can't have a gentleman caller in a pigsty! All my wedding silver has to be polished, the monogrammed table linen ought to be laundered! The windows have to be washed and fresh curtains put up. And how about clothes? We have to *wear* something, don't we?

TOM: Mother, this boy is no one to make a fuss over!

AMANDA: Do you realize he's the first young man we've introduced to your sister? It's terrible, dreadful, disgraceful that poor little sister has never received a single gentleman caller! Tom, come inside! (*She opens the screen door.*)

TOM: What for?

AMANDA: I want to ask you some things.

TOM: If you're going to make such a fuss, I'll call it off, I'll tell him not to come.

AMANDA: You certainly won't do anything of the kind. Nothing offends people worse than broken engagements. It simply means I'll have to work like a Turk! We won't be brilliant, but we'll pass inspection. Come on inside. (*Tom follows, groaning.*) Sit down.

TOM: Any particular place you would like me to sit?

AMANDA: Thank heavens I've got that new sofa! I'm also making payments on a floor lamp I'll have sent out! And put the chintz covers on, they'll brighten things up! Of course I'd hoped to have these walls repapered. . . . What is the young man's name?

TOM: His name is O'Connor.

AMANDA: That, of course, means fish — tomorrow is Friday!° I'll have that salmon loaf — with Durkee's dressing! What does he do? He works at the warehouse?

TOM: Of course! How else would I

AMANDA: Tom, he — doesn't drink?

TOM: Why do you ask me that?

AMANDA: Your father *did!*

TOM: Don't get started on that!

AMANDA: He *does* drink, then?

TOM: Not that I know of!

AMANDA: Make sure, be certain! The last thing I want for my daughter's a boy who drinks!

TOM: Aren't you being a little premature? Mr. O'Connor has not yet appeared on the scene!

---

fish . . . Friday: Until recent decades, Catholics were prohibited from eating meat on Fridays.

AMANDA: But will tomorrow. To meet your sister, and what do I know about his character? Nothing! Old maids are better off than wives of drunkards!

TOM: Oh, my God!

AMANDA: Be still!

TOM (*leaning forward to whisper*): Lots of fellows meet girls whom they don't marry!

AMANDA: Oh, talk sensibly, Tom — and don't be sarcastic! (*She has gotten a hairbrush.*)

TOM: What are you doing?

AMANDA: I'm brushing that cowlick down! What is this young man's position at the warehouse?

TOM (*submitting grimly to the brush and the interrogation*): This young man's position is that of a shipping clerk, Mother.

AMANDA: Sounds to me like a fairly responsible job, the sort of a job *you* would be in if you just had more *get-up*. What is his salary? Have you got any idea.

TOM: I would judge it to be approximately eighty-five dollars a month.

AMANDA: Well — not princely, but —

TOM: Twenty more than I make.

AMANDA: Yes, how well I know! But for a family man, eighty-five dollars a month is not much more than you can just get by on. . . .

TOM: Yes, but Mr. O'Connor is not a family man.

AMANDA: He might be, mightn't he? Some time in the future?

TOM: I see. Plans and provisions.

AMANDA: You are the only young man that I know of who ignores the fact that the future becomes the present, the present the past, and the past turns into everlasting regret if you don't plan for it!

TOM: I will think that over and see what I can make of it.

AMANDA: Don't be supercilious with your mother! Tell me some more about this — what do you call him?

TOM: James D. O'Connor. The D. is for Delaney.

AMANDA: Irish on *both* sides! *Gracious!* And doesn't drink?

TOM: Shall I call him up and ask him right this minute?

AMANDA: The only way to find out about those things is to make discreet inquiries at the proper moment. When I was a girl in Blue Mountain and it was suspected that a young man drank, the girl whose attentions he had been receiving, if any girl *was*, would sometimes speak to the minister of his church, or rather her father would if her father was living, and sort of feel him out on the young man's character. That is the way such things are discreetly handled to keep a young woman from making a tragic mistake!

TOM: Then how did you happen to make a tragic mistake?

AMANDA: That innocent look of your father's had everyone fooled! He *smiled* — the world was *enchanted!* No girl can do worse than put herself at the mercy of a handsome appearance! I hope that Mr. O'Connor is not too good-looking.

TOM: No, he's not too good-looking. He's covered with freckles and hasn't too much of a nose.

AMANDA: He's not right-down homely, though?

TOM: Not right-down homely. Just medium homely, I'd say.

AMANDA: Character's what to look for in a man.

TOM: That's what I've always said, Mother.

AMANDA: You've never said anything of the kind and I suspect you would never give it a thought.

TOM: Don't be suspicious of me.

AMANDA: At least I hope he's the type that's up and coming.

TOM: I think he really goes in for self-improvement.

AMANDA: What reason have you to think so?

TOM: He goes to night school.

AMANDA (*beaming*): Splendid! What does he do, I mean study?

TOM: Radio engineering and public speaking!

AMANDA: Then he has visions of being advanced in the world! Any young man who studies public speaking is aiming to have an executive job some day! And radio engineering? A thing for the future! Both of these facts are very illuminating. Those are the sort of things that a mother should know concerning any young man who comes to call on her daughter. Seriously or — not.

TOM: One little warning. He doesn't know about Laura. I didn't let on that we had dark ulterior motives. I just said, why don't you come have dinner with us? He said okay and that was the whole conversation.

AMANDA: I bet it was! You're eloquent as an oyster. However, he'll know about Laura when he gets here. When he sees how lovely and sweet and pretty she is, he'll thank his lucky stars he was asked to dinner.

TOM: Mother, you mustn't expect too much of Laura.

AMANDA: What do you mean?

TOM: Laura seems all those things to you and me because she's ours and we love her. We don't even notice she's crippled anymore.

AMANDA: Don't say crippled! You know that I never allow that word to be used!

TOM: But face facts, Mother. She is and — that's not all —

AMANDA: What do you mean not all?

TOM: Laura is very different from other girls.

AMANDA: I think the difference is all to her advantage.

TOM: Not quite all — in the eyes of others — strangers — she's terribly shy and lives in a world of her own and those things make her seem a little peculiar to people outside the house.

AMANDA: Don't say peculiar.

TOM: Face the facts. She is.

(*The dance-hall music changes to a tango that has a minor and somewhat ominous tone.*)

AMANDA: In what way is she peculiar — may I ask?

TOM (*gently*): She lives in a world of her own — a world of — little glass ornaments, Mother.... (*Gets up. Amanda remains holding brush, looking at him, troubled.*) She plays old phonograph records and — that's about all — (*He glances at himself in the mirror and crosses to door.*)

AMANDA (*sharply*): Where are you going?

TOM: I'm going to the movies. (*Out screen door.*)

AMANDA: Not to the movies, every night to the movies! (*Follows quickly to screen door.*) I don't believe you always go to the movies! (*He is gone. Amanda looks worriedly after him for a moment. Then vitality and optimism return and she turns from the door. Crossing to portieres.*) Laura! Laura! (*Laura answers from kitchenette.*)

LAURA: Yes, Mother.

AMANDA: Let those dishes go and come in front! (*Laura appears with dish towel. Gaily.*) Laura, come here and make a wish on the moon!

LAURA (*entering*). Moon — moon?

AMANDA: A little silver slipper of a moon. Look over your left shoulder, Laura, and make a wish! (*Laura looks faintly puzzled as if called out of sleep. Amanda seizes her shoulders and turns her at an angle by the door.*) Now! Now, darling, *wish!*

LAURA: What shall I wish for, Mother?

AMANDA (*her voice trembling and her eyes suddenly filling with tears*): Happiness! Good Fortune!

(*The violin rises and the stage dims out.*)

SCENE 6

(*Image: high school hero.*)

TOM: And so the following evening I brought Jim home to dinner. I had known Jim slightly in high school. In high school Jim was a hero. He had tremendous Irish good nature and vitality with the scrubbed and polished look of white chinaware. He seemed to move in a continual spotlight. He was a star in basketball, captain of the debating club, president of the senior class and the glee club and he sang the male lead in the annual light op-

eras. He was always running or bounding, never just walking. He seemed always at the point of defeating the law of gravity. He was shooting with such velocity through his adolescence that you would logically expect him to arrive at nothing short of the White House by the time he was thirty. But Jim apparently ran into more interference after his graduation from Soldan. His speed had definitely slowed. Six years after he left high school he was holding a job that wasn't much better than mine.

(*Image: clerk.*)

He was the only one at the warehouse with whom I was on friendly terms. I was valuable to him as someone who could remember his former glory, who had seen him win basketball games and the silver cup in debating. He knew of my secret practice of retiring to a cabinet of the washroom to work on poems when business was slack in the warehouse. He called me Shakespeare. And while the other boys in the warehouse regarded me with suspicious hostility, Jim took a humorous attitude toward me. Gradually his attitude affected the others, their hostility wore off and they also began to smile at me as people smile at an oddly fashioned dog who trots across their path at some distance.

I knew that Jim and Laura had known each other at Soldan, and I had heard Laura speak admiringly of his voice. I didn't know if Jim remembered her or not. In high school Laura had been as unobtrusive as Jim had been astonishing. If he did remember Laura, it was not as my sister, for when I asked him to dinner, he grinned and said, "You know, Shakespeare, I never thought of you as having folks!"

He was about to discover that I did....

(*Light up stage.*)

(*Legend on screen: "The Accent of a Coming Foot."*)

(*Friday evening. It is about five o'clock of a late spring evening which comes "scattering poems in the sky."*)

(*A delicate lemony light is in the Wingfield apartment.*)

(*Amanda has worked like a Turk in preparation for the gentleman caller. The results are astonishing. The new floor lamp with its rose-silk shade is in place, a colored paper lantern conceals the broken light fixture in the ceiling, new billowing white curtains are at the windows, chintz covers are on chairs and sofa, a pair of new sofa pillows make their initial appearance.*)

(*Open boxes and tissue paper are scattered on the floor.*)

(*Laura stands in the middle with lifted arms while Amanda crouches before her, adjusting the hem of the new dress, devout and ritualistic. The dress is colored and designed by memory. The arrangement of Laura's hair is changed; it is softer and more becoming. A fragile, unearthly prettiness has come out in Laura: she is like a piece of translucent glass touched by light, given a momentary radiance, not actual, not lasting.*)

AMANDA (*impatiently*): Why are you trembling?
LAURA: Mother, you've made me so nervous!
AMANDA: How have I made you nervous?
LAURA: By all this fuss! You make it seem so important!
AMANDA: I don't understand you, Laura. You couldn't be satisfied with just sitting home, and yet whenever I try to arrange something for you, you seem to resist it. (*She gets up.*) Now take a look at yourself. No, wait! Wait just a moment — I have an idea!
LAURA: What is it now?

(*Amanda produces two powder puffs which she wraps in handkerchiefs and stuffs in Laura's bosom.*)

LAURA: Mother, what are you doing?
AMANDA: They call them "Gay Deceivers"!
LAURA: I won't wear them!
AMANDA: You will!
LAURA: Why should I?
AMANDA: Because, to be painfully honest, your chest is flat.
LAURA: You make it seem like we were setting a trap.
AMANDA: All pretty girls are a trap, a pretty trap, and men expect them to be. (*Legend: "A Pretty Trap."*) Now look at yourself, young lady. This is the prettiest you will ever be! I've got to fix myself now! You're going to be surprised by your mother's appearance! (*She crosses through portieres, humming gaily.*)

(*Laura moves slowly to the long mirror and stares solemnly at herself.*)

(*A wind blows the white curtains inward in a slow, graceful motion and with a faint, sorrowful sighing.*)

AMANDA (*offstage*): It isn't dark enough yet. (*She turns slowly before the mirror with a troubled look.*)

(*Legend on screen: "This Is My Sister: Celebrate Her with Strings!" Music.*)

AMANDA (*laughing, off*): I'm going to show you something. I'm going to make a spectacular appearance!
LAURA: What is it, Mother?
AMANDA: Possess your soul in patience — you will see! Something I've resurrected from that old trunk! Styles haven't changed so terribly much after all.... (*She parts the portieres.*) Now just look at your mother! (*She wears a girlish frock of yellowed voile with a blue silk sash. She carries a*

bunch of jonquils — the legend of her youth is nearly revived. Feverishly.*) This is the dress in which I led the cotillion. Won the cakewalk twice at Sunset Hill, wore one spring to the Governor's ball in Jackson! See how I sashayed around the ballroom, Laura? (*She raises her skirt and does a mincing step around the room.*) I wore it on Sundays for my gentlemen callers! I had it on the day I met your father — I had malaria fever all that spring. The change of climate from East Tennessee to the Delta — weakened resistance — I had a little temperature all the time — not enough to be serious — just enough to make me restless and giddy! Invitations poured in — parties all over the Delta! — "Stay in bed," said Mother, "you have fever!" — but I just wouldn't. — I took quinine but kept on going, going! — Evenings, dances! — Afternoons, long, long rides! Picnics — lovely! — So lovely, that country in May. — All lacy with dogwood, literally flooded with jonquils! — That was the spring I had the craze for jonquils. Jonquils became an absolute obsession. Mother said, "Honey, there's no more room for jonquils." And still I kept on bringing in more jonquils. Whenever, wherever I saw them, I'd say, "Stop! Stop! I see jonquils!" I made the young men help me gather the jonquils! It was a joke, Amanda and her jonquils! Finally there were no more vases to hold them, every available space was filled with jonquils. No vases to hold them? All right, I'll hold them myself! And then I — (*She stops in front of the picture. Music.*) met your father! Malaria fever and jonquils and then — this — boy.... (*She switches on the rose-colored lamp.*) I hope they get here before it starts to rain. (*She crosses upstage and places the jonquils in bowl on table.*) I gave your brother a little extra change so he and Mr. O'Connor could take the service car home.
LAURA (*with altered look*): What did you say his name was?
AMANDA: O'Connor.
LAURA: What is his first name?
AMANDA: I don't remember. Oh, yes, I do. It was — Jim!

(*Laura sways slightly and catches hold of a chair.*)
(*Legend on screen: "Not Jim!"*)

LAURA (*faintly*): Not — Jim!
AMANDA: Yes, that was it, it was Jim! I've never known a Jim that wasn't nice!

(*Music: ominous.*)

LAURA: Are you sure his name is Jim O'Connor?
AMANDA: Yes. Why?
LAURA: Is he the one that Tom used to know in high school?

AMANDA: He didn't say so. I think he just got to know him at the warehouse.

LAURA: There was a Jim O'Connor we both knew in high school — (*Then, with effort.*) If that is the one that Tom is bringing to dinner — you'll have to excuse me, I won't come to the table.

AMANDA: What sort of nonsense is this?

LAURA: You asked me once if I'd ever liked a boy. Don't you remember I showed you this boy's picture?

AMANDA: You mean the boy you showed me in the yearbook?

LAURA: Yes, that boy.

AMANDA: Laura, Laura, were you in love with that boy?

LAURA: I don't know, Mother. All I know is I couldn't sit at the table if it was him!

AMANDA: It won't be him! It isn't the least bit likely. But whether it is or not, you will come to the table. You will not be excused.

LAURA: I'll have to be, Mother.

AMANDA: I don't intend to humor your silliness, Laura. I've had too much from you and your brother, both! So just sit down and compose yourself till they come. Tom has forgotten his key so you'll have to let them in, when they arrive.

LAURA (*panicky*): Oh, Mother — *you* answer the door!

AMANDA (*lightly*): I'll be in the kitchen — busy!

LAURA: Oh, Mother, please answer the door, don't make me do it!

AMANDA (*crossing into kitchenette*): I've got to fix the dressing for the salmon. Fuss, fuss — silliness! — over a gentleman caller!

(*Door swings shut. Laura is left alone.*)
    (*Legend: "Terror!"*)
(*She utters a low moan and turns off the lamp — sits stiffly on the edge of the sofa, knotting her fingers together.*)
    (*Legend on screen: "The Opening of a Door!"*)
    (*Tom and Jim appear on the fire escape steps and climb to landing. Hearing their approach, Laura rises with a panicky gesture. She retreats to the portieres.*)
    (*The doorbell. Laura catches her breath and touches her throat. Low drums.*)

AMANDA (*calling*): Laura, sweetheart! The door!

(*Laura stares at it without moving.*)

JIM: I think we just beat the rain.

TOM: Uh-huh. (*He rings again, nervously. Jim whistles and fishes for a cigarette.*)

AMANDA (*very, very gaily*): Laura, that is your brother and Mr. O'Connor! Will you let them in, darling?

(*Laura crosses toward kitchenette door.*)

LAURA (*breathlessly*): Mother — you go to the door!

(*Amanda steps out of kitchenette and stares furiously at Laura. She points imperiously at the door.*)

LAURA: Please, please!

AMANDA (*in a fierce whisper*): What is the matter with you, you silly thing?

LAURA (*desperately*): Please, you answer it, *please!*

AMANDA: I told you I wasn't going to humor you, Laura. Why have you chosen this moment to lose your mind?

LAURA: Please, please, please, you go!

AMANDA: You'll have to go to the door because I can't!

LAURA (*despairingly*): I can't either!

AMANDA: *Why?*

LAURA: I'm *sick!*

AMANDA: I'm sick, too — of your nonsense! Why can't you and your brother be normal people? Fantastic whims and behavior! (*Tom gives a long ring.*) Preposterous goings on! Can you give me one reason — (*Calls out lyrically.*) COMING! JUST ONE SECOND! — why should you be afraid to open a door? Now you answer it, Laura!

LAURA: Oh, oh, oh . . . (*She returns through the portieres. Darts to the victrola and winds it frantically and turns it on.*)

AMANDA: Laura Wingfield, you march right to that door!

LAURA: Yes — yes, Mother!

(*A faraway, scratchy rendition of "Dardanella" softens the air and gives her strength to move through it. She slips to the door and draws it cautiously open.*)
    (*Tom enters with the caller, Jim O'Connor.*)

TOM: Laura, this is Jim. Jim, this is my sister, Laura.

JIM (*stepping inside*): I didn't know that Shakespeare had a sister!

LAURA (*retreating stiff and trembling from the door*): How — how do you do?

JIM (*heartily extending his hand*): Okay!

(*Laura touches it hesitantly with hers.*)

JIM: Your hand's cold, Laura!

LAURA: Yes, well — I've been playing the victrola. . . .

JIM: Must have been playing classical music on it! You ought to play a little hot swing music to warm you up!

LAURA: Excuse me — I haven't finished playing the victrola. . . .

(*She turns awkwardly and hurries into the front room. She pauses a second by the victrola. Then catches her breath and darts through the portieres like a frightened deer.*)

JIM (*grinning*): What was the matter?

TOM: Oh — with Laura? Laura is — terribly shy.

JIM: Shy, huh? It's unusual to meet a shy girl nowa-

days. I don't believe you ever mentioned you had a
sister.

TOM: Well, now you know. I have one. Here is the
Post Dispatch. You want a piece of it?

JIM: Uh-huh.

TOM: What piece? The comics?

JIM: Sports! (*Glances at it.*) Ole Dizzy Dean is on his
bad behavior.

TOM (*disinterest*): Yeah? (*Lights cigarette and crosses
back to fire escape door.*)

JIM: Where are *you* going?

TOM: I'm going out on the terrace.

JIM (*goes after him*): You know, Shakespeare — I'm
going to sell you a bill of goods!

TOM: What goods?

JIM: A course I'm taking.

TOM: Huh?

JIM: In public speaking! You and me, we're not the
warehouse type.

TOM: Thanks — that's good news. But what has public speaking got to do with it?

JIM: It fits you for — executive positions!

TOM: Awww.

JIM: I tell you it's done a helluva lot for me.

(*Image: executive at desk.*)

TOM: In what respect?

JIM: In every! Ask yourself what is the difference between you an' me and men in the office down front?
Brains? — No! — Ability? — No! Then what? Just
one little thing —

TOM: What is that one little thing?

JIM: Primarily it amounts to — social poise! Being
able to square up to people and hold your own on
any social level!

AMANDA (*offstage*): Tom?

TOM: Yes, Mother?

AMANDA: Is that you and Mr. O'Connor?

TOM: Yes, Mother.

AMANDA: Well, you just make yourselves comfortable
in there.

TOM: Yes, Mother.

AMANDA: Ask Mr. O'Connor if he would like to wash
his hands.

JIM: Aw, — no — no — thank you — I took care of
that at the warehouse. Tom —

FAR LEFT: Amanda (Ruby
Dee) and Laura (Tonia Rowe)
in the 1989 Arena Stage
production of *The Glass
Menagerie,* directed by
Tazewell Thompson. LEFT:
Laura, Amanda, and Tom
(Jonathan Earl Peck). RIGHT:
Scene from *The Glass
Menagerie.*

TOM: Yes?

JIM: Mr. Mendoza was speaking to me about you.

TOM: Favorably?

JIM: What do you think?

TOM: Well —

JIM: You're going to be out of a job if you don't wake
up.

TOM: I am waking up —

JIM: You show no signs.

TOM: The signs are interior.

(*Image on screen: the sailing vessel with Jolly Roger
again.*)

TOM: I'm planning to change. (*He leans over the rail
speaking with quiet exhilaration. The incandescent
marquees and signs of the first-run movie houses
light his face from across the alley. He looks like a
voyager.*) I'm right at the point of committing myself to a future that doesn't include the warehouse
and Mr. Mendoza or even a night school course in
public speaking.

JIM: What are you gassing about?

TOM: I'm tired of the movies.

JIM: Movies!

TOM: Yes, movies! Look at them — (*A wave toward
the marvels of Grand Avenue.*) All of those glam-
orous people — having adventures — hogging it
all, gobbling the whole thing up! You know what
happens? People go to the *movies* instead of *moving!* Hollywood characters are supposed to have

all the adventures for everybody in America, while everybody in America sits in a dark room and watches them have them! Yes, until there's a war. That's when adventure becomes available to the masses! *Everyone's* dish, not only Gable's! Then the people in the dark room come out of the dark room to have some adventures themselves — Goody, goody! — It's our turn now, to go to the South Sea Island — to make a safari — to be exotic, far-off! — But I'm not patient. I don't want to wait till then. I'm tired of the *movies* and I am *about* to *move!*

JIM (*incredulously*): Move?

TOM: Yes.

JIM: When?

TOM: Soon!

JIM: Where? Where?

(*Theme three music seems to answer the question, while Tom thinks it over. He searches among his pockets.*)

TOM: I'm starting to boil inside. I know I seem dreamy, but inside — well, I'm boiling! Whenever I pick up a shoe, I shudder a little thinking how short life is and what I am doing! — Whatever that means. I know it doesn't mean shoes — except as something to wear on a traveler's feet! (*Finds paper.*) Look —

JIM: What?

TOM: I'm a member.

JIM (*reading*): The Union of Merchant Seamen.

TOM: I paid my dues this month, instead of the light bill.

JIM: You will regret it when they turn the lights off.

TOM: I won't be here.

JIM: How about your mother?

TOM: I'm like my father. The bastard son of a bastard! See how he grins? And he's been absent going on sixteen years!

JIM: You're just talking, you drip. How does your mother feel about it?

TOM: Shhh! — Here comes Mother! Mother is not acquainted with my plans!

AMANDA (*enters portieres*): Where are you all?

TOM: On the terrace, Mother.

(*They start inside. She advances to them. Tom is distinctly shocked at her appearance. Even Jim blinks a little. He is making his first contact with girlish Southern vivacity and in spite of the night school course in public speaking is somewhat thrown off the beam by the unexpected outlay of social charm.*)

(*Certain responses are attempted by Jim but are swept aside by Amanda's gay laughter and chatter. Tom is embarrassed but after the first shock Jim reacts very warmly. Grins and chuckles, is altogether won over.*)

(*Image: Amanda as a girl.*)

AMANDA (*coyly smiling, shaking her girlish ringlets*): Well, well, well, so this is Mr. O'Connor. Introductions entirely unnecessary. I've heard so much about you from my boy. I finally said to him, Tom — good gracious! — why don't you bring this paragon to supper? I'd like to meet this nice young man at the warehouse! — Instead of just hearing him sing your praises so much! I don't know why my son is so standoffish — that's not Southern behavior! Let's sit down and — I think we could stand a little more air in here! Tom, leave the door open. I felt a nice fresh breeze a moment ago. Where has it gone to? Mmm, so warm already! And not quite summer, even. We're going to burn up when summer really gets started. However, we're having — we're having a very light supper. I think light things are better fo' this time of year. The same as light clothes are. Light clothes an' light food are what warm weather calls fo'. You know our blood gets so thick during th' winter — it takes a while fo' us to *adjust* ou'selves! — when the season changes . . . It's come so quick this year. I wasn't prepared. All of a sudden — heavens! Already summer! — I ran to the trunk an' pulled out this light dress — Terribly old! Historical almost! But feels so good — so good an' co-ol, y'know. . . .

TOM: Mother —

AMANDA: Yes, honey?

TOM: How about — supper?

AMANDA: Honey, you go ask Sister if supper is ready! You know that Sister is in full charge of supper! Tell her you hungry boys are waiting for it. (*To Jim.*) Have you met Laura?

JIM: She —

AMANDA: Let you in? Oh, good, you've met already! It's rare for a girl as sweet an' pretty as Laura to be domestic! But Laura is, thank heavens, not only pretty but also very domestic. I'm not at all. I never was a bit. I never could make a thing but angel food cake. Well, in the South we had so many servants. Gone, gone, gone. All vestiges of gracious living! Gone completely! I wasn't prepared for what the future brought me. All of my gentlemen callers were sons of planters and so of course I assumed that I would be married to one and raise my family on a large piece of land with plenty of servants. But man proposes — and woman accepts the proposal! — To vary that old, old saying a little bit — I married no planter! I married a man who worked for the telephone company! — That gallantly smiling gentleman over there! (*Points to the picture.*) A telephone man who — fell in love with long distance! — Now he travels and I don't even know where! — But what am I going on for about my — tribulations! Tell me yours — I hope you don't have any! Tom?

TOM (*returning*): Yes, Mother?

AMANDA: Is supper nearly ready?

TOM: It looks to me like supper is on the table.

AMANDA: Let me look — (*She rises prettily and looks through portieres.*) Oh, lovely! — But where is Sister?

TOM: Laura is not feeling well and she says that she thinks she'd better not come to the table.

AMANDA: What? — Nonsense! — Laura? Oh, Laura!

LAURA (*offstage, faintly*): Yes, Mother.

AMANDA: You really must come to the table. We won't be seated until you come to the table! Come in, Mr. O'Connor. You sit over there, and I'll — Laura? Laura Wingfield! You're keeping us waiting, honey! We can't say grace until you come to the table!

(*The back door is pushed weakly open and Laura comes in. She is obviously quite faint, her lips trembling, her eyes wide and staring. She moves unsteadily toward the table.*)

(*Legend: "Terror!"*)

(*Outside a summer storm is coming abruptly. The white curtains billow inward at the windows and there is a sorrowful murmur and deep blue dusk.*)

(*Laura suddenly stumbles — she catches at a chair with a faint moan.*)

TOM: Laura!

AMANDA: Laura! (*There is a clap of thunder.*) (*Legend: "Ah!"*) (*Despairingly.*) Why, Laura, you *are* sick, darling! Tom, help your sister into the living room, dear! Sit in the living room, Laura — rest on the sofa. Well! (*To the gentleman caller.*) Standing over the hot stove made her ill! — I told her that it was just too warm this evening, but — (*Tom comes back in. Laura is on the sofa.*) Is Laura all right now?

TOM: Yes.

AMANDA: What *is* that? Rain? A nice cool rain has come up! (*She gives the gentleman caller a frightened look.*) I think we may — have grace — now . . . (*Tom looks at her stupidly.*) Tom, honey — you say grace!

TOM: Oh . . . "For these and all thy mercies — " (*They bow their heads, Amanda stealing a nervous glance at Jim. In the living room Laura, stretched on the sofa, clenches her hand to her lips, to hold back a shuddering sob.*) God's Holy Name be praised —

(*The scene dims out.*)

SCENE 7

(*A Souvenir*)

(*Half an hour later. Dinner is just being finished in the upstage area which is concealed by the drawn portieres.*)

(*As the curtain rises Laura is still huddled upon the sofa, her feet drawn under her, her head resting on a pale blue pillow, her eyes wide and mysteriously watchful. The new floor lamp with its shade of rose-colored silk gives a soft, becoming light to her face, bringing out the fragile, unearthly prettiness which usually escapes attention. There is a steady murmur of rain, but it is slackening and stops soon after the scene begins; the air outside becomes pale and luminous as the moon breaks out.*)

(*A moment after the curtain rises, the lights in both rooms flicker and go out.*)

JIM: Hey, there, Mr. Light Bulb!

(*Amanda laughs nervously.*)

(*Legend: "Suspension of a Public Service."*)

AMANDA: Where was Moses when the lights went out? Ha-ha. Do you know the answer to that one, Mr. O'Connor?

JIM: No, Ma'am, what's the answer?

AMANDA: In the dark! (*Jim laughs appreciably.*) Everybody sit still. I'll light the candles. Isn't it lucky we have them on the table? Where's a match? Which of you gentlemen can provide a match?

JIM: Here.

AMANDA: Thank you, sir.

JIM: Not at all, Ma'am!

AMANDA: I guess the fuse has burnt out. Mr. O'Connor, can you tell a burnt-out fuse? I know I can't and Tom is a total loss when it comes to mechanics. (*Sound: getting up: voices recede a little to kitchenette.*) Oh, be careful you don't bump into something. We don't want our gentleman caller to break his neck. Now wouldn't that be a fine howdy-do?

JIM: Ha-ha! Where is the fuse box?

AMANDA: Right here next to the stove. Can you see anything?

JIM: Just a minute.

AMANDA: Isn't electricity a mysterious thing? Wasn't it Benjamin Franklin who tied a key to a kite? We live in such a mysterious universe, don't we? Some people say that science clears up all the mysteries for us. In my opinion it only creates more! Have you found it yet?

JIM: No, Ma'am. All these fuses look okay to me.

AMANDA: Tom!

TOM: Yes, Mother?

AMANDA: That light bill I gave you several days ago. The one I told you we got the notices about?

TOM: Oh. — Yeah.

(*Legend: "Ha!"*)

AMANDA: You didn't neglect to pay it by any chance?

TOM: Why, I —

AMANDA: Didn't! I might have known it!

JIM: Shakespeare probably wrote a poem on that light bill, Mrs. Wingfield.

AMANDA: I might have known better than to trust him with it! There's such a high price for negligence in this world!

JIM: Maybe the poem will win a ten-dollar prize.

AMANDA: We'll just have to spend the remainder of the evening in the nineteenth century, before Mr. Edison made the Mazda lamp!

JIM: Candlelight is my favorite kind of light.

AMANDA: That shows you're romantic! But that's no excuse for Tom. Well, we got through dinner. Very considerate of them to let us get through dinner before they plunged us into everlasting darkness, wasn't it, Mr. O'Connor?

JIM: Ha-ha!

AMANDA: Tom, as a penalty for your carelessness you can help me with the dishes.

JIM: Let me give you a hand.

AMANDA: Indeed you will not!

JIM: I ought to be good for something.

AMANDA: Good for something? (*Her tone is rhapsodic.*) You? Why, Mr. O'Connor, nobody, *nobody's* given me this much entertainment in years — as you have!

JIM: Aw, now, Mrs. Wingfield!

AMANDA: I'm not exaggerating, not one bit! But Sister is all by her lonesome. You go keep her company in the parlor! I'll give you this lovely old candelabrum that used to be on the altar at the church of the Heavenly Rest. It was melted a little out of shape when the church burnt down. Lightning struck it one spring. Gypsy Jones was holding a revival at the time and he intimated that the church was destroyed because the Episcopalians gave card parties.

JIM: Ha-ha.

AMANDA: And how about coaxing Sister to drink a little wine? I think it would be good for her! Can you carry both at once?

JIM: Sure. I'm Superman!

AMANDA: Now, Thomas, get into this apron!

(*The door of kitchenette swings closed on Amanda's gay laughter; the flickering light approaches the portieres.*)

(*Laura sits up nervously as he enters. Her speech at first is low and breathless from the almost intolerable strain of being alone with a stranger.*)

(*The legend: "I Don't Suppose You Remember Me at All!"*)

(*In her first speeches in this scene, before Jim's warmth overcomes her paralyzing shyness, Laura's voice is thin and breathless as though she has just run up a steep flight of stairs.*)

(*Jim's attitude is gently humorous. In playing this scene it should be stressed that while the incident is apparently unimportant, it is to Laura the climax of her secret life.*)

JIM: Hello, there, Laura.

LAURA (*faintly*): Hello. (*She clears her throat.*)

JIM: How are you feeling now? Better?

LAURA: Yes. Yes, thank you.

JIM: This is for you. A little dandelion wine. (*He extends it toward her with extravagant gallantry.*)

LAURA: Thank you.

JIM: Drink it — but don't get drunk! (*He laughs heartily. Laura takes the glass uncertainly; laughs shyly.*) Where shall I set the candles?

LAURA: Oh — oh, anywhere . . .

JIM: How about here on the floor? Any objections?

LAURA: No.

JIM: I'll spread a newspaper under to catch the drippings. I like to sit on the floor. Mind if I do?

LAURA: Oh, no.

JIM: Give me a pillow?

LAURA: What?

JIM: A pillow!

LAURA: Oh . . . (*Hands him one quickly.*)

JIM: How about you? Don't you like to sit on the floor?

LAURA: Oh — yes.

JIM: Why don't you, then?

LAURA: I — will.

JIM: Take a pillow! (*Laura does. Sits on the other side of the candelabrum. Jim crosses his legs and smiles engagingly at her.*) I can't hardly see you sitting way over there.

LAURA: I can — see you.

JIM: I know, but that's not fair, I'm in the limelight. (*Laura moves her pillow closer.*) Good! Now I can see you! Comfortable?

LAURA: Yes.

JIM: So am I. Comfortable as a cow. Will you have some gum?

LAURA: No, thank you.

JIM: I think that I will indulge, with your permission. (*Musingly unwraps it and holds it up.*) Think of the fortune made by the guy that invented the first piece of chewing gum. Amazing, huh? The Wrigley Building is one of the sights of Chicago. — I saw it summer before last when I went up to the Century of Progress. Did you take in the Century of Progress?

LAURA: No, I didn't.

JIM: Well, it was quite a wonderful exposition. What impressed me most was the Hall of Science. Gives you an idea of what the future will be in America, even more wonderful than the present time is!

(*Pause. Smiling at her.*) Your brother tells me you're shy. Is that right, Laura?

LAURA: I — don't know.

JIM: I judge you to be an old-fashioned type of girl. Well, I think that's a pretty good type to be. Hope you don't think I'm being too personal — do you?

LAURA (*hastily, out of embarrassment*): I believe I *will* take a piece of gum, if you — don't mind. (*Clearing her throat.*) Mr. O'Connor, have you — kept up with your singing?

JIM: Singing? Me?

LAURA: Yes. I remember what a beautiful voice you had.

JIM: When did you hear me sing?

(*Voice offstage in the pause.*)

VOICE: (*offstage*): O blow, ye winds, heigh-ho,
      A-roving I will go!
         I'm off to my love
         With a boxing glove —
      Ten thousand miles away!

JIM: You say you've heard me sing?

LAURA: Oh, yes! Yes, very often . . . I — don't suppose you remember me — at all?

JIM (*smiling doubtfully*): You know I have an idea I've seen you before. I had that idea soon as you opened the door. It seemed almost like I was about to remember your name. But the name that I started to call you — wasn't a name! And so I stopped myself before I said it.

LAURA: Wasn't it — Blue Roses?

JIM (*Springs up. Grinning.*): Blue Roses! My gosh, yes — Blue Roses! That's what I had on my tongue when you opened the door! Isn't it funny what tricks your memory plays? I didn't connect you with the high school somehow or other. But that's where it was; it was high school. I didn't even know you were Shakespeare's sister! Gosh, I'm sorry.

LAURA: I didn't expect you to. You — barely knew me!

JIM: But we did have a speaking acquaintance, huh?

LAURA: Yes, we — spoke to each other.

JIM: When did you recognize me?

LAURA: Oh, right away!

JIM: Soon as I came in the door?

LAURA: When I heard your name I thought it was probably you. I knew that Tom used to know you a little in high school. So when you came in the door — Well, then I was — sure.

JIM: Why didn't you *say* something, then?

LAURA (*breathlessly*): I didn't know what to say, I was — too surprised!

JIM: For goodness' sakes! You know, this sure is funny!

LAURA: Yes! Yes, isn't it, though . . .

JIM: Didn't we have a class in something together?

LAURA: Yes, we did.

JIM: What class was that?

LAURA: It was — singing — Chorus!

JIM: Aw!

LAURA: I sat across the aisle from you in the Aud.

JIM: Aw.

LAURA: Mondays, Wednesdays, and Fridays.

JIM: Now I remember — you always came in late.

LAURA: Yes, it was so hard for me, getting upstairs. I had that brace on my leg — it clumped so loud!

JIM: I never heard any clumping.

LAURA (*wincing at the recollection*): To me it sounded like — thunder!

JIM: Well, well, well, I never even noticed.

LAURA: And everybody was seated before I came in. I had to walk in front of all those people. My seat was in the back row. I had to go clumping all the way up the aisle with everyone watching!

JIM: You shouldn't have been self-conscious.

LAURA: I know, but I was. It was always such a relief when the singing started.

JIM: Aw, yes, I've placed you now! I used to call you Blue Roses. How was it that I got started calling you that?

LAURA: I was out of school a little while with pleurosis. When I came back you asked me what was the matter. I said I had pleurosis — you thought I said Blue Roses. That's what you always called me after that!

JIM: I hope you didn't mind.

LAURA: Oh, no — I liked it. You see, I wasn't acquainted with many — people. . . .

JIM: As I remember you sort of stuck by yourself.

LAURA: I — I — never had much luck at — making friends.

JIM: I don't see why you wouldn't.

LAURA: Well, I — started out badly.

JIM: You mean being —

LAURA: Yes, it sort of — stood between me —

JIM: You shouldn't have let it!

LAURA: I know, but it did, and

JIM: You were shy with people!

LAURA: I tried not to be but never could —

JIM: Overcome it?

LAURA: No, I — I never could!

JIM: I guess being shy is something you have to work out of kind of gradually.

LAURA (*sorrowfully*): Yes — I guess it —

JIM: Takes time!

LAURA: Yes —

JIM: People are not so dreadful when you know them. That's what you have to remember! And everybody has problems, not just you, but practically everybody has got some problems. You think of yourself as having the only problems, as being the only one who is disappointed. But just look around you and you will see lots of people as disappointed as you are. For instance, I hoped when I was going to high school that I would be further along at this time, six years later, than I am now — You remember that wonderful write-up I had in *The Torch*?

LAURA: Yes! (*She rises and crosses to table.*)

JIM: It said I was bound to succeed in anything I went into! (*Laura returns with the annual.*) Holy Jeez! *The Torch!* (*He accepts it reverently. They smile across it with mutual wonder. Laura crouches beside him and they begin to turn through it. Laura's shyness is dissolving in his warmth.*)

LAURA: Here you are in *Pirates of Penzance*!

JIM (*wistfully*): I sang the baritone lead in that operetta.

LAURA (*rapidly*): So — *beautifully!*

JIM (*protesting*): Aw —

LAURA: Yes, yes — beautifully — beautifully!

JIM: You heard me?

LAURA: All three times!

JIM: No!

LAURA: Yes!

JIM: All three performances?

LAURA (*looking down*): Yes.

JIM: Why?

LAURA: I — wanted to ask you to — autograph my program.

JIM: Why didn't you ask me to?

LAURA: You were always surrounded by your own friends so much that I never had a chance to.

JIM: You should have just —

LAURA: Well, I — thought you might think I was —

JIM: Thought I might think you was — what?

LAURA: Oh —

JIM (*with reflective relish*): I was beleaguered by females in those days.

LAURA: You were terribly popular!

JIM: Yeah —

LAURA: You had such a — friendly way —

JIM: I was spoiled in high school.

LAURA: Everybody — liked you!

JIM: Including you?

LAURA: I — yes, I — I did, too — (*She gently closes the book in her lap.*)

JIM: Well, well, well! — Give me that program, Laura. (*She hands it to him. He signs it with a flourish.*) There you are — better late than never!

LAURA: Oh, I — what a — surprise!

JIM: My signature isn't worth very much right now. But some day — maybe — it will increase in value! Being disappointed is one thing and being discouraged is something else. I am disappointed but I am

not discouraged. I'm twenty-three years old. How old are you?

LAURA: I'll be twenty-four in June.

JIM: That's not old age!

LAURA: No, but —

JIM: You finished high school?

LAURA (*with difficulty*): I didn't go back.

JIM: You mean you dropped out?

LAURA: I made bad grades in my final examinations. (*She rises and replaces the book and the program. Her voice strained.*) How is — Emily Meisenbach getting along?

JIM: Oh, that kraut-head!

LAURA: Why do you call her that?

JIM: That's what she was.

LAURA: You're not still — going with her?

JIM: I never see her.

LAURA: It said in the Personal Section that you were — engaged!

JIM: I know, but I wasn't impressed by that — propaganda!

LAURA: It wasn't — the truth?

JIM: Only in Emily's optimistic opinion!

LAURA: Oh —

(*Legend: "What Have You Done since High School?"*)
    (*Jim lights a cigarette and leans indolently back on his elbows smiling at Laura with a warmth and charm which lights her inwardly with altar candles. She remains by the table and turns in her hands a piece of glass to cover her tumult.*)

JIM (*after several reflective puffs on a cigarette*): What have you done since high school? (*She seems not to hear him.*) Huh? (*Laura looks up.*) I said what have you done since high school, Laura?

LAURA: Nothing much.

JIM: You must have been doing something these six long years.

LAURA: Yes.

JIM: Well, then, such as what?

LAURA: I took a business course at business college —

JIM: How did that work out?

LAURA: Well, not very — well — I had to drop out, it gave me — indigestion —

(*Jim laughs gently.*)

JIM: What are you doing now?

LAURA: I don't do anything — much. Oh, please don't think I sit around doing nothing! My glass collection takes up a good deal of my time. Glass is something you have to take good care of.

JIM: What did you say — about glass?

LAURA: Collection I said — I have one — (*She clears her throat and turns away again, acutely shy.*)

JIM (*abruptly*): You know what I judge to be the trouble with you? Inferiority complex! Know what that is? That's what they call it when someone low-rates himself! I understand it because I had it, too. Although my case was not so aggravated as yours seems to be. I had it until I took up public speaking, developed my voice, and learned that I had an aptitude for science. Before that time I never thought of myself as being outstanding in any way whatsoever! Now I've never made a regular study of it, but I have a friend who says I can analyze people better than doctors that make a profession of it. I don't claim that to be necessarily true, but I can sure guess a person's psychology, Laura! (*Takes out his gum.*) Excuse me, Laura. I always take it out when the flavor is gone. I'll use this scrap of paper to wrap it in. I know how it is to get it stuck on a shoe. Yep — that's what I judge to be your principal trouble. A lack of confidence in yourself as a person. You don't have the proper amount of faith in yourself. I'm basing that fact on a number of your remarks and also on certain observations I've made. For instance that clumping you thought was so awful in high school. You say that you even dreaded to walk into class. You see what you did? You dropped out of school, you gave up an education because of a clump, which as far as I know was practically nonexistent! A little physical defect is what you have. Hardly noticeable even! Magnified thousands of times by imagination! You know what my strong advice to you is? Think of yourself as *superior* in some way!

LAURA: In what way would I think?

JIM: Why, man alive, Laura! Just look about you a little. What do you see? A world full of common people! All of 'em born and all of 'em going to die! Which of them has one-tenth of your good points! Or mine! Or anyone else's, as far as that goes — Gosh! Everybody excels in some one thing. Some in many! (*Unconsciously glances at himself in the mirror.*) All you've got to do is discover in what! Take me, for instance. (*He adjusts his tie at the mirror.*) My interest happens to lie in electro dynamics. I'm taking a course in radio engineering at night school, Laura, on top of a fairly responsible job at the warehouse. I'm taking that course and studying public speaking.

LAURA: Ohhhh.

JIM: Because I believe in the future of television! (*Turning back to her.*) I wish to be ready to go up right along with it. Therefore I'm planning to get in on the ground floor. In fact, I've already made the right connections and all that remains is for the industry itself to get under way! Full steam — (*His eyes are starry.*) Knowledge — Zzzzzp! Money —

Zzzzzzp! — *Power!* That's the cycle democracy is built on! (*His attitude is convincingly dynamic. Laura stares at him, even her shyness eclipsed in her absolute wonder. He suddenly grins.*) I guess you think I think a lot of myself!

LAURA: No — o-o-o, I —

JIM: Now how about you? Isn't there something you take more interest in than anything else?

LAURA: Well, I do — as I said — have my — glass collection —

(*A peal of girlish laughter from the kitchen.*)

JIM: I'm not right sure I know what you're talking about. What kind of glass is it?

LAURA: Little articles of it, they're ornaments mostly! Most of them are little animals made out of glass, the tiniest little animals in the world. Mother calls them a glass menagerie! Here's an example of one, if you'd like to see it! This one is one of the oldest. It's nearly thirteen. (*He stretches out his hand.*) (*Music: "The Glass Menagerie."*) Oh, be careful — if you breathe, it breaks!

JIM: I'd better not take it. I'm pretty clumsy with things.

LAURA: Go on, I trust you with him! (*Places it in his palm.*) There now — you're holding him gently! Hold him over the light, he loves the light! You see how the light shines through him?

JIM: It sure does shine!

LAURA: I shouldn't be partial, but he is my favorite one.

JIM: What kind of a thing is this one supposed to be?

LAURA: Haven't you noticed the single horn on his forehead?

JIM: A unicorn, huh?

LAURA: Mmm-hmmm!

JIM: Unicorns, aren't they extinct in the modern world?

LAURA: I know!

JIM: Poor little fellow, he must feel sort of lonesome.

LAURA (*smiling*): Well, if he does he doesn't complain about it. He stays on a shelf with some horses that don't have horns and all of them seem to get along nicely together.

JIM: How do you know?

LAURA (*lightly*): I haven't heard any arguments among them!

JIM (*grinning*): No arguments, huh? Well, that's a pretty good sign! Where shall I set him?

LAURA: Put him on the table. They all like a change of scenery once in a while!

JIM (*stretching*): Well, well, well, well — Look how big my shadow is when I stretch!

LAURA: Oh, oh, yes — it stretches across the ceiling!

JIM (*crossing to door*): I think it's stopped raining.

(*Opens fire escape door.*) Where does the music come from?

LAURA: From the Paradise Dance Hall across the alley.

JIM: How about cutting the rug a little, Miss Wingfield?

LAURA: Oh, I —

JIM: Or is your program filled up? Let me have a look at it. (*Grasps imaginary card.*) Why, every dance is taken! I'll just have to scratch some out. (*Waltz music: "La Golondrina."*) Ahhh, a waltz! (*He executes some sweeping turns by himself then holds his arms toward Laura.*)

LAURA (*breathlessly*): I — can't dance!

JIM: There you go, that inferiority stuff!

LAURA: I've never danced in my life!

JIM: Come on, try!

LAURA: Oh, but I'd step on you!

JIM: I'm not made out of glass.

LAURA: How — how — how do we start?

JIM: Just leave it to me. You hold your arms out a little.

LAURA: Like this?

JIM: A little bit higher. Right. Now don't tighten up, that's the main thing about it — relax.

LAURA (*laughing breathlessly*): It's hard not to.

JIM: Okay.

LAURA: I'm afraid you can't budge me.

JIM: What do you bet I can't? (*He swings her into motion.*)

LAURA: Goodness, yes, you can!

JIM: Let yourself go, now, Laura, just let yourself go.

LAURA: I'm —

JIM: Come on!

LAURA: Trying!

JIM: Not so stiff — Easy does it!

LAURA: I know but I'm —

JIM: Loosen th' backbone! There now, that's a lot better.

LAURA: Am I?

JIM: Lots, lots better! (*He moves her about the room in a clumsy waltz.*)

LAURA: Oh, my!

JIM: Ha-ha!

LAURA: Oh, my goodness!

JIM: Ha-ha-ha! (*They suddenly bump into the table. Jim stops.*) What did we hit on?

LAURA: Table.

JIM: Did something fall off it? I think —

LAURA: Yes.

JIM: I hope that it wasn't the little glass horse with the horn!

LAURA: Yes.

JIM: Aw, aw, aw. Is it broken?

LAURA: Now it is just like all the other horses.

JIM: It's lost its —

LAURA: Horn! It doesn't matter. Maybe it's a blessing in disguise.

JIM: You'll never forgive me. I bet that that was your favorite piece of glass.

LAURA: I don't have favorites much. It's no tragedy, Freckles. Glass breaks so easily. No matter how careful you are. The traffic jars the shelves and things fall off them.

JIM: Still I'm awfully sorry that I was the cause.

LAURA (*smiling*): I'll just imagine he had an operation. The horn was removed to make him feel less — freakish! (*They both laugh.*) Now he will feel more at home with the other horses, the ones that don't have horns . . .

JIM: Ha-ha, that's very funny! (*Suddenly serious.*) I'm glad to see that you have a sense of humor. You know — you're — well — very different! Surprisingly different from anyone else I know! (*His voice becomes soft and hesitant with a genuine feeling.*) Do you mind me telling you that? (*Laura is abashed beyond speech.*) I mean it in a nice way . . . (*Laura nods shyly, looking away.*) You make me feel sort of — I don't know how to put it! I'm usually pretty good at expressing things, but — This is something that I don't know how to say! (*Laura touches her throat and clears it — turns the broken unicorn in her hands.*) (*Even softer.*) Has anyone ever told you that you were pretty? (*Pause: Music.*) (*Laura looks up slowly, with wonder, and shakes her head.*) Well, you are! In a very different way from anyone else. And all the nicer because of the difference, too. (*His voice becomes low and husky. Laura turns away, nearly faint with the novelty of her emotions.*) I wish that you were my sister. I'd teach you to have some confidence in yourself. The different people are not like other people, but being different is nothing to be ashamed of. Because other people are not such wonderful people. They're one hundred times one thousand. You're one times one! They walk all over the earth. You just stay here. They're common as — weeds, but — you — well, you're — *Blue Roses!*

(*Image on screen: blue roses.*)
(*Music changes.*)

LAURA: But blue is wrong for — roses . . .

JIM: It's right for you — You're — pretty!

LAURA: In what respect am I pretty?

JIM: In all respects — believe me! Your eyes — your hair — are pretty! Your hands are pretty! (*He catches hold of her hand.*) You think I'm making this up because I'm invited to dinner and have to be nice. Oh, I could do that! I could put on an act for you, Laura, and say lots of things without being very sincere. But this time I am. I'm talking to you sincerely. I happened to notice you had this inferiority complex that keeps you from feeling comfortable with people. Somebody needs to build your confidence up and make you proud instead of shy and turning away and — blushing — Somebody ought to — Ought to — *kiss you, Laura! (His hand slips slowly up her arm to her shoulder.) (Music swells tumultuously.) (He suddenly turns her about and kisses her on the lips. When he releases her Laura sinks on the sofa with a bright, dazed look. Jim backs away and fishes in his pocket for a cigarette.) (Legend on screen: "Souvenir.")* Stumble-john! *(He lights the cigarette, avoiding her look. There is a peal of girlish laughter from Amanda in the kitchen. Laura slowly raises and opens her hand. It still contains the little broken glass animal. She looks at it with a tender, bewildered expression.)* Stumble-john! I shouldn't have done that — That was way off the beam. You don't smoke, do you? *(She looks up, smiling, not hearing the question. He sits beside her a little gingerly. She looks at him speechlessly — waiting. He coughs decorously and moves a little farther aside as he considers the situation and senses her feelings, dimly, with perturbation. Gently.)* Would you — care for a — mint? *(She doesn't seem to hear him but her look grows brighter even.)* Peppermint — Life Saver? My pocket's a regular drugstore — wherever I go . . . *(He pops a mint in his mouth. Then gulps and decides to make a clean breast of it. He speaks slowly and gingerly.)* Laura, you know, if I had a sister like you, I'd do the same thing as Tom. I'd bring out fellows and — introduce her to them. The right type of boys of a type to — appreciate her. Only — well — he made a mistake about me. Maybe I've got no call to be saying this. That may not have been the idea in having me over. But what if it was? There's nothing wrong about that. The only trouble is that in my case — I'm not in a situation to — do the right thing. I can't take down your number and say I'll phone. I can't call up next week and — ask for a date. I thought I had better explain the situation in case you misunderstood it and — hurt your feelings. . . . *(Pause. Slowly, very slowly, Laura's look changes, her eyes returning slowly from his to the ornament in her palm.)*

(Amanda utters another gay laugh in the kitchen.)

LAURA (*faintly*): You — won't — call again?
JIM: No, Laura, I can't. *(He rises from the sofa.)* As I was just explaining, I've — got strings on me, Laura, I've — been going steady! I go out all the time with a girl named Betty. She's a home-girl like you, and Catholic, and Irish, and in a great many ways we — get along fine. I met her last summer on a moonlight boat trip up the river to Alton, on the *Majestic.* Well — right away from the start it was — love! *(Legend: Love!) (Laura sways slightly forward and grips the arm of the sofa. He fails to notice, now enrapt in his own comfortable being.)* Being in love has made a new man of me! *(Leaning stiffly forward, clutching the arm of the sofa, Laura struggles visibly with her storm. But Jim is oblivious, she is a long way off.)* The power of love is really pretty tremendous! Love is something that — changes the whole world, Laura! *(The storm abates a little and Laura leans back. He notices her again.)* It happened that Betty's aunt took sick, she got a wire and had to go to Centralia. So Tom — when he asked me to dinner — I naturally just accepted the invitation, not knowing that you — that he — that I — (He stops awkwardly.) Huh — I'm a stumble-john! *(He flops back on the sofa. The holy candles in the altar of Laura's face have been snuffed out! There is a look of almost infinite desolation. Jim glances at her uneasily.)* I wish that you would — say something. *(She bites her lip which was trembling and then bravely smiles. She opens her hand again on the broken glass ornament. Then she gently takes his hand and raises it level with her own. She carefully places the unicorn in the palm of his hand, then pushes his fingers closed upon it.)* What are you — doing that for? You want me to have him? — Laura? *(She nods.)* What for?
LAURA: A — souvenir . . .

(She rises unsteadily and crouches beside the victrola to wind it up.)

(Legend on screen: "Things Have a Way of Turning out so Badly.")

(Or Image: "Gentleman Caller Waving Goodbye! — Gaily.")

(At this moment Amanda rushes brightly back in the front room. She bears a pitcher of fruit punch in an old-fashioned cut-glass pitcher and a plate of macaroons. The plate has a gold border and poppies painted on it.)

AMANDA: Well, well, well! Isn't the air delightful after the shower? I've made you children a little liquid refreshment. *(Turns gaily to the gentleman caller.)* Jim, do you know that song about lemonade?
"Lemonade, lemonade
     Made in the shade and stirred with a spade —
Good enough for any old maid!"
JIM (*uneasily*): Ha-ha! No — I never heard it.
AMANDA: Why, Laura! You look so serious!
JIM: We were having a serious conversation.
AMANDA: Good! Now you're better acquainted!
JIM (*uncertainly*): Ha-ha! Yes.
AMANDA: You modern young people are much more

serious-minded than my generation. I was so gay as a girl!

JIM: You haven't changed, Mrs. Wingfield.

AMANDA: Tonight I'm rejuvenated! The gaiety of the occasion, Mr. O'Connor! (*She tosses her head with a peal of laughter. Spills lemonade.*) Oooo! I'm baptizing myself!

JIM: Here — let me —

AMANDA (*setting the pitcher down*): There now. I discovered we had some maraschino cherries. I dumped them in, juice and all!

JIM: You shouldn't have gone to that trouble, Mrs. Wingfield.

AMANDA: Trouble, trouble? Why it was loads of fun! Didn't you hear me cutting up in the kitchen? I bet your ears were burning! I told Tom how out-done with him I was for keeping you to himself so long a time! He should have brought you over much, much sooner! Well, now that you've found your way, I want you to be a very frequent caller! Not just occasional but all the time. Oh, we're going to have a lot of gay times together! I see them coming! Mmm, just breathe that air! So fresh, and the moon's so pretty! I'll skip back out — I know where my place is when young folks are having a — serious conversation!

JIM: Oh, don't go out, Mrs. Wingfield. The fact of the matter is I've got to be going.

AMANDA: Going, now? You're joking! Why, it's only the shank of the evening, Mr. O'Connor!

JIM: Well, you know how it is.

AMANDA: You mean you're a young workingman and have to keep workingmen's hours. We'll let you off early tonight. But only on the condition that next time you stay later. What's the best night for you? Isn't Saturday night the best night for you workingmen?

JIM: I have a couple of time clocks to punch, Mrs. Wingfield. One at morning, another one at night!

AMANDA: My, but you *are* ambitious! You work at night, too?

JIM: No, Ma'am, not work but — Betty! (*He crosses deliberately to pick up his hat. The band at the Paradise Dance Hall goes into a tender waltz.*)

AMANDA: Betty? Betty? Who's — Betty! (*There is an ominous cracking sound in the sky.*)

JIM: Oh, just a girl. The girl I go steady with! (*He smiles charmingly. The sky falls.*)

(*Legend: "The Sky Falls."*)

AMANDA (*a long-drawn exhalation*): Ohhhh . . . Is it a serious romance, Mr. O'Connor?

JIM: We're going to be married the second Sunday in June.

AMANDA: Ohhhh — how nice! Tom didn't mention that you were engaged to be married.

JIM: The cat's not out of the bag at the warehouse yet. You know how they are. They call you Romeo and stuff like that. (*He stops at the oval mirror to put on his hat. He carefully shapes the brim and the crown to give a discreetly dashing effect.*) It's been a wonderful evening, Mrs. Wingfield. I guess this is what they mean by Southern hospitality.

AMANDA: It really wasn't anything at all.

JIM: I hope it don't seem like I'm rushing off. But I promised Betty I'd pick her up at the Wabash depot, an' by the time I get my jalopy down there her train'll be in. Some women are pretty upset if you keep 'em waiting.

AMANDA: Yes, I know — The tyranny of women! (*Extends her hand.*) Good-bye, Mr. O'Connor. I wish you luck — and happiness — and success! All three of them, and so does Laura! — Don't you, Laura?

LAURA: Yes!

JIM (*taking her hand*): Good-bye, Laura. I'm certainly going to treasure that souvenir. And don't you forget the good advice I gave you. (*Raises his voice to a cheery shout.*) So long, Shakespeare! Thanks again, ladies — Good night!

(*He grins and ducks jauntily out.*)

(*Still bravely grimacing, Amanda closes the door on the gentleman caller. Then she turns back to the room with a puzzled expression. She and Laura don't dare to face each other. Laura crouches beside the victrola to wind it.*)

AMANDA (*faintly*): Things have a way of turning out so badly. I don't believe that I would play the victrola. Well, well — well — Our gentleman caller was engaged to be married! Tom!

TOM (*from back*): Yes, Mother?

AMANDA: Come in here a minute. I want to tell you something awfully funny.

TOM (*enters with macaroon and a glass of the lemonade*): Has the gentleman caller gotten away already?

AMANDA: The gentleman caller has made an early departure. What a wonderful joke you played on us!

TOM: How do you mean?

AMANDA: You didn't mention that he was engaged to be married.

TOM: Jim? Engaged?

AMANDA: That's what he just informed us.

TOM: I'll be jiggered! I didn't know about that.

AMANDA: That seems very peculiar.

TOM: What's peculiar about it?

AMANDA: Didn't you call him your best friend down at the warehouse?

TOM: He is, but how did I know?

AMANDA: It seems extremely peculiar that you wouldn't know your best friend was going to be married!

TOM: The warehouse is where I work, not where I know things about people!

AMANDA: You don't know things anywhere! You live in a dream; you manufacture illusions! (*He crosses to door.*) Where are you going?

TOM: I'm going to the movies.

AMANDA: That's right, now that you've had us make such fools of ourselves. The effort, the preparations, all the expense! The new floor lamp, the rug, the clothes for Laura! All for what? To entertain some other girl's fiancé! Go to the movies, go! Don't think about us, a mother deserted, an unmarried sister who's crippled and has no job! Don't let anything interfere with your selfish pleasure! Just go, go, go — to the movies!

TOM: All right, I will! The more you shout about my selfishness to me the quicker I'll go, and I won't go to the movies!

AMANDA: Go, then! Then go to the moon — you selfish dreamer!

(*Tom smashes his glass on the floor. He plunges out on the fire escape, slamming the door. Laura screams — cut by door.*)

(*Dance hall music up. Tom goes to the rail and grips it desperately, lifting his face in the chill white moonlight penetrating the narrow abyss of the alley.*)

(*Legend on screen: "And so Good-bye . . . "*)

(*Tom's closing speech is timed with the interior pantomime. The interior scene is played as though viewed through soundproof glass. Amanda appears to be making a comforting speech to Laura who is huddled upon the sofa. Now that we cannot hear the mother's speech, her silliness is gone and she has dignity and tragic beauty. Laura's dark hair hides her face until at the end of the speech she lifts it to smile at her mother. Amanda's gestures are slow and graceful, almost dancelike, as she comforts the daughter. At the end of her speech she glances a moment at the*

father's picture — then withdraws through the portieres. At close of Tom's speech, Laura blows out the candles, ending the play.)

TOM: I didn't go to the moon, I went much further — for time is the longest distance between two places — Not long after that I was fired for writing a poem on the lid of a shoebox. I left Saint Louis. I descended the steps of this fire escape for a last time and followed, from then on, in my father's footsteps, attempting to find in motion what was lost in space — I traveled around a great deal. The cities swept about me like dead leaves, leaves that were brightly colored but torn away from the branches. I would have stopped, but I was pursued by something. It always came upon me unawares, taking me altogether by surprise. Perhaps it was a familiar bit of music. Perhaps it was only a piece of transparent glass — Perhaps I am walking along a street at night, in some strange city, before I have found companions. I pass the lighted window of a shop where perfume is sold. The window is filled with pieces of colored glass, tiny transparent bottles in delicate colors, like bits of a shattered rainbow. Then all at once my sister touches my shoulder. I turn around and look into her eyes . . . Oh, Laura, Laura, I tried to leave you behind me, but I am more faithful than I intended to be! I reach for a cigarette, I cross the street, I run into the movies or a bar, I buy a drink, I speak to the nearest stranger — anything that can blow your candles out! (*Laura bends over the candles.*) — for nowadays the world is lit by lightning! Blow out your candles, Laura — and so good-bye. . . .

(*She blows the candles out.*)
(*The scene dissolves.*)

CAT ON A HOT TIN ROOF

The title of the play comes from an offhand remark made by Tennessee Williams's father, Cornelius Williams, who told his wife that she sometimes made him "as nervous as a cat on a hot tin roof." In the play's first production Williams said that he saw his father in the character of Big Daddy. Reminiscence and family memory are as apparent in this play as in most of his work. The secret ingredient in the play, the secret that haunts Brick and torments Maggie, is homosexuality and Brick's relationship with his now-dead friend Skipper. Maggie seduced Skipper to find out what his relation with Brick was, and when he was unable to perform sexually with her, she felt she knew the truth. The theme of homosexuality extends to the previous inhabitants of Maggie and Brick's bedroom, the bachelors Jack Straw and Peter Ochello, the original owners of the plantation. Williams's note that the two "shared this room all their lives together" implies that their relationship was that of lovers. Williams had already become fully aware of his own homosexuality, although he revealed that personal element only obliquely in works such as *Cat on a Hot Tin Roof* until he "came out" during a television interview with David Frost in 1970.

Williams said in his *Memoirs* that this play was his favorite: "I believe that in *Cat* I reached beyond myself, in the second act, to a kind of crude eloquence of expression in Big Daddy that I have managed to give no other character of my creation." Critics have said that one reason Williams liked the play is that he was able to observe the unities of time, place, and action. Brick is confined to his room because he has broken his ankle in a drunken competition at the high school track. The central action of the play, the celebration of Big Daddy's sixty-fifth birthday, is thus brought to the bedroom, which is also at the center of one of the principal tensions in the play.

Big Daddy owns a cotton plantation and both his sons are a disappointment to him. Gooper, with his ambitious wife and his five "no-neck monsters," is weak and unappealing. Even though Gooper has become a lawyer and produced children in an effort to please his father, Big Daddy sees him as possessing none of the masculine qualities he expects in his heir. Brick, a former football player and Big Daddy's favorite, slipped into debilitating alcoholism after Skipper's death. At the time of the play he has no career and few prospects. Maggie sees that the only way she can secure Big Daddy's blessing in the form of Brick's inheritance is by having a child. And with Brick keeping a sexual distance from her, she has to find a way to help him over his grief.

Because Williams made Brick's homosexuality more or less ambiguous, some critics felt that the play's structure was inconclusive. For example, they reasoned that one sexual failure on the part of Skipper did not prove anything about his sexual preference. They also felt that Maggie and Brick's sexual efforts after the curtain falls on the last act may not be successful at all.

Williams's original version of the play — before it was performed — differed from his final version. Originally, Big Daddy did not appear after act 2, and Maggie and Brick did not vow to have a child or to get together at all. The play was changed because its first director, Elia Kazan, felt that Big Daddy was too brilliant a character to leave out of act 3. He argued with Williams until, against his will, Williams revised act 3 to imply a more positive ending, to bring back Big Daddy — who tells an elephant joke that caused the censor to complain in 1955 — and to make Maggie a softer, less acerbic, and much more appealing character. Williams later said that he agreed that the revision made the play stronger, although he preferred his original ending. He later published the play with two act 3s so that regional and other theaters could choose the ending they preferred.

Cat on a Hot Tin Roof in Performance

The play premiered at the Morosco Theater in New York in March 1955 with Burl Ives, then known best as a folk singer, as Big Daddy, Barbara Bel Geddes as Maggie, Ben Gazzara as Brick, and Mildred Dunnock as Big Mama. This powerful cast made the play a huge success. After 694 performances in New York, it toured for another 268 performances. It won Williams his second Pulitzer Prize and his third Drama Critics' Circle Award for best play of the season. Elia Kazan not only directed the play but worked hard to help Williams alter his conception. Williams felt that the play should have a realistic production, since in his mind it was a realistic play. Kazan saw it otherwise and introduced soft lighting and a dreamy setting that established the play as moderately expressionistic.

London theaters were banned from performing the play as written, but a theater club produced it to mixed reviews in 1956. The film version originally was to have Grace Kelly as Maggie, but Elizabeth Taylor got the role, and Paul Newman played Brick. The film version removed all suggestions of homosexuality, focusing instead on Brick's immaturity and his need to grow up to the responsibilities of marriage. It was a highly successful film for its time.

Numerous revivals of the play have appeared in many countries, including a production in Tokyo in 1970. Williams revised the ending once more — putting back the elephant joke — for a restaging of the play in 1974 in Stratford, Connecticut, and then took it to New York for twenty weeks with Elizabeth Ashley as Maggie and Keir Dullea as Brick. That version (which we use in this book) was made into a television production in 1984 with Rip Torn as Big Daddy, Kim Stanley as Big Mama, Tommy Lee Jones as Brick, and Jessica Lange as Maggie. TV critic Richard Zoglin said, "The net effect is to retain the beefed-up dimensions of Maggie and Big Daddy from Broadway, but to leave Brick, at the end, a little more stuck in what Williams describes as a 'state of spiritual despair.'" *Newsweek* described the 1990 New York production, with Howard Davies directing Kathleen Turner as Maggie, as "one of the strongest Tennessee Williams revivals ever on Broadway." Charles Durning's Big Daddy was called "a powerhouse performance."

Tennessee Williams *(1911–1983)*
CAT ON A HOT TIN ROOF

1955

Characters

MARGARET
BRICK
MAE, *sometimes called Sister Woman*
BIG MAMA
DIXIE, *a little girl*
BIG DADDY
REVEREND TOOKER
GOOPER, *sometimes called Brother Man*
DOCTOR BAUGH, *pronounced "Baw"*
LACEY, *a Negro servant*
SOOKEY, *another*
CHILDREN

Notes for the Designer

The set is the bed-sitting-room of a plantation home in the Mississippi Delta. It is along an upstairs gallery which probably runs around the entire house; it has two pairs of very wide doors opening onto the gallery, showing white balustrades against a fair summer sky that fades into dusk and night during the course of the play, which occupies precisely the time of its performance, excepting, of course, the fifteen minutes of intermission.

Perhaps the style of the room is not what you would expect in the home of the Delta's biggest cotton planter. It is Victorian with a touch of the Far East. It hasn't changed much since it was occupied by the original owners of the place, Jack Straw and Peter Ochello, a pair of old bachelors who shared this room all their lives together. In other words, the room must evoke some ghosts; it is gently and poetically haunted by a relationship that must have involved a tenderness which was uncommon. This may be irrelevant or unnecessary, but I once saw a reproduction of a faded photograph of the verandah of Robert Louis Stevenson's home on that Samoan Island where he spent his last years, and there was a quality of tender light on weathered wood, such as porch furniture made of bamboo and wicker, exposed to tropical suns and tropical rains, which came to mind when I thought about the set for this play, bringing also to mind the grace and comfort of light, the reassurance it gives, on a late and fair afternoon in summer, the way that no matter what, even dread of death, is gently touched and soothed by it. For the set is the background for a play that deals with human extremities of emotion, and it needs that softness behind it.

The bathroom door, showing only pale-blue tile and silver towel racks, is in one side wall; the hall door in the opposite wall. Two articles of furniture need mention: a big double bed which staging should make a functional part of the set as often as suitable, the surface of which should be slightly raked to make figures on it seen more easily; and against the wall space between the two huge double doors upstage: a monumental monstrosity peculiar to our times, a *huge* console combination of radio-phonograph (hi-fi with three speakers), TV set, *and* liquor cabinet, bearing and containing many glasses and bottles, all in one piece, which is a composition of muted silver tones, and the opalescent tones of reflecting glass, a chromatic link, this thing, between the sepia (tawny gold) tones of the interior and the cool (white and blue) tones of the gallery and sky. This piece of furniture (?!), this monument, is a very complete and compact little shrine to virtually all the comforts and illusions behind which we hide from such things as the characters in the play are faced with. . . .

The set should be far less realistic than I have so far implied in this description of it. I think the walls below the ceiling should dissolve mysteriously into air; the set should be roofed by the sky; stars and moon suggested by traces of milky pallor, as if they were observed through a telescope lens out of focus.

Anything else I can think of? Oh, yes, fanlights (transoms shaped like an open glass fan) above all the doors in the set, with panes of blue and amber, and above all, the designer should take as many pains to give the actors room to move about freely (to show their restlessness, their passion for breaking out) as if it were a set for a ballet.

An evening in summer. The action is continuous with two intermissions.

ACT 1

(*At the rise of the curtain someone is taking a shower in the bathroom, the door of which is half open. A pretty young woman, with anxious lines in her face, enters the bedroom and crosses to the bathroom door.*)

MARGARET (*shouting above roar of water*): One of those no-neck monsters hit me with a hot buttered biscuit so I have t' change!

(*Margaret's voice is both rapid and drawling. In her long speeches she has the vocal tricks of a priest delivering a liturgical chant, the lines are almost sung, always continuing a little beyond her breath so she has to gasp for another. Sometimes she intersperses the lines with a little wordless singing, such as "Dada-daaaa!"*)

(*Water turns off and Brick calls out to her, but is still unseen. A tone of politely feigned interest, masking indifference, or worse, is characteristic of his speech with Margaret.*)

BRICK: Wha'd you say, Maggie? Water was on s' loud I couldn't hearya. . . .
MARGARET: Well, I! — just remarked that! — one of th' no-neck monsters messed up m' lovely lace dress so I got t' — cha-a-ange. . . .

(*She opens and kicks shut drawers of the dresser.*)

BRICK: Why d'ya call Gooper's kiddies no-neck monsters?
MARGARET: Because they've got no necks! Isn't that a good enough reason?
BRICK: Don't they have any necks?
MARGARET: None visible. Their fat little heads are set on their fat little bodies without a bit of connection.
BRICK: That's too bad.

MARGARET: Yes, it's too bad because you can't wring their necks if they've got no necks to wring! Isn't that right, honey?

(*She steps out of her dress, stands in a slip of ivory satin and lace.*)

Yep, they're no-neck monsters, all no-neck people are monsters . . .

(*Children shriek downstairs.*)

Hear them? Hear them screaming? I don't know where their voice boxes are located since they don't have necks. I tell you I got so nervous at that table tonight I thought I would throw back my head and utter a scream you could hear across the Arkansas border an' parts of Louisiana an' Tennessee. I said to your charming sister-in-law, Mae, honey, couldn't you feed those precious little things at a separate table with an oilcloth cover? They make such a mess an' the lace cloth looks *so* pretty! She made enormous eyes at me and said, "Ohhh, noooooo! On Big Daddy's birthday? Why, he would never forgive me!" Well, I want you to know, Big Daddy hadn't been at the table two minutes with those five no-neck monsters slobbering and drooling over their food before he threw down his fork an' shouted, "Fo' God's sake, Gooper, why don't you put them pigs at a trough in th' kitchen?" — Well, I swear, I simply could have di-ieed!

Think of it, Brick, they've got five of them and number six is coming. They've brought the whole bunch down here like animals to display at a county fair. Why, they have those children doin' tricks all the time! "Junior, show Big Daddy how you do this, show Big Daddy how you do that, say your little piece fo' Big Daddy, Sister. Show your dimples, Sugar. Brother, show Big Daddy how you stand on your head!" — It goes on all the time, along with constant little remarks and innuendos about the fact that you and I have not produced any children, are totally childless and therefore totally useless! — Of course it's comical but it's also disgusting since it's so obvious what they're up to!

BRICK (*without interest*): What are they up to, Maggie?
MARGARET: Why you know what they're up to!
BRICK (*appearing*): No, I don't know what they're up to.

(*He stands there in the bathroom doorway drying his hair with a towel and hanging onto the towel rack because one ankle is broken, plastered and bound. He is still slim and firm as a boy. His liquor hasn't started tearing him down outside. He has the additional charm of that cool air of detachment that people have who have given up the struggle. But now and then, when disturbed, something flashes behind it, like lightning in a fair sky, which shows that at some deeper level he is far from peaceful. Perhaps in a stronger light he would show some signs of deliquescence, but the fading, still warm light from the gallery treats him gently.*)

MARGARET: I'll tell you what they're up to, boy of mine! — They're up to cutting you out of your father's estate, and —

(*She freezes momentarily before her next remark. Her voice drops as if it were somehow a personally embarrassing admission.*)

— Now we know that Big Daddy's dyin' of — cancer. . . .

(*There are voices on the lawn below: long-drawn calls across distance. Margaret raises her lovely bare arms and powders her armpits with a light sigh.*)
(*She adjusts the angle of a magnifying mirror to straighten an eyelash, then rises fretfully saying:*)

There's so much light in the room it —
BRICK (*softly but sharply*): Do we?
MARGARET: Do we what?
BRICK: Know Big Daddy's dyin' of cancer?
MARGARET: Got the report today.
BRICK: Oh . . .
MARGARET (*letting down bamboo blinds which cast long, gold-fretted shadows over the room*): Yep, got th' report just now . . . it didn't surprise me, Baby. . . .

(*Her voice has range, and music; sometimes it drops low as a boy's and you have a sudden image of her playing boy's games as a child.*)

I recognized the symptoms soon's we got here last spring and I'm willin' to bet you that Brother Man and his wife were pretty sure of it, too. That more than likely explains why their usual summer migration to the coolness of the Great Smokies was passed up this summer in favor of — hustlin' down here ev'ry whipstitch with their whole screamin' tribe! And why so many allusions have been made to Rainbow Hill lately. You know what Rainbow Hill is? Place that's famous for treatin' alcoholics an' dope fiends in the movies!
BRICK: I'm not in the movies.
MARGARET: No, and you don't take dope. Otherwise you're a perfect candidate for Rainbow Hill, Baby, and that's where they aim to ship you — over my dead body! Yep, over my dead body they'll ship you there, but nothing would please them better.

Then Brother Man could get a-hold of the purse strings and dole out remittances to us, maybe get power of attorney and sign checks for us and cut off our credit wherever, whenever he wanted! Son-of-a-bitch! — How'd you like that, Baby? — Well, you've been doin' just about ev'rything in your power to bring it about, you've just been doin' ev'rything you can think of to aid and abet them in this scheme of theirs! Quittin' work, devoting yourself to the occupation of drinkin'! — Breakin' your ankle last night on the high school athletic field: doin' what? Jumpin' hurdles? At two or three in the morning? Just fantastic! Got in the paper. *Clarksdale Register* carried a nice little item about it, human interest story about a well-known former athlete stagin' a one-man track meet on the Glorious Hill High School athletic field last night, but was slightly out of condition and didn't clear the first hurdle! Brother Man Gooper claims he exercised his influence t' keep it from goin' out over AP or UP or every goddamn "P."

But, Brick? You still have one big advantage!

(*During the above swift flood of words, Brick has reclined with contrapuntal leisure on the snowy surface of the bed and has rolled over carefully on his side or belly.*)

BRICK (*wryly*): Did you *say* something, Maggie?
MARGARET: Big Daddy dotes on you, honey. And he can't stand Brother Man and Brother Man's wife, that monster of fertility, Mae. Know how I know? By little expressions that flicker over his face when that woman is holding fo'th on one of her choice topics such as — how she refused twilight sleep!° — when the twins were delivered! Because she feels motherhood's an experience that a woman ought to experience fully! — in order to fully appreciate the wonder and beauty of it! HAH! — and how she made Brother Man come in an' stand beside her in the delivery room so he would not miss out on the "wonder and beauty" of it either! — producin' those no-neck monsters. . . .

(*A speech of this kind would be antipathetic from almost anybody but Margaret; she makes it oddly funny, because her eyes constantly twinkle and her voice shakes with laughter which is basically indulgent.*)

— Big Daddy shares my attitude toward those two! As for me, well — I give him a laugh now and then and he tolerates me. In fact! — I sometimes suspect that Big Daddy harbors a little unconscious "lech" fo' me. . . .

twilight sleep: Anesthesia.

BRICK: What makes you think that Big Daddy has a lech for you, Maggie?

MARGARET: Way he always drops his eyes down my body when I'm talkin' to him, drops his eyes to my boobs an' licks his old chops! Ha ha!

BRICK: That kind of talk is disgusting.

MARGARET: Did anyone ever tell you that you're an ass-aching Puritan, Brick?

I think it's mighty fine that that ole fellow, on the doorstep of death, still takes in my shape with what I think is deserved appreciation!

And you wanta know something else? Big Daddy didn't know how many little Maes and Goopers had been produced! "How many kids have you got?" he asked at the table, just like Brother Man and his wife were new acquaintances to him! Big Mama said he was jokin', but that ole boy wasn't jokin', Lord, no!

And when they infawmed him that they had five already and were turning out number six! — the news seemed to come as a sort of unpleasant surprise . . .

(*Children yell below.*)

Scream, monsters!

(*Turns to Brick with a sudden, gay, charming smile which fades as she notices that he is not looking at her but into fading gold space with a troubled expression.*)

(*It is constant rejection that makes her humor "bitchy."*)

Yes, you should of been at that supper-table, Baby.

(*Whenever she calls him "baby" the word is a soft caress.*)

Y'know, Big Daddy, bless his ole sweet soul, he's the dearest ole thing in the world, but he does hunch over his food as if he preferred not to notice anything else. Well, Mae an' Gooper were side by side at the table, direckly across from Big Daddy, watchin' his face like hawks while they jawed an' jabbered about the cuteness an' brillance of th' no-neck monsters!

(*She giggles with a hand fluttering at her throat and her breast and her long throat arched.*)

(*She comes downstage and recreates the scene with voice and gesture.*)

And the no-neck monsters were ranged around the table, some in high chairs and some on th' *Books of Knowledge,* all in fancy little paper caps in honor of Big Daddy's birthday, and all through dinner, well, I want you to know that Brother Man an' his partner never once, for one moment, stopped exchanging pokes an' pinches an' kicks an' signs an' signals! — Why, they were like a couple of cardsharps fleecing a sucker. — Even Big Mama, bless her ole sweet soul, she isn't th' quickest an' brightest thing in the world, she finally noticed, at last, an' said to Gooper, "Gooper, what are you an' Mae makin' all these signs at each other about?" — I swear t' goodness, I nearly choked on my chicken!

(*Margaret, back at the dressing table, still doesn't see Brick. He is watching her with a look that is not quite definable — Amused? shocked? contemptuous? — part of those and part of something else.*)

Y'know — your brother Gooper still cherishes the illusion he took a giant step up on the social ladder when he married Miss Mae Flynn of the Memphis Flynns.

But I have a piece of Spanish news for Gooper. The Flynns never had a thing in this world but money and they lost that, they were nothing at all but fairly successful climbers. Of course, Mae Flynn came out in Memphis eight years before I made my debut in Nashville, but I had friends at Ward-Belmont who came from Memphis and they used to come to see me and I used to go to see them for Christmas and spring vacations, and so I know who rates an' who doesn't rate in Memphis society. Why, y'know ole Papa Flynn, he barely escaped doing time in the Federal pen for shady manipulations on th' stock market when his chain stores crashed, and as for Mae having been a cotton carnival queen, as they remind us so often, lest we forget, well, that's one honor that I don't envy her for! — Sit on a brass throne on a tacky float an' ride down Main Street, smilin', bowin', and blowin' kisses to all the trash on the street —

(*She picks out a pair of jeweled sandals and rushes to the dressing table.*)

Why, year before last, when Susan McPheeters was singled out fo' that honor, y'know what happened to her? Y'know what happened to poor little Susie McPheeters?

BRICK (*absently*): No. What happened to little Susie McPheeters?

MARGARET: Somebody spit tobacco juice in her face.

BRICK (*dreamily*): Somebody spit tobacco juice in her face?

MARGARET: That's right, some old drunk leaned out of a window in the Hotel Gayoso and yelled, "Hey, Queen, hey, hey, there, Queenie!" Poor Susie looked up and flashed him a radiant smile and he shot out a squirt of tobacco juice right in poor Susie's face.

BRICK: Well, what d'you know about that.

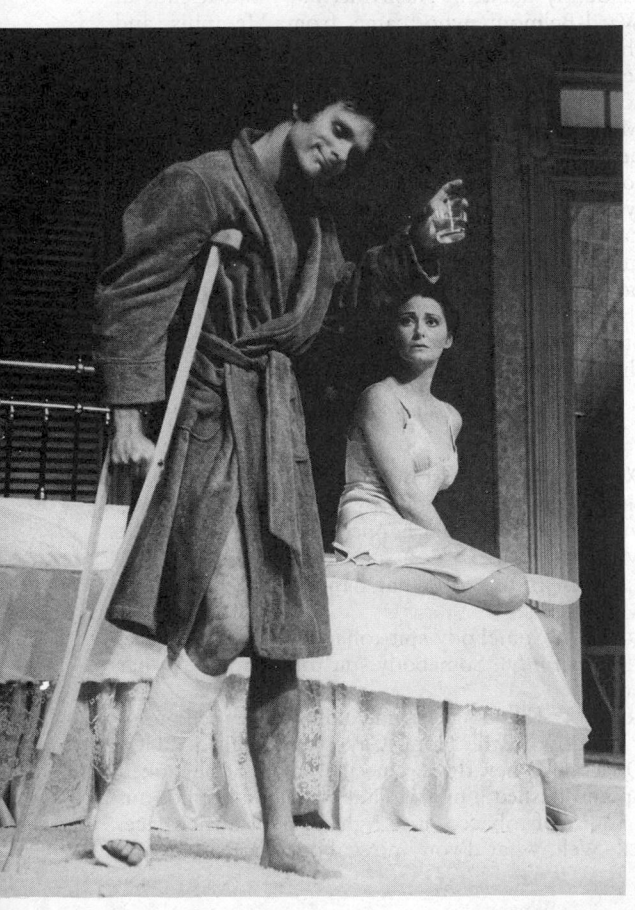

ABOVE LEFT: Maggie (Elizabeth
Ashley) in the 1974 American
Shakespeare Theater production
of *Cat on a Hot Tin Roof*. LEFT:
Brick (Keir Dullea) and Maggie.
ABOVE: Maggie and Big Daddy
(Fred Gwynne).

MARGARET (*gaily*): What do I know about it? I was there, I saw it!

BRICK (*absently*): Must have been kind of funny.

MARGARET: Susie didn't think so. Had hysterics. Screamed like a banshee. They had to stop th' parade an' remove her from her throne an' go on with —

(*She catches sight of him in the mirror, gasps slightly, wheels about to face him. Count ten.*)

— Why are you looking at me like that?

BRICK (*whistling softly, now*): Like what, Maggie?

MARGARET (*intensely, fearfully*): The way y' were lookin' at me just now, befo' I caught your eye in the mirror and you started t' whistle! I don't know how t' describe it but it froze my blood! — I've caught you lookin' at me like that so often lately. What are you thinkin' of when you look at me like that?

BRICK: I wasn't conscious of lookin' at you, Maggie.

MARGARET: Well, I was conscious of it! What were you thinkin'?

BRICK: I don't remember thinking of anything, Maggie.

MARGARET: Don't you think I know that — ? Don't you — ? — Think I know that — ?

BRICK (*cooly*): Know *what*, Maggie?

MARGARET (*struggling for expression*): That I've gone through this — *hideous!* — transformation, become — hard! Frantic!

(*Then she adds, almost tenderly:*)

— cruel!!
        That's what you've been observing in me lately. How could y' help but observe it? That's all right. I'm not — thin-skinned any more, can't afford t' be thin-skinned any more.

(*She is now recovering her power.*)

— But Brick? Brick?

BRICK: Did you say something?

MARGARET: I was *goin'* t' say something: that I get — lonely. Very!

BRICK: Ev'rybody gets that . . .

MARGARET: Living with someone you love can be lonelier — than living entirely *alone!* — if the one that y' love doesn't love you. . . .

(*There is a pause. Brick hobbles downstage and asks, without looking at her:*)

BRICK: Would you like to live alone, Maggie?

(*Another pause: then — after she has caught a quick, hurt breath:*)

MARGARET: No! — God! — I wouldn't!

(*Another gasping breath. She forcibly controls what must have been an impulse to cry out. We see her deliberately, very forcibly, going all the way back to the world in which you can talk about ordinary matters.*)

Did you have a nice shower?

BRICK: Uh-huh.

MARGARET: Was the water cool?

BRICK: No.

MARGARET: But it made y' feel fresh, huh?

BRICK: Fresher. . . .

MARGARET: I know something would make y' feel *much* fresher!

BRICK: What?

MARGARET: An alcohol rub. Or cologne, a rub with cologne!

BRICK: That's good after a workout but I haven't been workin' out, Maggie.

MARGARET: You've kept in good shape, though.

BRICK (*indifferently*): You think so, Maggie?

MARGARET: I always thought drinkin' men lost their looks, but I was plainly mistaken.

BRICK (*wryly*): Why, thanks, Maggie.

MARGARET: You're the only drinkin' man I know that it never seems t' put fat on.

BRICK: I'm gettin' softer, Maggie.

MARGARET: Well, sooner or later it's bound to soften you up. It was just beginning to soften up Skipper when —

(*She stops short.*)

I'm sorry. I never could keep my fingers off a sore — I wish you *would* lose your looks. If you did it would make the martyrdom of Saint Maggie a little more bearable. But no such goddamn luck. I actually believe you've gotten better looking since you've gone on the bottle. Yeah, a person who didn't know you would think you'd never had a tense nerve in your body or a strained muscle.

(*There are sounds of croquet on the lawn below: the click of mallets, light voices, near and distant.*)

Of course, you always had that detached quality as if you were playing a game without much concern over whether you won or lost, and now that you've lost the game, not lost but just quit playing, you have that rare sort of charm that usually only happens in very old or hopelessly sick people, the charm of the defeated. — You look so cool, so cool, so enviably cool.

REVEREND TOOKER (*offstage right*): Now looka here, boy, lemme show you how to get outa that!

MARGARET: They're playing croquet. The moon has appeared and it's white, just beginning to turn a little bit yellow. . . .

You were a wonderful lover. . . .

Such a wonderful person to go to bed with, and I think mostly because you were really indifferent to it. Isn't that right? Never had any anxiety about it, did it naturally, easily, slowly, with absolute confidence and perfect calm, more like opening a door for a lady or seating her at a table than giving expression to any longing for her. Your indifference made you wonderful at lovemaking — strange? — but true. . . .

REVEREND TOOKER: Oh! That's a beauty.

DOCTOR BAUGH: Yeah. I got you boxed.

MARGARET: You know, if I thought you would never, never, *never* make love to me again — I would go downstairs to the kitchen and pick out the longest and sharpest knife I could find and stick it straight into my heart, I swear that I would!

REVEREND TOOKER: Watch out, you're gonna miss it.

DOCTOR BAUGH: You just don't know me, boy!

MARGARET: But one thing I don't have is the charm of the defeated, my hat is still in the ring, and I am determined to win!

(*There is the sound of croquet mallets hitting croquet balls.*)

REVEREND TOOKER: Mmm — You're too slippery for me.

MARGARET: — What is the victory of a cat on a hot tin roof? — I wish I knew. . . .

Just staying on it, I guess, as long as she can. . . .

DOCTOR BAUGH: Jus' like an eel, boy, jus' like an eel!

(*More croquet sounds.*)

MARGARET: Later tonight I'm going to tell you I love you an' maybe by that time you'll be drunk enough to believe me. Yes, they're playing croquet. . . .

Big Daddy is dying of cancer. . . .

What were you thinking of when I caught you looking at me like that? Were you thinking of Skipper?

(*Brick takes up his crutch, rises.*)

Oh, excuse me, forgive me, but laws of silence don't work! No, laws of silence don't work. . . .

(*Brick crosses to the bar, takes a quick drink, and rubs his head with a towel.*)

Laws of silence don't work. . . .

When something is festering in your memory or your imagination, laws of silence don't work, it's just like shutting a door and locking it on a house on fire in hope of forgetting that the house is burning. But not facing a fire doesn't put it out. Silence about a thing just magnifies it. It grows and festers in silence, becomes malignant. . . .

(*He drops his crutch.*)

BRICK: Give me my crutch.

(*He has stopped rubbing his hair dry but still stands hanging onto the towel rack in a white towel-cloth robe.*)

MARGARET: Lean on me.

BRICK: No, just give me my crutch.

MARGARET: Lean on my shoulder.

BRICK: *I don't want to lean on your shoulder, I want my crutch!*

(*This is spoken like sudden lightning.*)

Are you going to give me my crutch or do I have to get down on my knees on the floor and —

MARGARET: *Here, here, take it, take it!*

(*She has thrust the crutch at him.*)

BRICK (*hobbling out*): Thanks . . .

MARGARET: We mustn't scream at each other, the walls in this house have ears. . . .

(*He hobbles directly to liquor cabinet to get a new drink.*)

— but that's the first time I've heard you raise your voice in a long time, Brick. A crack in the wall? — Of composure?

— I think that's a good sign. . . .

A sign of nerves in a player on the defensive!

(*Brick turns and smiles at her coolly over his fresh drink.*)

BRICK: It just hasn't happened yet, Maggie.

MARGARET: What?

BRICK: The click I get in my head when I've had enough of this stuff to make me peaceful. . . .

Will you do me a favor?

MARGARET: Maybe I will. What favor?

BRICK: Just, just keep your voice down!

MARGARET (*in a hoarse whisper*): I'll do you that favor, I'll speak in a whisper, if not shut up completely, if *you* will do *me* a favor and make that drink your last one till after the party.

BRICK: What party?

MARGARET: Big Daddy's birthday party.

BRICK: Is this Big Daddy's birthday?

MARGARET: You know this is Big Daddy's birthday!

BRICK: No, I don't, I forgot it.

MARGARET: Well, I remembered it for you . . .

(*They are both speaking as breathlessly as a pair of kids after a fight, drawing deep exhausted breaths and looking at each other with faraway eyes, shaking and panting together as if they had broken apart from a violent struggle.*)

BRICK: Good for you, Maggie.

MARGARET: You just have to scribble a few lines on this card.

BRICK: You scribble something, Maggie.

MARGARET: It's got to be your handwriting; it's your present, I've given him my present; it's got to be your handwriting!

(*The tension between them is building again, the voices becoming shrill once more.*)

BRICK: I didn't get him a present.

MARGARET: I got one for you.

BRICK: All right. You write the card, then.

MARGARET: And have him know you didn't remember his birthday?

BRICK: I didn't remember his birthday.

MARGARET: You don't have to prove you didn't!

BRICK: I don't want to fool him about it.

MARGARET: Just write "Love, Brick!" for God's —

BRICK: No.

MARGARET: You've *got* to!

BRICK: I don't have to do anything I don't want to do. You keep forgetting the conditions on which I agreed to stay on living with you.

MARGARET (*out before she knows it*): I'm not living with you. We occupy the same cage.

BRICK: You've got to remember the conditions agreed on.

SONNY (*offstage*): Mommy, give it to me. I had it first.

MAE: Hush.

MARGARET: They're impossible conditions!

BRICK: Then why don't you — ?

SONNY: I want it, I want it!

MAE: Get away!

MARGARET: HUSH! Who is out there? Is somebody at the door?

(*There are footsteps in hall.*)

MAE (*outside*): May I enter a moment?

MARGARET: Oh, *you!* Sure. Come in, Mae.

(*Mae enters bearing aloft the bow of a young lady's archery set.*)

MAE: Brick, is this thing yours?

MARGARET: Why, Sister Woman — that's my Diana Trophy. Won it at the intercollegiate archery contest on the Ole Miss campus.

MAE: It's a mighty dangerous thing to leave exposed round a house full of nawmal rid-blooded children attracted t'weapons.

MARGARET: "Nawmal rid-blooded children attracted t'weapons" ought t'be taught to keep their hands off things that don't belong to them.

MAE: Maggie, honey, if you had children of your own you'd know how funny that is. Will you please lock this up and put the key out of reach?

MARGARET: Sister Woman, nobody is plotting the destruction of your kiddies. — Brick and I still have our special archers' license. We're goin' deer-huntin' on Moon Lake as soon as the season starts. I love to run with dogs through chilly woods, run, run leap over obstructions —

(*She goes into the closet carrying the bow.*)

MAE: How's the injured ankle, Brick?

BRICK: Doesn't hurt. Just itches.

MAE: Oh, my! Brick — Brick, you should've been downstairs after supper! Kiddies put on a show. Polly played the piano, Buster an' Sonny drums, an' then they turned out the lights an' Dixie an' Trixie puhfawmed a toe dance in fairy costume with *spahkluhs!* Big Daddy just beamed! He just beamed!

MARGARET (*from the closet with a sharp laugh*): Oh, I bet. It breaks my heart that we missed it!

(*She reenters.*)

But Mae? Why did y'give dawgs' names to all your kiddies?

MAE: *Dogs'* names?

MARGARET (*sweetly*): Dixie, Trixie, Buster, Sonny, Polly! — Sounds like four dogs and a parrot . . .

MAE: Maggie?

(*Margaret turns with a smile.*)

Why are you so catty?

MARGARET: Cause I'm a cat! But why can't *you* take a joke, Sister Woman?

MAE: Nothin' pleases me more than a joke that's funny. You know the real names of our kiddies. Buster's real name is Robert. Sonny's real name is Saunders. Trixie's real name is Marlene and Dixie's —

(*Gooper downstairs calls for her. "Hey, Mae! Sister Woman, intermission is over!" — She rushes to door, saying:*)

Intermission is over! See ya later!

MARGARET: I wonder what Dixie's real name is?

BRICK: Maggie, being catty doesn't help things any . . .

MARGARET: I know! *WHY!* — Am I so catty? — Cause I'm consumed with envy an' eaten up with longing? — Brick, I'm going to lay out your beautiful Shantung silk suit from Rome and one of your monogrammed silk shirts. I'll put your cuff links in it, those lovely star sapphires I get you to wear so rarely. . . .

BRICK: I can't get trousers on over this plaster cast.

MARGARET: Yes, you can, I'll help you.

BRICK: I'm not going to get dressed, Maggie.

MARGARET: Will you just put on a pair of white silk pajamas?

BRICK: Yes, I'll do that, Maggie.

MARGARET: *Thank* you, thank you so *much!*

BRICK: Don't mention it.

MARGARET: *Oh, Brick!* How long does it have t' go on? This punishment? Haven't I done time enough, haven't I served my term, can't I apply for a — pardon?

BRICK: Maggie, you're spoiling my liquor. Lately your voice always sounds like you'd been running upstairs to warn somebody that the house was on fire!

MARGARET: Well, no wonder, no wonder. Y'know what I feel like, Brick?

> *I feel all the time like a cat on a hot tin roof!*

BRICK: Then jump off the roof, jump off it, cats can jump off roofs and land on their four feet uninjured!

MARGARET: Oh, yes!

BRICK: Do it! — fo' God's sake, do it . . .

MARGARET: Do what?

BRICK: Take a lover!

MARGARET: I can't see a man but you! Even with my eyes closed, I just see you! Why don't you get ugly, Brick, why don't you please get fat or ugly or something so I could stand it?

(*She rushes to hall door, opens it, listens.*)

> The concert is still going on! Bravo, no-necks, bravo!

(*She slams and locks door fiercely.*)

BRICK: What did you lock the door for?

MARGARET: To give us a little privacy for a while.

BRICK: You know better, Maggie.

MARGARET: No, I don't know better. . . .

(*She rushes to gallery doors, draws the rose-silk drapes across them.*)

BRICK: Don't make a fool of yourself.

MARGARET: I don't mind makin' a fool of myself over you!

BRICK: I mind, Maggie. I feel embarrassed for you.

MARGARET: Feel embarrassed! But don't continue my torture. I can't live on and on under these circumstances.

BRICK: You agreed to —

MARGARET: I know but —

BRICK: — Accept that condition!

MARGARET: *I CAN'T! CAN'T! CAN'T!*

(*She seizes his shoulder.*)

BRICK: Let go!

(*He breaks away from her and seizes the small boudoir chair and raises it like a lion-tamer facing a big circus cat.*)

(*Count five. She stares at him with her fist pressed to her mouth, then bursts into shrill, almost hysterical laughter. He remains grave for a moment, then grins and puts the chair down.*)

(*Big Mama calls through closed door.*)

BIG MAMA: Son? Son? Son?

BRICK: What is it, Big Mama?

BIG MAMA (*outside*): Oh, son! We got the most wonderful news about Big Daddy. I just had t' run up an' tell you right this —

(*She rattles the knob.*)

—What's this door doin', locked, faw? You all think there's robbers in the house?

MARGARET: Big Mama, Brick is dressin, he's not dressed yet.

BIG MAMA: That's all right, it won't be the first time I've seen Brick not dressed. Come on, open this door!

(*Margaret, with a grimace, goes to unlock and open the hall door, as Brick hobbles rapidly to the bathroom and kicks the door shut. Big Mama has disappeared from the hall.*)

MARGARET: Big Mama?

(*Big Mama appears through the opposite gallery doors behind Margaret, huffing and puffing like an old bulldog. She is a short, stout woman; her sixty years and 170 pounds have left her somewhat breathless most of the time; she's always tensed like a boxer, or rather, a Japanese wrestler. Her "family" was maybe a little superior to Big Daddy's, but not much. She wears a black or silver lace dress and at least half a million in flashy gems. She is very sincere.*)

BIG MAMA (*loudly, startling Margaret*): Here — I come through Gooper's and Mae's gall'ry door. Where's Brick? *Brick* — Hurry on out of there son, I just have a second and want to give you the news about Big Daddy. — I hate locked doors in a house . . .

MARGARET (*with affected lightness*): I've noticed you do, Big Mama, but people have got to have *some* moments of privacy, don't they?

BIG MAMA: No, ma'am, not in *my* house. (*Without pause.*) Whacha took off you' dress faw? I thought that little lace dress was so sweet on yuh, honey.

MARGARET: I thought it looked sweet on me, too, but one of m' cute little table-partners used it for a napkin so — !

BIG MAMA (*picking up stockings on floor*): What?

MARGARET: You know, Big Mama, Mae and Gooper's so touchy about those children — thanks, Big Mama . . .

(*Big Mama has thrust the picked-up stockings in Margaret's hand with a grunt.*)

— that you just don't dare to suggest there's any room for improvement in their —

BIG MAMA: Brick, hurry out! — Shoot, Maggie, you just don't like children.

MARGARET: I do SO like children! Adore them! — well brought up!

BIG MAMA (*gentle — loving*): Well, why don't you have some and bring them up well, then, instead of all the time pickin' on Gooper's an' Mae's?

GOOPER (*shouting up the stairs*): Hey, hey, Big Mama, Betsy an' Hugh got to go, waitin' t' tell yuh g'by!

BIG MAMA: Tell 'em to hold their hawses, I'll be right down in a jiffy!

GOOPER: Yes ma'am!

(*She turns to the bathroom door and calls out.*)

BIG MAMA: Son? Can you hear me in there?

(*There is a muffled answer.*)

We just got the full report from the laboratory at the Ochsner Clinic, completely negative, son, ev'rything negative, right on down the line! Nothin' a-tall's wrong with him but some little functional thing called a spastic colon. Can you hear me, son?

MARGARET: He can hear you, Big Mama.

BIG MAMA: Then why don't he say something? God Almighty, a piece of news like that should make him shout. It made *me* shout, I can tell you. I shouted and sobbed and fell right down on my knees! — Look!

(*She pulls up her skirt.*)

See the bruises where I hit my kneecaps? Took both doctors to haul me back on my feet!

(*She laughs — she always laughs like hell at herself.*)

Big Daddy was furious with me! But ain't that wonderful news?

(*Facing bathroom again, she continues:*)

After all the anxiety we been through to git a report like that on Big Daddy's birthday? Big Daddy tried to hide how much of a load that news took off his mind, but didn't fool *me*. He was mighty close to crying about it *himself*!

(*Good-byes are shouted downstairs, and she rushes to door.*)

GOOPER: Big Mama!

BIG MAMA: *Hold those people down there, don't let them go!* — Now, git dressed we're all comin' up to this room fo' Big Daddy's birthday party because of your ankle. — How's his ankle, Maggie?

MARGARET: Well, he broke it, Big Mama.

BIG MAMA: I know he broke it.

(*A phone is ringing in hall. A Negro voice answers: "Mistuh Polly's res'dence."*)

I mean does it hurt him much still.

MARGARET: I'm afraid I can't give you that information, Big Mama. You'll have to ask Brick if it hurts much still or not.

SOOKEY (*in the hall*): It's Memphis, Mizz Polly, it's Miss Sally in Memphis.

BIG MAMA: Awright, Sookey.

(*Big Mama rushes into the hall and is heard shouting on the phone:*)

Hello, Miss Sally. How are you, Miss Sally? — Yes, well, I was just gonna call you about it. *Shoot!* —

MARGARET: Brick, don't!

(*Big Mama raises her voice to a bellow.*)

BIG MAMA: *Miss Sally? Don't ever call me from the Gayoso Lobby, too much talk goes on in that hotel lobby, no wonder you can't hear me! Now listen, Miss Sally. They's nothin' serious wrong with Big Daddy. We got the report just now, they's nothin' wrong but a thing called a — spastic! SPASTIC! — colon . . .*

(*She appears at the hall door and calls to Margaret.*)

— Maggie, come out here and talk to that fool on the phone. I'm shouted breathless!

MARGARET (*goes out and is heard sweetly at phone*): Miss Sally? This is Brick's wife, Maggie. So nice to hear your voice. Can you hear *mine*? Well, good! — Big Mama just wanted you to know that they've got the report from the Ochsner Clinic and what Big Daddy has is a spastic colon. Yes. Spastic colon, Miss Sally. That's right, spastic colon. *G'bye, Miss Sally, hope I'll see you real soon!*

(*Hangs up a little before Miss Sally was probably ready to terminate the talk. She returns through the hall door.*)

She heard me perfectly. I've discovered with deaf people the thing to do is not shout at them but just enunciate clearly. My rich old Aunt Cornelia was deaf as the dead but I could make her hear me just by sayin' each word slowly, distinctly, close to her ear. I read her the *Commercial Appeal* ev'ry night, read her the classified ads in it, even, she never missed a word of it. But was she a mean ole thing! Know what I got when she died? Her unexpired subscriptions to five magazines and the Book-of-the-Month Club and a LIBRARY full of ev'ry dull book ever written! All else went to her hellcat of a sister . . . meaner than she was, even!

(*Big Mama has been straightening things up in the room during this speech.*)

BIG MAMA (*closing closet door on discarded clothes*): *Miss Sally sure is a case!* Big Daddy says she's always got her hand out fo' something. He's not mistaken. That poor ole thing always has her hand out fo' somethin'. I don't think Big Daddy gives her as much as he should.

GOOPER: Big Mama! Come on now! Betsy and Hugh can't wait no longer!

BIG MAMA (*shouting*): I'm comin'!

(*She starts out. At the hall door, turns and jerks a forefinger, first toward the bathroom door, then toward the liquor cabinet, meaning: "Has Brick been drinking?" Margaret pretends not to understand, cocks her head and raises her brows as if the pantomimic performance was completely mystifying to her.*)

(*Big Mama rushes back to Margaret:*)

Shoot! Stop playin' so dumb! — I mean has he been drinkin' that stuff much yet?

MARGARET (*with a little laugh*): Oh! I think he had a highball after supper.

BIG MAMA: Don't laugh about it! — Some single men stop drinkin' when they git married and others start! Brick never touched liquor before he — !

MARGARET (*crying out*): THAT'S NOT FAIR!

BIG MAMA: Fair or not fair I want to ask you a question, one question: D'you make Brick happy in bed?

MARGARET: Why don't you ask if he makes *me* happy in bed?

BIG MAMA: Because I know that —

MARGARET: *It works both ways!*

BIG MAMA: Something's not right! You're childless and my son drinks!

GOOPER: Come on, Big Mama!

(*Gooper has called her downstairs and she has rushed to the door on the line above. She turns at the door and points at the bed.*)

— When a marriage goes on the rocks, the rocks are *there*, right *there*!

MARGARET: *That's* —

(*Big Mama has swept out of the room and slammed the door.*)

— not — *fair* . . .

(*Margaret is alone, completely alone, and she feels it. She draws in, hunches her shoulders, raises her arms with fists clenched, shuts her eyes tight as a child about to be stabbed with a vaccination needle. When she opens her eyes again, what she sees is the long* oval mirror and she rushes straight to it, stares into it with a grimace and says: "Who are you?" — Then she crouches a little and answers herself in a different voice which is high, thin, mocking: "I am Maggie the Cat!" — Straightens quickly as bathroom door opens a little and Brick calls out to her.*)

BRICK: Has Big Mama gone?

MARGARET: She's gone.

(*He opens the bathroom door and hobbles out, with his liquor glass now empty, straight to the liquor cabinet. He is whistling softly. Margaret's head pivots on her long, slender throat to watch him.*)

(*She raises a hand uncertainly to the base of her throat, as if it was difficult for her to swallow, before she speaks:*)

You know, our sex life didn't just peter out in the usual way, it was cut off short, long before the natural time for it to, and it's going to revive again, just as sudden as that. I'm confident of it. That's what I'm keeping myself attractive for. For the time when you'll see me again like other men see me. Yes, like other men see me. They still see me, Brick, and they like what they see. Uh-huh. Some of them would give their —

Look, Brick!

(*She stands before the long oval mirror, touches her breast and then her hips with her two hands.*)

How high my body stays on me! — Nothing has fallen on me — not a fraction. . . .

(*Her voice is soft and trembling: a pleading child's. At this moment as he turns to glance at her — a look which is like a player passing a ball to another player, third down and goal to go — she has to capture the audience in a grip so tight that she can hold it till the first intermission without any lapse of attention.*)

Other men still want me. My face looks strained, sometimes, but I've kept my figure as well as you've kept yours, and men admire it. I still turn heads on the street. Why, last week in Memphis everywhere that I went men's eyes burned holes in my clothes, at the country club and in restaurants and department stores, there wasn't a man I met or walked by that didn't just eat me up with his eyes and turn around when I passed him and look back at me. Why, at Alice's party for her New York cousins, the best-lookin' man in the crowd — followed me upstairs and tried to force his way in the powder room with me, followed me to the door and tried to force his way in!

BRICK: Why didn't you let him, Maggie?

MARGARET: Because I'm not that common, for one

thing. Not that I wasn't almost tempted to. You like to know who it was? It was Sonny Boy Maxwell, that's who!

BRICK: Oh, yeah, Sonny Boy Maxwell, he was a good end-runner but had a little injury to his back and had to quit.

MARGARET: He has no injury now and has no wife and still has a lech for me!

BRICK: I see no reason to lock him out of a powder room in that case.

MARGARET: And have someone catch me at it? I'm not that stupid. Oh, I might sometime cheat on you with someone, since you're so insultingly eager to have me do it! — But if I do, you can be damned sure it will be in a place and a time where no one but me and the man could possibly know. Because I'm not going to give you any excuse to divorce me for being unfaithful or anything else....

BRICK: Maggie, I wouldn't divorce you for being unfaithful or anything else. Don't you know that? Hell. I'd be relieved to know that you'd found yourself a lover.

MARGARET: Well, I'm taking no chances. No, I'd rather stay on this hot tin roof.

BRICK: A hot tin roof's 'n uncomfo'table place t' stay on....

(*He starts to whistle softly.*)

MARGARET (*through his whistle*): Yeah, but I can stay on it just as long as I have to.

BRICK: You could leave me, Maggie.

(*He resumes whistle. She wheels about to glare at him.*)

MARGARET: *Don't want to and will not!* Besides if I did, you don't have a cent to pay for it but what you get from Big Daddy and he's dying of cancer!

(*For the first time a realization of Big Daddy's doom seems to penetrate to Brick's consciousness, visibly, and he looks at Margaret.*)

BRICK: Big Mama just said he *wasn't*, that the report was okay.

MARGARET: That's what she thinks because she got the same story that they gave Big Daddy. And was just as taken in by it as he was, poor ole things....

But tonight they're going to tell her the truth about it. When Big Daddy goes to bed, they're going to tell her that he is dying of cancer.

(*She slams the dresser drawer.*)

— It's malignant and it's terminal.

BRICK: Does Big Daddy know it?

MARGARET: Hell, do they *ever* know it? Nobody says, "You're dying." You have to fool them. They have to fool *themselves.*

BRICK: Why?

MARGARET: *Why?* Because human beings dream of life everlasting, that's the reason! But most of them want it on earth and not in heaven.

(*He gives a short, hard laugh at her touch of humor.*)

Well.... (*She touches up her mascara.*) That's how it is, anyhow.... (*She looks about.*) Where did I put down my cigarette? Don't want to burn up the home-place, at least not with Mae and Gooper and their five monsters in it!

(*She has found it and sucks at it greedily. Blows out smoke and continues:*)

So this is Big Daddy's last birthday. And Mae and Gooper, they know it, oh, *they* know it, all right. They got the first information from the Ochsner Clinic. That's why they rushed down here with their no-neck monsters. Because. Do you know something? Big Daddy's made no will? Big Daddy's never made out any will in his life, and so this campaign's afoot to impress him, forcibly as possible, with the fact that you drink and I've borne no children!

(*He continues to stare at her a moment, then mutters something sharp but not audible and hobbles rather rapidly out onto the long gallery in the fading, much faded, gold light.*)

MARGARET (*continuing her liturgical chant*): Y'know, I'm *fond* of Big Daddy, I am genuinely fond of that old man, I really *am*, you know....

BRICK (*faintly, vaguely*): Yes, I know you are....

MARGARET: I've always sort of admired him in spite of his coarseness, his four-letter words and so forth. Because Big Daddy *is* what he *is*, and he makes no bones about it. He hasn't turned gentleman farmer, he's still a Mississippi redneck, as much of a redneck as he must have been when he was just overseer here on the old Jack Straw and Peter Ochello place. But he got hold of it an' built it into th' biggest an' finest plantation in the Delta. — I've always *liked* Big Daddy....

(*She crosses to the proscenium.*)

Well, this is Big Daddy's last birthday. I'm sorry about it. But I'm facing the facts. It takes money to take care of a drinker and that's the office that I've been elected to lately.

BRICK: You don't have to take care of me.

MARGARET: Yes, I do. Two people in the same boat have got to take care of each other. At least you want money to buy more Echo Spring when this supply is exhausted, or will you be satisfied with a ten-cent beer?

Mae an' Gooper are plannin' to freeze us out of Big Daddy's estate because you drink and I'm childless. But we can defeat that plan. We're *going* to defeat that plan!

Brick, y'know, I've been so God damn disgustingly poor all my life! — That's the *truth*, Brick!

BRICK: I'm not sayin' it isn't.

MARGARET: Always had to suck up to people I couldn't stand because they had money and I was poor as Job's turkey. You don't know what that's like. Well, I'll tell you, it's like you would feel a thousand miles away from Echo Spring! — And had to get back to it on that broken ankle ... without a crutch!

That's how it feels to be as poor as Job's turkey and have to suck up to relatives that you hated because they had money and all you had was a bunch of hand-me-down clothes and a few old moldy three-percent government bonds. My daddy loved his liquor, he fell in love with his liquor the way you've fallen in love with Echo Spring! — And my poor Mama, having to maintain some semblance of social position, to keep appearances up, on an income of one hundred and fifty dollars a month on those old government bonds!

When I came out, the year that I made my debut, I had just two evening dresses! One Mother made me from a pattern in *Vogue*, the other a hand-me-down from a snotty rich cousin I hated!

— The dress that I married you in was my grandmother's weddin' gown. . . .

So that's why I'm like a cat on a hot tin roof!

(*Brick is still on the gallery. Someone below calls up to him in a warm Negro voice, "Hiya, Mistuh Brick, how yuh feelin'?" Brick raises his liquor glass as if that answered the question.*)

MARGARET: You can be young without money, but you can't be old without it. You've got to be old *with* money because to be old without it is just too awful, you've got to be one or the other, either *young* or *with money*, you can't be old and *without* it. — That's the *truth*, Brick. . . .

(*Brick whistles softly, vaguely.*)

Well, now I'm dressed, I'm all dressed, there's nothing else for me to do.

(*Forlornly, almost fearfully.*)

I'm dressed, all dressed, nothing else for me to do . . .

(*She moves about restlessly, aimlessly, and speaks, as if to herself.*)

What am I — ? Oh! — my bracelets. . . .

(*She starts working a collection of bracelets over her hands onto her wrists, about six on each, as she talks.*)

I've thought a whole lot about it and now I know when I made my mistake. Yes, I made my mistake when I told you the truth about that thing with Skipper. Never should have confessed it, a fatal error, tellin' you about that thing with Skipper.

BRICK: Maggie, shut up about Skipper. I mean it, Maggie; you got to shut up about Skipper.

MARGARET: You ought to understand that Skipper and I —

BRICK: You don't think I'm serious, Maggie? You're fooled by the fact that I am saying this quiet? Look, Maggie. What you're doing is a dangerous thing to do. You're — you're — you're — foolin' with something that — nobody ought to fool with.

MARGARET: This time I'm going to finish what I have to say to you. Skipper and I made love, if love you could call it, because it made both of us feel a little bit closer to you. You see, you son of a bitch, you asked too much of people, of me, of him, of all the unlucky poor damned sons of bitches that happen to love you, and there was a whole pack of them, yes, there was a pack of them besides me and Skipper, you asked too goddamn much of people that loved you, you — superior creature! — you godlike being! — And so we made love to each other to dream it was you, both of us! Yes, yes, yes! Truth, truth! What's so awful about it? I like it, I think the truth is — yeah! I shouldn't have told you. . . .

BRICK (*holding his head unnaturally still and uptilted a bit*): It was Skipper that told me about it. Not you, Maggie.

MARGARET: I told you!

BRICK: After he told me!

MARGARET: What does it matter who — ?

DIXIE: I got your mallet, I got your mallet.

TRIXIE: Give it to me, give it to me. IT's mine.

(*Brick turns suddenly out upon the gallery and calls:*)

BRICK: Little girl! Hey, little girl!

LITTLE GIRL (*at a distance*): What, Uncle Brick?

BRICK: Tell the folks to come up! — Bring everybody upstairs!

TRIXIE: It's mine, it's mine.

MARGARET: I can't stop myself! I'd go on telling you this in front of them all, if I had to!

BRICK: Little girl! Go on, go on, will you? Do what I told you, call them!

DIXIE: Okay.

MARGARET: Because it's got to be told and you, you! — you never let me!

(*She sobs, then controls herself, and continues almost calmly.*)

ABOVE: Kathleen Turner as Maggie in the 1990 Eugene O'Neill Theatre production of *Cat on a Hot Tin Roof*, directed by Howard Davies. BELOW: Brick (Daniel Hugh Kelly) and Maggie. (Photos by Michael Tighe.)

It was one of those beautiful, ideal things they tell about in the Greek legends, it couldn't be anything else, you being you, and that's what made it so sad, that's what made it so awful, because it was love that never could be carried through to anything satisfying or even talked about plainly.

BRICK: Maggie, you gotta stop this.

MARGARET: Brick, I tell you, you got to believe me, Brick, I *do* understand all about it! I — I think it was — *noble!* Can't you tell I'm sincere when I say I respect it? My only point, the only point that I'm making, is life has got to be allowed to continue even after the *dream* of life is — all — over. . . .

(*Brick is without his crutch. Leaning on furniture, he crosses to pick it up as she continues as if possessed by a will outside herself:*)

Why I remember when we double-dated at college, Gladys Fitzgerald and I and you and Skipper, it was more like a date between you and Skipper. Gladys and I were just sort of tagging along as if it was necessary to chaperone you! — to make a good public impression —

BRICK (*turns to face her, half lifting his crutch*): Maggie, you want me to hit you with this crutch? Don't you know I could kill you with this crutch?

MARGARET: Good Lord, man, d' you think I'd care if you did?

BRICK: One man has one great good true thing in his life. One great good thing which is true! — I had friendship with Skipper. — You are naming it dirty!

MARGARET: I'm not naming it dirty! I am naming it clean.

BRICK: Not love with you, Maggie, but friendship with Skipper was that one great true thing, and you are naming it dirty!

MARGARET: Then you haven't been listenin', not understood what I'm saying! I'm naming it so damn clean that it killed poor Skipper! — You two had something that had to be kept on ice, yes, incorruptible, yes! — and death was the only icebox where you could keep it. . . .

BRICK: I married you, Maggie. Why would I marry you, Maggie, if I was — ?

MARGARET: Brick, let me finish! — I know, believe me I know, that it was only Skipper that harbored even any *unconscious* desire for anything not perfectly pure between you two! — Now let me skip a little. You married me early that summer we graduated out of Ole Miss, and we were happy, weren't we, we were blissful, yes, hit heaven together ev'ry time that we loved! But that fall you an' Skipper turned down wonderful offers of jobs in order to keep on bein' football heroes — pro-football heroes. You organized the Dixie Stars that fall, so you could keep on bein' teammates forever! But somethin' was not right with it! — *Me included!* — between you. Skipper began hittin' the bottle . . . you got a spinal injury — couldn't play the Thanksgivin' game in Chicago, watched it on TV from a traction bed in Toledo. I joined Skipper. The Dixie Stars lost because poor Skipper was drunk. We drank together that night all night in the bar of the Blackstone and when cold day was comin' up over the Lake an' we were comin' out drunk to take a dizzy look at it, I said, "SKIPPER! STOP LOVIN' MY HUSBAND OR TELL HIM HE'S GOT TO LET YOU ADMIT IT TO HIM!" — one way or another!

HE SLAPPED ME HARD ON THE MOUTH! — then turned and ran without stopping once, I am sure, all the way back into his room at the Blackstone. . . .

— When I came to his room that night, with a little scratch like a shy little mouse at his door, he made that pitiful, ineffectual little attempt to prove that what I had said wasn't true. . . .

(*Brick strikes at her with crutch, a blow that shatters the gemlike lamp on the table.*)

— In this way, I destroyed him, by telling him truth that he and his world which he was born and raised in, yours and his world, had told him could not be told?

— From then on Skipper was nothing at all but a receptacle for liquor and drugs. . . .

— Who shot cock robin? I with my —

(*She throws back her head with tight shut eyes.*)

— merciful arrow!

(*Brick strikes at her; misses.*)

Missed me! — Sorry, — I'm not tryin' to whitewash my behavior, Christ, no! Brick, I'm not good. I don't know why people have to pretend to be good, nobody's good. The rich or the well-to-do can afford to respect moral patterns, conventional moral patterns, but I could never afford to, yeah, but — I'm honest! Give me credit for just that, will you *please?* — Born poor, raised poor, expect to die poor unless I manage to get us something out of what Big Daddy leaves when he dies of cancer! But Brick?! — *Skipper is dead! I'm alive!* Maggie the cat is —

(*Brick hops awkwardly forward and strikes at her again with his crutch.*)

— alive! I am alive, alive! I am . . .

(*He hurls the crutch at her, across the bed she took refuge behind, and pitches forward on the floor as she completes her speech.*)

— alive!

(*A little girl, Dixie, bursts into the room, wearing an Indian war bonnet and firing a cap pistol at Margaret and shouting: "Bang, bang, bang!"*)

(*Laughter downstairs floats through the open hall door. Margaret had crouched gasping to bed at child's entrance. She now rises and says with cool fury:*)

Little girl, your mother or someone should teach you — (*gasping*) — to knock at a door before you come into a room. Otherwise people might think that you — lack — good breeding. . . .

DIXIE: Yanh, yanh, yanh, what is Uncle Brick doin' on th' floor?

BRICK: I tried to kill your Aunt Maggie, but I failed — and I fell. Little girl, give me my crutch so I can get up off th' floor.

MARGARET: Yes, give your uncle his crutch, he's a cripple, honey, he broke his ankle last night jumping hurdles on the high school athletic field!

DIXIE: What were you jumping hurdles for, Uncle Brick?

BRICK: Because I used to jump them, and people like to do what they used to do, even after they've stopped being able to do it. . . .

MARGARET: That's right, that's your answer, now go away, little girl.

(*Dixie fires cap pistol at Margaret three times.*)

Stop, you stop that, monster! You little no-neck monster!

(*She seizes the cap pistol and hurls it through gallery doors.*)

DIXIE (*with a precocious instinct for the cruelest thing*): You're *jealous!* — You're just jealous because you can't have babies!

(*She sticks out her tongue at Margaret as she sashays past her with her stomach stuck out, to the gallery. Margaret slams the gallery doors and leans panting against them. There is a pause. Brick has replaced his spilt drink and sits, faraway, on the great four-poster bed.*)

MARGARET: You see? — they gloat over us being childless, even in front of their five little no-neck monsters!

(*Pauses. Voices approach on the stairs.*)

Brick? — I've been to a doctor in Memphis, a — a gynecologist. . . .

I've been completely examined, and there is no reason why we can't have a child whenever we want one. And this is my time by the calendar to conceive. Are you listening to me? Are you? Are you LISTENING TO ME!

BRICK: Yes. I hear you, Maggie.

(*His attention returns to her inflamed face.*)

— But how in hell on earth do you imagine — that you're going to have a child by a man that can't stand you?

MARGARET: That's a problem that I will have to work out.

(*She wheels about to face the hall door.*)

MAE (*offstage left*): Come on, Big Daddy. We're all goin' up to Brick's room.

(*From offstage left, voices: Reverend Tooker, Doctor Baugh, Mae.*)

MARGARET: *Here they come!*

(*The lights dim.*)

ACT 2

(*There is no lapse of time. Margaret and Brick are in the same positions they held at the end of act 1.*)

MARGARET (*at door*): *Here they come!*

(*Big Daddy appears first, a tall man with a fierce, anxious look, moving carefully not to betray his weakness even, or especially, to himself.*)

GOOPER: I read in the *Register* that you're getting a new memorial window.

(*Some of the people are approaching through the hall, others along the gallery: voices from both directions. Gooper and Reverend Tooker become visible outside gallery doors, and their voices come in clearly.*)

(*They pause outside as Gooper lights a cigar.*)

REVEREND TOOKER (*vivaciously*): Oh, but St. Paul's in Grenada has three memorial windows, and the latest one is a Tiffany stained-glass window that cost twenty-five hundred dollars, a picture of Christ the Good Shepherd with a Lamb in His arms.

MARGARET: Big Daddy.

BIG DADDY: Well, Brick.

BRICK: Hello Big Daddy. — Congratulations!

BIG DADDY: — Crap. . . .

GOOPER: Who give that window, Preach?

REVEREND TOOKER: Clyde Fletcher's widow. Also presented St. Paul's with a baptismal font.

GOOPER: Y'know what somebody ought t' give your church is a *coolin'* system, Preach.

MAE (*almost religiously*): — Let's see now, they've had their *tyyy*-phoid shots, and their tetanus shots, their diphtheria shots and their hepatitis shots and their polio shots, they got *those* shots every month from May through September, and — Gooper? Hey! Gooper! — What all have the kiddies been shot faw?

REVEREND TOOKER: Yes, siree, Bob! And y'know what Gus Hamma's family gave in his memory to the church at Two Rivers? A complete new stone parish-house with a basketball court in the basement and a —

BIG DADDY (*uttering a loud barking laugh which is far from truly mirthful*): Hey, Preach! What's all this talk about memorials, Preach? Y' think somebody's about t' kick off around here? 'S that it?

(*Startled by this interjection, Reverend Tooker decides to laugh at the question almost as loud as he can.*)

(*How he would answer the question we'll never know, as he's spared that embarrassment by the voice of Gooper's wife, Mae, rising high and clear as she appears with "Doc" Baugh, the family doctor, through the hall door.*)

MARGARET (*overlapping a bit*): Turn on the hi-fi, Brick! Let's have some music t' start off th' party with!

BRICK: You turn it on, Maggie.

(*The talk becomes so general that the room sounds like a great aviary of chattering birds. Only Brick remains unengaged, leaning upon the liquor cabinet with his faraway smile, an ice cube in a paper napkin with which he now and then rubs his forehead. He doesn't respond to Margaret's command. She bounds forward and stoops over the instrument panel of the console.*)

GOOPER: We gave 'em that thing for a third anniversary present, got three speakers in it.

(*The room is suddenly blasted by the climax of a Wagnerian opera or a Beethoven symphony.*)

BIG DADDY: *Turn that damn thing off!*

(*Almost instant silence, almost instantly broken by the shouting charge of Big Mama, entering through hall door like a charging rhino.*)

BIG MAMA: Wha's my Brick, wha's muh precious baby!!

BIG DADDY: *Sorry! Turn it back on!*

(*Everyone laughs very loud. Big Daddy is famous for his jokes at Big Mama's expense, and nobody laughs louder at these jokes than Big Mama herself, though*

sometimes they're pretty cruel and Big Mama has to pick up or fuss with something to cover the hurt that the loud laugh doesn't quite cover.)

(*On this occasion, a happy occasion because the dread in her heart has also been lifted by the false report on Big Daddy's condition, she giggles, grotesquely, coyly, in Big Daddy's direction and bears down upon Brick, all very quick and alive.*)

BIG MAMA: Here he is, here's my precious baby! What's that you've got in your hand? You put that liquor down, son, your hand was made fo' holdin' somethin' better than that!

GOOPER: Look at Brick put it down!

(*Brick has obeyed Big Mama by draining the glass and handing it to her. Again everyone laughs, some high, some low.*)

BIG MAMA: Oh, you bad boy, you, you're my bad little boy. Give Big Mama a kiss, you bad boy, you! — Look at him shy away, will you? Brick never liked bein' kissed or made a fuss over, I guess because he's always had too much of it!

Son, you turn that thing off!

(*Brick has switched on the TV set.*)

I can't stand TV, radio was bad enough but TV has gone it one better, I mean — (*plops wheezing in chair*) — one worse, ha ha! Now what'm I sittin' down here faw? I want t' sit next to my sweetheart on the sofa, hold hands with him and love him up a little!

(*Big Mama has on a black and white figured chiffon. The large irregular patterns, like the markings of some massive animal, the luster of her great diamonds and many pearls, the brilliants set in the silver frames of her glasses, her riotous voice, booming laugh, have dominated the room since she entered. Big Daddy has been regarding her with a steady grimace of chronic annoyance.*)

BIG MAMA (*still louder*): Preacher, Preacher, hey, Preach! Give me you' hand an' help me up from this chair!

REVEREND TOOKER: None of your tricks, Big Mama!

BIG MAMA: What tricks? You give me you' hand so I can get up an' —

(*Reverend Tooker extends her his hand. She grabs it and pulls him into her lap with a shrill laugh that spans an octave in two notes.*)

Ever seen a preacher in a fat lady's lap? Hey, hey, folks! Ever seen a preacher in a fat lady's lap?

(*Big Mama is notorious throughout the Delta for this sort of inelegant horseplay. Margaret looks on with*

*indulgent humor, sipping Dubonnet "on the rocks"
and watching Brick, but Mae and Gooper exchange
signs of humorless anxiety over these antics, the sort
of behavior which Mae thinks may account for their
failure to quite get in with the smartest young married
set in Memphis, despite all. One of the Negroes,
Lacey or Sookey, peeks in, cackling. They are waiting
for a sign to bring in the cake and champagne. But
Big Daddy's not amused. He doesn't understand why,
in spite of the infinite mental relief he's received from
the doctor's report, he still has these same old fox
teeth in his guts. "This spastic condition is something
else," he says to himself, but aloud he roars at Big
Mama:)*

BIG DADDY: *BIG MAMA, WILL YOU QUIT
    HORSIN'?* — You're too old an' too fat fo' that sort
    of crazy kid stuff an' besides a woman with your
    blood pressure   she had two hundred last spring! —
    is riskin' a stroke when you mess around like that....

(Mae blows on a pitch pipe.)

BIG MAMA: *Here comes Big Daddy's birthday!*

*(Negroes in white jackets enter with an enormous
birthday cake ablaze with candles and carrying buckets of champagne with satin ribbons about the bottle
necks.)*
    *(Mae and Gooper strike up song, and everybody,
including the Negroes and Children, joins in. Only
Brick remains aloof.)*

EVERYONE: Happy birthday to you.
    Happy birthday to you.
    Happy birthday, Big Daddy —

(Some sing: "Dear, Big Daddy!")

    Happy birthday to you.

(Some sing: "How old are you?")
    *(Mae has come down center and is organizing her
children like a chorus. She gives them a barely audible:
"One, two, three!" and they are off in the new tune.)*

CHILDREN: Skinamarinka — dinka — dink
    Skinamarinka — do
    We love you.
    Skinamarinka — dinka — dink
    Skinamarinka — do.

(All together, they turn to Big Daddy.)

    Big Daddy, you!

(They turn back front, like a musical comedy chorus.)

    We love you in the morning;
    We love you in the night.
    We love you when we're with you,

    And we love you out of sight.
    Skinamarinka — dinka — dink
    Skinamarinka — do.

(Mae turns to Big Mama.)

    Big Mama, too!

(Big Mama bursts into tears. The Negroes leave.)

BIG DADDY: Now Ida, what the hell is the matter with
    you?
MAE: She's just so happy.
BIG MAMA: I'm just so happy, Big Daddy, I have to
    cry or something.

(Sudden and loud in the hush:)

    Brick, do you know the wonderful news that Doc
    Baugh got from the clinic about Big Daddy? Big
    Daddy's one hundred percent!
MARGARET: Isn't that wonderful?
BIG MAMA: He's just one hundred percent. Passed the
    examination with flying colors. Now that we
    know there's nothing wrong with Big Daddy but a
    spastic colon, I can tell you something. I was wor-
    ried sick half out of my mind, for fear that Big
    Daddy might have a thing like —

*(Margaret cuts through this speech, jumping up and
exclaiming shrilly:)*

MARGARET: Brick, honey, aren't you going to give Big
    Daddy his birthday present?

*(Passing by him, she snatches his liquor glass from
him.)*
    (She picks up a fancily wrapped package.)

    Here it is, Big Daddy, this is from Brick!
BIG MAMA: This is the biggest birthday Big Daddy's
    ever had, a hundred presents and bushels of
    telegrams from —
MAE *(at same time)*: What is it, Brick?
GOOPER: I bet 500 to 50 that Brick don't *know* what
    it is.
BIG MAMA: The fun of presents is not knowing what
    they are till you open the package. Open your
    present, Big Daddy.
BIG DADDY: Open it you'self. I want to ask Brick
    somethin! Come here, Brick.
MARGARET. Big Daddy's callin' you, Brick.

(She is opening the package.)

BRICK: Tell Big Daddy I'm crippled.
BIG DADDY: I see you're crippled. I want to know
    how you got crippled.
MARGARET *(making diversionary tactics)*: Oh, look,
    oh, look, why, it's a cashmere robe!

(*She holds the robe up for all to see.*)

MAE: You sound surprised, Maggie.

MARGARET: I never saw one before.

MAE: That's funny. — Hah!

MARGARET (*turning on her fiercely, with a brilliant smile*): Why is it funny? All my family ever had was family — and luxuries such as cashmere robes still surprise me!

BIG DADDY (*ominously*): Quiet!

MAE (*heedless in her fury*): I don't see how you could be so surprised when you bought it yourself at Loewenstein's in Memphis last Saturday. You know how I know?

BIG DADDY: I said, Quiet!

MAE: — I know because the salesgirl that sold it to you waited on me and said, Oh, Mrs. Pollitt, your sister-in-law just bought a cashmere robe for your husband's father!

MARGARET: Sister Woman! Your talents are wasted as a housewife and mother, you really ought to be with the FBI or —

BIG DADDY: QUIET!

(*Reverend Tooker's reflexes are slower than the others'. He finishes a sentence after the bellow.*)

REVEREND TOOKER (*to Doc Baugh*): — the Stork and the Reaper are running neck and neck!

(*He starts to laugh gaily when he notices the silence and Big Daddy's glare. His laugh dies falsely.*)

BIG DADDY: Preacher, I hope I'm not butting in on more talk about memorial stained-glass windows, am I, Preacher?

(*Reverend Tooker laughs feebly, then coughs dryly in the embarrassed silence.*)

Preacher?

BIG MAMA: Now, Big Daddy, don't you pick on Preacher!

BIG DADDY (*raising his voice*): You ever hear that expression all hawk and no spit? You bring that expression to mind with that little dry cough of yours, all hawk an' no spit. . . .

(*The pause is broken only by a short startled laugh from Margaret, the only one there who is conscious of and amused by the grotesque.*)

MAE (*raising her arms and jangling her bracelets*): I wonder if the mosquitoes are active tonight?

BIG DADDY: What's that, Little Mama? Did you make some remark?

MAE: Yes, I said I wondered if the mosquitoes would eat us alive if we went out on the gallery for a while.

BIG DADDY: Well, if they do, I'll have your bones pulverized for fertilizer!

BIG MAMA (*quickly*): Last week we had an airplane spraying the place and I think it done some good, at least I haven't had a —

BIG DADDY (*cutting her speech*): Brick, they tell me, if what they tell me is true, that you done some jumping last night on the high school athletic field?

BIG MAMA: Brick, Big Daddy is talking to you, son.

BRICK (*smiling vaguely over his drink*): What was that, Big Daddy?

BIG DADDY: They said you done some jumping on the high school track field last night.

BRICK: That's what they told me, too.

BIG DADDY: Was it jumping or humping that you were doing out there? What were you doing out there at three A.M., layin' a woman on that cinder track?

BIG MAMA: Big Daddy, you are off the sick-list, now, and I'm not going to excuse you for talkin' so —

BIG DADDY: Quiet!

BIG MAMA: — *nasty* in front of Preacher and —

BIG DADDY: QUIET! — I ast you, Brick, if you was cuttin' you'self a piece o' poon-tang last night on that cinder track? I thought maybe you were chasin' poon-tang on that track an' tripped over something in the heat of the chase — 'sthat it?

(*Gooper laughs, loud and false, others nervously following suit. Big Mama stamps her foot, and purses her lips, crossing to Mae and whispering something to her as Brick meets his father's hard, intent, grinning stare with a slow, vague smile that he offers all situations from behind the screen of his liquor.*)

BRICK: No, sir, I don't think so. . . .

MAE (*at the same time, sweetly*): Reverend Tooker, let's you and I take a stroll on the widow's walk.

(*She and the preacher go out on the gallery as Big Daddy says:*)

BIG DADDY: Then what the hell were you doing out there at three o'clock in the morning?

BRICK: Jumping the hurdles, Big Daddy, runnin' and jumpin' the hurdles, but those high hurdles have gotten too high for me, now.

BIG DADDY: Cause you was drunk?

BRICK (*his vague smile fading a little*): Sober I wouldn't have tried to jump the *low* ones. . . .

BIG MAMA (*quickly*): Big Daddy, blow out the candles on your birthday cake!

MARGARET (*at the same time*): I want to propose a toast to Big Daddy Pollitt on his sixty-fifth birthday, the biggest cotton planter in —

BIG DADDY (*bellowing with fury and disgust*): *I told you to stop it, now stop it, quit this —* !

BIG MAMA (*coming in front of Big Daddy with the cake*): Big Daddy, I will not allow you to talk that way, not even on your birthday, I —

BIG DADDY: I'll talk like I want to on my birthday, Ida, or any other goddamn day of the year and anybody here that don't like it knows what they can do!

BIG MAMA: You don't mean that!

BIG DADDY What makes you think I don't mean it?

(*Meanwhile various discreet signals have been exchanged and Gooper has also gone out on the gallery.*)

BIG MAMA: I just know you don't mean it.

BIG DADDY: You don't know a goddamn thing and you never did!

BIG MAMA: Big Daddy, you don't mean that.

BIG DADDY: Oh, yes, I do, oh, yes, I do, I mean it! I put up with a whole lot of crap around here because I thought I was dying. And you thought I was dying and you started taking over, well, you can stop taking over now, Ida, because I'm not gonna die, you can just stop now this business of taking over because you're not taking over because I'm not dying, I went through the laboratory and the goddamn exploratory operation and there's nothing wrong with me but a spastic colon. And I'm not dying of cancer which you thought I was dying of. Ain't that so? Didn't you think that I was dying of cancer, Ida?

(*Almost everybody is out on the gallery but the two old people glaring at each other across the blazing cake.*)
(*Big Mama's chest heaves and she presses a fat fist to her mouth.*)
(*Big Daddy continues, hoarsely:*)

Ain't that so, Ida? Didn't you have an idea I was dying of cancer and now you could take control of this place and everything on it? I got that impression, I seemed to get that impression. Your loud voice everywhere, your fat old body butting in here and there!

BIG MAMA: Hush! The Preacher!

BIG DADDY: Fuck the goddamn preacher!

(*Big Mama gasps loudly and sits down on the sofa which is almost too small for her.*)

Did you hear what I said? I said fuck the goddamn preacher!

(*Somebody closes the gallery doors from outside just as there is a burst of fireworks and excited cries from the children.*)

BIG MAMA: I never seen you act like this before and I can't think what's got in you!

BIG DADDY: I went through all that laboratory and operation and all just so I would know if you or me was boss here! Well, now it turns out that I am and you ain't — and that's my birthday present — and my cake and champagne! — because for three years now you been gradually taking over. Bossing. Talking. Sashaying your fat old body around the place I made! I made this place! I was overseer on it! I was the overseer on the old Straw and Ochello plantation. I quit school at ten! I quit school at ten years old and went to work like a nigger in the fields. And I rose to be overseer of the Straw and Ochello plantation. And old Straw died and I was Ochello's partner and the place got bigger and bigger and bigger and bigger and bigger! I did all that myself with no goddamn help from you, and now you think you're just about to take over. Well, I am just about to tell you that you are not just about to take over, you are not just about to take over a God damn thing. Is that clear to you, Ida? Is that very plain to you, now? Is that understood completely? I been through the laboratory from A to Z. I've had the goddamn exploratory operation, and nothing is wrong with me but a spastic colon — made spastic, I guess, by *disgust!* By all the goddamn lies and liars that I have had to put up with and all the goddamn hypocrisy that I lived with all these forty years that we been livin' together!

Hey! Ida!! Blow out the candles on the birthday cake! Purse up your lips and draw a deep breath and blow out the goddamn candles on the cake!

BIG MAMA: Oh, Big Daddy, oh, oh, oh, Big Daddy!

BIG DADDY: What's the matter with you?

BIG MAMA: *In all these years you never believed that I loved you??*

BIG DADDY: Huh?

BIG MAMA: *And I did, I did so much, I did love you!* — I even loved your hate and your hardness, Big Daddy!

(*She sobs and rushes awkwardly out onto the gallery.*)

BIG DADDY (*to himself*): Wouldn't it be funny if that was true. . . .

(*A pause is followed by a burst of light in the sky from the fireworks.*)

BRICK! HEY, BRICK!

(*He stands over his blazing birthday cake.*)
(*After some moments, Brick hobbles in on his crutch, holding his glass.*)
(*Margaret follows him with a bright, anxious smile.*)

I didn't call you, Maggie. I called Brick.

MARGARET: I'm just delivering him to you.

(*She kisses Brick on the mouth which he immediately wipes with the back of his hand. She flies girlishly back out. Brick and his father are alone.*)

BIG DADDY: Why did you do that?

BRICK: Do what, Big Daddy?

BIG DADDY: Wipe her kiss off your mouth like she'd spit on you.

BRICK: I don't know. I wasn't conscious of it.

BIG DADDY: That woman of yours has a better shape on her than Gooper's but somehow or other they got the same look about them.

BRICK: What sort of look is that, Big Daddy?

BIG DADDY: I don't know how to describe it but it's the same look.

BRICK: They don't look peaceful, do they?

BIG DADDY: No, they sure in hell don't.

BRICK: They look nervous as cats?

BIG DADDY: That's right, they look nervous as cats.

BRICK: Nervous as a couple of cats on a hot tin roof?

BIG DADDY: That's right, boy, they look like a couple of cats on a hot tin roof. It's funny that you and Gooper being so different would pick out the same type of woman.

BRICK: Both of us married into society, Big Daddy.

BIG DADDY: Crap . . . I wonder what gives them both that look?

BRICK: Well. They're sittin' in the middle of a big piece of land, Big Daddy, twenty-eight thousand acres is a pretty big piece of land and so they're squaring off on it, each determined to knock off a bigger piece of it than the other whenever you let it go.

BIG DADDY: I got a surprise for those women. I'm not gonna let it go for a long time yet if that's what they're waiting for.

BRICK: That's right, Big Daddy. You just sit tight and let them scratch each other's eyes out. . . .

BIG DADDY: You bet your life I'm going to sit tight on it and let those sons of bitches scratch their eyes out, ha ha ha. . . .

But Gooper's wife's a good breeder, you got to admit she's fertile. Hell, at supper tonight she had them all at the table and they had to put a couple of extra leafs in the table to make room for them, she's got five head of them, now, and another one's comin'.

BRICK: Yep, number six is comin' . . .

BIG DADDY: Six hell, she'll probably drop a litter next time. Brick, you know, I swear to God, I don't know the way it happens.

BRICK: The way what happens, Big Daddy?

BIG DADDY: You git you a piece of land, by hook or crook, an' things start growin' on it, things accumulate on it, and the first thing you know it's completely out of hand, completely out of hand!

BRICK: Well, they say nature hates a vacuum, Big Daddy.

BIG DADDY: That's what they say, but sometimes I think that a vacuum is a hell of a lot better than some of the stuff that nature replaces it with. Is someone out there by that door?

GOOPER: Hey Mae.

BRICK: Yep.

BIG DADDY: Who?

(*He has lowered his voice.*)

BRICK: Someone int'rested in what we say to each other.

BIG DADDY: Gooper? — *GOOPER!*

(*After a discreet pause, Mae appears in the gallery door.*)

MAE: Did you call Gooper, Big Daddy?

BIG DADDY: Aw, it was you.

MAE: Do you want Gooper, Big Daddy?

BIG DADDY: No, and I don't want you. I want some privacy here, while I'm having a confidential talk with my son Brick. Now it's too hot in here to close them doors, but if I have to close those fuckin' doors in order to have a private talk with my son Brick, just let me know and I'll close 'em. Because I hate eavesdroppers, I don't like any kind of sneakin' an' spyin'.

MAE: Why, Big Daddy —

BIG DADDY: You stood on the wrong side of the moon, it threw your shadow!

MAE: I was just —

BIG DADDY: You was just nothing but *spyin'* an you *know* it!

MAE (*begins to sniff and sob*): Oh, Big Daddy, you're so unkind for some reason to those that really love you!

BIG DADDY: Shut up, shut up, shut up! I'm going to move you and Gooper out of that room next to this! It's none of your goddamn business what goes on in here at night between Brick an' Maggie. You listen at night like a couple of rutten peekhole spies and go and give a report on what you hear to Big Mama an' she comes to me and says they say such and such and so and so about what they heard goin' on between Brick an' Maggie, and Jesus, it makes me sick. I'm goin' to move you an' Gooper out of that room, I can't stand sneakin' an' spyin', it makes me puke. . . .

(*Mae throws back her head and rolls her eyes heavenward and extends her arms as if invoking God's pity for this unjust martyrdom; then she presses a handkerchief to her nose and flies from the room with a loud swish of skirts.*)

BRICK (*now at the liquor cabinet*): They listen, do they?

BIG DADDY: Yeah. They listen and give reports to Big

Mama on what goes on in here between you and Maggie. They say that —

(*He stops as if embarrassed.*)

— You won't sleep with her, that you sleep on the sofa. Is that true or not true? If you don't like Maggie, get rid of Maggie! — What are you doin' there now?

BRICK: Fresh'nin' up my drink.

BIG DADDY: Son, you know you got a real liquor problem?

BRICK: Yes, sir, yes, I know.

BIG DADDY: Is that why you quit sports-announcing, because of this liquor problem?

BRICK: Yes, sir, yes, sir, I guess so.

(*He smiles vaguely and amiably at his father across his replenished drink.*)

BIG DADDY: Son, don't guess about it, it's too important.

BRICK (*vaguely*): Yes, sir.

BIG DADDY: And listen to me, don't look at the damn chandelier. . . .

(*Pause. Big Daddy's voice is husky.*)

— Somethin' else we picked up at th' big fire-sale in Europe.

(*Another pause.*)

Life is important. There's nothing else to hold onto. A man that drinks is throwing his life away. Don't do it, hold onto your life. There's nothing else to hold onto. . . .

Sit down over here so we don't have to raise our voices, the walls have ears in this place.

BRICK (*hobbling over to sit on the sofa beside him*): All right, Big Daddy.

BIG DADDY: Quit! — how'd that come about? Some disappointment?

BRICK: I don't know. Do you?

BIG DADDY: I'm askin' you, God damn it! How in hell would I know if you don't?

BRICK: I just got out there and found that I had a mouth full of cotton. I was always two or three beats behind what was goin' on on the field and so I —

BIG DADDY: Quit!

BRICK (*amiably*): Yes, quit.

BIG DADDY: Son?

BRICK: Huh?

BIG DADDY (*inhales loudly and deeply from his cigar; then bends suddenly a little forward, exhaling loudly and raising a hand to his forehead*): Whew! — ha ha! — I took in too much smoke, it made me a little lightheaded. . . .

(*The mantel clock chimes.*)

Why is it so damn hard for people to talk?

BRICK: Yeah. . . .

(*The clock goes on sweetly chiming till it has completed the stroke of ten.*)

— Nice peaceful-soundin' clock, I like to hear it all night. . . .

(*He slides low and comfortable on the sofa; Big Daddy sits up straight and rigid with some unspoken anxiety. All his gestures are tense and jerky as he talks. He wheezes and pants and sniffs through his nervous speech, glancing quickly, shyly, from time to time, at his son.*)

BIG DADDY: We got that clock the summer we wint to Europe, me an' Big Mama on that damn Cook's Tour, never had such an awful time in my life, I'm tellin' you, son, those gooks over there, they gouge your eyeballs out in their grand hotels. And Big Mama bought more stuff than you could haul in a couple of boxcars, that's no crap. Everywhere she wint on this whirlwind tour, she bought, bought, bought. Why, half that stuff she bought is still crated up in the cellar, under water last spring!

(*He laughs.*)

That Europe is nothin' on earth but a great big auction, that's all it is, that bunch of old worn-out places, it's just a big fire-sale, the whole fuckin' thing, an' Big Mama wint wild in it, why, you couldn't hold that woman with a mule's harness! Bought, bought, bought! — lucky I'm a rich man, yes siree, Bob, an' half that stuff is mildewin' in th' basement. It's lucky I'm a rich man, it sure is lucky, well, I'm a rich man, Brick, yep, I'm a mighty rich man.

(*His eyes light up for a moment.*)

Y'know how much I'm worth? Guess, Brick! Guess how much I'm worth!

(*Brick smiles vaguely over his drink.*)

Close on ten million in cash an' blue-chip stocks, outside, mind you, of twenty-eight thousand acres of the richest land this side of the valley Nile!

But a man can't buy his life with it, he can't buy back his life with it when his life has been spent, that's one thing not offered in the Europe fire-sale or in the American markets or any markets on earth, a man can't buy his life with it, he can't buy back his life when his life is finished. . . .

That's a sobering thought, a very sobering thought, and that's a thought that I was turning over in my head, over and over and over — until today. . . .

I'm wiser and sadder, Brick, for this experience which I just gone through. They's one thing else that I remember in Europe.

BRICK: What is that, Big Daddy?

BIG DADDY: The hills around Barcelona in the country of Spain and the children running over those bare hills in their bare skins beggin' like starvin' dogs with howls and screeches, and how fat the priests are on the streets of Barcelona, so many of them and so fat and so pleasant, ha ha! — Y'know I could feed that country? I got money enough to feed that goddamn country, but the human animal is a selfish beast and I don't reckon the money I passed out there to those howling children in the hills around Barcelona would more than upholster the chairs in this room, I mean pay to put a new cover on this chair!

Hell, I threw them money like you'd scatter feed corn for chickens, I threw money at them just to get rid of them long enough to climb back into th' car and — drive away. . . .

And then in Morocco, them Arabs, why, I remember one day in Marrakech, that old walled Arab city, I set on a broken-down wall to have a cigar, it was fearful hot there and this Arab woman stood in the road and looked at me till I was embarrassed, she stood stock still in the dusty hot road and looked at me till I was embarrassed. But listen to this. She had a naked child with her, a little naked girl with her, barely able to toddle, and after a while she set this child on the ground and give her a push and whispered something to her.

This child come toward me, barely able t' walk, come toddling up to me and —

Jesus, it makes you sick t' remember a thing like this! It stuck out its hand and tried to unbutton my trousers!

That child was not yet five! Can you believe me? Or do you think that I am making this up? I wint back to the hotel and said to Big Mama, Git packed! We're clearing out of this country. . . .

BRICK: Big Daddy, you're on a talkin' jag tonight.

BIG DADDY (ignoring this remark): Yes, sir, that's how it is, the human animal is a beast that dies but the fact that he's dying don't give him pity for others, no, sir, it —
— Did you say something?

BRICK: Yes.

BIG DADDY: What?

BRICK: Hand me over that crutch so I can get up.

BIG DADDY: Where you goin?

BRICK: I'm takin' a little short trip to Echo Spring.

BIG DADDY: To where?

BRICK: Liquor cabinet. . . .

BIG DADDY: Yes, sir, boy —

(He hands Brick the crutch.)

— the human animal is a beast that dies and if he's got money he buys and buys and buys and I think the reason he buys everything he can buy is that in the back of his mind he has the crazy hope that one of his purchases will be life everlasting! — Which it never can be. . . . The human animal is a beast that —

BRICK (at the liquor cabinet): Big Daddy, you sure are shootin' th' breeze here tonight.

(There is a pause and voices are heard outside.)

BIG DADDY: I been quiet here lately, spoke not a word, just sat and stared into space. I had something heavy weighing on my mind but tonight that load was took off me. That's why I'm talking. — The sky looks diff'rent to me. . . .

BRICK: You know what I like to hear most?

BIG DADDY: What?

BRICK: Solid quiet. Perfect unbroken quiet.

BIG DADDY: Why?

BRICK: Because it's more peaceful.

BIG DADDY: Man, you'll hear a lot of that in the grave.

(He chuckles agreeably.)

BRICK: Are you through talkin' to me?

BIG DADDY: Why are you so anxious to shut me up?

BRICK: Well, sir, ever so often you say to me, Brick, I want to have a talk with you, but when we talk, it never materializes. Nothing is said. You sit in a chair and gas about this and that and I look like I listen. I try to look like I listen, but I don't listen, not much. Communication is — awful hard between people an' — somehow between you and me, it just don't — happen.

BIG DADDY: Have you ever been scared? I mean have you ever felt downright terror of something?

(He gets up.)

Just one moment.

(He looks off as if he were going to tell an important secret.)

Brick?

BRICK: What?

BIG DADDY: Son, I thought I had it!

BRICK: Had what? Had what, Big Daddy?

BIG DADDY: Cancer!

BRICK: Oh . . .

BIG DADDY: I thought the old man made out of bones had laid his cold and heavy hand on my shoulder!

BRICK: Well, Big Daddy, you kept a tight mouth about it.

BIG DADDY: A pig squeals. A man keeps a tight mouth about it, in spite of a man not having a pig's advantage.

BRICK: What advantage is that?

BIG DADDY: Ignorance — of mortality — is a comfort. A man don't have that comfort, he's the only living thing that conceives of death, that knows what it is. The others go without knowing which is the way that anything living should go, go without knowing, without any knowledge of it, and yet a pig squeals, but a man sometimes, he can keep a tight mouth about it. Sometimes he —

(*There is a deep, smoldering ferocity in the old man.*)

— can keep a tight mouth about it. I wonder if —

BRICK: What, Big Daddy?

BIG DADDY: A whiskey highball would injure this spastic condition?

BRICK: No, sir, it might do it good.

BIG DADDY (*grins suddenly, wolfishly*): Jesus, I can't tell you! The sky is open! Christ, it's open again! It's open, boy, it's open!

(*Brick looks down at his drink.*)

BRICK: You feel better, Big Daddy?

BIG DADDY: Better? Hell! I can breathe! — All of my life I been like a doubled up fist. . . .

(*He pours a drink.*)

— Poundin', smashin', drivin'! — now I'm going to loosen these doubled-up hands and touch things *easy* with them. . . .

(*He spreads his hands as if caressing the air.*)

You know what I'm contemplating?

BRICK (*vaguely*): No, sir. What are you contemplating?

BIG DADDY: Ha ha! — *Pleasure!* — pleasure with *women!*

(*Brick's smile fades a little but lingers.*)

— Yes, boy. I'll tell you something that you might not guess. I still have desire for women and this is my sixty fifth birthday.

BRICK: I think that's mighty remarkable, Big Daddy.

BIG DADDY: Remarkable?

BRICK: *Admirable*, Big Daddy.

BIG DADDY: You're damn right it is, remarkable and admirable both. I realize now that I never had me enough. I let many chances slip by because of scruples about it, scruples, convention — crap. . . . All that stuff is bull, bull, bull! — It took the shadow of death to make me see it. Now that shadow's lifted, I'm going to cut loose and have, what is it they call it, have me a — ball!

BRICK: A ball, huh?

BIG DADDY: That's right, a ball, a ball! Hell! — I slept with Big Mama till, let's see, five years ago, till I was sixty and she was fifty-eight, and never even liked her, never did!

(*The phone has been ringing down the hall. Big Mama enters, exclaiming:*)

BIG MAMA: Don't you men hear that phone ring? I heard it way out on the gall'ry.

BIG DADDY: There's five rooms off this front gall'ry that you could go through. Why do you go through this one?

(*Big Mama makes a playful face as she bustles out the hall door.*)

Hunh! — Why, when Big Mama goes out of a room, I can't remember what that woman looks like —

BIG MAMA: Hello.

BIG DADDY: — But when Big Mama comes back into the room, boy, then I see what she looks like, and I wish I didn't!

(*Bends over laughing at this joke till it hurts his guts and he straightens with a grimace. The laugh subsides to a chuckle as he puts the liquor glass a little distrustfully down the table.*)

BIG MAMA: Hello, Miss Sally.

(*Brick has risen and hobbled to the gallery doors.*)

BIG DADDY: Hey! Where you goin'?

BRICK: Out for a breather.

BIG DADDY: Not yet you ain't. Stay here till this talk is finished, young fellow.

BRICK: I thought it was finished, Big Daddy.

BIG DADDY: It ain't even begun.

BRICK: My mistake. Excuse me. I just wanted to feel that river breeze.

BIG DADDY: Set back down in that chair.

(*Big Mama's voice rises, carrying down the hall.*)

BIG MAMA: Miss Sally, you're a case! You're a caution, Miss Sally.

BIG DADDY: Jesus, she's talking to my old maid sister again.

BIG MAMA: Why didn't you give me a chance to explain it to you?

BIG DADDY: Brick, this stuff burns me.

BIG MAMA: Well, good-bye, now, Miss Sally. You come down real soon. Big Daddy's dying to see you.

BIG DADDY: Crap!

BIG MAMA: Yaiss, good-bye, Miss Sally. . . .

(*She hangs up and bellows with mirth. Big Daddy groans and covers his ears as she approaches.*)
    (*Bursting in:*)

Brick (Ben Gazzara) and Big Daddy (Burl Ives) in the original 1955 production of *Cat on a Hot Tin Roof,* directed by Elia Kazan.

Big Daddy, that was Miss Sally callin' from Memphis again! You know what she done, Big Daddy? She called her doctor in Memphis to git him to tell her what that spastic thing is! Ha-*HAAAA!* — And called back to tell me how relieved she was that — Hey! Let me in!

(*Big Daddy has been holding the door half closed against her.*)

BIG DADDY: Naw I ain't. I told you not to come and go through this room. You just back out and go through those five other rooms.

BIG MAMA: Big Daddy? Big Daddy? Oh, Big Daddy! — You didn't mean those things you said to me, did you?

(*He shuts door firmly against her but she still calls.*)

Sweetheart? Sweetheart? Big Daddy? You didn't mean those awful things you said to me? — I know

you didn't. I know you didn't mean those things in your heart. . . .

(*The childlike voice fades with a sob and her heavy footsteps retreat down the hall. Brick has risen once more on his crutches and starts for the gallery again.*)

BIG DADDY: All I ask of that woman is that she leave me alone. But she can't admit to herself that she makes me sick. That comes of having slept with her too many years. Should of quit much sooner but that old woman she never got enough of it — and I was good in bed . . . I never should of wasted so much of it on her. . . . They say you got just so many and each one is numbered. Well, I got a few left in me, a few, and I'm going to pick me a good one to spend 'em on! I'm going to pick me a choice one, I don't care how much she costs, I'll smother her in — minks! Ha ha! I'll strip her naked and smother her in minks and choke her with diamonds! Ha ha! I'll strip her naked and choke her with diamonds and smother her with minks and hump her from hell to breakfast. *Ha aha ha ha ha!*

MAE (*gaily at door*): Who's that laughin' in there?

GOOPER: Is Big Daddy laughin' in there?

BIG DADDY: Crap! — them two — *drips.* . . .

(*He goes over and touches Brick's shoulder.*)

Yes, son. Brick, boy. — I'm — *happy!* I'm happy, son, I'm happy!

(*He chokes a little and bites his under lip, pressing his head quickly, shyly against his son's head and then, coughing with embarrassment, goes uncertainly back to the table where he set down the glass. He drinks and makes a grimace as it burns his guts. Brick sighs and rises with effort.*)

What makes you so restless? Have you got ants in your britches?

BRICK: Yes, sir . . .

BIG DADDY: Why?

BRICK: — Something — hasn't — happened. . . .

BIG DADDY: Yeah? What is that!

BRICK (*sadly*): — the click. . . .

BIG DADDY: Did you say click?

BRICK: Yes, click.

BIG DADDY: What click?

BRICK: A click that I get in my head that makes me peaceful.

BIG DADDY: I sure in hell don't know what you're talking about, but it disturbs me.

BRICK: It's just a mechanical thing.

BIG DADDY: What is a mechanical thing?

BRICK: This click that I get in my head that makes me peaceful. I got to drink till I get it. It's just a mechanical thing, something like a — like a — like a —

BIG DADDY: Like a —

BRICK: Switch clicking off in my head, turning the hot light off and the cool night on and —

(*He looks up, smiling sadly.*)

— all of a sudden there's — peace!

BIG DADDY (*whistles long and soft with astonishment; he goes back to Brick and clasps his son's two shoulders*): Jesus! I didn't know it had gotten that bad with you. Why, boy, you're — *alcoholic!*

BRICK: That's the truth, Big Daddy. I'm alcoholic.

BIG DADDY: This shows how I — let things go!

BRICK: I have to hear that little click in my head that makes me peaceful. Usually I hear it sooner than this, sometimes as early as — noon, but —

— Today it's — dilatory. . . .

I just haven't got the right level of alcohol in my bloodstream yet!

(*This last statement is made with energy as he freshens his drink.*)

BIG DADDY: Uh — huh. Expecting death made me blind. I didn't have no idea that a son of mine was turning into a drunkard under my nose.

BRICK (*gently*): Well, now you do, Big Daddy, the news has penetrated.

BIG DADDY: UH-huh, yes, now I do, the news has — penetrated. . . .

BRICK: And so if you'll excuse me —

BIG DADDY: No, I won't excuse you.

BRICK: — I'd better sit by myself till I hear that click in my head, it's just a mechanical thing but it don't happen except when I'm alone or talking to no one. . . .

BIG DADDY: You got a long, long time to sit still, boy, and talk to no one, but now you're talkin' to me. At least I'm talking to you. And you set there and listen until I tell you the conversation is over!

BRICK: But this talk is like all the others we've ever had together in our lives! It's nowhere, nowhere! — it's — it's *painful*, Big Daddy. . . .

BIG DADDY: All right, then let it be painful, but don't you move from that chair! — I'm going to remove that crutch. . . .

(*He seizes the crutch and tosses it across room.*)

BRICK: I can hop on one foot, and if I fall, I can crawl!

BIG DADDY: If you ain't careful you're gonna crawl off this plantation and then, by Jesus, you'll have to hustle your drinks along Skid Row!

BRICK: That'll come, Big Daddy.

BIG DADDY: Naw, it won't. You're my son and I'm going to straighten you out; now that *I'm* straightened out, I'm going to straighten out you!

BRICK: Yeah?

BIG DADDY: Today the report come in from Ochsner Clinic. Y'know what they told me?

(*His face glows with triumph.*)

The only thing that they could detect with all the instruments of science in that great hospital is a little spastic condition of the colon! And nerves torn to pieces by all that worry about it.

(*A little girl bursts into room with a sparkler clutched in each fist, hops and shrieks like a monkey gone mad and rushes back out again as Big Daddy strikes at her.*)
(*Silence. The two men stare at each other. A woman laughs gaily outside.*)

I want you to know I breathed a sigh of relief almost as powerful as the Vicksburg tornado!

(*There is laughter outside, running footsteps, the soft, plushy sound and light of exploding rockets.*)

(*Brick stares at him soberly for a long moment; then makes a sort of startled sound in his nostrils and springs up on one foot and hops across the room to grab his crutch, swinging on the furniture for support. He gets the crutch and flees as if in horror for the gallery. His father seizes him by the sleeve of his white silk pajamas.*)

Stay here, you son of a bitch! — till I say go!

BRICK: I can't.

BIG DADDY: You sure in hell will, God damn it.

BRICK: No, I can't. We talk, you talk, in — circles! We get no where, no where! It's always the same, you say you want to talk to me and don't have a fuckin' thing to say to me!

BIG DADDY: Nothin' to say when I'm tellin' you I'm going to live when I thought I was dying?!

BRICK: Oh — *that!* — Is that what you have to say to me?

BIG DADDY: Why, you son of a bitch! Ain't that, ain't that — *important?!*

BRICK: Well, you said that, that's said, and now I —

BIG DADDY: Now you set back down.

BRICK: You're all balled up, you —

BIG DADDY: I ain't balled up!

BRICK: You are, you're all balled up!

BIG DADDY: Don't tell me what I am, you drunken whelp! I'm going to tear this coat sleeve off if you don't set down!

BRICK: Big Daddy —

BIG DADDY: Do what I tell you! I'm the boss here, now! I want you to know I'm back in the driver's seat now!

(*Big Mama rushes in, clutching her great heaving bosom.*)

BIG MAMA: Big Daddy!

BIG DADDY: What in hell do you want in here, Big Mama?

BIG MAMA: Oh, Big Daddy! Why are you shouting like that? I just cain't *stainnnnnnnd* — it. . . .

BIG DADDY (*raising the back of his hand above his head*): GIT! — outa here.

(*She rushes back out, sobbing.*)

BRICK (*softly, sadly*): Christ. . . .

BIG DADDY (*fiercely*): Yeah! Christ! — is right. . . .

(*Brick breaks loose and hobbles toward the gallery.*)
    (*Big Daddy jerks his crutch from under Brick so he steps with the injured ankle. He utters a hissing cry of anguish, clutches a chair and pulls it over on top of him on the floor.*)

Son of a — tub of — hog fat. . . .

BRICK: Big Daddy! Give me my crutch.

(*Big Daddy throws the crutch out of reach.*)

Give me that crutch, Big Daddy.

BIG DADDY: Why do you drink?

BRICK: Don't know, give me my crutch!

BIG DADDY: You better think why you drink or give up drinking!

BRICK: Will you please give me my crutch so I can get up off this floor?

BIG DADDY: First you answer my question. Why do you drink? Why are you throwing your life away, boy, like somethin' disgusting you picked up on the street?

BRICK (*getting onto his knees*): Big Daddy, I'm in pain, I stepped on that foot.

BIG DADDY: Good! I'm glad you're not too numb with the liquor in you to feel some pain!

BRICK: You — spilled my — drink . . .

BIG DADDY: I'll make a bargain with you. You tell me why you drink and I'll hand you one. I'll pour you the liquor myself and hand it to you.

BRICK: Why do I drink?

BIG DADDY: Yea! Why?

BRICK: Give me a drink and I'll tell you.

BIG DADDY: Tell me first!

BRICK: I'll tell you in one word.

BIG DADDY: What word?

BRICK: DISGUST!

(*The clock chimes softly, sweetly. Big Daddy gives it a short, outraged glance.*)

Now how about that drink?

BIG DADDY: What are you disgusted with? You got to tell me that, first. Otherwise being disgusted don't make no sense!

BRICK: Give me my crutch.

BIG DADDY: You heard me, you got to tell me what I asked you first.

BRICK: I told you, I said to kill my disgust!

BIG DADDY: DISGUST WITH WHAT!

BRICK: You strike a hard bargain.

BIG DADDY: What are you disgusted with? — an' I'll pass you the liquor.

BRICK: I can hop on one foot, and if I fall, I can crawl.

BIG DADDY: You want liquor that bad?

BRICK (*dragging himself up, clinging to bedstead*): Yeah, I want it that bad.

BIG DADDY: If I give you a drink, will you tell me what it is you're disgusted with, Brick?

BRICK: Yes, sir, I will try to.

(*The old man pours him a drink and solemnly passes it to him.*)
    (*There is silence as Brick drinks.*)

Have you ever heard the word "mendacity"?

BIG DADDY: Sure. Mendacity is one of them five dollar words that cheap politicians throw back and forth at each other.

BRICK: You know what it means?

BIG DADDY: Don't it mean lying and liars?

BRICK: Yes, sir, lying and liars.

BIG DADDY: Has someone been lying to you?

CHILDREN (*chanting in chorus offstage*):
We want Big Dad-dee!
We want Big Dad-dee!

(*Gooper appears in the gallery door.*)

GOOPER: Big Daddy, the kiddies are shouting for you out there.

BIG DADDY (*fiercely*): Keep out, Gooper!

GOOPER: 'Scuse *me!*

(*Big Daddy slams the doors after Gooper.*)

BIG DADDY: Who's been lying to you, has Margaret been lying to you, has your wife been lying to you about something, Brick?

BRICK: Not her. That wouldn't matter.

BIG DADDY: Then who's been lying to you, and what about?

BRICK: No one single person and no one lie. . . .

BIG DADDY: Then what, what then, for Christ's sake?

BRICK: — The whole, the whole — thing. . . .

BIG DADDY: Why are you rubbing your head? You got a headache?

BRICK: No, I'm tryin' to —

BIG DADDY: — Concentrate, but you can't because your brain's all soaked with liquor, is that the trouble? Wet brain!

(*He snatches the glass from Brick's hand.*)

What do you know about this mendacity thing? Hell! I could write a book on it! Don't you know that? I could write a book on it and still not cover the subject? Well, I could, I could write a goddamn book on it and still not cover the subject anywhere near enough!! — Think of all the lies I got to put up with! — Pretenses! Ain't that mendacity? Having to pretend stuff you don't think or feel or have any idea of? Having for instance to act like I care for Big Mama! — I haven't been able to stand the sight, sound, or smell of that woman for forty years now! — even when I *laid* her! — regular as a piston. . . .

Pretend to love that son of a bitch of a Gooper and his wife Mae and those five same screechers out there like parrots in a jungle? Jesus! Can't stand to look at 'em!

Church! — it bores the bejesus out of me but I go! — I go an' sit there and listen to the fool preacher!

Clubs! — Elks! Masons! Rotary! — *crap!*

(*A spasm of pain makes him clutch his belly. He sinks into a chair and his voice is softer and hoarser.*)

You I *do* like for some reason, did always have some kind of real feeling for — affection — respect — yes, always. . . .

You and being a success as a planter is all I ever had any devotion to in my whole life! — and that's the truth. . . .

I don't know why, but it is!

I've lived with mendacity! — Why can't *you* live with it? Hell, you *got* to live with it, there's nothing *else* to *live* with except mendacity, is there?

BRICK: Yes, sir. Yes, sir there is something else that you can live with!

BIG DADDY: What?

BRICK (*lifting his glass*): This! — Liquor. . . .

BIG DADDY: That's not living, that's dodging away from life.

BRICK: I want to dodge away from it.

BIG DADDY: Then why don't you kill yourself, man?

BRICK: I like to drink. . . .

BIG DADDY: Oh, God, I can't talk to you. . . .

BRICK: I'm sorry, Big Daddy.

BIG DADDY: Not as sorry as I am. I'll tell you something. A little while back when I thought my number was up —

(*This speech should have torrential pace and fury.*)

— before I found out it was just this — spastic — colon. I thought about you. Should I or should I not, if the jig was up, give you this place when I go — since I hate Gooper an' Mae an' know that they hate me, and since all five same monkeys are little Maes an' Goopers. — And I thought, No! — Then I thought, Yes! — I couldn't make up my mind. I hate Gooper and his five same monkeys and that bitch Mae! Why should I turn over twenty-eight thousand acres of the richest land this side of the valley Nile to not my kind? — But why in hell, on the other hand, Brick — should I subsidize a goddamn fool on the bottle? — Liked or not liked, well, maybe even — *loved!* — Why should I do that? — Subsidize worthless behavior? Rot? Corruption?

BRICK (*smiling*): I understand.

BIG DADDY: Well, if you do, you're smarter than I am, God damn it, because I don't understand. And this I will tell you frankly. I didn't make up my mind at all on that question and still to this day I ain't made out no will! — Well, now I don't *have* to. The pressure is gone. I can just wait and see if you pull yourself together or if you don't.

BRICK: That's right, Big Daddy.

BIG DADDY: You sound like you thought I was kidding.

BRICK (*rising*): No, sir, I know you're not kidding.

BIG DADDY: But you don't care — ?

BRICK (*hobbling toward the gallery door*): No, sir, I don't care. . . .

(*He stands in the gallery doorway as the night sky turns pink and green and gold with successive flashes of light.*)

BIG DADDY: *WAIT!* — Brick. . . .

(*His voice drops. Suddenly there is something shy, almost tender, in his restraining gesture.*)

Don't let's — leave it like this, like them other talks we've had, we've always — talked around things, we've — just talked around things for some fuckin' reason, I don't know what, it's always like something was left not spoken, something avoided because neither of us was honest enough with the — other. . . .

BRICK: I never lied to you, Big Daddy.

BIG DADDY: Did I ever to *you?*

BRICK: No, sir. . . .

BIG DADDY: Then there is at least two people that never lied to each other.

BRICK: But we've never *talked* to each other.

BIG DADDY: We can *now.*

BRICK: Big Daddy, there don't seem to be anything much to say.

BIG DADDY: You say that you drink to kill your disgust with lying.

BRICK: You said to give you a reason.

BIG DADDY: Is liquor the only thing that'll kill this disgust?

BRICK: Now. Yes.

BIG DADDY: But not once, huh?

BRICK: Not when I was still young an' believing. A drinking man's someone who wants to forget he isn't still young an' believing.

BIG DADDY: Believing what?

BRICK: Believing. . . .

BIG DADDY: Believing *what?*

BRICK (*stubbornly evasive*): Believing. . . .

BIG DADDY: I don't know what the hell you mean by believing and I don't think you know what you mean by believing, but if you still got sports in your blood, go back to sports announcing and —

BRICK: Sit in a glass box watching games I can't play? Describing what I can't do while players do it? Sweating out their disgust and confusion in contests I'm not fit for? Drinkin' a coke, half bourbon, so I can stand it? That's no goddamn good any more, no help — time just outran me, Big Daddy — got there first . . .

BIG DADDY: I think you're passing the buck.

BRICK: You know many drinkin' men?

BIG DADDY (*with a slight, charming smile*): I have known a fair number of that species.

BRICK: Could any of them tell you why he drank?

BIG DADDY: Yep, you're passin' the buck to things like time and disgust with "mendacity" and — crap! — if you got to use that kind of language about a thing, it's ninety-proof bull, and I'm not buying any.

BRICK: I had to give you a reason to get a drink!

BIG DADDY: You started drinkin' when your friend Skipper died.

(*Silence for five beats. Then Brick makes a startled movement, reaching for his crutch.*)

BRICK: What are you suggesting?

BIG DADDY: I'm suggesting nothing.

(*The shuffle and clop of Brick's rapid hobble away from his father's steady, grave attention.*)

— But Gooper an' Mae suggested that there was something not right exactly in your —

BRICK (*stopping short downstage as if backed to a wall*): "Not right"?

BIG DADDY: Not, well, exactly *normal* in your friendship with —

BRICK: They suggested that, too? I thought that was Maggie's suggestion.

(*Brick's detachment is at last broken through. His heart is accelerated; his forehead sweat-beaded; his breath becomes more rapid and his voice hoarse. The thing they're discussing, timidly and painfully on the side of Big Daddy, fiercely, violently on Brick's side, is the inadmissible thing that Skipper died to disavow between them. The fact that if it existed it had to be disavowed to "keep face" in the world they lived in, may be at the heart of the "mendacity" that Brick drinks to kill his disgust with. It may be the root of his collapse. Or maybe it is only a single manifestation of it, not even the most important. The bird that I hope to catch in the net of this play is not the solution of one man's psychological problem. I'm trying to catch the true quality of experience in a group of people, that cloudy, flickering, evanescent — fiercely charged! — interplay of live human beings in the thundercloud of a common crisis. Some mystery should be left in the revelation of character in a play, just as a great deal of mystery is always left in the revelation of character in life, even in one's own character to himself. This does not absolve the playwright of his duty to observe and probe as clearly and deeply as he legitimately can: But it should steer him away from "pat" conclusions, facile definitions which make a play just a play, not a snare for the truth of human experience.*)

(*The following scene should be played with great concentration, with most of the power leashed but palpable in what is left unspoken.*)

Who else's suggestion is it, is it *yours?* How many others thought that Skipper and I were —

BIG DADDY (*gently*): Now, hold on, hold on a minute, son. — I knocked around in my time.

BRICK: What's that got to do with —

BIG DADDY: I said "Hold on!" — I bummed, I bummed this country till I was —

BRICK: Whose suggestion, who else's suggestion is it?

BIG DADDY: Slept in hobo jungles and railroad Y's and flophouses in all cities before I —

BRICK: Oh, *you* think so, too, you call me your son and a queer. Oh! Maybe that's why you put Maggie and me in this room that was Jack Straw's and Peter Ochello's, in which that pair of old sisters slept in a double bed where both of 'em died!

BIG DADDY: *Now just don't go throwing rocks at —*

(*Suddenly Reverend Tooker appears in the gallery doors, his head slightly, playfully, fatuously cocked, with a practiced clergyman's smile, sincere as a birdcall blown on a hunter's whistle, the living embodiment of the pious, conventional lie.*)

(*Big Daddy gasps a little at this perfectly timed, but incongruous, apparition.*)

— What're you lookin' for, preacher?

REVEREND TOOKER: The gentleman's lavatory, ha ha! — heh, heh . . .

BIG DADDY (*with strained courtesy*): — Go back out and walk down to the other end of the gallery, Reverend Tooker, and use the bathroom connected with my bedroom, and if you can't find it, ask them where it is!

REVEREND TOOKER: Ah, thanks.

(*He goes out with a deprecatory chuckle.*)

BIG DADDY: It's hard to talk in this place . . .

BRICK: Son of a — !

BIG DADDY (*leaving a lot unspoken*): — I seen all things and understood a lot of them, till 1910. Christ, the year that — I had worn my shoes through, hocked my — I hopped off a yellow dog freight car half a mile down the road, slept in a wagon of cotton outside the gin — Jack Straw an' Peter Ochello took me in. Hired me to manage this place which grew into this one. — When Jack Straw died — why, old Peter Ochello quit eatin' like a dog does when its master's dead, and died, too!

BRICK: Christ!

BIG DADDY: I'm just saying I understand such —

BRICK (*violently*): Skipper is dead. I have not quit eating!

BIG DADDY: No, but you started drinking.

(*Brick wheels on his crutch and hurls his glass across the room shouting.*)

BRICK: YOU THINK SO, TOO?

(*Footsteps run on the gallery. There are women's calls.*)

(*Big Daddy goes toward the door.*)

(*Brick is transformed, as if a quiet mountain blew suddenly up in volcanic flame.*)

BRICK: You think so, too? You think so, too? You think me an' Skipper did, did, did! — *sodomy!* — together?

BIG DADDY: Hold — !

BRICK: That what you —

BIG DADDY: — *ON* — a minute!

BRICK: You think we did dirty things between us, Skipper an' —

BIG DADDY: Why are you shouting like that? Why are you —

BRICK: — Me, is that what you think of Skipper, is that —

BIG DADDY: — so excited? I don't think nothing. I don't know nothing. I'm simply telling you what —

BRICK: You think that Skipper and me were a pair of dirty old men?

BIG DADDY: Now that's —

BRICK: Straw? Ochello? A couple of —

BIG DADDY: Now just —

BRICK: — fucking sissies? Queers? Is that what you —

BIG DADDY: Shhh.

BRICK: — think?

(*He loses his balance and pitches to his knees without noticing the pain. He grabs the bed and drags himself up.*)

BIG DADDY: Jesus! — Whew. . . . Grab my hand!

BRICK: Naw, I don't want your hand. . . .

BIG DADDY: Well, I want yours. Git up!

(*He draws him up, keeps an arm about him with concern and affection.*)

You broken out in a sweat! You're panting like you'd run a race with —

BRICK (*freeing himself from his father's hold*): Big Daddy, you shock me, Big Daddy, you, you — *shock* me! Talkin' so —

(*He turns away from his father.*)

— casually! — about a — thing like that . . .

— Don't you know how people *feel* about things like that? How, how *disgusted* they are by things like that? Why, at Ole Miss when it was discovered a pledge to our fraternity, Skipper's and mine, did a, *attempted* to do a, unnatural thing with —

We not only dropped him like a hot rock! — We told him to git off the campus, and he did, he got! — All the way to —

(*He halts, breathless.*)

BIG DADDY: — Where?

BRICK: — North Africa, last I heard!

BIG DADDY: Well, I have come back from further away than that, I have just now returned from the other side of the moon, death's country, son, and I'm not easy to shock by anything here.

(*He comes downstage and faces out.*)

Always, anyhow, lived with too much space around me to be infected by ideas of other people. One thing you can grow on a big place more important than cotton! — is *tolerance!* — I grown it.

(*He returns toward Brick.*)

BRICK: Why can't exceptional friendship, *real, real, deep, deep friendship!* between two men be respected as something clean and decent without being thought of as —

BIG DADDY: It can, it is, for God's sake.

BRICK: — *Fairies.* . . .

(*In his utterance of this word, we gauge the wide and profound reach of the conventional mores he got from the world that crowned him with early laurel.*)

BIG DADDY: I told Mae an' Gooper —

BRICK: Frig Mae and Gooper, frig all dirty lies and liars! — Skipper and me had a clean, true thing between us! — had a clean friendship, practically all our lives, till Maggie got the idea you're talking about. Normal? No! — It was too rare to be normal, any true thing between two people is too rare to be normal. Oh, once in a while he put his hand on my shoulder or I'd put mine on his, oh, maybe even, when we were touring the country in pro-football an' shared hotel rooms we'd reach across the space between the two beds and shake hands to say goodnight, yeah, one or two times we —

BIG DADDY: Brick, nobody thinks that that's not normal!

BRICK: Well, they're mistaken, it was! It was a pure an' true thing an' that's not normal.

MAE (*offstage*): Big Daddy, they're startin' the fireworks.

(*They both stare straight at each other for a long moment. The tension breaks and both turn away as if tired.*)

BIG DADDY: Yeah, it's — hard t' — talk. . . .

BRICK: All right, then, let's — let it go. . . .

BIG DADDY: Why did Skipper crack up? Why have you?

(*Brick looks back at his father again. He has already decided, without knowing that he has made this decision, that he is going to tell his father that he is dying of cancer. Only this could even the score between them: one inadmissible thing in return for another.*)

BRICK (*ominously*): All right. You're asking for it, Big Daddy. We're finally going to have that real true talk you wanted. It's too late to stop it, now, we got to carry it through and cover every subject.

(*He hobbles back to the liquor cabinet.*)

Uh-huh.

(*He opens the ice bucket and picks up the silver tongs with slow admiration of their frosty brightness.*)

Maggie declares that Skipper and I went into pro-football after we left Ole Miss because we were scared to grow up . . .

(*He moves downstage with the shuffle and clop of a cripple on a crutch. As Margaret did when her speech became "recitative," he looks out into the house, commanding its attention by his direct, concentrated gaze — a broken, "tragically elegant" figure telling simply as much as he knows of "the Truth":*)

— Wanted to — keep on tossing — those long, long! — high, high! — passes that — couldn't be intercepted except by time, the aerial attack that made us famous! And so we did, we did, we kept it up for one season, that aerial attack, we held it high! — Yeah, but —

— that summer, Maggie, she laid the law down to me, said, Now or never, and so I married Maggie. . . .

BIG DADDY: How was Maggie in bed?

BRICK (*wryly*): Great! the greatest!

(*Big Daddy nods as if he thought so.*)

She went on the road that fall with the Dixie Stars. Oh, she made a great show of being the world's best sport. She wore a — wore a — tall bearskin cap! A shako, they call it, a dyed moleskin coat, a moleskin coat dyed red! — Cut up crazy! Rented hotel ballrooms for victory celebrations, wouldn't cancel them when it — turned out — defeat. . . .
      MAGGIE THE CAT! Ha ha!

(*Big Daddy nods.*)

— But Skipper, he had some fever which came back on him which doctors couldn't explain and I got that injury — turned out to be just a shadow on the X-ray plate — and a touch of bursitis. . . .
      I lay in a hospital bed, watched our games on TV, saw Maggie on the bench next to Skipper when he was hauled out of a game for stumbles, tumbles! — Burned me up the way she hung on his arm! — Y'know, I think that Maggie had always felt sort of left out because she and me never got any closer together than two people just get in bed, which is not much closer than two cats on a — fence humping. . . .

So! She took this time to work on poor dumb
Skipper. He was a less than average student at Ole
Miss, you know that, don't you?! — Poured in his
mind the dirty, false idea that what we were, him
and me, was a frustrated case of that ole pair of
sisters that lived in this room, Jack Straw and Peter Ochello! — He, poor Skipper, went to bed with
Maggie to prove it wasn't true, and when it didn't
work out, he thought it *was* true! — Skipper broke
in two like a rotten stick — nobody ever turned so
fast to a lush — or died of it so quick. . . .

— Now are you satisfied?

(*Big Daddy has listened to this story, dividing the
grain from the chaff. Now he looks at his son.*)

BIG DADDY: Are *you* satisfied?
BRICK: With what?
BIG DADDY: That half-ass story!
BRICK: What's half ass about it?
BIG DADDY: Something's left out of that story. What
did you leave out?

(*The phone has started ringing in the hall.*)

GOOPER (*offstage*): Hello.

(*As if it reminded him of something, Brick glances
suddenly toward the sound and says:*)

BRICK: Yes! — I left out a long-distance call which I
had from Skipper —
GOOPER: Speaking, go ahead.
BRICK: — In which he made a drunken confession to
me and on which I hung up!
GOOPER: No.
BRICK: — Last time we spoke to each other in our
lives . . .
GOOPER: No, sir.
BIG DADDY: You musta said something to him before
you hung up.
BRICK: What could I say to him?
BIG DADDY: Anything. Something.
BRICK: Nothing.
BIG DADDY: Just hung up?
BRICK: Just hung up.
BIG DADDY: Uh-huh. Anyhow now! — we have
tracked down the lie with which you're disgusted
and which you are drinking to kill your disgust
with, Brick. You been passing the buck. This dis-
gust with mendacity is disgust with yourself.

You! — dug the grave of your friend and
kicked him in it! — before you'd face truth with
him!
BRICK: *His* truth, not *mine!*
BIG DADDY: His truth, okay! But you wouldn't face it
with him!
BRICK: Who *can* face truth? Can *you?*

BIG DADDY: Now don't start passin' the rotten buck
again, boy!
BRICK: How about these birthday congratulations,
these many, many happy returns of the day, when
ev'rybody knows there won't be any except you!

(*Gooper, who has answered the hall phone, lets out a
high, shrill laugh; the voice becomes audible saying:
"No, no, you got it all wrong! Upside down! Are you
crazy?"*)
(*Brick suddenly catches his breath as he realizes
that he has made a shocking disclosure. He hobbles a
few paces, then freezes, and without looking at his father's shocked face says:*)

Let's, let's — go out, now, and — watch the fireworks. Come on, Big Daddy.

(*Big Daddy moves suddenly forward and grabs hold
of the boy's crutch like it was a weapon for which
they were fighting for possession.*)

BIG DADDY: Oh, no, no! No one's going out! What
did you start to say?
BRICK: I don't remember.
BIG DADDY: "Many happy returns when they know
there won't be any"?
BRICK: Aw, hell, Big Daddy, forget it. Come on out on
the gallery and look at the fireworks they're shooting off for your birthday. . . .
BIG DADDY: First you finish that remark you were
makin' before you cut off. "Many happy returns
when they know there won't be any"? — Ain't that
what you just said?
BRICK: Look, now. I can get around without that
crutch if I have to but it would be a lot easier on
the furniture an' glassware if I didn't have to go
swinging along like Tarzan of th' —
BIG DADDY: FINISH! WHAT YOU WAS SAYIN'!

(*An eerie green glow shows in sky behind him.*)

BRICK (*sucking the ice in his glass, speech becoming
thick*): Leave th' place to Gooper and Mae an'
their five little same little monkeys. All I want is —
BIG DADDY: "LEAVE TH' PLACE," did you say?
BRICK (*vaguely*): All twenty-eight thousand acres of
the richest land this side of the valley Nile.
BIG DADDY: Who said I was "leaving the place" to
Gooper or anybody? This is my sixty-fifth birthday! I got fifteen years or twenty years left in me!
I'll outlive *you!* I'll bury you an' have to pay for
your coffin!
BRICK: Sure. Many happy returns. Now let's go watch
the fireworks, come on, let's —
BIG DADDY: Lying, have they been lying? About the
report from th' — clinic? Did they, did they — find
something? — *Cancer.* Maybe?

BRICK: Mendacity is a system that we live in. Liquor is one way out an' death's the other. . . .

(*He takes the crutch from Big Daddy's loose grip and swings out on the gallery leaving the doors open.*)
(*A song, "Pick a Bale of Cotton," is heard.*)

MAE (*appearing in door*): Oh, Big Daddy, the field hands are singin' fo' you!

BRICK: I'm sorry, Big Daddy. My head don't work any more and it's hard for me to understand how anybody could care if he lived or died or was dying or cared about anything but whether or not there was liquor left in the bottle and so I said what I said without thinking. In some ways I'm no better than the others, in some ways worse because I'm less alive. Maybe it's being alive that makes them lie, and being almost *not* alive makes me sort of accidentally truthful — I don't know but — anyway — we've been friends . . .

   — And being friends is telling each other the truth. . . .

(*There is a pause.*)

   You told *me!* I told *you!*

BIG DADDY (*slowly and passionately*): CHRIST — DAMN —

GOOPER (*offstage*): Let her go!

(*Fireworks offstage right.*)

BIG DADDY: — ALL — LYING SONS OF — LYING BITCHES!

(*He straightens at last and crosses to the inside door. At the door he turns and looks back as if he had some desperate question he couldn't put into words. Then he nods reflectively and says in a hoarse voice:*)

   Yes, all liars, all liars, all lying dying liars!

(*This is said slowly, slowly, with a fierce revulsion. He goes on out.*)

   — Lying! Dying! Liars!

(*Brick remains motionless as the lights dim out and the curtain falls.*)

ACT 3

(*There is no lapse of time. Big Daddy is seen leaving as at the end of act 2.*)

BIG DADDY: ALL LYIN' — DYIN'! — LIARS! LIARS! — LIARS!

(*Margaret enters.*)

MARGARET: Brick, what in the name of God was goin' on in this room?

(*Dixie and Trixie enter through the doors and circle around Margaret shouting. Mae enters from the lower gallery window.*)

MAE: Dixie, Trixie, you quit that!

(*Gooper enters through the doors.*)

   Gooper, will y' please get these kiddies to bed right now!

GOOPER: Mae, you seen Big Mama?

MAE: Not yet.

(*Gooper and kids exit through the doors. Reverend Tooker enters through the windows.*)

REVEREND TOOKER: Those kiddies are so full of vitality. I think I'll have to be starting back to town.

MAE: Not yet, Preacher. You know we regard you as a member of this family, one of our closest an' dearest, so you just got t' be with us when Doc Baugh gives Big Mama th' actual truth about th' report from the clinic.

MARGARET: Where do you think you're going?

BRICK: Out for some air.

MARGARET: Why'd Big Daddy shout "Liars"?

MAE: Has Big Daddy gone to bed, Brick?

GOOPER (*entering*): Now where is that old lady?

REVEREND TOOKER: I'll look for her.

(*He exits to the gallery.*)

MAE: Cain'tcha find her, Gooper?

GOOPER: She's avoidin' this talk.

MAE: I think she senses somethin'.

MARGARET (*going out on the gallery to Brick*): Brick, they're goin' to tell Big Mama the truth about Big Daddy and she's goin' to need you.

DOCTOR BAUGH: This is going to be painful.

MAE: Painful things caint always be avoided.

REVEREND TOOKER: I see Big Mama.

GOOPER: Hey, Big Mama, come here.

MAE: Hush, Gooper, don't holler.

BIG MAMA (*entering*): Too much smell of burnt fireworks makes me feel a little bit sick at my stomach. — Where is Big Daddy?

MAE: That's what I want to know, where has Big Daddy gone?

BIG MAMA: He must have turned in, I reckon he went to baid . . .

GOOPER: Well, then, now we can talk.

BIG MAMA: What *is* this talk, *what* talk?

(*Margaret appears on the gallery, talking to Doctor Baugh.*)

MARGARET (*musically*): My family freed their slaves

ten years before abolition. My great-great-grandfather gave his slaves their freedom five years before the War between the States started!

MAE: Oh, for God's sake! Maggie's climbed back up in her family tree!

MARGARET (*sweetly*): What, Mae?

(*The pace must be very quick: great Southern animation.*)

BIG MAMA (*addressing them all*): I think Big Daddy was just worn out. He loves his family, he loves to have them around him, but it's a strain on his nerves. He wasn't himself tonight, Big Daddy wasn't himself, I could tell he was all worked up.

REVEREND TOOKER: I think he's remarkable.

BIG MAMA: Yaisss! Just remarkable. Did you all notice the food he ate at that table? Did you all notice the supper he put away? Why he ate like a hawss!

GOOPER: I hope he doesn't regret it.

BIG MAMA: What? Why that man — ate a huge piece of cawn bread with molasses on it! Helped himself twice to hoppin' John.

MARGARET: Big Daddy loves hoppin' John. — We had a real country dinner.

BIG MAMA (*overlapping Margaret*): Yaiss, he simply adores it! an' candied yams? Son? That man put away enough food at that table to stuff a *field* hand!

GOOPER (*with grim relish*): I hope he don't have to pay for it later on . . .

BIG MAMA (*fiercely*): What's *that,* Gooper?

MAE: Gooper says he hopes Big Daddy doesn't suffer tonight.

BIG MAMA: Oh, shoot, Gooper says, Gooper says! Why should Big Daddy suffer for satisfying a normal appetite? There's nothin' wrong with that man but nerves, he's sound as a dollar! And now he knows he is an' that's why he ate such a supper. He had a big load off his mind, knowin' he wasn't doomed t' — what he thought he was doomed to . . .

MARGARET (*sadly and sweetly*): Bless his old sweet soul . . .

BIG MAMA (*vaguely*): Yais, bless his heart, where's Brick?

MAE: Outside.

GOOPER: — Drinkin' . . .

BIG MAMA: I know he's drinkin'. Cain't I see he's drinkin' without you continually tellin' me that boy's drinkin'?

MARGARET: Good for you, Big Mama!

(*She applauds.*)

BIG MAMA: Other people *drink* and *have* drunk an' will *drink,* as long as they make that stuff an' put it in bottles.

MARGARET: That's the truth. I never trusted a man that didn't drink.

BIG MAMA: *Brick? Brick!*

MARGARET: He's still on the gall'ry. I'll go bring him in so we can talk.

BIG MAMA (*worriedly*): I don't know what this mysterious family conference is about.

(*Awkward silence. Big Mama looks from face to face, then belches slightly and mutters, "Excuse me . . ." She opens an ornamental fan suspended about her throat. A black lace fan to go with her black lace gown, and fans her wilting corsage, sniffing nervously and looking from face to face in the uncomfortable silence as Margaret calls "Brick?" and Brick sings to the moon on the gallery.*)

MARGARET: Brick, they're gonna tell Big Mama the truth an' she's gonna need you.

BIG MAMA: I don't know what's wrong here, you all have such long faces! Open that door on the hall and let some air circulate through here, will you please, Gooper?

MAE: I think we'd better leave that door closed, Big Mama, till after the talk.

MARGARET: Brick!

BIG MAMA: Reveren' Tooker, will *you* please open that door?

REVEREND TOOKER: I sure will, Big Mama.

MAE: I just didn't think we ought t' take any chance of Big Daddy hearin' a word of this discussion.

BIG MAMA: *I swan!* Nothing's going to be said in Big Daddy's house that he caint hear if he want to!

GOOPER: Well, Big Mama, it's —

(*Mae gives him a quick, hard poke to shut him up. He glares at her fiercely as she circles before him like a burlesque ballerina, raising her skinny bare arms over her head, jangling her bracelets, exclaiming:*)

MAE: *A breeze! A breeze!*

REVEREND TOOKER: I think this house is the coolest house in the Delta. — Did you all know that Halsey Banks's widow put air-conditioning units in the church and rectory at Friar's Point in memory of Halsey?

(*General conversation has resumed; everybody is chatting so that the stage sounds like a bird cage.*)

GOOPER: Too bad nobody cools your church off for you. I bet you sweat in that pulpit these hot Sundays, Reverend Tooker.

REVEREND TOOKER: Yes, my vestments are drenched. Last Sunday the gold in my chasuble faded into the purple.

GOOPER: Reveren', you musta been preachin' hell's fire last Sunday.

MAE (*at the same time to Doctor Baugh*): You reckon those vitamin B12 injections are what they're cracked up t' be, Doc Baugh?

DOCTOR BAUGH: Well, if you want to be stuck with something I guess they're as good to be stuck with as anything else.

BIG MAMA (*at the gallery door*): Maggie, Maggie, aren't you comin' with Brick?

MAE (*suddenly and loudly, creating a silence*): I have a strange feeling, I have a peculiar feeling!

BIG MAMA (*turning from the gallery*): What feeling?

MAE: That Brick said somethin' he shouldn't of said t' Big Daddy.

BIG MAMA: Now what on earth could Brick of said t' Big Daddy that he shouldn't say?

GOOPER: Big Mama, there's somethin' —

MAE: NOW, WAIT!

(*She rushes up to Big Mama and gives her a quick hug and kiss. Big Mama pushes her impatiently off.*)

DOCTOR BAUGH: In my day they had what they call the Keeley cure for heavy drinkers.

BIG MAMA: Shoot!

DOCTOR BAUGH: But now I understand they just take some kind of tablets.

GOOPER: They call them "Annie Bust" tablets.

BIG MAMA: *Brick* don't need to take *nothin'*.

(*Brick and Margaret appear in gallery doors, Big Mama unaware of his presence behind her.*)

That boy is just broken up over Skipper's death. You know how poor Skipper died. They gave him a big, big dose of that sodium amytal stuff at his home and then they called the ambulance and give him another big, big dose of it at the hospital and that and all of the alcohol in his system fo' months an' months just proved too much for his heart . . . I'm scared of needles! I'm more scared of a needle than the knife . . . I think more people have been needled out of this world than —

(*She stops short and wheels about.*)

Oh — here's Brick! My precious baby —

(*She turns upon Brick with short, fat arms extended, at the same time uttering a loud, short sob, which is both comic and touching. Brick smiles and bows slightly, making a burlesque gesture of gallantry for Margaret to pass before him into the room. Then he hobbles on his crutch directly to the liquor cabinet and there is absolute silence, with everybody looking at Brick as everybody has always looked at Brick when he spoke or moved or appeared. One by one he drops ice cubes in his glass, then suddenly, but not quickly, looks back over his shoulder with a wry, charming smile, and says:*)

BRICK: I'm sorry! Anyone else?

BIG MAMA (*sadly*): No, son. I *wish* you wouldn't!

BRICK: I wish I didn't have to, Big Mama, but I'm still waiting for that click in my head which makes it all smooth out!

BIG MAMA: Ow, Brick, you — BREAK MY HEART!

MARGARET (*at same time*): Brick, go sit with Big Mama!

BIG MAMA: I just cain't staiiiiii-nnnnnnnd-it . . .

(*She sobs.*)

MAE: Now that we're all assembled —

GOOPER: We kin talk . . .

BIG MAMA: Breaks my heart . . .

MARGARET: Sit with Big Mama, Brick, and hold her hand.

(*Big Mama sniffs very loudly three times, almost like three drumbeats in the pocket of silence.*)

BRICK: You do that, Maggie. I'm a restless cripple. I got to stay on my crutch.

(*Brick hobbles to the gallery door; leans there as if waiting.*)

(*Mae sits beside Big Mama, while Gooper moves in front and sits on the end of the couch, facing her. Reverend Tooker moves nervously into the space between them; on the other side, Doctor Baugh stands looking at nothing in particular and lights a cigar. Margaret turns away.*)

BIG MAMA: Why're you all *surroundin'* me — like this? Why're you all starin' at me like this an' makin' signs at each other?

(*Reverend Tooker steps back startled.*)

MAE: Calm yourself, Big Mama.

BIG MAMA: Calm you'self, *you'self*, Sister Woman. How could I calm myself with everyone starin' at me as if big drops of blood had broken out on m'face? What's this all about, annh! What?

(*Gooper coughs and takes a center position.*)

GOOPER: Now, Doc Baugh.

MAE: Doc Baugh?

GOOPER: Big Mama wants to know the complete truth about the report we got from the Ochsner Clinic.

MAE (*eagerly*): — on Big Daddy's condition!

GOOPER: Yais, on Big Daddy's condition, we got to face it.

DOCTOR BAUGH: Well . . .

BIG MAMA (*terrified, rising*): Is there? Something? Something that I? Don't — know?

(*In these few words, this startled, very soft, question, Big Mama reviews the history of her forty-five years with Big Daddy, her great, almost embarrassingly true-hearted and simple-minded devotion to Big Daddy, who must have had something Brick has, who made himself loved so much by the "simple expedient" of not loving enough to disturb his charming detachment, also once coupled, like Brick, with virile beauty.)*

(Big Mama has a dignity at this moment; she almost stops being fat.)

DOCTOR BAUGH *(after a pause, uncomfortably)*: Yes? — Well —
BIG MAMA: I!!! — want to — *knowwwwww . . .*

(Immediately she thrusts her fist to her mouth as if to deny that statement. Then for some curious reason, she snatches the withered corsage from her breast and hurls it on the floor and steps on it with her short, fat feet.)

Somebody must be lyin'! — I want to know!
MAE: Sit down, Big Mama, sit down on this sofa.
MARGARET: Brick, go sit with Big Mama.
BIG MAMA: *What is it, what is it?*
DOCTOR BAUGH: I never have seen a more thorough examination than Big Daddy Pollitt was given in all my experience with the Ochsner Clinic.
GOOPER: It's one of the best in the country.
MAE: It's THE best in the country — bar *none!*

(For some reason she gives Gooper a violent poke as she goes past him. He slaps at her hand without removing his eyes from his mother's face.)

DOCTOR BAUGH: Of course they were ninety-nine and nine-tenths percent sure before they even started.
BIG MAMA: Sure of what, sure of what, sure of — what? — what?

(She catches her breath in a startled sob. Mae kisses her quickly. She thrusts Mae fiercely away from her, staring at the Doctor.)

MAE: Mommy, be a brave girl!
BRICK *(in the doorway, softly)*: "By the light, by the light, Of the sil-ve-ry mo-oo-n . . . "
GOOPER: Shut up! — Brick.
BRICK: Sorry . . .

(He wanders out on the gallery.)

DOCTOR BAUGH: But now, you see, Big Mama, they cut a piece of this growth, a specimen of the tissue and —
BIG MAMA: Growth? You told Big Daddy —
DOCTOR BAUGH: Now wait.
BIG MAMA *(fiercely)*: You told me and Big Daddy there wasn't a thing wrong with him but —
MAE: Big Mama, they always —
GOOPER: Let Doc Baugh talk, will yuh?
BIG MAMA: — little spastic condition of —

(Her breath gives out in a sob.)

DOCTOR BAUGH: Yes, that's what we told Big Daddy. But we had this bit of tissue run through the laboratory and I'm sorry to say the test was positive on it. It's — well — malignant . . .

(Pause.)

BIG MAMA: — Cancer?! Cancer?!

(Doctor Baugh nods gravely. Big Mama gives a long gasping cry.)

MAE AND GOOPER: Now, now, now, Big Mama, you had to know . . .
BIG MAMA: WHY DIDN'T THEY CUT IT OUT OF HIM? HANH? HANH?
DOCTOR BAUGH: Involved too much, Big Mama, too many organs affected.
MAE: Big Mama, the liver's affected and so's the kidneys, both! It's gone way past what they call a —
GOOPER: A surgical risk.
MAE: — Uh-huh . . .

(Big Mama draws a breath like a dying gasp.)

REVEREND TOOKER: Tch, tch, tch, tch, tch!
DOCTOR BAUGH: Yes it's gone past the knife.
MAE: *That's why he's turned yellow, Mommy!*
BIG MAMA: *Git away from me, git away from me, Mae!*

(She rises abruptly.)

I want Brick! Where's Brick? Where is my only son?
MAE: Mama! Did she say "*only son*"?
GOOPER: What does that make *me?*
MAE: A sober responsible man with five precious children! — *Six!*
BIG MAMA: I want Brick to tell me! Brick! Brick!
MARGARET *(rising from her reflections in a corner)*: Brick was so upset he went back out.
BIG MAMA: *Brick!*
MARGARET: Mama, let *me* tell you!
BIG MAMA: No, no, leave me alone, you're not my blood!
GOOPER: *Mama, I'm your son!* Listen to *me!*
MAE: Gooper's your son, he's your first-born!
BIG MAMA: Gooper never liked Daddy.
MAE *(as if terribly shocked)*: *That's not TRUE!*

(There is a pause. The minister coughs and rises.)

REVEREND TOOKER *(to Mae)*: I think I'd better slip away at this point.

(Discreetly.)

Good night, good night, everybody, and God bless you all . . . on this place . . .

(*He slips out.*)

(*Mae coughs and points at Big Mama.*)

GOOPER: Well, Big Mama . . .

(*He sighs.*)

BIG MAMA: It's all a mistake, I know it's just a bad dream.

DOCTOR BAUGH: We're gonna keep Big Daddy as comfortable as we can.

BIG MAMA: Yes, it's just a bad dream, that's all it is, it's just an awful dream.

GOOPER: In my opinion Big Daddy is having some pain but won't admit that he has it.

BIG MAMA: Just a dream, a bad dream.

DOCTOR BAUGH: That's what lots of them do, they think if they don't admit they're having the pain they can sort of escape the fact of it.

GOOPER (*with relish*): Yes, they get sly about it, they get real sly about it.

MAE: Gooper and I think —

GOOPER: Shut up, Mae! Big Mama, I think — Big Daddy ought to be started on morphine.

BIG MAMA: Nobody's going to give Big Daddy morphine.

DOCTOR BAUGH: Now, Big Mama, when that pain strikes it's going to strike mighty hard and Big Daddy's going to need the needle to bear it.

BIG MAMA: I tell you, nobody's going to give him morphine.

MAE: Big Mama, you don't want to see Big Daddy suffer, you know you —

(*Gooper, standing beside her, gives her a savage poke.*)

DOCTOR BAUGH (*placing a package on the table*): I'm leaving this stuff here, so if there's a sudden attack you all won't have to send out for it.

MAE: I know how to give a hypo.

BIG MAMA: Nobody's gonna give Big Daddy morphine.

GOOPER: Mae took a course in nursing during the war.

MARGARET: Somehow I don't think Big Daddy would want Mae to give him a hypo.

MAE: You think he'd want *you* to do it?

DOCTOR BAUGH: Well . . .

(*Doctor Baugh rises.*)

GOOPER: Doctor Baugh is goin'.

DOCTOR BAUGH: Yes, I got to be goin'. Well, keep your chin up, Big Mama.

GOOPER (*with jocularity*): She's gonna keep *both* chins up, aren't you, Big Mama?

(*Big Mama sobs.*)

Now stop that, Big Mama.

GOOPER (*at the door with Doctor Baugh*): Well, Doc, we sure do appreciate all you done. I'm telling you, we're surely obligated to you for —

(*Doctor Baugh has gone out without a glance at him.*)

— I guess that doctor has got a lot on his mind but it wouldn't hurt him to act a little more human . . .

(*Big Mama sobs.*)

Now be a brave girl, Mommy.

BIG MAMA: It's not true, I know that it's just not true!

GOOPER: Mama, those tests are infallible!

BIG MAMA: Why are you so determined to see your father daid?

MAE: Big Mama!

MARGARET (*gently*): I know what Big Mama means.

MAE (*fiercely*): Oh, do you?

MARGARET (*quietly and very sadly*): Yes, I think I do.

MAE: For a newcomer in the family you sure do show a lot of understanding.

MARGARET: Understanding is needed on this place.

MAE: I guess you must have needed a lot of it in your family, Maggie, with your father's liquor problem and now you've got Brick with his!

MARGARET: Brick does not have a liquor problem at all. Brick is devoted to Big Daddy. This thing is a terrible strain on him.

BIG MAMA: Brick is Big Daddy's boy, but he drinks too much and it worries me and Big Daddy, and, Margaret, you've got to cooperate with us, you've got to cooperate with Big Daddy and me in getting Brick straightened out. Because it will break Big Daddy's heart if Brick don't pull himself together and take hold of things.

MAE: Take hold of *what* things, Big Mama?

BIG MAMA: The place.

(*There is a quick violent look between Mae and Gooper.*)

GOOPER: Big Mama, you've had a shock.

MAE: Yais, we've all had a shock, but . . .

GOOPER: Let's be realistic —

MAE: — Big Daddy would never, would *never*, be foolish enough to —

GOOPER: — put this place in irresponsible hands!

BIG MAMA: Big Daddy ain't going to leave the place in anybody's hands; Big Daddy is *not* going to die. I want you to get that in your heads, all of you!

MAE: Mommy, Mommy, Big Mama, we're just as hopeful an' optimistic as you are about Big Daddy's prospects, we have faith in *prayer* — but nevertheless there are certain matters that have to be discussed an' dealt with, because otherwise —

GOOPER: Eventualities have to be considered and

now's the time . . . Mae, will you please get my brief case out of our room?

MAE: Yes, honey.

(*She rises and goes out through the hall door.*)

GOOPER (*standing over Big Mama*): Now, Big Mom. What you said just now was not at all true and you know it. I've always loved Big Daddy in my own quiet way. I never made a show of it, and I know that Big Daddy has always been fond of me in a quiet way, too, and he never made a show of it neither.

(*Mae returns with Gooper's brief case.*)

MAE: Here's your brief case, Gooper, honey.

GOOPER (*handing the brief case back to her*): Thank you . . . Of cou'se, my relationship with Big Daddy is different from Brick's.

MAE: You're eight years older'n Brick an' always had t' carry a bigger load of th' responsibilities than Brick ever had t' carry. He never carried a thing in his life but a football or a highball.

GOOPER: Mae, will y' let me talk, please?

MAE: Yes, honey.

GOOPER: Now, a twenty-eight-thousand-acre plantation's a mighty big thing t' run.

MAE: Almost singlehanded.

(*Margaret has gone out onto the gallery and can be heard calling softly to Brick.*)

BIG MAMA: You never had to run this place! What are you talking about? As if Big Daddy was dead and in his grave, you had to run it? Why, you just helped him out with a few business details and had your law practice at the same time in Memphis!

MAE: Oh, Mommy, Mommy, Big Mommy! Let's be fair!

MARGARET: Brick!

MAE: Why, Gooper has given himself body and soul to keeping this place up for the past five years since Big Daddy's health started failing.

MARGARET: Brick!

MAE: Gooper won't say it, Gooper never thought of it as a duty, he just did it. And what did Brick do? Brick kept living in his past glory at college! Still a football player at twenty-seven!

MARGARET (*returning alone*): Who are you talking about now? Brick? A football player? He isn't a football player and you know it. Brick is a sports announcer on TV and one of the best-known ones in the country!

MAE: I'm talking about what he was.

MARGARET: Well, I wish you would just stop talking about my husband.

GOOPER: I've got a right to discuss my brother with other members of MY OWN family, which don't include *you*. Why don't you go out there and drink with Brick?

MARGARET: I've never seen such malice toward a brother.

GOOPER: How about his for me? Why, he can't stand to be in the same room with me!

MARGARET: This is a deliberate campaign of vilification for the most disgusting and sordid reason on earth, and I know what it is! It's *avarice, avarice, greed, greed!*

BIG MAMA: *Oh, I'll scream! I will scream in a moment unless this stops!*

(*Gooper has stalked up to Margaret with clenched fists at his sides as if he would strike her. Mae distorts her face again into a hideous grimace behind Margaret's back.*)

BIG MAMA (*sobs*): Margaret. Child. Come here. Sit next to Big Mama.

MARGARET: Precious Mommy. I'm sorry, I'm sorry, I — !

(*She bends her long graceful neck to press her forehead to Big Mama's bulging shoulder under its black chiffon.*)

MAE: How beautiful, how touching, this display of devotion! Do you know why she's childless? She's childless because that big beautiful athlete husband of hers won't go to bed with her!

GOOPER: You jest won't let me do this in a nice way, will yah? Aw right — I don't give a goddamn if Big Daddy likes me or don't like me or did or never did or will or will never! I'm just appealing to a sense of common decency and fair play. I'll tell you the truth. I've resented Big Daddy's partiality to Brick ever since Brick was born, and the way I've been treated like I was just barely good enough to spit on and sometimes not even good enough for that. Big Daddy is dying of cancer, and it's spread all through him and it's attacked all his vital organs including the kidneys and right now he is sinking into uremia, and you all know what uremia is, it's poisoning of the whole system due to the failure of the body to eliminate its poisons.

MARGARET (*to herself, downstage, hissingly*): Poisons, poisons! Venomous thoughts and words! In hearts and minds! — That's poisons!

GOOPER (*overlapping her*): I am asking for a square deal, and, by God, I expect to get one. But if I don't get one, if there's any peculiar shenanigans going on around here behind my back, well, I'm not a corporation lawyer for nothing, I know how to protect my own interests.

(*Brick enters from the gallery with a tranquil, blurred smile, carrying an empty glass with him.*)

BRICK: Storm coming up.
GOOPER: Oh! A late arrival!
MAE: Behold the conquering hero comes!
GOOPER: The fabulous Brick Pollitt! Remember him? — Who could forget him!
MAE: He looks like he's been injured in a game!
GOOPER: Yep, I'm afraid you'll have to warm the bench at the Sugar Bowl this year, Brick!

(*Mae laughs shrilly.*)

Or was it the Rose Bowl that he made that famous run in? —

(*Thunder.*)

MAE: The punch bowl, honey. It was in the punch bowl, the cut-glass punch bowl!
GOOPER: Oh, that's right, I'm getting the bowls mixed up!
MARGARET: Why don't you stop venting your malice and envy on a sick boy?
BIG MAMA: *Now you two hush, I mean it, hush, all of you, hush!*
DAISY, SOOKEY: Storm! Storm comin'! Storm! Storm!
LACEY: Brightie, close them shutters.
GOOPER: Lacey, put the top up on my Cadillac, will yuh?
LACEY: Yes, suh, Mistah Pollitt!
GOOPER (*at the same time*): Big Mama, you know it's necessary for me t' go back to Memphis in th' mornin' t' represent the Parker estate in a lawsuit.

(*Mae sits on the bed and arranges papers she has taken from the brief case.*)

BIG MAMA: Is it, Gooper?
MAE: Yaiss.
GOOPER: That's why I'm forced to — to bring up a problem that —
MAE: Somethin' that's too important t' be put off!
GOOPER: If Brick was sober, he ought to be in on this.
MARGARET: Brick is present; we're present.
GOOPER: Well, good. I will now give you this outline my partner, Tom Bullitt, an' me have drawn up — a sort of dummy — trusteeship.
MARGARET: Oh, that's it! You'll be in charge an dole out remittances, will you?
GOOPER: This we did as soon as we got the report on Big Daddy from th' Ochsner Laboratories. We did this thing, I mean we drew up this dummy outline with the advice and assistance of the Chairman of the Boa'd of Directors of th' Southern Plantahs Bank and Trust Company in Memphis, C. C. Bellowes, a man who handles estates for all th' prominent fam'lies in West Tennessee and th' Delta.

BIG MAMA: Gooper?
GOOPER (*crouching in front of Big Mama*): Now this is not — not final, or anything like it. This is just a preliminary outline. But it does provide a basis — a design — a — possible, feasible — *plan!*
MARGARET: Yes, I'll bet it's a plan.

(*Thunder.*)

MAE: It's a plan to protect the biggest estate in the Delta from irresponsibility an' —
BIG MAMA: Now you listen to me, all of you, you listen here! They's not goin' to be any more catty talk in my house! And Gooper, you put that away before I grab it out of your hand and tear it right up! I don't know what the hell's in it, and I don't want to know what the hell's in it. I'm talkin' in Big Daddy's language now; I'm his *wife,* not his *widow,* I'm still his *wife!* And I'm talkin' to you in his language an' —
GOOPER: Big Mama, what I have here is —
MAE (*at the same time*): Gooper explained that it's just a plan . . .
BIG MAMA: I don't care what you got there. Just put it back where it came from, an' don't let me see it again, not even the outside of the envelope of it! Is that understood? Basis! Plan! Preliminary! Design! I say — what is it Big Daddy always says when he's disgusted?
BRICK (*from the bar*): Big Daddy says "crap" when he's disgusted.
BIG MAMA (*rising*): That's right — CRAP! I say CRAP too, like Big Daddy!

(*Thunder.*)

MAE: Coarse language doesn't seem called for in this —
GOOPER: Somethin' in me is *deeply outraged* by hearin' you talk like this.
BIG MAMA: *Nobody's goin' to take nothin'!* — till Big Daddy lets go of it — maybe, just possibly, not — not even then! No, not even then!

(*Thunder.*)

MAE: Sookey, hurry up an' git that po'ch furniture covahed; want th' paint to come off?
GOOPER: Lacey, put mah car away!
LACEY: Caint, Mistah Pollitt, you got the keys!
GOOPER: Naw, you got 'em, man. Where th' keys to th' car, honey?
MAE: You got 'em in your pocket!
BRICK: "You can always hear me singin' this song, Show me the way to go home."

(*Thunder distantly.*)

BIG MAMA: Brick! Come here, Brick, I need you. Tonight Brick looks like he used to look when he

was a little boy, just like he did when he played
wild games and used to come home when I hollered
myself hoarse for him, all sweaty and pink cheeked
and sleepy, with his — red curls shining . . .

(*Brick draws aside as he does from all physical contact and continues the song in a whisper, opening the
ice bucket and dropping in the ice cubes one by one as
if he were mixing some important chemical formula.*)
(*Distant thunder.*)

Time goes by so fast. Nothin' can outrun it. Death
commences too early — almost before you're half
acquainted with life — you meet the other . . . Oh,
you know we just got to love each other an' stay
together, all of us, just as close as we can, especially now that such a *black* thing has come and
moved into this place without invitation.

(*Awkwardly embracing Brick, she presses her head to
his shoulder.*)
(*A dog howls offstage.*)

Oh, Brick, son of Big Daddy, Big Daddy does so
love you. Y'know what would be his fondest
dream come true? If before he passed on, if Big
Daddy has to pass on . . .

(*A dog howls.*)

. . . you give him a child of yours, a grandson as
much like his son as his son is like Big Daddy . . .
MARGARET: I know that's Big Daddy's dream.
BIG MAMA: That's his dream.
MAE: Such a pity that Maggie and Brick can't oblige.
BIG DADDY (*off downstage right on the gallery*): Looks
like the wind was takin' liberties with this place.
SERVANT (*offstage*): Yes, sir, Mr. Pollitt.
MARGARET (*crossing to the right door*): Big Daddy's
on the gall'ry.

(*Big Mama has turned toward the hall door at the
sound of Big Daddy's voice on the gallery.*)

BIG MAMA: I can't stay here. He'll see somethin' in my
eyes.

(*Big Daddy enters the room from upstage right.*)

BIG DADDY: Can I come in?

(*He puts his cigar in an ash tray.*)

MARGARET: Did the storm wake you up, Big Daddy?
BIG DADDY: Which stawm are you talkin' about — th'
one outside or th' hullballoo in here?

(*Gooper squeezes past Big Daddy.*)

GOOPER: 'Scuse me.

(*Mae tries to squeeze past Big Daddy to join Gooper,
but Big Daddy puts his arm firmly around her.*)

BIG DADDY: I heard some mighty loud talk. Sounded
like somethin' important was bein' discussed.
What was the powwow about?
MAE (*flustered*): Why — nothin', Big Daddy . . .
BIG DADDY (*crossing to extreme left center, taking Mae
with him*): What is that pregnant-lookin' envelope
you're puttin' back in your brief case, Gooper?
GOOPER (*at the foot of the bed, caught, as he stuffs
papers into envelope*): That? Nothin', suh —
nothin' much of anythin' at all . . .
BIG DADDY: Nothin'? It looks like a whole lot of
nothin'!

(*He turns upstage to the group.*)

You all know th' story about th' young married
couple —
GOOPER: Yes, sir!
BIG DADDY: Hello, Brick —
BRICK: Hello, Big Daddy.

(*The group is arranged in a semicircle above Big
Daddy, Margaret at the extreme right, then Mae and
Gooper, then Big Mama, with Brick at the left.*)

BIG DADDY: Young married couple took Junior out to
th' zoo one Sunday, inspected all of God's creatures in their cages, with satisfaction.
GOOPER: Satisfaction.
BIG DADDY (*crossing to upstage center, facing front*):
This afternoon was a warm afternoon in spring an'
that ole elephant had somethin' else on his mind
which was bigger'n peanuts. You know this story,
Brick?

(*Gooper nods.*)

BRICK: No, sir, I don't know it.
BIG DADDY: Y'see, in th' cage adjoinin' they was a
young female elephant in heat!
BIG MAMA (*at Big Daddy's shoulder*): Oh, Big Daddy!
BIG DADDY: What's the matter, preacher's gone, ain't
he? All right. That female elephant in the next cage
was permeatin' the atmosphere about her with a
powerful and excitin' odor of female fertility!
Huh! Ain't that a nice way to put it, Brick?
BRICK: Yes, sir, nothin' wrong with it.
BIG DADDY: Brick says th's nothin' wrong with it!
BIG MAMA: Oh, Big Daddy!
BIG DADDY (*crossing to downstage center*): So this ole
bull elephant still had a couple of fornications left
in him. He reared back his trunk an' got a whiff of
that elephant lady next door! — began to paw at
the dirt in his cage an' butt his head against the
separatin' partition and, first thing y'know, there
was a conspicuous change in his *profile* — very
conspicuous! Ain't I tellin' this story in decent language, Brick?

BRICK: Yes, sir, too fuckin' decent!

BIG DADDY: So, the little boy pointed at it and said, "What's that?" His mama said, "Oh, that's — nothin'!" — His papa said, "She's spoiled!"

(*Big Daddy crosses to Brick at left.*)

You didn't laugh at that story, Brick.

(*Big Mama crosses to downstage right crying. Margaret goes to her. Mae and Gooper hold upstage right center.*)

BRICK: No, sir, I didn't laugh at that story.

BIG DADDY: What is the smell in this room? Don't you notice it, Brick? Don't you notice a powerful and obnoxious odor of mendacity in this room?

BRICK: Yes, sir, I think I do, sir.

GOOPER: Mae, Mae . . .

BIG DADDY: There is nothing more powerful. Is there, Brick?

BRICK: No, sir. No, sir, there isn't, an' nothin' more obnoxious.

BIG DADDY: Brick agrees with me. The odor of mendacity is a powerful and obnoxious odor an' the stawm hasn't blown it away from this room yet. You notice it, Gooper?

GOOPER: What, sir?

BIG DADDY: How about you, Sister Woman? You notice the unpleasant odor of mendacity in this room?

MAE: Why, Big Daddy, I don't even know what that is.

BIG DADDY: You can smell it. Hell it smells like death!

(*Big Mama sobs. Big Daddy looks toward her.*)

What's wrong with that fat woman over there, loaded with diamonds? Hey, what's-you-name, what's the matter with you?

MARGARET (*crossing toward Big Daddy*): She had a slight dizzy spell, Big Daddy.

BIG DADDY: You better watch that, Big Mama. A stroke is a bad way to go.

MARGARET (*crossing to Big Daddy at center*): Oh, Brick, Big Daddy has on your birthday present to him, Brick, he has on your cashmere robe, the softest material I have ever felt.

BIG DADDY: Yeah, this is my soft birthday, Maggie . . . Not my gold or my silver birthday, but my soft birthday, everything's got to be soft for Big Daddy on this soft birthday.

(*Maggie kneels before Big Daddy at center.*)

MARGARET: Big Daddy's got on his Chinese slippers that I gave him, Brick. Big Daddy, I haven't given you my big present yet, but now I will, now's the time for me to present it to you! I have an announcement to make!

MAE: What? What kind of announcement?

GOOPER: A sports announcement, Maggie?

MARGARET: Announcement of life beginning! A child is coming, sired by Brick, and out of Maggie the Cat! I have Brick's child in my body, an' that's my birthday present to Big Daddy on this birthday!

(*Big Daddy looks at Brick who crosses behind Big Daddy to downstage portal, left.*)

BIG DADDY: Get up, girl, get up off your knees, girl.

(*Big Daddy helps Margaret to rise. He crosses above her, to her right, bites off the end of a fresh cigar, taken from his bathrobe pocket, as he studies Margaret.*)

Uh-huh, this girl has life in her body, that's no lie!

BIG MAMA: BIG DADDY'S DREAM COME TRUE!

BRICK: JESUS!

BIG DADDY (*crossing right below wicker stand*): Gooper, I want my lawyer in the mornin'.

BRICK: Where are you goin', Big Daddy?

BIG DADDY: Son, I'm goin' up on the roof, to the belvedere on th' roof to look over my kingdom before I give up my kingdom — twenty-eight thousand acres of th' richest land this side of the valley Nile!

(*He exits through right doors, and down right on the gallery.*)

BIG MAMA (*following*): Sweetheart, sweetheart, sweetheart — can I come with you?

(*She exits downstage right.*)

(*Margaret is downstage center in the mirror area. Mae has joined Gooper and she gives him a fierce poke, making a low hissing sound and a grimace of fury.*)

GOOPER (*pushing her aside*): Brick, could you possibly spare me one small shot of that liquor?

BRICK: Why, help yourself, Gooper boy.

GOOPER: I will.

MAE (*shrilly*): Of course we know that this is — a lie.

GOOPER: Be still, Mae.

MAE: I won't be still! I know she's made this up!

GOOPER: Goddamn it, I said shut up!

MARGARET: Gracious! I didn't know that my little announcement was going to provoke such a storm!

MAE: *That* woman isn't *pregnant!*

GOOPER: Who said she was?

MAE: *She* did.

GOOPER: The doctor didn't. Doc Baugh didn't.

MARGARET: I haven't gone to Doc Baugh.

GOOPER: Then who'd you go to, Maggie?

MARGARET: One of the best gynecologists in the South.

GOOPER: Uh huh, uh huh! — I see . . .

(*He takes out a pencil and notebook.*)

— May we have his name, please?

MARGARET: No, you may not, Mister Prosecuting Attorney!

MAE: He doesn't have any name, he doesn't exist!

MARGARET: Oh, he exists all right, and so does my child, Brick's baby!

MAE: You can't conceive a child by a man that won't sleep with you unless you think you're —

(*Brick has turned on the phonograph. A scat song cuts Mae's speech.*)

GOOPER: *Turn that off!*

MAE: We know it's a lie because we hear you in here; he won't sleep with you, we hear you! So don't imagine you're going to put a trick over on us, to fool a dying man with a —

(*A long drawn cry of agony and rage fills the house. Margaret turns the phonograph down to a whisper. The cry is repeated.*)

MAE: Did you hear that, Gooper, did you hear that?

GOOPER: Sounds like the pain has struck.

GOOPER: Come along and leave these lovebirds together in their nest!

(*He goes out first. Mae follows but turns at the door, contorting her face and hissing at Margaret.*)

MAE: *Liar!*

(*She slams the door.*)
    (*Margaret exhales with relief and moves a little unsteadily to catch hold of Brick's arm.*)

MARGARET: Thank you for — keeping still . . .

BRICK: O.K., Maggie.

MARGARET: It was gallant of you to save my face!

(*He now pours down three shots in quick succession and stands waiting, silent. All at once he turns with a smile and says:*)

BRICK: *There!*

MARGARET: What?

BRICK: The *click* . . .

(*His gratitude seems almost infinite as he hobbles out on the gallery with a drink. We hear his crutch as he swings out of sight. Then, at some distance, he begins singing to himself a peaceful song. Margaret holds the big pillow forlornly as if it were her only companion, for a few moments, then throws it on the bed. She rushes to the liquor cabinet, gathers all the bottles in her arms, turns about undecidedly, then runs out of*)

the room with them, leaving the door ajar on the dim yellow hall. Brick is heard hobbling back along the gallery, singing his peaceful song. He comes back in, sees the pillow on the bed, laughs lightly, sadly, picks it up. He has it under his arm as Margaret returns to the room. Margaret softly shuts the door and leans against it, smiling softly at Brick.*)

MARGARET: Brick, I used to think that you were stronger than me and I didn't want to be overpowered by you. But now, since you've taken to liquor — you know what? — I guess it's bad, but now I'm stronger than you and I can love you more truly! Don't move that pillow. I'll move it right back if you do! — Brick?

(*She turns out all the lamps but a single rose-silk-shaded one by the bed.*)

I really have been to a doctor and I know what to do and — Brick? — this is my time by the calendar to conceive?

BRICK: Yes, I understand, Maggie. But how are you going to conceive a child by a man in love with his liquor?

MARGARET: By locking his liquor up and making him satisfy my desire before I unlock it!

BRICK: Is that what you've done, Maggie?

MARGARET: Look and see. That cabinet's mighty empty compared to before!

BRICK: Well, I'll be a son of a —

(*He reaches for his crutch but she beats him to it and rushes out on the gallery, hurls the crutch over the rail, and comes back in, panting.*)

MARGARET: And so tonight we're going to make the lie true, and when that's done, I'll bring the liquor back here and we'll get drunk together, here, tonight, in this place that death has come into . . . — What do you say?

BRICK: I don't say anything. I guess there's nothing to say.

MARGARET: Oh, you weak people, you weak, beautiful people! — who give up with such grace. What you want is someone to —

(*She turns out the rose-silk lamp.*)

— take hold of you. — Gently, gently with love hand your life back to you, like somethin' gold you let go of. I do love you, Brick, I *do!*

BRICK (*smiling with charming sadness*): Wouldn't it be funny if that was true?

COMMENTARIES

Tennessee Williams has long been one of the fascinating figures of American drama. He was a forceful personality who charmed his friends and the public alike, although his life was often filled with uncertainties and unresolved problems. Some of his best work derived from his private agonies. His work was taken seriously almost from the first, and a body of criticism has developed around it, including biographies, personal reminiscences of collaborators, critical commentaries, and scholarship.

Among the commentaries included here is a sampling from his *Memoirs,* published in 1972, in which he discusses *The Glass Menagerie* and *Cat on a Hot Tin Roof.* Williams reflects on his role as author, what he calls "the professional side of my life." He talks about his reasons for liking *Cat on a Hot Tin Roof* best among his plays. His additional comments on what it is like to be a writer are brief, but loaded with meaning.

Donald Spoto, who wrote *The Kindness of Strangers: The Life of Tennessee Williams* (1985), tells about Laurette Taylor, who played the mother in the first production of *The Glass Menagerie.* Taylor, a powerful actress whose career had seemed finished when the part was offered to her, almost refused the role at first. But her interpretation established a point of reference to which later actresses had to pay homage. The *New York Times* review of *The Glass Menagerie* (included here as a commentary) describes Taylor's performance as "completely perfect." Spoto helps us understand the power of collaboration between actor and playwright that sometimes helps both expand their understanding of the work.

Benjamin Nelson explains that "*The Glass Menagerie* exhibits several of Williams's weaknesses as well as his strengths as a playwright." He discusses Williams's characterizations, especially of Laura and Amanda. He also points to "poetic passages" in the play that he feels are weaknesses. Ultimately, Nelson poses an interesting dramatic question: Is the play a tragedy? The search for an answer to this question involves a full consideration of the play's strengths and weaknesses, its success or failure.

Collaboration is the theme of Brenda Murphy's discussion of Williams's work with Elia Kazan, who directed *Cat on a Hot Tin Roof* and other works by Williams. She reveals that their collaboration was a clash of powerful personalities. Each had his own professional authority but different ideas. In the case of *Cat on a Hot Tin Roof,* their difficulties centered on Big Daddy, a character whose appeal and force onstage were so great that Kazan did not want him to disappear after act 2. Williams rewrote the ending under duress and much later admitted that Kazan was right. Murphy makes us aware of the extent to which theater is a collaboration, even when a play flows from the pen of a genius such as Williams.

Lewis Nichols (1903–1982)
REVIEW OF *THE GLASS MENAGERIE*   *1945*

Lewis Nichols's review of the New York premiere of The Glass Menagerie *focused on the stellar performance of Laurette Taylor, who played the Mother. Nichols also points out the quality of Williams's writing and his ear for "faintly sardonic dialogue." He saw the play as a superb vehicle for sublime acting.*

The theatre opened its Easter basket the night before and found it a particularly rich one. Preceded by warm and tender reports from Chicago, *The Glass Menagerie* opened at the Playhouse on Saturday, and immediately it was clear that for once the advance notes were not in error. Tennessee Williams' simple play forms the framework for some of the finest acting to be seen in many a day. "Memorable" is an overworked word, but that is the only one to describe Laurette Taylor's performance. March left the theatre like a lioness.

Miss Taylor's picture of a blowsy, impoverished woman who is living on memories of a flower-scented Southern past is completely perfect. It combines qualities of humor and human understanding. The Mother of the play is an amusing figure and a pathetic one. Aged, with two children, living in an apartment off an alley in St. Louis, she recalls her past glories, her seventeen suitors, the old and better life. She is a bit of a scold, a bit of a snob; her finery has worn threadbare, but she has kept it for occasions of state. Miss Taylor makes her a person known by any other name to everyone in her audience. That is art.

In the story the Mother is trying to do the best she can for her children. The son works in a warehouse, although he wants to go to far places. The daughter, a cripple, never has been able to finish school. She is shy, she spends her time collecting glass animals — the title comes from this — and playing old phonograph records. The Mother thinks it is time she is getting married, but there has never been a Gentleman Caller at the house. Finally the son brings home another man from the warehouse and out comes the finery and the heavy if bent candlestick. Even the Gentleman Caller fails. He is engaged to another girl.

Mr. Williams's play is not all of the same caliber. A strict perfectionist could easily find a good many flaws. There are some unconnected odds and ends which have little to do with the story: Snatches of talk about the war, bits of psychology, occasional moments of rather flowery writing. But Mr. Williams has a real ear for faintly sardonic dialogue, unexpected phrases and an affection for his characters. Miss Taylor takes these many good passages and makes them sing. She plays softly and part of the time seems to be mumbling — a mumble that can be heard at the top of the gallery. Her accents, like the author's phrases, are unexpected, her gestures are vague and fluttery. There is no doubt she was a Southern belle; there is no doubt she is a great actress.

Eddie Dowling, who is coproducer, and, with Margo Jones, codirector, has the double job of narrator and the player of The Son. The narration is like that of *Our Town* and *I Remember Mama* and it probably is not essential to *The Glass Menagerie*. In the play itself Mr. Dowling gives his quiet, easy performance. Julie Haydon, very ethereal and slight, is good as the daughter, as is Anthony Ross as the Gentleman Caller. The Caller had been the hero in high school, but he, too, had been unsuccessful. Jo Mielziner's setting fits the play, as does Paul Bowles's music. In fact, everything fits. *The Glass Menagerie,* like spring, is a pleasure to have in the neighborhood.

Donald Spoto (b. 1941)
LAURETTE TAYLOR IN *THE GLASS MENAGERIE*   1985

Before the part of Amanda Wingfield was offered to her, Laurette Taylor had thought her career as an actress was over. Donald Spoto, the biographer of Tennessee Williams, gives us a vision of how persistence and devotion to someone of genuine talent produced a legend in American acting.

That month [December 1944], the details moved together swiftly. [Actor-producer-director Eddie] Dowling, who had directed actress Julie Haydon in *The Time of Your Life,*° convinced her that (although she was thirty-four) she would be credible as the lame, fragile Laura, a character at least a decade younger. She, in turn, took the play to her friend and mentor (later her husband), the formidable critic George Jean Nathan, whose approval she felt obligatory. At the same time, the forty-nine-year-old Dowling announced — without a smile — that he would play young (twentyish) Tom, the shoe-warehouse clerk and aspiring poet; for the role of the gentleman caller, Anthony Ross was hired. The remaining role to be cast was Amanda Wingfield — the "little woman of great but confused vitality," as Williams described her in the play, "clinging frantically to another time and place." The role demanded not mere competence, but the nuances of dramatic greatness. Nathan suggested Laurette Taylor. Dowling and [Audrey] Wood [Williams's agent] and Williams saw his wisdom; they also panicked.

Laurette Taylor, then sixty, had been up to the 1930s one of the great ladies of the American stage. Those who had seen her in *Peg O'My Heart* (in 1912) or *The Furies* (in 1928) or *Outward Bound* (in 1938) knew her gifts. But for almost ten years she had herself become a woman of great but confused vitality, and a confirmed alcoholic.

At that time, Taylor was living in sad withdrawal from the theater, at a hotel on East 60th Street, where she was daily attended by a drama student named Eloise Sheldon. In return for acting lessons, the young woman cared for the practical details of Taylor's life and offered devoted companionship. The play reached Taylor by the circuitous route of Wood to Dowling to Haydon to Nathan to Sheldon to Taylor. It also bore a new title — *The Glass Menagerie.*

"Of course her first reaction was to turn it down," Eloise Sheldon Armen recalled years later; "she thought her career was over. But we prevailed on her to see that no one could bring this character to life the way she could." At last, with the loving encouragement of Eloise — "a small flame," as Laurette Taylor's daughter appreciatively wrote of the young student, "guiding [Taylor] back to the paths of everyday life" — she accepted the part. She did not, however, stop drinking, nor did she seem to give much attention to memorizing lines before or during rehearsals.

The Time of Your Life: A play (1939) by William Saroyan.

In November, Dowling (with, Williams insisted, Margo Jones as codirector) began rehearsals in New York prior to a scheduled Chicago tryout at the end of December. Terrified that something like the history of *Battle of Angels* would be repeated — not because of the new play's content (which could not have been more different) but because he no longer believed the play was anything but "rather dull, too nice" — Williams fled New York for St. Louis. There he was interviewed on his life and work and hopes by the drama critic of the *Star-Times,* a man named William Inge. The resulting article was full of inaccuracies, half-truths and Williams's typical alterations of personal history; the resulting friendship was much more intense and dramatic.

But Audrey and Dowling would not allow Williams to be an absentee author, and in December he was summoned to Chicago. The situation, he quickly realized, was as bleak as the fierce winter that had already descended.

First of all, Laurette Taylor — with only a week remaining before the December 26 premiere — attended the final rehearsals in what can only be called an alcoholic stupor, barely summarizing the dialogue and so broadly defining the woman's Southern accent and character that, as Williams wrote . . . , she made the play sound like the Aunt Jemima Pancake Hour. In addition, Jo Mielziner's stage designs were being followed with great difficulty, and the music Williams had commissioned from his old acquaintance Paul Bowles sounded harsh through the theater's crude sound system. Luggage had not arrived; a winter storm raged; the Civic Theatre was inconvenient to Chicago's main theater district; there was no budget for advertising or publicity; and everyone in the company (except Eddie Dowling and Julie Haydon) — cast, crew, author — submerged the fear of failure in strong drink. Margo Jones, Williams wrote . . . , was like a scoutmaster leading a wayward and desperate troop to their doom.

As late as Christmas Eve, the lines of the play had been neither "frozen" (fixed by the producer and playwright to be performed as written) nor completely memorized. Laurette Taylor managed only a martini mumble, Dowling was demanding rewrites, and the cast was stumbling into props and one another. "Mr. Dowling," Williams said quietly that night, "art is experience remembered in tranquillity. And I find no tranquillity in Chicago."

The night after Christmas, *The Glass Menagerie* was somehow performed for a small, diffident audience. By the afternoon of the twenty-seventh, the box office had taken in only four hundred dollars, and the producers prepared a closing notice. But then Audrey telephoned them to read two brief reviews: Critic Claudia Cassidy, writing in the *Chicago Daily Tribune,* said the play had "the stamina of success . . . [it] knows people and how they tick. . . . If it is your play, as it is mine, it reaches out . . . and you are caught in its spell." And Ashton Stevens, in the *Herald American,* said *The Glass Menagerie* "has the courage of true poetry couched in colloquial prose."

Before the end of that day, the mayor of Chicago, at the urging of the Civic Theatre's management, authorized a fifty-percent ticket subsidy for municipal employees. On the third night, Laurette Taylor was not simply discharging a half-formed role, she was creating a legend, she had begun to draw a more wonderful portrait than anyone could have imagined — not Eddie Dowling (who resented the critics' subsequent raves about her), not Tennessee Williams nor Audrey Wood, not anyone connected with the play.

"Actually," according to the playwright, "she directed many of the scenes, particularly the ones between mother and daughter, and she did a top-notch job.

She was continually working on her part, putting in little things and taking them out — almost every night in Chicago there was something new, but she never disturbed the central characterization. Everything she did was absolutely in character."

The closing notice was removed — not, however, because box-office business dramatically improved, but because Claudia Cassidy and Ashton Stevens had been championing the play, returning almost nightly and telling and writing about it almost daily. "It gripped players and audiences alike," Cassidy wrote on January 7, 1945, "and created one of those rare evenings in the theater that make 'stagestruck' an honorable word." By the middle of the month, no tickets were available. In an unusual example of journalistic salvation, a play was for once not lost but kept alive because of critical support.

Benjamin Nelson
PROBLEMS IN *THE GLASS MENAGERIE*   *1961*

Benjamin Nelson's analysis of Williams's play recognizes the power of the circumstances portrayed in the play. Nelson is concerned, however, that the characters, especially Laura, are not as fully and carefully drawn as they need to be to make the play truly powerful. He also criticizes Williams for creating a universe that "does not allow tragedy."

The Glass Menagerie exhibits several of Williams's weaknesses as well as his strengths as a playwright. The great strength of the play is of course the delicate, sympathetic, yet objective creation of meaningful people in a meaningful situation. Williams has caught a decisive and desperate moment in the lives of four individuals and given it illumination and a sense of deep meaning — no small feat for any writer.

His characterizations are not equally realized. He has been unable to create Laura on more than a single dimension, while Amanda is overwhelming in her multi-faceted delineation. On a more technical level the play manifests a doubt on the part of its author toward the power of the written word. As a backdrop for *The Glass Menagerie,* Williams originally wished to use a screen to register emotions and present images from the past, present, and future. For example, when Jim O'Connor confesses to the family that he is going steady with another girl, the legend on the screen is to read, "The Sky Falls." Fortunately, [actor-director] Eddie Dowling deleted these touches of the poet from his production, but the play still abounds with a number of pretentious statements on the part of Tom as Narrator.

I assume that the final scene between Amanda and Laura is played in pantomime because Williams wished to portray Amanda's dignity through her gestures and her daughter's reaction, rather than through the mother's speech, which during the course of the drama has been either shrill, simpering, or saucy. But in relegating this scene to background silence while Tom makes a self-conscious statement about drifting like a dead leaf "attempting to find in motion what was lost in space," he has substituted a painfully pretentious narration for what could have been an intense and luminous moment between the two women.

Again, on the credit side of the author, his play presents genuine situation, motivation, and, as Joseph Wood Krutch has noted, "a hard substantial core of shrewd observation and deft, economical characterization." But Mr. Krutch also noted that "this hard core is enveloped in a fuzzy haze of pretentious, sentimental, pseudopoetic verbiage."[1] In *The Glass Menagerie,* the strained lyricism runs parallel with dialogue that is fresh, alive, and highly characteristic, particularly in the speech of Amanda. This dialogue fortunately dominates the proceedings, but the excess of self-conscious "poetical" passages is quite apparent and is a fault of which Williams is to be guilty in much of his later work.

But the great weakness of *The Glass Menagerie* does not lie in its author's artistic or technical deficiencies. The weakness lies at the core of the play and evolves out of what is to become the playwright's hardening philosophical commitment. We can begin to comprehend this when we ask ourselves whether or not *The Glass Menagerie* is a tragedy. It presents a tragic situation and characters who, despite their moodiness and foolishness and self-deception, possess a sense of the tragic. With the possible exception of Laura, they are intensely genuine and the destruction of their dreams and aspirations bears the illusion of great importance. But the play is not a tragedy. The universe of *The Glass Menagerie* does not allow tragedy.

Everyone in the play is a failure and in the course of their drama they all perish a little. Amanda, the most heroic of the quartet, is pitiful but not tragic because from the outset she is doomed to failure despite her desperate struggle to right things. None of these people are given the opportunity to triumph against a fate which is as malignant as it is implacable. Their struggle is a rear-guard action against life, a continuous retreat. This retreat may be moving, pathetic, melodramatic, or boisterous, but it is always a withdrawal. After all, what is the world outside the glass menagerie?

> There was only hot swing music and liquor, dance halls, bars, and movies, and sex that hung in the gloom like a chandelier and flooded the world with brief, deceptive rainbows. . . . All the world was waiting for bombardments!   (p. 1044)

The world outside the Wingfield apartment is a world of illusions, also, even more deceptive and destructive than those held by Amanda and Laura. It is the world of *Stairs to the Roof* and this time the escape is not to a new star but into the individual and personal illusions fostered by each of the characters as his private defense against destruction. Jim waits for the day when his "zzzzzp!" will at last disperse his fear and uncertainty; Laura creates her own sparkling, cold world which gives the illusion of warmth but is as eternal in its unreality as the glass from which it is composed; Amanda strikes out with all her power against her fate by clinging to the past as to a shield; and Tom, recognizing the plight of his family, can do no more than drift away from them, rudderless, frightened, and never really as far from Amanda and Laura as he knows he should be.

Not one of these individuals can cope with his situation. They struggle and their hopes and the destruction of these hopes possess a sense of great importance because Williams has created genuine people in an intensely genuine situ-

---

[1]Joseph Wood Krutch, *The Nation* 14 April 1945:24.

ation, but they lack the completeness to truly cope with their dilemma. They are not responsible for what has happened to them and they are much too helpless to do more than delay the inevitable. And destruction is inevitable because it is implicit in the universe of Tennessee Williams.

> For the sins of the world are really only its partialities, and these are what sufferings must atone for. . . . The nature of man is full of such makeshift arrangements, devised by himself to cover his incompletion. He feels a part of himself to be like a missing wall or a room left unfurnished and he tries as well as he can to make up for it. The use of imagination, resorting to dreams or the loftier purpose of art, is a mask he devises to cover his incompletion. Or violence such as a war, between two men or among a number of nations, is also a blind and senseless compensation for that which is not yet formed in human nature. Then there is still another compensation. This one is found in the principle of atonement, the surrender of self to violent treatment by others with the idea of thereby cleansing one's self of his guilt.[2]

This statement emanates from the core of Williams's thought and is perhaps his most illuminating commentary about himself and his work. It represents a philosophy, or let us say an attitude toward man in his universe, which is to manifest itself in all his work. It is taken from his short story, "Desire and the Black Masseur," which deals with the final compensation cited in the above quotation: purification through violence. In this tale, a man atones for what the author feels is a cosmic fragmentation and guilt by allowing — and actually furthering — his destruction by a cannibal. In *Battle of Angels* and *The Purification*, we find this same kind of violent cleansing.

The Glass Menagerie is a far cry from any of these works; it is the most non-violent drama written by Williams. Nevertheless it adheres to the belief set forth in the short story. The underlying belief in *The Glass Menagerie* is that there is very little, if any, reason for living. Man is by nature incomplete because his universe is fragmented. There is nothing to be done about this condition because nothing *can* be done about it. Human guilt becomes a corollary of universal guilt and man's life is an atonement for the human condition. In each character in *The Glass Menagerie* there is a part "like a missing wall or a room left unfurnished and he tries as well as he can to make up for it." The mask devised by Laura and Amanda and Tom and Jim is "the use of imagination, resorting to dreams." The Wingfields are broken, fragmented people because "the sins of the world are really only its partialities." They are really not at all responsible for their condition, and thus are in no way able to cope with it. They are trapped in a determined universe. Without some kind of responsibility on the part of the protagonist there is opportunity neither for tragic elevation nor tragic fall. The Wingfields were doomed the moment they were born. At best their struggles will allow them to survive . . . for a time. They will never be allowed to triumph. Thus their struggles, their hopes, and even their eventual destruction can never move far beyond pathos. The beauty and magic of *The Glass Menagerie* is that this pathos is genuine, objective, and deeply moving.

---

[2] Williams, "Desire and the Black Masseur," *One Arm and Other Stories* (New York, 1948), 85.

Tennessee Williams (1911–1983)
MEMOIRS   *1972*

Tennessee Williams published Memoirs *in 1972, after establishing himself as one of the most successful American playwrights. The two excerpts included here concern his feelings about* Cat on a Hot Tin Roof *and his feelings about being a writer.*

Well, now, about plays, what about them? Plays are written and then, if they are lucky, they are performed, and if their luck still holds, which is not too frequently the case, their performance is so successful that both audience and critics at the first night are aware that they are being offered a dramatic work which is both honest and entertaining and also somehow capable of engaging their aesthetic appreciation.

I have never liked to talk about the professional side of my life. Am I afraid that it is a bird that will be startled away by discussion, as by a hawk's shadow? Something like that, I suppose.

People are always asking me, at those symposia to which I've been subjected in recent years, which is my favorite among the plays I have written, the number of which eludes my recollection, and I either say to them, "Always the latest" or I succumb to my instinct for the truth and say, "I suppose it must be the published version of *Cat on a Hot Tin Roof*."

That play comes closest to being both a work of art and a work of craft. It is really very well put together, in my opinion, and all its characters are amusing and credible and touching. Also it adheres to the valuable edict of Aristotle that a tragedy must have unity of time and place and magnitude of theme.

The set in *Cat* never changes and its running time is exactly the time of its action, meaning that one act, timewise, follows directly upon the other, and I know of no other modern American play in which this is accomplished.

However my reasons for liking *Cat* best are deeper than that. I believe that in *Cat* I reached beyond myself, in the second act, to a kind of crude eloquence of expression in Big Daddy that I have managed to give no other character of my creation.

The story of *Cat's* production in 1954 and the disaster that followed upon its enormous success must be told now.

[Director Elia] Kazan immediately shared Audrey's [Wood, Williams's agent] enthusiasm for *Cat* but he said that it was faulty in one act. I assumed that he meant the first act, but no, it was the third act. He wanted a more admirable heroine than the Maggie offered in the original script.

Inwardly I disagreed. I thought that in Maggie I had presented a very true and moving portrait of a young woman whose frustration in love and whose practicality drove her to the literal seduction of an unwilling young man. Seduction is too soft a word. Brick was literally forced back to bed by Maggie, when she confiscated his booze . . .

Then I also had to violate my own intuition by having Big Daddy re-enter the stage in Act Three. I saw nothing for him to do in that act when he re-entered and I did not think that it was dramatically proper that he should re-enter. Consequently I had him tell "the elephant story." This was assaulted by censors. I was told it must be removed. The material which I then had to put in its place was always offensive to me.

I would not tell you this except for the consequences to me as a writer after *Cat* had received its Critics' Award and its Pulitzer.

Even though I always go crazy on opening nights, the New York opening of *Cat* was particularly dreadful. I thought it was a failure, a distortion of what I had intended. After the show was over I thought I had heard coughs all during the performance. I suppose there weren't that many, probably the usual number. And it did become my biggest, my longest-running play. But after the show was over on opening night, Kazan said, "Let's go to my apartment until the reviews are out." He was totally confident that it would be a hit. I met Audrey Wood outside, and at the time I was totally dependent on her for any creative confidence; and so I said, "Audrey, we're all going up to the Kazans' to wait for the notices." She said, "Oh no, I have other plans." I was hurt, and said something mean. . . .

What is it like being a writer? I would say it is like being free.

I know that some writers aren't free, they are professionally employed, which is quite a different thing.

Professionally, they are probably better writers in the conventional sense of "better." They have an ear to the ground of best-seller demands: They please their publishers and presumably their public as well.

But they are not free and so they are not what I regard a true writer as being.

To be free is to have achieved your life.

It means any number of freedoms.

It means the freedom to stop when you please, to go where and when you please, it means to be voyager here and there, one who flees many hotels, sad or happy, without obstruction and without much regret.

It means the freedom of being. And someone has wisely observed, if you can't be yourself, what's the point of being anything at all?

I am not a frequent reader nor quoter of Scriptures and yet I love a piece of advice which occurs among them:

"Let thy light so shine among men that they see thy good works and glorify thy Father which is in heaven."

There is a New Journalism, there is a New Criticism, there is a new look and style of cinema and theater, of practically everything that we live with, but what I think we most need is a New Morality.

And I think we've arrived at a point where that is a necessity of continued and bearable existence.

Brenda Murphy (b. 1950)
TENNESSEE WILLIAMS AND ELIA KAZAN COLLABORATE ON *CAT*   1991

Theater is a collaborative art, and numerous plays have been altered because of suggestions of director or actor. The collaboration of Tennessee Williams and director Elia Kazan was special because both were powerful personalities and each respected the other. The Cat on a Hot Tin Roof *that we know is much different from the one that Williams first wrote. He was willing to make many of the creative changes suggested by Kazan.*

[Director Elia Kazan's] imagination stimulated by Big Daddy's rhetorical power, Kazan developed the production around the impetus of direct communication between the characters and the audience. At the beginning of Act 2, for example, he made a note to himself to have Big Daddy come downstage facing the audience and talk straight out to them while the others remained way upstage, even out on the gallery. Williams agreed with Kazan about the power of Big Daddy's character and the centrality of words in the play. In *Memoirs* he wrote, "In *Cat* I reached beyond myself, in the second act, to a kind of crude eloquence of expression in Big Daddy that I have managed to give no other character of my creation."[1]

Although Williams had incorporated the idea of addressing the audience in the "recitative" speeches of Maggie and Brick in the early scripts, he had not counted on what was in 1955 the radical concept that Kazan devised for the production. As Kazan noted in a later interview, the conventions of representational realism were so entrenched in the Broadway theater of the fifties that foregrounding the production's theatricality to the extent of having the characters address the audience directly had been considered anathema for many years. The last time he could remember it being done was in the production of *Our Town*° in 1938.[2]

Kazan's pride in this rejection of realistic convention and his continuing interest in subjectifying theatrical experience were evident in an interview he gave in the early sixties:

> I was busting out of the goddamned proscenium theater uptown. In *Cat on a Hot Tin Roof* I had everybody address the audience continually. Every time they had one of those long speeches they'd turn and say it to the audience. Nobody thought anything of it once we opened. But there was a hell of a lot of bitching about it before. . . . The whole second act of *Cat* was a long address by Burl Ives to the audience. I had him address various members of the audience . . . "what would *you* do?" is implicit in this kind of staging. It sucks the audience into the experience and emotion of that moment.[3]

Kazan wrote in his autobiography that he had to convince Williams to accept his notion of how Burl Ives would play the part of Big Daddy. When Kazan said he was going to bring Ives right down to the edge of the forestage, have him "look the audience right in the eye, and speak it directly to them," Williams protested that *Cat* was a realistic play, and should be kept within the representational conventions. When pressed by Kazan to say whether old cotton planters actually talked that eloquently and that long without interruption, Williams replied that they did. After all, who would dare interrupt them?[4] Nonetheless

[1]Tennessee Williams, *Memoirs* (Garden City: Doubleday, 1975).

[2]Michel Ciment, *Kazan on Kazan* (New York: Viking, 1974) 47.

[3]Quoted in Richard Schechner and Theodore Hoffman, " 'Look, There's the American Theatre': An Interview with Elia Kazan," *Tulane Drama Review,* 9 (Winter 1964): 71.

[4]Elia Kazan, *Elia Kazan: A Life* (New York: Knopf, 1988) 541–42.

Our Town: In this play by Thornton Wilder, a character called the Stage Manager speaks to the audience throughout the play.

Kazan pursued his concept for the production in the face of Williams's skepticism, if not his opposition.

The Design

When the central dynamic of the production had been established as direct communication between the characters and the audience, it had to imbue all the elements of the stage language. Here Kazan reports that he did run into opposition from Williams, who had a clear idea of what he thought the set should be like, an image that had evolved as he had revised the play. In the notes for the designer he prepared for the script preceding the November pre-rehearsal version, Williams described the basic plan of the set that was eventually used for the production: a bed–sitting room in a Mississippi Delta plantation, opening onto an upstairs gallery and showing white balustrades against a fair summer sky that fades into dusk and night during the course of the play. This is what is needed to support the action of the play which, as Williams was fond of pointing out, observed the unities of time and place, the action of the play being confined to the single set and occupying exactly the amount of time it took to enact on stage. The lighting was obviously crucial for this play, to show the passage of time that is a central thematic concern as well as a structural one.

Beyond this, however, Williams's original image of the set was strikingly different from the set Kazan and Jo Mielziner eventually devised between them. Williams described the room as Victorian, with a touch of the Far East, and poetically haunted by the tender relationship of Jack Straw and Peter Ochello. He noted that the room should not have changed much since Straw and Ochello's time. To suggest the style for the design, Williams referred the designer to the reproduction he had seen of a faded photograph of the verandah of Robert Louis Stevenson's home in Samoa: "There was a quality of tender light on weathered wood, such as porch-furniture made of bamboo and wicker, exposed to tropical suns and tropical rains, which came to mind when I thought about the set for this play" (RV xiii).° The photograph, he wrote, also brought to mind "the grace and comfort of light, the reassurance it gives, on a late and fair afternoon in summer, the way that no matter what, even dread of death, is gently touched and soothed by it. For the set is the background for a play that deals with human extremities of emotion and needs that softness behind it" (RV xiii).

Williams described in detail the big, slightly raked, double bed and the "entertainment center" that were the most significant objects in the set, and then he cautioned the designer, lest he feel that the previous description confined him to literal realism. As in the published "Note for the Designer," Williams envisioned that "the set should be far less realistic than I have so far implied in this description of it": The walls should dissolve mysteriously into the air below the ceiling; the set should be roofed by the sky; stars and moon suggested by traces of milky pallor, as if they were observed through a telescope lens out of focus (RV xiv). The original note, however, added the idea that a spiral nebula might be faintly suggested in order to suggest the "mystery of the cosmos," which Williams thought should be a visible presence in the play, almost as present as an actor in it. He also thought that the cloud effects and the sound effects for the windstorm in Act 3 should be as unrealistic as the set. As he revised the script, however, Williams began to reconceptualize the set as well. In November

RV: The reading version of the play (New York: New American Library, 1958), which has both versions of the third act.

he sent off a rewrite of the scene description suggesting that the room should appear to have been remodeled since Straw and Ochello's time, and now had an open, Japanese effect. The canopied bed, he suggested, could appear to have been removed from an Italian renaissance palazzo when Big Daddy and Big Mama raided Europe a few years previously.

When Kazan and Mielziner began talking about the design, their concept of a production that foregrounded the characters' rhetorical appeals to the audience became the central element in their discussion. Kazan has written:

> Jo Mielziner and I had read the play in the same way; we saw its great merit was its brilliant rhetoric and its theatricality. Jo didn't see the play as realistic any more than I did. If it was to be done realistically, I would have to contrive stage business to keep the old man talking those great second-act speeches turned out front and pretend that it was just another day in the life of the Pollitt family. This would, it seemed to me, amount to an apology to the audience for the glory of the author's language. It didn't seem like just another day in the life of a cotton planter's family to Jo or to me; it seemed like the best kind of theater, the kind we were interested in encouraging, the theater theatrical, not pretending any longer that an audience wasn't out there to be addressed but having a performer as great as Burl Ives acknowledge their presence at all times and even make eye contact with individuals.[5]

Accordingly, Kazan wrote, "I caused Jo to design our setting as I wished, a large, triangular platform, tipped toward the audience and holding only one piece of furniture, an ornate bed. This brought the play down to its essentials and made it impossible for it to be played any way except as I preferred."[6]

The set was not quite so spare as Kazan remembered it, but the central point of his statement, that the presentational impulse was the dominant aesthetic factor in creating the design, has been fully corroborated by Mielziner. In his memoir, Mielziner described their discussion about the design much as Kazan did. Asked how he thought the "elephant story" should be handled proxemically, Mielziner told Kazan that he thought it should receive as much emphasis as possible: "I suggested that we have an area of the stage on which Big Daddy could come down close to the audience and deliver the lines with dramatic force." Mielziner wrote that Kazan was delighted with his answer, and "from this discussion grew the idea of creating a stage within the stage. It would be steeply raked toward the audience with one corner actually jutting out over the footlights. In its final form it turned out to be a sort of thrust stage."[7]

Mielziner's design was a departure from the subjective realism he had employed in *Menagerie, Streetcar,* and *Summer and Smoke,* in that he did not try to suggest through the material elements of the stage language that the events unfolding on stage were filtered through the mind of one of the characters. Instead, the design of the set projected the action out toward the audience, forcing it to become involved as though it were one of the characters. Extremely spare, the set was composed of two platforms, a large diamond-shaped one, a corner of which projected beyond the proscenium, and a smaller rectangle a foot lower at stage right. There were no doors, such actions as opening doors and looking into the mirror being mimed in this production. The only items of furniture

[5]Kazan 542–43.
[6]Kazan 543.
[7]*Designing for Theatre: A Memoir and a Portfolio* (New York: Bram Hall House, 1965) 183.

Mielziner drew in his sketches were the primary material signifiers: the large bed, which signified both Maggie and Brick's failing marriage and the lingering memory of Straw and Ochello; the entertainment center, which signified both Brick's immediate goal of escape from reality and the vacuous materialism that Williams saw in the fifties; and the daybed, which signified Brick's withdrawal from Maggie, their marriage, and life in general. The actual set, however, also held a wicker night table and a large wicker armchair which could accommodate either Burl Ives or two of the other actors. The overall effect was of a large playing space down front where the actors could address the audience as if from a bare platform.

The lines of the design contributed to this effect. The perspective was such that the corner of the ceiling came down to a point slightly to the left of upstage center, helping to focus the audience's attention on the point of the diamond where the characters addressed the audience. Mielziner took Williams's hints to give lighting a central function in the play, running a scrim from floor to ceiling along two sides of the set with strips of black velour indicating the lines of the columns outside the windows of the room when the light of the moon was projected through them. To signify sunlight, slide projections of blinds were thrown on the scrims, while the gallery and the lawn beyond the windows were blocked out. When characters on the gallery or the lawn were to be seen, the lights behind the scrim were brought up, making the actors visible to the audience, as had been done with *Streetcar.*

Two follow-spots were used in the production. One, on the audience's left, highlighted Maggie throughout Act 1 and picked up Big Mama, Maggie, and Brick in Act 2, as they were in turn nominally being addressed by Big Daddy, who was downstage talking to the audience. In Act 3 the light again shone on Maggie almost without interruption. The follow-spot on the audience's right highlighted the characters Maggie was addressing in Act 1, chiefly Brick, as she had her turn at "recitative." It shone on Big Daddy throughout Act 2 and picked up Brick, Big Mama, Gooper, Mae, and Maggie at various times during Act 3, emphasizing a significant entrance or a significant reaction indexically as it occurred. Contributing to the generally "golden" look of the production's lighting, the follow-spots were amber except when a character went out onto the gallery, when they were changed to blue. The follow-spots not only helped to avoid confusion by focusing the audience's attention where Kazan wanted it to be, they also contributed to the foregrounding of the theatricality in the production by "framing" specific characters and pieces of action. Kazan stylized the composition of his stage picture in *Cat,* and encoded a great deal of meaning through gesture, movement, and pose in the production. Using the follow-spots to highlight these formal compositions emphasized that what was happening onstage was not real life but theater.

In designing the furniture, both Kazan and Mielziner took their cue from Williams's earlier description of the set, emphasizing the qualities he had seen in the Robert Louis Stevenson photograph. Kazan had underlined elements of this description in his copy of the script. Listed together, they indicate quite well the direction Mielziner took with the design after their conferences:

> Delta's biggest cotton planter
> Far East
> The room must evoke some ghosts
> Gently . . . poetically haunted by a relationship . . . a tenderness which was uncommon

> Samoan Island
> tender light on weathered wood
> Bamboo . . . wicker
> [the entertainment center] monument . . . very complete . . . compact little shrine . . .
> all the comforts . . . illusions . . . hide [written in the margin, "Brick hides"] such
> things as the characters in the play are faced with (RV xii–xiv)

From these suggestions came the old wicker headboard with its huge and fantastically shaped design of two cornucopias, the matching wicker furniture, the carpet with its lushly fertile design of oversized flowers and vines, and the one object in the room that competed with the fertility symbol of the bed for the audience's attention, the oversized bar, hi-fi, radio, and television with its sleekly modern fifties lines. This object realized Williams's description of a compact modern shrine to all the comforts and illusions of contemporary life and signified Brick's retreat from human contact.

Kazan has said more than once that Williams did not like the set that Mielziner finally developed for *Cat* because he thought his play should be performed realistically. Kazan has also indicated that the set was a material signifier of his aesthetic vision in opposition to Williams's:

> I had the setting I'd asked for; Jo had given me what I wanted. Tennessee had approved of it earlier, when he was ready to approve of damn near anything I asked for, because I was the director he wanted. Now the setting was up onstage, too late to change, and on that setting there was only one way for any human to conduct himself: "out front" it's called. Dear Tennessee was stuck with my vision, like it or not.[8]

[8]Kazan 543.

Arthur Miller

Arthur Miller (b. 1915) has been the dean of American playwrights since the opening of *Death of a Salesman* in 1949. His steady output as a writer and a playwright began with his first publications after college in 1939, when he worked in the New York Federal Theatre Project, a branch of the Works Progress Administration (WPA), Franklin D. Roosevelt's huge depression-era effort to put Americans back to work.

Miller, the son of a Jewish immigrant, was born and raised during his early years in the Harlem section of Manhattan and later in Brooklyn after his father's business failed. In high school Miller thought of himself more as an athlete than as a student, and he had trouble getting teachers' recommendations for college. After considerable struggle and waiting, he entered the University of Michigan, where his talent as a playwright emerged under the tutelage of Kenneth Rowe, his playwriting professor. His undergraduate plays won important university awards and he became noticed by the Theatre Guild, a highly respected theater founded to present excellent plays (not necessarily commercial successes). His career was under way.

From 1939 to 1947 Miller wrote radio plays, screenplays, articles, stories, and a novel. His work covered a wide range of material, much of it growing out of his childhood memories of a tightly knit and somewhat eccentric family that provided him with a large gallery of characters. But he also dealt with political issues and problems of anti-Semitism, which was widespread in the 1930s and 1940s. Miller's political concerns have been a constant presence in his work since his earliest writings.

All My Sons (1947) was his first successful play. It ran on Broadway for three hundred performances, a remarkable record for a serious drama. The story centers on a man who knowingly produces defective parts for airplanes and then blames the subsequent crashes on his business partner, who is ruined and imprisoned. When the guilty man's son finds out the truth, he confronts his father and rebukes him. Ultimately, the man realizes not only that he has lost his son because of his deceit but that the dead pilots were also "all my sons." The play won the New York Drama Critics' Circle Award.

Miller's next play, *Death of a Salesman* (1949), was written in six weeks. Focusing on the American ideal of business success, its conclusions were a challenge to standard American business values. Willy Loman, first performed by Lee J. Cobb, was intended to be a warning for Americans in the postwar period of the cost of growing wealth and affluence.

Miller's next play, *The Crucible* (1953), portrayed witch-hunts of seventeenth-century New England, but most people recognized the subtext: It was about contemporary anti-Communist witch-hunts. In the late 1940s and early 1950s the House Un-American Activities Committee (HUAC) held hearings to flush out suspected Communists from all areas of American life, particularly the arts. Many writers, artists, and performers came under close, often unfair, scrutiny by HUAC for their own political views and allegiances and were often asked to testify against their friends. Many were blacklisted — prevented from working in commercial theaters and movie companies — some were imprisoned for not testifying at others' trials, and some had their reputations and careers destroyed.

Arthur Miller was fearless in facing down HUAC, and he was convicted of contempt of court for not testifying against his friends. For a time he too was blacklisted, but his contempt citation was reversed and he was not imprisoned. Given his personal political stance during this dangerous time, it is not a surprise to find that he usually chooses to write about matters of social concern.

In the 1990s Miller has become the darling of the London stage while at the same time being somewhat neglected in the United States. His most recent full-scale play is *Broken Glass* (1994), which played in regional theater before going to a brief run on Broadway, then a longer run in London's West End. The play concerns a woman who becomes paralyzed in response to the German persecution of the Jews known as *Kristallnacht* (night of crystal) which took place on November 9, 1938, and which made it clear that Jews were no longer safe in Hitler's Germany. The event takes its name from the broken glass that resulted from the night of violent rampages against the Jews and destruction of Jewish property which resulted in 91 Jewish dead, hundreds injured, and 7,500 businesses and 177 synagogues gutted. The subject of the play is intense, significant, and still timely.

DEATH OF A SALESMAN

Death of a Salesman (1949) was a hit from its first performances and has remained at the center of modern American drama ever since. It has been successful in China, where there were no salesmen, and in Europe, where many salesmen dominate certain industries. Everywhere this play has touched the hearts and minds of its audiences. Its success is a phenomenon of American drama.

The play was first performed in an environment that must be called experimental. Miller had originally conceived of a model of a man's head as the stage setting. He has said: "The first image that occurred to me which was to result in *Death of a Salesman* was of an enormous face the height of the proscenium arch which would appear and then open up, and we would see the inside of a man's head. In fact, *The Inside of His Head* was the first title." This technique was not used, but when Miller worked with the director and producer of the first production, he helped develop a setting that became a model for the "American style" in drama. The multilevel set permitted the play to shift from Willy Loman and his wife, Linda, having a conversation in their kitchen to their son's bedroom on the second level of the house. The set permitted portions of the stage to be reserved for Willy's visions of his brother, Ben, and for scenes outside the house such as Willy's interlude with the woman in Boston.

In a way, the setup of the stage respected Miller's original plan, but instead of portraying a cross-section of Willy's head, it presented a metaphor for a cross-section of his life. The audience felt that they were looking in on more than a living room, as in the nineteenth-century Ibsenist approach; they were looking in on an entire house and an entire life.

Using a cross-section of a house as a metaphor was an especially important device in this play because of the play's allusions to Greek tragedy. The great Greek tragedies usually portray the destruction of a house — such as the house of Atreus — in which "house" stands for a whole family, not a building. When Shakespeare's Hamlet dies, for example, his entire line dies with him. The death in *Death of a Salesman* implies the destruction of a family holding certain beliefs that have been wrong from the start.

The life of the salesman has given Willy a sense of dignity and worth, and he imagines that the modern world has corrupted that sense by robbing salesmen of the value of their personality. He thinks that the modern world has failed him, but he is wrong. His original belief — that what counts is not *what* you know but *whom* you know and how well you are liked — lies at the heart of his failure. When the play opens, he already has failed at the traveling salesman's job because he can no longer drive to his assigned territory. He cannot sell what he needs to sell.

Willy has inculcated his beliefs in his sons, Happy and Biff, and both are as ineffectual as their father. Willy doted on Biff and encouraged him to become a high school football star at the expense of his studies. But when Biff cannot pass an important course and then his plans to make up the work are subverted by his disillusionment in his father, his dreams of a college football career vanish. He cannot change, cannot recover from this defeat. Happy, like his father, builds castles in the air and assumes somehow that he will be successful, though he has nothing to back himself up with. He wants the glory — and he spends time in fanciful imaginings, as Willy does — but he cannot do the basic work that makes it possible to achieve glory. Ironically, it is the "anemic" Bernard — who studies hard, stresses personal honesty and diligence, and never brags — who is successful.

Linda supports Willy's illusions, allowing him to be a fraud by sharing — or pretending to believe — in his dream. Willy has permitted himself to feel that integrity, honesty, and fidelity are not as important as being well liked.

The play ends with Willy still unable to face the deceptions he has perpetuated. He commits suicide, believing that his sons will be able to follow in his footsteps and succeed where he did not; he thinks that his insurance money will save the house and the family. What he does not realize is that his sons are no more capable than he is. They have been corrupted by his thinking, his values, his beliefs. And they cannot solve the problems that overwhelmed him.

Death of a Salesman has been given a privileged position in American drama because it is a modern tragedy. Aristotle felt that only characters of noble birth could be tragic heroes, but Miller confounds this theory, as John Millington Synge did, by showing the human integrity in even the lowliest characters. Miller's Willy Loman is not a peasant, nor is he noble in the savage way that Maurya is in *Riders to the Sea*. In fact, Miller took a frightening risk in producing a figure that we find hard to like. Willy wants to be well liked, but as an audience we find it difficult to like a person who whines, complains, and accepts petty immorality as a normal way of life. Despite his character, we are awed by his fate.

One Chinese commentator said, after the Chinese production, that China is filled with such dreamers as Willy. Certainly America has been filled with them. Willy stands as an aspect of our culture, commercial and otherwise, that is at the center of our reflection of ourselves. Perhaps we react so strongly to Willy because we are afraid that we might easily become a Willy Loman if we are not vigilant about our moral views, our psychological well-being, and the limits of our commitment to success. Willy Loman has mesmerized audiences in America in many different economic circumstances: prosperity, recession, rapid growth, and cautious development. No matter what those circumstances, we have looked at the play as if looking in a mirror. What we have seen has always involved us, although it has not always made us pleased with ourselves.

Death of a Salesman in Performance

Death of a Salesman opened on Broadway on February 10, 1949, and won virtually every prize available for drama, including the Pulitzer Prize and the New York Drama Critics' Circle Award for best play. It ran on Broadway for an incredible 742 performances. Elia Kazan, director, was instrumental in establishing the play's innovative staging. Lee J. Cobb was cast as Willy, Mildred Dunnock as Linda, Arthur Kennedy as Biff, and Cameron Mitchell as Happy. The London production in July 1949, with Paul Muni as Willy and Kevin McCarthy as Biff, lasted 204 performances. Robert Coleman said of the New York production: "An explosion of emotional dynamite was set off last evening in the Morosco [Theater]. . . . In fashioning *Death of a Salesman* for them, author Arthur Miller and director Elia Kazan have collaborated on as exciting and devastating a theatrical blast as the nerves of modern playgoers can stand." Of Cobb, Howard Barnes said, "Cobb contributes a mammoth and magnificent portrayal of the central character. In his hands the salesman's frustration and final suicide are a matter of tremendous import."

An all-black production was directed by Lee Sankowich in Baltimore in 1972. Miller, in the audience on that production's opening night, commented that the play had been well received in "many countries and cultures" and that the Baltimore production further underscored the universality of the play. George C. Scott was praised for the power of his performance as Willy in New York's Circle in the Square production in 1975. A Chinese production directed by Arthur Miller was enormously successful in the 1980s. In the most celebrated revival of the play Dustin Hoffman portrayed Willy, John Malkovich played Biff, and Michael Rudman directed at the Broadhurst Theatre in New York in 1984. The critic Benedict Nightingale said of that production: "Somewhere at the core of him [Willy] an elaborate battle is being fought between dishonesty and honesty, glitter and substance, appearance and reality, between the promises or supposed promises of society and the claims of the self, between what Willy professes to value and what, perhaps without knowing it, he actually does value." In 1985 Dustin Hoffman brought his production of Miller's play to television, where it was viewed by an estimated twenty-five million people.

Arthur Miller (b. 1915)

DEATH OF A SALESMAN   *1949*

CERTAIN PRIVATE CONVERSATIONS IN TWO ACTS AND A REQUIEM

Characters

WILLY LOMAN	UNCLE BEN
LINDA	HOWARD WAGNER
BIFF	JENNY
HAPPY	STANLEY
BERNARD	MISS FORSYTHE
THE WOMAN	LETTA
CHARLEY	

The action takes place in Willy Loman's house and yard and in various places he visits in the New York and Boston of today.

(Throughout the play, in the stage directions, left and right mean stage left and stage right.)

ACT I

(A melody is heard, played upon a flute. It is small and fine, telling of grass and trees and the horizon. The curtain rises.)

(Before us is the Salesman's house. We are aware of towering, angular shapes behind it, surrounding it on all sides. Only the blue light of the sky falls upon the house and forestage; the surrounding area shows an angry glow of orange. As more light appears, we see a solid vault of apartment houses around the small, fragile-seeming home. An air of the dream clings to the place, a dream rising out of reality. The kitchen at center seems actual enough, for there is a kitchen table with three chairs, and a refrigerator. But no other fixtures are seen. At the back of the kitchen there is a draped entrance, which leads to the living room. To the right of the kitchen, on a level raised two feet, is a bedroom furnished only with a brass bedstead and a straight chair. On a shelf over the bed a silver athletic trophy stands. A window opens onto the apartment house at the side.)

(Behind the kitchen, on a level raised six and a half feet, is the boys' bedroom, at present barely visible. Two beds are dimly seen, and at the back of the room a dormer window. [This bedroom is above the unseen living room.] At the left a stairway curves up to it from the kitchen.)

(The entire setting is wholly or, in some places, partially transparent. The roofline of the house is one-dimensional; under and over it we see the apartment buildings. Before the house lies an apron, curving beyond the forestage into the orchestra. This forward area serves as the back yard as well as the locale of all Willy's imaginings and of his city scenes. Whenever the action is in the present the actors observe the imaginary wall-lines, entering the house only through its door at the left. But in the scenes of the past these boundaries are broken, and characters enter or leave a room by stepping "through" a wall onto the forestage.)

(From the right, Willy Loman, the Salesman, enters, carrying two large sample cases. The flute plays on. He hears but is not aware of it. He is past sixty years of age, dressed quietly. Even as he crosses the stage to the doorway of the house, his exhaustion is apparent. He unlocks the door, comes into the kitchen, and thankfully lets his burden down, feeling the soreness of his palms. A word-sigh escapes his lips — it might be "Oh, boy, oh, boy." He closes the door then carries his cases out into the living room, through the draped kitchen doorway.)

(Linda, his wife, has stirred in her bed at the right. She gets out and puts on a robe, listening. Most often jovial, she has developed an iron repression of her exceptions to Willy's behavior — she more than loves him, she admires him, as though his mercurial nature, his temper, his massive dreams and little cruelties, served her only as sharp reminders of the turbulent longings within him, longings which she shares but lacks the temperament to utter and follow to their end.)

LINDA (*hearing Willy outside the bedroom, calls with some trepidation*): Willy!
WILLY: It's all right. I came back.
LINDA: Why? What happened? (*Slight pause.*) Did something happen, Willy?
WILLY: No, nothing happened.
LINDA: You didn't smash the car, did you?
WILLY (*with casual irritation*): I said nothing happened. Didn't you hear me?
LINDA: Don't you feel well?

WILLY: I'm tired to the death. (*The flute has faded away. He sits on the bed beside her, a little numb.*) I couldn't make it. I just couldn't make it, Linda.

LINDA (*very carefully, delicately*): Where were you all day? You look terrible.

WILLY: I got as far as a little above Yonkers. I stopped for a cup of coffee. Maybe it was the coffee.

LINDA: What?

WILLY (*after a pause*): I suddenly couldn't drive anymore. The car kept going off onto the shoulder, y'know?

LINDA (*helpfully*): Oh. Maybe it was the steering again. I don't think Angelo knows the Studebaker.

WILLY: No, it's me, it's me. Suddenly I realize I'm goin' sixty miles an hour and I don't remember the last five minutes. I'm — I can't seem to — keep my mind to it.

LINDA: Maybe it's your glasses. You never went for your new glasses.

WILLY: No, I see everything. I came back ten miles an hour. It took me nearly four hours from Yonkers.

LINDA (*resigned*): Well, you'll just have to take a rest, Willy, you can't continue this way.

WILLY: I just got back from Florida.

LINDA: But you didn't rest your mind. Your mind is overactive, and the mind is what counts, dear.

WILLY: I'll start out in the morning. Maybe I'll feel better in the morning. (*She is taking off his shoes.*) These goddam arch supports are killing me.

LINDA: Take an aspirin. Should I get you an aspirin? It'll soothe you.

WILLY (*with wonder*): I was driving along, you understand? And I was fine. I was even observing the scenery. You can imagine, me looking at scenery, on the road every week of my life. But it's so beautiful up there, Linda, the trees are so thick, and the sun is warm. I opened the windshield and just let the warm air bathe over me. And then all of a sudden I'm goin' off the road! I'm tellin' ya, I absolutely forgot I was driving. If I'd've gone the other way over the white line I might've killed somebody. So I went on again — and five minutes later I'm dreamin' again, and I nearly — (*He presses two fingers against his eyes.*) I have such thoughts, I have such strange thoughts.

LINDA: Willy, dear. Talk to them again. There's no reason why you can't work in New York.

WILLY: They don't need me in New York. I'm the New England man. I'm vital in New England.

LINDA: But you're sixty years old. They can't expect you to keep traveling every week.

WILLY: I'll have to send a wire to Portland. I'm supposed to see Brown and Morrison tomorrow morning at ten o'clock to show the line. Goddammit, I could sell them! (*He starts putting on his jacket.*)

LINDA (*taking the jacket from him*): Why don't you go down to the place tomorrow and tell Howard you've simply got to work in New York? You're too accommodating, dear.

WILLY: If old man Wagner was alive I'd a been in charge of New York now! That man was a prince, he was a masterful man. But that boy of his, that Howard, he don't appreciate. When I went north the first time, the Wagner Company didn't know where New England was!

LINDA: Why don't you tell those things to Howard, dear?

WILLY (*encouraged*): I will, I definitely will. Is there any cheese?

LINDA: I'll make you a sandwich.

WILLY: No, go to sleep. I'll take some milk. I'll be up right away. The boys in?

LINDA: They're sleeping. Happy took Biff on a date tonight.

WILLY (*interested*): That so?

LINDA: It was so nice to see them shaving together, one behind the other, in the bathroom. And going out together. You notice? The whole house smells of shaving lotion.

WILLY: Figure it out. Work a lifetime to pay off a house. You finally own it, and there's nobody to live in it.

LINDA: Well, dear, life is a casting off. It's always that way.

WILLY: No, no, some people — some people accomplish something. Did Biff say anything after I went this morning?

LINDA: You shouldn't have criticized him, Willy, especially after he just got off the train. You mustn't lose your temper with him.

WILLY: When the hell did I lose my temper? I simply asked him if he was making any money. Is that a criticism?

LINDA: But, dear, how could he make any money?

WILLY (*worried and angered*): There's such an undercurrent in him. He became a moody man. Did he apologize when I left this morning?

LINDA: He was crestfallen, Willy. You know how he admires you. I think if he finds himself, then you'll both be happier and not fight any more.

WILLY: How can he find himself on a farm? Is that a life? A farmhand? In the beginning, when he was young, I thought, well, a young man, it's good for him to tramp around, take a lot of different jobs. But it's more than ten years now and he has yet to make thirty-five dollars a week!

LINDA: He's finding himself, Willy.

WILLY: Not finding yourself at the age of thirty-four is a disgrace!

LINDA: Shh!

WILLY: The trouble is he's lazy, goddammit!

LINDA: Willy, please!

WILLY: Biff is a lazy bum!

LINDA: They're sleeping. Get something to eat. Go on down.

WILLY: Why did he come home? I would like to know what brought him home.

LINDA: I don't know. I think he's still lost, Willy. I think he's very lost.

WILLY: Biff Loman is lost. In the greatest country in the world a young man with such — personal attractiveness, gets lost. And such a hard worker. There's one thing about Biff — he's not lazy.

LINDA: Never.

WILLY (*with pity and resolve*): I'll see him in the morning; I'll have a nice talk with him. I'll get him a job selling. He could be big in no time. My God! Remember how they used to follow him around in high school? When he smiled at one of them their faces lit up. When he walked down the street . . . (*He loses himself in reminiscences.*)

LINDA (*trying to bring him out of it*): Willy, dear, I got a new kind of American-type cheese today. It's whipped.

WILLY: Why do you get American when I like Swiss?

LINDA: I just thought you'd like a change —

WILLY: I don't want a change! I want Swiss cheese. Why am I always being contradicted?

LINDA (*with a covering laugh*): I thought it would be a surprise.

WILLY: Why don't you open a window in here, for God's sake?

LINDA (*with infinite patience*): They're all open, dear.

WILLY: The way they boxed us in here. Bricks and windows, windows and bricks.

LINDA: We should've bought the land next door.

WILLY: The street is lined with cars. There's not a breath of fresh air in the neighborhood. The grass don't grow anymore, you can't raise a carrot in the back yard. They should've had a law against apartment houses. Remember those two beautiful elm trees out there? When I and Biff hung the swing between them?

LINDA: Yeah, like being a million miles from the city.

WILLY: They should've arrested the builder for cutting those down. They massacred the neighborhood. (*Lost.*) More and more I think of those days, Linda. This time of year it was lilac and wisteria. And then the peonies would come out, and the daffodils. What fragrance in this room!

LINDA: Well, after all, people had to move somewhere.

WILLY: No, there's more people now.

LINDA: I don't think there's more people. I think —

WILLY: There's more people! That's what's ruining this country! Population is getting out of control. The competition is maddening! Smell the stink from that apartment house! And another one on the other side . . . How can they whip cheese?

(*On Willy's last line, Biff and Happy raise themselves up in their beds, listening.*)

LINDA: Go down, try it. And be quiet.

WILLY (*turning to Linda, guiltily*): You're not worried about me, are you, sweetheart?

BIFF: What's the matter?

HAPPY: Listen!

LINDA: You've got too much on the ball to worry about.

WILLY: You're my foundation and my support, Linda.

LINDA: Just try to relax, dear. You make mountains out of molehills.

WILLY: I won't fight with him any more. If he wants to go back to Texas, let him go.

LINDA: He'll find his way.

WILLY: Sure. Certain men just don't get started till later in life. Like Thomas Edison, I think. Or B. F. Goodrich. One of them was deaf. (*He starts for the bedroom doorway.*) I'll put my money on Biff.

LINDA: And Willy — if it's warm Sunday we'll drive in the country. And we'll open the windshield, and take lunch.

WILLY: No, the windshields don't open on the new cars.

LINDA: But you opened it today.

WILLY: Me? I didn't. (*He stops.*) Now isn't that peculiar! Isn't that a remarkable — (*He breaks off in amazement and fright as the flute is heard distantly.*)

LINDA: What, darling?

WILLY: That is the most remarkable thing.

LINDA: What, dear?

WILLY: I was thinking of the Chevvy. (*Slight pause.*) Nineteen twenty-eight . . . when I had that red Chevvy — (*Breaks off.*) That funny? I coulda sworn I was driving that Chevvy today.

LINDA: Well, that's nothing. Something must've reminded you.

WILLY: Remarkable. Ts. Remember those days? The way Biff used to simonize that car? The dealer refused to believe there was eighty thousand miles on it. (*He shakes his head.*) Heh! (*To Linda.*) Close your eyes, I'll be right up. (*He walks out of the bedroom.*)

HAPPY (*to Biff*): Jesus, maybe he smashed up the car again!

LINDA (*calling after Willy*): Be careful on the stairs, dear! The cheese is on the middle shelf! (*She turns, goes over to the bed, takes his jacket, and goes out of the bedroom.*)

(*Light has risen on the boys' room. Unseen, Willy is heard talking to himself, "Eighty thousand miles," and a little laugh. Biff gets out of bed, comes downstage a bit, and stands attentively. Biff is two years older than his brother Happy, well built, but in these days bears a worn air and seems less self-assured. He has succeeded less, and his dreams are stronger and less acceptable than Happy's. Happy is tall, powerfully made. Sexuality is like a visible color on him, or a scent that many women have discovered. He, like his brother, is lost, but in a different way, for he has never allowed himself to turn his face toward defeat and is thus more confused and hard-skinned, although seemingly more content.*)

HAPPY (*getting out of bed*): He's going to get his license taken away if he keeps that up. I'm getting nervous about him, y'know, Biff?

BIFF: His eyes are going.

HAPPY: No, I've driven with him. He sees all right. He just doesn't keep his mind on it. I drove into the city with him last week. He stops at a green light and then it turns red and he goes. (*He laughs.*)

BIFF: Maybe he's color-blind.

HAPPY: Pop? Why he's got the finest eye for color in the business. You know that.

BIFF (*sitting down on his bed*): I'm going to sleep.

HAPPY: You're not still sour on Dad, are you, Biff?

BIFF: He's all right, I guess.

WILLY (*underneath them, in the living room*): Yes, sir, eighty thousand miles — eighty-two thousand!

BIFF: You smoking?

HAPPY (*holding out a pack of cigarettes*): Want one?

BIFF (*taking a cigarette*): I can never sleep when I smell it.

WILLY: What a simonizing job, heh!

HAPPY (*with deep sentiment*): Funny, Biff, y'know? Us sleeping in here again? The old beds. (*He pats his bed affectionately.*) All the talk that went across those two beds, huh? Our whole lives.

BIFF: Yeah. Lotta dreams and plans.

HAPPY (*with a deep and masculine laugh*): About five hundred women would like to know what was said in this room.

(*They share a soft laugh.*)

BIFF: Remember that big Betsy something — what the hell was her name — over on Bushwick Avenue?

HAPPY (*combing his hair*): With the collie dog!

BIFF: That's the one. I got you in there, remember?

HAPPY: Yeah, that was my first time — I think. Boy, there was a pig. (*They laugh, almost crudely.*) You taught me everything I know about women. Don't forget that.

BIFF: I bet you forgot how bashful you used to be. Especially with girls.

HAPPY: Oh, I still am, Biff.

BIFF: Oh, go on.

HAPPY: I just control it, that's all. I think I got less bashful and you got more so. What happened, Biff? Where's the old humor, the old confidence? (*He shakes Biff's knee. Biff gets up and moves restlessly about the room.*) What's the matter?

BIFF: Why does Dad mock me all the time?

HAPPY: He's not mocking you, he —

BIFF: Everything I say there's a twist of mockery on his face. I can't get near him.

HAPPY: He just wants you to make good, that's all. I wanted to talk to you about Dad for a long time, Biff. Something's — happening to him. He — talks to himself.

BIFF: I noticed that this morning. But he always mumbled.

HAPPY: But not so noticeable. It got so embarrassing I sent him to Florida. And you know something? Most of the time he's talking to you.

BIFF: What's he say about me?

HAPPY: I can't make it out.

BIFF: What's he say about me?

HAPPY: I think the fact that you're not settled, that you're still kind of up in the air . . .

BIFF: There's one or two other things depressing him, Happy.

HAPPY: What do you mean?

BIFF: Never mind. Just don't lay it all to me.

HAPPY: But I think if you just got started — I mean — is there any future for you out there?

BIFF: I tell ya, Hap, I don't know what the future is. I don't know — what I'm supposed to want.

HAPPY: What do you mean?

BIFF: Well, I spent six or seven years after high school trying to work myself up. Shipping clerk, salesman, business of one kind or another. And it's a measly manner of existence. To get on that subway on the hot mornings in summer. To devote your whole life to keeping stock, or making phone calls, or selling or buying. To suffer fifty weeks of the year for the sake of a two-week vacation, when all you really desire is to be outdoors, with your shirt off. And always to have to get ahead of the next fella. And still — that's how you build a future.

HAPPY: Well, you really enjoy it on a farm? Are you content out there?

BIFF (*with rising agitation*): Hap, I've had twenty or thirty different kinds of jobs since I left home before the war, and it always turns out the same. I just realized it lately. In Nebraska when I herded cattle, and the Dakotas, and Arizona, and now in Texas. It's why I came home now, I guess, because

I realized it. This farm I work on, it's spring there now, see? And they've got about fifteen new colts. There's nothing more inspiring or — beautiful than the sight of a mare and a new colt. And it's cool there now, see? Texas is cool now, and it's spring. And whenever spring comes to where I am, I suddenly get the feeling, my God, I'm not gettin' anywhere! What the hell am I doing, playing around with horses, twenty-eight dollars a week! I'm thirty-four years old, I oughta be makin' my future. That's when I come running home. And now, I get here, and I don't know what to do with myself. (*After a pause.*) I've always made a point of not wasting my life, and every time I come back here I know that all I've done is to waste my life.

HAPPY: You're a poet, you know that, Biff? You're a — you're an idealist!

BIFF: No, I'm mixed up very bad. Maybe I oughta get married. Maybe I oughta get stuck into something. Maybe that's my trouble. I'm like a boy. I'm not married, I'm not in business, I just — I'm like a boy. Are you content, Hap? You're a success, aren't you? Are you content?

HAPPY: Hell, no!

BIFF: Why? You're making money, aren't you?

HAPPY (*moving about with energy, expressiveness*): All I can do now is wait for the merchandise manager to die. And suppose I get to be merchandise manager? He's a good friend of mine, and he just built a terrific estate on Long Island. And he lived there about two months and sold it, and now he's building another one. He can't enjoy it once it's finished. And I know that's just what I would do. I don't know what the hell I'm workin' for. Sometimes I sit in my apartment — all alone. And I think of the rent I'm paying. And it's crazy. But then, it's what I always wanted. My own apartment, a car, and plenty of women. And still, goddammit, I'm lonely.

BIFF (*with enthusiasm*): Listen, why don't you come out West with me?

HAPPY: You and I, heh?

BIFF: Sure, maybe we could buy a ranch. Raise cattle, use our muscles. Men built like we are should be working out in the open.

HAPPY (*avidly*): The Loman Brothers, heh?

BIFF (*with vast affection*): Sure, we'd be known all over the counties!

HAPPY (*enthralled*): That's what I dream about, Biff. Sometimes I want to just rip my clothes off in the middle of the store and outbox that goddam merchandise manager. I mean I can outbox, outrun and outlift anybody in that store, and I have to take orders from those common, petty sons-of-bitches till I can't stand it anymore.

BIFF: I'm tellin' you, kid, if you were with me I'd be happy out there.

HAPPY (*enthused*): See, Biff, everybody around me is so false that I'm constantly lowering my ideals . . .

BIFF: Baby, together we'd stand up for one another, we'd have someone to trust.

HAPPY: If I were around you —

BIFF: Hap, the trouble is we weren't brought up to grub for money. I don't know how to do it.

HAPPY: Neither can I!

BIFF: Then let's go!

HAPPY: The only thing is — what can you make out there?

BIFF: But look at your friend. Builds an estate and then hasn't the peace of mind to live in it.

HAPPY: Yeah, but when he walks into the store the waves part in front of him. That's fifty-two thousand dollars a year coming through the revolving door, and I got more in my pinky finger than he's got in his head.

BIFF: Yeah, but you just said —

HAPPY: I gotta show some of those pompous, self-important executives over there that Hap Loman can make the grade. I want to walk into the store the way he walks in. Then I'll go with you, Biff. We'll be together yet, I swear. But take those two we had tonight. Now weren't they gorgeous creatures?

BIFF: Yeah, yeah, most gorgeous I've had in years.

HAPPY: I get that any time I want, Biff. Whenever I feel disgusted. The only trouble is, it gets like bowling or something. I just keep knockin' them over and it doesn't mean anything. You still run around a lot?

BIFF: Naa. I'd like to find a girl — steady, somebody with substance.

HAPPY: That's what I long for.

BIFF: Go on! You'd never come home.

HAPPY: I would! Somebody with character, with resistance! Like Mom, y'know? You're gonna call me a bastard when I tell you this. That girl Charlotte I was with tonight is engaged to be married in five weeks. (*He tries on his new hat.*)

BIFF: No kiddin'!

HAPPY: Sure, the guy's in line for the vice-presidency of the store. I don't know what gets into me, maybe I just have an overdeveloped sense of competition or something, but I went and ruined her, and furthermore I can't get rid of her. And he's the third executive I've done that to. Isn't that a crummy characteristic? And to top it all, I go to their weddings! (*Indignantly, but laughing.*) Like I'm not supposed to take bribes. Manufacturers offer me a hundred-dollar bill now and then to throw an order their way. You know how honest I am, but it's like this girl, see. I hate myself for it.

Because I don't want the girl, and, still, I take it and — I love it!

BIFF: Let's go to sleep.

HAPPY: I guess we didn't settle anything, heh?

BIFF: I just got one idea that I think I'm going to try.

HAPPY: What's that?

BIFF: Remember Bill Oliver?

HAPPY: Sure, Oliver is very big now. You want to work for him again?

BIFF: No, but when I quit he said something to me. He put his arm on my shoulder, and he said, "Biff, if you ever need anything, come to me."

HAPPY: I remember that. That sounds good.

BIFF: I think I'll go to see him. If I could get ten thousand or even seven or eight thousand dollars I could buy a beautiful ranch.

HAPPY: I bet he'd back you. 'Cause he thought highly of you, Biff. I mean, they all do. You're well liked, Biff. That's why I say to come back here, and we both have the apartment. And I'm tellin' you, Biff, any babe you want . . .

BIFF: No, with a ranch I could do the work I like and still be something. I just wonder though. I wonder if Oliver still thinks I stole that carton of basketballs.

HAPPY: Oh, he probably forgot that long ago. It's almost ten years. You're too sensitive. Anyway, he didn't really fire you.

BIFF: Well, I think he was going to. I think that's why I quit. I was never sure whether he knew or not. I know he thought the world of me, though. I was the only one he'd let lock up the place.

WILLY (below): You gonna wash the engine, Biff?

HAPPY: Shh!

(Biff looks at Happy, who is gazing down, listening. Willy is mumbling in the parlor.)

HAPPY: You hear that?

(They listen. Willy laughs warmly.)

BIFF (growing angry): Doesn't he know Mom can hear that?

WILLY: Don't get your sweater dirty, Biff!

(A look of pain crosses Biff's face.)

HAPPY: Isn't that terrible? Don't leave again, will you? You'll find a job here. You gotta stick around. I don't know what to do about him, it's getting embarrassing.

WILLY: What a simonizing job!

BIFF: Mom's hearing that!

WILLY: No kiddin', Biff, you got a date? Wonderful!

HAPPY: Go on to sleep. But talk to him in the morning, will you?

BIFF (reluctantly getting into bed): With her in the house. Brother!

HAPPY (getting into bed): I wish you'd have a good talk with him.

(The light on their room begins to fade.)

BIFF (to himself in bed): That selfish, stupid . . .

HAPPY: Sh . . . Sleep, Biff.

(Their light is out. Well before they have finished speaking, Willy's form is dimly seen below in the darkened kitchen. He opens the refrigerator, searches in there, and takes out a bottle of milk. The apartment houses are fading out, and the entire house and surroundings become covered with leaves. Music insinuates itself as the leaves appear.)

WILLY: Just wanna be careful with those girls, Biff, that's all. Don't make any promises. No promises of any kind. Because a girl, y'know, they always believe what you tell 'em, and you're very young, Biff, you're too young to be talking seriously to girls.

(Light rises on the kitchen. Willy, talking, shuts the refrigerator door and comes downstage to the kitchen table. He pours milk into a glass. He is totally immersed in himself, smiling faintly.)

WILLY: Too young entirely, Biff. You want to watch your schooling first. Then when you're all set, there'll be plenty of girls for a boy like you. (He smiles broadly at a kitchen chair.) That so? The girls pay for you? (He laughs.) Boy, you must really be makin' a hit.

(Willy is gradually addressing — physically — a point offstage, speaking through the wall of the kitchen, and his voice has been rising in volume to that of a normal conversation.)

WILLY: I been wondering why you polish the car so careful. Ha! Don't leave the hubcaps, boys. Get the chamois to the hubcaps. Happy, use newspaper on the windows, it's the easiest thing. Show him how to do it, Biff! You see, Happy? Pad it up, use it like a pad. That's it, that's it, good work. You're doin' all right, Hap. (He pauses, then nods in approbation for a few seconds, then looks upward.) Biff, first thing we gotta do when we get time is clip that big branch over the house. Afraid it's gonna fall in a storm and hit the roof. Tell you what. We get a rope and sling her around, and then we climb up there with a couple of saws and take her down. Soon as you finish the car, boys, I wanna see ye. I got a surprise for you, boys.

BIFF (offstage): Whatta ya got, Dad?

WILLY: No, you finish first. Never leave a job till you're finished — remember that. (Looking toward the "big trees.") Biff, up in Albany I saw a beautiful hammock. I think I'll buy it next trip, and we'll hang it right between those two elms. Wouldn't that be something? Just swingin' there under those branches. Boy, that would be . . .

(*Young Biff and Young Happy appear from the direction Willy was addressing. Happy carries rags and a pail of water. Biff, wearing a sweater with a block "S," carries a football.*)

BIFF (*pointing in the direction of the car offstage*): How's that, Pop, professional?

WILLY: Terrific. Terrific job, boys. Good work, Biff.

HAPPY: Where's the surprise, Pop?

WILLY: In the back seat of the car.

HAPPY: Boy! (*He runs off.*)

BIFF: What is it, Dad? Tell me, what'd you buy?

WILLY (*laughing, cuffs him*): Never mind, something I want you to have.

BIFF (*turns and starts off*): What is it, Hap?

HAPPY (*offstage*): It's a punching bag!

BIFF: Oh, Pop!

WILLY: It's got Gene Tunney's signature on it!

(*Happy runs onstage with a punching bag.*)

BIFF: Gee, how'd you know we wanted a punching bag?

WILLY: Well, it's the finest thing for the timing.

HAPPY (*lies down on his back and pedals with his feet*): I'm losing weight, you notice, Pop?

WILLY (*to Happy*): Jumping rope is good too.

BIFF: Did you see the new football I got?

WILLY (*examining the ball*): Where'd you get a new ball?

BIFF: The coach told me to practice my passing.

WILLY: That so? And he gave you the ball, heh?

BIFF: Well, I borrowed it from the locker room. (*He laughs confidentially.*)

WILLY (*laughing with him at the theft*): I want you to return that.

HAPPY: I told you he wouldn't like it!

BIFF (*angrily*): Well, I'm bringing it back!

WILLY (*stopping the incipient argument, to Happy*): Sure, he's gotta practice with a regulation ball, doesn't he? (*To Biff.*) Coach'll probably congratulate you on your initiative!

BIFF: Oh, he keeps congratulating my initiative all the time, Pop.

WILLY: That's because he likes you. If somebody else took that ball there'd be an uproar. So what's the report, boys, what's the report?

BIFF: Where'd you go this time, Dad? Gee we were lonesome for you.

WILLY (*pleased, puts an arm around each boy and they come down to the apron*): Lonesome, heh?

BIFF: Missed you every minute.

WILLY: Don't say? Tell you a secret, boys. Don't breathe it to a soul. Someday I'll have my own business, and I'll never have to leave home anymore.

HAPPY: Like Uncle Charley, heh?

WILLY: Bigger than Uncle Charley! Because Charley is not — liked. He's liked, but he's not — well liked.

BIFF: Where'd you go this time, Dad?

WILLY: Well, I got on the road, and I went north to Providence. Met the Mayor.

BIFF: The Mayor of Providence!

WILLY: He was sitting in the hotel lobby.

BIFF: What'd he say?

WILLY: He said, "Morning!" And I said, "You got a fine city here, Mayor." And then he had coffee with me. And then I went to Waterbury. Waterbury is a fine city. Big clock city, the famous Waterbury clock. Sold a nice bill there. And then Boston — Boston is the cradle of the Revolution. A fine city. And a couple of other towns in Mass., and on to Portland and Bangor and straight home!

BIFF: Gee, I'd love to go with you sometime, Dad.

WILLY: Soon as summer comes.

HAPPY: Promise?

WILLY: You and Hap and I, and I'll show you all the towns. America is full of beautiful towns and fine, upstanding people. And they know me, boys, they know me up and down New England. The finest people. And when I bring you fellas up, there'll be open sesame for all of us, 'cause one thing, boys: I have friends. I can park my car in any street in New England, and the cops protect it like their own. This summer, heh?

BIFF AND HAPPY (*together*): Yeah! You bet!

WILLY: We'll take our bathing suits.

HAPPY: We'll carry your bags, Pop!

WILLY: Oh, won't that be something! Me comin' into the Boston stores with you boys carryin' my bags. What a sensation!

(*Biff is prancing around, practicing passing the ball.*)

WILLY: You nervous, Biff, about the game?

BIFF: Not if you're gonna be there.

WILLY: What do they say about you in school, now that they made you captain?

HAPPY: There's a crowd of girls behind him every time the classes change.

BIFF (*taking Willy's hand*): This Saturday, Pop, this Saturday — just for you, I'm going to break through for a touchdown.

HAPPY: You're supposed to pass.

BIFF: I'm takin' one play for Pop. You watch me, Pop, and when I take off my helmet, that means I'm breakin' out. Then you watch me crash through that line!

WILLY (*kisses Biff*): Oh, wait'll I tell this in Boston!

(*Bernard enters in knickers. He is younger than Biff, earnest and loyal, a worried boy.*)

BERNARD: Biff, where are you? You're supposed to study with me today.

WILLY: Hey, looka Bernard. What're you lookin' so anemic about, Bernard?

BERNARD: He's gotta study, Uncle Willy. He's got Regents next week.

HAPPY (*tauntingly, spinning Bernard around*): Let's box, Bernard!

BERNARD: Biff! (*He gets away from Happy.*) Listen, Biff, I heard Mr. Birnbaum say that if you don't start studyin' math he's gonna flunk you, and you won't graduate. I heard him!

WILLY: You better study with him, Biff. Go ahead now.

BERNARD: I heard him!

BIFF: Oh, Pop, you didn't see my sneakers! (*He holds up a foot for Willy to look at.*)

WILLY: Hey, that's a beautiful job of printing!

BERNARD (*wiping his glasses*): Just because he printed University of Virginia on his sneakers doesn't mean they've got to graduate him, Uncle Willy!

WILLY (*angrily*): What're you talking about? With scholarships to three universities they're gonna flunk him?

BERNARD: But I heard Mr. Birnbaum say —

WILLY: Don't be a pest, Bernard! (*To his boys.*) What an anemic!

BERNARD: Okay, I'm waiting for you in my house, Biff.

(*Bernard goes off. The Lomans laugh.*)

WILLY: Bernard is not well liked, is he?

BIFF: He's liked, but he's not well liked.

HAPPY: That's right, Pop.

WILLY: That's just what I mean. Bernard can get the best marks in school, y'understand, but when he gets out in the business world, y'understand, you are going to be five times ahead of him. That's why I thank Almighty God you're both built like Adonises. Because the man who makes an appearance in the business world, the man who creates personal interest, is the man who gets ahead. Be liked and you will never want. You take me, for instance. I never have to wait in line to see a buyer. "Willy Loman is here!" That's all they have to know, and I go right through.

BIFF: Did you knock them dead, Pop?

WILLY: Knocked 'em cold in Providence, slaughtered 'em in Boston.

HAPPY (*on his back, pedaling again*): I'm losing weight, you notice, Pop?

(*Linda enters as of old, a ribbon in her hair, carrying a basket of washing.*)

LINDA (*with youthful energy*): Hello, dear!

WILLY: Sweetheart!

LINDA: How'd the Chevvy run?

WILLY: Chevrolet, Linda, is the greatest car ever built. (*To the boys.*) Since when do you let your mother carry wash up the stairs?

BIFF: Grab hold there, boy!

HAPPY: Where to, Mom?

LINDA: Hang them up on the line. And you better go down to your friends, Biff. The cellar is full of boys. They don't know what to do with themselves.

BIFF: Ah, when Pop comes home they can wait!

WILLY (*laughs appreciatively*): You better go down and tell them what to do, Biff.

BIFF: I think I'll have them sweep out the furnace room.

WILLY: Good work, Biff.

BIFF (*goes through wall-line of kitchen to doorway at back and calls down*): Fellas! Everybody sweep out the furnace room! I'll be right down!

VOICES: All right! Okay, Biff.

BIFF: George and Sam and Frank, come out back! We're hangin' up the wash! Come on, Hap, on the double! (*He and Happy carry out the basket.*)

LINDA: The way they obey him!

WILLY: Well, that's training, the training. I'm tellin' you, I was sellin' thousands and thousands, but I had to come home.

LINDA: Oh, the whole block'll be at that game. Did you sell anything?

WILLY: I did five hundred gross in Providence and seven hundred gross in Boston.

LINDA: No! Wait a minute, I've got a pencil. (*She pulls pencil and paper out of her apron pocket.*) That makes your commission . . . Two hundred — my God! Two hundred and twelve dollars!

WILLY: Well, I didn't figure it yet, but . . .

LINDA: How much did you do?

WILLY: Well, I — I did — about a hundred and eighty gross in Providence. Well, no — it came to — roughly two hundred gross on the whole trip.

LINDA (*without hesitation*): Two hundred gross. That's . . . (*She figures.*)

WILLY: The trouble was that three of the stores were half-closed for inventory in Boston. Otherwise I woulda broke records.

LINDA: Well, it makes seventy dollars and some pennies. That's very good.

WILLY: What do we owe?

LINDA: Well, on the first there's sixteen dollars on the refrigerator —

WILLY: Why sixteen?

LINDA: Well, the fan belt broke, so it was a dollar eighty.

WILLY: But it's brand new.

LINDA: Well, the man said that's the way it is. Till they work themselves in, y'know.

(*They move through the wall-line into the kitchen.*)

WILLY: I hope we didn't get stuck on that machine.

LINDA: They got the biggest ads of any of them!

WILLY: I know, it's a fine machine. What else?

LINDA: Well, there's nine-sixty for the washing machine. And for the vacuum cleaner there's three and a half due on the fifteenth. Then the roof, you got twenty-one dollars remaining.

WILLY: It don't leak, does it?

LINDA: No, they did a wonderful job. Then you owe Frank for the carburetor.

WILLY: I'm not going to pay that man! That goddam Chevrolet, they ought to prohibit the manufacture of that car!

LINDA: Well, you owe him three and a half. And odds and ends, comes to around a hundred and twenty dollars by the fifteenth.

WILLY: A hundred and twenty dollars! My God, if business don't pick up I don't know what I'm gonna do!

LINDA: Well, next week you'll do better.

WILLY: Oh, I'll knock 'em dead next week. I'll go to Hartford. I'm very well liked in Hartford. You know, the trouble is, Linda, people don't seem to take to me.

(*They move onto the forestage.*)

LINDA: Oh, don't be foolish.

WILLY: I know it when I walk in. They seem to laugh at me.

LINDA: Why? Why would they laugh at you? Don't talk that way, Willy.

(*Willy moves to the edge of the stage. Linda goes into the kitchen and starts to darn stockings.*)

WILLY: I don't know the reason for it, but they just pass me by. I'm not noticed.

LINDA: But you're doing wonderful, dear. You're making seventy to a hundred dollars a week.

WILLY: But I gotta be at it ten, twelve hours a day. Other men — I don't know — they do it easier. I don't know why — I can't stop myself — I talk too much. A man oughta come in with a few words. One thing about Charley. He's a man of few words, and they respect him.

LINDA: You don't talk too much, you're just lively.

WILLY (*smiling*): Well, I figure, what the hell, life is short, a couple of jokes. (*To himself.*) I joke too much! (*The smile goes.*)

LINDA: Why? You're —

WILLY: I'm fat. I'm very — foolish to look at, Linda. I didn't tell you, but Christmas time I happened to be calling on F. H. Stewarts, and a salesman I know, as I was going in to see the buyer I heard him say something about — walrus. And I — I cracked him right across the face. I won't take that. I simply will not take that. But they do laugh at me. I know that.

LINDA: Darling . . .

WILLY: I gotta overcome it. I know I gotta overcome it. I'm not dressing to advantage, maybe.

LINDA: Willy, darling, you're the handsomest man in the world —

WILLY: Oh, no, Linda.

LINDA: To me you are. (*Slight pause.*) The handsomest.

(*From the darkness is heard the laughter of a woman. Willy doesn't turn to it, but it continues through Linda's lines.*)

LINDA: And the boys, Willy. Few men are idolized by their children the way you are.

(*Music is heard as behind a scrim, to the left of the house, The Woman, dimly seen, is dressing.*)

WILLY (*with great feeling*): You're the best there is, Linda, you're a pal, you know that? On the road — on the road I want to grab you sometimes and just kiss the life outa you.

(*The laughter is loud now, and he moves into a brightening area at the left, where The Woman has come from behind the scrim and is standing, putting on her hat, looking into a "mirror" and laughing.*)

WILLY: 'Cause I get so lonely — especially when business is bad and there's nobody to talk to. I get the feeling that I'll never sell anything again, that I won't make a living for you, or a business, a business for the boys. (*He talks through The Woman's subsiding laughter; The Woman primps at the "mirror."*) There's so much I want to make for —

THE WOMAN: Me? You didn't make me, Willy. I picked you.

WILLY (*pleased*): You picked me?

THE WOMAN (*who is quite proper-looking, Willy's age*): I did. I've been sitting at that desk watching all the salesmen go by, day in, day out. But you've got such a sense of humor, and we do have such a good time together, don't we?

WILLY: Sure, sure. (*He takes her in his arms.*) Why do you have to go now?

THE WOMAN: It's two o'clock . . .

WILLY: No, come on in! (*He pulls her.*)

THE WOMAN: . . . my sisters'll be scandalized. When'll you be back?

WILLY: Oh, two weeks about. Will you come up again?

THE WOMAN: Sure thing. You do make me laugh. It's good for me. (*She squeezes his arm, kisses him.*) And I think you're a wonderful man.

WILLY: You picked me, heh?

THE WOMAN: Sure. Because you're so sweet. And such a kidder.

WILLY: Well, I'll see you next time I'm in Boston.

THE WOMAN: I'll put you right through to the buyers.

WILLY (*slapping her bottom*): Right. Well, bottoms up!

THE WOMAN (*slaps him gently and laughs*): You just kill me, Willy. (*He suddenly grabs her and kisses her roughly.*) You kill me. And thanks for the stockings. I love a lot of stockings. Well, good night.

WILLY: Good night. And keep your pores open!

THE WOMAN: Oh, Willy!

(*The Woman bursts out laughing, and Linda's laughter blends in. The Woman disappears into the dark. Now the area at the kitchen table brightens. Linda is sitting where she was at the kitchen table, but now is mending a pair of her silk stockings.*)

LINDA: You are, Willy. The handsomest man. You've got no reason to feel that —

WILLY (*coming out of The Woman's dimming area and going over to Linda*): I'll make it all up to you, Linda, I'll —

LINDA: There's nothing to make up, dear. You're doing fine, better than —

WILLY (*noticing her mending*): What's that?

LINDA: Just mending my stockings. They're so expensive —

WILLY (*angrily, taking them from her*): I won't have you mending stockings in this house! Now throw them out!

(*Linda puts the stockings in her pocket.*)

BERNARD (*entering on the run*): Where is he? If he doesn't study!

WILLY (*moving to the forestage, with great agitation*): You'll give him the answers!

BERNARD: I do, but I can't on a Regents! That's a state exam! They're liable to arrest me!

WILLY: Where is he? I'll whip him, I'll whip him!

LINDA: And he'd better give back that football, Willy, it's not nice.

WILLY: Biff! Where is he? Why is he taking everything?

LINDA: He's too rough with the girls, Willy. All the mothers are afraid of him!

WILLY: I'll whip him!

BERNARD: He's driving the car without a license!

(*The Woman's laugh is heard.*)

WILLY: Shut up!

LINDA: All the mothers —

WILLY: Shut up!

BERNARD (*backing quietly away and out*): Mr. Birnbaum says he's stuck up.

WILLY: Get outa here!

BERNARD: If he doesn't buckle down he'll flunk math! (*He goes off.*)

LINDA: He's right, Willy, you've gotta —

WILLY (*exploding at her*): There's nothing the matter with him! You want him to be a worm like Bernard? He's got spirit, personality . . .

(*As he speaks, Linda, almost in tears, exits into the living room. Willy is alone in the kitchen, wilting and staring. The leaves are gone. It is night again, and the apartment houses look down from behind.*)

WILLY: Loaded with it. Loaded! What is he stealing? He's giving it back, isn't he? Why is he stealing? What did I tell him? I never in my life told him anything but decent things.

(*Happy in pajamas has come down the stairs; Willy suddenly becomes aware of Happy's presence.*)

HAPPY: Let's go now, come on.

WILLY (*sitting down at the kitchen table*): Huh! Why did she have to wax the floors herself? Everytime she waxes the floors she keels over. She knows that!

HAPPY: Shh! Take it easy. What brought you back tonight?

WILLY: I got an awful scare. Nearly hit a kid in Yonkers. God! Why didn't I go to Alaska with my brother Ben that time! Ben! That man was a genius, that man was success incarnate! What a mistake! He begged me to go.

HAPPY: Well, there's no use in —

WILLY: You guys! There was a man started with the clothes on his back and ended up with diamond mines!

HAPPY: Boy, someday I'd like to know how he did it.

WILLY: What's the mystery? The man knew what he wanted and went out and got it! Walked into a jungle, and comes out, the age of twenty-one, and he's rich! The world is an oyster, but you don't crack it open on a mattress!

HAPPY: Pop, I told you I'm gonna retire you for life.

WILLY: You'll retire me for life on seventy goddam dollars a week? And your women and your car and your apartment, and you'll retire me for life! Christ's sake, I couldn't get past Yonkers today! Where are you guys, where are you? The woods are burning! I can't drive a car!

(*Charley has appeared in the doorway. He is a large man, slow of speech, laconic, immovable. In all he says, despite what he says, there is pity, and, now, trepidation. He has a robe over pajamas, slippers on his feet. He enters the kitchen.*)

CHARLEY: Everything all right?

HAPPY: Yeah, Charley, everything's . . .

WILLY: What's the matter?

CHARLEY: I heard some noise. I thought something happened. Can't we do something about the walls? You sneeze in here, and in my house hats blow off.

HAPPY: Let's go to bed, Dad. Come on.

(*Charley signals to Happy to go.*)

WILLY: You go ahead, I'm not tired at the moment.

HAPPY (*to Willy*): Take it easy, huh? (*He exits.*)

WILLY: What're you doin' up?

CHARLEY (*sitting down at the kitchen table opposite Willy*): Couldn't sleep good. I had a heartburn.

WILLY: Well, you don't know how to eat.

CHARLEY: I eat with my mouth.

WILLY: No, you're ignorant. You gotta know about vitamins and things like that.

CHARLEY: Come on, let's shoot. Tire you out a little.

WILLY (*hesitantly*): All right. You got cards?

CHARLEY (*taking a deck from his pocket*): Yeah, I got them. Someplace. What is it with those vitamins?

WILLY (*dealing*): They build up your bones. Chemistry.

CHARLEY: Yeah, but there's no bones in a heartburn.

WILLY: What are you talkin' about? Do you know the first thing about it?

CHARLEY: Don't get insulted.

WILLY: Don't talk about something you don't know anything about.

(*They are playing. Pause.*)

CHARLEY: What're you doin' home?

WILLY: A little trouble with the car.

CHARLEY: Oh. (*Pause.*) I'd like to take a trip to California.

WILLY: Don't say.

CHARLEY: You want a job?

WILLY: I got a job, I told you that. (*After a slight pause.*) What the hell are you offering me a job for?

CHARLEY: Don't get insulted.

WILLY: Don't insult me.

CHARLEY: I don't see no sense in it. You don't have to go on this way.

WILLY: I got a good job. (*Slight pause.*) What do you keep comin' in here for?

CHARLEY: You want me to go?

WILLY (*after a pause, withering*): I can't understand it. He's going back to Texas again. What the hell is that?

CHARLEY: Let him go.

WILLY: I got nothin' to give him, Charley, I'm clean, I'm clean.

CHARLEY: He won't starve. None a them starve. Forget about him.

WILLY: Then what have I got to remember?

CHARLEY: You take it too hard. To hell with it. When a deposit bottle is broken you don't get your nickel back.

WILLY: That's easy enough for you to say.

CHARLEY: That ain't easy for me to say.

WILLY: Did you see the ceiling I put up in the living room?

CHARLEY: Yeah, that's a piece of work. To put up a ceiling is a mystery to me. How do you do it?

WILLY: What's the difference?

CHARLEY: Well, talk about it.

WILLY: You gonna put up a ceiling?

CHARLEY: How could I put up a ceiling?

WILLY: Then what the hell are you bothering me for?

CHARLEY: You're insulted again.

WILLY: A man who can't handle tools is not a man. You're disgusting.

CHARLEY: Don't call me disgusting, Willy.

(*Uncle Ben, carrying a valise and an umbrella, enters the forestage from around the right corner of the house. He is a stolid man, in his sixties, with a mustache and an authoritative air. He is utterly certain of his destiny, and there is an aura of far places about him. He enters exactly as Willy speaks.*)

WILLY: I'm getting awfully tired, Ben.

(*Ben's music is heard. Ben looks around at everything.*)

CHARLEY: Good, keep playing; you'll sleep better. Did you call me Ben?

(*Ben looks at his watch.*)

WILLY: That's funny. For a second there you reminded me of my brother Ben.

BEN: I only have a few minutes. (*He strolls, inspecting the place. Willy and Charley continue playing.*)

CHARLEY: You never heard from him again, heh? Since that time?

WILLY: Didn't Linda tell you? Couple of weeks ago we got a letter from his wife in Africa. He died.

CHARLEY: That so.

BEN (*chuckling*): So this is Brooklyn, eh?

CHARLEY: Maybe you're in for some of his money.

WILLY: Naa, he had seven sons. There's just one opportunity I had with that man . . .

BEN: I must make a train, William. There are several properties I'm looking at in Alaska.

WILLY: Sure, sure! If I'd gone with him to Alaska that time, everything would've been totally different.

CHARLIE: Go on, you'd froze to death up there.

WILLY: What're you talking about?

BEN: Opportunity is tremendous in Alaska, William. Surprised you're not up there.

WILLY: Sure, tremendous.

CHARLEY: Heh?

WILLY: There was the only man I ever met who knew the answers.

CHARLEY: Who?

BEN: How are you all?

WILLY (*taking a pot, smiling*): Fine, fine.

CHARLEY: Pretty sharp tonight.

BEN: Is Mother living with you?

WILLY: No, she died a long time ago.

CHARLEY: Who?

BEN: That's too bad. Fine specimen of a lady, Mother.

WILLY (*to Charley*): Heh?

BEN: I'd hoped to see the old girl.

CHARLEY: Who died?

BEN: Heard anything from Father, have you?

WILLY (*unnerved*): What do you mean, who died?

CHARLEY (*taking a pot*): What're you talkin' about?

BEN (*looking at his watch*): William, it's half-past eight!

WILLY (*as though to dispel his confusion he angrily stops Charley's hand*): That's my build!

CHARLEY: I put the ace —

WILLY: If you don't know how to play the game I'm not gonna throw my money away on you!

CHARLEY (*rising*): It was my ace, for God's sake!

WILLY: I'm through, I'm through!

BEN: When did Mother die?

WILLY: Long ago. Since the beginning you never knew how to play cards.

CHARLEY (*picks up the cards and goes to the door*): All right! Next time I'll bring a deck with five aces.

WILLY: I don't play that kind of game!

CHARLEY (*turning to him*): You ought to be ashamed of yourself!

WILLY: Yeah?

CHARLEY: Yeah! (*He goes out.*)

WILLY (*slamming the door after him*): Ignoramus!

BEN (*as Willy comes toward him through the wall-line of the kitchen*): So you're William.

WILLY (*shaking Ben's hand*): Ben! I've been waiting for you so long! What's the answer? How did you do it?

BEN: Oh, there's a story in that.

(*Linda enters the forestage, as of old, carrying the wash basket.*)

LINDA: Is this Ben?

BEN (*gallantly*): How do you do, my dear.

LINDA: Where've you been all these years? Willy's always wondered why you —

WILLY (*pulling Ben away from her impatiently*): Where is Dad? Didn't you follow him? How did you get started?

BEN: Well, I don't know how much you remember.

WILLY: Well, I was just a baby, of course, only three or four years old —

BEN: Three years and eleven months.

WILLY: What a memory, Ben!

BEN: I have many enterprises, William, and I have never kept books.

WILLY: I remember I was sitting under the wagon in — was it Nebraska?

BEN: It was South Dakota, and I gave you a bunch of wild flowers.

WILLY: I remember you walking away down some open road.

BEN (*laughing*): I was going to find Father in Alaska.

WILLY: Where is he?

BEN: At that age I had a very faulty view of geography, William. I discovered after a few days that I was heading due south, so instead of Alaska, I ended up in Africa.

LINDA: Africa!

WILLY: The Gold Coast!

BEN: Principally diamond mines.

LINDA: Diamond mines!

BEN: Yes, my dear. But I've only a few minutes —

WILLY: No! Boys! Boys! (*Young Biff and Happy appear.*) Listen to this. This is your Uncle Ben, a great man! Tell my boys, Ben!

BEN: Why, boys, when I was seventeen I walked into the jungle, and when I was twenty-one I walked out. (*He laughs.*) And by God I was rich.

WILLY (*to the boys*): You see what I been talking about? The greatest things can happen!

BEN (*glancing at his watch*): I have an appointment in Ketchikan Tuesday week.

WILLY: No, Ben! Please tell about Dad. I want my boys to hear. I want them to know the kind of stock they spring from. All I remember is a man with a big beard, and I was in Mamma's lap, sitting around a fire, and some kind of high music.

BEN: His flute. He played the flute.

WILLY: Sure, the flute, that's right!

(*New music is heard, a high, rollicking tune.*)

BEN: Father was a very great and a very wild-hearted man. We would start in Boston, and he'd toss the whole family into the wagon, and then he'd drive the team right across the country; through Ohio, and Indiana, Michigan, Illinois, and all the Western states. And we'd stop in the towns and sell the flutes that he'd made on the way. Great inventor Father. With one gadget he made more in a week than a man like you could make in a lifetime.

WILLY: That's just the way I'm bringing them up, Ben — rugged, well liked, all-around.

BEN: Yeah? (*To Biff.*) Hit that, boy — hard as you can. (*He pounds his stomach.*)

BIFF: Oh, no, sir!

BEN (*taking boxing stance*): Come on, get to me! (*He laughs.*)

WILLY: Go to it, Biff! Go ahead, show him!

BIFF: Okay! (*He cocks his fists and starts in.*)

LINDA (*to Willy*): Why must he fight, dear?

BEN (*sparring with Biff*): Good boy! Good boy!

WILLY: How's that, Ben, heh?

HAPPY: Give him the left, Biff!

LINDA: Why are you fighting?

BEN: Good boy! (*Suddenly comes in, trips Biff, and stands over him, the point of his umbrella poised over Biff's eye.*)

LINDA: Look out, Biff!

BIFF: Gee!

BEN (*patting Biff's knee*): Never fight fair with a stranger, boy. You'll never get out of the jungle that way. (*Taking Linda's hand and bowing.*) It was an honor and a pleasure to meet you, Linda.

LINDA (*withdrawing her hand coldly, frightened*): Have a nice — trip.

BEN (*to Willy*): And good luck with your — what do you do?

WILLY: Selling.

BEN: Yes. Well . . . (*He raises his hand in farewell to all.*)

WILLY: No, Ben, I don't want you to think . . . (*He takes Ben's arm to show him.*) It's Brooklyn, I know, but we hunt too.

BEN: Really, now.

WILLY: Oh, sure, there's snakes and rabbits and — that's why I moved out here. Why, Biff can fell any one of these trees in no time! Boys! Go right over to where they're building the apartment house and get some sand. We're gonna rebuild the entire front stoop right now! Watch this, Ben!

BIFF: Yes, sir! On the double, Hap!

HAPPY (*as he and Biff run off*): I lost weight, Pop, you notice?

(*Charley enters in knickers, even before the boys are gone.*)

CHARLEY: Listen, if they steal any more from that building the watchman'll put the cops on them!

LINDA (*to Willy*): Don't let Biff . . .

(*Ben laughs lustily.*)

WILLY: You shoulda seen the lumber they brought home last week. At least a dozen six-by-tens worth all kinds a money.

CHARLEY: Listen, if that watchman —

WILLY: I gave them hell, understand. But I got a couple of fearless characters there.

CHARLEY: Willy, the jails are full of fearless characters.

BEN (*clapping Willy on the back, with a laugh at Charley*): And the stock exchange, friend!

WILLY (*joining in Ben's laughter*): Where are the rest of your pants?

CHARLEY: My wife bought them.

WILLY: Now all you need is a golf club and you can go upstairs and go to sleep. (*To Ben.*) Great athlete! Between him and his son Bernard they can't hammer a nail!

BERNARD (*rushing in*): The watchman's chasing Biff!

WILLY (*angrily*): Shut up! He's not stealing anything!

LINDA (*alarmed, hurrying off left*): Where is he? Biff, dear! (*She exits.*)

WILLY (*moving toward the left, away from Ben*): There's nothing wrong. What's the matter with you?

BEN: Nervy boy. Good!

WILLY (*laughing*): Oh, nerves of iron, that Biff!

CHARLEY: Don't know what it is. My New England man comes back and he's bleedin', they murdered him up there.

WILLY: It's contacts, Charley, I got important contacts!

CHARLEY (*sarcastically*): Glad to hear it, Willy. Come in later, we'll shoot a little casino. I'll take some of your Portland money. (*He laughs at Willy and exits.*)

WILLY (*turning to Ben*): Business is bad, it's murderous. But not for me, of course.

BEN: I'll stop by on my way back to Africa.

WILLY (*longingly*): Can't you stay a few days? You're just what I need, Ben, because I — I have a fine position here, but I — well, Dad left when I was such a baby and I never had a chance to talk to him and I still feel — kind of temporary about myself.

BEN: I'll be late for my train.

(*They are at opposite ends of the stage.*)

WILLY: Ben, my boys — can't we talk? They'd go into the jaws of hell for me, see, but I —

BEN: William, you're being first-rate with your boys. Outstanding, manly chaps!

WILLY (*hanging on to his words*): Oh, Ben, that's good to hear! Because sometimes I'm afraid that I'm not teaching them the right kind of — Ben, how should I teach them?

BEN (*giving great weight to each word, and with a certain vicious audacity*): William, when I walked into the jungle, I was seventeen. When I walked out I was twenty-one. And, by God, I was rich! (*He goes off into darkness around the right corner of the house.*)

WILLY: . . . was rich! That's just the spirit I want to imbue them with! To walk into a jungle! I was right! I was right! I was right!

(*Ben is gone, but Willy is still speaking to him as Linda, in nightgown and robe, enters the kitchen, glances around for Willy, then goes to the door of the house, looks out and sees him. Comes down to his left. He looks at her.*)

LINDA: Willy, dear? Willy?

WILLY: I was right!

LINDA: Did you have some cheese? (*He can't answer.*) It's very late, darling. Come to bed, heh?

WILLY (*looking straight up*): Gotta break your neck to see a star in this yard.

LINDA: You coming in?

WILLY: Whatever happened to that diamond watch fob? Remember? When Ben came from Africa that time? Didn't he give me a watch fob with a diamond in it?

LINDA: You pawned it, dear. Twelve, thirteen years ago. For Biff's radio correspondence course.

WILLY: Gee, that was a beautiful thing. I'll take a walk.

LINDA: But you're in your slippers.

WILLY (*starting to go around the house at the left*): I was right! I was! (*Half to Linda, as he goes, shaking his head.*) What a man! There was a man worth talking to. I was right!

LINDA (*calling after Willy*): But in your slippers, Willy!

(*Willy is almost gone when Biff, in his pajamas, comes down the stairs and enters the kitchen.*)

BIFF: What is he doing out there?

LINDA: Sh!

BIFF: God Almighty, Mom, how long has he been doing this?

LINDA: Don't, he'll hear you.

BIFF: What the hell is the matter with him?

LINDA: It'll pass by morning.

BIFF: Shouldn't we do anything?

LINDA: Oh, my dear, you should do a lot of things, but there's nothing to do, so go to sleep.

(*Happy comes down the stair and sits on the steps.*)

HAPPY: I never heard him so loud, Mom.

LINDA: Well, come around more often, you'll hear him. (*She sits down at the table and mends the lining of Willy's jacket.*)

BIFF: Why didn't you ever write me about this, Mom?

LINDA: How would I write to you? For over three months you had no address.

BIFF: I was on the move. But you know I thought of you all the time. You know that, don't you, pal?

LINDA: I know, dear, I know. But he likes to have a letter. Just to know that there's still a possibility for better things.

BIFF: He's not like this all the time, is he?

LINDA: It's when you come home he's always the worst.

BIFF: When I come home?

LINDA: When you write you're coming, he's all smiles and talks about the future, and — he's just wonderful. And then the closer you seem to come, the more shaky he gets, and then, by the time you get here, he's arguing, and he seems angry at you. I think it's just that maybe he can't bring himself to — to open up to you. Why are you so hateful to each other? Why is that?

BIFF (*evasively*): I'm not hateful, Mom.

LINDA: But you no sooner come in the door than you're fighting!

BIFF: I don't know why. I mean to change. I'm tryin', Mom, you understand?

LINDA: Are you home to stay now?

BIFF: I don't know. I want to look around, see what's goin'.

LINDA: Biff, you can't look around all your life, can you?

BIFF: I just can't take hold, Mom. I can't take hold of some kind of a life.

LINDA: Biff, a man is not a bird, to come and go with the springtime.

BIFF: Your hair . . . (*He touches her hair.*) Your hair got so gray.

LINDA: Oh, it's been gray since you were in high school. I just stopped dyeing it, that's all.

BIFF: Dye it again, will ye? I don't want my pal looking old. (*He smiles.*)

LINDA: You're such a boy! You think you can go away for a year and . . . You've got to get it into your head now that one day you'll knock on this door and there'll be strange people here —

BIFF: What are you talking about? You're not even sixty, Mom.

LINDA: But what about your father?

BIFF (*lamely*): Well, I meant him too.

HAPPY: He admires Pop.

LINDA: Biff, dear, if you don't have any feeling for him, then you can't have any feeling for me.

BIFF: Sure I can, Mom.

LINDA: No. You can't just come to see me, because I love him. (*With a threat, but only a threat, of tears.*) He's the dearest man in the world to me, and I won't have anyone making him feel unwanted and low and blue. You've got to make up your mind now, darling, there's no leeway any more. Either he's your father and you pay him that respect, or else you're not to come here. I know he's not easy to get along with — nobody knows that better than me — but . . .

WILLY (*from the left, with a laugh*): Hey, hey, Biffo!

BIFF (*starting to go out after Willy*): What the hell is the matter with him? (*Happy stops him.*)

LINDA: Don't — don't go near him!

BIFF: Stop making excuses for him! He always, always wiped the floor with you. Never had an ounce of respect for you.

HAPPY: He's always had respect for —

BIFF: What the hell do you know about it?

HAPPY (*surlily*): Just don't call him crazy!

BIFF: He's got no character — Charley wouldn't do this. Not in his own house — spewing out that vomit from his mind.

HAPPY: Charley never had to cope with what he's got to.

BIFF: People are worse off than Willy Loman. Believe me, I've seen them!

LINDA: Then make Charley your father, Biff. You can't do that, can you? I don't say he's a great man. Willy Loman never made a lot of money. His name was never in the paper. He's not the finest character that ever lived. But he's a human being, and a terrible thing is happening to him. So attention must be paid. He's not to be allowed to fall into his grave like an old dog. Attention, attention must be finally paid to such a person. You called him crazy —

BIFF: I didn't mean —

LINDA: No, a lot of people think he's lost his — balance. But you don't have to be very smart to know what his trouble is. The man is exhausted.

HAPPY: Sure!

LINDA: A small man can be just as exhausted as a great man. He works for a company thirty-six years this March, opens up unheard-of territories to their trademark, and now in his old age they take his salary away.

HAPPY (*indignantly*): I didn't know that, Mom.

LINDA: You never asked, my dear! Now that you get your spending money someplace else you don't trouble your mind with him.

HAPPY: But I gave you money last —

LINDA: Christmas time, fifty dollars! To fix the hot water it cost ninety-seven fifty! For five weeks he's been on straight commission, like a beginner, an unknown!

BIFF: Those ungrateful bastards!

LINDA: Are they any worse than his sons? When he brought them business, when he was young, they were glad to see him. But now his old friends, the old buyers that loved him so and always found some order to hand him in a pinch — they're all dead, retired. He used to be able to make six, seven calls a day in Boston. Now he takes his valises out of the car and puts them back and takes them out again and he's exhausted. Instead of walking he talks now. He drives seven hundred miles, and when he gets there no one knows him anymore, no one welcomes him. And what goes through a man's mind, driving seven hundred miles home without having earned a cent? Why shouldn't he talk to himself? Why? When he has to go to Charley and borrow fifty dollars a week and pretend to me that it's his pay? How long can that go on? How long? You see what I'm sitting here and waiting for? And you tell me he has no character? The man who never worked a day but for your benefit? When does he get the medal for that? Is this his reward — to turn around at the age of sixty-three and find his sons, who he loved better than his life, one a philandering bum —

HAPPY: Mom!

LINDA: That's all you are, my baby! (*To Biff.*) And you! What happened to the love you had for him? You were such pals! How you used to talk to him on the phone every night! How lonely he was till he could come home to you!

BIFF: All right, Mom. I'll live here in my room, and I'll get a job. I'll keep away from him, that's all.

LINDA: No, Biff. You can't stay here and fight all the time.

BIFF: He threw me out of this house, remember that.

LINDA: Why did he do that? I never knew why.

BIFF: Because I know he's a fake and he doesn't like anybody around who knows!

LINDA: Why a fake? In what way? What do you mean?

BIFF: Just don't lay it all at my feet. It's between me and him — that's all I have to say. I'll chip in from now on. He'll settle for half my pay check. He'll be all right. I'm going to bed. (*He starts for the stairs.*)

LINDA: He won't be all right.

BIFF (*turning on the stairs, furiously*): I hate this city and I'll stay here. Now what do you want?

LINDA: He's dying, Biff.

(*Happy turns quickly to her, shocked.*)

BIFF (*after a pause*): Why is he dying?

LINDA: He's been trying to kill himself.

BIFF (*with great horror*): How?

LINDA: I live from day to day.

BIFF: What're you talking about?

LINDA: Remember I wrote you that he smashed up the car again? In February?

BIFF: Well?

LINDA: The insurance inspector came. He said that they have evidence. That all these accidents in the last year — weren't — weren't — accidents.

HAPPY: How can they tell that? That's a lie.

LINDA: It seems there's a woman . . . (*She takes a breath as*)

BIFF (*sharply but contained*): What woman?

LINDA (*simultaneously*): . . . and this woman . . .

LINDA: What?

BIFF: Nothing. Go ahead.

LINDA: What did you say?

BIFF: Nothing. I just said what woman?

HAPPY: What about her?

LINDA: Well, it seems she was walking down the road and saw his car. She says that he wasn't driving fast at all, and that he didn't skid. She says he came to that little bridge, and then deliberately smashed into the railing, and it was only the shallowness of the water that saved him.

BIFF: Oh, no, he probably just fell asleep again.

LINDA: I don't think he fell asleep.

BIFF: Why not?

LINDA: Last month . . . (*With great difficulty.*) Oh, boys, it's so hard to say a thing like this! He's just a big stupid man to you, but I tell you there's more good in him than in many other people. (*She chokes, wipes her eyes.*) I was looking for a fuse. The lights blew out, and I went down the cellar. And behind the fuse box — it happened to fall out — was a length of rubber pipe — just short.

HAPPY: No kidding!

LINDA: There's a little attachment on the end of it. I knew right away. And sure enough, on the bottom of the water heater there's a new little nipple on the gas pipe.

HAPPY (*angrily*): That — jerk.

BIFF: Did you have it taken off?

LINDA: I'm — I'm ashamed to. How can I mention it to him? Every day I go down and take away that little rubber pipe. But, when he comes home, I put it back where it was. How can I insult him that way? I don't know what to do. I live from day to day, boys. I tell you, I know every thought in his mind. It sounds so old-fashioned and silly, but I tell you he put his whole life into you and you've turned your backs on him. (*She is bent over in the chair, weeping, her face in her hands.*) Biff, I swear to God! Biff, his life is in your hands!

HAPPY (*to Biff*): How do you like that damned fool!

BIFF (*kissing her*): All right, pal, all right. It's all settled now. I've been remiss. I know that, Mom. But now I'll stay, and I swear to you, I'll apply myself. (*Kneeling in front of her, in a fever of self-reproach.*) It's just — you see, Mom, I don't fit in business. Not that I won't try. I'll try, and I'll make good.

HAPPY: Sure you will. The trouble with you in business was you never tried to please people.

BIFF: I know, I —

HAPPY: Like when you worked for Harrison's. Bob Harrison said you were tops, and then you go and do some damn fool thing like whistling whole songs in the elevator like a comedian.

BIFF (*against Happy*): So what? I like to whistle sometimes.

HAPPY: You don't raise a guy to a responsible job who whistles in the elevator!

LINDA: Well, don't argue about it now.

HAPPY: Like when you'd go off and swim in the middle of the day instead of taking the line around.

BIFF (*his resentment rising*): Well, don't you run off? You take off sometimes, don't you? On a nice summer day?

HAPPY: Yeah, but I cover myself!

LINDA: Boys!

HAPPY: If I'm going to take a fade the boss can call any number where I'm supposed to be and they'll swear to him that I just left. I'll tell you something that I hate to say, Biff, but in the business world some of them think you're crazy.

BIFF (*angered*): Screw the business world!

HAPPY: All right, screw it! Great, but cover yourself!

LINDA: Hap, Hap!

BIFF: I don't care what they think! They've laughed at Dad for years, and you know why? Because we don't belong in this nuthouse of a city! We should be mixing cement on some open plain, or — or carpenters. A carpenter is allowed to whistle!

(*Willy walks in from the entrance of the house, at left.*)

WILLY: Even your grandfather was better than a carpenter. (*Pause. They watch him.*) You never grew up. Bernard does not whistle in the elevator, I assure you.

BIFF (*as though to laugh Willy out of it*): Yeah, but you do, Pop.

WILLY: I never in my life whistled in an elevator! And who in the business world thinks I'm crazy?

BIFF: I didn't mean it like that, Pop. Now don't make a whole thing out of it, will ye?

WILLY: Go back to the West! Be a carpenter, a cowboy, enjoy yourself!

LINDA: Willy, he was just saying —

WILLY: I heard what he said!

HAPPY (*trying to quiet Willy*): Hey, Pop, come on now . . .

WILLY (*continuing over Happy's line*): They laugh at me, heh? Go to Filene's, go to the Hub, go to Slattery's, Boston. Call out the name Willy Loman and see what happens! Big shot!

BIFF: All right, Pop.

WILLY: Big!

BIFF: All right!

WILLY: Why do you always insult me?

BIFF: I didn't say a word. (*To Linda.*) Did I say a word?

LINDA: He didn't say anything, Willy.

WILLY (*going to the doorway of the living room*): All right, good night, good night.

LINDA: Willy, dear, he just decided . . .

WILLY (*to Biff*): If you get tired hanging around tomorrow, paint the ceiling I put up in the living room.

BIFF: I'm leaving early tomorrow.

HAPPY: He's going to see Bill Oliver, Pop.

WILLY (*interestedly*): Oliver? For what?

BIFF (*with reserve, but trying, trying*): He always said he'd stake me. I'd like to go into business, so maybe I can take him up on it.

LINDA: Isn't that wonderful?

WILLY: Don't interrupt. What's wonderful about it? There's fifty men in the City of New York who'd stake him. (*To Biff.*) Sporting goods?

BIFF: I guess so. I know something about it and —

WILLY: He knows something about it! You know sporting goods better than Spalding, for God's sake! How much is he giving you?

BIFF: I don't know, I didn't even see him yet, but —

WILLY: Then what're you talkin' about?

BIFF (*getting angry*): Well, all I said was I'm gonna see him, that's all!

WILLY (*turning away*): Ah, you're counting your chickens again.

BIFF (*starting left for the stairs*): Oh, Jesus, I'm going to sleep!

WILLY (*calling after him*): Don't curse in this house!

BIFF (*turning*): Since when did you get so clean?

HAPPY (*trying to stop them*): Wait a . . .

WILLY: Don't use that language to me! I won't have it!

HAPPY (*grabbing Biff, shouts*): Wait a minute! I got an idea. I got a feasible idea. Come here, Biff, let's talk this over now, let's talk some sense here. When I was down in Florida last time, I thought of a great idea to sell sporting goods. It just came back to me. You and I, Biff — we have a line, the Loman Line. We train a couple of weeks, and put on a couple of exhibitions, see?

WILLY: That's an idea!

HAPPY: Wait! We form two basketball teams, see? Two water polo teams. We play each other. It's a million dollars' worth of publicity. Two brothers, see? The Loman Brothers. Displays in the Royal Palms — all the hotels. And banners over the ring and the basketball court: "Loman Brothers." Baby, we could sell sporting goods!

WILLY: That is a one-million-dollar idea!

LINDA: Marvelous!

BIFF: I'm in great shape as far as that's concerned.

HAPPY: And the beauty of it is, Biff, it wouldn't be like a business. We'd be out playin' ball again . . .

BIFF (*enthused*): Yeah, that's . . .

WILLY: Million-dollar . . .

HAPPY: And you wouldn't get fed up with it, Biff. It'd be the family again. There'd be the old honor, and comradeship, and if you wanted to go off for a swim or somethin' — well, you'd do it! Without some smart cooky gettin' up ahead of you!

WILLY: Lick the world! You guys together could absolutely lick the civilized world.

BIFF: I'll see Oliver tomorrow. Hap, if we could work that out . . .

LINDA: Maybe things are beginning to —

WILLY (*wildly enthused, to Linda*): Stop interrupting! (*To Biff.*) But don't wear sport jacket and slacks when you see Oliver.

BIFF: No, I'll —

WILLY: A business suit, and talk as little as possible, and don't crack any jokes.

BIFF: He did like me. Always liked me.

LINDA: He loved you!

WILLY (*to Linda*): Will you stop! (*To Biff.*) Walk in very serious. You are not applying for a boy's job. Money is to pass. Be quiet, fine, and serious. Everybody likes a kidder, but nobody lends him money.

HAPPY: I'll try to get some myself, Biff. I'm sure I can.

WILLY: I see great things for you kids, I think your troubles are over. But remember, start big and you'll end big. Ask for fifteen. How much you gonna ask for?

BIFF: Gee, I don't know —

WILLY: And don't say "Gee." "Gee" is a boy's word. A man walking in for fifteen thousand dollars does not say "Gee!"

BIFF: Ten, I think, would be top though.

WILLY: Don't be so modest. You always started too low. Walk in with a big laugh. Don't look worried. Start off with a couple of your good stories to lighten things up. It's not what you say, it's how you say it — because personality always wins the day.

LINDA: Oliver always thought the highest of him —

WILLY: Will you let me talk?

BIFF: Don't yell at her, Pop, will ye?

WILLY (*angrily*): I was talking, wasn't I?

BIFF: I don't like you yelling at her all the time, and I'm tellin' you, that's all.

WILLY: What're you, takin' over this house?

LINDA: Willy —

WILLY (*turning to her*): Don't take his side all the time, goddammit!

BIFF (*furiously*): Stop yelling at her!

WILLY (*suddenly pulling on his cheek, beaten down, guilt ridden*): Give my best to Bill Oliver — he may remember me. (*He exits through the living room doorway.*)

LINDA (*her voice subdued*): What'd you have to start

that for? (*Biff turns away.*) You see how sweet he was as soon as you talked hopefully? (*She goes over to Biff.*) Come up and say good night to him. Don't let him go to bed that way.

HAPPY: Come on, Biff, let's buck him up.

LINDA: Please, dear. Just say good night. It takes so little to make him happy. Come. (*She goes through the living room doorway, calling upstairs from within the living room.*) Your pajamas are hanging in the bathroom, Willy!

HAPPY (*looking toward where Linda went out*): What a woman! They broke the mold when they made her. You know that, Biff?

BIFF: He's off salary. My God, working on commission!

HAPPY: Well, let's face it: he's no hot-shot selling man. Except that sometimes, you have to admit, he's a sweet personality.

BIFF (*deciding*): Lend me ten bucks, will ye? I want to buy some new ties.

HAPPY: I'll take you to a place I know. Beautiful stuff. Wear one of my striped shirts tomorrow.

BIFF: She got gray. Mom got awful old. Gee, I'm gonna go in to Oliver tomorrow and knock him for a —

HAPPY: Come on up. Tell that to Dad. Let's give him a whirl. Come on.

BIFF (*steamed up*): You know, with ten thousand bucks, boy!

HAPPY (*as they go into the living room*): That's the talk, Biff, that's the first time I've heard the old confidence out of you! (*From within the living room, fading off.*) You're gonna live with me, kid, and any babe you want just say the word . . . (*The last lines are hardly heard. They are mounting the stairs to their parents' bedroom.*)

LINDA (*entering her bedroom and addressing Willy, who is in the bathroom. She is straightening the bed for him.*): Can you do anything about the shower? It drips.

WILLY (*from the bathroom*): All of a sudden everything falls to pieces. Goddam plumbing, oughta be sued, those people. I hardly finished putting it in and the thing . . . (*His words rumble off.*)

LINDA: I'm just wondering if Oliver will remember him. You think he might?

WILLY (*coming out of the bathroom in his pajamas*): Remember him? What's the matter with you, you crazy? If he'd've stayed with Oliver he'd be on top by now! Wait'll Oliver gets a look at him. You don't know the average caliber any more. The average young man today — (*he is getting into bed*) — is got a caliber of zero. Greatest thing in the world for him was to bum around.

(*Biff and Happy enter the bedroom. Slight pause.*)

WILLY (*stops short, looking at Biff*): Glad to hear it, boy.

HAPPY: He wanted to say good night to you, sport.

WILLY (*to Biff*): Yeah. Knock him dead, boy. What'd you want to tell me?

BIFF: Just take it easy, Pop. Good night. (*He turns to go.*)

WILLY (*unable to resist*): And if anything falls off the desk while you're talking to him — like a package or something — don't you pick it up. They have office boys for that.

LINDA: I'll make a big breakfast —

WILLY: Will you let me finish? (*To Biff.*) Tell him you were in the business in the West. Not farm work.

BIFF: All right, Dad.

LINDA: I think everything —

WILLY (*going right through her speech*): And don't undersell yourself. No less than fifteen thousand dollars.

BIFF (*unable to bear him*): Okay. Good night, Mom. (*He starts moving.*)

WILLY: Because you got a greatness in you, Biff, remember that. You got all kinds of greatness . . . (*He lies back, exhausted. Biff walks out.*)

LINDA (*calling after Biff*): Sleep well, darling!

HAPPY: I'm gonna get married, Mom. I wanted to tell you.

LINDA: Go to sleep, dear.

HAPPY (*going*): I just wanted to tell you.

WILLY: Keep up the good work. (*Happy exits.*) God . . . remember that Ebbets Field game? The championship of the city?

LINDA: Just rest. Should I sing to you?

WILLY: Yeah. Sing to me. (*Linda hums a soft lullaby.*) When that team came out — he was the tallest, remember?

LINDA: Oh, yes. And in gold.

(*Biff enters the darkened kitchen, takes a cigarette, and leaves the house. He comes downstage into a golden pool of light. He smokes, staring at the night.*)

WILLY: Like a young god. Hercules — something like that. And the sun, the sun all around him. Remember how he waved to me? Right up from the field, with the representatives of three colleges standing by? And the buyers I brought, and the cheers when he came out — Loman, Loman, Loman! God Almighty, he'll be great yet. A star like that, magnificent, can never really fade away!

(*The light on Willy is fading. The gas heater begins to glow through the kitchen wall, near the stairs, a blue flame beneath red coils.*)

LINDA (*timidly*): Willy dear, what has he got against you?

WILLY: I'm so tired. Don't talk anymore.

(*Biff slowly returns to the kitchen. He stops, stares toward the heater.*)

LINDA: Will you ask Howard to let you work in New York?

WILLY: First thing in the morning. Everything'll be all right.

(*Biff reaches behind the heater and draws out a length of rubber tubing. He is horrified and turns his head toward Willy's room, still dimly lit, from which the strains of Linda's desperate but monotonous humming rise.*)

WILLY (*staring through the window into the moonlight*): Gee, look at the moon moving between the buildings!

(*Biff wraps the tubing around his hand and quickly goes up the stairs.*)

ACT II

(*Music is heard, gay and bright. The curtain rises as the music fades away. Willy, in shirt sleeves is sitting at the kitchen table, sipping coffee, his hat in his lap. Linda is piling his cup when she can.*)

WILLY: Wonderful coffee. Meal in itself.

LINDA: Can I make you some eggs?

WILLY: No. Take a breath.

LINDA: You look so rested, dear.

WILLY: I slept like a dead one. First time in months. Imagine, sleeping till ten on a Tuesday morning. Boys left nice and early, heh?

LINDA: They were out of here by eight o'clock.

WILLY: Good work!

LINDA: It was so thrilling to see them leaving together. I can't get over the shaving lotion in this house!

WILLY (*smiling*): Mmm —

LINDA: Biff was very changed this morning. His whole attitude seemed to be hopeful. He couldn't wait to get downtown to see Oliver.

WILLY: He's heading for a change. There's no question, there simply are certain men that take longer to get — solidified. How did he dress?

LINDA: His blue suit. He's so handsome in that suit. He could be a — anything in that suit!

(*Willy gets up from the table. Linda holds his jacket for him.*)

WILLY: There's no question, no question at all. Gee, on the way home tonight I'd like to buy some seeds.

LINDA (*laughing*): That'd be wonderful. But not enough sun gets back there. Nothing'll grow any more.

WILLY: You wait, kid, before it's all over we're gonna get a little place out in the country, and I'll raise some vegetables, a couple of chickens . . .

LINDA: You'll do it yet, dear.

(*Willy walks out of his jacket. Linda follows him.*)

WILLY: And they'll get married, and come for a weekend. I'd build a little guest house. 'Cause I got so many fine tools, all I'd need would be a little lumber and some peace of mind.

LINDA (*joyfully*): I sewed the lining . . .

WILLY: I could build two guest houses, so they'd both come. Did he decide how much he's going to ask Oliver for?

LINDA (*getting him into the jacket*): He didn't mention it, but I imagine ten or fifteen thousand. You going to talk to Howard today?

WILLY: Yeah. I'll put it to him straight and simple. He'll just have to take me off the road.

LINDA: And Willy, don't forget to ask for a little advance, because we've got the insurance premium. It's the grace period now.

WILLY: That's a hundred . . . ?

LINDA: A hundred and eight, sixty-eight. Because we're a little short again.

WILLY: Why are we short?

LINDA: Well, you had the motor job on the car . . .

WILLY: That goddam Studebaker!

LINDA: And you got one more payment on the refrigerator . . .

WILLY: But it just broke again!

LINDA: Well, it's old, dear.

WILLY: I told you we should've bought a well-advertised machine. Charley bought a General Electric and it's twenty years old and it's still good, that son-of-a-bitch.

LINDA: But, Willy —

WILLY: Whoever heard of a Hastings refrigerator? Once in my life I would like to own something outright before it's broken! I'm always in a race with the junkyard! I just finished paying for the car and it's on its last legs. The refrigerator consumes belts like a goddamn maniac. They time those things. They time them so when you finally paid for them, they're used up.

LINDA (*buttoning up his jacket as he unbuttons it*): All told, about two hundred dollars would carry us, dear. But that includes the last payment on the mortgage. After this payment, Willy, the house belongs to us.

WILLY: It's twenty five years!

LINDA: Biff was nine years old when we bought it.

WILLY: Well, that's a great thing. To weather a twenty-five year mortgage is —

LINDA: It's an accomplishment.

WILLY: All the cement, the lumber, the reconstruction I put in this house! There ain't a crack to be found in it anymore.

LINDA: Well, it served its purpose.

WILLY: What purpose? Some stranger'll come along, move in, and that's that. If only Biff would take this house, and raise a family . . . (*He starts to go.*) Good-by, I'm late.

LINDA (*suddenly remembering*): Oh, I forgot! You're supposed to meet them for dinner.

WILLY: Me?

LINDA: At Frank's Chop House on Forty-eighth near Sixth Avenue.

WILLY: Is that so! How about you?

LINDA: No, just the three of you. They're gonna blow you to a big meal!

WILLY: Don't say! Who thought of that?

LINDA: Biff came to me this morning, Willy, and he said, "Tell Dad, we want to blow him to a big meal." Be there six o'clock. You and your two boys are going to have dinner.

WILLY: Gee whiz! That's really somethin'. I'm gonna knock Howard for a loop, kid. I'll get an advance, and I'll come home with a New York job. Goddammit, now I'm gonna do it!

LINDA: Oh, that's the spirit, Willy!

WILLY: I will never get behind a wheel the rest of my life!

LINDA: It's changing, Willy, I can feel it changing!

WILLY: Beyond a question. G'by, I'm late. (*He starts to go again.*)

LINDA (*calling after him as she runs to the kitchen table for a handkerchief*): You got your glasses?

WILLY (*feels for them, then comes back in*): Yeah, yeah, got my glasses.

LINDA (*giving him the handkerchief*): And a handkerchief.

WILLY: Yeah, handkerchief.

LINDA: And your saccharine?

WILLY: Yeah, my saccharine.

LINDA: Be careful on the subway stairs.

(*She kisses him, and a silk stocking is seen hanging from her hand. Willy notices it.*)

WILLY: Will you stop mending stockings? At least while I'm in the house. It gets me nervous. I can't tell you. Please.

(*Linda hides the stocking in her hand as she follows Willy across the forestage in front of the house.*)

LINDA: Remember, Frank's Chop House.

WILLY (*passing the apron*): Maybe beets would grow out there.

LINDA (*laughing*): But you tried so many times.

WILLY: Yeah. Well, don't work hard today. (*He disappears around the right corner of the house.*)

LINDA: Be careful!

(*As Willy vanishes, Linda waves to him. Suddenly the phone rings. She runs across the stage and into the kitchen and lifts it.*)

LINDA: Hello? Oh, Biff! I'm so glad you called, I just . . . Yes, sure, I just told him. Yes, he'll be there for dinner at six o'clock, I didn't forget. Listen, I was just dying to tell you. You know that little rubber pipe I told you about? That he connected to the gas heater? I finally decided to go down the cellar this morning and take it away and destroy it. But it's gone! Imagine? He took it away himself, it isn't there! (*She listens.*) When? Oh, then you took it. Oh — nothing, it's just that I'd hoped he'd taken it away himself. Oh, I'm not worried, darling, because this morning he left in such high spirits, it was like the old days! I'm not afraid any more. Did Mr. Oliver see you? . . . Well, you wait there then. And make a nice impression on him, darling. Just don't perspire too much before you see him. And have a nice time with Dad. He may have big news too! . . . That's right, a New York job. And be sweet to him tonight, dear. Be loving to him. Because he's only a little boat looking for a harbor. (*She is trembling with sorrow and joy.*) Oh, that's wonderful, Biff, you'll save his life. Thanks, darling. Just put your arm around him when he comes into the restaurant. Give him a smile. That's the boy . . . Good-by, dear. . . . You got your comb? . . . That's fine. Good-by, Biff dear.

(*In the middle of her speech, Howard Wagner, thirty-six, wheels in a small typewriter table on which is a wire-recording machine and proceeds to plug it in. This is on the left forestage. Light slowly fades on Linda as it rises on Howard. Howard is intent on threading the machine and only glances over his shoulder as Willy appears.*)

WILLY: Pst! Pst!

HOWARD: Hello, Willy, come in.

WILLY: Like to have a little talk with you, Howard.

HOWARD: Sorry to keep you waiting. I'll be with you in a minute.

WILLY: What's that, Howard?

HOWARD: Didn't you ever see one of these? Wire recorder.

WILLY: Oh. Can we talk a minute?

HOWARD: Records things. Just got delivery yesterday. Been driving me crazy, the most terrific machine I ever saw in my life. I was up all night with it.

WILLY: What do you do with it?

HOWARD: I bought it for dictation, but you can do anything with it. Listen to this. I had it home last night. Listen to what I picked up. The first one is my daughter. Get this. (*He flicks the switch and*

"Roll out the Barrel" is heard being whistled.) Listen to that kid whistle.

WILLY: That is lifelike, isn't it?

HOWARD: Seven years old. Get that tone.

WILLY: Ts, ts. Like to ask a little favor if you . . .

(*The whistling breaks off, and the voice of Howard's daughter is heard.*)

HIS DAUGHTER: Now you, Daddy.

HOWARD: She's crazy for me! (*Again the same song is whistled.*) That's me! Ha! (*He winks.*)

WILLY: You're very good!

(*The whistling breaks off again. The machine runs silent for a moment.*)

HOWARD: Sh! Get this now, this is my son.

HIS SON: "The capital of Alabama is Montgomery; the capital of Arizona is Phoenix; the capital of Arkansas is Little Rock; the capital of California is Sacramento . . ." (*and on, and on.*)

HOWARD (*holding up five fingers*): Five years old, Willy!

WILLY: He'll make an announcer some day!

HIS SON (*continuing*): "The capital . . ."

HOWARD: Get that — alphabetical order! (*The machine breaks off suddenly.*) Wait a minute. The maid kicked the plug out.

WILLY: It certainly is a —

HOWARD: Sh, for God's sake!

HIS SON: "It's nine o'clock, Bulova watch time. So I have to go to sleep."

WILLY: That really is —

HOWARD: Wait a minute! The next is my wife.

(*They wait.*)

HOWARD'S VOICE: "Go on, say something." (*Pause.*) "Well, you gonna talk?"

HIS WIFE: "I can't think of anything."

HOWARD'S VOICE: "Well, talk — it's turning."

HIS WIFE (*shyly, beaten*): "Hello." (*Silence.*) "Oh, Howard, I can't talk into this . . ."

HOWARD (*snapping the machine off*): That was my wife.

WILLY: That is a wonderful machine. Can we —

HOWARD: I tell you, Willy, I'm gonna take my camera, and my bandsaw, and all my hobbies, and out they go. This is the most fascinating relaxation I ever found.

WILLY: I think I'll get one myself.

HOWARD: Sure, they're only a hundred and a half. You can't do without it. Supposing you wanna hear Jack Benny, see? But you can't be at home at that hour. So you tell the maid to turn the radio on when Jack Benny comes on, and this automatically goes on with the radio . . .

WILLY: And when you come home you . . .

HOWARD: You can come home twelve o'clock, one o'clock, any time you like, and you get yourself a Coke and sit yourself down, throw the switch, and there's Jack Benny's program in the middle of the night!

WILLY: I'm definitely going to get one. Because lots of times I'm on the road, and I think to myself, what I must be missing on the radio!

HOWARD: Don't you have a radio in the car?

WILLY: Well, yeah, but who ever thinks of turning it on?

HOWARD: Say, aren't you supposed to be in Boston?

WILLY: That's what I want to talk to you about, Howard. You got a minute? (*He draws a chair in from the wing.*)

HOWARD: What happened? What're you doing here?

WILLY: Well . . .

HOWARD: You didn't crack up again, did you?

WILLY: Oh, no. No . . .

HOWARD: Geez, you had me worried there for a minute. What's the trouble?

WILLY: Well, tell you the truth, Howard. I've come to the decision that I'd rather not travel anymore.

HOWARD: Not travel! Well, what'll you do?

WILLY: Remember, Christmas time, when you had the party here? You said you'd try to think of some spot for me here in town.

HOWARD: With us?

WILLY: Well, sure.

HOWARD: Oh, yeah, yeah. I remember. Well, I couldn't think of anything for you, Willy.

WILLY: I tell ya, Howard. The kids are all grown up, y'know. I don't need much anymore. If I could take home — well, sixty-five dollars a week, I could swing it.

HOWARD: Yeah, but Willy, see I —

WILLY: I tell ya why, Howard. Speaking frankly and between the two of us, y'know — I'm just a little tired.

HOWARD: Oh, I could understand that, Willy. But you're a road man, Willy, and we do a road business. We've only got a half-dozen salesmen on the floor here.

WILLY: God knows, Howard, I never asked a favor of any man. But I was with the firm when your father used to carry you in here in his arms.

HOWARD: I know that, Willy, but —

WILLY: Your father came to me the day you were born and asked me what I thought of the name Howard, may he rest in peace.

HOWARD: I appreciate that, Willy, but there just is no spot here for you. If I had a spot I'd slam you right in, but I just don't have a single solitary spot.

(*He looks for his lighter. Willy has picked it up and gives it to him. Pause.*)

WILLY (*with increasing anger*): Howard, all I need to set my table is fifty dollars a week.

HOWARD: But where am I going to put you, kid?

WILLY: Look, it isn't a question of whether I can sell merchandise, is it?

HOWARD: No, but it's business, kid, and everybody's gotta pull his own weight.

WILLY (*desperately*): Just let me tell you a story, Howard —

HOWARD: 'Cause you gotta admit, business is business.

WILLY (*angrily*): Business is definitely business, but just listen for a minute. You don't understand this. When I was a boy — eighteen, nineteen — I was already on the road. And there was a question in my mind as to whether selling had a future for me. Because in those days I had a yearning to go to Alaska. See, there were three gold strikes in one month in Alaska, and I felt like going out. Just for the ride, you might say.

HOWARD (*barely interested*): Don't say.

WILLY: Oh, yeah, my father lived many years in Alaska. He was an adventurous man. We've got quite a little streak of self-reliance in our family. I thought I'd go out with my older brother and try to locate him, and maybe settle in the North with the old man. And I was almost decided to go, when I met a salesman in the Parker House. His name was Dave Singleman. And he was eighty-four years old, and he'd drummed merchandise in thirty-one states. And old Dave, he'd go up to his room, y'understand, put on his green velvet slippers — I'll never forget — and pick up his phone and call the buyers, and without ever leaving his room, at the age of eighty-four, he made his living. And when I saw that, I realized that selling was the greatest career a man could want. 'Cause what could be more satisfying than to be able to go, at the age of eighty-four, into twenty or thirty different cities, and pick up a phone, and be remembered and loved and helped by so many different people? Do you know? When he died — and by the way he died the death of a salesman, in his green velvet slippers in the smoker of the New York, New Haven and Hartford, going into Boston — when he died, hundreds of salesmen and buyers were at his funeral. Things were sad on a lotta trains for months after that. (*He stands up. Howard has not looked at him.*) In those days there was personality in it, Howard. There was respect and comradeship, and gratitude in it. Today, it's all cut and dried, and there's no chance for bringing friendship to bear — or personality. You see what I mean? They don't know me any more.

HOWARD (*moving away, to the right*): That's just the thing, Willy.

WILLY: If I had forty dollars a week — that's all I'd need. Forty dollars, Howard.

HOWARD: Kid, I can't take blood from a stone, I —

WILLY (*desperation is on him now*): Howard, the year Al Smith was nominated, your father came to me and —

HOWARD (*starting to go off*): I've got to see some people, kid.

WILLY (*stopping him*): I'm talking about your father! There were promises made across this desk! You mustn't tell me you've got people to see — I put thirty-four years into this firm, Howard, and now I can't pay my insurance! You can't eat the orange and throw the peel away — a man is not a piece of fruit! (*After a pause.*) Now pay attention. Your father — in 1928 I had a big year. I averaged a hundred and seventy dollars a week in commissions.

HOWARD (*impatiently*): Now, Willy, you never averaged —

WILLY (*banging his hand on the desk*): I averaged a hundred and seventy dollars a week in the year of 1928! And your father came to me — or rather I was in the office here — it was right over this desk — and he put his hand on my shoulder —

HOWARD (*getting up*): You'll have to excuse me, Willy, I gotta see some people. Pull yourself together. (*Going out.*) I'll be back in a little while.

(*On Howard's exit, the light on his chair grows very bright and strange.*)

WILLY: Pull myself together! What the hell did I say to him? My God, I was yelling at him! How could I? (*Willy breaks off, staring at the light, which occupies the chair, animating it. He approaches this chair, standing across the desk from it.*) Frank, Frank, don't you remember what you told me that time? How you put your hand on my shoulder, and Frank . . . (*He leans on the desk and as he speaks the dead man's name he accidentally switches on the recorder, and instantly*)

HOWARD'S SON: ". . . of New York is Albany. The capital of Ohio is Cincinnati, the capital of Rhode Island is . . ." (*The recitation continues.*)

WILLY (*leaping away with fright, shouting*): Ha! Howard! Howard! Howard!

HOWARD (*rushing in*): What happened?

WILLY (*pointing at the machine, which continues nasally, childishly, with the capital cities*): Shut it off! Shut it off!

HOWARD (*pulling the plug out*): Look, Willy . . .

WILLY (*pressing his hands to his eyes*): I gotta get myself some coffee. I'll get some coffee . . .

(*Willy starts to walk out. Howard stops him.*)

HOWARD (*rolling up the cord*): Willy, look . . .

WILLY: I'll go to Boston.

HOWARD: Willy, you can't go to Boston for us.

WILLY: Why can't I go?

HOWARD: I don't want you to represent us. I've been meaning to tell you for a long time now.

WILLY: Howard, are you firing me?

HOWARD: I think you need a good long rest, Willy.

WILLY: Howard —

HOWARD: And when you feel better, come back, and we'll see if we can work something out.

WILLY: But I gotta earn money, Howard. I'm in no position to —

HOWARD: Where are your sons? Why don't your sons give you a hand?

WILLY: They're working on a very big deal.

HOWARD: This is no time for false pride, Willy. You go to your sons and you tell them that you're tired. You've got two great boys, haven't you?

WILLY: Oh, no question, no question, but in the meantime . . .

HOWARD: Then that's that, heh?

WILLY: All right, I'll go to Boston tomorrow.

HOWARD: No, no.

WILLY: I can't throw myself on my sons. I'm not a cripple!

HOWARD: Look, kid, I'm busy this morning.

WILLY (*grasping Howard's arm*): Howard, you've got to let me go to Boston!

HOWARD (*hard, keeping himself under control*): I've got a line of people to see this morning. Sit down, take five minutes, and pull yourself together, and then go home, will ya? I need the office, Willy. (*He starts to go, turns, remembering the recorder, starts to push off the table holding the recorder.*) Oh, yeah. Whenever you can this week, stop by and drop off the samples. You'll feel better, Willy, and then come back and we'll talk. Pull yourself together, kid, there's people outside.

(*Howard exits, pushing the table off left. Willy stares into space, exhausted. Now the music is heard — Ben's music — first distantly, then closer, closer. As Willy speaks, Ben enters from the right. He carries valise and umbrella.*)

WILLY: Oh, Ben, how did you do it? What is the answer? Did you wind up the Alaska deal already?

BEN: Doesn't take much time if you know what you're doing. Just a short business trip. Boarding ship in an hour. Wanted to say good-by.

WILLY: Ben, I've got to talk to you.

BEN (*glancing at his watch*): Haven't the time, William.

WILLY (*crossing the apron to Ben*): Ben, nothing's working out. I don't know what to do.

BEN: Now, look here, William. I've bought timberland in Alaska and I need a man to look after things for me.

WILLY: God, timberland! Me and my boys in those grand outdoors!

BEN: You've a new continent at your doorstep, William. Get out of these cities, they're full of talk and time payments and courts of law. Screw on your fists and you can fight for a fortune up there.

WILLY: Yes, yes! Linda, Linda!

(*Linda enters as of old, with the wash.*)

LINDA: Oh, you're back?

BEN: I haven't much time.

WILLY: No, wait! Linda, he's got a proposition for me in Alaska.

LINDA: But you've got — (*To Ben.*) He's got a beautiful job here.

WILLY: But in Alaska, kid, I could —

LINDA: You're doing well enough, Willy!

BEN (*to Linda*): Enough for what, my dear?

LINDA (*frightened of Ben and angry at him*): Don't say those things to him! Enough to be happy right here, right now. (*To Willy, while Ben laughs.*) Why must everybody conquer the world? You're well liked, and the boys love you, and someday — (*To Ben*) — why, old man Wagner told him just the other day that if he keeps it up he'll be a member of the firm, didn't he, Willy?

WILLY: Sure, sure. I am building something with this firm, Ben, and if a man is building something he must be on the right track, mustn't he?

BEN: What are you building? Lay your hand on it. Where is it?

WILLY (*hesitantly*): That's true, Linda, there's nothing.

LINDA: Why? (*To Ben.*) There's a man eighty-four years old —

WILLY: That's right, Ben, that's right. When I look at that man I say, what is there to worry about?

BEN: Bah!

WILLY: It's true, Ben. All he has to do is go into any city, pick up the phone, and he's making his living and you know why?

BEN (*picking up his valise*): I've got to go.

WILLY (*holding Ben back*): Look at this boy!

(*Biff, in his high school sweater, enters carrying suitcase. Happy carries Biff's shoulder guards, gold helmet, and football pants.*)

WILLY: Without a penny to his name, three great universities are begging for him, and from there the sky's the limit, because it's not what you do, Ben. It's who you know and the smile on your face! It's contacts, Ben, contacts! The whole wealth of Alaska passes over the lunch table at the Commodore Hotel, and that's the wonder, the wonder of this country, that a man can end with diamonds here on the basis of being liked! (*He turns to Biff.*) And that's why when you get out on that field today it's important. Because thousands of people will be rooting for you and loving you. (*To Ben, who has again begun to leave.*) And Ben! when he walks into a business office his name will sound out like a bell and all the doors will open to him! I've seen it, Ben, I've seen it a thousand times! You can't feel it with your hand like timber, but it's there!

BEN: Good-by, William.

WILLY: Ben, am I right? Don't you think I'm right? I value your advice.

BEN: There's a new continent at your doorstep, William. You could walk out rich. Rich! (*He is gone.*)

WILLY: We'll do it here, Ben! You hear me? We're gonna do it here!

(*Young Bernard rushes in. The gay music of the Boys is heard.*)

BERNARD: Oh, gee, I was afraid you left already!

WILLY: Why? What time is it?

BERNARD: It's half-past one!

WILLY: Well, come on, everybody! Ebbets Field next stop! Where's the pennants? (*He rushes through the wall-line of the kitchen and out into the living room.*)

LINDA (*to Biff*): Did you pack fresh underwear?

BIFF (*who has been limbering up*): I want to go!

BERNARD: Biff, I'm carrying your helmet, ain't I?

HAPPY: No, I'm carrying the helmet.

BERNARD: Oh, Biff, you promised me.

HAPPY: I'm carrying the helmet.

BERNARD: How am I going to get in the locker room?

LINDA: Let him carry the shoulder guards. (*She puts her coat and hat on in the kitchen.*)

BERNARD: Can I, Biff? 'Cause I told everybody I'm going to be in the locker room.

HAPPY: In Ebbets Field it's the clubhouse.

BERNARD: I meant the clubhouse. Biff!

HAPPY: Biff!

BIFF (*grandly, after a slight pause*): Let him carry the shoulder guards.

HAPPY (*as he gives Bernard the shoulder guards*): Stay close to us now.

(*Willy rushes in with the pennants.*)

WILLY (*handing them out*): Everybody wave when Biff comes out on the field. (*Happy and Bernard run off.*) You set now, boy?

(*The music has died away.*)

BIFF: Ready to go, Pop. Every muscle is ready.

WILLY (*at the edge of the apron*): You realize what this means?

BIFF: That's right, Pop.

WILLY (*feeling Biff's muscles*): You're comin' home this afternoon captain of the All-Scholastic Championship Team of the City of New York.

BIFF: I got it, Pop. And remember, pal, when I take off my helmet, that touchdown is for you.

WILLY: Let's go! (*He is starting out, with his arm around Biff, when Charley enters, as of old, in knickers.*) I got no room for you, Charley.

CHARLEY: Room? For what?

WILLY: In the car.

CHARLEY: You goin' for a ride? I wanted to shoot some casino.

WILLY (*furiously*): Casino! (*Incredulously.*) Don't you realize what today is?

LINDA: Oh, he knows, Willy. He's just kidding you.

WILLY: That's nothing to kid about!

CHARLEY: No, Linda, what's goin' on?

LINDA: He's playing in Ebbets Field.

CHARLEY: Baseball in this weather?

WILLY: Don't talk to him. Come on, come on! (*He is pushing them out.*)

CHARLEY: Wait a minute, didn't you hear the news?

WILLY: What?

CHARLEY: Don't you listen to the radio? Ebbets Field just blew up.

WILLY: You go to hell! (*Charley laughs. Pushing them out.*) Come on, come on! We're late.

CHARLEY (*as they go*): Knock a homer, Biff, knock a homer!

WILLY (*the last to leave, turning to Charley*): I don't think that was funny, Charley. This is the greatest day of his life.

CHARLEY: Willy, when are you going to grow up?

WILLY: Yeah, heh? When this game is over, Charley, you'll be laughing out of the other side of your face. They'll be calling him another Red Grange. Twenty-five thousand a year.

CHARLEY (*kidding*): Is that so?

WILLY: Yeah, that's so.

CHARLEY: Well, then, I'm sorry, Willy. But tell me something.

WILLY: What?

CHARLEY: Who is Red Grange?

WILLY: Put up your hands. Goddam you, put up your hands!

(*Charley, chuckling, shakes his head and walks away, around the left corner of the stage. Willy follows him. The music rises to a mocking frenzy.*)

WILLY: Who the hell do you think you are, better than everybody else? You don't know everything, you big, ignorant, stupid . . . Put up your hands!

(*Light rises, on the right side of the forestage, on a small table in the reception room of Charley's office. Traffic sounds are heard. Bernard, now mature, sits whistling to himself. A pair of tennis rackets and an overnight bag are on the floor beside him.*)

WILLY (*offstage*): What are you walking away for? Don't walk away! If you're going to say something say it to my face! I know you laugh at me behind my back. You'll laugh out of the other side of your goddam face after this game. Touchdown! Touchdown! Eighty thousand people! Touchdown! Right between the goal posts.

(*Bernard is a quiet, earnest, but self-assured young man. Willy's voice is coming from right upstage now. Bernard lowers his feet off the table and listens. Jenny, his father's secretary, enters.*)

JENNY (*distressed*): Say, Bernard, will you go out in the hall?

BERNARD: What is that noise? Who is it?

JENNY: Mr. Loman. He just got off the elevator.

BERNARD (*getting up*): Who's he arguing with?

JENNY: Nobody. There's nobody with him. I can't deal with him anymore, and your father gets all upset everytime he comes. I've got a lot of typing to do, and your father's waiting to sign it. Will you see him?

WILLY (*entering*): Touchdown! Touch — (*He sees Jenny.*) Jenny, Jenny, good to see you. How're ya? Workin'? Or still honest?

JENNY: Fine. How've you been feeling?

WILLY: Not much any more, Jenny. Ha, ha! (*He is surprised to see the rackets.*)

BERNARD: Hello, Uncle Willy.

WILLY (*almost shocked*): Bernard! Well, look who's here! (*He comes quickly, guiltily, to Bernard and warmly shakes his hand.*)

BERNARD: How are you? Good to see you.

WILLY: What are you doing here?

BERNARD: Oh, just stopped by to see Pop. Get off my feet till my train leaves. I'm going to Washington in a few minutes.

WILLY: Is he in?

BERNARD: Yes, he's in his office with the accountant. Sit down.

WILLY (*sitting down*): What're you going to do in Washington?

BERNARD: Oh, just a case I've got there, Willy.

WILLY: That so? (*Indicating the rackets.*) You going to play tennis there?

BERNARD: I'm staying with a friend who's got a court.

WILLY: Don't say. His own tennis court. Must be fine people, I bet.

BERNARD: They are, very nice. Dad tells me Biff's in town.

WILLY (*with a big smile*): Yeah, Biff's in. Working on a very big deal, Bernard.

BERNARD: What's Biff doing?

WILLY: Well, he's been doing very big things in the West. But he decided to establish himself here. Very big. We're having dinner. Did I hear your wife had a boy?

BERNARD: That's right. Our second.

WILLY: Two boys! What do you know!

BERNARD: What kind of a deal has Biff got?

WILLY: Well, Bill Oliver — very big sporting-goods man — he wants Biff very badly. Called him in from the West. Long distance, carte blanche, special deliveries. Your friends have their own private tennis court?

BERNARD: You still with the old firm, Willy?

WILLY (*after a pause*): I'm — I'm overjoyed to see how you made the grade, Bernard, overjoyed. It's an encouraging thing to see a young man really — really — Looks very good for Biff — very — (*He breaks off, then.*) Bernard — (*He is so full of emotion, he breaks off again.*)

BERNARD: What is it, Willy?

WILLY (*small and alone*): What — what's the secret?

BERNARD: What secret?

WILLY: How — how did you? Why didn't he ever catch on?

BERNARD: I wouldn't know that, Willy.

WILLY (*confidentially, desperately*): You were his friend, his boyhood friend. There's something I don't understand about it. His life ended after that Ebbets Field game. From the age of seventeen nothing good ever happened to him.

BERNARD: He never trained himself for anything.

WILLY: But he did, he did. After high school he took so many correspondence courses. Radio mechanics; television; God knows what, and never made the slightest mark.

BERNARD (*taking off his glasses*): Willy, do you want to talk candidly?

WILLY (*rising, faces Bernard*): I regard you as a very brilliant man, Bernard. I value your advice.

BERNARD: Oh, the hell with the advice, Willy. I couldn't advise you. There's just one thing I've always wanted to ask you. When he was supposed to graduate, and the math teacher flunked him —

WILLY: Oh, that son-of-a-bitch ruined his life.

BERNARD: Yeah, but, Willy, all he had to do was go to summer school and make up that subject.

WILLY: That's right, that's right.

BERNARD: Did you tell him not to go to summer school?

WILLY: Me? I begged him to go. I ordered him to go!

BERNARD: Then why wouldn't he go?

WILLY: Why? Why! Bernard, that question has been trailing me like a ghost for the last fifteen years. He flunked the subject, and laid down and died like a hammer hit him!

BERNARD: Take it easy, kid.

WILLY: Let me talk to you — I got nobody to talk to. Bernard, Bernard, was it my fault? Y'see? It keeps going around in my mind, maybe I did something to him. I got nothing to give him.

BERNARD: Don't take it so hard.

WILLY: Why did he lay down? What is the story there? You were his friend!

BERNARD: Willy, I remember, it was June, and our grades came out. And he'd flunked math.

WILLY: That son-of-a-bitch!

BERNARD: No, it wasn't right then. Biff just got very angry, I remember, and he was ready to enroll in summer school.

WILLY (surprised): He was?

BERNARD: He wasn't beaten by it at all. But then, Willy, he disappeared from the block for almost a month. And I got the idea that he'd gone up to New England to see you. Did he have a talk with you then?

(Willy stares in silence.)

BERNARD: Willy?

WILLY (with a strong edge of resentment in his voice): Yeah, he came to Boston. What about it?

BERNARD: Well, just that when he came back — I'll never forget this, it always mystifies me. Because I'd thought so well of Biff, even though he'd always taken advantage of me. I loved him, Willy, y'know? And he came back after that month and took his sneakers — remember those sneakers with "University of Virginia" printed on them? He was so proud of those, wore them every day. And he took them down in the cellar, and burned them up in the furnace. We had a fist fight. It lasted at least half an hour. Just the two of us, punching each other down the cellar, and crying right through it. I've often thought of how strange it was that I knew he'd given up his life. What happened in Boston, Willy?

(Willy looks at him as at an intruder.)

BERNARD: I just bring it up because you asked me.

WILLY (angrily): Nothing. What do you mean, "What happened?" What's that got to do with anything?

BERNARD: Well, don't get sore.

WILLY: What are you trying to do, blame it on me? If a boy lays down is that my fault?

BERNARD: Now, Willy, don't get —

WILLY: Well, don't — don't talk to me that way! What does that mean, "What happened?"

(Charley enters. He is in his vest, and he carries a bottle of bourbon.)

CHARLEY: Hey, you're going to miss that train. (He waves the bottle.)

BERNARD: Yeah, I'm going. (He takes the bottle.) Thanks, Pop. (He picks up his rackets and bag.) Good-by, Willy, and don't worry about it. You know, "If at first you don't succeed . . ."

WILLY: Yes, I believe in that.

BERNARD: But sometimes, Willy, it's better for a man just to walk away.

WILLY: Walk away?

BERNARD: That's right.

WILLY: But if you can't walk away?

BERNARD (after a slight pause): I guess that's when it's tough. (Extending his hand.) Good-by, Willy.

WILLY (shaking Bernard's hand): Good-by, boy.

CHARLEY (an arm on Bernard's shoulder): How do you like this kid? Gonna argue a case in front of the Supreme Court.

BERNARD (protesting): Pop!

WILLY (genuinely shocked, pained, and happy): No! The Supreme Court!

BERNARD: I gotta run. 'By, Dad!

CHARLEY: Knock 'em dead, Bernard!

(Bernard goes off.)

WILLY (as Charley takes out his wallet): The Supreme Court! And he didn't even mention it!

CHARLEY (counting out money on the desk): He don't have to — he's gonna do it.

WILLY: And you never told him what to do, did you? You never took any interest in him.

CHARLEY: My salvation is that I never took any interest in anything. There's some money — fifty dollars. I got an accountant inside.

WILLY: Charley, look . . . (With difficulty.) I got my insurance to pay. If you can manage it — I need a hundred and ten dollars.

(Charley doesn't reply for a moment; merely stops moving.)

WILLY: I'd draw it from my bank but Linda would know, and I . . .

CHARLEY: Sit down, Willy.

WILLY (moving toward the chair): I'm keeping an account of everything, remember. I'll pay every penny back. (He sits.)

CHARLEY: Now listen to me, Willy.

WILLY: I want you to know I appreciate . . .

CHARLEY (sitting down on the table): Willy, what're you doin'? What the hell is goin' on in your head?

WILLY: Why? I'm simply . . .

CHARLEY: I offered you a job. You make fifty dollars a week. And I won't send you on the road.

WILLY: I've got a job.

CHARLEY: Without pay? What kind of a job is a job without pay? (He rises.) Now, look, kid, enough is enough. I'm no genius but I know when I'm being insulted.

WILLY: Insulted!

CHARLEY: Why don't you want to work for me?

WILLY: What's the matter with you? I've got a job.

CHARLEY: Then what're you walkin' in here every week for?

WILLY (*getting up*): Well, if you don't want me to walk in here —

CHARLEY: I'm offering you a job.

WILLY: I don't want your goddam job!

CHARLEY: When the hell are you going to grow up?

WILLY (*furiously*): You big ignoramus, if you say that to me again I'll rap you one! I don't care how big you are! (*He's ready to fight.*)

(*Pause.*)

CHARLEY (*kindly, going to him*): How much do you need, Willy?

WILLY: Charley, I'm strapped. I'm strapped. I don't know what to do. I was just fired.

CHARLEY: Howard fired you?

WILLY: That snotnose. Imagine that? I named him. I named him Howard.

CHARLEY: Willy, when're you gonna realize that them things don't mean anything? You named him Howard, but you can't sell that. The only thing you got in this world is what you can sell. And the funny thing is that you're a salesman, and you don't know that.

WILLY: I've always tried to think otherwise, I guess. I always felt that if a man was impressive, and well liked, that nothing —

CHARLEY: Why must everybody like you? Who liked J. P. Morgan?° Was he impressive? In a Turkish bath he'd look like a butcher. But with his pockets on he was very well liked. Now listen, Willy, I know you don't like me, and nobody can say I'm in love with you, but I'll give you a job because — just for the hell of it, put it that way. Now what do you say?

WILLY: I — I just can't work for you, Charley.

CHARLEY: What're you, jealous of me?

WILLY: I can't work for you, that's all, don't ask me why.

CHARLEY (*angered, takes out more bills*): You been jealous of me all your life, you dammed fool! Here, pay your insurance. (*He puts the money in Willy's hand.*)

WILLY: I'm keeping strict accounts.

CHARLEY: I've got some work to do. Take care of yourself. And pay your insurance.

J. P. Morgan: (1837–1913), wealthy financier and art collector whose money was made chiefly in banking, railroads, and steel.

WILLY (*moving to the right*): Funny, y'know? After all the highways, and the trains, and the appointments, and the years, you end up worth more dead than alive.

CHARLEY: Willy, nobody's worth nothin' dead. (*After a slight pause.*) Did you hear what I said?

(*Willy stands still, dreaming.*)

CHARLEY: Willy!

WILLY: Apologize to Bernard for me when you see him. I didn't mean to argue with him. He's a fine boy. They're all fine boys, and they'll end up big — all of them. Someday they'll all play tennis together. Wish me luck, Charley. He saw Bill Oliver today.

CHARLEY: Good luck.

WILLY (*on the verge of tears*): Charley, you're the only friend I got. Isn't that a remarkable thing? (*He goes out.*)

CHARLEY: Jesus!

(*Charley stares after him a moment and follows. All light blacks out. Suddenly raucous music is heard, and a red glow rises behind the screen at right. Stanley, a young waiter, appears, carrying a table, followed by Happy, who is carrying two chairs.*)

STANLEY (*putting the table down*): That's all right, Mr. Loman, I can handle it myself. (*He turns and takes the chairs from Happy and places them at the table.*)

HAPPY (*glancing around*): Oh, this is better.

STANLEY: Sure, in the front there you're in the middle of all kinds of noise. Whenever you got a party, Mr. Loman, you just tell me and I'll put you back here. Y'know, there's a lotta people they don't like it private, because when they go out they like to see a lotta action around them because they're sick and tired to stay in the house by theirself. But I know you, you ain't from Hackensack. You know what I mean?

HAPPY (*sitting down*): So how's it coming, Stanley?

STANLEY: Ah, it's a dog life. I only wish during the war they'd a took me in the Army. I coulda been dead by now.

HAPPY: My brother's back, Stanley.

STANLEY: Oh, he come back, heh? From the Far West.

HAPPY: Yeah, big cattle man, my brother, so treat him right. And my father's coming too.

STANLEY: Oh, your father too!

HAPPY: You got a couple of nice lobsters?

STANLEY: Hundred percent, big.

HAPPY: I want them with the claws.

STANLEY: Don't worry, I don't give you no mice. (*Happy laughs.*) How about some wine? It'll put a head on the meal.

HAPPY: No. You remember, Stanley, that recipe I brought you from overseas? With the champagne in it?

STANLEY: Oh, yeah, sure. I still got it tacked up yet in the kitchen. But that'll have to cost a buck apiece anyways.

HAPPY: That's all right.

STANLEY: What'd you, hit a number or somethin'?

HAPPY: No, it's a little celebration. My brother is — I think he pulled off a big deal today. I think we're going into business together.

STANLEY: Great! That's the best for you. Because a family business, you know what I mean? — that's the best.

HAPPY: That's what I think.

STANLEY: 'Cause what's the difference? Somebody steals? It's in the family. Know what I mean? (Sotto voce.°) Like this bartender here. The boss is goin' crazy what kinda leak he's got in the cash register. You put it in but it don't come out.

HAPPY (raising his head): Sh!

STANLEY: What?

HAPPY: You notice I wasn't lookin' right or left, was I?

STANLEY: No.

HAPPY: And my eyes are closed.

STANLEY: So what's the — ?

HAPPY: Strudel's comin'.

STANLEY (catching on, looks around): Ah, no, there's no —

(He breaks off as a furred, lavishly dressed girl enters and sits at the next table. Both follow her with their eyes.)

STANLEY: Geez, how'd ya know?

HAPPY: I got radar or something. (Staring directly at her profile.) Oooooooooo . . . Stanley.

STANLEY: I think that's for you, Mr. Loman.

HAPPY: Look at that mouth. Oh, God. And the binoculars.

STANLEY: Geez, you got a life, Mr. Loman.

HAPPY: Wait on her.

STANLEY (going to the girl's table): Would you like a menu, ma'am?

GIRL: I'm expecting someone, but I'd like a —

HAPPY: Why don't you bring her — excuse me, miss, do you mind? I sell champagne, and I'd like you to try my brand. Bring her a champagne, Stanley.

GIRL: That's awfully nice of you.

HAPPY: Don't mention it. It's all company money. (He laughs.)

GIRL: That's a charming product to be selling, isn't it?

Sotto voce: In a soft voice or stage whisper.

HAPPY: Oh, gets to be like everything else. Selling is selling, y'know.

GIRL: I suppose.

HAPPY: You don't happen to sell, do you?

GIRL: No, I don't sell.

HAPPY: Would you object to a compliment from a stranger? You ought to be on a magazine cover.

GIRL (looking at him a little archly): I have been.

(Stanley comes in with a glass of champagne.)

HAPPY: What'd I say before, Stanley? You see? She's a cover girl.

STANLEY: Oh, I could see, I could see.

HAPPY (to the Girl): What magazine?

GIRL: Oh, a lot of them. (She takes the drink.) Thank you.

HAPPY: You know what they say in France, don't you? "Champagne is the drink of the complexion" — Hya, Biff!

(Biff has entered and sits with Happy.)

BIFF: Hello, kid. Sorry I'm late.

HAPPY: I just got here. Uh, Miss — ?

GIRL: Forsythe.

HAPPY: Miss Forsythe, this is my brother.

BIFF: Is Dad here?

HAPPY: His name is Biff. You might've heard of him. Great football player.

GIRL: Really? What team?

HAPPY: Are you familiar with football?

GIRL: No, I'm afraid I'm not.

HAPPY: Biff is quarterback with the New York Giants.

GIRL: Well, that is nice, isn't it? (She drinks.)

HAPPY: Good health.

GIRL: I'm happy to meet you.

HAPPY: That's my name. Hap. It's really Harold, but at West Point they called me Happy.

GIRL (now really impressed): Oh, I see. How do you do? (She turns her profile.)

BIFF: Isn't Dad coming?

HAPPY: You want her?

BIFF: Oh, I could never make that.

HAPPY: I remember the time that idea would never come into your head. Where's the old confidence Biff?

BIFF: I just saw Oliver —

HAPPY: Wait a minute. I've got to see that old confidence again. Do you want her? She's on call.

BIFF: Oh, no. (He turns to look at the Girl.)

HAPPY: I'm telling you. Watch this. (Turning to the Girl): Honey? (She turns to him.) Are you busy?

GIRL: Well, I am . . . but I could make a phone call.

HAPPY: Do that, will you, honey? And see if you can get a friend. We'll be here for a while. Biff is one of the greatest football players in the country.

GIRL (standing up): Well, I'm certainly happy to meet you.

HAPPY: Come back soon.

GIRL: I'll try.

HAPPY: Don't try, honey, try hard.

(*The Girl exits. Stanley follows, shaking his head in bewildered admiration.*)

HAPPY: Isn't that a shame now? A beautiful girl like that? That's why I can't get married. There's not a good woman in a thousand. New York is loaded with them, kid!

BIFF: Hap, look —

HAPPY: I told you she was on call!

BIFF (*strangely unnerved*): Cut it out, will ya? I want to say something to you.

HAPPY: Did you see Oliver?

BIFF: I saw him all right. Now look, I want to tell Dad a couple of things and I want you to help me.

HAPPY: What? Is he going to back you?

BIFF: Are you crazy? You're out of your goddam head, you know that?

HAPPY: Why? What happened?

BIFF (*breathlessly*): I did a terrible thing today, Hap. It's been the strangest day I ever went through. I'm all numb, I swear.

HAPPY: You mean he wouldn't see you?

BIFF: Well, I waited six hours for him, see? All day. Kept sending my name in. Even tried to date his secretary so she'd get me to him, but no soap.

HAPPY: Because you're not showin' the old confidence Biff. He remembered you, didn't he?

BIFF (*stopping Happy with a gesture*): Finally, about five o'clock, he comes out. Didn't remember who I was or anything. I felt like such an idiot, Hap.

HAPPY: Did you tell him my Florida idea?

BIFF: He walked away. I saw him for one minute. I got so mad I could've torn the walls down! How the hell did I ever get the idea I was a salesman there? I even believed myself that I'd been a salesman for him! And then he gave me one look and — I realized what a ridiculous lie my whole life has been! We've been talking in a dream for fifteen years. I was a shipping clerk.

HAPPY: What'd you do?

BIFF (*with great tension and wonder*): Well, he left, see. And the secretary went out. I was all alone in the waiting room. I don't know what came over me, Hap. The next thing I know I'm in his office — paneled walls, everything. I can't explain it. I — Hap, I took his fountain pen.

HAPPY: Geez, did he catch you?

BIFF: I ran out. I ran down all eleven flights. I ran and ran and ran.

HAPPY: That was an awful dumb — what'd you do that for?

BIFF (*agonized*): I don't know, I just — wanted to take something, I don't know. You gotta help me, Hap. I'm gonna tell Pop.

HAPPY: You crazy? What for?

BIFF: Hap, he's got to understand that I'm not the man somebody lends that kind of money to. He thinks I've been spiting him all these years and it's eating him up.

HAPPY: That's just it. You tell him something nice.

BIFF: I can't.

HAPPY: Say you got a lunch date with Oliver tomorrow.

BIFF: So what do I do tomorrow?

HAPPY: You leave the house tomorrow and come back at night and say Oliver is thinking it over. And he thinks it over for a couple of weeks, and gradually it fades away and nobody's the worse.

BIFF: But it'll go on forever!

HAPPY: Dad is never so happy as when he's looking forward to something!

(*Willy enters.*)

HAPPY: Hello, scout!

WILLY: Gee, I haven't been here in years!

(*Stanley has followed Willy in and sets a chair for him. Stanley starts off but Happy stops him.*)

HAPPY: Stanley!

(*Stanley stands by, waiting for an order.*)

BIFF (*going to Willy with guilt, as to an invalid*): Sit down, Pop. You want a drink?

WILLY: Sure, I don't mind.

BIFF: Let's get a load on.

WILLY: You look worried.

BIFF: N-no. (*To Stanley.*) Scotch all around. Make it doubles.

STANLEY: Doubles, right. (*He goes.*)

WILLY: You had a couple already, didn't you?

BIFF: Just a couple, yeah.

WILLY: Well, what happened, boy? (*Nodding affirmatively, with a smile.*) Everything go all right?

BIFF (*takes a breath, then reaches out and grasps Willy's hand*): Pal . . . (*He is smiling bravely, and Willy is smiling too.*) I had an experience today.

HAPPY: Terrific, Pop.

WILLY: That so? What happened?

BIFF (*high, slightly alcoholic, above the earth*): I'm going to tell you everything from first to last. It's been a strange day. (*Silence. He looks around, composes himself as best he can, but his breath keeps breaking the rhythm of his voice.*) I had to wait quite a while for him, and —

WILLY: Oliver?

BIFF: Yeah, Oliver. All day, as a matter of cold fact.

And a lot of — instances — facts, Pop, facts about my life came back to me. Who was it, Pop? Who ever said I was a salesman with Oliver?

WILLY: Well, you were.

BIFF: No, Dad, I was a shipping clerk.

WILLY: But you were practically —

BIFF (*with determination*): Dad, I don't know who said it first, but I was never a salesman for Bill Oliver.

WILLY: What're you talking about?

BIFF: Let's hold on to the facts tonight, Pop. We're not going to get anywhere bullin' around. I was a shipping clerk.

WILLY (*angrily*): All right, now listen to me —

BIFF: Why don't you let me finish?

WILLY: I'm not interested in stories about the past or any crap of that kind because the woods are burning, boys, you understand? There's a big blaze going on all around. I was fired today.

BIFF (*shocked*): How could you be?

WILLY: I was fired, and I'm looking for a little good news to tell your mother, because the woman has waited and the woman has suffered. The gist of it is that I haven't got a story left in my head, Biff. So don't give me a lecture about facts and aspects. I am not interested. Now what've you got to say to me?

(*Stanley enters with three drinks. They wait until he leaves.*)

WILLY: Did you see Oliver?

BIFF: Jesus, Dad!

WILLY: You mean you didn't go up there?

HAPPY: Sure he went up there.

BIFF: I did. I — saw him. How could they fire you?

WILLY (*on the edge of his chair*): What kind of a welcome did he give you?

BIFF: He won't even let you work on commission?

WILLY: I'm out! (*Driving.*) So tell me, he gave you a warm welcome?

HAPPY: Sure, Pop, sure!

BIFF (*driven*): Well, it was kind of —

WILLY: I was wondering if he'd remember you. (*To Happy.*) Imagine, man doesn't see him for ten, twelve years and gives him that kind of a welcome!

HAPPY: Damn right!

BIFF (*trying to return to the offensive*): Pop, look —

WILLY: You know why he remembered you, don't you? Because you impressed him in those days.

BIFF: Let's talk quietly and get this down to the facts, huh?

WILLY (*as though Biff had been interrupting*): Well, what happened? It's great news, Biff. Did he take you into his office or'd you talk in the waiting room?

BIFF: Well, he came in, see, and —

WILLY (*with a big smile*): What'd he say? Betcha he threw his arm around you.

BIFF: Well, he kinda —

WILLY: He's a fine man. (*To Happy.*) Very hard man to see, y'know.

HAPPY (*agreeing*): Oh, I know.

WILLY (*to Biff*): Is that where you had the drinks?

BIFF: Yeah, he gave me a couple of — no, no!

HAPPY (*cutting in*): He told him my Florida idea.

WILLY: Don't interrupt. (*To Biff.*) How'd he react to the Florida idea?

BIFF: Dad, will you give me a minute to explain?

WILLY: I've been waiting for you to explain since I sat down here! What happened? He took you into his office and what?

BIFF: Well — I talked. And — and he listened, see.

WILLY: Famous for the way he listens, y'know. What was his answer?

BIFF: His answer was — (*He breaks off, suddenly angry.*) Dad, you're not letting me tell you what I want to tell you!

WILLY (*accusing, angered*): You didn't see him, did you?

BIFF: I did see him!

WILLY: What'd you insult him or something? You insulted him, didn't you?

BIFF: Listen, will you let me out of it, will you just let me out of it!

HAPPY: What the hell!

WILLY: Tell me what happened!

BIFF (*to Happy*): I can't talk to him!

(*A single trumpet note jars the ear. The light of green leaves stains the house, which holds the air of night and a dream. Young Bernard enters and knocks on the door of the house.*)

YOUNG BERNARD (*frantically*): Mrs. Loman, Mrs. Loman!

HAPPY: Tell him what happened!

BIFF (*to Happy*): Shut up and leave me alone!

WILLY: No, no! You had to go and flunk math!

BIFF: What math? What're you talking about?

YOUNG BERNARD: Mrs. Loman, Mrs. Loman!

(*Linda appears in the house, as of old.*)

WILLY (*wildly*): Math, math, math!

BIFF: Take it easy, Pop!

YOUNG BERNARD: Mrs. Loman!

WILLY (*furiously*): If you hadn't flunked you'd've been set by now!

BIFF: Now, look, I'm gonna tell you what happened, and you're going to listen to me.

YOUNG BERNARD: Mrs. Loman!

BIFF: I waited six hours —

HAPPY: What the hell are you saying?

BIFF: I kept sending in my name but he wouldn't see me. So finally he . . . (*He continues unheard as light fades low on the restaurant.*)

YOUNG BERNARD: Biff flunked math!

LINDA: No!

YOUNG BERNARD: Birnbaum flunked him! They won't graduate him!

LINDA: But they have to. He's gotta go to the university. Where is he? Biff! Biff!

YOUNG BERNARD: No, he left. He went to Grand Central.

LINDA: Grand — You mean he went to Boston!

YOUNG BERNARD: Is Uncle Willy in Boston?

LINDA: Oh, maybe Willy can talk to the teacher. Oh, the poor, poor boy!

(*Light on house area snaps out.*)

BIFF (*at the table, now audible, holding up a gold fountain pen*): . . . so I'm washed up with Oliver, you understand? Are you listening to me?

WILLY (*at a loss*): Yeah, sure. If you hadn't flunked —

BIFF: Flunked what? What're you talking about?

WILLY: Don't blame everything on me! I didn't flunk math — you did! What pen?

HAPPY: That was awful dumb, Biff, a pen like that is worth —

WILLY (*seeing the pen for the first time*): You took Oliver's pen?

BIFF (*weakening*): Dad, I just explained it to you.

WILLY: You stole Bill Oliver's fountain pen!

BIFF: I didn't exactly steal it! That's just what I've been explaining to you!

HAPPY: He had it in his hand and just then Oliver walked in, so he got nervous and stuck it in his pocket!

WILLY: My God, Biff!

BIFF: I never intended to do it, Dad!

OPERATOR'S VOICE: Standish Arms, good evening!

WILLY (*shouting*): I'm not in my room!

BIFF (*frightened*): Dad, what's the matter? (*He and Happy stand up.*)

OPERATOR: Ringing Mr. Loman for you!

WILLY: I'm not there, stop it!

BIFF (*horrified, gets down on one knee before Willy*): Dad, I'll make good, I'll make good. (*Willy tries to get to his feet. Biff holds him down.*) Sit down now.

WILLY: No, you're no good, you're no good for anything.

BIFF: I am, Dad, I'll find something else, you understand? Now don't worry about anything. (*He holds up Willy's face.*) Talk to me, Dad.

OPERATOR: Mr. Loman does not answer. Shall I page him?

WILLY (*attempting to stand, as though to rush and silence the Operator*): No, no, no!

HAPPY: He'll strike something, Pop.

WILLY: No, no . . .

BIFF (*desperately, standing over Willy*): Pop, listen! Listen to me! I'm telling you something good. Oliver talked to his partner about the Florida idea. You listening? He — he talked to his partner, and he came to me . . . I'm going to be all right, you hear? Dad, listen to me, he said it was just a question of the amount!

WILLY: Then you . . . got it?

HAPPY: He's gonna be terrific, Pop!

WILLY (*trying to stand*): Then you got it, haven't you? You got it! You got it!

BIFF (*agonized, holds Willy down*): No, no. Look, Pop. I'm supposed to have lunch with them tomorrow. I'm just telling you this so you'll know that I can still make an impression, Pop. And I'll make good somewhere, but I can't go tomorrow, see?

WILLY: Why not? You simply —

BIFF: But the pen, Pop!

WILLY: You give it to him and tell him it was an oversight!

HAPPY: Sure, have lunch tomorrow!

BIFF: I can't say that —

WILLY: You were doing a crossword puzzle and accidentally used his pen!

BIFF: Listen, kid, I took those balls years ago, now I walk in with his fountain pen? That clinches it, don't you see? I can't face him like that! I'll try elsewhere.

PAGE'S VOICE: Paging Mr. Loman!

WILLY: Don't you want to be anything?

BIFF: Pop, how can I go back?

WILLY: You don't want to be anything, is that what's behind it?

BIFF (*now angry at Willy for not crediting his sympathy*): Don't take it that way! You think it was easy walking into that office after what I'd done to him? A team of horses couldn't have dragged me back to Bill Oliver!

WILLY: Then why'd you go?

BIFF: Why did I go? Why did I go! Look at you! Look at what's become of you!

(*Off left, The Woman laughs.*)

WILLY: Biff, you're going to go to that lunch tomorrow, or —

BIFF: I can't go. I've got no appointment!

HAPPY: Biff, for . . . !

WILLY: Are you spiting me?

BIFF: Don't take it that way! Goddammit!

WILLY (*strikes Biff and falters away from the table*): You rotten little louse! Are you spiting me?

THE WOMAN: Someone's at the door, Willy!

BIFF: I'm no good, can't you see what I am?

HAPPY (*separating them*): Hey, you're in a restaurant! Now cut it out, both of you! (*The girls enter.*) Hello, girls, sit down.

(*The Woman laughs, off left.*)

MISS FORSYTHE: I guess we might as well. This is Letta.

THE WOMAN: Willy, are you going to wake up?

BIFF (*ignoring Willy*): How're ya, miss, sit down. What do you drink?

MISS FORSYTHE: Letta might not be able to stay long.

LETTA: I gotta get up very early tomorrow. I got jury duty. I'm so excited! Were you fellows ever on a jury?

BIFF: No, but I been in front of them! (*The girls laugh.*) This is my father.

LETTA: Isn't he cute? Sit down with us, Pop.

HAPPY: Sit him down, Biff!

BIFF (*going to him*): Come on, slugger, drink us under the table. To hell with it! Come on, sit down, pal.

(*On Biff's last insistence, Willy is about to sit.*)

THE WOMAN (*now urgently*): Willy, are you going to answer the door!

(*The Woman's call pulls Willy back. He starts right, befuddled.*)

BIFF: Hey, where are you going?

WILLY: Open the door.

BIFF: The door?

WILLY: The washroom . . . the door . . . where's the door?

BIFF (*leading Willy to the left*): Just go straight down.

(*Willy moves left.*)

THE WOMAN: Willy, Willy, are you going to get up, get up, get up, get up?

(*Willy exits left.*)

LETTA: I think it's sweet you bring your daddy along.

MISS FORSYTHE: Oh, he isn't really your father!

BIFF (*at left, turning to her resentfully*): Miss Forsythe, you've just seen a prince walk by. A fine, troubled prince. A hard-working, unappreciated prince. A pal, you understand? A good companion. Always for his boys.

LETTA: That's so sweet.

HAPPY: Well, girls, what's the program? We're wasting time. Come on, Biff. Gather round. Where would you like to go?

BIFF: Why don't you do something for him?

HAPPY: Me!

BIFF: Don't you give a damn for him, Hap?

HAPPY: What're you talking about? I'm the one who —

BIFF: I sense it, you don't give a good goddam about

him. (*He takes the rolled-up hose from his pocket and puts it on the table in front of Happy.*) Look what I found in the cellar, for Christ's sake. How can you bear to let it go on?

HAPPY: Me? Who goes away? Who runs off and —

BIFF: Yeah, but he doesn't mean anything to you. You could help him — I can't! Don't you understand what I'm talking about? He's going to kill himself, don't you know that?

HAPPY: Don't I know it! Me!

BIFF: Hap, help him! Jesus . . . help him . . . Help me, help me, I can't bear to look at his face! (*Ready to weep, he hurries out, up right.*)

HAPPY (*starting after him*): Where are you going?

MISS FORSYTHE: What's he so mad about?

HAPPY: Come on, girls, we'll catch up with him.

MISS FORSYTHE (*as Happy pushes her out*): Say, I don't like that temper of his!

HAPPY: He's just a little overstrung, he'll be all right!

WILLY (*off left, as The Woman laughs*): Don't answer! Don't answer!

LETTA: Don't you want to tell your father —

HAPPY: No, that's not my father. He's just a guy. Come on, we'll catch Biff, and, honey, we're going to paint this town! Stanley, where's the check! Hey, Stanley!

(*They exit. Stanley looks toward left.*)

STANLEY (*calling to Happy indignantly*): Mr. Loman! Mr. Loman!

(*Stanley picks up a chair and follows them off. Knocking is heard off left. The Woman enters, laughing. Willy follows her. She is in a black slip; he is buttoning his shirt. Raw, sensuous music accompanies their speech.*)

WILLY: Will you stop laughing? Will you stop?

THE WOMAN: Aren't you going to answer the door? He'll wake the whole hotel.

WILLY: I'm not expecting anybody.

THE WOMAN: Whyn't you have another drink, honey, and stop being so damn self-centered?

WILLY: I'm so lonely.

THE WOMAN: You know you ruined me, Willy? From now on, whenever you come to the office, I'll see that you go right through to the buyers. No waiting at my desk anymore, Willy. You ruined me.

WILLY: That's nice of you to say that.

THE WOMAN: Gee, you are self-centered! Why so sad? You are the saddest, self-centeredest soul I ever did see-saw. (*She laughs. He kisses her.*) Come on inside, drummer boy. It's silly to be dressing in the middle of the night. (*As knocking is heard.*) Aren't you going to answer the door?

WILLY: They're knocking on the wrong door.

THE WOMAN: But I felt the knocking. And he heard us talking in here. Maybe the hotel's on fire!

WILLY (*his terror rising*): It's a mistake.

THE WOMAN: Then tell him to go away!

WILLY: There's nobody there.

THE WOMAN: It's getting on my nerves, Willy. There's somebody standing out there and it's getting on my nerves!

WILLY (*pushing her away from him*): All right, stay in the bathroom here, and don't come out. I think there's a law in Massachusetts about it, so don't come out. It may be that new room clerk. He looked very mean. So don't come out. It's a mistake, there's no fire.

(*The knocking is heard again. He takes a few steps away from her, and she vanishes into the wing. The light follows him, and now he is facing Young Biff, who carries a suitcase. Biff steps toward him. The music is gone.*)

BIFF: Why didn't you answer?

WILLY: Biff! What are you doing in Boston?

BIFF: Why didn't you answer? I've been knocking for five minutes, I called you on the phone —

WILLY: I just heard you. I was in the bathroom and had the door shut. Did anything happen home?

BIFF: Dad — I let you down.

WILLY: What do you mean?

BIFF: Dad . . .

WILLY: Biffo, what's this about? (*Putting his arm around Biff.*) Come on, let's go downstairs and get you a malted.

BIFF: Dad, I flunked math.

WILLY: Not for the term?

BIFF: The term. I haven't got enough credits to graduate.

WILLY: You mean to say Bernard wouldn't give you the answers?

BIFF: He did, he tried, but I only got a sixty-one.

WILLY: And they wouldn't give you four points?

BIFF: Birnbaum refused absolutely. I begged him, Pop, but he won't give me those points. You gotta talk to him before they close the school. Because if he saw the kind of man you are, and you just talked to him in your way, I'm sure he'd come through for me. The class came right before practice, see, and I didn't go enough. Would you talk to him? He'd like you, Pop. You know the way you could talk.

WILLY: You're on. We'll drive right back.

BIFF: Oh, Dad, good work! I'm sure he'll change it for you!

WILLY: Go downstairs and tell the clerk I'm checkin' out. Go right down.

BIFF: Yes, sir! See, the reason he hates me, Pop — one day he was late for class so I got up at the blackboard and imitated him. I crossed my eyes and talked with a lithp.

WILLY (*laughing*): You did? The kids like it?

BIFF: They nearly died laughing!

WILLY: Yeah? What'd you do?

BIFF: The thquare root of thixthy twee is . . . (*Willy bursts out laughing; Biff joins.*) And in the middle of it he walked in!

(*Willy laughs and The Woman joins in offstage.*)

WILLY (*without hesitation*): Hurry downstairs and —

BIFF: Somebody in there?

WILLY: No, that was next door.

(*The Woman laughs offstage.*)

BIFF: Somebody got in your bathroom!

WILLY: No, it's the next room, there's a party —

THE WOMAN (*enters, laughing. She lisps this.*): Can I come in? There's something in the bathtub, Willy, and it's moving!

(*Willy looks at Biff, who is staring open-mouthed and horrified at The Woman.*)

WILLY: Ah — you better go back to your room. They must be finished painting by now. They're painting her room so I let her take a shower here. Go back, go back . . . (*He pushes her.*)

THE WOMAN (*resisting*): But I've got to get dressed, Willy, I can't —

WILLY: Get out of here! Go back, go back . . . (*Suddenly striving for the ordinary.*) This is Miss Francis, Biff, she's a buyer. They're painting her room. Go back, Miss Francis, go back . . .

THE WOMAN: But my clothes, I can't go out naked in the hall!

WILLY (*pushing her offstage*): Get outa here! Go back, go back!

(*Biff slowly sits down on his suitcase as the argument continues offstage.*)

THE WOMAN: Where's my stockings? You promised me stockings, Willy!

WILLY: I have no stockings here!

THE WOMAN: You had two boxes of size nine sheers for me, and I want them!

WILLY: Here, for God's sake, will you get outa here!

THE WOMAN (*enters holding a box of stockings*): I just hope there's nobody in the hall. That's all I hope. (*To Biff.*) Are you football or baseball?

BIFF: Football.

THE WOMAN (*angry, humiliated*): That's me too. G'night. (*She snatches her clothes from Willy, and walks out.*)

WILLY (*after a pause*): Well, better get going. I want to

get to the school first thing in the morning. Get my suits out of the closet. I'll get my valise. (*Biff doesn't move.*) What's the matter! (*Biff remains motionless, tears falling.*) She's a buyer. Buys for J. H. Simmons. She lives down the hall — they're painting. You don't imagine — (*He breaks off. After a pause.*) Now listen, pal, she's just a buyer. She sees merchandise in her room and they have to keep it looking just so . . . (*Pause. Assuming command.*) All right, get my suits. (*Biff doesn't move.*) Now stop crying and do as I say. I gave you an order. Biff, I gave you an order! Is that what you do when I give you an order? How dare you cry! (*Putting his arm around Biff.*) Now look, Biff, when you grow up you'll understand about these things. You mustn't — you mustn't overemphasize a thing like this. I'll see Birnbaum first thing in the morning.

BIFF: Never mind.

WILLY (*getting down beside Biff*): Never mind! He's going to give you those points. I'll see to it.

BIFF: He wouldn't listen to you.

WILLY: He certainly will listen to me. You need those points for the U. of Virginia.

BIFF: I'm not going there.

WILLY: Heh? If I can't get him to change that mark you'll make it up in summer school. You've got all summer to —

BIFF (*his weeping breaking from him*): Dad . . .

WILLY (*infected by it*): Oh, my boy . . .

BIFF: Dad . . .

WILLY: She's nothing to me, Biff. I was lonely, I was terribly lonely.

BIFF: You — you gave her Mama's stockings! (*His tears break through and he rises to go.*)

WILLY (*grabbing for Biff*): I gave you an order!

BIFF: Don't touch me, you — liar!

WILLY: Apologize for that!

BIFF: You fake! You phony little fake! You fake! (*Overcome, he turns quickly and weeping fully goes out with his suitcase. Willy is left on the floor on his knees.*)

WILLY: I gave you an order! Biff, come back here or I'll beat you! Come back here! I'll whip you!

(*Stanley comes quickly in from the right and stands in front of Willy.*)

WILLY (*shouts at Stanley*): I gave you an order . . .

STANLEY: Hey, let's pick it up, pick it up, Mr. Loman. (*He helps Willy to his feet.*) Your boys left with the chippies. They said they'll see you home.

(*A second waiter watches some distance away.*)

WILLY: But we were supposed to have dinner together.

(*Music is heard, Willy's theme.*)

STANLEY: Can you make it?

WILLY: I'll — sure, I can make it. (*Suddenly concerned about his clothes.*) Do I — I look all right?

STANLEY: Sure, you look all right. (*He flicks a speck off Willy's lapel.*)

WILLY: Here — here's a dollar.

STANLEY: Oh, your son paid me. It's all right.

WILLY (*putting it in Stanley's hand*): No, take it. You're a good boy.

STANLEY: Oh, no, you don't have to . . .

WILLY: Here — here's some more, I don't need it anymore. (*After a slight pause.*) Tell me — is there a seed store in the neighborhood?

STANLEY: Seeds? You mean like to plant?

(*As Willy turns, Stanley slips the money back into his jacket pocket.*)

WILLY: Yes. Carrots, peas . . .

STANLEY: Well, there's hardware stores on Sixth Avenue, but it may be too late now.

WILLY (*anxiously*): Oh, I'd better hurry. I've got to get some seeds. (*He starts off to the right.*) I've got to get some seeds, right away. Nothing's planted. I don't have a thing in the ground.

(*Willy hurries out as the light goes down. Stanley moves over to the right after him, watches him off. The other waiter has been staring at Willy.*)

STANLEY (*to the waiter*): Well, whatta you looking at?

(*The waiter picks up the chairs and moves off right. Stanley takes the table and follows him. The light fades on this area. There is a long pause, the sound of the flute coming over. The light gradually rises on the kitchen, which is empty. Happy appears at the door of the house, followed by Biff. Happy is carrying a large bunch of long-stemmed roses. He enters the kitchen, looks around for Linda. Not seeing her, he turns to Biff, who is just outside the house door, and makes a gesture with his hands, indicating "Not here, I guess." He looks into the living room and freezes. Inside, Linda, unseen, is seated, Willy's coat on her lap. She rises ominously and quietly and moves toward Happy, who backs up into the kitchen, afraid.*)

HAPPY: Hey, what're you doing up? (*Linda says nothing but moves toward him implacably.*) Where's Pop? (*He keeps backing to the right, and now Linda is in full view in the doorway to the living room.*) Is he sleeping?

LINDA: Where were you?

HAPPY (*trying to laugh it off*): We met two girls, Mom, very fine types. Here, we brought you some flowers. (*Offering them to her.*) Put them in your room, Ma.

(*She knocks them to the floor at Biff's feet. He has now come inside and closed the door behind him. She stares at Biff, silent.*)

HAPPY: Now what'd you do that for? Mom, I want you to have some flowers —

LINDA (*cutting Happy off, violently to Biff*): Don't you care whether he lives or dies?

HAPPY (*going to the stairs*): Come upstairs, Biff.

BIFF (*with a flare of disgust, to Happy*): Go away from me! (*To Linda.*) What do you mean, lives or dies? Nobody's dying around here, pal.

LINDA: Get out of my sight! Get out of here!

BIFF: I wanna see the boss.

LINDA: You're not going near him!

BIFF: Where is he? (*He moves into the living room and Linda follows.*)

LINDA (*shouting after Biff*): You invite him for dinner. He looks forward to it all day — (*Biff appears in his parents' bedroom, looks around, and exits*) — and then you desert him there. There's no stranger you'd do that to!

HAPPY: Why? He had a swell time with us. Listen, when I — (*Linda comes back into the kitchen*) — desert him I hope I don't outlive the day!

LINDA: Get out of here!

HAPPY: Now look, Mom . . .

LINDA: Did you have to go to women tonight? You and your lousy rotten whores!

(*Biff reenters the kitchen.*)

HAPPY: Mom, all we did was follow Biff around trying to cheer him up! (*To Biff.*) Boy, what a night you gave me!

LINDA: Get out of here, both of you, and don't come back! I don't want you tormenting him any more. Go on now, get your things together! (*To Biff.*) You can sleep in his apartment. (*She starts to pick up the flowers and stops herself.*) Pick up this stuff, I'm not your maid anymore. Pick it up, you bum, you!

(*Happy turns his back to her in refusal. Biff slowly moves over and gets down on his knees, picking up the flowers.*)

LINDA: You're a pair of animals! Not one, not another living soul would have had the cruelty to walk out on that man in a restaurant!

BIFF (*not looking at her*): Is that what he said?

LINDA: He didn't have to say anything. He was so humiliated he nearly limped when he came in.

HAPPY: But, Mom, he had a great time with us —

BIFF (*cutting him off violently*): Shut up!

(*Without another word, Happy goes upstairs.*)

LINDA: You! You didn't even go in to see if he was all right!

BIFF (*still on the floor in front of Linda, the flowers in his hand; with self-loathing*): No. Didn't. Didn't do a damned thing. How do you like that, heh? Left him babbling in a toilet.

LINDA: You louse. You . . .

BIFF: Now you hit it on the nose! (*He gets up, throws the flowers in the wastebasket.*) The scum of the earth, and you're looking at him!

LINDA: Get out of here!

BIFF: I gotta talk to the boss, Mom. Where is he?

LINDA: You're not going near him. Get out of this house!

BIFF (*with absolute assurance, determination*): No. We're gonna have an abrupt conversation, him and me.

LINDA: You're not talking to him.

(*Hammering is heard from outside the house, off right. Biff turns toward the noise.*)

LINDA (*suddenly pleading*): Will you please leave him alone?

BIFF: What's he doing out there?

LINDA: He's planting the garden!

BIFF (*quietly*): Now? Oh, my God!

(*Biff moves outside, Linda following. The light dies down on them and comes up on the center of the apron as Willy walks into it. He is carrying a flashlight, a hoe, and a handful of seed packets. He raps the top of the hoe sharply to fix it firmly, and then moves to the left, measuring off the distance with his foot. He holds the flashlight to look at the seed packets, reading off the instructions. He is in the blue of night.*)

WILLY: Carrots . . . quarter-inch apart. Rows . . . one-foot rows. (*He measures it off.*) One foot. (*He puts down a package and measures off.*) Beets. (*He puts down another package and measures again.*) Lettuce. (*He reads the package, puts it down.*) One foot — (*He breaks off as Ben appears at the right and moves slowly down to him.*) What a proposition, ts, ts. Terrific, terrific. 'Cause she's suffered, Ben, the woman has suffered. You understand me? A man can't go out the way he came in, Ben, a man has got to add up to something. You can't, you can't — (*Ben moves toward him as though to interrupt.*) You gotta consider, now. Don't answer so quick. Remember, it's a guaranteed twenty-thousand-dollar proposition. Now look, Ben, I want you to go through the ins and outs of this thing with me. I've got nobody to talk to, Ben, and the woman has suffered, you hear me?

BEN (*standing still, considering*): What's the proposition?

WILLY: It's twenty thousand dollars on the barrelhead. Guaranteed, gilt-edged, you understand?

BEN: You don't want to make a fool of yourself. They might not honor the policy.

WILLY: How can they dare refuse? Didn't I work like a coolie to meet every premium on the nose? And now they don't pay off? Impossible!

BEN: It's called a cowardly thing, William.

WILLY: Why? Does it take more guts to stand here the rest of my life ringing up a zero?

BEN (*yielding*): That's a point, William. (*He moves, thinking, turns.*) And twenty thousand — that is something one can feel with the hand, it is there.

WILLY (*now assured, with rising power*): Oh, Ben, that's the whole beauty of it! I see it like a diamond, shining in the dark, hard and rough, that I can pick up and touch in my hand. Not like — like an appointment! This would not be another damned-fool appointment, Ben, and it changes all the aspects. Because he thinks I'm nothing, see, and so he spites me. But the funeral — (*Straightening up.*) Ben, that funeral will be massive! They'll come from Maine, Massachusetts, Vermont, New Hampshire! All the old-timers with the strange license plates — that boy will be thunderstruck, Ben, because he never realized — I am known! Rhode Island, New York, New Jersey — I am known, Ben, and he'll see it with his eyes once and for all. He'll see what I am, Ben! He's in for a shock, that boy!

BEN (*coming down to the edge of the garden*): He'll call you a coward.

WILLY (*suddenly fearful*): No, that would be terrible.

BEN: Yes. And a damned fool.

WILLY: No, no, he mustn't, I won't have that! (*He is broken and desperate.*)

BEN: He'll hate you, William.

(*The gay music of the Boys is heard.*)

WILLY: Oh, Ben, how do we get back to all the great times? Used to be so full of light, and comradeship, the sleigh-riding in winter, and the ruddiness on his cheeks. And always some kind of good news coming up, always something nice coming up ahead. And never even let me carry the valises in the house, and simonizing, simonizing that little red car! Why, why can't I give him something and not have him hate me?

BEN: Let me think about it. (*He glances at his watch.*) I still have a little time. Remarkable proposition, but you've got to be sure you're not making a fool of yourself.

(*Ben drifts off upstage and goes out of sight. Biff comes down from the left.*)

WILLY (*suddenly conscious of Biff, turns and looks up at him, then begins picking up the packages of seeds in confusion*): Where the hell is that seed? (*Indignantly.*) You can't see nothing out here! They boxed in the whole goddam neighborhood!

BIFF: There are people all around here. Don't you realize that?

WILLY: I'm busy. Don't bother me.

BIFF (*taking the hoe from Willy*): I'm saying good-by to you, Pop. (*Willy looks at him, silent, unable to move.*) I'm not coming back any more.

WILLY: You're not going to see Oliver tomorrow?

BIFF: I've got no appointment, Dad.

WILLY: He put his arm around you, and you've got no appointment?

BIFF: Pop, get this now, will you? Everytime I've left it's been a fight that sent me out of here. Today I realized something about myself and I tried to explain it to you and I — I think I'm just not smart enough to make any sense out of it for you. To hell with whose fault it is or anything like that. (*He takes Willy's arm.*) Let's just wrap it up, heh? Come on in, we'll tell Mom. (*He gently tries to pull Willy to left.*)

WILLY (*frozen, immobile, with guilt in his voice*): No, I don't want to see her.

BIFF: Come on! (*He pulls again, and Willy tries to pull away.*)

WILLY (*highly nervous*): No, no, I don't want to see her.

BIFF (*tries to look into Willy's face, as if to find the answer there*): Why don't you want to see her?

WILLY (*more harshly now*): Don't bother me, will you?

BIFF: What do you mean, you don't want to see her? You don't want them calling you yellow, do you? This isn't your fault; it's me, I'm a bum. Now come inside! (*Willy strains to get away.*) Did you hear what I said to you?

(*Willy pulls away and quickly goes by himself into the house. Biff follows.*)

LINDA (*to Willy*): Did you plant, dear?

BIFF (*at the door, to Linda*): All right, we had it out. I'm going and I'm not writing any more.

LINDA (*going to Willy in the kitchen*): I think that's the best way, dear. 'Cause there's no use drawing it out, you'll just never get along.

(*Willy doesn't respond.*)

BIFF: People ask where I am and what I'm doing, you don't know, and you don't care. That way it'll be off your mind and you can start brightening up again. All right? That clears it, doesn't it? (*Willy is silent, and Biff goes to him.*) You gonna wish me luck, scout? (*He extends his hand.*) What do you say?

LINDA: Shake his hand, Willy.

WILLY (*turning to her, seething with hurt*): There's no necessity to mention the pen at all, y'know.

BIFF (*gently*): I've got no appointment, Dad.

WILLY (*erupting fiercely*): He put his arm around . . . ?

BIFF: Dad, you're never going to see what I am, so what's the use of arguing? If I strike oil I'll send you a check. Meantime forget I'm alive.

WILLY (*to Linda*): Spite, see?

BIFF: Shake hands, Dad.

WILLY: Not my hand.

BIFF: I was hoping not to go this way.

WILLY: Well, this is the way you're going. Good-by.

(*Biff looks at him a moment, then turns sharply and goes to the stairs.*)

WILLY (*stops him with*): May you rot in hell if you leave this house!

BIFF (*turning*): Exactly what is it that you want from me?

WILLY: I want you to know, on the train, in the mountains, in the valleys, wherever you go, that you cut down your life for spite!

BIFF: No, no.

WILLY: Spite, spite, is the word of your undoing! And

Dustin Hoffman as Willy Loman in the 1985 film version of *Death of a Salesman.*

when you're down and out, remember what did it. When you're rotting somewhere beside the railroad tracks, remember, and don't you dare blame it on me!

BIFF: I'm not blaming it on you!

WILLY: I won't take the rap for this, you hear?

(*Happy comes down the stairs and stands on the bottom step, watching.*)

BIFF: That's just what I'm telling you!

WILLY (*sinking into a chair at a table, with full accusation*): You're trying to put a knife in me — don't think I don't know what you're doing!

BIFF: All right, phony! Then let's lay it on the line. (*He whips the rubber tube out of his pocket and puts it on the table.*)

HAPPY: You crazy . . .

LINDA: Biff! (*She moves to grab the hose, but Biff holds it down with his hand.*)

BIFF: Leave it there! Don't move it!

WILLY (*not looking at it*): What is that?

BIFF: You know goddam well what that is.

WILLY (*caged, wanting to escape*): I never saw that.

BIFF: You saw it. The mice didn't bring it into the cellar! What is this supposed to do, make a hero out of you? This supposed to make me sorry for you?

WILLY: Never heard of it.

BIFF: There'll be no pity for you, you hear it? No pity!

WILLY (*to Linda*): You hear the spite!

BIFF: No, you're going to hear the truth — what you are and what I am!

LINDA: Stop it!

WILLY: Spite!

HAPPY (*coming down toward Biff*): You cut it now!

BIFF (*to Happy*): The man don't know who we are! The man is gonna know! (*To Willy.*) We never told the truth for ten minutes in this house!

HAPPY: We always told the truth!

BIFF (*turning on him*): You big blow, are you the assistant buyer? You're one of the two assistants to the assistant, aren't you?

HAPPY: Well, I'm practically . . .

BIFF: You're practically full of it! We all are! and I'm through with it. (*To Willy.*) Now hear this, Willy, this is me.

WILLY: I know you!

BIFF: You know why I had no address for three months? I stole a suit in Kansas City and I was in jail. (*To Linda, who is sobbing.*) Stop crying. I'm through with it.

(*Linda turns away from them, her hands covering her face.*)

WILLY: I suppose that's my fault!

BIFF: I stole myself out of every good job since high school!

WILLY: And whose fault is that?

BIFF: And I never got anywhere because you blew me so full of hot air I could never stand taking orders from anybody! That's whose fault it is!

WILLY: I hear that!

LINDA: Don't, Biff!

BIFF: It's goddam time you heard that! I had to be boss big shot in two weeks, and I'm through with it!

WILLY: Then hang yourself! For spite, hang yourself!

BIFF: No! Nobody's hanging himself, Willy! I ran down eleven flights with a pen in my hand today. And suddenly I stopped, you hear me? And in the middle of that office building, do you hear this? I stopped in the middle of that building and I saw — the sky. I saw the things that I love in this world. The work and the food and time to sit and smoke. And I looked at the pen and said to myself, what the hell am I grabbing this for? Why am I trying to become what I don't want to be? What am I doing in an office, making a contemptuous begging fool of myself, when all I want is out there, waiting for me the minute I say I know who I am! Why can't I say that, Willy? (*He tries to make Willy face him, but Willy pulls away and moves to the left.*)

WILLY (*with hatred, threateningly*): The door of your life is wide open!

BIFF: Pop! I'm a dime a dozen, and so are you!

WILLY (*turning on him in an uncontrolled outburst*): I am not a dime a dozen! I am Willy Loman, and you are Biff Loman!

(*Biff starts for Willy, but is blocked by Happy. In his fury, Biff seems on the verge of attacking his father.*)

BIFF: I am not a leader of men, Willy, and neither are you. You were never anything but a hard-working drummer who landed in the ash can like all the rest of them! I'm one dollar an hour, Willy! I tried seven states and couldn't raise it. A buck an hour! Do you gather my meaning? I'm not bringing home any prizes any more, and you're going to stop waiting for me to bring them home!

WILLY (*directly to Biff*): You vengeful, spiteful mutt!

(*Biff breaks from Happy. Willy, in fright, starts up the stairs. Biff grabs him.*)

BIFF (*at the peak of his fury*): Pop, I'm nothing! I'm nothing, Pop. Can't you understand that? There's no spite in it any more. I'm just what I am, that's all.

(*Biff's fury has spent itself and he breaks down, sobbing, holding on to Willy, who dumbly fumbles for Biff's face.*)

WILLY (*astonished*): What're you doing? What're you doing? (*To Linda.*) Why is he crying?

BIFF (*crying, broken*): Will you let me go, for Christ's

sake? Will you take that phony dream and burn it before something happens? (*Struggling to contain himself he pulls away and moves to the stairs.*) I'll go in the morning. Put him — put him to bed. (*Exhausted, Biff moves up the stairs to his room.*)

WILLY (*after a long pause, astonished, elevated*): Isn't that — isn't that remarkable? Biff — he likes me!

LINDA: He loves you, Willy!

HAPPY (*deeply moved*): Always did, Pop.

WILLY: Oh, Biff! (*Staring wildly.*) He cried! Cried to me. (*He is choking with his love, and now cries out his promise.*) That boy — that boy is going to be magnificent!

(*Ben appears in the light just outside the kitchen.*)

BEN: Yes, outstanding, with twenty thousand behind him.

LINDA (*sensing the racing of his mind, fearfully, carefully*): Now come to bed, Willy. It's all settled now.

WILLY (*finding it difficult not to rush out of the house*): Yes, we'll sleep. Come on. Go to sleep, Hap.

BEN: And it does take a great kind of a man to crack the jungle.

(*In accents of dread, Ben's idyllic music starts up.*)

HAPPY (*his arm around Linda*): I'm getting married, Pop, don't forget it. I'm changing everything. I'm gonna run that department before the year is up. You'll see, Mom. (*He kisses her.*)

BEN: The jungle is dark but full of diamonds, Willy.

(*Willy turns, moves, listening to Ben.*)

LINDA: Be good. You're both good boys, just act that way, that's all.

HAPPY: 'Night, Pop. (*He goes upstairs.*)

LINDA (*to Willy*): Come, dear.

BEN (*with greater force*): One must go in to fetch a diamond out.

WILLY (*to Linda, as he moves slowly along the edge of kitchen, toward the door*): I just want to get settled down, Linda. Let me sit alone for a little.

LINDA (*almost uttering her fear*): I want you upstairs.

WILLY (*taking her in his arms*): In a few minutes, Linda. I couldn't sleep right now. Go on, you look awful tired. (*He kisses her.*)

BEN: Not like an appointment at all. A diamond is rough and hard to the touch.

WILLY: Go on now. I'll be right up.

LINDA: I think this is the only way, Willy.

WILLY: Sure, it's the best thing.

BEN: Best thing!

WILLY: The only way. Everything is gonna be — go on, kid, get to bed. You look so tired.

LINDA: Come right up.

WILLY: Two minutes.

(*Linda goes into the living room, then reappears in her bedroom. Willy moves just outside the kitchen door.*)

WILLY: Loves me. (*Wonderingly.*) Always loved me. Isn't that a remarkable thing? Ben, he'll worship me for it!

BEN (*with promise*): It's dark there, but full of diamonds.

WILLY: Can you imagine that magnificence with twenty thousand dollars in his pocket?

LINDA (*calling from her room*): Willy! Come up!

WILLY (*calling into the kitchen*): Yes! yes. Coming! It's very smart, you realize that, don't you, sweetheart? Even Ben sees it. I gotta go, baby. 'By! 'By! (*Going over to Ben, almost dancing.*) Imagine? When the mail comes he'll be ahead of Bernard again!

BEN: A perfect proposition all around.

WILLY: Did you see how he cried to me? Oh, if I could kiss him, Ben!

BEN: Time, William, time!

WILLY: Oh, Ben, I always knew one way or another we were gonna make it, Biff and I!

BEN (*looking at his watch*): The boat. We'll be late. (*He moves slowly off into the darkness.*)

WILLY (*elegiacally, turning to the house*): Now when you kick off, boy, I want a seventy-yard boot, and get right down the field under the ball, and when you hit, hit low and hit hard, because it's important, boy. (*He swings around and faces the audience.*) There's all kinds of important people in the stands, and the first thing you know . . . (*Suddenly realizing he is alone.*) Ben! Ben, where do I . . . ? (*He makes a sudden movement of search.*) Ben, how do I . . . ?

LINDA (*calling*): Willy, you coming up?

WILLY (*uttering a gasp of fear, whirling about as if to quiet her*): Sh! (*He turns around as if to find his way; sounds, faces, voices, seem to be swarming in upon him and he flicks at them, crying, Sh! Sh! Suddenly music, faint and high, stops him. It rises in intensity, almost to an unbearable scream. He goes up and down on his toes, and rushes off around the house.*) Shhh!

LINDA: Willy?

(*There is no answer. Linda waits. Biff gets up off his bed. He is still in his clothes. Happy sits up. Biff stands listening.*)

LINDA (*with real fear*): Willy, answer me! Willy!

(*There is the sound of a car starting and moving away at full speed.*)

LINDA: No!

BIFF (*rushing down the stairs*): Pop!

(*As the car speeds off, the music crashes down in a frenzy of sound, which becomes the soft pulsation of a single cello string. Biff slowly returns to his bed-room. He and Happy gravely don their jackets. Linda slowly walks out of her room. The music has devel-oped into a dead march. The leaves of day are ap-pearing over everything. Charley and Bernard, somberly dressed, appear and knock on the kitchen door. Biff and Happy slowly descend the stairs to the kitchen as Charley and Bernard enter. All stop a mo-ment when Linda, in clothes of mourning, bearing a little bunch of roses, comes through the draped door-way into the kitchen. She goes to Charley and takes his arm. Now all move toward the audience, through the wall-line of the kitchen. At the limit of the apron, Linda lays down the flowers, kneels, and sits back on her heels. All stare down at the grave.)*

REQUIEM

CHARLEY: It's getting dark, Linda.

(Linda doesn't react. She stares at the grave.)

BIFF: How about it, Mom? Better get some rest, heh? They'll be closing the gate soon.

(Linda makes no move. Pause.)

HAPPY *(deeply angered)*: He had no right to do that. There was no necessity for it. We would've helped him.
CHARLEY *(grunting)*: Hmmm.
BIFF: Come along, Mom.
LINDA: Why didn't anybody come?
CHARLEY: It was a very nice funeral.
LINDA: But where are all the people he knew? Maybe they blame him.
CHARLEY: Naa. It's a rough world, Linda. They wouldn't blame him.
LINDA: I can't understand it. At this time especially. First time in thirty-five years we were just about free and clear. He only needed a little salary. He was even finished with the dentist.
CHARLEY: No man only needs a little salary.
LINDA: I can't understand it.
BIFF: There were a lot of nice days. When he'd come home from a trip; or on Sundays, making the stoop; finishing the cellar; putting on the new porch; when he built the extra bathroom; and put up the garage. You know something, Charley, there's more of him in that front stoop than in all the sales he ever made.
CHARLEY: Yeah. He was a happy man with a batch of cement.
LINDA: He was so wonderful with his hands.
BIFF: He had the wrong dreams. All, all, wrong.

HAPPY *(almost ready to fight Biff)*: Don't say that!
BIFF: He never knew who he was.
CHARLEY *(stopping Happy's movement and reply. To Biff)*: Nobody dast blame this man. You don't un-derstand: Willy was a salesman. And for a sales-man, there is no rock bottom to the life. He don't put a bolt to a nut, he don't tell you the law or give you medicine. He's a man way out there in the blue, riding on a smile and a shoeshine. And when they start not smiling back — that's an earthquake. And then you get yourself a couple of spots on your hat, and you're finished. Nobody dast blame this man. A salesman is got to dream, boy. It comes with the territory.
BIFF: Charley, the man didn't know who he was.
HAPPY *(infuriated)*: Don't say that!
BIFF: Why don't you come with me, Happy?
HAPPY: I'm not licked that easily. I'm staying right in this city, and I'm gonna beat this racket! *(He looks at Biff, his chin set.)* The Loman Brothers!
BIFF: I know who I am, kid.
HAPPY: All right, boy. I'm gonna show you and every-body else that Willy Loman did not die in vain. He had a good dream. It's the only dream you can have — to come out number-one man. He fought it out here, and this is where I'm gonna win it for him.
BIFF *(with a hopeless glance at Happy, bends toward his mother)*: Let's go, Mom.
LINDA: I'll be with you in a minute. Go on, Charley. *(He hesitates.)* I want to, just for a minute. I never had a chance to say good-by.

(Charley moves away, followed by Happy. Biff re-mains a slight distance up and left of Linda. She sits there, summoning herself. The flute begins, not far away, playing behind her speech.)

LINDA: Forgive me, dear. I can't cry. I don't know what it is, but I can't cry. I don't understand it. Why did you ever do that? Help me, Willy, I can't cry. It seems to me that you're just on another trip. I keep expecting you. Willy, dear, I can't cry. Why did you do it? I search and search and I search, and I can't understand it, Willy. I made the last payment on the house today. Today, dear. And there'll be nobody home. *(A sob rises in her throat.)* We're free and clear. *(Sobbing more fully, released.)* We're free. *(Biff comes slowly toward her.)* We're free . . . We're free . . .

(Biff lifts her to her feet and moves out up right with her in his arms. Linda sobs quietly. Bernard and Charley come together and follow them, followed by Happy. Only the music of the flute is left on the darkening stage as over the house the hard towers of the apartment buildings rise into sharp focus, and the curtain falls.)

COMMENTARIES

Arthur Miller (b. 1915)
IN MEMORIAM

1932

"In Memoriam," a short story about a salesman written in 1932 when Arthur Miller was seventeen, was published in 1995 after it was discovered in the Arthur Miller Archive at the University of Texas's Harry Ransom library. A note on the manuscript indicates that the real Schoenzeit threw himself in front of an elevated railway train the day after the incident the story records. While not providing the model for Death of a Salesman, *the story reminds us that Miller had experience with men like Willy Loman.*

Sitting here now, thinking of him, he seems to be a romantic figure, but really he wasn't. Yet I couldn't venture to call him "commonplace." I never knew him intimately, yet I feel as though I knew him more closely, more thoroughly, than I know myself. His was a salesman's profession, if one may describe such dignified slavery as a profession, and though he tried to interest himself in his work he never became entirely molded into the pot of that business. His emotions were displayed at the wrong times always, and he never quite knew when to laugh. Perhaps, if I may say so, he never was complete. He had lost something vital. There was an air of quiet solitude, of cryptic wondering about both him and his name.

Although he was ever simply and immaculately dressed, I always imagined he had been dressed by someone else.

When I first heard his name, I wondered if he hadn't forgotten some other and had merely been called this by men. His last name was Schoenzeit; the first I never learned, but it had to be Alfred. He always seemed to need that name. Especially when he sat at the small glass-topped table in my father's showroom, slowly perusing the columns of the *Times,* with tears of perspiration dotting the reddened ridge that his gray felt hat had made around his head. The shined, bulgy-toed shoes placed flatly and it seemed carefully on the carpet, his overcoat folded neatly on a chair, the bow of his tie stuck so perfectly into the crevice of a starched, rounded collar completed a setting where I am sure he never belonged.

Schoenzeit, as everyone called him, often was gay. I might add "happy," but of the last I shall never be sure. He laughed as superciliously as any of the others when someone was the object of a quip. But these occasions were rare and never lasted, as far as he was concerned. Always he returned to his fogged manner, and after the joke had faded from his mind the light which seemed to brighten his countenance, too, disappeared, and he was once more enigmatic and incomprehensible.

I had, on several occasions, been alone with him, and may truthfully say I deeply pitied such a dejected soul. At one time it was necessary for him to go to

1165

the Bronx to interview a large retail drygoods store, and I was instructed to carry his samples. It was late spring, the sky was cloudless and blue, a yellow sun was slowly warming the cool morning air, and the usual city hurriers were plying their trade.

I had six coats in my arms, holding them against my chest, while he walked, leaning very slightly forward, by my side. His feet must have hurt him, for he pointed them outward, laying them flat on the ground at every step. When walking, he seemed to be striving against a stiff wind, his eyebrows peaked together, forming tiny creases at the bridge of his nose. His hat, placed straight on his head, shaded his eyes, which gazed seekingly ahead.

It was necessary to walk from Eighth to Third Avenue in order to reach the Elevated, and he offered many times to rest. I must have looked tired, because he turned to me once and laughed, saying in his cracked yet resonant baritone, "Hard work, eh, kid? Some business . . ." Of course, I didn't admit my weariness, and pitching my head to one side, raising my eyebrows and smiling, assured him that I was enjoying it as much as he was.

In due time, we approached the El, and about a block away he slowly and lightly touched my arm and, still looking ahead, he asked, "Arthur, do you get paid from the firm for carfare?" He said this in a low tone, as though he were trying to hide his point until it was absolutely necessary to take the plunge.

I thought for a moment and answered, "Well, whenever I have to go anywhere out of walking distance I am given money to ride, but I have no standing allowance for such purposes." He seemed to falter, and flushed a trifle before answering, and for a second I felt both rage and pity for this decrepit soul, who, it seemed, aged many years as he turned to me. I knew then that he felt as though his life were ended, that he was merely being pushed by outside forces. And though his body went on as before, the soul inside had crumpled and broken beyond repair.

He was asking me now for carfare. I knew he would rather have been pulled apart by a tiger, but he was asking me for carfare, a nickel to hold out to a corpulent, uninterested machine for his fare. My heart bled for him at that moment, and as we mounted the long stairway to the trains I realized that as low and shakingly embarrassed as I felt, his senses were that much more tormented and destroyed. And I marvelled at his poise under the circumstances. The coats were warm now against me, and I was thankful to God himself for this refuge for my gawky body which, with the expression of my eyes, must reveal to him my sensations.

I tried as best I could to make this situation seem as if it were commonplace — I who had carried samples for so many salesmen. And when we reached the turnstile, I balanced my burden on one knee while I dipped my free hand into my pocket. Behind my throat, I cursed myself for not having the change. I turned from him in order to get the nickels required, and when I lifted my eyes to his figure I prayed, until my temples seemed to burst, for his salvation. At that moment, he looked so broken, so dejected and lost that I hastily lowered my gaze. He appeared to me then, as he stood there at the turnstile, like a small dog who has messed in the house, standing now, after his beating, waiting for his master to open the door to the back yard.

During the entire ride uptown, we two spoke but sparingly. The bright streets below changed constantly as we racketed past, and the windows of the houses facing the trains offered a haven for my confused and weary imagination.

He sold nothing that day and was profusely maltreated by the attending force at the buying office who, by virtue of their superior intelligence and ties to match, were vindicated even when they were consciously adding to the vicissitudes of a seller's life.

On the return trip, Alfred, as I subconsciously called him, became more voluble and questioned me as to my ambitions and my occupations in my leisure time. Upon hearing that I owned an old car, he immediately became interested and spoke a little less haltingly than was his wont. From constant rebuff, he was loath to venture an opinion, and often embarrassed us both by ending a bountiful conversation unexpectedly.

He accompanied me to my father's place and, placing his hand on the small of my back, patted me lightly, and said with a faint smile, "Thanks, Arthur — and I'll . . . see you tomorrow."

With that farewell, he was off into the crowd, and his restless body faded slowly into the dark overcoats of unknowns as it willingly shrank from my sight.

I never saw him again and had forgotten him entirely when I heard of his death.

"Schoenzeit is dead," and my only recollection of that second when I heard those words is a slow exhaling of my breath and a cool, soft, glowing smile within my soul.

Arthur Miller (b. 1915)
TRAGEDY AND THE COMMON MAN   1949

One of the curious debates that arose around Death of a Salesman *was the question of whether or not it was a genuine tragedy. One of the requirements for traditional tragedy is that the hero be of noble birth. Miller countered that notion with a clear statement of modern purpose regarding tragedy.*

In this age few tragedies are written. It has often been held that the lack is due to a paucity of heroes among us, or else that modern man has had the blood drawn out of his organs of belief by the skepticism of science, and the heroic attack on life cannot feed on an attitude of reserve and circumspection. For one reason or another, we are often held to be below tragedy — or tragedy above us. The inevitable conclusion is, of course, that the tragic mode is archaic, fit only for the very highly placed, the kings or the kingly, and where this admission is not made in so many words it is most often implied.

I believe that the common man is as apt a subject for tragedy in its highest sense as kings were. On the face of it this ought to be obvious in the light of modern psychiatry, which bases its analysis upon classic formulations, such as the Oedipus and Orestes complexes, for instance, which were enacted by royal beings, but which apply to everyone in similar emotional situations.

More simply, when the question of tragedy in art is not at issue, we never hesitate to attribute to the well-placed and the exalted the very same mental processes as the lowly. And finally, if the exaltation of tragic action were truly a property of the high-bred character alone, it is inconceivable that the mass of mankind should cherish tragedy above all other forms, let alone be capable of understanding it.

As a general rule, to which there may be exceptions unknown to me, I think the tragic feeling is evoked in us when we are in the presence of a character who is ready to lay down his life, if need be, to secure one thing — his sense of personal dignity. From Orestes to Hamlet, Medea to Macbeth, the underlying struggle is that of the individual attempting to gain his "rightful" position in his society.

Sometimes he is one who has been displaced from it, sometimes one who seeks to attain it for the first time, but the fateful wound from which the inevitable events spiral is the wound of indignity, and its dominant force is indignation. Tragedy, then, is the consequence of a man's total compulsion to evaluate himself justly.

In the sense of having been initiated by the hero himself, the tale always reveals what has been called his "tragic flaw," a failing that is not peculiar to grand or elevated characters. Nor is it necessarily a weakness. The flaw, or crack in the character, is really nothing — and need be nothing — but his inherent unwillingness to remain passive in the face of what he conceives to be a challenge to his dignity, his image of his rightful status. Only the passive, only those who accept their lot without active retaliation, are "flawless." Most of us are in that category.

But there are among us today, as there always have been, those who act against the scheme of things that degrades them, and in the process of action everything we have accepted out of fear or insensitivity or ignorance is shaken before us and examined, and from this total onslaught by an individual against the seemingly stable cosmos surrounding us — from this total examination of the "unchangeable" environment — comes the terror and the fear that is classically associated with tragedy.

More important, from this total questioning of what has previously been unquestioned, we learn. And such a process is not beyond the common man. In revolutions around the world, these past thirty years, he has demonstrated again and again this inner dynamic of all tragedy.

Insistence upon the rank of the tragic hero, or the so-called nobility of his character, is really but a clinging to the outward forms of tragedy. If rank or nobility of character was indispensable, then it would follow that the problems of those with rank were the particular problems of tragedy. But surely the right of one monarch to capture the domain from another no longer raises our passions, nor are our concepts of justice what they were to the mind of an Elizabethan king.

The quality in such plays that does shake us, however, derives from the underlying fear of being displaced, the disaster inherent in being torn away from our chosen image of what and who we are in this world. Among us today this fear is as strong, and perhaps stronger, than it ever was. In fact, it is the common man who knows this fear best.

Now, if it is true that tragedy is the consequence of a man's total compulsion to evaluate himself justly, his destruction in the attempt posits a wrong or an evil in his environment. And this is precisely the morality of tragedy and its lesson. The discovery of the moral law, which is what the enlightenment of tragedy consists of, is not the discovery of some abstract or metaphysical quantity.

The tragic right is a condition of life, a condition in which the human personality is able to flower and realize itself. The wrong is the condition which suppresses man, perverts the flowing out of his love and creative instinct. Tragedy enlightens — and it must, in that it points the heroic finger at the enemy of man's freedom. The thrust for freedom is the quality in tragedy which exalts. The revolutionary questioning of the stable environment is what terrifies. In no way is the common man debarred from such thoughts or such actions.

Seen in this light, our lack of tragedy may be partially accounted for by the turn which modern literature has taken toward the purely psychiatric view of life, or the purely sociological. If all our miseries, our indignities, are born and bred within our minds, then all action, let alone the heroic action, is obviously impossible.

And if society alone is responsible for the cramping of our lives, then the protagonist must needs be so pure and faultless as to force us to deny his validity as a character. From neither of these views can tragedy derive, simply because neither represents a balanced concept of life. Above all else, tragedy requires the finest appreciation by the writer of cause and effect.

No tragedy can therefore come about when its author fears to question absolutely everything, when he regards any institution, habit, or custom as being either everlasting, immutable, or inevitable. In the tragic view the need of man to wholly realize himself is the only fixed star, and whatever it is that hedges his nature and lowers it is ripe for attack and examination. Which is not to say that tragedy must preach revolution.

The Greeks could probe the very heavenly origin of their ways and return to confirm the rightness of laws. And Job could face God in anger, demanding his right, and end in submission. But for a moment everything is in suspension, nothing is accepted, and in this stretching and tearing apart of the cosmos, in the very action of so doing, the character gains "size," the tragic stature which is spuriously attached to the royal or the highborn in our minds. The commonest of men may take on that stature to the extent of his willingness to throw all he has into the contest, the battle to secure his rightful place in his world.

There is a misconception of tragedy with which I have been struck in review after review, and in many conversations with writers and readers alike. It is the idea that tragedy is of necessity allied to pessimism. Even the dictionary says nothing more about the word than that it means a story with a sad or unhappy ending. This impression is so firmly fixed that I almost hesitate to claim that in truth tragedy implies more optimism in its author than does comedy, and that its final result ought to be the reinforcement of the onlooker's brightest opinions of the human animal.

For, if it is true to say that in essence the tragic hero is intent upon claiming his whole due as a personality, and if this struggle must be total and without reservation, then it automatically demonstrates the indestructible will of man to achieve his humanity.

The possibility of victory must be there in tragedy. Where pathos rules, where pathos is finally derived, a character has fought a battle he could not possibly have won. The pathetic is achieved when the protagonist is, by virtue of his witlessness, his insensitivity, or the very air he gives off, incapable of grappling with a much superior force.

Pathos truly is the mode for the pessimist. But tragedy requires a nicer balance between what is possible and what is impossible. And it is curious, although edifying, that the plays we revere, century after century, are the tragedies. In them, and in them alone, lies the belief — optimistic, if you will — in the perfectibility of man.

It is time, I think, that we who are without kings, took up this bright thread of our history and followed it to the only place it can possibly lead in our time — the heart and spirit of the average man.

Richard Schickel (*b. 1933*)
REVIEW OF *DEATH OF A SALESMAN*   *1984*

Schickel's review is as much an appraisal of the play in all the phases of its existence as it is an appraisal of a single production. Dustin Hoffman receives praise for his fresh and original portrayal of Willy Loman, just as director Michael Rudman is lauded for his "reinvention" of the drama. But the main point is that thirty-five years after its original production, the play is still relevant, alive, and moving. Its meaning, as Miller puts it, depends on where you are and what year it is. Time has augmented, not withered its power.

"He's liked, but he's not — well liked."

"When I was 17 I walked into the jungle, and when I was 21 I walked out. And by God I was rich."

"He's a man way out there in the blue, riding on a smile and a shoeshine . . . A salesman is got to dream, boy. It comes with the territory."

And, above all, this: "So attention must be paid . . . Attention, attention must be finally paid to such a person."

To hear those lines spoken from a stage now, thirty-five years after they were first heard, is to realize how deeply they have insinuated themselves into the collective unconscious of modern America. We quote them without citing their original source, in some cases without knowing what that source is. And, again, not quite consciously, many of us live our lives differently than once we might have — defining success, failure, our relationships with our children, even our notions of what constitutes a worthwhile job in new ways. That is, in part, because more than a generation ago Arthur Miller invented an American dreamer named Willy Loman, put him in a play called *Death of a Salesman*, and invited us to watch him and his false, almost comic, near-to-tragic dream unravel.

Such was the cautionary power of this work that one's largest fear, approaching the new, palpitatingly anticipated Broadway production of *Salesman*, starring Dustin Hoffman in a role he admitted wanting to play since he began acting, only a decade after Miller finished writing it, was that we might have learned too well the lessons Willy taught. Perhaps familiarity might have rendered him irrelevant, a figure of nostalgic curiosity, conceivably, but of vastly diminished power to engage the emotions.

That fear turns out to be entirely groundless. For director Michael Rudman's fluid, driving production is not just a revival and a restaging, nor even a reinterpretation of the play, but a virtual reinvention of it. And Hoffman's performance as Willy is nothing short of a revelation. He has stripped away all the doomy portents that have encrusted the character over the years and brought him down to fighting weight, a scrappy, snappy little bantam, whom the audience may, if it wishes, choose to see as a victim, but who almost never sees himself that way. Not long ago, Arthur Miller said that "Willy is foolish and even ridiculous sometimes. He tells the most transparent lies, exaggerates mercilessly, and so on. But I want you to see that the impulses behind him are not foolish at all. He cannot bear reality, and since he can't do much to change it, he keeps changing his ideas of it."

It is this Willy that Hoffman plays with the demonic ferocity that is his glory as an actor. Shifting suddenly from time present to time past and back again, the play moves along a steadily darkening arc: Hoffman bobs and weaves on that line, shadowboxing the gathering shadows, hoping to the end for a T.K.O.° over reality. When the inevitable arrives, when he has lost his job, when it is clear that his sons have been ruined by his belief that success is just a matter of concealing the needle of sharp practice in a hand gloved by fraudulent gladness, his suicide is only in part dictated by despair. There is this insurance policy, and if Willy can contrive to make his demise look like an accident, then he will have achieved in death what he never could in life — a legacy for his family and, better still, that edge on the system for which he had always angled. When Hoffman makes his final exit, he actually does a little shimmy and shake, so eager is his salesman for this last but most promising road trip.

Yet exhilarating as this performance is, it does not dominate or distort Miller's vision. In fact, it frees it from the limits imposed by critics of the original production who tended to see Willy's fate determined almost solely by capitalist economics, and by later commentators who wondered whether the salesman could be regarded as a truly tragic figure, since he was not observed to fall from the great heights demanded of such characters by the laws of Aristotelian aesthetics. From the beginning, Miller told *Time* reporter Elaine Dutka, he had seen the play as two seemingly different entities. One was "a veritable encyclopedia of information about the man," which would permit actors and audiences alike to find their own sense of what moved him. The other was a kind of free-form poem, highly condensed emotionally and verbally, "a concentration through some kind of lens of my whole awareness of life up to that point." But here again, the problem of precise clarification was left up to performers and auditors. "What it 'means,'" said Miller, "depends on where on the face of the earth you are and what year it is."

He speaks from heartening experience. It has been claimed that not a night passes without *Salesman* being performed somewhere in the world, usually with success, mostly in venues where no one can possibly conceive of what America was like in 1949. For example, Miller's remarks about Willy's combative relationship with reality were contained in his advice to the players he directed last May in China (an experience he has wryly, and wisely, recounted in *Salesman in Beijing,* which the Viking Press will publish next month). To them he also insisted "the one red line connecting everyone in the play was a love for Willy." Even when the family are appalled by his self-delusions, they see "he is forever signaling to a future that he cannot describe and will not live to see, but he is in love with all the same."

T.K.O.: Technical knockout. A boxing term indicating a victory won through form and skill.

Such a man, obviously, has aspects of the universal about him. And so do his family: the patiently loving wife, played with unsentimental fortitude by Kate Reid in a performance in its way as awesome as Hoffman's; the sons who are Willy bifurcated, with Biff (John Malkovich) inheriting the dreaming genes, Happy (Stephen Lang) the gift of delusory gab, but with both lacking their father's annealing fire. Miller has said that at its heart *Salesman* is "a love story between a man and his son, and in a crazy way between both of them and America." As the wounded party in that triangle, Malkovich gives a subtly textured performance in which anguished puzzlement never gives way to self-pity. In that sense, at least, he remains this Willy's son. But all the actors in this brilliantly chosen cast are exemplary in their resistance to those easy generalizations that are often the curse of plays as ambitious, ambiguous and spacious as this one is.

One of the traditional arguments about *Salesman* is whether its diction is failed lyricism or failed realism. But it is neither: its first director, Elia Kazan, says it is written "just off the real." Miller's people are first- and second-generation Americans who have yet to achieve a perfect-pitch imitation of standard American brag, bluff and bluster; their language is thus a precise and moving metaphorical expression of the uneasiness with which they live in the American dream they have not quite assimilated. By touching this language with the accents of Brooklyn's old ethnic neighborhoods, this company simultaneously grounds the dialogue in the reality that formed Miller and his play, and grants his rhetoric, at last, the full weight, color and, yes, poetic power one sensed was waiting to be unlocked in it.

In the process the actors have unlocked, as well, the wild humor ("I laughed a lot when I wrote the play") that was also integral to Miller's first imaginings, yet was somehow lost to memory and lost on revivalists, who have mistaken glum sobriety for high seriousness. On the night of February 10, 1949, when *Salesman* opened on Broadway the first time, Arthur Kennedy, the original Biff, recalls wandering around in a daze between acts, encountering Miller, and asking him how he thought the play was going. "The issue is not in doubt," the playwright firmly replied; and now it seems even the last pockets of resistance must finally yield to his astonishing, youthful thirty-three-year-old confidence. What has arrived on Broadway is, assuredly, a classic of the modern theater. And one leaves it not with a sense of relief at a cultural duty properly discharged, but in that state of disarray and wonder that occurs when artists actually manage to act on the poet's simple, hard advice and "make it new."

Samuel Beckett

Samuel Beckett (1906–1989) was born in Dublin to an upper-middle-class Protestant family. After a privileged education at the Portora Royal School, he went to Trinity College, Dublin, where he studied French and Italian. He was an exceptionally good student and, in 1928 after graduation, went to Paris to teach English at the École Normale Supérieure, an unusual reward for good scholarship.

Beckett early on straddled two literary cultures: Irish and Anglo-Irish. Most of the literary energy in Ireland in the 1920s and 1930s was split between the essentially conservative Anglo-Irish Protestants, such as William Butler Yeats and Lady Gregory, and the more avant-garde Catholics, such as James Joyce, with whom Beckett formed an enduring personal and literary friendship in Paris. Although much younger than Joyce, Beckett developed a close artistic sympathy with him. Beckett's first published work (1929) was one of the earliest critical essays on Joyce's most radical literary composition, the not-yet-published *Finnegans Wake*.

When he was first in France, Beckett's reading of French philosophers, especially Descartes, exerted a strong influence on his work. Beckett's earliest writings appeared in Eugene Jolas's avant-garde literary journal *transition*, which put him in the center of Parisian literary activity in the late 1920s. After 1930, his series of short stories published under the title *More Pricks than Kicks* (1934) established him as an important writer. After settling in Paris in 1937, Beckett wrote the novel *Murphy* (1938), on a recognizably Irish theme of economic impoverishment, alienation, and inward meditation and spiritual complexity.

When World War II began in 1939, Beckett took up the cause of the French Resistance. His activity caught the eye of the Gestapo, and for two years he lay low in unoccupied France by working as a farmhand and also writing another novel, *Watt* (written in 1944 but published in 1953). After the war he took up residence again in Paris and began writing most of his work in French. His greatest novels were written in the five years after the war, and they are often referred to as his trilogy: *Molloy, Malone Dies,* and *The Unnamable*. These three novels are about men who have become disaffected with society and who have strange and compelling urgencies to be alone and to follow exacting and repetitive patterns of behavior. In a sense, they are archetypes of the kinds of heroes — if "heroes" can be used — that Beckett created in most of his work.

Beckett's first published play, *Waiting for Godot* (1952), was produced in Paris (1953), in London (1955), and in Miami (1956). From the first, its repetitive, whimsical, and sometimes nonsensical style established the play as a major postwar statement. In a barren setting, Vladimir and Estragon, two tramps who echo the comic vision of Charlie Chaplin, wait for Godot to come. They amuse themselves by doing vaudeville routines, but their loneliness and isolation are painfully apparent to the audience. Godot has promised to come, and as they wait, Vladimir and Estragon speculate on whether or not Godot will come.

The comic moments in the play, along with the enigma of Vladimir and Estragon's fruitless waiting, combined to capture the imagination of audiences and the press. They saw the play as a modern statement about the condition of humankind, although there was never any agreement on just what the statement was. Godot sends a boy to say that he will indeed come, but when the play ends, he has not arrived. The implication seems to be that he will never arrive. Most audiences saw Godot as a metaphor for God. Despite the critics' constant inquiries, Beckett was careful never to confirm the view that Godot was God and to keep Godot's identity open-ended.

The play itself was open-ended, as Beckett had hoped, and therefore could be interpreted in many ways. One was to see the play as a commentary on the futility of religion; another was to suggest that the play underscored the loneliness of humankind in an empty universe; yet a third implied that it was up to individuals, represented by the hapless Vladimir and Estragon, to shape the significance of their own lives, and their waiting represented that effort.

Many of the themes in *Waiting for Godot* are apparent in Beckett's later plays. The radio play *All That Fall* (1957) was followed by the very successful *Krapp's Last Tape* (1958). Also in 1957, *Endgame*, a play on the themes of the end of the world, was produced, followed in 1961 by *Happy Days*. Beckett experimented with minimalist approaches to drama, exemplified in *Act Without Words I* and *Act Without Words II*, both mime plays. Other plays experiment with minimalism in setting, props, and — in the mime plays — even words.

Beckett's plays reveal the deep influence of French postwar philosophers, such as Albert Camus and Jean-Paul Sartre, both existentialists. Their philosophy declares that people are not essentially good, bad, kind, or anything else, but what they make of themselves. Beckett's adaptation of existentialism sometimes borders on pessimism because his vision seems to negate many of the consolations of religious and secular philosophy. His style is antirealist, but the search for beliefs that are reasonable and plausible in a fundamentally absurd world and the plight of individuals who must make their own meanings is central to most of his work.

Beckett's view of the world is not cheerful. But his vision is consistent, honest, and sympathetic to the persistence of his characters, who endure even in the face of apparent defeat. The significance of Beckett's achievements was recognized in 1969 when he was awarded the Nobel Prize for literature.

ENDGAME

The title of this play derives from the game of chess, which has three different strategies to mark the opening, the middle game, and the endgame. The strategy of the endgame is based on the protection of the king and depends on very few pieces being left on the board — the king and sometimes a rook and a pawn. The moves in the endgame are always restricted, often repetitive, and limited by the fact that the king, if it can move at all, cannot move more than one space at a time. In Beckett's *Endgame* Hamm is the king and the central character in the drama; however, he cannot move or even stand by himself. His parents, Nagg and Nell, stuck immobile in ashcans, resemble rooks, who protect the king by controlling spaces forward, backward, and side to side but have little reason themselves to move. Clov, who most closely resembles a pawn, cannot sit down and is the only character in the play who can move. He is also the only means by which Hamm can move. Beckett has described Hamm as "a king in the chess game lost from the start."

World politics in 1957, when the play was written, were dominated by the threat of nuclear war and the possible extinction of the human race. The circumstances of *Endgame* suggest that the play portrays a version of the end of the world. Clov's description of the world outside the window implies desolation and grief. At one point as Clov looks out the window, Hamm tells him to use his "glass," his telescope, and to report back to him. Clov says all is "Zero," and Hamm asks, "All is what?" "In a word?" says Clov. "Is that what you want to know?" And in a moment he reports his one word: "Corpsed."

Unlike Hamm and Clov, who seem rooted only in the present, Nagg and Nell have a past. They remember rowing on Lake Como on an April afternoon after they were engaged. It was a moment in which Nell remembers she was happy. But they also remember the day they crashed on their tandem bicycle and lost their legs. Nagg recalls it was in the Ardennes forest on the road to Sedan. Beckett is making a distant allusion to the Ardennes, in France, site of the most appalling and murderous fighting in World War I, and to Sedan, the place of the most decisive French defeat by the Germans in the war of 1879.

Ruby Cohn and other critics have noted that the characters' names echo associations with hammers and nails: Nell is a homophone for *nail*; Hamm is a shortened form of *hammer*; Nagg is from the German *nagel*, for *nail*; and Clov is from the French *clou*, also for *nail*. The characters thus seem to be equipped to rebuild their society, but they refuse to do so. By using English, French, and German versions of *nail*, Beckett involves the principal combatants of modern European wars.

Some critics have observed that Beckett's drama often focuses on elements of play. Plays are play; life is play. In chess an endgame is played. In Beckett's drama characters' actions seem to be performed as if they were part of a game. Clov exercises great precision, for example, in placing Hamm exactly where he wishes to be. When Clov has done the rounds and moved Hamm's chair back to its position, Hamm says, "I feel a little too far to the left. Now I feel a little too far to the right." In a game of chess it would matter if he were too far to the left or right. In an endgame the king might move to one square and then move back again and again. The movements of Hamm and Clov are repetitious and meaningful only within the "system" of the drama and its space, just as all moves in an endgame are meaningful only within the "system" of the game of chess. Clov continually enters and exits with his ladder and looks out the windows, only to find that nothing has changed. He picks up the lids of Nagg and Nell's ashcans and replaces them several times. He pushes Hamm's chair along the wall, making minute adjustments, for no apparent reason, when he returns the chair to the center of the room. His moves are part of an endgame and *Endgame* is a play.

Beckett critic Ted Estess has said that "in Beckett's literature 'existence is play,'" implying a form of absurdity of the kind Martin Esslin talks about in his discussion of theater of the absurd. (See the commentary on pages 1207–9.) The absurd implies a nonmeaning, such as the meaningless movements of Hamm by Clov. The meaning of those moves is in the action itself, which strikes those in the audience as absurd. Beckett's use of the absurd helps him move away from the well-made play with its clearly marked beginning, middle, and end. In the process he pokes fun at that concept by embedding the end in the beginning of *Endgame.* As the lights go up and Clov removes the sheets from the ashcans and from Hamm in his chair, he intones to the audience: "Finished." The audience is meant to feel this irony: It is the endgame when the action — and the play — are expected to stop; but as Hamm says: "The end is in the beginning and yet you go on."

Endgame in Performance

Endgame was first produced in 1957. The year before, *Waiting for Godot* had been produced in Miami and New York, establishing Beckett as an important figure in modern experimental drama. *Endgame,* his next major play, satisfied the critics but baffled the public. The first London production was in French, at the Royal Court Theatre, which was known for producing experimental plays. Roger Blin directed. The first Paris production began three weeks later, April 26, 1957, in the Studio des Champs-Élysées. The New York production, directed by Beckett's friend and interpreter Alan Schneider, opened on January 28, 1958. A number of important revivals of the play have attested to its continuing power. In 1964 *Endgame* was produced at The Royal Shakespeare Company's Aldwych Theatre. Beckett himself directed the play at the Schiller Theatre in Berlin in September 1967. In the 1970 Open Theater Production at the Loeb Theater in Cambridge, Massachusetts, Joseph Chaikin as Hamm created a richly nuanced performance:

> Joseph Chaikin as the chairbound Hamm, throws an eerie light over the play. . . . He is sensual, domineering, crafty, and infinitely tender; he prattles and tells macabre stories and his dominion over the dwindling lives of his family is like the last hoarse gasp of King Lear over the strangled body of Cordelia.   (Samuel Hirsch, *Herald Traveler,* Boston, May 13, 1970)

Andre Gregory directed the play at the Manhattan Project in 1973. Clive Barnes noted the unusual staging of this production:

> Mr. Gregory has built himself a strange, bullring of a theater. It is hexagonal, and the audience is on two levels. The audience is placed in cubicles — each holding four chairs. Each cubicle is insulated from the stage and from the world by chicken wire.   (*New York Times,* February 9, 1973)

The Royal Court played it in English during its Beckett Festival in 1976. Beckett directed the play again in London at the Young Vic in January 1980 and then in Chicago's Goodman Theater with the San Quentin Workshop in September 1980. In 1984 JoAnn Akalaitis staged a controversial *Endgame* at the American Repertory Theatre in Cambridge, Massachusetts. She set the play in a burned-out subway tunnel and commissioned an eerie musical score by minimalist composer Philip Glass. Grove Press, Beckett's representative, complained that the production disregarded "the playwright's sparse, rigorous scenic demands" and added uncalled-for music. As one critic noted, Akalaitis had "simply, vividly visualized and auralized *Endgame*'s nuclear-holocaustal implications, at the expense of its chess and theatrical imagery" (Carolyn Clay, *Boston Phoenix,* December 18, 1984). The production was allowed to continue after the American Repertory Theatre agreed to include a program insert, signed by Beckett, "decrying the interpretation."

Samuel Beckett (1906–1989)

Endgame

A PLAY IN ONE ACT

1957

The Characters

Nagg	Hamm
Nell	Clov

(*Bare interior.*)
  (*Gray light.*)
  (*Left and right back, high up, two small windows, curtains drawn.*)

(*Front right, a door. Hanging near door, its face to wall, a picture.*)
  (*Front left, touching each other, covered with an old sheet, two ashbins.°*)
  (*Center, in an armchair on casters, covered with an old sheet, Hamm.*)

ashbins: trash cans

(Motionless by the door, his eyes fixed on Hamm, Clov. Very red face.)
(Brief tableau.)

(Clov goes and stands under window left. Stiff, staggering walk. He looks up at window left. He turns and looks at window right. He goes and stands under window right. He looks up at window right. He turns and looks at window left. He goes out, comes back immediately with a small stepladder, carries it over and sets it down under window left, gets up on it, draws back curtain. He gets down, takes six steps (for example) towards window right, goes back for ladder, carries it over and sets it down under window right, gets up on it, draws back curtain. He gets down, takes three steps towards window left, goes back for ladder, carries it over and sets it down under window left, gets up on it, looks out of window. Brief laugh. He gets down, takes one step towards window right, goes back for ladder, carries it over and sets it down under window right, gets up on it, looks out of window. Brief laugh. He gets down, goes with ladder towards ashbins, halts, turns, carries back ladder and sets it down under window right, goes to ashbins, removes sheet covering them, folds it over his arm. He raises one lid, stoops and looks into bin. Brief laugh. He closes lid. Same with other bin. He goes to Hamm, removes sheet covering him, folds it over his arm. In a dressing gown, a stiff toque° on his head, a large bloodstained handkerchief over his face, a whistle hanging from his neck, a rug over his knees, thick socks on his feet, Hamm seems to be asleep. Clov looks over him. Brief laugh. He goes to door, halts, turns towards auditorium.)

CLOV *(fixed gaze, tonelessly)*: Finished, it's finished, nearly finished, it must be nearly finished.

(Pause.)

Grain upon grain, one by one, and one day, suddenly, there's a heap, a little heap, the impossible heap.

(Pause.)

I can't be punished anymore.

(Pause.)

I'll go now to my kitchen, ten feet by ten feet by ten feet, and wait for him to whistle me.

(Pause.)

Nice dimensions, nice proportions, I'll lean on the table, and look at the wall, and wait for him to whistle me.

toque: A small, brimless, close-fitting hat.

(He remains a moment motionless, then goes out. He comes back immediately, goes to window right, takes up the ladder and carries it out. Pause. Hamm stirs. He yawns under the handkerchief. He removes the handkerchief from his face. Very red face. Black glasses.)

HAMM: Me — *(he yawns)* — to play.

(He holds the handkerchief spread out before him.)

Old stancher!°

(He takes off his glasses, wipes his eyes, his face, the glasses, puts them on again, folds the handkerchief and puts it back neatly in the breast pocket of his dressing gown. He clears his throat, joins the tips of his fingers.)

Can there be misery — *(he yawns)* — loftier than mine? No doubt. Formerly. But now?

(Pause.)

My father?

(Pause.)

My mother?

(Pause.)

My . . . dog?

(Pause.)

Oh I am willing to believe they suffer as much as such creatures can suffer. But does that mean their sufferings equal mine? No doubt.

(Pause.)

No, all is a — *(he yawns)* — bsolute, *(proudly)* the bigger a man is the fuller he is.

(Pause. Gloomily.)

And the emptier.

(He sniffs.)

Clov!

(Pause.)

No, alone.

(Pause.)

What dreams! Those forests!

(Pause.)

Enough, it's time it ended, in the shelter too.

stancher: The handkerchief, which stops, or stanches, the flow of blood.

(*Pause.*)

And yet I hesitate, I hesitate to . . . to end. Yes there it is, it's time it ended and yet I hesitate to — (*he yawns*) — to end.

(*Yawns.*)

God, I'm tired, I'd be better off in bed.

(*He whistles. Enter Clov immediately. He halts beside the chair.*)

You pollute the air!

(*Pause.*)

Get me ready, I'm going to bed.
CLOV: I've just got you up.
HAMM: And what of it?
CLOV: I can't be getting you up and putting you to bed every five minutes, I have things to do.

(*Pause.*)

HAMM: Did you ever see my eyes?
CLOV: No.
HAMM: Did you never have the curiosity, while I was sleeping, to take off my glasses and look at my eyes?
CLOV: Pulling back the lids?

(*Pause.*)

No.
HAMM: One of these days I'll show them to you.

(*Pause.*)

It seems they've gone all white.

(*Pause.*)

What time is it?
CLOV: The same as usual.
HAMM (*gesture towards window right*): Have you looked?
CLOV: Yes.
HAMM: Well?
CLOV: Zero.
HAMM: It'd need to rain.
CLOV: It won't rain.

(*Pause.*)

HAMM: Apart from that, how do you feel?
CLOV: I don't complain.
HAMM: You feel normal?
CLOV (*irritably*): I tell you I don't complain.
HAMM: I feel a little queer.

(*Pause.*)

Clov!
CLOV: Yes.

HAMM: Have you not had enough?
CLOV: Yes!

(*Pause.*)

Of what?
HAMM: Of this . . . this . . . thing.
CLOV: I always had.

(*Pause.*)

Not you?
HAMM (*gloomily*): Then there's no reason for it to change.
CLOV: It may end.

(*Pause.*)

All life long the same questions, the same answers.
HAMM: Get me ready.

(*Clov does not move.*)

Go and get the sheet.

(*Clov does not move.*)

Clov!
CLOV: Yes.
HAMM: I'll give you nothing more to eat.
CLOV: Then we'll die.
HAMM: I'll give you just enough to keep you from dying. You'll be hungry all the time.
CLOV: Then we won't die.

(*Pause.*)

I'll go and get the sheet.

(*He goes towards the door.*)

HAMM: No!

(*Clov halts.*)

I'll give you one biscuit per day.

(*Pause.*)

One and a half.

(*Pause.*)

Why do you stay with me?
CLOV: Why do you keep me?
HAMM: There's no one else.
CLOV: There's nowhere else.

(*Pause.*)

HAMM: You're leaving me all the same.
CLOV: I'm trying.
HAMM: You don't love me.
CLOV: No.
HAMM: You loved me once.
CLOV: Once!

HAMM: I've made you suffer too much.

(*Pause.*)

Haven't I?
CLOV: It's not that.
HAMM (*shocked*): I haven't made you suffer too much?
CLOV: Yes!
HAMM (*relieved*): Ah you gave me a fright!

(*Pause. Coldly.*)

Forgive me.

(*Pause. Louder.*)

I said, Forgive me.
CLOV: I heard you.

(*Pause.*)

Have you bled?
HAMM: Less.

(*Pause.*)

Is it not time for my painkiller?
CLOV: No.

(*Pause.*)

HAMM: How are your eyes?
CLOV: Bad.
HAMM: How are your legs?
CLOV: Bad.
HAMM: But you can move.
CLOV: Yes.
HAMM (*violently*): Then move!

(*Clov goes to back wall, leans against it with his forehead and hands.*)

Where are you?
CLOV: Here.
HAMM: Come back!

(*Clov returns to his place beside the chair.*)

Where are you?
CLOV: Here.
HAMM: Why don't you kill me?
CLOV: I don't know the combination of the cupboard.

(*Pause.*)

HAMM: Go and get two bicycle wheels.
CLOV: There are no more bicycle wheels.
HAMM: What have you done with your bicycle?
CLOV: I never had a bicycle.
HAMM: The thing is impossible.
CLOV: When there were still bicycles I wept to have one. I crawled at your feet. You told me to go to hell. Now there are none.

HAMM: And your rounds? When you inspected my paupers. Always on foot?
CLOV: Sometimes on horse.

(*The lid of one of the bins lifts and the hands of Nagg appear, gripping the rim. Then his head emerges. Nightcap. Very white face. Nagg yawns, then listens.*)

I'll leave you, I have things to do.
HAMM: In your kitchen?
CLOV: Yes.
HAMM: Outside of here it's death.

(*Pause.*)

All right, be off.

(*Exit Clov. Pause.*)

We're getting on.
NAGG: Me pap!
HAMM: Accursed progenitor!
NAGG: Me pap!
HAMM: The old folks at home! No decency left! Guzzle, guzzle, that's all they think of.

(*He whistles. Enter Clov. He halts beside the chair.*)

Well! I thought you were leaving me.
CLOV: Oh not just yet, not just yet.
NAGG: Me pap!
HAMM: Give him his pap.
CLOV: There's no more pap.
HAMM (*to Nagg*): Do you hear that? There's no more pap. You'll never get any more pap.
NAGG: I want me pap!
HAMM: Give him a biscuit.

(*Exit Clov.*)

Accursed fornicator! How are your stumps?
NAGG: Never mind me stumps.

(*Enter Clov with biscuit.*)

CLOV: I'm back again, with the biscuit.

(*He gives biscuit to Nagg who fingers it, sniffs it.*)

NAGG (*plaintively*): What is it?
CLOV: Spratt's medium.
NAGG (*as before*): It's hard! I can't!
HAMM: Bottle him!

(*Clov pushes Nagg back into the bin, closes the lid.*)

CLOV (*returning to his place beside the chair*): If age but knew!
HAMM: Sit on him!
CLOV: I can't sit.
HAMM: True. And I can't stand.
CLOV: So it is.
HAMM: Every man his speciality.

(*Pause.*)

No phone calls?

(*Pause.*)

Don't we laugh?

CLOV (*after reflection*): I don't feel like it.

HAMM (*after reflection*): Nor I.

(*Pause.*)

Clov!

CLOV: Yes.

HAMM: Nature has forgotten us.

CLOV: There's no more nature.

HAMM: No more nature! You exaggerate.

CLOV: In the vicinity.

HAMM: But we breathe, we change! We lose our hair, our teeth! Our bloom! Our ideals!

CLOV: Then she hasn't forgotten us.

HAMM: But you say there is none.

CLOV (*sadly*): No one that ever lived ever thought so crooked as we.

HAMM: We do what we can.

CLOV: We shouldn't.

(*Pause.*)

HAMM: You're a bit of all right, aren't you?

CLOV: A smithereen.

(*Pause.*)

HAMM: This is slow work.

(*Pause.*)

Is it not time for my painkiller?

CLOV: No.

(*Pause.*)

I'll leave you, I have things to do.

HAMM: In your kitchen?

CLOV: Yes.

HAMM: What, I'd like to know.

CLOV: I look at the wall.

HAMM: The wall! And what do you see on your wall? Mene, mene?° Naked bodies?

CLOV: I see my light dying.

HAMM: Your light dying! Listen to that! Well, it can die just as well here, *your* light. Take a look at me and then come back and tell me what you think of *your* light.

(*Pause.*)

CLOV: You shouldn't speak to me like that.

Mene, mene: The handwriting on the wall in Daniel 5:25 indicating the end of King Belshazzar's reign: "MENE, MENE, TEKEL, and PARSIN."

(*Pause.*)

HAMM (*coldly*): Forgive me.

(*Pause. Louder.*)

I said, Forgive me.

CLOV: I heard you.

(*The lid of Nagg's bin lifts. His hands appear, gripping the rim. Then his head emerges. In his mouth the biscuit. He listens.*)

HAMM: Did your seeds come up?

CLOV: No.

HAMM: Did you scratch round them to see if they had sprouted?

CLOV: They haven't sprouted.

HAMM: Perhaps it's still too early.

CLOV: If they were going to sprout they would have sprouted.

(*Violently.*)

They'll never sprout!

(*Pause. Nagg takes biscuit in his hand.*)

HAMM: This is not much fun.

(*Pause.*)

But that's always the way at the end of the day, isn't it, Clov?

CLOV: Always.

HAMM: It's the end of the day like any other day, isn't it, Clov?

CLOV: Looks like it.

(*Pause.*)

HAMM (*anguished*): What's happening, what's happening?

CLOV: Something is taking its course.

(*Pause.*)

HAMM: All right, be off.

(*He leans back in his chair, remains motionless. Clov does not move, heaves a great groaning sigh. Hamm sits up.*)

I thought I told you to be off.

CLOV: I'm trying.

(*He goes to door, halts.*)

Ever since I was whelped.

(*Exit Clov.*)

HAMM: We're getting on.

(*He leans back in his chair, remains motionless. Nagg knocks on the lid of the other bin. Pause. He knocks *harder. The lid lifts and the hands of Nell appear, gripping the rim. Then her head emerges. Lace cap. Very white face.*)

NELL: What is it, my pet?

(*Pause.*)

Time for love?

NAGG: Were you asleep?

NELL: Oh no!

NAGG: Kiss me.

NELL: We can't.

NAGG: Try.

(*Their heads strain towards each other, fail to meet, fall apart again.*)

NELL: Why this farce, day after day?

(*Pause.*)

NAGG: I've lost me tooth.

NELL: When?

NAGG: I had it yesterday.

NELL (*elegiac*): Ah yesterday!

(*They turn painfully towards each other.*)

NAGG: Can you see me?

NELL: Hardly. And you?

NAGG: What?

NELL: Can you see me?

NAGG: Hardly.

NELL: So much the better, so much the better.

NAGG: Don't say that.

(*Pause.*)

Our sight has failed.

NELL: Yes.

(*Pause. They turn away from each other.*)

NAGG: Can you hear me?

NELL: Yes. And you?

NAGG: Yes.

(*Pause.*)

Our hearing hasn't failed.

NELL: Our what?

NAGG: Our hearing.

NELL: No.

(*Pause.*)

Have you anything else to say to me?

NAGG: Do you remember —

NELL: No.

NAGG: When we crashed on our tandem and lost our shanks.

(*They laugh heartily.*)

NELL: It was in the Ardennes.

(*They laugh less heartily.*)

NAGG: On the road to Sedan.

(*They laugh still less heartily.*)

Are you cold?

NELL: Yes, perished. And you?

NAGG:

(*Pause.*)

I'm freezing.

(*Pause.*)

Do you want to go in?

NELL: Yes.

NAGG: Then go in.

(*Nell does not move.*)

Why don't you go in?

NELL: I don't know.

(*Pause.*)

NAGG: Has he changed your sawdust?

NELL: It isn't sawdust.

(*Pause. Wearily.*)

Can you not be a little accurate, Nagg?

NAGG: Your sand then. It's not important.

NELL: It is important.

(*Pause.*)

NAGG: It was sawdust once.

NELL: Once!

NAGG: And now it's sand.

(*Pause.*)

From the shore.

(*Pause. Impatiently.*)

Now it's sand he fetches from the shore.

NELL: Now it's sand.

NAGG: Has he changed yours?

NELL: No.

NAGG: Nor mine.

(*Pause.*)

I won't have it!

(*Pause. Holding up the biscuit.*)

Do you want a bit?

NELL: No.

(*Pause.*)

Of what?

NAGG: Biscuit. I've kept you half.

(*He looks at the biscuit. Proudly.*)

Three quarters. For you. Here.

(*He proffers the biscuit.*)

No?

(*Pause.*)

Do you not feel well?

HAMM (*wearily*): Quiet, quiet, you're keeping me awake.

(*Pause.*)

Talk softer.

(*Pause.*)

If I could sleep I might make love. I'd go into the woods. My eyes would see . . . the sky, the earth. I'd run, run, they wouldn't catch me.

(*Pause.*)

Nature!

(*Pause.*)

There's something dripping in my head.

(*Pause.*)

A heart, a heart in my head.

(*Pause.*)

NAGG (*soft*): Do you hear him? A heart in his head!

(*He chuckles cautiously.*)

NELL: One mustn't laugh at those things, Nagg. Why must you always laugh at them?

NAGG: Not so loud!

NELL (*without lowering her voice*): Nothing is funnier than unhappiness, I grant you that. But —

NAGG (*shocked*): Oh!

NELL: Yes, yes, it's the most comical thing in the world. And we laugh, we laugh, with a will, in the beginning. But it's always the same thing. Yes, it's like the funny story we have heard too often, we still find it funny, but we don't laugh anymore.

(*Pause.*)

Have you anything else to say to me?

NAGG: No.

NELL: Are you quite sure?

(*Pause.*)

Then I'll leave you.

NAGG: Do you not want your biscuit?

(*Pause.*)

I'll keep it for you.

(*Pause.*)

I thought you were going to leave me.

NELL: I am going to leave you.

NAGG: Could you give me a scratch before you go?

NELL: No.

(*Pause.*)

Where?

NAGG: In the back.

NELL: No.

(*Pause.*)

Rub yourself against the rim.

NAGG: It's lower down. In the hollow.

NELL: What hollow?

NAGG: The hollow!

(*Pause.*)

Could you not?

(*Pause.*)

Yesterday you scratched me there.

NELL (*elegiac*): Ah yesterday!

NAGG: Could you not?

(*Pause.*)

Would you like me to scratch you?

(*Pause.*)

Are you crying again?

NELL: I was trying.

(*Pause.*)

HAMM: Perhaps it's a little vein.

(*Pause.*)

NAGG: What was that he said?

NELL: Perhaps it's a little vein.

NAGG: What does that mean?

(*Pause.*)

That means nothing.

(*Pause.*)

Will I tell you the story of the tailor?

NELL: No.

(*Pause.*)

What for?

NAGG: To cheer you up.

NELL: It's not funny.

NAGG: It always made you laugh.

(*Pause.*)

The first time I thought you'd die.

NELL: It was on Lake Como.

(*Pause.*)

One April afternoon.

(*Pause.*)

Can you believe it?

NAGG: What?

NELL: That we once went out rowing on Lake Como.

(*Pause.*)

One April afternoon.

NAGG: We had got engaged the day before.

NELL: Engaged!

NAGG: You were in such fits that we capsized. By rights we should have been drowned.

NELL: It was because I felt happy.

NAGG (*indignant*): It was not, it was not, it was my story and nothing else. Happy! Don't you laugh at it still? Every time I tell it. Happy!

NELL: It was deep, deep. And you could see down to the bottom. So white. So clean.

NAGG: Let me tell it again.

(*Raconteur's voice.*)

An Englishman, needing a pair of striped trousers in a hurry for the New Year festivities, goes to his tailor who takes his measurements.

(*Tailor's voice.*)

"That's the lot, come back in four days, I'll have it ready." Good. Four days later.

(*Tailor's voice.*)

"So sorry, come back in a week, I've made a mess of the seat." Good, that's all right, a neat seat can be very ticklish. A week later.

(*Tailor's voice.*)

"Frightfully sorry, come back in ten days, I've made a hash of the crotch." Good, can't be helped, a snug crotch is always a teaser. Ten days later.

(*Tailor's voice.*)

"Dreadfully sorry, come back in a fortnight, I've made a balls of the fly." Good, at a pinch, a smart fly is a stiff proposition.

(*Pause. Normal voice.*)

I never told it worse.

(*Pause. Gloomy.*)

I tell this story worse and worse.

(*Pause. Raconteur's voice.*)

Well, to make it short, the bluebells are blowing and he ballockses the buttonholes.

(*Customer's voice.*)

"God damn you to hell, Sir, no, it's indecent, there are limits! In six days, do you hear me, six days, God made the world. Yes Sir, no less Sir, the WORLD! And you are not bloody well capable of making me a pair of trousers in three months!"

(*Tailor's voice, scandalized.*)

"But my dear Sir, my dear Sir, look — (*disdainful gesture, disgustedly*) — at the world — (*pause*) and look — (*loving gesture, proudly*) — at my TROUSERS!"

(*Pause. He looks at Nell who has remained impassive, her eyes unseeing, breaks into a high forced laugh, cuts it short, pokes his head towards Nell, launches his laugh again.*)

HAMM: Silence!

(*Nagg starts, cuts short his laugh.*)

NELL: You could see down to the bottom.

HAMM (*exasperated*): Have you not finished? Will you never finish?

(*With sudden fury.*)

Will this never finish?

(*Nagg disappears into his bin, closes the lid behind him. Nell does not move. Frenziedly.*)

My kingdom for a nightman!

(*He whistles. Enter Clov.*)

Clear away this muck! Chuck it in the sea!

(*Clov goes to bins, halts.*)

NELL: So white.

HAMM: What? What's she blathering about?

(*Clov stoops, takes Nell's hand, feels her pulse.*)

NELL (*to Clov*): Desert!

(*Clov lets go her hand, pushes her back in the bin, closes the lid.*)

CLOV (*returning to his place beside the chair*): She has no pulse.

HAMM: What was she driveling about?

CLOV: She told me to go away, into the desert.

HAMM: Damn busybody! Is that all?

CLOV: No.

HAMM: What else?

CLOV: I didn't understand.

HAMM: Have you bottled her?

CLOV: Yes.

HAMM: Are they both bottled?

CLOV: Yes.

HAMM: Screw down the lids.

(*Clov goes towards door.*)

Time enough.

(*Clov halts.*)

My anger subsides, I'd like to pee.
CLOV (*with alacrity*): I'll go and get the catheter.

(*He goes towards door.*)

HAMM: Time enough.

(*Clov halts.*)

Give me my painkiller.
CLOV: It's too soon.

(*Pause.*)

It's too soon on top of your tonic, it wouldn't act.
HAMM: In the morning they brace you up and in the
evening they calm you down. Unless it's the other
way round.

(*Pause.*)

That old doctor, he's dead naturally?
CLOV: He wasn't old.
HAMM: But he's dead?
CLOV: Naturally.

(*Pause.*)

You ask *me* that?

(*Pause.*)

HAMM: Take me for a little turn.

(*Clov goes behind the chair and pushes it forward.*)

Not too fast!

(*Clov pushes chair.*)

Right round the world!

(*Clov pushes chair.*)

Hug the walls, then back to the center again.

(*Clov pushes chair.*)

I was right in the center, wasn't I?
CLOV (*pushing*): Yes.
HAMM: We'd need a proper wheelchair. With big
wheels. Bicycle wheels!

(*Pause.*)

Are you hugging?
CLOV (*pushing*): Yes.
HAMM (*groping for wall*): It's a lie! Why do you lie to me?
CLOV (*bearing closer to wall*): There! There!

HAMM: Stop!

(*Clov stops chair close to back wall. Hamm lays his
hand against wall.*)

Old wall!

(*Pause.*)

Beyond is the . . . other hell.

(*Pause. Violently.*)

Closer! Closer! Up against!
CLOV: Take away your hand.

(*Hamm withdraws his hand. Clov rams chair against
wall.*)

There!

(*Hamm leans towards wall, applies his ear to it.*)

HAMM: Do you hear?

(*He strikes the wall with his knuckles.*)

Do you hear? Hollow bricks!

(*He strikes again.*)

All that's hollow!

(*Pause. He straightens up. Violently.*)

That's enough. Back!
CLOV: We haven't done the round.
HAMM: Back to my place!

(*Clov pushes chair back to center.*)

Is that my place?
CLOV: Yes, that's your place.
HAMM: Am I right in the center?
CLOV: I'll measure it.
HAMM: More or less! More or less!
CLOV (*moving chair slightly*): There!
HAMM: I'm more or less in the center?
CLOV: I'd say so.
HAMM: You'd say so! Put me right in the center!
CLOV: I'll go and get the tape.
HAMM: Roughly! Roughly!

(*Clov moves chair slightly.*)

Bang in the center!
CLOV: There!

(*Pause.*)

HAMM: I feel a little too far to the left.

(*Clov moves chair slightly.*)

Now I feel a little too far to the right.

(*Clov moves chair slightly.*)

I feel a little too far forward.

(*Clov moves chair slightly.*)

Now I feel a little too far back.

(*Clov moves chair slightly.*)

Don't stay there, (*i.e., behind the chair*) you give me the shivers.

(*Clov returns to his place beside the chair.*)

CLOV: If I could kill him I'd die happy.

(*Pause.*)

HAMM: What's the weather like?
CLOV: As usual.
HAMM: Look at the earth.
CLOV: I've looked.
HAMM: With the glass?
CLOV: No need of the glass.
HAMM: Look at it with the glass.
CLOV: I'll go and get the glass.

(*Exit Clov.*)

HAMM: No need of the glass!

(*Enter Clov with telescope.*)

CLOV: I'm back again, with the glass.

(*He goes to window right, looks up at it.*)

I need the steps.
HAMM: Why? Have you shrunk?

(*Exit Clov with telescope.*)

I don't like that, I don't like that.

(*Enter Clov with ladder, but without telescope.*)

CLOV: I'm back again, with the steps.

(*He sets down ladder under window right, gets up on it, realizes he has not the telescope, gets down.*)

I need the glass.

(*He goes towards door.*)

HAMM (*violently*): But you have the glass!
CLOV (*halting, violently*): No, I haven't the glass!

(*Exit Clov.*)

HAMM: This is deadly.

(*Enter Clov with telescope. He goes towards ladder.*)

CLOV: Things are livening up.

(*He gets up on ladder, raises the telescope, lets it fall.*)

I did it on purpose.

(*He gets down, picks up the telescope, turns it on auditorium.*)

I see . . . a multitude . . . in transports . . . of joy.

(*Pause.*)

That's what I call a magnifier.

(*He lowers the telescope, turns towards Hamm.*)

Well? Don't we laugh?
HAMM (*after reflection*): I don't.
CLOV (*after reflection*): Nor I.

(*He gets up on ladder, turns the telescope on the without.*)

Let's see.

(*He looks, moving the telescope.*)

Zero . . . (*he looks*) . . . zero . . . (*he looks*) . . . and zero.
HAMM: Nothing stirs. All is —
CLOV: Zer —
HAMM (*violently*): Wait till you're spoken to!

(*Normal voice.*)

All is . . . all is . . . all is what?

(*Violently.*)

All is what?
CLOV: What all is? In a word? Is that what you want to know? Just a moment.

(*He turns the telescope on the without, looks, lowers the telescope, turns towards Hamm.*)

Corpsed.

(*Pause.*)

Well? Content?
HAMM: Look at the sea.
CLOV: It's the same.
HAMM: Look at the ocean!

(*Clov gets down, takes a few steps towards window left, goes back for ladder, carries it over and sets it down under window left, gets up on it, turns the telescope on the without, looks at length. He starts, lowers the telescope, examines it, turns it again on the without.*)

CLOV: Never seen anything like that!
HAMM (*anxious*): What? A sail? A fin? Smoke?
CLOV (*looking*): The light is sunk.
HAMM (*relieved*): Pah! We all knew that.
CLOV (*looking*): There was a bit left.
HAMM: The base.
CLOV (*looking*): Yes.
HAMM: And now?
CLOV (*looking*): All gone.

HAMM: No gulls?
CLOV (*looking*): Gulls!
HAMM: And the horizon? Nothing on the horizon?
CLOV (*lowering the telescope, turning towards Hamm, exasperated*): What in God's name could there be on the horizon?

(*Pause.*)

HAMM: The waves, how are the waves?
CLOV: The waves?

(*He turns the telescope on the waves.*)

Lead.
HAMM: And the sun?
CLOV (*looking*): Zero.
HAMM: But it should be sinking. Look again.
CLOV (*looking*): Damn the sun.
HAMM: Is it night already then?
CLOV (*looking*): No.
HAMM: Then what is it?
CLOV (*looking*): Gray.

(*Lowering the telescope, turning towards Hamm, louder.*)

Gray!

(*Pause. Still louder.*)

GRRAY!

(*Pause. He gets down, approaches Hamm from behind, whispers in his ear.*)

HAMM (*starting*): Gray! Did I hear you say gray?
CLOV: Light black. From pole to pole.
HAMM: You exaggerate.

(*Pause.*)

Don't stay there, you give me the shivers.

(*Clov returns to his place beside the chair.*)

CLOV: Why this farce, day after day?
HAMM: Routine. One never knows.

(*Pause.*)

Last night I saw inside my breast. There was a big sore.
CLOV: Pah! You saw your heart.
HAMM: No, it was living.

(*Pause. Anguished.*)

Clov!
CLOV: Yes.
HAMM: What's happening?
CLOV: Something is taking its course.

(*Pause.*)

HAMM: Clov!
CLOV (*impatiently*): What is it?

HAMM: We're not beginning to . . . to . . . mean something?
CLOV: Mean something! You and I, mean something!

(*Brief laugh.*)

Ah that's a good one!
HAMM: I wonder.

(*Pause.*)

Imagine if a rational being came back to earth, wouldn't he be liable to get ideas into his head if he observed us long enough.

(*Voice of rational being.*)

Ah, good, now I see what it is, yes, now I understand what they're at!

(*Clov starts, drops the telescope and begins to scratch his belly with both hands. Normal voice.*)

And without going so far as that, we ourselves . . . (*with emotion*) . . . we ourselves . . . at certain moments . . .

(*Vehemently.*)

To think perhaps it won't all have been for nothing!
CLOV (*anguished, scratching himself*): I have a flea!
HAMM: A flea! Are there still fleas?
CLOV: On me there's one.

(*Scratching.*)

Unless it's a crablouse.
HAMM (*very perturbed*): But humanity might start from there all over again! Catch him, for the love of God!
CLOV: I'll go and get the powder.

(*Exit Clov.*)

HAMM: A flea! This is awful! What a day!

(*Enter Clov with a sprinkling tin.*)

CLOV: I'm back again, with the insecticide.
HAMM: Let him have it!

(*Clov loosens the top of his trousers, pulls it forward and shakes powder into the aperture. He stoops, looks, waits, starts, frenziedly shakes more powder, stoops, looks, waits.*)

CLOV: The bastard!
HAMM: Did you get him?
CLOV: Looks like it.

(*He drops the tin and adjusts his trousers.*)

Unless he's laying doggo.°

---

doggo: In hiding.

HAMM: Laying! Lying you mean. Unless he's *lying* doggo.

CLOV: Ah? One says lying? One doesn't say laying?

HAMM: Use your head, can't you. If he was laying we'd be bitched.

CLOV: Ah.

(*Pause.*)

What about that pee?

HAMM: I'm having it.

CLOV: Ah that's the spirit, that's the spirit!

(*Pause.*)

HAMM (*with ardor*): Let's go from here, the two of us!

South! You can make a raft and the currents will carry us away, far away, to other . . . mammals!

CLOV: God forbid!

HAMM: Alone, I'll embark alone! Get working on that raft immediately. Tomorrow I'll be gone forever.

CLOV (*hastening towards door*): I'll start straight away.

HAMM: Wait!

(*Clov halts.*)

Will there be sharks, do you think?

CLOV: Sharks? I don't know. If there are there will be.

(*He goes towards door.*)

HAMM: Wait!

RIGHT: Hamm (Alvin Epstein), seated, and Clov (Peter Evans) in the 1984 Harold Clurman Theatre production of *Endgame*, directed by Alvin Epstein. FAR RIGHT: Nell (Alice Drummond), Nagg (James Greene), Hamm, and Clov.

(*Clov halts.*)

Is it not yet time for my painkiller?
CLOV (*violently*): No!

(*He goes towards door.*)

HAMM: Wait!

(*Clov halts.*)

How are your eyes?
CLOV: Bad.
HAMM: But you can see.
CLOV: All I want.
HAMM: How are your legs
CLOV: Bad.
HAMM: But you can walk.
CLOV: I come . . . and go.
HAMM: In my house.

(*Pause. With prophetic relish.*)

One day you'll be blind, like me. You'll be sitting there, a speck in the void, in the dark, forever, like me.

(*Pause.*)

One day you'll say to yourself, I'm tired, I'll sit down, and you'll go and sit down. Then you'll say, I'm hungry, I'll get up and get something to eat. But you won't get up. You'll say, I shouldn't have sat down, but since I have I'll sit on a little longer, then I'll get up and get something to eat. But you won't get up and you won't get anything to eat.

(*Pause.*)

You'll look at the wall a while, then you'll say, I'll close my eyes, perhaps have a little sleep, after that I'll feel better, and you'll close them. And when you open them again there'll be no wall anymore.

(*Pause.*)

Infinite emptiness will be all around you, all the resurrected dead of all the ages wouldn't fill it, and there you'll be like a little bit of grit in the middle of the steppe.

(*Pause.*)

Yes, one day you'll know what it is, you'll be like me, except that you won't have anyone with you, because you won't have had pity on anyone and because there won't be anyone left to have pity on.

(*Pause.*)

CLOV: It's not certain.

(*Pause.*)

And there's one thing you forget.
HAMM: Ah?
CLOV: I can't sit down.
HAMM (*impatiently*): Well you'll lie down then, what the hell! Or you'll come to a standstill, simply stop and stand still, the way you are now. One day you'll say, I'm tired, I'll stop. What does the attitude matter?

(*Pause.*)

CLOV: So you all want me to leave you.
HAMM: Naturally.
CLOV: Then I'll leave you.
HAMM: You can't leave us.
CLOV: Then I won't leave you.

(*Pause.*)

HAMM: Why don't you finish us?

(*Pause.*)

I'll tell you the combination of the cupboard if you promise to finish me.
CLOV: I couldn't finish you.
HAMM: Then you won't finish me.

(*Pause.*)

CLOV: I'll leave you, I have things to do.
HAMM: Do you remember when you came here?
CLOV: No. Too small, you told me.
HAMM: Do you remember your father?
CLOV (*wearily*): Same answer.

(*Pause.*)

You've asked me these questions millions of times.
HAMM: I love the old questions.

(*With fervor.*)

Ah the old questions, the old answers, there's nothing like them!

(*Pause.*)

It was I was a father to you.
CLOV: Yes.

(*He looks at Hamm fixedly.*)

You were that to me.
HAMM: My house a home for you.
CLOV: Yes.

(*He looks about him.*)

This was that for me.
HAMM (*proudly*): But for me, (*gesture towards himself*) no father. But for Hamm, (*gesture towards surroundings*) no home.

(*Pause.*)

CLOV: I'll leave you.
HAMM: Did you ever think of one thmg?
CLOV: Never.
HAMM: That here we're down in a hole.

(*Pause.*)

But beyond the hills? Eh? Perhaps it's still green. Eh?

(*Pause.*)

Flora! Pomona!

(*Ecstatically.*)

Ceres!°

(*Pause,*)

Perhaps you won't need to go very far.
CLOV: I can't go very far.

(*Pause.*)

I'll leave you.
HAMM: Is my dog ready?
CLOV: He lacks a leg.
HAMM: Is he silky?
CLOV: He's a kind of Pomeranian.
HAMM: Go and get him.
CLOV: He lacks a leg.
HAMM: Go and get him!

(*Exit Clov.*)

We're getting on.

Flora . . . Pomona . . . Ceres: Goddesses of agricultural fertility.

(*Enter Clov holding by one of its three legs a black toy dog.*)

CLOV: Your dogs are here.

(*He hands the dog to Hamm who feels it, fondles it.*)

HAMM: He's white, isn't he?
CLOV: Nearly.
HAMM: What do you mean, nearly? Is he white or isn't he?
CLOV: He isn't.

(*Pause.*)

HAMM: You've forgotten the sex.
CLOV (*vexed*): But he isn't finished. The sex goes on at the end.

(*Pause.*)

HAMM: You haven't put on his ribbon.
CLOV (*angrily*): But he isn't finished, I tell you! First you finish your dog and then you put on his ribbon!

(*Pause.*)

HAMM: Can he stand?
CLOV: I don't know.
HAMM: Try.

(*He hands the dog to Clov who places it on the ground.*)

Well?
CLOV: Wait!

(*He squats down and tries to get the dog to stand on its three legs, fails, lets it go. The dog falls on its side.*)

HAMM (*impatiently*): Well?
CLOV: He's standing.
HAMM (*groping for the dog*): Where? Where is he?

(*Clov holds up the dog in a standing position.*)

CLOV: There.

(*He takes Hamm's hand and guides it towards the dog's head.*)

HAMM (*his hand on the dog's head*): Is he gazing at me?
CLOV: Yes.
HAMM (*proudly*): As if he were asking me to take him for a walk?
CLOV: If you like.
HAMM (*as before*): Or as if he were begging me for a bone.

(*He withdraws his hand.*)

Leave him like that, standing there imploring me.

(*Clov straightens up. The dog falls on its side.*)

CLOV: I'll leave you.
HAMM: Have you had your visions?
CLOV: Less.
HAMM: Is Mother Pegg's light on?
CLOV: Light! How could anyone's light be on?
HAMM: Extinguished!
CLOV: Naturally it's extinguished. If it's not on it's extinguished.
HAMM: No, I mean Mother Pegg.
CLOV: But naturally she's extinguished!

(*Pause.*)

What's the matter with you today?
HAMM: I'm taking my course.

(*Pause.*)

Is she buried?
CLOV: Buried! Who would have buried her?
HAMM: You.
CLOV: Me! Haven't I enough to do without burying people?
HAMM: But you'll bury me.
CLOV: No I won't bury you.

(*Pause.*)

HAMM: She was bonny once, like a flower of the field.

(*With reminiscent leer.*)

And a great one for the men!
CLOV: We too were bonny — once. It's a rare thing not to have been bonny — once.

(*Pause.*)

HAMM: Go and get the gaff.

(*Clov goes to door, halts.*)

CLOV: Do this, do that, and I do it. I never refuse. Why?
HAMM: You're not able to.
CLOV: Soon I won't do it anymore.
HAMM: You won't be able to anymore.

(*Exit Clov.*)

Ah the creatures, the creatures, everything has to be explained to them.

(*Enter Clov with gaff.*)

CLOV: Here's your gaff. Stick it up.

(*He gives the gaff to Hamm who, wielding it like a puntpole,° tries to move his chair.*)

puntpole: A pole used to propel a punt, a flat-bottomed boat, through the water.

HAMM: Did I move?

CLOV: No.

(*Hamm throws down the gaff.*)

HAMM: Go and get the oilcan.

CLOV: What for?

HAMM: To oil the casters.

CLOV: I oiled them yesterday.

HAMM: Yesterday! What does that mean? Yesterday!

CLOV (*violently*): That means that bloody awful day, long ago, before this bloody awful day. I use the words you taught me. If they don't mean anything anymore, teach me others. Or let me be silent.

(*Pause.*)

HAMM: I once knew a madman who thought the end of the world had come. He was a painter — and engraver. I had a great fondness for him. I used to go and see him, in the asylum. I'd take him by the hand and drag him to the window. Look! There! All that rising corn! And there! Look! The sails of the herring fleet! All that loveliness!

(*Pause.*)

He'd snatch away his hand and go back into his corner. Appalled. All he had seen was ashes.

(*Pause.*)

He alone had been spared.

(*Pause.*)

Forgotten.

(*Pause.*)

It appears the case is . . . was not so . . . so unusual.

CLOV: A madman? When was that?

HAMM: Oh way back, way back, you weren't in the land of the living.

CLOV: God be with the days!

(*Pause. Hamm raises his toque.*)

HAMM: I had a great fondness for him.

(*Pause. He puts on his toque again.*)

He was a painter — and engraver.

CLOV: There are so many terrible things.

HAMM: No, no, there are not so many now.

(*Pause.*)

Clov!

CLOV: Yes.

HAMM: Do you not think this has gone on long enough?

CLOV: Yes!

(*Pause.*)

What?

HAMM: This . . . this . . . thing.

CLOV: I've always thought so.

(*Pause.*)

You not?

HAMM (*gloomily*): Then it's a day like any other day.

CLOV: As long as it lasts.

(*Pause.*)

All life long the same inanities.

HAMM: I can't leave you.

CLOV: I know. And you can't follow me.

(*Pause.*)

HAMM: If you leave me how shall I know?

CLOV (*briskly*): Well you simply whistle me and if I don't come running it means I've left you.

(*Pause.*)

HAMM: You won't come and kiss me good-bye?

CLOV: Oh I shouldn't think so.

(*Pause.*)

HAMM: But you might be merely dead in your kitchen?

CLOV: The result would be the same.

HAMM: Yes, but how would I know, if you were merely dead in your kitchen?

CLOV: Well . . . sooner or later I'd start to stink.

HAMM: You stink already. The whole place stinks of corpses.

CLOV: The whole universe.

HAMM (*angrily*): To hell with the universe.

(*Pause.*)

Think of something.

CLOV: What?

HAMM: An idea, have an idea.

(*Angrily.*)

A bright idea!

CLOV: Ah good.

(*He starts pacing to and fro, his eyes fixed on the ground, his hands behind his back. He halts.*)

The pains in my legs! It's unbelievable! Soon I won't be able to think anymore.

HAMM: You won't be able to leave me.

(*Clov resumes his pacing.*)

What are you doing?

CLOV: Having an idea.

(*He paces.*)

Ah!

(*He halts.*)

HAMM: What a brain!

(*Pause.*)

Well?

CLOV: Wait!

(*He meditates. Not very convinced.*)

Yes . . .

(*Pause. More convinced.*)

Yes!

(*He raises his head.*)

I have it! I set the alarm.

(*Pause.*)

HAMM: This is perhaps not one of my bright days, but frankly —

CLOV: You whistle me. I don't come. The alarm rings. I'm gone. It doesn't ring. I'm dead.

(*Pause.*)

HAMM: Is it working?

(*Pause. Impatiently.*)

The alarm, is it working?

CLOV: Why wouldn't it be working?

HAMM: Because it's worked too much.

CLOV: But it's hardly worked at all.

HAMM (*angrily*): Then because it's worked too little!

CLOV: I'll go and see.

(*Exit Clov. Brief ring of alarm off. Enter Clov with alarm clock. He holds it against Hamm's ear and releases alarm. They listen to it ringing to the end. Pause.*)

Fit to wake the dead! Did you hear it?

HAMM: Vaguely.

CLOV: The end is terrific!

HAMM: I prefer the middle.

(*Pause.*)

Is it not time for my painkiller?

CLOV: No!

(*He goes to door, turns.*)

I'll leave you.

HAMM: It's time for my story. Do you want to listen to my story?

CLOV: No.

HAMM: Ask my father if he wants to listen to my story.

(*Clov goes to bins, raises the lid of Nagg's, stoops, looks into it. Pause. He straightens up.*)

CLOV: He's asleep.

HAMM: Wake him.

(*Clov stoops, wakes Nagg with the alarm. Unintelligible words. Clov straightens up.*)

CLOV: He doesn't want to listen to your story.

HAMM: I'll give him a bonbon.

(*Clov stoops. As before.*)

CLOV: He wants a sugarplum.

HAMM: He'll get a sugarplum.

(*Clov stoops. As before.*)

CLOV: It's a deal.

(*He goes towards door. Nagg's hands appear, gripping the rim. Then the head emerges. Clov reaches door, turns.*)

Do you believe in the life to come?

HAMM: Mine was always that.

(*Exit Clov.*)

Got him that time!

NAGG: I'm listening.

HAMM: Scoundrel! Why did you engender me?

NAGG: I didn't know.

HAMM: What? What didn't you know?

NAGG: That it'd be you.

(*Pause.*)

You'll give me a sugarplum?

HAMM: After the audition.

NAGG: You swear?

HAMM: Yes.

NAGG: On what?

HAMM: My honor.

(*Pause. They laugh heartily.*)

NAGG: Two.

HAMM: One.

NAGG: One for me and one for —

HAMM: One! Silence!

(*Pause.*)

Where was I?

(*Pause. Gloomily.*)

It's finished, we're finished.

(*Pause.*)

Nearly finished.

(*Pause.*)

There'll be no more speech.

(*Pause.*)

Something dripping in my head, ever since the fontanelles.°

(*Stifled hilarity of Nagg.*)

Splash, splash, always on the same spot.

(*Pause.*)

Perhaps it's a little vein.

(*Pause.*)

A little artery.

(*Pause. More animated.*)

Enough of that, it's story time, where was I?

(*Pause. Narrative tone.*)

The man came crawling towards me, on his belly. Pale, wonderfully pale and thin, he seemed on the point of —

(*Pause. Normal tone.*)

No, I've done that bit.

(*Pause. Narrative tone.*)

I calmly filled my pipe — the meerschaum, lit it with . . . let us say a vesta,° drew a few puffs. Aah!

(*Pause.*)

Well, what is it *you* want?

(*Pause.*)

It was an extraordinarily bitter day, I remember, zero by the thermometer. But considering it was Christmas Eve there was nothing . . . extraordinary about that. Seasonable weather, for once in a way.

(*Pause.*)

Well, what ill wind blows you my way? He raised his face to me, black with mingled dirt and tears.

(*Pause. Normal tone.*)

That should do it.

(*Narrative tone.*)

No no, don't look at me, don't look at me. He dropped his eyes and mumbled something, apologies I presume.

(*Pause.*)

I'm a busy man, you know, the final touches, before the festivities, you know what it is.

(*Pause. Forcibly.*)

Come on now, what is the object of this invasion?

(*Pause.*)

It was a glorious bright day, I remember, fifty by the heliometer,° but already the sun was sinking down into the . . . down among the dead.

(*Normal tone.*)

Nicely put, that.

(*Narrative tone.*)

Come on now, come on, present your petition and let me resume my labors.

(*Pause. Normal tone.*)

There's English for you. Ah well . . .

(*Narrative tone.*)

It was then he took the plunge. It's my little one, he said. Tsstss, a little one, that's bad. My little boy, he said, as if the sex mattered. Where did he come from? He named the hole. A good half-day, on horse. What are you insinuating? That the place is still inhabited? No, no, not a soul, except himself and the child — assuming he existed. Good. I inquired about the situation at Kov, beyond the gulf. Not a sinner. Good. And you expect me to believe you have left your little one back there, all alone, and alive into the bargain? Come now!

(*Pause.*)

It was a howling wild day, I remember, a hundred by the anemometer.° The wind was tearing up the dead pines and sweeping them . . . away.

(*Pause. Normal tone.*)

---

since the fontanelles: Since his embryonic development, when the membranes formed linking his skull bones in his infant head.
vesta: A wooden match.

heliometer: A telescope for measuring the apparent diameter of the sun.
anemometer: An instrument for measuring wind speed.

A bit feeble, that.

(*Narrative tone.*)

Come on, man, speak up, what is you want from me, I have to put up my holly.

(*Pause.*)

Well to make it short it finally transpired that what he wanted from me was . . . bread for his brat? Bread? But I have no bread, it doesn't agree with me. Good. Then perhaps a little corn?

(*Pause. Normal tone.*)

That should do it.

(*Narrative tone.*)

Corn, yes, I have corn, it's true, in my granaries. But use your head. I give you some corn, a pound, a pound and a half, you bring it back to your child and you make him — if he's still alive — a nice pot of porridge, (*Nagg reacts*) a nice pot and a half of porridge, full of nourishment. Good. The colors come back into his little cheeks — perhaps. And then?

(*Pause.*)

I lost patience.

(*Violently.*)

Use your head, can't you, use your head, you're on earth, there's no cure for that!

(*Pause.*)

It was an exceedingly dry day, I remember, zero by the hygrometer.° Ideal weather, for my lumbago.

(*Pause. Violently.*)

But what in God's name do you imagine? That the earth will awake in spring? That the rivers and seas will run with fish again? That there's manna in heaven still for imbeciles like you?

(*Pause.*)

Gradually I cooled down, sufficiently at least to ask him how long he had taken on the way. Three whole days. Good. In what condition he had left the child. Deep in sleep.

(*Forcibly.*)

But deep in what sleep, deep in what sleep already?

(*Pause.*)

---

hygrometer: Device for measuring humidity.

Well to make it short I finally offered to take him into my service. He had touched a chord. And then I imagined already that I wasn't much longer for this world.

(*He laughs. Pause.*)

Well?

(*Pause.*)

Well? Here if you were careful you might die a nice natural death, in peace and comfort.

(*Pause.*)

Well?

(*Pause.*)

In the end he asked me would I consent to take in the child as well — if he were still alive.

(*Pause.*)

It was the moment I was waiting for.

(*Pause.*)

Would I consent to take in the child . . .

(*Pause.*)

I can see him still, down on his knees, his hands flat on the ground, glaring at me with his mad eyes, in defiance of my wishes.

(*Pause. Normal tone.*)

I'll soon have finished with this story.

(*Pause.*)

Unless I bring in other characters.

(*Pause.*)

But where would I find them?

(*Pause.*)

Where would I look for them?

(*Pause. He whistles. Enter Clov.*)

Let us pray to God.

NAGG: Me sugarplum!

CLOV: There's a rat in the kitchen!

HAMM: A rat! Are there still rats?

CLOV: In the kitchen there's one.

HAMM: And you haven't exterminated him?

CLOV: Half. You disturbed us.

HAMM: He can't get away?

CLOV: No.

HAMM: You'll finish him later. Let us pray to God.

CLOV: Again!
NAGG: Me sugarplum!
HAMM: God first!

(*Pause.*)

Are you right?
CLOV (*resigned*): Off we go.
HAMM (*to Nagg*): And you?
NAGG (*clasping his hands, closing his eyes, in a gabble*): Our Father which art —
HAMM: Silence! In silence! Where are your manners?

(*Pause.*)

Off we go.

(*Attitudes of prayer. Silence. Abandoning his attitude, discouraged.*)

Well?
CLOV (*abandoning his attitude*): What a hope! And you?
HAMM: Sweet damn all!

(*To Nagg.*)

And you?
NAGG: Wait!

(*Pause. Abandoning his attitude.*)

Nothing doing!
HAMM: The bastard! He doesn't exist!
CLOV: Not yet.
NAGG: Me sugarplum!
HAMM: There are no more sugarplums!

(*Pause.*)

NAGG: It's natural. After all I'm your father. It's true if it hadn't been me it would have been someone else. But that's no excuse.

(*Pause.*)

Turkish Delight,° for example, which no longer exists, we all know that, there is nothing in the world I love more. And one day I'll ask you for some, in return for a kindness, and you'll promise it to me. One must live with the times.

(*Pause.*)

Whom did you call when you were a tiny boy, and were frightened, in the dark? Your mother? No. Me. We let you cry. Then we moved you out of earshot, so that we might sleep in peace.

(*Pause.*)

Turkish Delight: A gummy candy.

I was asleep, as happy as a king, and you woke me up to have me listen to you. It wasn't indispensable, you didn't really need to have me listen to you.

(*Pause.*)

I hope the day will come when you'll really need to have me listen to you, and need to hear my voice, any voice.

(*Pause.*)

Yes, I hope I'll live till then, to hear you calling me like when you were a tiny boy, and were frightened, in the dark, and I was your only hope.

(*Pause. Nagg knocks on lid of Nell's bin. Pause.*)

Nell!

(*Pause. He knocks louder. Pause. Louder.*)

Nell!

(*Pause. Nagg sinks back into his bin, closes the lid behind him. Pause.*)

HAMM: Our revels now are ended.

(*He gropes for the dog.*)

The dog's gone.
CLOV: He's not a real dog, he can't go.
HAMM (*groping*): He's not there.
CLOV: He's lain down.
HAMM: Give him up to me.

(*Clov picks up the dog and gives it to Hamm. Hamm holds it in his arms. Pause. Hamm throws away the dog.*)

Dirty brute!

(*Clov begins to pick up the objects lying on the ground.*)

What are you doing?
CLOV: Putting things in order.

(*He straightens up. Fervently.*)

I'm going to clear everything away!

(*He starts picking up again.*)

HAMM: Order!
CLOV (*straightening up*): I love order. It's my dream. A world where all would be silent and still and each thing in its last place, under the last dust.

(*He starts picking up again.*)

HAMM (*exasperated*): What in God's name do you think you are doing?

CLOV (*straightening up*): I'm doing my best to create a little order.

HAMM: Drop it!

(*Clov drops the objects he has picked up.*)

CLOV: After all, there or elsewhere.

(*He goes towards door.*)

HAMM (*irritably*): What's wrong with your feet?

CLOV: My feet?

HAMM: Tramp! Tramp!

CLOV: I must have put on my boots.

HAMM: Your slippers were hurting you?

(*Pause.*)

CLOV: I'll leave you.

HAMM: No!

CLOV: What is there to keep me here?

HAMM: The dialogue.

(*Pause.*)

I've got on with my story.

(*Pause.*)

I've got on with it well.

(*Pause. Irritably.*)

Ask me where I've got to.

CLOV: Oh, by the way, your story?

HAMM (*surprised*): What story?

CLOV: The one you've been telling yourself all your days.

HAMM: Ah you mean my chronicle?

CLOV: That's the one.

(*Pause.*)

HAMM (*angrily*): Keep going, can't you, keep going!

CLOV: You've got on with it, I hope.

HAMM (*modestly*): Oh not very far, not very far.

(*He sighs.*)

There are days like that, one isn't inspired.

(*Pause.*)

Nothing you can do about it, just wait for it to come.

(*Pause.*)

No forcing, no forcing, it's fatal.

(*Pause.*)

I've got on with it a little all the same.

(*Pause.*)

Technique, you know.

(*Pause. Irritably.*)

I say I've got on with it a little all the same.

CLOV (*admiringly*): Well I never! In spite of everything you were able to get on with it!

HAMM (*modestly*): Oh not very far, you know, not very far, but nevertheless, better than nothing.

CLOV: Better than nothing! Is it possible?

HAMM: I'll tell you how it goes. He comes crawling on his belly —

CLOV: Who?

HAMM: What?

CLOV: Who do you mean, he?

HAMM: Who do I mean! Yet another.

CLOV: Ah him! I wasn't sure.

HAMM: Crawling on his belly, whining for bread for his brat. He's offered a job as gardener. Before —

(*Clov bursts out laughing.*)

What is there so funny about that?

CLOV: A job as gardener!

HAMM: Is that what tickles you?

CLOV: It must be that.

HAMM: It wouldn't be the bread?

CLOV: Or the brat.

(*Pause.*)

HAMM: The whole thing is comical, I grant you that. What about having a good guffaw the two of us together?

CLOV (*after reflection*): I couldn't guffaw again today.

HAMM (*after reflection*): Nor I.

(*Pause.*)

I continue then. Before accepting with gratitude he asks if he may have his little boy with him.

CLOV: What age?

HAMM: Oh tiny.

CLOV: He would have climbed the trees.

HAMM: All the little odd jobs.

CLOV: And then he would have grown up.

HAMM: Very likely.

(*Pause.*)

CLOV: Keep going, can't you, keep going!

HAMM: That's all. I stopped there.

(*Pause.*)

CLOV: Do you see how it goes on.

HAMM: More or less.

CLOV: Will it not soon be the end?

HAMM: I'm afraid it will.

CLOV: Pah! You'll make up another.

HAMM: I don't know.

(*Pause.*)

I feel rather drained.

(*Pause.*)

The prolonged creative effort.

(*Pause.*)

If I could drag myself down to the sea! I'd make a pillow of sand for my head and the tide would come.
CLOV: There's no more tide.

(*Pause.*)

HAMM: Go and see is she dead.

(*Clov goes to bins, raises the lid of Nell's, stoops, looks into it. Pause.*)

CLOV: Looks like it.

(*He closes the lid, straightens up. Hamm raises his toque. Pause. He puts it on again.*)

HAMM (*with his hand to his toque*): And Nagg?

(*Clov raises lid of Nagg's bin, stoops, looks into it. Pause.*)

CLOV: Doesn't look like it.

(*He closes the lid, straightens up.*)

HAMM (*letting go his toque*): What's he doing?

(*Clov raises lid of Nagg's bin, stoops, looks into it. Pause.*)

CLOV: He's crying.

(*He closes lid, straightens up.*)

HAMM: Then he's living.

(*Pause.*)

Did you ever have an instant of happiness?
CLOV: Not to my knowledge.

(*Pause.*)

HAMM: Bring me under the window.

(*Clov goes towards chair.*)

I want to feel the light on my face.

(*Clov pushes chair.*)

Do you remember, in the beginning, when you took me for a turn? You used to hold the chair too high. At every step you nearly tipped me out.

(*With senile quaver.*)

Ah great fun, we had, the two of us, great fun.

(*Gloomily.*)

And then we got into the way of it.

(*Clov stops the chair under window right.*)

There already?

(*Pause. He tilts back his head.*)

Is it light?
CLOV: It isn't dark.
HAMM (*angrily*): I'm asking you is it light.
CLOV: Yes.

(*Pause.*)

HAMM: The curtain isn't closed?
CLOV: No.
HAMM: What window is it?
CLOV: The earth.
HAMM: I knew it!

(*Angrily.*)

But there's no light there! The other!

(*Clov pushes chair towards window left.*)

The earth!

(*Clov stops the chair under window left. Hamm tilts back his head.*)

That's what I call light!

(*Pause.*)

Feels like a ray of sunshine.

(*Pause.*)

No?
CLOV: No.
HAMM: It isn't a ray of sunshine I feel on my face?
CLOV: No.

(*Pause.*)

HAMM: Am I very white?

(*Pause. Angrily.*)

I'm asking you am I very white!
CLOV: Not more so than usual.

(*Pause.*)

HAMM: Open the window.
CLOV: What for?
HAMM: I want to hear the sea.
CLOV: You wouldn't hear it.
HAMM: Even if you opened the window?
CLOV: No.
HAMM: Then it's not worthwhile opening it?
CLOV: No.
HAMM (*violently*): Then open it!

RIGHT: Clov (John Bottoms) and Hamm (Ben Halley, Jr.), seated, in the 1984 American Repertory Theatre production of *Endgame,* directed by JoAnne Akalaitis. BELOW: Hamm and Clov.

(*Clov gets up on the ladder, opens the window. Pause.*)

Have you opened it?
CLOV: Yes.

(*Pause.*)

HAMM: You swear you've opened it?
CLOV: Yes.

(*Pause.*)

HAMM: Well . . . !

(*Pause.*)

It must be very calm.

(*Pause. Violently.*)

I'm asking you is it very calm!
CLOV: Yes.
HAMM: It's because there are no more navigators.

(*Pause.*)

You haven't much conversation all of a sudden. Do you not feel well?
CLOV: I'm cold.
HAMM: What month are we?

(*Pause.*)

Close the window, we're going back.

(*Clov closes the window, gets down, pushes the chair back to its place, remains standing behind it, head bowed.*)

Don't stay there, you give me the shivers!

(*Clov returns to his place beside the chair.*)

Father!

(*Pause. Louder.*)

Father!

(*Pause.*)

Go and see did he hear me.

(*Clov goes to Nagg's bin, raises the lid, stoops. Unintelligible words. Clov straightens up.*)

CLOV: Yes.
HAMM: Both times?

(*Clov stoops. As before.*)

CLOV: Once only.
HAMM: The first time or the second?

(*Clov stoops. As before.*)

CLOV: He doesn't know.
HAMM: It must have been the second.

CLOV: We'll never know.

(*He closes lid.*)

HAMM: Is he still crying?
CLOV: No.
HAMM: The dead go fast.

(*Pause.*)

What's he doing?
CLOV: Sucking his biscuit.
HAMM: Life goes on.

(*Clov returns to his place beside the chair.*)

Give me a rug,° I'm freezing.
CLOV: There are no more rugs.

(*Pause.*)

HAMM: Kiss me.

(*Pause.*)

Will you not kiss me?
CLOV: No.
HAMM: On the forehead.
CLOV: I won't kiss you anywhere.

(*Pause.*)

HAMM (*holding out his hand*): Give me your hand at least.

(*Pause.*)

Will you not give me your hand?
CLOV: I won't touch you.

(*Pause.*)

HAMM: Give me the dog.

(*Clov looks round for the dog.*)

No!
CLOV: Do you not want your dog?
HAMM: No.
CLOV: Then I'll leave you.
HAMM (*head bowed, absently*): That's right.

(*Clov goes to door, turns.*)

CLOV: If I don't kill that rat he'll die.
HAMM (*as before*): That's right.

(*Exit Clov. Pause.*)

Me to play.

(*He takes out his handkerchief, unfolds it, holds it spread out before him.*)

We're getting on.

---

rug: A small blanket to cover the lap, legs, and feet.

(*Pause.*)

You weep, and weep, for nothing, so as not to laugh, and little by little . . . you begin to grieve.

(*He folds the handkerchief, puts it back in his pocket, raises his head.*)

All those I might have helped.

(*Pause.*)

Helped!

(*Pause.*)

Saved.

(*Pause.*)

Saved!

(*Pause.*)

The place was crawling with them!

(*Pause. Violently.*)

Use your head, can't you, use your head, you're on earth, there's no cure for that!

(*Pause.*)

Get out of here and love one another! Lick your neighbor as yourself!

(*Pause. Calmer.*)

When it wasn't bread they wanted it was crumpets.

(*Pause. Violently.*)

Out of my sight and back to your petting parties!

(*Pause.*)

All that, all that!

(*Pause.*)

Not even a real dog!

(*Calmer.*)

The end is in the beginning and yet you go on.

(*Pause.*)

Perhaps I could go on with my story, end it and begin another.

(*Pause.*)

Perhaps I could throw myself out on the floor.

(*He pushes himself painfully off his seat, falls back again.*)

Dig my nails into the cracks and drag myself forward with my fingers.

(*Pause.*)

It will be the end and there I'll be, wondering what can have brought it on and wondering what can have . . . (*he hesitates*) . . . why it was so long coming.

(*Pause.*)

There I'll be, in the old shelter, alone against the silence and . . . (*he hesitates*) . . . the stillness. If I can hold my peace, and sit quiet, it will be all over with sound, and motion, all over and done with.

(*Pause.*)

I'll have called my father and I'll have called my . . . (*he hesitates*) . . . my son. And even twice, or three times, in case they shouldn't have heard me, the first time, or the second.

(*Pause.*)

I'll say to myself, He'll come back.

(*Pause.*)

And then?

(*Pause.*)

And then?

(*Pause.*)

He couldn't, he has gone too far.

(*Pause.*)

And then?

(*Pause. Very agitated.*)

All kinds of fantasies! That I'm being watched! A rat! Steps! Breath held and then . . .

(*He breathes out.*)

Then babble, babble, words, like the solitary child who turns himself into children, two, three, so as to be together, and whisper together, in the dark.

(*Pause.*)

Moment upon moment, pattering down, like the millet grains of . . . (*he hesitates*) . . . that old Greek, and all life long you wait for that to mount up to a life.

(*Pause. He opens his mouth to continue, renounces.*)

Ah let's get it over!

(*He whistles. Enter Clov with alarm clock. He halts beside the chair.*)

What? Neither gone nor dead?

CLOV: In spirit only.

HAMM: Which?

CLOV: Both.

HAMM: Gone from me you'd be dead.

CLOV: And vice versa.

HAMM: Outside of here it's death!

(*Pause.*)

And the rat?

CLOV: He's got away.

HAMM: He can't go far.

(*Pause. Anxious.*)

Eh?

CLOV: He doesn't need to go far.

(*Pause.*)

HAMM: Is it not time for my painkiller?

CLOV: Yes.

HAMM: Ah! At last! Give it to me! Quick!

(*Pause.*)

CLOV: There's no more painkiller.

(*Pause.*)

HAMM (*appalled*): Good. . . !

(*Pause.*)

No more painkiller!

CLOV: No more painkiller. You'll never get any more painkiller.

(*Pause.*)

HAMM: But the little round box. It was full!

CLOV: Yes. But now it's empty.

(*Pause. Clov starts to move about the room. He is looking for a place to put down the alarm clock.*)

HAMM (*soft*): What'll I do?

(*Pause. In a scream.*)

What'll I do?

(*Clov sees the picture, takes it down, stands it on the floor with its face to the wall, hangs up the alarm clock in its place.*)

What are you doing?

CLOV: Winding up.

HAMM: Look at the earth.

CLOV: Again!

HAMM: Since it's calling to you.

CLOV: Is your throat sore?

(*Pause.*)

Would you like a lozenge?

(*Pause.*)

No.

(*Pause.*)

Pity.

(*Clov goes, humming, towards window right, halts before it, looks up at it.*)

HAMM: Don't sing.

CLOV (*turning towards Hamm*): One hasn't the right to sing anymore?

HAMM: No.

CLOV: Then how can it end?

HAMM: You want it to end?

CLOV: I want to sing.

HAMM: I can't prevent you.

(*Pause. Clov turns towards window right.*)

CLOV: What did I do with that steps?

(*He looks around for ladder.*)

You didn't see that steps?

(*He sees it.*)

Ah, about time.

(*He goes towards window left.*)

Sometimes I wonder if I'm in my right mind. Then it passes over and I'm as lucid as before.

(*He gets up on ladder, looks out of window.*)

Christ, she's under water!

(*He looks.*)

How can that be?

(*He pokes forward his head, his hand above his eyes.*)

It hasn't rained.

(*He wipes the pane, looks. Pause.*)

Ah what a fool I am! I'm on the wrong side!

(*He gets down, takes a few steps towards window right.*)

Under water!

(*He goes back for ladder.*)

What a fool I am!

(*He carries ladder towards window right.*)

Sometimes I wonder if I'm in my right senses. Then it passes off and I'm as intelligent as ever.

(*He sets down ladder under window right, gets up on it, looks out of window. He turns towards Hamm.*)

Any particular sector you fancy? Or merely the whole thing?

HAMM: Whole thing.

CLOV: The general effect? Just a moment.

(*He looks out of window. Pause.*)

HAMM: Clov.

CLOV (*absorbed*): Mmm.

HAMM: Do you know what it is?

CLOV (*as before*): Mmm.

HAMM: I was never there.

(*Pause.*)

    Clov!

CLOV (*turning towards Hamm, exasperated*): What is it?

HAMM: I was never there.

CLOV: Lucky for you.

(*He looks out of window.*)

HAMM: Absent, always. It all happened without me. I don't know what's happened.

(*Pause.*)

    Do you know what's happened?

(*Pause.*)

    Clov!

CLOV (*turning towards Hamm, exasperated*): Do you want me to look at this muckheap, yes or no?

HAMM: Answer me first.

CLOV: What?

HAMM: Do you know what's happened?

CLOV: When? Where?

HAMM (*violently*): When! What's happened? Use your head, can't you! What has happened?

CLOV: What for Christ's sake does it matter?

(*He looks out of window.*)

HAMM: I don't know.

(*Pause. Clov turns towards Hamm.*)

CLOV (*harshly*): When old Mother Pegg asked you for oil for her lamp and you told her to get out to hell, you knew what was happening then, no?

(*Pause.*)

    You know what she died of, Mother Pegg? Of darkness.

HAMM (*feebly*): I hadn't any.

CLOV (*as before*): Yes, you had.

(*Pause.*)

HAMM: Have you the glass?

CLOV: No, it's clear enough as it is.

HAMM: Go and get it.

(*Pause. Clov casts up his eyes, brandishes his fists. He loses balance, clutches on to the ladder. He starts to get down, halts.*)

CLOV: There's one thing I'll never understand.

(*He gets down.*)

    Why I always obey you. Can you explain that to me?

HAMM: No. . . . Perhaps it's compassion.

(*Pause.*)

    A kind of great compassion.

(*Pause.*)

    Oh you won't find it easy, you won't find it easy.

(*Pause. Clov begins to move about the room in search of the telescope.*)

CLOV: I'm tired of our goings on, very tired.

(*He searches.*)

    You're not sitting on it?

(*He moves the chair, looks at the place where it stood, resumes his search.*)

HAMM (*anguished*): Don't leave me there!

(*Angrily Clov restores the chair to its place.*)

    Am I right in the center?

CLOV: You'd need a microscope to find this —

(*He sees the telescope.*)

    Ah, about time.

(*He picks up the telescope, gets up on the ladder, turns the telescope on the without.*)

HAMM: Give me the dog.

CLOV (*looking*): Quiet!

HAMM (*angrily*): Give me the dog!

(*Clov drops the telescope, clasps his hands to his head. Pause. He gets down precipitately, looks for the dog, sees it, picks it up, hastens towards Hamm and strikes him violently on the head with the dog.*)

CLOV: There's your dog for you!

(*The dog falls to the ground. Pause.*)

HAMM: He hit me!

CLOV: You drive me mad, I'm mad!

HAMM: If you must hit me, hit me with the axe.

(*Pause.*)

    Or with the gaff, hit me with the gaff. Not with the dog. With the gaff. Or with the axe.

(*Clov picks up the dog and gives it to Hamm who takes it in his arms.*)

CLOV (*imploringly*): Let's stop playing!
HAMM: Never!

(*Pause.*)

Put me in my coffin.
CLOV: There are no more coffins.
HAMM: Then let it end!

(*Clov goes towards ladder.*)

With a bang!

(*Clov gets up on ladder, gets down again, looks for telescope, sees it, picks it up, gets up ladder, raises telescope.*)

Of darkness! And me? Did anyone ever have pity on me?
CLOV (*lowering the telescope, turning towards Hamm*): What?

(*Pause.*)

Is it me you're referring to?
HAMM (*angrily*): An aside, ape! Did you never hear an aside before?

(*Pause.*)

I'm warming up for my last soliloquy.
CLOV: I warn you. I'm going to look at this filth since it's an order. But it's the last time.

(*He turns the telescope on the without.*)

Let's see.

(*He moves the telescope.*)

Nothing . . . nothing . . . good . . . good . . . nothing . . . goo —

(*He starts, lowers the telescope, examines it, turns it again on the without. Pause.*)

Bad luck to it!
HAMM: More complications!

(*Clov gets down.*)

Not an underplot, I trust.

(*Clov moves ladder nearer window, gets up on it, turns telescope on the without.*)

CLOV (*dismayed*): Looks like a small boy!
HAMM (*sarcastic*): A small . . . boy!
CLOV: I'll go and see.

(*He gets down, drops the telescope, goes towards door, turns.*)

I'll take the gaff.

(*He looks for the gaff, sees it, picks it up, hastens towards door.*)

HAMM: No!

(*Clov halts.*)

CLOV: No? A potential procreator?
HAMM: If he exists he'll die there or he'll come here. And if he doesn't . . .

(*Pause.*)

CLOV: You don't believe me? You think I'm inventing?

(*Pause.*)

HAMM: It's the end, Clov, we've come to the end. I don't need you anymore.

(*Pause.*)

CLOV: Lucky for you.

(*He goes towards door.*)

HAMM: Leave me the gaff.

(*Clov gives him the gaff, goes towards door, halts, looks at alarm clock, takes it down, looks round for a better place to put it, goes to bins, puts it on lid of Nagg's bin. Pause.*)

CLOV: I'll leave you.

(*He goes towards door.*)

HAMM: Before you go . . .

(*Clov halts near door.*)

. . . say something.
CLOV: There is nothing to say.
HAMM: A few words . . . to ponder . . . in my heart.
CLOV: Your heart!
HAMM: Yes.

(*Pause. Forcibly.*)

Yes!

(*Pause.*)

With the rest, in the end, the shadows, the murmurs, all the trouble, to end up with.

(*Pause.*)

Clov. . . . He never spoke to me. Then, in the end, before he went, without my having asked him, he spoke to me. He said . . .
CLOV (*despairingly*): Ah . . . !
HAMM: Something . . . from your heart.
CLOV: My heart!
HAMM: A few words . . . from your heart.

(*Pause.*)

CLOV (*fixed gaze, tonelessly, towards auditorium*): They said to me, That's love, yes, yes, not a doubt, now you see how —

HAMM: Articulate!

CLOV (*as before*): How easy it is. They said to me, That's friendship, yes, yes, no question, you've found it. They said to me, Here's the place, stop, raise your head and look at all that beauty. That order! They said to me, Come now, you're not a brute beast, think upon these things and you'll see how all becomes clear. And simple! They said to me, What skilled attention they get, all these dying of their wounds.

HAMM: Enough!

CLOV (*as before*): I say to myself — sometimes, Clov, you must learn to suffer better than that if you want them to weary of punishing you — one day. I say to myself — sometimes, Clov, you must be there better than that if you want them to let you go — one day. But I feel too old, and too far, to form new habits. Good, it'll never end, I'll never go.

(*Pause.*)

Then one day, suddenly, it ends, it changes, I don't understand, it dies, or it's me, I don't understand, that either. I ask the words that remain — sleeping, waking, morning, evening. They have nothing to say.

(*Pause.*)

I open the door of the cell and go. I am so bowed I only see my feet, if I open my eyes, and between my legs a little trail of black dust. I say to myself that the earth is extinguished, though I never saw it lit.

(*Pause.*)

It's easy going.

(*Pause.*)

When I fall I'll weep for happiness.

(*Pause. He goes towards door.*)

HAMM: Clov!

(*Clov halts, without turning.*)

Nothing.

(*Clov moves on.*)

Clov!

(*Clov halts, without turning.*)

CLOV: This is what we call making an exit.

HAMM: I'm obliged to you, Clov. For your services.

CLOV (*turning, sharply*): Ah pardon, it's I am obliged to you.

HAMM: It's we are obliged to each other.

(*Pause. Clov goes towards door.*)

One thing more.

(*Clov halts.*)

A last favor.

(*Exit Clov.*)

Cover me with the sheet.

(*Long pause.*)

No? Good.

(*Pause.*)

Me to play.

(*Pause. Wearily.*)

Old endgame lost of old, play and lose and have done with losing.

(*Pause. More animated.*)

Let me see.

(*Pause.*)

Ah yes!

(*He tries to move the chair, using the gaff as before. Enter Clov, dressed for the road. Panama hat, tweed coat, raincoat over his arm, umbrella, bag. He halts by the door and stands there, impassive and motionless, his eyes fixed on Hamm, till the end. Hamm gives up.*)

Good.

(*Pause.*)

Discard.

(*He throws away the gaff, makes to throw away the dog, thinks better of it.*)

Take it easy.

(*Pause.*)

And now?

(*Pause.*)

Raise hat.

(*He raises his toque.*)

Peace to our . . . arses.

(*Pause.*)

And put on again.

(*He puts on his toque.*)

Deuce.

(*Pause. He takes off his glasses.*)

Wipe.

(*He takes out his handkerchief and, without unfolding it, wipes his glasses.*)

And put on again.

(*He puts on his glasses, puts back the handkerchief in his pocket.*)

We're coming. A few more squirms like that and I'll call.

(*Pause.*)

A little poetry.

(*Pause.*)

You prayed —

(*Pause. He corrects himself.*)

You CRIED for night; it comes —

(*Pause. He corrects himself.*)

It FALLS: now cry in darkness.

(*He repeats, chanting.*)

You cried for night; it falls: now cry in darkness.

(*Pause.*)

Nicely put, that.

(*Pause.*)

And now?

(*Pause.*)

Moments for nothing, now as always, time was never and time is over, reckoning closed and story ended.

(*Pause. Narrative tone.*)

If he could have his child with him. . . .

(*Pause.*)

It was the moment I was waiting for.

(*Pause.*)

You don't want to abandon him? You want him to bloom while you are withering? Be there to solace your last million last moments?

(*Pause.*)

He doesn't realize, all he knows is hunger, and cold, and death to crown it all. But you! You ought to know what the earth is like, nowadays. Oh I put him before his responsibilities!

(*Pause. Normal tone.*)

Well, there we are, there I am, that's enough.

(*He raises the whistle to his lips, hesitates, drops it. Pause.*)

Yes, truly!

(*He whistles. Pause. Louder. Pause.*)

Good.

(*Pause.*)

Father!

(*Pause. Louder.*)

Father!

(*Pause.*)

Good.

(*Pause.*)

We're coming.

(*Pause.*)

And to end up with?

(*Pause.*)

Discard.

(*He throws away the dog. He tears the whistle from his neck.*)

With my compliments.

(*He throws whistle towards auditorium. Pause. He sniffs. Soft.*)

Clov!

(*Long pause.*)

No? Good.

(*He takes out the handkerchief.*)

Since that's the way we're playing it . . . (*he unfolds handkerchief*) . . . let's play it that way . . . (*he unfolds*) . . . and speak no more about it . . . (*he finishes unfolding*) . . . speak no more.

(*He holds handkerchief spread out before him.*)

Old stancher!

(*Pause.*)

You . . . remain.

(*Pause. He covers his face with handkerchief, lowers his arms to armrests, remains motionless.*)

(*Brief tableau.*)

COMMENTARIES

Martin Esslin (b. 1918)
THE THEATER OF THE ABSURD

1961

Martin Esslin is a drama critic whose work has had wide currency. He was the first to write extensively about the theater of the absurd, a term that has come to describe the plays of Samuel Beckett and a number of other post–World War II playwrights such as Eugène Ionesco and Harold Pinter. The question of what use playwrights make of the absurd and why it is an appropriate term to reflect the achievement of Beckett is explored briefly in this excerpt.

The Theater of the Absurd shows the world as an incomprehensible place. The spectators see the happenings on the stage entirely from the outside, without ever understanding the full meaning of these strange patterns of events, as newly arrived visitors might watch life in a country of which they have not yet mastered the language. The confrontation of the audience with characters and happenings which they are not quite able to comprehend makes it impossible for them to share the aspirations and emotions depicted in the play. Brecht's famous "Verfremdungseffekt" (alienation effect), the inhibition of any identification between spectator and actor, which Brecht could never successfully achieve in his own highly rational theater, really comes into its own in the Theater of the Absurd. It is impossible to identify oneself with characters one does not understand or whose motives remain a closed book, and so the distance between the public and the happenings on the stage can be maintained. Emotional identification with the characters is replaced by a puzzled, critical attention. For while the happenings on the stage are absurd, they yet remain recognizable as somehow related to real life with *its* absurdity, so that eventually the spectators are brought face to face with the irrational side of their existence. Thus, the absurd and fantastic goings-on of the Theater of the Absurd will, in the end, be found to reveal the irrationality of the human condition and the illusion of what we thought was its apparent logical structure.

If the dialogue in these plays consists of meaningless clichés and the mechanical, circular repetition of stereotyped phrases — how many meaningless clichés and stereotyped phrases do we use in our day-to-day conversation? If the characters change their personality halfway through the action, how consistent and truly integrated are the people we meet in our real life? And if people in these plays appear as mere marionettes, helpless puppets without any will of their own, passively at the mercy of blind fate and meaningless circumstance, do we, in fact, in our overorganized world, still possess any genuine initiative or power to decide our own destiny? The spectators of the Theater of the Absurd are thus confronted with a grotesquely heightened picture of their own world: a world without faith, meaning, and genuine freedom of will. In this sense, the Theater of the Absurd is the true theater of our time.

The theater of most previous epochs reflected an accepted moral order, a world whose aims and objectives were clearly present to the minds of all its public, whether it was the audience of the medieval mystery plays with their solidly accepted faith in the Christian world order or the audience of the drama of Ibsen, Shaw, or Hauptmann with their unquestioned belief in evolution and progress. To such audiences, right and wrong were never in doubt, nor did they question the then accepted goals of human endeavor. Our own time, at least in the Western world, wholly lacks such a generally accepted and completely integrated world picture. The decline of religious faith, the destruction of the belief in automatic social and biological progress, the discovery of vast areas of irrational and unconscious forces within the human psyche, the loss of a sense of control over rational human development in an age of totalitarianism and weapons of mass destruction, have all contributed to the erosion of the basis for a dramatic convention in which the action proceeds within a fixed and self-evident framework of generally accepted values. Faced with the vacuum left by the destruction of a universally accepted and unified set of beliefs, most serious playwrights have felt the need to fit their work into the frame of values and objectives expressed in one of the contemporary ideologies: Marxism, psychoanalysis, aestheticism, or nature worship. But these, in the eyes of a writer like Adamov, are nothing but superficial rationalizations which try to hide the depth of man's predicament, his loneliness and his anxiety. Or, as Ionesco puts it:

> As far as I am concerned, I believe sincerely in the poverty of the poor, I deplore it; it is real; it can become a subject for the theatre; I also believe in the anxieties and serious troubles the rich may suffer from; but it is neither in the misery of the former nor in the melancholia of the latter, that I, for one, find my dramatic subject matter. Theatre is for me the outward projection onto the stage of an inner world; it is in my dreams, in my anxieties, in my obscure desires, in my internal contradictions that I, for one, reserve for myself the right of finding my dramatic subject matter. As I am not alone in the world, as each of us, in the depth of his being, is at the same time part and parcel of all others, my dreams, my desires, my anxieties, my obsessions do not belong to me alone. They form part of an ancestral heritage, a very ancient storehouse which is a portion of the common property of all mankind. It is this, which, transcending their outward diversity, reunites all human beings and constitutes our profound common patrimony, the universal language.[1]

In other words, the commonly acceptable framework of beliefs and values of former epochs which has now been shattered is to be replaced by the community of dreams and desires of a collective unconscious. And, to quote Ionesco again:

> ... the new dramatist is one ... who tries to link up with what is most ancient: new language and subject matter in a dramatic structure which aims at being clearer, more stripped of inessentials and more purely theatrical; the rejection of traditionalism to rediscover tradition; a synthesis of knowledge and invention, of the real and imaginary, of the particular and the universal, or as they say now, of the individual and the collective. . . . By expressing my deepest obsessions, I express my deepest humanity. I become one with all others, spontaneously, over and above all the barriers of caste and different psychologies. I express my solitude and become one with all other solitudes.[2]

What is the tradition with which the Theater of the Absurd — at first sight the most revolutionary and radically new movement — is trying to link itself? It is in fact a very ancient and a very rich tradition, nourished from many and varied sources: the verbal exuberance and extravagant inventions of Rabelais, the

---

[1] Eugène Ionesco, "L'Impromptu de l'Alma," *Théâtre* II (Paris, 1958).
[2] Ionesco, "The Avant-Garde Theatre," *World Theatre* 8.3 (Autumn 1959).

age-old clowning of the Roman mimes and the Italian *Commedia dell'Arte,* the knock-about humor of circus clowns like Grock; the wild, archetypal symbolism of English nonsense verse, the baroque horror of Jacobean dramatists like Webster or Tourneur, the harsh, incisive, and often brutal tones of the German drama of Grabbe, Büchner, Kleist, and Wedekind with its delirious language and grotesque inventiveness; and the Nordic paranoia of the dreams and persecution fantasies of Strindberg.

Sidney Homan (b. 1938)
THE ENDING OF *ENDGAME*   1984

Sidney Homan's book Beckett's Theaters: Interpretations for Performance *concentrates on the production of Beckett's plays. His discussion of* Endgame *focuses on the performance aspects of movement in the final moments of the play. The question of death is central to the question of* Endgame.

Despite its seeming chaos on the surface, Hamm's last speech, that string of short phrases and snatches of dialogue much like that of Winnie in *Happy Days,* provides the most sustained insight into his playwright's mentality. In the words of the Unnamable,° it is the "end of the joke," the aesthetic painkiller if you will, as handy as that literal painkiller in the cupboard was not. Unseen, except by us, Clov constitutes the onstage audience of one. The speech itself is surely meant to contrast with Hamm's opening dialogue: This time Hamm is not discovered but rather constitutes *all* the stage, at least as far as he knows, and the speech is about endings rather than beginnings. The proper verbal constructions, in terms of his opening lines, would be something akin to "Me to play having played." No fear of mere "reveling" here.

Hamm's speech seems to be madness without matter. As with the scattered fragments in the closing lines of Eliot's *The Waste Land,* however, there is here an order and a depth of reference below the surface. Clov is absent, though he stands impassive upstage. The sheet with which he "discovered" Hamm at the opening is now useless. In a larger sense, Hamm has been revealed, the play itself representing his disclosure as a symbol. The removal of the sheet itself is thereby the stimulus for an aesthetic revelation. He is now moving toward the purely symbolic, and the chess metaphor comes to the fore, chess itself a symbolic enactment of literal battles and armies: "Me to play" and "Old endgame." Indeed, Hamm is moving toward the same sense of completeness found by Mr. Endon in *Murphy.* The King, the central piece, is now immobile at the center of the board, the word for both the theater and the field of chess pieces. Then "discard" the last life-support; the gaff is thrown away, though the dog, symbol of Hamm's artifice, is retained.

We see the artist now attempting to document the moment before human extinction. It is the process toward that movement, and not the actual event itself, defining the limits of our earthly inquiry.

Unnamable: Narrator of *The Unnamable* (1958), third in a trilogy of novels by Beckett.

Like Shakespeare, Beckett does not depict a hereafter. We may speculate on what will happen to Lear — can a pagan go to any sort of heaven? — but the Renaissance playwright, like the modern one, is content to show him approaching the end, promised or otherwise. There is a farewell here to the audience, obscene to be sure, and with that salute an identification with us as Hamm uses the plural possessive "our." The "You" who wants poetry, or the efficacy of prayer, or night to come is also the "you" that, in an absurdist or relative world, must cry in darkness. Again, we all die alone. Hamm's aesthetic consciousness, like that of the narrator in *Cascando,*° is now most acute: "Nicely put, that."

If relativity, both in terms of time itself and the mutability of all human things, relentlessly moves on, Hamm, now enveloped in his story, is about to make time run, to echo the Renaissance poet Marvell. The time is "over, reckoning closed and story ended." The wish for extinction, however, cannot hold as the life force, the final reference to the father and his starving son, is sounded. Hamm cannot shake off that memory. An invasion of his world, the story irritates the aesthetic fiber he has so closely woven. It is another world, with a past, with characters, and involving those issues of life and the sustenance of life that Hamm has otherwise so assiduously blocked out in his bomb shelter, in his circumscribed, lonely, inner world. The "Oh I put him before his responsibilities" sounds as much neurotic as convincing. Then with a *calm* — again, one of Beckett's favorite words — returning, Hamm reverses himself in the recognition that he is not alone, that he is part and parcel of all humanity, including us, including the fictive, or seemingly fictive father and his son: "Well, there we are, there I am, that's enough." This is something "truly," though the aesthetic inner world is itself in flux, only a momentary stay against reality, and yet Hamm will now be able to sustain this playwright-actor's posture at least until the end.

He approaches death with the same sense of "knowing" his story that several modern biblical scholars have attributed to Christ, an "actor" who plays the parts of a visitor to earth, prophet, crucified savior, and risen spirit. We approach now the closest thing to transcendence in Beckett, undercut, of course, by the fact that Hamm "*remains motionless*" as the curtain closes (he can no more leave his stage than Vladimir and Estragon can leave theirs). The dog is discarded, the last vestige of his creation; and then in a brilliant gesture he throws the whistle toward us, the audience — the "*auditorium.*" Though the isolation is illusory — again, Clov is backstage, visible to us if not to Hamm — for Hamm it is a convincing illusion. He is approaching the nonbeing sought by Nell in her vision of a silent, white ocean bottom, an empty world where nothingness is a fact, not a conceit, where we can cease to be like those talkative "political" artists who, in giving form to nothing, are bound to fail. In essence, Hamm is trying to give up the last hold on life, even if that "life" be the illusory existence of the stage world.

The transcendence itself is aborted. However much he would later cut away at the time scheme or the plot or the place of his plays (witness *Breath*), Beckett cannot present us with nothing: "Nothing" itself can be spoken of but not enacted. A bare stage is only a bare stage and not a play. Here Beckett is like Emily Dickinson in "I heard a fly buzz when I died," as she tries poetically to cross the thin boundary line between life and death and is frustrated in that attempt when

---

Cascando: Beckett's radio play for voice and music (1962), first broadcast in English by the BBC in 1964.

a fly intervenes between her eyes and the "light." Beckett is trying to go to the nonstate, if I may put it that way, of nonbeing. That is the way Hamm would "play it," so that he could "speak no more about it." I repeat his wish: "Speak no more." He seeks here not the failure of words, the very possibility that unnerves Winnie. Nor will he use words anymore to define nonbeing.

Now, without words and with the major character free of the tension in seeking physical life or death, we move to the level of mime. Our audience surrogate, the silent Clov, now sees Hamm hold the bloodied handkerchief before him and then cover his face. Two phrases act as glosses to the action. One is the descriptive "Old stancher," lest an audience member fail to identify properly the symbol, Hamm's Greek-like mask that is the physical correlative for his misery, for his suffering than which no one's is greater, as he reminds us early in the play. In effect, Hamm, like the figures in Greek myths, has passed through earthly existence and literally become a star. He has won his right to be a symbol, a symbol sustained by the play, a symbol that now wordlessly compresses all that he means, or has meant. This wretched piece of a costume, in effect, now equals the entire play. In Beckett, truly, the last shall be first. One also thinks of the handkerchief worn by Keaton in *Film,* and that used by Willie in *Happy Days,* though neither was so developed, nor so perfect a symbol of suffering.

The other phrase, a tantalizing one, is the closing "You . . . remain." Initially, it appears simply an appositive for "Old stancher," but I also take it as a reference to the audience. That is, Hamm has now *realized* his role; he has been elevated to a symbol. Our task has now just begun; we must leave the theater, refreshed by Beckett's mirror world, and must encounter the suffering anew. Outside of here it is hell, as the Beckett characters are fond of saying. We remain; we are the "mutes and audience" of the act to which Hamlet refers (V, II, 337).

The play closes beyond words, as Hamm covers his face with the handkerchief and, like the Auditor in *Not I,* lowers his arms and in a mockery of mime and its movements stops on the stage direction to remain "*motionless.*" Initiated by language, the play ends in silence, the "*Brief tableau,*" like that called for by Beckett in *The Unnamable. Curtain.* It will also start again; as Winnie observes, even if the glass breaks, it will be there whole tomorrow. Tomorrow the handkerchief will revert to the old sheet covering Hamm, that, with the bloodstained handkerchief, will in turn be removed, discovering another potential tragic hero — or "figure," if "hero" sounds too affirmative for some readers. The uncovering will allow theatrical life to flow again, the act of artistic creation, the long creative process to which Hamm himself refers, the informing of a vision and the production of a symbol — a symbol that, at the end, will remain with us, only to be undone the next day, the next performance. Curtain. . . .

Lorraine Hansberry

Lorraine Hansberry (1930–1965), like John Millington Synge, died tragically young. Her loss to the American stage is incalculable; her successes were only beginning, and at her death she seemed on the verge of a remarkable career.

Hansberry grew up in a middle-class black family in Chicago. Her father, who was successful in real estate, founded one of the first banks for blacks in Chicago. However, he spent much of his life trying to find a way to make a decent life for himself and his family in America. He eventually gave up on the United States and, when he died in 1945, he was scouting for a place in Mexico where he could move his family to live comfortably.

Lorraine Hansberry went to college after her father died, and her first ambition was to become a visual artist. She attended the Art Institute of Chicago and numerous other schools before moving to New York. Once there, she became interested in some drama groups and soon married the playwright Howard Nemiroff. She began writing, sharing parts of her first play with friends in her own living room. They helped raise money to stage the play and, with black director Lloyd Richards and little-known Sidney Poitier as Walter Lee Younger, *A Raisin in the Sun* (1959) thrust her into the drama spotlight.

In 1959, only twenty-nine years old, Hansberry was the most promising woman writing for the American stage. She was also the first black American to win the New York Drama Critics' Circle Award for the best play of the year. She died of cancer the day her second produced play, *The Sign in Sidney Brustein's Window,* closed. She had finished a third play, *Les Blancs,* which was brought to Broadway by Nemiroff in 1970. Neither of her other plays was as popular as *Raisin,* but the two later plays demonstrate a deepening concern for and understanding of some of the key issues of racial and sexual politics that interested her throughout her career.

The Sign in Sidney Brustein's Window's hero is a Jewish intellectual in the 1950s in Greenwich Village. Feeling that all the radical struggle of the 1930s has been lost, he agitates for personal involvement, for emotional and intellectual action. This idealistic play anticipates the political agitation in the United States during the mid-1960s and early 1970s. *Les Blancs* takes as its central character a black African intellectual, Tshembe, and explores his relationship to both Europe and Africa. In his uneasiness with both cultures he discovers that he cannot live outside his own history. *Les Blancs* reveals some of Hansberry's deep interest in Pan-Africanism and the search for a personal heritage.

A posthumous work was put together by Howard Nemiroff from Hansberry's notes, letters, and early writings. Titled *To Be Young, Gifted, and Black* (1971), it has helped solidify her achievements. Although we will never know just how Hansberry's career would have developed had she lived, her gifts were so remarkable that we can only lament that she is not writing for the stage today.

A RAISIN IN THE SUN

When produced on Broadway in 1959, *A Raisin in the Sun* was somewhat prophetic. Lorraine Hansberry's themes of blacks pressing forward with legitimate demands and expressing interest in their African heritage were to become primary themes of black culture in the 1960s, 1970s, and, indeed, to this day. The title of her play is from a poem by Langston Hughes, one of the poets of the Harlem Renaissance. It warns of the social explosions that might occur if society permits blacks to remain unequal and unfree.

The work appeared at the beginning of renewed political activity on the part of African Americans; it reveals its historical position in the use of the word *Negro,* which black activists rejected in the 1960s as an enslaving euphemism. This play illustrates the American dream as it is felt not just by African Americans but by all Americans: If you work hard and save your money, if you hold to the proper values and hope, then you can one day buy your own home and have the kind of space and privacy that permit people to live with dignity. Yet this very theme has plagued the play from the beginning: its apparent emphasis on middle-class, bourgeois values. On the surface, it seems to celebrate a mild form of consumerism — the desire for the house in the suburbs with the TV set inside to anesthetize its occupants. Hansberry was shocked when such criticisms, from black critics as well as white, were leveled against the play. She had written it very carefully to explore just those issues, but in a context that demonstrated that black families' needs paralleled white families' while also having a different dimension that most white families could not understand.

Hansberry was quick to admit that Walter Lee Younger was affected by the same craziness influencing all Americans who lusted after possessions and the power they might confer. Walter wants to take his father's insurance money to buy a liquor store in partnership with a con man. Lena Younger argues against her son's plan as a profanation of her husband's memory as well as an abuse of the American dream: She believes that the product of a liquor store will further poison the community. What she wants is not a consumer product. She wants the emblem of identity and security that she feels her family deserves.

Hansberry is painfully honest in this play. Walter Lee's weaknesses are recognizable. His male chauvinistic behavior undoes him. He is caught up in the old, failing pattern of male dominance over women. But none of the women in his life will tolerate his behavior. Hansberry also admits the social distinctions among African Americans. George Murchison is a young man from a wealthy black family, and when Beneatha tells Lena that she will not marry George, she says, "The only people in the world who are more snobbish than rich white people are rich colored people." Beneatha's desire to be a doctor is obviously not rooted in consumerism any more than in the middle-class need to be comfortable and rich.

The confusion brought to the family by a native African, Asagai, is realistically portrayed. In the early days of the Pan-African movement in the 1960s, blacks were often bemused by the way Africans presented themselves. Interest in Africa on the part of the American blacks was distorted by Tarzan movies and National Geographic ethnographic studies, none of which presented black Africans as role models. Therefore, the adjustment to black African pride — while made swiftly — was not without difficulties. The Youngers are presented as no more sophisticated about black Africans than the rest of black society would be.

The pride of the Younger family finally triumphs. When Walter Lee stands up for himself, he is not asserting his macho domination. He is asserting black manhood — a manhood that needs no domination over women. He is not expressing a desire for a big house — as he had done when he reflected on the possessions of his rich employer — but a desire to demonstrate to the Clybourne Park Improvement Association that the Youngers are not socially inferior and that they have a right to live wherever they choose.

A Raisin in the Sun in Performance

Lloyd Richards directed the first production at the Ethel Barrymore Theater in New York on March 11, 1959. The play won major prizes, and Sidney Poitier as a passionate Walter Lee Younger was a signal success. *New York Times* critic Brooks Atkinson said, "Since the performance is also honest and since Sidney Poitier is a candid actor, *A Raisin in the Sun* has vigor as well as veracity and is likely to destroy the complacency of any one who sees it." Critics were astonished that a first play could have the sophistication and depth they saw onstage.

The Theater Guild staged the play in 1960 in Boston with a different cast but the production received similar reviews. The film version, with most of the New York cast, was directed by Daniel Petrie in 1961. A revival in Chicago in 1983 at the Art Institute of Chicago — Hansberry's alma mater — was not altogether successful, but critics felt the text held up well. The Chicago revival, like the 1985 Merrimack Repertory Theater revival in Lowell, Massachusetts, demonstrated only that the play needs strong actors to have the desired impact. A twenty-fifth anniversary production was directed by Lloyd Richards at the Yale Repertory Theatre in 1983. This production was taken to New York in 1986 and enjoyed a successful run. The setting was a realistic interior, emphasizing the play's realistic style. Critic Mel Gussow felt the revival demonstrated that the play is "an enduring work of contemporary theater." The production also revealed that Hansberry's language had not become dated, nor had the social issues of the play become any less critical and important for the lapse of twenty-five years. Like the proletarian plays of Sean O'Casey, who inspired Lorraine Hansberry, this play continues to move us because its problems are serious and still remain.

Lorraine Hansberry *(1930–1965)*

A RAISIN IN THE SUN

1959

Harlem (A Dream Deferred)

What happens to a dream deferred?

> *Does it dry up*
> *like a raisin in the sun?*
> *Or fester like a sore —*
> *And then run?*
> *Does it stink like rotten meat?*

Or crust and sugar over —
like a syrupy sweet?

Maybe it just sags
like a heavy load.

Or does it explode?   — LANGSTON HUGHES

Characters

RUTH YOUNGER
TRAVIS YOUNGER
WALTER LEE YOUNGER *(brother)*
BENEATHA YOUNGER
LENA YOUNGER *(Mama)*
JOSEPH ASAGAI
GEORGE MURCHISON
MRS. JOHNSON
KARL LINDNER
BOBO
MOVING MEN

The action of the play is set in Chicago's Southside,
sometime between World War II and the present.

Act I
Scene I: *Friday morning.*
Scene II: *The following morning.*

Act II
Scene I: *Later, the same day.*
Scene II: *Friday night, a few weeks later.*
Scene III: *Moving day, one week later.*

Act III
An hour later.

ACT I • *Scene I*

(*The Younger living room would be a comfortable and well-ordered room if it were not for a number of indestructible contradictions to this state of being. Its furnishings are typical and undistinguished and their primary feature now is that they have clearly had to accommodate the living of too many people for too many years — and they are tired. Still, we can see that at some time, a time probably no longer remembered by the family [except perhaps for Mama], the furnishings of this room were actually selected with care and love and even hope — and brought to this apartment and arranged with taste and pride.*)

(*That was a long time ago. Now the once loved pattern of the couch upholstery has to fight to show itself from under acres of crocheted doilies and couch covers which have themselves finally come to be more important than the upholstery. And here a table or a chair has been moved to disguise the worn places in the carpet; but the carpet has fought back by showing its weariness, with depressing uniformity, elsewhere on its surface.*)

(*Weariness has, in fact, won in this room. Everything has been polished, washed, sat on, used, scrubbed too often. All pretenses but living itself have long since vanished from the very atmosphere of this room.*)

(*Moreover, a section of this room, for it is not really a room unto itself, though the landlord's lease would make it seem so, slopes backward to provide a small kitchen area, where the family prepares the meals that are eaten in the living room proper, which must also serve as dining room. The single window that has been provided for these "two" rooms is located in this kitchen area. The sole natural light the family may enjoy in the course of a day is only that which fights its way through this little window.*)

(*At left, a door leads to a bedroom which is shared by Mama and her daughter, Beneatha. At right, opposite, is a second room [which in the beginning of the life of this apartment was probably a breakfast room] which serves as a bedroom for Walter and his wife, Ruth.*)

(*Time: Sometime between World War II and the present.*)

(*Place: Chicago's Southside.*)

(*At rise: It is morning dark in the living room. Travis is asleep on the make-down bed at center. An alarm clock sounds from within the bedroom at right, and presently Ruth enters from that room and closes the door behind her. She crosses sleepily toward the window. As she passes her sleeping son she reaches down and shakes him a little. At the window she raises the shade and a dusky Southside morning light comes in feebly. She fills a pot with water and puts it on to boil. She calls to the boy, between yawns, in a slightly muffled voice.*)

(*Ruth is about thirty. We can see that she was a pretty girl, even exceptionally so, but now it is apparent that life has been little that she expected, and disappointment has already begun to hang in her face. In a few years, before thirty-five even, she will be known among her people as a "settled woman."*)

(*She crosses to her son and gives him a good, final, rousing shake.*)

RUTH: Come on now, boy, it's seven thirty! (*Her son sits up at last, in a stupor of sleepiness.*) I say hurry up, Travis! You ain't the only person in the world got to use a bathroom! (*The child, a sturdy, handsome little boy of ten or eleven, drags himself out of the bed and almost blindly takes his towels and "today's clothes" from drawers and a closet and goes out to the bathroom, which is in an outside hall and which is shared by another family or families on the same floor. Ruth crosses to the bedroom door at right and opens it and calls in to her husband.*) Walter Lee! . . . It's after seven thirty! Lemme see you do some waking up in there now! (*She waits.*) You better get up from there, man! It's after seven thirty I tell you. (*She waits again.*) All right, you just go ahead and lay there and next thing you know Travis be finished and Mr. Johnson'll be in there and you'll be fussing and cussing round here like a madman! And be late too! (*She waits, at the end of patience.*) Walter Lee — it's time for you to GET UP!

(*She waits another second and then starts to go into the bedroom, but is apparently satisfied that her husband has begun to get up. She stops, pulls the door to, and returns to the kitchen area. She wipes her face with a moist cloth and runs her fingers through her sleep-disheveled hair in a vain effort and ties an apron around her housecoat. The bedroom door at right opens and her husband stands in the doorway in his pajamas, which are rumpled and mismated. He is a lean, intense young man in his middle thirties, inclined to quick nervous movements and erratic speech habits — and always in his voice there is a quality of indictment.*)

WALTER: Is he out yet?

RUTH: What you mean *out*? He ain't hardly got in there good yet.

WALTER (*wandering in, still more oriented to sleep than to a new day*): Well, what was you doing all that yelling for if I can't even get in there yet? (*Stopping and thinking.*) Check coming today?

RUTH: They *said* Saturday and this is just Friday and I hopes to God you ain't going to get up here first thing this morning and start talking to me 'bout no money — 'cause I 'bout don't want to hear it.

WALTER: Something the matter with you this morning?

RUTH: No — I'm just sleepy as the devil. What kind of eggs you want?

WALTER: Not scrambled. (*Ruth starts to scramble eggs.*) Paper come? (*Ruth points impatiently to the rolled up Tribune on the table, and he gets it and spreads it out and vaguely reads the front page.*) Set off another bomb yesterday.

RUTH (*maximum indifference*): Did they?

WALTER (*looking up*): What's the matter with you?

RUTH: Ain't nothing the matter with me. And don't keep asking me that this morning.

WALTER: Ain't nobody bothering you. (*Reading the news of the day absently again.*) Say Colonel McCormick is sick.

RUTH (*affecting tea-party interest*): Is he now? Poor thing.

WALTER (*sighing and looking at his watch*): Oh, me. (*He waits.*) Now what is that boy doing in that bathroom all this time? He just going to have to start getting up earlier. I can't be being late to work on account of him fooling around in there.

RUTH (*turning on him*): Oh, no he ain't going to be getting up no earlier no such thing! It ain't his fault that he can't get to bed no earlier nights 'cause he got a bunch of crazy good-for-nothing clowns sitting up running their mouths in what is supposed to be his bedroom after ten o'clock at night . . .

WALTER: That's what you mad about, ain't it? The things I want to talk about with my friends just couldn't be important in your mind, could they?

(*He rises and finds a cigarette in her handbag on the table and crosses to the little window and looks out, smoking and deeply enjoying this first one.*)

RUTH (*almost matter of factly, a complaint too automatic to deserve emphasis*): Why you always got to smoke before you eat in the morning?

WALTER (*at the window*): Just look at 'em down there . . . Running and racing to work . . . (*He turns and faces his wife and watches her a moment at the stove, and then, suddenly.*) You look young this morning, baby.

RUTH (*indifferently*): Yeah?

WALTER: Just for a second — stirring them eggs. Just for a second it was — you looked real young again. (*He reaches for her; she crosses away. Then, drily.*) It's gone now — you look like yourself again!

RUTH: Man, if you don't shut up and leave me alone.

WALTER (*looking out to the street again*): First thing a man ought to learn in life is not to make love to no colored woman first thing in the morning. You all some eeeevil people at eight o'clock in the morning.

(*Travis appears in the hall doorway, almost fully dressed and quite wide awake now, his towels and pajamas across his shoulders. He opens the door and signals for his father to make the bathroom in a hurry.*)

TRAVIS (*watching the bathroom*): Daddy, come on!

(*Walter gets his bathroom utensils and flies out to the bathroom.*)

RUTH: Sit down and have your breakfast, Travis.

TRAVIS: Mama, this is Friday. (*Gleefully.*) Check coming tomorrow, huh?

RUTH: You get your mind off money and eat your breakfast.

TRAVIS (*eating*): This is the morning we supposed to bring the fifty cents to school.

RUTH: Well, I ain't got no fifty cents this morning.

TRAVIS: Teacher say we have to.

RUTH: I don't care what teacher say. I ain't got it. Eat your breakfast, Travis.

TRAVIS: I *am* eating.

RUTH: Hush up now and just eat!

(*The boy gives her an exasperated look for her lack of understanding and eats grudgingly.*)

TRAVIS: You think Grandmama would have it?

RUTH: No! And I want you to stop asking your grandmother for money, you hear me?

TRAVIS (*outraged*): Gaaaleee! I don't ask her, she just gimme it sometimes!

RUTH: Travis Willard Younger — I got too much on me this morning to be —

TRAVIS: Maybe Daddy —

RUTH: *Travis!*

(*The boy hushes abruptly. They are both quiet and tense for several seconds.*)

TRAVIS (*presently*): Could I maybe go carry some groceries in front of the supermarket for a little while after school then?

RUTH: Just hush, I said. (*Travis jabs his spoon into his cereal bowl viciously and rests his head in anger upon his fists.*) If you through eating, you can get over there and make up your bed.

(*The boy obeys stiffly and crosses the room, almost mechanically, to the bed and more or less folds the bedding into a heap, then angrily gets his books and cap.*)

TRAVIS (*sulking and standing apart from her unnaturally*): I'm gone.

RUTH (*looking up from the stove to inspect him automatically*): Come here. (*He crosses to her and she studies his head.*) If you don't take this comb and fix this here head, you better! (*Travis puts down his books with a great sigh of oppression and crosses to the mirror. His mother mutters under her breath about his "slubbornness."*) 'Bout to march out of here with that head looking just like chickens slept in it! I just don't know where you get your slubborn ways . . . And get your jacket, too. Looks chilly out this morning.

TRAVIS (*with conspicuously brushed hair and jacket*): I'm gone.

RUTH: Get carfare and milk money — (*waving one finger*) — and not a single penny for no caps, you hear me?

TRAVIS (*with sullen politeness*): Yes'm.

(*He turns in outrage to leave. His mother watches after him as in his frustration he approaches the door almost comically. When she speaks to him, her voice has become a very gentle tease.*)

RUTH (*mocking; as she thinks he would say it*): Oh, Mama makes me so mad sometimes, I don't know what to do! (*She waits and continues to his back as he stands stock-still in front of the door.*) I wouldn't kiss that woman good-bye for nothing in this world this morning! (*The boy finally turns around and rolls his eyes at her, knowing the mood has changed and he is vindicated; he does not, however, move toward her yet.*) Not for nothing in this world! (*She finally laughs aloud at him and holds out her arms to him and we see that it is a way between them, very old and practiced. He crosses to her and allows her to embrace him warmly but keeps his face fixed with masculine rigidity. She holds him back from her presently and looks at him and runs her fingers over the features of his face. With utter gentleness —*) Now — whose little old angry man are you?

TRAVIS (*the masculinity and gruffness start to fade at last*): Aw gaalee — Mama . . .

RUTH (*mimicking*): Aw — gaaaaalleeeee, Mama! (*She pushes him, with rough playfulness and finality, toward the door.*) Get on out of here or you going to be late.

TRAVIS (*in the face of love, new aggressiveness*): Mama, could I *please* go carry groceries?

RUTH: Honey, it's starting to get so cold evenings.

WALTER (*coming in from the bathroom and drawing a make-believe gun from a make-believe holster and shooting at his son*): What is it he wants to do?

RUTH: Go carry groceries after school at the supermarket.

WALTER: Well, let him go . . .

TRAVIS (*quickly, to the ally*): I *have* to — she won't gimme the fifty cents . . .

WALTER (*to his wife only*): Why not?

RUTH (*simply, and with flavor*): 'Cause we don't have it.

WALTER (*to Ruth only*): What you tell the boy things like that for? (*Reaching down into his pants with a rather important gesture.*) Here, son —

(*He hands the boy the coin, but his eyes are directed to his wife's. Travis takes the money happily.*)

TRAVIS: Thanks, Daddy.

(*He starts out. Ruth watches both of them with murder in her eyes. Walter stands and stares back at her with defiance and suddenly reaches into his pocket again on an afterthought.*)

WALTER (*without even looking at his son, still staring hard at his wife*): In fact, here's another fifty cents . . . Buy yourself some fruit today — or take a taxicab to school or something!

TRAVIS: Whoopee —

(*He leaps up and clasps his father around the middle with his legs, and they face each other in mutual appreciation; slowly Walter Lee peeks around the boy to catch the violent rays from his wife's eyes and draws his head back as if shot.*)

WALTER: You better get down now — and get to school, man.

TRAVIS (*at the door*): O.K. Good-bye.

(*He exits.*)

WALTER (*after him, pointing with pride*): That's my boy. (*She looks at him in disgust and turns back to her work.*) You know what I was thinking 'bout in the bathroom this morning?

RUTH: No.

WALTER: How come you always try to be so pleasant!

RUTH: What is there to be pleasant 'bout!

WALTER: You want to know what I was thinking 'bout in the bathroom or not!

RUTH: I know what you thinking 'bout.

WALTER (*ignoring her*): 'Bout what me and Willy Harris was talking about last night.

RUTH (*immediately — a refrain*): Willy Harris is a good-for-nothing loudmouth.

WALTER: Anybody who talks to me has got to be a good-for-nothing loudmouth, ain't he? And what you know about who is just a good-for-nothing loudmouth? Charlie Atkins was just a "good-for-nothing loudmouth" too, wasn't he! When he wanted me to go in the dry-cleaning business with him. And now — he's grossing a hundred thousand a year. A hundred thousand dollars a year! You still call *him* a loudmouth!

RUTH (*bitterly*): Oh, Walter Lee . . .

(*She folds her head on her arms over the table.*)

WALTER (*rising and coming to her and standing over her*): You tired, ain't you? Tired of everything. Me, the boy, the way we live — this beat-up hole — everything. Ain't you? (*She doesn't look up, doesn't answer.*) So tired — moaning and groaning all the time, but you wouldn't do nothing to help, would you? You couldn't be on my side that long for nothing, could you?

RUTH: Walter, please leave me alone.

WALTER: A man needs for a woman to back him up . . .

RUTH: Walter —

WALTER: Mama would listen to you. You know she listen to you more than she do me and Bennie. She think more of you. All you have to do is just sit down with her when you drinking your coffee one morning and talking 'bout things like you do and — (*He sits down beside her and demonstrates graphically what he thinks her methods and tone should be.*) — you just sip your coffee, see, and say easy like that you been thinking 'bout that deal Walter Lee is so interested in, 'bout the store and all, and sip some more coffee, like what you saying ain't really that important to you — And the next thing you know, she be listening good and asking you questions and when I come home — I can tell her the details. This ain't no fly-by-night proposition, baby. I mean we figured it out, me and Willy and Bobo.

RUTH (*with a frown*): Bobo?

WALTER: Yeah. You see, this little liquor store we got in mind cost seventy-five thousand and we figured the initial investment on the place be 'bout thirty thousand, see. That be ten thousand each. Course, there's a couple of hundred you got to pay so's you don't spend your life just waiting for them clowns to let your license get approved —

RUTH: You mean graft?

WALTER (*frowning impatiently*): Don't call it that. See there, that just goes to show you what women understand about the world. Baby, don't *nothing* happen for you in this world 'less you pay *somebody* off!

RUTH: Walter, leave me alone! (*She raises her head and stares at him vigorously — then says, more quietly.*) Eat your eggs, they gonna be cold.

WALTER (*straightening up from her and looking off*): That's it. There you are. Man say to his woman: I got me a dream. His woman say: Eat your eggs. (*Sadly, but gaining in power.*) Man say: I got to take hold of this here world, baby! And a woman will say: Eat your eggs and go to work. (*Passionately now.*) Man say: I got to change my life, I'm choking to death, baby! And his woman say — (*in utter anguish as he brings his fists down on his thighs*) — Your eggs is getting cold!

RUTH (*softly*): Walter, that ain't none of our money.

WALTER (*not listening at all or even looking at her*): This morning, I was lookin' in the mirror and thinking about it . . . I'm thirty-five years old; I been married eleven years and I got a boy who sleeps in the living room — (*very, very quietly*) — and all I got to give him is stories about how rich white people live . . .

RUTH: Eat your eggs, Walter.

WALTER (*slams the table and jumps up*): — DAMN MY EGGS — DAMN ALL THE EGGS THAT EVER WAS!

RUTH: Then go to work.

WALTER (*looking up at her*): See — I'm trying to talk to you 'bout myself — (*shaking his head with the repetition*) — and all you can say is eat them eggs and go to work.

RUTH (*wearily*): Honey, you never say nothing new. I listen to you every day, every night and every morning, and you never say nothing new. (*Shrugging.*) So you would rather *be* Mr. Arnold than be his chauffeur. So — I would *rather* be living in Buckingham Palace.

WALTER: That is just what is wrong with the colored woman in this world . . . Don't understand about building their men up and making 'em feel like they somebody. Like they can do something.

RUTH (*drily, but to hurt*): There *are* colored men who do things.

WALTER: No thanks to the colored woman.

RUTH: Well, being a colored woman, I guess I can't help myself none.

(*She rises and gets the ironing board and sets it up and attacks a huge pile of rough-dried clothes, sprinkling them in preparation for the ironing and then rolling them into tight fat balls.*)

WALTER (*mumbling*): We one group of men tied to a race of women with small minds!

(*His sister Beneatha enters. She is about twenty, as slim and intense as her brother. She is not as pretty as her sister-in-law, but her lean, almost intellectual face has a handsomeness of its own. She wears a bright red flannel nightie, and her thick hair stands wildly about her head. Her speech is a mixture of many things; it is different from the rest of the family's insofar as education has permeated her sense of English — and perhaps the Midwest rather than the South has finally — at last — won out in her inflection; but not altogether, because over all of it is a soft slurring and transformed use of vowels which is the decided influence of the Southside. She passes through the room without looking at either Ruth or Walter and goes to the outside door and looks, a little blindly, out to the bathroom. She sees that it has been lost to the Johnsons. She closes the door with a sleepy vengeance and crosses to the table and sits down a little defeated.*)

BENEATHA: I am going to start timing those people.

WALTER: You should get up earlier.

BENEATHA (*Her face in her hands. She is still fighting the urge to go back to bed.*): Really — would you suggest dawn? Where's the paper?

WALTER (*pushing the paper across the table to her as he studies her almost clinically, as though he has never seen her before*): You a horrible-looking chick at this hour.

BENEATHA (*drily*): Good morning, everybody.

WALTER (*senselessly*): How is school coming?

BENEATHA (*in the same spirit*): Lovely. Lovely. And you know, biology is the greatest. (*Looking up at him.*) I dissected something that looked just like you yesterday.

WALTER: I just wondered if you've made up your mind and everything.

BENEATHA (*gaining in sharpness and impatience*): And what did I answer yesterday morning — and the day before that?

RUTH (*from the ironing board, like someone disinterested and old*): Don't be so nasty, Bennie.

BENEATHA (*still to her brother*): And the day before that and the day before that!

WALTER (*defensively*): I'm interested in you. Something wrong with that? Ain't many girls who decide —

WALTER AND BENEATHA (*in unison*): — "to be a doctor."

(*Silence.*)

WALTER: Have we figured out yet just exactly how much medical school is going to cost?

RUTH: Walter Lee, why don't you leave that girl alone and get out of here to work?

BENEATHA (*exits to the bathroom and bangs on the door*): Come on out of there, please!

Ester Rolle as Lena Younger comforts her daughter-in-law Ruth in the Huntington Theatre Company's 1994 production of *A Raisin in the Sun.* Also in the scene are Marguerite Hannah as Ruth and B. W. Gonzalez as Beneatha.

(*She comes back into the room.*)

WALTER (*looking at his sister intently*): You know the check is coming tomorrow.

BENEATHA (*turning on him with a sharpness all her own*): That money belongs to Mama, Walter, and it's for her to decide how she wants to use it. I don't care if she wants to buy a house or a rocketship or just nail it up somewhere and look at it. It's hers. Not ours — *hers.*

WALTER (*bitterly*): Now ain't that fine! You just got your mother's interest at heart, ain't you, girl? You such a nice girl — but if Mama got that money she can always take a few thousand and help you through school too — can't she?

BENEATHA: I have never asked anyone around here to do anything for me!

WALTER: No! And the line between asking and just accepting when the time comes is big and wide — ain't it!

BENEATHA (*with fury*): What do you want from me, Brother — that I quit school or just drop dead, which!

WALTER: I don't want nothing but for you to stop acting holy 'round here. Me and Ruth done made some sacrifices for you — why can't you do something for the family?

RUTH: Walter, don't be dragging me in it.

WALTER: You are in it — Don't you get up and go work in somebody's kitchen for the last three years to help put clothes on her back?

RUTH: Oh, Walter — that's not fair . . .

WALTER: It ain't that nobody expects you to get on your knees and say thank you, Brother; thank you, Ruth; thank you, Mama — and thank you, Travis, for wearing the same pair of shoes for two semesters —

BENEATHA (*dropping to her knees*): Well — I *do* — all right? — thank everybody! And forgive me for ever wanting to be anything at all! (*Pursuing him on her knees across the floor.*) FORGIVE ME, FORGIVE ME, FORGIVE ME!

RUTH: Please stop it! Your mama'll hear you.

WALTER: Who the hell told you you had to be a doctor? If you so crazy 'bout messing 'round with sick people — then go be a nurse like other women — or just get married and be quiet . . .

BENEATHA: Well — you finally got it said . . . It took you three years but you finally got it said. Walter, give up; leave me alone — it's Mama's money.

WALTER: *He was my father, too!*

BENEATHA: So what? He was mine, too — and Travis' grandfather — but the insurance money belongs to Mama. Picking on me is not going to make her give it to you to invest in any liquor stores — (*under breath, dropping into a chair*) — and I for one say, God bless Mama for that!

WALTER (*to Ruth*): See — did you hear? Did you hear!

RUTH: Honey, please go to work.

WALTER: Nobody in this house is ever going to understand me.

BENEATHA: Because you're a nut.

WALTER: Who's a nut?

BENEATHA: You — you are a nut. Thee is mad, boy.

WALTER (*looking at his wife and his sister from the door, very sadly*): The world's most backward race of people, and that's a fact.

BENEATHA (*turning slowly in her chair*): And then there are all those prophets who would lead us out of the wilderness — (*Walter slams out of the house*) — into the swamps!

RUTH: Bennie, why you always gotta be pickin' on your brother? Can't you be a little sweeter sometimes? (*Door opens. Walter walks in. He fumbles with his cap, starts to speak, clears throat, looks everywhere but at Ruth. Finally.*)

WALTER (*to Ruth*): I need some money for carfare.

RUTH (*looks at him, then warms; teasing, but tenderly*): Fifty cents? (*She goes to her bag and gets money.*) Here — take a taxi!

(*Walter exits. Mama enters. She is a woman in her early sixties, full-bodied and strong. She is one of those women of a certain grace and beauty who wear it so unobtrusively that it takes a while to notice. Her dark brown face is surrounded by the total whiteness of her hair, and, being a woman who has adjusted to many things in life and overcome many more, her face is full of strength. She has, we can see, wit and faith of a kind that keep her eyes lit and full of interest and expectancy. She is, in a word, a beautiful woman. Her bearing is perhaps most like the noble bearing of the women of the Hereros of Southwest Africa — rather as if she imagines that as she walks she still bears a basket or a vessel upon her head. Her speech, on the other hand, is as careless as her carriage is precise — she is inclined to slur everything — but her voice is perhaps not so much quiet as simply soft.*)

MAMA: Who that 'round here slamming doors at this hour?

(*She crosses through the room, goes to the window, opens it, and brings in a feeble little plant growing doggedly in a small pot on the window sill. She feels the dirt and puts it back out.*)

RUTH: That was Walter Lee. He and Bennie was at it again.

MAMA: My children and they tempers. Lord, if this little old plant don't get more sun than it's been getting it ain't never going to see spring again. (*She turns from the window.*) What's the matter with you this morning, Ruth? You looks right peaked. You aiming to iron all them things? Leave some for me. I'll get to 'em this afternoon. Bennie honey, it's too drafty for you to be sitting 'round half dressed. Where's your robe?

BENEATHA: In the cleaners.

MAMA: Well, go get mine and put it on.

BENEATHA: I'm not cold, Mama, honest.

MAMA: I know — but you so thin . . .

BENEATHA (*irritably*): Mama, I'm not cold.

MAMA (*seeing the make-down bed as Travis has left it*): Lord have mercy, look at that poor bed. Bless his heart — he tries, don't he?

(*She moves to the bed Travis has sloppily made up.*)

RUTH: No — he don't half try at all 'cause he knows you going to come along behind him and fix everything. That's just how come he don't know how to do nothing right now — you done spoiled that boy so.

MAMA (*folding bedding*): Well — he's a little boy. Ain't supposed to know 'bout housekeeping. My baby, that's what he is. What you fix for his breakfast this morning?

RUTH (*angrily*): I feed my son, Lena!

MAMA: I ain't meddling — (*Under breath; busybody-ish.*) I just noticed all last week he had cold cereal, and when it starts getting this chilly in the fall a child ought to have some hot grits or something when he goes out in the cold —

RUTH (*furious*): I gave him hot oats — is that all right!

MAMA: I ain't meddling. (*Pause.*) Put a lot of nice butter on it? (*Ruth shoots her an angry look and does not reply.*) He likes lots of butter.

RUTH (*exasperated*): Lena —

MAMA (*To Beneatha. Mama is inclined to wander conversationally sometimes.*): What was you and your brother fussing 'bout this morning?

BENEATHA: It's not important, Mama.

(*She gets up and goes to look out at the bathroom, which is apparently free, and she picks up her towels and rushes out.*)

MAMA: What was they fighting about?

RUTH: Now you know as well as I do.

MAMA (*shaking her head*): Brother still worrying hisself sick about that money?

RUTH: You know he is.

MAMA: You had breakfast?

RUTH: Some coffee.

MAMA: Girl, you better start eating and looking after yourself better. You almost thin as Travis.

RUTH: Lena —

MAMA: Un-hunh?

RUTH: What are you going to do with it?

MAMA: Now don't you start, child. It's too early in the morning to be talking about money. It ain't Christian.

RUTH: It's just that he got his heart set on that store —

MAMA: You mean that liquor store that Willy Harris want him to invest in?

RUTH: Yes —

MAMA: We ain't no business people, Ruth. We just plain working folks.

RUTH: Ain't nobody business people till they go into business. Walter Lee say colored people ain't never going to start getting ahead till they start gambling on some different kinds of things in the world — investments and things.

MAMA: What done got into you, girl? Walter Lee done finally sold you on investing.

RUTH: No. Mama, something is happening between Walter and me. I don't know what it is — but he needs something — something I can't give him anymore. He needs this chance, Lena.

MAMA (*frowning deeply*): But liquor, honey —

RUTH: Well — like Walter say — I spec people going to always be drinking themselves some liquor.

MAMA: Well — whether they drinks it or not ain't none of my business. But whether I go into business selling it to 'em *is*, and I don't want that on my ledger this late in life. (*Stopping suddenly and studying her daughter-in-law.*) Ruth Younger, what's the matter with you today? You look like you could fall over right there.

RUTH: I'm tired.

MAMA: Then you better stay home from work today.

RUTH: I can't stay home. She'd be calling up the agency and screaming at them, "My girl didn't come in today — send me somebody! My girl didn't come in!" Oh, she just have a fit . . .

MAMA: Well, let her have it. I'll just call her up and say you got the flu —

RUTH (*laughing*): Why the flu?

MAMA: 'Cause it sounds respectable to 'em. Something white people get, too. They know 'bout the flu. Otherwise they think you been cut up or something when you tell 'em you sick.

RUTH: I got to go in. We need the money.

MAMA: Somebody would of thought my children done all but starved to death the way they talk about money here late. Child, we got a great big old check coming tomorrow.

RUTH (*sincerely, but also self-righteously*): Now that's your money. It ain't got nothing to do with me. We all feel like that — Walter and Bennie and me — even Travis.

MAMA (*thoughtfully, and suddenly very far away*): Ten thousand dollars —

RUTH: Sure is wonderful.

MAMA: Ten thousand dollars.

RUTH: You know what you should do, Miss Lena? You should take yourself a trip somewhere. To Europe or South America or someplace —

MAMA (*throwing up her hands at the thought*): Oh, child!

RUTH: I'm serious. Just pack up and leave! Go on away and enjoy yourself some. Forget about the family and have yourself a ball for once in your life —

MAMA (*drily*): You sound like I'm just about ready to die. Who'd go with me? What I look like wandering 'round Europe by myself?

RUTH: Shoot — these here rich white women do it all the time. They don't think nothing of packing up they suitcases and piling on one of them big steamships and — swoosh! — they gone, child.

MAMA: Something always told me I wasn't no rich white woman.

RUTH: Well — what are you going to do with it then?

MAMA: I ain't rightly decided. (*Thinking. She speaks now with emphasis.*) Some of it got to be put away for Beneatha and her schoolin' — and ain't nothing going to touch that part of it. Nothing. (*She waits several seconds, trying to make up her mind about something, and looks at Ruth a little tentatively before going on.*) Been thinking that we maybe could meet the notes on a little old two-story somewhere, with a yard where Travis could play in the summertime, if we use part of the insurance for a down payment and everybody kind of pitch in. I could maybe take on a little day work again, few days a week —

RUTH (*studying her mother-in-law furtively and concentrating on her ironing, anxious to encourage without seeming to*): Well, Lord knows, we've put enough rent into this here rat trap to pay for four houses by now . . .

MAMA (*looking up at the words "rat trap" and then looking around and leaning back and sighing — in a suddenly reflective mood —*): "Rat trap" — yes, that's all it is. (*Smiling.*) I remember just as well the day me and Big Walter moved in here. Hadn't been married but two weeks and wasn't planning on living here no more than a year. (*She shakes her head at the dissolved dream.*) We was going to set away, little by little, don't you know, and buy a little place out in Morgan Park. We had even picked out the house. (*Chuckling a little.*) Looks right dumpy today. But Lord, child, you should know, all the dreams I had 'bout buying that house and fixing it up and making me a little garden in the back — (*She waits and stops smiling.*) And didn't none of it happen.

(*Dropping her hands in a futile gesture.*)

RUTH (*keeps her head down, ironing*): Yes, life can be a barrel of disappointments, sometimes.

MAMA: Honey, Big Walter would come in here some nights back then and slump down on that couch there and just look at the rug, and look at me and look at the rug and then back at me — and I'd know he was down then . . . really down. (*After a second very long and thoughtful pause; she is seeing back to times that only she can see.*) And then, Lord, when I lost that baby — little Claude — I almost thought I was going to lose Big Walter too. Oh, that man grieved hisself! He was one man to love his children.

RUTH: Ain't nothin' can tear at you like losin' your baby.

MAMA: I guess that's how come that man finally worked hisself to death like he done. Like he was fighting his own war with this here world that took his baby from him.

RUTH: He sure was a fine man, all right. I always liked Mr. Younger.

MAMA: Crazy 'bout his children! God knows there was plenty wrong with Walter Younger — hard-headed, mean, kind of wild with women — plenty wrong with him. But he sure loved his children. Always wanted them to have something — be something. That's where Brother gets all these notions, I reckon. Big Walter used to say, he'd get right wet in the eyes sometimes, lean his head back with the water standing in his eyes and say, "Seem like God didn't see fit to give the black man nothing but dreams — but He did give us children to make them dreams seem worthwhile." (*She smiles.*) He could talk like that, don't you know.

RUTH: Yes, he sure could. He was a good man, Mr. Younger.

MAMA: Yes, a fine man — just couldn't never catch up with his dreams, that's all.

(*Beneatha comes in, brushing her hair and looking up to the ceiling, where the sound of a vacuum cleaner has started up.*)

BENEATHA: What could be so dirty on that woman's rugs that she has to vacuum them every single day?

RUTH: I wish certain young women 'round here who I could name would take inspiration about certain rugs in a certain apartment I could also mention.

BENEATHA (*shrugging*): How much cleaning can a house need, for Christ's sakes.

MAMA (*not liking the Lord's name used thus*): Bennie!

RUTH: Just listen to her — just listen!

BENEATHA: Oh, God!

MAMA: If you use the Lord's name just one more time —

BENEATHA (*a bit of a whine*): Oh, Mama —

RUTH: Fresh — just fresh as salt, this girl!

BENEATHA (*drily*): Well — if the salt loses its savor —

MAMA: Now that will do. I just ain't going to have you 'round here reciting the scriptures in vain — you hear me?

BENEATHA: How did I manage to get on everybody's wrong side by just walking into a room?

RUTH: If you weren't so fresh —

BENEATHA: Ruth, I'm twenty years old.

MAMA: What time you be home from school today?

BENEATHA: Kind of late. (*With enthusiasm.*) Madeline is going to start my guitar lessons today.

(*Mama and Ruth look up with the same expression.*)

MAMA: Your *what* kind of lessons?

BENEATHA: Guitar.

RUTH: Oh, Father!

MAMA: How come you done taken it in your mind to learn to play the guitar?

BENEATHA: I just want to, that's all.

MAMA (*smiling*): Lord, child, don't you know what to

do with yourself? How long it going to be before you get tired of this now — like you got tired of that little play-acting group you joined last year? (*Looking at Ruth.*) And what was it the year before that?

RUTH: The horseback-riding club for which she bought that fifty-five-dollar riding habit that's been hanging in the closet ever since!

MAMA (*to Beneatha*): Why you got to flit so from one thing to another, baby?

BENEATHA (*sharply*): I just want to learn to play the guitar. Is there anything wrong with that?

MAMA: Ain't nobody trying to stop you. I just wonders sometimes why you has to flit so from one thing to another all the time. You ain't never done nothing with all that camera equipment you brought home —

BENEATHA: I don't flit! I — I experiment with different forms of expression —

RUTH: Like riding a horse?

BENEATHA: — People have to express themselves one way or another.

MAMA: What is it you want to express?

BENEATHA (*angrily*): Me! (*Mama and Ruth look at each other and burst into raucous laughter.*) Don't worry — I don't expect you to understand.

MAMA (*to change the subject*): Who you going out with tomorrow night?

BENEATHA (*with displeasure*): George Murchison again.

MAMA (*pleased*): Oh — you getting a little sweet on him?

RUTH: You ask me, this child ain't sweet on nobody but herself — (*Under breath.*) Express herself!

(*They laugh.*)

BENEATHA: Oh — I like George all right, Mama. I mean I like him enough to go out with him and stuff, but —

RUTH (*for devilment*): What does *and stuff* mean?

BENEATHA: Mind your own business.

MAMA: Stop picking at her now, Ruth. (*She chuckles — then a suspicious sudden look at her daughter as she turns in her chair for emphasis.*) What DOES it mean?

BENEATHA (*wearily*): Oh, I just mean I couldn't ever really be serious about George. He's — he's so shallow.

RUTH: Shallow — what do you mean he's shallow? He's *Rich!*

MAMA: Hush, Ruth.

BENEATHA: I know he's rich. He knows he's rich, too.

RUTH: Well — what other qualities a man got to have to satisfy you, little girl?

BENEATHA: You wouldn't even begin to understand. Anybody who married Walter could not possibly understand.

MAMA (*outraged*): What kind of way is that to talk about your brother?

BENEATHA: Brother is a flip — let's face it.

MAMA (*to Ruth, helplessly*): What's a flip?

RUTH (*glad to add kindling*): She's saying he's crazy.

BENEATHA: Not crazy. Brother isn't really crazy yet — he — he's an elaborate neurotic.

MAMA: Hush your mouth!

BENEATHA: As for George. Well. George looks good — he's got a beautiful car and he takes me to nice places and, as my sister-in-law says, he is probably the richest boy I will ever get to know and I even like him sometimes — but if the Youngers are sitting around waiting to see if their little Bennie is going to tie up the family with the Murchisons, they are wasting their time.

RUTH: You mean you wouldn't marry George Murchison if he asked you someday? That pretty, rich thing? Honey, I knew you was odd —

BENEATHA: No I would not marry him if all I felt for him was what I feel now. Besides, George's family wouldn't really like it.

MAMA: Why not?

BENEATHA: Oh, Mama — The Murchisons are honest-to-God-real-*live*-rich colored people, and the only people in the world who are more snobbish than rich white people are rich colored people. I thought everybody knew that. I've met Mrs. Murchison. She's a scene!

MAMA: You must not dislike people 'cause they well off, honey.

BENEATHA: Why not? It makes just as much sense as disliking people 'cause they are poor, and lots of people do that.

RUTH (*A wisdom-of-the-ages manner. To Mama.*): Well, she'll get over some of this —

BENEATHA: Get over it? What are you talking about, Ruth? Listen, I'm going to be a doctor. I'm not worried about who I'm going to marry yet — if I ever get married.

MAMA AND RUTH: *If!*

MAMA: Now, Bennie —

BENEATHA: Oh, I probably will . . . but first I'm going to be a doctor, and George, for one, still thinks that's pretty funny. I couldn't be bothered with that. I am going to be a doctor and everybody around here better understand that!

MAMA (*kindly*): 'Course you going to be a doctor, honey, God willing.

BENEATHA (*drily*): God hasn't got a thing to do with it.

MAMA: Beneatha — that just wasn't necessary.

BENEATHA: Well — neither is God. I get sick of hearing about God.

MAMA: Beneatha!

BENEATHA: I mean it! I'm just tired of hearing about

God all the time. What has He got to do with anything? Does he pay tuition?

MAMA: You 'bout to get your fresh little jaw slapped!

RUTH: That's just what she needs, all right!

BENEATHA: Why? Why can't I say what I want to
around here, like everybody else?

MAMA: It don't sound nice for a young girl to say
things like that — you wasn't brought up that way.
Me and your father went to trouble to get you and
Brother to church every Sunday.

BENEATHA: Mama, you don't understand. It's all a
matter of ideas, and God is just one idea I don't
accept. It's not important. I am not going out and
be immoral or commit crimes because I don't believe in God. I don't even think about it. It's just
that I get tired of Him getting credit for all the
things the human race achieves through its own
stubborn effort. There simply is no blasted
God — there is only man and it is *he* who makes
miracles!

(*Mama absorbs this speech, studies her daughter and
rises slowly and crosses to Beneatha and slaps her
powerfully across the face. After, there is only silence
and the daughter drops her eyes from her mother's
face, and Mama is very tall before her.*)

MAMA: Now — you say after me, in my mother's
house there is still God. (*There is a long pause and
Beneatha stares at the floor wordlessly. Mama repeats the phrase with precision and cool emotion.*)
In my mother's house there is still God.

BENEATHA: In my mother's house there is still God.

(*A long pause.*)

MAMA (*Walking away from Beneatha, too disturbed
for triumphant posture. Stopping and turning back
to her daughter.*): There are some ideas we ain't going to have in this house. Not long as I am at the
head of this family.

BENEATHA: Yes, ma'am.

(*Mama walks out of the room.*)

RUTH (*almost gently, with profound understanding*):
You think you a woman, Bennie — but you still a
little girl. What you did was childish — so you got
treated like a child.

BENEATHA: I see. (*Quietly.*) I also see that everybody
thinks it's all right for Mama to be a tyrant. But all
the tyranny in the world will never put a God in
the heavens!

(*She picks up her books and goes out. Pause.*)

RUTH (*goes to Mama's door*): She said she was sorry.

MAMA (*coming out, going to her plant*): They frightens me, Ruth. My children.

RUTH: You got good children, Lena. They just a little
off sometimes — but they're good.

MAMA: No — there's something come down between
me and them that don't let us understand each
other and I don't know what it is. One done almost lost his mind thinking 'bout money all the
time and the other done commence to talk about
things I can't seem to understand in no form or
fashion. What is it that's changing, Ruth.

RUTH (*soothingly, older than her years*): Now . . . you
taking it all too seriously. You just got strong-
willed children and it takes a strong woman like
you to keep 'em in hand.

MAMA (*looking at her plant and sprinkling a little
water on it*): They spirited all right, my children.
Got to admit they got spirit — Bennie and Walter.
Like this little old plant that ain't never had
enough sunshine or nothing — and look at it . . .

(*She has her back to Ruth, who has had to stop ironing and lean against something and put the back of
her hand to her forehead.*)

RUTH (*trying to keep Mama from noticing*): You . . .
sure . . . loves that little old thing, don't you? . . .

MAMA: Well, I always wanted me a garden like I used
to see sometimes at the back of the houses down
home. This plant is close as I ever got to having
one. (*She looks out of the window as she replaces
the plant.*) Lord, ain't nothing as dreary as the
view from this window on a dreary day, is there?
Why ain't you singing this morning, Ruth? Sing
that "No Ways Tired." That song always lifts me
up so — (*She turns at last to see that Ruth has
slipped quietly to the floor, in a state of semicon-
sciousness.*) Ruth! Ruth honey — what's the matter with you . . . Ruth!

Scene II

(*It is the following morning; a Saturday morning, and
house cleaning is in progress at the Youngers'. Furniture has been shoved hither and yon and Mama is giving the kitchen-area walls a washing down. Beneatha,
in dungarees, with a handkerchief tied around her
face, is spraying insecticide into the cracks in the
walls. As they work, the radio is on and a Southside
disk jockey program is inappropriately filling the
house with a rather exotic saxophone blues. Travis,
the sole idle one, is leaning on his arms, looking out
of the window.*)

TRAVIS: Grandmama, that stuff Bennie is using smells
awful. Can I go downstairs, please?

MAMA: Did you get all them chores done already? I
ain't seen you doing much.

TRAVIS: Yes'm — finished early. Where did Mama go this morning?

MAMA (*looking at Beneatha*): She had to go on a little errand.

(*The phone rings. Beneatha runs to answer it and reaches it before Walter, who has entered from bedroom.*)

TRAVIS: Where?

MAMA: To tend to her business.

BENEATHA: Haylo . . . (*Disappointed.*) Yes, he is. (*She tosses the phone to Walter, who barely catches it.*) It's Willie Harris again.

WALTER (*as privately as possible under Mama's gaze*): Hello, Willie. Did you get the papers from the lawyer? . . . No, not yet. I told you the mailman doesn't get here till ten-thirty . . . No, I'll come there . . . Yeah! Right away. (*He hangs up and goes for his coat.*)

BENEATHA: Brother, where did Ruth go?

WALTER (*as he exits*): How should I know!

TRAVIS: Aw come on, Grandma. Can I go outside?

MAMA: Oh, I guess so. You stay right in front of the house, though, and keep a good lookout for the postman.

TRAVIS: Yes'm. (*He darts into bedroom for stickball and bat, reenters, and sees Beneatha on her knees spraying under sofa with behind upraised. He edges closer to the target, takes aim, and lets her have it. She screams.*) Leave them poor little cockroaches alone, they ain't bothering you none! (*He runs as she swings the spraygun at him viciously and playfully.*) Grandma! Grandma!

MAMA: Look out there, girl, before you be spilling some of that stuff on that child!

TRAVIS (*safely behind the bastion of Mama*): That's right — look out, now! (*He exits.*)

BENEATHA (*drily*): I can't imagine that it would hurt him — it has never hurt the roaches.

MAMA: Well, little boys' hides ain't as tough as Southside roaches. You better get over there behind the bureau. I seen one marching out of there like Napoleon yesterday.

BENEATHA: There's really only one way to get rid of them, Mama —

MAMA: How?

BENEATHA: Set fire to this building! Mama, where did Ruth go?

MAMA (*looking at her with meaning*): To the doctor, I think.

BENEATHA: The doctor? What's the matter? (*They exchange glances.*) You don't think —

MAMA (*with her sense of drama*): Now I ain't saying what I think. But I ain't never been wrong 'bout a woman neither.

(*The phone rings.*)

BENEATHA (*at the phone*): Hay-lo . . . (*Pause, and a moment of recognition.*) Well — when did you get back! . . . And how was it? . . . Of course I've missed you — in my way . . . This morning? No . . . house cleaning and all that and Mama hates it if I let people come over when the house is like this . . . You *have?* Well, that's different . . . What is it — Oh, what the hell, come on over . . . Right, see you then. *Arrivederci.*

(*She hangs up.*)

MAMA (*who has listened vigorously, as is her habit*): Who is that you inviting over here with this house looking like this? You ain't got the pride you was born with!

BENEATHA: Asagai doesn't care how houses look, Mama — he's an intellectual.

MAMA: *Who?*

BENEATHA: Asagai — Joseph Asagai. He's an African boy I met on campus. He's been studying in Canada all summer.

MAMA: What's his name?

BENEATHA: Asagai, Joseph. Ah-sah-guy . . . He's from Nigeria.

MAMA: Oh, that's the little country that was founded by slaves way back . . .

BENEATHA: No, Mama — that's Liberia.

MAMA: I don't think I never met no African before.

BENEATHA: Well, do me a favor and don't ask him a whole lot of ignorant questions about Africans. I mean, do they wear clothes and all that —

MAMA: Well, now, I guess if you think we so ignorant 'round here maybe you shouldn't bring your friends here —

BENEATHA: It's just that people ask such crazy things. All anyone seems to know about when it comes to Africa is Tarzan —

MAMA (*indignantly*): Why should I know anything about Africa?

BENEATHA: Why do you give money at church for the missionary work?

MAMA: Well, that's to help save people.

BENEATHA: You mean save them from *heathenism* —

MAMA (*innocently*): Yes.

BENEATHA: I'm afraid they need more salvation from the British and the French.

(*Ruth comes in forlornly and pulls off her coat with dejection. They both turn to look at her.*)

RUTH (*dispiritedly*): Well, I guess from all the happy faces — everybody knows.

BENEATHA: You pregnant?

MAMA: Lord have mercy, I sure hope it's a little old girl. Travis ought to have a sister.

(*Beneatha and Ruth give her a hopeless look for this grandmotherly enthusiasm.*)

BENEATHA: How far along are you?

RUTH: Two months.

BENEATHA: Did you mean to? I mean did you plan it or was it an accident?

MAMA: What do you know about planning or not planning?

BENEATHA: Oh, Mama.

RUTH (*wearily*): She's twenty years old, Lena.

BENEATHA: Did you plan it, Ruth?

RUTH: Mind your own business.

BENEATHA: It is my business — where is he going to live, on the *roof*? (*There is silence following the remark as the three women react to the sense of it.*) Gee — I didn't mean that, Ruth, honest. Gee, I don't feel like that at all. I — I think it is wonderful.

RUTH (*dully*): Wonderful.

BENEATHA: Yes — really.

MAMA (*looking at Ruth, worried*): Doctor say everything going to be all right?

RUTH (*far away*): Yes — she says everything is going to be fine . . .

MAMA (*immediately suspicious*): "She" — What doctor you went to?

(*Ruth folds over, near hysteria.*)

MAMA (*worriedly hovering over Ruth*): Ruth honey — what's the matter with you — you sick?

(*Ruth has her fists clenched on her thighs and is fighting hard to suppress a scream that seems to be rising in her.*)

BENEATHA: What's the matter with her, Mama?

MAMA (*working her fingers in Ruth's shoulders to relax her*): She be all right. Women gets right depressed sometimes when they get her way. (*Speaking softly, expertly, rapidly.*) Now you just relax. That's right . . . just lean back, don't think 'bout nothing at all . . . nothing at all —

RUTH: I'm all right . . .

(*The glassy-eyed look melts and then she collapses into a fit of heavy sobbing. The bell rings.*)

BENEATHA: Oh, my God — that must be Asagai.

MAMA (*to Ruth*): Come on now, honey. You need to lie down and rest awhile . . . then have some nice hot food.

(*They exit, Ruth's weight on her mother-in-law. Beneatha, herself profoundly disturbed, opens the door to admit a rather dramatic-looking young man with a large package.*)

ASAGAI: Hello, Alaiyo —

BENEATHA (*holding the door open and regarding him with pleasure*): Hello . . . (*Long pause.*) Well — come in. And please excuse everything. My mother was very upset about my letting anyone come here with the place like this.

ASAGAI (*coming into the room*): You look disturbed too . . . Is something wrong?

BENEATHA (*still at the door, absently*): Yes . . . we've all got acute ghetto-itus. (*She smiles and comes toward him, finding a cigarette and sitting.*) So — sit down! No! Wait! (*She whips the spraygun off sofa where she had left it and puts the cushions back. At last perches on arm of sofa. He sits.*) So, how was Canada?

ASAGAI (*a sophisticate*): Canadian.

BENEATHA (*looking at him*): Asagai, I'm very glad you are back.

ASAGAI (*looking back at her in turn*): Are you really?

BENEATHA: Yes — very.

ASAGAI: Why? — you were quite glad when I went away. What happened?

BENEATHA: You went away.

ASAGAI: Ahhhhhhhh.

BENEATHA: Before — you wanted to be so serious before there was time.

ASAGAI: How much time must there be before one knows what one feels?

BENEATHA (*Stalling this particular conversation. Her hands pressed together, in a deliberately childish gesture.*): What did you bring me?

ASAGAI (*handing her the package*): Open it and see.

BENEATHA (*eagerly opening the package and drawing out some records and the colorful robes of a Nigerian woman*): Oh, Asagai! . . . You got them for me! . . . How beautiful . . . and the records too! (*She lifts out the robes and runs to the mirror with them and holds the drapery up in front of herself.*)

ASAGAI (*coming to her at the mirror*): I shall have to teach you how to drape it properly. (*He flings the material about her for the moment and stands back to look at her.*) Ah — Oh-pay-gay-day, oh-gbah-mu-shay. (*A Yoruba exclamation for admiration.*) You wear it well . . . very well . . . mutilated hair and all.

BENEATHA (*turning suddenly*): My hair — what's wrong with my hair?

ASAGAI (*shrugging*): Were you born with it like that?

BENEATHA (*reaching up to touch it*): No . . . of course not.

(*She looks back to the mirror, disturbed.*)

ASAGAI (*smiling*): How then?

BENEATHA: You know perfectly well how . . . as crinkly as yours . . . that's how.

ASAGAI: And it is ugly to you that way?

BENEATHA (*quickly*): Oh, no — not ugly . . . (*More slowly, apologetically.*) But it's so hard to manage when it's, well — raw.

ASAGAI: And so to accommodate that — you mutilate it every week?

BENEATHA: It's not mutilation!

ASAGAI (*laughing aloud at her seriousness*): Oh . . . please! I am only teasing you because you are so very serious about these things. (*He stands back from her and folds his arms across his chest as he watches her pulling at her hair and frowning in the mirror.*) Do you remember the first time you met me at school? . . . (*He laughs.*) You came up to me and you said — and I thought you were the most serious little thing I had ever seen — you said: (*He imitates her.*) "Mr. Asagai — I want very much to talk with you. About Africa. You see, Mr. Asagai, I am looking for my *identity!*"

(*He laughs.*)

BENEATHA (*turning to him, not laughing*): Yes —

(*Her face is quizzical, profoundly disturbed.*)

ASAGAI (*still teasing and reaching out and taking her face in his hands and turning her profile to him*): Well . . . it is true that this is not so much a profile of a Hollywood queen as perhaps a queen of the Nile — (*A mock dismissal of the importance of the question.*) But what does it matter? Assimilationism is so popular in your country.

BENEATHA (*wheeling, passionately, sharply*): I am not an assimilationist!

ASAGAI (*the protest hangs in the room for a moment and Asagai studies her, his laughter fading*): Such a serious one. (*There is a pause.*) So — you like the robes? You must take excellent care of them — they are from my sister's personal wardrobe.

BENEATHA (*with incredulity*): You — you sent all the way home — for me?

ASAGAI (*with charm*): For you — I would do much more . . . Well, that is what I came for. I must go.

BENEATHA: Will you call me Monday?

ASAGAI: Yes . . . We have a great deal to talk about. I mean about identity and time and all that.

BENEATHA: Time?

ASAGAI: Yes. About how much time one needs to know what one feels.

BENEATHA: You see! You never understood that there is more than one kind of feeling which can exist between a man and a woman — or, at least, there should be.

ASAGAI (*shaking his head negatively but gently*): No. Between a man and a woman there need be only one kind of feeling. I have that for you . . . Now even . . . right this moment . . .

BENEATHA: I know — and by itself — it won't do. I can find that anywhere.

ASAGAI: For a woman it should be enough.

BENEATHA: I know — because that's what it says in all the novels that men write. But it isn't. Go ahead and laugh — but I'm not interested in being someone's little episode in America or — (*with feminine vengeance*) — one of them! (*Asagai has burst into laughter again.*) That's funny as hell, huh!

ASAGAI: It's just that every American girl I have known has said that to me. White — black — in this you are all the same. And the same speech, too!

BENEATHA (*angrily*): Yuk, yuk, yuk!

ASAGAI: It's how you can be sure that the world's most liberated women are not liberated at all. You all talk about it too much!

(*Mama enters and is immediately all social charm because of the presence of a guest.*)

BENEATHA: Oh — Mama — this is Mr. Asagai.

MAMA: How do you do?

ASAGAI (*total politeness to an elder*): How do you do, Mrs. Younger. Please forgive me for coming at such an outrageous hour on a Saturday.

MAMA: Well, you are quite welcome. I just hope you understand that our house don't always look like this. (*Chatterish.*) You must come again. I would love to hear all about — (*not sure of the name*) — your country. I think it's so sad the way our American Negroes don't know nothing about Africa 'cept Tarzan and all that. And all that money they pour into these churches when they ought to be helping you people over there drive out them French and Englishmen done taken away your land.

(*The mother flashes a slightly superior look at her daughter upon completion of the recitation.*)

ASAGAI (*taken aback by this sudden and acutely unrelated expression of sympathy*): Yes . . . yes . . .

MAMA (*smiling at him suddenly and relaxing and looking him over*): How many miles is it from here to where you come from?

ASAGAI: Many thousands.

MAMA (*looking at him as she would Walter*): I bet you don't half look after yourself, being away from your mama either. I spec you better come 'round here from time to time to get yourself some decent home-cooked meals . . .

ASAGAI (*moved*): Thank you. Thank you very much.

(*They are all quiet, then —*) Well . . . I must go. I will call you Monday, Alaiyo.

MAMA: What's that he call you?

ASAGAI: Oh — "Alaiyo." I hope you don't mind. It is what you would call a nickname, I think. It is a Yoruba word. I am a Yoruba.

MAMA (*looking at Beneatha*): I — I thought he was from — (*Uncertain.*)

ASAGAI (*understanding*): Nigeria is my country. Yoruba is my tribal origin —

BENEATHA: You didn't tell us what Alaiyo means . . . for all I know, you might be calling me Little Idiot or something . . .

ASAGAI: Well . . . let me see . . . I do not know how just to explain it . . . The sense of a thing can be so different when it changes languages.

BENEATHA: You're evading.

ASAGAI: No — really it is difficult . . . (*Thinking.*) It means . . . it means One for Whom Bread — Food — Is Not Enough. (*He looks at her.*) Is that all right?

BENEATHA (*understanding, softly*): Thank you.

MAMA (*looking from one to the other and not understanding any of it*): Well . . . that's nice . . . You must come see us again — Mr. ——

ASAGAI: Ah-sah-guy . . .

MAMA: Yes . . . Do come again.

ASAGAI: Good-bye.

(*He exits.*)

MAMA (*after him*): Lord, that's a pretty thing just went out here! (*Insinuatingly, to her daughter.*) Yes, I guess I see why we done commence to get so interested in Africa 'round here. Missionaries my aunt Jenny!

(*She exits.*)

BENEATHA: Oh, Mama! . . .

(*She picks up the Nigerian dress and holds it up to her in front of the mirror again. She sets the headdress on haphazardly and then notices her hair again and clutches at it and then replaces the headdress and frowns at herself. Then she starts to wriggle in front of the mirror as she thinks a Nigerian woman might. Travis enters and stands regarding her.*)

TRAVIS: What's the matter, girl, you cracking up?

BENEATHA: Shut up.

(*She pulls the headdress off and looks at herself in the mirror and clutches at her hair again and squinches her eyes as if trying to imagine something. Then, suddenly, she gets her raincoat and kerchief and hurriedly prepares for going out.*)

MAMA (*coming back into the room*): She's resting now. Travis, baby, run next door and ask Miss Johnson to please let me have a little kitchen cleanser. This here can is empty as Jacob's kettle.

TRAVIS: I just came in.

MAMA: Do as you told. (*He exits and she looks at her daughter.*) Where you going?

BENEATHA (*halting at the door*): To become a queen of the Nile!

(*She exits in a breathless blaze of glory. Ruth appears in the bedroom doorway.*)

MAMA: Who told you to get up?

RUTH: Ain't nothing wrong with me to be lying in no bed for. Where did Bennie go?

MAMA (*drumming her fingers*): Far as I could make out — to Egypt. (*Ruth just looks at her.*) What time is it getting to?

RUTH: Ten twenty. And the mailman going to ring that bell this morning just like he done every morning for the last umpteen years.

(*Travis comes in with the cleanser can.*)

TRAVIS: She say to tell you that she don't have much.

MAMA (*angrily*): Lord, some people I could name sure is tight-fisted! (*Directing her grandson.*) Mark two cans of cleanser down on the list there. If she that hard up for kitchen cleanser, I sure don't want to forget to get her none!

RUTH: Lena — maybe the woman is just short on cleanser —

MAMA (*not listening*): — Much baking powder as she done borrowed from me all these years, she could of done gone into the baking business!

(*The bell sounds suddenly and sharply and all three are stunned — serious and silent — mid-speech. In spite of all the other conversations and distractions of the morning, this is what they have been waiting for, even Travis, who looks helplessly from his mother to his grandmother. Ruth is the first to come to life again.*)

RUTH (*to Travis*): Get down them steps, boy!

(*Travis snaps to life and flies out to get the mail.*)

MAMA (*her eyes wide, her hand to her breast*): You mean it done really come?

RUTH (*excited*): Oh, Miss Lena!

MAMA (*collecting herself*): Well . . . I don't know what we all so excited about 'round here for. We known it was coming for months.

RUTH: That's a whole lot different from having it come and being able to hold it in your hands . . . a piece of paper worth ten thousand dollars . . . (*Travis bursts back into the room. He holds the envelope high above his head, like a little dancer, his face is radiant and he is breathless. He moves to his grand-*

mother with sudden slow ceremony and puts the envelope into her hands. She accepts it, and then merely holds it and looks at it.) Come on! Open it . . . Lord have mercy, I wish Walter Lee was here!

TRAVIS: Open it, Grandmama!

MAMA (*staring at it*): Now you all be quiet. It's just a check.

RUTH: Open it . . .

MAMA (*still staring at it*): Now don't act silly . . . We ain't never been no people to act silly 'bout no money —

RUTH (*swiftly*): We ain't never had none before — OPEN IT!

(*Mama finally makes a good strong tear and pulls out the thin blue slice of paper and inspects it closely. The boy and his mother study it raptly over Mama's shoulders.*)

MAMA: *Travis!* (*She is counting off with doubt.*) Is that the right number of zeros.

TRAVIS: Yes'm . . . ten thousand dollars. Gaalee, Grandmama, you rich.

MAMA (*She holds the check away from her, still looking at it. Slowly her face sobers into a mask of unhappiness.*): Ten thousand dollars. (*She hands it to Ruth.*) Put it away somewhere, Ruth. (*She does not look at Ruth; her eyes seem to be seeing something somewhere very far off.*) Ten thousand dollars they give you. Ten thousand dollars.

TRAVIS (*to his mother, sincerely*): What's the matter with Grandmama — don't she want to be rich?

RUTH (*distractedly*): You go on out and play now, baby. (*Travis exits. Mama starts wiping dishes absently, humming intently to herself. Ruth turns to her, with kind exasperation.*) You've gone and got yourself upset.

MAMA (*not looking at her*): I spec if it wasn't for you all . . . I would just put that money away or give it to the church or something.

RUTH: Now what kind of talk is that. Mr. Younger would just be plain mad if he could hear you talking foolish like that.

MAMA (*stopping and staring off*): Yes . . . he sure would. (*Sighing.*) We got enough to do with that money, all right. (*She halts then, and turns and looks at her daughter-in-law hard; Ruth avoids her eyes and Mama wipes her hands with finality and starts to speak firmly to Ruth.*) Where did you go today, girl?

RUTH: To the doctor.

MAMA (*impatiently*): Now, Ruth . . . you know better than that. Old Doctor Jones is strange enough in his way but there ain't nothing 'bout him make somebody slip and call him "she" — like you done this morning.

RUTH: Well, that's what happened — my tongue slipped.

MAMA: You went to see that woman, didn't you?

RUTH (*defensively, giving herself away*): What woman you talking about?

MAMA (*angrily*): That woman who —

(*Walter enters in great excitement.*)

WALTER: Did it come?

MAMA (*quietly*): Can't you give people a Christian greeting before you start asking about money?

WALTER (*to Ruth*): Did it come? (*Ruth unfolds the check and lays it quietly before him, watching him intently with thoughts of her own. Walter sits down and grasps it close and counts off the zeros.*) Ten thousand dollars — (*He turns suddenly, frantically to his mother and draws some papers out of his breast pocket.*) Mama — look. Old Willy Harris put everything on paper —

MAMA: Son — I think you ought to talk to your wife . . . I'll go on out and leave you alone if you want —

WALTER: I can talk to her later — Mama, look —

MAMA: Son —

WALTER: WILL SOMEBODY PLEASE LISTEN TO ME TODAY!

MAMA (*quietly*): I don't 'low no yellin' in this house, Walter Lee, and you know it — (*Walter stares at them in frustration and starts to speak several times.*) And there ain't going to be no investing in no liquor stores.

WALTER: But, Mama, you ain't even looked at it.

MAMA: I don't aim to have to speak on that again.

(*A long pause.*)

WALTER: You ain't looked at it and you don't aim to have to speak on that again? You ain't even looked at it and *you* have decided — (*Crumpling his papers.*) Well, *you* tell that to my boy tonight when you put him to sleep on the living room couch . . . (*Turning to Mama and speaking directly to her.*) Yeah — and tell it to my wife, Mama, tomorrow when she has to go out of here to look after somebody else's kids. And tell it to *me*, Mama, every time we need a new pair of curtains and I have to watch *you* go out and work in somebody's kitchen. Yeah, you tell me then!

(*Walter starts out.*)

RUTH: Where you going?

WALTER: I'm going out!

RUTH: Where?

WALTER: Just out of this house somewhere —

RUTH (*getting her coat*): I'll come too.

WALTER: I don't want you to come!

RUTH: I got something to talk to you about, Walter.

WALTER: That's too bad.

MAMA (*still quietly*): Walter Lee — (*She waits and he finally turns and looks at her.*) Sit down.

WALTER: I'm a grown man, Mama.

MAMA: Ain't nobody said you wasn't grown. But you still in my house and my presence. And as long as you are — you'll talk to your wife civil. Now sit down.

RUTH (*suddenly*): Oh, let him go on out and drink himself to death! He makes me sick to my stomach! (*She flings her coat against him and exits to bedroom.*)

WALTER (*violently flinging the coat after her*): And you turn mine too, baby! (*The door slams behind her.*) That was my biggest mistake —

MAMA (*still quietly*): Walter, what is the matter with you?

WALTER: Matter with me? Ain't nothing the matter with *me!*

MAMA: Yes there is. Something eating you up like a crazy man. Something more than me not giving you this money. The past few years I been watching it happen to you. You get all nervous acting and kind of wild in the eyes — (*Walter jumps up impatiently at her words.*) I said sit there now, I'm talking to you!

WALTER: Mama — I don't need no nagging at me today.

MAMA: Seem like you getting to a place where you always tied up in some kind of knot about something. But if anybody ask you 'bout it you just yell at 'em and bust out the house and go out and drink somewheres. Walter Lee, people can't live with that. Ruth's a good, patient girl in her way — but you getting to be too much. Boy, don't make the mistake of driving that girl away from you.

WALTER: Why — what she do for me?

MAMA: She loves you.

WALTER: Mama — I'm going out. I want to go off somewhere and be by myself for a while.

MAMA: I'm sorry 'bout your liquor store, son. It just wasn't the thing for us to do. That's what I want to tell you about —

WALTER: I got to go out, Mama —

(*He rises.*)

MAMA: It's dangerous, son.

WALTER: What's dangerous?

MAMA: When a man goes outside his home to look for peace.

WALTER (*beseechingly*): Then why can't there never be no peace in this house then?

MAMA: You done found it in some other house?

WALTER: No — there ain't no woman! Why do women always think there's a woman somewhere when a man gets restless. (*Picks up the check.*) Do you know what this money means to me? Do you know what this money can do for us? (*Puts it back.*) Mama — Mama — I want so many things . . .

MAMA: Yes, son —

WALTER: I want so many things that they are driving me kind of crazy . . . Mama — look at me.

MAMA: I'm looking at you. You a good-looking boy. You got a job, a nice wife, a fine boy and —

WALTER: A job. (*Looks at her.*) Mama, a job? I open and close car doors all day long. I drive a man around in his limousine and I say, "Yes, sir, no, sir; very good, sir; shall I take the Drive, sir?" Mama, that ain't no kind of job . . . that ain't nothing at all. (*Very quietly.*) Mama, I don't know if I can make you understand.

MAMA: Understand what, baby?

WALTER (*quietly*): Sometimes it's like I can see the future stretched out in front of me — just plain as day. The future, Mama. Hanging over there at the edge of my days. Just waiting for me — a big, looming blank space — full of *nothing.* Just waiting for *me.* But it don't have to be. (*Pause. Kneeling beside her chair.*) Mama — sometimes when I'm downtown and I pass them cool, quiet-looking restaurants where them white boys are sitting back and talking 'bout things . . . sitting there turning deals worth millions of dollars . . . sometimes I see guys don't look much older than me —

MAMA: Son — how come you talk so much 'bout money?

WALTER (*with immense passion*): Because it is life, Mama!

MAMA (*quietly*): Oh — (*Very quietly.*) So now it's life. Money is life. Once upon a time freedom used to be life — now it's money. I guess the world really do change . . .

WALTER: No — it was always money, Mama. We just didn't know about it.

MAMA: No . . . something has changed. (*She looks at him.*) You something new, boy. In my time we was worried about not being lynched and getting to the North if we could and how to stay alive and still have a pinch of dignity too . . . Now here come you and Beneatha — talking 'bout things we ain't never even thought about hardly, me and your daddy. You ain't satisfied or proud of nothing we done. I mean that you had a home, that we kept you out of trouble till you was grown, that you don't have to ride to work on the back of nobody's streetcar — You my children — but how different we done become.

WALTER (*A long beat. He pats her hand and gets up.*):

You just don't understand, Mama, you just don't understand.

MAMA: Son — do you know your wife is expecting another baby? (*Walter stands, stunned, and absorbs what his mother has said.*) That's what she wanted to talk to you about. (*Walter sinks down into a chair.*) This ain't for me to be telling — but you ought to know. (*She waits.*) I think Ruth is thinking 'bout getting rid of that child.

WALTER (*slowly understanding*): — No — no — Ruth wouldn't do that.

MAMA: When the world gets ugly enough — a woman will do anything for her family. *The part that's already living.*

WALTER: You don't know Ruth, Mama, if you think she would do that.

(*Ruth opens the bedroom door and stands there a little limp.*)

RUTH (*beaten*): Yes I would too, Walter. (*Pause.*) I gave her a five-dollar down payment.

(*There is total silence as the man stares at his wife and the mother stares at her son.*)

MAMA (*presently*): Well — (*Tightly.*) Well — son, I'm waiting to hear you say something . . . (*She waits.*) I'm waiting to hear how you be your father's son. Be the man he was . . . (*Pause. The silence shouts.*) Your wife says she going to destroy your child. And I'm waiting to hear you talk like him and say we a people who give children life, not who destroys them — (*She rises.*) I'm waiting to see you stand up and look like your daddy and say we done give up one baby to poverty and that we ain't going to give up nary another one . . . I'm waiting.

WALTER: Ruth — (*He can say nothing.*)

MAMA: If you a son of mine, tell her! (*Walter picks up his keys and his coat and walks out. She continues, bitterly.*) You . . . you are a disgrace to your father's memory. Somebody get me my hat!

ACT II • *Scene 1*

(*Time: Later the same day.*)

(*At rise: Ruth is ironing again. She has the radio going. Presently Beneatha's bedroom door opens and Ruth's mouth falls and she puts down the iron in fascination.*)

RUTH: What have we got on tonight!

BENEATHA (*emerging grandly from the doorway so that we can see her thoroughly robed in the costume Asagai brought*): You are looking at what a well-dressed Nigerian woman wears — (*She pa-*

rades for Ruth, her hair completely hidden by the headdress; she is coquettishly fanning herself with an ornate oriental fan, mistakenly more like Butterfly° than any Nigerian that ever was.*) Isn't it beautiful? (*She promenades to the radio and, with an arrogant flourish, turns off the good loud blues that is playing.*) Enough of this assimilationist junk! (*Ruth follows her with her eyes as she goes to the phonograph and puts on a record and turns and waits ceremoniously for the music to come up. Then, with a shout —*) OCOMOGOSIAY!

(*Ruth jumps. The music comes up, a lovely Nigerian melody. Beneatha listens, enraptured, her eyes far away — "back to the past." She begins to dance. Ruth is dumfounded.*)

RUTH: What kind of dance is that?

BENEATHA: A folk dance.

RUTH (*Pearl Bailey*): What kind of folks do that, honey?

BENEATHA: It's from Nigeria. It's a dance of welcome.

RUTH: Who you welcoming?

BENEATHA: The men back to the village.

RUTH: Where they been?

BENEATHA: How should I know — out hunting or something. Anyway, they are coming back now . . .

RUTH: Well, that's good.

BENEATHA (*with the record*): Alundi, alundi
Alundi alunya
Jop pu a jeepua
Ang gu sooooooooooo

Ai yai yue . . .
Ayehaye — alundi . . .

(*Walter comes in during this performance; he has obviously been drinking. He leans against the door heavily and watches his sister, at first with distaste. Then his eyes look off — "back to the past" — as he lifts both his fists to the roof, screaming.*)

WALTER: YEAH . . . AND ETHIOPIA STRETCH FORTH HER HANDS AGAIN! . . .

RUTH (*drily, looking at him*): Yes — and Africa sure is claiming her own tonight. (*She gives them both up and starts ironing again.*)

WALTER (*all in a drunken, dramatic shout*): Shut up! . . . I'm digging them drums . . . them drums move me! . . . (*He makes his weaving way to his wife's face and leans in close to her.*) In my *heart of hearts* — (*he thumps his chest*) — I am much warrior!

Butterfly: Madame Butterfly, the title character in the opera by Puccini, set in China.

RUTH (*without even looking up*): In your heart of hearts you are much drunkard.

WALTER (*coming away from her and starting to wander around the room, shouting*): Me and Jomo . . . (*Intently, in his sister's face. She has stopped dancing to watch him in this unknown mood.*) That's my man, Kenyatta. (*Shouting and thumping his chest.*) FLAMING SPEAR! HOT DAMN! (*He is suddenly in possession of an imaginary spear and actively spearing enemies all over the room.*) OCOMOGOSIAY . . .

BENEATHA (*to encourage Walter, thoroughly caught up with this side of him*): OCOMOGOSIAY, FLAMING SPEAR!

WALTER: THE LION IS WAKING . . . OWIMOWEH! (*He pulls his shirt open and leaps up on the table and gestures with his spear.*)

BENEATHA: OWIMOWEH!

WALTER (*On the table, very far gone, his eyes pure glass sheets. He sees what we cannot, that he is a leader of his people, a great chief, a descendant of Chaka, and that the hour to march has come.*): Listen, my black brothers —

BENEATHA: OCOMOGOSIAY!

WALTER: — Do you hear the waters rushing against the shores of the coastlands —

BENEATHA: OCOMOGOSIAY!

WALTER: — Do you hear the screeching of the cocks in yonder hills beyond where the chiefs meet in council for the coming of the mighty war —

BENEATHA: OCOMOGOSIAY!

(*And now the lighting shifts subtly to suggest the world of Walter's imagination, and the mood shifts from pure comedy. It is the inner Walter speaking: the Southside chauffeur has assumed an unexpected majesty.*)

WALTER: — Do you hear the beating of the wings of the birds flying low over the mountains and the low places of our land —

BENEATHA: OCOMOGOSIAY!

WALTER: — Do you hear the singing of the women singing the war songs of our fathers to the babies in the great houses? Singing the sweet war songs! (*The doorbell rings.*) OH, DO YOU HEAR, MY BLACK BROTHERS!

BENEATHA (*completely gone*): We hear you, Flaming Spear —

(*Ruth shuts off the phonograph and opens the door. George Murchison enters.*)

WALTER: Telling us to prepare for the GREATNESS OF THE TIME! (*Lights back to normal. He turns and sees George.*) Black Brother!

(*He extends his hand for the fraternal clasp.*)

GEORGE: Black Brother, hell!

RUTH (*having had enough, and embarrassed for the family*): Beneatha, you got company — what's the matter with you? Walter Lee Younger, get down off that table and stop acting like a fool . . .

(*Walter comes down off the table suddenly and makes a quick exit to the bathroom.*)

RUTH: He's had a little to drink . . . I don't know what her excuse is.

GEORGE (*to Beneatha*): Look honey, we're going *to* the theater — we're not going to be *in* it . . . so go change, huh?

(*Beneatha looks at him and slowly, ceremoniously, lifts her hands and pulls off the headdress. Her hair is close-cropped and unstraightened. George freezes midsentence and Ruth's eyes all but fall out of her head.*)

GEORGE: What in the name of —

RUTH (*touching Beneatha's hair*): Girl, you done lost your natural mind? Look at your head!

GEORGE: What have you done to your head — I mean your hair!

BENEATHA: Nothing — except cut it off.

RUTH: Now that's the truth — it's what ain't been done to it! You expect this boy to go out with you with your head all nappy like that?

BENEATHA (*looking at George*): That's up to George. If he's ashamed of his heritage —

GEORGE: Oh, don't be so proud of yourself, Bennie — just because you look eccentric.

BENEATHA: How can something that's natural be eccentric?

GEORGE: That's what being eccentric means — being natural. Get dressed.

BENEATHA: I don't like that, George.

RUTH: Why must you and your brother make an argument out of everything people say?

BENEATHA: Because I hate assimilationist Negroes!

RUTH: Will somebody please tell me what assimilawhoever means!

GEORGE: Oh, it's just a college girl's way of calling people Uncle Toms — but that isn't what it means at all.

RUTH: Well, what does it mean?

BENEATHA (*cutting George off and staring at him as she replies to Ruth*): It means someone who is willing to give up his own culture and submerge himself completely in the dominant, and in this case *oppressive* culture!

GEORGE: Oh, dear, dear, dear! Here we go! A lecture on the African past! On our Great West African Heritage! In one second we will hear all about the great Ashanti empires; the great Songhay civilizations; and the great sculpture of Bénin — and then some poetry in the Bantu — and the whole monologue will end with the word *heritage!* (*Nastily.*) Let's face it, baby, your heritage is nothing but a bunch of raggedy-assed spirituals and some grass huts!

BENEATHA: GRASS HUTS! (*Ruth crosses to her and forcibly pushes her toward the bedroom.*) See there . . . you are standing there in your splendid ignorance talking about people who were the first to smelt iron on the face of the earth! (*Ruth is pushing her through the door.*) The Ashanti were performing surgical operations when the English — (*Ruth pulls the door to, with Beneatha on the other side, and smiles graciously at George. Beneatha opens the door and shouts the end of the sentence defiantly at George*) — were still tatooing themselves with blue dragons! (*She goes back inside.*)

RUTH: Have a seat, George. (*They both sit. Ruth folds her hands rather primly on her lap, determined to demonstrate the civilization of the family.*) Warm, ain't it? I mean for September. (*Pause.*) Just like they always say about Chicago weather: If it's too hot or cold for you, just wait a minute and it'll change. (*She smiles happily at this cliché of clichés.*) Everybody say it's got to do with them bombs and things they keep setting off. (*Pause.*) Would you like a nice cold beer?

GEORGE: No, thank you. I don't care for beer. (*He looks at his watch.*) I hope she hurries up.

RUTH: What time is the show?

GEORGE: It's an eight-thirty curtain. That's just Chicago, though. In New York standard curtain time is eight forty.

(*He is rather proud of this knowledge.*)

RUTH (*properly appreciating it*): You get to New York a lot?

GEORGE (*offhand*): Few times a year.

RUTH: Oh — that's nice. I've never been to New York.

(*Walter enters. We feel he has relieved himself, but the edge of unreality is still with him.*)

WALTER: New York ain't got nothing Chicago ain't. Just a bunch of hustling people all squeezed up together — being "Eastern."

(*He turns his face into a screw of displeasure.*)

GEORGE: Oh — you've been?

WALTER: *Plenty* of times.

RUTH (*shocked at the lie*): Walter Lee Younger!

WALTER (*staring her down*): Plenty! (*Pause.*) What we got to drink in this house? Why don't you offer this man some refreshment. (*To George.*) They don't know how to entertain people in this house, man.

GEORGE: Thank you — I don't really care for anything.

WALTER (*feeling his head; sobriety coming*): Where's Mama?

RUTH: She ain't come back yet.

WALTER (*looking Murchison over from head to toe, scrutinizing his carefully casual tweed sports jacket over cashmere V-neck sweater over soft eyelet shirt and tie, and soft slacks, finished off with white buckskin shoes*): Why all you college boys wear them faggoty-looking white shoes?

RUTH: Walter Lee!

(*George Murchison ignores the remark.*)

WALTER (*to Ruth*): Well, they look crazy as hell — white shoes, cold as it is.

RUTH (*crushed*): You have to excuse him —

WALTER: No he don't! Excuse me for what? What you always excusing me for! I'll excuse myself when I needs to be excused! (*A pause.*) They look as funny as them black knee socks Beneatha wears out of here all the time.

RUTH: It's the college *style*, Walter.

WALTER: Style, hell. She looks like she got burnt legs or something!

RUTH: Oh, Walter —

WALTER (*an irritable mimic*): Oh, Walter! Oh, Walter! (*To Murchison.*) How's your old man making out? I understand you all going to buy that big hotel on the Drive? (*He finds a beer in the refrigerator, wanders over to Murchison, sipping and wiping his lips with the back of his hand, and straddling a chair backward to talk to the other man.*) Shrewd move. Your old man is all right, man. (*Tapping his head and half winking for emphasis.*) I mean he knows how to operate. I mean he thinks *big*, you know what I mean, I mean for a *home*, you know? But I think he's kind of running out of ideas now. I'd like to talk to him. Listen, man, I got some plans that could turn this city upside down. I mean think like he does. *Big*. Invest big, gamble big, hell, lose *big* if you have to, you know what I mean. It's hard to find a man on this whole Southside who understands my kind of thinking — you dig? (*He scrutinizes Murchison again, drinks his beer, squints his eyes, and leans in close, confidential, man to man.*) Me and you ought to sit down and talk sometimes, man. Man, I got me some ideas . . .

MURCHISON (*with boredom*): Yeah — sometimes we'll have to do that, Walter.

WALTER (*understanding the indifference, and offended*): Yeah — well, when you get the time, man. I know you a busy little boy.

RUTH: Walter, please —

WALTER (*bitterly, hurt*): I know ain't nothing in this world as busy as you colored college boys with your fraternity pins and white shoes . . .

RUTH (*covering her face with humiliation*): Oh, Walter Lee —

WALTER: I see you all all the time — with the books tucked under your arms — going to your (*British A — a mimic*) "clahsses." And for what! What the hell you learning over there? Filling up your heads — (*counting off on his fingers*) — with the sociology and the psychology — but they teaching you how to be a man? How to take over and run the world? They teaching you how to run a rubber plantation or a steel mill? Naw — just to talk proper and read books and wear them faggoty-looking white shoes . . .

GEORGE (*looking at him with distaste, a little above it all*): You're all wacked up with bitterness, man.

WALTER (*intently, almost quietly, between the teeth, glaring at the boy*): And you — ain't you bitter, man? Ain't you just about had it yet? Don't you see no stars gleaming that you can't reach out and grab? You happy? — You contented son-of-a-bitch — you happy? You got it made? Bitter? Man, I'm a volcano. Bitter? Here I am a giant — surrounded by ants! Ants who can't even understand what it is the giant is talking about.

RUTH (*passionately and suddenly*): Oh, Walter — ain't you with nobody!

WALTER (*violently*): No! 'Cause ain't nobody with me! Not even my own mother!

RUTH: Walter, that's a terrible thing to say!

(*Beneatha enters, dressed for the evening in a cocktail dress and earrings, hair natural.*)

GEORGE: Well — hey — (*Crosses to Beneatha; thoughtful, with emphasis, since this is a reversal.*) You look great!

WALTER (*seeing his sister's hair for the first time*): What's the matter with your head?

BENEATHA (*tired of the jokes now*): I cut it off, Brother.

WALTER (*coming close to inspect it and walking around her*): Well, I'll be damned. So that's what they mean by the African bush . . .

BENEATHA: Ha ha. Let's go, George.

GEORGE (*looking at her*): You know something? I like it. It's sharp. I mean it really is. (*Helps her into her wrap.*)

RUTH: Yes — I think so, too. (*She goes to the mirror and starts to clutch at her hair.*)

WALTER: Oh no! You leave yours alone, baby. You might turn out to have a pin-shaped head or something!

BENEATHA: See you all later.

RUTH: Have a nice time.

GEORGE: Thanks. Good night. (*Half out the door, he reopens it. To Walter.*) Good night, Prometheus!°

(*Beneatha and George exit.*)

WALTER (*to Ruth*): Who is Prometheus?

RUTH: I don't know. Don't worry about it.

WALTER (*in fury, pointing after George*): See there — they get to a point where they can't insult you man to man — they got to go talk about something ain't nobody never heard of!

RUTH: How do you know it was an insult? (*To humor him.*) Maybe Prometheus is a nice fellow.

WALTER: Prometheus! I bet there ain't even no such thing! I bet that simple-minded clown —

RUTH: Walter —

(*She stops what she is doing and looks at him.*)

WALTER (*yelling*): Don't start!

RUTH: Start what?

WALTER: Your nagging! Where was I? Who was I with? How much money did I spend?

RUTH (*plaintively*): Walter Lee — why don't we just try to talk about it . . .

WALTER (*not listening*): I been out talking with people who understand me. People who care about the things I got on my mind.

RUTH (*wearily*): I guess that means people like Willy Harris.

WALTER: Yes, people like Willy Harris.

RUTH (*with a sudden flash of impatience*): Why don't you all just hurry up and go into the banking business and stop talking about it!

WALTER: Why? You want to know why? 'Cause we all tied up in a race of people that don't know how to do nothing but moan, pray, and have babies!

(*The line is too bitter even for him and he looks at her and sits down.*)

RUTH: Oh, Walter . . . (*Softly.*) Honey, why can't you stop fighting me?

WALTER (*without thinking*): Who's fighting you? Who even cares about you?

(*This line begins the retardation of his mood.*)

RUTH: Well — (*She waits a long time, and then with resignation starts to put away her things.*) I guess I might as well go on to bed . . . (*More or less to herself.*) I don't know where we lost it . . . but we have . . . (*Then, to him.*) I — I'm sorry about this new baby, Walter. I guess maybe I better go on and

Prometheus: A shrewd and inventive god noted for stealing fire from the heavens and giving it to humans.

do what I started . . . I guess I just didn't realize how bad things was with us . . . I guess I just didn't really realize — (*She starts out to the bedroom and stops.*) You want some hot milk?

WALTER: Hot milk?

RUTH: Yes — hot milk.

WALTER: Why hot milk?

RUTH: 'Cause after all that liquor you come home with you ought to have something hot in your stomach.

WALTER: I don't want no milk.

RUTH: You want some coffee then?

WALTER: No, I don't want no coffee. I don't want nothing hot to drink. (*Almost plaintively.*) Why you always trying to give me something to eat?

RUTH (*standing and looking at him helplessly*): What else can I give you, Walter Lee Younger?

(*She stands and looks at him and presently turns to go out again. He lifts his head and watches her going away from him in a new mood which began to emerge when he asked her "Who cares about you?"*)

WALTER: It's been rough, ain't it, baby? (*She hears and stops but does not turn around and he continues to her back.*) I guess between two people there ain't never as much understood as folks generally thinks there is. I mean like between me and you — (*She turns to face him.*) How we gets to the place where we scared to talk softness to each other. (*He waits, thinking hard himself.*) Why you think it got to be like that? (*He is thoughtful, almost as a child would be.*) Ruth, what is it gets into people ought to be close?

RUTH: I don't know, honey. I think about it a lot.

WALTER: On account of you and me, you mean? The way things are with us. The way something done come down between us.

RUTH: There ain't so much between us, Walter . . . Not when you come to me and try to talk to me. Try to be with me . . . a little even.

WALTER (*total honesty*): Sometimes . . . sometimes . . . I don't even know how to try.

RUTH: Walter —

WALTER: Yes?

RUTH (*coming to him, gently and with misgiving, but coming to him*): Honey . . . life don't have to be like this. I mean sometimes people can do things so that things are better . . . You remember how we used to talk when Travis was born . . . about the way we were going to live . . . the kind of house . . . (*She is stroking his head.*) Well, it's all starting to slip away from us . . .

(*He turns her to him and they look at each other and*

kiss, *tenderly and hungrily. The door opens and Mama enters — Walter breaks away and jumps up. A beat.*)

WALTER: Mama, where have you been?

MAMA: My — them steps is longer than they used to be. Whew! (*She sits down and ignores him.*) How you feeling this evening, Ruth?

(*Ruth shrugs, disturbed at having been interrupted and watching her husband knowingly.*)

WALTER: Mama, where have you been all day?

MAMA (*still ignoring him and leaning on the table and changing to more comfortable shoes*): Where's Travis?

RUTH: I let him go out earlier and he ain't come back yet. Boy, is he going to get it!

WALTER: Mama!

MAMA (*as if she has heard him for the first time*): Yes, son?

WALTER: Where did you go this afternoon?

MAMA: I went downtown to tend to some business that I had to tend to.

WALTER: What kind of business?

MAMA: You know better than to question me like a child, Brother.

WALTER (*rising and bending over the table*): Where were you, Mama? (*Bringing his fists down and shouting.*) Mama, you didn't go do something with that insurance money, something crazy?

(*The front door opens slowly, interrupting him, and Travis peeks his head in, less than hopefully.*)

TRAVIS (*to his mother*): Mama, I —

RUTH: "Mama I" nothing! You're going to get it, boy! Get on in that bedroom and get yourself ready!

TRAVIS: But I —

MAMA: Why don't you all never let the child explain hisself.

RUTH: Keep out of it now, Lena.

(*Mama clamps her lips together, and Ruth advances toward her son menacingly.*)

RUTH: A thousand times I have told you not to go off like that —

MAMA (*holding out her arms to her grandson*): Well — at least let me tell him something. I want him to be the first one to hear . . . Come here, Travis. (*The boy obeys, gladly.*) Travis — (*she takes him by the shoulder and looks into his face*) — you know that money we got in the mail this morning?

TRAVIS: Yes'm —

MAMA: Well — what you think your grandmama gone and done with that money?

TRAVIS: I don't know, Grandmama.

MAMA (*putting her finger on his nose for emphasis*): She went out and she bought you a house! (*The explosion comes from Walter at the end of the revelation and he jumps up and turns away from all of them in a fury. Mama continues, to Travis.*) You glad about the house? It's going to be yours when you get to be a man.

TRAVIS: Yeah — I always wanted to live in a house.

MAMA: All right, gimme some sugar then — (*Travis puts his arms around her neck as she watches her son over the boy's shoulder. Then, to Travis, after the embrace.*) Now when you say your prayers tonight, you thank God and your grandfather — 'cause it was him who give you the house — in his way.

RUTH (*taking the boy from Mama and pushing him toward the bedroom*): Now you get out of here and get ready for your beating.

TRAVIS: Aw, Mama —

RUTH: Get on in there — (*Closing the door behind him and turning radiantly to her mother-in-law.*) So you went and did it!

MAMA (*quietly, looking at her son with pain*): Yes, I did.

RUTH (*raising both arms classically*): PRAISE GOD! (*Looks at Walter a moment, who says nothing. She crosses rapidly to her husband.*) Please, honey — let me be glad . . . you be glad too. (*She has laid her hands on his shoulders, but he shakes himself free of her roughly, without turning to face her.*) Oh, Walter . . . a home . . . a home. (*She comes back to Mama.*) Well — where is it? How big is it? How much it going to cost?

MAMA: Well —

RUTH: When we moving?

MAMA (*smiling at her*): First of the month.

RUTH (*throwing back her head with jubilance*): Praise God!

MAMA (*tentatively, still looking at her son's back turned against her and Ruth*): It's — it's a nice house too . . . (*She cannot help speaking directly to him. An imploring quality in her voice, her manner, makes her almost like a girl now.*) Three bedrooms — nice big one for you and Ruth . . . Me and Beneatha still have to share our room, but Travis have one of his own and (*with difficulty*) I figure if the — new baby — is a boy, we could get one of them double-decker outfits . . . And there's a yard with a little patch of dirt where I could maybe get to grow me a few flowers . . . And a nice big basement . . .

RUTH: Walter honey, be glad —

MAMA (*still to his back, fingering things on the table*): 'Course I don't want to make it sound fancier than it is . . . It's just a plain little old house — but it's made good and solid — and it will be ours. Walter Lee — it makes a difference in a man when he can walk on floors that belong to him . . .

RUTH: Where is it?

MAMA (*frightened at this telling*): Well — well — it's out there in Clybourne Park —

(*Ruth's radiance fades abruptly, and Walter finally turns slowly to face his mother with incredulity and hostility.*)

RUTH: Where?

MAMA (*matter-of-factly*): Four o six Clybourne Street, Clybourne Park.

RUTH: Clybourne Park? Mama, there ain't no colored people living in Clybourne Park.

MAMA (*almost idiotically*): Well, I guess there's going to be some now.

WALTER (*bitterly*): So that's the peace and comfort you went out and bought for us today!

MAMA (*raising her eyes to meet his finally*): Son — I just tried to find the nicest place for the least amount of money for my family.

RUTH (*trying to recover from the shock*): Well — well — 'course I ain't one never been 'fraid of no crackers,° mind you — but — well, wasn't there no other houses nowhere?

MAMA: Them houses they put up for colored in them areas way out all seem to cost twice as much as other houses. I did the best I could.

RUTH (*struck senseless with the news, in its various degrees of goodness and trouble, she sits a moment, her fists propping her chin in thought, and then she starts to rise, bringing her fists down with vigor, the radiance spreading from cheek to cheek again*): Well — well — All I can say is — if this is my time in life — MY TIME — to say good-bye — (*and she builds with momentum as she starts to circle the room with an exuberant, almost tearfully happy release*) — to these Goddamned cracking walls! — (*she pounds the walls*) — and these marching roaches! — (*she wipes at an imaginary army of marching roaches*) — and this cramped little closet which ain't now or never was no kitchen! . . . then I say it loud and good, HALLELUJAH! AND GOOD-BYE MISERY . . . I DON'T NEVER WANT TO SEE YOUR UGLY FACE AGAIN! (*She laughs joyously, having practically destroyed the apartment, and flings her arms up and lets them come down happily, slowly, reflectively, over her abdomen, aware for the first*

---

crackers: White people, often used to refer disparagingly to poor whites.

time perhaps that the life therein pulses with happiness and not despair.) Lena?

MAMA (*moved, watching her happiness*): Yes, honey?

RUTH (*looking off*): Is there — is there a whole lot of sunlight?

MAMA (*understanding*): Yes, child, there's a whole lot of sunlight.

(*Long pause.*)

RUTH (*collecting herself and going to the door of the room Travis is in*): Well — I guess I better see 'bout Travis. (*To Mama.*) Lord, I sure don't feel like whipping nobody today!

(*She exits.*)

MAMA (*the mother and son are left alone now and the mother waits a long time, considering deeply, before she speaks*): Son — you — you understand what I done, don't you? (*Walter is silent and sullen.*) I — I just seen my family falling apart today . . . just falling to pieces in front of my eyes . . . We couldn't of gone on like we was today. We was going backwards 'stead of forwards — talking 'bout killing babies and wishing each other was dead . . . When it gets like that in life — you just got to do something different, push on out and do something bigger . . . (*She waits.*) I wish you say something, son . . . I wish you'd say how deep inside you you think I done the right thing —

WALTER (*crossing slowly to his bedroom door and finally turning there and speaking measuredly*): What you need me to say you done right for? *You* the head of this family. You run our lives like you want to. It was your money and you did what you wanted with it. So what you need for me to say it was all right for? (*Bitterly, to hurt her as deeply as he knows is possible.*) So you butchered up a dream of mine — you — who always talking 'bout your children's dreams . . .

MAMA: Walter Lee —

(*He just closes the door behind him. Mama sits alone, thinking heavily.*)

Scene II

(*Time: Friday night. A few weeks later.*)

(*At rise: Packing crates mark the intention of the family to move. Beneatha and George come in, presumably from an evening out again.*)

GEORGE: O.K. . . . O.K., whatever you say . . . (*They both sit on the couch. He tries to kiss her. She moves away.*) Look, we've had a nice evening; let's not spoil it, huh? . . .

(*He again turns her head and tries to nuzzle in and she turns away from him, not with distaste but with momentary lack of interest; in a mood to pursue what they were talking about.*)

BENEATHA: I'm *trying* to talk to you.

GEORGE: We always talk.

BENEATHA: Yes — and I love to talk.

GEORGE (*exasperated; rising*): I know it and I don't mind it sometimes . . . I want you to cut it out, see — The moody stuff, I mean. I don't like it. You're a nice-looking girl . . . all over. That's all you need, honey, forget the atmosphere. Guys aren't going to go for the atmosphere — they're going to go for what they see. Be glad for that. Drop the Garbo routine. It doesn't go with you. As for myself, I want a nice — (*groping*) — simple (*thoughtfully*) — sophisticated girl . . . not a poet O.K.?

(*He starts to kiss her, she rebuffs him again, and he jumps up.*)

BENEATHA: Why are you angry, George?

GEORGE: Because this is stupid! I don't go out with you to discuss the nature of "quiet desperation" or to hear all about your thoughts — because the world will go on thinking what it thinks regardless —

BENEATHA: Then why read books? Why go to school?

GEORGE (*with artificial patience, counting on his fingers*): It's simple. You read books — to learn facts — to get grades — to pass the course — to get a degree. That's all — it has nothing to do with thoughts.

(*A long pause.*)

BENEATHA: I see. (*He starts to sit.*) Good night, George.

(*George looks at her a little oddly and starts to exit. He meets Mama coming in.*)

GEORGE: Oh — hello, Mrs. Younger.

MAMA: Hello, George, how you feeling?

GEORGE: Fine — fine, how are you?

MAMA: Oh, a little tired. You know them steps can get you after a day's work. You all have a nice time tonight?

GEORGE: Yes — a fine time. A fine time.

MAMA: Well, good night.

GEORGE: Good night. (*He exits. Mama closes the door behind her.*)

MAMA: Hello, honey. What you sitting like that for?

BENEATHA: I'm just sitting.

MAMA: Didn't you have a nice time?

BENEATHA: No.

MAMA: No? What's the matter?

BENEATHA: Mama, George is a fool — honest. (*She rises.*)

MAMA (*Hustling around unloading the packages she has entered with. She stops.*): Is he, baby?

BENEATHA: Yes.

(*Beneatha makes up Travis's bed as she talks.*)

MAMA: You sure?

BENEATHA: Yes.

MAMA: Well — I guess you better not waste your time with no fools.

(*Beneatha looks up at her mother, watching her put groceries in the refrigerator. Finally she gathers up her things and starts into the bedroom. At the door she stops and looks back at her mother.*)

BENEATHA: Mama —

MAMA: Yes, baby —

BENEATHA: Thank you.

MAMA: For what?

BENEATHA: For understanding me this time.

(*She exits quickly and the mother stands, smiling a little, looking at the place where Beneatha just stood. Ruth enters.*)

RUTH: Now don't you fool with any of this stuff, Lena —

MAMA: Oh, I just thought I'd sort a few things out. Is Brother here?

RUTH: Yes.

MAMA (*with concern*): Is he —

RUTH (*reading her eyes*): Yes.

(*Mama is silent and someone knocks on the door. Mama and Ruth exchange weary and knowing glances and Ruth opens it to admit the neighbor, Mrs. Johnson,° who is a rather squeaky wide-eyed lady of no particular age, with a newspaper under her arm.*)

MAMA (*changing her expression to acute delight and a ringing cheerful greeting*): Oh — hello there, Johnson.

JOHNSON (*this is a woman who decided long ago to be enthusiastic about* EVERYTHING *in life and she is inclined to wave her wrist vigorously at the height of her exclamatory comments*): Hello there, yourself! H'you this evening, Ruth?

RUTH (*not much of a deceptive type*): Fine, Mis' Johnson, h'you?

JOHNSON: Fine. (*Reaching out quickly, playfully, and patting Ruth's stomach.*) Ain't you starting to poke out none yet! (*She mugs with delight at the over-familiar remark and her eyes dart around looking at the crates and packing preparation; Mama's face is a cold sheet of endurance.*) Oh, ain't we getting ready round here, though! Yessir! Lookathere! I'm telling you the Youngers is really getting ready to "move on up a little higher!" — Bless God!

MAMA (*a little drily, doubting the total sincerity of the Blesser*): Bless God.

JOHNSON: He's good, ain't He?

MAMA: Oh yes, He's good.

JOHNSON: I mean sometimes He works in mysterious ways . . . but He works, don't He!

MAMA (*the same*): Yes, he does.

JOHNSON: I'm just sooooooo happy for y'all. And this here child — (*about Ruth*) looks like she could just pop open with happiness, don't she. Where's all the rest of the family?

MAMA: Bennie's gone to bed —

JOHNSON: Ain't no . . . (*the implication is pregnancy*) sickness done hit you — I hope . . . ?

MAMA: No — she just tired. She was out this evening.

JOHNSON (*all is a coo, an emphatic coo*): Aw — ain't that lovely. She still going out with the little Murchison boy?

MAMA (*drily*): Ummmm huh.

JOHNSON: That's lovely. You sure got lovely children, Younger. Me and Isaiah talks all the time 'bout what fine children you was blessed with. We sure do.

MAMA: Ruth, give Mis' Johnson a piece of sweet potato pie and some milk.

JOHNSON: Oh honey, I can't stay hardly a minute — I just dropped in to see if there was anything I could do. (*Accepting the food easily.*) I guess y'all seen the news what's all over the colored paper this week . . .

MAMA: No — didn't get mine yet this week.

JOHNSON (*lifting her head and blinking with the spirit of catastrophe*): You mean you ain't read 'bout them colored people that was bombed out their place out there?

(*Ruth straightens with concern and takes the paper and reads it. Johnson notices her and feeds commentary.*)

JOHNSON: Ain't it something how bad these here white folks is getting here in Chicago! Lord, getting so you think you right down in Mississippi! (*With a tremendous and rather insincere sense of melodrama.*) 'Course I thinks it's wonderful how our folks keeps on pushing out. You hear some of these Negroes round here talking 'bout how they don't go where they ain't wanted and all that — but not me, honey! (*This is a lie.*) Wilhemenia

Othella Johnson goes anywhere, any time she feels like it! (*With head movement for emphasis.*) Yes I do! Why if we left it up to these here crackers the poor niggers wouldn't have nothing — (*She clasps her hand over her mouth.*) Oh, I always forgets you don't 'low that word in your house.

MAMA (*quietly, looking at her*): No — I don't 'low it.

JOHNSON (*vigorously again*): Me neither! I was just telling Isaiah yesterday when he come using it in front of me — I said, "Isaiah, it's just like Mis' Younger says all the time —"

MAMA: Don't you want some more pie?

JOHNSON: No — no thank you; this was lovely. I got to get on over home and have my midnight coffee. I hear some people say it don't let them sleep but I finds I can't close my eyes right lessen I done had that laaaast cup of coffee . . . (*She waits. A beat. Undaunted.*) My Good-night coffee, I calls it!

MAMA (*with much eye-rolling and communication between herself and Ruth*): Ruth, why don't you give Mis' Johnson some coffee.

(*Ruth gives Mama an unpleasant look for her kindness.*)

JOHNSON (*accepting the coffee*): Where's Brother tonight?

MAMA: He's lying down.

JOHNSON: Mmmmmmm, he sure gets his beauty rest, don't he? Good-looking man. Sure is a good-looking man! (*Reaching out to pat Ruth's stomach again.*) I guess that's how come we keep on having babies around here. (*She winks at Mama.*) One thing 'bout Brother, he always know how to have a *good* time. And soooooo ambitious! I bet it was his idea y'all moving out to Clybourne Park. Lord — I bet this time next month y'all's names will have been in the papers plenty — (*Holding up her hands to mark off each word of the headline she can see in front of her.*) "NEGROS INVADE CLYBOURNE PARK — BOMBED!"

MAMA (*she and Ruth look at the woman in amazement*): We ain't exactly moving out there to get bombed.

JOHNSON: Oh, honey — you know I'm praying to God every day that don't nothing like that happen! But you have to think of life like it is — and these here Chicago peckerwoods is some baaaad peckerwoods.

MAMA (*wearily*): We done thought about all that Mis' Johnson.

(*Beneatha comes out of the bedroom in her robe and passes through to the bathroom. Mrs. Johnson turns.*)

JOHNSON: Hello there, Bennie!

BENEATHA (*crisply*): Hello, Mrs. Johnson.

JOHNSON: How is school?

BENEATHA (*crisply*): Fine, thank you. (*She goes out.*)

JOHNSON (*insulted*): Getting so she don't have much to say to nobody.

MAMA: The child was on her way to the bathroom.

JOHNSON: I know — but sometimes she act like ain't got time to pass the time of day with nobody ain't been to college. Oh — I ain't criticizing her none. It's just — you know how some of our young people gets when they get a little education. (*Mama and Ruth say nothing, just look at her.*) Yes — well. Well, I guess I better get on home. (*Unmoving.*) 'Course I can understand how she must be proud and everything — being the only one in the family to make something of herself. I know just being a chauffeur ain't never satisfied Brother none. He shouldn't feel like that, though. Ain't nothing wrong with being a chauffeur.

MAMA: There's plenty wrong with it.

JOHNSON: What?

MAMA: Plenty. My husband always said being any kind of a servant wasn't a fit thing for a man to have to be. He always said a man's hands was made to make things, or to turn the earth with — not to drive nobody's car for 'em — or — (*she looks at her own hands*) carry they slop jars. And my boy is just like him — he wasn't meant to wait on nobody.

JOHNSON (*rising, somewhat offended*): Mmmmmmmmm. The Youngers is too much for me! (*She looks around.*) You sure one proud-acting bunch of colored folks. Well — I always thinks like Booker T. Washington said that time — "Education has spoiled many a good plow hand" —

MAMA: Is that what old Booker T. said?

JOHNSON: He sure did.

MAMA: Well, it sounds just like him. The fool.

JOHNSON (*indignantly*): Well — he was one of our great men.

MAMA: Who said so?

JOHNSON (*nonplussed*): You know, me and you ain't never agreed about some things, Lena Younger. I guess I better be going —

RUTH (*quickly*): Good night.

JOHNSON: Good night. Oh — (*Thrusting it at her.*) You can keep the paper! (*With a trill.*) 'Night.

MAMA: Good night, Mis' Johnson.

(*Mrs. Johnson exits.*)

RUTH: If ignorance was gold . . .

MAMA: Shush. Don't talk about folks behind their backs.

RUTH: You do.

MAMA: I'm old and corrupted. (*Beneatha enters.*) You

was rude to Mis' Johnson, Beneatha, and I don't like it at all.

BENEATHA (*at her door*): Mama, if there are two things we, as a people, have got to overcome, one is the Klu Klux Klan — and the other is Mrs. Johnson. (*She exits.*)

MAMA: Smart aleck.

(*The phone rings.*)

RUTH: I'll get it.

MAMA: Lord, ain't this a popular place tonight.

RUTH (*at the phone*): Hello — Just a minute. (*Goes to door.*) Walter, it's Mrs. Arnold. (*Waits. Goes back to the phone. Tense.*) Hello. Yes, this is his wife speaking . . . He's lying down now. Yes . . . well, he'll be in tomorrow. He's been very sick. Yes — I know we should have called, but we were so sure he'd be able to come in today. Yes — yes, I'm very sorry. Yes . . . Thank you very much. (*She hangs up. Walter is standing in the doorway of the bedroom behind her.*) That was Mrs. Arnold.

WALTER (*indifferently*): Was it?

RUTH: She said if you don't come in tomorrow that they are getting a new man . . .

WALTER: Ain't that sad — ain't that crying sad.

RUTH: She said Mr. Arnold has had to take a cab for three days . . . Walter, you ain't been to work for three days! (*This is a revelation to her.*) Where you been, Walter Lee Younger? (*Walter looks at her and starts to laugh.*) You're going to lose your job.

WALTER: That's right . . . (*He turns on the radio.*)

RUTH: Oh, Walter, and with your mother working like a dog every day —

(*A steamy, deep blues pours into the room.*)

WALTER: That's sad too — Everything is sad.

MAMA: What you been doing for these three days, son?

WALTER: Mama — you don't know all the things a man what got leisure can find to do in this city . . . What's this — Friday night? Well — Wednesday I borrowed Willy Harris's car and I went for a drive . . . just me and myself and I drove and drove . . . Way out . . . way past South Chicago, and I parked the car and I sat and looked at the steel mills all day long. I just sat in the car and looked at them big black chimneys for hours. Then I drove back and I went to the Green Hat. (*Pause.*) And Thursday — Thursday I borrowed the car again and I got in it and I pointed it the other way and I drove the other way — for hours — way, way up to Wisconsin, and I looked at the farms. I just drove and looked at the farms. Then I drove back and I went to the Green Hat. (*Pause.*) And today — today I didn't get the car. Today I just

walked. All over the Southside. And I looked at the Negroes and they looked at me and finally I just sat down on the curb at Thirty-ninth and South Parkway and I just sat there and watched the Negroes go by. And then I went to the Green Hat. You all sad? You all depressed? And you know where I am going right now —

(*Ruth goes out quietly.*)

MAMA: Oh, Big Walter, is this the harvest of our days?

WALTER: You know what I like about the Green Hat? I like this little cat they got there who blows a sax . . . He blows. He talks to me. He ain't but 'bout five feet tall and he's got a conked head and his eyes is always closed and he's all music —

MAMA (*rising and getting some papers out of her handbag*): Walter —

WALTER: And there's this other guy who plays the piano . . . and they got a sound. I mean they can work on some music . . . They got the best little combo in the world in the Green Hat . . . You can just sit there and drink and listen to them three men play and you realize that don't nothing matter worth a damn, but just being there —

MAMA: I've helped do it to you, haven't I, son? Walter I been wrong.

WALTER: Naw — you ain't never been wrong about nothing, Mama.

MAMA: Listen to me, now. I say I been wrong, son. That I been doing to you what the rest of the world been doing to you. (*She turns off the radio.*) Walter — (*She stops and he looks up slowly at her and she meets his eyes pleadingly.*) What you ain't never understood is that I ain't got nothing, don't own nothing, ain't never really wanted nothing that wasn't for you. There ain't nothing as precious to me . . . There ain't nothing worth holding on to, money, dreams, nothing else — if it means — if it means it's going to destroy my boy. (*She takes an envelope out of her handbag and puts it in front of him and he watches her without speaking or moving.*) I paid the man thirty-five hundred dollars down on the house. That leaves sixty-five hundred dollars. Monday morning I want you to take this money and take three thousand dollars and put it in a savings account for Beneatha's medical schooling. The rest you put in a checking account — with your name on it. And from now on any penny that come out of it or that go in it is for you to look after. For you to decide. (*She drops her hands a little helplessly.*) It ain't much, but it's all I got in the world and I'm putting it in your hands. I'm telling you to be the head of this family from now on like you supposed to be.

WALTER (*stares at the money*): You trust me like that, Mama?

MAMA: I ain't never stop trusting you. Like I ain't never stop loving you.

(*She goes out, and Walter sits looking at the money on the table. Finally, in a decisive gesture, he gets up and, in mingled joy and desperation, picks up the money. At the same moment, Travis enters for bed.*)

TRAVIS: What's the matter, Daddy? You drunk?

WALTER (*sweetly, more sweetly than we have ever known him*): No, Daddy ain't drunk. Daddy ain't going to never be drunk again . . .

TRAVIS: Well, good night, Daddy.

(*The father has come from behind the couch and leans over, embracing his son.*)

WALTER: Son, I feel like talking to you tonight.

TRAVIS: About what?

WALTER: Oh, about a lot of things. About you and what kind of man you going to be when you grow up. . . . Son — son, what do you want to be when you grow up?

TRAVIS: A bus driver.

WALTER (*laughing a little*): A what? Man, that ain't nothing to want to be!

TRAVIS: Why not?

WALTER: 'Cause, man — it ain't big enough — you know what I mean.

TRAVIS: I don't know then. I can't make up my mind. Sometimes Mama asks me that too. And sometimes when I tell her I just want to be like you — she says she don't want me to be like that and sometimes she says she does. . . .

WALTER (*gathering him up in his arms*): You know what, Travis? In seven years you going to be seventeen years old. And things is going to be very different with us in seven years Travis. . . . One day when you are seventeen I'll come home — home from my office downtown somewhere —

TRAVIS: You don't work in no office, Daddy.

WALTER: No — but after tonight. After what your daddy gonna do tonight, there's going to be offices — a whole lot of offices. . . .

TRAVIS: What you gonna do tonight, Daddy?

WALTER: You wouldn't understand yet, son, but your daddy's gonna make a transaction . . . a business transaction that's going to change our lives. . . . That's how come one day when you 'bout seventeen years old I'll come home and I'll be pretty tired, you know what I mean, after a day of conferences and secretaries getting things wrong the way they do . . . 'cause an executive's life is hell man — (*The more he talks the farther away he*

gets.*) And I'll pull the car up on the driveway . . . just a plain black Chrysler, I think, with white walls — no — black tires. More elegant. Rich people don't have to be flashy . . . though I'll have to get something a little sportier for Ruth — maybe a Cadillac convertible to do her shopping in. . . . And I'll come up the steps to the house and the gardener will be clipping away at the hedges and he'll say, "Good evening, Mr. Younger." And I'll say, "Hello, Jefferson, how are you this evening?" And I'll go inside and Ruth will come downstairs and meet me at the door and we'll kiss each other and she'll take my arm and we'll go up to your room to see you sitting on the floor with the catalogues of all the great schools in America around you. . . . All the great schools in the world! And — and I'll say, all right son — it's your seventeenth birthday, what is it you've decided? . . . Just tell me where you want to go to school and you'll *go*. Just tell me, what it is you want to be — and you'll *be* it. . . . Whatever you want to be — Yessir! (*He holds his arms open for Travis.*) You just name it, son . . . (*Travis leaps into them*) and I hand you the world!

(*Walter's voice has risen in pitch and hysterical promise and on the last line he lifts Travis high.*)

Scene III

(*Time: Saturday, moving day, one week later.*)

(*Before the curtain rises, Ruth's voice, a strident, dramatic church alto, cuts through the silence.*)

(*It is, in the darkness, a triumphant surge, a penetrating statement of expectation: "Oh, Lord, I don't feel no ways tired! Children, oh, glory hallelujah!"*)

(*As the curtain rises we see that Ruth is alone in the living room, finishing up the family's packing. It is moving day. She is nailing crates and tying cartons. Beneatha enters, carrying a guitar case, and watches her exuberant sister-in-law.*)

RUTH: Hey!

BENEATHA (*putting away the case*): Hi.

RUTH (*pointing at a package*): Honey — look in that package there and see what I found on sale this morning at the South Center. (*Ruth gets up and moves to the package and draws out some curtains.*) Lookahere — hand-turned hems!

BENEATHA: How do you know the window size out there?

RUTH (*who hadn't thought of that*): Oh — Well, they bound to fit something in the whole house. Anyhow, they was too good a bargain to pass up. (*Ruth slaps her head, suddenly remembering some-*

thing.) Oh, Bennie — I meant to put a special note on that carton over there. That's your mama's good china and she wants 'em to be very careful with it.

BENEATHA: I'll do it.

(*Beneatha finds a piece of paper and starts to draw large letters on it.*)

RUTH: You know what I'm going to do soon as I get in that new house?

BENEATHA: What?

RUTH: Honey — I'm going to run me a tub of water up to here . . . (*With her fingers practically up to her nostrils.*) And I'm going to get in it — and I am going to sit . . . and sit . . . and sit in that hot water and the first person who knocks to tell *me* to hurry up and come out —

BENEATHA: Gets shot at sunrise.

RUTH (*laughing happily*): You said it, sister! (*Noticing how large Beneatha is absent-mindedly making the note.*) Honey, they ain't going to read that from no airplane.

BENEATHA (*laughing herself*): I guess I always think things have more emphasis if they are big, somehow.

RUTH (*looking up at her and smiling*): You and your brother seem to have that as a philosophy of life. Lord, that man — done changed so 'round here. You know — you know what we did last night? Me and Walter Lee?

BENEATHA: What?

RUTH (*smiling to herself*): We went to the movies. (*Looking at Beneatha to see if she understands.*) We went to the movies. You know the last time me and Walter went to the movies together?

BENEATHA: No.

RUTH: Me neither. That's how long it been. (*Smiling again.*) But we went last night. The picture wasn't much good, but that didn't seem to matter. We went — and we held hands.

BENEATHA: Oh, Lord!

RUTH: We held hands — and you know what?

BENEATHA: What?

RUTH: When we come out of the show it was late and dark and all the stores and things was closed up . . . and it was kind of chilly and there wasn't many people on the streets . . . and we was still holding hands, me and Walter.

BENEATHA: You're killing me.

(*Walter enters with a large package. His happiness is deep in him; he cannot keep still with his newfound exuberance. He is singing and wiggling and snapping his fingers. He puts his package in a corner and puts a phonograph record which he has brought in with*

him, *on the record player. As the music, soulful and sensuous, comes up he dances over to Ruth and tries to get her to dance with him. She gives in at last to his raunchiness and in a fit of giggling allows herself to be drawn into his mood. They dip and she melts into his arms in a classic, body-melding "slow drag."*)

BENEATHA (*regarding them a long time as they dance, then drawing in her breath for a deeply exaggerated comment which she does not particularly mean*): Talk about — olddddddddddd — fashionedddddddd — Negroes!

WALTER (*stopping momentarily*): What kind of Negroes?

(*He says this in fun. He is not angry with her today, nor with anyone. He starts to dance with his wife again.*)

BENEATHA: Old-fashioned.

WALTER (*as he dances with Ruth*): You know, when these *New Negroes* have their convention — (*pointing at his sister*) — that is going to be the chairman of the Committee on Unending Agitation. (*He goes on dancing, then stops.*) Race, race, race! . . . Girl, I do believe you are the first person in the history of the entire human race to successfully brainwash yourself. (*Beneatha breaks up and he goes on dancing. He stops again, enjoying his tease.*) Damn, even the N double A C P takes a holiday sometimes! (*Beneatha and Ruth laugh. He dances with Ruth some more and starts to laugh and stops and pantomimes someone over an operating table.*) I can just see that chick someday looking down at some poor cat on an operating table and before she starts to slice him, she says . . . (*pulling his sleeves back maliciously*) "By the way, what are your views on civil rights down there? . . ."

(*He laughs at her again and starts to dance happily. The bell sounds.*)

BENEATHA: Sticks and stones may break my bones but . . . words will never hurt me!

(*Beneatha goes to the door and opens it as Walter and Ruth go on with the clowning. Beneatha is somewhat surprised to see a quiet-looking middle-aged white man in a business suit holding his hat and a briefcase in his hand and consulting a small piece of paper.*)

MAN: Uh — how do you do, miss. I am looking for a Mrs. — (*he looks at the slip of paper*) Mrs. Lena Younger? (*He stops short, struck dumb at the sight of the oblivious Walter and Ruth.*)

BENEATHA (*smoothing her hair with slight embarrassment*): Oh — yes, that's my mother. Excuse me.

(*She closes the door and turns to quiet the other two.*) Ruth! Brother! (*Enunciating precisely but soundlessly: "There's a white man at the door!" They stop dancing, Ruth cuts off the phonograph, Beneatha opens the door. The man casts a curious quick glance at all of them.*) Uh — come in please.

MAN (*coming in*): Thank you.

BENEATHA: My mother isn't here just now. Is it business?

MAN: Yes . . . well, of a sort.

WALTER (*freely, the Man of the House*): Have a seat. I'm Mrs. Younger's son. I look after most of her business matters.

(*Ruth and Beneatha exchange amused glances.*)

MAN (*regarding Walter, and sitting*): Well — My name is Karl Lindner . . .

WALTER (*stretching out his hand*): Walter Younger. This is my wife — (*Ruth nods politely*) — and my sister.

LINDNER: How do you do.

WALTER (*amiably, as he sits himself easily on a chair, leaning forward on his knees with interest and looking expectantly into the newcomer's face*): What can we do for you, Mr. Lindner!

LINDNER (*some minor shuffling of the hat and briefcase on his knees*): Well — I am a representative of the Clybourne Park Improvement Association —

WALTER (*pointing*): Why don't you sit your things on the floor?

LINDNER: Oh — yes. Thank you. (*He slides the briefcase and hat under the chair.*) And as I was saying — I am from the Clybourne Park Improvement Association and we have had it brought to our attention at the last meeting that you people — or at least your mother — has bought a piece of residential property at — (*he digs for the slip of paper again*) — four o six Clybourne Street . . .

WALTER: That's right. Care for something to drink? Ruth, get Mr. Lindner a beer.

LINDNER (*upset for some reason*): Oh — no, really. I mean thank you very much, but no thank you.

RUTH: (*innocently*): Some coffee?

LINDNER: Thank you, nothing at all.

(*Beneatha is watching the man carefully.*)

LINDNER: Well, I don't know how much you folks know about our organization. (*He is a gentle man; thoughtful and somewhat labored in his manner.*) It is one of these community organizations set up to look after — oh, you know, things like block upkeep and special projects and we also have what we call our New Neighbors Orientation Committee . . .

BENEATHA (*drily*): Yes — and what do they do?

LINDNER (*turning a little to her and then returning the main force to Walter*): Well — it's what you might call a sort of welcoming committee, I guess. I mean they, we — I'm the chairman of the committee — go around and see the new people who move into the neighborhood and sort of give them the low-down on the way we do things out in Clybourne Park.

BENEATHA (*with appreciation of the two meanings, which escape Ruth and Walter*): Un-huh.

LINDNER: And we also have the category of what the association calls — (*he looks elsewhere*) — uh — special community problems . . .

BENEATHA: Yes — and what are some of those?

WALTER: Girl, let the man talk.

LINDNER (*with understated relief*): Thank you. I would sort of like to explain this thing in my own way. I mean I want to explain to you in a certain way.

WALTER: Go ahead.

LINDNER: Yes. Well. I'm going to try to get right to the point. I'm sure we'll all appreciate that in the long run.

BENEATHA: Yes.

WALTER: Be still now!

LINDNER: Well —

RUTH (*still innocently*): Would you like another chair — you don't look comfortable.

LINDNER (*more frustrated than annoyed*): No, thank you very much. Please. Well — to get right to the point I — (*a great breath, and he is off at last*) I am sure you people must be aware of some of the incidents which have happened in various parts of the city when colored people have moved into certain areas — (*Beneatha exhales heavily and starts tossing a piece of fruit up and down in the air.*) Well — because we have what I think is going to be a unique type of organization in American community life — not only do we deplore that kind of thing — but we are trying to do something about it. (*Beneatha stops tossing and turns with a new and quizzical interest to the man.*) We feel — (*gaining confidence in his mission because of the interest in the faces of the people he is talking to*) — we feel that most of the trouble in this world, when you come right down to it — (*he hits his knee for emphasis*) — most of the trouble exists because people just don't sit down and talk to each other.

RUTH (*nodding as she might in church, pleased with the remark*): You can say that again, mister.

LINDNER (*more encouraged by such affirmation*): That we don't try hard enough in this world to understand the other fellow's problem. The other guy's point of view.

RUTH: Now that's right.

(*Beneatha and Walter merely watch and listen with genuine interest.*)

LINDNER: Yes — that's the way we feel out in Clybourne Park. And that's why I was elected to come here this afternoon and talk to you people. Friendly like, you know, the way people should talk to each other and see if we couldn't find some way to work this thing out. As I say, the whole business is a matter of *caring* about the other fellow. Anybody can see that you are a nice family of folks, hard-working and honest I'm sure. (*Beneatha frowns slightly, quizzically, her head tilted regarding him.*) Today everybody knows what it means to be on the outside of *something*. And of course, there is always somebody who is out to take advantage of people who don't always understand.

WALTER: What do you mean?

LINDNER: Well — you see our community is made up of people who've worked hard as the dickens for years to build up that little community. They're not rich and fancy people; just hard-working, honest people who don't really have much but those little homes and a dream of the kind of community they want to raise their children in. Now, I don't say we are perfect and there is a lot wrong in some of the things they want. But you've got to admit that a man, right or wrong, has the right to want to have the neighborhood he lives in a certain kind of way. And at the moment the overwhelming majority of our people out there feel that people get along better, take more of a common interest in the life of the community, when they share a common background. I want you to believe me when I tell you that race prejudice simply doesn't enter into it. It is a matter of the people of Clybourne Park believing, rightly or wrongly, as I say, that for the happiness of all concerned that our Negro families are happier when they live in their *own* communities.

BENEATHA (*with a grand and bitter gesture*): This, friends, is the Welcoming Committee!

WALTER (*dumfounded, looking at Lindner*): Is this what you came marching all the way over here to tell us?

LINDNER: Well, now we've been having a fine conversation. I hope you'll hear me all the way through.

WALTER (*tightly*): Go ahead, man.

LINDNER: You see — in the face of all the things I have said, we are prepared to make your family a very generous offer . . .

BENEATHA: Thirty pieces and not a coin less!

WALTER: Yeah!

LINDNER (*putting on his glasses and drawing a form out of the briefcase*): Our association is prepared, through the collective effort of our people, to buy the house from you at a financial gain to your family.

RUTH: Lord have mercy, ain't this the living gall!

WALTER: All right, you through?

LINDNER: Well, I want to give you the exact terms of the financial arrangement —

WALTER: We don't want to hear no exact terms of no arrangements. I want to know if you got any more to tell us 'bout getting together?

LINDNER (*taking off his glasses*): Well — I don't suppose that you feel . . .

WALTER: Never mind how I feel — you got any more to say 'bout how people ought to sit down and talk to each other? . . . Get out of my house, man.

(*He turns his back and walks to the door.*)

LINDNER (*looking around at the hostile faces and reaching and assembling his hat and briefcase*): Well — I don't understand why you people are reacting this way. What do you think you are going to gain by moving into a neighborhood where you just aren't wanted and where some elements — well — people can get awful worked up when they feel that their whole way of life and everything they've ever worked for is threatened.

WALTER: Get out.

LINDNER (*at the door, holding a small card*): Well — I'm sorry it went like this.

WALTER: Get out.

LINDNER (*almost sadly regarding Walter*): You just can't force people to change their hearts, son.

(*He turns and puts his card on a table and exits. Walter pushes the door to with stinging hatred, and stands looking at it. Ruth just sits and Beneatha just stands. They say nothing. Mama and Travis enter.*)

MAMA: Well — this all the packing got done since I left out of here this morning. I testify before God that my children got all the energy of the *dead*! What time the moving men due?

BENEATHA: Four o'clock. You had a caller, Mama.

(*She is smiling, teasingly.*)

MAMA: Sure enough — who?

BENEATHA (*her arms folded saucily*): The Welcoming Committee.

(*Walter and Ruth giggle.*)

MAMA (*innocently*): Who?

BENEATHA: The Welcoming Committee. They said they're sure going to be glad to see you when you get there.

WALTER (*devilishly*): Yeah, they said they can't hardly wait to see your face.

(*Laughter.*)

MAMA (*sensing their facetiousness*): What's the matter with you all?

WALTER: Ain't nothing the matter with us. We just telling you 'bout the gentleman who came to see you this afternoon. From the Clybourne Park Improvement Association.

MAMA: What he want?

RUTH (*in the same mood as Beneatha and Walter*): To welcome you, honey.

WALTER: He said they can't hardly wait. He said the one thing they don't have, that they just *dying* to have out there is a fine family of fine colored people! (*To Ruth and Beneatha.*) Ain't that right!

RUTH (*mockingly*): Yeah! He left his card —

BENEATHA (*handing card to Mama*): In case.

(*Mama reads and throws it on the floor — understanding and looking off as she draws her chair up to the table on which she has put her plant and some sticks and some cord.*)

MAMA: Father, give us strength. (*Knowingly — and without fun.*) Did he threaten us?

BENEATHA: Oh — Mama — they don't do it like that anymore. He talked Brotherhood. He said everybody ought to learn how to sit down and hate each other with good Christian fellowship.

(*She and Walter shake hands to ridicule the remark.*)

MAMA (*sadly*): Lord, protect us . . .

RUTH: You should hear the money those folks raised to buy the house from us. All we paid and then some.

BENEATHA: What they think we going to do — eat 'em?

RUTH: No, honey, marry 'em.

MAMA (*shaking her head*): Lord, Lord, Lord . . .

RUTH: Well — that's the way the crackers crumble. (*A beat.*) Joke.

BENEATHA (*laughingly noticing what her mother is doing*): Mama, what are you doing?

MAMA: Fixing my plant so it won't get hurt none on the way . . .

BENEATHA: Mama, you going to take *that* to the new house?

MAMA: Un-huh —

BENEATHA: That raggedy-looking old thing?

MAMA (*stopping and looking at her*): It expresses ME!

RUTH (*with delight, to Beneatha*): So there, Miss Thing!

(*Walter comes to Mama suddenly and bends down behind her and squeezes her in his arms with all his strength. She is overwhelmed by the suddenness of it and, though delighted, her manner is like that of Ruth and Travis.*)

MAMA: Look out now, boy! You make me mess up my thing here!

WALTER (*his face lit, he slips down on his knees beside her, his arms still about her*): Mama . . . you know what it means to climb up in the chariot?

MAMA (*gruffly, very happy*): Get on away from me now . . .

RUTH (*near the gift-wrapped package, trying to catch Walter's eye*): Psst —

WALTER: What the old song say, Mama . . .

RUTH: Walter — Now?

(*She is pointing at the package.*)

WALTER (*speaking the lines, sweetly, playfully, in his mother's face*): I got wings . . . you got wings . . . All God's Children got wings . . .

MAMA: Boy — get out of my face and do some work . . .

WALTER: When I get to heaven gonna put on my wings,
Gonna fly all over God's heaven . . .

BENEATHA (*teasingly, from across the room*): Everybody talking 'bout heaven ain't going there!

WALTER (*to Ruth, who is carrying the box across to them*): I don't know, you think we ought to give her that . . . Seems to me she ain't been very appreciative around here.

MAMA (*eyeing the box, which is obviously a gift*): What is that?

WALTER (*taking it from Ruth and putting it on the table in front of Mama*): Well — what you all think? Should we give it to her?

RUTH: Oh — she was pretty good today.

MAMA: I'll good you —

(*She turns her eyes to the box again.*)

BENEATHA: Open it, Mama.

(*She stands up, looks at it, turns, and looks at all of them, and then presses her hands together and does not open the package.*)

WALTER (*sweetly*): Open it, Mama. It's for you. (*Mama looks in his eyes. It is the first present in her life without its being Christmas. Slowly she opens her package and lifts out, one by one, a brand-new sparkling set of gardening tools. Walter continues, prodding.*) Ruth made up the note — read it . . .

MAMA (*picking up the card and adjusting her glasses*): "To our own Mrs. Miniver — Love from Brother, Ruth and Beneatha." Ain't that lovely . . .

TRAVIS (*tugging at his father's sleeve*): Daddy, can I give her mine now?

WALTER: All right, son. (*Travis flies to get his gift.*)

MAMA: Now I don't have to use my knives and forks no more . . .

WALTER: Travis didn't want to go in with the rest of us, Mama. He got his own. (*Somewhat amused.*) We don't know what it is . . .

TRAVIS (*racing back in the room with a large hatbox and putting it in front of his grandmother*): Here!

MAMA: Lord have mercy, baby. You done gone and bought your grandmother a hat?

TRAVIS (*very proud*): Open it!

(*She does and lifts out an elaborate, but very elaborate, wide gardening hat, and all the adults break up at the sight of it.*)

RUTH: Travis, honey, what is that?

TRAVIS (*who thinks it is beautiful and appropriate*): It's a gardening hat! Like the ladies always have on in the magazines when they work in their gardens.

BENEATHA (*giggling fiercely*): Travis — we were trying to make Mama Mrs. Miniver — not Scarlett O'Hara!

MAMA (*indignantly*): What's the matter with you all! This here is a beautiful hat! (*Absurdly.*) I always wanted me one just like it!

(*She pops it on her head to prove it to her grandson, and the hat is ludicrous and considerably oversized.*)

RUTH: Hot dog! Go, Mama!

WALTER (*doubled over with laughter*): I'm sorry, Mama — but you look like you ready to go out and chop you some cotton sure enough!

(*They all laugh except Mama, out of deference to Travis's feelings.*)

MAMA (*gathering the boy up to her*): Bless your heart — this is the prettiest hat I ever owned — (*Walter, Ruth, and Beneatha chime in — noisily, festively, and insincerely congratulating Travis on his gift.*) What are we all standing around here for? We ain't finished packin' yet. Bennie, you ain't packed one book.

(*The bell rings.*)

BENEATHA: That couldn't be the movers . . . it's not hardly two good yet —

(*Beneatha goes into her room. Mama starts for door.*)

WALTER (*turning, stiffening*): Wait — wait — I'll get it.

(*He stands and looks at the door.*)

MAMA: You expecting company, son?

WALTER (*just looking at the door*): Yeah — yeah . . .

(*Mama looks at Ruth, and they exchange innocent and unfrightened glances.*)

MAMA (*not understanding*): Well, let them in, son.

BENEATHA (*from her room*): We need some more string.

MAMA: Travis — you run to the hardware and get me some string cord.

(*Mama goes out and Walter turns and looks at Ruth. Travis goes to a dish for money.*)

RUTH: Why don't you answer the door, man?

WALTER (*suddenly bounding across the floor to embrace her*): 'Cause sometimes it hard to let the future begin! (*Stooping down in her face.*)
I got wings! You got wings!
All God's children got wings!

(*He crosses to the door and throws it open. Standing there is a very slight little man in a not too prosperous business suit and with haunted frightened eyes and a hat pulled down tightly, brim up, around his forehead. Travis passes between the men and exits. Walter leans deep in the man's face, still in his jubilance.*) When I get to heaven gonna put on my wings, Gonna fly all over God's heaven . . .
(*The little man just stares at him.*) Heaven —
(*Suddenly he stops and looks past the little man into the empty hallway.*) Where's Willy, man?

BOBO: He ain't with me.

WALTER (*not disturbed*): Oh — come on in. You know my wife.

BOBO (*dumbly, taking off his hat*): Yes — h'you, Miss Ruth.

RUTH (*quietly, a mood apart from her husband already, seeing Bobo*): Hello, Bobo.

WALTER: You right on time today . . . Right on time. That's the way! (*He slaps Bobo on his back.*) Sit down . . . lemme hear.

(*Ruth stands stiffly and quietly in back of them, as though somehow she senses death, her eyes fixed on her husband.*)

BOBO (*his frightened eyes on the floor, his hat in his hands*): Could I please get a drink of water, before I tell you about it, Walter Lee?

(*Walter does not take his eyes off the man. Ruth goes blindly to the tap and gets a glass of water and brings it to Bobo.*)

WALTER: There ain't nothing wrong, is there?

BOBO: Lemme tell you —

WALTER: Man — didn't nothing go wrong?

BOBO: Lemme tell you — Walter Lee. (*Looking at Ruth and talking to her more than to Walter.*) You know how it was. I got to tell you how it was. I mean first I got to tell you how it was all the way . . . I mean about the money I put in, Walter Lee . . .

WALTER (*with taut agitation now*): What about the money you put in?

BOBO: Well — it wasn't much as we told you — me and Willy — (*He stops.*) I'm sorry, Walter. I got a bad feeling about it. I got a real bad feeling about it . . .

WALTER: Man, what you telling me about all this for? . . . Tell me what happened in Springfield . . .

BOBO: Springfield.

RUTH (*like a dead woman*): What was supposed to happen in Springfield?

BOBO (*to her*): This deal that me and Walter went into with Willy — Me and Willy was going to go down to Springfield and spread some money 'round so's we wouldn't have to wait so long for the liquor license . . . That's what we were going to do. Everybody said that was the way you had to do, you understand, Miss Ruth?

WALTER: Man — what happened down there?

BOBO (*a pitiful man, near tears*): I'm trying to tell you, Walter.

WALTER (*screaming at him suddenly*): THEN TELL ME, GODDAMMIT . . . WHAT'S THE MATTER WITH YOU?

BOBO: Man . . . I didn't go to no Springfield, yesterday.

WALTER (*halted, life hanging in the moment*): Why not?

BOBO (*the long way, the hard way to tell*): 'Cause I didn't have no reasons to . . .

WALTER: Man, what are you talking about!

BOBO: I'm talking about the fact that when I got to the train station yesterday morning — eight o'clock like we planned . . . Man — *Willy didn't never show up.*

WALTER: Why . . . where was he . . . where is he?

BOBO: That's what I'm trying to tell you . . . I don't know . . . I waited six hours . . . I called his house . . . and I waited . . . six hours . . . I waited in that train station six hours . . . (*Breaking into tears.*) That was all the extra money I had in the world . . . (*Looking up at Walter with the tears running down his face.*) Man, Willy is gone.

WALTER: Gone, what you mean Willy is gone? Gone where? You mean he went by himself. You mean he went off to Springfield by himself — to take care of getting the license — (*Turns and looks anxiously at Ruth.*) You mean maybe he didn't want too many people in on the business down there? (*Looks to Ruth again, as before.*) You know Willy got his own ways. (*Looks back to Bobo.*) Maybe you was late yesterday and he just went on down there without you. Maybe — maybe — he's been callin' you at home tryin' to tell you what hap-

pened or something. Maybe — maybe — he just got sick. He's somewhere — he's got to be somewhere. We just got to find him — me and you got to find him. (*Grabs Bobo senselessly by the collar and starts to shake him.*) We got to!

BOBO (*in sudden angry, frightened agony*): What's the matter with you, Walter! *When a cat take off with your money he don't leave you no road maps!*

WALTER (*turning madly, as though he is looking for Willy in the very room*): Willy! . . . Willy . . . don't do it . . . Please don't do it . . . Man, not with that money . . . Man, please, not with that money . . . Oh, God . . . Don't let it be true . . . (*He is wandering around, crying out for Willy and looking for him or perhaps for help from God.*) Man . . . I trusted you . . . Man, I put my life in your hands . . . (*He starts to crumple down on the floor as Ruth just covers her face in horror. Mama opens the door and comes into the room, with Beneatha behind her.*) Man . . . (*He starts to pound the floor with his fists, sobbing wildly.*) THAT MONEY IS MADE OUT MY FATHER'S FLESH ——

BOBO (*standing over him helplessly*): I'm sorry, Walter . . . (*Only Walter's sobs reply. Bobo puts on his hat.*) I had my life staked on this deal, too . . .

(*He exits.*)

MAMA (*to Walter*): Son — (*She goes to him, bends down to him, talks to his bent head.*) Son . . . Is it gone? Son, I gave you sixty-five hundred dollars. Is it gone? All of it? Beneatha's money too?

WALTER (*lifting his head slowly*): Mama . . . I never . . . went to the bank at all . . .

MAMA (*not wanting to believe him*): You mean . . . your sister's school money . . . you used that too . . . Walter? . . .

WALTER: Yessss! All of it . . . It's all gone . . .

(*There is total silence. Ruth stands with her face covered with her hands; Beneatha leans forlornly against a wall, fingering a piece of red ribbon from the mother's gift. Mama stops and looks at her son without recognition and then, quite without thinking about it, starts to beat him senselessly in the face. Beneatha goes to them and stops it.*)

BENEATHA: Mama!

(*Mama stops and looks at both of her children and rises slowly and wanders vaguely, aimlessly away from them.*)

MAMA: I seen . . . him . . . night after night . . . come in . . . and look at that rug . . . and then look at me . . . the red showing in his eyes . . . the veins moving in his head . . . I seen him grow thin and old before he was forty . . . working and working and working like somebody's old horse . . . killing himself . . . and you — you give it all away in a day — (*She raises her arms to strike him again.*)

BENEATHA: Mama —

MAMA: Oh, God . . . (*She looks up to Him.*) Look down here — and show me the strength.

BENEATHA: Mama —

MAMA (*folding over*): Strength . . .

BENEATHA (*plaintively*): Mama . . .

MAMA: Strength!

ACT III

(*An hour later.*)

(*At curtain, there is a sullen light of gloom in the living room, gray light not unlike that which began the first scene of act I. At left we can see Walter within his room, alone with himself. He is stretched out on the bed, his shirt out and open, his arms under his head. He does not smoke, he does not cry out, he merely lies there, looking up at the ceiling, much as if he were alone in the world.*)

(*In the living room Beneatha sits at the table, still surrounded by the now almost ominous packing crates. She sits looking off. We feel that this is a mood struck perhaps an hour before, and it lingers now, full of the empty sound of profound disappointment. We see on a line from her brother's bedroom the sameness of their attitudes. Presently the bell rings and Beneatha rises without ambition or interest in answering. It is Asagai, smiling broadly, striding into the room with energy and happy expectation and conversation.*)

ASAGAI: I came over . . . I had some free time. I thought I might help with the packing. Ah, I like the look of packing crates! A household in preparation for a journey! It depresses some people . . . but for me . . . it is another feeling. Something full of the flow of life, do you understand? Movement, progress . . . It makes me think of Africa.

BENEATHA: Africa!

ASAGAI: What kind of a mood is this? Have I told you how deeply you move me?

BENEATHA: He gave away the money, Asagai . . .

ASAGAI: Who gave away what money?

BENEATHA: The insurance money. My brother gave it away.

ASAGAI: Gave it away?

BENEATHA: He made an investment! With a man even Travis wouldn't have trusted with his most worn-out marbles.

ASAGAI: And it's gone?

BENEATHA: Gone!

ASAGAI: I'm very sorry . . . And you, now?

BENEATHA: Me? . . . Me? . . . Me, I'm nothing . . . Me. When I was very small . . . we used to take our sleds out in the wintertime and the only hills we had were the ice-covered stone steps of some houses down the street. And we used to fill them in with snow and make them smooth and slide down them all day . . . and it was very dangerous, you know . . . far too steep . . . and sure enough one day a kid named Rufus came down too fast and hit the sidewalk and we saw his face just split open right there in front of us . . . And I remember standing there looking at his bloody open face thinking that was the end of Rufus. But the ambulance came and they took him to the hospital and they fixed the broken bones and they sewed it all up . . . and the next time I saw Rufus he just had a little line down the middle of his face . . . I never got over that . . .

ASAGAI: What?

BENEATHA: That that was what one person could do for another, fix him up — sew up the problem, make him all right again. That was the most marvelous thing in the world . . . I wanted to do that. I always thought it was the one concrete thing in the world that a human being could do. Fix up the sick, you know — and make them whole again. This was truly being God . . .

ASAGAI: You wanted to be God?

BENEATHA: No — I wanted to cure. It used to be so important to me. I wanted to cure. It used to matter. I used to care. I mean about people and how their bodies hurt . . .

ASAGAI: And you've stopped caring?

BENEATHA: Yes — I think so.

ASAGAI: Why?

BENEATHA (*bitterly*): Because it doesn't seem deep enough, close enough to what ails mankind! It was a child's way of seeing things — or an idealist's.

ASAGAI: Children see things very well sometimes — and idealists even better.

BENEATHA: I know that's what you think. Because you are still where I left off. You with all your talk and dreams about Africa! You still think you can patch up the world. Cure the Great Sore of Colonialism — (*loftily, mocking it*) with the Penicillin of Independence —!

ASAGAI: Yes!

BENEATHA: Independence *and then what?* What about all the crooks and thieves and just plain idiots who will come into power and steal and plunder the same as before — only now they will be black and do it in the name of the new Independence — WHAT ABOUT THEM?!

ASAGAI: That will be the problem for another time. First we must get there.

BENEATHA: And where does it end?

ASAGAI: End? Who even spoke of an end? To life? To living?

BENEATHA: An end to misery! To stupidity! Don't you see there isn't any real progress, Asagai, there is only one large circle that we march in, around and around, each of us with our own little picture in front of us — our own little mirage that we think is the future.

ASAGAI: That is the mistake.

BENEATHA: What?

ASAGAI: What you just said — about the circle. It isn't a circle — it is simply a long line — as in geometry, you know, one that reaches into infinity. And because we cannot see the end — we also cannot see how it changes. And it is very odd but those who see the changes — who dream, who will not give up — are called idealists . . . and those who see only the circle — we call *them* the "realists"!

BENEATHA: Asagai, while I was sleeping in that bed in there, people went out and took the future right out of my hands! And nobody asked me, nobody consulted me — they just went out and changed my life!

ASAGAI: Was it your money?

BENEATHA: What?

ASAGAI: Was it your money he gave away?

BENEATHA: It belonged to all of us.

ASAGAI: But did you earn it? Would you have had it at all if your father had not died?

BENEATHA: No.

ASAGAI: Then isn't there something wrong in a house — in a world — where all dreams, good or bad, must depend on the death of a man? I never thought to see *you* like this, Alaiyo. You! Your brother made a mistake and you are grateful to him so that now you can give up the ailing human race on account of it! You talk about what good is struggle, what good is anything! Where are we all going and why are we bothering!

BENEATHA: AND YOU CANNOT ANSWER IT!

ASAGAI (*shouting over her*): I LIVE THE ANSWER! (*Pause.*) In my village at home it is the exceptional man who can even read a newspaper . . . or who ever sees a book at all. I will go home and much of what I will have to say will seem strange to the people of my village. But I will teach and work and things will happen, slowly and swiftly. At times it will seem that nothing changes at all . . . and then again the sudden dramatic events which make history leap into the future. And then quiet again. Retrogression even. Guns, murder, revolution. And I even will have moments when I wonder if the quiet was not better than all that death and hatred. But I will look about my village at the illiteracy and disease and ignorance and I will not wonder long. And perhaps . . . perhaps I will be a great man . . . I mean perhaps I will hold on to the substance of truth and find my way always with the right course . . . and perhaps for it I will be butchered in my bed some night by the servants of empire . . .

BENEATHA: *The martyr!*

ASAGAI (*he smiles*): . . . or perhaps I shall live to be a very old man, respected and esteemed in my new nation . . . And perhaps I shall hold office and this is what I'm trying to tell you, Alaiyo: Perhaps the things I believe now for my country will be wrong and outmoded, and I will not understand and do terrible things to have things my way or merely to keep my power. Don't you see that there will be young men and women — not British soldiers then, but my own black countrymen — to step out of the shadows some evening and slit my then useless throat? Don't you see they have always been there . . . that they always will be. And that such a thing as my own death will be an advance? They who might kill me even . . . actually replenish all that I was.

BENEATHA: Oh, Asagai, I know all that.

ASAGAI: Good! Then stop moaning and groaning and tell me what you plan to do.

BENEATHA: Do?

ASAGAI: I have a bit of a suggestion.

BENEATHA: What?

ASAGAI (*rather quietly for him*): That when it is all over — that you come home with me —

BENEATHA (*staring at him and crossing away with exasperation*): Oh — Asagai — at this moment you decide to be romantic!

ASAGAI (*quickly understanding the misunderstanding*): My dear, young creature of the New World — I do not mean across the city — I mean across the ocean: home — to Africa.

BENEATHA (*slowly understanding and turning to him with murmured amazement*): To Africa?

ASAGAI: Yes! . . . (*Smiling and lifting his arms playfully.*) Three hundred years later the African Prince rose up out of the seas and swept the maiden back across the middle passage over which her ancestors had come —

BENEATHA (*unable to play*): To — to Nigeria?

ASAGAI: Nigeria. Home. (*Coming to her with genuine romantic flippancy.*) I will show you our mountains and our stars; and give you cool drinks from gourds and teach you the old songs and the ways of our people — and, in time, we will pretend that — (*very softly*) — you have only been away for a day. Say that you'll come — (*He swings her around and takes her full in his arms in a kiss which proceeds to passion.*)

BENEATHA (*pulling away suddenly*): You're getting me all mixed up —

ASAGAI: Why?

BENEATHA: Too many things — too many things have happened today. I must sit down and think. I don't know what I feel about anything right this minute.

(*She promptly sits down and props her chin on her fist.*)

ASAGAI (*charmed*): All right, I shall leave you. No — don't get up. (*Touching her, gently, sweetly.*) Just sit awhile and think . . . Never be afraid to sit awhile and think. (*He goes to door and looks at her.*) How often I have looked at you and said, "Ah — so this is what the New World hath finally wrought . . ."

(*He exits. Beneatha sits on alone. Presently Walter enters from his room and starts to rummage through things, feverishly looking for something. She looks up and turns in her seat.*)

BENEATHA (*hissingly*): Yes — just look at what the New World hath wrought! . . . Just look! (*She gestures with bitter disgust.*) There he is! *Monsieur le petit bourgeois noir*° — himself! There he is — Symbol of a Rising Class! Entrepreneur! Titan° of the system! (*Walter ignores her completely and continues frantically and destructively looking for something and hurling things to floor and tearing things out of their place in his search. Beneatha ignores the eccentricity of his actions and goes on with the monologue of insult.*) Did you dream of yachts on Lake Michigan, Brother? Did you see yourself on that Great Day sitting down at the Conference Table, surrounded by all the mighty bald-headed men in America? All halted, waiting, breathless, waiting for your pronouncements on industry? Waiting for you — Chairman of the Board! (*Walter finds what he is looking for — a small piece of white paper — and pushes it in his pocket and puts on his coat and rushes out without ever having looked at her. She shouts after him.*) I look at you and I see the final triumph of stupidity in the world!

(*The door slams and she returns to just sitting again. Ruth comes quickly out of Mama's room.*)

RUTH: Who was that?

BENEATHA: Your husband.

RUTH: Where did he go?

BENEATHA: Who knows — maybe he has an appointment at U.S. Steel.

RUTH (*anxiously, with frightened eyes*): You didn't say nothing bad to him, did you?

BENEATHA: Bad? Say anything bad to him? No — I told him he was a sweet boy and full of dreams and everything is strictly peachy keen, as the ofay° kids say!

(*Mama enters from her bedroom. She is lost, vague, trying to catch hold, to make some sense of her former command of the world, but it still eludes her. A sense of waste overwhelms her gait; a measure of apology rides on her shoulders. She goes to her plant, which has remained on the table, looks at it, picks it up and takes it to the window sill and sits it outside, and she stands and looks at it a long moment. Then she closes the window, straightens her body with effort, and turns around to her children.*)

MAMA: Well — ain't it a mess in here, though? (*A false cheerfulness, a beginning of something.*) I guess we all better stop moping around and get some work done. All this unpacking and everything we got to do. (*Ruth raises her head slowly in response to the sense of the line; and Beneatha in similar manner turns very slowly to look at her mother.*) One of you all better call the moving people and tell 'em not to come.

RUTH: Tell 'em not to come?

MAMA: Of course, baby. Ain't no need in 'em coming all the way here and having to go back. They charges for that too. (*She sits down, fingers to her brow, thinking.*) Lord, ever since I was a little girl, I always remembers people saying, "Lena — Lena Eggleston, you aims too high all the time. You needs to slow down and see life a little more like it is. Just slow down some." That's what they always used to say down home — "Lord, that Lena Eggleston is a high-minded thing. She'll get her due one day!"

RUTH: No, Lena . . .

MAMA: Me and Big Walter just didn't never learn right.

RUTH: Lena, no! We gotta go. Bennie — tell her . . . (*She rises and crosses to Beneatha with her arms outstretched. Beneatha doesn't respond.*) Tell her we can still move . . . the notes ain't but a hundred and twenty-five a month. We got four grown people in this house — we can work . . .

MAMA (*to herself*): Just aimed too high all the time —

Monsieur . . . noir: Mr. Black Middle Class.
Titan: Person of great power; originally, a god.

ofay: White person, usually used disparagingly.

RUTH (*turning and going to Mama fast — the words pouring out with urgency and desperation*): Lena — I'll work . . . I'll work twenty hours a day in all the kitchens in Chicago . . . I'll strap my baby on my back if I have to and scrub all the floors in America and wash all the sheets in America if I have to — but we got to MOVE! We got to get OUT OF HERE!!

(*Mama reaches out absently and pats Ruth's hand.*)

MAMA: No — I sees things differently now. Been thinking 'bout some of the things we could do to fix this place up some. I seen a second-hand bureau over on Maxwell Street just the other day that could fit right there. (*She points to where the new furniture might go. Ruth wanders away from her.*) Would need some new handles on it and then a little varnish and it look like something brand-new. And — we can put up them new curtains in the kitchen . . . Why this place be looking fine. Cheer us all up so that we forget trouble ever come . . . (*To Ruth.*) And you could get some nice screens to put up in your room round the baby's bassinet . . . (*She looks at both of them, pleadingly.*) Sometimes you just got to know when to give up some things . . . and hold on to what you got. . . .

(*Walter enters from the outside, looking spent and leaning against the door, his coat hanging from him.*)

MAMA: Where you been, son?

WALTER (*breathing hard*): Made a call.

MAMA: To who, son?

WALTER: To The Man. (*He heads for his room.*)

MAMA: What man, baby?

WALTER (*stops in the door*): The Man, Mama. Don't you know who The Man is?

RUTH: Walter Lee?

WALTER: *The Man.* Like the guys in the streets say — The Man. Captain Boss — Mistuh Charley . . . Old Cap'n Please Mr. Bossman . . .

BENEATHA (*suddenly*): Lindner!

WALTER: That's right! That's good. I told him to come right over.

BENEATHA (*fiercely, understanding*): For what? What do you want to see him for!

WALTER (*looking at his sister*): We going to do business with him.

MAMA: What you talking 'bout, son?

WALTER: Talking 'bout life, Mama. You all always telling me to see life like it is. Well — I laid in there on my back today . . . and I figured it out. Life just like it is. Who gets and who don't get. (*He sits down with his coat on and laughs.*) Mama, you know it's all divided up. Life is. Sure enough. Between the takers and the "tooken." (*He laughs.*)

I've figured it out finally. (*He looks around at them.*) Yeah. Some of us always getting "tooken." (*He laughs.*) People like Willy Harris, they don't never get "tooken." And you know why the rest of us do? 'Cause we all mixed up. Mixed up bad. We get to looking 'round for the right and the wrong; and we worry about it and cry about it and stay up nights trying to figure out 'bout the wrong and the right of things all the time . . . And all the time, man, them takers is out there operating, just taking and taking. Willy Harris? Shoot — Willy Harris don't even count. He don't even count in the big scheme of things. But I'll say one thing for old Willy Harris . . . he's taught me something. He's taught me to keep my eye on what counts in this world. Yeah — (*Shouting out a little.*) Thanks, Willy!

RUTH: What did you call that man for, Walter Lee?

WALTER: Called him to tell him to come on over to the show. Gonna put on a show for the man. Just what he wants to see. You see, Mama, the man came here today and he told us that them people out there where you want us to move — well they so upset they willing to pay us *not* to move! (*He laughs again.*) And — and oh, Mama — you would of been proud of the way me and Ruth and Bennie acted. We told him to get out . . . Lord have mercy! We told the man to get out! Oh, we was some proud folks this afternoon, yeah. (*He lights a cigarette.*) We were still full of that old-time stuff . . .

RUTH (*coming toward him slowly*): You talking 'bout taking them people's money to keep us from moving in that house?

WALTER: I ain't just talking 'bout it, baby — I'm telling you that's what's going to happen!

BENEATHA: Oh, God! Where is the bottom! Where is the real honest-to-God bottom so he can't go any farther!

WALTER: See — that's the old stuff. You and that boy that was here today. You all want everybody to carry a flag and a spear and sing some marching songs, huh? You wanna spend your life looking into things and trying to find the right and the wrong part, huh? Yeah. You know what's going to happen to that boy someday — he'll find himself sitting in a dungeon, locked in forever — and the takers will have the key! Forget it, baby! There ain't no causes — there ain't nothing but taking in this world, and he who takes most is smartest — and it don't make a damn bit of difference *how*.

MAMA: You making something inside me cry, son. Some awful pain inside me.

WALTER: Don't cry, Mama. Understand. That white man is going to walk in that door able to write checks for more money than we ever had. It's important to him and I'm going to help him . . . I'm going to put on the show, Mama.

MAMA: Son — I come from five generations of people who was slaves and sharecroppers — but ain't nobody in my family never let nobody pay 'em no money that was a way of telling us we wasn't fit to walk the earth. We ain't never been that poor. (*Raising her eyes and looking at him.*) We ain't never been that — dead inside.

BENEATHA: Well — we are dead now. All the talk about dreams and sunlight that goes on in this house. It's all dead now.

WALTER: What's the matter with you all! I didn't make this world! It was give to me this way! Hell, yes, I want me some yachts someday! Yes, I want to hang some real pearls 'round my wife's neck. Ain't she supposed to wear no pearls? Somebody tell me — tell me, who decides which women is suppose to wear pearls in this world. I tell you I am a *man* — and I think my wife should wear some pearls in this world!

(*This last line hangs a good while and Walter begins to move about the room. The word "Man" has penetrated his consciousness; he mumbles it to himself repeatedly between strange agitated pauses as he moves about.*)

MAMA: Baby, how you going to feel on the inside?

WALTER: Fine! . . . Going to feel fine . . . a man . . .

MAMA: You won't have nothing left then, Walter Lee.

WALTER (*coming to her*): I'm going to feel fine, Mama. I'm going to look that son-of-a-bitch in the eyes and say — (*he falters*) — and say, "All right, Mr. Lindner — (*he falters even more*) — that's *your* neighborhood out there! You got the right to keep it like you want! You got the right to have it like you want! Just write the check and — the house is yours." And — and I am going to say — (*His voice almost breaks.*) "And you — you people just put the money in my hand and you won't have to live next to this bunch of stinking niggers! . . ." (*He straightens up and moves away from his mother, walking around the room.*) And maybe — maybe I'll just get down on my black knees . . . (*He does so; Ruth and Bennie and Mama watch him in frozen horror.*) "Captain, Mistuh, Bossman — (*Groveling and grinning and wringing his hands in profoundly anguished imitation of the slow-witted movie stereotype.*) A-hee-hee-hee! Oh, yassuh boss! Yasssssuh! Great white — (*voice breaking, he forces himself to go on*) — Father, just gi' ussen de money, fo' God's sake, and we's — we's ain't gwine come out deh and dirty up yo' white folks neighborhood . . ." (*He breaks down completely.*) And I'll feel fine! Fine! FINE! (*He gets up and goes into the bedroom.*)

BENEATHA: That is not a man. That is nothing but a toothless rat.

MAMA: Yes — death done come in this here house. (*She is nodding, slowly, reflectively.*) Done come walking in my house on the lips of my children. You what supposed to be my beginning again. You — what supposed to be my harvest. (*To Beneatha.*) You — you mourning your brother?

BENEATHA: He's no brother of mine.

MAMA: What you say?

BENEATHA: I said that that individual in that room is no brother of mine.

MAMA: That's what I thought you said. You feeling like you better than he is today? (*Beneatha does not answer.*) Yes? What you tell him a minute ago? That he wasn't a man? Yes? You give him up for me? You done wrote his epitaph too — like the rest of the world? Well, who give you the privilege?

BENEATHA: Be on my side for once! You saw what he just did, Mama! You saw him — down on his knees. Wasn't it you who taught me to despise any man who would do that? Do what he's going to do?

MAMA: Yes — I taught you that. Me and your daddy. But I thought I taught you something else too . . . I thought I taught you to love him.

BENEATHA: Love him? There is nothing left to love.

MAMA: There is *always* something left to love. And if you ain't learned that, you ain't learned nothing. (*Looking at her.*) Have you cried for that boy today? I don't mean for yourself and for the family 'cause we lost the money. I mean for him: what he been through and what it done to him. Child, when do you think is the time to love somebody the most? When they done good and made things easy for everybody? Well then, you ain't through learning — because that ain't the time at all. It's when he's at his lowest and can't believe in hisself 'cause the world done whipped him so! When you starts measuring somebody, measure him right, child, measure him right. Make sure you done taken into account what hills and valleys he come through before he got to wherever he is.

(*Travis bursts into the room at the end of the speech, leaving the door open.*)

TRAVIS: Grandmama — the moving men are downstairs! The truck just pulled up.

MAMA (*turning and looking at him*): Are they, baby? They downstairs?

(*She sighs and sits. Lindner appears in the doorway. He peers in and knocks lightly, to gain attention, and comes in. All turn to look at him.*)

LINDNER (*hat and briefcase in hand*): Uh — hello . . .

(*Ruth crosses mechanically to the bedroom door and opens it and lets it swing open freely and slowly as the lights come up on Walter within, still in his coat, sitting at the far corner of the room. He looks up and out through the room to Lindner.*)

RUTH: He's here.

(*A long minute passes and Walter slowly gets up.*)

LINDNER (*coming to the table with efficiency, putting his briefcase on the table and starting to unfold papers and unscrew fountain pens*): Well, I certainly was glad to hear from you people. (*Walter has begun the trek out of the room, slowly and awkwardly, rather like a small boy, passing the back of his sleeve across his mouth from time to time.*) Life can really be so much simpler than people let it be most of the time. Well — with whom do I negotiate? You, Mrs. Younger, or your son here? (*Mama sits with her hands folded on her lap and her eyes closed as Walter advances. Travis goes closer to Lindner and looks at the papers curiously.*) Just some official papers, sonny.

RUTH: Travis, you go downstairs —

MAMA (*opening her eyes and looking into Walter's*): No, Travis, you stay right here. And you make him understand what you doing, Walter Lee. You teach him good. Like Willy Harris taught you. You show where our five generations done come to. (*Walter looks from her to the boy, who grins at him innocently.*) Go ahead, son — (*She folds her hands and closes her eyes.*) Go ahead.

WALTER (*at last crosses to Lindner, who is reviewing the contract*): Well, Mr. Lindner. (*Beneatha turns away.*) We called you — (*there is a profound, simple groping quality in his speech*) — because, well, me and my family (*he looks around and shifts from one foot to the other*) Well — we are very plain people . . .

LINDNER: Yes —

WALTER: I mean — I have worked as a chauffeur most of my life — and my wife here, she does domestic work in people's kitchens. So does my mother. I mean — we are plain people . . .

LINDNER: Yes, Mr. Younger —

WALTER (*really like a small boy, looking down at his shoes and then up at the man*): And — uh — well, my father, well, he was a laborer most of his life. . . .

LINDNER (*absolutely confused*): Uh, yes — yes, I understand. (*He turns back to the contract.*)

WALTER (*a beat; staring at him*): And my father — (*With sudden intensity.*) My father almost *beat a man to death* once because this man called him a bad name or something, you know what I mean?

LINDNER (*looking up, frozen*): No, no, I'm afraid I don't —

WALTER (*A beat. The tension hangs; then Walter steps back from it.*): Yeah. Well — what I mean is that we come from people who had a lot of *pride.* I mean — we are very proud people. And that's my sister over there and she's going to be a doctor — and we are very proud —

LINDNER: Well — I am sure that is very nice, but —

WALTER: What I am telling you is that we called you over here to tell you that we are very proud and that this — (*Signaling to Travis.*) Travis, come here. (*Travis crosses and Walter draws him before him facing the man.*) This is my son, and he makes the sixth generation of our family in this country. And we have all thought about your offer —

LINDNER: Well, good . . . good —

WALTER: And we have decided to move into our house because my father — my father — he earned it for us brick by brick. (*Mama has her eyes closed and is rocking back and forth as though she were in church, with her head nodding the Amen yes.*) We don't want to make no trouble for nobody or fight no causes, and we will try to be good neighbors. And that's *all* we got to say about that. (*He looks the man absolutely in the eyes.*) We don't want your money. (*He turns and walks away.*)

LINDNER (*looking around at all of them*): I take it then — that you have decided to occupy . . .

BENEATHA: That's what the man said.

LINDNER (*to Mama in her reverie*): Then I would like to appeal to you, Mrs. Younger. You are older and wiser and understand things better I am sure . . .

MAMA: I am afraid you don't understand. My son said we was going to move and there ain't nothing left for me to say. (*Briskly.*) You know how these young folks is nowadays, mister. Can't do a thing with 'em! (*As he opens his mouth, she rises.*) Goodbye.

LINDNER (*folding up his materials*): Well — if you are that final about it . . . there is nothing left for me to say. (*He finishes, almost ignored by the family, who are concentrating on Walter Lee. At the door Lindner halts and looks around.*) I sure hope you people know what you're getting into.

(*He shakes his head and exits.*)

RUTH (*looking around and coming to life*): Well, for God's sake — if the moving men are here — LET'S GET THE HELL OUT OF HERE!

MAMA (*into action*): Ain't it the truth! Look at all this here mess. Ruth, put Travis's good jacket on him . . . Walter Lee, fix your tie and tuck your shirt in, you look like somebody's hoodlum! Lord have mercy, where is my plant? (*She flies to get it amid the general bustling of the family, who are deliberately trying to ignore the nobility of the past moment.*) You all start on down . . . Travis child, don't go empty-handed . . . Ruth, where did I put that box with my skillets in it? I want to be in charge of it myself . . . I'm going to make us the biggest dinner we ever ate tonight . . . Beneatha, what's the matter with them stockings? Pull them things up, girl . . .

(*The family starts to file out as two moving men appear and begin to carry out the heavier pieces of furniture, bumping into the family as they move about.*)

BENEATHA: Mama, Asagai asked me to marry him today and go to Africa —
MAMA (*in the middle of her getting-ready activity*): He did? You ain't old enough to marry nobody — (*Seeing the moving men lifting one of her chairs precariously.*) Darling, that ain't no bale of cotton, please handle it so we can sit in it again! I had that chair twenty-five years . . .

(*The movers sigh with exasperation and go on with their work.*)

BENEATHA (*girlishly and unreasonably trying to pursue the conversation*): To go to Africa, Mama — be a doctor in Africa . . .
MAMA (*distracted*): Yes, baby —
WALTER: *Africa!* What he want you to go to Africa for?
BENEATHA: To practice there . . .
WALTER: Girl, if you don't get all them silly ideas out your head! You better marry yourself a man with some loot . . .

BENEATHA (*angrily, precisely as in the first scene of the play*): What have you got to do with who I marry!
WALTER: Plenty. Now I think George Murchison —
BENEATHA: *George Murchison!* I wouldn't marry him if he was Adam and I was Eve!

(*Walter and Beneatha go out yelling at each other vigorously and the anger is loud and real till their voices diminish. Ruth stands at the door and turns to Mama and smiles knowingly.*)

MAMA (*fixing her hat at last*): Yeah — they something all right, my children . . .
RUTH: Yeah — they're something. Let's go, Lena.
MAMA (*stalling, starting to look around at the house*): Yes — I'm coming. Ruth —
RUTH: Yes?
MAMA (*quietly, woman to woman*): He finally come into his manhood today, didn't he? Kind of like a rainbow after the rain . . .
RUTH (*biting her lip lest her own pride explode in front of Mama*): Yes, Lena.

(*Walter's voice calls for them raucously.*)

WALTER (*offstage*): Y'all come on! These people charges by the hour you know!
MAMA (*waving Ruth out vaguely*): All right, honey — go on down. I be down directly.

(*Ruth hesitates, then exits. Mama stands, at last alone in the living room, her plant on the table before her as the lights start to come down. She looks around at all the walls and ceilings and suddenly, despite herself, while the children call below, a great heaving thing rises in her and she puts her fist to her mouth to stifle it, takes a final desperate look, pulls her coat about her, pats her hat, and goes out. The lights dim down. The door opens and she comes back in, grabs her plant, and goes out for the last time.*)

COMMENTARY

Brooks Atkinson (1894–1984)
REVIEW OF *A RAISIN IN THE SUN*   *1959*

It is clear from this review that Atkinson felt the "craftsmanship" of the play could have been more polished, but it is also clear that he was struck by the honesty of the entire enterprise. His praise for Sidney Poitier, who played Walter Lee Younger, and his praise for the director Lloyd Richards emphasize the eloquence and directness of their work.

In *A Raisin in the Sun,* which opened at the Ethel Barrymore last evening, Lorraine Hansberry touched on some serious problems. No doubt, her feelings about them are as strong as any one's.

But she has not tipped her play to prove one thing or another. The play is honest. She has told the inner as well as the outer truth about a Negro family in the southside of Chicago at the present time. Since the performance is also honest and since Sidney Poitier is a candid actor, *A Raisin in the Sun* has vigor as well as veracity and is likely to destroy the complacency of any one who sees it.

The family consists of a firm-minded widow, her daughter, her restless son and his wife and son. The mother has brought up her family in a tenement that is small, battered but personable. All the mother wants is that her children adhere to the code of honor and self-respect that she inherited from her parents.

The son is dreaming of success in a business deal. And the daughter, who is race-conscious, wants to become a physician and heal the wounds of her people. After a long delay the widow receives $10,000 as the premium on her husband's life insurance. The money projects the family into a series of situations that test their individual characters.

What the situations are does not matter at the moment. For *A Raisin in the Sun* is a play about human beings who want, on the one hand, to preserve their family pride and, on the other hand, to break out of the poverty that seems to be their fate. Not having any axe to grind, Miss Hansberry has a wide range of topics to write about — some of them hilarious, some of them painful in the extreme.

You might, in fact, regard *A Raisin in the Sun* as a Negro *The Cherry Orchard*. Although the social scale of the characters is different, the knowledge of how character is controlled by environment is much the same, and the alternation of humor and pathos is similar.

If there are occasional crudities in the craftsmanship, they are redeemed by the honesty of the writing. And also by the rousing honesty of the stage work. For Lloyd Richards has selected an admirable cast and directed a bold and stirring performance.

Mr. Poitier is a remarkable actor with enormous power that is always under control. Cast as the restless son, he vividly communicates the tumult of a high-strung young man. He is as eloquent when he has nothing to say as when he has

1257

a pungent line to speak. He can convey devious processes of thought as graphically as he can clown and dance.

As the matriarch, Claudia McNeil gives a heroic performance. Although the character is simple, Miss McNeil gives it nobility of spirit. Diana Sands's amusing portrait of the overintellectualized daughter; Ivan Dixon's quiet, sagacious student from Nigeria; Ruby Dee's young wife burdened with problems; Louis Gossett's supercilious suitor; John Fiedler's timid white man, who speaks sanctimonious platitudes — bring variety and excitement to a first-rate performance.

All the crises and comic sequences take place inside Ralph Alswang's set, which depicts both the poverty and the taste of the family. Like the play, it is honest. That is Miss Hansberry's personal contribution to an explosive situation in which simple honesty is the most difficult thing in the world. And also the most illuminating.

Contemporary Drama

Experimentation

The experimentation in drama in the first half of the twentieth century has continued in contemporary drama. The achievements of Tennessee Williams, Arthur Miller, Samuel Beckett, and other mid-century playwrights encouraged later playwrights to experiment more daringly. Mixing media such as film, video, opera, rock, and other music with live actors is still an option for playwrights at the end of the twentieth century; however, most contemporary plays celebrated by critics and audiences have been relatively traditional. They build on the achievement of nineteenth-century realism and twentieth-century expressionism.

Harold Pinter's distinctive style, developed in the late 1950s and early 1960s, is connected with some of the absurdist experiments in drama. His dialogue is acerbic, repetitive, sometimes apparently aimless. However, he is able to produce intense emotional situations, such as that in *The Dumb Waiter* (1957), in which two "hit men" wait for instructions in a basement room. *The Caretaker* (1959) and *The Homecoming* (1965), his first commercial successes, established him as a major figure in modern theater. He has also been important as a screenwriter of such films as *The Quiller Memorandum* (1966), *The French Lieutenant's Woman* (1981), and *The Handmaid's Tale* (1990). *Betrayal* (1978) is one of his most recent full-length plays. His experiments with time and sequence in that play have inspired other playwrights to experiment with the backward movement of action.

Most of the interesting experimental theater was done in groups such as Richard Schechner's Performance Group, which created what Schechner called ENVIRONMENTAL THEATER in New York City in the late 1960s, and Jerzy Grotowski's Polish Laboratory Theatre in Wroclaw, Poland, during the same period. Ensembles like the Bread and Puppet Theatre, San Francisco Mime Troupe, and El Teatro Campesino on the West Coast combined a radical political message with theatrical experimentation. The work of these groups is effective primarily at the level of performance; their texts are not representative of their impact on audiences.

Theater of Cruelty

The ensembles of the 1960s and 1970s were strongly influenced by the work of Antonin Artaud (1896–1948), French actor, director, and a theorist of theater. In creating what came to be known as the THEATER OF CRUELTY, he insisted on removing the comforting distance between actors and audience. Thus the audience was involved in a direct, virtually physical fashion with the dramatic action. Artaud designed theater to be a total experience — a sensational spectacle that did not depend on coherent plot or development. He concentrated on what he called a total theater that emphasized movement, gesture, music, sound, light and other nonverbal elements to intensify the experience.

Artaud's manifestos collected in a work called *The Theater and Its Double* (1938) inspired some of the most important theater practitioners working today, including Peter Brook and Robert Wilson, among others. Artaud's notion of a "serious" theater is at the root of his influence:

> Our long habit of seeking diversion has made us forget the idea of a serious theater, which, overturning all our preconceptions, inspires us with the fiery magnetism of its images and acts upon us like a spiritual therapeutics whose touch can never be forgotten.
>
> Everything that acts is a cruelty. It is upon this idea of extreme action, pushed beyond all limits, that theater must be rebuilt.

Artaud compared the theater artist he envisioned to a victim "burnt at the stake, signaling through the flames."

Environmental Theater

Richard Schechner's most famous production, based on Euripides' *The Bacchae,* was *Dionysus in 69* (1968), in which Pentheus is torn to pieces in an impassioned frenzy. Part of the point of Schechner's production was to inspire the audience so much that they would take to the stage, becoming indistinguishable from the actors. *Dionysus in 69* was an effort to draw on the same spiritual energies tapped by Greek drama by connecting with the feasts of Dionysus, god of wine and ecstasy. The play was a spontaneous and partly improvised performance piece rather than a text meant to be read. At one point the audience and actors disrobed in a simulation of a Greek religious orgy and Schechner's goal of involving audience and actors in a pagan ritual was realized night after night during the run.

In a similar way Julian Beck and Judith Malina's Living Theatre maintained a special relationship with the audience. Beck's plays were designed to break down the absolutes of dramatic space and audience space by having the actors roam through the audience and interact apparently at random with audience members. *Paradise Now* (1968) is his best-known play. Like Schechner's *Dionysus in 69*, it was essentially a performance piece. Certain segments were improvised; therefore, as a reading text, it has relatively little power.

"Poor Theater"

Jerzy Grotowski called his work "poor theater" because it was meant to contrast with the "rich theater" of the commercial stage, with its expensive lighting, decorated stages, rich costumes, numerous props, and elaborate settings. Grotowski's Laboratory Theatre, begun in 1959, relied on preexisting texts but interpreted them broadly through a total reconception of their meaning. For example, Grotowski's *Akropolis* (1962; revised frequently from 1963 to 1975) adapted an older Polish drama by Stanislaw Wyspiański (1904) and reset it in modern times in Auschwitz with the actors, dressed in ragged sackcloth prison uniforms, looking wretched and starving. At the end of the play the prisoners follow a headless puppet-corpse, Christ, into an afterlife. They march in an eerie ritual procession offstage into the waiting prison camp ovens.

Grotowski's theater has been influential worldwide. When the Polish government clamped down on the Solidarity° movement in the late 1970s, Grotowski left Poland. After 1970 Grotowski shifted his focus from public performances to small, intense group workshops and, more recently, to the ritual performances of cultures from all over the world. The first phase of his work with the Laboratory Theatre has remained the most influential. One of his actors, Richard Cieslak, traveled widely training people in Grotowski's methods.

Theater of Images

Robert Wilson experimented in the 1970s, 1980s, and 1990s with repetitive narratives that sometimes take eight hours to perform. His multimedia dramas involve huge casts and ordinarily cover an immense historic range (Figure 10). One of his most extraordinary successes was *Einstein on the Beach* (1976), an opera written in collaboration with composer Philip Glass. Eight hours long, it was originally produced in a conventional theater, but it uses dramatic techniques that involve extensive patterns of repetition, the creation of enigmatic and evocative images, and characters who are cartoonlike caricatures of historical people. The overall effect is hypnotic; one of the points of Wilson's work seems to be to induce a trancelike state in his audience. In 1994 Wilson produced a monologue version of *Hamlet* which received some acclaim.

New Ensembles and Gay and Lesbian Theater

Some of the most energetic theater of the period beginning in the 1960s has come from groups who have been excluded at times from representation in mainstream theater. Gays, lesbians, and some black groups have been virtually ignored by commercial theater and as a result have formed their own collectives and groups.

The Ridiculous Theatrical Company, founded by Charles Ludlam

Solidarity: A labor organizing movement in Communist Poland led by Lech Walesa.

Figure 10. Multimedia effects in Robert Wilson's *CIVIL warS*.

(1940–1987) in 1969, produced a formidable body of work rooted in the homosexual community of New York. Its influence spread to many parts of the world. One of Ludlam's catchphrases was "plays without the stink of art." His plays were often ridiculously funny. *Bluebeard* (1970), for example, focused on creating a third gender by inventing a third genital. *Camille* (1973), starring Ludlam himself in the title role, hilariously spoofed not only Dumas's play but most of the "Hallmark card" conventions about romantic love. A gifted female impersonator, Ludlam played Hedda Gabler at the American Ibsen Theatre in Pittsburgh. The Ridiculous Theatrical Company continues Ludlam's tradition, with his partner Everett Quinton producing Ludlam's plays as well as new plays in his tradition. One reason for the development of gay theater in the United States and Great Britain in the 1960s was the decriminalization of homosexuality beginning in 1967 in Boston. Depiction of homosexual love onstage waited even longer, until the Gay Workshop's plays in London beginning in 1976.

Lesbian theatrical groups have sprung up in the United States and Great Britain. They often merge with women's theater groups and deal with issues such as male violence, societal restrictions on women, and women's opportunities. A number of important collectives, such as the Rhode Island Women's Theater and At the Foot of the Mountain in Minneapolis treated general women's issues in the 1970s. Groups such as Medusa's Revenge (founded 1976) and Atlanta's Red Dyke Theater (1974) were more centered on lesbian experience. These last two groups disbanded after a few years of successful productions. Megan Terry's Omaha Magic Theater, founded with Joanne Schmidman, has been a long-lasting theater focusing on women's issues. Other groups such as Spiderwoman, consisting of three Native American sisters, and the highly successful Split Britches consider Cafe WOW in New York's East Village to be the home of lesbian theater. Gay and lesbian theater groups have often been concerned with erasing stereotypes while also celebrating gay and lesbian lifestyles. Plays that once may have been thought appropriate only for such groups — such as Martin Sherman's (b. 1938) *Bent* (1977) and Larry Kramer's (b. 1936) *The Normal Heart* (1985) — are now shown in theaters worldwide.

Many of the most-praised recent plays have addressed the issues of AIDS and its ravaging of the gay community. The first openly gay play was Mart Crowley's *The Boys in the Band* (1968), a popular success produced just after the repeal of a New York law prohibiting homosexuality from being represented on stage. Harvey Fierstein's *Torch Song Trilogy* (1982) was named best play of the year and appeared several years later on television. *As Is* by William M. Hoffman (1985) has been described by Don Shewey as the "best gay play anyone has written on AIDS yet." Tony Kushner dazzled New York with *Angels in America Part One: Millennium Approaches* (1992) and *Part Two: Perestroika* (1992). This two-part drama approached the problems of gay life in America both on a personal and a public, political level. The plays are called a "fantasia" and use a free-form, nonrealistic style of presentation.

Important women playwrights have made their mark in contemporary theater, with plays such as María Irene Fornés's *Fefu and Her Friends* (1977), a sprawling play featuring women in roles traditionally reserved for men. It has become a cult classic, with many productions in regional theaters. Her *The Conduct of Life* (1985) is a cruel parody of macho values in a Latin American dictatorship. It won an Obie Award for best play of the year. Caryl Churchill has been a dominant figure in British drama since the first production of *Cloud Nine* (1979), a drama that critiques colonialism and gender stereotyping. *Top Girls* (1982) is one of her most successful plays. It centers on an employment agency for women but has as its premise the introduction of famous women from the past of several cultures. It is a powerful feminist statement. *Fen* (1983), *Serious Money* (1987), and *The Skriker* (1994) have solidified her reputation as an experimental, powerful dramatist. Marsha Norman's *Getting Out* (1977), *'night Mother* (1982), and *The Secret Garden* (1991) have been produced to considerable acclaim. Norman has become an important presence in American drama. Emily Mann's *Execution of Justice* (1983) centered on the trial of Dan White, who murdered Harvey Milk, San Francisco's openly gay mayor. Anne Devlin's *Ourselves Alone* (1986); Lynn Siefert's *Coyote Ugly* (1986); Tina Howe's *Painting Churches* (1982); and Suzan-Lori Parks's *The Death of the Last Black Man in the Whole Entire World* (1990), *The America Play* (1993), and *Venus* (1996) have all added stature to the position of women in contemporary theater.

Through the 1970s and 1980s numerous black theatrical groups developed in many parts of the world. An important Afro-Caribbean theater group was formed in the Keskidee Center in North London, with Edgar White (b. 1947) as one of its directors. White's plays are often centered in Caribbean mystical experiences, including Rastafarianism. *The Nine Night* (1983), produced in London, focuses on a Jamaican funeral tradition designed to help the deceased enter the gates of heaven.

Experiments with Theater Space

Drama around the world has developed alternatives to the proscenium theater. Theater in the round, which seats audiences on all sides of the actors, has been exceptionally powerful for certain plays. Peter Weiss's *Persecution and Assassination of Jean-Paul Marat as Performed by the Inmates of the Asylum of Charenton Under the Direction of the Marquis de Sade* (1964) was especially effective in this format. Other theatrical experiments explored the power of spaces one would not have thought appropriate for drama. For example, Wladimir Pereira Cardoso designed an elaborate welded-steel set for a production of Jean Genet's *The Balcony* in the Ruth Escobar Theater in São Paulo, Brazil. The set was a huge suspended cone in which people sat looking inward while the actors were suspended in the spherical space before them. The production was first staged in 1969 and was seen through 1971 and most of 1972 by many thousands of people. The set was constructed of eighty tons of iron assembled like a trellis and requiring 500,000 welds. The entire insides of the theater were torn out to accommodate the new set. The audience of 250 was seated on circular platforms and the actors moved through the space on ramps, on suspended cables, and on moving platforms. The same theater produced *The Voyage,* an adaptation of an epic poem, *The Lusiads,* about the origin of Portuguese people. That set used open welded platforms suggesting ships' decks. In Dubrovnik, Yugoslavia, a replica of Columbus's *Santa Maria* — built much larger than the original — was used to stage Miroslav Krleza's expressionist play *Christopher Columbus,* written in 1917. The ship was docked in Dubrovnik Harbor for the performances.

Richard Foreman's Ontological-Hysteric Theatre performs in a loft in New York City with all audience members facing in the same direction. This is not fundamentally different from the traditional proscenium theater, but the open loft space and the visible movements of actors offstage create a new relationship to the action. Foreman's work, such as *Sophia = (Wisdom)* (1970 and later), which has been performed in many parts, has none of the usually accepted narrative clues to its action. However, it aims to explore hitherto hidden aspects of experience, such as sexual taboos and unorthodox relationships. The relationship of the author to the performance is also experimental in his theater, since he directs his actors, often using a loud buzzer, as if they were extensions of his will. His work, begun in the 1960s, has continued into the 1990s.

Experimentation Within the Tradition

It is too soon to assess the direction in which current drama is heading, but playwrights still use traditional staging and traditional techniques. Marsha Norman, who wrote *'night, Mother*, has said that her plays are "wildly traditional. I'm a purist about structure. Plays are like plane rides. You [the audience] buy the ticket and you have to get where the ticket takes you. Or else you've been had."

Wole Soyinka's experimentation has spanned two traditions, modern European theater and modern ritual theater of the Yoruba people in Nigeria. Yoruba plays develop from religious celebrations and annual festivals and include music and dance. Soyinka's plays, including *The Strong Breed*, concern themselves with African traditions and African issues, but they often explore mythic forces that link European and African culture. His plays have been produced throughout the world and have demonstrated the universality of community and the individual anxiety it sometimes breeds. Soyinka has also written on Yoruba tragedy and has interpreted, translated, and produced Greek tragedy.

Sam Shepard, one of the most prolific modern playwrights, experiments with his material, much of which premiered in small theaters in Greenwich Village, such as the La Mama Experimental Theater Club. But his most widely known plays, among them *Buried Child* (1978), are produced easily on conventional stages. Shepard's work is wide-ranging and challenging. His language is coarse, a representation of the way he has heard people speak, and the violence he portrays onstage is strong enough to alienate many in the audience. Shepard, important as he is, has not found a popular commercial audience for his plays. At root, his work is always experimental.

Manuel Puig (1932–1990), a novelist, playwright, and film director, is best known for *Kiss of the Spider Woman* (1981), a novel before Puig turned it into a two-person drama. He also directed the film, starring William Hurt and Raul Julia, which made the play known around the world. The homosexual issues raised in the play, along with the questions of political repression in Latin America, have made it one of the most timely of modern plays.

Athol Fugard, a South African, writes powerful plays that also work well on conventional proscenium stages. Like Shepard's, his subject matter is not the kind that permits an audience to sit back relaxed and appreciate the drama with a sense of detachment. Instead, the plays usually disturb audiences. His primary subject matter is the devastation — for blacks and whites — caused by apartheid in South Africa. Fugard's work with black actors in South Africa produced a vital experimental theater out of which his best early work grew.

The Blood Knot (1961) and *Boesman and Lena* (1969), part of a trilogy on South Africa, are based on the theme of racial discrimination. But other plays, such as *A Lesson from Aloes* (1978) and *My Children! My Africa!* (1989), are involved with problems of individuals in relation to their political world. Fugard is in many ways a traditional playwright, except for his subject matter. His characters are thoroughly developed, but with great economy; in *"MASTER HAROLD" . . . and the boys,* for example, we are given a deep understanding of Hally and Sam, whose relationship, past, present, and future, is the center of the play. Fugard is not writing the well-made play, any more than the other contemporary playwrights in this collection are. There is nothing "mechanical" in Fugard's work but rather a sense of organic growth, of actions arising from perceptible conditions and historical circumstances. These contribute to the sense of integrity that his plays communicate.

Some of Caryl Churchill's plays, emphasizing themes of socialism, colonialism, and feminism, were developed in workshops and collaborations with actors and directors. When writing a play, she experiments early in the first stages by spending time in the environments her plays depict. When she worked on *Top Girls* (1982) she came up with the idea of setting the action in an employment agency after she had talked with many people whose lives are wrapped up in business. For *Serious Money* (1987), she and the group developing the play spent time at the London Stock Exchange, absorbing the atmosphere of frenetic buying and selling.

Though she claims to be a traditionalist, Marsha Norman has written experimental plays. Her first success, *Getting Out* (1977), portrays the same character at two periods in her life — as an adolescent and as an adult — on separate parts of the stage at the same time. The effect is startling, but the structure of the play is clear and simple: Arlene is trying to start life over after leaving prison, while Arlie, her younger, rebellious self, is still with her, commenting on what she is doing. The play ends with a reconciliation of the two parts of the character.

Norman's *'night, Mother* is another traditionally structured play. It respects the Aristotelian unities of time, place, and action, and it is confrontational. Thelma and her daughter, Jessie, are in a power struggle over Jessie's right to commit suicide. The technique is naturalistic, and the play's subject matter, as in the plays of Strindberg and Ibsen, is discomforting to its contemporary audiences.

August Wilson has been working on a series of ten plays on the subject of black life in twentieth-century America. So far he has written six of those plays, and each of the first four won the New York Drama Critics' Circle Award for best play of the year. Wilson's plays show the pain endured by blacks in an America that is supposed to be the land of opportunity. Like Arthur Miller in *Death of a Salesman* and Lorraine Hansberry in *A Raisin in the Sun,* Wilson explores the nature and consequences of the American dream, especially for those effectively excluded from this dream. Blacks' frustration, exploitation, and suffering are presented in powerful characters such as Troy Maxson in *Fences* (1985). Troy is a garbage man who was a star baseball player at a time when blacks could play only in their own league. (The major leagues were exclusively white until 1947, when Jackie Robinson joined the Brooklyn Dodgers and the game began to be integrated.) The play centers on Maxson's anger, but it also shows his pride for his family and his concerns for his son's growing up into a world in which he must empower himself to achieve what he most wants for himself.

Cory, Troy's son, does not see the same kind of discrimination and has not felt the unfairness that was Troy's primary experience in growing up. He does not understand the world from Troy Maxson's point of view. Showing the world as Troy Maxson sees it is one of the functions of the play.

All of Wilson's plays have explored the way the heritage of blacks enables them to live intelligently in the present, with understanding and dignity. People in his plays have lost touch with the past and, for that reason, risk a loss of self-understanding.

Wilson's plays have a naturalistic surface, but they also allude to the supernatural, as in *The Piano Lesson* (1990). Some of the roots of this tradition are in the black church and some in African religion, a source shared by Soyinka and Wilson, among others. Wilson's effects are achieved in a proscenium theater, using traditional methods of DRA-MATURGY, the craft or techniques of dramatic composition. Much of the powerful and lasting drama of the 1980s and 1990s has followed a similar technical path. Contemporary dramatists are by no means shy of experimentation, but they are also sensitive to the continuing resources of the traditional stage as it was conceived by Chekhov and Ibsen and Miller.

Among the current playwrights, David Henry Hwang has been active in writing for both stage and film. His work has often centered on Chinese-Americans and problems encountered in their experiences in the United States. Hwang has sensitized audiences to subjects about which playwrights had hitherto been silent. His first success, *F. O. B.* (1980) focused on how new immigrants were viewed by Chinese-Americans who had already assimilated. The play's title is an acronym for "fresh off the boat." Hwang's most successful play, *M. Butterfly* (1987), is about a romance between a French diplomat and a transvestite Chinese opera singer.

Anna Deavere Smith works in a very different way from most of the playwrights in this book. She is a performance artist who not only writes her material but appears in it as well. *Twilight: Los Angeles, 1992* is comprised of interviews with people in many different walks of life in Los Angeles in the aftermath of the riots and burnings following the Rodney King verdict in 1992. She gathers these interviews, shapes them, and then adopts the persona of the interviewee to enact the scene. Her subject matter is usually a socially stimulated crisis. To an extent David Mamet responds to a social situation in *Oleanna* (1992). The characters, a male college professor and a female student, at first adopt an ordinary teacher-student relationship; eventually, though, that relationship alters. Mamet explores the questions of power alongside issues of sexual harassment. As the lines he draws shift back and forth, the audience never knows exactly how clear the lines are meant to be. The issues in the play are thus controversial, subject to a number of different interpretations.

Tony Kushner's two-part drama *Angels in America: Millennium Approaches* (1992) and *Perestroika* (1992) represents an effort to explore issues in modern American history, with an emphasis on religion, politics, and a variety of hysterias. The plays explore homophobia, red-baiting politics, and the impact of AIDS on contemporary society. The open, dynamic structure of the play is enormously powerful. The entire drama lasts six and a half hours and has been seen not only in San Francisco, where it opened, but also in New York, London, Europe, and in regional theaters throughout the United States. Kushner is one of the most energetic of American playwrights, and the scope and success of his work portend exciting new directions in contemporary theater.

Wole Soyinka

Wole Soyinka (b. 1934) is one of Nigeria's several important writers to achieve international fame, winning the Nobel Prize for literature in 1986. His work includes novels, poems, and plays, but he admits that "there is no question at all that I think the Nobel Prize is for my drama."

Soyinka studied at University College, Ibadan, Nigeria, and began his literary career as an undergraduate, publishing poetry in the distinguished African literary magazine *Black Orpheus*. His work, especially his drama, has been an investigation of political, religious, and other forces in Nigerian culture. *The Swamp Dwellers* (1958) is a powerful play condemning African superstition. *The Lion and the Jewel* (1959) offers a comic view of Nigerian attitudes toward European values left over from the colonial period. Among his other plays are *The Trials of Brother Jero* (1960), about a corrupt evangelist, and *Kongi's Harvest* (1964). *A Dance of the Forests* (1960) was written to celebrate Nigerian independence, but it also alerted people to Nigeria's past violence and warned against its return.

Nigeria went through a bitter civil war in 1967, and Soyinka's political sympathies led to a term in prison, where he was placed in solitary confinement. He continued his writing, even smuggling poems out of prison to give hope to his political allies. Interestingly, he criticized his own tribe, the Yoruba, for murdering members of the Ibo during the war against Biafra.

Soyinka studied at the University of Leeds after his schooling in Ibadan. Most of his writing is in English, but he still writes some of his poetry in his tribal language, Yoruba. He has recommended Swahili as the national language of Nigeria. Soyinka has spoken out against cultural parochialism, including its manifestation in the negritude movement, which rejects white culture as a form of pollution. He expressed his philosophy to another great African writer, Leopold Senghor: "A tiger is not forever shouting about his tigritude"; a duiker antelope does not have to "prove his duikertude; you will know him by his elegant leap."

Soyinka has been chairman of the drama department at Ife University as well as of his own University College, Ibadan. He has also lectured in Cambridge, England, and in universities in North America. One of his most recent works, *A Play of Giants* (1984), is a scathing attack on abuse of power, indicting African tyrants such as Idi Amin, Jean-Bedel Bokassa, and others.

For all of his criticism of Nigerian politics, Soyinka has rooted his work in the religion and folklore of the Yoruba people. Ifa, the Yoruba religion, depends on a complex cosmology that sees experience as layered in interactive animal, mineral, and vegetable spheres. African critic Femi Osofisan has described Yoruba cosmology as holding "coeval the three historical, actual and prospective planes of entity; . . . the animal and vegetable essences are correspondent; . . . the acknowledged deities are both anthropomorphic and symbiotic, each fusing in his personality a series of antinomies." Osofisan also notes "the comprehensive union of religious and secular intuition in the traditional Yoruba." Ifa plays a role in *The Strong Breed,* but the play is nonetheless understandable to those unfamiliar with the religion. Soyinka must be thought of as a traditional dramatist, writing in the tradition of his Yoruba people but reaching a worldwide audience.

THE STRONG BREED

The Strong Breed (1962), written at a time of political uncertainty in Nigeria, examines the interrelationship of ritual and community in African culture, describing one process by which a society renews itself. The "strong breed" are those men capable of the sacrifice needed annually to purify the community of its sins and to allow it to start over again. The community's sacrifice signals the beginning of a new year.

As the new year approaches, the elders of the community, Jaguna and Oroge, search for the appropriate "carrier" who can bear the burden of the community's guilt. The tradition in their community is to choose a stranger. Despite the elders' reluctance, Eman, one of the strong breed who has exiled himself from his own community, seems a logical choice until another outsider, the idiot Ifada, comes on the scene. Ifada seems heaven-sent to serve the community, but when he is chosen, he protests in terrified confusion. Eman explains to Jaguna and Oroge that no community should force a carrier to perform unwillingly. If he is unwilling, the guilt will not be carried away. Eman then offers himself as a willing sacrifice in Ifada's place.

The mythic pattern of sacrifice and renewal is basic to much Yoruba myth. Part of the tradition of Yoruba ritual drama is the reenactment of myths that resemble Eman's willing sacrifice. These are celebrated annually on the feast of Obatala, the god of creation. *The Strong Breed* has also been connected to ritual tragedies enacted in honor of Ogun, who suffers greatly for the good of the community.

The Strong Breed is informed by Soyinka's studies of Greek tragedy. Like Greek tragic figures, Soyinka's strong breed are genetically linked — they are fathers and sons who inherit their fathers' power. Soyinka's *The Bacchae of Euripides* (1973) deals with inspiration, intoxication, and a form of hysteria that affects a mass of people. *Death and the King's Horseman* (1976), centering on death, also explores Greek themes of fate and inevitability. Soyinka demonstrates the universality of Greek themes in both European and African experience.

Certain patterns link Eman with Oedipus. Once Eman is identified by his father as one of the strong breed, he prepares himself for his mission by leaving his community. Like Oedipus, he unwittingly goes to another community where he ultimately must be sacrificed. Eman also resembles Christ: He is a teacher and healer; he refuses to exploit those around him; he lifts up the weak and has empathy for everyone, including the idiot Ifada. And, like Christ, those for whom he sacrifices himself do not hold him in high regard.

Despite its Greek and Christian overtones, the story is grounded in Yoruba tradition, with its initiation rites and concepts of heredity, community, and sacrifice. Soyinka's stagecraft includes traditional Yoruba music and dance as well as traditional Yoruba images, such as the effigy — the carrier doll — and the appearance of the human carrier in the form of Ifada. Soyinka demonstrates that everything in the past is part of the present by overlaying the ghosts of Omae, the woman Eman was to marry; his father (the Old Man); his tutor; and the priest. The past shapes the present just as his father's blood runs in his veins and shapes everything he does as a man.

The play leaves us wondering if Eman's sacrifice was wasteful or redeeming. Is the community led by Jaguna and Oroge worth dying for? Will Eman's death benefit Sunma, Ifada, and the Girl who betrayed him to his killers? Or does Eman die only because he is one of the strong breed, whose mission is to serve as the sacrifice for the community? Even the latter interpretation might imply a positive ending for the play, although it would be a different ending than suggesting that Eman has died *for* this village and thus has secured its renewal. Yoruba tradition implies that even if the community is unworthy, it shares in purification by the sacrifice of the willing. The subtlety of the issues in this play invites multiple interpretations.

The Strong Breed in Performance

In Ibadan in 1963, Soyinka created a twenty-five-minute version of *The Strong Breed* that omitted the flashbacks at the end of the play when Eman's past returns to him. This was done for Esso World Theatre and was included in the film *Culture in Transition*. The play was produced in its full-length version in 1964 at the Greenwich Mews Theatre in New York, and it has been performed by theater groups in several African nations. An African university theater group produced the play in its full-length version in Malawi in 1976 with Anthony Nazombe as Eman.

Wole Soyinka (b. 1934)
THE STRONG BREED

1962

Characters

EMAN, *a stranger*
SUNMA, *Jaguna's daughter*
IFADA, *an idiot*
A GIRL
JAGUNA
OROGE
ATTENDANT STALWARTS, *the villagers*

From Eman's past:
OLD MAN, *his father*
OMAE, *his betrothed*
TUTOR
PRIEST
ATTENDANTS, *the villagers*

The scenes are described briefly, but very often a darkened stage with lit areas will not only suffice but is necessary. Except for the one indicated place, there can be no break in the action. A distracting scene change would be ruinous.

(A mud house, with space in front of it. Eman, in light buba and trousers stands at the window, looking out. Inside, Sunma is clearing the table of what looks like a modest clinic, putting the things away in a cupboard. Another rough table in the room is piled with exercise books, two or three worn textbooks, etc. Sunma appears agitated. Outside, just below the window crouches Ifada. He looks up with a shy smile from time to time, waiting for Eman to notice him.)

SUNMA (*hesitant*): You will have to make up your mind soon, Eman. The lorry leaves very shortly.

(As Eman does not answer, Sunma continues her work, more nervously. Two villagers, obvious travelers, pass hurriedly in front of the house, the man has a small raffia sack, the woman a cloth-covered basket, the man enters first, turns and urges the woman who is just emerging to hurry.)

SUNMA (*seeing them, her tone is more intense*): Eman, are we going or aren't we? You will leave it till too late.

EMAN (*quietly*): There is still time — if you want to go.

SUNMA: If I want to go . . . and you?

(Eman makes no reply.)

SUNMA (*bitterly*): You don't really want to leave here. You never want to go away — even for a minute.

(Ifada continues his antics. Eman eventually pats him on the head and the boy grins happily. Leaps up suddenly and returns with a basket of oranges which he offers to Eman.)

EMAN: My gift for today's festival enh?

(Ifada nods, grinning.)

EMAN: They look ripe — that's a change.

SUNMA (*she has gone inside the room. Looks round the door*): Did you call me?

EMAN: No. (*She goes back.*) And what will you do tonight, Ifada? Will you take part in the dancing? Or perhaps you will mount your own masquerade?

(Ifada shakes his head, regretfully.)

EMAN: You won't? So you haven't any? But you would like to own one.

(Ifada nods eagerly.)

EMAN: Then why don't you make your own?

(Ifada stares, puzzled by this idea.)

EMAN: Sunma will let you have some cloth you know. And bits of wool . . .

SUNMA (*coming out*): Who are you talking to, Eman?

EMAN: Ifada. I am trying to persuade him to join the young maskers.

SUNMA (*losing control*): What does he want here? Why is he hanging round us?

EMAN (*amazed*): What . . . ? I said Ifada, Ifada.

SUNMA: Just tell him to go away. Let him go and play somewhere else!

EMAN: What is this? Hasn't he always played here?

SUNMA: I don't want him here. (*Rushes to the window.*) Get away, idiot. Don't bring your foolish face here anymore, do you hear? Go on, go away from here . . .

EMAN (*restraining her*): Control yourself, Sunma. What on earth has got into you?

(Ifada, hurt and bewildered, backs slowly away.)

SUNMA: He comes crawling round here like some horrible insect. I never want to lay my eyes on him again.

EMAN: I don't understand. It *is* Ifada you know. Ifada! The unfortunate one who runs errands for you and doesn't hurt a soul.

SUNMA: I cannot bear the sight of him.

EMAN: You can't do what? It can't be two days since he last fetched water for you.

SUNMA: What else can he do except that? He is useless. Just because we have been kind to him . . . Others would have put him in an asylum.

EMAN: You are not making sense. He is not a madman, he is just a little more unlucky than other children. (*Looks keenly at her.*) But what is the matter?

SUNMA: It's nothing. I only wish we had sent him off to one of those places for creatures like him.

EMAN: He is quite happy here. He doesn't bother anyone and he makes himself useful.

SUNMA: Useful! Is that one of any use to anybody? Boys of his age are already earning a living but all he can do is hang around and drool at the mouth.

EMAN: But he does work. You know he does a lot for you.

SUNMA: Does he? And what about the farm you started for him! Does he ever work on it? Or have you forgotten that it was really for Ifada you cleared that bush. Now you have to go and work it yourself. You spend all your time on it and you have no room for anything else.

EMAN: That wasn't his fault. I should first have asked him if he was fond of farming.

SUNMA: Oh, so he can choose? As if he shouldn't be thankful for being allowed to live.

EMAN: Sunma!

SUNMA: He does not like farming but he knows how to feast his dumb mouth on the fruits.

EMAN: But I want him to. I encourage him.

SUNMA: Well keep him. I don't want to see him anymore.

EMAN (*after some moments*): But why? You cannot be telling all the truth. What has he done?

SUNMA: The sight of him fills me with revulsion.

EMAN (*goes to her and holds her*): What really is it? (*Sunma avoids his eyes.*) It is almost as if you are forcing yourself to hate him. Why?

SUNMA: That is not true. Why should I?

EMAN: Then what is the secret? You've even played with him before.

SUNMA: I have always merely tolerated him. But I cannot anymore. Suddenly my disgust won't take him anymore. Perhaps . . . perhaps it is the new year. Yes, yes, it must be the new year.

EMAN: I don't believe that.

SUNMA: It must be. I am a woman, and these things matter. I don't want a misshape near me. Surely for one day in the year, I may demand some wholesomeness.

EMAN: I do not understand you.

(*Sunma is silent.*)

It was cruel of you. And to Ifada who is so helpless and alone. We are the only friends he has.

SUNMA: No, just you. I have told you, with me it has always been only an act of kindness. And now I haven't any pity left for him.

EMAN: No. He is not a wholesome being.

(*He turns back to looking through the window.*)

SUNMA (*half-pleading*): Ifada can rouse your pity. And yet if anything, I need more kindness from you. Every time my weakness betrays me, you close your mind against me . . . Eman . . . Eman . . .

(*A Girl comes in view, dragging an effigy° by a rope attached to one of its legs. She stands for a while gazing at Eman. Ifada, who has crept back shyly to his accustomed position, becomes somewhat excited when he sees the effigy. The Girl is unsmiling. She possesses in fact a kind of inscrutability which does not make her hard but is unsettling.*)

GIRL: Is the teacher in?

EMAN (*smiling*): No.

GIRL: Where is he gone?

EMAN: I don't really know. Shall I ask?

GIRL: Yes, do.

EMAN (*turning slightly*): Sunma, a girl outside wants to know . . .

(*Sunma turns away, goes into the inside room.*)

effigy: Doll in a human shape.

EMAN: Oh. (*Returns to the Girl, but his slight gaiety is lost.*) There is no one at home who can tell me.

GIRL: Why are you not in?

EMAN: I don't really know. Maybe I went somewhere.

GIRL: All right. I will wait until you get back.

(*She pulls the effigy to her, sits down.*)

EMAN (*slowly regaining his amusement*): So you are all ready for the new year.

GIRL (*without turning round*): I am not going to the festival.

EMAN: Then why have you got that?

GIRL: Do you mean my carrier? I am unwell you know. My mother says it will take away my sickness with the old year.

EMAN: Won't you share the carrier with your playmates?

GIRL: Oh, no. Don't you know I play alone? The other children won't come near me. Their mothers would beat them.

EMAN: But I have never seen you here. Why don't you come to the clinic?

GIRL: My mother said No.

(*Gets up, begins to move off.*)

EMAN: You are not going away?

GIRL: I must not stay talking to you. If my mother caught me . . .

EMAN: All right, tell me what you want before you go.

GIRL (*stops. For some moments she remains silent*): I must have some clothes for my carrier.

EMAN: Is that all? You wait a moment.

(*Sunma comes out as he takes down a buba from the wall. She goes to the window and glares almost with hatred at the Girl. The Girl retreats hastily, still impassive.*)

By the way, Sunma, do you know who that girl is?

SUNMA: I hope you don't really mean to give her that.

EMAN: Why not? I hardly ever use it.

SUNMA: Just the same, don't give it to her. She is not a child. She is as evil as the rest of them.

EMAN: What has got into you today?

SUNMA: All right, all right. Do what you wish.

(*She withdraws. Baffled, Eman returns to the window.*)

EMAN: Here . . . will this do? Come and look at it.

GIRL: Throw it.

EMAN: What is the matter? I am not going to eat you.

GIRL: No one lets me come near them.

EMAN: But I am not afraid of catching your disease.

GIRL: Throw it.

(*Eman shrugs and tosses the buba. She takes it with-*

out a word and slips it on the effigy, completely absorbed in the task. Eman watches for a while, then joins Sunma in the inner room.)

GIRL (*after a long, cool survey of Ifada*): You have a head like a spider's egg, and your mouth dribbles like a roof. But there is no one else. Would you like to play?

(*Ifada nods eagerly, quite excited.*)

GIRL: You will have to get a stick.

(*Ifada rushes around, finds a big stick, and whirls it aloft, bearing down on the carrier.*)

GIRL: Wait. I don't want you to spoil it. If it gets torn I shall drive you away. Now, let me see how you are going to beat it.

(*Ifada hits it gently.*)

GIRL: You may hit harder than that. As long as there is something left to hang at the end.

(*She appraises him up and down.*)

You are not very tall . . . will you be able to hang it from a tree?

(*Ifada nods, grinning happily.*)

GIRL: You will hang it up and I will set fire to it. (*Then, with surprising venom.*) But just because you are helping me, don't think it is going to cure you. I am the one who will get well at midnight, do you understand? It is my carrier and it is for me alone.

(*She pulls at the rope to make sure that it is well attached to the leg.*)

Well don't stand there drooling. Let's go.

(*She begins to walk off, dragging the effigy in the dust. Ifada remains where he is for some moments, seemingly puzzled. Then his face breaks into a large grin and he leaps after the procession, belaboring the effigy with all his strength. The stage remains empty for some moments. Then the horn of a lorry is sounded and Sunma rushes out. The hooting continues for some time with a rhythmic pattern. Eman comes out.*)

EMAN: I am going to the village . . . I shan't be back before nightfall.
SUNMA (*blankly*): Yes.
EMAN (*hesitates*): Well what do you want me to do?
SUNMA: The lorry was hooting just now.
EMAN: I didn't hear it.
SUNMA: It will leave in a few minutes. And you did promise we could go away.
EMAN: I promised nothing. Will you go home by yourself or shall I come back for you?

SUNMA: You don't even want me here?
EMAN: But you have to go home haven't you?
SUNMA: I had hoped we would watch the new year together — in some other place.
EMAN: Why do you continue to distress yourself?
SUNMA: Because you will not listen to me. Why do you continue to stay where nobody wants you?
EMAN: That is not true.
SUNMA: It is. You are wasting your life on people who really want you out of their way.
EMAN: You don't know what you are saying.
SUNMA: You think they love you? Do you think they care at all for what you — or I — do for them?
EMAN: *Them?* These are your own people. Sometimes you talk as if you were a stranger too.
SUNMA: I wonder if I really sprang from here. I know they are evil and I am not. From the oldest to the smallest child, they are nourished in evil and unwholesomeness in which I have no part.
EMAN: You knew this when you returned?
SUNMA: You reproach me then for trying at all?
EMAN: I reproach you with nothing? But you must leave me out of your plans. I can have no part in them.
SUNMA (*nearly pleading*): Once I could have run away. I would have gone and never looked back.
EMAN: I cannot listen when you talk like that.
SUNMA: I swear to you, I do not mind what happens afterwards. But you must help me tear myself away from here. I can no longer do it by myself . . . It is only a little thing. And we have worked so hard this past year . . . surely we can go away for a week . . . even a few days would be enough.
EMAN: I have told you, Sunma . . .
SUNMA (*desperately*): Two days, Eman. Only two days.
EMAN (*distressed*): But I tell you I have no wish to go.
SUNMA (*suddenly angry*): Are you so afraid then?
EMAN: Me? Afraid of what?
SUNMA: You think you will not want to come back.
EMAN (*pitying*): You cannot dare me that way.
SUNMA: Then why won't you leave here, even for an hour? If you are so sure that your life is settled here, why are you afraid to do this thing for me? What is so wrong that you will not go into the next town for a day or two?
EMAN: I don't want to. I do not have to persuade you or myself about anything. I simply have no desire to go away.
SUNMA (*his quiet confidence appears to incense her*): You are afraid. You accuse me of losing my sense of mission, but you are afraid to put yours to the test.
EMAN: You are wrong, Sunma. I have no sense of mission. But I have found peace here and I am content with that.

SUNMA: I haven't. For a while I thought that too, but I found there could be no peace in the midst of so much cruelty. Eman, tonight at least, the last night of the old year . . .

EMAN: No, Sunma. I find this too distressing; you should go home now.

SUNMA: It is the time for making changes in one's life, Eman. Let's breathe in the new year away from here.

EMAN: You are hurting yourself.

SUNMA: Tonight. Only tonight. We will come back tomorrow, as early as you like. But let us go away for this one night. Don't let another year break on me in this place . . . you don't know how important it is to me, but I will tell you, I will tell you on the way . . . but we must not be here today, Eman, do this one thing for me.

EMAN (*sadly*): I cannot.

SUNMA (*suddenly calm*): I was a fool to think it would be otherwise. The whole village may use you as they will but for me there is nothing. Sometimes I think you believe that doing anything for me makes you unfaithful to some part of your life. If it was a woman then I pity her for what she must have suffered.

(*Eman winces and hardens slowly. Sunma notices nothing.*)

Keeping faith with so much is slowly making you inhuman. (*Seeing the change in Eman.*) Eman. Eman. What is it?

(*As she goes toward him, Eman goes into the house.*)

SUNMA (*apprehensive, follows him*): What did I say? Eman, forgive me, forgive me please.

(*Eman remains facing into the slow darkness of the room. Sunma, distressed, cannot decide what to do.*)

I swear I didn't know . . . I would not have said it for all the world.

(*A lorry is heard taking off somewhere nearby. The sound comes up and slowly fades away into the distance. Sunma starts visibly, goes slowly to the window.*)

SUNMA (*as the sound dies off, to herself*): What happens now?

EMAN (*joining her at the window*): What did you say?

SUNMA: Nothing.

EMAN: Was that not the lorry going off?

SUNMA: It was.

EMAN: I am sorry I couldn't help you.

(*Sunma, about to speak, changes her mind.*)

EMAN: I think you ought to go home now.

SUNMA: No, don't send me away. It's the least you can do for me. Let me stay here until all the noise is over.

EMAN: But are you not needed at home? You have a part in the festival.

SUNMA: I have renounced it; I am Jaguna's eldest daughter only in name.

EMAN: Renouncing one's self is not so easy — surely you know that.

SUNMA: I don't want to talk about it. Will you at least let us be together tonight?

EMAN: But . . .

SUNMA: Unless you are afraid my father will accuse you of harboring me.

EMAN: All right, we will go out together.

SUNMA: Go out? I want us to stay here.

EMAN: When there is so much going on outside?

SUNMA: Someday you will wish that you went away when I tried to make you.

EMAN: Are we going back to that?

SUNMA: No. I promise you I will not recall it again. But you must know that it was also for your sake that I tried to get us away.

EMAN: For me? How?

SUNMA: By yourself you can do nothing here. Have you not noticed how tightly we shut out strangers? Even if you lived here for a lifetime, you would remain a stranger.

EMAN: Perhaps that is what I like. There is peace in being a stranger.

SUNMA: For a while perhaps. But they would reject you in the end. I tell you it is only I who stand between you and contempt. And because of this you have earned their hatred. I don't know why I say this now, except that somehow, I feel that it no longer matters. It is only I who have stood between you and much humiliation.

EMAN: Think carefully before you say any more. I am incapable of feeling indebted to you. This will make no difference at all.

SUNMA: I ask for nothing. But you must know it all the same. It is true I hadn't the strength to go by myself. And I must confess this now, if you had come with me, I would have done everything to keep you from returning.

EMAN: I know that.

SUNMA: You see, I bare myself to you. For days I had thought it over, this was to be a new beginning for us. And I placed my fate wholly in your hands. Now the thought will not leave me, I have a feeling which will not be shaken off, that in some way, you have tonight totally destroyed my life.

EMAN: You are depressed, you don't know what you are saying.

SUNMA: Don't think I am accusing you. I say all this only because I cannot help it.

EMAN: We must not remain shut up here. Let us go and be part of the living.

SUNMA: No. Leave them alone.

EMAN: Surely you don't want to stay indoors when the whole town is alive with rejoicing.

SUNMA: Rejoicing! Is that what it seems to you? No, let us remain here. Whatever happens I must not go out until all this is over.

(*There is silence. It has grown much darker.*)

EMAN: I shall light the lamp.

SUNMA (*eager to do something*): No, let me do it.

(*She goes into the inner room.*)

(*Eman paces the room, stops by a shelf and toys with the seeds in an "ayo" board, takes down the whole board and places it on a table, playing by himself.*)

(*The Girl is now seen coming back, still dragging her "carrier." Ifada brings up the rear as before. As he comes round the corner of the house two men emerge from the shadows. A sack is thrown over Ifada's head, the rope is pulled tight rendering him instantly helpless. The Girl has reached the front of the house before she turns round at the sound of scuffle. She is in time to see Ifada thrown over the shoulders and borne away. Her face betraying no emotion at all, the Girl backs slowly away, turns and flees, leaving the "carrier" behind. Sunma enters, carrying two kerosene lamps. She hangs one up from the wall.*)

EMAN: One is enough.

SUNMA: I want to leave one outside.

(*She goes out, hangs the lamp from a nail just above the door. As she turns she sees the effigy and gasps. Eman rushes out.*)

EMAN: What is it? Oh, is that what frightened you?

SUNMA: I thought . . . I didn't really see it properly.

(*Eman goes towards the object, stoops to pick it up.*)

EMAN: It must belong to that sick girl.

SUNMA: Don't touch it.

EMAN: Let's keep it for her.

SUNMA: Leave it alone. Don't touch it, Eman.

EMAN (*shrugs and goes back*): You are very nervous.

SUNMA: Let's go in.

EMAN: Wait. (*He detains her by the door, under the lamp.*) I know there is something more than you've told me. What are you afraid of tonight?

SUNMA: I was only scared by that thing. There is nothing else.

EMAN: I am not blind, Sunma. It is true I would not run away when you wanted me to, but that doesn't mean I do not feel things. What does tonight really mean that it makes you so helpless?

SUNMA: It is only a mood. And your indifference to me . . . let's go in.

(*Eman moves aside and she enters; he remains there for a moment and then follows.*)

(*She fiddles with the lamp, looks vaguely round the room, then goes and shuts the door, bolting it. When she turns, it is to meet Eman's eyes, questioning.*)

SUNMA: There is a cold wind coming in.

(*Eman keeps his gaze on her.*)

SUNMA: It *was* getting cold.

(*She moves guiltily to the table and stands by the "ayo" board, rearranging the seeds. Eman remains where he is a few moments, then brings a stool and sits opposite her. She sits down also and they begin to play in silence.*)

SUNMA: What brought you here at all, Eman? And what makes you stay?

(*There is another silence.*)

SUNMA: I am not trying to share your life. I know you too well by now. But at least we have worked together since you came. Is there nothing at all I deserve to know?

EMAN: Let me continue a stranger — especially to you. Those who have much to give fulfill themselves only in total loneliness.

SUNMA: Then there is no love in what you do.

EMAN: There is. Love comes to me more easily with strangers.

SUNMA: That is unnatural.

EMAN: Not for me. I know I find consummation only when I have spent myself for a total stranger.

SUNMA: It seems unnatural to me. But then I am a woman. I have a woman's longings and weaknesses. And the ties of blood are very strong in me.

EMAN (*smiling*): You think I have cut loose from all these — ties of blood.

SUNMA: Sometimes you are so inhuman.

EMAN: I don't know what that means. But I am very much my father's son.

(*They play in silence. Suddenly Eman pauses, listening.*)

EMAN: Did you hear that?

SUNMA (*quickly*): I heard nothing . . . it's your turn.

EMAN: Perhaps some of the mummers are coming this way.

(*Eman, about to play, leaps up suddenly.*)

SUNMA: What is it? Don't you want to play anymore?

(*Eman moves to the door.*)

SUNMA: No. Don't go out, Eman.

EMAN: If it's the dancers, I want to ask them to stay. At least we won't have to miss everything.

SUNMA: No, no. Don't open the door. Let us keep out everyone tonight.

(*A terrified and disordered figure bursts suddenly round the corner, past the window, and begins hammering at the door. It is Ifada. Desperate with terror, he pounds madly at the door, dumb-moaning all the while.*)

EMAN: Isn't that Ifada?

SUNMA: They are only fooling about. Don't pay any attention.

EMAN (*looks round the window*): That is Ifada. (*Begins to unbolt the door.*)

SUNMA (*pulling at his hands*): It is only a trick they are playing on you. Don't take any notice, Eman.

EMAN: What are you saying? The boy is out of his senses with fear.

SUNMA: No, no. Don't interfere, Eman. For God's sake, don't interfere.

EMAN: Do you know something of this then?

SUNMA: You are a stranger here, Eman. Just leave us alone and go your own way. There is nothing you can do.

EMAN (*he tries to push her out of the way but she clings fiercely to him*): Have you gone mad? I tell you the boy must come in.

SUNMA: Why won't you listen to me, Eman? I tell you it's none of your business. For your own sake, do as I say.

(*Eman pushes her off, unbolts the door. Ifada rushes in, clasps Eman round the knees, dumb-moaning against his legs.*)

EMAN (*manages to rebolt the door*): What is it, Ifada? What is the matter?

(*Shouts and voices are heard coming nearer the house.*)

SUNMA: Before it's too late, let him go. For once, Eman, believe what I tell you. Don't harbor him or you will regret it all your life.

(*Eman tries to calm Ifada who becomes more and more abject as the outside voices get nearer.*)

EMAN: What have they done to him? At least tell me that. What is going on, Sunma?

SUNMA (*with sudden venom*): Monster! Could you not take yourself somewhere else?

EMAN: Stop talking like that.

SUNMA: He could have run into the bush couldn't he? Toad! Why must he follow us with his own disasters!

VOICES OUTSIDE: It's here . . . Round the back . . .

Spread, spread . . . this way . . . no, head him off . . . use the bush path and head him off . . . get some more lights . . .

(*Eman listens. Lifts Ifada bodily and carries him into the inner room. Returns at once, shutting the door behind him.*)

SUNMA (*slumps into a chair, resigned*): You always follow your own way.

JAGUNA (*comes round the corner followed by Oroge and three men, one bearing a torch*): I knew he would come here.

OROGE: I hope our friend won't make trouble.

JAGUNA: He had better not. You, recall all the men and tell them to surround the house.

OROGE: But he may not be in the house after all.

JAGUNA: I know he is here . . . (*to the men*) . . . go on, do as I say.

(*He bangs on the door.*)

Teacher, open your door . . . you two, stay by the door. If I need you I will call you.

(*Eman opens the door.*)

JAGUNA (*speaks as he enters*): We know he is here.

EMAN: Who?

JAGUNA: Don't let us waste time. We are grown men, teacher. You understand me and I understand you. But we must take back the boy.

EMAN: This is my house.

JAGUNA: Daughter, you'd better tell your friend. I don't think he quite knows our ways. Tell him why he must give up the boy.

SUNMA: Father, I . . .

JAGUNA: Are you going to tell him or aren't you?

SUNMA: Father, I beg you, leave us alone tonight . . .

JAGUNA: I thought you might be a hindrance. Go home then if you will not use your sense.

SUNMA: But there are other ways . . .

JAGUNA (*turning to the men*): See that she gets home. I no longer trust her. If she gives trouble carry her. And see that the women stay with her until all this is over.

(*Sunma departs, accompanied by one of the men.*)

JAGUNA: Now, teacher . . .

OROGE (*restrains him*): You see, Mister Eman, it is like this. Right now, nobody knows that Ifada has taken refuge here. No one except us and our men — and they know how to keep their mouths shut. We don't want to have to burn down the house you see, but if the word gets around, we would have no choice.

JAGUNA: In fact, it may be too late already. A carrier should end up in the bush, not in a house. Anyone who doesn't guard his door when the carrier goes by has himself to blame. A contaminated house should be burnt down.

OROGE: But we are willing to let it pass. Only, you must bring him out quickly.

EMAN: All right. But at least you will let me ask you something.

JAGUNA: What is there to ask? Don't you understand what we have told you?

EMAN: Yes. But why did you pick on a helpless boy. Obviously he is not willing.

JAGUNA: What is the man talking about? Ifada is a godsend. Does he have to be willing?

EMAN: In my home, we believe that a man should be willing.

OROGE: Mister Eman, I don't think you quite understand. This is not a simple matter at all. I don't know what you do, but here, it is not a cheap task for anybody. No one in his senses would do such a job. Why do you think we give refuge to idiots like him? We don't know where he came from. One morning, he is simply there, just like that. From nowhere at all. You see, there is a purpose in that.

JAGUNA: We only waste time.

OROGE: Jaguna, be patient. After all, the man has been with us for some time now and deserves to know. The evil of the old year is no light thing to load on any man's head.

EMAN: I know something about that.

OROGE: You do? (*Turns to Jaguna who snorts impatiently.*) You see I told you so didn't I? From the moment you came I saw you were one of the knowing ones.

JAGUNA: Then let him behave like a man and give back the boy.

EMAN: It is you who are not behaving like men.

JAGUNA (*advances aggressively*): That is a quick mouth you have . . .

OROGE: Patience, Jaguna . . . if you want the new year to cushion the land there must be no deeds of anger. What did you mean, my friend?

EMAN: It is a simple thing. A village which cannot produce its own carrier contains no men.

JAGUNA: Enough. Let there be no more talk or this business will be ruined by some rashness. You . . . come inside. Bring the boy out, he must be in the room there.

EMAN: Wait.

(*The men hesitate.*)

JAGUNA (*hitting the nearer one and propelling him forward*): Go on. Have you changed masters now that you listen to what he says?

OROGE (*sadly*): I am sorry you would not understand, Mister Eman. But you ought to know that no car-

rier may return to the village. If he does, the people will stone him to death. It has happened before. Surely it is too much to ask a man to give up his own soil.

EMAN: I know others who have done more.

(*Ifada is brought out, abjectly dumb-moaning.*)

EMAN: You can see him with your own eyes. Does it really have meaning to use one as unwilling as that.

OROGE (*smiling*): He shall be willing. Not only willing but actually joyous. I am the one who prepares them all, and I have seen worse. This one escaped before I began to prepare him for the event. But you will see him later tonight, the most joyous creature in the festival. Then perhaps you will understand.

EMAN: Then it is only a deceit. Do you believe the spirit of a new year is so easily fooled?

JAGUNA: Take him out. (*The men carry out Ifada.*) You see, it is so easy to talk. You say there are no men in this village because they cannot provide a willing carrier. And yet I heard Oroge tell you we only use strangers. There is only one other stranger in the village, but I have not heard him offer himself (*spits*). It is so easy to talk is it not?

(*He turns his back on him.*)

(*They go off, taking Ifada with them, limp and silent. The only sign of life is that he strains his neck to keep his eyes on Eman till the very moment that he disappears from sight. Eman remains where they left him, staring after the group.*)

(*A blackout lasting no more than a minute. The lights come up slowly and Ifada is seen returning to the house. He stops at the window and looks in. Seeing no one, he bangs on the sill. Appears surprised that there is no response. He slithers down on his favorite spot, then sees the effigy still lying where the Girl had dropped it in her flight. After some hesitation, he goes towards it, begins to strip it of the clothing. Just then the Girl comes in.*)

GIRL: Hey, leave that alone. You know it's mine.

(*Ifada pauses, then speeds up his action.*)

GIRL: I said it is mine. Leave it where you found it.

(*She rushes at him and begins to struggle for possession of the carrier.*)

GIRL: Thief! Thief! Let it go, it is mine. Let it go. You animal, just because I let you play with it. Idiot! Idiot!

(*The struggle becomes quite violent. The Girl is hanging to the effigy and Ifada lifts her with it, flinging her all about. The Girl hangs on grimly.*)

GIRL: You are spoiling it . . . why don't you get your own? Thief! Let it go, you thief!

(*Sunma comes in walking very fast, throwing apprehensive glances over her shoulder. Seeing the two children, she becomes immediately angry. Advances on them.*)

SUNMA: So you've made this place your playground. Get away, you untrained pigs. Get out of here.

(*Ifada flees at once, the Girl retreats also, retaining possession of the "carrier."*)
(*Sunma goes to the door. She has her hand on the door when the significance of Ifada's presence strikes her for the first time. She stands rooted to the spot, then turns slowly round.*)

SUNMA: Ifada! What are you doing here?

(*Ifada is bewildered. Sunma turns suddenly and rushes into the house, flying into the inner room and out again.*)

Eman! Eman! Eman!

(*She rushes outside.*)

Where did he go? Where did they take him?

(*Ifada distressed, points. Sunma seizes him by the arm, drags him off.*)

Take me there at once. God help you if we are too late. You loathsome thing, if you have let him suffer . . .

(*Her voice fades into other shouts, running footsteps, banged tins, bells, dogs, etc., rising in volume.*)

(*It is a narrow passageway between two mud houses. At the far end one man after another is seen running across the entry, the noise dying off gradually.*)
(*About halfway down the passage, Eman is crouching against the wall, tense with apprehension. As the noise dies off, he seems to relax, but the alert hunted look is still in his eyes, which are ringed in a reddish color. The rest of his body has been whitened with a floury substance. He is naked down to the waist, wears a baggy pair of trousers, calf-length, and around both feet are bangles.*)

EMAN: I will simply stay here till dawn. I have done enough.

(*A window is thrown open and a woman empties some slop from a pail. With a startled cry Eman leaps aside to avoid it and the woman puts out her head.*)

WOMAN: Oh, my head. What have I done! Forgive me, neighbor. . . . Eh, it's the carrier!

(*Very rapidly she clears her throat and spits on him, flings the pail at him, and runs off, shouting.*)

He's here. The carrier is hiding in the passage. Quickly, I have found the carrier!

(*The cry is taken up and Eman flees down the passage. Shortly afterwards his pursuers come pouring down the passage in full cry. After the last of them come Jaguna and Oroge.*)

OROGE: Wait, wait. I cannot go so fast.
JAGUNA: We will rest a little then. We can do nothing anyway.
OROGE: If only he had let me prepare him.
JAGUNA: They are the ones who break first, these fools who think they were born to carry suffering like a hat. What are we to do now?
OROGE: When they catch him I must prepare him.
JAGUNA: He? It will be impossible now. There can be no joy left in that one.
OROGE: Still, it took him by surprise. He was not expecting what he met.
JAGUNA: Why then did he refuse to listen? Did he think he was coming to sit down to a feast? He had not even gone through one compound before he bolted. Did he think he was taken round the people to be blessed? A woman, that is all he is.
OROGE: No, no. He took the beating well enough. I think he is the kind who would let himself be beaten from night till dawn and not utter a sound. He would let himself be stoned until he dropped dead.
JAGUNA: Then what made him run like a coward?
OROGE: I don't know. I don't really know. It is a night of curses, Jaguna. It is not many unprepared minds will remain unhinged under the load.
JAGUNA: We must find him. It is a poor beginning for a year when our own curses remain hovering over our homes because the carrier refused to take them.

(*They go. The scene changes. Eman is crouching beside some shrubs, torn and bleeding.*)

EMAN: They are even guarding my house . . . as if I would go there, but I need water . . . they could at least grant me that . . . I can be thirsty too . . . (*He pricks his ears.*) . . . there must be a stream nearby . . . (*As he looks round him, his eyes widen at a scene he encounters.*)

(*An Old Man, short and vigorous looking, is seated on a stool. He also is wearing calf-length baggy trousers, white. On his head, a white cap. An attendant is engaged in rubbing his body with oil. Round his eyes, two white rings have already been marked.*)

OLD MAN: Have they prepared the boat?
ATTENDANT: They are making the last sacrifice.
OLD MAN: Good. Did you send for my son?

ATTENDANT: He's on his way.

OLD MAN: I have never met the carrying of the boat with such a heavy heart. I hope nothing comes of it.

ATTENDANT: The gods will not desert us on that account.

OLD MAN: A man should be at his strongest when he takes the boat, my friend. To be weighed down inside and out is not a wise thing. I hope when the moment comes I shall have found my strength.

(*Enter Eman, a wrapper round his waist and a danski° over it.*)

OLD MAN: I meant to wait until after my journey to the river, but my mind is so burdened with my own grief and yours I could not delay it. You know I must have all my strength. But I sit here, feeling it all eaten slowly away by my unspoken grief. It helps to say it out. It even helps to cry sometimes.

(*He signals to the attendant to leave them.*)

Come nearer . . . we will never meet again, son. Not on this side of the flesh. What I do not know is whether you will return to take my place.

EMAN: I will never come back.

OLD MAN: Do you know what you are saying? Ours is a strong breed, my son. It is only a strong breed that can take this boat to the river year after year and wax stronger on it. I have taken down each year's evils for over twenty years. I hoped you would follow me.

EMAN: My life here died with Omae.

OLD MAN: Omae died giving birth to your child and you think the world is ended. Eman, my pain did not begin when Omae died. Since you sent her to stay with me, son, I lived with the burden of knowing that this child would die bearing your son.

EMAN: Father . . .

OLD MAN: Don't you know it was the same with you? And me? No woman survives the bearing of the strong ones. Son, it is not the mouth of the boaster that says he belongs to the strong breed. It is the tongue that is red with pain and black with sorrow. Twelve years you were away my son, and for those twelve years I knew the love of an old man for his daughter and the pain of a man helplessly awaiting his loss.

EMAN: I wish I had stayed away. I wish I never came back to meet her.

OLD MAN: It had to be. But you know now what slowly ate away my strength. I awaited your return with love and fear. Forgive me then if I say that

danski: A brief Yoruba garment.

your grief is light. It will pass. This grief may drive you now from home. But you must return.

EMAN: You do not understand. It is not grief alone.

OLD MAN: What is it then? Tell me, I can still learn.

EMAN: I was away twelve years. I changed much in that time.

OLD MAN: I am listening.

EMAN: I am unfitted for your work, father. I wish to say no more. But I am totally unfitted for your call.

OLD MAN: It is only time you need, son. Stay longer and you will answer the urge of your blood.

EMAN: That I stayed at all was because of Omae. I did not expect to find her waiting. I would have taken her away, but hard as you claim to be, it would have killed you. And I was a tired man. I needed peace. Because Omae was peace, I stayed. Now nothing holds me here.

OLD MAN: Other men would rot and die doing this task year after year. It is strong medicine which only we can take. Our blood is strong like no other. Anything you do in life must be less than this, son.

EMAN: That is not true, father.

OLD MAN: I tell you it is true. Your own blood will betray you, son, because you cannot hold it back. If you make it do less than this, it will rush to your head and burst it open. I say what I know, my son.

EMAN: There are other tasks in life, father. This one is not for me. There are even greater things you know nothing of.

OLD MAN: I am very sad. You only go to give to others what rightly belongs to us. You will use your strength among thieves. They are thieves because they take what is ours, they have no claim of blood to it. They will even lack the knowledge to use it wisely. Truth is my companion at this moment, my son. I know everything I say will surely bring the sadness of truth.

EMAN: I am going, father.

OLD MAN: Call my attendant. And be with me in your strength for this last journey. A-ah, did you hear that? It came out without my knowing it; this is indeed my last journey. But I am not afraid.

(*Eman goes out. A few moments later, the attendant enters.*)

ATTENDANT: The boat is ready.

OLD MAN: So am I.

(*He sits perfectly still for several moments. Drumming begins somewhere in the distance, and the Old Man sways his head almost imperceptibly. Two men come in bearing a miniature boat, containing an indefinable mound. They rush it in and set it briskly down near the Old Man, and stand well back. The Old Man gets up slowly, the Attendant watching him keenly.*)

He signs to the men, who lift the boat quickly onto the Old Man's head. As soon as it touches his head, he holds it down with both hands and runs off, the men give him a start, then follow at a trot.)

(As the last man disappears Oroge limps in and comes face to face with Eman — as carrier — who is now seen still standing beside the shrubs, staring into the scene he has just witnessed. Oroge, struck by the look on Eman's face, looks anxiously behind him to see what has engaged Eman's attention. Eman notices him then, and the pair stare at each other. Jaguna enters, sees him and shouts, "Here he is," rushes at Eman who is whipped back to the immediate and flees, Jaguna in pursuit. Three or four others enter and follow them. Oroge remains where he is, thoughtful.)

JAGUNA (*reenters*): They have closed in on him now, we'll get him this time.

OROGE: It is nearly midnight.

JAGUNA: You were standing there looking at him as if he was some strange spirit. Why didn't you shout?

OROGE: You shouted didn't you? Did that catch him?

JAGUNA: Don't worry. We have him now. But things have taken a bad turn. It is no longer enough to drive him past every house. There is too much contamination about already.

OROGE (*not listening*): He saw something. Why may I not know what it was?

JAGUNA: What are you talking about?

OROGE: Hm. What is it?

JAGUNA: I said there is too much harm done already. The year will demand more from this carrier than we thought.

OROGE: What do you mean?

JAGUNA: Do we have to talk with the full mouth?

OROGE: S-sh . . . look!

(Jaguna turns just in time to see Sunma fly at him, clawing at his face like a crazed tigress.)

SUNMA: Murderer! What are you doing to him. Murderer! Murderer!

(Jaguna finds himself struggling really hard to keep off his daughter; he succeeds in pushing her off and striking her so hard on the face that she falls to her knees. He moves on her to hit her again.)

OROGE (*comes between*): Think what you are doing, Jaguna, she is your daughter.

JAGUNA: My daughter! Does this one look like my daughter? Let me cripple the harlot for life.

OROGE: That is a wicked thought, Jaguna.

JAGUNA: Don't come between me and her.

OROGE: Nothing in anger — do you forget what tonight is?

JAGUNA: Can you blame me for forgetting?

(Draws his hand across his cheek — it is covered with blood.)

OROGE: This is an unhappy night for us all. I fear what is to come of it.

JAGUNA: Let's go. I cannot restrain myself in this creature's presence. My own daughter . . . and for a stranger . . .

(They go off, Ifada, who came in with Sunma and had stood apart, horror-stricken, comes shyly forward. He helps Sunma up. They go off, he holding Sunma bent and sobbing.)

(Enter Eman — as carrier. He is physically present in the bounds of this next scene, a side of a round thatched hut. A young girl, about fourteen, runs in, stops beside the hut. She looks carefully to see that she is not observed, puts her mouth to a little hole in the wall.)

OMAE: Eman . . . Eman . . .

(Eman — as carrier — responds, as he does throughout the scene, but they are unaware of him.)

EMAN (*from inside*): Who is it?

OMAE: It is me, Omae.

EMAN: How dare you come here!

(Two hands appear at the hole and pushing outwards, create a much larger hole through which Eman puts out his head. It is Eman as a boy, the same age as the girl.)

Go away at once. Are you trying to get me into trouble!

OMAE: What is the matter?

EMAN: You. Go away.

OMAE: But I came to see you.

EMAN: Are you deaf? I say I don't want to see you. Now go before my tutor catches you.

OMAE: All right. Come out.

EMAN: Do what!

OMAE: Come out.

EMAN: You must be mad.

OMAE (*sits on the ground*): All right, if you don't come out I shall simply stay here until your tutor arrives.

EMAN (*about to explode, thinks better of it and the head disappears. A moment later he emerges from behind the hut*): What sort of a devil has got into you?

OMAE: None. I just wanted to see you.

EMAN (*his mimicry is nearly hysterical*): "None. I just wanted to see you." Do you think this place is the stream where you can go and molest innocent people?

OMAE (*coyly*): Aren't you glad to see me?

EMAN: I am not.

OMAE: Why?

EMAN: Why? Do you really ask me why? Because you are a woman and a most troublesome woman. Don't you know anything about this at all. We are not meant to see any woman. So go away before more harm's done.

OMAE (*flirtatious*): What is so secret about it anyway? What do they teach you?

EMAN: Nothing any woman can understand.

OMAE: Ha ha. You think we don't know eh? You've all come to be circumcised.

EMAN: Shut up. You don't know anything.

OMAE: Just think, all this time you haven't been circumcised, and you dared make eyes at us women.

EMAN: Thank you — woman. Now go.

OMAE: Do they give you enough to eat?

EMAN (*testily*): No. We are so hungry that when silly girls like you turn up, we eat them.

OMAE (*feigning tears*): Oh, oh, oh, he's abusing me. He's abusing me.

EMAN (*alarmed*): Don't try that here. Go quickly if you are going to cry.

OMAE: All right, I won't cry.

EMAN: Cry or no cry, go away and leave me alone. What do you think will happen if my tutor turns up now?

OMAE: He won't.

EMAN (*mimicking*): "He won't." I suppose you are his wife and he tells you where he goes. In fact this is just the time he comes round to our huts. He could be at the next hut this very moment.

OMAE: Ha-ha. You're lying. I left him by the stream, pinching the girls' bottoms. Is that the sort of thing he teaches you?

EMAN: Don't say anything against him or I shall beat you. Isn't it you loose girls who tease him, wiggling your bottoms under his nose?

OMAE (*going tearful again*): A-ah, so I am one of the loose girls eh?

EMAN: Now don't start accusing me of things I didn't say.

OMAE: But you said it. You said it.

EMAN: I didn't. Look, Omae, someone will hear you and I'll be in disgrace. Why don't you go before anything happens.

OMAE: It's all right. My friends have promised to hold your old rascal tutor till I get back.

EMAN: Then you go back right now. I have work to do. (*Going in.*)

OMAE (*runs after and tries to hold him. Eman leaps back, genuinely scared*): What is the matter? I was not going to bite you.

EMAN: Do you know what you nearly did? You almost touched me!

OMAE: Well?

EMAN: Well! Isn't it enough that you let me set my eyes on you? Must you now totally pollute me with your touch? Don't you understand anything?

OMAE: Oh, that.

EMAN (*nearly screaming*): It is not "oh that." Do you think this is only a joke or a little visit like spending the night with your grandmother? This is an important period of my life. Look, these huts, we built them with our own hands. Every boy builds his own. We learn things, do you understand? And we spend much time just thinking. At least, I do. It is the first time I have had nothing to do except think. Don't you see, I am becoming a man. For the first time, I understand that I have a life to fulfill. Has that thought ever worried you?

OMAE: You are frightening me.

EMAN: There. That is all you can say. And what use will that be when a man finds himself alone — like that? (*Points to the hut.*) A man must go on his own, go where no one can help him, and test his strength. Because he may find himself one day sitting alone in a wall as round as that. In there, my mind could hold no other thought. I may never have such moments again to myself. Don't dare to come and steal any more of it.

OMAE (*this time, genuinely tearful*): Oh, I know you hate me. You only want to drive me away.

EMAN (*impatiently*): Yes, yes, I know I hate you — but go.

OMAE (*going, all tears. Wipes her eyes, suddenly all mischief*): Eman.

EMAN: What now?

OMAE: I only want to ask one thing . . . do you promise to tell me?

EMAN: Well, what is it?

OMAE (*gleefully*): Does it hurt?

(*She turns instantly and flees, landing straight into the arms of the returning tutor.*)

TUTOR: Te-he-he . . . what have we here? What little mouse leaps straight into the beak of the wise old owl eh?

(*Omae struggles to free herself, flies to the opposite side, grimacing with distaste.*)

TUTOR: I suppose you merely came to pick some fruits eh? You did not sneak here to see any of my children.

OMAE: Yes, I came to steal your fruits.

TUTOR: Te-he-he . . . I thought so. And that dutiful son of mine over there. He saw you and came to chase you off my fruit trees didn't he? Te-he-he . . . I'm sure he did, isn't that so, my young Eman?

EMAN: I was talking to her.

TUTOR: Indeed you were. Now be good enough to go

into your hut until I decide your punishment. (*Eman withdraws.*) Te-he-he . . . now now, my little daughter, you need not be afraid of me.

OMAE (*spiritedly*): I am not.

TUTOR: Good. Very good. We ought to be friendly. (*His voice becomes leering.*) Now this is nothing to worry you, my daughter . . . a very small thing indeed. Although of course if I were to let it slip that your young Eman had broken a strong taboo, it might go hard on him you know. I am sure you would not like that to happen, would you?

OMAE: No.

TUTOR: Good. You are sensible, my girl. Can you wash clothes?

OMAE: Yes.

TUTOR: Good. If you will come with me now to my hut, I shall give you some clothes to wash, and then we will forget all about this matter eh? Well, come on.

OMAE: I shall wait here. You go and bring the clothes.

TUTOR: Eh? What is that? Now now, don't make me angry. You should know better than to talk back at your elders. Come now.

(*He takes her by the arm and tries to drag her off.*)

OMAE: No no, I won't come to your hut. Leave me. Leave me alone, you shameless old man.

TUTOR: If you don't come I shall disgrace the whole family of Eman, and yours too.

(*Eman reenters with a small bundle.*)

EMAN: Leave her alone. Let us go, Omae.

TUTOR: And where do you think you are going?

EMAN: Home.

TUTOR: Te-he-he . . . As easy as that eh? You think you can leave here any time you please? Get right back inside that hut!

(*Eman takes Omae by the arm and begins to walk off.*)

TUTOR: Come back at once.

(*He goes after him and raises his stick. Eman catches it, wrenches it from him, and throws it away.*)

OMAE (*hopping delightedly*): Kill him. Beat him to death.

TUTOR: Help! Help! He is killing me! Help!

(*Alarmed, Eman clamps his hand over his mouth.*)

EMAN: Old tutor, I don't mean you any harm, but you mustn't try to harm me either. (*He removes his hand.*)

TUTOR: You think you can get away with your crime. My report shall reach the elders before you ever get into town.

EMAN: You are afraid of what I will say about you? Don't worry. Only if you try to shame me, then I will speak. I am not going back to the village anyway. Just tell them I have gone, no more. If you say one word more than that I shall hear of it the same day and I shall come back.

TUTOR: You are telling me what to do? But don't think to come back next year because I will drive you away. Don't think to come back here even ten years from now. And don't send your children.

(*Goes off with threatening gestures.*)

EMAN: I won't come back.

OMAE: Smoked vulture! But Eman, he says you cannot return next year. What will you do?

EMAN: It is a small thing one can do in the big towns.

OMAE: I thought you were going to beat him that time. Why didn't you crack his dirty hide?

EMAN: Listen carefully, Omae . . . I am going on a journey.

OMAE: Come on. Tell me about it on the way.

EMAN: No, I go that way. I cannot return to the village.

OMAE: Because of that wretched man? Anyway you will first talk to your father.

EMAN: Go and see him for me. Tell him I have gone away for some time. I think he will know.

OMAE: But, Eman . . .

EMAN: I haven't finished. You will go and live with him till I get back. I have spoken to him about you. Look after him!

OMAE: But what is this journey? When will you come back?

EMAN: I don't know. But this is a good moment to go. Nothing ties me down.

OMAE: But, Eman, you want to leave me.

EMAN: Don't forget all I said. I don't know how long I will be. Stay in my father's house as long as you remember me. When you become tired of waiting, you must do as you please. You understand? You must do as you please.

OMAE: I cannot understand anything, Eman. I don't know where you are going or why. Suppose you never came back! Don't go, Eman. Don't leave me by myself.

EMAN: I must go. Now let me see you on your way.

OMAE: I shall come with you.

EMAN: Come with me! And who will look after you? Me? You will only be in my way, you know that! You will hold me back and I shall desert you in a strange place. Go home and do as I say. Take care of my father and let him take care of you.

(*He starts going but Omae clings to him.*)

OMAE: But, Eman, stay the night at least. You will

only lose your way. Your father, Eman, what will he say? I won't remember what you said . . . come back to the village . . . I cannot return alone, Eman . . . come with me as far as the crossroads.

(*His face set, Eman strides off and Omae loses balance as he increases his pace. Falling, she quickly wraps her arms around his ankle, but Eman continues unchecked, dragging her along.*)

OMAE: Don't go, Eman . . . Eman, don't leave me, don't leave me . . . don't leave your Omae . . . don't go, Eman . . . don't leave your Omae . . .

(*Eman — as carrier — makes a nervous move as if he intends to go after the vanished pair. He stops but continues to stare at the point where he last saw them. There is stillness for a while. Then the Girl enters from the same place and remains looking at Eman. Startled, Eman looks apprehensively round him. The Girl goes nearer but keeps beyond arm's length.*)

GIRL: Are you the carrier?
EMAN: Yes. I am Eman.
GIRL: Why are you hiding?
EMAN: I really came for a drink of water . . . er . . . is there anyone in front of the house?
GIRL: No.
EMAN: But there might be people in the house. Did you hear voices?
GIRL: There is no one here.
EMAN: Good. Thank you. (*He is about to go, stops suddenly.*) Er . . . would you . . . you will find a cup on the table. Could you bring me the water out here? The water pot is in a corner.

(*The Girl goes. She enters the house, then, watching Eman carefully, slips out and runs off.*)

EMAN (*sitting*): Perhaps they have all gone home. It will be good to rest. (*He hears voices and listens hard.*) Too late. (*Moves cautiously nearer the house.*) Quickly, girl, I can hear people coming. Hurry up. (*Looks through the window.*) Where are you? Where is she? (*The truth dawns on him suddenly and he moves off, sadly.*)

(*Enter Jaguna and Oroge, led by the Girl.*)

GIRL (*pointing*): He was there.
JAGUNA: Ay, he's gone now. He is a sly one is your friend. But it won't save him forever.
OROGE: What was he doing when you saw him?
GIRL: He asked me for a drink of water.
JAGUNA: } Ah! (*They look at each other.*)
OROGE: }
OROGE: We should have thought of that.
JAGUNA: He is surely finished now. If only we had thought of it earlier.

OROGE: It is not too late. There is still an hour before midnight.
JAGUNA: We must call back all the men. Now we need only wait for him — in the right place.
OROGE: Everyone must be told. We don't want anyone heading him off again.
JAGUNA: And it works so well. This is surely the help of the gods themselves, Oroge. Don't you know at once what is on the path to the stream?
OROGE: The sacred trees.
JAGUNA: I tell you it is the very hand of the gods. Let us go.

(*An overgrown part of the village. Eman wanders in, aimlessly, seemingly uncaring of discovery. Beyond him, an area lights up, revealing a group of people clustered round a spot, all the heads are bowed. One figure stands away and separate from them. Even as Eman looks, the group breaks up and the people disperse, coming down and past him. Only three people are left, a man [Eman] whose back is turned, the village priest, and the isolated one. They stand on opposite sides of the grave, the man on the mound of earth. The Priest walks round to the man's side and lays a hand on his shoulder.*)

PRIEST: Come.
EMAN: I will. Give me a few moments here alone.
PRIEST: Be comforted.

(*They fall silent.*)

EMAN: I was gone twelve years but she waited. She whom I thought had too much of the laughing child in her. Twelve years I was a pilgrim, seeking the vain shrine of secret strength. And all the time, strange knowledge, this silent strength of my child-woman.
PRIEST: We all saw it. It was a lesson to us; we did not know that such goodness could be found among us.
EMAN: Then why? Why the wasted years if she had to perish giving birth to my child? (*They are both silent.*) I do not really know for what great meaning I searched. When I returned, I could not be certain I had found it. Until I reached my home and I found her a full-grown woman, still a child at heart. When I grew to believe it, I thought, this, after all, is what I sought. It was here all the time. And I threw away my new-gained knowledge. I buried the part of me that was formed in strange places. I made a home in my birthplace.
PRIEST: That was as it should be.
EMAN: Any truth of that was killed in the cruelty of her brief happiness.
PRIEST (*looks up and sees the figure standing away from them, the child in his arms. He is totally still*): Your father — he is over there.

EMAN: I knew he would come. Has he my son with
him?

PRIEST: Yes.

EMAN: He will let no one take the child. Go and comfort him, priest. He loved Omae like a daughter,
and you all know how well she looked after him.
You see how strong we really are. In his heart of
hearts the old man's love really awaited a daughter.
Go and comfort him. His grief is more than mine.

(*The Priest goes. The Old Man has stood well away
from the burial group. His face is hard and his gaze
unswerving from the grave. The Priest goes to him,
pauses, but sees that he can make no dent in the man's
grief. Bowed, he goes on his way.*)

(*Eman, as carrier, walking towards the graveside,
the other Eman having gone. His feet sink into the
mound and he breaks slowly onto his knees, scooping
up the sand in his hands and pouring it on his head.
The scene blacks out slowly.*)

(*Enter Jaguna and Oroge.*)

OROGE: We have only a little time.

JAGUNA: He will come. All the wells are guarded.
There is only the stream left him. The animal must
come to drink.

OROGE: You are sure it will not fail — the trap, I
mean.

JAGUNA: When Jaguna sets the trap, even elephants
pay homage — their trunks downwards and one
leg up in the sky. When the carrier steps on the
fallen twigs, it is up in the sacred trees with him.

OROGE: I shall breathe again when this long night is
over.

(*They go out.*)

(*Enter Eman — as carrier — from the same direction as the last two entered. In front of him is a still figure, the Old Man as he was, carrying the dwarf boat.*)

EMAN (*joyfully*): Father.

(*The figure does not turn round.*)

EMAN: It is your son, Eman. (*He moves nearer.*) Don't
you want to look at me? It is I, Eman. (*He moves
nearer still.*)

OLD MAN: You are coming too close. Don't you
know what I carry on my head?

EMAN: But, Father, I am your son.

OLD MAN: Then go back. We cannot give the two of
us.

EMAN: Tell me first where you are going.

OLD MAN: Do *you* ask that? Where else but to the
river?

EMAN (*visibly relieved*): I only wanted to be sure. My

throat is burning. I have been looking for the
stream all night.

OLD MAN: It is the other way.

EMAN: But you said . . .

OLD MAN: I take the longer way, you know how I
must do this. It is quicker if you take the other
way. Go now.

EMAN: No, I will only get lost again. I shall go with
you.

OLD MAN: Go back, my son. Go back.

EMAN: Why? Won't you even look at me?

OLD MAN: Listen to your father. Go back.

EMAN: But, father!

(*He makes to hold him. Instantly the old man breaks
into a rapid trot. Eman hesitates, then follows, his
strength nearly gone.*)

EMAN: Wait, father. I am coming with you . . .
wait . . . wait for me, father . . .

(*There is a sound of twigs breaking, of a sudden trembling in the branches. Then silence.*)

(*The front of Eman's house. The effigy is hanging
from the sheaves. Enter Sunma, still supported by
Ifada, she stands transfixed as she sees the hanging
figure. Ifada appears to go mad, rushes at the object,
and tears it down. Sunma, her last bit of will gone,
crumbles against the wall. Some distance away from
them, partly hidden, stands the Girl, impassively
watching. Ifada hugs the effigy to him, stands above
Sunma. The Girl remains where she is, observing.*)

(*Almost at once, the villagers begin to return, subdued and guilty.*)

(*They walk across the front, skirting the house as
widely as they can. No word is exchanged. Jaguna
and Oroge eventually appear. Jaguna, who is leading,
sees Sunma as soon as he comes in view. He stops at
once, retreating slightly.*)

OROGE (*almost whispering*): What is it?

JAGUNA: The viper.

(*Oroge looks cautiously at the woman.*)

OROGE: I don't think she will even see you.

JAGUNA: Are you sure? I am in no frame of mind for
another meeting with her.

OROGE: Let's go home.

JAGUNA: I am sick to the heart of the cowardice I have
seen tonight.

OROGE: That is the nature of men.

JAGUNA: Then it is a sorry world to live in. We did it
for them. It was all for their own common good.
What did it benefit me whether the man lived or
died. But did you see them? One and all they looked
up at the man and words died in their throats.

OROGE: It was no common sight.

JAGUNA: Women could not have behaved so shame-fully. One by one they crept off like sick dogs. Not one could raise a curse.

OROGE: It was not only him they fled. Do you see how unattended we are?

JAGUNA: There are those who will pay for this night's work!

OROGE: Ay, let us go home.

(*They go off. Sunma, Ifada, and the Girl remain as they are, the light fading slowly on them.*)

COMMENTARY

Lewis Nkosi (b. 1935)

INTERVIEW WITH WOLE SOYINKA   1962

This early interview with Soyinka was taped in Lagos, Nigeria, in August 1962, while The Strong Breed *was very fresh in his mind. In fact, it had not yet had its first publication, which in Nigeria was in 1963. Nkosi in the interview highlights the impact of Bertolt Brecht's theater on Soyinka's writing.*

Nkosi: Well, Wole Soyinka, could you tell us what set you off on this road to writing?

Soyinka: I suppose that requires really going back a bit. I would say I began writing seriously, or rather taking myself seriously, taking my *writing* seriously about three, four years ago, but I can only presume that I have always been interested in writing. In school I wrote the usual little sketches for production, the occasional verse, you know, the short story, etc., and I think about 1951 I had the great excitement of having a short story of mine broadcast on the Nigerian Broadcasting Service and that was sort of my first public performance.

Nkosi: What schools did you attend?

Soyinka: I went to Government School, Ibadan; after that I spent a couple of years in the University College, Ibadan.

Nkosi: You have now published drama or rather you've had some plays produced?

Soyinka: Yes, "produced" is the correct word. I haven't had any plays published although some are in print right now and will come out shortly.

Nkosi: Could you tell us what those plays are?

Soyinka: There is *The Lion and the Jewel* which was the first play I wrote.

Nkosi: No, the second.

Soyinka: The first one I sent up, I suppose like most people do, is the *A Dance of Forests* which I wrote in 1960 and timed it for the Independence Celebrations; there is the *House of Banigeji* which has never been performed. And I have written about four one-acts including *The Trials of Brother Jero* which was done quite recently in Nigeria.

Nkosi: The *A Dance of the Forests* won you a prize, didn't it?

Soyinka: Yes, Nigerian Independence competition prize 1960.

Nkosi: Have you got any particular authors that have influenced you most?

Soyinka: This is a very difficult question for me because I am not aware of any conscious influence on my work, but I can say that if I wanted to aim at any particular kind of theater, I think, however subconsciously, I might aim at Brecht's kind of theater, which I admire tremendously, just his complete freedom with the medium of the theater.

Nkosi: In your last play, *A Dance of the Forests,* which caused a lot of people a tremendous amount of agony trying to figure out just exactly what it was trying to do — they felt that there were some hidden meanings contained in lots of symbolism which they couldn't gather. Now as you're the author, we are lucky to have you here, and we think that you probably might enlighten us about just what you were trying to say in that work of yours.

Soyinka: Well, let me say first of all that I think that my prime duty as a playwright is to provide excellent theater; in other words, I think that I have only one commitment to the public, and that is to my audience and that is to make sure they do not leave the theater bored. I don't believe that I have any obligation to enlighten, to instruct, to teach: I don't possess that sense of duty or didacticism — very much unlike Brecht for instance, for, you see, what I like in Brecht is his sort of theater, its liveliness and freedom, not so much his purpose or intentions. I believe my primary duty is just to see that I provide excellent theater for the audience. But inevitably, it is just common sense to say that one just cannot write about just nothing. In *A Dance of the Forests,* I was very much conscious of all the potentialities of existing theatrical idioms in Nigeria and I only know that there was one thing which motivated, maybe, guided the form and the shape of the play or the eventual fate of the characters. I use this word "motivated" quite cautiously because I do not think I consciously tried to preach or bring out, you know, a series of symbolisms at all, but the main thing was the realization that human beings are just destructive all over the world. I think this is it — I have thought about this again and again but during the production — I produced it myself — and in trying to see the play take shape on the stage, I find that the main thing is my own personal conviction or observation that human beings are simply cannibals all over the world so that their main preoccupation seems to be eating up one another. This I think is the main thing I would say was in the back of my mind when I wrote it.

Nkosi: Yes, that sounds very much like Tennessee Williams's idea of the world conscious of the evil.

Soyinka: Well, I don't sort of regard it so much as . . .

Nkosi: The ferocity of human beings.

Soyinka: Yes, the carnivorous nature of. . . .

Nkosi: Yes, I wonder whether now — have you pursued this theme in the other plays or are the other plays different?

Soyinka: . . . Fundamentally, I think they're different. I think that sort of semiconsciously the moment I realize I'm pursuing a theme again, it seems to ring a bell warning that I have preceded myself somewhere; I have such a feeling about this that I shirk from it but I would say there are traces of it in my other plays — in, for instance, my favorite one-act play which is *The Strong Breed.* I think this one is also very much mixed up with the whole element of sacrifice, so contrasting the idea of selfishness with willing self-sacrifice as opposed to the other general cannibalism of human beings.

Sam Shepard

Samuel Shepard Rogers VII was born in Illinois in 1943, but his father was a career man in the army, and like most "army brats," Shepard found himself essentially uprooted, moving from base to base around the country. If he has roots as a writer, they are clearly in the American West, but not necessarily the West created by writers of westerns, comic books, and second-rate movies. Shepard's plays often have a surreal quality, as if they are set in a world of the imagination rather than in a real place like Paris, Texas.

Shepard is one of America's most important playwrights. He has won numerous awards, including ten Obie Awards (given to off-Broadway plays) between 1966 and 1979, an Obie Award for sustained achievement in 1980, the New York Drama Critics' Circle Award for *A Lie of the Mind* in 1985, and a Pulitzer Prize for *Buried Child* in 1979. His work has been produced primarily in the experimental theater of downtown New York in places such as La Mama and in regional theaters throughout the United States known for artistic integrity but not for reaching a broad spectrum of theatergoers. In his way Shepard has been an underground playwright who has won the respect of most theater people, including the best playwrights.

Shepard's love for, and frustrations with, music have found their way into a major theme of his work. He plays drums and guitar and has never realized an early desire for a career in rock music. But the subversive qualities of rock and jazz — their implicit critique of middle-class life — appear in his plays in his analyses of the middle-class family. His primary themes center on the family and its complications, the nature of the person alone, and the myth of the Old West. In each theme Shepard expresses a deep sense of longing and of loss, emotions that his audiences have found significant.

Because his father began to drink and family life became intolerable, Shepard left home after a year at college and toured with the Bishops Company Repertory Players. At nineteen he wound up in New York working in one of the best jazz clubs of the day, the Village Gate. During this time in Greenwich Village he began to write one-act plays with extraordinary energy. Like Jack Kerouac, he almost never revised his work. He wrote it in a burst of energy and then had it performed to audiences whose admiration grew.

In the 1970s Shepard began acting in major motion pictures. One of the ironies of his life is that he became a matinee idol after appearing in movies such as *The Right Stuff, Fool for Love, Country,* and *Crimes of the Heart.* The critic Harry Haun said of him, "He is the Recluse as Superstar, the man who has arrived on his own terms, carefully sculpting a special myth for himself."

His output for the stage has been prodigious, with dozens of one-act plays, and he has a central body of work that has gained him an enviable reputation. *Operation Sidewinder* (1970) was performed at the Vivian Beaumont Theater — a public theater at Lincoln Center in New York City — to mixed reviews. The play, set in the West, involves a giant mechanical snake designed to make contact with outer space travelers; it includes Hopi snake dances and military scenes. *The Tooth of Crime* (1972) is about turf wars between an aging rock star and an up-and-coming young star. Its brutality and directness make it intense, exciting, and revealing of the California rock-and-roll scene in the early 1970s.

Curse of the Starving Class (1977) and *Buried Child* (1978) both helped solidify Shepard's reputation. *Suicide in B-flat* (1976) and *True West* (1980) only made it clearer that his work was developing in a consistent vein of black humor and dark criticism of the sanctity of family life. *A Lie of the Mind* (1985), like *Buried Child,* is about disturbed family life. It is filled with secrets: incest, murder, and sin. *New York Times* critic Mel Gussow said that it explores "the damage that one does to filial, fraternal, and marital bonds." Incest — or potential incest — is also a theme in *Fool for Love* (1983), in which Shepard starred on film. The play is set in the West and contains all the themes for which his work is known.

Shepard began his work with a sense of the West drawn from popular literature, reshaped it, and produced it in a new form. If the American West has a reality that survived its mythicization in the dime novel and John Wayne's movies, then Shepard is partly responsible for the way we now see it.

BURIED CHILD

Buried Child won the Pulitzer Prize for drama in 1979. The play was developed in an intense collaborative effort with cast, crew, director, and playwright using a process of give-and-take that has generally pleased Sam Shepard. In some cases he has turned down offers of major commercial productions of his plays because they would preclude that kind of collaborative atmosphere.

Critics have seen this play as loosely related to *Curse of the Starving Class* (1977) and *True West* (1980), forming a "family" trilogy. The three plays are very different in style, but they all offer a view of the American family that is painfully distant from the sentimental idealism of popular magazines of the 1940s and 1950s. Shepard emphasizes the rootlessness of the family, its emotional chill, and its capacity for violence.

Buried Child is beguilingly ordinary at first glance. The simple interior is dominated by a television set and an old sofa. Vince's girlfriend Shelly, who is visiting for the first time, had imagined that the house would resemble a Norman Rockwell painting — that is, a stereotypical American home. It falls short of that, but the living room is nonetheless a recognizable, low-key, ordinary room that might be found anywhere in middle America. However, beginning with the unexceptional setting, the ordinariness of Tilden's walking in with an armful of corn, and Dodge's wracking cough, Shepard builds a portrait of an extraordinary family.

Dodge's one-track alcoholic mind seems a minor aberration at first. And Halie's nagging seems comparatively normal. Even Tilden's distant relationship with his father seems close to ordinary. But when Vince and Shelly walk in and Vince identifies himself first to his grandfather and then to his father — whom he does not expect to find here — we begin to see that something is very odd. Neither grandfather nor father recognizes him. Eventually, as we watch Shepard explore the family relationships, we begin to sense that the surface ordinariness hides a deeper structure, one that is built on myth.

The play draws on agricultural myth similar to that in *Oedipus Rex*, which begins with a curse on the land. Like *Oedipus*, it includes the theme of incest. The crops have failed and there has been no rain. Yet Tilden walks in with an armful of corn, which Halie thinks he must have stolen. Critics have compared Tilden with the corn god, a symbol of renewal. Shepard adds to that the sense of doom visited upon the family as if its genes carried destruction. As in Wole Soyinka's *The Strong Breed*, responsibility is transmitted from father to son. Those who are of the strong breed do not escape their fate. In the terms of *The Strong Breed*, Vince can be thought of as a "carrier," willing or unwilling. When Dodge bequeaths the house to Vince, he seals Vince's fate.

Certainly during the course of the play we begin to see that a change is at hand. The rains have come. Halie, who doubted the existence of the corn, calls down at the end of the play: "It's like a paradise out there, Dodge. You oughta' take a look. A miracle." But the "old king," Dodge, is dead. Vince has come to take his place.

Buried Child in Performance

Buried Child was first produced at the Magic Theatre in San Francisco in June 1978. Later that year it was transferred to the Theater for the New City in Greenwich Village. In May 1979 it was awarded the Pulitzer Prize.

About the Yale Repertory Theatre production of 1979, *New York Times* critic Mel Gussow said, "The tone of the play is almost surrealistic. Like a figure out of Ionesco, the father brings in armloads of fresh vegetables from a garden that has been barren for years." In commenting on the New York and Yale productions of the play, he said that they ended with "a dirge for the decline of traditional values, a wake for the American dream."

In 1980 the Trinity Repertory Company in Providence produced the play, directed by Adrian Hall, the director of the Yale production. It contrasted with the New York production in that the sets and lighting were "slicker," more detailed, and more subtle. One critic labeled the first production of *Buried Child* a "Gothic comedy," and that description has affected subsequent productions. For example, the MIT student production in 1985 aimed at Gothic effects: dark colors, suspense, and other staple ingredients of horror films. Productions of that sort remind us that on one level, at least, the play is about a haunted house. Shepard had to wait until 1996 to see *Buried Child* on Broadway. Gary Sinese, who had worked with Shepard in the Steppenwolf Theater in Chicago, directed the play in its production at the Brooks Atkinson Theater. Leo Burmester played Bradley, James Gammon played Dodge, and Terry Kinney played Tilden. Ben Brantley in the *New York Times* described *Buried Child* as "an inspired revival," and went on to say that the work "emerges as a play for the ages."

Sam Shepard (b. 1943)
BURIED CHILD

1978

While the rain of your fingertips falls,
while the rain of your bones falls,

and your laughter and marrow fall down,
you come flying.   — PABLO NERUDA

Characters

DODGE, *in his seventies*
HALIE, *his wife, mid-sixties*
TILDEN, *their oldest son*
BRADLEY, *their next oldest son, an amputee*
VINCE, *Tilden's son*
SHELLY, *Vince's girlfriend*
FATHER DEWIS, *a Protestant minister*

ACT I

Scene: *Day. Old wooden staircase down left with pale, frayed carpet laid down on the steps. The stairs lead offstage left up into the wings with no landing. Up right is an old, dark green sofa with the stuffing coming out in spots. Stage right of the sofa is an upright lamp with a faded yellow shade and a small night table with several small bottles of pills on it. Down right of the sofa, with the screen facing the sofa, is a large, old-fashioned brown TV. A flickering blue light comes from the screen, but no image, no sound. In the dark, the light of the lamp and the TV slowly brighten in the black space. The space behind the sofa, upstage, is a large, screened-in porch with a board floor. A solid interior door to stage right of the sofa, leading into the room onstage; and another screen door up left, leading from the porch to the outside. Beyond that are the shapes of dark elm trees.*

Gradually the form of Dodge is made out, sitting on the couch, facing the TV, the blue light flickering on his face. He wears a well-worn T-shirt, suspenders, khaki work pants, and brown slippers. He's covered himself in an old brown blanket. He's very thin and sickly looking, in his late seventies. He just stares at the TV. More light fills the stage softly. The sound of light rain. Dodge slowly tilts his head back and stares at the ceiling for a while, listening to the rain. He lowers his head again and stares at the TV. He turns his head slowly to the left and stares at the cushion of the sofa next to the one he's sitting on. He pulls his left arm out from under the blanket, slides his hand under the cushion, and pulls out a bottle of whiskey. He looks down left toward the staircase, listens, then uncaps the bottle, takes a long swig, and caps it again. He puts the bottle back under the cushion and stares at the TV. He starts to cough slowly and softly. The coughing gradually builds. He holds one hand to his mouth and tries to stifle it. The coughing gets louder, then suddenly stops when he hears the sound of his wife's voice coming from the top of the staircase.*

HALIE'S VOICE: Dodge?

(*Dodge just stares at the TV. Long pause. He stifles two short coughs.*)

HALIE'S VOICE: Dodge! You want a pill, Dodge?

(*He doesn't answer. Takes the bottle out again and takes another long swig. Puts the bottle back, stares at TV, pulls blanket up around his neck.*)

HALIE'S VOICE: You know what it is, don't you? It's the rain! Weather. That's it. Every time. Every time you get like this, it's the rain. No sooner does the rain start then you start. (*Pause.*) Dodge?

(*He makes no reply. Pulls a pack of cigarettes out from his sweater and lights one. Stares at TV. Pause.*)

HALIE'S VOICE: You should see it coming down up here. Just coming down in sheets. Blue sheets. The bridge is pretty near flooded. What's it like down there? Dodge?

(*Dodge turns his head back over his left shoulder and takes a look out through the porch. He turns back to the TV.*)

DODGE (*to himself*): Catastrophic.
HALIE'S VOICE: What? What'd you say, Dodge?
DODGE (*louder*): It looks like rain to me! Plain old rain!
HALIE'S VOICE: Rain? Of course it's rain! Are you having a seizure or something! Dodge? (*Pause.*) I'm coming down there in about five minutes if you don't answer me!
DODGE: Don't come down.
HALIE'S VOICE: What!
DODGE (*louder*): Don't come down!

(*He has another coughing attack. Stops.*)

HALIE'S VOICE: You should take a pill for that! I don't see why you just don't take a pill. Be done with it once and for all. Put a stop to it.

(*He takes bottle out again. Another swig. Returns bottle.*)

HALIE'S VOICE: It's not Christian, but it works. It's not necessarily Christian, that is. We don't know. There's some things the ministers can't even answer. I, personally, can't see anything wrong with it. Pain is pain. Pure and simple. Suffering is a different matter. That's entirely different. A pill seems as good an answer as any. Dodge? (*Pause.*) Dodge, are you watching baseball?

DODGE: No.

HALIE'S VOICE: What?

DODGE (*louder*): No!

HALIE'S VOICE: What're you watching? You shouldn't be watching anything that'll get you excited! No horse racing!

DODGE: They don't race on Sundays.

HALIE'S VOICE: What?

DODGE (*louder*): They don't race on Sundays!

HALIE'S VOICE: Well they shouldn't race on Sundays.

DODGE: Well they don't!

HALIE'S VOICE: Good. I'm amazed they still have that kind of legislation. That's amazing.

DODGE: Yeah, it's amazing.

HALIE'S VOICE: What?

DODGE (*louder*): It is amazing!

HALIE'S VOICE: It is. It truly is. I would've thought these days they'd be racing on Christmas even. A big flashing Christmas tree right down at the finish line.

DODGE (*shakes his head*): No.

HALIE'S VOICE: They used to race on New Year's! I remember that.

DODGE: They never raced on New Year's!

HALIE'S VOICE: Sometimes they did.

DODGE: They never did!

HALIE'S VOICE: Before we were married they did!

(*Dodge waves his hand in disgust at the staircase. Leans back in sofa. Stares at TV.*)

HALIE'S VOICE: I went once. With a man.

DODGE (*mimicking her*): Oh, a "man."

HALIE'S VOICE: What?

DODGE: Nothing!

HALIE'S VOICE: A wonderful man. A breeder.

DODGE: A what?

HALIE'S VOICE: A breeder! A horse breeder! Thoroughbreds.

DODGE: Oh, thoroughbreds. Wonderful.

HALIE'S VOICE: That's right. He knew everything there was to know.

DODGE: I bet he taught you a thing or two, huh? Gave you a good turn around the old stable!

HALIE'S VOICE: Knew everything there was to know about horses. We won bookoos of money that day.

DODGE: What?

HALIE'S VOICE: Money! We won every race I think.

DODGE: Bookoos?

HALIE'S VOICE: Every single race.

DODGE: Bookoos of money?

HALIE'S VOICE: It was one of those kind of days.

DODGE: New Year's!

HALIE'S VOICE: Yes! It might've been Florida. Or California! One of those two.

DODGE: Can I take my pick?

HALIE'S VOICE: It was Florida!

DODGE: Aha!

HALIE'S VOICE: Wonderful! Absolutely wonderful! The sun was just gleaming. Flamingos. Bougainvilleas. Palm trees.

DODGE (*to himself, mimicking her*): Bougainvilleas. Palm trees.

HALIE'S VOICE: Everything was dancing with life! There were all kinds of people from everywhere. Everyone was dressed to the nines. Not like today. Not like they dress today.

DODGE: When was this anyway?

HALIE'S VOICE: This was long before I knew you.

DODGE: Must've been.

HALIE'S VOICE: Long before. I was escorted.

DODGE: To Florida?

HALIE'S VOICE: Yes. Or it might've been California. I'm not sure which.

DODGE: All that way you were escorted?

HALIE'S VOICE: Yes.

DODGE: And he never laid a finger on you, I suppose? (*Long silence.*) Halie?

(*No answer. Long pause.*)

HALIE'S VOICE: Are you going out today?

DODGE (*gesturing toward rain*): In this?

HALIE'S VOICE: I'm just asking a simple question.

DODGE: I rarely go out in the bright sunshine, why would I go out in this?

HALIE'S VOICE: I'm just asking because I'm not doing any shopping today. And if you need anything you should ask Tilden.

DODGE: Tilden's not here!

HALIE'S VOICE: He's in the kitchen.

(*Dodge looks toward stage left, then back toward TV.*)

DODGE: All right.

HALIE'S VOICE: What?

DODGE (*louder*): All right!

HALIE'S VOICE: Don't scream. It'll only get your coughing started.

DODGE: All right.

HALIE'S VOICE: Just tell Tilden what you want and he'll get it. (*Pause.*) Bradley should be over later.

DODGE: Bradley?

HALIE'S VOICE: Yes. To cut your hair.

DODGE: My hair? I don't need my hair cut!

HALIE'S VOICE: It won't hurt!

DODGE: I don't need it!

HALIE'S VOICE: It's been more than two weeks, Dodge.

DODGE: I don't need it!

HALIE'S VOICE: I have to meet Father Dewis for lunch.

DODGE: You tell Bradley that if he shows up here with those clippers, I'll kill him!

HALIE'S VOICE: I won't be very late. No later than four at the very latest.

DODGE: You tell him! Last time he left me almost bald! And I wasn't even awake! I was sleeping! I woke up and he'd already left!

HALIE'S VOICE: That's not my fault!

DODGE: You put him up to it!

HALIE'S VOICE: I never did!

DODGE: You did too! You had some fancy, stupid meeting planned! Time to dress up the corpse for company! Lower the ears a little! Put up a little front! Surprised you didn't tape a pipe to my mouth while you were at it! That woulda' looked nice! Huh? A pipe? Maybe a bowler hat! Maybe a copy of the *Wall Street Journal* casually placed on my lap!

HALIE'S VOICE: You always imagine the worst things of people!

DODGE: That's not the worst! That's the least of the worst!

HALIE'S VOICE: I don't need to hear it! All day long I hear things like that and I don't need to hear more.

DODGE: You better tell him!

HALIE'S VOICE: You tell him yourself! He's your own son. You should be able to talk to your own son.

DODGE: Not while I'm sleeping! He cut my hair while I was sleeping!

HALIE'S VOICE: Well, he won't do it again.

DODGE: There's no guarantee.

HALIE'S VOICE: I promise he won't do it without your consent.

DODGE (*after pause*): There's no reason for him to even come over here.

HALIE'S VOICE: He feels responsible.

DODGE: For my hair?

HALIE'S VOICE: For your appearance.

DODGE: My appearance is out of his domain! It's even

out of mine! In fact, it's disappeared! I'm an invisible man!

HALIE'S VOICE: Don't be ridiculous.

DODGE: He better not try it. That's all I've got to say.

HALIE'S VOICE: Tilden will watch out for you.

DODGE: Tilden won't protect me from Bradley!

HALIE'S VOICE: Tilden's the oldest. He'll protect you.

DODGE: Tilden can't even protect himself!

HALIE'S VOICE: Not so loud! He'll hear you. He's right in the kitchen.

DODGE (*yelling off left*): Tilden!

HALIE'S VOICE: Dodge, what are you trying to do?

DODGE (*yelling off left*): Tilden, get in here!

HALIE'S VOICE: Why do you enjoy stirring things up?

DODGE: I don't enjoy anything!

HALIE'S VOICE: That's a terrible thing to say.

DODGE: Tilden!

HALIE'S VOICE: That's the kind of statement that leads people right to the end of their rope.

DODGE: Tilden!

HALIE'S VOICE: It's no wonder people turn to Christ!

DODGE: TILDEN!!

HALIE'S VOICE: It's no wonder the messengers of God's word are shouted down in public places!

DODGE: TILDEN!!!!

(*Dodge goes into a violent, spasmodic coughing attack as Tilden enters from stage left, his arms loaded with fresh ears of corn. Tilden is Dodge's oldest son, late forties, wears heavy construction boots, covered with mud, dark green work pants, a plaid shirt, and a faded brown windbreaker. He has a butch haircut, wet from the rain. Something about him is profoundly burned out and displaced. He stops center stage with the ears of corn in his arms and just stares at Dodge until he slowly finishes his coughing attack. Dodge looks up at him slowly. He stares at the corn. Long pause as they watch each other.*)

HALIE'S VOICE: Dodge, if you don't take that pill nobody's going to force you.

(*The two men ignore the voice.*)

DODGE (*to Tilden*): Where'd you get that?

TILDEN: Picked it.

DODGE: You picked all that?

(*Tilden nods.*)

DODGE: You expecting company?

TILDEN: No.

DODGE: Where'd you pick it from?

TILDEN: Right out back.

DODGE: Out back where!

TILDEN: Right out in back.

DODGE: There's nothing out there!

TILDEN: There's corn.

DODGE: There hasn't been corn out there since about nineteen thirty-five! That's the last time I planted corn out there!

TILDEN: It's out there now.

DODGE (*yelling at stairs*): Halie!

HALIE'S VOICE: Yes dear!

DODGE: Tilden's brought a whole bunch of corn in here! There's no corn out in back is there?

TILDEN (*to himself*): There's tons of corn.

HALIE'S VOICE: Not that I know of!

DODGE: That's what I thought.

HALIE'S VOICE: Not since about nineteen thirty-five!

DODGE (*to Tilden*): That's right. Nineteen thirty-five.

TILDEN: It's out there now.

DODGE: You go and take that corn back to wherever you got it from!

TILDEN (*after pause, staring at Dodge*): It's picked. I picked it all in the rain. Once it's picked you can't put it back.

DODGE: I haven't had trouble with neighbors here for fifty-seven years. I don't even know who the neighbors are! And I don't wanna know! Now go put that corn back where it came from!

(*Tilden stares at Dodge, then walks slowly over to him and dumps all the corn on Dodge's lap and steps back. Dodge stares at the corn, then back to Tilden. Long pause.*)

DODGE: Are you having trouble here, Tilden? Are you in some kind of trouble?

TILDEN: I'm not in any trouble.

DODGE: You can tell me if you are. I'm still your father.

TILDEN: I know you're still my father.

DODGE: I know you had a little trouble back in New Mexico. That's why you came out here.

TILDEN: I never had any trouble.

DODGE: Tilden, your mother told me all about it.

TILDEN: What'd she tell you?

(*Tilden pulls some chewing tobacco out of his jacket and bites off a plug.*)

DODGE: I don't have to repeat what she told me! She told me all about it!

TILDEN: Can I bring my chair in from the kitchen?

DODGE: What?

TILDEN: Can I bring in my chair from the kitchen?

DODGE: Sure. Bring your chair in.

(*Tilden exits left. Dodge pushes all the corn off his lap onto the floor. He pulls the blanket off angrily and tosses it at one end of the sofa, pulls out the bottle and takes another swig. Tilden enters again from left with a milking stool and a pail. Dodge hides the bottle quickly under the cushion before Tilden sees it.*)

Tilden sets the stool down by the sofa, sits on it, puts the pail in front of him on the floor. Tilden starts picking up the ears of corn one at a time and husking them. He throws the husks and silk in the center of the stage and drops the ears into the pail each time he cleans one. He repeats this process as they talk.)

DODGE (*after pause*): Sure is nice looking corn.

TILDEN: It's the best.

DODGE: Hybrid?

TILDEN: What?

DODGE: Some kinda fancy hybrid?

TILDEN: You planted it. I don't know what it is.

DODGE (*pause*): Tilden, look, you can't stay here forever. You know that, don't you?

TILDEN (*spits in spittoon*): I'm not.

DODGE: I know you're not. I'm not worried about that. That's not the reason I brought it up.

TILDEN: What's the reason?

DODGE: The reason is I'm wondering what you're gonna do.

TILDEN: You're not worried about me, are you?

DODGE: I'm not worried about you.

TILDEN: You weren't worried about me when I wasn't here. When I was in New Mexico.

DODGE: No, I wasn't worried about you then either.

TILDEN: You shoulda worried about me then.

DODGE: Why's that? You didn't do anything down there, did you?

TILDEN: I didn't do anything.

DODGE: Then why should I have worried about you?

TILDEN: Because I was lonely.

DODGE: Because you were lonely?

TILDEN: Yeah. I was more lonely than I've ever been before.

DODGE: Why was that?

TILDEN (*pause*): Could I have some of that whiskey you've got?

DODGE: What whiskey? I haven't got any whiskey.

TILDEN: You've got some under the sofa.

DODGE: I haven't got anything under the sofa! Now mind your own damn business! Jesus God, you come into the house outa the middle of nowhere, haven't heard or seen you in twenty years and suddenly you're making accusations.

TILDEN: I'm not making accusations.

DODGE: You're accusing me of hoarding whiskey under the sofa!

TILDEN: I'm not accusing you.

DODGE: You just got through telling me I had whiskey under the sofa!

HALIE'S VOICE: Dodge?

DODGE (*to Tilden*): Now she knows about it!

TILDEN: She doesn't know about it.

HALIE'S VOICE: Dodge, are you talking to yourself down there?

DODGE: I'm talking to Tilden!

HALIE'S VOICE: Tilden's down there?

DODGE: He's right here!

HALIE'S VOICE: What?

DODGE (*louder*): He's right here!

HALIE'S VOICE: What's he doing?

DODGE (*to Tilden*): Don't answer her.

TILDEN (*to Dodge*): I'm not doing anything wrong.

DODGE: I know you're not.

HALIE'S VOICE: What's he doing down there!

DODGE (*to Tilden*): Don't answer.

TILDEN: I'm not.

HALIE'S VOICE: Dodge!

(*The men sit in silence. Dodge lights a cigarette. Tilden keeps husking corn, spits tobacco now and then in spittoon.*)

HALIE'S VOICE: Dodge! He's not drinking anything, is he? You see to it that he doesn't drink anything! You've gotta watch out for him. It's our responsibility. He can't look after himself anymore, so we have to do it. Nobody else will do it. We can't just send him away somewhere. If we had lots of money we could sent him away. But we don't. We never will. That's why we have to stay healthy. You and me. Nobody's going to look after us. Bradley can't look after us. Bradley can hardly look after himself. I was always hoping that Tilden would look out for Bradley when they got older. After Bradley lost his leg. Tilden's the oldest. I always thought he'd be the one to take responsibility. I had no idea in the world that Tilden would be so much trouble. Who would've dreamed. Tilden was an All-American, don't forget. Don't forget that. Fullback. Or quarterback. I forget which.

TILDEN (*to himself*): Fullback. (*Still husking.*)

HALIE'S VOICE: Then when Tilden turned out to be so much trouble, I put all my hopes on Ansel. Of course Ansel wasn't as handsome, but he was smart. He was the smartest probably. I think he probably was. Smarter than Bradley, that's for sure. Didn't go and chop his leg off with a chain saw. Smart enough not to go and do that. I think he was smarter than Tilden too. Especially after Tilden got in all that trouble. Doesn't take brains to go to jail. Anybody knows that. Course then when Ansel died that left us all alone. Same as being alone. No different. Same as if they'd all died. He was the smartest. He could've earned lots of money. Lots and lots of money.

(*Halie enters slowly from the top of the staircase as she continues talking. Just her feet are seen at first as she makes her way down the stairs, a step at a time. She appears dressed completely in black, as though in mourning. Black handbag, hat with a veil, and pulling on elbow-length black gloves. She is about sixty-five with pure white hair. She remains absorbed in what she's saying as she descends the stairs and doesn't really notice the two men who continue sitting there as they were before she came down, smoking and husking.*)

HALIE: He would've took care of us, too. He would've seen to it that we were repaid. He was like that. He was a hero. Don't forget that. A genuine hero. Brave. Strong. And very intelligent. Ansel could've been a great man. One of the greatest. I only regret that he didn't die in action. It's not fitting for a man like that to die in a motel room. A soldier. He could've won a medal. He could've been decorated for valor. I've talked to Father Dewis about putting up a plaque for Ansel. He thinks it's a good idea. He agrees. He knew Ansel when he used to play basketball. Went to every game. Ansel was his favorite player. He even recommended to the City Council that they put up a statue of Ansel. A big, tall statue with a basketball in one hand and a rifle in the other. That's how much he thinks of Ansel.

(*Halie reaches the stage and begins to wander around, still absorbed in pulling on her gloves, brushing lint off her dress, and continuously talking to herself as the men just sit.*)

HALIE: Of course, he'd still be alive today if he hadn't married into the Catholics. The Mob. How in the world he never opened his eyes to that is beyond me. Just beyond me. Everyone around him could see the truth. Even Tilden. Tilden told him time and again. Catholic women are the Devil incarnate. He wouldn't listen. He was blind with love. Blind. I knew. Everyone knew. The wedding was more like a funeral. You remember? All those Italians. All that horrible black, greasy hair. The smell of cheap cologne. I think even the priest was wearing a pistol. When he gave her the ring I knew he was a dead man. I knew it. As soon as he gave her the ring. But then it was the honeymoon that killed him. The honeymoon. I knew he'd never come back from the honeymoon. I kissed him and he felt like a corpse. All white. Cold. Icy blue lips. He never used to kiss like that. Never before. I knew then that she'd cursed him. Taken his soul. I saw it in her eyes. She smiled at me with that Catholic sneer of hers. She told me with her eyes that she'd murder him in his bed. Murder my son. She told me. And there was nothing I could do. Absolutely nothing. He was going with her, thinking he was free. Thinking it was love. What could I do? I couldn't tell him she was a witch. I couldn't tell him that. He'd have turned on me. Hated me. I couldn't stand him hating me and then dying before he ever saw me again. Hating me in his death bed. Hating me and loving her! How could I do that? I had to let him go. I had to. I watched him leave. I watched him throw gardenias as he helped her into the limousine. I watched his face disappear behind the glass.

(*She stops abruptly and stares at the corn husks. She looks around the space as though just waking up. She turns and looks hard at Tilden and Dodge who continue sitting calmly. She looks again at the corn husks.*)

HALIE (*pointing to the husks*): What's this in my house! (*Kicks husks.*) What's all this!

(*Tilden stops husking and stares at her.*)

HALIE (*to Dodge*): And you encourage him!

(*Dodge pulls blanket over him again.*)

DODGE: You're going out in the rain?

HALIE: It's not raining.

(*Tilden starts husking again.*)

DODGE: Not in Florida it's not.

HALIE: We're not in Florida!

DODGE: It's not raining at the race track.

HALIE: Have you been taking those pills? Those pills always make you talk crazy. Tilden, has he been taking those pills?

TILDEN: He hasn't took anything.

HALIE (*to Dodge*): What've you been taking?

DODGE: It's not raining in California or Florida or the race track. Only in Illinois. This is the only place it's raining. All over the rest of the world it's bright golden sunshine.

(*Halie goes to the night table next to the sofa and checks the bottle of pills.*)

HALIE: Which ones did you take? Tilden, you must've seen him take something.

TILDEN: He never took a thing.

HALIE: Then why's he talking crazy?

TILDEN: I've been here the whole time.

HALIE: Then you've both been taking something!

TILDEN: I've just been husking the corn.

HALIE: Where'd you get that corn anyway? Why is the house suddenly full of corn?

DODGE: Bumper crop!

HALIE (*moving center*): We haven't had corn here for over thirty years.

TILDEN: The whole back lot's full of corn. Far as the eye can see.

DODGE (*to Halie*): Things keep happening while

you're upstairs, ya know. The world doesn't stop just because you're upstairs. Corn keeps growing. Rain keeps raining.

HALIE: I'm not unaware of the world around me! Thank you very much. It so happens that I have an overall view from the upstairs. The back yard's in plain view of my window. And there's no corn to speak of. Absolutely none!

DODGE: Tilden wouldn't lie. If he says there's corn, there's corn.

HALIE: What's the meaning of this corn, Tilden!

TILDEN: It's a mystery to me. I was out in back there. And the rain was coming down. And I didn't feel like coming back inside. I didn't feel the cold so much. I didn't mind the wet. So I was just walking. I was muddy but I didn't mind the mud so much. And I looked up. And I saw this stand of corn. In fact I was standing in it. So, I was standing in it.

HALIE: There isn't any corn outside, Tilden! There's no corn! Now, you must've either stolen this corn or you bought it.

DODGE: He doesn't have any money.

HALIE (*to Tilden*): So you stole it!

TILDEN: I didn't steal it. I don't want to get kicked out of Illinois. I was kicked out of New Mexico and I don't want to get kicked out of Illinois.

HALIE: You're going to get kicked out of this house, Tilden, if you don't tell me where you got that corn!

(*Tilden starts crying softly to himself but keeps husking corn. Pause.*)

DODGE (*to Halie*): Why'd you have to tell him that? Who cares where he got the corn? Why'd you have to go and tell him that?

HALIE (*to Dodge*): It's your fault you know! You're the one that's behind all this! I suppose you thought it'd be funny! Some joke! Cover the house with corn husks. You better get this cleaned up before Bradley sees it.

DODGE: Bradley's not getting in the front door!

HALIE (*kicking husks, striding back and forth*): Bradley's going to be very upset when he sees this. He doesn't like to see the house in disarray. He can't stand it when one thing is out of place. The slightest thing. You know how he gets.

DODGE: Bradley doesn't even live here!

HALIE: It's his home as much as ours. He was born in this house!

DODGE: He was born in a hog wallow.

HALIE: Don't you say that! Don't you ever say that!

DODGE: He was born in a goddamn hog wallow! That's where he was born and that's where he belongs! He doesn't belong in this house!

HALIE (*she stops*): I don't know what's come over

you, Dodge. I don't know what in the world's come over you. You've become an evil man. You used to be a good man.

DODGE: Six of one, a half dozen of another.

HALIE: You sit here day and night, festering away! Decomposing! Smelling up the house with your putrid body! Hacking your head off till all hours of the morning! Thinking up mean, evil, stupid things to say about your own flesh and blood!

DODGE: He's not my flesh and blood! My flesh and blood's buried in the back yard!

(*They freeze. Long pause. The men stare at her.*)

HALIE (*quietly*): That's enough, Dodge. That's quite enough. I'm going out now. I'm going to have lunch with Father Dewis. I'm going to ask him about a monument. A statue. At least a plaque.

(*She crosses to the door up right. She stops.*)

HALIE: If you need anything, ask Tilden. He's the oldest. I've left some money on the kitchen table.

DODGE: I don't need anything.

HALIE: No, I suppose not. (*She opens the door and looks out through porch.*) Still raining. I love the smell just after it stops. The ground. I won't be too late.

(*She goes out door and closes it. She's still visible on the porch as she crosses toward stage left screen door. She stops in the middle of the porch, speaks to Dodge but doesn't turn to him.*)

HALIE: Dodge, tell Tilden not to go out in the back lot anymore. I don't want him back there in the rain.

DODGE: You tell him. He's sitting right here.

HALIE: He never listens to me, Dodge. He's never listened to me in the past.

DODGE: I'll tell him.

HALIE: We have to watch him just like we used to now. Just like we always have. He's still a child.

DODGE: I'll watch him.

HALIE: Good.

(*She crosses to screen door, left, takes an umbrella off a hook, and goes out the door. The door slams behind her. Long pause. Tilden husks corn, stares at pail. Dodge lights a cigarette, stares at TV.*)

TILDEN (*still husking*): You shouldn't a told her that.

DODGE (*staring at TV*): What?

TILDEN: What you told her. You know.

DODGE: What do you know about it?

TILDEN: I know. I know all about it. We all know.

DODGE: So what difference does it make? Everybody knows, everybody's forgot.

TILDEN: She hasn't forgot.

DODGE: She should've forgot.

TILDEN: It's different for a woman. She couldn't forget that. How could she forget that?

DODGE: I don't want to talk about it!

TILDEN: What do you want to talk about?

DODGE: I don't want to talk about anything! I don't want to talk about troubles or what happened fifty years ago or thirty years ago or the race track or Florida or the last time I seeded the corn! I don't want to talk!

TILDEN: You don't wanna die, do you?

DODGE: No, I don't wanna die either.

TILDEN: Well, you gotta talk or you'll die.

DODGE: Who told you that?

TILDEN: That's what I know. I found that out in New Mexico. I thought I was dying but I just lost my voice.

DODGE: Were you with somebody?

TILDEN: I was alone. I thought I was dead.

DODGE: Might as well have been. What'd you come back here for?

TILDEN: I didn't know where to go.

DODGE: You're a grown man. You shouldn't be needing your parents at your age. It's unnatural. There's nothing we can do for you now anyway. Couldn't you make a living down there? Couldn't you find some way to make a living? Support yourself? What'd'ya come back here for? You expect us to feed you forever?

TILDEN: I didn't know where else to go.

DODGE: I never went back to my parents. Never. Never even had the urge. I was independent. Always independent. Always found a way.

TILDEN: I didn't know what to do. I couldn't figure anything out.

DODGE: There's nothing to figure out. You just forge ahead. What's there to figure out?

(*Tilden stands.*)

TILDEN: I don't know.

DODGE: Where are you going?

TILDEN: Out back.

DODGE: You're not supposed to go out there. You heard what she said. Don't play deaf with me!

TILDEN: I like it out there.

DODGE: In the rain?

TILDEN: Especially in the rain. I like the feeling of it. Feels like it always did.

DODGE: You're supposed to watch out for me. Get me things when I need them.

TILDEN: What do you need?

DODGE: I don't need anything! But I might. I might need something any second. Any second now. I can't be left alone for a minute!

(*Dodge starts to cough.*)

TILDEN: I'll be right outside. You can just yell.

DODGE (*between coughs*): No! It's too far! You can't go out there! It's too far! You might not ever hear me!

TILDEN (*moving to pills*): Why don't you take a pill? You want a pill?

(*Dodge coughs more violently, throws himself back against sofa, clutches his throat. Tilden stands by helplessly.*)

DODGE: Water! Get me some water!

(*Tilden rushes off left. Dodge reaches out for the pills, knocking some bottles to the floor, coughing in spasms. He grabs a small bottle, takes out pills, and swallows them. Tilden rushes back on with a glass of water. Dodge takes it and drinks, his coughing subsides.*)

TILDEN: You all right now?

(*Dodge nods. Drinks more water. Tilden moves in closer to him. Dodge sets glass of water on the night table. His coughing is almost gone.*)

TILDEN: Why don't you lay down for a while? Just rest a little.

(*Tilden helps Dodge lay down on the sofa. Covers him with blanket.*)

DODGE: You're not going outside, are you?

TILDEN: No.

DODGE: I don't want to wake up and find you not here.

TILDEN: I'll be here.

(*Tilden tucks blanket around Dodge.*)

DODGE: You'll stay right here?

TILDEN: I'll stay in my chair.

DODGE: That's not a chair. That's my old milking stool.

TILDEN: I know.

DODGE: Don't call it a chair.

TILDEN: I won't.

(*Tilden tries to take Dodge's baseball cap off.*)

DODGE: What're you doing! Leave that on me! Don't take that offa me! That's my cap!

(*Tilden leaves the cap on Dodge.*)

TILDEN: I know.

DODGE: Bradley'll shave my head if I don't have that on. That's my cap.

TILDEN: I know it is.

DODGE: Don't take my cap off.

TILDEN: I won't.

DODGE: You stay right here now.

TILDEN (*sits on stool*): I will.

DODGE: Don't go outside. There's nothing out there.

TILDEN: I won't.

DODGE: Everything's in here. Everything you need. Money's on the table. TV. Is the TV on?

TILDEN: Yeah.

DODGE: Turn it off! Turn the damn thing off! What's it doing on?

TILDEN (*shuts off TV, light goes out*): You left it on.

DODGE: Well, turn it off.

TILDEN (*sits on stool again*): It's off.

DODGE: Leave it off.

TILDEN: I will.

DODGE: When I fall asleep you can turn it on.

TILDEN: Okay.

DODGE: You can watch the ball game. Red Sox. You like the Red Sox don't you?

TILDEN: Yeah.

DODGE: You can watch the Red Sox. Pee Wee Reese. Pee Wee Reese. You remember Pee Wee Reese?

TILDEN: No.

DODGE: Was he with the Red Sox?

TILDEN: I don't know.

DODGE: Pee Wee Reese. (*Falling asleep.*) You can watch the Cardinals. You remember Stan Musial.

TILDEN: No.

DODGE: Stan Musial. (*Falling into sleep.*) Bases loaded. Top a' the sixth. Bases loaded. Runner on first and third. Big fat knuckle ball. Floater. Big as a blimp. Cracko! Ball just took off like a rocket. Just pulverized. I marked it. Marked it with my eyes. Straight between the clock and the Burma Shave ad. I was the first kid out there. First kid. I had to fight hard for that ball. I wouldn't give it up. They almost tore the ears right off me. But I wouldn't give it up.

(*Dodge falls into deep sleep. Tilden just sits staring at him for a while. Slowly he leans toward the sofa, checking to see if Dodge is well asleep. He reaches slowly under the cushion and pulls out the bottle of booze. Dodge sleeps soundly. Tilden stands quietly, staring at Dodge as he uncaps the bottle and takes a long drink. He caps the bottle and sticks it in his hip pocket. He looks around at the husks on the floor and then back to Dodge. He moves center stage and gathers an armload of corn husks then crosses back to the sofa. He stands holding the husks over Dodge and looking down at him he gently spreads the corn husks over the whole length of Dodge's body. He stands back and looks at Dodge. Pulls out bottle, takes another drink, returns bottle to his hip pocket. He gathers more husks and repeats the procedure until the floor is clean of corn husks and Dodge is completely covered in them except for his head. Tilden takes another long drink, stares at Dodge sleeping, then quietly exits stage left.*)

Long pause as the sound of rain continues. Dodge
sleeps on. The figure of Bradley appears up left, outside
the screen porch door. He holds a wet newspaper over
his head as a protection from the rain. He seems to be
struggling with the door, then slips and almost falls to
the ground. Dodge sleeps on, undisturbed.)

BRADLEY: Sonuvabitch! Sonuvagoddamnbitch!

(Bradley recovers his footing and makes it through
the screen door onto the porch. He throws the newspaper down, shakes the water out of his hair, and
brushes the rain off of his shoulders. He is a big man
dressed in a gray sweatshirt, black suspenders, baggy
dark blue pants, and black janitor's shoes. His left leg
is wooden, having been amputated above the knee.
He moves with an exaggerated, almost mechanical
limp. The squeaking sounds of leather and metal accompany his walk coming from the harness and
hinges of the false leg. His arms and shoulders are extremely powerful and muscular due to a lifetime dependency on the upper torso doing all the work for
the legs. He is about five years younger than Tilden.
He moves laboriously to the stage right door and enters, closing the door behind him. He doesn't notice
Dodge at first. He moves toward the staircase.)

BRADLEY (calling to upstairs): Mom!

(He stops and listens. Turns upstage and sees Dodge
sleeping. Notices corn husks. He moves slowly toward sofa. Stops next to pail and looks into it. Looks
at husks. Dodge stays asleep. Talks to himself.)

BRADLEY: What in the hell is this?

(He looks at Dodge's sleeping face and shakes his head
in disgust. He pulls out a pair of black electric hair
clippers from his pocket. Unwinds the cord and crosses
to the lamp. He jabs his wooden leg behind the knee,
causing it to bend at the joint and awkwardly kneels to
plug the cord into a floor outlet. He pulls himself to his
feet again by using the sofa as leverage. He moves to
Dodge's head and again jabs his false leg. Goes down
on one knee. He violently knocks away some of the
corn husks, and then jerks off Dodge's baseball cap
and throws it down center stage. Dodge stays asleep.
Bradley switches on the clippers. Lights start dimming.
Bradley cuts Dodge's hair while he sleeps. Lights dim
slowly to black with the sound of clippers and rain.)

ACT 2

Scene: Same set as act 1. Night. Sound of rain. Dodge
still asleep on sofa. His hair is cut extremely short and
in places the scalp is cut and bleeding. His cap is still

center stage. All the corn and husks, pail and milking
stool have been cleared away. The lights come up to
the sound of a young girl laughing offstage left.
Dodge remains asleep. Shelly and Vince appear up left
outside the screen porch door sharing the shelter of
Vince's overcoat above their heads. Shelly is about
nineteen, black hair, very beautiful. She wears tight
jeans, high heels, purple T-shirt, and a short rabbit fur
coat. Her makeup is exaggerated and her hair has
been curled. Vince is Tilden's son, about twenty-two,
wears a plaid shirt, jeans, dark glasses, cowboy boots
and carries a black saxophone case. They shake the
rain off themselves as they enter the porch through
the screen door.

SHELLY (laughing, gesturing to house): This is it? I
don't believe this is it!

VINCE: This is it.

SHELLY: This is the house?

VINCE: This is the house.

SHELLY: I don't believe it!

VINCE: How come?

SHELLY: It's like a Norman Rockwell cover or something.

VINCE: What's a' matter with that? It's American.

SHELLY: Where's the milkman and the little dog?
What's the little dog's name? Spot. Spot and Jane.
Dick and Jane and Spot.

VINCE: Knock it off.

SHELLY: Dick and Jane and Spot and Mom and Dad
and Junior and Sissy!

(She laughs. Slaps her knee.)

VINCE: Come on! It's my heritage. What dya' expect?

(She laughs more hysterically, out of control.)

SHELLY: "And Tuffy and Toto and Dooda and Bonzo
all went down one day to the corner grocery store
to buy a big bag of licorice for Mr. Marshall's
pussy cat!"

(She laughs so hard she falls to her knees holding her
stomach. Vince stands there looking at her.)

VINCE: Shelly, will you get up!

(She keeps laughing. Staggers to her feet. Turning in
circles holding her stomach.)

SHELLY (continuing her story in kid's voice): "Mr.
Marshall was on vacation. He had no idea that the
four little boys had taken such a liking to his little
kitty cat."

VINCE: Have some respect, would ya'!

SHELLY (trying to control herself): I'm sorry.

VINCE: Pull yourself together.

SHELLY (salutes him): Yes, sir.

Vince and Shelly in a scene from *Buried Child.*

(*She giggles.*)

VINCE: Jesus Christ, Shelly.
SHELLY (*pause, smiling*): And Mr. Marshall —
VINCE: Cut it out.

(*She stops. Stands there staring at him. Stifles a giggle.*)

VINCE (*after pause*): Are you finished?
SHELLY: Oh brother!
VINCE: I don't wanna go in there with you acting like an idiot.
SHELLY: Thanks.
VINCE: Well, I don't.
SHELLY: I won't embarrass you. Don't worry.
VINCE: I'm not worried.
SHELLY: You are too.
VINCE: Shelly, look, I just don't wanna go in there with you giggling your head off. They might think something's wrong with you.
SHELLY: There is.
VINCE: There is not!
SHELLY: Something's definitely wrong with me.
VINCE: There is not!
SHELLY: There's something wrong with you too.

VINCE: There's nothing wrong with me either!
SHELLY: You wanna know what's wrong with you?
VINCE: What?

(*Shelly laughs.*)

VINCE (*crosses back left toward screen door*): I'm leaving!
SHELLY (*stops laughing*): Wait! Stop. Stop! (*Vince stops.*) What's wrong with you is that you take the situation too seriously.
VINCE: I just don't want to have them think that I've suddenly arrived out of the middle of nowhere completely deranged.
SHELLY: What do you want them to think then?
VINCE (*pause*): Nothing. Let's go in.

(*He crosses porch toward stage right interior door. Shelly follows him. The stage right door opens slowly. Vince sticks his head in, doesn't notice Dodge sleeping. Calls out toward staircase.*)

VINCE: Grandma!

(*Shelly breaks into laughter, unseen behind Vince. Vince pulls his head back outside and pulls door shut. We hear their voices again without seeing them.*)

SHELLY'S VOICE (*stops laughing*): I'm sorry. I'm sorry, Vince. I really am. I really am sorry. I won't do it again. I couldn't help it.

VINCE'S VOICE: It's not all that funny.

SHELLY'S VOICE: I know it's not. I'm sorry.

VINCE'S VOICE: I mean this is a tense situation for me! I haven't seen them for over six years. I don't know what to expect.

SHELLY'S VOICE: I know. I won't do it again.

VINCE'S VOICE: Can't you bite your tongue or something?

SHELLY'S VOICE: Just don't say Grandma, okay? (*She giggles, stops.*) I mean if you say "Grandma," I don't know if I can stop myself.

VINCE'S VOICE: Well try!

SHELLY'S VOICE: Okay. Sorry.

(*Door opens again. Vince sticks his head in then enters. Shelly follows behind him. Vince crosses to staircase, sets down saxophone case and overcoat, looks up staircase. Shelly notices Dodge's baseball cap. Crosses to it. Picks it up and puts it on her head. Vince goes up the stairs and disappears at the top. Shelly watches him, then turns and sees Dodge on the sofa. She takes off the baseball cap.*)

VINCE'S VOICE (*from above stairs*): Grandma!

(*Shelly crosses over to Dodge slowly and stands next to him. She stands at his head, reaches out slowly, and touches one of the cuts. The second she touches his head, Dodge jerks up to a sitting position on the sofa, eyes open. Shelly gasps. Dodge looks at her, sees his cap in her hands, quickly puts his hand to his bare head. He glares at Shelly, then whips the cap out of her hands and puts it on. Shelly backs away from him. Dodge stares at her.*)

SHELLY: I'm uh — with Vince.

(*Dodge just glares at her.*)

SHELLY: He's upstairs.

(*Dodge looks at the staircase, then back to Shelly.*)

SHELLY (*calling upstairs*): Vince!

VINCE'S VOICE: Just a second!

SHELLY: You better get down here!

VINCE'S VOICE: Just a minute! I'm looking at the pictures.

(*Dodge keeps staring at her.*)

SHELLY (*to Dodge*): We just got here. Pouring rain on the freeway so we thought we'd stop by. I mean Vince was planning on stopping anyway. He wanted to see you. He said he hadn't seen you in a long time.

(*Pause. Dodge just keeps staring at her.*)

SHELLY: We were going all the way through to New Mexico. To see his father. I guess his father lives out there. We thought we'd stop by and see you on the way. Kill two birds with one stone, you know? (*She laughs, Dodge stares, she stops laughing.*) I mean Vince has this thing about his family now. I guess it's a new thing with him. I kind of find it hard to relate to. But he feels it's important. You know. I mean he feels he wants to get to know you all again. After all this time.

(*Pause, Dodge just stares at her. She moves nervously to staircase and yells up to Vince.*)

SHELLY: Vince, will you come down here please!

(*Vince comes halfway down the stairs.*)

VINCE: I guess they went out for a while.

(*Shelly points to sofa and Dodge. Vince turns and sees Dodge. He comes all the way down staircase and crosses to Dodge. Shelly stays behind near staircase, keeping her distance.*)

VINCE: Grandpa?

(*Dodge looks up at him, not recognizing him.*)

DODGE: Did you bring the whiskey?

(*Vince looks back at Shelly, then back to Dodge.*)

VINCE: Grandpa, it's Vince. I'm Vince. Tilden's son. You remember?

(*Dodge stares at him.*)

DODGE: You didn't do what you told me. You didn't stay here with me.

VINCE: Grandpa, I haven't been here until just now. I just got here.

DODGE: You left. You went outside like we told you not to do. You went out there in back. In the rain.

(*Vince looks back at Shelly. She moves slowly toward sofa.*)

SHELLY: Is he okay?

VINCE: I don't know. (*Takes off his shades.*) Look, Grandpa, don't you remember me? Vince. Your Grandson.

(*Dodge stares at him, then takes off his baseball cap.*)

DODGE (*points to his head*): See what happens when you leave me alone? See that? That's what happens.

(*Vince looks at his head. Vince reaches out to touch his head. Dodge slaps his hand away with the cap and puts it back on his head.*)

VINCE: What's going on, Grandpa? Where's Halie?

DODGE: Don't worry about her. She won't be back for days. She says she'll be back but she won't be. (*He starts laughing.*) There's life in the old girl yet! (*Stops laughing.*)

VINCE: How did you do that to your head?

DODGE: I didn't do it! Don't be ridiculous!

VINCE: Well, who did then?

(*Pause. Dodge stares at Vince.*)

DODGE: Who do you think did it? Who do you think?

(*Shelly moves toward Vince.*)

SHELLY: Vince, maybe we oughta' go. I don't like this. I mean this isn't my idea of a good time.

VINCE (*to Shelly*): Just a second. (*To Dodge.*) Grandpa, look, I just got here. I just now got here. I haven't been here for six years. I don't know anything that's happened.

(*Pause. Dodge stares at him.*)

DODGE: You don't know anything?

VINCE: No.

DODGE: Well, that's good. That's good. It's much better not to know anything. Much, much better.

VINCE: Isn't there anybody here with you?

(*Dodge turns slowly and looks off to stage left.*)

DODGE: Tilden's here.

VINCE: No, Grandpa, Tilden's in New Mexico. That's where I was going. I'm going out there to see him.

(*Dodge turns slowly back to Vince.*)

DODGE: Tilden's here.

(*Vince backs away and joins Shelly. Dodge stares at them.*)

SHELLY: Vince, why don't we spend the night in a motel and come back in the morning? We could have breakfast. Maybe everything would be different.

VINCE: Don't be scared. There's nothing to be scared of. He's just old.

SHELLY: I'm not scared!

DODGE: You two are not my idea of the perfect couple!

SHELLY (*after pause*): Oh really? Why's that?

VINCE: Shh! Don't aggravate him.

DODGE: There's something wrong between the two of you. Something not compatible.

VINCE: Grandpa, where did Halie go? Maybe we should call her.

DODGE: What are you talking about? Do you know what you're talking about? Are you just talking for the sake of talking? Lubricating the gums?

VINCE: I'm trying to figure out what's going on here!

DODGE: Is that it?

VINCE: Yes. I mean I expected everything to be different.

DODGE: Who are you to expect anything? Who are you supposed to be?

VINCE: I'm Vince! Your Grandson!

DODGE: Vince. My Grandson.

VINCE: Tilden's son.

DODGE: Tilden's son, Vince.

VINCE: You haven't seen me for a long time.

DODGE: When was the last time?

VINCE: I don't remember.

DODGE: You don't remember?

VINCE: No.

DODGE: You don't remember. How am I supposed to remember if you don't remember?

SHELLY: Vince, come on. This isn't going to work out.

VINCE (*to Shelly*): Just take it easy.

SHELLY: I'm taking it easy! He doesn't even know who you are!

VINCE (*crossing toward Dodge*): Grandpa, look —

DODGE: Stay where you are! Keep your distance!

(*Vince stops. Looks back at Shelly, then to Dodge.*)

SHELLY: Vince, this is really making me nervous. I mean he doesn't even want us here. He doesn't even like us.

DODGE: She's a beautiful girl.

VINCE: Thanks.

DODGE: Very Beautiful Girl.

SHELLY: Oh my God.

DODGE (*to Shelly*): What's your name?

SHELLY: Shelly.

DODGE: Shelly. That's a man's name isn't it?

SHELLY: Not in this case.

DODGE (*to Vince*): She's a smart-ass too.

SHELLY: Vince! Can we go?

DODGE: She wants to go. She just got here and she wants to go.

VINCE: This is kind of strange for her.

DODGE: She'll get used to it. (*To Shelly.*) What part of the country do you come from?

SHELLY: Originally?

DODGE: That's right. Originally. At the very start.

SHELLY: L.A.

DODGE: L.A. Stupid country.

SHELLY: I can't stand this, Vince! This is really unbelievable!

DODGE: It's stupid! L.A. is stupid! So is Florida! All

those Sunshine States. They're all stupid! Do you know why they're stupid?

SHELLY: Illuminate me.

DODGE: I'll tell you why. Because they're full of smart-asses! That's why.

(*Shelly turns her back to Dodge, crosses to staircase, and sits on bottom step.*)

DODGE (*to Vince*): Now she's insulted.

VINCE: Well, you weren't very polite.

DODGE: She's insulted! Look at her! In my house she's insulted! She's over there sulking because I insulted her!

SHELLY (*to Vince*): This is really terrific. This is wonderful. And you were worried about me making the right first impression!

DODGE (*to Vince*): She's a fireball, isn't she? Regular fireball. I had some a' them in my day. Temporary stuff. Never lasted more than a week.

VINCE: Grandpa —

DODGE: Stop calling me Grandpa will ya'! It's sickening. "Grandpa." I'm nobody's Grandpa!

(*Dodge starts feeling around under the cushion for the bottle of whiskey. Shelly gets up from the staircase.*)

SHELLY (*to Vince*): Maybe you've got the wrong house. Did you ever think of that? Maybe this is the wrong address!

VINCE: It's not the wrong address! I recognize the yard.

SHELLY: Yeah, but do you recognize the people? He says he's not your Grandfather.

DODGE (*digging for bottle*): Where's that bottle!

VINCE: He's just sick of something. I don't know what's happened to him.

DODGE: Where's my goddamn bottle!

(*Dodge gets up from sofa and starts tearing the cushions off it and throwing them downstage, looking for the whiskey.*)

SHELLY: Can't we just drive on to New Mexico? This is terrible, Vince! I don't want to stay here. In this house. I thought it was going to be turkey dinners and apple pie and all that kinda stuff.

VINCE: Well, I hate to disappoint you!

SHELLY: I'm not disappointed! I'm fuckin' terrified! I wanna' go!

(*Dodge yells toward stage left.*)

DODGE: Tilden! Tilden!

(*Dodge keeps ripping away at the sofa looking for his bottle, he knocks over the night stand with the bottles. Vince and Shelly watch as he starts ripping the stuffing out of the sofa.*)

VINCE (*to Shelly*): He's lost his mind or something. I've got to try to help him.

SHELLY: You help him! I'm leaving!

(*Shelly starts to leave. Vince grabs her. They struggle as Dodge keeps ripping away at the sofa and yelling.*)

DODGE: Tilden! Tilden, get your ass in here! Tilden!

SHELLY: Let go of me!

VINCE: You're not going anywhere! You're going to stay right here!

SHELLY: Let go of me, you sonuvabitch! I'm not your property!

(*Suddenly Tilden walks on from stage left just as he did before. This time his arms are full of carrots. Dodge, Vince, and Shelly stop suddenly when they see him. They all stare at Tilden as he crosses slowly center stage with the carrots and stops. Dodge sits on sofa, exhausted.*)

DODGE (*panting, to Tilden*): Where in the hell have you been?

TILDEN: Out back.

DODGE: Where's my bottle?

TILDEN: Gone.

(*Tilden and Vince stare at each other. Shelly backs away.*)

DODGE (*to Tilden*): You stole my bottle!

VINCE (*to Tilden*): Dad?

(*Tilden just stares at Vince.*)

DODGE: You had no right to steal my bottle! No right at all!

VINCE (*to Tilden*): It's Vince. I'm Vince.

(*Tilden stares at Vince, then looks at Dodge, then turns to Shelly.*)

TILDEN (*after pause*): I picked these carrots. If anybody wants any carrots, I picked 'em.

SHELLY (*to Vince*): This is your father?

VINCE (*to Tilden*): Dad, what're you doing here?

(*Tilden just stares at Vince, holding carrots, Dodge pulls the blanket back over himself.*)

DODGE (*to Tilden*): You're going to have to get me another bottle! You gotta get me a bottle before Halie comes back! There's money on the table. (*Points to stage left kitchen.*)

TILDEN (*shaking his head*): I'm not going down there. Into town.

(*Shelly crosses to Tilden. Tilden stares at her.*)

SHELLY (*to Tilden*): Are you Vince's father?

TILDEN (*to Shelly*): Vince?

SHELLY (*pointing to Vince*): This is supposed to be your son! Is he your son? Do you recognize him? I'm just along for the ride here. I thought everybody knew each other!

(*Tilden stares at Vince. Dodge wraps himself up in the blanket and sits on sofa staring at the floor.*)

TILDEN: I had a son once but we buried him.

(*Dodge quickly looks at Tilden. Shelly looks to Vince.*)

DODGE: You shut up about that! You don't know anything about that!

VINCE: Dad, I thought you were in New Mexico. We were going to drive down there and see you.

TILDEN: Long way to drive.

DODGE (*to Tilden*): You don't know anything about that! That happened before you were born! Long before!

VINCE: What's happened, Dad? What's going on here? I thought everything was all right. What's happened to Halie?

TILDEN: She left.

SHELLY (*to Tilden*): Do you want me to take those carrots for you?

(*Tilden stares at her. She moves in close to him. Holds out her arms. Tilden stares at her arms then slowly dumps the carrots into her arms. Shelly stands there holding the carrots.*)

TILDEN (*to Shelly*): You like carrots?

SHELLY: Sure. I like all kinds of vegetables.

DODGE (*to Tilden*): You gotta get me a bottle before Halie comes back!

(*Dodge hits sofa with his fist. Vince crosses up to Dodge and tries to console him. Shelly and Tilden stay facing each other.*)

TILDEN (*to Shelly*): Back yard's full of carrots. Corn. Potatoes.

SHELLY: You're Vince's father, right?

TILDEN: All kinds of vegetables. You like vegetables?

SHELLY (*laughs*): Yeah. I love vegetables.

TILDEN: We could cook these carrots, ya' know. You could cut 'em up and we could cook 'em.

SHELLY: All right.

TILDEN: I'll get you a pail and a knife.

SHELLY: Okay.

TILDEN: I'll be right back. Don't go.

(*Tilden exits offstage left. Shelly stands center, arms full of carrots. Vince stands next to Dodge. Shelly looks toward Vince, then down at the carrots.*)

DODGE (*to Vince*): You could get me a bottle. (*Pointing off left.*) There's money on the table.

VINCE: Grandpa, why don't you lay down for a while?

DODGE: I don't wanna lay down for a while! Every time I lay down something happens! (*Whips off his cap, points at his head.*) Look what happens! That's what happens! (*Pulls his cap back on.*) You go lie down and see what happens to you! See how you like it! They'll steal your bottle! They'll cut your hair! They'll murder your children! That's what'll happen.

VINCE: Just relax for a while.

DODGE (*pause*): You could get me a bottle, ya' know. There's nothing stopping you from getting me a bottle.

SHELLY: Why don't you get him a bottle, Vince? Maybe it would help everybody identify each other.

DODGE (*pointing to Shelly*): There, see? She thinks you should get me a bottle.

(*Vince crosses to Shelly.*)

VINCE: What're you doing with those carrots?

SHELLY: I'm waiting for your father.

DODGE: She thinks you should get me a bottle!

VINCE: Shelly, put the carrots down, will ya'! We gotta deal with the situation here! I'm gonna need your help.

SHELLY: I'm helping.

VINCE: You're only adding to the problem! You're making things worse! Put the carrots down!

(*Vince tries to knock the carrots out of her arms. She turns away from him, protecting the carrots.*)

SHELLY: Get away from me! Stop it!

(*Vince stands back from her. She turns to him still holding the carrots.*)

VINCE (*to Shelly*): Why are you doing this! Are you trying to make fun of me? This is my family, you know!

SHELLY: You coulda' fooled me! I'd just as soon not be here myself. I'd just as soon be a thousand miles from here. I'd rather be anywhere but here. You're the one who wants to stay. So I'll stay. I'll stay and I'll cut the carrots. And I'll cook the carrots. And I'll do whatever I have to do to survive. Just to make it through this.

VINCE: Put the carrots down, Shelly.

(*Tilden enters from left with pail, milking stool, and a knife. He sets the stool and pail center stage for Shelly. Shelly looks at Vince, then sits down on stool, sets the carrots on the floor, and takes the knife from Tilden. She looks at Vince again, then picks up a carrot, cuts the ends off, scrapes it, and drops it in pail. She repeats this; Vince glares at her. She smiles.*)

DODGE: She could get me a bottle. She's the type a' girl that could get me a bottle. Easy. She'd go down there. Slink up to the counter. They'd probably give her two bottles for the price of one. She could do that.

(*Shelly laughs. Keeps cutting carrots. Vince crosses up to Dodge, looks at him. Tilden watches Shelly's hands. Long pause.*)

VINCE (*to Dodge*): I haven't changed that much. I mean physically. Physically I'm just about the same. Same size. Same weight. Everything's the same.

(*Dodge keeps staring at Shelly while Vince talks to him.*)

DODGE: She's a beautiful girl. Exceptional.

(*Vince moves in front of Dodge to block his view of Shelly. Dodge keeps craning his head around to see her as Vince demonstrates tricks from his past.*)

VINCE: Look. Look at this. Do you remember this? I used to bend my thumb behind my knuckles. You remember? I used to do it at the dinner table.

(*Vince bends a thumb behind his knuckles for Dodge and holds it out to him. Dodge takes a short glance then looks back at Shelly. Vince shifts position and shows him something else.*)

VINCE: What about this?

(*Vince curls his lips back and starts drumming on his teeth with his fingernails making little tapping sounds. Dodge watches awhile. Tilden turns toward the sound. Vince keeps it up. He sees Tilden taking notice and crosses to Tilden as he drums on his teeth. Dodge turns TV on, watches it.*)

VINCE: You remember this, Dad?

(*Vince keeps on drumming for Tilden. Tilden watches awhile, fascinated, then turns back to Shelly. Vince keeps up the drumming on his teeth, crosses back to Dodge doing it. Shelly keeps working on carrots, talking to Tilden.*)

SHELLY (*to Tilden*): He drives me crazy with that sometimes.

VINCE (*to Dodge*): I know! Here's one you'll remember. You used to kick me out of the house for this one.

(*Vince pulls his shirt out of his belt and holds it tucked under his chin with his stomach exposed. He grabs the flesh on either side of his belly button and pushes it in and out to make it look like a mouth talking. He watches his belly button and makes a deep sounding cartoon voice to synchronize with the movement. He demonstrates it to Dodge, then*

crosses down to Tilden doing it. Both Dodge and Tilden take short, uninterested glances then ignore him.)

VINCE (*deep cartoon voice*): "Hello. How are you? I'm fine. Thank you very much. It's so good to see you looking well this fine Sunday morning. I was going down to the hardware store to fetch a pail of water."

SHELLY: Vince, don't be pathetic, will ya!

(*Vince stops. Tucks his shirt back in.*)

SHELLY: Jesus Christ. They're not gonna play. Can't you see that?

(*Shelly keeps cutting carrots. Vince slowly moves toward Tilden. Tilden keeps watching Shelly. Dodge watches TV.*)

VINCE (*to Shelly*): I don't get it. I really don't get it. Maybe it's me. Maybe I forgot something.

DODGE (*from sofa*): You forgot to get me a bottle! That's what you forgot. Anybody in this house could get me a bottle. Anybody! But nobody will. Nobody understands the urgency! Peelin carrots is more important. Playin piano on your teeth! Well I hope you all remember this when you get up in years. When you find yourself immobilized. Dependent on the whims of others.

(*Vince moves up toward Dodge. Pause as he looks at him.*)

VINCE: I'll get you a bottle.

DODGE: You will?

VINCE: Sure.

(*Shelly stands holding knife and carrot.*)

SHELLY: You're not going to leave me here, are you?

VINCE (*moving to her*): You suggested it! You said, "Why don't I go get him a bottle?" So I'll go get him a bottle!

SHELLY: But I can't stay here.

VINCE: What is going on! A minute ago you were ready to cut carrots all night!

SHELLY: That was only if you stayed. Something to keep me busy, so I wouldn't be so nervous. I don't want to stay here alone.

DODGE: Don't let her talk you out of it! She's a bad influence. I could see it the minute she stepped in here.

SHELLY (*to Dodge*): You were asleep!

TILDEN (*to Shelly*): Don't you want to cut carrots anymore?

SHELLY: Sure. Sure I do.

(*Shelly sits back down on stool and continues cutting carrots. Pause. Vince moves around, stroking his hair,*

staring at Dodge and Tilden. Vince and Shelly exchange glances. Dodge watches TV.)

VINCE: Boy! This is amazing. This is truly amazing.
(Keeps moving around.) What is this anyway? Am I
in a time warp or something? Have I committed an
unpardonable offense? It's true, I'm not married.
(Shelly looks at him, then back to carrots.) But I'm
also not divorced. I have been known to plunge into
sinful infatuation with the Alto Saxophone. Sucking on number 5 reeds deep into the wee wee hours.

SHELLY: Vince, what are you doing that for? They
don't care about any of that. They just don't recognize you, that's all.

VINCE: How could they not recognize me! How in the
hell could they not recognize me! I'm their son!

DODGE (watching TV): You're no son of mine. I've
had sons in my time and you're not one of 'em.

(Long pause. Vince stares at Dodge, then looks at
Tilden. He turns to Shelly.)

VINCE: Shelly, I gotta go out for a while. I just gotta
go out. I'll get a bottle and I'll come right back.
You'll be okay here. Really.

SHELLY: I don't know if I can handle this, Vince.

VINCE: I just gotta think or something. I don't know.
I gotta put this all together.

SHELLY: Can't we just go?

VINCE: No! I gotta find out what's going on.

SHELLY: Look, you think you're bad off, what about
me? Not only don't they recognize me but I've
never seen them before in my life. I don't know
who these guys are. They could be anybody!

VINCE: They're not anybody!

SHELLY: That's what you say.

VINCE: They're my family for Christ's sake! I should
know who my own family is! Now give me a
break. It won't take that long. I'll just go out and
I'll come right back. Nothing'll happen. I promise.

(Shelly stares at him. Pause.)

SHELLY: All right.

VINCE: Thanks. (He crosses up to Dodge.) I'm gonna
go out now, Grandpa, and I'll pick you up a bottle.
Okay?

DODGE: Change of heart huh? (Pointing off left.)
Money's on the table. In the kitchen.

(Vince moves toward Shelly.)

VINCE (to Shelly): You be all right?

SHELLY (cutting carrots): Sure. I'm fine. I'll just keep
real busy while you're gone.

(Vince looks at Tilden who keeps staring down at
Shelly's hands.)

DODGE: Persistence, see? That's what it takes. Persis-

tence. Persistence, fortitude, and determination.
Those are the three virtues. You stick with those
three and you can't go wrong.

VINCE (to Tilden): You want anything, Dad?

TILDEN (looks up at Vince): Me?

VINCE: From the store? I'm gonna get Grandpa a
bottle.

TILDEN: He's not supposed to drink. Halie wouldn't
like it.

VINCE: He wants a bottle.

TILDEN: He's not supposed to drink.

DODGE (to Vince): Don't negotiate with him! Don't
make any transactions until you've spoken to me
first! He'll steal you blind!

VINCE (to Dodge): Tilden says you're not supposed to
drink.

DODGE: Tilden's lost his marbles! Look at him! He's
around the bend. Take a look at him.

(Vince stares at Tilden. Tilden watches Shelly's hands
as she keeps cutting carrots.)

DODGE: Now look at me. Look here at me!

(Vince looks back to Dodge.)

DODGE: Now, between the two of us, who do you
think is more trustworthy? Him or me? Can you
trust a man who keeps bringing in vegetables from
out of nowhere? Take a look at him.

(Vince looks back at Tilden.)

SHELLY: Go get the bottle, Vince.

VINCE (to Shelly): You sure you'll be all right?

SHELLY: I'll be fine. I feel right at home now.

VINCE: You do?

SHELLY: I'm fine. Now that I've got the carrots everything is all right.

VINCE: I'll be right back.

(Vince crosses stage left.)

DODGE: Where are you going?

VINCE: I'm going to get the money.

DODGE: Then where are you going?

VINCE: Liquor store.

DODGE: Don't go anyplace else. Don't go off some
place and drink. Come right back here.

VINCE: I will.

(Vince exits stage left.)

DODGE (calling after Vince): You've got responsibility
now! And don't go out the back way either! Come
out through this way! I wanna' see you when you
leave! Don't go out the back!

VINCE'S VOICE (off left): I won't!

(Dodge turns and looks at Tilden and Shelly.)

DODGE: Untrustworthy. Probably drown himself if he went out the back. Fall right in a hole. I'd never get my bottle.

SHELLY: I wouldn't worry about Vince. He can take care of himself.

DODGE: Oh he can, huh? Independent.

(*Vince comes on again from stage left with two dollars in his hand. He crosses stage right past Dodge.*)

DODGE (*to Vince*): You got the money?

VINCE: Yeah. Two bucks.

DODGE: Two bucks. Two bucks is two bucks. Don't sneer.

VINCE: What kind do you want?

DODGE: Whiskey! Gold Star Sour Mash. Use your own discretion.

VINCE: Okay.

(*Vince crosses to stage right door. Opens it. Stops when he hears Tilden.*)

TILDEN (*to Vince*): You drove all the way from New Mexico?

(*Vince turns and looks at Tilden. They stare at each other. Vince shakes his head, goes out the door, crosses porch, and exits out screen door. Tilden watches him go. Pause.*)

SHELLY: You really don't recognize him? Either one of you?

(*Tilden turns again and stares at Shelly's hands as she cuts carrots.*)

DODGE (*watching TV*): Recognize who?

SHELLY: Vince.

DODGE: What's to recognize?

(*Dodge lights a cigarette, coughs slightly, and stares at TV.*)

SHELLY: It'd be cruel if you recognized him and didn't tell him. Wouldn't be fair.

(*Dodge just stares at TV, smoking.*)

TILDEN: I thought I recognized him. I thought I recognized something about him.

SHELLY: You did?

TILDEN: I thought I saw a face inside his face.

SHELLY: Well, it was probably that you saw what he used to look like. You haven't seen him for six years.

TILDEN: I haven't?

SHELLY: That's what he says.

(*Tilden moves around in front of her as she continues with carrots.*)

TILDEN: Where was it I saw him last?

SHELLY: I don't know. I've only known him for a few months. He doesn't tell me everything.

TILDEN: He doesn't?

SHELLY: Not stuff like that.

TILDEN: What does he tell you?

SHELLY: You mean in general?

TILDEN: Yeah.

(*Tilden moves around behind her.*)

SHELLY: Well, he tells me all kinds of things.

TILDEN: Like what?

SHELLY: I don't know! I mean I can't just come right out and tell you how he feels.

TILDEN: How come?

(*Tilden keeps moving around her slowly in a circle.*)

SHELLY: Because it's stuff he told me privately!

TILDEN: And you can't tell me?

SHELLY: I don't even know you!

DODGE: Tilden, go out in the kitchen and make me some coffee! Leave the girl alone.

SHELLY (*to Dodge*): He's all right.

(*Tilden ignores Dodge, keeps moving around Shelly. He stares at her hair and coat. Dodge stares at TV.*)

TILDEN: You mean you can't tell me anything?

SHELLY: I can tell you some things. I mean we can have a conversation.

TILDEN: We can?

SHELLY: Sure. We're having a conversation right now.

TILDEN: We are?

SHELLY: Yes. That's what we're doing.

TILDEN: But there's certain things you can't tell me, right?

SHELLY: Right.

TILDEN: There's certain things I can't tell you either.

SHELLY: How come?

TILDEN: I don't know. Nobody's supposed to hear it.

SHELLY: Well, you can tell me anything you want to.

TILDEN: I can?

SHELLY: Sure.

TILDEN: It might not be very nice.

SHELLY: That's all right. I've been around.

TILDEN: It might be awful.

SHELLY: Well, can't you tell me anything nice?

(*Tilden stops in front of her and stares at her coat. Shelly looks back at him. Long pause.*)

TILDEN (*after pause*): Can I touch your coat?

SHELLY: My coat? (*She looks at her coat then back to Tilden.*) Sure.

TILDEN: You don't mind?

SHELLY: No. Go ahead.

(*Shelly holds her arm out for Tilden to touch. Dodge stays fixed on TV. Tilden moves in slowly toward*

Shelly, staring at her arm. He reaches out very slowly and touches her arm, feels the fur gently, then draws his hand back. Shelly keeps her arm out.)

SHELLY: It's rabbit.
TILDEN: Rabbit.

(He reaches out again very slowly and touches the fur on her arm then pulls back his hand again. Shelly drops her arm.)

SHELLY: My arm was getting tired.
TILDEN: Can I hold it?
SHELLY (*pause*): The coat? Sure.

(Shelly takes off her coat and hands it to Tilden. Tilden takes it slowly, feels the fur, then puts it on. Shelly watches as Tilden strokes the fur slowly. He smiles at her. She goes back to cutting carrots.)

SHELLY: You can have it if you want.
TILDEN: I can?
SHELLY: Yeah. I've got a raincoat in the car. That's all I need.
TILDEN: You've got a car?
SHELLY: Vince does.

(Tilden walks around stroking the fur and smiling at the coat. Shelly watches him when he's not looking. Dodge sticks with TV, stretches out on sofa wrapped in blanket.)

TILDEN (*as he walks around*): I had a car once! I had a white car! I drove. I went everywhere. I went to the mountains. I drove in the snow.
SHELLY: That must've been fun.
TILDEN (*still moving, feeling coat*): I drove all day long sometimes. Across the desert. Way out across the desert. I drove past towns. Anywhere. Past palm trees. Lightning. Anything. I would drive through it. I would drive through it and I would stop and I would look around and I would drive on. I would get back in and drive! I loved to drive. There was nothing I loved more. Nothing I dreamed of was better than driving.
DODGE (*eyes on TV*): Pipe down, would ya'!

(Tilden stops. Stares at Shelly.)

SHELLY: Do you do much driving now?
TILDEN: Now? Now? I don't drive now.
SHELLY: How come?
TILDEN: I'm grown up now.
SHELLY: Grown up?
TILDEN: I'm not a kid.
SHELLY: You don't have to be a kid to drive.
TILDEN: It wasn't driving then.
SHELLY: What was it?
TILDEN: Adventure. I went everywhere.
SHELLY: Well, you can still do that.

TILDEN: Not now.
SHELLY: Why not?
TILDEN: I just told you. You don't understand anything. If I told you something you wouldn't understand it.
SHELLY: Told me what?
TILDEN: Told you something that's true.
SHELLY: Like what?
TILDEN: Like a baby. Like a little tiny baby.
SHELLY: Like when you were little?
TILDEN: If I told you you'd make me give your coat back.
SHELLY: I won't. I promise. Tell me.
TILDEN: I can't. Dodge won't let me.
SHELLY: He won't hear you. It's okay.

(Pause. Tilden stares at her. Moves slightly toward her.)

TILDEN: We had a baby. (*Motioning to Dodge.*) He did. Dodge did. Could pick it up with one hand. Put it in the other. Little baby. Dodge killed it.

(Shelly stands.)

TILDEN: Don't stand up. Don't stand up!

(Shelly sits again. Dodge sits up on sofa and looks at them.)

TILDEN: Dodge drowned it.
SHELLY: Don't tell me anymore! Okay?

(Tilden moves closer to her. Dodge takes more interest.)

DODGE: Tilden? You leave that girl alone!
TILDEN (*pays no attention*): Never told Halie. Never told anybody. Just drowned it.
DODGE (*shuts off TV*): Tilden!
TILDEN: Nobody could find it. Just disappeared. Cops looked for it. Neighbors. Nobody could find it.

(Dodge struggles to get up from sofa.)

DODGE: Tilden, what're you telling her! Tilden!

(Dodge keeps struggling until he's standing.)

TILDEN: Finally everybody just gave up. Just stopped looking. Everybody had a different answer. Kidnap. Murder. Accident. Some kind of accident.

(Dodge struggles to walk toward Tilden and falls. Tilden ignores him.)

DODGE: Tilden, you shut up! You shut up about it!

(Dodge starts coughing on the floor. Shelly watches him from the stool.)

TILDEN: Little tiny baby just disappeared. It's not hard. It's so small. Almost invisible.

(*Shelly makes a move to help Dodge. Tilden firmly pushes her back down on the stool. Dodge keeps coughing.*)

TILDEN: He said he had his reasons. Said it went a long way back. But he wouldn't tell anybody.
DODGE: Tilden! Don't tell her anything! Don't tell her!
TILDEN: He's the only one who knows where it's buried. The only one. Like a secret buried treasure. Won't tell any of us. Won't tell me or mother or even Bradley. Especially Bradley. Bradley tried to force it out of him but he wouldn't tell. Wouldn't even tell why he did it. One night he just did it.

(*Dodge's coughing subsides. Shelly stays on stool staring at Dodge. Tilden slowly takes Shelly's coat off and holds it out to her. Long pause. Shelly sits there trembling.*)

TILDEN: You probably want your coat back now.

(*Shelly stares at coat but doesn't move to take it. The sound of Bradley's leg squeaking is heard off left. The others on stage remain still. Bradley appears up left outside the screen door wearing a yellow rain slicker. He enters through screen door, crosses porch to stage right door and enters stage. Closes door. Takes off rain slicker and shakes it out. He sees all the others and stops. Tilden turns to him. Bradley stares at Shelly. Dodge remains on floor.*)

BRADLEY: What's going on here? (*Motioning to Shelly.*) Who's that?

(*Shelly stands, moves back away from Bradley as he crosses toward her. He stops next to Tilden. He sees coat in Tilden's hand and grabs it away from him.*)

BRADLEY: Who's she supposed to be?
TILDEN: She's driving to New Mexico.

(*Bradley stares at her. Shelly is frozen. Bradley limps over to her with the coat in his fist. He stops in front of her.*)

BRADLEY (*to Shelly, after pause*): Vacation?

(*Shelly shakes her head "no," trembling.*)

BRADLEY (*to Shelly, motioning to Tilden*): You taking him with you?

(*Shelly shakes her head "no." Bradley crosses back to Tilden.*)

BRADLEY: You oughta'. No use leaving him here. Doesn't do a lick a' work. Doesn't raise a finger. (*Stopping, to Tilden.*) Do ya'. (*To Shelly.*) 'Course he used to be an All-American. Quarterback or fullback or somethin'. He tell you that?

(*Shelly shakes her head "no."*)

BRADLEY: Yeah, he used to be a big deal. Wore lettermen's sweaters. Had medals hanging all around his neck. Real purty. Big deal. (*He laughs to himself, notices Dodge on floor, crosses to him, stops.*) This one too. (*To Shelly.*) You'd never think it to look at him, would ya'? All bony and wasted away.

(*Shelly shakes her head again. Bradley stares at her, crosses back to her, clenching the coat in his fist. He stops in front of Shelly.*)

BRADLEY: Women like that kinda' thing, don't they?
SHELLY: What?
BRADLEY: Importance. Importance in a man?
SHELLY: I don't know.
BRADLEY: Yeah. You know, you know. Don't give me that. (*Moves closer to Shelly.*) You're with Tilden?
SHELLY: No.
BRADLEY (*turning to Tilden*): Tilden! She with you?

(*Tilden doesn't answer. Stares at floor.*)

BRADLEY: Tilden!

(*Tilden suddenly bolts and runs off up stage left. Bradley laughs. Talks to Shelly. Dodge starts moving his lips silently as though talking to someone invisible on the floor.*)

BRADLEY (*laughing*): Scared to death! He was always scared!

(*Bradley stops laughing. Stares at Shelly.*)

BRADLEY: You're scared too, right? (*Laughs again.*) You're scared and you don't even know me. (*Stops laughing.*) You don't gotta be scared.

(*Shelly looks at Dodge on the floor.*)

SHELLY: Can't we do something for him?
BRADLEY (*looking at Dodge*): We could shoot him. (*Laughs.*) We could drown him! What about drowning him?
SHELLY: Shut up!

(*Bradley stops laughing. Moves in closer to Shelly. She freezes. Bradley speaks slowly and deliberately.*)

BRADLEY: Hey! Missus. Don't talk to me like that. Don't talk to me in that tone a' voice. There was a time when I had to take that tone a' voice from pretty near everyone. (*Motioning to Dodge.*) Him, for one! Him and that half brain that just ran outa' here. They don't talk to me like that now. Not anymore. Everything's turned around now. Full circle. Isn't that funny?
SHELLY: I'm sorry.
BRADLEY: Open your mouth.

SHELLY: What?

BRADLEY (*motioning for her to open her mouth*): Open up.

(*She opens her mouth slightly.*)

BRADLEY: Wider.

(*She opens her mouth wider.*)

BRADLEY: Keep it like that.

(*She does. Stares at Bradley. With his free hand he puts his fingers into her mouth. She tries to pull away.*)

BRADLEY: Just stay put!

(*She freezes. He keeps his fingers in her mouth. Stares at her. Pause. He pulls his hand out. She closes her mouth, keeps her eyes on him. Bradley smiles. He looks at Dodge on the floor and crosses over to him. Shelly watches him closely. Bradley stands over Dodge and smiles at Shelly. He holds her coat up in both hands over Dodge, keeps smiling at Shelly. He looks down at Dodge, then drops the coat so that it lands on Dodge and covers his head. Bradley keeps his hands up in the position of holding the coat, looks over at Shelly, and smiles. The lights black out.*)

ACT 3

Scene: *Same set. Morning. Bright sun. No sound of rain. Everything has been cleared up again. No sign of carrots. No pail. No stool. Vince's saxophone case and overcoat are still at the foot of the staircase. Bradley is asleep on the sofa under Dodge's blanket. His head toward stage left. Bradley's wooden leg is leaning against the sofa right by his head. The shoe is left on it. The harness hangs down. Dodge is sitting on the foor, propped up against the TV set facing stage left wearing his baseball cap. Shelly's rabbit fur coat covers his chest and shoulders. He stares off toward stage left. He seems weaker and more disoriented. The lights rise slowly to the sound of birds and remain for a while in silence on the two men. Bradley sleeps very soundly. Dodge hardly moves. Shelly appears from stage left with a big smile, slowly crossing toward Dodge balancing a steaming cup of broth in a saucer. Dodge just stares at her as she gets close to him.*

SHELLY (*as she crosses*): This is going to make all the difference in the world, Grandpa. You don't mind me calling you Grandpa, do you? I mean I know you minded when Vince called you that but you don't even know him.

DODGE: He skipped town with my money, ya' know. I'm gonna hold you as collateral.

SHELLY: He'll be back. Don't you worry.

(*She kneels down next to Dodge and puts the cup and saucer in his lap.*)

DODGE: It's morning already! Not only didn't I get my bottle but he's got my two bucks!

SHELLY: Try to drink this, okay? Don't spill it.

DODGE: What is it?

SHELLY: Beef bouillon. It'll warm you up.

DODGE: Bouillon! I don't want any goddamn bouillon! Get that stuff away from me!

SHELLY: I just got through making it.

DODGE: I don't care if you just spent all week making it! I ain't drinking it!

SHELLY: Well, what am I supposed to do with it then? I'm trying to help you out. Besides, it's good for you.

DODGE: Get it away from me!

(*Shelly stands up with cup and saucer.*)

DODGE: What do you know what's good for me anyway?

(*She looks at Dodge, then turns away from him, crossing to staircase, sits on bottom step, and drinks the bouillon. Dodge stares at her.*)

DODGE: You know what'd be good for me?

SHELLY: What?

DODGE: A little massage. A little contact.

SHELLY: Oh no. I've had enough contact for a while. Thanks anyway.

(*She keeps sipping bouillon, stays sitting. Pause as Dodge stares at her.*)

DODGE: Why not? You got nothing better to do. That fella's not gonna be back here. You're not expecting him to show up again, are you?

SHELLY: Sure. He'll show up. He left his horn here.

DODGE: His horn? (*Laughs.*) You're his horn?

SHELLY: Very funny.

DODGE: He's run off with my money! He's not coming back here.

SHELLY: He'll be back.

DODGE: You're a funny chicken, you know that?

SHELLY: Thanks.

DODGE: Full of faith. Hope. Faith and hope. You're all alike, you hopers. If it's not God then it's a man. If it's not a man then it's a woman. If it's not a woman then it's the land or the future of some kind. Some kind of future.

(*Pause.*)

SHELLY (*looking toward porch*): I'm glad it stopped raining.

DODGE (*looks toward porch then back to her*): That's what I mean. See, you're glad it stopped raining. Now you think everything's gonna be different. Just 'cause the sun comes out.

SHELLY: It's already different. Last night I was scared.

DODGE: Scared a' what?

SHELLY: Just scared.

DODGE: Bradley? (*Looks at Bradley.*) He's a pushover. 'Specially now. All ya' gotta do is take his leg and throw it out the back door. Helpless. Totally helpless.

(*Shelly turns and stares at Bradley's wooden leg, then looks at Dodge. She sips bouillon.*)

SHELLY: You'd do that?

DODGE: Me? I've hardly got the strength to breathe.

SHELLY: But you'd actually do it if you could?

DODGE: Don't be so easily shocked, girlie. There's nothing a man can't do. You dream it up and he can do it. Anything.

SHELLY: You've tried I guess.

DODGE: Don't sit there sippin' your bouillon and judging me! This is my house!

SHELLY: I forgot.

DODGE: You forgot? Whose house did you think it was?

SHELLY: Mine.

(*Dodge just stares at her. Long pause. She sips from cup.*)

SHELLY: I know it's not mine but I had that feeling.

DODGE: What feeling?

SHELLY: The feeling that nobody lives here but me. I mean everybody's gone. You're here, but it doesn't seem like you're supposed to be. (*Pointing to Bradley.*) Doesn't seem like he's supposed to be here either. I don't know what it is. It's the house or something. Something familiar. Like I know my way around here. Did you ever get that feeling?

(*Dodge stares at her in silence. Pause.*)

DODGE: No. No, I never did.

(*Shelly gets up. Moves around space holding cup.*)

SHELLY: Last night I went to sleep up there in that room.

DODGE: What room?

SHELLY: That room up there with all the pictures. All the crosses on the wall.

DODGE: Halie's room?

SHELLY: Yeah. Whoever "Halie" is.

DODGE: She's my wife.

SHELLY: So you remember her?

DODGE: Whad'ya mean! 'Course I remember her! She's only been gone for a day — half a day. However long it's been.

SHELLY: Do you remember her when her hair was bright red? Standing in front of an apple tree?

DODGE: What is this, the third degree or something! Who're you to be askin' me personal questions about my wife!

SHELLY: You never look at those pictures up there?

DODGE: What pictures!

SHELLY: Your whole life's up there hanging on the wall. Somebody who looks just like you. Somebody who looks just like you used to look.

DODGE: That isn't me! That never was me! This is me. Right here. This is it. The whole shootin' match, sittin' right in front of you.

SHELLY: So the past never happened as far as you're concerned?

DODGE: The past? Jesus Christ. The past. What do you know about the past?

SHELLY: Not much. I know there was a farm.

(*Pause.*)

DODGE: A farm?

SHELLY: There's a picture of a farm. A big farm. A bull. Wheat. Corn.

DODGE: Corn?

SHELLY: All the kids are standing out in the corn. They're all waving these big straw hats. One of them doesn't have a hat.

DODGE: Which one was that?

SHELLY: There's a baby. A baby in a woman's arms. The same woman with the red hair. She looks lost standing out there. Like she doesn't know how she got there.

DODGE: She knows! I told her a hundred times it wasn't gonna' be the city! I gave her plenty a' warning.

SHELLY: She's looking down at the baby like it was somebody else's. Like it didn't even belong to her.

DODGE: That's about enough outa' you! You got some funny ideas. Some damn funny ideas. You think just because people propagate they have to love their offspring? You never seen a bitch eat her puppies? Where are you from anyway?

SHELLY: L.A. We already went through that.

DODGE: That's right, L.A. I remember.

SHELLY: Stupid country.

DODGE: That's right! No wonder.

(*Pause.*)

SHELLY: What's happened to this family anyway?

DODGE: You're in no position to ask! What do you care? You some kinda' Social Worker?

SHELLY: I'm Vince's friend.

DODGE: Vince's friend! That's rich. That's really rich.

"Vince"! "Mr. Vince"! "Mr. Thief" is more like it! His name doesn't mean a hoot in hell to me. Not a tinkle in the well. You know how many kids I've spawned? Not to mention Grand kids and Great Grand kids and Great Great Grand kids after them?

SHELLY: And you don't remember any of them?

DODGE: What's to remember? Halie's the one with the family album. She's the one you should talk to. She'll set you straight on the heritage if that's what you're interested in. She's traced it all the way back to the grave.

SHELLY: What do you mean?

DODGE: What do you think I mean? How far back can you go? A long line of corpses! There's not a living soul behind me. Not a one. Who's holding me in their memory? Who gives a damn about bones in the ground?

SHELLY: Was Tilden telling the truth?

(*Dodge stops short. Stares at Shelly. Shakes his head. He looks off stage left.*)

SHELLY: Was he?

(*Dodge's tone changes drastically.*)

DODGE: Tilden? (*Turns to Shelly, calmly.*) Where is Tilden?

SHELLY: Last night. Was he telling the truth about the baby?

(*Pause.*)

DODGE (*turns toward stage left*): What's happened to Tilden? Why isn't Tilden here?

SHELLY: Bradley chased him out.

DODGE (*looking at Bradley asleep*): Bradley? Why is he on my sofa? (*Turns back to Shelly.*) Have I been here all night? On the floor?

SHELLY: He wouldn't leave. I hid outside until he fell asleep.

DODGE: Outside? Is Tilden outside? He shouldn't be out there in the rain. He'll get himself into trouble. He doesn't know his way around here anymore. Not like he used to. He went out West and got himself into trouble. Got himself into bad trouble. We don't want any of that around here.

SHELLY: What did he do?

(*Pause.*)

DODGE (*quietly stares at Shelly*): Tilden? He got mixed up. That's what he did. We can't afford to leave him alone. Not now.

(*Sound of Halie laughing comes from off left. Shelly stands, looking in direction of voice, holding cup and saucer, doesn't know whether to stay or run.*)

DODGE (*motioning to Shelly*): Sit down! Sit back down!

(*Shelly sits. Sound of Halie's laughter again.*)

DODGE (*to Shelly in a heavy whisper, pulling coat up around him*): Don't leave me alone now! Promise me? Don't go off and leave me alone. I need somebody here with me. Tilden's gone now and I need someone. Don't leave me! Promise!

SHELLY (*sitting*): I won't.

(*Halie appears outside the screen porch door, up left with Father Dewis. She is wearing a bright yellow dress, no hat, white gloves and her arms are full of yellow roses. Father Dewis is dressed in traditional black suit, white clerical collar, and shirt. He is a very distinguished gray-haired man in his sixties. They are both slightly drunk and feeling giddy. As they enter the porch through the screen door, Dodge pulls the rabbit fur coat over his head and hides. Shelly stands again. Dodge drops the coat and whispers intensely to Shelly. Neither Halie nor Father Dewis are aware of the people inside the house.*)

DODGE (*to Shelly in a strong whisper*): You promised!

(*Shelly sits on stairs again. Dodge pulls coat back over his head. Halie and Father Dewis talk on the porch as they cross toward stage right interior door.*)

HALIE: Oh, Father! That's terrible! That's absolutely terrible. Aren't you afraid of being punished?

(*She giggles.*)

DEWIS: Not by the Italians. They're too busy punishing each other.

(*They both break out in giggles.*)

HALIE: What about God?

DEWIS: Well, prayerfully, God only hears what he wants to. That's just between you and me of course. In our heart of hearts we know we're every bit as wicked as the Catholics.

(*They giggle again and reach the stage right door.*)

HALIE: Father, I never heard you talk like this in Sunday sermon.

DEWIS: Well, I save all my best jokes for private company. Pearls before swine, you know.

(*They enter the room laughing and stop when they see Shelly. Shelly stands. Halie closes the door behind Father Dewis. Dodge's voice is heard under the coat, talking to Shelly.*)

DODGE (*under coat, to Shelly*): Sit down, sit down! Don't let 'em buffalo you!

(*Shelly sits on stair again. Halie looks at Dodge on the floor, then looks at Bradley asleep on sofa and sees his wooden leg. She lets out a shriek of embarrassment for Father Dewis.*)

HALIE: Oh my gracious! What in the name of Judas Priest is going on in this house!

(*She hands over the roses to Father Dewis.*)

HALIE: Excuse me, Father.

(*Halie crosses to Dodge, whips the coat off him, and covers the wooden leg with it. Bradley stays asleep.*)

HALIE: You can't leave this house for a second without the Devil blowing in through the front door!

DODGE: Gimme back that coat! Gimme back that goddamn coat before I freeze to death!

HALIE: You're not going to freeze! The sun's out in case you hadn't noticed!

DODGE: Gimme back that coat! That coat's for live flesh not dead wood!

(*Halie whips the blanket off Bradley and throws it on Dodge. Dodge covers his head again with blanket. Bradley's amputated leg can be faked by having half of it under a cushion of the sofa. He's fully clothed. Bradley sits up with a jerk when the blanket comes off him.*)

HALIE (*as she tosses blanket*): Here! Use this! It's yours anyway! Can't you take care of yourself for once!

BRADLEY (*yelling at Halie*): Gimme that blanket! Gimme back that blanket! That's my blanket!

(*Halie crosses back toward Father Dewis who just stands there with the roses. Bradley thrashes helplessly on the sofa trying to reach blanket. Dodge hides himself deeper in blanket. Shelly looks on from staircase still holding cup and saucer.*)

HALIE: Believe me, Father, this is not what I had in mind when I invited you in.

DEWIS: Oh, no apologies please. I wouldn't be in the ministry if I couldn't face real life.

(*He laughs self-consciously. Halie notices Shelly again and crosses over to her. Shelly stays sitting. Halie stops and stares at her.*)

BRADLEY: I want my blanket back! Gimme my blanket!

(*Halie turns toward Bradley and silences him.*)

HALIE: Shut up, Bradley! Right this minute! I've had enough!

(*Bradley slowly recoils, lies back down on sofa, turns his back toward Halie and whimpers softly. Halie directs her attention to Shelly again. Pause.*)

HALIE (*to Shelly*): What're you doing with my cup and saucer?

SHELLY (*looking at cup, back to Halie*): I made some bouillon for Dodge.

HALIE: For Dodge?

SHELLY: Yeah.

HALIE: Well, did he drink it?

SHELLY: No.

HALIE: Did you drink it?

SHELLY: Yes.

(*Halie stares at her. Long pause. She turns abruptly away from Shelly and crosses back to Father Dewis.*)

HALIE: Father, there's a stranger in my house. What would you advise? What would be the Christian thing?

DEWIS (*squirming*): Oh, well . . . I . . . I really —

HALIE: We still have some whiskey, don't we?

(*Dodge slowly pulls the blanket down off his head and looks toward Father Dewis. Shelly stands.*)

SHELLY: Listen, I don't drink or anything. I just —

(*Halie turns toward Shelly viciously.*)

HALIE: You sit back down!

(*Shelly sits again on stair. Halie turns again to Dewis.*)

HALIE: I think we have plenty of whiskey left! Don't we, Father?

DEWIS: Well, yes. I think so. You'll have to get it. My hands are full.

(*Halie giggles. Reaches into Dewis's pockets, searching for bottle. She smells the roses as she searches. Dewis stands stiffy. Dodge watches Halie closely as she looks for bottle.*)

HALIE: The most incredible things, roses! Aren't they incredible, Father?

DEWIS: Yes. Yes, they are.

HALIE: They almost cover the stench of sin in this house. Just magnificent! The smell. We'll have to put some at the foot of Ansel's statue. On the day of the unveiling.

(*Halie finds a silver flask of whiskey in Dewis's vest pocket. She pulls it out. Dodge looks on eagerly. Halie crosses to Dodge, opens the flask, and takes a sip.*)

HALIE (*to Dodge*): Ansel's getting a statue, Dodge. Did you know that? Not a plaque but a real live statue. A full bronze. Tip to toe. A basketball in one hand and a rifle in the other.

BRADLEY (*his back to Halie*): He never played basketball!

HALIE: You shut up, Bradley! You shut up about Ansel! Ansel played basketball better than anyone! And you know it! He was an All-American! There's no reason to take the glory away from others

(*Halie turns away from Bradley, crosses back toward Dewis, sipping on the flask and smiling.*)

HALIE (*to Dewis*): Ansel was a great basketball player. One of the greatest.

DEWIS: I remember Ansel.

HALIE: Of course! You remember. You remember how he could play. (*She turns toward Shelly.*) Of course nowadays they play a different brand of basketball. More vicious. Isn't that right, dear?

SHELLY: I don't know.

(*Halie crosses to Shelly, sipping on flask. She stops in front of Shelly.*)

HALIE: Much, much more vicious. They smash into each other. They knock each other's teeth out. There's blood all over the court. Savages.

(*Halie takes the cup from Shelly and pours whiskey into it.*)

HALIE: They don't train like they used to. Not at all. They allow themselves to run amuck. Drugs and women. Women mostly.

(*Halie hands the cup of whiskey back to Shelly slowly. Shelly takes it.*)

HALIE: Mostly women. Girls. Sad, pathetic little girls. (*She crosses back to Father Dewis.*) It's just a reflection of the times, don't you think, Father? An indication of where we stand?

DEWIS: I suppose so, yes.

HALIE: Yes. A sort of bad omen. Our youth becoming monsters.

DEWIS: Well, I uh —

HALIE: Oh you can disagree with me if you want to, Father. I'm open to debate. I think argument only enriches both sides of the question don't you? (*She moves toward Dodge.*) I suppose, in the long run, it doesn't matter. When you see the way things deteriorate before your very eyes. Everything running downhill. It's kind of silly to even think about youth.

DEWIS: No, I don't think so. I think it's important to believe in certain things.

HALIE: Yes. Yes, I know what you mean. I think that's right. I think that's true. (*She looks at Dodge.*) Certain basic things. We can't shake certain basic things. We might end up crazy. Like my husband. You can see it in his eyes. You can see how mad he is.

(*Dodge covers his head with the blanket again. Halie takes a single rose from Dewis and moves slowly over to Dodge.*)

HALIE: We can't not believe in something. We can't

stop believing. We just end up dying if we stop. Just end up dead.

(*Halie throws the rose gently onto Dodge's blanket. It lands between his knees and stays there! Long pause as Halie stares at the rose. Shelly stands suddenly. Halie doesn't turn to her but keeps staring at rose.*)

SHELLY (*to Halie*): Don't you wanna' know who I am! Don't you wanna know what I'm doing here! I'm not dead!

(*Shelly crosses toward Halie. Halie turns slowly toward her.*)

HALIE: Did you drink your whiskey?

SHELLY: No! And I'm not going to either!

HALIE: Well, that's a firm stand. It's good to have a firm stand.

SHELLY: I don't have any stand at all. I'm just trying to put all this together.

(*Halie laughs and crosses back to Dewis.*)

HALIE (*to Dewis*): Surprises, surprises! Did you have any idea we'd be returning to this?

SHELLY: I came here with your grandson for a little visit! A little innocent friendly visit.

HALIE: My grandson?

SHELLY: Yes! That's right. The one no one remembers.

HALIE (*to Dewis*): This is getting a little far-fetched.

SHELLY: I told him it was stupid to come back here. To try to pick up from where he left off.

HALIE: Where was that?

SHELLY: Wherever he was when he left here! Six years ago! Ten years ago! Whenever it was. I told him nobody cares.

HALIE: Didn't he listen?

SHELLY: No! No, he didn't. We had to stop off at every tiny little meatball town that he remembered from his boyhood! Every stupid little donut shop he ever kissed a girl in. Every drive-in. Every drag strip. Every football field he ever broke a bone on.

HALIE (*suddenly alarmed, to Dodge*): Where's Tilden?

SHELLY: Don't ignore me!

HALIE: Dodge! Where's Tilden gone?

(*Shelly moves violently toward Halie.*)

SHELLY (*to Halie*): I'm talking to you!

(*Bradley sits up fast on the sofa, Shelly backs away.*)

BRADLEY (*to Shelly*): Don't you yell at my mother!

HALIE: Dodge! (*She kicks Dodge.*) I told you not to let Tilden out of your sight! Where's he gone to?

DODGE: Gimme a drink and I'll tell ya'.

DEWIS: Halie, maybe this isn't the right time for a visit.

(*Halie crosses back to Dewis.*)

HALIE (*to Dewis*): I never should've left. I never, never should've left! Tilden could be anywhere by now! Anywhere! He's not in control of his faculties. Dodge knew that. I told him when I left here. I told him specifically to watch out for Tilden.

(*Bradley reaches down, grabs Dodge's blanket, and yanks it off him. He lays down on sofa and pulls the blanket over his head.*)

DODGE: He's got my blanket again! He's got my blanket!

HALIE (*turning to Bradley*): Bradley! Bradley, put that blanket back!

(*Halie moves toward Bradley. Shelly suddenly throws the cup and saucer against the stage right door. Dewis ducks. The cup and saucer smash into pieces. Halie stops, turns toward Shelly. Everyone freezes. Bradley slowly pulls his head out from under blanket, looks toward stage right door, then to Shelly. Shelly stares at Halie. Dewis cowers with roses. Shelly moves slowly toward Halie. Long pause. Shelly speaks softly.*)

SHELLY (*to Halie*): I don't like being ignored. I don't like being treated like I'm not here. I didn't like it when I was a kid and I still don't like it.

BRADLEY (*sitting up on sofa*): We don't have to tell you anything, girl. Not a thing. You're not the police, are you? You're not the government. You're just some prostitute that Tilden brought in here.

HALIE: Language! I won't have that language in my house!

SHELLY (*to Bradley*): You stuck your hand in my mouth and you call me a prostitute!

HALIE: Bradley! Did you put your hand in her mouth? I'm ashamed of you. I can't leave you alone for a minute.

BRADLEY: I never did. She's lying!

DEWIS: Halie, I think I'll be running along now. I'll just put the roses in the kitchen.

(*Dewis moves toward stage left. Halie stops him.*)

HALIE: Don't go now, Father! Not now.

BRADLEY: I never did anything, Mom! I never touched her! She propositioned me! And I turned her down. I turned her down flat!

(*Shelly suddenly grabs her coat off the wooden leg and takes both the leg and coat downstage, away from Bradley.*)

BRADLEY: Mom! Mom! She's got my leg! She's taken my leg! I never did anything to her! She's stolen my leg!

(*Bradley reaches pathetically in the air for his leg. Shelly sets it down for a second, puts on her coat fast,*

and picks the leg up again. Dodge starts coughing softly.*)

HALIE (*to Shelly*): I think we've had about enough of you, young lady. Just about enough. I don't know where you came from or what you're doing here but you're no longer welcome in this house.

SHELLY (*laughs, holds leg*): No longer welcome!

BRADLEY: Mom! That's my leg! Get my leg back! I can't do anything without my leg.

(*Bradley keeps making whimpering sounds and reaching for his leg.*)

HALIE: Give my son back his leg. Right this very minute!

(*Dodge starts laughing softly to himself in between coughs.*)

HALIE (*to Dewis*): Father, do something about this, would you! I'm not about to be terrorized in my own house!

BRADLEY: Gimme back my leg!

HALIE: Oh, shut up, Bradley! Just shut up! You don't need your leg now! Just lay down and shut up!

(*Bradley whimpers. Lays down and pulls blanket around him. He keeps one arm outside blanket, reaching out toward his wooden leg. Dewis cautiously approaches Shelly with the roses in his arms. Shelly clutches the wooden leg to her chest as though she's kidnaped it.*)

DEWIS (*to Shelly*): Now, honestly dear, wouldn't it be better to try to talk things out? Try to use some reason?

SHELLY: There isn't any reason here! I can't find a reason for anything.

DEWIS: There's nothing to be afraid of. These are all good people. All righteous people.

SHELLY: I'm not afraid!

DEWIS: But this isn't your house. You have to have some respect.

SHELLY: You're the strangers here, not me.

HALIE: This has gone far enough!

DEWIS: Halie, please. Let me handle this.

SHELLY: Don't come near me! Don't anyone come near me. I don't need any words from you. I'm not threatening anybody. I don't even know what I'm doing here. You all say you don't remember Vince, okay, maybe you don't. Maybe it's Vince that's crazy. Maybe he's made this whole family thing up. I don't even care anymore. I was just coming along for the ride. I thought it'd be a nice gesture. Besides, I was curious. He made all of you sound familiar to me. Every one of you. For every name, I had an image. Every time he'd tell me a name, I'd see the person. In fact, each of you was so clear in my mind that I actually believed it was you. I really believed when I walked through that door that the people who lived here would turn out to he the same people in my imagination. But I don't recognize any of you. Not one. Not even the slightest resemblance.

DEWIS: Well, you can hardly blame others for not fulfilling your hallucination.

SHELLY: It was no hallucination! It was more like a prophecy. You believe in prophecy, don't you?

HALIE: Father, there's no point in talking to her any further. We're just going to have to call the police.

BRADLEY: No! Don't get the police in here. We don't want the police in here. This is our home.

SHELLY: That's right. Bradley's right. Don't you usually settle your affairs in private? Don't you usually take them out in the dark? Out in the back?

BRADLEY: You stay out of our lives! You have no business interfering!

SHELLY: I don't have any business period. I got nothing to lose.

(*She moves around, staring at each of them.*)

BRADLEY: You don't know what we've been through. You don't know anything!

SHELLY: I know you've got a secret. You've all got a secret. It's so secret in fact, you're all convinced it never happened.

(*Halie moves to Dewis.*)

HALIE: Oh, my God, Father!

DODGE (*laughing to himself*): She thinks she's going to get it out of us. She thinks she's going to uncover the truth of the matter. Like a detective or something.

BRADLEY: I'm not telling her anything! Nothing's wrong here! Nothin's ever been wrong! Everything's the way it's supposed to be! Nothing ever happened that's bad! Everything is all right here! We're all good people!

DODGE: She thinks she's gonna suddenly bring everything out into the open after all these years.

DEWIS (*to Shelly*): Can't you see that these people want to be left in peace? Don't you have any mercy? They haven't done anything to you.

DODGE: She wants to get to the bottom of it. (*To Shelly.*) That's it, isn't it? You'd like to get right down to bedrock? You want me to tell ya'? You want me to tell ya' what happened? I'll tell ya'. I might as well.

BRADLEY: No! Don't listen to him. He doesn't remember anything!

DODGE: I remember the whole thing from start to finish. I remember the day he was born.

(*Pause.*)

HALIE: Dodge, if you tell this thing — if you tell this, you'll be dead to me. You'll be just as good as dead.

DODGE: That won't be such a big change, Halie. See this girl, this girl here, she wants to know. She wants to know something more. And I got this feeling that it doesn't make a bit a' difference. I'd sooner tell it to a stranger than anybody else.

BRADLEY (*to Dodge*): We made a pact! We made a pact between us! You can't break that now!

DODGE: I don't remember any pact.

BRADLEY (*to Shelly*): See, he doesn't remember anything. I'm the only one in the family who remembers. The only one. And I'll never tell you!

SHELLY: I'm not so sure I want to find out now.

DODGE (*laughing to himself*): Listen to her! Now she's runnin' scared!

SHELLY: I'm not scared!

(*Dodge stops laughing, long pause. Dodge stares at her.*)

DODGE: You're not, huh? Well, that's good. Because I'm not either. See, we were a well-established family once. Well-established. All the boys were grown. The farm was producing enough milk to fill Lake Michigan twice over. Me and Halie here were pointed toward what looked like the middle part of our life. Everything was settled with us. All we had to do was ride it out. Then Halie got pregnant again. Outa' the middle a' nowhere, she got pregnant. We weren't planning on havin' any more boys. We had enough boys already. In fact, we hadn't been sleepin' in the same bed for about six years.

HALIE (*moving toward stairs*): I'm not listening to this! I don't have to listen to this!

DODGE (*stops Halie*): Where are you going! Upstairs! You'll just be listenin' to it upstairs! You go outside, you'll be listenin' to it outside. Might as well stay here and listen to it.

(*Halie stays by stairs.*)

BRADLEY: If I had my leg you wouldn't be saying this. You'd never get away with it if I had my leg.

DODGE (*pointing to Shelly*): She's got your leg. (*Laughs.*) She's gonna keep your leg too. (*To Shelly.*) She wants to hear this. Don't you?

SHELLY: I don't know.

DODGE: Well even if ya' don't I'm gonna' tell ya'. (*Pause.*) Halie had this kid. This baby boy. She had it. I let her have it on her own. All the other boys I had had the best doctors, best nurses, everything. This one I let her have by herself. This one hurt real bad. Almost killed her, but she had it anyway. It lived, see. It lived. It wanted to grow up in this family. It wanted to be just like us. It wanted to be

a part of us. It wanted to pretend that I was its father. She wanted me to believe in it. Even when
everyone around us knew. Everyone. All our boys
knew. Tilden knew.

HALIE: You shut up! Bradley, make him shut up!

BRADLEY: I can't.

DODGE: Tilden was the one who knew. Better than
any of us. He'd walk for miles with that kid in his
arms. Halie let him take it. All night sometimes.
He'd walk all night out there in the pasture with
it. Talkin' to it. Singin' to it. Used to hear him
singing to it. He'd make up stories. He'd tell that
kid all kinds a' stories. Even when he knew it
couldn't understand him. Couldn't understand a
word he was sayin'. Never would understand him.
We couldn't let a thing like that continue. We
couldn't allow that to grow up right in the middle
of our lives. It made everything we'd accomplished
look like it was nothin'. Everything was canceled
out by this one mistake. This one weakness.

SHELLY: So you killed him?

DODGE: I killed it. I drowned it. Just like the runt of a
litter. Just drowned it.

(*Halie moves toward Bradley.*)

HALIE (*to Bradley*): Ansel would've stopped him!
Ansel would've stopped him from telling these lies!
He was a hero! A man! A whole man! What's hap-
pened to the men in this family! Where are the men!

(*Suddenly Vince comes crashing through the screen
porch door up left, tearing it off its hinges. Everyone
but Dodge and Bradley back away from the porch and
stare at Vince who has landed on his stomach on
the porch in a drunken stupor. He is singing loudly to
himself and hauls himself slowly to his feet. He has a
paper shopping bag full of empty booze bottles. He
takes them out one at a time as he sings and smashes
them at the opposite end of the porch, behind the solid
interior door, stage right. Shelly moves slowly toward
stage right, holding wooden leg and watching Vince.*)

VINCE (*singing loudly as he hurls bottles*): "From the
Halls of Montezuma to the Shores of Tripoli. We
will fight our country's battles on the land and on
the sea."

(*He punctuates the words "Montezuma," "Tripoli,"
"battles," and "sea" with a smashed bottle each. He
stops throwing for a second, stares toward stage right
of the porch, shades his eyes with his hand as though
looking across to a battlefield, then cups his hands
around his mouth and yells across the space of the
porch to an imaginary army. The others watch in terror and expectation.*)

VINCE (*to imagined army*): Have you had enough

over there! 'Cause there's a lot more here where
that came from! (*Pointing to paper bag full of bottles.*) A helluva lot more! We got enough over here
to blow ya' from here to Kingdomcome!

(*He takes another bottle, makes high whistling sound
of a bomb, and throws it toward stage right porch.
Sound of bottle smashing against wall. This should be
the actual smashing of bottles and not tape sound. He
keeps yelling and heaving bottles one after another.*)

  (*Vince stops for a while, breathing heavily from
exhaustion. Long silence as the others watch him.
Shelly approaches tentatively in Vince's direction, still
holding Bradley's wooden leg.*)

SHELLY (*after silence*): Vince?

(*Vince turns toward her. Peers through screen.*)

VINCE: Who? What? Vince who? Who's that in there?

(*Vince pushes his face against the screen from the
porch and stares in at everyone.*)

DODGE: Where's my goddamn bottle!

VINCE (*looking in at Dodge*): What? Who is that?

DODGE: It's me! Your Grandfather! Don't play stupid
with me! Where's my two bucks!

VINCE: Your two bucks?

(*Halie moves away from Dewis, upstage, peers out at
Vince, trying to recognize him.*)

HALIE: Vincent? Is that you, Vincent?

(*Shelly stares at Halie, then looks out at Vince.*)

VINCE (*from porch*): Vincent who? What is this! Who
are you people?

SHELLY (*to Halie*): Hey, wait a minute. Wait a minute!
What's going on?

HALIE (*moving closer to porch screen*): We thought
you were a murderer or something. Barging in
through the door like that.

VINCE: I am a murderer! Don't underestimate me for
a minute! I'm the Midnight Strangler! I devour
whole families in a single gulp!

(*Vince grabs another bottle and smashes it on the
porch. Halie backs away.*)

SHELLY (*approaching Halie*): You mean you know
who he is?

HALIE: Of course I know who he is! That's more than
I can say for you.

BRADLEY (*sitting up on sofa*): You get off our front
porch, you creep! What're you doing out there
breaking bottles? Who are these foreigners anyway! Where did they come from?

VINCE: Maybe I should come in there and break
them!

HALIE (*moving toward porch*): Don't you dare! Vincent, what's got into you! Why are you acting like this?

VINCE: Maybe I should come in there and usurp your territory!

(*Halie turns back toward Dewis and crosses to him.*)

HALIE (*to Dewis*): Father, why are you just standing around here when everything's falling apart? Can't you rectify this situation?

(*Dodge laughs, coughs.*)

DEWIS: I'm just a guest here, Halie. I don't know what my position is exactly. This is outside my parish anyway.

(*Vince starts throwing more bottles as things continue.*)

BRADLEY: If I had my leg I'd rectify it! I'd rectify him all over the goddamn highway! I'd pull his ears out if I could reach him!

(*Bradley sticks his fist through the screening of the porch and reaches out for Vince, grabbing at him and missing. Vince jumps away from Bradley's hand.*)

VINCE: Aaaah! Our lines have been penetrated! Tentacles animals! Beasts from the deep!

(*Vince strikes out at Bradley's hand with a bottle. Bradley pulls his hand back inside.*)

SHELLY: Vince! Knock it off, will ya! I want to get out of here!

(*Vince pushes his face against screen, looks in at Shelly.*)

VINCE (*to Shelly*): Have they got you prisoner in there, dear? Such a sweet young thing too. All her life in front of her. Nipped in the bud.

SHELLY: I'm coming out there, Vince! I'm coming out there and I want us to get in the car and drive away from here. Anywhere. Just away from here.

(*Shelly moves toward Vince's saxophone case and overcoat. She sets down the wooden leg, downstage left, and picks up the saxophone case and overcoat. Vince watches her through the screen.*)

VINCE (*to Shelly*): We'll have to negotiate. Make some kind of a deal. Prisoner exchange or something. A few of theirs for one of ours. Small price to pay if you ask me.

(*Shelly crosses toward stage right door with overcoat and case.*)

SHELLY: Just go and get the car! I'm coming out there now. We're going to leave.

VINCE: Don't come out here! Don't you dare come out here!

(*Shelly stops short of the door, stage right.*)

SHELLY: How come?

VINCE: Off limits! Verboten! This is taboo territory. No man or woman has ever crossed the line and lived to tell the tale!

SHELLY: I'll take my chances.

(*Shelly moves to stage right door and opens it. Vince pulls out a big folding hunting knife and pulls open the blade. He jabs the blade into the screen and starts cutting a hole big enough to climb through. Bradley cowers in a corner of the sofa as Vince rips at the screen.*)

VINCE (*as he cuts screen*): Don't come out here! I'm warning you! You'll disintegrate!

(*Dewis takes Halie by the arm and pulls her toward staircase.*)

DEWIS: Halie, maybe we should go upstairs until this blows over.

HALIE: I don't understand it. I just don't understand it. He was the sweetest little boy!

(*Dewis drops the roses beside the wooden leg at the foot of the staircase, then escorts Halie quickly up the stairs. Halie keeps looking back at Vince as they climb the stairs.*)

HALIE: There wasn't a mean bone in his body. Everyone loved Vincent. Everyone. He was the perfect baby.

DEWIS: He'll be all right after a while. He's just had a few too many that's all.

HALIE: He used to sing in his sleep. He'd sing. In the middle of the night. The sweetest voice. Like an angel. (*She stops for a moment.*) I used to lie awake listening to it. I used to lie awake thinking it was all right if I died. Because Vincent was an angel. A guardian angel. He'd watch over us. He'd watch over all of us.

(*Dewis takes her all the way up the stairs. They disappear above. Vince is now climbing through the porch screen onto the sofa. Bradley crashes off the sofa, holding tight to his blanket, keeping it wrapped around him. Shelly is outside on the porch. Vince holds the knife in his teeth once he gets the hole wide enough to climb through. Bradley starts crawling slowly toward his wooden leg, reaching out for it.*)

DODGE (*to Vince*): Go ahead! Take over the house! Take over the whole goddamn house! You can have it! It's yours. It's been a pain in the neck ever since the very first mortgage. I'm gonna die any second now. Any second. You won't even notice. So I'll settle my affairs once and for all.

(*As Dodge proclaims his last will and testament, Vince climbs into the room, knife in mouth, and strides slowly around the space, inspecting his inheritance. He casually notices Bradley as he crawls toward his leg. Vince moves to the leg and keeps pushing it with his foot so that it's out of Bradley's reach, then goes on with his inspection. He picks up the roses and carries them around smelling them. Shelly can be seen outside on the porch, moving slowly center and staring in at Vince. Vince ignores her.*)

DODGE: The house goes to my Grandson, Vincent. All the furnishings, accoutrements, and paraphernalia therein. Everything tacked to the walls or otherwise resting under this roof. My tools — namely my hand saw, my skill saw, my drill press, my chain saw, my lathe, my electric sander, all go to my eldest son, Tilden. That is, if he ever shows up again. My shed and gasoline powered equipment, namely my tractor, my dozer, my hand tiller plus all the attachments and riggings for the above mentioned machinery, namely my spring tooth harrow, my deep plows, my disk plows, my automatic fertilizing equipment, my reaper, my swathe, my seeder, my John Deere Harvester, my post hole digger, my jackhammer, my lathe — (*to himself*) Did I mention my lathe? I already mentioned my lathe — my Bennie Goodman records, my harnesses, my bits, my halters, my brace, my rough rasp, my forge, my welding equipment, my shoeing nails, my levels and bevels, my milking stool — no, not my milking stool — my hammers and chisels, my hinges, my cattle gates, my barbed wire, self-tapping augers, my horse hair ropes, and all related materials are to be pushed into a gigantic heap and set ablaze in the very center of my fields. When the blaze is at its highest, preferably on a cold, windless night, my body is to be pitched into the middle of it and burned till nothing remains but ash.

(*Pause. Vince takes the knife out of his mouth and smells the roses. He's facing toward audience and doesn't turn around to Shelly. He folds up knife and pockets it.*)

SHELLY (*from porch*): I'm leaving, Vince. Whether you come or not, I'm leaving.

VINCE (*smelling roses*): Just put my horn on the couch there before you take off.

SHELLY (*moving toward hole in screen*): You're not coming?

(*Vince stays downstage, turns, and looks at her.*)

VINCE: I just inherited a house.

SHELLY (*through hole, from porch*): You want to stay here?

VINCE (*as he pushes Bradley's leg out of reach*): I've gotta carry on the line. I've gotta see to it that things keep rolling.

(*Bradley looks up at him from floor, keeps pulling himself toward his leg. Vince keeps moving it.*)

SHELLY: What happened to you, Vince? You just disappeared.

VINCE (*pause, delivers speech front*): I was gonna run last night. I was gonna run and keep right on running. I drove all night. Clear to the Iowa border. The old man's two bucks sitting right on the seat beside me. It never stopped raining the whole time. Never stopped once. I could see myself in the windshield. My face. My eyes. I studied my face. Studied everything about it. As though I was looking at another man. As though I could see his whole race behind him. Like a mummy's face. I saw him dead and alive at the same time. In the same breath. In the windshield, I watched him breathe as though he was frozen in time. And every breath marked him. Marked him forever without him knowing. And then his face changed. His face became his father's face. Same bones. Same eyes. Same nose. Same breath. And his father's face changed to his grandfather's face. And it went on like that. Changing. Clear on back to faces I'd never seen before but still recognized. Still recognized the bones underneath. The eyes. The breath. The mouth. I followed my family clear into Iowa. Every last one. Straight into the Corn Belt and further. Straight back as far as they'd take me. Then it all dissolved. Everything dissolved.

(*Shelly stares at him for a while then reaches through the hole in the screen and sets the saxophone case and Vince's overcoat on the sofa. She looks at Vince again.*)

SHELLY: Bye, Vince.

(*She exits left off the porch. Vince watches her go. Bradley tries to make a lunge for his wooden leg. Vince quickly picks it up and dangles it over Bradley's head like a carrot. Bradley keeps making desperate grabs at the leg. Dewis comes down the staircase and stops halfway, staring at Vince and Bradley. Vince looks up at Dewis and smiles. He keeps moving backwards with the leg toward upstage left as Bradley crawls after him.*)

VINCE (*to Dewis as he continues torturing Bradley*): Oh, excuse me, Father. Just getting rid of some of the vermin in the house. This is my house now, ya' know? All mine. Everything. Except for the power tools and stuff. I'm gonna get all new equipment anyway. New plows, new tractor, everything. All brand new. (*Vince teases Bradley closer to the up left corner of the stage.*) Start right off on the ground floor.

(*Vince throws Bradley's wooden leg far offstage left. Bradley follows his leg offstage, pulling himself along on the ground, whimpering. As Bradley exits, Vince pulls the blanket off him and throws it over his own shoulder. He crosses toward Dewis with the blanket and smells the roses. Dewis comes to the bottom of the stairs.*)

DEWIS: You'd better go up and see your Grandmother.

VINCE (*looking up stairs, back to Dewis*): My Grandmother? There's nobody else in this house. Except for you. And you're leaving, aren't you?

(*Dewis crosses toward stage right door. He turns back to Vince.*)

DEWIS: She's going to need someone. I can't help her. I don't know what to do. I don't know what my position is. I just came in for some tea. I had no idea there was any trouble. No idea at all.

(*Vince just stares at him. Dewis goes out the door, crosses porch, and exits left. Vince listens to him leaving. He smells roses, looks up the staircase, then smells roses again. He turns and looks upstage at Dodge. He crosses up to him and bends over looking at Dodge's open eyes. Dodge is dead. His death should have come completely unnoticed by the audience. Vince covers Dodge's body with the blanket, then covers his head. He sits on the sofa, smelling roses and staring at Dodge's body. Long pause. Vince places the roses on Dodge's chest, then lays down on the sofa, arms folded behind his head, staring at the ceiling. His body is in the same relationship to Dodge's. After a while Halie's voice is heard coming* from above the staircase. The lights start to dim almost imperceptively as Halie speaks. Vince keeps staring at the ceiling.*)

HALIE'S VOICE: Dodge? Is that you, Dodge? Tilden was right about the corn, you know. I've never seen such corn. Have you taken a look at it lately? Tall as a man already. This early in the year. Carrots too. Potatoes. Peas. It's like a paradise out there, Dodge. You oughta' take a look. A miracle. I've never seen it like this. Maybe the rain did something. Maybe it was the rain.

(*As Halie keeps talking offstage, Tilden appears from stage left, dripping with mud from the knees down. His arms and hands are covered with mud. In his hands he carries the corpse of a small child at chest level, staring down at it. The corpse mainly consists of bones wrapped in muddy, rotten cloth. He moves slowly downstage toward the staircase, ignoring Vince on the sofa. Vince keeps staring at the ceiling as though Tilden wasn't there. As Halie's voice continues, Tilden slowly makes his way up the stairs. His eyes never leave the corpse of the child. The lights keep fading.*)

HALIE'S VOICE: Good hard rain. Takes everything straight down deep to the roots. The rest takes care of itself. You can't force a thing to grow. You can't interfere with it. It's all hidden. It's all unseen. You just gotta wait till it pops up out of the ground. Tiny little shoot. Tiny little white shoot. All hairy and fragile. Strong though. Strong enough to break the earth even. It's a miracle, Dodge. I've never seen a crop like this in my whole life. Maybe it's the sun. Maybe that's it. Maybe it's the sun.

(*Tilden disappears above. Silence. Lights go to black.*)

Harold Pinter

Harold Pinter (b. 1930) has written plays for the commercial stage, radio, and television as well as film scripts produced by some of the best directors of his time. Pinter was born into relatively humble circumstances in East London, but his early schooling distinguished him, and he eventually enrolled in London's prestigious Royal Academy of Dramatic Arts to study acting. When he finished his studies, he joined a company, toured for several years, and began to write for the stage. His previous writing efforts had been in prose: short stories and a long novel, *The Dwarfs* (1956), purportedly autobiographical, but never finished and not published until 1990. Produced as a radio play in 1960, it expresses some of the themes of his best work: the disintegration of a mind and the cruelty of people to their fellow beings.

In 1957 Pinter wrote three important plays, the one-act *The Room* and *The Dumb Waiter* and the full-length *The Birthday Party* (finished in 1958). All were well received. They established his method in dialogue and to a large extent the style that has dominated his work. The critic Martin Esslin, who coined the term "theater of the absurd," saw in Pinter's work an absurdist strain, especially in the nihilism — the belief in nothing — that sometimes shows up in his work. Pinter's characters usually reveal no spiritual awareness and no longing for spiritual values.

Pinter's dialogue sometimes has qualities of aimlessness, at least on the surface. But always the dialogue penetrates the unconsciousness of the audience and reveals the nature of the characters and their situation. Even the repetitious dialogue makes the audience more aware of the limitations and the pain of the circumstances in which Pinter's people find themselves.

Early reaction to the plays sometimes saw the aimless dialogue and the absurdist qualities as shortcomings rather than as indictments of the social order from which the plays arose. Yet the brutality of his characters to one another, their lack of sympathy for one another, and their demands for dominance have all become hallmarks of late-twentieth-century life.

The first of Pinter's plays to catch the attention of the general theater public was the commercially produced *The Caretaker* (1960), a play about two brothers, one of whom, Aston, invites a bewildered and all but mentally destroyed tramp, Davies, to become a caretaker in his room. Davies hardly knows who he is. His identity is essentially reduced to nothing by his soul-destroying life, and he speaks in broken language, especially when he is trying to explain that he left his identity papers in his beloved Sidcup — some fifteen years before — and that if they could find those papers, he would know where he was born and who he was. At the end of the play the younger brother, Mick, torments Davies, demanding that he leave, twisting his arm, verbally abusing him, but then relenting. The play ends with the shards of a life, as Davies says: "Listen...if I...go down...if I was to...get my papers...would you...would you let...would you...if I got down...and got my...(*Long silence.*)"

Pinter's *The Homecoming* (1965) has a brutal, shocking quality. A professor returns to England from America with his wife, and it becomes clear that he plans to return to America but that his wife will stay on as a mistress to his father and his brothers. The matter-of-factness with which the situation is treated and the way the relationships are portrayed provide part of the play's shock value.

In 1968 his play *Landscape* was censored for the use of obscenities, but eventually it and another short play, *Silence*, were produced in London in 1969 and in New York in 1970. *Old Times* was produced in London and in New York in 1971. Throughout the 1970s Pinter directed many plays by other playwrights and acted in films and on stage. *The Hothouse*, which has been revived in 1995, was first produced in Hampstead in 1980. He later directed it himself in Providence, Rhode Island. He wrote the screenplay for *Betrayal* in 1982, when he also wrote the screenplay for *The French Lieutenant's Woman*, which received an Academy Award nomination for best film. In 1992 he adapted Kazuo Ishiguro's novel *Remains of the Day* for the screen and also wrote the screenplay for Franz Kafka's *The Trial*. Both he and his wife, Lady Antonia Fraser, were very active through the eighties and early nineties on behalf of writers in countries that emerged from Eastern Europe's economic and political shifts.

BETRAYAL

Unlike many of his plays, in which people are specifically brutal toward one another, *Betrayal* shows people in an extraordinarily civil, although complex, relationship. The play concerns the betrayal of husbands and wives in adulterous relationships, but it also explores the power relations between the genders as well as the relationship between male friends. Jerry and Robert, best friends from college, are now business associates; Jerry, as literary agent, finds authors for Robert, who is a publisher. At first, the betrayal seems to have been committed by Jerry, the best man at Robert's marriage to Emma. As the play progresses, however, we see many levels of betrayal, including some appearing in the literature that Jerry promotes and Robert rejects, such as Spinks's novel, which Emma enjoys. Pinter examines the relationship of all three characters in great detail, revealing that Robert knew about Emma's affair with Jerry but never mentioned a word to Jerry. Indeed, Robert and Jerry continued to have civilized lunches, to drink together at bars, and generally enjoy each other's company as if nothing had happened. All the while and unknown to Emma and Jerry, Robert was himself having affairs. Part of the cruel fun of the play is watching the reactions of characters as they discover that such behavior had been going on without their knowledge.

The structure of the play is unusual. At first, it seems to progress normally, with the date 1977 displayed prominently at the top of the stage during the first two scenes, which follow chronologically. After those scenes, however, the play moves backward in time. During the first production in London this effect was powerful, if only because it was so unexpected. Pinter puts the audience into a special relationship with the characters and their circumstances because the audience understands the implied ironies in much of the dialogue, as for example in Robert's going off to read Yeats on the island of Torcello. Not only had Robert and Jerry discussed Yeats as undergraduates, but Yeats, the Irish poet, had also been "betrayed" by the one he loved, Maud Gonne, and had "betrayed" her in turn. It is especially ironic for Robert to tell Jerry that his early morning hours alone on Torcello were the high point of his trip to Venice, since it was the evening before that he had first discovered Emma and Jerry's affair.

The dialogue is pure Pinter. The speeches are very short at first, the words simple, often only one syllable, and often questions or observations are repeated in what seems an almost needless fashion. Yet the dialogue accretes and the significance of things that seem casual and almost irrelevant grows until we catch the innuendo and understand the deeper implications. One useful experience is going back to the opening scene after reading through the play. The emotional coolness of that scene is a powerful counterpoint to the intense closing scene of the play.

Betrayal in Performance

Betrayal was produced first at the National Theatre in London in 1978, then in New York in 1979. In London Michael Gambon was Jerry, Penelope Wilton was Emma, and Daniel Massey was Robert. In New York Raul Julia played Jerry, Blythe Danner was Emma, and Roy Scheider was Robert. Both productions were highly successful. The staging for both was similar, with realistic sets for the opening scene in the restaurant and the following scenes in the flat. The film, which opened in February 1983, followed the structure of the play itself and stayed close to the original dialogue. Ben Kingsley was Robert; Jeremy Irons was Jerry; and a relative unknown, Patricia Hodge, played Emma. Of the film Vincent Canby said, "The writing is superb, and so quintessentially Pinter that it sometimes comes close to sounding like parody, though, in the screenplay, there's not one predictable line or gesture."

The play has been revived several times in London, first in 1983, then again at the Almeida Theater in 1991. It has also been produced regionally in the United States and seems to have proved itself as a popular work in repertory.

Harold Pinter *(b. 1930)*

BETRAYAL

1978

Characters

EMMA
JERRY
ROBERT
A WAITER

In 1977 Emma is 38, Jerry and Robert are 40.

1977

Scene 1

Pub. 1977. Spring. *Noon.*

Emma is sitting at a corner table. Jerry approaches with drinks, a pint of bitter for him, a glass of wine for her.

He sits. They smile, toast each other silently, drink. He sits back and looks at her.

JERRY: Well . . .
EMMA: How are you?
JERRY: All right.
EMMA: You look well.
JERRY: Well, I'm not all that well, really.
EMMA: Why? What's the matter?
JERRY: Hangover.

(He raises his glass.)

Cheers.

(He drinks.)

How are you?
EMMA: I'm fine.

(She looks round the bar, back at him.)

Just like old times.
JERRY: Mmn. It's been a long time.
EMMA: Yes.

(*Pause.*)

I thought of you the other day.
JERRY: Good God. Why?

(*She laughs.*)

JERRY: Why?
EMMA: Well, it's nice, sometimes, to think back. Isn't it?
JERRY: Absolutely.

(*Pause.*)

How's everything?
EMMA: Oh, not too bad.

(*Pause.*)

Do you know how long it is since we met?
JERRY: Well I came to that private view, when was it — ?
EMMA: No, I don't mean that.
JERRY: Oh you mean alone?
EMMA: Yes.
JERRY: Uuh . . .
EMMA: Two years.
JERRY: Yes, I thought it must be. Mmnn.

(*Pause.*)

EMMA: Long time.
JERRY: Yes. It is.

(*Pause.*)

How's it going? The Gallery?
EMMA: How do you think it's going?
JERRY: Well. Very well, I would say.
EMMA: I'm glad you think so. Well, it is, actually. I enjoy it.
JERRY: Funny lot, painters, aren't they?
EMMA: They're not at all funny.
JERRY: Aren't they? What a pity.

(*Pause.*)

How's Robert?
EMMA: When did you last see him?
JERRY: I haven't seen him for months. Don't know why. Why?
EMMA: Why what?
JERRY: Why did you ask when I last saw him?
EMMA: I just wondered. How's Sam?
JERRY: You mean Judith.
EMMA: Do I?
JERRY: You remember the form. I ask about your husband, you ask about my wife.
EMMA: Yes, of course. How is your wife?
JERRY: All right.

(*Pause.*)

EMMA: Sam must be . . . tall.
JERRY: He is tall. Quite tall. Does a lot of running. He's a long distance runner. He wants to be a zoologist.
EMMA: No, really? Good. And Sarah?
JERRY: She's ten.
EMMA: God. I suppose she must be.
JERRY: Yes, she must be.

(*Pause.*)

Ned's five, isn't he?
EMMA: You remember.
JERRY: Well, I would remember that.

(*Pause.*)

EMMA: Yes.

(*Pause.*)

You're all right, though?
JERRY: Oh . . . yes, sure.

(*Pause.*)

EMMA: Ever think of me?
JERRY: I don't need to think of you.
EMMA: Oh?
JERRY: I don't need to *think* of you.

(*Pause.*)

Anyway I'm all right. How are you?
EMMA: Fine, really. All right.
JERRY: You're looking very pretty.
EMMA: Really? Thank you. I'm glad to see you.
JERRY: So am I. I mean to see you.
EMMA: You think of me sometimes?
JERRY: I think of you sometimes.

(*Pause.*)

I saw Charlotte the other day.
EMMA: No? Where? She didn't mention it.
JERRY: She didn't see me. In the street.
EMMA: But you haven't seen her for years.
JERRY: I recognised her.
EMMA: How could you? How could you know?
JERRY: I did.
EMMA: What did she look like?
JERRY: You.
EMMA: No, what did you think of her, really?
JERRY: I thought she was lovely.
EMMA: Yes. She's very . . . She's smashing. She's thirteen.

(*Pause.*)

Do you remember that time . . . oh god it was . . . when you picked her up and threw her up and caught her?
JERRY: She was very light.

EMMA: She remembers that, you know.
JERRY: Really?
EMMA: Mmnn. Being thrown up.
JERRY: What a memory.

(*Pause.*)

She doesn't know . . . about us, does she?
EMMA: Of course not. She just remembers you, as an old friend.
JERRY: That's right.

(*Pause.*)

Yes, everyone was there that day, standing around, your husband, my wife, all the kids, I remember.
EMMA: What day?
JERRY: When I threw her up. It was in your kitchen.
EMMA: It was in your kitchen.

(*Silence.*)

JERRY: Darling.
EMMA: Don't say that.

(*Pause.*)

It all . . .
JERRY: Seems such a long time ago.
EMMA: Does it?
JERRY: Same again?

(*He takes the glasses, goes to the bar. She sits still. He returns, with the drinks, sits.*)

EMMA: I thought of you the other day.

(*Pause.*)

I was driving through Kilburn. Suddenly I saw where I was. I just stopped, and then I turned down Kinsale Drive and drove into Wessex Grove. I drove past the house and then stopped about fifty yards further on, like we used to do, do you remember?
JERRY: Yes.
EMMA: People were coming out of the house. They walked up the road.
JERRY: What sort of people?
EMMA: Oh . . . young people. Then I got out of the car and went up the steps. I looked at the bells, you know, the names on the bells. I looked for our name.

(*Pause.*)

JERRY: Green.

(*Pause.*)

Couldn't see it, eh?
EMMA: No.
JERRY: That's because we're not there any more. We haven't been there for years.

EMMA: No we haven't.

(*Pause.*)

JERRY: I hear you're seeing a bit of Casey.
EMMA: What?
JERRY: Casey. I just heard you were . . . seeing a bit of him.
EMMA: Where did you hear that?
JERRY: Oh . . . people . . . talking.
EMMA: Christ.
JERRY: The funny thing was that the only thing I really felt was irritation, I mean irritation that nobody gossiped about us like that, in the old days. I nearly said, now look, she may be having the occasional drink with Casey, who cares, but she and I had an affair for seven years and none of you bastards had the faintest idea it was happening.

(*Pause.*)

EMMA: I wonder. I wonder if everyone knew, all the time.
JERRY: Don't be silly. We were brilliant. Nobody knew. Who ever went to Kilburn in those days? Just you and me.

(*Pause.*)

Anyway, what's all this about you and Casey?
EMMA: What do you mean?
JERRY: What's going on?
EMMA: We have the occasional drink.
JERRY: I thought you didn't admire his work.
EMMA: I've changed. Or his work has changed. Are you jealous?
JERRY: Of what?

(*Pause.*)

I couldn't be jealous of Casey. I'm his agent. I advised him about his divorce. I read all his first drafts. I persuaded your husband to publish his first novel. I escort him to Oxford to speak at the Union. He's my . . . he's my boy. I discovered him when he was a poet, and that's a bloody long time ago now.

(*Pause.*)

He's even taken me down to Southampton to meet his Mum and Dad. I couldn't be jealous of Casey. Anyway it's not as if we're having an affair now, is it? We haven't seen each other for years. Really, I'm very happy if you're happy.

(*Pause.*)

What about Robert?

(*Pause.*)

EMMA: Well . . . I think we're going to separate.

JERRY: Oh?

EMMA: We had a long talk . . . last night.

JERRY: Last night?

EMMA: You know what I found out . . . last night? He's betrayed me for years. He's had . . . other women for years.

JERRY: No? Good Lord.

(*Pause.*)

But we betrayed him for years.

EMMA: And he betrayed me for years.

JERRY: Well I never knew that.

EMMA: Nor did I.

(*Pause.*)

JERRY: Does Casey know about this?

EMMA: I wish you wouldn't keep calling him Casey. His name is Roger.

JERRY: Yes. Roger.

EMMA: I phoned *you*. I don't know why.

JERRY: What a funny thing. We were such close friends, weren't we? Robert and me, even though I haven't seen him for a few months, but through all those years, all the drinks, all the lunches . . . we had together, I never even gleaned . . . I never suspected . . . that there was anyone else . . . in his life but you. Never. For example, when you're with a fellow in a pub, or a restaurant, for example, from time to time he pops out for a piss, you see, who doesn't, but what I mean is, if he's making a crafty telephone call, you can sort of sense it, you see, you can sense the pip pip pips. Well, I never did that with Robert. He never made any pip pip telephone calls in any pub I was ever with him in. The funny thing is that it was me who made the pip pip calls — to you, when I left him boozing at the bar. That's the funny thing.

(*Pause.*)

When did he tell you all this?

EMMA: Last night. I think we were up all night.

(*Pause.*)

JERRY: You talked all night?

EMMA: Yes. Oh yes.

(*Pause.*)

JERRY: I didn't come into it, did I?

EMMA: What?

JERRY: I just —

EMMA: I just phoned you this morning, you know, that's all, because I . . . because we're old friends . . . I've been up all night . . . the whole thing's finished . . . I suddenly felt I wanted to see you.

JERRY: Well, look, I'm happy to see you. I am. I'm sorry . . . about . . .

EMMA: Do you remember? I mean, you do remember?

JERRY: I remember.

(*Pause.*)

EMMA: You couldn't really afford Wessex Grove when we took it, could you?

JERRY: Oh, love finds a way.

EMMA: I bought the curtains.

JERRY: You found a way.

EMMA: Listen, I didn't want to see you for nostalgia, I mean what's the point? I just wanted to see how you were. Truly. How are you?

JERRY: Oh what does it matter?

(*Pause.*)

You didn't tell Robert about me last night, did you?

EMMA: I had to.

(*Pause.*)

He told me everything. I told him everything. We were up . . . all night. At one point Ned came down. I had to take him up to bed, had to put him back to bed. Then I went down again. I think it was the voices woke him up. You know . . .

JERRY: You told him everything?

EMMA: I had to.

JERRY: You told him everything . . . about us?

EMMA: I had to.

(*Pause.*)

JERRY: But he's my oldest friend. I mean, I picked his own daughter up in my own arms and threw her up and caught her, in my kitchen. He watched me do it.

EMMA: It doesn't matter. It's all gone.

JERRY: Is it? What has?

EMMA: It's all all over.

(*She drinks.*)

1977

LATER

Scene 2

Jerry's House. Study. 1977. Spring. *Jerry sitting. Robert standing, with glass.*

JERRY: It's good of you to come.

ROBERT: Not at all.

JERRY: Yes, yes, I know it was difficult . . . I know . . . the kids . . .

ROBERT: It's all right. It sounded urgent.
JERRY: Well . . . You found someone, did you?
ROBERT: What?
JERRY: For the kids.
ROBERT: Yes, yes. Honestly. Everything's in order. Anyway, Charlotte's not a baby.
JERRY: No.

(*Pause.*)

Are you going to sit down?
ROBERT: Well, I might, yes, in a minute.

(*Pause.*)

JERRY: Judith's at the hospital . . . on night duty. The kids are . . . here . . . upstairs.
ROBERT: Uh-huh.
JERRY: I must speak to you. It's important.
ROBERT: Speak.
JERRY: Yes.

(*Pause.*)

ROBERT: You look quite rough.

(*Pause.*)

What's the trouble?

(*Pause.*)

It's not about you and Emma, is it?

(*Pause.*)

I know all about that.
JERRY: Yes. So I've . . . been told.
ROBERT: Ah.

(*Pause.*)

Well, it's not very important, is it? Been over for years, hasn't it?
JERRY: It is important.
ROBERT: Really? Why?

(*Jerry stands, walks about.*)

JERRY: I thought I was going to go mad.
ROBERT: When?
JERRY: This evening. Just now. Wondering whether to phone you. I had to phone you. It took me . . . two hours to phone you. And then you were with the kids . . . I thought I wasn't going to be able to see you . . . I thought I'd go mad. I'm very grateful to you . . . for coming.
ROBERT: Oh for God's sake! Look, what exactly do you want to say?

(*Pause.*)
(*Jerry sits.*)

JERRY: I don't know why she told you. I don't know

how she could tell you. I just don't understand. Listen, I know you've got . . . look, I saw her today . . . we had a drink . . . I haven't seen her for . . . she told me, you know, that you're in trouble, both of you . . . and so on. I know that. I mean I'm sorry.
ROBERT: Don't be sorry.
JERRY: Why not?

(*Pause.*)

The fact is I can't understand . . . why she thought it necessary . . . after all these years . . . to tell you . . . so suddenly . . . last night . . .
ROBERT: Last night?
JERRY: Without consulting me. Without even warning me. After all, you and me . . .
ROBERT: She didn't tell me last night.
JERRY: What do you mean?

(*Pause.*)

I know about last night. She told me about it. You were up all night, weren't you?
ROBERT: That's correct.
JERRY: And she told you . . . last night . . . about her and me. Did she not?
ROBERT: No, she didn't. She didn't tell me about you and her last night. She told me about you and her four years ago.

(*Pause.*)

So she didn't have to tell me again last night. Because I knew. And she knew I knew because she told me herself four years ago.

(*Silence.*)

JERRY: What?
ROBERT: I think I will sit down.

(*He sits.*)

I thought you knew.
JERRY: Knew what?
ROBERT: That I knew. That I've known for years. I thought you knew that.
JERRY: You thought I knew?
ROBERT: She said you didn't. But I didn't believe that.

(*Pause.*)

Anyway I think I thought you knew. But you say you didn't?
JERRY: She told you . . . when?
ROBERT: Well, I found out. That's what happened. I told her I'd found out and then she . . . confirmed . . . the facts.
JERRY: When?
ROBERT: Oh, a long time ago, Jerry.

(*Pause.*)

JERRY: But we've seen each other . . . a great deal . . . over the last four years. We've had lunch.

ROBERT: Never played squash though.

JERRY: I was your best friend.

ROBERT: Well, yes, sure.

(*Jerry stares at him and then holds his head in his hands.*)

Oh, don't get upset. There's no point.

(*Silence.*)

(*Jerry sits up.*)

JERRY: Why didn't she tell me?

ROBERT: Well, I'm not her, old boy.

JERRY: Why didn't you tell me?

(*Pause.*)

ROBERT: I thought you might know.

JERRY: But you didn't know for *certain*, did you? You didn't *know*!

ROBERT: No.

JERRY: Then why didn't you tell me?

(*Pause.*)

ROBERT: Tell you what?

JERRY: That you knew. You bastard.

ROBERT: Oh, don't call me a bastard, Jerry.

(*Pause.*)

JERRY: What are we going to do?

ROBERT: You and I are not going to do anything. My marriage is finished. I've just got to make proper arrangements, that's all. About the children.

(*Pause.*)

JERRY: You hadn't thought of telling Judith?

ROBERT: Telling Judith what? Oh, about you and Emma. You mean she never knew? Are you quite sure?

(*Pause.*)

No, I hadn't thought of telling Judith, actually. You don't seem to understand. You don't seem to understand that I don't give a shit about any of this. It's true I've hit Emma once or twice. But that wasn't to defend a principle. I wasn't inspired to do it from any kind of moral standpoint. I just felt like giving her a good bashing. The old itch . . . you understand.

(*Pause.*)

JERRY: But you betrayed her for years, didn't you?

ROBERT: Oh yes.

JERRY: And she never knew about it. Did she?

ROBERT: Didn't she?

(*Pause.*)

JERRY: I didn't.

ROBERT: No, you didn't know very much about anything, really, did you?

(*Pause.*)

JERRY: No.

ROBERT: Yes you did.

JERRY: Yes I did. I lived with her.

ROBERT: Yes. In the afternoons.

JERRY: Sometimes very long ones. For seven years.

ROBERT: Yes, you certainly knew all there was to know about that. About the seven years of afternoons. I don't know anything about that.

(*Pause.*)

I hope she looked after you all right.

(*Silence.*)

JERRY: We used to like each other.

ROBERT: We still do.

(*Pause.*)

I bumped into old Casey the other day. I believe he's having an affair with my wife. We haven't played squash for years, Casey and me. We used to have a damn good game.

JERRY: He's put on weight.

ROBERT: Yes, I thought that.

JERRY: He's over the hill.

ROBERT: Is he?

JERRY: Don't you think so?

ROBERT: In what respect?

JERRY: His work. His books.

ROBERT: Oh his books. His art. Yes his art does seem to be falling away, doesn't it?

JERRY: Still sells.

ROBERT: Oh, sells very well. Sells very well indeed. Very good for us. For you and me.

JERRY: Yes.

ROBERT: Someone was telling me — who was it — must have been someone in the publicity department — the other day — that when Casey went up to York to sign his latest book, in a bookshop, you know, with Barbara Spring, you know, the populace queued for hours to get his signature on his book, while one old lady and a dog queued to get Barbara Spring's signature, on her book. I happen to think that Barbara Spring . . . is good, don't you?

JERRY: Yes.

(*Pause.*)

ROBERT: Still, we both do very well out of Casey, don't we?
JERRY: Very well.

(*Pause.*)

ROBERT: Have you read any good books lately?
JERRY: I've been reading Yeats.
ROBERT: Ah. Yeats. Yes.

(*Pause.*)

JERRY: You read Yeats on Torcello once.
ROBERT: On Torcello?
JERRY: Don't you remember? Years ago. You went over to Torcello in the dawn, alone. And read Yeats.
ROBERT: So I did. I told you that, yes.

(*Pause.*)

Yes.

(*Pause.*)

Where are you going this summer, you and the family?
JERRY: The Lake District.

1975

Scene 3

Flat. 1975. Winter. *Jerry and Emma. They are sitting. Silence.*

JERRY: What do you want to do then?

(*Pause.*)

EMMA: I don't quite know what we're doing, any more, that's all.
JERRY: Mmnn.

(*Pause.*)

EMMA: I mean, this flat . . .
JERRY: Yes.
EMMA: Can you actually remember when we were last here?
JERRY: In the summer, was it?
EMMA: Well, was it?
JERRY: I know it seems —
EMMA: It was the beginning of September.
JERRY: Well, that's summer, isn't it?
EMMA: It was actually extremely cold. It was early autumn.
JERRY: It's pretty cold now.

EMMA: We were going to get another electric fire.
JERRY: Yes, I never got that.
EMMA: Not much point in getting it if we're never here.
JERRY: We're here now.
EMMA: Not really.

(*Silence.*)

JERRY: Well, things have changed. You've been so busy, your job, and everything.
EMMA: Well, I know. But I mean, I like it. I want to do it.
JERRY: No, it's great. It's marvellous for you. But you're not —
EMMA: If you're running a gallery you've got to run it, you've got to be there.
JERRY: But you're not free in the afternoons. Are you?
EMMA: No.
JERRY: So how can we meet?
EMMA: But look at the times you're out of the country. You're never here.
JERRY: But when I am here you're not free in the afternoons. So we can never meet.
EMMA: We can meet for lunch.
JERRY: We can meet for lunch but we can't come all the way out here for a quick lunch. I'm too old for that.
EMMA: I didn't suggest that.

(*Pause.*)

You see, in the past . . . we were inventive, we were determined, it was . . . it seemed impossible to meet . . . impossible . . . and yet we did. We met here, we took this flat and we met in this flat because we wanted to.
JERRY: It would not matter how much we wanted to if you're not free in the afternoons and I'm in America.

(*Silence.*)

Nights have always been out of the question and you know it. I have a family.
EMMA: I have a family too.
JERRY: I know that perfectly well. I might remind you that your husband is my oldest friend.
EMMA: What do you mean by that?
JERRY: I don't *mean* anything by it.
EMMA: But what are you trying to say by saying that?
JERRY: Jesus. I'm not *trying* to say anything. I've said precisely what I wanted to say.
EMMA: I see.

(*Pause.*)

The fact is that in the old days we used our imagination and we'd take a night and make an arrangement and go to an hotel.

JERRY: Yes. We did.

(*Pause.*)

But that was . . . in the main . . . before we got this flat.

EMMA: We haven't spent many nights . . . in this flat.

JERRY: No.

(*Pause.*)

Not many nights anywhere, really.

(*Silence.*)

EMMA: Can you afford . . . to keep it going, month after month?

JERRY: Oh . . .

EMMA: It's a waste. Nobody comes here. I just can't bear to think about it, actually. Just . . . empty. All day and night. Day after day and night after night. I mean the crockery and the curtains and the bedspread and everything. And the tablecloth I brought from Venice. (*Laughs.*) It's ridiculous.

(*Pause.*)

It's just . . . an empty home.

JERRY: It's not a home.

(*Pause.*)

I know . . . I know what you wanted . . . but it could never . . . actually be a home. You have a home. I have a home. With curtains, etcetera. And children. Two children in two homes. There are no children here, so it's not the same kind of home.

EMMA: It was never intended to be the same kind of home. Was it?

(*Pause.*)

You didn't ever see it as a home, in any sense, did you?

JERRY: No, I saw it as a flat . . . you know.

EMMA: For fucking.

JERRY: No, for loving.

EMMA: Well, there's not much of that left, is there?

(*Silence.*)

JERRY: I don't think we don't love each other.

(*Pause.*)

EMMA: Ah well.

(*Pause.*)

What will you do about all the . . . furniture?

JERRY: What?

EMMA: The contents.

(*Silence.*)

JERRY: You know we can do something very simple, if we want to do it.

EMMA: You mean sell it to Mrs. Banks for a small sum and . . . and she can let it as a furnished flat?

JERRY: That's right. Wasn't the bed here?

EMMA: What?

JERRY: Wasn't it?

EMMA: We bought the bed. We bought everything. We bought the bed together.

JERRY: Ah. Yes.

(*Emma stands.*)

EMMA: You'll make all the arrangements, then? With Mrs Banks?

(*Pause.*)

I don't want anything. Nowhere I can put it, you see. I have a home, with tablecloths and all the rest of it.

JERRY: I'll go into it, with Mrs. Banks. There'll be a few quid, you know, so . . .

EMMA: No, I don't want any *cash*, thank you very much.

(*Silence. She puts coat on.*)

I'm going now.

(*He turns, looks at her.*)

Oh here's my key.

(*Takes out keyring, tries to take key from ring.*)

Oh Christ.

(*Struggles to take key from ring.
Throws him the ring.*)

You take it off.

(*He catches it, looks at her.*)

Can you just do it please? I'm picking up Charlotte from school. I'm taking her shopping.

(*He takes key off.*)

Do you realise this is an afternoon? It's the Gallery's afternoon off. That's why I'm here. We close every Thursday afternoon. Can I have my keyring?

(*He gives it to her.*)

Thanks. Listen. I think we've made absolutely the right decision.

(*She goes.*)

(*He stands.*)

1974

Scene 4

Robert and Emma's House. Living room. 1974. Autumn. *Robert pouring a drink for Jerry. He goes to the door.*

ROBERT: Emma! Jerry's here!
EMMA (*off*): Who?
ROBERT: Jerry.
EMMA: I'll be down.

(*Robert gives the drink to Jerry.*)

JERRY: Cheers.
ROBERT: Cheers. She's just putting Ned to bed. I should think he'll be off in a minute.
JERRY: Off where?
ROBERT: Dreamland.
JERRY: Ah. Yes, how is your sleep these days?
ROBERT: What?
JERRY: Do you still have bad nights? With Ned, I mean?
ROBERT: Oh, I see. Well, no. No, it's getting better. But you know what they say?
JERRY: What?
ROBERT: They say boys are worse than girls.
JERRY: Worse?
ROBERT: Babies. They say boy babies cry more than girl babies.
JERRY: Do they?
ROBERT: You didn't find that to be the case?
JERRY: Uh . . . yes, I think we did. Did you?
ROBERT: Yes. What do you make of it? Why do you think that is?
JERRY: Well, I suppose . . . boys are more anxious.
ROBERT: Boy babies?
JERRY: Yes.
ROBERT: What the hell are they anxious about . . . at their age? Do you think?
JERRY: Well . . . facing the world, I suppose, leaving the womb, all that.
ROBERT: But what about girl babies? They leave the womb too.
JERRY: That's true. It's also true that nobody talks much about girl babies leaving the womb. Do they?
ROBERT: I am prepared to do so.
JERRY: I see. Well, what have you got to say?
ROBERT: I was asking you a question.
JERRY: What was it?
ROBERT: Why do you assert that boy babies find leaving the womb more of a problem than girl babies?
JERRY: Have I made such an assertion?
ROBERT: You went on to make a further assertion, to

the effect that boy babies are more anxious about facing the world than girl babies.
JERRY: Do you yourself believe that to be the case?
ROBERT: I do, yes.

(*Pause.*)

JERRY: Why do you think it is?
ROBERT: I have no answer.

(*Pause.*)

JERRY: Do you think it might have something to do with the difference between the sexes?

(*Pause.*)

ROBERT: Good God, you're right. That must be it.

(*Emma comes in.*)

EMMA: Hullo. Surprise.
JERRY: I was having tea with Casey.
EMMA: Where?
JERRY: Just around the corner.
EMMA: I thought he lived in . . . Hampstead or somewhere.
ROBERT: You're out of date.
EMMA: Am I?
JERRY: He's left Susannah. He's living alone round the corner.
EMMA: Oh.
ROBERT: Writing a novel about a man who leaves his wife and three children and goes to live alone on the other side of London to write a novel about a man who leaves his wife and three children —
EMMA: I hope it's better than the last one.
ROBERT: The last one? Ah, the last one. Wasn't that the one about the man who lived in a big house in Hampstead with his wife and three children and is writing a novel about — ?
JERRY (*to Emma*): Why didn't you like it?
EMMA: I've told you actually.
JERRY: I think it's the best thing he's written.
EMMA: It may be the best thing he's *written* but it's still bloody dishonest.
JERRY: Dishonest? In what way dishonest?
EMMA: I've told you, actually.
JERRY: Have you?
ROBERT: Yes, she has. Once when we were all having dinner, I remember, you, me, Emma and Judith, where was it, Emma gave a dissertation over the pudding about dishonesty in Casey with reference to his last novel. *Drying Out.* It was most stimulating. Judith had to leave unfortunately in the middle of it for her night shift at the hospital. How is Judith, by the way?
JERRY: Very well.

(*Pause.*)

ROBERT: When are we going to play squash?

JERRY: You're too good.

ROBERT: Not at all. I'm not good at all. I'm just fitter than you.

JERRY: But why? Why are you fitter than me?

ROBERT: Because I play squash.

JERRY: Oh, you're playing? Regularly?

ROBERT: Mmnn.

JERRY: With whom?

ROBERT: Casey, actually.

JERRY: Casey? Good Lord. What's he like?

ROBERT: He's a brutally honest squash player. No, really, we haven't played for years. We must play. You were rather good.

JERRY: Yes, I was quite good. All right. I'll give you a ring.

ROBERT: Why don't you?

JERRY: We'll make a date.

ROBERT: Right.

JERRY: Yes. We must do that.

ROBERT: And then I'll take you to lunch.

JERRY: No, no. I'll take you to lunch.

ROBERT: The man who wins buys the lunch.

EMMA: Can I watch?

(*Pause.*)

ROBERT: What?

EMMA: Why can't I watch and then take you both to lunch?

ROBERT: Well, to be brutally honest, we wouldn't actually want a woman around, would we, Jerry? I mean a game of squash isn't simply a game of squash, it's rather more than that. You see, first there's the game. And then there's the shower. And then there's the pint. And then there's lunch. After all, you've been at it. You've had your battle. What you want is your pint and your lunch. You really don't want a woman buying you lunch. You don't actually want a woman within a mile of the place, any of the places, really. You don't want her in the squash court, you don't want her in the shower, or the pub, or the restaurant. You see, at lunch you want to talk about squash, or cricket, or books, or even women, with your friend, and be able to warm to your theme without fear of improper interruption. That's what it's all about. What do you think, Jerry?

JERRY: I haven't played squash for years.

(*Pause.*)

ROBERT: Well, let's play next week.

JERRY: I can't next week. I'm in New York.

EMMA: Are you?

JERRY: I'm going over with one of my more celebrated writers, actually.

EMMA: Who?

JERRY: Casey. Someone wants to film that novel of his you didn't like. We're going over to discuss it. It was a question of them coming over here or us going over there. Casey thought he deserved the trip.

EMMA: What about you?

JERRY: What?

EMMA: Do you deserve the trip?

ROBERT: Judith going?

JERRY: No. He can't go alone. We'll have that game of squash when I get back. A week, or at the most ten days.

ROBERT: Lovely.

JERRY (*to Emma*): Bye. Thanks for the drink.

EMMA: Bye.

(*Robert and Jerry leave.*
She remains still.)

(*Robert returns. He kisses her. She responds. She breaks away, puts her head on his shoulder, cries quietly. He holds her.*)

1973

Scene 5

Hotel Room. Venice. 1973. Summer. *Emma on bed reading. Robert at window looking out. She looks up at him, then back at the book.*

EMMA: It's Torcello tomorrow, isn't it?

ROBERT: What?

EMMA: We're going to Torcello tomorrow, aren't we?

ROBERT: Yes. That's right.

EMMA: That'll be lovely.

ROBERT: Mmn.

EMMA: I can't wait.

(*Pause.*)

ROBERT: Book good?

EMMA: Mmn. Yes.

ROBERT: What is it?

EMMA: This new book. This man Spinks.

ROBERT: Oh that. Jerry was telling me about it.

EMMA: Jerry? Was he?

ROBERT: He was telling me about it at lunch last week.

EMMA: Really? Does he like it?

ROBERT: Spinks is his boy. He discovered him.

EMMA: Oh. I didn't know that.

ROBERT: Unsolicited manuscript.

(*Pause.*)

You think it's good, do you?

EMMA: Yes, I do. I'm enjoying it.

ROBERT: Jerry thinks it's good too. You should have lunch with us one day and chat about it.

EMMA: Is that absolutely necessary?

(*Pause.*)

It's not as good as all that.

ROBERT: You mean it's not good enough for you to have lunch with Jerry and me and chat about it?

EMMA: What the hell are you talking about?

ROBERT: I must read it again myself, now it's in hard covers.

EMMA: Again?

ROBERT: Jerry wanted us to publish it.

EMMA: Oh, really?

ROBERT: Well, naturally. Anyway, I turned it down.

EMMA: Why?

ROBERT: Oh . . . not much more to say on that subject, really, is there?

EMMA: What do you consider the subject to be?

ROBERT: Betrayal.

EMMA: No, it isn't.

ROBERT: Isn't it? What is it then?

EMMA: I haven't finished it yet. I'll let you know.

ROBERT: Well, do let me know.

(*Pause.*)

Of course, I could be thinking of the wrong book.

(*Silence.*)

By the way, I went into American Express yesterday.

(*She looks up.*)

EMMA: Oh?

ROBERT: Yes. I went to cash some travellers cheques. You get a much better rate there, you see, than you do in an hotel.

EMMA: Oh, do you?

ROBERT: Oh yes. Anyway, there was a letter there for you. They asked me if you were any relation and I said yes. So they asked me if I wanted to take it. I mean, they gave it to me. But I said no, I would leave it. Did you get it?

EMMA: Yes.

ROBERT: I suppose you popped in when you were out shopping yesterday evening?

EMMA: That's right.

ROBERT: Oh well, I'm glad you got it.

(*Pause.*)

To be honest, I was amazed that they suggested I take it. It could never happen in England. But these Italians . . . so free and easy. I mean, just because

my name is Downs and your name is Downs doesn't mean that we're the Mr. and Mrs. Downs that they, in their laughing Mediterranean way, assume we are. We could be, and in fact are vastly more likely to be, total strangers. So let's say I, whom they laughingly assume to be your husband, had taken the letter, having declared myself to be your husband but in truth being a total stranger, and opened it, and read it, out of nothing more than idle curiosity, and then thrown it in a canal, you would never have received it and would have been deprived of your legal right to open your own mail, and all this because of Venetian *je m'en foutisme.*° I've a good mind to write to the Doge of Venice about it.

(*Pause.*)

That's what stopped me taking it, by the way, and bringing it to you, the thought that I could very easily be a total stranger.

(*Pause.*)

What they of course did not know, and had no way of knowing, was that I am your husband.

EMMA: Pretty inefficient bunch.

ROBERT: Only in a laughing Mediterranean way.

(*Pause.*)

EMMA: It was from Jerry.

ROBERT: Yes, I recognised the handwriting.

(*Pause.*)

How is he?

EMMA: Okay.

ROBERT: Good. And Judith?

EMMA: Fine.

(*Pause.*)

ROBERT: What about the kids?

EMMA: I don't think he mentioned them.

ROBERT: They're probably all right, then. If they were ill or something he'd have probably mentioned it.

(*Pause.*)

Any other news?

EMMA: No.

(*Silence.*)

ROBERT: Are you looking forward to Torcello?

(*Pause.*)

je m'en foutisme: Vulgar phrase indicating a lax attitude.

How many times have we been to Torcello? Twice. I remember how you loved it, the first time I took you there. You fell in love with it. That was about ten years ago, wasn't it? About . . . six months after we were married. Yes. Do you remember? I wonder if you'll like it as much tomorrow.

(*Pause.*)

What do you think of Jerry as a letter writer?

(*She laughs shortly.*)

You're trembling. Are you cold?
EMMA: No.
ROBERT: He used to write to me at one time. Long letters about Ford Madox Ford. I used to write to him too, come to think of it. Long letters about . . . oh, W. B. Yeats, I suppose. That was the time when we were both editors of poetry magazines. Him at Cambridge, me at Oxford. Did you know that? We were bright young men. And close friends. Well, we still are close friends. All that was long before I met you. Long before he met you. I've been trying to remember when I introduced him to you. I simply can't remember. I take it I *did* introduce him to you? Yes. But when? Can you remember?
EMMA: No.
ROBERT: You can't?
EMMA: No.
ROBERT: How odd.

(*Pause.*)

He wasn't best man at our wedding, was he?
EMMA: You know he was.
ROBERT: Ah yes. Well, that's probably when I introduced him to you.

(*Pause.*)

Was there any message for me, in his letter?

(*Pause.*)

I mean in the line of business, to do with the world of publishing. Has he discovered any new and original talent? He's quite talented at uncovering talent, old Jerry.
EMMA: No message.
ROBERT: No message. Not even his love?

(*Silence.*)

EMMA: We're lovers.
ROBERT: Ah. Yes. I thought it might be something like that, something along those lines.
EMMA: When?
ROBERT: What?
EMMA: When did you think?

ROBERT: Yesterday. Only yesterday. When I saw his handwriting on the letter. Before yesterday I was quite ignorant.
EMMA: Ah.

(*Pause.*)

I'm sorry.
ROBERT: *Sorry?*

(*Silence.*)

Where does it . . . take place? Must be a bit awkward. I mean we've got two kids, he's got two kids, not to mention a wife . . .
EMMA: We have a flat.
ROBERT: Ah. I see.

(*Pause.*)

Nice?

(*Pause.*)

A flat. It's quite well established then, your . . . uh . . . affair?
EMMA: Yes.
ROBERT: How long?
EMMA: Some time.
ROBERT: Yes, but how long exactly?
EMMA: Five years.
ROBERT: *Five years?*

(*Pause.*)

Ned is one year old.

(*Pause.*)

Did you hear what I said?
EMMA: Yes. He's your son. Jerry was in America. For two months.

(*Silence.*)

ROBERT: Did he write to you from America?
EMMA: Of course. And I wrote to him.
ROBERT: Did you tell him that Ned had been conceived?
EMMA: Not by letter.
ROBERT: But when you did tell him, was he happy to know I was to be a father?

(*Pause.*)

I've always liked Jerry. To be honest, I've always liked him rather more than I've liked you. Maybe I should have had an affair with him myself.

(*Silence.*)

Tell me, are you looking forward to our trip to Torcello?

1973
LATER

Scene 6

Flat. 1973. Summer. *Emma and Jerry standing, kissing. She is holding a basket and a parcel.*

EMMA: Darling.
JERRY: Darling.

(*He continues to hold her. She laughs.*)

EMMA: I must put this down.

(*She puts basket on table.*)

JERRY: What's in it?
EMMA: Lunch.
JERRY: What?
EMMA: Things you like.

(*He pours wine.*)

   How do I look?
JERRY: Beautiful.
EMMA: Do I look well?
JERRY: You do.

(*He gives her wine.*)

EMMA (*sipping*): Mmmnn.
JERRY: How was it?
EMMA: It was lovely.
JERRY: Did you go to Torcello?
EMMA: No.
JERRY: Why not?
EMMA: Oh, I don't know. The speedboats were on strike, or something.
JERRY: On strike?
EMMA: Yes. On the day we were going.
JERRY: Ah. What about the gondolas?
EMMA: You can't take a gondola to Torcello.
JERRY: Well, they used to in the old days, didn't they? Before they had speedboats. How do you think they got over there?
EMMA: It would take hours.
JERRY: Yes, I suppose so.

(*Pause.*)

   I got your letter.
EMMA: Good.
JERRY: Get mine?
EMMA: Of course. Miss me?
JERRY: Yes. Actually, I haven't been well.
EMMA: What?
JERRY: Oh nothing. A bug.

(*She kisses him.*)

EMMA: I missed you.

(*She turns away, looks about.*)

   You haven't been here . . . at all?
JERRY: No.
EMMA: Needs Hoovering.°
JERRY: Later.

(*Pause.*)

   I spoke to Robert this morning.
EMMA: Oh?
JERRY: I'm taking him to lunch on Thursday.
EMMA: Thursday? Why?
JERRY: Well, it's my turn.
EMMA: No, I meant why are you taking him to lunch?
JERRY: Because it's my turn. Last time he took me to lunch.
EMMA: You know what I mean.
JERRY: No. What?
EMMA: What is the subject or point of your lunch?
JERRY: No subject or point. We've just been doing it for years. His turn, followed by my turn.
EMMA: You've misunderstood me.
JERRY: Have I? How?
EMMA: Well, quite simply, you often do meet, or have lunch, to discuss a particular writer or a particular book, don't you? So to those meetings, or lunches, there is a point or a subject.
JERRY: Well, there isn't to this one.

(*Pause.*)

EMMA: You haven't discovered any new writers, while I've been away?
JERRY: No. Sam fell off his bike.
EMMA: No.
JERRY: He was knocked out. He was out for about a minute.
EMMA: Were you with him?
JERRY: No. Judith. He's all right. And then I got this bug.
EMMA: Oh dear.
JERRY: So I've had time for nothing.
EMMA: Everything will be better, now I'm back.
JERRY: Yes.
EMMA: Oh, I read that Spinks, the book you gave me.
JERRY: What do you think?
EMMA: Excellent.
JERRY: Robert hated it. He wouldn't publish it.
EMMA: What's he like?
JERRY: Who?
EMMA: Spinks.
JERRY: Spinks? He's a very thin bloke. About fifty.

Hoovering: vacuuming.

Wears dark glasses day and night. He lives alone, in a furnished room. Quite like this one, actually. He's . . . unfussed.

EMMA: Furnished rooms suit him?

JERRY: Yes.

EMMA: They suit me too. And you? Do you still like it? Our home?

JERRY: It's marvellous not to have a telephone.

EMMA: And marvellous to have me?

JERRY: You're all right.

EMMA: I cook and slave for you.

JERRY: You do.

EMMA: I bought something in Venice — for the house.

(*She opens the parcel, takes out a tablecloth. Puts it on the table.*)

Do you like it?

JERRY: It's lovely.

(*Pause.*)

EMMA: Do you think we'll ever go to Venice together?

(*Pause.*)

No. Probably not.

(*Pause.*)

JERRY: You don't think I should see Robert for lunch on Thursday, or on Friday, for that matter?

EMMA: Why do you say that?

JERRY: You don't think I should see him at all?

EMMA: I didn't say that. How can you not see him? Don't be silly.

(*Pause.*)

JERRY: I had a terrible panic when you were away. I was sorting out a contract, in my office, with some lawyers. I suddenly couldn't remember what I'd done with your letter. I couldn't remember putting it in the safe. I said I had to look for something in the safe. I opened the safe. It wasn't there. I had to go on with the damn contract . . . I kept seeing it lying somewhere in the house, being picked up . . .

EMMA: Did you find it?

JERRY: It was in the pocket of a jacket — in my wardrobe — at home.

EMMA: God.

JERRY: Something else happened a few months ago — I didn't tell you. We had a drink one evening. Well, we had our drink, and I got home about eight, walked in the door, Judith said, hello, you're a bit late. Sorry, I said, I was having a drink with Spinks. Spinks? she said, how odd, he's just phoned, five minutes ago, wanted to speak to you, he didn't mention he'd just seen you. You know old Spinks, I said, not exactly forthcoming, is he?

He'd probably remembered something he'd meant to say but hadn't. I'll ring him later. I went up to see the kids and then we all had dinner.

(*Pause.*)

Listen. Do you remember, when was it, a few years ago, we were all in your kitchen, must have been Christmas or something, do you remember, all the kids were running about and suddenly I picked Charlotte up and lifted her high up, high up, and then down and up. Do you remember how she laughed?

EMMA: Everyone laughed.

JERRY: She was so light. And there was your husband and my wife and all the kids, all standing and laughing in your kitchen. I can't get rid of it.

EMMA: It was your kitchen, actually.

(*He takes her hand. They stand. They go to the bed and lie down.*)

Why shouldn't you throw her up?

(*She caresses him. They embrace.*)

1973
LATER

Scene 7

Restaurant. 1973. Summer. *Robert at table drinking white wine. The waiter brings Jerry to the table. Jerry sits.*

JERRY: Hullo, Robert.

ROBERT: Hullo.

JERRY (*to the waiter*): I'd like a Scotch on the rocks.

WAITER: With water?

JERRY: What?

WAITER: You want it with water?

JERRY: No. No water. Just on the rocks.

WAITER: Certainly signore.

ROBERT: Scotch? You don't usually drink Scotch at lunchtime.

JERRY: I've had a bug, actually.

ROBERT: Ah.

JERRY: And the only thing to get rid of this bug was Scotch — at lunchtime as well as at night. So I'm still drinking Scotch at lunchtime in case it comes back.

ROBERT: Like an apple a day.

JERRY: Precisely.

(*Waiter brings Scotch on rocks.*)

Cheers.

ROBERT: Cheers.
WAITER: The menus, signori.

(*He passes the menus, goes.*)

ROBERT: How are you? Apart from the bug?
JERRY: Fine.
ROBERT: Ready for some squash?
JERRY: When I've got rid of the bug, yes.
ROBERT: I thought you had got rid of it.
JERRY: Why do you think I'm still drinking Scotch at lunchtime?
ROBERT: Oh yes. We really must play. We haven't played for years.
JERRY: How old are you now, then?
ROBERT: Thirty six.
JERRY: That means I'm thirty six as well.
ROBERT: If you're a day.
JERRY: Bit violent, squash.
ROBERT: Ring me. We'll have a game.
JERRY: How was Venice?
WAITER: Ready to order, signori?
ROBERT: What'll you have?

(*Jerry looks at him, briefly, then back to the menu.*)

JERRY: I'll have melone. And Piccata al limone with a green salad.
WAITER: Insalata verde. Prosciutto e melone?
JERRY: No. Just melone. On the rocks.
ROBERT: I'll have prosciutto and melone. Fried scampi. And spinach.
WAITER: E spinaci. Grazie, signore.
ROBERT: And a bottle of Corvo Bianco straight away.
WAITER: Si, signore. Molte grazie.

(*He goes.*)

JERRY: Is he the one who's always been here or is it his son?
ROBERT: You mean has his son always been here?
JERRY: No, is *he* his son? I mean, is he the son of the one who's always been here?
ROBERT: No, he's his father.
JERRY: Ah. Is he?
ROBERT: He's the one who speaks wonderful Italian.
JERRY: Yes. Your Italian's pretty good, isn't it?
ROBERT: No. Not at all.
JERRY: Yes it is.
ROBERT: No, it's Emma's Italian which is very good. Emma's Italian is very good.
JERRY: Is it? I didn't know that.

(*Waiter with bottle.*)

WAITER: Corvo Bianco, signore.
ROBERT: Thank you.
JERRY: How was it, anyway? Venice.
WAITER: Venice, signore? Beautiful. A most beautiful

place of Italy. You see that painting on the wall? Is Venice.
ROBERT: So it is.
WAITER: You know what is none of in Venice?
JERRY: What?
WAITER: Traffico.

(*He goes, smiling.*)

ROBERT: Cheers.
JERRY: Cheers.
ROBERT: When were you last there?
JERRY: Oh, years.
ROBERT: How's Judith?
JERRY: What? Oh, you know, okay. Busy.
ROBERT: And the kids?
JERRY: All right. Sam fell off —
ROBERT: What?
JERRY: No, no, nothing. So how was it?
ROBERT: You used to go there with Judith, didn't you?
JERRY: Yes, but we haven't been there for years.

(*Pause.*)

How about Charlotte? Did she enjoy it?
ROBERT: I think she did.

(*Pause.*)

I did.
JERRY: Good.
ROBERT: I went for a trip to Torcello.
JERRY: Oh, really? Lovely place.
ROBERT: Incredible day. I got up very early and — whoomp — right across the lagoon — to Torcello. Not a soul stirring.
JERRY: What's the "whoomp"?
ROBERT: Speedboat.
JERRY: Ah. I thought —
ROBERT: What?
JERRY: It's so long ago, I'm obviously wrong. I thought one went to Torcello by gondola.
ROBERT: It would take hours. No, no, — whoomp — across the lagoon in the dawn.
JERRY: Sounds good.
ROBERT: I was quite alone.
JERRY: Where was Emma?
ROBERT: I think asleep.
JERRY: Ah.
ROBERT: I was alone for hours, as a matter of fact, on the island. Highpoint, actually, of the whole trip.
JERRY: Was it? Well, it sounds marvellous.
ROBERT: Yes. I sat on the grass and read Yeats.
JERRY: Yeats on Torcello?
ROBERT: They went well together.

(*Waiter with food.*)

WAITER: One melone. One prosciutto e melone.

ROBERT: Prosciutto for me.

WAITER: Buon appetito.

ROBERT: Emma read that novel of that chum of
yours — what's his name?

JERRY: I don't know. What?

ROBERT: Spinks.

JERRY: Oh Spinks. Yes. The one you didn't like.

ROBERT: The one I wouldn't publish.

JERRY: I remember. Did Emma like it?

ROBERT: She seemed to be madly in love with it.

JERRY: Good.

ROBERT: You like it yourself, do you?

JERRY: I do.

ROBERT: And it's very successful?

JERRY: It is.

ROBERT: Tell me, do you think that makes me a publisher of unique critical judgement or a foolish
publisher?

JERRY: A foolish publisher.

ROBERT: I agree with you. I am a very foolish publisher.

JERRY: No you're not. What are you talking about?
You're a good publisher. What are you talking
about?

ROBERT: I'm a bad publisher because I hate books. Or
to be more precise, prose. Or to be even more precise, modern prose, I mean modern novels, first
novels and second novels, all that promise and sensibility it falls upon me to judge, to put the firm's
money on, and then to push for the third novel, see
it done, see the dust jacket done, see the dinner for
the national literary editors done, see the signing in
Hatchards done, see the lucky author cook himself
to death, all in the name of literature. You know
what you and Emma have in common? You love
literature. I mean you love modern prose literature, I mean you love the new novel by the new
Casey or Spinks. It gives you both a thrill.

JERRY: You must be pissed.

ROBERT: Really? You mean you don't think it gives
Emma a thrill?

JERRY: How do I know? She's your wife.

(*Pause.*)

ROBERT: Yes. Yes. You're quite right. I shouldn't have
to consult you. I shouldn't have to consult anyone.

JERRY: I'd like some more wine.

ROBERT: Yes, yes. Waiter! Another bottle of Corvo
Bianco. And where's our lunch? This place is going
to pot. Mind you, it's worse in Venice. They really
don't give a fuck there. I'm not drunk. You can't
get drunk on Corvo Bianco. Mind you . . . last
night . . . I was up late . . . I hate brandy . . . it
stinks of modern literature. No, look, I'm sorry . . .

(*Waiter with bottle.*)

WAITER: Corvo Bianco.

ROBERT: Same glass. Where's our lunch?

WAITER: It comes.

ROBERT: I'll pour.

(*Waiter goes, with melon plates.*)

No, look, I'm sorry, have another drink. I'll tell
you what it is, it's just that I can't bear being back
in London. I was happy, such a rare thing, not in
Venice, I don't mean that, I mean on Torcello,
when I walked about Torcello in the early morning, alone, I was happy, I wanted to stay there forever.

JERRY: We all . . .

ROBERT: Yes, we all . . . feel that sometimes. Oh you
do yourself, do you?

(*Pause.*)

I mean there's nothing really wrong, you see. I've
got the family. Emma and I are very good together.
I think the world of her. And I actually consider
Casey to be a first rate writer.

JERRY: Do you really?

ROBERT: First rate. I'm proud to publish him and you
discovered him and that was very clever of you.

JERRY: Thanks.

ROBERT: You've got a good nose and you care and I
respect that in you. So does Emma. We often talk
about it.

JERRY: How is Emma?

ROBERT: Very well. You must come and have a drink
sometime. She'd love to see you.

1971

Scene 8

Flat. 1971. Summer. *Flat empty. Kitchen door open.
Table set; crockery, glasses, bottle of wine.*
Jerry comes in through front door, with key.

JERRY: Hullo.

(*Emma's voice from kitchen.*)

EMMA: Hullo.

(*Emma comes out of kitchen. She is wearing an
apron.*)

EMMA: I've only just got here. I meant to be here ages
ago. I'm making this stew. It'll be hours.

(*He kisses her.*)

Are you starving?

JERRY: Yes.

(*He kisses her.*)

EMMA: No really. I'll never do it. You sit down. I'll get it on.

JERRY: What a lovely apron.

EMMA: Good.

(*She kisses him, goes into kitchen.*)
(*She calls. He pours wine.*)

EMMA: What have you been doing?

JERRY: Just walked through the park.

EMMA: What was it like?

JERRY: Beautiful. Empty. A slight mist.

(*Pause.*)

I sat down for a bit, under a tree. It was very quiet. I just looked at the Serpentine.

(*Pause.*)

EMMA: And then?

JERRY: Then I got a taxi to Wessex Grove. Number 31. And I climbed the steps and opened the front door and then climbed the stairs and opened this door and found you in a new apron cooking a stew.

(*Emma comes out of the kitchen.*)

EMMA: It's on.

JERRY: Which is now on.

(*Emma pours herself a vodka.*)

JERRY: Vodka? At lunchtime?

EMMA: Just feel like one.

(*She drinks.*)

I ran into Judith yesterday. Did she tell you?

JERRY: No, she didn't.

(*Pause.*)

Where?

EMMA: Lunch.

JERRY: Lunch?

EMMA: She didn't tell you?

JERRY: No.

EMMA: That's funny.

JERRY: What do you mean, lunch? Where?

EMMA: At Fortnum and Mason's.

JERRY: Fortnum and Mason's? What the hell was she doing at Fortnum and Mason's?

EMMA: She was lunching with a lady.

JERRY: A lady?

EMMA: Yes.

(*Pause.*)

JERRY: Fortnum and Mason's is a long way from the hospital.

EMMA: Of course it isn't.

JERRY: Well . . . I suppose not.

(*Pause.*)

And you?

EMMA: Me?

JERRY: What were you doing at Fortnum and Mason's?

EMMA: Lunching with my sister.

JERRY: Ah.

(*Pause.*)

EMMA: Judith . . . didn't tell you?

JERRY: I haven't really seen her. I was out late last night, with Casey. And she was out early this morning.

(*Pause.*)

EMMA: Do you think she knows?

JERRY: Knows?

EMMA: Does she know? About us?

JERRY: No.

EMMA: Are you sure?

JERRY: She's too busy. At the hospital. And then the kids. She doesn't go in for . . . speculation.

EMMA: But what about clues? Isn't she interested . . . to follow clues?

JERRY: What clues?

EMMA: Well, there must be some . . . available to her . . . to pick up.

JERRY: There are none . . . available to her.

EMMA: Oh. Well . . . good.

(*Pause.*)

JERRY: She has an admirer.

EMMA: Really?

JERRY: Another doctor. He takes her for drinks. It's . . . irritating. I mean, she says that's all there is to it. He likes her, she's fond of him, etcetera, etcetera . . . perhaps that's what I find irritating. I don't know exactly what's going on.

EMMA: Oh, why shouldn't she have an admirer? I have an admirer.

JERRY: Who?

EMMA: Uuh . . . you, I think.

JERRY: Ah. Yes.

(*He takes her hand.*)

I'm more than that.

(*Pause.*)

EMMA: Tell me . . . have you ever thought . . . of changing your life?

JERRY: Changing?

EMMA: Mmnn.

(*Pause.*)

JERRY: It's impossible.

(*Pause.*)

EMMA: Do you think she's being unfaithful to you?
JERRY: No. I don't know.
EMMA: When you were in America, just now, for instance?
JERRY: No.
EMMA: Have you ever been unfaithful?
JERRY: To whom?
EMMA: To me, of course.
JERRY: No.

(*Pause.*)

Have you . . . to me?
EMMA: No.

(*Pause.*)

If she was, what would you do?
JERRY: She isn't. She's busy. She's got lots to do. She's a very good doctor. She likes her life. She loves the kids.
EMMA: Ah.
JERRY: She loves me.

(*Pause.*)

EMMA: Ah.

(*Silence.*)

JERRY: All that means something.
EMMA: It certainly does.
JERRY: But I adore you.

(*Pause.*)

I adore you.

(*Emma takes his hand.*)

EMMA: Yes.

(*Pause.*)

Listen. There's something I have to tell you.
JERRY: What?
EMMA: I'm pregnant. It was when you were in America.

(*Pause.*)

It wasn't anyone else. It was my husband.

(*Pause.*)

JERRY: Yes. Yes, of course.

(*Pause.*)

I'm very happy for you.

1968

Scene 9

Robert and Emma's House. Bedroom. 1968. Winter.
The room is dimly lit. Jerry is sitting in the shadows. Faint music through the door.
The door opens. Light. Music. Emma comes in, closes the door. She goes towards the mirror, sees Jerry.

EMMA: Good God.
JERRY: I've been waiting for you.
EMMA: What do you mean?
JERRY: I knew you'd come.

(*He drinks.*)

EMMA: I've just come in to comb my hair.

(*He stands.*)

JERRY: I knew you'd have to. I knew you'd have to comb your hair. I knew you'd have to get away from the party.

(*She goes to the mirror, combs her hair.*
He watches her.)

You're a beautiful hostess.
EMMA: Aren't you enjoying the party?
JERRY: You're beautiful.

(*He goes to her.*)

Listen. I've been watching you all night. I must tell you, I want to tell you, I have to tell you —
EMMA: Please —
JERRY: You're incredible.
EMMA: You're drunk.
JERRY: Nevertheless.

(*He holds her.*)

EMMA: Jerry.
JERRY: I was best man at your wedding. I saw you in white. I watched you glide by in white.
EMMA: I wasn't in white.
JERRY: You know what should have happened?
EMMA: What?
JERRY: I should have had you, in your white, before the wedding. I should have blackened you, in your white wedding dress, blackened you in your bridal dress, before ushering you into your wedding, as your best man.
EMMA: My husband's best man. Your best friend's best man.
JERRY: No. Your best man.
EMMA: I must get back.

JERRY: You're lovely. I'm crazy about you. All these words I'm using, don't you see, they've never been said before. Can't you see? I'm crazy about you. It's a whirlwind. Have you ever been to the Sahara Desert? Listen to me. It's true. Listen. You overwhelm me. You're so lovely.

EMMA: I'm not.

JERRY: You're so beautiful. Look at the way you look at me.

EMMA: I'm not . . . looking at you. Please.

JERRY: Look at the way you're looking at me. I can't wait for you, I'm bowled over, I'm totally knocked out, you dazzle me, you jewel, my jewel, I can't ever sleep again, no, listen, it's the truth, I won't walk, I'll be a cripple, I'll descend, I'll diminish, into total paralysis, my life is in your hands, that's what you're banishing me to, a state of catatonia, do you know the state of catatonia? do you? do you? the state of . . . where the reigning prince is the prince of emptiness, the prince of absence, the prince of desolation. I love you.

EMMA: My husband is at the other side of that door.

JERRY: Everyone knows. The world knows. It knows. But they'll never know, they'll never know, they're in a different world. I adore you. I'm madly in love with you. I can't believe that what anyone is at this moment saying has ever happened has ever happened. Nothing has ever happened. Nothing. This is the only thing that has ever happened. Your eyes kill me. I'm lost. You're wonderful.

EMMA: No.

JERRY: Yes.

(*He kisses her.*
She breaks away.
He kisses her.)

(*Laughter off.*
She breaks away.
Door opens. Robert.)

EMMA: Your best friend is drunk.

JERRY: As you are my best and oldest friend and, in the present instance, my host, I decided to take this opportunity to tell your wife how beautiful she was.

ROBERT: Quite right.

JERRY: It is quite right, to . . . to face up to the facts . . . and to offer a token, without blush, a token of one's unalloyed appreciation, no holds barred.

ROBERT: Absolutely.

JERRY: And how wonderful for you that this is so, that this is the case, that her beauty is the case.

ROBERT: Quite right.

(*Jerry moves to Robert and takes hold of his elbow.*)

JERRY: I speak as your oldest friend. Your best man.

ROBERT: You are, actually.

(*He clasps Jerry's shoulder, briefly, turns, leaves the room.*)

(*Emma moves towards the door. Jerry grasps her arm. She stops still.*)

(*They stand still, looking at each other.*)

COMMENTARY

Katherine H. Burkman (b. 1934)
HAROLD PINTER'S *BETRAYAL*: Life Before Death — and After   *1982*

Burkman's interest lies in the interplay of the characters and the dimensions of their betrayal of each other. She is concerned with Robert and Jerry's relationship and the role that Emma plays in their lives. The apparent simplicity of the play is belied by the complexities that lie beneath the surface, and Burkman's approach is to help reveal the play's depths.

In scene five of Harold Pinter's *Betrayal*, just before Robert learns from his wife Emma that she has betrayed him for five years with his best friend Jerry, they discuss the book she is reading. It is a book that her publisher husband has, he tells her, refused to publish himself, despite the urging of Jerry (the author's agent, Robert's friend, and Emma's lover) because there isn't "much more to say on that subject."[1] He considers the subject to be betrayal. Emma does not think the book is about betrayal, but she hasn't finished reading it yet; she promises to let Robert know what it is about when she is done.

In this nicely self-reflexive moment, Pinter invites us to look beneath the cross currents of this play's love affairs for what remains the primary subject in all of his dramas — renewal. In *A Slight Ache* and *The Homecoming* Pinter's depiction of women disposing of their husbands and taking on new partners had all of the ritual connotations attendant on Sir James Frazer's fertility goddesses in *The Golden Bough*. The prototype of these goddesses is Diana in the Grove of Nemi, who must unite with the new god-king-priest of her grove when he defeats the old, just as spring must follow winter — if spring is to follow winter.[2] One may look in vain in *Betrayal* for the lush summer setting of *A Slight Ache* (1959) in which Flora assumes a new mate who will understand and nourish the garden with which her old mate could no longer connect, just as one may look in vain for the environmental alternatives that attend Ruth, whose disposal of her husband and assumption of his family in *The Homecoming* (1965) is a desperate choice of life in the English jungle over death in the American desert. Still, the battle in *Betrayal* (1978) is a desperate one, its issue is renewal, and its strategies may be detected and charted as they operate beneath the seemingly casual game of betrayal in which the characters are ostensibly engaged.

Betrayal does not end, as do *A Slight Ache* and *The Homecoming,* with the breakup of a marriage; we learn at the very beginning that Emma and Robert's marriage is over. Emma returns in scene one to her now ex-lover Jerry, ostensibly to tell him the news. Lest Jerry have any doubts, Robert confirms that the marriage is over in scene two. The rest of the play, with the exception of scenes five, six, and seven, moves backward in time, exploring the life of the now dead triangle and ending at the triangle's inception or birth; the final tableau reveals Robert's intrusion on the scene of Jerry's first "pass" at Emma.

This backward narrative or exploration of the triangle's life before death may seem at times like an autopsy on characters who have never been very fully alive. "Instead of suffering hell-fire and damnation," writes one critic, "the char-

---

[1] Harold Pinter, *Betrayal* (New York: Grove Press, Inc., 1978), p. 78. All subsequent quotations from the play are from this edition as reprinted in *The Bedford Introduction to Drama*, Third Edition, and are hereafter given parenthetically in the body of the essay.
[2] Sir James George Frazer, *The Golden Bough*, abr. ed. in 1 vol. (New York: The Macmillan Co., 1951), p. 823.

acters simply fall apart from each other; their personal relationships disintegrate."[3] For others the characters fail to arouse our "concern or compassion."[4] It seems to me, however, that Pinter continues in his best tradition here to give us a vision of "life honed to the injured bone."[5] Combining his surgical precision and black humor with a haunting compassion, Pinter probes not only into the triangle's life before death, but for its life in death, and after. Without some form of death, after all, there can be no renewal.

There is little doubt in the opening scenes of the play that the relationships in the triangle are coming to an end, yet there is a kind of life that still bristles in what is now supposedly dead. Why, for example, has Emma sought out Jerry at this point in time? Not apparently to rekindle their affair; it has been over for two years and she is involved with somebody else, Casey, a writer whom Jerry has discovered and Robert has published. What Emma seems to need to share with Jerry is not even any great sense of loss over the end of her marriage. Rather, it is her sense of being betrayed.

> EMMA: You know what I found out . . . last night? He's betrayed me for years. He's had . . . other women for years.
> JERRY: No? Good Lord.
>
> (*Pause.*)
>
>   But we betrayed him for years.
> EMMA: And he betrayed me for years.
> JERRY: Well I never knew that.
> EMMA: Nor did I.
>
> (*Pause.*)
>
> JERRY: Does Casey know about this?   [p. 1329]

Emma, it seems, is still involved enough with both husband and lover to care that she has been betrayed by the one and to share that sense of betrayal with the other. Jerry, in turn, is involved enough with Emma to be jealous of her current affair with his protégé, Casey, a jealousy which exudes from his flagrant denials. "I couldn't be jealous of Casey. I'm his agent. I advised him about his divorce. I read all his first drafts. I persuaded your husband to publish his first novel. I escort him to Oxford to speak at the Union. He's my . . . He's my boy . . ." (p. 1328).

Jerry also cares enough about Robert to be deeply concerned that Emma has told her husband about their affair in the previous night's conversation during which they decided to terminate their marriage. He is even more deeply dismayed in the following scene when he discovers that Emma has not, as she implied, told Robert about their affair the previous night but had told him four years ago. And even worse, in Jerry's eyes, is Robert's betrayal of him by continuing to pretend not to know.

> JERRY: Then why didn't you tell me?
>
> (*Pause.*)

---

[3] *Wall Street Journal*, 11 January 1980, quoted in *New York Theatre Critics' Review*, 41 (1980) 392.

[4] John Beaufort, *The Christian Science Monitor*, 11 January 1980, p. 19.

[5] Walter Kerr, "Play: Pinter's 'Betrayal,' Story of an Affair," *New York Times*, 7 January 1980, quoted in *New York Theatre Critics' Review*, 41 (1980) 390.

ROBERT: Tell you what?
JERRY: That you knew. You bastard.
ROBERT: Oh, don't call me a bastard, Jerry. [p. 1331]

Robert too, it appears, despite his constant disclaimers about caring, cares. "You don't seem to understand that I don't give a shit about any of this," Robert points out in unconvincing tones to Jerry. "It's true I've hit Emma once or twice. But that wasn't to defend a principle. I wasn't inspired to do it from any kind of moral standpoint. I just felt like giving her a good bashing. The old itch . . . you understand" (p. 1331).

At the end of the first scene, when Emma tells Jerry, "It doesn't matter. It's all gone," and he replies, "Is it? What has?" (p. 1329), we share Jerry's confusion. The relationships in the triangle may be terminating, but the members of the triangle are still very much caught up in the anguish and complexities of their mutual betrayals; there is life in their dying. As Pinter moves us backward in time, however, the confusion clears up and we discover not only further betrayals and betrayals within betrayals but more of the rules of the game, the nature of the players, and the stakes of the battle that the game conceals and reveals. As in so many of Pinter's plays, much remains unstated; the characters are "subtly inarticulate, almost to the point of code."[6] However, if one can detect what is being said "underneath what is said," filling in the pauses and the silences as well, one can crack the code and come to know almost too much.[7]

Major clues to the life principle of the triangle lie in Robert's reaction to Emma's fifth scene confession of the affair with Jerry. He has become suspicious when asked at American Express to deliver a letter to his wife and has recognized the handwriting as Jerry's. Pretending to be incensed at the Italians who in their "laughing Mediterranean way" may have given the letter to a stranger with the same name, he has declined to deliver the letter. "That's what stopped me taking it, by the way," he explains to Emma, "and bringing it to you, the thought that I could very easily be a total stranger" (p. 1336). That husband and wife have become strangers is clear to both of them, and Robert expresses his bitterness when speaking of their planned trip from Venice to Torcello: "How many times have we been to Torcello? Twice. I remember how you loved it, the first time I took you there. You fell in love with it. That was about ten years ago, wasn't it? About . . . six months after we were married. Yes. Do you remember? I wonder if you'll like it as much tomorrow" (p. 1337).

Robert continues turning the ironical knife, reminding Emma that Jerry was best man at their wedding as he pushes her to confession. When confession comes, however, Robert is not so much shocked at the fact, which we later find out he has probably guessed much earlier, but at the arrangements that have attended the betrayal and its time span — five years of meeting in a flat. He wonders too if Ned, their four-year-old, is his. When reassured that Jerry was away at the time, Robert drives home to Emma the doubleness of her betrayal.

[6] Clive Barnes, "Pinter's back with 'Betrayal,' " *New York Post*, quoted in *New York Theatre Critics' Review*, 41 (1980) 392.
[7] Harold Pinter, quoted in Katherine H. Burkman, *The Dramatic World of Harold Pinter: Its Basis in Ritual* (Ohio: Ohio State University Press, 1971), p. 9.

ROBERT: Did you tell him that Ned had been conceived?

EMMA: Not by letter.

ROBERT: But when you did tell him, was he happy to know I was to be a father?

(*Pause.*)

I've always liked Jerry. To be honest, I've always liked him rather more than I've liked you. Maybe I should have had an affair with him myself.

(*Silence.*)

Tell me, are you looking forward to our trip to Torcello?   [p. 1337]

One wonders why Robert even needs to hit Emma when he is capable of such verbal thrusts.[8] Understandably bitter over what he considers Emma's double role as whore — betraying him with Jerry but also betraying Jerry with him by having their child — Robert's "honest" admission that he has always liked Jerry better than Emma provides a key for her behavior and for his.

In an interview with Mel Gussow, Pinter noted that, "the play is about a nine-year relationship between two men who are best friends."[9] The nature of that friendship would seem to be a classical example of what René Girard calls triangular desire, a situation in which two men, through the mechanism of imitative desire, wish to possess the same woman. Imitative desire, as defined by Girard, is universal in human relationships and need not necessarily involve homosexuality or latent homosexuality, though it may: "The impulse toward the object is ultimately an impulse toward the mediator . . ."[10] What occurs is that one man (Jerry, in this case) desires another woman (Robert's) because the other man desires her. Robert, in turn, not only becomes the internal mediator of Jerry's desire (internal rather than external because of the nearness and involvement of the men in each other's sphere of action), but offers a case of what Girard calls double mediation as he founds his own desire on that of his disciple/rival. "The person who is mediator without realizing it may himself be incapable of spontaneous desire. Thus he will be tempted to copy the copy of his own desire . . . We now have a subject-mediator and a mediator-subject, a model-disciple and a disciple-model."[11] Because of the nearness of the mediators to each other, the object of desire, Emma, becomes less real; she becomes more and more a mere object to the men.[12]

Evidence in the play, other than Robert's stated preference for Jerry, suggests that Emma, who seems to be doing the most betraying, is actually the triangle's major victim, a prize or object for which the men vie mostly because of their in-

[8] Robert certainly knows how to fight back better than Teddy did in *The Homecoming*; Teddy weakly protests to Ruth as she leans toward taking on his family by reminding her that he has taken her to Venice.

[9] Mel Gussow, "An Interview with Harold Pinter," *Sunday New York Times*, 30 December 1979, quoted in The Goodman Theatre of the Art Institute of Chicago program for their production of *Betrayal*, January 16–February 22, 1981, p. 17.

[10] René Girard, *Deceit, Desire, and the Novel: Self and Other in Literary Structure*, trans. Yvonne Freccero (Maryland: The Johns Hopkins University Press, 1965), pp. 9–10.

[11] Girard, p. 99.

[12] "The closer the mediator comes, the greater his role becomes and the smaller that of the object." Girard, p. 45.

terest in each other.[13] In scene four, for example, when Jerry drops in to see Robert and Emma, having just had tea with Casey around the corner, Emma is pointedly excluded by Robert when she offers to come and watch them play squash and treat them to lunch. "Well to be brutally honest," Robert informs his wife, "we wouldn't actually want a woman around, would we, Jerry?" (p. 1335). This is not only an exclusion of Emma from the battle they are engaged in, even though she may be the spoils of that battle, it is a triple put down of her. They have just discussed Casey's novel — which Emma has considered dishonest — hence the barb in Robert's, "Well to be brutally honest." Robert has also just told Jerry that Emma has given her reaction to Casey's work when the two couples had dinner together, at which ". . . Emma gave a dissertation over the pudding about dishonesty in Casey with reference to his last novel" (p. 1334). Robert excludes Emma from lunch, mocks her daring to call another dishonest, and clearly objects to a woman interrupting male talk about books and giving her own opinions on them.

One could excuse Robert's behavior on the ground that he has learned in the next scene (going backwards in time) of the extent of Emma's affair with Jerry and is obviously very angry. But there is an implication in the speech that Emma has really been an interruption in his relationship with Jerry with whom he still intends to "play." His subtextual sparring with Jerry over playing squash is fraught with his knowledge of the affair, though neither Jerry nor the audience knows at this point that Robert knows. Robert challenges Jerry to the game, assures Jerry that he is not better than he, as Jerry fears, only fitter from practice with Casey; he then reminds Jerry that he used to be good, almost suggesting to him that he is no longer a worthy opponent in their current war, as Casey is. Jerry counters by putting off "playing" with Robert since he must accompany Casey to New York to talk about film rights to the novel Emma has called dishonest, a neat put-down of Robert (Casey is *his*) and of Emma, whose judgment must be faulty if Casey has become so successful.

Actually, despite his invitations to Jerry to play squash, part of Robert's game involves not playing squash with him. When Jerry expresses his dismay in scene two at the way their friendship has continued over the years despite Robert's knowledge of the affair, Robert remarks, "Never played squash though" (p. 1331). Later in the scene he also mentions bumping into Casey recently. "I believe he's having an affair with my wife. We haven't played squash for years, Casey and me. We used to have a damn good game" (p. 1331). Invitations to the contrary, apparently Robert draws the line at playing squash with his wife's lovers, but he is nostalgic over the loss of this strictly masculine activity.

While Jerry's war with Robert, like Robert's war with Jerry, seems to be of more interest to him than his love for Emma, the quality of that love is suspect from the beginning-ending and at the ending-beginning — as well as in the middle. As Emma tries to get some support from Jerry in the opening scene (doubtless the affairs Robert has confessed to are symbolic to her of what she must always have sensed, his lack of involvement with her), Jerry is really only concerned with her betrayal of him by telling Robert of their affair. "But he's my

---

[13] One is reminded of Pinter's play, *The Collection,* in which Stella tells her husband James that she has had a one night affair with a dress designer, apparently in an effort to get her husband's fuller attention. Her effort backfires as the husband becomes vindictively interested in his wife's alleged lover, who is a homosexual.

oldest friend," Jerry protests. "I mean, I picked his own daughter up in my arms and threw her up and caught her, in my kitchen. He watched me do it" (p. 1329). Later in the play, though earlier in time, when Jerry and Emma are breaking up their flat and their relationship, they speak of family obligations that have prevented them from meeting at night. "I might remind you," Jerry says testily to Emma, "that your husband is my oldest friend" (p. 1332), a remark that particularly offends her. Even when their affair is ostensibly at its height and Emma questions Jerry about his wife Judith's possible betrayal of him, Emma says to Jerry, "Oh, why shouldn't she have an admirer? I have an admirer" (p. 1342). When Jerry wants to know who that admirer is, Emma responds, "Uuh . . . you, I think" (p. 1342). Jerry's absentmindedness about Emma reveals her almost peripheral value for him in the drama of triangular desire and doubtless stems from the narcissistic quality of his initial attraction for her which we learn about when he first professes that love at the play's end. "You're so beautiful," Jerry says to her. "Look at the way you look at me" (p. 1344). Without her, he suggests, he will be "where the reigning prince is the prince of emptiness, the prince of absence, the prince of desolation" (p. 1344). With her, he is there too.

Betrayal is, in fact, a play in which the beginning is not only the ending, but the ending of the affair is suggested in its beginning at the play's end. Looking closely at the final conversation and movements among the three major characters at the end of the play, one gets a sense that at some level, despite the bitterness in his scene five discovery, Robert senses a good deal about the incipient affair before it really gets underway and that what the men are entering into is their own peculiar brand of squash, which they enjoy far more for sharing the sport than for Emma, the prize. In the concluding scene Emma assures Robert, as he enters and interrupts Jerry's lovemaking, that his "best friend is drunk," after which Jerry, admiring Emma's beauty, takes Robert by the elbow and assures him that he speaks "as your oldest friend. Your best man." When Robert replies, "You are, actually" (p. 1344), he leaves the room and leaves Emma to Jerry. The real passion here, restrained and understated, is between the two men, best friends become best enemies, both willing to sacrifice Emma for the fray — and in it. "Bit violent, squash," Jerry remarks of the game at one point in the play "Ring me. We'll have a game" (p. 1340) Robert replies.

If Jerry actually has any kind of passionate feelings for Emma, they are hostile feelings and relate back to Robert. Recalling how he was best man at her wedding at which he remembers her in white, a color which she denies having worn, he tells Emma of his fantasy: "I should have had you in your white, before the wedding. I should have blackened you in your white wedding dress, blackened you in your bridal dress, before ushering you into your wedding as your best man" (p. 1343). Jerry's dream is not one of possessing Emma — he doesn't even recall the color of her dress properly. It is a dream of desecrating her virginity, blackening her whiteness, and then, rather than keeping her for himself, delivering her to Robert as damaged goods.

In terms of her relationship with the men, Emma seems to be very much like her daughter Charlotte who was thrown up in the air as a child and caught by Jerry in the midst of both Emma's and Jerry's families. The image is a central one. Emma first brings up the incident in scene one after Jerry tells her he has seen Charlotte on the street and recognized her because she looks like Emma. Jerry recalls throwing Charlotte up in the air in Emma's kitchen, which Emma corrects — it was in his kitchen. At the end of scene one, then, when he is dismayed that Emma has told Robert of their now dead affair, he again recalls throwing Charlotte up in front of Robert, this time in his own kitchen. He is suggesting, I think, that Robert trusted him with his daughter, or given the earlier connection Jerry made between Charlotte and Emma, with his wife. The memory is brought up again in scene six with Jerry reverting (not exactly reverting since it is earlier in time) to the idea that he threw Charlotte up in Robert's kitchen and Emma correcting him when she has returned from Venice and the affair is still going forward. They have been discussing the possibility that Judith could easily have found them out (Robert, Emma knows and we know from scene five, has found out) but the memory is a pleasant one here, emphasizing the friendship of both families and Emma's trust of Jerry. "Why shouldn't you throw her up?" (p. 1339) Emma asks as they embrace. . . .

Manuel Puig

Manuel Puig (1932–1990) was born and raised in General Vallegas, a small Argentinian town in the rural pampas. His early years were dominated by memories of the films he saw, as he said, almost every night. These films of the 1940s were largely American — sentimental, popular entertainment featuring actors such as Cary Grant, Clark Gable, and Marlene Dietrich. The suspense and detective films, which became known as *film noir* (literally "black film") because so much of their footage was at night or in darkness, merged in his imagination with the serials that continued from one moment of suspense to another. When he finally turned to writing, these images and narratives were the inspiration for some of his richest material.

Puig's parents were relatively comfortable — his father was a businessman and his mother a chemist — and eventually they moved the family to Buenos Aires. In 1950 Puig went to the university to study architecture, but eventually left to study film directing in Rome. He worked with some directors at Cinecittà in the 1950s and then again in 1961–1962, but then began a brief odyssey in which he held many different jobs, from Spanish instructor to translator to dishwasher to clerk for Air France in New York City.

His novel, *Betrayed by Rita Hayworth,* was begun in 1962 and finished in 1965 but problems with censors in Argentina delayed publication until 1968, when it won a prize from the French publication *Le Monde* as one of the best foreign novels. The story is about Toto, a boy who lives through myriad fantasies centering on the films he has seen. He develops a strong connection with his mother, who is also enjoying these films. The novel is to some extent a portrait of an artist growing up as a homosexual. Toto's questioning centers on gender roles, sexual identity, and the macho attitudes and behaviors expected of men in his culture. The novel established Puig as an important writer.

He followed with *Heartbreak Tango* (1969), a novel modeled on popular forms of fiction, especially the detective novel. Many critics see this book and others that refer directly to popular films and forms as parodies, but Puig said that he respected such popular forms and was primarily interested in writing in them as well as possible. *Heartbreak Tango* is marked by breaks with strict chronology and by the use of various kinds of dialogues, letters, documents, and lyrics from popular dances. It helped establish him as a leader among experimental writers of his generation.

While Puig's career is primarily that of the novelist, at the end of his life he was writing more specifically for the stage. Ironically, films led him to write a novel; then his writing of *The Kiss of the Spider Woman* (novel version, 1976; play adaptation, 1981) led him back to film in the version by Brazilian director Hector Babenco (1985). Puig published the play in 1983 and won the American Library Association award in 1985 for "most promising playwright." His next work for the stage, *Mystery of the Rose Bouquet* (1985), was produced in London in 1987, and two years later in Los Angeles. In 1990 Puig died in Mexico of a sudden heart attack during surgery. At the time of his death he was working on the book for the highly acclaimed musical version of *Kiss of the Spider Woman* that was produced in 1992.

Puig had lived in Argentina, England, Rome, Paris, Sweden, New York, and Brazil, virtually a citizen of the world. Unfortunately, the rule of Juan Perón, dictator of Argentina during 1946–1955 and 1973–1974, made life in his own country dangerous for Puig. Puig's politics and Peron's did not match; with the threat of possible imprisonment and torture over his head, Puig was forced to live much of his life in exile.

KISS OF THE SPIDER WOMAN

Politics and homosexuality, two of Puig's favorite themes, dominate the play. Valentin is the political prisoner, a Marxist bent on changing society. Molina is a homosexual window-dresser absorbed by images of sentimental, popular movies of the 1940s and bent on getting out of jail to help his mother. Puig spent a great deal of time researching the novel and play, not only examining old films but also interviewing many political prisoners from the infamous Villa Devoto prison in Buenos Aires before he left Argentina for New York in 1973. He wanted to make his play accurate in describing the suffering of many Argentinians.

Molina opens the play in the dark, as if they were at the movies, by spinning a tale that comes from an old film, describing the scene carefully, analyzing the characters and situation. Valentin interrupts him with questions and comments. Eventually, though, the spell is broken and their attention focuses on the sordidness of their tiny cell. During their conversation the differences in their personalities become more and more evident. Valentin, completely absorbed by his Marxist ideals, is suspicious of a mind that "oozed sentiment," but he appreciates Molina's cooking. He also reveals that while he needs a woman he does not believe in monogamy; Molina tells him, "It's my dream. . . . The only thing I want is to live forever with a wonderful man."

Despite Molina's being lured with a promise of early release to secure secrets from Valentin, Molina begins to feel close to his cellmate. Valentin, initially repulsed by Molina's constant reference to himself as a woman, eventually finds that sexual contact is not disgusting to him. The center of the play is the growing affection that Valentin and Molina have for one another as human beings. Molina is not interested in politics — all he wants is to get out of prison to help his mother. Valentin, repulsed by homosexuality, is committed to a macho ideal of manliness in which the man enjoys domination in the home and sexual pleasures abroad. But these differences melt under the pressure of the prison and its impending terrors. The ending of the play is perhaps sentimental, but it may also be realistic. The tensions built up in dialogue that veers from the banal to the philosophical are compressed and intensified by the claustrophobia of their cell. It becomes a crucible in which their personalities are forged anew.

**Kiss of the
Spider Woman
in Performance**

The first production was in Spain in 1981, *El beso de la mujer araña.* The first English translation, by Allan Baker, was produced at the Bush Theatre in London in 1985. It was produced again at the Cast Theatre in 1987, then at the Yale Repertory Theatre in 1989. All these productions were successful, but they were overshadowed by the film starring Raul Julia and William Hurt. Hurt won an Academy Award in 1985 for his performance. The musical version played on Broadway for two years, starring a number of prominent actresses, among them Chita Rivera and Vanessa Williams.

Manuel Puig (1932–1990)

KISS OF THE SPIDER WOMAN

1981

TRANSLATED BY ALLAN BAKER

ACT 1 • *Scene 1*

(*A small cell in the Villa Devoto prison in Buenos Aires. The stage is in total darkness. Suddenly two overhead white spots light up the heads of the two men. They are sitting down, looking in opposite directions.*)

MOLINA: You can see there's something special about her, that she's not any ordinary woman. Quite young . . . and her face more round than oval, with a little pointy chin like a cat's.

VALENTIN: And her eyes?

MOLINA: Most probably green. She looks up at the model, the black panther lying down in its cage in the zoo. But she scratches her pencil against the sketch pad, and the panther sees her.

VALENTIN: How come it didn't smell her before?

MOLINA (*deliberately not answering*): But who's that behind her? Someone trying to light a cigarette, but the wind blows out the match.

VALENTIN: Who is it?

MOLINA: Hold on. She flusters. He's no matinée idol, but he's nice-looking, in a hat with a low brim. He touches the brim like he's saluting and says the drawing is terrific. She fiddles with the curls of her fringe.

VALENTIN: Go on.

MOLINA: He can tell she's a foreigner by her accent. She tells him that she came to New York when the war broke out. He asks her if she's homesick. And

then it's like a cloud passes across her eyes and she tells him she comes from the mountains, some place not far from Transylvania.

VALENTIN: Where Dracula comes from.

MOLINA: The next day he's in his office with some colleagues — he's an architect — and this girl, another architect he works with — and when the clock strikes three he just wants to drop everything and go to the zoo. It's right across the street. And the architect girl asks him why he's so happy. Deep down, she's really in love with him, no use her pretending otherwise.

VALENTIN: Is she a dog?

MOLINA: No, nothing out of this world: chestnut hair, but pleasant enough. But the other one, the one at the zoo, Irene — no, Irina — has disappeared. As time goes by he just can't get her out of his mind until one day he's walking down this fashionable avenue and he notices something in the window of an art gallery. They're pictures by an artist who only paints . . . panthers. The guy goes in, and there's Irina being congratulated by all the guests. And I don't remember what comes next.

VALENTIN: Try to remember.

MOLINA: Hold on a sec . . . Okay . . . then the architect goes up and congratulates her too. She drops the critics and walks off with him. He tells her that he just happened to be passing by, really he was on his way to buy a present.

VALENTIN: For the girl architect.

MOLINA: Now he's wondering if he's got enough money with him to buy two presents. And he stops outside a shop, and she gets a really funny feeling when she sees what kind of a shop it is. There are all different kinds of birds in little cages, sipping fresh water from their bowls.

VALENTIN: Excuse me . . . is there any water in the bottle?

MOLINA: Yes, I filled it up when they let us out to the lavatory.

(*The white light which up till now has lit just their heads widens to fully light both actors: we see the cell for the first time.*)

VALENTIN: That's okay then.

MOLINA: Do you want some? It's nice and cool.

VALENTIN: No, or we won't have enough for tea in the morning.

MOLINA: Don't exaggerate. We've got enough to last all day.

VALENTIN: Don't spoil me. I forgot to fetch some when they let us out to shower. If it wasn't for you, we wouldn't have any.

MOLINA: Look, there's plenty . . . Anyway, when they go inside that shop it's like — I don't know what — it's like the devil just came in. The birds, blind with fear, hurl themselves against the wire mesh and hurt their wings. She grabs his hand and drags him outside. Straight away the birds calm down. She asks him to let her go home. When he comes back into the shop, the birds are chirruping and singing just like normal and he buys one for the other girl's birthday. And then . . . it's no good, I can't remember what happens next, I'm pooped.

VALENTIN: Just a little more.

MOLINA: When I'm sleepy, my memory goes. I'll carry on with the morning tea.

VALENTIN: No, it's better at night. During the day I don't want to bother with this trivia. There are more important things . . .

(*Molina says nothing.*)

If I'm not reading and I'm keeping quiet, it's because I'm thinking. But don't take it wrong.

(*Molina is upset by Valentin's remark.*)

MOLINA (*with almost concealed irony*): I shan't bother you. You can count on that!

VALENTIN: I see you understand. See you in the morning.

(*He settles down to sleep.*)

MOLINA: Till tomorrow. Pleasant dreams of Irina.

(*Molina settles down too, but he is troubled by something.*)

VALENTIN: I prefer the architect girl.

MOLINA: I'd already sussed that.

Scene 2

(*Molina and Valentin are sitting in different positions. They do not look at one another. Only their heads are lit; seconds later the night light comes on.*)

MOLINA: So they go on seeing each other and they fall in love. She pampers him, cuddles up in his arms, but when he wants to hold her tight and kiss her she slips away from him. She asks him not to kiss her but to let her kiss him with her full lips, but she keeps her mouth shut tight.

(*Valentin is about to interrupt, but Molina forges ahead.*)

So, on their next date they go to this quaint restaurant. He tells her she's prettier than ever in her shimmering black blouse. But she's lost her appetite, she can't manage a thing, and they leave. It's snowing gently. The noise of the city is muffled, but far away you can just hear the growling of wild animals. The zoo's close, that's why. Barely in a whisper she says she's afraid to return to her house and spend the night alone. He hails a taxi, and they go to his house. It's a huge place, all *fin-de-siècle* decor; it used to be his mother's.

VALENTIN: And what does he do?

MOLINA: Nothing. He lights up his pipe and looks over at her. You always guessed he had a kind heart.

VALENTIN: I'd like to ask you something: how do you picture his mother?

MOLINA: So you can make fun of her?

VALENTIN: I swear I won't.

MOLINA: I don't know . . . someone really charming. She made her husband happy and her children too. She's always well groomed.

VALENTIN: And do you picture her scrubbing floors?

MOLINA: No, she's always impeccable. The high-necked dress hides the wrinkles round her throat.

VALENTIN: Always impeccable. With servants. People with no other choice than to fetch and carry for her. And, of course, she was happy with her husband who also exploited her in his turn, kept her locked up in the house like a slave, waiting for him . . .

MOLINA: . . . listen . . .

VALENTIN: . . . waiting for him to come home every night from his chambers or his surgery. And she condoned the system, fed all this crap to her son, and now he trips over the panther-woman. Serves him right.

MOLINA (*irritated*): Why did you have to bring up all

that . . . ? I'd forgotten all about this dump while I was telling you the movie.

VALENTIN: I'd forgotten about it too.

MOLINA: Well, then . . . why d'you have to go and break the spell?

VALENTIN: I don't know what you want me to say.

MOLINA: That I have your permission to escape from reality . . . Why should I make myself more depressed than I am already? What's the point in making myself more unhappy . . . ? Otherwise, I'll just go crazy, like Charlotte of Mexico. Though I'd rather be Christina of Sweden, since at least that way I'll end up a queen.

VALENTIN: No, be serious, you're right, being in here can drive you crazy, and not just because it gets you down . . . but because you can alienate yourself just the way you do. This habit of yours, only thinking about the nice things as you call it, that has its own dangers.

MOLINA: That's nonsense . . . How?

VALENTIN: Escaping from reality all the time the way you do becomes a vice, like taking drugs or something. Because, listen to me, reality, *your* reality, isn't only this cell. I mean, if you're reading or studying something, you can transcend whatever cell you're in, do you understand me? That's why I read, that's why I study every day.

MOLINA: Politics . . . I don't know what's become of the world, look where it's got us . . . you and all those politicians . . .

VALENTIN: Stop wingeing° like a nineteenth-century housewife . . . You're not a housewife, and this isn't the nineteenth century. Tell me a little more of the movie, have we much more to go?

MOLINA: Yes, lots . . . Why did I get lumbered with you and not the panther-woman's boyfriend?

VALENTIN: That's another story and one that doesn't interest me.

MOLINA: Frightened to talk about it?

VALENTIN: It bores me. I know all about it — even though you've never said a word.

MOLINA: Fine. I told you I was put away for gross indecency. There's nothing more to add. So don't come the psychologist with me.

VALENTIN (*shielding himself behind humor*): Admit that you like him because he smokes a pipe.

MOLINA: No, it's not that, it's because he's gentle and understanding.

VALENTIN: His mother castrated him, that's all.

MOLINA: I like him and that's that. And you like the architect girl — she's not exactly manning the barricades.

VALENTIN: I prefer her to the panther-woman, that's for sure. But the guy with the pipe won't suit you.

wingeing: Whining.

MOLINA: Why not?

VALENTIN: Your intentions aren't exactly chaste, are they?

MOLINA: Certainly not.

VALENTIN: Exactly. He likes Irina because she's frigid and he doesn't have to pounce on her, and that's why he takes her to the house where his mother is still present even if she is dead.

MOLINA (*getting angrier and angrier*): Continue.

VALENTIN: If he's still kept all his mother's things, it's because he wants to remain a child. He doesn't bring home a woman but a child to play with.

MOLINA: That's all in your head. I don't even know if the place is his mother's — I said that because I liked the place, and since I saw antiques in there, I told you it belonged to his mother. For all I know, he rents it furnished.

VALENTIN: So you're making up half the movie?

MOLINA: I'm not, I swear. But — you know — there are some things I add to fill it out for you. The house, for example. And, in any case, don't forget I'm a window-dresser, and that's almost like being an interior designer . . . Anyway . . . she begins to tell him her story, and I don't remember all the details, but I do remember that in her village, a long time ago, there used to be panther-women. And these tales frightened her a lot when she was a little girl.

VALENTIN: And the birds . . . ? Why were they afraid of her?

MOLINA: That's what the architect asks her. And what does she say? She doesn't say anything! And the scene ends with him in pyjamas and a dressing-gown, good quality, no pattern, something serviceable — and he looks at her sleeping on the sofa from his bedroom door, and he lights up his pipe and stands there, all thoughtful.

VALENTIN: Do you know what I like about it? That it's like an allegory of women's fear of submitting to the male, because when it comes to sex, the animal part takes over. You see?

(*Molina doesn't approve of Valentin's comments.*)

MOLINA: Irina wakes up, it's morning already.

VALENTIN: She wakes up because of the cold, like us.

MOLINA (*irritated*): I knew you were going to say that . . . She wakes up because there's a canary singing in its cage. At first she's afraid to go near it, but the little bird is chirpy so she dares to move a little closer. She heaves a sigh of relief because the bird isn't frightened of her. And then she makes breakfast . . . toast and cereals and pancakes . . .

VALENTIN: Don't mention food.

MOLINA: . . . and pancakes . . .

VALENTIN: I'm serious. Neither food nor women.

MOLINA: She wakes him up and he's all happy to see

her settling in, and so he asks her to stay there forever and be his wife. And she says, yes, from the
bottom of her heart, and she looks around and the
curtains look so beautiful to her, they're made of
thick dark velvet. (*Aggressively.*) And now you can
fully appreciate the *fin-de-siècle* decor. Then Irina
asks him if he truly wants her to be his wife to give
her just a little more time, just long enough for her
to get over her fears.

VALENTIN: You can see what's going on with her, can't
you?

MOLINA: Hold on. He agrees and they get married.
And on their wedding night she sleeps in the bed
and he sleeps on the couch.

VALENTIN: Looking at his mother's ornaments. Admit
it, it's your ideal home, isn't it?

MOLINA: Of course it is! Now you're going to tell me
what they all say.

VALENTIN: What d'you mean? What do they all say?

MOLINA: They're all the same, they all tell me the
same thing.

VALENTIN: What?

MOLINA: That I was fussed over as a kid and that's
why I'm like I am now, that I was clinging to my
mother's skirts, but it's never too late to straighten
out, and all I need is a good woman because
there's nothing better than a good woman.

VALENTIN: And that's what they all tell you?

MOLINA: And this is what I tell them . . . You're dead
right . . . ! And since there's nothing better than a
good woman . . . I want to be one! So spare me the
advice please, because I know what I feel like, and
it's all as clear as day to me.

VALENTIN: I don't see it as clear — at least, not the
way you've just put it.

MOLINA: I don't need you telling me what's what — if
you want I'll go on with the picture, if not, ciao . . .
I'll just whisper it to myself, and arrivederci,
Sparafucile!

VALENTIN: Who's Sparafucile?

MOLINA: You don't have a clue about opera. He's the
hatchet-man in *Rigoletto* . . . Where were we?

VALENTIN: The wedding night. He hasn't laid a finger
on her.

MOLINA: And I forgot to tell you that they'd agreed
she'd go and see a psychoanalyst.

VALENTIN: Excuse me again . . . don't get upset.

MOLINA: What is it?

VALENTIN (*less communicative than ever, sombre*): I
can't keep my mind on the story.

MOLINA: Is it boring you?

VALENTIN: No, it's not that. It's . . . My head is in a
state.

(*He talks more to himself than to Molina.*)

I just want to be quiet for a while. I don't know if

this has ever happened to you, that you're just
about to understand something, you've got the end
of the thread and if you don't yank it now . . .
you'll lose it.

MOLINA: Why do you like the architect girl?

VALENTIN: It has to come out some way or other . . .
(*Self-contemptuous.*) Weakness, I mean . . .

MOLINA: Ttt . . . it's not weakness.

VALENTIN (*bitter, impersonally*): Funny how you just
can't avoid getting attached to something. It's . . .
it's as if the mind just oozed sentiment constantly.

MOLINA: Is that what you believe?

VALENTIN: Like a leaky tap. Drips falling over anything.

MOLINA: Anything?

VALENTIN: You can't stop the drips.

MOLINA: And you don't want to be reminded of your
girlfriend, is that it?

VALENTIN (*mistrustful*): How do you know whether I
have a girlfriend?

MOLINA: It's only natural.

VALENTIN: I can't help it . . . I get attached to anything
that reminds me of her. Anyway, I'd do better to
get my mind on what I ought to, right?

MOLINA: Yank the thread.

VALENTIN: Exactly.

MOLINA: And if you get it all in a tangle, Missy
Valentina, you'll flunk needlework.

VALENTIN: Don't worry on my account.

MOLINA: Okay, I won't say another word.

VALENTIN: And don't call me Valentina. I'm not a
woman.

MOLINA: How should I know?

VALENTIN: I'm sorry, Molina, but I don't give demon-
strations.

MOLINA: I wasn't asking for one.

Scene 3

(*Night. The prison light is on. Molina and Valentin
are sitting on the floor eating.*)

VALENTIN (*speaking as soon as he finishes his last
mouthful*): You're a good cook.

MOLINA: Thank you, Valentin.

VALENTIN: It could cause problems later on. I'm getting spoiled.

MOLINA: You're crazy. Live for today!

VALENTIN: I don't believe in that live for today crap.
We haven't earned that paradise yet.

MOLINA: Do you believe in heaven and hell?

VALENTIN: Hold on a minute. If we're going to have a
discussion, then we need a framework. Otherwise
you'll just ramble on.

MOLINA: I'm not going to ramble.

VALENTIN: Okay, I'll state an opening proposition. Let me put it to you like this.

MOLINA: Put it any way you like.

VALENTIN: I can't live just for today. All I do is determined by the ongoing political struggle, d'you get me? Everything that I endure here, which is bad enough . . . is nothing if you compare it to torture . . . but you don't know what that's like.

MOLINA: I can imagine.

VALENTIN: No, Molina, you can't imagine what it's like . . . Well, anyway, I can put up with all this because there's a blueprint. The essential thing is the social revolution, and the pleasures of the senses come second. The greatest pleasure, well, it's knowing that I'm part of the most noble cause . . . my ideas, for instance . . .

(*The prison lights go out. The blue nighttime light stays on.*)

It's eight . . .

MOLINA: What do you mean, "your ideas"?

VALENTIN: My ideals. Marxism. And that good feeling is one I can experience anywhere, even here in this cell, and even in torture. And that's my strength.

MOLINA: And what about your girlfriend?

VALENTIN: That has to be second too. And I'm second for her. Because she also knows what's most important.

(*Molina remains silent.*)

You don't look convinced.

MOLINA: Don't mind me. I'm going to turn in soon.

VALENTIN: You're mad. What about the panther-woman?

MOLINA: Tomorrow.

VALENTIN: What's up?

MOLINA: Look, Valentin, that's me. I get hurt easy. I cooked that food for you, with my supplies, and worse still I give you half my avocado — which is my favorite and could have eaten tomorrow . . . Result? You throw it in my face that I'm spoiling you . . .

VALENTIN: Don't be so soft! It's just like a . . .

MOLINA: Say it!

VALENTIN: Say what?

MOLINA: I know what you were going to say, Valentin.

VALENTIN: Cut it out.

MOLINA: "It's just like a woman." That's what you were going to say.

VALENTIN: Yes.

MOLINA: And what's wrong with being soft like a woman? Why can't a man — or whatever — a dog, or a fairy — why can't he be sensitive if he feels like it?

VALENTIN: In excess, it can get in a man's way.

MOLINA: In the way of what? Of torturing someone?

VALENTIN: No, of getting rid of the torturers.

MOLINA: But if all men were like women, then there'd be no torturers.

VALENTIN: And what would you do without men?

MOLINA: You're right. They're brutes, but I need them.

VALENTIN: Molina . . . you just said that if all men were like women, there'd be no torturers. You've got a point there; kind of weird, but a point at least.

MOLINA: The way you say things. (*Imitating Valentin.*) "A point at least."

VALENTIN: I'm sorry I upset you.

MOLINA: I'm not upset.

VALENTIN: Well, cheer up then. Don't sulk, man.

MOLINA: Man? What man? Where . . . ? Tell me so he won't get away . . . ! Do you want me to go on with the picture?

VALENTIN (*trying to hide he finds this funny*): Start.

MOLINA: Irina goes along to the psychoanalyst who's a ladykiller, real handsome.

VALENTIN: Tell me what you mean by real handsome. I'd like to know.

MOLINA: Well, if you're really interested, he isn't my type at all.

VALENTIN: Who's the actor?

MOLINA: I don't remember. Too skinny for my taste. With a pencil moustache. But there's something about him, so full of himself, he just puts you off. And he puts off Irina. She skips the next appointment, she lies to her husband, and instead of going to the doctor's she puts on that black fleecy coat and goes along to the zoo, to look at the panther. The keeper comes along, opens the cage, throws in the meat and closes the door again. But he's absent-minded and leaves the key in the lock. Irina sneaks up to the door and puts her hand on the key. And she just stands there, musing, rapt in her thoughts.

VALENTIN: What does she do then?

MOLINA: That's all for tonight. I'll continue tomorrow.

VALENTIN: At least, let me ask you something.

MOLINA: What?

VALENTIN: Who do you identify with? Irina or the architect girl?

MOLINA: With Irina — who do you think? *Moi* — always with the leading lady.

VALENTIN: Continue.

MOLINA: What about you? I guess you're stuck because the guy is such a wimp.

VALENTIN: Don't laugh — with the psychoanalyst. But I didn't say anything about your choice, so don't mock mine . . . You know something? I'm finding it hard to keep my mind on it.

MOLINA: What's the problem?

VALENTIN: Nothing.

MOLINA: Come on, open up a little.

VALENTIN: When you said the girl was there in front of the cage, I imagined it was my girl who was in danger.

MOLINA: I understand.

VALENTIN: I shouldn't be telling you this, Molina. But I guess you've figured it all out for yourself anyhow. My girl is in the organization too.

MOLINA: So what?

VALENTIN: It's only that I don't want to burden you with information it's better you don't know.

MOLINA: With me, it's not a woman, a girlfriend, I mean. It's my mother. She's got blood pressure and a weak heart.

VALENTIN: People can live for years with that.

MOLINA: Sure, but they don't need more aggravation, Valentin. Imagine the shame of having a son inside — and why.

VALENTIN: Look, the worst has already happened, hasn't it?

MOLINA: Yes, but the risk is ever-present inside her. It's that dodgy heart.

VALENTIN: She's waiting for you. Eight years'll fly by, what with remission and all that . . .

MOLINA (*a little contrived*): Tell me about your girlfriend if you like . . .

VALENTIN: I'd give anything to hold her in my arms right now.

MOLINA: It won't be long. You're not in for life.

VALENTIN: Something might happen to her.

MOLINA: Write to her, tell her not to take chances, that you need her.

VALENTIN: Never. Impossible. If you think like that, you'll never change anything in the world.

MOLINA (*not realizing he's mocking Valentin*): And you think you're going to change the world?

VALENTIN: Yes, and I don't care that you laugh. It makes people laugh to hear this, but what I have to do before anything is to change the world.

MOLINA: Sure, but you can't do it all at once, *and* on your own.

VALENTIN: But I'm not on my own — that's it! I'm with her and all those other people who think like we do. That's the end of the thread that slips through my fingers . . . I'm not apart from my comrades — I'm with them, right now . . . ! It doesn't matter whether I can see them or not.

MOLINA (*with a slight drawl, sceptically*): If that makes you feel good, terrific!

VALENTIN: Christ, what a moron!

MOLINA: Sticks and stones . . .

VALENTIN: Don't provoke me, then. I'm not some loudmouth who just spouts off about politics in a bar. The proof is that I'm in here.

MOLINA: I'm sorry.

VALENTIN: It's okay . . .

MOLINA (*pretending not to pry*): You were going to tell me something . . . about your girlfriend.

VALENTIN: We'd better drop that.

MOLINA: As you like.

VALENTIN: Why it gets me so upset, I can't fathom.

MOLINA: Better not, then, if it upsets you . . .

VALENTIN: The one thing I shouldn't tell you is her name.

MOLINA: What sort of girl is she?

VALENTIN: She's twenty-four, two years younger than me.

MOLINA: Thirteen years younger than me . . . No, I tell a lie, sixteen.

VALENTIN: She was always politically conscious. First it was . . . well, I needn't be shy with you, at first it was because of the sexual revolution.

MOLINA (*bracing himself for some saucy tidbit*): I mustn't miss this bit.

VALENTIN: She comes from a bourgeois family, not really wealthy, but comfortably off. But as a kid and all through her adolescence she had to watch her parents destroy each other. Her father cheating her mother, you know what I mean?

MOLINA: No, I don't.

VALENTIN: Cheating her by not telling her he needed other relationships. I don't hold with monogamy.

MOLINA: But it's beautiful when a couple love each other for ever and ever.

VALENTIN: Is that what you'd like?

MOLINA: It's my dream.

VALENTIN: Why do you like men, then?

MOLINA: What's that got to do with it? I want to marry a man — to love and to cherish, for ever and ever.

VALENTIN: So, basically, you're just a bourgeois man?

MOLINA: A bourgeois lady, please.

VALENTIN: If you were a woman, you'd think otherwise.

MOLINA: The only thing I want is to live forever with a wonderful man.

VALENTIN: And that's impossible because . . . well, if he's a man, he wants a woman . . . you'll always be living in a fool's paradise.

MOLINA: Go on about your girlfriend. I don't want to talk about me.

VALENTIN: She was brought up to be the lady of the house. Piano lessons, French, drawing . . . I'll tell you the rest tomorrow, Molina . . . I want to think about something I was studying today.

MOLINA: Now you're getting your own back.

VALENTIN: No, silly. I'm tired, too.

MOLINA: I'm not sleepy at all.

Scene 4

(*Night. The prison lights are on. Valentin is engrossed in a book. Molina restless, is flicking through a magazine he already knows backwards.*)

VALENTIN (*lifting his head from the book*): Why are they late with dinner? Next door had it ages ago.

MOLINA (*ironic*): Is *that* all you're studying tonight? I'm not hungry, thank goodness.

VALENTIN: That's unusual. Don't you feel well?

MOLINA: No, it's just my nerves.

VALENTIN: Listen . . . I think they're coming.

MOLINA: Better hide the magazines or else they'll pinch them.

VALENTIN: I'm famished.

MOLINA: Please, Valentin, promise me you won't make a scene with the guards.

VALENTIN: No.

(*Through the grille in the other door come two plates of porridge — one visibly more loaded than the other. Molina looks at Valentin.*)

    Porridge.

MOLINA: Yes.

(*Molina looks at the two plates which Valentin has collected from the hatch.*)

(*Exchanging an enigmatic glance with the invisible guard.*)

    Thank you.

VALENTIN (*to the guard*): What about this one? Why's it got less? (*To Molina.*) I didn't say anything for your sake. Otherwise I'd have thrown it in his face, this bloody glue.

MOLINA: What's the use of complaining?

VALENTIN: One plate's only got half as much as the other. That bastard guard, he's out of his fucking mind.

MOLINA: It's okay, Valentin, I'll take the small portion.

VALENTIN (*serving Molina the larger one*): No, you like porridge, you always lap it up.

MOLINA: Skip the chivalry. You have it.

VALENTIN: I told you no.

MOLINA: Why should I have the big one?

VALENTIN: Because I know you like porridge.

MOLINA: But I'm not hungry.

VALENTIN: Eat it, it'll do you good.

(*Valentin starts eating from the small plate.*)

MOLINA: No.

VALENTIN: It's not too bad today.

MOLINA: I don't want it.

VALENTIN: Afraid of putting on weight?

MOLINA: No.

VALENTIN: Get stuck in then. This porridge à la glue isn't so bad today. This small plate is plenty for me.

(*Molina starts eating.*)

MOLINA (*overcoming his resistance: his voice nostalgic now*): Thursday. Ladies' day. The cinema in my neighborhood used to show a romantic triple feature on Thursdays. Years ago now.

VALENTIN: Is that where you saw the panther-woman?

MOLINA: No, that was in a smart little cinema in that German neighborhood where all those posh houses with gardens are. My house was near there, but in the run-down part. Every Monday they'd show a German-language feature. Even during the war. They still do.

VALENTIN: Nazi propaganda films.

MOLINA: But the musical numbers were fabulous!

VALENTIN: You're touched.

(*He finishes his dinner.*)

    They'll be turning off the lights soon, that's it for studying today. (*Unconsciously authoritarian.*) You can go on with the film now — Irina's hand was on the key in the lock.

MOLINA (*picking at his porridge*): She takes the key out of the lock and gives it back to the keeper. The old fellow thanks her, and she goes back home to wait for her husband. She's all out to kiss him, on the mouth this time.

VALENTIN (*absorbed*): Mmmm . . .

MOLINA: Irina calls him up at his office, it's getting late, and the girl architect answers. Irina slams down the phone. She's eaten up with jealousy. She paces up and down the apartment like a caged beast, and when she walks by the canary she notices it's frenetically flapping its wings. She can't control herself, and she opens the little door and puts her hand right inside the cage. The little bird drops stone dead before she even touches it. Irina panics and flees from the house, looking for her husband, but, of course, she has to go past the bar on the corner and she sees them both inside. And she just wants to tear the other woman to shreds. Irina only wears black clothes, but she's never again worn that blouse he liked so much, the one in the restaurant scene, the one with all the rhinestones.

VALENTIN: What are they?

MOLINA (*shocked*): Rhinestones! I don't believe this! You don't know . . . ?

VALENTIN: Not a clue.

MOLINA: They're like diamonds only worthless; little pieces of glass that shine.

(*At this moment the cell light goes out.*)

VALENTIN: I'm going to turn in early tonight. I've had enough of all this drivel.

MOLINA (*overreacting, but deeply hurt*): Thank goodness there's no light so I don't have to see your face. Don't ever speak another word to me!

(*Note: The production must establish that when the blue light is on — meaning nighttime — Molina and Valentin cannot see each other, and so are free to express themselves as they like in gestures and body language.*)

VALENTIN: I'm sorry . . .

(*Molina stays silent.*)

Really, I'm sorry, I didn't think you'd get so upset.

MOLINA: You upset me because it's one of my favorite movies, you can't know . . .

(*He starts to cry.*)

. . . you didn't see it.

VALENTIN: Are you crazy? It's nothing to cry about.

MOLINA: I'll . . . I'll cry if I feel like it.

VALENTIN: Suit yourself . . . I'm very sorry.

MOLINA: And don't get the idea you've made me cry. It's because today's my mother's birthday and I'm dying to be with her . . . and not with you. (*Pause.*) Ay . . . ! Ay . . . ! I don't feel well.

VALENTIN: What's wrong?

MOLINA: Ay . . . ! Ay . . . !

VALENTIN: What is it? What's the matter?

MOLINA: The girl's fucked!

VALENTIN: Which girl?

MOLINA: Me, dummy. It's my stomach.

VALENTIN: Do you want to throw up?

MOLINA: The pain's lower down. It's in my guts.

VALENTIN: I'll call the guard, okay?

MOLINA: No, it'll pass, Valentin.

VALENTIN: The food didn't do any harm to me.

MOLINA: I bet it's my nerves. I've been on edge all day. I think it's letting up now.

VALENTIN: Try to relax. Relax your arms and legs, let them go loose.

MOLINA: Yes, that's better. I think it's going.

VALENTIN: Do you want to go to sleep?

MOLINA: I don' know . . . Ugh! It's awful . . .

VALENTIN: Maybe it'd be better if you talk, it'll take your mind off the pain.

MOLINA: You mean the movie?

VALENTIN: Where had we got to?

MOLINA: Afraid I'm going to croak before we get to the end?

VALENTIN: This is for your benefit. We broke off when they were in the bar on the corner.

MOLINA: Okay . . . The two of them get up together to leave, and Irina takes cover behind a tree. The architect girl decides to take the shortcut home through the park. He told her everything while they were in the bar, that Irina doesn't make love to him, that she has nightmares about panther-women and all. The other girl, who'd just got used to the idea that she'd lost him, now begins to think maybe she has a chance again. So she's walking along, and then you hear heels clicking behind her. She turns round and sees the silhouette of a woman. And then the clicking gets faster and now, right, the girl begins to get frightened, because you know what it's like when you've been talking about scary things . . . But she's right in the middle of the park, and if she starts to run she'll be in even worse trouble . . . and, then, suddenly, you can't hear the human footsteps any more . . . Ay . . . ! Ay . . . ! It's still hurting me.

Scene 5

(*Day. Valentin is lying down, doubled-up with stomach pains. Molina stands looking on at him.*)

VALENTIN: You can't imagine how much it hurts. Like a stabbing pain.

MOLINA: Just what I had two days ago.

VALENTIN: And each time it gets worse, Molina.

MOLINA: You should go to the clinic.

VALENTIN: Don't be thick, I already told you I don't want to go.

MOLINA: They'll only give you a little Seconol. It can't harm you.

VALENTIN: Of course it can; you can get hooked on it. You don't have a clue.

MOLINA: About what?

VALENTIN: Nothing.

MOLINA: Go on, tell me. Don't be like that.

VALENTIN: It happened to one of my comrades once. They got him hooked, his will-power just went. A political prisoner can't afford to end up in prison hospital. You follow me? Never. Once you're in there they come along and interrogate you and you have no resistance . . . Ay . . . ! Ay . . . ! It feels like my guts are splitting open. Aaargh!

MOLINA: I told you not to gobble down your food like that.

VALENTIN (*raising himself with difficulty*): You were right. I'm ready to burst.

MOLINA: Stretch out a little.

VALENTIN: No, I don't want to sleep, I had nightmares all last night and this morning.

MOLINA (*relenting, like a middle-class housewife*): I swore I wouldn't tell you another film. I'll probably go to hell for breaking my word.

VALENTIN: Ay . . . ! Oh, fucking hell . . . !

(*Molina hesitates.*)

You carry on. Pay no attention if I groan.

MOLINA: I'll tell you another movie, one for tummy-ache. Now, you seemed keen on those German movies, am I right?

VALENTIN: In their propaganda machine . . . but, listen, go on with the panther-woman. We left off where the architect girl stopped hearing the human footsteps behind her in the park.

MOLINA: Well . . . she's shaking with fear, she won't dare turn around in case she sees the panther. She stops for a second to see if she still can't hear the woman's footsteps, but there's nothing, absolute silence, and then suddenly she begins to notice this rustling noise coming from the bushes being stirred by the wind . . . or maybe by something else . . .

(*Molina imitates the actions he describes.*)

And she turns round with a start.

VALENTIN: I think I want to go to the toilet again.

MOLINA: Shall I call them to open up?

VALENTIN: They'll catch on that I'm ill.

MOLINA: They're not going to whip you into hospital for a dose of the runs.

VALENTIN: It'll go away, carry on with the story.

MOLINA: Okay . . . (*repeating the same actions*) . . . she turns around with a start . . .

VALENTIN: Ay . . . ! Ay . . . ! The pain . . .

MOLINA (*suddenly*): Tell me something: you never told me why your mother doesn't bring you any food.

VALENTIN: She's a difficult woman. That's why I don't talk about her. She could never stand my ideas — she believes she's entitled to everything she's got, her family's got a certain position to keep up.

MOLINA: The family name.

VALENTIN: Only second league, but a name all the same.

MOLINA: Let her know that she can bring you a week's supplies at a time. You're only spiting yourself.

VALENTIN: If I'm in here it's because I brought it on myself, it's got nothing to do with her.

MOLINA: My mother didn't visit lately 'cos she's ill, did I tell you?

VALENTIN: You never mentioned it.

MOLINA: She thinks she's going to recover from one minute to the next. She won't let anyone but her bring me food, so I'm in a pickle.

VALENTIN: If you could get out of this hole, she'd improve, right?

MOLINA: You're a mind-reader . . . Okay, let's get on

with it. (*Repeating the same actions as before.*) She turns round with a start.

VALENTIN: Ay . . . ! Ay . . . ! What have I gone and done? I'm sorry.

MOLINA: No, no . . . hold still, don't clean yourself with the sheet, wait a second.

VALENTIN: No, not your shirt . . .

MOLINA: Here, take it, wipe yourself with it. You'll need the sheet to keep warm.

VALENTIN: No, you haven't got a change of shirt.

MOLINA: Wait . . . get up, that way it won't go through . . . like this . . . mind it doesn't soil the sheet.

VALENTIN: Did it go through?

MOLINA: Your underpants held it in. Here, take them off . . .

VALENTIN: I'm embarrassed . . .

MOLINA: Didn't you say you have to be a man . . . ? So what's all this about being embarrassed?

VALENTIN: Wrap my underpants up well, Molina, so they don't smell.

MOLINA: I know how to handle this. You see . . . all wrapped up in the shirt. It'll be easier to wash than the sheet. Take the toilet paper.

VALENTIN: No, not yours. You'll have none left.

MOLINA: You never had any. So cut it out.

VALENTIN: Thank you.

(*He takes the tissue and wipes himself and hands the roll back to Molina.*)

MOLINA: You're welcome. Relax a little, you're shaking.

VALENTIN: It's with rage. I could cry . . . I'm furious for letting myself get caught.

MOLINA: Calm down. Pull yourself together.

(*Valentin watches Molina wrap the shirt and soiled tissue in a newspaper.*)

VALENTIN: Good idea . . . so it won't smell, eh?

MOLINA: Clever, isn't it?

VALENTIN: I'm freezing.

(*Molina is meanwhile lighting the stove and putting water on to boil.*)

MOLINA: I'm just making some tea. We're down to the last little bag. It's camomile, good for the nerves.

VALENTIN: No, leave it, it'll go away now.

MOLINA: Don't be silly.

VALENTIN: You're crazy — you're using up all your supplies.

MOLINA: I'll be getting more soon.

VALENTIN: But your mother's sick and can't come.

MOLINA: I'll continue. (*With irony, repeating the same gestures as before but without the same élan.*) She turns round with a start. The rustling noise gets nearer, and she lets rip with a desperate scream, when . . . whack! The door of the bus opens in front of her. The driver saw her standing there and stopped for her . . . The tea's almost ready.

(*Molina pours the hot water.*)

VALENTIN: Thanks. I mean that sincerely. And I want to apologize . . . sometimes I get too rough and hurt people without thinking.

MOLINA: Don't talk nonsense.

VALENTIN: Instead of a film, I want to tell you something real. About me. I lied to you when I told you about my girlfriend. I was talking about another one, someone I loved very much. I didn't tell you the truth about my real girlfriend, you'd like her a lot, she's just a sweet and simple kid, but really courageous.

MOLINA: Please don't tell me anything about her. I don't want to know anything about your political business.

VALENTIN: Don't be dumb. Who's going to question you about me?

MOLINA: They might interrogate me.

VALENTIN (*finishing his tea; much improved*): You trust me, don't you?

MOLINA: Yes . . .

VALENTIN: Well, then . . . Inside here it's got to be share and share alike.

MOLINA: It's not that . . .

(*Valentin lies down on the pillow, relaxing.*)

VALENTIN: There's nothing worse than feeling bad about having hurt someone. And I hurt her, I forced her to join the organization when she wasn't ready for it; she's very . . . unsophisticated.

MOLINA: But don't tell me any more now. I'm doing the telling for the moment. Where were we? Where did we stop . . . ?

(*Hearing no response, Molina looks at Valentin, who has fallen asleep.*)

How did it continue? What comes next?

(*Molina feels proud of having helped his fellow cell-mate.*)

Scene 6

(*Daylight. Both Molina and Valentin are stretched out on their beds, lost in a private sorrow. In the distance we hear a bolero tune.*
Molina is singing softly.)

MOLINA: My love, I write to you again

The night brings an urge to inquire
If you, too, dear, recall the tender pain
And the sad dreams our love would inspire.

VALENTIN: What's that you're singing?

MOLINA: A bolero. "My Letter."

VALENTIN: Only you would go for that stuff.

MOLINA: What's wrong with it?

VALENTIN: It's romantic eyewash, that's what. You're daft.

MOLINA: I'm sorry. I think I've put my foot in it.

VALENTIN: In what?

MOLINA: Well, after you got that letter, you were really down in the dumps, and here I am singing about sad love letters.

VALENTIN: It was some bad news. You can read it if you like.

MOLINA: Better not.

VALENTIN: Don't start all that again; no one's going to ask you anything. Besides, they read it through before I did.

(*He unfolds the letter and reads it as he talks.*)

MOLINA: The handwriting's like hens' tracks.

VALENTIN: She didn't have much education . . . One of the comrades was killed, and now she's leader of the group. It's all written in code.

MOLINA: Ah . . .

VALENTIN: And she writes that she's having relations with another of the lads, just like I told her.

MOLINA: What relations?

VALENTIN: She was missing me too much. In the organization we take an oath not to get too involved with someone because it can paralyze you when you go into action.

MOLINA: Into action?

VALENTIN: Direct action. Risking your life . . . We can't afford to worry about someone who wants us to go on living because it makes you scared of dying. Well, maybe not scared exactly, but you hate the suffering it'll cause others. And that's why she's having a relationship with another comrade.

MOLINA: You said that your girlfriend wasn't really the one you told me about.

VALENTIN: Damn, staring at this letter has made me dizzy again.

MOLINA: You're still weak.

VALENTIN: I'm shivering and I feel queasy.

(*He covers himself with the sheet.*)

MOLINA: I told you not to start taking food again.

VALENTIN: But I was famished.

(*Molina helps Valentin wrap up well.*)

MOLINA: You were getting better yesterday, and then you went and ate and got sick again. And today it's the same story. Promise me you won't touch a thing tomorrow.

VALENTIN: The girl I told you about, the bourgeois one, she joined the organization with me, but she dropped out and tried to persuade me to split with her.

MOLINA: Why?

VALENTIN: She loved life too much and she was happy just to be with me, that's all she wanted. So we had to break up.

MOLINA: Because you loved each other too much.

VALENTIN: You make it sound like one of your boleros.

MOLINA: Listen, tough guy, haven't you cottoned on yet? Those songs are full of really deep truths, and that's why I like them. The truth is you mock them because they're too close to home. You laugh to keep from crying. . . . As a tango says.

VALENTIN: I was lying low for a while in that guy's flat, the one they killed. With his wife and kid. I even used to change the kid's nappies . . . And do you want to know what the worst of it is? I can't write to a single one of them without blowing them to the police.

MOLINA: Not even your girlfriend?

VALENTIN (*struggling to hold back his tears*): Oh, God . . . ! What a mess . . . ! It's all so sad! Give me your hand, Molina. Squeeze hard . . .

MOLINA: Hold it tight.

VALENTIN: There's something else. It's wrecking me. It's shameful, awful . . .

MOLINA: Tell me, get it off your chest.

VALENTIN: It's . . . the girl I want to hear from, the one I want to have next to me right now and hug and kiss . . . it's not the one in the movement, but the other one . . . Marta, that's her name . . .

MOLINA: If that's what you feel deep down . . . Oh, I forgot, if your stomach feels real empty, there's a few digestives I'd forgotten all about.

(*Without taking his hand from Valentin's he reaches for the packet of digestives.*)

VALENTIN: For all I shoot my mouth off about progress . . . when it comes to women, what I really like is a woman with class, and I'm just like all the reactionary sons-of-bitches that killed my comrade . . . The same, exactly the same . . .

MOLINA: That's not true . . .

VALENTIN: And sometimes I think maybe I don't even love Marta because of who she is but because she's got . . . class . . . I'm just like all the other class-conscious sons-of-bitches . . . in the world.

GUARD'S VOICE: Luis Alberto Molina! To the visiting room!

(*Valentin and Molina let go of each others hand as if*

caught in a shameful act. The cell door opens and Molina exits, but not before he's managed to slip the biscuits under Valentin's blanket. Hereafter, the dialogue is on prerecorded tape. Meanwhile, Valentin remains onstage and takes the biscuits from under his covers, manages to find just three at the bottom of the large packet and begins to eat them, one at a time, savoring each one.)

WARDEN'S VOICE: Stop shaking, man, no one's going to do anything to you.

MOLINA'S VOICE: I had a bad stomachache before, sir, but I'm fine now.

WARDEN'S VOICE: You've got nothing to be afraid of. We've made it look like you've had a visitor. The other one won't suspect a thing.

MOLINA'S VOICE: No, he won't suspect anything.

WARDEN'S VOICE: At home last night I had dinner with your benefactor, and he had some good news for you. Your mother is on the road to recovery . . . It seems the chance of your pardon is doing her good . . .

MOLINA'S VOICE: Are you sure?

WARDEN'S VOICE: What's the matter with you? Why are you trembling . . . ? You should be jubilant . . . Well, have you got any news for me yet? Has he told you anything? Is he opening up to you yet?

MOLINA'S VOICE: No, sir, not so far. You have to take these things a step at a time.

WARDEN'S VOICE: Didn't it help at all when we weakened him physically?

MOLINA'S VOICE: I had to eat the first plate of fixed food myself.

WARDEN'S VOICE: You shouldn't have done that.

MOLINA'S VOICE: The truth is he doesn't like porridge, and since one portion was bigger than the other . . . he insisted I ate it. If I'd refused, he might have got suspicious. You told me, sir, that the doctored food would be on the newest plate, but they made a mistake piling it high like that.

WARDEN'S VOICE: Ah, well, in that case, I'm obliged to you, Molina. I'm sorry about the mistake.

MOLINA'S VOICE: Now you should let him get some of his strength back.

WARDEN'S VOICE (*irritated*): That's for us to decide. We know what we're doing. And when you get back to your cell, say you had a visit from your mother. That'll explain why you're so excited.

MOLINA'S VOICE: No, I couldn't say that, she always brings me a food parcel.

WARDEN'S VOICE: Okay, we'll send out for some groceries. Think of it as a reward for the trouble with the porridge. Poor Molina!

MOLINA'S VOICE: Thank you, Warden.

WARDEN'S VOICE: Reel off a list of what she usually brings. (*Pause.*) Now!

MOLINA'S VOICE: To you?

WARDEN'S VOICE: Yes, and be quick about it, I've got work to catch up with.

MOLINA'S VOICE (*as the curtain falls*): Condensed milk, a can of peaches . . . two roast chickens . . . a big bag of sugar . . . two packs of tea, one breakfast, one camomile . . . powdered milk, a bar of soap — bathsize — oh, let me think a second, my mind's a complete blank . . .

ACT 2 • *Scene 1*

(*Lighting as in the previous scene. The cell door opens, and Molina enters with a shopping bag.*)

MOLINA: Look what I've got!

VALENTIN: No! Your mother's been!

MOLINA: Yes!

VALENTIN: So she's better now?

MOLINA: A little better . . . and look what she brought me. Oops! Sorry, brought us!

VALENTIN (*secretly flattered*): No, it's for you. Cut the nonsense.

MOLINA: Shut it, you're the invalid. The chickens are for you, they'll get you back on your feet.

VALENTIN: No, I won't let you do this.

MOLINA: It's no sacrifice. I can go without the chicken if it means I don't have to put up with your pong . . . No, listen, I'm being serious now, you've got to stop eating this pig-swill they serve in here. At least for a day or two.

VALENTIN: You think so?

MOLINA: And then when you're better . . . Close your eyes.

(*Valentin closes his eyes, and Molina places a large tin in one of his hands.*)

Three guesses . . .

VALENTIN: Ahem . . . er . . . er . . .

(*Enjoying the game, Molina places an identical tin in Valentin's other hand.*)

MOLINA: The weight ought to help you . . .

VALENTIN: Heavy all right . . . I give up.

MOLINA: Open your eyes.

VALENTIN: Condensed milk!

MOLINA: But you can't have it yet, not until you're better. And this is for both of us.

VALENTIN: Marvelous.

MOLINA: First . . . we'll have a cup of camomile tea because my nerves are shot, and you can have a drumstick, no, better not, it's only five . . . Anyway, we can have tea and some biscuits, they're even lighter than those digestives.

VALENTIN: Please, can't I have one right away?

MOLINA: Why not! But just with a little marmalade . . . ! Luckily, everything she brought is easy to get down so it won't give you any trouble. Except for the condensed milk, for the time being.

VALENTIN: Oh, Molina, I'm wilting with hunger. Why won't you let me have that chicken leg now?

(*Molina hesitates a moment.*)

MOLINA: Here . . .

VALENTIN (*wolfing down the chicken.*): Honest, I really was beginning to feel bad . . .

(*He devours the chicken*)

Thanks . . .

MOLINA: You're welcome.

VALENTIN (*with his mouth full*): But there's just one thing missing to round off the picnic.

MOLINA: Tut, and I thought I was supposed to be the pervert here.

VALENTIN: Stop fooling around! What we need is a movie . . .

MOLINA: Ah! Well, never mind . . . Now there's a scene where Irina has a completely new hairstyle.

VALENTIN: Oh, I'm sorry, I don't feel too good, it's that dizziness again.

MOLINA: Are you positive?

VALENTIN: Yes, it's been threatening all night.

MOLINA: But it can't be the chicken. Maybe you're imagining it.

VALENTIN: I felt full up all of a sudden.

MOLINA: That's because you wolfed it down without even chewing.

VALENTIN: And this itching is driving me wild. I don't know when I last had a bath.

MOLINA: Don't even think about that. That freezing water in your present state! (*Pause.*) Anyway, she looks stunning here, you can see her reflection in a window pane; it's drizzling and all the drops are running down the glass. She's got raven black hair and it's all scooped up in a bun. Let me describe it to you . . .

VALENTIN: It's all scooped up, okay, never mind the silly details . . .

MOLINA: Silly, my foot! And she's got a rhinestone flower in her hair.

VALENTIN (*very agitated now because of his itch*): I know what rhinestones are, so you can save your breath!

MOLINA: My, you are touchy today!

VALENTIN: Can I ask you something?

MOLINA: Go ahead.

VALENTIN: I feel all screwed up — and confused. If it's not too much trouble, I'd like to dictate a letter to her. Would you mind taking it down . . . ? I get dizzy if I try to focus my eyes too hard.

MOLINA: Let me get a pencil.

VALENTIN: You're very kind to me.

MOLINA: We'll do a rough draft first on a bit of paper.

VALENTIN: Here, take my pen-case.

MOLINA: Wait till I sharpen this pencil.

VALENTIN (*short-tempered*): I told you! Use one of mine!

MOLINA: Okay, don't blow your top!

VALENTIN: I'm sorry, it's just that everything is going black.

MOLINA: Okay, ready, shoot . . .

VALENTIN (*very sad*): Dear Marta . . . you don't expect this letter . . . In your case, it won't endanger you . . . I'm feeling . . . lonely, I need you, I want to be . . . near you . . . I want you to give me . . . a word of encouragement.

MOLINA: . . . "of encouragement" . . .

VALENTIN: . . . in this moment I couldn't face my comrades, I'd be ashamed of being so weak . . . I have sores all over inside, I need somebody to pour some honey . . . over my wounds . . . And only you could understand . . . because you too were brought up in a nice clean house to enjoy life to the full . . . I can't accept becoming a martyr, it makes me angry to be one . . . or, it isn't that, I see it clearer now . . . I'm afraid because I'm sick, horribly afraid of dying . . . that it may just end here, that my life has amounted to nothing more than this, I never exploited anyone . . . and ever since I had any sense, I've been struggling against the exploitation of my fellow man . . .

MOLINA: Go on.

VALENTIN: Where was I?

MOLINA: "My fellow man" . . .

VALENTIN: . . . because I want to go out into the street one day and not die. And sometimes I get this idea that never ever again will I be able to touch a woman, and I can't accept it, and when I think of women I only see you, and what a relief it would be to believe that right until I finish writing this letter you'll be thinking of me . . . and that you'll be running your hands over your body I so well remember . . .

MOLINA: Hold on, don't go so fast.

VALENTIN: . . . over your body I so well remember, and you'll be thinking that it's my hand . . . it would be as if I were touching you, darling . . . because there's still something of me inside you, isn't that so? Just as your own scent has stayed in my nose . . . beneath my fingertips lies a sort of memory of your skin, do you understand me? Although it's not a matter of understanding . . . it's a matter of believing, and sometimes I'm convinced that I

took something of you with me . . . and that I haven't lost it, and then sometimes not, I feel there's just me all alone in this cell . . .

(*Pause.*)

MOLINA: Yes . . . "all alone in this cell" . . . Go on.

VALENTIN: . . . because nothing leaves any trace, and my luck in having had such happiness with you, of spending those nights and afternoons and mornings of sheer enjoyment, none of this is any use now, just the opposite, it all turns against me, because I miss you madly, and all I can feel is the torture of my loneliness, and in my nose there is only the stench of this cell, and of myself . . . and I can't have a wash because I'm ill, really weak, and the cold water would give me pneumonia, and beneath my fingertips what I feel is the chill of my fear of death, I can feel it in my joints . . . what a terrible thing to lose hope, and that's what's happened to me . . .

MOLINA: I'm sorry for butting in . . .

VALENTIN: What is it?

MOLINA: When you finish dictating the letter, there's something I want to say.

VALENTIN (*wound up*): What?

MOLINA: Because if you take one of those freezing showers, it'll kill you.

VALENTIN (*almost hysterical*): And . . . ? So what? Tell me, for Christ's sake.

MOLINA: I could help you to get cleaned up. You see, we've got the hot water we were going to use to boil the potatoes and we've got two towels, so we lather one of them and you do your front and I'll do the back and then you can dry yourself with the other towel.

VALENTIN: And then I'd stop itching?

MOLINA: Sure. And we'd clean up a bit at a time so you won't catch cold.

VALENTIN: And you'll help me?

MOLINA: Of course I will.

VALENTIN: When?

MOLINA: Now, if you like. The water's boiling, we can mix it with a little cold water.

(*Molina starts to do this. Valentin can't believe in such happiness.*)

VALENTIN: And I'd be able to get to sleep without scratching?

MOLINA: Take your shirt off. I'll put some more water on.

(*He mixes the hot and cold water.*)

VALENTIN: But you're using up all your paraffin.

MOLINA: I don't mind.

VALENTIN: Give me the letter, Molina.

MOLINA: What for?

VALENTIN: Just hand it over.

MOLINA: Here.

(*Molina gives Valentin the letter. Valentin starts to tear it up.*)

What are you doing?

VALENTIN: This.

(*He tears the letter into quarters.*)

Let's not mention it again.

MOLINA: As you like . . .

VALENTIN: It's wrong to get carried away like that by despair.

MOLINA: But it's good to get it into the open. You said so yourself.

VALENTIN: But it's bad for me. I have to learn to restrain myself. (*Pause.*) Listen, I mean it, one day I'll thank you properly for all this.

(*Molina puts more water on the stove.*)

Are you going to waste all that water?

MOLINA: Yes . . . and don't be daft, there's no need to thank me.

(*Molina signals to Valentin to turn around.*)

VALENTIN: Tell me, how does the movie end? Just the last scene.

MOLINA (*scrubbing Valentin's back*): It's either all or nothing.

VALENTIN: Why?

MOLINA: Because of the details. Her hairdo is very important, it's the style that women wear, or used to wear, when they wanted to show that this was a crucial moment in their lives, because the hair all scooped up in a bun, which left the neck bare, gave the woman's face a certain nobility.

(*Valentin, despite the tensions and turmoil of this difficult day, changes his expression and smiles.*)

Why have you got that mocking little grin on your face? I don't see anything to laugh at.

VALENTIN: Because my back doesn't itch any more!

Scene 2

(*Day. Molina is tidying up his belongings with extreme care so as not to wake Valentin. Valentin, nevertheless, wakes up. Both of them are charged with renewed energy, and the dialogue begins at its normal pace but accelerates rapidly into tenseness.*)

VALENTIN: Good morning.

MOLINA: Good morning.

VALENTIN: What's the time?

MOLINA: Ten past ten. I call my mother "ten past ten," the poor dear, because of the way her feet stick out when she walks.

VALENTIN: It's late.

MOLINA: When they brought the tea round, you just turned over and carried on sleeping.

VALENTIN: What were you saying about your old lady?

MOLINA: Look who's still sleeping. Nothing. Sleep well?

VALENTIN: I feel a lot better.

MOLINA: You don't feel dizzy?

VALENTIN: Lying in bed, no.

MOLINA: Great — why don't you try to walk a little?

VALENTIN: No, you'll laugh.

MOLINA: At what?

VALENTIN: Something that happens to a normal healthy man when he wakes up in the morning with too much energy.

MOLINA: You've got a hard-on? Well, God bless . . .

VALENTIN: But look away, please. I get embarrassed . . .

(*He gets up to wash his face with water from the jug. Molina puts his hand over his eyes and looks away.*)

MOLINA: My eyes are shut tight.

VALENTIN: It's all thanks to your food. My legs are a bit shaky still, but I don't feel queasy. You can look now.

(*He gets back into bed.*)

I'll lie down a bit more now.

MOLINA (*overprotective and smothering*): I'll put the water on for tea.

VALENTIN: No, just reheat the crap they brought us this morning.

MOLINA: I threw it out when I went to the loo. You must look after yourself properly if you want to get better.

VALENTIN: It embarrasses me to use up your things. I'm better now.

MOLINA: Button it.

VALENTIN: No, listen . . .

MOLINA: Listen nothing. My mother's bringing stuff again.

VALENTIN: Okay, thanks, but just for today.

(*He collects his books together.*)

MOLINA: And no reading. Rest . . . ! I'll start another film while I'm making the tea.

VALENTIN: I'd better try and study, if I can, now that I'm on form.

(*He starts to read.*)

MOLINA: Won't it be too tiring?

VALENTIN: I'll give it a go.

MOLINA: You're a real fanatic.

VALENTIN (*throwing the book to the ground as his tenseness increases*): I can't . . . the words are jumping around.

MOLINA: I told you so. Are you feeling dizzy?

VALENTIN: Only when I try to read.

MOLINA: You know what it is? It's probably just a temporary weakness — if you have a ham sandwich you'll be right as rain.

VALENTIN: Do you think so?

MOLINA: Sure, and then later, after you've had lunch and another little snooze, you'll feel up to studying again.

VALENTIN: I feel lazy as hell. I'll just lie down.

MOLINA (*schoolmistressy*): No, lying in bed only weakens the constitution; you'd be better standing or at least sitting up.

(*Molina hands Valentin his tea.*)

VALENTIN: This is the last day I'm taking any more of this.

MOLINA (*mistress of the situation*): Ha! Ha! I already told the guard not to bring you any more tea in the morning.

VALENTIN: Listen, you decide what you want for yourself, but I want them to bring me the tea even if it is horse's piss.

MOLINA: You don't know the first thing about a healthy diet.

VALENTIN (*trying to control himself*): I'm not joking, Molina, I don't like other people controlling my life.

MOLINA (*counting on his fingers*): Today is Wednesday . . . everything will hang on what happens on Monday. That's what my lawyer says. I don't believe in appeals and all that, but if there's someone who can pull a few strings, maybe there's a chance.

VALENTIN: I hope so.

MOLINA (*with concealed cunning, as he makes more tea*): If they let me out . . . who knows who you'll get as a cell-mate?

VALENTIN: Haven't you had breakfast yet?

MOLINA: I didn't want to disturb you. You were sleeping.

(*He takes Valentin's cup to refill it.*)

Will you join me in another cup?

VALENTIN: No, thanks.

(*Molina opens a new packet, not letting Valentin see.*)

MOLINA: Tell me, what are you going to study later on?

VALENTIN: What are you doing?

MOLINA: A surprise. Tell me what you're reading.

VALENTIN: Nothing . . .

MOLINA: Cat got your tongue . . . ? And now . . . we untie the mystery parcel . . . which I had hidden about my person . . . and, what have we got here . . . ? something that goes a treat with tea . . . a cherry madeira!

VALENTIN: No, thanks.

MOLINA: What d'you mean "no" . . . ? The kettle's on . . . Oh, I know why not — you want to go to the loo. Ask them to open up, and then fly back here.

VALENTIN: For Christ's sake, don't tell me what to do!

(*Molina squeezes Valentin's chin.*)

MOLINA: Oh, come on, let me pamper you a little.

VALENTIN: That's enough . . . you prick!

MOLINA: Are you crazy . . . ? What's the matter with you?

(*Valentin hurls the teacup and the cake against the wall.*)

VALENTIN: Shut your fucking trap!

MOLINA: The cake . . .

(*Valentin is silent.*)

Look what you've done . . . If the stove's broke, we're done for . . . (*Pause.*) . . . and the saucer . . . (*Pause.*) . . . and the tea . . .

VALENTIN: I'm sorry . . .

(*Molina is silent now.*)

I lost control . . . I'm really sorry.

(*Molina remains silent.*)

The stove is okay; but the paraffin spilled.

(*Molina still doesn't answer.*)

. . . I'm sorry I got carried away, forgive me . . .

MOLINA (*deeply wounded*): There's nothing to forgive.

VALENTIN: There is. A lot.

MOLINA: Forget it. Nothing happened.

VALENTIN: It did, I'm dying with shame.

(*Molina says nothing.*)

. . . I behaved like an animal . . . Look, I'll call the guard and fill up the bottle while I'm at it. We're almost out of water . . . Molina, please look at me. Raise your head.

(*Molina remains silent.*)

GUARD'S VOICE: Luis Alberto Molina. To the visiting room!

(*The door opens and Molina exits. The recorded dialogue begins as soon as Molina moves towards the door. Molina returns with the provisions to find Valentin picking up the things he has just thrown on the floor. Molina starts to unpack the shopping bag. The recorded dialogue is heard while the action takes place onstage.*)

WARDEN'S VOICE: Today's Monday, Molina, what have you got for me?

MOLINA'S VOICE: Nothing, I'm afraid, sir.

WARDEN'S VOICE: Indeed.

MOLINA'S VOICE: But he's taking me more into his confidence.

WARDEN'S VOICE: The problem is they're putting pressure on me, Molina. From the top: from the President's private office. You understand what I'm saying to you, Molina? They want to try interrogation again. Less carrot, more stick.

MOLINA'S VOICE: Not that, sir. It'd be even worse if you lost him in interrogation.

WARDEN'S VOICE: That's what I tell them, but they won't listen.

MOLINA'S VOICE: Just one more week, sir. Please. I have an idea . . .

WARDEN'S VOICE: What?

MOLINA'S VOICE: He's a hard nut, but he has an emotional side.

WARDEN'S VOICE: So?

MOLINA'S VOICE: Well, if the guard were to come and say they're moving me to another block in a week's time because of the appeal, that might really soften him up.

WARDEN'S VOICE: What are you driving at?

MOLINA'S VOICE: Nothing, I swear. It's just a hunch. If he thinks I'm leaving soon, he'll feel like opening up even more with me. Prisoners are like that, sir . . . when one of their pals is leaving, they feel more defenseless than ever.

(*At this moment Molina is back in the cell, and he takes out the food as the warden's voice mentions each item. Valentin looks at Molina.*)

WARDEN'S VOICE: Guard, take this down: two roast chickens, four baked apples, one carton of coleslaw, one pound of bacon, one pound of cooked ham, four French loaves, four pieces of crystalized fruit . . .

(*The recorded voice begins to fade out.*)

. . . a carton of orange juice, two cherry madeiras . . .

(*Molina is very calm and sad; he is still upset by Valentin's remarks.*)

MOLINA: This is the bacon and this one's the ham. I'm going to make a sandwich while the bread's fresh. You fix yourself whatever you want.

VALENTIN (*deeply ashamed*): Thank you.

MOLINA (*reserved and calm*): I'm going to cut this roll

in half and spread it with butter and have a sandwich. And a baked apple.

VALENTIN: Sounds delicious.

MOLINA: If you'd like some of the chicken while it's still warm, go ahead. Feel free.

VALENTIN: Thank you, Molina.

MOLINA: We'll each fend for ourselves. Then I won't get on your nerves.

VALENTIN: If that's what you prefer.

MOLINA: There's some crystalized fruit, too. All I ask is that you leave me the pumpkin. Otherwise, take what you want.

VALENTIN (*finding it hard to apologize*): I'm still embarrassed . . . because of that tantrum.

MOLINA: Don't be silly.

VALENTIN: If I got annoyed with you . . . it was because you were kind to me . . . and I didn't want . . . to treat you the same way.

MOLINA: Look, I've been thinking too, and I remembered something you once said, right . . . ? That when you're involved in a struggle like that, well, it's not too convenient to get fond of someone. Well, fond is maybe going too far . . . or, why not? Fond as a friend.

VALENTIN: That's a very noble way of looking at it.

MOLINA: You see, sometimes I do understand what you tell me.

VALENTIN: But are we so fettered by the world outside that we can't act like human beings just for a minute . . . ?

MOLINA: I don't follow.

VALENTIN: Our persecutors are on the outside, not inside this cell . . . The problem is I'm so brainwashed that it freaks me out when someone is nice to me without asking anything in return.

MOLINA: I don't know about that . . .

VALENTIN: About what?

MOLINA: Don't get me wrong, but if I'm nice to you, well, it's because I want you to be my friend . . . and why not admit it? I want your affection. Just like I treat my mother well because she's a good person and I want her to love me. And you're a good person too, and unselfish because you're risking your life for an ideal . . . that I don't understand but, all the same, it's not just for yourself . . . Don't look away like that, are you embarrassed?

VALENTIN: A bit.

(*He looks Molina in the face.*)

MOLINA: And that's why I respect you and have warm feelings toward you . . . and why I want you to like me . . . because, you see, my mother's love is the only good thing I've felt in my life, because she likes me . . . just the way I am.

VALENTIN (*pointing to the loaf Molina put aside*): Can I cut the loaf for you?

MOLINA: Of course . . .

VALENTIN (*cutting the loaf*): And did you never have good friends that meant a lot to you?

MOLINA: My friends were all . . . screaming queens, like me, we never really count on each other because . . . how can I express it? — because we know we're so easily frightened off. We're always looking, you know, for friendship, or whatever, with somebody more serious, with a man, you see? And that just doesn't happen, right? Because what a man wants is a woman.

VALENTIN (*taking a slice of ham for Molina's sandwich*): And are all homosexuals like that?

MOLINA: Oh no, there are some who fall in love with each other. But me and my friends, we're women. One hundred percent. We don't go in for those little games. We're normal women; *we* only go to bed with men.

VALENTIN (*too absorbed to see the funny side of this*): Butter?

MOLINA: Yes, thanks. There's something I have to tell you.

VALENTIN: Of course, the movie . . .

MOLINA (*with cunning, but nervous all the same*): My lawyer said things were looking up.

VALENTIN: What a creep I am! I didn't ask you.

MOLINA: And when there's an appeal pending, the prisoner gets moved to another block in the prison. They'll probably shift me within a week or so.

VALENTIN (*upset by this but dissimulating*): That's terrific . . . You ought to be pleased.

MOLINA: I don't want to dwell on it too much, build my hopes . . . Have some coleslaw.

VALENTIN: Should I?

MOLINA: It's very good.

VALENTIN: Your news made me lose my appetite.

(*He gets up.*)

MOLINA: Pretend I didn't say anything, nothing's settled yet.

VALENTIN: No, it all looks good for you, we should be happy.

MOLINA: Have some salad.

VALENTIN: I don't know what's wrong, but all of a sudden I don't feel too good.

MOLINA: Is your stomach hurting?

VALENTIN: No . . . it's my head. I'm all confused.

MOLINA: About what?

VALENTIN: Let me rest for a while.

(*Valentin sits down again, resting his head in his palms. The light changes to indicate a shift to a dif-*ferent *time — the two characters stay where they are: there is a special tension, a hypersensitivity in the air.*)

MOLINA: The guy is all muddled up, he doesn't know how to handle this freaky wife of his. She comes in, sees that he's dead serious and goes to the bathroom to put away her shoes, all dirty with mud. He says he went to the doctor's to look for her and found out that she didn't go anymore. Then she breaks into tears and tells him that she's just what she always feared, a madwoman with hallucinations or even worse, a panther-woman. Then he gives in and takes her in his arms, and you were right, she's really just a little girl for him, because when he sees her so defenseless and lost, he feels again he loves her with all his heart and tells her that everything will sort itself out . . .

(*Molina sighs deeply.*)

Ahhh . . . !

VALENTIN: What a sigh!

MOLINA: Life is so difficult . . .

VALENTIN: What's the matter?

MOLINA: I don't know, I'm afraid of building up my hopes of getting out of here . . . and that I'll get put in some other cell and spend my life there with God knows what sort of creep.

VALENTIN: Don't lose sight of this. Your mother's health is the most precious thing to you, right?

MOLINA: Yes . . .

VALENTIN: Think about her recovery. Period!

(*Molina laughs involuntarily in his distress.*)

MOLINA: I don't want to think about it.

VALENTIN: What's wrong?

MOLINA: Nothing!

VALENTIN: Don't bury your head in the pillow . . . Are you hiding something from me?

MOLINA: It's . . .

VALENTIN: It's what . . . ? Look, when you get out of here, you're going to be a free man. You can join a political organization if you like.

MOLINA: You're crazy! They won't trust a fag.

VALENTIN: But I can tell you who to speak to . . .

MOLINA (*suddenly forceful, raising his head from the pillow*): Promise me on whatever you hold most dear, never, never, you understand, never tell me anything about your comrades.

VALENTIN: But who would ever think you're seeing them?

MOLINA: They could interrogate me, whatever, but if I know nothing, I say nothing.

VALENTIN: In any case, there are all kinds of groups,

Raul Julia (left) and
William Hurt in the film
version of *Kiss of the
Spider Woman* directed by
Hector Babenco.

of political action; there are even some who just sit and talk. When you get out, things'll be different.

MOLINA: Things *won't* be different. That's the worst of it.

VALENTIN: How many times have I seen you cry? Come on, you annoy me with your snivelling.

MOLINA: It's just that I can't take any more . . . I've had nothing but bad luck . . . always.

(*The prison light goes out.*)

VALENTIN: Lights out already . . . ? In the first place, you must join a group, avoid being alone.

MOLINA: I don't understand any of that . . . (*suddenly grave*) . . . and I don't believe in it much either.

VALENTIN (*tough*): Then like it or lump it.

MOLINA (*still crying a little*): Let's . . . skip it.

VALENTIN (*conciliatory*): Come on, don't be like that . . .

(*He pats Molina on the back affectionately.*)

MOLINA: I'm asking you . . . please don't touch me.

VALENTIN: Can't a friend pat you on the back?

MOLINA: It makes it worse . . .

VALENTIN: Why . . . ? Tell me what's troubling you . . .

MOLINA (*with deep, deep feeling*): I'm so tired, Valentin . . . I'm tired of suffering. I hurt all over inside.

VALENTIN: Where does it hurt you?

MOLINA: Inside my chest and my throat . . . Why does sadness always get you there? It's choking me, like a knot . . .

VALENTIN: It's true, that's where people always feel it.

(*Molina is quiet.*)

Is it hurting you a lot, this knot?

MOLINA: Yes.

VALENTIN: Is it here?

MOLINA: Yes.

VALENTIN: Want me to stroke it . . . here?

MOLINA: Yes.

(*Short pause.*)

VALENTIN: This is relaxing . . .

MOLINA: Why relaxing, Valentin?

VALENTIN: Not to think about myself for a while. Thinking about you, that you need me, and I can be of some use to you.

MOLINA: You're always looking for explanations . . . You're crazy.

VALENTIN: I don't want events to get the better of me. I want to know why they happen.

MOLINA: Can I touch you?

VALENTIN: Yes . . .

MOLINA: I want to touch that mole — the little round one over your eye.

(*Molina touches the mole.*)

You're very kind.

VALENTIN: No, you're the one who's kind.

MOLINA: If you like, you can do what you want with me . . . because I want it too . . . If it won't disgust you . . .

VALENTIN: Don't say that — let's not say anything.

(*Valentin goes under Molina's top sheet.*)

Shift a bit closer to the wall . . . (*Pause.*) You can't see a thing, it's so dark.

MOLINA: Gently . . . (*Pause.*) No, it hurts too much like that. (*Pause.*) Slowly please . . . (*Pause.*) That's it . . . (*Pause.*) . . . thanks . . .

VALENTIN: Thank you, too. Are you feeling better?

MOLINA: Yes. And what about you, Valentin?

VALENTIN: Don't ask me . . . I don't know anything anymore . . .

MOLINA: Oh . . . it's beautiful . . .

VALENTIN: Don't say anything . . . not for now . . .

MOLINA: It's just that I feel . . . such strange things . . . Without thinking, I just lifted my hand to my eye, looking for that mole.

VALENTIN: What mole . . . ? I'm the one with the mole, not you.

MOLINA: I know, but I just lifted up my hand . . . to touch the mole . . . I don't have.

VALENTIN: Ssh, try and keep quiet for a while . . .

MOLINA: And do you know what else I felt, but only for a minute, no longer . . . ?

VALENTIN: Tell me, but keep still, like that . . .

MOLINA: For just a minute, it felt like I wasn't here . . . not in here, nor anywhere else . . . (*Pause.*) It felt like I wasn't here, there was just you . . . Or that I wasn't me any more. As if I was . . . you.

Scene 3

(*Day. Molina and Valentin are in their beds.*)

VALENTIN: Good morning.

(*He's reinvigorated, happy. Molina is also highly charged.*)

MOLINA: Good morning, Valentin.

VALENTIN: Did you sleep well?

MOLINA: Yes. (*Calmly, not insisting.*) Would you like tea or coffee?

VALENTIN: Coffee. To wake me up well — and study. Try to get back into the swing of things . . . What about you? Is the gloom over? Or not?

MOLINA: Yes it is, but I feel groggy. I can't think . . . my mind's blank.

VALENTIN: I don't want to think about anything either, so I'm going to read. That'll keep my mind off things.

MOLINA: Off what? Feeling guilty about what happened?

VALENTIN: I'm more and more convinced that sex is innocence itself.

MOLINA: Can I ask you a favor . . . ? Can we not analyze anything, just for today.

VALENTIN: Whatever you like.

MOLINA: I feel . . . fine and I don't want anything to rob me of that feeling. I haven't felt so good since I was a kid. Since my mother bought me some toy.

VALENTIN: Do you remember what toy you liked most?

MOLINA: A doll.

VALENTIN: Ay!

(*He starts to laugh.*)

MOLINA: What's funny about that?

VALENTIN: As a psychologist I would starve.

MOLINA: Why?

VALENTIN: Nothing . . . I was just wondering if there was any link between your favorite toy and . . . me.

MOLINA (*playing along*): It was your own fault for asking.

VALENTIN: Are you sure it wasn't a boy doll?

MOLINA: Absolutely. She had blonde braids and a little Tyrolese folk dress.

(*They laugh together, unselfconsciously.*)

VALENTIN: One question . . . Physically, you're as much a man as I am.

MOLINA: Ummm . . .

VALENTIN: Why then don't you behave like a man . . . ? I don't mean with women if you're not attracted to them, but with another man?

MOLINA: It's not me. I only enjoy myself like that.

VALENTIN: Well, if you like being a woman . . . you shouldn't feel diminished because of that.

(*Molina doesn't answer.*)

I mean you shouldn't feel you owe anyone, or feel obliged to them because that's what you happen to feel like . . . You shouldn't yield . . .

MOLINA: But if a man is . . . my husband, he has to be boss to feel good. That's only natural.

VALENTIN: No, the man and the woman should be equal partners inside the home. Otherwise, it's exploitation. Don't you see?

MOLINA: But there's no thrill like that.

VALENTIN: What?

MOLINA: Since you want to know about it . . . the thrill is that when a man embraces you, you're a little bit afraid.

VALENTIN: Who put that idea into your head? That's all crap.

MOLINA: But it's what I feel.

VALENTIN: No, it's not what you feel, it's what you've been taught to feel. Being a woman doesn't make you . . . how shall I say . . . ? A martyr. And if I didn't think it would hurt like hell, I'd ask you to do it to me, to show you that all this business about being macho doesn't give anyone rights over another person.

MOLINA (*now disturbed*): This is getting us nowhere.

VALENTIN: On the contrary, I want to talk about it.

MOLINA: Well, I don't, so that's it. I'm begging you, no more, please.

VALENTIN: As you like.

MOLINA: There is something I want to tell you, though . . . When you were here it was like I wasn't myself, it was such a relief. And then later, when you were back in your bed . . . I still wasn't me, it's so strange, I can't explain.

VALENTIN: Tell me . . . try . . .

MOLINA: Don't rush me, I have to concentrate . . . Yes . . . when I was alone in my bed, and I was no longer you, I still felt like I was somebody else, neither male nor female . . . what I felt was . . .

VALENTIN: . . . out of danger . . .

MOLINA: Yes! That's it, exactly. How did you know?

VALENTIN: Because it's just what I felt too.

MOLINA: Valentin, why should we feel like that?

VALENTIN: I don't know . . .

MOLINA: Valentin . . .

VALENTIN: Mmm . . .

MOLINA: I'm going to tell you something, but promise me you won't laugh.

VALENTIN: Tell me.

MOLINA: When you come to my bed, afterwards . . . I hope I'll never wake up anymore once I've fallen asleep. I'd be sorry for my mother, sure, because she'd be on her own . . . but if it was just me, then I wouldn't want to wake ever again. And this isn't just some half-baked notion that I've just dreamed up either, no, it's the honest truth . . .

VALENTIN: But first you have to finish the movie.

GUARD'S VOICE: Prisoner Luis Alberto Molina! To the visiting room!

WARDEN'S VOICE: Put me through to your boss, please . . . How's it going? Nothing this end. Yes, that's why I called. He's on his way here now . . . Yes, they need the information, I'm aware of that . . . and if Molina still hasn't found out anything, what should I do with him . . . ? Are you sure . . . ? Let him out . . . But why . . . ? Yes, of course, there's no time to lose. Quite, and if the other one gives him a message, Molina will lead us straight to the group . . . I've got it, yes, we'll give him just enough time for the other to pass on the message . . . The tricky thing will be if Molina catches on that he's under surveillance . . . It's hard to anticipate the reactions of someone like Molina: a pervert after all.

(*The cell door opens and Molina comes back in totally deflated.*)

MOLINA: Poor Valentin, you're looking at my hands.

VALENTIN: I didn't mean to.

MOLINA: Your eyes gave you away, poor love . . .

VALENTIN: Such language . . .

MOLINA: I didn't get a parcel. You'll have to forgive me . . . Ay! Valentin . . .

VALENTIN: What's wrong.

MOLINA: Ay, you can't imagine . . .

VALENTIN: What's up. Tell me.

MOLINA: I'm going.

VALENTIN: To another cell . . .

MOLINA: No, they're releasing me.

VALENTIN: No.

MOLINA: I'm out on parole.

VALENTIN (*exploding with unexpected happiness*): But that's incredible!

(*Molina is confused by the way Valentin is taking this.*)

MOLINA: You're very kind to be so pleased for me.

VALENTIN: I'm happy for you too, of course . . . but, it's terrific! And I guarantee there's not the slightest risk.

MOLINA: What are you saying?

VALENTIN: Listen . . . I had to get urgent information out to my people, and I was dying with frustration because I couldn't do anything about it. I was racking my brains trying to find a way . . . And you come and serve it to me on a plate.

MOLINA (*as if he'd just had an electric shock*): I can't do that, you're out of your head.

VALENTIN: You'll memorize it in a minute. That's how easy it is. All you have to do is tell them that Number Three Command has been knocked out and they have to go to Corrientes for new orders.

MOLINA: No, I'm on parole, they can lock me up again for anything.

VALENTIN: I give you my word there's no risk.

MOLINA: I'm pleading with you. I don't want to hear another word. Not who they are or where they are. Nothing.

VALENTIN: Don't you want me to get out one day too?

MOLINA: Of here?

VALENTIN: Yes, to be free.

MOLINA: There's nothing I want more. But listen to me, I'm telling you this for your own good . . . I'm not good at this sort of thing, if they catch me, I'll spill everything.

VALENTIN: I'll answer for my comrades. You just have to wait a few days and then call from a public telephone, and make an appointment with someone in some bogus place.

MOLINA: What do you mean "a bogus place"?

VALENTIN: You just give them a name in code, let's

say the Ritz cinema, and that means a certain
bench in a particular square.

MOLINA: I'm frightened.

VALENTIN: You won't be when I explain the procedure to you.

MOLINA: But if the phone's tapped, I'll get in trouble.

VALENTIN: Not from a public call-box and if you disguise your voice. It's the easiest thing in the world,
I'll show you how to do it. There are millions of
ways — a sweet in your mouth, or a toothpick under your tongue . . .

MOLINA: No.

VALENTIN: We'll discuss it later.

MOLINA: No!

VALENTIN: Whatever you say.

*(Molina flops on the bed, all done in, and buries his
face in the pillow.)*

Look at me please.

MOLINA *(not looking at Valentin)*: I made a promise,
I don't know who to, maybe God, even though I
don't much believe in that.

VALENTIN: Yes . . .

MOLINA: I swore that I'd sacrifice anything if I could
only get out of here and look after my mother. And
my wish has come true.

VALENTIN: It was very generous of you to put someone else first.

MOLINA: But where's the justice in it? I always get left
with nothing . . .

VALENTIN: You have your mother and she needs you.
You have to assume that responsibility.

MOLINA: Listen, my mother's already had her life,
she's lived, been married, had a child . . . She's old
now, and her life is almost finished . . .

VALENTIN: But she's still alive . . .

MOLINA: And so am I . . . But when is my life going to
begin . . . ? When is it my turn for something good
to happen? To have something for myself?

VALENTIN: You can start a new life outside . . .

MOLINA: All I want is to stay with you . . .

(Valentin doesn't say anything.)

Doesn't that embarrass you?

VALENTIN: No . . . er, well, yes . . .

MOLINA: Yes what?

VALENTIN: That . . . it makes me a little embarrassed . . . Molina, try to understand this. Everything in a man's life, which may be short or long,
is only temporary. Nothing lasts forever.

MOLINA: Maybe . . . but why can't it last a little
longer, just that at least . . . ? If I can relay the information, will you get out sooner?

VALENTIN: It's a way of helping the cause.

MOLINA: But you won't get out sooner. You just think
it'll bring the revolution a bit closer.

VALENTIN: Yes, Molinita . . . Don't dwell on it, we'll
discuss it later.

MOLINA: There's no time left to discuss.

VALENTIN: Besides, you have to finish the panther
movie.

MOLINA: It's a sad ending.

VALENTIN: How?

MOLINA: She's a flawed woman . . . *(With his usual
irony.)* All we flawed women come to a sad ending.

VALENTIN *(laughing)*: And the psychoanalyst? Does
he get her in the end?

MOLINA: She gets him! And good! No, it's not so terrible, she just tears him to pieces.

VALENTIN: Does she kill him?

MOLINA: In the movie, yes. In real life, no.

VALENTIN: Tell me.

MOLINA: Let's see. Irina goes from bad to worse, she's
insanely jealous of the other girl and tries to kill
her. But the other one's lucky like hell, and she gets
away. Then one day the husband, who's at his
wits' end now, arranges to meet the psychoanalyst
at their house while she's out. But things get all
muddled up, and when the psychoanalyst arrives,
she's there on her own. He tries to take advantage
of the situation and throws himself at her and
kisses her. And right there she turns into a panther.
By the time the husband gets home, the guy's bled
to death. Meanwhile, Irina has made it to the zoo,
and she sidles up to the panther's cage. She's all
alone, in the night. That afternoon she got the key
when the keeper left it in the lock. It's like Irina's in
another world. The husband is on his way with the
cops at top speed. Irina opens the panther's cage,
and it pounces on her and mortally wounds her
with the first blow. The animal is scared away by
the police siren, it dashes out into the street, a car
runs over it and kills it.

VALENTIN: I'm going to miss you, Molinita.

MOLINA: The movies, at least.

VALENTIN: At least.

MOLINA: I want to ask you for a going-away present.
Something that we never did, although we got up
to worse.

VALENTIN: What?

MOLINA: A kiss.

VALENTIN: It's true. We never did.

MOLINA: But right at the end, just as I'm leaving.

VALENTIN: Okay.

MOLINA: I'm curious . . . Did the idea of kissing me
disgust you?

VALENTIN: Ummm . . . Maybe I was afraid you'd turn
into a panther.

MOLINA: I'm not the panther-woman.

VALENTIN: I know.

MOLINA: It's not fun to be a panther-woman, no one can kiss you. Or anything else.

VALENTIN: You're the spider woman who traps men in her web.

MOLINA (*flattered*): How sweet! I like that!

VALENTIN: And now it's your turn to promise me something: that you'll make people respect you, that you won't let anybody take advantage of you . . . Promise me you won't let anybody degrade you.

GUARD'S VOICE: Prisoner Luis Alberto Molina, be ready with your belongings!

MOLINA: Valentin . . .

VALENTIN: What?

MOLINA: Nothing, it doesn't matter . . . (*Pause.*) Valentin . . .

VALENTIN: What is it?

MOLINA: Rubbish, skip it.

VALENTIN: Do you want . . . ?

MOLINA: What?

VALENTIN: The kiss.

MOLINA: No, it was something else.

VALENTIN: Don't you want your kiss now?

MOLINA: Yes, if it won't disgust you.

VALENTIN: Don't get me mad.

(*He walks over to Molina and timidly gives him a kiss on the mouth.*)

MOLINA: Thank you.

VALENTIN: Thank you.

(*Long pause.*)

MOLINA: And now give me the number of your comrades.

VALENTIN: If you want.

MOLINA: I'll get the message to them.

VALENTIN: Okay . . . Is that what you wanted to ask?

MOLINA: Yes.

(*Valentin kisses Molina one more time.*)

VALENTIN: You don't know how happy you've made me. It's 323–1025.

(*Bolero music starts playing; it chokes Valentin's voice as he gives his instructions. Molina and Valentin separate slowly. Molina puts all his belongings into a duffel bag. They are now openly broken-hearted: Molina can hardly keep his mind on what he's doing. Valentin looks at him in total helplessness. Their taped voices are heard as all this action takes place onstage.*)

MOLINA'S VOICE: What happened to me, Valentin, when I got out of here?

VALENTIN'S VOICE: The police kept you under constant surveillance, listened in on your phone, everything. The first call you got was from an uncle, your godfather; he told you not to dally with minors again. You told him what he deserved, that he should go to hell, because in jail you'd learned what dignity was. Your friends telephoned and you called each other Greta and Marlene and Marilyn, and the police thought maybe it was a secret code. You got a job as a window dresser, and then finally one day you called my comrades. You took your mother to the movies and bought her some fashion magazines. And one day you went to meet my friends, but the police were shadowing you and they arrested you. My friends opened fire and killed you from their getaway car as you'd asked them to if the police caught you. And that was all . . . And what about me, Molina, what happened to me?

MOLINA'S VOICE: They tortured you a lot . . . and then your wounds turned septic. A nurse took pity on you and secretly he gave you some morphine, and you had a dream.

VALENTIN'S VOICE: About what?

MOLINA'S VOICE: You dreamed that inside you, in your chest, you were carrying Marta and that you'd never ever be apart from one another. And she asked you if you regretted what happened to me, my death, which she said was your fault.

VALENTIN'S VOICE: And what did I answer her?

MOLINA'S VOICE: You replied that I had died for a noble and selfless ideal. And she said that wasn't true, she said that I had sacrificed myself just so I could die like the heroine in a movie. And you said that only I knew the answer. And you dreamed you were very hungry when you escaped from prison and that you ended up on a savage island, and in the middle of the jungle you met a spider woman who gave you food to eat. And she was so lonely there in the jungle, but you had to carry on with your struggle and go back to join your comrades, and your strength was restored by the food the spider woman gave you.

VALENTIN'S VOICE: And, at the end, did I get away from the police, or did they catch up with me?

MOLINA'S VOICE: No, at the end you left the island, you were glad to be reunited with your comrades in the struggle, because it was a short dream, but a pleasant one . . .

(*The door opens: Molina and Valentin embrace one another with infinite sadness. Molina exits. The door closes behind him.*)

Caryl Churchill

Caryl Churchill (b. 1938) is in many ways a conventional middle-class citizen. She was born in London to a comfortable family: Her father was a political cartoonist and her mother a model. During World War II, her family emigrated to Canada, and much of her growing up was done in Montreal. She returned to England for college, taking her degree in English literature at Oxford in Lady Margaret Hall.

Churchill says that through all these years she did all the right things. She was a proper intellectual, a proper student, a proper person. She began writing plays in Oxford, where they were produced by students. After college, she married David Harter, also from Oxford, who became a lawyer in London. She raised three sons and at the same time tried to keep alive her dream of being a writer. Most of her early work was written for radio, and many of the plays were short. With so many children in the house, she says, it was difficult to sustain a long project.

Churchill's social conscience has been a significant part of her playwriting and her life. She found herself sometimes depressed by the dullness of the middle-class life demanded of the wife of a barrister, and much of her early drama is satire directed at what many people thought was an enviable lifestyle.

In the early 1970s her husband left a very lucrative practice and has since devoted himself to helping the poor at a nearby legal aid center. She has become involved in theater groups, among them a group of women called Monstrous Regiment. She is closely aligned with the Royal Court Theatre in London, noted for producing satiric, biting, experimental drama with a punch.

Her first play staged at the Royal Court Theatre was a farcical but serious play called *Owners* (1972). It attacks the way that the concept of ownership destroys potential relationships. Churchill's basic socialist views are very apparent in the play, which is a critique of the values that most capitalists take for granted: being aggressive, getting ahead, doing well. Although this play is not explicitly feminist, Churchill combines socialism and feminism in most of her plays, thus producing an often unusual approach to her subject matter. *Owners* has been criticized for its Brechtian use of disconnected scenes and its loose plot, but when it was produced off Broadway in 1973 it marked Churchill as a serious playwright.

After a year as a playwright in residence at the Royal Court Theatre, Churchill produced *Objections to Sex and Violence* (1975). The play was not immensely successful but it introduced themes of feminism into her work. Among other themes, the play examines in depth the domination of women by men and the relationship of violence to sex roles.

In 1976 Churchill produced *Vinegar Tom,* a play about witch hunts set in the seventeenth century. After researching witch trials, Churchill concluded that women were convenient scapegoats for men when times became difficult. A companion play also set in the seventeenth century is *Light Shining in Buckinghamshire,* which studies revolutions. The play was developed by the Joint Stock Theatre Group and produced at the Royal Court Theatre to uniformly positive reviews.

Her first play to receive wide notice was *Cloud Nine* (1979). It treats several themes simultaneously, among them colonization. The first act is set in the Victorian era in a British colony of Africa. The play is broadly satirical, involving farcical moments in the relationships of colonialist and native, master/servant, and man/woman. Churchill cast certain parts of the play in a cross-gender fashion: a woman plays a sensitive schoolboy, a man plays an unfulfilled wife. The effect is both comic and instructive, since one of her most important purposes is to cast some light on gender distinctions. She said that she saw "parallels between the way colonizers treat the colonized and the way men tended to treat women in our own society." *Cloud Nine* was produced in the Lucille Lortel Theatre, where it ran for two years off Broadway and won an Obie award.

Top Girls (1982) played at the Royal Court Theatre in London and at the Public Theatre in New York, where the reviews were mixed. The play, essentially feminist in theme, was praised in England for being "the best British play ever from a woman dramatist." *Fen* (1983) was also warmly praised by critics and audiences alike. A study of the effects of poverty on women, the play was developed with the Joint Stock Theatre Group and researched in the area of England called the Fens, where women work the fields and most of the people are poor.

Churchill's *Serious Money* (1987) is a verse play (like her first Oxford play) about the London stock market. It ran on Broadway to exceptional acclaim, partly because it played just after the stock market crash of October 1987. The play is a satiric study of those for whom only greed and getting ahead matter. Its success indicates that Caryl Churchill has been recognized as a major writer.

TOP GIRLS

Top Girls (1982), commissioned by the Royal Court Theatre in London, was first performed there under the direction of Max Stafford-Clark. Like many of the explosive Royal Court playwrights, Churchill had produced experimental, socially conscious plays that challenged the normal London and Broadway styles of production. She had established herself as a serious, significant writer.

The play has been produced in England and America by both important commercial theaters and smaller experimental and regional theaters. Although it is widely considered a feminist drama, Churchill is quick to point out that the play is often misunderstood; it is a critique not only of the dominance of males in the workplace but also of women who are satisfied to dominate the workplace in their turn and behave essentially like males. Churchill, an ardent socialist as well as a feminist, has said that *Top Girls* is an indictment of people, male or female, who get ahead at the cost of their humanity and their capacity to care for others.

The play opens with important legendary women gathering to share Marlene's celebration of her promotion with the Top Girls employment agency. The assembled group includes Pope Joan, a woman who posed as a man and became pope; Lady Nijo, a Japanese courtesan of the thirteenth century; Isabella Bird, a Victorian traveler who had many interesting adventures; Dull Gret, a figure from a Brueghel painting who led an attack on hell; and Patient Griselda, the obedient wife who inspired Chaucer.

Churchill creates characters who could be from a medieval allegory: Pope Joan succeeds by imitating a man physically; Lady Nijo succeeds by satisfying men; Isabella Bird attracts attention by displacing men (who were the legendary travelers); and Dull Gret and Patient Griselda, allegorical characters borrowed from other works of art, have their own ways of getting on in a "man's" world. Marlene is also allegorical: she stands for the woman who will succeed at all costs, including abandoning her own daughter.

Churchill alludes to medieval practice in another way. It was common in medieval poetic literature to tell stories about important historical and biblical women (as well as men). Such collections included incisive portraits of Eve, Cleopatra, the Witch of Endor, and Delilah. In the misogynist medieval period, such compilations of "top girls" focused on women who had caused scandal and harm to society. Such literature portrayed "bad girls."

One would think that the tables would be turned at the hands of a modern feminist, but Churchill's analysis is subtle. She demonstrates that Marlene and the other contemporary women have settled for demeaning themselves rather than demanding to re-create themselves. Most of the women in act II — Marlene, her coworkers, clients, and family — reveal their callousness, their indifference, and their basic incapacity to love. Marlene is unable to feel deeply even about those closest to her — her sister, her mother, and her daughter.

The ending of the play is a study of family relations. The failure of the two sisters is part of the message of the play. Marlene has paid an extraordinary price for her success. The play leaves us with the question of whether Marlene sees what she has done to herself and to her daughter and her sister. The play does not pull punches; it tries to illuminate the ways in which we make ourselves less human, less fulfilled, when we are driven to a success that is illusory and values that are false.

Top Girls in Performance

Max Stafford Clark, the longtime director of London's Royal Court Theatre, helped Churchill develop the play and directed its first production in August 1982. With sixteen characters and seven actors, a good deal of multiple role-playing was required, for example, Deborah Finley played the roles of Isabella Bird, Joyce, and Mrs. Kidd, while Lindsay Duncan played Lady Nijo and Win. Gwen Taylor, who played Marlene, was the only actor not to play more than one role. This casting method is one of Churchill's frequent devices, as is the technique of having characters speak while other characters are talking.

Churchill originally wanted the play produced in three acts. However, consideration for the time taken by two intervals persuaded her to break the play into two acts, ending act one at what was originally act two, scene two. The production at the Royal Court Theatre was successful and drew good reviews. The play was then taken to Joseph Papp's Public Theatre in New York later in 1982 and led the *New York Time*'s Frank Rich to say, "*Top Girls* remains one of the few plays this season that allows its audience to watch a truly original theatrical mind at work." After its New York run, the play returned to the Royal Court Theatre in 1983. *Top Girls* has been produced in regional theaters in the United States, England, and elsewhere to considerable acclaim.

Caryl Churchill (b. 1938)
Top Girls
1982

Characters

MARLENE
WAITRESS/KIT/SHONA
ISABELLA BIRD/JOYCE/MRS. KIDD
LADY NIJO/WIN
DULL GRET/ANGIE
POPE JOAN/LOUISE
PATIENT GRISELDA/NELL/JEANINE

Act I
Scene I: *A Restaurant.*
Scene II: *Top Girls' Employment Agency, London.*
Scene III: *Joyce's backyard in Suffolk.*

Act II
Scene I: *Top Girls' Employment Agency.*
Scene II: *A Year Earlier. Joyce's kitchen.*

Production Note: *The seating order for Act I, Scene I in the original production at the Royal Court was (from right) Gret, Nijo, Marlene, Joan, Griselda, Isabella.*

The Characters

ISABELLA BIRD (1831–1904): Lived in Edinburgh, traveled extensively between the ages of forty and seventy.

LADY NIJO (b. 1258): Japanese, was an Emperor's courtesan and later a Buddhist nun who traveled on foot through Japan.

DULL GRET: Is the subject of the Brueghel painting *Dulle Griet*, in which a woman in an apron and armor leads a crowd of women charging through hell and fighting the devils.

POPE JOAN: Disguised as a man, is thought to have been pope between 854 and 856.

PATIENT GRISELDA: Is the obedient wife whose story is told by Chaucer in "The Clerk's Tale" of *The Canterbury Tales.*

The Layout: *A speech usually follows the one immediately before it but: (1) When one character starts speaking before the other has finished, the point of interruption is marked/. E.g.,*

ISABELLA: This is the Emperor of Japan? / I once met the Emperor of Morocco.
NIJO: In fact he was the ex-Emperor.

(2) A character sometimes continues speaking right through another's speech. E.g.,

ISABELLA: When I was forty I thought my life was over. / Oh I was pitiful. I was
NIJO: I didn't say I felt it for twenty years. Not every minute.
ISABELLA: sent on a cruise for my health and felt even worse. Pains in my bones, pins and needles . . . etc.

(3) Sometimes a speech follows on from a speech earlier than the one immediately before it, and continuity is marked*. E.g.,

GRISELDA: I'd seen him riding by, we all had. And he'd seen me in the fields with the sheep.*
ISABELLA: I would have been well suited to minding sheep.
NIJO: And Mr. Nugent went riding by.
ISABELLA: Of course not, Nijo, I mean a healthy life in the open air.
JOAN: *He just rode up while you were minding the sheep and asked you to marry him?

where "in the fields with the sheep" is the cue to both "I would have been" and "He just rode up."

ACT I • Scene I

(Restaurant. Saturday night. There is a table with a white cloth set for dinner with six places. The lights come up on Marlene and the Waitress.)

MARLENE: Excellent, yes, table for six. One of them's going to be late but we won't wait. I'd like a bottle of Frascati straight away if you've got one really cold. *(The Waitress goes. Isabella Bird arrives.)* Here we are. Isabella.
ISABELLA: Congratulations, my dear.
MARLENE: Well, it's a step. It makes for a party. I haven't time for a holiday. I'd like to go somewhere exotic like you but I can't get away. I don't

know how you could bear to leave Hawaii. / I'd like to lie

ISABELLA: I did think of settling.

MARLENE: in the sun forever, except of course I can't bear sitting still.

ISABELLA: I sent for my sister Hennie to come and join me. I said, Hennie we'll live here forever and help the natives. You can buy two sirloins of beef for what a pound of chops cost in Edinburgh. And Hennie wrote back, the dear, that yes, she would come to Hawaii if I wished, but I said she had far better stay where she was. Hennie was suited to life in Tobermory.

MARLENE: Poor Hennie.

ISABELLA: Do you have a sister?

MARLENE: Yes in fact.

ISABELLA: Hennie was happy. She was good. I did miss its face, my own pet. But I couldn't stay in Scotland. I loathed the constant murk.

(Lady Nijo arrives.)

MARLENE *(seeing her)*: Ah! Nijo! *(The Waitress enters with the wine.)*

NIJO: Marlene! *(To Isabella.)* So excited when Marlene told me / you were coming.

ISABELLA: I'm delighted / to meet you.

MARLENE: I think a drink while we wait for the others. I think a drink anyway. What a week. *(Marlene seats Nijo. The Waitress pours the wine.)*

NIJO: It was always the men who used to get so drunk I'd be one of the maidens, passing the sake.

ISABELLA: I've had sake.° Small hot drink. Quite fortifying after a day in the wet.

NIJO: One night my father proposed three rounds of three cups, which was normal, and then the Emperor should have said three rounds of three cups, but he said three rounds of nine cups, so you can imagine. Then the Emperor passed his sake cup to my father and said, "Let the wild goose come to me this spring."

MARLENE: Let the what?

NIJO: It's a literary allusion to a tenth-century epic, / His Majesty was very cultured.

ISABELLA: This is the Emperor of Japan? / I once met the Emperor of Morocco.

NIJO: In fact he was the ex-Emperor.

MARLENE: But he wasn't old? / Did you, Isabella?

NIJO: Twenty-nine.

ISABELLA: Oh it's a long story.

MARLENE: Twenty-nine's an excellent age.

NIJO: Well I was only fourteen and I knew he meant something but I didn't know what. He sent me an

---

sake: Japanese rice wine.

---

eight-layered gown and I sent it back. So when the time came I did nothing but cry. My thin gowns were badly ripped. But even that morning when he left / he'd a green

MARLENE: Are you saying he raped you?

NIJO: robe with a scarlet lining and very heavily embroidered trousers, I already felt different about him. It made me uneasy. No, of course not, Marlene, I belonged to him, it was what I was brought up for from a baby. I soon found I was sad if he stayed away. It was depressing day after day not knowing when he would come. I never enjoyed taking other women to him.

ISABELLA: I certainly never saw my father drunk. He was a clergyman. / And I didn't get married till I was fifty. *(The Waitress brings the menus.)*

NIJO: Oh, my father was a very religious man. Just before he died he said to me, "Serve His Majesty, be respectful, if you lose his favor enter holy orders."

MARLENE: But he meant stay in a convent, not go wandering round the country.

NIJO: Priests were often vagrants, so why not a nun? You think I shouldn't? / I still did what my father wanted.

MARLENE: No no, I think you should. / I think it was wonderful.

(Dull Gret arrives.)

ISABELLA: I tried to do what my father wanted.

MARLENE: Gret, good. Nijo. Gret / I know Griselda's going to be late, but should we wait for Joan? / Let's get you a drink.

ISABELLA: Hello, Gret! *(She continues to Nijo.)* I tried to be a clergyman's daughter. Needlework, music, charitable schemes. I had a tumor removed from my spine and spent a great deal of time on the sofa. I studied the metaphysical poets and hymnology. / I thought I enjoyed intellectual pursuits.

NIJO: Ah, you like poetry. I come of a line of eight generations of poets. Father had a poem / in the anthology.

ISABELLA: My father taught me Latin although I was a girl. / But really I was

MARLENE: They didn't have Latin at my school.

ISABELLA: more suited to manual work. Cooking, washing, mending, riding horses. / Better than reading

NIJO: Oh but I'm sure you're very clever.

ISABELLA: books, eh Gret? A rough life in the open air.

NIJO: I can't say I enjoyed my rough life. What I enjoyed most was being the Emperor's favorite / and wearing thin silk.

ISABELLA: Did you have any horses, Gret?

GRET: Pig.

(*Pope Joan arrives.*)

MARLENE: Oh Joan, thank God, we can order. Do you know everyone? We were just talking about learning Latin and being clever girls. Joan was by way of an infant prodigy. Of course you were. What excited you when you were ten?

JOAN: Because angels are without matter they are not individuals. Every angel is a species.

MARLENE: There you are. (*They laugh. They look at the menus.*)

ISABELLA: Yes, I forgot all my Latin. But my father was the mainspring of my life and when he died I was so grieved. I'll have the chicken, please, / and the soup.

NIJO: Of course you were grieved. My father was saying his prayers and he dozed off in the sun. So I touched his knee to rouse him. "I wonder what will happen," he said, and then he was dead before he finished the sentence. / If he'd

MARLENE: What a shock.

NIJO: died saying his prayers he would have gone straight to heaven. / Waldorf salad.

JOAN: Death is the return of all creatures to God.

NIJO: I shouldn't have woken him.

JOAN: Damnation only means ignorance of the truth. I was always attracted by the teachings of John the Scot, though he was inclined to confuse / God and the world.

ISABELLA: Grief always overwhelmed me at the time.

MARLENE: What I fancy is a rare steak. Gret?

ISABELLA: I am of course a member of the / Church of England.

MARLENE: Gret?

GRET: Potatoes.

MARLENE: I haven't been to church for years. / I like Christmas carols.

ISABELLA: Good works matter more than church attendance.

MARLENE: Make that two steaks and a lot of potatoes. Rare. But I don't do good works either.

JOAN: Canelloni, please, / and a salad.

ISABELLA: Well, I tried, but oh dear. Hennie did good works.

NIJO: The first half of my life was all sin and the second / all repentance.*

MARLENE: Oh what about starters?

GRET: Soup.

JOAN: *And which did you like best?

MARLENE: Were your travels just a penance? Avocado vinaigrette. Didn't you / enjoy yourself?

JOAN: Nothing to start with for me, thank you.

NIJO: Yes, but I was very unhappy. / It hurt to remember the past.

MARLENE: And the wine list.

NIJO: I think that was repentance.

MARLENE: Well I wonder.

NIJO: I might have just been homesick.

MARLENE: Or angry.

NIJO: Not angry, no, / why angry?

GRET: Can we have some more bread?

MARLENE: Don't you get angry? I get angry.

NIJO: But what about?

MARLENE: Yes let's have two more Frascati. And some more bread, please. (*The Waitress exits.*)

ISABELLA: I tried to understand Buddhism when I was in Japan but all this birth and death succeeding each other through eternities just filled me with the most profound melancholy. I do like something more active.

NIJO: You couldn't say I was inactive. I walked every day for twenty years.

ISABELLA: I don't mean walking. / I mean in the head.

NIJO: I vowed to copy five Mahayana sutras. / Do you know how long they are?

MARLENE: I don't think religious beliefs are something we have in common. Activity yes. (*Gret empties the bread basket into her apron.*)

NIJO: My head was active. / My head ached.

JOAN: It's no good being active in heresy.

ISABELLA: What heresy? She's calling the Church of England / a heresy.

JOAN: There are some very attractive / heresies.

NIJO: I had never heard of Christianity. Never / heard of it. Barbarians.

MARLENE: Well I'm not a Christian. / And I'm not a Buddhist.

ISABELLA: You have heard of it?

MARLENE: We don't all have to believe the same.

ISABELLA: I knew coming to dinner with a Pope we should keep off religion.

JOAN: I always enjoy a theological argument. But I won't try to convert you, I'm not a missionary. Anyway I'm a heresy myself.

ISABELLA: There are some barbaric practices in the east.

NIJO: Barbaric?

ISABELLA: Among the lower classes.

NIJO: I wouldn't know.

ISABELLA: Well theology always made my head ache.

MARLENE: Oh good, some food. (*The Waitress brings the first course, serves it during the following, then exits.*)

NIJO: How else could I have left the court if I wasn't a nun? When father died I had only His Majesty. So when I fell out of favor I had nothing. Religion is a kind of nothing / and I dedicated what was left of me to nothing.

ISABELLA: That's what I mean about Buddhism. It doesn't brace.

MARLENE: Come on, Nijo, have some wine.

NIJO: Haven't you ever felt like that? You've all felt / like that. Nothing will ever happen again. I am dead already.

ISABELLA: You thought your life was over but it wasn't.

JOAN: You wish it was over.

GRET: Sad.

MARLENE: Yes, when I first came to London I sometimes . . . and when I got back from America I did. But only for a few hours. Not twenty years.

ISABELLA: When I was forty I thought my life was over. / Oh I was pitiful. I was sent

NIJO: I didn't say I felt it for twenty years. Not every minute.

ISABELLA: on a cruise for my health and I felt even worse. Pains in my bones, pins and needles in my hands, swelling behind the ears, and — oh, stupidity. I shook all over, indefinable terror. And Australia seemed to me a hideous country, the acacias stank like drains. / I

NIJO: You were homesick. (*Gret steals a bottle of wine.*)

ISABELLA: had a photograph taken for Hennie but I told her I wouldn't send it, my hair had fallen out and my clothes were crooked, I looked completely insane and suicidal.

NIJO: So did I, exactly, dressed as a nun. / I was wearing walking shoes for the first time.

ISABELLA: I longed to go home, / but home to what? Houses are so perfectly dismal.*

NIJO: I longed to go back ten years.

MARLENE: *I thought traveling cheered you both up.

ISABELLA: Oh it did / of course. It was on

NIJO: I'm not a cheerful person, Marlene. I just laugh a lot.

ISABELLA: the trip from Australia to the Sandwich Isles, I fell in love with the sea. There were rats in the cabin and ants in the food but suddenly it was like a new world. I woke up every morning happy, knowing there would be nothing to annoy me. No nervousness. No dressing.

NIJO: Don't you like getting dressed? I adored my clothes. / When I was chosen

MARLENE: You had prettier colors than Isabella.

NIJO: to give sake to His Majesty's brother, the Emperor Kameyana, on his formal visit, I wore raw silk pleated trousers and a seven-layered gown in shades of red, and two outer garments, / yellow lined with green

MARLENE: Yes, all that silk must have been very — (*The Waitress enters, clears the first course and exits.*)

JOAN: I dressed as a boy when I left home.*

NIJO: and a light green jacket. Lady Betto had a five-layered gown in shades of green and purple.

ISABELLA: *You dressed as a boy?

MARLENE: Of course, / for safety.

JOAN: It was easy, I was only twelve. / Also women weren't allowed in the library. We wanted to study in Athens.

MARLENE: You ran away alone?

JOAN: No, not alone, I went with my friend. / He was

NIJO: Ah, an elopement.

JOAN: sixteen but I thought I knew more science than he did and almost as much philosophy.

ISABELLA: Well I always traveled as a lady and I repudiated strongly any suggestion in the press that I was other than feminine.

MARLENE: I don't wear trousers in the office. / I could but I don't.

ISABELLA: There was no great danger to a woman of my age and appearance.

MARLENE: And you got away with it, Joan?

JOAN: I did then. (*The Waitress brings in the main course.*)

MARLENE: And nobody noticed anything?

JOAN: They noticed I was a very clever boy. / And

MARLENE: I couldn't have kept pretending for so long.

JOAN: when I shared a bed with my friend, that was ordinary — two poor students in a lodging house. I think I forgot I was pretending.

ISABELLA: Rocky Mountain Jim, Mr. Nugent, showed me no disrespect. He found it interesting, I think, that I could make scones and also lasso cattle. Indeed he declared his love for me, which was most distressing.

NIJO: What did he say? / We always sent poems first.

MARLENE: What did you say?

ISABELLA: I urged him to give up whiskey, / but he said it was too late.

MARLENE: Oh Isabella.

ISABELLA: He had lived alone in the mountains for many years.

MARLENE: But did you — ? (*The Waitress goes.*)

ISABELLA: Mr. Nugent was a man that any woman might love but none could marry. I came back to England.

NIJO: Did you write him a poem when you left? / Snow on the mountains. My sleeves

MARLENE: Did you never see him again?

ISABELLA: No, never.

NIJO: are wet with tears. In England no tears, no snow.

ISABELLA: Well, I say never. One morning very early in Switzerland, it was a year later, I had a vision of him as I last saw him / in his trapper's clothes with his

NIJO: A ghost!

ISABELLA: hair round his face, and that was the day, / I learned later, he died with a

NIJO: Ah!

ISABELLA: bullet in his brain. / He just bowed to me and vanished.

MARLENE: Oh Isabella.

NIJO: When your lover dies — One of my lovers died. / The priest Ariake.

JOAN: My friend died. Have we all got dead lovers?

MARLENE: Not me, sorry.

NIJO (*to Isabella*): I wasn't a nun, I was still at court, but he was a priest, and when he came to me he dedicated his whole life to hell. / He knew that when he died he would fall into one of the three lower realms. And he died, he did die.

JOAN (*to Marlene*): I'd quarreled with him over the teachings of John the Scot, who held that our ignorance of God is the same as his ignorance of himself. He only knows what he creates because he creates everything he knows but he himself is above being — do you follow?

MARLENE: No, but go on.

NIJO: I couldn't bear to think / in what shape would he be reborn.*

JOAN: St. Augustine maintained that the Neo-Platonic Ideas are indivisible

ISABELLA: *Buddhism is really most uncomfortable.

JOAN: from God, but I agreed with John that the created world is essences derived from Ideas which derived from God. As Denys the Areopagite said — the pseudo-Denys — first we give God a name, then deny it, / then reconcile the contradiction

NIJO: In what shape would he return?

JOAN: by looking beyond / those terms —

MARLENE: Sorry, what? Denys said what?

JOAN: Well we disagreed about it, we quarreled. And next day he was ill, / I was so annoyed with him

NIJO: Misery in this life and worse in the next, all because of me.

JOAN: all the time I was nursing him I kept going over the arguments in my mind. Matter is not a means of knowing the essence. The source of the species is the Idea. But then I realized he'd never understand my arguments again, and that night he died. John the Scot held that the individual disintegrates / and there is no personal immortality.

ISABELLA: I wouldn't have you think I was in love with Jim Nugent. It was yearning to save him that I felt.

MARLENE (*to Joan*): So what did you do?

JOAN: First I decided to stay a man. I was used to it. And I wanted to devote my life to learning. Do you know why I went to Rome? Italian men didn't have beards.

ISABELLA: The loves of my life were Hennie, my own pet, and my dear husband the doctor, who nursed Hennie in her last illness. I knew it would be terrible when Hennie died but I didn't know how terrible. I felt half of myself had gone. How could I go on my travels without that sweet soul waiting at home for my letters? It was Doctor Bishop's devotion to her in her last illness that made me decide to marry him. He and Hennie had the same sweet character. I had not.

NIJO: I thought His Majesty had sweet character because when he found out about Ariake he was so kind. But really it was because he no longer cared for me. One night he even sent me out to a man who had been pursuing me. / He lay awake on the other side of the screens and listened.

ISABELLA: I did wish marriage had seemed more of a step. I tried very hard to cope with the ordinary drudgery of life. I was ill again with carbuncles on the spine and nervous prostration. I ordered a tricycle, that was my idea of adventure then. And John himself fell ill, with erysipelas and anemia. I began to love him with my whole heart but it was too late. He was a skeleton with transparent white hands. I wheeled him on various seafronts in a bathchair. And he faded and left me. There was nothing in my life. The doctors said I had gout / and my heart was much affected.

NIJO: There was nothing in my life, nothing, without the Emperor's favor. The Empress had always been my enemy, Marlene, she said I had no right to wear three-layered gowns. / But I was the adopted daughter of my grandfather the Prime Minister. I had been publicly granted permission to wear thin silk.

JOAN: There was nothing in my life except my studies. I was obsessed with pursuit of the truth. I taught at the Greek School in Rome, which St. Augustine had made famous. I was poor, I worked hard, I spoke apparently brilliantly, I was still very young, I was a stranger, suddenly I was quite famous, I was everyone's favorite. Huge crowds came to hear me. The day after they made me cardinal I fell ill and lay two weeks without speaking, full of terror and regret. / But then I got up determined to

MARLENE: Yes, success is very . . .

JOAN: go on. I was seized again / with a desperate longing for the absolute.

ISABELLA: Yes, yes, to go on. I sat in Tobermory among Hennie's flowers and sewed a complete outfit in Jaeger flannel. / I was fifty-six years old.

NIJO: Out of favor but I didn't die. I left on foot, nobody saw me go. For the next twenty years I walked through Japan.

GRET: Walking is good. (*Meanwhile, the Waitress enters, pours lots of wine, then shows Marlene the empty bottle.*)

JOAN: Pope Leo died and I was chosen. All right then. I would be Pope. I would know God. I would know everything.

ISABELLA: I determined to leave my grief behind and set off for Tibet.

MARLENE: Magnificent all of you. We need some more wine, please, two bottles I think, Griselda isn't even here yet, and I want to drink a toast to you all. (*The Waitress exits.*)

ISABELLA: To yourself surely, / we're here to celebrate your success.

NIJO: Yes, Marlene.

JOAN: Yes, what is it exactly, Marlene?

MARLENE: Well it's not Pope but it is managing director.*

JOAN: And you find work for people.

MARLENE: Yes, an employment agency.

NIJO: *Over all the women you work with. And the men.

ISABELLA: And very well deserved too. I'm sure it's just the beginning of something extraordinary.

MARLENE: Well it's worth a party.

ISABELLA: To Marlene.*

MARLENE: And all of us.

JOAN: *Marlene.

NIJO: Marlene.

GRET: Marlene.

MARLENE: We've all come a long way. To our courage and the way we changed our lives and our extraordinary achievements. (*They laugh and drink a toast.*)

ISABELLA: Such adventures. We were crossing a mountain pass at seven thousand feet, the cook was all to pieces, the muleteers suffered fever and snow blindness. But even though my spine was agony I managed very well.*

MARLENE: Wonderful.

NIJO: *Once I was ill for four months lying alone at an inn. Nobody to offer a horse to Buddha. I had to live for myself, and I did live.

ISABELLA: Of course you did. It was far worse returning to Tobermory. I always felt dull when I was stationary. / That's why I could never stay anywhere.

NIJO: Yes, that's it exactly. New sights. The shrine by the beach, the moon shining on the sea. The goddess had vowed to save all living things. / She would even save the fishes. I was full of hope.

JOAN: I had thought the Pope would know everything. I thought God would speak to me directly. But of course he knew I was a woman.

MARLENE: But nobody else even suspected? (*The Waitress brings more wine and then exits.*)

JOAN: In the end I did take a lover again.*

ISABELLA: In the Vatican?

GRET: *Keep you warm.

NIJO: *Ah, lover.

MARLENE: *Good for you.

JOAN: He was one of my chamberlains. There are such a lot of servants when you're Pope. The food's very good. And I realized I did know the truth. Because whatever the Pope says, that's true.

NIJO: What was he like, the chamberlain?*

GRET: Big cock.

ISABELLA: Oh, Gret.

MARLENE: *Did he fancy you when he thought you were a fella?

NIJO: What was he like?

JOAN: He could keep a secret.

MARLENE: So you did know everything.

JOAN: Yes, I enjoyed being Pope. I consecrated bishops and let people kiss my feet. I received the King of England when he came to submit to the church. Unfortunately there were earthquakes, and some village reported it had rained blood, and in France there was a plague of giant grasshoppers, but I don't think that can have been my fault, do you?* (*Laughter.*) The grasshoppers fell on the English Channel / and were washed up on shore.

NIJO: I once went to sea. It was very lonely. I realized it made very little difference where I went.

JOAN: and their bodies rotted and poisoned the air and everyone in those parts died. (*Laughter.*)

ISABELLA: *Such superstition! I was nearly murdered in China by a howling mob. They thought the barbarians ate babies and put them under railway sleepers to make the tracks steady, and ground up their eyes to make the lenses of cameras. / So they were shouting,

MARLENE: And you had a camera!

ISABELLA: "Child-eater, child-eater." Some people tried to sell girl babies to Europeans for cameras or stew! (*Laughter.*)

MARLENE: So apart from the grasshoppers it was a great success.

JOAN: Yes, if it hadn't been for the baby I expect I'd have lived to an old age like Theodora of Alexandria, who lived as a monk. She was accused by a girl / who fell in love with her of being the father of her child and —

NIJO: But tell us what happened to your baby. I had some babies.

MARLENE: Didn't you think of getting rid of it?

JOAN: Wouldn't that be a worse sin than having it? / But a Pope with a child was about as bad as possible.

MARLENE: I don't know, you're the Pope.

JOAN: But I wouldn't have known how to get rid of it.

MARLENE: Other Popes had children, surely.

JOAN: They didn't give birth to them.

NIJO: Well you were a woman.

JOAN: Exactly and I shouldn't have been a woman. Woman, children, and lunatics can't be Pope.

Royal Court production of *Top Girls* in 1983 with the following cast (from left to right): Lindsay Duncan as Lady Nijo, Carole Hayman as Dull Gret, Gwen Taylor as Marlene, and Selina Cadell as Pope Joan.

MARLENE: So the only thing to do / was to get rid of it somehow.

NIJO: You had to have it adopted secretly.

JOAN: But I didn't know what was happening. I thought I was getting fatter, but then I was eating more and sitting about, the life of a Pope is quite luxurious. I don't think I'd spoken to a woman since I was twelve. The chamberlain was the one who realized.

MARLENE: And by then it was too late.

JOAN: Oh I didn't want to pay attention. It was easier to do nothing.

NIJO: But you had to plan for having it. You had to say you were ill and go away.

JOAN: That's what I should have done I suppose.

MARLENE: Did you want them to find out?

NIJO: I too was often in embarrassing situations, there's no need for a scandal. My first child was His Majesty's, which unfortunately died, but my second was Akebono's. I was seventeen. He was in love with me when I was thirteen, he was very up-set when I had to go the Emperor, it was very romantic, a lot of poems. Now His Majesty hadn't been near me for two months so he thought I was four months pregnant when I was really six, so when I reached the ninth month / I announced I was seriously ill,

JOAN: I never knew what month it was.

NIJO: and Akebono announced he had gone on a religious retreat. He held me round the waist and lifted me up as the baby was born. He cut the cord with a short sword, wrapped the baby in white and took it away. It was only a girl but I was sorry to lose it. Then I told the Emperor that the baby had miscarried because of my illness, and there you are. The danger was past.

JOAN: But, Nijo, I wasn't used to having a woman's body.

ISABELLA: So what happened?

JOAN: I didn't know of course that it was near the time. It was Rogation Day, there was always a procession. I was on the horse dressed in my robes and a cross was carried in front of me, and all the cardinals were following, and all the clergy of Rome, and a huge crowd of people. / We set off from St. Peter's to go

MARLENE: Total Pope. (*Gret pours the wine and steals the bottle.*)

JOAN: to St. John's. I had felt a slight pain earlier, I thought it was something I'd eaten, and then it came back, and came back more often. I thought when this is over I'll go to bed. There were still long gaps when I felt perfectly all right and I didn't want to attract attention to myself and spoil the ceremony. Then I suddenly realized what it must be. I had to last out till I could get home and hide. Then something changed, my breath started to catch, I couldn't plan things properly anymore. We were in a little street that goes between St. Clement's and the Colosseum, and I just had to get off the horse and sit down for a minute. Great waves of pressure were going through my body, I heard sounds like a cow lowing, they came out of my mouth. Far away I heard people screaming, "The Pope is ill, the Pope is dying." And the baby just slid out on to the road.*

MARLENE: The cardinals / won't have known where to put themselves.

NIJO: Oh dear, Joan, what a thing to do! In the street!

ISABELLA: *How embarrassing.

GRET: In a field, yah. (*They are laughing.*)

JOAN: One of the cardinals said, "The Antichrist!" and fell over in a faint. (*They all laugh.*)

MARLENE: So what did they do? They weren't best pleased.

JOAN: They took me by the feet and dragged me out of town and stoned me to death. (*They stop laughing.*)

MARLENE: Joan, how horrible.

JOAN: I don't really remember.

NIJO: And the child died too?

JOAN: Oh yes, I think so, yes. (*The Waitress enters to clear the plates. Pause. They start talking very quietly.*)

ISABELLA (*to Joan*): I never had any children. I was very fond of horses.

NIJO (*to Marlene*): I saw my daughter once. She was three years old. She wore a plum-red / small sleeved gown. Akebono's wife

ISABELLA: Birdie was my favorite. A little Indian bay mare I rode in the Rocky Mountains.

NIJO: had taken the child because her own died. Everyone thought I was just a visitor. She was being brought up carefully so she could be sent to the palace like I was. (*Gret steals her empty plate.*)

ISABELLA: Legs of iron and always cheerful, and such a pretty face. If a stranger led her she reared up like a bronco.

NIJO: I never saw my third child after he was born, the son of Ariake the priest. Ariake held him on his lap the day he was born and talked to him as if he could understand, and cried. My fourth child was Ariake's too. Ariake died before he was born. I didn't want to see anyone, I stayed alone in the hills. It was a boy again, my third son. But oddly enough I felt nothing for him.

MARLENE: How many children did you have, Gret?

GRET: Ten.

ISABELLA: Whenever I came back to England I felt I had so much to atone for. Hennie and John were so good. I did no good in my life. I spent years in self-gratification. So I hurled myself into committees, I nursed the people of Tobermory in the epidemic of influenza, I lectured the Young Women's Christian Association on Thrift. I talked and talked explaining how the East was corrupt and vicious. My travels must do good to someone besides myself. I wore myself out with good causes.

MARLENE (*pause*): Oh God, why are we all so miserable?

JOAN (*pause*): The procession never went down that street again.

MARLENE: They rerouted it specially?

JOAN: Yes they had to go all round to avoid it. And they introduced a pierced chair.

MARLENE: A pierced chair?

JOAN: Yes, a chair made out of solid marble with a hole in the seat / and it was

MARLENE: You're not serious.

JOAN: in the Chapel of the Savior, and after he was elected the Pope had to sit in it.

MARLENE: And someone looked up his skirts? / Not really!

ISABELLA: What an extraordinary thing.

JOAN: Two of the clergy / made sure he was a man.

NIJO: On their hands and knees!

MARLENE: A pierced chair!

GRET: Balls!

(*Griselda arrives unnoticed.*)

NIJO: Why couldn't he just pull up his robe?

JOAN: He had to sit there and look dignified.

MARLENE: You could have made all your chamberlains sit in it.*

GRET: Big one. Small one.

NIJO: Very useful chair at court.

ISABELLA: *Or the Laird of Tobermory in his kilt.

(*They are quite drunk. They get the giggles. Marlene notices Griselda and gets up to welcome her. The others go on talking and laughing. Gret crosses to Joan and Isabella and pours them wine from her stolen bottles. The Waitress gives out the menus.*)

MARLENE: Griselda! / There you are. Do you want to eat?

GRISELDA: I'm sorry I'm so late. No, no, don't bother.

MARLENE: Of course it's no bother. / Have you eaten?

GRISELDA: No really, I'm not hungry.

MARLENE: Well have some pudding.

GRISELDA: I never eat pudding.

MARLENE: Griselda, I hope you're not anorexic. We're having pudding, I am, and getting nice and fat.

GRISELDA: Oh if everyone is. I don't mind.

MARLENE: Now who do you know? This is Joan who was Pope in the ninth century, and Isabella Bird, the Victorian traveler, and Lady Nijo from Japan, Emperor's concubine and Buddhist nun, thirteenth century, nearer your own time, and Gret who was painted by Brueghel. Griselda's in Boccaccio and Petrarch and Chaucer because of her extraordinary marriage. I'd like profiteroles because they're disgusting.

JOAN: Zabaglione, please.

ISABELLA: Apple pie / and cream.

NIJO: What's this?

MARLENE: Zabaglione, it's Italian, it's what Joan's having, / it's delicious.

NIJO: A Roman Catholic / dessert? Yes please.

MARLENE: Gret?

GRET: Cake.

GRISELDA: Just cheese and biscuits, thank you. (*The Waitress exits.*)

MARLENE: Yes, Griselda's life is like a fairy story, except it starts with marrying the prince.

GRISELDA: He's only a marquis, Marlene.

MARLENE: Well everyone for miles around is his liege and he'd absolute lord of life and death and you were the poor but beautiful peasant girl and he whisked you off. / Near enough a prince.

NIJO: How old were you?

GRISELDA: Fifteen.

NIJO: I was brought up in court circles and it was still a shock. Had you ever seen him before?

GRISELDA: I'd seen him riding by, we all had. And he'd seen me in the fields with the sheep.*

ISABELLA: I would have been well suited to minding sheep.

NIJO: And Mr. Nugent riding by.

ISABELLA: Of course not, Nijo, I mean a healthy life in the open air.

JOAN: *He just rode up while you were minding the sheep and asked you to marry him?

GRISELDA: No, no, it was on the wedding day. I was waiting outside the door to see the procession. Everyone wanted him to get married so there'd be an heir to look after us when he died, / and at last he

MARLENE: I don't think Walter wanted to get married. It is Walter? Yes.

GRISELDA: announced a day for the wedding but nobody knew who the bride was, we thought it must be a foreign princess, we were longing to see her. Then the carriage stopped outside our cottage and we couldn't see the bride anywhere. And he came and spoke to my father.

NIJO: And your father told you to serve the Prince.

GRISELDA: My father could hardly speak. The Marquis said it wasn't an order, I could say no, but if I said yes I must always obey him in everything.

MARLENE: That's when you should have suspected.

GRISELDA: But of course a wife must obey her husband. / And of course I must obey the Marquis.*

ISABELLA: I swore to obey dear John, of course, but it didn't seem to arise. Naturally I wouldn't have wanted to go abroad while I was married.

MARLENE: *Then why bother to mention it at all? He'd got a thing about it, that's why.

GRISELDA: I'd rather obey the Marquis than a boy from the village.

MARLENE: Yes, that's a point.

JOAN: I never obeyed anyone. They all obeyed me.

NIJO: And what did you wear? He didn't make you get married in your own clothes? That would be perverse.*

MARLENE: Oh, you wait.

GRISELDA: *He had ladies with him who undressed me and they had a white silk dress and jewels for my hair.

MARLENE: And at first he seemed perfectly normal?

GRISELDA: Marlene, you're always so critical of him. / Of course he was normal, he was very kind.

MARLENE: But, Griselda, come on, he took your baby.

GRISELDA: Walter found it hard to believe I loved him. He couldn't believe I would always obey him. He had to prove it.

MARLENE: I don't think Walter likes women.

GRISELDA: I'm sure he loved me, Marlene, all the time.

MARLENE: He just had a funny way / of showing it.

GRISELDA: It was hard for him too.

JOAN: How do you mean he took away your baby?

NIJO: Was it a boy?

GRISELDA: No, the first one was a girl.

NIJO: Even so it's hard when they take it away. Did you see it at all?

GRISELDA: Oh yes, she was six weeks old.

NIJO: Much better to do it straight away.

ISABELLA: But why did your husband take the child?

GRISELDA: He said all the people hated me because I was just one of them. And now I had a child they were restless. So he had to get rid of the child to keep them quiet. But he said he wouldn't snatch her, I had to agree and obey and give her up. So when I was feeding her a man came in and took her away. I thought he was going to kill her even before he was out of the room.

MARLENE: But you let him take her? You didn't struggle?

GRISELDA: I asked him to give her back so I could kiss her. And I asked him to bury her where no animals could dig her up. / It was Walter's child to do what he

ISABELLA: Oh, my dear.

GRISELDA: liked with.*

MARLENE: Walter was bonkers.

GRET: Bastard.

ISABELLA: *But surely, murder.

GRISELDA: I had promised.

MARLENE: I can't stand this. I'm going for a pee.

(*Marlene goes out. The Waitress brings the dessert, serves it during the following, then exits*)

NIJO: No, I understand. Of course you had to, he was your life. And were you in favor after that?

GRISELDA: Oh yes, we were very happy together. We never spoke about what had happened.

ISABELLA: I can see you were doing what you thought was your duty. But didn't it make you ill?

GRISELDA: No, I was very well, thank you.

NIJO: And you had another child?

GRISELDA: Not for four years, but then I did, yes, a boy.

NIJO: Ah a boy. / So it all ended happily.

GRISELDA: Yes he was pleased. I kept my son till he was two years old. A peasant's grandson. It made the people angry. Walter explained.

ISABELLA: But surely he wouldn't kill his children / just because —

GRISELDA: Oh it wasn't true. Walter would never give in to the people. He wanted to see if I loved him enough.

JOAN: He killed his children / to see if you loved him enough?

NIJO: Was it easier the second time or harder?

GRISELDA: It was always easy because I always knew I would do what he said. (*Pause. They start to eat.*)

ISABELLA: I hope you didn't have any more children.

GRISELDA: Oh no, no more. It was twelve years till he tested me again.

ISABELLA: So whatever did he do this time? / My poor John, I never loved him enough, and he would never have dreamt . . .

GRISELDA: He sent me away. He said the people wanted him to marry someone else who'd give him an heir and he'd got special permission from the Pope. So I said I'd go home to my father. I came with nothing / so I went with nothing. I took

NIJO: Better to leave if your master doesn't want you.

GRISELDA: off my clothes. He let me keep a slip so he wouldn't be shamed. And I walked home barefoot.

My father came out in tears. Everyone was crying except me.

NIJO: At least your father wasn't dead. / I had nobody.

ISABELLA: Well it can be a relief to come home. I loved to see Hennie's sweet face again.

GRISELDA: Oh yes, I was perfectly content. And quite soon he sent for me again.

JOAN: I don't think I would have gone.

GRISELDA: But he told me to come. I had to obey him. He wanted me to help prepare his wedding. He was getting married to a young girl from France / and nobody except me knew how to arrange things the way he liked them.

NIJO: It's always hard taking him another woman. (*Marlene comes back.*)

JOAN: I didn't live a woman's life. I don't understand it.

GRISELDA: The girl was sixteen and far more beautiful than me. I could see why he loved her. / She had her younger brother with her as a page. (*The Waitress enters.*)

MARLENE: Oh God, I can't bear it. I want some coffee. Six coffees. Six brandies. / Double brandies. Straightaway. (*The Waitress exits.*)

GRISELDA: They all went into the feast I'd prepared. And he stayed behind and put his arms round me and kissed me. / I felt half asleep with the shock.

NIJO: Oh, like a dream.

MARLENE. And he said, "This is your daughter and your son."

GRISELDA: Yes.

JOAN: What?

NIJO: Oh. Oh I see. You got them back.

ISABELLA: I did think it was remarkably barbaric to kill them but you learn not to say anything. / So he had them brought up secretly I suppose.

MARLENE: Walter's a monster. Weren't you angry? What did you do?

GRISELDA: Well I fainted. Then I cried and kissed the children. / Everyone was making a fuss of me.

NIJO: But did you feel anything for them?

GRISELDA: What?

NIJO: Did you feel anything for the children?

GRISELDA: Of course, I loved them.

JOAN: So you forgave him and lived with him?

GRISELDA: He suffered so much all those years.

ISABELLA: Hennie had the same sweet nature.

NIJO: So they dressed you again?

GRISELDA: Cloth of gold.

JOAN: I can't forgive anything.

MARLENE: You really are exceptional, Griselda.

NIJO: Nobody gave me back my children. (*She cries.*)

(*The Waitress brings the brandies and then exits. During the following, Joan goes to Nijo.*)

ISABELLA: I can never be like Hennie. I was always so busy in England, a kind of business I detested. The very presence of people exhausted my emotional reserves. I could not be like Hennie however I tried. I tried and was as ill as could be. The doctor suggested a steel net to support my head, the weight of my own head was too much for my diseased spine. It is dangerous to put oneself in depressing circumstances. Why should I do it?

JOAN (to Nijo): Don't cry.

NIJO: My father and the Emperor both died in the autumn. So much pain.

JOAN: Yes, but don't cry.

NIJO: They wouldn't let me into the palace when he was dying. I hid in the room with his coffin, then I couldn't find where I'd left my shoes, I ran after the funeral procession in bare feet, I couldn't keep up. When I got there it was over, a few wisps of smoke in the sky, that's all that was left of him. What I want to know is, if I'd still been at court, would I have been allowed to wear full mourning?

MARLENE: I'm sure you would.

NIJO: Why do you say that? You don't know anything about it. Would I have been allowed to wear full mourning?

ISABELLA: How can people live in this dim pale island and wear our hideous clothes? I cannot and will not live the life of a lady.

NIJO: I'll tell you something that made me angry. I was eighteen, at the Full Moon Ceremony. They make a special rice gruel and stir it with their sticks, and then they beat their women across the loins so they'll have sons and not daughters. So the Emperor beat us all / very hard as

MARLENE: What a sod. (The Waitress enters with the coffees.)

NIJO: usual — that's not it, Marlene, that's normal, what made us angry he told his attendants they could beat us too. Well they had a wonderful time. / So Lady Genki and I made a plan, and the ladies

MARLENE: I'd like another brandy, please. Better make it six. (The Waitress exits.)

NIJO: all hid in his rooms, and Lady Mashimizu stood guard with a stick at the door, and when His Majesty came in Genki seized him and I beat him till he cried out and promised he would never order anyone to hit us again. Afterward there was a terrible fuss. The nobles were horrified. "We wouldn't even dream of stepping on Your Majesty's shadow." And I had hit him with a stick. Yes, I hit him with a stick.

(The Waitress brings the brandy bottle and tops up the glasses. Joan crosses in front of the table and back to her place while drunkenly reciting:)

JOAN: Suave, mari magno turantibus aequora ventis,
   e terra magnum alterius spectare laborem;
   non quia vexari quemquamst iucunda voluptas,
   sed quibus ipse malis careas quia cernere suave est.
   Suave etiam belli certamina magna tueri
   per campos instructa tua sine parse pericli.
   Sed nil dulcius est, bene quam munita tenere
   edita doctrine sapientum temple serena, /
   despicere uncle queas alios passimque videre
   errare atque viam palantis quaerere vitae,

GRISELDA: I do think — I do wonder — it would have been nicer if Walter hadn't had to.

ISABELLA: Why should I? Why should I?

MARLENE: Of course not.

NIJO: I hit him with a stick.

JOAN: certare ingenio, contendere nobilitate,
   noctes atque dies niti praestante labore
   ad summas emergere opes rerumque potiri.
   O miseras hominum mentis, / o pectora caeca!*°

ISABELLA: O miseras!

NIJO: *Pectora caeca!

JOAN: qualibus in tenebris vitae quantisque periclis
   degitur hoc aevi quodcumquest! / none videre
   nil aliud sibi naturam latrare, nisi utqui
   corpore seiunctus dolor absit, mente fruatur° . . .
   (She subsides.)

GRET: We come to hell through a big mouth. Hell's black and red. / It's

MARLENE (to Joan): Shut up, pet.

Suave, . . . o pectora caeca!: Joan's speech is from the Second Book of On the Nature of Things by Titus Lucretius Carus (97?–54 B.C.), the Latin poet and philosopher. The following translation of the passage is by Cyril Bailey: Sweet it is, when on the great sea the winds are buffeting the waters, to gaze from the land on another's great struggles; not because it is pleasure or joy that any one should be distressed, but because it is sweet to perceive from what misfortune you yourself are free. Sweet is it too, to behold great contests of war in full array over the plains, when you have no part in the danger. But nothing is more gladdening than to dwell in the calm high places, firmly embattled on the heights by the teaching of the wise, whence you can look down on others, and see them wandering hither and thither, going astray as they seek the way of life, in strife matching their wits or rival claims of birth, struggling night and day by surpassing effort to rise up to the height of power and gain possession of the world. Ah! miserable minds of men, blind hearts!

qualibus . . . fruatur: In what darkness of life, in what great dangers ye spend this little span of years! to think that ye should not see that nature cries aloud for nothing else but that pain may be kept far sundered from the body, and that, withdrawn from care and fear, she may enjoy in mind the sense of pleasure!

GRISELDA: Hush, please.

ISABELLA: Listen, she's been to hell.

GRET: like the village where I come from. There's a river and a bridge and houses. There's places on fire like when the soldiers come. There's a big devil sat on a roof with a big hole in his arse and he's scooping stuff out of it with a big ladle and it's falling down on us, and it's money, so a lot of the women stop and get some. But most of us is fighting the devils. There's lots of little devils, our size, and we get them down all right and give them a beating. There's lots of funny creatures round your feet, you don't like to look, like rats and lizards, and nasty things, a bum with a face, and fish with legs, and faces on things that don't have faces on. But they don't hurt, you just keep going. Well we'd had worse, you see, we'd had the Spanish. We'd all had family killed. My big son die on a wheel. Birds eat him. My baby, a soldier run her through with a sword. I'd had enough, I was mad, I hate the bastards. I come out of my front door that morning and shout till my neighbors come out and I said, "Come on, we're going where the evil come from and pay the bastards out." And they all come out just as they was / from baking or

NIJO: All the ladies come.

GRET: washing in their aprons, and we push down the street and the ground opens up and we go through a big mouth into a street just like ours but in hell. I've got a sword in my hand from somewhere and I fill a basket with gold cups they drink out of down there. You just keep running on and fighting, / you didn't stop for nothing. Oh we give them devils such a beating.*

NIJO: Take that, take that.

JOAN: *Something something something mortisque timores
tum vacuum pectus° — damn.
Quod si ridicula —
something something on and on and on
and something splendorem purpureai.

ISABELLA: I thought I would have a last jaunt up the west river in China. Why not? But the doctors were so very grave I just went to Morocco. The sea was so wild I had to be landed by ship's crane in a coal bucket. / My horse was a terror to me, a powerful black charger.

GRET: Coal bucket good.

JOAN: nos in luce timemus

Something . . . pectus: Fragments from Lucretius meaning "the dread of death leaves your heart empty . . ."

something
terrorem°

(*Nijo is laughing and crying. Joan gets up and is sick. Griselda looks after her.*)

GRISELDA: Can I have some water, please? (*The Waitress exits.*)

ISABELLA: So off I went to visit the Berber sheikhs in full blue trousers and great brass spurs. I was the only European woman ever to have seen the Emperor of Morocco. I was (*the Waitress brings the water*) seventy years old. What lengths to go to for a last chance of joy. I knew my return of vigor was only temporary, but how marvelous while it lasted.

Scene II

(*"Top Girls" Employment Agency. Monday morning. The lights come up on Marlene and Jeanine.*)

MARLENE: Right, Jeanine, you are Jeanine aren't you? Let's have a look. O's and A's°. / No A's, all those

JEANINE: Six O's.

MARLENE: O's you probably could have got an A. / Speeds, not brilliant, not too bad.

JEANINE: I wanted to go to work.

MARLENE: Well, Jeanine, what's your present job like?

JEANINE: I'm a secretary.

MARLENE: Secretary or typist?

JEANINE: I did start as a typist but the last six months I've been a secretary.

MARLENE: To?

JEANINE: To three of them, really, they share me. There's Mr. Ashford, he's the office manager, and Mr. Philly / is sales, and —

Quod . . . purpureai. . . . nos in luce . . . terrorem: Fragments from the following passage by Lucretius: But if we see that these thoughts are mere mirth and mockery, and in very truth the fears of men and the cares that dog them fear not the clash of arms nor the weapons of war, but pass boldly among kings and lords of the world, nor dread the glitter that comes from gold nor the bright sheen of the purple robe, can you doubt that all such power belongs to reason alone, above all when the whole of life is but a struggle in darkness? For even as children tremble and fear everything in blinding darkness, so we sometimes dread in the light things that are no whit more to be feared than what children shudder at in the dark.

O's and A's: O-level and A-level examinations in the British education system. An O-level is a public examination for secondary-school students testing basic knowledge in various subjects; it is required before advancement to more specialized courses of study. A-level exams require advanced knowledge in a subject and are taken at the end of secondary school, usually two years after O-levels.

MARLENE: Quite a small place?

JEANINE: A bit small.

MARLENE: Friendly?

JEANINE: Oh it's friendly enough.

MARLENE: Prospects?

JEANINE: I don't think so, that's the trouble. Miss Lewis is secretary to the managing director and she's been there forever, and Mrs. Bradford / is —

MARLENE: So you want a job with better prospects?

JEANINE: I want a change.

MARLENE: So you'll take anything comparable?

JEANINE: No, I do want prospects. I want more money.

MARLENE: You're getting — ?

JEANINE: Hundred.

MARLENE: It's not bad you know. You're what? Twenty?

JEANINE: I'm saving to get married.

MARLENE: Does that mean you don't want a long-term job, Jeanine?

JEANINE: I might do.

MARLENE: Because where do the prospects come in? No kids for a bit?

JEANINE: Oh no, not kids, not yet.

MARLENE: So you won't tell them you're getting married?

JEANINE: Had I better not?

MARLENE: It would probably help.

JEANINE: I'm not wearing a ring. We thought we wouldn't spend on a ring.

MARLENE: Saves taking it off.

JEANINE: I wouldn't take it off.

MARLENE: There's no need to mention it when you go for an interview. / Now, Jeanine, do you have a feel

JEANINE: But what if they ask?

MARLENE: for any particular kind of company?

JEANINE: I thought advertising.

MARLENE: People often do think advertising. I have got a few vacancies but I think they're looking for something glossier.

JEANINE: You mean how I dress? / I can

MARLENE: I mean experience.

JEANINE: dress different. I dress like this on purpose for where I am now.

MARLENE: I have a marketing department here of a knitwear manufacturer. / Marketing is near enough

JEANINE: Knitwear?

MARLENE: advertising. Secretary to the marketing manager, he's thirty-five, married, I've sent him a girl before and she was happy, left to have a baby, you won't want to mention marriage there. He's very fair I think, good at his job, you won't have to nurse him along. Hundred and ten, so that's better than you're doing now.

JEANINE: I don't know.

MARLENE: I've a fairly small concern here, father and two sons, you'd have more say potentially, secretarial and reception duties, only a hundred but the job's going to grow with the concern and then you'll be in at the top with new girls coming in underneath you.

JEANINE: What is it they do?

MARLENE: Lampshades. / This would be my first choice for you.

JEANINE: Just lampshades?

MARLENE: There's plenty of different kinds of lampshade. So we'll send you there, shall we, and the knitwear second choice. Are you free to go for an interview any day they call you?

JEANINE: I'd like to travel.

MARLENE: We don't have any foreign clients. You'd have to go elsewhere.

JEANINE: Yes I know. I don't really . . . I just mean . . .

MARLENE: Does your fiancé want to travel?

JEANINE: I'd like a job where I was here in London and with him and everything but now and then — I expect it's silly. Are there jobs like that?

MARLENE: There's personal assistant to a top executive in a multinational. If that's the idea you need to be planning ahead. Is that where you want to be in ten years?

JEANINE: I might not be alive in ten years.

MARLENE: Yes but you will be. You'll have children.

JEANINE: I can't think about ten years.

MARLENE: You haven't got the speeds anyway. So I'll send you to these two shall I? You haven't been to any other agency? Just so we don't get crossed wires. Now, Jeanine, I want you to get one of these jobs, all right? If I send you that means I'm putting myself on the line for you. Your presentation's OK, you look fine, just be confident and go in there convinced that this is the best job for you and you're the best person for the job. If you don't believe it they won't believe it.

JEANINE: Do you believe it?

MARLENE: I think you could make me believe it if you put your mind to it.

JEANINE: Yes, all right.

Scene III

(*Joyce's back yard. Sunday afternoon. The house with a back door is upstage. Downstage is a shelter made of junk, made by children. The lights come up on two girls, Angie and Kit, who are squashed together in the shelter. Angie is sixteen, Kit is twelve. They cannot be seen from the house.*)

JOYCE (*off, calling from the house*): Angie. Angie, are you out there?

(*Silence. They keep still and wait. When nothing else happens they relax.*)

ANGIE: Wish she was dead.

KIT: Wanna watch *The Exterminator*?

ANGIE: You're sitting on my leg.

KIT: There's nothing on telly. We can have an ice cream. Angie?

ANGIE: Shall I tell you something?

KIT: Do you wanna watch *The Exterminator*?

ANGIE: It's X, innit?

KIT: I can get into Xs.

ANGIE: Shall I tell you something?

KIT: We'll go to something else. We'll go to Ipswich. What's on the Odeon?

ANGIE: She won't let me, will she.

KIT: Don't tell her.

ANGIE: I've no money.

KIT: I'll pay.

ANGIE: She'll moan though, won't she.

KIT: I'll ask her for you if you like.

ANGIE: I've no money, I don't want you to pay.

KIT: I'll ask her.

ANGIE: She don't like you.

KIT: I still got three pounds birthday money. Did she say she don't like me? I'll go by myself then.

ANGIE: Your mum don't let you. I got to take you.

KIT: She won't know.

ANGIE: You'd be scared who'd sit next to you.

KIT: No I wouldn't. She does like me anyway. Tell me then.

ANGIE: Tell you what?

KIT: It's you she doesn't like.

ANGIE: Well I don't like her so tough shit.

JOYCE (*off*): Angie. Angie. Angie. I know you're out there. I'm not coming out after you. You come in here. (*Silence. Nothing happens.*)

ANGIE: Last night when I was in bed. I been thinking yesterday could I make things move. You know, make things move by thinking about them without touching them. Last night I was in bed and suddenly a picture fell down off the wall.

KIT: What picture?

ANGIE: My gran, that picture. Not the poster. The photograph in the frame.

KIT: Had you done something to make it fall down?

ANGIE: I must have done.

KIT: But were you thinking about it?

ANGIE: Not about it, but about something.

KIT: I don't think that's very good.

ANGIE: You know the kitten?

KIT: Which one?

ANGIE:: There only is one. The dead one.

KIT: What about it?

ANGIE: I heard it last night.

KIT: Where?

ANGIE: Out here. In the dark. What if I left you here in the dark all night?

KIT: You couldn't. I'd go home.

ANGIE: You couldn't.

KIT: I'd / go home.

ANGIE: No you couldn't, not if I said.

KIT: I could.

ANGIE: Then you wouldn't see anything. You'd just be ignorant.

KIT: I can see in the daytime.

ANGIE: No you can't. You can't hear it in the daytime.

KIT: I don't want to hear it.

ANGIE: You're scared that's all.

KIT: I'm not scared of anything.

ANGIE: You're scared of blood.

KIT: It's not the same kitten anyway. You just heard an old cat, / you just heard some old cat.

ANGIE: You don't know what I heard. Or what I saw. You don't know nothing because you're a baby.

KIT: You're sitting on me.

ANGIE: Mind my hair / you silly cunt.

KIT: Stupid fucking cow, I hate you.

ANGIE: I don't care if you do.

KIT: You're horrible.

ANGIE: I'm going to kill my mother and you're going to watch.

KIT: I'm not playing.

ANGIE: You're scared of blood. (*Kit puts her hand under dress, brings it out with blood on her finger.*)

KIT: There, see, I got my own blood, so. (*Angie takes Kit's hand and licks her finger.*)

ANGIE: Now I'm a cannibal. I might turn into a vampire now.

KIT: That picture wasn't nailed up right.

ANGIE: You'll have to do that when I get mine.

KIT: I don't have to.

ANGIE: You're scared.

KIT: I'll do it, I might do it. I don't have to just because you say. I'll be sick on you.

ANGIE: I don't care if you are sick on me, I don't mind sick. I don't mind blood. If I don't get away from here I'm going to die.

KIT: I'm going home.

ANGIE. You can't go through the house. She'll see you.

KIT: I won't tell her.

ANGIE: Oh great, fine.

KIT: I'll say I was by myself. I'll tell her you're at my house and I'm going there to get you.

ANGIE: She knows I'm here, stupid.

KIT: Then why can't I go through the house?

ANGIE: Because I said not.

KIT: My mum don't like you anyway.

ANGIE: I don't want her to like me. She's a slag.

KIT: She is not.

ANGIE: She does it with everyone.

KIT: She does not.

ANGIE: You don't even know what it is.

KIT: Yes I do.

ANGIE: Tell me then.

KIT: We get it all at school, cleverclogs. It's on television. You haven't done it.

ANGIE: How do you know?

KIT: Because I know you haven't.

ANGIE: You know wrong then because I have.

KIT: Who with?

ANGIE: I'm not telling you / who with.

KIT: You haven't anyway.

ANGIE: How do you know?

KIT: Who with?

ANGIE: I'm not telling you.

KIT: You said you told me everything.

ANGIE: I was lying wasn't I.

KIT: Who with? You can't tell me who with because / you never —

ANGIE: Sh.

(*Joyce has come out of the house. She stops halfway across the yard and listens. They listen.*)

JOYCE: You there Angie? Kit? You there Kitty? Want a cup of tea? I've got some chocolate biscuits. Come on now I'll put the kettle on. Want a choccy biccy, Angie? (*They all listen and wait.*) Fucking rotten little cunt. You can stay there and die. I'll lock the door.

(*They all wait. Joyce goes back to the house. Angie and Kit sit in silence for a while.*)

KIT: When there's a war, where's the safest place?

ANGIE: Nowhere.

KIT: New Zealand is, my mum said. Your skin's burned right off. Shall we go to New Zealand?

ANGIE: I'm not staying here.

KIT: Shall we go to New Zealand?

ANGIE: You're not old enough.

KIT: You're not old enough.

ANGIE: I'm old enough to get married.

KIT: You don't want to get married.

ANGIE: No but I'm old enough.

KIT: I'd find out where they were going to drop it and stand right in the place.

ANGIE: You couldn't find out.

KIT: Better than walking round with your skin dragging on the ground. Eugh. / Would you like walking round with your skin dragging on the ground?

ANGIE: You couldn't find out, stupid, it's a secret.

KIT: Where are you going?

ANGIE: I'm not telling you.

KIT: Why?

ANGIE: It's a secret.

KIT: But you tell me all your secrets.

ANGIE: Not the true secrets.

KIT: Yes you do.

ANGIE: No I don't.

KIT: I want to go somewhere away from the war.

ANGIE: Just forget the war.

KIT: I can't.

ANGIE: You have to. It's so boring.

KIT: I'll remember it at night.

ANGIE: I'm going to do something else anyway.

KIT: What? Angie, come on. Angie.

ANGIE: It's a true secret.

KIT: It can't be worse than the kitten. And killing your mother. And the war.

ANGIE: Well I'm not telling you so you can die for all I care.

KIT: My mother says there's something wrong with you playing with someone my age. She says why haven't you got friends your own age. People your own age know there's something funny about you. She says you're a bad influence. She says she's going to speak to your mother. (*Angie twists Kit's arm till she cries out.*)

ANGIE: Say you're a liar.

KIT: She said it not me.

ANGIE: Say you eat shit.

KIT: You can't make me. (*Angie lets go.*)

ANGIE: I don't care anyway. I'm leaving.

KIT: Go on then.

ANGIE: You'll all wake up one morning and find I've gone.

KIT: Go on then.

ANGIE: You'll wake up one morning and find I've gone.

KIT: Good.

ANGIE: I'm not telling you when.

KIT: Go on then.

ANGIE: I'm sorry I hurt you.

KIT: I'm tired.

ANGIE: Do you like me?

KIT: I don't know.

ANGIE: You do like me.

KIT: I'm going home. (*She gets up.*)

ANGIE: No you're not.

KIT: I'm tired.

ANGIE: She'll see you.

KIT: She'll give me a chocolate biscuit.

ANGIE: Kitty.

KIT: Tell me where you're going.

ANGIE: Sit down.

KIT (*sitting down again*): Go on then.

ANGIE: Swear?

KIT: Swear.

ANGIE: I'm going to London. To see my aunt.
KIT: And what?
ANGIE: That's it.
KIT: I see my aunt all the time.
ANGIE: I don't see my aunt.
KIT: What's so special?
ANGIE: It is special. She's special.
KIT: Why?
ANGIE: She is.
KIT: Why?
ANGIE: She is.
KIT: Why?
ANGIE: My mother hates her.
KIT: Why?
ANGIE: Because she does.
KIT: Perhaps she's not very nice.
ANGIE: She is nice.
KIT: How do you know?
ANGIE: Because I know her.
KIT: You said you never see her.
ANGIE: I saw her last year. You saw her.
KIT: Did I?
ANGIE: Never mind.
KIT: I remember her. That aunt. What's so special?
ANGIE: She gets people jobs.
KIT: What's so special?
ANGIE: I think I'm my aunt's child. I think my mother's really my aunt.
KIT: Why?
ANGIE: Because she goes to America, now shut up.
KIT: I've been to London.
ANGIE: Now give us a cuddle and shut up because I'm sick.
KIT: You're sitting on my arm.

(*They curl up in each other's arms. Silence. Joyce comes out of the house and comes up to them quietly.*)

JOYCE: Come on.
KIT: Oh hello.
JOYCE: Time you went home.
KIT: We want to go to the Odeon.
JOYCE: What time?
KIT: Don't know.
JOYCE: What's on?
KIT: Don't know.
JOYCE: Don't know much do you?
KIT: That all right then?
JOYCE: Angie's got to clean her room first.
ANGIE: No I don't.
JOYCE: Yes you do, it's a pigsty.
ANGIE: Well I'm not.
JOYCE: Then you're not going. I don't care.
ANGIE: Well I am going.
JOYCE: You've no money, have you?
ANGIE: Kit's paying anyway.

JOYCE: No she's not.
KIT: I'll help you with your room.
JOYCE: That's nice.
ANGIE: No you won't. You wait here.
KIT: Hurry then.
ANGIE: I'm not hurrying. You just wait. (*Angie goes slowly into the house. Silence.*)
JOYCE: I don't know. (*Silence.*) How's school then?
KIT: All right.
JOYCE: What are you now? Third year?
KIT: Second year.
JOYCE: Your mum says you're good at English. (*Silence.*) Maybe Angie should've stayed on.
KIT: She didn't like it.
JOYCE: I didn't like it. And look at me. If your face fits at school it's going to fit other places too. It wouldn't make no difference to Angie. She's not going to get a job when jobs are hard to get. I'd be sorry for anyone in charge of her. She'd better get married. I don't know who'd have her, mind. She's one of those girls might never leave home. What do you want to be when you grow up, Kit?
KIT: Physicist.
JOYCE: What?
KIT: Nuclear physicist.
JOYCE: Whatever for?
KIT: I could, I'm clever.
JOYCE: I know you're clever, pet. (*Silence.*) I'll make a cup of tea. (*Silence.*) Looks like it's going to rain. (*Silence.*) Don't you have friends your own age?
KIT: Yes.
JOYCE: Well then.
KIT: I'm old for my age.
JOYCE: And Angie's simple is she? She's not simple.
KIT: I love Angie.
JOYCE: She's clever in her own way.
KIT: You can't stop me.
JOYCE: I don't want to.
KIT: You can't, so.
JOYCE: Don't be cheeky, Kitty. She's always kind to little children.
KIT: She's coming so you better leave me alone.

(*Angie comes out. She has changed into an old best dress, slightly small for her.*)

JOYCE: What you put that on for? Have you done your room? You can't clean you room in that.
ANGIE: I looked in the cupboard and it was there.
JOYCE: Of course it was there, it's meant to be there. Is that why it was a surprise, finding something in the right place? I should think she's surprised, wouldn't you, Kit, to find something in her room in the right place.
ANGIE: I decided to wear it.
JOYCE: Not today, why? To clean your room? You're

not going to the pictures till you've done your room. You can put your dress on after if you like. (*Angie picks up a brick.*) Have you done your room? You're not getting out of it, you know.

KIT: Angie, let's go.

JOYCE: She's not going till she's done her room.

KIT: It's starting to rain.

JOYCE: Come on, come on then. Hurry and do your room, Angie, and then you can go to the cinema with Kit. Oh it's wet, come on. We'll look up the time in the paper. Does your mother know, Kit, it's going to be a late night for you, isn't it? Hurry up, Angie. You'll spoil your dress. You make me sick. (*Joyce and Kit run into the house. Angie stays where she is. There is the sound of rain. Kit comes out of the house.*)

KIT (*shouting*): Angie. Angie, come on, you'll get wet. (*She comes back to Angie.*)

ANGIE: I put on this dress to kill my mother.

KIT: I suppose you thought you'd do it with a brick.

ANGIE: You can kill people with a brick. (*She puts the brick down.*)

KIT: Well you didn't, so.

ACT II • *Scene 1*

(*"Top Girls" Employment Agency. Monday morning. There are three desks in the main office and a separate small interviewing area. The lights come up in the main office on Win and Nell who have just arrived for work.*)

NELL: Coffee coffee coffee coffee / coffee.

WIN: The roses were smashing. / Mermaid.

NELL: Ohhh.

WIN: Iceberg. He taught me all their names. (*Nell has some coffee now.*)

NELL: Ah. Now then.

WIN: He has one of the finest rose gardens in West Sussex. He exhibits.

NELL: He what?

WIN: His wife was visiting her mother. It was like living together.

NELL: Crafty, you never said.

WIN: He rang on Saturday morning.

NELL: Lucky you were free.

WIN: That's what I told him.

NELL: Did you hell.

WIN: Have you ever seen a really beautiful rose garden?

NELL: I don't like flowers. / I like swimming pools.

WIN: Marilyn. Esther's Baby. They're all called after birds.

NELL: Our friend's late. Celebrating all weekend I bet you.

WIN: I'd call a rose Elvis. Or John Conteh.

NELL: Is Howard in yet?

WIN: If he is he'll be bleeping us with a problem.

NELL: Howard can just hang on to himself.

WIN: Howard's really cut up.

NELL: Howard thinks because he's a fella the job was his as of right. Our Marlene's got far more balls than Howard and that's that.

WIN: Poor little bugger.

NELL: He'll live.

WIN: He'll move on.

NELL: I wouldn't mind a change of air myself.

WIN: Serious?

NELL: I've never been a staying-put lady. Pastures new.

WIN: So who's the pirate?

NELL: There's nothing definite.

WIN: Inquiries?

NELL: There's always inquiries. I'd think I'd got bad breath if there stopped being inquiries. Most of them can't afford me. Or you.

WIN: I'm all right for the time being. Unless I go to Australia.

NELL: There's not a lot of room upward.

WIN: Marlene's filled it up.

NELL: Good luck to her. Unless there's some prospects moneywise.

WIN: You can but ask.

NELL: Can always but ask.

WIN: So what have we got? I've got a Mr. Holden I saw last week.

NELL: Any use?

WIN: Pushy. Bit of a cowboy.

NELL: Goodlooker?

WIN: Good dresser.

NELL: High flyer?

WIN: That's his general idea certainly but I'm not sure he's got it up there.

NELL: Prestel wants six flyers and I've only seen two and a half.

WIN: He's making a bomb on the road but he thinks it's time for an office. I sent him to IBM but he didn't get it.

NELL: Prestel's on the road.

WIN: He's not overbright.

NELL: Can he handle an office?

WIN: Provided his secretary can punctuate he should go far.

NELL: Bear Prestel in mind then, I might put my head round the door. I've got that poor little nerd I should never had said I could help. Tender heart me.

WIN: Tender like old boots. How old?

NELL: Yes well forty-five.

WIN: Say no more.

NELL: He knows his place, he's not after calling himself a manager, he's just a poor little bod wants a better commission and a bit of sunshine.

WIN: Don't we all.

NELL: He's just got to relocate. He's got a bungalow in Dymchurch.

WIN: And his wife says.

NELL: The lady wife wouldn't care to relocate. She's going through the change.

WIN: It's his funeral, don't waste your time.

NELL: I don't waste a lot.

WIN: Good weekend you?

NELL: You could say.

WIN: Which one?

NELL: One Friday, one Saturday.

WIN: Aye — aye.

NELL: Sunday night I watched telly.

WIN: Which of them do you like best really?

NELL: Sunday was best, I like the Ovaltine.

WIN: Holden, Barker, Gardner, Duke.

NELL: I've a lady here thinks she can sell.

WIN: Taking her on?

NELL: She's had some jobs.

WIN: Services?

NELL: No, quite heavy stuff, electric.

WIN: Tough bird like us.

NELL: We could do with a few more here.

WIN: There's nothing going here.

NELL: No but I always want the tough ones when I see them. Hang on to them.

WIN: I think we're plenty.

NELL: Derek asked me to marry him again.

WIN: He doesn't know when he's beaten.

NELL: I told him I'm not going to play house, not even in Ascot.

WIN: Mind you, you could play house.

NELL: If I chose to play house I would play house ace.

WIN: You could marry him and go on working.

NELL: I could go on working and not marry him.

(*Marlene arrives.*)

MARLENE: Morning ladies. (*Win and Nell cheer and whistle.*) Mind my head.

NELL: Coffee coffee coffee.

WIN: We're tactfully not mentioning you're late.

MARLENE: Fucking tube.

WIN: We've heard that one.

NELL: We've used that one.

WIN: It's the top executive doesn't come in as early as the poor working girl.

MARLENE: Pass the sugar and shut your face, pet.

WIN: Well I'm delighted.

NELL: Howard's looking sick.

WIN: Howard is sick. He's got ulcers and heart. He told me.

NELL: He'll have to stop then, won't he?

WIN: Stop what?

NELL: Smoking, drinking, shouting. Working.

WIN: Well, working.

NELL: We're just looking through the day.

MARLENE: I'm doing some of Pam's ladies. They've been piling up while she's away.

NELL: Half a dozen little girls and an arts graduate who can't type.

WIN: I spent the whole weekend at his place in Sussex.

NELL: She fancies his rose garden.

WIN: I had to lie down in the back of the car so the neighbors wouldn't see me go in.

NELL: You're kidding.

WIN: It was funny.

NELL: Fuck that for a joke.

WIN: It was funny.

MARLENE: Anyway they'd see you in the garden.

WIN: The garden has extremely high walls.

NELL: I think I'll tell the wife.

WIN: Like hell.

NELL: She might leave him and you could have the rose garden.

WIN: The minute it's not a secret I'm out on my ear.

NELL: Don't know why you bother.

WIN: Bit of fun.

NELL: I think it's time you went to Australia.

WIN: I think it's pushy Mr. Holden time.

NELL: If you've any really pretty bastards, Marlene, I want some for Prestel.

MARLENE: I might have one this afternoon. This morning it's all Pam's secretarial.

NELL: Not long now and you'll be upstairs watching over us all.

MARLENE: Do you feel bad about it?

NELL: I don't like coming second.

MARLENE: Who does?

WIN: We'd rather it was you than Howard. We're glad for you, aren't we, Nell?

NELL: Oh yes. Aces.

(*Louise enters the interviewing area. The lights crossfade to Win and Louise in the interviewing area. Nell exits.*)

WIN: Now, Louise, hello, I have your details here. You've been very loyal to the one job I see.

LOUISE: Yes I have.

WIN: Twenty-one years is a long time in one place.

LOUISE: I feel it is. I feel it's time to move on.

WIN: And you are what age now?

LOUISE: I'm in my early forties.

WIN: Exactly?

LOUISE: Forty-six.

WIN: It's not necessarily a handicap, well it is of

course we have to face that, but it's not necessarily a disabling handicap, experience does count for something.

LOUISE: I hope so.

WIN: Now between ourselves is there any trouble, any reason why you're leaving that wouldn't appear on the form?

LOUISE: Nothing like that.

WIN: Like what?

LOUISE: Nothing at all.

WIN: No long-term understandings come to a sudden end, making for an insupportable atmosphere?

LOUISE: I've always completely avoided anything like that at all.

WIN: No personality clashes with your immediate superiors or inferiors?

LOUISE: I've always taken care to get on very well with everyone.

WIN: I only ask because it can affect the reference and it also affects your motivation, I want to be quite clear why you're moving on. So I take it the job itself no longer satisfies you. Is it the money?

LOUISE: It's partly the money. It's not so much the money.

WIN: Nine thousand is very respectable. Have you dependents?

LOUISE: No, no dependents. My mother died.

WIN: So why are you making a change?

LOUISE: Other people make changes.

WIN: But why are you, now, after spending most of your life in the one place?

LOUISE: There you are, I've lived for that company, I've given my life really you could say because I haven't had a great deal of social life, I've worked in the evenings. I haven't had office entanglements for the very reason you just mentioned and if you are committed to your work you don't move in many other circles. I had management status from the age of twenty-seven and you'll appreciate what that means. I've built up a department. And there it is, it works extremely well, and I feel I'm stuck there. I've spent twenty years in middle management. I've seen young men who I trained go on, in my own company or elsewhere, to higher things. Nobody notices me, I don't expect it, I don't attract attention by making mistakes, everybody takes it for granted that my work is perfect. They will notice me when I go, they will be sorry I think to lose me, they will offer me more money of course, I will refuse. They will see when I've gone what I was doing for them.

WIN: If they offer you more money you won't stay?

LOUISE: No I won't.

WIN: Are you the only woman?

LOUISE: Apart from the girls of course, yes. There

was one, she was my assistant, it was the only time I took on a young woman assistant, I always had my doubts. I don't care greatly for working with women, I think I pass as a man at work. But I did take on this young woman, her qualifications were excellent, and she did well, she got a department of her own, and left the company for a competitor where she's now on the board and good luck to her. She has a different style, she's a new kind of attractive well dressed — I don't mean I don't dress properly. But there is a kind of woman who is thirty now who grew up in a different climate. They are not so careful. They take themselves for granted. I have had to justify my existence every minute, and I have done so, I have proved — well.

WIN: Let's face it, vacancies are ones where you'll be in competition with younger men. And there are companies that will value your experience enough that you'll be in with a chance. There are also fields that are easier for a woman, there is a cosmetic company here where your experience might be relevant. It's eight and a half, I don't know if that appeals.

LOUISE: I've proved I can earn money. It's more important to get away. I feel it's now or never. I sometimes / think

WIN: You shouldn't talk too much at an interview.

LOUISE: I don't. I don't normally talk about myself. I know very well how to handle myself in an office situation. I only talk to you because it seems to me this is different, it's your job to understand me, surely. You asked the questions.

WIN: I think I understand you sufficiently.

LOUISE: Well good, that's good.

WIN: Do you drink?

LOUISE: Certainly not. I'm not a teetotaler, I think that's very suspect, it's seen as being an alcoholic if you're teetotal. What do you mean? I don't drink. Why?

WIN: I drink.

LOUISE: I don't.

WIN: Good for you.

(*The lights crossfade to the main office with Marlene sitting at her desk. Win and Louise exit. Angie arrives in the main office.*)

ANGIE: Hello.

MARLENE: Have you an appointment?

ANGIE: It's me. I've come.

MARLENE: What? It's not Angie?

ANGIE: It was hard to find this place. I got lost.

MARLENE: How did you get past the receptionist? The girl on the desk, didn't she try to stop you?

ANGIE: What desk?

MARLENE: Never mind.

ANGIE: I just walked in. I was looking for you.

MARLENE: Well you found me.

ANGIE: Yes.

MARLENE: So where's your mum? Are you up in town for the day?

ANGIE: Not really.

MARLENE: Sit down. Do you feel all right?

ANGIE: Yes thank you.

MARLENE: So where's Joyce?

ANGIE: She's at home.

MARLENE: Did you come up on a school trip then?

ANGIE: I've left school.

MARLENE: Did you come up with a friend?

ANGIE: No. There's just me.

MARLENE: You came up by yourself, that's fun. What have you been doing? Shopping? Tower of London?

ANGIE: No, I just come here. I come to you.

MARLENE: That's very nice of you to think of paying your aunty a visit. There's not many nieces make that the first port of call. Would you like a cup of coffee?

ANGIE: No thank you.

MARLENE: Tea, orange?

ANGIE: No thank you.

MARLENE: Do you feel all right?

ANGIE: Yes thank you.

MARLENE: Are you tired from the journey?

ANGIE: Yes, I'm tired from the journey.

MARLENE: You sit there for a bit then. How's Joyce?

ANGIE: She's all right.

MARLENE: Same as ever.

ANGIE: Oh yes.

MARLENE: Unfortunately you've picked a day when I'm rather busy, if there's ever a day when I'm not, or I'd take you out to lunch and we'd go to Madame Tussaud's. We could go shopping. What time do you have to be back? Have you got a day return?

ANGIE: No.

MARLENE: So what train are you going back on?

ANGIE: I came on the bus.

MARLENE: So what bus are you going back on? Are you staying the night?

ANGIE: Yes.

MARLENE: Who are you staying with? Do you want me to put you up for the night, is that it?

ANGIE: Yes please.

MARLENE: I haven't got a spare bed.

ANGIE: I can sleep on the floor.

MARLENE: You can sleep on the sofa.

ANGIE: Yes please.

MARLENE: I do think Joyce might have phoned me. It's like her.

ANGIE: This is where you work is it?

MARLENE: It's where I have been working the last two years but I'm going to move into another office.

ANGIE: It's lovely.

MARLENE: My new office is nicer than this. There's just the one big desk in it for me.

ANGIE: Can I see it?

MARLENE: Not now, no, there's someone else in it now. But he's leaving at the end of next week and I'm going to do his job.

ANGIE: Is that good?

MARLENE: Yes, it's very good.

ANGIE: Are you going to be in charge?

MARLENE: Yes I am.

ANGIE: I knew you would be.

MARLENE: How did you know?

ANGIE: I knew you'd be in charge of everything.

MARLENE: Not quite everything.

ANGIE: You will be.

MARLENE: Well we'll see.

ANGIE: Can I see it next week then?

MARLENE: Will you still be here next week?

ANGIE: Yes.

MARLENE: Don't you have to go home?

ANGIE: No.

MARLENE: Why not?

ANGIE: It's all right.

MARLENE: Is it all right?

ANGIE: Yes, don't worry about it.

MARLENE: Does Joyce know where you are?

ANGIE: Yes of course she does.

MARLENE: Well does she?

ANGIE: Don't worry about it.

MARLENE: How long are you planning to stay with me then?

ANGIE: You know when you came to see us last year?

MARLENE: Yes, that was nice wasn't it.

ANGIE: That was the best day of my whole life.

MARLENE: So how long are you planning to stay?

ANGIE: Don't you want me?

MARLENE: Yes yes, I just wondered.

ANGIE: I won't stay if you don't want me.

MARLENE: No, of course you can stay.

ANGIE: I'll sleep on the floor. I won't be any bother.

MARLENE: Don't get upset.

ANGIE: I'm not, I'm not. Don't worry about it.

(*Mrs. Kidd comes in.*)

MRS. KIDD: Excuse me.

MARLENE: Yes.

MRS. KIDD: Excuse me.

MARLENE: Can I help you?

MRS. KIDD: Excuse me bursting in on you like this but I have to talk to you.

MARLENE: I am engaged at the moment. / If you could go to reception —

MRS. KIDD: I'm Rosemary Kidd, Howard's wife, you don't recognize me but we did meet, I remember you of course / but you wouldn't —

MARLENE: Yes of course, Mrs. Kidd, I'm sorry, we did meet. Howard's about somewhere I expect, have you looked in his office?

MRS. KIDD: Howard's not about, no. I'm afraid it's you I've come to see if I could have a minute or two.

MARLENE: I do have an appointment in five minutes.

MRS. KIDD: This won't take five minutes. I'm very sorry. It is a matter of some urgency.

MARLENE: Well of course. What can I do for you?

MRS. KIDD: I just wanted a chat, an informal chat. It's not something I can simply — I'm sorry if I'm interrupting your work. I know office work isn't like housework / which is all interruptions.

MARLENE: No no, this is my niece. Angie. Mrs. Kidd.

MRS. KIDD: Very pleased to meet you.

ANGIE: Very well thank you.

MRS. KIDD: Howard's not in today.

MARLENE: Isn't he?

MRS. KIDD: He's feeling poorly.

MARLENE: I didn't know. I'm sorry to hear that.

MRS. KIDD: The fact is he's in a state of shock. About what's happened.

MARLENE: What has happened?

MRS. KIDD: You should know if anyone. I'm referring to you been appointed managing director instead of Howard. He hasn't been at all well all weekend. He hasn't slept for three nights. I haven't slept.

MARLENE: I'm sorry to hear that, Mrs. Kidd. Has he thought of taking sleeping pills?

MRS. KIDD: It's very hard when someone has worked all these years.

MARLENE: Business life is full of little setbacks. I'm sure Howard knows that. He'll bounce back in a day or two. We all bounce back.

MRS. KIDD: If you could see him you'd know what I'm talking about. What's it going to do to him working for a woman? I think if it was a man he'd get over it as something normal.

MARLENE: I think he's going to have to get over it.

MRS. KIDD: It's me that bears the brunt. I'm not the one that's been promoted. I put him first every inch of the way. And now what do I get? You women this, you women that. It's not my fault. You're going to have to be very careful how you handle him. He's very hurt.

MARLENE: Naturally I'll be tactful and pleasant to him, you don't start pushing someone around. I'll consult him over any decisions affecting his department. But that's no different, Mrs. Kidd, from any of my other colleagues.

MRS. KIDD: I think it is different, because he's a man.

MARLENE: I'm not quite sure why you came to see me.

MRS. KIDD: I had to do something.

MARLENE: Well you've done it, you've seen me. I think that's probably all we've time for. I'm sorry he's been taking it out on you. He really is a shit, Howard.

MRS. KIDD: But he's got a family to support. He's got three children. It's only fair.

MARLENE: Are you suggesting I give up the job to him then?

MRS. KIDD: It had crossed my mind if you were unavailable after all for some reason, he would be the natural second choice I think, don't you? I'm not asking.

MARLENE: Good.

MRS. KIDD: You mustn't tell him I came. He's very proud.

MARLENE: If he doesn't like what's happening here he can go and work somewhere else.

MRS. KIDD: Is that a threat?

MARLENE: I'm sorry but I do have some work to do.

MRS. KIDD: It's not that easy, a man of Howard's age. You don't care. I thought he was going too far but he's right. You're one of these ballbreakers, / that's what you

MARLENE: I'm sorry but I do have some work to do.

MRS. KIDD: are. You'll end up miserable and lonely. You're not natural.

MARLENE: Could you please piss off?

MRS. KIDD: I thought if I saw you at least I'd be doing something. (*Mrs. Kidd goes.*)

MARLENE: I've got to go and do some work now. Will you come back later?

ANGIE: I think you were wonderful.

MARLENE: I've got to go and do some work now.

ANGIE: You told her to piss off.

MARLENE: Will you come back later?

ANGIE: Can't I stay here?

MARLENE: Don't you want to go sightseeing?

ANGIE: I'd rather stay here.

MARLENE: You can stay here I suppose, if it's not boring.

ANGIE: It's where I most want to be in the world.

MARLENE: I'll see you later then.

(*Marlene goes. Shona and Nell enter the interviewing area. Angie sits at Win's desk. The lights crossfade to Nell and Shona in the interviewing area.*)

NELL: Is this right? You are Shona?

SHONA: Yeh.

NELL: It says here you're twenty-nine.

SHONA: Yeh.

NELL: Too many late nights, me. So you've been where you are for four years, Shona, you're earn-

ing six basic and three commission. So what's the
problem?

SHONA: No problem.

NELL: Why do you want a change?

SHONA: Just a change.

NELL: Change of product, change of area?

SHONA: Both.

NELL: But you're happy on the road?

SHONA: I like driving.

NELL: You're not after management status?

SHONA: I would like management status.

NELL: You'd be interested in titular management status but not come off the road?

SHONA: I want to be on the road, yeh.

NELL: So how many calls have you been making a
day?

SHONA: Six.

NELL: And what proportion of those are successful?

SHONA: Six.

NELL: That's hard to believe.

SHONA: Four.

NELL: You find it easy to get the initial interest do
you?

SHONA: Oh yeh, I get plenty of initial interest.

NELL: And what about closing?

SHONA: I close, don't I?

NELL: Because that's what an employer is going to
have doubts about with a lady as I needn't tell you,
whether she's got the guts to push through to a
closing situation. They think we're too nice. They
think we listen to the buyer's doubts. They think
we consider his needs and his feelings.

SHONA: I never consider people's feelings.

NELL: I was selling for six years, I can sell anything,
I've sold in three continents, and I'm jolly as they
come but I'm not very nice.

SHONA: I'm not very nice.

NELL: What sort of time do you have on the road
with the other reps? Get on all right? Handle the
chat?

SHONA: I get on. Keep myself to myself.

NELL: Fairly much of a loner are you?

SHONA: Sometimes.

NELL: So what field are you interested in?

SHONA: Computers.

NELL: That's a top field as you know and you'll be up
against some very slick fellas there, there's some
very pretty boys in computers, it's an American-
style field.

SHONA: That's why I want to do it.

NELL: Video systems appeal? That's a high-flying situation.

SHONA: Video systems appeal OK.

NELL: Because Prestel have half a dozen vacancies
I'm looking to fill at the moment. We're talking in

the area of ten to fifteen thousand here and up-
wards.

SHONA: Sounds OK.

NELL: I've half a mind to go for it myself. But it's
good money here if you've got the top clients.
Could you fancy it do you think?

SHONA: Work here?

NELL: I'm not in a position to offer, there's nothing officially going just now, but we're always on the
lookout. There's not that many of us. We could
keep in touch.

SHONA: I like driving.

NELL: So the Prestel appeals.

SHONA: Yeh.

NELL: What about ties?

SHONA: No ties.

NELL: So relocation wouldn't be a problem.

SHONA: No problem.

NELL: So just fill me in a bit more could you about
what you've been doing.

SHONA: What I've been doing. It's all down there.

NELL: The bare facts are down here but I've got to
present you to an employer.

SHONA: I'm twenty-nine years old.

NELL: So it says here.

SHONA: We look young. Youngness runs in the family
in our family.

NELL: So just describe your present job for me.

SHONA: My present job at present. I have a car. I have
a Porsche. I go up the M1 a lot. Burn up the M1 a
lot. Straight up the M1 in the fast lane to where
the clients are, Staffordshire, Yorkshire, I do a lot
in Yorkshire. I'm selling electric things. Like dish-
washers, washing machines, stainless steel tubs
are a feature and the reliability of the program. After sales service, we offer a very good after sales
service, spare parts, plenty of spare parts. And
fridges, I sell a lot of fridges specially in the summer. People want to buy fridges in the summer because of the heat melting the butter and you get fed
up standing the milk in a basin of cold water with
a cloth over, stands to reason people don't want to
do that in this day and age. So I sell a lot of them.
Big ones with big freezers. Big freezers. And I stay
in hotels at night when I'm away from home. On
my expense account. I stay in various hotels. They
know me, the ones I go to. I check in, have a bath,
have a shower. Then I go down to the bar, have a
gin and tonic, have a chat. Then I go into the dining room and have dinner. I usually have fillet
steak and mushrooms, I like mushrooms. I like
smoked salmon very much. I like having a salad on
the side. Green salad. I don't like tomatoes.

NELL: Christ what a waste of time.

SHONA: Beg your pardon?

NELL: Not a word of this is true, is it?
SHONA: How do you mean?
NELL: You just filled in the form with a pack of lies.
SHONA: Not exactly.
NELL: How old are you?
SHONA: Twenty-nine.
NELL: Nineteen?
SHONA: Twenty-one.
NELL: And what jobs have you done? Have you done any?
SHONA: I could though, I bet you.

(*The lights crossfade to the main office with Angie sitting as before. Win comes in to the main office. Shona and Nell exit.*)

WIN: Who's sitting in my chair?
ANGIE: What? Sorry.
WIN: Who's been eating my porridge?
ANGIE: What?
WIN: It's all right, I saw Marlene. Angie, isn't it? I'm Win. And I'm not going out for lunch because I'm knackered. I'm going to set me down here and have a yogurt. Do you like yogurt?
ANGIE: No.
WIN: That's good because I've only got one. Are you hungry?
ANGIE: No.
WIN: There's a café on the corner.
ANGIE: No thank you. Do you work here?
WIN: How did you guess?
ANGIE: Because you look as if you might work here and you're sitting at the desk. Have you always worked here?
WIN: No I was headhunted. That means I was working for another outfit like this and this lot came and offered me more money. I broke my contract, there was a hell of a stink. There's not many top ladies about. Your aunty's a smashing bird.
ANGIE: Yes I know.
MARLENE: Fan are you? Fan of your aunty's?
ANGIE: Do you think I could work here?
WIN: Not at the moment.
ANGIE: How do I start?
WIN: What can you do?
ANGIE: I don't know. Nothing.
WIN: Type?
ANGIE: Not very well. The letters jump up when I do capitals. I was going to do a CSE° in commerce but I didn't.
WIN: What have you got?
ANGIE: What?
WIN: CSE's, O's.

CSE: Certificate of Secondary Education.

ANGIE: Nothing, none of that. Did you do all that?
WIN: Oh yes, all that, and a science degree funnily enough. I started out doing medical research but there's no money in it. I thought I'd go abroad. Did you know they sell Coca Cola in Russia and Pepsi-Cola in China? You don't have to be qualified as much as you might think. Men are awful bullshitters, they like to make out jobs are harder than they are. Any job I ever did I started doing it better than the rest of the crowd and they didn't like it. So I'd get unpopular and I'd have a drink to cheer myself up. I lived with a fella and supported him for four years, he couldn't get work. After that I went to California. I like the sunshine. Americans know how to live. This country's too slow. Then I went to Mexico, still in sales, but it's no country for a single lady. I came home, went bonkers for a bit, thought I was five different people, got over that all right, the psychiatrist said I was perfectly sane and highly intelligent. Got married in a moment of weakness and he's inside now, he's been inside four years, and I've not been to see him too much this last year. I like this better than sales, I'm not really that aggressive. I started thinking sales was a good job if you want to meet people, but you're meeting people that don't want to meet you. It's no good if you like being liked. Here your clients want to meet you because you're the one doing them some good. They hope. (*Angie has fallen asleep. Nell comes in.*)
NELL: You're talking to yourself, sunshine.
WIN: So what's new?
NELL: Who is this?
WIN: Marlene's little niece.
NELL: What's she got, brother, sister? She never talks about her family.
WIN: I was telling her my life story.
NELL: Violins?
WIN: No, success story.
NELL.: You've heard Howard's had a heart attack?
WIN: No, when?
NELL: I heard just now. He hadn't come in, he was at home, he's gone to hospital. He's not dead. His wife was here, she rushed off in a cab.
WIN: Too much butter, too much smoke. We must send him some flowers. (*Marlene comes in.*) You've heard about Howard?
MARLENE: Poor sod.
NELL: Lucky he didn't get the job if that's what his health's like.
MARLENE: Is she asleep?
WIN: She wants to work here.
MARLENE: Packer in Tesco more like.
WIN: She's a nice kid. Isn't she?
MARLENE: She's a bit thick. She's a bit funny.

WIN: She thinks you're wonderful.

MARLENE: She's not going to make it.

Scene II

(Joyce's kitchen. Sunday evening, a year earlier. The lights come up on Joyce, Angie, and Marlene. Marlene is taking presents out of bright carrier bag. Angie has already opened a box of chocolates.)

MARLENE: Just a few little things. / I've

JOYCE: There's no need.

MARLENE: no memory for birthdays have I, and Christmas seems to slip by. So I think I owe Angie a few presents.

JOYCE: What do you say?

ANGIE: Thank you very much. Thank you very much, Aunty Marlene. (*She opens a present. It is the dress from Act I, new.*) Oh look, Mum, isn't it lovely?

MARLENE: I don't know if it's the right size. She's grown up since I saw her. / I knew she was always

ANGIE: Isn't it lovely?

MARLENE: tall for her age.

JOYCE: She's a big lump.

MARLENE: Hold it up, Angie, let's see.

ANGIE: I'll put it on, shall I?

MARLENE: Yes, try it on.

JOYCE: Go on to your room then, we don't want / a strip show thank you.

ANGIE: Of course I'm going to my room, what do you think. Look, Mum, here's something for you. Open it, go on. What is it? Can I open it for you?

JOYCE: Yes, you open it, pet.

ANGIE: Don't you want to open it yourself? / Go on.

JOYCE: I don't mind, you can do it.

ANGIE: It's something hard. It's — what is it? A bottle. Drink is it? No, it's what? Perfume, look. What a lot. Open it, look, let's smell it. Oh it's strong. It's lovely. Put it on me. How do you do it? Put it on me.

JOYCE: You're too young.

ANGIE: I can play wearing it like dressing up.

JOYCE: And you're too old for that. Here, give it here, I'll do it, you'll tip the whole bottle over yourself / and we'll have you smelling all summer.

ANGIE: Put it on you. Do I smell? Put it on Aunty too. Put it on Aunty too. Let's all smell.

MARLENE: I didn't know what you'd like.

JOYCE: There's no danger I'd have it already, / that's one thing.

ANGIE: Now we all smell the same.

MARLENE: It's a bit of nonsense.

JOYCE: It's very kind of you Marlene, you shouldn't.

ANGIE: Now I'll put on the dress and then we'll see. (*Angie goes.*)

JOYCE: You've caught me on the hop with the place in the mess. / If you'd let me

MARLENE: That doesn't matter.

JOYCE: know you was coming I'd have got something in to eat. We had our dinner dinnertime. We're just going to have a cup of tea. You could have an egg.

MARLENE: No, I'm not hungry. Tea's fine.

JOYCE: I don't expect you take sugar.

MARLENE: Why not?

JOYCE: You take care of yourself.

MARLENE: How do you mean you didn't know I was coming?

JOYCE: You could have written. I know we're not on the phone but we're not completely in the dark ages, / we do have a postman.

MARLENE: But you asked me to come.

JOYCE: How did I ask you to come?

MARLENE: Angie said when she phoned up.

JOYCE: Angie phoned up, did she.

MARLENE: Was it just Angie's idea?

JOYCE: What did she say?

MARLENE: She said you wanted me to come and see you. / It was a couple of

JOYCE: Ha.

MARLENE: weeks ago. How was I to know that's a ridiculous idea? My diary's always full a couple of weeks ahead so we fixed it for this weekend. I was meant to get here earlier but I was held up. She gave me messages from you.

JOYCE: Didn't you wonder why I didn't phone you myself?

MARLENE: She said you didn't like using the phone. You're shy on the phone and can't use it. I don't know what you're like, do I?

JOYCE: Are there people who can't use the phone?

MARLENE: I expect so.

JOYCE: I haven't met any.

MARLENE: Why should I think she was lying?

JOYCE: Because she's like what she's like.

MARLENE: How do I know / what she's like?

JOYCE: It's not my fault you don't know what she's like. You never come and see her.

MARLENE: Well I have now / and you don't seem over the moon.*

JOYCE: Good. *Well I'd have got a cake if she'd told me. (*Pause.*)

MARLENE: I did wonder why you wanted to see me.

JOYCE: I didn't want to see you.

MARLENE: Yes, I know. Shall I go?

JOYCE: I don't mind seeing you.

MARLENE: Great, I feel really welcome.

JOYCE: You can come and see Angie any time you like, I'm not stopping you. / You

MARLENE: Ta ever so.

JOYCE: know where we are. You're the one went away,

not me. I'm right here where I was. And will be a few years yet I shouldn't wonder.

MARLENE: All right. All right. (*Joyce gives Marlene a cup of tea.*)

JOYCE: Tea.

MARLENE: Sugar? (*Joyce passes Marlene the sugar.*) It's very quiet down here.

JOYCE: I expect you'd notice it.

MARLENE: The air smells different too.

JOYCE: That's the scent.

MARLENE: No, I mean walking down the lane.

JOYCE: What sort of air you get in London then?

(*Angie comes in, wearing the dress. It fits.*)

MARLENE: Oh, very pretty. / You do look pretty, Angie.

JOYCE: That fits all right.

MARLENE: Do you like the color?

ANGIE: Beautiful. Beautiful.

JOYCE: You better take it off, / you'll get it dirty.

ANGIE: I want to wear it. I want to wear it.

MARLENE: It is for wearing after all. You can't just hang it up and look at it.

ANGIE: I love it.

JOYCE: Well if you must you must.

ANGIE: If someone asks me what's my favorite color I'll tell them it's this. Thank you very much Aunty Marlene.

MARLENE: You didn't tell your mum you asked me down.

ANGIE: I wanted it to be a surprise.

JOYCE: I'll give you a surprise / one of these days.

ANGIE: I thought you'd like to see her. She hasn't been here since I was nine. People do see their aunts.

MARLENE: Is it that long? Doesn't time fly.

ANGIE: I wanted to.

JOYCE: I'm not cross.

ANGIE: Are you glad?

JOYCE: I smell nicer anyhow, don't I?

(*Kit comes in without saying anything, as if she lived there.*)

MARLENE: I think it was a good idea, Angie, about time. We are sisters after all. It's a pity to let that go.

JOYCE: This is Kitty, / who lives up the road. This is Angie's Aunty Marlene.

KIT: What's that?

ANGIE: It's a present. Do you like it?

KIT: It's all right. / Are you coming out?*

MARLENE: Hello, Kitty.

ANGIE: *No.

KIT: What's that smell?

ANGIE: It's a present.

KIT: It's horrible. Come on.*

MARLENE: Have a chocolate.

ANGIE: *No, I'm busy.

KIT: Coming out later?

ANGIE: No.

KIT (*to Marlene*): Hello. (*Kit goes without a chocolate.*)

JOYCE: She's a little girl Angie sometimes plays with because she's the only child lives really close. She's like a little sister to her really. Angie's good with little children.

MARLENE: Do you want to work with children, Angie? / Be a teacher or a nursery nurse?

JOYCE: I don't think she's ever thought of it.

MARLENE: What do you want to do?

JOYCE: She hasn't an idea in her head what she wants to do. / Lucky to get anything.

MARLENE: Angie?

JOYCE: She's not clever like you. (*Pause.*)

MARLENE: I'm not clever, just pushy.

JOYCE: True enough. (*Marlene takes a bottle of whiskey out of the bag.*) I don't drink spirits.

ANGIE: You do at Christmas.

JOYCE: It's not Christmas, is it?

ANGIE: It's better than Christmas.

MARLENE: Glasses?

JOYCE: Just a small one then.

MARLENE: Do you want some, Angie?

ANGIE: I can't, can I?

JOYCE: Taste it if you want. You won't like it. (*Angie tastes it.*)

ANGIE: Mmm.

MARLENE: We got drunk together the night your grandfather died.

JOYCE: We did not get drunk.

MARLENE: I got drunk. You were just overcome with grief.

JOYCE: I still keep up the grave with flowers.

MARLENE: Do you really?

JOYCE: Why wouldn't I?

MARLENE: Have you seen Mother?

JOYCE: Of course I've seen Mother.

MARLENE: I mean lately.

JOYCE: Of course I've seen her lately, I go every Thursday.

MARLENE (*to Angie*): Do you remember your grandfather?

ANGIE: He got me out of the bath one night in a towel.

MARLENE: Did he? I don't think he ever gave me a bath. Did he give you a bath, Joyce? He probably got soft in his old age. Did you like him?

ANGIE: Yes of course.

MARLENE: Why?

ANGIE: What?

MARLENE: So what's the news? How's Mrs. Paisley? Still going crazily? / And Dorothy. What happened to Dorothy?*

ANGIE: Who's Mrs. Paisley?

JOYCE: *She went to Canada.

MARLENE: Did she? What to do?

JOYCE: I don't know. She just went to Canada.

MARLENE: Well / good for her.

ANGIE: Mr. Connolly killed his wife.

MARLENE: What, Connolly at Whitegates?

ANGIE: They found her body in the garden. / Under the cabbages.

MARLENE: He was always so proper.

JOYCE: Stuck up git, Connolly. Best lawyer money could buy but he couldn't get out of it. She was carrying on with Matthew.

MARLENE: How old's Matthew then?

JOYCE: Twenty-one. / He's got a motorbike.

MARLENE: I think he's about six.

ANGIE: How can he be six? He's six years older than me. / If he was six I'd be nothing, I'd be just born this minute.

JOYCE: Your aunty knows that, she's just being silly. She means it's so long since she's been here she's forgotten about Matthew.

ANGIE: You were here for my birthday when I was nine. I had a pink cake. Kit was only five then, she was four, she hadn't started school yet. She could read already when she went to school. You remember my birthday? / You remember me?

MARLENE: Yes, I remember the cake.

ANGIE: You remember me?

MARLENE: Yes, I remember you.

ANGIE: And Mum and Dad was there, and Kit was.

MARLENE: Yes, how is your dad? Where is he tonight? Up the pub?

JOYCE: No, he's not here.

MARLENE: I can see he's not here.

JOYCE: He moved out.

MARLENE: What? When did he? / Just recently?*

ANGIE: Didn't you know that? You don't know much.

JOYCE: *No, it must be three years ago. Don't be rude, Angie.

ANGIE: I'm not, am I, Aunty? What else don't you know?

JOYCE: You was in America or somewhere. You sent a postcard.

ANGIE: I've got that in my room. It's the Grand Canyon. Do you want to see it? Shall I get it? I can get it for you.

MARLENE: Yes, all right. (*Angie goes.*)

JOYCE: You could be married with twins for all I know. You must have affairs and break up and I don't need to know about any of that so I don't see what the fuss is about.

MARLENE: What fuss? (*Angie comes back with the postcard.*)

ANGIE: "Driving across the states for a new job in L.A. It's a long way but the car goes very fast. It's very hot. Wish you were here. Love from Aunty Marlene."

JOYCE: Did you make a lot of money?

MARLENE: I spent a lot.

ANGIE: I want to go to America. Will you take me?

JOYCE: She's not going to America, she's been to America, stupid.

ANGIE: She might go again, stupid. It's not something you do once. People who go keep going all the time, back and forth on jets. They go on Concorde and Laker and get jet lag. Will you take me?

MARLENE: I'm not planning a trip.

ANGIE: Will you let me know?

JOYCE: Angie, / you're getting silly.

ANGIE: I want to be American.

JOYCE: It's time you were in bed.

ANGIE: No it's not. / I don't have to go to bed at all tonight.

JOYCE: School in the morning.

ANGIE: I'll wake up.

JOYCE: Come on now, you know how you get.

ANGIE: How do I get? / I don't get anyhow.*

JOYCE: Angie. *Are you staying the night?

MARLENE: Yes, if that's all right. / I'll see you in the morning.

ANGIE: You can have my bed. I'll sleep on the sofa.

JOYCE: You will not, you'll sleep in your bed. / Think

ANGIE: Mum.

JOYCE: I can't see through that? I can just see you going to sleep / with us talking.

ANGIE: I would, I would go to sleep, I'd love that.

JOYCE: I'm going to get cross, Angie.

ANGIE: I want to show her something.

JOYCE: Then bed.

ANGIE: It's a secret.

JOYCE: Then I expect it's in your room so off you go. Give us a shout when you're ready for bed and your aunty'll be up and see you.

ANGIE: Will you?

MARLENE: Yes of course. (*Angie goes. Silence.*) It's cold tonight.

JOYCE: Will you be all right on the sofa? You can / have my bed.

MARLENE: The sofa's fine.

JOYCE: Yes the forecast said rain tonight but it's held off.

MARLENE: I was going to walk down to the estuary but I've left it a bit late. Is it just the same?

JOYCE: They cut down the hedges a few years back. Is that since you were here?

MARLENE: But it's not changed down the end, all the mud? And the reeds? We used to pick them up when they were bigger than us. Are there still lap-wings?

JOYCE: You get strangers walking there on a Sunday. I expect they're looking at the mud and the lap-wings, yes.

MARLENE: You could have left.

JOYCE: Who says I wanted to leave?

MARLENE: Stop getting at me then, you're really boring.

JOYCE: How could I have left?

MARLENE: Did you want to?

JOYCE: I said how, / how could I?

MARLENE: If you'd wanted to you'd have done it.

JOYCE: Christ.

MARLENE: Are we getting drunk?

JOYCE: Do you want something to eat?

MARLENE: No, I'm getting drunk.

JOYCE: Funny time to visit, Sunday evening.

MARLENE: I came this morning. I spent the day —

ANGIE (*off*): Aunty! Aunty Marlene!

MARLENE: I'd better go.

JOYCE: Go on then.

MARLENE: All right.

ANGIE (*off*): Aunty! Can you hear me? I'm ready.

(*Marlene goes. Joyce goes on sitting, clears up, sits again. Marlene comes back.*)

JOYCE: So what's the secret?

MARLENE: It's a secret.

JOYCE: I know what it is anyway.

MARLENE: I bet you don't. You always said that.

JOYCE: It's her exercise book.

MARLENE: Yes, but you don't know what's in it.

JOYCE: It's some game, some secret society she has with Kit.

MARLENE: You don't know the password. You don't know the code.

JOYCE: You're really in it, aren't you. Can you do the handshake?

MARLENE: She didn't mention a handshake.

JOYCE: I thought they'd have a special handshake. She spends hours writing that but she's useless at school. She copies things out of books about black magic, and politicians out of the paper. It's a bit childish.

MARLENE: I think it's a plot to take over the world.

JOYCE: She's been in the remedial class the last two years.

MARLENE: I came up this morning and spent the day in Ipswich. I went to see Mother.

JOYCE: Did she recognize you?

MARLENE: Are you trying to be funny?

JOYCE: No, she does wander.

MARLENE: She wasn't wandering at all, she was very lucid thank you.

JOYCE: You were very lucky then.

MARLENE: Fucking awful life she's had.

JOYCE: Don't tell me.

MARLENE: Fucking waste.

JOYCE: Don't talk to me.

MARLENE: Why shouldn't I talk? Why shouldn't I talk to you? / Isn't she my mother too?

JOYCE: Look, you've left, you've gone away, / we can do without you.

MARLENE: I left home, so what, I left home. People do leave home / it is normal.

JOYCE: We understand that, we can do without you.

MARLENE: We weren't happy. Were you happy?

JOYCE: Don't come back.

MARLENE: So it's just your mother is it, your child, you never wanted me round, / you were jealous

JOYCE: Here we go.

MARLENE: of me because I was the little one and I was clever.

JOYCE: I'm not clever enough for all this psychology / if that's what it is.

MARLENE: Why can't I visit my own family / without

JOYCE: Aah.

MARLENE: all this?

JOYCE: Just don't go on about Mum's life when you haven't been to see her for how many years. / I go

MARLENE: It's up to me.

JOYCE: and see her every week.

MARLENE: Then don't go and see her every week.

JOYCE: Somebody has to.

MARLENE: No they don't. / Why do they?

JOYCE: How would I feel if I didn't go?

MARLENE: A lot better.

JOYCE: I hope you feel better.

MARLENE: It's up to me.

JOYCE: You couldn't get out of here fast enough. (*Pause.*)

MARLENE: Of course I couldn't get out of here fast enough. What was I going to do? Marry a dairy-man who'd come home pissed? / Don't you fucking this

JOYCE: Christ.

MARLENE: fucking that fucking bitch fucking tell me what to fucking do fucking.

JOYCE: I don't know how you could leave your own child.

MARLENE: You were quick enough to take her.

JOYCE: What does that mean?

MARLENE: You were quick enough to take her.

JOYCE: Or what? Have her put in a home? Have some stranger / take her would you rather?

MARLENE: You couldn't have one so you took mine.

JOYCE: I didn't know that then.

MARLENE: Like hell, / married three years.

JOYCE: I didn't know that. Plenty of people / take that long.

MARLENE: Well it turned out lucky for you, didn't it?

JOYCE: Turned out all right for you by the look of you. You'd be getting a few less thousand a year.

MARLENE: Not necessarily.

JOYCE: You'd be stuck here / like you said.

MARLENE: I could have taken her with me.

JOYCE: You didn't want to take her with you. It's no good coming back now, Marlene, / and saying —

MARLENE: I know a managing director who's got two children, she breastfeeds in the board room, she pays a hundred pounds a week on domestic help alone and she can afford that because she's an extremely high-powered lady earning a great deal of money.

JOYCE: So what's that got to do with you at the age of seventeen?

MARLENE: Just because you were married and had somewhere to live —

JOYCE: You could have lived at home. / Or live

MARLENE: Don't be stupid.

JOYCE: with me and Frank. / You

MARLENE: You never suggested.

JOYCE: said you weren't keeping it. You shouldn't have had it / if you wasn't

MARLENE: Here we go.

JOYCE: going to keep it. You was the most stupid, / for someone so clever you was the most stupid, get yourself pregnant, not go to the doctor, not tell.

MARLENE: You wanted it, you said you were glad, I remember the day, you said I'm glad you never got rid of it, I'll look after it, you said that down by the river. So what are you saying, sunshine, you don't want her?

JOYCE: Course I'm not saying that.

MARLENE: Because I'll take her, / wake her up and pack now.

JOYCE: You wouldn't know how to begin to look after her.

MARLENE: Don't you want her?

JOYCE: Course I do, she's my child.

MARLENE: Then what are you going on about / why did I have her?

JOYCE: You said I got her off you / when you didn't —

MARLENE: I said you were lucky / the way it —

JOYCE: Have a child now if you want one. You're not old.

MARLENE: I might do.

JOYCE: Good. (Pause.)

MARLENE: I've been on the pill so long / I'm probably sterile.

JOYCE: Listen when Angie was six months I did get pregnant and I lost it because I was so tired looking after your fucking baby / because she cried so

MARLENE: You never told me.

JOYCE: much — yes I did tell you — / and the doctor

MARLENE: Well I forgot.

JOYCE: said if I'd sat down all day with my feet up I'd've kept it / and that's the only chance I ever had because after that —

MARLENE: I've had two abortions, are you interested? Shall I tell you about them? Well I won't, it's boring, it wasn't a problem. I don't like messy talk about blood / and what a bad time we all had. I

JOYCE: If I hadn't had your baby. The doctor said.

MARLENE: don't want a baby. I don't want to talk about gynecology.

JOYCE: Then stop trying to get Angie off of me.

MARLENE: I come down here after six years. All night you've been saying I don't come often enough. If I don't come for another six years she'll be twenty-one, will that be OK?

JOYCE: That'll be fine, yes, six years would suit me fine. (Pause.)

MARLENE: I was afraid of this. I only came because I thought you wanted . . . I just want . . . (She cries.)

JOYCE: Don't grizzle, Marlene, for God's sake. Marly? Come on, pet. Love you really. Fucking stop it, will you? (She goes to Marlene.)

MARLENE: No, let me cry. I like it. (They laugh, Marlene begins to stop crying.) I knew I'd cry if I wasn't careful.

JOYCE: Everyone's always crying in this house. Nobody takes any notice.

MARLENE: You've been wonderful looking after Angie.

JOYCE: Don't get carried away.

MARLENE: I can't write letters but I do think of you.

JOYCE: You're getting drunk. I'm going to make some tea.

MARLENE: Love you. (Joyce goes to make tea.)

JOYCE: I can see why you'd want to leave. It's a dump here.

MARLENE: So what's this about you and Frank?

JOYCE: He was always carrying on, wasn't he. And if I wanted to go out in the evening he'd go mad, even if it was nothing, a class, I was going to go to an evening class. So he had this girlfriend, only twenty-two poor cow, and I said go on, off you go, hoppit. I don't think he even likes her.

MARLENE: So what about money?

JOYCE: I've always said I don't want your money.

MARLENE: No, does he send you money?

JOYCE: I've got four different cleaning jobs. Adds up. There's not a lot round here.

MARLENE: Does Angie miss him?

JOYCE: She doesn't say.

MARLENE: Does she see him?

JOYCE: He was never that fond of her to be honest.

MARLENE: He tried to kiss me once. When you were engaged.

JOYCE: Did you fancy him?

MARLENE: No, he looked like a fish.

JOYCE: He was lovely then.

MARLENE: Ugh.

JOYCE: Well I fancied him. For about three years.

MARLENE: Have you got someone else?

JOYCE: There's not a lot round here. Mind you, the minute you're on your own, you'd be amazed how your friends' husbands drop by. I'd sooner do without.

MARLENE: I don't see why you couldn't take my money.

JOYCE: I do, so don't bother about it.

MARLENE: Only got to ask.

JOYCE: So what about you? Good job?

MARLENE: Good for a laugh. / Got back

JOYCE: Good for more than a laugh I should think.

MARLENE: from the US of A a bit wiped out and slotted into this speedy employment agency and still there.

JOYCE: You can always find yourself work then?

MARLENE: That's right.

JOYCE: And men?

MARLENE: Oh there's always men.

JOYCE: No one special?

MARLENE: There's fellas who like to be seen with a high-flying lady. Shows they've got something really good in their pants. But they can't take the day to day. They're waiting for me to turn into the little woman. Or maybe I'm just horrible of course.

JOYCE: Who needs them.

MARLENE: Who needs them. Well I do. But I need adventures more. So on on into the sunset. I think the eighties are going to be stupendous.

JOYCE: Who for?

MARLENE: For me. / I think I'm going up up up.

JOYCE: Oh for you. Yes, I'm sure they will.

MARLENE: And for the country, come to that. Get the economy back on its feet and whoosh. She's a tough lady, Maggie. I'd give her a job. / She just needs to hang

JOYCE: You voted for them, did you?

MARLENE: in there. This country needs to stop whining. / Monetarism is not

JOYCE: Drink your tea and shut up, pet.

MARLENE: stupid. It takes time, determination. No more slop. / And

JOYCE: Well I think they're filthy bastards.

MARLENE: who's got to drive it on? First woman prime minister. Terrifico. Aces. Right on. / You must admit. Certainly gets my vote.

JOYCE: What good's first woman if it's her? I suppose you'd have liked Hitler if he was a woman. Ms. Hitler. Got a lot done, Hitlerina. / Great adventures.

MARLENE: Bosses still walking on the worker's faces? Still dadda's little parrot? Haven't you learned to think for yourself? I believe in the individual. Look at me.

JOYCE: I am looking at you.

MARLENE: Come on, Joyce, we're not going to quarrel over politics.

JOYCE: We are though.

MARLENE: Forget I mentioned it. Not a word about the slimy unions will cross my lips. (*Pause.*)

JOYCE: You say Mother had a wasted life.

MARLENE: Yes I do. Married to that bastard.

JOYCE: What sort of life did he have? /

MARLENE: Violent life?

JOYCE: Working in the fields like an animal. / Why

MARLENE: Come off it.

JOYCE: wouldn't he want a drink? You want a drink. He couldn't afford whiskey.

MARLENE: I don't want to talk about him.

JOYCE: You started, I was talking about her. She had a rotten life because she had nothing. She went hungry.

MARLENE: She was hungry because he drank the money. / He used to hit her.

JOYCE: It's not all down to him / Their

MARLENE: She didn't hit him.

JOYCE: lives were rubbish. They were treated like rubbish. He's dead and she'll die soon and what sort of life / did they have?

MARLENE: I saw him one night. I came down.

JOYCE: Do you think I didn't? / They

MARLENE: I still have dreams.

JOYCE: didn't get to America and drive across it in a fast car. / Bad nights, they had bad days.

MARLENE: America, America, you're jealous. / I had to get out, I knew when I

JOYCE: Jealous?

MARLENE: was thirteen, out of their house, out of them, never let that happen to me, / never let him, make my own way, out.

JOYCE: Jealous of what you've done, you'd be ashamed of me if I came to your office, your smart friends, wouldn't you, I'm ashamed of you, think of nothing but yourself, you've got on, nothing's changed for most people, / has it?

MARLENE: I hate the working class / which is what

JOYCE: Yes you do.

MARLENE: you're going to go on about now, it doesn't exist any more, it means lazy and stupid. / I don't

JOYCE: Come on, now we're getting it.

MARLENE: like the way they talk. I don't like beer guts and football vomit and saucy tits / and brothers and sisters —

JOYCE: I spit when I see a Rolls Royce, scratch it with my ring / Mercedes it was.

MARLENE: Oh very mature —

JOYCE: I hate the cows I work for / and their dirty dishes with blanquette of fucking veau.

MARLENE: and I will not be pulled down to their level by a flying picket and I won't be sent to Siberia / or a loony bin just because I'm original. And I support

JOYCE: No, you'll be on a yacht, you'll be head of Coca Cola and you wait, the eighties is going to be stupendous all right because we'll get you lot off our backs —

MARLENE: Reagan even if he is a lousy movie star because the reds are swarming up his map and I want to be free in a free world —

JOYCE: What? / What?

MARLENE: I know what I mean / by that — not shut up here.

JOYCE: So don't be round here when it happens because if someone's kicking you I'll just laugh. (*Silence.*)

MARLENE: I don't mean anything personal. I don't believe in class. Anyone can do anything if they've got what it takes.

JOYCE: And if they haven't?

MARLENE: If they're stupid or lazy or frightened, I'm not going to help them get a job, why should I?

JOYCE: What about Angie?

MARLENE: What about Angie?

JOYCE: She's stupid, lazy, and frightened, so what about her?

MARLENE: You run her down too much. She'll be all right.

JOYCE: I don't expect so, no. I expect her children will say what a wasted life she had. If she has children. Because nothing's changed and it won't with them in.

MARLENE: Them, them. / Us and them?

JOYCE: And you're one of them.

MARLENE: And you're us, wonderful us, and Angie's us / and Mum and Dad's us.

JOYCE: Yes, that's right, and you're them.

MARLENE: Come on, Joyce, what a night. You've got what it takes.

JOYCE: I know I have.

MARLENE: I didn't really mean all that.

JOYCE: I did.

MARLENE: But we're friends anyway.

JOYCE: I don't think so, no.

MARLENE: Well it's lovely to be out in the country. I really must make the effort to come more often. I want to go to sleep. I want to go to sleep. (*Joyce gets blankets for the sofa.*)

JOYCE: Goodnight then. I hope you'll be warm enough.

MARLENE: Goodnight. Joyce —

JOYCE: No, pet. Sorry. (*Joyce goes. Marlene sits wrapped in a blanket and has another drink. Angie comes in.*)

ANGIE: Mum?

MARLENE: Angie? What's the matter?

ANGIE: Mum?

MARLENE: No, she's gone to bed. It's Aunty Marlene.

ANGIE: Frightening.

MARLENE: Did you have a bad dream? What happened in it? Well you're awake now, aren't you, pet?

ANGIE: Frightening.

COMMENTARY

Kathleen Betsko, Rachel Koenig, and Emily Mann
AN INTERVIEW WITH CARYL CHURCHILL   1984

Kathleen Betsko and Rachel Koenig interviewed Caryl Churchill in New York on February 25, 1984, but found their tape was incomplete. Luckily, Emily Mann, a playwright, was able to complete the interview with Churchill at London's Riverside Studio on November 23, 1984. The excerpts presented here

combine the two sessions, emphasizing Top Girls *and some of the interesting responses to Churchill's drama.*

Interviewer: Is there a female aesthetic? And we'd like you to wrap this question up once and for all. [Laughter]

Churchill: I don't see how you can tell until there are so many plays by women that you can begin to see what they have in common that's different from the way men have written, and there are still relatively so few. And we have things in common with male playwrights who are worried about similar things in their particular country and who have worked in the same theaters with the same directors. So it's hard to separate out and think of "women playwrights" rather than just "playwrights." Though I do remember before I wrote *Top Girls* thinking about women barristers — how they were in a minority and had to imitate men to succeed — and I was thinking of them as different from me. And then I thought, "Wait a minute, my whole concept of what plays might be is from plays written by men. I don't have to put on a wig, speak in a special voice, but how far do I assume things that have been defined by men?" There isn't a simple answer to that. And I remember long before that thinking of the "maleness" of the traditional structure of plays, with conflict and building in a certain way to a climax. But it's not something I think about very often. Playwriting will change not just because more women are doing it but because more women are doing other things as well. And of course men will be influenced by that too. So maybe you'll still be no nearer to defining a female aesthetic.

Interviewer: Some of the playwrights we've interviewed suggest there are no "lost masterpieces" and that "the cream will rise to the top" in terms of women's writing for the stage.

Churchill: Most theaters are still controlled by men and people do tend to be able to see promise in people who are like themselves. Women directors have pointed out to me how established men tend to take a young male director under their wing, and seem to feel more uncomfortable with a woman director because they can't quite see where she is, because they weren't like that at her age. I think the same thing can happen with writers: If you're at the stage where you are promising but not doing it all that well yet, it's perhaps easier for a man choosing plays to see the potential in a man writer. I don't know about "lost masterpieces" but people don't usually start out writing masterpieces and women may have less chance of getting started. Having productions does seem to make people write better.

Interviewer: Has the political climate for women dramatists changed drastically since you began writing plays?

Churchill: I began writing plays in 1958, and I don't think I knew of any other women playwrights then. Luckily, I didn't think about it. Do you know Tillie Olsen's book *Silences*? She says that at different times, whole categories of people are enabled to write. You tend to think of your own development only having to do with yourself and it's exciting to discover it in a historical context. When I began it was quite hard for any playwrights to get started in London. The English Stage Company had just started a policy of doing new writing at the Royal Court, but that was almost the only place. I had student productions at first, and then wrote for radio. In the late sixties and early seventies there was a surge of fringe theaters and interest in new writing, starting with the Theatre Upstairs and the Royal Court, and that was the first place to do a professional stage production of one of my plays, *Owners,* in 1972. For a while, a lot of writers were getting produced for the first time, though far fewer women than men. Gradually during the seventies the number of women increased, coming partly through fringe theaters and partly through women's theater groups. In the last five years there seem to be far more women playwrights and some theaters are more open to them, though others still aren't. At the moment, because of the financial cuts, it's again become quite hard for all playwrights. Theaters are having to do co-productions with other theaters because they haven't enough money to do a whole year's work on their grants, so it means one new play gets done instead of two. The Royal Court, for instance, can now only afford to do four new plays in the main house instead of eight. But I get the impression life is even harder for playwrights in the United States than in England because of there not being a subsidized theater.

Interviewer: In Laurie Stone's *Village Voice* interview [March 1, 1983], you talked about women becoming Coca-Cola executives and you said, "Well, that's not what I mean by feminism." What exactly do you mean by feminism?

Churchill: When I was in the States in '79 I talked to some women who were saying how well things were going for women in America now with far more top executives being women, and I was struck by the difference between that and the feminism I was used to in England, which is far more closely connected with socialism. And that was one of the ideas behind writing *Top Girls,* that achieving things isn't necessarily good, it matters *what* you achieve.

Thatcher° had just become prime minister; there was talk about whether it was an advance to have a woman prime minister if it was someone with policies like hers: She may be a woman but she isn't a sister, she may be a sister but she isn't a comrade. And, in fact, things have got much worse for women under Thatcher. So that's the context of that remark. I do find it hard to conceive of a right-wing feminism. Of course, socialism and feminism aren't synonymous, but I feel strongly about both and wouldn't be interested in a form of one that didn't include the other.

Interviewer: Do you think it's odd, given the fact that there is at best indifference, at worst hostility, to political plays in America, that your works are so popular here?

Churchill: Is it true that on the whole plays here tend to be more family-centered, personal, individual-centered?

Interviewer: Yes, more psychological.

Churchill: Whereas I've been quite heavily exposed to a tradition of looking at the larger context of groups of people. It doesn't mean you don't look at families or individuals within that, but you are also looking at bigger things. Like with the kind of work Joint Stock Theatre Group has done, where you go and research a subject and where you have a lot of characters, even if played by only a few people. It tends to open things out.

Interviewer: The critics do ask, "Where are the American plays with the larger social issues?" Unfortunately, when one comes along our own critics usually turn thumbs down if the politics are overt. An overt political position is considered poor craft or preaching. . . .

Interviewer: Does the playwright have an obligation to take a moral and political stance?

Thatcher: Margaret (Hilda) Thatcher (b. 1925), British Prime Minister, 1979–1990, and a strong political conservative.

Churchill: It's almost impossible not to take one, whether you intend to or not. Most plays can be looked at from a political perspective and have said something, even if it isn't what you set out to say. If you wrote a West End comedy relying on conventional sexist jokes, that's taking a moral and political stance, though the person who wrote it might say, "I was just writing an entertaining show." Whatever you do your point of view is going to show somewhere. It usually only gets noticed and called "political" if it's against the status quo. There are times when I feel I want to deal with immediate issues and times when I don't. I do like the stuff of theater, in the same way people who are painting like paint; and of course when you say "moral and political" that doesn't have to imply reaching people logically or overtly, because theater can reach people on all kinds of other levels too. Sometimes one side or the other is going to have more weight. Sometimes it's going to be about images, more like a dream to people, and sometimes it's going to be more like reading an article. And there's room for all that. But either way, the issues you feel strongly about are going to come through, and they're going to be a moral and political stance in some form. Sometimes more explicitly, sometimes less. . . .

Mann: Let's talk about your play *Top Girls*.

Churchill: When I wrote *Top Girls* I was writing it by myself and not for a company. I wanted to write about women doing different kinds of work and didn't feel I knew enough about it. Then I thought, this is ridiculous, if you were with a company you'd go out and talk to people, so I did. Which is how I came up with the employment agency in the second act.

Mann: Are there specific characters in *Top Girls* that have their real life counterparts?

Churchill: Quite a few of the things Win tells Angie about her life are things different people said to me. And of course the dead women at the dinner are all based on someone [from art, literature or history]. But apart from that, it's imaginary.

Mann: Tell me about the ways in which *Top Girls* has been misunderstood.

Churchill: What I was intending to do was make it first look as though it was celebrating the achievements of women and then — by showing the main character, Marlene, being successful in a very competitive, destructive, capitalist way — ask, what kind of achievement is that? The idea was that it would start out looking like a feminist play and turn into a socialist one, as well. And I think on the whole it's mostly been understood like that. A lot of people have latched on to Marlene leaving her child, which interestingly was something that came very late. Originally the idea was just that Marlene was "writing off" her niece, Angie, because she'd never make it; I didn't yet have the plot idea that Angie was actually Marlene's own child. Of course women are pressured to make choices between working and having children in a way that men aren't, so it *is* relevant, but it isn't the main point of it.

There's another thing that I've recently discovered with other productions of *Top Girls*. In Greece, for example, where fewer women go out to work, the attitude from some men seeing it was, apparently, that the women in the play who'd gone out to work weren't very nice, weren't happy, and they abandoned their children. They felt the play was obviously saying women *shouldn't* go out to work — they took it to mean what they were wanting to say about women themselves, which is depressing. Highly depressing. [laughter] Another example of its being open to misunderstanding was a production in Cologne, Germany, where the women characters were played as miserable and quarrelsome and competitive at the dinner, and the women in the office were neurotic and incapable. The waitress slunk about in a catsuit like a bunnygirl and Win changed her clothes on stage in the office. It just turned into a complete travesty of what it was supposed to be. So that's the sort of moment when you think you'd rather write novels, because the productions can't be changed.

Mann: I don't know whether we're safer in the theater or not. . . .

Churchill: With a play you do leave more room for other things and that's one of the attractions, that people can keep coming to it fresh and doing it differently.

Athol Fugard

Athol Fugard (b. 1932) was an actor before becoming a playwright. In 1956 he began working with a theater group called the Serpent Company in Cape Town, South Africa. The group included both black and white actors as participants at a time when racial mixing was illegal. Fugard's wife, the actress Sheila Meiring, stimulated his interest in theater in 1956 and in developing the theater company, which sustained itself to produce fine plays and to make a contribution to world drama.

Fugard, who is white, met Zakes Mokae, a black musician and actor, in the early days of the Serpent players, and the two collaborated on several works. Mokae has said that the tradition in Africa was not so much for a solitary playwright to compose a work that others would act out as it was for people to develop a communal approach to drama, crafting a dramatic piece through their interaction. To some extent, Fugard in his early efforts did just that. He worked with actors, watched the developments among them, and then shaped the drama accordingly.

In 1960 he began to write a two-person play called *The Blood Knot* while he was in England trying to establish a theater group there. This play was part of a trilogy called *The Family,* with *Hello and Goodbye* (1965) and *Boesman and Lena* (1969). *The Blood Knot* was given its first performance in Dorkay House in Johannesburg late in 1961. As Fugard has said, the entire production, which starred Fugard and Mokae, was put together so quickly that the government never had time to stop it. The play is about two brothers, one black, the other light-skinned enough to pass for white. It is exceptionally powerful, and in the play's first performances in Johannesburg, it was a sensation. It toured South Africa and had a revival in New Haven and in New York in 1984 and 1985.

While they toured South Africa, Fugard and Mokae were victims of the country's apartheid policies. They could not travel in the same train car: Fugard went first class and Mokae had to go in the special cars for blacks. After *The Blood Knot*'s success the government passed laws making it all but impossible to have black and white actors working together on the stage, but that policy has now changed.

Fugard has had a considerable number of plays produced in New York and London in recent years. *Sizwe Banzi Is Dead* (1972), written with John Kani and Winston Ntshona, is about a man who exchanges identity with a corpse as a way of avoiding the racial laws of South

Africa; it was well received. *The Island* (1975), also written with Kani and Ntshona, starred the latter two black actors, who have become associated with Fugard and his work. They portray prisoners who, while putting on *Antigone*, become immersed in the political themes of the play, seeing it as an example of the political repression they experience in their own lives.

His plays *A Lesson from Aloes* (1978) and *The Road to Mecca* (1984) were successful in their first American productions at the Yale Repertory Theatre and on Broadway. Fugard's works are not always concerned with racial problems, but they usually center on political issues and the stress that individuals feel in trying to be themselves in an intolerant society.

The situation in South Africa has improved since "*MASTER HAROLD*" . . . *and the boys* was first produced in 1982. Apartheid has been abolished, and the government is in the hands of the African National Congress, led by Nelson Mandela. The shift has been more successful than white South Africans expected, although political tensions still exist. Fugard's attachment and commitment to South Africa remain deep and lifelong. He has been criticized by black writers for dealing with themes they feel belong to them, while also being criticized by whites for his sympathies toward blacks. In the new South Africa some of these problems have begun to sort themselves out. Fugard's latest play, *Valley Song* (1996), produced at London's Royal Court Theatre, explores the problems and the promise of the new South Africa.

"MASTER HAROLD"...
AND THE BOYS

Athol Fugard has said that *"MASTER HAROLD"... and the boys* (1982) is a very personal play in which he exorcises personal guilt (Fugard's entire name is Athol Harold Lannigan Fugard). As a white South African he has written numerous plays that represent the racial circumstances of life in that troubled nation. This play has won international distinction and has made a reputation for its stars, especially Zakes Mokae, with whom Fugard has worked for more than thirty years.

Hally reveals throughout the play (which is set in 1950) that he is more attached emotionally to Sam, the black waiter who has befriended him, than he is even to his own parents, owners of the restaurant. His attitude toward his father is complicated by his father's alcoholism and confinement. At that time in South Africa even such an alcoholic was considered automatically superior to a black man such as Sam, who is intelligent, quick, thoughtful, and generous. When Hally reveals his anxiety about his father, Sam warns him that it is dishonorable to treat one's father the way he does, but Sam's presumption in admonishing Hally triggers Hally's mean outburst toward him.

Zakes Mokae, who created the role of Sam in the first performance of the play at the Yale Repertory Theatre, has commented extensively about his role and the character of Sam. He has observed that some black audience members called out during a performance that he should beat Hally up the minute Hally demands that Sam call him Master Harold. But other black audience members spoke with him after the performance and agreed that, because Sam had never taken that kind of stand against Harold or his father, he was getting what he deserved. Mokae himself has pointed out that Sam is probably not living in Port Elizabeth legally and that to have taken action, even if he wanted to, would have ended with his removal from the town into exile.

Zakes Mokae understands the character from his perspective as a black South African, and he realizes Sam's limits. But he has said that in his version of the play Sam would give Hally a beating and "suffer the consequences." He points out, however, that he is an urban South African, unlike Sam, and his attitude is quite different from anything that Sam would have understood. As an urban black, Mokae could not have been sent into exile, although he could certainly have been punished, for beating a white boy.

On the question of whether the play made a positive contribution to white-black relations in South Africa, Mokae feels that a play cannot change people's minds. Audiences were not likely to seek to change the government of South Africa simply because they had seen a play. But at the same time, he feels that it was productive to talk about the apartheid and racial distrust in South Africa.

Unfortunately, the government of South Africa decided that the play was too inflammatory for performance in its country, and it was banned briefly from performance in Johannesburg and other theatrical centers in South Africa. This suggests that while Zakes Mokae did not feel that one play would have much impact on injustices in South Africa, it is likely that the government feared otherwise.

In an important way, "MASTER HAROLD" . . . and the boys is a personal statement by Fugard that establishes the extent to which apartheid damages even a person sympathetic to black rights. It is astonishing in retrospect to think, as his interviewer, Heinrich von Staden, once said, that Hally could grow up to be Athol himself. If this is true, then it is also true that the play is hopeful.

One sign of hope is that the violence in the play is restrained. Sam does not beat Hally for humiliating him, although he probably would like to. And no one in the play makes a move to be physically threatening to Sam. However faint, these are signs of hope. And as Zakes Mokae has said about the situation in his homeland, "One is always optimistic. It can't go on forever." He was right. On June 5, 1991, parliament abandoned apartheid and South Africa had a new beginning.

"MASTER HAROLD" . . . and the boys in Performance

The world premiere of "MASTER HAROLD" . . . and the boys was at the Yale Repertory Theatre in March 1982. Fugard himself directed the play, with Zakes Mokae as Sam, Danny Glover as Willie, and Željko Ivanek as Hally. It was the first of his plays to premiere outside South Africa. Fugard chose New Haven in part because the play's setting was so personal that he feared it might disturb his brother and sister if it were produced first in South Africa. The setting was a bright tea room — a restaurant that serves light meals — interpreted to look like the tea room Fugard's mother actually ran in Port Elizabeth when he was a child. The space was open, the walls a whitish hue, everything simple and plain in decoration.

New York Times critic Frank Rich reviewed the premiere, saying, "'MASTER HAROLD' . . . and the boys is only an anecdote, really, and it's often as warm and musical as the men's dance. But somewhere along the way it rises up and breaks over the audience like a storm." Alan Stern of the *Boston Phoenix* linked the play with Greek tragedy:

> One reason for the play's potency is that, as in Greek tragedy, the events seem preordained — they're the by-product of social forces and human nature. Even as he spits in Sam's face, Hally realizes the magnitude of his action, that he is the one who will be harmed by it. And yet he can't help himself. Power cor-

rupts, and in a society that sanctions the domination of one man — or set of men — over another, all relationships, even the promising ones, are poisoned.

Zakes Mokae and Danny Glover starred in the Broadway production in May 1982. After a brief period in which it was banned, the play was produced in Johannesburg, South Africa, in March 1983 with a South African cast. Joseph Lelyveld, in the *New York Times,* said of that production: "Athol Fugard's confessional drama about a white adolescent's initiation in the uses of racial power has come home to South Africa, and it left its multiracial audience . . . visibly shaken and stunned. . . . Many, blacks and whites, were crying."

The play was televised in 1984 with Matthew Broderick as Hally. It has had revivals in 1985 by the Trinity Repertory Company in Providence, in 1986 by the Boston Shakespeare Company in Boston, and in 1987 at the American Stage Festival in Milford, New Hampshire. These productions, although without Fugard's direction and without a "star" cast, had the same effect on their audiences as the major productions in New York and Johannesburg. Clifford Gallo in the *Boston Globe* called the American Stage production "a devastating look at the loss of racial innocence in a nation where political and social inequality are the norm."

Athol Fugard (b. 1932)
"MASTER HAROLD" . . . AND THE BOYS   *1982*

Characters

WILLIE
SAM
HALLY

(*The St. George's Park Tea Room on a wet and windy Port Elizabeth afternoon.*)

(*Tables and chairs have been cleared and are stacked on one side except for one which stands apart with a single chair. On this table a knife, fork, spoon and side plate in anticipation of a simple meal, together with a pile of comic books.*)

(*Other elements: a serving counter with a few stale cakes under glass and a not very impressive display of sweets, cigarettes and cool drinks, etc.; a few cardboard advertising handouts — Cadbury's Chocolate, Coca-Cola — and a blackboard on which an untrained hand has chalked up the prices of Tea, Coffee, Scones, Milkshakes — all flavors — and Cool Drinks; a few sad ferns in pots; a telephone; an old-style jukebox.*)

(*There is an entrance on one side and an exit into a kitchen on the other.*)

(*Leaning on the solitary table, his head cupped in one hand as he pages through one of the comic books, is Sam. A black man in his mid-forties. He wears the white coat of a waiter. Behind him on his knees, mopping down the floor with a bucket of water and a rag, is Willie. Also black and about the same age as Sam. He has his sleeves and trousers rolled up.*)

(*The year: 1950.*)

WILLIE (*singing as he works*): "She was scandalizin' my name,
She took my money
She called me honey
But she was scandalizin' my name.
Called it love but was playin' a game. . . ."

(*He gets up and moves the bucket. Stands thinking for a moment, then, raising his arms to hold an imaginary partner, he launches into an intricate ballroom dance step. Although a mildly comic figure, he reveals a reasonable degree of accomplishment.)*

Hey, Sam.

(Sam, absorbed in the comic book, does not respond.)

Hey, Boet° Sam!

(Sam looks up.)

I'm getting it. The quickstep. Look now and tell me. *(He repeats the step.)* Well?

SAM *(encouragingly)*: Show me again.

WILLIE: Okay, count for me.

SAM: Ready?

WILLIE: Ready.

SAM: Five, six, seven, eight. . . . *(Willie starts to dance.)* A-n-d one two three four . . . and one two three four. . . . *(Ad libbing as Willie dances.)* Your shoulders, Willie . . . your shoulders! Don't look down! Look happy, Willie! Relax, Willie!

WILLIE *(desperate but still dancing)*: I am relax.

SAM: No, you're not.

WILLIE *(he falters)*: Ag no man, Sam! Mustn't talk. You make me make mistakes.

SAM: But you're stiff.

WILLIE: Yesterday I'm not straight . . . today I'm too stiff!

SAM: Well, you are. You asked me and I'm telling you.

WILLIE: Where?

SAM: Everywhere. Try to glide through it.

WILLIE: Glide?

SAM: Ja, make it smooth. And give it more style. It must look like you're enjoying yourself.

WILLIE *(emphatically)*: I wasn't.

SAM: Exactly.

WILLIE: How can I enjoy myself? Not straight, too stiff and now it's also glide, give it more style, make it smooth. . . . Haai! Is hard to remember all those things, Boet Sam.

SAM: That's your trouble. You're trying too hard.

WILLIE: I try hard because it *is* hard.

SAM: But don't let me see it. The secret is to make it look easy. Ballroom must look happy, Willie, not like hard work. It must. . . . Ja! . . . it must look like romance.

WILLIE: Now another one! What's romance?

SAM: Love story with happy ending. A handsome man in tails, and in his arms, smiling at him, a beautiful lady in evening dress!

WILLIE: Fred Astaire, Ginger Rogers.

SAM: You got it. Tapdance or ballroom, it's the same. Romance. In two weeks' time when the judges look at you and Hilda, they must see a man and a woman who are dancing their way to a happy ending. What I saw was you holding her like you were frightened she was going to run away.

Boet: Brother.

WILLIE: Ja! Because that is what she wants to do! I got no romance left for Hilda anymore, Boet Sam.

SAM: Then pretend. When you put your arms around Hilda, imagine she is Ginger Rogers.

WILLIE: With no teeth? You try.

SAM: Well, just remember, there's only two weeks left.

WILLIE: I know, I know! *(To the jukebox.)* I do it better with music. You got sixpence for Sarah Vaughan?

SAM: That's a slow foxtrot. You're practicing the quickstep.

WILLIE: I'll practice slow foxtrot.

SAM *(shaking his head)*: It's your turn to put money in the jukebox.

WILLIE: I only got bus fare to go home. *(He returns disconsolately to his work.)* Love story and happy ending! She's doing it all right, Boet Sam, but is not me she's giving happy endings. Fuckin' whore! Three nights now she doesn't come practice. I wind up gramophone, I get record ready and I sit and wait. What happens? Nothing. Ten o'clock I start dancing with my pillow. You try and practice romance by yourself, Boet Sam. Struesgod, she doesn't come tonight I take back my dress and ballroom shoes and I find me new partner. Size twenty-six. Shoes size seven. And now she's also making trouble for me with the baby again. Reports me to Child Wellfed, that I'm not giving her money. She lies! Every week I am giving her money for milk. And how do I know is my baby? Only his hair looks like me. She's fucking around all the time I turn my back. Hilda Samuels is a bitch! *(Pause.)* Hey, Sam!

SAM: Ja.

WILLIE: You listening?

SAM: Ja.

WILLIE: So what you say?

SAM: About Hilda?

WILLIE: Ja.

SAM: When did you last give her a hiding?

WILLIE *(reluctantly)*: Sunday night.

SAM: And today is Thursday.

WILLIE *(he knows what's coming)*: Okay.

SAM: Hiding on Sunday night, then Monday, Tuesday, and Wednesday she doesn't come to practice . . . and you are asking me why?

WILLIE: I said okay, Boet Sam!

SAM: You hit her too much. One day she's going to leave you for good.

WILLIE: So? She makes me the hell-in too much.

SAM *(emphasizing his point)*: *Too* much and *too* hard. You had the same trouble with Eunice.

WILLIE: Because she also make the hell-in, Boet Sam. She never got the steps right. Even the waltz.

SAM: Beating her up every time she makes a mistake in the waltz? *(Shaking his head.)* No, Willie! That takes the pleasure out of ballroom dancing.

WILLIE: Hilda is not too bad with the waltz, Boet Sam. Is the quickstep where the trouble starts.

SAM (*teasing him gently*): How's your pillow with the quickstep?

WILLIE (*ignoring the tease*): Good! And why? Because it got no legs. That's her trouble. She can't move them quick enough, Boet Sam. I start the record and before halfway Count Basie is already winning. Only time we catch up with him is when gramophone runs down. (*Sam laughs.*) Haaikona, Boet Sam, is not funny.

SAM (*snapping his fingers*): I got it! Give her a handicap.

WILLIE: What's that?

SAM: Give her a ten-second start and then let Count Basie go. Then I put my money on her. Hot favorite in the Ballroom Stakes: Hilda Samuels ridden by Willie Malopo.

WILLIE (*turning away*): I'm not talking to you no more.

SAM (*relenting*): Sorry, Willie. . . .

WILLIE: It's finish between us.

SAM: Okay, okay . . . I'll stop.

WILLIE: You can also fuck off.

SAM: Willie, listen! I want to help you!

WILLIE: No more jokes?

SAM: I promise.

WILLIE: Okay. Help me.

SAM (*his turn to hold an imaginary partner*): Look and learn. Feet together. Back straight. Body relaxed. Right hand placed gently in the small of her back and wait for the music. Don't start worrying about making mistakes or the judges or the other competitors. It's just you, Hilda and the music, and you're going to have a good time. What Count Basie do you play?

WILLIE: "You the cream in my coffee, you the salt in my stew."

SAM: Right. Give it to me in strict tempo.

WILLIE: Ready?

SAM: Ready.

WILLIE: A-n-d . . . (*Singing.*)

"You the cream in my coffee.
You the salt in my stew.
You will always be my necessity.
I'd be lost without you. . . ." (*etc.*)

(*Sam launches into the quickstep. He is obviously a much more accomplished dancer than Willie. Hally enters. A seventeen-year-old white boy. Wet raincoat and school case. He stops and watches Sam. The demonstration comes to an end with a flourish. Applause from Hally and Willie.*)

HALLY: Bravo! No question about it. First place goes to Mr. Sam Semela.

WILLIE (*in total agreement*): You was gliding with style, Boet Sam.

HALLY (*cheerfully*): How's it, chaps?

SAM: Okay, Hally.

WILLIE (*springing to attention like a soldier and saluting*): At your service, Master Harold!

HALLY: Not long to the big event, hey!

SAM: Two weeks.

HALLY: You nervous?

SAM: No.

HALLY: Think you stand a chance?

SAM: Let's just say I'm ready to go out there and dance.

HALLY: It looked like it. What about you, Willie?

(*Willie groans.*)

What's the matter?

SAM: He's got leg trouble.

HALLY (*innocently*): Oh, sorry to hear that, Willie.

WILLIE: Boet Sam! You promised. (*Willie returns to his work.*)

(*Hally deposits his school case and takes off his raincoat. His clothes are a little neglected and untidy: black blazer with school badge, gray flannel trousers in need of an ironing, khaki shirt and tie, black shoes. Sam has fetched a towel for Hally to dry his hair.*)

HALLY: God, what a lousy bloody day. It's coming down cats and dogs out there. Bad for business, chaps. . . . (*Conspiratorial whisper.*) . . . but it also means we're in for a nice quiet afternoon.

SAM: You can speak loud. Your Mom's not here.

HALLY: Out shopping?

SAM: No. The hospital.

HALLY: But it's Thursday. There's no visiting on Thursday afternoons. Is my Dad okay?

SAM: Sounds like it. In fact, I think he's going home.

HALLY (*stopped short by Sam's remark*): What do you mean?

SAM: The hospital phoned.

HALLY: To say what?

SAM: I don't know. I just heard your Mom talking.

HALLY: So what makes you say he's going home?

SAM: It sounded as if they were telling her to come and fetch him.

(*Hally thinks about what Sam has said for a few seconds.*)

HALLY: When did she leave?

SAM: About an hour ago. She said she would phone you. Want to eat?

(*Hally doesn't respond.*)

Hally, want your lunch?

HALLY: I suppose so. (*His mood has changed.*) What's on the menu? . . . as if I don't know.

SAM: Soup, followed by meat pie and gravy.

HALLY: Today's?

SAM: No.

HALLY: And the soup?

SAM: Nourishing pea soup.

HALLY: Just the soup. (*The pile of comic books on the table.*) And these?

SAM: For your Dad. Mr. Kempston brought them.

HALLY: You haven't been reading them, have you?

SAM: Just looking.

HALLY (*examining the comics*): *Jungle Jim . . . Batman and Robin . . . Tarzan . . .* God, what rubbish! Mental pollution. Take them away.

(*Sam exits waltzing into the kitchen. Hally turns to Willie.*)

HALLY: Did you hear my Mom talking on the telephone, Willie?

WILLIE: No, Master Hally. I was at the back.

HALLY: And she didn't say anything to you before she left?

WILLIE: She said I must clean the floors.

HALLY: I mean about my Dad.

WILLIE: She didn't say nothing to me about him, Master Hally.

HALLY (*with conviction*): No! It can't be. They said he needed at least another three weeks of treatment. Sam's definitely made a mistake. (*Rummages through his school case, finds a book and settles down at the table to read.*) So, Willie!

WILLIE: Yes, Master Hally! Schooling okay today?

HALLY: Yes, okay. . . . (*He thinks about it.*) . . . No, not really. Ag, what's the difference? I don't care. And Sam says you've got problems.

WILLIE: Big problems.

HALLY: Which leg is sore?

(*Willie groans.*)

Both legs.

WILLIE: There is nothing wrong with my legs. Sam is just making jokes.

HALLY: So then you *will* be in the competition.

WILLIE: Only if I can find a partner.

HALLY: But what about Hilda?

SAM (*returning with a bowl of soup*): She's the one who's got trouble with her legs.

HALLY: What sort of trouble, Willie?

SAM: From the way he describes it, I think the lady has gone a bit lame.

HALLY: Good God! Have you taken her to see a doctor?

SAM: I think a vet would be better.

HALLY: What do you mean?

SAM: What do you call it again when a racehorse goes very fast?

HALLY: Gallop?

SAM: That's it!

WILLIE: Boet Sam!

HALLY: "A gallop down the homestretch to the winning post." But what's that got to do with Hilda?

SAM: Count Basie always gets there first.

(*Willie lets fly with his slop rag. It misses Sam and hits Hally.*)

HALLY (*furious*): For Christ's sake, Willie! What the hell do you think you're doing?

National Theatre of London's 1983 production of *"MASTER HAROLD" . . . and the boys* with (l. to r.) Ramolao Makene as Willie, Duart Sylwain as Hally, and John Kani as Sam.

WILLIE: Sorry, Master Hally, but it's him. . . .

HALLY: Act your bloody age! (*Hurls the rag back at Willie.*) Cut out the nonsense now and get on with your work. And you too, Sam. Stop fooling around.

(*Sam moves away.*)

No. Hang on. I haven't finished! Tell me exactly what my Mom said.

SAM: I have. "When Hally comes, tell him I've gone to the hospital and I'll phone him."

HALLY: She didn't say anything about taking my Dad home?

SAM: No. It's just that when she was talking on the phone. . . .

HALLY (*interrupting him*): No, Sam. They can't be discharging him. She would have said so if they were. In any case, we saw him last night and he wasn't in good shape at all. Staff nurse even said there was talk about taking more X-rays. And now suddenly today he's better? If anything, it sounds more like a bad turn to me . . . which I sincerely hope it isn't. Hang on . . . how long ago did you say she left?

SAM: Just before two . . . (*His wrist watch.*) . . . hour and a half.

HALLY: I know how to settle it. (*Behind the counter to the telephone. Talking as he dials.*) Let's give her ten minutes to get to the hospital, ten minutes to load him up, another ten, at the most, to get home, and another ten to get him inside. Forty minutes. They should have been home for at least half an hour already. (*Pause — he waits with the receiver to his ear.*) No reply, chaps. And you know why? Because she's at his bedside in hospital helping him pull through a bad turn. You definitely heard wrong.

SAM: Okay.

(*As far as Hally is concerned, the matter is settled. He returns to his table, sits down, and divides his attention between the book and his soup. Sam is at his school case and picks up a textbook.*)

Modern Graded Mathematics for Standards Nine and Ten. (*Opens it at random and laughs at something he sees.*) Who is this supposed to be?

HALLY: Old fart-face Prentice.

SAM: Teacher?

HALLY: Thinks he is. And believe me, that is not a bad likeness.

SAM: Has he seen it?

HALLY: Yes.

SAM: What did he say?

HALLY: Tried to be clever, as usual. Said I was no Leonardo da Vinci and that bad art had to be punished. So, six of the best, and his are bloody good.

SAM: On your bum?

HALLY: Where else? The days when I got them on my hands are gone forever, Sam.

SAM: With your trousers down!

HALLY: No. He's not quite that barbaric.

SAM: That's the way they do it in jail.

HALLY (*flicker of morbid interest*): Really?

SAM: Ja. When the magistrate sentences you to "strokes with a light cane."

HALLY: Go on.

SAM: They make you lie down on a bench. One policeman pulls down your trousers and holds your ankles, another one pulls your shirt over your head and holds your arms. . . .

HALLY: Thank you! That's enough.

SAM: . . . and the one that gives you the strokes talks to you gently and for a long time between each one. (*He laughs.*)

HALLY: I've heard enough, Sam! Jesus! It's a bloody awful world when you come to think of it. People can be real bastards.

SAM: That's the way it is, Hally.

HALLY: It doesn't *have* to be that way. There is something called progress, you know. We don't exactly burn people at the stake anymore.

SAM: Like Joan of Arc.

HALLY: Correct. If she was captured today, she'd be given a fair trial.

SAM: And then the death sentence.

HALLY (*a world-weary sigh*): I know, I know! I oscillate between hope and despair for this world as well, Sam. But things will change, you wait and see. One day somebody is going to get up and give history a kick up the backside and get it going again.

SAM: Like who?

HALLY (*after thought*): They're called social reformers. Every age, Sam, has got its social reformer. My history book is full of them.

SAM: So where's ours?

HALLY: Good question. And I hate to say it, but the answer is: I don't know. Maybe he hasn't even been born yet. Or is still only a babe in arms at his mother's breast. God, what a thought.

SAM: So we just go on waiting.

HALLY: Ja, looks like it. (*Back to his soup and the book.*)

SAM (*reading from the textbook*): "Introduction: In some mathematical problems only the magnitude. . . ." (*He mispronounces the word "magnitude."*)

HALLY (*correcting him without looking up*): Magnitude.

SAM: What's it mean?

HALLY: How big it is. The size of the thing.

SAM (*reading*): ". . . magnitude of the quantities is of importance. In other problems we need to know whether these quantities are negative or positive. For example, whether there is a debit or credit bank balance . . ."

HALLY: Whether you're broke or not.

SAM: ". . . whether the temperature is above or below Zero. . . ."

HALLY: Naught degrees. Cheerful state of affairs! No cash and you're freezing to death. Mathematics won't get you out of that one.

SAM: "All these quantities are called . . ." (*spelling the word*) . . . s-c-a-l. . . .

HALLY: Scalars.

SAM: Scalars! (*Shaking his head with a laugh.*) You understand all that?

HALLY (*turning a page*): No. And I don't intend to try.

SAM: So what happens when the exams come?

HALLY: Failing a maths exam isn't the end of the world, Sam. How many times have I told you that examination results don't measure intelligence?

SAM: I would say about as many times as you've failed one of them.

HALLY (*mirthlessly*): Ha, ha, ha.

SAM (*simultaneously*): Ha, ha, ha.

HALLY: Just remember Winston Churchill didn't do particularly well at school.

SAM: You've also told me that one many times.

HALLY: Well, it just so happens to be the truth.

SAM (*enjoying the word*): Magnitude! Magnitude! Show me how to use it.

HALLY (*after thought*): An intrepid social reformer will not be daunted by the magnitude of the task he has undertaken.

SAM (*impressed*): Couple of jaw-breakers in there!

HALLY: I gave you three for the price of one. Intrepid, daunted, and magnitude. I did that once in an exam. Put five of the words I had to explain in one sentence. It was half a page long.

SAM: Well, I'll put my money on you in the English exam.

HALLY: Piece of cake. Eighty percent without even trying.

SAM (*another textbook from Hally's case*): And history?

HALLY: So-so. I'll scrape through. In the fifties if I'm lucky.

SAM: You didn't do too badly last year.

HALLY: Because we had World War One. That at least has some action. You try to find that in the South African Parliamentary system.

SAM (*reading from the history textbook*): "Napoleon and the principle of equality." Hey! This sounds interesting. "After concluding peace with Britain in 1802, Napoleon used a brief period of calm to in-sti-tute . . ."

HALLY: Introduce.

SAM: ". . . many reforms. Napoleon regarded all people as equal before the law and wanted them to have equal opportunities for advancement. All ves-ti-ges of the feu-dal sys-tem with its oppression of the poor were abol-ished." Vestiges, feudal system, and abolished. I'm all right on oppression.

HALLY: I'm thinking. He swept away . . . abol-ished . . . the last remains . . . vestiges . . . of the bad old days . . . feudal system.

SAM: Ha! There's the social reformer we're waiting for. He sounds like a man of some magnitude.

HALLY: I'm not so sure about that. It's a damn good title for a book, though. A man of magnitude!

SAM: He sounds pretty big to me, Hally.

HALLY: Don't confuse historical significance with greatness. But maybe I'm being a bit prejudiced. Have a look in there and you'll see he's two chapters long. And hell! . . . has he only got dates, Sam, all of which you've got to remember! This campaign and that campaign, and then, because of all the fighting, the next thing is we get Peace Treaties all over the place. And what's the end of the story? Battle of Waterloo, which he loses. Wasn't worth it. No, I don't know about him as a man of magnitude.

SAM: Then who would you say was?

HALLY: To answer that, we need a definition of greatness, and I suppose that would be somebody who . . . somebody who benefited all mankind.

SAM: Right. But like who?

HALLY (*he speaks with total conviction*): Charles Darwin. Remember him? That big book from the library. *The Origin of the Species.*

SAM: Him?

HALLY: Yes. For his Theory of Evolution.

SAM: You didn't finish it.

HALLY: I ran out of time. I didn't finish it because my two weeks was up. But I'm going to take it out again after I've digested what I read. It's safe. I've hidden it away in the Theology section. Nobody ever goes in there. And anyway who are you to talk? You hardly even looked at it.

SAM: I tried. I looked at the chapters in the beginning and I saw one called "The Struggle for an Existence." Ah ha, I thought. At last! But what did I get? Something called the mistiltoe which needs the apple tree and there's too many seeds and all are going to die except one . . . ! No, Hally.

HALLY (*intellectually outraged*): What do you mean, No! The poor man had to start somewhere. For God's sake, Sam, he revolutionized science. Now we know.

SAM: What?

HALLY: Where we come from and what it all means.

SAM: And that's a benefit to mankind? Anyway, I still don't believe it.

HALLY: God, you're impossible. I showed it to you in black and white.

SAM: Doesn't mean I got to believe it.

HALLY: It's the likes of you that kept the Inquisition in business. It's called bigotry. Anyway, that's my man of magnitude. Charles Darwin! Who's yours?

SAM (*without hesitation*): Abraham Lincoln.

HALLY: I might have guessed as much. Don't get sentimental, Sam. You've never been a slave, you know. And anyway we freed your ancestors here in

South Africa long before the Americans. But if you want to thank somebody on their behalf, do it to Mr. William Wilberforce.° Come on. Try again. I want a real genius.

(*Now enjoying himself, and so is Sam. Hally goes behind the counter and helps himself to a chocolate.*)

SAM: William Shakespeare.

HALLY (*no enthusiasm*): Oh. So you're also one of them, are you? You're basing that opinion on only one play, you know. You've only read my *Julius Caesar* and even I don't understand half of what they're talking about. They should do what they did with the old Bible: bring the language up to date.

SAM: That's all you've got. It's also the only one *you've* read.

HALLY: I know. I admit it. That's why I suggest we reserve our judgment until we've checked up on a few others. I've got a feeling, though, that by the end of this year one is going to be enough for me, and I can give you the names of twenty-nine other chaps in the Standard Nine class of the Port Elizabeth Technical College who feel the same. But if you want him, you can have him. My turn now. (*Pacing.*) This is a damned good exercise, you know! It started off looking like a simple question and here it's got us really probing into the intellectual heritage of our civilization.

SAM: So who is it going to be?

HALLY: My next man ... and he gets the title on two scores: social reform and literary genius ... is Leo Nikolaevich Tolstoy.

SAM: That Russian.

HALLY: Correct. Remember the picture of him I showed you?

SAM: With the long beard.

HALLY (*trying to look like Tolstoy*): And those burning, visionary eyes. My God, the face of a social prophet if ever I saw one! And remember my words when I showed it to you? Here's a *man,* Sam!

SAM: Those were words, Hally.

HALLY: Not many intellectuals are prepared to shovel manure with the peasants and then go home and write a "little book" called *War and Peace.* Incidentally, Sam, he was somebody else who, to quote, "... did not distinguish himself scholastically."

SAM: Meaning?

HALLY: He was also no good at school.

SAM: Like you and Winston Churchill.

HALLY (*mirthlessly*): Ha, ha, ha.

SAM (*simultaneously*): Ha, ha, ha.

Mr. William Wilberforce: (1759–1833), British statesman who supported a bill outlawing the slave trade and suppressing slavery in the British Empire.

HALLY: Don't get clever, Sam. That man freed his serfs of his own free will.

SAM: No argument. He was a somebody, all right. I accept him.

HALLY: I'm sure Count Tolstoy will be very pleased to hear that. Your turn. Shoot. (*Another chocolate from behind the counter.*) I'm waiting, Sam.

SAM: I've got him.

HALLY: Good. Submit your candidate for examination.

SAM: Jesus.

HALLY (*stopped dead in his tracks*): Who?

SAM: Jesus Christ.

HALLY: Oh, come on, Sam!

SAM: The Messiah.

HALLY: Ja, but still ... No, Sam. Don't let's get started on religion. We'll just spend the whole afternoon arguing again. Suppose I turn around and say Mohammed?

SAM: All right.

HALLY: You can't have them both on the same list!

SAM: Why not? You like Mohammed, I like Jesus.

HALLY: I *don't* like Mohammed. I never have. I was merely being hypothetical. As far as I'm concerned, the Koran is as bad as the Bible. No. Religion is out! I'm not going to waste my time again arguing with you about the existence of God. You know perfectly well I'm an atheist ... and I've got homework to do.

SAM: Okay, I take him back.

HALLY: You've got time for one more name.

SAM (*after thought*): I've got one I know we'll agree on. A simple straightforward great Man of Magnitude ... and no arguments. And *he* really *did* benefit all mankind.

HALLY: I wonder. After your last contribution I'm beginning to doubt whether anything in the way of an intellectual agreement is possible between the two of us. Who is he?

SAM: Guess.

HALLY: Socrates? Alexandre Dumas? Karl Marx, Dostoevsky? Nietzsche?

(*Sam shakes his head after each name.*)

Give me a clue.

SAM: The letter *P* is important. . . .

HALLY: Plato!

SAM: . . . and his name begins with an *F.*

HALLY: I've got it. Freud and Psychology.

SAM: No. I didn't understand him.

HALLY: That makes two of us.

SAM: Think of moldy apricot jam.

HALLY (*after a delighted laugh*): Penicillin and Sir Alexander Fleming! And the title of the book: *The Microbe Hunters.* (*Delighted.*) Splendid, Sam! Splendid. For once we are in total agreement. The major breakthrough in medical science in the

Twentieth Century. If it wasn't for him, we might have lost the Second World War. It's deeply gratifying, Sam, to know that I haven't been wasting my time in talking to you. (*Strutting around proudly.*) Tolstoy may have educated his peasants, but I've educated you.

SAM: Standard Four to Standard Nine.

HALLY: Have we been at it as long as that?

SAM: Yep. And my first lesson was geography.

HALLY (*intrigued*): Really? I don't remember.

SAM: My room there at the back of the old Jubilee Boarding House. I had just started working for your Mom. Little boy in short trousers walks in one afternoon and asks me seriously: "Sam, do you want to see South Africa?" Hey man! Sure I wanted to see South Africa!

HALLY: Was that me?

SAM: . . . So the next thing I'm looking at a map you had just done for homework. It was your first one and you were very proud of yourself.

HALLY: Go on.

SAM: Then came my first lesson. "Repeat after me, Sam: Gold in the Transvaal, mealies in the Free State, sugar in Natal, and grapes in the Cape." I still know it!

HALLY: Well, I'll be buggered. So that's how it all started.

SAM: And your next map was one with all the rivers and the mountains they came from. The Orange the Vaal, the Limpopo, the Zambezi. . . .

HALLY: You've got a phenomenal memory!

SAM: You should be grateful. That is why you started passing your exams. You tried to be better than me.

(*They laugh together. Willie is attracted by the laughter and joins them.*)

HALLY: The old Jubilee Boarding House. Sixteen rooms with board and lodging, rent in advance and one week's notice. I haven't thought about it for donkey's years . . . and I don't think that's an accident. God, was I glad when we sold it and moved out. Those years are not remembered as the happiest ones of an unhappy childhood.

WILLIE (*knocking on the table and trying to imitate a woman's voice*): "Hally, are you there?"

HALLY: Who's that supposed to be?

WILLIE: "What you doing in there, Hally? Come out at once!"

HALLY (*to Sam*): What's he talking about?

SAM: Don't you remember?

WILLIE: "Sam, Willie . . . is he in there with you boys?"

SAM: Hiding away in our room when your mother was looking for you.

HALLY (*another good laugh*): Of course! I used to crawl and hide under your bed! But finish the story, Willie. Then what used to happen? You

chaps would give the game away by telling her I was in there with you. So much for friendship.

SAM: We couldn't lie to her. She knew.

HALLY: Which meant I got another rowing for hanging around the "servants' quarters." I think I spent more time in there with you chaps than anywhere else in that dump. And do you blame me? Nothing but bloody misery wherever you went. Somebody was always complaining about the food, or my mother was having a fight with Micky Nash because she'd caught her with a petty officer in her room. Maud Meiring was another one. Remember those two? They were prostitutes, you know. Soldiers and sailors from the troopships. Bottom fell out of the business when the war ended. God, the flotsam and jetsam that life washed up on our shores! No joking, if it wasn't for your room, I would have been the first certified ten-year-old in medical history. Ja, the memories are coming back now. Walking home from school and thinking: "What can I do this afternoon?" Try out a few ideas, but sooner or later I'd end up in there with you fellows. I bet you I could still find my way to your room with my eyes closed. (*He does exactly that.*) Down the corridor . . . telephone on the right, which my Mom keeps locked because somebody is using it on the sly and not paying . . . past the kitchen and unappetizing cooking smells . . . around the corner into the backyard, hold my breath again because there are more smells coming when I pass your lavatory, then into that little passageway, first door on the right and into your room. How's that?

SAM: Good. But, as usual, you forgot to knock.

HALLY: Like that time I barged in and caught you and Cynthia . . . at it. Remember? God, was I embarrassed! I didn't know what was going on at first.

SAM: Ja, that taught you a lesson.

HALLY: And about a lot more than knocking on doors, I'll have you know, and I don't mean geography either. Hell, Sam, couldn't you have waited until it was dark?

SAM: No.

HALLY: Was it that urgent?

SAM: Yes, and if you don't believe me, wait until your time comes.

HALLY: No, thank you. I am not interested in girls. (*Back to his memories. . . . Using a few chairs he re-creates the room as he lists the items.*) A gray little room with a cold cement floor. Your bed against that wall . . . and I now know why the mattress sags so much! . . . Willie's bed . . . it's propped up on bricks because one leg is broken . . . that wobbly little table with the washbasin and jug of water . . . Yes! . . . stuck to the wall above it are

some pin-up pictures from magazines. Joe
Louis. . . .

WILLIE: Brown Bomber. World Title. (*Boxing pose.*)
Three rounds and knockout.

HALLY: Against who?

SAM: Max Schmeling.

HALLY: Correct. I can also remember Fred Astaire and
Ginger Rogers, and Rita Hayworth in a bathing
costume which always made me hot and bothered
when I looked at it. Under Willie's bed is an old
suitcase with all his clothes in a mess, which is why
I never hide there. Your things are neat and tidy in
a trunk next to your bed, and on it there is a picture of you and Cynthia in your ballroom clothes,
your first silver cup for third place in a competition
and an old radio which doesn't work anymore.
Have I left out anything?

SAM: No.

HALLY: Right, so much for the stage directions. Now
the characters. (*Sam and Willie move to their appropriate positions in the bedroom.*) Willie is in
bed, under his blankets with his clothes on, complaining nonstop about something, but we can't
make out a word of what he's saying because he's
got his head under the blankets as well. You're on
your bed trimming your toenails with a knife —
not a very edifying sight — and as for me. . . .
What am I doing?

SAM: You're sitting on the floor giving Willie a lecture
about being a good loser while you get the
checkerboard and pieces ready for a game. Then
you go to Willie's bed, pull off the blankets and
make him play with you first because you know
you're going to win, and that gives you the second
game with me.

HALLY: And you certainly were a bad loser, Willie!

WILLIE: Haai!

HALLY: Wasn't he, Sam? And so slow! A game with
you almost took the whole afternoon. Thank God
I gave up trying to teach you how to play chess.

WILLIE: You and Sam cheated.

HALLY: I never saw Sam cheat, and mine were mostly
the mistakes of youth.

WILLIE: Then how is it you two was always winning?

HALLY: Have you ever considered the possibility,
Willie, that it was because we were better than you?

WILLIE: Every time better?

HALLY: Not every time. There were occasions when
we deliberately let you win a game so that you
would stop sulking and go on playing with us. Sam
used to wink at me when you weren't looking to
show me it was time to let you win.

WILLIE: So then you two didn't play fair.

HALLY: It was for your benefit, Mr. Malopo, which is
more than being fair. It was an act of self-sacrifice.

(*To Sam.*) But you know what my best memory is,
don't you?

SAM: No.

HALLY: Come on, guess. If your memory is so good,
you must remember it as well.

SAM: We got up to a lot of tricks in there, Hally.

HALLY: This one was special, Sam.

SAM: I'm listening.

HALLY: It started off looking like another of those useless nothing-to-do afternoons. I'd already been
down to Main Street looking for adventure, but
nothing had happened. I didn't feel like climbing
trees in the Donkin Park or pretending I was a private eye and following a stranger . . . so as usual:
See what's cooking in Sam's room. This time it was
you on the floor. You had two thin pieces of wood
and you were smoothing them down with a knife.
It didn't look particularly interesting, but when I
asked you what you were doing, you just said,
"Wait and see, Hally. Wait . . . and see" . . . in that
secret sort of way of yours, so I knew there was a
surprise coming. You teased me, you bugger, by
being deliberately slow and not answering my
questions!

(*Sam laughs.*)

And whistling while you worked away! God, it
was infuriating! I could have brained you! It was
only when you tied them together in a cross and
put that down on the brown paper that I realized
what you were doing. "Sam is making a kite?"
And when I asked you and you said, "Yes". . . !
(*Shaking his head with disbelief.*) The sheer audacity of it took my breath away. I mean, seriously,
what the hell does a black man know about flying
a kite? I'll be honest with you, Sam, I had no hopes
for it. If you think I was excited and happy, you
got another guess coming. In fact, I was shit-scared
that we were going to make fools of ourselves.
When we left the boarding house to go up onto the
hill, I was praying quietly that there wouldn't be
any other kids around to laugh at us.

SAM (*enjoying the memory as much as Hally*): Ja, I
could see that.

HALLY: I made it obvious, did I?

SAM: Ja. You refused to carry it.

HALLY: Do you blame me? Can you remember what
the poor thing looked like? Tomato-box wood and
brown paper! Flour and water for glue! Two of my
mother's old stockings for a tail, and then all those
bits and pieces of string you made me tie together
so that we could fly it! Hell, no, that was now only
asking for a miracle to happen.

SAM: Then the big argument when I told you to hold
the string and run with it when I let go.

HALLY: I was prepared to run, all right, but straight back to the boarding house.

SAM (*knowing what's coming*): So what happened?

HALLY: Come on, Sam, you remember as well as I do.

SAM: I want to hear it from you.

(*Hally pauses. He wants to be as accurate as possible.*)

HALLY: You went a little distance from me down the hill, you held it up ready to let it go. . . . "This is it," I thought. "Like everything else in my life, here comes another fiasco." Then you shouted, "Go, Hally!" and I started to run. (*Another pause.*) I don't know how to describe it, Sam. Ja! The miracle happened! I was running, waiting for it to crash to the ground, but instead suddenly there was something alive behind me at the end of the string, tugging at it as if it wanted to be free. I looked back . . . (*Shakes his head.*) . . . I still can't believe my eyes. It was flying! Looping around and trying to climb even higher into the sky. You shouted to me to let it have more string. I did, until there was none left and I was just holding that piece of wood we had tied it to. You came up and joined me. You were laughing.

SAM: So were you. And shouting, "It works, Sam! We've done it!"

HALLY: And we had! I was so proud of us! It was the most splendid thing I had ever seen. I wished there were hundreds of kids around to watch us. The part that scared me, though, was when you showed me how to make it dive down to the ground and then just when it was on the point of crashing, swoop up again!

SAM: You didn't want to try yourself.

HALLY: Of course not! I would have been suicidal if anything had happened to it. Watching you do it made me nervous enough. I was quite happy just to see it up there with its tail fluttering behind it. You left me after that, didn't you? You explained how to get it down, we tied it to the bench so that I could sit and watch it, and you went away. I wanted you to stay, you know. I was a little scared of having to look after it by myself.

SAM (*quietly*): I had work to do, Hally.

HALLY: It was sort of sad bringing it down, Sam. And it looked sad again when it was lying there on the ground. Like something that had lost its soul. Just tomato-box wood, brown paper and two of my mother's old stockings! But, hell, I'll never forget that first moment when I saw it up there. I had a stiff neck the next day from looking up so much.

(*Sam laughs. Hally turns to him with a question he never thought of asking before.*)

Why did you make that kite, Sam?

SAM (*evenly*): I can't remember.

HALLY: Truly?

SAM: Too long ago, Hally.

HALLY: Ja, I suppose it was. It's time for another one, you know.

SAM: Why do you say that?

HALLY: Because it feels like that. Wouldn't be a good day to fly it, though.

SAM: No. You can't fly kites on rainy days.

HALLY (*He studies Sam. Their memories have made him conscious of the man's presence in his life.*): How old are you, Sam?

SAM: Two score and five.

HALLY: Strange, isn't it?

SAM: What?

HALLY: Me and you.

SAM: What's strange about it?

HALLY: Little white boy in short trousers and a black man old enough to be his father flying a kite. It's not every day you see that.

SAM: But why strange? Because the one is white and the other black?

HALLY: I don't know. Would have been just as strange, I suppose, if it had been me and my Dad . . . cripple man and a little boy! Nope! There's no chance of me flying a kite without it being strange. (*Simple statement of fact — no self-pity.*) There's a nice little short story there. "The Kite-Flyers." But we'd have to find a twist in the ending.

SAM: Twist?

HALLY: Yes. Something unexpected. The way it ended with us was too straightforward . . . me on the bench and you going back to work. There's no drama in that.

WILLIE: And me?

HALLY: You?

WILLIE: Yes me.

HALLY: You want to get into the story as well, do you? I got it! Change the title: "Afternoons in Sam's Room" . . . expand it and tell all the stories. It's on its way to being a novel. Our days in the old Jubilee. Sad in a way that they're over. I almost wish we were still in that little room.

SAM: We're still together.

HALLY: That's true. It's just that life felt the right size in there . . . not too big and not too small. Wasn't so hard to work up a bit of courage. It's got so bloody complicated since then.

(*The telephone rings. Sam answers it.*)

SAM: St. George's Park Tea Room . . . Hello, Madam . . . Yes, Madam, he's here. . . . Hally, it's your mother.

HALLY: Where is she phoning from?

SAM: Sounds like the hospital. It's a public telephone.

HALLY (*relieved*). You see! I told you. (*The telephone.*) Hello, Mom . . . Yes . . . Yes no fine. Everything's under control here. How's things with poor old Dad? . . . Has he had a bad turn? . . . What? . . . Oh, God! . . . Yes, Sam told me, but I was sure he'd made a mistake. But what's this all about, Mom? He didn't look at all good last night. How can he get better so quickly? . . . Then very obviously you must say no. Be firm with him. You're the boss. . . . You know what it's going to be like if he comes home. . . . Well then, don't blame me when I fail my exams at the end of the year. . . . Yes! How am I expected to be fresh for school when I spend half the night massaging his gammy leg? . . . So am I! . . . So tell him a white lie. Say Dr. Colley wants more X-rays of his stump. Or bribe him. We'll sneak in double tots of brandy in future. . . . What? . . . Order him to get back into bed at once! If he's going to behave like a child, treat him like one. . . . All right, Mom! I was just trying to . . . I'm sorry. . . . I said I'm sorry. . . . Quick, give me your number. I'll phone you back. (*He hangs up and waits a few seconds.*) Here we go again! (*He dials.*) I'm sorry, Mom. . . . Okay. . . . But now listen to me carefully. All it needs is for you to put your foot down. Don't take no for an answer. . . . Did you hear me? And whatever you do, don't discuss it with him. . . . Because I'm frightened you'll give in to him. . . . Yes, Sam gave me lunch. . . . I ate all of it! . . . No, Mom not a soul. It's still raining here. . . . Right, I'll tell them. I'll just do some homework and then lock up. . . . But remember now, Mom. Don't listen to anything he says. And phone me back and let me know what happens. . . . Okay. Bye, Mom. (*He hangs up. The men are staring at him.*) My Mom says that when you're finished with the floors you must do the windows. (*Pause.*) Don't misunderstand me, chaps. All I want is for him to get better. And if he was, I'd be the first person to say: "Bring him home." But he's not, and we can't give him the medical care and attention he needs at home. That's what hospitals are there for. (*Brusquely.*) So don't just stand there! Get on with it!

(*Sam clears Hally's table.*)

You heard right. My Dad wants to go home.

SAM: Is he better?

HALLY (*sharply*): No! How the hell can he be better when last night he was groaning with pain? This is not an age of miracles!

SAM: Then he should stay in hospital.

HALLY (*seething with irritation and frustration*): Tell me something I don't know, Sam. What the hell do you think I was saying to my Mom? All I can say is fuck-it-all.

SAM: I'm sure he'll listen to your Mom.

HALLY: You don't know what she's up against. He's already packed his shaving kit and pajamas and is sitting on his bed with his crutches, dressed and ready to go. I know him when he gets in that mood. If she tries to reason with him, we've had it. She's no match for him when it comes to a battle of words. He'll tie her up in knots. (*Trying to hide his true feelings.*)

SAM: I suppose it gets lonely for him in there.

HALLY: With all the patients and nurses around? Regular visits from the Salvation Army? Balls! It's ten times worse for him at home. I'm at school and my mother is here in the business all day.

SAM: He's at least got you at night.

HALLY (*before he can stop himself*): And we've got him! Please! I don't want to talk about it anymore. (*Unpacks his school case, slamming down books on the table.*) Life is just a plain bloody mess, that's all. And people are fools.

SAM: Come on, Hally.

HALLY: Yes, they are! They bloody well deserve what they get.

SAM: Then don't complain.

HALLY: Don't try to be clever, Sam. It doesn't suit you. Anybody who thinks there's nothing wrong with this world needs to have his head examined. Just when things are going along all right, without fail someone or something will come along and spoil everything. Somebody should write that down as a fundamental law of the Universe. The principle of perpetual disappointment. If there is a God who created this world, he should scrap it and try again.

SAM: All right, Hally, all right. What you got for homework?

HALLY: Bullshit, as usual. (*Opens an exercise book and reads.*) "Write five hundred words describing an annual event of cultural or historical significance."

SAM: That should be easy enough for you.

HALLY: And also plain bloody boring. You know what he wants, don't you? One of their useless old ceremonies. The commemoration of the landing of the 1820 Settlers, or if it's going to be culture, Carols by Candlelight every Christmas.

SAM: It's an impressive sight. Make a good description, Hally. All those candles glowing in the dark and the people singing hymns.

HALLY: And it's called religious hysteria. (*Intense irritation.*) Please, Sam! Just leave me alone and let me get on with it. I'm not in the mood for games this afternoon. And remember my Mom's orders . . . you're to help Willie with the windows. Come on now, I don't want any more nonsense in here.

SAM: Okay, Hally, okay.

(*Hally settles down to his homework; determined preparations . . . pen, ruler, exercise book, dictionary, another cake . . . all of which will lead to nothing.*)

(*Sam waltzes over to Willie and starts to replace tables and chairs. He practices a ballroom step while doing so. Willie watches. When Sam is finished, Willie tries.*)

Good! But just a little bit quicker on the turn and only move in to her after she's crossed over. What about this one?

(*Another step. When Sam is finished, Willie again has a go.*)

Much better. See what happens when you just relax and enjoy yourself? Remember that in two weeks' time and you'll be all right.

WILLIE: But I haven't got partner, Boet Sam.

SAM: Maybe Hilda will turn up tonight.

WILLIE: No, Boet Sam. (*Reluctantly.*) I gave her a good hiding.

SAM: You mean a bad one.

WILLIE: Good bad one.

SAM: Then you mustn't complain either. Now you pay the price for losing your temper.

WILLIE: I also pay two pounds ten shilling entrance fee.

SAM: They'll refund you if you withdraw now.

WILLIE (*appalled*): You mean, don't dance?

SAM: Yes.

WILLIE: No! I wait too long and I practice too hard. If I find me new partner, you think I can be ready in two weeks? I ask Madam for my leave now and we practice every day.

SAM: Quickstep nonstop for two weeks. World record, Willie, but you'll be mad at the end.

WILLIE: No jokes, Boet Sam.

SAM: I'm not joking.

WILLIE: So then what?

SAM: Find Hilda. Say you're sorry and promise you won't beat her again.

WILLIE: No.

SAM: Then withdraw. Try again next year.

WILLIE: No.

SAM: Then I give up.

WILLIE: Haaikona, Boet Sam, you can't.

SAM: What do you mean, I can't? I'm telling you: I give up.

WILLIE (*adamant*): No! (*Accusingly.*) It was you who start me ballroom dancing.

SAM: So?

WILLIE: Before that I use to be happy. And is you and Miriam who bring me to Hilda and say here's partner for you.

SAM: What are you saying, Willie?

WILLIE: You!

SAM: But me what? To blame?

WILLIE: Yes.

SAM: Willie . . . ? (*Bursts into laughter.*)

WILLIE: And now all you do is make jokes at me. You wait. When Miriam leaves you is my turn to laugh. Ha! Ha! Ha!

SAM (*he can't take Willie seriously any longer*): She can leave me tonight! I know what to do. (*Bowing before an imaginary partner.*) May I have the pleasure? (*He dances and sings.*)
"Just a fellow with his pillow . . .
Dancin' like a willow . . .
In an autumn breeze. . . ."

WILLIE: There you go again!

(*Sam goes on dancing and singing.*)

Boet Sam!

SAM: There's the answer to your problem! Judges' announcement in two weeks' time: "Ladies and gentlemen, the winner in the open section . . . Mr. Willie Malopo and his pillow!"

(*This is too much for a now really angry Willie. He goes for Sam, but the latter is too quick for him and puts Hally's table between the two of them.*)

HALLY (*exploding*): For Christ's sake, you two!

WILLIE (*still trying to get at Sam*): I donner you, Sam! Struesgod!

SAM (*still laughing*): Sorry, Willie . . . Sorry. . . .

HALLY: Sam! Willie! (*Grabs his ruler and gives Willie a vicious whack on the bum.*) How the hell am I supposed to concentrate with the two of you behaving like bloody children!

WILLIE: Hit him too!

HALLY: Shut up, Willie.

WILLIE: He started jokes again.

HALLY: Get back to your work. You too, Sam. (*His ruler.*) Do you want another one, Willie?

(*Sam and Willie return to their work. Hally uses the opportunity to escape from his unsuccessful attempt at homework. He struts around like a little despot, ruler in hand, giving vent to his anger and frustration.*)

Suppose a customer had walked in then? Or the Park Superintendent. And seen the two of you behaving like a pair of hooligans. That would have been the end of my mother's license, you know. And your jobs? Well, this is the end of it. From now on there will be no more of your ballroom nonsense in here. This is a business establishment, not a bloody New Brighton dancing school. I've been far too lenient with the two of you. (*Behind the counter for a green cool drink and a dollop of ice cream. He keeps up his tirade as he prepares it.*) But what really makes me bitter is that I allow you chaps a little freedom in here when business is bad and what do you do with it? The foxtrot! Specially you, Sam. There's more to life than trotting around a dance floor and I thought at least you knew it.

SAM: It's a harmless pleasure, Hally. It doesn't hurt anybody.

HALLY: It's also a rather simple one, you know.

SAM: You reckon so? Have you ever tried?

HALLY: Of course not.

SAM: Why don't you? Now.

HALLY: What do you mean? Me dance?

SAM: Yes. I'll show you a simple step — the waltz — then you try it.

HALLY: What will that prove?

SAM: That it might not be as easy as you think.

HALLY: I didn't say it was easy. I said it was simple — like in simple-minded, meaning mentally retarded. You can't exactly say it challenges the intellect.

SAM: It does other things.

HALLY: Such as?

SAM: Make people happy.

HALLY (*the glass in his hand*): So do American cream sodas with ice cream. For God's sake, Sam, you're not asking me to take ballroom dancing serious, are you?

SAM: Yes.

HALLY (*sigh of defeat*): Oh, well, so much for trying to give you a decent education. I've obviously achieved nothing.

SAM: You still haven't told me what's wrong with admiring something that's beautiful and then trying to do it yourself.

HALLY: Nothing. But we happen to be talking about a foxtrot, not a thing of beauty.

SAM: But that is just what I'm saying. If you were to see two champions doing, two masters of the art . . . !

HALLY: Oh God, I give up. So now it's also art!

SAM: Ja.

HALLY: There's a limit, Sam. Don't confuse art and entertainment.

SAM: So then what is art?

HALLY: You want a definition?

SAM: Ja.

HALLY (*He realizes he has got to be careful. He gives the matter a lot of thought before answering.*): Philosophers have been trying to do that for centuries. What is Art? What is Life? But basically I suppose it's . . . the giving of meaning to matter.

SAM: Nothing to do with beautiful?

HALLY: It goes beyond that. It's the giving of form to the formless.

SAM: Ja, well, maybe it's not art, then. But I still say it's beautiful.

HALLY: I'm sure the word you mean to use is entertaining.

SAM (*adamant*): No. Beautiful. And if you want proof come along to the Centenary Hall in New Brighton in two weeks' time.

(*The mention of the Centenary Hall draws Willie over to them.*)

HALLY: What for? I've seen the two of you prancing around in here often enough.

SAM (*he laughs*): This isn't the real thing, Hally. We're just playing around in here.

HALLY: So? I can use my imagination.

SAM: And what do you get?

HALLY: A lot of people dancing around and having a so-called good time.

SAM: That all?

HALLY: Well, basically it is that, surely.

SAM: No, it isn't. Your imagination hasn't helped you at all. There's a lot more to it than that. We're getting ready for the championships, Hally, not just another dance. There's going to be a lot of people, all right, and they're going to have a good time, but they'll only be spectators, sitting around and watching. It's just the competitors out there on the dance floor. Party decorations and fancy lights all around the walls! The ladies in beautiful evening dresses!

HALLY: My mother's got one of those, Sam, and, quite frankly, it's an embarrassment every time she wears it.

SAM (*undeterred*): Your imagination left out the excitement.

(*Hally scoffs.*)

Oh, yes. The finalists are not going to be out there just to have a good time. One of those couples will be the 1950 Eastern Province Champions. And your imagination left out the music.

WILLIE: Mr. Elijah Gladman Guzana and his Orchestral Jazzonions.

SAM: The sound of the big band, Hally. Trombone, trumpet, tenor and alto sax. And then, finally, your imagination also left out the climax of the evening when the dancing is finished, the judges have stopped whispering among themselves and the Master of Ceremonies collects their scorecards and goes up onto the stage to announce the winners.

HALLY: All right. So you make it sound like a bit of a do. It's an occasion. Satisfied?

SAM (*victory*): So you admit that!

HALLY: Emotionally yes, intellectually no.

SAM: Well, I don't know what you mean by that, all I'm telling you is that it is going to be *the* event of the year in New Brighton. It's been sold out for two weeks already. There's only standing room left. We've got competitors coming from Kingwilliamstown, East London, Port Alfred.

(*Hally starts pacing thoughtfully.*)

HALLY: Tell me a bit more.

SAM: I thought you weren't interested . . . intellectually.

HALLY (*mysteriously*): I've got my reasons.

SAM: What do you want to know?

HALLY: It takes place every year?

SAM: Yes. But only every third year in New Brighton. It's East London's turn to have the championships next year.

HALLY: Which, I suppose, makes it an even more significant event.

SAM: Ah ha! We're getting somewhere. Our "occasion" is now a "significant event."

HALLY: I wonder.

SAM: What?

HALLY: I wonder if I would get away with it.

SAM: But what?

HALLY (*to the table and his exercise book*): "Write five hundred words describing an annual event of cultural or historical significance." Would I be stretching poetic license a little too far if I called your ballroom championships a cultural event?

SAM: You mean . . . ?

HALLY: You think we could get five hundred words out of it, Sam?

SAM: Victor Sylvester has written a whole book on ballroom dancing.

WILLIE: You going to write about it, Master Hally?

HALLY: Yes, gentlemen, that is precisely what I am considering doing. Old Doc Bromely — he's my English teacher — is going to argue with me, of course. He doesn't like natives. But I'll point out to him that in strict anthropological terms the culture of a primitive black society includes its dancing and singing. To put my thesis in a nutshell: The war-dance has been replaced by the waltz. But it still amounts to the same thing: the release of primitive emotions through movement. Shall we give it a go?

SAM: I'm ready.

WILLIE: Me also.

HALLY: Ha! This will teach the old bugger a lesson. (*Decision taken.*) Right. Let's get ourselves organized. (*This means another cake on the table. He sits.*) I think you've given me enough general atmosphere, Sam, but to build the tension and suspense I need facts. (*Pencil poised.*)

WILLIE: Give him facts, Boet Sam.

HALLY: What you called the climax . . . how many finalists?

SAM: Six couples.

HALLY (*making notes*): Go on. Give me the picture.

SAM: Spectators seated right around the hall. (*Willie becomes a spectator.*)

HALLY: . . . and it's a full house.

SAM: At one end, on the stage, Gladman and his Orchestral Jazzonions. At the other end is a long table with the three judges. The six finalists go onto the dance floor and take up their positions. When they are ready and the spectators have settled down, the Master of Ceremonies goes to the microphone. To start with, he makes some jokes to get people laughing. . . .

HALLY: Good touch. (*As he writes.*) ". . . creating a relaxed atmosphere which will change to one of tension and drama as the climax is approached."

SAM (*onto a chair to act out the M.C.*): "Ladies and gentlemen, we come now to the great moment you have all been waiting for this evening. . . . The finals of the 1950 Eastern Province Open Ballroom Dancing Championships. But first let me introduce the finalists! Mr. and Mrs. Welcome Tchabalala from Kingwilliamstown . . ."

WILLIE (*he applauds after every name*): Is when the people clap their hands and whistle and make a lot of noise, Master Hally.

SAM: "Mr. Mulligan Njikelane and Miss Nomhle Nkonyeni of Grahamstown; Mr. and Mrs. Norman Nchinga from Port Alfred; Mr. Fats Bokolane and Miss Dina Plaatjies from East London; Mr. Sipho Dugu and Mrs. Mable Magada from Peddie; and from New Brighton our very own Mr. Willie Malopo and Miss Hilda Samuels."

(*Willie can't believe his ears. He abandons his role as spectator and scrambles into position as a finalist.*)

WILLIE: Relaxed and ready to romance!

SAM: The applause dies down. When everybody is silent, Gladman lifts up his sax, nods at the Orchestral Jazzonions. . . .

WILLIE: Play the jukebox please, Boet Sam!

SAM: I also only got bus fare, Willie.

HALLY: Hold it, everybody. (*Heads for the cash register behind the counter.*) How much is in the till, Sam?

SAM: Three shillings. Hally . . . Your Mom counted it before she left.

(*Hally hesitates.*)

HALLY: Sorry, Willie. You know how she carried on the last time I did it. We'll just have to pool our combined imaginations and hope for the best. (*Returns to the table.*) Back to work. How are the points scored, Sam?

SAM: Maximum of ten points each for individual style, deportment, rhythm, and general appearance.

WILLIE: Must I start?

HALLY: Hold it for a second, Willie. And penalties?

SAM: For what?

HALLY: For doing something wrong. Say you stumble or bump into somebody . . . do they take off any points?

SAM (*aghast*): Hally . . . !

HALLY: When you're dancing. If you and your partner collide into another couple.

(*Hally can get no further. Sam has collapsed with laughter. He explains to Willie.*)

SAM: If me and Miriam bump into you and Hilda. . . .

(*Willie joins him in another good laugh.*)

Hally, Hally . . . !

HALLY (*perplexed*): Why? What did I say?

SAM: There's no collisions out there, Hally. Nobody trips or stumbles or bumps into anybody else. That's what that moment is all about. To be one of those finalists on that dance floor is like . . . like being in a dream about a world in which accidents don't happen.

HALLY (*genuinely moved by Sam's image*): Jesus, Sam! That's beautiful!

WILLIE (*can endure waiting no longer*): I'm starting!

(*Willie dances while Sam talks.*)

SAM: Of course it is. That's what I've been trying to say to you all afternoon. And it's beautiful because that is what we want life to be like. But instead, like you said, Hally, we're bumping into each other all the time. Look at the three of us this afternoon: I've bumped into Willie, the two of us have bumped into you, you've bumped into your mother, she bumping into your Dad. . . . None of us knows the steps and there's no music playing. And it doesn't stop with us. The whole world is doing it all the time. Open a newspaper and what do you read? America has bumped into Russia, England is bumping into India, rich man bumps into poor man. Those are big collisions, Hally. They make for a lot of bruises. People get hurt in all that bumping, and we're sick and tired of it now. It's been going on for too long. Are we never going to get it right? . . . Learn to dance life like champions instead of always being just a bunch of beginners at it?

HALLY (*deep and sincere admiration of the man*): You've got a vision, Sam!

SAM: Not just me. What I'm saying to you is that everybody's got it. That's why there's only standing room left for the Centenary Hall in two weeks' time. For as long as the music lasts, we are going to see six couples get it right, the way we want life to be.

HALLY: But is that the best we can do, Sam . . . watch six finalists dreaming about the way it should be?

SAM: I don't know. But it starts with that. Without the dream we won't know what we're going for. And anyway I reckon there are a few people who have got past just dreaming about it and are trying for something real. Remember that thing we read once in the paper about the Mahatma Gandhi? Going without food to stop those riots in India?

HALLY: You're right. He certainly was trying to teach people to get the steps right.

SAM: And the Pope.

HALLY: Yes, he's another one. Our old General Smuts° as well, you know. He's also out there dancing. You know, Sam, when you come to think of it, that's what the United Nations boils down to . . . a dancing school for politicians!

SAM: And let's hope they learn.

HALLY (*a little surge of hope*): You're right. We mustn't despair. Maybe there's some hope for mankind after all. Keep it up, Willie. (*Back to his table with determination.*) This is a lot bigger than I thought. So what have we got? Yes, our title: "A World Without Collisions."

SAM: That sounds good! "A World Without Collisions."

HALLY: Subtitle: "Global Politics on the Dance Floor." No. A bit too heavy, hey? What about "Ballroom Dancing as a Political Vision"?

(*The telephone rings. Sam answers it.*)

SAM: St. George's Park Tea Room . . . Yes, Madam . . . Hally, it's your Mom.

HALLY (*back to reality*): Oh, God, yes! I'd forgotten all about that. Shit! Remember my words, Sam? Just when you're enjoying yourself, someone or something will come along and wreck everything.

SAM: You haven't heard what she's got to say yet.

HALLY: Public telephone?

SAM: No.

HALLY: Does she sound happy or unhappy?

SAM: I couldn't tell. (*Pause.*) She's waiting, Hally.

HALLY (*to the telephone*): Hello, Mom . . . No, everything is okay here. Just doing my homework. . . . What's your news? . . . You've what? . . . (*Pause. He takes the receiver away from his ear for a few seconds. In the course of Hally's telephone conversation, Sam and Willie discreetly position the stacked tables and chairs. Hally places the receiver back to his ear.*) Yes, I'm still here. Oh, well, I give up now. Why did you do it, Mom? . . . Well, I just hope you know what you've let us in for. . . . (*Loudly.*) I said I hope you know what you've let us in for! It's the end of the peace and quiet we've been having. (*Softly.*) Where is he? (*Normal voice.*) He can't hear us from in there. But for God's sake, Mom, what happened? I told you to be firm with him. . . . Then

General Smuts: (1870–1950), South African statesman who fought the British in the Boer War in 1899, was instrumental in forming the Union of South Africa in 1910, and was active in the creation of the United Nations.

you and the nurses should have held him down, taken his crutches away. . . . I know only too well he's my father! . . . I'm not being disrespectful, but I'm sick and tired of emptying stinking chamber pots full of phlegm and piss. . . . Yes, I do! When you're not there, he asks *me* to do it. . . . If you really want to know the truth, that's why I've got no appetite for my food. . . . Yes! There's a lot of things you don't know about. For your information, I still haven't got that science textbook I need. And you know why? He borrowed the money you gave me for it. . . . Because I didn't want to start another fight between you two. . . . He says that every time. . . . All right, Mom! (*Viciously.*) Then just remember to start hiding your bag away again, because he'll be at your purse before long for money for booze. And when he's well enough to come down here, you better keep an eye on the till as well, because that is also going to develop a leak. . . . Then don't complain to me when he starts his old tricks. . . . Yes, you do. I get it from you on one side and from him on the other, and it makes life hell for me. I'm not going to be the peacemaker anymore. I'm warning you now: when the two of you start fighting again, I'm leaving home. . . . Mom, if you start crying, I'm going to put down the receiver. . . . Okay. . . . (*Lowering his voice to a vicious whisper.*) Okay, Mom. I heard you. (*Desperate.*) No. . . . Because I don't want to. I'll see him when I get home! Mom! . . . (*Pause. When he speaks again, his tone changes completely. It is not simply pretense. We sense a genuine emotional conflict.*) Welcome home, chum! . . . What's that? . . . Don't be silly, Dad. You being home is just about the best news in the world. . . . I bet you are. Bloody depressing there with everybody going on about their ailments, hey! . . . How you feeling? . . . Good. . . . Here as well, pal. Coming down cats and dogs. . . . That's right. Just the day for a kip° and a toss in your old Uncle Ned. . . . Everything's just hunky-dory on my side, Dad. . . . Well, to start with, there's a nice pile of comics for you on the counter. . . . Yes, old Kemple brought them in. *Batman and Robin, Submariner* . . . just your cup of tea. . . . I will. . . . Yes, we'll spin a few yarns tonight. . . . Okay, chum, see you in a little while. . . . No, I promise. I'll come straight home. . . . (*Pause — his mother comes back on the phone.*) Mom? Okay. I'll lock up now. . . . What? . . . Oh, the brandy . . . Yes, I'll remember! . . . I'll put it in my suitcase now, for God's sake. I know well enough what will happen if he doesn't get it. . . . (*Places a bottle of brandy on the counter.*) I *was* kind to him, Mom. I didn't say any-

kip: Nap.

thing nasty! . . . All right. Bye. (*End of telephone conversation. A desolate Hally doesn't move. A strained silence.*)

SAM (*quietly*): That sounded like a bad bump, Hally.

HALLY (*Having a hard time controlling his emotions. He speaks carefully.*): Mind your own business, Sam.

SAM: Sorry. I wasn't trying to interfere. Shall we carry on? Hally? (*He indicates the exercise book. No response from Hally.*)

WILLIE (*also trying*): Tell him about when they give out the cups, Boet Sam.

SAM: Ja! That's another big moment. The presentation of the cups after the winners have been announced. You've got to put that in.

(*Still no response from Hally.*)

WILLIE: A big silver one, Master Hally, called floating trophy for the champions.

SAM: We always invite some big-shot personality to hand them over. Guest of honor this year is going to be His Holiness Bishop Jabulani of the All African Free Zionist Church.

(*Hally gets up abruptly, goes to his table, and tears up the page he was writing on.*)

HALLY: So much for a bloody world without collisions.

SAM: Too bad. It was on its way to being a good composition.

HALLY: Let's stop bullshitting ourselves, Sam.

SAM: Have we been doing that?

HALLY: Yes! That's what all our talk about a decent world has been . . . just so much bullshit.

SAM: We did say it was still only a dream.

HALLY: And a bloody useless one at that. Life's a fuckup and it's never going to change.

SAM: Ja, maybe that's true.

HALLY: There's no maybe about it. It's a blunt and brutal fact. All we've done this afternoon is waste our time.

SAM: Not if we'd got your homework done.

HALLY: I don't give a shit about my homework, so, for Christ's sake, just shut up about it. (*Slamming books viciously into his school case.*) Hurry up now and finish your work. I want to lock up and get out of here. (*Pause.*) And then go where? Home-sweet-fucking-home. Jesus, I hate that word.

(*Hally goes to the counter to put the brandy bottle and comics in his school case. After a moment's hesitation, he smashes the bottle of brandy. He abandons all further attempts to hide his feelings. Sam and Willie work away as unobtrusively as possible.*)

Do you want to know what is really wrong with your lovely little dream, Sam? It's not just that we

are all bad dancers. That does happen to be perfectly true, but there's more to it than just that.
You left out the cripples.

SAM: Hally!

HALLY (*now totally reckless*): Ja! Can't leave them
out, Sam. That's why we always end up on our
backsides on the dance floor. They're also out there
dancing . . . like a bunch of broken spiders trying
to do the quickstep! (*An ugly attempt at laughter.*)
When you come to think of it, it's a bloody comical sight. I mean, it's bad enough on two legs . . .
but one and a pair of crutches! Hell, no, Sam.
That's guaranteed to turn that dance floor into a
shambles. Why you shaking your head? Picture it,
man. For once this afternoon let's use our imaginations sensibly.

SAM: Be careful, Hally.

HALLY: Of what? The truth? I seem to be the only one
around here who is prepared to face it. We've had
the pretty dream, it's time now to wake up and
have a good long look at the way things really are.
Nobody knows the steps, there's no music, the
cripples are also out there tripping up everybody
and trying to get into the act, and it's all called the
All-Com-ers-How-to-Make-a-Fuckup-of-Life Championships. (*Another ugly laugh.*) Hang on, Sam!
The best bit is still coming. Do you know what the
winner's trophy is? A beautiful big chamber pot
with roses on the side, and it's full to the brim with
piss. And guess who I think is going to be this
year's winner.

SAM (*almost shouting*): Stop now!

HALLY (*suddenly appalled by how far he has gone*):
Why?

SAM: Hally? It's your father you're talking about.

HALLY: So?

SAM: Do you know what you've been saying?

(*Hally can't answer. He is rigid with shame. Sam
speaks to him sternly.*)

No, Hally, you mustn't do it. Take back those
words and ask for forgiveness! It's a terrible sin for
a son to mock his father with jokes like that. You'll
be punished if you carry on. Your father is your father, even if he is a . . . cripple man.

WILLIE: Yes, Master Hally. Is true what Sam say.

SAM: I understand how you are feeling, Hally, but
even so. . . .

HALLY: No, you don't!

SAM: I think I do.

HALLY: And I'm telling you you don't. Nobody does.
(*Speaking carefully as his shame turns to rage at
Sam.*) It's your turn to be careful, Sam. Very careful! You're treading on dangerous ground. Leave
me and my father alone.

SAM: I'm not the one who's been saying things about
him.

HALLY: What goes on between me and my Dad is
none of your business!

SAM: Then don't tell me about it. If that's all you've
got to say about him, I don't want to hear.

(*For a moment Hally is at loss for a response.*)

HALLY: Just get on with your bloody work and shut up.

SAM: Swearing at me won't help you.

HALLY: Yes, it does! Mind your own fucking business
and shut up!

SAM: Okay. If that's the way you want it, I'll stop trying.

(*He turns away. This infuriates Hally even more.*)

HALLY: Good. Because what you've been trying to do is
meddle in something you know nothing about. All
that concerns you in here, Sam, is to try and do what
you get paid for — keep the place clean and serve
the customers. In plain words, just get on with your
job. My mother is right. She's always warning me
about allowing you to get too familiar. Well, this
time you've gone too far. It's going to stop right now.

(*No response from Sam.*)

You're only a servant in here, and don't forget it.

(*Still no response. Hally is trying hard to get one.*)

And as far as my father is concerned, all you need
to remember is that he is your boss.

SAM (*needled at last*): No, he isn't. I get paid by your
mother.

HALLY: Don't argue with me, Sam!

SAM: Then don't say he's my boss.

HALLY: He's a white man and that's good enough for you.

SAM: I'll try to forget you said that.

HALLY: Don't! Because you won't be doing me a favor
if you do. I'm telling you to remember it.

(*A pause. Sam pulls himself together and makes one
last effort.*)

SAM: Hally, Hally . . . ! Come on now. Let's stop before it's too late. You're right. We *are* on dangerous ground. If we're not careful, somebody is
going to get hurt.

HALLY: It won't be me.

SAM: Don't be so sure.

HALLY: I don't know what you're talking about, Sam.

SAM: Yes, you do.

HALLY (*furious*): Jesus, I wish you would stop trying
to tell me what I do and what I don't know.

(*Sam gives up. He turns to Willie.*)

SAM: Let's finish up.

HALLY: Don't turn your back on me! I haven't finished talking.

(*He grabs Sam by the arm and tries to make him turn around. Sam reacts with a flash of anger.*)

SAM: Don't do that, Hally! (*Facing the boy.*) All right, I'm listening. Well? What do you want to say to me?

HALLY (*pause as Hally looks for something to say*): To begin with, why don't you also start calling me Master Harold, like Willie.

SAM: Do you mean that?

HALLY: Why the hell do you think I said it?

SAM: And if I don't?

HALLY: You might just lose your job.

SAM (*quietly and very carefully*): If you make me say it once, I'll never call you anything else again.

HALLY: So? (*The boy confronts the man.*) Is that meant to be a threat?

SAM: Just telling you what will happen if you make me do that. You must decide what it means to you.

HALLY: Well, I have. It's good news. Because that is exactly what Master Harold wants from now on. Think of it as a little lesson in respect, Sam, that's long overdue, and I hope you remember it as well as you do your geography. I can tell you now that somebody who will be glad to hear I've finally given it to you will be my Dad. Yes! He agrees with my Mom. He's always going on about it as well. "You must teach the boys to show you more respect, my son."

SAM: So now you can stop complaining about going home. Everybody is going to be happy tonight.

HALLY: That's perfectly correct. You see, you mustn't get the wrong idea about me and my Dad, Sam. We also have our good times together. Some bloody good laughs. He's got a marvelous sense of humor. Want to know what our favorite joke is? He gives out a big groan, you see, and says: "It's not fair, is it, Hally?" Then I have to ask: "What, chum?" And then he says: "A nigger's arse" . . . and we both have a good laugh.

(*The men stare at him with disbelief.*)

What's the matter, Willie? Don't you catch the joke? You always were a bit slow on the uptake. It's what is called a pun. You see, fair means both light in color and to be just and decent. (*He turns to Sam.*) I thought *you* would catch it, Sam.

SAM: Oh ja, I catch it all right.

HALLY: But it doesn't appeal to your sense of humor.

SAM: Do you really laugh?

HALLY: Of course.

SAM: To please him? Make him feel good?

HALLY: No, for heavens sake! I laugh because I think it's a bloody good joke.

SAM: You're really trying hard to be ugly, aren't you? And why drag poor old Willie into it? He's done nothing to you but show you the respect you want so badly. That's also not being fair, you know . . . and *I* mean just or decent.

WILLIE: It's all right, Sam. Leave it now.

SAM: It's me you're after. You should just have said "Sam's arse" . . . because that's the one you're trying to kick. Anyway, how do you know it's not fair? You've never seen it. Do you want to? (*He drops his trousers and underpants and presents his backside for Hally's inspection.*) Have a good look. A real Basuto arse . . . which is about as nigger as they can come. Satisfied? (*Trousers up.*) Now you can make your Dad even happier when you go home tonight. Tell him I showed you my arse and he is quite right. It's not fair. And if it will give him an even better laugh next time, I'll also let *him* have a look. Come, Willie, let's finish up and go.

(*Sam and Willie start to tidy up the tea room. Hally doesn't move. He waits for a moment when Sam passes him.*)

HALLY (*quietly*): Sam . . .

(*Sam stops and looks expectantly at the boy. Hally spits in his face. A long and heartfelt groan from Willie. For a few seconds Sam doesn't move.*)

SAM (*taking out a handkerchief and wiping his face*): It's all right, Willie.

(*To Hally.*)

Ja, well, you've done it . . . Master Harold. Yes, I'll start calling you that from now on. It won't be difficult anymore. You've hurt yourself, Master Harold. I saw it coming. I warned you, but you wouldn't listen. You've just hurt yourself *bad.* And you're a coward, Master Harold. The face you should be spitting in is your father's . . . but you used mine, because you think you're safe inside your fair skin . . . and this time I don't mean just or decent. (*Pause, then moving violently toward Hally.*) Should I hit him, Willie?

WILLIE (*stopping Sam*): No, Boet Sam.

SAM (*violently*): Why not?

WILLIE: It won't help, Boet Sam.

SAM: I don't want to help! I want to hurt him.

WILLIE: You also hurt yourself.

SAM: And if he had done it to you, Willie?

WILLIE: Me? Spit at me like I was a dog? (*A thought that had not occurred to him before. He looks at Hally.*) Ja. Then I want to hit him. I want to hit him hard!

(*A dangerous few seconds as the men stand staring at the boy. Willie turns away, shaking his head.*)

But maybe all I do is go cry at the back. He's little

boy, Boet Sam. Little *white* boy. Long trousers now, but he's still little boy.

SAM (*his violence ebbing away into defeat as quickly as it flooded*): You're right. So go on, then: groan again, Willie. You do it better than me. (*To Hally.*) You don't know all of what you've just done . . . Master Harold. It's not just that you've made me feel dirtier than I've ever been in my life . . . I mean, how do I wash off yours and your father's filth? . . . I've also failed. A long time ago I promised myself I was going to try and do something, but you've just shown me . . . Master Harold . . . that I've failed. (*Pause.*) I've also got a memory of a little white boy when he was still wearing short trousers and a black man, but they're not flying a kite. It was the old Jubilee days, after dinner one night. I was in my room. You came in and just stood against the wall, looking down at the ground, and only after I'd asked you what you wanted, what was wrong, I don't know how many times, did you speak and even then so softly I almost didn't hear you. "Sam, please help me to go and fetch my Dad." Remember? He was dead drunk on the floor of the Central Hotel Bar. They'd phoned for your Mom, but you were the only one at home. And do you remember how we did it? You went in first by yourself to ask permission for me to go into the bar. Then I loaded him onto my back like a baby and carried him back to the boarding house with you following behind carrying his crutches. (*Shaking his head as he remembers.*) A crowded Main Street with all the people watching a little white boy following his drunk father on a nigger's back! I felt for that little boy . . . Master Harold. I felt for him. After that we still had to clean him up, remember? He'd messed in his trousers, so we had to clean him up and get him into bed.

HALLY (*great pain*): I love him, Sam.

SAM: I know you do. That's why I tried to stop you from saying these things about him. It would have been so simple if you could have just despised him for being a weak man. But he's your father. You love him and you're ashamed of him. You're ashamed of so much! . . . And now that's going to include yourself. That was the promise I made to myself: to try and stop that happening. (*Pause.*) After we got him to bed you came back with me to my room and sat in a corner and carried on just looking down at the ground. And for days after that! You hadn't done anything wrong, but you went around as if you owed the world an apology for being alive. I didn't like seeing that! That's not the way a boy grows up to be a man! . . . But the

one person who should have been teaching you what that means was the cause of your shame. If you really want to know, that's why I made you that kite. I wanted you to look up, be proud of something, of yourself . . . (*bitter smile at the memory*) . . . and you certainly were that when I left you with it up there on the hill. Oh, ja . . . something else! . . . If you ever do write it as a short story, there *was* a twist in our ending. I couldn't sit down there and stay with you. It was a "Whites Only" bench. You were too young, too excited to notice then. But not anymore. If you're not careful . . . Master Harold . . . you're going to be sitting up there by yourself for a long time to come, and there won't be a kite in the sky. (*Sam has got nothing more to say. He exits into the kitchen, taking off his waiter's jacket.*)

WILLIE: Is bad. Is all bad in here now.

HALLY (*books into his school case, raincoat on*): Willie . . . (*It is difficult to speak.*) Will you lock up for me and look after the keys?

WILLIE: Okay.

(*Sam returns. Hally goes behind the counter and collects the few coins in the cash register. As he starts to leave. . . .*)

SAM: Don't forget the comic books.

(*Hally returns to the counter and puts them in his case. He starts to leave again.*)

SAM (*to the retreating back of the boy*): Stop . . . Hally. . . .

(*Hally stops, but doesn't turn to face him.*)

Hally . . . I've got no right to tell you what being a man means if I don't behave like one myself, and I'm not doing so well at that this afternoon. Should we try again, Hally?

HALLY: Try what?

SAM: Fly another kite, I suppose. It worked once, and this time I need it as much as you do.

HALLY: It's still raining, Sam. You can't fly kites on rainy days, remember.

SAM: So what do we do? Hope for better weather tomorrow?

HALLY (*helpless gesture*): I don't know. I don't know anything anymore.

SAM: You sure of that, Hally? Because it would be pretty hopeless if that was true. It would mean nothing has been learnt in here this afternoon, and there was a hell of a lot of teaching going on . . . one way or the other. But anyway, I don't believe you. I reckon there's one thing you know. You don't *have* to sit up there by yourself. You know what that bench means now, and you can leave it any time you choose. All you've got to do is stand up and walk away from it.

(Hally leaves. Willie goes up quietly to Sam.)

WILLIE: Is okay, Boet Sam. You see. Is . . . *(he can't find any better words)* . . . is going to be okay tomorrow. *(Changing his tone.)* Hey, Boet Sam! *(He is trying hard.)* You right. I think about it and you right. Tonight I find Hilda and say sorry. And make promise I won't beat her no more. You hear me, Boet Sam?

SAM: I hear you, Willie.

WILLIE: And when we practice I relax and romance with her from beginning to end. Nonstop! You watch! Two weeks' time: "First prize for promising newcomers: Mr. Willie Malopo and Miss Hilda Samuels." *(Sudden impulse.)* To hell with it! I walk home. *(He goes to the jukebox, puts in a coin and selects a record. The machine comes to life in the gray twilight, blushing its way through a spectrum of soft, romantic colors.)* How did you say it, Boet Sam? Let's dream. *(Willie sways with the music and gestures for Sam to dance.)*

(Sarah Vaughan sings.)

"Little man you're crying,
I know why you're blue,
Someone took your kiddy car away;
Better go to sleep now,
Little man you've had a busy day." *(etc., etc.)*
You lead. I follow.

(The men dance together.)

"Johnny won your marbles,
Tell you what we'll do;
Dad will get you new ones right away;
Better go to sleep now,
Little man you've had a busy day."

COMMENTARIES

Heinrich von Staden (b. 1939)
INTERVIEW WITH ATHOL FUGARD   *1982*

When "MASTER HAROLD". . . and the boys *was first produced at the Yale Repertory Theatre, Athol Fugard had the chance to respond to some questions about its significance to him. He revealed that the play was deeply personal and that through it he had been able to exorcise a demon that had haunted him for some time. In this interview Fugard detailed his involvement with South African drama and black actors in South Africa. He also commented on the extent to which censorship and other political pressures in South Africa made it difficult for his work to be produced in his own country.*

von Staden: The bombs of fiction — Athol, aren't they more explosive than TNT?

Fugard: I'd like to believe that. You understand I've got to be careful about that one. I've got to be careful about flattering myself about the potency of the one area of activity which I've got, which is theater and being a writer.

von Staden: How often have there been productions of your plays for non-segregated audiences in South Africa?

Fugard: I've had to change my tactics in terms of that over the years. At a period when the policy on segregated audiences in South Africa was rigid and very strictly enforced, I had to make a decision whether to take on an act of silence, just be silent because I couldn't go into a theater that was decent in my terms, or whether to take on the compromising circumstances of segregated audiences simply because I felt that if a play has got something to say, at least say it. And there were years when I decided to do the latter. I did perform before segregated audiences. In a sense I regret that decision now. I think I might possibly have looked after myself — and maybe the situation — better by not accepting that compromise. But I did.

von Staden: But do you think you had a genuine choice at that time?

Fugard: I had a choice between silence or being heard.

von Staden: Let me ask you along similar lines, when you are writing a play or a novel like *Tsotsi,* do you sense constraints on the way you are writing in view of the fact that certain things are anathema to the government, also in fiction?

Fugard: I would like to believe that I have operated at the table at which I sit and write, that I have operated totally without self-censorship. Maybe some awareness of what is possible and is not possible has operated subconsciously and is deciding choices I make in terms of what I favor. I think it may be pertinent to the conversation we are having, that *"MASTER HAROLD" . . . and the boys* is the first play of mine in twenty-four years of writing that will have its premiere outside of South Africa. And one of the reasons why I'm doing that this time is that there are elements in *"MASTER HAROLD" . . . and the boys* that might have run into censorship problems. . . .

von Staden: Here you are, a person who, critics say, has achieved exceptional insight into human nature, and you never obtained a university degree. What institutions, what processes do you think contributed most to the insights you have?

Fugard: Well, I think to be a South African is in a way to be at a university that teaches you about that. The South African experience is certainly one in which, if you're prepared to keep your eyes open and look, you're going to see a lot of suffering. But then, in terms of personal specifics, I suppose for me there was a very, very important relationship, a friendship, with a black man in what I suppose is any person's most formative and definitive years, the age between eleven, ten up until the age of twenty-one. It was a black man in Port Elizabeth, and my play *"MASTER HAROLD" . . . and the boys* reflects something of that friendship, tries to talk about it, look at it. I left South Africa, hitchhiked through the African continent, ended up as a sailor on a ship which, apart from the officers and engineers, had a totally nonwhite, had a totally black crew, and I was a sailor in a totally black crew. There was that, I think I can't nail down any one specific traumatic incident as being totally decisive. But I could be certain that *"MASTER HAROLD" . . . and the boys* deals with one specific moment which I'm trying to exorcise out of my soul.

von Staden: In all of your plays and in the novel you always have a South African setting. Yet your plays and your novels, though so rooted in the specifics of the South African situation, seem to have a tremendous appeal to audiences that are largely ignorant of the situation there. To what do you ascribe that?

Fugard: You take a chance. As a storyteller one year ago, I took a chance . . . I realized that it was finally time to deal with the story of a seventeen-year-old boy and his friendship with two black men. And it's a gamble. There's no formula. There is no way that you can make or decide or guarantee before the event that that story is going to resonate outside of its specific context. You just take a bloody chance.

Athol Fugard (b. 1932)
FROM NOTEBOOKS 1960–1977

Like most playwrights, Athol Fugard is a journal writer. In his notebooks he has written scraps of memory that have special meaning to him. In one entry for March 1961, long before he began to write "MASTER HAROLD" . . . and the boys (1982), he describes one of his childhood memories. It concerns the real-life Sam, and it reveals — very painfully — exactly what the personal crime was that his play deals with. His gesture of contempt for the man who was like a grandfather to him became a demon that had to be exorcised.

Sam Semela — Basuto — with the family fifteen years. Meeting him again when he visited Mom set off string of memories.

The kite which he produced for me one day during those early years when Mom ran the Jubilee Hotel and he was a waiter there. He had made it himself: brown paper, its ribs fashioned from thin strips of tomato-box plank which he had smoothed down, a paste of flour and water for glue. I was surprised and bewildered that he had made it for me.

I vaguely recall shyly "haunting" the servants' quarters in the well of the hotel — cold, cement-gray world — the pungent mystery of the dark little rooms — a world I didn't understand. Frightened to enter any of the rooms. Sam, broad-faced, broader based — he smelled of woodsmoke. The "kaffir smell" of South Africa is the smell of poverty — woodsmoke and sweat.

Later, when he worked for her at the Park café, Mom gave him the sack: ". . . he became careless. He came late for work. His work went to hell. He didn't seem to care no more." I was about thirteen and served behind the counter while he waited on table.

Realize now he was the most significant — the only — friend of my boyhood years. On terrible windy days when no one came to swim or walk in the park, we would sit together and talk. Or I was reading — Introductions to Eastern Philosophy or Plato and Socrates — and when I had finished he would take the book back to New Brighton.

Can't remember now what precipitated it, but one day there was a rare quarrel between Sam and myself. In a truculent silence we closed the café, Sam set off home to New Brighton on foot and I followed a few minutes later on my bike. I saw him walking ahead of me and, coming out of a spasm of acute loneliness, as I rode up behind him I called his name, he turned in mid-stride to look back and, as I cycled past, I spat in his face. Don't suppose I will ever deal with the shame that overwhelmed me the second after I had done that.

Now he is thin. We had a long talk. He told about the old woman ("Ma") whom he and his wife have taken in to look after their house while he goes to work — he teaches ballroom dancing. "Ma" insists on behaving like a domestic — making Sam feel guilty and embarrassed. She brings him an early morning cup of coffee. Sam: "No, Ma, you mustn't, man." Ma: "I must." Sam: "Look, Ma, if I want it, I can make it." Ma: "No, I must."

Occasionally, when she is doing something, Sam feels like a cup of tea but is too embarrassed to ask her, and daren't make one for himself. Similarly, with his washing. After three days or a week away in other towns, giving dancing lessons, he comes back with underclothes that are very dirty. He is too shy to give them out to be washed so washes them himself. When Ma sees this she goes and complains to Sam's wife that he doesn't trust her, that it's all wrong for him to do the washing.

Of tsotsis,° he said: "They grab a old man, stick him with a knife, and ransack him. And so he must go to hospital and his kids is starving with hungry." Of others: "He's got some little moneys. So he is facing starvation for the weekend."

Of township snobs, he says there are the educational ones: "If you haven't been to the big school, like Fort Hare, what you say isn't true." And the money ones: "If you aren't selling shops or got a business or a big car, man, you're nothing."

Sam's incredible theory about the likeness of those "with the true seed of love." Starts with Plato and Socrates — they were round. "Man is being shrinking all the time. An Abe Lincoln, him too, taller, but that's because man is shrinking." Basically, those with the true seed of love look the same — "It's in the eyes."

He spoke admiringly of one man, a black lawyer in East London, an educated man — university background — who was utterly without snobbery, looking down on no one — any man, educated or ignorant, rich or poor, was another *man* to him, another human being, to be respected, taken seriously, to be talked to, listened to.

"They" won't allow Sam any longer to earn a living as a dancing teacher. "You must get a job!" One of his fellow teachers was forced to work at Fraser's Quarries.

---

tsotis: Gang members.

David Henry Hwang

Born in 1957, David Henry Hwang was raised in California's San Gabriel Valley by Asian-born parents. His father, a native of Shanghai, is a successful banker; his mother, born in the Philippines, is a professor of piano. As a child, Hwang was a proficient violinist, and today his sister makes a living as a cellist. Hwang plays jazz violin occasionally and has appeared on friends' albums. While art and music were influential as he grew, so too was his awareness of his ethnic roots; his interest in Asian-American experience developed out of personal observation. Up to now, much of his focus in drama has been on assimilation and on the power of Chinese culture, but he is also aware that he has other issues to explore in his writing.

Hwang's first play, *F. O. B.* (1980), was written while an undergraduate at Stanford. The title of the play is an acronym standing for "Fresh Off the Boat," and the play examines the problems of immigrant assimilation. It is set in a restaurant in Chinatown with college-age characters who all reveal difficulties in fitting into the American way of life. Assimilated immigrants make fun of a young man who has just arrived from China. Hwang strips off the social pretensions of those who feel that getting ahead calls for abandoning their roots and humiliating others. The play, developed at the O'Neill Playwright's Conference, was then brought to the Public Theater in New York by Joseph Papp. It won a 1981 Obie Award for best play.

The Dance and the Railroad (1981) was developed in New York with the assurance that Joseph Papp would produce it. Hwang worked with actor John Lone, who had trained in Chinese opera in Hong Kong and who starred in the play. Hwang says that he tried to learn from Lone everything he could about the history and tradition of Chinese opera. This play demonstrates the need to understand and participate in the traditions of one's culture. The dance and operatic forms that Lone practices and values are at first rejected by Ma, the other central character in the play, but eventually win him over.

Hwang's other plays are *Family Devotions* (1981), *The House of Sleeping Beauties* (1983), *The Sound of a Voice* (1983), *Rich Relations* (1986), and *M. Butterfly* (1987), for which he is best known. *M. Butterfly* has been an international success, winning a Tony award for best play in 1988. The story of a French diplomat's affair with a Chinese actress in the Peking Opera, it culminates in the astonishing discovery that the actress is not a woman, but a man. Further, their relationship, based on a true story of a more than decade-long affair, includes touches of espionage and intrigue. Hwang read the story in the *New York Times* and began writing shortly afterward, avoiding further research into the strange relationship so that he would have a free hand in developing his material. The setting of the play is somewhat surrealist, with allusions to Peking opera and to the Italian opera *Madame Butterfly* by Puccini.

Hwang's activity since *M. Butterfly* has included more plays, films, and an opera libretto. He collaborated with Philip Glass on *1000 Airplanes on the Roof* (1988), a science fiction musical; and on *The Voyage* (1992), Glass's full-length opera. Hwang's *Bondage* (1992), a one-act play that premiered at the Humana Theatre Festival, explores the psychology of sadomasochism. Hwang's parody of *Miss Saigon,* called *Face Value* (1993), desentimentalizes the popular treatment of Vietnam. His film *Golden Gate* (1994) was based on a story he heard about Chinese immigrants arrested for sending money back to China. Among the projects he has been working on recently are a screenplay based on Dostoevsky's *The Idiot* and a screenplay of A. S. Byatt's novel *Possession.*

THE DANCE AND THE RAILROAD

The setting of the play is 1867, a time when Chinese labor was used for building the transcontinental railroads connecting the east and west coasts of the United States. Among the drama's themes are the degenerative effects that gambling, drinking, and other vices have on the Chinese laborers. Lone, who has been in the United States for two years, talks of his fellow workers as dead men. Ma, on the other hand, has been out of China only a few weeks and has a much more optimistic view of life.

Ma believes that he will return to China rich enough to have twenty wives and that the gold in the mountain will be his, enough so that he will never have to work again. Lone knows better. The two men begin wary of each other but eventually share their stories and their feelings. Lone, who has trained as a child in Chinese opera, teaches Ma traditional movments, gestures, and techniques. Ma is an eager pupil who learns quickly but is involved in a painful strike of the Chinese workers against their bosses. Lone feels that they have little chance of winning, but Ma is ever confident. Once they win — a compromised victory, but a victory — Ma expresses the desire to act in an opera about himself. Lone at first resists but eventually gives in, and they enact Ma's story of the lengthy sea voyage to the United States and his ultimate struggle for dignity. At the end of the play Ma, by reason of his accepting traditional discipline and of seeing that the world in which they now live has worthwhile opportunities, emerges as a stronger, more forward-looking character than when he first appeared.

The clash between the old world and the new, between cultural tradition and cultural innovation, is at the heart of the drama. So, too, is the search for the individual's dignity in a world filled with traps and illusions. At the end of the drama we wonder which of the characters is truly liberated.

The Dance and the Railroad in Performance

The Dance and the Railroad got a Drama Desk Award nomination and the CINE Golden Eagle award for 1983. It was produced off Broadway in New York by the New Federal Theater and was subsequently telecast on the Arts and Entertainment cable network in 1982. Directed by John Lone, it starred Lone and Tzi Ma. Hwang, who has said that he is lazy about creating names, used the actors' real names for the characters in the play. His work with Lone to learn some of the history, tradition, and technique of Chinese opera has also been useful in his subsequent plays. The New Federal Theater production used a simple backdrop, with the actors wearing simple white costumes. Lone's acrobatic skill in the scenes in which the two characters practice Chinese operatic techniques was especially compelling and gave the performance a special quality. *The Dance and the Railroad* was produced along with Hwang's one-act play, *The House of Sleeping Beauties,* under the title *Broken Promises* in London in 1987.

David Henry Hwang (b. 1957)
THE DANCE AND THE RAILROAD

1981

Characters

LONE, *twenty years old, Chinaman railroad worker*
MA, *eighteen years old, Chinaman railroad worker*

Place: *A mountain top near the transcontinental railroad.*
Time: *June, 1867.*

SCENE 1

(*Afternoon. A mountain top. Lone, sitting on a rock, rotating his head so that it twirls his pigtail like a fan. He jumps to the ground, practices opera steps. Ma enters, cautiously, watches from a hidden spot. Ma approaches Lone.*)

LONE: So, there are insects hiding in the bushes.
MA: Hey, listen, we haven't met, but . . .
LONE: I don't spend time with insects.

(*Lone whips his hair into Ma's face; Ma backs off; Lone pursues him, swiping at Ma with his hair.*)

MA: What the . . . ? Cut it out! (*Ma pushes Lone away.*)
LONE: Don't push me.
MA: What was that for?
LONE: Don't ever push me again.
MA: You mess like that, you're gonna get pushed.
LONE: Don't push me.
MA: You started it. I just wanted to watch.
LONE: "You just wanted to watch." Did you ask my permission?
MA: What?
LONE: Did you?
MA: C'mon.

LONE: You can't expect to get in for free.
MA: Listen. I got some stuff you'll wanna hear.
LONE: You think so?
MA: Yeah. Some advice.
LONE: Advice? How old are you, anyway?
MA: Eighteen.
LONE: A child.
MA: Yeah. Right. A child. But listen . . .
LONE: A child who tries to advise a grown man . . .
MA: Listen, you got this kind of attitude.
LONE: . . . is a child who will never grow up.
MA: You know, the Chinamen down at camp, they can't stand it.
LONE: Oh?
MA: Yeah. You gotta watch yourself. You know what they say?
LONE: No. Tell me.
MA: They call you, "Prince of the Mountain." Like you're too good to spend time with them.
LONE: Perceptive of them.
MA: After all, you never sing songs, never tell stories. They say you act like your spit is too clean for them, and they got ways to fix that.
LONE: Is that so?
MA: Like they're gonna bury you in the shitbuckets, so you'll have more to clean than your nails.
LONE: But I don't shit.
MA: Or they're gonna cut out your tongue, since you never speak to them.
LONE: There's no one here worth talking to.
MA: Cut it out, Lone. Look, I'm trying to help you, all right? I got a solution.
LONE: So young yet so clever.
MA: That stuff you're doing—it's beautiful. Why don't you do it for the guys at camp? Help us celebrate?

LONE: What will "this stuff" help celebrate?

MA: C'mon. The strike, of course. Guys on a railroad gang, we gotta stick together, you know.

LONE: This is something to celebrate?

MA: Yeah. Yesterday, the weak-kneed Chinamen: they were running around like chickens without a head: "The white devils are sending their soldiers! Shoot us all!" But now, look . . . day four, see? Still in one piece. Those soldiers . . . we've never seen a gun or a bullet.

LONE: So you're all warrior-spirits, huh?

MA: They're scared of us, Lone . . . that's what it means.

LONE: I appreciate your advice. Tell you what . . . you go down . . .

MA: Yeah?

LONE: Down to the camp.

MA: Okay.

LONE: To where the men are.

MA: Yeah?

LONE: Sit there . . .

MA: Yeah?

LONE: And wait for me.

MA: Okay. (*Pause.*) That's it? What do you think I am?

LONE: I think you're an insect interrupting my practice. So fly away. Go home.

MA: Look, I didn't come here to get laughed at.

LONE: No, I suppose you didn't.

MA: So just stay up here. By yourself. You deserve it.

LONE: I do.

MA: And don't expect any more help from me.

LONE: I haven't gotten any yet.

MA: If one day, you wake up and your head is buried in the shitcan . . .

LONE: Yes?

MA: You can't find your body, your tongue is cut out . . .

LONE: Yes.

MA: Don't worry 'cuz I'll be there.

LONE: Oh.

MA: To make sure your mother's head is sitting right next to yours. (*Ma exits.*)

LONE: His head is too big for this mountain.

(*Lone returns to practicing.*)

SCENE 2

(*Mountain top. Afternoon, the next day. Lone is practicing. Ma enters.*)

MA: Hey.

LONE: You? Again?

MA: I forgive you.

LONE: You . . . what?

MA: For making fun of me yesterday. I forgive you.

LONE: You can't . . .

MA: No. Don't thank me.

LONE: You can't forgive me.

MA: No. Don't mention it.

LONE: You . . . I never asked for your forgiveness.

MA: I know. That's just the kinda guy I am.

LONE: This is ridiculous. Why don't you leave? Go down to your friends and play soldiers, sing songs, tell stories.

MA: Ah! See? That's just it. I got other ways I wanna spend my time. Will you teach me the opera?

LONE: What?

MA: I wanna learn it. I dreamt about it all last night.

LONE: No.

MA: The dance, the opera . . . I can do it.

LONE: You think so?

MA: Yeah. When I get outa here, I wanna go back to China and perform.

LONE: You want to become an actor?

MA: Well, I wanna perform.

LONE: Don't you remember the story about the three sons whose parents send them away to learn a trade? After three years, they return. The first one says, "I have become a coppersmith." The parents say, "Good. Second son, what have you become?" "I've become a silversmith." "Good . . . and youngest son . . . what about you?" "I have become an actor." When the parents hear that their son has become only an actor, they are very sad. The mother beats her head against the ground until the ground, out of pity, opens up and swallows her. The father is so angry, he can't even speak, and the anger builds up inside him until it blows his body to pieces — little bits of his skin are found hanging from trees days later. You don't know how you endanger your relatives by becoming an actor.

MA: Well, I don't wanna become an "actor." That sounds terrible. I just wanna perform. Look, I'll be rich by the time I get out of here, right?

LONE: Oh?

MA: Sure. By the time I go back to China, I'll ride in gold sedan chairs, with twenty wives fanning me all around.

LONE: Twenty wives? This boy is ambitious.

MA: I'll give out pigs on New Years and keep a stable of small birds to give to any woman who pleases me. And in my spare time, I'll perform.

LONE: Between your twenty wives and your birds, where will you find a free moment?

MA: I'll play Kwan Kung and tell stories of what life was like in the Gold Mountain.

LONE: Ma, just how long have you been in "America"?

MA: Huh? About four weeks.

LONE: You are a big dreamer.

MA: Well, all us Chinamen here are — right? Men with little dreams have little brains to match. They walk with their eyes down, trying to find extra grains of rice on the ground.

LONE: So, you know all about "America"? Tell me, what kind of stories will you tell?

MA: I'll say, "We laid tracks like soldiers. Mountains? We hung from cliffs in baskets and the winds blew us like birds. Snow? We lived underground like moles for days at a time. Deserts? We . . ."

LONE: Wait. Wait. How do you know these things after only four weeks?

MA: They told me — the other Chinamen on the gang. We've been telling stories ever since the strike began.

LONE: They make it sound like it's very enjoyable.

MA: They said it is.

LONE: Oh? And you believe them?

John Lone (left) and Tzi Ma in the 1981 New York Skakespeare Festival production of *The Dance and the Railroad.*

MA: They're my friends. Living underground in winter — sounds exciting, huh?

LONE: Did they say anything about the cold?

MA: Oh, I already know about that. They told me about the mild winters and the warm snow.

LONE: Warm snow?

MA: When I go home, I'll bring some back to show my brothers.

LONE: Bring some . . . On the boat?

MA: They'll be shocked . . . they never seen American snow before.

LONE: You can't. By the time you get snow to the boat, it'll have melted, evaporated, and returned as rain already.

MA: No.

LONE: No?

MA: Stupid.

LONE: Me?

MA: You been here awhile, haven't you?

LONE: Yes. Two years.

MA: Then how come you're so stupid? This is the Gold Mountain. The snow here doesn't melt. It's not wet.

LONE: That's what they told you?

MA: Yeah. It's true.

LONE: Did anyone show you any of this snow?

MA: No. It's not winter.

LONE: So where does it go?

MA: Huh?

LONE: Where does it go? If it doesn't melt, what happens to it?

MA: The snow? I dunno. I guess it just stays around.

LONE: So where is it? Do you see any?

MA: Here? Well, no, but . . . (*Pause.*) This is probably one of those places where it doesn't snow—even in winter.

LONE: Oh.

MA: Anyway, what's the use of me telling you what you already know? Hey, c'mon . . . teach me some of that stuff. Look . . . I've been practicing the walk . . . how's this? (*Ma waddles awkwardly.*)

LONE: You look like a duck in heat.

MA: Hey . . . it's a start, isn't it?

LONE: Tell you what — you want to play some *Die Siu*?

MA: *Die Siu?* Sure.

LONE: You know, I'm pretty good.

MA: Hey, I play with the guys at camp. You can't be any better than Lee . . . he's really got it down.

(*Lone pulls out a case with two dice.*)

LONE: I used to play 'til morning.

MA: Hey, us too. We see the sun start to rise, and say, "Hey, if we go to sleep now, we'll never get up for work." So we just keep playing.

LONE: (*Holding out dice.*) *Die* or *Siu*?

MA: *Siu.*

LONE: You sure?

MA: Yeah!

LONE: All right. (*He rolls.*) *Die!*

MA: *Siu!* (*They see the result.*) Not bad.

(*They continue taking turns rolling through the following section; Ma always loses.*)

LONE: I haven't touched these in two years.

MA: I gotta practice more . . .

LONE: Have you lost much money?

MA: Huh? So what?

LONE: Oh, you have gold hidden in all your shirt linings, huh?

MA: Here in "America" . . . losing is no problem. You know . . . End of the Year Bonus?

LONE: Oh, right.

MA: After I get that, I'll laugh at what I lost.

LONE: Lee told you there was a bonus, right?

MA: How'd you know?

LONE: When I arrived here, Lee told me there was a bonus, too.

MA: Lee teach you how to play?

LONE: Him? He talked to me a lot.

MA: Look, why don't you come down and start playing with the guys again?

LONE: The "guys."

MA: Before we start playing, Lee uses a stick to write "Kill!" in the dirt.

LONE: You seem to live for your nights with "the guys."

MA: What's life without friends, huh?

LONE: Well, why do *you* think I stopped playing?

MA: Hey, maybe you were the one getting killed, huh?

LONE: What?

MA: Hey, just kidding.

LONE: Who's getting killed here?

MA: Just a joke.

LONE: That's not a joke, it's blasphemy.

MA: Look, obviously you stopped playing 'cause you wanted to practice the opera.

LONE: Do you understand that discipline?

MA: But, I mean, you don't have to overdo it either. You don't have to beat 'em like dirt. I mean, who are you trying to impress?

(*Pause; Lone throws dice into the bushes.*)

LONE: Oooops. Better go see who won.

MA: Hey! C'mon! Help me look!

LONE: If you find them, they are yours.

MA: You serious?

LONE: Yes.

MA: (*Finds the dice.*) Here.

LONE: Who won?

MA: I didn't check.

LONE: Well, no matter. Keep the dice. Take them, and go play with your friends.

MA: Here. (*He offers them to Lone.*) A present.

LONE: A present? This isn't a present!

MA: They're mine, aren't they? You gave them to me, right?

LONE: Well, yes, but . . .

MA: So now I'm giving them to you.

LONE: You can't give me a present. I don't want them.

MA: You wanted them enough to keep them two years.

LONE: I'd forgotten I had them.

MA: See, I know, Lone. You wanna get rid of me. But you can't. I'm paying for lessons.

LONE: With my dice.

MA: Mine now. (*He offers them again.*) Here.

(*Pause; Lone runs Ma's hand across his forehead.*)

LONE: Feel this.

MA: Hey!

LONE: Pretty wet, huh?

MA: Big deal.

LONE: Well, it's not from playing *Die Siu.*

MA: I know how to sweat. I wouldn't be here if I didn't.

LONE: Yes, but are you willing to sweat after you've finished sweating? Are you willing to come up after you've spent the whole day chipping half an inch off a rock, and punish your body some more?

MA: Yeah. Even after work, I still . . .

LONE: No, you don't. You want to gamble, and tell dirty stories, and dress up like women to do shows.

MA: Hey, I never did that.

LONE: You've only been here a month. (*Pause.*) And what about "the guys"? They're not going to treat you so well once you stop playing with them. Are you willing to work all day listening to them whisper, "That one — let's put spiders in his soup."

MA: They won't do that to me. With you, it's different.

LONE: Is it?

MA: You don't have to act that way.

LONE: What way?

MA: Like you're so much better than them.

LONE: No. You haven't even begun to understand. To practice every day, you must have a fear to force you up here.

MA: A fear? No — it's 'cause what you're doing is beautiful.

LONE: No.

MA: I've seen it.

LONE: It's ugly to practice when the mountain has turned your muscles to ice. When my body hurts too much to come here, I look at the other Chinamen and think, "They are dead. Their muscles work only because the white man forces them." I live because I can still force my muscles to work for me. Say it — "They are dead."

MA: No. They're my friends.

LONE: Well, then, take your dice down to your friends.

MA: But I want to learn . . .

LONE: This is your first lesson.

MA: Look, it shouldn't matter . . .

LONE: It does.

MA: It shouldn't matter what I think.

LONE: Attitude is everything.

MA: But as long as I come up, do the exercises . . .

LONE: I'm not going to waste time on a quitter.

MA: I'm not!

LONE: Then say it — "They are dead men."

MA: I can't.

LONE: Then you will never have the dedication.

MA: That doesn't prove anything.

LONE: I will not teach a dead man.

MA: What?

LONE: If you can't see it, then you're dead too.

MA: Don't start pinning . . .

LONE: Say it!

MA: All right.

LONE: What?

MA: All right. I'm one of them. I'm a dead man too.

(*Pause.*)

LONE: I thought as much. So, go. You have your friends.

MA: But I don't have a teacher.

LONE: I don't think you need both.

MA: Are you sure?

LONE: I'm being questioned by a child.

(*Lone returns to practicing; silence.*)

MA: Look, Lone, I'll come up here every night — after work . . . I'll spend my time practicing, okay? (*Pause.*) But I'm not gonna say that they're dead. Look at them. They're on strike; dead men don't go on strike, Lone. The white devils — they try and stick us with a ten-hour day. We want a return to eight hours and also a fourteen-dollar-a-month raise. I learned the demon English — listen: "Eight hour a day good for white man, alla same good for Chinaman." These are the demands of live Chinamen, Lone. Dead men don't complain.

LONE: All right, this is something new. But no one can judge the Chinamen 'til after the strike.

MA: They say we'll hold out for months if we have to. The smart men will live on what we've hoarded.

LONE: A Chinaman's mouth can swallow the earth. (*He takes the dice.*) While the strike is on, I'll teach you.

MA: And afterwards?

LONE: Afterwards — we'll decide then whether these are dead or live men.

MA: When can we start?

LONE: We've already begun. Give me your hand.

SCENE 3

(*Late afternoon, four days later. Lone and Ma are doing physical exercises.*)

MA: How long will it be before I can play Kwan Kung?

LONE: How long before a dog can play the violin?

MA: Old Ah Hong — have you heard him play the violin?

LONE: Yes. Now he should take his violin and give it to a dog.

MA: I think he sounds okay.

LONE: I think he caused that avalanche last winter.

MA: He used to play for weddings back home.

LONE: Ah Hong?

MA: That's what he said.

LONE: You probably heard wrong.

MA: No.

LONE: He probably said he played for funerals.

MA: He's been playing for the guys down at camp.

LONE: He should play for the white devils — that will end this stupid strike.

MA: Yang told me for sure — it'll be over by tomorrow.

LONE: Eight days already. And Yang doesn't know anything.

MA: He said they're already down to an eight-hour day and five dollars raise at the bargaining sessions.

LONE: Yang eats too much opium.

MA: That doesn't mean he's wrong about this.

LONE: You can't trust him. One time — last year — he went around camp looking in everybody's eyes and saying, "Your nails are too long. They're hurting my eyes." This went on for a week. Finally, all the men clipped their nails, made a big pile, which they wrapped in leaves and gave to him. Yang used the nails to season his food . . . he put it in his soup, sprinkled it on his rice, and never said a word about it again. Now tell me — are you going to trust a man who eats other men's fingernails?

MA: Well, all I know is we won't go back to work until they meet all our demands. Listen, teach me some Kwan Kung steps.

LONE: I should have expected this. A boy who wants to have twenty wives is the type who demands more than he can handle.

MA: Just a few.

LONE: It takes years before an actor can play Kwan Kung.

MA: I can do it. Back home I would spend a lot of time watching the opera when it came to town. Everytime I'd see Kwan Kung, I'd say, "Yeah. That's me. The God of Fighters. The God of Adventurers. We have the same kind of spirit."

LONE: I tell you, if you work very hard, when you return to China, you can perhaps be the Second Clown.

MA: Second Clown?

LONE: If you work hard.

MA: What's the Second Clown?

LONE: You can play the p'i p'a, and dance and jump all over.

MA: I'll buy them.

LONE: Excuse me?

MA: I'm going to be rich, remember? I'll buy a troupe and force them to let me play Kwan Kung.

LONE: I hope you have enough money, then, to pay audiences to sit through your show.

MA: You mean, I'm going to have to practice here every night . . . and in return, all I can play is the Second Clown?

LONE: If you work hard.

MA: Am I that bad? Maybe I shouldn't even try to do this. Maybe I should just go down.

LONE: It's not you. Everyone must earn the right to play Kwan Kung. I entered Opera school when I was ten years old. My parents decided to sell me for ten years to this Opera company. I lived with eighty other boys and we slept in bunks four beds high and hid our candy and rice cakes from each other. After eight years, I was studying to play Kwan Kung.

MA: Eight years?

LONE: I was one of the best in my class. One day, I was summoned by my master, who told me I was to go home for two days, because my mother had fallen very ill and was dying. When I arrived home, mother was standing at the door waiting, not sick at all. Her first words to me, the son away for eight years, were, "You've been playing while your village has starved. You must go to the Gold Mountain and work."

MA: And you never returned to school?

LONE: I went from a room with eighty boys to a ship with three hundred men. So, you see, it does not come easily to play Kwan Kung.

MA: Did you want to play Kwan Kung?

LONE: What a foolish question!

MA: Well, you're better off this way.

LONE: What?

MA: Actors — they don't make much money. Here, you make a bundle, then go back and be an actor again. Best of both worlds.

LONE: "Best of both worlds."

MA: Yeah!

(*Lone drops to the floor, begins imitating a duck, waddling and quacking.*)

MA: Lone? What are you doing? (*Lone quacks.*) You're a duck? (*Lone quacks.*) I can see that. (*Lone quacks.*) Is this an exercise? Am I supposed to do this? (*Lone quacks.*) This is dumb. I never seen Kwan Kung waddle. (*Lone quacks.*) Okay. All right I'll do it. (*Ma and Lone quack and waddle.*) You know, I never realized before how uncomfortable a duck's life is. And you have to listen to yourself quacking all day. Go crazy! (*Lone stands up straight.*) Now, what was that all about?

LONE: No, no. Stay down there, duck.

MA: What's the . . .

LONE (*prompting*): "Quack, quack, quack."

MA: I don't . . .

LONE: Act your species!

MA: I'm not a duck!

LONE: Nothing worse than a duck that doesn't know his place.

MA: All right. (*Mechanically.*) Quack, quack.

LONE: More.

MA: Quack.

LONE: More!

MA: Quack, quack, quack!

(*Ma now continues quacking, as Lone gives commands.*)

LONE: Louder! It's your mating call! Think of your twenty duck wives! Good! Louder! Project! More! Don't slow down! Put your tails feathers into it! They can't hear you!

(*Ma is now quacking up a storm. Lone exits, unnoticed by Ma.*)

MA: Quack! Quack! Quack! Quack. Quack . . . quack. (*He looks around.*) Quack . . . quack . . . Lone? . . . Lone? (*He waddles around the stage looking.*) Lone, where are you? Where'd you go? (*He stops, scratches his left leg with his right foot.*) C'mon — stop playing around. What is this? (*Lone enters as a tiger, unseen by Ma.*) Look, let's call it a day, okay? I'm getting hungry. (*Ma turns around, notices Lone right before Lone is to bite him.*) Aaaaah! Quack, quack, quack! (*They face off, in character as animals. Duck-Ma is terrified.*)

LONE: Grrrr!

MA (*as a cry for help*): Quack, quack, quack!

(*Lone pounces on Ma. They struggle, in character. Ma is quacking madly, eyes tightly closed. Lone stands up straight. Ma continues to quack, his eyes still closed.*)

MA: Quack, quack, quack!

LONE (*louder*): Stand up.

MA (*opening his eyes*): Oh.

LONE: What are you?

MA: Huh?

LONE: A Chinaman or a duck?

MA: Huh? Gimme a second to remember.

LONE: You like being a duck?

MA: My feet fell asleep.

LONE: You change forms so easily.

MA: You said to.

LONE: What else could you turn into?

MA: Well, you scared me — sneaking up like that.

LONE: Perhaps a rock. That would be useful. When the men need to rest, they can sit on you.

MA: I got carried away.

LONE: Let's try . . . a locust. Can you become a locust?

MA: No. Let's cut this, okay?

LONE: Here. It's easy. You just have to know how to hop.

MA: You're not gonna get me . . .

LONE: Like this. (*He demonstrates.*)

MA: Forget it, Lone.

LONE: I'm a locust. (*He begins jumping towards Ma.*)

MA: Hey! Get away!

LONE: I devour whole fields.

MA: Stop it.

LONE: I starve babies before they are born.

MA: Hey, look, stop it!

LONE: I cause famines and destroy villages.

MA: I'm warning you! Get away!

LONE: What are you going to do? You can't kill a locust.

MA: You're not a locust.

LONE: You kill one, and another sits on your hand.

MA: Stop following me.

LONE: Locusts always trouble people. If not, we'd feel useless. Now, if you became a locust, too . . .

MA: I'm not going to become a locust.

LONE: Just stick your teeth! Out!

MA: I'm not gonna be a bug! It's stupid!

LONE: No man who's just been a duck has the right to call anything stupid.

MA: I thought you were trying to teach me something.

LONE: I am. Go ahead.

MA: All right. There. That look right?

LONE: Your legs should be a little lower. Lower! There. That's adequate. So, how does it feel to be a locust? (*Lone gets up.*)

MA: I dunno. How long do I have to do this?

LONE: Could you do it for three years?

MA: Three years? Don't be . . .

LONE: You couldn't, could you? Could you be a duck for that long?

MA: Look, I wasn't born to be either of those.

LONE: Exactly. Well, I wasn't born to work on a railroad, either. "Best of both worlds." How can you be such an insect?

(*Pause.*)

MA: Lone . . .

LONE: Stay down there! Don't move! I've never told anyone my story — the story of my parents kidnapping me from school. All the time we were crossing the ocean, the last two years here — I've kept my mouth shut. To you, I finally tell it. And all you can say is, "Best of both worlds." You're a bug to me, a locust. You think you understand the dedication one must have to be in the opera? You think it's the same as working on a railroad.

MA: Lone, all I was saying is that you'll go back too, and . . .

LONE: You're no longer a student of mine.

MA: What?

LONE: You have no dedication.

MA: Lone, I'm sorry.

LONE: Get up.

MA: I'm honored that you told me that.

LONE: Get up.

MA: No.

LONE: No?

MA: I don't want to. I want to talk.

LONE: Well, I've learned from the past. You're stubborn. You don't go. All right. Stay there. If you want to prove to me that you're dedicated, be a locust 'til morning. I'll go.

MA: Lone, I'm really honored that you told me.

LONE: I'll return in the morning. (*Lone exits.*)

MA: Lone? Lone — that's ridiculous. You think I'm gonna stay like this? If you'do, you're crazy. Lone? Come back here.

SCENE 4

(*Night. Ma, alone, as a locust.*)

MA: Locusts travel in huge swarms, so large that when they cross the sky, they block out the sun, like a storm. Second Uncle — back home — when he was a young man, his whole crop got wiped out by locusts one year. In the famine that followed, Second Uncle lost his eldest son and his second wife — the one he married for love. Even to this day, we look around before saying the word "locust" — to make sure Second Uncle is out of hearing range. About eight years ago, my brother and I discovered Second Uncle's cave in back of the stream near our house. We saw him come out of it one day around noon. Later, just before the sun went down, we sneaked in. We only looked once. Inside, there must have been hundreds — maybe five hundred or more — grasshoppers in huge bamboo cages — and around them — stacks of grasshopper legs, grasshopper heads, grasshopper antennae, grasshoppers with one leg still trying to hop but toppling like trees coughing, grasshoppers wrapped around sharp branches rolling from side to side, grasshopper legs cut off grasshopper bodies then tied around grasshoppers and tightened 'til grasshoppers died. Every conceivable kind of grasshopper in every conceivable stage of life and death, subject to every conceivable grasshopper torture. We ran out quickly, my brother and I — we knew an evil place by the thickness of the air. Now, I think of Second Uncle. How sad that the locusts forced him to take out his agony on innocent grasshoppers. What if Second Uncle could see me now? Would he cut off my legs? He might as well. I can barely feel them. But then again, Second Uncle never tortured actual locusts, just weak grasshoppers.

SCENE 5

(*Night. Ma still as a locust. Chinese gongs, drums, in the distance, then getting closer. It is just before dawn.*)

LONE (*off, singing*):
"Hit your hardest,
Pound out your tears.
The more you try,
The more you'll cry
At how little I've moved
And how large I loom
By the time the sun goes down."

MA: You look rested.

LONE: Me?

MA: Well, you sound rested.

LONE: No, not at all.

MA: Maybe I'm just comparing you to me.

LONE: I didn't even close my eyes all last night.

MA: Aw, Lone, you didn't have to stay up for me. You coulda' just come up here and . . .

LONE: For you?

MA: . . . apologized and everything woulda' been . . .

LONE: I didn't stay up for you.

MA: Huh? You didn't?

LONE: No.

MA: Oh. (*Beat.*) You sure?

LONE: Positive. I was thinking, that's all.

MA: About me?

LONE: Well . . .

MA: Even a little?

LONE: I was thinking about the Chinamen . . . and
you. Get up, Ma.

MA: Aw, do I have to? I've gotten to know these
grasshoppers real well.

LONE: Get up. I have a lot to tell you.

MA: What'll they think? They take me in even though
I'm a little large, then they find out I'm a human
being. I stepped on their kids. No trust. Gimme a
hand, will you? (*Lone helps Ma up, but Ma's legs
can't support him.*) Aw, shit. My legs are coming
off. (*He lies down and tries to straighten them
out.*)

LONE: I have many surprises. First, you will play
Kwan Kung.

MA: My legs will be sent home without me. What'll
my family think? Come to port to meet me, and all
they get is two legs.

LONE: Did you hear me?

MA: Hold on. I can't be in agony and listen to Chinese at the same time.

LONE: Did you hear my first surprise?

MA: No. I'm too busy screaming.

LONE: I said, you'll play Kwan Kung.

MA: Kwan Kung?

LONE: Yes.

MA: Me?

LONE: Yes.

MA: Without legs?

LONE: What?

MA: That might be good.

LONE: Stop that!

MA: I'll become a legend. Like the blind man who defended Amoy.

LONE: Didn't you hear?

MA: "The legless man who played Kwan Kung."

LONE: Isn't that what you want? To play Kwan Kung?

MA: No, I just wanna sleep.

LONE: No, you don't. Look. Here. I brought you
something.

MA: Food?

LONE: Here. Some rice.

MA: Thanks, Lone. And duck?

LONE: Just a little.

MA: Where'd you get the duck?

LONE: Just bones and skin.

MA: We don't have duck. And the white devils have
been blockading the food.

LONE: Sing — he had some left over.

MA: Sing? That thief?

LONE: And something to go with it.

MA: What? (*Lone reveals a bottle.*) Lone, where did
you find whiskey?

LONE: You know, Sing — he has almost anything.

MA: Yeah. For a price.

LONE: Once, even some thousand-day-old eggs.

MA: He's a thief. That's what they told me.

LONE: Not if you're his friend.

MA: Sing don't have any real friends. Everyone talks
about him bein' tied in to the head of the Klan in
San Francisco. Lone, you didn't have to do this.
Here. Have some.

LONE: I had plenty.

MA: Don't gimme that. This cost you plenty, Lone.

LONE: Well, I thought if we were going to celebrate,
we should do it as well as we would at home.

MA: Celebrate? What for? Wait.

LONE: Ma, the strike is over.

MA: Shit, I knew it. And we won, right?

LONE: Yes, the Chinamen have won. They can do
more than just talk.

MA: I told you. Didn't I tell you?

LONE: Yes. Yes, you did.

MA: Yang told me it was gonna be done. He said

LONE: Yes, I remember.

MA: Didn't I tell you? Huh?

LONE: Ma, eat your duck.

MA: Nine days. In nine days, we civilized the white
devils. I knew it, I knew we'd hold out 'til their
ears started twitching. So that's where you got the
duck, right? At the celebration?

LONE: No, there wasn't a celebration.

MA: Huh? You sure? The Chinamen — they look for
any excuse to party.

LONE: But I thought we should celebrate.

MA: Well, that's for sure.

LONE: So you will play Kwan Kung.

MA: God, nine days. Shit, it's finally done. Well, we'll
show them how to party. Make noise. Jump off
rocks. Make the mountain shake.

LONE: We'll wash your body, to prepare you for the
role.

MA: What role?

LONE: Kwan Kung. I've been telling you.

MA: I don't wanna play Kwan Kung.

LONE: You've shown the dedication required to become my student, so . . .

MA: Lone, you think I stayed up last night 'cause I
wanted to play Kwan Kung?

LONE: You said you were like him.

MA: I am. Kwan Kung stayed up all night once to
prove his loyalty. Well, now I have too. Lone, I'm
honored that you told me your story.

LONE: Yes. . . . That is like Kwan Kung.

MA: Good. So let's do an opera about me.

LONE: What?

MA: You wanna party or what?

LONE: About you?

MA: You said I was like Kwan Kung, didn't you?

LONE: Yes, but . . .

MA: Well, look at the operas he's got. I ain't even got one.

LONE: Still, you can't . . .

MA: You tell, me, is that fair?

LONE: You can't do an opera about yourself.

MA: I just won a victory, didn't I? I deserve an opera in my honor.

LONE: But, it's not traditional.

MA: Traditional? Lone, you gotta figure any way I could do Kwan Kung wasn't gonna be traditional anyway. I may be as good a guy as him, but he's a better dancer. (*He sings.*)
"Old Kwan Kung, just sits about
'Til the dime store fighters have had it out.
Then he pitches his peach pit,
Combs his beard,
Draws his sword,
And they scatter in fear."

LONE: What are you talking about?

MA: I just won a great victory. I get — what'cha call it? — poetic license. C'mon. Hit the gong. I'll immortalize my story.

LONE: I refuse. This goes against all my training. I try and give you your wish and . . .

MA: Do it. Gimme my wish. Hit the gongs.

LONE: I never . . . I can't.

MA: Can't what? Don't think I'm worth an opera? (*Beat.*) No. I guess not. I forgot — you think I'm just one of those dead men.

(*Silence. Lone pulls out a gong. Ma gets into position. Lone hits the gong. They do the following in a mock Chinese opera style.*)

MA: I am Ma. Yesterday, I was kicked out of my house by my three elder brothers, calling me the lazy dreamer of the family. I am sitting here in front of the temple trying to decide how I will avenge this indignity. Here comes the poorest beggar in this village. (*He cues Lone.*) He is called Fleaman because his body is the most popular meeting place for fleas from around the province.

LONE (*singing*):
"Fleas in love,
Find your happiness
In the gray scraps of my suit."

MA: Hello, Flea . . .

LONE (*continuing*):
"Fleas in need,
Shield your families

In the gray hairs of my beard."

MA: Hello, Flea . . .

(*Lone cuts Ma off, continues an extended improvised aria.*)

MA: Hello, Fleaman.

LONE: Hello, Ma. Are you interested in providing a home for these fleas?

MA: No!

LONE: This couple here — seeking to start a new home. Housing today is so hard to find. How about your left arm?

MA: I may have plenty of my own fleas in time. I have been thrown out by my elder brothers.

LONE: Are you seeking revenge? A flea epidemic on your house? (*To a flea.*) Get back there. You should be asleep. Your mother will worry.

MA: Nothing would make my brothers angrier than seeing me rich.

LONE: Rich? After the bad crops of the last three years, even the fleas are thinking of moving north.

MA: I heard a white devil talk yesterday.

LONE: Oh — with hair the color of a sick chicken and eyes round as eggs? The fleas and I call him Chicken-Laying-an-Egg.

MA: He said we can make our fortunes on the Gold Mountain, where work is play and the sun scares off snow.

LONE: Don't listen to chicken-brains.

MA: Why not? He said gold grows like weeds.

LONE: I have heard that it is slavery.

MA: Slavery? What do you know, Fleaman? Who told you? The fleas? Yes, I will go to Gold Mountain.

(*They pick up fighting sticks and do a water-crossing dance. When the dance ends, they stoop next to each other and rock.*)

MA: I have been in the bottom of this boat for thirty-six days now. Tang, how many have died?

LONE: Not me. I'll live through this ride.

MA: I didn't ask how you are.

LONE: But why's the Gold Mountain so far?

MA: We left with three hundred and three.

LONE: My family's depending on me.

MA: So tell me how many have died?

LONE: I'll be the last one alive.

MA: That's not what I wanted to know.

LONE: I'll find some fresh air in this hole.

MA: I asked, how many have died.

LONE: Is that a crack in the side?

MA: Are you listening to me?

LONE: If I had some air . . .

MA: I asked, don't you see . . . ?

LONE: The crack — over there.

MA: Will you answer me please?

LONE: I need to get out.
MA: The rest here agree . . .
LONE: I can't stand the smell.
MA: That a hundred eighty . . .
LONE: I can't see the air.
MA: Of us will not see . . .
LONE: And I can't die.
MA: Our Gold Mountain dream.

(*Lone/Tang dies; Ma throws his body off board. The boat docks. Ma exits, walks through the streets. He picks up one of the fighting sticks, while Lone becomes the mountain.*)

MA: I have been given my pickaxe. Now, I will attack the mountain.

(*Ma does a dance of labor. Lone sings.*)

LONE:

"Hit your hardest,
Pound out your tears.
The more you try,
The more you'll cry
At how little I've moved
And how large I loom
By the time the sun goes down."

(*Dance stops.*)

MA: This Mountain is clever. But why shouldn't it be? It's fighting for its life, like we fight for ours.

(*The Mountain [Lone] picks up a stick. Ma and the Mountain do a battle dance. The dance ends.*)

MA: This mountain not only defends itself — it also attacks. It turns our strength against us. (*Lone does Ma's labor dance, while Ma plants explosives in mid-air. Dance ends.*) The mountain has survived for millions of years. Its wisdom is immense.

(*Lone and Ma begin a second battle dance. This one ends with them working the battle sticks together. Lone breaks away, does a warrior strut.*)

LONE: I am a white devil! Listen to my stupid language: "Wha Che Doo Doo Blah Blah." Look at my wide eyes — like I have drunk seventy-two pots of tea. Look at my funny hair — twisting, turning, like a snake telling lies. (*To Ma.*) Bla Bla Doo Doo Tee Tee.
MA: We don't understand English.
LONE (*angry*): Bla Bla Doo Doo Tee Tee!
MA (*with Chinese accent*): Please you-ah spcak-ah Chinee?
LONE: Oh. Work — uh — one — two — more — work — two —

MA: Two hours more? Stupid demons. As confused as your hair. We will strike!

(*Ma is on strike.*)

MA (*in broken English*): Eight hours day good for white man, alla same good for Chinaman.
LONE: The strike is over! We've won!
MA: I knew we would.
LONE: We forced the white devil to act civilized.
MA: Tamed the barbarians!
LONE: Did you think . . .
MA: Who woulda' thought?
LONE: . . . it could be done?
MA: Who?
LONE: But who?
MA: Who could tame them?
MA AND LONE: Only a Chinaman? (*They laugh.*)
LONE: Well, c'mon.
MA: Let's celebrate!
LONE: We have.
MA: Oh.
LONE: Back to work.
MA: But we've won the strike.
LONE: I know. Congratulations! And now . . .
MA: . . . back to work?
LONE: Right.
MA: No.
LONE: But the strike is over.

(*Lone tosses Ma a stick; they resume their stick battle as before, but Ma is heard over Lone's singing.*)

LONE: "Hit your hardest,	MA: Wait.
Pound out your tears.	I'm tired of this!
The more you try,	How do we end it?
The more you'll cry	Let's stop now, all right?
At how little I've moved	Look, I said enough!
And how large I loom	
By the time the sun goes down."	

(*Ma tosses his stick away, but Lone is already aiming a blow towards it, so that Lone hits Ma instead and knocks him down.*)

MA: Oh! Shit . . .
LONE: I'm sorry! Are you all right?
MA: Yeah. I guess.
LONE: Why'd you let go? You can't just do that.
MA: I'm bleeding.
LONE: That was stupid . . . Where?
MA: Here.
LONE: No.

MA: Ow!

LONE: There will probably be a bump.

MA: I dunno.

LONE: What?

MA: I dunno why I let go.

LONE: It was stupid.

MA: But how were we going to end the opera?

LONE: Here. (*He applies whiskey to Ma's bruise.*) I don't know.

MA: Why didn't we just end it with the celebration? Ow! Careful.

LONE: Sorry. But Ma, the celebration's not the end. We're returning to work. Today. At dawn.

MA: What?

LONE: We've already lost nine days of work. But we got eight hours.

MA: Today? That's terrible.

LONE: What do you think we're here for? But they listened to our demands. We're getting a raise.

MA: Right. Fourteen dollars.

LONE: No. Eight.

MA: What?

LONE: We had to compromise. We got an eight dollar raise.

MA: But we wanted fourteen! Why didn't we get fourteen?

LONE: It was the best deal they could get. Congratulations.

MA: Congratulations? Look, Lone, I'm sick of you making fun of the Chinamen.

LONE: Ma, I'm not. For the first time. I was wrong. We got eight dollars.

MA: We wanted fourteen.

LONE: But we got eight hours.

MA: We'll go back on strike.

LONE: Why?

MA: We could hold out for months.

LONE: And lose all that work?

MA: But we just gave in.

LONE: You're being ridiculous. We got eight hours. Besides, it's already been decided.

MA: I didn't decide. I wasn't there. You made me stay up here.

LONE: The heads of the gangs decide.

MA: And that's it?

LONE: It's done.

MA: Back to work? That's what they decided? Lone, I don't want to go back to work.

LONE: Who does?

MA: I forgot what it's like.

LONE: You'll pick up the technique again soon enough.

MA: I mean, what it's like to have them telling you what to do all the time. Using up your strength.

LONE: I thought you said even after work, you still feel good.

MA: Some days. But others . . . (*Pause.*) I get so frustrated sometimes. At the rock. The rock doesn't give in. It's not human. I wanna claw it with my fingers, but that would just rip them up. I wanna throw myself head first onto it, but it'd just knock my skull open. The rock would knock my skull open, then just sit there, smiling, still, like nothing had happened like a faceless Buddha. (*Pause.*) Lone, when do I get out of here?

LONE: Well, the railroad may get finished.

MA: It'll never get finished.

LONE: . . . or you may get rich.

MA: Rich. Right. This is the Gold Mountain. (*Pause.*) Lone, has anyone ever gone home rich from here?

LONE: Yes. Some.

MA: But most?

LONE: Most . . . do go home.

(*Beat.*)

MA: Do you still have the fear?

LONE: The fear?

MA: That you'll become like them — dead men?

LONE: Maybe I was wrong about them.

MA: Well, I do. You wanted me to say it before, I can say it now: "They are dead men." Their greatest accomplishment was to win a strike that's gotten us nothing.

LONE: They're sending money home.

MA: No.

LONE: It's not much, I know, but it's something.

MA: Lone, I'm not even doing that. If I don't get rich here, I might as well die here. Let my brothers laugh in peace.

LONE: Ma, you're too soft to get rich here, naïve — you believed the snow was warm.

MA: I've got to change myself. Toughen up. Take no shit. Count my change. Learn to gamble. Learn to win. Learn to stare. Learn to deny. Learn to look at men with opaque eyes.

LONE: You want to do that?

MA: I will. 'Cause I've got the fear. You've given it to me.

(*Pause.*)

LONE: Will I see you here tonight?

MA: Tonight?

LONE: I just thought I'd ask.

MA: I'm sorry, Lone. I haven't got time to be the Second Clown.

LONE: I thought you might not.

MA: Sorry.

LONE: You could have been a . . . fair actor.

MA: You coming down? I gotta get ready for work. This is gonna be a terrible day. My legs are sore and my arms are outa' practice.

LONE: You go first. I'm going to practice some before work. There's still time.

MA: Practice? But you said you lost your fear. And you said that's what brings you up here.

LONE: I guess I was wrong about that, too. Today, I am dancing for no reason at all.

MA: Do whatever you want. See you down at camp.

LONE: Could you do me a favor?

MA: A favor?

LONE: Could you take this down so I don't have to take it all?

MA: Well, okay. (*Pause.*) But this is the last time.

LONE: Of course, Ma. (*Ma exits.*) See you soon. The last time. I suppose so.

(*Lone resumes practicing. The sun begins to rise. Lone jumps up on a rock, twirls his long pigtail as in the first scene. The sun continues rising until Lone is seen only in shadow.*)

Marsha Norman

Marsha Norman was born in Louisville, Kentucky, in 1947. Because her mother was a deeply religious woman, she did not allow television in her house, and radios, though available, were never used. Movies were also forbidden. But Norman explains that her mother "did not know the dangers of books because she didn't read," so books were Marsha Norman's world for most of her childhood.

But they were not the only influence. Norman spent much of her youth playing the piano, and she enjoyed the children's productions of the Actors' Theatre of Louisville. The Actors' Theatre and its director, Jon Jory, later became influential on Norman's early career as a writer.

Norman has said many times that the best thing for a writer is to be able to see drama during childhood. She has intense memories of *The Glass Menagerie*, Peter Shaffer's *The Royal Hunt of the Sun,* which is about the last day of Montezuma's life, and Archibald MacLeish's *J.B.*, an adaptation of the Book of Job. The vigor and the violence of these plays were explicitly attractive to her. Some of the excitement of that kind of theatricality is present in her first play, *Getting Out* (1977), which had its first performance at the Actors' Theatre.

Norman was a philosophy major at Agnes Scott College in Georgia, but she spent a good deal of her energy in theater there. Yet when she left college she did not expect to do any writing. As she said, she was sure that she would have to work at something else for a living. But a combination of circumstances changed that.

Norman had worked with disturbed teenagers in a Kentucky state hospital and had met a thirteen-year-old girl who was violent, reckless, and frightening. Later when she was working in children's TV in Louisville, Jon Jory offered to commission her to write a play, but initially she was not interested. When she talked over her feelings, Jory advised her to reflect on a moment when she was truly frightened. It was then that she remembered the thirteen-year-old girl, and thus began the gestation of *Getting Out*.

Her unusual approach in that play was to present two views of the same woman: Arlie as an imprisoned adolescent and Arlene as an adult trying to begin a reasonable life for herself in a shabby apartment. The two parts of the character share the stage simultaneously. The ultimate problem is how Arlene will learn to integrate the separate parts of her personality. It is a very effective work and ran for eight months off Broadway after a successful opening with the Actors' Theatre.

Norman also wrote some one-act plays for the Actors' Theatre — *The Laundromat* and *The Pool Hall* — and a full-length play, *Circus Valentine* (1979). She won the Pulitzer Prize for *'night, Mother* (1983), currently her most internationally successful play. *Traveler in the Dark* (1984) premiered at the American Repertory Theatre in Cambridge, Massachusetts, starring Sam Waterston as a cancer surgeon suffering from the strain of guilt. She also wrote the script for *The Secret Garden* (1990), a prize-winning Broadway musical.

Norman has frequently talked about the structure of her plays, which follow a very traditional pattern. She has linked them often to a "ski lift. When you get in it, you must feel absolutely secure; you must know that this thing can hold you up." Her sense of the play as resembling a machine is based in part on her awareness of the audience's needs and expectations. She has said that a good play should follow several simple rules: "You must state the issue at the beginning of the play. The audience must know what is at stake; they must know when they will be able to go home."

Norman is deeply concerned with giving language to those who are inarticulate. The most important characters in her best plays have been women who would not have been able to express themselves clearly without someone like Marsha Norman to give them a voice. Such an ambition may owe something to her youthful desire "to save the world," the same desire that led her to work in the Kentucky hospital that provided the material for her first play.

'NIGHT, MOTHER

Marsha Norman's best-known and most successful play, 'night, Mother (1983), has won numerous awards, including the Pulitzer Prize. Its subject — a middle-aged woman's determination to commit suicide and leave her mother behind — is not the uplifting fare usually offered to Broadway audiences. Such a play would seem to spell horror for a New York theater; while it ran for ten months after a shaky start, Norman had to accept a 50 percent reduction in her standard royalties to keep the play open.

Her strategy in the play was to face the issue of suicide squarely and directly. She chose not to have Jessie deal with her decision alone and merely leave a note, as had been done in many such plays in the past. Rather, she chose to make the play a dialogue, with Jessie having to confront the one person who loves her most and who most wants her to live and to give up her thoughts of killing herself.

Norman also made the play more difficult for popular audiences because she did not take the obvious path of giving Jessie a terminal disease, as some plays had done. She felt it was imperative that the issues of life and death, of personal choice and motive, be explored directly onstage, with the characters facing as squarely as possible the ramifications of their choices.

The ethical issues that suicide raises are naturally complex, and the play does not broach them directly. But such issues are always in the minds of the audience. In no sense does the play offer anyone reasons for committing suicide. Jessie's discussion with her mother is not equivalent to a debate: She has made up her mind based on her personal feelings about life, and she makes her decision seem inevitable.

Jessie is not a deep thinker, not a reflective person, and she does not concern herself with spiritual issues in making her decision. Her last evening's concerns are limited to the physical, material, and psychological comfort of her mother.

'night, Mother in Performance

'night, Mother opened on March 31, 1983, at New York's Golden Theater. Kathy Bates played the daughter, Jessie, and Anne Pitoniak played Thelma, her mother. Bates and Pitoniak were voted best actresses of the year by the Critics' Outer Circle, and the play was awarded the Pulitzer. The play ran for 388 performances.

Before its New York opening, the play premiered at the American Repertory Theatre under Robert Brustein's aegis in January 1983. Of that production Frank Rich, *New York Times* critic, said, "'night, Mother . . . is one of the most disturbing American plays of recent seasons. You can pick at it and argue with it, but you can't hide from its bruising impact." The fact that it premiered in Boston distinguished the play because it was the first time a playwright received a Pulitzer for a non–New York production. When the play moved to New York, Rich again reviewed it for the *Times,* praising "the superb actresses" and "the brilliant, unerring choreographic hand of the director Tom Moore."

In 1986 the film version appeared, with Tom Moore directing, Sissy Spacek as Jessie, and Anne Bancroft as Thelma. Some reviews complained of Moore's "busy-ness."

In a short time, the play had appeared in productions in thirty-six countries in Europe, South America, Scandinavia, and Africa. Marsha Norman has commented on the differences in the languages and the actresses in various national productions in her interview with David Savran on pp. 1481–82. *'night, Mother* has become a universal play, one that absorbs cultural differences and speaks to people everywhere.

Marsha Norman (b. 1947)
'NIGHT MOTHER

1983

Characters

JESSIE CATES, *in her late thirties or early forties, is pale and vaguely unsteady physically. It is only in the last year that Jessie has gained control of her mind and body, and tonight she is determined to hold on to that control. She wears pants and a long black sweater with deep pockets, which contain scraps of paper, and there may be a pencil behind her ear or a pen clipped to one of the pockets of the sweater.*

As a rule, Jessie doesn't feel much like talking. Other people have rarely found her quirky sense of humor amusing. She has a peaceful energy on this night, a sense of purpose, but is clearly aware of the time passing moment by moment. Oddly enough, Jessie has never been as communicative or as enjoyable as she is on this evening, but we must know she has not always been this way. There is a familiarity between these two women that comes from having lived together for a long time. There is a shorthand to the talk and a sense of routine comfort in the way they relate to each other physically. Naturally, there are also routine aggravations.

THELMA CATES, MAMA, *is Jessie's mother, in her late fifties or early sixties. She has begun to feel her age and so takes it easy when she can, or when it*

serves her purpose to let someone help her. But she speaks quickly and enjoys talking. She believes that things are what she says they are. Her sturdiness is more a mental quality than a physical one, finally. She is chatty and nosy, and this is her house.*

(The play takes place in a relatively new house built way out on a country road, with a living room and connecting kitchen, and a center hall that leads off to the bedrooms. A pull cord in the hall ceiling releases a ladder which leads to the attic. One of these bedrooms opens directly onto the hall, and its entry should be visible to everyone in the audience. It should be, in fact, the focal point of the entire set, and the lighting should make it disappear completely at times and draw the entire set into it at others. It is a point of both threat and promise. It is an ordinary door that opens onto absolute nothingness. That door is the point of all the action, and the utmost care should be given to its design and construction.)

(The living room is cluttered with magazines and needlework catalogues, ashtrays and candy dishes. Examples of Mama's needlework are everywhere — pillows, afghans, and quilts, doilies and rugs, and they are quite nice examples. The house is more comfortable than messy, but there is quite a lot to keep in

place here. It is more personal than charming. It is not quaint. Under no circumstances should the set and its dressing make a judgment about the intelligence or taste of Jessie and Mama. It should simply indicate that they are very specific real people who happen to live in a particular part of the country. Heavy accents, which would further distance the audience from Jessie and Mama, are also wrong.)

(The time is the present, with the action beginning about 8:15. Clocks onstage in the kitchen and on a table in the living room should run throughout the performance and be visible to the audience.)

(Mama stretches to reach the cupcakes in a cabinet in the kitchen. She can't see them, but she can feel around for them, and she's eager to have one, so she's working pretty hard at it. This may be the most serious exercise Mama ever gets. She finds a cupcake, the coconut-covered, raspberry-and-marshmallow-filled kind known as a snowball, but sees that there's one missing from the package. She calls to Jessie, who is apparently somewhere else in the house.)

MAMA (*unwrapping the cupcake*): Jessie, it's the last snowball, sugar. Put it on the list, O.K.? And we're out of Hershey bars, and where's that peanut brittle? I think maybe Dawson's been in it again. I ought to put a big mirror on the refrigerator door. That'll keep him out of my treats, won't it? You hear me, honey? (*Then more to herself.*) I hate it when the coconut falls off. Why does the coconut fall off?

(Jessie enters from her bedroom, carrying a stack of newspapers.)

JESSIE: We got any old towels?

MAMA: There you are!

JESSIE (*holding a towel that was on the stack of newspapers*): Towels you don't want anymore. (*Picking up Mama's snowball wrapper.*) How about this swimming towel Loretta gave us? Beach towel, that's the name of it. You want it? (*Mama shakes her head no.*)

MAMA: What have you been doing in there?

JESSIE: And a big piece of plastic like a rubber sheet or something. Garbage bags would do if there's enough.

MAMA: Don't go making a big mess, Jessie. It's eight o'clock already.

JESSIE: Maybe an old blanket or towels we got in a soap box sometime?

MAMA: I said don't make a mess. Your hair is black enough, hon.

JESSIE (*continuing to search the kitchen cabinets, finding two or three more towels to add to her stack*): It's not for my hair, Mama. What about some old

pillows anywhere, or a foam cushion out of a yard chair would be real good.

MAMA: You haven't forgot what night it is, have you? (*Holding up her fingernails.*) They're all chipped, see? I've been waiting all week, Jess. It's Saturday night, sugar.

JESSIE: I know. I got it on the schedule.

MAMA (*crossing to the living room*): You want me to wash 'em now or are you making your mess first? (*Looking at the snowball.*) We're out of these. Did I say that already?

JESSIE: There's more coming tomorrow. I ordered you a whole case.

MAMA (*checking the TV Guide*): A whole case will go stale, Jessie.

JESSIE: They can go in the freezer till you're ready for them. Where's Daddy's gun?

MAMA: In the attic.

JESSIE: Where in the attic? I looked your whole nap and couldn't find it anywhere.

MAMA: One of his shoeboxes, I think.

JESSIE: Full of shoes. I looked already.

MAMA: Well, you didn't look good enough, then. There's that box from the ones he wore to the hospital. When he died, they told me I could have them back, but I never did like those shoes.

JESSIE (*pulling them out of her pocket*): I found the bullets. They were in an old milk can.

MAMA (*as Jessie starts for the hall*): Dawson took the shotgun, didn't he? Hand me that basket, hon.

JESSIE (*getting the basket for her*): Dawson better not've taken that pistol.

MAMA (*stopping her again*): Now my glasses, please. (*Jessie returns to get the glasses.*) I told him to take those rubber boots, too, but he said they were for fishing. I told him to take up fishing.

(Jessie reaches for the cleaning spray and cleans Mama's glasses for her)

JESSIE: He's just too lazy to climb up there, Mama. Or maybe he's just being smart. That floor's not very steady.

MAMA (*getting out a piece of knitting*): It's not a floor at all, hon, it's a board now and then. Measure this for me. I need six inches.

JESSIE (*as she measures*): Dawson could probably use some of those clothes up there. Somebody should have them. You ought to call the Salvation Army before the whole thing falls in on you. Six inches exactly.

MAMA: It's plenty safe! As long as you don't go up there.

JESSIE (*turning to go again*): I'm careful.

MAMA: What do you want the gun for, Jess?

JESSIE (*Not returning this time. Opening the ladder in*

the hall.): Protection. (*She steadies the ladder as Mama talks.*)

MAMA: You take the TV way too serious, hon. I've never seen a criminal in my life. This is way too far to come for what's out here to steal. Never seen a one.

JESSIE (*taking her first step up*): Except for Ricky.

MAMA: Ricky is mixed up. That's not a crime.

JESSIE: Get your hands washed. I'll be right back. And get 'em real dry. You dry your hands till I get back or it's no go, all right?

MAMA: I thought Dawson told you not to go up those stairs.

JESSIE (*going up*): He did.

MAMA: I don't like the idea of a gun, Jess.

JESSIE (*calling down from the attic*): Which shoebox, do you remember?

MAMA: Black.

JESSIE: The box was black?

MAMA: The shoes were black.

JESSIE: That doesn't help much, Mother.

MAMA: I'm not trying to help, sugar. (*No answer.*) We don't have anything anybody'd want, Jessie. I mean, I don't even want what we got, Jessie.

JESSIE: Neither do I. Wash your hands. (*Mama gets up and crosses to stand under the ladder.*)

MAMA: You come down from there before you have a fit. I can't come up and get you, you know.

JESSIE: I know.

MAMA: We'll just hand it over to them when they come, how's that? Whatever they want, the criminals.

JESSIE: That's a good idea, Mama.

MAMA: Ricky will grow out of this and be a real fine boy, Jess. But I have to tell you, I wouldn't want Ricky to know we had a gun in the house.

JESSIE: Here it is. I found it.

MAMA: It's just something Ricky's going through. Maybe he's in with some bad people. He just needs some time, sugar. He'll get back in school or get a job or one day you'll get a call and he'll say he's sorry for all the trouble he's caused and invite you out for supper someplace dress-up.

JESSIE (*coming back down the steps*): Don't worry. It's not for him, it's for me.

MAMA: I didn't think you would shoot your own boy, Jessie. I know you've felt like it, well, we've all felt like shooting somebody, but we don't do it. I just don't think we need . . .

JESSIE (*interrupting*): Your hands aren't washed. Do you want a manicure or not?

MAMA: Yes, I do, but . . .

JESSIE (*crossing to the chair*): Then wash your hands and don't talk to me anymore about Ricky. Those two rings he took were the last valuable things I

had, so now he's started in on other people, door to door. I hope they put him away sometime. I'd turn him in myself if I knew where he was.

MAMA: You don't mean that.

JESSIE: Every word. Wash your hands and that's the last time I'm telling you.

(*Jessie sits down with the gun and starts cleaning it, pushing the cylinder out, checking to see that the chambers and barrel are empty, then putting some oil on a small patch of cloth and pushing it through the barrel with the push rod that was in the box. Mama goes to the kitchen and washes her hands, as instructed, trying not to show her concern about the gun.*)

MAMA: I shoulda got you to bring down that milk can. Agnes Fletcher sold hers to somebody with a flea market for forty dollars apiece.

JESSIE: I'll go back and get it in a minute. There's a wagon wheel up there, too. There's even a churn. I'll get it all if you want.

MAMA (*coming over, now, taking over now*): What are you doing?

JESSIE: The barrel has to be clean, Mama. Old powder, dust gets in it . . .

MAMA: What for?

JESSIE: I told you.

MAMA (*reaching for the gun*): And I told you, we don't get criminals out here.

JESSIE (*quickly pulling it to her*): And I told you . . . (*Then trying to be calm.*) The gun is for me.

MAMA: Well, you can have it if you want. When I die, you'll get it all, anyway.

JESSIE: I'm going to kill myself, Mama.

MAMA (*returning to the sofa*): Very funny. Very funny.

JESSIE: I am.

MAMA: You are not! Don't even say such a thing, Jessie.

JESSIE: How would you know if I didn't say it? You want it to be a surprise? You're lying there in your bed or maybe you're just brushing your teeth and you hear this . . . noise down the hall?

MAMA: Kill yourself.

JESSIE: Shoot myself. In a couple of hours.

MAMA: It must be time for your medicine.

JESSIE: Took it already.

MAMA: What's the matter with you?

JESSIE: Not a thing. Feel fine.

MAMA: You feel fine. You're just going to kill yourself.

JESSIE: Waited until I felt good enough, in fact.

MAMA: Don't make jokes, Jessie. I'm too old for jokes.

JESSIE: It's not a joke, Mama.

(*Mama watches for a moment in silence.*)

MAMA: That gun's no good, you know. He broke it right before he died. He dropped it in the mud one day.

JESSIE: Seems O.K. (*She spins the chamber, cocks the pistol, and pulls the trigger. The gun is not yet loaded, so all we hear is the click, but it will definitely work. It's also obvious that Jessie knows her way around a gun. Mama cannot speak.*) I had Cecil's all ready in there, just in case I couldn't find this one, but I'd rather use Daddy's.

MAMA: Those bullets are at least fifteen years old.

JESSIE (*pulling out another box*): These are from last week.

MAMA: Where did you get those?

JESSIE: Feed store Dawson told me about.

MAMA: Dawson!

JESSIE: I told him I was worried about prowlers. He said he thought it was a good idea. He told me what kind to ask for.

MAMA: If he had any idea . . .

JESSIE: He took it as a compliment. He thought I might be taking an interest in things. He got through telling me all about the bullets and then he said we ought to talk like this more often.

MAMA: And where was I while this was going on?

JESSIE: On the phone with Agnes. About the milk can, I guess. Anyway, I asked Dawson if he thought they'd send me some bullets and he said he'd just call for me, because he knew they'd send them if he told them to. And he was absolutely right. Here they are.

MAMA: How could he do that?

JESSIE: Just trying to help, Mama.

MAMA: And then I told you where the gun was.

JESSIE (*smiling, enjoying this joke*): See? Everybody's doing what they can.

MAMA: You told me it was for protection!

JESSIE: It *is*! I'm still doing your nails, though. Want to try that new Chinaberry color?

MAMA: Well, I'm calling Dawson right now. We'll just see what he has to say about this little stunt.

JESSIE: Dawson doesn't have any more to do with this.

MAMA: He's your brother.

JESSIE: And that's all.

MAMA (*stands up, moves toward the phone*): Dawson will put a stop to this. Yes he will. He'll take the gun away.

JESSIE: If you call him, I'll just have to do it before he gets here. Soon as you hang up the phone, I'll just walk in the bedroom and lock the door. Dawson will get here just in time to help you clean up. Go ahead, call him. Then call the police. Then call the funeral home. Then call Loretta and see if *she'll* do your nails.

MAMA: You will not! This is crazy talk, Jessie!

(*Mama goes directly to the telephone and starts to dial, but Jessie is fast, coming up behind her and taking the receiver out of her hand, putting it back down.*)

JESSIE (*firm and quiet*): I said no. This is private. Dawson is not invited.

MAMA: Just me.

JESSIE: I don't want anybody else over here. Just you and me. If Dawson comes over, it'll make me feel stupid for not doing it ten years ago.

MAMA: I think we better call the doctor. Or how about the ambulance. You like that one driver, I know. What's his name, Timmy? Get you somebody to talk to.

JESSIE (*going back to her chair*): I'm through talking, Mama. You're it. No more.

MAMA: We're just going to sit around like every other night in the world and then you're going to kill yourself? (*Jessie doesn't answer.*) You'll miss. (*Again there is no response.*) You'll just wind up a vegetable. How would you like that? Shoot your ear off? You know what the doctor said about getting excited. You'll cock the pistol and have a fit.

JESSIE: I think I can kill myself, Mama.

MAMA: You're not going to kill yourself, Jessie. You're not even upset! (*Jessie smiles, or laughs quietly, and Mama tries a different approach.*) People don't really kill themselves, Jessie. No, mam, doesn't make sense, unless you're retarded or deranged, and you're as normal as they come, Jessie, for the most part. We're all *afraid* to die.

JESSIE: I'm not, Mama. I'm cold all the time, anyway.

MAMA: That's ridiculous.

JESSIE: It's exactly what I want. It's dark and quiet.

MAMA: So is the back yard, Jessie! Close your eyes. Stuff cotton in your ears. Take a nap! It's quiet in your room. I'll leave the TV off all night.

JESSIE: So quiet I don't know it's quiet. So nobody can get me.

MAMA: You don't know what dead is like. It might not be quiet at all. What if it's like an alarm clock and you can't wake up so you can't shut it off. Ever.

JESSIE: Dead is everybody and everything I ever knew, gone. Dead is dead quiet.

MAMA: It's a sin. You'll go to hell.

JESSIE: Uh-huh.

MAMA: You will!

JESSIE: Jesus was a suicide, if you ask me.

MAMA: You'll go to hell just for saying that. Jessie!

JESSIE (*with genuine surprise*): I didn't know I thought that.

MAMA: Jessie!

(*Jessie doesn't answer. She puts the now-loaded gun*

Kathy Bates and Anne Pitoniak in the American Repertory Theatre's 1983 production of *'night, Mother.*

back in the box and crosses to the kitchen. But Mama is afraid she's headed for the bedroom.)

MAMA (*in a panic*): You can't use my towels! They're my towels. I've had them for a long time. I like my towels.

JESSIE: I asked you if you wanted that swimming towel and you said you didn't.

MAMA: And you can't use your father's gun, either. It's mine now, too. And you can't do it in my house.

JESSIE: Oh, come on.

MAMA: No. You can't do it. I won't let you. The house is in my name.

JESSIE: I have to go in the bedroom and lock the door behind me so they won't arrest you for killing me. They'll probably test your hands for gunpowder, anyway, but you'll pass.

MAMA: Not in my house!

JESSIE: If I'd known you were going to act like this, I wouldn't have told you.

MAMA: How am I supposed to act? Tell you to go ahead? O.K. by me, sugar? Might try it myself. What took you so long?

JESSIE: There's just no point in fighting me over it, that's all. Want some coffee?

MAMA: Your birthday's coming up, Jessie. Don't you want to know what we got you?

JESSIE: You got me dusting powder, Loretta got me a new housecoat, pink probably, and Dawson got me new slippers, too small, but they go with the robe, he'll say. (*Mama cannot speak.*) Right? (*Apparently Jessie is right.*) Be back in a minute.

(*Jessie takes the gun box, puts it on top of the stack of towels and garbage bags, and takes them into her bedroom. Mama, alone for a moment, goes to the phone, picks up the receiver, looks toward the bedroom, starts to dial, and then replaces the receiver in its cradle as Jessie walks back into the room. Jessie wonders, silently. They have lived together for so long there is very rarely any reason for one to ask what the other was about to do.)*

MAMA: I started to, but I didn't. I didn't call him.

JESSIE: Good. Thank you.

MAMA (*starting over, a new approach*): What's this all about, Jessie?

JESSIE: About?

(*Jessie now begins the next task she had "on the schedule," which is refilling all the candy jars, taking the empty papers out of the boxes of chocolates, etc. Mama generally snitches when Jessie does this. Not tonight, though. Nevertheless, Jessie offers.*)

MAMA: What did I do?

JESSIE: Nothing. Want a caramel?

MAMA (*ignoring the candy*): You're mad at me.

JESSIE: Not a bit. I am worried about you, but I'm going to do what I can before I go. We're not just going to sit around tonight. I made a list of things.

MAMA: What things?

JESSIE: How the washer works. Things like that.

MAMA: I know how the washer works. You put the clothes in. You put the soap in. You turn it on. You wait.

JESSIE: You do something else. You don't just wait.

MAMA: Whatever else you find to do, you're still mainly waiting. The waiting's the worst part of it. The waiting's what you pay somebody else to do, if you can.

JESSIE (*nodding*): O.K. Where do we keep the soap?

MAMA: I could find it.

JESSIE: See?

MAMA: If you're mad about doing the wash, we can get Loretta to do it.

JESSIE: Oh now, that might be worth staying to see.

MAMA: She'd never in her life, would she?

JESSIE: Nope.

MAMA: What's the matter with her?

JESSIE: She thinks she's better than we are. She's not.

MAMA: Maybe if she didn't wear that yellow all the time.

JESSIE: The washer repair number is on a little card taped to the side of the machine.

MAMA: Loretta doesn't ever have to come over here again. Dawson can just leave her at home when he comes. And we don't ever have to see Dawson either if he bothers you. Does he bother you?

JESSIE: Sure he does. Be sure you clean out the lint tray every time you use the dryer. But don't ever put your house shoes in, it'll melt the soles.

MAMA: What does Dawson do, that bothers you?

JESSIE: He just calls me Jess like he knows who he's talking to. He's always wondering what I do all day. I mean, I wonder that myself, but it's my day, so it's mine to wonder about, not his.

MAMA: Family is just accident, Jessie. It's nothing personal, hon. They don't mean to get on your nerves. They don't even mean to be your family, they just are.

JESSIE: They know too much.

MAMA: About what?

JESSIE: They know things about you, and they learned it before you had a chance to say whether you wanted them to know it or not. They were there when it happened and it don't belong to them, it belongs to you, only they got it. Like my mail-order bra got delivered to their house.

MAMA: By accident!

JESSIE: All the same . . . they opened it. They saw the little rosebuds on it. (*Offering her another candy.*) Chewy mint?

MAMA (*shaking her head no*): What do they know about you? I'll tell them never to talk about it again. Is it Ricky or Cecil or your fits or your hair is falling out or you drink too much coffee or you never go out of the house or what?

JESSIE: I just don't like their talk. The account at the grocery is in Dawson's name when you call. The number's on a whole list of numbers on the back cover of the phone book.

MAMA: Well! Now we're getting somewhere. They're none of them ever setting foot in this house again.

JESSIE: It's not them, Mother. I wouldn't kill myself just to get away from them.

MAMA: You leave the room when they come over, anyway.

JESSIE: I stay as long as I can. Besides, it's you they come to see.

MAMA: That's because I stay in the room when they come.

JESSIE: It's not them.

MAMA: Then what is it?

JESSIE (*checking the list on her note pad*): The grocery won't deliver on Saturday anymore. And if you want your order the same day, you have to call before ten. And they won't deliver less than fifteen dollars' worth. What I do is tell them what we need and tell them to add on cigarettes until it gets to fifteen dollars.

MAMA: It's Ricky. You're trying to get through to him.

JESSIE: If I thought I could do that, I would stay.

MAMA: Make him sorry he hurt you, then. That's it, isn't it?

JESSIE: He's hurt me, I've hurt him. We're about even.

MAMA: You'll be telling him killing is O.K. with you, you know. Want him to start killing next? Nothing wrong with it. Mom did it.

JESSIE: Only a matter of time, anyway, Mama. When the call comes, you let Dawson handle it.

MAMA: Honey, nothing says those calls are always going to be some new trouble he's into. You could get one that he's got a job, that he's getting married, or how about he's joined the army, wouldn't that be nice?

JESSIE: If you call the Sweet Tooth before you call the grocery, that Susie will take your fudge next door to the grocery and it'll all come out together. Be sure you talk to Susie, though. She won't let them put it in the bottom of a sack like that one time, remember?

MAMA: Ricky could come over, you know. What if he calls us?

JESSIE: It's not Ricky, Mama.

MAMA: Or anybody could call us, Jessie.

JESSIE: Not on Saturday night, Mama.

MAMA: Then what is it? Are you sick? If your gums are swelling again, we can get you to the dentist in the morning.

JESSIE: No. Can you order your medicine or do you want Dawson to? I've got a note to him. I'll add that to it if you want.

MAMA: Your eyes don't look right. I thought so yesterday.

JESSIE: That was just the ragweed. I'm not sick.

MAMA: Epilepsy is sick, Jessie.

JESSIE: It won't kill me. (*A pause.*) If it would, I wouldn't have to.

MAMA: You don't *have* to.

JESSIE: No, I don't. That's what I like about it.

MAMA: Well, I won't let you!

JESSIE: It's not up to you.

MAMA: Jessie!

JESSIE: I want to hang a big sign around my neck, like Daddy's on the barn. GONE FISHING.

MAMA: You don't like it here.

JESSIE (*smiling*): Exactly.

MAMA: I meant here in my house.

JESSIE: I know you did.

MAMA: You never should have moved back in here with me. If you'd kept your little house or found another place when Cecil left you, you'd have made some new friends at least. Had a life to lead. Had your own things around you. Give Ricky a place to come see you. You never should've come here.

JESSIE: Maybe.

MAMA: But I didn't force you, did I?

JESSIE: If it was a mistake, we made it together. You took me in. I appreciate that.

MAMA: You didn't have any business being by yourself right then, but I can see how you might want a place of your own. A grown woman should . . .

JESSIE: Mama . . . I'm just not having a very good time and I don't have any reason to think it'll get anything but worse. I'm tired. I'm hurt. I'm sad. I feel used.

MAMA: Tired of what?

JESSIE: It all.

MAMA: What does that mean?

JESSIE: I can't say it any better.

MAMA: Well, you'll have to say it better because I'm not letting you alone till you do. What were those other things? Hurt . . . (*Before Jessie can answer.*) You had this all ready to say to me, didn't you? Did you write this down? How long have you been thinking about this?

JESSIE: Off and on, ten years. On all the time, since Christmas.

MAMA: What happened at Christmas?

JESSIE: Nothing.

MAMA: So why Christmas?

JESSIE: That's it. On the nose.

(*A pause. Mama knows exactly what Jessie means. She was there, too, after all.*)

JESSIE (*putting the candy sacks away*): See where all this is? Red hots up front, sour balls and horehound mixed together in this one sack. New packages of toffee and licorice right in back there.

MAMA: Go back to your list. You're hurt by what?

JESSIE (*Mama knows perfectly well*): Mama . . .

MAMA: O.K. Sad about what? There's nothing real sad going on right now. If it was after your divorce or something, that would make sense.

JESSIE (*looking at her list, then opening the drawer*): Now, this drawer has everything in it that there's no better place for. Extension cords, batteries for the radio, extra lighters, sandpaper, masking tape, Elmer's glue, thumbtacks, that kind of stuff. The mousetraps are under the sink, but you call Dawson if you've got one and let him do it.

MAMA: Sad about what?

JESSIE: The way things are.

MAMA: Not good enough. What things?

JESSIE: Oh, everything from you and me to Red China.

MAMA: I think we can leave the Chinese out of this.

JESSIE (*crosses back into the living room*): There's extra light bulbs in a box in the hall closet. And we've got a couple of packages of fuses in the fuse box. There's candles and matches in the top of the broom closet, but if the lights go out, just call Dawson and sit tight. But don't open the refrigerator door. Things will stay cool in there as long as you keep the door shut.

MAMA: I asked you a question.

JESSIE: I read the paper. I don't like how things are.

And they're not any better out there than they are in here.

MAMA: If you're doing this because of the newspapers, I can sure fix that!

JESSIE: There's just more of it on TV.

MAMA (*kicking the television set*): Take it out, then!

JESSIE: You wouldn't do that.

MAMA: Watch me.

JESSIE: What would you do all day?

MAMA (*desperately*): Sing. (*Jessie laughs.*) I would, too. You want to watch? I'll sing till morning to keep you alive, Jessie, please!

JESSIE: No. (*Then affectionately.*) It's a funny idea, though. What do you sing?

MAMA (*has no idea how to answer this*): We've got a good life here!

JESSIE (*going back into the kitchen*): I called this morning and canceled the papers, except for Sunday, for your puzzles; you'll still get that one.

MAMA: Let's get another dog, Jessie! You liked a big dog, now, didn't you? That King dog, didn't you?

JESSIE (*washing her hands*): I did like that King dog, yes.

MAMA: I'm so dumb. He's the one run under the tractor.

JESSIE: That makes him dumb, not you.

MAMA: For bringing it up.

JESSIE: It's O.K. Handi-Wipes and sponges under the sink.

MAMA: We could get a new dog and keep him in the house. Dogs are cheap!

JESSIE (*getting big pill jars out of the cabinet*): No.

MAMA: Something for you to take care of.

JESSIE: I've had you, Mama.

MAMA (*frantically starting to fill pill bottles*): You do too much for me. I can fill pill bottles all day Jessie, and change the shelf paper and wash the floor when I get through. You just watch me. You don't have to do another thing in this house if you don't want to. You don't have to take care of me, Jessie.

JESSIE: I know that. You've just been letting me do it so I'll have something to do, haven't you?

MAMA (*realizing this was a mistake*): I don't do it as well as you. I just meant if it tires you out or makes you feel used . . .

JESSIE: Mama, I know you used to ride the bus. Riding the bus and it's hot and bumpy and crowded and too noisy and more than anything in the world you want to get off and the only reason in the world you don't get off is it's still fifty blocks from where you're going? Well, I can get off right now if I want to, because even if I ride fifty more years and get off then, it's the same place when I step down to it. Whenever I feel like it, I can get off. As soon as I've had enough, it's my stop. I've had enough.

MAMA: You're feeling sorry for yourself!

JESSIE: The plumber's helper is under the sink, too.

MAMA: You're not having a good time! Whoever promised you a good time? Do you think I've had a good time?

JESSIE: I think you're pretty happy, yeah. You have things you like to do.

MAMA: Like what?

JESSIE: Like crochet.

MAMA: I'll teach you to crochet.

JESSIE: I can't do any of that nice work, Mama.

MAMA: Good time don't come looking for you, Jessie. You could work some puzzles or put in a garden or go to the store. Let's call a taxi and go to the A&P!

JESSIE: I shopped you up for about two weeks already. You're not going to need toilet paper till Thanksgiving.

MAMA (*interrupting*): You're acting like some little brat, Jessie. You're mad and everybody's boring and you don't have anything to do and you don't like me and you don't like going out and you don't like staying in and you never talk on the phone and you don't watch TV and you're miserable and it's your own sweet fault.

JESSIE: And it's time I did something about it.

MAMA: Not something like killing yourself. Something like . . . buying us all new dishes! I'd like that. Or maybe the doctor would let you get a driver's license now, or I know what let's do right this minute, let's rearrange the furniture.

JESSIE: I'll do that. If you want. I always thought if the TV was somewhere else, you wouldn't get such a glare on it during the day. I'll do whatever you want before I go.

MAMA (*badly frightened by those words*): You could get a job!

JESSIE: I took that telephone sales job and I didn't even make enough money to pay the phone bill, and I tried to work at the gift shop at the hospital and they said I made people real uncomfortable smiling at them the way I did.

MAMA: You could keep books. You kept your dad's books.

JESSIE: But nobody ever checked them.

MAMA: When he died, they checked them.

JESSIE: And that's when they took the books away from me.

MAMA: That's because without him there wasn't any business, Jessie!

JESSIE (*putting the pill bottles away*): You know I couldn't work. I can't do anything. I've never been around people my whole life except when I went to the hospital. I could have a seizure any time.

What good would a job do? The kind of job I could get would make me feel worse.

MAMA: Jessie!

JESSIE: It's true!

MAMA: It's what you think is true!

JESSIE (*struck by the clarity of that*): That's right. It's what I think is true.

MAMA (*hysterically*): But I can't do anything about that!

JESSIE (*quietly*): No. You can't. (*Mama slumps, if not physically, at least emotionally.*) And I can't do anything either, about my life, to change it, make it better, make me feel better about it. Like it better, make it work. But I can stop it. Shut it down, turn it off like the radio when there's nothing on I want to listen to. It's all I really have that belongs to me and I'm going to say what happens to it. And it's going to stop. And I'm going to stop it. So. Let's just have a good time.

MAMA: Have a good time.

JESSIE: We can't go on fussing all night. I mean, I could ask you things I always wanted to know and you could make me some hot chocolate. The old way.

MAMA (*in despair*): It takes cocoa, Jessie.

JESSIE (*gets it out of the cabinet*): I bought cocoa, Mama. And I'd like to have a caramel apple and do your nails.

MAMA: You didn't eat a bite of supper.

JESSIE: Does that mean I can't have a caramel apple?

MAMA: Of course not. I mean . . . (*Smiling a little.*) Of course you can have a caramel apple.

JESSIE: I thought I could.

MAMA: I make the best caramel apples in the world.

JESSIE: I know you do.

MAMA: Or used to. And you don't get cocoa like mine anywhere anymore.

JESSIE: It takes time, I know, but . . .

MAMA: The salt is the trick.

JESSIE: Trouble and everything.

MAMA (*backing away toward the stove*): It's no trouble. What trouble? You put it in the pan and stir it up. All right. Fine. Caramel apples. Cocoa. O.K.

(*Jessie walks to the counter to retrieve her cigarettes as Mama looks for the right pan. There are brief near-smiles, and maybe Mama clears her throat. We have a truce, for the moment. A genuine but nevertheless uneasy one. Jessie, who has been in constant motion since the beginning, now seems content to sit.*)

(*Mama starts looking for a pan to make the cocoa, getting out all the pans in the cabinets in the process. It looks like she's making a mess on purpose so Jessie will have to put them all away again. Mama is buying time, or trying to, and entertaining.*)

JESSIE: You talk to Agnes today?

MAMA: She's calling me from a pay phone this week. God only knows why. She has a perfectly good Trimline at home.

JESSIE (*laughing*): Well, how is she?

MAMA: How is she every day, Jessie? Nuts.

JESSIE: Is she really crazy or just silly?

MAMA: No, she's really crazy. She was probably using the pay phone because she had another little fire problem at home.

JESSIE: Mother . . .

MAMA: I'm serious! Agnes Fletcher's burned down every house she ever lived in. Eight fires, and she's due for a new one any day now.

JESSIE (*laughing*): No!

MAMA: Wouldn't surprise me a bit.

JESSIE (*laughing*): Why didn't you tell me this before? Why isn't she locked up somewhere?

MAMA: 'Cause nobody ever got hurt, I guess. Agnes woke everybody up to watch the fires as soon as she set 'em. One time she set out porch chairs and served lemonade.

JESSIE (*shaking her head*): Real lemonade?

MAMA: The houses they lived in, you knew they were going to fall down anyway, so why wait for it, is all I could ever make out about it. Agnes likes a feeling of accomplishment.

JESSIE: Good for her.

MAMA (*finding the pan she wants*): Why are you asking about Agnes? One cup or two?

JESSIE: One. She's your friend. No marshmallows.

MAMA (*getting the milk, etc.*): You have to have marshmallows. That's the old way, Jess. Two or three? Three is better.

JESSIE: Three, then. Her whole house burns up? Her clothes and pillows and everything? I'm not sure I believe this.

MAMA: When she was a girl, Jess, not now. Long time ago. But she's still got it in her, I'm sure of it.

JESSIE: She wouldn't burn her house down now. Where would she go? She can't get Buster to build her a new one, he's dead. How could she burn it up?

MAMA: Be exciting, though, if she did. You never know.

JESSIE: You do too know, Mama. She wouldn't do it.

MAMA (*forced to admit, but reluctant*): I guess not.

JESSIE: What else? Why does she wear all those whistles around her neck?

MAMA: Why does she have a house full of birds?

JESSIE: I didn't know she had a house full of birds!

MAMA: Well, she does. And she says they just follow her home. Well, I know for a fact she's still paying on the last parrot she bought. You gotta keep your life filled up, she says. She says a lot of stupid things. (*Jessie laughs, Mama continues, convinced she's getting somewhere.*) It's all that okra she eats.

You can't just willy-nilly eat okra two meals a day and expect to get away with it. Made her crazy.

JESSIE: She really eats okra twice a day? Where does she get it in the winter?

MAMA: Well, she eats it a lot. Maybe not two meals, but . . .

JESSIE: More than the average person.

MAMA (*beginning to get irritated*): I don't know how much okra the average person eats.

JESSIE: Do you know how much okra Agnes eats?

MAMA: No.

JESSIE: How many birds does she have?

MAMA: Two.

JESSIE: Then what are the whistles for?

MAMA: They're not real whistles. Just little plastic ones on a necklace she won playing Bingo, and I only told you about it because I thought I might get a laugh out of you for once even if it wasn't the truth, Jessie. Things don't have to be true to talk about 'em, you know.

JESSIE: Why won't she come over here?

(*Mama is suddenly quiet, but the cocoa and milk are in the pan now, so she lights the stove and starts stirring.*)

MAMA: Well now, what a good idea. We should've had more cocoa. Cocoa is perfect.

JESSIE: Except you don't like milk.

MAMA (*another attempt, but not as energetic*): I hate milk. Coats your throat as bad as okra. Something just downright disgusting about it.

JESSIE: It's because of me, isn't it?

MAMA: No, Jess.

JESSIE: Yes, Mama.

MAMA: O.K. Yes, then, but she's crazy. She's as crazy as they come. She's a lunatic.

JESSIE: What is it exactly? Did I say something, sometime? Or did she see me have a fit and's afraid I might have another one if she came over, or what?

MAMA: I guess.

JESSIE: You guess what? What's she ever said? She must've given you some reason.

MAMA: Your hands are cold.

JESSIE: What difference does that make?

MAMA: "Like a corpse," she says, "and I'm gonna be one soon enough as it is."

JESSIE: That's crazy.

MAMA: That's Agnes. "Jessie's shook the hand of death and I can't take the chance it's catching, Thelma, so I ain't comin' over, and you can understand or not, but I ain't comin'. I'll come up the driveway, but that's as far as I go."

JESSIE (*laughing, relieved*): I thought she didn't like

me! She's scared of me! How about that! Scared of me.

MAMA: I could make her come over here, Jessie. I could call her up right now and she could bring the birds and come visit. I didn't know you ever thought about her at all. I'll tell her she just has to come and she'll come, all right. She owes me one.

JESSIE: No, that's all right. I just wondered about it. When I'm in the hospital, does she come over here?

MAMA: Her kitchen is just a tiny thing. When she comes over here, she feels like . . . (*Toning it down a little.*) Well, we all like a change of scene, don't we?

JESSIE (*playing along*): Sure we do. Plus there's no birds diving around.

MAMA: I hate those birds. She says I don't understand them. What's there to understand about birds?

JESSIE: Why Agnes likes them, for one thing. Why they stay with her when they could be outside with the other birds. What their singing means. How they fly. What they think Agnes is.

MAMA: Why do you have to know so much about things, Jessie? There's just not that much *to* things that I could ever see.

JESSIE: That you could ever *tell*, you mean. You didn't have to lie to me about Agnes.

MAMA: I didn't lie. You never asked before!

JESSIE: You lied about setting fire to all those houses and about how many birds she has and how much okra she eats and why she won't come over here. If I have to keep dragging the truth out of you, this is going to take all night.

MAMA: That's fine with me. I'm not a bit sleepy.

JESSIE: Mama . . .

MAMA: All right. Ask me whatever you want. Here.

(*They come to an awkward stop, as the cocoa is ready and Mama pours it into the cups Jessie has set on the table.*)

JESSIE (*as Mama takes her first sip*): Did you love Daddy?

MAMA: No.

JESSIE (*pleased that Mama understands the rules better now*): I didn't think so. Were you really fifteen when you married him?

MAMA: The way he told it? I'm sitting in the mud, he comes along, drags me in the kitchen, "She's been there ever since"?

JESSIE: Yes.

MAMA: No. It was a big fat lie, the whole thing. He just thought it was funnier that way. God, this milk in here.

JESSIE: The cocoa helps.

MAMA (*pleased that they agree on this, at least*): Not

enough, though, does it? You can still taste it, can't you?

JESSIE: Yeah, it's pretty bad. I thought it was my memory that was bad, but it's not. It's the milk, all right.

MAMA: It's a real waste of chocolate. You don't have to finish it.

JESSIE (*putting her cup down*): Thanks, though.

MAMA: I should've known not to make it. I knew you wouldn't like it. You never did like it.

JESSIE: You didn't ever love him, or he did something and you stopped loving him, or what?

MAMA: He felt sorry for me. He wanted a plain country woman and that's what he married, and then he held it against me the rest of my life like I was supposed to change and surprise him somehow. Like I remember this one day he was standing on the porch and I told him to get a shirt on and he went in and got one and then he said, real peaceful, but to the point, "You're right, Thelma. If God had meant for people to go around without any clothes on, they'd have been born that way."

JESSIE (*sees Mama's hurt*): He didn't mean anything by that, Mama.

MAMA: He never said a word he didn't have to, Jessie. That was probably all he'd said to me all day, Jessie. So if he said it, there was something to it, but I never did figure that one out. What did that mean?

JESSIE: I don't know. I liked him better than you did, but I didn't know him any better.

MAMA: How could I love him, Jessie. I didn't have a thing he wanted. (*Jessie doesn't answer.*) He got his share, though. You loved him enough for both of us. You followed him around like some . . . Jessie, all the man ever did was farm and sit . . . and try to think of somebody to sell the farm to.

JESSIE: Or make me a boyfriend out of pipe cleaners and sit back and smile like the stick man was about to dance and wasn't I going to get a kick out of that. Or sit up with a sick cow all night and leave me a chain of sleepy stick elephants on my bed in the morning.

MAMA: Or just sit.

JESSIE: I liked him sitting. Big old faded blue man in the chair. Quiet.

MAMA: Agnes gets more talk out of her birds than I got from the two of you. He could've had that GONE FISHING sign around his neck in that chair. I saw him stare off at the water. I saw him look at the weather rolling in. I got where I could practically see the boat myself. But you, you knew what he was thinking about and you're going to tell me.

JESSIE: I don't know, Mama! His life, I guess. His corn. His boots. Us. Things. You know.

MAMA: No, I don't know, Jessie! You had those quiet little conversations after supper every night. What were you whispering about?

JESSIE: We weren't whispering, you were just across the room.

MAMA: What did you talk about?

JESSIE: We talked about why black socks are warmer than blue socks. Is that something to go tell Mother? You were just jealous because I'd rather talk to him than wash the dishes with you.

MAMA: I was jealous because you'd rather talk to him than anything! (*Jessie reaches across the table for the small clock and starts to wind it.*) If I had died instead of him, he wouldn't have taken you in like I did.

JESSIE: I wouldn't have expected him to.

MAMA: Then what would you have done?

JESSIE: Come visit.

MAMA: Oh, I see. He died and left you stuck with me and you're mad about it.

JESSIE (*getting up from the table*): Not anymore. He didn't mean to. I didn't have to come here. We've been through this.

MAMA: He felt sorry for you, too, Jessie, don't kid yourself about that. He said you were a runt and he said it from the day you were born and he said you didn't have a chance.

JESSIE (*getting the canister of sugar and starting to refill the sugar bowl*): I know he loved me.

MAMA: What if he did? It didn't change anything.

JESSIE: It didn't have to. I miss him.

MAMA: He never really went fishing, you know. Never once. His tackle box was full of chewing tobacco and all he ever did was drive out to the lake and sit in his car. Dawson told me. And Bennie at the bait shop, he told Dawson. They all laughed about it. And he'd come back from fishing and all he'd have to show for it was . . . a whole pipe-cleaner *family* — chickens, pigs, a dog with a bad leg — it was creepy strange. It made me sick to look at them and I hid his pipe cleaners a couple of times but he always had more somewhere.

JESSIE: I thought it might be better for you after he died. You'd get interested in things. Breathe better. Change somehow.

MAMA: Into what? The Queen? A clerk in a shoe store? Why should I? Because he said to? Because you said to? (*Jessie shakes her head.*) Well I wasn't here for his entertainment and I'm not here for yours either, Jessie. I don't know what I'm here for, but then I don't think about it. (*Realizing what all this means.*) But I bet you wouldn't be killing yourself if he were still alive. That's a fine thing to figure out, isn't it?

JESSIE (*filling the honey jar now*): That's not true.

MAMA: Oh no? Then what were you asking about him for? Why did you want to know if I loved him?

JESSIE: I didn't think you did, that's all.

MAMA: Fine then. You were right. Do you feel better now?

JESSIE (*cleaning the honey jar carefully*): It feels good to be right about it.

MAMA: It didn't matter whether I loved him. It didn't matter to me and it didn't matter to him. And it didn't mean we didn't get along. It wasn't important. We didn't talk about it. (*Sweeping the pots off the cabinet.*) Take all these pots out to the porch!

JESSIE: What for?

MAMA: Just leave me this one pan. (*She jerks the silverware drawer open.*) Get me one knife, one fork, one big spoon, and the can opener, and put them out where I can get them. (*Starts throwing knives and forks in one of the pans.*)

JESSIE: Don't do that! I just straightened that drawer!

MAMA (*throwing the pan in the sink*): And throw out all the plates and cups. I'll use paper. Loretta can have what she wants and Dawson can sell the rest.

JESSIE (*calmly*): What are you doing?

MAMA: I'm not going to cook. I never liked it, anyway. I like candy. Wrapped in plastic or coming in sacks. And tuna. I like tuna. I'll eat tuna, thank you.

JESSIE (*taking the pan out of the sink*): What if you want to make apple butter? You can't make apple butter in that little pan. What if you leave carrots on cooking and burn up that pan?

MAMA: I don't like carrots.

JESSIE: What if the strawberries are good this year and you want to go picking with Agnes.

MAMA: I'll tell her to bring a pan. You said you would do whatever I wanted! I don't want a bunch of pans cluttering up my cabinets I can't get down to, anyway. Throw them out. Every last one.

JESSIE (*gathering up the pots*): I'm putting them all back in. I'm not taking them to the porch. If you want them, they'll be here. You'll bend down and get them, like you got the one for the cocoa. And if somebody else comes over here to cook, they'll have something to cook in, and that's the end of it!

MAMA: Who's going to come cook here?

JESSIE: Agnes.

MAMA: In my pots. Not on your life.

JESSIE: There's no reason why the two of you couldn't just live here together. Be cheaper for both of you and somebody to talk to. And if the birds bothered you, well, one day when Agnes is out getting her hair done, you could take them all for a walk!

MAMA (*as Jessie straightens the silverware*): So that's why you're pestering me about Agnes. You think you can rest easy if you get me a new babysitter? Well, I don't want to live with Agnes. I barely want to talk with Agnes. She's just around. We go back, that's all. I'm not letting Agnes near this place. You don't get off as easy as that, child.

JESSIE: O.K., then. It's just something to think about.

MAMA: I don't like things to think about. I like things to go on.

JESSIE (*closing the silverware drawer*): I want to know what Daddy said to you the night he died. You came storming out of his room and said I could wait it out with him if I wanted to, but you were going to watch *Gunsmoke*. What did he say to you?

MAMA: He didn't have *anything* to say to me, Jessie. That's why I left. He didn't say a thing. It was his last chance not to talk to me and he took full advantage of it.

JESSIE (*after a moment*): I'm sorry you didn't love him. Sorry for you, I mean. He seemed like a nice man.

MAMA (*as Jessie walks to the refrigerator*): Ready for your apple now?

JESSIE: Soon as I'm through here, Mama.

MAMA: You won't like the apple, either. It'll be just like the cocoa. You never liked eating at all, did you? Any of it! What have you been living on all these years, toothpaste?

JESSIE (*as she starts to clean out the refrigerator*): Now, you know the milkman comes on Wednesdays and Saturdays, and he leaves the order blank in an egg box, and you give the bills to Dawson once a month.

MAMA: Do they still make that orangeade?

JESSIE: It's not orangeade, it's just orange.

MAMA: I'm going to get some. I thought they stopped making it. You just stopped ordering it.

JESSIE: You should drink milk.

MAMA: Not anymore, I'm not. That hot chocolate was the last. Hooray.

JESSIE (*getting the garbage can from under the sink*): I told them to keep delivering a quart a week no matter what you said. I told them you'd run out of Cokes and you'd have to drink it. I told them I knew you wouldn't pour it on the ground...

MAMA (*finishing her sentence*): And you told them you weren't going to be ordering anymore?

JESSIE: I told them I was taking a little holiday and to look after you.

MAMA: And they didn't think something was funny about that? You who doesn't go to the front steps? You, who only sees the driveway looking down from a stretcher passed out cold?

JESSIE (*enjoying this, but not laughing*): They said it

was about time, but why didn't I take you with me? And I said I didn't think you'd want to go and they said, "Yeah, everybody's got their own idea of vacation."

MAMA: I guess you think that's funny.

JESSIE (*pulling jars out of the refrigerator*): You know there never was any reason to call the ambulance for me. All they ever did for me in the emergency room was let me wake up. I could've done that here. Now, I'll just call them out and you say yes or no. I know you like pickles. Ketchup?

MAMA: Keep it.

JESSIE: We've had this since last Fourth of July.

MAMA: Keep the ketchup. Keep it all.

JESSIE: Are you going to drink ketchup from the bottle or what? How can you want your food and not want your pots to cook it in? This stuff will all spoil in here, Mother.

MAMA: Nothing I ever did was good enough for you and I want to know why.

JESSIE: That's not true.

MAMA: And I want to know why you've lived here this long feeling the way you do.

JESSIE: You have no earthly idea how I feel.

MAMA: Well, how could I? You're real far back there, Jessie.

JESSIE: Back where?

MAMA: What's it like over there, where you are? Do people always say the right thing or get whatever they want, or what?

JESSIE: What are you talking about?

MAMA: Why do you read the newspaper? Why don't you wear that sweater I made for you? Do you remember how I used to look, or am I just any old woman now? When you have a fit, do you see stars or what? How did you fall off the horse, really? Why did Cecil leave you? Where did you put my old glasses?

JESSIE (*stunned by Mama's intensity*): They're in the bottom drawer of your dresser in an old Milk of Magnesia box. Cecil left me because he made me choose between him and smoking.

MAMA: Jessie, I know he wasn't that dumb.

JESSIE: I never understood why he hated it so much when it's so good. Smoking is the only thing I know that's always just what you think it's going to be. Just like it was the last time, right there when you want it and real quiet.

MAMA: Your fits made him sick and you know it.

JESSIE: Say seizures, not fits. Seizures.

MAMA: It's the same thing. A seizure in the hospital is a fit at home.

JESSIE: They didn't bother him at all. Except he did feel responsible for it. It *was* his idea to go horse-

back riding that day. It was his idea I could do *anything* if I just made up my mind to. I fell off the horse because I didn't know how to hold on. Cecil left for pretty much the same reason.

MAMA: He had a girl, Jessie. I walked right in on them in the toolshed.

JESSIE (*after a moment*): O.K. That's fair. (*Lighting another cigarette.*) Was she very pretty?

MAMA: She was Agnes's girl, Carlene. Judge for yourself.

JESSIE (*as she walks to the living room*): I guess you and Agnes had a good talk about that, huh?

MAMA: I never thought he was good enough for you. They moved here from Tennessee, you know.

JESSIE: What are you talking about? You liked him better than I did. You flirted him out here to build your porch or I'd never even met him at all. You thought maybe he'd help you out around the place, come in and get some coffee and talk to you. God knows what you thought. All that curly hair.

MAMA: He's the best carpenter I ever saw. That little house of yours will still be standing at the end of the world, Jessie.

JESSIE: You didn't need a porch, Mama.

MAMA: All right! I wanted you to have a husband.

JESSIE: And I couldn't get one on my own, of course.

MAMA: How were you going to get a husband never opening your mouth to a living soul?

JESSIE: So I was quiet about it, so what?

MAMA: So I should have let you just sit here? Sit like your daddy? Sit here?

JESSIE: Maybe.

MAMA: Well, I didn't think so.

JESSIE: Well, what did you know?

MAMA: I never said I knew much. How was I supposed to learn anything living out here? I didn't know enough to do half the things I did in my life. Things happen. You do what you can about them and you see what happens next. I married you off to the wrong man, I admit that. So I took you in when he left. I'm sorry.

JESSIE: He wasn't the wrong man.

MAMA: He didn't love you, Jessie, or he wouldn't have left.

JESSIE: He wasn't the wrong man, Mama. I loved Cecil so much. And I tried to get more exercise and I tried to stay awake. I tried to learn to ride a horse. And I tried to stay outside with him, but he always knew I was trying, so it didn't work.

MAMA: He was a selfish man. He told me once he hated to see people move into his houses after he built them. He knew they'd mess them up.

JESSIE: I loved that bridge he built over the creek in back of the house. It didn't have to be anything special, a couple of boards would have been just fine, but he used that yellow pine and rubbed it so smooth . . .

MAMA: He had responsibilities here. He had a wife and son here and he failed you.

JESSIE: Or that baby bed he built for Ricky. I told him he didn't have to spend so much time on it, but he said it had to last, and the thing ended up weighing two hundred pounds and I couldn't move it. I said, "How long does a baby bed have to last, anyway?" But maybe he thought if it was strong enough, it might keep Ricky a baby.

MAMA: Ricky is too much like Cecil.

JESSIE: He is not. Ricky is as much like me as it's possible for any human to be. We even wear the same size pants. These are his, I think.

MAMA: That's just the same size. That's not you're the same person.

JESSIE: I see it on his face. I hear it when he talks. We look out at the world and we see the same thing: Not Fair. And the only difference between us is Ricky's out there trying to get even. And he knows not to trust anybody and he got it straight from me. And he knows not to try to get work, and guess where he got that. He walks around like there's loose boards in the floor, and you know who laid that floor, I did.

MAMA: Ricky isn't through yet. You don't know how he'll turn out!

JESSIE (going back to the kitchen): Yes I do and so did Cecil. Ricky is the two of us together for all time in too small a space. And we're tearing each other apart, like always, inside that boy, and if you don't see it, then you're just blind.

MAMA: Give him time, Jess.

JESSIE: Oh, he'll have plenty of that. Five years for forgery, ten years for armed assault . . .

MAMA (furious): Stop that! (Then pleading.) Jessie, Cecil might be ready to try it again, honey, that happens sometimes. Go downtown. Find him. Talk to him. He didn't know what he had in you. Maybe he sees things different now, but you're not going to know that till you go see him. Or call him up! Right now! He might be home.

JESSIE: And say what? Nothing's changed, Cecil, I'd just like to look at you, if you don't mind? No. He loved me, Mama. He just didn't know how things fall down around me like they do. I think he did the right thing. He gave himself another chance, that's all. But I did beg him to take me with him. I did tell him I would leave Ricky and you and everything I loved out here if only he would take me with him, but he couldn't and I understood that. (Pause.) I wrote that note I showed you. I wrote it. Not Cecil. I said "I'm sorry, Jessie, I can't

fix it all for you." I said I'd always love me, not Cecil. But that's how he felt.

MAMA: Then he should've taken you with him!

JESSIE (picking up the garbage bag she has filled): Mama, you don't pack your garbage when you move.

MAMA: You will not call yourself garbage, Jessie.

JESSIE (taking the bag to the big garbage can near the back door): Just a way of saying it, Mama. Thinking about my list, that's all. (Opening the can, putting the garbage in, then securing the lid.) Well, a little more than that. I was trying to say it's all right that Cecil left. It was . . . a relief in a way. I never was what he wanted to see, so it was better when he wasn't looking at me all the time.

MAMA: I'll make your apple now.

JESSIE: No thanks. You get the manicure stuff and I'll be right there.

(Jessie ties up the big garbage bag in the can and replaces the small garbage bag under the sink, all the time trying desperately to regain her calm. Mama watches, from a distance, her hand reaching unconsciously for the phone. Then she has a better idea. Or rather she thinks of the only other thing left and is willing to try it. Maybe she is even convinced it will work.)

MAMA: Jessie, I think your daddy had little . . .

JESSIE (interrupting her): Garbage night is Tuesday. Put it out as late as you can. The Davises' dogs get in it if you don't. (Replacing the garbage bag in the can under the sink.) And keep ordering the heavy black bags. It doesn't pay to buy the cheap ones. And I've got all the ties here with the hammers and all. Take them out of the box as soon as you open a new one and put them in this drawer. They'll get lost if you don't, and rubber bands or something else won't work.

MAMA: I think your daddy had fits too. I think he sat in his chair and had little fits. I read this a long time ago in a magazine, how little fits go, just little blackouts where maybe their eyes don't even close and people just call them "thinking spells."

JESSIE (getting the slipcover out of the laundry basket): I don't think you want this manicure we've been looking forward to. I washed this cover for the sofa, but it'll take both of us to get it back on.

MAMA: I watched his eyes. I know that's what it was. The magazine said some people don't even know they've had one.

JESSIE: Daddy would've known if he'd had fits, Mama.

MAMA: The lady in this story had kept track of hers and she'd had eighty thousand of them in the last eleven years.

JESSIE: Next time you wash this cover, it'll dry better if you put it on wet.

MAMA: Jessie, listen to what I'm telling you. This lady had anywhere between five and five hundred fits a day and they lasted maybe fifteen seconds apiece, so that out of her life, she'd only lost about two weeks altogether, and she had a full-time secretary job and an IQ of 120.

JESSIE (*amused by Mama's approach*): You want to talk about fits, is that it?

MAMA: Yes. I do. I want to say . . .

JESSIE (*interrupting*): Most of the time I wouldn't even know I'd had one, except I wake up with different clothes on, feeling like I've been run over. Sometimes I feel my head start to turn around or hear myself scream. And sometimes there *is* this dizzy stupid feeling a little before it, but if the TV's on, well, it's easy to miss.

(*As Jessie and Mama replace the slipcover on the sofa and the afghan on the chair, the physical struggle somehow mirrors the emotional one in the conversation.*)

MAMA: I can tell when you're about to have one. Your eyes get this big! But, Jessie, you haven't . . .

JESSIE (*taking charge of this*): What do they look like? The seizures.

MAMA (*reluctant*): Different each time, Jess.

JESSIE: O.K. Pick one, then. A good one. I think I want to know now.

MAMA: There's not much to tell. You just . . . crumple, in a heap, like a puppet and somebody cut the strings all at once, or like the firing squad in some Mexican movie, you just slide down the wall, you know. You don't know what happens? How can you not know what happens?

JESSIE: I'm busy.

MAMA: That's not funny.

JESSIE: I'm not laughing. My head turns around and I fall down and then what?

MAMA: Well, your chest squeezes in and out, and you sound like you're gagging, sucking air in and out like you can't breathe.

JESSIE: Do it for me. Make the sound for me.

MAMA: I will not. It's awful-sounding.

JESSIE: Yeah. It felt like it might be. What's next?

MAMA: Your mouth bites down and I have to get your tongue out of the way fast, so you don't bite yourself.

JESSIE: Or you. I bite you, too, don't I?

MAMA: You got me once real good. I had to get a tetanus! But I know what to watch for now. And then you turn blue and the jerks start up. Like I'm standing there poking you with a cattle prod or you're sticking your finger in a light socket as fast as you can . . .

JESSIE: Foaming like a mad dog the whole time.

MAMA: It's bubbling, Jess, not foam like the washer overflowed, for God's sake; it's bubbling like a baby spitting up. I go get a wet washcloth, that's all. And then the jerks slow down and you wet yourself and it's over. Two minutes tops.

JESSIE: How do I get to the bed?

MAMA: How do you think?

JESSIE: I'm too heavy for you now. How do you do it?

MAMA: I call Dawson. But I get you cleaned up before he gets here and I make him leave before you wake up.

JESSIE: You could just leave me on the floor.

MAMA: I want you to wake up someplace nice, O.K.? (*Then making a real effort.*) But, Jessie, and this is the reason I even brought this up! You haven't had a seizure for a solid year. A whole year, do you realize that?

JESSIE: Yeah, the phenobarb's about right now, I guess.

MAMA: You bet it is. You might never have another one, ever! You might be through with it for all time!

JESSIE: Could be.

MAMA: You are. I know you are!

JESSIE: I sure am feeling good. I really am. The double vision's gone and my gums aren't swelling. No rashes or anything. I'm feeling as good as I ever felt in my life. I'm even feeling like worrying or getting mad and I'm not afraid it will start a fit if I do, I just go ahead.

MAMA: Of course you do! You can even scream at me, if you want to. I can take it. You don't have to act like you're just visiting here, Jessie. This is your house, too.

JESSIE: The best part is, my memory's back.

MAMA: Your memory's always been good. When couldn't you remember things? You're always reminding me what . . .

JESSIE: Because I've made lists for everything. But now I remember what things mean on my lists. I see "dish towels," and I used to wonder whether I was supposed to wash them, buy them, or look for them because I wouldn't remember where I put them after I washed them, but now I know it means wrap them up, they're a present for Loretta's birthday.

MAMA (*finished with the sofa now*): You used to go looking for your lists, too, I've noticed that. You always know where they are now! (*Then suddenly worried.*) Loretta's birthday isn't coming up, is it?

JESSIE: I made a list of all the birthdays for you. I even put yours on it. (*A small smile.*) So you can call Loretta and remind her.

MAMA: Let's take Loretta to Howard Johnson's and have those fried clams. I *know* you love that clam roll.

JESSIE (*slight pause*): I won't be here, Mama.

MAMA: What have we just been talking about? You'll be here. You're well, Jessie. You're starting all over. You said it yourself. You're remembering things and . . .

JESSIE: I won't be here. If I'd ever had a year like this, to think straight and all, before now, I'd be gone already.

MAMA (*not pleading, commanding*): No, Jessie.

JESSIE (*folding the rest of the laundry*): Yes, Mama. Once I started remembering, I could see what it all added up to.

MAMA: The fits are over!

JESSIE: It's not the fits, Mama.

MAMA: Then it's me for giving them to you, but I didn't do it!

JESSIE: It's not the fits! You said it yourself, the medicine takes care of the fits.

MAMA (*interrupting*): Your daddy gave you those fits, Jessie. He passed it down to you like your green eyes and your straight hair. It's not my fault!

JESSIE: So what if he had little fits? It's not inherited. I fell off the horse. It was an accident.

MAMA: The horse wasn't the first time, Jessie. You had a fit when you were five years old.

JESSIE: I did not.

MAMA: You did! You were eating a popsicle and down you went. He gave it to you. It's *his* fault, not mine.

JESSIE: Well, you took your time telling me.

MAMA: How do you tell that to a five-year-old?

JESSIE: What did the doctor say?

MAMA: He said kids have them all the time. He said there wasn't anything to do but wait for another one.

JESSIE: But I didn't have another one.

(*Now there is a real silence.*)

JESSIE: You mean to tell me I had fits all the time as a kid and you just told me I fell down or something and it wasn't till I had the fit when Cecil was looking that anybody bothered to find out what was the matter with me?

MAMA: It wasn't *all the time,* Jessie. And they changed when you started to school. More like your daddy's. Oh, that was some swell time, sitting here with the two of you turning off and on like light bulbs some nights.

JESSIE: How many fits did I have?

MAMA: You never hurt yourself. I never let you out of my sight. I caught you every time.

JESSIE: But you didn't tell anybody.

MAMA: It was none of their business.

JESSIE: You were ashamed.

MAMA: I didn't want anybody to know. Least of all you.

JESSIE: Least of all me. Oh, right. That was mine to know, Mama, not yours. Did Daddy know?

MAMA: He thought you were . . . you fell down a lot. That's what he thought. You were careless. Or maybe he thought I beat you. I don't know what he thought. He didn't think about it.

JESSIE: Because you didn't tell him!

MAMA: If I told him about you, I'd have to tell him about him!

JESSIE: I don't like this. I don't like this one bit.

MAMA: I didn't think you'd like it. That's why I didn't tell you.

JESSIE: If I'd known I was an epileptic, Mama, I wouldn't have ridden any horses.

MAMA: Make you feel like a freak, is that what I should have done?

JESSIE: Just get the manicure tray and sit down!

MAMA (*throwing it to the floor*): I don't want a manicure!

JESSIE: Doesn't look like you do, no.

MAMA: Maybe I did drop you, you don't know.

JESSIE: If you say you didn't, you didn't.

MAMA (*beginning to break down*): Maybe I fed you the wrong thing. Maybe you had a fever sometime and I didn't know it soon enough. Maybe it's a punishment.

JESSIE: For what?

MAMA: I don't know. Because of how I felt about your father. Because I didn't want any more children. Because I smoked too much or didn't eat right when I was carrying you. It has to be something I did.

JESSIE: It does not. It's just a sickness, not a curse. Epilepsy doesn't mean anything. It just is.

MAMA: I'm not talking about the fits here, Jessie! I'm talking about this killing yourself. It has to be me that's the matter here. You wouldn't be doing this if it wasn't. I didn't tell you things or I married you off to the wrong man or I took you in and let your life get away from you or all of it put together. I don't know what I did, but I did it, I know. This is all my fault, Jessie, but I don't know what to do about it now!

JESSIE (*exasperated at having to say this again*): It doesn't have anything to do with you!

MAMA: Everything you do has to do with me, Jessie. You can't do *anything,* wash your face or cut your finger, without doing it to me. That's right! You might as well kill me as you, Jessie, it's the same thing. This has to do with me, Jessie.

JESSIE: Then what if it does! What if it has everything to do with you! What if you are all I have and you're not enough? What if I could take all the rest of it if only I didn't have you here? What if the only way I can get away from you for good is to kill myself? What if it is? I can *still* do it!

MAMA (*in desperate tears*): Don't leave me, Jessie!

(*Jessie stands for a moment, then turns for the bedroom.*) No! (*She grabs Jessie's arm.*)

JESSIE (*carefully taking her arm away*): I have a box of things I want people to have. I'm just going to go get it for you. You . . . just rest a minute.

(*Jessie is gone. Mama heads for the telephone, but she can't even pick up the receiver this time and, instead, stoops to clean up the bottles that have spilled out of the manicure tray.*)

(*Jessie returns, carrying a box that groceries were delivered in. It probably says Hershey Kisses or Starkist Tuna. Mama is still down on the floor cleaning up, hoping that maybe if she just makes it look nice enough, Jessie will stay.*)

MAMA: Jessie, how can I live here without you? I need you! You're supposed to tell me to stand up straight and say how nice I look in my pink dress, and drink my milk. You're supposed to go around and lock up so I know we're safe for the night, and when I wake up, you're supposed to be out there making the coffee and watching me get older every day, and you're supposed to help me die when the time comes. I can't do that by myself, Jessie. I'm not like you, Jessie. I hate the quiet and I don't want to die and I don't want you to go, Jessie. How can I . . . (*Has to stop a moment.*) How can I get up every day knowing you had to kill yourself to make it stop hurting and I was here all the time and I never even saw it. And then you gave me this chance to make it better, convince you to stay alive, and I couldn't do it. How can I live with myself after this, Jessie?

JESSIE: I only told you so I could explain it, so you wouldn't blame yourself, so you wouldn't feel bad. There wasn't anything you could say to change my mind. I didn't want you to save me. I just wanted you to know.

MAMA: Stay with me just a little longer. Just a few more years. I don't have that many more to go, Jessie. And as soon as I'm dead, you can do whatever you want. Maybe with me gone, you'll have all the quiet you want, right here in the house. And maybe one day you'll put in some begonias up the walk and get just the right rain for them all summer. And Ricky will be married by then and he'll bring your grandbabies over and you can sneak them a piece of candy when their daddy's not looking and then be real glad when they've gone home and left you to your quiet again.

JESSIE: Don't you see, Mama, everything I do winds up like this. How could I think you would understand? How could I think you would want a manicure? We could hold hands for an hour and then I could go shoot myself? I'm sorry about tonight, Mama, but it's exactly why I'm doing it.

MAMA: If you've got the guts to kill yourself, Jessie, you've got the guts to stay alive.

JESSIE: I know that. So it's really just a matter of where I'd rather be.

MAMA: Look, maybe I can't think of what you should do, but that doesn't mean there isn't something that would help. *You* find it. *You* think of it. You can keep trying. You can get brave and try some more. You don't have to give up!

JESSIE: I'm *not* giving up! This *is* the other thing I'm trying. And I'm sure there are some other things that might work, but *might* work isn't good enough anymore. I need something that *will* work. *This* will work. That's why I picked it.

MAMA: But something might happen. Something that could change everything. Who knows what it might be, but it might be worth waiting for! (*Jessie doesn't respond.*) Try it for two more weeks. We could have more talks like tonight.

JESSIE: No, Mama.

MAMA: I'll pay more attention to you. Tell the truth when you ask me. Let you have your say.

JESSIE: No, Mama! We wouldn't have more talks like tonight, because it's this next part that's made this last part so good, Mama. No, Mama. *This* is how I have my say. This is how I say what I thought about it *all* and I say no. To Dawson and Loretta and the Red Chinese and epilepsy and Ricky and Cecil and you. And me. And hope. I say no! (*Then going to Mama on the sofa.*) Just let me go easy, Mama.

MAMA: How can I let you go?

JESSIE: You can because you have to. It's what you've always done.

MAMA: You are my child!

JESSIE: I am what became of your child. (*Mama cannot answer.*) I found an old baby picture of me. And it was somebody else, not me. It was somebody pink and fat who never heard of sick or lonely, somebody who cried and got fed, and reached up and got held and kicked but didn't hurt anybody, and slept whenever she wanted to, just by closing her eyes. Somebody who mainly just laid there and laughed at the colors waving around over her head and chewed on a polka-dot whale and woke up knowing some new trick nearly every day, and rolled over and drooled on the sheet and felt your hand pulling my quilt back up over me. That's who I started out and this is who is left. (*There is no self-pity here.*) That's what this is about. It's somebody I lost, all right, it's my own self. Who I never was. Or who I tried to be and never got there. Somebody I waited for who never came. And never will. So, see, it doesn't much matter what else happens in the world or in this house, even. I'm what was worth waiting for and I didn't make it. Me . . . who might have made a difference to me . . . I'm not going to show up, so there's no reason to stay, except to keep you company, and that's . . . not reason enough because I'm not . . . very good company. (*Pause.*) Am I.

MAMA (*knowing she must tell the truth*): No. And neither am I.

JESSIE: I had this strange little thought, well, maybe it's not so strange. Anyway after Christmas, after I decided to do this, I would wonder, sometimes, what might keep me here, what might be worth staying for, and you know what it was? It was maybe if there was something I really liked, like maybe if I really liked rice pudding or cornflakes for breakfast or something, that might be enough.

MAMA: Rice pudding is good.

JESSIE: Not to me.

MAMA: And you're not afraid?

JESSIE: Afraid of what?

MAMA: I'm afraid of it, for me, I mean. When my time comes. I know it's coming, but . . .

JESSIE: You don't know when. Like in a scary movie.

MAMA: Yeah, sneaking up on me like some killer on the loose, hiding out in the back yard just waiting for me to have my hands full someday and how am I supposed to protect myself anyhow when I don't know what it looks like and I don't know how he sounds coming up behind me like that or if it will hurt or take very long or what I don't get done before it happens.

JESSIE: You've got plenty of time left.

MAMA: I forget what for, right now.

JESSIE: For whatever happens, I don't know. For the rest of your life. For Agnes burning down one more house or Dawson losing his hair or . . .

MAMA (*quickly*): Jessie, I can't just sit here and say O.K., kill yourself if you want to.

JESSIE: Sure you can. You just did. Say it again.

MAMA (*really startled*): Jessie! (*Quiet horror.*) How dare you! (*Furious.*) How dare you! You think you can just leave whenever you want, like you're watching television here? No, you can't, Jessie. You make me feel like a fool for being alive, child, and you are so wrong! I like it here, and I will stay here until they make me go, until they drag me screaming and I mean screeching into my grave, and you're real smart to get away before then because, I mean, honey, you've never heard noise like that in your life. (*Jessie turns away.*) Who am I talking to? You're gone already, aren't you? I'm looking right through you! I can't stop you because you're already gone! I guess you think they'll all have to talk about you now! I guess you think this will really confuse them. Oh yes, ever since Christmas you've been laughing to yourself and thinking, "Boy, are they all in for a surprise." Well,

nobody's going to be a bit surprised, sweetheart. This is just like you. Do it the hard way, that's my girl, all right. (*Jessie gets up and goes into the kitchen, but Mama follows her.*) You know who they're going to feel sorry for? Me! How about that! Not you, me! They're going to be *ashamed* of you. Yes. *Ashamed!* If somebody asks Dawson about it, he'll change the subject as fast as he can. He'll talk about how much he has to pay to park his car these days.

JESSIE: Leave me alone.

MAMA: It's the truth!

JESSIE: I should've just left you a note!

MAMA (*screaming*): Yes! (*Then suddenly understanding what she has said, nearly paralyzed by the thought of it, she turns slowly to face Jessie, nearly whispering.*) No. No. I . . . might not have thought of all the things you've said.

JESSIE: It's O.K., Mama.

(*Mama is nearly unconscious from the emotional devastation of these last few moments. She sits down at the kitchen table, hurt and angry and desperately afraid. But she looks almost numb. She is so far beyond what is known as pain that she is virtually unreachable and Jessie knows this, and talks quietly, watching for signs of recovery.*)

JESSIE (*washes her hands in the sink*): I remember you liked that preacher who did Daddy's, so if you want to ask him to do the service, that's O.K. with me.

MAMA (*not an answer, just a word*): What.

JESSIE (*putting on hand lotion as she talks*): And pick some songs you like or let Agnes pick, she'll know exactly which ones. Oh, and I had your dress cleaned that you wore to Daddy's. You looked real good in that.

MAMA: I don't remember, hon.

JESSIE And it won't be so bad once your friends start coming to the funeral home. You'll probably see people you haven't seen for years, but I thought about what you should say to get you over that nervous part when they first come in.

MAMA (*simply repeating*): Come in.

JESSIE: Take them up to see their flowers, they'd like that. And when they say, "I'm so sorry, Thelma," you just say, "I appreciate your coming, Connie." And then ask how their garden was this summer or what they're doing for Thanksgiving or how their children . . .

MAMA: I don't think I should ask about their children. I'll talk about what they have on, that's always good. And I'll have some crochet work with me.

JESSIE: And Agnes will be there, so you might not have to talk at all.

MAMA: Maybe if Connie Richards does come, I can

get her to tell me where she gets that Irish yarn, she calls it. I know it doesn't come from Ireland. I think it just comes with a green wrapper.

JESSIE: And be sure to invite enough people home afterward so you get enough food to feed them all and have some left for you. But don't let anybody take anything home, especially Loretta.

MAMA: Loretta will get all the food set up, honey. It's only fair to let her have some macaroni or something.

JESSIE: No, Mama. You have to be more selfish from now on. (*Sitting at the table with Mama.*) Now, somebody's bound to ask you why I did it and you just say you don't know. That you loved me and you know I loved you and we just sat around tonight like every other night of our lives, and then I came over and kissed you and said, "'Night, Mother," and you heard me close my bedroom door and the next thing you heard was the shot. And whatever reasons I had, well, you guess I just took them with me.

MAMA (*quietly*): It was something personal.

JESSIE: Good. That's good, Mama.

MAMA: That's what I'll say, then.

JESSIE: Personal. Yeah.

MAMA: Is that what I tell Dawson and Loretta, too? We sat around, you kissed me, "'Night, Mother"? They'll want to know more, Jessie. They won't believe it.

JESSIE: Well, then, tell them what we did. I filled up the candy jars. I cleaned out the refrigerator. We made some hot chocolate and put the cover back on the sofa. You had no idea. All right? I really think it's better that way. If they know we talked about it, they really won't understand how you let me go.

MAMA: I guess not.

JESSIE: It's private. Tonight is private, yours and mine, and I don't want anybody else to have any of it.

MAMA: O.K., then.

JESSIE (*standing behind Mama now, holding her shoulders*): Now, when you hear the shot, I don't want you to come in. First of all, you won't be able to get in by yourself, but I don't want you trying. Call Dawson, then call the police, and then call Agnes. And then you'll need something to do till somebody gets here, so wash the hot-chocolate pan. You wash that pan till you hear the doorbell ring and I don't care if it's an hour, you keep washing that pan.

MAMA: I'll make my calls and then I'll just sit. I won't need something to do. What will the police say?

JESSIE: They'll do that gunpowder test, I guess, and ask you what happened, and by that time, the ambulance will be here and they'll come in and get me and you know how that goes. You stay out here with Dawson and Loretta. You keep Dawson out here. I want the police in the room first, not Dawson, O.K.?

MAMA: What if Dawson and Loretta want me to go home with them?

JESSIE (*returning to the living room*): That's up to you.

MAMA: I think I'll stay here. All they've got is Sanka.

JESSIE: Maybe Agnes could come stay with you for a few days.

MAMA (*standing up, looking into the living room*): I'd rather be by myself, I think. (*Walking toward the box Jessie brought in earlier.*) You want me to give people those things?

JESSIE (*they sit down on the sofa, Jessie holding the box on her lap*): I want Loretta to have my little calculator. Dawson bought it for himself, you know, but then he saw one he liked better and he couldn't bring both of them home with Loretta counting every penny the way she does, so he gave the first one to me. Be funny for her to have it now, don't you think? And all my house slippers are in a sack for her in my closet. Tell her I know they'll fit and I've never worn any of them, and make sure Dawson hears you tell her that. I'm glad he loves Loretta so much, but I wish he knew not everybody has her size feet.

MAMA (*taking the calculator*): O.K.

JESSIE (*reaching into the box again*): This letter is for Dawson, but it's mostly about you, so read it if you want. There's a list of presents for you for at least twenty more Christmases and birthdays, so if you want anything special you better add it to this list before you give it to him. Or if you want to be surprised, just don't read that page. This Christmas, you're getting mostly stuff for the house, like a new rug in your bathroom and needlework, but next Christmas, you're really going to cost him next Christmas. I think you'll like it a lot and you'd never think of it.

MAMA: And you think he'll go for it?

JESSIE: I think he'll feel like a real jerk if he doesn't. Me telling him to, like this and all. Now, this number's where you call Cecil. I called it last week and he answered, so I know he still lives there.

MAMA: What do you want me to tell him?

JESSIE: Tell him we talked about him and I only had good things to say about him, but mainly tell him to find Ricky and tell him what I did, and tell Ricky you have something for him, out here, from me, and to come get it. (*Pulls a sack out of the box.*)

MAMA (*the sack feels empty*): What is it?

JESSIE (*taking it off*): My watch. (*Putting it in the sack and taking a ribbon out of the sack to tie around the top of it.*)

MAMA: He'll sell it!

JESSIE: That's the idea. I appreciate him not stealing it already. I'd like to buy him a good meal.

MAMA: He'll buy dope with it!

JESSIE: Well, then, I hope he gets some good dope with it, Mama. And the rest of this is for you. (*Handing Mama the box now. Mama picks up the things and looks at them.*)

MAMA (*surprised and pleased*): When did you do all this? During my naps, I guess.

JESSIE: I guess. I tried to be quiet about it. (*As Mama is puzzled by the presents.*) Those are just little presents. For whenever you need one. They're not bought presents, just things I thought you might like to look at, pictures or things you think you've lost. Things you didn't know you had, even. You'll see.

MAMA: I'm not sure I want them. They'll make me think of you.

JESSIE: No they won't. They're just things, like a free tube of toothpaste I found hanging on the door one day.

MAMA: Oh. All right, then.

JESSIE: Well, maybe there's one nice present in there somewhere. It's Granny's ring she gave me and I thought you might like to have it, but I didn't think you'd wear it if I gave it to you right now.

MAMA (*taking the box to a table nearby*): No. Probably not. (*Turning back to face her.*) I'm ready for my manicure, I guess. Want me to wash my hands again?

JESSIE (*standing up*): It's time for me to go, Mama.

MAMA (*starting for her*): No, Jessie, you've got all night!

JESSIE (*as Mama grabs her*): No, Mama.

MAMA: It's not even ten o'clock.

JESSIE (*very calm*): Let me go, Mama.

MAMA: I can't. You can't go. You can't do this. You didn't say it would be so soon, Jessie. I'm scared. I love you.

JESSIE (*takes her hands away*): Let go of me, Mama. I've said everything I had to say.

MAMA (*standing still a minute*): You said you wanted to do my nails.

JESSIE (*taking a small step backward*): I can't. It's too late.

MAMA: It's not too late!

JESSIE: I don't want you to wake Dawson and Loretta when you call. I want them to still be up and dressed so they can get right over.

MAMA (*as Jessie backs up, Mama moves in on her, but carefully*): They wake up fast, Jessie, if they have to. They don't matter here, Jessie. You do. I do. We're not through yet. We've got a lot of things to take care of here. I don't know where my prescriptions are and you didn't tell me what to tell Dr. Davis when he calls or how much you want

me to tell Ricky or who I call to rake the leaves or . . .

JESSIE: Don't try and stop me, Mama, you can't do it.

MAMA (*grabbing her again, this time hard*): I can too! I'll stand in front of this hall and you can't get past me. (*They struggle.*) You'll have to knock me down to get away from me, Jessie. I'm not about to let you . . .

(*Mama struggles with Jessie at the door and in the struggle Jessie gets away from her and —)*

JESSIE (*almost a whisper*): 'Night, Mother. (*She vanishes into her bedroom and we hear the door lock just as Mama gets to it.*)

MAMA (*screams*): Jessie! (*Pounding on the door.*) Jessie, you let me in there. Don't you do this, Jessie. I'm not going to stop screaming until you open this door, Jessie. Jessie! Jessie! What if I don't do any of the things you told me to do! I'll tell Cecil what a miserable man he was to make you feel the way he did and I'll give Ricky's watch to Dawson if I feel like it and the only way you can make sure I do what you want is you come out here and make me, Jessie! (*Pounding again.*) Jessie! Stop this! I didn't know! I was here with you all the time. How could I know you were so alone?

(*And Mama stops for a moment, breathless and frantic, putting her ear to the door, and when she doesn't hear anything, she stands up straight again and screams once more.*)

Jessie! Please!

(*And we hear the shot, and it sounds like an answer, it sounds like No.*)

(*Mama collapses against the door, tears streaming down her face, but not screaming anymore. In shock now.*)

Jessie, Jessie, child . . . Forgive me. (*Pause.*) I thought you were mine.

(*And she leaves the door and makes her way through the living room, around the furniture, as though she didn't know where it was, not knowing what to do. Finally, she goes to the stove in the kitchen and picks up the hot-chocolate pan and carries it with her to the telephone and holds on to it while she dials the number. She looks down at the pan, holding it tight like her life depended on it. She hears Loretta answer.*)

MAMA: Loretta, let me talk to Dawson, honey.

COMMENTARY

David Savran (*b. 1950*)
INTERVIEW WITH MARSHA NORMAN   1988

As Marsha Norman said during an interview, her dissatisfaction with other plays about suicide led her to be very direct in her own play and to confront the issue directly. Here she discusses how that decision changed her entire concept of the play and helped her shape the dramatic action.

Savran: How do you begin a play? With an outline, a character, a line of dialogue?

Norman: . . . With '*night, Mother* I knew I wanted to tell the story of this woman who kills herself, but I didn't have any idea how. At the time, in '81, there were a number of other plays on the subject. But I kept saying that these plays — particularly *Whose Life Is It Anyway?* — are tantrums. I wanted to put somebody in the room with this woman, somebody who cares deeply, wildly, madly, who will fight this person to the death to save her own life. This is a gladiator contest where the point is to keep the other person alive. And once I had that, I had all these parallels — gladiators and world heavyweight boxing championships — and I understood immediately how this has to work. You have to have a closed ring, nobody can get out or in, you can have only two people.

I knew going into '*night, Mother* that it was going to be the most treacherous act of my writing life. So I went to the world of music. I was in a mad Glenn Gould state at the time — I've spent my life at the piano. Okay, I thought, what if I do a little sonata form, a three-act play with no intermission? You can actually feel the moment when the orchestra stops and the conductor raises his hands and Jessie says, "You talked to Agnes today," and the second movement starts. The second movement ends when Jessie goes in to get the box of presents, Mama just having said, "Don't leave me, Jessie." The actors would come on stage knowing, "We don't have to go all the way to the end. We just have to get to the Agnes section." And then you start in on Agnes and think, "Great, I'll just get to 'Don't leave me, Jessie,' then I can take a breath" — this is from Mama's point of view — "and get down and wash the floor." And then all they have to do is go to the end. '*night, Mother* would be undoable if it weren't for that. People would fall out of it all the time. But they don't. So I think that if you don't have structure, you might as well not have anything to put in it. If you don't have the bookshelves, you don't have the books.

I have a great trick during that period of thinking about the play. I say, "I'm not writing until I absolutely have to, till I can no longer contain it." I build up the piece in a pressure cooker, as it were. All that time I'm writing myself notes in the form of questions. What did Daddy do? How long ago did he die? Where did he die? What did he ever do for Jessie? Those kinds of questions. Curiously enough, you'll find that just from asking the questions, you'll get all the answers during the next weeks. It's internal research into the lives of these people. From those questions will come lines of dialogue — you begin to hear the voicing, what they can talk about, what they think is funny. The first line of dialogue I wrote for *'night, Mother* was Jessie's line "We got any old towels?" As soon as I wrote it down, I understood that it was a ritual piece, that Jessie was coming in to celebrate this requiem mass, that she has these stacks of towels: here are the witnesses, the household objects. She comes in as though she is the altar boy.

I wait until I cannot avoid it anymore and by that time, I already know what the beginning is, because of all this scribbling down. Then it's really very easy. I keep two kinds of notebooks, one that has structure and information in it and the other that has my own thoughts — "Can we really have this? What about that? What would happen if this?" I have a wonderful piece of paper upstairs that says, "Have I written something that anybody will want to see? Have I written something that will last? Have I written something that will humiliate me?" This comes from a pretty grim moment in the writing of *'night, Mother.* I thought, "What is this that I've written?" Humiliation is easily a possibility.

Savran: What is the European reaction to *'night, Mother*?

Norman: *'night, Mother* is done all over the world. Any list that New Guinea is on is a long list. It's still running in Spain, four and a half years later, with all of the jokes taken out. Curiously enough, my work has always been popular in Eastern Europe. But this time I've caught the Mediterranean crowd. What strikes you as you watch it in a foreign country, in another language, is that the play seems to contain this other culture. In Italy you get enormous "Mama mia" Mamas, and the Jessies are always Ariels, little sprites. In Scandinavian countries it's quite the opposite. The mothers are really small, like the old woman who lived in the shoe, and the daughters are Valkyries, towering over these little Mamas. In the Latin American countries Mama and Jessie look like sisters.

María Irene Fornés

Born in Havana, Cuba, in 1930, Fornés was fifteen when she arrived in the United States. Originally a painter and a designer of textiles, it was not until she lived with the critic Susan Sontag that Fornés was encouraged to begin writing and became a playwright. Fornés has won six Obies for her plays in off-Broadway theaters. Despite her fame and status as a cult figure among women's groups, she has yet to achieve a major position in contemporary theater comparable to, say, August Wilson, because most of her work remains experimental and outside the mainstream of popular theater.

Fornés's first success was *Promenade* (1965), a musical that garnered her the first of her Obie awards. The play was described by reviewer Phyllis Mael as a zany satire focusing on "unrequited love, the abuse of power, the injustice of those who are supposed to uphold the law, and the illogical and random nature of life." The play, like many of Fornés's pieces, lacks a standard plot, and therefore has been criticized for having a "thin" story line. But *New York Times* critic Clive Barnes felt there would be many in the audience who would "glory in the show's dexterity, wit and compassion."

Fefu and Her Friends (1977) followed as the first work to find a major audience. Between these two plays, Fornés worked steadily producing plays in the Judson Poets' Theatre, at La Mama Experimental Theater in New York, and in theaters in London, Havana, and San Francisco. *Fefu* is a feminist play that has no definite plot line, but does have a mordant humor and a relentless pace. It is structured in short, intense scenes, moving from indoor to outdoor locations, with a second act that takes place in three different places simultaneously. In one production the audience needed to move physically to each of these locations. The effect is unsettling on the one hand, but expansive on the other. The play's focus is on the uneven treatment of women in a society dominated by men. The play has a cartoonlike quality but also a seriousness that may make some in the audience uncomfortable.

Mud (1983), produced in the Padua Hills Festival in Claremont, California, focuses on a domestic triangle with an abused woman. It is a dark, unsettling play, with a violent ending involving a gun. Fornés makes use of guns in many of her plays, including *Fefu*; some critics see the gun as an important emblem in her work. Among her later plays are *The Trial of Joan of Arc on a Matter of Faith* (1986), *The Mothers* (1986), *Abingdon Square* (1987), and *And What of the Night?* (1990).

THE CONDUCT OF LIFE

The Conduct of Life (1985), called Fornés's "most terrifying play," was developed in a workshop setting in Padua Hills. It was sketched out first at the California Institute of the Arts in an outdoor production that was rambling, intensely visual, and spatially immense. Later, when Fornés brought the play inside, the staging was altered profoundly and much of the dialogue revised.

Fornés said the play came out of an exercise she used in the classroom. "What came was mostly an image. I saw a girl — a mulatto girl — wearing a little pink slip and a soldier who was wearing an undershirt, military breeches and boots." Her vision of these two figures was in a hotel room after the girl's boyfriend had been arrested. The girl had seduced the soldier in order to help free her boyfriend. The intensity of the image helped Fornés develop it into a play.

The Conduct of Life deals with torture and interrogation, which obviously corrupts the spirit of those who inflict it. Orlando's drive for power and his commitment to the "ideal" of maximum power is stated baldly at the beginning of the play. He claims that his sexuality must be repressed if he is to achieve his goals. Leticia's relationship to her husband Orlando is somewhat shaky as the play opens. Orlando warns her that she is not in his will; he informs the audience that when he retires from the military he may marry again for power and shove Leticia aside. Meanwhile, her concerns for life and for innocence are revealed in her dislike of hunting and in her willingness to place herself between the hunter and the deer.

Nena, a prisoner in the basement of their house, is an embodiment of that hypothetical deer — a mere child. When Orlando visits her, he rapes her viciously; but sex is only one expression of his twisted nature: He is a sadist. Leticia tries not to face the reality of Nena's situation, but eventually the truth comes out.

The pacing and structure of the play are wrenching. At first the conversation seems to center on conventional issues, ordinary moments of life. The servant Olimpia and Nena are innocent in their way, living simple lives. Nena has come from the streets, where her grandfather still lives. She is powerless. Leticia seems in some ways unfocused, unsure of herself and her situation. As the play progresses, things begin to seem out of joint. The continuity of scenes is purposefully uncertain, their disjunction suggesting a parallel mental disjunction. Orlando acts as if he is paranoid, defending himself against charges that he behaved too cruelly in the death of a man he interrogated. These charges resulted in his loss of a promotion.

Orlando's behavior toward women becomes increasingly cruel, vicious, and violent. His opening attitude toward Leticia is bad enough, telling the audience how he will push her aside, but his sexual assault of Nena is sadistically brutal. Orlando becomes more and more depraved by his work, and the work becomes more and more frightening. Bodies are left in the streets torn, bleeding, disfigured so as to frighten the people. The "ideals" that Orlando speaks about in the opening scene are realized in a most horrifying fashion.

The Conduct of Life in Performance

The Conduct of Life was originally developed in workshop form in California. The California production was expansive — very different from the printed version. The play was then moved to New York's Theater for a New City in February of 1985; this production was directed by the playwright. The set utilized two levels, and the transition from scene to scene was accomplished by lighting that faded slowly like "punctuation marks." The reviews expressed some uncertainties about the nature of the play and its form, although the central issues of torture and violence in Latin America came through clearly.

The Conduct of Life, directed by Francesca Joseph, was produced in London at the Gate Theatre in 1988. The London reviews recognized the seriousness of the play's subject and the intensity and importance of the play as a work of art. Sabine Durrant in the *Independent* called it "a brave and powerful show," but Helen Rose in *Time Out* complained of missing plot links, as if she expected the play to be conventionally structured. Nicholas de Jongh in the *Guardian* said, "We are left, after watching Richard Lintern's chilling performance as Orlando and Annabelle Lanyon's pitiful, quaking, assaulted young girl, to try to relate the political and the personal world."

María Irene Fornés (b. 1930)
THE CONDUCT OF LIFE

1985

Characters

ORLANDO, *an army lieutenant at the start of the play.*
  A lieutenant commander soon after.
LETICIA, *his wife, ten years his elder.*
ALEJO, *a lieutenant commander. Their friend.*
NENA, *a destitute girl of twelve.*
OLIMPIA, *a middle-aged, somewhat retarded servant.*

Time and Place: *The present. A Latin American country.*

To Julian Beck°
in Memory of his courageous life
(1925–1985)

(The floor is divided in four horizontal planes. Downstage is the living room, which is about ten feet deep.

Julian Beck: With Julian Malina, Beck developed The Living Theatre, an influential experimental group flourishing off Broadway in the 1960s and 1970s.

Center stage, eighteen inches high, is the dining room, which is about ten feet deep. Further upstage, eighteen inches high, is a hallway which is about four feet deep. At each end of the hallway there is a door. The one to the right leads to the servants' quarters, the one to the left to the cellar. Upstage, three feet lower than the hallway (the same level as the living room), is the cellar, which is twenty feet wide and sixteen feet deep. Most of the cellar is occupied by two platforms, which are eight feet wide, eight feet deep, and three feet high. There is a space four feet wide around each platform. Upstage of the cellar are steps leading upstairs. Approximately ten feet above the cellar is another level, extending from the extreme left to the extreme right, which represents a warehouse. There is a door on the left of the warehouse. On the left and the right of the living room there are archways that lead to hallways or antechambers. The floors of these hallways are the same level as the dining room. On the left and the right of the dining room there is a second set of archways that lead to hallways or antechambers, the floors of which are the same level as the hallways. All along the edge of each level there is a step that leads to the next level. All floors and steps are black marble. In the living room there are two chairs. One is to the left, next to a table with a telephone on it. The other is to the right. In the dining room there are a large green marble table and three chairs. On the right cellar platform there is a mattress, on the left cellar platform there is a chair. In the warehouse there is a table and a chair to the left, and a chair and some crates and boxes to the right.)

SCENE 1

(Before the lights come up one hears Orlando doing jumping-jacks. He is in the upper left corner of the dining room. A light slowly comes up on him. He wears military breeches held by suspenders, and riding boots. He continues doing jumping-jacks as long as the actor can endure it. When he stops, the lights come up on the center area. There is a chair upstage of the table. There is a linen towel on the left side of the table. Orlando dries his face with the towel and sits as he puts the towel around his neck.)

ORLANDO: Thirty-three and I'm still a lieutenant. In two years I'll receive a promotion or I'll leave the military. I promise I will not spend time feeling sorry for myself. — Instead I will study the situation and draw an effective plan of action. I must eliminate all obstacles. — I will make the acquaintance of people in high power. If I cannot achieve this on my own merit, I will marry a woman in

high circles. Leticia must not be an obstacle. — Man must have an ideal, mine is to achieve maximum power. That is my destiny. — No other interest will deter me from this. — My sexual drive is detrimental to my ideals. I must no longer be overwhelmed by sexual passion or I will be degraded beyond hope of recovery.

(Lights fade to black.)

SCENE 2

(Alejo sits to the right of the dining-room table. Orlando stands to Alejo's left. He is now a lieutenant commander. He wears an army tunic, breeches, and boots. Leticia stands to the left. She wears a dress that suggests 1940s fashion.)

LETICIA: What! Me go hunting? Do you think I'm going to shoot a deer, the most beautiful animal in the world? Do you think I'm going to destroy a deer? On the contrary, I would run in the field and scream and wave my arms like a mad woman and try to scare them away so the hunters could not reach them. I'd run in front of the bullets and let the mad hunters kill me — stand in the way of the bullets — stop the bullets with my body. I don't see how anyone can shoot a deer.

ORLANDO *(to Alejo)*: Do you understand that? You, who are her friend, can you understand that? You don't think that is madness? She's mad. Tell her that — she'll think it's you who's mad. *(To Leticia.)* Hunting is a sport! A skill! Don't talk about something you know nothing about. Must you have an opinion about every damn thing! Can't you keep your mouth shut when you don't know what you're talking about? *(He exits right.)*

LETICIA: He told me that he didn't love me, and that his sole relationship to me was simply a marital one. What he means is that I am to keep this house, and he is to provide for it. That's what he said. That explains why he treats me the way he treats me. I never understood why he did, but now it's clear. He doesn't love me. I thought he loved me and that he stayed with me because he loved me and that's why I didn't understand his behavior. But now I know, because he told me that he sees me as a person who runs the house. I never understood that because I would have never — if he had said, "Would you marry me to run my house even if I don't love you." I would have never — I would have never believed what I was hearing. I would have never believed that these words were coming out of his mouth. Because I loved him.

(*Orlando has reentered. Leticia sees him and exits left. Orlando sits center.*)

ORLANDO: I didn't say any of that. I told her that she's not my heir. That's what I said. I told her that she's not in my will, and she will not receive a penny of my money if I die. That's what I said. I didn't say anything about running the house. I said she will not inherit a penny from me because I would be humiliated by how she'd put it to use. She is capable of foolishness beyond belief. Ask her what she would do if she were rich and could do anything she wants with her money.

(*Leticia reenters.*)

LETICIA: I would distribute it among the poor.
ORLANDO: She has no respect for money.
LETICIA: That is not true. If I had money I would give it to those who need it. I know what money is, what money can do. It can feed people, it can put a roof over their heads. Money can do that. It can clothe them. What do you know about money? What does it mean to you? What do you do with money? Buy rifles? To shoot deer?
ORLANDO: You're foolish! — You're foolish! You're a foolish woman! (*He exits. His voice becomes faint as he walks into the distance.*) Foolish! Foolish! Foolish!
LETICIA: He has no respect for me. He is insensitive. He doesn't listen. You cannot reach him. He is deaf. He is an animal. Nothing touches him except sensuality. He responds to food, to the flesh. To music sometimes, if it is romantic. To the moon. He is romantic but he is not aware of what you are feeling. I can't change him. — I'll tell you why I asked you to come. Because I want something from you. — I want you to educate me. I want to study. I want to study so I am not an ignorant person. I want to go to the university. I want to be knowledgeable. I'm tired of being ignored. I want to study political science. Is political science what diplomats study? Is that what it is? You have to teach me elemental things because I never finished grammar school. I would have to study a great deal. A great deal so I could enter the university. I would have to go through all the subjects. I would like to be a woman who speaks in a group and have others listen.
ALEJO: Why do you want to worry about any of that? What's the use? Do you think you can change anything? Do you think anyone can change anything?
LETICIA: Why not? (*Pause.*) Do you think I'm crazy? — He can't help it. — Do you think I'm crazy? — Because I love him?

(*He looks away. Lights fade to black.*)

SCENE 3

(*Orlando enters the warehouse holding Nena close to him. She wears a gray overlarge uniform. She is barefoot. She resists him. She is tearful and frightened. She pulls away and runs to the right wall. He follows her.*)

ORLANDO (*softly*): You called me a snake.
NENA: No, I didn't.

(*He tries to reach her. She pushes his hands away from her.*)

I was kidding. — I swear I was kidding.

(*He grabs her and pushes her against the wall. He pushes his pelvis against her. He moves to the chair dragging her with him. She gets away from him and crawls to the left. He goes after her. She goes behind the table. He goes after her. She goes under the table. He grabs her foot and pulls her out toward the downstage side. He opens his fly and pushes his pelvis against her. She screams. Lights fade to black.*)

SCENE 4

(*Olimpia is wiping crumbs off the dining-room table. She wears a plain gray uniform. Leticia sits to the left of the table facing front. She wears a dressing gown. She writes in a notebook. There is some silverware on the table. Olimpia has a speech defect.*)

LETICIA: Let's do this.
OLIMPIA: Okay. (*She continues wiping the table*)
LETICIA (*still writing*): What are you doing?
OLIMPIA: I'm doing what I always do.
LETICIA: Let's do this.
OLIMPIA (*in a mumble*): As soon as I finish doing this. You can't just ask me to do what you want me to do, and interrupt what I'm doing. I don't stop from the time I wake up in the morning to the time I go to sleep. You can't interrupt me whenever you want, not if you want me to get to the end of my work. I wake up at 5:30. I wash. I put on my clothes and make my bed. I go to the kitchen. I get the milk and the bread from outside and I put them on the counter. I open the icebox. I put one bottle in and take the butter out. I leave the other bottle on the counter. I shut the refrigerator door. I take the pan that I use for water and put water in it. I know how much. I put the pan on the stove, light the stove, cover it. I take the top off the milk and pour it in the milk pan except for a little. (*Indicating with her finger.*) Like this. For the cat. I put the pan on the stove, light the stove. I put coffee in the thing. I know how much.

I light the oven and put bread in it. I come here, get the tablecloth and I lay it on the table. I shout "Breakfast." I get the napkins. I take the cups, the saucers, and the silver out and set the table. I go to the kitchen. I put the tray on the counter, put the butter on the tray. The water and the milk are getting hot. I pick up the cat's dish. I wash it. I pour the milk I left in the bottle in the milk dish. I put it on the floor for the cat. I shout "Breakfast." The water boils. I pour it in the thing. When the milk boils I turn off the gas and cover the milk. I get the bread from the oven. I slice it down the middle and butter it. Then I cut it in pieces (*indicating*) this big. I set a piece aside for me. I put the rest of the bread in the bread dish and shout "Breakfast." I pour the coffee in the coffee pot and the milk in the milk pitcher, except I leave (*indicating*) this much for me. I put them on the tray and bring them here. If you're not in the dining room I call again. "Breakfast." I go to the kitchen, I fill the milk pan with water and let it soak. I pour my coffee, sit at the counter and eat my breakfast. I go upstairs to make your bed and clean your bathroom. I come down here to meet you and figure out what you want for lunch and dinner. And try to get you to think quickly so I can run to the market and get it bought before all the fresh stuff is bought up. Then, I start the day.

LETICIA: So?

OLIMPIA: So I need a steam pot.

LETICIA: What is a steam pot?

OLIMPIA: A pressure cooker.

LETICIA: And you want a steam pot? Don't you have enough pots?

OLIMPIA: No.

LETICIA: Why do you want a steam pot?

OLIMPIA: It cooks faster.

LETICIA: How much is it?

OLIMPIA: Expensive.

LETICIA: How much?

OLIMPIA: Twenty.

LETICIA: Too expensive.

(*Olimpia throws the silver on the floor. Leticia turns her eyes up to the ceiling.*)

Why do you want one more pot?

OLIMPIA: I don't have a steam pot.

LETICIA: A pressure cooker.

OLIMPIA: A pressure cooker.

LETICIA: You have too many pots.

(*Olimpia goes to the kitchen and returns with an aluminum pan. She shows it to Leticia.*)

OLIMPIA: Look at this.

(*Leticia looks at it.*)

LETICIA: What?

(*Olimpia hits the pan against the back of a chair, breaking off a piece of it.*)

OLIMPIA: It's no good.

LETICIA: All right! (*She takes money from her pocket and gives it to Olimpia.*) Here. Buy it! — What are we having for lunch?

OLIMPIA: Fish.

LETICIA: I don't like fish. — What else?

OLIMPIA: Boiled plantains.

LETICIA: Make something I like.

OLIMPIA: Avocados.

(*Leticia looks at Olimpia with resentment.*)

LETICIA: Why can't you make something I like?

OLIMPIA: Avocados.

LETICIA: Something that needs cooking.

OLIMPIA: Bread pudding.

LETICIA: And for dinner?

OLIMPIA: Pot roast.

LETICIA: What else?

OLIMPIA: Rice.

LETICIA: What else?

OLIMPIA: Salad.

LETICIA: What kind?

OLIMPIA: Avocado.

LETICIA: Again.

(*Olimpia looks at Leticia.*)

OLIMPIA: You like avocados.

LETICIA: Not again. — Tomatoes. (*Olimpia mumbles.*) What's wrong with tomatoes besides that you don't like them? (*Olimpia mumbles.*) Get some. (*Olimpia mumbles.*) What does that mean? (*Olimpia doesn't answer.*) Buy tomatoes. — What else?

OLIMPIA: That's all.

LETICIA: We need a green.

OLIMPIA: Watercress.

LETICIA: What else.

OLIMPIA: Nothing.

LETICIA: For dessert.

OLIMPIA: Bread pudding.

LETICIA: Again.

OLIMPIA: Why not?

LETICIA: Make a flan.

OLIMPIA: No flan.

LETICIA: Why not?

OLIMPIA: No good.

LETICIA: Why no good? — Buy some fruit then.

OLIMPIA: What kind?

LETICIA: Pineapple. (*Olimpia shakes her head.*) Why not? (*Olimpia shakes her head.*) Mango.

OLIMPIA: No mango.

LETICIA: Buy some fruit! That's all. Don't forget bread.

(*Leticia hands Olimpia money. Olimpia holds her hand out for more. Leticia hands her one more bill. Lights fade to black.*)

SCENE 5

(*The warehouse table is propped against the door. The chair on the left faces right. The door is pushed and the table falls to the floor. Orlando enters. He wears an undershirt with short sleeves, breeches with suspenders and boots. He looks around the room for Nena. Believing she has escaped, he becomes still and downcast. He turns to the door and stands there for a moment. He takes a few steps to the right and stands there for a moment staring fixedly. He hears a sound from behind the boxes, walks to them and takes a box off. Nena is there. Her head is covered with a blanket. He pulls the blanket off. Nena is motionless and staring into space. He looks at her for a while, then walks to the chair and sits facing right staring into space. A few moments pass. Lights fade to black.*)

SCENE 6

(*Leticia speaks on the telephone to Mona.*)

LETICIA: Since they moved him to the new department he's different. (*Brief pause.*) He's distracted. I don't know where he goes in his mind. He doesn't listen to me. He worries. When I talk to him he doesn't listen. He's thinking about the job. He says he worries. What is there to worry about? Do you think there is anything to worry about? (*Brief pause.*) What meeting? (*Brief pause.*) Oh, sure. When is it? (*Brief pause.*) At what time? What do you mean I knew? No one told me. — I don't remember. Would you pick me up? (*Brief pause.*) At 1:00? Isn't 1:00 early? (*Brief pause.*) Orlando may still be home at 1:00. Sometimes he's here a little longer than usual. After lunch he sits and smokes. Don't you think 1:30 will give us enough time? (*Brief pause.*) No. I can't leave while he's smoking . . . I'd rather not. I'd rather wait till he leaves. (*Brief pause.*) 1:30, then. Thank you, Mona. (*Brief pause.*) See you then. Bye.

(*Leticia puts down the receiver and walks to the stage right area. Orlando's voice is heard offstage left. He and Alejo enter halfway through the following speech.*)

ORLANDO: He made loud sounds, not high-pitched like a horse. He sounded like a whale, like a wounded whale. He was pouring liquid from everywhere, his mouth, his nose, his eyes. He was

not a horse but a sexual organ. — Helpless. A viscera. — Screaming. Making strange sounds. He collapsed on top of her. She wanted him off but he collapsed on top of her and stayed there on top of her. Like gum. He looked more like a whale than a horse. A seal. His muscles were soft. What does it feel like to be without shape like that. Without pride. She was indifferent. He stayed there for a while and then lifted himself off her and to the ground. (*Pause.*) He looked like a horse again.

LETICIA: Alejo, how are you?

(*Alejo kisses Leticia's hand.*)

ORLANDO (*as he walks to the living room*): Alejo is staying for dinner. (*He sits left facing front.*)
LETICIA: Would you like some coffee?
ALEJO: Yes, thank you.
LETICIA: Would you like some coffee, Orlando?
ORLANDO: Yes, thank you.
LETICIA (*in a loud voice towards the kitchen*): Olimpia . . .
OLIMPIA: What?
LETICIA: Coffee . . .

(*Leticia sits to the right of the table. Alejo sits center.*)

ALEJO: Have you heard?
LETICIA: Yes, he's dead and I'm glad he's dead. An evil man. I knew he'd be killed. Who killed him?
ALEJO: Someone who knew him.
LETICIA: What is there to gain? So he's murdered. Someone else will do the job. Nothing will change. To destroy them all is to say we destroy us all.
ALEJO: Do you think we're all rotten?
LETICIA: Yes.
ORLANDO: A bad germ?
LETICIA: Yes.
ORLANDO: In our hearts?
LETICIA: Yes. — In our eyes.
ORLANDO: You're silly.
LETICIA: We're blind. We can't see beyond an arm's reach. We don't believe our life will last beyond the day. We only know what we have in our hand to put in our mouth, to put in our stomach, and to put in our pocket. We take care of our pocket, but not of our country. We take care of our stomachs but not of our hungry. We are primitive. We don't believe in the future. Each night when the sun goes down we think that's the end of life — so we have one last fling. We don't think we have a future. We don't think we have a country. Ask anybody, "Do you have a country?" They'll say, "Yes." Ask them, "What is your country?" They'll say, "My bed, my dinner plate." But, things can change. They can. I have changed. You have changed. He has changed.
ALEJO: Look at me. I used to be an idealist. Now I

don't have any feeling for anything. I used to be strong, healthy, I looked at the future with hope.

LETICIA: Now you don't?

ALEJO: Now I don't. I know what viciousness is.

ORLANDO: What is viciousness?

ALEJO: You.

ORLANDO: Me?

ALEJO: The way you tortured Felo.

ORLANDO: I never tortured Felo.

ALEJO: You did.

ORLANDO: Boys play that way. You did too.

ALEJO: I didn't.

ORLANDO: He was repulsive to us.

ALEJO: I never hurt him.

ORLANDO: Well, you never stopped me.

ALEJO: I didn't know how to stop you. I didn't know anyone could behave the way you did. It frightened me. It changed me. I became hopeless.

(*Orlando walks to the dining room.*)

ORLANDO: You were always hopeless.

(*Orlando exits. Olimpia enters carrying three demitasse coffees on a tray. She places them on the table and exits.*)

ALEJO: I am sexually impotent. I have no feelings. Things pass through me which resemble feelings but I know they are not. I'm impotent.

LETICIA: Nonsense.

ALEJO: It's not nonsense. How can you say it's nonsense? — How can one live in a world that festers the way ours does and take any pleasure in life?

(*Lights fade to black.*)

SCENE 7

(*Nena and Orlando stand against the wall in the warehouse. She is fully dressed. He is barechested. He pushes his pelvis against her gently. His lips touch her face as he speaks. The words are inaudible to the audience. On the table there is a tin plate with food and a tin cup with milk.*)

ORLANDO: Look this way. I'm going to do something to you.

(*She makes a move away from him.*)

Don't do that. Don't move away. (*As he slides his hand along her side.*) I just want to put my hand here like this. (*He puts his lips on hers softly and speaks at the same time.*) Don't hold your lips so tight. Make them soft. Let them loose. So I can do this. (*She whimpers.*) Don't cry. I won't hurt you.

This is all I'm going to do to you. Just hold your lips soft. Be nice. Be a nice girl. (*He pushes against her and reaches an orgasm. He remains motionless for a moment; then steps away from her still leaning his hand on the wall.*) Go eat. I brought you food.

(*She goes to the table. He sits on the floor and watches her eat. She eats voraciously. She looks at the milk.*)

Drink it. It's milk. It's good for you.

(*She drinks the milk, then continues eating. Lights fade to black.*)

SCENE 8

(*Leticia stands left of the dining-room table. She speaks words she has memorized. Olimpia sits to the left of the table. She holds a book close to her eyes. Her head moves from left to right along the written words as she mumbles the sound of imaginary words. She continues doing this through the rest of the scene.*)

LETICIA: The impact of war is felt particularly in the economic realm. The destruction of property, private as well as public, may paralyze the country. Foreign investment is virtually . . . (*To Olimpia.*) Is that right? (*Pause.*) Is that right!

OLIMPIA: Wait a moment. (*She continues mumbling and moving her head.*)

LETICIA: What for? (*Pause.*) You can't read. (*Pause.*) You can't read!

OLIMPIA: Wait a moment. (*She continues mumbling and moving her head.*)

LETICIA (*slapping the book out of Olimpia's hand*): Why are you pretending you can read?

(*Olimpia slaps Leticia's hands. They slap each other's hands. Lights fade to black.*)

SCENE 9

(*Orlando sits in the living room. He smokes. He faces front and is thoughtful. Leticia and Olimpia are in the dining room. Leticia wears a hat and jacket. She tries to put a leather strap through the loops of a suitcase. There is a smaller piece of luggage on the floor.*)

LETICIA: This strap is too wide. It doesn't fit through the loop. (*Orlando doesn't reply.*) Is this the right strap? Is this the strap that came with this suitcase? Did the strap that came with the suitcase break? If so, where is it? And when did it break? Why doesn't this strap fit the suitcase and how did it get here? Did you buy this strap, Orlando?

ORLANDO: I may have.

LETICIA: It doesn't fit.

ORLANDO: Hm.

LETICIA: It doesn't fit through the loops.

ORLANDO: Just strap it outside the loops.

(*Leticia stands. Olimpia tries to put the strap through the loop.*)

LETICIA: No. You're supposed to put it through the loops. That's what the loops are for. What happened to the other strap?

ORLANDO: It broke.

LETICIA: How?

ORLANDO: I used it for something.

LETICIA: What! (*He looks at her.*) You should have gotten me one that fit. What did you use it for? — Look at that.

ORLANDO: Strap it outside the loops.

LETICIA: That wouldn't look right.

ORLANDO (*going to look at the suitcase*): Why do you need the straps?

LETICIA: Because they come with it.

ORLANDO: You don't need them.

LETICIA: And travel like this?

ORLANDO: Use another suitcase.

LETICIA: What other suitcase. I don't have another.

(*Orlando looks at his watch.*)

ORLANDO: You're going to miss your plane.

LETICIA: I'm not going. I'm not traveling like this.

ORLANDO: Go without it. I'll send it to you.

LETICIA: You'll get new luggage, repack it and send it to me? — All right. (*She starts to exit left.*) It's nice to travel light. (*Offstage.*) Do I have everything? — Come, Olimpia.

(*Olimpia follows with the suitcases. Orlando takes the larger suitcase from Olimpia. She exits. Orlando puts the suitcase down on the floor. He goes up the hallway and exits through the left door. A moment later he enters holding Nena close to him. She is pale, disheveled and has black circles around her eyes. She has a high fever and is almost unconscious. Her dress is torn and soiled. She is barefoot. He carries a new cotton dress on his arm. He takes her to the chair in the living room. He takes off the soiled dress and puts the new dress on her over a soiled slip.*)

ORLANDO: That's nice. You look nice.

(*Leticia's voice is heard. He hurriedly takes Nena out the door, closes it, and leans on it.*)

LETICIA (*offstage*): It would take but a second. You run to the garage and get the little suitcase and I'll take out the things I need.

(*Leticia and Olimpia reenter left. Olimpia exits right.*)

Hurry. Hurry. It would take but a second. (*Seeing Orlando.*) Orlando, I came back because I couldn't leave without anything at all. I came to get a few things because I have a smaller suitcase where I can take a few things.

(*Leticia puts the suitcase she left behind on the table and opens it. Olimpia reenters right with a small suitcase.*)

OLIMPIA: Here.

LETICIA (*taking out the things she mentions*): A pair of shoes. A nightgown. A robe. Underwear. A dress. A sweater.

OLIMPIA (*overlapping Leticia's lines, packing the things she mentions in the small suitcase*): A robe. A dress. A nightgown. Underwear. A sweater. A pair of shoes.

(*Leticia closes the large suitcase. Olimpia closes the small suitcase.*)

LETICIA (*starting to exit*): Good-bye.

OLIMPIA (*following Leticia*): Good-bye.

ORLANDO: Good-bye.

(*Lights fade to black.*)

SCENE 10

(*In the cellar, Nena is curled up on the mattress. Orlando sits on the mattress using Nena as a back support. Alejo sits on the chair. He holds a green paper in his hand. Olimpia sweeps the floor.*)

ORLANDO: Tell them to check him. See if there's a scratch on him. There's not a scratch on that body. Why the fuss! Who was he and who's making a fuss? Why is he so important?

ALEJO: He was in deep. He knew names.

ORLANDO: I was never told that. But it wouldn't have mattered if they had because he died before I touched him.

ALEJO: You have to go to headquarters. They want you there.

ORLANDO: He came in screaming and he wouldn't stop. I had to wait for him to stop screaming before I could even pose a question to him. He wouldn't stop. I had put the poker to his neck to see if he would stop. Just to see if he would shut up. He just opened his eyes wide and started shaking and screamed even louder and fell over dead. Maybe he took something. I didn't do anything to him. If I didn't get anything from him it's because he died before I could get to him. He died of fear, not from anything I did to him. Tell them to do an autopsy. I'm telling you the truth. That's the truth. Why the fuss.

ALEJO (*starting to put the paper in his pocket*): I'll tell them what you said.

ORLANDO: Let me see that.

(*Alejo takes it to him. Orlando looks at it and puts it back in Alejo's hands.*)

Okay so it's a trap. So what side are you on? (*Pause. Alejo says nothing.*) So what do they want? (*Pause.*) Who's going to question me? That's funny. That's very funny. They want to question me. They want to punch my eyes out? I knew something was wrong because they were getting nervous. Antonio was getting nervous. I went to him and I asked him if something was wrong. He said, no, nothing was wrong. But I could tell something was wrong. He looked at Velez and Velez looked back at him. They are stupid. They want to conceal something from me and they look at each other right in front of me, as if I'm blind, as if I can't tell that they are worried about something. As if there's something happening right in front of my nose but I'm blind and I can't see it. (*He grabs the paper from Alejo's hand.*) You understand? (*He goes up the steps.*)

OLIMPIA: Like an alligator, big mouth and no brains. Lots of teeth but no brains. All tongue.

(*Orlando enters through the left hallway door, and sits at the dining-room table. Alejo enters a few moments later. He stands to the right.*)

ORLANDO: What kind of way is this to treat me? — After what I've done for them? — Is this a way to treat me? — I'll come up . . . as soon as I can — I haven't been well. — Okay. I'll come up. I get depressed because things are bad and they are not going to improve. There's something malignant in the world. Destructiveness, aggressiveness. — Greed. People take what is not theirs. There is greed. I am depressed, disillusioned . . . with life . . . with work . . . family. I don't see hope. (*He sits. He speaks more to himself than to Alejo.*) Some people get a cut in a finger and die. Because their veins are right next to their skin. There are people who, if you punch them in their stomach, the skin around the stomach bursts and the bowels fall out. Other people, you cut them open and you don't see any veins. You can't find their intestines. There are people who don't even bleed. There are people who bleed like pigs. There are people who have the nerves right on their skins. You touch them and they scream. They have their vital organs close to the surface. You hit them and they burst an organ. I didn't even touch this one and he died. He died of fear.

(*Lights fade to black.*)

SCENE 11

(*Nena, Alejo and Olimpia sit cross-legged on the mattress. Nena sits right, Alejo center, Olimpia left. Nena and Olimpia play patty-cake. Orlando enters. He goes close to them.*)

ORLANDO: What are you doing?

OLIMPIA: I'm playing with her.

ORLANDO (*to Alejo*): What are you doing here? (*Alejo looks at him as a reply. He speaks sarcastically.*) They're playing patty-cake. (*He goes near Nena.*) So? (*Short pause. Nena giggles.*) Stop laughing!

(*Nena is frightened. Olimpia holds her.*)

OLIMPIA: Why do you have to spoil everything. We were having a good time.

ORLANDO: Shut up! (*Nena whimpers.*) Stop whimpering. I can't stand your whimpering. I can't stand it. (*Timidly, she tries to speak words as she whimpers.*) Speak up. I can't hear you! She's crazy! Take her to the crazy house!

OLIMPIA: She's not crazy! She's a baby!

ORLANDO: She's not a baby! She's crazy! You think she's a baby? She's older than you think! How old do you think she is. — Don't tell me that.

OLIMPIA: She's sick. Don't you see she's sick? Let her cry! (*To Nena.*) Cry!

ORLANDO: You drive me crazy too with your . . .

(*Orlando imitates Olimpia's speech defect. She punches him repeatedly.*)

OLIMPIA: You drive me crazy! (*He pushes her off.*) You drive me crazy! You are a bastard! One day I'm going to kill you when you're asleep! I'm going to open you up and cut your entrails and feed them to the snakes. (*She tries to strangle him.*) I'm going to tear your heart out and feed it to the dogs! I'm going to cut your head open and have the cats eat your brain! (*Reaching for his fly.*) I'm going to cut your peepee and hang it on a tree and feed it to the birds!

ORLANDO: Get off me! I'm getting rid of you too! (*He starts to exit.*) I can't stand you!

OLIMPIA: Oh, yeah! I'm getting rid of you.

ORLANDO: I can't stand you!

OLIMPIA: I can't stand you!

ORLANDO: Meddler! (*To Alejo.*) I can't stand you either. (*He exits.*)

OLIMPIA (*going to the stairs.*): Tell the boss! Tell her! She won't get rid of me! She'll get rid of you! What good are you! Tell her! (*She goes to Nena.*) Don't pay any attention to him. He's a coward. — You're pretty.

(*Orlando enters through the hallway left door. He sits*

center at the dining-room table and leans his head on it. Leticia enters. He turns to look at her.)

LETICIA: You didn't send it.

(*Lights fade to black.*)

SCENE 12

(*Leticia sits next to the phone. Without holding the phone, she speaks to an imaginary Mona.*)

LETICIA: I walk through the house and I know where he's made love to her I think I hear his voice making love to her. Saying the same things he says to me, the same words. (*There is a pause.*) There is someone here. He keeps someone here in the house. (*Pause.*) I don't dare look. (*Pause.*) No, there's nothing I can do. I can't do anything.

(*Leticia walks to the hallway. She hears footsteps. She moves rapidly to the left and hides behind a pillar. Olimpia enters from right. She takes a few steps down the hallway. She carries a plate of food. She sees Leticia and stops. She takes a few steps in various directions, then stops.*)

OLIMPIA: Here kitty, kitty.

(*Leticia walks to Olimpia, looks closely at the plate, then up at her.*)

LETICIA: What is it?
OLIMPIA: Food.
LETICIA: Who is it for?

(*Olimpia turns her eyes away and doesn't answer. Leticia decides to go to the cellar door. She stops halfway there.*)

　　Who is it?
OLIMPIA: A cat.

(*Leticia opens the cellar door.*)

LETICIA: It's not a cat. I'm going down. (*She opens the door to the cellar and starts to go down.*) I want to see who is there.
ORLANDO (*offstage from the cellar*): What is it you want?

(*Lights fade to black.*)

SCENE 13

(*Orlando lies back in the chair in the cellar. His legs are outstretched. His eyes are bloodshot. His tunic is*

open. Nena is curled on the floor. Orlando speaks quietly. He is deeply absorbed.*)

ORLANDO: What I do to you is out of love. Out of want. It's not what you think. I wish you didn't have to be hurt. I don't do it out of hatred. It is not out of rage. It is love. It is a quiet feeling. It's a pleasure. It is quiet and it pierces my insides in the most internal way. It is my most private self. And this I give to you. — Don't be afraid. — It is a desire to destroy and to see things destroyed and to see the inside of them. — It's my nature. I must hide this from others. But I don't feel remorse. I was born this way and I must have this. — I need love. I wish you did not feel hurt and recoil from me.

(*Lights fade to black.*)

SCENE 14

(*Orlando sits to the right and Leticia sits to the left of the table.*)

LETICIA: Don't make her scream.

(*There is a pause.*)

ORLANDO: You're crazy.
LETICIA: Don't I give you enough?
ORLANDO (*he's calm*): Don't start.
LETICIA: How long is she going to be here?
ORLANDO: Not long.
LETICIA: Don't make her cry. (*He looks at her.*) I can't stand it. (*Pause.*) Why do you make her scream?
ORLANDO: I don't make her scream.
LETICIA: She screams.
ORLANDO: I can't help it.

(*Pause.*)

LETICIA: I tell you I can't stand it. I'm going to ask Mona to come and stay with me.
ORLANDO: No.
LETICIA: I want someone here with me.
ORLANDO: I don't want her here.
LETICIA: Why not?
ORLANDO: I don't.
LETICIA: I need someone here with me.
ORLANDO: Not now.
LETICIA: When?
ORLANDO: Soon enough. — She's going to stay here for a while. She's going to work for us. She'll be a servant here.
LETICIA: . . . No.
ORLANDO: She's going to be a servant here.

(*Lights fade to black.*)

SCENE 15

(*Olimpia and Nena are sitting at the dining-room table. They are separating stones and other matter from dried beans.*)

NENA: I used to clean beans when I was in the home. And also string beans. I also pressed clothes. The days were long. Some girls did hand sewing. They spent the day doing that. I didn't like it. When I did that, the day was even longer and there were times when I couldn't move even if I tried. And they said I couldn't go there anymore, that I had to stay in the yard. I didn't mind sitting in the yard looking at the birds. I went to the laundry room and watched the women work. They let me go in and sit there. And they showed me how to press. I like to press because my mind wanders and I find satisfaction. I can iron all day. I like the way the wrinkles come out and things look nice. It's a miracle isn't it? I could earn a living pressing clothes. And I could find my grandpa and take care of him.

OLIMPIA: Where is your grandpa?

NENA: I don't know.

(*They work a little in silence.*)

He sleeps in the streets. Because he's too old to remember where he lives. He needs a person to take care of him. And I can take care of him. But I don't know where he is. — He doesn't know where I am. — He doesn't know who he is. He's too old. He doesn't know anything about himself. He only knows how to beg. And he knows that only because he's hungry. He walks around and begs for food. He forgets to go home. He lives in the camp for the homeless and he has his own box. It's not an ugly box like the others. It is a real box. I used to live there with him. He took me with him when my mother died till they took me to the home. It is a big box. It's big enough for two. I could sleep in the front where it's cold. And he could sleep in the back where it's warmer. And he could lean on me. The floor is hard for him because he's skinny and it's hard on his poor bones. He could sleep on top of me if that would make him feel comfortable. I wouldn't mind. Except that he may pee on me because he pees in his pants. He doesn't know not to. He is incontinent. He can't hold it. His box was a little smelly. But that doesn't matter because I could clean it. All I would need is some soap. I could get plenty of water from the public faucet. And I could borrow a brush. You know how clean I could get it? As clean as new. You know what I would do? I would make holes in the floor so the pee would go down to the ground. And you know what else I would do?

OLIMPIA: What?

NENA: I would get straw and put it on the floor for him and for me and it would make it comfortable and clean and warm. How do you like that? Just as I did for my goat.

OLIMPIA: You have a goat?

NENA: . . . I did.

OLIMPIA: What happened to him?

NENA: He died. They killed him and ate him. Just like they did Christ.

OLIMPIA: Nobody ate Christ.

NENA: . . . I thought they did. My goat was eaten though. — In the home we had clean sheets. But that doesn't help. You can't sleep on clean sheets, not if there isn't someone watching over you while you sleep. And since my ma died there just wasn't anyone watching over me. Except you. — Aren't you? In the home they said guardian angels watch your sleep, but I didn't see any there. There weren't any. One day I heard my grandpa calling me and I went to look for him. And I didn't find him. I got tired and I slept in the street, and I was hungry and I was crying. And then he came to me and he spoke to me very softly so as not to scare me and he said he would give me something to eat and he said he would help me look for my grandpa. And he put me in the back of his van. . . . And he took me to a place. And he hurt me. I fought with him but I stopped fighting — because I couldn't fight anymore and he did things to me. And he locked me in. And sometimes he brought me food and sometimes he didn't. And he did things to me. And he beat me. And he hung me on the wall. And I got sick. And sometimes he brought me medicine. And then he said he had to take me somewhere. And he brought me here. And I am glad to be here because you are here. I only wish my grandpa were here too. He doesn't beat me so much anymore.

OLIMPIA: Why does he beat you? I hear him at night. He goes down the steps and I hear you cry. Why does he beat you?

NENA: Because I'm dirty.

OLIMPIA: You are not dirty.

NENA: I am. That's why he beats me. The dirt won't go away from inside me. — He comes downstairs when I'm sleeping and I hear him coming and it frightens me. And he takes the covers off me and I don't move because I'm frightened and because I feel cold and I think I'm going to die. And he puts his hand on me and he recites poetry. And he is almost naked. He wears a robe but he leaves it open and he feels himself as he recites. He touches himself and he touches his stomach and his breast and his behind. He puts his fingers in my parts and he keeps reciting. Then he turns me on my stomach and puts himself inside me. And he says I belong to him. (*There is a pause.*) I want to conduct each day of my life in the best possible way. I should value the things I have. And I should value all those who are near me. And I should value the kindness that others bestow upon me. And if someone should treat me unkindly, I should not blind myself with rage, but I should see them and receive them, since maybe they are in worse pain than me.

(*Lights fade to black.*)

SCENE 16

(*Leticia speaks on the telephone with Mona. She speaks rapidly.*)

LETICIA: He is violent. He has become more so. I sense it. I feel it in him. — I understand his thoughts. I know what he thinks. — I raised him. I practically did. He was a boy when I met him. I saw him grow. I was the first woman he loved. That's how young he was. I have to look after him, make sure he doesn't get into trouble. He's not wise. He's trusting. They are changing him. — He tortures people. I know he does. He tells me he doesn't but I know he does. I know it. How could I not. Sometimes he comes from headquarters and his hands are shaking. Why should he shake? What do they do there? — He should transfer. Why do that? He says he doesn't do it himself. That the officers don't do it. He says that people are not being tortured. That that is questionable. — Everybody knows it. How could he not know it when everybody knows it. Sometimes you see blood in the streets. Haven't you seen it? Why do they leave the bodies in the streets — how evil, to frighten people? They tear their fingernails off and their poor hands are bloody and destroyed. And they mangle their genitals and expose them and they tear their eyes out and you can see the empty eyesockets in the skull. How awful, Mona. He mustn't do it. I don't care if I don't have anything! What's money! I don't need a house as big as this! He's doing it for money! What other reason could he have! What other reason could he have!! He shouldn't do it. I cannot look at him without thinking of it. He's doing it. I know he's doing it. — Shhhh! I hear steps. I'll call you later. Bye, Mona. I'll talk to you.

(*She hangs up the receiver. Lights fade to black.*)

SCENE 17

(*The living room. Olimpia sits to the right, Nena to the left.*)

OLIMPIA: I don't wear high heels because they hurt my feet. I used to have a pair but they hurt my feet and also (*pointing to her calf*) here in my legs. So I don't wear them anymore even if they were pretty. Did you ever wear high heels? (*Nena shakes her head.*) Do you have ingrown nails? (*Nena looks at her questioningly.*) Nails that grow twisted into the flesh. (*Nena shakes her head.*) I don't either. Do you have sugar in the blood? (*Nena shakes her head.*) My mother had sugar in the blood and that's what she died of but she lived to be eighty-six which is very old even if she had many things wrong with her. She had glaucoma and high blood pressure.

(*Leticia enters and sits center at the table. Nena starts to get up. Olimpia signals her to be still. Leticia is not concerned with them.*)

LETICIA: So, what are you talking about?
OLIMPIA: Ingrown nails.

(*Nena turns to Leticia to make sure she may remain seated there. Leticia is involved with her own thoughts. Nena turns front. Lights fade to black.*)

SCENE 18

(*Orlando is sleeping on the dining-room table. The telephone rings. He speaks as someone having a nightmare.*)

ORLANDO: Ah! Ah! Ah! Get off me! Get off! I said get off!

(*Leticia enters.*)

LETICIA (*going to him*): Orlando! What's the matter! What are you doing here!
ORLANDO: Get off me! Ah! Ah! Ah! Get off me!
LETICIA: Why are you sleeping here! On the table. (*Holding him close to her.*) Wake up.
ORLANDO: Let go of me. (*He slaps her hands as she tries to reach him.*) Get away from me. (*He goes to the floor on his knees. He staggers to the telephone.*) Yes. Yes, it's me. — You did? — So? — It's true then. — What's the name? — Yes, sure. — Thanks. — Sure.

(*Orlando hangs up the receiver. He turns to look at Leticia. Lights fade to black.*)

SCENE 19

(*Two chairs are placed side by side facing front in the center of the living room. Leticia sits on the right. Orlando stands in the down left corner. Nena sits to the left of the dining-room table facing front. She covers her face. Olimpia stands behind her, holding Nena and leaning her head on her.*)

ORLANDO: Talk.

LETICIA: I cant talk like this.

ORLANDO: Why not?

LETICIA: In front of everyone.

ORLANDO: Why not?

LETICIA: It is personal. I don't need the whole world to know.

ORLANDO: Why not?

LETICIA: Because it's private. My life is private.

ORLANDO: Are you ashamed?

LETICIA: Yes, I am ashamed!

ORLANDO: What of . . . ? What of . . . ? — I want you to tell us — about your lover.

LETICIA: I don't have a lover.

(*Orlando grabs Leticia by the hair. Olimpia holds on to Nena. Olimpia and Nena hide their faces.*)

ORLANDO: You have a lover.

LETICIA: That's a lie.

ORLANDO (*moving closer to Leticia*): It's not a lie. Come on tell us. (*He pulls her hair.*) What's his name? (*Leticia emits a sound of pain. He pulls harder, leans toward her and speaks in a low tone.*) What's his name?

LETICIA: Albertico.

(*Orlando takes a moment to release Leticia.*)

ORLANDO: Tell us about it.

(*There is silence. Orlando pulls Leticia's hair.*)

LETICIA: All right.

(*Orlando releases Leticia.*)

ORLANDO: What's his name?

LETICIA: Albertico.

ORLANDO: Go on. (*Pause.*) Sit up! (*She does.*) Albertico what?

LETICIA: Estévez.

(*Orlando sits next to Leticia.*)

ORLANDO: Go on. (*Silence.*) Where did you first meet him?

LETICIA: At . . . I . . .

ORLANDO (*he grabs Leticia by the hair*): In my office.

LETICIA: Yes.

ORLANDO: Don't lie. — When?

LETICIA: You know when.

ORLANDO: When! (*Silence.*) How did you meet him?

LETICIA: You introduced him to me.

(*Orlando lets Leticia go.*)

ORLANDO: What else? (*Silence.*) Who is he!

LETICIA: He's a lieutenant.

ORLANDO (*he stands*): When did you meet with him?

LETICIA: Last week.

ORLANDO: When!

LETICIA: Last week.

ORLANDO: When!

LETICIA: Last week. I said last week.

ORLANDO: Where did you meet him?

LETICIA: . . . In a house of rendezvous . . .

ORLANDO: How did you arrange it?

LETICIA: . . . I wrote to him

ORLANDO: Did he approach you?

LETICIA: No.

ORLANDO: Did he!

LETICIA: No.

ORLANDO (*He grabs Leticia's hair again.*): He did! How!

LETICIA: I approached him.

ORLANDO: How!

LETICIA (*aggressively*): I looked at him! I looked at him! I looked at him!

(*Orlando lets Leticia go.*)

ORLANDO: When did you look at him?

LETICIA: Please stop . . . !

ORLANDO: Where! When!

LETICIA: In your office!

ORLANDO: When?

LETICIA: I asked him to meet me!

ORLANDO: What did he say?

LETICIA (*aggressively*): He walked away. He walked away! He walked away! I asked him to meet me.

ORLANDO: What was he like?

LETICIA: . . . Oh . . .

ORLANDO: Was he tender? Was he tender to you!

(*Leticia doesn't answer. Orlando put his hand inside her blouse. She lets out an excruciating scream. He lets her go and walks to the right of the dining room. She goes to the telephone table, opens the drawer, takes a gun and shoots Orlando. Orlando falls dead. Nena runs to downstage of the table. Leticia is disconcerted, then puts the revolver in Nena's hand, hoping she will take the blame. Leticia steps away from Nena.*)

LETICIA: Please . . .

(*Nena is in a state of terror and numb acceptance. She looks at the gun. Then, up. The lights fade.*)

COMMENTARY

David Savran (b. 1950)

INTERVIEW WITH MARÍA IRENE FORNÉS 1987

David Savran, a Canadian drama professor, uncovers some of Fornés's views of politics in the Americas. The interview, conducted in 1987, came at a painful time in Latin American politics and at a time when the media presented the United States as experiencing a period of selfishness and self-satisfaction. Fornés's insights into The Conduct of Life *resulted from her own deep personal concerns.*

Savran: Are there any favorites among your plays?

Fornés: There are favorites but usually it's the one that I'm working on, the one that I don't really understand yet. Like when you're in love, it means you don't really understand the person. When you understand the person, it's *a* love, rather than *in* love. I think *Fefu* is a very beautiful play. I did it in Minneapolis in May, and working with it again, I find it's a very moving play without being sentimental. Men who are more feminine in their nature, more artistic, feel it as deeply as women. There are some men who don't know what's happening. They say, "What? Is there a play there? Is there anybody on the stage?" *Mud* I think is a little jewel.

I'm worried about *The Conduct of Life* because I only did it once. When I do a play once I feel that I don't yet understand it fully. And I worry whether it would work as well if I didn't direct it. I knew *Mud* would work. I saw one production of it which wasn't good and yet it worked. But *Conduct of Life* may have a strange soul to it.

Savran: How so?

Fornés: I don't know how it reads. Recently there was a reading of it at Los Angeles Theatre Center. I got a call from the director. He wanted to talk about casting, so I said, "Please, above all, Orlando should look like a very ordinary person, a nice guy. You meet him and he's like someone who works in an office and has a nice job." And he said, "Fine." For Leticia he said he had a very strong woman. Then he asked, "How old is Olimpia?" I said, "Olimpia's a middle-aged woman." He had cast a young girl. I said, "She's a housekeeper, a woman who cleans. She's short and heavy." An attractive girl would throw the balance of the play. I don't even know if the play would work.

He was thinking, too, of women being oppressed. All those women are strong. Nena is a strong woman, a strong child. It's not just women being oppressed. When you have a nut, a crazy person like that, everybody's oppressed. It's the oppression of a sadist. It has nothing to do with women. So a playwright has to be careful. I thought it was so obvious that Olimpia is an illiterate housekeeper that I didn't specify that she's middle-aged, overweight and unattractive. How can you say Olimpia's being oppressed? She runs the house! A servant is a

1497

job like any other. You work. When you go to work in an office, are you oppressed? You think that everybody should be a boss?

Savran: People like to draw a clear line between victim and victimizer. It's frightening for people to recognize their role in the maintenance of this system.

Fornés: I don't think Olimpia, Nena and Leticia are maintaining the situation. I remember shortly after the Castro takeover there was a group of Cuban exile artists. They wanted me to go to meetings, to have readings, and they said, "It's not political." So I went. They had readings of poetry and discussions of painting and stuff like that. Then one day they passed an anti-Castro manifesto around that we were supposed to sign. It talked about the Red monster and the language was extreme. I said, "No, I don't want to sign." They were indignant and asked, "Are you in favor of Castro?" I said, "Not really. I'm not in favor of Castro but I'm not against him either. I don't know enough." And they said, "If you're not against him, you're for him." I'm not for him and don't tell me what I am because I know what I am. It's like saying if people don't fight the system, then they are for the system. That's not so. People have to survive. If you don't go out and get a gun and shoot the general, it doesn't mean you're supporting the system.

Leticia is in love with Orlando, but I don't think she's a masochist. She discovers horrible things, that he's in love with a child. She discovers what he is and she shoots him, because she cannot live around him. Before that she has enough information to realize what he is, but she cannot face it. But that doesn't mean that she's supporting the system. There is an oppressor in that play, but it's not Orlando, who is just a peon in the political system. It's the generals.

I don't think everybody there is supporting the system. What are they going to do? Olimpia has a job. She has to survive. You think she's going to say, "You son of a bitch. I'm not going to work in this house anymore. I'm going to go out and starve." We can do that in this country. Here, if Olimpia leaves a job, she's employed the next day somewhere else, because she's a good housekeeper and knows how to cook. But not in other places. So you cannot say, if you don't fight it, you're with it.

Savran: It may not be true in Latin America where survival is the bottom line. But in this country so many people are passively complicit with an oppressive regime. That's a very serious problem.

Fornés: Are you supporting Reagan because you don't go out and shoot him?

Savran: No.

Fornés: Do you know how many people in other countries think that you are? Because you are going around with your little tape recorder and doing your little interviews instead of fighting.

Savran: There are ways of being politically active besides picking up a gun.

Fornés: Leticia is just an ordinary woman who doesn't know anything. She's just in love with this guy. She's not political. She's not even intelligent. And Olimpia is an imbecile! Do you expect her to be political? And Nena? You expect her to be political? I expect you to be political. I expect me to be. We're supposed to be. It's been going on how many years now?

Savran: Six.

Fornés: It's getting worse and worse. There isn't even a strong opposition as there was in the sixties. I would say that we are parties to this, but not them. We have the knowledge, the intelligence, the perspective. We know what's right and what's wrong.

Savran: What does this mean then in terms of bringing about social change, for people who don't have the perspective we have?

Fornés: They cannot bring about social change. They don't know what's possible.

Savran: What can they do?

Fornés: The only thing they can do is act emotionally. Leticia acts emotionally. She kills Orlando. Not because he has betrayed her, but because he attacks her physically. When he does, she shoots him.

August Wilson

August Wilson was born in Pittsburgh in 1945, the son of a white father who never lived with his family and a black mother who had come from North Carolina to a Pittsburgh slum, where she worked to keep her family together. Wilson's early childhood was spent in an environment very similar to that of his play *Fences,* and Troy Maxson seems to be patterned somewhat on Wilson's stepfather.

Wilson's writing is rooted to a large extent in music, specifically the blues. As a poet, writing over several years, Wilson found himself interested in the speech patterns and rhythms that were familiar to him from black neighborhoods, but the value of those patterns became clearer to him when he grew older and moved from Pittsburgh to Minneapolis. From a distance, he was able to see more clearly what had attracted him to the language and to begin to use the language more fully in his work.

In the 1960s and 1970s Wilson became involved in the civil rights movement and began to describe himself as a black nationalist, a term he has said he feels comfortable with. He began writing plays in the 1960s in Pittsburgh and then took a job in St. Paul writing dramatic skits for the Science Museum of Minnesota. He founded the Playwrights Center in Minneapolis and began writing a play, *Jitney,* about a gypsy cab station, which was produced in 1982. *Fullerton Street,* about Pittsburgh, was another play written in this early period. Wilson's first commercial success, *Ma Rainey's Black Bottom,* eventually premiered at the Yale Repertory Theatre in 1984 and then went to Broadway, where it enjoyed 275 performances and won the New York Drama Critics' Circle Award.

Ma Rainey's Black Bottom was the first of a planned sequence of ten plays based on the black American experience. As Wilson said, "I think the black Americans have the most dramatic story of all mankind to tell." The concept of such a vast project echoes O'Neill's projected group of eleven plays based on the Irish-American experience. (Unfortunately, O'Neill destroyed all but *A Touch of the Poet* in his series.) Wilson's project, however, is ongoing and intense and so far has produced some of the most successful plays in the recent American theater.

Ma Rainey is about the legendary black blues singer who preceded Bessie Smith and Billie Holiday. The play is about the way in which she was exploited by white managers and recording executives and the way in which she knowingly dealt with her exploitation. In the cast of the play are several black musicians in the backup band. Levee, the trumpet player, has a dream of leading his own band and establishing himself as an important jazz musician. But he is haunted by memories of seeing his mother raped by a gang of white men when he was a boy. He wants to "improve" the session he's playing by making the old jazz tune "Black Bottom" swing in the new jazz style, but Ma Rainey keeps him in tow and demands that they play the tune in the old way. Levee finally cracks under the pressure, and the play ends painfully.

Fences opened at the Yale Repertory Theatre in 1985 and in New York in early 1987, where it won the Pulitzer Prize as well as the New York Drama Critics' Circle Award. This long-running success established Wilson firmly as an important writer. *Joe Turner's Come and Gone* opened at the Yale Repertory Theatre in late 1986 and moved to New York in early 1988, where it too has been hailed as an important play, winning its author the New York Drama Critics' Circle Award. Set in a rooming house in Pittsburgh in 1911, *Joe Turner* is a study of the children of former slaves. They have come north to find work, and some of them have been found by the legendary bounty hunter Joe Turner. As a study of a people in transition, the play is a quiet masterpiece. It incorporates a number of important African traditions, especially religious rituals of healing as performed by Bynum, the "bone man," a seer and a medicine man. In this play and others, Wilson makes a special effort to highlight the elements of African heritage that white society strips away from blacks.

The next play in Wilson's projected series, *The Piano Lesson*, which premiered at the Yale Repertory Theatre in 1987, also portrays the complexity of black attitudes toward the past and black heritage. The piano represents two kinds of culture: the white culture that produced the musical instrument and the black culture, in the form of Papa Boy Willie, who carved into it images from black Africa. The central question in the play is whether Boy Willie should sell the piano and use the money for a down payment on land and therefore on the future. Or should he follow his sister Berniece's advice and keep it because it is too precious to sell? The conflict is deep and the play ultimately focuses on a profound moment of spiritual exorcism. How one exorcises the past — how one lives with it or without it — is a central theme in Wilson's work.

The next play, *Two Trains Running*, is set in 1969, in the decade that saw the Vietnam War, racial and political riots, and the assassinations of both Kennedys, Malcolm X, and Martin Luther King, Jr. The play premiered at the Yale Repertory Theatre in 1990 and opened on Broadway at the Walter Kerr Theater in April 1992, directed by Lloyd Richards. The characters remain in Memphis Lee's diner — scheduled for demolition — throughout the play. The two trains in the title are heading to Africa and to the old South, but the characters are immobile and seem indifferent to both of them. Wilson moved away from the careful structure of the well-made play in this work and produced an open-ended conclusion, leaving the racial and philosophical tensions unresolved.

Seven Guitars (1996), Wilson's latest play in the series, takes place in a backyard in Pittsburgh in 1948 on the eve of the landmark boxing match between Joe Louis and "Jersey" Joe Walcott. The play focuses on a blues musician, Floyd Barton, who hopes to regain his lost love, put his band back together, and move to Chicago to make his second recording. *Seven Guitars* emphasizes the blues, especially in its long first act, with Barton's friends gathered in his backyard to mourn his death and the loss of his talent. People did much the same when Joe Louis, the "Brown Bomber," lost his fight, a loss that punctuated the end of an era. The second act focuses on Hedley, a West Indian boarder, whom critic Margo Jefferson describes as "half madman and half prophet." Hedley recites a litany of racial injustices and gives voice to a torrent of wrongs. Hedley's voice is a counterpoint to the blues; he gives us a powerful range of responses to the condition of being black in Pittsburgh in the late 1940s.

FENCES

Fences (1985), like most of August Wilson's recent plays, was directed by Lloyd Richards, who also directed the first production of Lorraine Hansberry's *A Raisin in the Sun*. Richards was, until 1991, the dean of the School of Drama at Yale University and ran the Yale Repertory Theatre, where he directed all of the plays Wilson has written in his projected ten-play cycle about black American life.

Fences presents a slice of life in a black tenement in Pittsburgh in the 1950s. Its main character, Troy Maxson, is a garbage collector who has taken great pride in keeping his family together and providing for them. When the play opens, he and his friend Bono are talking about Troy's challenge to the company and the union about blacks' ability to do the same "easy" work that whites do. Troy's rebellion and frustration set the tone of the entire play: He is looking for his rights and, at age fifty-three, he has missed many opportunities to get what he deserves.

Troy's struggle for fairness becomes virtually mythic as he describes his wrestling with death during a bout with pneumonia in 1941. He describes a three-day struggle in which he eventually overcame his foe. Troy — a good baseball player who was relegated to the Negro leagues — sees death as nothing but a fastball, and he could always deal with a fastball. Both Bono and Troy's wife, Rose, show an intense admiration for him as he describes his ordeal.

The father-son relationship that begins to take a central role in the drama is complicated by strong feelings of pride and independence on both sides. Troy's son Cory wants to play football and Troy wants him to work on the fence he's mending. Cory's youthful enthusiasm probably echoes Troy's own youthful innocence, but Troy resents it in Cory, seeing it as partly responsible for his own predicament. Cory cannot see his father's point of view and feels that he is exempt from the kind of prejudice his father suffered.

The agony of the father-son relationship, their misperceptions of each other, persist through the play. Rose's capacity to cope with the deepest of Troy's anxieties — his fear of death — is one of her most important achievements in the play. At the end of the play Rose demands that Cory give Troy the respect he deserves, although Cory's anger and inexperience make it all but impossible for him to see his father as anything other than an oppressor. Cory feels that he must say no to his father once, but Rose will not let him deny his father. When the play ends with Gabe's fantastic ritualistic dance, the audience feels a sense of closure, of spiritual finish.

Fences in Performance

Like many of America's best plays, *Fences* began in a workshop production. Its first version was performed in a reading without full production — no sets, no full lighting, actors working "on book" instead of fully memorizing the play — in the summer of 1983 at the Eugene O'Neill Center in Waterford, Connecticut. This early version was four hours long.

Once Wilson found the focus of his play, it premiered in 1985 at the Yale Repertory Theatre in New Haven. Lloyd Richards, then dean of Yale Drama School, directed this as well as the New York production. The New York opening on March 27, 1987, starred Mary Alice, James Earl Jones, and Ray Anranha, the cast from New Haven. Frank Rich in the *New York Times* praised James Earl Jones, congratulating him on finding "what may be the best role of his career." He also said, "*Fences* leaves no doubt that Mr. Wilson is a major writer, combining a poet's ear for vernacular with a robust sense of humor (political and sexual), a sure instinct for crackling dramatic incident and a passionate commitment to a great subject."

From the first, *Fences* was recognized as an important play. It won four Tony Awards: best play, best actor, best supporting actress, and best director. It also won the New York Drama Critics' Circle Award for best play. Before the New York production, it had traveled to Chicago, San Francisco, and Seattle. It has been performed numerous times since, with the 1990 Stage West production in Springfield, Massachusetts, among the most recent.

August Wilson (b. 1946)

FENCES

1987

Characters

TROY MAXSON
JIM BONO, *Troy's friend*
ROSE, *Troy's wife*
LYONS, *Troy's oldest son by previous marriage*
GABRIEL, *Troy's brother*
CORY, *Troy and Rose's son*
RAYNELL, *Troy's daughter*

Setting: *The setting is the yard which fronts the only entrance to the Maxson household, an ancient two-story brick house set back off a small alley in a big-city neighborhood. The entrance to the house is gained by two or three steps leading to a wooden porch badly in need of paint.*

A relatively recent addition to the house and running its full width, the porch lacks congruence. It is a sturdy porch with a flat roof. One or two chairs of dubious value sit at one end where the kitchen window opens onto the porch. An old-fashioned icebox stands silent guard at the opposite end.

The yard is a small dirt yard, partially fenced, except for the last scene, with a wooden sawhorse, a pile of lumber, and other fence-building equipment set off to the side. Opposite is a tree from which hangs a ball made of rags. A baseball bat leans against the tree. Two oil drums serve as garbage receptacles and sit near the house at right to complete the setting.

The Play: *Near the turn of the century, the destitute of Europe sprang on the city with tenacious claws* *and an honest and solid dream. The city devoured them. They swelled its belly until it burst into a thousand furnaces and sewing machines, a thousand butcher shops and bakers' ovens, a thousand churches and hospitals and funeral parlors and money-lenders. The city grew. It nourished itself and offered each man a partnership limited only by his talent, his guile, and his willingness and capacity for hard work. For the immigrants of Europe, a dream dared and won true.*

The descendants of African slaves were offered no such welcome or participation. They came from places called the Carolinas and the Virginias, Georgia, Alabama, Mississippi, and Tennessee. They came strong, eager, searching. The city rejected them and they fled and settled along the riverbanks and under bridges in shallow, ramshackle houses made of sticks and tarpaper. They collected rags and wood. They sold the use of their muscles and their bodies. They cleaned houses and washed clothes, they shined shoes, and in quiet desperation and vengeful pride, they stole, and lived in pursuit of their own dream. That they could breathe free, finally, and stand to meet life with the force of dignity and whatever eloquence the heart could call upon.

By 1957, the hard-won victories of the European immigrants had solidified the industrial might of America. War had been confronted and won with new energies that used loyalty and patriotism as its fuel. Life was rich, full, and flourishing. The Milwaukee Braves won the World Series, and the hot winds of change that would make the sixties a turbulent, racing, dangerous, and provocative decade had not yet begun to blow full.

ACT I • *Scene I*

(It is 1957. Troy and Bono enter the yard, engaged in conversation. Troy is fifty-three years old, a large man with thick, heavy hands; it is this largeness that he strives to fill out and make an accommodation with. Together with his blackness, his largeness informs his sensibilities and the choices he has made in his life.)

(Of the two men, Bono is obviously the follower. His commitment to their friendship of thirty-odd years is rooted in his admiration of Troy's honesty, capacity for hard work, and his strength, which Bono seeks to emulate.)

(It is Friday night, payday, and the one night of the week the two men engage in a ritual of talk and drink. Troy is usually the most talkative and at times he can be crude and almost vulgar, though he is capable of rising to profound heights of expression. The

men carry lunch buckets and wear or carry burlap aprons and are dressed in clothes suitable to their jobs as garbage collectors.)

BONO: Troy, you ought to stop that lying!

TROY: I ain't lying! The nigger had a watermelon this big.

(He indicates with his hands.)

Talking about . . . "What watermelon, Mr. Rand?" I liked to fell out! "What watermelon, Mr. Rand?" . . . And it sitting there big as life.

BONO: What did Mr. Rand say?

TROY: Ain't said nothing. Figure if the nigger too dumb to know he carrying a watermelon, he wasn't gonna get much sense out of him. Trying to hide that great big old watermelon under his coat. Afraid to let the white man see him carry it home.

BONO: I'm like you . . . I ain't got no time for them kind of people.

TROY: Now what he look like getting mad cause he see the man from the union talking to Mr. Rand?

BONO: He come to me talking about . . . "Maxson gonna get us fired." I told him to get away from me with that. He walked away from me calling you a troublemaker. What Mr. Rand say?

TROY: Ain't said nothing. He told me to go down the Commissioner's office next Friday. They called me down there to see them.

BONO: Well, as long as you got your complaint filed, they can't fire you. That's what one of them white fellows tell me.

TROY: I ain't worried about them firing me. They gonna fire me cause I asked a question? That's all I did. I went to Mr. Rand and asked him, "Why? Why you got the white mens driving and the colored lifting?" Told him "what's the matter, don't I count? You think only white fellows got sense enough to drive a truck. That ain't no paper job! Hell, anybody can drive a truck. How come you got all whites driving and the colored lifting?" He told me "take it to the union." Well, hell, that's what I done! Now they wanna come up with this pack of lies.

BONO: I told Brownie if the man come and ask him any questions . . . just tell the truth! It ain't nothing but something they done trumped up on you cause you filed a complaint on them.

TROY: Brownie don't understand nothing. All I want them to do is change the job description. Give everybody a chance to drive the truck. Brownie can't see that. He ain't got that much sense.

BONO: How you figure he be making out with that gal be up at Taylors' all the time . . . that Alberta gal?

TROY: Same as you and me. Getting just as much as we is. Which is to say nothing.

BONO: It is, huh? I figure you doing a little better than me . . . and I ain't saying what I'm doing.

TROY: Aw, nigger, look here . . . I know you. If you had got anywhere near that gal, twenty minutes later you be looking to tell somebody. And the first one you gonna tell . . . that you gonna want to brag to . . . is gonna be me.

BONO: I ain't saying that. I see where you be eyeing her.

TROY: I eye all the women. I don't miss nothing. Don't never let nobody tell you Troy Maxson don't eye the women.

BONO: You been doing more than eyeing her. You done bought her a drink or two.

TROY: Hell yeah, I bought her a drink! What that mean? I bought you one, too. What that mean cause I buy her a drink? I'm just being polite.

BONO: It's all right to buy her one drink. That's what you call being polite. But when you wanna be buying two or three . . . that's what you call eyeing her.

TROY: Look here, as long as you known me . . . you ever known me to chase after women?

BONO: Hell yeah! Long as I done known you. You forgetting I knew you when.

TROY: Naw, I'm talking about since I been married to Rose?

BONO: Oh, not since you been married to Rose. Now, that's the truth, there. I can say that.

TROY: All right then! Case closed.

BONO: I see you be walking up around Alberta's house. You supposed to be at Taylors' and you be walking up around there.

TROY: What you watching where I'm walking for? I ain't watching after you.

BONO: I seen you walking around there more than once.

TROY: Hell, you liable to see me walking anywhere! That don't mean nothing cause you see me walking around there.

BONO: Where she come from anyway? She just kinda showed up one day.

TROY: Tallahassee. You can look at her and tell she one of them Florida gals. They got some big healthy women down there. Grow them right up out the ground. Got a little bit of Indian in her. Most of them niggers down in Florida got some Indian in them.

BONO: I don't know about that Indian part. But she damn sure big and healthy. Woman wear some big stockings. Got them great big old legs and hips as wide as the Mississippi River.

TROY: Legs don't mean nothing. You don't do nothing but push them out of the way. But them hips cushion the ride!

BONO: Troy, you ain't got no sense.

TROY: It's the truth! Like you riding on Goodyears!

(*Rose enters from the house. She is ten years younger than Troy, her devotion to him stems from her recognition of the possibilities of her life without him: a succession of abusive men and their babies, a life of partying and running the streets, the Church, or aloneness with its attendant pain and frustration. She recognizes Troy's spirit as a fine and illuminating one and she either ignores or forgives his faults, only some of which she recognizes. Though she doesn't drink, her presence is an integral part of the Friday night rituals. She alternates between the porch and the kitchen, where supper preparations are under way.*)

ROSE: What you all out here getting into?

TROY: What you worried about what we getting into for? This is men talk, woman.

ROSE: What I care what you all talking about? Bono, you gonna stay for supper?

BONO: No, I thank you, Rose. But Lucille say she cooking up a pot of pigfeet.

TROY: Pigfeet! Hell, I'm going home with you! Might even stay the night if you got some pigfeet. You got something in there to top them pigfeet, Rose?

ROSE: I'm cooking up some chicken. I got some chicken and collard greens.

TROY: Well, go on back in the house and let me and Bono finish what we was talking about. This is men talk. I got some talk for you later. You know what kind of talk I mean. You go on and powder it up.

ROSE: Troy Maxson, don't you start that now!

TROY (*puts his arm around her*): Aw, woman . . . come here. Look here, Bono . . . when I met this woman . . . I got out that place, say, "Hitch up my pony, saddle up my mare . . . there's a woman out there for me somewhere. I looked here. Looked there. Saw Rose and latched on to her." I latched on to her and told her — I'm gonna tell you the truth — I told her, "Baby, I don't wanna marry, I just wanna be your man." Rose told me . . . tell him what you told me, Rose.

ROSE: I told him if he wasn't the marrying kind, then move out the way so the marrying kind could find me.

TROY: That's what she told me. "Nigger, you in my way. You blocking the view! Move out the way so I can find me a husband." I thought it over two or three days. Come back —

ROSE: Ain't no two or three days nothing. You was back the same night.

TROY: Come back, told her . . . "Okay, baby . . . but I'm gonna buy me a banty rooster and put him out there in the backyard . . . and when he see a stranger come, he'll flap his wings and crow . . ."

Look here, Bono, I could watch the front door by myself . . . it was that back door I was worried about.

ROSE: Troy, you ought not talk like that. Troy ain't doing nothing but telling a lie.

TROY: Only thing is . . . when we first got married . . . forget the rooster . . . we ain't had no yard!

BONO: I hear you tell it. Me and Lucille was staying down there on Logan Street. Had two rooms with the outhouse in the back. I ain't mind the outhouse none. But when that goddamn wind blow through there in the winter . . . that's what I'm talking about! To this day I wonder why in the hell I ever stayed down there for six long years. But see, I didn't know I could do no better. I thought only white folks had inside toilets and things.

ROSE: There's a lot of people don't know they can do no better than they doing now. That's just something you got to learn. A lot of folks still shop at Bella's.

TROY: Ain't nothing wrong with shopping at Bella's. She got fresh food.

ROSE: I ain't said nothing about if she got fresh food. I'm talking about what she charge. She charge ten cents more than the A&P.

TROY: The A&P ain't never done nothing for me. I spends my money where I'm treated right. I go down to Bella, say, "I need a loaf of bread, I'll pay you Friday." She give it to me. What sense that make when I got money to go and spend it somewhere else and ignore the person who done right by me? That ain't in the Bible.

ROSE: We ain't talking about what's in the Bible. What sense it make to shop there when she overcharge?

TROY: You shop where you want to. I'll do my shopping where the people been good to me.

ROSE: Well, I don't think it's right for her to overcharge. That's all I was saying.

BONO: Look here . . . I got to get on. Lucille going be raising all kind of hell.

TROY: Where you going, nigger? We ain't finished this pint. Come here, finish this pint.

BONO: Well, hell, I am . . . if you ever turn the bottle loose.

TROY (*hands him the bottle*): The only thing I say about the A&P is I'm glad Cory got that job down there. Help him take care of his school clothes and things. Gabe done moved out and things getting tight around here. He got that job. . . . He can start to look out for himself.

ROSE: Cory done went and got recruited by a college football team.

TROY: I told that boy about that football stuff. The white man ain't gonna let him get nowhere with that football. I told him when he first come to me

with it. Now you come telling me he done went and got more tied up in it. He ought to go and get recruited in how to fix cars or something where he can make a living.

ROSE: He ain't talking about making no living playing football. It's just something the boys in school do. They gonna send a recruiter by to talk to you. He'll tell you he ain't talking about making no living playing football. It's a honor to be recruited.

TROY: It ain't gonna get him nowhere. Bono'll tell you that.

BONO: If he be like you in the sports . . . he's gonna be all right. Ain't but two men ever played baseball as good as you. That's Babe Ruth and Josh Gibson.° Them's the only two men ever hit more home runs than you.

TROY: What it ever get me? Ain't got a pot to piss in or a window to throw it out of.

ROSE: Times have changed since you was playing baseball, Troy. That was before the war. Times have changed a lot since then.

TROY: How in hell they done changed?

ROSE: They got lots of colored boys playing ball now. Baseball and football.

BONO: You right about that, Rose. Times have changed, Troy. You just come along too early.

TROY: There ought not never have been no time called too early! Now you take that fellow . . . what's that fellow they had playing right field for the Yankees back then? You know who I'm talking about, Bono. Used to play right field for the Yankees.

ROSE: Selkirk?

TROY: Selkirk! That's it! Man batting .269, understand? .269. What kind of sense that make? I was hitting .432 with thirty-seven home runs! Man batting .269 and playing right field for the Yankees! I saw Josh Gibson's daughter yesterday. She walking around with raggedy shoes on her feet. Now I bet you Selkirk's daughter ain't walking around with raggedy shoes on her feet! I bet you that!

ROSE: They got a lot of colored baseball players now. Jackie Robinson was the first. Folks had to wait for Jackie Robinson.

TROY: I done seen a hundred niggers play baseball better than Jackie Robinson. Hell, I know some teams Jackie Robinson couldn't even make! What you talking about Jackie Robinson. Jackie Robinson wasn't nobody. I'm talking about if you could play ball then they ought to have let you play.

Josh Gibson: (1911–1947), powerful black baseball player known in the 1930s as the Babe Ruth of the Negro leagues.

Don't care what color you were. Come telling me I come along too early. If you could play . . . then they ought to have let you play.

(*Troy takes a long drink from the bottle.*)

ROSE: You gonna drink yourself to death. You don't need to be drinking like that.

TROY: Death ain't nothing. I done seen him. Done wrassled with him. You can't tell me nothing about death. Death ain't nothing but a fastball on the outside corner. And you know what I'll do to that! Lookee here, Bono . . . am I lying? You get one of them fastballs, about waist high, over the outside corner of the plate where you can get the meat of the bat on it . . . and good god! You can kiss it goodbye. Now, am I lying?

BONO: Naw, you telling the truth there. I seen you do it.

TROY: If I'm lying . . . that 450 feet worth of lying!

(*Pause.*)

That's all death is to me. A fastball on the outside corner.

ROSE: I don't know why you want to get on talking about death.

TROY: Ain't nothing wrong with talking about death. That's part of life. Everybody gonna die. You gonna die, I'm gonna die. Bono's gonna die. Hell, we all gonna die.

ROSE: But you ain't got to talk about it. I don't like to talk about it.

TROY: You the one brought it up. Me and Bono was talking about baseball . . . you tell me I'm gonna drink myself to death. Ain't that right, Bono? You know I don't drink this but one night out of the week. That's Friday night. I'm gonna drink just enough to where I can handle it. Then I cuts it loose. I leave it alone. So don't you worry about me drinking myself to death. 'Cause I ain't worried about Death. I done seen him. I done wrestled with him.

Look here, Bono . . . I looked up one day and Death was marching straight at me. Like Soldiers on Parade! The Army of Death was marching straight at me. The middle of July, 1941. It got real cold just like it be winter. It seem like Death himself reached out and touched me on the shoulder. He touch me just like I touch you. I got cold as ice and Death standing there grinning at me.

ROSE: Troy, why don't you hush that talk.

TROY: I say . . . What you want, Mr. Death? You be wanting me? You done brought your army to be getting me? I looked him dead in the eye. I wasn't fearing nothing. I was ready to tangle. Just like I'm ready to tangle now. The Bible say be ever vigilant.

That's why I don't get but so drunk. I got to keep watch.

ROSE: Troy was right down there in Mercy Hospital. You remember he had pneumonia? Laying there with a fever talking plumb out of his head.

TROY: Death standing there staring at me . . . carrying that sickle in his hand. Finally he say, "You want bound over for another year?" See, just like that . . . "You want bound over for another year?" I told him, "Bound over hell! Let's settle this now!"

It seem like he kinda fell back when I said that, and all the cold went out of me. I reached down and grabbed that sickle and threw it just as far as I could throw it . . . and me and him commenced to wrestling.

We wrestled for three days and three nights. I can't say where I found the strength from. Every time it seemed like he was gonna get the best of me, I'd reach way down deep inside myself and find the strength to do him one better.

ROSE: Every time Troy tell that story he find different ways to tell it. Different things to make up about it.

TROY: I ain't making up nothing. I'm telling you the facts of what happened. I wrestled with Death for three days and three nights and I'm standing here to tell you about it.

(*Pause.*)

All right. At the end of the third night we done weakened each other to where we can't hardly move. Death stood up, throwed on his robe . . . had him a white robe with a hood on it. He throwed on that robe and went off to look for his sickle. Say, "I'll be back." Just like that. "I'll be back." I told him, say, "Yeah, but . . . you gonna have to find me!" I wasn't no fool. I wan't going looking for him. Death ain't nothing to play with. And I know he's gonna get me. I know I got to join his army . . . his camp followers. But as long as I keep my strength and see him coming . . . as long as I keep up my vigilance . . . he's gonna have to fight to get me. I ain't going easy.

BONO: Well, look here, since you got to keep up your vigilance . . . let me have the bottle.

TROY: Aw hell, I shouldn't have told you that part. I should have left out that part.

ROSE: Troy be talking that stuff and half the time don't even know what he be talking about.

TROY: Bono know me better than that.

BONO: That's right. I know you. I know you got some Uncle Remus° in your blood. You got more stories than the devil got sinners.

Uncle Remus: Black storyteller who recounts traditional black tales in the book by Joel Chandler Harris.

TROY: Aw hell, I done seen him too! Done talked with the devil.

ROSE: Troy, don't nobody wanna be hearing all that stuff.

(*Lyons enters the yard from the street. Thirty-four years old, Troy's son by a previous marriage, he sports a neatly trimmed goatee, sport coat, white shirt, tieless and buttoned at the collar. Though he fancies himself a musician, he is more caught up in the rituals and "idea" of being a musician than in the actual practice of the music. He has come to borrow money from Troy, and while he knows he will be successful, he is uncertain as to what extent his lifestyle will be held up to scrutiny and ridicule.*)

LYONS: Hey, Pop.

TROY: What you come "Hey, Popping" me for?

LYONS: How you doing, Rose?

(*He kisses her.*)

Mr. Bono. How you doing?

BONO: Hey, Lyons . . . how you been?

TROY: He must have been doing all right. I ain't seen him around here last week.

ROSE: Troy, leave your boy alone. He come by to see you and you wanna start all that nonsense.

TROY: I ain't bothering Lyons.

(*Offers him the bottle.*)

Here . . . get you a drink. We got an understanding. I know why he come by to see me and he know I know.

LYONS: Come on, Pop . . . I just stopped by to say hi . . . see how you was doing.

TROY: You ain't stopped by yesterday.

ROSE: You gonna stay for supper, Lyons? I got some chicken cooking in the oven.

LYONS: No, Rose . . . thanks. I was just in the neighborhood and thought I'd stop by for a minute.

TROY: You was in the neighborhood all right, nigger. You telling the truth there. You was in the neighborhood cause it's my payday.

LYONS: Well, hell, since you mentioned it . . . let me have ten dollars.

TROY: I'll be damned! I'll die and go to hell and play blackjack with the devil before I give you ten dollars.

BONO: That's what I wanna know about . . . that devil you done seen.

LYONS: What . . . Pop done seen the devil? You too much, Pops.

TROY: Yeah, I done seen him. Talked to him too!

ROSE: You ain't seen no devil. I done told you that man ain't had nothing to do with the devil. Anything you can't understand, you want to call it the devil.

TROY: Look here, Bono . . . I went down to see Hertzberger about some furniture. Got three rooms for two-ninety-eight. That what it say on the radio. "Three rooms . . . two-ninety-eight." Even made up a little song about it. Go down there . . . man tell me I can't get no credit. I'm working every day and can't get no credit. What to do? I got an empty house with some raggedy furniture in it. Cory ain't got no bed. He's sleeping on a pile of rags on the floor. Working every day and can't get no credit. Come back here — Rose'll tell you — madder than hell. Sit down . . . try to figure what I'm gonna do. Come a knock on the door. Ain't been living here but three days. Who know I'm here? Open the door . . . devil standing there bigger than life. White fellow . . . got on good clothes and everything. Standing there with a clipboard in his hand. I ain't had to say nothing. First words come out of his mouth was . . . "I understand you need some furniture and can't get no credit." I liked to fell over. He say, "I'll give you all the credit you want, but you got to pay the interest on it." I told him, "Give me three rooms worth and charge whatever you want." Next day a truck pulled up here and two men unloaded them three rooms. Man what drove the truck give me a book. Say send ten dollars, first of every month to the address in the book and everything will be all right. Say if I miss a payment the devil was coming back and it'll be hell to pay. That was fifteen years ago. To this day . . . the first of the month I send my ten dollars, Rose'll tell you.

ROSE: Troy lying.

TROY: I ain't never seen that man since. Now you tell me who else that could have been but the devil? I ain't sold my soul or nothing like that, you understand. Naw, I wouldn't have truck with the devil about nothing like that. I got my furniture and pays my ten dollars the first of the month just like clockwork.

BONO: How long you say you been paying this ten dollars a month?

TROY: Fifteen years!

BONO: Hell, ain't you finished paying for it yet? How much the man done charged you.

TROY: Ah hell, I done paid for it. I done paid for it ten times over! The fact is I'm scared to stop paying it.

ROSE: Troy lying. We got that furniture from Mr. Glickman. He ain't paying no ten dollars a month to nobody.

TROY: Aw hell, woman. Bono know I ain't that big a fool.

LYONS: I was just getting ready to say . . . I know where there's a bridge for sale.

TROY: Look here, I'll tell you this . . . it don't matter

to me if he was the devil. It don't matter if the devil give credit. Somebody has got to give it.

ROSE: It ought to matter. You going around talking about having truck with the devil . . . God's the one you gonna have to answer to. He's the one gonna be at the Judgment.

LYONS: Yeah, well, look here, Pop . . . let me have that ten dollars. I'll give it back to you. Bonnie got a job working at the hospital.

TROY: What I tell you, Bono? The only time I see this nigger is when he wants something. That's the only time I see him.

LYONS: Come on, Pop, Mr. Bono don't want to hear all that. Let me have the ten dollars. I told you Bonnie working.

TROY: What that mean to me? "Bonnie working." I don't care if she working. Go ask her for the ten dollars if she working. Talking about "Bonnie working." Why ain't you working?

LYONS: Aw, Pop, you know I can't find no decent job. Where am I gonna get a job at? You know I can't get no job.

TROY: I told you I know some people down there. I can get you on the rubbish if you want to work. I told you that the last time you came by here asking me for something.

LYONS: Naw, Pop . . . thanks. That ain't for me. I don't wanna be carrying nobody's rubbish. I don't wanna be punching nobody's time clock.

TROY: What's the matter, you too good to carry people's rubbish? Where you think that ten dollars you talking about come from? I'm just supposed to haul people's rubbish and give my money to you cause you too lazy to work. You too lazy to work and wanna know why you ain't got what I got.

ROSE: What hospital Bonnie working at? Mercy?

LYONS: She's down at Passavant working in the laundry.

TROY: I ain't got nothing as it is. I give you that ten dollars and I got to eat beans the rest of the week. Naw . . . you ain't getting no ten dollars here.

LYONS: You ain't got to be eating no beans. I don't know why you wanna say that.

TROY: I ain't got no extra money. Gabe done moved over to Miss Pearl's paying her the rent and things done got tight around here. I can't afford to be giving you every payday.

LYONS: I ain't asked you to give me nothing. I asked you to loan me ten dollars. I know you got ten dollars.

TROY: Yeah, I got it. You know why I got it? Cause I don't throw my money away out there in the streets. You living the fast life . . . wanna be a musician . . . running around in them clubs and things . . . then, you learn to take care of yourself.

You ain't gonna find me going and asking nobody for nothing. I done spent too many years without.

LYONS: You and me is two different people, Pop.

TROY: I done learned my mistake and learned to do what's right by it. You still trying to get something for nothing. Life don't owe you nothing. You owe it to yourself. Ask Bono. He'll tell you I'm right.

LYONS: You got your way of dealing with the world . . . I got mine. The only thing that matters to me is the music.

TROY: Yeah, I can see that! It don't matter how you gonna eat . . . where your next dollar is coming from. You telling the truth there.

LYONS: I know I got to eat. But I got to live too. I need something that gonna help me to get out of the bed in the morning. Make me feel like I belong in the world. I don't bother nobody. I just stay with my music cause that's the only way I can find to live in the world. Otherwise there ain't no telling what I might do. Now I don't come criticizing you and how you live. I just come by to ask you for ten dollars. I don't wanna hear all that about how I live.

TROY: Boy, your mamma did a hell of a job raising you.

LYONS: You can't change me, Pop. I'm thirty-four years old. If you wanted to change me, you should have been there when I was growing up. I come by to see you . . . ask for ten dollars and you want to talk about how I was raised. You don't know nothing about how I was raised.

ROSE: Let the boy have ten dollars, Troy.

TROY (*to Lyons*): What the hell you looking at me for? I ain't got no ten dollars. You know what I do with my money.

(*To Rose.*)

Give him ten dollars if you want him to have it.

ROSE: I will. Just as soon as you turn it loose.

TROY (*handing Rose the money*): There it is. Seventy-six dollars and forty-two cents. You see this, Bono? Now, I ain't gonna get but six of that back.

ROSE: You ought to stop telling that lie. Here, Lyons. (*She hands him the money.*)

LYONS: Thanks, Rose. Look . . . I got to run . . . I'll see you later.

TROY: Wait a minute. You gonna say, "thanks, Rose" and ain't gonna look to see where she got that ten dollars from? See how they do me, Bono?

LYONS: I know she got it from you, Pop. Thanks. I'll give it back to you.

TROY: There he go telling another lie. Time I see that ten dollars . . . he'll be owing me thirty more.

LYONS: See you, Mr. Bono.

BONO: Take care, Lyons!

LYONS: Thanks, Pop. I'll see you again.

(*Lyons exits the yard.*)

TROY: I don't know why he don't go and get him a decent job and take care of that woman he got.

BONO: He'll be all right, Troy. The boy is still young.

TROY: The *boy* is thirty-four years old.

ROSE: Let's not get off into all that.

BONO: Look here . . . I got to be going. I got to be getting on. Lucille gonna be waiting.

TROY (*puts his arm around Rose*): See this woman, Bono? I love this woman. I love this woman so much it hurts. I love her so much . . . I done run out of ways of loving her. So I got to go back to basics. Don't you come by my house Monday morning talking about time to go to work . . . 'cause I'm still gonna be stroking!

ROSE: Troy! Stop it now!

BONO: I ain't paying him no mind, Rose. That ain't nothing but gin-talk. Go on, Troy. I'll see you Monday.

TROY: Don't you come by my house, nigger! I done told you what I'm gonna be doing.

(*The lights go down to black.*)

Scene II

(*The lights come up on Rose hanging up clothes. She hums and sings softly to herself. It is the following morning.*)

ROSE (*sings*): Jesus, be a fence all around me every day

Jesus, I want you to protect me as I travel on my way.

Jesus, be a fence all around me every day.

(*Troy enters from the house.*)

Jesus, I want you to protect me

As I travel on my way.

(*To Troy.*) 'Morning. You ready for breakfast? I can fix it soon as I finish hanging up these clothes?

TROY: I got the coffee on. That'll be all right. I'll just drink some of that this morning.

ROSE: That 651 hit yesterday. That's the second time this month. Miss Pearl hit for a dollar . . . seem like those that need the least always get lucky. Poor folks can't get nothing.

TROY: Them numbers don't know nobody. I don't know why you fool with them. You and Lyons both.

ROSE: It's something to do.

TROY: You ain't doing nothing but throwing your money away.

ROSE: Troy, you know I don't play foolishly. I just play a nickel here and a nickel there.

TROY: That's two nickels you done thrown away.

ROSE: Now I hit sometimes . . . that makes up for it. It always comes in handy when I do hit. I don't hear you complaining then.

TROY: I ain't complaining now. I just say it's foolish. Trying to guess out of six hundred ways which way the number gonna come. If I had all the money niggers, these Negroes, throw away on numbers for one week — just one week — I'd be a rich man.

ROSE: Well, you wishing and calling it foolish ain't gonna stop folks from playing numbers. That's one thing for sure. Besides . . . some good things come from playing numbers. Look where Pope done bought him that restaurant off of numbers.

TROY: I can't stand niggers like that. Man ain't had two dimes to rub together. He walking around with his shoes all run over bumming money for cigarettes. All right. Got lucky there and hit the numbers . . .

ROSE: Troy, I know all about it.

TROY: Had good sense, I'll say that for him. He ain't throwed his money away. I seen niggers hit the numbers and go through two thousand dollars in four days. Man bought him that restaurant down there . . . fixed it up real nice . . . and then didn't want nobody to come in it! A Negro go in there and can't get no kind of service. I seen a white fellow come in there and order a bowl of stew. Pope picked all the meat out the pot for him. Man ain't had nothing but a bowl of meat! Negro come behind him and ain't got nothing but the potatoes and carrots. Talking about what numbers do for people, you picked a wrong example. Ain't done nothing but make a worser fool out of him than he was before.

ROSE: Troy, you ought to stop worrying about what happened at work yesterday.

TROY: I ain't worried. Just told me to be down there at the Commissioner's office on Friday. Everybody think they gonna fire me. I ain't worried about them firing me. You ain't got to worry about that.

(*Pause.*)

Where's Cory? Cory in the house? (*Calls.*) Cory?

ROSE: He gone out.

TROY: Out, huh? He gone out 'cause he know I want him to help me with this fence. I know how he is. That boy scared of work.

(*Gabriel enters. He comes halfway down the alley and, hearing Troy's voice, stops.*)

TROY (*continues*): He ain't done a lick of work in his life.

ROSE: He had to go to football practice. Coach wanted them to get in a little extra practice before the season start.

TROY: I got his practice . . . running out of here before he get his chores done.

ROSE: Troy, what is wrong with you this morning? Don't nothing set right with you. Go on back in there and go to bed . . . get up on the other side.

TROY: Why something got to be wrong with me? I ain't said nothing wrong with me.

ROSE: You got something to say about everything. First it's the numbers . . . then it's the way the man runs his restaurant . . . then you done got on Cory. What's it gonna be next? Take a look up there and see if the weather suits you . . . or is it gonna be how you gonna put up the fence with the clothes hanging in the yard.

TROY: You hit the nail on the head then.

ROSE: I know you like I know the back of my hand. Go on in there and get you some coffee . . . see if that straighten you up. 'Cause you ain't right this morning.

(*Troy starts into the house and sees Gabriel. Gabriel starts singing. Troy's brother, he is seven years younger than Troy. Injured in World War II, he has a metal plate in his head. He carries an old trumpet tied around his waist and believes with every fiber of his being that he is the Archangel Gabriel. He carries a chipped basket with an assortment of discarded fruits and vegetables he has picked up in the strip district and which he attempts to sell.*)

GABRIEL (*singing*): Yes, ma'am, I got plums
You ask me how I sell them
Oh ten cents apiece
Three for a quarter
Come and buy now
'Cause I'm here today
And tomorrow I'll be gone

(*Gabriel enters.*)

Hey, Rose!

ROSE: How you doing, Gabe?

GABRIEL: There's Troy . . . Hey, Troy!

TROY: Hey, Gabe.

(*Exit into kitchen.*)

ROSE (*to Gabriel*): What you got there?

GABRIEL: You know what I got, Rose. I got fruits and vegetables.

ROSE (*looking in basket*): Where's all these plums you talking about?

GABRIEL: I ain't got no plums today, Rose. I was just

singing that. Have some tomorrow. Put me in a big order for plums. Have enough plums tomorrow for St. Peter and everybody.

(*Troy reenters from kitchen, crosses to steps.*)
(*To Rose.*)

Troy's mad at me.

TROY: I ain't mad at you. What I got to be mad at you about? You ain't done nothing to me.

GABRIEL: I just moved over to Miss Pearl's to keep out from in your way. I ain't mean no harm by it.

TROY: Who said anything about that? I ain't said anything about that.

GABRIEL: You ain't mad at me, is you?

TROY: Naw . . . I ain't mad at you, Gabe. If I was mad at you I'd tell you about it.

GABRIEL: Got me two rooms. In the basement. Got my own door too. Wanna see my key?

(*He holds up a key.*)

That's my own key! Ain't nobody else got a key like that. That's my key! My two rooms!

TROY: Well, that's good, Gabe. You got your own key . . . that's good.

ROSE: You hungry, Gabe? I was just fixing to cook Troy his breakfast.

GABRIEL: I'll take some biscuits. You got some biscuits? Did you know when I was in heaven . . . every morning me and St. Peter would sit down by the gate and eat some big fat biscuits? Oh, yeah! We had us a good time. We'd sit there and eat us them biscuits and then St. Peter would go off to sleep and tell me to wake him up when it's time to open the gates for the judgment.

ROSE: Well, come on . . . I'll make up a batch of biscuits.

(*Rose exits into the house.*)

GABRIEL: Troy . . . St. Peter got your name in the book. I seen it. It say . . . Troy Maxson. I say . . . I know him! He got the same name like what I got. That's my brother!

TROY: How many times you gonna tell me that, Gabe?

GABRIEL: Ain't got my name in the book. Don't have to have my name. I done died and went to heaven. He got your name though. One morning St. Peter was looking at his book . . . marking it up for the judgment . . . and he let me see your name. Got it in there under M. Got Rose's name . . . I ain't seen it like I seen yours . . . but I know it's in there. He got a great big book. Got everybody's name what was ever been born. That's what he told me. But I seen your name. Seen it with my own eyes.

TROY: Go on in the house there. Rose going to fix you something to eat.

GABRIEL: Oh, I ain't hungry. I done had breakfast with Aunt Jemimah. She come by and cooked me up a whole mess of flapjacks. Remember how we used to eat them flapjacks?

TROY: Go on in the house and get you something to eat now.

GABRIEL: I got to go sell my plums. I done sold some tomatoes. Got me two quarters. Wanna see?

(*He shows Troy his quarters.*)

I'm gonna save them and buy me a new horn so St. Peter can hear me when it's time to open the gates.

(*Gabriel stops suddenly. Listens.*)

Hear that? That's the hellhounds. I got to chase them out of here. Go on get out of here! Get out!

(*Gabriel exits singing.*)

Better get ready for the judgment
Better get ready for the judgment
My Lord is coming down

(*Rose enters from the house.*)

TROY: He gone off somewhere.

GABRIEL (*offstage*): Better get ready for the judgment
Better get ready for the judgment morning
Better get ready for the judgment
My God is coming down

ROSE: He ain't eating right. Miss Pearl say she can't get him to eat nothing.

TROY: What you want me to do about it, Rose? I done did everything I can for the man. I can't make him get well. Man got half his head blown away . . . what you expect?

ROSE: Seem like something ought to be done to help him.

TROY: Man don't bother nobody. He just mixed up from that metal plate he got in his head. Ain't no sense for him to go back into the hospital.

ROSE: Least he be eating right. They can help him take care of himself.

TROY: Don't nobody wanna be locked up, Rose. What you wanna lock him up for? Man go over there and fight the war . . . messin' around with them Japs, get half his head blown off . . . and they give him a lousy three thousand dollars. And I had to swoop down on that.

ROSE: Is you fixing to go into that again?

TROY: That's the only way I got a roof over my head . . . cause of that metal plate.

ROSE: Ain't no sense you blaming yourself for nothing. Gabe wasn't in no condition to manage that money. You done what was right by him. Can't no-body say you ain't done what was right by him. Look how long you took care of him . . . till he wanted to have his own place and moved over there with Miss Pearl.

TROY: That ain't what I'm saying, woman! I'm just stating the facts. If my brother didn't have that metal plate in his head . . . I wouldn't have a pot to piss in or a window to throw it out of. And I'm fifty-three years old. Now see if you can understand that!

(*Troy gets up from the porch and starts to exit the yard.*)

ROSE: Where you going off to? You been running out of here every Saturday for weeks. I thought you was gonna work on this fence?

TROY: I'm gonna walk down to Taylors'. Listen to the ball game. I'll be back in a bit. I'll work on it when I get back.

(*He exits the yard. The lights go to black.*)

Scene III

(*The lights come up on the yard. It is four hours later. Rose is taking down the clothes from the line. Cory enters carrying his football equipment.*)

ROSE: Your daddy like to had a fit with you running out of here this morning without doing your chores.

CORY: I told you I had to go to practice.

ROSE: He say you were supposed to help him with this fence.

CORY: He been saying that the last four or five Saturdays, and then he don't never do nothing but go down to Taylors'. Did you tell him about the recruiter?

ROSE: Yeah, I told him.

CORY: What he say?

ROSE: He ain't said nothing too much. You get in there and get started on your chores before he gets back. Go on and scrub down them steps before he gets back here hollering and carrying on.

CORY: I'm hungry. What you got to eat, Mama?

ROSE: Go on and get started on your chores. I got some meat loaf in there. Go on and make you a sandwich . . . and don't leave no mess in there.

(*Cory exits into the house. Rose continues to take down the clothes. Troy enters the yard and sneaks up and grabs her from behind.*)

Troy! Go on, now. You liked to scared me to death. What was the score of the game? Lucille had me on the phone and I couldn't keep up with it.

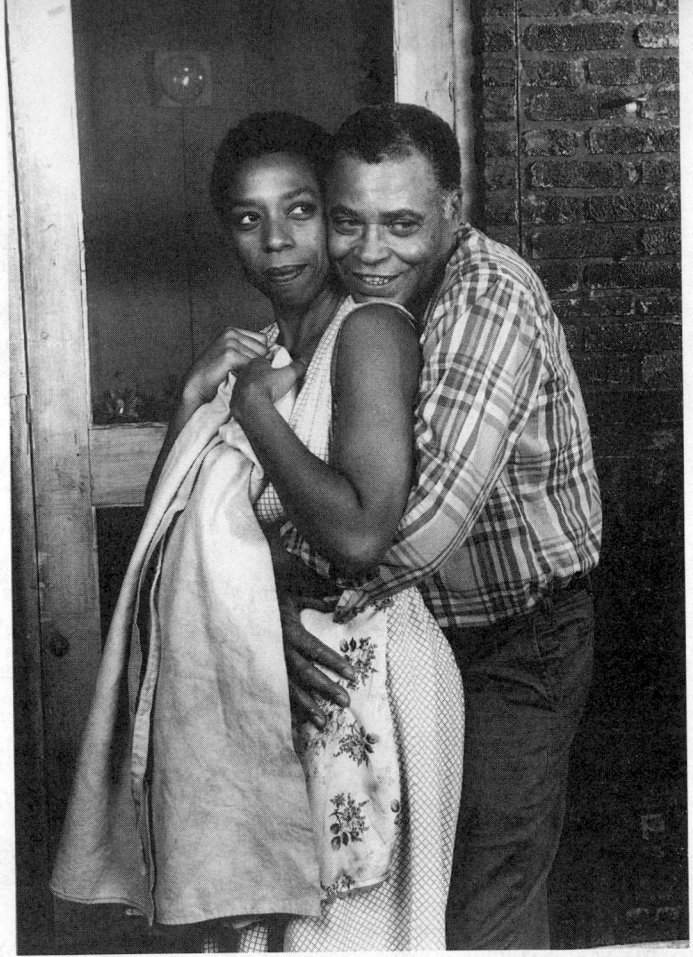

RIGHT: Lynn Thigpen and James Earl Jones in the 1987 production of *Fences*. FAR RIGHT: James Earl Jones as Troy Maxson in *Fences*. BELOW FAR RIGHT: Jones and Courtney Vance as his son Cory.

TROY: What I care about the game? Come here, woman. (*He tries to kiss her.*)

ROSE: I thought you went down Taylors' to listen to the game. Go on, Troy! You supposed to be putting up this fence.

TROY (*attempting to kiss her again*): I'll put it up when I finish with what is at hand.

ROSE: Go on, Troy. I ain't studying you.

TROY (*chasing after her*): I'm studying you . . . fixing to do my homework!

ROSE: Troy, you better leave me alone.

TROY: Where's Cory? That boy brought his butt home yet?

ROSE: He's in the house doing his chores.

TROY (*calling*): Cory! Get your butt out here, boy!

(*Rose exits into the house with the laundry. Troy goes over to the pile of wood, picks up a board, and starts sawing. Cory enters from the house.*)

TROY: You just now coming in here from leaving this morning?

CORY: Yeah, I had to go to football practice.

TROY: Yeah, what?

CORY: Yessir.

TROY: I ain't but two seconds off you noway. The garbage sitting in there overflowing . . . you ain't done none of your chores . . . and you come in here talking about "Yeah."

CORY: I was just getting ready to do my chores now, Pop . . .

TROY: Your first chore is to help me with this fence on Saturday. Everything else come after that. Now get that saw and cut them boards.

(*Cory takes the saw and begins cutting the boards. Troy continues working. There is a long pause.*)

CORY: Hey, Pop . . . why don't you buy a TV?

TROY: What I want with a TV? What I want one of them for?

CORY: Everybody got one. Earl, Ba Bra . . . Jesse!

TROY: I ain't asked you who had one. I say what I want with one?

CORY: So you can watch it. They got lots of things on

TV. Baseball games and everything. We could watch the World Series.

TROY: Yeah . . . and how much this TV cost?

CORY: I don't know. They got them on sale for around two hundred dollars.

TROY: Two hundred dollars, huh?

CORY: That ain't that much, Pop.

TROY: Naw, it's just two hundred dollars. See that roof you got over your head at night? Let me tell you something about that roof. It's been over ten years since that roof was last tarred. See now . . . the snow come this winter and sit up there on that roof like it is . . . and it's gonna seep inside. It's just gonna be a little bit . . . ain't gonna hardly notice it. Then the next thing you know, it's gonna be leaking all over the house. Then the wood rot from all that water and you gonna need a whole new roof. Now, how much you think it cost to get that roof tarred?

CORY: I don't know.

TROY: Two hundred and sixty-four dollars . . . cash money. While you thinking about a TV, I got to be thinking about the roof . . . and whatever else go wrong around here. Now if you had two hundred dollars, what would you do . . . fix the roof or buy a TV?

CORY: I'd buy a TV. Then when the roof started to leak . . . when it needed fixing . . . I'd fix it.

TROY: Where you gonna get the money from? You done spent it for a TV. You gonna sit up and watch the water run all over your brand new TV.

CORY: Aw, Pop. You got money. I know you do.

TROY: Where I got it at, huh?

CORY: You got it in the bank.

TROY: You wanna see my bankbook? You wanna see that seventy-three dollars and twenty-two cents I got sitting up in there.

CORY: You ain't got to pay for it all at one time. You can put a down payment on it and carry it on home with you.

TROY: Not me. I ain't gonna owe nobody nothing if I can help it. Miss a payment and they come and snatch it right out your house. Then what you got? Now, soon as I get two hundred dollars clear, then I'll buy a TV. Right now, as soon as I get two hundred and sixty-four dollars, I'm gonna have this roof tarred.

CORY: Aw . . . Pop!

TROY: You go on and get you two hundred dollars and buy one if ya want it. I got better things to do with my money.

CORY: I can't get no two hundred dollars. I ain't never seen two hundred dollars.

TROY: I'll tell you what . . . you get you a hundred dollars and I'll put the other hundred with it.

CORY: All right, I'm gonna show you.

TROY: You gonna show me how you can cut them boards right now.

(Cory begins to cut the boards. There is a long pause.)

CORY: The Pirates won today. That makes five in a row.

TROY: I ain't thinking about the Pirates. Got an all-white team. Got that boy . . . that Puerto Rican boy . . . Clemente. Don't even half-play him. That boy could be something if they give him a chance. Play him one day and sit him on the bench the next.

CORY: He gets a lot of chances to play.

TROY: I'm talking about playing regular. Playing every day so you can get your timing. That's what I'm talking about.

CORY: They got some white guys on the team that don't play every day. You can't play everybody at the same time.

TROY: If they got a white fellow sitting on the bench . . . you can bet your last dollar he can't play! The colored guy got to be twice as good before he get on the team. That's why I don't want you to get all tied up in them sports. Man on the team and what it get him? They got colored on the team and don't use them. Same as not having them. All them teams the same.

CORY: The Braves got Hank Aaron and Wes Covington. Hank Aaron hit two home runs today. That makes forty-three.

TROY: Hank Aaron ain't nobody. That's what you supposed to do. That's how you supposed to play the game. Ain't nothing to it. It's just a matter of timing . . . getting the right follow-through. Hell, I can hit forty-three home runs right now!

CORY: Not off no major-league pitching, you couldn't.

TROY: We had better pitching in the Negro leagues. I hit seven home runs off of Satchel Paige.° You can't get no better than that!

CORY: Sandy Koufax. He's leading the league in strikeouts.

TROY: I ain't thinking of no Sandy Koufax.

CORY: You got Warren Spahn and Lew Burdette. I bet you couldn't hit no home runs off of Warren Spahn.

TROY: I'm through with it now. You go on and cut them boards.

(Pause.)

Your mama tell me you done got recruited by a college football team? Is that right?

CORY: Yeah. Coach Zellman say the recruiter gonna be coming by to talk to you. Get you to sign the permission papers.

TROY: I thought you supposed to be working down there at the A&P. Ain't you suppose to be working down there after school?

CORY: Mr. Stawicki say he gonna hold my job for me until after the football season. Say starting next week I can work weekends.

TROY: I thought we had an understanding about this football stuff? You suppose to keep up with your chores and hold that job down at the A&P. Ain't been around here all day on a Saturday. Ain't none of your chores done . . . and now you telling me you done quit your job.

CORY: I'm gonna be working weekends.

TROY: You damn right you are! And ain't no need for nobody coming around here to talk to me about signing nothing.

CORY: Hey, Pop . . . you can't do that. He's coming all the way from North Carolina.

TROY: I don't care where he coming from. The white man ain't gonna let you get nowhere with that football noway. You go on and get your book-learning so you can work yourself up in that A&P or learn how to fix cars or build houses or something, get you a trade. That way you have something can't nobody take away from you. You go on and learn how to put your hands to some good use. Besides hauling people's garbage.

CORY: I get good grades, Pop. That's why the re-

Satchel Paige: (1906–1982), legendary black pitcher in the Negro leagues.

cruiter wants to talk with you. You got to keep up your grades to get recruited. This way I'll be going to college. I'll get a chance . . .

TROY: First you gonna get your butt down there to the A&P and get your job back.

CORY: Mr. Stawicki done already hired somebody else 'cause I told him I was playing football.

TROY: You a bigger fool than I thought . . . to let somebody take away your job so you can play some football. Where you gonna get your money to take out your girlfriend and whatnot? What kind of foolishness is that to let somebody take away your job?

CORY: I'm still gonna be working weekends.

TROY: Naw . . . naw. You getting your butt out of here and finding you another job.

CORY: Come on, Pop! I got to practice. I can't work after school and play football too. The team needs me. That's what Coach Zellman say . . .

TROY: I don't care what nobody else say. I'm the boss . . . you understand? I'm the boss around here. I do the only saying what counts.

CORY: Come on, Pop!

TROY: I asked you . . . did you understand?

CORY: Yeah . . .

TROY: What?!

CORY: Yessir.

TROY: You go on down there to that A&P and see if you can get your job back. If you can't do both . . . then you quit the football team. You've got to take the crookeds with the straights.

CORY: Yessir.

(*Pause.*)

Can I ask you a question?

TROY: What the hell you wanna ask me? Mr. Stawicki the one you got the questions for.

CORY: How come you ain't never liked me?

TROY: Liked you? Who the hell say I got to like you? What law is there say I got to like you? Wanna stand up in my face and ask a damn fool-ass question like that. Talking about liking somebody. Come here, boy, when I talk to you.

(*Cory comes over to where Troy is working. He stands slouched over and Troy shoves him on his shoulder.*)

Straighten up, goddammit! I asked you a question . . . what law is there say I got to like you?

CORY: None.

TROY: Well, all right then! Don't you eat every day?

(*Pause.*)

Answer me when I talk to you! Don't you eat every day?

CORY: Yeah.

TROY: Nigger, as long as you in my house, you put that sir on the end of it when you talk to me!

CORY: Yes . . . sir.

TROY: You eat every day.

CORY: Yessir!

TROY: Got a roof over your head.

CORY: Yessir!

TROY: Got clothes on your back.

CORY: Yessir.

TROY: Why you think that is?

CORY: Cause of you.

TROY: Ah, hell I know it's 'cause of me . . . but why do you think that is?

CORY (*hesitant*): Cause you like me.

TROY: Like you? I go out of here every morning . . . bust my butt . . . putting up with them crackers° every day . . . cause I like you? You about the biggest fool I ever saw.

(*Pause.*)

It's my job. It's my responsibility! You understand that? A man got to take care of his family. You live in my house . . . sleep you behind on my bed-clothes . . . fill you belly up with my food . . . cause you my son. You my flesh and blood. Not 'cause I like you! Cause it's my duty to take care of you. I owe a responsibility to you! Let's get this straight right here . . . before it go along any further . . . I ain't got to like you. Mr. Rand don't give me my money come payday cause he likes me. He gives me cause he owe me. I done give you everything I had to give you. I gave you your life! Me and your mama worked that out between us. And liking your black ass wasn't part of the bargain. Don't you try and go through life worrying about if somebody like you or not. You best be making sure they doing right by you. You understand what I'm saying, boy?

CORY: Yessir.

TROY: Then get the hell out of my face, and get on down to that A&P.

(*Rose has been standing behind the screen door for much of the scene. She enters as Cory exits.*)

ROSE: Why don't you let the boy go ahead and play football, Troy? Ain't no harm in that. He's just try-ing to be like you with the sports.

TROY: I don't want him to be like me! I want him to move as far away from my life as he can get. You the only decent thing that ever happened to me. I wish him that. But I don't wish him a thing else

---

crackers: White people, often used to refer disparagingly to poor whites.

from my life. I decided seventeen years ago that boy wasn't getting involved in no sports. Not after what they did to me in the sports.

ROSE: Troy, why don't you admit you was too old to play in the major leagues? For once . . . why don't you admit that?

TROY: What do you mean too old? Don't come telling me I was too old. I just wasn't the right color. Hell, I'm fifty-three years old and can do better than Selkirk's .269 right now!

ROSE: How's was you gonna play ball when you were over forty? Sometimes I can't get no sense out of you.

TROY: I got good sense, woman. I got sense enough not to let my boy get hurt over playing no sports. You been mothering that boy too much. Worried about if people like him.

ROSE: Everything that boy do . . . he do for you. He wants you to say "Good job, son." That's all.

TROY: Rose, I ain't got time for that. He's alive. He's healthy. He's got to make his own way. I made mine. Ain't nobody gonna hold his hand when he get out there in that world.

ROSE: Times have changed from when you was young, Troy. People change. The world's changing around you and you can't even see it.

TROY (*slow, methodical*): Woman . . . I do the best I can do. I come in here every Friday. I carry a sack of potatoes and a bucket of lard. You all line up at the door with your hands out. I give you the lint from my pockets. I give you my sweat and my blood. I ain't got no tears. I done spent them. We go upstairs in that room at night . . . and I fall down on you and try to blast a hole into forever. I get up Monday morning . . . find my lunch on the table. I go out. Make my way. Find my strength to carry me through to the next Friday.

(*Pause.*)

That's all I got, Rose. That's all I got to give. I can't give nothing else.

(*Troy exits into the house. The lights go down to black.*)

Scene IV

(*It is Friday. Two weeks later. Cory starts out of the house with his football equipment. The phone rings.*)

CORY (*calling*): I got it!

(*He answers the phone and stands in the screen door talking.*)

Hello? Hey, Jesse. Naw . . . I was just getting ready to leave now.

ROSE (*calling*): Cory!

CORY: I told you, man, them spikes is all tore up. You can use them if you want, but they ain't no good. Earl got some spikes.

ROSE (*calling*): Cory!

CORY (*calling to Rose*): Mam? I'm talking to Jesse.

(*Into phone.*)

When she say that? (*Pause.*) Aw, you lying, man. I'm gonna tell her you said that.

ROSE (*calling*): Cory, don't you go nowhere!

CORY: I got to go to the game, Ma!

(*Into the phone.*)

Yeah, hey, look, I'll talk to you later. Yeah, I'll meet you over Earl's house. Later. Bye, Ma.

(*Cory exits the house and starts out the yard.*)

ROSE: Cory, where you going off to? You got that stuff all pulled out and thrown all over your room.

CORY (*in the yard*): I was looking for my spikes. Jesse wanted to borrow my spikes.

ROSE: Get up there and get that cleaned up before your daddy get back in here.

CORY: I got to go to the game! I'll clean it up *when I get back.*

(*Cory exits.*)

ROSE: That's all he need to do is see that room all messed up.

(*Rose exits into the house. Troy and Bono enter the yard. Troy is dressed in clothes other than his work clothes.*)

BONO: He told him the same thing he told you. Take it to the union.

TROY: Brownie ain't got that much sense. Man wasn't thinking about nothing. He wait until I confront them on it . . . then he wanna come crying seniority.

(*Calls.*)

Hey, Rose!

BONO: I wish I could have seen Mr. Rand's face when he told you.

TROY: He couldn't get it out of his mouth! Liked to bit his tongue! When they called me down there to the Commissioner's office . . . he thought they was gonna fire me. Like everybody else.

BONO: I didn't think they was gonna fire you. I thought they was gonna put you on the warning paper.

TROY: Hey, Rose!

(*To Bono.*)

Yeah, Mr. Rand like to bit his tongue.

(*Troy breaks the seal on the bottle, takes a drink, and hands it to Bono.*)

BONO: I see you run right down to Taylors' and told that Alberta gal.

TROY (*calling*): Hey, Rose! (*To Bono.*) I told everybody. Hey, Rose! I went down there to cash my check.

ROSE (*entering from the house*): Hush all that hollering, man! I know you out here. What they say down there at the Commissioner's office?

TROY: You supposed to come when I call you, woman. Bono'll tell you that.

(*To Bono.*)

Don't Lucille come when you call her?

ROSE: Man, hush your mouth. I ain't no dog . . . talk about "come when you call me."

TROY (*puts his arm around Rose*): You hear this Bono? I had me an old dog used to get uppity like that. You say, "C'mere, Blue!" . . . and he just lay there and look at you. End up getting a stick and chasing him away trying to make him come.

ROSE: I ain't studying you and your dog. I remember you used to sing that old song.

TROY (*he sings*): Hear it ring! Hear it ring! I had a dog his name was Blue.

ROSE: Don't nobody wanna hear you sing that old song.

TROY (*sings*): You know Blue was mighty true.

ROSE: Used to have Cory running around here singing that song.

BONO: Hell, I remember that song myself.

TROY (*sings*): You know Blue was a good old dog. Blue treed a possum in a hollow log.
That was my daddy's song. My daddy made up that song.

ROSE: I don't care who made it up. Don't nobody wanna hear you sing it.

TROY (*makes a song like calling a dog*): Come here, woman.

ROSE: You come in here carrying on, I reckon they ain't fired you. What they say down there at the Commissioner's office?

TROY: Look here, Rose . . . Mr. Rand called me into his office today when I got back from talking to them people down there . . . it come from up top . . . he called me in and told me they was making me a driver.

ROSE: Troy, you kidding!

TROY: No I ain't. Ask Bono.

ROSE: Well, that's great, Troy. Now you don't have to hassle them people no more.

(*Lyons enters from the street.*)

TROY: Aw hell, I wasn't looking to see you today. I thought you was in jail. Got it all over the front page of the *Courier* about them raiding Sefus' place . . . where you be hanging out with all them thugs.

LYONS: Hey, Pop . . . that ain't got nothing to do with me. I don't go down there gambling. I go down there to sit in with the band. I ain't got nothing to do with the gambling part. They got some good music down there.

TROY: They got some rogues . . . is what they got.

LYONS: How you been, Mr. Bono? Hi, Rose.

BONO: I see where you playing down at the Crawford Grill tonight.

ROSE: How come you ain't brought Bonnie like I told you. You should have brought Bonnie with you, she ain't been over in a month of Sundays.

LYONS: I was just in the neighborhood . . . thought I'd stop by.

TROY: Here he come . . .

BONO: Your daddy got a promotion on the rubbish. He's gonna be the first colored driver. Ain't got to do nothing but sit up there and read the paper like them white fellows.

LYONS: Hey, Pop . . . if you knew how to read you'd be all right.

BONO: Naw . . . naw . . . you mean if the nigger knew how to *drive* he'd be all right. Been fighting with them people about driving and ain't even got a license. Mr. Rand know you ain't got no driver's license?

TROY: Driving ain't nothing. All you do is point the truck where you want it to go. Driving ain't nothing.

BONO: Do Mr. Rand know you ain't got no driver's license? That's what I'm talking about. I ain't asked if driving was easy. I asked if Mr. Rand know you ain't got no driver's license.

TROY: He ain't got to know. The man ain't got to know my business. Time he find out, I have two or three driver's licenses.

LYON (*going into his pocket*): Say, look here, Pop . . .

TROY: I knew it was coming. Didn't I tell you, Bono? I know what kind of "Look here, Pop" that was. The nigger fixing to ask me for some money. It's Friday night. It's my payday. All them rogues down there on the avenue . . . the ones that ain't in jail . . . and Lyons is hopping in his shoes to get down there with them.

LYONS: See, Pop . . . if you give somebody else a chance to talk sometime, you'd see that I was fixing to pay you back your ten dollars like I told you. Here . . . I told you I'd pay you when Bonnie got paid.

TROY: Naw . . . you go ahead and keep that ten dollars. Put it in the bank. The next time you feel like you wanna come by here and ask me for something . . . you go on down there and get that.

LYONS: Here's your ten dollars, Pop. I told you I don't want you to give me nothing. I just wanted to borrow ten dollars.

TROY: Naw . . . you go on and keep that for the next time you want to ask me.

LYONS: Come on, Pop . . . here go your ten dollars.

ROSE: Why don't you go on and let the boy pay you back, Troy?

LYONS: Here you go, Rose. If you don't take it I'm gonna have to hear about it for the next six months.

(*He hands her the money.*)

ROSE: You can hand yours over here too, Troy.

TROY: You see this, Bono. You see how they do me.

BONO: Yeah, Lucille do me the same way.

(*Gabriel is heard singing offstage. He enters.*)

GABRIEL: Better get ready for the Judgment! Better get ready for . . . Hey! . . . Hey! . . . There's Troy's boy!

LYONS: How are you doing, Uncle Gabe?

GABRIEL: Lyons . . . The King of the Jungle! Rose . . . hey, Rose. Got a flower for you.

(*He takes a rose from his pocket.*)

Picked it myself. That's the same rose like you is!

ROSE: That's right nice of you, Gabe.

LYONS: What you been doing, Uncle Gabe?

GABRIEL: Oh, I been chasing hellhounds and waiting on the time to tell St. Peter to open the gates.

LYONS: You been chasing hellhounds, huh? Well . . . you doing the right thing, Uncle Gabe. Somebody got to chase them.

GABRIEL: Oh, yeah . . . I know it. The devil's strong. The devil ain't no pushover. Hellhounds snipping at everybody's heels. But I got my trumpet waiting on the judgment time.

LYONS: Waiting on the Battle of Armageddon, huh?

GABRIEL: Ain't gonna be too much of a battle when God get to waving that Judgment sword. But the people's gonna have a hell of a time trying to get into heaven if them gates ain't open.

LYONS (*putting his arm around Gabriel*): You hear this, Pop. Uncle Gabe, you all right!

GABRIEL (*laughing with Lyons*): Lyons! King of the Jungle.

ROSE: You gonna stay for supper, Gabe. Want me to fix you a plate?

GABRIEL: I'll take a sandwich, Rose. Don't want no plate. Just wanna eat with my hands. I'll take a sandwich.

ROSE: How about you, Lyons? You staying? Got some short ribs cooking.

LYONS: Naw, I won't eat nothing till after we finished playing.

(*Pause.*)

You ought to come down and listen to me play, Pop.

TROY: I don't like that Chinese music. All that noise.

ROSE: Go on in the house and wash up, Gabe . . . I'll fix you a sandwich.

GABRIEL (*to Lyons, as he exits*): Troy's mad at me.

LYONS: What you mad at Uncle Gabe for, Pop.

ROSE: He thinks Troy's mad at him cause he moved over to Miss Pearl's.

TROY: I ain't mad at the man. He can live where he want to live at.

LYONS: What he move over there for? Miss Pearl don't like nobody.

ROSE: She don't mind him none. She treats him real nice. She just don't allow all that singing.

TROY: She don't mind that rent he be paying . . . that's what she don't mind.

ROSE: Troy, I ain't going through that with you no more. He's over there cause he want to have his own place. He can come and go as he please.

TROY: Hell, he could come and go as he please here. I wasn't stopping him. I ain't put no rules on him.

ROSE: It ain't the same thing, Troy. And you know it.

(*Gabriel comes to the door.*)

Now, that's the last I wanna hear about that. I don't wanna hear nothing else about Gabe and Miss Pearl. And next week . . .

GABRIEL: I'm ready for my sandwich, Rose.

ROSE: And next week . . . when that recruiter come from that school . . . I want you to sign that paper and go on and let Cory play football. Then that'll be the last I have to hear about that.

TROY (*to Rose as she exits into the house*): I ain't thinking about Cory nothing.

LYONS: What . . . Cory got recruited? What school he going to?

TROY: That boy walking around here smelling his piss . . . thinking he's grown. Thinking he's gonna do what he want, irrespective of what I say. Look here, Bono . . . I left the Commissioner's office and went down to the A&P . . . that boy ain't working down there. He lying to me. Telling me he got his job back . . . telling me he working weekends . . . telling me he working after school . . . Mr. Stawicki tell me he ain't working down there at all!

LYONS: Cory just growing up. He's just busting at the seams trying to fill out your shoes.

TROY: I don't care what he's doing. When he get to

the point where he wanna disobey me . . . then it's time for him to move on. Bono'll tell you that. I bet he ain't never disobeyed his daddy without paying the consequences.

BONO: I ain't never had a chance. My daddy came on through . . . but I ain't never knew him to see him . . . or what he had on his mind or where he went. Just moving on through. Searching out the New Land. That's what the old folks used to call it. See a fellow moving around from place to place . . . woman to woman . . . called it searching out the New Land. I can't say if he ever found it. I come along, didn't want no kids. Didn't know if I was gonna be in one place long enough to fix on them right as their daddy. I figured I was going searching too. As it turned out I been hooked up with Lucille near about as long as your daddy been with Rose. Going on sixteen years.

TROY: Sometimes I wish I hadn't known my daddy. He ain't cared nothing about no kids. A kid to him wasn't nothing. All he wanted was for you to learn how to walk so he could start you to working. When it come time for eating . . . he ate first. If there was anything left over, that's what you got. Man would sit down and eat two chickens and give you the wing.

LYONS: You ought to stop that, Pop. Everybody feed their kids. No matter how hard times is . . . everybody care about their kids. Make sure they have something to eat.

TROY: The only thing my daddy cared about was getting them bales of cotton in to Mr. Lubin. That's the only thing that mattered to him. Sometimes I used to wonder why he was living. Wonder why the devil hadn't come and got him. "Get them bales of cotton in to Mr. Lubin" and find out he owe him money . . .

LYONS: He should have just went on and left when he saw he couldn't get nowhere. That's what I would have done.

TROY: How he gonna leave with eleven kids? And where he gonna go? He ain't knew how to do nothing but farm. No, he was trapped and I think he knew it. But I'll say this for him . . . he felt a responsibility toward us. Maybe he ain't treated us the way I felt he should have . . . but without that responsibility he could have walked off and left us . . . made his own way.

BONO: A lot of them did. Back in those days what you talking about . . . they walk out their front door and just take on down one road or another and keep on walking.

LYONS: There you go! That's what I'm talking about.

BONO: Just keep on walking till you come to something else. Ain't you never heard of nobody having the walking blues? Well, that's what you call it when you just take off like that.

TROY: My daddy ain't had them walking blues! What you talking about? He stayed right there with his family. But he was just as evil as he could be. My mama couldn't stand him. Couldn't stand that evilness. She run off when I was about eight. She sneaked off one night after he had gone to sleep. Told me she was coming back for me. I ain't never seen her no more. All his women run off and left him. He wasn't good for nobody.

When my turn come to head out, I was fourteen and got to sniffing around Joe Canewell's daughter. Had us an old mule we called Greyboy. My daddy sent me out to do some plowing and I tied up Greyboy and went to fooling around with Joe Canewell's daughter. We done found us a nice little spot, got real cozy with each other. She about thirteen and we done figured we was grown anyway . . . so we down there enjoying ourselves . . . ain't thinking about nothing. We didn't know Greyboy had got loose and wandered back to the house and my daddy was looking for me. We down there by the creek enjoying ourselves when my daddy come up on us. Surprised us. He had them leather straps off the mule and commenced to whupping me like there was no tomorrow. I jumped up, mad and embarrassed. I was scared of my daddy. When he commenced to whupping on me . . . quite naturally I run to get out of the way.

(*Pause.*)

Now I thought he was mad cause I ain't done my work. But I see where he was chasing me off so he could have the gal for himself. When I see what the matter of it was, I lost all fear of my daddy. Right there is where I become a man . . . at fourteen years of age.

(*Pause.*)

Now it was my turn to run him off. I picked up them same reins that he had used on me. I picked up them reins and commenced to whupping on him. The gal jumped up and run off . . . and when my daddy turned to face me, I could see why the devil had never come to get him . . . cause he was the devil himself. I don't know what happened. When I woke up, I was laying right there by the creek, and Blue . . . this old dog we had . . . was licking my face. I thought I was blind. I couldn't see nothing. Both my eyes were swollen shut. I layed there and cried. I didn't know what I was gonna do. The only thing I knew was the time had come for me to leave my daddy's house. And right there the world suddenly got big. And it was a long time before I could cut it down to where I could handle it.

Part of that cutting down was when I got to the place where I could feel him kicking in my blood and knew that the only thing that separated us was the matter of a few years.

(*Gabriel enters from the house with a sandwich.*)

LYONS: What you got there, Uncle Gabe?

GABRIEL: Got me a ham sandwich. Rose gave me a ham sandwich.

TROY: I don't know what happened to him. I done lost touch with everybody except Gabriel. But I hope he's dead. I hope he found some peace.

LYONS: That's a heavy story, Pop. I didn't know you left home when you was fourteen.

TROY: And didn't know nothing. The only part of the world I knew was the forty-two acres of Mr. Lubin's land. That's all I knew about life.

LYONS: Fourteen's kinda young to be out on your own. (*Phone rings.*) I don't even think I was ready to be out on my own at fourteen. I don't know what I would have done.

TROY: I got up from the creek and walked on down to Mobile. I was through with farming. Figured I could do better in the city. So I walked the two hundred miles to Mobile.

LYONS: Wait a minute . . . you ain't walked no two hundred miles, Pop. Ain't nobody gonna walk no two hundred miles. You talking about some walking there.

BONO: That's the only way you got anywhere back in them days.

LYONS: Shhh. Damn if I wouldn't have hitched a ride with somebody!

TROY: Who you gonna hitch it with? They ain't had no cars and things like they got now. We talking about 1918.

ROSE (*entering*): What you all out here getting into?

TROY (*to Rose*): I'm telling Lyons how good he got it. He don't know nothing about this I'm talking.

ROSE: Lyons, that was Bonnie on the phone. She say you supposed to pick her up.

LYONS: Yeah, okay, Rose.

TROY: I walked on down to Mobile and hitched up with some of them fellows that was heading this way. Got up here and found out . . . not only couldn't you get a job . . . you couldn't find no place to live. I thought I was in freedom. Shhh. Colored folks living down there on the riverbanks in whatever kind of shelter they could find for themselves. Right down there under the Brady Street Bridge. Living in shacks made of sticks and tarpaper. Messed around there and went from bad to worse. Started stealing. First it was food. Then I

figured, hell, if I steal money I can buy me some food. Buy me some shoes too! One thing led to another. Met your mama. I was young and anxious to be a man. Met your mama and had you. What I do that for? Now I got to worry about feeding you and her. Got to steal three times as much. Went out one day looking for somebody to rob . . . that's what I was, a robber. I'll tell you the truth. I'm ashamed of it today. But it's the truth. Went to rob this fellow . . . pulled out my knife . . . and he pulled out a gun. Shot me in the chest. It felt just like somebody had taken a hot branding iron and laid it on me. When he shot me I jumped at him with my knife. They told me I killed him and they put me in the penitentiary and locked me up for fifteen years. That's where I met Bono. That's where I learned how to play baseball. Got out that place and your mama had taken you and went on to make life without me. Fifteen years was a long time for her to wait. But that fifteen years cured me of that robbing stuff. Rose'll tell you. She asked me when I met her if I had gotten all that foolishness out of my system. And I told her, "Baby, it's you and baseball all what count with me." You hear me, Bono? I meant it too. She say "Which one comes first?" I told her, "Baby, ain't no doubt it's baseball . . . but you stick and get old with me and we'll both outlive this baseball." Am I right, Rose? And it's true.

ROSE: Man, hush your mouth. You ain't said no such thing. Talking about, "Baby, you know you'll always be number one with me." That's what you was talking.

TROY: You hear that, Bono. That's why I love her.

BONO: Rose'll keep you straight. You get off the track, she'll straighten you up.

ROSE: Lyons, you better get on up and get Bonnie. She waiting on you.

LYONS (*gets up to go*): Hey, Pop, why don't you come on down to the Grill and hear me play?

TROY: I ain't going down there. I'm too old to be sitting around in them clubs.

BONO: You got to be good to play down at the Grill.

LYONS: Come on, Pop . . .

TROY: I got to get up in the morning.

LYONS: You ain't got to stay long.

TROY: Naw, I'm gonna get my supper and go on to bed.

LYONS: Well, I got to go. I'll see you again.

TROY: Don't you come around my house on my payday.

ROSE: Pick up the phone and let somebody know you coming. And bring Bonnie with you. You know I'm always glad to see her.

LYONS: Yeah, I'll do that, Rose. You take care now. See you, Pop. See you, Mr. Bono. See you, Uncle Gabe.

GABRIEL: Lyons! King of the Jungle!

(*Lyons exits.*)

TROY: Is supper ready, woman? Me and you got some business to take care of. I'm gonna tear it up too.

ROSE: Troy, I done told you now!

TROY (*puts his arm around Bono*): Aw hell, woman . . . this is Bono. Bono like family. I done known this nigger since . . . how long I done know you?

BONO: It's been a long time.

TROY: I done known this nigger since Skippy was a pup. Me and him done been through some times.

BONO: You sure right about that.

TROY: Hell, I done know him longer than I known you. And we still standing shoulder to shoulder. Hey, look here, Bono . . . a man can't ask for no more than that.

(*Drinks to him.*)

I love you, nigger.

BONO: Hell, I love you too . . . but I got to get home see my woman. You got yours in hand. I got to go get mine.

(*Bono starts to exit as Cory enters the yard, dressed in his football uniform. He gives Troy a hard, uncompromising look.*)

CORY: What you do that for, Pop?

(*He throws his helmet down in the direction of Troy.*)

ROSE: What's the matter? Cory . . . what's the matter?

CORY: Papa done went up to the school and told Coach Zellman I can't play football no more. Wouldn't even let me play the game. Told him to tell the recruiter not to come.

ROSE: Troy . . .

TROY: What you Troying me for. Yeah, I did it. And the boy know why I did it.

CORY: Why you wanna do that to me? That was the one chance I had.

ROSE: Ain't nothing wrong with Cory playing football, Troy.

TROY: The boy lied to me. I told the nigger if he wanna play football . . . to keep up his chores and hold down that job at the A&P. That was the conditions. Stopped down there to see Mr. Stawicki . . .

CORY: I can't work after school during the football season, Pop! I tried to tell you that Mr. Stawicki's holding my job for me. You don't never want to listen to nobody. And then you wanna go and do this to me!

TROY: I ain't done nothing to you. You done it to yourself.

CORY: Just cause you didn't have a chance! You just scared I'm gonna be better than you, that's all.

TROY: Come here.

ROSE: Troy . . .

(*Cory reluctantly crosses over to Troy.*)

TROY: All right! See. You done made a mistake.

CORY: I didn't even do nothing!

TROY: I'm gonna tell you what your mistake was. See . . . you swung at the ball and didn't hit it. That's strike one. See, you in the batter's box now. You swung and you missed. That's strike one. Don't you strike out!

(*Lights fade to black.*)

ACT II • Scene I

(*The following morning. Cory is at the tree hitting the ball with the bat. He tries to mimic Troy, but his swing is awkward, less sure. Rose enters from the house.*)

ROSE: Cory, I want you to help me with this cupboard.

CORY: I ain't quitting the team. I don't care what Poppa say.

ROSE: I'll talk to him when he gets back. He had to go see about your Uncle Gabe. The police done arrested him. Say he was disturbing the peace. He'll be back directly. Come on in here and help me clean out the top of this cupboard.

(*Cory exits into the house. Rose sees Troy and Bono coming down the alley.*)

Troy . . . what they say down there?

TROY: Ain't said nothing. I give them fifty dollars and they let him go. I'll talk to you about it. Where's Cory.

ROSE: He's in there helping me clean out these cupboards.

TROY: Tell him to get his butt out here.

(*Troy and Bono go over to the pile of wood. Bono picks up the saw and begins sawing.*)

TROY (*to Bono*): All they want is the money. That makes six or seven times I done went down there and got him. See me coming they stick out their hands.

BONO: Yeah. I know what you mean. That's all they care about . . . that money. They don't care about what's right.

(*Pause.*)

Nigger, why you got to go and get some hard wood? You ain't doing nothing but building a little old fence. Get you some soft pine wood. That's all you need.

TROY: I know what I'm doing. This is outside wood. You put pine wood inside the house. Pine wood is inside wood. This here is outside wood. Now you tell me where the fence is gonna be?

BONO: You don't need this wood. You can put it up with pine wood and it'll stand as long as you gonna be here looking at it.

TROY: How you know how long I'm gonna be here, nigger? Hell, I might just live forever. Live longer than old man Horsely.

BONO: That's what Magee used to say.

TROY: Magee's a damn fool. Now you tell me who you ever heard of gonna pull their own teeth with a pair of rusty pliers.

BONO: The old folks . . . my granddaddy used to pull his teeth with pliers. They ain't had no dentists for the colored folks back then.

TROY: Get clean pliers! You understand? Clean pliers! Sterilize them! Besides we ain't living back then. All Magee had to do was walk over to Doc Gold-blum's.

BONO: I see where you and that Tallahassee gal . . . that Alberta . . . I see where you all done got tight.

TROY: What you mean "got tight"?

BONO: I see where you be laughing and joking with her all the time.

TROY: I laughs and jokes with all of them, Bono. You know me.

BONO: That ain't the kind of laughing and joking I'm talking about.

(Cory enters from the house.)

CORY: How you doing, Mr. Bono?

TROY: Cory? Get that saw from Bono and cut some wood. He talking about the wood's too hard to cut. Stand back there, Jim, and let that young boy show you how it's done.

BONO: He's sure welcome to it.

(Cory takes the saw and begins to cut the wood.)

Whew-e-e! Look at that. Big old strong boy. Look like Joe Louis. Hell, must be getting old the way I'm watching that boy whip through that wood.

CORY: I don't see why Mama want a fence around the yard noways.

TROY: Damn if I know either. What the hell she keeping out with it? She ain't got nothing nobody want.

BONO: Some people build fences to keep people out . . . and other people build fences to keep people in. Rose wants to hold on to you all. She loves you.

TROY: Hell, nigger, I don't need nobody to tell me my wife loves me, Cory . . . go on in the house and see if you can find that other saw.

CORY: Where's it at?

TROY: I said find it! Look for it till you find it!

(Cory exits into the house.)

What's that supposed to mean? Wanna keep us in?

BONO: Troy . . . I done known you seem like damn near my whole life. You and Rose both. I done know both of you all for a long time. I remember when you met Rose. When you was hitting them baseball out the park. A lot of them old gals was after you then. You had the pick of the litter. When you picked Rose, I was happy for you. That was the first time I knew you had any sense. I said . . . My man Troy knows what he's doing . . . I'm gonna follow this nigger . . . he might take me somewhere. I been following you too. I done learned a whole heap of things about life watching you. I done learned how to tell where the shit lies. How to tell it from the alfalfa. You done learned me a lot of things. You showed me how to not make the same mistakes . . . to take life as it comes along and keep putting one foot in front of the other.

(Pause.)

Rose a good woman, Troy.

TROY: Hell, nigger, I know she a good woman. I been married to her for eighteen years. What you got on your mind, Bono?

BONO: I just say she a good woman. Just like I say anything. I ain't got to have nothing on my mind.

TROY: You just gonna say she a good woman and leave it hanging out there like that? Why you telling me she a good woman?

BONO: She loves you, Troy. Rose loves you.

TROY: You saying I don't measure up. That's what you trying to say. I don't measure up cause I'm seeing this other gal. I know what you trying to say.

BONO: I know what Rose means to you, Troy. I'm just trying to say I don't want to see you mess up.

TROY: Yeah, I appreciate that, Bono. If you was messing around on Lucille I'd be telling you the same thing.

BONO: Well, that's all I got to say. I just say that because I love you both.

TROY: Hell, you know me . . . I wasn't out there looking for nothing. You can't find a better woman than Rose. I know that. But seems like this woman just stuck onto me where I can't shake her loose. I done wrestled with it, tried to throw her off me . . . but she just stuck on tighter. Now she's stuck on for good.

BONO: You's in control . . . that's what you tell me all the time. You responsible for what you do.

TROY: I ain't ducking the responsibility of it. As long as it sets right in my heart . . . then I'm okay.

Cause that's all I listen to. It'll tell me right from wrong every time. And I ain't talking about doing Rose no bad turn. I love Rose. She done carried me a long ways and I love and respect her for that.

BONO: I know you do. That's why I don't want to see you hurt her. But what you gonna do when she find out? What you got then? If you try and juggle both of them . . . sooner or later you gonna drop one of them. That's common sense.

TROY: Yeah, I hear what you saying, Bono. I been trying to figure a way to work it out.

BONO: Work it out right, Troy. I don't want to be getting all up between you and Rose's business . . . but work it so it come out right.

TROY: Ah hell, I get all up between you and Lucille's business. When you gonna get that woman that refrigerator she been wanting? Don't tell me you ain't got no money now. I know who your banker is. Mellon don't need that money bad as Lucille want that refrigerator. I'll tell you that.

BONO: Tell you what I'll do . . . when you finish building this fence for Rose . . . I'll buy Lucille that refrigerator.

TROY: You done stuck your foot in your mouth now!

(Troy grabs up a board and begins to saw. Bono starts to walk out the yard.)

Hey, nigger . . . where you going?

BONO: I'm going home. I know you don't expect me to help you now. I'm protecting my money. I wanna see you put that fence up by yourself. That's what I want to see. You'll be here another six months without me.

TROY: Nigger, you ain't right.

BONO: When it comes to my money . . . I'm right as fireworks on the Fourth of July.

TROY: All right, we gonna see now. You better get out your bankbook.

(Bono exits, and Troy continues to work. Rose enters from the house.)

ROSE: What they say down there? What's happening with Gabe?

TROY: I went down there and got him out. Cost me fifty dollars. Say he was disturbing the peace. Judge set up a hearing for him in three weeks. Say to show cause why he shouldn't be recommitted.

ROSE: What was he doing that cause them to arrest him?

TROY: Some kids was teasing him and he run them off home. Say he was howling and carrying on. Some folks seen him and called the police. That's all it was.

ROSE: Well, what's you say? What'd you tell the judge?

TROY: Told him I'd look after him. It didn't make no sense to recommit the man. He stuck out his big greasy palm and told me to give him fifty dollars and take him on home.

ROSE: Where's he at now? Where'd he go off to?

TROY: He's gone on about his business. He don't need nobody to hold his hand.

ROSE: Well, I don't know. Seem like that would be the best place for him if they did put him into the hospital. I know what you're gonna say. But that's what I think would be best.

TROY: The man done had his life ruined fighting for what? And they wanna take and lock him up. Let him be free. He don't bother nobody.

ROSE: Well, everybody got their own way of looking at it I guess. Come on and get your lunch. I got a bowl of lima beans and some cornbread in the oven. Come on get something to eat. Ain't no sense you fretting over Gabe.

(Rose turns to go into the house.)

TROY: Rose . . . got something to tell you.

ROSE: Well, come on . . . wait till I get this food on the table.

TROY: Rose!

(She stops and turns around.)

I don't know how to say this.

(Pause.)

I can't explain it none. It just sort of grows on you till it gets out of hand. It starts out like a little bush . . . and the next thing you know it's a whole forest.

ROSE: Troy . . . what is you talking about?

TROY: I'm talking, woman, let me talk. I'm trying to find a way to tell you . . . I'm gonna be a daddy. I'm gonna be somebody's daddy.

ROSE: Troy . . . you're not telling me this? You're gonna be . . . what?

TROY: Rose . . . now . . . see . . .

ROSE: You telling me you gonna be somebody's daddy? You telling your *wife* this?

(Gabriel enters from the street. He carries a rose in his hand.)

GABRIEL: Hey, Troy! Hey, Rose!

ROSE: I have to wait eighteen years to hear something like this.

GABRIEL: Hey, Rose . . . I got a flower for you.

(He hands it to her.)

That's a rose. Same rose like you is.

ROSE: Thanks, Gabe.

GABRIEL: Troy, you ain't mad at me is you? Them bad mens come and put me away. You ain't mad at me is you?

TROY: Naw, Gabe, I ain't mad at you.

ROSE: Eighteen years and you wanna come with this.

GABRIEL (*takes a quarter out of his pocket*): See what I got? Got a brand new quarter.

TROY: Rose . . . it's just . . .

ROSE: Ain't nothing you can say, Troy. Ain't no way of explaining that.

GABRIEL: Fellow that give me this quarter had a whole mess of them. I'm gonna keep this quarter till it stop shining.

ROSE: Gabe, go on in the house there. I got some watermelon in the frigidaire. Go on and get you a piece.

GABRIEL: Say, Rose . . . you know I was chasing hell-hounds and them bad mens come and get me and take me away. Troy helped me. He come down there and told them they better let me go before he beat them up. Yeah, he did!

ROSE: You go on and get you a piece of watermelon, Gabe. Them bad mens is gone now.

GABRIEL: Okay, Rose . . . gonna get me some watermelon. The kind with the stripes on it.

(*Gabriel exits into the house.*)

ROSE: Why, Troy? Why? After all these years to come dragging this in to me now. It don't make no sense at your age. I could have expected this ten or fifteen years ago, but not now.

TROY: Age ain't got nothing to do with it, Rose.

ROSE: I done tried to be everything a wife should be. Everything a wife could be. Been married eighteen years and I got to live to see the day you tell me you been seeing another woman and done fathered a child by her. And you know I ain't never wanted no half nothing in my family. My whole family is half. Everybody got different fathers and mothers . . . my two sisters and my brother. Can't hardly tell who's who. Can't never sit down and talk about Papa and Mama. It's your papa and your mama and my papa and my mama . . .

TROY: Rose . . . stop it now.

ROSE: I ain't never wanted that for none of my children. And now you wanna drag your behind in here and tell me something like this.

TROY: You ought to know. It's time for you to know.

ROSE: Well, I don't want to know, goddamn it!

TROY: I can't just make it go away. It's done now. I can't wish the circumstance of the thing away.

ROSE: And you don't want to either. Maybe you want to wish me and my boy away. Maybe that's what you want? Well, you can't wish us away. I've got eighteen years of my life invested in you. You ought to have stayed upstairs in my bed where you belong.

TROY: Rose . . . now listen to me . . . we can get a handle on this thing. We can talk this out . . . come to an understanding.

ROSE: All of a sudden it's "we." Where was "we" at when you was down there rolling around with some godforsaken woman? "We" should have come to an understanding before you started making a damn fool of yourself. You're a day late and a dollar short when it comes to an understanding with me.

TROY: It's just . . . She gives me a different idea . . . a different understanding about myself. I can step out of this house and get away from the pressures and problems . . . be a different man. I ain't got to wonder how I'm gonna pay the bills or get the roof fixed. I can just be a part of myself that I ain't never been.

ROSE: What I want to know . . . is do you plan to continue seeing her. That's all you can say to me.

TROY: I can sit up in her house and laugh. Do you understand what I'm saying. I can laugh out loud . . . and it feels good. It reaches all the way down to the bottom of my shoes.

(*Pause.*)

Rose, I can't give that up.

ROSE: Maybe you ought to go on and stay down there with her . . . if she's a better woman than me.

TROY: It ain't about nobody being a better woman or nothing. Rose, you ain't the blame. A man couldn't ask for no woman to be a better woman than you've been. I'm responsible for it. I done locked myself into a pattern trying to take care of you all that I forgot about myself.

ROSE: What the hell was I there for? That was my job, not somebody else's.

TROY: Rose, I done tried all my life to live decent . . . to live a clean . . . hard . . . useful life. I tried to be a good husband to you. In every way I knew how. Maybe I come into the world backwards, I don't know. But . . . you born with two strikes on you before you come to the plate. You got to guard it closely . . . always looking for the curve ball on the inside corner. You can't afford to let none get past you. You can't afford a call strike. If you going down . . . you going down swinging. Everything lined up against you. What you gonna do. I fooled them, Rose. I bunted. When I found you and Cory and a halfway decent job . . . I was safe. Couldn't nothing touch me. I wasn't gonna strike out no more. I wasn't going back to the penitentiary. I wasn't gonna lay in the streets with a bottle of wine. I was safe. I had me a family. A job. I wasn't gonna get that last strike. I was on first looking for one of them boys to knock me in. To get me home.

ROSE: You should have stayed in my bed, Troy.

TROY: Then when I saw that gal . . . she firmed up my backbone. And I got to thinking that if I tried . . . I just might be able to steal second. Do you understand after eighteen years I wanted to steal second.

ROSE: You should have held me tight. You should have grabbed me and held on.

TROY: I stood on first base for eighteen years and I thought . . . well, goddamn it . . . go on for it!

ROSE: We're not talking about baseball! We're talking about you going off to lay in bed with another woman . . . and then bring it home to me. That's what we're talking about. We ain't talking about no baseball.

TROY: Rose, you're not listening to me. I'm trying the best I can to explain it to you. It's not easy for me to admit that I been standing in the same place for eighteen years.

ROSE: I been standing with you! I been right here with you, Troy. I got a life too. I gave eighteen years of my life to stand in the same spot with you. Don't you think I ever wanted other things? Don't you think I had dreams and hopes? What about my life? What about me. Don't you think it ever crossed my mind to want to know other men? That I wanted to lay up somewhere and forget about my responsibilities? That I wanted someone to make me laugh so I could feel good? You not the only one who's got wants and needs. But I held on to you, Troy. I took all my feelings, my wants and needs, my dreams . . . and I buried them inside you. I planted a seed and watched and prayed over it. I planted myself inside you and waited to bloom. And it didn't take me no eighteen years to find out the soil was hard and rocky and it wasn't never gonna bloom.

But I held on to you, Troy. I held you tighter. You was my husband. I owed you everything I had. Every part of me I could find to give you. And upstairs in that room . . . with the darkness falling in on me . . . I gave everything I had to try and erase the doubt that you wasn't the finest man in the world. And wherever you was going . . . I wanted to be there with you. Cause you was my husband. Cause that's the only way I was gonna survive as your wife. You always talking about what you give . . . and what you don't have to give. But you take too. You take . . . and don't even know nobody's giving!

(Rose turns to exit into the house; Troy grabs her arm.)

TROY: You say I take and don't give!

ROSE: Troy! You're hurting me!

TROY: You say I take and don't give.

ROSE: Troy . . . you're hurting my arm! Let go!

TROY: I done give you everything I got. Don't you tell that lie on me.

ROSE: Troy!

TROY: Don't you tell that lie on me!

(Cory enters from the house.)

CORY: Mama!

ROSE: Troy. You're hurting me.

TROY: Don't you tell me about no taking and giving.

(Cory comes up behind Troy and grabs him. Troy, surprised, is thrown off balance just as Cory throws a glancing blow that catches him on the chest and knocks him down. Troy is stunned, as is Cory.)

ROSE: Troy. Troy. No!

(Troy gets to his feet and starts at Cory.)

Troy . . . no. Please! Troy!

(Rose pulls on Troy to hold him back. Troy stops himself.)

TROY *(to Cory):* All right. That's strike two. You stay away from around me, boy. Don't you strike out. You living with a full count. Don't you strike out.

(Troy exits out the yard as the lights go down.)

Scene II

(It is six months later, early afternoon. Troy enters from the house and starts to exit the yard. Rose enters from the house.)

ROSE: Troy, I want to talk to you.

TROY: All of a sudden, after all this time, you want to talk to me, huh? You ain't wanted to talk to me for months. You ain't wanted to talk to me last night. You ain't wanted no part of me then. What you wanna talk to me about now?

ROSE: Tomorrow's Friday.

TROY: I know what day tomorrow is. You think I don't know tomorrow's Friday? My whole life I ain't done nothing but look to see Friday coming and you got to tell me it's Friday.

ROSE: I want to know if you're coming home.

TROY: I always come home, Rose. You know that. There ain't never been a night I ain't come home.

ROSE: That ain't what I mean . . . and you know it. I want to know if you're coming straight home after work.

TROY: I figure I'd cash my check . . . hang out at Taylors' with the boys . . . maybe play a game of checkers . . .

ROSE: Troy, I can't live like this. I won't live like this. You livin' on borrowed time with me. It's been going on six months now you ain't been coming home.

TROY: I be here every night. Every night of the year. That's 365 days.

ROSE: I want you to come home tomorrow after work.

TROY: Rose . . . I don't mess up my pay. You know that now. I take my pay and I give it to you. I don't have no money but what you give me back. I just want to have a little time to myself . . . a little time to enjoy life.

ROSE: What about me? When's my time to enjoy life?

TROY: I don't know what to tell you, Rose. I'm doing the best I can.

ROSE: You ain't been home from work but time enough to change your clothes and run out . . . and you wanna call that the best you can do?

TROY: I'm going over to the hospital to see Alberta. She went into the hospital this afternoon. Look like she might have the baby early. I won't be gone long.

ROSE: Well, you ought to know. They went over to Miss Pearl's and got Gabe today. She said you told them to go ahead and lock him up.

TROY: I ain't said no such thing. Whoever told you that is telling a lie. Pearl ain't doing nothing but telling a big fat lie.

ROSE: She ain't had to tell me. I read it on the papers.

TROY: I ain't told them nothing of the kind.

ROSE: I saw it right there on the papers.

TROY: What it say, huh?

ROSE: It said you told them to take him.

TROY: Then they screwed that up, just the way they screw up everything. I ain't worried about what they got on the paper.

ROSE: Say the government send part of his check to the hospital and the other part to you.

TROY: I ain't got nothing to do with that if that's the way it works. I ain't made up the rules about how it work.

ROSE: You did Gabe just like you did Cory. You wouldn't sign the paper for Cory . . . but you signed for Gabe. You signed that paper.

(The telephone is heard ringing inside the house.)

TROY: I told you I ain't signed nothing, woman! The only thing I signed was the release form. Hell, I can't read, I don't know what they had on that paper! I ain't signed nothing about sending Gabe away.

ROSE: I said send him to the hospital . . . you said let him be free . . . now you done went down there

and signed him to the hospital for half his money. You went back on yourself, Troy. You gonna have to answer for that.

TROY: See now . . . you been over there talking to Miss Pearl. She done got mad cause she ain't getting Gabe's rent money. That's all it is. She's liable to say anything.

ROSE: Troy, I seen where you signed the paper.

TROY: You ain't seen nothing I signed. What she doing got papers on my brother anyway? Miss Pearl telling a big fat lie. And I'm gonna tell her about it too! You ain't seen nothing I signed. Say . . . you ain't seen nothing I signed.

(Rose exits into the house to answer the telephone. Presently she returns.)

ROSE: Troy . . . that was the hospital. Alberta had the baby.

TROY: What she have? What is it?

ROSE: It's a girl.

TROY: I better get on down to the hospital to see her.

ROSE: Troy . . .

TROY: Rose . . . I got to go see her now. That's only right . . . what's the matter . . . the baby's all right, ain't it?

ROSE: Alberta died having the baby.

TROY: Died . . . you say she's dead? Alberta's dead?

ROSE: They said they done all they could. They couldn't do nothing for her.

TROY: The baby? How's the baby?

ROSE: They say it's healthy. I wonder who's gonna bury her.

TROY: She had family, Rose. She wasn't living in the world by herself.

ROSE: I know she wasn't living in the world by herself.

TROY: Next thing you gonna want to know if she had any insurance.

ROSE: Troy, you ain't got to talk like that.

TROY: That's the first thing that jumped out your mouth. "Who's gonna bury her?" Like I'm fixing to take on that task for myself.

ROSE: I am your wife. Don't push me away.

TROY: I ain't pushing nobody away. Just give me some space. That's all. Just give me some room to breathe.

(Rose exits into the house. Troy walks about the yard.)

TROY (with a quiet rage that threatens to consume him): All right . . . Mr. Death. See now . . . I'm gonna tell you what I'm gonna do. I'm gonna take and build me a fence around this yard. See? I'm gonna build me a fence around what belongs to me. And then I want you to stay on the other side.

See? You stay over there until you're ready for me. Then you come on. Bring your army. Bring your sickle. Bring your wrestling clothes. I ain't gonna fall down on my vigilance this time. You ain't gonna sneak up on me no more. When you ready for me . . . when the top of your list say Troy Maxson . . . that's when you come around here. You come up and knock on the front door. Ain't nobody else got nothing to do with this. This is between you and me. Man to man. You stay on the other side of that fence until you ready for me. Then you come up and knock on the front door. Anytime you want. I'll be ready for you.

(The lights go down to black.)

Scene III

(The lights come up on the porch. It is late evening three days later. Rose sits listening to the ball game waiting for Troy. The final out of the game is made and Rose switches off the radio. Troy enters the yard carrying an infant wrapped in blankets. He stands back from the house and calls.)

(Rose enters and stands on the porch. There is a long, awkward silence, the weight of which grows heavier with each passing second.)

TROY: Rose . . . I'm standing here with my daughter in my arms. She ain't but a wee bittie little old thing. She don't know nothing about grownups' business. She innocent . . . and she ain't got no mama.

ROSE: What you telling me for, Troy?

(She turns and exits into the house.)

TROY: Well . . . I guess we'll just sit out here on the porch.

(He sits down on the porch. There is an awkward indelicateness about the way he handles the baby. His largeness engulfs and seems to swallow it. He speaks loud enough for Rose to hear.)

A man's got to do what's right for him. I ain't sorry for nothing I done. It felt right in my heart.

(To the baby.)

What you smiling at? Your daddy's a big man. Got these great big old hands. But sometimes he's scared. And right now your daddy's scared cause we sitting out here and ain't got no home. Oh, I been homeless before. I ain't had no little baby with me. But I been homeless. You just be out on the road by your lonesome and you see one of

them trains coming and you just kinda go like this . . .

(He sings as a lullaby.)

Please, Mr. Engineer let a man ride the line
Please, Mr. Engineer let a man ride the line
I ain't got no ticket please let me ride the blinds

(Rose enters from the house. Troy hearing her steps behind him, stands and faces her.)

She's my daughter, Rose. My own flesh and blood. I can't deny her no more than I can deny them boys.

(Pause.)

You and them boys is my family. You and them and this child is all I got in the world. So I guess what I'm saying is . . . I'd appreciate it if you'd help me take care of her.

ROSE: Okay, Troy . . . you're right. I'll take care of your baby for you . . . cause . . . like you say . . . she's innocent . . . and you can't visit the sins of the father upon the child. A motherless child has got a hard time.

(She takes the baby from him.)

From right now . . . this child got a mother. But you a womanless man.

(Rose turns and exits into the house with the baby. Lights go down to black.)

Scene IV

(It is two months later. Lyons enters from the street. He knocks on the door and calls.)

LYONS: Hey, Rose! *(Pause.)* Rose!

ROSE *(from inside the house)*: Stop that yelling. You gonna wake up Raynell. I just got her to sleep.

LYONS: I just stopped by to pay Papa this twenty dollars I owe him. Where's Papa at?

ROSE: He should be here in a minute. I'm getting ready to go down to the church. Sit down and wait on him.

LYONS: I got to go pick up Bonnie over her mother's house.

ROSE: Well, sit it down there on the table. He'll get it.

LYONS *(enters the house and sets the money on the table)*: Tell Papa I said thanks. I'll see you again.

ROSE: All right, Lyons. We'll see you.

(Lyons starts to exit as Cory enters.)

CORY: Hey, Lyons.

LYONS: What's happening, Cory. Say man, I'm sorry I

missed your graduation. You know I had a gig and couldn't get away. Otherwise, I would have been there, man. So what you doing?

CORY: I'm trying to find a job.

LYONS: Yeah I know how that go, man. It's rough out here. Jobs are scarce.

CORY: Yeah, I know.

LYONS: Look here, I got to run. Talk to Papa . . . he know some people. He'll be able to help get you a job. Talk to him . . . see what he say.

CORY: Yeah . . . all right, Lyons.

LYONS: You take care. I'll talk to you soon. We'll find some time to talk.

(*Lyons exits the yard. Cory wanders over to the tree, picks up the bat, and assumes a batting stance. He studies an imaginary pitcher and swings. Dissatisfied with the result, he tries again. Troy enters. They eye each other for a beat. Cory puts the bat down and exits the yard. Troy starts into the house as Rose exits with Raynell. She is carrying a cake.*)

TROY: I'm coming in and everybody's going out.

ROSE: I'm taking this cake down to the church for the bake sale. Lyons was by to see you. He stopped by to pay you your twenty dollars. It's laying in there on the table.

TROY (*going into his pocket*): Well . . . here go this money.

ROSE: Put it in there on the table, Troy. I'll get it.

TROY: What time you coming back?

ROSE: Ain't no use in you studying me. It don't matter what time I come back.

TROY: I just asked you a question, woman. What's the matter . . . can't I ask you a question?

ROSE: Troy, I don't want to go into it. Your dinner's in there on the stove. All you got to do is heat it up. And don't you be eating the rest of them cakes in there. I'm coming back for them. We having a bake sale at the church tomorrow.

(*Rose exits the yard. Troy sits down on the steps, takes a pint bottle from his pocket, opens it, and drinks. He begins to sing.*)

TROY: Hear it ring! Hear it ring!
    Had an old dog his name was Blue
    You know Blue was mighty true
    You know Blue as a good old dog
    Blue trees a possum in a hollow log
    You know from that he was a good old dog

(*Bono enters the yard.*)

BONO: Hey, Troy.

TROY: Hey, what's happening, Bono?

BONO: I just thought I'd stop by to see you.

TROY: What you stop by and see me for? You ain't stopped by in a month of Sundays. Hell, I must owe you money or something.

BONO: Since you got your promotion I can't keep up with you. Used to see you every day. Now I don't even know what route you working.

TROY: They keep switching me around. Got me out in Greentree now . . . hauling white folks' garbage.

BONO: Greentree, huh? You lucky, at least you ain't got to be lifting them barrels. Damn if they ain't getting heavier. I'm gonna put in my two years and call it quits.

TROY: I'm thinking about retiring myself.

BONO: You got it easy. You can *drive* for another five years.

TROY: It ain't the same, Bono. It ain't like working the back of the truck. Ain't got nobody to talk to . . . feel like you working by yourself. Naw, I'm thinking about retiring. How's Lucille?

BONO: She all right. Her arthritis get to acting up on her sometime. Saw Rose on my way in. She going down to the church, huh?

TROY: Yeah, she took up going down there. All them preachers looking for somebody to fatten their pockets.

(*Pause.*)

    Got some gin here.

BONO: Naw, thanks. I just stopped by to say hello.

TROY: Hell, nigger . . . you can take a drink. I ain't never known you to say no to a drink. You ain't got to work tomorrow.

BONO: I just stopped by. I'm fixing to go over to Skinner's. We got us a domino game going over his house every Friday.

TROY: Nigger, you can't play no dominoes. I used to whup you four games out of five.

BONO: Well, that learned me. I'm getting better.

TROY: Yeah? Well, that's all right.

BONO: Look here . . . I got to be getting on. Stop by sometime, huh?

TROY: Yeah, I'll do that, Bono. Lucille told Rose you bought her a new refrigerator.

BONO: Yeah, Rose told Lucille you had finally built your fence . . . so I figured we'd call it even.

TROY: I knew you would.

BONO: Yeah . . . okay. I'll be talking to you.

TROY: Yeah, take care, Bono. Good to see you. I'm gonna stop over.

BONO: Yeah. Okay, Troy.

(*Bono exits. Troy drinks from the bottle.*)

TROY: Old Blue died and I dig his grave
    Let him down with a golden chain
    Every night when I hear old Blue bark

I know Blue treed a possum in Noah's Ark.
Hear it ring! Hear it ring!

(*Cory enters the yard. They eye each other for a beat. Troy is sitting in the middle of the steps. Cory walks over.*)

CORY: I got to get by.

TROY: Say what? What's you say?

CORY: You in my way. I got to get by.

TROY: You got to get by where? This is my house. Bought and paid for. In full. Took me fifteen years. And if you wanna go in my house and I'm sitting on the steps . . . you say excuse me. Like your mama taught you.

CORY: Come on, Pop . . . I got to get by.

(*Cory starts to maneuver his way past Troy. Troy grabs his leg and shoves him back.*)

TROY: You just gonna walk over top of me?

CORY: I live here too!

TROY (*advancing toward him*): You just gonna walk over top of me in my own house?

CORY: I ain't scared of you.

TROY: I ain't asked if you was scared of me. I asked you if you was fixing to walk over top of me in my own house? That's the question. You ain't gonna say excuse me? You just gonna walk over top of me?

CORY: If you wanna put it like that.

TROY: How else am I gonna put it?

CORY: I was walking by you to go into the house cause you sitting on the steps drunk, singing to yourself. You can put it like that.

TROY: Without saying excuse me???

(*Cory doesn't respond.*)

I asked you a question. Without saying excuse me???

CORY: I ain't got to say excuse me to you. You don't count around here no more.

TROY: Oh, I see . . . I don't count around here no more. You ain't got to say excuse me to your daddy. All of a sudden you done got so grown that your daddy don't count around here no more . . . Around here in his own house and yard that he done paid for with the sweat of his brow. You done got so grown to where you gonna take over. You gonna take over my house. Is that right? You gonna wear my pants. You gonna go in there and stretch out on my bed. You ain't got to say excuse me cause I don't count around here no more. Is that right?

CORY: That's right. You always talking this dumb stuff. Now, why don't you just get out my way.

TROY: I guess you got someplace to sleep and some-

thing to put in your belly. You got that, huh? You got that? That's what you need. You got that, huh?

CORY: You don't know what I got. You ain't got to worry about what I got.

TROY: You right! You one hundred percent right! I done spent the last seventeen years worrying about what you got. Now it's your turn, see? I'll tell you what to do. You grown . . . we done established that. You a man. Now, let's see you act like one. Turn your behind around and walk out this yard. And when you get out there in the alley . . . you can forget about this house. See? 'Cause this is my house. You go on and be a man and get your own house. You can forget about this. 'Cause this is mine. You go on and get yours 'cause I'm through with doing for you.

CORY: You talking about what you did for me . . . what'd you ever give me?

TROY: Them feet and bones! That pumping heart, nigger! I give you more than anybody else is ever gonna give you.

CORY: You ain't never gave me nothing! You ain't never done nothing but hold me back. Afraid I was gonna be better than you. All you ever did was try and make me scared of you. I used to tremble every time you called my name. Every time I heard your footsteps in the house. Wondering all the time . . . what's Papa gonna say if I do this? . . . What's he gonna say if I do that? . . . What's Papa gonna say if I turn on the radio? And Mama, too . . . she tries . . . but she's scared of you.

TROY: You leave your mama out of this. She ain't got nothing to do with this.

CORY: I don't know how she stand you . . . after what you did to her.

TROY: I told you to leave your mama out of this!

(*He advances toward Cory.*)

CORY: What you gonna do . . . give me a whupping? You can't whup me no more. You're too old. You just an old man.

TROY (*shoves him on his shoulder*): Nigger! That's what you are. You just another nigger on the street to me!

CORY: You crazy! You know that?

TROY: Go on now! You got the devil in you. Get on away from me!

CORY: You just a crazy old man . . . talking about I got the devil in me.

TROY: Yeah, I'm crazy! If you don't get on the other side of that yard . . . I'm gonna show you how crazy I am! Go on . . . get the hell out of my yard.

CORY: It ain't your yard. You took Uncle Gabe's money he got from the army to buy this house and then you put him out.

TROY (*Troy advances on Cory*): Get your black ass out of my yard!

(*Troy's advance backs Cory up against the tree. Cory grabs up the bat.*)

CORY: I ain't going nowhere! Come on . . . put me out! I ain't scared of you.
TROY: That's my bat!
CORY: Come on!
TROY: Put my bat down!
CORY: Come on, put me out.

(*Cory swings at Troy, who backs across the yard.*)

What's the matter? You so bad . . . put me out!

(*Troy advances toward Cory.*)

CORY (*backing up*): Come on! Come on!
TROY: You're gonna have to use it! You wanna draw that bat back on me . . . you're gonna have to use it.
CORY: Come on! . . . Come on!

(*Cory swings the bat at Troy a second time. He misses. Troy continues to advance toward him.*)

TROY: You're gonna have to kill me! You wanna draw that bat back on me. You're gonna have to kill me.

(*Cory, backed up against the tree, can go no farther. Troy taunts him. He sticks out his head and offers him a target.*)

Come on! Come on!

(*Cory is unable to swing the bat. Troy grabs it.*)

TROY: Then I'll show you.

(*Cory and Troy struggle over the bat. The struggle is fierce and fully engaged. Troy ultimately is the stronger and takes the bat from Cory and stands over him ready to swing. He stops himself.*)

Go on and get away from around my house.

(*Cory, stung by his defeat, picks himself up, walks slowly out of the yard and up the alley.*)

CORY: Tell Mama I'll be back for my things.
TROY: They'll be on the other side of that fence.

(*Cory exits.*)

TROY: I can't taste nothing. Helluljah! I can't taste nothing no more. (*Troy assumes a batting posture and begins to taunt Death, the fastball on the outside corner.*) Come on! It's between you and me now! Come on! Anytime you want! Come on! I be ready for you . . . but I ain't gonna be easy.

(*The lights go down on the scene.*)

Scene V

(*The time is 1965. The lights come up in the yard. It is the morning of Troy's funeral. A funeral plaque with a light hangs beside the door. There is a small garden plot off to the side. There is noise and activity in the house as Rose, Gabriel, and Bono have gathered. The door opens and Raynell, seven years old, enters dressed in a flannel nightgown. She crosses to the garden and pokes around with a stick. Rose calls from the house.*)

ROSE: Raynell!
RAYNELL: Mam?
ROSE: What you doing out there?
RAYNELL: Nothing.

(*Rose comes to the door.*)

ROSE: Girl, get in here and get dressed. What you doing?
RAYNELL: Seeing if my garden growed.
ROSE: I told you it ain't gonna grow overnight. You got to wait.
RAYNELL: It don't look like it never gonna grow. Dag!
ROSE: I told you a watched pot never boils. Get in here and get dressed.
RAYNELL: This ain't even no pot, Mama.
ROSE: You just have to give it a chance. It'll grow. Now you come on and do what I told you. We got to be getting ready. This ain't no morning to be playing around. You hear me?
RAYNELL: Yes, mam.

(*Rose exits into the house. Raynell continues to poke at her garden with a stick. Cory enters. He is dressed in a Marine corporal's uniform, and carries a duffel bag. His posture is that of a military man, and his speech has a clipped sternness.*)

CORY (*to Raynell*): Hi.

(*Pause.*)

I bet your name is Raynell.
RAYNELL: Uh huh.
CORY: Is your mama home?

(*Raynell runs up on the porch and calls through the screen door.*)

RAYNELL: Mama . . . there's some man out here. Mama?

(*Rose comes to the door.*)

ROSE: Cory? Lord have mercy! Look here, you all!

(*Rose and Cory embrace in a tearful reunion as Bono and Lyons enter from the house dressed in funeral clothes.*)

BONO: Aw, looka here . . .

ROSE: Done got all grown up!

CORY: Don't cry, Mama. What you crying about?

ROSE: I'm just so glad you made it.

CORY: Hey Lyons. How you doing, Mr. Bono.

(*Lyons goes to embrace Cory.*)

LYONS: Look at you, man. Look at you. Don't he look good, Rose. Got them Corporal stripes.

ROSE: What took you so long.

CORY: You know how the Marines are, Mama. They got to get all their paperwork straight before they let you do anything.

ROSE: Well, I'm sure glad you made it. They let Lyons come. Your Uncle Gabe's still in the hospital. They don't know if they gonna let him out or not. I just talked to them a little while ago.

LYONS: A Corporal in the United States Marines.

BONO: Your daddy knew you had it in you. He used to tell me all the time.

LYONS: Don't he look good, Mr. Bono?

BONO: Yeah, he remind me of Troy when I first met him.

(*Pause.*)

Say, Rose, Lucille's down at the church with the choir. I'm gonna go down and get the pallbearers lined up. I'll be back to get you all.

ROSE: Thanks, Jim.

CORY: See you, Mr. Bono.

LYONS (*with his arm around Raynell*): Cory . . . look at Raynell. Ain't she precious? She gonna break a whole lot of hearts.

ROSE: Raynell, come and say hello to your brother. This is your brother, Cory. You remember Cory.

RAYNELL: No, Mam.

CORY: She don't remember me, Mama.

ROSE: Well, we talk about you. She heard us talk about you. (*To Raynell.*) This is your brother, Cory. Come on and say hello.

RAYNELL: Hi.

CORY: Hi. So you're Raynell. Mama told me a lot about you.

ROSE: You all come on into the house and let me fix you some breakfast. Keep up your strength.

CORY: I ain't hungry, Mama.

LYONS: You can fix me something, Rose. I'll be in there in a minute.

ROSE: Cory, you sure you don't want nothing. I know they ain't feeding you right.

CORY: No, Mama . . . thanks. I don't feel like eating. I'll get something later.

ROSE: Raynell . . . get on upstairs and get that dress on like I told you.

(*Rose and Raynell exit into the house.*)

LYONS: So . . . I hear you thinking about getting married.

CORY: Yeah, I done found the right one, Lyons. It's about time.

LYONS: Me and Bonnie been split up about four years now. About the time Papa retired. I guess she just got tired of all them changes I was putting her through.

(*Pause.*)

I always knew you was gonna make something out yourself. Your head was always in the right direction. So . . . you gonna stay in . . . make it a career . . . put in your twenty years?

CORY: I don't know. I got six already, I think that's enough.

LYONS: Stick with Uncle Sam and retire early. Ain't nothing out here. I guess Rose told you what happened with me. They got me down the workhouse. I thought I was being slick cashing other people's checks.

CORY: How much time you doing?

LYONS: They give me three years. I got that beat now. I ain't got but nine more months. It ain't so bad. You learn to deal with it like anything else. You got to take the crookeds with the straights. That's what Papa used to say. He used to say that when he struck out. I seen him strike out three times in a row . . . and the next time up he hit the ball over the grandstand. Right out there in Homestead Field. He wasn't satisfied hitting in the seats . . . he want to hit it over everything! After the game he had two hundred people standing around waiting to shake his hand. You got to take the crookeds with the straights. Yeah, Papa was something else.

CORY: You still playing?

LYONS: Cory . . . you know I'm gonna do that. There's some fellows down there we got us a band . . . we gonna try and stay together when we get out . . . but yeah, I'm still playing. It still helps me to get out of bed in the morning. As long as it do that I'm gonna be right there playing and trying to make some sense out of it.

ROSE (*calling*): Lyons, I got these eggs in the pan.

LYONS: Let me go on and get these eggs, man. Get ready to go bury Papa.

(*Pause.*)

How you doing? You doing all right?

(*Cory nods. Lyons touches him on the shoulder and they share a moment of silent grief. Lyons exits into the house. Cory wanders about the yard. Raynell enters.*)

RAYNELL: Hi.

CORY: Hi.

RAYNELL: Did you used to sleep in my room?

CORY: Yeah . . . that used to be my room.

RAYNELL: That's what Papa call it. "Cory's room." It got your football in the closet.

(*Rose comes to the door.*)

ROSE: Raynell, get in there and get them good shoes on.

RAYNELL: Mama, can't I wear these. Them other one hurt my feet.

ROSE: Well, they just gonna have to hurt your feet for a while. You ain't said they hurt your feet when you went down to the store and got them.

RAYNELL: They didn't hurt then. My feet done got bigger.

ROSE: Don't you give me no backtalk now. You get in there and get them shoes on.

(*Raynell exits into the house.*)

Ain't too much changed. He still got that piece of rag tied to that tree. He was out here swinging that bat. I was just ready to go back in the house. He swung that bat and then he just fell over. Seem like he swung it and stood there with this grin on his face . . . and then he just fell over. They carried him on down to the hospital, but I knew there wasn't no need . . . why don't you come on in the house?

CORY: Mama . . . I got something to tell you. I don't know how to tell you this . . . but I've got to tell you . . . I'm not going to Papa's funeral.

ROSE: Boy, hush your mouth. That's your daddy you talking about. I don't want hear that kind of talk this morning. I done raised you to come to this? You standing there all healthy and grown talking about you ain't going to your daddy's funeral?

CORY: Mama . . . listen . . .

ROSE: I don't want to hear it, Cory. You just get that thought out of your head.

CORY: I can't drag Papa with me everywhere I go. I've got to say no to him. One time in my life I've got to say no.

ROSE: Don't nobody have to listen to nothing like that. I know you and your daddy ain't seen eye to eye, but I ain't got to listen to that kind of talk this morning. Whatever was between you and your daddy . . . the time has come to put it aside. Just take it and set it over there on the shelf and forget about it. Disrespecting your daddy ain't gonna make you a man, Cory. You got to find a way to come to that on your own. Not going to your daddy's funeral ain't gonna make you a man.

CORY: The whole time I was growing up . . . living in his house . . . Papa was like a shadow that followed you everywhere. It weighed on you and sunk into your flesh. It would wrap around you and lay there until you couldn't tell which one was you anymore. That shadow digging in your flesh. Trying to crawl in. Trying to live through you. Everywhere I looked, Troy Maxson was staring back at me . . . hiding under the bed . . . in the closet. I'm just saying I've got to find a way to get rid of that shadow, Mama.

ROSE: You just like him. You got him in you good.

CORY: Don't tell me that, Mama.

ROSE: You Troy Maxson all over again.

CORY: I don't want to be Troy Maxson. I want to be me.

ROSE: You can't be nobody but who you are, Cory. That shadow wasn't nothing but you growing into yourself. You either got to grow into it or cut it down to fit you. But that's all you got to make life with. That's all you got to measure yourself against that world out there. Your daddy wanted you to be everything he wasn't . . . and at the same time he tried to make you into everything he was. I don't know if he was right or wrong . . . but I do know he meant to do more good than he meant to do harm. He wasn't always right. Sometimes when he touched he bruised. And sometimes when he took me in his arms he cut.

When I first met your daddy I thought . . . Here is a man I can lay down with and make a baby. That's the first thing I thought when I seen him. I was thirty years old and had done seen my share of men. But when he walked up to me and said "I can dance a waltz that'll make you dizzy," I thought, Rose Lee, here is a man that you can open yourself up to and be filled to bursting. Here is a man that can fill all them empty spaces you been tipping around the edges of. One of them empty spaces was being somebody's mother.

I married your daddy and settled down to cooking his supper and keeping clean sheets on the bed. When your daddy walked through the house he was so big he filled it up. That was my first mistake. Not to make him leave some room for me. For my part in the matter. But at that time I wanted that. I wanted a house that I could sing in. And that's what your daddy gave me. I didn't know to keep up his strength I had to give up little pieces of mine. I did that. I took on his life as mine and mixed up the pieces so that you couldn't hardly tell which was which anymore. It was my choice. It was my life and I didn't have to live it like that. But that's what life offered me in the way of being a woman and I took it. I grabbed hold of it with both hands.

By the time Raynell came into the house, me

and your daddy had done lost touch with one another. I didn't want to make my blessing off of nobody's misfortune . . . but I took on to Raynell like she was all them babies I had wanted and never had.

(*The phone rings.*)

Like I'd been blessed to relive a part of my life. And if the Lord see fit to keep up my strength . . . I'm gonna do her just like your daddy did you . . . I'm gonna give her the best of what's in me.

RAYNELL (*entering, still with her old shoes*): Mama . . . Reverend Tollivier on the phone.

(*Rose exits into the house.*)

RAYNELL: Hi.

CORY: Hi.

RAYNELL: You in the Army or the Marines?

CORY: Marines.

RAYNELL: Papa said it was the Army. Did you know Blue?

CORY: Blue? Who's Blue?

RAYNELL: Papa's dog what he sing about all the time.

CORY (*singing*): Hear it ring! Hear it ring!
I had a dog his name was Blue
You know Blue was mighty true
You know Blue was a good old dog
Blue treed a possum in a hollow log
You know from that he was a good old dog.
Hear it ring! Hear it ring!

(*Raynell joins in singing.*)

CORY AND RAYNELL: Blue treed a possum out on a limb
Blue looked at me and I looked at him
Grabbed that possum and put him in a sack
Blue stayed there till I came back
Old Blue's feets was big and round
Never allowed a possum to touch the ground.

Old Blue died and I dug his grave
I dug his grave with a silver spade
Let him down with a golden chain
And every night I call his name
Go on Blue, you good dog you
Go on Blue, you good dog you

RAYNELL: Blue laid down and died like a man
Blue laid down and died . . .

BOTH: Blue laid down and died like a man
Now he's treeing possums in the Promised Land

I'm gonna tell you this to let you know
Blue's gone where the good dogs go
When I hear old Blue bark
When I hear old Blue bark
Blue treed a possum in Noah's Ark
Blue treed a possum in Noah's Ark.

(*Rose comes to the screen door.*)

ROSE: Cory, we gonna be ready to go in a minute.

CORY (*to Raynell*): You go on in the house and change them shoes like Mama told you so we can go to Papa's funeral.

RAYNELL: Okay, I'll be back.

(*Raynell exits into the house. Cory gets up and crosses over to the tree. Rose stands in the screen door watching him. Gabriel enters from the alley.*)

GABRIEL (*calling*): Hey, Rose!

ROSE: Gabe?

GABRIEL: I'm here, Rose. Hey Rose, I'm here!

(*Rose enters from the house.*)

ROSE: Lord . . . Look here, Lyons!

LYONS: See, I told you, Rose . . . I told you they'd let him come.

CORY: How you doing, Uncle Gabe?

LYONS: How you doing, Uncle Gabe?

GABRIEL: Hey, Rose. It's time. It's time to tell St. Peter to open the gates. Troy, you ready? You ready, Troy. I'm gonna tell St. Peter to open the gates. You get ready now.

(*Gabriel, with great fanfare, braces himself to blow. The trumpet is without a mouthpiece. He puts the end of it into his mouth and blows with great force, like a man who has been waiting some twenty-odd years for this single moment. No sound comes out of the trumpet. He braces himself and blows again with the same result. A third time he blows. There is a weight of impossible description that falls away and leaves him bare and exposed to a frightful realization. It is a trauma that a sane and normal mind would be unable to withstand. He begins to dance. A slow, strange dance, eerie and life-giving. A dance of atavistic signature and ritual. Lyons attempts to embrace him. Gabriel pushes Lyons away. He begins to howl in what is an attempt at song, or perhaps a song turning back into itself in an attempt at speech. He finishes his dance and the gates of heaven stand open as wide as God's closet.*)

That's the way that go!

THE PIANO LESSON

One of Wilson's most eloquent and lyrical plays, *The Piano Lesson* won Wilson his second Pulitzer Prize. Centering on the history of an African-American family, it reaches back to slavery days in the South even while set in Pittsburgh sometime in the first half of the twentieth century. The Charles family memory goes back to the time when Doaker's grandmother, Berniece (Doaker's niece is also Berniece) and Doaker's father, Boy Charles, at age nine, were traded for a piano. Soon enough, Ophelia Sutter, whose husband had owned Berniece and Willie Boy, wanted them back but could not have them. Instead, Willie Boy, Berniece's husband, a slave remaining on the Sutter land, carved on the piano the images of Berniece, Boy Charles, and many other people in their family so that Ophelia would have both the piano and the likenesses of the slaves she missed.

The piano itself remains powerful and symbolic throughout the play. The history of the family, connected with agriculture and the Sutter land — which the Charles' originally worked and now have a chance to purchase — is related also to the industrial development of the South. Doaker talks about having laid the tracks for the railroad, particularly the Yellow Dog, their nickname for a specific line. Willie Boy's son, Boy Charles, (who was the father of Berniece and Boy Willie), decided in 1911 to take that piano from the Sutters when they were out of the house. He said, "it was the story of our whole family and as long as Sutter had it . . . he had us. Say we was still in slavery." When Sutter returned he tracked Boy Charles to a railroad car which was mysteriously set on fire. The five people who died in the blaze became known as the Ghosts of the Yellow Dog, avenging themselves by the doctrine of an eye for an eye. These ghosts supposedly claimed about a dozen men, including Mr. Sutter, whose death before the opening of the play results in Boy Willie's sensing the opportunity to change his life by buying Sutter's land.

The central struggle between siblings Berniece and Boy Willie is over their different sense of the value of the piano. Berniece does not play the piano, although she knows how, as we learn at the end of the play. Her daughter Maretha plays simple tunes. For Berniece the piano represents the struggle, the pain of the family. For Boy Willie it can be sold to help him realize his ambitions. Whether or not he would truly have an opportunity to free himself by owning Sutter's land is a question that is raised in the course of the play. Some critics have seen the symbolism of the piano as connected to the loss of African-American family history on the one hand and as the absence of economic opportunity on the other. Each side of the struggle is clear in its purposes, and each side makes a fairly reasonable claim on the power and value of the piano; however, it is clear that only one side can eventually win.

In terms of style, the play borrows from the tradition known as magical realism. The texture of the play is carefully realistic, with earthy, natural, recognizable dialogue. The situation is believable. But adding the magical elements of the Ghosts of the Yellow Dog and Sutter's ghost moves the play into another dimension. Onstage the actors project the influence of a force at the appropriate moments of Sutter's presence. Although he is never physically seen, his actuality rivals that of the ghost in *Hamlet*. The concept of ghosts may seem unreasonable to the modern imagination, but Wilson raises the issue into a haunting; thus we realize that the past, bearing the power of slavery and its consequences, haunt the present and seems to shape the future.

The structure of the play is especially interesting. Key details, such as the origin of the piano, the history of the family, the meaning of the Ghosts of the Yellow Dog, and the role of Sutter in the family fortunes are only slowly revealed. Berniece and Boy Willie's relationship is unclear at first. The dialogue seems almost casual in the beginning, but key issues repeat themselves; eventually, lengthy speeches by Doaker and Berniece provide the background that makes the important elements of the play come clear. By the end of the play, through the agency of Avery's religious faith and Berniece's song, calling on the core of her ancestral family, the ghost of Sutter is exorcised.

The Piano Lesson in Performance

The play was developed in workshop at the Eugene O'Neill Center in New London, Connecticut, in the summer of 1987. It opened at the Yale Repertory theater in November 1987, with Lloyd Richards as director. Starletta DuPois played Berniece, Samuel L. Jackson was Boy Willie, and Carl Gordon played Doaker. The production used a single set, Doaker's parlor, with a staircase running up the rear wall of the stage. A light shining from the top of the stairs was used to simulate the presence of Sutter's ghost. The play then moved to Boston in January 1988 with some of the same cast, then to New York's Walter Kerr Theatre on Broadway in April 1990. Charles S. Dutton replaced Jackson as Boy Willie, and S. Epatha Merkerson replaced DuPois as Berniece. The response of New York critics was virtually unanimous in seeing this play as among the most important plays of the year. It was described as Wilson's most "accomplished work to date." The play won the Pulitzer Prize for 1990, the New York Drama Critics' Circle Award for best new play, and the Drama Desk Award for best play.

New York Times critic Frank Rich said of the New York production, "Like all Wilson protagonists, both the brother and sister must take a journey, at times a supernatural one, to the past if they are to seize the future. They cannot be reconciled with each other until they have had a reconciliation with the identity that is etched in their family tree, as in the piano, with blood."

August Wilson *(b. 1945)*
THE PIANO LESSON

1987

Gin my cotton
Sell my seed
Buy my baby
Everything she need — SKIP JAMES

Characters

DOAKER
BOY WILLIE
LYMON
BERNIECE
MARETHA
AVERY
WINING BOY
GRACE

The Setting: *The action of the play takes place in the kitchen and parlor of the house where Doaker Charles lives with his niece, Berniece, and her eleven-year-old daughter, Maretha. The house is sparsely furnished, and although there is evidence of a woman's touch, there is a lack of warmth and vigor. Berniece and Maretha occupy the upstairs rooms. Doaker's room is prominent and opens onto the kitchen. Dominating the parlor is an old upright piano. On the legs of the piano, carved in the manner of African sculpture, are mask-like figures resembling totems. The carvings are rendered with a grace and power of invention that lifts them out of the realm of craftsmanship and into the realm of art. At left is a staircase leading to the upstairs.*

ACT 1 • *Scene 1*

(*The lights come up on the Charles household. It is five o'clock in the morning. The dawn is beginning to announce itself, but there is something in the air that belongs to the night. A stillness that is a portent, a gathering, a coming together of something akin to a storm. There is a loud knock at the door.*)

BOY WILLIE (*off stage, calling*): Hey, Doaker . . . Doaker!

(*He knocks again and calls.*)

Hey, Doaker! Hey, Berniece! Berniece!

(*Doaker enters from his room. He is a tall, thin man of forty-seven, with severe features, who has for all intents and purposes retired from the world though he works full-time as a railroad cook.*)

DOAKER: Who is it?
BOY WILLIE: Open the door, nigger! It's me . . . Boy Willie!
DOAKER: Who?
BOY WILLIE: Boy Willie! Open the door!

(*Doaker opens the door and Boy Willie and Lymon enter. Boy Willie is thirty years old. He has an infectious grin and a boyishness that is apt for his name. He is brash and impulsive, talkative and somewhat crude in speech and manner. Lymon is twenty-nine. Boy Willie's partner, he talks little, and then with a straightforwardness that is often disarming.*)

DOAKER: What you doing up here?
BOY WILLIE: I told you, Lymon. Lymon talking about you might be sleep. This is Lymon. You remember Lymon Jackson from down home? This my Uncle Doaker.

DOAKER: What you doing up here? I couldn't figure out who that was. I thought you was still down in Mississippi.

BOY WILLIE: Me and Lymon selling watermelons. We got a truck out there. Got a whole truckload of watermelons. We brought them up here to sell. Where's Berniece?

(Calls.)

Hey, Berniece!

DOAKER: Berniece up there sleep.

BOY WILLIE: Well, let her get up.

(Calls.)

Hey, Berniece!

DOAKER: She got to go to work in the morning.

BOY WILLIE: Well she can get up and say hi. It's been three years since I seen her.

(Calls.)

Hey, Berniece! It's me . . . Boy Willie.

DOAKER: Berniece don't like all that hollering now. She got to work in the morning.

BOY WILLIE: She can go on back to bed. Me and Lymon been riding two days in that truck . . . the least she can do is get up and say hi.

DOAKER (looking out the window): Where you all get that truck from?

BOY WILLIE: It's Lymon's. I told him let's get a load of watermelons and bring them up here.

LYMON: Boy Willie say he going back, but I'm gonna stay. See what it's like up here.

BOY WILLIE: You gonna carry me down there first.

LYMON: I told you I ain't going back down there and take a chance on that truck breaking down again. You can take the train. Hey, tell him Doaker, he can take the train back. After we sell them watermelons he have enough money he can buy him a whole railroad car.

DOAKER: You got all them watermelons stacked up there no wonder the truck broke down. I'm surprised you made it this far with a load like that. Where you break down at?

BOY WILLIE: We broke down three times! It took us two and a half days to get here. It's a good thing we picked them watermelons fresh.

LYMON: We broke down twice in West Virginia. The first time was just as soon as we got out of Sunflower. About forty miles out she broke down. We got it going and got all the way to West Virginia before she broke down again.

BOY WILLIE: We had to walk about five miles for some water.

LYMON: It got a hole in the radiator but it runs pretty good. You have to pump the brakes sometime before they catch. Boy Willie have his door open and be ready to jump when that happens.

BOY WILLIE: Lymon think that's funny. I told the nigger I give him ten dollars to get the brakes fixed. But he thinks that funny.

LYMON: They don't need fixing. All you got to do is pump them till they catch.

(Berniece enters on the stairs. Thirty-five years old, with an eleven-year-old daughter, she is still in mourning for her husband after three years.)

BERNIECE: What you doing all that hollering for?

BOY WILLIE: Hey, Berniece. Doaker said you was sleep. I said at least you could get up and say hi.

BERNIECE: It's five o'clock in the morning and you come in here with all this noise. You can't come like normal folks. You got to bring all that noise with you.

BOY WILLIE: Hell, I ain't done nothing but come in and say hi. I ain't got in the house good.

BERNIECE: That's what I'm talking about. You start all that hollering and carry on as soon as you hit the door.

BOY WILLIE: Aw hell, woman, I was glad to see Doaker. You ain't had to come down if you didn't want to. I come eighteen hundred miles to see my sister I figure she might want to get up and say hi. Other than that you can go back upstairs. What you got, Doaker? Where your bottle? Me and Lymon want a drink.

(To Berniece.)

This is Lymon. You remember Lymon Jackson from down home.

LYMON: How you doing, Berniece. You look just like I thought you looked.

BERNIECE: Why you all got to come in hollering and carrying on? Waking the neighbors with all that noise.

BOY WILLIE: They can come over and join the party. We fixing to have a party. Doaker, where your bottle? Me and Lymon celebrating. The Ghosts of the Yellow Dog got Sutter.

BERNIECE: Say what?

BOY WILLIE: Ask Lymon, they found him the next morning. Say he drowned in his well.

DOAKER: When this happen, Boy Willie?

BOY WILLIE: About three weeks ago. Me and Lymon was over in Stoner County when we heard about it. We laughed. We thought it was funny. A great big old three-hundred-and-forty-pound man gonna fall down his well.

LYMON: It remind me of Humpty Dumpty.

BOY WILLIE: Everybody say the Ghosts of the Yellow Dog pushed him.

BERNIECE: I don't want to hear that nonsense. Somebody down there pushing them people in their
wells.

DOAKER: What was you and Lymon doing over in
Stoner County?

BOY WILLIE: We was down there working. Lymon got
some people down there.

LYMON: My cousin got some land down there. We
was helping him.

BOY WILLIE: Got near about a hundred acres. He got
it set up real nice. Me and Lymon was down there
chopping down trees. We was using Lymon's truck
to haul the wood. Me and Lymon used to haul
wood all around them parts.

(*To Berniece.*)

Me and Lymon got a truckload of watermelons
out there.

(*Berniece crosses to the window to the parlor.*)

Doaker, where your bottle? I know you got a bottle stuck up in your room. Come on, me and Lymon want a drink.

(*Doaker exits into his room.*)

BERNIECE: Where you all get that truck from?

BOY WILLIE: I told you it's Lymon's.

BERNIECE: Where you get the truck from, Lymon?

LYMON: I bought it.

BERNIECE: Where he get that truck from, Boy Willie?

BOY WILLIE: He told you he bought it. Bought it for a
hundred and twenty dollars. I can't say where he
got that hundred and twenty dollars from . . . but
he bought that old piece of truck from Henry
Porter. (*To Lymon.*) Where you get that hundred
and twenty dollars from, nigger?

LYMON: I got it like you get yours. I know how to
take care of money.

(*Doaker brings a bottle and sets it on the table.*)

BOY WILLIE: Aw hell, Doaker got some of that good
whiskey. Don't give Lymon none of that. He ain't
used to good whiskey. He liable to get sick.

LYMON: I done had good whiskey before.

BOY WILLIE: Lymon bought that truck so he have him
a place to sleep. He down there wasn't doing no
work or nothing. Sheriff looking for him. He
bought that truck to keep away from the sheriff.
Got Stovall looking for him too. He down there
sleeping in that truck ducking and dodging both of
them. I told him come on let's go up and see my
sister.

BERNIECE: What the sheriff looking for you for, Lymon?

BOY WILLIE: The man don't want you to know all his
business. He's my company. He ain't asking you no
questions.

LYMON: It wasn't nothing. It was just a misunderstanding.

BERNIECE: He in my house. You say the sheriff looking for him, I wanna know what he looking for
him for. Otherwise you all can go back out there
and be where nobody don't have to ask you nothing.

LYMON: It was just a misunderstanding. Sometimes
me and the sheriff we don't think alike. So we just
got crossed on each other.

BERNIECE: Might be looking for him about that truck.
He might have stole that truck.

BOY WILLIE: We ain't stole no truck, woman. I told
you Lymon bought it.

DOAKER: Boy Willie and Lymon got more sense than
to ride all the way up here in a stolen truck with a
load of watermelons. Now they might have stole
them watermelons, but I don't believe they stole
that truck.

BOY WILLIE: You don't even know the man good and
you calling him a thief. And we ain't stole them
watermelons either. Them old man Pitterford's watermelons. He give me and Lymon all we could
load for ten dollars.

DOAKER: No wonder you got them stacked up out
there. You must have five hundred watermelons
stacked up out there.

BERNIECE: Boy Willie, when you and Lymon planning
on going back?

BOY WILLIE: Lymon say he staying. As soon as we sell
them watermelons I'm going on back.

BERNIECE (*starts to exit up the stairs*): That's what
you need to do. And you need to do it quick.
Come in here disrupting the house. I don't want all
that loud carrying on around here. I'm surprised
you ain't woke Maretha up.

BOY WILLIE: I was fixing to get her now.

(*Calls.*)

Hey, Maretha!

DOAKER: Berniece don't like all that hollering now.

BERNIECE: Don't you wake that child up!

BOY WILLIE: You going up there . . . wake her up and
tell her her uncle's here. I ain't seen her in three
years. Wake her up and send her down here. She
can go back to bed.

BERNIECE: I ain't waking that child up . . . and don't
you be making all that noise. You and Lymon need
to sell them watermelons and go on back.

(*Berniece exits up the stairs.*)

BOY WILLIE: I see Berniece still try to be stuck up.

DOAKER: Berniece alright. She don't want you making all that noise. Maretha up there sleep. Let her sleep until she get up. She can see you then.

BOY WILLIE: I ain't thinking about Berniece. You hear from Wining Boy? You know Cleotha died?

DOAKER: Yeah, I heard that. He come by here about a year ago. Had a whole sack of money. He stayed here about two weeks. Ain't offered nothing. Berniece asked him for three dollars to buy some food and he got mad and left.

LYMON: Who's Wining Boy?

BOY WILLIE: That's my uncle. That's Doaker's brother. You heard me talk about Wining Boy. He play piano. He done made some records and everything. He still doing that, Doaker?

DOAKER: He made one or two records a long time ago. That's the only ones I ever known him to make. If you let him tell it he a big recording star.

BOY WILLIE: He stopped down home about two years ago. That's what I hear. I don't know. Me and Lymon was up on Parchman Farm doing them three years.

DOAKER: He don't never stay in one place. Now, he been here about eight months ago. Back in the winter. Now, you subject not to see him for another two years. It's liable to be that long before he stop by.

BOY WILLIE: If he had a whole sack of money you liable never to see him. You ain't gonna see him until he get broke. Just as soon as that sack of money is gone you look up and he be on your doorstep.

LYMON (*noticing the piano*): Is that the piano?

BOY WILLIE: Yeah . . . look here, Lymon. See how it's carved up real nice and polished and everything? You never find you another piano like that.

LYMON: Yeah, that look real nice.

BOY WILLIE: I told you. See how it's polished? My mama used to polish it every day. See all them pictures carved on it? That's what I was talking about. You can get a nice price for that piano.

LYMON: That's all Boy Willie talked about the whole trip up here. I got tired of hearing him talk about the piano.

BOY WILLIE: All you want to talk about is women. You ought to hear this nigger, Doaker. Talking about all the women he gonna get when he get up here. He ain't had none down there but he gonna get a hundred when he get up here.

DOAKER: How your people doing down there, Lymon?

LYMON: They alright. They still there. I come up here to see what it's like up here. Boy Willie trying to get me to go back and farm with him.

BOY WILLIE: Sutter's brother selling the land. He say

he gonna sell it to me. That's why I come up here. I got one part of it. Sell them watermelons and get me another part. Get Berniece to sell that piano and I'll have the third part.

DOAKER: Berniece ain't gonna sell that piano.

BOY WILLIE: I'm gonna talk to her. When she see I got a chance to get Sutter's land she'll come around.

DOAKER: You can put that thought out your mind. Berniece ain't gonna sell that piano.

BOY WILLIE: I'm gonna talk to her. She been playing on it?

DOAKER: You know she won't touch that piano. I ain't never known her to touch it since Mama Ola died. That's over seven years now. She say it got blood on it. She got Maretha playing on it though. Say Maretha can go on and do everything she can't do. Got her in an extra school down at the Irene Kaufman Settlement House. She want Maretha to grow up and be a schoolteacher. Say she good enough she can teach on the piano.

BOY WILLIE: Maretha don't need to be playing on no piano. She can play on the guitar.

DOAKER: How much land Sutter got left?

BOY WILLIE: Got a hundred acres. Good land. He done sold it piece by piece, he kept the good part for himself. Now he got to give that up. His brother come down from Chicago for the funeral . . . he up there in Chicago got some kind of business with soda fountain equipment. He anxious to sell the land, Doaker. He don't want to be bothered with it. He called me to him and said cause of how long our families done known each other and how we been good friends and all, say he wanted to sell the land to me. Say he'd rather see me with it than Jim Stovall. Told me he'd let me have it for two thousand dollars cash money. He don't know I found out the most Stovall would give him for it was fifteen hundred dollars. He trying to get that extra five hundred out of me telling me he doing me a favor. I thanked him just as nice. Told him what a good man Sutter was and how he had my sympathy and all. Told him to give me two weeks. He said he'd wait on me. That's why I come up here. Sell them watermelons. Get Berniece to sell that piano. Put them two parts with the part I done saved. Walk in there. Tip my hat. Lay my money down on the table. Get my deed and walk on out. This time I get to keep all the cotton. Hire me some men to work it for me. Gin my cotton. Get my seed. And I'll see you again next year. Might even plant some tobacco or some oats.

DOAKER: You gonna have a hard time trying to get Berniece to sell that piano. You know Avery Brown from down there don't you? He up here now. He followed Berniece up here trying to get her to marry him after Crawley got killed. He been up here about two years. He call himself a preacher now.

BOY WILLIE: I know Avery. I know him from when he used to work on the Willshaw place. Lymon know him too.

DOAKER: He after Berniece to marry him. She keep telling him no but he won't give up. He keep pressing her on it.

BOY WILLIE: Avery think all white men is bigshots. He don't know there some white men ain't got as much as he got.

DOAKER: He supposed to come past here this morning. Berniece going down to the bank with him to see if he can get a loan to start his church. That's why I know Berniece ain't gonna sell that piano. He tried to get her to sell it to help him start his church. Sent the man around and everything.

BOY WILLIE: What man?

DOAKER: Some white fellow was going around to all the colored people's houses looking to buy up musical instruments. He'd buy anything. Drums. Guitars. Harmonicas. Pianos. Avery sent him past here. He looked at the piano and got excited. Offered her a nice price. She turned him down and got on Avery for sending him past. The man kept on her about two weeks. He seen where she wasn't gonna sell it, he gave her his number and told her if she ever wanted to sell it to call him first. Say he'd go one better than what anybody else would give her for it.

BOY WILLIE: How much he offer her for it?

DOAKER: Now you know me. She didn't say and I didn't ask. I just know it was a nice price.

LYMON: All you got to do is find out who he is and tell him somebody else wanna buy it from you. Tell him you can't make up your mind who to sell it to, and if he like Doaker say, he'll give you anything you want for it.

BOY WILLIE: That's what I'm gonna do. I'm gonna find out who he is from Avery.

DOAKER: It ain't gonna do you no good. Berniece ain't gonna sell that piano.

BOY WILLIE: She ain't got to sell it. I'm gonna sell it. I own just as much of it as she does.

BERNIECE (offstage, hollers): Doaker! Go on get away. Doaker!

DOAKER (calling): Berniece?

(Doaker and Boy Willie rush to the stairs, Boy Willie runs up the stairs, passing Berniece as she enters, running.)

DOAKER: Berniece, what's the matter? You alright? What's the matter?

(Berniece tries to catch her breath. She is unable to speak.)

DOAKER: That's alright. Take your time. You alright. What's the matter?

(He calls.)

Hey, Boy Willie?

BOY WILLIE (offstage): Ain't nobody up here.

BERNIECE: Sutter . . . Sutter's standing at the top of the steps.

DOAKER (calls): Boy Willie!

(Lymon crosses to the stairs and looks up. Boy Willie enters from the stairs.)

BOY WILLIE: Hey Doaker, what's wrong with her? Berniece, what's wrong? Who was you talking to?

DOAKER: She say she seen Sutter's ghost standing at the top of the stairs.

BOY WILLIE: Seen what? Sutter? She ain't seen no Sutter.

BERNIECE: He was standing right up there.

BOY WILLIE (entering on the stairs): That's all in Berniece's head. Ain't nobody up there. Go on up there, Doaker.

DOAKER: I'll take your word for it. Berniece talking about what she seen. She say Sutter's ghost standing at the top of the steps. She ain't just make all that up.

BOY WILLIE: She up there dreaming. She ain't seen no ghost.

LYMON: You want a glass of water, Berniece? Get her a glass of water, Boy Willie.

BOY WILLIE: She don't need no water. She ain't seen nothing. Go on up there and look. Ain't nobody up there but Maretha.

DOAKER: Let Berniece tell it.

BOY WILLIE: I ain't stopping her from telling it.

DOAKER: What happened, Berniece?

BERNIECE: I come out my room to come back down here and Sutter was standing there in the hall.

BOY WILLIE: What he look like?

BERNIECE: He look like Sutter. He look like he always look.

BOY WILLIE: Sutter couldn't find his way from Big Sandy to Little Sandy. How he gonna find his way all the way up here to Pittsburgh? Sutter ain't never even heard of Pittsburgh.

DOAKER: Go on, Berniece.

BERNIECE: Just standing there with the blue suit on.

BOY WILLIE: The man ain't never left Marlin County when he was living . . . and he's gonna come all the way up here now that he's dead?

DOAKER: Let her finish. I want to hear what she got to say.

BOY WILLIE: I'll tell you this. If Berniece had seen him like she think she seen him she'd still be running.

DOAKER: Go on, Berniece. Don't pay Boy Willie no mind.

BERNIECE: He was standing there . . . had his hand on top of his head. Look like he might have thought if he took his hand down his head might have fallen off.

LYMON: Did he have on a hat?

BERNIECE: Just had on that blue suit . . . I told him to go away and he just stood there looking at me . . . calling Boy Willie's name.

BOY WILLIE: What he calling my name for?

BERNIECE: I believe you pushed him in the well.

BOY WILLIE: Now what kind of sense that make? You telling me I'm gonna go out there and hide in the weeds with all them dogs and things he got around there . . . I'm gonna hide and wait till I catch him looking down his well just right . . . then I'm gonna run over and push him in. A great big old three-hundred-and-forty-pound man.

BERNIECE: Well, what he calling your name for?

BOY WILLIE: He bending over looking down his well, woman . . . how he know who pushed him? It could have been anybody. Where was you when Sutter fell in his well? Where was Doaker? Me and Lymon was over in Stoner County. Tell her, Lymon. The Ghosts of the Yellow Dog got Sutter. That's what happened to him.

BERNIECE: You can talk all that Ghosts of the Yellow Dog stuff if you want. I know better.

LYMON: The Ghosts of the Yellow Dog pushed him. That's what the people say. They found him in his well and all the people say it must be the Ghosts of the Yellow Dog. Just like all them other men.

BOY WILLIE: Come talking about he looking for me. What he come all the way up here for? If he looking for me all he got to do is wait. He could have saved himself a trip if he looking for me. That ain't nothing but in Berniece's head. Ain't no telling what she liable to come up with next.

BERNIECE: Boy Willie, I want you and Lymon to go ahead and leave my house. Just go on somewhere. You don't do nothing but bring trouble with you everywhere you go. If it wasn't for you Crawley would still be alive.

BOY WILLIE: Crawley what? I ain't had nothing to do with Crawley getting killed. Crawley three time seven. He had his own mind.

BERNIECE: Just go on and leave. Let Sutter go somewhere else looking for you.

BOY WILLIE: I'm leaving. Soon as we sell them watermelons. Other than that I ain't going nowhere. Hell, I just got here. Talking about Sutter looking for me. Sutter was looking for that piano. That's

what he was looking for. He had to die to find out where that piano was at . . . If I was you I'd get rid of it. That's the way to get rid of Sutter's ghost. Get rid of that piano.

BERNIECE: I want you and Lymon to go on and take all this confusion out of my house!

BOY WILLIE: Hey, tell her, Doaker. What kind of sense that make? I told you, Lymon, as soon as Berniece see me she was gonna start something. Didn't I tell you that? Now she done made up that story about Sutter just so she could tell me to leave her house. Well, hell, I ain't going nowhere till I sell them watermelons.

BERNIECE: Well why don't you go out there and sell them! Sell them and go on back!

BOY WILLIE: We waiting till the people get up.

LYMON: Boy Willie say if you get out there too early and wake the people up they get mad at you and won't buy nothing from you.

DOAKER: You won't be waiting long. You done let the sun catch up with you. This the time everybody be getting up around here.

BERNIECE: Come on, Doaker, walk up here with me. Let me get Maretha up and get her started. I got to get ready myself. Boy Willie, just go on out there and sell them watermelons and you and Lymon leave my house.

(Berniece and Doaker exit up the stairs.)

BOY WILLIE *(calling after them):* If you see Sutter up there . . . tell him I'm down here waiting on him.

LYMON: What if she see him again?

BOY WILLIE: That's all in her head. There ain't no ghost up there.

(Calls.)

Hey, Doaker . . . I told you ain't nothing up there.

LYMON: I'm glad he didn't say he was looking for me.

BOY WILLIE: I wish I would see Sutter's ghost. Give me a chance to put a whupping on him.

LYMON: You ought to stay up here with me. You be down there working his land . . . he might come looking for you all the time.

BOY WILLIE: I ain't thinking about Sutter. And I ain't thinking about staying up here. You stay up here. I'm going back and get Sutter's land. You think you ain't got to work up here. You think this the land of milk and honey. But I ain't scared of work. I'm going back and farm every acre of that land.

(Doaker enters from the stairs.)

I told you there ain't nothing up there, Doaker. Berniece dreaming all that.

DOAKER: I believe Berniece seen something. Berniece levelheaded. She ain't just made all that up. She

ABOVE FAR LEFT: Alliance Theatre's 1991–92 production of *The Piano Lesson* with (from left to right) Thomas Byrd, Gary Yates, Ellis Williams, and Denise Burse-Mickelbury (seated). BELOW FAR LEFT: Broadway production of *The Piano Lesson* at the Walter Kerr Theatre (1990), with the following cast (from left to right): Lou Myers, Rocky Carroll, Charles S. Dutton, and Carl Gordon. NEAR LEFT: Charles S. Dutton (left) and Lou Myers in the Broadway production of *The Piano Lesson*. BELOW: Charles S. Dutton (behind the piano), Tommy Lee Hollis, and S. Epatha Merkerson.

say Sutter had on a suit. I don't believe she ever
seen Sutter in a suit. I believe that's what he was
buried in, and that's what Berniece saw.

BOY WILLIE: Well, let her keep on seeing him then. As
long as he don't mess with me.

(*Doaker starts to cook his breakfast.*)

I heard about you, Doaker. They say you got all
the women looking out for you down home. They
be looking to see you coming. Say you got a different one every two weeks. Say they be fighting
one another for you to stay with them.

(*To Lymon.*)

Look at him, Lymon. He know it's true.

DOAKER: I ain't thinking about no women. They
never get me tied up with them. After Coreen I
ain't got no use for them. I stay up on Jack Slattery's place when I be down there. All them
women want is somebody with a steady payday.

BOY WILLIE: That ain't what I hear. I hear every two
weeks the women all put on their dresses and line
up at the railroad station.

DOAKER: I don't get down there but once a month. I
used to go down there every two weeks but they
keep switching me around. They keep switching all
the fellows around.

BOY WILLIE: Doaker can't turn that railroad loose. He
was working the railroad when I was walking
around crying for sugartit. My mama used to brag
on him.

DOAKER: I'm cooking now, but I used to line track. I
pieced together the Yellow Dog stitch by stitch.
Rail by rail. Line track all up around there. I lined
track all up around Sunflower and Clarksdale.
Wining Boy worked with me. He helped put in
some of that track. He'd work it for six months
and quit. Go back to playing piano and gambling.

BOY WILLIE: How long you been with the railroad
now?

DOAKER: Twenty-seven years. Now, I'll tell you something about the railroad. What I done learned after
twenty-seven years. See, you got North. You got
West. You look over here you got South. Over
there you got East. Now, you can start from anywhere. Don't care where you at. You got to go one
of them four ways. And whichever way you decide
to go they got a railroad that will take you there.
Now, that's something simple. You think anybody
would be able to understand that. But you'd be
surprised how many people trying to go North get
on a train going West. They think the train's supposed to go where they going rather than where
it's going.

Now, why people going? Their sister's sick.
They leaving before they kill somebody . . . and
they sitting across from somebody who's leaving to
keep from getting killed. They leaving cause they
can't get satisfied. They going to meet someone. I
wish I had a dollar for every time that someone
wasn't at the station to meet them. I done seen that
a lot. In between the time they sent the telegram
and the time the person get there . . . they done forgot all about them.

They got so many trains out there they have a
hard time keeping them from running into each
other. Got trains going every whichaway. Got people on all of them. Somebody going where somebody just left. If everybody stay in one place I
believe this would be a better world. Now what I
done learned after twenty-seven years of railroad-
ing is this . . . if the train stays on the track . . . it's
going to get where it's going. It might not be where
you going. If it ain't, then all you got to do is sit
and wait cause the train's coming back to get you.
The train don't never stop. It'll come back every
time. Now I'll tell you another thing . . .

BOY WILLIE: What you cooking over there, Doaker?
Me and Lymon's hungry.

DOAKER: Go on down there to Wylie and Kirkpatrick
to Eddie's restaurant. Coffee cost a nickel and you
can get two eggs, sausage, and grits for fifteen
cents. He even give you a biscuit with it.

BOY WILLIE: That look good what you got. Give me a
little piece of that grilled bread.

DOAKER: Here . . . go on take the whole piece.

BOY WILLIE: Here you go, Lymon . . . you want a
piece?

(*He gives Lymon a piece of toast. Maretha enters
from the stairs.*)

BOY WILLIE: Hey, sugar. Come here and give me a
hug. Come on give Uncle Boy Willie a hug. Don't
be shy. Look at her, Doaker. She done got bigger.
Ain't she got big?

DOAKER: Yeah, she getting up there.

BOY WILLIE: How you doing, sugar?

MARETHA: Fine.

BOY WILLIE: You was just a little old thing last time I
seen you. You remember me, don't you? This your
Uncle Boy Willie from down South. That there's
Lymon. He my friend. We come up here to sell watermelons. You like watermelons?

(*Maretha nods.*)

We got a whole truckload out front. You can have
as many as you want. What you been doing?

MARETHA: Nothing.

BOY WILLIE: Don't be shy now. Look at you getting all big. How old is you?

MARETHA: Eleven. I'm gonna be twelve soon.

BOY WILLIE: You like it up here? You like the North?

MARETHA: It's alright.

BOY WILLIE: That there's Lymon. Did you say hi to Lymon?

MARETHA: Hi.

LYMON: How you doing? You look just like your mama. I remember you when you was wearing diapers.

BOY WILLIE: You gonna come down South and see me? Uncle Boy Willie gonna get him a farm. Gonna get a great big old farm. Come down there and I'll teach you how to ride a mule. Teach you how to kill a chicken, too.

MARETHA: I seen my mama do that.

BOY WILLIE: Ain't nothing to it. You just grab him by his neck and twist it. Get you a real good grip and then you just wring his neck and throw him in the pot. Cook him up. Then you got some good eating. What you like to eat? What kind of food you like?

MARETHA: I like everything . . . except I don't like no black-eyed peas.

BOY WILLIE: Uncle Doaker tell me your mama got you playing that piano. Come on play something for me.

(*Boy Willie crosses over to the piano followed by Maretha.*)

Show me what you can do. Come on now. Here . . . Uncle Boy Willie give you a dime . . . show me what you can do. Don't be bashful now. That dime say you can't be bashful.

(*Maretha plays. It is something any beginner first learns.*)

Here, let me show you something.

(*Boy Willie sits and plays a simple boogie-woogie.*)

See that? See what I'm doing? That's what you call the boogie-woogie. See now . . . you can get up and dance to that. That's how good it sound. It sound like you wanna dance. You can dance to that. It'll hold you up. Whatever kind of dance you wanna do you can dance to that right there. See that? See how it go? Ain't nothing to it. Go on you do it.

MARETHA: I got to read it on the paper.

BOY WILLIE: You don't need no paper. Go on. Do just like that there.

BERNIECE: Maretha! You get up here and get ready to go so you be on time. Ain't no need you trying to take advantage of company.

MARETHA: I got to go.

BOY WILLIE: Uncle Boy Willie gonna get you a guitar. Let Uncle Doaker teach you how to play that. You don't need to read no paper to play the guitar. Your mama told you about that piano? You know how them pictures got on there?

MARETHA: She say it just always been like that since she got it.

BOY WILLIE: You hear that, Doaker? And you sitting up here in the house with Berniece.

DOAKER: I ain't got nothing to do with that. I don't get in the way of Berniece's raising her.

BOY WILLIE: You tell your mama to tell you about that piano. You ask her how them pictures got on there. If she don't tell you I'll tell you.

BERNIECE: Maretha!

MARETHA: I got to get ready to go.

BOY WILLIE: She getting big, Doaker. You remember her, Lymon?

LYMON: She used to be real little.

(*There is a knock on the door. Doaker goes to answer it. Avery enters. Thirty-eight years old, honest and ambitious, he has taken to the city like a fish to water, finding in it opportunities for growth and advancement that did not exist for him in the rural South. He is dressed in a suit and tie with a gold cross around his neck. He carries a small Bible.*)

DOAKER: Hey, Avery, come on in. Berniece upstairs.

BOY WILLIE: Look at him . . . look at him . . . he don't know what to say. He wasn't expecting to see me.

AVERY: Hey, Boy Willie. What you doing up here?

BOY WILLIE: Look at him, Lymon.

AVERY: Is that Lymon? Lymon Jackson?

BOY WILLIE: Yeah, you know Lymon.

DOAKER: Berniece be ready in a minute, Avery.

BOY WILLIE: Doaker say you a preacher now. What . . . we supposed to call you Reverend? You used to be plain old Avery. When you get to be a preacher, nigger?

LYMON: Avery say he gonna be a preacher so he don't have to work.

BOY WILLIE: I remember when you was down there on the Willshaw place planting cotton. You wasn't thinking about no Reverend then.

AVERY: That must be your truck out there. I saw that truck with them watermelons, I was trying to figure out what it was doing in front of the house.

BOY WILLIE: Yeah, me and Lymon selling watermelons. That's Lymon's truck.

DOAKER: Berniece say you all going down to the bank.

AVERY: Yeah, they give me a half day off work. I got an appointment to talk to the bank about getting a loan to start my church.

BOY WILLIE: Lymon say preachers don't have to work. Where you working at, nigger?

DOAKER: Avery got him one of them good jobs. He working at one of them skyscrapers downtown.

AVERY: I'm working down there at the Gulf Building running an elevator. Got a pension and everything. They even give you a turkey on Thanksgiving.

LYMON: How you know the rope ain't gonna break? Ain't you scared the rope's gonna break?

AVERY: That's steel. They got steel cables hold it up. It take a whole lot of breaking to break that steel. Naw, I ain't worried about nothing like that. It ain't nothing but a little old elevator. Now, I wouldn't get in none of them airplanes. You couldn't pay me to do nothing like that.

LYMON: That be fun. I'd rather do that than ride in one of them elevators.

BOY WILLIE: How many of them watermelons you wanna buy?

AVERY: I thought you was gonna give me one seeing as how you got a whole truck full.

BOY WILLIE: You can get one, get two. I'll give you two for a dollar.

AVERY: I can't eat but one. How much are they?

BOY WILLIE: Aw, nigger, you know I'll give you a watermelon. Go on, take as many as you want. Just leave some for me and Lymon to sell.

AVERY: I don't want but one.

BOY WILLIE: How you get to be a preacher, Avery? I might want to be a preacher one day. Have everybody call me Reverend Boy Willie.

AVERY: It come to me in a dream. God called me and told me he wanted me to be a shepherd for his flock. That's what I'm gonna call my church . . . The Good Shepherd Church of God in Christ.

DOAKER: Tell him what you told me. Tell him about the three hobos.

AVERY: Boy Willie don't want to hear all that.

LYMON: I do. Lots a people say your dreams can come true.

AVERY: Naw. You don't want to hear all that.

DOAKER: Go on. I told him you was a preacher. He didn't want to believe me. Tell him about the three hobos.

AVERY: Well, it come to me in a dream. See . . . I was sitting out in this railroad yard watching the trains go by. The train stopped and these three hobos got off. They told me they had come from Nazareth and was on their way to Jerusalem. They had three candles. They gave me one and told me to light it . . . but to be careful that it didn't go out. Next thing I knew I was standing in front of this house. Something told me to go knock on the door. This old woman opened the door and said they had been waiting on me. Then she led me into this room. It was a big room and it was full of all kinds of different people. They looked like anybody else except they all had sheep heads and was making noise like sheep make. I heard somebody call my name. I looked around and there was these same three hobos. They told me to take off my clothes and they give me a blue robe with gold thread. They washed my feet and combed my hair. Then they showed me these three doors and told me to pick one.

I went through one of them doors and that flame leapt off that candle and it seemed like my whole head caught fire. I looked around and there was four or five other men standing there with these same blue robes on. Then we heard a voice tell us to look out across this valley. We looked out and saw the valley was full of wolves. The voice told us that these sheep people that I had seen in the other room had to go over to the other side of this valley and somebody had to take them. Then I heard another voice say, "Who shall I send?" Next thing I knew I said, "Here I am. Send me." That's when I met Jesus. He say, "If you go, I'll go with you." Something told me to say, "Come on. Let's go." That's when I woke up. My head still felt like it was on fire . . . but I had a peace about myself that was hard to explain. I knew right then that I had been filled with the Holy Ghost and called to be a servant of the Lord. It took me a while before I could accept that. But then a lot of little ways God showed me that it was true. So I became a preacher.

LYMON: I see why you gonna call it the Good Shepherd Church. You dreaming about them sheep people. I can see that easy.

BOY WILLIE: Doaker say you sent some white man past the house to look at that piano. Say he was going around to all the colored people's houses looking to buy up musical instruments.

AVERY: Yeah, but Berniece didn't want to sell that piano. After she told me about it . . . I could see why she didn't want to sell it.

BOY WILLIE: What's this man's name?

AVERY: Oh, that's a while back now. I done forgot his name. He give Berniece a card with his name and telephone number on it, but I believe she throwed it away.

(*Berniece and Maretha enter from the stairs.*)

BERNIECE: Maretha, run back upstairs and get my pocketbook. And wipe that hair grease off your forehead. Go ahead, hurry up.

(*Maretha exits up the stairs.*)

How you doing, Avery? You done got all dressed up. You look nice. Boy Willie, I thought you and Lymon was going to sell them watermelons.

BOY WILLIE: Lymon done got sleepy. We liable to get some sleep first.

LYMON: I ain't sleepy.

DOAKER: As many watermelons as you got stacked up on that truck out there, you ought to have been gone.

BOY WILLIE: We gonna go in a minute. We going.

BERNIECE: Doaker. I'm gonna stop down there on Logan Street. You want anything?

DOAKER: You can pick up some ham hocks if you going down there. See if you can get the smoked ones. If they ain't got that get the fresh ones. Don't get the ones that got all that fat under the skin. Look for the long ones. They nice and lean.

(*He gives her a dollar.*)

Don't get the short ones lessen they smoked. If you got to get the fresh ones make sure that they the long ones. If they ain't got them smoked then go ahead and get the short ones.

(*Pause.*)

You may as well get some turnip greens while you down there. I got some buttermilk . . . if you pick up some cornmeal I'll make me some cornbread and cook up them turnip greens.

(*Maretha enters from the stairs.*)

MARETHA: We gonna take the streetcar?

BERNIECE: Me and Avery gonna drop you off at the settlement house. You mind them people down there. Don't be going down there showing your color. Boy Willie, I done told you what to do. I'll see you later, Doaker.

AVERY: I'll be seeing you again, Boy Willie.

BOY WILLIE: Hey, Berniece . . . what's the name of that man Avery sent past say he want to buy the piano?

BERNIECE: I knew it. I knew it when I first seen you. I knew you was up to something.

BOY WILLIE: Sutter's brother say he selling the land to me. He waiting on me now. Told me he'd give me two weeks. I got one part. Sell them watermelons get me another part. Then we can sell that piano and I'll have the third part.

BERNIECE: I ain't selling that piano, Boy Willie. If that's why you come up here you can just forget about it.

(*To Doaker.*)

Doaker, I'll see you later. Boy Willie ain't nothing but a whole lot of mouth. I ain't paying him no mind. If he come up here thinking he gonna sell that piano then he done come up here for nothing.

(*Berniece, Avery, and Maretha exit the front door.*)

BOY WILLIE: Hey, Lymon! You ready to go sell these watermelons.

(*Boy Willie and Lymon start to exit. At the door Boy Willie turns to Doaker.*)

Hey, Doaker . . . if Berniece don't want to sell that piano . . . I'm gonna cut it in half and go on and sell my half.

(*Boy Willie and Lymon exit.*)

(*The lights go down on the scene.*)

Scene 2

(*The lights come up on the kitchen. It is three days later. Wining Boy sits at the kitchen table. There is a half-empty pint bottle on the table. Doaker busies himself washing pots. Wining Boy is fifty-six years old. Doaker's older brother, he tries to present the image of a successful musician and gambler, but his music, his clothes, and even his manner of presentation are old. He is a man who looking back over his life continues to live it with an odd mixture of zest and sorrow.*)

WINING BOY: So the Ghosts of the Yellow Dog got Sutter. That just go to show you I believe I always lived right. They say every dog gonna have his day and time it go around it sure come back to you. I done seen that a thousand times. I know the truth of that. But I'll tell you outright . . . if I see Sutter's ghost I'll be on the first thing I find that got wheels on it.

(*Doaker enters from his room.*)

DOAKER: Wining Boy!

WINING BOY: And I'll tell you another thing . . . Berniece ain't gonna sell that piano.

DOAKER: That's what she told him. He say he gonna cut it in half and go on and sell his half. They been around here three days trying to sell them watermelons. They trying to get out to where the white folks live but the truck keep breaking down. They go a block or two and it break down again. They trying to get out to Squirrel Hill and can't get around the corner. He say soon as he can get that truck empty to where he can set the piano up in there he gonna take it out of here and go sell it.

WINING BOY: What about them boys Sutter got? How come they ain't farming that land?

DOAKER: One of them going to school. He left down there and come North to school. The other one ain't got as much sense as that frying pan over yonder. That is the dumbest white man I ever seen. He'd stand in the river and watch it rise till it drown him.

WINING BOY: Other than seeing Sutter's ghost how's Berniece doing?

DOAKER: She doing alright. She still got Crawley on her mind. He been dead three years but she still holding on to him. She need to go out here and let one of these fellows grab a whole handful of whatever she got. She act like it done got precious.

WINING BOY: They always told me any fish will bite if you got good bait.

DOAKER: She stuck up on it. She think it's better than she is. I believe she messing around with Avery. They got something going. He a preacher now. If you let him tell it the Holy Ghost sat on his head and heaven opened up with thunder and lightning and God was calling his name. Told him to go out and preach and tend to his flock. That's what he gonna call his church. The Good Shepherd Church.

WINING BOY: They had that joker down in Spear walking around talking about he Jesus Christ. He gonna live the life of Christ. Went through the Last Supper and everything. Rented him a mule on Palm Sunday and rode through the town. Did everything . . . talking about he Christ. He did everything until they got up to that crucifixion part. Got up to that part and told everybody to go home and quit pretending. He got up to the crucifixion part and changed his mind. Had a whole bunch of folks come down there to see him get nailed to the cross. I don't know who's the worse fool. Him or them. Had all them folks come down there . . . even carried the cross up this little hill. People standing around waiting to see him get nailed to the cross and he stop everything and preach a little sermon and told everybody to go home. Had enough nerve to tell them to come to church on Easter Sunday to celebrate his resurrection.

DOAKER: I'm surprised Avery ain't thought about that. He trying every little thing to get him a congregation together. They meeting over at his house till he get him a church.

WINING BOY: Ain't nothing wrong with being a preacher. You got the preacher on one hand and the gambler on the other. Sometimes there ain't too much difference in them.

DOAKER: How long you been in Kansas City?

WINING BOY: Since I left here. I got tied up with some old gal down there.

(*Pause.*)

You know Cleotha died.

DOAKER: Yeah, I heard that last time I was down there. I was sorry to hear that.

WINING BOY: One of her friends wrote and told me. I got the letter right here.

(*He takes the letter out of his pocket.*)

I was down in Kansas City and she wrote and told me Cleotha had died. Name of Willa Bryant. She say she know cousin Rupert.

(*He opens the letter and reads.*)

Dear Wining Boy: I am writing this letter to let you know Miss Cleotha Holman passed on Saturday the first of May she departed this world in the loving arms of her sister Miss Alberta Samuels. I know you would want to know this and am writing as a friend of Cleotha. There have been many hardships since last you seen her but she survived them all and to the end was a good woman whom I hope have God's grace and is in His Paradise. Your cousin Rupert Bates is my friend also and he give me your address and I pray this reaches you about Cleotha. Miss Willa Bryant. A friend.

(*He folds the letter and returns it to his pocket.*)

They was nailing her coffin shut by the time I heard about it. I never knew she was sick. I believe it was that yellow jaundice. That's what killed her mama.

DOAKER: Cleotha wasn't but forty-some.

WINING BOY: She was forty-six. I got ten years on her. I met her when she was sixteen. You remember I used to run around there. Couldn't nothing keep me still. Much as I loved Cleotha I loved to ramble. Couldn't nothing keep me still. We got married and we used to fight about it all the time. Then one day she asked me to leave. Told me she loved me before I left. Told me, Wining Boy, you got a home as long as I got mine. And I believe in my heart I always felt that and that kept me safe.

DOAKER: Cleotha always did have a nice way about her.

WINING BOY: Man that woman was something. I used to thank the Lord. Many a night I sat up and looked out over my life. Said, well, I had Cleotha.

When it didn't look like there was nothing else for me, I said, thank God, at least I had that. If ever I go anywhere in this life I done known a good woman. And that used to hold me till the next morning.

(*Pause.*)

What you got? Give me a little nip. I know you got something stuck up in your room.

DOAKER: I ain't seen you walk in here and put nothing on the table. You done sat there and drank up your whiskey. Now you talking about what you got.

WINING BOY: I got plenty money. Give me a little nip.

(*Doaker carries a glass into his room and returns with it half-filled. He sets it on the table in front of Wining Boy.*)

WINING BOY: You hear from Coreen?

DOAKER: She up in New York. I let her go from my mind.

WINING BOY: She was something back then. She wasn't too pretty but she had a way of looking at you made you know there was a whole lot of woman there. You got married and snatched her out from under us and we all got mad at you.

DOAKER: She up in New York City. That's what I hear.

(*The door opens and Boy Willie and Lymon enter.*)

BOY WILLIE: Aw hell . . . look here! We was just talking about you. Doaker say you left out of here with a whole sack of money. I told him we wasn't going see you till you got broke.

WINING BOY: What you mean broke? I got a whole pocketful of money.

DOAKER: Did you all get that truck fixed?

BOY WILLIE: We got it running and got halfway out there on Centre and it broke down again. Lymon went out there and messed it up some more. Fellow told us we got to wait till tomorrow to get it fixed. Say he have it running like new. Lymon going back down there and sleep in the truck so the people don't take the watermelons.

LYMON: Lymon nothing. You go down there and sleep in it.

BOY WILLIE: You was sleeping in it down home, nigger! I don't know nothing about sleeping in no truck.

LYMON: I ain't sleeping in no truck.

BOY WILLIE: They can take all the watermelons. I don't care. Wining Boy, where you coming from? Where you been?

WINING BOY: I been down in Kansas City.

BOY WILLIE: You remember Lymon? Lymon Jackson.

WINING BOY: Yeah, I used to know his daddy.

BOY WILLIE: Doaker say you don't never leave no address with nobody. Say he got to depend on your whim. See when it strike you to pay a visit.

WINING BOY: I got four or five addresses.

BOY WILLIE: Doaker say Berniece asked you for three dollars and you got mad and left.

WINING BOY: Berniece try and rule over you too much for me. That's why I left. It wasn't about no three dollars.

BOY WILLIE: Where you getting all these sacks of money from? I need to be with you. Doaker say you had a whole sack of money . . . turn some of it loose.

WINING BOY: I was just fixing to ask you for five dollars.

BOY WILLIE: I ain't got no money. I'm trying to get some. Doaker tell you about Sutter? The Ghosts of the Yellow Dog got him about three weeks ago. Berniece done seen his ghost and everything. He right upstairs.

(*Calls.*)

Hey Sutter! Wining Boy's here. Come on, get a drink!

WINING BOY: How many that make the Ghosts of the Yellow Dog done got?

BOY WILLIE: Must be about nine or ten, eleven or twelve. I don't know.

DOAKER: You got Ed Saunders. Howard Peterson. Charlie Webb.

WINING BOY: Robert Smith. That fellow that shot Becky's boy . . . say he was stealing peaches . . .

DOAKER: You talking about Bob Mallory.

BOY WILLIE: Berniece say she don't believe all that about the Ghosts of the Yellow Dog.

WINING BOY: She ain't got to believe. You go ask them white folks in Sunflower County if they believe. You go ask Sutter if he believe. I don't care if Berniece believe or not. I done been to where the Southern cross the Yellow Dog and called out their names. They talk back to you, too.

LYMON: What they sound like? The wind or something?

BOY WILLIE: You done been there for real, Wining Boy?

WINING BOY: Nineteen thirty. July of nineteen thirty I stood right there on that spot. It didn't look like nothing was going right in my life. I said everything can't go wrong all the time . . . let me go down there and call on the Ghosts of the Yellow Dog, see if they can help me. I went down there and right there where them two railroads cross each other . . . I stood right there on that spot and called out their names. They talk back to you, too.

LYMON: People say you can ask them questions. They talk to you like that?

WINING BOY: A lot of things you got to find out on your own. I can't say how they talked to nobody else. But to me it just filled me up in a strange sort of way to be standing there on that spot. I didn't want to leave. It felt like the longer I stood there the bigger I got. I seen the train coming and it seem like I was bigger than the train. I started not to move. But something told me to go ahead and get on out the way. The train passed and I started to go back up there and stand some more. But something told me not to do it. I walked away from there feeling like a king. Went on and had a stroke of luck that run on for three years. So I don't care if Berniece believe or not. Berniece ain't got to believe. I know cause I been there. Now Doaker'll tell you about the Ghosts of the Yellow Dog.

DOAKER: I don't try and talk that stuff with Berniece. Avery got her all tied up in that church. She just think it's a whole lot of nonsense.

BOY WILLIE: Berniece don't believe in nothing. She just think she believe. She believe in anything if it's convenient for her to believe. But when that convenience run out then she ain't got nothing to stand on.

WINING BOY: Let's not get on Berniece now. Doaker tell me you talking about selling that piano.

BOY WILLIE: Yeah . . . hey, Doaker, I got the name of that man Avery was talking about. The man what's fixing the truck gave me his name. Everybody know him. Say he buy up anything you can make music with. I got his name and his telephone number. Hey, Wining Boy, Sutter's brother say he selling the land to me. I got one part. Sell them watermelons get me the second part. Then . . . soon as I get them watermelons out that truck I'm gonna take and sell that piano and get the third part.

DOAKER: That land ain't worth nothing no more. The smart white man's up here in these cities. He cut the land loose and step back and watch you and the dumb white man argue over it.

WINING BOY: How you know Sutter's brother ain't sold it already? You talking about selling the piano and the man's liable to sold the land two or three times.

BOY WILLIE: He say he waiting on me. He say he give me two weeks. That's two weeks from Friday. Say if I ain't back by then he might gonna sell it to somebody else. He say he wanna see me with it.

WINING BOY: You know as well as I know the man gonna sell the land to the first one walk up and hand him the money.

BOY WILLIE: That's just who I'm gonna be. Look, you ain't gotta know he waiting on me. I know. Okay. I know what the man told me. Stovall already done tried to buy the land from him and he told him no. The man say he waiting on me . . . he waiting on me. Hey, Doaker . . . give me a drink. I see Wining Boy got his glass.

(*Doaker exits into his room.*)

Wining Boy, what you doing in Kansas City? What they got down there?

LYMON: I hear they got some nice-looking women in Kansas City. I sure like to go down there and find out.

WINING BOY: Man, the women down there is something else.

(*Doaker enters with a bottle of whiskey. He sets it on the table with some glasses.*)

DOAKER: You wanna sit up here and drink up my whiskey, leave a dollar on the table when you get up.

BOY WILLIE: You ain't doing nothing but showing your hospitality. I know we ain't got to pay for your hospitality.

WINING BOY: Doaker say they had you and Lymon down on the Parchman Farm. Had you on my old stomping grounds.

BOY WILLIE: Me and Lymon was down there hauling wood for Jim Miller and keeping us a little bit to sell. Some white fellows tried to run us off of it. That's when Crawley got killed. They put me and Lymon in the penitentiary.

LYMON: They ambushed us right there where that road dip down and around that bend in the creek. Crawley tried to fight them. Me and Boy Willie got away but the sheriff got us. Say we was stealing wood. They shot me in my stomach.

BOY WILLIE: They looking for Lymon down there now. They rounded him up and put him in jail for not working.

LYMON: Fined me a hundred dollars. Mr. Stovall come and paid my hundred dollars and the judge say I got to work for him to pay him back his hundred dollars. I told them I'd rather take my thirty days but they wouldn't let me do that.

BOY WILLIE: As soon as Stovall turned his back, Lymon was gone. He down there living in that truck dodging the sheriff and Stovall. He got both of them looking for him. So I brought him up here.

LYMON: I told Boy Willie I'm gonna stay up here. I ain't going back with him.

BOY WILLIE: Ain't nobody twisting your arm to make you go back. You can do what you want to do.

WINING BOY: I'll go back with you. I'm on my way

down there. You gonna take the train? I'm gonna take the train.

LYMON: They treat you better up here.

BOY WILLIE: I ain't worried about nobody mistreating me. They treat you like you let them treat you. They mistreat me I mistreat them right back. Ain't no difference in me and the white man.

WINING BOY: Ain't no difference as far as how somebody supposed to treat you. I agree with that. But I'll tell you the difference between the colored man and the white man. Alright. Now you take and eat some berries. They taste real good to you. So you say I'm gonna go out and get me a whole pot of these berries and cook them up to make a pie or whatever. But you ain't looked to see them berries is sitting in the white fellow's yard. Ain't got no fence around them. You figure anybody want something they'd fence it in. Alright. Now the white man come along and say that's my land. Therefore everything that grow on it belong to me. He tell the sheriff, "I want you to put this nigger in jail as a warning to all the other niggers. Otherwise first thing you know these niggers have everything that belong to us."

BOY WILLIE: I'd come back at night and haul off his whole patch while he was sleep.

WINING BOY: Alright. Now Mr. So and So, he sell the land to you. And he come to you and say, "John, you own the land. It's all yours now. But them is my berries. And come time to pick them I'm gonna send my boys over. You got the land . . . but them berries, I'm gonna keep them. They mine." And he go and fix it with the law that them is his berries. Now that's the difference between the colored man and the white man. The colored man can't fix nothing with the law.

BOY WILLIE: I don't go by what the law say. The law's liable to say anything. I go by if it's right or not. It don't matter to me what the law say. I take and look at it for myself.

LYMON: That's why you gonna end up back down there on the Parchman Farm.

BOY WILLIE: I ain't thinking about no Parchman Farm. You liable to go back before me.

LYMON: They work you too hard down there. All that weeding and hoeing and chopping down trees. I didn't like all that.

WINING BOY: You ain't got to like your job on Parchman. Hey, tell him, Doaker, the only one got to like his job is the waterboy.

DOAKER: If he don't like his job he need to set that bucket down.

BOY WILLIE: That's what they told Lymon. They had Lymon on water and everybody got mad at him cause he was lazy.

LYMON: That water was heavy.

BOY WILLIE: They had Lymon down there singing:

(*Sings.*)

> O Lord Berta Berta O Lord gal oh-ah
> O Lord Berta Berta O Lord gal well

(*Lymon and Wining Boy join in.*)

> Go 'head marry don't you wait on me oh-ah
> Go 'head marry don't you wait on me well
> Might not want you when I go free oh-ah
> Might not want you when I go free well

BOY WILLIE: Come on, Doaker. Doaker know this one.

(*As Doaker joins in the men stamp and clap to keep time. They sing in harmony with great fervor and style.*)

> O Lord Berta Berta O Lord gal oh-ah
> O Lord Berta Berta O Lord gal well
>
> Raise them up higher, let them drop on down oh-ah
> Raise them up higher, let them drop on down well
> Don't know the difference when the sun go down oh-ah
> Don't know the difference when the sun go down well
>
> Berta in Meridan and she living at ease oh-ah
> Berta in Meridan and she living at ease well
> I'm on old Parchman, got to work or leave oh-ah
> I'm on old Parchman, got to work or leave well
>
> O Alberta, Berta, O Lord gal oh-ah
> O Alberta, Berta, O Lord gal well
>
> When you marry, don't marry no farming man oh-ah
> When you marry, don't marry no farming man well
> Everyday Monday, hoe handle in your hand oh-ah
> Everyday Monday, hoe handle in your hand well
>
> When you marry, marry a railroad man, oh-ah
> When you marry, marry a railroad man, well
> Everyday Sunday, dollar in your hand oh-ah
> Everyday Sunday, dollar in your hand well
>
> O Alberta, Berta, O Lord gal oh-ah
> O Alberta, Berta, O Lord gal well

BOY WILLIE: Doaker like that part. He like that railroad part.

LYMON: Doaker sound like Tangleye. He can't sing a lick.

BOY WILLIE: Hey, Doaker, they still talk about you down on Parchman. They ask me, "You Doaker

Boy's nephew?" I say, "Yeah, me and him is family." They treated me alright soon as I told them that. Say, "Yeah, he my uncle."

DOAKER: I don't never want to see none of them niggers no more.

BOY WILLIE: I don't want to see them either. Hey, Wining Boy, come on play some piano. You a piano player, play some piano. Lymon wanna hear you.

WINING BOY: I give that piano up. That was the best thing that ever happened to me, getting rid of that piano. That piano got so big and I'm carrying it around on my back. I don't wish that on nobody. See, you think it's all fun being a recording star. Got to carrying that piano around and man did I get slow. Got just like molasses. The world just slipping by me and I'm walking around with that piano. Alright. Now, there ain't but so many places you can go. Only so many road wide enough for you and that piano. And that piano get heavier and heavier. Go to a place and they find out you play piano, the first thing they want to do is give you a drink, find you a piano, and sit you right down. And that's where you gonna be for the next eight hours. They ain't gonna let you get up! Now, the first three or four years of that is fun. You can't get enough whiskey and you can't get enough women and you don't never get tired of playing that piano. But that only last so long. You look up one day and you hate the whiskey, and you hate the women, and you hate the piano. But that's all you got. You can't do nothing else. All you know how to do is play that piano. Now, who am I? Am I me? Or am I the piano player? Sometime it seem like the only thing to do is shoot the piano player cause he the cause of all the trouble I'm having.

DOAKER: What you gonna do when your troubles get like mine?

LYMON: If I knew how to play it, I'd play it. That's a nice piano.

BOY WILLIE: Whoever playing better play quick. Sutter's brother say he waiting on me. I sell them watermelons. Get Berniece to sell that piano. Put them two parts with the part I done saved . . .

WINING BOY: Berniece ain't gonna sell that piano. I don't see why you don't know that.

BOY WILLIE: What she gonna do with it? She ain't doing nothing but letting it sit up there and rot. That piano ain't doing nobody no good.

LYMON: That's a nice piano. If I had it I'd sell it. Unless I knew how to play like Wining Boy. You can get a nice price for that piano.

DOAKER: Now I'm gonna tell you something, Lymon don't know this . . . but I'm gonna tell you why me

and Wining Boy say Berniece ain't gonna sell that piano.

BOY WILLIE: She ain't got to sell it! I'm gonna sell it! Berniece ain't got no more rights to that piano than I do.

DOAKER: I'm talking to the man . . . let me talk to the man. See, now . . . to understand why we say that . . . to understand about that piano . . . you got to go back to slavery time. See, our family was owned by a fellow named Robert Sutter. That was Sutter's grandfather. Alright. The piano was owned by a fellow named Joel Nolander. He was one of the Nolander brothers from down in Georgia. It was coming up on Sutter's wedding anniversary and he was looking to buy his wife . . . Miss Ophelia was her name . . . he was looking to buy her an anniversary present. Only thing with him . . . he ain't had no money. But he had some niggers. So he asked Mr. Nolander to see if maybe he could trade off some of his niggers for that piano. Told him he would give him one and a half niggers for it. That's the way he told him. Say he could have one full grown and one half grown. Mr. Nolander agreed only he say he had to pick them. He didn't want Sutter to give him just any old nigger. He say he wanted to have the pick of the litter. So Sutter lined up his niggers and Mr. Nolander looked them over and out of the whole bunch he picked my grandmother . . . her name was Berniece . . . same like Berniece . . . and he picked my daddy when he wasn't nothing but a little boy nine years old. They made the trade-off and Miss Ophelia was so happy with that piano that it got to be just about all she would do was play on that piano.

WINING BOY: Just get up in the morning, get all dressed up and sit down and play on that piano.

DOAKER: Alright. Time go along. Time go along. Miss Ophelia got to missing my grandmother . . . the way she would cook and clean the house and talk to her and what not. And she missed having my daddy around the house to fetch things for her. So she asked to see if maybe she could trade back that piano and get her niggers back. Mr. Nolander said no. Said a deal was a deal. Him and Sutter had a big falling out about it and Miss Ophelia took sick to the bed. Wouldn't get out of the bed in the morning. She just lay there. The doctor said she was wasting away.

WINING BOY: That's when Sutter called our granddaddy up to the house.

DOAKER: Now, our granddaddy's name was Boy Willie. That's who Boy Willie's named after . . . only they called him Willie Boy. Now, he was a worker of wood. He could make you anything you wanted out of wood. He'd make you a desk. A table. A lamp. Anything you wanted. Them white fellows around there used to come up to Mr. Sutter and get him to make all kinds of things for them. Then they'd pay Mr. Sutter a nice price. See, everything my granddaddy made Mr. Sutter owned cause he owned him. That's why when Mr. Nolander offered to buy him to keep the family together Mr. Sutter wouldn't sell him. Told Mr. Nolander he didn't have enough money to buy him. Now . . . am I telling it right, Wining Boy?

WINING BOY: You telling it.

DOAKER: Sutter called him up to the house and told him to carve my grandmother and my daddy's picture on the piano for Miss Ophelia. And he took and carved this . . .

(*Doaker crosses over to the piano.*)

See that right there? That's my grandmother, Berniece. She looked just like that. And he put a picture of my daddy when he wasn't nothing but a little boy the way he remembered him. He made them up out of his memory. Only thing . . . he didn't stop there. He carved all this. He got a picture of his mama . . . Mama Esther . . . and his daddy, Boy Charles.

WINING BOY: That was the first Boy Charles.

DOAKER: Then he put on the side here all kinds of things. See that? That's when him and Mama Berniece got married. They called it jumping the broom. That's how you got married in them days. Then he got here when my daddy was born . . . and here he got Mama Esther's funeral . . . and down here he got Mr. Nolander taking Mama Berniece and my daddy away down to his place in Georgia. He got all kinds of things what happened with our family. When Mr. Sutter seen the piano with all them carvings on it he got mad. He didn't ask for all that. But see . . . there wasn't nothing he could do about it. When Miss Ophelia seen it . . . she got excited. Now she had her piano and her niggers too. She took back to playing it and played on it right up till the day she died. Alright . . . now see, our brother Boy Charles . . . that's Berniece and Boy Willie's daddy . . . he was the oldest of us three boys. He's dead now. But he would have been fifty-seven if he had lived. He died in 1911 when he was thirty-one years old. Boy Charles used to talk about that piano all the time. He never could get it off his mind. Two or three months go by and he be talking about it again. He be talking about taking it out of Sutter's house. Say it was the story of our whole family and as long as Sutter had it . . . he had us. Say we was still in slavery. Me and Wining Boy tried to talk him out of it but it wouldn't do any good. Soon as he quiet down

about it he'd start up again. We seen where he wasn't gonna get it off his mind . . . so, on the Fourth of July, 1911 . . . when Sutter was at the picnic what the county give every year . . . me and Wining Boy went on down there with him and took that piano out of Sutter's house. We put it on a wagon and me and Wining Boy carried it over into the next county with Mama Ola's people. Boy Charles decided to stay around there and wait until Sutter got home to make it look like business as usual.

Now, I don't know what happened when Sutter came home and found that piano gone. But somebody went up to Boy Charles's house and set it on fire. But he wasn't in there. He must have seen them coming cause he went down and caught the 3:57 Yellow Dog. He didn't know they was gonna come down and stop the train. Stopped the train and found Boy Charles in the boxcar with four of them hobos. Must have got mad when they couldn't find the piano cause they set the boxcar afire and killed everybody. Now, nobody know who done that. Some people say it was Sutter cause it was his piano. Some people say it was Sheriff Carter. Some people say it was Robert Smith and Ed Saunders. But don't nobody know for sure. It was about two months after that that Ed Saunders fell down his well. Just upped and fell down his well for no reason. People say it was the ghost of them men who burned up in the boxcar that pushed him in his well. They started calling them the Ghosts of the Yellow Dog. Now, that's how all that got started and that why we say Berniece ain't gonna sell that piano. Cause her daddy died over it.

BOY WILLIE: All that's in the past. If my daddy had seen where he could have traded that piano in for some land of his own, it wouldn't be sitting up here now. He spent his whole life farming on somebody else's land. I ain't gonna do that. See, he couldn't do no better. When he come along he ain't had nothing he could build on. His daddy ain't had nothing to give him. The only thing my daddy had to give me was that piano. And he died over giving me that. I ain't gonna let it sit up there and rot without trying to do something with it. If Berniece can't see that, then I'm gonna go ahead and sell my half. And you and Wining Boy know I'm right.

DOAKER: Ain't nobody said nothing about who's right and who's wrong. I was just telling the man about the piano. I was telling him why we say Berniece ain't gonna sell it.

LYMON: Yeah, I can see why you say that now. I told Boy Willie he ought to stay up here with me.

BOY WILLIE: You stay! I'm going back! That's what

I'm gonna do with my life! Why I got to come up here and learn to do something I don't know how to do when I already know how to farm? You stay up here and make your own way if that's what you want to do. I'm going back and live my life the way I want to live it.

(*Wining Boy gets up and crosses to the piano.*)

WINING BOY: Let's see what we got here. I ain't played on this thing for a while.
DOAKER: You can stop telling that. You was playing on it the last time you was through here. We couldn't get you off of it. Go on and play something.

(*Wining Boy sits down at the piano and plays and sings. The song is one which has put many dimes and quarters in his pocket, long ago, in dimly remembered towns and way stations. He plays badly, without hesitation, and sings in a forceful voice.*)

WINING BOY: (*Singing.*)

I am a rambling gambling man
I gambled in many towns
I rambled this wide world over
I rambled this world around
I had my ups and downs in life
And bitter times I saw
But I never knew what misery was
Till I lit on old Arkansas.

I started out one morning
to meet that early train
He said, "You better work for me
I have some land to drain.
I'll give you fifty cents a day,
Your washing, board and all
And you shall be a different man
In the state of Arkansas."

I worked six months for the rascal
Joe Herrin was his name
He fed me old corn dodgers
They was hard as any rock
My tooth is all got loosened
And my knees begin to knock
That was the kind of hash I got
In the state of Arkansas.

Traveling man
I've traveled all around this world
Traveling man
I've traveled from land to land
Traveling man
I've traveled all around this world
Well it ain't no use
writing no news
I'm a traveling man.

(*The door opens and Berniece enters with Maretha.*)

BERNIECE: Is that . . . Lord, I know that ain't Wining Boy sitting there.
WINING BOY: Hey, Berniece.
BERNIECE: You all had this planned. You and Boy Willie had this planned.
WINING BOY: I didn't know he was gonna be here. I'm on my way down home. I stopped by to see you and Doaker first.
DOAKER: I told the nigger he left out of here with that sack of money, we thought we might never see him again. Boy Willie say he wasn't gonna see him till he got broke. I looked up and seen him sitting on the doorstep asking for two dollars. Look at him laughing. He know it's the truth.
BERNIECE: Boy Willie, I didn't see that truck out there. I thought you was out selling watermelons.
BOY WILLIE: We done sold them all. Sold the truck too.
BERNIECE: I don't want to go through none of your stuff. I done told you to go back where you belong.
BOY WILLIE: I was just teasing you, woman. You can't take no teasing?
BERNIECE: Wining Boy, when you get here?
WINING BOY: A little while ago. I took the train from Kansas City.
BERNIECE: Let me go upstairs and change and then I'll cook you something to eat.
BOY WILLIE: You ain't cooked me nothing when I come.
BERNIECE: Boy Willie, go on and leave me alone. Come on, Maretha, get up here and change your clothes before you get them dirty.

(*Berniece exits up the stairs, followed by Maretha.*)

WINING BOY: Maretha sure getting big, ain't she, Doaker. And just as pretty as she want to be. I didn't know Crawley had it in him.

(*Boy Willie crosses to the piano.*)

BOY WILLIE: Hey, Lymon . . . get up on the other side of this piano and let me see something.
WINING BOY: Boy Willie, what is you doing?
BOY WILLIE: I'm seeing how heavy this piano is. Get up over there, Lymon.
WINING BOY: Go on and leave that piano alone. You ain't taking that piano out of here and selling it.
BOY WILLIE: Just as soon as I get them watermelons out that truck.
WINING BOY: Well, I got something to say about that.
BOY WILLIE: This my daddy's piano.
WINING BOY: He ain't took it by himself. Me and Doaker helped him.
BOY WILLIE: He died by himself. Where was you and Doaker at then? Don't come telling me nothing

about this piano. This is me and Berniece's piano. Am I right, Doaker?

DOAKER: Yeah, you right.

BOY WILLIE: Let's see if we can lift it up, Lymon. Get a good grip on it and pick it up on your end. Ready? Lift!

(*As they start to move the piano, the sound of Sutter's Ghost is heard. Doaker is the only one to hear it. With difficulty they move the piano a little bit so it is out of place.*)

BOY WILLIE: What you think?

LYMON: It's heavy . . . but you can move it. Only it ain't gonna be easy.

BOY WILLIE: It wasn't that heavy to me. Okay, let's put it back.

(*The sound of Sutter's Ghost is heard again. They all hear it as Berniece enters on the stairs.*)

BERNIECE: Boy Willie . . . you gonna play around with me one too many times. And then God's gonna bless you and West is gonna dress you. Now set that piano back over there. I done told you a hundred times I ain't selling that piano.

BOY WILLIE: I'm trying to get me some land, woman. I need that piano to get me some money so I can buy Sutter's land.

BERNIECE: Money can't buy what that piano cost. You can't sell your soul for money. It won't go with the buyer. It'll shrivel and shrink to know that you ain't taken on to it. But it won't go with the buyer.

BOY WILLIE: I ain't talking about all that, woman. I ain't talking about selling my soul. I'm talking about trading that piece of wood for some land. Get something under your feet. Land the only thing God ain't making no more of. You can always get you another piano. I'm talking about some land. What you get something out the ground from. That's what I'm talking about. You can't do nothing with that piano but sit up there and look at it.

BERNIECE: That's just what I'm gonna do. Wining Boy, you want me to fry you some pork chops?

BOY WILLIE: Now, I'm gonna tell you the way I see it. The only thing that make that piano worth something is them carvings Papa Willie Boy put on there. That's what make it worth something. That was my great-granddaddy. Papa Boy Charles brought that piano into the house. Now, I'm supposed to build on what they left me. You can't do nothing with that piano sitting up here in the house. That's just like if I let them watermelons sit out there and rot. I'd be a fool. Alright now, if you say to me, Boy Willie, I'm using that piano. I give out lessons on it and that help me make my rent or

whatever. Then that be something else. I'd have to go on and say, well, Berniece using that piano. She building on it. Let her go on and use it. I got to find another way to get Sutter's land. But Doaker say you ain't touched that piano the whole time it's been up here. So why you wanna stand in my way? See, you just looking at the sentimental value. See, that's good. That's alright. I take my hat off whenever somebody say my daddy's name. But I ain't gonna be no fool about no sentimental value. You can sit up here and look at the piano for the next hundred years and it's just gonna be a piano. You can't make more than that. Now I want to get Sutter's land with that piano. I get Sutter's land and I can go down and cash in the crop and get my seed. As long as I got the land and the seed then I'm alright. I can always get me a little something else. Cause that land give back to you. I can make me another crop and cash that in. I still got the land and the seed. But that piano don't put out nothing else. You ain't got nothing working for you. Now, the kind of man my daddy was he would have understood that. I'm sorry you can't see it that way. But that's why I'm gonna take that piano out of here and sell it.

BERNIECE: You ain't taking that piano out of my house.

(*She crosses to the piano.*)

Look at this piano. Look at it. Mama Ola polished this piano with her tears for seventeen years. For seventeen years she rubbed on it till her hands bled. Then she rubbed the blood in . . . mixed it up with the rest of the blood on it. Every day that God breathed life into her body she rubbed and cleaned and polished and prayed over it. "Play something for me, Berniece. Play something for me, Berniece." Every day. "I cleaned it up for you, play something for me, Berniece." You always talking about your daddy but you ain't never stopped to look at what his foolishness cost your mama. Seventeen years' worth of cold nights and an empty bed. For what? For a piano? For a piece of wood? To get even with somebody? I look at you and you're all the same. You, Papa Boy Charles, Wining Boy, Doaker, Crawley . . . you're all alike. All this thieving and killing and thieving and killing. And what it ever lead to? More killing and more thieving. I ain't never seen it come to nothing. People getting burned up. People getting shot. People falling down their wells. It don't never stop.

DOAKER: Come on now, Berniece, ain't no need in getting upset.

BOY WILLIE: I done a little bit of stealing here and

there, but I ain't never killed nobody. I can't be speaking for nobody else. You all got to speak for yourself, but I ain't never killed nobody.

BERNIECE: You killed Crawley just as sure as if you pulled the trigger.

BOY WILLIE: See, that's ignorant. That's downright foolish for you to say something like that. You ain't doing nothing but showing your ignorance. If the nigger was here I'd whup his ass for getting me and Lymon shot at.

BERNIECE: Crawley ain't knew about the wood.

BOY WILLIE: We told the man about the wood. Ask Lymon. He knew all about the wood. He seen we was sneaking it. Why else we gonna be out there at night? Don't come telling me Crawley ain't knew about the wood. Them fellows come up on us and Crawley tried to bully them. Me and Lymon seen the sheriff with them and give in. Wasn't no sense in getting killed over fifty dollars' worth of wood.

BERNIECE: Crawley ain't knew you stole that wood.

BOY WILLIE: We ain't stole no wood. Me and Lymon was hauling wood for Jim Miller and keeping us a little bit on the side. We dumped our little bit down there by the creek till we had enough to make a load. Some fellows seen us and we figured we better get it before they did. We come up there and got Crawley to help us load it. Figured we'd cut him in. Crawley trying to keep the wolf from his door . . . we was trying to help him.

LYMON: Me and Boy Willie told him about the wood. We told him some fellows might be trying to beat us to it. He say let me go back and get my thirty-eight. That's what caused all the trouble.

BOY WILLIE: If Crawley ain't had the gun he'd be alive today.

LYMON: We had it about half loaded when they come up on us. We seen the sheriff with them and we tried to get away. We ducked around near the bend in the creek . . . but they was down there too. Boy Willie say let's give in. But Crawley pulled out his gun and started shooting. That's when they started shooting back.

BERNIECE: All I know is Crawley would be alive if you hadn't come up there and got him.

BOY WILLIE: I ain't had nothing to do with Crawley getting killed. That was his own fault.

BERNIECE: Crawley's dead and in the ground and you still walking around here eating. That's all I know. He went off to load some wood with you and ain't never come back.

BOY WILLIE: I told you, woman . . . I ain't had nothing to do with . . .

BERNIECE: He ain't here, is he? He ain't here!

(Berniece hits Boy Willie.)

I said he ain't here. Is he?

(Berniece continues to hit Boy Willie, who doesn't move to defend himself, other than back up and turning his head so that most of the blows fall on his chest and arms.)

DOAKER (grabbing Berniece): Come on, Berniece . . . let it go, it ain't his fault.

BERNIECE: He ain't here, is he? Is he?

BOY WILLIE: I told you I ain't responsible for Crawley.

BERNIECE: He ain't here.

BOY WILLIE: Come on now, Berniece . . . don't do this now. Doaker get her. I ain't had nothing to do with Crawley . . .

BERNIECE: You come up there and got him!

BOY WILLIE: I done told you now. Doaker, get her. I ain't playing.

DOAKER: Come on. Berniece.

(Maretha is heard screaming upstairs. It is a scream of stark terror.)

MARETHA: Mama! . . . Mama!

(The lights go down to black. End of Act One.)

ACT 2 • Scene 1

(The lights come up on the kitchen. It is the following morning. Doaker is ironing the pants to his uniform. He has a pot cooking on the stove at the same time. He is singing a song. The song provides him with the rhythm for his work and he moves about the kitchen with the ease born of many years as a railroad cook.)

DOAKER:

Gonna leave Jackson Mississippi
and go to Memphis
and double back to Jackson
Come on down to Hattiesburg
Change cars on the Y. D.
coming through the territory to Meridian
and Meridian to Greenville
and Greenville to Memphis
I'm on my way and I know where

Change cars on the Katy
Leaving Jackson
and going through Clarksdale
Hello Winona!
Courtland!
Bateville!
Como!
Senitobia!
Lewisberg!

Sunflower!
Glendora!
Sharkey!
And double back to Jackson
Hello Greenwood
I'm on my way Memphis
Clarksdale
Moorhead
Indianola
Can a highball pass through?
Highball on through sir
Grand Carson!
Thirty First Street Depot
Fourth Street Depot
Memphis!

(*Wining Boy enters carrying a suit of clothes.*)

DOAKER: I thought you took that suit to the pawn-shop?

WINING BOY: I went down there and the man tell me the suit is too old. Look at this suit. This is one hundred percent silk! How a silk suit gonna get too old? I know what it was he just didn't want to give me five dollars for it. Best he wanna give me is three dollars. I figure a silk suit is worth five dollars all over the world. I wasn't gonna part with it for no three dollars so I brought it back.

DOAKER: They got another pawnshop up on Wylie.

WINING BOY: I carried it up there. He say he don't take no clothes. Only thing he take is guns and radios. Maybe a guitar or two. Where's Berniece?

DOAKER: Berniece still at work. Boy Willie went down there to meet Lymon this morning. I guess they got that truck fixed, they been out there all day and ain't come back yet. Maretha scared to sleep up there now. Berniece don't know, but I seen Sutter before she did.

WINING BOY: Say what?

DOAKER: About three weeks ago. I had just come back from down there. Sutter couldn't have been dead more than three days. He was sitting over there at the piano. I come out to go to work . . . and he was sitting right there. Had his hand on top of his head just like Berniece said. I believe he broke his neck when he fell in the well. I kept quiet about it. I didn't see no reason to upset Berniece.

WINING BOY: Did he say anything? Did he say he was looking for Boy Willie?

DOAKER: He was just sitting there. He ain't said nothing. I went on out the door and left him sitting there. I figure as long as he was on the other side of the room everything be alright. I don't know what I would have done if he had started walking toward me.

WINING BOY: Berniece say he was calling Boy Willie's name.

DOAKER: I ain't heard him say nothing. He was just sitting there when I seen him. But I don't believe Boy Willie pushed him in the well. Sutter here cause of that piano. I heard him playing on it one time. I thought it was Berniece but then she don't play that kind of music. I come out here and ain't seen nobody, but them piano keys was moving a mile a minute. Berniece need to go on and get rid of it. It ain't done nothing but cause trouble.

WINING BOY: I agree with Berniece. Boy Charles ain't took it to give it back. He took it cause he figure he had more right to it than Sutter did. If Sutter can't understand that . . . then that's just the way that go. Sutter dead and in the ground . . . don't care where his ghost is. He can hover around and play on the piano all he want. I want to see him carry it out the house. That's what I want to see. What time Berniece get home? I don't see how I let her get away from me this morning.

DOAKER: You up there sleep. Berniece leave out of here early in the morning. She out there in Squirrel Hill cleaning house for some bigshot down there at the steel mill. They don't like you to come late. You come late they won't give you your carfare. What kind of business you got with Berniece?

WINING BOY: My business. I ain't asked you what kind of business you got.

DOAKER: Berniece ain't got no money. If that's why you was trying to catch her. She having a hard enough time trying to get by as it is. If she go ahead and marry Avery . . . he working every day . . . she go ahead and marry him they could do alright for themselves. But as it stands she ain't got no money.

WINING BOY: Well, let me have five dollars.

DOAKER: I just give you a dollar before you left out of here. You ain't gonna take my five dollars out there and gamble and drink it up.

WINING BOY: Aw, nigger, give me five dollars. I'll give it back to you.

DOAKER: You wasn't looking to give me five dollars when you had that sack of money. You wasn't looking to throw nothing my way. Now you wanna come in here and borrow five dollars. If you going back with Boy Willie you need to be trying to figure out how you gonna get train fare.

WINING BOY: That's why I need the five dollars. If I had five dollars I could get me some money.

(*Doaker goes into his pocket.*)

Make it seven.

DOAKER: You take this five dollars . . . and you bring my money back here too.

(*Boy Willie and Lymon enter. They are happy and excited. They have money in all of their pockets and are anxious to count it.*)

DOAKER: How'd you do out there?

BOY WILLIE: They was lining up for them.

LYMON: Me and Boy Willie couldn't sell them fast enough. Time we got one sold we'd sell another.

BOY WILLIE: I seen what was happening and told Lymon to up the price on them.

LYMON: Boy Willie say charge them a quarter more. They didn't care. A couple of people give me a dollar and told me to keep the change.

BOY WILLIE: One fellow bought five. I say now what he gonna do with five watermelons? He can't eat them all. I sold him the five and asked him did he want to buy five more.

LYMON: I ain't never seen nobody snatch a dollar fast as Boy Willie.

BOY WILLIE: One lady asked me say, "Is they sweet?" I told her say, "Lady, where we grow these watermelons we put sugar in the ground." You know, she believed me. Talking about she had never heard of that before. Lymon was laughing his head off. I told her, "Oh, yeah, we put the sugar right in the ground with the seed." She say, "Well, give me another one." Them white folks is something else . . . ain't they, Lymon?

LYMON: Soon as you holler watermelons they come right out their door. Then they go and get their neighbors. Look like they having a contest to see who can buy the most.

WINING BOY: I got something for Lymon.

(*Wining Boy goes to get his suit. Boy Willie and Lymon continue to count their money.*)

BOY WILLIE: I know you got more than that. You ain't sold all them watermelons for that little bit of money.

LYMON: I'm still looking. That ain't all you got either. Where's all them quarters?

BOY WILLIE: You let me worry about the quarters. Just put the money on the table.

WINING BOY (*entering with his suit*): Look here, Lymon . . . see this? Look at his eyes getting big. He ain't never seen a suit like this. This is one hundred percent silk. Go ahead . . . put it on. See if it fit you.

(*Lymon tries the suit coat on.*)

Look at that. Feel it. That's one hundred percent genuine silk. I got that in Chicago. You can't get clothes like that nowhere but New York and Chicago. You can't get clothes like that in Pittsburgh. These folks in Pittsburgh ain't never seen clothes like that.

LYMON: This is nice, feel real nice and smooth.

WINING BOY: That's a fifty-five-dollar suit. That's the kind of suit the bigshots wear. You need a pistol and a pocketful of money to wear that suit. I'll let you have it for three dollars. The women will fall out their windows they see you in a suit like that. Give me three dollars and go on and wear it down the street and get you a woman.

BOY WILLIE: That looks nice, Lymon. Put the pants on. Let me see it with the pants.

(*Lymon begins to try on the pants.*)

WINING BOY: Look at that . . . see how it fits you? Give me three dollars and go on and take it. Look at that, Doaker . . . don't he look nice?

DOAKER: Yeah . . . that's a nice suit.

WINING BOY: Got a shirt to go with it. Cost you an extra dollar. Four dollars you got the whole deal.

LYMON: How this look, Boy Willie?

BOY WILLIE: That look nice . . . if you like that kind of thing. I don't like them dress-up kind of clothes. If you like it, look real nice.

WINING BOY: That's the kind of suit you need for up here in the North.

LYMON: Four dollars for everything? The suit and the shirt?

WINING BOY: That's cheap. I should be charging you twenty dollars. I give you a break cause you a homeboy. That's the only way I let you have it for four dollars.

LYMON (*going into his pocket*): Okay . . . here go the four dollars.

WINING BOY: You got some shoes? What size you wear?

LYMON: Size nine.

WINING BOY: That's what size I got! Size nine. I let you have them for three dollars.

LYMON: Where they at? Let me see them.

WINING BOY: They real nice shoes, too. Got a nice tip to them. Got pointy toe just like you want.

(*Wining Boy goes to get his shoes.*)

LYMON: Come on, Boy Willie, let's go out tonight. I wanna see what it looks like up here. Maybe we go to a picture show. Hey, Doaker, they got picture shows up here?

DOAKER: The Rhumba Theater. Right down there on Fullerton Street. Can't miss it. Got the speakers outside on the sidewalk. You can hear it a block away. Boy Willie know where it's at.

(*Doaker exits into his room.*)

LYMON: Let's go to the picture show, Boy Willie. Let's go find some women.

BOY WILLIE: Hey, Lymon, how many of them water-

melons would you say we got left? We got just under a half a load . . . right?

LYMON: About that much. Maybe a little more.

BOY WILLIE: You think that piano will fit up in there?

LYMON: If we stack them watermelons you can sit it
up in the front there.

BOY WILLIE: I'm gonna call that man tomorrow.

WINING BOY (*returns with his shoes*): Here you go . . .
size nine. Put them on. Cost you three dollars.
That's a Florsheim shoe. That's the kind Staggerlee
wore.

LYMON (*trying on the shoes*): You sure these size
nine?

WINING BOY: You can look at my feet and see we
wear the same size. Man, you put on that suit and
them shoes and you got something there. You
ready for whatever's out there. But is they ready
for you? With them shoes on you be the King of
the Walk. Have everybody stop to look at your
shoes. Wishing they had a pair. I'll give you a
break. Go on and take them for two dollars.

(*Lymon pays Wining Boy two dollars.*)

LYMON: Come on, Boy Willie . . . let's go find some
women. I'm gonna go upstairs and get ready. I'll
be ready to go in a minute. Ain't you gonna get
dressed?

BOY WILLIE: I'm gonna wear what I got on. I ain't
dressing up for these city niggers.

(*Lymon exits up the stairs.*)

That's all Lymon think about is women.

WINING BOY: His daddy was the same way. I used to
run around with him. I know his mama too. Two
strokes back and I would have been his daddy! His
daddy's dead now . . . but I got the nigger out of
jail one time. They was fixing to name him Daniel
and walk him through the Lion's Den. He got in a
tussle with one of them white fellows and the sheriff lit on him like white on rice. That's how the
whole thing come about between me and Lymon's
mama. She knew me and his daddy used to run together and he got in jail and she went down there
and took the sheriff a hundred dollars. Don't get
me to lying about where she got it from. I don't
know. The sheriff looked at that hundred dollars
and turned his nose up Told her, say, "That ain't
gonna do him no good. You got to put another
hundred on top of that." She come up there and
got me where I was playing at this saloon . . . said
she had all but fifty dollars and asked me if I could
help. Now the way I figured it . . . without that
fifty dollars the sheriff was gonna turn him over to
Parchman. The sheriff turn him over to Parchman
it be three years before anybody see him again.

Now I'm gonna say it right . . . I will give anybody
fifty dollars to keep them out of jail for three years.
I give her the fifty dollars and she told me to come
over to the house. I ain't asked her. I figure if she
was nice enough to invite me I ought to go. I ain't
had to say a word. She invited me over just as nice.
Say, "Why don't you come over to the house?" She
ain't had to say nothing else. Them words rolled
off her tongue just as nice. I went on down there
and sat about three hours. Started to leave and
changed my mind. She grabbed hold to me and
say, "Baby, it's all night long." That was one of the
shortest nights I have ever spent on this earth! I
could have used another eight hours. Lymon's
daddy didn't even say nothing to me when he got
out. He just looked at me funny. He had a good
notion something had happened between me an'
her. L. D. Jackson. That was one bad-luck nigger.
Got killed at some dance. Fellow walked in and
shot him thinking he was somebody else.

(*Doaker enters from his room.*)

Hey, Doaker, you remember L. D. Jackson?

DOAKER: That's Lymon's daddy. That was one bad-
luck nigger.

BOY WILLIE: Look like you ready to railroad some.

DOAKER: Yeah, I got to make that run.

(*Lymon enters from the stairs. He is dressed in his
new suit and shoes, to which he has added a cheap
straw hat.*)

LYMON: How I look?

WINING BOY: You look like a million dollars. Don't
he look good, Doaker? Come on, let's play some
cards. You wanna play some cards?

BOY WILLIE: We ain't gonna play no cards with you.
Me and Lymon gonna find some women. Hey, Lymon, don't play no cards with Wining Boy. He'll
take all your money.

WINING BOY (*to Lymon*): You got a magic suit there.
You can get you a woman easy with that suit . . .
but you got to know the magic words. You know
the magic words to get you a woman?

LYMON: I just talk to them to see if I like them and
they like me.

WINING BOY: You just walk right up to them and say,
"If you got the harbor I got the ship." If that don't
work ask them if you can put them in your pocket.
The first thing they gonna say is, "It's too small."
That's when you look them dead in the eye and
say, "Baby, ain't nothing small about me." If that
don't work then you move on to another one. Am
I telling him right, Doaker?

DOAKER: That man don't need you to tell him nothing
about no women. These women these days ain't

gonna fall for that kind of stuff. You got to buy them a present. That's what they looking for these days.

BOY WILLIE: Come on, I'm ready. You ready, Lymon? Come on, let's go find some women.

WINING BOY: Here, let me walk out with you. I wanna see the women fall out their window when they see Lymon.

(*They all exit and the lights go down on the scene.*)

Scene 2

(*The lights come up on the kitchen. It is late evening of the same day. Berniece has set a tub for her bath in the kitchen. She is heating up water on the stove. There is a knock at the door.*)

BERNIECE: Who is it?

AVERY: It's me, Avery.

(*Berniece opens the door and lets him in.*)

BERNIECE: Avery, come on in. I was just fixing to take my bath.

AVERY: Where Boy Willie? I see that truck out there almost empty. They done sold almost all them watermelons.

BERNIECE: They was gone when I come home. I don't know where they went off to. Boy Willie around here about to drive me crazy.

AVERY: They sell them watermelons . . . he'll be gone soon.

BERNIECE: What Mr. Cohen say about letting you have the place?

AVERY: He say he'll let me have it for thirty dollars a month. I talked him out of thirty-five and he say he'll let me have it for thirty.

BERNIECE: That's a nice spot next to Benny Diamond's store.

AVERY: Berniece . . . I be at home and I get to thinking you up here an' I'm down there. I get to thinking how that look to have a preacher that ain't married. It makes for a better congregation if the preacher was settled down and married.

BERNIECE: Avery . . . not now. I was fixing to take my bath.

AVERY: You know how I feel about you, Berniece. Now . . . I done got the place from Mr. Cohen. I get the money from the bank and I can fix it up real nice. They give me a ten cents a hour raise down there on the job . . . now Berniece, I ain't got much in the way of comforts. I got a hole in my pockets near about as far as money is concerned. I ain't never found no way through life to a woman I care about like I care about you. I need that. I

need somebody on my bond side. I need a woman that fits in my hand.

BERNIECE: Avery, I ain't ready to get married now.

AVERY: You too young a woman to close up, Berniece.

BERNIECE: I ain't said nothing about closing up. I got a lot of woman left in me.

AVERY: Where's it at? When's the last time you looked at it?

BERNIECE (*stunned by his remark*): That's a nasty thing to say. And you call yourself a preacher.

AVERY: Anytime I get anywhere near you . . . you push me away.

BERNIECE: I got enough on my hands with Maretha. I got enough people to love and take care of.

AVERY: Who you got to love you? Can't nobody get close enough to you. Doaker can't half say nothing to you. You jump all over Boy Willie. Who you got to love you, Berniece?

BERNIECE: You trying to tell me a woman can't be nothing without a man. But you alright, huh? You can just walk out of here without me — without a woman — and still be a man. That's alright. Ain't nobody gonna ask you, "Avery, who you got to love you?" That's alright for you. But everybody gonna be worried about Berniece. "How Berniece gonna take care of herself? How she gonna raise that child without a man? Wonder what she do with herself. How she gonna live like that?" Everybody got all kinds of questions for Berniece. Everybody telling me I can't be a woman unless I got a man. Well, you tell me, Avery — you know — how much woman am I?

AVERY: It wasn't me, Berniece. You can't blame me for nobody else. I'll own up to my own shortcomings. But you can't blame me for Crawley or nobody else.

BERNIECE: I ain't blaming nobody for nothing. I'm just stating the facts.

AVERY: How long you gonna carry Crawley with you, Berniece? It's been over three years. At some point you got to let go and go on. Life's got all kinds of twists and turns. That don't mean you stop living. That don't mean you cut yourself off from life. You can't go through life carrying Crawley's ghost with you. Crawley's been dead three years. Three years, Berniece.

BERNIECE: I know how long Crawley's been dead. You ain't got to tell me that. I just ain't ready to get married right now.

AVERY: What is you ready for, Berniece? You just gonna drift along from day to day. Life is more than making it from one day to another. You gonna look up one day and it's all gonna be past you. Life's gonna be gone out of your hands — there won't be enough to make nothing with. I'm standing here now, Berniece — but I don't know how much longer I'm gonna be standing here waiting on you.

BERNIECE: Avery, I told you . . . when you get your church we'll sit down and talk about this. I got too many other things to deal with right now. Boy Willie and the piano . . . and Sutter's ghost. I thought I might have been seeing things, but Maretha done seen Sutter's ghost, too.

AVERY: When this happen, Berniece?

BERNIECE: Right after I came home yesterday. Me and Boy Willie was arguing about the piano and Sutter's ghost was standing at the top of the stairs. Maretha scared to sleep up there now. Maybe if you bless the house he'll go away.

AVERY: I don't know, Berniece. I don't know if I should fool around with something like that.

BERNIECE: I can't have Maretha scared to go to sleep up there. Seem like if you bless the house he would go away.

AVERY: You might have to be a special kind of preacher to do something like that.

BERNIECE: I keep telling myself when Boy Willie leave he'll go on and leave with him. I believe Boy Willie pushed him in the well.

AVERY: That's been going on down there a long time. The Ghosts of the Yellow Dog been pushing people in their wells long before Boy Willie got grown.

BERNIECE: Somebody down there pushing them people in their wells. They ain't just upped and fell. Ain't no wind pushed nobody in their well.

AVERY: Oh, I don't know. God works in mysterious ways.

BERNIECE: He ain't pushed nobody in their wells.

AVERY: He caused it to happen. God is the Great Causer. He can do anything. He parted the Red Sea. He say I will smite my enemies. Reverend Thompson used to preach on the Ghosts of the Yellow Dog as the hand of God.

BERNIECE: I don't care who preached what. Somebody down there pushing them people in their wells. Somebody like Boy Willie. I can see him doing something like that. You ain't gonna tell me that Sutter just upped and fell in his well. I believe Boy Willie pushed him so he could get his land.

AVERY: What Doaker say about Boy Willie selling the piano?

BERNIECE: Doaker don't want no part of that piano. He ain't never wanted no part of it. He blames himself for not staying behind with Papa Boy Charles. He washed his hands of that piano a long time ago. He didn't want me to bring it up here — but I wasn't gonna leave it down there.

AVERY: Well, it seems to me somebody ought to be able to talk to Boy Willie.

BERNIECE: You can't talk to Boy Willie. He been that way all his life. Mama Ola had her hands full trying to talk to him. He don't listen to nobody. He just like my daddy. He get his mind fixed on something and can't nobody turn him from it.

AVERY: You ought to start a choir at the church. Maybe if he seen you was doing something with it — if you told him you was gonna put it in my church — maybe he'd see it different. You ought to put it down in the church and start a choir. The Bible say "Make a joyful noise unto the Lord." Maybe if Boy Willie see you was doing something with it he'd see it different.

BERNIECE: I done told you I don't play on that piano. Ain't no need in you to keep talking this choir stuff. When my mama died I shut the top on that piano and I ain't never opened it since. I was only playing it for her. When my daddy died seem like all her life went into that piano. She used to have me playing on it . . . had Miss Eula come in and teach me . . . say when I played it she could hear my daddy talking to her. I used to think them pictures came alive and walked through the house. Sometime late at night I could hear my mama talking to them. I said that wasn't gonna happen to me. I don't play that piano cause I don't want to wake them spirits. They never be walking around in this house.

AVERY: You got to put all that behind you, Berniece.

BERNIECE: I got Maretha playing on it. She don't know nothing about it. Let her go on and be a schoolteacher or something. She don't have to carry all of that with her. She got a chance I didn't have. I ain't gonna burden her with that piano.

AVERY: You got to put all of that behind you, Berniece. That's the same thing like Crawley. Everybody got stones in their passway. You got to step over them or walk around them. You picking them up and carrying them with you. All you got to do is set them down by the side of the road. You ain't got to carry them with you. You can walk over there right now and play that piano. You can walk over there right now and God will walk over there with you. Right now you can set that sack of stones down by the side of the road and walk away from it. You don't have to carry it with you. You can do it right now.

(*Avery crosses over to the piano and raises the lid.*)

Come on, Berniece . . . set it down and walk away from it. Come on, play "Old Ship of Zion." Walk over here and claim it as an instrument of the Lord. You can walk over here right now and make it into a celebration.

(*Berniece moves toward the piano.*)

BERNIECE: Avery . . . I done told you I don't want to play that piano. Now or no other time.

AVERY: The Bible say, "The Lord is my refuge . . . and my strength!" With the strength of God you can put the past behind you, Berniece. With the strength of God you can do anything! God got a bright tomorrow. God don't ask what you done . . . God ask what you gonna do. The strength of God can move mountains! God's got a bright tomorrow for you . . . all you got to do is walk over here and claim it.

BERNIECE: Avery, just go on and let me finish my bath. I'll see you tomorrow.

AVERY: Okay, Berniece. I'm gonna go home. I'm gonna go home and read up on my Bible. And tomorrow . . . if the good Lord give me strength tomorrow . . . I'm gonna come by and bless the house . . . and show you the power of the Lord.

(*Avery crosses to the door.*)

It's gonna be alright, Berniece. God say he will soothe the troubled waters. I'll come by tomorrow and bless the house.

(*The lights go down to black.*)

Scene 3

(*Several hours later. The house is dark. Berniece has retired for the night. Boy Willie enters the darkened house with Grace.*)

BOY WILLIE: Come on in. This my sister's house. My sister live here. Come on, I ain't gonna bite you.

GRACE: Put some light on. I can't see.

BOY WILLIE: You don't need to see nothing, baby. This here is all you need to see. All you need to do is see me. If you can't see me you can feel me in the dark. How's that, sugar?

(*He attempts to kiss her.*)

GRACE: Go on now . . . wait!

BOY WILLIE: Just give me one little old kiss.

GRACE (*pushing him away*): Come on, now. Where I'm gonna sleep at?

BOY WILLIE: We got to sleep out here on the couch. Come on, my sister don't mind. Lymon come back he just got to sleep on the floor. He run off with Dolly somewhere he better stay there. Come on, sugar.

GRACE: Wait now . . . you ain't told me nothing about no couch. I thought you had a bed. Both of us can't sleep on that little old couch.

BOY WILLIE: It don't make no difference. We can sleep on the floor. Let Lymon sleep on the couch.

GRACE: You ain't told me nothing about no couch.

BOY WILLIE: What difference it make? You just wanna be with me.

GRACE: I don't want to be with you on no couch. Ain't you got no bed?

BOY WILLIE: You don't need no bed, woman. My granddaddy used to take women on the backs of horses. What you need a bed for? You just want to be with me.

GRACE: You sure is country. I didn't know you was this country.

BOY WILLIE: There's a lot of things you don't know about me. Come on, let me show you what this country boy can do.

GRACE: Let's go to my place. I got a room with a bed if Leroy don't come back there.

BOY WILLIE: Who's Leroy? You ain't said nothing about no Leroy.

GRACE: He used to be my man. He ain't coming back. He gone off with some other gal.

BOY WILLIE: You let him have your key?

GRACE: He ain't coming back.

BOY WILLIE: Did you let him have your key?

GRACE: He got a key but he ain't coming back. He took off with some other gal.

BOY WILLIE: I don't wanna go nowhere he might come. Let's stay here. Come on, sugar.

(*He pulls her over to the couch.*)

Let me heist your hood and check your oil. See if your battery needs charged.

(*He pulls her to him. They kiss and tug at each other's clothing. In their anxiety they knock over a lamp.*)

BERNIECE: Who's that . . . Wining Boy?

BOY WILLIE: It's me . . . Boy Willie. Go on back to sleep. Everything's alright.

(*To Grace.*)

That's my sister. Everything's alright, Berniece. Go on back to sleep.

BERNIECE: What you doing down there? What you done knocked over?

BOY WILLIE: It wasn't nothing. Everything's alright. Go on back to sleep.

(*To Grace.*)

That's my sister. We alright. She gone back to sleep.

(*They begin to kiss. Berniece enters from the stairs dressed in a nightgown. She cuts on the light.*)

BERNIECE: Boy Willie, what you doing down here?

BOY WILLIE: It was just that there lamp. It ain't

broke. It's okay. Everything's alright. Go on back to bed.

BERNIECE: Boy Willie, I don't allow that in my house. You gonna have to take your company someplace else.

BOY WILLIE: It's alright. We ain't doing nothing. We just sitting here talking. This here is Grace. That's my sister Berniece.

BERNIECE: You know I don't allow that kind of stuff in my house.

BOY WILLIE: Allow what? We just sitting here talking.

BERNIECE: Well, your company gonna have to leave. Come back and talk in the morning.

BOY WILLIE: Go on back upstairs now.

BERNIECE: I got an eleven-year-old girl upstairs. I can't allow that around here.

BOY WILLIE: Ain't nobody said nothing about that. I told you we just talking.

GRACE: Come on . . . let's go to my place. Ain't nobody got to tell me to leave but once.

BOY WILLIE: You ain't got to be like that, Berniece.

BERNIECE: I'm sorry, Miss. But he know I don't allow that in here.

GRACE: You ain't got to tell me but once. I don't stay nowhere I ain't wanted.

BOY WILLIE: I don't know why you want to embarrass me in front of my company.

GRACE: Come on, take me home.

BERNIECE: Go on, Boy Willie. Just go on with your company.

(*Boy Willie and Grace exit. Berniece puts the light on in the kitchen and puts on the teakettle. Presently there is a knock at the door. Berniece goes to answer it. Berniece opens the door. Lymon enters.*)

LYMON: How you doing, Berniece? I thought you'd be asleep. Boy Willie been back here?

BERNIECE: He just left out of here a minute ago.

LYMON: I went out to see a picture show and never got there. We always end up doing something else. I was with this woman she just wanted to drink up all my money. So I left her there and came back looking for Boy Willie.

BERNIECE: You just missed him. He just left out of here.

LYMON: They got some nice-looking women in this city. I'm gonna like it up here real good. I like seeing them with their dresses on. Got them high heels. I like that. Make them look like they real precious. Boy Willie met a real nice one today. I wish I had met her before he did.

BERNIECE: He come by here with some woman a little while ago. I told him to go on and take all that out of my house.

LYMON: What she look like, the woman he was with?

Was she a brown-skinned woman about this high? Nice and healthy? Got nice hips on her?

BERNIECE: She had on a red dress.

LYMON: That's her! That's Grace. She real nice. Laugh a lot. Lot of fun to be with. She don't be trying to put on. Some of these woman act like they the Queen of Sheba. I don't like them kind. Grace ain't like that. She real nice with herself.

BERNIECE: I don't know what she was like. He come in here all drunk knocking over the lamp, and making all kind of noise. I told them to take that somewhere else. I can't really say what she was like.

LYMON: She real nice. I seen her before he did. I was trying not to act like I seen her. I wanted to look at her a while before I said something. She seen me when I come into the saloon. I tried to act like I didn't see her. Time I looked around Boy Willie was talking to her. She was talking to him kept looking at me. That's when her friend Dolly came. I asked her if she wanted to go to the picture show. She told me to buy her a drink while she thought about it. Next thing I knew she done had three drinks talking about she too tired to go. I bought her another drink, then I left. Boy Willie was gone and I thought he might have come back here. Doaker gone, huh? He say he had to make a trip.

BERNIECE: Yeah, he gone on his trip. This is when I can usually get me some peace and quiet, Maretha asleep.

LYMON: She look just like you. Got them big eyes. I remember her when she was in diapers.

BERNIECE: Time just keep on. It go on with or without you. She going on twelve.

LYMON: She sure is pretty. I like kids.

BERNIECE: Boy Willie say you staying . . . what you gonna do up here in this big city? You thought about that?

LYMON: They never get me back down there. The sheriff looking for me. All because they gonna try and make me work for somebody when I don't want to. They gonna try and make me work for Stovall when he don't pay nothing. It ain't like that up here. Up here you more or less do what you want. I figure I find me a job and try to get set up and then see what the year brings. I tried to do that two or three times down there . . . but it never would work out. I was always in the wrong place.

BERNIECE: This ain't a bad city once you get to know your way around.

LYMON: Up here is different. I'm gonna get me a job unloading boxcars or something. One fellow told me say he know a place. I'm gonna go over there with him next week. Me and Boy Willie finish selling them watermelons I'll have enough money to hold me for a while. But I'm gonna go over there and see what kind of jobs they have.

BERNIECE: You shouldn't have too much trouble finding a job. It's all in how you present yourself. See now, Boy Willie couldn't get no job up here. Somebody hire him they got a pack of trouble on their hands. Soon as they find that out they fire him. He don't want to do nothing unless he do it his way.

LYMON: I know. I told him let's go to the picture show first and see if there was any women down there. They might get tired of sitting at home and walk down to the picture show. He say he wanna look around first. We never did get down there. We tried a couple of places and then we went to this saloon where he met Grace. I tried to meet her before he did but he beat me to her. We left Wining Boy sitting down there running his mouth. He told me if I wear this suit I'd find me a woman. He was almost right.

BERNIECE: You don't need to be out there in them saloons. Ain't no telling what you liable to run into out there. This one liable to cut you as quick as that one shoot you. You don't need to be out there. You start out that fast life you can't keep it up. It makes you old quick. I don't know what them women out there be thinking about.

LYMON: Mostly they be lonely and looking for somebody to spend the night with them. Sometimes it matters who it is and sometimes it don't. I used to be the same way. Now it got to matter. That's why I'm here now. Dolly liable not to even recognize me if she sees me again. I don't like women like that. I like my women to be with me in a nice and easy way. That way we can both enjoy ourselves. The way I see it we the only two people like us in the world. We got to see how we fit together. A woman that don't want to take the time to do that I don't bother with. Used to. Used to bother with all of them. Then I woke up one time with this woman and I didn't know who she was. She was the prettiest woman I had ever seen in my life. I spent the whole night with her and didn't even know it. I had never taken the time to look at her. I guess she kinda knew I ain't never really looked at her. She must have known that cause she ain't wanted to see me no more. If she had wanted to see me I believe we might have got married. How come you ain't married? It seem like to me you would be married. I remember Avery from down home. I used to call him plain old Avery. Now he Reverend Avery. That's kinda funny about him becoming a preacher. I like when he told about how that come to him in a dream

about them sheep people and them hobos. Nothing ever come to me in a dream like that. I just dream about women. Can't never seem to find the right one.

BERNIECE: She out there somewhere. You just got to get yourself ready to meet her. That's what I'm trying to do. Avery's alright. I ain't really got nobody in mind.

LYMON: I get me a job and a little place and get set up to where I can make a woman comfortable I might get married. Avery's nice. You ought to go ahead and get married. You be a preacher's wife you won't have to work. I hate living by myself. I didn't want to be no strain on my mama so I left home when I was about sixteen. Everything I tried seem like it just didn't work out. Now I'm trying this.

BERNIECE: You keep trying it'll work out for you.

LYMON: You ever go down there to the picture show?

BERNIECE: I don't go in for all that.

LYMON: Ain't nothing wrong with it. It ain't like gambling and sinning. I went to one down in Jackson once. It was fun.

BERNIECE: I just stay home most of the time. Take care of Maretha.

LYMON: It's getting kind of late. I don't know where Boy Willie went off to. He's liable not to come back. I'm gonna take off these shoes. My feet hurt. Was you in bed? I don't mean to be keeping you up.

BERNIECE: You ain't keeping me up. I couldn't sleep after that Boy Willie woke me up.

LYMON: You got on that nightgown. I likes women when they wear them fancy nightclothes and all. It makes their skin look real pretty.

BERNIECE: I got this at the five-and-ten-cents store. It ain't so fancy.

LYMON: I don't too often get to see a woman dressed like that.

(There is a long pause. Lymon takes off his suit coat.)

Well, I'm gonna sleep here on the couch. I'm supposed to sleep on the floor but I don't reckon Boy Willie's coming back tonight. Wining Boy sold me this suit. Told me it was a magic suit. I'm gonna put it on again tomorrow. Maybe it bring me a woman like he say.

(He goes into his coat pocket and takes out a small bottle of perfume.)

I almost forgot I had this. Some man sold me this for a dollar. Say it come from Paris. This is the same kind of perfume the Queen of France wear. That's what he told me. I don't know if it's true or not. I smelled it. It smelled good to me. Here . . .

smell it see if you like it. I was gonna give it to
Dolly. But I didn't like her too much.

BERNIECE (*takes the bottle*): It smells nice.

LYMON: I was gonna give it to Dolly if she had went
to the picture with me. Go on, you take it.

BERNIECE: I can't take it. Here . . . go on you keep it.
You'll find somebody to give it to.

LYMON: I wanna give it to you. Make you smell nice.

(*He takes the bottle and puts perfume behind
Berniece's ear.*)

They tell me you supposed to put it right here behind your ear. Say if you put it there you smell nice
all day.

(*Berniece stiffens at his touch. Lymon bends down to
smell her.*)

There . . . you smell real good now.

(*He kisses her neck.*)

You smell real good for Lymon.

(*He kisses her again. Berniece returns the kiss, then
breaks the embrace and crosses to the stairs. She turns
and they look silently at each other. Lymon hands her
the bottle of perfume. Berniece exits up the stairs. Lymon picks up his suit coat and strokes it lovingly with
the full knowledge that it is indeed a magic suit. The
lights go down on the scene.*)

Scene 4

(*It is late the next morning. The lights come up on the
parlor. Lymon is asleep on the sofa. Boy Willie enters
the front door.*)

BOY WILLIE: Hey, Lymon! Lymon, come on get up.

LYMON: Leave me alone.

BOY WILLIE: Come on, get up, nigger! Wake up, Lymon.

LYMON: What you want?

BOY WILLIE: Come on, let's go. I done called the man
about the piano.

LYMON: What piano?

BOY WILLIE (*dumps Lymon on the floor*): Come on,
get up!

LYMON: Why you leave, I looked around and you was
gone.

BOY WILLIE: I come back here with Grace, then I
went looking for you. I figured you'd be with
Dolly.

LYMON: She just want to drink and spend up your
money. I come on back here looking for you to see
if you wanted to go to the picture show.

BOY WILLIE: I been up at Grace's house. Some

named Leroy come by but I had a chair up against
the door. He got mad when he couldn't get in. He
went off somewhere and I got out of there before
he could come back. Berniece got mad when we
came here.

LYMON: She say you was knocking over the lamp
busting up the place.

BOY WILLIE: That was Grace doing all that.

LYMON: Wining Boy seen Sutter's ghost last night.

BOY WILLIE: Wining Boy's liable to see anything. I'm
surprised he found the right house. Come on, I
done called the man about the piano.

LYMON: What he say?

BOY WILLIE: He say to bring it on out. I told him I
was calling for my sister, Miss Berniece Charles. I
told him some man wanted to buy it for eleven
hundred dollars and asked him if he would go any
better. He said yeah, he would give me eleven hundred and fifty dollars for it if it was the same piano. I described it to him again and he told me to
bring it out.

LYMON: Why didn't you tell him to come and pick it
up?

BOY WILLIE: I didn't want to have no problem with
Berniece. This way we just take it on out there and
it be out the way. He want to charge twenty-five
dollars to pick it up.

LYMON: You should have told him the man was
gonna give you twelve hundred for it.

BOY WILLIE: I figure I was taking a chance with that
eleven hundred. If I had told him twelve hundred
he might have run off. Now I wish I had told him
twelve-fifty. It's hard to figure out white folks
sometimes.

LYMON: You might have been able to tell him anything. White folks got a lot of money.

BOY WILLIE: Come on, let's get it loaded before
Berniece come back. Get that end over there. All
you got to do is pick it up on that side. Don't
worry about this side. You wanna stretch you'
back for a minute?

LYMON: I'm ready.

BOY WILLIE: Get a real good grip on it now.

(*The sound of Sutter's Ghost is heard. They do not
hear it.*)

LYMON: I got this end. You get that end.

BOY WILLIE: Wait till I say ready now. Alright. You
got it good? You got a grip on it?

LYMON: Yeah, I got it. You lift up on that end.

BOY WILLIE: Ready? Lift!

(*The piano will not budge.*)

LYMON: Man, this piano is heavy! It's gonna take
more than me and you to move this piano.

BOY WILLIE: We can do it. Come on — we did it before.

LYMON: Nigger — you crazy! That piano weighs five hundred pounds!

BOY WILLIE: I got three hundred pounds of it! I know you can carry two hundred pounds! You be lifting them cotton sacks! Come on lift this piano!

(*They try to move the piano again without success.*)

LYMON: It's stuck. Something holding it.

BOY WILLIE: How the piano gonna be stuck? We just moved it. Slide you' end out.

LYMON: Naw — we gonna need two or three more people. How this big old piano get in the house?

BOY WILLIE: I don't know how it got in the house. I know how it's going out though! You get on this end. I'll carry three hundred and fifty pounds of it. All you got to do is slide your end out. Ready?

(*They switch sides and try again without success. Doaker enters from his room as they try to push and shove it.*)

LYMON: Hey, Doaker . . . how this piano get in the house?

DOAKER: Boy Willie, what you doing?

BOY WILLIE: I'm carrying this piano out the house. What it look like I'm doing? Come on, Lymon, let's try again.

DOAKER: Go on let the piano sit there till Berniece come home.

BOY WILLIE: You ain't got nothing to do with this, Doaker. This my business.

DOAKER: This is my house, nigger! I ain't gonna let you or nobody else carry nothing out of it. You ain't gonna carry nothing out of here without my permission!

BOY WILLIE: This is my piano. I don't need your permission to carry my belongings out of your house. This is mine. This ain't got nothing to do with you.

DOAKER: I say leave it over there till Berniece come home. She got part of it too. Leave it set there till you see what she say.

BOY WILLIE: I don't care what Berniece say. Come on, Lymon. I got this side.

DOAKER: Go on and cut it half in two if you want to. Just leave Berniece's half sitting over there. I can't tell you what to do with your piano. But I can't let you take her half out of here.

BOY WILLIE: Go on, Doaker. You ain't got nothing to do with this. I don't want you starting nothing now. Just go on and leave me alone. Come on, Lymon. I got this end.

(*Doaker goes into his room. Boy Willie and Lymon prepare to move the piano.*)

LYMON: How we gonna get it in the truck?

BOY WILLIE: Don't worry about how we gonna get it on the truck. You got to get it out the house first.

LYMON: It's gonna take more than me and you to move this piano.

BOY WILLIE: Just lift up on that end, nigger!

(*Doaker comes to the doorway of his room and stands.*)

DOAKER (*quietly with authority*): Leave that piano set over there till Berniece come back. I don't care what you do with it then. But you gonna leave it sit over there right now.

BOY WILLIE: Alright . . . I'm gonna tell you this, Doaker. I'm going out of here . . . I'm gonna get me some rope . . . find me a plank and some wheels . . . and I'm coming back. Then I'm gonna carry that piano out of here . . . sell it and give Berniece half the money. See . . . now that's what I'm gonna do. And you . . . or nobody else is gonna stop me. Come on, Lymon . . . let's go get some rope and stuff. I'll be back, Doaker.

(*Boy Willie and Lymon exit. The lights go down on the scene.*)

Scene 5

(*The lights come up. Boy Willie sits on the sofa, screwing casters on a wooden plank. Maretha is sitting on the piano stool. Doaker sits at the table playing solitaire.*)

BOY WILLIE (*to Maretha*): Then after that them white folks down around there started falling down their wells. You ever seen a well? A well got a wall around it. It's hard to fall down a well. You got to be leaning way over. Couldn't nobody figure out too much what was making these fellows fall down their well . . . so everybody says the Ghosts of the Yellow Dog must have pushed them. That's what everybody called them four men what got burned up in the boxcar.

MARETHA: Why they call them that?

BOY WILLIE: Cause the Yazoo Delta railroad got yellow boxcars. Sometime the way the whistle blow sound like an old dog howling so the people call it the Yellow Dog.

MARETHA: Anybody ever see the Ghosts?

BOY WILLIE: I told you they like the wind. Can you see the wind?

MARETHA: No.

BOY WILLIE: They like the wind you can't see them. But sometimes you be in trouble they might be around to help you. They say if you go where the

Southern cross the Yellow Dog . . . you go to where them two railroads cross each other . . . and call out their names . . . they say they talk back to you. I don't know, I ain't never done that. But Uncle Wining Boy he say he been down there and talked to them. You have to ask him about that part.

(Berniece has entered from the front door.)

BERNIECE: Maretha, you go on and get ready for me to do your hair.

(Maretha crosses to the steps.)

Boy Willie, I done told you to leave my house.

(To Maretha.)

Go on, Maretha.

(Maretha is hesitant about going up the stairs.)

BOY WILLIE: Don't be scared. Here, I'll go up there with you. If we see Sutter's ghost I'll put a whupping on him. Come on, Uncle Boy Willie going with you.

(Boy Willie and Maretha exit up the stairs.)

BERNIECE: Doaker — what is going on here?

DOAKER: I come home and him and Lymon was moving the piano. I told them to leave it over there till you got home. He went out and got that board and them wheels. He say he gonna take that piano out of here and ain't nobody gonna stop him.

BERNIECE: I ain't playing with Boy Willie. I got Crawley's gun upstairs. He don't know but I'm through with it. Where Lymon go?

DOAKER: Boy Willie sent him for some rope just before you come in.

BERNIECE: I ain't studying Boy Willie or Lymon — or the rope. Boy Willie ain't taking that piano out this house. That's all there is to it.

(Boy Willie and Maretha enter on the stairs. Maretha carries a hot comb and a can of hair grease. Boy Willie crosses over and continues to screw the wheels on the board.)

MARETHA: Mama, all the hair grease is gone. There ain't but this little bit left.

BERNIECE *(gives her a dollar)*: Here . . . run across the street and get another can. You come straight back, too. Don't you be playing around out there. And watch the cars. Be careful when you cross the street.

(Maretha exits out the front door.)

Boy Willie, I done told you to leave my house.

BOY WILLIE: I ain't in you' house. I'm in Doaker's house. If he ask me to leave then I'll go on and leave. But consider me done left your part.

BERNIECE: Doaker, tell him to leave. Tell him to go on.

DOAKER: Boy Willie ain't done nothing for me to put him out of the house. I told you if you can't get along just go on and don't have nothing to do with each other.

BOY WILLIE: I ain't thinking about Berniece.

(He gets up and draws a line across the floor with his foot.)

There! Now I'm out of your part of the house. Consider me done left your part. Soon as Lymon come back with that rope. I'm gonna take that piano out of here and sell it.

BERNIECE: You ain't gonna touch that piano.

BOY WILLIE: Carry it out of here just as big and bold. Do like my daddy would have done come time to get Sutter's land.

BERNIECE: I got something to make you leave it over there.

BOY WILLIE: It's got to come better than this thirty-two-twenty.

DOAKER: Why don't you stop all that! Boy Willie, go on and leave her alone. You know how Berniece get. Why you wanna sit there and pick with her?

BOY WILLIE: I ain't picking with her. I told her the truth. She the one talking about what she got. I just told her what she better have.

BERNIECE: That's alright, Doaker. Leave him alone.

BOY WILLIE: She trying to scare me. Hell, I ain't scared of dying. I look around and see people dying every day. You got to die to make room for somebody else. I had a dog that died. Wasn't nothing but a puppy. I picked it up and put it in a bag and carried it up there to Reverend C. L. Thompson's church. I carried it up there and prayed and asked Jesus to make it live like he did the man in the Bible. I prayed real hard. Knelt down and everything. Say ask in Jesus' name. Well, I must have called Jesus' name two hundred times. I called his name till my mouth got sore. I got up and looked in the bag and the dog still dead. It ain't moved a muscle! I say, "Well, ain't nothing precious." And then I went out and killed me a cat. That's when I discovered the power of death. See, a nigger that ain't afraid to die is the worse kind of nigger for the white man. He can't hold that power over you. That's what I learned when I killed that cat. I got the power of death too. I can command him. I can call him up. The white man don't like to see that. He don't like for you to stand up and look him square in the eye and say, "I got it too." Then he got to deal with you square up.

BERNIECE: That's why I don't talk to him, Doaker. You try and talk to him and that's the only kind of stuff that comes out his mouth.

DOAKER: You say Avery went home to get his Bible?

BOY WILLIE: What Avery gonna do? Avery can't do nothing with me. I wish Avery would say something to me about this piano.

DOAKER: Berniece ain't said about that. Avery went home to get his Bible. He coming by to bless the house see if he can get rid of Sutter's ghost.

BOY WILLIE: Ain't nothing but a house full of ghosts down there at the church. What Avery look like chasing away somebody's ghost?

(Maretha enters the front door.)

BERNIECE: Light that stove and set that comb over there to get hot. Get something to put around your shoulders.

BOY WILLIE: The Bible say an eye for an eye, a tooth for a tooth, and a life for a life. Tit for tat. But you and Avery don't want to believe that. You gonna pass up that part and pretend it ain't in there. Everything else you gonna agree with. But if you gonna agree with part of it you got to agree with all of it. You can't do nothing halfway. You gonna go at the Bible halfway. You gonna act like that part ain't in there. But you pull out the Bible and open it and see what it say. Ask Avery. He a preacher. He'll tell you it's in there. He the Good Shepherd. Unless he gonna shepherd you to heaven with half the Bible.

BERNIECE: Maretha, bring me that comb. Make sure it's hot.

(Maretha brings the comb. Berniece begins to do her hair.)

BOY WILLIE: I will say this for Avery. He done figured out a path to go through life. I don't agree with it. But he done fixed it so he can go right through it real smooth. Hell, he liable to end up with a million dollars that he done got from selling bread and wine.

MARETHA: OWWWWWW!

BERNIECE: Be still, Maretha. If you was a boy I wouldn't be going through this.

BOY WILLIE: Don't you tell that girl that. Why you wanna tell her that?

BERNIECE: You ain't got nothing to do with this child.

BOY WILLIE: Telling her you wished she was a boy. How's that gonna make her feel?

BERNIECE: Boy Willie, go on and leave me alone.

DOAKER: Why don't you leave her alone? What you got to pick with her for? Why don't you go on out and see what's out there in the streets? Have something to tell the fellows down home.

BOY WILLIE: I'm waiting on Lymon to get back with that truck. Why don't you go on out and see what's out there in the streets? You ain't got to work tomorrow. Talking about me . . . why don't you go out there? It's Friday night.

DOAKER: I got to stay around here and keep you all from killing one another.

BOY WILLIE: You ain't got to worry about me. I'm gonna be here just as long as it takes Lymon to get back here with that truck. You ought to be talking to Berniece. Sitting up there telling Maretha she wished she was a boy. What kind of thing is that to tell a child? If you want to tell her something tell her about that piano. You ain't even told her about that piano. Like that's something to be ashamed of. Like she supposed to go off and hide somewhere about that piano. You ought to mark down on the calendar the day that Papa Boy Charles brought that piano into the house. You ought to mark that day down and draw a circle around it . . . and every year when it come up throw a party. Have a celebration. If you did that she wouldn't have no problem in life. She could walk around here with her head held high. I'm talking about a big party!

Invite everybody! Mark that day down with a special meaning. That way she know where she at in the world. You got her going out here thinking she wrong in the world. Like there ain't no part of it belong to her.

BERNIECE: Let me take care of my child. When you get one of your own then you can teach it what you want to teach it.

(Doaker exits into his room.)

BOY WILLIE: What I want to bring a child into this world for? Why I wanna bring somebody else into all this for? I'll tell you this . . . If I was Rockefeller I'd have forty or fifty. I'd make one every day. Cause they gonna start out in life with all the advantages. I ain't got no advantages to offer nobody. Many is the time I looked at my daddy and seen him staring off at his hands. I got a little older I know what he was thinking. He sitting there saying, "I got these big old hands but what I'm gonna do with them? Best I can do is make a fifty-acre crop for Mr. Stovall. Got these big old hands capable of doing anything. I can take and build something with these hands. But where's the tools? All I got is these hands. Unless I go out here and kill me somebody and take what they got . . . it's a long row to hoe for me to get something of my own. So what I'm gonna do with these big old hands? What would you do?"

See now . . . if he had his own land he wouldn't

have felt that way. If he had something under his feet that belonged to him he could stand up taller. That's what I'm talking about. Hell, the land is there for everybody. All you got to do is figure out how to get you a piece. Ain't no mystery to life. You just got to go out and meet it square on. If you got a piece of land you'll find everything else fall right into place. You can stand right up next to the white man and talk about the price of cotton . . . the weather, and anything else you want to talk about. If you teach that girl that she living at the bottom of life, she's gonna grow up and hate you.

BERNIECE: I'm gonna teach her the truth. That's just where she living. Only she ain't got to stay there.

(To Maretha.)

Turn you' head over to the other side.

BOY WILLIE: This might be your bottom but it ain't mine. I'm living at the top of life. I ain't gonna just take my life and throw it away at the bottom. I'm in the world like everybody else. The way I see it everybody else got to come up a little taste to be where I am.

BERNIECE: You right at the bottom with the rest of us.

BOY WILLIE: I'll tell you this . . . and ain't a living soul can put a come back on it. If you believe that's where you at then you gonna act that way. If you act that way then that's where you gonna be. It's as simple as that. Ain't no mystery to life. I don't know how you come to believe that stuff. Crawley didn't think like that. He wasn't living at the bottom of life. Papa Boy Charles and Mama Ola wasn't living at the bottom of life. You ain't never heard them say nothing like that. They would have taken a strap to you if they heard you say something like that.

(Doaker enters from his room.)

Hey, Doaker . . . Berniece say the colored folks is living at the bottom of life. I tried to tell her if she think that . . . that's where she gonna be. You think you living at the bottom of life? Is that how you see yourself?

DOAKER: I'm just living the best way I know how. I ain't thinking about no top or no bottom.

BOY WILLIE: That's what I tried to tell Berniece. I don't know where she got that from. That sound like something Avery would say. Avery think cause the white man give him a turkey for Thanksgiving that makes him better than everybody else. That's gonna raise him out of the bottom of life. I don't need nobody to give me a turkey. I can get my own turkey. All you have to do is get out my way. I'll get me two or three turkeys.

BERNIECE: You can't even get a chicken let alone two

or three turkeys. Talking about get out your way. Ain't nobody in your way.

(To Maretha.)

Straighten your head, Maretha! Don't be bending down like that. Hold your head up!

(To Boy Willie.)

All you got going for you is talk. You' whole life that's all you ever had going for you.

BOY WILLIE: See now . . . I'll tell you something about me. I done strung along and strung along. Going this way and that. Whatever way would lead me to a moment of peace. That's all I want. To be as easy with everything. But I wasn't born to that. I was born to a time of fire.

  The world ain't wanted no part of me. I could see that since I was about seven. The world say it's better off without me. See, Berniece accept that. She trying to come up to where she can prove something to the world. Hell, the world a better place cause of me. I don't see it like Berniece. I got a heart that beats here and it beats just as loud as the next fellow's. Don't care if he black or white. Sometime it beats louder. When it beats louder, then everybody can hear it. Some people get scared of that. Like Berniece. Some people get scared to hear a nigger's heart beating. They think you ought to lay low with that heart. Make it beat quiet and go along with everything the way it is. But my mama ain't birthed me for nothing. So what I got to do? I got to mark my passing on the road. Just like you write on a tree, "Boy Willie was here."

  That's all I'm trying to do with that piano. Trying to put my mark on the road. Like my daddy done. My heart say for me to sell that piano and get me some land so I can make a life for myself to live in my own way. Other than that I ain't thinking about nothing Berniece got to say.

(There is a knock at the door. Boy Willie crosses to it and yanks it open thinking it is Lymon. Avery enters. He carries a Bible.)

BOY WILLIE: Where you been, nigger? Aw . . . I thought you was Lymon. Hey, Berniece, look who's here.

BERNIECE: Come on in, Avery. Don't you pay Boy Willie no mind.

BOY WILLIE: Hey . . . Hey, Avery . . . tell me this . . . can you get to heaven with half the Bible?

BERNIECE: Boy Willie . . . I done told you to leave me alone.

BOY WILLIE: I just ask the man a question. He can answer. He don't need you to speak for him. Avery . . . if you only believe on half the Bible and

don't want to accept the other half . . . you think
God let you in heaven? Or do you got to have the
whole Bible? Tell Berniece . . . if you only believe in
part of it . . . when you see God he gonna ask you
why you ain't believed in the other part . . . then he
gonna send you straight to Hell.

AVERY: You got to be born again. Jesus say unless a
man be born again he cannot come unto the Father
and who so ever heareth my words and believeth
them not shall be cast into a fiery pit.

BOY WILLIE: That's what I was trying to tell Berniece.
You got to believe in it all. You can't go at nothing
halfway. She think she going to heaven with half
the Bible.

(To Berniece.)

You hear that . . . Jesus say you got to believe in it
all.

BERNIECE: You keep messing with me.

BOY WILLIE: I ain't thinking about you.

DOAKER: Come on in, Avery, and have a seat. Don't
pay neither one of them no mind. They been arguing all day.

BERNIECE: Come on in, Avery.

AVERY: How's everybody in here?

BERNIECE: Here, set this comb back over there on that
stove.

(To Avery.)

Don't pay Boy Willie no mind. He been around here
bothering me since I come home from work.

BOY WILLIE: Boy Willie ain't bothering you. Boy
Willie ain't bothering nobody. I'm just waiting on
Lymon to get back. I ain't thinking about you. You
heard the man say I was right and you still don't
want to believe it. You just wanna go and make up
anythin'. Well there's Avery . . . there's the
preacher . . . go on and ask him.

AVERY: Berniece believe in the Bible. She been baptized.

BOY WILLIE: What about that part that say an eye for
an eye a tooth for a tooth and a life for a life? Ain't
that in there?

DOAKER: What they say down there at the bank, Avery?

AVERY: Oh, they talked to me real nice. I told
Berniece . . . they say maybe they let me borrow
the money. They done talked to my boss down at
work and everything.

DOAKER: That's what I told Berniece. You working
every day you ought to be able to borrow some
money.

AVERY: I'm getting more people in my congregation
every day. Berniece says she gonna be the Dea-

coness. I get me my church I can get married and
settled down. That's what I told Berniece.

DOAKER: That be nice. You all ought to go ahead and
get married. Berniece don't need to be by herself. I
tell her that all the time.

BERNIECE: I ain't said nothing about getting married. I
said I was thinking about it.

DOAKER: Avery get him his church you all can make it
nice.

(To Avery.)

Berniece said you was coming by to bless the
house.

AVERY: Yeah, I done read up on my Bible. She asked
me to come by and see if I can get rid of Sutter's
ghost.

BOY WILLIE: Ain't no ghost in this house. That's all in
Berniece's head. Go on up there and see if you see
him. I'll give you a hundred dollars if you see him.
That's all in her imagination.

DOAKER: Well, let her find that out then. If Avery
blessing the house is gonna make her feel better . . .
what you got to do with it?

AVERY: Berniece say Maretha seen him too. I don't
know, but I found a part in the Bible to bless the
house. If he is here then that ought to make him go.

BOY WILLIE: You worse than Berniece believing all
that stuff. Talking about . . . if he here. Go on up
there and find out. I been up there I ain't seen him.
If you reading from that Bible gonna make him
leave out of Berniece imagination, well, you might
be right. But if you talking about . . .

DOAKER: Boy Willie, why don't you just be quiet?
Getting all up in the man's business. This ain't got
nothing to do with you. Let him go ahead and do
what he gonna do.

BOY WILLIE: I ain't stopping him. Avery ain't got no
power to do nothing.

AVERY: Oh, I ain't got no power. God got the power!
God got power over everything in His creation.
God can do anything. God say, "As I commandeth
so it shall be." God said, "Let there be light," and
there was light. He made the world in six days and
rested on the seventh. God's got a wonderful
power. He got power over life and death. Jesus
raised Lazareth from the dead. They was getting
ready to bury him and Jesus told him say, "Rise up
and walk." He got up and walked and the people
made great rejoicing at the power of God. I ain't
worried about him chasing away a little old ghost!

*(There is a knock at the door. Boy Willie goes to an-
swer it. Lymon enters carrying a coil of rope.)*

BOY WILLIE: Where you been? I been waiting on you
and you run off somewhere.

LYMON: I ran into Grace. I stopped and bought her drink. She say she gonna go to the picture show with me.

BOY WILLIE: I ain't thinking about no Grace nothing.

LYMON: Hi, Berniece.

BOY WILLIE: Give me that rope and get up on this side of the piano.

DOAKER: Boy Willie, don't start nothing now. Leave the piano alone.

BOY WILLIE: Get that board there, Lymon. Stay out of this, Doaker.

(*Berniece exits up the stairs.*)

DOAKER: You just can't take the piano. How you gonna take the piano? Berniece ain't said nothing about selling that piano.

BOY WILLIE: She ain't got to say nothing. Come on, Lymon. We got to lift one end at a time up on the board. You got to watch so that the board don't slide up under there.

LYMON: What we gonna do with the rope?

BOY WILLIE: Let me worry about the rope. You just get up on this side over here with me.

(*Berniece enters from the stairs. She has her hand in her pocket where she has Crawley's gun.*)

AVERY: Boy Willie . . . Berniece . . . why don't you all sit down and talk this out now?

BERNIECE: Ain't nothing to talk out.

BOY WILLIE: I'm through talking to Berniece. You can talk to Berniece till you get blue in the face, and it don't make no difference. Get up on that side, Lymon. Throw that rope around there and tie it to the leg.

LYMON: Wait a minute . . . wait a minute, Boy Willie. Berniece got to say. Hey, Berniece . . . did you tell Boy Willie he could take this piano?

BERNIECE: Boy Willie ain't taking nothing out of my house but himself. Now you let him go ahead and try.

BOY WILLIE: Come on, Lymon, get up on this side with me.

(*Lymon stands undecided.*)

Come on, nigger! What you standing there for?

LYMON: Maybe Berniece is right, Boy Willie. Maybe you shouldn't sell it.

AVERY: You all ought to sit down and talk it out. See if you can come to an agreement.

DOAKER: That's what I been trying to tell them. Seem like one of them ought to respect the other one's wishes.

BERNIECE: I wish Boy Willie would go on and leave my house. That's what I wish. Now, he can respect that. Cause he's leaving here one way or another.

BOY WILLIE: What you mean one way or another? What's that supposed to mean? I ain't scared of no gun.

DOAKER: Come on, Berniece, leave him alone with that.

BOY WILLIE: I don't care what Berniece say. I'm selling my half. I can't help it if her half got to go along with it. It ain't like I'm trying to cheat her out of her half. Come on, Lymon.

LYMON: Berniece . . . I got to do this . . . Boy Willie say he gonna give you half of the money . . . say he want to get Sutter's land.

BERNIECE: Go on, Lymon. Just go on . . . I done told Boy Willie what to do.

BOY WILLIE: Here, Lymon . . . put that rope up over there.

LYMON: Boy Willie, you sure you want to do this? The way I figure it . . . I might be wrong . . . but I figure she gonna shoot you first.

BOY WILLIE: She just gonna have to shoot me.

BERNIECE: Maretha, get on out the way. Get her out the way, Doaker.

DOAKER: Go on, do what your mama told you.

BERNIECE: Put her in your room.

(*Maretha exits to Doaker's room. Boy Willie and Lymon try to lift the piano. The door opens and Wining Boy enters. He has been drinking.*)

WINING BOY: Man, these niggers around here! I stopped down there at Seefus. . . . These folks standing around talking about Patchneck Red's coming. They jumping back and getting off the sidewalk talking about Patchneck Red this and Patchneck Red that. Come to find out . . . you know who they was talking about? Old John D. from up around Tyler! Used to run around with Otis Smith. He got everybody scared of him. Calling him Patchneck Red. They don't know I whupped the nigger's head in one time.

BOY WILLIE: Just make sure that board don't slide, Lymon.

LYMON: I got this side. You watch that side.

WINING BOY: Hey, Boy Willie, what you got? I know you got a pint stuck up in your coat.

BOY WILLIE: Wining Boy, get out the way!

WINING BOY: Hey, Doaker. What you got? Gimme a drink. I want a drink.

DOAKER: It look like you had enough of whatever it was. Come talking about "What you got?" You ought to be trying to find somewhere to lay down.

WINING BOY: I ain't worried about no place to lay down. I can always find me a place to lay down in Berniece's house. Ain't that right, Berniece?

BERNIECE: Wining Boy, sit down somewhere. You

been out there drinking all day. Come in here smelling like an old polecat. Sit on down there, you don't need nothing to drink.

DOAKER: You know Berniece don't like all that drinking.

WINING BOY: I ain't disrespecting Berniece. Berniece, am I disrespecting you? I'm just trying to be nice. I been with strangers all day and they treated me like family. I come in here to family and you treat me like a stranger. I don't need your whiskey. I can buy my own. I wanted your company, not your whiskey.

DOAKER: Nigger, why don't you go upstairs and lay down? You don't need nothing to drink.

WINING BOY: I ain't thinking about no laying down. Me and Boy Willie fixing to party. Ain't that right, Boy Willie? Tell him. I'm fixing to play me some piano. Watch this.

(*Wining Boy sits down at the piano.*)

BOY WILLIE: Come on, Wining Boy! Me and Lymon fixing to move the piano.

WINING BOY: Wait a minute . . . wait a minute. This a song I wrote for Cleotha. I wrote this song in memory of Cleotha.

(*He begins to play and sing.*)

Hey little woman what's the matter with you now
Had a storm last night and blowed the line all down

Tell me how long
Is I got to wait
Can I get it now
Or must I hesitate

It takes a hesitating stocking in her hesitating shoe
It takes a hesitating woman wanna sing the blues

Tell me how long
Is I got to wait
Can I kiss you now
Or must I hesitate.

BOY WILLIE: Come on, Wining Boy, get up! Get up, Wining Boy! Me and Lymon's fixing to move the piano.

WINING BOY: Naw . . . Naw . . . you ain't gonna move this piano!

BOY WILLIE: Get out the way, Wining Boy.

(*Wining Boy, his back to the piano, spreads his arms out over the piano.*)

WINING BOY: You ain't taking this piano out the house. You got to take me with it!

BOY WILLIE: Get on out the way, Wining Boy! Doaker get him!

(*There is a knock on the door.*)

BERNIECE: I got him, Doaker. Come on, Wining Boy. I done told Boy Willie he ain't taking the piano.

(*Berniece tries to take Wining Boy away from the piano.*)

WINING BOY: He got to take me with it!

(*Doaker goes to answer the door. Grace enters.*)

GRACE: Is Lymon here?

DOAKER: Lymon.

WINING BOY: He ain't taking that piano.

BERNIECE: I ain't gonna let him take it.

GRACE: I thought you was coming back. I ain't gonna sit in that truck all day.

LYMON: I told you I was coming back.

GRACE: (*Sees Boy Willie.*) Oh, hi, Boy Willie. Lymon told me you was gone back down South.

LYMON: I said he was going back. I didn't say he had left already.

GRACE: That's what you told me.

BERNIECE: Lymon, you got to take your company someplace else.

LYMON: Berniece, this is Grace. That there is Berniece. That's Boy Willie's sister.

GRACE: Nice to meet you.

(*To Lymon.*)

I ain't gonna sit out in that truck all day. You told me you was gonna take me to the movie.

LYMON: I told you I had something to do first. You supposed to wait on me.

BERNIECE: Lymon, just go on and leave. Take Grace or whoever with you. Just go on get out my house.

BOY WILLIE: You gonna help me move this piano first, nigger!

LYMON: (*To Grace.*) I got to help Boy Willie move the piano first.

(*Everybody but Grace suddenly senses Sutter's presence.*)

GRACE: I ain't waiting on you. Told me you was coming right back. Now you got to move a piano. You just like all the other men.

(*Grace now senses something.*)

Something ain't right here. I knew I shouldn't have come back up in this house.

(*Grace exits.*)

LYMON: Hey, Grace! I'll be right back, Boy Willie.

BOY WILLIE: Where you going, nigger?

LYMON: I'll be back. I got to take Grace home.

BOY WILLIE: Come on, let's move the piano first!

LYMON: I got to take Grace home. I told you I'll be back.

(*Lymon exits. Boy Willie exits and calls after him.*)

BOY WILLIE: Come on, Lymon! Hey . . . Lymon! Lymon . . . come on!

(*Again, the presence of Sutter is felt.*)

WINING BOY: Hey, Doaker, did you feel that? Hey, Berniece . . . did you get cold? Hey, Doaker . . .
DOAKER: What you calling me for?
WINING BOY: I believe that's Sutter.
DOAKER: Well, let him stay up there. As long as he don't mess with me.
BERNIECE: Avery, go on and bless the house.
DOAKER: You need to bless that piano. That's what you need to bless. It ain't done nothing but cause trouble. If you gonna bless anything go on and bless that.
WINING BOY: Hey, Doaker, if he gonna bless something let him bless everything. The kitchen . . . the upstairs. Go on and bless it all.
BOY WILLIE: Ain't no ghost in this house. He need to bless Berniece's head. That's what he need to bless.
AVERY: Seem like that piano's causing all the trouble. I can bless that. Berniece, put me some water in that bottle.

(*Avery takes a small bottle from his pocket and hands it to Berniece, who goes into the kitchen to get water. Avery takes a candle from his pocket and lights it. He gives it to Berniece as she gives him the water.*)

Hold this candle. Whatever you do make sure it don't go out.

O Holy Father we gather here this evening in the Holy Name to cast out the spirit of one James Sutter. May this vial of water be empowered with thy spirit. May each drop of it be a weapon and a shield against the presence of all evil and may it be a cleansing and blessing of this humble abode.

Just as Our Father taught us how to pray so He say, "I will prepare a table for you in the midst of mine enemies," and in His hands we place ourselves to come unto his presence. Where there is Good so shall it cause Evil to scatter to the Four Winds.

(*He throws water at the piano at each commandment.*)

AVERY: Get thee behind me, Satan! Get thee behind the face of Righteousness as we Glorify His Holy Name! Get thee behind the Hammer of Truth that breaketh down the Wall of Falsehood! Father. Father. Praise. Praise. We ask in Jesus' name and call forth the power of the Holy Spirit as it is written . . .

(*He opens the Bible and reads from it.*)

I will sprinkle clean water upon thee and ye shall be clean.
BOY WILLIE: All this old preaching stuff. Hell, just tell him to leave.

(*Avery continues reading throughout Boy Willie's outburst.*)

AVERY: I will sprinkle clean water upon you and you shall be clean: from all your uncleanliness, and from all your idols, will I cleanse you. A new heart also will I give you, and a new spirit will I put within you: and I will take out of your flesh the heart of stone, and I will give you a heart of flesh. And I will put my spirit within you, and cause you to walk in my statutes, and ye shall keep my judgments, and do them.

(*Boy Willie grabs a pot of water from the stove and begins to fling it around the room.*)

BOY WILLIE: Hey Sutter! Sutter! Get your ass out this house! Sutter! Come on and get some of this water! You done drowned in the well, come on and get some more of this water!

(*Boy Willie is working himself into a frenzy as he runs around the room throwing water and calling Sutter's name. Avery continues reading.*)

BOY WILLIE: Come on, Sutter!

(*He starts up the stairs.*)

Come on, get some water! Come on, Sutter!

(*The sound of Sutter's Ghost is heard. As Boy Willie approaches the steps he is suddenly thrown back by the unseen force, which is choking him. As he struggles he frees himself, then dashes up the stairs.*)

BOY WILLIE: Come on, Sutter!
AVERY (*continuing*): A new heart also will I give you and a new spirit will I put within you: and I will take out of your flesh the heart of stone, and I will give you a heart of flesh. And I will put my spirit within you, and cause you to walk in my statutes, and ye shall keep my judgments, and do them.

(*There are loud sounds heard from upstairs as Boy Willie begins to wrestle with Sutter's Ghost. It is a life-and-death struggle fraught with perils and faultless terror. Boy Willie is thrown down the stairs. Avery is stunned into silence. Boy Willie picks himself up and dashes back upstairs.*)

AVERY: Berniece, I can't do it.

(*There are more sounds heard from upstairs. Doaker and Wining Boy stare at one another in stunned disbe-*)

lief. It is in this moment, from somewhere old, that Berniece realizes what she must do. She crosses to the piano. She begins to play. The song is found piece by piece. It is an old urge to song that is both a commandment and a plea. With each repetition it gains in strength. It is intended as an exorcism and a dressing for battle. A rustle of wind blowing across two continents.)

BERNIECE (*singing*):
  I want you to help me
  I want you to help me
  I want you to help me
  I want you to help me
  I want you to help me
  I want you to help me
  Mama Berniece
  I want you to help me
  Mama Esther
  I want you to help me
  Papa Boy Charles
  I want you to help me
  Mama Ola
  I want you to help me

  I want you to help me
  I want you to help me
  I want you to help me
  I want you to help me
  I want you to help me
  I want you to help me
  I want you to help me
  I want you to help me

(The sound of a train approaching is heard. The noise upstairs subsides.)

BOY WILLIE: Come on, Sutter! Come back, Sutter!

(Berniece begins to chant:)

BERNIECE:
  Thank you.
  Thank you.
  Thank you.

(A calm comes over the house. Maretha enters from Doaker's room. Boy Willie enters on the stairs. He pauses a moment to watch Berniece at the piano.)

BERNIECE:
  Thank you.
  Thank you.
BOY WILLIE: Wining Boy, you ready to go back down home? Hey, Doaker, what time the train leave?
DOAKER: You still got time to make it.

(Maretha crosses and embraces Boy Willie.)

BOY WILLIE: Hey Berniece . . . if you and Maretha don't keep playing on that piano . . . ain't no telling . . . me and Sutter both liable to be back.

(He exits.)

BERNIECE: Thank you.

(The lights go down to black.)

COMMENTARIES

David Savran (b. 1950)
INTERVIEW WITH AUGUST WILSON   1987

    August Wilson is interested not only in the characters in his plays but also in their political circumstances. One of his primary efforts has been to help strip away the black male stereotypes so that his audiences can see his people as he sees them. In this interview he discusses the social conditions of black Americans and the relationship between Troy Maxson and his son Cory. Wilson's views about their relationship may be surprising, since he interprets it in a way that differs from many of the critics' interpretations.

Savran: In reading *Fences,* I came to view Troy more and more critically as the play progressed, sharing Rose's point of view. We see that Troy has been crippled by his father. That's being replayed in Troy's relationship with Cory. Do you think there's a way out of that cycle?

Wilson: Surely. First of all, we're all like our parents. The things we are taught early in life, how to respond to the world, our sense of morality — everything, we get from them. Now you can take that legacy and do with it anything you want to do. It's in your hands. Cory is Troy's son. How can he be Troy's son without sharing Troy's values? I was trying to get at why Troy made the choices he made, how they have influenced his values and how he attempts to pass those along to his son. Each generation gives the succeeding generation what they think they need. One question in the play is "Are the tools we are given sufficient to compete in a world that is different from the one our parents knew?" I think they are — it's just that we have to do different things with the tools. That's all Troy has to give. Troy's flaw is that he does not recognize that the world was changing. That's because he spent fifteen years in a penitentiary.

As African-Americans, we should demand to participate in society as Africans. That's the way out of the vicious cycle of poverty and neglect that exists in 1987 in America, where you have a huge percentage of blacks living in the equivalent of South African townships, in housing projects. No one is inviting these people to participate in society. Look at the poverty levels — $8,500 for a family of four, if you have $8,501 you're not counted. Those statistics would go up enormously if we had an honest assessment of the cost of living in America. I don't know how anybody can support a family of four on $8,500. What I'm saying is that 85 or 90 percent of blacks in America are living in abject poverty and, for the most part, are crowded into what amount to concentration camps. The situation for blacks in America is worse than it was forty years ago. Some sociologists will tell you about the tremendous progress we've made. They didn't put me out when I walked in the door. And you can always point to someone who works on Wall Street, or is a doctor. But they don't count in the larger scheme of things.

Savran: Do you have any idea how these political changes could take place?

Wilson: I'm not sure. I know that blacks must be allowed their cultural differences. I think the process of assimilation to white American society was a big mistake. We don't want to be like you. Blacks living in housing projects are isolated from the society, for the most part — living as they choose, as Africans. Only they don't realize the value in what they're doing because they have accepted their victimization. They've marked themselves as victims. Once they recognize that, they can begin to move through society in a different manner, from a stronger position, and claim what is theirs.

Savran: A project of yours is to point up what happens when oppression is internalized.

Wilson: Yes, transfer of aggression to the wrong target. I think it's interesting that the two roads open to blacks for "full participation" are entertainment and sports. *Ma Rainey* and *Fences,* and I didn't plan it that way. I don't think that they're the correct roads. I think Troy's right. Now with the benefit of historical perspective, I can say that the athletic scholarship was actually a way of exploiting. Now you've got two million kids who think they're going to play in the NBA. In the sixties the universities made a lot of money off of athletics. You had kids playing for free who, by and large, were not getting educated, were taking courses in basketweaving. Some of them could barely read.

Savran: Troy may be right about that issue, but it seems that he has passed on certain destructive traits in spite of himself. Take the hostility between father and son.

Wilson: I think every generation says to the previous generation: you're in my way, I've got to get by. The father-son conflict is actually a normal generational conflict that happens all the time.

Savran: So it's a healthy and a good thing?

Wilson: Oh, sure. Troy is seeing this boy walk around, smelling his piss. Two men cannot live in the same household. Troy would have been tremendously disappointed if Cory had not challenged him. Troy knows that this boy has to go out and do battle with that world: "So I had best prepare him because I know that's a harsh, cruel place out there. But that's going to be easy compared to what he's getting here. Ain't nobody gonna whip your ass like I'm gonna whip it." He has a tremendous love for the kid. But he's not going to say, "I love you," he's going to demonstrate it. He's carrying garbage for seventeen years just for the kid. The only world Troy knows is the one that he made. Cory's going to go on to find another one, he's going to arrive at the same place as Troy. I think one of the most important lines in the play is when Troy is talking about his father: "I got to the place where I could feel him kicking in my blood and knew that the only thing that separated us was the matter of a few years."

Hopefully, Cory will do things a bit differently with his son. For Troy, sports was not the way to go, the white man wouldn't let him get away with that. "Get you a job, with your hands, something that nobody can take away from you." The idea of school — he doesn't know what that is. That's for white folks. Very few blacks had paperwork jobs. But if you knew how to fix cars, you could always make some money. That's what Troy wants for Cory. There aren't many people who ever jumped up in Troy's face. So he's proud of the kid at the same time that he expresses a hurt that all men feel. You got to cut your kid loose at some point. There's that sense of loss and separation. You find out how Troy left his father's house and you see how Cory leaves his house. I suspect with Cory it will repeat with some differences and maybe, after five or six generations, they'll find a different way to do it.

Savran: Where Cory ends up is very ambiguous, as a marine in 1965.

Wilson: Yes. For the average black kid on the street, that was an alternative. You went into the army because you could learn how to do something. I can remember my parents talking about the son of some friends: "He's in the navy. He *did* something" — as opposed to standing on the street corner, shooting drugs, drinking wine, and robbing stores. Lyons says to Cory, "I always knew you were going to make something out of yourself." It really wounds me. He's a corporal in the marines. For blacks, that is a sense of accomplishment. Therein lies one of the tragedies of blacks in America. Cory says, "I don't know. I put in six years. That's enough." Anyone who goes into the army and makes a career out of it is a loser. They sit there and are nurtured by the army and they don't have to confront life. Then they get out of the army and find there's nothing to do. They didn't learn any skills. And if they did, they can't find a job. Four months later, they're shooting dope. In the sixties a whole bunch of blacks went over, fought and died in the Vietnam War. The survivors came back to the same street corners and found out nothing had changed. They still couldn't get a job.

At the end of *Fences* every person, with the exception of Raynell, is institutionalized. Rose is in a church. Lyons is in a penitentiary. Gabriel's in a mental hospital and Cory's in the marines. The only free person is the girl, Troy's daughter, the hope for the future. That was conscious on my part because in '57 that's what I saw. Blacks have relied on institutions which are really foreign — except for the black church, which has been our saving grace. I have some problems with it but I recognize it as a central social organization and sometimes an economic organization for the black community. I would like to see blacks develop their own institutions that respond to their needs.

Frank Rich (b. 1949)
REVIEW OF *FENCES*   1987

Frank Rich, the New York Times *critic, reviews* Fences *in context with August Wilson's other plays. Rich criticizes the old-fashioned structure of the plot which he characterizes as "clunky," but he also admits that the play is "gripping," especially in the second act. Rich focuses on the struggle between father and son, which he sees as meaningful to "theatergoers from all kinds of families."*

To hear his wife tell it, Troy Maxson, the middle-aged Pittsburgh sanitation worker at the center of *Fences,* is "so big" that he fills up his tenement house just by walking through it. Needless to say, that description could also apply to James Earl Jones, the actor who has found what may be the best role of his career in August Wilson's new play, at the 46th Street Theater. But the remarkable stature of the character — and of the performance — is not a matter of sheer size. If Mr Jones's Troy is a mountainous man prone to tyrannical eruptions of rage, he is also a dignified, delicate figure capable of cradling a tiny baby, of pleading gravely to his wife for understanding, of standing still to stare death unflinchingly in the eye. A black man, a free man, a descendant of slaves, a menial laborer, a father, a husband, a lover — Mr. Jones's Troy embraces all the contradictions of being black and male and American in his time.

That time is 1957 — three decades after the period of Mr. Wilson's previous and extraordinary *Ma Rainey's Black Bottom.* For blacks like Troy in the industrial North of *Fences,* social and economic equality is more a legal principle than a reality: the Maxson's slum neighborhood, a panorama of grimy brick and smokestack-blighted sky in James D. Sandefur's eloquent design, is a cauldron of busted promises, waiting to boil over. The conflagration is still a decade away — the streetlights burn like the first sparks of distant insurrection — so Mr. Wilson writes about the pain of an extended family lost in the wilderness of de facto segregation and barren hope.

It speaks of the power of the play — and of the cast assembled by the director, Lloyd Richards — that Mr. Jones's patriarch doesn't devour the rest of *Fences* so much as become the life force that at once nurtures and stunts the characters who share his blood. The strongest countervailing player is his wife,

Rose, luminously acted by Mary Alice. Rose is a quiet woman who, as she says, "planted herself" in the "hard and rocky" soil of her husband. But she never bloomed: marriage brought frustration and betrayal in equal measure with affection.

Even so, Ms. Alice's performance emphasizes strength over self-pity, open anger over festering bitterness. The actress finds the spiritual quotient in the acceptance that accompanies Rose's love for a scarred, profoundly complicated man. It's rare to find a marriage of any sort presented on stage with such balance — let alone one in which the husband has fathered children by three different women. Mr. Wilson grants both partners the right to want to escape the responsibilities of their domestic drudgery while affirming their respective claims to forgiveness.

The other primary relationship of *Fences* is that of Troy to his son Cory (Courtney B. Vance) — a promising 17-year-old football player being courted by a college recruiter. Troy himself was once a baseball player in the Negro Leagues — early enough to hit homers off Satchel Paige, too early to benefit from Jackie Robinson's breakthrough — and his bitter, long-ago disappointment leads him to decree a different future for his son. But while Troy wants Cory to settle for a workhorse trade guaranteeing a weekly paycheck, the boy resists. The younger Maxson is somehow convinced that the dreams of his black generation need not end in the city's mean alleys with the carting of white men's garbage.

The struggle between father and son over conflicting visions of black identity, aspirations and values is the play's narrative fulcrum, and a paradigm of violent divisions that would later tear apart a society. As written, the conflict is also a didactic one, reminiscent of old-fashioned plays, black and white, about disputes between first-generation American parents and their rebellious children.

In *Ma Rainey* — set at a blues recording session — Mr. Wilson's characters were firecrackers exploding in a bottle, pursuing jagged theatrical riffs reflective of their music and of their intimacy with the Afro-American experience that gave birth to that music. The relative tameness of *Fences* — with its laboriously worked-out titular metaphor, its slow-fused Act I exposition — is as much an expression of its period as its predecessor was of the hotter 20s. Intentionally or not — and perhaps to the satisfaction of those who found the more esthetically daring *Ma Rainey* too "plotless" — Mr. Wilson invokes the clunkier dramaturgy of Odets, Miller and Hansberry on this occasion.

Such formulaic theatrical tidiness, while exasperating at times, proves a minor price for the gripping second act (strengthened since the play's Yale debut in 1985) and for the scattered virtuoso passages throughout. Like *Ma Rainey* and the latest Wilson work seen at Yale (*Joe Turner's Come and Gone,* also promised for New York), *Fences* leaves no doubt that Mr. Wilson is a major writer, combining a poet's ear for vernacular with a robust sense of humor (political and sexual), a sure instinct for crackling dramatic incident and a passionate commitment to a great subject.

Mr. Wilson continues to see history as fully as he sees his characters. In one scene, Troy and his oldest friend (played with brimming warmth by Ray Aranha) weave an autobiographical "talking blues" — a front-porch storytelling jaunt from the antebellum plantation through the pre-industrial urban South, jail and northward migration. *Fences* is pointedly bracketed by two disparate wars that swallowed up black manhood, and, as always with Mr. Wilson, is as keenly cognizant of its characters' bonds to Africa, however muted here, as their bondage to white America. One hears the cadences of a centuries-old heritage in Mr. Jones's efforts to shout down the devil. It is a frayed scrap of timeless blues singing, unpretty but unquenchable, that proves the over-powering cathartic link among the disparate branches of the Maxson family tree.

Under the exemplary guidance of Mr. Richards — whose staging falters only in the awkward scene transitions — the entire cast is impressive, including Frankie R. Faison in the problematic (but finally devastating) role of a brain-damaged, horn-playing uncle named Gabriel, and Charles Brown, as a Maxson son who falls into the sociological crack separating the play's two principal generations. As Cory, Courtney B. Vance is not only formidable in challenging Mr. Jones to a psychological (and sometimes physical) kill-or-be-killed battle for supremacy but also seems to grow into Troy's vocal timbre and visage by the final scene. Like most sons, Mr. Vance just can't elude "the shadow" of his father, no matter how hard he tries. Such is the long shadow Mr. Jones's father casts in *Fences* that theatergoers from all kinds of families may find him impossible to escape.

Michael Morales (b. 1965)

GHOSTS ON THE PIANO: AUGUST WILSON
AND THE REPRESENTATION OF BLACK AMERICAN
HISTORY   *1994*

Morales sees the piano in The Piano Lesson *as an artifact with roots in African culture. Certain African artifacts carry a cultural memory in much the way that the piano does for the Charles family. By examining the piano in relation to "devices used to preserve the oral history of several African civilizations," Morales demonstrates the innate complexity of the piano as symbol.*

Using *The Piano Lesson* as the example, both the literal and the metaphoric functions of the piano serve to elucidate Wilson's framing of black American history as an active relation (kinship bond) between the living and the dead. The piano provides the key links to the past in what I argue are its interrelated, dual ritual functions. First, it functions as a mnemonic device for the transmission of oral history; and second, it functions as a sacred ancestral altar, bridging the world of the living to that of the dead.

The piano parallels similar devices used to preserve the oral history of several African civilizations, such as the memory boards (*lukasa*) of the Luba and the brass plaques of Benin. While controversy still exists about the precise representational intention of many of the brass plaques of Benin, accounts of nineteenth-century visitors to the kingdom attest to their historiographic function.[1] These plaques, which covered the supporting pillars of the royal palace,

---

[1] Ben-Amos, Paula. "History and Art in Benin," in *The Art of Power / The Power of Art: Studies in Benin Iconography,* edited by Paula Ben-Amos and Arnold Rubin. Los Angeles: Museum of Cultural History at UCLA, 1983, pp. 13–14.

represented in relief major events of the Benin kingdom, the daily court life, and the lineage of rulers.[2] Even though art historians may disagree as to whether some of the representations are of individual kings or of more general signifiers of a royal line, it is clear that the plaques served as a pictorial repository of lineage history and provided a stable mechanism to maintain the narrative of origin and cultural assumptions upon which the ruling class justified itself. In many respects, the carvings on the piano in *The Piano Lesson*, though no longer serving a sacral kingship and a royal order, function similarly to this Benin tradition by pictorially preserving important events of the family's history as well as the images of the ancestors themselves. While the example of Luba traditions are not specifically pictorial, as are the carvings on the piano, they are especially close to the historiographic function of the piano because they preserve history through the integration of the narrative with the plastic arts and music.[3] The communal oral historians of the Luba, known as the *men of memory*, sculpture concave boards (*lukasa*) implanted with a design of cowries and beads to help them accurately retain the lineage history and recall major historical events.[4] The design of the cowries, although not writing per se, contains specific patterns that help the historians to replicate the lineage history. The correct retention of history from generation to generation is further assured by the tonal and rhythmic patterns of the narrative itself, which can be played on the two-tone slit gong or the signal drum.[5] While the actual narrative may change according to the individual performance and situation, the rhythms of the music and the patterns of the boards help maintain the historical continuity upon which the social order depends. In *The Piano Lesson*, Doaker plays a similar role to the *men of memory* as he recalls three generations of his own lineage history in order to explain to Lymon why Berniece will not sell the piano. Boy Willie also assumes this role when he begins to recount the history of the piano carvings to Maretha in order to give her a sense of pride, and he explains to Berniece that with knowledge of the piano Maretha "could walk around here with her head held high" [p. 1570]. The piano is both the slit gong and the memory board, contained in one site in the family living room, and the music played on that piano, from Boy Willie's improvised boogie-woogie to Wining Boy's "Rambling Gambling Man," reach, like the style of the carvings, across the middle passage back to Africa — to the original ancestors and their gods. The images carved on the piano preserve a narrative-generating, visual memory that connects the family to their own ancestors who brought those rhythms and styles from Africa and transformed them in the context of slave life.

While this function of the piano may seem to be purely historical, the connections established between the past and present through the piano are represented in metaphysical dimensions. Within the imaginative world of the play, the piano also serves as a site of direct mystical connections with the ancestors,

---

[2] Ibid., p. 14; Blackmun, Barbara Winston. "Wall Plaque of a Junior Titleholder Carrying an Ekpokin." In *The Art of Power / The Power of Art: Studies in Benin Iconography*, edited by Paula Ben-Amos and Arnold Rubin. Los Angeles: Museum of Cultural History at UCLA, 1983, p. 84.

[3] Reefe, Thomas Q. *The Rainbow and the Kings: A History of the Luba Empire to 1891*. Berkeley: University of California Press, 1981, pp. 10, 40.

[4] Ibid., p. 39.

[5] Ibid., p. 10.

functioning similarly to sacred ancestral shrines or altars in many traditional African cultures. In the terms of Yoruba cosmography it is an *orita meta,* a crossroad between the world of the living and that of the dead. For the Yoruba, ancestral shrines are key links between the two worlds, where descendants may contact their ancestors for protection, support, and guidance.[6] Of all the characters in the play, Berniece is closest to fully realizing this aspect of the piano, even though concurrently she distances herself from the piano more than any other character does:

> I used to think those pictures came alive and walked through the house. Sometimes late at night I could hear my mama talking to them. I said that wasn't going to happen to me. I don't play that piano because I don't want to wake them spirits. They never be walking around in this house. [p. 1563]

Berniece believes in the mystical power of the piano, recognizing it as the site of connection to her ancestral spirits, but at the same time she denies those spirits access to her life.

The blood sacrifices made over the piano intensify its sacral properties and parallel similar African practices of pouring blood, meal, and urine over sacred representations of the ancestors or gods in order to feed them and maintain their spiritual existence. The piano initially becomes family property with the human sacrifice of Boy Willie's and Berniece's father, who is burned alive in the Yellow Dog railway car. Subsequently, as Berniece recounts, Mama Ola, her mother, makes daily sacrifice at the altar of the piano:

> You ain't taking that piano out of my house. Look at this piano. Look at it. Mama Ola polished this piano with her tears for seventeen years. For seventeen years she rubbed on it till her hands bled. Then she rubbed the blood in . . . mixed it up with the rest of the blood on it. Every day that God breathed life into her body she rubbed and cleaned and polished and prayed over it. "Play something for me, Berniece. Play something for me, Berniece." Every day. "I cleaned it up for you, play something for me, Berniece." [p. 1557]

For Mama Ola the piano becomes a shrine to her murdered husband, where she pours the libations of her own blood and tears. It is a cleansing ritual that is consummated daily with music, and the piano becomes the prayer site where Mama Ola connects with her deceased husband and tragic past. But upon her death and with the eventual transference of the piano to Pittsburgh, the next generation loses this sacral connection to the piano and it becomes the source of internecine conflict.

Berniece shuts the piano in order to forget her past, and the family shrine becomes moribund except for the childish tinkering of Maretha and the occasional bursts of life that come with Wining Boy's visits. While it is easy to sympathize with Berniece's desire to forget her painful memories, if we draw the parallel between the piano and African ritual practice, the spiritual and physical consequences of forgetting her past and not using the piano are very serious. In the parallel context of most African ancestral worship, neglect of the ancestors and the ancestral altars results in loss of their protection and threatens the destruc-

[6] Drewel, Henry John, and John Pemberton III, with Rowland Abiodeen. Edited by Allen Wardell. *Yoruba: Nine Centuries of African Art and Thought.* New York: Center for African Art, 1989, p. 15.

tion of the entire community.[7] As a Yoruba diviner explains: "If a person neglects his or her shrine (by not offering prayers or gifts) the spirits will leave . . . all you are seeing is the images . . . the person has relegated the deities to mere idols, ordinary images" (parenthesis added).[8] Ritual neglect of the ancestors not only results in the loss of ancestral protection from forces destructive to living members of the lineage, but it also threatens the very existence of the ancestors who require the food of sacrifice to maintain their existence in the realm of the dead.[9] The kinship between the living and the dead is a symbiotic relation — mutually beneficial or self-destructive — and it must be carried on in order to guarantee the continuation of the lineage. The ancestors are still members of the lineage, an active part of the clan, and after a period of time most of the ancestors will reenter the world of the living by reincarnation back into the lineage, thus completing a cycle of life and death that ensures the continuity and survival of their own kinship line.[10] Any break in this cycle has potentially catastrophic effects.

Within the play, a lack of sacral connection to the piano eventually threatens fratricide when Boy Willie attempts to remove the piano from Doaker's home against Berniece's will. This loss of ritual connection also allows the invasion of Doaker's home by Sutter's ghost, who begins to play his own songs on the piano. Doaker and Berniece ask Avery to perform a Christian exorcism of the ghost, but that only seems to feed Sutter's power rather than diminish it. Boy Willie, the consummate materialist, then tries to fight the ghost physically. But it is only when Berniece calls upon the protective spirits of her ancestors that the family finally can exorcise Sutter from their house:

(It is in this moment, from somewhere old, that Berniece realizes what she must do. She crosses to the piano. She begins to play. The song is found piece by piece. It is an old urge to song that is both a commandment and a plea. With each repetition it gains in strength. It is intended as an exorcism and a dressing for battle. A rustle of wind blowing across two continents.)

BERNIECE (*singing*):

>I want you to help me
>I want you to help me
>I want you to help me . . .
>Mama Berniece
>I want you to help me
>Mama Esther
>I want you to help me
>Papa Boy Charles
>I want you to help me
>Mama Ola
>I want you to help me . . .

(The sound of a train approaching is heard. The noise upstairs subsides.)
[p. 1576]

[7] Sharevskaya, B. J. *The Religious Traditions of Tropical Africa in Contemporary Focus.* Budapest: Center for Afro-Asian Research of the Hungarian Academy of Sciences, 1973, p. 74.

[8] Drewel, *Yoruba*, p. 26.

[9] Sharevskaya, *Religious Traditions of Tropical Africa*, p. 54.

[10] Ibid., Drewel, *Yoruba*, p. 15.

It is important to note that this was not Berniece's song in the original productions or in the play's first publication in *Theater*. By the time the play reached Broadway and was published in soft cover, Wilson changed the song and the ending. Berniece's original song was "Oh, Lord I want you to help me," repeated fourteen times in succession, and the play ended with Boy Willie chasing Sutter's ghost up the stairs.[11] The change in song from a call to God to an appeal to the ancestors strengthens the African ritual properties of the play and simultaneously distances Berniece from a Christian context. The success of this appeal in defeating Sutter and Boy Willie's final warning further emphasize the piano's ritual power and the necessity of keeping the ancestors alive with the food of music. As he leaves, Boy Willie threatens. "Hey Berniece... if you and Maretha don't keep playing that piano... ain't no telling... me and Sutter both liable to be back." [p. 1576]

[11] Wilson, August. *The Piano Lesson, Theater,* 1987, p. 68.

Suzan-Lori Parks

Suzan-Lori Parks (b. 1964) was named by Mel Gussow in the *New York Times* as the "year's most promising playwright" in 1989. She lives in New York City and teaches as writer-in-residence at the New School for Social Research. Her work has been supported by grants from numerous agencies, including the Rockefeller and Ford foundations and the National Endowment for the Arts, from which she has received a playwriting fellowship twice. She also received a MacArthur Award in 1986. Her work has been seen primarily in off-Broadway theaters in New York as well as important regional theaters.

Parks was the child of an army officer and therefore grew up in several different locations. She says, "I've heard horrible stories about 12-step groups for army people. But I had a great childhood. My parents were really into experiencing the places we lived." She lived, for example, in a small town in Germany and attended German schools, studying in German. She went to Hampshire College, where she studied writing with James Baldwin. After that experience she went to London for a year to study acting. "It really made a difference in my writing. It dawned on me that a lot of people write with ideas in mind.... But I never really have ideas, per se. I have these movements, these gestures. Then I figure out how to put those gestures into words."

She is aware of being influenced by a number of important literary figures, among them Gertrude Stein, James Joyce, William Faulkner, and Samuel Beckett, but there are echoes of other writers such as Shakespeare and Richard Wright in *The Death of the Last Black Man in the Whole Entire World*. Parks's approach to language is partly vernacular as she attempts to reproduce speech both as it is spoken and as her audience assumes it may be spoken. But she is interested in the hypnotic and musical value of words, which accounts for much of the patterning of repetition that marks her work.

Her plays have been performed in the BACA (Brooklyn Arts Council Association) Downtown Theater, Manhattan Theater Club, and the Joseph Papp Public Theater in Manhattan. Her early short plays are *Betting on the Dust Commander, Fishes, The Sinners' Place,* and *The America Play.* Her full-length play *Imperceptible Mutabilities in the Third Kingdom,* directed by her long-time collaborator Liz Diamond, won the Obie Award for the best off-Broadway play of 1990. One section of *Mutabilities* takes place on Emancipation Day in 1865 and is played in whiteface by African American actors. Another section, "Greeks," makes reference to her own family, with a character called

Mr. Sergeant Smith. Parts of the play have been described as "like a choral poem."

Parks has produced a film, *Anemone Me* (1990), that has been shown in New York. Her *Devotees in the Garden of Love* (1992) premiered at the Actors Theatre of Louisville, Kentucky. Her latest play, *Venus* (1996), was a coproduction of the Joseph Papp Public Theater and Yale Repertory Theatre. It was directed by Richard Foreman, the founder of the Ontological-Hysteric Theater. The play focuses on the life of a black woman brought to England as the Venus Hottentot, a sideshow freak displaying "an intensely ugly figure, distorted beyond all European notions of beauty." The authorities put an end to the sideshow, and Parks explores this mysterious woman's life. Parks has also written *Girl 6* (1996), a film directed by Spike Lee. She is an energetic, carefully focused, and clearly directed playwright with a special interest in the language of speech and the language of gesture — in almost equal measure.

THE DEATH OF THE LAST BLACK MAN IN THE WHOLE ENTIRE WORLD

The Death of the Last Black Man in the Whole Entire World (1990) is not a straight-line narrative, nor is it situational in the manner of the Scribean well-made play. It consists of several sections:

Overture

Panel I: Thuh Holy Ghost

Panel II: First Chorus

Panel III: Thuh Lonesome 3some

Panel IV: Second Chorus

Panel V: In thuh Garden of HooDoo It

Final Chorus

The first production of the play, at the Brooklyn Arts Council Association (BACA) Downtown Theater, was directed by Liz Diamond in close collaboration with Suzan-Lori Parks. Although Parks's text provides no conventional stage directions, the BACA production created very powerful visual images in the staging and costuming. In Panels I, III, and IV the name of the panel was projected on the back of the stage, lighted brightly enough to be read, like the caption of a cartoon panel. The visual emblems that dominated the panels were powerful: an electric chair in "Thuh Holy Ghost," with Black Man, wearing only a pair of white jockey shorts, rising from a black catafalque to find himself seated in the chair with a metal helmet to facilitate the flow of electricity through his body. This emblem was duplicated: While one actor sat in the chair, another played his part downstage getting solace from Black Woman, who anointed him and washed his feet in the traditional Christian fashion.

In "Thuh Lonesome 3some" the emblem was three watermelons borne by Black Man with Watermelon, who struggles to understand the role these melons play in his life. The biblical references to melons in paradise ironically underpin this section. In "In thuh Garden of HooDoo It," another emblem of death, the lynched man, dangled over the action. Again, the Black Man was duplicated downstage with a noose around his neck and with a dead tree limb dragged onto the stage. In each instance the Black Man dies a different death, but he cannot die without the accompanying spirits telling their story.

Liz Diamond, the director, explained, "These are figures, not characters, and their function as figures must be understood." One of Diamond's greatest challenges was in bringing these figures onstage so the audience would understand that they are not "realistic" characters. They are epic types that Diamond calls spirits who will not let Black Man die before he hears them impart their wisdom. The figures come from many sources: And Bigger and Bigger and Bigger from Richard Wright's *Native Son*; Ham from the Bible; Black Man with Watermelon and Black Woman with Fried Drumstick from black folklore; Queen-then-Pharaoh Hatshepsut from history; Prunes and Prisms, an image of the black prom queen; and Voice on thuh Tee V, a contemporary image.

Each of these figures was costumed appropriately in the Diamond production. Hatshepsut wore the squared-off headdress found on the Sphinx with a gold pleated full-length dress. Black Man with Watermelon wore overalls; Black Woman wore a black matronly dress and later a black veil of mourning. Bigger wore a gold zoot suit; Voice on thuh Tee V wore a trench coat and carried a microphone. Ham, one of the most compelling figures, wore a multicolored shawl and headdress and carried a long staff. The inspiration for his character, as Parks and Diamond observed, was the "Times Square Prophet," a homeless wanderer who rants as if he were a holy man.

Ham's major section, Panel IV, is dominated by his biblical "voice." In the Bible, when Ham saw his father Noah's nakedness, he was condemned, and his progeny were forever black as a result. As Parks has said, "Ham doesn't get a chance to respond" in the Bible. But Parks provides Ham's response with a parody of the Bible's series of "begets." The figure Before Columbus was costumed like an African villager in an abbadan obie, an African tunic, and comments on the world when it was "flat." These figures are the stereotypes of blacks as created in the Western European imagination, beginning with the Bible.

Parks hears language as much as she sees it. Therefore in her text she spells words as she wants them to be heard and signifies meanings that sometimes transcend the limits of individual words. She adds the syllable -ed to a word such as *died,* and the result is a new word, in this case *dieded.* The effect is both ironic and rhythmically powerful and reinforcing. That kind of syllabic repetition also complements the repetition of important phrases, such as "You should write that down. You should write that down and hide it under uh rock." Much of history has been written down and hidden under rocks only to be discovered and deciphered by later generations. The point is to get it down in language somehow, to tell the story so that the future will know.

Music was used judiciously throughout the Yale performance, including a saxophone with a jazz riff, but no songs. A gong sounded to signal important moments like the string breaking in *The Cherry Orchard.* Subtle rhythmic effects are achieved with the repetition of words and phrases, and time becomes as plastic as space. The time of the play encompasses ancient Egypt, biblical Judea, the coming of Columbus, slavery in the American South, lynchings in the post–Civil War era, and contemporary electrocutions of blacks. *Last Black Man* is nothing if not inclusive.

The Death of the Last Black Man in the Whole Entire World in Performance

The Death of the Last Black Man in the Whole Entire World premiered in the BACA Downtown Theater in New York in September 1990. It was revived in a larger, full-scale production at the Yale Repertory Theatre Winterfest Program in early 1992. Audiences responded positively to a production that was more avant-garde than most drama being shown in regional theaters, and reviewers hailed Parks as an exciting new voice in theater.

Suzan-Lori Parks *(b. 1964)*

THE DEATH OF THE LAST BLACK MAN IN THE WHOLE ENTIRE WORLD

1990

When I die
I wont stay
Dead. — BOB KAUFMAN

The Figures

BLACK MAN WITH WATERMELON
BLACK WOMAN WITH FRIED DRUMSTICK
LOTS OF GREASE AND LOTS OF PORK
YES AND GREENS BLACK-EYED PEAS CORNBREAD
QUEEN-THEN-PHARAOH HATSHEPSUT
BEFORE COLUMBUS
OLD MAN RIVER JORDAN
HAM
AND BIGGER AND BIGGER AND BIGGER
PRUNES AND PRISMS
VOICE ON THUH TEE V

The Sections

Overture

Panel I: *Thuh Holy Ghost*
Panel II: *First Chorus*
Panel III: *Thuh Lonesome 3some*
Panel IV: *Second Chorus*

Panel V: *In thuh Garden of HooDoo It*
Final Chorus

The action takes place in the present.

OVERTURE

BLACK MAN WITH WATERMELON: The black man moves his hands.

(*a bell sounds twice*)

LOTS OF GREASE AND LOTS OF PORK: Lots of grease and lots of pork.
QUEEN-THEN-PHARAOH HATSHEPSUT: Queen-then-Pharaoh Hatshepsut.
AND BIGGER AND BIGGER AND BIGGER: And Bigger and Bigger and Bigger.
PRUNES AND PRISMS: Prunes and Prisms.
HAM: Ham.
VOICE ON THUH TEE V: Voice on thuh Tee V.
OLD MAN RIVER JORDAN: Old Man River Jordan.
YES AND GREENS BLACK-EYED PEAS CORNBREAD: Yes and Greens Black-Eyed Peas Cornbread.

BEFORE COLUMBUS: Before Columbus.

(*a bell sounds once*)

BLACK MAN WITH WATERMELON: The black man moves his hands.

QUEEN-THEN-PHARAOH HATSHEPSUT: Not yet. Let Queen-then-Pharaoh Hatshepsut tell you when.

LOTS OF GREASE AND LOTS OF PORK: This is the death of the last black man in the whole entire world.

(*a bell sounds three times*)

BLACK WOMAN WITH FRIED DRUMSTICK: Yesterday today next summer tomorrow just uh moment uh-goh in 1317 dieded thuh last black man in thuh whole entire world. Uh! Oh. Don't be uhlarmed. Do not be afeared. It was painless. Uh painless passin. He falls twenty-three floors to his death. 23 floors from uh passin ship from space tuh splat on thuh pavement. He have uh head he been keepin under thuh Tee V. On his bottom pantry shelf. He have uh head that hurts. Don't fit right. Put it on tuh go tuh thuh store and it pinched him when he walks his thoughts don't got room. Why dieded he huh? Where he gonna go now that he done dieded? Where he gonna go tuh wash his hands?

YES AND GREENS BLACK-EYED PEAS CORNBREAD: You should write that down and you should hide it under a rock. This is the death of the last black man in the whole entire world.

LOTS OF GREASE AND LOTS OF PORK/PRUNES AND PRISMS: Not yet —

BLACK MAN WITH WATERMELON: The black man moves. His hands —

QUEEN-THEN-PHARAOH HATSHEPSUT: You are too young to move. Let me move it for you.

BLACK MAN WITH WATERMELON: The black man moves his hands. — He moves his hands round. Back. Back. Back tuh that.

LOTS OF GREASE AND LOTS OF PORK: (Not dat).

BLACK MAN WITH WATERMELON: When thuh worl usta be roun. Thuh worl usta be *roun.*

BLACK WOMAN WITH FRIED DRUMSTICK: Uh roun worl. Uh roun? Thuh worl? When was this.

QUEEN-THEN-PHARAOH HATSHEPSUT: Columbus. Before.

BEFORE COLUMBUS: Before. Columbus.

YES AND GREENS BLACK-EYED PEAS CORNBREAD: Before Columbus.

BLACK MAN WITH WATERMELON: HHH. HA!

QUEEN-THEN-PHARAOH HATSHEPSUT: Before Columbus thuh worl usta be *roun* they put uh /d/ on thuh end of roun makin round. Thusly they set in motion thuh end. Without that /d/ we coulda gone on spinnin for ever. Thuh /d/ thing ended things ended.

YES AND GREENS BLACK-EYED PEAS CORNBREAD: Before Columbus:

(*a bell sounds twice*)

BEFORE COLUMBUS: The popular thinking of the day back in them days was that the world was flat. They thought the world was flat. Back then when they thought the world was flat they were afeared and stayed at home. They wanted to go out back then when they thought the world was flat but the water had in it dragons of which meaning these dragons they were afeared back then when they thought the world was flat. They stayed at home. Them thinking the world was flat kept it roun. Them thinking the sun revolved around the earth kept them satellite-like. They figured out the truth and scurried out. Figuring out the truth put them in their place and they scurried out to put us in ours.

YES AND GREENS BLACK-EYED PEAS CORNBREAD: Mmmm. Yes. You should write this down. You should hide this under a rock.

LOTS OF GREASE AND LOTS OF PORK/PRUNES AND PRISMS: Not yet —

BLACK MAN WITH WATERMELON: The black man bursts into flames. The black man bursts into blames. Whose fault is it?

ALL: Ain't mines.

BLACK MAN WITH WATERMELON: Whose fault is it?

ALL: Ain't mines.

BLACK WOMAN WITH FRIED DRUMSTICK: I can't remember back that far.

QUEEN-THEN-PHARAOH HATSHEPSUT: And besides, I wasn't even there.

BLACK MAN WITH WATERMELON: Ha ha ha. The black man laughs out loud.

ALL (*except Ham*): HAM-BONE-HAM-BONE-WHERE-YOU-BEEN-ROUN-THUH-WORL-N-BACK-UH-*GAIN.*

YES AND GREENS BLACK-EYED PEAS CORNBREAD: Whatcha seen hambone girl?

BLACK WOMAN WITH FRIED DRUMSTICK: Didn't see you. I saw thuh worl.

QUEEN-THEN-PHARAOH HATSHEPSUT: I was there.

LOTS OF GREASE AND LOTS OF PORK: Didn't see you.

BLACK WOMAN WITH FRIED DRUMSTICK: I was there.

BLACK MAN WITH WATERMELON: Didn't see you. The black man moves his hands.

QUEEN-THEN-PHARAOH HATSHEPSUT: We are too young to see. Let them see it for you. We are too young to rule. Let them rule it for you. We are too young to have. Let them have it for you. You are too young to write. Let them — let them. Do it. Before you.

BLACK MAN WITH WATERMELON: The black man moves his hands.

YES AND GREENS BLACK-EYED PEAS CORNBREAD: You should write it down because if you dont write it down then they will come along and tell the future that we did not exist. You should write it down and you should hide it under a rock. You should write down the past and you should write down the present and in what in the future you should write it down. It will be of us but you should mention them from time to time so that in the future when they come along and know that they exist. You should hide it all under a rock so that in the future when they come along they will say that the rock did not exist.

BLACK WOMAN WITH FRIED DRUMSTICK: We getting somewheres. We getting down. Down down down down down down down down —

QUEEN-THEN-PHARAOH HATSHEPSUT: I saw Columbus comin. / I saw Columbus comin goin over tuh visit you. "To borrow a cup of sugar," so he said. I waved my hands in warnin. You waved back. I aint seen you since.

LOTS OF GREASE AND LOTS OF PORK: In the future when they came along I meeting them. On thuh coast. Uh! Thuh Coast! I — was — so — polite. But in thuh dirt, I wrote: "Ha. Ha. Ha."

ALL: Ha. Ha. Ha. Ha. Ha. Ha. Ha. Ha. Ha. Ha. Ha. Ha. Ha. Ha. Ha. Ha. HHHHHHHHHHHHHHHH.

BLACK MAN WITH WATERMELON: Thuh black man he move. He move he hans.

(a bell sounds once)

PANEL I: THUH HOLY GHOST

BLACK MAN WITH WATERMELON: Saint mines. Saint mines. Iduhnt it Nope: iduhnt. Saint mines cause everythin I calls mines got uh print uh me someway on it in it dont got uh print uh me someway on it so saint mines. Duhduhnt so saint: huh.

BLACK WOMAN WITH FRIED DRUMSTICK: Hen.

BLACK MAN WITH WATERMELON: Huh. Huh?

BLACK WOMAN WITH FRIED DRUMSTICK: Hen. Hen?

BLACK MAN WITH WATERMELON: Who gived birth tuh this I wonder. Who gived birth tuh this. I wonder.

BLACK WOMAN WITH FRIED DRUMSTICK: You comed back. Comin backs somethin in itself. You comed back.

BLACK MAN WITH WATERMELON: This does not belong tuh me. Somebody planted this on me. On me in my hands.

BLACK WOMAN WITH FRIED DRUMSTICK: Cold compress. Cold compress then some hen. Lean back. You comed back. Lean back.

BLACK MAN WITH WATERMELON: Who gived birth tuh this I wonder who.

BLACK WOMAN WITH FRIED DRUMSTICK: Comin for you. Came for you: that they done did. Comin for tuh take you. Told me tuh pack up your clothes. Told me tuh cut my bed in 2 from double tuh single. Cut off thuh bed-foot where your feets had rested. Told me tuh do that too. Burry your ring in his hidin spot under thuh porch! That they told me too to do. Didnt have uh ring so I didnt do diddly. They told and told and told: proper instructions for thuh burial proper attire for thuh mournin. They told and told and told: I didnt do squat. Awe on that. You comed back. You got uhway. Knew you would. Hen?

BLACK MAN WITH WATERMELON: Who gived birth tuh this I wonder. Who? Not me. Saint mines.

BLACK WOMAN WITH FRIED DRUMSTICK: Killed every hen on thuh block. You comed back. Knew you would. Knew you would came back. Knew you will wanted uh good big hen dinner in waitin. Every hen on thuh block.

BLACK MAN WITH WATERMELON: Saint mines.

BLACK WOMAN WITH FRIED DRUMSTICK: Strutted down on up thuh road with my axe. By-myself-with-my-axe. Got tuh thuh street top 93 dyin hen din hand. Dropped thuh axe. Tooked tuh stranglin. 93 dyin hen din hand with no heads let em loose tuh run down tuh towards home infront of me. Flipped thuh necks of thuh next 23 more odd. Slinged um over my shoulders. Hens of thuh neighbors now in my pots. Feathers of thuh hens of thuh neighbors stucked in our mattress. They told and told and told. On me. Huh. Awe on that. Hen? You got uhway. Knew you would.

BLACK MAN WITH WATERMELON: Who gived birth tuh me I wonder.

BLACK WOMAN WITH FRIED DRUMSTICK: They dont speak tuh us no more. They pass by our porch but they dont nod. You been comed back goin on 9 years not even heard from thuh neighbors uh congratulation. Uh alienationed dum. Uh guess. Huh. Hen? *WE AINT GOT NO FRIENDS,* — sweetheart.

BLACK MAN WITH WATERMELON: *SWEET-HEART.*

BLACK WOMAN WITH FRIED DRUMSTICK: Hen!!

BLACK MAN WITH WATERMELON: Aint hungry.

BLACK WOMAN WITH FRIED DRUMSTICK: Hen.

BLACK MAN WITH WATERMELON: Aint eaten in years.

BLACK WOMAN WITH FRIED DRUMSTICK: Hen?

BLACK MAN WITH WATERMELON: Last meal I had was my last-mans-meal.

BLACK WOMAN WITH FRIED DRUMSTICK: You got uhway. Knew you would.

BLACK MAN WITH WATERMELON: This thing dont look like me!

BLACK WOMAN WITH FRIED DRUMSTICK: It dont. Do it. Should it? Hen: eat it.

BLACK MAN WITH WATERMELON: I kin tell whats mines by whets gots my looks. Ssmymethod. Try it by testin it and it turns out true. Every time. Fool proofly. Look down at my foot and wonder if its mine. Foot mine? I kin ask it and foot answers back with uh "yes Sir" — not like you and me say "yes Sir" but uh "yes Sir" peculiar tuh thuh foot. Foot mine? I kin ask it and through uh look that looks like my looks thuh foot gives me back uh "yes Sir." Ssmymethod. Try by thuh test tuh pass for true. Move on tuh thuh uther foot. Foot mine? And uh nother "yes Sir" so feets mine is understood. Got uh forearm thats up for question check myself out teeth by tooth. Melon mine? —. Dont look like me.

BLACK WOMAN WITH FRIED DRUMSTICK: Hen mine? Gobble it up and it will be. You got uhway. Fixed uh good big hen dinner for you. Get yourself uh mouthful afore it rots.

BLACK MAN WITH WATERMELON: Was we green and stripe-dly when we first comed out?

BLACK WOMAN WITH FRIED DRUMSTICK: Uh huhn. Thuh features comes later. Later comes after now.

BLACK MAN WITH WATERMELON: Oh. Later comes now: melon mine?

BLACK WOMAN WITH FRIED DRUMSTICK: They comed for you and tooked you. That was yesterday. Today you sit in your chair where you sat yesterday and thuh day afore yesterday afore they comed and tooked you. Things today is just as they are yesterday cept nothin is familiar cause it was such uh long time uhgoh.

BLACK MAN WITH WATERMELON: Later oughta be now by now huh?: melon mine?

BLACK WOMAN WITH FRIED DRUMSTICK: Thuh chair was portable. They take it from county tuh county. Only got one. Can only eliminate one at uh time. Woulda fried you right here on thuh front porch but we dont got enough electric. No onessgot enough electric. Not on our block. Dont believe in havin enough. Put thuh Chair in thuh middle of thuh City. Outdoors. In thuh square. Folks come tuh watch with picnic baskets. — Hen?

BLACK MAN WITH WATERMELON: Sweetheart?

BLACK WOMAN WITH FRIED DRUMSTICK: They juiced you some, huh?

BLACK MAN WITH WATERMELON: Just uh squirt. Sweetheart.

BLACK WOMAN WITH FRIED DRUMSTICK: Humpty Dumpty.

BLACK MAN WITH WATERMELON: Melon mines?

BLACK WOMAN WITH FRIED DRUMSTICK: Humpty damn Dumpty actin like thuh Holy Ghost. You got

uhway. Thuh lights dimmed but you got uhway. Knew you would.

BLACK MAN WITH WATERMELON: They juiced me some.

BLACK WOMAN WITH FRIED DRUMSTICK: Just uh squirt.

BLACK MAN WITH WATERMELON: They had theirselves uh extender chord. Fry uh man in thuh town square needs uh extender tuh reach em thuh electric Hook up thuh chair tuh thuh power. Extender: 49 foot in length. Closer tuh thuh power I never been. Flip on up thuh go switch. Huh! Juice begins its course.

BLACK WOMAN WITH FRIED DRUMSTICK: Humpty damn Dumpty.

BLACK MAN WITH WATERMELON: Thuh straps they have on me are leathern. See thuh cord waggin full with uh jump-juice try me tuh wiggle from thuh waggin but belt leathern straps: width thickly. One round each forearm. Forearm mines? 2 cross thuh chest. Chest is mines: and it explodin. One for my left hand fingers left strapted too. Right was done thuh same. Jump-juice meets me-mine juices I do uh slow soft shoe like on water. Town crier cries uh moan. Felt my nappy head go frizzly. Town follows thuh crier in uh sorta sing-uhlong-song.

BLACK WOMAN WITH FRIED DRUMSTICK: Then you got uhway. Got uhway in comed back.

BLACK MAN WITH WATERMELON: Uh extender chord 49 foot in length. Turned on thuh up switch in I started runnin. First 49 foot I was runnin they was still juicin.

BLACK WOMAN WITH FRIED DRUMSTICK: And they chase-ted you.

BLACK MAN WITH WATERMELON: — Melon mines?

BLACK WOMAN WITH FRIED DRUMSTICK: When you broked tuh seek your freedom they followed after, huh?

BLACK MAN WITH WATERMELON: Later oughta be now by now, huh?

BLACK WOMAN WITH FRIED DRUMSTICK: You comed back.

BLACK MAN WITH WATERMELON: — Not exactly.

BLACK WOMAN WITH FRIED DRUMSTICK: They comed for you tuh take you. Tooked you uhway: that they done did. You got uhway. Thuh lights dimmed. Had us uh brownout. You got past that. You comed back.

BLACK MAN WITH WATERMELON: Turned on thuh juice on me in me in I started runnin. First just runnin then runnin towards home. Couldnt find us. Think I got lost. Saw us on up uhhead but I flew over thuh yard. Couldnt stop. Think I overshot.

BLACK WOMAN WITH FRIED DRUMSTICK: Killed every hen on thuh block. Made you uh —

BLACK MAN WITH WATERMELON: Make me uh space 6 feet by 6 feet by 6. Make it big and mark it so as

I wont miss it. If you would please, sweetness, uh mass grave-site. Theres company comin soonish. I would like tuh get up and go. I would like tuh move my hands.

BLACK WOMAN WITH FRIED DRUMSTICK: You comed back.

BLACK MAN WITH WATERMELON: Overshot. Overshot. I would like tuh move my hands.

BLACK WOMAN WITH FRIED DRUMSTICK: Cold compress?

BLACK MAN WITH WATERMELON: Sweetheart.

BLACK WOMAN WITH FRIED DRUMSTICK: How uhbout uh hen leg?

BLACK MAN WITH WATERMELON: Nothanks. Justate.

BLACK WOMAN WITH FRIED DRUMSTICK: Just ate?

BLACK MAN WITH WATERMELON: Justate. Thatsright. 6 by 6 by 6. Thatsright.

BLACK WOMAN WITH FRIED DRUMSTICK: Oh. —. They eat their own yuh know.

BLACK MAN WITH WATERMELON: HooDoo.

BLACK WOMAN WITH FRIED DRUMSTICK: Hen do. Saw it on thuh Tee V.

BLACK MAN WITH WATERMELON: Aint that nice.

(a bell sounds once)

PANEL II: FIRST CHORUS

BLACK MAN WITH WATERMELON: 6 by 6 by 6.

ALL: THATS RIGHT.

BLACK WOMAN WITH FRIED DRUMSTICK: Oh. They eat their own you know.

ALL: HOODOO.

BLACK WOMAN WITH FRIED DRUMSTICK: Hen do. Saw it on thuh Tee V.

ALL: Aint that nice.

AND BIGGER AND BIGGER AND BIGGER: WILL SOMEBODY TAKE THESE STRAPS OFF UH ME PLEASE? I WOULD LIKE TUH MOVE MY HANDS.

PRUNES AND PRISMS: Prunes and prisms will begin: prunes and prisms prunes and prisms prunes and prisms and prunes and prisms: 23.

VOICE ON THUH TEE V: Good evening. I'm Broad Caster. Headlining tonight: the news: is Gamble Major, the absolutely last living negro man in the whole entire known world — is dead. Major Gamble, born a slave, taught himself the rudiments of education to become a spearhead in the Civil Rights Movement. He was 38 years old. News of Major's death sparked controlled displays of jubilation in all corners of the world.

PRUNES AND PRISMS: Oh no no: world is roun.

AND BIGGER AND BIGGER AND BIGGER: WILL SOMEBODY TAKE THESE STRAPS OFF UH ME

PLEASE? I WOULD LIKE TUH MOVE MY HANDS.

(a bell sounds 4 times)

LOTS OF GREASE AND LOTS OF PORK: This is the death of the last black man in the whole entire world.

PRUNES AND PRISMS: Not yet —

VOICE ON THUH TEE V: Good evening. Broad Caster. Head line tonight: Gamble Major, the absolutely last living negro man in the whole known entire world is dead. Gamble Major born a slave rose to become a spearhead in the Civil Rights Movement. He was 38 years old. The Civil Rights Movement. He was 38 years old.

AND BIGGER AND BIGGER AND BIGGER: WILL SOMEBODY TAKE THESE STRAPS OFF UH ME PLEASE? I WOULD LIKE TUH MOVE MY HANDS.

LOTS OF GREASE AND LOTS OF PORK: This is the death of the last black man in the whole entire world.

(a bell sounds 3 times)

PRUNES AND PRISMS: Prunes and prisms prunes and prisms prunes and prisms prunes and prisms.

QUEEN-THEN-PHARAOH HATSHEPSUT: Yesterday tuhday next summer tuhmorrow just uh moment uhgoh in 1317 dieded thuh last black man in thuh whole entire world. Uh! Oh. Dont be uhlarmed. Do not be afeared. It was painless. Uh painless passin. He falls 23 floors to his death.

PRUNES AND PRISMS: No.

QUEEN-THEN-PHARAOH HATSHEPSUT: 23 floors from uh passin ship from space tuh splat on thuh pavement.

PRUNES AND PRISMS: No.

QUEEN-THEN-PHARAOH HATSHEPSUT: He have uh head he been keepin under thuh Tee V. On his bottom pantry shelf.

PRUNES AND PRISMS: No.

QUEEN-THEN-PHARAOH HATSHEPSUT: He have uh head that hurts. Dont fit right. Put it on tuh go tuh thuh store in it pinched him when he walks his thoughts dont got room. Why dieded he huh?

PRUNES AND PRISMS: No.

QUEEN-THEN-PHARAOH HATSHEPSUT: Where he gonna go now that he done dieded?

PRUNES AND PRISMS: No.

BLACK WOMAN WITH FRIED DRUMSTICK: Where he gonna go tuh wash his hands?

CHORUS: You should write that down. You should write that down and you should hide it under uh rock.

VOICE ON THUH TEE V: Good evening. Broad Caster. Headlinin tonight: thuh news:

OLD MAN RIVER JORDAN: Tell you of uh news. Last news. Last news of thuh last man. Last man had last words say hearin it. He spoked uh speech spoked hisself uh chatter-tooth babble "ya-oh-may/chuh-naw" dribblin down his lips tuh puddle in his lap. Dribblin by droppletts. Drop by drop. Last news. News flashes then drops. Thuh last drop was uh all uhlone drop. Singular. Thuh last drop started it off it all. Started off with uh drop. Started off with uh jungle. Started sproutin in his spittle growin leaves off of his mines and thuh vines say drippin doin it. Last news leads tuh thuh first news. He is dead he crosses thuh river. He jumps in thuh puddle have his clothing: ON. On thuh other side thuh mountin yo he dripply wet with soppin. Do drop be dripted? I say "yes."

BLACK MAN WITH WATERMELON: Dont leave me hear. Dont leave me. Hear?

QUEEN-THEN-PHARAOH HATSHEPSUT: Where he gonna go tuh wash his dribblin hands?

PRUNES AND PRISMS: Where he gonna go tuh dry his dripplin clothes?

YES AND GREENS BLACK-EYED PEAS CORNBREAD: Did you write it down? On uh little slip uh paper stick thuh slip in thuh river afore you slip in that way you keep your clothes dry, man.

PRUNES AND PRISMS: Aintcha heard uh that trick?

BEFORE COLUMBUS: That tricks thuh method.

QUEEN-THEN-PHARAOH HATSHEPSUT: They used it on uhlong uhgoh still works every time.

OLD MAN RIVER JORDAN: He jumped in thuh water without uh word for partin come out drippley wet with soppin. Do drop be dripted? I say "do."

BLACK MAN WITH WATERMELON: In you all theres kin. You all kin. Kin gave thuh first permission kin be givin it now still. Some things is all thuh ways gonna be uh continuin sort of uh some thing. Some things go on and on till they dont stop. I am sop- pin wet. I left my scent behind in uh bundle of old clothing that was not thrown out. Left thuh scent in thuh clothin in thuh clothin on uh rooftop. Dogs surround my house and laugh. They are mockin thuh scent that I left behind. I jumped in thuh water without uh word. I jumped in thuh wa- ter without uh smell. I am in thuh river and in my skin is soppin wet. I would like tuh stay afloat now. I would like tuh move my hands.

AND BIGGER AND BIGGER AND BIGGER: Would some- body take these straps off uh me please? I would like tuh move my hands.

BLACK MAN WITH WATERMELON: Now kin kin I move my hands?

QUEEN-THEN-PHARAOH HATSHEPSUT: My black man my subject man my man uh all mens my my my no no not yes no not yes thuh hands. Let Queen-then-

Pharaoh Hatshepsut tell you when. She is I am. An I am she passing by with her train. Pulling it be- hind her on uh plastic chain. Ooooh who! Oooooh who! Where you gonna go now, now that you done dieded?

CHORUS: Ha ha ha.

PRUNES AND PRISMS: Say "prunes and prisms" 40 times each day and you'll cure your big lips. Prunes and prisms prunes and prisms prunes and prisms: 19.

QUEEN-THEN-PHARAOH HATSHEPSUT: An I am Sheba- like she be me am passin on by she with her train. Pullin it behind / he on uh plastic chain. Ooch who! Ooch who! Come uhlong. Come uhlong.

BLACK WOMAN WITH FRIED DRUMSTICK: Say he was waitin on the right time.

AND BIGGER AND BIGGER AND BIGGER: Say he was waitin in thuh wrong line.

BLACK MAN WITH WATERMELON: I jumped in thuh river without a word. My kin are soppin wet.

QUEEN-THEN-PHARAOH HATSHEPSUT: Come uhlong. Come uhlong.

PRUNES AND PRISMS: Prunes and prisms prunes and prisms.

LOTS OF GREASE AND LOTS OF PORK: This is the death of the last black man in the whole entire world.

PRUNES AND PRISMS: Not yet.

LOTS OF GREASE AND LOTS OF PORK: Back tuh when thuh worl usta be roun.

QUEEN-THEN-PHARAOH HATSHEPSUT: Come uhlong come uhlong get on board come uhlong.

OLD MAN RIVER JORDAN: Back tuh that. Yes.

YES AND GREENS BLACK-EYED PEAS CORNBREAD: Back tuh then thuh worl usta be roun.

OLD MAN RIVER JORDAN: Uhcross thuh river in back tuh that. Yes. Do in diddly dip didded thuh drop. Out to thuh river uhlong to thuh sea. Long thuh long coast. Skirtin. Yes. Skirtin back tuh that. Come up back flip take uhway like thuh waves do. Far uhway. Uhway tuh where they dont speak thuh language and where they dont want tuh. Huh. Go on back tuh that.

YES AND GREENS BLACK-EYED PEAS CORNBREAD: Awe on uh interior before uh demarcation made it mapped. Awe on uh interior with out uh road- word called macadam. Awe onin uh interior that was uh whole was once. Awe on uh whole roun worl uh roun worl with uh river.

OLD MAN RIVER JORDAN: In thuh interior was uh river. Huh. Back tuh that.

CHORUS: The river was roun as thuh worl was. Roun.

OLD MAN RIVER JORDAN: He hacks his way through thuh tall grass. Tall grass scratch. Width: thickly. Grasses thickly comin from all angles at it. He runs along thuh path worn out by uh 9 million paddin bare footed feet. Uh path overgrown cause it aint

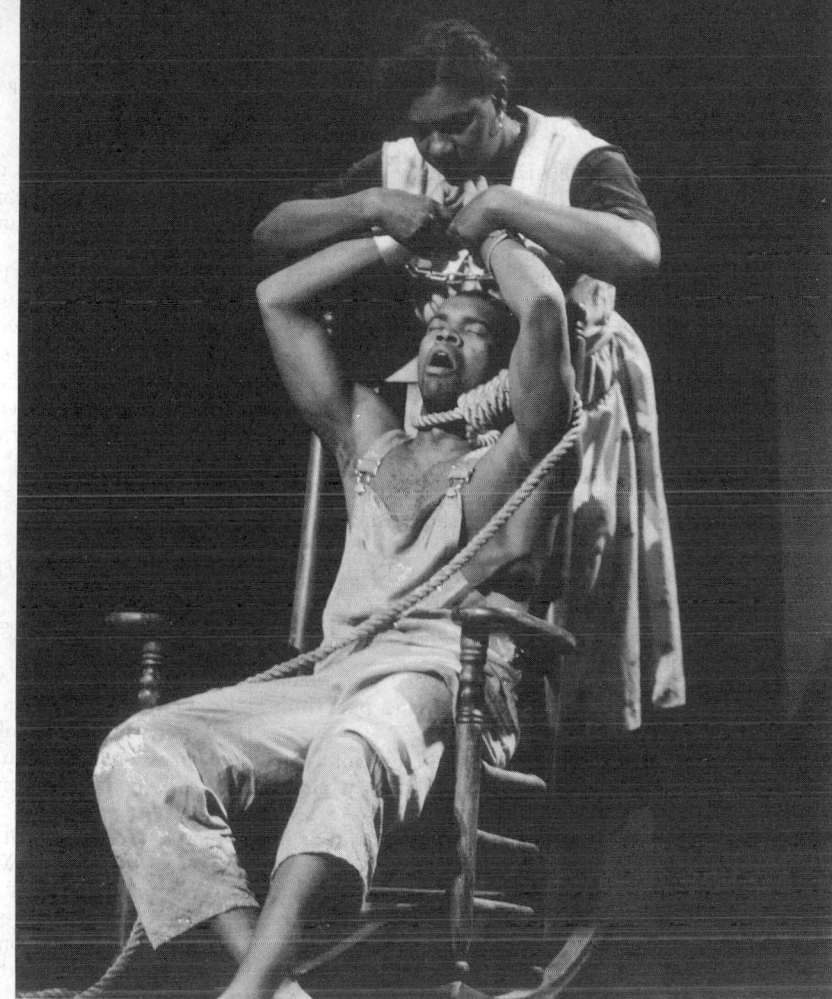

LEFT: Panel II: Prunes and Prisms (Karen A. Bishop), Black Woman with Fried Drumstick (Fanni Green), And Bigger and Bigger and Bigger (Michael Potts), Yes and Greens Black-Eyed Peas Cornbread (Melody J. Garrett), Old Man River Jordan (Ron Brice), and Black Man with Watermelon (Leon Addison Brown) in the 1992 Yale Repertory Theatre Winterfest production of *Last Black Man*. BELOW LEFT: Final Chorus: Black Man with Watermelon and And Bigger and Bigger and Bigger. RIGHT: Panel III: Black Man with Watermelon and Black Woman with Fried Drumstick.

as all as happened as of yet. Tuh be extracted from thuh jungle first he gotta go in hide.

BLACK MAN WITH WATERMELON: Chaseted me outa thuh trees now they tree me. Thuh dogs come out from their hidin spots under thuh porch and give me uhway. Thuh hidin spot was under thuh porch of uh house that werent there as of yet. Thuh dogs give me uhway by uh laugh aimed at my scent.

AND BIGGER AND BIGGER AND BIGGER: HA HA HA. Thats how thuh laugh sorta like be wentin.

PRUNES AND PRISMS: Where he gonna go now now that he done dieded?

QUEEN-THEN-PHARAOH HATSHEPSUT: Where he gonna go tuh move his hands?

BLACK MAN WITH WATERMELON: I. I. I would like tuh move my hands.

YES AND GREENS BLACK-EYED PEAS CORNBREAD: Back tuh when thuh worl usta be roun.

LOTS OF GREASE AND LOTS OF PORK: Uh roun. Thuh worl? Uh roun worl? When was this?

OLD MAN RIVER JORDAN: Columbus. Before.

PRUNES AND PRISMS: Before Columbus?

AND BIGGER AND BIGGER AND BIGGER: Ha!

QUEEN-THEN-PHARAOH HATSHEPSUT: Before Columbus thuh worl usta be roun. They put uh /d/ on thuh end of roun makin roun*d*. Thusly they set in motion thuh enduh. Without that /d/ we could uh gone on spinnin forever. Thuh /d/ thing endiduh things endiduh.

BEFORE COLUMBUS:. Before Columbus.

(*a bell sounds once*)

BEFORE COLUMBUS: Thuh popular thinkin kin of thuh day back then in them days was that thuh worl was flat. They thought thuh worl was flat. Back then kin in them days when they thought thuh worl was flat they were afeared and stayed at home. They wanted tuh go out back then when they thought thuh worl was flat but thuh water had in it dragons.

AND BIGGER AND BIGGER AND BIGGER: Not lurkin in thuh sea but lurkin in thuh street, see? Sir name Tom-us and Bigger be my christian name. Rise up out of uh made up story in grown Bigger and Bigger. Too big for my own name. Nostrils: flarin. Width: thickly. Breath: fire-laden and smellin badly.

1597

BLACK WOMAN WITH FRIED DRUMSTICK: Huh. Whif-fit.

BEFORE COLUMBUS: Dragons, of which meanin these dragons they were afeared back then. When they thought thuh worl was flat. They stayed at home. Them thinkin thuh worl was flat kept it roun. Them thinkin thuh sun revolved uhroun thuh earth kin kept them satellite-like. They figured out thuh truth and scurried out. Figurin out thuh truth kin put them in their place and they scurried out tuh put us in ours.

YES AND GREENS BLACK-EYED PEAS CORNBREAD: Mmmmm. Yes. You should write that down. You should write that down and you should hide it un-der uh rock.

BEFORE COLUMBUS: Thuh earthsgettin level with thuh land land HO and thuh lands gettin level with thuh sea.

PRUNES AND PRISMS: Not yet —

QUEEN-THEN-PHARAOH HATSHEPSUT: An I am Sheba she be me. Youll mutter thuh words and part thuh waves and come uhlong come uhlong.

AND BIGGER AND BIGGER AND BIGGER: I would like tuh fit in back in thuh storybook from which I camed.

BLACK MAN WITH WATERMELON: My text was writ in water. I would like tuh drink it down.

QUEEN-THEN-PHARAOH HATSHEPSUT: Down tuh float drown tuh float down. My son erased his mothers mark.

AND BIGGER AND BIGGER AND BIGGER: I am grown too big for thuh word thats me.

PRUNES AND PRISMS: Prunes and prisms prunes and prisms prunes and prisms: 14.

QUEEN-THEN-PHARAOH HATSHEPSUT: An I am Sheba me am (She be doo be wah waaaah doo wah). Come uhlong come on uhlong on.

BEFORE COLUMBUS: Before Columbus directs thuh traffic: left right left right.

PRUNES AND PRISMS: Prunes and prisms prunes and prisms.

QUEEN-THEN-PHARAOH HATSHEPSUT: I left my mark on all I made. My son erase his mothers mark.

BLACK WOMAN WITH FRIED DRUMSTICK: Where you gonna go now now that you done dieded.

AND BIGGER AND BIGGER AND BIGGER: Would some-body take these straps offuh me please? Gaw. I would like tuh drink in drown —

BEFORE COLUMBUS: There is uh tiny land mass just above my reach.

LOTS OF GREASE AND LOTS OF PORK: There is uh tiny land mass just outside of my vocabulary.

OLD MAN RIVER JORDAN: Do in dip diddly did-did thuh drop? Drop do it be dripted? Uh huh.

BEFORE COLUMBUS: Land:

AND BIGGER AND BIGGER AND BIGGER: HO!

QUEEN-THEN-PHARAOH HATSHEPSUT: I saw Columbus comin Before Columbus comin/goin over tuh meet you —

BEFORE COLUMBUS: Thuh first time I saw it. It was huge. Thuh green sea becomes uh hillside. Uh hill-side populated with some peoples I will name. Thuh first time I saw it it was uh was-huge once one. Huh. It has been gettin smaller ever since.

QUEEN-THEN-PHARAOH HATSHEPSUT: Land:

BLACK MAN WITH WATERMELON: HO!

(*a bell sounds once*)

PANEL III: THUH LONESOME 3SOME

(NOTE: *indicates a glottal stop and choking sound*)

BLACK MAN WITH WATERMELON: It must have rained. Gaw.* Must-uh-rained-on-down-us-why. Aint that somethin. Must uh rained! Gaw. Our crops have prospered. Must uh rained why aint that somethin why aint that somethin-somethin gaw somethin: nice.

BLACK WOMAN WITH FRIED DRUMSTICK: Funny.

BLACK MAN WITH WATERMELON: Gaw. Callin on it spose we did: gaw — thuh uhrainin gaw huh? Gaw gaw. Lookie look-see gaw: where there were rivlets now there are some. Gaw. Cement tuh mudment accomplished with uh gaw uh flick of my wrist gaw. Huh. Look here now there is uh gaw uh wormlett. Came out tuhday. In my stools gaw gaw gaw gaw they all out tuhday. Come out tuh breathe gaw dontcha? Sure ya dontcha sure gaw ya dontcha sure ya dontcha do yell gaw. Gaw. Our one melon has given intuh 3. Callin what it gived birth callin it gaw. 3 August hams out uh my hands now surroundin me an is all of um mines? GAW. Uh huhn. Gaw gaw. Cant breathe.

BLACK WOMAN WITH FRIED DRUMSTICK: Funny how they break when I dropped em. Thought they was past that. Huh. 3 broke in uh row. Guess mmm on uh roll uh some sort, huh. Hell. Huh. Whiffit.

BLACK MAN WITH WATERMELON: Gaw. Gaw. Cant breathe.

BLACK WOMAN WITH FRIED DRUMSTICK: Some things still hold. Huh. Uh old rayed eggull break after droppin most likely. Huh. 4 in uh row. Awe on that.

BLACK MAN WITH WATERMELON: Gaw. Cant breathe you.

BLACK WOMAN WITH FRIED DRUMSTICK: You dont need to. No need for breathin for you no more, huh? 5. 6. Mm making uh history. 7-hhh 8-hhh mm makin uh mess. Huh. Whiffit.

BLACK MAN WITH WATERMELON: Gaw. Gaw loosen my collar. No air in here.

BLACK WOMAN WITH FRIED DRUMSTICK: 7ssgot uh red dot. Awe on that.

BLACK MAN WITH WATERMELON: Sweetheart —. SWEETHEART?!

BLACK WOMAN WITH FRIED DRUMSTICK: 9. Chuh. Funny. Funny. Somethin still holdin on. Let me loosen your collar for you you comed home after uh hard days work. Your suit: tied. Days work was runnin from them we know aint chase-ted you. You comed back home after uh hard days work such uh hard days work that now you cant breathe, you. Now.

BLACK MAN WITH WATERMELON: Dont take it off just loosen it. Dont move thuh tree branch let thuh tree branch be.

BLACK WOMAN WITH FRIED DRUMSTICK: Your days work aint like any others day work: you bring your tree branch home. Let me loosen thuh tie let me loosen thuh neck-lace let me loosen up thuh noose that stringed him up let me leave thuh tree branch be. Let me rub your wrists.

BLACK MAN WITH WATERMELON: Gaw. Gaw.

BLACK WOMAN WITH FRIED DRUMSTICK: Some things still hold. Wrung thuh necks of them hens and they still give eggs. Huh: Like you. Still sproutin feathers even after they fried. Huh: like you too. 10. Chuh. Eggs still break. Thuh mess makes uh stain. Thuh stain makes uh mark. Whiffit. Whiffit.

BLACK MAN WITH WATERMELON: Put me on uh platform tuh wait for uh train. Uh who who uh who who uh where ya gonna go now —. Platform hitched with horses / steeds. Steeds runned off in left me there swingin. It had begun tuh rain. Hands behind my back. This time tied. I had heard of uh word called scaffold and thought that perhaps they just might build me one of um but uh uhn naw just outa my vocabulary but uh uhn new trees come cheaply.

BLACK WOMAN WITH FRIED DRUMSTICK: 8. 9. I aint hungry. 9. 10. You dont eat. Dont need to.

BLACK MAN WITH WATERMELON: Swingin from front tuh back uhgain. Back tuh — back tuh that was how I be wentin. Chin on my chest hangin down in restin eyes each on eyein my 2 feets. Left on thuh right one right one on thuh left. Crossed eyin. It was difficult tuh breathe. Toes uncrossin then crossin for luck. With my eyes. Gaw. It had begun tuh rain. Oh. Gaw. Ever so lightly. Blood came on up. you know: tough. Like riggamartins-stiffly only — isolated. They some of em pointed they some looked quick in an then they looked uhway. It had begun tuh rain. I hung on out tuh dry. They puttin uhway their picnic baskets. Ever so lightly gaw gaw it had begun tuh rain. They pullin out their umbrellas in hidedid up their eyes. Oh.

BLACK WOMAN WITH FRIED DRUMSTICK: I aint hungry you dont eat 12 13 and thuh floor will shine. Look: there we are. You in me. Reflectin. Hello! Dont move —.

BLACK MAN WITH WATERMELON: It had begun tuh rain. Now: huh. Sky flew open and thuh light went ZAP. Tree bowed over till thuh branch said BROKE. Uhround my necklace my neck uhround my neck my tree branch. In full bloom. It had begun tuh rain. Feet hit thuh ground in I started runnin. I was wet right through intuh through. I was uh wet that dont get dry. Draggin on my tree branch on back tuh home.

BLACK WOMAN WITH FRIED DRUMSTICK: On back tuh that.

BLACK MAN WITH WATERMELON: Gaw. What was that?

BLACK WOMAN WITH FRIED DRUMSTICK: "On back tuh that?" Huh. Somethin I figured. Huh. Chuh. Lord. Who! Whiffit.

BLACK MAN WITH WATERMELON: When I dieded they cut me down. Didnt have no need for me no more. They let me go.

BLACK WOMAN WITH FRIED DRUMSTICK: Thuh lights dimmed in thats what saved you. Lightnin comed down zappin trees from thuh sky. You got uhway.

BLACK MAN WITH WATERMELON: Not exactly.

BLACK WOMAN WITH FRIED DRUMSTICK: Oh. I see.

BLACK MAN WITH WATERMELON: They tired of me. Pulled me out of thuh trees then treed me then tired of me. Thats how it has gone. Thats how it be wentin.

BLACK WOMAN WITH FRIED DRUMSTICK: Oh. I see. Youve been dismissed. But-where-to? Must be somewhere else tuh go aside from just go gone. Huh. Whiffit: huh. You smell.

BLACK MAN WITH WATERMELON: Maybe I should bathe.

BLACK WOMAN WITH FRIED DRUMSTICK: I call those 3 thuh lonesome 3some. Maybe we should pray.

BLACK MAN WITH WATERMELON: Thuh lonesome 3some. Spose theyll do.

(a bell sounds twice)

PANEL IV: SECOND CHORUS

OLD MAN RIVER JORDAN: Come in look tuh looksee.

VOICE ON THUH TEE V: Good evening this is thuh news. A small sliver of uh tree branch has been found in *The Death of the Last Black Man.* Upon careful examination thuh small sliver of thuh treed branch what was found has been found tuh be uh fosilized bone fragment. With this finding authorities claim they are hot on his tail.

PRUNES AND PRISMS: Uh small sliver of uh treed branch growed from-tuh uh bone.

AND BIGGER AND BIGGER AND BIGGER: WILL SOMEBODY WILL THIS ROPE FROM ROUND MY NECK GOD DAMN I WOULD LIKE TUH TAKE MY BREATH BY RIGHTS GAW GAW.

LOTS OF GREASE AND LOTS OF PORK: This is the death of the last black man in the whole entire world.

(a bell sounds slowly twice)

BLACK MAN WITH WATERMELON: I had heard of uh word called scaffold and had hopes they just might maybe build me one by uh uh new gaw —

HAM: There was uh tree with your name on it.

BLACK MAN WITH WATERMELON: Jumpin out of uh tree they chase me tree me back tuh thuh tree. Thats where I be came from. Thats where I be wentin.

YES AND GREENS BLACK-EYED PEAS CORNBREAD: Someone ought tuh. Write that down.

LOTS OF GREASE AND LOTS OF PORK: There is a page dog eared at "Histree" hidin just outside my word hoard. Wheres he gonna come to now that he done gone from.

QUEEN-THEN-PHARAOH HATSHEPSUT: Wheres he gonna go come to now that he gonna go gone on?

OLD MAN RIVER JORDAN: For that you must ask Ham.

BLACK WOMAN WITH FRIED DRUMSTICK: Hen?

LOTS OF GREASE AND LOTS OF PORK: HAM.

QUEEN-THEN-PHARAOH HATSHEPSUT: Ham.

PRUNES AND PRISMS: Hmmmm.

(a bell sounds twice)

HAM: Ham's Begotten Tree (catchin up to um *in media res* that is we takin off from where we stopped up last time). Huh. NOW: She goned begotten One who in turn begotten Ours. Ours laughed one day uhloud in from thuh sound hittin thuh air smakity sprung up I, you, n He, She, It. They turned in engaged in simple multiplication thus tuh spawn of theirselves one We one You and one called They (They in certain conversation known as "Them" and in other certain conversation a.k.a. "Us"). Now very simply: Wassername she finally gave intuh It and tugether they broughted forth uh wildish one called simply Yo. Yo gone be wentin much too long without hisself uh comb in from thuh frizzly that resulted comed one called You (polite form). You (polite) birthed herself Mister, Miss Maam and Sir who in his later years with That

brought forth Yuh Fathuh. Thuh fact that That was uh mother tuh Yuh Fathuh didnt stop them 2 relations from havin relations. Those strange relations between That thuh mother and Yuh Fathuh thuh son brought forth uh odd lot: called: Yes Massuh, Yes Missy, Yes Maam n Yes Suh Mistuh Suh which goes tuh show that relations with your relations produces complications. Thuh children of That and Yuh Fathuh aside from being plain peculiar was all cross-eyed. This defect enhanced their multiplicative possibilities, for example. Yes Suh Mistuh Suh breeded with hisself n gived us Wassername (thuh 2nd), and Wassernickname (2 twins in birth joindid at thuh lip). Thuh 2 twins lived next door tuh one called Uhnother bringin forth Themuhns, She (thuh 2nd) Auntie, Cousin, and Bro who makeshifted continuous compensations for his loud and odiforous bodily emissions by all thuh time saying excuse me n through his graciousness brought forth They (polite) who had mixed feelins with She (thuh 2nd) thus bringin forth Ussin who then went on tuh have MeMines.

YES AND GREENS BLACK-EYED PEAS CORNBREAD: Thuh list goes on in on.

HAM: MeMines gived out 2 offspring one she called Mines after herself thuh uther she called Themuhns named after all them who comed before. Themuhns married outside thuh tribe joinin herself with uh man they called WhoDat. Themuhns n WhoDat brough forth only one child called WhoDatDere. Mines joined up with Wasshisname and from that union come AllYall.

BEFORE COLUMBUS: All us?

HAM: No. AllYall.

LOTS OF GREASE AND LOTS OF PORK: This list goes on in on.

HAM: Ah yes: Yo suddenly if by majic again became productive in after uh lapse of some great time came back intuh circulation to wiggled uhbout with Yes Missy (one of thuh cross-eyed daughters of That and Yuh Fathuh). Yo in Yes Missy begottin ThissunRightHere, Us, ThatOne, She (thuh 3rd) and one called Uncle (who from birth was gifted with great singin and dancin capabilities which helped him make his way in life but tended tuh bring shame on his family).

BEFORE COLUMBUS/BLACK MAN WITH WATERMELON: Shame on his family.

LOTS OF GREASE/BLACK MAN WITH WATERMELON: Shame on his family.

AND BIGGER AND BIGGER/BLACK MAN WITH WATERMELON: Shamed on his family gaw.

YES AND GREENS BLACK-EYED PEAS CORNBREAD: Write that down.

OLD MAN RIVER JORDAN: (Ham seed his daddy Noah neckked. From that seed, comed AllYall.)

(*a bell sounds twice*)

AND BIGGER AND BIGGER AND BIGGER: (Will somebody please will this rope —)

VOICE ON THUH TEE V: Good evening. This is thuh news: Whose fault is it?

BLACK MAN WITH WATERMELON: Saint mines.

VOICE ON THUH TEE V: Whose fault iszit??!

CHORUS: Saint mines!

OLD MAN RIVER JORDAN: I cant re-member back that far. (Ham can — but uh uh new gaw — Ham wuduhnt there, huh.)

CHORUS: HAM BONE HAM BONE WHERE YOU BEEN ROUN THUH WORL N BACK A-GAIN.

QUEEN-THEN-PHARAOH HATSHEPSUT: Whatcha seen. Hambone girl?

BLACK WOMAN WITH FRIED DRUMSTICK: Didnt see you. I saw thuh worl.

HAM: I was there.

PRUNES AND PRISMS: Didnt see you.

HAM: I WAS THERE.

VOICE ON THUH TEE V: Didnt see you.

BLACK MAN WITH WATERMELON / AND BIGGER: THUH BLACK MAN. HE MOOOVE.

CHORUS: HAM BONE HAM BONE WHATCHA DO? GOT UH CHANCE N FAIRLY FLEW.

BLACK WOMAN WITH FRIED DRUMSTICK: Over thuh front yard.

BLACK MAN WITH WATERMELON: Overshot.

CHORUS: 6 BY 6 BY 6.

BLACK MAN WITH WATERMELON: Thats right.

AND BIGGER AND BIGGER AND BIGGER: WILL SOMEBODY WILL THIS ROPE —

CHORUS: Good evening. This is the news.

VOICE ON THUH TEE V: Whose fault is it?

ALL: Saint mines!

VOICE ON THUH TEE V: Whose fault iszit?

HAM: SAINT MINES!

(*a bell rings twice*)

—. Ham. Is. Not. Tuh. BLAME! WhoDatDere joinded with one called Sir 9th generation of thuh first Sir son of You (polite) thuh first daughter of You WhoDatDere with thuh 9th Sir begettin forth him —

BLACK MAN WITH WATERMELON: Ham?!

ALL (*except Ham*): HIM!

BLACK WOMAN WITH FRIED DRUMSTICK: sold.

HAM: SOLD! allyall[9-0] not tuh be confused w/allus[12] joined w/allthem[3] in from that union comed forth wasshisname[21] SOLD wassername[19] still by thuh reputation uh thistree one uh thuh 2 twins loses her sight through fiddlin n falls w/ugly old yuh-fathuh[4] given she[8] SOLD whodat[33] pairs w/you[23] (still polite) of which nothinmuch comes nothinmuch now nothinmuch[6] pairs with ycssuhmistuh-suh[17] tuh drop one called yo now yo[9-0] still who gone be wentin now w/elle gived us el SOLD let us not forget ye[1-2-5] w/ thee[3] givin us thou[9-2] who w/thuh they who switches their designation in certain conversation yes they[10] broughted forth onemore[2] at thuh same time in thuh same row right next door we have datone[12] w/ disonc[14] droppin off duhutherone[2-2] SOLD let us not forget du and sie let us not forget yesssuhmassuhsuh[38] w/thou[8] who gived up memines[3-0] SOLD we are now rollin through thuh long division gimmie uh gimmie uh gimmie uh squared off route round it off round it off n round it out w/sistuh[4-3] who lives with one called saintmines[9] givin forth one uh year how it got there callin it jessgrew callin it saintmines callin it whatdat whatdat whatdat SOLD.

BLACK MAN WITH WATERMELON: Thuh list goes on and on. Dont it.

CHORUS: Ham Bone Ham Bone Ham Bone Ham Bone

BEFORE COLUMBUS: Left right left right.

QUEEN-THEN-PHARAOH HATSHEPSUT: Left left left whose left . . . ?

(*a bell sounds twice*)

LOTS OF GREASE AND LOTS OF PORK: This is the death of the last black man in the whole entire world.

PANEL V: IN THUH GARDEN OF HOODOO IT

BLACK WOMAN WITH FRIED DRUMSTICK: Somethins turnin. Huh. Whatizit. — Mercy. Mercy. Huh. Chew on this. Ssuh feather. Sswhatchashud be eatin now ya no. Ssuhfeather: stuffin. Chew on it. Huh. Feathers sprouted from thuh fried hens — dont ask me how. Somethins out uh whack. Somethins out uh rights. Your arms still on your elbows. I'm still here. Whensit gonna end. Soon. Huh. Mercy. Thuh Tree. Springtime. And harvest. Huh. Somethins turnin. So many melons. Huh. From one tuh 3 tuh many. Must be nature. Gnaw on this. Gnaw on this, huh? Gnaw on this awe on that.

BLACK MAN WITH WATERMELON: Aint eatable.

BLACK WOMAN WITH FRIED DRUMSTICK: I know.

BLACK MAN WITH WATERMELON: Aint eatable aint it. Nope. Nope.

BLACK WOMAN WITH FRIED DRUMSTICK: Somethins turnin. Huh. Whatizit.

BLACK MAN WITH WATERMELON: Aint eatable so I

[9]: The numbers in Ham's speech are chanted by several actors together as if they were auction prices or verses of the Bible.

RIGHT: Panel IV: Black Woman with Fried Drumstick, Before Columbus (Leo V. Finnie III), And Bigger and Bigger and Bigger (top), Ham (Reg E. Cathey) (center), Black Man with Watermelon (bottom), Yes and Greens Black-Eyed Peas Cornbread, and Lots of Grease and Lots of Pork (Darryl Theirse).
MIDDLE RIGHT: Final Chorus: Queen-then-Pharaoh Hatshepsut (Pamala Tyson).
FAR RIGHT: Final Chorus: Black Woman with Fried Drumstick.

out in out ought not aint be eatin it aint that right. Yep. Nope. Yep. Uh huhn.

BLACK WOMAN WITH FRIED DRUMSTICK: Huh. Whatizit.

BLACK MAN WITH WATERMELON: I remember what I like. I remember what my likes tuh eat when I be in thuh eatin mode.

BLACK WOMAN WITH FRIED DRUMSTICK: Chew on this.

BLACK MAN WITH WATERMELON: When I be in thuh eatin mode.

BLACK WOMAN WITH FRIED DRUMSTICK: Swallow it down. I know. Gimmie your pit. Needs bathin.

BLACK MAN WITH WATERMELON: Choice between peas and corns — my feets —. Choice: peas. Choice between peas and greens choice: greens.

Choice between greens and potatoes choice: potatoes. Yams. Boiled or mashed choice: mashed. Aaah. Mmm. My likenesses.

BLACK WOMAN WITH FRIED DRUMSTICK: Mercy. Turns —

BLACK MAN WITH WATERMELON: My likenesses! My feets! Aaah! SWEET-HEART. Aaah! SPRING-TIME!

BLACK WOMAN WITH FRIED DRUMSTICK: Spring-time.

BLACK MAN WITH WATERMELON: SPRING-TIME!

BLACK WOMAN WITH FRIED DRUMSTICK: Mercy. Turns —

BLACK MAN WITH WATERMELON: I remembers what I likes. I remembers what I likes tuh eat when I bein in had been in thuh eatin mode. Bein in had been: now in then. I be eatin hen. Hen.

BLACK WOMAN WITH FRIED DRUMSTICK: Huh?

BLACK MAN WITH WATERMELON: HEN!

BLACK WOMAN WITH FRIED DRUMSTICK: Hen?

BLACK MAN WITH WATERMELON: Hen. Huh. My meals. Aaaah: my meals. *BRACH-A-LEE.*

BLACK WOMAN WITH FRIED DRUMSTICK: Whatizit. Huh. — GNAW ON THIS! Good. Uhther pit?

BLACK MAN WITH WATERMELON: We sittin on this porch right now aint we. Uh huhn. Aaah. Yes. Sittin right here right now on it in it ainthuh first time either iduhnt it. Yep. Nope. Once we was here once wuhduhnt we. Yep. Yep. Once we being here. Uh huhn. Huh. There is uh Now and there is uh Then. Ssall there is. (I bein in uh Now: uh Now bein in uh Then; I bein, in Now in Then, in I will be. I was be too but that uh Then thats past. That me that was be is uh me has-been. Thuh Then that was be is uh has-been-Then too. Thuh me-has-been sits in thuh be-me: we sit on this porch. Same porch. Same me. Thuh Then that been somehow sits in thuh Then that will be: same Thens. I swing from uh tree. You cut me down and bring me back. Home. Here. I fly over thuh yard. I fly over thuh yard in all over. Them thens stays fixed. Fixed Thens. Thuh Thems stays fixed too. Thuh Thems that come and take me and thuh Thems that greet me and then them Thems that send me back here. Home. Stays fixed. Them do.)

BLACK WOMAN WITH FRIED DRUMSTICK: Your feets.

BLACK MAN WITH WATERMELON: I: be. You: is. It: be. He, She: thats us. (Thats it.) We: thats he in she: you aroun me: us be here. You: still is. They: be. Melon. Melon. Melon: mines. I remember all my lookuhlikes. You. You. Remember me.

BLACK WOMAN WITH FRIED DRUMSTICK: Gnaw on this then swallow it down. Youll have your fill then we'll put you in your suit coat.

BLACK MAN WITH WATERMELON: Thuh suit coat I picked out? Thuh stripely one? HA! Peas. Choice: BRACH-A-LEE.

BLACK WOMAN WITH FRIED DRUMSTICK: Chew and swallow please.

BLACK MAN WITH WATERMELON: Thuh stripely one with thuh fancy patch pockets!

BLACK WOMAN WITH FRIED DRUMSTICK: Sweetheart.

BLACK MAN WITH WATERMELON: SPRING-TIME.

BLACK WOMAN WITH FRIED DRUMSTICK: Sweetheart.

BLACK MAN WITH WATERMELON: SPRING-TIME.

BLACK WOMAN WITH FRIED DRUMSTICK: This could go on forever.

BLACK MAN WITH WATERMELON: Lets. Hope. Not.

BLACK WOMAN WITH FRIED DRUMSTICK: — Sweetheart.

BLACK MAN WITH WATERMELON: SPRING-TIME.

BLACK WOMAN WITH FRIED DRUMSTICK: Sweetheart.

BLACK MAN WITH WATERMELON: SPRING-TIME.

BLACK WOMAN WITH FRIED DRUMSTICK: This could go on forever.

BLACK MAN WITH WATERMELON: Lets. Hope. Not.

BLACK WOMAN WITH FRIED DRUMSTICK: Must be somewhere else tuh go aside from just go gone.

BLACK MAN WITH WATERMELON: 6 by 6 by 6.

BLACK WOMAN WITH FRIED DRUMSTICK: Thats right.

BLACK MAN WITH WATERMELON: Rock reads "HooDoo."

BLACK WOMAN WITH FRIED DRUMSTICK: Now you know. Know now dontcha. Somethins turnin —.

BLACK MAN WITH WATERMELON: Who do? Them do. Aint that nice. Huh. Miss me. Remember me. Missmemissmewhatsmyname.

BLACK WOMAN WITH FRIED DRUMSTICK: Aaaaaah?

BLACK MAN WITH WATERMELON: Remember me. AAAH.

BLACK WOMAN WITH FRIED DRUMSTICK: Thats it. Open wide. Here it comes. Stuffin.

BLACK MAN WITH WATERMELON: Yeeeech.

BLACK WOMAN WITH FRIED DRUMSTICK: Eat uh-nother. Hear. I eat one. You eat one more.

BLACK MAN WITH WATERMELON: Stuffed. Time tuh go.

BLACK WOMAN WITH FRIED DRUMSTICK: Not yet!

BLACK MAN WITH WATERMELON: I got uhway?

BLACK WOMAN WITH FRIED DRUMSTICK: Huh?

BLACK MAN WITH WATERMELON: I got uhway?

BLACK WOMAN WITH FRIED DRUMSTICK: Nope. Yep. Nope. Nope.

BLACK MAN WITH WATERMELON: Miss me.

BLACK WOMAN WITH FRIED DRUMSTICK: Miss me.

BLACK MAN WITH WATERMELON: Re-member me.

BLACK WOMAN WITH FRIED DRUMSTICK: Re-member me.

BLACK MAN WITH WATERMELON: My hands are on my wrists. Arms on elbows. Looks: old fashioned. Nothin fancy there. Toes curl up not down. My feets-now clean. Still got all my teeth. Re-member me.

BLACK WOMAN WITH FRIED DRUMSTICK: Re-member me.

BLACK MAN WITH WATERMELON: Call on me some-time.

BLACK WOMAN WITH FRIED DRUMSTICK: Call on me sometime. Hear? Hear? Thuh dirt itself turns itself. So many melons. From one tuh 3 tuh many. Look at um all. Ssuh garden. Awe on that. Winter processin back tuh back with spring-time. They roll on by us that way. Uh whole line gone roun. Chuh. Thuh worl he roun. Moves that way so they say. You comed back. Yep. Nope. Well. Well. Build uh well.

(a bell sounds twice)

FINAL CHORUS

ALL: "YES. OH, ME? CHUM, NO —"

VOICE ON THUH TEE V: Good morning. This is thuh news:

BLACK WOMAN WITH FRIED DRUMSTICK: Somethins turnin. Thuh page.

(a bell sounds twice)

LOTS OF GREASE AND LOTS OF PORK: This is the death of the last black man in the whole entire worl

PRUNES AND PRISMS: 19.

OLD MAN RIVER JORDAN: Uh blank page turnin with thuh sound of it. Thuh sound of movie hands.

BLACK WOMAN WITH FRIED DRUMSTICK: Yesterday today next summer tomorrow just uh moment uh-goh in 1317 dieded thuh last black man in thuh whole entire world. Uh! Oh. Dont be uhlarmed. Do not he afeared. It was painless. Uh painless passin. He falls twenty-three floors to his death.

CHORUS: yes.

BLACK WOMAN WITH FRIED DRUMSTICK: 23 floors from uh passin ship from space tuh splat on thuh pavement.

CHORUS: yes.

BLACK WOMAN WITH FRIED DRUMSTICK: He have uh head he been keepin under thuh Tee V.

CHORUS: yes.

BLACK WOMAN WITH FRIED DRUMSTICK: On his bottom pantry shelf.

CHORUS: yes.

BLACK WOMAN WITH FRIED DRUMSTICK: He have uh head that hurts. Dont fit right. Put it on tuh go tuh thuh store in it pinched him when he walks his thoughts dont got room. He diediduh he did, huh.

CHORUS: yes.

BLACK WOMAN WITH FRIED DRUMSTICK: Where he gonna go now now now now now that he done diediduh?

CHORUS: yes.

BLACK WOMAN WITH FRIED DRUMSTICK: Where he gonna go tuh. WASH.

PRUNES AND PRISMS: Somethins turnin. Thuh page.

AND BIGGER AND BIGGER AND BIGGER: Somethins burnin. Thuh tongue.

BLACK MAN WITH WATERMELON: Thuh tongue itself burns.

OLD MAN RIVER JORDAN: He jumps in thuh river. These words for partin.

YES AND GREENS BLACK-EYED PEAS CORNBREAD: And you will write them down.

(a bell sounds 3 times)

BEFORE COLUMBUS: All these boats passed by my coast.

PRUNES AND PRISMS: Somethins turnin. Thuh page.

QUEEN-THEN-PHARAOH HATSHEPSUT: I saw Columbus comin / I saw Columbus comin goin —

QUEEN-THEN-PHARAOH HATSHEPSUT/BEFORE COLUMBUS: Left left left whose left ... ?

AND BIGGER AND BIGGER/BLACK MAN WITH WATERMELON: Somethins burnin. Thuh page.

BEFORE COLUMBUS: All those boats passed by me. My coast fell in-to-the-sea. All thuh boats. They stopped for me.

OLD MAN RIVER JORDAN: Land: HO!

QUEEN-THEN-PHARAOH HATSHEPSUT: I waved my hands in warnin. You waved back.

BLACK WOMAN WITH FRIED DRUMSTICK: Somethins burnin. Thuh page.

QUEEN-THEN-PHARAOH HATSHEPSUT: I have-not seen you since.

ALL: oh!

LOTS OF GREASE AND LOTS OF PORK: This is the death of the last black man in the whole entire worl

OLD MAN RIVER JORDAN: Do in diddley dip die-die thuh drop. Do drop he dripted? Why, of course.

AND BIGGER AND BIGGER AND BIGGER: Somethins burnin. Thuh tongue.

BLACK MAN WITH WATERMELON: The tongue itself hums itself.

HAM: ... And from that seed comed All Us.

BLACK WOMAN WITH FRIED DRUMSTICK: Thuh page.

ALL: 6 BY 6 BY 6.

BLACK WOMAN WITH FRIED DRUMSTICK: Thats right.

(a bell sounds twice)

BEFORE COLUMBUS: LAND: HO!

YES AND GREENS BLACK-EYED PEAS CORNBREAD: You will write it down because if you dont write it down then we will come along and tell the future that we did not exist. You will write it down and you will carve it out of a rock.

(pause)

You will write down thuh past and you will write down thuh present and in what in thuh future. You will write it down.

(pause)

It will be of us but you will mention them from time to time so that in the future when they come along theyll know how they exist.

(pause)

It will be for us but you will mention them from time to time so that in the future when they come along theyll know why they exist.

(pause)

You will carve it all out of a rock so that in the future when they come along we will know that the rock did yes exist.

BLACK WOMAN WITH FRIED DRUMSTICK: Down down down down down down down down —

LOTS OF GREASE AND LOTS OF PORK: This is the death of the last black man in the whole entire worl

PRUNES AND PRISMS: Somethins turnin. Thuh page.

OLD MAN RIVER JORDAN: Thuh last news of thuh last man:

VOICE ON THUH TEE V: Good mornin. This is thuh last news:

BLACK MAN WITH WATERMELON: Miss me.

BLACK WOMAN WITH FRIED DRUMSTICK: Miss me.

BLACK MAN WITH WATERMELON: Re-member me.

BLACK WOMAN WITH FRIED DRUMSTICK: Re-member me. Call on me sometime. Call on me sometime. Hear? Hear?

HAM: In thuh future when they came along I meeting them. On thuh coast. Uuuuhh! My coast! I — was — so — po-lite! But. In thuh rock. I wrote: ha ha ha.

ALL: Ha. Ha. Ha. Ha. Ha. Ha. Ha. Ha. Ha. Ha. Ha. Ha. Ha. Ha. HHHHHHHHHHHH. HA!

BLACK WOMAN WITH FRIED DRUMSTICK: Thuh black man he move. He move. He hans.

(a bell sounds once)

ALL: Hold it. Hold it. Hold it. Hold it. Hold it. Hold it. Hold it.

COMMENTARIES

The following interviews with Suzan-Lori Parks and Liz Diamond resulted from a meeting following the Yale production of *The Last Black Man* in February 1992. After discussing the play in production, I asked the author and director to respond to a number of questions that would give them a chance to explore issues of interest to those who would read the play but probably not see it in production. I gave them the questions to consider at home, and they returned their responses. Both interviews give us insight into the issues of space and time and of theme and style in this play and into the opportunities available to playwright and director when approaching a fresh script in a style that is innovative and exciting.

Lee A. Jacobus (b. 1935)
INTERVIEW WITH SUZAN-LORI PARKS   1992

Jacobus: Your play takes a long view of history and in a way has a profound narrative scope. But the play also avoids the beginning-middle-end approach to storytelling. How would you describe your approach to narrative structure — particularly in relation to time — in *The Death of the Last Black Man in the Whole Entire World?*

Parks: I start with "knowns" and I get to thinking — not merely sitting at my desk and scratching my head — but I get to listening, I get to watching, hearing, seeing. If time is more curved than flat, then a plot line of a play can be more curved. Then we can refigure "plot." Things may happen over and over again with slight changes. Words may come back to us again and again. Jazz musicians have been doing this for years. They call it "repetition and revision."

Jacobus: You describe the sections of your play as "Panels" and "Choruses." What do these terms mean to you and what should they mean to your audience?

Parks: "Panels" and "Choruses" are two different words that I use to denote two different kinds of experience or attack. In a Panel there are only the two of them, the Black Man with Watermelon and the Black Woman with Fried Drumstick; during the Panels we see them at various points of confusion — which are the same points of confusion over and over again refigured with different variables. The idea of this comes partly from the Stations of the Cross — the tableaux of Christ which hang in churches. The Choruses are the spaces between those tableaux — if you've seen those Stations hanging in a church you know that between them hangs — nothing. A blank space. So the Choruses are figuring the blank space between. That's why the Choruses are so weird. They're coming out of that blank, unspoken, unfigured space and all eleven figures are onstage.

There are Greek choruses. There are choruses in pop songs. Unlike the choruses in most songs, however, my Choruses work differently. Think of a well-known song — "America the Beautiful" for example. The verses contain the information or meat, the choruses the fun, the fat, the gravy. The power of the chorus comes not from the presentation of new information but from its repeating. In *Last Black Man* this is what I'm exploring with certain speeches such as the "Yesterday today next summer tomorrow . . ." speech or the "You should write that down . . ." line. In terms of the Panels and Choruses, where you'd expect the Chorus to simply repeat, Liz [Diamond, the director] discovered early in rehearsal that it is in the Panels where actions are repeated (the Black Man comes back; he is dead; the Black Woman must manage; she is alive), and the Choruses were where the really new information is presented, where the action really happens. With *Last Black Man* I'm using elements of traditional song structure and inverting, subverting, converting those elements.

Jacobus: Your figures have some interesting names, such as Lots of Grease and Lots of Pork. Could you tell us how you visualized some of them onstage?

Parks: I saw them as human — I didn't imagine that Lots of Grease and Lots of Pork would go through the play dressed up as a pork chop — that *would* be avant-garde, wouldn't it? The most important thing about the figures is that they are *figures* and not *characters*. They are *signs* of something and not people just like people we know. *Figures* help to cue the shape of the play. This is epic theater. This is a play where one stands for a thousand. Epic is a state of existence which, I think, comes very naturally out of the day-to-day African American existence — we're a people who are often honored or damned because of the actions of one of our group. One of us stands for all of us. Those are epic stakes.

Also important is where these figures come from: Prunes and Prisms comes from a line in Joyce's *Ulysses*; And Bigger and Bigger and Bigger spins out of Wright's *Native Son*; Ham is the biblical Ham; Queen-then-Pharaoh Hatshepsut really was once.

So. The figures aren't real people but they're voices briefly embodied — embodied for the duration of the play. Part of Liz's preset [the stage setting before the play begins] was an audio track of the figures whispering their names. Those whispers helped create the feeling of *Last Black Man* as a visitation.

Jacobus: You've got a new play in production and you have been very productive in the last several years. What are the sources of your inspiration as a playwright? What directions do you feel yourself heading in?

Parks: What inspires? *Inspirare:* to breathe. What keeps me breathing? What keeps me going? I have good friends. Good friends who read my work and encourage me. Working with Liz Diamond is always a joy — we've done five shows together now and we both keep getting better. What else? I listen to music: Ornette Coleman, Sarah Vaughan, Bach, Wagner, Dionne Warwick. I do karate. Read read read all the time. I work hard. I play with words. Spelling casts a spell. I think the world is telling us. Telling us telling us something that is present but not written down. As a child I wanted to be a geologist. Writing is like digging. So in this play they write it down and they lower him down. Into the ground. I have often thought that I could read the shape of my whole life through this play. So where am I heading? Well. I've done about ten plays now. I finished writing this play in 1990. I've written three more since then. None of the new plays are like this one. So much for predictable trajectory. In all of my work I'm concerned with space and time and the phenomenon of moving through them. Hopefully I'll write more. Hopefully stay sharp. *Awake.* Looking at this play — it's such an extravaganza, such a pageant — you'd figure the writer's next work would be maybe an opera. Yep. She would either write an opera or move to Las Vegas.

Lee A. Jacobus (b. 1935)
INTERVIEW WITH LIZ DIAMOND

1992

Jacobus: Some people have commented on the fact that Suzan-Lori Parks provided no stage directions for *The Last Black Man in the Whole Entire World.* What were the problems — and the opportunities — that resulted from her decision?

Diamond: It is somewhat misleading to say that Suzan-Lori wrote no stage directions. In a conventional sense it is true that the director will not find acres of parenthetical notes describing the stage setting and stage action as envisioned by the playwright. Nevertheless, a close reading of the text reveals that Suzan-Lori has some very specific ideas about how the dramatic action of the text should be played. "In thuh Garden of HooDoo It," Panel V of the play, begins with a speech by Black Woman with Fried Drumstick, who observes:

> Somethins turnin. Huh. Whatizit. — Mercy. Mercy. Huh. Chew on this. Ssuh feather. Sswhatchashud be eatin now ya no. Ssuhfeather stuffin. Chew on it. Huh. Feathers sprouted from thuh fried hens — dont ask me how. Somethins out uh whack. Somethins out uh rights. Your arms still on your elbows. I'm still here. Whensit gonna end. Soon. Huh. Mercy. Thuh Tree. Springtime. And harvest. Huh. Somethins turnin. So many melons. Huh. From one tuh 3 tuh many. Must be nature. Gnaw on this. Gnaw on this, huh? Gnaw on this awe on that.

At the top of the speech Black Woman senses that something is different . . . the atmosphere, the emotional temperature of the play has changed. She senses it has something to do with mercy. Has it been bestowed? Does she sense a new atmosphere of forgiveness is in the air? She gives up trying to articulate what she senses for the moment with a "huh." And then moves on to the task at hand, which is, quite simply, to feed her beloved Black Man feathers which have mysteriously appeared. She must stuff him. Now, a director may or may not feel obliged to follow the stage direction that, I would argue, is quite explicitly embedded in the text. Nevertheless, it is there, and, I think, well worth exploring in rehearsal. In our production at the Yale Repertory Theatre, we did in fact have the Black Woman gently feed the Black Man feathers, then bathe him, in preparation for his final burial. These simple activities, in the context of the larger dramatic action of the text — to tell the Black Man's story and then to lay him to rest — achieved a metaphorical resonance that reinforced the text itself.

There is no doubt that I enjoyed and exercised a great deal of creative control over the visual and aural landscape of *The Death of the Last Black Man* by virtue of the fact that Suzan-Lori chose not to dictate details of set, costume, lighting, and sound. But the major design decisions I made — for example, to set the play in a highly ceremonial, ecclesiastical setting, a sort of surreal cathedral / burial ground, with a treelike pulpit and a huge black sarcophagus at the center that served as both coffin and altar, scaffold and auction block — all grew out of my reading of the play. I saw *Last Black Man* as a highly ritualized and presentational mourning and celebration of the death of the last black man in the whole entire world. Another director may well come along whose reading makes entirely different visual demands.

I do not believe that one reading is as good as another; a director's reading of the play not only must be internally coherent but must serve to open up the text to the spectator's understanding. The importance — or possibility — of honoring authorial intention in a stage production is a thorny issue better left to the critics. But a close reading of the text, a passionate hunt for every visual, aural clue the text has to offer — from its layout on the page, to punctuation (or lack of it), to scene titles, to spelling, to character names — all of this must be sharply observed for clues as to rhythm, tempo, and potential meaning.

Jacobus: One of your jobs as director was to help audiences see that the figures who appeared onstage to the Black Man and Black Woman were spirits. How did you solve the problem?

Diamond: Of course, one might first ask: Are those "figures," as they are called in the text, spirits? It doesn't explicitly state anywhere that Queen-then-Pharaoh Hatshepsut, Ham, etc. are any less real than the Black Man or Black Woman. But an offhand remark made by Suzan-Lori during one of our script conferences — "By the way, you could say that the only living human being onstage is the Black Woman. Everyone else is dead, some more than others, but dead" — suggested that something might be called for to help the audience discover that there is indeed a hierarchy of the dead in this play, moving in descending order from the biblical Ham, who "died" thousands of years ago, to the Voice on thuh Tee V, who perhaps died yesterday. But visually insisting on ghosts can get a bit silly in a play as stylistically unbound by the conventions of naturalism as is *The Death of the Last Black Man in the Whole Entire World.* So we decided (the costume designer, Caryn Neman, and myself) on "celestial" versions of each figure's own earthly dress. We put them all in what we called high church drag — the gold and glitter of the ultimate high mass, but kept each figure's costume pieces specific to the historic period or social role implied by their title. Thus Yes and Greens Black-Eyed Peas Cornbread wore the rags and pigtails of the pickaninny to be found in the racist cartoons and caricatures of the slave period but glowed with the gold and the glitter of the Promised Land. In contrast, the Black Woman wore a quite conventional black dress, the sort of garment any widow might wear to her husband's funeral.

Jacobus: Could you talk about your collaboration with Suzan-Lori in directing this play? Is it more or less difficult for the director when the playwright is in rehearsal?

Diamond: One of the many reasons Suzan-Lori and I love collaborating on a production is that we don't mess around in each other's business. She writes the play; I direct it. At the same time, we talk constantly. Before rehearsals begin, we read the play aloud together, with Suzan-Lori pointing out specific rhythmic requirements as they come up. She helps me decode the many and rich historic and fictional references woven into the text. She suggests books to read, artworks to examine, music to listen to. I try to avoid asking what a passage means, because I prefer to make those discoveries myself. I share with her my initial impressions, early hints as to where it all might take place, and obsessions begin to emerge as I read the play over and over. I listen carefully to her responses and to her elaborations on ideas I propose for setting, sound, action, etc. We cast the play together and I keep her abreast of the evolving design decisions. She attends the first read-through of the play. And then she does an amazing thing: She leaves us alone until the first run-through, which may be two or three weeks later. I consider the space she gives me and the actors — to make our own discoveries — an incredible gift, a little scary, and very smart. She understands our need to ask whatever comes into our heads, to try out all kinds of crazy solutions, and that it will be easier on everyone if the playwright is absent. By the time she comes back, of course, there is something reasonably coherent for her to respond to. She and I are likely to be in close touch by phone throughout the process, with me proposing textual changes as they come up in rehearsal, and with Suzan-Lori helping me untangle whatever staging knots I may be struggling with. It should be clear that what I am describing is an ongoing dialogue, one that thrives, I think, because we trust each other's judgment and taste, because we have so much fun tossing ideas back and forth and because we both get such a huge kick out of sitting in the back of the theater watching this *thing* we've created actually come to life.

Having a playwright come to rehearsal, in particular to that first run-through, is, of course, a terrifying moment for everyone. The writer is wondering: Will this play hold up? The director is wondering: Will this staging hold up? The actor is wondering: Am I about to be fired? But this atmosphere of near total paranoia is broken with the uttering of the first line of text, as private anxieties give way to this immense, collective rooting for the play to fly. The joy of working with Suzan-Lori is that when it's over, we collectively celebrate what works and collectively get to work on what doesn't. It is usually abundantly clear where the problems are, if not how to solve them, and very little ego gets in the way of just diving in and fixing them.

Alisa Solomon
LANGUAGE IN *LAST BLACK MAN*   1990

Alisa Solomon focuses on Suzan-Lori Parks's use of language, particularly repetition, and on influences from jazz, which also depends on choruses, verses, and refrains of the kind Parks has written. The connection between American jazz and African ritual is one of Parks's most important inspirations.

Parks's plays look like long, dialogic poems. There are no stage directions and little in the way of moorings for the unsuspecting director. But, Parks insists, movement is contained in the speech itself. Often leaving out punctuation that would delineate formal pauses, she lets words run together to find their own rhythms. And with a nod to Zora Neale Hurston's seamless welding of the "folkloric" and the "literary," Parks makes music of everyday usage. Even the way a word is spelled can imply stage action: "Thuh," she says, slumping, "makes the body do something very different" — and here she straightens up — "than 'The.'"

What's more, for African-Americans, the difference can mean the difference between work and unemployment, even between life and death. . . .

Parks goes even further in her experiments with language in her second major play, *The Death of the Last Black Man in the Whole Entire World.* If *Imperceptible Mutabilities* showed African-Americans in a perpetual state of middle passage, their identity hidden somewhere in the ocean-sized, centuries-old hyphen separating African from American, *Death of the Last Black Man,* with humor and pointedness, takes on the American side of the divide, confronting stereotypes and dismantling cultural myths.

Here, again, Parks addresses the themes of self-narration, the way language can confer autonomy, the gaps between image and reality, white America's denial of African-American history. But this play is even more complex in approach, more inventive in style, and, surprisingly — because its experiments are so formal — more passionate.

There's little that could be called plot here. Indeed, the idea of sequence is subverted again and again. Time itself is subverted, past and future conflated into the simultaneity of the theatrical present. When did the last black man die? "Yesterday tuhday next summer tuhmorrow just a moment ughoh in 1317."

Instead of relying on logical sequence, Parks creates a sense of progression through repetition. Her language gathers momentum through what Gertrude Stein called "the natural way to count . . . not that one and one make two but to go on counting by one and one. . . . One and one and one and one and one." Parks does not drive her plays with the mechanism of suspense: if there's any eagerness to find out what will happen next, it comes not from the hurtling forward of an event into its consequences, but from the variations she builds on established patterns.

Stein is one clear influence on this style; the other is jazz. Through listening to jazz, with its solos sculpted around revisions of a repeated theme, Parks says she's recently realized "how much this method is an integral part of the African and African-American literary and oral traditions."

In a note to other members of BACA's New Works Project — a workshop for writers and directors — Parks explains what intrigues her about this technique:

Repetition — we accept it in poetry and call it incremental refrain. For the most part incremental refrain creates a weight and a rhythm. In dramatic writing it does the same — yes, but we want to get to the CLIMAX. Where does repetition fit? First, it's not just repetition, but repetition with *revision.* And in drama, change is the thing. Characters refigure their words. Secondly, a text based on the concept of repetition and revision is one which breaks from the text which we are told to write — the text which cleanly ARCS. Thirdly, Rep and Rev texts create a real challenge for the actor and director as they create a physical life appropriate to the text. In such pieces we are not moving from A–B but rather, for example, from A–A–A–B–A. Through such movement, we refigure A. And if we wish to continue to call this movement FORWARD PROGRESSION, which I think it is, then we refigure the concept of forward progression.

Subverting sequence changes the meaning of consequence. The teleological nature of naturalistic drama virtually requires some kind of huge event that brings on catastrophe — or at least consequences that the action of the play seeks to expose and explain. "If you stick to that kind of writing," Parks says, "then all you can write is plays about black men being killed by policemen, as if to indict society, you need a Big Event. But on stage, as in physics, an event doesn't have to be big to be a big deal. In the theater, someone can simply turn their hand palm up and that is an event."

In *Death of the Last Black Man,* history itself refuses to be linear or sequential. For Parks, history is round — or perhaps, roun'. "The worl usta be *roun*," the Black Man with Watermelon says, "before Columbus." And then, Queen-then-Pharaoh Hatshepsut explains, "they put uh 'd' on thuh end of roun making round. Thusly they set in motion thuh end. Without that 'd' we coulda gone on spinnin for ever. The 'd' thing ended things ended." More than that, [Before Columbus] replies, "Them thinking the world was flat kept it roun. Them thinking the sun revolved around the earth kept them satellite-like. They figured out the truth and scurried out. Figuring out the truth put them in their place and they scurried out to put us in ours. [Yes and Greens Black-Eyed Peas Cornbread adds] Mmm. Yes. You should write this down. You should hide this under a rock."

The consequences Parks is concerned with are those that resulted from that "d" being appended to the roun worl. In one sequence, the Black Man appears with a noose around his neck, dragging a tree branch behind him. Over and over in the play this last black man *almost* dies: We hear of him falling from a ship, bursting into flames, being plucked from his homeland, being auctioned at the block. And in another extended sequence, he tells the Black Woman how he escaped from electrocution, even after "Jump-juice meets me-mine juices I do uh slow soft shoe like on water. Town crier cries uh moan. Felt my nappy head go frizzly." All these deaths — or near-deaths — are offset by a celebration of births, presented as a ritualized series of begets: "MeMines gived out 2 offspring one she called Mines after herself thuh uther she called Themuhns named after all them who comed before." But these generically named offspring are a dubious blessing; this resurgence is given theatrical extension by an onstage proliferation of watermelons.

Still, the play implies, the greatest death of the Black Man is his being written out of history. Over and over, speakers advise each other, "You should write it down because if you don't write it down then they will come along and tell the future that we did not exist." Gradually, it seems the characters learn this lesson. By the play's end, they have gathered into "uh multitude," recognizing the pull of their own "Nature, History, Gravity." In a triumphant finale, the chorus's "And we will lay us down" gives way to the Black Man and Black Woman's "And we will write us down."

This, of course, is precisely what Suzan-Lori Parks, young, gifted, and African-American, has been doing, capturing the contradictions and crises contained in her own project. As she is increasingly recognized, she too — as she well knows — will run the risk of seeing white institutions want to fix that flattening -d onto her roun writing. In the *New York Times*, Mel Gussow called Parks the most promising playwright of the year; *Imperceptible Mutabilities* won an Obie Award from *The Village Voice* last spring. . . . Meanwhile, the Women's Project has commissioned a play from Parks, and regional theaters are considering productions of *Imperceptible Mutabilities* — though, Parks quips, "If they decide to do it, it will have to be in February so people can have an explanation for it." She's referring, of course, to Black History Month.

David Mamet

The title of one of David Mamet's plays, *A Life in the Theatre* (1977), may have been autobiographically inspired. Mamet has spent his life — from high school onward — in the theater, as actor, director, playwright, and screenwriter. Born in Chicago in 1947, he graduated with an English major from Goddard College in Vermont where he wrote several plays, including his undergraduate thesis, *Camel* (1968). *Sexual Perversity in Chicago* (1975), Mamet's first resounding commercial success, was first drafted when he was at Goddard. In the same year, *American Buffalo* premiered in the Goodman Theatre in Chicago, beginning a series of productions around the country. The Broadway production was not especially well received, but it was the first American play produced at London's new National Theatre in 1978. After a 1980 revival in New Haven's Long Wharf Theater with Al Pacino as Teach, it moved to Circle in the Square in New York in 1981 and then to Broadway in 1983. A study of petty thieves living a darkly comic underground life, *American Buffalo* has become one of Mamet's most highly regarded plays.

His much-acclaimed *Glengarry Glen Ross* (1983) premiered in London at the National Theatre, then moved to Broadway the following year, where it won the Pulitzer Prize and many other awards. This tale of scheming real estate salesmen derives in part from Mamet's experience working in a real estate office as a young man. The portrait of avarice and deceit is an indictment of one aspect of American business. *Glengarry Glen Ross* was eventually revised for film.

In the 1980s and 1990s Mamet wrote many stage plays, radio plays, and film scripts. He adapted Chekhov's *The Cherry Orchard* (1985), wrote *Goldberg Street* for radio performance, and wrote the screenplays for *The Untouchables* (1987), *House of Games* (1987), nominated for a Golden Globe Award, *Things Change* (1988), and *Homocide* (1991). *Speed The Plow* (1988) opened on Broadway with Madonna playing a secretary from a temp agency. It draws on Mamet's experience in the film industry and explores the insecurities and double-dealing of those who make decisions about producing movies. More recently, his play *The Cryptogram* (1994) was produced first in London in June 1994, then in February 1995 at the American Repertory Theatre in Boston. The New York production was at the Westside Arts Theater in March 1995.

In the early 1970s Mamet was deeply involved in Chicago's St.

Nicholas Theatre Company, a group that gathered to produce a variety of plays, including some of his own. William H. Macy, Steven Schacter, and Patricia Cox were the principal actors, and others joined with them. Soon, however, Mamet's responsibilities as a writer and his occasional stints as a university professor at Goddard and elsewhere forced him to leave Chicago and center himself in New York. Currently living in Vermont, he does most of his writing in a small cabin on his property.

OLEANNA

The title of the play is ironic, referring to a folksong that yearns for a utopian community, Oleanna, in Wisconsin. There is nothing utopian about the play. It was first produced in a small off-Broadway theater in 1992, running for more than 250 performances and stirring an enormous amount of controversy. Shortly before the play was produced, the nation had been transfixed by Senate hearings on Anita Hill's accusation that Clarence Thomas, a Supreme Court nominee, sexually harassed her. Both held to stories that contradicted the other, and the nation took sides without knowing which was correct. *Oleanna* was not, according to Mamet, inspired by the hearings but as many reviewers pointed out, certainly profited from them.

The play concerns a professor in his interchange with a female student who is having trouble in his course. When we first see him, John's tenure has been approved, but not fully confirmed by the university. Carol, when we first meet her, is tentative, uncertain, and struggles with some of John's vocabulary. John is confident, swaggering, a bit condescending, generally enjoying being in a position of considerable power. Mamet explores the relationship as it begins to reverse itself. At the end of the play Carol, now heading an unnamed group of feminists, interprets the early events in such a way as to file charges of sexual harassment and rape against John and petitions to have his tenure denied.

All the while this grappling ensues, the telephone (critic Clive Barnes referred it to as the third actor onstage) rings incessantly with news from John's wife and real estate agent concerning the house they are trying to buy, now that they are confident that tenure will be awarded. The struggle of ideas between professor and student, the concerns for power, and the issues of patriarchy and sexual harassment become manifest in John's ultimate realization that the price for what he has done (if only he could understand what he has done) is the loss of his house and an ultimate threat to his family and his security.

The audience is in a privileged position because it has seen the events of the first two scenes of the play. John expresses a desire to help Carol and offers her an A if she will retake as a tutorial the course she failed. He reassures her when she says she cannot understand anything. He even good-naturedly criticizes the entire institution of education as a "warehousing of the young." He innocently embraces her in a show of confidence. But all these gestures, once Carol goes on the attack in act 2, are seen to have an entirely different significance than anything John seems to have intended. As Michael Feingold said in his review, "*Oleanna* is a tragedy built as a series of audience traps; the minute you get suckered into thinking it says one thing, you're likely to find it saying the exact opposite." The point is that from one position — that of power — a gesture will mean one thing; from another position — that of powerlessness — a gesture will take on another meaning. The audience, with good reason to distrust both John and Carol, given their obvious character flaws, is left to decide the meaning of events.

Oleanna in Performance

In production, whether in New York, New Haven, Croton Falls, or London, the play induced audiences to cry out in response to lines and to stand around afterward under marquees in forceful argument over the issues and outcome of the events. Whatever one may say about the flaws of the play — overreliance on the telephone, annoying stuttering dialogue, an unlikely reversal of Carol from a woman who misunderstood common words to a spokesperson for a coalition using complex language — it charged members of the audience. The feelings of frustration onstage seemed to find resonance in observers quick and ready to respond.

Mamet's treatment of women in his earlier plays has sometimes drawn fire. In discussing *Oleanna*, Otis Guernsey, Jr., said that both Pinter and Mamet "seem to view women as ultimately unfathomable." Yet Guernsey felt that Mamet's direction of *Oleanna* "was a galvanizing theatrical experience." Not all critics agreed. Alisa Solomon in the *Village Voice* scorned it as a "twisted little play" in which the student is vilified and the professor made an object of sympathy. Jan Stuart in *New York Newsday* called it "scurrilous," and said, "*Oleanna* is loathsome and riveting in the way that only Mamet plays can be." Clive Barnes called it "a pretentious flop." Other critics saw it as powerful. David Sterritt in the *Christian Science Monitor* called it "a searing new play." David Patrick Stearns in *USA Today* said the play "gets under your skin and itches there for days."

The staging of the play depends on tightness of quarters. John's office is tight, small, uncluttered. The New Haven production used stark white surfaces and bright lighting, while the New York production seemed dingier, with an office that held obviously used furniture. The lighting was simple, even, and somewhat harsh. One reason given for choosing New York's small Orpheum Theatre was that it is itself somewhat small, virtually claustrophobic.

After its New York premiere the play was produced in London and regionally throughout the United States before being made into a film in 1994. A 1995 production in Croton Falls, New York, garnered exceptionally strong reviews, indicating that the play does not depend on star quality. As a curious note, the programs for the original production depicted a bull's-eye target, some with John's and some with Carol's face in the center. Mamet was clearly aware of the drama's potential for controversy.

David Mamet *(b. 1947)*

OLEANNA

1992

The want of fresh air does not seem much to affect the happiness of children in a London alley: the greater part of them sing and play as though they were on a moor in Scotland. So the absence of a genial mental atmosphere is not commonly recognized by children who have never known it. Young people have a marvelous faculty of either dying or adapting themselves to circumstances. Even if they are unhappy — very unhappy — it is astonishing how easily they can be prevented from finding

it out, or at any rate from attributing it to any other cause than their own sinfulness. —The Way of All Flesh
SAMUEL BUTLER

"Oh, to be in Oleanna,
That's where I would rather be
Than be bound in Norway
And drag the chains of slavery." — FOLK SONG

Characters

CAROL, *a woman of twenty*
JOHN, *a man in his forties*

The play takes place in John's office.

ACT 1

(John is talking on the phone. Carol is seated across the desk from him.)

JOHN *(on phone):* And what about the land. *(Pause.)* The land. And what about the land? *(Pause.)* What about it? *(Pause.)* No. I don't understand. Well, yes, I'm I'm . . . no, I'm *sure* it's signif . . . I'm sure it's significant. *(Pause.)* Because it's significant to mmmmmm . . . did you call Jerry? *(Pause.)* Because . . . no, no, no, no, no. What did they say . . . ? Did you speak to the *real* estate . . . where *is* she . . . ? Well, well, all right. Where are her notes? Where are the notes we took with her. *(Pause.)* I thought you were? No. No, I'm sorry, I didn't mean that, I just thought that I saw you, when we were there . . . what . . . ? I thought I saw you with a *pencil.* WHY NOW? is what I'm say . . . well, that's why I say "call Jerry." Well, I can't right now, be . . . no, I *didn't* schedule any . . . Grace: I *didn't* . . . I'm well aware . . . Look: Look. Did you call Jerry? Will you call Jerry . . . ? Because I can't now. I'll be there, I'm sure I'll be there in fifteen, in twenty. I intend to. No, we aren't *going* to lose the, we aren't *going* to lose the house. Look: Look, I'm not minimizing it. The "easement." Did she say "easement"? *(Pause.)* What did she *say*; *is* it a "term of art," are we *bound* by it . . . I'm sorry . . . *(Pause.)* are: we: yes. *Bound* by . . . Look: *(he*

checks his watch) before the other side *goes home,* all right? "a term of art." Because: that's right *(Pause.)* The yard for the boy. Well, that's the whole . . . Look: I'm going to meet you there . . . *(He checks his watch.)* Is the realtor there? All right, tell her to show you the basement again. Look at the *this* because . . . Bec . . . I'm leaving in, I'm leaving in ten or fifteen . . . Yes. No, no, I'll meet you at the new . . . That's a good. If he thinks it's necc . . . you tell Jerry to meet . . . All right? We *aren't* going to lose the deposit. All right? I'm sure it's going to be . . . *(Pause.)* I hope so. *(Pause.)* I love you, too. *(Pause.)* I love you, too. As soon as . . . I will.

(He hangs up.) (He bends over the desk and makes a note.) (He looks up.) (To Carol): I'm sorry . . .

CAROL *(pause):* What is a "term of art"?

JOHN *(pause):* I'm sorry . . . ?

CAROL *(pause):* What is a "term of art"?

JOHN: Is that what you want to talk about?

CAROL: . . . to talk about . . . ?

JOHN: Let's take the mysticism out of it, shall we? Carol? *(Pause.)* Don't you think? I'll tell you: when you have some "thing." Which must be broached. *(Pause.)* Don't you think . . . ? *(Pause.)*

CAROL: . . . don't I think . . . ?

JOHN: Mmm?

CAROL: . . . did I . . . ?

JOHN: . . . what?

CAROL: Did . . . did I . . . did I say something wr . . .

JOHN *(pause):* No. I'm sorry. No. You're right. I'm very sorry. I'm somewhat rushed. As you see. I'm sorry. You're right. *(Pause.)* What is a "term of art"? It seems to mean a *term,* which has come, through its use, to mean something *more specific* than the words would, to someone *not acquainted* with them . . . indicate. That, I believe, is what a "term of art," would mean. *(Pause.)*

CAROL: You don't know what it means . . . ?

JOHN: I'm not sure that I know what it means. It's one of those things, perhaps you've had them, that, you look them up, or have someone explain them to you, and you say "aha," and, you immediately *forget* what . . .

CAROL: You don't do that.

JOHN: . . . I . . . ?

CAROL: You don't do . . .

JOHN: . . . I don't, what . . . ?

CAROL: . . . for . . .

JOHN: . . . I don't for . . .

CAROL: . . . no . . .

JOHN: . . . forget things? Everybody does that.

CAROL: No, they don't.

JOHN: They don't . . .

CAROL: No.

JOHN (*pause*): No. Everybody does that.

CAROL: Why would they do that . . . ?

JOHN: Because. I don't know. Because it doesn't interest them.

CAROL: No.

JOHN: I think so, though. (*Pause.*) I'm sorry that I was distracted.

CAROL: You don't have to say that to me.

JOHN: You paid me the compliment, or the "obeisance" — all right — of coming in here . . . All right. *Carol.* I find that I am at a *standstill.* I find that I . . .

CAROL: . . . what . . .

JOHN: . . . one moment. In regard to your . . . to your . . .

CAROL: Oh, oh. You're buying a new house!

JOHN: No, let's get on with it.

CAROL: "get on"? (*Pause.*)

JOHN: I know how . . . *believe* me. I know how . . . potentially *humiliating* these . . . I have no desire to . . . I have no desire other than to help you. But (*he picks up some papers on his desk*) I won't even say "but." I'll say that as I go back over the . . .

CAROL: I'm just, I'm just trying to . . .

JOHN: . . . no, it will not do.

CAROL: . . . what? What will . . . ?

JOHN: No. I see, I see what you, it . . . (*He gestures to the papers.*) but your work . . .

CAROL: I'm just: I sit in class I . . . (*She holds up her notebook.*) I take notes . . .

JOHN (*simultaneously with* "notes"): Yes. I understand. What I am trying to *tell* you is that some, some basic . . .

CAROL: . . . I . . .

JOHN: . . . one moment: some basic missed communi . . .

CAROL: I'm doing what I'm told. I bought your book, I read your . . .

JOHN: No, I'm sure you . . .

CAROL: No, no, no. I'm doing what I'm told. It's *difficult* for me. It's *difficult* . . .

JOHN: . . . but . . .

CAROL: I don't . . . lots of the *language* . . .

JOHN: . . . please . . .

CAROL: The *language*, the "things" that you say . . .

JOHN: I'm sorry. No. I don't think that that's true.

CAROL: It *is* true. I . . .

JOHN: I think . . .

CAROL: It *is* true.

JOHN: . . . I . . .

CAROL: Why would I . . . ?

JOHN: I'll tell you why: you're an incredibly bright girl.

CAROL: . . . I . . .

JOHN: You're an incredibly . . . you have no problem with the . . . Who's kidding who?

CAROL: . . . I . . .

JOHN: No. No. I'll tell you why. I'll tell . . . I think you're *angry,* I . . .

CAROL: . . . why would I . . .

JOHN: . . . wait one moment. I . . .

CAROL: It is true. I have *problems* . . .

JOHN: . . . every . . .

CAROL: . . . I come from a different *social* . . .

JOHN: . . . ev . . .

CAROL: a different economic . . .

JOHN: . . . Look:

CAROL: No. I: when I *came* to this school:

JOHN: Yes. Quite . . . (*Pause.*)

CAROL: . . . does that mean nothing . . . ?

JOHN: . . . but look: look . . .

CAROL: . . . I . . .

JOHN (*picks up paper*): Here: Please: Sit down. (*Pause.*) Sit down. (*Reads from her paper.*) "I think that the ideas contained in this work express the author's feelings in a way that he intended, based on his results." What can that mean? Do you see? What . . .

CAROL: I, the best that I . . .

JOHN: I'm saying, that perhaps this course . . .

CAROL: No, no, no, you can't, you can't . . . I have to . . .

JOHN: . . . how . . .

CAROL: . . . I have to pass it . . .

JOHN: Carol, I:

CAROL: I *have* to pass this course, I . . .

JOHN: Well.

CAROL: . . . don't you . . .

JOHN: Either the . . .

CAROL: . . . I . . .

JOHN: . . . either the, I . . . either the *criteria* for judging progress in the class are . . .

CAROL: No, no, no, no, I have to pass it.

JOHN: Now, look: I'm a human being, I . . .

CAROL: I did what you told me. I did, I did everything that, I read your *book,* you told me to buy your book and read it. Everything you *say* I . . . (*She gestures to her notebook.*) (*The phone rings.*) I do. . . . Ev . . .

JOHN: . . . look:

CAROL: . . . everything I'm told . . .

JOHN: Look. Look. I'm not your *father.* (*Pause.*)

CAROL: What?

JOHN: I'm.

CAROL: Did I say you were my father?

JOHN: . . . no . . .

CAROL: Why did you say that . . . ?

JOHN: I . . .

CAROL: . . . why . . . ?

JOHN: . . . in class I . . . (*He picks up the phone.*) (*Into phone:*) Hello. I can't talk now. Jerry? Yes? I underst . . . I can't talk now. I know . . . I know . . . Jerry. I can't *talk* now. Yes, I. Call me back in . . . Thank you. (*He hangs up.*) (*To Carol.*) What do you want me to do? We are two people, all right? Both of whom have subscribed to . . .

CAROL: No, no . . .

JOHN: . . . certain arbitrary . . .

CAROL: No. You have to help me.

JOHN: Certain institutional . . . you tell me what you want me to do. . . . You tell me what you want me to . . .

CAROL: How can I go back and tell them the *grades* that I . . .

ABOVE AND BELOW: Mary McCann and William H. Macy in the 1993 New York production of *Oleanna.*

JOHN: . . . what can I do . . . ?

CAROL: *Teach* me. *Teach* me.

JOHN: . . . I'm trying to teach you.

CAROL: I read your book. I read it. I don't under . . .

JOHN: . . . you don't understand it.

CAROL: No.

JOHN: Well, perhaps it's not well *written* . . .

CAROL (*simultaneously with* "written"): No. No. No. I want to *understand* it.

JOHN: What don't you understand? (*Pause.*)

CAROL: *Any* of it. What you're trying to say. When you talk about . . .

JOHN: . . . yes . . . ? (*She consults her notes.*)

CAROL: "Virtual warehousing of the young" . . .

JOHN: "Virtual warehousing of the young." If we artificially prolong adolescence . . .

CAROL: . . . and about "The Curse of Modern Education."

JOHN: . . . well . . .

CAROL: I don't . . .

JOHN: Look. It's just a *course*, it's just a *book*, it's just a . . .

CAROL: No. No. There are *people* out there. People who came *here*. To know something they didn't *know*. Who *came* here. To be *helped*. To be *helped*. So someone would *help* them. To *do* something. To *know* something. To get, what do they say? "To get on in the world." How can I do that if I don't, if I fail? But I don't *understand*. I don't *understand*. I don't understand what anything means . . . and I walk around. From morning 'til night: with this one thought in my head. I'm *stupid*.

JOHN: No one thinks you're stupid.

CAROL: No? What am I . . . ?

JOHN: I . . .

CAROL: . . . what am I, then?

JOHN: I think you're angry. Many people are. I have a *telephone* call that I have to make. And an *appointment*, which is rather *pressing*; though I sympathize with your concerns, and though I wish I had the time, this was not a previously scheduled meeting and I . . .

CAROL: . . . you think I'm nothing . . .

JOHN: . . . have an appointment with a *realtor*, and with my wife and . . .

CAROL: You think that I'm stupid.

JOHN: No. I certainly don't.

CAROL: You said it.

JOHN: No. I did not.

CAROL: You did.

JOHN: When?

CAROL: . . . you . . .

JOHN: No. I never did, or never would say that to a student, and . . .

CAROL: You said, "What can that mean?" (*Pause.*) "What can that mean?" . . . (*Pause.*)

JOHN: . . . and what did that mean to you . . . ?

CAROL: That meant I'm stupid. And I'll never learn. That's what that meant. And you're right.

JOHN: . . . I . . .

CAROL: But then. But then, what am I doing here . . . ?

JOHN: . . . if you thought that I . . .

CAROL: . . . when nobody wants me, and . . .

JOHN: . . . if you interpreted . . .

CAROL: Nobody *tells* me anything. And I *sit* there . . . in the *corner*. In the *back*. And everybody's talking about "this" all the time. And "concepts," and "precepts" and, and, and, and, and, WHAT IN THE WORLD ARE YOU *TALKING* ABOUT? And I read your book. And they said, "Fine, go in that class." Because you talked about responsibility to the young. I DON'T KNOW WHAT IT MEANS AND I'M *FAILING* . . .

JOHN: May . . .

CAROL: No, you're right. "Oh, hell." I failed. Flunk me out of it. It's garbage. Everything I do. "The ideas contained in this work express the author's feelings." That's right. That's right. I know I'm stupid. I know what I am. (*Pause.*) I know what I am, Professor. You don't have to tell me. (*Pause.*) It's pathetic. Isn't it?

JOHN: . . . Aha . . . (*Pause.*) Sit down. Sit down. Please. (*Pause.*) Please sit down.

CAROL: Why?

JOHN: I want to talk to you.

CAROL: Why?

JOHN: Just sit down. (*Pause.*) Please. Sit down. Will you, please . . . ? (*Pause. She does so.*) Thank you.

CAROL: What?

JOHN: I want to tell you something.

CAROL (*pause*): What?

JOHN: Well, I know what you're talking about.

CAROL: No. You don't.

JOHN: I think I do. (*Pause.*)

CAROL: How can you?

JOHN: I'll tell you a story about myself. (*Pause.*) Do you mind? (*Pause.*) I was raised to think myself stupid. That's what I want to tell you. (*Pause.*)

CAROL: What do you mean?

JOHN: Just what I said. I was brought up, and my earliest, and most persistent memories are of being told that I was stupid. "You have such *intelligence*. Why must you behave so *stupidly*?" Or, "Can't you *understand*? Can't you *understand*?" And I could *not* understand. I could *not* understand.

CAROL: What?

JOHN: The simplest problem. Was beyond me. It was a mystery.

CAROL: What was a mystery?

JOHN: How people learn. How *I* could learn. Which is what I've been speaking of in class. And of *course* you can't hear it. Carol. Of *course* you can't. (*Pause.*) I used to speak of "real people," and wonder what the *real* people did. The *real* people. Who were they? *They* were the people other than myself. The *good* people. The *capable* people. The people who could do the things, *I* could not do: learn, study, retain . . . all that *garbage* — which is what I have been talking of in class, and that's *exactly* what I have been talking of — If you are told. . . . Listen to this. If the young child is told he cannot understand. Then he takes it as a *description* of himself. What am I? I am *that which can not understand.* And I saw you out there, when we were speaking of the concepts of . . .

CAROL: I can't understand any of them.

JOHN: Well, then, that's *my* fault. That's not your fault. And that is not verbiage. That's what I firmly hold to be the truth. And I am sorry, and I owe you an apology.

CAROL: Why?

JOHN: And I suppose that I have had some *things* on my mind. . . . We're buying a *house,* and . . .

CAROL: People said that you were stupid . . . ?

JOHN: Yes.

CAROL: When?

JOHN: I'll tell you when. Through my life. In my childhood; and, perhaps, they stopped. But I heard them continue.

CAROL: And what did they say?

JOHN: They said I was incompetent. Do you see? And when I'm tested, the, the, the *feelings* of my youth about the *very subject of learning* come up. And I . . . I become, I feel "unworthy," and "unprepared." . . .

CAROL: . . . yes.

JOHN: . . . eh?

CAROL: . . . yes.

JOHN: And I feel that I must fail. (*Pause.*)

CAROL: . . . but then you *do* fail. (*Pause.*) You have to. (*Pause.*) Don't you?

JOHN: A *pilot.* Flying a plane. The pilot is flying the plane. He thinks: Oh, my *God,* my mind's been drifting! Oh, my God! What kind of a cursed imbecile am I, that I, with this so precious cargo of *Life* in my charge, would allow my attention to wander. Why was I born? How deluded are those who put their trust in me, . . . et cetera, so on, and he crashes the plane.

CAROL (*pause*): He could just . . .

JOHN: That's right.

CAROL: He could say:

JOHN: My attention *wandered* for a moment . . .

CAROL: . . . uh huh . . .

JOHN: I had a *thought* I did not like . . . but now:

CAROL: . . . but now it's . . .

JOHN: That's what I'm telling you. It's time to put my attention . . . see: it is not: this is what I learned. It is Not Magic. Yes. Yes. *You.* You are going to be frightened. When faced with what may or may not be but which you are going to perceive as a test. You will become frightened. And you will say: "I am incapable of . . . " and everything *in* you will think these two things. "I must. But I can't." And you will think: Why was I born to be the laughingstock of a world in which everyone is better than I? In which I am entitled to nothing. Where I can not learn.

(*Pause.*)

CAROL: Is that . . . (*Pause.*) Is that what I have . . . ?

JOHN: Well. I don't know if I'd put it that way. Listen: I'm talking to you as I'd talk to my son. Because that's what I'd like him to have that I never had. I'm talking to you the way I wish that someone had talked to me. I don't know how to do it, other than to be *personal,* . . . but . . .

CAROL: Why would you want to be personal with me?

JOHN: Well, you see? That's what I'm saying. We can only interpret the behavior of others through the screen we . . . (*The phone rings.*) Through . . . (*To phone.*) Hello . . . ? (*To Carol.*) Through the screen we create. (*To phone.*) Hello. (*To Carol.*) Excuse me a moment. (*To phone.*) Hello? No, I can't talk nnn . . . I know I did. In a few . . . I'm . . . is he coming to the . . . yes. I talked to him. We'll meet you at the No, because I'm with a *student.* It's going to be fff . . . This is important, too. I'm with a *student,* Jerry's going to . . . Listen: the sooner I get off, the sooner I'll be down, all right. I love you. Listen, listen, I said "I love you," it's going to work *out* with the, because I feel that it is, I'll be right down. All right? Well, then it's going to take as long as it takes. (*He hangs up.*) (*To Carol.*) I'm sorry.

CAROL: What was that?

JOHN: There are some problems, as there usually are, about the final agreements for the new house.

CAROL: You're buying a new house.

JOHN: That's right.

CAROL: Because of your promotion.

JOHN: Well, I suppose that that's right.

CAROL: Why did you stay here with me?

JOHN: Stay here.

CAROL: Yes. When you should have gone.

JOHN: Because I like you.

CAROL: You like me.

JOHN: Yes.

CAROL: Why?

JOHN: Why? Well? Perhaps we're similar. (*Pause.*) Yes. (*Pause.*)

CAROL: You said "everyone has problems."

JOHN: Everyone has problems.

CAROL: Do they?

JOHN: Certainly.

CAROL: You do?

JOHN: Yes.

CAROL: What are they?

JOHN: Well. (*Pause.*) Well, you're perfectly right. (*Pause.*) If we're going to take off the Artificial *Stricture,* of "Teacher," and "Student," why should *my* problems be any more a mystery than your own? Of *course* I have problems. As you saw.

CAROL: . . . with what?

JOHN: With my *wife* . . . with *work* . . .

CAROL: With work?

JOHN: Yes. And, and, perhaps my problems are, do you see? *Similar* to yours.

CAROL: Would you tell me?

JOHN: All right. (*Pause.*) I came *late* to teaching. And I found it Artificial. The notion of "I know and you do not"; and I saw an *exploitation* in the education process. I told you. I hated school, I hated teachers. I hated everyone who was in the position of a "boss" because I *knew* — I didn't *think,* mind you, I *knew* I was going to fail. Because I was a fuckup. I was just no goddamned good. When I . . . late in life . . . (*Pause.*) When I *got out from under* . . . when I worked my way out of the need to fail. When I . . .

CAROL: How do you do that? (*Pause.*)

JOHN: You have to look at what you are, and what you feel, and how you act. And, finally, you have to look at how you act. And say: If that's what I *did,* that must be how I think of myself.

CAROL: I don't understand.

JOHN: If I fail all the time, it must be that I think of myself as a failure. If I do not want to think of myself as a failure, perhaps I should begin by *succeeding* now and again. Look. The tests, you see, which you encounter, in school, in college, in life, were designed, in the most part, for idiots. *By* idiots. There is no need to fail at them. They are not a test of your worth. They are a test of your ability to retain and spout back misinformation. Of *course* you fail them. They're *nonsense.* And I . . .

CAROL: . . . no . . .

JOHN: Yes. They're *garbage.* They're a *joke.* Look at me. Look at me. The Tenure Committee. The Tenure Committee. Come to judge me. The Bad Tenure Committee.

The "Test." Do you see? They put me to the test. Why, they had people voting on me I wouldn't employ to wax my car. And yet, I go before the Great Tenure Committee, and I have an urge, to *vomit,* to, to, to puke my *badness* on the table, to show them: "I'm no good. Why would you pick *me?*"

CAROL: They granted you tenure.

JOHN: Oh no, they announced it, but they haven't *signed.* Do you see? "At any moment . . . "

CAROL: . . . mmm . . .

JOHN: "They might not *sign*" . . . I might not . . . the *house* might not go through . . . Eh? Eh? They'll find out my "dark secret." (*Pause.*)

CAROL: . . . what is it . . . ?

JOHN: There *isn't* one. But *they* will find an index of my badness . . .

CAROL: Index?

JOHN: A " . . . pointer." A "Pointer." You see? Do you see? I *understand* you. I. Know. That. Feeling. Am I entitled to my job, and my nice *home,* and my *wife,* and my *family,* and so on. This is what I'm saying: That theory of education which, that *theory:*

CAROL: I . . . I . . . (*Pause.*)

JOHN: What?

CAROL: I . . .

JOHN: What?

CAROL: I want to know about my grade. (*Long pause.*)

JOHN: Of course you do.

CAROL: Is that bad?

JOHN: No.

CAROL: Is it bad that I asked you that?

JOHN: No.

CAROL: Did I upset you?

JOHN: No. And I apologize. Of *course* you want to know about your grade. And, of course, you can't concentrate on anyth . . . (*The telephone starts to ring.*) Wait a moment.

CAROL: I should go.

JOHN: I'll make you a deal.

CAROL: No, you have to . . .

JOHN: Let it ring. I'll make you a deal. You stay here. We'll start the whole course over. I'm going to say it was not you, it was I who was not paying attention. We'll start the whole course over. Your grade is an "A." Your final grade is an "A." (*The phone stops ringing.*)

CAROL: But the class is only half over . . .

JOHN (*simultaneously with "over"*): Your grade for the whole term is an "A." If you will come back and meet with me. A few more times. Your grade's an "A." Forget about the paper. You didn't like it, you didn't like writing it. It's not important. What's important is that I awake your interest, if I can, and that I answer your questions. Let's start over. (*Pause.*)

CAROL: Over. With what?

JOHN: Say this is the beginning.

CAROL: The beginning.

JOHN: Yes.

CAROL: Of what?

JOHN: Of the class.

CAROL: But we can't start over.

JOHN: I say we can. (*Pause.*) I say we can.

CAROL: But I don't believe it.

JOHN: Yes, I know that. But it's true. What is The Class but you and me? (*Pause.*)

CAROL: There are rules.

JOHN: Well. We'll break them.

CAROL: How can we?

JOHN: We won't tell anybody.

CAROL: Is that all right?

JOHN: I say that it's fine.

CAROL: Why would you do this for me?

JOHN: I like you. Is that so difficult for you to . . .

CAROL: Um . . .

JOHN: There's no one here but you and me. (*Pause.*)

CAROL: All right. I did not understand. When you referred . . .

JOHN: All right, yes?

CAROL: When you referred to hazing.

JOHN: Hazing.

CAROL: You wrote, in your book. About the comparative . . . the comparative . . . (*She checks her notes.*)

JOHN: Are you checking your notes . . . ?

CAROL: Yes.

JOHN: Tell me in your own . . .

CAROL: I want to make sure that I have it right.

JOHN: No. Of course. You want to be exact.

CAROL: I want to know everything that went on.

JOHN: . . . that's good.

CAROL: . . . so I . . .

JOHN: That's very good. But I was suggesting, many times, that that which we wish to retain is retained oftentimes, I think, *better* with less expenditure of effort.

CAROL (*of notes*): Here it is: you wrote of *hazing*.

JOHN: . . . that's correct. Now: I said "hazing." It means ritualized annoyance. We shove this book at you, we say read it. Now, you say you've read it? I think that you're *lying*. I'll *grill* you, and when I find you've lied, you'll be disgraced, and your life will be ruined. It's a sick game. Why do we do it? Does it educate? In no sense. Well, then, what is higher education? It is something-other-than-useful.

CAROL: What is "something-other-than-useful?"

JOHN: It has become a ritual, it has become an article of faith. That all must be subjected to, or to put it differently, that all are entitled to Higher Education. And my point . . .

CAROL: You disagree with that?

JOHN: Well, let's address that. What do you think?

CAROL: I don't know.

JOHN: What do you think, though? (*Pause.*)

CAROL: I don't know.

JOHN: I spoke of it in class. Do you remember my example?

CAROL: Justice.

JOHN: Yes. Can you repeat it to me? (*She looks down at her notebook.*) Without your notes? I ask you as a favor to me, so that I can see if my idea was interesting.

CAROL: You said "justice" . . .

JOHN: Yes?

CAROL: . . . that all are entitled . . . (*Pause.*) I . . . I . . . I . . .

JOHN: Yes. To a speedy trial. To a fair trial. But they needn't be given a trial *at all* unless they stand accused. Eh? Justice is their right, should they choose to avail themselves of it, they should have a fair trial. It does not follow, of necessity, a person's life is incomplete without a trial in it. Do you see?

My point is a confusion between equity and *utility* arose. So we confound the *usefulness* of higher education with our, granted, right to equal access to the same. We, in effect, create a *prejudice* toward it, completely independent of . . .

CAROL: . . . that it is prejudice that we should go to school?

JOHN: Exactly. (*Pause.*)

CAROL: How can you say that? How . . .

JOHN: Good. Good. *Good.* That's right! Speak up! What is a prejudice? An unreasoned belief. We are all subject to it. None of us is not. When it is threatened, or opposed, we feel anger, and feel, do we not? As you do now. Do you not? Good.

CAROL: . . . but how can you . . .

JOHN: . . . let us examine. Good.

CAROL: How . . .

JOHN: Good. Good. When . . .

CAROL: I'M SPEAKING . . . (*Pause.*)

JOHN: I'm sorry.

CAROL: How can you . . .

JOHN: . . . I beg your pardon.

CAROL: That's all right.

JOHN: I beg your pardon.

CAROL: That's all right.

JOHN: I'm sorry I interrupted you.

CAROL: That's all right.

JOHN: You were saying?

CAROL: I was saying . . . I was saying . . . (*She checks her notes.*) How can you say in a class. Say in a college class, that college education is prejudice?

JOHN: I said that our predilection for it . . .

CAROL: Predilection . . .

JOHN: . . . you know what that means.

CAROL: Does it mean "liking"?

JOHN: Yes.

CAROL: But how can you say that? That College . . .

JOHN: . . . that's my *job*, don't you know.

CAROL: What is?

JOHN: To provoke you.

CAROL: No.

JOHN: Oh. Yes, though.

CAROL: To provoke me?

JOHN: That's right.

CAROL: To make me mad?

JOHN: That's right. To force you . . .

CAROL: . . . to make me mad is your job?

JOHN: To force you to . . . listen (*Pause.*) Ah. (*Pause.*) When I was young somebody told me, are you ready, the rich copulate less often than the poor. But when they do, they take more of their clothes off. Years. Years, mind you, I would compare experiences of my own to this dictum, saying, aha, this fits the norm, or ah, this is a variation from it. What did it mean? Nothing. It was some jerk thing, some school kid told me that took up room inside my head. (*Pause.*)

Somebody told *you*, and you hold it as an article of faith, that higher education is an unassailable good. This notion is so dear to you that when I question it you become angry. Good. Good, I say. Are not those the very things which we should question? I say college education, since the war, has become so a matter of course, and such a fashionable necessity, for those either of or aspiring *to* to the new vast middle class, that we *espouse* it, as a matter of right, and have ceased to ask, "What is it good for?" (*Pause.*)

What might be some reasons for pursuit of higher education?

One: A love of learning.

Two: The wish for mastery of a skill.

Three: For economic betterment.

(*Stops. Makes a note.*)

CAROL: I'm keeping you.

JOHN: One moment. I have to make a note . . .

CAROL: It's something that I said?

JOHN: No, we're buying a house.

CAROL: You're buying the new house.

JOHN: To go with the tenure. That's right. Nice *house*, close to the *private school* . . . (*He continues making his note.*) . . . We were talking of economic bet-

terment (*Carol writes in her notebook*) . . . I was thinking of the School Tax. (*He continues writing.*) (*To himself.*) . . . *where is it written* that I have to send my child to public school. . . . Is it a law that I have to improve the City Schools at the expense of my own interest? And, is this not simply *The White Man's Burden?* Good. And (*looks up to Carol*) . . . does this interest you?

CAROL: No. I'm taking notes . . .

JOHN: You don't have to take notes, you know, you can just listen.

CAROL: I want to make sure I remember it. (*Pause.*)

JOHN: I'm not lecturing you, I'm just trying to tell you some things I think.

CAROL: What do you think?

JOHN: Should all kids go to college? *Why* . . .

CAROL (*pause*): To learn.

JOHN: But if he does not learn.

CAROL: If the child does not learn?

JOHN: Then why is he in college? Because he was told it was his "right"?

CAROL: Some might find college instructive.

JOHN: I would hope so.

CAROL: But how do they feel? Being told they are wasting their time?

JOHN: I don't think I'm telling them that.

CAROL: You said that education was "prolonged and systematic hazing."

JOHN: Yes. It can be so.

CAROL: . . . if education is so *bad*, why do you do it?

JOHN: I do it because I love it. (*Pause.*) Let's. . . . I suggest you look at the demographics, wage-earning capacity, college- and noncollege-educated men and women, 1855 to 1980, and let's see if we can wring some worth from the statistics. Eh? And . . .

CAROL: No.

JOHN: What?

CAROL: I can't understand them.

JOHN: . . . you . . . ?

CAROL: . . . the "charts." The *Concepts*, the . . .

JOHN: "Charts" are simply . . .

CAROL: When I leave here . . .

JOHN: Charts, do you see . . .

CAROL: No, I can't . . .

JOHN: You can, though.

CAROL: NO, NO — I DON'T UNDERSTAND. DO YOU SEE??? I DON'T *UNDERSTAND* . . .

JOHN: What?

CAROL: *Any* of it. *Any* of it. I'm *smiling* in class, I'm *smiling*, the whole time. What are you *talking* about? What is everyone *talking* about? I don't *understand*. I don't know what it *means*. I don't know what it means to *be* here . . . you tell me I'm intelligent, and then you tell me I should not be *here*, what do you *want* with me? What does it *mean*? Who should I *listen* to . . . I . . .

(*He goes over to her and puts his arm around her shoulder.*)

NO! (*She walks away from him.*)

JOHN: Sshhhh.

CAROL: No, I don't under . . .

JOHN: Sshhhhh.

CAROL: I don't know what you're *saying* . . .

JOHN: Sshhhhh. It's all right.

CAROL: . . . I have no . . .

JOHN: Sshhhhh. Sshhhhh. Let it go a moment. (*Pause.*) Sshhhhh . . . let it go. (*Pause.*) Just let it go. (*Pause.*) Just let it go. It's all right. (*Pause.*) Sshhhhh. (*Pause.*) I understand . . . (*Pause.*) What do you feel?

CAROL: I feel bad.

JOHN: I know. It's all right.

CAROL: I . . . (*Pause.*)

JOHN: What?

CAROL: I . . .

JOHN: What? Tell me.

CAROL: I don't understand you.

JOHN: I know. It's all right.

CAROL: I . . .

JOHN: What? (*Pause.*) What? *Tell* me.

CAROL: I can't tell you.

JOHN: No, you must.

CAROL: I can't.

JOHN: No. Tell me. (*Pause.*)

CAROL: I'm bad. (*Pause.*) Oh, God. (*Pause.*)

JOHN: It's all right.

CAROL: I'm . . .

JOHN: It's all right.

CAROL: I can't talk about this.

JOHN: It's all right. Tell me.

CAROL: Why do you want to know this?

JOHN: I don't want to know. I want to know whatever you . . .

CAROL: I always . . .

JOHN: . . . good . . .

CAROL: I always . . . all my life . . . I have never told anyone this . . .

JOHN: Yes. Go on. (*Pause.*) Go on.

CAROL: All of my life . . . (*The phone rings.*) (*Pause. John goes to the phone and picks it up.*)

JOHN (*into phone*): I can't talk now. (*Pause.*) What? (*Pause.*) Hmm. (*Pause.*) All right, I . . . I. Can't. Talk. Now. No, no, no, I *Know* I did, but . . . What? Hello. What? She *what*? She *can't*, she said the agreement is void? How, how is the agreement *void*? *That's Our House.*

I have the *paper*; when we come down, next week, with the payment, and the paper, that house

is . . . wait, wait, wait, wait, wait, wait, wait: Did Jerry . . . is Jerry there? (*Pause.*) Is *she* there . . . ? Does she have a *lawyer* . . . ? How the *hell*, how the *Hell*. That is . . . it's a question, you said, of the *easement*. I don't underst . . . it's not the *whole agreement*. It's just the *easement*, why would she? Put, put, put, *Jerry* on. (*Pause.*) Jer, *Jerry*: What the *Hell* . . . that's my *house*. That's . . . Well, I'm, no, no, no, I'm *not* coming ddd . . . List, *Listen*, screw her. You *tell* her. You, listen: I want you to take *Grace*, you take Grace, and get out of that house. You *leave* her there. Her and her lawyer, and you *tell* them, we'll see them in court next . . . no. No. Leave her there, leave her to *stew* in it: You tell her, we're *getting* that house, and we are going to . . . No. I'm *not* coming down. I'll be damned if I'll sit in the same rrr . . . the *next*, you tell her the next time I *see* her is in court . . . I . . . (*Pause.*) What? (*Pause.*) What? I don't understand. (*Pause.*) Well, what about the house? (*Pause.*) There isn't any problem with the hhh . . . (*Pause.*) No, no, no, that's all right. All ri . . . All right . . . (*Pause.*) Of course. Tha . . . Thank you. No, I will. Right away. (*He hangs up.*) (*Pause*)

CAROL: What is it? (*Pause.*)

JOHN: It's a surprise party.

CAROL: It is.

JOHN: Yes.

CAROL: A party for you.

JOHN: Yes.

CAROL: Is it your birthday?

JOHN: No.

CAROL: What is it?

JOHN: The tenure announcement.

CAROL: The tenure announcement.

JOHN: They're throwing a party for us in our new house.

CAROL: Your new house.

JOHN: The house that we're buying.

CAROL: You have to go.

JOHN: It seems that I do.

CAROL (*pause*): They're proud of you.

JOHN: Well, there are those who would say it's a form of aggression.

CAROL: What is?

JOHN: A surprise.

ACT 2

(*John and Carol seated across the desk from each other.*)

JOHN: You see, (*pause*) I love to teach. And flatter myself I am *skilled* at it. And I love the, the aspect of *performance*. I think I must confess that.

When I found I loved to teach I swore that I would not become that cold, rigid automaton of an instructor which I had encountered as a child.

Now, I was not unconscious that it was given me to err upon the other side. And, so, I asked and *ask* myself if I engaged in heterodoxy, I will not say "gratuitously" for I do not care to posit orthodoxy as a given good — but, "to the detriment of, of my students." (*Pause.*)

As I said. When the possibility of tenure opened, and, of course, I'd long pursued it, I was, of course *happy,* and *covetous* of it.

I asked myself if I was wrong to covet it. And thought about it long, and, I hope, truthfully, and saw in myself several things in, I think, no particular order. (*Pause.*)

That I *would* pursue it. That I *desired* it, that I was not pure of longing for security, and that that, perhaps, was not reprehensible in me. That I had duties *beyond* the school, and that my duty to my home, for instance, was, or should be, if it were not, of an equal weight. That tenure, and security, and yes, and *comfort,* were not, of themselves, to be scorned; and were even worthy of honorable pursuit. And that it was given me. Here, in this place, which I enjoy, and in which I find comfort, to assure myself of — as far as it rests in The Material — a continuation of that joy and comfort. In exchange for what? Teaching. Which I love.

What was the price of this security? To obtain *tenure.* Which tenure the committee is in the process of granting me. And on the basis of which I contracted to purchase a house. Now, as you don't have your own family, at this point, you may not know what that means. But to me it is important. A home. A Good Home. To raise my family. Now: The Tenure Committee will meet. This is the process, and a *good* process. Under which the school has functioned for quite a long time. They will meet, and hear your complaint — which you have the right to make; and they will dismiss it. They will *dismiss* your complaint; and, in the intervening period, I will lose my house. I will not be able to close on my house. I will lose my *deposit,* and the home I'd picked out for my wife and son will go by the boards. Now: I see I have angered you. I understand your anger at teachers. I was angry with mine. I felt hurt and humiliated by them. Which is one of the reasons that I went into education.

CAROL: What do you want of me?

JOHN (*pause*): I was hurt. When I received the report. Of the tenure committee. I was shocked. And I was hurt. No, I don't mean to subject you to my weak sensibilities. All right. Finally, I didn't understand.

Then I thought: Is it not always at those points at which we reckon ourselves unassailable that we are most vulnerable and . . . (*Pause.*) Yes. All right. You find me pedantic. Yes. I am. By nature, by *birth,* by profession, I don't know . . . I'm always looking for a *paradigm* for . . .

CAROL: I don't know what a paradigm is.

JOHN: It's a model.

CAROL: Then why can't you use that word? (*Pause.*)

JOHN: If it is important to you. Yes, all right. I was looking for a model. To continue: I feel that one point . . .

CAROL: I . . .

JOHN: One second . . . upon which I am unassailable is my unflinching concern for my students' dignity. I asked you here to . . . in the spirit of *investigation,* to ask you . . . to ask . . . (*Pause.*) What have I done to you? (*Pause.*) And, and, I suppose, how I can make amends. Can we not settle this now? It's pointless, really, and I want to know.

CAROL: What you can do to force me to retract?

JOHN: That is not what I meant at all.

CAROL: To bribe me, to convince me . . .

JOHN: . . . No.

CAROL: To retract . . .

JOHN: That is not what I meant at all. I think that you know it is not.

CAROL: That is not what I know. I *wish* I . . .

JOHN: I do not want to . . . you wish what?

CAROL: No, you said what amends can you make. To force me to retract.

JOHN: That is not what I said.

CAROL: I have my notes.

JOHN: Look. Look. The Stoics say . . .

CAROL: The Stoics?

JOHN: The Stoical Philosophers say if you remove the phrase "I have been injured," you have removed the injury. Now: Think: I know that you're upset. Just tell me. Literally. Literally: what wrong have I done you?

CAROL: Whatever you have done to me — to the extent that you've done it to *me,* do you know, rather than to me as a *student,* and, so, to the student body, is contained in my report. To the tenure committee.

JOHN: Well, all right. (*Pause.*) Let's see. (*He reads.*) I find that I am sexist. That I am *elitist.* I'm not sure I know what that means, other than it's a derogatory word, meaning "bad." That I . . . That I insist on wasting time, in nonprescribed, in self-aggrandizing and theatrical *diversions* from the prescribed *text* . . . that these have taken both sexist and pornographic forms . . . here we find listed . . . (*Pause.*) Here we find listed . . . instances "... closeted with a student" . . . "Told a rambling, sexually explicit story, in which the frequency and attitudes of fornication of the poor and rich are, it would seem, the central point . . . moved to *embrace* said student and . . . all part of a pattern . . ." (*Pause.*)

(*He reads.*) That I used the phrase "The White Man's Burden" . . . that I told you how I'd asked you to my room because I quote like you. (*Pause.*)

(*He reads.*) "He said he 'liked' me. That he 'liked being with me.' He'd let me write my examination paper over, if I could come back oftener to see him in his office." (*Pause.*) (*To Carol.*) It's *ludicrous.* Don't you know that? It's not *necessary.* It's going to *humiliate* you, and it's going to cost me my *house,* and . . .

CAROL: It's "*ludicrous* . . ."?

(*John picks up the report and reads again.*)

JOHN: "He told me he had problems with his wife; and that he wanted to take off the artificial stricture of Teacher and Student. He put his arm around me . . ."

CAROL: Do you deny it? Can you deny it . . . ? Do you see? (*Pause.*) Don't you see? You don't see, do you?

JOHN: I don't see . . .

CAROL: You think, you think you can deny that these things happened; or, if they *did,* if they *did,* that they meant what you *said* they meant. Don't you see? You drag me in here, you drag us, to listen to you "go on"; and "go on" about this, or that, or we don't "express" ourselves very well. We don't say what we mean. Don't we? Don't we? We *do* say what we mean. And you say that "I don't understand you . . . ": Then *you* . . . (*Points.*)

JOHN: "Consult the Report"?

CAROL: . . . that's right.

JOHN: You see. You see. Can't you. . . . You see what I'm saying? Can't you tell me in your own words?

CAROL: Those are my own words. (*Pause.*)

JOHN (*he reads*): "He told me that if I would stay alone with him in his office, he would change my grade to an A." (*To Carol.*) What have I done to you? Oh. My God, are you so hurt?

CAROL: What I "feel" is irrelevant. (*Pause.*)

JOHN: Do you know that I tried to help you?

CAROL: What I know I have reported.

JOHN: I would like to help you now. I would. Before this escalates.

CAROL (*simultaneously with* "escalates"): You see. I don't think that I need your help. I don't think I need anything you have.

JOHN: I feel . . .

CAROL: I don't *care* what you feel. Do you see? DO YOU SEE? You can't *do* that anymore. You. Do.

Not. Have. The. Power. Did you misuse it? *Someone* did. Are you part of that group? *Yes. Yes.* You Are. You've *done* these things. And to say, and to say, "Oh. Let me help you with your problem . . ."

JOHN: Yes. I understand. I understand. You're *hurt.* You're *angry.* Yes. I think your *anger* is *betraying* you. Down a path which helps no one.

CAROL: I don't *care* what you think.

JOHN: You don't? (*Pause.*) But you talk of *rights.* Don't you see? *I* have rights too. Do you see? I have a *house* . . . part of the *real* world; and The Tenure Committee, Good Men and True . . .

CAROL: . . . Professor . . .

JOHN: . . . Please: *Also* part of that world: you understand? This is my *life.* I'm not a *bogeyman.* I don't "stand" for something, I . . .

CAROL: . . . Professor . . .

JOHN: . . . I . . .

CAROL: Professor. I came here as a *favor.* At your personal request. Perhaps I should not have done so. But I did. On my behalf, and on behalf of my group. And you speak of the tenure committee, one of whose members is a woman, as you know. And though you might call it Good Fun, or An Historical Phrase, or An Oversight, or, All of the Above, to refer to the committee as Good Men and True, it is a demeaning remark. It is a sexist remark, and to overlook it is to countenance continuation of that method of thought. It's a remark . . .

JOHN: OH COME ON. Come on. . . . Sufficient to deprive a family of . . .

CAROL: Sufficient? Sufficient? Sufficient? Yes. It is a *fact* . . . and that story, which I quote, is *vile* and *classist,* and *manipulative* and *pornographic.* It . . .

JOHN: . . . it's pornographic . . . ?

CAROL: What gives you the *right.* Yes. To speak to a *woman* in your private . . . Yes. Yes. I'm sorry. I'm sorry. You feel yourself empowered . . . you say so yourself. To *strut.* To *posture.* To "perform." To "Call me in here . . . " Eh? You say that higher education is a joke. And treat it as such, you *treat* it as such. And *confess* to a taste to play the *Patriarch* in your class. To grant *this.* To deny *that.* To embrace your students.

JOHN: How can you assert. How can you stand there and . . .

CAROL: How can you *deny* it. You did it to me. *Here.* You *did* . . . . You *confess.* You love the Power. To *deviate.* To *invent,* to transgress . . . to *transgress* whatever norms have been established for us. And you think it's charming to "question" in yourself this taste to mock and destroy. But you should question it. Professor. And you pick those things which you feel *advance* you: publication, *tenure,* and the steps to get them you call "harmless rituals." And you perform those steps. Although you say it is hypocrisy. But to the aspirations of your students. Of *hardworking students,* who come here, who *slave* to come here — you have no idea what it cost me to come to this school — you *mock* us. You call education "hazing," and from your so-protected, so-elitist seat you hold our confusion as a *joke,* and our hopes and efforts with it. Then you sit there and say "what have I done?" And ask me to understand that *you* have aspirations too. But I tell you. I tell you. That you are vile. And that you are exploitative. And if you possess one ounce of that inner honesty you describe in your book, you can look in yourself and see those things that I see. And you can find revulsion equal to my own. Good day. (*She prepares to leave the room.*)

JOHN: Wait a second, will you, just one moment. (*Pause.*) Nice day today.

CAROL: What?

JOHN: You said "Good day." I think that it is a nice day today.

CAROL: *Is* it?

JOHN: Yes, I think it is.

CAROL: And why is that important?

JOHN: Because it is the essence of all human communication. I say something conventional, you respond, and the information we exchange is not about the "weather," but that we both agree to converse. In effect, we agree that we are both human. (*Pause.*)

I'm not a . . . "exploiter," and you're not a . . . "deranged," what? *Revolutionary* . . . that we may, that we may have . . . positions, and that we may have . . . desires, which are in *conflict,* but that we're just human. (*Pause.*) That means that sometimes we're *imperfect.* (*Pause.*) Often we're in conflict . . . (*Pause.) Much* of what we do, you're right, in the name of "principles" is *self-serving* . . . much of what we do is *conventional.* (*Pause.*) You're right. (*Pause.*) You said you came in the class because you wanted to learn about *education.* I don't know that I can teach you about education. But I know that I can tell you what I *think* about education, and then *you* decide. And you don't have to fight with me. *I'm* not the subject. (*Pause.*) And where I'm *wrong* . . . perhaps it's not your job to "fix" me. I don't want to fix *you.* I would like to tell you what I *think,* because that *is* my job, conventional as it is, and flawed as I may be. And then, if you can show me some better *form,* then we can proceed from there. But, just like "nice day, isn't it . . . ?" I don't think we can proceed until we accept that each of us is human. (*Pause.*) And we still can have difficulties. We *will* have them . . . that's all right too. (*Pause.*) Now:

CAROL: . . . wait . . .

JOHN: Yes. I want to hear it.

CAROL: . . . the . . .

JOHN: Yes. Tell me frankly.

CAROL: . . . my position . . .

JOHN: I want to hear it. In your own words. What you want. And what you feel.

CAROL: . . . I . . .

JOHN: . . . yes . . .

CAROL: My Group.

JOHN: Your "Group" . . . ? (*Pause.*)

CAROL: The people I've been talking to . . .

JOHN: There's no shame in that. Everybody needs advisers. Everyone needs to expose themselves. To various points of view. It's not wrong. It's essential. Good. Good. Now: You and I . . . (*The phone rings.*)

You and I . . .

(*He hesitates for a moment, and then picks it up.*) (*Into phone.*) Hello. (*Pause.*) Um . . . no, I know they do. (*Pause.*) I know she does. Tell her that I . . . can I call you back? . . . Then tell her that I think it's going to be fine. (*Pause.*) Tell her just, just hold on, I'll . . . can I get back to you? . . . Well . . . no, no, no, we're *taking* the house . . . we're . . . no, no, nn . . . no, she will nnn, it's not a *question* of refunding the dep . . . no . . . it's not a *question* of the deposit . . . will you call Jerry? Babe, baby, will you just call Jerry? Tell him, nnn . . . tell him they, well, they're to keep the deposit, because the deal, be . . . because the deal is going to go *through* . . . because I know . . . be . . . will you please? Just *trust* me. Be . . . well, I'm dealing with the complaint. Yes. Right *Now.* Which is why I . . . yes, no, no, it's really, I can't *talk* about it now. Call Jerry, and I can't talk now. Ff . . . fine. Gg . . . good-bye. (*Hangs up.*) (*Pause*) I'm sorry we were interrupted.

CAROL: No . . .

JOHN: I . . . I was saying:

CAROL: You said that we should agree to talk about my complaint.

JOHN: That's correct.

CAROL: But we *are* talking about it.

JOHN: Well, that's correct too. You see? This is the *gist* of education.

CAROL: No, no. I mean, we're talking about it at the Tenure Committee Hearing. (*Pause.*)

JOHN: Yes, but I'm saying: we can talk about it *now,* as easily as . . .

CAROL: No. I think that we should stick to the process . . .

JOHN: . . . wait a . . .

CAROL: . . . the "conventional" process. As you said. (*She gets up.*) And you're right, I'm sorry if I was, um, if I was "discourteous" to you. You're right.

JOHN: Wait, wait a . . .

CAROL: I really should go.

JOHN: Now, look, granted. I have an interest. In the status quo. All right? Everyone does. But what I'm saying is that the *committee* . . .

CAROL: Professor, you're right. Just don't impinge on me. We'll take our differences, and . . .

JOHN: You're going to make a . . . look, look, look, you're going to . . .

CAROL: I shouldn't have come here. They told me . . .

JOHN: One moment. No. No. There are *norms,* here, and there's no reason. Look: I'm trying to *save* you . . .

CAROL: No one *asked* you to . . . you're trying to save *me?* Do me the courtesy to . . .

JOHN: I *am* doing you the courtesy. I'm talking *straight* to you. We can settle this *now.* And I want you to sit *down* and . . .

CAROL: You must excuse me . . . (*She starts to leave the room.*)

JOHN: Sit down, it seems we each have a . . . . Wait one moment. Wait one moment . . . just do me the courtesy to . . .

(*He restrains her from leaving.*)

CAROL: LET ME GO.

JOHN: I have no desire to *hold* you, I just want to *talk* to you . . .

CAROL: LET ME GO. LET ME GO. WOULD SOMEBODY *HELP* ME? WOULD SOMEBODY *HELP* ME PLEASE . . . ?

ACT 3

(*At rise, Carol and John are seated.*)

JOHN: I have asked you here. (*Pause.*) I have asked you here against, against my . . .

CAROL: I was most surprised you asked me.

JOHN: . . . against my better *judgment,* against . . .

CAROL: I was most surprised . . .

JOHN: . . . against the . . . yes. I'm sure.

CAROL: . . . If you would like me to leave, I'll leave. I'll go right now . . . (*She rises.*)

JOHN: Let us begin *correctly,* may we? I feel . . .

CAROL: That is what I wished to do. That's why I came here, but now . . .

JOHN: . . . I feel . . .

CAROL: But now perhaps you'd like me to leave . . .

JOHN: I don't want you to leave. I asked you to come . . .

CAROL: I didn't have to come here.

JOHN: No. (*Pause.*) Thank you.

CAROL: All right. (*Pause.*) (*She sits down.*)

JOHN: Although I feel that it *profits,* it would *profit* you something, to . . .

CAROL: . . . what I . . .

JOHN: If you would hear me out, if you would hear me out.

CAROL: I came here to, the court officers told me not to come.

JOHN: . . . the "court" officers . . . ?

CAROL: I was shocked that you asked.

JOHN: . . . wait . . .

CAROL: Yes. But I did *not* come here to hear what it "profits" me.

JOHN: The "court" officers . . .

CAROL: . . . no, no, perhaps I should leave . . . (*She gets up.*)

JOHN: Wait.

CAROL: No. I shouldn't have . . .

JOHN: . . . wait. Wait. Wait a moment.

CAROL: Yes? What is it you want? (*Pause.*) What is it you want?

JOHN: I'd like you to stay.

CAROL: You want me to stay.

JOHN: Yes.

CAROL: You do.

JOHN: Yes. (*Pause.*) Yes. I would like to have you hear me out. If you would. (*Pause.*) Would you please? If you would do that I would be in your debt. (*Pause.*) (*She sits.*) Thank You. (*Pause.*)

CAROL: What is it you wish to tell me?

JOHN: All right. I cannot . . . (*Pause.*) I cannot help but feel you are owed an apology. (*Pause.*) (*Of papers in his hands.*) I have read. (*Pause.*) And reread these accusations.

CAROL: What "accusations"?

JOHN: The, the tenure comm . . . what other accusations . . . ?

CAROL: The tenure committee . . . ?

JOHN: Yes.

CAROL: Excuse me, but those are not accusations. They have been *proved.* They are facts.

JOHN: . . . I . . .

CAROL: No. Those are not "accusations."

JOHN: . . . those?

CAROL: . . . the committee (*The phone starts to ring.*) the committee has . . .

JOHN: . . . All right . . .

CAROL: . . . those are not accusations. The Tenure Committee.

JOHN: ALL RIGHT. ALL RIGHT. ALL RIGHT. (*He picks up the phone.*) Hello. Yes. No. I'm here. Tell Mister . . . No, I can't talk to him now . . . I'm sure he has, but I'm fff . . . I know . . . No, I have no time t . . . tell Mister . . . tell Mist . . . tell Jerry that I'm *fine* and that I'll call him right aw . . . (*Pause.*) My wife . . . Yes. I'm sure she has. Yes, thank you.

Yes, I'll call her too. I cannot talk to you now. (*He hangs up.*) (*Pause.*) All right. It was good of you to come. Thank you. I have studied. I have spent some time studying the indictment.

CAROL: You will have to explain that word to me.

JOHN: An "indictment" . . .

CAROL: Yes.

JOHN: Is a "bill of particulars." A . . .

CAROL: Ah right. Yes.

JOHN: In which is alleged . . .

CAROL: No. I cannot allow that. I cannot allow that. Nothing is alleged. Everything is proved . . .

JOHN: Please, wait a sec . . .

CAROL: I cannot *come* to allow . . .

JOHN: If I may . . . If I may, from whatever you feel is "established," by . . .

CAROL: The issue here is not what I "feel." It is not my "feelings," but the feelings of women. And men. Your superiors, who've been "polled," do you see? To whom *evidence* has been presented, who have *ruled,* do you see? Who have weighed the testimony and the evidence, and have *ruled,* do you see? That you are *negligent.* That you are *guilty,* that you are found *wanting,* and in *error*; and are *not,* for the reasons so-told, to be given tenure. That you are to be disciplined. For facts. For *facts.* Not "alleged," what is the word? But *proved.* Do you see? *By your own actions.*

That is what the tenure committee has said. That is what my lawyer said. For what you did in class. For what you did *in this office.*

JOHN: They're going to discharge me.

CAROL: As full well they should. You don't understand? You're angry? What has *led* you to this place? Not your sex. Not your race. Not your class. YOUR OWN ACTIONS. And you're *angry.* You *ask* me here. What *do* you want? You want to "charm" me. You want to "convince" me. You want me to recant. I will *not* recant. Why should I . . . ? What I say is right. You tell me, you are going to tell me that you have a wife and child. You are going to say that you have a career and that you've worked for twenty years for this. Do you know what you've *worked* for? *Power.* For *power.* Do you understand? And you sit there, and you tell me *stories.* About your *house,* about all the private *schools,* and about *privilege,* and how you are entitled. To *buy,* to *spend,* to *mock,* to *summon.* All your stories. All your silly weak *guilt,* it's all about *privilege*; and you won't know it. Don't you see? You worked twenty years for the right to *insult* me. And you feel entitled to be *paid* for it. Your Home. Your Wife . . . Your sweet "deposit" on your house . . .

JOHN: Don't you have feelings?

CAROL: That's my point. You see? Don't you have feelings? Your final argument. What is it that has no feelings. *Animals.* I don't take your side, you question if I'm Human.

JOHN: Don't you have feelings?

CAROL: I have a responsibility. I . . .

JOHN: . . . to . . . ?

CAROL: To? This institution. To the *students.* To my *group.*

JOHN: . . . your "group." . . .

CAROL: Because I speak, yes, not for myself. But for the group; for those who suffer what I suffer. On behalf of whom, even if I, were, inclined, to what, forgive? Forget? What? Overlook your . . .

JOHN: . . . my behavior?

CAROL: . . . it would be wrong.

JOHN: Even if you were inclined to "forgive" me.

CAROL: It would be wrong.

JOHN: And what would transpire.

CAROL: Transpire?

JOHN: Yes.

CAROL: "Happen?"

JOHN: Yes.

CAROL: Then *say* it. For Christ's sake. Who the *hell* do you think that you are? You want a post. You want unlimited power. To do and to say what you want. As it pleases you — Testing, Questioning, Flirting . . .

JOHN: I never . . .

CAROL: Excuse me, one moment, will you?

(*She reads from her notes.*)

The twelfth: "Have a good day, dear."

The fifteenth: "Now, don't *you* look fetching . . . "

April seventeenth: "If you girls would come over here . . . " I saw you. I saw you, Professor. For two semesters sit there, stand there and exploit our, as you thought, "paternal prerogative," and what is that but rape; I swear to God. You asked me in here to explain something to me, as a child, that I did not understand. But I came to explain something to you. You Are Not God. You ask me why I came? I came here to instruct you.

(*She produces his book.*)

And your book? You think you're going to show me some "light"? You "*maverick.*" Outside of tradition. No, no, (*She reads from the book's liner notes.*) "*of that fine tradition of *inquiry.* Of Polite *skepticism*" . . . and you say you believe in free intellectual discourse. YOU BELIEVE IN NOTHING. YOU BELIEVE IN NOTHING AT ALL.

JOHN: I believe in freedom of thought.

CAROL: Isn't that fine. *Do* you?

JOHN: Yes. I do.

CAROL: Then why do you question, for one moment,

the committee's decision refusing your tenure? Why do you question your suspension? You believe in what *you call* freedom of thought. Then, fine. *You* believe in freedom-of-thought *and* a home, and, *and* prerogatives for your kid, *and* tenure. And I'm going to tell you. You believe *not* in "freedom of thought," but in an elitist, in, in a protected hierarchy which rewards you. And for whom you are the clown. And you mock and exploit the system which pays your rent. You're wrong. I'm not wrong. You're wrong. You think that I'm full of hatred. I know what you think I am.

JOHN: Do you?

CAROL: You think I'm a, of course I do. You think I am a frightened, repressed, confused, I don't know, abandoned young thing of some doubtful sexuality, who wants, power and revenge. (*Pause.*) *Don't you? (Pause.)*

JOHN: Yes. I do. (*Pause.*)

CAROL: Isn't that better? And I feel that that is the first moment which you've treated me with respect. For you told me the truth. (*Pause.*) I did not come here, as you are assured, to gloat. Why would I want to gloat? I've profited nothing from your, your, as you say, your "misfortune." I came here, as you did me the honor to *ask* me here, I came here to *tell* you something.

   (*Pause.*) That I think . . . that I think you've been wrong. That I think you've been terribly wrong. Do you hate me now? (*Pause.*)

JOHN: Yes.

CAROL: Why do you hate me? Because you think me wrong? No. Because I have, you think, *power* over you. Listen to me. Listen to me, Professor. (*Pause.*) It is the power that you hate. So deeply that, that any atmosphere of free discussion is impossible. It's not "unlikely." It's *impossible*. Isn't it?

JOHN: Yes.

CAROL: *Isn't* it . . . ?

JOHN: Yes. I suppose.

CAROL: Now. The thing which you find so cruel is the selfsame process of selection I, and my group, go through *every day of our lives*. In admittance to school. In our tests, in our class rankings. . . . Is it unfair? I can't tell you. But, if it is fair. Or even if it is "unfortunate but necessary" for us, then, by God, so must it be for you. (*Pause.*) You write of your "responsibility to the young." Treat us with respect, and that will *show* you your responsibility. You write that education is just hazing. (*Pause.*) But we worked to get to this school. (*Pause.*) And some of us. (*Pause.*) Overcame prejudices. Economic, sexual, you cannot begin to imagine. And endured humiliations I *pray* that you and those you love never will encounter. (*Pause.*) To gain

admittance here. To pursue that same dream of security *you* pursue. We, who, who are, at any moment, in danger of being deprived of it. By . . .

JOHN: . . . by . . . ?

CAROL: By the administration. By the teachers. By *you*. By, say, one low grade, that keeps us out of graduate school; by one, say, one capricious or inventive answer on our parts, which, perhaps, you don't find amusing. Now you *know*, do you see? What it is to be subject to that power. (*Pause.*)

JOHN: I don't understand. (*Pause.*)

CAROL: My charges are not trivial. You see that in the haste, I think, with which they were accepted. A *joke* you have told, with a sexist tinge. The language you use, a verbal or physical caress, yes, yes, I know, you say that it is meaningless. I understand. I differ from you. To lay a hand on someone's shoulder.

JOHN: It was devoid of sexual content.

CAROL: I say it was not. I SAY IT WAS NOT. Don't you begin to *see* . . . ? Don't you begin to understand? IT'S NOT FOR YOU TO SAY.

JOHN: I take your point, and I see there is much good in what you refer to.

CAROL: . . . do you think so . . . ?

JOHN: . . . but, and this is not to say that I cannot change, in those things in which I am deficient . . . But, the . . .

CAROL: Do you hold yourself harmless from the charge of sexual exploitativeness . . . ? (*Pause.*)

JOHN: Well, I . . . I . . . I . . . You know I, as I said. I . . . think I am not too old to *learn*, and I *can* learn, I . . .

CAROL: Do you hold yourself innocent of the charge of . . .

JOHN: . . . wait, wait, wait . . . All right, let's go back to . . .

CAROL: YOU FOOL. Who do you think I am? To come here and be taken in by a *smile*. You little yapping fool. You think I want "revenge." I don't want revenge. I WANT UNDERSTANDING.

JOHN: . . . do you?

CAROL: I do. (*Pause.*)

JOHN: What's the use. It's over.

CAROL: Is it? What is?

JOHN: My job.

CAROL: Oh. Your job. That's what you want to talk about. (*Pause.*) (*She starts to leave the room. She steps and turns back to him.*) All right. (*Pause.*) What if it were possible that my Group withdraws its complaint. (*Pause.*)

JOHN: What?

CAROL: That's right. (*Pause.*)

JOHN: Why.

CAROL: Well, let's say as an act of friendship.

JOHN: An act of friendship.

CAROL: Yes. (*Pause.*)

JOHN: In exchange for what.

CAROL: Yes. But I don't think, "exchange." Not "in exchange." For what do we derive from it? (*Pause.*)

JOHN: "Derive."

CAROL: Yes.

JOHN (*pause*): Nothing. (*Pause.*)

CAROL: That's right. We derive nothing. (*Pause.*) Do you see that?

JOHN: Yes.

CAROL: That is a little word, Professor. "Yes." "I see that." But you will.

JOHN: And you might speak to the committee . . . ?

CAROL: To the committee?

JOHN: Yes.

CAROL: Well. Of course. That's on your mind. We might.

JOHN: "If" what?

CAROL: "Given" what. Perhaps. I think that that is more friendly.

JOHN: GIVEN WHAT?

CAROL: And, believe me, I understand your rage. It is not that I don't feel it. But I do not see that it is deserved, so I do not resent it. . . . All right. I have a list.

JOHN: . . . a list.

CAROL: Here is a list of books, which we . . .

JOHN: . . . a list of books . . . ?

CAROL: That's right. Which we find questionable.

JOHN: What?

CAROL: Is this so bizarre . . . ?

JOHN: I can't believe . . .

CAROL: It's not necessary you believe it.

JOHN: Academic freedom . . .

CAROL: Someone chooses the books. If you can choose them, others can. What are you, "God"?

JOHN: . . . no, no, the "dangerous." . . .

CAROL: You have an agenda, we have an agenda. I am not interested in your feelings or your motivation, but your actions. If you would like me to speak to the Tenure Committee, here is my list. You are a Free Person, you decide. (*Pause.*)

JOHN: Give me the list. (*She does so. He reads.*)

CAROL: I think you'll find . . .

JOHN: I'm capable of reading it. Thank you.

CAROL: We have a number of *texts* we need re . . .

JOHN: I see that.

CAROL: We're amenable to . . .

JOHN: Aha. Well, let me look over the . . . (*He reads.*)

CAROL: I think that . . .

JOHN: LOOK. I'm reading your demands. All right?! (*He reads.*) (*Pause.*) You want to ban my book?

CAROL: We do not . . .

JOHN (*of list*): It says here . . .

CAROL: . . . We want it removed from inclusion as a representative example of the university.

JOHN: Get out of here.

CAROL: If you put aside the issues of personalities.

JOHN: Get the fuck out of my office.

CAROL: No, I think I would reconsider.

JOHN: . . . you think you can.

CAROL: We can and we *will*. Do you want our support? That is the only quest . . .

JOHN: . . . to ban my *book* . . . ?

CAROL: . . . that is correct . . .

JOHN: . . . this . . . this is a *university* . . . we . . .

CAROL: . . . and we have a statement . . . which we need you to . . . (*She hands him a sheet of paper.*)

JOHN: No, no. It's out of the question. I'm sorry. I don't know what I was thinking of. I want to tell you something. I'm a teacher. I am a teacher. Eh? It's my *name* on the door, and *I* teach the class, and that's what I do. I've got a book with my name on it. And my son will *see* that *book* someday. And I have a respon . . . No, I'm sorry I have a *responsibility* . . . to *myself*, to my *son*, to my *profession.* . . . I haven't been *home* for two days, do you know that? Thinking this out.

CAROL: . . . you haven't?

JOHN: I've been, no. If it's of interest to you. I've been in a *hotel. Thinking.* (*The phone starts ringing.*) *Thinking* . . .

CAROL: . . . you haven't been home?

JOHN: . . . *thinking*, do you see.

CAROL: Oh.

JOHN: And, and, I owe you a debt, I see that now. (*Pause.*) You're *dangerous*, you're *wrong* and it's my *job* . . . to say no to you. That's my job. You are absolutely right. You want to ban my book? Go to *hell*, and they can do whatever they want to me.

CAROL: . . . you haven't been home in two days . . .

JOHN: I think I told you that.

CAROL: . . . you'd better get that phone. (*Pause.*) I think that you should pick up the phone. (*Pause.*)

(*John picks up the phone.*)

JOHN (*on phone*): Yes. (*Pause.*) Yes. Wh . . . I. I. I had to be away. All ri . . . did they wor . . . did they worry ab . . . No. I'm all right, now, Jerry. I'm f . . . I got a little turned *around*, but I'm *sitting* here and . . . I've got it figured out. I'm fine. I'm fine don't worry about me. I got a little bit mixed up. But I am not sure that it's not a blessing. It cost me my job? Fine. Then the job was not worth having. Tell Grace that I'm coming home and everything is fff . . . (*Pause.*) What? (*Pause.*) What? (*Pause.*) What do you *mean*? WHAT? Jerry . . . Jerry. They . . . Who, who, what can they do . . . ?

(*Pause.*) NO. (*Pause.*) NO. They can't do th...
What do you mean? (*Pause.*) But how... (*Pause.*)
She's, she's, she's *here* with me. To... Jerry. I don't
underst... (*Pause.*) (*He hangs up.*) (*To Carol.*)
What does this mean?

CAROL: I thought you knew.

JOHN: What. (*Pause.*) What does it mean. (*Pause.*)

CAROL: You tried to rape me. (*Pause.*) According to
the law. (*Pause.*)

JOHN: ... what...?

CAROL: You tried to rape me. I was leaving this office,
you "pressed" yourself into me. You "pressed"
your body into me.

JOHN: ... I...

CAROL: My Group has told your lawyer that we may
pursue criminal charges.

JOHN: ... no...

CAROL: ... under the statute. I am told. It was battery.

JOHN: ... no...

CAROL: Yes. And attempted rape. That's right.
(*Pause.*)

JOHN: I think that you should go.

CAROL: Of course. I thought you knew.

JOHN: I have to talk to my lawyer.

CAROL: Yes. Perhaps you should.
(*The phone rings again.*) (*Pause.*)

JOHN (*Picks up phone. Into phone.*): Hello? I...
Hello...? I... Yes, he just called. No... I. I can't
talk to you now, Baby. (*To Carol.*) Get out.

CAROL: ... your wife...?

JOHN: ... who it is is no concern of yours. Get out.
(*To phone.*) No, no, it's going to be all right. I. I
can't talk now, Baby. (*To Carol.*) Get out of here.

CAROL: I'm going.

JOHN: Good.

CAROL (*exiting*): ... and don't call your wife "baby."

JOHN: What?

CAROL: Don't call your wife baby. You heard what I
said.

(*Carol starts to leave the room. John grabs her and
begins to beat her.*)

JOHN: You vicious little bitch. You think you can
come in here with your political correctness and
destroy my life?

(*He knocks her to the floor.*)

After how I treated you...? You should be...
Rape you...? Are you kidding me...?

(*He picks up a chair, raises it above his head, and
advances on her.*)

I wouldn't touch you with a ten-foot pole. You little *cunt...*

(*She cowers on the floor below him. Pause. He
looks down at her. He lowers the chair. He moves
to his desk, and arranges the papers on it. Pause.
He looks over at her.*)

... well...

(*Pause. She looks at him.*)

CAROL: Yes. That's right.

(*She looks away from him, and lowers her head.
To herself:*) ... yes. That's right.

Tony Kushner

Tony Kushner was born in 1956 in New York City, but his family soon moved to Louisiana, where his father ran the family lumberyard. His parents were classical musicians, and their home was filled with art. Kushner dates his interest in theater to early memories of seeing his mother onstage. He also recollects from childhood "fairly clear memories of being gay since I was six." He did not, however, "come out" until after he had tried psychotherapy to change his sexual orientation.

After finishing his undergraduate education at Columbia University, Kushner studied directing in graduate school at New York University, partly because he was not confident of his chances to become a playwright. Among his early plays are *Yes, Yes, No, No* (1985), a children's play produced in St. Louis; *Stella* (1987), an adaptation from Goethe produced in New York; *A Bright Room Called Day* (1987), produced in San Francisco; *The Illusion* (1988), adapted from Corneille, produced in New York, then in Hartford in 1990. He worked with Argentinian playwright Ariel Dorfman to adapt Dorfman's *Widows*, produced in Los Angeles in 1991. *A Bright Room Called Day*, about left-wing politics in Nazi Germany, was not well reviewed after its New York production in 1991. Frank Rich, for example, said that it was "an early front-runner for the most infuriating play of 1991." But some people saw in it the power that was to show up later in his work. The Eureka Theater in San Francisco commissioned him to write a play that ultimately turned out to be *Angels in America: A Gay Fantasia on National Themes* (1992), the play that catapulted him to international prominence.

Among Kushner's current projects is a series of three plays which he describes as having money as its subject — meaning, in part, the effects of economics, in the forms of both poverty and wealth, on individuals. The first of these plays, to be titled *Henry Box Brown*, centers on the true story of a black American who escaped slavery by being smuggled out of the South in a crate. Brown eventually made his way to England where he joined with a number of other former slaves in producing dramatic "panoramas" intended to discourage the English from buying slave-picked cotton, on which their textile industry largely relied. Kushner has said, "I've always been drawn to writing historical characters. . . . The best stories are the ones you find in history."

Angels in America: Millennium Approaches

Kushner began work on the play shortly after Oskar Eustis of Eureka Theater commissioned a two-and-a-half hour play with songs. Once Kushner got a presentable version, he showed it to Eustis and realized that, even incomplete, it was already longer than a one-evening play. Eventually, *Millennium Approaches* and *Perestroika,* the second part of *Angels* (not included here), grew to be more than seven hours long. Although the two parts are thematically linked and contain many of the same characters, both parts of *Angels* stand on their own as complete plays. Kushner said that he never expected to see his play produced anywhere but in a small theater in San Francisco; certainly he never expected it to be a smash hit on Broadway. It won the 1993 Pulitzer Prize for drama, another surprise.

Angels in America has epic Brechtian proportions. Kushner has said that he set out to write a play on "AIDS, Mormons, and Roy Cohn." He chose AIDS because it is a scourge that has especially destroyed large numbers of the gay community. He chose Mormons because he saw in them a group that valued goodness and godliness but that could not tolerate gays. He chose Roy Cohn because when Cohn was an aid to Senator McCarthy during the anti-Communist hysteria of the 1950s, he persecuted gays although he was himself a closet homosexual. His homosexuality did not become public until he contracted AIDS and died in 1986. In Cohn, Kushner had found a villain whose rapacious individualism and unquenchable thirst for power helped symbolize the selfishness of the 1980s. In its New York production Ron Liebman was an overbearingly powerful Cohn, shouting orders, raising hypocrisy to an art form, with depths of contempt matching a profound love of power.

Kushner indicated that his play was a "fantasia on national themes," and it certainly lives up to its title. Kushner set his play in 1985, during the second term of Ronald Reagan. He critiques the values of the Reagan years and politics in general. Jews, WASPs, and Mormons all suffer under his scrutiny. Moreover, he goes beyond national themes and introduces cosmological themes, notably with the introduction of an angel descending through the ceiling at the end of *Millennium Approaches.*

The play focuses as well on problems of individuals. Cohn's friend and protégé Joe Pitt works for the Reagan administration and struggles with his growing awareness that he is gay. A conservative Mormon, Joe faces honestly and painfully these complex, threatening feelings. Harper, Joe's wife, relies on pills, listens all day to talk shows, and has no job, but thinks of herself as part of a traditional marriage and fights to hold on to it. Louis Ironson, a liberal but not profoundly political homosexual, is partnered with Prior Walter, dying from AIDS. Louis has hidden his sexuality from his family and finds it impossible to stay with Prior as his lover's illness worsens. Kushner makes sure that we see all these sets of people interrelated throughout the play, despite their distinctness and the unlikeliness of their ever knowing one another.

Though the scope of the play is enormous, its focus is essentially on politics. Kushner's own views contrast sharply with Cohn's conservative politics, and he is surprised that both conservatives and liberals found the play rewarding, since Kushner felt it to be a pointed attack on conservative values.

Angels in America: Millennium Approaches in Performance

The premiere of the play was in a workshop version in 1991 in the Eureka Theater in San Francisco. Its first full-scale production came in July 1992 at London's Royal National Theatre, where it was a sensation. Some reviewers speculated that in London the way was prepared for this play by the political theater of Caryl Churchill and other playwrights such as David Hare and David Edgar. The audiences were enormously enthusiastic, and the positive reviews the play received attracted attention in the United States. Despite Kushner's relatively unknown status, the two parts of the drama (over seven hours long) were staged in the Mark Taper Forum in Los Angeles in 1992, directed by Oskar Eustis. *Millennium Approaches* appeared on Broadway in April 1993 at the Walter Kerr Theater, directed by George C. Wolfe. Frank Rich gave it a strong, positive review and said, "When first seen a year or so ago, the play seemed defined by its anger at the reigning political establishment, which tended to reward the Roy Cohns and ignore the Prior Walters. Mr. Kushner has not revised the text since — a crony of Cohn's still boasts of a Republican lock on the White House until the year 2000 — but the shift in Washington has had the subliminal effect of making *Angels in America* seem more focused on what happens next than on the past."

The second part of the work, *Perestroika*, arrived on Broadway in November 1993. Frank Rich in the *New York Times* said it was "also a true millennial work of art, uplifting, hugely comic and pantheistically religious in a very American style." After its Broadway run, the play moved to regional theaters, touring throughout the United States. The staging of the drama includes moments that may be described as magical realism featuring ghosts, hallucinations, and other illusions. But Kushner has said, "The play benefits from a pared-down style of presentation, with minimal scenery and scene shifts done rapidly (no blackouts!), employing the cast as well as stagehands — which makes for an actor-driven event, as this must be." He said that it was not a problem if "wires showed," "but the magic should at the same time be thoroughly amazing."

Tony Kushner (b. 1956)

ANGELS IN AMERICA: MILLENNIUM APPROACHES   *1992*
A GAY FANTASIA ON NATIONAL THEMES

Characters

ROY M. COHN, *a successful New York lawyer and unofficial power broker*

JOSEPH PORTER PITT, *chief clerk for Justice Theodore Wilson of the Federal Court of Appeals, Second Circuit*

HARPER AMATY PITT, *Joe's wife, an agoraphobic with a mild Valium addiction*

LOUIS IRONSON, *a word processor working for the Second Circuit Court of Appeals*

PRIOR WALTER, *Louis's boyfriend. Occasionally works as a club designer or caterer, otherwise lives very modestly but with great style off a small trust fund.*

HANNAH PORTER PITT, *Joe's mother, currently residing in Salt Lake City, living off her deceased husband's army pension*

BELIZE, *a former drag queen and former lover of Prior's. A registered nurse. Belize's name was originally Norman Arriaga; Belize is a drag name that stuck.*

THE ANGEL, *four divine emanations, Fluor, Phosphor, Lumen and Candle; manifest in One: the Continental Principality of America. She has magnificent steel-gray wings.*

Other Characters in Part One

RABBI ISISOR CHEMELWITZ, *an orthodox Jewish rabbi, played by the actor playing Hannah*

MR. LIES, *Harper's imaginary friend, a travel agent, who in style of dress and speech suggests a jazz musician; he always wears a large lapel badge emblazoned "IOTA" (The International Order of Travel Agents). He is played by the actor playing Belize.*

THE MAN IN THE PARK, *played by the actor playing Prior*

THE VOICE, *the voice of The Angel*

HENRY, *Roy's doctor, played by the actor playing Hannah*

EMILY, *a nurse, played by the actor playing The Angel*

MARTIN HELLER, *a Reagan Administration Justice*

Department flackman, *played by the actor playing Harper*

SISTER ELLA CHAPTER, *a Salt Lake City real-estate saleswoman, played by the actor playing the Angel*

PRIOR 1, *the ghost of a dead Prior Walter from the 13th century, played by the actor playing Joe. He is blunt, gloomy medieval farmer with a gutteral Yorkshire accent.*

PRIOR 2, *the ghost of a dead Prior Walter from the 17th century, played by the actor playing Roy. He is a Londoner, sophisticated, with a High British accent.*

THE ESKIMO, *played by the actor playing Joe*

THE WOMAN IN THE SOUTH BRONX, *played by the actor playing the Angel*

ETHEL ROSENBERG, *played by the actor playing Hannah*

Playwright's Notes

A Disclaimer: Roy M. Cohn, the character, is based on the late Roy M. Cohn (1927–1986), who was all too real; for the most part the acts attributed to the character Roy, such as his illegal conferences with Judge Kaufmann during the trial of Ethel Rosenberg, are to be found in the historical record. But this Roy is a work of dramatic fiction; his words are my invention, and liberties have been taken.

A Note about the Staging: The play benefits from a pared-down style of presentation, with minimal scenery and scene shifts done rapidly (no blackouts!), employing the cast as well as stagehands — which makes for an actor-driven event, as this must be. The moments of magic — the appearance and disappearance of Mr. Lies and the ghosts, the Book hallucination, and the ending — are to be fully realized, as bits of wonderful theatrical illusion — which means it's OK if the wires show, and maybe it's good that they do, but the magic should at the same time be thoroughly amazing.

In a murderous time
the heart breaks and breaks
and lives by breaking.

— STANLEY KUNITZ
"THE TESTING-TREE"

ACT 1
BAD NEWS • *October–November 1985*

Scene 1

(*The last days of October. Rabbi Isidor Chemelwitz alone onstage with a small coffin. It is a rough pine box with two wooden pegs, one at the foot and one at the head, holding the lid in place. A prayer shawl embroidered with a Star of David is draped over the lid, and by the head a yarzheit candle is burning.*)

RABBI ISIDOR CHEMELWITZ (*he speaks sonorously, with a heavy Eastern European accent, unapologetically consulting a sheet of notes for the family names*): Hello and good morning. I am Rabbi Isidor Chemelwitz of the Bronx Home for Aged Hebrews. We are here this morning to pay respects at the passing of Sarah Ironson, devoted wife of Benjamin Ironson, also deceased, loving and caring mother of her sons Morris, Abraham, and Samuel, and her daughters Esther and Rachel; beloved grandmother of Max, Mark, Louis, Lisa, Maria . . . uh . . . Lesley, Angela, Doris, Luke and Eric. (*Looks more closely at paper.*) Eric? This is a Jewish name? (*Shrugs.*) Eric. A large and loving family. We assemble that we may mourn collectively this good and righteous woman.
(*He looks at the coffin.*)
This woman. I did not know this woman. I cannot accurately describe her attributes, nor do justice to her dimensions. She was. . . . Well, in the Bronx Home of Aged Hebrews are many like this, the old, and to many I speak but not to be frank with this one. She preferred silence. So I do not know her and yet I know her. She was . . .
(*he touches the coffin*)
. . . not a person but a whole kind of person, the ones who crossed the ocean, who brought with us to America the villages of Russia and Lithuania — and how we struggled, and how we fought, for the family, for the Jewish home, so that you would not grow up *here,* in this strange place, in the melting pot where nothing melted. Descendants of this immigrant woman, you do not grow up in America, you and your children and their children with the goyische names. You do not live in America. No such place exists. Your clay is the clay of some Litvak shtetl, your air the air of the steppes — because she carried the old world on her back across the ocean, in a boat, and she put it down on Grand Concourse Avenue, or in Flatbush, and she worked that earth into your bones, and you pass it to your children, this ancient, ancient culture and home.

(*Little pause.*)
You can never make that crossing that she made, for such Great Voyages in this world do not any more exist. But every day of your lives the miles that voyage between that place and this one you cross. Every day. You understand me? In you that journey is.
So . . .
She was the last of the Mohicans, this one was. Pretty soon . . . all the old will be dead.

Scene 2

(*Same day. Roy and Joe in Roy's office. Roy at an impressive desk, bare except for a very elaborate phone system, rows and rows of flashing buttons which bleep and beep and whistle incessantly, making chaotic music underneath Roy's conversations. Joe is sitting, waiting. Roy conducts business with great energy, impatience and sensual abandon: gesticulating, shouting, cajoling, crooning, playing the phone, receiver and hold button with virtuosity and love.*)

ROY (*hitting a button*): Hold. (*To Joe.*) I wish I was an octopus, a fucking octopus. Eight loving arms and all those suckers. Know what I mean?
JOE: No, I . . .
ROY (*gesturing to a deli platter of little sandwiches on his desk*): You want lunch?
JOE: No, that's OK really I just . . .
ROY (*hitting a button*): Ailene? Roy Cohn. Now what kind of a greeting is. . . . I thought we were friends, Ai. . . . Look Mrs. Soffer you don't have to get. . . . You're upset. You're yelling. You'll aggravate your condition, you shouldn't yell, you'll pop little blood vessels in your face if you yell. . . . No that was a joke, Mrs. Soffer, I was joking. . . . I already apologized sixteen times for that, Mrs. Soffer, you . . . (*While she's fulminating, Roy covers the mouthpiece with his hand and talks to Joe.*) This'll take a minute, *eat* already, what is this tasty sandwich here it's — (*he takes a bite of a sandwich.*) Mmmmm, liver or some. . . . Here.

(*He pitches the sandwich to Joe, who catches it and returns it to the platter.*)

ROY (*back to Mrs. Soffer*): Uh huh, uh huh. . . . No, I already told you, it wasn't a vacation, it was business, Mrs. Soffer, I have clients in Haiti, Mrs. Soffer, I. . . . Listen, Ailene, YOU THINK I'M THE ONLY GODDAM LAWYER IN HISTORY EVER MISSED A COURT DATE? Don't make such a big fucking. . . . Hold. (*He hits the hold button.*) You HAG!

JOE: If this is a bad time . . .

ROY: *Bad* time? This is a *good* time! (*Button.*) Baby doll, get me. . . . Oh fuck, wait . . . (*Button, button.*) Hello? Yah. Sorry to keep you holding, Judge Hollins, I. . . . Oh Mrs. Hollins, sorry dear deep voice you got. Enjoying your visit? (*Hand over mouthpiece again, to Joe.*) She sounds like a truck-driver and he sounds like Kate Smith, very confusing. Nixon appointed him, all the geeks are Nixon appointees . . . (*To Mrs. Hollins.*) Yeah yeah right good so how many tickets dear? Seven. For what, *Cats, 42nd Street,* what? No you wouldn't like *La Cage,* trust me, I know. Oh for godsake. . . . Hold. (*Button, button.*) Baby doll, seven for *Cats* or something, anything hard to get, I don't give a fuck what and neither will they. (*Button; to Joe.*) You see *La Cage?*

JOE: No, I . . .

ROY: Fabulous. Best thing on Broadway. Maybe ever. (*Button.*) Who? Aw, Jesus H. Christ, Harry, *no,* Harry, Judge John Francis Grimes, Manhattan Family Court. Do I have to do every goddam thing myself? *Touch* the bastard, Harry, and don't call me on this line again, I told you not to . . .

JOE (*starting to get up*): Roy, uh, should I wait outside or . . .

ROY (*to Joe*): Oh sit. (*To Harry.*) You hold. I pay you to hold fuck you Harry you jerk. (*Button.*) Half-wit dick-brain. (*Instantly philosophical.*) I see the universe, Joe, as a kind of sandstorm in outer space with winds of mega-hurricane velocity, but instead of grains of sand it's shards and splinters of glass. You ever feel that way? Ever have one of those days?

JOE: I'm not sure I . . .

ROY: So how's life in Appeals? How's the Judge?

JOE: He sends his best.

ROY: He's a good man. Loyal. Not the brightest man on the bench, but he has manners. And a nice head of silver hair.

JOE: He gives me a lot of responsibility.

ROY: Yeah, like writing his decisions and signing his name.

JOE: Well . . .

ROY: He's a nice guy. And you cover admirably.

JOE: Well, thanks, Roy, I . . .

ROY (*button*): Yah? Who is *this?* Well who the fuck are *you?* Hold — (*button*) Harry? Eighty-seven grand, something like that. Fuck him. Eat me. New Jersey, chain of porno film stores in, uh, Wee-hawken. That's — Harry, that's the beauty of the law. (*Button.*) So, baby doll, what? *Cats?* Bleah. (*Button.*) *Cats!* It's about cats. Singing cats, you'll love it. Eight o'clock, the theatre's always at eight. (*Button.*) Fucking tourists. (*Button, then to Joe.*)

Oh live a little, Joe, *eat* something for Christ sake —

JOE: Um, Roy, could you . . .

ROY: What? (*To Harry.*) Hold a minute. (*Button.*) Mrs. Soffer? Mrs. . . . (*Button.*) God-fucking-dammit to hell, where is . . .

JOE (*overlapping*): Roy, I'd really appreciate it if . . .

ROY (*overlapping*): Well she was here a minute ago, baby doll, see if . . .

(*The phone starts making three different beeping sounds, all at once.*)

ROY (*smashing buttons*): Jesus fuck this goddam thing . . .

JOE (*overlapping*): I really wish you wouldn't . . .

ROY (*overlapping*): Baby doll? Ring the *Post* get me Suzy see if . . .

(*The phone starts whistling loudly.*)

ROY: CHRIST!

JOE: *Roy.*

ROY (*into receiver*): Hold. (*Button; to Joe.*) *What?*

JOE: Could you please not take the Lord's name in vain

(*Pause.*)

I'm sorry. But please. At least while I'm . . .

ROY (*laughs, then*): Right. Sorry. Fuck.

Only in America. (*Punches a button.*) Baby doll, tell 'em all to fuck off. Tell 'em I died. You handle Mrs. Soffer. Tell her it's on the way. Tell her I'm schtupping the judge. I'll call her back. I *will* call her. I *know* how much I borrowed. She's got four hundred times that stuffed up her. . . . Yeah, tell her I said that. (*Button. The phone is silent.*)

So, Joe.

JOE: I'm sorry Roy, I just . . .

ROY: No no no no, principles count, I respect principles, I'm not religious but I like God and God likes me. Baptist, Catholic?

JOE: Mormon.

ROY: Mormon. Delectable. Absolutely. Only in America. So, Joe. Whattya think?

JOE: It's . . . well . . .

ROY: Crazy life.

JOE: Chaotic.

ROY: Well but God bless chaos. Right?

JOE: Ummm . . .

ROY: Huh. Mormons. I knew Mormons, in, um, Nevada.

JOE: Utah, mostly.

ROY: No, these Mormons were in Vegas.

So. So, how'd you like to go to Washington and work for the Justice Department?

JOE: Sorry?

ROY: How'd you like to go to Washington and work

for the Justice Department? All I gotta do is pick up the phone, talk to Ed, and you're in.

JOE: In . . . what, exactly?

ROY: Associate Assistant Something Big. Internal Affairs, heart of the woods, something nice with clout.

JOE: Ed . . . ?

ROY: Meese. The Attorney General.

JOE: Oh.

ROY: I just have to pick up the phone . . .

JOE: I have to think.

ROY: Of course.

> (*Pause.*)

> It's a great time to be in Washington, Joe.

JOE: Roy, it's incredibly exciting . . .

ROY: And it would mean something to me. You understand?

(*Little pause.*)

JOE: I . . . can't say how much I appreciate this Roy, I'm sort of . . . well, stunned, I mean. . . . Thanks, Roy. But I have to give it some thought. I have to ask my wife.

ROY: Your wife. Of course.

JOE: But I really appreciate . . .

ROY: Of course. Talk to your wife.

Scene 3

(*Later that day. Harper at home, alone. She is listening to the radio and talking to herself, as she often does. She speaks to the audience.*)

HARPER: People who are lonely, people left alone, sit talking nonsense to the air, imagining . . . beautiful systems dying, old fixed orders spiraling apart . . .

 When you look at the ozone layer, from outside, from a spaceship, it looks like a pale blue halo, a gentle, shimmering aureole encircling the atmosphere encircling the earth. Thirty miles above our heads, a thin layer of three-atom oxygen molecules, product of photosynthesis, which explains the fussy vegetable preference for visible light, its rejection of darker rays and emanations. Danger from without. It's a kind of gift, from God, the crowning touch to the creation of the world: guardian angels, hands linked, make a spherical net, a blue-green nesting orb, a shell of safety for life itself. But everywhere, things are collapsing, lies surfacing, systems of defense giving way. . . . This is why, Joe, this is why I shouldn't be left alone.

> (*Little pause.*)

> I'd like to go traveling. Leave you behind to worry. I'll send postcards with strange stamps and tantalizing messages on the back. "Later maybe." "Nevermore . . ."

(*Mr. Lies, a travel agent, appears.*)

HARPER Oh! You startled me!

MR. LIES: Cash, check or credit card?

HARPER: I remember you. You're from Salt Lake. You sold us the plane tickets when we flew here. What are you doing in Brooklyn?

MR. LIES: You said you wanted to travel . . .

HARPER: And here you are. How thoughtful.

MR. LIES: Mr. Lies. Of the International Order of Travel Agents. We mobilize the globe, we set people adrift, we stir the populace and send nomads eddying across the planet. We are adepts of motion, acolytes of the flux. Cash, check or credit card. Name your destination.

HARPER: Antarctica, maybe. I want to see the hole in the ozone. I heard on the radio . . .

MR. LIES (*he has a computer terminal in his briefcase*): I can arrange a guided tour. Now?

HARPER: Soon. Maybe soon. I'm not safe here you see. Things aren't right with me. Weird stuff happens . . .

MR. LIES: Like?

HARPER: Well, like you, for instance. Just appearing. Or last week . . . well never mind.

 People are like planets, you need a thick skin. Things get to me, Joe stays away and now. . . . Well look. My dreams are talking back to me.

MR. LIES: It's the price of rootlessness. Motion sickness. The only cure: to keep moving.

HARPER: I'm undecided. I feel . . . that something's going to give. It's 1985. Fifteen years till the third millennium. Maybe Christ will come again. Maybe seeds will be planted, maybe there'll be harvests then, maybe early figs to eat, maybe new life, maybe fresh blood, maybe companionship and love and protection, safety from what's outside, maybe the door will hold, or maybe . . . maybe the troubles will come, and the end will come, and the sky will collapse and there will be terrible rains and showers of poison light, or maybe my life is really fine, maybe Joe loves me and I'm only crazy thinking otherwise, or maybe not, maybe it's even worse than I know, maybe . . . I want to know, maybe I don't. The suspense, Mr. Lies, it's killing me.

MR. LIES: I suggest a vacation.

HARPER (*hearing something*): That was the elevator. Oh God, I should fix myself up, I. . . . You have to go, you shouldn't be here . . . you aren't even real.

MR. LIES: Call me when you decide . . .

HARPER: Go!

(*The Travel Agent vanishes as Joe enters.*)

JOE: Buddy?
    Buddy? Sorry I'm late. I was just . . . out. Walking. Are you mad?
HARPER: I got a little anxious.
JOE: Buddy kiss.

(*They kiss.*)

JOE: Nothing to get anxious about.
    So. So how'd you like to move to Washington?

Scene 4

(*Same day. Louis and Prior outside the funeral home, sitting on a bench, both dressed in funereal finery, talking. The funeral service for Sarah Ironson has just concluded and Louis is about to leave for the cemetery.*)

LOUIS: My grandmother actually saw Emma Goldman speak. In Yiddish. But all Grandma could remember was that she spoke well and wore a hat.
    What a weird service. That rabbi . . .
PRIOR: A definite find. Get his number when you go to the graveyard. I want him to bury me.
LOUIS: Better head out there. Everyone gets to put dirt on the coffin once it's lowered in.
PRIOR: Oooh. Cemetery fun. Don't want to miss that.
LOUIS: It's an old Jewish custom to express love. Here, Grandma, have a shovelful. Latecomers run the risk of finding the grave completely filled.
    She was pretty crazy. She was up there in that home for ten years, talking to herself. I never visited. She looked too much like my mother.
PRIOR (*hugs him*): Poor Louis. I'm sorry your grandma is dead.
LOUIS: Tiny little coffin, huh?
    Sorry I didn't introduce you to. . . . I always get so closety at these family things.
PRIOR: Butch. You get butch. (*Imitating.*) "Hi Cousin Doris, you don't remember me I'm Lou, Rachel's boy." Lou, not Louis, because if you say Louis they'll hear the sibilant S.
LOUIS: I don't have a . . .
PRIOR: I don't blame you, hiding. Bloodlines. Jewish curses are the worst. I personally would dissolve if anyone ever looked me in the eye and said "Feh." Fortunately WASPs don't say "Feh." Oh and by the way, darling, cousin Doris is a dyke.
LOUIS: No.
    Really?
PRIOR: You don't notice anything. If I hadn't spent the last four years fellating you I'd swear you were straight.
LOUIS: You're in a pissy mood. Cat still missing?

(*Little pause.*)

PRIOR: Not a furball in sight. It's your fault.
LOUIS: It is?
PRIOR: I warned you, Louis. Names are important. Call an animal "Little Sheba" and you can't expect it to stick around. Besides, it's a dog's name.
LOUIS: I wanted a dog in the first place, not a cat. He sprayed my books.
PRIOR: He was a female cat.
LOUIS: Cats are stupid, high-strung predators. Babylonians sealed them up in bricks. Dogs have brains.
PRIOR: Cats have intuition.
LOUIS: A sharp dog is as smart as a really dull two-year-old child.
PRIOR: Cats know when something's wrong.
LOUIS: Only if you stop feeding them.
PRIOR: They know. That's why Sheba left, because she knew.
LOUIS: Knew what?

(*Pause.*)

PRIOR: I did my best Shirley Booth this morning, floppy slippers, housecoat, curlers, can of Little Friskies; "Come back, Little Sheba, come back. . . ." To no avail. Le chat, elle ne reviendra jamais, jamais . . . °
    (*He removes his jacket, rolls up his sleeve, shows Louis a dark-purple spot on the underside of his arm near the shoulder.*)
    See.
LOUIS: That's just a burst blood vessel.
PRIOR: Not according to the best medical authorities.
LOUIS: What?
    (*Pause.*)
    Tell me.
PRIOR: K.S., baby. Lesion number one. Lookit. The wine-dark kiss of the angel of death.
LOUIS (*very softly, holding Prior's arm*): Oh please . . .
PRIOR: I'm a lesionnaire. The Foreign Lesion. The American Lesion. Lesionnaire's disease.
LOUIS: Stop.
PRIOR: My troubles are lesion.
LOUIS: Will you *stop*.
PRIOR: Don't you think I'm handling this well?
    I'm going to die.
LOUIS: Bullshit.
PRIOR: Let go of my arm.
LOUIS: No.
PRIOR: Let go.
LOUIS (*grabbing Prior, embracing him ferociously*): No.
PRIOR: I can't find a way to spare you baby. No wall

Le chat . . . jamais: The cat will never return, ever.

like the wall of hard scientific fact. K.S. Wham. Bang your head on that.

LOUIS: Fuck you. (*Letting go.*) Fuck you fuck you fuck you.

PRIOR: Now that's what I like to hear. A mature reaction.

> Let's go see if the cat's come home.
> Louis?

LOUIS: When did you find this?

PRIOR: I couldn't tell you.

LOUIS: Why?

PRIOR: I was scared, Lou.

LOUIS: Of what?

PRIOR: That you'll leave me.

LOUIS: Oh.

(*Little pause.*)

PRIOR: Bad timing, funeral and all, but I figured as long as we're on the subject of death . . .

LOUIS: I have to go bury my grandma.

PRIOR: Lou?

> (*Pause.*)
> Then you'll come home?

LOUIS: Then I'll come home.

Scene 5

(*Same day, later on. Split scene: Joe and Harper at home; Louis at the cemetery with Rabbi Isidor Chemelwitz and the little coffin.*)

HARPER: Washington?

JOE: It's an incredible honor, buddy, and . . .

HARPER: I have to think.

JOE: Of course.

HARPER: Say no.

JOE: You said you were going to think about it.

HARPER: I don't want to move to Washington.

JOE: Well I do.

HARPER: It's a giant cemetery, huge white graves and mausoleums everywhere.

JOE: We could live in Maryland. Or Georgetown.

HARPER: We're happy here.

JOE: That's not really true, buddy, we . . .

HARPER: Well happy enough! Pretend-happy. That's better than nothing.

JOE: It's time to make some changes, Harper.

HARPER: No changes. Why?

JOE: I've been chief clerk for four years. I make twenty-nine thousand dollars a year. That's ridiculous. I graduated fourth in my class and I make less than anyone I know. And I'm . . . I'm tired of being a clerk, I want to go where something good is happening.

HARPER: Nothing good happens in Washington. We'll forget church teachings and buy furniture at . . . at *Conran's* and become yuppies. I have too much to do here.

JOE: Like what?

HARPER: I *do* have things . . .

JOE: What things?

HARPER: I have to finish painting the bedroom.

JOE: You've been painting in there for over a year.

HARPER: I know, I. . . . It just isn't done because I never get time to finish it.

JOE: Oh that's . . . that doesn't make sense. You have all the time in the world. You could finish it when I'm at work.

HARPER: I'm afraid to go in there alone.

JOE: Afraid of what?

HARPER: I heard someone in there. Metal scraping on the wall. A man with a knife, maybe.

JOE: There's no one in the bedroom, Harper.

HARPER: Not now.

JOE: Not this morning either.

HARPER: How do you know? You were at work this morning. There's something creepy about this place. Remember *Rosemary's Baby*?

JOE: *Rosemary's Baby*?

HARPER: Our apartment looks like that one. Wasn't that apartment in Brooklyn?

JOE: No, it was . . .

HARPER: Well, it looked like this. It did.

JOE: Then let's move.

HARPER: Georgetown's worse. *The Exorcist* was in Georgetown.

JOE: The devil, everywhere you turn, huh, buddy.

HARPER: Yeah. Everywhere.

JOE: How many pills today, buddy?

HARPER: None. One. Three. Only three.

LOUIS (*pointing at the coffin*): Why are there just two little wooden pegs holding the lid down?

RABBI ISIDOR CHEMELWITZ: So she can get out easier if she wants to.

LOUIS: I hope she stays put.

> I pretended for years that she was already dead. When they called to say she had died it was a surprise. I abandoned her.

RABBI ISIDOR CHEMELWITZ: "Sharfer vi di tson fun a shlang iz an umdankbar kind!"

LOUIS: I don't speak Yiddish.

RABBI ISIDOR CHEMELWITZ: Sharper than the serpent's tooth is the ingratitude of children. Shakespeare. *King Lear.*

LOUIS: Rabbi, what does the Holy Writ say about someone who abandons someone he loves at a time of great need?

RABBI ISIDOR CHEMELWITZ: Why would a person do such a thing?

LOUIS: Because he has to.

Maybe because this person's sense of the world, that it will change for the better with struggle, maybe a person who has this neo-Hegelian positivist sense of constant historical progress towards happiness or perfection or something, who feels very powerful because he feels connected to these forces, moving uphill all the time . . . maybe that person can't, um, incorporate sickness into his sense of how things are supposed to go. Maybe vomit . . . and sores and disease . . . really frighten him, maybe . . . he isn't so good with death.

RABBI ISIDOR CHEMELWITZ: The Holy Scriptures have nothing to say about such a person.

LOUIS: Rabbi, I'm afraid of the crimes I may commit.

RABBI ISIDOR CHEMELWITZ: Please, mister. I'm a sick old rabbi facing a long drive home to the Bronx. You want to confess, better you should find a priest.

LOUIS: But I'm not a Catholic, I'm a Jew.

RABBI ISIDOR CHEMELWITZ: Worse luck for you, bubbulah. Catholics believe in forgiveness. Jews believe in Guilt. (*He pats the coffin tenderly.*)

LOUIS: You just make sure those pegs are in good and tight.

RABBI ISIDOR CHEMELWITZ: Don't worry, mister. The life she had, she'll stay put. She's better off.

JOE: Look, I know this is scary for you. But try to understand what it means to me. Will you try?

HARPER: Yes.

JOE: Good. Really try.

I think things are starting to change in the world.

HARPER: But I don't want . . .

JOE: Wait. For the good. Change for the good. America has rediscovered itself. Its sacred position among nations. And people aren't ashamed of that like they used to be. This is a great thing. The truth restored. Law restored. That's what President Reagan's done, Harper. He says "Truth exists and can be spoken proudly." And the country responds to him. We become better. More good. I need to be a part of that, I need something big to lift me up. I mean, six years ago the world seemed in decline, horrible, hopeless, full of unsolvable problems and crime and confusion and hunger and . . .

HARPER: But it still seems that way. More now than before. They say the ozone layer is . . .

JOE: Harper . . .

HARPER: And today out the window on Atlantic Avenue there was a schizophrenic traffic cop who was making these . . .

JOE: Stop it! I'm trying to make a point.

HARPER: So am I.

JOE: You aren't even making sense, you . . .

HARPER: My point is the world seems just as . . .

JOE: It only seems that way to you because you never go out in the world, Harper, and you have emotional problems.

HARPER: I do so get out in the world.

JOE: You don't. You stay in all day, fretting about imaginary . . .

HARPER: I get out. I do. You don't know what I do.

JOE: You don't stay in all day.

HARPER: No.

JOE: Well. . . . Yes you do.

HARPER: That's what you think.

JOE: Where do you go?

HARPER: Where do *you* go? When you walk.

(*Pause, then angrily.*) And I DO NOT have emotional problems.

JOE: I'm sorry.

HARPER: And if I do have emotional problems it's from living with you. Or . . .

JOE: I'm sorry buddy, I didn't mean to . . .

HARPER: Or if you do think I do then you should never have married me. You have all these secrets and lies.

JOE: I want to be married to you, Harper.

HARPER: You shouldn't. You never should.

(*Pause.*)

Hey buddy. Hey buddy.

JOE: Buddy kiss . . .

(*They kiss.*)

HARPER: I heard on the radio how to give a blowjob.

JOE: What?

HARPER: You want to try?

JOE: You really shouldn't listen to stuff like that.

HARPER: Mormons can give blowjobs.

JOE: *Harper.*

HARPER (*imitating his tone*): *Joe.*

It was a little Jewish lady with a German accent.

This is a good time. For me to make a baby.

(*Little pause. Joe turns away.*)

HARPER: Then they went on to a program about holes in the ozone layer. Over Antarctica. Skin burns, birds go blind, icebergs melt. The world's coming to an end.

Scene 6

(*First week of November. In the men's room of the offices of the Brooklyn Federal Court of Appeals; Louis is crying over the sink; Joe enters.*)

JOE: Oh, um. . . . Morning.

LOUIS: Good morning, counselor.

JOE (*he watches Louis cry*): Sorry, I . . . I don't know your name.

LOUIS: Don't bother. Word processor. The lowest of the low.

JOE (*holding out hand*): Joe Pitt. I'm with Justice Wilson . . .

LOUIS: Oh, I know that. Counselor Pitt. Chief Clerk.

JOE: Were you . . . are you OK?

LOUIS: Oh, yeah. Thanks. What a nice man.

JOE: Not so nice.

LOUIS: What?

JOE: Not so nice. Nothing. You sure you're . . .

LOUIS: Life sucks shit. Life . . . just sucks shit.

JOE: What's wrong?

LOUIS: Run in my nylons.

JOE: Sorry . . . ?

LOUIS: Forget it. Look, thanks for asking.

JOE: Well . . .

LOUIS: I mean it really is nice of you.
(*He starts crying again.*)
Sorry, sorry, sick friend . . .

JOE: Oh, I'm sorry.

LOUIS: Yeah, yeah, well, that's sweet.
Three of your colleagues have preceded you to this baleful sight and you're the first one to ask. The others just opened the door, saw me, and fled. I hope they had to pee real bad.

JOE (*handing him a wad of toilet paper*): They just didn't want to intrude.

LOUIS: Hah. Reaganite heartless macho asshole lawyers.

JOE: Oh, that's unfair.

LOUIS: What is? Heartless? Macho? Reaganite? Lawyer?

JOE: I voted for Reagan.

LOUIS: You did?

JOE: Twice.

LOUIS: Twice? Well, oh boy. A Gay Republican.

JOE: Excuse me?

LOUIS: Nothing.

JOE: I'm not . . .
Forget it.

LOUIS: Republican? Not Republican? Or . . .

JOE: What?

LOUIS: What?

JOE: Not gay. I'm not gay.

LOUIS: Oh. Sorry.
(*Blows his nose loudly.*) It's just . . .

JOE: Yes?

LOUIS: Well, sometimes you can tell from the way a person sounds that . . . I mean you *sound* like a . . .

JOE: No I don't. Like what?

LOUIS: Like a Republican.

(*Little pause. Joe knows he's being teased; Louis knows he knows. Joe decides to be a little brave.*)

JOE (*making sure no one else is around*): Do I? Sound like a . . . ?

LOUIS: What? Like a . . . ? Republican, or . . . ? Do *I*?

JOE: Do you what?

LOUIS: Sound like a . . . ?

JOE: Like a . . . ?
I'm . . . confused.

LOUIS: Yes.
My name is Louis. But all my friends call me Louise. I work in Word Processing. Thanks for the toilet paper.

(*Louis offers Joe his hand, Joe reaches, Louis feints and pecks Joe on the cheek, then exits.*)

Scene 7

(*A week later. Mutual dream scene. Prior is at a fantastic makeup table, having a dream, applying the face. Harper is having a pill-induced hallucination. She has these from time to time. For some reason, Prior has appeared in this one. Or Harper has appeared in Priors dream. It is bewildering.*)

PRIOR (*alone, putting on makeup, then examining the results in the mirror; to the audience*): "I'm ready for my closeup, Mr. DeMille."
One wants to move through life with elegance and grace, blossoming infrequently but with exquisite taste, and perfect timing, like a rare bloom, a zebra orchid. . . . One wants. . . . But one so seldom gets what one wants, does one? No. One does not. One gets fucked. Over. One . . . dies at thirty, robbed of . . . decades of majesty.
Fuck this shit. Fuck this shit.
(*He almost crumbles; he pulls himself together; he studies his handiwork in the mirror.*)
I look like a corpse. A corpsette. Oh my queen; you know you've hit rock-bottom when even drag is a drag.

(*Harper appears.*)

HARPER: Are you. . . . Who are you?

PRIOR: Who are you?

HARPER: What are you doing in my hallucination?

PRIOR: I'm not in your hallucination. You're in my dream.

HARPER: You're wearing makeup.

PRIOR: So are you.

HARPER: But you're a man.

PRIOR (*feigning dismay, shock, he mimes slashing his throat with his lipstick and dies, fabulously tragic. Then*): The hands and feet give it away.

HARPER: There must be some mistake here. I don't

recognize you. You're not. . . . Are you my . . . some sort of imaginary friend?

PRIOR: No. Aren't you too old to have imaginary friends?

HARPER: I have emotional problems. I took too many pills. Why are you wearing makeup?

PRIOR: I was in the process of applying the face, trying to make myself feel better — I swiped the new fall colors at the Clinique counter at Macy's. (*Showing her.*)

HARPER: You stole these?

PRIOR: I was out of cash; it was an emotional emergency!

HARPER: Joe will be so angry. I promised him. No more pills.

PRIOR: These pills you keep alluding to?

HARPER: Valium. I take Valium. Lots of Valium.

PRIOR: And you're dancing as fast as you can.

HARPER: I'm not *addicted*. I don't believe in addiction, and I never . . . well, I *never* drink. And I *never* take drugs.

PRIOR: Well, smell *you,* Nancy Drew.

HARPER: Except Valium.

PRIOR: Except Valium; in wee fistfuls.

HARPER: It's terrible. Mormons are not supposed to be addicted to anything. I'm a Mormon.

PRIOR: I'm a homosexual.

HARPER: Oh! In my church we don't believe in homosexuals.

PRIOR: In my church we don't believe in Mormons.

HARPER: What church do . . . oh! (*She laughs.*) I get it.
  I don't understand this. If I didn't ever see you before and I don't think I did then I don't think you should be here, in this hallucination, because in my experience the mind, which is where hallucinations come from, shouldn't be able to make up anything that wasn't there to start with, that didn't enter it from experience, from the real world. Imagination can't create anything new, can it? It only recycles bits and pieces from the world and reassembles them into visions. . . . Am I making sense right now?

PRIOR: Given the circumstances, yes.

HARPER: So when we think we've escaped the unbearable ordinariness and, well, untruthfulness of our lives, it's really only the same old ordinariness and falseness rearranged into the appearance of novelty and truth. Nothing unknown is knowable. Don't you think it's depressing?

PRIOR: The limitations of the imagination?

HARPER: Yes.

PRIOR: It's something you learn after your second theme party: It's All Been Done Before.

HARPER: The world. Finite. Terribly, terribly. . . . Well . . .

This is the most depressing hallucination I've ever had.

PRIOR: Apologies. I do try to be amusing.

HARPER: Oh, well, don't apologize, you. . . . I can't expect someone who's really sick to entertain me.

PRIOR: How on earth did you know . . .

HARPER: Oh that happens. This is the very threshhold of revelation sometimes. You can see things . . . how sick you are. Do you see anything about me?

PRIOR: Yes.

HARPER: What?

PRIOR: You are amazingly unhappy.

HARPER: Oh big deal. You meet a Valium addict and you figure out she's unhappy. That doesn't count. Of course I. . . . Something else. Something surprising.

PRIOR: Something surprising.

HARPER: Yes.

PRIOR: Your husband's a homo.

(*Pause.*)

HARPER: Oh, ridiculous.
  (*Pause, then very quietly.*)
  Really?

PRIOR (*shrugs*): Threshhold of revelation.

HARPER: Well I don't like your revelations. I don't think you intuit well at all. Joe's a very normal man, he . . .
  Oh God. Oh God. He. . . . Do homos take, like, lots of long walks?

PRIOR: Yes. We do. In stretch pants with lavender coifs. I just looked at you, and there was . . .

HARPER: A sort of blue streak of recognition.

PRIOR: Yes.

HARPER: Like you knew me incredibly well.

PRIOR: Yes.

HARPER: Yes.
  I have to go now, get back, something just . . . fell apart.
  Oh God, I feel so sad . . .

PRIOR: I . . . I'm sorry. I usually say, "Fuck the truth," but mostly, the truth fucks you.

HARPER: I see something else about you . . .

PRIOR: Oh?

HARPER: Deep inside you, there's a part of you, the most inner part, entirely free of disease. I can see that.

PRIOR: Is that. . . . That isn't true.

HARPER: Threshhold of revelation.
  Home . . .

(*She vanishes.*)

PRIOR: People come and go so quickly here . . .
  (*To himself in the mirror.*) I don't think there's

any uninfected part of me. My heart is pumping polluted blood. I feel dirty.

(*He begins to wipe makeup off with his hands, smearing it around. A large gray feather falls from up above. Prior stops smearing the makeup and looks at the feather. He goes to it and picks it up.*)

A VOICE (*it is an incredibly beautiful voice*): Look up!
PRIOR (*looking up, not seeing anyone*): Hello?
A VOICE: Look up!
PRIOR: Who is that?
A VOICE: Prepare the way!
PRIOR: I don't see any . . .

(*There is a dramatic change in lighting, from above.*)

A VOICE:
>Look up, look up,
>prepare the way
>the infinite descent
>A breath in air
>floating down
>Glory to . . .

(*Silence.*)

PRIOR: Hello? Is that it? Helloooo!
>What the fuck . . . ? (*He holds himself.*)
>Poor me. Poor poor me. Why me? Why poor poor me? Oh I don't feel good right now. I really don't.

Scene 8

(*That night. Split scene: Harper and Joe at home; Prior and Louis in bed.*)

HARPER: Where were you?
JOE: Out.
HARPER: Where?
JOE: Just out. Thinking.
HARPER: It's late.
JOE: I had a lot to think about.
HARPER: I burned dinner.
JOE: Sorry.
HARPER: Not my dinner. My dinner was fine. Your dinner. I put it back in the oven and turned everything up as high as it could go and I watched till it burned black. It's still hot. Very hot. Want it?
JOE: You didn't have to do that.
HARPER: I know. It just seemed like the kind of thing a mentally deranged sex-starved pill-popping housewife would do.
JOE: Uh huh.
HARPER: So I did it. Who knows anymore what I have to do?
JOE: How many pills?

HARPER: A bunch. Don't change the subject.
JOE: I won't talk to you when you . . .
HARPER: No. No. Don't do that! I'm . . . I'm fine, pills are not the problem, not our problem, I WANT TO KNOW WHERE YOU'VE BEEN! I WANT TO KNOW WHAT'S GOING ON!
JOE: Going on with what? The job?
HARPER: Not the job.
JOE: I said I need more time.
HARPER: Not the job!
JOE: Mr. Cohn, I talked to him on the phone, he said I had to hurry . . .
HARPER: Not the . . .
JOE: But I can't get you to talk sensibly about anything so . . .
HARPER: SHUT UP!
JOE: Then what?
HARPER: Stick to the subject.
JOE: I don't know what that is. You have something you want to ask me? Ask me. Go.
HARPER: I . . . can't. I'm scared of you.
JOE: I'm tired, I'm going to bed.
HARPER: Tell me without making me ask. Please.
JOE: This is crazy, I'm not . . .
HARPER: When you come through the door at night your face is never exactly the way I remembered it. I get surprised by something . . . mean and hard about the way you look. Even the weight of you in the bed at night, the way you breathe in your sleep seems unfamiliar.
>You terrify me.
JOE (*cold*): I know who you are.
HARPER: Yes. I'm the enemy. That's easy. That doesn't change.
>You think you're the only one who hates sex; I do; I hate it with you; I do. I dream that you batter away at me till all my joints come apart, like wax, and I fall into pieces. It's like a punishment. It was wrong of me to marry you. I knew you . . . (*She stops herself.*) It's a sin, and it's killing us both.
JOE: I can always tell when you've taken pills because it makes you red-faced and sweaty and frankly that's very often why I don't want to . . .
HARPER: Because . . .
JOE: Well, you aren't pretty. Not like this.
HARPER: I have something to ask you.
JOE: Then ASK! ASK! What in hell are you . . .
HARPER: Are you a homo?
>(*Pause.*)
>Are you? If you try to walk out right now I'll put your dinner back in the oven and turn it up so high the whole building will fill with smoke and everyone in it will asphyxiate. So help me God I will.
>Now answer the question.

JOE: What if I . . .

(*Small pause.*)

HARPER: Then tell me, please. And we'll see.
JOE: No. I'm not.
    I don't see what difference it makes.

LOUIS: Jews don't have any clear textual guide to the
    afterlife; even that it exists. I don't think much
    about it. I see it as a perpetual rainy Thursday af-
    ternoon in March. Dead leaves.
PRIOR: Feeugh. Very Greco-Roman.
LOUIS: Well for us it's not the verdict that counts,
    it's the act of judgment. That's why I could never be
    a lawyer. In court all that matters is the verdict.
PRIOR: You could never be a lawyer because you are
    oversexed. You're too distracted.
LOUIS: Not distracted; *abstracted.* I'm trying to make
    a point:
PRIOR: Namely:
LOUIS: It's the judge in his or her chambers, weighing,
    books open, pondering the evidence, ranging freely
    over categories: good, evil, innocent, guilty; the
    judge in the chamber of circumspection, not the
    judge on the bench with the gavel. The shaping of
    the law, not its execution.
PRIOR: The point, dear, the point . . .
LOUIS: That it should be the questions and shape of a
    life, its total complexity gathered, arranged and
    considered, which matters in the end, not some
    stamp of salvation or damnation which disperses
    all the complexity in some unsatisfying little deci-
    sion — the balancing of the scales . . .
PRIOR: I like this; very zen; it's . . . reassuringly incom-
    prehensible and useless. We who are about to die
    thank you.
LOUIS: You are not about to die.
PRIOR: It's not going well, really . . . two new lesions.
    My leg hurts. There's protein in my urine, the doctor
    says, but who knows what the fuck that portends.
    Anyway it shouldn't be there, the protein. My butt is
    chapped from diarrhea and yesterday I shat blood.
LOUIS: I really hate this. You don't tell me . . .
PRIOR: You get too upset, I wind up comforting you.
    It's easier . . .
LOUIS: Oh thanks.
PRIOR: If it's bad I'll tell you.
LOUIS: Shitting blood sounds bad to me.
PRIOR: And I'm telling you.
LOUIS: And I'm handling it.
PRIOR: Tell me some more about justice.
LOUIS: I *am* handling it.
PRIOR: Well Louis you win Trooper of the Month.

(*Louis starts to cry.*)

PRIOR: I take it back. You aren't Trooper of the Month.
    This isn't working . . .
    Tell me some more about justice.
LOUIS: You are not about to die.
PRIOR: Justice . . .
LOUIS: . . . is an immensity, a confusing vastness. Jus-
    tice is God.
    Prior?
PRIOR: Hmmm?
LOUIS: You love me.
PRIOR: Yes.

LOUIS: What if I walked out on this?
    Would you hate me forever?

(*Prior kisses Louis on the forehead.*)

PRIOR: Yes.

JOE: I think we ought to pray. Ask God for help. Ask
    him together . . .
HARPER: God won't talk to me. I have to make up
    people to talk to me.
JOE: You have to keep asking.
HARPER: I forgot the question.
    Oh yeah. God, is my husband a . . .
JOE (*scary*): Stop it. Stop it. I'm warning you.
    Does it make any difference? That I might be
    one thing deep within, no matter how wrong or
    ugly that thing is, so long as I have fought, with
    everything I have, to kill it. What do you want
    from me? What do you want from me, Harper?
    More than that? For God's sake, there's nothing
    left, I'm a shell. There's nothing left to kill.
    As long as my behavior is what I know it has to
    be. Decent. Correct. That alone in the eyes of God.
HARPER: No, no, not that, that's Utah talk, Mormon
    talk, I hate it, Joe, tell me, say it . . .
JOE: All I will say is that I am a very good man who
    has worked very hard to become good and you
    want to destroy that. You want to destroy me, but
    I am not going to let you do that.

(*Pause.*)

HARPER: I'm going to have a baby.
JOE: Liar.
HARPER: You liar.
    A baby born addicted to pills. A baby who does
    not dream but who hallucinates, who stares up at
    us with big mirror eyes and who does not know
    who we are.

(*Pause.*)

JOE: Are you really . . .
HARPER: No. Yes. No. Yes. Get away from me.
    Now we both have a secret.

PRIOR: One of my ancestors was a ship's captain who made money bringing whale oil to Europe and returning with immigrants — Irish mostly, packed in tight, so many dollars per head. The last ship he captained foundered off the coast of Nova Scotia in a winter tempest and sank to the bottom. He went down with the ship — la Grande Geste — but his crew took seventy women and kids in the ship's only longboat, this big, open rowboat, and when the weather got too rough, and they thought the boat was overcrowded, the crew started lifting people up and hurling them into the sea. Until they got the ballast right. They walked up and down the longboat, eyes to the waterline, and when the boat rode low in the water they'd grab the nearest passenger and throw them into the sea. The boat was leaky, see; seventy people; they arrived in Halifax with nine people on board.

LOUIS: Jesus.

PRIOR: I think about that story a lot now. People in a boat, waiting, terrified, while implacable, unsmiling men, irresistibly strong, seize . . . maybe the person next to you, maybe you, and with no warning at all, with time only for a quick intake of air you are pitched into freezing, turbulent water and salt and darkness to drown.

   I like your cosmology, baby. While time is running out I find myself drawn to anything that's suspended, that lacks an ending — but it seems to me that it lets you off scot-free.

LOUIS: What do you mean?

PRIOR: No judgment, no guilt or responsibility.

LOUIS: For me.

PRIOR: For anyone. It was an editorial "you."

LOUIS: Please get better. Please.
   Please don't get any sicker.

Scene 9

(*Third week in November. Roy and Henry, his doctor, in Henry's office.*)

HENRY: Nobody knows what causes it. And nobody knows how to cure it. The best theory is that we blame a retrovirus, the Human Immunodeficiency Virus. Its presence is made known to us by the useless antibodies which appear in reaction to its entrance into the bloodstream through a cut, or an orifice. The antibodies are powerless to protect the body against it. Why, we don't know. The body's immune system ceases to function. Sometimes the body even attacks itself. At any rate it's left open to a whole horror house of infections from microbes which it usually defends against.

Like Kaposi's sarcomas. These lesions. Or your throat problem. Or the glands.

We think it may also be able to slip past the blood-brain barrier into the brain. Which is of course very bad news.

And it's fatal in we don't know what percent of people with suppressed immune responses.

(*Pause.*)

ROY: This is very interesting, Mr. Wizard, but why the fuck are you telling me this?

(*Pause.*)

HENRY: Well, I have just removed one of three lesions which biopsy results will probably tell us is a Kaposi's sarcoma lesion. And you have a pronounced swelling of glands in your neck, groin, and armpits — lymphadenopathy is another sign. And you have oral candidiasis and maybe a little more fungus under the fingernails of two digits on your right hand. So that's why . . .

ROY: This disease . . .

HENRY: Syndrome.

ROY: Whatever. It afflicts mostly homosexuals and drug addicts.

HENRY: Mostly. Hemophiliacs are also at risk.

ROY: Homosexuals and drug addicts. So why are you implying that I . . .
   (*Pause.*)
   What are you implying, Henry?

HENRY: I don't . . .

ROY: I'm not a drug addict.

HENRY: Oh come on Roy.

ROY: What, what, come on Roy what? Do you think I'm a junkie, Henry, do you see tracks?

HENRY: This is absurd.

ROY: Say it.

HENRY: Say what?

ROY: Say, "Roy Cohn, you are a . . ."

HENRY: Roy.

ROY: "You are a. . . ." Go on. Not "Roy Cohn you are a drug fiend." "Roy Marcus Cohn, you are a . . ."
   Go on, Henry, it starts with an "H."

HENRY: Oh I'm not going to . . .

ROY: *With an "H,"* Henry, and it isn't "Hemophiliac." Come on . . .

HENRY: What are you doing, Roy?

ROY: No, say it. I mean it. Say: "Roy Cohn, you are a homosexual."
   (*Pause.*)
   And I will proceed, systematically, to destroy your reputation and your practice and your career in New York State, Henry. Which you know I can do.

(*Pause.*)

HENRY: Roy, you have been seeing me since 1958. Apart from the facelifts I have treated you for everything from syphilis . . .

ROY: From a whore in Dallas.

HENRY: From syphilis to venereal warts. In your rectum. Which you may have gotten from a whore in Dallas, but it wasn't a female whore.

(*Pause.*)

ROY: So say it.

HENRY: Roy Cohn, you are . . .

You have had sex with men, many many times, Roy, and one of them, or any number of them, has made you very sick. You have AIDS.

ROY: AIDS.

Your problem, Henry, is that you are hung up on words, on labels, that you believe they mean what they seem to mean. AIDS. Homosexual. Gay. Lesbian. You think these are names that tell you who someone sleeps with, but they don't tell you that.

HENRY: No?

ROY: No. Like all labels they tell you one thing and one thing only: where does an individual so identified fit in the food chain, in the pecking order? Not ideology, or sexual taste, but something much simpler: clout. Not who I fuck or who fucks me, but who will pick up the phone when I call, who owes me favors. This is what a label refers to. Now to someone who does not understand this, homosexual is what I am because I have sex with men. But really this is wrong. Homosexuals are not men who sleep with other men. Homosexuals are men who in fifteen years of trying cannot get a pissant antidiscrimination bill through City Council. Homosexuals are men who know nobody and who nobody knows. Who have zero clout. Does this sound like me, Henry?

HENRY: No.

ROY: No. I have clout. A lot. I can pick up this phone, punch fifteen numbers, and you know who will be on the other end in under five minutes, Henry?

HENRY: The President.

ROY: Even better, Henry. His wife.

HENRY: I'm impressed.

ROY: I don't want you to be impressed. I want you to understand. This is not sophistry. And this is not hypocrisy. This is reality. I have sex with men. But unlike nearly every other man of whom this is true, I bring the guy I'm screwing to the White House and President Reagan smiles at us and shakes his hand. Because *what* I am is defined entirely by *who* I am. Roy Cohn is not a homosexual. Roy Cohn is

a heterosexual man, Henry, who fucks around with guys.

HENRY: OK, Roy.

ROY: And what is my diagnosis, Henry?

HENRY: You have AIDS, Roy.

ROY: No, Henry, no. AIDS is what homosexuals have. I have liver cancer.

(*Pause.*)

HENRY: Well, whatever the fuck you have, Roy, it's very serious, and I haven't got a damn thing for you. The NIH in Bethesda has a new drug called AZT with a two-year waiting list that not even I can get you onto. So get on the phone, Roy, and dial the fifteen numbers, and tell the First Lady you need in on an experimental treatment for liver cancer, because you can call it any damn thing you want, Roy, but what it boils down to is very bad news.

ACT 2
IN VITRO • *December 1985–January 1986*

Scene 1

(*Night, the third week in December. Prior alone on the floor of his bedroom; he is much worse.*)

PRIOR: Louis, Louis, please wake up, oh God.

(*Louis runs in.*)

PRIOR: I think something horrible is wrong with me I can't breathe . . .

LOUIS (*starting to exit*): I'm calling the ambulance.

PRIOR: No, wait, I . . .

LOUIS: *Wait?* Are you fucking crazy? Oh God you're on fire, your head is on fire.

PRIOR: It hurts, it hurts . . .

LOUIS: I'm calling the ambulance.

PRIOR: I don't want to go to the hospital, I don't want to go to the hospital please let me lie here, just . . .

LOUIS: No, no, God, Prior, stand up . . .

PRIOR: DON'T TOUCH MY LEG!

LOUIS: We have to . . . oh God this is so crazy.

PRIOR: I'll be OK if I just lie here Lou, really, if I can only sleep a little . . .

(*Louis exits.*)

PRIOR: Louis?

NO! NO! Don't call, you'll send me there and I won't come back, please, please Louis I'm begging, baby, please . . .

(*Screams.*) LOUIS!!

LOUIS (*from off; hysterical*): WILL YOU SHUT THE FUCK UP!

PRIOR (*trying to stand*): Aaaah. I have . . . to go to the bathroom. Wait. Wait, just . . . oh. Oh God. (*He shits himself.*)

LOUIS (*entering*): Prior? They'll be here in . . . Oh my God.

PRIOR: I'm sorry, I'm sorry.

LOUIS: What did . . . ? What?

PRIOR: I had an accident.

(*Louis goes to him.*)

LOUIS: This is blood.

PRIOR: Maybe you shouldn't touch it . . . me. . . . I . . . (*He faints.*)

LOUIS (*quietly*): Oh help. Oh help. Oh God oh God oh God help me I can't I can't I can't.

Scene 2

(*Same night. Harper is sitting at home, all alone, with no lights on. We can barely see her. Joe enters, but he doesn't turn on the lights.*)

JOE: Why are you sitting in the dark? Turn on the light.

HARPER: *No.* I heard the sounds in the bedroom again. I know someone was in there.

JOE: No one was.

HARPER: Maybe actually in the bed, under the covers with a knife.
　　Oh, boy. Joe. I, um, I'm thinking of going away. By which I mean: I think I'm going off again. You . . . you know what I mean?

JOE: Please don't. Stay. We can fix it. I pray for that. This is my fault, but I can correct it. You have to try too . . .

(*He turns on the light. She turns it off again.*)

HARPER: When you pray, what do you pray for?

JOE: I pray for God to crush me, break me up into little pieces and start all over again.

HARPER: Oh. Please. Don't pray for that.

JOE: I had a book of Bible stories when I was a kid. There was a picture I'd look at twenty times every day: Jacob wrestles with the angel. I don't really remember the story, or why the wrestling — just the picture. Jacob is young and very strong. The angel is . . . a beautiful man, with golden hair and wings, of course. I still dream about it. Many nights. I'm. . . . It's me. In that struggle. Fierce, and unfair. The angel is not human, and it holds nothing back, so how could anyone human win, what kind of a fight is that? It's not just. Losing means

your soul thrown down in the dust, your heart torn out from God's. But you can't not lose.

HARPER: In the whole entire world, you are the only person, the only person I love or have ever loved. And I love you terribly. Terribly. That's what's so awfully, irreducibly real. I can make up anything but I can't dream that away.

JOE: Are you . . . are you really going to have a baby?

HARPER: It's my time, and there's no blood. I don't really know. I suppose it wouldn't be a great thing. Maybe I'm just not bleeding because I take too many pills. Maybe I'll give birth to a pill. That would give a new meaning to pill-popping, huh?
　　I think you should go to Washington. Alone. Change, like you said.

JOE: I'm not going to leave you, Harper.

HARPER: Well maybe not. But I'm going to leave you.

Scene 3

(*One AM, the next morning. Louis and a nurse, Emily, are sitting in Prior's room in the hospital.*)

EMILY: He'll be all right now.

LOUIS: No he won't.

EMILY: No. I guess not. I gave him something that makes him sleep.

LOUIS: Deep asleep?

EMILY: Orbiting the moons of Jupiter.

LOUIS: A good place to be.

EMILY: Anyplace better than here. You his . . . uh?

LOUIS: Yes. I'm his uh.

EMILY: This must be hell for you.

LOUIS: It is. Hell. The After Life. Which is not at all like a rainy afternoon in March, by the way, Prior. A lot more vivid than I'd expected. Dead leaves, but the crunchy kind. Sharp, dry air. The kind of long, luxurious dying feeling that breaks your heart.

EMILY: Yeah, well we all get to break our hearts on this one.
　　He seems like a nice guy. Cute.

LOUIS: Not like this.
　　Yes, he is. Was. Whatever.

EMILY: Weird name. Prior Walter. Like, "The Walter before this one."

LOUIS: Lots of Walters before this one. Prior is an old old family name in an old old family. The Walters go back to the Mayflower and beyond. Back to the Norman Conquest. He says there's a Prior Walter stitched into the Bayeux tapestry.

EMILY: Is that impressive?

LOUIS: Well, it's old. Very old. Which in some circles equals impressive.

EMILY: Not in my circle. What's the name of the tapestry?

LOUIS: The Bayeux tapestry. Embroidered by La Reine Mathilde.

EMILY: I'll tell my mother. She embroiders. Drives me nuts.

LOUIS: Manual therapy for anxious hands.

EMILY: Maybe you should try it.

LOUIS: Mathilde stitched while William the Conqueror was off to war. She was capable of ... more than loyalty. Devotion.

She waited for him, she stitched for years. And if he had come back broken and defeated from war, she would have loved him even more. And if he had returned mutilated, ugly, full of infection and horror, she would still have loved him; fed by pity, by a sharing of pain, she would love him even more, and even more, and she would never, never have prayed to God, please let him die if he can't return to me whole and healthy and able to live a normal life.... If he had died, she would have buried her heart with him.

So what the fuck is the matter with me?

(*Little pause.*)

Will he sleep through the night?

EMILY: At least.

LOUIS: I'm going.

EMILY: Its one AM. Where do you have to go at ...

LOUIS: I know what time it is. A walk. Night air, good for the.... The park.

EMILY: Be careful.

LOUIS: Yeah. Danger.

Tell him, if he wakes up and you're still on, tell him goodbye, tell him I had to go.

Scene 4

(*An hour later. Split scene. Joe and Roy in a fancy [straight] bar; Louis and a Man in the Rambles in Central Park. Joe and Roy are sitting at the bar; the place is brightly lit. Joe has a plate of food in front of him but he isn't eating. Roy occasionally reaches over the table and forks small bites off Joe's plate. Roy is drinking heavily, Joe not at all. Louis and the Man are eyeing each other, each alternating interest and indifference.*)

JOE: The pills were something she started when she miscarried or ... no, she took some before that. She had a really bad time at home, when she was a kid, her home was really bad. I think a lot of drinking and physical stuff. She doesn't talk about that, instead she talks about ... the sky falling down, people with knives hiding under sofas. Monsters. Mormons. Everyone thinks Mormons don't come from homes like that, we aren't supposed to behave that way, but we do. It's not lying,

or being two-faced. Everyone tries very hard to live up to God's strictures, which are very ... um ...

ROY: Strict.

JOE: I shouldn't be bothering you with this.

ROY: No, please. Heart to heart. Want another.... What is that, seltzer?

JOE: The failure to measure up hits people very hard. From such a strong desire to be good they feel very far from goodness when they fail.

What scares me is that maybe what I really love in her is the part of her that's farthest from the light, from God's love; maybe I was drawn to that in the first place. And I'm keeping it alive because I need it.

ROY: Why would you need it?

JOE: There are things.... I don't know how well we know ourselves. I mean, what if? I know I married her because she ... because I loved it that she was always wrong, always doing something wrong, like one step out of step. In Salt Lake City that stands out. I never stood out, on the outside, but inside, it was hard for me. To pass.

ROY: Pass?

JOE: Yeah.

ROY: Pass as what?

JOE: Oh. Well.... As someone cheerful and strong. Those who love God with an open heart unclouded by secrets and struggles are cheerful; God's easy simple love for them shows in how strong and happy they are. The saints.

ROY: But you had secrets? Secret struggles ...

JOE: I wanted to be one of the elect, one of the Blessed. You feel you ought to be, that the blemishes are yours by choice, which of course they aren't. Harper's sorrow, that really deep sorrow, she didn't choose that. But it's there.

ROY: You didn't put it there.

JOE: No.

ROY: You sound like you think you did.

JOE: I am responsible for her.

ROY: Because she's your wife.

JOE: That. And I do love her.

ROY: Whatever. She's your wife. And so there are obligations. To her. But also to yourself.

JOE: She'd fall apart in Washington.

ROY: Then let her stay here.

JOE: She'll fall apart if I leave her.

ROY: Then bring her to Washington.

JOE: I just can't, Roy. She needs me.

ROY: Listen, Joe. I'm the best divorce lawyer in the business.

(*Little pause.*)

JOE: Can't Washington wait?

ROY: You do what you need to do, Joe. What *you* need. *You.* Let her life go where it wants to go.

You'll both be better for that. *Somebody* should get what they want.

MAN: What do you want?
LOUIS: I want you to fuck me, hurt me, make me bleed.
MAN: I want to.
LOUIS: Yeah?
MAN: I want to hurt you.
LOUIS: Fuck me.
MAN: Yeah?
LOUIS: Hard.
MAN: Yeah? You been a bad boy?

(*Pause. Louis laughs, softly.*)

LOUIS: Very bad. Very bad.
MAN: You need to be punished, boy?
LOUIS: Yes. I do.
MAN: Yes what?

(*Little pause.*)

LOUIS: Um, I . . .
MAN: Yes *what,* boy?
LOUIS: Oh. Yes sir.
MAN: I want you to take me to your place, boy.
LOUIS: No, I can't do that.
MAN: No *what?*
LOUIS: No sir, I can't, I . . .
    I don't live alone, sir.
MAN: Your lover know you're out with a man tonight, boy?
LOUIS: No sir, he . . .
    My lover doesn't know.
MAN: Your lover know you . . .
LOUIS: Let's change the subject, OK? Can we go to your place?
MAN: I live with my parents.
LOUIS: Oh.

ROY: Everyone who makes it in this world makes it because somebody older and more powerful takes an interest. The most precious asset in life, I think, is the ability to be a good son. You have that, Joe. Somebody who can be a good son to a father who pushes them farther than they would otherwise go. I've had many fathers, I owe my life to them, powerful, powerful men. Walter Winchell, Edgar Hoover. Joe McCarthy most of all. He valued me because I am a good lawyer, but he loved me because I was and am a good son. He was a very difficult man, very guarded and cagey; I brought out something tender in him. He would have died for me. And me for him. Does this embarrass you?
JOE: I had a hard time with my father.
ROY: Well sometimes that's the way. Then you have to find other fathers, substitutes, I don't know. The father-son relationship is central to life. Women are for birth, beginning, but the father is continuance. The son offers the father his life as a vessel for carrying forth his father's dream. Your father's living?
JOE: Um, dead.
ROY: He was . . . what? A difficult man?
JOE: He was in the military. He could be very unfair. And cold.
ROY: But he loved you.
JOE: I don't know.
ROY: No, no, Joe, he did, I know this. Sometimes a father's love has to be very, very hard, unfair even, cold to make his son grow strong in a world like this. This isn't a good world.

MAN: Here, then.
LOUIS: I. . . . Do you have a rubber?
MAN: I don't use rubbers.
LOUIS: You should. (*He takes one from his coat pocket.*) Here.
MAN: I don't use them.
LOUIS: Forget it, then. (*He starts to leave.*)
MAN: No, wait.
    Put it on me. Boy.
LOUIS: Forget it, I have to get back. Home. I must be going crazy.
MAN: Oh come on please he won't find out.
LOUIS: It's cold. Too cold.
MAN: It's never too cold, let me warm you up. Please?

(*They begin to fuck.*)

MAN: Relax.
LOUIS (*a small laugh*): Not a chance.
MAN: It . . .
LOUIS: What?
MAN: I think it broke. The rubber. You want me to keep going? (*Little pause.*) Pull out? Should I . . .
LOUIS: Keep going.
    Infect me.
    I don't care. I don't care.

(*Pause. The Man pulls out.*)

MAN: I . . . um, look, I'm sorry, but I think I want to go.
LOUIS: Yeah.
    Give my best to mom and dad.

(*The Man slaps him.*)

LOUIS: Ow!

(*They stare at each other.*)

LOUIS: It was a joke.

(*The Man leaves.*)

ROY: How long have we known each other?
JOE: Since 1980.

ROY: Right. A long time. I feel close to you, Joe. Do I advise you well?

JOE: You've been an incredible friend, Roy, I . . .

ROY: I want to be family. Familia, as my Italian friends call it. La Familia. A lovely word. It's important for me to help you, like I was helped.

JOE: I owe practically everything to you, Roy.

ROY: I'm dying, Joe. Cancer.

JOE: Oh my God.

ROY: Please. Let me finish.

 Few people know this and I'm telling you this only because. . . . I'm not afraid of death. What can death bring that I haven't faced? I've lived; life is the worst. (*Gently mocking himself.*) Listen to me, I'm a philosopher.

 Joe. You must do this. You must must must. Love; that's a trap. Responsibility; that's a trap too. Like a father to a son I tell you this: Life is full of horror; nobody escapes, nobody; save yourself. Whatever pulls on you, whatever needs from you, threatens you. Don't be afraid; people are so afraid; don't be afraid to live in the raw wind, naked, alone. . . . Learn at least this: What you are capable of. Let nothing stand in your way.

Scene 5

(*Three days later. Prior and Belize in Prior's hospital room. Prior is very sick but improving. Belize has just arrived.*)

PRIOR: Miss Thing.

BELIZE: Ma cherie bichette.

PRIOR: Stella.

BELIZE: Stella for star. Let me see. (*Scrutinizing Prior.*) You look like shit, why yes indeed you do, comme la merde!°

PRIOR: Merci.

BELIZE (*taking little plastic bottles from his bag, handing them to Prior*): Not to despair, Belle Reeve. Lookie! Magic goop!

PRIOR (*opening a bottle, sniffing*): Pooh! What kinda crap is that?

BELIZE: Beats me. Let's rub it on your poor blistered body and see what it does.

PRIOR: This is not Western medicine, these bottles . . .

BELIZE: Voodoo cream. From the botanica° 'round the block.

PRIOR: And you a registered nurse.

BELIZE (*sniffing it*): Beeswax and cheap perfume. Cut

with Jergen's Lotion. Full of good vibes and love from some little black Cubana witch in Miami.

PRIOR: Get that trash away from me, I am immune-suppressed.

BELIZE: I *am* a health professional. I *know* what I'm doing.

PRIOR: It stinks. Any word from Louis?

(*Pause. Belize starts giving Prior a gentle massage.*)

PRIOR: Gone.

BELIZE: He'll be back. I know the type. Likes to keep a girl on edge.

PRIOR: It's been . . .

(*Pause.*)

BELIZE (*trying to jog his memory*): How long?

PRIOR: I don't remember.

BELIZE: How long have you been here?

PRIOR (*getting suddenly upset*): I don't remember, I don't give a fuck. I want Louis. I want my fucking boyfriend, where the fuck is he? I'm dying, I'm dying, where's Louis?

BELIZE: Shhhh, shhh . . .

PRIOR: This is a very strange drug, this drug. Emotional lability, for starters.

BELIZE: Save a tab or two for me.

PRIOR: Oh no, not this drug, ce n'est pas pour la joyeux noël et la bonne année, this drug she is serious poisonous chemistry, ma pauvre bichette.°

 And not just disorienting. I hear things. Voices.

BELIZE: Voices.

PRIOR: A voice.

BELIZE: Saying what?

(*Pause.*)

PRIOR: I'm not supposed to tell.

BELIZE: You better tell the doctor. Or I will.

PRIOR: No no don't. Please. I want the voice; it's wonderful. It's all that's keeping me alive. I don't want to talk to some intern about it.

 You know what happens? When I hear it, I get hard.

BELIZE: Oh my.

PRIOR: Comme ça. (*He uses his arm to demonstrate.*) And you know I am slow to rise.

BELIZE: My jaw aches at the memory.

PRIOR: And would you deny me this little solace — betray my concupiscence to Florence Nightingale's storm troopers?

BELIZE: Perish the thought, ma bébé.°

---

comme la merde: Like shit.
botanica: Shop that sells magic charms and herbs.

ce n'est pas . . . bichette: This drug isn't for a merry Christmas or a happy new year . . . my poor little bitch.
ma bébé: My baby.

PRIOR: They'd change the drug just to spoil the fun.

BELIZE: You and your boner can depend on me.

PRIOR: Je t'adore, ma belle nègre.°

BELIZE: All this girl-talk shit is politically incorrect, you know. We should have dropped it back when we gave up drag.

PRIOR: I'm sick, I get to be politically incorrect if it makes me feel better. You sound like Lou.

(*Little pause.*)

Well, at least I have the satisfaction of knowing he's in anguish somewhere. I loved his anguish. Watching him stick his head up his asshole and eat his guts out over some relatively minor moral conundrum — it was the best show in town. But Mother warned me: if they get overwhelmed by the little things . . .

BELIZE: They'll be belly-up bustville when something big comes along.

PRIOR: Mother warned me.

BELIZE: And they do come along.

PRIOR: But I didn't listen.

BELIZE: No. (*Doing Hepburn.*) Men are beasts.

PRIOR (*also Hepburn*): The absolute lowest.

BELIZE: I have to go. If I want to spend my whole lonely life looking after white people I can get underpaid to do it.

PRIOR: You're just a Christian martyr.

BELIZE: Whatever happens, baby, I will be here for you.

PRIOR: Je t'aime.°

BELIZE: Je t'aime. Don't go crazy on me, girlfriend, I already got enough crazy queens for one lifetime. For two. I can't be bothering with dementia.

PRIOR: I promise.

BELIZE (*touching him; softly*): Ouch.

PRIOR: Ouch. Indeed.

BELIZE: Why'd they have to pick on you?

And eat more, girlfriend, you really do look like shit.

(*Belize leaves.*)

PRIOR (*after waiting a beat*): He's gone.

Are you still . . .

VOICE: I can't stay. I will return.

PRIOR: Are you one of those "Follow me to the other side" voices?

VOICE: No. I am no nightbird. I am a messenger . . .

PRIOR: You have a beautiful voice, it sounds . . . like a viola, like a perfectly tuned, tight string, balanced, the truth. . . . Stay with me.

VOICE: Not now. Soon I will return, I will reveal my-self to you; I am glorious, glorious; my heart, my countenance and my message. You must prepare.

PRIOR: For what? I don't want to . . .

VOICE: No death, no:

A marvelous work and a wonder we undertake, an edifice awry we sink plumb and straighten, a great Lie we abolish, a great error correct, with the rule, sword and broom of Truth!

PRIOR: What are you talking about, I . . .

VOICE:

I am on my way; when I am manifest, our Work begins:

Prepare for the parting of the air,

The breath, the ascent,

Glory to . . .

Scene 6

(*The second week of January. Martin, Roy and Joe in a fancy Manhattan restaurant.*)

MARTIN: It's a revolution in Washington, Joe. We have a new agenda and finally a real leader. They got back the Senate but we have the courts. By the nineties the Supreme Court will be block-solid Republican appointees, and the Federal bench — Republican judges like land mines, everywhere, everywhere they turn. Affirmative action? Take it to court. Boom! Land mine. And we'll get our way on just about everything: abortion, defense, Central America, family values, a live investment climate. We have the White House locked till the year 2000. And beyond. A permanent fix on the Oval Office? It's possible. By '92 we'll get the Senate back, and in ten years the South is going to give us the House. It's really the end of Liberalism. The end of New Deal Socialism. The end of ipso facto secular humanism. The dawning of a genuinely American political personality. Modeled on Ronald Wilson Reagan.

JOE: It sounds great, Mr. Heller.

MARTIN: Martin. And Justice is the hub. Especially since Ed Meese took over. He doesn't specialize in Fine Points of the Law. He's a flatfoot, a cop. He reminds me of Teddy Roosevelt.

JOE: I can't wait to meet him.

MARTIN: Too bad, Joe, he's been dead for sixty years!

(*There is a little awkwardness. Joe doesn't respond.*)

MARTIN: Teddy Roosevelt. You said you wanted to. . . . Little joke. It reminds me of the story about the . . .

ROY (*smiling, but nasty*): Aw shut the fuck up Martin.

(*To Joe.*) You see that? Mr. Heller here is one of the mighty, Joseph, in D.C. he sitteth on the right

---

Je t'adore . . . nègre: I adore you, my beautiful negro.

Je t'aime: I love you.

hand of the man who sitteth on the right hand of The Man. And yet I can say "shut the fuck up" and he will take no offense. Loyalty. He . . .
  Martin?
MARTIN: Yes, Roy?
ROY: Rub my back.
MARTIN: Roy . . .
ROY: No no really, a sore spot, I get them all the time now, these. . . . Rub it for me darling, would you do that for me?

(*Martin rubs Roy's back. They both look at Joe.*)

ROY (*to Joe*): How do you think a handful of Bolsheviks turned St. Petersburg into Leningrad in one afternoon? *Comrades.* Who do for each other. Marx and Engels. Lenin and Trotsky. Josef Stalin and Franklin Delano Roosevelt.

(*Martin laughs.*)

ROY: *Comrades,* right Martin?
MARTIN: This man, Joe, is a Saint of the Right.
JOE: I know, Mr. Heller, I . . .
ROY: And you see what I mean, Martin? He's special, right?
MARTIN: Don't embarrass him, Roy.
ROY: Gravity, decency, smarts! His strength is as the strength of ten because his heart is pure! *And* he's a Royboy, one hundred percent.
MARTIN: We're on the move, Joe. On the move.
JOE: Mr. Heller, I . . .
MARTIN (*ending backrub*): We can't wait any longer for an answer.

(*Little pause.*)

JOE: Oh. Um, I . . .
ROY: Joe's a married man, Martin.
MARTIN: Aha.
ROY: With a wife. She doesn't care to go to D.C., and so Joe cannot go. And keeps us dangling. We've seen that kind of thing before, haven't we? These men and their wives.
MARTIN: Oh yes. Beware.
JOE: I really can't discuss this under . . .
MARTIN: Then *don't* discuss. Say yes, Joe.
ROY: Now.
MARTIN: Say yes I will.
ROY: Now.
  Now. I'll hold my breath till you do, I'm turning blue waiting. . . . *Now,* goddammit!
MARTIN: Roy, calm down, it's not . . .
ROY: Aw, fuck it. (*He takes a letter from his jacket pocket, hands it to Joe.*)
  Read. Came today.

(*Joe reads the first paragraph, then looks up.*)

JOE: Roy. This is . . . Roy, this is terrible.
ROY: You're telling me.
  A letter from the New York State Bar Association, Martin.
  They're gonna try and disbar me.
MARTIN: Oh my.
JOE: Why?
ROY: Why, Martin?
MARTIN: Revenge.
ROY: The whole Establishment. Their little rules. Because I know no rules. Because I don't see the Law as a dead and arbitrary collection of antiquated dictums, thou shall, thou shalt not, because, because I know the Law's a pliable, breathing, sweating . . . *organ,* because, because . . .
MARTIN: Because he borrowed half a million from one of his clients.
ROY: Yeah, well, there's that.
MARTIN: *And* he forgot to *return* it.
JOE: Roy, that's. . . . You borrowed money from a client?
ROY: I'm deeply ashamed.

(*Little pause.*)

JOE (*very sympathetic*): Roy, you know how much I admire you. Well I mean I know you have unorthodox ways, but I'm sure you only did what you thought at the time you needed to do. And I have faith that . . .
ROY: Not so damp, please. I'll deny it was a loan. She's got no paperwork. Can't prove a fucking thing.

(*Little pause. Martin studies the menu.*)

JOE (*handing back the letter, more official in tone*): Roy I really appreciate your telling me this, and I'll do whatever I can to help.
ROY (*holding up a hand, then, carefully*): I'll tell you what you can do.
  I'm about to be tried, Joe, by a jury that is not a jury of my peers. The disbarment committee: genteel gentleman Brahmin lawyers, country-club men. I offend them, to these men . . . I'm what, Martin, some sort of filthy little Jewish troll?
MARTIN: Oh well, I wouldn't go so far as . . .
ROY: Oh well I would.
  Very fancy lawyers, these disbarment committee lawyers, fancy lawyers with fancy corporate clients and complicated cases. Antitrust suits. Deregulation. Environmental control. Complex cases like these need Justice Department cooperation like flowers need the sun. Wouldn't you say that's an accurate assessment, Martin?
MARTIN: I'm not here, Roy. I'm not hearing any of this.

ROY: No. Of course not.
Without the light of the sun, Joe, these cases, and the fancy lawyers who represent them, will wither and die.
A well-placed friend, someone in the Justice Department, say, can turn off the sun. Cast a deep shadow on my behalf. Make them shiver in the cold. If they overstep. They would fear that.

(*Pause.*)

JOE: Roy. I don't understand.
ROY: You do.

(*Pause.*)

JOE: You're not asking me to . . .
ROY: Sssshhhh. Careful.
JOE (*a beat, then*): Even if I said yes to the job, it would be illegal to interfere. With the hearings. It's unethical. No. I can't.
ROY: Un-ethical.
Would you excuse us, Martin?
MARTIN: Excuse you?
ROY: Take a walk, Martin. For real.

(*Martin leaves.*)

ROY: Un-ethical. Are you trying to embarrass me in front of my friend?
JOE: Well it is unethical, I can't . . .
ROY: Boy, you are really something. What the fuck do you think this is, Sunday School?
JOE: No, but Roy this is . . .
ROY: This is . . . this is gastric juices churning, this is enzymes and acids, this is intestinal is what this is, bowel movement and blood-red meat — this stinks, this is *politics*, Joe, the game of being alive. And you think you're. . . . What? Above that? Above alive is what? Dead! In the clouds! You're on earth, goddammit! Plant a foot, stay a while.
I'm sick. They smell I'm weak. They want blood this time. I must have eyes in Justice. In Justice you will protect me.
JOE: Why can't Mr. Heller . . .
ROY: Grow up, Joe. The administration can't get involved.
JOE: But I'd be part of the administration. The same as him.
ROY: Not the same. Martin's Ed's man. And Ed's Reagan's man. So Martin's Reagan's man.
And you're mine.
(*Little pause. He holds up the letter.*)
This will never be. Understand me?
(*He tears the letter up.*)
I'm gonna be a lawyer, Joe, I'm gonna be a lawyer, Joe, I'm gonna be a goddam motherfuck-ing legally licensed member of the bar lawyer, just like my daddy was, till my last bitter day on earth, Joseph, until the day I die.

(*Martin returns.*)

ROY: Ah, Martin's back.
MARTIN: So are we agreed?
ROY: Joe?

(*Little pause.*)

JOE: I will think about it.
(*To Roy.*) I will.
ROY: Huh.
MARTIN: It's the fear of what comes after the doing that makes the doing hard to do.
ROY: Amen.
MARTIN: But you can almost always live with the consequences.

Scene 7

(*That afternoon. On the granite steps outside the Hall of Justice, Brooklyn. It is cold and sunny. A Sabrett wagon is selling hot dogs. Louis, in a shabby overcoat, is sitting on the steps contemplatively eating one. Joe enters with three hot dogs and a can of Coke.*)

JOE: Can I . . . ?
LOUIS: Oh sure. Sure. Crazy cold sun.
JOE (*sitting*): Have to make the best of it.
How's your friend?
LOUIS: My . . . ? Oh. He's worse. My friend is worse.
JOE: I'm sorry.
LOUIS: Yeah, well. Thanks for asking. It's nice. You're nice. I can't believe you voted for Reagan.
JOE: I hope he gets better.
LOUIS: Reagan?
JOE: Your friend.
LOUIS: He won't. Neither will Reagan.
JOE: Let's not talk politics, OK?
LOUIS (*pointing to Joe's lunch*): You're eating *three* of those?
JOE: Well . . . I'm . . . hungry.
LOUIS: They're really terrible for you. Full of rat-poo and beetle legs and wood shavings 'n' shit.
JOE: Huh.
LOUIS: And . . . um . . . irridium, I think. Something toxic.
JOE: You're eating one.
LOUIS: Yeah, well, the shape, I can't help myself, plus I'm *trying* to commit suicide, what's your excuse?
JOE: I don't have an excuse. I just have Pepto-Bismol.

(*Joe takes a bottle of Pepto-Bismol and chugs it. Louis shudders audibly.*)

JOE: Yeah I know but then I wash it down with Coke.

(*He does this. Louis mimes barfing in Joes lap. Joe pushes Louis's head away.*)

JOE: Are you *always* like this?

LOUIS: I've been worrying a lot about his kids.

JOE: Whose?

LOUIS: Reagan's. Maureen and Mike and little orphan Patti and Miss Ron Reagan Jr., the you-should-pardon-the-expression heterosexual.

JOE: Ron Reagan Jr. is *not*. . . . You shouldn't just make these assumptions about people. How do you know? About him? What he is? You don't know.

LOUIS (*doing Tallulah*): Well darling he never sucked *my* cock but . . .

JOE: Look, if you're going to get vulgar . . .

LOUIS: No no really I mean. . . . What's it like to be the child of the Zeitgeist? To have the American Animus as your dad? It's not really a *family*, the Reagans, I read *People*, there aren't any connections there, no love, they don't ever even speak to each other except through their agents. So what's it like to be Reagan's kid? Enquiring minds want to know.

JOE: You can't believe everything you . . .

LOUIS (*looking away*): But . . . I think we all know what that's like. Nowadays. No connections. No responsibilities. All of us . . . falling through the cracks that separate what we owe to our selves and . . . and what we owe to love.

JOE: You just. . . . Whatever you feel like saying or doing, you don't care, you just . . . do it.

LOUIS: Do what?

JOE: It. Whatever. Whatever it is you want to do.

LOUIS: Are you trying to tell me something?

(*Little pause, sexual. They stare at each other. Joe looks away.*)

JOE: No, I'm just observing that you . . .

LOUIS: Impulsive.

JOE: Yes, I mean it must be scary, you . . .

LOUIS (*shrugs*): Land of the free. Home of the brave. Call me irresponsible.

JOE: It's kind of terrifying.

LOUIS: Yeah, well, freedom is. Heartless, too.

JOE: Oh you're not heartless.

LOUIS: You don't know.
      Finish your weenie.

(*He pats Joe on the knee, starts to leave.*)

JOE: Um . . .

(*Louis turns, looks at him. Joe searches for something to say.*)

JOE: Yesterday was Sunday but I've been a little unfocused recently and I thought it was Monday. So I came here like I was going to work. And the whole place was empty. And at first I couldn't figure out why, and I had this moment of incredible . . . fear and also. . . . It just flashed through my mind: The whole Hall of Justice, it's empty, it's deserted, it's gone out of business. Forever. The people that make it run have up and abandoned it.

LOUIS (*looking at the building*): Creepy.

JOE: Well yes but. I felt that I was going to scream. Not because it was creepy, but because the emptiness felt so *fast*.
      And . . . well, good. A . . . happy scream.
      I just wondered what a thing it would be . . . if overnight everything you owe anything to, justice, or love, had really gone away. Free.
      It would be . . . heartless terror. Yes. Terrible, and . . .
      Very great. To shed your skin, every old skin, one by one and then walk away, unencumbered, into the morning.
      (*Little pause. He looks at the building.*)
      I can't go in there today.

LOUIS: Then don't.

JOE (*not really hearing Louis*): I can't go in, I need . . .
      (*He looks for what he needs. He takes a swig of Pepto-Bismol*)
      I can't be this anymore. I need . . . a change, I should just . . .

LOUIS (*not a come-on, necessarily; he doesn't want to be alone*): Want some company? For whatever?

(*Pause. Joe looks at Louis and looks away, afraid. Louis shrugs.*)

LOUIS: Sometimes, even if it scares you to death, you have to be willing to break the law. Know what I mean?

(*Another little pause.*)

JOE: Yes.

(*Another little pause.*)

LOUIS: I moved out. I moved out on my . . .
      I haven't been sleeping well.

JOE: Me neither.

(*Louis goes up to Joe, licks his napkin and dabs at Joes mouth.*)

LOUIS: Antacid moustache.
      (*Points to the building.*) Maybe the court won't convene. Ever again. Maybe we are free. To do whatever.
      Children of the new morning, criminal minds.

Selfish and greedy and loveless and blind. Reagan's children.

    You're scared. So am I. Everybody is in the land of the free. God help us all.

Scene 8

(*Late that night. Joe at a payphone phoning Hannah at home in Salt Lake City.*)

JOE: Mom?

HANNAH: Joe?

JOE: Hi.

HANNAH: You're calling from the street. It's . . . it must be four in the morning. What's happened?

JOE: Nothing, nothing, I . . .

HANNAH: It's Harper. Is Harper. . . . Joe? Joe?

JOE: Yeah, hi. No, Harper's fine. Well, no, she's . . . not fine. How are you, Mom?

HANNAH: What's happened?

JOE: I just wanted to talk to you. I, uh, wanted to try something out on you.

HANNAH: Joe, you haven't . . . have you been drinking, Joe?

JOE: Yes ma'am. I'm drunk.

HANNAH: That isn't like you.

JOE: No. I mean, who's to say?

HANNAH: Why are you out on the street at four AM? In that crazy city. It's dangerous.

JOE: Actually, Mom, I'm not on the street. I'm near the boathouse in the park.

HANNAH: What park?

JOE: Central Park.

HANNAH: CENTRAL PARK! Oh my Lord. What on earth are you doing in Central Park at this time of night? Are you . . .
    Joe, I think you ought to go home right now. Call me from home.
    (*Little pause.*)
    Joe?

JOE: I come here to watch, Mom. Sometimes. Just to watch.

HANNAH: Watch what? What's there to watch at four in the . . .

JOE: Mom, did Dad love me?

HANNAH: What?

JOE: Did he?

HANNAH: You ought to go home and call from there.

JOE: Answer.

HANNAH: Oh now really. This is maudlin. I don't like this conversation.

JOE: Yeah, well, it gets worse from here on.

(*Pause.*)

HANNAH: Joe?

JOE: Mom. Momma. I'm a homosexual, Momma.
    Boy, did that come out awkward.
    (*Pause.*)
    Hello? Hello?
    I'm a homosexual.
    (*Pause.*)
    Please, Momma. Say something.

HANNAH: You're old enough to understand that your father didn't love you without being ridiculous about it.

JOE: What?

HANNAH: You're ridiculous. You're being ridiculous.

JOE: I'm . . .
    What?

HANNAH: You really ought to go home now to your wife. I need to go to bed. This phone call. . . . We will just forget this phone call.

JOE: Mom.

HANNAH: No more talk. Tonight. This . . .
    (*Suddenly very angry.*) Drinking is a sin! A sin! I raised you better than that. (*She hangs up.*)

Scene 9

(*The following morning, early. Split scene: Harper and Joe at home; Louis and Prior in Prior's hospital room. Joe and Louis have just entered. This should be fast and obviously furious; overlapping is fine; the proceedings may be a little confusing but not the final results.*)

HARPER: Oh God. Home. The moment of truth has arrived.

JOE: Harper.

LOUIS: I'm going to move out.

PRIOR: The fuck you are.

JOE: Harper. Please listen. I still love you very much. You're still my best buddy; I'm not going to leave you.

HARPER: No, I don't like the sound of this. I'm leaving.

LOUIS: I'm leaving.
    I already have.

JOE: Please listen. Stay. This is really hard. We have to talk.

HARPER: We are talking. Aren't we. Now please shut up. OK?

PRIOR: Bastard. Sneaking off while I'm flat out here, that's low. If I could get up now I'd beat the holy shit out of you.

JOE: Did you take pills? How many?

HARPER: No pills. Bad for the . . . (*Pats stomach.*)

JOE: You aren't pregnant. I called your gynecologist.

HARPER: I'm seeing a new gynecologist.

PRIOR: You have no right to do this.

LOUIS: Oh, that's ridiculous.

PRIOR: No right. It's criminal.

JOE: Forget about that. Just listen. You want the truth. This is the truth.

I knew this when I married you. I've known this I guess for as long as I've known anything, but... I don't know, I thought maybe that with enough effort and will I could change myself...but I can't...

PRIOR: Criminal.

LOUIS: There oughta be a law.

PRIOR: There is a law. You'll see.

JOE: I'm losing ground here, I go walking, you want to know where I walk, I... go to the park, or up and down 53rd Street, or places where.... And I keep swearing I won't go walking again, but I just can't.

LOUIS: I need some privacy.

PRIOR: That's new.

LOUIS: Everything's new, Prior.

JOE: I try to tighten my heart into a knot, a snarl, I try to learn to live dead, just numb, but then I see someone I want, and it's like a nail, like a hot spike right through my chest, and I know I'm losing.

PRIOR: Apartment too small for three? Louis and Prior comfy but not Louis and Prior and Prior's disease?

LOUIS: Something like that.

I won't be judged by you. This isn't a crime, just — the inevitable consequence of people who run out of — whose limitations....

PRIOR: Bang bang bang. The court will come to order.

LOUIS: I mean let's talk practicalities, schedules; I'll come over if you want, spend nights with you when I can, I can...

PRIOR: Has the jury reached a verdict?

LOUIS: I'm doing the best I can.

PRIOR: Pathetic. Who cares?

JOE: My whole life has conspired to bring me to this place, and I can't despise my whole life. I think I believed when I met you I could save you, you at least if not myself, but...

I don't have any sexual feelings for you, Harper. And I don't think I ever did.

(*Little pause.*)

HARPER: I think you should go.

JOE: Where?

HARPER: Washington. Doesn't matter.

JOE: What are you talking about?

HARPER: Without me.

Without me, Joe. Isn't that what you want to hear?

(*Little pause.*)

JOE: You.

LOUIS: You can love someone and fail them. You can love someone and not be able to...

PRIOR: You *can,* theoretically, yes. A person can, maybe an editorial "you" can love, Louis, but not *you,* specifically you, I don't know, I think you are excluded from that general category.

HARPER: You were going to save me, but the whole time you were spinning a lie. I just don't understand that.

PRIOR: A person could theoretically love and maybe many do but we both know now you can't.

LOUIS: I do.

PRIOR: You can't even say it.

LOUIS: I love you, Prior.

PRIOR: I repeat. Who cares?

HARPER: This is so scary, I want this to stop, to go back...

PRIOR: We have reached a verdict, your honor. This man's heart is deficient. He loves, but his love is worth nothing.

JOE: Harper...

HARPER: Mr. Lies, I want to get away from here. Far away. Right now. Before he starts talking again. Please, please...

JOE: As long as I've known you Harper you've been afraid of...Of men hiding under the bed, men hiding under the sofa, men with knives.

PRIOR (*shattered; almost pleading; trying to reach him*): I'm dying! You stupid fuck! Do you know what that is! Love! Do you know what love means? We lived together four-and-a-half years, you animal, you idiot.

LOUIS: I have to find some way to save myself.

JOE: Who are these men? I never understood it. Now I know.

HARPER: What?

JOE: It's me.

HARPER: It is?

PRIOR: GET OUT OF MY ROOM!

JOE: I'm the man with the knives.

HARPER: You are?

PRIOR: If I could get up now I'd kill you. I would. Go away. Go away or I'll scream.

HARPER: Oh God...

JOE: I'm sorry...

HARPER: It is you.

LOUIS: Please don't scream.

PRIOR: Go.

HARPER: I recognize you now.

LOUIS: Please...

JOE: Oh. Wait, I. . . . Oh!

(*He covers his mouth with his hand, gags, and removes his hand, red with blood.*)

I'm bleeding.

(*Prior screams.*)

HARPER: Mr. Lies.

MR. LIES (*appearing, dressed in antarctic explorer's apparel*): Right here.

HARPER: I want to go away. I can't see him anymore.

MR. LIES: Where?

HARPER: Anywhere. Far away.

MR. LIES: Absolutamento.

(*Harper and Mr. Lies vanish. Joe looks up, sees that she's gone.*)

PRIOR (*closing his eyes*): When I open my eyes you'll be gone.

(*Louis leaves.*)

JOE: Harper?

PRIOR (*opening his eyes*): Huh. It worked.

JOE (*calling*): Harper?

PRIOR: I hurt all over. I wish I was dead.

Scene 10

(*The same day, sunset. Hannah and Sister Ella Chapter, a real-estate saleswoman, Hannah Pitt's closest friend, in front of Hannah's house in Salt Lake City.*)

SISTER ELLA CHAPTER: Look at that view! A view of heaven. Like the living city of heaven, isn't it, it just fairly glimmers in the sun.

HANNAH: Glimmers.

SISTER ELLA CHAPTER: Even the stone and brick it just glimmers and glitters like heaven in the sunshine. Such a nice view you get, perched up on a canyon rim. Some kind of beautiful place.

HANNAH: It's just Salt Lake, and you're selling the house *for* me, not *to* me.

SISTER ELLA CHAPTER: I like to work up an enthusiasm for my properties.

HANNAH: Just get me a good price.

SISTER ELLA CHAPTER: Well, the market's off.

HANNAH: At least fifty.

SISTER ELLA CHAPTER: Forty'd be more like it.

HANNAH: Fifty.

SISTER ELLA CHAPTER: Wish you'd wait a bit.

HANNAH: Well I can't.

SISTER ELLA CHAPTER: Wish you would. You're about the only friend I got.

HANNAH: Oh well now.

SISTER ELLA CHAPTER: Know why I decided to like you? I decided to like you 'cause you're the only unfriendly Mormon I ever met.

HANNAH: Your wig is crooked.

SISTER ELLA CHAPTER: Fix it.

(*Hannah straightens Sister Ella's wig.*)

SISTER ELLA CHAPTER: New York City. All they got there is tiny rooms.

I always thought: People ought to stay put. That's why I got my license to sell real estate. It's a way of saying: Have a house! Stay put! It's a way of saying traveling's no good. Plus I needed the cash. (*She takes a pack of cigarettes out of her purse, lights one, offers pack to Hannah.*)

HANNAH: Not out here, anyone could come by.

There's been days I've stood at this ledge and thought about stepping over.

It's a hard place, Salt Lake: baked dry. Abundant energy; not much intelligence. That's a combination that can wear a body out. No harm looking someplace else. I don't need much room.

My sister-in-law Libby thinks there's radon gas in the basement.

SISTER ELLA CHAPTER: Is there gas in the . . .

HANNAH: Of course not. Libby's a fool.

SISTER ELLA CHAPTER: 'Cause I'd have to include that in the description.

HANNAH: There's no gas, Ella. (*Little pause.*) Give a puff. (*She takes a furtive drag of Ella's cigarette.*) Put it away now.

SISTER ELLA CHAPTER: So I guess it's goodbye.

HANNAH: You'll be all right, Ella, I wasn't ever much of a friend.

SISTER ELLA CHAPTER: I'll say something but don't laugh, OK?

This is the home of saints, the godliest place on earth, they say, and I think they're right. That mean there's no evil here? No. Evil's everywhere. Sin's everywhere. But this . . . is the spring of sweet water in the desert, the desert flower. Every step a Believer takes away from here is a step fraught with peril. I fear for you, Hannah Pitt, because you are my friend. Stay put. This is the right home of saints.

HANNAH: Latter-day saints.

SISTER ELLA CHAPTER: Only kind left.

HANNAH: But still. Late in the day . . . for saints and everyone. That's all. That's all.

Fifty thousand dollars for the house, Sister Ella Chapter; don't undersell. It's an impressive view.

ACT 3
NOT-YET-CONSCIOUS, FORWARD DAWNING • *January 1986*

Scene 1

(*Late night, three days after the end of act 2. The stage is completely dark. Prior is in bed in his apart-*

ment, having a nightmare. He wakes up, sits up and
switches on a nightlight. He looks at his clock. Seated
by the table near the bed is a man dressed in the clothing of a 13th-century British squire.)

PRIOR (terrified): Who are you?
PRIOR 1: My name is Prior Walter.

(Pause.)

PRIOR: My name is Prior Walter.
PRIOR 1: I know that.
PRIOR: Explain.
PRIOR 1: You're alive. I'm not. We have the same
   name. What do you want me to explain?
PRIOR: A ghost?
PRIOR 1: An ancestor.
PRIOR: Not the Prior Walter? The Bayeux tapestry
   Prior Walter?
PRIOR 1: His great-great grandson. The fifth of the
   name.
PRIOR: I'm the thirty-fourth, I think.
PRIOR 1: Actually the thirty-second.
PRIOR: Not according to Mother.
PRIOR 1: She's including the two bastards, then; I say
   leave them out. I say no room for bastards. The lit-
   tle things you swallow . . .
PRIOR: Pills.
PRIOR 1: Pills. For the pestilence. I too . . .
PRIOR: Pestilence. . . . You too what?
PRIOR 1: The pestilence in my time was much worse
   than now. Whole villages of empty houses. You
   could look outdoors and see Death walking in the
   morning, dew dampening the ragged hem of his
   black robe. Plain as I see you now.
PRIOR: You died of the plague.
PRIOR 1: The spotty monster. Like you, alone.
PRIOR: I'm not alone.
PRIOR 1: You have no wife, no children.
PRIOR: I'm gay.
PRIOR 1: So? Be gay, dance in your altogether for all I
   care, what's that to do with not having children?
PRIOR: Gay homosexual, not bonny, blithe and . . .
   never mind.
PRIOR 1: I had twelve. When I died.

(The second ghost appears, this one dressed in the
clothing of an elegant 17th-century Londoner.)

PRIOR 1 (pointing to Prior 2): And I was three years
   younger than him.

(Prior sees the new ghost, screams.)

PRIOR: Oh God another one.
PRIOR 2: Prior Walter. Prior to you by some seventeen
   others.
PRIOR 1: He's counting the bastards.
PRIOR: Are we having a convention?

PRIOR 2: We've been sent to declare her fabulous in-
   cipience. They love a well-paved entrance with lots
   of heralds, and . . .
PRIOR 1: The messenger come. Prepare the way. The
   infinite descent, a breath in air . . .
PRIOR 2: They chose us, I suspect, because of the mortal affinities. In a family as long-descended as the
   Walters there are bound to be a few carried off by
   plague.
PRIOR 1: The spotty monster.
PRIOR 2: Black Jack. Came from a water pump, half
   the city of London, can you imagine? His came
   from fleas. Yours, I understand, is the lamentable
   consequence of venery . . .
PRIOR 1: Fleas on rats, but who knew that?
PRIOR: Am I going to die?
PRIOR 2: We aren't allowed to discuss . . .
PRIOR 1: When you do, you don't get ancestors to
   help you through it. You may be surrounded by
   children but you die alone.
PRIOR: I'm afraid.
PRIOR 1: You should be. There aren't even torches,
   and the path's rocky, dark and steep.
PRIOR 2: Don't alarm him. There's good news before
   there's bad.
     We two come to strew rose petal and palm leaf
   before the triumphal procession. Prophet. Seer.
   Revelator. It's a great honor for the family.
PRIOR 1: He hasn't got a family.
PRIOR 2: I meant for the Walters, for the family in the
   larger sense.
PRIOR (singing):
     All I want is a room somewhere,
     Far away from the cold night air . . .
PRIOR 2 (putting a hand on Prior's forehead): Calm,
   calm, this is no brain fever . . .

(Prior calms down, but keeps his eyes closed. The
lights begin to change. Distant Glorious Music.)

PRIOR 1 (low chant):
     Adonai, Adonai,
     Olam ha-yichud,
     Zefirot, Zazahot,
     Ha-adam, ha-gadol
     Daughter of Light,
     Daughter of Splendors,
     Fluor! Phosphor!
     Lumen! Candle!
PRIOR 2 (simultaneously):
     Even now,
     From the mirror-bright halls of heaven,
     Across the cold and lifeless infinity of space,
     The Messenger comes
     Trailing orbs of light,
     Fabulous, incipient,

Oh Prophet,
To you . . .
PRIOR 1 AND PRIOR 2:
　　Prepare, prepare,
　　The Infinite Descent,
　　A breath, a feather,
　　Glory to . . .

(*They vanish.*)

Scene 2

(*The next day. Split scene. Louis and Belize in a coffee shop. Prior is at the outpatient clinic at the hospital with Emily, the nurse; she has him on a pentamidine IV drip.*)

LOUIS: Why has democracy succeeded in America? Of course by succeeded I mean comparatively, not literally, not in the present, but what makes for the prospect of some sort of radical democracy spreading outward and growing up? Why does the power that was once so carefully preserved at the top of the pyramid by the original framers of the Constitution seem drawn inexorably downward and outward in spite of the best effort of the Right to stop this? I mean it's the really hard thing about being Left in this country, the American Left can't help but trip over all these petrified little fetishes: freedom, that's the worst; you know, *Jeane Kirkpatrick*° for God's sake will go on and on about freedom and so what does that mean, the word freedom, when she talks about it, or human rights; you have Bush talking about human rights, and so what are these people talking about, they might as well be talking about the mating habits of Venusians, these people don't begin to know what, ontologically, freedom is or human rights, like they see these bourgeois property-based Rights-of-Man-type rights but that's not enfranchisement, not democracy, not what's implicit, what's potential within the idea, not the idea with blood in it. That's just liberalism, the worst kind of liberalism, really, bourgeois tolerance, and what I think is that what AIDS shows us is the limits of tolerance, that it's not enough to be tolerated, because when the shit hits the fan you find out how much tolerance is worth. Nothing. And underneath all the tolerance is intense, passionate hatred.

Jeane Kirkpatrick: Former U.S. ambassador to the United Nations. Kirkpatrick now teaches at Georgetown University and remains a member of the American Enterprise Institute for Public Policy and Research, a conservative think tank.

BELIZE: Uh huh.
LOUIS: Well don't you think that's true?
BELIZE: Uh huh. It is.
LOUIS: *Power* is the object, not being tolerated. Fuck assimilation. But I mean in spite of all this the thing about America, I think, is that ultimately we're different from every other nation on earth, in that, with people here of every race, we can't. . . . Ultimately what defines us isn't race, but politics. Not like any European country where there's an insurmountable fact of a kind of racial, or ethnic, monopoly, or monolith, like all Dutchmen, I mean Dutch people, are well, Dutch, and the Jews of Europe were never Europeans, just a small problem. Facing the monolith. But here there are so many small problems, it's really just a collection of small problems, the monolith is missing. Oh, I mean, of course I suppose there's the monolith of White America. White Straight Male America.
BELIZE: Which is not unimpressive, even among monoliths.
LOUIS: Well, no, but when the race thing gets taken care of, and I don't mean to minimalize how major it is, I mean I know it is, this is a really, really incredibly racist country but it's like, well, the British. I mean, all these blue-eyed pink people. And it's just weird, you know, I mean I'm not all that Jewish-looking, or . . . well, maybe I am but, you know, in New York, everyone is . . . well, not everyone, but so many are but so but in England, in London I walk into bars and I feel like Sid the Yid, you know I mean like Woody Allen in *Annie Hall,* with the payess and the gabardine coat, like never, never anywhere so much — I mean, not actively despised, not like they're Germans, who I think are still terribly anti-Semitic, and racist too, I mean black-racist, they pretend otherwise but, anyway, in London, there's just . . . and at one point I met this black gay guy from Jamaica who talked with a lilt but he said his family'd been living in London since before the Civil War — the American one — and how the English never let him forget for a minute that he wasn't blue-eyed and pink and I said yeah, me too, these people are anti-Semites and he said yeah but the British Jews have the clothing business all sewed up and blacks there can't get a foothold. And it was an incredibly awkward moment of just. . . . I mean there we were, in this bar that was gay but it was a *pub,* you know, the beams and the plaster and those horrible little, like, two-day-old fish and egg sandwiches — and just so British, so *old,* and I felt, well, there's no way out of this because both of us are, right now, too much immersed in this history, hope is dissolved in the sheer age of this place,

where race is what counts and there's no real hope of change — it's the racial destiny of the Brits that matters to them, not their political destiny, whereas in America . . .

BELIZE: Here in America race doesn't count.

LOUIS: No, no, that's not. . . . I mean you *can't* be hearing that . . .

BELIZE: I . . .

LOUIS: It's — look, race, yes, but ultimately race here is a political question, right? Racists just try to use race here as a tool in a political struggle. It's not really about race. Like the spiritualists try to use that stuff, are you enlightened, are you centered, channeled, whatever, this reaching out for a spiritual past in a country where no indigenous spirits exist — only the Indians, I mean Native American spirits and we killed them off so now, there are no gods here, no ghosts and spirits in America, there are no angels in America, no spiritual past, no racial past, there's only the political, and the decoys and the ploys to maneuver around the inescapable battle of politics, the shifting downwards and outwards of political power to the people . . .

BELIZE: POWER to the People! AMEN! (*Looking at his watch.*) OH MY GOODNESS! Will you look at the time, I gotta . . .

LOUIS: Do you. . . . You think this is, what, racist or naive or something?

BELIZE: Well it's certainly *something*. Look, I just remembered I have an appointment . . .

LOUIS: What? I mean I really don't want to, like, speak from some position of privilege and . . .

BELIZE: I'm sitting here, thinking, eventually he's *got* to run out of steam, so I let you rattle on and on saying about maybe seven or eight things I find really offensive.

LOUIS: What?

BELIZE: But I know you, Louis, and I know the guilt fueling this peculiar tirade is obviously already swollen bigger than your hemorrhoids.

LOUIS: I don't have hemorrhoids.

BELIZE: I hear different. May I finish?

LOUIS: Yes, but I don't have hemorrhoids.

BELIZE: So finally, when I . . .

LOUIS: Prior told you, he's an asshole, he shouldn't have . . .

BELIZE: You promised, Louis. Prior is not a subject.

LOUIS: You brought him up.

BELIZE: I brought up hemorrhoids.

LOUIS: So it's indirect. Passive-aggressive.

BELIZE: Unlike, I suppose, banging me over the head with your theory that America doesn't have a race problem.

LOUIS: Oh be fair I never said that.

BELIZE: Not exactly, but . . .

LOUIS: I said . . .

BELIZE: . . . but it was close enough, because if it'd been that blunt I'd've just walked out and . . .

LOUIS: You deliberately misinterpreted! I . . .

BELIZE: Stop interrupting! I haven't been able to . . .

LOUIS: Just let me . . .

BELIZE: NO! What, *talk*? You've been running your mouth nonstop since I got here, yaddadda yaddadda blah blah blah, up the hill, down the hill, playing with your MONOLITH . . .

LOUIS (*overlapping*): Well, you could have joined in at any time instead of . . .

BELIZE (*continuing over Louis*): . . . and girlfriend it is truly an *awesome* spectacle but I got better things to do with my time than sit here listening to this racist bullshit just because I feel sorry for you that . . .

LOUIS: I am not a racist!

BELIZE: Oh come on . . .

LOUIS: So maybe I am a racist but . . .

BELIZE: Oh I really hate that! It's no fun picking on you Louis; you're so guilty, it's like throwing darts at a glob of jello, there's no satisfying hits, just quivering, the darts just blop in and vanish.

LOUIS: I just think when you are discussing lines of oppression it gets very complicated and . . .

BELIZE: Oh is that a fact? You know, we black drag queens have a rather intimate knowledge of the complexity of the lines of . . .

LOUIS: *Ex*-black drag queen.

BELIZE: Actually ex-ex.

LOUIS: You're doing drag again?

BELIZE: I don't. . . . Maybe. I don't have to tell you. Maybe.

LOUIS: I think it's sexist.

BELIZE: I didn't ask you.

LOUIS: Well it is. The gay community, I think, has to adopt the same attitude towards drag as black women have to take towards black women blues singers.

BELIZE: Oh my we *are* walking dangerous tonight.

LOUIS: Well, it's all internalized oppression, right, I mean the masochism, the stereotypes, the . . .

BELIZE: Louis, are you deliberately trying to make me hate you?

LOUIS: No, I . . .

BELIZE: I mean, are you deliberately transforming yourself into an arrogant, sexual-political Stalinist-slash-racist flag-waving thug for my benefit?

(*Pause.*)

LOUIS: You know what I think?

BELIZE: What?

LOUIS: You hate me because I'm a Jew.

BELIZE: I'm leaving.

LOUIS: It's true.

BELIZE: You have no basis except your . . .

Louis, it's good to know you haven't changed; you are still an honorary citizen of the Twilight Zone, and after your pale, pale white polemics on behalf of racial insensitivity you have a flaming *fuck* of a lot of nerve calling me an anti-Semite. Now I really gotta go.

LOUIS: You called me Lou the Jew.

BELIZE: That was a joke.

LOUIS: I didn't think it was funny. It was hostile.

BELIZE: It was three years ago.

LOUIS: So?

BELIZE: You just called yourself Sid the Yid.

LOUIS: That's not the same thing.

BELIZE: Sid the Yid is different from Lou the Jew.

LOUIS: Yes.

BELIZE: Someday you'll have to explain that to me, but right now . . .

You hate me because you hate black people.

LOUIS: I do not. But I do think most black people are anti-Semitic.

BELIZE: "Most black people." *That's* racist, Louis, and *I* think most Jews . . .

LOUIS: Louis Farrakhan.

BELIZE: Ed Koch.

LOUIS: Jesse Jackson.

BELIZE: Jackson. Oh really, Louis, this is . . .

LOUIS: Hymietown! Hymietown!

BELIZE: Louis, you voted for Jesse Jackson. You send checks to the Rainbow Coalition.

LOUIS: I'm ambivalent. The checks bounced.

BELIZE: All your checks bounce, Louis; you're ambivalent about everything.

LOUIS: What's that supposed to mean?

BELIZE: You may be dumber than shit but I refuse to believe you can't figure it out. Try.

LOUIS: I was never ambivalent about Prior. I love him. I do. I really do.

BELIZE: Nobody said different.

LOUIS: Love and ambivalence are. . . . Real love isn't ambivalent.

BELIZE: "Real love isn't ambivalent." I'd swear that's a line from my favorite bestselling paperback novel, *In Love with the Night Mysterious,* except I don't think you ever read it.

(*Pause.*)

LOUIS: I never read it, no.

BELIZE: You ought to. Instead of spending the rest of your life trying to get through *Democracy in America.* It's about this white woman whose Daddy owns a plantation in the Deep South in the years before the Civil War — the American one — and her name is Margaret, and she's in love with her Daddy's number-one slave, and his name is Thaddeus, and she's married but her white slave-owner husband has AIDS: Antebellum Insufficiently Developed Sexorgans. And there's a lot of hot stuff going down when Margaret and Thaddeus can catch a spare torrid ten under the cotton-picking moon, and then of course the Yankees come, and they set the slaves free, and the slaves string up old Daddy, and so on. Historical fiction. Somewhere in there I recall Margaret and Thaddeus find the time to discuss the nature of love; her face is reflecting the flames of the burning plantation — you know, the way white people do — and his black face is dark in the night and she says to him, "Thaddeus, real love isn't ever ambivalent."

(*Little pause. Emily enters and turns off IV drip.*)

BELIZE: Thaddeus looks at her; he's contemplating her thesis; and he isn't sure he agrees.

EMILY (*removing IV drip from Prior's arm*): Treatment number . . . (*consulting chart*) four.

PRIOR: Pharmaceutical miracle. Lazarus breathes again.

LOUIS: Is he. . . . How bad is he?

BELIZE: You want the laundry list?

EMILY: Shirt off, let's check the . . .

(*Prior takes his shirt off. She examines his lesions.*)

BELIZE: There's the weight problem and the shit problem and the morale problem.

EMILY: Only six. That's good. Pants.

(*He drops his pants. He's naked. She examines.*)

BELIZE: And. He thinks he's going crazy.

EMILY: Looking good. What else?

PRIOR: Ankles sore and swollen, but the leg's better. The nausea's mostly gone with the little orange pills. BM's pure liquid but not bloody anymore, for now, my eye doctor says everything's OK, for now, my dentist says "Yuck!" when he sees my fuzzy tongue, and now he wears little condoms on his thumb and forefinger. And a mask. So what? My dermatologist is in Hawaii and my mother . . . well leave my mother out of it. Which is usually where my mother is, out of it. My glands are like walnuts, my weight's holding steady for week two, and a friend died two days ago of bird tuberculosis; bird tuberculosis; that scared me and I didn't go to the funeral today because he was an Irish Catholic and it's probably open casket and I'm afraid of . . . something, the bird TB or seeing him or. . . . So I guess I'm doing OK. Except for of course I'm going nuts.

EMILY: We ran the toxoplasmosis series and there's no indication . . .

PRIOR: I know, I know, but I feel like something terrifying is on its way, you know, like a missile from outer space, and it's plummeting down towards the earth, and I'm ground zero, and . . . I am generally known where I am known as one cool, collected queen. And I am ruffled.

EMILY: There's really nothing to worry about. I think that shochen bamromim hamtzeh menucho nechono al kanfey haschino.

PRIOR: What?

EMILY: Everything's fine. Bemaalos k'doshim ut'horim kezohar horokeea mazhirim . . .

PRIOR: Oh I don't understand what you're . . .

EMILY: Es nishmas Prior sheholoch leolomoh, baavur shenodvoo z'dokoh b'ad hazkoras nishmosoh.

PRIOR: Why are you doing that?! Stop it! Stop it!

EMILY: Stop what?

PRIOR: You were just . . . weren't you just speaking in Hebrew or something.

EMILY: *Hebrew?* (*Laughs.*) I'm basically Italian-American. No. I didn't speak in Hebrew.

PRIOR: Oh no, oh God please I really think I . . .

EMILY: Look, I'm sorry, I have a waiting room full of. . . . I think you're one of the lucky ones, you'll live for years, probably — you're pretty healthy for someone with no immune system. Are you seeing someone? Loneliness is a danger. A therapist?

PRIOR: No, I don't need to see anyone, I just . . .

EMILY: Well think about it. You aren't going crazy. You're just under a lot of stress. No wonder . . . (*She starts to write in his chart.*)

(*Suddenly there is an astonishing blaze of light, a huge chord sounded by a gigantic choir, and a great book with steel pages mounted atop a molten-red pillar pops up from the stage floor. The book opens; there is a large Aleph inscribed on its pages, which bursts into flames. Immediately the book slams shut and disappears instantly under the floor as the lights become normal again. Emily notices none of this, writing. Prior is agog.*)

EMILY (*laughing, exiting*): Hebrew . . .

(*Prior flees.*)

LOUIS: Help me.

BELIZE: I beg your pardon?

LOUIS: You're a nurse, give me something, I . . . don't know what to do anymore, I. . . . Last week at work I screwed up the Xerox machine like permanently and so I . . . then I tripped on the subway steps and my glasses broke and I cut my forehead, here, see, and now I can't see much and my forehead . . . it's like the Mark of Cain,° stu-

pid, right, but it won't heal and every morning I see it and I think, Biblical things, Mark of Cain, Judas Iscariot° and his silver and his noose, people who . . . in betraying what they love betray what's truest in themselves, I feel . . . nothing but cold for myself, just cold, and every night I miss him, I miss him so much but then . . . those sores, and the smell and . . . where I thought it was going. . . . I could be . . . I could be . . . sick too, maybe I'm sick too. I don't know.

Belize. Tell him I love him. Can you do that?

BELIZE: I've thought about it for a very long time, and I still don't understand what love is. Justice is simple. Democracy is simple. Those things are unambivalent. But love is very hard. And it goes bad for you if you violate the hard law of love.

LOUIS: I'm dying.

BELIZE: He's dying. You just wish you were.

Oh cheer up, Louis. Look at that heavy sky out there.

LOUIS: Purple.

BELIZE: *Purple?* Boy, what kind of a homosexual are you, anyway? That's not purple, Mary, that color up there is (*very grand*) mauve.

All day today it's felt like Thanksgiving. Soon, this . . . ruination will be blanketed white. You can smell it — can you smell it?

LOUIS: Smell what?

BELIZE: Softness, compliance, forgiveness, grace.

LOUIS: No . . .

BELIZE: I can't help you learn that. I can't help you, Louis. You're not my business. (*He exits.*)

(*Louis puts his head in his hands, inadvertently touching his cut forehead.*)

LOUIS: Ow FUCK! (*He stands slowly, looks towards where Belize exited.*) Smell what?

(*He looks both ways to be sure no one is watching, then inhales deeply, and is surprised.*) Huh. Snow.

Scene 3

(*Same day. Harper in a very white, cold place, with a brilliant blue sky above; a delicate snowfall. She is dressed in a beautiful snowsuit. The sound of the sea, faint.*)

HARPER: Snow! Ice! Mountains of ice! Where am I? I . . .

I feel better, I do, I . . . feel better. There are ice

Mark of Cain: In Genesis Cain murdered his brother Abel and subsequently was marked on his forehead by God.

Judas Iscariot: An apostle, Judas betrayed Jesus for thirty pieces of silver.

crystals in my lungs, wonderful and sharp. And the snow smells like cold, crushed peaches. And there's something . . . some current of blood in the wind, how strange, it has that iron taste.

MR. LIES: Ozone.

HARPER: Ozone! Wow! Where am I?

MR. LIES: The Kingdom of Ice, the bottommost part of the world.

HARPER (*looking around, then realizing*): Antarctica. This is Antarctica!

MR. LIES: Cold shelter for the shattered. No sorrow here, tears freeze.

HARPER: Antarctica, Antarctica, oh boy oh boy, LOOK at this, I. . . . Wow, I must've really snapped the tether, huh?

MR. LIES: Apparently

HARPER: That's great. I want to stay here forever. Set up camp. Build things. Build a city, an enormous city made up of frontier forts, dark wood and green roofs and high gates made of pointed logs and bonfires burning on every street corner. I should build by a river. Where are the forests?

MR. LIES: No timber here. Too cold. Ice, no trees.

HARPER: Oh details! I'm sick of details! I'll plant them and grow them. I'll live off caribou fat, I'll melt it over the bonfires and drink it from long, curved goat-horn cups. It'll be great. I want to make a new world here. So that I never have to go home again.

MR. LIES: As long as it lasts. Ice has a way of melting . . .

HARPER: No. Forever. I can have anything I want here — maybe even companionship, someone who has . . . desire for me. You, maybe.

MR. LIES: It's against the by-laws of the International Order of Travel Agents to get involved with clients. Rules are rules. Anyway, I'm not the one you really want.

HARPER: There isn't anyone . . . maybe an Eskimo. Who could ice-fish for food. And help me build a nest for when the baby comes.

MR. LIES: There are no Eskimo in Antarctica. And you're not really pregnant. You made that up.

HARPER: Well all of this is made up. So if the snow feels cold I'm pregnant. Right? Here, I can be pregnant. And I can have any kind of a baby I want.

MR. LIES: This is a retreat, a vacuum, its virtue is that it lacks everything; deep-freeze for feelings. You can be numb and safe here, that's what you came for. Respect the delicate ecology of your delusions.

HARPER: You mean like no Eskimo in Antarctica.

MR. LIES: Correcto. Ice and snow, no Eskimo. Even hallucinations have laws.

HARPER: Well then who's that?

(*The Eskimo appears.*)

MR. LIES: An Eskimo.

HARPER: An antarctic Eskimo. A fisher of the polar deep.

MR. LIES: There's something wrong with this picture.

(*The Eskimo beckons.*)

HARPER: I'm going to like this place. It's my own National Geographic Special! Oh! Oh! (*She holds her stomach.*) I think . . . I think I felt her kicking. Maybe I'll give birth to a baby covered with thick white fur, and that way she won't be cold. My breasts will be full of hot cocoa so she doesn't get chilly. And if it gets really cold, she'll have a pouch I can crawl into. Like a marsupial. We'll mend together. That's what we'll do; we'll mend.

Scene 4

(*Same day. An abandoned lot in the South Bronx. A homeless Woman is standing near an oil drum in which a fire is burning. Snowfall. Trash around. Hannah enters dragging two heavy suitcases.*)

HANNAH: Excuse me? I said excuse me? Can you tell me where I am? Is this Brooklyn? Do you know a Pineapple Street? Is there some sort of bus or train or . . . ?

I'm lost, I just arrived from Salt Lake. City. Utah? I took the bus that I was told to take and I got off — well it was the very last stop, so I had to get off, and I *asked* the driver was this Brooklyn, and he nodded yes but he was from one of those foreign countries where they think it's good manners to nod at everything even if you have no idea what it is you're nodding at, and in truth I think he spoke no English at all, which I think would make him ineligible for employment on public transportation. The public being English-speaking, mostly. Do you speak English?

(*The Woman nods.*)

HANNAH: I was supposed to be met at the airport by my son. He didn't show and I don't wait more than three and three-quarters hours for *anyone.* I should have been patient, I guess, I. . . . Is this . . .

WOMAN: Bronx.

HANNAH: Is that. . . . The *Bronx?* Well how in the name of Heaven did I get to the Bronx when the bus driver said —

WOMAN (*talking to herself*): Slurp slurp slurp will you STOP that disgusting slurping! YOU DIS-

GUSTING SLURPING FEEDING ANIMAL!
Feeding yourself, just feeding yourself, what would
it matter, to you or to ANYONE, if you just
stopped. Feeding. And DIED?

(*Pause.*)

HANNAH: Can you just tell me where I . . .
WOMAN: Why was the Kosciusko Bridge named after
a Polack?
HANNAH: I don't know what you're . . .
WOMAN: That was a joke.
HANNAH: Well what's the punchline?
WOMAN: I don't know.
HANNAH (*looking around desperately*): Oh for pete's
sake, is there anyone else who . . .
WOMAN (*again, to herself*): Stand further off you fat
loathsome whore, you can't have any more of this
soup, slurp slurp slurp you animal, and the — I
know you'll just go pee it all away and where will
you do that? Behind what bush? It's FUCKING
COLD out here and I . . .
    Oh that's right, because it was supposed to have
been a tunnel!
    That's not very funny.
    Have you read the prophecies of Nostradamus?
HANNAH: Who?
WOMAN: Some guy I went out with once somewhere,
Nostradamus. Prophet, outcast, eyes like. . . .
Scary shit, he . . .
HANNAH: Shut up. Please. Now I want you to stop
jabbering for a minute and pull your wits together
and tell me how to get to Brooklyn. Because you
know! And you are going to tell me! Because there
is no one else around to tell me and I am wet and
cold and I am very angry! So I am sorry you're
psychotic but just make the effort — take a deep
breath — DO IT!

(*Hannah and the Woman breathe together.*)

HANNAH: That's good. Now exhale.

(*They do.*)

HANNAH: Good. Now how do I get to Brooklyn?
WOMAN: Don't know. Never been. Sorry. Want some
soup?
HANNAH: Manhattan? Maybe you know . . . I don't
suppose you know the location of the Mormon
Visitor's . . .
WOMAN: 65th and Broadway.
HANNAH: How do you . . .
WOMAN: Go there all the time. Free movies. Boring,
but you can stay all day.
HANNAH: Well. . . . So how do I.
WOMAN: Take the D Train. Next block make a right.
HANNAH: Thank you.

WOMAN: Oh yeah. In the new century I think we will
all be insane.

Scene 5

(*Same day. Joe and Roy in the study of Roy's brown-
stone. Roy is wearing an elegant bathrobe. He has
made a considerable effort to look well. He isn't well,
and he hasn't succeeded much in looking it.*)

JOE: I can't. The answer's no. I'm sorry.
ROY: Oh, well, apologies . . .
    I can't see that there's anyone asking for apolo-
gies.

(*Pause.*)

JOE: I'm sorry, Roy.
ROY: Oh, well, apologies.
JOE: My wife is missing, Roy. My mother's coming
from Salt Lake to . . . to help look, I guess. I'm
supposed to be at the airport now, picking her up
but. . . . I just spent two days in a hospital, Roy,
with a bleeding ulcer, I was spitting up blood.
ROY: Blood, huh? Look, I'm very busy here and . . .
JOE: It's just a job.
ROY: A job? A *job*? *Washington*! Dumb Utah Mormon hick shit!
JOE: Roy . . .
ROY: *WASHINGTON!* When Washington called me
I was younger than you, you think I said "Aw fuck
no I can't go I got two fingers up my asshole and a
little moral nosebleed to boot!" When Washington
calls you my pretty young punk friend you go or
you can go fuck yourself sideways 'cause the train
has pulled out of the station, and you are *out*,
nowhere, out in the cold. Fuck you, Mary Jane, get
outta here.
JOE: Just let me . . .
ROY: Explain? Ephemera. You broke my heart. Explain that. Explain that.
JOE: I love you, Roy.
    There's so much that I want, to be . . . what you
see in me, I want to be a participant in the world,
in your world, Roy, I want to be capable of that,
I've tried, really I have but . . . I can't do this. Not
because I don't believe in you, but because I believe
in you so much, in what you stand for, at heart,
the order, the decency. I would give anything to
protect you, but. . . . There are laws I can't break.
It's too ingrained. It's not me. There's enough damage I've already done.
    Maybe you were right, maybe I'm dead.
ROY: You're not dead, boy, you're a sissy.

You love me; that's moving, I'm moved. It's nice to be loved. I warned you about her, didn't I, Joe? But you don't listen to me, why, because you say Roy is smart and Roy's a friend but Roy . . . well, he isn't nice, and you wanna be nice. Right? A nice, nice man!

(*Little pause.*)

You know what my greatest accomplishment was, Joe, in my life, what I am able to look back on and be proudest of? And I have helped make Presidents and unmake them and mayors and more goddam judges than anyone in NYC ever — AND several million dollars, tax-free — and what do you think means the most to me?

You ever hear of Ethel Rosenberg? Huh, Joe, huh?

JOE: Well, yeah, I guess I. . . . Yes.

ROY: Yes. Yes. You have heard of Ethel Rosenberg. Yes. Maybe you even read about her in the history books.

If it wasn't for me, Joe, Ethel Rosenberg would be alive today, writing some personal-advice column for *Ms.* magazine. She isn't. Because during the trial, Joe, I was on the phone every day, talking with the judge . . .

JOE: Roy . . .

ROY: Every day, doing what I do best, talking on the telephone, making sure that timid Yid nebbish on the bench did his duty to America, to history. That sweet unprepossessing woman, two kids, boo-hoo-hoo, reminded us all of our little Jewish mamas — she came this close to getting life; I pleaded till I wept to put her in the chair. Me. I did that. I would have fucking pulled the switch if they'd have let me. Why? Because I fucking hate traitors. Because I fucking hate communists. Was it legal? Fuck legal. Am I a nice man? Fuck nice. They say terrible things about me in the *Nation.* Fuck the *Nation.* You want to be Nice, or you want to be Effective? Make the law, or subject to it. Choose. Your wife chose. A week from today, she'll be back. SHE knows how to get what SHE wants. Maybe I ought to send *her* to Washington.

JOE: I don't believe you.

ROY: Gospel.

JOE: You can't possibly mean what you're saying.

Roy, you were the Assistant United States Attorney on the Rosenberg case, ex-parte communication with the judge during the trial would be . . . censurable, at least, probably conspiracy and . . . in a case that resulted in execution, it's . . .

ROY: What? Murder?

JOE: You're not well is all.

ROY: What do you mean, not well? Who's not well?

(*Pause.*)

JOE: You said . . .

ROY: No I didn't. I said what?

JOE: Roy, you have cancer.

ROY: No I don't.

(*Pause.*)

JOE: You told me you were dying.

ROY: What the fuck are you talking about, Joe? I never said that. I'm in perfect health. There's not a goddam thing wrong with me.
   (*He smiles.*)
   Shake?

(*Joe hesitates. He holds out his hand to Roy. Roy pulls Joe into a close, strong clinch.*)

ROY (*more to himself than to Joe*): It's OK that you hurt me because I love you, baby Joe. That's why I'm so rough on you.

(*Roy releases Joe. Joe backs away a step or two.*)

ROY: Prodigal son. The world will wipe its dirty hands all over you.

JOE: It already has, Roy.

ROY: Now go.

(*Roy shoves Joe, hard. Joe turns to leave. Roy stops him, turns him around.*)

ROY (*smoothing Joe's lapels, tenderly*): I'll always be here, waiting for you . . .
   (*Then again, with sudden violence, he pulls Joe close, violently.*)
   What did you want from me, what was all this, what do you want, treacherous ungrateful little . . .

(*Joe, very close to belting Roy, grabs him by the front of his robe, and propels him across the length of the room. He holds Roy at arm's length, the other arm ready to hit.*)

ROY (*laughing softly, almost pleading to be hit*): Transgress a little, Joseph.

(*Joe releases Roy.*)

ROY: There are so many laws; find one you can break.

(*Joe hesitates, then leaves, backing out. When Joe has gone, Roy doubles over in great pain, which he's been hiding throughout the scene with Joe.*)

ROY: Ah, Christ . . .
   Andy! Andy! Get in here! Andy!

(*The door opens, but it isn't Andy. A small Jewish Woman dressed modestly in a fifties hat and coat stands in the doorway. The room darkens.*)

ROY: Who the fuck are you? The new nurse?

(*The figure in the doorway says nothing. She stares at*

Roy. *A pause. Roy looks at her carefully, gets up, crosses to her. He crosses back to the chair, sits heavily.*)

ROY: Aw, fuck. Ethel.

ETHEL ROSENBERG (*her manner is friendly, her voice is ice-cold*): You don't look good, Roy.

ROY: Well, Ethel. I don't feel good.

ETHEL ROSENBERG: But you lost a lot of weight. That suits you. You were heavy back then. Zaftig, mit hips.

ROY: I haven't been that heavy since 1960. We were all heavier back then, before the body thing started. Now I look like a skeleton. They stare.

ETHEL ROSENBERG: The shit's really hit the fan, huh, Roy?

(*Little pause. Roy nods.*)

ETHEL ROSENBERG: Well the fun's just started.

ROY: What is this, Ethel, Halloween? You trying to scare me?

(*Ethel says nothing.*)

ROY: Well you're wasting your time! I'm scarier than you any day of the week! So beat it, Ethel! BOOO! BETTER DEAD THAN RED! Somebody trying to shake me up? HAH HAH! From the throne of God in heaven to the belly of hell, you can all fuck yourselves and then go jump in the lake because I'M NOT AFRAID OF YOU OR DEATH OR HELL OR ANYTHING!

ETHEL ROSENBERG: Be seeing you soon, Roy. Julius sends his regards.

ROY: Yeah, well send this to Julius!

(*He flips the bird in her direction, stands and moves towards her. Halfway across the room he slumps to the floor, breathing laboriously, in pain.*)

ETHEL ROSENBERG: You're a very sick man, Roy.

ROY: Oh God . . . ANDY!

ETHEL ROSENBERG: Hmmm. He doesn't hear you, I guess. We should call the ambulance.
    (*She goes to the phone.*)
    Hah! Buttons! Such things they got now.
    What do I dial, Roy?

(*Pause. Roy looks at her, then:*)

ROY: 911

ETHEL ROSENBERG (*dials the phone*): It sings!
    (*Imitating dial tones.*) La la la . . .
    Huh.
    Yes, you should please send an ambulance to the home of Mister Roy Cohn, the famous lawyer.
    What's the address, Roy?

ROY (*a beat, then*): 244 East 87th.

ETHEL ROSENBERG: 244 East 87th Street. No apartment number, he's got the whole building.
    My name? (*A beat.*) Ethel Greenglass Rosenberg.
    (*Small smile.*) Me? No I'm not related to Mr. Cohn. An old friend.
    (*She hangs up.*)
    They said a minute.

ROY: I have all the time in the world.

ETHEL ROSENBERG: You're immortal.

ROY: I'm immortal. Ethel. (*He forces himself to stand.*)
    I have *forced* my way into history. I ain't never gonna die.

ETHEL ROSENBERG (*a little laugh, then*): History is about to crack wide open. Millennium approaches.

Scene 6

(*Late that night. Prior's bedroom. Prior 1 watching Prior in bed, who is staring back at him, terrified. Tonight Prior 1 is dressed in weird alchemical robes and hat over his historical clothing and he carries a long palm-leaf bundle.*)

PRIOR 1: Tonight's the night! Aren't you excited? Tonight she arrives! Right through the roof! Ha-adam, Ha-gadol . . .

PRIOR 2 (*appearing, similarly attired*): Lumen! Phosphor! Fluor! Candle! An unending billowing of scarlet and . . .

PRIOR: Look. Garlic. A mirror. Holy water. A crucifix. FUCK OFF! Get the fuck out of my room! GO!

PRIOR 1 (*to Prior 2*): Hard as a hickory knob, I'll bet.

PRIOR 2: We all tumesce when they approach. We wax full, like moons.

PRIOR 1: Dance.

PRIOR: Dance?

PRIOR 1: Stand up, dammit, give us your hands, dance!

PRIOR 2: Listen . . .

(*A lone oboe begins to play a little dance tune.*)

PRIOR 2: Delightful sound. Care to dance?

PRIOR: Please leave me alone, please just let me sleep . . .

PRIOR 2: Ah, he wants someone familiar. A partner who knows his steps. (*To Prior.*) Close your eyes. Imagine . . .

PRIOR: I don't . . .

PRIOR 2: Hush. Close your eyes.

(*Prior does.*)

PRIOR 2: Now open them.

(*Prior does. Louis appears. He looks gorgeous. The music builds gradually into a full-blooded, romantic dance tune.*)

PRIOR: Lou.

LOUIS: Dance with me.

PRIOR: I can't, my leg, it hurts at night . . .
Are you . . . a ghost, Lou?

LOUIS: No. Just spectral. Lost to myself. Sitting all day on cold park benches. Wishing I could be with you. Dance with me, babe . . .

(*Prior stands up. The leg stops hurting. They begin to dance. The music is beautiful.*)

PRIOR 1 (*to Prior 2*): Hah. Now I see why he's got no children. He's a sodomite.

PRIOR 2: Oh be quiet, you medieval gnome, and let them dance.

PRIOR 1: I'm not interfering, I've done my bit. Hooray, hooray, the messenger's come, now I'm blowing off. I don't like it here.

(*Prior 1 vanishes.*)

PRIOR 2: The twentieth century. Oh dear, the world has gotten so terribly, terribly old.

(*Prior 2 vanishes. Louis and Prior waltz happily. Lights fade back to normal. Louis vanishes.*
Prior dances alone.
Then suddenly, the sound of wings fills the room.*)

Scene 7

(*Split scene. Prior alone in his apartment; Louis alone in the park.*
Again, a sound of beating wings.*)

PRIOR: Oh don't come in here don't come in . . . LOUIS!!
No. My name is Prior Walter, I am . . . the scion of an ancient line, I am . . . abandoned I . . . no, my name is . . . is . . . Prior and I live . . . *here and now,* and . . . in the dark, in the dark, the Recording Angel opens its hundred eyes and snaps the spine of the Book of Life and . . . hush! Hush!
I'm talking nonsense, I . . .
No more mad scene, hush, hush.

(*Louis in the park on a bench. Joe approaches, stands at a distance. They stare at each other, then Louis turns away.*)

LOUIS: Do you know the story of Lazarus?

JOE: Lazarus?

LOUIS: Lazarus. I can't remember what happens, exactly.

JOE: I don't. . . . Well, he was dead, Lazarus, and Jesus breathed life into him. He brought him back from death.

LOUIS: Come here often?

JOE: No. Yes. Yes.

LOUIS: Back from the dead. You believe that really happened?

JOE: I don't know anymore what I believe.

LOUIS: This is quite a coincidence. Us meeting.

JOE: I followed you.
From work. I . . . followed you here.

(*Pause.*)

LOUIS: You followed me.
You probably saw me that day in the washroom and thought: there's a sweet guy, sensitive, cries for friends in trouble.

JOE: Yes.

LEFT: Ron Liebman as Roy Cohn in the Broadway production of *Angels in America: Millennium Approaches.* RIGHT: Scene from the end of *Angels in America: Millennium Approaches.*

LOUIS: You thought maybe I'll cry for you.
JOE: Yes.
LOUIS: Well I fooled you. Crocodile tears. Nothing . . .
    (*He touches his heart, shrugs.*)

(*Joe reaches tentatively to touch Louis's face.*)

LOUIS (*pulling back*): What are you doing? Don't do that.
JOE (*withdrawing his hand*): Sorry. I'm sorry.
LOUIS: I'm . . . just not . . . I think, if you touch me, your hand might fall off or something. Worse things have happened to people who have touched me.
JOE: Please.
    Oh, boy . . .

Can I . . .
    I . . . want . . . to touch you. Can I please just touch you . . . um, here?
    (*He puts his hand on one side of Louis's face. He holds it there.*)
    I'm going to hell for doing this.
LOUIS: Big deal. You think it could be any worse than New York City?
    (*He puts his hand on Joe's hand. He takes Joe's hand away from his face, holds it for a moment, then*) Come on.
JOE: Where?
LOUIS: Home. With me.
JOE: This makes no sense. I mean I don't know you.

LOUIS: Likewise.

JOE: And what you do know about me you don't like.

LOUIS: The Republican stuff?

JOE: Yeah, well for starters.

LOUIS: I don't not like that. I *hate* that.

JOE: So why on earth should we . . .

(*Louis goes to Joe and kisses him.*)

LOUIS: Strange bedfellows. I don't know. I never made it with one of the damned before.

    I would really rather not have to spend tonight alone.

JOE: I'm a pretty terrible person, Louis.

LOUIS: Lou.

JOE: No, I really really am. I don't think I deserve being loved.

LOUIS: There? See? We already have a lot in common.

(*Louis stands, begins to walk away. He turns, looks back at Joe. Joe follows. They exit.*)

(*Prior listens. At first no sound, then once again, the sound of beating wings, frighteningly near.*)

PRIOR: That sound, that sound, it . . . . What is that, like birds or something, like a *really* big bird, I'm frightened, I . . . no, no fear, find the anger, find the . . . anger, my blood is clean, my brain is fine, I can handle pressure, I am a gay man and I am used to pressure, to trouble, I am tough and strong and . . . . Oh. Oh my goodness. I . . . (*He is washed over by an intense sexual feeling.*) Ooohhhh. . . . I'm hot, I'm . . . so . . . aw Jeez what is going on here I . . . must have a fever I . . .

(*The bedside lamp flickers wildly as the bed begins to roll forward and back. There is a deep bass creaking and groaning from the bedroom ceiling, like the timbers of a ship under immense stress, and from above a fine rain of plaster dust.*)

PRIOR: OH!

    PLEASE, OH PLEASE! Something's coming in here, I'm scared, I don't like this at all, something's approaching and I. . . . OH!

(*There is a great blaze of triumphal music, heralding. The light turns an extraordinary harsh, cold, pale blue, then a rich, brilliant warm golden color, then a hot, bilious green, and then finally a spectacular royal purple. Then silence.*)

PRIOR (*an awestruck whisper*): God almighty . . .

    Very Steven Spielberg.

(*A sound, like a plummeting meteor, tears down from very, very far above the earth, hurtling at an incredible velocity towards the bedroom; the light seems to be sucked out of the room as the projectile approaches; as the room reaches darkness, we hear a terrifying CRASH as something immense strikes earth; the whole building shudders and a part of the bedroom ceiling, lots of plaster and lathe and wiring, crashes to the floor. And then in a shower of unearthly white light, spreading great opalescent gray-silver wings, the Angel descends into the room and floats above the bed.*)

ANGEL:

    Greetings, Prophet;
    The Great Work begins:
    The Messenger has arrived.

(*Blackout.*)

COMMENTARY

Andrea Bernstein
INTERVIEW WITH TONY KUSHNER

1995

Andrea Bernstein, a freelance cultural critic, engaged Tony Kushner in a discussion of the politics in his plays. Kushner's responses to her questions establish his credentials as a left-thinking critic of contemporary political life. His discussion of his work is centered much more in political reality than it is in dramatic technique or concern for theater. Yet, Kushner is able to zero in on the dramatic moment and present contemporary politics as a dialectical struggle.

Tony Kushner, a gay Jewish socialist who was raised in Louisiana, won a Pulitzer Prize and two Tony Awards for his two-part, seven-hour Broadway production of *Angels in America: A Gay Fantasia on National Themes*. Other plays, *A Bright Room Called Day* (1985) and *Slavs!* (1994), are also concerned with the moral responsibilities of people in politically repressive times. Such concerns may be especially relevant in America today, where, as he observes: "What used to be called liberal is now called radical, what used to be called radical is now called insane, what used to be called reactionary is now called moderate, and what used to be called insane is now called solid conservative thinking."

Q: Angels in America opened on Broadway just months after the Clinton inauguration. It ends with a very hopeful speech about healing. Do you still feel that hope?

A: You have to have hope. It's irresponsible to give *false* hope, which I think a lot of playwrights are guilty of. But I also think it's irresponsible to simply be a nihilist, which quite a lot of playwrights, especially playwrights younger than me, have become guilty of. I don't believe you would bother to write a play if you really had no hope. That passage was one of the very first things I ever wrote when I was working on *Angels*. I read it to the woman who I was originally writing the part of the angel for, who died of breast cancer before the play was finished. In one of my last conversations with her, she told me that she thought about that image a lot and that she hoped I would include it in the play. I think I wouldn't have included it otherwise, but I'm glad I did now.

Q: Angels in America was a political play — and that's something Americans and critics frequently resist. How did you overcome that resistance?

A: What I found in the audience response is a huge hunger for political issues and political discussion. So I always wonder: Is it that Americans don't like politics, or is it that so much theater that is political isn't well-done? One of the things I learned in *Slavs!* is that it's much easier to talk about being gay than it is to talk about being a socialist. People are afraid of socialism, and plays that deal with economics are scarier to them. I'll learn more about that — my next three plays are all about money.

Also, *Angels* is very entertaining. It does things formally that are new, and people were excited by the size and the scope. It's a good play and that makes all the difference.

Thelma and Louise, for instance, is a really terrific movie, and genuinely left in its political sensibilities. It's well-made, so the fact that it is unquestionably coming from a feminist perspective didn't make it absolutely marginal the way you would expect such a film to be. It had guns — that probably helped.

Q: People loved *Forrest Gump,* too.

A: People shouldn't trust artists and they shouldn't trust art. Part of the fun of art is that it invites you to interpret it.

There's a very complicated relationship between form and content and between aesthetics and politics. Good politics will produce good aesthetics, really good politics will produce really good aesthetics, and really good aesthetics, if somebody's really asking the hard questions and answering them honestly, they'll probably produce truth, which is to say progressive politics.

Q: Is it hard to write characters that are not caricatures and to overcome the barrier that people have about listening to politics from a character on stage?

A: I think that a character's politics have to live in the same sort of relationship to the character's psyche that people's politics live in relationship to their own psyches. People are never consistent. People will always do surprising things, both good and bad, and the way that people surprise themselves and their audience are the most interesting moments of human behavior. The space between what we'd like to be and what we actually are is where you find out the most interesting things.

Q: Do you see your plays as part of a political movement?

A: I do. I would hate to write anything that wasn't. I would like my plays to be of use to progressive people. I think preaching to the converted is exactly what art ought to do.

I am happiest when people who are politically engaged in the world say, "Your play meant a lot to me; it helped me think about something, or made me feel like I wasn't the only person who felt this way."

It's the way you feel when you go to a demo, which is the only way to keep sane a lot of the time. You need to remind yourself there are many bodies who are as angry about something as you are.

When I teach writing, I always tell my students you should assume that the audience you're writing for is smarter than you. You can't write if you don't think they're on your side, because then you start to yell at them or preach down to them.

Q: The character Prelapsarianov — the "world's oldest living Bolshevik" — gives the same speech in both *Angels* and *Slavs!*: "How are we to proceed without theory? Is it enough to reject the past, is it wise to move forward in this blind fashion, without the cold brilliant light of theory to guide the way? . . . You who live in this sour little age cannot imagine the sheer grandeur of the prospect we gazed upon."

A: In both *Perestroika* [part two of *Angels*] and *Slavs!,* the whole play proceeds from the question: If you don't know where you're going, can you move? And do you even have a choice, or do you just dive in and work it out as you're going?

That speech came out of a fight I had with my friend Oskar Eustis about

Gorbachev. Oskar's point, which became the basis of Prelapsarianov's speech, is that if you don't have a theory to start with — Gorbachev pretended to be about democratic socialism but actually sort of was and sort of wasn't; he was also sort of about preserving the Communist Party power elite — what do you do? It's one of those big conundrums.

Q: So what *do* you do?

A: You can't stay back. The fundamental question is: Are we made by history or do we make history — and the answer is yes. I was rereading Marx's *Eighteenth Brumaire of Louis Bonaparte* recently. The whole tradition in socialist struggle is looking to the past for an antecedent form upon which the present revolutionary response is to be modeled. We may need to stop doing that.

Q: Why does the play *Slavs!* end with the question: "What is to be done?"

A: I wanted someone to ask the question: What if this really is the end of history? What if there really is literally nothing to be done, and we're simply stuck with capitalism — although I don't really think it is a possibility.

I still believe in a dialectical ordering of the universe. There is a dynamic principle at work it isn't always mechanically moving things toward the good, but there's always either some sort of progress or decay. And there's too much misery in the world. That is not something that can hold.

Q: What do you think is to be done?

A: I'm 38 now. One of the painful rites of passage that everyone on the left goes through is to realize it's a lifelong struggle. What we're dealing with from Nixon on as a counter-reaction to the '60s is a very widespread, long-term historical trend. It's going to take many years and probably a few decades to reverse. People need to be willing to take an issue that they feel passionately about, address themselves to it as extensively as they are capable of and build common cause between issue groups.

Everybody on the left needs to start talking about how to create, first on local levels and eventually on a national level, a third party or at least a party that could establish some kind of position in Congress. That's the eternal dream of the left.

Q: You think there's no hope for revitalizing the Democratic Party?

A: It's a waste of time at this point. There's a famous story about Paul Wellstone refusing to shake Jesse Helms' hand and being chastised by everyone in the Senate because he wouldn't do it — he was told this is a gentlemen's club where we're all colleagues. That's what's wrong.

Q: One of the characters in *A Bright Room Called Day* keeps saying — as Nazism progressively snatches power and the Weimar Republic falls — that each turn for the worse would be the essential spur for people to rise up and oppose fascism. That didn't happen. Do you see parallels today?

A: You don't want to be opportunistic about it and say, "Oh, goody, millions of people are going to be thrown out of their homes — now we'll really get things cooking." It's like people saying the AIDS epidemic helped organize the gay and lesbian community.

Q: Speaking of which, there's a lot of discussion now about the second wave of the AIDS epidemic, and about gay men not practicing safer sex. Where do you weigh in?

A: It's very difficult to ask people to abstain from pleasure indefinitely, especially sexual erotic pleasure, which is so incredibly important to human beings and the enjoyment of which among homosexuals is so much of a political battlefield. There is absolutely no question that safer sex is not as gratifying and that given all the despair and the unbelievably imponderable weight of loss that the community has had to deal with, self-destructive behaviors are going to be engaged in.

Q: Do you think the gay community should be discussing this publicly?

A: Of course it's going to be discussed publicly. But you have to be smart. When you make a public utterance you are responsible for being responsible. We're still an embattled community, and if you're stupid about it you'll give aid to the enemy.

Q: Do you have that conundrum as a playwright?

A: You have to say: What am I feeding into? I think you should ask yourself that question and then make the decision based on the answers you come up with. I regret having made the only black person in *Angels* a nurse; that was an inept thing to do.

I was very scared about writing a play where there's a couple, one has AIDS and the other walks out. I thought, this is transgressive and scary and am I going to become public enemy number one in the gay community for having written a character like Louis?

On the other hand, you have to be willing to scare the horses. You have to be interesting and you have to be daring and you have to be willing to write things that shock. Shock is part of art. Art that's polite is not much fun.

Anna Deavere Smith

Anna Deavere Smith was born in 1950. Besides teaching at Stanford University where she is the Ann O'Day Maples Professor of the Arts, she is a poet, director, playwright, and a notable actor, appearing most recently in the film *American President* (1996). She has also taught at Carnegie-Mellon University, Yale University, New York University, in the Drama Division of the University of Southern California, and at American Conservatory Theatre, her alma mater.

She is at work on a series of theatrical pieces that she calls *On the Road: A Search for American Character,* the first of which was produced in Berkeley, California, in 1983, followed by *Aye, Aye, Aye, I'm Integrated,* a 1984 off-Broadway production. She has also done a one-woman show called *A Birthday Card and Aunt Julia's Shoes.* Her sensational *Fires in the Mirror: Crown Heights, Brooklyn, and Other Identities* (1991), the thirteenth work in the *On the Road* series, was a one-woman show in which she played all the roles. It won the Obie award, was a runner-up for the Pulitzer Prize in drama in 1992, and was shown on the Public Broadcasting System in 1993.

Smith became nationally known for *Fires in the Mirror* and for developing what the *New York Times* called "documentary theater, which has the immediacy of live drama and the fluidity of film." Smith's technique is to interview many people connected with a traumatic social event; she then refines their dialogue and enacts it herself, using a minimum of makeup, wigs, costumes, and props. She relies heavily on her body language, on gesture and speech pattern, and on facial expression to create character. In the sense Smith is as much a performance artist as a playwright, and her dynamic approach to the roles convinces the audience she has "become" the parts she plays, from gang members to city officials, from prostitutes to housewifes. She portrays African-American men, Asian merchants, white suburbanites — and all convincingly.

TWILIGHT: LOS ANGELES, 1992

Twilight: Los Angeles, 1992 opened at the Joseph Papp Public Theater in New York in 1994 and moved to the Cort Theater on Broadway. The play focuses on the riots in Los Angeles set off when a jury handed down a not-guilty verdict for the white policemen who were videotaped beating Rodney King, an African American, after they pulled him over for a traffic violation. Emotions ran high across the country in response to the beating, and most people were astonished at the verdict. When the verdict was read, South-Central Los Angeles erupted into one of the worst riots in the United States since the 1960s.

Just as Rodney King had become a symbol of police violence toward African Americans, a white truck driver named Reginald Denny became a symbol of the innocent bystander. During these riots Denny was beaten by a mob; his assault was captured on film from a news helicopter. In both cases TV replays stirred public emotions — both men were at the center of intense drama.

Anna Deavere Smith had confronted similar material when she wrote *Fires in the Mirror*, which centered on the death of a black child killed in an automobile accident in which the driver responsible for the accident was a Hasidic Jew. That incident was followed by a riot in which a Jewish Talmudic student was stabbed and killed by a group of blacks. Smith's method of talking with people on all sides of a dispute was developed for that play, and it yields fascinating results in *Twilight: Los Angeles, 1992*.

Part of the excitement of the work is missing when we read it on the page, but the material Smith transforms for the drama is extraordinary in itself. She recorded interviews with Latinos, African-American gang members, the police, people in the Hollywood power structure, store-owners who had been burned out and shot, and Reginald Denny himself. The entire play, from which the following is excerpted, includes the edited transcripts of interviews with forty-six people. Smith played all of them in the course of the drama.

Part of the power of this play lies in the language of the characters. It is diverse, sometimes unclear and confused — mirroring the thinking of the speaker — and it sometimes reveals the limitations of people attempting to confront issues that would give professional sociologists pause. As one critic has said, most of the speakers seem shocked, traumatized by what has happened. Many are filled with hatred: against African Americans, against whites, against Latinos, against Asians, against non-Asians, against police, against citizens. Others speak as if they feel guilty for what happened. Others resent the attention that Reginald Denny, a survivor, received from celebrities such as Jesse Jackson and Arsenio Hall and from the press in general. Others see themselves as victims and have a difficult time fathoming why they should be singled out. Smith's characters cover an amazing range of possible responses.

Smith delivers each speech as a monologue — a risky technique, because the creative tension developed when a second person is present onstage is unavailable to her. She carries it off not only by her acting but also by the power of her subject matter. The sheer variety — and the consistency of the reappearance of the characters — is spellbinding.

Twilight: Los Angeles, 1992 in Performance

George C. Wolfe, the director of the Joseph Papp Public Theater in New York directed the first production and used a number of multimedia effects to intensify the action. The video of Rodney King's beating was projected on the back of the stage, first in slow motion, then later at regular speed. Other videos showed the burning and looting of Los Angeles. The beating of Reginald Denny, as filmed from the air by a television crew in a helicopter, was also shown in its entirety. As Smith changed characters, a projection identified the character and offered a telling fragment from the character's speech, such as Stanley K. Sheinbaum's "Hammer," highlighting his description of seeing an African-American woman driving a BMW waving a hammer outside the driver's side window. The entire Public Theater run was sold out and the play was moved to Broadway in May 1994 where it ran for five weeks. Smith has also toured in regional theater to considerable acclaim. One of the most recent performances was held at New Haven's Long Wharf Theatre in 1996 and was directed by Sharon Ott of the Berkeley Repertory Theatre.

Robert Brustein commented in his review that he felt the multimedia effects of George C. Wolfe were "probably more appropriate for the coming Broadway move than for the stage of the Public. But it leaves us with a shocking sense of how America's hopes for racial harmony were left burning in the ashes of South-Central L.A."

Anna Deavere Smith (b. 1950)

FROM TWILIGHT: LOS ANGELES, 1992   *1994*

THESE CURIOUS PEOPLE

STANLEY K. SHEINBAUM, *former president, Los Angeles Police Commission*

(*A beautiful house in Brentwood. There is art on all the walls. The art has a real spirit to it. These are the paintings by his wife, Betty Sheinbaum. There is a large living room, an office off the living room which you can see. It is mostly made of wood, lots of papers and books. The office of a writer. There are glass windows that look out on a pool, a garden, a view. Behind us is a kitchen where his wife, Betty, was, but eventually she leaves. Stanley is sitting at a round wooden table with a cup of coffee. He is in a striped shirt and khaki pants and loafers. He has a beard. He is tall, and about seventy-three years old. He seems gruff, but when he smiles or laughs, his face lights up the room. It's very unusual. He has the smile and laugh of a highly spiritual, joyous, old woman, like a grandmother who has really been around. There is a bird inside the house which occasionally chirps.*)

Very
interesting thing happened.
Like a week and a half (*very thoughtfully trying to
    remember*),
Maxine Waters° calls me up —
You know who she is?
We're very good friends —
she calls me up and she says,
"Ya gotta come with me.
I been going down to Nickerson Gardens
and
the cops come in and break up these gang meetings
and these are gang meetings
for the purpose of truces."
(*I was momentarily distracted.*)
Pay attention.
The next Saturday afternoon,
the next day even,

I go down with her,
uh,
to,
uh,
Nickerson Gardens
(*an abrupt stop, and
second pause, as if he's forgotten something for a
    moment*)
and I see a whole bunch of, uh,
police car
sirens and the lights
and I say, "What the hell's going on here?"
So sure enough, I pull in there
(*three-second pause*).
We pull in there
and, uh,
I ask a cop what's going on
and he says,
"Well, we got a call for help."
There's a gang meeting over there.
There's a community park there and there's a gym
and I go down to the . . .
we go down to the gang meeting
and half of 'em
outside of the
gym
and half of 'em
inside
and here's about a hundred cops lined up over here
and about another hundred
over here
and, uh,
I go
into the, uh,
into the group of gang members who were outside.
Even Maxine got scared by this.
I gotta tell you I was brought up in Harlem.
I just have a feel for what I can do and what I can't
    do
and I did that.
And I spent about
two, two
hours talkin' to these guys.
Some of these guys were ready to kill me.
(*A bird chirps loudly; maybe this is a parakeet or an
    inside bird.*)
I'm the police commissioner

Maxine Waters: Then-congressional representative from South-Central Los Angeles and currently a senator from California (see p. 1694).

and therefore a cop
and therefore all the things that went along with be-
    ing a cop.
It was a very interesting experience, God knows.
One guy who was really disheveled and disjointed
and disfigured
opens up his whole body
and it's clear he's been shot across . . .
not in that . . . not in that day,
months or years before,
and, you know,
these guys have been through the wars down there
and,
you know, I hung around long enough that I could
    talk to them,
get some insights.
But the cops were mad,
they were really mad
that I would go talk to them
and not talk to them
and I knew that if I went and talked to them
I'd have bigger problems here
But I also knew as I was doing this,
I knew they were gonna be pissed.
Two days I got a letter
and I was . . .
the letter really pleased me in some way.
It was very respectful.
"You went in and talked to our enemy."
Gangs are their enemy.
And so
I marched down to Seventy-seventh
and, uh,
I said, "Fuck you,
I can come in here
anytime I want and talk to you."
Yeah, at roll call.
I said, uh,
"This is a shot I had at talking to these
curious people
about whom I know nothing
and I wanna learn.
Don't you want me to learn about 'em?"
You know, that kind of thing.
At the same time, I had been on this kick,
as I told you before, of . . .
of fighting for what's right for the cops,
because they haven't gotten what they should.
I mean, this city has abused both sides.
The city has abused the cops.
Don't ever forget that.
If you want me to give you an hour on that, I'll give
    you an hour on
that.
Uh,

and at the end,
uh,
I knew I hadn't won when they said,
"So which side are you on?"
When I said, I said, it's . . .
my answer was
"Why do I have to be on a side?"
Yu, yuh, yeh know.
Why do I have to be on a side?
There's a problem here.

WHEN I FINALLY GOT MY VISION/NIGHTCLOTHES

MICHAEL ZINZUN, *representative, Coalition Against Police Abuse*

(*In his office at Coalition Against Police Abuse. There are very bloody and disturbing photographs of victims of police abuse. The most disturbing one was a man with part of his skull blown off and part of his body in the chest area blown off, so that you can see the organs. There is a large white banner with a black circle and a panther. The black panther is the image from the Black Panther Party. Above the circle is "All Power to the People." At the bottom is "Support Our Youth, Support the Truce."*)

I witnessed police abuse.
It was
about one o'clock in the morning
and, um,
I was asleep,
like
so many of the other neighbors,
and I hear this guy calling out for help.
So myself and other people came out in socks
and gowns
and, you know,
nightclothes
and we came out so quickly we saw the police had
    this brother
handcuffed
and they was beatin' the shit out of him!
You see,
Eugene Rivers was his name
and, uh,
we had our community center here
and they was doin' it right across the street from
    it.
So I went out there 'long with other people and we
    demanded they stop.

They tried to hide him by draggin' him away and we
    followed him
and told him they gonna stop.
They singled me out.
They began Macing the crowd, sayin' it was hostile.
They began
shootin' the Mace to get everybody back.
They singled me out.
I was handcuffed.
Um,
when I got Maced I moved back
but as I was goin' back I didn't go back to the center,
I ended up goin' around this . . .
it was a darkened
unlit area.
And when I finally got my vision
I said I ain't goin' this way with them police behind
    me,
so I turned back around, and when I did,
they Maced me again
and I went down on one knee
and all I could do was feel all these police stompin'
    on my back.
(*He is smiling.*)
And I was thinkin' . . . I said
why, sure am glad they got them soft walkin' shoes
    on,
because when the patrolmen, you know, they have
    them cushions,
so every stomp,
it wasn't a direct hard old . . .
yeah
type thing.
So
then they handcuffed me.
I said they . . .
well,
I,
I can take this
we'll deal with this tamarr [sic],
and they handcuffed me.
And then one of them lifted my
head up —
I was on my stomach —
he lifted me from behind
and hit me with a billy club
and struck me in the
side of the head,
which give me about forty stitches —
the straight billy club,
it wasn't a
P-28, the one with the side handle.
Now, I thought in my mind, said hunh,
they couldn't even knock me out,
they in trouble now.

You see what I'm sayin'?
'Cause I knew what we were gonna do,
'cause I dealt with police abuse
and I knew how to organize.
I say they couldn't even knock me out,
and so as I was layin' there
they was all standin' around me.
They still was Macing, the crowd was gettin' larger
    and larger and
larger
and more police was comin'.
One these pigs stepped outta the crowd with his flash-
    light,
caught me right in my eye,
and you can still see the stitches (*he lowers his lid and
    shows it*)
and
exploded the optic nerve to the brain,
ya see,
and boom (*he snaps his fingers*)
that was it.
I couldn't see no more since then.
I mean, they . . .
they took me to the hospital
and the doctor said, "Well, we can sew this eyelid up
    and these
stitches here
but
I don't think we can do nothin' for that eye."
So when I got out I got a CAT scan,
you know,
and
they said,
"It's gone."
So I still didn't understand it but I said
well,
I'm just gonna keep strugglin'.
We mobilized
to the point where we were able
to get two officers fired,
two officers had to go to trial,
and
the city on an eye
had to cough up one point two million dollars
and so
that's why
I am able to be here every day,
because that money's bein' used to further the strug-
    gle.
I ain't got no big Cadillac,
I ain't got no gold . . .
I ain't got no
expensive shoes or clothes.
What we do have

is an opportunity to keep struggling and to do
        research and to
organize.

CARMEN

ANGELA KING, *aunt of Rodney King*

*(A shop in Pasadena. A very, very rainy day. We are
sitting in the back of the shop. She insists that my assistant, Kishisha Jefferson, join us, because she
thought it was not good to make Kishisha sit in the car
in the rain. We are in the back of her shop. There are
work tables with paints, etc. She makes T-shirts. The
shop itself is a boutique with clothing for men,
women, and children. Some of the clothing is Afro-
centric in design, other items are more mainstream.
She is a powerful looking woman with a direct gaze
and wavy hair, and a warmth that is natural, even
when it is not intended. She looks as though she has
Native American ancestry. She is wearing a white
sweater, a long skirt, and boots. She smokes a cigarette. There is an iron gate at the main door that is
painted white. There is a small television in the back
where we are. She lives in an area behind where we are
sitting. The interview was actually scheduled for the
day before, but she was reluctant to speak with me,
because when I arrived Kishisha was in the car.
[Kishisha normally drove me to, but did not attend,
each interview.] It is ironic that now at the rescheduled
time, she insists that Kishisha join us.)*

Our life is something like,
uh,
what's the name of that picture
with Dorothy Dandridge
when she was like
a prostitute and the guy she met was in the Air
        Force — the service?
Carmen.
Dorothy Dandridge
and Harry Belafonte —
that was us.
How they partied a lot,
and the guy in in the Air Force,
the way he was conservative,
was my father.
We were brought up
for about five or six years like that.
The part where she was . . .
she got in some trouble,
the way my mom,

she cut my father:
They were at the NCO° club,
they got to drinkin',
and they went to jail out on the base.
She stabbed him —
oh yeah, honey —
he had a scar on his neck.
She went to jail behind that.
We were twelve or thirteen years old.
It seems like it should have been in a movie:
separated and
livin' in different homes
and then joinin' back together in different homes
and reuniting.
My brother and I were only two that stayed together,
and that brother was the father of Rodney.
Things that we did
like goin fishin',
and then on Franklin,
the Sacramento River,
and then . . .
I ain't never seen nothing like it in my life.
It was me, Rodney, Paul, and Sam,
Rodney's friend,
and I looked up and Rodney was down in the
        water —
had his pants rolled,
feet and all,
like these Africans —
done caught him a big old
trout
by his —
with his hands.
That was the worst mess I seen.
Got him like this here:
"I got him, I got him!
I got a big . . .
'bout that big . . . "
I said, "Boy, you sure you ain't got some African in
        you?"
Ooh,
yeah,
I'm talkin 'bout them wild Africans,
not one them well raised ones.
Like with a fish hook?
But to see somebody down in the water with the
        pants rolled up
like this here . . .
I said "Get out of there you scaring 'em, you scaring
        um!"

NCO: Acronym for noncommissioned officers, that is, below the rank of lieutenant.

"Naw, I got this one, I got this one!"
And comin' up there with this big old trout.
Hand fishin'!
He was the only one I saw down in there in that
    water,
him and this other guy, this big Mexican guy,
Sam?
And he's the only one I seen catch fish like that.
The rest of 'em got poles.
Down in there with them pants up like that.
That remind me of what I see in Africa somewhere.
I ain't never seen nobody fish with their hands.
Talkin' bout "I ain't got time to wait."
That's why I call him greedy.
I'm 'a ask him does he remember that.
He oughta remember it, he was bout sixteen or sev-
    enteen years old.
Um, Um, Um . . .
He — Glen,
Rodney —
went through three plastic surgeons
just to look like Rodney again.
Galen called to say cops done beat Glen up, talkin
    about Rodney,
I said "What?"
And when I was just turning the channels,
I saw this white car . . .
And he looked just like his father.
I don't know if it's when you lose a life
it comes back in somebody else.
Oh, you should have seen him.
It's a hell of a look.
I, I mean you wouldn't have known him
to look at him now.
I tell him he's got a lot to be thankful for —
a hell of a lot:
He couldn't talk,
just, "Der, der, der."
I said, Goddamn!
I was right here
when it happened.
You want me to tell it?
Ah . . .
(*She starts crying;*
she makes about seven sobs.)
Oh, man.
It just came out.
(*She gets up and goes away to the door. The hammer-*
ing is louder. There are two hammers, in different
places, as if above or next door. The hammers really
sound like a dialogue, and there are cars outside, and
rain. The dripping is very close.)
Ah.
It comes up every now and then.
Don't worry.

Just burst out . . .
Um . . .
I told you this whole thing is too much.
It's hurting an' then you're happy,
'specially when I get to thinking about such treacher-
    ous people out there.
We weren't raised like this.
We weren't raised with no black and white thing.
We were raised with all kinds of friends:
Mexicans, Indians, Blacks, Whites, Chinese.
You never would have known that something like
    this would happen to us.
And now it's such a shock.
And then the media,
and then, uh,
"What the hell did you get on there tellin' them
    people?"
I said,
"Leave me the hell alone," —
this is the other end of the family —
"them people wants to know.
I'm not gonna keep my doors closed up."
I'm arguin' with them.
"Well tell them this here,
and the next time you get on there,
you tell these people this"
I'm not tellin' these people a damn thing —
all this here went through my damn mind.
I get up here,
"Well Mrs. King so and so and so and so."
Um hum, yeah.
And then they . . .
You know I get up here,
"Oh should I say this should I say that?"
Just a mess, the whole thing.
The media came to me 'cause I was a relative
of Rodney's
and his mother
Dessa wasn't gonna talk —
they didn't because of they religion,
they didn't want to get involved in a political . . .
whatever this thing was.
But I didn't give a damn if it was the president's . . .
whatever it was,
my brother's son out there was lookin' like hell,
that I saw in that bed, and I was gonna fight for
    every bit of
our justice
and fairness.
I didn't care nothin' 'bout no religious . . .
You know, the President,
he's the top thing,
you know, they cared about him;
that's the way I cared about Glen,
you know, Rodney.

That's the way I feel,
you know, a higher sorts.
It could have been my mother.
But I'm not gonna say that.
You see how everybody rave when something
      happens with the
President of the United States?
Okay, here's a nobody,
but the way they beat him,
this is the way I felt towards him.
You understand what I'm sayin' now?
You do? (*really making sure that I mean what I say*)
Alright.
(*a breath, and more speed as she proceeds*)
That's the way I felt.
I didn't give a damn about no religious
nothin' else,
I wanted justice,
and I wanted whatever
them things had comin' to them done to them,
regardless — you can call it revenge or whatever, but
what I saw on that video,
on that TV,
that was a
mess.
And I just heard him holler,
that's what got me 'while ago.
And then they say,
"Motorist."
And then I look and saw that white car,
and then I saw him out on that ground,
I heard him hollerin',
I recognized him
out on that ground.
Um . . .
Um . . .
That Koon —
that's the one in that whole trial —
that man showed no kind of remorse at all,
you know that?
He sit there like, "It ain't no big thing,
and I
will do it again."
That's the way he looked.
You ever seen him?
And he smile at you.
I don't know how,
I don't *even* know how . . .
the nerve,
the audacity.
And even Briseno,
he's gonna get on there . . .
that's what I'm tellin'
Rodney:
"They tryin'

to do everything they possibly can — *anything* they
      can —
to make you look bad to the people.
Because of what they had,
that, you know,
what's been done to them —
they've been embarrassed,
and they caught them,
you know, on video,
beatin' you like that,
and the public saw it,
they tryin' to do anything they can to discredit you.
You need to get somewhere and sit down."
I didn't hear nobody mention
about 'em having a bug.
It was like a screw
about the size of my thumb
on the bumper —
on the Blazer —
and they were trailin' him everywhere he went.
This is how they knew
where he was goin',
or how
every time you turn around Rodney King's encounter
      with the law
they had a *screw*.
This is how they had him tagged down.
Uhm hum. Uhm hum.
Right after that Hollywood incident
with that prostitute
and on the phone,
I can hear the echo.
And when I hang up someone is still there.
And then most of the time
I be talkin' crazy anyway
so it doesn't matter.
And why? I have no idea.
But they say there's nothing they can do about the
      taps.
I've called the telephone company
but
something — it being interfered with the federal gov-
      ernment,
so it wasn't nothin' they could do about it.
But I know one thing:
Half the things I said to them on there —
it's been goin' on for a while —
I drop through profanity,
I do,
'cause I get on there, I be wantin' to talk and relax,
      you know, and here something click up and click
      up
and that's when I get started.
I do.
'Cause you have to stop and catch yourself,

Anna Deavere Smith in *Twilight: Los Angeles, 1992.*

you can't just talk comfortable.
Yeah.

YOUR HEADS IN SHAME

ANONYMOUS MAN, *juror in Simi Valley trial*

(*A house in Simi Valley. Fall. Halloween decorations
are up. Dusk. Low lamplight. A slender, soft-spoken
man in glasses. His young daughter and wife greeted
me as well. Quietness.*)

As soon as we went
into the courtroom with the verdicts

there were
plainclothes policemen everywhere.
You know, I knew that
there would be people unhappy with the verdict,
but I didn't expect near
what happened.
If I had known
what was going to happen,
I mean, it's not,
it's not fair to say I would have voted a different
way.
I wouldn't have —
that's not our justice system —
but I would have written a note to the judge saying,
"I can't do this,"
because of
what it put my family through.
Excuse me.
(*Crying.*)
So anyway,
we started going out to the bus
and the police said
right away,
"If there's rocks and bottles, don't worry
the glass on the bus is bulletproof."
And then I noticed a huge mob scene,
and it's a sheriff's bus that they lock prisoners in.
We got to the hotel and there were some obnoxious
    reporters out
there
already, trying to get interviews.
And, you know, the police were trying to get us into
    the bus and cover
our faces,
and,
and this reporter said,
"Why are you hiding your heads in shame? Do you
    know that buildings
are burning
and people are dying in South L.A.
because of you?"
And twenty minutes later I got home
and the same obnoxious reporter was at the door
and my wife was saying, "He doesn't want to talk to
    anybody,"
and she kept saying,
"The people wanna know,
the people wanna know,"
and trying to get her foot in the door.
And I said, "Listen, I don't wanna talk to anybody.
    My wife has made
that clear."
And I,
you know, slammed the door in her face.
And so she pulled two houses down
and started

filming our house.
And watching on the TV
and seeing all the political leaders,
Mayor Bradley
and President Bush,
condemning our verdicts.
I mean, the jurors as a group, we tossed around:
was this a setup of some sort?
We just feel like we were pawns that were thrown
     away by the
system.
I mean,
the judge,
most of the jurors
feel like when he was reading the verdicts
he . . .
we thought we could sense a look of disdain on his
     face,
and he also had said
beforehand
that after the verdicts came out
he would like to come up and talk to us,
but after we gave the verdicts
he sent someone up and said he didn't really want
     to
do that then.
And plus, he had the right and power to
withhold our names for a period of time
and he did not do that,
he released them right away.
I think it was apparent that we would be harassed
and I got quite a few threats.
I got threatening letters and threatening phone
     calls.
I think he just wanted to separate himself . . .
A lot of newspapers published our addresses too.
The *New York Times* published the values of our
     homes.
They were released in papers all across the country.
We didn't answer the phone,
because it was just every three minutes . . .
We've been portrayed as white racists.
One of the most disturbing things, and a lot of the
     jurors
said that
the thing that bothered them that they received in
     the mail
more
than anything else,
more than the threats, was a letter from the KKK
saying,
"We support you, and if you need our help, if you
     want to join
our organization,
we'd welcome you into our fold."
And we all just were:

No, oh!
God!

"DON'T SHOOT"

RICHARD KIM, *appliance store owner*

(*Morning. August 1993. A Korean-American man in his thirties. He is dressed in khakis, a white shirt, and a tie. We are sitting in the back of his electronics store, which is quite large. We are in a room with very expensive stereo equipment.*)

We waited for about half an hour
and then my father showed up with a neighbor.
He told me what had happened.
There was no police officer to be found anywhere.
We came back here.
We started calling all the police stations and the
     hospitals to see if
anybody had checked in
if they fit the description.
Unfortunately we can't get any kind of answer from
     anybody.
While that was happening, a neighbor called and
     said you better
come down here because
there are hundreds of people and your store's being
     looted
at this time.
So we packed up our van, four people, five people,
     including
myself, and we headed down there.
I already knew people were carrying guns,
already knew my mother was shot at that corner.
So it was like going to war.
That's the only thing I can say.
By the time we got there
at this time
there are hundreds of people at our store.
At that time when we were approaching the store
I realized there are gunshots going on.
As I was approaching the store
one person was carrying to the side —
obviously he was wounded —
and our neighbor,
he was a car dealership and he was trying to hold
     down the store,
trying to keep the people back,
and I can see one person still at the corner by the
     door
with a shotgun and I looked at across the street.
There are at least three or four people with hand-
     guns firing back.
There was exchange of fire going on.

So I pulled our van — I was driving —
I pulled our van in between our store entrance,
in between the person firing at me in front of the
    store,
and I got out and my first thought was I could use
    the van to block
the bullets from hitting the guy in front of the store.
I yelled for everybody to stop shooting, yelled,
"Don't shoot!"
For a split second, they stopped shooting.
And across the street
I looked, could see three people, they looked at me,
    and they pointed the
guns at me.
And they were so close
I could see the barrels of the guns.
And . . . I knew they were going to start firing.
I got a gut feeling.
And I ducked.
And . . . they started firing at the van.
And . . . I came around the van, to the back.
And . . . we had a rifle inside the van.
And . . . I pulled it out,
pulled the trigger,
and it just clicked, because there was no bullet in the
    chamber.
So I went back,
put the bullet in the chamber, and returned fire at the
    people firing
at us.
I wasn't aiming to hurt anybody.
More or less trying to disperse the people.
I was firing at the general direction that the gunfire
    was coming from.
When that happened, people dispersed.
I guess the people firing at me decided it wasn't
    worth it and they all
took off.
Everybody just went "pa-chew."

BUBBLE GUM MACHINE MAN

ALLEN COOPER, A.K.A. BIG AL, *ex-gang
member, ex-convict, activist in national truce
movement*

(*He is wearing an odd cap with a button, and buttons
on his shirt. In a gym in Nickerson Gardens, 5:30
P.M.*)

The L.A. Four they committed a crime of what?
Assault
and battery?
And what did the government dig for?

What did they dig for?
Stoppin' traffic of a truck?
Are they sure that truck belonged in that area?
Did they check to see if that truck qualified to fit on
    that city street?
No, they didn't check that.
That wasn't a highway or nothin';
that was a boulevard.
He was turnin' off a residential street!
You gotta understand, it may have been a
intimidation move,
OK,
drivin' into a location that is at a uprising.
And I guess he's at a point tryin' to prove he can get
past.
Any other commonsense person
woulda went around.
But we're not basin' our life on Reginald Denny;
neither are we basin' our lives on Rodney King.
Only thing we're expressing through the Rodney
    King —
through Reginald Denny beating —
it shows how
a black person gets treated in his community.
And it was once brought to the light
and shown
and then we still . . . we see no belief,
because they never handled, from the top of the
    level, the way it
should have been handled,
because they handled like a soap opera.
That's all that
really was.
If you put twenty hidden cameras
in the country jail system,
you got people beat worse than that
point blank.
Some jails got things
called
the red room
and the blue room,
you get what they call an attitude adjustment.
What Rodney King . . .
It been —
it's been twenty, thirty years,
and people suffered beatings from law enforcement.
It ain't nothin' new.
It was just brought to the light this time.
But then it showed what —
it showed that it doesn't mean a thing,
It doesn't mean a thing.
Now if that was an officer down there gettin' beat,
it would a been a real national riot thing —
you hear me?
Just imagine how many people woulda been out
    there

clappin';
it wouldn't a been no sad sorry, hot . . .
it woulda been a happy hot line.
Everybody makin' emotion out of somethin':
Rotney King, Rotney King, Rotney King.
It's not Rotney King.
It's the ghetto.
I was at one of these swap meets
and a bubble gum machine man pulled a gun out.
Now what a bubble gum machine man doin' with a
     pistol?
Who wanna rob a bubble gum machine?
Because we live here, the conditions are so
enormous and so dangerous,
that they have to be qualified to carry a firearm.
What is the purpose?
You got to live here to express this point, you got to
     live
here to see what's goin' on.
You gotta look at history, baby,
you gotta look at history.
It wasn't . . .
Anything is never a problem 'til the black man gets
     his
          hands on it.
It was good for the NRA
to have fully automatic weapons,
but when the Afro-American people got hold of 'em,
it was a crime!
Aww . . .
He's a problem
in the neighborhood;
he has a AK 47 assault weapon.
We didn't bring them guns here.
We didn't make up —
they was put here for a reason:
to entrap us!
Point blank.
You gotta look at history, baby,
you gotta look at history.
This Reginald Denny thing is a joke.
It's joke.
That's just a delusion to the real
problem.

A WEIRD COMMON THREAD IN OUR LIVES

REGINALD DENNY

(*In the office of Johnnie Cochran, his lawyer. A conference room. Walls are lined with law books. Denny
is wearing a baseball hat and T-shirt. His friend, a
man, is there with a little girl. One of Cochran's assis-*

*tants, a young black woman attorney, sits in on the in-
terview. Denny is upbeat, speaks loudly. Morning,
May 1993.*)

Every single day
I must make this trip to Inglewood — no problem —
and I get off the freeway like usual,
taking up as much space as I can in the truck.
People don't like that.
Because I have to.
That little turn onto Florence
is pretty tricky,
it's really a tight turn.
I take two lanes to do it in
and
it was just like a scene
out of a movie.
Total confusion and chaos.
I was just in awe.
And the thing that I remember most vivid —
broken glass
on the ground.
And for a split second I was goin'
check this out,
and the truck in front of me —
and I found out later —
the truck in front of me,
medical supplies goin' to Daniel Freeman!°
(*He laughs.*)
Kind of a
ironic thing!
And the, uh,
the strange thing was
that what everyone thought was a fire extinguisher
I got clubbed with,
it was a bottle of oxygen,
'cause the guy had medical supplies.
I mean,
does anyone know
what a riot looks like?
I mean, I'm sure they do now.
I didn't have a clue of what one looked like
and
I didn't know that the verdict had come down.
I didn't pay any attention
to that,
because that
was somebody else's problem
I guess I thought
at the time.
It didn't have anything to do with me.
I didn't usually pay too much attention of what was
     going on in

Daniel Freeman: A hospital in South-Central Los Angeles.

California
or in America or anything
and, uh,
I couldn't for the life of me figure out what was
     goin' on.
Strange things do happen on that street.
Every now and again police busting somebody.
That was a street that was never . . .
I mean, it was always an exciting . . .
we,
lot of guys looked forward to going down that street
'cause there was always something going on, it
     seemed
like,
and the cool thing was I'd buy those cookies
from
these guys
on the corner,
and I think they're, uh,
Moslems?
And they sell cookies
or cakes,
the best-tasting stuff,
and whatever they were selling that day,
and it was always usually a surprise,
but it was very well known
that it was a good surprise!
Heck, a good way to munch!
But when I knew something was wrong was when
     they bashed in the
right window of
my truck.
That's the end of what I remember as far as anything
until five or six days later.
They say I was in a coma.
And I still couldn't figure out,
you know,
how I got here.
And
It was quite a few weeks after I was in the hospital
that they even let on that there was a riot,
because the doctor didn't feel it
was something I needed to know.
Morphine is what they were givin me for pain,
and it was just an interesting time.
But I've never been in an operating room.
It was like . . .
this is just . . .
I 'member like in a movie
they flip on the big lights
and they're really in there.
(*He laughs.*)
I was just goin' "God"
and seein' doctors around with masks on
and I still didn't know why I was still there

and next thing
I know I wake up a few days later.
I think when it really dawned on me
that something big might have happened
was when important people wanted to come in and
     say hi.
The person that I remember that wanted to come in
     and see me,
the first person that I was even aware of who wanted
     to see me,
was Reverend Jesse Jackson,
and I'm just thinkin':
not this guy,
that's the dude I see on TV all the time.
And then it was a couple days later that
Arsenio Hall came to see me
and he just poked his head in, said hello,
and, uh,
I couldn't say nothin' to him.
And then, about then I started to, uh,
started to get it.
And by the time I left Daniel Freeman I knew what
     happened,
except they wouldn't let me watch it on TV.
I mean, they completely controlled that remote-
     control thing.
They just had it on a movie station.
And if I hadn't seen some of the stuff,
you know, of me doin' a few things after everything
     was done,
like climbing back into the truck,
and talking to Titus and Bobby and Terry and Lee —
that's the four people
who came to my rescue,
you know — they're telling me stuff that I would
     never
even have known.
Terry
I met only because she came as a surprise guest visit
     to the hospital.
That was an emotional time.
How does one say that
someone
saved
my life?
How does a person,
how do I
express enough
thanks
for someone risking their
neck?
And then I was kind of . . .
I don't know if "afraid" is the word,
I was just a little,
felt a little awkward meeting people

who
saved me.
Meeting them was not like meeting
a stranger,
but it was like
meeting a
buddy.
There was a weird common thread in our lives
That's an extraordinary event,
and here is four people —
the ones in the helicopter —
and they just stuck with it,
and then you got four people
who seen it on TV
and said enough's enough
and came to my rescue.
They tell me
I drove the truck for what? About a hundred or so
    feet.
The doctors say there's *fight* or *flight* syndrome.
And I guess I was in *flight!*
And it's been seventeen years since I got outta high
    school!
I been driving semis,
it's almost second nature,
but Bobby Green
saw that I was gettin' nowhere fast and she just
    jumped in and
scooted me over
and drove the truck.
By this time
it was tons of glass and blood everywhere,
'cause I've seen pictures of what I looked like
when I first went into surgery,
and I mean it was a pretty
bloody mess.
And they showed me my hair,
when they cut off my hair
they gave it to me in a plastic bag.
And it was just
long hair and
glass and blood.
Lee —
that's a woman —
Lee Euell,
she told me
she just
cradled me.
There's no
passenger seat in the truck
and here I am just kind of on my knees in the middle
    of the floor
and, uh,
Lee's just covered with blood,
and Titus is on one side,

'cause Bobby couldn't see out the window.
The front windshield was so badly broken
it was hard to see.
And Titus is standing on the running board telling
    Bobby where to go,
and then Terry,
Titus's girlfriend,
she's in front of the truck
weaving through traffic,
dodging toward cars
to get them to
kind of move out of the way,
to get them to clear a path,
and next stop was
Daniel Freeman Hospital!
Someday when I,
uh,
get a house,
I'm gonna have one of the rooms
and it's just gonna be
of all the riot stuff
and it won't be a
blood-and-guts
memorial,
it's not gonna be a sad,
it's gonna be a happy room.
It's gonna be . . .
Of all the crazy things that I've got,
all the,
the
love and compassion
and the funny notes
and the letters from faraway places,
just framed, placed,
framed things,
where a person will walk in
and just have a good old time in there.
It'll just be
fun to be in there,
just like a fun thing,
and there won't be
a color problem
in this room.
You take the toughest
white guy
who thinks he's a bad-ass
and
thinks he's better than any other race in town,
get him in a position where he needs help,
he'll take the help
from no matter who the color of the guy
    across . . .
because he's so self-
centered and -serving,
he'll take it

and then
soon as he's better
he'll turn around
and rag on 'em.
I know that for a fact.
Give me what I need and shove off.
It's crazy, it's nuts.
That's the person I'd like to shake and go,
"Uuuh,
you fool,
you selfish little shit" —
those kind of words.
"Uhhh, man, you *nut*."
(*Pause and intense stare, low-key.*)
I don't know what I want.
I just want people to wake up.
It's not a color, it's a person.
So this room,
it's just gonna be
people,
just a wild place,
it's gonna be a blast.
One day,
Lord
willing, it'll happen.

GODZILLA

ANONYMOUS MAN #2 (Hollywood Agent)

(*Morning. A good looking man in shirt and tie and fine shoes. A chic office in an agency in Beverly Hills. We are sitting on a sofa.*)

There was still the uneasiness that was growing
when the fuse was still burning,
but
it was
business as usual.
Basically,
you got
such-and-so on line one,
such-and-so on line two.
Traffic,
Wilshire,
Santa Monica.
Bunch of us hadda go to lunch at the
the Grill
in Beverly Hills.
Um,
gain major
show business dead center business restaurant,
kinda loud but genteel.
The . . . there was an incipient panic —

you could just feel —
the tension
in the
restaurant
it
was palpable,
it was tangible,
you could cut it with a knife.
All anyone was talking
about, you could hear little bits
of information —
did ya hear?
did ya hear?
It's like we were transmitting
thoughts
to each other
all across the restaurant,
we were transmitting thoughts to each other.
All the,
frankly, the
white
upper class,
upper middle class —
whatever your,
the
definition is —
white successful . . .
spending too much money,
too, ya know, too good a restaurant,
that kinda thing.
We were just
getting ourselves into a frenzy,
which I think a lot of it
involved
guilt,
just generic guilt.
When we drove back,
and it's about a ten-minute drive,
talking about the need
for guns
to protect ourselves,
it had just gone from there to there.
But I'm tellin' you, nothin' happened!
I don't mean somebody in the restaurant
had a fight
or somebody screamed at someone —
nothing, just,
ya know,
Caesar salad,
da-de-da,
ya know,
but the whole
bit
went
like that.
We walked in

from the underground garage into here and we
   looked at each other
and we could see people
running around
instead of . . . like,
people walk fast in this business
but now they were, they were like
running,
and
we looked at ourselves —
"we gotta close the office."
So we had gone from
"I'm a little nervous"
to "We gotta close the office,
shut down."
This is a business
we don't shut down.
Memo goes
out saying:
"Office closed for the day.
Everyone please leave
the office."
And *then*
I remember somebody said:
"Did you hear?
They're burning down
the Beverly Center."
By the way, *they* . . .
No no no, it's . . .
There is no *who*.
Whaddya mean, *who*?
No, just *they*.
That's fair enough.
"Did you hear *they* are burning down the Beverly
   Center?"
Oh, okay, *they* . . .
Ya know what I mean?
It almost didn't matter who,
it's irrelevant.
Somebody.
It's not *us!*
That was one of the highlights for me.
So I'm looking outside
and the traffic is far worse
and people were basically fleeing the office
and we were closing all the blinds
and this is about,
um,
I guess about four o'clock.
The vision of all these yuppies
and aging or aged yuppies,
Armani suits,
and, you know,
fleeing like
wild-eyed . . .
All you needed was Godzilla behind them,

you know,
like this . . .
chasing them out of the building,
that's really it.
Aaah, aaah.
(*He laughs, a very hearty laugh.*)
Still,
still,
nothing had happened —
I don't mean to tell you that bombs were
   exploding —
nothing, zero.
So we,
I was one of the last to leave,
as usual,
and the roads were so packed it
it must be like
they were leaving
Hiroshima
or something,
Dresden . . .
I've never been in a war or . . .
just the daily war of . . .
(*Intercom beeps.*)
Who's that?
Do you need me?
One sec. (*He leaves, then returns.*)
Where was I?
Yeah.
What, what was, was
"I deserve it,"
you know,
was I, was I getting
my . . .
when I was *fearing*
for
safety
or my family or something . . .
those moments.
Because the panic was so high
that, oh my God,
I was almost thinking:
"Did I deserve this,
do I, do I deserve it?"
I thought me, personally — no,
me, generically,
maybe so.
Even though I, I . . .
what's provoked it —
the spark —
was the verdict,
which was
ab*surd*.
But that was just the spark —
this had been set
for years before.

But maybe,
not maybe,
but, uh, the
system
plays unequally,
and the people who were
the, they,
who were burning down the Beverly Center
had been victims of the system.
Whether well-intentioned or not,
somebody got the short shrift,
and they did,
and I started to
absorb a little guilt
and say, uh,
"I deserve,
I deserve it!"
I don't mean I deserve to get my house burned
    down.
The us
did
not in . . .
not,
I like to think, not intentionally,
but
maybe so,
there's just . . .
it's so
awful out there.
it was so *heart*breaking,
seeing those . . .
the devastation that went on
and people reduced to burning down their own
    neighborhoods.
Burning down our neighborhoods
I could see.
But burning down their own —
that was more dramatic
to me.

THE UNHEARD

MAXINE WATERS, *Congresswoman, 35th District*

(*This interview is from a speech that she gave at the
First African Methodist Episcopal Church, just after
Daryl Gates had resigned and soon after the upheaval. FAME is a center for political activity in L.A.
Many movie stars go there. On any Sunday you are
sure to see Arsenio Hall and others. Barbra Streisand
contributed money to the church after the unrest. It is
a very colorful church, with an enormous mural and a
huge choir with very exciting music. People line up to*

*go in to the services the way they line up for the the-
ater or a concert.*)

   (*Maxine Waters is a very elegant, confident congresswoman, with a big smile, a fierce bite, and a lot of
guts. Her area is in South-Central. She is a brilliant orator. Her speech is punctuated by organ music and applause. Sometimes the audience goes absolutely wild.*)

First
African
Methodist Episcopal Church.
You all here got it going on.
I didn't know this is what you did at twelve o'clock
    on Sunday.
Methodist,
Baptist,
Church of God and Christ all rolled into one.
There was an insurrection in this city before
and if I remember correctly
it was sparked by police brutality.
We had a Kerner Commission report.
It talked about what was wrong with our society.
It talked about institutionalized racism.
It talked about a lack of services,
lack of government responsive to the people.
Today, as we stand here in 1992,
if you go back and read the report
it seems as though we are talking about what that
    report cited
some twenty years ago still exists today.
Mr. President,
THEY'RE HUNGRY IN THE BRONX TONIGHT,
THEY'RE HUNGRY IN ATLANTA TONIGHT,
THEY'RE HUNGRY IN ST. LOUIS TONIGHT.
Mr. President,
our children's lives are at stake.
We want to deal with the young men who have been
    dropped off of
America's agenda.
Just hangin' out,
chillin',
nothin' to do,
nowhere to go.
They don't show up on anybody's statistics.
They're not in school,
they have never been employed,
they don't really live anywhere.
They move from grandmama
to mama to girlfriend.
They're on general relief and
they're sleepin' under bridges.
Mr. President,
Mr. Governor,
and anybody else who wants to listen:
Everybody in the street was not a thug
or a hood.

For politicians who think
everybody in the street
who committed a petty crime,
stealing some Pampers
for the baby,
a new pair of shoes . . .
We know you're not supposed to steal,
but the times are such,
the environment is such,
that good people reacted in strange ways. They are
     not all crooks and
criminals.
If they are,
Mr. President,
what about your violations?
Oh yes.
We're angry,
and yes,
this Rodney King incident.
The verdict.
Oh, it was more than a slap in the face.
It kind of reached in and grabbed you right here in
     the heart
and it pulled at you
and it hurts so bad.
They want me to march out into Watts,
as the black so-called leadership did in the sixties,
and say, "Cool it, baby,
cool it."
I am sorry.
I know how to talk to my people.
I know how to tell them not to put their lives at risk.
I know how to say don't put other people's lives at
     risk.
But, journalists,
don't you dare dictate to me
about what I'm supposed to say.
It's not nice to display anger.
I am angry.
It is all right to be angry.
It is unfortunate what people do when they are
     frustrated and angry.
The fact of the matter is,
whether we like it or not,
riot
is the voice of the unheard.

IT'S AWFUL HARD TO BREAK AWAY

DARYL GATES, *former chief of Los Angeles Police
Department and current talk show host*

(*In a lounge at the radio station where he does a talk
show. He is in great physical shape and is wearing a
tight-fitting golf shirt and jeans. There is the sound of a
Xerox machine. This is my second interview with him.*)

First of all, I . . . I don't think it was a fund-raiser.
I don't think it was a fund-raiser at all.
It was a group of
people
who were in opposition
to Proposition F.
We're talking about long-term support.
We're talking about people who
came out and supported me right from the beginning
of this controversy,
when people were trying to get me to retire and
     everything.
Real strong supporters
of mine
and they were supporting
a no against Prop . . .
Proposition F.
And they begged me to be there
and I said I would and this is before we knew the . . .
     the,
uh, verdicts were coming in
and I didn't wanna go.
I didn't like those things, I don't like them at all,
but
strong supporters and I said I'll drop by for a little
     while,
I'll drop by,
and, um, so I had a commitment
and I'm a person who tries very hard to keep
     commitments
and somewhere along the way
better sense
should have
prevailed.
Not because it would have changed
the course of . . . of events in any way, shape, or
     form, it wouldn't have.
I was in constant contact with my office.
I have radio beepers, telephones,
uh,
a portable telephone . . .
telephone in my car,
just about everything you'd need
to communicate anywhere within our power.
But somewhere along the line
I should have said
my commitment to them is
not as important as my overall commitment to
     the . . . to the city.
When I . . . when I thought things were getting
to the point that I had . . . we were having some
     serious problems,

I was almost there.
My intent was to drop in say, "Hey,
I think we got a . . . a, uh,
riot blossoming.
I can't stay. I gotta get out of here."
And that's basically what I did.
The problem was
I was further away.
I thought it was in Bel Air. It turned out to be Pacific
    Palisades.
And my driver kept saying,
"We're almost there, we're almost there."
You know, he was kinda . . .
he wasn't sure of the distance either.
"We're almost there, Chief, we're almost there."
My intent was
to say, "Hey, I . . . I gotta get outta here," say hi,
and that's what I intended to do,
and it's awful hard to
break away.
I kept walking toward the door, walking toward the
    door.
People want a picture.
Shake your hand.
And it took longer than I thought it was
and I've criticized myself
from the very beginning. I've never, uh, I've never,
    uh,
justified that in any way, shape, or form.
I said it was wrong. I shouldn't have . . . I should
    have
    turned around.
I know better.
Would it have made any difference
if I had closeted myself in . . . in my office and did
    nothing?
I never would have been criticized.
But the very fact
that it gave that . . . that
perception of a fund-raiser,
and I know
in the minds of some
that's a big
cocktail party
and
it wasn't that at all, eh,
but, eh, in somebody's home
and there weren't that many people there at all
and anyway . . .
But I shouldn't have gone!
If for no other reason
than it's given
so many people
who wanted it
an opportunity to carp

and to criticize,
for . . . for
I should have been smarter.
I'm usually smart enough to realize hey,
I know I'll be criticized for that,
and I'm not going to give them the opportunity.
But for some
reason I didn't and, uh . . .
I think a lot of people who have . . . have
looked at me as being, uh,
stubborn and
obstinate
because I wouldn't compromise
and I was not going to be forced out of the depart-
    ment
and I believed it would be overall harmful to the
    department to be
forced out
and I think
the department was demoralized anyway
and I think it would just have absolutely
totally demoralized 'em.
And when I stood up,
they said, "Hey,
by golly, uh,
uh,
he's saying a lot of things that
I'd like to say."
And some of them were just shaking with anger
    because
    they were
being accused of things
that
they wouldn't think of doing and
didn't do
and they know the people around them,
their partners, wouldn't have done those types of
    things.
I don't think there's anyone who doesn't feel and
    isn't sensitive to
what is being said about them
day in and day out.
All you gotta do is pick up a newspaper and see
    what's being said
about you in the *Los Angeles Times*
and the . . . and, and the . . . and in the electronic
    media.
I mean, it was day in and day out.
Editorials
and all kinds of things.
I mean, the community activists
and most of them were really nasty
politicians,
nasty. I mean, they weren't so . . .
Nobody likes to read those types of things and more

importantly
no one wants their friends and family
to read those kinds of things and I mean, uh, uh, it's
     a terribly difficult
thing to endure
and when people hear it over and over and over
     again.
And I make speeches
on college campuses all across the country
and I swear
I have a group,
mostly African Americans,
and I swear
I am the symbol
of police oppression
in the United States,
if not the world.
I am.
Me!
And I ask them:
Who told you this?
What gave you this idea?
You don't know me.
You don't have any idea
what I've done.
Forty-three years in law enforcement,
no one has said that about me,
no one.
And suddenly
I am the symbol
of police oppression
and it's a tough thing to deal with,
a very tough thing.
You know,
just prior
to this,
in a poll
taken by a legitimate pollster,
the individual
with the greatest credibility
in the state of California —
I can't say the state
of California,
but the southern
part of the state of California —
was me.
The most popular Republican in Los Angeles
and Los Angeles County
was me.
I got more support
than
Ronald Reagan,
George Deukmejian,
what other Republicans,
Pete Wilson.

I got more support,
and suddenly!
suddenly!
I am the symbol.
And, you know,
on the day
that the Rodney thing [sic],
thing
happened,
the
President of the United States
was declaring me a national hero
for the work that I had done
in drugs
and narcotics
and the work that I had done with kids
and a lot of those kids were black kids.
And suddenly,
suddenly,
I am the symbol
of police oppression.
Just because some officers
whacked Rodney King
out in Foothill Division
while I was in Washington, D.C.

ASK SADDAM HUSSEIN

ELAINE BROWN, *former head of the Black
Panther Party; author,* A Taste of Power

*(A pretty black woman in her early fifties. She is in a
town outside of Paris, France, on the phone. It is 5
P.M. France time. Spring.)*

I think people do have, uh,
some other image
of the Black Panther Party than the guns.
The young men, of course, are attracted
to the guns,
but what I tell them is this:
Did you know Jonathan Jackson?
Because I did,
and Jonathan Jackson was seventeen years old.
He was probably one of the most brilliant young
     men
that you could meet.
He happened to be a science genius.
He was not a gang member, by the way,
but Jonathan Jackson
went to a courtroom by himself
and took over for that one glorious minute
in the name of
revolution and the freedom of his brother

and other people who were in prison
and died that day.
My question to you,
seventeen-year-old young brother with a gun in your
hand,
tough and strong and beautiful as you are:
Do you think it would be better
if Jonathan Jackson were alive today
or that he died
that day in Marin County?
Me personally,
I'd rather know Jonathan Jackson.
That's what I'd rather do,
and I'd rather him be alive today,
to be among the leadership that we do not have,
than to be dead and in his grave at seventeen years
old.
I'm talking merely about strategy,
not swashbuckling.
I think that this idea of picking up the gun and going
into the street
without a
plan and without
any more rhyme or reason than rage
is bizarre and so, uh . . .
And it's foolish
because it will, uh . . .
I think that
all one has to do
is ask, to ask the Vietnamese
or Saddam Hussein
about the power and weaponry
and the arsenal of the United States government and
its willingness to
use it
to get to understanding what this is about.
You are not facing a,
you know, some little Nicaraguan clique
here.
You are not in Havana in 1950 something.
This is the United States of America.
There isn't another *country,*
there isn't another *community*
that is more organized and armed.
Uh,
not only is it naive,
it is foolish if one is talking
about jumping out into the street
and waving a gun,
because you not that bad,
you see what I'm saying?
You just not that bad.
You *think* you bad,
but I say again,
ask Saddam Hussein

about who is bad
and you'll get the answer.
So what I am saying is:
Be conscious of what you are doing.
If you just want to die
and become a poster,
go ahead and do that —
we will all put you on the wall with all the rest of
the people.
But if you want to effect change for your people
and you are serious about it,
that doesn't mean throw down your gun.
Matter of fact, I would def . . . definitely never tell
anybody to do that,
not black and in America.
But if you want a gun,
I hope you can shoot
and I hope you know who to shoot
and I hope you know how to not go to jail for having done that
and then let that be the end of that.
But if you are talking about a war
against the United States government,
then you better talk to Saddam Hussein
and you better talk to the Vietnamese people
and the Nicaraguans
and El Salvadorans
and people in South Africa
and people in other countries in Southeast Asia
and ask those motherfuckers
what this country is capable of doing.
So all I am saying is:
I'm saying that
if you are *committed,*
if you seriously make a *commitment,*
because . . .
and that commitment
must be based not on hate but on love.
And that's the other thing.
My theme is
that love of your people.
Then you gonna have to realize that this may have
to be a lifetime
commitment
and that the longer you live,
the more you can do.
So don't get hung up
on your own ego
and your own image
and pumping up your muscles
and putting on a black beret
or some kinda Malcolm X hat or whatever other
regalia
and symbolic vestment you can put on your
body.

Think in terms of what
are you going to do
for black people.
I'm saying that these
are the long haul,
because then you might be talkin' about
bein' in a better position for a so-called
armed struggle.
At this point you talkin' about a piss-poor,
ragtag, unorganized, poorly armed
and poorly, poorly,
uh-uhm,
poorly led
army
and we will be twenty more years
trying to figure out what happened to Martin,
    Malcolm,
and the Black Panther Party.°

TWILIGHT #1

HOMI BHABHA, *literary critic/writer/scholar*

*(Phone interview. He was in England. I was in L.A.
He is part Persian, lived in India. Has a beautiful
British accent.)*

This twilight moment
is an in-between moment.
It's the moment of dusk.
It's the moment of ambivalence
and ambiguity.
The inclarity,
the enigma,
the ambivalences,
in what happened in the L.A.
uprisings
are precisely what we want to get hold of.
It's exactly the moment
when the L.A. uprisings could be something
else
than it was
seen to be,
or maybe something
other than it was seen to be.

Martin ... Black Panther Party: Martin Luther King, Jr.
(1929–1968) and Malcolm X (1925–1965) were civil rights
leaders. The Black Panther Party was a militant organization
fighting for African American civil and political rights. King
and Malcolm X were assassinated; the Black Panther Party
was hunted by the FBI and local police.

I think when we look at it in twilight
we learn
to . . .
we learn three things:
one, we learn that the hard outlines of what we see in
    daylight
that make it easy for us to order
daylight
disappear.
So we begin to see its boundaries in a much more
    faded way.
That fuzziness of twilight
allows us to see the intersections
of the event with a number of other things that
    daylight obscures for
us,
to use a paradox.
We have to interpret more in
twilight,
we have to make ourselves
part of the act,
we have to interpret,
we have to project more.
But also the thing itself
in twilight
challenges us
to
be aware
of how we are projecting onto the event itself.
We are part of
producing the event,
whereas, to use the daylight
metaphor,
there we somehow think
the event and its clarity
as it is presented to us,
and we have to just react to it.
Not that we're participating in its clarity:
it's more interpretive,
it's more creative.

SWALLOWING THE BITTERNESS

MRS. YOUNG-SOON HAN, *former liquor store
owner*

*(A house on Sycamore Street in Los Angeles just
south of Beverly. A tree-lined street. A quiet street. It's
in an area where many Hasidic Jews live as well as
yuppie types. Mrs. Young-Soon Han's living room is
impeccable. Dark pink-and-apricot rug and sofa and
chairs. The sofa and chairs are made of a velour. On
the back of the sofa and chairs is a Korean design. A
kind of circle with lines in it, a geometric design.*

There is a glass coffee table in front of the sofa. There is nothing on the coffee table. There is a mantel with a bookcase, and a lot of books. The mantel has about thirty trophies. These are her nephew's. They may be for soccer. On the wall behind the sofa area, a series of citations and awards. These are her ex-husband's. They are civic awards. There are a couple of pictures of her husband shaking hands with official-looking people and accepting awards. In this area is also a large painting of Jesus Christ. There is another religious painting over the archway to the dining room. There are some objects hanging on the side of the archway. Long strips and oval shapes. It is very quiet. When we first came in, the television was on, but she turned it off.)

(She is sitting on the floor and leaning on the coffee table. When she hits her hand on the table, it sounds very much like a drum. I am accompanied by two Korean-American graduate students from UCLA.)

Until last year
I believed America is the best.
I still believe it.
I don't deny that now
because I'm a victim,
but
as
the year ends in '92
and we were still in turmoil
and having all the financial problems
and mental problems.
Then a couple months ago
I really realized that
Korean immigrants were left out
from this
society and we were nothing.
What is our right?
Is it because we are Korean?
Is it because we have no politicians?
Is it because we don't
speak good English?
Why?
Why do we have to be left out?
(She is hitting her hand on the coffee table.)
We are not qualified to have medical treatment.
We are not qualified to get, uh,
food stamp
(she hits the table once),
not GR
(hits the table once),
no welfare
(hits the table once).
Anything.
Many Afro-Americans
(two quick hits)

who never worked
(one hit),
they get
at least minimum amount
(one hit)
of money
(one hit)
to survive
(one hit).
We don't get any!
(large hit with full hand spread)
Because we have a car
(one hit)
and we have a house.
(Pause six seconds.)
And we are high taxpayers.
(One hit.)
(Pause fourteen seconds.)
Where do I finda [sic] justice?
Okay, Black people
probably
believe they won
by the trial?
Even some complains only half right?
justice was there.
But I watched the television
that Sunday morning,
early morning as they started.
I started watch it all day.
They were having party and then they celebrated,
all of South-Central,
all the churches.
They finally found that justice exists
in this society.
Then where is the victims' rights?
They got their rights.
By destroying innocent Korean merchants . . .
They have a lot of respect,
as I do,
for
Dr. Martin King?
He is the only model for Black community.
I don't care Jesse Jackson.
But
he was the model
of nonviolence.
Nonviolence?
They like to have hiseh [sic] spirits.
What about last year?
They destroyed innocent people.
(Five-second pause.)
And I wonder if that is really justice
(and a very soft "uh" after "justice," like "justicah," but very quick)
to get their rights
in this way.

(*Thirteen-second pause.*)
I waseh swallowing the bitternesseh,
sitting here alone
and watching them.
They became all hilarious
(*three-second pause*)
and, uh,
in a way I was happy for them
and I felt glad for them.
At leasteh they got something back, you know.
Just let's forget Korean victims or other victims
who are destroyed by them.
They have fought
for their rights
(*one hit simultaneous with the word "rights"*)
over two centuries
(*one hit simultaneous with "centuries"*)
and I have a lot of sympathy and understanding for
     them.
Because of their effort and sacrificing,
other minorities, like Hispanic
or Asians,
maybe we have to suffer more
by mainstream.
You know,
that's why I understand,
and then
I like to be part of their
'joyment.
But . . .
That's why I had mixed feeling
as soon as I heard the verdict.
I wish I could
live together
with eh [sic] Blacks,
but after the riots
there were too much differences.
The fire is still there —
how do you call it? —
igni . . .
igniting fire.
(*She says a Korean phrase phonetically: "Dashi yun
     gi ga nuh."*)
It's still dere.
It canuh
burst out anytime.

LIMBO/TWILIGHT #2

TWILIGHT BEY, *organizer of gang truce*

(*In a Denny's restaurant in a shopping center. Saturday morning, February 1993. He is a gang member.
He is short, graceful, very dark skinned. He is soft-
spoken and even in his delivery. He is very confident.*)

Twilight Bey,
that's my name.
When I was
twelve and thirteen,
I stayed out until, they say,
until the sun come up.
Every night, you know,
and that was my thing.
I was a
watchdog.
You know, I stayed up in the neighborhood,
make sure we wasn't being rolled on and everything,
and when people
came into light
a what I knew,
a lot a people said,
"Well, Twilight, you know,
you a lot smarter and you have a lot more wisdom
     than those
twice your age."
And what I did, you know,
I was
at home writing one night
and I was writing my name
and I just looked at it and it came ta me:
"twi,"
abbreviation
of the word "twice."
You take a way the "ce."
You have the last word,
"light."
"Light" is a word that symbolizes knowledge, know-
     ing,
wisdom,
within the Koran and the Holy Bible.
Twilight.
I have twice the knowledge of those my age,
twice the understanding of those my age.
So twilight
is
that time
between day and night.
Limbo,
I call it limbo.
So a lot of times when I've brought up ideas to my
     homeboys,
they say,
"Twilight,
that's before your time,
that's something you can't do now."
When I talked about the truce back in 1988,
that was something they considered before its time,
yet
in 1992
we made it
realistic.

So to me it's like I'm stuck in limbo,
like the sun is stuck between night and day
in the twilight hours.
You know,
I'm in an area not many people exist.
Nighttime to me
is like a lack of sun,
and I don't affiliate
darkness with anything negative.
I affiliate
darkness with what was first,
because it was first,
and then relative to my complexion.
I am a dark individual,
and with me stuck in limbo,
I see darkness as myself.
I see the light as knowledge and the wisdom of the
    world and
understanding others,
and in order for me to be a, to be a true human
    being,
I can't forever dwell in darkness,
I can't forever dwell in the idea,
of just identifying with people like me and under-
    standing me and mine.
So I'm up twenty-four hours, it feels like,

and, you know,
what I see at nighttime
is,
like,
little kids
between the ages of
eight and eleven
out at three in the morning.
They beatin' up a old man on the bus stop,
a homeless old man.
You know,
I see these things.
I tell 'em, "Hey, man, what ya all doin'?
Whyn't ya go on home?
What ya doin' out this time of night?"
You know,
and then when I'm in my own neighborhood, I'm
    driving through and I
see the living dead, as we call them,
the base heads,
the people who are so addicted on crack,
if they need a hit they be up all night doin' whatever
    they have to do
to make the money to get the hit.
It's like gettin' a total dose
of what goes on in the daytime creates at night.

Writing About Drama

Why Write About Drama?

The act of writing involves making a commitment to ideas, and that commitment helps clarify your thinking. Your writing forces you to examine the details, the elements of a play that might otherwise pass unnoticed, and it helps you develop creative interpretations that enrich your appreciation of the plays you read. Besides deepening your own understanding, your writing can contribute to that of your peers and readers, as the commentaries in this book are meant to do.

Since every reader of plays has a unique experience and background, every reader can contribute something to the experience and awareness of others. You will see things that others do not. You will interpret things in a way that others will not. Naturally, every reader's aim is to respect the text, but it is not reasonable to think that there is only one way to interpret a text. Nor is it reasonable to think that only a few people can give "correct" interpretations. One of the most interesting aspects of writing about drama is that it is usually preceded by discussion, through which a range of possible interpretations begins to appear. When you start to write, you commit yourself to working with certain ideas, and you begin to deepen your thinking about those ideas as you write.

Conventions in Writing Criticism About Drama

Ordinarily, when you are asked to write about a play, you are expected to produce a critical and analytical study. A critical essay will go beyond any subjective experience and include a discussion of what the play achieves and how it does so. If you have a choice, you should choose a play that you admire and enjoy. If you have special background material on that play, such as a playbill or newspaper article, or if you have seen a production, these aids will be especially useful to you in writing.

For a critical study you will need to go far beyond retelling the events of the play. You may have to describe what you feel happens in a given scene or moment in a play, but simply rewriting the plot of the play in your own words does not constitute an interpretation. A critical reading

1703

of the play demands that you isolate evidence and comment on it. For example, you may want to quote passages of dialogue or stage direction to point out an idea that plays a key role in the drama. When you do so, quote in moderation. A critical essay that is merely a string of quotations linked together with a small amount of your commentary will not suffice. Further, make sure that the quotations you use are illustrations of your point; explain clearly their importance to your discussion.

Approaches to Criticism

Many critical approaches are available to the reader of drama. One approach might emphasize the response of audience members or readers, recognizing that the audience brings a great deal to the play even before the action begins. The audience's or reader's previous experience with drama influences expectations about what will happen on stage and about how the central characters will behave. Personal and cultural biases also influence how an audience member reacts to the unfolding drama. Reader response criticism pays close attention to these responses and to what causes them.

Another critical approach might treat the play as the coherent work of a playwright who intends the audience to perceive certain meanings in the play. This approach assumes that a careful analysis, or close reading, of the play will reveal the author's meanings. Either approach can lead to engaging essays on drama. In the pages that follow, you will find directions on how to pay attention to your responses as an audience member or reader and advice about how to read a play with close attention to dialogue, images, and patterns of action.

Reader Response to Criticism

Response criticism depends on a full experience of the text — a good understanding of its meaning as well as of its conventions of staging and performance.

Your responses to various elements of the drama, whether to the characters, the setting, the theme, or the dialogue, may change and grow as you see a play or read it through. You might have a very different reaction to a play during a second reading or viewing of it. Keeping a careful record of your responses as you read is a first step in response criticism.

There is, however, a big difference between recording your responses and examining them. Douglas Atkins of the University of Kansas speaks not only of reader response in criticism, but of reader responsibility, by which he means that readers have the responsibility to respond on more than a superficial level when they read drama. This book helps you reach deeper critical levels because you can read each play in light of the history of drama. The book also gives you important background material and commentary from the playwrights and from professional critics. Reading such criticism helps you understand what the critic's role is and what a critic can say about drama.

Reading drama in a historical perspective is important because it can highlight similarities between plays of different eras. Anyone who has read *Oedipus Rex* and *Antigone* will be better prepared to respond to *Hamlet*. In addition to the history and criticism of drama presented in this book, the variety of style, subject matter, and scope of the plays gives you the opportunity to read and respond to a broad range of drama. The more plays you read carefully, the better you will become at responding to drama and writing about it.

When you write response criticism, keep these guidelines in mind:

1. As you read, make note of the important effects the text has on you. Annotate in the margins moments that are especially effective. Do you find yourself alarmed, disturbed, sympathetic, or unsympathetic to a character? Do you sense suspense, or are you confused about what is happening? Do you feel personally involved with the action, or is it very distant? Do you find the situation funny? What overall response do you find yourself giving the play?

2. By analyzing the following two elements of your response, establish why the play had the effects you observe. Do you think it would have those effects on others? Have you observed that it does?

First, determine what it is about the play that causes you to have the response you do. Is it the structure of the play, the way the characters behave, their talk? Is it an unusual use of language, allusions to literature you know (or don't know)? Is the society portrayed especially familiar (or especially unfamiliar) to you? What does the author seem to expect the audience to know before the play begins?

Second, determine what it is about you, the reader, that causes you to respond as you do. Were you prepared for the dramatic conventions of the play, in terms of its genre as tragedy, comedy, tragicomedy or in terms of its place in the history of drama? How does your preparation affect your response? Did you have difficulty interpreting the language of the play because of unfamiliarity? Are you especially responsive to certain kinds of plays because of familiarity?

3. What do your responses to the play tell you about your own limitations, your own expertise, your own values, and your own attitudes toward social behavior, uses of language, and your sense of what is "normal"? Be sure to be willing to face your limitations as well as your strengths.[1]

Reader response criticism is flexible and useful in the way it allows you to explore possible interpretations of a text. Everyone is capable of responding to drama and everyone's response will differ depending on his or her preparation and background.

Close Reading   Analyzing a play by close reading means examining the text in detail, looking for patterns that might not be evident with a less attentive ap-

---

[1] Adapted from Kathleen McCormick, "Theory in the Reader: Bleich, Holland, and Beyond," *College English* 47 (1985): 838.

proach to the text. Annotation is the key to close reading, since the critic's job is to keep track of elements in the play that, innocent though they may seem alone, imply a greater significance when seen together.

Close reading implies rereading, since you do not know the first time through a text just what will be meaningful as the play unfolds, and you will want to read it again to confirm and deepen your impressions. You will usually make only a few discoveries the first time through. However, it is important to annotate the text even the first time you read it.

In annotating a play try following these guidelines:

1. Underline all the speeches and images you think are important. Look for dialogue that you think reveals the play's themes, the true nature of the characters, and the position of the playwright.

2. Watch for repetition of imagery (such as the garden and weed imagery in *Hamlet*) and keep track of it through annotation. Do the same for repeated ideas in the dialogue and for repeated comments on government or religion or psychology. Such repetitions will reveal their importance to the playwright.

3. Color-code or number-code various patterns in the text; then gather them either in photocopies or in lists for examination before you begin to plan your essay.

Criticism that uses the techniques of close reading pays very careful attention to the elements of drama — plot, characterization, setting, dialogue (use of language), movement, and theme — which were discussed earlier in relation to Lady Gregory's *The Rising of the Moon*. As you read a play, keep track of its chief elements because often they will give you useful ideas for your paper. You may find it helpful to refer to the earlier discussion of the elements in *The Rising of the Moon* since a short critical essay about that play is presented here.

Annotating the special use of any of the elements will help you decide how important they are and whether a close study of them can contribute to an interesting interpretation of the play. You may not want to discuss all the elements in an essay, or if you do, only one may be truly dominant, but you should be aware of them in any play you write about.

From Prewriting to Final Draft: A Sample Essay on *The Rising of the Moon*

Most good writing results from good planning. When you write criticism about drama, consider these important stages:

1. When possible, choose a play that you enjoy.
2. Annotate the play very carefully.
3. Spend time prewriting.
4. Write a good first draft, then revise for content, organization, style, and mechanics.

The essay on Lady Gregory's *The Rising of the Moon* at the end of this section involved several stages of writing. First, the writer read and annotated the play. In the process of doing so, she noticed the unusual stage direction beginning the play, *Moonlight,* and noticed also that when the two policemen leave the Sergeant they take the lantern, but the Sergeant reminds them that it is very lonely waiting there "with nothing but the moon." Second, she used the stage directions regarding moonlight to guide her in several important techniques of prewriting, including brainstorming, clustering, freewriting, drafting a trial thesis, and outlining.

The first stage, brainstorming, involved listing ideas, words, or phrases suggested by reading the play. The idea of moonlight and the moon recurred often. Then the writer practiced clustering: beginning with *moon,* a key term developed from brainstorming, then radiating from it all the associations that naturally suggested themselves.

Next the student chose the term *romance,* because it had generated a number of responses, and performed a freewriting exercise around that term. Freewriting is a technique in which a writer takes four or five minutes to write whatever comes to mind. The technique is designed to be done quickly so the conscious censor has to be turned off. Anything you write in freewriting may be useful because you may produce ideas you did not know you had.

The following passage is part of the freewriting exercise the student wrote using *romance* as a key term. The passage is also an example of invisible writing because the writing was done on a computer and the

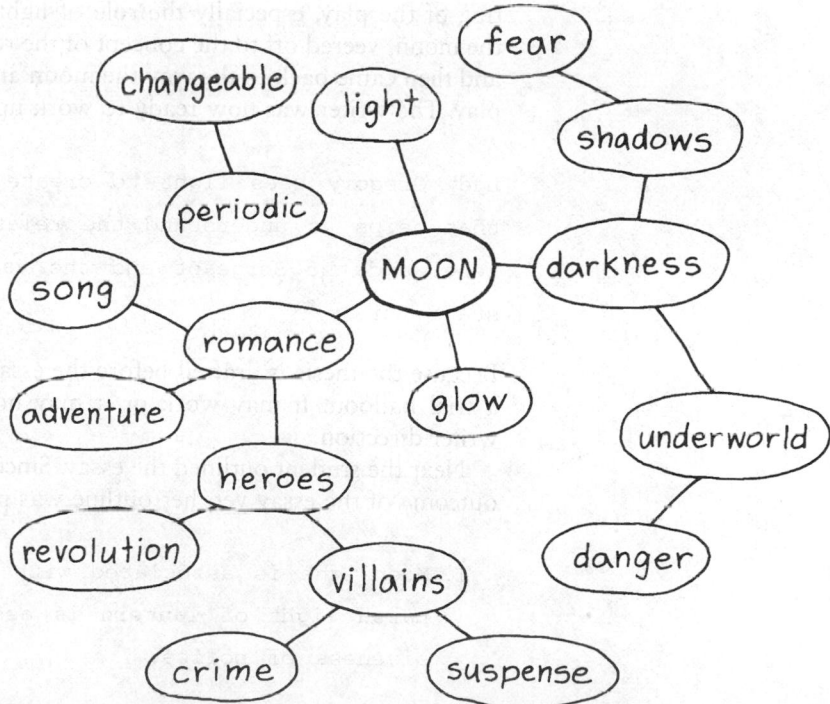

writer turned off the monitor so that she could not censor or erase what she was writing. The writer could only go forward, as fast as possible.

```
The setting of the play is completely romantic. In a
lot of ways the play wouldn't work in a different set-
ting. When you think about it the moon in the title is
what makes all the action possible. Moon associated
with darkness, underworld, world of fairies, so the
moon is what makes all the action possible. Moon makes
Sergeant look at things differently. The moon is the
rebel moon--that's what title means. Rebel moon is ris-
ing, always rising. So the world the policeman lives
in--sun lights up everything in practical and nonroman-
tic way--is like lantern that second policeman brings to
dockside. It shows things in a harsh light. Moon shows
things in soft light. Without the moon there would be
a different play.
```

The freewriting gave the writer a new direction — discussing the setting of the play, especially the role of light. The clustering began with the moon, veered off to the concept of the romantic elements in the play, and then came back to the way the moon and the lantern function in the play. The writer was now ready to work up a trial thesis:

```
Lady Gregory uses light to create a romantic setting
that helps us understand the relationship between the
rebel and the Sergeant and the values that they each
stand for.
```

Because the thesis is drafted before the essay is written, the thesis is like a trial balloon. It may work or it may not. At this point it gives the writer direction.

Next the student outlined the essay. Since the writer did not know the outcome of the essay yet, her outline was necessarily sketchy:

```
I. Moonlight is associated with romance and rebellion;
   harsh light of lantern is associated with repres-
   siveness of police.
```

    A. Rebel is associated with romance.

    B. Sergeant is associated with practicality and the
       law.

  II. Without the lantern the Sergeant is under the in-
     fluence of the romantic moon and the rebel.

    A. Sergeant feels resentment about his job.

    B. Rebel sings forbidden song and Sergeant reveals
       his former sympathies.

    C. Sergeant admits he was romantic when young.

 III. Sergeant must choose between moon and lantern.

    A. Sergeant seems ready to arrest rebel.

    B. When police return with lantern the Sergeant
       sends them away.

    C. Rebel escapes and Sergeant remains in moonlight.

The prewriting strategies of brainstorming, clustering, freewriting, drafting a thesis, and outlining helped the student generate ideas and material for her first draft. After writing this draft, she revised it carefully for organization, clarity of ideas, expression, punctuation, and format. What follows is her final draft.

Andrea James

Professor Jacobus

English 233

19 October 19--

    The Use of Light in The Rising of the Moon

    Lady Gregory uses light imagery in The Rising of the Moon to contrast rebellion and repressiveness. Her initial stage direction is basic: Moonlight. She suggests some of the values associated with moonlight, such as rebellion and romance, caution and secrecy, daring exploits, and even the underworld. All these are set against the policemen, who are governed not by the moon, which casts shadows and makes the world look mag-

ical, but by the lantern, which casts a harsh light
that even the Sergeant eventually rejects.

The ballad singer, the rebel, is associated with
romance from the start: "Dark hair--dark eyes, smooth
face. . . . There isn't another man in Ireland would have
broken jail the way he did" (27-28). He is dark, handsome, and recklessly brave. The Sergeant, by contrast,
is a practical man, no romantic. He sees that he might
have a chance to arrest the rebel and gain the reward
for his capture if he stays right on the quay, a
likely place for the rebel to escape from. But he unknowingly spoils his chances by refusing to keep the
lantern the policemen offer. He tells the policemen,
"You can take the lantern. Don't be too long now. It's
very lonesome here with nothing but the moon" (28).
What he does not realize is that with the lantern as
his guiding light, he will behave like a proper
Sergeant. But with the moon to guide him, he will side
with the rebel.

It takes only a few minutes for the rebel to show
up on the scene. At first, the Sergeant is very tough
and abrupt with the rebel, who is disguised as "Jimmy
Walsh, a ballad singer." The rebel tells the Sergeant
that he is a traveler, that he is from Ennis, and that
he has been to Cork. Unlike the Sergeant, who has
stayed in one place and is a family man, the ballad
singer appears to be a romantic figure, in the sense
that he follows his mind to go where he wants to,
sings what he wants to, and does what he wants to.

When the ballad singer begins singing, the Sergeant
reacts badly, telling the singer, "Stop that noise"
(28). Maybe he is envious of the ballad singer's freedom. When the Sergeant tries to make the rebel leave,
the rebel instead begins telling stories about the man
the Sergeant is looking for. He reminds the Sergeant of

deeds done that would frighten anyone. "It was after the time of the attack on the police barrack at Kilmallock. . . . Moonlight . . . just like this" (29). The moonlight of the tale and the moonlight of the setting combine to add mystery and suspense to the situation.

The effect of the rebel's talk--and of the moonlight--is to make the Sergeant feel sorry for himself in a thankless job. "It's little we get but abuse from the people, and no choice but to obey our orders," he says bitterly while sitting on the barrel sharing a pipe with the singer (29). When the rebel sings an illegal song, the Sergeant corrects a few words, revealing his former sympathies with the people. The rebel realizes this, telling the Sergeant, "It was with the people you were, and not with the law you were, when you were a young man" (30). The Sergeant admits that when he was young he too was a romantic, but now that he is older he is practical and law-abiding: "Well, if I was foolish then, that time's gone. . . . I have my duties and I know them" (30).

Pulled by his past and his present, the Sergeant is suddenly forced to choose when the ballad singer's signal to his friend reveals the singer's identity to the Sergeant. He must decide whether his heart is with the world of moonlight or the world of the lantern. He seizes the rebel's hat and wig and seems about to arrest him when the policemen, with their lantern, come back. The Sergeant orders the policemen back to the station, and they offer to leave the lantern with him. But the Sergeant refuses. We know that he will not turn the rebel in. He has chosen the world of moonlight, of the rebel.

Before they leave the policemen try to make the world of the lantern seem the right choice. Policeman B says:

>Well, I thought it might be a comfort to you.
>I often think when I have it in my hand and
>can be flashing it about into every dark cor-
>ner (doing so) that it's the same as being
>beside the fire at home, and the bits of bog-
>wood blazing up now and again. (Flashes it
>about, now on the barrel, now on Sergeant.)
>(31)

The Sergeant reacts furiously and tells them to get
out--"yourselves and your lantern!"

The play ends with the Sergeant giving the hat
and wig back to the rebel, obviously having chosen the
side of the people. When the rebel leaves, the Sergeant
wonders if he himself was crazy for losing his chance
at the reward. But as the curtain goes down, the
Sergeant is still in the moonlight.

How to Write a Review

What Is the Purpose of a Review?

A review is more than a critical essay because it covers the actual performance of a play. As a reviewer you write after digesting an evening's entertainment and observing how actors and a director present a production for your enjoyment. Your responsibility is to respond both to the production and to the text of the play; thus, you will discuss the quality of the acting, the effectiveness of the setting, the interpretation of the text, and the power of the direction.

Reviews of plays ordinarily appear in daily newspapers or in weekly or semiweekly publications timely enough to help a prospective playgoer decide on whether or not to see the play. Considering the cost of tickets in contemporary theater, the best reviewers can perform a valuable service by letting readers know what they feel is most worth seeing. Regular reviewers, such as Frank Rich and Vincent Canby in the *New York Times*, John Simon in *Newsweek*, and John Lahr in *The New Yorker*, develop their own following because playgoers know from experience whether or not they can rely on these reviewers judgments.

Another purpose of theater reviews is to set a standard to which producers aspire. Criticism can promote excellence because experienced and demanding critics force producers of drama to maintain high standards. The power of theater critics in major cities is legendary: more than a few plays have closed prematurely after savage reviews in London, New York, Chicago, and elsewhere. Knowing that they risk close examination by knowledgeable reviewers convinces writers, directors, actors, and producers to do their best.

What You Need to
Write a Good Review

The best reviewers ordinarily bring three qualities to their work: experience in the theater, a knowledge of theatrical history, and a sensitivity to dramatic production. Some reviewers have had experience onstage as actors or as production assistants. They are familiar with the process of preparing a play for the stage and in some cases may actually have written for the stage. Reviewers without such experience have, instead, spent hours in the theater watching plays; their rich experience of seeing a variety of plays enables them to make useful comparisons.

Knowledge of the basics of theater history is fundamental equipment for a good reviewer. New plays that borrow from the traditions of the Greek chorus, or plays that emulate medieval pageants or nineteenth-century melodrama need reviewers who understand their sources. Suzan-Lori Parks, for example, admits responding to the influence of Bertolt Brecht and Samuel Beckett. While expecting her audience to recognize some of that influence, she knows that her reviewers will spot most or all of it. This book is structured around the history of drama so that readers will better understand drama's roots and evolution. In that sense this book is an aid in helping a theater enthusiast to become a competent reviewer.

Besides knowing the history of drama, the reviewer needs also to be extremely well read. Some reviewers, for example, have not had the opportunity to see all of Shakespeare's plays, but a good reviewer will have read most of them and can refer to them as necessary. The same will be true of the plays of Bernard Shaw, as many have not been produced in the last dozen years or so. In the case of contemporary playwrights, it is common for a reviewer to refer to the playwright's earlier work in order to put the current production in a useful context. A knowledgeable reviewer knows not only the history of theater but also the work of other playwrights that may be relevant to the play under review.

Most of us have enough sensitivity to dramatic productions to write adequate reviews. The most sensitive reviewers will pay close attention to the suitability of the acting almost as a matter of first importance, especially if the play is well known. Most contemporary reviews single out actors and comment on their performance in some detail. Reviewers usually know the work of the most busy actors and in some cases they will make comparisons with earlier roles. They will also indicate whether or not the actor has developed further as an artist or has perhaps walked mechanically through the part. The reviewer's sensitivity to individual actors is developed in part from past experience and therefore from having a benchmark against which to match a performance. Curiosity about an actor's performance sometimes drives a review, as in John Lahr's examination of Ralph Fiennes's acting in *Hamlet* (pp. 485–88), which was the main focus of his essay on the play.

Obviously, neither John Lahr nor any other reviewer is going to review *Hamlet* with an eye toward telling us that it is a good or bad play; the history of criticism has already done that. The reviewer of *Hamlet*, like the reviewer of any of Shakespeare's great plays, will aim to tell us about the quality of the acting or the effectiveness of the setting, as in Clive Barnes's review of *A Midsummer Night's Dream* (pp. 475–76). Being sensitive to the effective use of lighting, props, costumes, and stage design is essential for any reviewer, but it is probably even more essential for a reviewer of classic theater.

Preparing to Review a Classic Play

If you have the opportunity to review a play that is well established — like most of the plays in this collection — you need special preparation. Besides having read the text before seeing the play, you need to imagine how the play should be staged. Once you understand what the play is about and what its implications may be, you then need to consult reviews or descriptions of early productions. You may do so by referring to the index of any major newspaper or to *New York Theatre Critics' Reviews*, which includes multiple reviews of important productions over the years. The point is simply to come to the experience of the drama as a fully informed viewer. Knowing how the play has been staged in the past will help you see the innovations and special interpretation of the current production.

Preparing to Review a New Play

Sometime you may have the opportunity to review a new play — one that playgoers, including the reviewers, have not had the chance to read in advance. In that case you need to pay special attention to the text, taking notes when necessary, to follow the development of the drama's ideas and issues. You are still responsible for commenting on the acting and the production, but in the case of a new play, your responsibility shifts to preparing the prospective audience to understand and respond to the play. They will need to know what the play is about, how it presents the primary issues in the drama, and what is at stake. You may need to tell something of the plot, but always with an eye toward not giving too much away, especially if the play involves suspense. Ask yourself how much the reader needs to know in order to decide whether or not to see the play.

Reviewers of new plays usually include a special commentary on a new or relatively unknown playwright. The most important information here would be any previous work of the playwright. The best reviewers will have seen that work and are prepared to relate it to the new play at hand. Reviewers of August Wilson, for example, spent time in the late 1980s establishing his credentials as a playwright. Now, when a new play of his is produced, reviewers usually attempt to describe how the new play fits into the growing body of his work. Since Wilson is in the process of writing a series of plays on African American life centering on specific decades of this century, the reviewer does the reader a service by explaining how a new play fits into his overall scheme.

Guidelines for Writing Reviews

Good reviewers approach the job of writing reviews from many different angles. Some of the reviews in this book begin with a generalization on the theme. Some begin with a personal observation about the play at hand or a personal experience in the theater. Others begin with a note on the background of the playwright, the actors, or the director. There is no one way to write a review, but the following suggestions can help you to structure your reaction.

1. If you are reviewing a professionally produced play, request a press kit from the theater. These kits usually include a great deal of information that could interest readers.

2. In your review provide any necessary background on a playwright who is contemporary or relatively unknown. The press kit should contain some information; if not, the program may do so. Check with the press representative or with the box office manager to see if the playwright is in the house and, before the play begins, ask to arrange an interview.

Sample Reviews

You can learn a great deal from some of the reviews in this book. Clive Barnes's review of *Hedda Gabler* (pp. 729–30) is exemplary in many ways. First, Barnes clearly enjoyed the production and lets us know at the very start. He praises the director, Trevor Nunn, after praising the star, Glenda Jackson, who has been regarded as one of the most commanding Heddas in contemporary theater. In his first two paragraphs Barnes makes us aware that he regards the production as a landmark.

Barnes emphasizes the humor in the play, which he admits does not always come across. He goes so far as to describe Hedda's life as a "grotesque farce," and clarifies Ibsen's humor as satirical, ending with a "final stroke of tragic irony." His concern for the actors' interpretation of the text centers on "The production's bitter and emphatic insistence upon Ibsen's sardonic mockery of convention." The review focuses on Ibsen as a critic of "bourgeois parochialism."

Most importantly, perhaps, is the fact that Barnes attempts not only to describe the quality of this production, but to analyze the play itself as he writes. You finish the review knowing that Barnes liked the play, the actors, and the production. He convinces us that even if we have seen *Hedda Gabler* before, this production is special enough for us to see it again because this is a fresh new interpretation.

Because August Wilson's *Fences* (1987) was completely unknown to his readers, Frank Rich had a different task in his review. He takes special care to discuss the details of the play's narrative and to comment on

Wilson's other work, much of which may not be familiar to his audience. Rich carefully establishes the time period of the play, 1957, and the neighborhood in which it is set. He then goes on to examine the "mountainous" stature of Troy Maxson, played by James Earl Jones in what Rich feels may be one of his best roles. The struggle between Troy, the one-time player in the Negro baseball leagues, and his son, who is being courted by college football coaches, is central to the drama, and Rich helps us understand its import and its relevance to life in general, not just the play.

Rich reviews each of the main actors: James Earl Jones, Courtney Vance, Mary Alice, and Ray Aranha, clarifying the strength of their work. However, Rich also qualifies his praise of the play by suggesting that Wilson's earlier play, *Ma Rainey's Black Bottom* is "more aesthetically daring." Yet, that does not stop him from approving the power of Wilson's use of the "talking blues," and "Mr. Jones's efforts to shout down the devil." Rich ends with a useful comment on Lloyd Richards's direction and the dominant struggle, both psychological and physical, between father and son that ends the play. Rich leaves the reader with no question about the importance of going to see *Fences*.

Analysis of any of the other reviews in this book will show variations on the structure of Barnes and Rich. When you write your own review, be sure to set up a checklist based on the one that follows here:

Author and title of play

What the play is about

The play's main issues

Actors

Setting

Description of the action

Direction

Theater and dates of performance

Your recommendation

Take the list to the theater with you and keep your notes on it. When you begin writing your review look at some of the tips in this discussion and some of the reviews elsewhere in this book. Your review should provide your readers a valuable service.

Greek Drama Timeline

	THEATER	POLITICAL	SOCIAL/CULTURAL
900 B.C.			**9th c.:** Age of the Homeric epic; *The Iliad, The Odyssey.*
800			**776:** First Olympian Festival (predecessor of the modern Olympic games). Only one event is featured: a footrace of approximately 200 meters.
600	**534:** First contest for best tragedy is held in Athens as part of the annual City Dionysia, a major religious festival. The winning playwright (and actor) is Thespis. **c. 501:** Satyr plays are added to the City Dionysia play competition. Each playwright now has to present a trilogy of tragedies and a satyr play.	**594:** Solon, the law-giver, is elected archon of Athens. **525–405:** Persians conquer Egypt.	
500	**487–486:** Comedy is introduced as a dramatic form in the City Dionysia. **c. 471:** Aeschylus introduces the second actor in the performance of tragedy at the City Dionysia. **c. 468:** Sophocles is credited with introducing the third actor in the performance of tragedies at the City Dionysia. **458:** First performance of Aeschylus's trilogy the *Oresteia* at the City Dionysia.	**490:** Persians invade Greece. Athenians defeat the Persians in the Battle of Marathon; war continues intermittently until peace is established in 449. **462–429:** Periclean Athens.	

	THEATER	POLITICAL	SOCIAL/CULTURAL
	458: *Skene,* or scene house, is introduced in Greek theater.		
	c. 441: First performance of Sophocles' *Antigone* at the City Dionysia.		
	431: First performance of Euripides' *Medea* at the City Dionysia.		
	c. 430–425: First performance of Sophocles' *Oedipus Rex* at the City Dionysia.	**431:** Peloponnesian War begins; Athens is defeated in 404. Thucydides records the events in his history *The Peloponnesian War.*	
	411: First performance of Aristophanes' *Lysistrata.*		
400	**400–c. 320:** Era of Middle Comedy, which concentrates on more accurately portraying daily life rather than the more fantastic plots of Old Comedy (Aristophanes).	**395:** Corinthian War begins. Athens joins with Corinth, Thebes, and Argos to attack Sparta. Athens emerges from the ten-year war a partially restored power.	**399:** Socrates is tried and executed for corrupting the youth of Athens.
			c. 373: Plato writes *Republic.*
	336–300: Era of New Comedy. Menander and others move further away from Aristophanes; stock characters are common.	**332:** Alexander the Great conquers Egypt.	
		321: Alexander the Great dies of a fever at age thirty-three.	
	335–323: Aristotle writes *Poetics.*		
300	**277:** Artists of Dionysus, a performing artists' guild, is formed.		

Roman Drama Timeline

	THEATER	POLITICAL	SOCIAL/CULTURAL
800 B.C.			**753:** Rome is founded.
600			**6th c.:** Circus Maximus is constructed for chariot races and athletic contests. **509–27:** Roman Republic.
500			**450:** Roman law is codified in the Twelve Tables.
300	**3rd c.:** Atellan farce, lively improvised scenarios based on domestic life, is imported from southern Italy to Rome. **240:** Ludi Romani, a festival in honor of Jupiter, incorporates comedy and tragedy for the first time. The festival, established by the elder Tarquin, Etruscan ruler of Rome, already included chariot races, boxing matches, and other popular entertainments. The plays performed at the festival in 240 are probably translations or imitations of Greek plays. **205–184:** Titus Maccius Plautus writes his plays, including *The Twin Menaechmi.*	**264–241:** First Punic War with Carthage. **218–201:** Second Punic War.	**c. 300:** Roman consul Appius Claudius Crassus builds the Appian Way, which stretches from Rome to Capua.
200	**160:** Publius Terentius Afer (Terence) writes *The Brothers.* **c. 126– c. 62:** Roscius, a popular Roman actor.	**c. 146:** Rome completes its conquest of Greece.	**186:** Wild animals are exhibited at the Circus Maximus. Contests between wild animals and humans begin shortly hereafter. **106–43:** Cicero, Roman orator.

	THEATER	POLITICAL	SOCIAL/CULTURAL
			105: Gladiatorial contests become part of state festivals.
100	1st c.: Theaters are built throughout the Roman Empire.	69 B.C. Cleopatra born. She reigns as queen of Egypt from 51 to 49 and from 48 to her death in 30.	70–19: Virgil (P. Virgilius Maro), poet and author of the *Aeneid*.
	90: Vitruvius writes *De Architectura*, a treatise on Roman architecture that discusses theater architecture in Greece and Rome.	60: First Triumvirate (Pompey, Crassus, and Julius Caesar) rules Rome.	46: Julius Caesar stages the first *naumachia* (mock sea battle).
	55: The first permanent stone theater is built in Rome.	45: Julius Caesar is declared dictator by Roman Senate.	43 B.C.–A.D. 17: Ovid (Publius Ovidius Naso), poet and author of the *Metamorphoses*.
	4 B.C.–A.D. 65: Seneca. Dates for his plays, including *Medea*, are unknown. Seneca commits suicide after suffering a decline in power and influence.	44: On the Ides of March Caesar is assassinated.	22: Roman pantomime, a predecessor of modern ballet, is introduced by Pylades and Bathyllus.
		43–28: Second Triumvirate (Antony, Lepidus, and Octavius) rules Rome.	19: Horace (65–8 B.C.) writes *Ars Poetica*.
		27 B.C.–A.D. 476: Roman Empire.	
		27: Gaius Octavius, Julius Caesar's grand-nephew, becomes first emperor of the Roman Empire, assuming the name Augustus.	
A.D. 1		14: Augustus dies, and his stepson Tiberius becomes emperor.	c. 30: Crucifixion of Jesus.
		37: Tiberius's grand-nephew Gaius Caesar (Caligula) is named emperor.	64: Much of Rome is destroyed by fire. Nero blames the fire on Rome's increasing Christian population and initiates the first large-scale persecution of Christians in Rome.
		41: Caligula is assassinated by his own guards; his wife and young daughter are also murdered. Caligula's uncle Claudius is named emperor.	
		54: Claudius is allegedly poisoned by his wife, Julia Agrippina. Claudius's	

	THEATER	POLITICAL	SOCIAL/CULTURAL
		stepson Nero is named emperor.	
		68: Nero commits suicide.	79: Mount Vesuvius erupts, destroying Pompeii.
		69: Vespasian is named emperor. He is succeeded by his son Titus.	80: The Colosseum is completed.
100	197–202: Tertullian writes *De Spectaculis*, denouncing the theater as anti-Christian.	117: Hadrian becomes emperor.	
		120: Hadrian commissions the building of the Pantheon ("the place of all gods").	
		138: Hadrian dies and is succeeded by Antoninus Pius and then by Marcus Aurelius.	
400			c. 400: In part because of the rise of Christianity, state festivals honoring pagan gods cease in Rome.
			404: Gladiatorial contests are abolished.
500			523: Wild animal contests are abolished.

Medieval Drama Timeline

	THEATER	POLITICAL	SOCIAL/CULTURAL
400		476: The fall of Rome and beginning of the Dark Ages.	
500	500–1000: Traveling performers proliferate in Europe.		570–632: Muhammed, founder of Islam.
700		768–814: Reign of Charlemagne in France.	

	THEATER	POLITICAL	SOCIAL/CULTURAL
800	**9th c.:** Beginnings of liturgical drama.		
900	**925:** Earliest extant Easter trope.		
	965–975: Compilation of the *Regularis Concordia* (Monastic Agreement) by Ethelwold, bishop of Winchester, England. The *Regularis Concordia* contains the text of the earliest extant playlet in Europe, with directions for its performance.		
	970: Plays of Hrosvitha, a German nun and the first known female playwright. The six plays are modeled on the comedies of Terence but deal with serious religious matters.		
1000		**1066:** Norman conquest of Britain.	**c. 800–1000:** *Beowulf*, one of the first long poems written in English.
		1096: Crusades begin.	
1100	**12th c.:** Religious plays are first performed outside the church.		
1200	**1276–1277:** French poet Adam de la Halle writes *The Play of the Greenwood*, the oldest extant medieval secular drama.		**1264:** First celebration of the feast of Corpus Christi.
1300	**14th c.:** Beginnings of *noh* drama in Japan.		**c. 1302:** Dante's *Divine Comedy*.
	c. 1375: *The Second Shepherds' Play*, part of the English Wakefield cycle.		**c. 1387:** Chaucer's *Canterbury Tales*.
1400	**c. 1425:** *The Castle of Perseverance*, English morality play.	**1481:** Spanish Inquisition.	**c. 1450:** Gutenberg invents movable type.
	1429: Rediscovery of Plautus's plays in Italy.	**1483–1485:** Reign of Richard III. Richard maintains a company of actors at court, which	**1492:** Columbus sets sail across the Atlantic.

	THEATER	POLITICAL	SOCIAL/CULTURAL
	c. 1470: *Pierre Pathelin,* most renowned of medieval French farces. **c. 1495:** *Everyman,* best-known English morality play.	tours surrounding towns when not needed by His Majesty. **1485–1509:** Reign of Henry VII, first of the Tudor rulers. Like Richard III, Henry maintains a company of actors.	
1500	**1527:** Henry VIII builds a House of Revels in which to stage court entertainments. **1548:** Production of plays is forbidden in Paris. **1558:** Elizabeth I forbids performance of all religious plays.	**1509–1547:** Reign of Henry VIII. **1534:** Henry VIII breaks with the Roman Catholic Church. Drama is used as a political instrument to attack or defend opposing viewpoints. **1558–1603:** Reign of Elizabeth I.	**1545–1563:** Council of Trent is convened by the Catholic Church to solidify its control over expressions of church doctrine. Medieval religious plays, while still immensely popular, are deemed provocative and controversial.

Renaissance Drama Timeline

	THEATER	POLITICAL	SOCIAL/CULTURAL
1300	**1377–1446:** Filippo Brunelleschi, an Italian architect, develops vanishing-point perspective, which allows theatrical scenery to be drawn in realistic proportions.		
1400	**1414:** Rediscovery of Vitruvius's *De Architectura* (90 B.C.) in Italy. After its publication in 1486, the treatise has a significant influence on the development of staging practices.		**c. 1466–1536:** Desiderius Erasmus, Dutch humanist. **1469–1527:** Niccolò Machiavelli, who writes the political treatise *The Prince* in 1513 and the comedy *Mandragola* sometime between 1513 and 1520.

	THEATER	POLITICAL	SOCIAL/CULTURAL
			1473–1543: Nicolaus Copernicus, founder of modern astronomy.
1500	**1508:** Vernacular drama begins in Italy with Ludovico Ariosto's *The Casket*.	**1534:** Henry VIII (reigned 1509–1547) breaks with the Roman Catholic Church.	
	1508: Opening of the Hôtel de Bourgogne, a permanent theater building, in Paris.	**1547:** Ivan IV (the Terrible) becomes czar of Russia.	**1547–1616:** Miguel de Cervantes, best known for the novel *Don Quixote*, writes many plays.
	1550–1650: Golden Age of Spanish drama. The two principal playwrights are Lope de Vega (1562–1635) and Pedro Calderón de la Barca (1600–1681).	**1553–1558:** Reign of Mary I in England. The country returns temporarily to Catholicism.	
	1558–1594: Playwright Thomas Kyd, author of *The Spanish Tragedy* (c. 1587).	**1558–1603:** Reign of Elizabeth I in England. Protestantism becomes the religion of the realm. England emerges as a world power.	
	1562: First English tragedy, *Gorboduc,* performed at the Inns of Court.		**1561–1626:** Francis Bacon, English philosopher and statesman.
	1564–1593: Christopher Marlowe, author of *Doctor Faustus* (c. 1588), *Tamburlaine* (1590), and *Edward II* (c. 1592).		
	1564–1616: William Shakespeare.		**1564–1642:** Galileo Galilei, Italian astronomer.
	c. 1568: Formation of the Italian *commedia dell'arte* company I Gelosi.		
	1572–1637: Playwright Ben Jonson, author of *Volpone* (1605) and *Bartholomew Fair* (1614).	**1572:** Saint Bartholomew's Day Massacre in France; thousands of Protestants are killed.	
	1574: The Earl of Leicester's Men, the first important acting troupe in London, is licensed.		

	THEATER	POLITICAL	SOCIAL/CULTURAL
	1576: James Burbage builds the Theatre, a public building specifically for the performance of plays. Blackfriars, London's first private theater, is also built.		
	1577: John Northbrooke publishes *A Treatise against Dicing, Dancing, Plays, and Interludes,* one of several tracts attacking the growing professional theater.		**1577–1580:** Sir Francis Drake sails around the world.
	1580–1627: Playwright Thomas Middleton, author of *A Chaste Maid in Cheapside* (1630) and *The Changeling* (with William Rowley, 1622).		
	1584: Completion of the Teatro Olimpico in Vicenza, Italy, designed by architect Andrea Palladio (1508–1580).		**1583:** Sir Philip Sidney's *Defence of Poesy* argues for literature's importance in teaching morality and virtue.
	1586?–c. 1640: Playwright John Ford, author of *'Tis Pity She's a Whore* (1633).	**1587:** The Catholic Mary Stuart, queen of Scotland, is executed in England.	
	1595–1596: Shakespeare's comedy *A Midsummer Night's Dream.*	**1588:** The English fleet defeats the Spanish Armada.	
	1599: The Globe theatre is built in London.		
1600	**1600 1601:** Shakespeare's *Hamlet.*	**1603:** Death of Elizabeth I. James VI of Scotland, son of Mary Stuart, becomes James I of England.	**1602:** Establishment of the Dutch East India Company for trade with the Far East.
	1606–1684: French playwright Pierre Corneille, author of *Le Cid* (1636).	**1605:** The Gunpowder Plot, an attempt to blow up the English Parliament and James I, is uncovered.	**1607:** Founding of Jamestown, Virginia, the first permanent English settlement across the Atlantic.
	1611–1612: Shakespeare's *The Tempest.*		**1611:** King James Bible is published.

	THEATER	POLITICAL	SOCIAL/CULTURAL
	1633: First performance of the Oberammergau Passion play in Germany.	**1618–1648:** The Thirty Years' War is initiated by a Protestant revolt in Bohemia against the authority of the Holy Roman emperor.	**1620:** Pilgrims land at Plymouth Rock, Massachusetts.
		1625: Death of James I. His son becomes Charles I of England.	
	1642: English Parliament closes the theaters.	**1642:** Beginning of civil war in England.	
		1643: Louis XIV ascends the throne of France at age four.	
		1649: Charles I is beheaded in England.	

Late Seventeenth- and Eighteenth-Century Drama Timeline

	THEATER	POLITICAL	SOCIAL/CULTURAL
1600	**1600–1681:** Spanish playwright Pedro Calderón de la Barca, author of *Life Is a Dream* (1635) and *The Wonder-Working Magician* (1637).		
	1606–1684: French playwright Pierre Corneille, author of *Le Cid* (1636).		
	1622–1673: Molière (born Jean Baptiste Poquelin), French dramatist and actor, author of *The Misanthrope* (1666), *Tartuffe* (1667), and *The Learned Ladies* (1672).		
	c. 1634–1691: Sir George Etherege, author of *Love in a Tub* and *The Man of Mode* (1676).		

	THEATER	POLITICAL	SOCIAL/CULTURAL
	1635–1710: Thomas Betterton, perhaps the Restoration's most important actor.		
	1639–1699: Jean Baptiste Racine, French playwright, author of *Phaedre* (1677).		
	1640–1689: Aphra Behn, first professional woman playwright in the English theater, author of *The Rover* (1677–1680).	**1643:** Louis XIV becomes king of France at age four.	
	1640–1716: William Wycherley, author of *The Plain Dealer* (1677) and *The Country Wife* (1675).		
	1650–1687: Nell Gwynne, English actress and mistress of Charles II.		
	1656: First use of Italianate scenery in England in a production of *The Siege of Rhodes*, designed by John Webb.		
	1658: Molière's troupe, the Illustre Théâtre, is invited to perform at the court of Louis XIV. The company is subsequently given permission to remain in Paris, as the Troupe de Monsieur, and allowed to use the Petit Bourbon for public performances.		
	1660: Theatrical activity resumes in London (after being halted in 1642) when Charles II issues patents to Thomas Killigrew and William Davenant. Women are permitted on the English stage for the first time.	**1660:** Restoration of the English monarchy and end of the Commonwealth. Charles II, son of the executed Charles I, is crowned.	

	THEATER	POLITICAL	SOCIAL/CULTURAL
	1664: Fukui Yagozaemon writes *The Outcast's Revenge,* the first full-length *kabuki* play, in Japan.		**1665:** Plague devastates London.
	1670–1729: William Congreve, author of *Love for Love* (1695) and *The Way of the World* (1700).	**1682:** Louis XIV moves the French court to Versailles.	**1666:** Great Fire of London.
	1680: Opening of the Comédie Française, the first national theater, in Paris.	**1682–1725:** Peter the Great reigns as czar of Russia.	
	1695–1715: Proliferation of female playwrights in England. Thirty-seven new plays by women are produced on the London stage during this period by playwrights such as Mary Pix (1666–1706), Susanna Centlivre (c. 1670–1723), Mary Delarivière Manley (c. 1672–1724), and Catharine Trotter (1679–1749).	**1685:** Death of Charles II; his brother James II is crowned.	
		1685: Louis XIV revokes the Edict of Nantes; persecution of the Huguenots (French Protestants) ensues.	**1687:** Isaac Newton, English scientist, publishes *Mathematical Principles.*
		1688: William of Orange invades England with the encouragement of prominent Protestants, who fear James II's Catholicism. James flees to France and then England; William III and Mary II (daughter of James II) are crowned in 1689.	**1692:** Witchcraft trials in Salem, Massachusetts.
	1698: Jeremy Collier's *A Short View of the Immorality and Profaneness of the English Stage,* the most effective of several attacks on the theater published at the turn of the century.		**1694–1778:** François Marie Arouet de Voltaire, French author often described as the embodiment of the Enlightenment.
		1690: An Irish uprising in favor of James II is suppressed by William III at the Battle of the Boyne.	
1700	**1707–1793:** Carlo Goldoni, Italian playwright, author of *The Servant of Two Masters* (1743).		**1709–1784:** Samuel Johnson, English lexicographer, critic, and poet.
	1717–1779: David Garrick, greatest English actor of the eighteenth century and owner and manager of the Drury Lane Theatre in London.	**1715:** Death of Louis XIV, France's Sun King.	
	1720–1806: Carlo Gozzi, Italian playwright, author of *King Stag* (1762) and *Turandot* (1762).		

	THEATER	POLITICAL	SOCIAL/CULTURAL
	1728: John Gay (1685–1732) writes *The Beggar's Opera,* arguably the most popular English play of the eighteenth century.		**1726:** Jonathan Swift writes *Gulliver's Travels.*
	1729–1781: Gotthold Ephraim Lessing, Germany's first important playwright, author of *Minna von Barnhelm* (1767) and *Emilia Galotti* (1772).		
	1737: The Licensing Act in England prohibits the performance of any play not previously licensed by the Lord Chamberlain. A number of such laws regulating theatrical activity are enacted throughout the eighteenth century.	**1740:** Frederick the Great becomes king of Prussia. **1756:** Frederick begins the Seven Years' War, which pits Prussia and Great Britain against Russia, Austria, and France.	
	1749–1832: Johann Wolfgang von Goethe, German writer. His early works include the play *Götz von Berlichingen* (1773) and the novel *The Sorrows of Young Werther* (1774).	**1762:** Catherine the Great (b. 1729) becomes empress of Russia after overthrowing her husband, Peter III; she reigns until her death in 1796.	
	1751–1816: Richard Brinsley Sheridan, playwright and statesman, author of *The School for Scandal* (1777).		**1751:** Denis Diderot, French writer and philosopher, publishes the first volume of his *Encyclopédie.*
	1762: English actor-manager David Garrick prohibits audience members from sitting on the stage.		**1756–1791:** Wolfgang Amadeus Mozart, Austrian composer, who produced the operas *Marriage of Figaro* (1786) and *Don Giovanni* (1787).
	1767–1787: *Sturm und Drang* period in German drama featuring the work of Goethe, Schiller, and others who rebelled against eighteenth-century rationalism.		**1759–1797:** Mary Wollstonecraft, English writer and early feminist, author of *Vindication of the Rights of Woman* (1792).
	c. 1769: Spectators banned from sitting on the stage in Paris.		

Nineteenth-Century Drama Timeline

	THEATER	POLITICAL	SOCIAL/CULTURAL
1700	**1757–1823:** John Philip Kemble, one of the great English actors of the nineteenth century.	**1773:** Boston Tea Party.	
		1775: American War of Independence begins at Concord, Massachusetts.	
	1759–1805: Friedrich von Schiller, German playwright, author of *The Robbers* (1781) and *Maria Stuart* (1800).	**1776:** Signing of the Declaration of Independence.	
		1788: The U.S. Constitution is ratified.	
	1761–1819: August Friedrich Ferdinand von Kotzebue, German playwright and one of the early developers of melodrama.	**1789:** French revolutionaries storm the Bastille as the French Revolution sweeps over French society.	
	1773–1844: Guilbert de Pixérécourt, French playwright generally credited with originating the melodrama.	**1793:** Louis XVI and his queen, Marie Antoinette, are guillotined. The Reign of Terror, a purge instituted by the revolutionary government of France, claims thirty-five thousand lives in one year.	
	1791–1861: Eugène Scribe, French playwright and developer of the "well-made" play, author of *Adrienne Lecouvreur* (1849).	**1799:** Napoleon Bonaparte overthrows the Directory of France, the moderate government that replaced the government of the Terror.	
1800	**1806–1872:** Edwin Forrest, America's first great native-born actor. Other legendary American actors of the century include Charlotte Cushman (1816–1876), Joseph Jefferson III (1829–1905), and Edwin Booth (1833–1893).	**1804:** Napoleon I (1769–1821) declares himself emperor of France.	**1805:** Gas lighting is introduced in Great Britain.
		1805: Admiral Horatio Nelson's victory over Napoleon at Trafalgar establishes the supremacy of British naval forces.	
	1808 and 1832: German writer Johann Wolfgang von Goethe (1749–1832) produces his masterpiece, *Faust* (in two parts).		

	THEATER	POLITICAL	SOCIAL/CULTURAL
	1809–1852: Nikolai Gogol, Russian playwright, author of *The Inspector General* (1836).		
	1813–1837: George Büchner, German playwright, author of *Danton's Death* (1835) and *Woyzeck* (1836).	**1815:** Napoleon is decisively defeated at the Battle of Waterloo.	
	1816: Chestnut Street Theater in Philadelphia is the first theater to illuminate its stage with gas lighting.	**1818:** Shaka ascends the Zulu throne in Southern Africa and initiates a period of military reform; he is assassinated in 1828.	
	1822–1890: Dion Boucicault, Irish-American actor and writer of popular melodramas, among them *The Octoroon* (1859) and *The Colleen Bawn* (1860).	**1821:** Mexico declares its independence.	
	1828–1906: Henrik Ibsen, Norwegian playwright. Among his best-known works are *A Doll House* (1879) and *Hedda Gabler* (1890).		
	c. 1830: Beginnings of Peking (Beijing) Opera in China.		
	1830: *Hernani,* by the French novelist and playwright Victor Hugo (1802–1885), traditionally marks the beginning of French romanticism.		
	1837: William Charles Macready (1793–1873), an English actor, is the first to use the limelight (or Drummond light), a prototype of the spotlight. By the 1850s, the limelight is being widely used.	**1837:** Queen Victoria begins her sixty-four-year reign in England.	
	1840–1902: Émile Zola, French writer and promoter of naturalism in literature. Among his	**1839:** Beginning of the First Opium War between England and China. The war ends in 1842 with the Treaty of Nanjing, which turns over Hong Kong to England and opens several Chinese ports to Western trade.	

THEATER	POLITICAL	SOCIAL/CULTURAL
works is the novel (also a play) *Thérèse Raquin* (1873).		
1849: Astor Place Riot in New York, a result of the rivalry between the actors William Charles Macready and Edwin Forrest; twenty-two people are killed.	**1848:** Revolutions break out across Europe, sparked by nationalism, liberalism, or socialism. All are suppressed within a year.	**1848:** Karl Marx, German political philosopher, writes *The Communist Manifesto*, with Friedrich Engels.
1849–1923: Sarah Bernhardt, born in France, perhaps the greatest actress of the nineteenth century.		**1848:** Gold is discovered in California.
1849–1912: August Strindberg, Swedish playwright. Among his works are *Miss Julie* (1888) and *The Dream Play* (1902).		
1852: George Aiken produces a theatrical adaptation of Harriet Beecher Stowe's novel *Uncle Tom's Cabin* in Troy, New York.	**1852:** Napoleon III declares himself emperor of France and rules until 1871.	
1854–1900: Oscar Wilde, English writer. His plays include *A Woman of No Importance* (1893) and *The Importance of Being Earnest* (1895).		**1854–1856:** Scottish explorer David Livingstone crosses Africa.
1856–1950: Bernard Shaw, Irish playwright. Among his works are *Mrs. Warren's Profession* (1898), *Major Barbara* (1905), and *Pygmalion* (1912).		
1859–1924: Eleanora Duse, great Italian-born actress.		**1859:** Charles Darwin, English naturalist, publishes *On the Origin of Species*.
1860–1904: Anton Chekhov, Russian writer, author of *The Seagull* (1896) and *The Cherry Orchard* (1903).	**1861:** Unification of Italy under Victor Emmanuel II.	
	1861–1865: Civil War in the United States.	

	THEATER	POLITICAL	SOCIAL/CULTURAL
	1866: George II, Duke of Saxe-Meiningen (in what is now Germany), establishes a theater company that becomes highly influential because of its historically accurate and realistic costuming, staging, and acting.	**1862:** Otto von Bismarck is appointed prime minister of Prussia. **1865:** Abraham Lincoln is assassinated by the actor John Wilkes Booth at Ford's Theatre in Washington, D.C., during a performance of *Our American Cousin*.	
	1870–1900: Golden Age of Peking (Beijing) Opera.		**1869:** Completion of the first transcontinental railroad in the United States. Opening of the Suez Canal.
	1871–1896: Gilbert and Sullivan (the playwright William Schwenck Gilbert and the composer Arthur Seymour Sullivan) write their comic operas, among them *H.M.S. Pinafore* (1878) and *The Pirates of Penzance* (1879).	**1871:** German Empire is founded under Kaiser Wilhelm I.	
	1876: Opening of Richard Wagner's Festival Theater in Bayreuth, Germany. Wagner (1813–1883), a German composer, puts into practice his theory of the *Gesamtkunstwerk* ("master artwork"), which combines elements of spoken drama, rhythmic movement, and music under the unifying hand of the author-composer. Among his works is the four-part *Der Ring des Nibelungen* (1853–1874).	**1876:** At the Battle of the Little Bighorn, the Sioux defeat General George Custer's troops.	**1879:** Thomas Edison invents the lightbulb.
	1881: The Savoy Theatre is the first theater in London to be completely illuminated by electric light.		
	1887: Théâtre Libre is founded in Paris by André Antoine to pursue naturalism in subject matter and staging.		

	THEATER	POLITICAL	SOCIAL/CULTURAL
	1889: Freie Bühne (Free Stage) is founded in Berlin under Otto Brahm's direction. Like the Théâtre Libre, it fosters increased realism in theatrical production.		
	1890–1930: Vaudeville becomes one of the most popular forms of entertainment in the United States.	**1890:** The Battle at Wounded Knee ends the American Indians' wars of resistance; two hundred Indians are killed by the U.S. army.	
	1896: The first revolving stage is installed by Karl Lautenschlager at the Residenz Theater in Munich.		
	1898: The Moscow Art Theatre is founded under the direction of Konstantin Stanislavsky and Vladimir Nemirovich-Danchenko.	**1899–1902:** The Boer War (South African War) ends in British supremacy in South Africa.	
	1898: The Irish Literary Society is founded by William Butler Yeats (1865–1939) and Lady Augusta Gregory (1863–1935). The group leads the way in creating an indigenous Irish theater.		
1900	**1904:** The Abbey Theatre, evolved from the Irish Literary Society founded by Yeats and Lady Gregory, opens in Dublin.	**1900:** Boxer Rebellion attempts to curtail Western commercial interests in China.	

Twentieth-Century Drama Timeline

(This timeline combines events covered in the last two parts of the book, "Drama in the Early and Mid-Twentieth Century" and "Contemporary Drama.")

	THEATER	POLITICAL	SOCIAL/CULTURAL
1850	**1854–1931:** David Belasco, American producer. Belasco uses pictorial realism in staging and creates "stars" on the New York stage.		
	1862–1928: Adolphe Appia, influential Swiss designer. Appia explains his theories of theatrical production in *The Staging of Wagner's Musical Dramas* (1895), *Music and Stage Setting* (1899), and *The Work of Living Art* (1921).		
	1865–1932: Minnie Maddern Fiske, American actress, one of the first proponents of Ibsen on the New York stage. Fiske strives for a more natural acting style and emphasizes ensemble playing.		
	1871–1909: John Millington Synge, Irish playwright, author of *Riders to the Sea* (1904) and *The Playboy of the Western World* (1907).		
	1872–1966: Edward Gordon Craig, influential English theatrical designer, and son of the great actress Ellen Terry. His publications include *On the Art of the Theater* (1911) and the periodical *The Mask* (1908–1929).		
	1873–1943: Max Reinhardt, Austrian director, producer, and theorist.		

	THEATER	POLITICAL	SOCIAL/CULTURAL
	1880–1964: Sean O'Casey, Irish playwright, author of *Juno and the Paycock* (1924) and *The Plough and the Stars* (1926).		
	1887–1954: Robert Edmond Jones, revolutionary American scenic designer. Other important designers of the period include Lee Simonson (1888–1967) and Norman Bel Geddes (1893–1958).		
	1888–1953: Eugene O'Neill, American playwright. Among his works are *Desire under the Elms* (1924), *Mourning Becomes Electra* (1931), and *Long Day's Journey into Night* (1939–1941).		
	1898–1956: Bertolt Brecht, German playwright, author of *The Threepenny Opera* (a musical in collaboration with German composer Kurt Weill, 1928), *Mother Courage* (1941), and *The Good Woman of Setzuan* (1943).		
1900	**1905–1984:** Lillian Hellman, American playwright, author of *The Children's Hour* (1934) and *The Little Foxes* (1939). Other important American female playwrights of the period include Rachel Crothers (1876–1958), Zona Gale (1874–1938), and Susan Glaspell (1876–1948).	**1901:** Queen Victoria of England dies and is succeeded by her son Edward VII.	**1900:** Sigmund Freud writes *The Interpretation of Dreams*. **1903:** Wilbur and Orville Wright's first flight. **1905:** The first movie theater in the United States opens in New York City. By 1909 there are eight thousand movie theaters across the country. **1906:** An earthquake and subsequent fire ravage San Francisco.
	1906–1989: Samuel Beckett, Irish playwright who wrote some of his		

	THEATER	POLITICAL	SOCIAL/CULTURAL
	plays in French. Among his works are *Waiting for Godot* (1952) and *Endgame* (1957).		**1909:** Sergei Diaghilev, Russian producer, forms the Ballets Russes in Paris.
	1911–1983: Tennessee Williams, American playwright, author of *The Glass Menagerie* (1945), *A Streetcar Named Desire* (1947), and *Cat on a Hot Tin Roof* (1955).		**1912:** The ocean liner *Titanic* sinks, killing 1,513 passengers.
	1915: Arthur Miller, American playwright, born. Among his works are *Death of a Salesman* (1949) and *The Crucible* (1953).	**1914:** World War I begins with the assassination of Austrian Archduke Franz Ferdinand in Sarajevo.	**1914:** The Panama Canal is completed. **1915:** D. W. Griffith's film *The Birth of a Nation* is released.
	1915: George Cram Cook, Eugene O'Neill, and Susan Glaspell found the Provincetown Players in Provincetown, Massachusetts.	**1916:** The Easter Rising in Ireland is suppressed by the British.	
	1917: J. L. Williams's *Why Marry?* receives the first Pulitzer Prize for drama.	**1917:** Russian Revolution overthrows the czar and establishes Bolshevik control under V. I. Lenin.	
	1918: Formation of the Theater Guild in New York City.	**1918:** End of the Ottoman Empire and World War I.	
	1919: Actors Equity Association is officially recognized as a union in the United States.	**1919:** Treaty of Versailles formally ends World War I.	**1919:** The Bauhaus, an influential school of art and architecture, is established by Walter Gropius in Germany.
	1920: Théâtre National Populaire is founded in Paris.	**1920:** Passage of the Nineteenth Amendment to the U.S. Constitution gives women the right to vote.	**1920:** Beginning of Prohibition in the United States.
	1921: Italian playwright Luigi Pirandello (1867–1936) writes *Six Characters in Search of an Author.*	**1921:** Southern Ireland gains its independence from Great Britain and becomes the Republic of Ireland.	
	1923–1924: Moscow Art Theater visits the United States for the first time.	**1922:** Fascist dictator Benito Mussolini gains power in Italy.	**1923:** Tokyo is devastated by a major earthquake.
	1927: Neil Simon born; becomes Broadway's	**c. 1928:** Joseph Stalin comes to power in the Soviet Union.	

	THEATER	POLITICAL	SOCIAL/CULTURAL
	most successful playwright after 1960. His plays include *The Odd Couple* (1965), *Chapter Two* (1979), and *Biloxi Blues* (1984).	**1929:** U.S. stock market crash; beginning of the Great Depression.	
	1930: María Irene Fornés, Cuban playwright, born. Among her works are *Fefu and Her Friends* (1977) and *The Conduct of Life* (1985).		
	1930: Harold Pinter, English playwright and screenwriter, born. Among his works are *The Caretaker* (1960), *The Homecoming* (1965), and *Betrayal* (1978).		
	1931: The Group Theatre is founded by Harold Clurman, Cheryl Crawford, and Lee Strasberg; it operates for ten years.		
	1932: Athol Fugard, South African playwright, born. Among his works are *The Blood Knot* (1961) and *"MASTER HAROLD" . . . and the boys* (1982).	**1933:** Adolf Hitler comes to power in Germany.	
	1934: Wole Soyinka, Nigerian playwright, born. His works include *The Strong Breed* (1962) and *A Play of Giants* (1985).		
	1934: Socialist realism is declared the official artistic policy in Soviet theater.		
	1935: The American plays *Dead End* by Sidney Kingsley, *Winterset* by Maxwell Anderson, and *Waiting for Lefty* by Clifford Odets are produced.	**1935:** Introduction of the Nuremberg laws in Nazi Germany, under which German Jews are deprived of their citizenship and civil rights.	

	THEATER	POLITICAL	SOCIAL/CULTURAL
	1935–1939: Federal Theatre Project operates in the United States under the auspices of the Works Progress Administration.	**1936–1939:** Civil War in Spain results in Generalissimo Francisco Franco's consolidation of power.	
	1936: Federico García Lorca, Spanish playwright, writes *The House of Bernarda Alba*.		
	1937: Peter Stein, influential German director, born. Among his important productions are *Peer Gynt* (1971) and the *Oresteia* (1980).		
	1938: Antonin Artaud, French playwright and theorist, writes *The Theater and Its Double*.		
	1938: Caryl Churchill, English playwright, born. Among her works are *Cloud 9* (1979) and *Top Girls* (1982).	**1939:** England and France declare war on Germany and its allies.	
	1943: Sam Shepard, American playwright and actor, born. His works include *Buried Child* (1978) and *True West* (1980).	**1940:** Germany invades France.	
		1941: Japan attacks Pearl Harbor; the United States enters World War II.	
		1944: Allies liberate France.	
	1945: August Wilson, African-American playwright, born. Besides the Pulitzer Prize–winning *Piano Lesson* (1987), he has written *Fences* (1985).	**1945:** The United States drops atomic bombs on Hiroshima and Nagasaki, Japan.	
	1946: The Living Theatre is founded by Judith Malina and Julian Beck.	**1945:** Hitler commits suicide in Berlin, and Germany signs an unconditional surrender.	
	1947: David Mamet, American playwright, born. His works include *Glengarry Glen Ross* (1983) and *Oleanna* (1992).		

	THEATER	POLITICAL	SOCIAL/CULTURAL
	1947: Marsha Norman, American playwright, born. Among her plays are *Getting Out* (1977) and the Pulitzer Prize–winning *'night, Mother* (1983).		
	1947: Actors Studio is founded in New York City by Robert Lewis, Elia Kazan, and Cheryl Crawford. Lee Strasberg assumes control by 1948.	**1948:** Republic of Israel is proclaimed by Jewish leaders in Palestine.	
	1947: Beginning of the regional theater movement in the United States. Margo Jones opens an arena theater in Dallas, and Nina Vance founds the Alley Theatre in Houston. The Arena Stage opens in 1949 in Washington, D.C.; regional theaters proliferate after 1950; others include the Guthrie Theatre in Minneapolis (1963) and the Actors Theatre of Louisville (1964).	**1948:** Indian leader Mahatma Gandhi is assassinated.	
	1949: Berliner Ensemble is founded in East Berlin.	**1949:** Mao Zedong announces the establishment of the People's Republic of China.	
1950	**1951:** Anna Deavere Smith, African-American playwright and actress, born. Among her works are *Fires in the Mirror* (1991) and *Twilight: Los Angeles, 1992* (1994).	**1950:** U.S. Senator Joseph McCarthy begins his war on communism by investigating the alleged "un-American activities" of hundreds of U.S. citizens.	
	1954: Joseph Papp founds the New York Shakespeare Festival.	**1953:** Joseph Stalin dies.	
	1956: John Osborne's *Look Back in Anger* is produced in London.	**1958–69:** Charles de Gaulle rules as president of France.	
	1956: Tony Kushner, American playwright, born. He is best known	**1962:** The cold war reaches one of its tensest moments in a United States–Soviet Union confrontation over Soviet nuclear missile bases in Cuba.	

THEATER	POLITICAL	SOCIAL/CULTURAL
for the plays *Angels in America, Parts 1 and 2* (1991–1993).	**1962:** The first U.S. combat troops are sent to fight in South Vietnam.	
1959: Lorraine Hansberry writes *A Raisin in the Sun.*	**1963:** President John F. Kennedy is assassinated in Dallas.	
1959: Jerzy Grotowski establishes the Laboratory Theater in Poland. In 1968 he publishes *Towards a Poor Theatre.*	**1967:** In the Six-Day War, Israel responds to Arab provocation by capturing territory from Egypt, Syria, and Jordan.	
1960s: Off-Off-Broadway flourishes with the formation of such groups as Café Cino (1958), La Mama ETC (1962), Open Theatre (1963), and the Performance Group (1967).	**1968:** American civil rights leader Martin Luther King, Jr. is assassinated.	
	1968: Student uprisings occur throughout France.	
1961: Peter Schumann founds the Bread and Puppet Theatre, an influential political ensemble, in the United States.	**1972:** U.S. President Richard Nixon and Soviet leader Leonid Brezhnev sign the strategic arms limitation treaty (SALT).	
1963: National Theatre is established in London under the direction of Laurence Olivier.	**1973:** U.S. troops are withdrawn from Vietnam.	
1964: Ariane Mnouchkine forms the Théâtre du Soleil in France.	**1974:** President Nixon resigns from office as a result of the Watergate scandal.	
1964: Peter Brook's production of Peter Weiss's *Marat/Sade* opens at the Royal Shakespeare Company.	**1975:** Spanish dictator Francisco Franco dies.	**1965:** National Endowment for the Arts is established by the U.S. government.
1968: The Negro Ensemble Company is established in the United States under the direction of Douglas Turner Ward.	**1976:** Chinese Communist leader Mao Zedong dies. Deng Xiaoping emerges as the new Chinese leader in 1978.	
1968: The Living Theatre produces its highly influential experimental work, *Paradise Now.*	**1979:** After the overthrow of Shah Mohammad Reza Pahlevi, the Ayatollah Khomeini establishes the Islamic Republic of Iran.	
1968: Theatrical censorship, in place since the	**1980:** Iran-Iraq War begins when Iraq invades Iran; the war lasts for eight years.	**1969:** U.S. astronaut Neil Armstrong walks on the moon.

	THEATER	POLITICAL	SOCIAL/CULTURAL
	Licensing Act of 1737, is finally abolished in England.	**1981:** General Idi Amin begins his eight-year reign of terror in Uganda.	**1969:** New York City police raid a gay bar, the Stonewall Inn, and the resulting three-day protest becomes a symbol for the emerging gay rights movement.
	1968: *Hair!*, the first rock musical, hits Broadway; it is followed by *Jesus Christ Superstar* in 1971.	**1981:** Egyptian leader Anwar Sadat is assassinated by Muslim extremists.	
	1968: The Performance Group produces *Dionysus in 69* under the direction of Richard Schechner.	**1982:** Martial law is declared in Poland by Communist leaders fearful of the Solidarity movement.	**1982:** Wisconsin becomes the first state to include gays and lesbians as protected citizens under civil rights legislation.
	1970: Peter Brook's acclaimed production of *A Midsummer Night's Dream* opens at the Royal Shakespeare Company.	**1985:** Mikhail Gorbachev becomes the leader of the Soviet Union and institutes a policy of *glasnost* (openness).	**1986:** In *Bowers v. Hardwick,* the U.S. Supreme Court upholds the constitutionality of the Georgia state law against sodomy.
	1975: Michael Bennett's musical *A Chorus Line* opens on Broadway; it runs until 1990.	**1989:** Student demonstration in Beijing's Tiananmen Square results in bloodshed.	**1986:** The U.S. space shuttle *Challenger* explodes seconds after liftoff, killing all seven on board.
	1979: Stephen Sondheim's *Sweeney Todd* opens on Broadway. Other musicals by the prolific composer include *Sunday in the Park with George* (1984), *Into the Woods* (1987), and *Passion* (1995).	**1989:** The Solidarity trade union wins free elections in Poland.	
	1985: Manuel Puig's *Kiss of the Spider Woman* opens in London; the film version, starring William Hurt and Raul Julia, is also released.	**1989:** Communism crumbles in Eastern Europe; peaceful revolutions liberate East Germany, Bulgaria, and Czechoslovakia. Hungary announces a multiparty democracy, Nicolae Ceauşescu is removed from power in Romania after a brief struggle, and the Berlin Wall is torn down.	
	1987: The immensely popular Broadway adaptation of Victor Hugo's *Les Misérables* opens.	**1990:** Iraq invades Kuwait; as a result, the Gulf War begins in 1991.	**1990:** Attacks against the National Endowment for the Arts begin in earnest when a few controversial awards are brought to the public's attention.
	1990s: In a proliferation of Shakespeare on film, new versions of *Hamlet, Henry V, Much Ado about Nothing, Othello,* and *Richard III* are released.	**1990:** Playwright Václav Havel is elected leader of Czechoslovakia.	**mid-1990s:** *Internet* and *World Wide Web* become household words.
		1990: South African nationalist leader Nelson Mandela is released from prison.	

	THEATER	POLITICAL	SOCIAL/CULTURAL
	1996: Jonathan Larson's *Rent*, a musical based on Puccini's *La Bohème*, wins the Pulitzer Prize.	**1991:** Collapse of the Soviet Union. U.S. President Bush officially recognizes the twelve new countries created as a result. **1994:** Nelson Mandela is elected the first black president of South Africa. **1995:** Israeli leader Yitzhak Rabin is assassinated.	**1995:** The already minuscule budget of the National Endowment for the Arts is significantly slashed by the newly elected Republican Congress. The Public Broadcasting Corporation and the National Endowment for the Humanities also come under fire. **1996:** In *Rome v. Evans*, the U.S. Supreme Court rules that the equal protection clause of the Constitution applies to lesbians and gay men.

Glossary of Dramatic Terms

Act. A major division in the action of a play. Most plays from the Elizabethan era until the nineteenth century were divided into five acts by the playwrights or by later editors. In the nineteenth century many writers began to write four-act plays. Today one-, two-, and three-act plays are most common.

Action. What happens in a play; the events that make up the **plot**.

Agon. The Greek word for contest. In Greek tragedy the *agon* was often a formal debate in which the **chorus** divided and took the sides of the disputants.

Alienation effect. In his **epic theater**, Bertolt Brecht (1898–1956) tried to make the familiar unfamiliar (or to alienate it) to show the audience that familiar, seemingly "natural," and therefore unalterable social conditions could be changed. Different devices achieved the alienation effect by calling attention to the theater as theater — stage lights brought in front of the curtain, musicians put onstage instead of hidden in an orchestra pit, placards indicating scene changes and interrupting the linear flow of the action, actors distancing themselves from their characters to invite the audience to analyze and criticize the characters instead of empathizing with them. These alienating devices prevented the audience from losing itself in the illusion of reality. (See **epic theater.**)

Allegory. A literary work that is coherent on at least two levels simultaneously: a literal level consisting of recognizable characters and events and an allegorical level in which the literal characters and events represent moral, political, religious, or other ideas and meanings.

Anagnorisis. Greek term for a character's discovery or recognition of someone or something previously unknown. *Anagnorisis* often paves the way for a reversal of fortune (see *peripeteia*). An example in *Oedipus Rex* is Oedipus's discovery of his true identity.

Antagonist. A character or force in conflict with the **protagonist.** The antagonist is often another character but may also be an intangible force such as nature or society. The dramatic conflict can also take the form of a struggle with the protagonist's own character.

Anticlimax. See **plot.**

Antimasque. See **masque.**

Antistrophe. The second of the three parts of the verse ode sung by the **chorus** in Greek drama. While singing the **strophe** the chorus moves in a dance rhythm from right to left; during the antistrophe it moves from left to right back to its original position. The third part, the **epode,** was sung standing still.

Apron stage. The apron is the part of the stage extending in front of the **proscenium arch.** A stage is an apron stage if all or most of it is in front of any framing structures. The Elizabethan stage, which the audience surrounded on three sides, is an example of an apron stage.

Arena stage. A stage surrounded on all sides by the audience, actors make exits and entrances through the aisles. Usually used in **theater in the round.**

Arras. A curtain hung at the back of the Elizabethan playhouse to partition off an alcove or booth. The curtain could be pulled back to reveal a room or a cave.

Aside. A short speech made by a character to the audience which, by **convention,** the other characters onstage cannot hear.

Atellan farce. Broad and sometimes coarse popular humor indigenous to the town of Atella in Italy. By the third century B.C., the Romans had imported the Atellan farce, which they continued to modify and develop.

Blank verse. An unrhymed verse form often used in writing drama. Blank verse is composed of ten-syllable lines accented on the second, fourth, sixth eighth, and tenth syllables (**iambic pentameter**).

Bombast. A loud, pompous speech whose inflated diction is disproportionate to the subject matter it expresses.

Bourgeois drama. Drama that treats middle-class subject matter or characters rather than the lives of the rich and powerful.

Braggart soldier. A **stock character** in comedy who is usually cowardly, parasitical, pompous, and easily victimized by practical jokers. Sir John Falstaff in Shakespeare's *Henry IV* (parts 1, 2) is an example of this type.

Burla (plural, *burle*). Jests or practical jokes that were part of the comic **stage business** in the *commedia dell'arte.*

Buskin. A thick-soled boot possibly worn by Greek tragedians to increase their stature. Later called a *cothornus.*

Catastrophe. See **plot.**

Catharsis. The feeling of emotional purgation or release that, according to Aristotle, an audience should feel after watching a tragedy.

Ceremonial drama. Egyptian passion play about the god Osiris.

Character. Any person appearing in a drama or narrative.

Stock character. A stereotypical character type whose behavior, qualities, or beliefs conform to familiar dramatic **conventions,** such as the clever servant or the **braggart soldier.** (Also called *type character.*)

Chiton. Greek tunic worn by Roman actors.

Choregos. An influential citizen chosen to pay for the training and costuming of the **chorus** in Greek drama competitions. He probably also paid for the musicians and met other financial production demands not paid for by the state.

Chorus. A masked group that sang and danced in Greek tragedy. The chorus usually chanted in uni-

son, offering advice and commentary on the action but rarely participating. See also **strophe, antistrophe,** and **epode.**

City Dionysia. See **Dionysus.**

Climax. See **plot.**

Closet drama. A drama, usually in verse, meant for reading rather than for performance. Percy Bysshe Shelley's *Prometheus Unbound* and John Milton's *Samson Agonistes* are examples.

Comedy. A type of drama intended to interest and amuse rather than to concern the audience deeply. Although characters experience various discomfitures, the audience feels confident that they will overcome their ill fortune and find happiness at the end.

Comedy of humors. Form of comedy developed by Ben Jonson in the seventeenth century in which characters' actions are determined by the preponderance in their systems of one of the four bodily fluids or humors — blood, phlegm, choler (yellow bile), and melancholy (black bile). Characters' dispositions are exaggerated and stereotyped; common types are the melancholic and the belligerent bully.

Comedy of manners. Realistic, often satiric comedy concerned with the manners and conventions of high society. Usually refers to the Restoration comedies of late seventeenth-century England, which feature witty dialogue or **repartee.** An example is William Congreve's *The Way of the World.*

Drawing room comedy. A type of comedy of manners concerned with life in polite society. The action generally takes place in a drawing room.

Farce. A short dramatic work that depends on exaggerated, improbable situations, incongruities, coarse wit, and horseplay for its comic effect.

High comedy. Comedy that appeals to the intellect, often focusing on the pretensions, foolishness, and incongruity of human behavior. **Comedy of manners** with its witty dialogue is a type of high comedy.

Low comedy. Comedy that lacks the intellectual appeal of **high comedy,** depending instead on boisterous buffoonery, "gags," and jokes for its comic effect.

New Comedy. Emerging between the fourth and third centuries B.C. in ancient Greece, New Comedy replaced the farcical **Old Comedy.** New Comedy, usually associated with Menander, is witty and intellectually engaging; it is often thought of as the first **high comedy.**

Old Comedy. Greek comedy of the fifth century B.C. that uses bawdy farce to attack satirically social, religious, and political institutions. Old Comedy is usually associated with Aristophanes.

Sentimental comedy. Comedy populated by stereotypical virtuous **protagonists** and villainous **antagonists** that resolves the domestic trials of middle-class people in a pat, happy ending.

Slapstick. Low comedy that involves little plot or character development but consists of physical horseplay or practical jokes.

Comic relief. The use of humorous characters, speeches, or scenes in an otherwise serious or tragic drama.

Commedia dell'arte. Italian **low comedy** dating from around the mid-sixteenth century in which professional actors playing **stock characters** improvised dialogue to fit a given **scenario.**

Complication. See **plot.**

Conflict. See **plot.**

Convention. Any feature of a literary work that has become standardized over time, such as the **aside** or the **stock character.** Often refers to an unrealistic device (such as Danish characters speaking English in *Hamlet*) that the audience tacitly agrees to accept.

Coryphaeus. See *koryphaios.*

Cosmic irony. See **irony.**

Cothurnes. See **buskin.**

Craft play. Medieval sacred drama based on Old and New Testament stories. Craft plays were performed outside the church by members of a particular trade guild, and their subject matter often reflected the guild's trade. The fisherman's guild, for example, might present the story of Noah and the flood.

Crisis. Same as **climax.** See **plot.**

Cycle. A group of medieval **mystery plays** written in the vernacular (the language in common use rather than Latin) for performance outside the church. Cycles, each of which treated biblical stories from creation through the last judgment, are named after the town in which they were produced. Most extant mystery plays are from the York, Chester, Wakefield (Towneley), and N-Town cycles.

Decorum. A quality that exists when the style of a work is appropriate to the speaker, the occasion, and the subject matter. Kings should speak in a "high style" and clowns in a "low style," according to many Renaissance authors. Decorum was a guiding critical principle in **neoclassicism.**

Defamiliarization effect (*Verfremdungseffkt*). See **alienation effect.**

Denouement. See **plot.**

Deus ex machina. Latin for "a god out of a machine." In Greek drama, a mechanical device called a *mechane* could lower "gods" onto the stage to solve the seemingly unsolvable problems of mortal characters. Also used to describe a playwright's use of a forced or improbable solution to plot complications — for example, the discovery of a lost will or inheritance that will pay off the evil landlord.

Dialogue. Spoken interchange or conversation between two or more characters. Also see **soliloquy.**

Diction. A playwright's choice of words or the match between language and subject matter. Also refers collectively to an actor's phrasing, enunciation, and manner of speaking.

Dionysus. Greek nature god of wine, mystic revelry, and irrational impulse. Greek tragedy probably sprang from dramatized ritual choral celebrations in his honor.

City Dionysia. (Also called Great or Greater Dionysia.) The most important of the four Athenian festivals in honor of Dionysus. This spring festival sponsored the first tragedy competitions; comedy was associated with the winter festival, the Lenaea.

Director. The person responsible for a play's interpretation and staging and for the guidance of the actors.

Disguising. Medieval entertainment featuring a masked procession of actors performing short plays in pantomime; probably the origin of the court **masque.**

Dithyramb. Ancient Greek choral hymn sung and danced to honor **Dionysus;** originally divided into an improvised story sung by a choral leader and a traditional refrain sung by the **chorus.** Believed by some to be the origin of Greek tragedy.

Domestic tragedy. A serious play usually focusing on the family and depicting the fall of a middle-class **protagonist** rather than of a powerful or noble hero. Also called *bourgeois tragedy.* An example is Arthur Miller's *Death of a Salesman,* which traces the emotional collapse and eventual suicide of Willy Loman, a traveling salesman.

Double plot. See **plot.**

Drama. A play written in prose or verse that tells a story through **dialogue** and actions performed by actors impersonating the characters of the story.

Dramatic illusion. The illusion of reality created by drama and accepted by the audience for the duration of the play.

Dramatic irony. See **irony.**

Dramatist. The author of a play; playwright.

Dramaturge. One who represents the playwright and guides the production. In some cases, the dramaturge researches different aspects of the production or earlier productions of the play.

Dramaturgy. The art of writing plays.

Drawing room comedy. See **comedy.**

Empathy. The sense of feeling *with* a character. (Distinct from sympathy, which is feeling *for* a character.)

Ensemble acting. Performance by a group of actors, usually members of a **repertory** company, in which the integrated acting of all members is emphasized over individual star performances. The famous nineteenth-century director Konstantin Stanislavsky promoted this type of acting in the Moscow Art Theatre.

Environmental theater. A term used by Richard Schechner, director of the Performance Group in the late 1960s and early 1970s, to describe his work and the work of other theater companies, including the Bread and Puppet Theatre, Open Theatre, and Living Theatre. He also used the term to describe the indigenous theater of Africa and Asia. Environmental theater occupies the whole of a performance space; it is not confined to a stage separated from the audience. Action can take place in and around the audience, and audience members are often encouraged to participate in the theater event.

Epic theater. A type of theater first associated with German director Erwin Piscator (1893–1966). Bertolt Brecht (1898–1956) used the term to distinguish his own theater from the "dramatic" theater that created the illusion of reality and invited the audience to identify and empathize with the characters. Brecht criticized the dramatic theater for encouraging the audience to believe that social conditions were "natural" and therefore unalterable. According to Brecht, the theater should show human beings as dependent on certain political and economic factors and at the same time as capable of altering them. "The spectator is given the chance to criticize human behavior from a social point of view, and the scene is played as a piece of history," he wrote. Epic theater calls attention to itself as theater, bringing the stage lights in front of the curtain and interrupting the linear flow of the action to help the audience analyze the action and characters onstage. (See **alienation effect.**)

Epilogue. A final speech added to the end of a play. An example is Puck's "If we shadows have offended . . ." speech that ends Shakespeare's *A Midsummer Night's Dream.*

Epitasis. Ancient term for the **rising action** of a **plot.** (See also **plot.**)

Epode. The third of three parts of the verse ode sung by the **chorus** in a Greek drama. The epode follows the **strophe** and **antistrophe.**

Exodos. The concluding scene, which includes the exit of all characters and the **chorus,** of a Greek drama.

Exposition. See **plot.**

Expressionism. Early twentieth-century literary movement in Germany that posited that art should represent powerful emotional states and moods. Expressionists abandon **realism** and **verisimilitude,** producing distorted, nightmarish images of the individual unconscious.

Falling action. See **plot.**

Farce. See **comedy.**

First Folio. The first collected edition of thirty-six of Shakespeare's plays, collected by two of his fellow actors and published posthumously in 1623.

Foil. A character who, through difference or similarity, brings out a particular aspect of another character. Laertes, reacting to the death of his father, acts as a foil for Hamlet.

Foreshadowing. Ominous hints of events to come that help to create an air of suspense in a drama.

Frons scaena. The elaborately decorated facade of the *scaena* or stage house used in presenting Roman drama. (Also called *scaena frons.*)

Hamartia. An error or wrong act through which the fortunes of the **protagonist** are reversed in a tragedy.

High comedy. See **comedy.**

History play. A drama set in a time other than that in which it was written. The term usually refers to Elizabethan drama, such as Shakespeare's Henry plays, that draws its plots from English historical materials such as Holinshed's *Chronicles.*

Hubris (or *hybris*). Excessive pride or ambition. In ancient Greek tragedy *hubris* often causes the **protagonist's** fall.

Humor character. A stereotyped character in the **comedy of humors** (see **comedy**). Clever plots often play on the character's personality distortions (caused by an imbalance of humors), revealing his or her absurdity.

Iambic pentameter. A poetic meter that divides a line into five parts (or feet), each part containing an unaccented syllable followed by an accented syllable.

The line "When I consider everything that grows" is an example of iambic pentameter verse.

Imitation. See *mimesis*.

Impressionism. A highly personal style of writing in which the author presents characters, scenes, or moods as they appear to him or her at a particular moment rather than striving for an objectively realistic description.

Interlude. A short play, usually either farcical or moralistic, performed between the courses of a feast or between the acts of a longer play. The interlude thrived during the late fifteenth and early sixteenth centuries in England.

Irony. The use of words to suggest a meaning that is the opposite of the literal meaning, as in "I can't wait to take the exam." Irony is present in a literary work that gives expression to contradictory attitudes or impulses to entertain ambiguity or to maintain detachment.

Cosmic irony. Irony present when destiny or the gods seem to be in favor of the **protagonist** but are actually engineering his or her downfall. (Same as *irony of fate*.)

Dramatic irony. Irony present when the outcome of an event or situation is the opposite of what a character expects.

Tragic irony. Irony that exists when a character's lack of complete knowledge or understanding (which the audience possesses) results in his or her fall or has tragic consequences for loved ones. An example from *Oedipus Rex* is Oedipus's declaration that he will stop at nothing to banish King Laios's murderer, whom the audience knows to be Oedipus himself.

Jongleur. A French term for early medieval musical entertainers who recited lyrics, ballads, and stories. Forerunners of the minstrel.

Koryphaios. The leader of the **chorus** in Greek drama.

Kothurnus. See **buskin**.

Lazzo (plural, *lazzi*). Comic routines or **stage business** associated with the stock situations and characters of the Italian *commedia dell'arte*. A scenario might, for example, call for the *lazzo* of fear.

Liturgical drama. Short dramatized sections of the medieval church service. Some scholars believe that these playlets evolved into the vernacular **mystery plays**, which were performed outside the church by lay people.

Low comedy. See **comedy**.

Mansion. Scenic structures used in medieval drama to indicate the locale or scene of the action. Man-sions were areas inside the church used for performing liturgical drama; later more elaborate structures were built on pageant wagons to present **mystery plays** outside the church.

Mask. A covering used to disguise or ornament the face; used by actors in Greek drama and revived in the later *commedia dell'arte* and court **masque** to heighten dramatic effect.

Masque (also *mask*). A short but elaborately staged court drama, often mythological and allegorical, principally acted and danced by masked courtiers. (Professional actors often performed the major speaking and singing roles.) Popular in England during the late sixteenth and early seventeenth centuries, masques were often commissioned to honor a particular person or occasion. Ben Jonson was the most important masque writer; the genre's most elaborate sets and costumes were designed by Jonson's occasional partner Inigo Jones.

Antimasque. A parody of the court **masque** developed by Ben Jonson featuring broad humor, grotesque characters, and ludicrous actions.

Melodrama. A suspenseful play filled with situations that appeal to the audience's emotions. Justice triumphs in a happy ending: the good characters (completely virtuous) are rewarded and the bad characters (thoroughly villainous) are punished.

Method acting. A naturalistic technique of acting developed by the Russian director Konstantin Stanislavsky and adapted for American actors by Lee Strasberg, among others. The Method actor identifies with the **character** he or she portrays and experiences the emotions called for by the play in an effort to render the character with emotional **verisimilitude**.

Mimesis. The Greek word for imitation. Aristotle used the term to define the role of art as an imitation of an action.

Miracle play. A type of medieval sacred drama that depicts the lives of saints, focusing especially on the miracles performed by saints.

Mise-en-scène. The stage setting of a play, including the use of scenery, props, and stage movement.

Moira. Greek word for fate.

Morality play. Didactic late medieval drama (flourishing in England c. 1400–1550) that uses **allegory** to dramatize some aspects of the Christian moral life. Abstract qualities or entities such as Virtue, Vice, Good Deeds, Knowledge, and Death are cast as characters who discuss with the **protagonist** issues related to salvation and the afterlife. *Everyman* is an example.

Motivation. The reasons for a character's actions in a drama. For drama to be effective, the audience must believe that a character's actions are justified and plausible given what they know about him or her.

Mouth of hell. A stage prop in medieval drama suggesting the entrance to hell. Often in the shape of an open-mouthed monster's head, the mouth of hell was positioned over a smoke-and-fire-belching pit in the stage that appeared to swallow up sinners.

Mystery play. A sacred medieval play dramatizing biblical events such as the creation, the fall of Adam and Eve, and Christ's birth and resurrection. The genre probably evolved from **liturgical drama**; mystery plays were often incorporated into larger **cycles** of plays.

Naturalism. Literary philosophy popularized during the nineteenth century that casts art's role as the scientifically accurate reflection of a "slice of life." Naturalism is aligned with the belief that each person is a product of heredity and environment driven by internal and external forces beyond his or her control. August Strindberg's *Miss Julie*, with its focus on reality's sordidness and humankind's powerlessness, draws on naturalism.

Neoclassicism. A movement in sixteenth-century Italy and seventeenth-century France to revive and emulate classical attitudes toward art based on principles of order, harmony, unity, restrained wit, and **decorum.** The neoclassical movement in France gave rise to a corresponding movement in England during the late seventeenth and eighteenth centuries.

New Comedy. See **comedy.**

Ode. A dignified Greek three-part song sung by the **chorus** in Greek drama. The parts are the **strophe,** the **antistrophe,** and the **epode.**

Old Comedy. See **comedy.**

Orchestra. Literally the "dancing place"; the circular stage where the Greek **chorus** performed.

Pageant. A movable stage or wagon (often called a pageant wagon) on which a set was built for the performance of medieval drama. The term can also refer to the spectacle itself.

Pallium. Long white cloak or mantle worn by Greek actors or Romans in Greek-based plays.

Pantomime. Silent acting using facial expression, body movement, and gesture to convey the plot and the characters' feelings.

Parodos. The often stately entrance song of the **chorus** in Greek drama. The term also refers to the aisles (plural, *parodoi*) on either side of the orchestra by which the chorus entered the Greek theater.

Pastoral drama. A dramatic form glorifying shepherds and rural life in an idealized natural setting; usually implies a negative comparison to urban life.

Pathos. The quality of evoking pity.

Peripeteia. A reversal of fortune, for better or worse, for the **protagonist.** Used especially to describe the main character's fall in Greek tragedy.

Phallus. An appendage meant to suggest the penis added to the front of blatantly comic male characters' costumes in some Greek comedy; associated chiefly with the Greek **satyr play.**

Play. A literary genre whose plot is usually presented dramatically by actors portraying characters before an audience.

Play-within-the-play. A brief secondary drama presented to or by the characters of a play that reflects or comments on the larger work. An example is the Pyramus and Thisby episode in Shakespeare's *A Midsummer Night's Dream.*

Plot. The events of a play or narrative. The sequence and relative importance a **dramatist** assigns to these events.

Anticlimax. An unexpectedly trivial or significant conclusion to a series of significant events; an unsatisfying resolution that often occurs in place of a conventional **climax.**

Catastrophe. The outcome or conclusion of a play; usually applied specifically to tragedy. (**Denouement** is a parallel term applied to both comedy and tragedy.)

Climax. The turning point in a drama's action, preceded by the **rising action** and followed by the **falling action.** Same as **crisis.**

Complication. The part of the plot preceding the **climax** that establishes the entanglements to be untangled in the **denouement.** Part of the **rising action.**

Conflict. The struggle between the **protagonist** and the **antagonist** that propels the **rising action** of the plot and is resolved in the **denouement.**

Denouement. The "unknotting" of the plot's **complication;** the resolution of a drama's action. See **catastrophe.**

Double plot. A dramatic structure in which two related plots function simultaneously.

Exposition. The presentation of essential information, especially about events that have occurred prior to the first scene of a play. The exposition appears early in the play and initiates the **rising action.**

Falling action. The events of the plot following the **climax** and ending in the **catastrophe** or resolution.

Rising action. The events of the plot leading up to the **climax.**

Subplot. A secondary plot intertwined with the main plot, often reflecting or commenting on the main plot.

Underplot. Same as **subplot.**

Problem play. A drama that argues a point or presents a problem (usually a social problem). Ibsen is a notable writer of problem plays.

Prologos. In Greek drama, an introductory scene for actor or actors that precedes the entrance of the **chorus.** This **convention** has evolved into the modern dramatic introductory monologue or **prologue.**

Prologue. A preface or introduction preceding the play proper.

Proscaena. The space in front of the *scaena* in a Roman theater.

Proscenium arch. An arched structure over the front of the stage from which a curtain often hangs. The arch frames the action onstage and separates the audience from the action.

Proskenion. The playing space in front of the *skene* or scene house in Greek drama.

Protagonist. The main character in a drama. This character is usually the most interesting and sympathetic and is the person involved in the **conflict** driving the **plot.**

Protasis. Classical term for the introductory act or **exposition** of a drama.

Psychomachia. Psychological struggle; a war of souls.

Quem Quaeritis **trope.** A brief dramatized section of the medieval church's Easter liturgy. The oldest extant **trope** and the probable origin of liturgical drama, it enacts the visit of the three Marys to Christ's empty tomb (*quem quaeritis* means "whom do you seek?" in Latin).

Rising action. See **plot.**

Realism. The literary philosophy holding that art should accurately reproduce an image of life. Avoiding the use of dramatic **conventions** such as asides and soliloquies, it depicts ordinary people in ordinary situations. Ibsen's *A Doll House* is an example of realism in drama.

Recognition. See *anagnorisis.*

Repartee. Witty and pointed verbal exchanges usually found in the **comedy of manners.**

Repertory. A theater company or group of actors that presents a set of plays alternately throughout a season. The term also refers to the set of plays itself.

Restoration comedy. A type of **comedy of manners** that developed in England in the late seventeenth century. Often features **repartee** in the service of complex romantic plots. William Congreve's *The Way of the World* is an example.

Revenge tragedy. Sensational tragedy popularized during the Elizabethan age that is notable for bloody plots involving such elements as murder, ghosts, insanity, and crimes of lust.

Reversal. See *peripeteia.*

Riposte. A quick or sharp reply; similar to **repartee.**

Rising action. See **plot.**

Ritual. Repeated formalized or ceremonial practices, many of which have their roots in primitive cultures. Certain theorists hold that primitive ritual evolved into drama.

Satire. A work that makes fun of a social institution or human foible, often in an intellectually sophisticated way, to persuade the audience to share the author's views. Molière's *The Misanthrope* contains social satire.

Satyr play. A comic play performed after the tragic trilogy in Greek tragedy competitions. The satyr play provided **comic relief** and was usually a farcical, boisterous treatment of mythological material.

Scaena. The stage house in Roman drama; the facade of the *scaena* (called the *frons scaena*) was often elaborately ornamented.

Scenario. The plot outline around which professional actors of the *commedia dell'arte* improvised their plays. Most scenarios specified the action's sequence and the entrances of the main characters.

Scene. Division of an **act** in a drama. By traditional definition a scene has no major shift in place or time frame, and it is performed by a static group of actors onstage (in French drama, if an actor enters or exits, the group is altered and the scene, technically, should change). The term also refers to the physical surroundings or locale in which a play's action is set.

Scenery. The backdrop and set (furniture and so on) onstage that suggest to the audience the surroundings in which a play's **action** takes place.

Scenography. Painting of backdrops and hangings.

Senecan tragedy. Tragic drama modeled on plays written by Seneca. The genre usually has five acts and features a chorus; it is notable for its thematic concern with bloodshed, revenge, and unnatural crimes. (See also **revenge tragedy.**)

Sentimental. Refers to tender emotions in excess of what the situation calls for.

Setting. All details of time, location, and environment relating to a play.

Skene. The building or scene house in the Greek theater that probably began as a dressing room and eventually was incorporated into the action as part of the scenery.

Slapstick. See **comedy**.

Slice of life. See **naturalism**.

Social problem play. Same as **problem play**.

Sock. Derived from the Latin *soccus,* the term refers to a light slipper or sock worn by Roman comic actors.

Soliloquy. A speech in which an actor, usually alone onstage, utters his or her thoughts aloud, revealing personal feelings. Hamlet's "To be, or not to be" speech is an example.

Spectacle. In Aristotle's terms, the costumes and scenery in a drama — the elements that appeal to the eye.

Stage business. Minor physical action, including an actor's posture and facial expression, and the use of props, all of which make up a particular interpretation of a character.

Stichomythia. Dialogue in which two speakers engage in a verbal duel in alternating lines.

Stock character. See **character**.

Strophe. The first of three parts of the verse **ode** sung by the Greek **chorus**. While singing the strophe the chorus moves in a dancelike pattern from right to left. See also **antistrophe** and **epode**.

Subplot. See **plot**.

Subtext. A level of meaning implicit in or underlying the surface meaning of a text.

Surrealism. A literary movement flourishing in France during the early twentieth century that valued the unwilled expression of the unconscious (usually as revealed in dreams) over a rendering of "reality" structured by the conscious mind.

Suspense. The sense of tension aroused by an audience's uncertainty about the resolution of dramatic conflicts.

Suspension of disbelief. An audience's willingness to accept the world of the drama as reality during the course of a play.

Symbolism. A literary device in which an object, event, or action is used to suggest a meaning beyond its literal meaning. The guns in *Hedda Gabler* have a symbolic function.

Theater. The building in which a play is performed. Also used to refer to drama as an art form.

Theater in the round. The presentation of a play on an **arena stage** surrounded by the audience.

Theater of the absurd. A type of twentieth-century drama presenting the human condition as meaningless, absurd, and illogical. An example of the genre is Samuel Beckett's *Waiting for Godot.*

Theater of cruelty. A type of drama created by Antonin Artaud in the 1930s that uses shock techniques to expose the audience's primitive obsessions with cruelty and sexuality. The purpose was to overwhelm spectators' rational minds, leading them to understand and even participate in the cycle of cruelty and ritual purgation dramatized in the performance.

Three unities. Aristotle noted that a play's action usually occurs in one day or a little more and that the plot should reveal clearly ordered actions and incidents moving toward the plot's resolution. Later scholars and critics, especially those in the neoclassical tradition, interpreted Aristotle's ideas as rules (unity of time and unity of action) and added a third, unity of place (a play's action should occur in a single locale).

Thrust stage. A stage extending beyond the **proscenium arch**, usually surrounded on three sides by the audience.

Tiring house. From "attiring house," the backstage space in Elizabethan public theaters used for storage and as a dressing room. The term also refers to the changing space beneath the medieval pageant wagon.

Total theater. A concept of the theater as an experience synthesizing all the expressive arts including music, dance, lighting, and so on.

Tragedy. Serious drama in which a **protagonist,** traditionally of noble position, suffers a series of unhappy events culminating in a **catastrophe** such as death or spiritual breakdown. Shakespeare's *Hamlet,* which ends with the prince's death, is an example of Elizabethan tragedy.

Tragicomedy. A play that combines elements of tragedy and comedy. Chekhov's *The Cherry Orchard* is an example. Tragicomedies often include a serious plot in which the expected tragic **catastrophe** is replaced by a happy ending.

Trope. Interpolation into or expansion of an existing medieval liturgical text. These expansions, such as the *Quem Quaeritis* trope, gave rise to **liturgical drama.**

Type character. See **character**.

Underplot. See **plot**.

Unity. The sense that the events of a play and the actions of the characters follow one another naturally to form one complete action. Unity is present when characters' behavior seems **motivated** and the work is perceived to be a connected artistic whole. See also **three unities.**

Verfremdungseffkt. German term coined by Bertolt Brecht to mean "alienation." See also **alienation effect.**

Verisimilitude. The degree to which a dramatic representation approximates an appearance of reality.

Well-made play. Drama that relies for effect on the suspense generated by its logical, cleverly constructed plot rather than on characterization. Plots often involve a withheld secret, a battle of wits between hero and villain, and a resolution in which the secret is revealed and the **protagonist** saved. The plays of Eugène Scribe (1791–1861) have defined the type.

Selected Bibliography

Selected References for Periods of Drama

GREEK DRAMA

Aylen, Leo. *The Greek Theater*. Rutherford: Fairleigh Dickinson UP, 1985.

Bieber, Margaret. *The History of the Greek and Roman Theater*. 2nd ed. Princeton: Princeton UP, 1961.

Hamilton, Edith. *The Greek Way*. New York: Norton, 1983.

Havelock, Eric. "The Double Vision of Greek Tragedy." *Hudson Review* 37 (1984): 244–70.

Kitto, H. D. F. *Greek Tragedy: A Literary Study*. 3rd ed. London: Methuen, 1966.

———. *Form and Meaning in Drama: A Study of Six Greek Plays and of "Hamlet."* 2nd ed. New York: Barnes, 1968.

Knox, Bernard M. *Word and Action: Essays on the Ancient Theater*. Baltimore: Johns Hopkins UP, 1979.

Pickard-Cambridge, Arthur W. *Dramatic Festivals of Athens*. 2nd ed. Revised by John Gould and D. M. Lewis. Oxford: Clarendon, 1962.

Steiner, George. *The Death of Tragedy*. New York: Knopf, 1961.

Taplin, Oliver. *Greek Tragedy in Action*. Berkeley: U of California P, 1978.

Trendall, A. D., and T. B. L. Webster. *Illustrations of Greek Drama*. London: Phaidon, 1971.

Vickers, Brian. *Towards Greek Tragedy: Drama, Myth, Society*. London: Longman, 1973.

Walcot, Peter. *Greek Drama in Its Theatrical and Social Context*. Cardiff: U of Wales P, 1976.

Walton, Michael J. *Living Greek Theater: A Handbook of Classical Performance and Modern Production*. New York: Greenwood, 1987.

Webster, T. B. L. *Greek Theater Production*. 2nd ed. London: Methuen, 1970.

Winkler, John J., and Froma I. Zeitlin. *Nothing to Do with Dionysus?: Athenian Drama in Its Social Context*. Princeton: Princeton UP, 1990.

ROMAN DRAMA

Beare, William. *The Roman Stage*. 3rd ed. London: Methuen, 1969.

Bieber, Margaret. *The History of the Greek and Roman Theater*. 2nd ed. Princeton: Princeton UP, 1961.

Duckworth, George E. *The Nature of Roman Comedy: A Study in Popular Entertainment*. Princeton: Princeton UP, 1952.

Hunter, R. L. *The New Comedy of Greece and Rome*. New York: Cambridge UP, 1985.

Kenney, E. J., ed. *The Cambridge History of Classical Literature*. 2 vols. New York: Cambridge UP, 1982.

Konstan, David. *Roman Comedy*. Ithaca: Cornell UP, 1983.

Segal, Erich. *Roman Laughter*. Cambridge: Harvard UP, 1968.

Wiles, David. *The Masks of Menander: Sign and Meaning in Greek and Roman Performances*. New York: Cambridge UP, 1991.

MEDIEVAL DRAMA

Axton, Richard. *European Drama of the Early Middle Ages*. London: Hutchinson, 1974.

Bevington, David, ed. *Medieval Drama*. Boston: Houghton, 1975.

Briscoe, Marianne G., and John C. Coldewey. *Contexts for Early English Drama*. Bloomington: Indiana UP, 1989.

Chambers, Edmund K. *English Literature at the Close of the Middle Ages.* Oxford: Clarendon, 1945.
———. *The Medieval Stage.* 2 vols. London: Oxford UP, 1967.

Craig, Hardin. *English Religious Drama of the Middle Ages.* 1968. Westport: Greenwood, 1978.

Davidson, Clifford, et al., eds. *Drama in the Middle Ages.* New York: AMS, 1982.

Elliott, John R. *Playing God: Medieval Mysteries on the Modern Stage.* Toronto: U Toronto P, 1989.

Gassner, John, ed. *Medieval and Tudor Drama.* New York: Bantam, 1971.

Hardison, O. B., Jr. *Christian Rite and Christian Drama in the Middle Ages: Essays in the Origin and Early History of Modern Drama.* Baltimore: Johns Hopkins UP, 1965.

Spinrad, Phoebe. *The Summons of Death on the Medieval and Renaissance English Stage.* Columbus: Ohio State UP, 1987.

Vince, Ronald W. *Ancient and Medieval Theatre: A Historiographical Handbook.* Westport: Greenwood, 1984.

Wickham, Glynne. *The Medieval Theatre.* 3rd ed. New York: Cambridge UP, 1987.

Woolf, Rosemary. *The English Mystery Plays.* Berkeley: U of California P, 1972.

RENAISSANCE DRAMA

Adams, John C. *The Globe Playhouse.* 2nd ed. New York: Barnes, 1961.

Altman, Joel B. *The Tudor Play of Mind: Rhetorical Inquiry and the Development of Elizabethan Drama.* Berkeley: U of California P, 1978.

Bevington, David. *From Mankind to Marlowe: Growth of Structure in the Popular Drama of Tudor England.* Cambridge: Harvard UP, 1962.

Bradbrook, Muriel C. *The Growth and Structure of Elizabethan Comedy.* London: Chatto, 1955.

Braunmuller, A. R., and Michael Hattaway. *The Cambridge Companion to Renaissance Drama.* New York: Cambridge UP, 1990.

Bush, Douglas. *The Renaissance and English Humanism.* Toronto: U of Toronto P, 1939.

Bushnell, Rebecca W. *Tragedies of Tyrants: Political Thought and Theater in the English Renaissance.* Ithaca: Cornell UP, 1990.

Chambers, E. K. *The Elizabethan Stage.* 4 vols. Oxford: Clarendon, 1923.

Farnham, W. *The Medieval Heritage of Elizabethan Tragedy.* Berkeley: U of California P, 1936.

Hussey, Maurice. *The World of Shakespeare and His Contemporaries: A Visual Approach.* New York: Viking, 1972.

Kernodle, George. *From Art to Theatre: Form and Convention in the Renaissance.* Chicago: U of Chicago P, 1944.

Lea, Kathleen M. *Italian Popular Comedy: A Study of the Commedia dell'Arte, 1560–1620.* 2 vols. Oxford: Clarendon, 1934.

Loomba, Ania. *Gender, Race, and Renaissance Drama.* New York: Manchester UP, 1989.

McLuskie, Kathleen. *Renaissance Dramatists.* Atlantic Highlands: Humanities Intl., 1989.

Nicoll, Allardyce. *The World of Harlequin.* Cambridge: Cambridge UP, 1963.

Rose, Mary Beth. *The Expense of Spirit: Love and Sexuality in English Renaissance Drama.* Ithaca: Cornell UP, 1988.

Tetzell, Kurt von Rosador. "The Power of Magic: From Endimion to *The Tempest.*" *Shakespeare Survey* 43 (1991): 1–13.

Waith, Eugene M. *Patterns and Perspectives in English Renaissance Drama.* Newark: U of Delaware P, 1988.

Welsford, Enid. *The Court Masque.* Cambridge: Cambridge UP, 1927.

Wind, Edgar. *Pagan Mysteries in the Renaissance.* New Haven: Yale UP, 1958.

Woodbridge, Linda. *Woman and the English Renaissance: Literature and the Nature of Womankind, 1540–1620.* Urbana: U of Illinois P, 1984.

Yates, Frances A. *Theatre of the World.* Chicago: U of Chicago P, 1969.

LATE SEVENTEENTH- AND EIGHTEENTH-CENTURY DRAMA

Barber, Charles L. *The Idea of Honour in the English Drama, 1591–1700.* Stockholm: Göteborg, 1957.

Cox, Jeffrey N. *In the Shadows of Romance.* Athens: Ohio UP, 1987.

Grene, Nicholas. *Shakespeare, Jonson, Molière: The Comic Contract.* Totowa: Barnes, 1980.

Holland, Norman N. *The First Modern Comedies: The Significance of Etherege, Wycherley, and Congreve.* Cambridge: Harvard UP, 1959.

Hume, Robert. *The Rakish Stage: Studies in English Drama, 1660–1800.* Carbondale: Southern Illinois UP, 1983.

Loftis, John, ed. *Restoration Drama.* New York: Oxford UP, 1966.

Lynch, Kathleen M. *The Social Mode of Restoration Comedy.* New York: Farrar, 1975.

Marshall, Geoffrey. *Restoration Serious Drama.* Norman: U of Oklahoma P, 1975.

Nicoll, Allardyce. *A History of Restoration Drama, 1600–1700.* New York: Cambridge UP, 1923.

Peters, Julie Stone. "'Things Govern'd by Words': Late 17th-Century Comedy and the Reformers." *English Studies* 68 (1987): 142–53.

Powell, Jocelyn. *Restoration Theatre Production.* Boston: Routledge, 1984.

Price, Cecil. *Theatre in the Age of Garrick.* Oxford: Oxford UP, 1973.

Richards, K. R., ed. *Essays on the Eighteenth Century English Stage.* London: Methuen, 1972.

Rothstein, Eric. *The Designs of Carolean Comedy.* Carbondale: Southern Illinois UP, 1988.

Stynan, J. L. *Restoration Comedy in Performance.* New York: Cambridge UP, 1986.

Turnell, Martin. *The Classical Movement: Studies in Corneille, Molière, and Racine.* New York: New Directions, 1948.

NINETEENTH-CENTURY DRAMA THROUGH THE TURN OF THE CENTURY

Bentley, Eric. *The Playwright as Thinker: A Study of Drama in Modern Times.* New York: Harcourt, 1967.

Bogard, Travis, ed. *Modern Drama: Essays in Criticism.* New York: Oxford UP, 1965.

Booth, Michael. *English Melodrama.* London: Jenkins, 1965.

Brustein, Robert. *The Theatre of Revolt.* Boston: Little, 1964.

Cole, Toby, ed. *Playwrights on Playwriting: The Meaning and Making of Modern Drama from Ibsen to Ionesco.* New York: Hill, 1960.

Driver, Tom Faw. *Romantic Quest and Modern Query: A History of the Modern Theatre.* New York: Delacorte, 1970.

Finney, Gail. *Women in Modern Drama: Freud, Feminism, and European Theater at the Turn of the Century.* Ithaca: Cornell UP, 1989.

Fisher, Judith L., and Stephen Watt, eds. *When They Weren't Doing Shakespeare: Essays on Nineteenth-century British and American Theatre.* Athens: U of Georgia P, 1989.

Gilman, Richard. *The Making of Modern Drama: A Study of Buchner, Ibsen, Strindberg, Chekhov, Pirandello, Brecht, Beckett, Handke.* New York: Farrar, 1974.

Stynan, J. L. *Modern Drama in Theory and Practice.* 3 vols. New York: Cambridge UP, 1980.

Valency, Maurice Jacques. *The Flower and the Castle: An Introduction to Modern Drama.* New York: Schocken, 1982.

Whitaker, Thomas R. *Fields of Play in Modern Drama.* Princeton: Princeton UP, 1977.

Williams, Raymond. *Drama from Ibsen to Eliot.* New York: Oxford UP, 1953.

DRAMA IN THE EARLY AND MID-TWENTIETH CENTURY

Artaud, Antonin. *The Theatre and Its Double.* Trans. Mary C. Richards. New York: Grove, 1958.

Bentley, Eric. *The Theatre of Commitment and Other Essays on Drama in Our Society.* New York: Atheneum, 1967.

Blau, Herbert, *The Impossible Theatre: A Manifesto.* New York: Macmillan, 1964.

Brater, Enoch, and Ruby Cohn, eds. *Around the Absurd: Essays on Modern and Postmodern Drama.* Ann Arbor: U of Michigan P, 1990.

Bogard, Travis, and William I. Oliver, eds. *Modern Drama: Essays in Criticism.* New York: Oxford UP, 1965.

Brockett, Oscar G. *History of the Theatre.* 5th ed. Boston: Allyn, 1987.

Brook, Peter. *The Empty Space.* New York: Avon, 1968.

Cohn, Ruby. *From Desire to Godot: Pocket Theater of Postwar Paris.* Berkeley: U of California P, 1987.

Davidson, Clifford, C. J. Gianakaris, and John H. Stroupe, eds. *Drama in the Twentieth Century: Comparative and Critical Essays.* New York: AMS, 1984.

Esslin, Martin. *The Theatre of the Absurd.* Woodstock, NY: Overlook, 1973.

Gassner, John. *Theatre at the Crossroads.* New York: Holt, 1960.

Goldberg, RosaLee. *Performance: Live Art 1909 to the Present.* New York: Abrams, 1979.

Kernan, Alvin B., ed. *The Modern American Theater: A Collection of Critical Essays.* Englewood Cliffs: Prentice, 1967.

Kirby, Michael. *A Formalist Theatre.* Philadelphia: U of Pennsylvania P, 1987.

Orr, John. *Tragic Drama and Modern Society: Studies in Social and Literary Theory of Drama from 1870 to the Present.* New York: Macmillan, 1981.

Piscator, Erwin. *The Political Theatre: A History, 1914–1929.* Trans. Hugh Rorrison. London: Eyre Methuen, 1980.

Roose-Evans, James. *Experimental Theatre: From Stanislavsky to Today.* Rev. ed. London: Studio Vista, 1973.

Smith, Wendy. *Real Life Drama: The Group Theatre and America, 1931–1940.* New York: Knopf, 1990.

Szilassy, Zolt N. *American Theater of the 1960s.* Carbondale: U of Illinois P, 1986.

CONTEMPORARY DRAMA

Betsko, Kathleen, and Rachel Koenig. *Interviews with Contemporary Women Playwrights.* New York: Beech Tree, 1987.

Blau, Herbert. *Eye of Prey: Subversions of the Postmodern.* Bloomington: Indiana UP, 1987.

Blumenthal, Eileen. *Joseph Chaikin: Exploring at the Boundaries of Theatre.* New York: Cambridge UP, 1984.

Brecht, Stefan. *The Theatre of Visions: Robert Wilson.* Frankfurt am Main: Suhrkamp, 1978.

Cheney, Sheldon. *New Movement in the Theatre.* Westport: Greenwood, 1971.

The Drama Review [journal]. New York U.

Grotowski, Jerzy. *Towards a Poor Theatre.* New York: Simon, 1968.

Hart, Lynda, ed. *Making a Spectacle: Feminist Essays on Contemporary Women's Theatre.* Ann Arbor: U of Michigan P, 1989.

Hayman, Ronald. *Theatre and Anti-Theatre: New Movements Since Beckett.* New York: Oxford UP, 1979.

Hill, Errol, ed. *The Theatre of Black Americans.* 2 vols. Englewood Cliffs: Prentice, 1980.

Inverso, MaryBeth. *The Gothic Impulse in Contemporary Drama.* Ann Arbor: U of Michigan P, 1990.

Lahr, John. *Up Against the Fourth Wall: Essays on Modern Theatre.* New York: Grove, 1968.

Marranca, Bonnie, ed. *The Theatre of Images.* New York: Drama Book Specialists, 1977.

Orr, John. *Tragicomedy and Contemporary Culture: Play and Performance from Beckett to Shepard.* Ann Arbor: U of Michigan P, 1990.

Parker, Dorothy. *Essays on Modern American Drama: Williams, Miller, Albee, and Shepard.* Toronto: U of Toronto P, 1987.

Savran, David. *In Their Own Words: Contemporary American Playwrights.* New York: Theatre Communications Group, 1988.

Schechner, Richard. *Environmental Theater.* New York: Hawthorn, 1973.

Wellworth, George E. *The Theater of Protest and Paradox.* New York: New York UP, 1971.

Selected References for Playwrights and Plays

AESCHYLUS

Brooks, Otis. *Cosmos and Tragedy: An Essay on the Meaning of Aeschylus.* Chapel Hill: U of North Carolina P, 1981.

Gannon, J. F. "Aeschylus's *Agamemnon.*" *Classical Quarterly.* 39.1 (1989): 254–57.

Harrington, J. C. *Aeschylus.* New Haven: Yale UP, 1986.

Ireland, S. *Aeschylus, Greece and Rome.* 1947. Classical Association 18. Oxford: Clarendon, 1986.

Konishi, H. "Agamemnon's Reason for Yielding." *American Journal of Philology* 110 (1989): 210–22.

Podlecki, Anthony J. *The Political Background of Aeschylean Tragedy.* Ann Arbor: U of Michigan P, 1966.

Rosenmeyer, Thomas G. *The Art of Aeschylus.* Berkeley: U of California P, 1982.

Spatz, Lois. *Aeschylus.* Twayne's World Authors Series 675. Boston: Twayne, 1982.

Thalmann, W. G. "Aeschylus's Physiology of the Emotions." *American Journal of Philology* 107 (1986): 489–511.

Thomson, George Derwent. *Aeschylus and Athens: A Study in the Social Origins of Drama.* 2nd ed. London: Lawrence & Wishart, 1967.

Winnington-Ingram, R. P. [Reginald Pepys]. *Studies in Aeschylus.* New York: Cambridge UP, 1983.

ARISTOPHANES

Dane, Joseph A. *Parody: Critical Concepts Versus Literary Practices, Aristophanes to Sterne.* Norman: U of Oklahoma P, 1988.

Deardon, C. W. *The Stage of Aristophanes.* London: Athlone, 1976.

Dover, K. J. *Aristophanic Comedy.* Berkeley: U of California P, 1972.

Gruber, William E. "The Wild Men of Comedy: Transformations in the Comic Hero from Aristophanes to Pirandello." *Genre* 14.2 (1981): 207–27.

Harriott, Rosemary. *Aristophanes: Poet and Dramatist.* Baltimore: Johns Hopkins UP, 1986.

Henderson, Jeffrey. *Aristophanes' "Lysistrata."* New York: Oxford UP, 1987.

McLeish, Kenneth. *The Theatre of Aristophanes.* New York: Taplinger, 1980.

Murray, Gilbert. *Aristophanes.* Oxford: Clarendon, 1933.

Reckford, Kenneth. *Aristophanes' Old-and-New Comedy.* Chapel Hill: U of North Carolina P, 1987.

Ussher, Robert Glenn. *Aristophanes.* New York: Oxford UP, 1979.

SAMUEL BECKETT

Astro, Alan. *Understanding Beckett.* Columbia: U of South Carolina P, 1990.

Athanason, Arthur N. *"Endgame": The Ashbin Play.* New York: Twayne, 1993.

Beja, Morris, S. E. Gontarski, and Pierre Astier, eds. *Samuel Beckett: Humanistic Perspectives.* Columbus: Ohio State UP, 1983.

Ben-Zvi, Linda, ed. *Women in Beckett: Performance and Critical Perspectives.* Urbana: U of Illinois P, 1990.

Bloom, Harold. *Samuel Beckett's "Endgame."* New York: Chelsea, 1988.

Brater, Enoch, ed. *Beckett at 80: Beckett in Context.* New York: Oxford UP, 1986.

———. *Why Beckett: With 122 Illustrations.* New York: Thames, 1989.

Bryden, Mary. "The Sacrificial Victim of Beckett's *Endgame.*" *Literature and Theology* 4.2 (1990): 219–25.

Buning, Marius, and Lois Oppenheim, eds. *Beckett in the 1990s.* Amsterdam: Rodopi, 1993.

Burkman, Katherine. *Myth and Ritual in the Plays of Samuel Beckett.* Rutherford: Fairleigh Dickinson UP, 1987.

Butler, Lance S., and Robin J. Davis, eds. *Rethinking Beckett: A Collection of Critical Essays.* New York: St. Martin's, 1990.

Cohn, Ruby. *Just Play: Beckett's Theater.* Princeton: Princeton UP, 1980.

———, ed. *Samuel Beckett: A Collection of Criticism.* New York: McGraw, 1975.

Connor, Steven, ed. *Gender in Transition:* Waiting for Godot *and* Endgame. New York: St. Martin's, 1992.

Dearlove, J. E. *Accommodating the Chaos: Samuel Beckett's Nonrelational Art.* Durham: Duke UP, 1982.

Doll, Mary Aswell. *Beckett and Myth: An Archetypal Approach.* Syracuse: Syracuse UP, 1988.

Esslin, Martin, ed. *Samuel Beckett: A Collection of Critical Essays.* Englewood Cliffs: Prentice, 1965.

Fletcher, Beryl S., et al. *A Student's Guide to the Plays of Samuel Beckett.* 2nd ed. Boston: Faber, 1985.

Fletcher, John. *Beckett, the Playwright.* New York: Hill, 1985.

Gidal, Peter. *Understanding Beckett.* New York: St. Martin's, 1986.

Gontarski, S. E. *On Beckett: Essays and Criticism.* New York: Grove, 1986.

Kenner, Hugh. *A Reader's Guide to Samuel Beckett.* New York: Farrar, 1973.

Lawley, Paul. "Adoption in *Endgame.*" *Modern Drama* 31 (1988): 529–35.

Lyons, Charles R. *Samuel Beckett.* New York: Grove, 1983.

Noguchi, Rei. "Style and Strategy in *Endgame.*" *Journal of Beckett Studies* 9 (1984): 101–11.

O'Dair, Sharon K. "'The Contentless Passion of an Unfruitful Wind': Irony and Laughter in *Endgame.*" *Criticism* 28.2 (1986): 165–78.

Popovic, Poll. "Beckett's *Endgame* as a Bond of Dependency." *European Studies Journal* 11.1 (1994): 35–47.

Rosen, Steven J. *Samuel Beckett and the Pessimistic Tradition.* New Brunswick: Rutgers UP, 1976.

Smith, Joseph H., ed. *The World of Samuel Beckett.* Baltimore: Johns Hopkins UP, 1991.

Aphra Behn

Armistid, J. M. *Four Restoration Playwrights: A Reference Guide to Thomas Shadwell, Aphra Behn, Nathaniel Lee, and Thomas Otway.* Boston: Hall, 1984.

DeRitter, Jones. "*The Gypsy, The Rover,* and the Wanderer: Aphra Behn's Revision of Thomas Killigrew." *Restoration: Studies in English Literary Culture, 1660–1700* 10.2 (1986): 82–92.

Gallagher, Catherine. "Who Was That Masked Woman? The Prostitute and the Playwright in the Comedies of Aphra Behn." *Last Laughs.* Ed. Gina Barreca. New York: Gordon, 1989. 23–42.

Goreau, Angeline. "'Last Night's Rambles': Restoration Literature and the War Between the Sexes." *The Sexual Dimension in Literature.* Ed. Alan Bold. Totowa: Barnes, 1982.

Jones, Jane. "New Light on the Background and Early Life of Aphra Behn." *Notes and Queries* 37 (1990): 288–93.

Link, Frederick M. *Aphra Behn.* Boston: Twayne, 1969.

Lussier, Mark. "'The Vile Mercandize of Fortune': Women, Economy, and Desire in Aphra Behn." *Women's Studies* 18.4 (1991): 379–93.

Mendelson, Sara Heller. *The Mental World of Stuart Women: Three Studies.* Amherst: U of Massachusetts P, 1987.

Munns, Jessica. "'I by a Double Right Thy Bounties Claim': Aphra Behn and Sexual Space." *Curtain Calls: British and American Women and the Theater, 1660–1820.* Ed. Mary Anne Schofield and Cecilia Macheski. Athens: Ohio UP, 1991.

Musser, Joseph F., Jr. "'Imposing Nought but Constancy in Love': Aphra Behn Snares *The Rover.*" *Restoration: Studies in English Literary Culture, 1660–1700* 3.1 (1979): 17–25.

Todd, Janet. *Aphra Behn Studies.* Cambridge: Cambridge UP, 1996.

Wiseman, S. J. *Aphra Behn.* Plymouth: Northcote House, 1996.

Bertolt Brecht

Beckley, Richard. "Brecht: The Reality and the Ideal." *Gestus* 2.1 (1986): 37–46.

Brecht, Bertolt. *Brecht on Theatre: The Development of an Aesthetic.* Ed. and trans. John Willett. New York: Hill, 1964.

Brown, Russell E. *Intimacy and Intimidation: Three Essays on Bertolt Brecht.* Stuttgart: Steiner, 1990.

Bryant-Bertail, Sarah. "Women, Space, Ideology: *Mutter Courage und Ihre Kinder.*" *The Brecht Yearbook* 12 (1983): 43–61.

Cima, Gay Gibson, Maarten Van Dijk, Liz Diamond, et al. "Brecht/'Brecht': A Symposium." *Theater* 25.2 (1994): 24–41.

Crouch, Paul H. "A Definition 'of Drama: Illustrated Through a Structural Analysis of *Mother Courage and Her Children.*" *Gestus* 1.1 (1985): 64–74.

Demetz, Peter, ed. *Brecht: A Collection of Critical Essays.* Englewood Cliffs: Prentice, 1962.

Docherty, Brian, ed. *Twentieth-Century European Drama.* New York: St. Martin's, 1994.

Esslin, Martin. *Brecht: The Man and His Works.* Garden City: Doubleday, 1971.

Ewen, Frederick. *Bertolt Brecht: His Life, His Art and His Times.* New York: Citadel, 1967.

Fuegi, John. *Bertolt Brecht: Chaos, According to Plan.* New York: Cambridge UP, 1987.

———. *Brecht and Company: Sex, Politics, and the Making of Modern Drama.* New York: Grove, 1994.

Gleitman, Claire. "All in the Family: *Mother Courage* and the Ideology in the Gestus." *Comparative Drama* 25.2 (1991): 147–67.

Gray, Ronald. *Bertolt Brecht.* New York: Grove, 1967.

Hill, Claude. *Bertolt Brecht.* New York: Twayne, 1975.

Kleber, Pia, and Colin Visser, eds. *Re-Interpreting Brecht: His Influence on Contemporary Drama and Film.* Cambridge: Cambridge UP, 1990.

Lug, Sieglinde. "The 'Good' Woman Demystified." *Communications from the International Brecht Society* 14.1 (1984): 3–16.

Mews, Siegfried, comp. *Critical Essays on Bertolt Brecht.* Boston: Hall, 1989.

Munk, Erika, ed. "On Brecht." *Theater* 25.2 (1994): 9–55.

Reinelt, Janelle. "Approaching the Postmodernist Threshold: Samuel Beckett and Bertolt Brecht." *Journal of Comparative Literature and Aesthetics* 11 (1988): 1–2, 75–83.

Rouse, John. "Brecht and the Contradictory Actor." *Theatre Journal* 36.1 (1984): 25–41.

Schoeps, Karl Heinz. *Bertolt Brecht: Life, Work, and Criticism.* Fredericton: York, 1989.

Silberman, Marc. "A Postmodernized Brecht?" *Theatre Journal* 45.1 (1993): 1–19.

Spalter, Max. *Brecht's Tradition.* Baltimore: Johns Hopkins UP, 1967.

Speirs, Ronald. *Bertolt Brecht.* New York: St. Martin's, 1987.

Thomson, Peter, and Glendyr Sachs, eds. *The Cambridge Companion to Brecht.* Cambridge: Cambridge UP, 1994.

Willett, John. *Brecht in Context: Contemporary Approaches.* London: Methuen, 1984.

———. *The Theatre of Bertolt Brecht.* New York, 1959.

Willits, Ross D. "The Through-line of Meaning in *Mother Courage* and Brecht." *Text and Presentation.* Ed. Karelisa Hartigan. Lanham, MD: UP of America, 1989.

ANTON CHEKHOV

Barricelli, Jean-Pierre, ed. *Chekhov's Great Plays: A Critical Anthology.* New York: New York UP, 1981.

———. "Counterpoint of the Snapping String: Chekhov's *The Cherry Orchard.*" *Chekhov's Great Plays: A Critical Anthology.* New York: New York UP, 1981. 111–28.

Bely, Andrei. "*The Cherry Orchard.*" *Russian Dramatic Theory from Pushkin to the Symbolists: An Anthology.* Ed. and trans. L. Senelick. Austin: U of Texas P, 1981. 89–92.

Deer, Irving. "Speech as Action in Chekhov's *The Cherry Orchard.*" *Educational Theatre Journal* 10 (1959): 30–34.

Eekman, Thomas A. *Critical Essays on Anton Chekhov.* Boston: Hall, 1989.

Emeljanow, Victor. *Chekhov: The Critical Heritage.* Boston: Routledge, 1981.

Hahn, Beverly. "Chekhov's *The Cherry Orchard.*" *Critical Review* 16 (1973): 56–72.

Hingley, Ronald. *Chekhov: A Biographical and Critical Study.* New York: Barnes, 1966.

Jackson, Robert Louis. *Chekhov: A Collection of Critical Essays.* Englewood Cliffs: Prentice, 1967.

Karlinsky, Simon, and Michael Heim, eds. *Anton Chekhov's Life and Thought: Selected Letters and Commentary.* Berkeley: U of California P, 1975.

Magarshak, David. *Chekhov the Dramatist.* New York: Hill, 1960.

Meister, Charles. *Chekhov Criticism 1880 through 1986.* New York: McFarland, 1988.

Peace, Richard. *Chekhov: A Study of the Four Major Plays.* New Haven: Yale UP, 1983.

Remaley, Peter B. "Chekhov's *The Cherry Orchard.*" *South Atlantic Bulletin* 38 (1973): 16–20.

Russell, Robert, and Andrew Barratt, eds. *Russian Theatre in the Age of Modernism.* New York: St. Martin's, 1990.

Stanislavsky, Konstantin. *My Life in Art.* New York: Routledge Chapman and Hall, 1924.

Stynan, J. L. *Chekhov in Performance.* Cambridge: Cambridge UP, 1971.

Toumanova, Princess Nina Andronikova. *Anton Chekhov: The Voice of Twilight Russia.* New York: Columbia UP, 1960.

Valency, Maurice. *The Breaking String: The Plays of Anton Chekhov.* New York: Oxford UP, 1966.

Welleck, Rene, and Nonna D. Welleck, eds. *Chekhov: New Perspectives.* Englewood Cliffs: Prentice, 1984.

Williams, Lee J. *Anton Chekhov, the Iconoclast.* Scranton: U of Scranton P, 1989.

CARYL CHURCHILL

Acheson, James, ed. *British and Irish Drama Since 1960.* Houndmills: Macmillan, 1993.

Brater, Enoch, and Ruby Cohn, eds. *Feminine Focus: The New Women Playwrights.* Oxford: Oxford UP, 1989.

Fitzsimmons, Linda. "'I Won't Turn Back for You or Anyone': Caryl Churchill's Socialist-Feminist Theatre." *Essays in Theatre* 6.1 (1987): 19–29.

Keyssar, Helene. "The Dramas of Caryl Churchill: The Politics of Possibility." *Massachusetts Review* 24.1 (1983): 198–216.

Marohl, Joseph. "De-Realised Women: Performance and Identity in Churchill's *Top Girls*: Essays from *Modern Drama*." *Contemporary British Drama 1970–1990.* Ed. Hersh Zeifman and Cynthia Zimmerman. Toronto: U of Toronto P, 1993. 307–22.

Nischik, Reingard M. "Betrayal Psychohistorically: The Representation of Emotions in the British Drama of Manners." *Anglistentag 1991 Dusseldorf.* Ed. Wilhelm B. Busse. Tubingen: Niemeyer, 1992. 189–204.

Randall, Phyllis R., ed. *Caryl Churchill: A Casebook.* New York: Garland, 1988.

Swanson, Michael. "Mother/Daughter Relationships in Three Plays by Caryl Churchill." *Theatre Studies* (1984–1986): 31–32, 49–46.

Vanden-Heuvel, Michael. "Performing Gender(s)." *Contemporary Literature* 35.4 (1994): 804–13.

WILLIAM CONGREVE

Braverman, Richard. "Capital Relations and *The Way of the World*." *ELH* 52.1 (1985): 133–58.

Dobree, Bonamy. *Congreve.* London: British Council, 1963.

Hodges, John C. *Congreve the Man: A Biography.* London: Oxford UP, 1941.

Kroll, Richard. "Discourse and Power in *The Way of the World*." *ELH* 53.4 (1986): 727–58.

Love, Harold. *Congreve.* Oxford: Blackwell, 1974.

Lynch, Kathleen M. *The Social Mode of Restoration Comedy.* New York: Macmillan, 1926.

Markley, Robert. *Two-Edged Weapons: Style and Ideology in the Comedies of Etherege, Wycherley, and Congreve.* New York: Oxford UP, 1988.

Morris, Brian, ed. *Congreve: A Collection of Critical Studies.* London: Benn, 1972.

Mueschke, Paul and Carol. *A New View of Congreve's* The Way of the World. Ann Arbor: U of Michigan P, 1958.

Novak, Maximilian. *William Congreve.* Boston: Twayne, 1971.

Peters, Julie Stone. *Congreve: The Drama, and the Printed Word.* Stanford: Stanford UP, 1990.

Van Voris, W. *The Cultivated Stance: The Designs of Congreve's Plays.* Dublin: Dolmen, 1965.

Williams, Aubrey Lake. *An Approach to Congreve.* New Haven: Yale UP, 1979.

EURIPIDES

Barlow, Shirley Anne. "Stereotype and Reversal in Euripides' *Medea*." *Greece & Rome* 36 (1989): 158–71.

Burian, Peter, ed. *Directions in Euripidean Criticism.* Durham: Duke UP, 1985.

Collard, Christopher. *Euripides.* New York: Oxford UP, 1981.

Foley, Helene P. "Medea's Divided Self." *Classical Antiquity* 8 (1989): 61–85.

———. *Ritual Irony: Poetry and Sacrifice in Euripides.* Ithaca: Cornell UP, 1985.

Halleran, Michael P. *Stagecraft in Euripides.* Totowa: Barnes, 1985.

Keane, Ellen Marie, Judith P. Saunders, and Ellen S. Silber. "Female Outlaws: Exploring Ethical Choice Through Literature." *Women's Voices.* Ed. Lorna D. Edmundson. Littleton, MA: Copley, 1987.

Meagher, Robert E. *Mortal Vision: The Wisdom of Euripides.* New York: St. Martin's, 1989.

Michelini, Ann N. *Euripides and the Tragic Tradition.* Madison: U of Wisconsin P, 1987.

O'Connor, E. A. M. E. *Aspects of Human Sacrifice in the Tragedies of Euripides.* Amsterdam: Grüner, 1987.

Pucci, Pietro. *The Violence of Pity in Euripides' "Medea."* Ithaca: Cornell UP, 1980.

Segal, Erich, ed. *Euripides: A Collection of Critical Essays.* Englewood Cliffs: Prentice, 1968.

Stoeckl, Ula. "The Medea Myth in Contemporary Cinema." *Film Criticism* 10 (1985): 47–51.

Tuana, Nancy. "Medea: With the Eyes of the Lost Goddess." *Soundings: An Interdisciplinary Journal* 68.2 (1985): 253–72.

Whitman, Cedric Hubbell. *Euripides and the Full Circle of Myth.* Cambridge: Harvard UP, 1974.

EVERYMAN

Bevington, David M. *From Mankind to Marlowe: Growth of Structure in the Popular Drama of Tudor England.* Cambridge: Harvard UP, 1962.

Cawley, A. C. *Everyman.* Manchester: Manchester UP, 1977.

———, ed. *"Everyman" and Medieval Miracle Plays.* New York: Dutton, 1977.

Cunningham, John. "Comedic and Liturgical Restoration in *Everyman*." *Drama in the Middle Ages: Comparative and Critical Essays.* Second Series. Ed. Clifford Davidson and John H. Stroupe. New York: AMS, 1990.

Garner, Stanton B., Jr. "Theatricality in Mankind and *Everyman*." *Studies in Philology* 84.3 (1987): 272–85.

Gilman, Donald, ed. *"Everyman" and Company: Essays on the Theme and Structure of the European Moral Play.* New York: AMS, 1989.

Munson, William. "Knowing and Doing in *Everyman*." *The Chaucer Review* 19.3 (1985): 252–71.

Ryan, Lawrence V. "Doctrine and Dramatic Structure in *Everyman*." *Mississippi Quarterly* 14 (1961): 3–13.

Spinrad, Phoebe S. "The Last Temptation of Everyman." *Philological Quarterly* 64.2 (1985): 185–94.

Tanner, Ron. "Humor in *Everyman* and the Middle English Morality Play." *Philological Quarterly* 70 (1991): 149–61.

White, D. Jerry. *Early English Drama: "Everyman" to 1580, A Reference Guide.* Boston: Hall, 1986.

MARÍA IRENE FORNÉS

Brater, Enoch, and Ruby Cohn, eds. *Feminine Focus: The New Women Playwrights.* Oxford: Oxford UP, 1989.

Cummings, Scott. "Seeing with Clarity: The Visions of María Irene Fornés." *Theater* 17.1 (1985): 51–56.

France, Anna Kay, ed. *Voices of Identity and Transformation.* Metuchen, NJ: Scarecrow, 1993.

Gruber, William A. *Missing Persons: Character and Characterization in Modern Drama.* Athens: U of Georgia P, 1994.

Kintz, Linda. "Permeable Boundaries: Femininity, Fascism, and Violence: Fornés' *The Conduct of Life*." *Gestos* 6.11 (1991): 79–89.

O'Malley, Lurana Donnels. "Pressing Clothes/Snapping Beans/Reading Books: María Fornés's Women's Work." *Studies in American Drama 1945–Present* 4 (1989): 103–17.

Schlueter, June, ed. *Modern American Drama: The Female Canon.* Rutherford: Fairleigh Dickinson UP, 1990.

Wolf, Stacy. "Re/Presenting Gender, Re/Presenting Violence: Feminism, Form and the Plays of María Irene Fornés." *Theatre Studies* 37 (1992): 17–31.

ATHOL FUGARD

Benson, Mary. "Keeping an Appointment with the Future: The Theatre of Athol Fugard." *Theatre Quarterly* 7 (1977/78): 77–83.

Bragg, Melvyn. "Athol Fugard, Playwright — A Conversation with Melvyn Bragg." *Listener* 5 Dec. 1974: 734.

Collins, Michael. "The Sabotage of Love: Athol Fugard's Recent Plays." *World Literature Today* 57.3 (1983): 369–71.

Daymond, M. J., J. A. Jacobs, and Margaret Lenta, eds. *Momentum: On Recent South African Writing.* Pietermaritzburg: U of Natal P, 1984.

Durbach, Errol. " *'MASTER HAROLD'. . . and the boys*: Athol Fugard and the Psychopathology of Apartheid." *Modern Drama* 30.4 (1987): 505–13.

Fugard, Athol. "Fugard on Actors, Actors on Fugard." *Theatre Quarterly* 7 (1977/78): 83–7.

———. "Fugard on Fugard." *Yale Theatre* 1 (Winter 1973): 41–54.

———. "Letter from Athol Fugard." *Classic* 1 (1966): 78–80.

———. *Notebooks 1960–1977.* New York: Knopf, 1983.

Gray, Stephen, ed. *Athol Fugard.* Southern Africa Literature Series 1. Johannesburg: McGraw, 1982.

Heywood, Christopher. *Aspects of South African Literature.* London: Heinemann, 1976.

Jordan, John O. "Life in the Theatre: Politics and Romance in *'MASTER HAROLD'. . . and the boys*." *Twentieth-Century Literature* 39.4 (1993): 461–72.

Kavanagh, Robert Mshengu. *Theatre and Cultural Struggle in South Africa.* London: Zed, 1985.

Post, Robert M. "Racism in Athol Fugard's *'MASTER HAROLD'. . . and the boys*." *World Literature Written in English* 30.1 (1990): 97–102.

Roberts, Sheila. "'No Lessons Learnt': Reading the Texts of *A Lesson from Aloes* and *'MASTER HAROLD'. . . and the boys*." *English in Africa* 9.2 (1982): 27–33.

Seidenspinner, Margarete. *Exploring the Labyrinth: Athol Fugard's Approach to South African Drama.* Essen: Verlag Die Blaue Eule, 1986.

Vandenbrouke, Russell. *Truths the Hand Can Touch: The Theatre of Athol Fugard.* New York: Theatre Communications Group, 1985.

Walder, Dennis. *Athol Fugard.* New York: Grove, 1985.

Wertheim, Albert. "Ballroom Dancing, Kites and Politics: Athol Fugard's *'MASTER HAROLD'. . . and the boys*." *SPAN* 30 (1990): 141–55.

Susan Glaspell

Abramson, Doris, María Irene Fornés, Carolee Schneemann, et al. "Women in the Theatre." *Centerpoint: A Journal of Interdisciplinary Studies* 3.11 (1980): 31–37.

Ben-Zvi, Linda. "Susan Glaspell's Contributions to Contemporary Women Playwrights." *Feminine Focus: The New Women Playwrights.* Ed. Enoch Brater and Ruby Cohn. Oxford: Oxford UP, 1989.

———. "'Murder, She Wrote': The Genesis of Susan Glaspell's *Trifles.*" *Theatre Journal* 44.2 (1992): 141–62.

Dymkowski, Christine. "On the Edge: The Plays of Susan Glaspell." *Modern Drama* 31.1 (1988): 91–105.

Mael, Phyllis. "*Trifles:* The Path to Sisterhood." *Literature-Film Quarterly* 17.4 (1989): 281–84.

Makowsky, Veronica. *Susan Glaspell's Century of American Women: A Critical Interpretation of Her Work.* New York: Oxford UP, 1993.

Mustazza, Leonard. "Generic Translation and Thematic Shift in Susan Glaspell's *Trifles* and 'A Jury of Her Peers.'" *Studies in Short Fiction* 26.4 (1989): 489–96.

Noe, Marcia. "Region As Metaphor in the Plays of Susan Glaspell." *Western Illinois Regional Studies* 4.1 (1981): 77–85.

———. "Reconfiguring the Subject/Recuperating Realism: Susan Glaspell's Unseen Woman." *American Drama* 4.2 (1995): 36–54.

Oziebolo, Barbara. "Rebellion and Rejection: The Plays of Susan Glaspell." *Modern American Drama: The Female Canon.* Ed. June Schlueter. Rutherford: Fairleigh Dickinson UP, 1990.

Smith, Beverly A. "'Women's Work — Trifles? The Skill and Insights of Susan Glaspell." *International Journal of Women's Studies* 5.2 (1982): 172–84.

Lady Gregory (Isabella Augusta Gregory)

Adams, Hazard. *Lady Gregory.* Lewisburg: Bucknell UP, 1973.

Coxhead, Elizabeth. *Lady Gregory: A Literary Portrait.* New York: Harcourt, 1961.

Gregory, Isabella Augusta. *Lady Gregory's Journals, 1910–1930.* New York: Oxford UP, 1978.

———. *Our Irish Theatre.* Gerrards Cross: Smythe, 1972.

Kohfeldt, Mary Lou. *Lady Gregory: The Woman Behind the Irish Renaissance.* New York: Atheneum, 1985.

Kopper, E. A., Jr. "Lady Gregory's *The Rising of the Moon.*" *Explicator* 47 (1989): 29–31.

Maxwell, D. E. S. *A Critical History of Modern Irish Drama: 1891–1980.* New York: Cambridge UP, 1984.

O'Connor, Ulick. *All the Olympians.* New York: Atheneum, 1984.

Owens, C'il'n D., and Joan N. Radner. *Irish Drama: 1900–1980.* Washington: Catholic U of America P, 1990.

Saddlemyer, Ann. *In Defense of Lady Gregory, Playwright.* Dublin: Dolmen, 1966.

———. *Lady Gregory, Fifty Years After.* Totowa: Barnes, 1987.

Lorraine Hansberry

Brown, Lloyd W. "Lorraine Hansberry as Ironist: A Reappraisal of *A Raisin in the Sun.*" *Journal of Black Studies* 4 (March 1974): 237–47.

Carter, Steven R. *Hansberry's Drama: Commitment and Complexity.* Urbana: U of Illinois P, 1991.

Cheney, Anne. *Lorraine Hansberry.* Boston: Twayne, 1984.

Freedman, Morris. *American Drama in Social Context.* Carbondale: Southern Illinois UP, 1971.

Keyssar, Helene. "Rites and Responsibilities: The Drama of Black American Women." *The New Women Playwrights.* Ed. Enoch Brater and Ruby Cohn. Oxford: Oxford UP, 1989. 226–40.

McKelly, James C. "Hymns of Sedition: Portraits of the Artist in Contemporary African-American Drama." *Arizona Quarterly* 48.1 (1992): 87–107.

Miller, Jeanne-Marie A. "Images of Black Women in Plays by Black Playwrights." *CLA Journal* 20 (June 1977): 498–99.

Nemiroff, Robert. *To Be Young, Gifted, and Black: A Portrait of Lorraine Hansberry in Her Own Words.* Englewood Cliffs: Prentice, 1969.

Scheader, Catherine. *They Found a Way: Lorraine Hansberry.* Chicago: Children's, 1978.

Schlueter, June, ed. *Modern American Drama: The Female Canon.* Rutherford: Fairleigh Dickinson UP, 1990.

Seaton, Sandra. "*A Raisin in the Sun:* A Study in Afro-American Culture." *Midwestern Miscellany* 20 (1992): 40–49.

Washington, J. Charles. "*A Raisin in the Sun* Revisited." *Black American Literature Forum* 22.1 (1988): 109–24.

Weales, Gerald. "Lorraine Hansberry." *Contemporary Dramatists.* Ed. D. L. Kirkpatrick. 4th ed. Chicago: St. James, 1988. 653–54.

Wilkerson, Margaret B. "Excavating Our History: The Importance of Biographies of Women of Color." *Black American Forum* 24.1 (1990): 73–84.

Williams, Mance. *Black Theatre in the 1960s and 1970s*. Westport: Greenwood, 1985.

DAVID HENRY HWANG

DiGaetani, John Louis. "*M. Butterfly:* An Interview with David Henry Hwang." *The Drama Review* 33.3 (Fall 1989): 141–53.

Hwang, David Henry. "Evolving a Multicultural Tradition." *MELUS* 16.3 (1989–90): 16–19.

Skloot, Robert. "Breaking the Butterfly: The Politics of David Henry Hwang." *Modern Drama* 33.1 (1990): 59–66.

Street, Douglas. *David Henry Hwang*. (Western Writers Series no. 90) Boise: Boise State U, 1989.

HENRIK IBSEN

List of Plays

Catiline, 1850
Grouse in Justedal, 1850
The Burial Mound, 1850
Norma, 1851
St. John's Eve, 1853
Lady Inger of Østraat, 1855
The Feast at Solhoug, 1856
Olaf Liljekrans, 1857
The Vikings at Helgeland, 1857
Love's Comedy, 1862
The Pretenders, 1864
Brand, 1866
Peer Gynt, 1867
The League of Youth, 1869
Emperor and Galilean, 1873
The Pillars of Society, 1877
A Doll House, 1879
Quicksands, 1880
Ghosts, 1881
The Child Wife, 1882
An Enemy of the People, 1882
The Wild Duck, 1884
Rosmersholm, 1886
The Lady from the Sea, 1888
Hedda Gabler, 1890
The Master Builder, 1892
Little Eyolf, 1894
John Gabriel Borkman, 1896
When We Dead Awaken, 1899

Ackerman, Gretchen P. *Ibsen and the English Stage, 1889–1903*. New York: Garland, 1987.

Chamberlain, John S. *Ibsen: The Open Vision*. London: Athlone, 1982.

Egan, Michael, ed. *Ibsen: The Critical Heritage*. London: Routledge, 1972.

Fjelde, Rolf, ed. *Ibsen: A Collection of Critical Essays*. Englewood Cliffs: Prentice, 1965.

Gaskell, Ronald. *Drama and Reality: The European Theatre Since Ibsen*. London: Routledge, 1972.

Lebowitz, Naomi. *Ibsen and the Great World*. Baton Rouge: Louisiana UP, 1990.

McFarlane, James, ed. *Discussions of Henrik Ibsen*. Boston: Heath, 1962.

Marker, Frederick J. *Ibsen's Lively Art: A Performance Study of the Major Plays*. New York: Cambridge UP, 1989.

Meyer, Michael, *Henrik Ibsen: A Biography*. 3 vols. Garden City: Doubleday, 1971.

Noreng, Harald, et al., eds. *Contemporary Approaches to Ibsen*. Oslo: Universitetsforlaget, 1977.

Northam, John. *Ibsen: A Critical Study*. Cambridge: Cambridge UP, 1973.

Shaw, Bernard. *The Quintessence of Ibsenism*. New York: Hill, 1957.

Thomas, David. *Henrik Ibsen*. New York: Grove, 1984.

Ibsen's *A Doll House*

Andreas-Salomé, Lou. *Ibsen's Heroines*. Ed. and trans. Siegfried Mandel. Austrian/German Culture Series. Redding Ridge, CT: Black Swan, 1985.

Bradbrook, M. C. "*A Doll's House* and the Unweaving of the Web." *Women and Literature, 1779–1982*. Vol. 2. Totowa: Barnes, 1982. 81–92. 2 vols.

Downs, R. B. "Birth of the New Woman." *Molders of the Modern Mind*. New York: Barnes, 1961. 311–14.

Durbach, Errol. "*A Doll's House*": *Ibsen's Myth of Transformation*. Boston: Twayne, 1991.

Gassner, John. "An Ibsen Revival: Too Much Doll." *Dramatic Soundings*. New York: Crown, 1968. 290–94.

Hardwick, Elizabeth. "*A Doll's House.*" *Seduction and Betrayal*. New York: Random, 1974. 33–48.

Ibsen, Henrik. "*Doll's House*" [Ibsen's notes on *A Doll House*]. *Playwrights on Playwriting*. Ed. Toby Cole. New York: Hill, 1960. 151–54.

Sprinchorn, E. M. "Ibsen and the Actors." *Ibsen and the Theatre*. Ed. Errol Durbach. New York: New York UP, 1980. 118–30.

Ibsen's *Hedda Gabler*

Ackley, Katherine Anne. "A Rage to Live: The Violent Life and Death of Hedda Gabler." *Women and Violence in Literature: An Essay Collection*. Ed.

Katherine Anne Ackley. New York: Garland, 1990. 163–73.

Braunmuller, A. R. "Hedda Gabler and the Sources of Symbolism." *Drama and Symbolism.* Ed. James Redmond. New York: Cambridge UP, 1982. 57–70.

Fuchs, Elinor. "Mythic Structure in Hedda Gabler: The Mask Behind the Face." *Comparative Drama* 19.3 (1985): 209–21.

Ibsen, Henrik. *"Hedda Gabler"* [Ibsen's notes on *Hedda Gabler*]. *Playwrights on Playwriting.* Ed. Toby Cole. New York: Hill, 1960. 156–70.

Low, Lisa Elaine. "In Defense of Hedda." *Massachusetts Studies in English* 8.3 (1982): 43–49.

Lyons, Charles R. *"Hedda Gabler": Gender, Role, and World.* Boston: Twayne, 1991.

Mayer, H. "Judith as Bourgeois Heroine." *Outsiders.* Cambridge: MIT P, 1982. 53–75.

Olsen, Stein Haugom. "Why Does Hedda Gabler Marry Jorgen Tesman?" *Modern Drama* 28 (1985): 591–610.

Suzman, Janet. *"Hedda Gabler:* The Play in Performance." *Ibsen and the Theatre.* Ed. Errol Durbach. New York: New York UP, 1980. 83–104.

Tynan, Kenneth. *"Hedda Gabler." Curtains.* New York: Atheneum, 1961. 77–78.

Watson, George J. "Ibsen and Miller: The Individual and Society." *Drama: An Introduction.* New York: St. Martin's, 1983. 112–31.

TONY KUSHNER

Arons, Wendy. "'Preaching to the Converted?' — 'You Couldn't Possibly Do Any Better!': An Interview with Tony Kushner." *Communications from the International Brecht Society* 23.2 (1994): 51–59.

Kiefer, Daniel. *"Angels in America* and the Failure of Revelation." *American Drama* 4.1 (1994): 21–38.

Lowenthal, Michael. "On Art, Angels, and 'Postmodern Fascism.'" *Harvard Gay and Lesbian Review* 2.2 (1995): 10–12.

Posnock, Ross. "Roy Cohn in *America." Raritan* 13.3 (1994): 64–77.

Rogoff, Gordon. "Angels in America, Devils in the Wings." *Theater* 24.2 (1993): 21–29.

Steyn, Mark. "Communism Is Dead: Long Live the King." *The New Criterion:* 13.6 (Feb. 1995): 49–53.

FEDERICO GARCÍA LORCA

Anderson, Andrew. "On Broadway, Off Broadway: García Lorca and the New York Theatre, 1929–1930." *Gestos* 8.16 (1993): 135–48.

Duran, Manuel, and Francesca Colecchia, eds. *Lorca's Legacy: Essays on Lorca's Life, Poetry, and Theatre.* New York: Lang, 1991.

Fitzpatrick, Tim, and Sean Batten. "Watching the Watchers Watch: Some Implications of Audience Attention Patterns." *Gestos* 6.12 (1991): 11–31.

Franco, Adolfo M., ed. *National Symposium on Hispanic Theatre April 22–24, 1982.* Cedar Falls: U of Northern Iowa, 1985.

Gabriele, John P. "Of Mothers and Freedom: Adela's Struggle for Freedom in *La Casa de Bernardo Alba." Symposium* 47.3 (1993): 188–99.

Harvard, Robert, ed. *Lorca: Poet and Playwright.* Cardiff: U of Wales, 1992.

Klein, Dennis A. Blood Wedding, Yerma, *and* The House of Bernarda Alba: *García Lorca's Tragic Trilogy.* Boston: Twayne, 1991.

Lanters, Jose. "The Theatre of Thomas Murphy and Federico García Lorca." *Modern Drama* 36.4 (1993): 481–89.

Parilla, Catherine Arturi. *A Theory for Reading Dramatic Texts: Selected Texts by Pirandello and García Lorca.* New York: Lang, 1995.

Rees, Margaret A., ed. *Leeds Papers on Hispanic Drama.* Leeds: Trinity and All Saints College, 1991.

Soufas, C. Christopher, Jr. "Dialectics of Vision: Pictorial vs. Photographic Representation in Lorca's *La Casa de Bernarda Alba." Ojancano* 5 (1991): 52–66.

Wellington, Beth. *Reflections on Lorca's Private Mythology: "Once Five Years Pass" and the Rural Plays.* New York: Lang, 1993.

DAVID MAMET

Almansi, Guido. "David Mamet: A Virtuoso of Invective." *Critical Angles: European Views of Contemporary American Literature.* Ed. Marc Chenetier. Carbondale: Southern Illinois UP, 1986.

Blumberg, Marcia. "Eloquent Stammering in the Fog: O'Neill's Heritage in Mamet." *Perspectives on O'Neill: New Essays.* Ed. Shyamal Bagchee. Victoria: U of Victoria P, 1988. 97–111.

Dean, Anne. *David Mamet: Language As Dramatic Action.* Rutherford: Fairleigh Dickinson UP, 1990.

Ditsky, John. "'He Lets You See the Thought There': The Theater of David Mamet." *Kansas Quarterly* 12.4 (1980): 25–34.

Gale, Stephen H. "David Mamet: The Plays, 1972–1980." *Essays on Contemporary American Drama.* Ed. Hedwig Bock and Albert Wertheim. Munich: Hueber, 1981.

Hubert, Liebler Pascale. "Dominance and Anguish: The Teacher-Student Relationship in the Plays of David Mamet." *Modern Drama* 31.4 (1988): 557–570.

Jacobs, Dorothy H. "Working Worlds in David Mamet's Dramas." *Midwestern Miscellany* 14 (1986): 47–57.

Kane, Leslie, ed. *David Mamet: A Casebook.* New York: Garland, 1991.

Lundon, Edward. "Mamet and Mystery." *Publications of the Mississippi Philological Association* (1988): 106–14.

MacLeod, Christine. "The Politics of Gender, Language and Hierarchy in Mamet's *Oleanna.*" *Journal of American Studies* 29.2 (1995): 199–213.

Maufort, Marc. "Narrative Patterns in the Plays of David Mamet." *BELL* (1991): 112–19.

Mc Donough, Carla J. "Every Fear Hides a Wish: Unstable Masculinity in Mamet's Drama." *Theatre Journal* 44.2 (1992): 195–205.

Mufson, Daniel. "The Critical Eye: Sexual Perversity in Viragos." *Theater* 24.1 (1993): 111–13.

Roudané, Matthew. "An Interview with David Mamet." *Studies in American Drama 1945–Present* 1 (1986): 73–81.

Zinman, Toby Silerman. "Jewish Aporia: The Rhythm of Talking in Mamet." *Theatre Journal* 44.2 (1992): 207–15.

Christopher Marlowe

Bartels, Emily C. "Authorizing Subversion: Strategies of Power in Marlowe's *Doctor Faustus.*" *Renaissance Papers* (1989): 65–74.

Birrenger, Johannes. "Between Body and Language: 'Writing' The Damnation of Faust." *Theatre Journal* 36.3 (1984): 301–20.

———. "The Demonic Flight of Doctor Faustus: Hope or Escape?" *Massachusetts Studies in English* 8.3 (1982): 17–26.

Bloom, Harold, ed. *Christopher Marlowe.* New York: Chelsea, 1986.

———. *Christopher Marlowe's "Doctor Faustus."* New York: Chelsea, 1988.

Cole, Douglas. *Suffering and Evil in the Plays of Christopher Marlowe.* Princeton: Princeton UP, 1962.

Cox, John D. "Devils and Power in Marlowe and Shakespeare." *Yearbook of English Studies* 23 (1993): 46–64.

Cutts, John P. *The Left Hand of God.* Haddonfield, NJ: Haddonfield, 1973.

Danson, Lawrence. "Christopher Marlowe: The Questioner." *English Literary Renaissance* 12.2 (1982): 3–29.

Ellis-Fermor, Una Mary. *Christopher Marlowe.* Hamden, CT: Anchor, 1967.

Farnham, Willard, comp. *Twentieth-Century Interpretation of Doctor Faustus: A Collection of Critical Essays.* Englewood Cliffs: Prentice, 1969.

Friedenreich, Kenneth, Roma Gill, and Constance Kuriyama, eds. *New Essays on Christopher Marlowe.* New York: AMS, 1988.

Godshalk, W. L. *The Marlovian World Picture.* The Hague: Mouton, 1974.

Golden, Kenneth. "Myth, Psychology and Marlowe's *Doctor Faustus.*" *College Literature* 12.3 (1985): 202–10.

Honigmann, Ernst. "Ten Problems in *Doctor Faustus.*" *The Arts of Performance in Elizabethan and Early Stuart Drama.* Eds. Murray Biggs et al. Edinburgh: Edinburgh UP, 1991. 173–191.

Jones, John Henry, ed. *The English Faust Book: A Critical Edition Based on the Text of 1592.* Cambridge: Cambridge UP, 1994.

Keefer, Michael H. "History and the Canon: the Case of *Doctor Faustus.*" *University of Toronto Quarterly* 56.4 (1987): 498–522.

Leech, Clifford, ed. *Marlowe: A Collection of Critical Essays.* Englewood Cliffs: Prentice, 1964.

Levin, Harry. *The Overreacher, A Study of Christopher Marlowe.* Boston: Beacon, 1964.

McAlindon, T. *"Doctor Faustus": Divine in Show.* New York: Twayne, 1994.

———. "The Ironic Vision: Diction and Theme in Marlowe's *Doctor Faustus.*" *Review of English Studies* 32.126 (1981): 129–41.

Marlowe, Christopher. *Complete Plays.* Ed., intro, and notes Irving Ribner. New York: Odyssey, 1963.

Ricks, Christopher. "*Doctor Faustus* and Hell on Earth." *Essays in Criticism* 35.2 (1985): 101–20.

Spinrad, Phoebe. "The Dilettante's Lie in *Doctor Faustus.*" *Texas Studies in Language and Literature* 24.3 (1982): 243–54.

Steane, J. B. *Marlowe: A Critical Study.* Cambridge: Cambridge UP, 1964.

Stover, David F. "The Individualism of Doctor Faustus." *North Dakota Quarterly* 57.4 (1989): 146–61.

Warren, Michael J. "Doctor Faustus: The Old Man in the Text." *English Literary Renaissance* 11.2 (1981): 111–47.

Arthur Miller

Anderson, M. C. "*Death of a Salesman*: A Consideration of Willy Loman's Role in Twentieth-Century Tragedy." *CRUX* 20.2 (1986): 25–29.

August, Eugene R. "*Death of a Salesman*: A Men's Studies Approach." *Western Ohio Journal* 7.1 (1986): 53–71.

Babcock, Granger. "'What's the Secret?': Willy Loman as Desiring Machine." *American Drama* 2.1 (1992): 59–83.

Bloom, Harold, ed. *Arthur Miller's "Death of a Salesman."* New York: Chelsea, 1988.

———. *Willy Loman.* New York: Chelsea, 1990.

Brucher, Richard T. "Willy Loman and the Soul of a New Machine: Technology and the Common Man." *Journal of American Studies* 17.3 (1983): 325–36.

Carson, Neil. *Arthur Miller.* London: Macmillan; 1982.

Centola, Steven R. "Family Values in *Death of a Salesman*." *College Language Association Journal* 37.1 (1993): 29–41.

Corrigan, Robert W., ed. *Arthur Miller: A Collection of Critical Essays.* Englewood Cliffs: Prentice, 1969.

Gelb, Phillip. "*Death of a Salesman*: A Symposium." *Tulane Drama Review* 2 (1958): 20–21.

Hadomi, Leah. "Fantasy and Reality: Dramatic Rhythm in *Death of a Salesman*." *Modern Drama* 31.2 (1988): 157–74.

Hagopian, John V. "Arthur Miller: The Salesman's Two Cases." *Modern Drama* 6 (1963): 117–25.

Harder, Harry. "*Death of a Salesman*: An American Classic." *Censored Books: Critical Viewpoints.* Ed. Nicholas J. Karolides, Lee Burress, and John M. Kean. Metuchen, NJ: Scarecrow, 1993.

Hayman, Ronald. *Arthur Miller.* New York: Ungar, 1972.

Huftel, Sheila. *Arthur Miller: The Burning Glass.* New York: Citadel, 1965.

Koon, Helene Wickham. *Twentieth Century Interpretations of "Death of a Salesman."* Englewood Cliffs: Prentice, 1983.

Martin, Robert A., ed. *Arthur Miller: New Perspectives.* Englewood Cliffs: Prentice, 1982.

Miller, Arthur. *Collected Plays.* New York: Viking, 1957.

———. *The Theater Essays of Arthur Miller.* Ed. and intro. Robert A. Martin. New York: Viking, 1978.

———. *Timebends: A Life.* New York: Grove, 1987.

Roudane, Matthew C., ed. *Conversations with Arthur Miller.* Jackson: UP of Mississippi, 1987.

Schlueter, June, and James K. Flanagan. *Arthur Miller.* New York: Ungar, 1987.

Schockley, John S. "*Death of a Salesman* and American Leadership: Life Imitates Art." *Journal of American Culture* 17.2 (1994): 49–56.

Stanton, Kay. "Women and the American Dream of *Death of a Salesman*." *Feminist Rereadings of Modern American Drama.* Ed. June Schlueter. Rutherford: Fairleigh Dickinson UP, 1989.

Vidal, Gore, et al. "*Death of a Salesman*: A Symposium." *Tulane Drama Review* 2 (May 1958): 63–69.

MOLIÈRE (JEAN BAPTISTE POQUELIN)

Bermel, Albert. *Molière's Theatrical Bounty: A New View of the Plays.* Carbondale: Southern Illinois UP, 1990.

Gaines, James F. *Molière's Theater.* Columbus: Ohio State UP, 1984.

Gross, Nathan. *From Gesture to Idea: Esthetics and Ethics in Molière's Comedy.* New York: Columbia UP, 1982.

Guicharnaud, Jacques. *Molière: A Collection of Critical Essays.* Englewood Cliffs: Prentice, 1964.

Hall, H. Gaston. *Comedy in Context: Essays on Molière.* Jackson: UP of Mississippi, 1984.

Jagendorf, Zvi. *The Happy End of Comedy: Jonson, Molière, and Shakespeare.* Newark: U of Delaware P, 1984.

Knutson, Harold C. *The Triumph of Wit: Molière and Restoration Comedy.* Columbus: Ohio State UP, 1988.

Molière. *Tartuffe: Comedy in Five Acts.* Trans. Richard Wilbur. New York: Harcourt, 1963.

Walker, Hallam. *Molière.* Rev. ed. Boston: Twayne, 1990.

MARSHA NORMAN

Betsko, Kathleen, and Rachel Koenig. "Marsha Norman." *Interviews with Contemporary Women Playwrights.* New York: Beech Tree, 1987.

Browder, Sally. "'I Thought You Were Mine': Marsha Norman's *'night, Mother.*" *Mother Puzzles: Daughters and Mothers in Contemporary American Literature.* Ed. Mickey Pearlman. Westport: Greenwood, 1989.

Brustein, Robert. "Robert Brustein on Theater." *New Republic* 2 May 1983: 25–26.

Burkman, Katherine H. "The Demeter Myth and Doubling in Marsha Norman's *'night, Mother.*" *Modern American Drama: The Female Canon.* Ed. June Schlueter. Rutherford: Fairleigh Dickinson UP, 1990. 254–63.

Demastes, William. "Jessie and Thelma Revisited: Conceptual Challenge in *'night, Mother.*" *Modern Drama* 36.1 (1993): 109–19.

Denby, David. "Stranger in a Strange Land." *Atlantic* Jan. 1985: 44–45.

DiGaetani, John L., ed. *A Search for a Postmodern Theater: Interviews with Contemporary Playwrights.* New York: Greenwood, 1991.

Forte, Jeanie. "Realism, Narrative and the Feminist Playwright: A Problem of Perception." *Modern Drama* 32.1 (1989): 115–27.

Gill, Brendan. "The Theatre." *New Yorker* 11 April 1983: 109+.

Gilman, Richard. "Theater." *Nation* 7 May 1983: 586.

Greiff, Louis K. "Fathers, Daughters, and Spiritual Sisters: Marsha Norman's *'night, Mother* and Tennessee Williams's *The Glass Menagerie*." *Text and Performance Quarterly* 9.3 (1989): 224–28.

Gussow, Mel. "Women Playwrights: New Voices in the Theatre." *New York Times Magazine* 1 May 1983: 22–40.

Hart, Lynda. "Doing Time: Hunger for Power in Marsha Norman's Plays." *Southern Quarterly* 25.3 (1987): 67–69.

Kane, Leslie. "The Way Out, the Way In: Paths to Self in the Plays of Marsha Norman." *Feminine Focus: The New Women Playwrights.* Ed. Enoch Brater and Ruby Cohn. Oxford: Oxford UP, 1989. 255–74.

Kauffmann, Stanley. "More Trick than Tragedy." *Saturday Review* Oct. 1983: 47–48.

Sauvage, Leo. "Different Kinds of Kin." *New Leader* 18 April 1983: 21–22.

Savran, David. *In Their Own Words.* New York: Theater Communications Group, 1988.

Smith, Raynette Halvorsen. "' *'night, Mother'* and *'True West'*: Mirror Images of Violence and Gender." *Violence in Drama.* Ed. James Redmond. Cambridge: Cambridge UP, 1991.

Spencer, Jenny S. "Norman's *'night, Mother*: Psychodrama of Female Identity." *Modern Drama* 30.3 (1987): 364–75.

Stone, Elizabeth. "Playwright Marsha Norman: An Optimist Writes About Suicide, Confinement, and Despair." *Ms.* July 1983: 56–59.

Weales, Gerald. "Really 'Going On.'" *Commonweal* 17 June 1983: 370–71.

Wolfe, Irmgard H. "Marsha Norman: A Classified Bibliography." *Studies in American Drama, 1945–Present* 3 (1988): 148–75.

EUGENE O'NEILL

Ahuja, Chaman. *Tragedy, Modern Temper, and O'Neill.* Atlantic Highlands: Humanities, 1984.

Berlin, Normand. *Eugene O'Neill.* New York: Grove, 1987.

Bogard, Travis. *Contour in Time: The Plays of Eugene O'Neill.* New York: Oxford UP, 1988.

Cargill, Oscar, N. Bryllion Fagan, and William J. Fisher, eds. *O'Neill and His Plays: Four Decades of Criticism.* New York: New York UP, 1961.

Gassner, John, ed. *O'Neill: A Collection of Critical Essays.* Englewood Cliffs: Prentice, 1964.

Floyd, Virginia. *The Plays of Eugene O'Neill: A New Assessment.* New York: Ungar, 1985.

Leech, Clifford. *Eugene O'Neill.* New York: Grove, 1963.

Maufort, Marc, ed. *Eugene O'Neill and the Emergence of American Drama.* Atlanta: Rodopi, 1989.

Miller, Jordan Yale. *Eugene O'Neill and American Criticism: A Bibliographical Checklist.* 2nd ed. Hamden: Anchor, 1973.

Moorton, Richard F., Jr. *Eugene O'Neill's Century: Centennial Views on America's Foremost Critic.* New York: Greenwood, 1991.

O'Neill, Eugene. *The Plays of Eugene O'Neill.* 3 vols. New York: Modern Library, 1982.

———. *Long Day's Journey into Night.* New Haven: Yale UP, 1956.

Porter, Laurin. *The Banished Prince: Time, Memory, and Ritual in the Late Plays of Eugene O'Neill.* Ann Arbor: UMI Research, 1988.

Ranald, Margaret Loftus. *The Eugene O'Neill Companion.* Westport: Greenwood, 1984.

Wainscott, Ronald Harold. *Staging O'Neill: The Experimental Years, 1920–1934.* New Haven: Yale UP, 1988.

SUZAN-LORI PARKS

Carr, C. Rev. of *Imperceptible Mutabilities in the Third Kingdom.* *Artforum* Nov. 1989: 154.

Gussow, Mel. Rev. of *The Death of the Last Black Man in the Whole Entire World.* *New York Times* 25 Sept. 1990: C15.

———. Rev. of *Imperceptible Mutabilities in the Third Kingdom.* *New York Times* 20 Sept. 1989: C24.

Holden, Stephen. Rev. of *Betting on the Dust Commander.* *New York Times* 26 June 1991: C12.

HAROLD PINTER

Barnett, Claudia. "The Metadramatic Prison of *Betrayal.*" *The Pinter Review: Annual Essays* (1992–93):69–72.

Bloom, Harold, ed. *Harold Pinter.* New York: Chelsea, 1987.

Bold, Alan, ed. *Harold Pinter: You Never Heard Such Silence.* Critical Studies Series. Totowa: Barnes, 1985.

Burkman, Katherine H. *The Dramatic World of Harold Pinter.* Columbia: Ohio State UP, 1971.

———. "Harold Pinter's *Betrayal*: Life Before Death — And After." *Theatre Journal* 34.4 (1982): 505–18.

Conklin, Robert. "*Old Times* and *Betrayal* as Rorschach Test." *The Pinter Review* (1992–93): 69–72.

Deer, Harriet. "Melodramatic Problematics in Pinter's Film of *Betrayal*." *The Pinter Review* (1990): 61–70.

Diamond, Elin. *Pinter's Comic Play*. Lewisburg: Bucknell UP, 1985.

Dukore, Bernard F. *Harold Pinter*. 2nd ed. New York: Macmillan, 1988.

Esslin, Martin. *Pinter: The Playwright*. New York: Methuen, 1984.

Gaggi, Silvio. "Pinter's *Betrayal*: Problems of Language or Grand Metatheatre?" *Theatre Journal* 33.4 (1981): 504–16.

Gale, Steven H., ed. *Critical Essays on Harold Pinter*. Boston: Hall, 1990.

———. *Harold Pinter: Critical Approaches*. Rutherford: Fairleigh Dickinson UP, 1986.

Ganz, Arthur F., ed. *Pinter: A Collection of Critical Essays*. Englewood Cliffs: Prentice, 1979.

Gordon, Lois, ed. *Harold Pinter: A Casebook*. New York: Garland, 1990.

Hayman, Ronald. *Harold Pinter*. New York: Ungar, 1973.

Hinchliffe, Arnold P. *Harold Pinter*. Boston: Twayne, 1981.

Kerr, Walter. *Harold Pinter*. New York: Columbia UP, 1967.

Mayberry, Bob. *Theatre of Discord: Dissonance in Beckett, Albee, and Pinter*. Rutherford: Fairleigh Dickinson UP, 1989.

Pinter, Harold. *Complete Works*. 3 vols. New York: Grove, 1977–78.

Quigley, Austin E. *The Pinter Problem*. Princeton: Princeton UP, 1975.

Strunk, Volker. *Harold Pinter: Towards a Poetics of His Plays*. New York: Lang, 1989.

Sykes, Arlene. *Harold Pinter*. New York: Humanities, 1970.

Wells, Linda. "A Discourse on Failed Love: Harold Pinter's *Betrayal*." *Modern Language Studies* 13.1 (1983): 22–30.

Woodroffe, Graham. "From Kinsale Drive to Wessex Grove: A Psychoanalytical Study of Harold Pinter's *Betrayal*." *Literature and Psychology* 35.3 (1989): 43–63.

Zeifman, Hersh, and Cynthia Zimmerman, eds. *Contemporary British Drama 1970–90*. Toronto: U of Toronto P, 1993.

LUIGI PIRANDELLO

Bassnett, Susan. *File on Pirandello*. London: Methuen, 1989.

Bassnett-McGuire, Susan. *Luigi Pirandello*. New York: Grove, 1983.

Bentley, Eric. *The Pirandello Commentaries*. Evanston: Northwestern UP, 1986.

Bloom, Harold. *Luigi Pirandello*. New York: Chelsea, 1989.

Büdel, Oscar. *Pirandello*. New York: Hillary, 1969.

Cambon, Glauco, ed. *Pirandello: A Collection of Critical Essays*. Englewood Cliffs: Prentice, 1967.

Caputi, Anthony. *Pirandello and the Crisis of Modern Consciousness*. Urbana: U of Illinois P, 1988.

Guidice, Gaspare. *Pirandello: A Biography*. Trans. Alastair Hamilton. New York: Oxford UP, 1975.

Mariani, Umberto. "The 'Pirandellian' Character." *Canadian Journal of Italian Studies* 12.38–39 (1989): 1–9.

Oliver, Roger W. *Dreams of Passion: The Theater of Luigi Pirandello*. New York: New York UP, 1979.

Paolucci, Anne. *Pirandello's Theater*. Carbondale: Southern Illinois UP, 1974.

Pirandello, Luigi. *Naked Masks, Five Plays*. Ed. Eric Bentley. New York: Dutton, 1952.

———. *Short Stories*. Ed. and trans. Frederick May. New York: Oxford UP, 1965.

Ragusa, Olga. "Comparative Perspectives on Pirandello." *Atenea* 8.1 (1988): 19–36.

Starkie, Walter. *Luigi Pirandello, 1867–1936*. 3rd ed. Berkeley: U of California P, 1965.

Stone, Jennifer. *Pirandello's Naked Prompt: The Structure of Repetition in Modernism*. Ravenna: Longo Editore, 1989.

PLAUTUS

Segal, Erich. *Roman Laughter: The Comedy of Plautus*. New York: Oxford UP, 1987.

Slater, Niall W. *Plautus in Performance: The Theater of the Mind*. Princeton: Princeton UP, 1985.

MANUEL PUIG

Iversen, Eric. "Deviance and Form in the Prison-House of Culture: A Reading of Manuel Puig's *Kiss of the Spider Woman*." *Postscript* 11 (1994): 75–82.

"Kiss of the Spider Woman." *London Theatre Record* 5.19 (1–24 Sept., 1985): 939–43.

"Kiss of the Spider Woman." *New York Theatre Critics' Reviews* 10 (1993): 191–200.

Tittler, Jonathan. *Manuel Puig*. Twayne's World Authors Series. New York: Twayne, 1993.

SENECA

Fairweather, Janet. *Seneca the Elder*. New York: Cambridge UP, 1981.

Tarrant, R. J. *Seneca's "Thyestes."* Atlanta: Scholars, 1985.

WILLIAM SHAKESPEARE

List of Plays

Comedies
The Comedy of Errors, 1592–94
The Taming of the Shrew, 1593–94
The Two Gentlemen of Verona, 1594
Love's Labor's Lost, 1594–95
A Midsummer Night's Dream, 1595–96
The Merchant of Venice, 1596–97
The Merry Wives of Windsor, 1597
Much Ado About Nothing, 1598–99
As You Like It, 1599
Twelfth Night, or What You Will, 1601–02
All's Well That Ends Well, 1602–03
Measure for Measure, 1604

Histories
Henry the Sixth, Part One, 1589–90
Henry the Sixth, Part Two, 1590–91
Henry the Sixth, Part Three, 1590–91
Richard the Third, 1592–93
King John, 1594–96
Richard the Second, 1595
Henry the Fourth, Part One, 1596–97
Henry the Fourth, Part Two, 1598
Henry the Fifth, 1599
Henry the Eighth, 1612–13

Tragedies
The Tragedy of Titus Andronicus, 1593
The Tragedy of Romeo and Juliet, 1595–96
The Tragedy of Julius Caesar, 1599
The Tragedy of Hamlet, 1600–01
The History of Troilus and Cressida, 1601–02
The Tragedy of Othello, the Moor of Venice, 1604
The Tragedy of King Lear, 1605
The Tragedy of Macbeth, 1606
The Tragedy of Antony and Cleopatra, 1606
The Tragedy of Coriolanus, 1607
The Life of Timon of Athens, 1607

Romances
Pericles, Prince of Tyre, 1607–08
Cymbeline, 1609–10
The Winter's Tale, 1610–11
The Tempest, 1611
Two Noble Kinsmen, 1613

Bamber, Linda. *Comic Women, Tragic Men: A Study of Gender and Genre in Shakespeare*. Stanford: Stanford UP, 1982.

Barber, C. L. *Shakespeare's Festive Comedy*. Princeton: Princeton UP, 1968.

Bradley, A. C. *Shakespearean Tragedy*. New York: Meridian, 1955.

Bullough, Geoffrey, ed. *Narrative and Dramatic Sources of Shakespeare*. 8 vols. New York: Columbia UP, 1957–75.

Chute, Marchette. *Shakespeare of London*. New York: Dutton, 1949.

Doran, Madeleine. *Shakespeare's Dramatic Language*. Madison: U of Wisconsin P, 1976.

Drakakis, John, ed. *Alternative Shakespeares*. New York: Methuen, 1985.

Dusinberre, Juliet. *Shakespeare and the Nature of Women*. London: Macmillan, 1975.

Dutton, Richard. *Shakespeare: A Literary Life*. New York: St. Martin's, 1989.

Eagleton, Terry. *William Shakespeare*. New York: Blackwell, 1986.

Erikson, Peter. *Rewriting Shakespeare, Rewriting Ourselves*. Berkeley: U of California P, 1991.

Frye, Northrop. *On Shakespeare*. New Haven: Yale UP, 1986.

Goddard, Harold C. *The Meaning of Shakespeare*. Chicago: U of Chicago P, 1951.

Grady, Hugh. *The Modernist Shakespeare: Critical Texts in a Material World*. New York: Oxford UP, 1991.

Granville-Barker, H. *Prefaces to Shakespeare*. Princeton: Princeton UP, 1946.

Greene, G., et al., eds. *The Women's Part: Feminist Criticism of Shakespeare*. Urbana: U of Illinois P, 1980.

Ioppolo, Grace. *Revising Shakespeare*. Cambridge: Harvard UP, 1991.

Jardine, Lisa. *Still Harping on Daughters: Women and Drama in the Age of Shakespeare*. Totowa: Barnes, 1983.

Kermode, Frank, ed. *Four Centuries of Shakespearean Criticism*. New York: Avon, 1974.

Kott, Jan. *Shakespeare Our Contemporary*. New York: Norton, 1974.

Righter, Anne. *Shakespeare and the Idea of the Play*. London: Chatto, 1962.

Schoenbaum, Samuel. *William Shakespeare: A Documentary Life*. New York: Oxford UP, 1975.

Schwartz, Murray M., and Coppelia Kahn, eds. *Representing Shakespeare: New Psychoanalytic Essays*. Baltimore: Johns Hopkins UP, 1981.

Scott, Michael. *Shakespeare and the Modern Dramatist*. New York: St. Martin's, 1989.

Shakespeare Quarterly. Annual Bibliography.
Shakespeare Survey.

Shakespeare's *Hamlet*

Berkoff, Steven. *I Am Hamlet*. New York: Grove, 1990.

Bloom, Harold, ed. *William Shakespeare's "Hamlet."* New York: Chelsea, 1986.

Calderwood, James. *To Be and Not to Be: Negation and Metadrama in "Hamlet."* New York: Columbia UP, 1983.

Cantor, Paul A. *Shakespeare, Hamlet.* New York: Cambridge UP, 1989.

Charney, Maurice. *Hamlet's Fictions.* New York: Routledge, 1988.

Cohen, Michael. *"Hamlet" in My Mind's Eye.* Athens: U of Georgia P, 1989.

Frye, Northrop. *Fools of Time: Studies in Shakespearean Tragedy.* Buffalo: U of Toronto P, 1973.

Jones, Ernest. *Hamlet and Oedipus.* New York: Norton, 1976.

Lacan, Jacques. "Desire and the Interpretation of Desire in *Hamlet.*" *Literature and Psychoanalysis: The Question of Reading Otherwise.* Ed. Shoshana Felman. Baltimore: Johns Hopkins UP, 1982.

Levin, Harry. *The Question of Hamlet.* New York: Oxford UP, 1959.

Mack, Maynard. "The World of Hamlet." *Yale Review* 41 (1952): 502–23.

Mills, John A. *"Hamlet" on Stage: The Great Tradition.* Westport: Greenwood, 1985.

Prosser, Eleanor. *Hamlet and Revenge.* Stanford: Stanford UP, 1967.

Ribner, Irving. *Patterns in Shakespearean Tragedy.* New York: Barnes, 1960.

Shakespeare Survey 9 (1956).

Showalter, Elaine. "Representing Ophelia: Women, Madness, and the Responsibilities of Feminist Criticism." *Shakespeare and the Question of Theory.* Ed. Patricia Parker and Geoffrey Hartman. New York: Methuen, 1985.

Trewin, J. C. *Five and Eighty Hamlets.* New York: New Amsterdam, 1987.

Wilson, John Dover. *What Happens in "Hamlet."* Cambridge: Cambridge UP, 1967.

Shakespeare's *A Midsummer Night's Dream*

Bevington, David. "But We Are Spirits of Another Sort: The Dark of Love and Magic in *A Midsummer Night's Dream.*" *Medieval and Renaissance Studies* 7 (1975): 80–92.

Bloom, Harold, ed. *William Shakespeare's "A Midsummer Night's Dream."* New York: Chelsea, 1987.

Brown, John Russell. *Shakespeare and His Comedies.* London: Methuen, 1968.

Doran, Madeleine. "Pyramus and Thisbe Once More." *Essays on Shakespeare and Elizabethan Drama in Honor of Hardin Craig.* Ed. Richard Hosley. Columbia: U of Missouri P, 1962. 449–62.

Garber, Marjorie. *Dream in Shakespeare: From Metaphor to Metamorphosis.* New Haven: Yale UP, 1974.

Girard, Rene. "Myth and Ritual in Shakespeare: *A Midsummer Night's Dream.*" *Textual Strategies: Perspectives in Post-Structuralist Criticism.* Ithaca: Cornell UP, 1979.

Kermode, Frank. "The Mature Comedies." *Early Shakespeare.* Ed. John Russell Brown and Bernard Harris. Stratford-upon-Avon Studies 3. London: Edward Arnold, 1961. 211–27.

Latham, Minor White. *The Elizabethan Fairies: The Fairies of Folklore and the Fairies of Shakespeare.* New York: Columbia UP, 1930.

Legatt, Alexander. *"A Midsummer Night's Dream": Shakespeare's Comedy of Love.* London: Methuen, 1974.

Montrose, Louis Adrian. "'Shaping Fantasies': Figurations of Gender and Power in Elizabethan Culture." *Representations* 1.2 (1983): 61–94.

Schanzer, Ernest. "The Central Theme of *A Midsummer Night's Dream.*" *University of Toronto Quarterly* 20 (1957): 233–38.

Shelbourne, David. *The Making of "A Midsummer Night's Dream."* London: Methuen, 1982.

Young. David P. *Something of Great Constancy: The Art of "A Midsummmer Night's Dream."* New Haven: Yale UP, 1966.

Shakespeare's *The Tempest*

Brockbank, J. Philip. "*The Tempest*: Conventions of Art and Empire." *Later Shakespeare.* Ed. John Russell Brown and Bernard Harris. Stratford-upon-Avon Studies 8. New York: St. Martin's, 1966.

Brown, Paul. "'This Thing of Darkness I Acknowledge Mine': *The Tempest* and the Discourse of Colonialism." *Political Shakespeare: New Essays.* Ed. Jonathan Dollimore and Alan Sinfield. Manchester: Manchester UP, 1985.

Felperin, Howard. "Undream's Shores: *The Tempest* Shakespearean Romance." Princeton: Princeton UP, 1972.

Fiedler, Leslie A. "The New World Savage as Stranger; or, 'Tis New to Thee.'" *The Stranger in Shakespeare.* New York: Stein, 1979.

Frye, Northrop. *A Natural Perspective: The Development of Shakespeare's Comedy and Romance.* New York: Columbia UP, 1965.

Greenblatt, Stephen. *Shakespearean Negotiations.* Berkeley: U of California P, 1988.

Griffiths, Trevor R. "'This Island's Mine': Caliban and Colonialism." *Yearbook of English Studies* 13 (1983): 159–80.

James, D. G. *The Dream of Prospero.* Oxford: Clarendon, 1967.

Kermode, Frank. *"The Tempest." William Shakespeare: The Final Plays.* London: Longman, 1963.

Kernan, Alvin B. "'The Great Globe Itself': The Public Playhouse and the Ideal Theater of *The Tempest." The Playwright as Magician: Shakespeare's Image of the Poet in the English Public Theater.* New Haven: Yale UP, 1979.

Marbane, John S. *Renaissance Magic and the Return of the Golden Age: The Occult Tradition and Marlowe, Jonson, and Shakespeare.* Lincoln: U of Nebraska P, 1989.

Orgel, Stephen. "New Uses of Adversity: Tragic Experience in *The Tempest." Essays in Shakespearean Criticism.* Ed. James L. Calderwood and Harold Toliver. Englewood Cliffs: Prentice, 1970.

———. "Prospero's Wife." *Rewriting the Renaissance: The Discourse of Sexual Difference in Early Modern Europe.* Ed. Margaret W. Ferguson, Maureen Quilligan, and Catherine R. Stimpson. Chicago: U of Chicago P, 1986.

Payne, Michael. "Magic and Politics in *The Tempest." Shakespeare and the Triple Play: From Study to Stage to Classroom.* Ed. Sidney Homan. Lewisburg: Bucknell UP, 1988.

Skura, Meredith Anne. "Discourse and the Individual: The Case of Colonialism in *The Tempest." Shakespeare Quarterly* 40 (1989): 42–69.

Summers, Joseph. *Dreams of Love and Power.* Oxford: Clarendon, 1984.

Schwartz, Murray M., and Coppelia Kahn, eds. *Representing Shakespeare: New Psychoanalytic Essays.* Baltimore: Johns Hopkins UP, 1980.

William, David. *"The Tempest on Stage." Jacobean Theater.* Ed. John Russell Brown and Bernard Harris. Stratford-upon-Avon Studies 1. New York: St. Martin's, 1960.

BERNARD SHAW

Adams, Elsie B. "Heartless, Heartbroken, and Heartfelt: A Recurrent Theme in the Plays of George Bernard Shaw." *English Literature in Transition* 25.1 (1982): 4–9.

Bentley, Eric. *Bernard Shaw.* 2nd ed. London: Methuen, 1967.

Berst, Charles A. *Bernard Shaw and the Art of Drama.* Urbana: U of Illinois P, 1973.

Bloom, Harold, ed. *George Bernard Shaw.* New York: Chelsea, 1987.

———. *George Bernard Shaw's "Pygmalion."* New York: Chelsea, 1988.

Bloomfield, Zachary. "America's Response to George Bernard Shaw: A Study of Professional Productions." *Theatre Studies* 36 (1991): 5–17.

Bosha, Francis J. "William James's Unpublished Correspondence with Bernard Shaw." *Notes and Queries* 37 (1990): 432–33.

Bower, Anne. "Tyranny, Telling, Learning: Teaching the Female Student." *West Virginia Philological Papers* 36 (1990): 38–45.

Brown, John Ivor. *Shaw in His Time.* London: Nelson, 1965.

Eldred, Janet Carey, and Peter Mortenson. "Reading Literary Narratives." *College English* 54.5 (1992): 50–53.

Evans, T. F. *Shaw: The Critical Heritage.* Boston: Routledge, 1976.

Gainor, J. Ellen. "G. B. S. and the New Woman." *New England Theatre Journal* 1.1 (1990): 1–17.

———. *Shaw's Daughters: Dramatic and Narrative Constructions of Gender.* Ann Arbor: U of Michigan P, 1991.

Ganz, Arthur F. *George Bernard Shaw.* New York: Grove, 1983.

Gibbs, A. M. *The Art and Mind of Shaw: Essays in Criticism.* New York: St. Martin's, 1983.

———, ed. *Shaw: Interviews and Recollections.* Iowa City: U of Iowa P, 1990.

Gordon, David J. *Bernard Shaw and the Comic Sublime.* New York: St. Martin's, 1990.

Greene, Nicholas. *Bernard Shaw: A Critical View.* New York: St. Martin's, 1984.

Kauffmann, Stanley. "The Late Beginner: Bernard Shaw Becoming a Dramatist." *South Atlantic Quarterly* 91.2 (1992): 289–301.

Kaufman, R. J., ed. *G. B. Shaw: A Collection of Critical Essays.* Englewood Cliffs: Prentice, 1965.

May, Keith M. *Ibsen and Shaw.* New York: St. Martin's, 1985.

Miller, J. Hillis. *Versions of "Pygmalion."* Cambridge: Harvard UP, 1990.

Muggleston, Lynda. "Shaw, Subjective Inequality, and the Social Meanings of Language in *Pygmalion." Review of English Studies* 44.175 (1993): 373–85.

Shaw, Bernard. *An Autobiography.* Ed. Stanley Weintraub. 2 vols. New York: Weybright, 1969.

———. *Collected Letters.* Ed. Dan H. Laurence. New York: Dodd, 1972.

———. *Complete Plays with Prefaces.* New York: Dodd, 1962.

———. *Plays and Players: Essays on the Theatre.* Ed. A. C. Ward. New York: Oxford UP, 1963.

———. *Shaw on Shakespeare: An Anthology of Bernard Shaw's Writings on the Plays and Production of Shakespeare.* Ed. Edwin Wilson. New York: Dutton, 1961.

Silver, Arnold. *Bernard Shaw: The Darker Side.* Stanford: Stanford UP, 1982.

Valency, Maurice. *The Cart and the Trumpet: The Plays of George Bernard Shaw.* New York: Schocken, 1983.

Weintraub, Stanley. *The Unexpected Shaw: Biographical Approaches to G.B.S. and His Work.* New York: Ungar, 1982.

Wisenthal, J.L. "Wilde, Shaw and the Play of Conversation." *Modern Drama* 37.1 (1994): 206–19.

Yorks, Samuel A. *The Evolution of Bernard Shaw.* Washington: UP of America, 1981.

SAM SHEPARD

Auerbach, Doris. *Sam Shepard, Arthur Kopit, and the Off-Broadway Theatre.* Twayne's United States Author Series 432. Boston: Twayne, 1982.

Cima, Gay Gibson. "*Buried Child.*" *Theatre Journal* 35 (Dec. 1983): 559–60.

Cohn, Ruby. *New American Dramatists: 1960–1980.* New York: Grove, 1982.

Cott, Jonathan. "The Rolling Stone Interview: Sam Shepard." *Rolling Stone* 18 Dec. 1986–1 Jan. 1987: 166–72+.

Falk, Florence. "The Role of Performance in Sam Shepard's Plays." *Theatre Journal* May 1981: 182–98.

Gilman, Richard. Introduction. *Sam Shepard: Seven Plays.* New York: Bantam, 1981. ix–xiv.

Hart, Lynda. *Sam Shepard's Metaphorical Stages.* Westport: Greenwood, 1987.

King, Kimball, ed. *Sam Shepard: A Casebook.* New York: Garland, 1988.

Marranca, Bonnie, ed. *American Dreams: The Imagination of Sam Shepard.* New York: Performing Arts Journal, 1981.

Mottram, Ron. *Inner Landscapes: The Theater of Sam Shepard.* Columbia: U of Missouri P, 1984.

Mustazza, Leonard. "Women's Roles in Sam Shepard's *Buried Child.*" *Literature in Performance* 5.2 (1985): 36–41.

Nash, Thomas. "Sam Shepard's *Buried Child*: The Ironic Use of Folklore." *Modern Drama* 26 (1983): 486–91.

Orbison, Tucker. "Authorization and Subversion of Myth in Shepard's *Buried Child.*" *Modern Drama* 37.3 (1994): 509–20.

———. "Mythic Levels in Sam Shepard's *True West.*" *Modern Drama* 27 (Dec. 1984): 506–19.

Oumano, Ellen. *Sam Shepard: The Life and Work of an American Dreamer.* New York: St. Martin's, 1986.

Radel, Nicholas F. "What's the Meaning of This Corn, Tilden?: Mimesis in Sam Shepard's *Buried Child.*" *From the Bard to Broadway.* Ed. V. Hartigan-Karelisa. Lanham, MD: UP of America, 1987. 177–189.

Sessums, Kevin. "Geography of a Horse Dreamer: Playwright, Actor, and Movie Director Sam Shepard." *Interview* Sept. 1988: 70–78.

Shea, Laura. "The Sacrificial Crisis in Sam Shepard's *Buried Child.*" *Theatre Annual* 44 (1989–90): 1–9.

Shepard, Sam. "Metaphors, Mad Dogs, and Old-Time Cowboys." *Theatre Quarterly* 15 (Aug.–Oct. 1974): 3–16.

———. "Visualization, Language, and the Inner Library." *Drama Review* 4 (Dec. 1977): 49–58.

Shewey, Don. *Sam Shepard.* New York: Dell, 1985.

Steinke, Lauri B. "Visiting the Inequities of the Fathers upon the Children: Spiritual Retribution in Shepard's Family Trilogy and *Fool for Love.*" *Publications of the Arkansas Philological Association* 19.2 (1993): 73–84.

Whiting, Charles G. "Digging Up *Buried Child.*" *Modern Drama* 31.4 (1986): 548–56.

Wilson, Ann. "Fool of Desire: the Spectator to the Plays of Sam Shepard." *Modern Drama* 30.1 (1987): 46–57.

Wilson, Ann, ed. *Rereading Shepard: Contemporary Critical Essays on the Plays of Sam Shepard.* New York: St. Martin's, 1993.

ANNA DEAVERE SMITH

Lyons, Charles L. "Anna Deavere Smith: Perspectives on Her Performance within the Context of Critical Theory." *Journal of Dramatic Theory and Criticism* 9.1 (1994): 43–66.

SOPHOCLES

List of Plays (Sophocles wrote in the fifth century b.c. The exact dates for his plays are unknown.)

Oedipus Rex
Antigone
Oedipus at Colonus
Philoctetes
Ajax
Trachiniae
Elektra
Ichneutai
Aleadae

Bloom, Harold, ed. *Sophocles.* New York: Chelsea, 1990.

Bowra, Sir Maurice. *Sophoclean Tragedy.* Oxford: Clarendon, 1944.

Burton, Reginald William Boteler. *The Chorus in Sophocles' Tragedies.* New York: Oxford UP, 1980.

Bushnell, Rebecca. *Prophesying Tragedy: Sign and Voice in Sophocles' Theban Plays.* Ithaca: Cornell UP, 1988.

Buxton, R. G. A. *Sophocles.* New York: Clarendon, 1984.

Gardiner, Cynthia P. *The Sophoclean Chorus: A Study of Character and Function.* Iowa City: U of Iowa P, 1987.

Kitto, H. D. F. *Sophocles: Dramatist and Philosopher.* London: Oxford UP, 1958.

Knox, Bernard M. *Sophocles at Thebes: Sophocles' Tragic Hero and His Time.* New York: Norton, 1971.

Reinhardt, Karl. *Sophokles.* Trans. D. and H. Harvey. New York: Barnes, 1978.

Scodel, Ruth. *Sophocles.* Boston: Twayne, 1984.

Segal, Charles. *Tragedy and Civilization: An Interpretation of Sophocles.* Cambridge: Harvard UP, 1981.

Waldock, A. J. A. *Sophocles the Dramatist.* Cambridge: Cambridge UP, 1951.

Wiles, David. *The Masks of Menander: Sign and Meaning in Greek and Roman Performances.* Cambridge: Cambridge UP, 1991.

Winnington-Ingram, R. P. *Sophocles: An Interpretation.* New York: Cambridge UP, 1980.

Woodard, T. M, ed. *Sophocles: A Collection of Critical Essays.* Englewood Cliffs: Prentice, 1966.

Sophocles' *Oedipus Rex*

Bloom, Harold *Sophocles' "Oedipus Rex."* New York: Chelsea, 1988.

Cameron, Alister. *The Identity of Oedipus the King: Five Essays on the "Oedipus Tyrannus."* New York: New York UP, 1968.

Edmonds, Lowell. *Oedipus: The Ancient Legend and Its Later Analogues.* Baltimore: Johns Hopkins UP, 1985.

Fergusson, Francis. *The Idea of a Theater.* Princeton: Princeton UP, 1949.

O'Brien, M. J., ed. *Twentieth Century Interpretations of "Oedipus Rex."* Englewood Cliffs: Prentice, 1968.

Rudnytsky, Peter L. *Freud and Oedipus.* New York: Columbia UP, 1987.

Tonelli, Franco. "Sophocles' *Oedipus* and the Tale of the Theatre." Speculum Artium Series 12. Ravenna: Longo Editore, 1983.

Verhoeff, Han, and Harly Sonne. "Does Oedipus Have His Complex?" *Style* 18.3 (1984): 261-83.

Sophocles' *Antigone*

Brown, Andrew. *A New Companion to Greek Tragedy.* Totowa: Barnes, 1983.

Goheen, R. F. *The Imagerey of Sophocles' "Antigone": A Study of Poetic Language and Structure.* Princeton: Princeton UP, 1951.

Joseph, Gerhard. "The *Antigone* as Cultural Touchstone: Matthew Arnold, Hegel, George Eliot, Virginia Woolf, and Margaret Drabble." *PLMA* 96 (1981): 22–35.

Linforth, I. M. *Antigone and Creon.* Berkeley: U of California P, 1961.

Steiner, George. *Antigones.* New York: Clarendon, 1984.

WOLE SOYINKA

Gibbs, James. "The BBC Became a Glutton for Punishment: Wole Soyinka's Dealings with the BBC (1953–1959)." *Crisis and Creativity in the New Literatures in English: Cross/Cultures.* Ed. Geoffrey Davis and Hena Maes-Jelinek. Amsterdam: Rodopi, 1990. 205–17.

———. *Critical Perspectives on Wole Soyinka.* Washington: Three Continents, 1980.

———. "'Marrying Earth to Heaven': A Nobel Laureate at the End of the Eighties." *International Literature in English: Essays on the Major Writers.* Ed. Robert L. Ross. New York: Garland, 1991.

———. *Wole Soyinka.* New York: Grove, 1986.

Hepburn, Joan. "Mediators of Ritual Closure." *Black American Literature Forum* 22.3 (1988): 576–614.

Jones, Eldred D. *The Writing of Wole Soyinka.* Portsmouth: Heinemann, 1988.

Katrak, Ketu H. *Wole Soyinka and Modern Tragedy: A Study of Dramatic Theory and Practice.* Westport: Greenwood, 1986.

King, Bruce, ed. *Post-Colonial English Drama: Commonwealth Drama Since 1960.* New York: St. Martin's, 1992.

Larsen, Stephan. *A Writer and His Gods: A Study of the Importance of Yoruba Myths and Religious Ideas to the Writing of Wole Soyinka.* Stockholm: U of Stockholm P, 1983.

Lindfors, Bernth. "Beating the White Man at His Own Game: Nigerian Reactions to the Nobel Prize in Literature." *Literary Criterion* 25.1 (1990): 43–59.

Maduakor, Obi. *Wole Soyinka: An Introduction to His Writings.* New York: Garland, 1987.

Maja-Pearce, Adewale. *Who's Afraid of Wole Soyinka? Essays on Censorship.* London: Heinemann, 1991.

———, ed. *Wole Soyinka: An Appraisal.* Oxford: Heinemann, 1994.

Moody, David. "The Prodigal Father: Discursive Rupture in the Plays of Wole Soyinka." *ARIEL* 23.1 (1992): 25–38.

Ndiava, Marieme. "Female Stereotypes in Wole Soyinka's *The Strong Breed* and *The Lion and the Jewel.*" *Bridges* 5 (1993): 19–24.

Ogbaa, Kalu, ed. *The Gong and the Flute: African Literary Development and Celebration.* Westport: Greenwood, 1994.

Olaniva, Tejumola. "Dramatizing Postcoloniality: Wole Soyinka and Derek Walcott." *Theatre Journal* 44.4 (1992): 485–99.

Omotoso, Kole. *Achebe or Soyinka? A Re-Interpretation and a Study in Contrasts.* Oxford: Zell, 1994.

Soyinka, Wole. *Ake: The Years of Childhood.* New York: Random, 1981.

———. *Isara: A Voyage Round Essay.* New York: Random, 1989.

———. *The Man Died: The Prison Notes of Wole Soyinka.* London: Collings, 1972.

———. "Twice Bitten: The Fate of Africa's Culture Producers." *PMLA* 105.1 (1990): 110–120.

Wright, Derek. "Ritual and Revolution: Soyinka's Dramatic Theory." *ARIEL* 23.1 (1992): 39–53.

———. *Wole Soyinka Revisited.* New York: Twayne, 1993.

August Strindberg

Carlson, Harry Gilbert. *Strindberg and the Poetry of Myth.* Berkeley: U of California P, 1982.

Lally, M. L. K. "Strindberg's *Miss Julie.*" *Explicator* 48.3 (1990): 196–98.

Lucas, F. L. *The Drama of Ibsen and Strindberg.* London: Cassell, 1962.

Parker, Brian. "Strindberg's *Miss Julie* and the Legend of Salome." *Modern Drama* 32 (1989): 469–84.

Reinert, Otto, ed. *Strindberg: A Collection of Critical Essays.* Englewood Cliffs: Prentice, 1971.

Robinson, Michael. "August Strindberg: His True Life?" *Scandinavica* 28.2 (1989): 185–91.

Shideler, Ross. "The Absent Authority: From Darwin to Nora and Julie." *Space and Boundaries in Literature.* Proc. of the 12th Congress of the Intl. Comparative Lit. Assn. Ed. Roger Bauer and Donwe Fokkema. Munich: Iudicium, 1990.

Sprinchorn, Evert. *Strindberg as Dramatist.* New Haven: Yale UP, 1982.

Steene, Birgitta. *The Greatest Fire: A Study of August Strindberg.* Carbondale: Southern Illinois UP, 1973.

Stockenstrom, Goran, ed. *Strindberg's Dramaturgy.* Minneapolis: U of Minnesota P, 1988.

Tornqvist, Egil. *Strindberg's "Miss Julie": A Play and Its Transpositions.* Norwich, Eng.: Norvik, 1988.

John Millington Synge

Benson, Eugene. *J. M. Synge.* New York: Grove, 1983.

Corkery, Daniel. *Synge and Anglo-Irish Literature.* Cork: Cork UP, 1955.

Gerstenberger, Donna Lorine. *John Millington Synge.* Rev. ed. Boston: Twayne, 1990.

Greene, David H., and Edward M. Stephens. *John Millington Synge, 1871–1909.* Rev. ed. New York: New York UP, 1989.

Kiberd, Declan. *Synge and the Irish Language.* London: Macmillan, 1979.

King, Mary C. *The Drama of J. M. Synge.* Syracuse: Syracuse UP, 1985.

Kopper, Edward A. *A John Millington Synge Literary Companion.* New York: Greenwood, 1988.

Price, Alan. *Synge and Anglo-Irish Drama.* London: Methuen, 1961.

Skelton, Robin. *J. M. Synge and His World.* New York: Viking, 1971.

———. *The Writings of J. M. Synge.* London: Thames, 1971.

Terence

Forehand, Walter. *Terence.* Boston: Twayne, 1985.

Goldberg, Sander M. *Understanding Terence.* Princeton: Princeton UP, 1986.

Oscar Wilde

Bloom, Harold. *Oscar Wilde's "The Importance of Being Earnest."* New York: Chelsea, 1988.

Byrne, Patrick. *The Wildes of Merrion Square: The Family of Oscar Wilde.* New York: Staples, 1953.

Cohen, Ed. "Writing Gone Wild: Homoerotic Desire in the Closet of Representation." *PMLA* 102 (1987): 801–13.

Cohen, Philip K. *The Moral Vision of Oscar Wilde.* Rutherford: Fairleigh Dickinson UP, 1978.

Ellmann, Richard. *Oscar Wilde.* New York: Knopf, 1988.

———. *Oscar Wilde: A Collection of Critical Essays.* Englewood Cliffs: Prentice, 1969.

Erikson, Donald. *Oscar Wilde.* Boston: Twayne, 1977.

Gagnier, Regenia. *Idylls of the Marketplace: Oscar Wilde and the Victorian Public.* Stanford: Stanford UP, 1986.

Haley, Bruce. "Wilde's 'Decadence' and the Positivist Tradition." *Victorian Studies* 28 (1985): 215–29.

Hart-Davis, Rupert, ed. *Letters of Oscar Wilde.* New York: Harcourt, 1962.

———. *More Letters of Oscar Wilde.* New York: Vanguard, 1985.

Hodge, James H. *Famous Trials.* Baltimore: Penguin, 1963.

Mikhail, E. H. *Oscar Wilde: Interviews and Recollections.* New York: Barnes, 1979.

Miller, Robert Keith. *Oscar Wilde.* New York: Ungar, 1982.

Poznar, Walter. "Life and Play in Wilde's *The Impor-*

tance of Being Earnest." *Midwest Quarterly* 30.4 (1989): 515–28.

San Juan, Epifanio. *The Art of Oscar Wilde*. Princeton: Princeton UP, 1963.

Smith, Philip E., and Michael S. Heffland, eds. *Oscar Wilde's Oxford Notebooks*. New York: Oxford UP, 1989.

Sullivan, Kevin. *Oscar Wilde*. Columbia Essays on Modern Writers 64. New York: Columbia UP, 1972.

Weintraub, Stanley. *The Literary Criticism of Oscar Wilde*. Lincoln: U of Nebraska P, 1968.

Wilde, Oscar. *The Complete Works*. New York: Doubleday, 1923.

———. *The Plays of Oscar Wilde*. New York: Random, 1980.

TENNESSEE WILLIAMS

List of Plays

American Blues, 1939 (published 1948)
Battle of Angels, 1940 (published 1945)
The Glass Menagerie, 1944
A Streetcar Named Desire, 1947
Summer and Smoke, 1947
The Rose Tatoo, 1950
Camino Real, 1953
Cat on a Hot Tin Roof, 1955
Orpheus Descending, 1957
Suddenly Last Summer, 1958
Sweet Bird of Youth, 1959
Period of Adjustment, 1960
The Night of the Iguana, 1962
The Milk Train Doesn't Stop Here Anymore, 1963
The Eccentricities of a Nightingale, 1965
The Seven Descents of Myrtle, 1968
In the Bar of a Tokyo Hotel, 1969
Small Craft Warnings, 1972
A Lovely Sunday for Creve Coeur, 1979
Clothes for a Summer Hotel, 1980

Aisbong, Emmanuel B. *Tennessee Williams: The Tragic Tension*. Elms Court: Stockwell, 1978.

Boxill, Roger. *Tennessee Williams*. New York: St. Martin's, 1987.

Bruhm, Steven. "Blackmailed by Sex: Tennessee Williams and the Economics of Desire." *Modern Drama* 34.4 (1991): 528–37.

Devlin, Albert J., ed. *Conversations with Tennessee Williams*. Jackson: UP of Mississippi, 1986.

Donahue, Francis. *The Dramatic World of Tennessee Williams*. New York: Ungar, 1964.

Falk, Signi Lenea. *Tennessee Williams*. 2nd ed. Boston: Twayne, 1978.

Hayman, Ronald. *Tennessee Williams: Everyone Else Is an Audience*. New Haven: Yale UP, 1993.

Koprince, Susan. "Tennessee Williams's Unseen Characters." *The Southern Quarterly* 33.1 (1994): 87–95.

Leavitt, Richard Freeman, ed. *The World of Tennessee Williams*. New York: Putnam's, 1978.

Parker, R. B., ed. *"The Glass Menagerie": A Collection of Critical Essays*. Englewood Cliffs: Prentice, 1983.

Savran, David. "'By coming suddenly into a room that I thought was empty': Mapping the Closet with Tennessee Williams." *Studies in the Literary Imagination* 24.2 (1991): 57–74.

———. *Communists, Cowboys and Queers: The Politics of Masculinity in the Work of Arthur Miller and Tennessee Williams*. Minneapolis: U of Minnesota P, 1992.

Spoto, Donald. *The Kindness of Strangers: The Life of Tennessee Williams*. Boston: Little, 1985.

Stanton, Stephen, ed. *Tennessee Williams: A Collection of Critical Essays*. Englewood Cliffs: Prentice, 1977.

Thompson, Judith. *Tennessee Williams' Plays: Memory, Myth, and Symbol*. New York: Lang, 1987.

Wilhelmi, Nancy O. "The Language of Power and Powerlessness: Verbal Combat in the Plays of Tennessee Williams." *The Text and Beyond: Essays in Literary Linguistics*. Ed. Cynthia Goldin-Bernstein. Tuscaloosa: U of Alabama P, 1994.

Williams, Dakin, with Shepherd Mead. *Tennessee Williams: An Intimate Biography*. New York: Arbor, 1983.

Williams, Tennessee. *Memoirs*. Garden City: Doubleday, 1975.

Williams's *Cat on a Hot Tin Roof*

Atkinson, Brooks. "Williams' 'Tin Roof.'" *New York Times* 3 Apr. 1955: B1.

Huzzard, Jere. "Williams' *Cat on a Hot Tin Roof*." *Explicator* 43.2 (1985): 46–47.

Inge, Thomas M. "The South, Tragedy and Comedy in Tennessee Williams's *Cat on a Hot Tin Roof*." *The United States South: Regionalism and Identity*. Ed. Tjebbe Westendorp. Rome: Bulzoni, 1991.

Kalem, T. E. "Fate Strikes the Delta." *Time* 6 Dec. 1976: 97–98.

"London Sees Cat; Opinion Is Divided." *New York Times* 31 Jan. 1958: 24.

Mayberry, Susan Neal. "A Study of Illusion and the Grotesque in Tennessee Williams' *Cat on a Hot Tin Roof*." *Southern Studies* 22.4 (1983): 359–65.

Rev. of *Cat on a Hot Tin Roof*. *New York Theatre Critics' Reviews* 20 Mar. 1955: 342–43.

Rev. of *Cat on a Hot Tin Roof*. *New York Theatre Critics' Reviews* 25 Sept. 1974: 242–46.

Williams's *The Glass Menagerie*

Beaurline, Lester A. "*The Glass Menagerie* from Story to Play." *Modern Drama* 8 (1965): 143–49.

Bloom, Harold. *Tennessee Williams's "The Glass Menagerie."* New York: Chelsea, 1988.

Greiff, Louis K. "Fathers, Daughters, and Spiritual Sisters: Marsha Norman's *'night, Mother* and Tennessee Williams's *The Glass Menagerie.*" *Text and Performance Quarterly* 9.3 (1989): 224–28.

Jones, John H. "The Missing Link: The Father in *The Glass Menagerie.*" *Notes on Mississippi Writers* 20.1 (1988): 29–38.

Kolin, Philip C. "The Black and Multi-Racial Productions of Tennessee Williams's *The Glass Menagerie.*" *Journal of Dramatic Theory and Criticism* 9.2 (1995): 96–128.

Levy, Eric P. "Through Soundproof Glass: The Prison of Self-Consciousness in *The Glass Menagerie.*" *Modern Drama* 36.4 (1993): 529–37.

Parker, R. B. "The Circle Closed: A Psychological Reading of *The Glass Menagerie* and the Two Character Play." *Modern Drama* 28 (1985): 517–34.

Presley, Delma Eugene. *"The Glass Menagerie": An American Memory*. Boston: Twayne, 1990.

Reynolds, James. "The Failure of Technology in *The Glass Menagerie.*" *Modern Drama* 34.4 (1991): 522–27.

Thierfelder, William R. "Williams's *The Glass Menagerie.*" *Explicator* 48.4 (1990): 284–85.

Usui, Masami. "'A World of Her Own' in Tennessee Williams's *The Glass Menagerie.*" *Studies in Culture and the Humanities* 1 (1992): 21–37.

AUGUST WILSON

List of Plays

Recycle, 1973
The Coldest Day of the Year, 1976
The Homecoming, 1976
Eskimo Song Duel, 1979
Black Bart and the Sacred Hills, 1980
Fullerton Street, 1980
Jitney!, 1982
Ma Rainey's Black Bottom, 1984
The Janitor, 1985
Fences, 1985
Joe Turner's Come and Gone, 1987
The Piano Lesson, 1988
Two Trains Running, 1990
Seven Guitars, 1995

Arthur, Thomas H. "Looking for My Relatives: The Political Implications of 'Family' in Selected Works of Athol Fugard and August Wilson." *South African Theatre Journal* 6.2 (1992): 5–16.

DiGaetani, John L. *A Search for a Postmodern Theater: Interviews with Contemporary Playwrights.* New York: Greenwood, 1991.

Freedman, Samuel G. "A Voice from the Streets." *New York Times Magazine* 15 Mar. 1987: 33+.

———. "Wilson's New *Fences* Nurtures a Partnership." *New York Times* 5 May 1985, sec. I: 80.

Gerard, Jeremy. "Waterford to Broadway: Well-Traveled *Fences.*" *New York Times* 9 Apr. 1987, sec. III: 21.

Henderson, Heather. "Building *Fences*: An Interview with Mary Alice and James Earl Jones." *Yale Theater* 12 (Summer/Fall 1985): 67–70.

Kelley, Kevin. "August Wilson an Heir to O'Neill." *Boston Globe* 24 Jan. 1988: A1+.

Nadel, Alan, ed. *May All Your Fences Have Gates: Essays on the Drama of August Wilson.* Iowa City: U of Iowa P, 1994.

Pereira, Kim. *August Wilson and the African American Odyssey.* Urbana: U of Illinois P, 1995.

Plum, Jay. "Blues, History and the Dramaturgy of August Wilson." *African American Review* 27.4 (1993): 561–67.

Rich, Frank. "Theater: Family Ties in Wilson's *Fences.*" *New York Times* 27 Mar. 1987, sec. II: 1.

Shannon, Sandra, "Blues, History, and Dramaturgy: An Interview with August Wilson." *African American Review* 27.4 (1993): 539–59.

———. "Conversing with the Past: *Joe Turner's Come and Gone* and *The Piano Lesson.*" *CEA Magazine* 4.1 (1991): 33–42.

Selected List of Film, Video, and Audiocassette Resources

The following is a list of audiovisual resources to supplement the teaching of plays in *The Bedford Introduction to Drama*. The resources are listed alphabetically by playwright.

The films and videos marked with an asterisk (*) are available for rental from member institutions of the Consortium of College and University Media Centers. For further information, consult *Media Sources: Consortium of College and University Media Centers*, 1st ed. on CD-ROM.

Many of the videos are available for rental from local video outlets. Others are available through a distributor. Check the Directory of Distributors at the end of this list for information.

AESCHYLUS

Aeschylus, *Agamemnon*
2 cassettes.
Dramatization, abridged version.
Distributed by Sounddeluxe Audio Publishing.

Aeschylus and the Death of Tragedy
1 cassette (80 min.), 1963.
Walter Kaufmann.
Kaufmann argues that although Aeschylus is generally considered the creator of tragedy, his worldview contains central elements that are usually associated with the death of tragedy in our time. The *Oresteia* trilogy is examined.
Distributed by Audio-Forum.

*Aeschylus, *The Oresteia*
230 min., 1985.

VHS, Beta, 3/4" U-matic cassette.
Directed by Peter Hall. The National Theatre of Great Britain perform Aeschylus's classic dramas, each available separately.
Distributed by Films for the Humanities and Sciences.

ANONYMOUS

*Anonymous, *Everyman*
25 min., color, 1971. 16 mm film.
Abridged by H. Frances Clark.
Distributed by Coronet/MTI Film & Video.

Anonymous, *Everyman*
53 min., color, 1991.
VHS.
Produced in conjunction with medieval literature scholar Howard Schless of Columbia University. Authentically staged in period costume.
Distributed by Insight Media.

Anonymous, *Everyman* [recording]
1 cassette.
Dramatization performed by Burgess Meredith and Terrence Kilburn.
Distributed by HarperCollins Publishers.

ARISTOPHANES

Aristophanes, *Lysistrata*
97 min., color, 1987.
VHS.
A contemporary adaptation, shot on location at the Acropolis. In Greek with English subtitles.
Distributed by Insight Media.

Aristophanes, *Lysistrata* [recording]
2 cassettes.
Dramatization of Dudley Fitts's translation. Performed by Hermione Gingold and Stanley Holloway.
Distributed by HarperCollins Publishers.

SAMUEL BECKETT

Samuel Beckett, *Beckett Festival of Radio Plays* [recording] 1989
Features a collection of five plays written for the radio: *All That Fall, Embers, Words and Music, Cascando,* and *Rough for Radio.*
Distributed by Spoken Arts.

*The History of the Drama
History of the Drama Series, No.10.
48 min., 16 mm film (2 reels), 1975.
Mainly on Beckett.

Samuel Beckett
80 min., color, 1989.
Beta, VHS, 3/4″ U-matic cassette.
An autobiographical portrait of Beckett's artistic life through his work.
Distributed by Films for the Humanities and Sciences.

BERTOLT BRECHT

*Bertolt Brecht
55 min., color, 1989.
Beta, VHS, 3/4″ U-matic cassette.
A biographical portrait of Brecht through his works.
Distributed by Films for the Humanities and Sciences.

Gisela May: Reflections on the Theater of Brecht
30 min., color, 1979.
Beta, VHS, 1/2″ open reel (EIAJ), 3/4″ U-matic cassette, 2″ quadraplex open reel.
Gisela May of the Berliner Ensemble performs excerpts from Brecht's plays.
Distributed by the New York State Education Department.

*The Theatre of Bertolt Brecht, as Performed by the Berliner Ensemble
Slide collection: 46 color slides and guide, 1973.
Presents photographs of the sets of twenty plays by Brecht produced between 1949 and 1969 by the Berliner Ensemble.

ANTON CHEKHOV

*Anton Chekhov, The Cherry Orchard, Part 1: Chekhov, Innovator of Modern Drama
21 min., color and B/W, 1968.

Beta, VHS, 3/4″ U-matic cassette, 16 mm film.
Important scenes with discussion led by Norris Houghton.
Distributed by Encyclopedia Britannica Educational Corp.

*Anton Chekhov, The Cherry Orchard, Part II: Comedy or Tragedy?
21 min., color and B/W, 1967.
Beta, VHS, 3/4″ U-matic cassette, 16 mm film.
Important scenes with discussion led by Norris Houghton. Covers Chekhov's technique of dramatization of interior actions and examines the notion of subtext.
Distributed by Encyclopedia Britannica Educational Corp.

Anton Chekhov, *The Cherry Orchard* [recording]
3 cassettes.
Translated by Leonid Kipnis and performed by Jessica Tandy and Hume Cronyn.
Distributed by HarperCollins Publishers.

*Anton Chekhov: A Writer's Life
37 min., B/W, 1974.
Beta, VHS, 3/4″ U-matic cassette.
A biographical portrait of the playwright.
Distributed by Films for the Humanities and Sciences.

Chekhov [recording]
12 cassettes (90 min. each), 1989.
By Henri Troyat, read by Wolfram Kandinsky.
A biography of the writer.
Distributed by Books on Tape, Inc.

Chekhov: Humanity's Advocate [recording]
1 cassette (46 min.), 1968.
By Ernest J. Simmons. Explores various facets of Chekhov's works and his artistic principles. Classics of Russian Literature Series.
Distributed by Audio-Forum.

WILLIAM CONGREVE

*William Congreve, The Way of the World
60 min., color, 1978.
Beta, VHS, 3/4″ U-matic cassette.
Hosted by Jose Ferrer and Anna Russell. Focuses on main characters and eliminates some subplots.
Distributed by Films, Inc. PMI.

William Congreve, *The Way of the World* [recording]
3 cassettes.
Performed by Helen Burns and Edward Hardwicke.
Distributed by HarperCollins Publishers.

EURIPIDES

Euripides, *Medea*
118 min., color, 1970.
Beta, VHS.
With Maria Callas, Guiseppi Gentile, and Laurent Tarzieff. Directed by Pier Paolo Passolini. In Italian with English subtitles.
Distributed by Video Artists International.

Euripides, *Medea*
70 min., color, 1979.
Beta, VHS.
With Marina Goderdzishvili and Vladimir Julukhadze. A free adaptation for ballet.
Distributed by Kultur Video.

Euripides, *Medea*
90 min., color, 1982.
Beta, VHS, 3/4″ U-matic cassette.
With Zoe Caldwell and Judith Anderson. A Kennedy Center production based on poet Robinson Jeffers's version.
Distributed by Films for the Humanities and Sciences.

*Euripides, *Medea*
100 min., color, 1986.
VHS.
Performed by the New York Greek Drama Company in ancient Greek with English subtitles.

Euripides, *Medea* [recording]
2 cassettes.
Translated by Rex Warner. Performed by Judith Anderson and Anthony Quayle.
Distributed by HarperCollins Publishers.

ATHOL FUGARD

Athol Fugard: White South African Playwright
Fresh Air with Terry Gross (series) [recording].
1 cassette (30 min.).
Distributed by Spoken Arts.

Athol Fugard, *"MASTER HAROLD" . . . and the boys*
90 min., color, 1984.
Beta, VHS.
With Matthew Broderick. A made-for-cable production.
Distributed by Video Learning Library, Warner Home Video.

*Athol Fugard, *"MASTER HAROLD" . . . and the boys*
90 min., 1986.
VHS.
Starring Matthew Broderick, Zakes Mokae, and John Kani.

LORRAINE HANSBERRY

Lorraine Hansberry, *A Raisin in the Sun*
128 min., B/W, 1961.
Beta, VHS.
With Sidney Poitier, Claudia McNeil, and Ruby Dee. Directed by Daniel Petrie.
Distributed by Columbia Tristar.

Lorraine Hansberry, *A Raisin in the Sun*
171 min., color, 1989.
Beta, VHS.
With Danny Glover, Esther Rolle, and Starletta DuPois. Directed by Bill Duke. An American Playhouse, made-for-television production.
Distributed by Chuck Fries Productions.

Lorraine Hansberry, *A Raisin in the Sun* [recording]
3 cassettes.
Dramatization performed by Ossie Davis and Ruby Dee.
Distributed by HarperCollins Publishers.

Black Theatre Movement from "A Raisin in the Sun" to the Present
130 min., color, 1979.
16 mm film.
Traces the Black Theatre Movement from its roots in Hansberry's play to the black plays and musicals on Broadway in the late 1970s. Includes interviews with performers, writers, and directors as well as footage from plays and theater pieces from around the country.

Lorraine Hansberry: The Black Experience in the Creation of Drama
35 min., color, 1975.
Beta, VHS, 3/4″ U-matic cassette.
With Sidney Poitier, Ruby Dee, and Al Freeman, Jr. Narrated by Claudia McNeil. A profile of the playwright's life and work.
Distributed by Films for the Humanities and Sciences.

Lorraine Hansberry Speaks Out: Art and the Black Revolution [recording]
1 cassette.
By Lorraine Hansberry, edited by Robert Nemiroff.
Distributed by HarperCollins Publishers.

A Raisin in the Sun
9 min., color, 1969.
16 mm film.
An introduction to the racial problems dealt with in the play.
Distributed by Phoenix/BFA Films.

Lorraine Hansberry, To Be Young, Gifted, and Black
90 min., color, 1972.

Beta, VHS, 1/2″ open reel (EIAJ), 3/4N U-matic cassette, 16 mm film.

With Ruby Dee, Al Freeman, Jr., Claudia McNeil, Barbara Barrie, Lauren Jones, Roy Scheider, and Blythe Danner. A play about the life of Lorraine Hansberry.

Distributed by the Indiana University Audio-Visual Center.

HENRIK IBSEN

Henrik Ibsen, *A Doll's House*
89 min., B/W, 1959.
Beta, VHS, 3/4″ U-matic cassette.
With Julie Harris, Christopher Plummer, Jason Robards, Hume Cronyn, Eileen Heckart, and Richard Thomas. An original television production.
Distributed by MGM/UA Home Entertainment.

*Henrik Ibsen, *A Doll's House*
98 min., color, 1973.
VHS, 16 mm film.
With Jane Fonda, Edward Fox, Trevor Howard, and David Warner. Screenplay by David Mercer.
Distributed by Prism Entertainment.

Henrik Ibsen, *A Doll's House*
39 min., color, 1977.
Beta, VHS, 3/4″ U-matic cassette.
With Claire Bloom.
Distributed by AIMS Media.

Henrik Ibsen, *A Doll's House* [recording]
3 cassettes.
Translated by Christopher Hampton and performed by Claire Bloom and Donald Madden.
Distributed by HarperCollins Publishers.

A Doll's House, Part I: The Distinction of Illusion
34 min. color, 1968.
Beta, VHS, 3/4″ U-matic cassette, 16 mm film.
Norris Houghton discusses the subsurface tensions in the play.
Distributed by Encyclopedia Britannica Educational Corp.

A Doll's House, Part II: Ibsen's Themes
29 min., color 1968.
Beta, VHS, 3/4″ U-matic cassette, 16 mm film.
Norris Houghton examines the cast of characters and the themes in the play.
Distributed by Encyclopedia Britannica Educational Corp.

Henrik Ibsen, *Hedda*
102 min., color, 1975.

Beta, VHS.
With Glenda Jackson, Peter Eyre, and Timothy West. Directed by Trevor Nunn.
Distributed by Fox Video.

Henrik Ibsen, *Hedda Gabler* (Also known as *The Theater of Social Problems*.)
60 min., color, 1976.
VHS, 3/4″ U-matic cassette, 16 mm film.
Narrated by Irene Worth.
Distributed by Films for the Humanities and Sciences.

Henrik Ibsen, *Hedda Gabler* [recording]
3 cassettes.
Translated by Michael Meyer. Performed by Joan Plowright and Anthony Quale.
Distributed by HarperCollins Publishers.

Henrik Ibsen, *Hedda Gabler* [recording]
3 cassettes.
Unabridged version. Performed by Eva Gallienne.
Distributed by Random House, Inc.

Ibsen's Life and Times, Part I: Youth and Self-Imposed Exile
28 min., color.
VHS.
The conflict between individual and society is illustrated in scenes from *Ghosts*, featuring Beatrice Straight as Mrs. Alving. Includes a biographical segment on the playwright.
Distributed by Insight Media.

Ibsen's Life and Times, Part II: The Later Years
24 min., color.
VHS.
Includes scenes from *The Master Builder* and *Lady from the Sea*, emphasizing the realism in Ibsen's plays. A biographical segment includes on-location footage.
Distributed by Insight Media.

FEDERICO GARCÍA LORCA

Spanish Treasury of Drama
3 cassettes, 1992.
Distributed by Audio-Forum.

Spanish Treasury of Drama
1 cassette, 1994 (vol. 2).
Distributed by Audio-Forum.

Spanish Treasury of Drama
1 cassette, 1994 (vol. 3).
Distributed by Audio-Forum.

DAVID MAMET

*Mamet
29 min.
VHS.
Series: Emerging Playwrights #5.
Richard Barr interviews David Mamet.

Mamet, *Oleanna*
90 min., 1994.
VHS.
With William Macy and Debra Eisenstadt. Directed by David Mamet.
Distributed by Hallmark Home Entertainment.

CHRISTOPHER MARLOWE

Christopher Marlowe, *Doctor Faustus*
93 min., 1968.
VHS, Beta.
Adaptation of Marlowe's classic. With Richard Burton and Elizabeth Taylor. Directed by Richard Burton and Neville Coghill.
Distributed by Columbia Tristar Video.

Hearing Great Poetry: From Chaucer to Milton [recording]
1 cassette.
Read by Mark Van Doren. Performed by Hurd Hatfield and Frank Silvera. Includes *The Tragical History of Doctor Faustus*.
Distributed by HarperCollins Publishers.

Tragical History of Doctor Faustus [recording]
1 cassette
Dramatization. With Frank Silvera and Julian Barry.
Distributed by HarperCollins Publishers.

ARTHUR MILLER

Arthur Miller, *Death of a Salesman*
135 min., color, 1985.
Beta, VHS.
With Dustin Hoffman, John Malkovich, Charles Durning, and Stephen Lang. Directed by Volker Schlondorff. A made-for-television adaptation of the play.
Distributed by Video Learning Library.

Arthur Miller, *Death of a Salesman* [recording]
3 cassettes.
Performed by Lee J. Cobb and Mildred Dunnock.
Distributed by HarperCollins Publishers.

Arthur Miller, *Death of a Salesman* [recording]
1 cassette, 1986.
Dramatization performed by Paul Douglas.
Distributed by Sounddeluxe Audio Publishing.

Private Conversations on the Set of Death of a Salesman
82 min., color, 1985.
Beta, VHS.
With Arthur Miller, Dustin Hoffman, Volker Schlondorff, John Malkovich, and Jon Polito. This PBS documentary presents heated discussions among actors, director, and playwright. Various interpretations of the play emerge, and viewers gain insight into how each party contributed to the final production.
Distributed by Video Learning Library.

MOLIÈRE

Molière, *Le Misanthrope*
160 min., color, 1986.
Beta, VHS, 3/4" U-matic cassette.
In French with English subtitles.
Distributed by Films for the Humanities and Sciences.

Molière, *The Misanthrope* [recording]
2 cassettes.
Translated by Richard Wilbur. Performed by Richard Easton and Sydney Walker.
Distributed by HarperCollins Publishers.

Molière
112 min., color, 1990.
Beta, VHS.
With Anthony Sher. Mikhail Bulgakov's comedy/drama of the playwright's life.
Distributed by Turner Home Entertainment Company.

MARSHA NORMAN

Marsha Norman, *'night, Mother*
97 min., color, 1986.
Beta, VHS, laser optical videodisc.
With Sissy Spacek and Anne Bancroft. Directed by Tom Moore.
Distributed by MCA/Universal Home Video.

HAROLD PINTER

Harold Pinter, *Betrayal*
95 min., color, 1983.
VHS.
With Ben Kingsley, Patricia Hodge, and Jeremy Irons. Directed by David Jones.
Distributed by CBS/Fox Video. (See local retailer.)

Harold Pinter with Benedict Nightingale
55 min., 1989.
VHS.
Interview with Pinter.

LUIGI PIRANDELLO

Luigi Pirandello, *Six Characters in Search of an Author*
52 min., color, 1976.
Beta, VHS, 3/4" U-matic cassette, 16 mm film.
Joseph Heller discusses the boundaries between reality and fiction.
Distributed by Films for the Humanities and Sciences.

*Luigi Pirandello, *Six Characters in Search of an Author*
60 min., color, 1978.
Beta, VHS, 3/4" U-matic cassette.
Hosted by Jose Ferrer. As an accompaniment to the play, Ossie Davis discusses Pirandello's work in the theater.
Distributed by Films, Inc. PMI.

MANUEL PUIG

Manuel Puig, *Kiss of the Spider Woman*
119 min., color, 1985.
VHS, Beta.
With William Hurt and Raul Julia. Directed by Hector Babenco.
Distributed by Columbia Tristar Home Entertainment, Baker and Taylor Video, and New Line Home video.

WILLIAM SHAKESPEARE

Hamlet

*William Shakespeare, *Hamlet*
153 min., B/W, 1948.
VHS and 16 mm film.
With Laurence Olivier, Basil Sydney, Felix Aylmer, Jean Simmons, Stanley Holloway, Peter Cushing, and Christopher Lee. Voice of John Gielgud. Directed by Olivier. Photographed in Denmark. Cut scenes include all of Rosencrantz and Guildenstern. Emphasizes Oedipal implications in the play.
Distributed by Paramount Home Video.

*William Shakespeare, *Hamlet*
115 min., color, 1969.
With Nicol Williamson. Directed by Tony Richardson.

*William Shakespeare, *Hamlet*
150 min., color, 1979.
Beta, VHS, 3/4" U-matic cassette, other formats by arrangement. Directed by Derek Jacobi.
Distributed by Time-Life Video.

William Shakespeare, *Hamlet*
135 min., color, 1990.
VHS.
With Mel Gibson, Glenn Close, Alan Bates, Paul Scofield, Ian Holm, and Helena Bonham-Carter. Directed by Franco Zeffirelli.
Distributed by Warner Home Video.

William Shakespeare, *Hamlet* [recording]
4 cassettes.
Performed by Paul Scofield and Diana Wynyard.
Distributed by HarperCollins Publishers.

William Shakespeare, *Hamlet* [recording]
4 cassettes.
Performed by Ronald Pickup and Robert Lang.
Distributed by Audio-Forum.

William Shakespeare, *Hamlet* [recording]
2 cassettes (180 min.), 1988.
With Ronald Pickup and Angela Pleasance. Music by Malcolm Clarke, BBC Audio Collection.
Distributed by Sounddeluxe Audio Publishing.

Approaches to Hamlet
45 min., color, 1979.
Beta, VHS, 3/4" U-matic cassette, 16 mm film.
Includes footage of the four greatest Hamlets of this century: John Barrymore, Laurence Olivier, John Gielgud, and Nicol Williamson. Shows a young actor learning the role. Narrated by Gielgud.
Distributed by Films for the Humanities and Sciences.

Hamlet: The Age of Elizabeth, I
30 min., color, 1979.
Beta, VHS, 3/4" U-matic cassette, 16 mm film.
An Introduction to Elizabethan theater.
Distributed by Encyclopedia Britannica Educational Corp.

Hamlet: What Happens in Hamlet, II
30 min., color, B/W, 1959.
Beta, VHS, 3/4" U-matic cassette, 16 mm film.
Analyzes the play as a ghost story, a detective story, and a revenge story. Uses scenes from acts I, III, and V to introduce the principal characters and to present the structure of each substory.
Distributed by Encyclopedia Britannica Educational Corp.

Hamlet: The Poisoned Kingdom, III
30 min., color, 1959.
Beta, VHS, 3/4" U-matic cassette, 16 mm film.
Observes that poisoning in the play is both literal and figurative and affects all the characters.
Distributed by Encyclopedia Britannica Educational Corp.

Hamlet: The Readiness Is All, IV
30 min., color, 1959.
Beta, VHS, 3/4" U-matic cassette, 16 mm film.
Hamlet is presented as a coming-of-age story.
Distributed by Encyclopedia Britannica Educational Corp.

Hamlet: The Trouble with Hamlet
23 min., color, 1969.
16 mm film.
Emphasizes Hamlet's existential dilemma.

The Tragedie of Hamlet: Prince of Denmark
22 min., color, 1988.
VHS.
Actors depict Shakespeare and his contemporary
Richard Burbage rehearsing the play. "Shake-
speare" gives a line-by-line analysis of scenes from
the play along with insight into plot and character.
Part of the Shakespeare in Rehearsal Series.
Distributed by Coronet/MTI Film & Video.

A Midsummer Night's Dream
William Shakespeare, *A Midsummer Night's Dream*
111 min., B/W, 1963.
Beta, VHS.
With Patrick Allen, Eira Heath, Cyril Luckham, Tony
Bateman, and Jill Bennett. A live BBC-TV perfor-
mance, with Mendelssohn's incidental music.
Distributed by Video Yesteryear.

*William Shakespeare, *A Midsummer Night's Dream*
120 min., 1968.
Beta, VHS, 16 mm film.
With Diana Rigg and David Warner. Directed by Peter
Hall. A Royal Shakespeare Company performance.

*William Shakespeare, *A Midsummer Night's Dream*
120 min., color, 1982.
Beta, VHS.
With Helen Mirren, Peter McEnery, and Brian Glover.
Distributed by Time-Life Video.

*William Shakespeare, *A Midsummer Night's Dream*
165 min., color, 1983.
Beta, VHS, 3/4" U-matic cassette.
With William Hurt and Michelle Shay. A lively inter-
pretation by Joseph Papp.
Distributed by Films for the Humanities and Sciences.

William Shakespeare, *A Midsummer Night's Dream*
194 min., color, 1987.
Beta, VHS.
With Ileana Cotrubas, James Bowman, and Curt Ap-
pelgren. Directed by Peter Hall. A performance of
the Benjamin Britten opera, taped at the Glynde-
bourne Festival Opera.
Distributed by Home Vision & Public Media Video.

*William Shakespeare, *A Midsummer Night's Dream*
[recording]
1 cassette.
Dramatization by the Folio Theatre Players.
Distributed by Sounddeluxe Audio Publishing.

William Shakespeare, *A Midsummer Night's Dream*
[recording]
3 cassettes (text included).
Dramatization performed by Paul Scofield and Joy
Parker.
Distributed by HarperCollins Publishers.

William Shakespeare, *A Midsummer Night's Dream*
[recording]
2 cassettes (120 min.).
Performed by Robert Helpmann and Moira Shearer.
An Old Vic production.
Distributed by Durkin Hayes Publishing.

*A Midsummer Night's Dream: Introduction to the
Play*
14 min., B/W, 1954.
Key scenes from the play, with a discussion of char-
acters and language.
Distributed by Coronet/MTI Film & Video.

The Tempest
*William Shakespeare, *The Tempest*
76 min., color, 1963.
Beta, VHS, 3/4" U-matic cassette.
With Maurice Evans, Richard Burton, Roddy Mc-
Dowall, Lee Remick, and Tom Poston. Directed
by George Schaefer.
Distributed by Films for the Humanities and Sciences.

*William Shakespeare, *The Tempest*
150 min., color, 1980.
Beta, VHS, 3/4" U-matic cassette, other formats by
arrangement.
Distributed by Time-Life Video.

*William Shakespeare, *The Tempest*
126 min., color, 1983. Two cassettes.
Beta, VHS, 3/4" U-matic cassette.
With Efrem Zimbalist, Jr., William H. Basset, Ted
Sorrel, Kay E. Kuter, Edward Edwards, Nicholas
Hammond, and Ron Palillo. Directed by William
Woodman. Puts American actors on an artist's re-
creation of the Globe Theatre stage.
Distributed by Kultur Video and by Encyclopedia
Britannica Educational Corp.

William Shakespeare, *The Tempest* [recording]
1 cassette.
Dramatization performed by the Folio Theatre Players.
Distributed by Spoken Arts.

William Shakespeare, *The Tempest* [recording]
3 cassettes (text included).
Dramatization performed by Michael Redgrave and
Vanessa Redgrave.
Distributed by HarperCollins Publishers.

Tempest
140 min., color, 1982.
Beta, VHS (stereo).
A modern version with John Cassavetes, Gena
    Rowlands, Susan Sarandon, Vittorio Gassman,
    and Raul Julia. Directed by Paul Mazursky.
    A New York architect abandons city life to
    go live on a barren Greek island with his
    daughter.
Distributed by Columbia Tristar Home Video.

*Prospero's Books
130 min., color, 1992.
With John Gielgud, Erland Josephson, Michael
    Clark, Tom Bell, and Kenneth Cranham. Directed
    by Peter Greenaway. A loose interpretation of *The
    Tempest* with sumptuous visuals.
Distributed by Fox Video.

*The Tempest: O Brave New World
23 min., color, 1969.
16 mm film.
Explores the problem of evil in the play.
Distributed by Spoken Arts.

General
*Behind the Scenes Views of Shakespeare: Shake-
    speare and His Theater* [recording]
1 cassette (60 min.).
Read by Daniel Seltzer. Explores Shakespeare and
    the characteristics of his works, suggesting how to
    watch a play.
Distributed by Spoken Arts.

*Behind the Scenes Views of Shakespeare: Shake-
    speare in Our Time* [recording]
1 cassette (60 min.).
Read by Maynard Mack, Jr.
Discusses Shakespeare from a modern perspective
    and considers to what extent he is and is not our
    contemporary.
Distributed by Spoken Arts.

*Behind the Scenes Views of Shakespeare: Shake-
    speare the Man* [recording]
1 cassette (60 min.).
Portrays Shakespeare as reflected in his work and
    in the facts and myths about his life that have
    survived.
Distributed by Spoken Arts.

**The Life and Times of William Shakespeare 1: The
    Historical Setting*
25 min., color, 1978.
VHS.
An overview of Elizabethan England.

**The Life and Times of William Shakespeare 2: Eng-
    lish Drama*
20 min., color, 1978.
VHS.
History of drama from the Greeks to Shakespeare's
    time.

**The Life and Times of William Shakespeare 3:
    Stratford Years*
18 min., color, 1978.
VHS.
Deals with Shakespeare's early life.

**The Life and Times of William Shakespeare 4: Lon-
    don Years*
33 min., color, 1978.
VHS.
A history of the center of the English-speaking world.

**The Life and Times of William Shakespeare 5:
    Globe Theatre*
27 min., color, 1978.
VHS.
A study of the Globe and Elizabethan theater.

*Shakespeare and the Globe
31 min., color, 1985.
VHS.
A survey of Shakespeare's life, work, and cultural
    milieu.
Distributed by Films for the Humanities and Sciences.

*Shakespeare and His Stage
46 min., color, 1975.
VHS, 16 mm film.
Provides a montage of Shakespearean background,
    including scenes from *Hamlet* and the preparation
    of various actors for the role.
Distributed by Films for the Humanities and Sciences.

*Shakespeare and His Theatre
55 min., color.
VHS, 16 mm film.
A history of Shakespeare's life and times.
Distributed by The Media Guild.

*Shakespeare's Heritage
29 min., color, 1988.
16 mm film.
Narrated by Anthony Quayle. Explores Stratford
    and the life of the playwright.
Distributed by Encyclopedia Britannica Educational
    Corp.

*Shakespeare's Theater
13 min., color, 1946.
16 mm film.

Re-creates the experience of going to a play at the Globe Theatre in Shakespeare's time.
Distributed by the Indiana University Audio-Visual Center.

Shakespeare's Theater
28 min., B/W, 1952.
16 mm film.
Hosted by Frank Baxter. A discussion of the evolution of Elizabethan theater and the original staging of Shakespeare's plays.

Shakespeare's Theater: The Globe Playhouse
18 min., B/W, 1953.
16 mm film.
Provides a model of the Globe Theatre and a discussion of original staging of some of Shakespeare's plays.
Distributed by the University of California Extension Center for Media and Independent Learning.

Shakespeare's World and Shakespeare's London
29 min., B/W, 1952.
16 mm film.
Hosted by Frank Baxter. Re-creates the climate of Elizabethan England that allowed Shakespeare's genius to flourish.
Distributed by Films, Inc. PMI.

The Two Traditions
50 min., color, 1983.
VHS.
Deals with the problem of overcoming barriers of time and culture to make Shakespeare relevant today. Examples from *Hamlet, Coriolanus, The Merchant of Venice,* and *Othello.* Part of the Playing Shakespeare Series.
Distributed by Films for the Humanities and Sciences.

Understanding Shakespeare: His Sources
20 min., color, 1972.
Beta, VHS, 3/4" U-matic cassette, 16 mm film, other formats by arrangement.
Examines how Shakespeare's plays grew out of sources available to him and how he enhanced the material with his own imagination.
Distributed by Coronet/MTI Film & Video.

BERNARD SHAW

George Bernard Shaw
16 min., B/W, 1956.
16 mm film.
A biographical tribute, with anecdotes and comments by Dame Sybil Thorndike, Wendy Hiller, and Colin Wilson; sketches by Felix Topolski; highlights from Shaw's plays and opinions; and interviews with the playwright.
Distributed by Phoenix/BFA Films.

George Bernard Shaw
26 min., B/W, 1964.
16 mm film.
Narrated by Mike Wallace. A biographical portrait of Shaw the playwright and Shaw the man.
Distributed by CRM.

My Fair Lady
170 min., color, 1964.
With Rex Harrison and Audrey Hepburn. Directed by George Cukor. Colorful production of Lerner and Lowe's musical version of *Pygmalion.*
Distributed by CBS/Fox Video, and by Facets Multimedia.

Bernard Shaw, *Pygmalion*
96 min. B/W, 1938.
VHS, Beta, LV.
With Leslie Howard, Wendy Hiller, and Anthony Asquith. Directed by Leslie Howard. Shaw aided in writing the filmscript.
Distributed by Columbia Tristar Home Video, and Sultan Entertainment.

Bernard Shaw, *Pygmalion* [recording]
3 cassettes.
Dramatization.
Distributed by HarperCollins Publishers.

Pygmalion by George Bernard Shaw
96 min., B/W.
VHS.
Adaptation by W. P. Liscomb and Cecil Lewis.

The Seven Ages of George Bernard Shaw [recording]
4 cassettes.
Unabridged version read by Margaret Webster. Discusses Shaw as comedian, satirist, iconoclast, social reformer, crusader, philosopher, and critic.
Distributed by Random House, Inc.

ANNA DEAVERE SMITH

Anna Deavere Smith, *Fires in the Mirror*
82 min., 1993.
VHS.
An American Playhouse Production.
Dramatized exploration of a 1991 racial conflict in Brooklyn, NY, with a performance of eighteen parts by Anne Deavere Smith.
Distributed by PBS Video.

The Rodney King Case: What the Jury Saw in California vs Powell.
116 min., 1992.
VHS.

A condensed version of the Los Angeles police brutality case involving Rodney King, the results of which sparked the 1992 Los Angeles riots.
Distributed by MPI Media Group, Facets Multimedia, and Professional Media Service Corp.

SOPHOCLES

Sophocles, *Antigone*
88 min., B/W, 1962.
16 mm film.
With Irene Papas. Directed by George Tzavellas. In Greek with English subtitles.
Distributed by Films, Inc. PMI.

*Sophocles, *Antigone*
120 min., 1987.
Beta, VHS, 3/4″ U-matic cassette.
With Juliet Stevenson, John Shrapnel, and John Gielgud. Staged version.
Distributed by Films for the Humanities and Sciences.

Sophocles, *Antigone* [recording]
2 cassettes.
Dramatization of the Fitts and Fitzgerald translation. Performed by Dorothy Tutin and Max Adrian.
Distributed by HarperCollins Publishers.

Sophocles, *Antigone* [recording]
2 cassettes (60 min.).
Translated and adapted by Bernard Mayes.
Distributed by Sounddeluxe Audio Publishing.

Sophocles, *Oedipus Rex*
20 min., color, 1957.
Beta, VHS, 3/4″ U-matic cassette.
A performance in which all the actors are deaf.
Distributed by Gallaudet Media Distribution.

*Sophocles, *Oedipus Rex*
87 min., color, 1957.
VHS, 16 mm film.
With Douglas Campbell, Douglas Rain, Eric House, and Eleanor Stuart. Based on William Butler Yeats's translation. Directed by Tyrone Guthrie. Contained and highly structured rendering by the Stratford (Ontario) Festival Players.
Distributed by Water Bearer Films.

Sophocles, *Oedipus the King*
97 min., color, 1967.
VHS.
With Donald Sutherland, Christopher Plummer, Lilli Palmer, Orson Welles, Cyril Cusack, Richard Johnson, and Roger Livesey. Directed by Philip Saville. Simplified version of the play, filmed in

Greece using an old amphitheater as background for much of the action.
Distributed by Crossroads Video.

*Sophocles, *Oedipus the King*
45 min., color, 1975.
Beta, VHS, 3/4″ U-matic cassette, 16 mm film.
With Anthony Quayle, James Mason, Claire Bloom, and Ian Richardson. A production by the Athens Classical Theatre Company, with an English soundtrack.
Distributed by Films for the Humanities and Sciences.

Sophocles, *Oedipus Tyrannus*
60 min., color, 1978.
Beta, VHS, 3/4″ U-matic cassette.
Hosted by Jose Ferrer. Begins when Oedipus is informed of the death of his father. Expository portion shows scenes of Greek theaters and recounts Aristotle's definition of tragedy.
Distributed by Films, Inc. PMI.

Sophocles, *Oedipus the King*
120 min., color, 1987.
VHS.
With John Gielgud, Michael Pennington, and Claire Bloom.
Distributed by Films for the Humanities and Sciences.

Sophocles, *Oedipus Rex* [recording]
2 cassettes.
Translated by William Butler Yeats. Performed by Douglas Campbell and Eric House.
Distributed by HarperCollins Publishers.

Sophocles, *Oedipus Rex* [recording]
2 cassettes (100 min.).
Translated and adapted by Bernard Mayes.
Distributed by Sounddeluxe Audio Publishing.

*Sophocles, *Oedipus at Colonus*
120 min., color, 1987.
Beta, VHS, 3/4″ U-matic cassette.
With Anthony Quayle, Juliet Stevenson, and Kenneth Haigh. Staged version.
Distributed by Films for the Humanities and Sciences.

Oedipus Rex: Age of Sophocles, I
31 min., color and B/W, 1959.
Beta, VHS, 3/4″ U-matic cassette, 16 mm film.
Discusses Greek civilization, the classic Greek theater, and the theme of fundamental human nature.
Distributed by Encyclopedia Britannica Educational Corp.

Oedipus Rex: The Character of Oedipus, II
31 min., color and B/W, 1959.

Beta, VHS, 3/4″ U-matic cassette, 16 mm film.
Debates whether Oedipus's trouble is a result of character flaws or of fate.
Distributed by Encyclopedia Britannica Educational Corp.

Oedipus Rex: Man and God, III
30 min., color and B/W, 1959.
Beta, VHS, 3/4″ U-matic cassette, 16 mm film.
Deals with the idea that Oedipus, although a worldly ruler, cannot overcome the gods and his destiny.
Distributed by Encyclopedia Britannica Educational Corp.

Oedipus Rex: Recovery of Oedipus, IV
30 min., color and B/W, 1959.
Beta, VHS, 3/4″ U-matic cassette, 16 mm film.
Deals with the place of human beings in the great chain of existence — midway between the animals and God.
Distributed by Encyclopedia Britannica Educational Corp.

WOLE SOYINKA

Wole Soyinka
50 min., color, 1985.
VI IS, 3/4″ U-matic cassette.
An interview with the playwright, who discusses political and cultural life in Africa and the United States and what it means to be an artist.
Distributed by The Roland Collection.

* *Wole Soyinka*
50 min., 1989.
VHS.
Series: Writers in Conversation (#29).
Soyinka lectures on creative traditions and the "climate of terror" in which they are born. Also discusses the growth of contemporary African self-awareness.

AUGUST STRINDBERG

August Strindberg, Miss Julie
60 min., color, 1978.
Beta, VHS, 3/1″ U-matic cassette. Ancillary materials available.
With Patrick Stewart and Lisa Harrow. Hosted by Jose Ferrer. Opens with the rehearsal of a crucial scene and closes with a full-dress production of the play. In between, the actors show different ways of interpreting a scene.
Distributed by Films, Inc. PMI.

August Strindberg, *Strindberg's "Miss Julie": Royal Shakespeare Company*
120 min., color, 1990.
Beta, VHS.
Distributed by Mastervision, Inc.

JOHN MILLINGTON SYNGE

John Millington Synge, *Riders to the Sea* [recording]
1 cassette.
Recorded with *In the Shadow of the Glen*.
Distributed by Spoken Arts.

OSCAR WILDE

Oscar Wilde, The Importance of Being Earnest
95 min., color, 1952.
Beta, VHS.
With Michael Redgrave, Edith Evans, Margaret Rutherford, Michael Dennison, and Joan Greenwood. Directed by Anthony Asquith. Staged version.
Distributed by Paramount Home Video.

Oscar Wilde, *The Importance of Being Earnest*
99 min., color, 1980.
3/4″ U-matic cassette.
A BBC production.
Distributed by Time-Life Video.

Oscar Wilde, *The Importance of Being Earnest*
2 cassettes (120 min.), 1980.
Unabridged dramatization performed by John Gielgud and Edith Evans.
Distributed by Durkin Hayes Publishing.

Oscar Wilde, *The Importance of Being Earnest* [recording]
2 cassettes.
Performed by Lynn Redgrave and Gladys Cooper.
Distributed by HarperCollins Publishers.

TENNESSEE WILLIAMS

Tennessee Williams, Cat on a Hot Tin Roof
108 min., color, 1958.
With Paul Newman, Burl Ives, Elizabeth Taylor, and Jack Carson. Directed by Richard Brooks.
Distributed by MGM/UA Home Video.

Tennessee Williams, *Cat on a Hot Tin Roof*
148 min., color, 1984.
With Jessica Lange, Tommy Lee Jones, and Rip Torn. Directed by Jack Hofsiss.
Distributed by Live Entertainment Video.

Tennessee Williams, *The Glass Menagerie*
134 min., color, 1987.
With Joanne Woodward, Karen Allen, John
    Malkovich, and James Naughton. Directed by
    Paul Newman.
Distributed by MCA/Universal Home Video.

Tennessee Williams, *The Glass Menagerie* [recording]
1 cassette (60 min.), 1980.
Abridged dramatization performed by Helen Hayes
    and Montgomery Clift. Radio Series.
Distributed by Sounddeluxe Audio Publishing.

Tennessee Williams, *The Glass Menagerie* [recording]
2 cassettes.
Performed by Montgomery Clift and Julie Harris.
Distributed by HarperCollins Publishers.

Tennessee Williams, *The Glass Menagerie* [recording]
Read by Tennessee Williams. Includes "The Yellow
    Bird" (short story) and poems.
Distributed by American Audio Prose Library.

Tennessee Williams, *Tennessee Williams Reads "The
    Glass Menagerie" and Others* [recording]
1 cassette.
Read by Tennessee Williams. Includes *The Glass
    Menagerie* (opening monologue and closing scene);
    "Cried the Fox"; "The Eyes"; "The Summer
    Belvedere"; "Some Poems Meant for Music";
    "Little Horse"; "Which Is My Little Boy"; "Little
    One"; "Gold-Tooth Blues"; "Kitchen-Door Blues";
    "Heavenly Grass"; and "The Yellow Bird."
Distributed by HarperCollins Publishers.

In the Country of Tennessee Williams
30 min., color, 1977.
Beta, VHS, 1/2" reel, 3/4" U-matic cassette, 2" Quad.
A one-act play about how Williams developed as a
    writer.
Distributed by the New York State Education De-
    partment.

General Resources

Black Theatre: The Making of a Movement
113 min., 1978.
VHS.
Documentary look at black theater born of the Civil
    Rights activism of the 1950s, 60s, and 70s.
Distributed by California Newsreel.

A Day at the Globe
30 min., color.
VHS.

Starts with a brief overview of early drama and of
    seventeenth-century England and then discusses
    the Globe Theatre, using still images. Explains
    how actors, artisans, and other company mem-
    bers prepared for performances. Also presents
    dramatic readings, period costumes, music, and
    sound effects, helping students envision how
    Shakespearean drama actually looked.
Distributed by Insight Media.

*Drama Comes of Age
30 min., B/W, 1957.
16 mm film.
Discusses the Shakespearean theater and neoclassical
    drama. Demonstrates early realism with a scene
    from *Hedda Gabler*.
Distributed by the Indiana University Audio-Visual
    Center.

*Drama: How It Began
30 min., B/W, 1957.
16 mm film.
Discusses the early beginnings of the theater. Ex-
    plains the techniques of the Greek theater and
    how playwriting developed. Illustrates the chorus
    technique with a scene from *Oedipus the King*.
Distributed by the Indiana University Audio-Visual
    Center.

The Elizabethan Age
30 min., color.
VHS.
A discussion of the resurgence of enthusiasm for the
    arts and letters that swept seventeenth-century
    England. Uses original sources.
Distributed by Insight Media.

*The Greek Theater: Greece 478–336 B.C.
26 min., color, 1979.
16 mm film.
Professor Eric Handley of University College and the
    Institute for Classical Studies, London, discusses
    the classical Greek theater, focusing on the the-
    aters at Epidaurus and Athens. Contrasts the an-
    cient and modern theatrical experiences and
    discusses such aspects of drama as costume, act-
    ing, and the function of the chorus.
Distributed by The Media Guild.

Greek Tragedy [recording]
1 cassette.
Works of Euripides and Sophocles. Performed by
    Katina Paxinou and Alexis Minotis.
Distributed by HarperCollins Publishers.

*Interviews with Playwrights: Sophocles, Shakespeare,
    O'Neill.*
Frances Carter.

3 cassettes, 1977.
Dramatization. Set includes study guide.
Distributed by Contemporary Drama Service & Meriwether Publishing.

*Literary Visions [videorecording]
116 min.
Four programs, each 29 minutes (Nos. 19–22).
Includes discussion of plot and structure in classical and contemporary theater; interpretation of dramatic language.

Old Globe: A Theatre Reborn
30 min., color, 1984.
Beta, VHS, 3/4″ U-matic cassette.
With Bing Crosby and Bob Hope. A documentary following the travels of the old theater, from Elizabethan England to the present. Features USO footage from World War II.
Distributed by San Diego State University.

On Contemporary Theatre
1 cassette (45 min.), 1969.
Theater critic John Simon discusses contemporary plays and playwrights.
Distributed by Audio-Forum.

*The Renaissance Stage [videorecording]
30 min., color, 1990.
Traces the earliest Renaissance attempts to stage classical drama through application of medieval concepts of production.

The Theatre in Ancient Greece
26 min., color, 1989.
Beta, VHS, 3/4″ U-matic cassette.
Program explores ancient theater design, the origins of tragedy, the audience, the comparative role of the writer/director and actors, and the use of landscape in many plays. Examines the theaters of Herodus, Atticus, Epidaurus, Corinth, and numerous others.
Distributed by Films for the Humanities and Sciences.

Directory of Distributors

AIMS Media Inc.
9710 DeSoto Ave.
Chatsworth, CA 91311-9409
(818) 773-4300
(800) 367-2467

American Audio Prose Library
P O. Box 842

Columbia, MO 65205
(314) 443-0361
(800) 447-2275

Audio-Forum
96 Broad St.
Guilford, CT 06437
(203) 453-9794
(800) 243-1234

Baker & Taylor Entertainment
100 Business Ctr. Dr.
Pittsburgh, PA 15205
(800) 775-2600

Books on Tape, Inc.
P.O. Box 7900
Newport Beach, CA 92658
(714) 548-5525
(800) 626-3333

California Newsreel
149 9th St., Suite 420
San Francisco, CA 94103
(415) 621-6196

Chuck Fries Productions
6922 Hollywood Blvd., 12th floor
Los Angeles, CA 90028
(213) 466-2266

Columbia Tristar
See local retailer.

Contemporary Drama Service & Meriwether Publishing
885 Elkton Dr.
Colorado Springs, CO 80907
(719) 594-4422

Coronet/MTI Film & Video
4350 Equity Dr.
Columbus, OH 43228
(800) 777-8100

CRM
2215 Faraday Ave.
Carlsbad, CA 92008
(800) 421-0833

Crossroads Video
15 Buckminster Ln.
Manhasset, NY 11030
(516) 365-3715

Durkin Hayes Publishing
1 Colomba Dr.
Niagara Falls, NY 14305
(716) 298-5150
(800) 962-5200

Canadian address:
3312 Mainway
Burlington, ON
CN L7M 7A7
(416) 335-0393

Encyclopedia Britannica Educational Corp.
310 South Michigan Ave.
Chicago, IL 60604
(800) 621-3900

Facets Multimedia, Inc.
1517 W. Fullerton Ave.
Chicago, IL 60614
(312) 281-9075

Films for the Humanities and Sciences
12 Perrine Rd.
Monmouth Junction, NJ 08852
(800) 257-5126

Films, Inc. PMI
5547 North Ravenswood Ave.
Chicago, IL 60640-1199
(312) 878-2600
(800) 323-4222

Fox Video
See local retailer.

Gallaudet Media Distribution
Gallaudet University Library
800 Florida Ave. NE
Washington, DC 20020-3695

Hallmark Home Entertainment
See local retailer.

HarperCollins Publishers
P.O. Box 588
Dunmore, PA 18512
(717) 343-4761
(800) 242-7737
(800) 982-4377 (in Pennsylvania)

Home Vision & Public Media Video
5547 Ravenswood Ave.
Chicago, IL 60640-1199
(800) 826-3456

Indiana University Instructional Support Services
Bloomington, Indiana 47405-5901
(800) 552-8620

Insight Media
2162 Broadway
New York, NY 10024
(212) 721-6316

Kultur Video
195 Hwy. No. 36

West Long Branch, NJ 07764
(800) 458-5887

Live Entertainment Video
15400 Sherman Way
P.O. Box 10124
Van Nuys, CA 91410-0124
(818) 988-5060

Mastervision, Inc.
969 Park Ave.
New York, NY 10028
(212) 879-0448

MCA/Universal Home Video
See local distributor.

MGM/UA Home Entertainment
See local retailer.

The Media Guild
11722 Sorrento Valley Rd., Suite E
San Diego, CA 92121
(800) 886-9191

MPI Media Group
16101 S. 108th Ave.
Orland Park, IL 60462
(708) 460-0555

New Line Home Video
116 N. Robertson Blvd.
Los Angeles, CA 90048
(310) 967-6670

New York State Education Department
Media Distribution Network
Rm. 7-C—CEC
Empire State Plaza
Albany, NY 12230
(518) 474-3168

Paramount Home Video
See local distributor.

PBS Video
1320 Braddock Pl.
Alexandria, VA 22314
(800) 344-3337

Phoenix/BFA Films
2349 Chaffee Dr.
St. Louis, MO 63146
(800) 221-1274

Prism Entertainment
1888 Century Park, E.
Suite 350
Los Angeles, CA 90067
(310) 277-3270

Professional Media Service Corp.
19122 S. Vermont Ave.
Gardena, CA 90248
(800) 223-7672

Random House, Inc.
400 Hahn Rd.
Westminster, MD 21157
(800) 733-3000

The Roland Collection
22-D Hollywood Ave.
Hohokus, NJ 07423
(800) 597-6526

San Diego State University
Media Technology Services
San Diego, CA 92182
(619) 594-5910

Sounddeluxe
Box H
Novato City, CA 94949
(800) 227-2020

Spoken Arts
P.O. Box 100
New Rochelle, NY 10802-0100
(800) 326-4090

Time-Life Video and Television
1450 East Parham Rd.
Richmond, VA 23280
(800) 621-7026

Turner Home Entertainment Co.
See local retailer.

University of California Extension Center for Media
    & Independent Learning
2000 Center St., 4th Fl.
Berkeley, CA 94704
(510) 642-0460

Video Artists International
P.O. Box 158
Linwood Plaza
Suit 301
Fort Lee, NJ 07024
(201) 944-0099
(800) 477-7146

Video Learning Library
15838 N. 62nd St., Suite 100
Scottsdale, AZ 85254

Video Yesteryear
Box C
Sandy Hook, CT 06482
(203) 426-2574
(800) 243-0987

Warner Home Video
See local retailer.

Water Bearer Films
205 West End Ave.
Suite 24H
New York, NY 10023
(212) 580-8185
(800) 551-8304

Acknowledgments (continued from p. iv)

sional, amateur, motion picture, recitation, lecturing, performance, public reading, radio broadcasting, and television are strictly reserved. Inquiries on all rights should be addressed to Harcourt Brace and Company, Permissions Department, Orlando, FL 32887–67777. *Photos:* © Martha Swope (pp. 141–42, 147–48).

"Poetics: Comedy and Epic and Tragedy" by Aristotle, from *Poetics,* translated by Gerald F. Else, (1967). Reprinted by permission of The University of Michigan Press.

Excerpt from *The Structural Study of Myth* by Claude Lévi-Strauss. Reprinted from *The Bibliographical and Special Series of the American Folklore Society, Vol. 5,* (1955).

"Review of *Oedipus Tyrannus*" by Brooks Atkinson. Copyright © 1952 by The New York Times Company. Reprinted by permission.

"Emotion and Meaning in Greek Tragedy," excerpt from *Greek Tragedy in Action* by Oliver Taplin. Reprinted by permission of Methuen & Co.

"Principal Constants of Conflict in *Antigone,*" excerpt from *Antigones* by George Steiner. Copyright © 1984 by George Steiner. Reprinted by permission of Oxford University Press.

Excerpt from *Antigone* by Jean Anouilh, adapted and translated by Lewis Galantière. Copyright 1946 by Random House, Inc. and renewed 1974 by Lewis Galantière. Reprinted by permission of Random House, Inc.

Medea is reprinted from *Three Plays of Euripides: Alcestis, Medea, The Bacchae,* translated by Paul Roche, with the permission of W. W. Norton & Company, Inc. Copyright © 1974 by Paul Roche. *Photo:* © Joan Marcus (p. 210).

"Review of *Medea*" by John Simon from "Murder, She Wrought" by John Simon. Copyright © 1994 K-III Magazine Corporation. All rights reserved. Reprinted by permission of *New York* Magazine.

Lysistrata translated by Dudley Fitts. Copyright 1954 by Harcourt Brace and Company and renewed 1982 by Cornelia Fitts, Daniel H. Fitts, and Deborah W. Fitts. Reprinted by permission of the publisher. CAUTION: All rights, including professional, amateur, motion picture, recitation, lecturing, public reading, radio broadcasting, and television are strictly reserved. Inquiries on all rights should be addressed to Harcourt Brace and Company, Orlando, Florida 32887. *Photo:* Spingold Theatre, Brandeis University (p. 234).

"Review of *Lysistrata*" by Brooks Atkinson. Copyright © 1930 by The New York Times Company. Reprinted by permission.

Roman Drama

Figure 2. Theater of Marcellus from *The History of the Greek and Roman Theater* by Margarete Bieber. Copyright 1939, 1961 by Princeton University Press. Fig. 641 (after Peruzzi; redrawn by Mrs. Wadhams). Reprinted by permission of Princeton University Press.

Excerpt from *The Twin Menaechmi* from *Six Plays of Plautus* by Plautus, translated by Lionel Casson. Translation copyright © 1963 by Lionel Casson. Reprinted by permission of Doubleday, a division of Bantam Doubleday Dell Publishing Group, Inc.

Excerpt from *The Brothers* from *The Mother-in-Law* by Terence from *Comedies of Terence,* translated by Robert Graves. Reprinted by permission of A.P. Watt LTD on behalf of The Trustees of the Robert Graves Copyright Trust.

Excerpt from *Thyestes* by Seneca from *The Complete Roman Drama* by George E. Duckworth. Copyright 1942 and renewed 1970 by Random House, Inc. Reprinted by permission of Random House, Inc.

Medieval Drama

Figure 3. Pageant wagon from *Early English Stages 1300 to 1660* by Glynne William Gladstone Wickham. Reprinted by permission of Columbia University Press and Routledge & Kegan Paul Ltd.

Everyman edited by A.C. Cawley. Reprinted from the Everyman's Library edition, 1974, with footnotes by A.C. Cawley, by permission of David Campbell Publishers Ltd. *Photo:* The Guthrie Theater (p. 274).

Renaissance Drama

Figure 4. Teatro Olimpico in Vicenza, Italy, Alinari/Art Resource New York.

Figure 5. Perspective setting designed by Peruzzi, Scala/Art Resource New York.

Figure 6. Swan Theatre from *Essai sur L'Histoire du Théâtre* by Germain Bapst. Reprinted by courtesy of the Trustees of the Boston Public Library.

Doctor Faustus by Christopher Marlowe from *Doctor Faustus, Text and Major Criticism,* edited with notes by Irving Ribner. Copyright © 1985. Reprinted by permission of Prentice-Hall, Inc. Upper Saddle River, NJ. *Photo:* Donald Cooper © Photostage (p. 302).

Excerpt from Ernst Honigmann's "Ten Problems in *Dr. Faustus*" in *The Arts of Performance in Elizabethan and Early Stuart Drama,* ed. Murray Biggs et al (Edinburgh, 1991) reprinted by permission of Edinburgh University Press.

A Midsummer Night's Dream, Hamlet, and *The Tempest* by William Shakespeare from *The Complete Works of Shakespeare,* 4th Edition by David Bevington. Copyright © 1992 by HarperCollins Publishers, Inc. Reprinted by permission. *Photos:* Richard M. Feldman (pp. 338–39, 384–85, 446);

Osterreichisches Theatermuseum (p. 356); © Martha Swope (pp. 350–51, 436); Donald Cooper © Photostage (pp. 400–401); Michal Daniel (p. 437); Guthrie Theater (pp. 458–59).

"Masque Elements in *A Midsummer Night's Dream*" by Enid Welsford, from *The Court Masque* by Enid Welsford. Cambridge: Cambridge University Press; New York: The Macmillan Company, 1927. Reprinted by permission of Cambridge University Press.

"Broken Nuptials," excerpt from *Broken Nuptials in Shakespeare's Plays* by Carol Thomas Neely. Reprinted by permission of Yale University Press.

"On *A Midsummer Night's Dream*" by Linda Bamber. Reprinted from *Comic Women, Tragic Men: A Study of Gender and Genre in Shakespeare* by Linda Bamber with the permission of the publishers, Stanford University Press. Copyright © 1982 by the Board of Trustees of the Leland Stanford Junior University.

"The Play Is the Message . . ." by Peter Brook from *The Shifting Point* by Peter Brook. Copyright © 1987 by Peter Brook. Reprinted by permission of HarperCollins Publishers, Inc.

"Review of *A Midsummer Night's Dream*" by Clive Barnes. Copyright © 1970 by The New York Times Company. Reprinted by permission.

"Hamlet and His Problems" from "Hamlet" in *Selected Essays* by T.S. Eliot, copyright 1950 by Harcourt Brace and Company, renewed 1978 by Esme Valerie Eliot. Reprinted by permission of Harcourt Brace and Company and Faber and Faber Ltd.

"Review of *Hamlet*" from "Matinee Idolatry" in *Light Fantastic* by John Lahr. Copyright © 1996 by John Lahr. Reprinted by permission of The Dial Press/Dell Publishing, a division of Bantam, Doubleday Dell Publishing Group, Inc.

"*The Tempest* and the New World" by Stephen J. Greenblatt from *Learning to Curse* by Stephen J. Greenblatt. Reprinted by permission of the author.

"Review of *The Tempest*" by Ben Brantley. Copyright © 1995 by The New York Times Company. Reprinted by permission.

Late Seventeenth- and Eighteenth-Century Drama

Figure 7. Early Restoration Theater, illustration by Peter Kahn. From *The Frolicks; or, The Lawyer Cheated* by Elizabeth Polwhele, edited by Judith Milhous and Robert D. Hume, Cornell University Press, 1977. Used by permission of the publisher, Cornell University Press.

The Misanthrope translated by Richard Wilbur, copyright © 1955 and renewed 1983 by Richard Wilbur, reprinted by permission of Harcourt Brace and Company. CAUTION: Professionals and amateurs are hereby warned that this translation, being fully protected under the copyright laws of the United States, the British Commonwealth, including Canada, and all other countries which are signatories to the Universal Copyright Convention, is subject to royalty. All rights, including professional, amateur, motion picture, recitation, lecturing, public reading, radio broadcasting, and television, are strictly reserved. Particular emphasis is laid on the question of readings, permission for which must be secured from the author's agent in writing. Inquiries on professional rights (except for amateur rights) should be addressed to Mr. Gilbert Parker, Curtis Brown, Ltd., Ten Astor Place, New York, NY 10003. The amateur acting rights of *The Misanthrope* are controlled exclusively by the Dramatists Play Service, Inc., 440 Park Avenue South, New York, NY 10016. No amateur performance of the play may be given without obtaining in advance the written permission of the Dramatists Play Service, Inc. and paying the requisite fee. Translation rights should be addressed to Harcourt Brace and Company, Permissions Department, Orlando, Florida 32887. *Photo.* Courtesy of the Williamstown Theatre Festival. Photo by Michael C. Durling (p. 514).

"Alceste's Love for Célimène," excerpt from *Men and Masks* by Lionel Gossman. Reprinted by permission of Johns Hopkins University Press.

The Rover; or, The Banished Cavaliers. Photo: Courtesy of the Williamstown Theatre Festival. Photo by Nina Krieger (p. 544).

"On Aphra Behn," excerpt from *A Room of One's Own* by Virginia Woolf. Copyright © 1929 by Harcourt Brace and Company and renewed 1957 by Leonard Woolf. Reprinted by permission of the publisher.

"Courtship and Marriage in *The Rover*," excerpt from *Virtue of Necessity: English Women's Writing* by Elaine Hobby. Copyright © Elaine Hobby 1988. Reprinted by permission of The University of Michigan Press.

The Way of the World. Photos: © Richard Feldman (p. 591); Spingold Theatre, Brandeis University (p. 601).

"Review of *The Way of the World*" by Howard Taubman. Copyright © 1965 by The New York Times Company. Reprinted by permission.

Nineteenth-Century Drama Through the Turn of the Century

Figure 8. Realistic setting in Anton Chekhov's *The Cherry Orchard*, Harvard Theatre Collection.

Photos: Realistic stage setting of Ibsen's *The Wild Duck*, Bibliotheque de l'Arsenal, Paris (p. 636); Edvard Munch's stage design for Ibsen's *Ghosts*, Munch Museum, Oslo Photo: Munch Museum (p. 637).

A Doll House and *Hedda Gabler* from *The Complete Major Prose Plays of Henrik Ibsen* by Henrik Ibsen, translated by Rolf Fjelde. Translation copyright © 1965, 1970, 1978, by Rolf Fjelde. Used by permission of Dutton Signet, a division of Penguin Books USA Inc. *Photos:* © 1992 Martha Swope (pp. 648–49); Donald Cooper © Photostage (pp. 656–57, 686, 692–93); © T. Charles Erickson (pp. 700–701).

"*A Doll's House*: Ibsen the Moralist" by Muriel C. Bradbrook from *Ibsen the Norwegian* by Muriel C. Bradbrook. Reprinted by permission of Random Century.

"Notes for *Hedda Gabler*," selection from Ibsen's Notes on *Hedda Gabler* translated by Evert Sprinchorn, from *Playwrights on Playwriting*, edited by Toby Cole. Copyright © 1960 and renewal copyright © 1988 by Toby Cole. Reprinted by permission of Hill and Wang, a division of Farrar, Straus and Giroux, Inc.

"Thematic Symbols in *Hedda Gabler*" by Caroline Mayerson. Reprinted by permission of the author.

"On *Hedda Gabler*," excerpt from "Ibsen Read Anew" by Jan Kott from *The Theatre of Essence and Other Essays* by Jan Kott. Copyright © 1984 by Jan Kott. Reprinted by permission of the author.

Review of *A Doll House*" ("Godfather of Women's Lib") by T. E. Kalem. Copyright © 1971 Time Inc. Reprinted by permission.

"Review of *Hedda Gabler*" by Clive Barnes. Copyright © 1970 by The New York Times Company. Reprinted by permission.

Miss Julie by August Strindberg, and excerpt from the "Preface to *Miss Julie*" from *Strindberg: Five Plays*, Harry Carlson, editor and translator. Copyright © 1983 The Regents of the University of California. Reprinted by permission of the University of California Press. *Photo:* Donald Cooper © Photostage (p. 742).

The Importance of Being Earnest. Photo: © Richard Feldman (p. 766).

"An Unpublished Letter from Oscar Wilde on *The Importance of Being Earnest*" from "The Making of *The Importance of Being Earnest*" by Peter Raby. *Times Literary Supplement* No. 4629, December 1991. Reprinted by permission of Peter Raby. Oscar Wilde's letter to George Alexander is reprinted by permission of Merlin Holland.

The Cherry Orchard by Anton Chekhov from *The Major Plays of Anton Chekhov* by Anton Chekhov, translated by Ann Dunnigan. Translation copyright © 1964 by Ann Dunnigan. Used by permission of New American Library, a division of Penguin Books USA Inc. *Photos:* © Richard Feldman (p. 801).

"From *Letters of Anton Chekhov*," two letters from *Letters of Anton Chekhov* translated by Michael Henry Heim with Simon Karlinsky. Copyright © 1973 by Harper & Row Publishers, Inc. Reprinted by permission of HarperCollins Publishers, Inc.

Excerpt from "Recollections" by Maxim Gorky from *Reminiscences of Tolstoy, Chekhov and Andreyev* by Maxim Gorky. Reprinted by permission of Random Century.

"Review of *The Cherry Orchard*" by John Corbin. Copyright © 1923 by The New York Times Company. Reprinted by permission.

"On Chekhov" by Peter Brook from *The Shifting Point* by Peter Brook. Copyright © 1987 by Peter Brook. Reprinted by permission of HarperCollins Publishers, Inc.

Pygmalion and the Preface to *Pygmalion* by Bernard Shaw is reprinted by permission of The Society of Authors on behalf of the Estate of Bernard Shaw. *Photo:* Donald Cooper © Photostage (p. 833).

"Higgins and Shaw," excerpt from *Bernard Shaw: The Darker Side* by Arnold Silver with the permission of the publishers, Stanford University Press. Copyright © 1982 by the Board of Trustees of the Leland Stanford Junior University.

"Patriarchy in *Pygmalion*," excerpt from *Shaw's Daughters*. Copyright © 1991 by J. Ellen Gainor. Reprinted by permission of the University of Michigan Press.

Drama in the Early and Mid-Twentieth Century

Figure 9: Expressionistic setting in Arthur Miller's *Death of a Salesman*, the Billy Rose Theatre Collection of New York Public Library for the Performing Arts/Astor, Lenox, and Tilden Foundations.

Trifles by Susan Glaspell is reprinted by permission of Daphne C. Cook.

Six Characters in Search of An Author copyright 1922 by E. P. Dutton. Renewed 1950 in the names of Stefano, Fausto and Lietta Pirandello. From *Naked Masks: Five Plays* by Luigi Pirandello, edited by Eric Bentley. Translation copyright 1922, 1952 by E.P. Dutton. Renewed 1950 in the names of Stefano, Fausto and Lietta Pirandello. Introduction copyright 1952, © renewed 1980 by Eric Bentley. Used by permission of Dutton Signet, a division of Penguin Books USA Inc. *Photo:* © Richard Feldman (p. 915).

"Review of *Six Characters in Search of an Author*" by John Corbin. Copyright © 1922 by The New York Times Company. Reprinted by permission.

Desire Under the Elms by Eugene O'Neill. Copyright 1924 and renewed 1952 by Eugene O'Neill. Reprinted from *The Plays of Eugene O'Neill* by Eugene O'Neill by permission of Random House, Inc. *Photo:* © T. Charles Erickson (p. 952).

"Review of *Desire Under the Elms*" by Stark Young. Copyright © 1924 by The New York Times Company. Reprinted by permission.

The House of Bernarda Alba by Frederico García Lorca from *Three Tragedies*. Copyright © 1947 by New Directions Publishing Corp. Reprinted by permission of New Directions Publishing Corp. *Photo:* © Carol Rosegg (p. 976).

"Religion in *The House of Bernarda Alba*" by John Gilmour in "The Cross of Pain and Death: Religion in the Rural Tragedies" from *Lorca: Poet and Playwright*, edited by Robert Harvard. Copyright © 1992. Reprinted by permission of St. Martin's Press, Inc.

Mother Courage and Her Children by Bertolt Brecht. Copyright © 1940 by Arvid Englind Teaterforlag, a.b., renewed June 1967 by Stefan S. Brecht; copyright © 1949 by Suhrkamp Verlag, Frankfurt am Main. Translation copyright © 1980 Stefan S. Brecht. Reprinted from *Mother Courage and Her Children* by Bertolt Brecht. Reprinted by permission of Arcade Publishing Inc., New York, New York and Reed Books, London. *Photo:* Photofest (p. 1000).

The Glass Menagerie by Tennessee Williams. Copyright 1945 by Tennessee Williams and Edwina D. Williams and renewed 1973 by Tennessee Williams. Reprinted by permission of Random House, Inc. *Photos:* Estate of Jo Mielziner, used by permission (p. 1040); The Billy Rose Theatre Collection of the New York Public Library for the Performing Arts/Astor, Lenox, and Tilden Foundations (pp. 1040–41); Joan Marcus/Arena Stage (pp. 1050–51).

Cat on a Hot Tin Roof by Tennessee Williams. Copyright © 1954, 1955, 1971, 1975 by Tennessee Williams. Reprinted by permission of New Directions Publishing Corporation. *Photos:* © 1992 Martha Swope (p. 1068); © Michael Tighe/Visages 1992 (p. 1077); Fred Fehl/The Billy Rose Theatre Collection of the New York Public Library for the Performing Arts/Astor, Lenox, and Tilden Foundations (p. 1088).

"Review of *The Glass Menagerie*" by Lewis Nichols. Copyright © 1945 by The New York Times Company. Reprinted by permission.

"Laurette Taylor in *The Glass Menagerie*," excerpt from *The Kindness of Strangers: The Life of Tennessee Williams* by Donald Spoto. Copyright © 1985 by Donald Spoto. Reprinted by permission of Little, Brown and Company.

"Problems in *The Glass Menagerie*," by Benjamin Nelson. Excerpt from *Tennessee Williams: The Man and His Work* by Benjamin Nelson (New York: 1961). Reprinted by permission of the author.

"Memoirs," excerpt from *Tennessee Williams: Memoirs* by Tennessee Williams. Copyright © 1972, 1975 by Tennessee Williams. Reprinted by permission of Doubleday, a division of Bantam Doubleday Dell Publishing Group, Inc.

"Tennessee Williams and Elia Kazan Collaborate on *Cat*," excerpt from *Tennessee Williams and Elia Kazan: A Collaboration in the Theatre* by Brenda Murphy. Copyright © 1991 by Cambridge University Press. Reprinted by permission of Cambridge University Press.

Death of a Salesman by Arthur Miller. Copyright 1949, renewed © 1977 by Arthur Miller. All rights reserved. Used by permission of Viking Penguin, a division of Penguin Books USA Inc. *Photo:* Photofest (p. 1161).

"In Memoriam" by Arthur Miller is reprinted by permission of the author and International Creative Management, Inc. Copyright © 1995 by Arthur Miller. First appeared in *The New Yorker*.

"Tragedy and the Common Man," excerpt from *The Theatre Essays of Arthur Miller* by Arthur Miller, edited by Robert A. Martin. Copyright 1949, renewed © 1977 by Arthur Miller. Used by permission of Viking Penguin, a division of Penguin Books USA Inc.

"Review of *Death of a Salesman*" ("Rebirth of an American Dream") by Richard Schickel. Copyright © 1984 Time Inc. Reprinted by permission.

Endgame by Samuel Beckett. Copyright © 1958 by Grove Press, Inc.; copyright renewed © 1986 by Samuel Beckett. Used by permission of Grove Press, Inc. *Photos:* © 1992 Martha Swope (pp. 1188–89); Richard M. Feldman (p. 1199).

Excerpt from "The Theatre of the Absurd" by Martin Esslin. Reprinted by permission of the author.

"The Ending of *Endgame*," excerpt from *Beckett's Theaters: Interpretations for Performance* by Sidney Homan (Bucknell University Press). Reprinted by permission of Associated University Presses.

A Raisin in the Sun by Lorraine Hansberry. Copyright © 1958 by Robert Nemiroff, as an unpublished work. Copyright © 1959, 1966, 1984 by Robert Nemiroff. Reprinted by permission of Random House, Inc. *Photo:* © Richard Feldman (p. 1221).

"Harlem (Dream Deferred)" by Langston Hughes from *The Panther and the Lash* by Langston Hughes. Copyright 1951 by Langston Hughes. Reprinted by permission of Alfred A. Knopf, Inc.

"Review of *A Raisin in the Sun*" by Brooks Atkinson. Copyright © 1959 by The New York Times Company. Reprinted by permission.

Contemporary Drama

Figure 10. Multimedia effects in Robert Wilson's *CIVIL warS*, Richard M. Feldman.

The Strong Breed by Wole Soyinka. Copyright © Oxford University Press 1964. Reprinted from *Wole Soyinka: Collected Plays 1* (1973) by permission of Oxford University Press.

"Interview with Wole Soyinka," excerpt from *African Writers Talking: A Collection of Radio Interviews*, edited by Cosmo Pieterse and Dennis Duerden (New York: Holmes & Meier, 1972). Copyright © 1972 by Cosmo Pieterse and Dennis Duerden. Reprinted by permission of the publisher.

Buried Child by Sam Shepard, copyright © 1979 by Sam Shepard from *Seven Plays* by Sam Shepard. Used by permission of Bantam Books, a division of Bantam Doubleday Dell Publishing Group, Inc. *Photo:* © Richard Feldman (p. 1302).

Betrayal by Harold Pinter copyright © 1978 by H. Pinter Ltd. Reprinted by permission of Grove/Atlantic, Inc. and Faber and Faber, Ltd.

"Harold Pinter's *Betrayal*: Life Before Death—and After" from *Theatre Journal* (December 1982). Reprinted by permission of Johns Hopkins University Press.

Angels in America, Part One: Millennium Approaches by Tony Kushner. Copyright © 1993 by Tony Kushner. Reprinted by permission of Theatre Communications Group, Inc. *Photos:* © Joan Marcus (pp.1670–71).

"Interview with Tony Kushner" by Andrea Bernstein reprinted with permission from *Mother Jones* magazine, © 1995, Foundation for National Progress.

Excerpts from *Twilight: Los Angeles, 1992* by Anna Deavere Smith. Copyright © 1994 by Anna Deavere Smith. Used by permission of Doubleday, a division of Bantam Doubleday Dell Publishing Group, Inc. *Photo:* William Gibson/Martha Swope Studios (p. 1686).